ATHLET
1995
THE INTERNATIONAL TRACK AND FIELD ANNUAL

ASSOCIATION OF
TRACK & FIELD STATISTICIANS
EDITED BY PETER MATTHEWS

SPORTSBOOKS

Published by SportsBooks Ltd

SportsBooks Limited
PO Box 422A
Surbiton
Surrey
KT5 9YP
0181 226 0831

This publication incorporates the ATFS Annual.

Photographs supplied by Mark Shearman, 22 Grovelands Road, Purley, Surrey, CR8 4LA.
Tel: 0181-660-0156 Fax: 0181-660-3437

British Library Cataloguing in Publication Data

Athletics: the international track and
field annual – 1995
1. Athletics. Track & Field events –
Serials
1. International athletics annual (London)
796.4'2'05

ISBN 1 899807 00 4

Printed and bound in Great Britain by BPC Wheatons, Exeter

CONTENTS

CONTENTS

INTRODUCTION

IT HAS been another fascinating year of athletics – and the details are recorded in this Annual. I know from my correspondence and from my travels to athletics meetings around the world that this book is keenly awaited by athletics enthusiasts. It is also a matter of great pride for me that it will be used extensively by representatives of the media to help them with the background for their reporting of meetings and events. Over the past decade I have become accustomed to looking around the press, radio and television stands at major championships and most especially in the press centres to see, to my delight, scores of copies being used.

I trust that this volume will meet all your expectations, There are no major changes this year in the contents – the base of which remains the detailed ATFS year lists, augmented by all-time lists. The proliferation of major events means that the championships section is the largest ever, and this has meant that I was unable to include a few articles that enthusiasts had submitted to me. My apologies to those people, but I must concentrate on the essential items of record.

As ever it has been hard work meeting my self-imposed deadlines, themselves very tight indeed if we are to meet a publishing schedule to get the book out before the summer season. Even with a cut off date of the end of March 1995 some information from 1994 remains outstanding. However, with the exception of Chinese performances (only top tens were received in time), I do not expect too many serious omissions. The most important missing national lists came, through the good offices of Nejat Kök, just in time – those of the Ukraine, but I still urge present or potential contributors to make sure that our compilers receive results and ranking lists in good time, and not too late for inclusion. Mel Watman and I will continue to publish all marks from around the world that make the ATFS standards (world top 150-200 level) in *Athletics International*. in the 30 annual issues of our newsletter. I would like to pay especial thanks to contributors to this most vital source of information on international results and to the other important magazines and newsletters published in various countries.

In addition to the contributors shown on the acknowledgements page, I am also most grateful to Randall Northam (Sports Books), who has taken over as publisher this year. His experience as an athletics writer and former editor of the much-missed *Athletics Today* as well as his practical lay-out expertise has been invaluable. I now wish him well in successfully marketing this book, so that its continued publication will be both assured and successful. And finally my most sincere thanks go to Mobil, whose sponsorship of this book has enabled us to present the book in this form for the past ten editions. This started when Jim Dunaway introduced me to Fran Michelman of Mobil at the World Cup in Canberra in 1985, so both deserve our warm-est appreciation.

As I write at the end of the compilation process we have already had two world championships in 1995 – Indoors and Cross-country – and we all look forward to the undoubted highlight of the coming year – the 5th IAAF World Championships in Athletics – in Göteborg, Sweden in August. Great deeds from there and elsewhere will be in Athletics 1996. Work on that starts here!

Peter Matthews

ABBREVIATIONS

Meeting Abbreviations

The following abbreviations have been used for meetings with, in parentheses, the first year that they were held.

AAA (GBR) Amateur Athletic Association Championships (1880)
AAU (USA) Amateur Athletic Union Championships (1888) (now TAC)
AfCh African Championships (1979)
AfG African Games (1965) (or AfrG)
AmCp America's Cup (World Cup Trial)
APM Adriaan Paulen Memorial, Hengelo
Arena Arena International, Bern, Switzerland
AsiC Asian Championships (1973)
AsiG Asian Games (1951)
ASV Weltklasse in Köln, ASV club meeting (1934)
Athl Athletissima, Lausanne (1976)
Balk Balkan Games (1929)
Barr (Cuba) Barrientos Memorial (1950)
BGP Budapest Grand Prix (1978) (now HGP)
Bisl Bislett Games, Oslo
BNP BNP meeting, Paris, Lille or Villeneuve d'Ascq
CAC Central American and Caribbean Championships (1967)
CAG Central American and Caribbean Games (1926)
CalR California Relays (1942)
CISM International Military Championships (1946)
CG Commonwealth Games (1930)
DNG DN Galan, Stockholm (1966)
Drake Drake Relays (1910)
Drz Druzhba/Friendship Games
EC European Championships (1934)
ECCp European Clubs Cup (1975)
ECp European Cup - track & field (1965), multi-events (1973)
ECp23 European Under 23 Cup (1992)
EI European Indoor Championships (1970, Games 1966-9)
EJ European Junior Championships (1970)
EsC Eschborn Cup - Women's World Race Walking Cup (1979)
Expo Expo 92 meeting, Sevilla
FBK Fanny Blankers-Koen meeting, Hengelo (now APM)
FlaR Florida Relays (1939)
FOT (USA) Final Olympic Trials (1920)
GGala Golden Gala, Roma (from 1980), Verona (1988), Pescara (1989), Bologna (1990)
GO Golden Oval, Dresden
GPB Bratislva Grand Prix (formerly PTS) (1990)
GPF IAAF Grand Prix final (1985)
GS Golden Spike, Ostrava (1969)
Gugl Gugl Internationales, Linz (1988)
GWG Goodwill Games (1986)
HB Hanns Braun Memorial, München (1930)
Herc Herculis, Monte Carlo, Monaco (1987)
HGP Hungalu Budapest Grand Prix
IAAF International Amateur Athletic Federation
IAAFg IAAF Golden events (1978)
IAC IAC meeting (1968), formerly Coke meeting
IbAm Ibero-American Championships (1983)
Int International meeting
ISTAF Internationales Stadionfest, Berlin (1921)
Izv (URS) Izvestia Cup
Jen Bruce Jenner Classic, San Jose (1979)
Jer Harry Jerome Track Classic (1984)
JO Jesse Owens Memorial (1981)
JP Jan Popper Memorial (1987), formerly Journalists' Lath, Praha
-j Junior, championships or international match
KansR Kansas Relays, Lawrence (1923)
King Martin Luther King Games (1969)
Kuso Janusz Kusocinski Memorial (1954)
Kuts Vladimir Kuts Memorial
LAT Los Angeles Times indoors (1960, from 1968 at Inglewood)
LB Liberty Bell, Philadelphia
LT Lugano Trophy, IAAF World Race Walking Cup (1961)
MAI Malmö AI Galan, Sweden (formerly Idag) (1958)
Mal Malinowski Memorial, Poland
McV McVitie's Challenge, Crystal Palace, London (1985-9), Sheffield (1990-1)
Mast Masters pole vault, Grenoble (1987)
McD McDonald's Games, Sheffield (1992)
MedG Mediterranean Games (1951)
Mill Millrose Games, New York indoors (1908)
MSR Mt. San Antonio College Relays (1959)
NC National Championships
NC-j National Junior Championships
NC-y National Youth Championships
NCAA National Collegiate Athletic Association Championships (1921)
Nik Nikaïa, Nice (1976)
ND Nina Dumbadze Memorial
NM Narodna Mladezhe, Sofia (1955)
NP National Cup
Nurmi Paavo Nurmi Games (1957)
NYG New York Games (1989)
OD (GDR) Olympischer Tag (Olympic Day)
OG Olympic Games (1896)
OT Olympic Trials
PAm Pan American Games (1951)
PennR Pennsylvania Relays (1895)

Pepsi Pepsi Cola Invitational
PG Parcelforce Games, formerly Peugeot (Talbot) Games (1980), Royal Mail Parcels Games 1989-90, Parcelforce Games 1991
PO Pre Olympic Meet
Prav (URS) Pravda Cup
PTS Pravda Televízia Slovnaft, Bratislava (1957) (now GPB)
Pre Steve Prefontaine Memorial (1976)
RomIC Romanian International Championships (1948)
Ros Evzen Rosicky Memorial, Praha (1947)
R-W Rot-Weiss meeting, Koblenz
SACh South American Championships (1919) (or SoAmC)
SEAG South East Asia Games
SGP Softeland Grand Prix (walking)
Slovn Slovnaft '92, Bratislava (formerly PTS) (1990)
Spart (URS) Spartakiad (1956)
S&W S & W Invitational, Modesto (previously CalR)
TAC (USA) The Athletics Congress Championships (1980-91)
TexR Texas Relays (1925)
Toto Toto International Super Meet, Tokyo
TSB TSB International, Crystal Palace, London (Formerly PG)
USOF US Olympic Festival
VD Ivo Van Damme Memorial, Brussels (1977)
Veniz Venizelia, Khania, Crete
WA West Athletic Meet (AUT/BEL/DEN/HOL/IRL/POR/SPA/SWZ)
WAAA (GBR) Women's Amateur Athletic Association Championships (1922-91)
WCh World Championships (1983)
WCp World Cup - track & field (1977), marathon (1985)
WG World Games, Helsinki (1961)
WI World Indoor Championships (1987), World Indoor Games (1985)
WJ World Junior Championships (1986)
WK Weltklasse, Zürich (1962)
WPT World Cup Trials (1977)
WUG World University Games (1923)
Znam Znamenskiy Brothers Memorial (1958)

Dual and triangular matches are indicated by "v" (versus) followed by the name(s) of the opposition. Quadrangular and larger inter-nation matches are denoted by the number of nations and -N; viz 8-N designates an 8-nation meeting.

Events

C-C cross-country
Dec decathlon
DT discus
h hurdles
Hep heptathlon
HJ high jump
HT hammer
JT javelin
LJ long jump
Mar marathon
Pen pentathlon
PV pole vault
R relay
SP shot
St steeplechase
TJ triple jump
W walk
Wt weight

Miscellaneous abbreviations

+ Intermediate time in longer race
= Tie (ex-aequo)
A Made at an altitude of 1000m or higher
b date of birth
D Made in decathlon competition
dnf did not finish
dnq did not qualify
dns did not start
exh exhibition
h heat
H Made in heptathlon competition
hr hour
i indoors
kg kilograms
km kilometres
m metres
M mile
m/s metres per second
mx Made in mixed men's and women's race
O Made in octathlon
P Made in pentathlon
pb personal best
Q Made in qualifying round
qf quarter final (or q in lists)
r Race number in a series of races
sf semi final (or s in lists)
w wind assisted
y yards
* Converted time from yards to metres:
For 200m: 220 yards less 0.11 second
For 400m: 440 yards less 0.26 second
For 110mh: 120yh plus 0.03 second

Countries

ALB Albania
ALG Algeria
ANG Anguilla
ANO Angola (ANG)
ANT Antigua
ARG Argentina
ARM Armenia
AUS Australia
AUT Austria
AZE Azerbaijan
BAH Bahamas
BAR Barbados
BEL Belgium
BER Bermuda
BHR Bahrain (BHN)
BKF Burkina Faso
BLR Belarus
BOL Bolivia
BRA Brazil
BSH Bosnia Hercegovina
BUL Bulgaria
BUR Burundi
CAF Central African Republic
CAN Canada
CAY Cayman Islands
CGO Congo (CON)
CHI Chile (CHL)
CHN People's Republic of China
CIV Ivory Coast (IVC)
CMR Cameroon (CAM)
COL Colombia
CRC Costa Rica
CRO Croatia
CUB Cuba
CYP Cyprus
DEN Denmark
DJI Djibouti
DMN Dominica
DOM Dominican Republic
ECU Ecuador
EGY Egypt
Eng England
ESA El Salvador
ESP Spain (SPA)
EST Estonia
ETH Ethiopia
FIJ Fiji
FIN Finland
FRA France
FRG Federal Republic of Germany (1948-90)
GAB Gabon
GAM The Gambia
GBR United Kingdom of Great Britain & Northern Ireland (UK)
GDR German Democratic Republic (1948-90)
GEO Georgia
GER Germany (pre 1948 and from 1991)
GHA Ghana
GRE Greece
GRN Grenada
GUA Guatemala
GUY Guyana
HAI Haiti
HLG Hong Kong
HOL Holland (Netherlands) (now NED)
HON Honduras
HUN Hungary
INA Indonesia
IND India
IRL Ireland (IRE)
IRN Iran
IRQ Iraq
ISL Iceland (ICE)
ISR Israel
ISV US Virgin Islands (UVI)
ITA Italy
JAM Jamaica
JOR Jordan
JPN Japan (JAP)
KEN Kenya
KGZ Kirgizstan
KOR Korea (SKO)
KUW Kuwait
KZK Kazakhstan
LAT Latvia
LES Lesotho
LIE Liechtenstein
LIT Lithuania
LUX Luxembourg
MAD Madagascar
MAR Morocco (MOR)
MAS Malaysia
MAW Malawi
MEX Mexico
MNT Montserrat
MOL Moldova
MON Monaco
MOZ Mozambique
MRI Mauritius (MAU)
MYA Myanmar (formerly BIR Burma)
NAM Namibia
NCA Nicaragua (NIC)
NED Netherlands (changed from HOL)
NEP Nepal
NGR Nigeria (NIG)
NGU Papua New Guinea (PNG)
NI Northern Ireland
NOR Norway
NZL New Zealand (NZ)
OMA Oman
PAK Pakistan
PAN Panama
PAR Paraguay
PER Peru
PHI Philippines
POL Poland
POR Portugal
PRK North Korea (Korean PDR) (NKO)
PUR Puerto Rico (PR)
QAT Qatar
ROM Romania
RSA South Africa
RUS Russia
RWA Rwanda
SAU Saudi Arabia
Sco Scotland
SEN Sénégal
SEY Seychelles
SIN Singapore
SLE Sierra Leone
SLO Slovenia
SOM Somalia
SRI Sri Lanka
STL St Lucia
SUD Sudan
SUI Switzerland (SWZ)
SUR Surinam
SVK Slovakia
SWE Sweden
SYR Syria
TAN Tanzania
TCH Czech Repbublic (formerly Czechoslovakia) (CS)
THA Thailand
TJK Tadjikistan
TKM Turkmenistan
TPE Taiwan (Chinese Taipeh) (TAI)
TRI Trinidad & Tobago
TUN Tunisia
TUR Turkey
UAE United Arab Emirates
UGA Uganda
UKR Ukraine
URS Soviet Union (SU) (to 1991)
URU Uruguay
USA United States
UZB Uzbekistan
VEN Venezuela
Wal Wales
YUG Yugoslavia
ZAI Zaïre
ZAM Zambia
ZIM Zimbabwe

Notes

1 *These are mostly IAAF (and usually IOC) abbreviations. In Annuals prior to 1992 ATFS abbreviations were used. Where these differ from those formerly used the ATFS ones are shown in brackets. There are also some additional ones.*

2 *Other IAAF members not shown, as athletes not included in lists in this book*

ACKNOWLEDGEMENTS

FOR THIS the 11th ATFS Annual that I have edited, I am once again most grateful for the help of many people, most of them ATFS members and I would like to thank all those who contributed to a greater or lesser extent. The main compilers collect information from a wide range of sources, of which the most important are the major magazines and newsletters devoted to the sport, and the end of year national lists produced by dedicated individuals and by national federations.

During the year Mel Watman and I publish all marks that we know about to ATFS standards in *Athletics International* , and we are now producing 30 issues per year This can thus serve as a base from which the lists in this book can be compiled, together with the major magazines that are published around the world, such as *Track & Field News* (USA) with its results spin-off *Track Newsletter*, and *Leichtathletik* (Germany). Then there are an increasing number of invaluable results and statistics bulletins, with particular spheres of interest such as Yves Pinaud's *Lettre de l'Athlétism*, Sergey Tikhonov's Russian newsletter *Legkaya Atletika*, and *Atletismo en España* by Francisco J Ascorbe and José Luis Hernández.

Many of the national contributors to *Athletics International* are included in the acknowledgments list below. In order to ensure that the record of 1995 is as complete as possible I urge results contribution worldwide to AI and then in turn our lists in *Athletics 1996* will be as comprehensive as we can make them. These 1994 lists are as detailed as I can make them, although there are still some disappointments - at the time of writing no information had been received from Ukraine and only top tens have been received from China, so that in events such as the walks and women's shot we are missing many athletes.

Some ancillary details (such as wind speeds) are missing. Nonetheless I am confident that our annual lists are the most comprehensive that we have ever published.

The lists this year started with those produced in late 1994 by Richard Hymans, who as usual compiled the men's index, and later I received main bulk of the lists compiled by Alfons Juck and Jirí Havlín, who had the help of Robert Blaho and Dr Zdenék Jebavy (walks), Milan Urban (heptathlon), Vaclav Klvana (decathlon) and Miroslav Ondruska (women's jumping events).

Marco Buccellato produced deep world lists, which were a most useful check, and other major help in general came from Winfried Kramer and Heinrich Hubbelling who work so hard to get information from countries where we do not have regular correspondents.

Further information on specific areas was provided by: *Records* Bob Sparks, *Juniors* Milan Skocovsky and Lionel Peters,*Marathon* Dr. David E Martin, *Ultrarunning* Andy Milroy, *Indoor marks* Ed Gordon, *Walks* Emmerich Götze, *Men's middle and long distance events* Ian Smith, *Long jump* Francisco Ascorbe, *Heptathlon* Milan Urban, *Men's pentathlon* Dr Hans-Peter Car.

The following specialists supplied information for their respective areas and countries: *Africa*: Yves Pinaud; *Argentina* Eduardo Biscayart,*Asia*: Heinrich Hubbeling; *Australia*: Paul Jenes; *Austria*: Erich Kamper and Karl Graf; *Belgium*: André de Hooghe and Alain Monet; *Brazil* José C Gonçalves; *Bulgaria*: Grigor Khristov and Alexander Vangelov; *CAC & Trinidad & Tobago*: Bernard Linley; *Canada*: Cecil Smith; *China*: Gao Dianmin;*Cuba*: Basilio Fuentes; *Croatia* Mladen Delic;*Czech Republic* Milan Skocovsky and Milan Urban; *Denmark*: Erik Laursen; *Estonia*: Erlend Teemägi; *Finland*: Juhani Jalava, Mirko Jalava and Matti Hannus; *France*: Yves Pinaud; *Germany*: Klaus Amrhein, Ederhard Vollmer; *Greece*: Karolos Sargologos and Thomas Constas; *Hungary*: Gabriel Szabó and Zoltán Subert; *India*: Ranjit Bhatia; *Ireland*: Liam Hennessy; *Israel*: David Eiger; *Italy*: Raul Leoni, Ottavio Castellini and Silvio Garavaglia; *Jamaica*: Richard Ashenheim; *Japan*: Yoshimasa Noguchi, Seichi Tanabe, Naoshi Ito and Isao Sugawara; *Latvia*: Andris Stagis; *Liechtenstein:* Robert Schumacher; Luxembourg Georges Klepper, *Netherlands*: Louis Weisscher; *New Zealand*: Barry Hunt and Peter Heidenstrom; *Norway*: Tore Johansen, Bjarte Bogstad, Stein Fossen, Hans T Halvorsen, Jan Jørgen Moe, Jo Nesse and Bernt Solaas *Poland*: Tadeusz Wolejko; *Portugal*: Luis Lopes; *Romania* Vladimir Simionescu; *Russia*: Sergey Tikhonov; *Slovakia* Alfons Juck; *South Africa*: Gert le Roux, Hans Prinsloo and Riël Hauman; *South America*: Luis Vinker; *Spain*: José Maria Garcia, José Luis Hernández, Manuel Villuendas, Francisco Ascorbe; *Sweden*: A.Lennart Julin and Owe Fröberg; *Switzerland*: Fulvio Regli and Alberto Bordoli; *Syria and Arab world*: Fouad Habbash; *UK*: Peter Matthews and Ian Hodge; *USA*: Scott Davis and FAST, *Track Newsletter*, Roger Cass and Hal Bateman; *Yugoslavia*: Ozren Karamata. Also national federation lists from Belarus, Iceland, Luxembourg.

General assistance: Patrice Bertignon, Roberto Quercetani, Silvio Garavaglia, Carlos Fernández, Pino Mappa, Luigi Mengoni, Nejat Kök and Palle Lassen. Computer expertise: Rob Whittingham. My apologies to anybody whose name I may have missed.

Finally a very special thanks to Fulvio Regli, who has told me that, having celebrated his 70th birthday last year, that he has made his last contribution to the ATFS Annual. Throughout the history of the ATFS Annual he has been a tower of strength. He and Roberto Quercetini produced its foreruner with the 50 Best European Performances of 1949 and they went on to be the General Editors of the 1951to 1955 International Athletics Annuals.

Peter Matthews

MEMBERS OF THE ATFS
(ASSOCIATION OF TRACK AND FIELD STATISTICIANS)

Executive Committee
President
Bob Sparks GBR
Secretary General
Scott Davis USA
Treasurer
Palle Lassen DEN
Past Presidents
Rooney Magnusson Swe
Dr Don Potts USA
Dr Roberto Quercetani ITA
Committee
Jiří Havlín TCH
Paul Jenes AUS
A.Lennart Julin SWE
Nejat Kök TUR
Peter J Matthews GBR
Yves Pinaud FRA
Luis R Vinker ARG-SAm
Area representatives
Gert le Roux RSA-Afr
Bernard Linley TRN-CAC
Tatsumi Senda JPN-Asi

Members *As at 1 Feb 1995*
Argentina
Ruben Aguilera
Edgardo Fontana
Luis R.Vinker

Australia
Ron Casey
Paul Jenes
Stephen Lock
Fletcher McEwen
Ray McFadden
Michael J McLaughlin
David Tarbotton

Austria
Karl Graf
Erich Kamper (HM)
Dr Georg Werthner

Belgium
André de Hooghe
Alain Monet
Bermuda
Robert Oliver

Brazil
José C Gonçalves
Ulf Lagerström

British Virgin Islands
Reynold O'Neal

Bulgaria
Georgi Kabarov
Grigor Khristov
Alexander Vangelov

Canada
Paul F Houde
Bill McNulty
Tom MacWilliam
Ted Radcliffe
Cecil Smith

Chile
J Francisco Baraona

China
Gao Dianmin

Croatia
Mladen Delic

Cuba
Prof. Jesús Argüelles
Basilio Fuentes
Severo Nieto

Cyprus
Antonios Dracos

Czech Republic
Milos Alter
Vladimir Braun
Svatopluk Dubský
Ludek Follprecht
Pavel Formánek
Přemysl Hartman
Jiří Havlín
Stanislav Hrnčiř
Dr Vladimír Jorda
Vaclav Klvaňa
Otto Kudelka
Franti šek Macák
Miroslav Malý
Karel Míšek
Miroslav Ondruška
Josef Potuček
Milan Skočovský
Dr Lubomír Slavíček
Jiří Stavjař
Vladimit Takačev (P)
Milan Urban
Vladimír Višek
Josef Zdychynec

Denmark
Palle Lassen
Valborg Lassen
Erik Laursen
Egon Rasmussen
Emanuel Rose

Ecuador
Ramiro Almeida
Fausto Mendoza

Estonia
Leo Heinla
Jaan Otsason
Eugen Piisang
Ants Teder
Erlend Teemägi

Finland
Matti Hannus
Juhani Jalava
Erkki Kiilunen
Asko Koski
Esa Laitinen
Pekka Rinne (P)
Esko Saarinen
Arvo Siltanen
Björn-Johan Weckman (HM)

France
André Alberty
Patrice Bertignon
Alain Bouillé
Jacques Carmelli
Jean-Louis Absin de Cassière
Vincenzo Guglielmelli
André Halphen
Guy Kerfant
Gérard Leconte
Robert Pariente (HM)
Jean-Claude Patinaud
Yves Pinaud
Daniel Urien

Georgia
Yevgeniy Gagua

Germany
Walter Abmayr
Klaus Amrhein
Dr Hans-Peter Car
Werner Gessner
Emmerich Götze
Max Heilrath
Raymund Herdt
Heinrich Hubbeling
Dieter Huhn
Heinz Klatt
Winfried Kramer
Rolf von der Laage
Dr Karl Lennartz
Jürgen Martin
Ekkehard zur Megede
Reinhard Müller
Axel Schäfer
Fritz Steinmetz (HM)
Otto Verhoeven

Greece
Akis Andrikopoulos
Angelos Cocconis
John A Kyriacos
Karolos Sargologos
Leandros J Slavis
Charalambos Zannias (P)

Hungary
Endre Jahlich
György Lévai
Zoltán Subert
Gabriel Szabó
Dr István Zahumenszky

India
Ranjit Bhatia
Rameshchandra G Kharkar
R Murali Krishnan
Norris Pritam

Iran
Fred Sahebjam

Ireland
Fionnbar Callanan
Liam Hennessy
Tony O'Donoghue

Israel
David Eiger
Moshe Genuth
Prof. Uri Goldbourt

Italy
Marco Buccellato
Ottavio Castellini
Lucio Celletti
Prof. Paulo de Bartolomeis
Gianni Galeotti
Tiziano Gambalonga
Silvio Garavaglia
Michelangelo Granata
Raul Leoni
Fabio Majocchi
Giorgio Malisani
Gabriele Manfredini
Giuseppe Mappa
Salvatore Massara
Danilo Massone
Gianni Menicatti
Matteo Piombo
Dr Roberto Quercetani (HM)
Dr Giorgio Rizzoli
Mauro Rossi
Carlo Santi
Pier Paulo Temeroli

Jamaica
Richard G Ashenheim

Japan
Atsushi Hoshino
Naoshi Ito
Wakaki Maeda
Yoshimasa Noguchi
Tatsumi Senda
Isao Sugawara
Seiichi Tanabe

Latvia
Andris Stagis

Malaysia
Balwant Singh Kler
Datuk Gurbaksh Singh Kler

Mexico
Prof. Jorge Molina Celis

Netherlands
Anton de Groot
Nic Lemmens
Louis Weisscher

New Zealand
Barry Hunt
Dr Hugh Morton

Norway
Hans T Halvorsen
Tore Johansen
Jan Jørgen Moe
Ingmund Ofstad
Einar Otto Øren
Ole Petter Sandvig
Bernt A Solaas
Magne Teigen

Papua New Guinea
Bob Snow

Philippines
Col Romulo A Constantino
Sy Yinchow

Poland
Marek Drzewowski
Wojciech Gaczkowski
Zygmunt Gluszek
Daniel Grinberg
Henryk Kurzynski
Zbigniew Lojewski
Leszek Luftman (P)
Adam Parczewski
Henryk Paskal
Maciej Petruczenko
Stefan J K Pietkiewicz
Jozef Pliszkiewicz
Janusz Rozum
Marian Ryakowski
Maciej Rychwalski
Leslaw Skinder
Tadeusz Smolarski
Wlodzmierz Szymanski
Janusz Wasko
Edward Wiecek
Tadeusz Wolejko

Portugal
Luis Leite
Luis O Lopes

Romania
Adrian Ionescu
Nicolae Marasescu
Romeo Vilara
Tudor Vornicu

Russia
Vladimir Andreyev
Nikolay Ivanov
Rostislav V Orlov
Vladimir A Otkalenko (HM)
Vladimir Spychkov
Sergey Tikhonov

Singapore
Ong Teong Cheng

Slovakia
Róbert Blaho
Peter Horváth
Alfons Juck
Ladislav Krnač
Marián Malek

South Africa
Naomi Beinart
Riël Haumann
De Villiers Lamprecht
Gert J J le Roux
Harry Lombaard
Allister Matthews
Hans Prinsloo
John van Wyk
Fritz Vermaak

Spain
Andres de Acuña
Juan-Manuel Alonso
Francisco Ascorbe
Felix Capilla
Josep Corominas
Pedro Escamilla
José María García
Ignacio Romo
Alberto Sánchez
Manuel Villuendas

Sweden
Mats Åkesson
Owe Fröberg
Jöran Hedberg
A.Lennart Julin
Ove Karlsson
Rooney Magnusson (HM)
Stig L Nilsson (HM)
Ture Widlund

Switzerland
Alberto Bordoli
Antonin Heyda
Fulvio Regli (HM)

Syria
Fouad Habbash

Trinidad & Tobago
Bernard A Linley

Turkey
Turhan Göker
Nejat Kök
Cüneyt E Koryürek
I Süreyya Yigit

Ukraine
Leonid Epshteyn
Anatoliy K Kashcheyev

UK
Ian Buchanan
Mark Butler
Mark Cawte
Justin Clouder
Eric L Cowe
Leslie J Crouch
Dr David P Dallman
Stan Greenberg
Roger W H Gynn
Ian M M Hodge
Andrew Huxtable (HM)
Richard Hymans
Tony Isaacs
Alan Lindop
Peter H Lovesey
Tim Lynch-Staunton
Norris D McWhirter (HM)
David Martin
Peter V Martin
Peter J Matthews
Stuart Mazdon
Ted O'Neill
Lionel Peters
Ian R Smith
Bob Sparks
M David Terry
Melvyn F Watman
Rob Whittingham

USA
Jon W Alquist
David A Batchelor
Hal Bateman
Jed Brickner
Dave Carey
Tom Casacky
Roger Cass
Pete Cava
Gene Cherry
Scott S Davis
Wally Donovan
James O Dunaway
Tom Feuer
Edward C Gordon
Robert Hersh
Jeff Hollobaugh
Mike Hubbard
David Johnson
Michael Kennedy
Dr Clifford E Larrabee
Frank Litsky
Roar Lund (P)
Steven McPeek
Dr Bill Mallon
Dr David E Martin
Alan Mazursky
Cordner B Nelson
Rich Perelman
Jack Pfeifer
Martin A Post
Dr Donald H Potts (HM)
Shawn Price
Stan Saplin
Kevin Saylors
Alan Sigmon
James I Spier
Carol R Swenson
Michael Takaha
Robert Womack
Frank Zarnowski

Yugoslavia
Olga Acic
Ozren Karamata

In Memoriam -died in 1994
Albert D Nelson USA
Heinz Vogel (HM)
died in 1995
Jean Creuzé

DRUG BANS

Automatic disqualification for athletes found to have used anabolic steroids was introduced by the IAAF from 1 January 1975. The first athlete to be disqualified from a major competition had been Eduard de Noorlander (Ned), sixth in the 1969 European decathlon, and drugs testing had been introduced at the Olympic Games in 1972. In addition to testing at competitions, random testing out of competition has been introduced by several national federations in recent years.

In 1990 the IAAF Doping Commission produced procedural guidelines for doping controls. Copies of their booklet are available from the IAAF. At the IAAF Congress held in Tokyo in August 1991 it was determined that for serious doping offences athletes would henceforth receive a minimum four year suspension.

Surprise out-of-competition testing has produced a higher proportion of positive tests, and the number of these was doubled in 1994 compared to 1993, with a concentration on top athletes.

The following cases were reported of athletes failing drug tests in 1994

Suspension: Life - life ban, 4y = 4 years, 3m = 3 months, P = pending hearing

Name	*Date*	*Suspension*
Men		
Vadim Bavikin ISR	Apr	4y
Alexei Bazarov ISR	25 Jul	4y
József Belak HUN	26 Feb	P
Martin Bremer GER	2 Oct	4y
Marcus Browning GBR	31 Jul	4y
Abdel Chaghrouchini FRA	20 Feb	3m
Angus Cooper NZL	5 Mar	3m
Hassan Darwish EGY	29 Jun	4y
Tritto Domenico ITA	21 May	4y
Horace Dove-Edwin SLE	26 Aug	P
Andrey Dydalin RUS	27 Feb	3m
Paul Edwards GBR	14 Aug	4y
Freddy Fernando Carza ECU		
Robert Foster JAM	26 Aug	P
Mike Gravelle USA		
Gheorge Guset ROM	17 Jun	4y
Claus-Peter Heinbach GER	22 Jan	4y
Hu Gangjun CHN	17 Apr	3m
Chidi Imoh NGR	11 Jun	4y
Sergey Kirmasov RUS	23 May	4y
Kalman Konya HUN	4 Jun	4y
Jean-Pierre Lautredoux FRA	20 Feb	2y
Colin Mackenzie GBR	24 Jul	3m
José Luis Molina CRC	28 May	3m
Aston Morgan JAM		
Aham Okeke NOR	12 Jul	3m
	Dec	
Piotr Perzylo POL	4 Jun	3m
Vladimir Piskunov UKR	25 Jul	4y
James Shelton USA		4y
Sergey Sokov BLR		3m
Stavros Tsitouras GRE	28 Mar	4y
Majej Urban TCH	2 Jun	P
Solomon Wariso GBR	1 Jul	3m
Tim Williams USA	10 Mar	4y
Mohammed Zouak MAR	5 Jun	4y
Women		
Olga Bogoslovskaya RUS	5 Jun	4y
Sofia Bozhanova BUL	8 Aug	4y
Dai Yan CHN M or F?	11 Jul	4y
Christa Eschenbach GER	4 Jun	3m
Han Qing CHN	14 Oct	4y
Ulrike Heidelmann GER	17 Jul	4y
Gea Johnson USA		
Hedvika Korosak SVK	12 Jun	4y
Ella Kovacs ROM	18 Jun	3m
Liu Wanjie CHN	11 Jul	4y
Yelena Lysak RUS	30 Jul	4y
Vladimira Malátová TCH	29 May	4y
Dalia Matuseviciene LIT		
Diane Modahl GBR	18 Jun	4y
Magdalena Nedelcu ROM	17 Jun	P
Doina Nugent IRL	15 May	3m
Florina Pana ROM	19 Apr	4y
Qiu Qiaoping CHN	26 Sep	P
Agnieszka Stanczyk POL	19 Mar	4y
Sun Caiyun CHN	1 Mar	3m
Petra Vaideanu ROM	19 Apr	4y
Jocelyne Villeton FRA	26 Jun	3m
Natalya Voronova RUS	1 Jun	3m

The above 2 year bans given by national federation under investigation by the IAAF.

To add to 1993

Men		
Ezekiel Bitok KEN	12 Dec	3m
Calvin Harrison USA	Jul	3m
Juan Vincente Trull ESP	24 Oct	4y
Steve Wotaw USA	10 Oct	3m
Women		
Mariana Florea ROM		P

Peter Gordon GBR, included on the 1993, was reinstated and exonerated in 1994.

DIARY OF 1994

By Mel Watman and Peter Matthews

Chronological survey of highlights in major events in the world of track and field athletics during the year.

JANUARY

14 – Moscow, Russia. The first world indoor record of the year went to Inna Lasovskaya, who triple jumped 14.61 to smash the mark of 14.47 by Inessa Kravets.

22 – Ludwigshafen, Germany. Nicole Rieger set a European indoor pole vault record of 3.91.

Auckland, New Zealand. Daniela Costian threw the discus 68.72 for a Commonwealth record.

23 – Tokyo Half Marathon, Japan. After a great battle with Dionicio Ceron (60:28), world champion Vincent Rousseau set a European half marathon best of 60:23. The 10k mark was reached in 28:06, 20k in 57:15.

27 – Moscow, Russia. Inna Lasovskaya claimed her second world indoor triple jump record of the month, with 14.78 – a mark superior to her outdoor personal best of 14.70.

28 – Clermont-Ferrand, France. Six days after her previous exploit, Nicole Rieger raised the European indoor pole vault record to 4.00.

29 – GBR v Russia, Glasgow. Britain won the men's match 74-63, Russia the women's 74-41. Linford Christie's win at 60m over Colin Jackson, 6.56 to 6.57, was the highlight.

30 – Osaka Marathon, Japan. In the closest ever top marathon, Tomoe Abe just held off Nobuko Fujimura, both credited with a Japanese women's record of 2:26:09, with Junko Asari third one second behind. Seven Japanese finished inside 2:28:30, all with personal bests.

FEBRUARY

1 – Moscow, Russia. Irina Privalova easily defeated Merlene Ottey over 50m, 6.03 to 6.18, trimming her own official world indoor record of 6.04. In 1993 Privalova had a time of 6.00 ruled out by the IAAF as the timing camera was not properly aligned with the finish line.

4 – Moscow, Russia. Merlene Ottey (33), appointed a roving ambassador by the Jamaican Government, bounced back by winning a 50m race in a world record 6.00. At the same meeting a Russian team of Natalya Zaytseva, Olga Kuznyetsova, Yelena Afanasyeva and 41 year-old Yekaterina Podkopayeva set a world 4x800m record of 8:18.71 (2:04.7 average) while Yelena Lysak triple jumped 13.91 for a world junior indoor best.

Millrose Games, New York. Greg Foster returned from a short 'retirement' to win the 60mh, his 10th win at this meeting.

Wuppertal, Germany. Javier Sotomayor won the high jump to music contest at 2.40, from Steve Smith's Commonwealth record 2.38.

6 – Grenoble, France. As with the women, it was a Russian triple jumper who claimed the first men's world indoor record of the season. Leonid Voloshin leapt 17.77 at to add 1cm to Mike Conley's 1987 mark. It surpassed his all-time (outdoor) best of 17.75.

Inna Lasovskaya: the first world indoor record of the year

9 – Ghent, Belgium. Colin Jackson, whose previous best was 7.41 in 1989, clocked 7.38 for a European indoor 60m hurdles record.
11 – Madrid, Spain. At this super-fast sprint venue, Irina Privalova just missed Merlene Ottey's new world indoor 50m figures with her European record of 6.01. Five days earlier, in Vienna, she had been unofficially timed at 5.99 on the way to a 6.95 60m time.
12 – UK v USA, Glasgow. Britain won the men's match 79-60 and the women's 69-59. Colin Jackson equalled the world indoor record 60m hurdles 7.36. The time was originally announced as 7.35 but closer scrutiny of the photo added 1/100th to match Greg Foster's controversial 1987 mark.
13 – Liévin, France. Inna Lasovskaya claimed her third world indoor record of the season by triple jumping 14.90. Irina Privalova beat Merlene Ottey (7.02) in a 6.93 60m, just 1/100th outside her own world record, and followed with a 22.16 200m to miss her European record also by a hundredth.

Tokyo Marathon, Japan. Steve Moneghetti with 2:08:55 had his first marathon win for four years, from Vincent Rousseau, who set a Belgian record of 2:09:08.
18/19 – AAA Indoor Championships, Birmingham. Mike Rosswess handed Linford Christie his first loss to a British athlete at 60m for six years. Both ran 6.56, with Colin Jackson third at 6.57.
19 – Sydney, Australia. Debbie Sosimenko set her third Commonwealth hammer record of the year with 62.38.
20 – Allston, Massachusetts, USA, Eamonn Coghlan (41) became the oldest sub-four minute miler with an indoor time of 3:58.15. The previous world veteran's record indoors was his own 4:01.39. The Irishman still holds the absolute record with 3:49.78 in 1983.

Landau, Germany. Nicole Rieger raised her European indoor pole vault record to 4.01.
23 – Sochi, Russia. Olga Kuzenkova improved her world hammer record from 65.40 to 66.84.
25 – Bucharest, Romania. Mihaela Melinte (18) threw the hammer 65.48, a world junior record.
26 – Dortmund, Germany. Rieger again, with a vault of 4.02.

MARCH

1 – Karlsruhe, Germany. Linford Christie, faster than ever before indoors approaching his 34th birthday, set a European 60m record of 6.48. Nicole Rieger cleared 4.08 at the second attempt for a world pole vault record. China's Sun Caiyun (holder of the outdoor record of 4.11 and previous indoor mark of 4.07) cleared 4.08 at the third try but was disqualified (3-month ban) for a drugs offence and lost a share in the new record.
4-5 – US Indoor Championships, Atlanta. Held out of New York for the first time since 1969, there was a record championships attendance of 19,080 on the Saturday. There were American records from Gwen Torrence in heat (22.84) and final (22.74) of the 200m and from Jackie Joyner-Kersee, 7.13 long jump. Torrence also won the 60m, but JJK fell when leading the 60mh.
6 – Sindelfingen, Germany. Colin Jackson obliterated the world indoor 60m hurdles record of 7.36 with the startling time of 7.30. This was just a few kilometres from Stuttgart where he set the world 110m hurdles record of 12.91.

Los Angeles Marathon, USA. Paul Pilkington was supposed to be the hare but after reaching halfway well clear in 65:13 and feeling good he decided to keep going. He finished 39 sec clear in 2:12:13 and instead of picking up $3000 as pacemaker he pocketed $27,000 plus a Mercedes!
11/12 – European Indoor Championships, Paris (Bercy). There was a record participation of 529 athletes from 40 nations. Colin Jackson completed an unique 60m/60m hurdles double. His flat time of 6.49 was 1/100th outside Linford Christie's newly established European record. His two golds helped Britain to its highest ever tally of five victories, but the most successful team was Russia's with nine titles – among them Inna Lasovskaya's 14.88 triple jump, just 2cm short of her pending world record. Yekaterina Podkopayeva, the 1500m winner, became at 41 the oldest athlete ever to win a major international track championship, while Nelli Cooman took advantage of Irina Privalova's absence to notch up her sixth European 60m title. Jackson was one of only five athletes who would go on to strike gold also at the outdoor European Championships in Helsinki five months later, the others being Du'aine Ladejo, Mikhail Shchennikov, Fernanda Ribeiro and Heike Drechsler, who won her 4th indoor long jump title. *For first six at each event see pages 606-7 of Athletics 1994.*

NCAA Indoor Championships, Indianapolis, USA. The University of Arkansas men's team won for the 11th successive year and the Louisiana State women's team had their fifth win in eight years. Lawrence Johnson's collegiate record 5.83 pole vault was the top mark. Erick Walder won the long jump and triple jump for the third successive year.

20 – Kyongju, Korea. Manuel Matias clocked the fastest marathon time of the year so far, a personal best of 2:08:33, but had only one second to spare over the 1993 winner, Kim Wan-ki.

26 – IAAF World Cross Country Championships, Budapest, HUN. For the first time ever one country (Kenya) supplied the winners of all four races through William Sigei, Helen Chepngeno and the juniors Philip Mosima (17) and Sally Barsosio (16). Kenya also won three of the team titles, with Portugal taking the senior women's honours. The overwhelming African presence was most apparent in the senior men's race, the first 12 places being filled by Africans. Winners of the World Cross Challenge, based on points accumulated during the winter, were Haile Gebrselassie and Catherina McKiernan. *For leading results see page 607 of Athletics 1994.*

Helen Chepngeno: helped Kenya supply all four winners at the World Cross

APRIL

2 – Franconville, France. Thierry Toutain set a European 50km track walk record of 3:45:24.2.

7 – **Chinese Walks Championships**, Beijing. Bo Lingtang won the 20km in a time of 1:18:03.3. This was at first thought to be a world track record, but it transpired that the race was on the road. Gao Hongmiao's 41:37.9 was the women's fastest 10k time of 1994.

16 – New Orleans, USA. William Sigei was credited with a world 10k road best of 27:24 on a point-to-point course.

El Paso, Texas, USA. Obadele Thompson (18) of Barbados was timed at 10.08 for 100m at high altitude (1130m) for a world junior record, finishing third in a race won by Olapade Adeniken in an African record-equalling 9.95. The tailwind was 1.9m/sec.

16-17 – Mt. San Antonio College Relays, Walnut, California, USA. A Santa Monica Track Club team of Michael Marsh (20.0), Leroy Burrell (19.6), Floyd Heard (19.7) and Carl Lewis (19.4) set a world 4x200m record of 1:18.68. Their previous mark of 1:19.11 was also bettered by a World All-Stars team, for whom Britain's John Regis was timed at 19.1 on the anchor leg for the fastest split on record.

17 – IAAF World Road Relay (Ekiden) Championship, Litochoro, Greece. African men's teams filled the first four places over the marathon distance, with Morocco winning by almost a minute from Ethiopia with a severely under-strength Kenya third. In the women's race Russia ran out easy winners ahead of Ethiopia.

London Marathon, GBR The world's top marathon runner of 1993, Dionicio Ceron, was hoping to run close to 2:07, but high winds on the day persuaded him to bide his time and concentrate on victory in good time (2:08:53). With the late withdrawal of the Chinese, the women's race became a dawdle with Katrin Dörre of Germany winning the event for a third successive year but in a time (2:32:34) that was the slowest in the race's history.

Rotterdam Marathon, Netherlands. Later in the day, on the course which is widely accepted as the world's fastest, Vincent Rousseau posted a time of 2:07:51, the world's quickest since 1988. The Belgian covered the first half in 64:55, the second in 62:56. It was his third sub-2:10 in the space of six months. Miyoko Asahina was first woman home in the Japanese record time of 2:25:52.

18 – Boston Marathon, USA. An advantageous wind as well as the overall slightly downhill course led to fast times galore. Cosmas Ndeti, a surprise winner in 1993 in 2:09:33, this time registered a course record of

2:07:15 (62:15 for the second half!) to become the fifth fastest marathoner in history, while close behind Andrés Espinosa became the sixth quickest with 2:07:19. Jackson Kipngok, who had run 2:16:33 in his only previous marathon, clocked 2:08:08 just ahead of Hwang Young-cho, who, in his first race since winning the Olympic title, ran his best ever time of 2:08:09. A record number of 11 men broke 2:10. Uta Pippig of Germany put together halves of 70:48 and 70:57 for a time (2:21:45) that has only ever been surpassed by Ingrid Kristiansen (2:21:06) and Joan Benoit (2:21:21), both in 1985. Olympic champion Valentina Yegorova smashed the Russian record with 2:23:33 and South Africa's Elana Meyer made her debut in third place with an African record of 2:25:15.
28-30 – Penn Relays, Philadelphia, USA. The 100th running of this famous meeting. There was a record attendance of 43,830 on the Saturday.

MAY

6 – London, GBR. Fourteen world mile record holders from Sydney Wooderson (1937) to Noureddine Morceli (1994) attended a gala dinner at the Grosvenor House Hotel to celebrate the 40th anniversary of Roger Bannister's first sub-four minute mile.
7 – Fana, Norway. Bernardo Segura of Mexico smashed the world record for the 20k track walk with a time of 1:17:25.6. On the way he covered 15,577.3m in the hour, the best on record. Mexico lost a world record at the same meeting when Raúl González's 1979 50k figures were broken by René Piller of France with 3:41:28.2.
14-15 – Copa America (America's Cup), Manaus, Brazil. *See Championships section for winners.*
19-21 – US Junior Colleges Championships, Odessa, Texas Tim Montgomery (19), whose fastest 100m time last year was 10.61, was timed in a sensational 9.96 (1.7m wind), but it was not forwarded for ratification as a world junior record as the track was found to be 4cm short and the wind gauge was incorrectly placed on the outside of the track where it would be more sheltered by stands. Second was Daniel Effiong at 9.98.

Spot the world mile record breaker. The stars at the Bannister Memorial dinner are (front): Roger Bannister; (second row from left) John Landy, Seb Coe, Noureddine Morceli, Sydney Wooderson; (third row) Filbert Bayi, Peter Snell, Derek Ibbotson; (fourth row) Herb Elliott, Arne Andersson, Michel Jazy (back row) John Walker, Jim Ryun and Steve Cram

21 – São Paulo, Brazil. The first IAAF/Mobil Grand Prix meeting of the year. There were nine world leading performances, including a 5.92 pole vault by Dean Starkey.
22 – New York Games, USA. Long jumping outdoors for the first time in 1994, Jackie Joyner-Kersee produced an American record of 7.49 (1.3m wind) for the second longest leap in history, 3cm below the world record. Carl Lewis won his first long jump competition since the 1992 Olympics at 8.45w.
28 – Bruce Jenner Classic, San José, USA. Gail Devers said that she "got sluggish" in the middle of her 100m race, but she still ran a remarkable 10.77w (+2.3m/s). Daniel Effiong ran the fastest time of 1994 so far at 200m with a Nigerian record 20.10 (-0.2 wind) and Jackie Joyner-Kersee maintained her brilliant form by long jumping 7.30.
28-29 – Götzis, Austria. Eduard Hämäläinen won the decathlon for the second successive year with 8735 (adding 11 points to his best) from Henrik Dagård 8359. Sabine Braun won the heptathlon with 6665 from Larisa Turchinskaya 6596 and Rita Ináncsi 6573.
29 – European Men's Clubs Cup, Malaga, Spain. Winner Larios Madrid (Spain) *See Championships section for details.*

European Women's Clubs Cup, Schwechat, Austria. Winner Levski Sofia (Bulgaria). *See Championships section for details.*

La Courneuve, France. Paul Tergat ran 42:12 for 15k for a world road best.
31 – Comrades Marathon, Durban to Pietermaritzburg, South Africa. Former US marathon great Alberto Salazar made a remarkable comeback to win this 86.7km (53.87 miles) race (uphill this year) in 5:38:39. First women was Valentina Lyakhova 6:41:23.

JUNE

1 – Bratislava, Slovakia. The women's world triple jump record came under threat as Inessa Kravets jumped 14.91 (+1.4m) in the third round, but was passed in the fifth round by Inna Lasovskaya whose personal best 14.94 (+0.2m) moved her to fourth on the world all-time list. Biryukova was third with 14.62 and second and third were world bests for those places. World bests for the year so far were set at 400mh by Samuel Matete (48.24) and Sally Gunnell (54.74).
1-4 – NCAA Championships, Boise, Idaho, USA. Led by Erick Walder's LJ/TJ double, the University of Arkansas won the men's title for the third successive year with 83 points, from UTEP 45 and Tennessee 38. Louisiana State won a record 8th successive women's title with 86 from Texas 43 and UCLA 42. At 831m altitude. Holli Hyche won the 100m in 11.23, after a world leading 11.03 semi, but after a 22.41 heat eased down in the 200m down when she felt her hamstring tightening and was beaten by Merlene Frazer (22.49w). There were third successive titles for José Parrilla (800m), Walder (LJ) and Brent Noon (SP). *See USA section for winners.*
1-5 – Chinese Championships, Beijing. Ren Ruiping (19) added 7cm to her own world junior triple jump record with a leap of 14.36 on the first day. *See China section for winners.*
4 – Hengelo, Netherlands. Haile Gebrselassie became Ethiopia's first world record breaker on the track when breaking Said Aouita's 1987 5000m mark of 12:58.39 with a time of 12:56.96. His kilometre splits were 2:36.6, 5:13.7, 7:50.9 and 10:28.3, with the final kilometre covered in a searing 2:28.7 (last three laps of 60.4, 60.6 and 57.9).

Prefontaine Classic. Eugene, USA. Sergey Bubka's 5.95 vault was the best ever in the USA.
5 – Lahti, Finland. Mick Hill won the Golden Javelin event with 86.36 from Juha Laukkanen 85.54 and Gavin Lovegrove 85.46.

Sevilla, Spain. Javier Sotomayor recorded the best high jump of 1994, 2.42, at this Grand Prix II meeting, before taking two attempts at a world record 2.46. Other top marks included 17.86w (+5.7) triple jump by Denis Kapustin, 83.00 hammer by Igor Astapkovich, and world bests to date of 12.65 for 100mh by Svetla Dimitrova and 71.40 javelin by Natalya Shikolenko.
7 – Innsbruck, Austria. Kareem Streete-Thompson beat Mike Powell, 8.33 to 8.32, after Powell had won 34 successive long jump competitions from 1992.
8 – Golden Gala, Rome, Italy. Seven world-leading marks for 1994 were recorded: Samson Kitur 400m in 44.32, Johnny Gray, just 11 days away from his 34th birthday, ran 1:43.73 for 800m, his 23rd time under 1:44, Vénuste Niyongabo took the 1500m in a Burundi record of 3:35.10, Eliud Barngetuny 3000m steeplechase 8:17.06, Samuel Matete 400mh 48.11 and Svetla Dimitrova 100mh 12.64.
10 – **St Denis**, France. Haile Gebrselassie fell victim to Khalid Skah's deadly kick as the Moroccan edged past the Ethiopian entering the final straight to win the 5000m by a stride in 13:10.51. At 200m Frank Fredericks beat Michael Johnson, 20.45 to 20.49, and Marie-José

Pérec outdipped Gwen Torrence, 22.61 to 22.63.
10 – **Monte Carlo**, Monaco. Official opening of the IAAF's new offices.
11-12 – **Japanese Championships**, Tokyo, Japan. The Kenyan Daniel Njenga set a world junior 3000m steeplechase record of 8:19.21. *See Japan section for winners.*

AAA Championships ,Sheffield. Linford Christie took advantage of strong wind assistance to run 10.03w in his semi-final and then clocked the fastest 100m ever in Britain under any conditions with 9.91w (+3.7). It was his seventh AAA 100m title, to tie the event record set by E McDonald Bailey and his 25th national title, including indoors and UKs. That is the record for a man, but is left behind by the women's record, which Judy Oakes extended to 33 with her 12th AAA shot title, in her second week of return from retirement. Commonwealth records were established by Kate Staples (3.65 PV) and Michelle Griffith (14.08 TJ). *See UK section for winners.*
12 – Duisburg, Germany. Nicole Rieger became the first European woman to vault 4 metres outdoors, clearing precisely that height.
14-18 – US Championships, Knoxville, Tennessee. Scott Huffman added a centimetre to Joe Dial's 1987 US record with a first-time clearance at 5.97. Also setting US records were Lance Deal (82.50 hammer) and Sheila Hudson-Strudwick (14.23 triple jump). The most exciting contest of a poorly attended meeting, missing many top US athletes, was the long jump. Kareem Streete-Thompson jumped 8.64w in the second round to head Mike Powell (8.51 fourth round) until, with his final leap, the world record holder landed at 8.68w. Jackie Joyner-Kersee completed a double with 12.88 100mh and 7.14w LJ (her 6th title). Dan O'Brien amassed the second best ever first day decathlon score of 4738, and after nine events was 14 points ahead of his world record pace with 8238. However, dehydration in the hot, thundery conditions slowed him to 5:16.42 in the 1500m and 8707 points, as against the 4:44.29 he needed to break his record of 8891. Hollis Conway won his 5th successive HJ title. *See USA section for winners.*
18 – Russian Under-23 Championships, Voronezh. The European women's vault record was raised to 4.01 by Marina Andreyeva.

25/26 – **European Cup Super League**, Birmingham. Germany scored a double triumph in this now annual contest. The men's team won by a record margin over Britain, 121 points to 106.5, with Russia third on 101, but the women's competition could hardly have been much closer as Germany totalled 98 points to Britain's 97 and Russia's 95. Germany and Britain thus qualified for the World Cup, the first time for Britain's women's team. That feat was later marred when Diane Modahl, winner of the 800m here, was found to have failed a drugs test earlier at Lisbon on 18 June, and Britain were relegated to third. Russia paid dearly for the mistakes of Radion Gataullin, who failed to clear a height in the pole vault, and Vera Sychugova who slipped from first to fifth on the second leg of the 4x400m relay by neglecting to cut in from lane five until near the end of her stint. Linford Christie won a sprint double (the 100m for the fifth time) and brought his number of individual cup final victories to a record seven, while Heike Drechsler had her fifth long jump success. Andrey Moruyev won the javelin with a Russian record 87.34.

Heike Drechsler: won a fifth European Cup long jump

European Cup - First League at Valencia, Spain and **Second League** groups at Dublin IRE, Istanbul TUR and Ljubljana SLO. *See Championships section for details.*

26 – IAU 100km World Challenge, Lake Saroma, Japan. Individual winners were the Russians Aleksey Volgin 6:22:43 and Valentina Shatyayeva 7:34:58. Team winners were Germany (men) and Russia (women).

29 – Lucerne, Switzerland. Derrick Adkins ran a world leading 48.06 for 400mh.

World Games, Helsinki, Finland. Jan Zelezny broke the stadium record twice with javelin throws of 88.00 and 88.04, and Vebjørn Rodal set a Norwegian 800m record of 1:44.30.

JULY

1 – Gateshead Games, GBR. Jan Zelezny produced the best javelin throw of the year to date with 91.68.

1-3 – German Championships, Erfurt. Heike Drechsler won her tenth national outdoor long jump title. *See Germany section for winners.*

2/3 – European Cups for Combined Events. In the Super League at Vénissieux, the French men and Russian women triumphed. The individual winners were Christian Plaziat (8505 decathlon) and Svetlana Moskalets (6507 heptathlon). The First League match was at Bressanone, Italy and Second League matches were held at København, Denmark and Tallinn, Estonia. *See Championships section for details.*

3 – Kokemäki, Finland. Sari Essayah set a European women's 5000m walk record of 20:34.76.

4 – Linz, Austria. After a 9.98 heat, Davidson Ezinwa scored a notable 100m victory in the Grand Prix II meeting in the African record time of 9.94. Dennis Mitchell was second in 9.97, while Linford Christie (10.01 heat) was third in 10.03 after having been left at the start. Former Canadian Mark McKoy celebrated the granting of his eligibility to represent Austria by clocking a 1994 world 110mh best of 13.15 in his new home town. Derrick Adkins continued his 400mh improvement, to a 1994 world best of 47.70, and Kareem Streete-Thompson long jumped 8.63.

6 – Athletissima '94, Lausanne, Switzerland. Burrell reclaimed the world 100m record with 9.85 (+1.2m wind). Despite a modest start he won by a metre and a half from Davidson Ezinwa (who had set an African record of 9.94 two days earlier) and Dennis Mitchell, both 9.99. Irina Privalova set a European women's record of 10.77 (+0.9m). Frank Fredericks matched the fastest 200m time of the year (20.10) and there were new world bests for 1994 from Maicel Malone with 50.05 for 400m, Sally Gunnell, 54.06 for 400mh, and Haile Gebrselassie with 27:15.00 for 10,000m.

8 – TSB Challenge, Edinburgh, GBR. Sonia O'Sullivan became the first Irish woman to set an official world record as she covered 2000m in 5:25.36, with Yvonne Murray also inside Maricica Puica's old figures of 5:28.69 with her Commonwealth record of 5:26.93.

Villeneuve d'Ascq, France. Noureddine Morceli ran 1500m in 3:30.61, but only just won as Vénuste Niyongabo improved from 3:35.10 to a startling 3:30.66. Khalid Skah's 5000m in 13:00.54 moved him to no. 4 of all time. With South Africa back in the Commonwealth, pole vaulter Okkert Brits became, with a 5.85 pole vault, the first RSA athlete for over 30 years to claim a Commonwealth record.

9 – Tuusula, Finland. Sari Essayah lowered her European women's 5000m walk record to 20:28.62.

9-10 – Balkan Games, Trikala, Greece. *See Championships section for winners.*

11-13 – Francophone Games, Bondoufle, France. Khalid Skah won his first steeplechase

Sonia O'Sullivan: the first Irish woman to set an official world record

since 1990 in 8:19.30. *See Championships section for winners.*

12 - DN Galan, Stockholm, Sweden. Diamonds worth c.$10,000 each were on offer for stadium records, and these went to Dennis Mitchell, 100m 9.97, Jeff Williams, 200m 20.19, Irina Privalova, 100m 10.90 and 200m 22.02. There were also world leading marks from Moses Kiptanui, 3000mSt 8:09.16, and Yelena Romanova, 5000m 15:05.94.

15 - TSB Games, Crystal Palace. London GBR. Tatyana Kazankina's 1984 European 3000m record of 8:22.62, unapproached as a world record until the astonishing Chinese National Games of 1993, fell to Sonia O'Sullivan. Reaching halfway in 4:10.9 as against the Russian's corresponding 4:13.2, the Irish runner produced a 62 sec last lap for a time of 8:21.64. Natalya Shikolenko tied her world leading javelin mark of 71.40.

18 - Nikaïa, Nice, France. Sonia O'Sullivan continued her great sequence of races with an Irish 1500m record of 3:59.10. Even more remarkable was the 3:59.78 behind her of Yekaterina Podkopayeva at the age of 42. It was her fastest for a decade. There were world-leading marks for 1994 also in the 3000m, Paul Bitok 7:34.36, and women's 400mh, where Kim Batten, with a pb 53.72, defeated Sally Gunnell, 53.91, for the first time. Vénuste Niyongabo again ran brilliantly to win the 1500m in 3:30.95.

20 - GBR v USA, Gateshead. The US won both matches: men 206-180, women 168-152.

20-24 - IAAF World Junior Championships, Lisbon, Portugal. Contested by a record total of 1218 athletes from 143 nations. Double gold medal winners at individual events were Daniel Komen of Kenya (5000/10,000m) and Yelena Lysak of Russia (long/triple jump) although the latter went on to fail a drugs test at the European Under-23 Cup a week later. Lysak had a great competition with Ren Ruiping, winning with 14.47w to 14.36w. Vladislav Piskunov, at 16 the youngest winner, was stripped of the hammer gold medal when he tested positive at the meeting. *See Championships section for medallists.*

22 - Bislett Games, Oslo, Norway. The legendary status of Oslo's Bislett Stadium was further enhanced when, for the second year running, the world 10,000m record was shattered. In 1993 Yobes Ondieki ran a barrier-breaking 26:58.38, and this time fellow Kenyan William Sigei registered 26:52.23. Paul Donovan led through 3000m (2:41.34, 5:23.74 and 8:05.41),

William Sigei: set an astonishing world 10,000m record in Oslo

then William Mutwol took over for splits of 10:50.56 and 13:32.71. After that Sigei proceeded to cover the second half in an astonishing 13:19.52, his last lap taking just 56.91. 6k 16:14.08, 7k 18:53.76, 8k 21:35.95, 9k 24:18.46. The crowd were delighted with six Norwegian records, including 1:43.50 for Vebjørn Rodal at 800m behind Wilson Kipketer's world leading 1:43.29. Vénuste Niyongabo had a clear win in the Dream Mile in 3:48.94 and Sonia O'Sullivan set yet another Irish record, 4:17.25 in the mile. A great duel between Jackie Joyner-Kersee and Heike Drechsler in the long jump had JJK opening with 7.26, Drechsler 7.29 in the 5th round, only for the American to respond immediately with 7.33w. Dennis Mitchell, 9.94, beat Jon Drummond, 9.99, at 100m.

24-29 - Goodwill Games, St Petersburg, Russia. Many of the world's elite competed, but it was little known Marina Pluzhnikova who accounted for the only world best with 6:11.84 for the women's 2000m steeplechase. There were world leading marks from Noureddine Morceli, mile 3:48.67, Michael Johnson, 200m 20.10 and Sally Gunnell. 400mh

53.51. Dan O'Brien again looked set to break his world decathlon record of 8891, only to ruin his final score with a pedestrian 1500m. He scored 4736 on the first day, including a pb high jump of 2.20, and needed 4:40.92 to break the record but was let down by a time of 5:10.94 for a total of 8715. *See Championships section for medallists.*

30 – Hechtel, Belgium. For the second successive year there was a world 2 miles best at this meeting. In 1993 it was 8:12.17 by Khalid Skah, this time it was 8:09.01 by Moses Kiptanui although even the new mark is markedly inferior to the record at 3000m. Lyubov Gurina, a few days short of her 37th birthday, moved to the top of the world 800m list for 1994 with a 1:56.53 800m, a world veteran's record.

30/31 – European Under-23 Cup, Ostrava, Czech Republic. Germany (men) and Russia (women) were winners of the top league. *See Championships section for details.*

31 – Sestriere, Italy. Benefiting from the 2037m altitude at this Alpine resort Sergey Bubka set his 17th world outdoor pole vault record. He cleared 6.14 with plenty to spare to claim the Ferrari Spider 348 (worth some $120,000) on offer to anyone setting a world record. Counting indoors, it was his 35th world record; he had two attempts at 5.70 followed by first time clearances at 5.90 and 6.14 before calling it a day. Falling just short of the prize was Jackie Joyner-Kersee with her second 7.49 US record long jump of the year, while in the men's event Mike Powell defeated Carl Lewis, 8.95w to 8.72w. Heike Dreschler won the women's event with 7.39w. John Regis defeated Frank Fredericks in a UK record 200m of 19.87 (+1.8) and Colin Jackson won the hurdles in 12.94 (+2.8) for his sixth sub-13.00 mark in all conditions.

AUGUST

2 – Gatorade Herculis Grand Prix, Monaco. Arguably the greatest performance of the year came from Noureddine Morceli, who had gone so close to Moses Kiptanui's world 3000m record of 7:28.96 in this stadium in 1993. He made no mistake this time. Passing 1000m in 2:29.5 and 2000m in 5:01.3, and leading throughout an amazing 2:23.8 final kilometre, the Algerian finished in 7:25.11, for an average of 59.34 per lap. The improvement to the record of 3.85 sec was the biggest since Kip Keino in 1965. Michael Johnson won the 200m in 19.94, the fastest sea level time of 1994, to beat John Regis 20.01 and Marie-José Pérec, ran a world-leading 49.95 for 400m, but, weeks later, was disqualified as she clearly stepped out of her lane on the final turn. Svetla Dimitrova tied the world lead for 100mh with 12.53.

7-14 – European Championships, Helsinki, Finland. Russia, competing as such for the first time, was the most successful nation with a total of 25 medals, of which ten were gold. Their included Irina Privalova, who gained a sprint double, and Radion Gataullin who pole vaulted 6.00 in Sergey Bubka's much remarked upon absence. Germany had the next most medals (15) but Britain – with six – was the second highest ranked in terms of gold medals. Linford Christie emulated Valeriy Borzov's three 100m titles, Colin Jackson and Sally Gunnell added to their hurdling laurels, Du'aine Ladejo took the 400m and anchored the 4x400m relay team, and Steve Backley retained his javelin title. Sonia O'Sullivan won the 3000m to become Ireland's first ever European champion, but in the longer events it was the Spanish and Portuguese who were dominant. Of the record total of 44 competing teams, 24 came away with at least one medal. In all ten world-leading marks for 1994 were recorded. The total attendance at the afternoon sessions was 254,500 with an additional 26,500 tickets sold for the morning sessions. *See Championships section for report and results.*

12/13 – USA v Africa, Durham, North Carolina. The USA won both matches: 79-69 men and 68-46 women. Highlights were excellent sprint victories by Dennis Mitchell (9.94), Michael Johnson (44.32), Gwen Torrence (10.87/21.85) and the US women's relay team who ran a year's best 42.45.

17 – Weltklasse, Zürich, Switzerland. The meeting was hampered by torrential rain at times but it did not deter Linford Christie and Noureddine Morceli. Christie made light of the downpour and 1.4m headwind to trounce the best 100m field of the year in 10.05, while Morceli, in his first major 5000m, uncorked an astonishing 52.2 last lap for victory in 13:03.85. Maria Mutola set an African 800m record of 1:55.19, the world's fastest since 1989. Moses Kiptanui ran the year's fastest 3000m steeplechase with 8:08.80.

19 – Van Damme Memorial, Brussels, Belgium. Quite the most entertaining race was the women's 1500m. The two favourites, Sonia O'Sullivan and Hassiba Boulmerka, were so preoccupied with each other that they allowed Yvonne Graham to build up a 40m lead by the bell, believing she was just the pacemaker. The former Yvonne Mai of the GDR, now married to Jamaican 400m hurdler Winthrop Graham, had other ideas and held on to win in a Jamaican record of 4:04.35! Gwen Torrence ran a pb 100m of 10.83 to beat Merlene Ottey and Irina Privalova.

21 – Köln, Germany. Dieter Baumann provided the highlight for the crowd by winning the 3000m in 7:34.69.

22-28 – Commonwealth Games, Victoria, British Columbia, Canada. Linford Christie produced the most outstanding performance with 9.91 for 100m, the second quickest of his career and a mark that only two others, Leroy Burrell and Carl Lewis, have ever bettered under legal conditions. That was one of nine winning marks which were superior to those at the European Championships. Welshman Colin Jackson equalled his Helsinki winning time of 13.08. Namibia, competing in the Games for the first time, had a winner in Frank Fredericks (19.97 200m) but South Africa – back for the first time since 1958 – failed to strike gold. Okkert Brits, a huge favourite to win the pole vault, did not register a clearance and Elana Meyer was outsprinted by Yvonne Murray (in her first race at the distance since 1985) in the 10,000m. Cathy Freeman, 200m and 400m, was the only double champion, becoming the first Australian Aboriginal athlete to win a Commonwealth title. Kenya left behind most of their celebrated runners but still amassed five victories to rank behind Australia (12) and England (11). *See Championships section for report and results.*

28 – Rieti, Italy. Benson Koech became the fastest ever teenager at 800m with a 1:43.17 victory, the world's fastest of 1994. Noureddine Morceli won the 5000m in 13:07.88 and Jon Drummond ran his third 9.99 100m of the summer.

30 – ISTAF, Berlin, Germany. Colin Jackson (110mh 13.02) and Mike Powell (LJ 8.20) they shared 20 kilogram gold bars worth in total about $240,000 for winning at all of the "Golden Four" meetings (earlier Oslo, Zürich and Brussels). Dieter Baumann outkicked Khalid Skah to win the 5000m in 13:12.47 and Sergey Bubka won the vault at 6.05, the 23rd competition in his career in which he has achieved this height or higher. Michael Johnson extended his win streak at 400m to 36 and his 44.04 was the fastest time of 1994 to that date. Merlene Ottey returned to her best to beat Gwen Torrence and Irina Privalova at 200m in 22.07.

SEPTEMBER

1-4 – South American Junior Championships, Santa Fé, Argentina. *See Championships section for winners.*

3 – IAAF/Mobil Grand Prix Final ,Paris, France. At the beautiful refurbished Charléty Stadium, the unstoppable Noureddine Morceli produced a 51.8 last lap to win the 1500m and to clinch the overall men's title worth $100,000, despite bronchitis in the week leading up to the meeting. The women's award, determined by scoring tables, went to Jackie Joyner-Kersee, who won the long jump with 7.21. World bests for 1994 came from Merlene Ottey, who at 34 tied her own Commonwealth 100m record of 10.78, Mike Conley triple jump (outdoors) 17.68 and Marie José Pérec, 400m 49.77.

4 – McDonald's Games, Sheffield, GBR. Jan Zelezny showed his liking for the stadium, where he had set the world record a year earlier, with the best javelin throw of the year, 91.82.

ICMR Mountain Racing World Cup, Berchtesgaden, Germany. *See Championships section for leading results.*

6 – Madrid, Spain. Michael Johnson became the first ever to break 44 sec for 400m five times with a 43.90 victory. It was his 37th successive win in 400m finals, indoors or out. Colin Jackson ran the 110mh in a yearly leading 12.99.

9-11 – World Cup, Crystal Palace, London Africa's men, fielding an immensely strong track team (plus Okkert Brits in the pole vault), retained the title, with Britain finishing a close second and thus avenging their European Cup defeat by Germany. The USA, three times Cup winners, were represented by a disappointingly weak team and finished sixth, their lowest ever. On the women's side, the Europe Select team ran out comfortable winners, thanks to a massive contribution by Irina Privalova who won the 100m and 400m (a late replacement for Marie-José Pérec) and placed second to Merlene Ottey in the 200m. Cup records were broken by Javier Sotomayor, Brits, Yoelbi Quesada, Hassiba Boulmerka, Anna Biryukova and Elana Meyer, whose 10,000m time of 30:52.51 – like Brits' 5.90 vault – also broke the Commonwealth and African records. *See Championships section for results.*

10/11 – Talence, France. Dan O'Brien, with a score of 8710, became the first to score over 8700 three times in the same year. Heike Drechsler, who last contested the heptathlon in 1981 when, aged 16, she set a world junior record of 5812, made a stunning return after 13 years with a score of 6741, the year's best.

15 – TOTO meeting, Tokyo, Japan. Colin Jackson ended his season with a season's best of 12.98, his fifth legal sub-13 whereas the rest of the world's hurdlers put together can point to only four. Linford Christie beat Dennis Mitchell at 100m, 10.02 to 10.15, to bring the season's record between them to 4-3 in Christie's favour.
17-20 – Asian Junior Championships, Jakarta, Indonesia. *See Championships section for winners.*
24 – World Half Marathon Championships, Oslo, Norway. Khalid Skah, who beat German Silva by one second, and Elana Meyer who broke away at 5km to win clearly, took world half marathon titles over an undulating course in Oslo. Kenya and Romania were the team champions. 215 athletes from 48 countries took part. *See Championships section for leading results.*
25 – Berlin Marathon, Germany. Winners were Antonio Pinto and Katrin Dörre in personal bests of 2:08:31 and 2:25:15.

OCTOBER

2 – 5th Avenue Mile, New York, USA. Jason Pyrah was the men's winner in 3:52.3 and Regina Jacobs the women's in 4:27.8.
9-16 – Asian Games, Hiroshima, Japan. China, with 23 golds, dominated. Wang Junxia won the 10,000m in a world year best of 30:50.34, with a staggering 14:50.34 second 5000m. *See Championships section for medallists.*
22 – Guangzhou, China. Sun Caiyun cleared 4.12, a mark she matched at the same venue on November 25. for unofficial world women's pole vault records.
27-30 – Ibero-American Championships, Mar del Plata, Argentina. Ximena Restrepo won four gold medals, 200m, 400m and both relays for Colombia, but Brazil was the most successful nation. *See Championships section for winners.*
30 – Chicago Marathon. Luis dos Santos (2:11:16) became the first runner to win this race in two successive years since Steve Jones in 1984-5.

Catherina McKiernan: inaugural European Cross Country champion

NOVEMBER

6 – New York Marathon, USA. German Silva won in 2:11:21 despite going off course with about 800m to go, while in her first marathon Tecla Lorupe took the women's event with a Kenyan record of 2:27:37. There were a world record 29,543 finishers.
22-27 – South American (Odesur) Games, Valencia, Venezuela. Ximena Restrepo starred with a South American record 56.05 for 400mh, a season's best 51.31 for 400m and a third gold on Colombia's sprint relay team. *See Championships section for winners.*
23 – Chiba Ekiden, Japan. Men's winners were Ethiopia in 2:00:28 from Japan 2:00:57, and women's Japan by nearly three minutes in 2:15:31.
27 – Bolbec, France. The first race of the 1994/5 IAAF World Cross Challenge series. There was a Kenyan 1-2 in the men's race from Shem Kororia and James Kariuki, while in the women's Fernanda Ribeiro beat defending champion Catherina McKiernan.

DECEMBER

4 – Fukuoka Marathon. Japan. Tanzania's Boay Akonay won in 2:09:45 from Manuel Matias 2:09:50.
10 – European Cross Country Championships, Alnwick, GBR. Inaugural individual champions were Paulo Guerra and Catherina McKiernan, while the team winners were Portugal (men) and Romania (women). *See Championships section for leading results.*

REVIEW OF 1994

By Peter Matthews

The leading contenders for male athlete of the year in 1994 were Colin Jackson, Noureddine Morceli and Javier Sotomayor. Jackson was undefeated at high hurdles events, winning 18 finals at 110mh, having earlier won nine finals at 60mh indoors. Morceli, although racing more sparingly than usual, excelled at a wide range of distances and smashed the world record for 3000m, and Sotomayor was in a class of his own at the high jump, although his otherwise perfect record was slightly spoiled by his no height in poor weather in Zürich.

Noureddine Morceli in 1994

All wins except for his 800m race

Event	*Date*	*Venue - meeting*	*Time*
3000m	19 Jun	Narbonne	7:34.74
1500m	8 Jul	Villeneuve d'Ascq	3:30.61
1500m	12 Jul	Stockholm - DNG	3:34.09
1500m	15 Jul	London - TSB	3:34.72
1M	27 Jul	St Peterburg - GWG	3:48.67
3000m	2 Aug	Monte Carlo	7:25.11
		(2000m)	5:01.3
5000m	17 Aug	Zürich - WK	13:03.85
800m	21 Aug	Köln - ASV	1:44.89 (3rd)
5000m	28 Aug	Rieti	13:07.88
1500m	3 Sep	Paris - GPF	3:40.89
1500m	10 Sep	London - WCp	3:34.70

100 METRES

LEROY BURRELL regained the world record with a powerful run in Lausanne. However his season lacked depth of performances to support that, and he was beaten by Dennis

The IAAF conducted their usual world-wide poll, inviting people in the world of athletics to select their top tens of 1994. The result for men is shown, followed by my own selections and in the final column those of the international experts polled by *Track & Field News*:

IAAF position	*pts*	*PJM*	*T&FN*
1. Noureddine Morceli	3203	2	1
2. Javier Sotomayor	2721	3	3
3. Sergey Bubka	1982	8	4
4. Colin Jackson	1856	1	2
5. Linford Christie	1704	6	-
6. Leroy Burrell	1699	-	-
7. William Sigei	1654	7	7
8. Haile Gebrselasie	1445	9	
9. Dan O'Brien	807	5	6
10. Michael Johnson	804	4	5
11. Mike Powell	556		
12. Khalid Skah	495		
13. Wilson Kipketer	405		
14. Moses Kiptanui	337		10
15. Samuel Matete	267		
16. Dennis Mitchell	217		
17. Mike Conley	212		
18. Andrey Abduvaliyev	114		
19. Mikhail Shchennikov	102		
20. Dieter Baumann	78		
Jan Zelezny			8
Vénuste Niyongabo		10	9

Geir Moen, a national record as well as gold

Mitchell at the Goodwill Games and was a poor 7th in Zürich when troubled by a foot injury. The top 100m runners of the previous two years, Linford Christie, and Mitchell were closely matched. Both won the major titles they sought, Mitchell the US, Goodwill and Grand Prix, Christie the AAA, European Cup, European and Commonwealth. Mitchell had the best times, with five sub 10.00 times to Christie's three (inc. 1 wa).

Date and meeting		Christie	Mitchell
4 Jul	Linz	10.03 3rd	9.97 1st
Christie left at start by fast gun			
17 Aug	Zürich	10.05 1st	10.23 4th
19 Aug	Brussels	10.03 1st	10.12 2nd
30 Aug	Berlin B	10.03 1st	10.04 2nd
30 Aug	Berlin A	10.01 2nd	10.00 1st
3 Sep	Paris GPF	10.13 2nd	10.12 1st
15 Sep	Tokyo	10.02 1st	10.15 2nd

The edge was just with Christie on a 4-3 win-loss record, and he is the only rational candidate for number one ranking because of his clear margin of superiority at the peak of the season in Zürich and Brussels, when he left Mitchell a metre down. Jon Drummond raced consistently well; while he lost 2-11 to Mitchell and 1-4 to Burrell, he was 3-4 against Christie. Andre Cason was only 6th in the US Champs and Goodwill Games, but beat Olapade Adeniken 3-1 in July.

Davidson Ezinwa was under 10.00 three times in early July, riding the fast gun to beat Mitchell and Christie (who was left at the start) in Linz, and although he faded at the end of the year he had a 2-1 advantage over the year's best newcomer to the rankings, Donovan Bailey. Unfortunately Bailey was restricted to the relay at the Commonwealth Games, where Michael Green and Frank Fredericks picked up the medals behind Christie and Adeniken was 6th (after a positive drugs test had cost Horace Dove-Edwin his sensational silver). Bailey beat Adeniken 4-1 and Green 5-0.

Daniel Effiong was fast in the USA, but was disappointing in the major European races and was 5th in the US v Africa won by Mitchell from Drummond and Adeniken.

Carl Lewis ran 10.04 in his first race of the year and 10.14 to beat Fredericks and Bailey in Rome, but was otherwise outside 10.20; after a record 14 successive years in the top ten he is unranked for the first time since 1979.

1. Christie, 2. Mitchell, 3. Burrell,
4. Drummond, 5. Ezinwa, 6. Cason,
7. Fredericks, 8. Bailey, 9. Adeniken,
10. Green

200 METRES

MICHAEL JOHNSON is back at the top, as he was in 1990 and 1991. He lost to Frank Fredericks at St Denis and was 4th at Lausanne, behind Fredericks, John Regis and Daniel Effiong, but then he won six major races, beating Fredericks at the Goodwill Games, Monaco (his season's best 19.94) and Tokyo. He also won in Zürich from Effiong, Jeff Williams and Geir Moen. The latter took the European title from Vladislav Dologodin, with Regis missing that race through injury. Regis, came back, however, for second in the Commonwealth Games behind Fredericks and had run the year's fastest time, 19.87 at the high altitude of Sestriere ahead of Fredericks and Kevin Braunskill. Fredericks beat Regis 5-3 and Regis beat Effiong 2-1.

Braunskill and Williams were only 5th and 6th at the US Championships, surprisingly won by Ron Clark, but they were the next best Americans, with Williams winning in Edinburgh and beating Fredericks and Olapade Adeniken in Stockholm; he was 2-0 up on Moen.

The World Junior champion Tony Wheeler also had good results with 3rd at the NCAAs and a win in the US Olympic Festival.

1. Johnson, 2. Fredericks, 3. Regis, 4. Effiong, 5. Williams, 6. Adeniken, 7. Moen, 8. Dologodin, 9. Braunskill, 10. Wheeler

400 METRES

MICHAEL JOHNSON took his win streak at 400m to 37 since 1989, with two races indoors and three out. His smallest winning margin in his three outdoors was 0.53 when he won the US - Africa race in 44.32 from Antonio Pettigrew 44.88. He won in 44.04 in Berlin from Steve Lewis 44.73, and with Roger Black and Samson Kitur following outside 45 secs, and then ran the year's best 43.90 in Madrid from Sunday Bada 44.96.

Derek Mills had never ranked in the top ten before, but after only 5th in his semi at the US Champs, had a marvellous time in Europe, losing only two of his 1 races there. Overall he beat the US champion Pettigrew 3-1, Kitur 4-0, Steve Lewis 3-0 and Du'aine Ladejo 3-1.

The Grand Prix order was Mills, Pettigrew, Kitur, Black, Andrew Valmon, Darnell Hall, Ladejo. The British pair of Ladejo and Black were closely matched, 3-3 on the year, but Ladejo won the Europeans when these two were well ahead of the rest of the field, and was also 2nd in the Commonwealth Games, when he was surprised by Charles Gitonga, and at the Goodwill Games, although there video evidence seemed to indicate that the verdict should have gone to him and not to Quincy Watts. Mills was 3rd and Lewis 6th in that race.

Steve Lewis finished the season well, but lost twice to Watts, who had only four races in 1994. Valmon was below his usual form, but edges into the rankings in a season where the overall standard was down, as he beat US 2nd placer Jason Rouser 2-1 and Greg Haughton 1-0. Bada, Commonwealth 3rd, ran poorly in mid-season but finished well and just edges Haughton and Rouser, with each of whom he was 1-1.

1. Johnson, 2. Mills, 3. Pettigrew, 4. Kitur, 5. Ladejo, 6. Watts, 7. Lewis, 8. Black, 9. Valmon, 10. Bada

800 METRES

WILSON KIPKETER, not ranked previously, had a great season. He ran eight sub 1:45 times to the next best of three by seven men, and had

Michael Johnson: took 400m win streak to 37

13 wins and two seconds. His only losses were in Helsinki, when Vebjørn Rodal ran his first Norwegian record of the year 1:44.30, and in Brussels to Patrick Konchellah. However Kipketer beat both these men 2-1. At the Bislett Games he ran 1:43.29 to Rodal's second record 1:43.50, and won again in Zürich, when Konchellah was 2nd and Rodal had his one poor race of the year to place 8th. Kipketer also won in Berlin, when Benson Koech was second and Konchellah third. Konchellah was 1st or 2nd in all his other races and was Kenyan and Commonwealth champion. Koech ran this distance infrequently, but produced the year's fastest time, 1:43.17 in Rieti well ahead of William Tanui 1:44.18.

As in 1993, when there were five in the top seven, Kenyans were again dominant, with 8 of the 15 men to better 1:44.5 in 1994. Andrea Benvenuti beat Rodal to take the European title, but his season was perhaps too thin to rank above the Norwegian. The top American was Mark Everett, who won the US title and the US - Africa match from Tanui and Nixon Kiprotich, but was well beaten by Atle Douglas and Rodal at Edinburgh. Johnny Gray was, as ever, inconsistent, but ran two sub 1:44 times - in New York when he was well ahead of Benvenuti and for third place in Oslo - to take his career record to 24, well ahead of the second best (10 Joaquim Cruz).

Tanui beat Gray 2-1 and Kiprotich 4-2, and David Kiptoo beat Gray 3-0. Just missing out on the top ten were Atle Douglas, only 8th in the Europeans and beaten 3-0 by Kiprotich, Sammy Langat, who was 2-2 v Kiptoo, and James Tengelei.

1. Kipketer, 2. P Konchellah, 3. Rodal,
4. Koech, 5. Everett, 6. Benvenuti,
7. Tanui, 8. Kiptoo, 9. Gray, 10. Kiprotich

1500 METRES

NOUREDDINE MORCELI is number one for the fifth successive year, but he was chased hard by Vénuste Niyongabo. Morceli won all his six races at 1500m or 1 mile in 1994 and ran 3:30.61 in his first race, at Villeneuve d'Ascq, needing to run fast as Niyongabo was 2nd in 3:30.66, following earlier Burundian records of 3:35.18 and 3:35.10. Niyongabo went on to a series of impressive wins, including the Dream Mile in 3:48.94, but had to give best to Morceli at the Grand Prix final.

Abdi Bile did not win a race, but always ran well to retain his third ranking, beating Mohamed Suleiman 3-2, including at the Dream Mile, where the order behind Niyongabo was Bile, Steve Holman, Suleiman, David Kibet, and with 3rd place to 6th at the Grand Prix final.

Fermín Cacho had a moderate season, except that he won his main target, the Europeans, and he was also a good third in Brussels, behind Niyongabo and the exciting newcomer Azzedine Sediki, with Bile 4th, Holman 5th and Benson Koech 6th. The latter improved over 8 seconds when he ran 3:32.71 for 2nd at Nice behind Niyongabo, and also won for Africa v USA, before 3rd in the Zürich mile behind Andrey Bulkovskiy and Holman. In Köln the order was Niyongabo, Suleiman, Sediki, Bile and Koech, but Sediki was only 12th in the Grand Prix. Matthew Yates started poorly and did not make the British teams for the major championships, but was 2nd in Berlin, and 4th at the Grand Prix final and beat Atoi Boru 4-0.

Reuben Chesang is the most difficult to rank. he was unbeaten and took the Kenyan and Commonwealth titles, but did not meet any of the top names, as the other Kenyans passed those championships.

1. Morceli, 2. Niyongabo, 3. Bile,
4. Suleiman, 5. Sediki, 6. Holman,
7. Cacho, 8. Koech, 9. Yates, 10. Boru

Vénuste Niyongabo: chased Morceli hard

3000 METRES

NOUREDDINE MORCELI took the huge margin of 3.85 secs off the world record with his 7:25.11 in Monaco, where he had missed Kiptanui's mark by just 0.28 secs in 1993. In this race Haile Gebrselassie was second in 7:37.49 and Abdellah Béhar and Jim Spivey also ran under 7:40.

The best depth of times came from two other races: Nice, where Paul Bitok won in 7:34.26, and Aloÿs Nizigama, Moses Kiptanui and Bob Kennedy ran 7:35s with Spivey 5th in 7:41.09, and Köln, where Dieter Baumann won in 7:34.60 and Kiptanui, Khalid Skah, Kennedy and Salah Hissou followed under 7:39. Bitok was only 14th in this race, but had also won for Africa v USA at 3000m, well ahead of Kiptanui.

Kiptanui added the world best at 2 miles, with 8:09.01 (worth about 7:35 for 3000m) at Hechtel, the previous best was Skah's 8:12.17 at the same venue in 1993. There was another good 2 miles at Göteborg when Marc Davis beat Skah 8:12.74 to 8:12.92.

5000 METRES

FOUR MEN could have claims to rank as the world number one at 5000m in 1994: Haile Gebrselassie, Khalid Skah, Noureddine Morceli and Dieter Baumann.

Gebrselassie took the world record down to 12:56.96 with a superb run at Hengelo on 4 June. He was then, however, beaten 13:10.79 to 13:10.71 by Khalid Skah at St Denis, and was 4th behind the Kenyans William Sigei, Paul Bitok and Simon Chemoiywo at the London Grand Prix. Skah was just outside 13 minutes with big wins at Villeneuve d'Ascq (13:00.54), where Bob Kennedy, Worku Bikila and Brahim Lahlafi also broke 13:10, and Oslo (13:01.89), where there were sub 13:05 times behind him from Kennedy, Lahlafi and Salah Hissou. Then came Zürich and a devastating last lap clinching a brilliant victory for Noureddine Morceli in 13:03.85, with Fita Bayissa 2nd and Skah 3rd four seconds behind. Bikila, Lahlafi, Kennedy, Sigei and Ismael Kirui filled places 4th to 8th. Morceli won again at Rieti, beating Hissou and Chemoiywo.

Joining Morceli with an unbeaten record was Baumann, winner of the European Cup and German and European titles. His only sub-13:20 time or indeed race against the top men was at Berlin, when he beat Skah and Khalid Boulami, who went on to second in the Grand Prix behind Skah. In that race Moses Kiptanui, Hissou, Lahlafi, Aloÿs Nizigama, Kennedy and Worku were 3rd to 8th, with Fita Bayissa 9th after falling, Kirui 10th and Chemoiywo and Sigei tailed off 11th and 12th.

Rob Denmark was second in the Europeans and won the Commonwealth, but there he did not have to face the top Kenyans. although he beat Philemon Hanneck, who went on to beat Nizigama in Tokyo.

1. Morceli, 2. Skah, 3. Baumann,
4. Gebrselasie, 5. Kennedy, 6. Hissou,
7. Bikila, 8. Boulami, 9. Lahlafi, 10. Bayissa

10,000 METRES

WILLIAM SIGEI ran sensationally to smash the world record in Oslo; his 26:52.23 was especially remarkable for his 13:19.52 second 5000m. Sigei won his other two 10,000m track races at high altitude in Nairobi.

Haile Gebrselassie ran the year's second fastest time, 27:15.00 in Lausanne, but the list of the year's fastest times is dominated by two races: Oslo and Brussels. In the former William Kiptum and Armando Quintanilla were under 27:20, with Aloÿs Nizigama, Paul Tergat, Mathias Ntawalikura and Ondoro Osoro under 27:45. In Brussels Gebrselassie won in 27:20.39 and Salah Hissou, Nizigama, Tergat and Osoro broke 27:30, with Ntawalikura 6th and Vincent Rousseau, who had been second in the Europeans behind Abel Antón, 7th.

Khalid Skah won the World Cup in 27:38.74, an extraordinary time in appalling conditions, but as none of the other top men were in that race it makes him difficult to rank. The other race in which many of the fastest men met was the Kenyan Armed Forces Championship, won by Sigei in 28:27,5, from Kiptum, Joseph Kariuki, and Osoro with Tergat 6th. Hissou won the Francophone Games title, Quintanilla the Ibero-American title and Nizigama had two wins in Japan.

1. Sigei, 2. Gebrselassie, 3. Nizigama,
4. Kiptum, 5. Quintanilla, 6. Hissou,
7. Skah, 8. Tergat, 9. Osoro,
10. Ntawalikura

MARATHON

THE HIGHLY favourable conditions for the Boston marathon, a following wind with the overall downhill course, despite those hills,, make comparison of times and performances even more difficult than usual. Five of the year's six fastest times came from Boston. Cosmas N'Deti won in 2:07:15 from Andrés Espinosa, Jackson Kipngok, Hwang Young-cho and Arturo Barrios with Boay Akonay 6th.

Dieter Baumann wins the European title from a despairing Rob Denmark

Ndeti later dropped out at Chicago, Kipngok, who had been 6th at Orlando, was 6th in Berlin, Hwang won the Asian title, and Akonay won at Fukuoka with Espinosa 4th.

Vincent Rousseau won the Rotterdam marathon in 2:07:51 and went on to win in Brussels before failing to finish in New York. He had started the year with 2:09:01 in Tokyo, behind Steve Moneghetti's 2:08:55. Moneghetti's Commonwealth Games win is enough to give him the top ranking for the year.

The 1993 number one Dionicio Ceron continued his success, winning in London in 2:08:53, but then lost his position as world's best as he trailed in 16th in Fukuoka. The quality of his London win was reinforced, however, as 2nd placed Abebe Mekonnen had been 5th in Tokyo and went on to 2nd in Berlin, and 3rd placed German Silva won in New York.

Martin Fíz, who had been 12th in Boston, led a Spanish 1-2-3 in the European Championships. There António Pinto was only 9th, but he had been 2nd in Paris and was the winner in Berlin in 2:08:31.

The next fastest race had been in Kyongju, Korea, won by Manuel Matias in 2:08:33, one second head of Kim Wan-ki. Matias was 7th in the Europeans, but returned to place 2nd at Fukuoka.

1. Moneghetti, 2. Rousseau, 3. Silva,
4. Matias, 5. N'Deti, 6. Akonay, 7. Cerón,
8. Espinosa, 9. Hwang Young-cho,
10. Mekonnen

Steve Moneghetti: Commonwealth champion

3000 METRES STEEPLECHASE

MOSES KIPTANUI ranks first for the fourth successive year, running second to Matthew Birir at St Denis and then running under 8:10 three times, the fastest times of the year, in Stockholm, Zürich and Berlin, before rounding off his season with a win in the World Cup.

As usual the Kenyans were dominant, taking six of the top six placings in these rankings and seven in the top ten. Their 10th fastest was 14th in the world. Eliud Barngetuny and Richard Kosgei were 4-4 in their clashes, but the former had seven under 8:18 to five by Kosgei. The best races for depth of quality were at Berlin, Stockholm and Monaco. Stockholm was the first of these and there Kiptanui won in 8::09.16 from William Mutwol, Barngetuny, Mark Croghan, Kosgei and Patrick Sang. Barngetuny won at Monaco in 8:10.84, with Sang, Mutwol, Angelo Carosi, Bernard Barmasai and Matthew Birir under 8:15. Kiptanui again ran 8:09.16 to win in Berlin, where there were season's best under 8:12 from 2nd to 4th: Kosgei, Croghan and Abdelaziz Sahere, with Sang matching his Monaco time of 8:12.16 and Birir 6th, Alessandro Lambruschini won the European title from Carosi despite falling over, and also won at the European Cup, but he had to give best to the top Kenyans, losing 1-3 to Kosgei for instance, but he beat Sang 2-0.

The American champion, Croghan, had a fine year and although he was 1-3 down to both Kosgei and Barngetuny, beat Birir 3-0.

Johnstone Kipkoech won the Commonwealth title from Gideon Chirchir, but did not run in Europe after a win over Sang in Duisburg in June. Sahere is another who is difficult to rank, as he had only three races, dropping out at Villeneuve d'Ascq, before 4th in Zürich, behind Kiptanui, Barngetuny and Croghan and ahead of Birir and Sang, and 4th at Berlin.

1. Kiptanui, 2. Barngetuny, 3. Kosgei,
4. Croghan, 5. Kipkoech, 6. Birir,
7. Sahere, 8. Lambruschini, 9. Sang,
10. Mutwol

110 METRES HURDLES

COLIN JACKSON was top for the third successive year and once again had the greatest ever year at the event with 11 times under 13.20 and winning all his 18 finals. He retained both Commonwealth and European titles.

The closest that anyone came to defeating him was the 0.03 seconds behind that Tony Jarrett was at the Goodwill Games. Mark Crear and Mark McKoy were, however, the next best, McKoy winning the first three times they met and Crear the next four. Crear ahead on win-loss 4-3.

At the Europeans Florian Schwarthoff was 2nd, Jarrett 3rd, but Jarrett had a 4-2 advantage overall and went on to 2nd in the Commonwealth. Jarrett also won the World Cup from Allen Johnson, who beat Schwarthoff 5-1 and Jarrett 5-4, with Emilio Valle 3rd, Schwarthoff 4th and Li Tong 5th.

Reading beat Johnson 4-2, but ended his season in July due to a hamstring strain, while Johnson went on to run well at the major European meetings. Courtney Hawkins had been 4th in the US Champs behind Crear, Robert Reading and Johnson and was 2-2 with Valle, but had slightly better times. Jack Pierce just did enough for 10th ranking.

1. Jackson, 2. Crear, 3. McKoy, 4. Jarrett, 5. Johnson, 6. Reading, 7. Schwarthoff, 8. Hawkins, 9. Valle, 10. Pierce

Greatest seasons at 110mh

Name	Year	Under 13.10	Under 13.20
Colin Jackson	1994	9 + 2w	11 + 2w
Colin Jackson	1992	6	15
Roger Kingdom	1988	4	9 + 1w
Renaldo Nehemiah	1981	4 + 1w	5 + 2w
Colin Jackson	1993	3 + 2w	11 + 2w
Roger Kingdom	1989	2 + 1w	7 + 2w
Colin Jackson	1990	2	6 + 2w
Greg Foster	1991	2	6
Tony Dees	1992	2	5
Colin Jackson	1989	2w	4 + 4w
Mark McKoy	1992	1w	6 + 1w

400 METRES HURDLES

KEVIN YOUNG ended his season after just two meetings, after failing to make the final of the US Championship, but in his absence Samuel Matete and Derrick Adkins contested the position of World number one. Adkins started best but Matete, as with his finish, came through to have an overall edge 6-5 as he won their last three clashes. Matete's overall record

Colin Jackson: two titles and 16 races unbeaten

read 19 wins (plus two in Commonwealth Games prelims), 4 2nd places and 1 3rd. He ran five times under 48.00 and 22 under 49.00. Adkins's record: 16 wins, 4 2nd, 1 3rd, 1 4th; with 8 times under 48.00 and 21 under 49.00.

The only other man to beat Matete was Sven Nylander who was 2nd in the Lille GP, and Adkins was beaten by Stéphane Diagana, who split Matete and Adkins in Berlin, and by Oleg Tverdokhleb and Nylander behind Matete in Brussels.

There was a fine race in the Europeans, with the gold and silver medallists, Tverdokhleb and Nylander setting national records, 48.06 and 48.22 and the favourite Diagana 3rd in 48.23. Pedro Rodrigues improved his Portuguese record in each round of the championships to place 4th in 48.77, but had little other form in 1994 and went out in the heats of the NCAAs, won by Octavius Terry, who was also 2nd in the US Championships. Winston Graham was, as ever, consistently a threat; he was 1-6 down to Diagana but beat Nylander 5-4.

Danny Harris was released from his drugs ban by TAC and competed in six meetings, including four Grand Prix events, before the IAAF realised that he was still banned by them. At the end of the year the IAAF Council reinstated him. He is omitted from these rankings in which his form would have warranted 7th place.

The top six are well ahead of the rest and the final places are shown only after very conflicting form made a ranking exceedingly difficult. Edgar Itt was much the fastest with his 48.48 to win the German title and he was 5th in the Europeans. Shunji Karube was the best of the three Japanese to run in the low 49s as he won both Japanese and Asian titles.

1. Matete, 2. Adkins, 3. Tverdokhleb,
4. Nylander, 5. Diagana, 6. Graham, 7. Itt,
8. Terry, 9. Dollendorf, 10. Karube

HIGH JUMP

JAVIER SOTOMAYOR was once again a class apart at the top, with a record nine meetings (including two indoors) at 2.40 or better, 22 over 2.35 and 30 of his 33 competitions at 2.30 or higher. His one blemish was his no height in bad conditions in Zürich after a streak of 30 successive wins.

Troy Kemp had the next best record, beating the European champion Steinar Hoen 7-3 outdoors. After improving his British record to 2.38 indoors Steve Smith lost much of the outdoor season through injury, but showed his competitive resilience with European and Commonwealth silver medals and was 4-4 v Hoen. Smith's great rival Tim Forsyth beat him to the Commonwealth gold and had a 6-1 advantage on win-loss, but amazingly at every single one of these seven competitions Forsyth and Smith cleared the same height. Hoen beat Forsyth 9-2. Another fine competitor Artur Partyka shared the European silver with Smith, but was way below this form in most other meetings outdoors. Håkon Särnblom was 4th and Dragutin Topic 5th= at the Europeans, but the latter had the best overall record, also beating Hollis Conway 4-2 and Jean-Claude Gicquel, who had won the European Indoor silver behind Dalton Grant, 7-1. Gicquel beat Conway 6-3 and Grant 3-2. With Conway and Tony Barton just missing the top ten, there was no US jumper in the rankings. Grant was European Indoor champion at 2.37, from Gicquel 2.35 and Wolf-Hendrik Beyer 2.33, with Hoen 4th. Both Grant and Beyer were much more effective indoors than out.

Gilmar Mayo made four improvements on the South American record from 2.30 to 2.33.

1. Sotomayor, 2. Kemp, 3. Hoen,
4. Forsyth, 5. Smith, 6. Topic, 7. Särnblom,
8. Gicquel, 9. Mayo, 10. Grant
Including indoors: the last four places:
7. Grant, 8. Gicquel, 9. Beyer,
10, Särnblom

POLE VAULT

SERGEY BUBKA was again supreme, achieving his 18th world record at the high altitude of Sestriere. He passed the Europeans, at which Radion Gataullin matched the best ever clearance in a major championships of 6.00 to win a great competition. Igor Trandenkov was 2nd, Jean Galfione 3rd, Philippe Collet 4th and Denis Petushinsky 5th, Maksim Tarasov also missed the Europeans, but was second to Trandenkov at the Goodwill Games, with Bubka only third. The Americans showed improved form, with Scott Huffman's record 5.97 to take the US title. Dean Starkey was 2nd at 5.70 that day, but had two meetings over 5.90 and nine over 5.80 and was 9-7 v Huffman, who was over 5.80 four times, overall.

Bubka had the most 5.80-plus comp-etitions, 19 (including 5 indoors) and other leaders were Gataulin 10 (3 indoors), Galfione 10 (3), Trandenkov 8 (1). Pat Manson and Kory Tarpenning were closely matched, 4-4 on win-loss, both having an advantage over Petushinskiy. Okkert Brits added eight African

Javier Sotomayor: a class apart

records in 1994, culminating in a magnificent 5.90 to win the World Cup from Galfione. Brits was beaten 5-2 by Starkey but was 4-1 up on Huffman.

1. S Bubka, 2. Gataullin, 3. Trandenkov,
4. Starkey, 5. Brits, 6. Galfione, 7. Tarasov,
8. Huffman, 9. Manson, 10. Tarpenning
Adding indoors: Tarpenning up to 8th.

LONG JUMP

MIKE POWELL was again the world's best, winning once indoors and 15 out of 17 outdoors. Kareem Streete-Thompson beat him in Lausanne, when these two were followed by Stanislav Tarasenko, Ivaylo Mladenov and Roland McGhee in the best quality event of the year apart from Sestriere, and Powell also lost on count-back to Huang Geng in his final event at Tokyo.

After a year away from the event Carl Lewis returned but only jumped twice, winning in New York from Streete-Thompson, and placing second to Powell with 8.72w at Sestriere. There Powell used wind assistance and high altitude to leap to 8.95, with Streete-Thompson 3rd at 8.58w. The top five rankings went to Americans; Walder and McGhee both jumped 8.34 at the NCAAs, the former taking the title, and although both failed (8th and no jumps) at the US Championships they had a string of good performances with McGhee ahead 3-2 on win-loss and maintaining his form better in Europe.

Mladenov won a low quality but closely contested Europeans from Milan Gombala and Kostas Koukodimos, but the latter had much better jumps earlier in the year and 6th placer Tarasenko beat Mladenov 5-2. Dietmar Haaf won the European Indoor title from Koukodimos, Bogdan Tudor, Mladenov and Tarasenko, and the German title outdoors, but thereafter lost form.

1. Powell, 2. Lewis, 3. Streete-Thompson,
4. McGhee, 5. Walder, 6. Koukodimos,
7. Tarasenko, 8. Mladenov, 9. Bentley,
10. Huang Geng
Adding indoors: 4. Walder, 5. McGhee,
6. Koukodimos, 7. Mladenov, 8. Tarasenko,
9. Haaf, 10. Bentley

TRIPLE JUMP

MIKE CONLEY retained his top ranking. He won 8 of his 13 competitions outdoors, jumping over 17.20 on each occasion except for 10th with 15.23 at his first meeting at Duisburg and 13.90 in the Kuts meeting. Leonid Voloshin improved the world indoor record to 17.72 in Grenoble and won also at Liévin and the European Indoors, but he did not compete outdoors through injury.

Denis Kapustin: European champion and Cup winner

Denis Kapustin won both the European Cup and Championships, at which Serge Hélan and Maris Bruziks won the other medals, and he had the longest jump of the year, 17.86w at Seville when he beat Vladimir Melikhov and Yoelbi Quesada, who later excelled to win the World Cup by a huge margin. Kenny Harrison was over 17m in seven of his eight competitions and beat Conley in the US - Africa match and at the Goodwill Games, where the Americans were followed by Oleg Sakirkin, later Asian champion, and Gennadiy Markov, 5th in the Europeans. Sakirkin beat Vasiliy Sokov 4-0 and Bruziks 4-1. Although behind Julian Golley and Jonathan Edwards at the Commonwealth Games, Brian Wellman had an excellent record against the leading jumpers and had nine competitions over 17m.

1. Conley, 2. Harrison, 3. Kapustin,
4. Quesada, 5. Wellman, 6. Sakirkin,
7. Hélan, 8. Bruziks, 9. Sokov, 10. Markov
Adding indoors: 7. Voloshin, 8. Sokov,
9. Hélan, 10. Bruziks

SHOT

THE AMERICANS dominated world shot putting in 1994, with their top five men taking the top five places. A sixth, Brent Noon, also ranked but was difficult to place, as although he was NCAA champion and 3rd in the US Champs behind C J Hunter and Randy Barnes and ahead of Jim Doehring and Kevin Toth, he competed rarely and not at all in Europe. Hunter was 3-3 v Barnes, but just takes top ranking. His other victories included the Goodwill Games, with Barnes 2nd, and the World Cup, while Barnes won the Grand Prix Final from Hunter, Tafralis, Doehring and Toth. with Dragan Peric 6th and Paulo Dal Soglio 7th the best Europeans.

Doehring was 3-3 with Barnes and beat Tafralis 4-2 and Toth 4-2, and Toth, who had won the US indoor title with 21.25, the year's longest throw, was 3-3 with Tafralis. Aleksandr Klimenko won the European title from Bagach, whom he beat 2-1 overall.

Bagach won the European Indoor title from Peric and Petur Gudmundsson, who was only 7th outdoors, but beat Dal Soglio 2-1. The latter's series of 20m plus throws might just give him the edge on outdoor form alone

1. Hunter, 2. Barnes, 3. Doehring, 4. Toth,
5. Tafralis, 6. Klimenko, 7. Bagach,
8. Noon, 9. Peric, 10. Dal Soglio.
Adding indoors: 10. Gudmundsson

Vladimir Dubrovshchik: profited from Lars Reidel's injury

DISCUS

LARS RIEDEL looked set to retain his top ranking with 10 wins in 12 meetings, beating his compatriot Jürgen Schult 7-1, but he was unable to contest the European final through an injury which ended his season.

Vladimir Dubrovshchik won in Helsinki from Dmitriy Shevchenko, with Schult 3rd, Nick Sweeney 4th, Attila Horváth 5th and Vladimir Zinchenko 6th, and went on to win the World Cup from Alexis Elizalde and Adewale Olukoju. Although beaten by Horváth in the European Cup first league, the young Belarussian did just enough for top ranking.

Horváth produced much the year's longest throw, but did not fare so well in the major meetings, placing 3rd at the Goodwill Games behind Shevchenko and Sergey Lyakhov and 5th in Cologne behind Shevchenko, Lyakhov, Zinchenko and Elizalde. Shevchenko won four of his five meetings, and threw 64 something in each. Lyakhov beat Schult 4-2, but was only 9th at the Europeans.

1. Dubrovshchik, 2. Riedel, 3. Shevchenko,
4. Schult, 5. Horváth, 6. Lyakhov,
7. Sweeney, 8. Zinchenko, 9. Elizalde,
10. Olukoju

HAMMER

ANDREY ABDUVALIYEV and Igor Astapkovich are 1st and 2nd as in 1993, but this time the Tajikistani was clearly the best with a 6-3 win-loss advantage. Vasiliy Sidorenko beat Astapkovich to win the European title, as Heinz Weis, Igor Nikulin and Tibor Gécsek were 3rd to 5th.

Sidorenko had also won at the European Cup from Andrey Skvaryuk and Christoph Epalle, but was 2-2 with US champion Lance Deal. At the Goodwill Games Deal beat Sidorenko by 8 cm, with Yuriy Sedykh 3rd and Abduvaliyev, in his only poor result of the year, 4th.

Most of the world's best met at the Berlin Grand Prix: 1. Abduvaliyev, 2, Astapkovich, 3. Sidorenko, 4, Weis, 5, Deal, 6. Nikulin. Sidorenko was 6cm ahead of Deal at the Grand Prix final in 3rd and 4th places, but Deal's fine 2nd place to Abduvaliyev at the World Cup, when Weis was 3rd and Sidorenko far behind 4th, just gives the American third ranking.

1. Abduvaliyev, 2. Astapkovich, 3. Deal,
4. Sidorenko, 5. Weis, 6. Nikulin,
7. Gécsek, 8. Sedykh, 9. Skvaruk,
10. Epalle

JAVELIN

JAN ZELEZNY was only third in the Europeans behind Steve Backley and Seppo Räty, but he won 17 of his 20 competitions and had the four best competitions of the year, all over 91m. European 5th placer Raymond Hecht was the only other man over 90m, but he was a place behind Patrik Bodén in Helsinki and lost 6-7 to him overall. Backley made a magnificent return from injury to retain not only the Europeans, but also the Commonwealth title, where, as in 1990, he was followed by Mick Hill, 6th in the Europeans, and Gavin Lovegrove. Backley added a third major win at the World Cup, with Hecht, Lovegrove and Bodén 2nd to 4th.

Andrey Moruyev set a Russian record to win the European Cup javelin ahead of Hecht, Hill and Bodén, and although only 9th in the Europeans, had a fine year. Most of the world's best competed at Sheffield where Zelezny's 91.82 was the year's leading throw. behind him the order was Moruyev, Backley, Hecht, Donald Sild, Dag Wennlund and Hill.

Räty had a fine Europeans but otherwise did very little; he was only 9th in the Finnish Championships, won by Juha Laukkanen, and 4th behind Harri Hakkarainen, Wennlund and Bodén in the Finland - Sweden match.

Wennlund beat Vladimir Sasimovich, 8th in Europe, 8-3 and the latter was 6-2 v Lovegrove and 2-1 v Hakkarainen. Lovegrove beat Hakkarainen 3-1.

1. Zelezny, 2. Backley, 3. Bodén, 4. Hecht, 5. Moruyev, 6. Hill, 7. Wennlund, 8. Räty, 9. Sasimovich, 10. Lovegrove

DECATHLON

DAN O'BRIEN won the US title and then at the Goodwill Games and in Talence, scoring just over 8700 on each occasion. Eduard Hämäläinen achieved the year's top score, 8735, at Götzis, but then crashed out in the hurdles when looking likely to win the Europeans, and finished 2nd, 251 points behind O'Brien at Talence.

Alain Blondel became the European champion from Henrik Dagård, Lev Lobodin, Christian Plaziat and Stefan Schmid, and was third at Talence, where he was followed by 4. Dagård, 5. Steve Fritz, 6. Schmid, 7. William Motti. Dagård had a great year, with three Swedish records, 8359 2nd at Götzis, then 8362 Europeans and 8403 Talance, with 8347 for 2nd in the European Cup behind Plaziat (3. Tomás Dvorák, 4. Blondel). Fritz was second to O'Brien in the US Champs and Goodwill Games. At Götzis 3rd was Schmid and 4th was Michael Smith, who went on to retain his Commonwealth title.

1. O'Brien, 2. Hämäläinen, 3. Blondel, 4. Dagård, 5. Fritz, 6. Plaziat, 7. Schmid, 8. Smith, 9. Janvrin, 10. Lobodin

20 KILOMETRES WALK

BERNARDO SEGURA set a world track record at Fana, won the Goodwill Games and the Pan-American Cup, but his record was spoilt by third in his opening race at Puebla to Daniel Garcia and Jefferson Pérez. A slightly better record, perhaps, is that of Mikhail Shchennikov who won in Barcelona from Yevgeniy Misyulya and Igor Kollár, and at La Coruña from Valentin Massana, Robert Korzeniowski and Garcia. At L'Hospitalet Garcia and Massana beat Shchennikov, but the Russian won the most important race, the Europeans. The order behind him was: Misyulya, Massana, Giovanni Di Benedictis and Mikhail Orlov; the last two were difficult to rank as this was their only 20k of the year.

Garcia beat Misyulya at Eisenhüttenstadt. Bo Lingtang won the Chinese title from Tan Mingjun, Chen Shaoguo and Li Mingcai, but Chen beat Bo to take the Asian title and Li won the September Chinese race.

1. Shchennikov, 2. Segura, 3. D Garcia, 4. Misyulya, 5. Massana, 6. Bo, 7. Chen, 8. Tan, 9. Li, 10. De Benedictis

50 KILOMETRES WALK

THE European Championships was much the most important race of the year, with Valeriy Spitsyn, Thierry Toutain and Giovanni Perricelli taking the medals. On the track Toutain had set a European record, which was improved by the world record at Fana of his compatriot René Piller, who was disqualified in Helsinki. Valentin Massana, who contested the 20k in Helsinki, recorded the year's fastest time in winning the Spanish title from Jesús Garcia, who was 4th in the Europeans.

Valentin Kononen was much favoured to bring Finland a gold in Helsinki, but after being in contention faded to 7th, with Robert Korzeniowski 5th and German Skurygin 6th. Carlos Mercenario won the Pan-American Cup, but in a slow time.

1. Spitsyn, 2. Toutain, 3. Perricelli, 4. Massana, 5. J Garcia, 6. Piller, 7. Korzeniowski, 8. Skurygin, 9. Kononen, 10. Blazek

WOMEN ATHLETES OF 1994

100 METRES

MERLENE OTTEY, Irina Privalova and Gwen Torrence were again very closely matched. Torrence had the best record with 13 wins from 15 finals at 100m and 6 times under 10.90 to one each for the other two. Privalova won 7 of 13 and Ottey, who missed much of the season through injury but tied her own 4 year-old Commonwealth record in the Grand Prix final, 4 of 8. Privalova set a European record 10.77 in her first 100m race of the year in Lausanne, beating Torrence and Ottey, but Torrence beat her on the remaining five occasions that they met.

Zhanna Tarnopolskaya was runner-up to Privalova in the Europeans and lost only to the big three prior to her Grand Prix Final 5th, a place behind Carlette Guidry, whom she had earlier beaten five times. Gail Devers contested only two meetings in 1994, but after a speedy 10.77w at San José, two metres ahead of Guidry; she again beat Guidry to win the US title. Guidry was 5-4 up on Juliet Cuthbert.

NCAA champion Holli Hyche ran a series of fast times in the USA, but was moderate in Europe, although she beat Commonwealth champion Mary Onyali and was 1-1 with Cuban champion Liliana Allen, who beat Onyali 2-1, including in the World Cup. Allen also beat Cheryl Taplin, 3rd in the US Champs, 2-0. Taplin had a 3-2 edge on Onyali, but the latter's clear margin in the US - Africa match, 2nd in 11.06 to Taplin's 5th 11.39, is enough to give her the final rankings place.

1. Torrence, 2. Ottey, 3. Privalova, 4. Tarnopolskaya, 5. Devers, 6. Guidry-White, 7. Cuthbert, 8. Allen, 9. Hyche, 10. Onyali

THE IAAF conducted their usual world-wide poll, inviting people in the world of athletics to select their top tens of 1994. The result for women is shown, followed by my own selections and in the final column those of the international experts polled by *Track & Field News*:

IAAF position, name, points		*PJM*	*T&FN*
1. Jackie Joyner-Kersee	3067	2	1
2. Irina Privalova	2356	-	11
3. Sonia O'Sullivan	2320	1	3
4. Sally Gunnell	2305	3	4
5. Heike Drechsler	1931	4	6
6. Marie-José Pérec	1794	5	7
7. Maria Mutola	1779	6	2
8. Gwen Torrence	1490	7	5
9. Merlene Ottey	1263	8	12
10. Trine Hattestad	733		13
11. Elana Meyer	684		
12. Uta Pippig	607	-	8
13. Svetla Dimitrova	468	10	9
14. Ilke Wyludda	405		10
15. Fernanda Ribeiro	211		
16. Inna Lasovskaya	196		14
17. Anna Biryukova	165		
18. Sari Essayah	139		
19. Natalya Shikolenko	134		
20. Inessa Kravets	93		17
Yekaterina Podkopayeva			15
Britta Bilac			16
Yvonne Murray			18
Wang Junxia		9	19

Jackie Joyner-Kersee ranked no. 1 by the IAAF and Track & Field News but behind Sonia O'Sullivan by Peter Matthews

Torrence v Ottey v Privalova in 1994

Date	*Venue*	*Event*	*Torrence*	*Ottey*	*Privalova*
6 Jul	Lausanne	100m	2. 10.85	3. 10.95	1. 10.77
17 Aug	Zürich	200m	2. 22.16	3. 22.41	1. 22.15
19 Aug	Brussels	100m	1. 10.83	2. 10.92	3. 11.07
30 Aug	Berlin	200m	2. 22.15	1. 22.07	3. 22.37
3 Sep	Paris (GPF)	100m	2. 10.82	1. 10.78	3. 11.02

200 METRES

THE TOP three sprinters ranked in the same order as the 100m. Once again Gwen Torrence had the best set of marks, six times under 22.20 to three and one windy by Irina Privalova and one by Merlene Ottey, and the best win-loss record, although it was even closer here than in the 100m. Torrence beat Privalova 3-2 and was 1-1 v Ottey, who beat Privalova 2-1.

The Australian record went three times, first to Melinda Gainsford when beating Cathy Freeman, but Freeman improved that time twice and beat Gainsford on the next four times they met, including at the Commonwealth Games, when Mary Onyali split them to take the silver medal. Freeman also beat the US champion Carlette Guidry 2-0, while Guidry was 5-1 up on Dannette Young and 2-0 on Onyali, and Young beat Onyali 2-1. Marie-José Pérec ran only four 200m races, but all under 23 seconds and was 2-1 up on Young. She was, however, 6th in Zürich, a place behind the European silver medallist Zhanna Tarno-pol-skaya (Freeman was 4th).

Holli Hyche ran 11 times under 23 seconds, including 2 indoors, but narrowly misses 10th ranking, which goes to Galina Malchugina, who started well but lost form somewhat after a busy season, which included an impressive European indoor gold medal and the outdoor bronze.

1. Torrence, 2. Ottey, 3. Privalova, 4. Freeman, 5. Guidry-White, 6. Young, 7. Onyali, 8. Tarnopolskaya, 9. Pérec, 10. Malchugina

400 METRES

MARIE-JOSÉ PÉREC was unbeaten at 400m in 1994, as she had been in 1991 and 1992, not running the event in 1993, and was the one woman to break 50 seconds; although she lost her 49.95 at Monaco due to running inside her lane. She took the Grand Prix title in fine style in 49.77 and also won the European title. Behind her in Paris were Cathy Freeman, who improved her Australian record to 50.04, having won the Commonwealth title two weeks earlier, and Maicel Malone, thus giving Freeman a vital 3-2 edge over Malone, who was clearly the best of the US trio completed by Jearl Miles , whom she beat 7-1 and Natasha Kaiser-Brown, whom she beat 6-3. The order of this trio is easily determined by Miles 8-2 over Kaiser-Brown.

The best American, however, was again Gwen Torrence, who easily beat both Malone and Miles in Lille. However Torrence ran only one other minor 400m race, and like Irina Privalova, who ran only once, but then beat Commonwealth silver medallist Fatima Yusuf (2nd) and Miles (3rd) at the World Cup, is difficult to rank.

Sandie Richards took the Commonwealth bronze, but was 2-3 down to Pauline Davis overall. Ma Yuqin won Chinese and Asian titles, but did not meet any of the world's best.

1. Pérec, 2. Freeman, 3. Malone, 4. Miles, 5. Kaiser-Brown, 6. Torrence, 7. Privalova, 8. Yusuf, 9. Davis, 10. Richards

Marie-José Pérec: unbeaten at 400m in 1994

800 METRES

MARIA MUTOLA extended her unbeaten run which dates back to 21 Aug 1992. She won four races indoors and seven outdoors with a pb 1:55.19 in Zürich and was a class apart from the rest of the world.

Lyubov Gurina won the European title, but shared the time of 1:58.55 with Natalya Dukhnova, who had beaten her in their first three clashes. Dukhnova, however, was behind Gurina, 2nd to 4th, in Köln, a race won by Mutola with Joetta Clark 4th.

The top three were well clear, but the overall standard was poor compared to recent years, and in looking for the 4th ranked athlete I have gone beyond the top ten on times to Yekaterina Podkopayeva, who won four of her five outdoor races and who beat both Gurina and Luciana Mendes, South American champion and World Cup second placer, 2-0. European bronze medallist Lyudmila Rogachova ran the event only four times, but was also second to Mutola at the Goodwill Games. Joetta Clark was 5th there and at the World Cup and although she ran three 1:58 times her competitive record was too patchy for a ranking.

Qu Yunxia was untroubled in winning the Chinese and Asian titles, but only needed to run 1:59s to do so. Patricia Djaté set a French record when third in Zürich behind Mutola and Dukhnova, ahead of Clark, but was beaten by Kelly Holmes at Sheffield. Holmes was also 1-1 v Ellen van Langen, in the latter's only sub 2-minute race before her season was cut short by injury but who had won all her five previous races.

1. Mutola, 2. Gurina, 3. Dukhnova,
4. Podkopayeva, 5. Rogachova,
6. Mendes, 7. Qu, 8. Holmes, 9. Djaté,
10. van Langen

Yekaterina Popkopayeva: amazing veteran

1500 METRES

THE AMAZING super-veteran Yekaterina Popkopayeva, was only third in the sprint finish which decided the European title, behind Lyudmila Rogachova and Kelly Holmes, but is ranked first with a 3-2 advantage over Sonia O'Sullivan, 3-1 over Angela Chalmers and 7-1 over Rogachova. Podkopayeva had 11 wins outdoors and three indoors with three seconds and two thirds.

Win-loss records sorted out the rest of the top places too, with O'Sullivan 2-1 up on Chalmers and 5-0 over Rogachova. Chalmers beat Hassiba Boulmerka in the first two of the last three big races of the year, at Berlin and Paris, before Boulmerka reversed the placings in the World Cup.

The Russians Rogachova and Lyubov Kremlyova were 4-4 and Kremlyova beat the Commonwealth champion Kelly Holmes, who had a great first season at the event, 2-1. Yvonne Murray only ran three races at 1500m or 1 mile, but she was but narrowly beaten by Holmes at the AAAs and after winning v the USA was second in Oslo to O'Sullivan.

Lyubov Gurina and Yvonne Graham ran some good times, with the former ahead on the one occasion they met. Graham delighted the crowd by winning at Brussels, when she was the designated pacemaker, building up such a lead that the pack, led by Boulmerka, could not catch her. Just as at 800m Qu Yunxia won both Chinese and Asian titles, but did not meet her European rivals.

1. Podkopayeva, 2. O'Sullivan,
3. Chalmers, 4. Boulmerka, 5. Rogachova,
6. Kremlyova, 7. Holmes, 8. Murray,
9. Gurina, 10. Graham.

3000 METRES

Sonia O'Sullivan broke the European record when winning the London Grand Prix, with Yvonne Murray and Angela Chalmers follow-

Wang Junxia: no non-Asian competition but a different class

ing, well ahead of Annette Peters 4th. This came a week after O'Sullivan set a world record 5:25.36 for 2000m at Edinburgh, with Murray, 5:26.93, also inside the old record. O'Sullivan and Murray again finished 1st and 2nd at the Europeans, where the World Junior champion Gabriela Szabo took the bronze medal, with Russian champion Olga Churbanova 4th, European Cup winner Lyudmila Borisova 5th and Alison Wyeth 6th. Chalmers went on to win the Commonwealth title, and Murray the World Cup from Meagher.

Yelena Romanova won all her four races, including the Goodwill Games, but passed the Europeans and did not break 8:40. Fernanda Ribeiro won the European Indoor title and was a fine second at the Goodwill Games, with Peters 3rd, Borisova 4th and Churbanova 5th, but was only third in the European Cup first league and was also beaten by Churbanova at the Kuts Memorial. Tenth ranking was contested by Yvonne Graham, 3rd at Rome and Nice, Wyeth and Meagher, with the latter's 2nd to Wyeth's third at the Commonwealth giving her the edge.

1. O'Sullivan, 2. Murray, 3. Chalmers,
4. Romanova, 5. Peters, 6. Szabo,
7. Churbanova, 8. Borisova, 9. Ribeiro,
10. Meagher.

5,000 METRES

THIS EVENT replaces the 3000m as the standard event in future, and a ranking is attempted although this was not a championship event in 1994. It was, however, a Grand Prix event and the 30 best performances of the year were dominated by four races: 9 from Köln, 7 from Berlin, 6 from Paris and 4 from Stockholm, where Yelena Romanova ran the year's fastest time (apart that is from Wang Junxia's astonishing second 5000m in 14:50.34 in the Asian 10,000m). Second in Stockholm was Catherina McKiernan who was also third at Berlin, behind Alison Wyeth and Kathrin Wessel, and fifth in the Grand Prix Final, won by Sonia O'Sullivan from Lyudmila Borisova, Wyeth and Yvonne Graham. O'Sullivan had also won in Köln, when she was followed in 2nd to 5th places by Borisova, Graham, Annette Peters and Wessel. Tired from a great season O'Sullivan was well beaten in Tokyo by Fernanda Ribeiro. Daria Nauer set a Swiss record when 4th in Berlin and Wessel was also 6th in the Grand Prix final.

1. O'Sullivan, 2. Borisova, 3. Wyeth,
4. Romanova, 5. Graham, 6. Ribeiro,
7. McKiernan, 8. Peters, 9. Wessel,
10. Nauer.

10,000 METRES

Wang Junxia did not meet non-Asians, but remained a class apart as she took the Chinese and Asian titles, with Dong Li in second place in both races. The only other runner to break 31 minutes was Elana Meyer, who ran a brilliant race at the World Cup to beat Fernanda Ribeiro, who had won the European title from Conceição Ferreira, Daria Nauer, Kathrin Wessel, Cristina Misaros and Maria Guida.

The problem in attempting a ranking is that Meyer was decisively beaten by Yvonne Murray at the Commonwealth Games. Murray could undoubtedly have run much faster than her 31:56.97 which was only 17th on the year list, and there is a case for ranking her second, but I felt that one race in a relatively slow time was not enough. Zhong Huandi is another difficult to place as she ran only in Japan, but won all her three races in good times. Ferreira also won the Iberian 10k and the European Cup I, in which Nauer was 4th. Catherina McKiernan set an Irish record in her European Cup race but failed to finish at the Europeans.

1. Wang, 2. Meyer, 3. Ribeiro, 4. Ferreira,
5. Dong, 6. Murray, 7. Zhong, 8. Nauer,
9. Wessel, 10. McKiernan

Sally Gunnell: two titles for a clean sweep

MARATHON

WHILE THE Boston conditions were highly favourable, nonetheless Uta Pippig's 2:21:45 was the performance of the year. She had nearly two minutes to spare over Valentina Yegorova, who went on to win the Tokyo marathon, and a further two minutes over Elana Meyer. Although she dropped out of the European marathon, won by Manuela Machado, Katrin Dörre had two big wins, London and Berlin.

Apart from Boston the greatest depth of fast times was at Osaka, where the first two, Tomoe Abe and Nobuki Fujimura, tied the Japanese record and Junko Asari was only a second behind. Miyoko Asahina was 5th in 2:27:51, but three months later improved the record to 2:25:52 when she won in Rotterdam. Fujimura was later only third in the Asian Games, won by Zhong Huandi. As impressive as any was the smooth run by Tecla Lorupe to win the New York marathon on her début at the distance. Olga Appell won both Los Angeles and Hokkaido marathons, although she was only 6th in New York.

1. Pippig, 2. Yegorova, 3. Dörre,
4. Asahina, 5. Abe, 6. Fujimura, 7. Asari,
8. Lorupe, 9. Meyer, 10. Appell

100 METRES HURDLES.

SVETLA DIMITROVA was the clear number one, with 13 wins and 2 seconds in her 15 races. The first loss was to her compatriot Yordanka Donkova in Dijon, and the second quite a shock, when she was pipped by Aliuska López at the World Cup. Overall Dimitrova beat Donkova 8-1 and Yulia Graudyn. Donkova beat Graudyn on the first four occasions that they met, but then lost the next seven, including at the Europeans where these two took silver and bronze behind Dimitrova. Sharing the fastest 'legal' time of the year with Dimitrova was Tatyana Reshetnikova, but she was 5th in the Europeans, a place down to Brigita Bukovec, whom she beat 6-3, and a place ahead of Julia Baumann.

Win-loss records in the middle section of the top ten: Bukovec 3-3 v Baumann, 5-3 v López, 3-1 v Michelle Freeman; Baumann 3-2 v López, 4-0 v Freeman; López 7-1 v Freeman. Freeman won the Commonwealth title from Jackie Agyepong, who had earlier surprised to win the European Cup. Agyepong just misses out on a ranking to Asian champion Olga Shishigina, whom she was behind at the Goodwill Games. Jackie Joyner-Kersee won the US title and at the US - Africa match.

1. Dimitrova, 2. Graudyn, 3. Donkova,
4. Reshetnikova, 5. Bukovec, 6. Baumann,
7. López, 8. Freeman, 9. Joyner-Kersee,
10. Shishigina

400 METRES HURDLES

SALLY GUNNELL won European and Commonwealth titles to complete a clean sweep of major titles and won 10 of 11 finals. Her one loss was at Nice to Kim Batten, whom she beat on the other four occasions they met. Russian champion Anna Knoroz was the year's third fastest, and was third at the Goodwill Games behind Gunnell and Batten, with Olga Nazarova 4th. Silvia Rieger was 2nd at the Europeans with Knoroz 3rd, Heike Meissner 4th, Tatyana Kurochkina 5th and Tatyana Tereshchuk 6th, but Meissner beat Rieger 4-2.

Deon Hemmings and Debbie Ann Parris took the other Commonwealth medals. Hemmings did not meet Rieger but lost 2-1 to Meissner. Tereshchuk won the Ukrainian title and was second to Gunnell at the European Cup, ahead of Kurochkina, Vera Ordina and Meissner.

1. Gunnell, 2. Batten, 3. Knoroz,
4. Meissner, 5. Rieger, 6. Hemmings,
7. Tereshchuk, 8. Kurochkina, 9. Nazarova,
10. Parris

HIGH JUMP

IN RECENT years Stefka Kostadinova and Heike Henkel have dominated world high jumping. Both their seasons were however affected by pregnancy in 1994. Kostadinova jumped 2.00 indoors and won the European Indoor title, but only had three outdoor competitions in May with a best of 1.96. Henkel came back after the birth of her baby, but although she had a best of 1.95 the Europeans came too soon for her to get back amongst the best. Also missing the outdoor season was Alina Astafei, who produced the year's best jumps of 2.02 and 2.01 indoors, but who was banned by the Romanian federation for refusing selection for the European Indoors. She now lives in Germany and will compete for them in future.

Outdoors three women each cleared 2.00 once: Silvia Costa, Inga Babakova and the ex-East German, now Slovenian, Britta Bilac, who took the European title with 2.00 and won at the World Cup. Bilac had much the best overall record, with all the other leading jumpers compiling inconsistent records, and there was very little between them.

Costa beat Yelena Gulyayeva, the European 2nd, 3-0 although twice at the same height, but lost at her only meeting with Babakova, European 4th. Alison Inverarity won the Commonwealth title, but her record was marred by her 7th at the World Cup. Shevchik was 3-1 v Hanne Haugland outdoors, and 1-1 indoors, including 4th to 6th at the European Indoor, but was only 9th outdoors.

1. Bilac, 2. Costa, 3. Gulyayeva,
4. Babakova, 5. Inverarity, 6. Shevchik,
7. Haugland, 8. Topchina, 9. Zhdanova,
10. Waller
Adding indoors: 4. Astafei, 5. Babakova,
6. Kostadinova, 7. Inverarity, 8. Shevchik,
9. Haugland, 10. Topchina.

Britta Bilac: took advantage of absentees

POLE VAULT

AFTER Nicole Rieger had cleared successive European bests of 4.00, 4.01 and 4.02 in earlier meetings, she improved the world indoor best to 4.08 at Karlsruhe. So too, did Sun Caiyun, but she tested positive for stimulants and therefore was disqualified and suffered a three-month ban. She came back, however, to win at the Goodwill Games, the first time the event had been held at a major meeting. from Svetlana Abramova, the German champion Andrea Müller, and Marina Andreyeva, and late in the year cleared 4.12 twice at Guangzhou. News of these marks came through after the IAAF had recognised 4.05 as the inaugural world outdoor record and Rieger's 4.08 indoors. At the time of writing it was not clear whether the new marks would be able to be ratified. Rieger set outdoor European bests at 3.96 and 4.00 before Marina Andreyeva took over at 4.01.

LONG JUMP

JACKIE JOYNER-KERSEE and Heike Drechsler renewed their rivalry. They were well ahead of the rest of the world, except for Inessa Kravets, who won at Zürich in a competition much affected by heavy rain, with 7.09 to 7.01 Drechsler and 6.95 JJK, and who was second at the Grand Prix Final won by JJK, with Drechsler a tired third. Zürich was JJK's only outdoor loss of the year in ten competitions, headed by her US record 7.49 at both New York and Sestriere. She beat Drechsler 5-1 outdoors, but was well beaten by her German rival indoors at Maebashi. Drechsler won all seven long jump competitions indoors and 19 of 26 outdoors. She was second six times and third once and was over 7 metres six times indoors and 15 outdoors. She lost once to Mirela Dulgheru and twice to Kravets, whom she beat once indoors and seven times outdoors.

JJK v Drechsler career record

Date	*Venue*	*Drechsler*	*JJK*
25 Jun 83	Los Angeles - US v GDR	1 6.65	3 6.61
21 Aug 85	Zürich - WK	1 7.39	2 7.24
28 Feb 86	New York - TAC	1 7.03	2 6.97
5 Sep 86	Brussels - VD	1 7.23	2 7.12
4 Sep 87	Roma - WCh	3 7.13	1 7.36
29 Sep 88	Seoul - OG	2 7.22	1 7.40
9 Sep 90	Rieti	1 7.17	2 7.12
25 Aug 91	Tokyo - WCh	2 7.29	1 7.32
7 Aug 92	Barcelona - OG	1 7.14	3 7.07
27 Aug 93	Berlin - ISTAF	2 7.07	1 7.08
28 Aug 93	Innsbruck	1 7.02	2 7.01
13 Feb 94	Maebashi	1 7.15	2 6.55
22 Jul 94	Oslo - Bisl	2 7.29	1 7.33w
31 Jul 94	Sestriere (A)	2 7.39w	1 7.49
17 Aug 94	Zürich - WK	2 7.01	3 6.95
19 Aug 94	Brussels - VD	2 7.01	1 7.11
21 Aug 94	Köln	2 7.00	1 7.10
3 Sep 94	Paris - GPF	3 6.88	1 7.21

Kravets lost only to the big two apart from her third at the European Indoors, won by Drechsler from Ljudmila Ninova.

In the European Championships Fiona May was 3rd, Renata Nielsen 4th and Ninova 5th, with Agata Karczmarek 6th and Irina Mushailova 7th, but Ninova was the best of this group overall, beating May 7-3 and Nielsen 6-5, with May 5-3 up on Nielsen.

Mushailova started with 6.89 for 3rd at Villeneuve d'Ascq behind Drechsler and Kravets and then jumped 7.20 to win the Russian title, but after that her best was 6.77 for third at the Goodwill Games behind Drechsler and Svetlana Moskalets. The Cuban champion Niurka Montalvo was 2nd in the World Cup won by Kravets, where she was well ahead of Commonwealth champion Nicole Boegman, 5th, but the 4th placer Yao Weili won the Asian title at 6.91 and had two other competitions over 6.80.

1. Joyner-Kersee, 2. Drechsler, 3. Kravets,
4. Ninova, 5. May, 6. Nielsen,
7. Karczmarek, 8. Mushailova,
9. Moskalets, 10. Yao

TRIPLE JUMP

INDOORS Inna Lasovskaya was supreme, winning all her seven competitions with world indoor records at 14.61, 14.78 and 14.90 before her European title. Outdoors Lasovskaya swapped wins with Inessa Kravets, but both were passed in the last two months of the season by the European Indoor silver medallist Anna Biryukova, who won her last five competitions, including Goodwill Games, Europeans and World Cup.

Overall Lasovskaya was 3-2 ahead of Biryukova outdoors (2-0 indoors) and was only two centimetres behind at the Europeans. Kravets was third at the Europeans, losing 1-3 to Lasovskaya (0-2 indoors) and 2-3 to Biryukova (0-2 indoors), The two European Championships had much the highest standards in depth with six women exceeding 14.30 in each. third placer Sofia Bozhanova was 3rd and 4th at these events, before losing the latter place on a positive drugs test, Sarka Kaspárková was 4th and 6th, Kravets 6th and 3rd and Iva Prandzheva 5th indoors, but no jumping outdoors. Yolanda Chen, who had been second to Lasovskaya in the Russian Championships, was 4th and Rodica Petrescu 5th outdoors.

The best non-Europeans were the former world record holder Sheila Hudson-Strudwick, the world junior champion (after Yelena Lysak disqualified) Ren Ruiping, and Cuban champion Niurka Montalvo. They finished 2nd, 3rd and 5th respectively at the World Cup, with the German champion Helga Radtke, 7th and 8th in the two Europeans, 6th.

1. Lasovskaya, 2. Biryukova, 3. Kravets,
4. Chen, 5. Petrescu, 6. Hudson-Strudwick,
7. Ren, 8. Montalvo, 9. Kaspárková,
10. Radtke, dq (4) Bozhanova.
Adding indoors: 7. Kaspárková, 8. Ren.
9. Radtke, 10. Chistyakova

SHOT

VALENTINA FEDYUSHINA led the year lists with 20.82 indoors and was second in the outdoor lists with the 20.56 with which she won the Ukrainian title in May. She was second in the European Cup to Astrid Kumbernuss, but was not over 19m thereafter.

The Chinese throwers Sui Xinmei and Huang Zhihong were the only women over 20m more than once outdoors. Zhang Luihong beat Sui to win the Chinese title with Cheng Xiaoyan, who later won the World Junior title 3rd, also over 20m. Sui, however, had the best throw, 20.74, and won both Goodwill Games and Asian titles, beating Zhang by over a metre on the latter occasion. Huang was second in the Goodwill Games, followed by Svetla Mitkova, Anna Romanova, Larisa Peleshenko and Kathrin Neimke, and won the World Cup from Belsis Laza, Kumbernuss and Viktoriya Pavlysh. The latter, who had been second in the Ukraine Champs, was a surprise European Champion, from Kumbernuss, Mitkova, Stephanie Storp, Peleshenko, Neimke, Fedysuhina and Romanova.

Indoors Kumbernuss won the European title from Peleshenko, Mitkova and Romanova, with Fedyushina having no valid throws.

1. Sui, 2. Huang, 3. Kumbernuss, 4. Zhang,
5. Pavlysh, 6. Mitkova, 7. Storp,
8. Peleshenko, 9. Neimke, 10, Cheng.
Adding indoors: 10. Fedyushina

DISCUS

ALTHOUGH NOT back to her 70m plus throwing of old, Ilke Wyludda was the world number one. She won 11 and was second 3 times of her 14 competitions. Barbara Echevarría, Manuela Tirneci and Ellina Zvereva each beat her once. Zvereva was second to Wyludda in the Europeans and World Cup and third behind Wyludda and Olga Nikishina in the European Cup. Zvereva also beat Daniela Costian, who had the world's longest throw of the year, 6-1 and Echevarría 6-2. In turn Costian was 7-2 up on Echevarría and beat the European third placer Mette Bergmann 5-0, while Bergmann led Echevarría 4-0, so the top five places are clear-cut.

The European 4th and 5th placers were Nicoleta Grasu and Olga Chernyavskaya, with the win-loss record 4-3 to Grasu. Ukrainian champion Nikishina was only 10th and Polish champion Renata Katewicz failed to make the final in Helsinki, but the latter had enough good performances to make up the top ten with Asian champion Min Chunfeng. Just missing ranking places were the Germans Franka Dietzsch and Jana Lauren, who were 4-4 in their clashes. The Chinese champion Qiu Qiaoping is not ranked as she later suffered a drugs disqualification.

1. Wyludda, 2. Zvereva, 3. Costian,
4. Bergmann, 5. Echevarría, 6. Grasu,
7. Chernyavskaya, 8. Nikishina,
9. Katewicz, 10. Min

HAMMER

OLGA KUZENKOVA improved her world best to 66.84 in February, won the Russian title and was unbeaten in 1994, with six meetings over 63m. Unbeaten, too, was Mihaela Melinte who took the world junior best to 65.48. It emerged later in the year that Svetlana Sudak had improved the world best to 67.34 in Minsk, although that was not able to be ratified. She lost to Kuzenkova in April at the one meeting of the top women. Debbie Sosimenko set three Commonwealth bests to 62.38, and the Ukrainian champion Marina Pirog threw 62.22.

Ilke Wyludda: back on top if not back to her best

JAVELIN

TRINE HATTESTAD remained the world number one; her 1994 record being 14 wins and four second places. She beat her great rival Natalya Shikolenko 5-3, but the latter's injury at the Europeans spoiled a potentially fascinating clash.

Shikolenko had the year's two longest throws, 71.40 at both Seville and London, and won the European Cup and Grand Prix final, while Hattestad had the next four best competitions. Karen Forkel, 2nd in the Europeans and 3rd in the World Cup was the only other woman to beat Hattestad, winning at Lehrte in their last competition of the year.

The dominance of these three women is shown by the fact that of the best 31 performances in 1994: Shikolenko had 13, Hattestad 10, Forkel 5, Felicea Tilea 2 and Claudia Isaila 1. While Isaila was 4-4 with Tilea 4-3, she was only 11th at the Europeans while Tilea was 3rd.

Tatyana Shikolenko did not compete in Helsinki, but had a consistent record in the major meetings, beating Commonwealth champion Louise McPaul 3-1.

There was little to choose between the last three ranked or other contenders, such as Jette Jeppesen and Sueli dos Santos. Tanja Damaske, 6th in the Europeans, was the most consistent, while Kinga Zsigmond beat Yekaterina Ivakina 2-1.

1. Hattestad, 2. N Shikolenko, 3. Forkel,
4. Tilea, 5. Isaila, 6. T Shikolenko,
7. McPaul, 8. Damaske, 9. Zsigmond,
10. Ivakina

HEPTATHLON

THE MOST exciting development in the heptathlon was the return to the event for the first time for 13 years of Heike Drechsler. She excelled to beat many of the world's best at Talence with the year's best score of 6741. Behind her the order was 2. Nathalie Teppe, 3. Larisa Turchinskaya, 4. Urszula Wlodarczyk, 5. Svetlana Moskalets, 6. Tiina Rattyä, 7. Irina Tyukhay.

Missing from that event, however, were Jackie Joyner-Kersee and Sabine Braun. JJK won her one heptathlon of 1994 at the Goodwill Games from Turchinskaya and Ghada Shouaa, who later won the Asian title.

Braun did not meet the two all-time greats, but takes top ranking due to two wins: Götzis and the Europeans. At the former the order behind her was 2. Turchinskaya, 3. Rita Ináncsi, 4. Moskalets, 5. Beatrice Mau-Repnak, 6. Tyukhay.

Moskalets went on to win the European Combined Events super league from Teppe and Peggy Beer, and at the Europeans, Ináncsi, the winner of the Cup B competition, was 2nd, Wlodarczyk 3rd, Teppe 4th, Moskalets 5th and Beer 6th. Wlodarczyk was 2-1 v Moskalets and 2-2 v Teppe, but loses ground as her best score was 6322, twice bettered by Shouaa.

1. Braun, 2. Drechsler, 3. Joyner-Kersee,
4. Ináncsi, 5. Turchinskaya, 6. Moskalets,
7. Teppe, 8. Shouaa, 9. Wlodarczyk,
10. Beer

10 KILOMETRES WALK

AS THE top walkers did not meet this is an event which is very difficult to rank. The fastest time of the year was 41:38 by Gao Hongmiao in Beijing and later in the year she also won the Asian title in the much slower time of 44:11.

Gu Yan was second in both those races and her form could be compared with the Europeans as she won in Fana from Italian champion Elisabeta Perrone with Yelena Arshintseva 3rd, although was only 11th at Sesto SG.

The second and third fastest times came at Livorno from Annarita Sidoti and Perrone with Larisa Ramazanova 3rd and Beate Gummelt 4th. These four were respectively 2nd, 7th, 5th and 8th at the Europeans.

The European champion Sari Essayah has the best claim to be world number one, as she also won at Eisenhüttenstadt and the Finnish title, although she was third at the Goodwill Games behind Olympiada Ivanova and Yelena Sayko. Ivanova, who had two other wins, and Sayko were only 4th and 5th in the Russian Championships, won by Arshintseva.

With good series of races were Yelena Nikolayeva, 2nd at Sesto, 1st at La Coruña and 3rd in Europe, and Arshintseva, who after two fast times in Russia was 3rd at Sesto, 9th Livorno and 4th Europe.

1. Essayah, 2. Sidoti, 3. Nikolayeva,
4. Gao, 5. Gu, 6. Arshintseva, 7. Perrone,
8, Ivanova, 9. Sayko, 10. Ramazanova,

Cross-Country - National Champions 1994

	MEN	WOMEN
Australia	Wayne Larden	Sue Mahony
Austria	Michael Buchleitner	Gudrun Pflüger
Belgium	Vincent Rousseau	Liève Slegers
Canada (Nov)	Jeff Schiebler	Leah Pells
Czech Republic	Michel Kucera	Sourková
Denmark	Klaus PHansen	Dorthe Rasmussen
England	David Lewis	Paula Radcliffe
Finland	Risto Ulmala	Annemari Sandell
France	Mohamed Essaïd	Maria Rebelo
Germany	Stephan Freigang	Claudia Lokar
Hungary	Imre Berkovics	Éva Doczi
Ireland	Peter Matthews	Catherina McKiernan
Israel	Dev Kremer	Nili Avramski
Italy	Umberto Pusterla	Maria Guida
Kenya	William Sigei	Tecla Lorupe
Luxembourg	Jean-Pierre Ernzen	Danièle Kaber
Netherlands	Tonnie Dirks	Grete Koens
New Zealand	Richard Potts	Sharon Clode
Northern Ireland	Dermot Donnelly	Teresa Duffy
Norway	Terje Næss	Christin Sørum
Portugal	Domingos Castro	Conceição Ferreira
Russia	Farid Khayrullin	Olga Churbanova
Scotland	Chris Robison	Susan Ridley
Slovenia	Izudin Hrapic	Helena Javornik
South Africa (Oct)	Jacques Van Rensburg	Zola Pieterse
Spain	Juan Carlos Adán	Julia Vaquero
Sweden	Jonny Danielson	Malin Ewerlöf
Switzerland	Markus Graf	Daria Nauer
UK Trials	Steve Tunstall	Paula Radcliffe
US Trials	Bob Kennedy	Lucy Nusrala
USA (Nov)	Reuben Reina	Olga Appell
Wales	Justin Hobbs	Wendy Ore
Yugoslavia	Borislav Devic	Olivera Jevtic
Balkan	Goran Raicevic YUG	Gogirlea ROM
European Clubs	Domingos Castro POR	Albertina Dias POR
NCAA (Nov)	Martin Keino KEN	Jennifer Rhines
South America	Salvador Guerra ECU	Carmen de Oliveira BRA
World Students	Spencer Duval GBR	Iulia Negura ROM
Team	GBR	GBR

Where countries have national championships over more than one distance the winners of the event over c.10-12 km for men, or 5-8km for women are listed.

Classic races - 1994		
Durham 1/1	Haile Gebrselassie ETH	Paula Radcliffe GBR
Mallusk 8/1	Ismael Kirui KEN	Paula Radcliffe GBR
Fuensalida 9/1	Ondoro Osoro KEN	Sally Barsosio KEN
Sevilla 23/1	William Sigei KEN	Yelena Romanova RUS
San Sebastián 31/1	Haile Gebrselassie ETH	Yelena Romanova RUS
Hannut 6/2	Ruddy Walem BEL	Isabel Delagrange BEL
Tourcoing 6/2	Ezekiel Bitok KEN	Zola Pieterse RSA
Faro 13/2	Ondoro Osoro KEN	Catherina McKiernan
Diekirch 20/2	Tendai Chimusasa ZIM	Catherina McKiernan
Chiba 20/2	Gert Thys RSA	Galyamova RUS
San Vittore Olona 5/3	Fita Bayissa ETH	Albertina Dias POR
Lidingöloppet 30k 2/10	Benson Masya KEN	Tecla Lorupe KEN

IAAF Cross-country Challenge

See *Athletics 1994* page 607 for the top 5 men and women in the 1993/4 series.

1994/5 Series	1	2	3
Men			
Bolbec 27/11	S Kororia	Jas. Kariuki	S Sghir
Alger 4/12 (n/s)	E Barngetuny	Jas. Kariuki	W Mutwol
Brussels 18/12	F Bayissa	P Guerra	H Gebrselasie
Durham 31/12	I Kirui	A Pearson	S Hissou
Belfast 7/1	I Kirui	P Hanneck	James Kariuki
Amorebieta 15/1	P Guerra	I Kirui	M Fiz
Sevilla 22/1	A Gómez	Dom. Castro	S Hissou
San Sebastián 29/1	P Guerra	S Hissou	J C Adan
Tourcoing 4/2	L Chege	S Rono	L Zeroual
Algarve 12/2	P Guerra	O Osoro	Dom. Castro
Diekirch 19/2	D Lewis	R Walem	D Clarke
Chiba 19/2	D Njenga	S Makaya	A Mezgebu
Nairobi 25/2	P Tergat	S Chemoiwyo	I Kirui
San Vittore 4/3	F Bayissa	P Tergat	S Hissou
Women			
Bolbec 27/11	F Ribeiro	C McKiernan	M Keszeg
Alger 4/12 (n/s)	R Cheruiyot	C Kirui	L Kremlyova
Brussels 18/12	D Tulu	R Cheruiyot	C McKiernan
Durham 31/12	R Cheruiyot	C McKiernan	P Radcliffe
Belfast 7/1	R Cheruiyot	C Kirui	E Fidatov
Amorebieta 15/1	R Cheruiyot	A Dias	C Kirui
Sevilla 22/1	C McKiernan	F Ribeiro	H Kimaiyo
San Sebastián 29/1	E Fidatov	Z Ouaziz	C Lokar
Tourcoing 4/2	G Szabo	C McKiernan	E Fidatov
Algarve 12/2	G Szabo	F Ribeiro	P Radcliffe
Diekirch 19/2	G Szabo	J Koech	R Martin
Chiba 19/2	T Chidu	I Negura	W Wanjiru
Nairobi 25/2	R Cheruiyot	S Barsosio	M Ngotho
San Vittore 4/3	A Dias	C Kirui	M Ernstdóttir

EUROPEAN CC CHAMPIONSHIPS

At Alnwick, GBR December 10

Men

1. Paulo Guerra POR	27:43
2. Domingos Castro POR	27:59
3. Antonio Serrano ESP	28:03
4. Carlos Adán ESP	28:06
5. Abdellah Béhar FRA	28:08
6. Luca Barzaghi ITA	28:10
7. José M Garcia ESP	28:11
8. António Pinto POR	28:12
9. Alberto Maravilha POR	28:13
10. Mustapha Essaïd FRA	28:19
11. Andrew Pearson GBR	28:20
12. João Junqueira POR	28:21
13. Alejandro Gómez ESP	28:22
14. Barry Royden GBR	28:23
15. Carsten Jørgensen DEN	28:24

Team:1. POR 20, 2. ESP 27, 3. FRA 50, 4. GBR 77, 5. ITA 84, 6. HOL 132, 7. RUS 146, 8. IRL 152, 9. GER 167, 10. BEL 170. 18 nations placed.

Women

1. Catherina McKiernan IRL	14:29
2. Julia Vacquero ESP	14:30
3. Elena Fidatov ROM	14:36
4. Alla Zhilyayeva RUS	14:45
5. Maria Rebelo FRA	14:46
6. Fernanda Ribeiro POR	14:47
7. Mariana Chirila ROM	14:48
8. Liève Slegers BEL	14:49
9. Blandine Ducret FRA	14:50
10. Tamara Koba UKR	14:51
11. Carla Sacramento POR	14:52
12. Ana Dias POR	14:54
13. Flavia Gaviglio ITA	14:54
14. Farida Fates FRA	14:55
15. Nina Belikhova RUS	14:55

Team: 1. ROM 26, 2. FRA 28, 3. POR 29, 4. ESP 45, 5. ITA 62, 6. BEL 64, 7. RUS 73, 8. IRL 75, 9. GBR 84, 10. UKR 91. 16 nations placed.

1994 MARATHON REVIEW

By Dr David E Martin

FAST TIMES, exciting competition, changing citizenships, rabbits who win, and impressive débuts all combined with the influence of several major regional championships to highlight the year's activities. And the inevitable loss of one of the event's great leaders brought all who follow the event much closer together for the future.

A preview of fast times to come when three Japanese athletes entered the track together for a final 'sprint' around the stadium at the Osaka International Ladies marathon in January. It was a primary selection race for the October Asian Games. Indeed the selectors were impressed, with the first two finishers equalling 2:26:09 (Tomoe Abe and Nobuko Fujimura), and the third (Junko Asari) a second behind. All bettered their national record! It was a study in contrasts, with Abe being coached at sea level by one of the famous Soh brothers, the other two being trained by Tsugumichi Suzuki at altitude.

In March the Los Angeles marathon, known as much for Hollywood glitz as for excellence in the front ranks, caught global attention. The USA's Paul Pilkington had been hired to set a quick first-half pace. His assignment was 1:05:00, and he came through in 1:05:02, nearly a minute ahead of the pack. With a personal best 2:11:13 to his credit, and feeling wonderful despite the fast pace in warm weather, instead of dropping out as rabbits often do, he continued on to victory. Earning in addition to his 'rabbiting fee' a Mercedes and a $37,000 pay-day, he then went on to notoriety on American TV talk shows as 'the rabbit paid to lose who went on to win'. In the women's race, Olga Appell, formerly Mexican but who had recently achieved American citizenship in part to provide her with athletics opportunities being denied her as a Mexican, broke the 2:30 barrier to start a stunning year of track, road racing, and cross country victories. Later in the year, her countryman Arturo Barrios, residing in the USA since 1986, would do the same, giving the USA two outstanding new talents on the world athletics scene. (Barrios ran Boston as a Mexican, New York as an American).

The men began their year on a quick note as well, in April, with Belgium's Vincent Rousseau scoring the first sub-2:08:00 performance since Beijing '88. His 2:07:51 Rotterdam win on a cold windy day was a new European record. Nearly as impressive was the companion women's victory by Miyoko Asahina (2:25:52), only 11 weeks following her fifth place at Osaka (2:27:51). Across the English Channel, in London, even nastier weather conditions produced performances similar in quality, but not quite so fast. Dionicio Cerón, who won Rotterdam the year previous, reinforced Mexico's claim as one of the leading producers of great marathon talent.

His 2:08:53 victory required a punishing struggle into headwinds gusting to 40 km/hr for most of the final 5 km – but still he covered that distance at a pace faster than 3 minutes/km! On the women's side, two great stars of the sport, Lisa Ondieki and the former Katrin Dörre (now married to her coach Wolfgang Heinig) duelled essentially alone, after a hoped-for top-level Chinese team opted not to come. Heinig surged at 24 miles and went unchallenged, making it three London wins in a row.

The following day, across the Atlantic in Boston, it was also windy and cool, but for much of the route the breeze favourably assisted the runners. Both men's and women's course records fell as Kenya's Cosmus Ndeti duelled Andrés Espinosa to a 4-second victory in 2:07:15, and Uta Pippig improved by 4:39 upon her '93 New York personal best with 2:21:45. The USA's Bob Kempainen ran his nation's fastest time ever, dethroning the legendary Alberto Salazar, yet he only placed seventh (2:08:47), so deep was the quality and so fast the times. South Africa's Elana Meyer placed third in 2:25:15 – a début time surpassed only by some of the Chinese women in '93 at Tianjin.

As is usual in a year with major international area championships, athletes must either achieve specific qualifying times or else perform well enough to satisfy selection committees, or both, in order to compete for their nation. Three major regional championships influenced the planning of a large number of the world's top athletes: the European Championships, the Commonwealth Games (both in August), and the Asian Games (October).

Thus, while the big-city glamour races effectively served to help select some participating athletes for their teams, other athletes contented themselves with either their national championships or lesser-known races in hopefully favourable conditions.

One example was Kenya's Angelina Kanana, who débuted at Hamburg in late April. As a road racer living in Germany along with many other Kenyans who have found good coaching and competition in that part of the world, her move to the longer distance was not unexpected. Her victory in a major international race was a first for a black African woman. She qualified for her Commonwealth Games team. Three weeks later, her Canadian competitors selected themselves onto their team in Toronto, Carole Rouillard leading that group across the line with 2:32:49. Steve Moneghetti secured his Commonwealth Australian team berth in February with a brilliant win (2:08:55) over Rousseau (2:09:08) at Tokyo. Hu Gangjun scored a Chinese national record 2:10:28 at Rotterdam, just behind Rousseau, to capture a spot on his nation's Asian Games team. Results of drug control, however, showed a positive test for ephedrine, resulting in his disqualification and a three-month suspension from competition.

Often the marathon races at these major regional championship races are boring affairs for spectators, due to very small fields that soon get strung out along the route, and somewhat slowish performances due to warm summer weather. Not so this year – Helsinki and Victoria provided exciting competitions, with the sizeable crowds rewarded well for their interest. In Helsinki for the European Championships, it was a Spanish sweep for the men. Martin Fíz had visited Helsinki the year previous to learn the course, and got a psychological boost by winning their city marathon as part of his training stay. Wisely, for these championships, held on a warm humid day, he started conservatively, and then confidently led his Spanish teammates (Diego Garcia and Alberto Juzdado) to the front in the closing stages. A roughly 10 km loop done four times around the stadium environs gave spectators excellent vantage points as the race progressed.

For the women's race a week later, it was a continuation of the Portuguese grip on the women's top spot. Rosa Mota's reign over this event began with the first women's race at Athens in 1982, and continued through Stuttgart and Split. Mota was absent from Helsinki, but telephoned Manuela Machado the day previous, to wish her good luck and dispense some wisdom. Machado had run a personal-best 32:09 for 10 km on the track three weeks previous, so she was both fit and confident. Taking the lead at 20 km, she never was challenged.

In Victoria the two marathons were staged only a day apart, but in terms of weather they might as well have been a year apart. The women started at dawn on a cool, clear, crisp day, while the men weathered a thunderstorm with heat and humidity so unbearable that it seemed like the Caribbean! Kenya's Kanana took the lead at 5 km, but erred in pace judgement, fading to fifth as two Canadians from Québec (Carole Rouillard and Lizanne Bussières) made headlines throughout their country with gold and silver medals. Steve Moneghetti completed his Commonwealth medal collection with the gold, surviving the 20 km-long rain deluge and even finishing with freshness in his stride.

Proudly he raised high his six-month-old daughter Emma to a drenched and delighted crowd. Almost lost in this excitement was his countryman Sean Quilty, much less experienced, but who ran brilliantly in the final stages, moving up through the pack to capture the silver. Steve had earned a bronze at Brisbane, and a silver at Auckland; he had run far faster on other occasions, but this was his finest hour.

The fall European and American marathon circuits also provided quality, excitement, and intrigue. The always-fast Berlin marathon was so again. Katrin Heinig recovered well enough from London to achieve a personal best of 2:25:15 at the age of 32, nearly four minutes ahead of second place. In somewhat similar fashion to the women, Kenya's Sammy

Nyangincha, ninth at Boston with 2:09:15, recovered well enough to take second at Berlin with a fine 2:08:50, only 19 seconds away from Portuguese winner António Pinto.

The October Asian Games in Hiroshima were hot and humid, and the marathons were challenging. The Japanese had tested their new marathon course in April (a modified downhill version of the '85 World Cup route), achieving fast times but in cool weather. Only seven women started the championships race, and six finished, with China earning gold (Zhong Huandi) and silver medals; Japan's Fujimura took the bronze. Sixteen men started, including the now-reinstated Hu Gangjun. Barcelona gold medallist Hwang Young-Cho (fourth at Boston) took the gold medal for Korea, with Hu dropping to fourth. Three weeks later, however, at Beijing, Hu once again set a Chinese marathon record, this time with 2:10:56.

On the same day as these Asian Games marathons (October 9), and as final preparations for the 25th New York City marathon were proceeding like clockwork, its leader, Fred Lebow, who most experts in the sport have acclaimed as the father of the mass marathon movement, lost his several-year fight with lingering brain cancer. Way back in 1976 it wasn't his idea to change the New York City marathon route from its loops through Central Park to a course that sprawled through all five boroughs of the city. But it was indeed his genius to make the event successful. Indeed, not only was it successful beyond his or anyone else's imagination, but also it united the city in sport. Lebow improved upon his race with every year, but as well, travelled the world to encourage other cities worldwide – from Cairo to Moscow and far beyond – that yes, they too could do it, and it would be good for their city's teeming masses to participate – by running or cheering. This 25th edition of the New York race proceeded with him still there in spirit. A life-size statue was at the finish line, and as runners approached, they crossed a large white segment of pavement on which was painted in blue a heartfelt message of 'Fred, This One's For You.' A record 29,735 finished the race, compared to 25,194 at London.

Who won? For the men the finale became a spirited battle among two Mexicans, German Silva and Benjamin Paredes racing almost side-by-side. With half a mile to go, Silva erroneously followed an on-course vehicle making a quick exit to avoid the finish area. Paredes immediately quickened his pace. Silva sensed his error in time, and physiologists will use this example for years to come to illustrate how his accompanying surge of adrenaline gave him an overpowering burst of speed. He caught Paredes and passed him on the final straightaway to win by two seconds – the closest in race history.

The women's race was just as impressive. Kenya's Tecla Lorupe, now following in Angelina Kanana's footsteps, living in Germany and moving up from shorter-distance road-racing to the marathon, did it successfully. Thirty seconds behind the lead women's pack at the first mile, she surged powerfully in the second half to win by more than two minutes.

Identifying the year's best marathoner is never easy, and '94 was no exception. In this author's opinion, however, for the women, Uta Pippig won out over Valentina Yegorova. Pippig's world-leading time was aided by Boston's windy point-to-point course. It was her only marathon, but she very decisively overpowered the deepest field assembled anywhere during the year. Yegorova was runner-up in that race, and returned to form in November to defeat a good field at Tokyo. For the men, clearly Steve Moneghetti and Vincent Rousseau were at the top. Rousseau's world-leading 2:07:51 at Rotterdam and a fine second place 2:09:08 at Tokyo were hard to beat. But Moneghetti did that, beating him at Tokyo and then taking the Commonwealth Games gold medal. Rousseau later attempted New York but did not finish.

Ending the year, once again on a note epitomising the spirit of global mass participation as well as high-level competition occurring side-by-side, was the story at Honolulu. The race had the second largest number of finishers anywhere in the world, 25,801. But 32,768 had registered, nearly two-thirds from Japan, an ocean away!

That was the scene back in the pack – celebrating the challenge of enduring 42,195 meters of running. Course conditions? You guessed it – strong and gusty winds, along with high humidity. Benson Masya (17th at Boston) claimed his third victory, capping an exceptionally excellent year of road racing. And Carla Beurskens, now 42 years old, took her eighth women's title. Times for these and a selected potpourri of big city races and various championships are in the accompanying event summary.

1994 MARATHON SUMMARY

Date	Venue	Men's Winner	Time	Women's Winner	Time
12 Jan	Tiberias	Ahmed Hussein ETH	2:14:52	Liora Leibovitz ISR	2:51:36
16 Jan	Ho Chi Minh	Douglas Kurtis USA	2:26:19	Lucy Ramwell GBR	2:56:15
16 Jan	Houston	Colin Moore GBR	2:13:34	Alevtina Naumova RUS	2:34:47
16 Jan	Lake Buena Vista	Leonid Shvetsov RUS	2:14:27	Judit Nagy HUN	2:32:32
29 Jan	Kathmandu	Purna Akshya NEP	2:27:50	Susan Bitzer GER	3:06:50
30 Jan	Marrakesh	Mukhamet Nazhipov RUS	2:12:07	Adriana Barbu ROM	2:29:21
30 Jan	Osaka	Women only		Tomoe Abe JPN	2:26:09
5 Feb	Las Vegas	Michael Dudley USA	2:16:54	Kathlene Bowman USA	2:40:14
6 Feb	Oita	Hajime Nakatomi JPN	2:11:28	Men only	
6 Feb	Valencia	Yevgeniy Zarakovsky RUS	2:16:20	Zinaida Semyonova RUS	2:34:08
13 Feb	Tokyo	Steve Moneghetti AUS	2:08:55	Men only	
27 Feb	Sevilla	José Apalanza ESP	2:16:09	Ana Isabel Alonso ESP	2:33:18
5 Mar	East London	Daniel Radebe RSA	2:15:06	Grace de Oliveira RSA	2:46:00
6 Mar	Hiroshima	Kenichi Suzuki JPN	2:11:05	Men only	
6 Mar	Los Angeles	Paul Pilkington USA	2:12:13	Olga Appell USA	2:28:12
13 Mar	Barcelona	Benito Ojeda ESP	2:15:14	Marina Ivanova RUS	2:40:30
13 Mar	Hong Kong	Reinhold Walk GER	2:53:39	Ingrid Tippelt GER	3:44:18
13 Mar	Nagoya	Women only		Eriko Asai JPN	2:30:30
14 Mar	Tel Aviv	Gezahegn Bira ETH	2:19:37	Czeslawa Mentlewicz POL	2:40:44
20 Mar	Kyongju	Manuel Matias POR	2:08:33	Lee Mi-kyung KOR	2:35:44
20 Mar	Vigarano	Marco Di Lieto ITA	2:19:41	Dana Hajna TCH	2:48:47
3 Apr	Huangshan	Han Zongmin CHN	2:18:27	Ren Xiujuan CHN	2:38:23
9 Apr	Antwerpen	Eddy Hellebuyck BEL	2:11:50	Marie-Chr. Christiaens BEL	2:40:54
10 Apr	Canberra	Allan Carman AUS	2:19:39	Susan Hobson AUS	2:32:57
10 Apr	Wien	Joaquim Silva POR	2:10:42	Sissel Grottenberg NOR	2:36:17
17 Apr	London	Dionicio Cerón MEX	2:08:53	Katrin Dörre GER	2:32:34
17 Apr	Rotterdam	Vincent Rousseau BEL	2:07:51	Miyoko Asahina JPN	2:25:52
18 Apr	Boston	Cosmus Ndeti KEN	2:07:15	Uta Pippig GER	2:21:45
21 Apr	Brasilia, SAmCh	Luiz Carlos Da Silva BRA	2:22:07	S Cordeiro de Souza BRA	2:56:20
24 Apr	Beograd	Vladimir Bukhanov UKR	2:12:28	Cristina Pomacu ROM	2:33:09
24 Apr	Carmel	Chad Bennion USA	2:24:36	Kim Goff USA	2:52:01
24 Apr	Hamburg	Eduard Tukhbatulin RUS	2:12:58	Angelina Kanana KEN	2:29:59
24 Apr	Kaliningrad	Anatoliy Archakov RUS	2:14:08	Larisa Zyusko RUS	2:39:31
24 Apr	Madrid	Abdelkader Al Mouaziz MAR	2:17:39	Marina Ivanova RUS	2:43:48
24 Apr	Paris	Said Ermili MAR	2:10:56	Mari Tanigawa JPN	2:27:55
24 Apr	Santiago	Valmir Carvalho BRA	2:16:25	N Freitas da Costa BRA	2:49:59
24 Apr	Torino	Michael Kipkiai KEN	2:10:08	Laura Fogli ITA	2:31:45
27 Apr	Kastoria	Marian Gigea ROM	2:16:31	Lidia Slavuteanu ROM	2:32:38
30 Apr	Rotorua	Paul Smith NZL	2:19:12	Nyla Carroll NZL	2:37:37
1 May	Pittsburgh	Abel Gisemba KEN	2:13:51	Tammy Slusser USA	2:37:14
1 May	Vancouver	Makoto Sasaki JPN	2:17:24	Enikó Fehér HUN	2:46:24
15 May	Munchen	Gidamis Shahanga TAN	2:17:27	Svetlana Kazatkina RUS	2:53:45
15 May	Pardubice	Juma Mynampanda TAN	2:17:32	Alena Peterková TCH	2:31:47
15 May	Toronto	Peter Maher CAN	2:16:07	Carole Rouillard CAN	2:32:49
15 May	Wroclaw	Tadeusz Lawicki POL	2:24:09	Ewa Kepa POL	3:03:21
22 May	København	Joel Kipchumba KEN	2:20:20	Svetlana Kazatkina RUS	2:50:56
29 May	Hannover	Simon Qamunga TAN	2:14:48	Suzana Ciric YUG	2:33:00
29 May	Porto Alegre	Luis Carlos da Silva BRA	2:12:59	Cleuza Irineu BRA	2:43:31
4 Jun	Stockholm	Tesfaye Bekele ETH	2:14:06	Irina Sklyarenko UKR	2:40:34

5 Jun	Enschede	Piotr Poblocki POL	2:13:01	Franca Fiacconi ITA	2:37:43
5 Jun	Melbourne	Manabu Kawagoe JPN	2:18:58	Winnie Lai-Chu Ng HKG	2:47:37
12 Jun	Caen	Jean-Marie Gehen FRA	2:14:30	Valentina Lunegova RUS	2:40:41
18 Jun	Duluth	Donald Johns USA	2:18:19	Linda Somers USA	2:33:42
19 Jun	Mombasa	Zackaria Nyambaso KEN	2:12:49	Linah Chepyator KEN	2:56:04
26 Jun	Tallinn	Pavelas Fedorenko LIT	2:21:21	Tatyana Ivanova RUS	2:56:02
2 Jul	Tromso	Terje Hole NOR	2:23:49	Anita Bergdal NOR	2:54:55
3 Jul	Turku	Noriaki Kiguchi JPN	2:18:58	Svetlana Nechayeva RUS	2:43:48
11 Jul	Bondoufle	Taieb Mansouri TUN	2:17:18	Cindy New CAN	2:54:14
17 Jul	Surfers Paradise	Hajime Nakatomi JPN	2:15:05	Yuko Yamazoe JPN	2:43:20
31 Jul	San Francisco	Patrick Muturi KEN	2:17:34	Karolina Szabó HUN	2:44:34
6 Aug	Helsinki	Zerihun Gizaw ETH	2:20:18	Sylvia Renz GER	2:41:30
6 Aug	Omsk	Rustam Shagiyev RUS	2:17:05	Nadyezhda Ilyina RUS	2:33:49
14/7 Aug	Helsinki, EC	Martin Fíz ESP	2:10:31	Manuela Machado POR	2:29:54
21 Aug	Reykjavik	Pavel Kryska TCH	2:22:41	Kim Goff USA	2:47:23
28/27 Aug	Victoria, CG	Steve Moneghetti AUS	2:11:49	Carole Rouillard CAN	2:30:41
28 Aug	Hokkaido	Eric Wainaina KEN	2:15:03	Olga Appell USA	2:36:33
28 Aug	Sydney	Zithulele Sinqe RSA	2:14:13	Tammy Slusser USA	2:38:29
3 Sep	Moskva	Anatoliy Archakov RUS	2:18:27	Valentina Shatyeyeva RUS	2:44:10
4 Sep	Arusha	Benedict Ako TAN	2:17:40	Blanka James TAN	2:56:33
18 Sep	Bruxelles	Vincent Rousseau BEL	2:12:59	Karin Andersen DEN	3:03:02
25 Sep	Amsterdam	Tesfaye Eticha ETH	2:15:56	Barbara Kamp GER	2:51:57
25 Sep	Berlin	Antonio Pinto POR	2:08:31	Katrin Dörre GER	2:25:15
25 Sep	Buenos Aires	Clair Wathier BRA	2:14:02	Euseli de Assis BRA	2:47:57
25 Sep	Warszawa	Wieslaw Lenda POL	2:17:50	Yelena Tsukhlo BLS	2:42:36
2 Oct	Kosice	Petr Pipa SVK	2:15:03	Ludmila Melicherová SVK	2:40:27
2 Oct	Portland	Masato Yonehara JPN	2:18:41	Elizabeth Brim USA	2:52:41
2 Oct	Saint Paul	Pablo Sierra ESP	2:11:35	Suzana Ciric YUG	2:34:04
9 Oct	Eindhoven	Adugna Atnafa ETH	2:11:37	Jeanne Jansen HOL	2:45:03
9 Oct	Heraklion	Toomas Tarm EST	2:27:42	Maria Belyaeva RUS	2:43:57
9 Oct	Hiroshima	Hwang Young-cho KOR	2:11:13	Zhong Huandi CHN	2:29:32
9 Oct	Istanbul	Bigboy Goromonzi ZIM	2:24:58	Serap Aktas TUR	2:46:42
9 Oct	Venezia	Tena Negere ETH	2:10:50	Ornella Ferrara ITA	2:32:16
16 Oct	Lausanne	Nada Saktay TAN	2:16:09	Natalya Galushko BLS	2:41:38
23 Oct	Carpi	Roberto Crosio ITA	2:12:04	Simona Viola ITA	2:36:07
23 Oct	Frankfurt	Terje Næss NOR	2:13:19	Franziska Moser SUI	2:27:44
23 Oct	Reims	Vanderlei Lima BRA	2:11:06	Stefania Statkuvene LIT	2:32:22
30 Oct	Beijing	Hu Gangjun CHN	2:10:56	Wang Junxia CHN	2:31:11
30 Oct	Dublin	Steve Brace GBR	2:17:13	Linda Rushmere GBR	2:40:17
30 Oct	Chicago	Luis Antonio Santos BRA	2:11:16	Kristy Johnston USA	2:31:34
6 Nov	New York	German Silva MEX	2:11:21	Tecla Lorupe KEN	2:27:37
20 Nov	Habana	Alberto Cuba CUB	2:13:37	Yesenia Centeno CUB	2:44:12
20 Nov	Tokyo	Women only		Valentina Yegorova RUS	2:30:09
27 Nov	Bangkok	Shungea KEN	2:22::04	Ren Xiumei CHN	2:49:21
27 Nov	Kawaguchi	Andrzej Krzyscin POL	2:16:33	Yoko Okuda JPN	2:46:30
27 Nov	Lisboa	Zbigniew Nadolski POL	2:11:57	Adriana Barbu ROM	2:32:56
4 Dec	Abidjan, Afr Ch	Andries Pilusa RSA	2:25:13	Men only	
4 Dec	Firenze	Clair Wathier BRA	2:14:03	Dana Hajná TCH	2:41:34
4 Dec	Macau	Paulo Catarino POR	2:15:28	Li Yemei CHN	2:38:18
4 Dec	Sacramento	Graeme Fell CAN	2:16:13	Jennifer Martin USA	2:36:19
4 Dec	Fukuoka	Boay Akonay TAN	2:09:45	Men only	
4 Dec	Calvia	D Morano ESP	2:20:14	Valentina Shatyayeva RUS	2:56:18
11 Dec	Honolulu	Benson Masya KEN	2:15:04	Carla Beurskens HOL	2:37:06

1994 ROAD RACE REVIEW

By Dr David E Martin

ROAD RACING enjoys a unique charm in athletics in that the world's best athletes can line up beside the masses – sometimes numbering 50,000 or more – to determine who is the best on the day. As such, these sporting events become as much a social event for the community hosting them as they do an athletic spectacle. Whether it be simply one stop of many for an international-class athlete using road-racing to earn an income, or the single race of the year that a serious fitness devotee aspires to complete – road racing has become a mainstream fabric of cities and towns particularly in Europe, the Americas, South Africa, Japan, and Oceania, with increasing activities developing in other regions as well. In a real sense it could be said that road-racing celebrated its centennial. In Hamilton, Ontario, Canada, on March 27, Sammy Nyangincha and May Allison won the 100th edition of the 30 kilometre Around the Bay road race – an event older than the 1896 Olympic marathon in Athens, and as with the Boston marathon, still going strong.

For the mega-races, such as the 50,000-participant Peachtree Road Race in Atlanta, lucrative sponsorship money is required to supplement race entry fees in order to stage such events. For others not quite so large, a large prize-money purse must still be obtained from somewhere to make the event attractive to participation by a large number of the world's élite. Thus, the spectrum of road races is extremely wide-ranging – from local events providing little more than a shirt for participation to extravaganzas that are televised nationally. And changing corporate whims as well as race organisational decisions cause new races to develop, long-standing races to fold, and new twists to alter the event's flavour. Road racing in more ways than one is a microcosm of the sport business world.

Many top athletes have found road racing so satisfying that they have essentially abandoned cross country and track in favour of doing it year-round. However, this is by no means the only path to road-racing success. Others begin the year by developing a strong endurance base through cross country competition. This provides a stepping stone for further sharpening of skills that permit quality road racing later on. Still others have added a third level of structure, that being to move from cross country through road-racing into another fine-tuning phase that permits excellent track running mid-year.

From this pinnacle of fitness, if the athletes have been careful to ensure adequate rest breaks, a strong road-race season can develop out of the second half of the year. As can thus be imagined, the skill of a road-racer is as much determined by knowing when to rest and recover as it is knowing when to race. Unlike the track specialists, who have two definite seasons – indoor and outdoor – and who often opt only for one supreme period of great

Benson Maysa: top road racer of the year

fitness, the continual stimulus placed upon road athletes to accept globe-trotting invitations for racing promotes more than its fair share of mediocrity and injury. The majority of road races – both the very lucrative in terms of potential prize winnings and the small local events that can serve almost as training runs for the super-élite – are in Europe and North America, so it is quite logical that athletes specialising in road racing would either reside in these regions, or travel there periodically for training and a racing block. Kenyan male runners continue to mount the victory podium for the major races more than any other national group, although their women are quickly rising to the forefront as well. Many have found it to their advantage to to based in Europe (notably Germany) or in the United States (notably the New England area). Along with the already-mentioned proximity to racing opportunities, favourable sport club and coaching arrangements as well as better travel dynamics, make these locales more desirable than central Africa.

The accompanying summary of winners at just a very small sampling of the world's top-level road races provides a flavour for the diversity of distances and locales. It is, of course, tempting to compile such lists even more in depth, with a view toward identifying the 'road racer of the year' as is done with track athletes. However, because a sizeable number of these athletes so successfully mix all of the various components of running excellence – cross country, road- racing, track, and marathoning – simply separating out road-racing achievements may not adequately indicate their excellence as a distance runner.

Just a few examples will suffice to illustrate this point, and at the same time focus on the top stars of road racing. Clearly the one athlete of '94 who most successfully devoted his days to being the best pure road racer was Kenya's Benson Masya. He achieved a spectacular ten-week peak of fitness starting early in July. He achieved clear victories over deep fields of athletes in hot weather over challenging courses: The Peachtree 10K, The Utica Boilermaker 15K, the Bix 7-mile, the George Sheehan 10K Classic, the 7.1 mile Falmouth Road Race, the Bobby Crim 10 mile, the inaugural Cobb 10K Classic – all in the United States – and then he won the Great North Run half marathon in England. No one in history had ever won so many of these events all in one season. But he was excellent before this period, winning the City-Pier-City half marathon in Den Haag in March, placing 17th at the Boston marathon in April, finishing a fine seventh at the 2,000 m altitude Bolder Boulder 10K race in late May, and preparing for the Peachtree with a 5K road win at Indianapolis. He continued to compete during the fall, winning the 30 km Lidingöloppet cross country race in Stockholm early in October. As if he needed more, his third victory at the Honolulu marathon in December certainly gave him the title of 1994 King of the Roads.

For the women, there was Kenya's Tecla Lorupe, who resided for much of the year in Germany. From March through November she raced, in Europe and in the United States. And she won – big races and small, nearly all with excellent international women's fields. In the springtime of Europe she won three half marathons, in Holland and at Lisboa and Paris. In May, after sharpening her quickness at the Darmstadt 5K, she tried the United States circuit, winning the Bay-to-Breakers 12K in May. After winning a road 10K in Casablanca as a quality training effort (32:29), she went to Moscow and won the Goodwill Games track 10,000 with a fine 31:52.39 in hot windy conditions. Then it was back to the USA a week later,

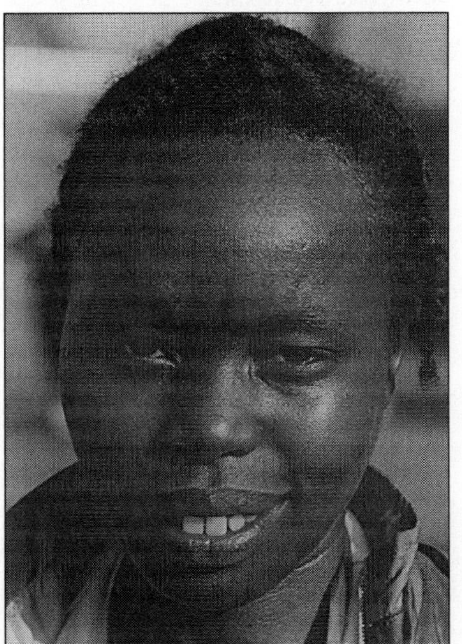

Tecla Lorupe: won in Europe and the USA

beating by 25 seconds Uta Pippig's '93 course record at the Bix 7-mile in Iowa. After another brief break, she began a five-week racing block starting in early September. She was fifth (33:31) in the uphill Atlanta Cobb 10 km race, runner-up (52:43) to Hellen Kimaiyo (52:28) at the 10th 10 mile running of the loop between the two town squares of Amsterdam and Zaandam, winner of the prestigious half marathon from Remich to Grevenmacher along the Mosel River, and she capped the series with a win on the 30 km Stockholm Lidingöloppet cross country course. Then came a five-week break which prepared her both mentally and physically for her debut at the marathon distance in New York.

However, other superb road-racing athletes preferred to mix racing surfaces, and did it well. South Africa's Elana Meyer used road racing in January and February in Japan and the USA to help her fitness for cross country (where she was sixth at the world championships in March). She then débuted at the marathon in Boston, finishing a sparkling third (2:25:15). A justifiable break then let her prepare for her important track season during August/September. She represented her country well in the Commonwealth Games, silver medal at 10,000 (32:06.02), and her continent in the World Cup 10,000 (30:52.51). Two weeks later, in mid-September she used this track sharpness to win the IAAF World Half Marathon Championships on the streets of Oslo. A quick trip to the east coast of the USA in October then put her back on the roads to 'dash for cash' in addition to glory as she crossed the finish tape first in Boston at the USA national 10K road championships (31:39). One week later she gave another hint of her range of talent with a world best 5K road performance (15:10) at nearby Providence.

Elana Meyer: mixed her surfaces well

But among the men there was Kenya's William Sigei – in a class by himself. Early on he ranked second in the IAAF's World Cross Challenge Series, and then won the World Cross Country Championships in March. But then, he applied the fitness from his cross country training to a very brief foray onto the American road circuit. In two weeks time he had two world bests: at 10 miles at the Cherry Blossom Classic in Washington, and at 10 km at the Crescent City Classic in New Orleans. He then disappeared as quickly as he arrived, having a greater interest in a wonderful summer on the European track circuit. He did just that, giving a hint of what might follow with an altitude-affected 28:04.5 10,000 m track victory at his national championships. Along with several other top-quality European track results, his crowning achievement was a world record for 10,000 m in Oslo (26:52.23) in July.

Road racing as a sport continues to grow and prosper. New circuits, new races, new athletes, and new ideas fill a sport that seems always changing. An increasing popularity of inner-city loop courses – made for television – are attractive to both sponsors and athletes – Germany has a wide variety of so-called 'city-laufen,' and the idea is being copied elsewhere. The USA recently announced a 'PRO Circuit' of 13 top-level races as an outgrowth of the long-successful Association of Road Racing Athletes (ARRA). Prize money payouts are expected to total more than $1 million. In addition to this is a new 'US Men's Road Grand Prix Circuit,' involving other events, and open to all athletes but with prize money ($250,000) available only to USA men. In England, the BUPA-sponsored series of well-established longer- distance road races continues successfully. Whoever the sponsors and whatever the weather or length of the event, road racing is here to stay, being ever more enriched by the resourcefulness of its participants.

1994 ROAD RACE SUMMARY

9 Jan	Manaus	Manaus 10K	*Simon Chemoiywo KEN 27:48	*Carmen de Oliveira BRA 33:03
23 Jan	Tokyo	City 1/2 Mar	Vincent Rousseau BEL 60:23	Junko Kataoka JPN 68:41
5 Feb	Las Vegas	1/2 Mar	Paul Pilkington USA 62:37	Nadia Prasad FRA 69:05
6 Feb	Coamo	San Blas 1/2 Mar	*Lameck Aguta KEN 62:55	
19 Feb	Freeport	Grand Bahama 5K	Philemon Hanneck ZIM 13:35	Anne Marie Letko USA 15:42
26 Feb	Tampa	Gasparilla 15K	*Philemon Hanneck ZIM 42:35	Elana Meyer RSA 48:11
6 Mar	Frankfurt	1/2 Mar	*Andrew Eyapan KEN 62:38	*Claudia Metzner GER 72:25
12 Mar	Jacksonville	River Run 15K	Todd Williams USA 43:42	Anne Marie Letko USA 49:27
13 Mar	Lisboa	Lisboa 1/2 Mar	Andrés Espinosa MEX 61:34	Tecla Lorupe KEN 69:27
20 Mar	Kyoto	Kyoto 1/2 Mar	*Valdenor Dos Santos BRA 61:53	*Uta Pippig GER 67:59
27 Mar	Carlsbad	Carlsbad 5K	Josphat Machuka KEN 13:21	Colleen de Reuck RSA 15:20
27 Mar	Den Haag	City-Pier-City 1/2 Mar	Benson Masya KEN 62:00	Jane Salumáe EST 70:10
27 Mar	Hamilton	Around The Bay 30K	*Sammy Nyangincha KEN 1:32:55	May Allison CAN 1:50:54
27 Mar	Paris	Paris 1/2 Mar	Said Ermili MAR 61:58	Tecla Lorupe KEN 70:47
10 Apr	Berlin	Berlin 1/2 Mar	Tendai Chimusasa ZIM 61:45	Kathrin Wessel GER 70:47
10 Apr	Washington	Cherry Blossom 10M	#William Sigei KEN 46:01	Helen Chepngeno KEN 54:05
16 Apr	Milano	Stramilano 1/2 Mar	Paul Tergat KEN 60:13	Maria Guida ITA 70:19
16 Apr	New Orleans	Crescent City 110K	#William Sigei KEN 27:24	Judi St. Hilaire USA 32:26
1 May	Spokane	Bloomsday 12K	Josphat Machuka KEN 3:59	Olga Appell USA 38:45
7 May	Göteborg	1/2 Mar	Onesmo Ludago KEN 63:08	Ritva Lemettinen FIN 73:04
8 May	Berlin	25km von Berlin	Tendai Chimusassa ZIM 1:14:45	Alena Peterková TCH 1:25:46
8 May	Darmstadt	Nike Frauenlauf		Tecla Lorupe KEN 15:47
15 May	Cleveland	Revco 10K	Yobes Ondieki KEN 28:30	Nadia Prasad FRA 32:01
15 May	San Francisco	Bay to Breakers 12K	Ismail Kirui KEN 34:03	Tecla Lorupe KEN 39:10
29 May	La Courneuve	15K	#Paul Tergat KEN 42:12	Fernanda Ribeiro POR 48:45
30 May	Boulder	Bolder Boulder 10K	Armando Quintanilla MEX 29:31	Nadia Prasad FRA 33:28
18 Jun	Peoria	Steamboat Classic 4M	Lameck Aguta KEN17:43	Jane Omoro KEN 20:31
4 Jul	Atlanta	Peachtree 10K	Benson Masya KEN 28:01	Anne Marie Letko USA 31:57
10 Jul	Utica	Boilermaker 15K	*Benson Masya KEN 42:57	Delilah Asiago KEN 50:24
17 Jul	Sapporo	1/2 Mar	Tadesse Gebre ETH 64:29	Mari Tanigawa JPN 73:53
30 Jul	Davenport	Bix 7 Mile	*Benson Masya KEN 31:56	*Tecla Lorupe KEN 36:02
13 Aug	Red Bank	Sheehan Classic	Benson Masya KEN 28:29	Gwyn Coogan USA 33:00
21 Aug	Falmouth	Falmouth 7.1M	Benson Masya KEN 31:59	Laura Mykytok USA 37:01
27 Aug	Bojano	La Matesina 10K	Paul Tergat KEN 28:11	
27 Aug	Flint	Bobby Crim 10 Mile	Benson Masya KEN 46:22	Anne Marie Letko USA 53:42
4 Sep	Buenos Aires	1/2 Mar	Ronaldo Da Costa BRA 61:05	Solange de Souza BRA 72:21 05
Sep	Marietta	Cobb 10K Classic	*Benson Masya KEN 28:55	*Jane Omoro KEN 32:24
17 Sep	Zürich	Greifenseelauf 1/2 Mar	Wilson Omwoyo KEN 61:53	Rosa Mota POR 71:11
18 Sep	South Shields	Gt North Run 1/2 Mar	Benson Masya KEN 60:02	Rosanna Munerotto ITA 71:29
19 Sep	Philadelphia	Distance Run 1/2 Mar	William Koech KEN 62:04	Anne Marie Letko USA 70:03
24 Sep	Oslo	IAAF World 12 Mar	Khalid Skah MAR 60:27	Elana Meyer RSA 68:36
25 Sep	Grevenmacher	Route du Vin 12 Mar	Julius Korir KEN 61:28	Tecla Lorupe KEN 70:38
2 Oct	Breda	1/2 Mar	Simon Lopuyet KEN 61:58	Joyce Chepchumba KEN 72:03
16 Oct	Chula Vista	Barrios Invit. 10K	*Philemon Hanneck ZIM 27:59	*Nadia Prasad FRA 31:38
16 Oct	Providence	Downtown 5K	Stephen Nyamu KEN 13:49	#Elana Meyer RSA 15:10
29 Oct	Tulsa	Tulsa Run 15K	*Stephen Nyamu KEN 42:51	Delilah Asiago KEN 48:59
5 Nov	Barnsley	Barnsley 10K	Simon Lopuyet KEN 28:36	*Joyce Chepchumba KEN 32:26
20 Nov	Nijmegen	Zevenheuvelenloop 15K	*Haile GebrselassieETH 43:00	*Liz McColgan GBR 49:56
18 Dec	Orlando	12 Mar	Keith Brantly USA 63:02	Kim Jones USA 74:38
18 Dec	Zürich	9.1k/6.8k	Carsten Eich GER 25:50	Tecla Lorupe KEN 21:11
31 Dec	São Paulo	São Silvestre 10k	Ronaldo da Costa BRA 44:11	Derartu Tulu ETH 51:17

* = Course Record, # = World Best

1994 ULTRA SUMMARY

by Andy Milroy

NINETY NINETY four saw yet another fascinating year in the ongoing development of Ultrarunning. There was an influx of new talent attracted by the growth in international competition, particularly in the 100km. New areas of the world became involved over an increasingly widening spectrum of Ultra events as Ultrarunning continued its expansion and development, becoming a truly world sport.

The World 100km Challenge in 1994 was held at Saroma in Northern Japan, the first time the event had been held in Asia. Virtually all the major 100km runners participated and the race saw the greatest number of male runners ever under seven hours (24). A newcomer, Aleksey Volgin (RUS), in his second ever 100km, won with 6:22:43; (he does however have a background as a world class 50km walker.) Jaroslav Janicki (POL) in second, Kazimierz Bak (GER) in third, and Shaun Meiklejohn (RSA) in fourth all ran under 6:30, a feat that only nine men had achieved prior to this race on certified courses. (All four were unknown internationally before this year, and had only run a handful of 100kms between them prior to the World Challenge. In the women's race at least experience told and Valentina Shatyayeva, second in last year's event, won clearly with 7:34:58.

The year for the men in the 100km event had really started in April with the French and Russian championships. Konstantin Santalov (RUS) won the French in 6:36:38, and then six days later had a real fight on his hands in the Russian. On a short, flat, out and back course measured by surveyor's wheel I understand, Santalov emerged the exhausted winner after a torrid battle with Volgin. The times recorded were remarkable – 6:16:21 to 6:18:49 with Aleksey Kononov being given 6:22:20 in third. Obviously the competition for places in the World Challenge team in the world's greatest Ultrarunning nation is going to be fierce, but no measurement details have been received yet, and thus the reliability of these times remains uncertain.

Later that month Bak, a former Pole, now a naturalised German, blazed his way into the record books on his 100km debut, setting a new German best of 6:27:59 at Rodenbach, (setting a 50km best en route!) The next major mark came in June, when Jean-Paul Praet (BEL) produced his usual strong performance to win at Torhout with 6:29:42.

The first major 100km after the World Challenge was the International event in Victoria, Canada (Aug 31) which incorporated the IAU North American and Canadian Championships. The race was won by Stefan Fekner (CAN) in 6:54:31. The next significant event was the European Championships at Winschoten in September. The two Polish athletes, Jaroslav Janicki and Andrzej Magier, had figured highly in the World Challenge, but with no other Polish runners in Japan, had failed to secure the team title. They made sure of this at Winschoten, running in together in a time of 6:33:43. with teammate Damien Bregula also going under 7 hours. In early October at the Santa Cruz de Bezana 100km, Volgin produced his slowest time to date, a mere 6:27: 43, to win easily. In November a new international 100km was held at São Paulo in Brazil. The race was won by José Da Silva (BRA) in 6:33:02, the fastest time ever recorded in the Americas. I am still awaiting details of the course measurement.

Apart from the World Challenge, the top runners seldom met head-to -head. Santalov was dominant early in the year, but was then sidelined by injury. The other major figures were Volgin, Janicki and Bak. Volgin was beaten by Santalov in early April, on his 100km debut, but went on to win at Saroma when the latter was forced to retire with leg problems, and then won well again in Spain late in the year. Janicki finished second to Volgin at Saroma, and was adjudged the winner at the European Championships at Winschoten. Bak won two 100km races, but finished third at Saroma. Their positions at, Saroma, I feel, reflect fairly their world rankings for 1994. For the second year running five men ran under 6:30 on certified courses. The number of performances and actual performers under seven hours was however somewhat down on 1993 record numbers.

However the women continued to progress by leaps and bounds in the 100km. In February, Donna Perkins had run 7:33:46 on her 100km debut in the US national championships. In the Russian championships in April, Irma Petrova won with 7:22:55. At Torhout, Belgium, in June, Alciro Lario (POR) made a very strong debut with 7:34:27. The World Challenge, won by Shatyayev in 7:34, from Trudi Thomson (GBR) in 7:4-2, saw the greatest number of, women ever under 8 hours (8) as well as the most ever under 8:10 and 8:20. The European Championships was won by Valentina Lyakhova (RUS) with 7:36:39 who three weeks later showed her incredible resilience when she produced the best time in the world for 1994 (7:22:18) at Amiens. Former holder of the world road best, Birgit Lennartz-Lohrengel ran 7:38:14 in the German championships on the same day. In October, Maria Bak, wife of Kazimierz, seized the, family spotlight with 7:30:32 at Kalisz in Poland, for the second best mark of the year. Amidst these highlights, other newcomers made their marks. Mary Morgan, Maria Ostrovskaya, Anni Loenstad and Rae Bisschoff set new national bests under 8 hours for Australia, Ukraine, Demnark and South Africa, and runners like Olive (FRA), Duryea (USA), Drescher (GER), Evans (CAN) and Reymann (FRA) broke through into world class.

Ranking the top women is not easy. Valentina Shatyayeva won the World Challenge, and also ran 7: 57 later in the year. Valentina Lyakhova won the European Championships and also ran the fastest time in the world. Trudi Thomson ran second in the World Challenge in her only 100km of the year; Maria Bak ran under 8 hours three times including the second best time of the year. However, the World Challenge was by far the toughest competition of the year. I would rank the women: Shatyayeva first, Lyakhova second, Thomson third and Bak fourth.

The improvement in depth in the 100km over the year was once again relatively greater among the women than the men. Eighteen women ran under 8 hours, and 44 under 8:30. (13 and 35 in 1993; 10 and 29 in 1992.)

It was a vintage year for the 24 hour event. Anatoly Kruglikov ran 270.296km to win in Podolsk indoors in Russia in February, from Nasibula Khusnulin's 269.560km. In May in the major international championships of the year, the European Challenge in Szeged, Hungary, Janos Bogár won on home soil with 261.122km, with Jean Pierre Guyomarch (FRA) second with 254.013km. Bogár's mark was to be the best road mark in the world until August, when Paul Beckers (BEL) covered 262,758km at Torhout. However, 1994 marked the resurgence of the track event. in August, at Podolsk once again, this time outdoors, Kruglikov went over 270km again with a fine 271.200km (for fourth place on the all time list) with Eduard Khirov running 268.975km in second (for fifth), and Mikhail Yeremisov 264.400km (for eighth). In October yet another runner went over 260km on the track when Seigi Arita (JPN) covered 262. 238km at Arcueil in France.

For the third year running Sigrid Lomsky (GER) won the European 24 hour Challenge, this year covering 231.482km. This mark was to be surpassed by Marie Bertrand in the French Championships in September, breaking through into world class with a fine 231.510km. These were to be the top marks of the year, with Sue Ellen Trapp's 220.125km (136.7 miles) in the US Championships the nearest contender.

The World No. 1 has to be Kruglikov, with Bogar second. Lomsky remains the top woman, her 231km in the extreme heat of Szeged was the top competitive mark of 1994.

The 24 hour took a major step forward in its development in 1994. The European Challenge saw the strongest team event yet, and major international events were held in China and Brazil for the first time, with continental records being set in the latter race. There were eight men's marks over 260km by seven athletes, the best ever tally in a year.

For the first time for some years the top 48 hour race was not Surgères. At Köln on a road loop, Tomás Rusek (CZE) ran 403.622km to win. The best track mark, though, was at Surgères – Jean-Gilles Boussiquet produced 394.170km to win. The first woman was Susan Olsen (USA) with 348.939km (for second place on the world all-time track list and third on the absolute best list behind Hilary Walker and Sue Ellen Trapp).

Six day races this year were held in the USA, Ukraine, France and Australia. The top mark was indoors at La Rochelle, won by Stu Mittleman (USA) with 863km.

For some, even running for six days is not long enough. Gary Parsons (AUS) set a new world 1000 mile track best of 13d 17h 37m 21s at Nanango, Australia in March. The longest race on a certified road course is the 1300 miler held in New York in September/October; it was yet again dominated by women, Antana

Locs (CAN) won with Suprabha Beckford (USA) second. There were no male finishers.The top man was Argentinian Nicola Sinisgalli who set a South American 1000 mile best. The 1000 mile race for women held in conjunction with the 1300 miles, was won by Silvia Andonie (MEX) in 14:18:52:38. The longest race of the year was the TransAmerica Footrace of some 4707km in 64 daily stages. It was won by István Sipos (HUN) in 517:43:02, (it may be remembered that Sipos holds the world road best for 2000km.) The five finishers included two Japanese.

The classic non-standard events still appeal to many. The London to Brighton was won by Shaun Meiklejohn (RSA) in a record time for the new longer 88km course of 6:01:02. The first woman was Jackie Leake (GBR) in 7:06:22.

The Comrades was won from the front by a novice ultrarunner called Alberto Salazar! Perhaps the major American marathon star of the1980s, Salazar had long been sidelined by physical problems which now seem to be resolved. He is apparently interested in being part of the 1995 US 100km team for the Winschoten World Challenge in Holland. Nick Bester (RSA) was second some four minutes behind. The women's race was dominated by the Russian women after Frith van der Merwe retired with an injury. Valentina Lyakhova won in 63:42:18 from Valentina Shatyayeva, with Marta Vass (HUN) third.

The longest of the classic events is the Spartathlon, 240km from Athens to Sparta in Greece, to commemorate Pheidippides' famous run. James Zarei (GBR) was first in 26:15, (ironically he was born in Iran), well clear of Ronald Teunisse (HOL). The first woman was Helga Backhaus (GER) in 30:41.

Some runners prefer stage, races, and there were some notable events in 1994. In a fiercely contested seven day 617km stage event in Tasmania, Yiannis Kouros (GRE) returned to competitive ultras. He faced the redoubtable Kruglikov, Bogár and Santalov among a stellar field. Kruglikov won by half an hour from the legendary Greek runner.

Eleanor Robinson faced Irina Petrova, 25 years younger, as well as the more mature Sigrid Lomsky. Robinson emerged as winner when Petrov retired. In October another five day stage race 344km from Vienna to Budapest took place. Bogár had a tough tussle with Santalov but emerged as winner by eight minutes. (Kruglikov finished sixth) In the women's race after Lyakhova won the first day, Robinson proceeded to dominate the event and won by an hour and a half, from Agnes Bozan (HUN).

The World Ultrarunning scene continues to develop year by year. Naturally with Lake Saroma in northern Japan hosting the World Challenge, Asia became a focal area. In May the first international 24 Hour track race to be held in China took place at Guangzhou, with runners from China, Japan, Hong Kong and Singapore. The media coverage was considerable and millions saw the race on television.

Following a 250km road race from Nagoya to Kanazawa, Rune Larsson (SWE) described Japan as a sleeping giant of ultrarunning. This year the giant has begun to stir. There were four Japanese runners under 7 hours in the World Challenge in Hokkaido, and their team finished second overall. Following the success of that event, a second 100km race has been held at Nakamura in southern Japan. A thousand runners entered this inaugural race, and a further 200 took part in a 60km race held in conjunction with it (60% of the field were novices.) The Japanese have in fact shown considerable interest in ultrarunning for years. The Spartathlon always attracts Japanese runners and the TransAmerica race is sponsored by a Japanese company. The emergence of Seigi Arita as a major 24 hour performer is sure to strengthen and.develop their interest in ultras still further.

Another growth area in 1994 has been Latin America. There has been a 50km in Cuba, and the major Brazilian 100km moved to São Paulo and attracted an international field, as did a later 24 hour event there. Another 24 was held in Argentina, and also a 48 hour race. Argentinian and Mexican runners have competed successfully in several multi-day races in the United States, setting continental and national best performances. (The Mexican Tarahumara Indians again dominated the Leadville 100 mile trail race in Colorado).

With the growing influx of new talent and the continued global development of the sport, Ultrarunning looks set for a lively future. In the traditional heartlands of the sport, the Russians are still dominant, but the Germans and French are in contention, with the Americans, French and now Japanese coming through strongly. The British and South Africans will bounce back through the sheer depth of their ultra traditions. Add to that the wild cards from Australasia, Latin America and Africa and life will be very interesting ...

OBITUARIES

See *Athletics 1994* for obituaries of Robert Bobin, Patrick El Mabrouk, Jack Metcalfe, Bert Nelson, Arthur Porritt, Helen Stephens and Cliff Temple.

Dave ALBRITTON (USA) (b. 13 Apr 1913 Danville, Alabama) on 15 May at Dayton, Ohio. The Olympic high jump silver medallist in 1936 behind his teammate Cornelius Johnson. Both men had improved the world record to 2.076m on their second jumps at this height at the US Olympic Trials in New York on 12 July 1936. Although he never again jumped so high Albritton had a long career, placing in the first three nine times in the AAU championships outdoors, winning in 1937, 1945, 1947 and 1950, 2nd 1938, 3rd 1936, 1939, 1944 and 1949. A pioneer straddler, he was also AAU indoor champion in 1944 and NCAA champion (tied) each year 1936-8. He was a teammate of Jesse Owens both at East Tech high school, Cleveland and at Ohio State University, and served for 12 years as a state legislator in Ohio.
Progression at high jump (position on world list): 1935- 1.98 (9=), 1936- 2.076 (1), 1937- 2.048 (3), 1938- 2.05 (1=), 1939- 2.007 (3=), 1940- 1.943 (42=), 1944- 2.007 (4=), 1945- 1.975 (11=), 1946- 2.003 (5=), 1947- 1.98 (14=), 1948- 2.038 (2=), 1949- 1.93i, 1950- 1.969 (29=).

Mal ANDREWS (USA) (b. 11 Sep 1933) on 16 April. At long jump he was 2nd in the NCAA, with pb 7.71 (1956), 7.72w (1955). He was 4th at the US Olympic Trials in 1956. Coached at Cal State Hayward.

John Joe BARRY (Ireland) (b. 5 Oct 1925) on 9 December. A charismatic runner, who never fulfilled his potential. In 1948 ran in the heats of the 1500m and 5000m at the Olympics. His best year was 1949, when he ranked 9th in the world at 5000m, won the AAA 3 miles and set Irish records at 1 mile 4:08.6, 2 miles 8:59.0 and 3 miles 13:56.2. He went to Villanova University and won the 1950 AAU mile indoors.

Jim BELLWOOD (New Zealand) at the age of 82. He coached more than 150 New Zealand senior champions, including such notable athletes as Yvette Williams and Val Young.

Ray CONGER (USA) (b. 12 Nov 1903) on 23 October in Brookline Village, Pennsylvania. He was 10th in the 1928 Olympic 1500m, having set a US record 3:55.0 to win the Olympic Trials, He won the 1927 NCAA mile title in a meeting record 4:17.6 while at Iowa State and was AAU champion at 1500m three times, 1927-8 and 1930. pbs: 1500m 3:55.0 (1928), 1M 4:13.2i (1929).

Georges DAMITIO (France) (b. 20 May 1924) on 7 September when an aircraft he was piloting crashed into the sea. At the 1948 Olympics he was 5th in the high jump and 6th in the long jump. In 1949 with 2.02 he became the first Frenchman to high jump 2 metres, having set the previous record at 1.97 in 1948. He appeared in 30 internationals for France 1946-55 and was French champion at high jump 1947-9 and 1951-3 and long jump 1947. pb LJ 7.35 (1947).

José Romão DA SILVA (Brazil) (b. 23 Apr 1948) on 12 January in São Paulo in an accident in a warm-up football game. He was the first Brazilian to become world class at distance running, putting an end to the myth that this was impossible at home due to climatic conditions. He set 25 national records from 1500m to 10,000m in his career, 1969 to 1980 and in 1975 was South American champion and 2nd at the Pan-American Games at the steeplechase. South American records: 3000m 7:53.0 (1975), 3000m St 8:35.8 (1975); pbs: 1500m 3:44.4 (1976), 5000m 13:43.6 (1975), 10,000m 29:04.2 (1975).

Maria DOLLINGER (Germany) (b. 28 Oct 1910) on 10 August. She set an unofficial world record for 800m when winning the 1931 German title with 2:16.8, and four relay world records, at 3 x 800m in 1931 and three at 4 x 100m, including in the heats of the 1936 Olympics, when the baton was dropped in the final. She also set German records at 100m: 11.9 '34 and 11.8 '35 and five at 200m from 25.7 '30 to 25.2 '32. Her best 200m was 24.9 '34 and long jump 5.48 '34. At the Women's World Games she was 2nd at 800m in 1930, and 1st at 4 x 100m, 4th 100m and 6th 200m in 1934, and she was German champion at 100m 1932, 200m 1931, 1933; 800m 1929-31.

Her daughter Brunhilde Hendrix won an Olympic silver medal at 4 x 100m in 1960.

José María ELORRIAGA (Spain) (b. 3 Feb 1931) on 12 August. Spanish hammer champion 1957-9 and 1963, with 4 Spanish records to 57.52 (1962).

Ivan FUQUA (USA) (b. 9 Aug 1909 Decatur, Illinois) on 14 January. He ran the opening leg in 47.1 for the US team that took the gold medal in a world record time of 3:08.2 at the 1932 Olympics in Los Angeles. The same team had run a world record 3:11.8 in their heat. From Denver AC and Indiana University, he had been 5th at the 1932 US Olympic Trials and was the AAU champion for 400m in 1933 and 1934. He coached at Connecticut State and after war service in the navy, ending with the rank of lieutenant commander, he was head coach at Brown 1947-73.

Progression at 400m (position on world list): 1929- 49.1* (42=) and 48.6* est, 1932- 47.6 (9=), 1933- 47.0* (3), 1934- 47.2* (3), 1935- 47.6 (9) (*440y less 0.3 sec). pb 200m 21.2 (1933).

Bert GARDINER (Australia) at age of 92. National walks champion 1925, national selector for 20 years and life member of Athletics Australia. Father of Bob Gardiner, 1970 Commonwealth 20 miles walk silver medallist and 5th 1964 Olympic 50km walk.

Reinaldo GORNO (Argentina) (b. 18 Jul 1918 Yapeyu, Corrientes) in Buenos Aires on April 10. In January he was shot by a gang of thieves who attacked the sports complex where he worked and, despite five operations, died from the effects. At the marathon he won silver medals at the 1951 Pan-American Games and at the 1952 Olympics. He won major marathons at Enschede 1954 and Nakamura 1955, the latter in his best time of 2:24:55. At South American Championships he won the cross-country title in 1945 and was second at 10,000m 1941 (pb 31:39.6) and 1945 and half marathon 1952.

(Dame) **Marea HARTMAN** (UK) on 29 August at the age of 74. The most influential administrator in British women's athletics history. Having run for Spartan Ladies she became WAAA honorary treasurer in 1950, and served for many years as secretary as well as British team manager and chairman of the IAAF Women's Commission.. When the WAAA merged with the AAA she was elected the first president of the AAA of England. Awarded the MBE in 1967 and the CBE in 1978, she was made a Dame for her distinguished services to athletics in 1994.

Alan HELFFRICH (USA) (b. 7 Aug 1900 New York) at State College, Pennsylvania in June. Gold medallist at 4x400m at the 1924 Olympics in a world record time of 3:16.0 and AAU champion at 880y 1921-2 and 1925. At the US Olympic Trials he was 5th at 880yin 1920 and 7th at 400m in 1924. pbs: 440y 50.1 (1924), 880y 1:54.8 (1921). Graduate of Penn State University, for whom he won the NCAA 880y in 1922 and 1923 and the IC4A 880y in 1923 and 440y in 1924, and with whose team he set a world record at 4 x 880y in 1923.

Ralph HILL (USA) (b. 26 Dec 1908) in Klamath Falls, Oregon on 17 October. He had an epic race against Lauri Lehtinen in the 1932 Olympic 5000m. In the home straight he tried to pass the Finn on either side, but Lehtinen held him off by weaving across the track. A call for Lehtinen's disqualification was disallowed and announcer Bill Henry went into history when he calmed spectators on the verge of rioting by saying "Remember please, these people are our guests". Both men were given the Olympic record time of 14:30.0. Hill, who had earlier won the AAU 5000m in 14:55.7, took Lehtinen's hindrance with supreme sportsmanship and no protest was made. The world's fastest miler of 1930 with 4:12.4, Hill was second in the NCAA mile in 1931 and graduated from the University of Oregon in business studies. He became a farmer. Other pbs: 2M 9:23.4 (1932), 3M 14:23.3 (1932).

Clarence HOUSER (USA) (b. 25 Sep 1901 Winnigan, Mo.) on 1 October in Gardena, California at the age of 93. He won both shot and discus at the 1924 Olympics and retained his discus title in 1928. While at the University of Southern California he won the NCAA discus title in 1926, in which year he set a world discus record of 48.20m. He won AAU titles at shot in 1921 and 1925, with third places in 1923 and 1926, and at discus in 1925, 1926 and 1928, with 2nd in 1922 and 3rd in 1923. He became a dentist, practicing in Palm Springs.

Partial progression at SP, DT: 1921- 14.32, 43.63; 1922- 44.35, 1923- 14.04+, 45.02+; 1924- 14.99, 46.16; 1925- 15.26, 47.70; 1926- 15.42, 48.20; 1928- 47.70, 1929- 46.40, 1931- 44.40.

Rafael ILLÁN (Spain) (b. 27 Nov 1970) on 20 October by a train. pb 5000m 13:39.32 '93.

Rudolf JOHANSSON (Sweden) (b. 12 Apr 1899) on 28 November. Swedish champion at 800m in 1926 and 4th in his semi-final at the 1924 Olympic Games. In 1923 he was the third equal fastest European at 1:54.9.

Oluyemi KAYODE (Nigeria) (b. 7 Jul 1968) in a car crash in Arizona in October. He had been a student at Brigham Young University, USA and was 2nd in the NCAA 200m in 1993. In 1992 he was 7th at 200m and won a silver medal at the sprint relay at the Olympic Games and was also 4th in the World Cup 200m. pbs: 100m 10.17 '92, 200m 20.22 '92, 20.18Aw '93.

Don LASH (USA) (b. 15 Aug 1914) on 19 September. Known as "The Iron Man", he won the US cross-country title for a record seven successive years 1934-40. On the track he set a US record of 31:06.9 to win the AAU 10,000m in 1936 and returned the next day to win the 5000m. In 1940 he was 2nd at 5k after winning at 10k. Indoors he was AAU champion at 5000m in 1938 and 1939 and in 1940 he was 2nd in 13:55.0 to Greg Rice, 13:52.3, when both men broke the world indoor record for 3 miles in New York. He won the 1936 NCAA 5000m while at Indiana University and set world records at 2 miles both outdoors, 8:58.3 in 1936, and indoors, 8:58.0 in 1937. Winner of the Sullivan Award in 1938
Other pbs: 1500m 3:52.8 (1937), 1M 4:07.2 (1937), 3000m 8:22.8 (1936), 3M out 14:27.0 (1937); 5000m 14:30.9i (1939), 14:56.0 (1940).

Fred LEBOW (USA) (b. Fischel Lebowitz 3 Jun 1932 in Arad, Romania) on 8 October at age 62 after a 4 $^1{}_2$-year battle against brain cancer. He will always be remembered for the New York Marathon, which he organised annually from 1970, The dramatic growth of the race began in 1976, when to celebrate the US Bicentennial the course was changed from being run around Central Park to a route through all five boroughs of the city. That year the race attracted 2090 starters, a figure that rose rapidly to 14,496 in 1981, the year of the first London Marathon, a race inspired by New York's success, and to the record number of 29,543 finishers in 1994. After making his fortune in the garment business, Lebow built the New York Road Runners Club from 270 beginners to an organisation of over 31.000 runners and 100 events each year. He was also the inspiration behind the Fifth Avenue Mile and the annual New York Games. He ran 69 marathons, with a best time of 3:19.

Albert MARTINEAU (GB) (b. 24 Dec 1914) on 3 May. Fifth in 1948 Olympic 50km walk, with a best of 4:39:40 that year when he was 3rd in the RWA Championships.

Ira MURCHISON (USA) (b. 6 Feb 1933 Chicago) on 28 March. In 1956 after twice equalling the world record for 100m with 10.2 he broke it with 10.1 at the International Military Championships in Berlin. He was then 4th at 100m and earned a gold medal as he led off the world record setting US 4 x 100m relay team at the Melbourne Olympics. After military service he returned to Western Michigan and at the NCAA 100y shared the world record time of 9.3 when second to Bobby Joe Morrow in 1957 and won the title in 1958. Just 5 ft 4 in (1.63m) tall he was an explosive starter and ideally suited to indoor sprints, running 6.1 for 60y three times in 1957-8 and winning the 1957 AAU title. He continued sprinting despite surgery for a diseased colon in 1959 and won the 100m bronze and took gold at 4 x 100m at the 1963 Pan-American Games. From 1986 he was an assistant coach at Chicago State.

Progression at 100y and 100m (position on world list): 1948- 10.3y, 1949- 10.3y, 1950- 10.0y, 1951- 9.6yw, 1952- 9.6yw, 1953- 9.6y (9=), 1954- 9.6y (8=), 1955- 10.4 (5=), 1956- 9.4yw, 10.1 (1=); 1957- 9.3y (1=), 10.3 (4=); 1958- 9.4y (2=), 10.2 (1=); 1959- 9.4yw, 10.2 (2=); 1960- 10.4 (40=), 1961- 9.4y (7=), 1962- 9.5y (27=)/9.3w, 1963- 10.3 (4=). pb 220y 21.2 (1958).

Åke ÖDMARK (Sweden) (b. 29 Oct 1916) on 4 September. In 1941 he became first Swedish high jumper to clear 2 metres, having also set a Swedish record at 1.99 in 1939. He was Swedish champion in 1939 and 1940 and was 12th at the 1936 Olympics and 4th at the 1938 Europeans. He was the winner in four international matches.

Stig OLDÉN (Sweden) (b. 8 Jun 1922) on 13 September. The Swedish champion at javelin in 1949 and second at the 1947 World University Games. pb 68.84 (1949).

Walter PEKTOR (Austria) (b. 30 Sep 1945) on 23 December. Austrian javelin champion nine times, 1964-8, 1971 and 1974-6, he succeeded his father Dr Erwin Pektor as Austrian record holder with ten records, from 71.31 in 1964 to 82.16 in the qualifying round at the 1968 Olympic Games, which he followed with 10th place in the final

Borivoj POJEZDNY (Czech) (b. 30 Apr 1930) of a heart attack in a road race in Prague on September 25. Won the CS cross-country title 1957. pbs: 5000m 14:26.2 (1956), 3000mSt 9:21.4 (1957).

Krasimir RACIC (Croatia) (b. 15 Aug 1932) on June 19, having been hit by a car while cycling to Zagreb stadium on June 15. At the hammer he was 6th at the 1956 Olympics and also competed in 1960 and was 18th in 1954 and 10th in 1958 at the Europeans. Yugoslav champion in 1954, 1957 and 1959, having set Yugoslav records from 60.28 in 1955 to 62.80 in 1956, his best throw was 63.89 in 1960. The top Croatian statistician, he produced the first two statistical handbooks for his new nation, and provided much help to ATFS members for some 30 years.

Onni RAJASAARI (Finland) (b. 2 Mar 1910 Hanko) on 12 November at Hanko. An economist by profession, he won the European triple jump in 1938, having been third in 1934. At the Olympics he was 11th in 1932 and 12th in 1936, was Finnish champion at TJ 1933-9, with 2nd place 1940, 1942-3, and 4th 1945, and won the long jump in 1938. His best triple jump of 15.52 at Lahti in 1939 was never recognised as a European record, but lasted as a Finnish record until 1956. Long jump best 7.05 (1936).

Progression at TJ (position on world lists): 1929- 14.28 (27=), 1930- 14.88 (4), 1931- 14.65 (12), 1932- 15.16 (6), 1933- 15.09 (5=), 1934- 15.03 (12), 1935- 15.28 (7), 1936- 15.19 (11=), 1937- 15.29 (3), 1938- 15.32 (5), 1939- 15.52 (4), 1940- 15.22 (6), 1941- 14.27 (49), 1942- 14.56 (12), 1943- 14.45 (13), 1945- 14.21 (35=).

Norman READ (New Zealand) (b. 13 Aug 1931) on 22 May during a cycle race. English-born Read won New Zealand's first Olympic walking gold, when he was the surprise champion at 50km in 1956, three years after he had emigrated. His fastest time at this distance was 4:21.23 in 1960 and that year he was a notable 5th at 20km in the Olympics, but did not finish at 50km. In 1966 he was third in the inaugural Commonwealth 20 miles event and won 10 NZ titles at 50km and 6 at 20km. He was appointed president of Athletics NZ in 1993.

Simon ROBERT NAALI (Tanzania) (b.9 Mar 1966) after being hit by a car while on a training run in Moshi, Tanzania in August. His brother Thomas had been hurt in a car crash just a week earlier. Simon was the Commonwealth gold medallist of 1990 in his fastest ever time of 2:10:38, and 11th in the 1993 World Championships. His major marathon wins were: Dar es Salaam 1987, Arusha 1989, Honolulu 1989-90, Rouen 1993. Other pbs: 3000m 8:07.53 (1988), 5000m 13:47.67 (1988), 10000m 29:04.0 (1989), Half Mar 61:44 (1990).

Wilma RUDOLPH (USA) (b. 23 Jun 1940) on 12 Nov 1994 at Brentwood, Tennessee. A heroine of the 1960 Olympics when she was triple sprint gold medallist with 100m, 200m and relay. In 1956 she had won Olympic bronze on the US sprint relay team, but did not qualify from the heats of the 200m. She missed the 1958 season through the birth of her first child, but reached world class in 1959, when she was second at 100m and took relay gold at the Pan-American Games, and won the first of four successive US titles at 100m/100y. She was AAU indoor champion at 50y 1959-60 and 220y 1960 and set her first world record when she won the 1960 outdoor title with 22.9 for 200m. She added the 100m world record with 11.3 (11.41 automatic timing) in the Olympic semi-final, running a wind-aided 11.0 (11.18) in the final. She set further world records with 11.3 and 11.2 for 100m in 1961 (her fifth US record from 11.5 in 1960) and on the US 4 x 100m teams at the Olympics and in 1961 against the USSR and indoors twice at 60y in 1961. She was the 1961 Sullivan Award winner. The 20th of 22 children, she lost the use of her left leg for a while after suffering from double pneumonia and scarlet fever at the age of four and had to wear a leg brace until she was 8. She formed the Wilma Rudolph Foundation to work with underprivileged children. Married names Ward and Eldridge.

Progression at 100m, 200m (position on world lists): 1955- -, 1956- 11.7 (22=), 24.2 (14=); 1957- ?, 1959- 11.8 (25=), 1960- 11.3/11.0w (1), 22.9 (1); 1961- 11.2 (1), 1962- 11.4 (1=). Best 100y 10.6 (1960).

Rabia Abdul SALAM (Malaysia) (b. 5 Nov 1973) died, apparently from poisoning at Kajang, Malaysia on 25 February. She had won the silver medal at the 1993 Asian Championships at 400m in a national record time of 52.56 just a month after her 20th birthday.

Georg SALLEN (Germany) (b. 25 Nov 1927) on 18 February. He was the World Student champion at 400mh in 1951, in which year he set his pb of 53.2. 400m pb 48.4 (1949).

Archie SAN ROMANI (USA) (b. 17 Sep 1912) on 7 November at Fresno, California. Fourth in the 1936 Olympic 1500m, he set world records at 4 x 1 mile that year and at 2000m with 5:16.8 in 1937. He won the NCAA title for Emporia State University at 1 mile in 1935 and at 1500m in 1936 and ran for NY Curb Exchange AA. He won the AAU indoor 1500m in 1937 and outdoors he was 2nd in 1936 and 3rd in 1935 and 1938.

Progression at 1500m, 1M (position on world lists): 1935- 3;57.2 (24=), 4;19.1 (32=); 1936- 3:49.9 (4), 4:09.0 (1); 1937- 3;50.3 (2=), 4:07.2 (2=); 1938- 3:50.9 (4), 4:10.4 (4); 1939- 4:11.7 (7=), 1940- 4:10 M est. pb 3000m 8:27.4i (1938).

Herbert SCHADE (Germany) (b. 26 May 1922 Solingen) on 1 March in Solingen. The Olympic bronze medallist at 5000m in 1952, he went on to place 12th at 5000m and 9th at 10,000m in 1956, At the Europeans he was 4th at 5000m in 1954 and he won eight German titles: 5000m 1950-1, 1954-5; 10,000m 1951-2, 1954, 1956. German records with bests: 2000m 5:23.2 (1950), 3000m (3) 8:13.2 (1952), 5000m (5) 14:06.6 (1952), 10,000m (3) 29:24.8 (1951).

Progression (position on world lists) at 5000m, 10,000m: 1941- 16:16.0, 1947- 15:45.4, 1948- 14:47.0, 1949- 14:46.8, 1950- 14:22.8, 30:10.6; 1951- 14:15.4, 29:42.2; 1952- 14:06.6, 29:24.8; 1953- 14:15.6, 30:58.4; 1954- 14:14.2, 29:30.0; 1955- 14:11.6, 29:39.0; 1956- 14:12.8, 29:35.4; 1957- 14:14.4, 29:29.2; 1958- 14:17.4, 29:48.6. pb 1500m 3:53.4 (1952).

Tollien SCHUURMAN (Netherlands) (b. 20 Jan 1913) on 29 January at Apeldoorn. She set world records at 100m, 12.0 in 1930 and 11.9 in 1932, with five further unratified 11.9 times 1932-3 and an unratified world 200m best of 24.6 in 1933. National records: 80m 10.3 (1931), 100y 11.2 (1931), 200m 24.6 (1933). Dutch champion 100m 1930-1, 1933-4; 200m 1931, 1933-4; LJ 1933-4. She made her international début at 17 at the Women's World Games 1930, when she was 2nd at 100m and 200m to Stanislawa Walasiewicz. At the 1932 Olympics she was 4th in her semi-final at 100m and ran on the 4th placed sprint relay team.

Petar SEGEDIN (YUG) (b.14 Sep 1926) on 14 October. Ranked in the world top three in the steeplechase 1949-51 and 1951, he was 6th at the 1948 Olympics and 2nd in the 1950 Europeans, but went out in the heats of the 1952 Olympics. He was Balkan champion 1953-4 and Yugoslav champion seven times at 3000mSt and 5000m with four more titles at cross-country. He set five YUG records at each of 3000mSt and 5000m, with bests of 8:47.8 (1953) and 14:37.6 (1950), and also set a 3000m record in 1949. Other pbs: 3000m 8:27.4 (1953), 10,000m 30:48.4 (1955).

Aleksandar STEVANOVIC (YUG) (b. 21 Feb 1920) on 30 January. Balkan champion at 100m 1938 and 1940, with three relay golds and five other medals at these Games 1938-47.

Woodrow **'Woody' STRODE** (USA) (b. 1914) on December 31. While at UCLA he was 4th in the NCAA and 3rd in the AAU shot with a pb of 15.71 all in 1938 before turning to pro football. He became a well-known character actor, including roles in Sergeant Rutledge and Spartacus.

Herbie TOWERS (New Zealand) on 28 January. Past president of Athletics New Zealand and a member of the organising committee of the 1950 Commonwealth Games in 1950. MBE 1963, OBE 1978.

Lolésio TUITA (France) (b. 15 Jul 1943). A Wallis & Futuna islander he competed in 19 internationals for France, had a javelin best of 81.70 in 1973, was 11th at the 1972 Olympics and was French champion in 1970, 1972-3 and 1976.

Vilmos VARJU (Hungary) (b. 10 Jun 1937 Gyula) on 17 February in Budapest. The European shot champion of 1962 and 1966, with 7th in 1958, 7th in 1969 and 4th in 1971 as well as winning the first indoor title in 1966. He was 3rd at the 1964 Olympic Games and 8th in 1972. He set European records at 18.67 in 1860 and 19.62 in 1966 amongst 17 Hungarian records, a record for any one men's event, from 16.63 in 1958 to 20.45 in 1971. He competed in 49 internationals for Hungary and was their champion 13 times, 1958-60 and 1963-72.

Progression at shot (position in world lists): 1956- 13.38, 1957- 15.42, 1958- 16.96 (31), 1959- 18.20 (8), 1960- 18.67 (8), 1961- 18.44 (9), 1962- 19.11 (5), 1963- 19.42 (2), 1964- 19.39 (3), 1965- 19.10 (6), 1966- 19.62 (5), 1967- 19.54 (7), 1968- 19.61 (14), 1969- 18.97 (33), 1970- 19.72 (15), 1971- 20.45 (8), 1972- 20.17 (8), 1973- 18.32, 1974- 18.41, 1975- 16.61, 1976- 14.57.

Heinz VOGEL (Germany) (b. 24 Oct 1922) on

15 May in Berlin. Highly respected editor for many years of *Leichtathletik*, for which magazine he worked from 1949, and a long-time member of the ATFS.

William John **'Bill' WALTERS** (RSA) (b.31 Jul 1907) on 15 July. He won the silver medal at 440y and bronze at 220y at the 1930 Empire Games and at the 1932 Olympics was 4th at 400m and 6th at 200m. South African champion at 220y 1929, 1932-3 and 440y 1932-3, his pbs were: 200m 21.5 (1932), 400m 48.2 (1932).

Charles **'Chic' WARNER** (USA) (b. 14 Jan 1905) on May 3. Third in the NCAA 120y hurdles and second in the AAU in 1926 in his senior year at Illinois and winner of the AAU title in 1927 in 14.6, he had a distinguished coaching career, chiefly at Penn State. He then served as the first director of the USTFF.

Alex WILSON (Canada) (b. 1 Dec 1907) on 10 Oct in South Bend, Illinois. Having won an Olympic bronze on Canada's 4 x 400m relay team at the 1928 Olympics, when he also ran in the 400m and 800m, he won medals at all three events in 1932. First he took the silver at 800m, when he ran 1:49.9 behind Tom Hampson's world record 1:49.7 (the old record was 1:50.0 by Ben Eastman), the bronze at 400m in 47.4 and another bronze at 4 x 400m. In 1930 he had won the Canadian 440y and took a complete set of medals at the Empire Games: 1st 440y, 2nd 4 x 440y, 3rd 880y. His best 440y was 47.6 in 1932.

Having graduated from Notre Dame University, for whom he was 2nd in the NCAA 880y 1931 and winner at 400m in 1932, he was athletics director and track coach at Loyola University, Chicago 1932-50 before returning to Notre Dame to coach 1950-72.

Fred WILT (USA) (b.14 Dec 1920) in Anderson, Indiana on September 5. A top American distance runner of the 1940s, he became even better known as a coach (to such runners as Buddy Edelen) and author of influential books, most notably *How They Train* (1959). He also edited the magazine *Track Technique* for over 20 years from 1960. Before war service in the Navy he won the 1941 NCAA 2 miles for Indiana. Later he won nine AAU titles: 5000m 1949-51, 10,000m 1949, cross-country 1949, 1952-3, indoor 1 mile 1951, 1954. In both 1948 and 1952 he was 4th at 5000m and 2nd at 10,000m at the US Olympic Trials, placing 11th and 21st respectively at 10,000m at the Games. A leading figure on the US indoor circuit as a miler, he set a world indoor 2 miles best with 8:50.7 in 1952. Winner of the Sullivan Award in 1950

US Records: 3000m 8:12.2 (1950), 2M 8:54.5 (1951), 5000m 14:26.8 (1951). Other pbs: 1500m 3:53.1 (1949), 1M 4:08.5i/4:10.3 (1951), 10,000m 31:04.0 (1952).

Pete ZAREMBA (USA) (b.7 Apr 1909) in Kingwood, Texas. The 1932 Olympic bronze medallist at the hammer and the IC4A champion for New York University in 1932 and 1933. He was also AAU 2nd in 1932 and 1934. pb 51.98 for 4th on the world list in 1932.

Died in 1993

Erwin GILLMEISTER (Germany) (b. 11 Jul 1907) on 26 Nov 1993 in München. He ran on the German 4 x 100m teams that won the gold medal at the inaugural European Championships of 1934 and the bronze at the 1936 Olympics. In 1934 he first ran the 100m in his pb of 10.5 and had set a 200m best of 21.3 in 1929.

Note: **Prof. Dr. August KIRSCH** (Germany) (b. 14 Sep 1925).

Dr. **Friedrich-Wilhelm TARNOGROCKI** (Germany) (b. 4 Sep 1904) on 22 December. After second place at the 1928 German Championships in his pb of 1:54.4 he ran in the 1928 Olympics at 800m, being eliminated in the heats.

Died in 1995

Godfrey BROWN (GBR) (b. 21 Feb 1915 Bankura, India) on February 4. At the 1936 Olympics he anchored Britain to a famous victory in the 4x400m relay in a European record 3:09.0, having earlier won the silver medal at 400m in 46.68, a European record and which lasted as a British record until 1958. In a desperately close finish, Archie Williams (USA) won in 46.66. A week after the Games, Brown was timed at 45.9 for a 440y relay leg. He won the 1937 World Student Games 400m, with gold at both relays and the 1938 European 400m, with silver at 4 x 400m and bronze at 4 x 100m. AAA champion 440y 1936 and 1938, 880y 1939. Other bests: 100y 9.9 and downhill 9.7 (1936), 880y 1:52.2 (1937).

Nora CALLEBOUT (later **COATES**) (UK) (b.29 Apr 1895) on 26 January in her 100th year.

She won the 100y at the first Women's World Games in 1922 and was a member of the winning UK sprint relay team that set a world record time of 51.8 for 4 x 110y. Best times: 60m 7.8e (1922), 80m 10.6 (1925), 100y 11.6 (1922), 220y 27.2e (1922), 300m 45.4 (1922).

Jean CREUZÉ (b.5 Feb 1912) on 10 January at the age of 82 in Colombes. A meticulous and thorough researcher, his contributions, most particularly for his specialist era 1880-1940, played an important part in books published on French athletics for many years.

Hannes KOCH (Germany) (b. 12 Feb 1935) in January. GDR champion at 50km walk 1959 and 1961, and 2nd 1960, he was 17th at 20km at the 1960 Olympics and 7th at 50km at the 1962 Europeans. pbs: 20kmW 1:29:52 (1960), 50kmW 4:19:00.4 (1959).

Gösta LEANDERSSON (Sweden) (b. 22 Apr 1918) on 28 January from injuries suffered in a traffic accident. At the marathon he was 5th in 1946 and 4th in 1950 at the Europeans. He won Boston in 1949 (3rd in 1953), Kosice 1948 and 19650 (2nd in 1946), and the Swedish title four times, 1945 and 1948-50. He also won the Swedish 25km in 1945 and 1949. Almost exclusively a road runner he had a track 10,000m best of 31:32.4 in 1945.

Thompson MAGAWANA (S.Africa) (b. 23 Mar 1959) on 1 January of pneumonia. The 1980 South African marathon champion, with a best time of 2:10:39 in 1985, he ran world road best times for 30 miles, 2:37:31, and 50 kilometres, 2:43:38, in 1988.

Gisela MAUERMAYER (Germany) (b. 24 Nov 1913 München) on 9 January. A marvellous all-round athlete, Mauermayer won at least 86 consecutive discus contests between 1935 and 1949 (second best by a woman at any event) and set ten world records, seven in 1935 starting with 44.34 and three in 1936 culminating in 48.31. She also set three world records at the pentathlon, in 1933, 1934 and 1938, and a German shot record of 14.38m in 1934.

She won the discus at the 1936 Olympics and 1938 Europeans, when she also took the shot silver, won the shot and pentathlon at the 1934 Women's World Games, and won 20 German titles between 1933 and 1942: SP 1934, 1937-42; DT 1934-43, Pen 1933-4, 1938. Other bests 100m 12.4, HJ 1.56, LJ 5.84 (1938).

Olga MODRACHOVÁ - DAVIDOVÁ (TCH) (b. 9 May 1930) at Brno on 30 January. She won two European bronze medals: pentathlon in 1950, high jump in 1954 (9th pentathlon), and was 5th n the 1958 European pentathlon. With the pentathlon not then an Olympic event. she was 5th in 1952 and 10th in 1956 at high jump. She won a record 27 Czechoslovak national titles, 12 at high jump 1949-60, 7 pentathlon 1949-51, 1954-5, 1957-8; 3 at 200m 1950-2, 100m 1951-2, 80mh 1950-1, long jump 1955. She set ten CS pentathlon records from 1949 to her best in 1958 of 44.84 (1954 Tables), seven at high jump from 1.60 in 1951 to 1.69 in 1955, and CS records at 80mh 11.7 (1951) and LJ 5.70 (1954). She improved at long jump to 5.82 (1955) and her other pbs were: 100m 12.4 (1951), 200m 25.2 (1958).

Heinz OBERBECK (Germany) (b. 20 Aug 1931) on 26 January. Third in the 1954 European decathlon, with a best score (on the 1952 tables) of 6412 points in 1956. Second in the FRG decathlon championships in 1952, 1954 and 1956 and winner of the long jump 1954.

Robert 'Scotty' RANKINE (Canada) (b.6 Jan 1909) on 10 January. During a racing career from 1930 to 1953, he won 250 of his 350 races, including Canadian championships from 3 miles to the marathon. At the Empire Games 3 miles and 6 miles he was 4th and 2nd in 1934 and 2nd and 3rd respectively in 1938. He was 11th at 5000m at the 1932 Olympics and also ran in 1936. He was in the top seven in the Boston marathon three times.

Ian TOMLINSON (Australia) (b. 27 Feb 1936) on 26 January in Melbourne of cancer. Commonwealth champion at triple jump in 1958 and 1962, when he was also 4th and 6th respectively at long jump. He was 9th in the 1960 Olympic TJ and was AUS champion at LJ 1963 and TJ 1957-9, 1962, 1964-5. pbs: LJ 7.71 (1964), TJ 16.28 (1962).

Robert VINTOUSKY (France) (b. 19 Jun 1902) in January. He made 34 international appearances for France at the pole vault 1926-39, including the Olympic Games of 1928. He was French champion in 1933 and 1935 and set five national records from 3.75 in 1926 to 3.90 in 1928. His pb was 3.93 in 1931 and 1937.

WORLD CHAMPIONSHIPS

THE 5th IAAF World Championships in Athletics will be held in Göteborg, Sweden on 4-13 August 1995. The Ullevi Stadium, originally built for the Football World Cup in 1958, has been reconstructed especially for these championships. Athletics events at the Olympic Games have had world championship status, but the first championships for athletics alone were staged in 1983.

Year	*Venue*	*Athletes*	*Nations*
1983	Helsinki, FIN	1572	153
1987	Rome, ITA	1741	157
1991	Tokyo, JPN	1551	164
1993	Stuttgart, GER	1624	187

Previous Champions
MEN
100m
1983 Carl Lewis USA 10.07
1987 Carl Lewis USA 9.93 *
1991 Carl Lewis USA 9.86
1993 Linford Christie GBR 9.87
**Ben Johnson CAN won in 9.83, but following his admission of drug taking had his world record,and title stripped from him by the IAAF*

200m
1983 Calvin Smith USA 20.14
1987 Calvin Smith USA 20.16
1991 Michael Johnson USA 20.01
1993 Frank Fredericks NAM 19.85

400m
1983 Bert Cameron JAM 45.05
1987 Thomas Schönlebe GDR 44.33
1991 Antonio Pettigrew USA 44.57
1993 Michael Johnson USA 43.65
800m
1983 Willi Wülbeck FRG 1:43.65
1987 Billy Konchellah KEN 1:43.06
1991 Billy Konchellah KEN 1:43.99
1993 Paul Ruto KEN 1:44.71
1500m
1983 Steve Cram GBR 3:41.59
1987 Abdi Bile SOM 3:36.80
1991 Noureddine Morceli ALG 3:32.84
1993 Noureddine Morceli ALG 3:34.24
5000m
1983 Eamonn Coghlan IRL 13:28.53
1987 Saïd Aouita MAR 13:26.44
1991 Yobes Ondieki KEN 13:14.45
1993 Ismael Kirui KEN 13:02.75
10 000m
1983 Alberto Cova ITA 28:01.04
1987 Paul Kipkoech KEN 27:38.63
1991 Moses Tanui KEN 27:38.74
1993 Haile Gebresilassie ETH 27:46.02
Marathon
1983 Rob de Castella AUS 2:10:03
1987 Douglas Wakiihuri KEN 2:11:48
1991 Hiromi Taniguchi JPN 2:14:57
1993 Mark Plaatjes USA 2:13:57
3000m steeplechase
1983 Patriz Ilg FRG 8:15.06

Carl Lewis: winning in Helsinki 1983

1987 Francesco Panetta ITA 8:08.57
1991 Moses Kiptanui KEN 8:12.59
1993 Moses Kiptanui KEN 8:06.36

110m hurdles

1983 Greg Foster USA 13.42
1987 Greg Foster USA 13.21
1991 Greg Foster USA 13.06
1993 Colin Jackson GBR 12.91

400m hurdles

1983 Edwin Moses USA 47.50
1987 Edwin Moses USA 47.46
1991 Samuel Matete ZAM 47.64
1993 Kevin Young USA 47.18

High jump

1983 Gennadiy Avdeyenko URS 2.32
1987 Patrik Sjöberg SWE 2.38
1991 Charles Austin USA 2.38
1993 Javier Sotomayor CUB 2.40

Pole vault

1983 Sergey Bubka URS 5.70
1987 Sergey Bubka URS 5.85
1991 Sergey Bubka URS 5.92
1993 Sergey Bubka UKR 6.00

Long jump

1983 Carl Lewis USA 8.55
1987 Carl Lewis USA 8.67
1991 Mike Powell USA 8.95
1993 Mike Powell USA 8.59

Triple jump

1983 Zdzislaw Hoffmann POL 17.42
1987 Khristo Markov BUL 17.92
1991 Kenny Harrison USA 17.78
1993 Mike Conley USA 17.86

Shot

1983 Edward Sarul POL 21.39
1987 Werner Günthör SUI 22.23
1991 Werner Günthör SUI 21.67
1993 Werner Günthör SUI 21.97

Discus

1983 Imrich Bugár TCH 67.72
1987 Jürgen Schult GDR 68.74
1991 Lars Riedel GER 66.20
1993 Lars Riedel GER 67.72

Hammer

1983 Sergey Litvinov URS 82.68
1987 Sergey Litvinov URS 83.06
1991 Yuriy Sedykh URS 81.70
1993 Andrey Abduvaliyev TJK 81.64

Javelin

1983 Detlef Michel GDR 89.48 (old spec.)
1987 Seppo Räty FIN 83.54
1991 Kimmo Kinnunen FIN 90.82
1993 Jan Zelezny TCH 85.98

Decathlon

1983 Daley Thompson GBR 8714
1987 Torsten Voss GDR 8680
1991 Dan O'Brien USA 8812
1993 Dan O'Brien USA 8817

4x100m relay

1983 USA 37.86
1987 USA 37.90
1991 USA 37.50
1993 USA 37.48 (37.40 sf CBP)

4x400m relay

1983 USSR 3:00.79
1987 USA 2:57.29
1991 Great Britain 2:57.53
1993 USA 2:54.29

20km walk

1983 Ernesto Canto MEX 1:20:49
1987 Maurizio Damilano ITA 1:20:45
1991 Maurizio Damilano ITA 1:19:37
1993 Valentin Massana ESP 1:22:31

50km walk

1983 Ronald Weigel GDR 3:43:08
1987 Hartwig Gauder GDR 3:40:53
1991 Aleksandr Potashov URS 3:53:09
1993 Jesús Angel Garcia ESP 3:41:41

WOMEN

100m

1983 Marlies Göhr GDR 10.97
1987 Silke Gladisch GDR 10.90
1991 Katrin Krabbe GER 10.99
1993 Gail Devers USA 1`0.82

200m

1983 Marita Koch GDR 22.13
1987 Silke Gladisch GDR 21.74
1991 Katrin Krabbe GER 22.09
1993 Merlene Ottey JAM 21.98

400m

1983 Jarmila Kratochvílová TCH 47.99
1987 Olga Bryzgina URS 49.38
1991 Marie-José Pérec FRA 49.13
1993 Jearl Miles USA 49.82

800m

1983 Jarmila Kratochvílová TCH 1:54.68
1987 Sigrun Wodars GDR 1:55.26
1991 Lilia Nurutdinova URS 1:57.50
1993 Maria Mutola MOZ 1:55.43

1500m

1983 Mary Decker USA 4:00.90
1987 Tatyana Samolenko URS 3:58.56
1991 Hassiba Boulmerka ALG 4:02.21
1993 Liu Dong CHN 4:00.50

3000m

1983 Mary Decker USA 8:34.62
1987 Tatyana Samolenko URS 8:38.73
1991 Tatyana Dorovskikh URS 8:35.82
1993 Qu Yunxia CHN 8:28.71

5000m

Replaces the 3000m in 1995.

10 000m (first held 1987)
1987 Ingrid Kristiansen NOR 31:05.85
1991 Liz McColgan GBR 31:14.31
1993 Wang Junxia CHN 30:49.30
Marathon
1983 Grete Waitz NOR 2:28:09
1987 Rosa Mota POR 2:25:17
1991 Wanda Panfil POL 2:29:53
1993 Junko Asara JPN 2:30:03
100m hurdles
1983 Bettine Jahn GDR 12.35
1987 Ginka Zagorcheva BUL 12.34
1991 Lyudmila Narozhilenko URS 12.59
1993 Gail Devers USA 12.46
400m hurdles
1983 Yekaterina Fesenko URS 54.14
1987 Sabine Busch GDR 53.62
1991 Tatyana Ledovskaya URS 53.11
1993 Sally Gunnell GBR 52.74
High jump
1983 Tamara Bykova URS 2.01
1987 Stefka Kostadinova BUL 2.09
1991 Heike Henkel GER 2.05
1993 Ioamnet Quintero CUB 1.99
Long jump
1983 Heike Daute GDR 7.27w
1987 Jackie Joyner-Kersee USA 7.36
1991 Jackie Joyner-Kersee USA 7.32
1993 Heike Drechsler (née Daute) GER 7.11
Triple jump (first held 1993)
1993 Ana Biryukova RUS 15.09
Shot
1983 Helena Fibingerová TCH 21.05
1987 Natalya Lisovskaya URS 21.24
1991 Huang Zhihong CHN 20.83
1993 Huang Zhihong CHN 20.57
Discus
1983 Martina Opitz GDR 68.94
1987 Martina Hellmann (née Opitz) GDR 71.62
1991 Tsvetanka Khristova BUL 71.02
1993 Olga Burova RUS 67.40
Javelin
1983 Tiina Lillak FIN 70.82
1987 Fatima Whitbread GBR 76.64
1991 Xu Demei CHN 68.78
1993 Trine Hattestad NOR 69.18
Heptathlon
1983 Ramona Neubert GDR 6770
1987 Jackie Joyner-Kersee USA 7128
1991 Sabine Braun GER 6672
1993 Jackie Joyner-Kersee USA 6837
10km walk (first held 1987)
1987 Irina Strakhova URS 44:12
1991 Alina Ivanova URS 42:57
1993 Sari Essayah FIN 42:59
4x100m relay
1983 GDR 41.76
1987 USA 41.58
1991 Jamaica 41.94
1993 Russia 41.49
4x400m relay
1983 GDR 3:19.73
1987 GDR 3:18.63
1991 USSR 3:18.43
1993 USA 3:16.79

Winners of the most medals
10 Carl Lewis USA gold 100m, LJ & 4x100mR 1983; 100m, LJ & 4x100mR 1987, 100m & 4x100mR 1991; silver LJ 1991; bronze 200m 1993
10 Merlene Ottey JAM gold 4x100mR 1991, 200m 1993; silver 200m 1983, 100m 1993; bronze 4x100mR 1983, 100m & 200m 1983 & 1987, 4x100mR 1993
6 Heike Daute/Drechsler GDR/GER gold LJ 1983 & 1993; silver 100m 1987, LJ 1991; bronze LJ 1987, 4x100mR 1991
6 Gwen Torrence USA gold 4x400mR 1993; silver 100m 1991, 200m 1991 & 1993, 4x100mR 1993; bronze 100m 1993
5 Calvin Smith USA gold 200m & 4x100mR 1983, 200m 1987, 4x100m 1993; silver 100m 1983
5 John Regis GBR gold 4x400mR 1991; silver 200m, 4x100mR 1993; bronze 200m 1987, 4x100mR 1991

Winners of the most gold medals
8 Carl Lewis *as above*
4 Sergey Bubka PV 1983, 1987, 1991, 1993
4 Jackie Joyner-Kersee USA LJ 1987 & 1991, Hep 1991 & 1993
4 Calvin Smith *as above*

Oldest world champions - Men
36yr 77d Yuriy Sedykh HT 1991
34yr 140d Maurizio Damilano 20kmW 1991
34yr 30 d Helena Fibingerová SP 1983

Oldest medallist
40yr 71d John Powell USA 2nd DT 1987
Oldest women's medallist
37yr 34d Maricica Puica ROM 2nd 3000m 1987
36yr 11d Lyubov Gurina RUS 2nd 800m 1993

Youngest gold medallists:
17yr 88d Nicole Mitchell JAM 4x100mR 1991
18y 177d Ismael Kirui KEN 10000m 1993
18yr 241d Heike Daute GDR LJ 1983

Timetable of Finals 1995

Saturday, 5 August
15.10 Marathon W
17.25 Shot W
Prelims:
men - 100m, 400m, 800m, 10,00m, TJ, HT;
women - 400m, 100mh, LJ, SP

Sunday, 6 August
09.30 Decathlon 100m
10.20 Decathlon LJ
12.30 Decathlon SP
14.00 20 kilometres walk
14.15 Hammer
16.15 Decathlon HJ
16.50 Long jump W
18.10 100 metres hurdles W
18.55 100 metres
19.35 Decathlon 400m
Prelims:
men - 100m, 400m, 800m, HJ;
women - 100m, 400m, 1500m,10,000m, 100mh, JT

Monday, 7 August
09.30 Decathlon 110mh
10.15 Decathlon DT
12.30 Decathlon PV
15.30 Decathlon JT
17.20 Triple jump
17.25 10 kilometres walk W
19.25 100 metres W
20.40 Decathlon 1500m
Prelims:
men - 400m, 3000mSt, 400mh;
women - 100m, 1500m

Tuesday, 8 August
16.30 High jump
17.35 Javelin W
17.45 800 metres
18.05 400 metres W
19.05 10000 metres
Prelims:
men - 400mh, SP;
women - 400mh, TJ

Wednesday, 9 August
09.30 Heptathlon W 100mh
10.30 Heptathlon W HJ
16.45 Heptathlon W SP
17.25 1500 metres W
18.20 400 metres
18.30 Shot
19.10 10000 metres W
19.55 Heptathlon W 200m
Prelims:
men - 3000mSt, PV, DT;
women - 200m, 400mh

Thursday, 10 August
09.45 Heptathlon W LJ
15.15 Heptathlon W JT
15.45 50 kilometres walk
16.55 Triple jump W
17.05 400 metres hurdles
18.35 200 metres W
18.55 Heptathlon W 800m
Prelims:
men - 200m, 1500m, 5000m;
women - 200m, 800m, 5000m, DT

Friday, 11 August
16.15 Pole vault
17.30 3000m steeplechase
17.50 Discus
18.50 400 metres hurdles W
19.45 200 metres
Prelims:
men - 200m, 1500m, 5000m, 110mh, LJ, JT;
women - 800m, HJ

Saturday, 12 August
14.00 Marathon
17.00 Discus W
17.40 Long jump
18.50 5000 metres W
20.05 110 metres hurdles
Prelims:
men - 110mh, 4x100m, 4x400m;
women - 4x100m, 4x400m

Sunday, 13 August
15.15 High Jump W
16.00 Javelin
16.05 4 x 100 metres relay W
16.20 1500 metres
16.35 4 x 100 metres relay
16.55 800 metres W
17.15 5000 metres
17.55 4 x 400 metres relay W
18.30 4 x 400 metres relay

W women's events

WORLD JUNIOR CHAMPIONSHIPS

MEDALS were won by athletes from a record 39 countries in 1994, when the Championships were held at Estadio Universitario, Lisbon, Portugal on 19-24 July.

MEN

100 Metres (Jul 21) (+1.2)

1.	Deji Aliu	NGR	10.21
2.	Jason Gardener	GBR	10.25
3.	Deworski Odom	USA	10.26
4.	Obadele Thompson	BAR	10.29
5.	Carlton Chambers	CAN	10.30
6.	Ibrahim Meité	CIV	10.34
7.	Eric Frempong-Manso	CAN	10.37
8.	Julian Golding	GBR	10.46

Daniel Komen: won 5000 and 10,000

200 Metres (23 Jul) (+1.7)

1.	Anthony Wheeler	USA	20.62
2.	Deji Aliu	NGR	20.88
3.	Ian Mackie	GBR	20.95
4.	Eric Frempong-Manso	CAN	21.01
5.	Mark Keddell	NZL	21.02
6.	Han Chaoming	CHN	21.08
7.	Ibrahim Meité	CIV	21.24
8.	Bryan Howard	USA	21.25

400 Metres (22 Jul)

1.	Michael McDonald	JAM	45.83
2.	Ramon Clay	USA	46.13
3.	Shaun Farrell	NZL	46.31
4.	Mark Hylton	GBR	46.37
5.	Desmond Johnson	USA	46.38
6.	Riaan Dempers	RSA	47.31
7=	Kunle Adejuyigbe	NGR	47.62
7=	Rohan McDonald	JAM	47.62

800 Metres (22 Jul)

1.	Paul Byrne	AUS	1:47.42
2.	Japhet Kimutai	KEN	1:48.22
3.	Alain Miranda	CUB	1:48.24
4.	Julius Achon	UGA	1:48.85
5.	Peter Biwott	KEN	1:49.09
6.	Abako Bekele	ETH	1:49.63
7.	David Krummenacker	USA	1:49.80
8.	Abdul. Hasan Abdulla	QAT	1:55.67

1500 Metres (24 Jul)

1.	Julius Achon	UGA	3:39.78
2.	André Bucher	SUI	3:40.46

Championships have been held

Venue	*Dates*	*Athletes*	*Nations*
Athens, Greece	16-20 July 1986	1188	143
Sudbury, Canada	27-31 July 1988	1052	122
Plovdiv, Bulgaria	8-12 Aug 1990	1033	86
Seoul, Korea	16-20 Sep 1992	988	90
Lisbon, Portugal	20-24 Jul 1994	1218	143

1179 competitors - 701 men, 478 women from 143 nations.

Medal Table

	Gold	Silver	Bronze
USA	5	8	4
Russia	5	1	3
Kenya	3	4	3
Romania	3	2	0
Germany	3	3	2
South Africa	3	0	0
GB & NI	2	1	5
Australia	2	1	0
Jamaica	2	1	0
Nigeria	2	1	0
Finland	1	2	4
Japan	1	1	3
PR of China	1	1	1
Ukraine	1	1	1
Switzerland	1	1	0
Norway	1	0	1
Brazil	1	0	0
Mexico	1	0	0
Netherlands	1	0	0
Poland	1	0	0
Slovenia	1	0	0
Uganda	1	0	0
Sweden	0	2	1
Spain	0	2	0
Cuba	0	3	2
Italy	0	1	2
Belarus	0	1	1
Ethiopia	0	1	1
Hungary	0	1	1
Ireland	0	1	0
Argentina	0	1	0
Portugal	0	1	0
France	0	0	2
Canada	0	0	1
New Zealand	0	0	1
Czech Republic	0	0	1
Ghana	0	0	1
Morocco	0	0	1
Slovakia	0	0	1

3. Philip Mosima KEN 3:41.09
4. Reyes Estévez ESP 3:42.98
5. Michael Power AUS 3:43.86
6. Paul Cleary AUS 3:44.64
7. Alexandru Vasile ROM 3:44.78
8. Bruno Witchalls GBR 3:45.11

5000 Metres (24 Jul)
1. Daniel Komen KEN 13:45.37
2. Regasa Habte ETH 13:49.70
3. Giuliano Battocletti ITA 13:51.16
4. Pablo Olmedo MEX 13:55.19
5. Kenji Takao JPN 14:02.55
6. Samir Moussaoui ALG 14:03.75
7. Benoit Zwierzchlewski FRA 14:04.34
8. Valeriy Kuzmin RUS 14:04.50

10,000 Metres (20 Jul)
1. Daniel Komen KEN 28:29.74
2. Kenji Takao JPN 28:55.24
3. Michitane Noda JPN 29:00.55
4. Regasa Habte ETH 29:04.57
5. Alemayehu Tekaligh ETH 29:06.03
6. Ko Jung-won KOR 29:17.23
7. Simone Zanon ITA 29:21.00
8. Ivan Pérez ESP 29:36.15

20 Kilometres Road Race (24 Jul)
1. Clodoaldo Silva BRA 63:21
2. Carlos García ESP 63:38
3. Antonello Landi ITA 63:40
4. Isidoro Martínez MEX 64:05
5. José Maria Prieto ESP 64:11
6. Hriso. Athanassiou GRE 64:18
7. Zsolt Bacskay HUN 64:24
8. Mohammad Akdy SAU 64:25

3000 Metres Steeplechase (23 Jul)
1. Paul Chemase KEN 8:31.51
2. Julius Chelule KEN 8:33.64
3. Irba Lakhal MAR 8:34.42
4. Luciano Di Pardo ITA 8:48.11
5. Wordofa Lemma ETH 8:48.66
6. José Luis Blanco ESP 8:49.85
7. Christian Knoblich GER 8:49.99
8. César Pérez ESP 8:52.45

110 Metres Hurdles (22 Jul) (+2.1)
1. Frank Busemann GER 13.47w
2. Dudley Dorival USA 13.65
3. Darius Pemberton USA 13.93
4. Sven Pieters BEL 14.00
5. Anier García CUB 14.05
6. Andrey Kislykh RUS 14.21
7. Filip Bickel GER 14.23
8. Andrey Vinitskiy UKR 14.31

400 Metres Hurdles (22 Jul)

1.	Gennadiy Gorbenko	UKR	50.56
2.	Miklos Roth	HUN	50.85
3.	Noel Levy	GBR	50.94
4.	Robert Jarábek	SVK	50.95
5.	Mohammed Al Beshi	SAU	51.70
6.	Kevin James	JAM	51.90
7.	Andrey Shcheglov	RUS	51.99
8.	Jaco Jonker	RSA	53.65

High Jump (24 Jul)

1.	Jagan Hames	AUS	2.23
2.	Antoine Burke	IRL	2.20
3.	Mika Polku	FIN	2.20
4.	Attila Zsivótzky	HUN	2.20
5.	Roland Stark	GER	2.15
6.	Oskari Frîsen	FIN	2.15
7=	Shunichi Kobayashi	JPN	2.10
7=	Stefan Holm	SWE	2.10

Pole Vault (22 Jul)

1.	Viktor Chistyakov	RUS	5.60
2.	Dmitriy Markov	BLS	5.50
3.	Taoufik Lachheb	FRA	5.30
4.	Przemyslaw Gurin	POL	5.30
5.	Eric Boxley	USA	5.30
6.	Martin Lorenci	SLO	5.20
7.	Adam Kolasa	POL	5.10
8.	Jurij Rovan	SLO	5.10

Long Jump (21 Jul)

1.	Gregor Cankar	SLO	8.04w
2.	Bogdan Tarus	ROM	8.01
3.	Shigeru Tagawa	JPN	7.85w
4.	Andrew Channer	CAN	7.79w
5.	Darius Pemberton	USA	7.77w
6.	Olivier Borderan	FRA	7.74
7.	Andrej Benda	SVK	7.72w
8.	Carlos Calado	POR	7.56w

Triple Jump (24 Jul)

1.	Onochie Achike	GBR	16.67w
2.	Leonard Cobb	USA	16.65
3.	Ronald Servius	FRA	16.55w
4.	Sergey Izmaylov	UKR	16.42w
5.	César Javier Rizo	CUB	16.24
6.	Carlos Calado	POR	16.14w
7.	Vyacheslav Taranov	RUS	16.05
8.	Jason Wight	AUS	15.96

Shot (23 Jul)

1.	Adam Nelson	USA	18.34
2.	Andreas Gustafsson	SWE	17.95
3.	Ville Tiisanoja	FIN	17.90
4.	Leif Dolonen Larsen	NOR	17.75
5.	Pavol Pankuch	SVK	17.16
6.	Conny Karlsson	FIN	17.08
7.	Gunnar Pfingsten	GER	16.95
8.	Christian Nehme	GER	16.63

Discus (21 Jul)

1.	Frantz Kruger	RSA	58.22
2.	Julio Piñero	ARG	57.80
3.	Timo Sinervo	FIN	56.76
4.	Andzej Krawczyk	POL	55.68
5.	Li Shaojie	CHN	55.58
6.	Robert Fazekas	HUN	53.24
7.	Doug Reynolds	USA	53.04
8.	Jason Tunks	CAN	52.44

Hammer (23 Jul)

1.	Szymon Ziolkowski	POL	70.44
2.	Igor Tugay	UKR	70.08
3.	Sergey Vasilyev	RUS	66.14
4.	Tapio Kolunsarka	FIN	65.08
5.	Vadim Devyatovskiy	BLS	64.70
6.	Norbert Horváth	HUN	63.60
7.	Yosnel Montes	CUB	62.78
8.	Steve Harnapp	GER	62.22

Vladimir Piskunov UKR finished first with 71.66, but was disqualified on a positive drugs test.

Javelin (24 Jul)

1.	Marius Corbett	RSA	77.98
2.	Matti Närhi	FIN	74.92
3.	Isbel Luaces	CUB	72.82
4.	Sergey Voynov	UZB	72.74
5.	Christian Nicolay	GER	72.48
6.	Pietari Skyttä	FIN	72.06
7.	Toru Ue	JPN	69.48
8.	Kiyoshi Ishiba	JPN	68.56

Decathlon (20/21 Jul)

1.	Benjamin Jensen	NOR	7676
2.	Klaus Isekenmeier	GER	7298
3.	Glenn Lindqvist	FIN	7288
4.	Alf-Gerrit Christiansen	GER	7228
5.	Thomas Tebbich	AUS	7125
6.	Gines Hidalgo	ESP	7097
7.	Arnaud Humbey	FRA	7008
8.	Tage Peterson	USA	6973

10,000 Metres Walk (21 Jul)

1.	Jorge Segura	MEX	40:26.93
2.	Yevgeniy Shmalyuk	RUS	40:32.72
3.	Artur Meleskevich	BLS	40:35.52
4.	Sebastiano Catania	ITA	40:58.46
5.	Daisuke Ikeshima	JPN	41:01.97
6.	Alejandro López	MEX	41:28.14
7.	Oleg Ishutkin	RUS	41:46.30
8.	Dion Russell	AUS	41:50.70

4 x 100 Metres Relay (24 Jul)

1.	Great Britain & NI	GBR	39.60
2.	United States	USA	39.76
3.	Canada	CAN	39.90
4.	Japan	JPN	40.03
5.	France	FRA	40.38
6.	Germany	GER	40.45
7.	Jamaica	JAM	40.72
8.	Norway	NOR	41.79

4 x 400 Metres Relay (Jul 24)

1.	United States	USA	3:03.32
2.	Jamaica	JAM	3:04.12
3.	Great Britain & NI	GBR	3:06.59
4.	New Zealand	NZL	3:07.25
5.	Japan	JPN	3:08.06
6.	Germany	GER	3:08.77
7.	Nigeria	NGR	3:09.68
8.	Cuba	CUB	3:10.30

WOMEN

100 Metres (Jul 21) (+2.0)

1.	Sabrina Kelly	USA	11.36
2.	Aspen Burkett	USA	11.40
3.	Philomina Mensah	GHA	11.43
4.	Ekaterini Thanou	GRE	11.46
5.	Debbie Ferguson	BAH	11.48
6.	Kerry-Ann Richards	JAM	11.56
7.	Frédérique Bangue	FRA	11.57
8.	Daynelki Pérez	CUB	11.58

200 Metres (22 Jul) (+2.2)

1.	Heide Seyerling	RSA	22.80w CB
2.	LaKeisha Backus	USA	22.86
3.	Tatyana Tkalich	UKR	23.35
4.	Debbie Ferguson	BAH	23.59
5.	Sylvianne Félix	FRA	23.61
6.	Fabé Dia	FRA	23.67
7.	Huang Mei	CHN	24.11
dq	Astia Walker	JAM	(23.19)

400 Metres (22 Jul)

1.	Olabisi Afolabi	NGR	51.97
2.	Monique Hennagan	USA	52.25
3.	Hana Benesová	TCH	52.60
4.	Li Yajun	CHN	52.62
5.	Tracey Barnes	JAM	53.46
6.	Tamsyn Lewis	AUS	53.51
7.	Cicely Scott	USA	53.57
dnf	Claudine Williams	JAM	-

800 Metres (22 Jul)

1.	Miaoara Cosulianu	ROM	2:04.95
2.	Jackline Maranga	KEN	2:05.05
3.	Ware Kutre	ETH	2:05.17
4.	Grazyna Penc	POL	2:05.66
5.	Lyudmila Voronicheva	RUS	2:06.66
6.	Kumiko Okamoto	JPN	2:07.09
7.	Eleonora Berlanda	ITA	2:07.26
8.	Szilvia Csocsanszky	HUN	2:10.75

1500 Metres (24 Jul)

1.	Anita Weyermann	SUI	4:13.97
2.	Marta Domínguez	ESP	4:14.59
3.	Atsumi Yashima	JPN	4:15.84
4.	Rose Cheruiyot	KEN	4:17.12
5.	Ware Kutre	ETH	4:17.39
6.	Irina Nedelenko	UKR	4:18.47
7.	Lidia Chojecka	POL	4:18.70
8.	Heather DeGeest	CAN	4:19.07

3000 Metres (22 Jul)

1.	Gabriela Szabo	ROM	8:47.40
2.	Susie Power	AUS	8:56.93
3.	Sally Barsosio	KEN	8:59.34
4.	Annemari Sandell	FIN	9:04.10
5.	Pamela Chepchumba	KEN	9:13.33
6.	Chiemi Takahashi	JPN	9:14.22
7.	Lu Jing	CHN	9:15.98
8.	Miwa Sugawara	JPN	9:16.57

10,000 Metres (24 Jul)

1.	Yoko Yamazaki	JPN	32:34.11
2.	Jackline Okemwa	KEN	33:19.51
3.	Jebiwott Keitany	KEN	33:35.98
4.	Maria Singeorzan	ROM	33:49.19
5.	Abate Birhan	ETH	34:13.58
6.	Lu Jing	CHN	34:33.87
7.	Erika Olivera	CHI	34:36.96
8.	Adriana Chirita	ROM	34:41.87

100 Metres Hurdles (22 Jul) (+0.5)

1.	Kirsten Bolm	GER	13.26
2.	LaTasha Colander	USA	13.30
3.	Diane Allahgreen	GBR	13.31
4.	Chen Zhenghong	CHN	13.59
5.	Ingvild Larsen	NOR	13.66
6.	Carmen Banks	USA	13.72
7.	Nikola Spinová	TCH	13.74
dn	Astia Walker	JAM	-

400 Metres Hurdles (22 Jul)

1.	Ionela Târlea	ROM	56.25
2.	Virna De Angeli	ITA	56.93
3.	Emma Holmqvist	SWE	57.23
4.	Zhu Wei	CHN	58.10
5.	Rebecca Campbell	AUS	58.60
6.	Kelly Oliveira	BRA	59.15
7.	Claudia Salvarani	ITA	59.39
8.	Ikiko Yamagata	JPN	59.39

High Jump (23 Jul)

1.	Olga Kaliturina	RUS	1.88
2.	Kajsa Bergqvist	SWE	1.88
3=	Lenka Riháková	SVK	1.88
3=	Amy Acuff	USA	1.88
5.	Helen Sanzenbacher	GER	1.85
6.	Viktoriya Stepina	UKR	1.85
7=	Yekat Aleksandrova	RUS	1.80
7=	Dora Györfy	HUN	1.80
7=	Amewu Mensah	GER	1.80
7=	Emelie Färdigh	SWE	1.80

Long Jump (23 Jul)

1.	Yelena Lysak	RUS	6.72w
2.	Heli Koivula	FIN	6.64w
3.	Ingvild Larsen	NOR	6.39w
4.	Magdalena Khristova	BUL	6.39w
5.	Kirsten Bolm	GER	6.33w
6.	Franziska Hofmann	SUI	6.32
7.	Angela Henry	USA	6.27
8.	Lacena Golding	JAM	6.27

Triple Jump (21 Jul)

1.	Yelena Lysak	RUS	14.43w CB
2.	Ren Ruiping	CHN	14.36w (14.34 CR)
3.	Tatyana Lebedeva	RUS	13.62
4.	Suzette Lee	JAM	13.41
5.	Olga Cepero	CUB	13.32w
6.	Cosmina Boaje	ROM	13.12w
7.	Aneta Sadach	POL	13.01
8.	Daniela Bologa	ROM	12.88w

Shot (21 Jul)

1.	Cheng Xiaoyan	CHN	18.76 CR
2.	Yumileidi Cumba	CUB	18.09
3.	Claudia Mues	GER	17.07
4.	Corrie de Bruin	HOL	16.79
5.	Shang Xiaoli	CHN	16.74
6.	Nadine Kleinert	GER	16.70
7.	Alina Pupo	CUB	16.15
8.	Anna Rauhala	FIN	15.71

Discus (24 Jul)

1.	Corrie de Bruin	HOL	55.18
2.	Sabine Sievers	GER	54.86
3.	Suzy Powell	USA	52.62
4.	Claudia Mues	GER	52.60
5.	Olga Tsander	BLS	51.90
6.	Yu Qingmei	CHN	51.32
7.	Veerle Blondeel	BEL	51.28
8.	Monique Nacsa	AUS	50.06

Javelin (22 Jul)

1.	Taina Uppa	FIN	59.02
2.	María Caridad Alvarez	CUB	58.26
3.	Reka Kovács	HUN	55.88
4.	Odaliz Palma	CUB	55.74
5.	Christina Scherwin	DEN	55.70
6.	Wang Yang	CHN	53.26
7.	Angeliki Tsiolakoudi	GRE	53.16
8.	Mirela Manjani	ALB	52.22

Heptathlon

1.	Kathleen Gutjahr	GER	5918
2.	Regula Cardeñas	CUB	5834
3.	Ding Ying	CHN	5785
4.	Diana Koritskaya	RUS	5616
5.	Deborah den Boer	HOL	5604
6.	Vera Ináncsi	HUN	5596
7.	Deborah Feltrin	ITA	5575
8.	Annelies De Meester	BEL	5521

5000 Metres Walk

1.	Irina Stankina	RUS	21:05.41 CR
2.	Susana Feitór	POR	21:12.87
3.	Natalya Trofimova	RUS	21:24.71
4.	María Vasco	ESP	21:41.47
5.	Song Lijuan	CHN	22:03.69
6.	Yuka Kamioka	JPN	22:06.47
7.	Eva Pérez	ESP	22:23.31
8.	Liu Hongyu	CHN	22:23.69

4 x 100 Metres Relay (24 Jul)

1.	Jamaica	JAM	44.01
2.	Germany	GER	44.78
3.	Great Britain & NI	GBR	45.08
4.	Bulgaria	BUL	45.22
5.	Italy	ITA	45.48
6.	New Zealand	NZL	45.57
dq	South Africa	RSA	(45.53)
dnf	Spain	ESP	-

4 x 400 Metres Relay (24 Jul)

1.	United States	USA	3:32.08
2.	Romania	ROM	3:36.59
3.	Germany	GER	3:36.65
4.	Russia	RUS	3:37.41
5.	Finland	FIN	3:37.55
6.	South Africa	RSA	3:37.93
7.	Cuba	CUB	3:37.95
8.	Great Britain & NI	GBR	3:39.80

CR Championships record, CB = Championhip best (wind assisted)

7TH IAAF/MOBIL WORLDCUP

7th IAAF/Mobil World Cup In Athletics At Crystal Palace National Sports Centre, London 9-11 Sep 1994

MEN

1.	Africa	116
2.	Great Britain & NI	111
3.	Americas	95
4.	Europe	91
5.	Germany	85.5
6.	United States	78
7.	Asia	75
8.	Oceania	62.5

100 Metres (9 Sep) (-0.3)

1.	Linford Christie	GBR	10.21
2.	Olapade Adeniken	AFR/NGR	10.25
3.	Talal Mansour	ASI/QAT	10.31
4.	Aleks Porkhomovskiy	EUR/RUS	10.40
5.	Augustine Nketia	OCE/NZL	10.42
6.	André da Silva	AME/BRA	10.49
7.	Marc Blume	GER	10.52
8.	Vince Henderson	USA	10.63

200 Metres (11 Sep) (-1.4)

1.	John Regis	GBR	20.45
2.	Frank Fredericks	AFR/NAM	20.55
3.	Geir Moen	EUR/NOR	20.72
4.	Ron Clark	USA	21.00
5.	Robert Kurnicki	GER	21.02
6=	Ivan García	AME/CUB	21.10
	Damien Marsh	OCE/AUS	21.10
8.	Huang Danwei	ASI/CHN	21.23

400 Metres (10 Sep)

1.	Antonio Pettigrew	USA	45.26
2.	Du'aine Ladejo	GBR	45.44
3.	Inaldo Sena	AME/BRA	45.67
4.	Ibrahim Ismail	ASI/QAT	45.74
5.	Matthias Rusterholz	EUR/SUI	45.92
6.	Samson Kitur	AFR/KEN	45.98
7.	Paul Greene	OCE/AUS	46.29
8.	Daniel Bittner	GER	46.73

800 Metres (9 Sep)

1.	Mark Everett	USA	1:46.02
2.	William Tanui	AFR/KEN	1:46.84
3.	Craig Winrow	GBR	1:47.16
4.	Brendan Hanigan	OCE/AUS	1:47.41
5.	Nico Motchebon	GER	1:47.67
6.	Tomás de Teresa	EUR/ESP	1:48.04
7.	José Luiz Barbosa	AME/BRA	1:48.26
8.	Kim Yong-hwan	ASI/KOR	1:51.88

1500 Metres (10 Sep)

1.	Noureddine Morceli	AFR/ALG	3:34.70
2.	Rüdiger Stenzel	GER	3:40.04
3.	Mohamed Suleiman	ASI/QAT	3:40.52
4.	Jason Pyrah	USA	3:41.55
5.	Gary Lough	GBR	3:44.10
6.	José Valente	AME/BRA	3:44.32
7.	Isaac Viciosa	EUR/ESP	3:47.22
8.	Richard Potts	OCE/NZL	3:54.09

5000 Metres (11 Sep)

1.	Brahim Lahlafi	AFR/MAR	13:27.96
2.	John Nuttall	GBR	13:32.47
3.	Martin Bremer	GER	13:33.57
4.	Robbie Johnston	OCE/NZL	13:37.13

Anontio Pettigrew: won 400 for USA

Yoelvis Quesada: World Indoor title followed his World Cup victory

5.	Bahadur Prasad	ASI/IND	13:37.20
6.	Gabino Apolonio	AME/MEX	13:51.73
7.	Abel Antón	EUR/ESP	13:55.02
8.	Dan Mayer	USA	14:07.65

10,000 Metres (9 Sep)

1.	Khalid Skah	AFR/MAR	27:38.74
2.	Antonio Silio	AME/ARG	28:16.54
3.	Rob Denmark	GBR	28:20.65
4.	Stéphane Franke	GER	28:32.07
5.	Olayan Al-Qahtani	ASI/SAU	28:41.21
6.	Robert Stefko	EUR/SVK	28:45.32
7.	Phillip Clode	OCE/NZL	29:19.87
8.	Jim Westpahl	USA	29:22.39

3000 Metres Steeplechase (10 Sep)

1.	Moses Kiptanui	AFR/KEN	8:28.28
2.	Sa'ad. Shad Al-Asmari	ASI/SAU	8:35.74
3.	Aless. Lambruschini	EUR/ITA	8:40.34
4.	Colin Walker	GBR	8:41.14
5.	Martin Strege	GER	8:45.18
6.	Ricardo Vera	AME/URU	8:58.80
7.	Dan Reese	USA	9:15.16
8.	Peter Brett	OCE/AUS	9:19.11

110 Metres Hurdles (11 Sep) (-1.6)

1.	Tony Jarrett	GBR	13.23
2.	Allen Johnson	USA	13.29
3.	Emilio Valle	AME/CUB	13.45
4.	Florian Schwarthoff	GER	13.47
5.	Li Tong	ASI/CHN	13.59
6.	Kyle Vander-Kuyp	OCE/AUS	13.71
7.	Kehinde Aladefa	AFR/NGR	14.03
8.	Antti Haapakoski	EUR/FIN	14.11

400 Metres Hurdles (9 Sep)

1.	Samuel Matete	AFR/ZAM	48.77
2.	Oleg Tverdokhleb	EUR/UKR	49.26
3.	Eronildo de Araujo	AME/BRA	49.62
4.	Olaf Hense	GER	49.97
5.	Kazuhiko Yamazaki	ASI/JPN	50.22
6.	Gary Cadogan	GBR	50.48
7.	Rohan Robinson	OCE/AUS	51.12
8.	Marco Morgan	USA	53.58

High Jump (11 Sep)

1.	Javier Sotomayor	AME/CUB	2.40 CR
2.	Tim Forsyth	OCE/AUS	2.28
3.	Steve Smith	GBR	2.28
4.	Steinar Hoen	EUR/NOR	2.25
5.	Wolfgang Kreissig	GER	2.20
6.	Yoshiteru Kaihoko	ASI/JPN	2.20
7.	Khemraj Naiko	AFR/MRI	2.15
8.	Jeff Wylie	USA	2.15

Pole Vault (10 Sep)

1.	Okkert Brits	AFR/RSA	5.90 CR
2.	Jean Galfione	EUR/FRA	5.75
3.	Alberto Manzano	AME/CUB	5.40
4.	Andrej Tiwontschik	GER	5.40
5.	Scott Huffman	USA	5.40
6.	Grigoriy Yegorov	ASI/KZK	5.40
7.	James Miller	OCE/AUS	5.20
-	Neil Winter	GBR	nh

Long Jump (9 Sep)

1.	Fred Salle	GBR	8.10
2.	Douglas de Souza	AME/BRA	7.96
3.	Dion Bentley	USA	7.93
4.	Obinna Eregbu	AFR/NGR	7.87
5.	Georg Ackermann	GER	7.84
6.	Tetsuya Shida	ASI/JPN	7.72
7.	David Culbert	OCE/AUS	7.59
8.	Milan Gombala	EUR/TCH	7.37

Triple Jump (10 Sep)

1.	Yoelvis Quesada	AME/CUB	17.61 CR
2.	Julian Golley	GBR	17.06
3.	Oleg Sakirkin	ASI/KZK	16.81
4.	Lotfi Khaida	AFR/ALG	16.75w
5.	Serge Hélan	EUR/FRA	16.67w
6.	Reggie Jones	USA	16.41w
7.	Wolfgang Knabe	GER	16.07
8.	Andrew Murphy	OCE/AUS	15.86w

Shot (9 Sep)

1.	C J Hunter	USA	19.92
2.	Aleksandr Klimenko	EUR/UKR	19.16
3.	Courtney Ireland	OCE/NZL	18.93
4.	Sven Buder	GER	18.88
5.	Burger Lambrechts	AFR/RSA	18.08
6.	Carlos Fandino	AME/CUB	18.04
7.	Bilal Saad Mubarak	ASI/QAT	17.40
8.	Nigel Spratley	GBR	17.20

Discus (10 Sep)

1.	Vladimir Dubrovshchik	EUR/BLS	64.54
2.	Alexis Elizalde	AME/CUB	61.50
3.	Adewale Olukoju	AFR/NGR	60.22
4.	Werner Reiterer	OCE/AUS	60.22
5.	Jürgen Schult	GER	58.86
6.	Mike Gravelle	USA	56.76
7.	Robert Weir	GBR	55.86

Hammer (10 Sep)

1.	Andrey Abduvaliyev	ASI/TJK	81.72
2.	Lance Deal	USA	81.14
3.	Heinz Weis	GER	80.32
4.	Vasiliy Sidorenko	EUR/RUS	76.34
5.	Alberto Sánchez	AME/CUB	74.72
6.	Sean Carlin	OCE/AUS	74.54
7.	Hakim Toumi	AFR/ALG	69.38
8.	Paul Head	GBR	68.38

Javelin (11 Sep)

1.	Steve Backley	GBR	85.02
2.	Raymond Hecht	GER	84.36
3.	Gavin Lovegrove	OCE/NZL	82.28
4.	Patrik Bodén	EUR/SWE	80.86
5.	Louis Fouché	AFR/RSA	76.98
6.	Zhang Lianbiao	ASI/CHN	76.96
7.	Emeterio González	AME/CUB	76.42
8.	Todd Riech	USA	70.28

4 x 100 Metres Relay (Sep 10)

1.	Great Britain & NI	38.46
2.	Africa	38.97
3.	United States	39.33
4.	Americas	39.39
5.	Europe (France)	39.46
6.	Asia (PR of China)	55.58
dq	Germany	-
dnf	Oceania	-

4 x 400 Metres Relay (11 Sep)

1.	Great Britain & NI	3:01.34
2.	Africa	3:02.66
3.	Europe	3:03.26
4.	Germany	3:04.15
5.	Americas	3:04.28
6.	Oceania	3:05.70
7.	Asia	3:12.38

WOMEN

Overall Team Standings

		Original	Recalculated
1.	Europe	111	115
2.	Americas	98	104
3.	Germany	79	87
4.	Africa	78	85
5.	Asia	67	74
6.	Oceania	57	68
7.	USA	48	60
	Great Britain & NI	73	-

The British women's team competed and finished 5th, but as a consequence of the drugs disqualification of Diane Modahl at an earlier meeting the points she had earned at the European Cup were forfeited. As a result the British team were demoted from 2nd to 3rd and thus would not have qualified for the World Cup. Their points were thus removed from the World Cup by the IAAF in December 1994. In the results that follow the British performances are shown, but these placings were later discounted.

Irina Privalova: first and second

100 Metres (10 Sep) (-1.7)

1.	Irina Privalova	EUR/RUS	11.32
2.	Liliana Allen	AME/CUB	11.50
3.	Mary Onyali	AFR/NGR	11.52
4.	Melinda Gainsford	OCE/AUS	11.55
5.	Melanie Paschke	GER	11.64
6.	Liu Xiaomei	ASI/CHN	11.66
7.	Sheila Echols	USA	11.81
(7.	Paula Thomas	GBR	11.67)

200 Metres (9 Sep) (-1.7)

1.	Merlene Ottey	AME/JAM	22.23
2.	Irina Privalova	EUR/RUS	22.51
3.	Cathy Freeman	OCE/AUS	22.72
4.	Mary Onyali	AFR/NGR	22.82
5.	Chen Zhaojing	ASI/CHN	23.20
6.	Melanie Paschke	GER	23.32
7.	Chryste Gaines	USA	24.21
(6.	Paula Thomas	GBR	23.22)

400 Metres (11 Sep)

1.	Irina Privalova	EUR/RUS	50.62
2.	Fatima Yusuf	AFR/NGR	50.80
3.	Jearl Miles	USA	51.24
4.	Julia Duporty	AME/CUB	52.48
5.	Zhang Hangyun	ASI/CHN	52.79
6.	Kylie Hanigan	OCE/AUS	53.82
7.	Anja Rücker	GER	54.21
(4.	Phylis Smith	GBR	51.36)

800 Metres (10 Sep)

1.	Maria Mutola	AFR/MOZ	1:58.27
2.	Luciana Mendes	AME/BRA	2:00.13
3.	Natalya Dukhnova	EUR/BLS	2:02.81
4.	Kati Kovacs	GER	2:03.32
5.	Joetta Clark	USA	2:03.76
6.	Lisa Lightfoot	OCE/AUS	2:03.88
7.	Chen Xuehui	ASI/CHN	2:09.82
(7.	Cathy Dawson	GBR	2:04.13)

1500 Metres (9 Sep)

1.	Hassiba Boulmerka	AFR/ALG	4:01.05 CR
2.	Angela Chalmers	AME/CAN	4:01.73
3.	Margaret Leaney	OCE/AUS	4:12.16
4.	Sonia O'Sullivan	EUR/IRL	4:12.30
5.	Kathy Franey	USA	4:21.48
6.	Antje Beggerow	GER	4:23.65
7	Liu Jing	ASI/CHN	4:34.02
(3.	Kelly Holmes	GBR	4:10.81)

3000 Metres (11 Sep)

1.	Robyn Meagher	AME/CAN	9:05.81
2.	Gabriela Szabo	EUR/ROM	9:15.16
3.	Liu Jianying	ASI/CHN	9:15.39
4.	Susie Power	OCE/AUS	9:16.01
5.	Dörte Köster	GER	9:23.32
6.	Cassie McWilliam	USA	9:26.50
7.	Gwen Griffiths	AFR/RSA	9:31.91
(1.	Yvonne Murray	GBR	8:56.81)

Maria Mutola

10,000 Metres (10 Sep)

1.	Elana Meyer	AFR/RSA	30:52.51 CR
2.	Fernanda Ribeiro	EUR/POR	31:04.25
3.	Wei Li	ASI/CHN	32:37.94
4.	Claudia Dreher	GER	33:04.79
5.	Anne Cross	OCE/AUS	33:40.75
6.	Laura LaMena-Coll	USA	33:43.66
7.	Paola Cabrera	AME/MEX	34:41.22
(5.	Suzanne Rigg	GBR	33:38.14)

100 Metres Hurdles (10 Sep) (-0.9)

1.	Aliuska López	AME/CUB	12.91
2.	Svetla Dimitrova	EUR/BUL	12.95
4.	Nicole Ramalalanirina	AFR/MAD	13.24
5.	Kristin Patzwahl	GER	13.68
6.	Luo Bin	ASI/CHN	13.89
7.	Sherlese Taylor	USA	14.10
8.	Rachel Links	OCE/AUS	14.14
(3.	Jackie Agyepong	GBR	13.02)

400 Metres Hurdles (9 Sep)

1.	Silvia Rieger	GER	56.14
2.	Anna Knoroz	EUR/RUS	56.63

3.	Donalda Duprey	AME/CAN	56.67
4.	Nezha Bidouane	AFR/MAR	57.35
5.	Natalya Torshina	ASI/KZK	57.60
6.	Tonya Lee	USA	59.61
7.	Rebecca Campbell	OCE/AUS	60.96
(1.	Sally Gunnell	GBR	54.80)

High Jump (9 Sep)

1.	Britta Bilac	EUR/SLO	1.91
2.	Charmaine Weavers	AFR/RSA	1.91
3.	Silvia Costa	AME/CUB	1.91
4.	Heike Balck	GER	1.88
5.	Svetlana Zalevskaya	ASI/KZK	1.85
6.	Alison Inverarity	OCE/AUS	1.85
7.	Karol Damon	USA	1.80
(6.	Debbie Marti	GBR	1.85)

Long Jump (11 Sep)

1.	Inessa Kravets	EUR/UKR	7.00
2.	Niurka Montalvo	AME/CUB	6.70
3.	C Opara-Thompson	AFR/NGR	6.66
4.	Yao Weili	ASI/CHN	6.60
5.	Sabine Braun	GER	6.54
6.	Nicole Boegman	OCE/AUS	6.45
7.	Sheila Echols	USA	6.23
(6.	Yinka Idowu	GBR	6.51)

Triple Jump (9 Sep)

1.	Anna Biryukova	EUR/RUS	14.46 CR
2.	Sh. Hudson-Strudwick	USA	14.00
3.	Ren Ruiping	ASI/CHN	13.84
4.	Niurka Montalvo	AME/CUB	13.64
5.	Helga Radtke	GER	13.47
6.	Tania Dixon	OCE/NZL	12.55
7.	Hasna Atiallah	AFR/MAR	12.44
(4.	Michelle Griffith	GBR	13.70)

Shot (10 Sep)

1.	Huang Zhihong	ASI/CHN	19.45
2.	Belsy Laza	AME/CUB	19.07
3.	Astrid Kumbernuss	GER	18.89
4.	Viktoriya Pavlysh	EUR/UKR	18.67
5.	Dawn Dumble	USA	15.63
6.	Fouzia Fatihi	AFR/MAR	15.48
7.	Lisa-Marie Vizaniari	OCE/AUS	15.23
(5.	Judy Oakes	GBR	17.92)

Discus (11 Sep)

1.	Ilke Wyludda	GER	65.30
2.	Ellina Zvereva	EUR/BLS	63.86
3.	Daniela Costian	OCE/AUS	63.38
4.	Barbara Echevarría	AME/CUB	62.90
5.	Qiu Qiaoping	ASI/CHN	57.92
6.	Connie Price-Smith	USA	57.04
7.	Lisette Etsebeth	AFR/RSA	51.54
(7.	Jackie McKernan	GBR	56.28)

Javelin (9 Sep)

1.	Trine Hattestad	EUR/NOR	66.48
2.	Isel López	AME/CUB	61.40
3.	Karen Forkel	GER	61.26
4.	Louise McPaul	OCE/AUS	59.92
5.	Zhang Li	ASI/CHN	58.82
6.	Donna Mayhew	USA	51.50
7.	Ronah Dwinger	AFR/RSA	49.02
(6.	Sharon Gibson	GBR	53.32)

4 x 100 Metres Relay (11 Sep)

1.	Africa (Nigeria)	42.92
2.	Germany	43.22
3.	Oceania	43.36
4.	Asia (PR of China)	43.63
5.	United States	43.79
6.	Europe	43.99
7.	Americas	44.26
(8.	Great Britain & NI	44.45)

4 x 400 Metres Relay (9 Sep)

1.	Germany	3:27.59
2.	Americas	3:27.91
3.	Europe (France)	3:29.07
4.	United States	3:30.99
5.	Oceania (Australia)	3:31.63
6.	Asia	3:40.89
dq	Africa	-
(1.	Great Britain & NI	3:27.36)

The Algerian hammer thrower Hakim Toumi set a new record by competing in five World Cups. His record: 8th 1981, 5th 1985, 8th 1989, 7th 1992, 7th 1994.

Anna Biryukova

IAAF WORLD HALF MARATHON CHAMPIONSHIPS 1994

At Oslo, Norway, September 24

Men

1.	Khalid Skah NOR	60:27
2.	German Silva MEX	60:28
3.	Ronaldo da Costa BRA	60:54
4.	Godfrey Kiprotich KEN	61:01
5.	Sam Kororia KEN	61:16
6.	Andrew Masai KEN	61:19
7.	Tendai Chimusasa ZIM	61:26
8,	Fackson Nkandu ZAM	61:30
9.	Moses Tanui KEN	61:35
10.	Rolando Rodes ECU	61:36
11.	Paul Tergat KEN	61:37
12.	Martin Pitayo MEX	61:38
13.	Badilu Kibret ETH	61:40
14.	Benjamin Paredes MEX	61:41
15.	Carsten Eich GER	61:44
16.	Kamel Kohil ALG	61:50
17.	Addis Abede ETH	62:14
18.	Salah Hissou MAR	62:20
19.	Samson Dingani ZIM	62:21
20.	Meshack Mogotsi RSA	62:26

121 finished.

Men's team: 1. KEN 3:03:36, 2. MEX 3:03:47, 3. MAR 3:05:58, 4. ZIM, 5. ETH, 6. BRA, 7. RUS, 98. POR, 9. GER, 10. FRA, 11. RSA, 12. GBR, 13. ALG, 14. DJI, 15. ZAM, 16. JPN, 17. USA, 18. KGZ, 19. ISR, 20. SUI; 28 nations placed.

Women

1.	Elana Meyer RSA	68:36
2.	Iulia Negura ROM	69:15
3.	Anuta Catuna ROM	69:35
4.	Albertina Dias POR	69:57
5.	Elena Fidatov ROM	70:13
6.	Hilde Stavik NOR	70:21
7.	Merlene Renders BEL	70:29
8.	Brynhild Synstnes NOR	70:34
9.	Adriana Barbu ROM	70:38
10.	Mari Tanigawa JPN	70:43
11.	Fatima Roba ETH	70:49
12.	Natalya Galushko BLS	71:00
13.	Alena Peterková TCH	71:02
14.	Alla Zhilyayeva RUS	71:16
15.	Nicole Levéque FRA	71:54
16.	Klara Kashapova RUS	72:04
17.	Martha Ernstdóttir ISL	72:15
18.	Stella Castro COL	72:23
19.	Mineko Watanabe JPN	72:26
20.	Yukari Komatsu JPN	72:30

85 finished.

Women's team: 1. ROM 3:29:03, 2. NOR 3:33:36, 3. JPN 3:35:39, 4. POR, 5. RUS, 6. RSA, 7. ETH, 8. BLS, 9. GBR, 10. FRA, 11. AUS, 12. USA, 13. KZK, 14. MEX, 15. HUN, 16. SWE, 17. Isl.

Previous Winners - IAAF Women's World Road Race Championship

Held at 10km 1983-4 and 15km 1985-91.

	Team	*Individual*	
1983	USA	Wendy Sly (UK)	32:23
1984	UK	Aurora Cunha (Por)	33:04

Khalid Skah: won in his adopted home town

1985	UK	Aurora Cunha (Por)	49:17
1986	USSR	Aurora Cunha (Por)	48:31
1987	Portugal	Ingrid Kristiansen (Nor)	47:17
1988	USSR	Ingrid Kristiansen (Nor)	48:24
1989	China	Wang Xiuting (Chn)	49:34
1990	Portugal	Iulia Negura (Rom)	50:12
1991	Germany	Iulia Negura (Rom)	48:42

Previous Winners - IAAF World Half Marathon Championships

First held 1992 and to be held annually to 1996, from when the Half Marathon will alternate every two years with the World Road Race Championships.

	Team	*Individual*	
Men			
1992	Kenya	Benson Masya (Ken)	60:24
1993	Kenya	Vincent Rousseau (Bel)	61:06
Women			
1992	Japan	Liz McColgan (UK)	68:53
1993	Romania	M Conceição Ferreira (Por)	70:07

IAAF WORLD ROAD RELAY CHAMPIONSHIPS

At Litochoro, Greece April 16/17

Men

1. Morocco 1:57:56 (Brahim Jabbour 13:35, Larbi Khattabi 28:44, Hicham El Guerrouj 13:43, Salah Hissou 27:57, Brahim Boutayeb 13:53, Khalid Skah 20:04)

2. Ethiopia 1:58:51 (Worku Bikila 13:30, Badilu Kibret 28:36, Abraham Assefa 14:17, Fita Bayissa 28:52, Chala Kelele 14:09, Hai;le Gebresilasie 19:27)

3. Kenya 2:00:51 (Peter Ndirangu 13:40, Joseph Kibor 28:19, Clement Kiprotich 14:16, Paul Yego 29:56, John Kiprono 13:55, Simon Rono 20:45)

4. ZIM 2:01:42, 5. GBR 2:02:12, 6. ITA 2:02:39, 7. JPN 2:02:52, 8. BRA 2:03:23, 9. RUS 2:03:40, 10. TCH 2:04:58, 11. USA 2:05:03, 12. BUL 2:05:25, 13. UKR 2:05:26, 14. DEN 2:05:35, 15. KZK 2:07:07, 27 teams finished.

Women

1. Russia 2:17:19 (Tatyana Pentukova 16:12, Natalya Galyamova 32:59, Yelena Kopytova 15:45, Natalya Solominskaya 33:21, Yelena Romanova 15:48, Olga Churbanova 23:14)

2. Ethiopia 2:19:09 (Askale Bireca 16:05, Deratu Tulu 32:26, Leila Aman 16:31, Gadise Edato 33:47, Berhan Dagne 16:13, Asha Gigi 24:07)

3, Romania 2:19:18 (Daniela Bran 16:29, Alina Tecuta 33:17, Mariana Chirila 16:02, Anula Catuna 33:16, Florina Pana 16:49, Iulia Negura 23:25)

4. ITA 2:19:23, 5. USA 2:19:40, 6. UKR 2:20:15, 7. CHN 2:21:05, 8. GBR 2:21:52, 9. DEN 2:23:33, 10. MEX 2:26:42, 11. BUL 2:29:45, 12. GRE 2:37:00, 13. ALB 2:49:44.

First held in 1992 in Funchal, Madeira, Portugal. Contested by teams of six, running stages of 5km, 10km, 5km, 10km, 5km, 7.195km to make up the marathon distance.

1992 winners: Men: Kenya 2:00:02, **Women**: Portugal 2:20:14.

IAAF WORLD CUP MARATHON

There have been five World Cup marathons and from now on they will be incorporated in the World Championship marathon.

	Team		Individual	
	Men	Women	Men	Women
1985	Djibouti	Italy	Ahmed Salah DJI 2:08:09	Katrin Dörre GDR 2:33:30
1987	Italy	USSR	Ahmed Salah DJI 2:10:55	Zoya Invanova USSR 2:30:39
1989	Ethiopia	USSR	Metaferia Zeleke ETH 2:10:28	Sue Marchiano USA 2:30:48
1991	GBR	USSR	Yakov Tolstikova URS 2:09:17	Rosa Mota POR 2:26:14
1993	Ethiopia	China	Richard Nerurkar GBR 2:10:03	Wang Junxia CHN 2:28:16

IAAF WORLD RACE WALKING CUP

THIS competition is held biennially for the Lugano Trophy (men) and the Eschborn Cup (women). In 1995 it was due to be held at Beijing, China on 29-30 April.

Lugano, Switzerland was the first venue for this competition, which was then for men's European teams; the first team from the rest of the world to take part was the USA in 1967. From 1977 the event has been officially recognised by the IAAF with the above name.

Until 1985 there was a final contested by nations from each continent, with additional European nations qualifying for the final from three qualifying matches, but from 1987 in New York, when competitors from a record 35 nations took part, there has been one event.

LUGANO CUP
Winning teams

5 GDR 1965, 1967, 1970, 1973, 1985
4 USSR 1975, 1983, 1987, 1989
3 Mexico 1977, 1979, 1993
2 United Kingdom 1961, 1963
2 Italy 1981, 1991

Individual winners - 20 kilometres

1961	Ken Matthews (UK)	1:30:54
1963	Ken Matthews (UK)	1:30:10
1965	Dieter Lindner (GDR)	1:29:10
1967	Nikolay Smaga (SU)	1:28:39
1970	Hans-Georg Reimann (GDR)	1:26:55
1973	Hans-Georg Reimann (GDR)	1:29:31
1975	Karl-Heinz Stadtmüller (GDR)	1:26:12
1977	Daniel Bautista (Mex)	1:24:03
1979	Daniel Bautista (Mex)	1:18:49
1981	Ernesto Canto (Mex)	1:23:52
1983	Jozef Pribilinec (Cs)	1:19:30
1985	José Marin (Spa)	1:21:42
1987	Carlos Mercenario (Mex)	1:19:24
1989	Frants Kostyukevich (SU)	1:20:21
1991	Mikhail Shchennikov (SU)	1:20:43
1993	Daniel Garcia (Mex)	1:24:26

Individual winners - 50 kilometres

1961	Abdon Pamich (Ita)	4:25:38
1963	István Havasi (Hun)	4:17:16
1965	Christoph Höhne (GDR)	4:03:14
1967	Christoph Höhne (GDR)	4:09:09
1970	Christoph Höhne (GDR)	4:04:36
1973	Bernard Kannenberg (FRG)	3:56:51
1975	Yevgeniy Lyungin (SU)	4:03:42
1977	Raúl Gonzalez (Mex)	4:04:17
1979	Martín Bermudez (Mex)	3:43:36
1981	Raúl Gonzalez (Mex)	3:48:30
1983	Raúl Gonzalez (Mex)	3:45:37
1985	Hartwig Gauder (GDR)	3:47:31
1987	Ronald Weigel (GDR)	3:42:52
1989	Simon Baker (Aus)	3:43:13
1991	Carlos Mercenario (Mex)	3:42:03
1993	Carlos Mercenario (Mex)	3:50:28

Most individual wins

3 Christoph Höhne (GDR) 50km 1965, 1967, 1970
3 Raúl Gonzalez (Mex) 50km 1977, 1981, 1983
3 Carlos Mercenario (Mex) 20k 1987, 50km 1991, 1993

Most finals:

9 Bo Gustafsson (Swe)
8 Sandro Bellucci (Ita) 20km 1977-85 (best 3rd 1981), 50km 1987-91
8 Maurizio Damilano (Ita) 20km 1977-91 (best 2nd 1985)
8 Hartwig Gauder (GDR/Ger) 20km 1975-9, 50km 1981-93
7 Gerhard Weidner (FRG) 50km 1965-77 (best 2nd 1975)

ESCHBORN CUP

In 1975 a women's race over 5km was held in conjunction with the Lugano Trophy races. This event was maintained and when held at Eschborn in 1979 a Cup was introduced for the team competition. The distance was increased to 10km from 1983. A record 26 nations contested the 1989 competition.

Winning teams

4 USSR 1981, 1987, 1989, 1991
2 China 1983, 1985
1 United Kingdom 1979
1 Italy 1993

Individual winners
5 kilometres

1979 Marion Fawkes (UK) 22:51
1981 Siw Gustavsson (Swe) 22:57

10 kilometres

1983 Xu Yongjiu (Chn) 45:14
1985 Yan Hong (Chn) 46:22
1987 Olga Krishtop (SU) 43:22
1989 Beate Anders (GDR) 43:08
1991 Irina Strakhova (SU) 43:55
1993 Wang Yan (Chn) 45:10

WORLD UNIVERSITY GAMES

THE 'Universiade' or World Student Games, organised by the Fédération Internationale du Sport Universitaire (FISU), is well established as one of the world's most important multi-sport meetings. The 1995 events are to be held at Fukuoka, Japan.

The first 'International Universities' Games was held in 1924 in Warsaw, organised by the Confédération Internationale des Etudiants (CIE). From 1951 to 1962 rival Games were staged by FISU and the UIE. The latter, Communist inspired, were known as the World Youth Games from 1954 and these had the higher standards. From 1963, however, the Games merged and are now held biennially.

Championship best performances after 1993

MEN

100m	10.07	Lee McRae USA	1985
	9.97w	Andrés Simon CUB (ht)	1985
200m	19.72	Pietro Mennea ITA	1979
400m	44.98	Harald Schmid FRG	1979
800m	1:43.44	Alberto Juantorena CUB	1977
1500m	3:38.43	Saïd Aouita MAR	1981
5000m	13:39.04	Stefano Mai ITA	1989
10000m	28:15.84	Stephan Freigang GER	1991
Mar	2:12:19	Kennedy Manyisa KEN	1993
3000mSt	8:21.26	John Gregorek USA	1981
110mh	13.21	Alejandro Casañas CUB	1977
400mh	48.44	Harry Schulting HOL	1979
HJ	2.41	Igor Paklin URS	1985
PV	5.80	István Bagyula HUN	1991
LJ	8.21	Yusuf Ali NGR	1983
	8.23w	László Szalma HUN	1981
TJ	17.86	Charlie Simpkins USA	1985
SP	21.13	Remigius Machura TCH*	1985
	20.85	Alessandro Andrei ITA	1985
DT	69.46	Luís Delis CUB	1983
HT	80.56	Igor Astapkovich URS	1989
JT	87.42	Steve Backley GBR	1991
(old)	89.52	Dainis Kula URS	1981
Dec	8348	Siegfried Wentz FRG	1987
4x100m	38.42	Italy	1979
4x400m	3:00.98	USA	1979
20kmW	1:22:01	Robert Korzeniowski POL	1993

Women

100m	11.00	Marlies Göhr GDR	1979
200m	21.91	Marita Koch GDR	1979
400m	50.35	Maria Pinigina URS	1979
800m	1:56.88	Slobodanka Colovic YUG	1987
1500m	4:01.32	Paula Ivan ROM	1987
3000m	8:44.09	Paula Ivan ROM	1989
10000m	31:46.43	Viorica Ghican ROM	1989
Mar	2:35:09	Irina Bogacheva URS	1989
100mh	12.62	Lucyna Langer POL	1979
400mh	54.97	Yekaterina Fesenko URS	1983
HJ	2.01	Silvia Costa CUB	1985
LJ	7.04	Irina Valyukevich URS	1985
	7.06w	Anisoara Cusmir ROM	1983
TJ	14.20	Li Huirong CHN	1991
SP	20.82	Nadyezhda Chizhova URS	1973
DT	67.96	Tsvetanka Khristova BUL	1987
JT	71.82	Ivonne Leal CUB	1985
Hep	6847	Larisa Nikitina URS	1989
4x100m	42.40	USA	1989
4x400m	3:24.97	USSR	1983
5kmW	21:51.50	Li Sujie CHN	1987
	20:44R	Ileana Salvador ITA	1989
10kmW	44:04	Sari Essayah FIN	1991

** Later found to have had a positive drugs test at the preceding European Cup Final.*

17 world records have been set in these meetings from 1933: 3:49.2 at 1500m by Luigi Beccali ITA and 14.4 at 110mh by John Morriss USA, to 1985: 2.41m high jump by Igor Paklin.

COMMONWEALTH GAMES 1995

At Victoria, British Columbia, Canada 22-28 August

ENGLAND'S ATHLETES accumulated the most medals (35), with Australia next best on 22, although the Australians won 12 gold to England's 11. Kenya won five titles despite leaving out their biggest stars, Canada four, Nigeria three, Jamaica and Wales two, Namibia, Zambia and Scotland one each. In overall medal terms, Canada finished third with 16, followed by Nigeria (11), Kenya (10), Jamaica (8) and New Zealand and South Africa (in their first Games since 1958) with five apiece.

The standard of performance varied wildly, the 100m final being one of the greatest ever races for depth while the pole vault, for instance, was won with a Games record that would not have sufficed to qualify for the European final. However, in nine events the winning mark was superior to that recorded in Helsinki, while Colin Jackson clocked the identical time of 13.08 in both championships.

Dates given in brackets after the heading for each event are those of the final.
* Games record

MEN

100 METRES (23rd, wind +1.9)

CHRISTIE, after 10.39, 10.02 and 9.98 in preliminary rounds, ran the second quickest legal time of the year and his second fastest ever with 9.91. bettering his 1990 Games records of 9.93w and 10.02. Fredericks ran 10.14, 10.04 and 10.01w in qualifying. Dove-Edwin finished an unexpected second, improving from a pre-Games 10.34 to 10.17, 10.10 and 10.02! His overnight rise from obscurity caught the world's imagination, but a few days later he was revealed to have failed a drugs test for stenozolol. The standard was exceptional and times of 10.17w (Terry Williams) and 10.19 (Damien Marsh) failed to make the final. Gus Nketia, who ran for Ghana in the 1990 Games, took the NZ record from 10.42 to 10.11 in his first round heat.

1. Linford Christie ENG 9.91*
2. Michael Green JAM 10.05
3. Frank Fredericks NAM 10.06
4. Ato Boldon TRI 10.07
5. Glenroy Gilbert CAN 10.11
6. Olapade Adeniken NGR 10.11
7. Gus Nketia NZL 10.42

dq Horace Dove-Edwin SLE (positive drugs test) (10.02)

200 METRES (26th, wind +1.5)

THE GAMES records of 20.43 and 20.10w were swept away. Regis ran 20.36 in his quarter-final, and improved in the final to 20.25 but he was well beaten by the strong finish of Fredericks (in Namibia's Games début). These two won their semis - Fredericks 20.43 and Regis 20.65.

1. Frank Fredericks NAM 19.97*
2. John Regis ENG 20.25
3. Daniel Effiong NGR 20.40
4. Damien Marsh AUS 20.54
5. Terry Williams ENG 20.62
6. Oluyemi Kayode NGR 20.64
7. Steve Brimacombe AUS 20.67
8. Troy Douglas BER 20.71

400 METRES (23rd)

FOUR RACES in two days was a tough schedule, as European champion Ladejo was to discover. He ran a relaxed looking 45.20 semi but in the final some four hours later he faltered after leading into the finishing straight. Kenyan champion Gitonga (drawn in the outside lane) finished strongly to win in a pb of 45.00.

1. Charles Gitonga KEN 45.00
2. Du'aine Ladejo ENG 45.11
3. Sunday Bada NGR 45.45
4. Paul Greene AUS 45.50
5. Patrick Delice TRI 45.89
6. Eswort Coombs STV 45.96
7. Neil da Silva TRI 46.27
8. Bobang Phiri RSA 46.35

800 METRES (26th)

PATRICK KONCHELLAH, younger brother of two-time world champion Billy, dominated the race. His team-mate Serem led through 200m in 25.06 and 52.11 before fading to sixth, while Sepeng dashed ahead approaching 600m (1:19.54) but had no response to the Kenyan's strong kick. Sepeng became South Africa's first ever black medallist in Commonwealth Games athletics and Ngidhi took Zimbabwe's first medal since 1962 when the country competed as Southern Rhodesia.

1. Patrick Konchellah KEN 1:45.18
2. Hezekiel Sepeng RSA 1:45.76
3. Savieri Ngidhi ZIM 1:46.06
4. Craig Winrow ENG 1:46.91
5. Brendan Hanigan AUS 1:47.24
6. William Serem KEN 1:47.30
7. Martin Steele ENG 1:48.04
8. Tom McKean SCO 1:50.81

1500 METRES (28th)

CHESANG, only the second Kenyan to win this title (after Kip Keino in 1962), kicked home with a 54 sec last lap after race leader splits for Julius Achon 56.67, Tanui 1:58.12 and 2:56.73. Simon Doyle, fastest man in the field, was hampered by injury and failed to reach the final.

1. Reuben Chesang KEN 3:36.70
2. Kevin Sullivan CAN 3:36.78
3. John Mayock ENG 3:37.22
4. Whaddon Niewoudt RSA 3:37.96
5. Julius Tanui KEN 3:38.10
6. Brian Treacy NIR 3:38.93
7. Steve Green JAM 3:39.19
8. Kevin McKay ENG 3:39.72

5000 METRES (24th)

SECOND TO Baumann in Helsinki after being boxed in at a crucial moment, Denmark this time escaped before it was too late and produced a victorious sub-26 last 200, holding off Hanneck with Nuttall and Brown making it three Englishmen in the first four. Kenyans Laban Chege and Sum paid the price for their extravagant opening, 1000m 2:31.49. Chege was on his own at 2000m in 5:15.02, but was caught by the pack at 3000m in 8:02.82, and finished 9th in 13:47.34. World junior CC champion Mosima led at 4000m in 10:50.51 and at the bell in 11:55.66.

1. Rob Denmark ENG 13:23.00
2. Philemon Hanneck ZIM 13:23.20
3. John Nuttall ENG 13:23.54
4. Jon Brown ENG 13:23.96
5. Philip Mosima KEN 13:24.07
6. Jon Wyatt NZL 13:35.46
7. Paul Sum KEN 13:39.53
8. Justin Hobbs WAL 13:45.53

10,000 METRES (27th)

DOUBLE world junior champion Daniel Komen ruined his chances with a first lap of 57.42! That put him 50m clear and at 1000m (2:36.48) he was nearly 100m ahead. Slowing drastically, his lead at halfway, reached in a very ordinary 14:23.54, was down to 30m as Chimusasa led the pursuit. Aguta swept into the lead just before 6km and a 64.66 lap enabled him to open a sizeable gap over Chimusasa which by the finish stretched to 60m. The barefoot Zambian, Nkanda, was third while Komen struggled in ninth in 29:37.91. The winning time was the slowest since the event went metric in 1970. For the first time since 1938 no UK runner medalled.

1. Lameck Aguta KEN 28:38.22
2. Tendai Chimusasa ZIM 28:47.72
3. Fackson Nkandu ZAM 28:51.72
4. Martin Jones ENG 29:08.53
5. Peter Fonseca CAN 29:14.85
6. Eamonn Martin ENG 29:15.81
7. Mu. Ramachandran MAS 29:30.19
8. Paul Patrick AUS 29:35.95

Reuben Chesang: only the second Kenyan to win the Commonwealth 1500m

MARATHON (28th)

MONEGHETTI, the only truly world class runner in the field, was a runaway winner. He revelled in the rain and after a cautious first half of 67:36 covered the second half in 64:13 for the widest winning margin since Jack Holden in 1950. He just ran increasingly faster as the 5k splits show: 16:27, 16:14, 15:44, 15:44, 15:33, 15:17, 15:16, 14:58, 6:36 (2.195k), breaking away from the rest after 30km.

1. Steve Moneghetti AUS 2:11:49
2. Sean Quilty AUS 2:14:57
3. Mark Hudspith ENG 2:15:11
4. Dale Rixon WAL 2:16:15
5. Pat Carroll AUS 2:16:27
6. Nicolas Kioko KEN 2:16:37
7. Carey Nelson CAN 2:16:52
8. Colin Moore ENG 2:18:07

3000M STEEPLECHASE (23rd)

CHIRCHIR and Kipkoech set a cracking pace, reaching 1000m in 2:39.27 and 2000m in 5:26.10. Walker attempted to stay close to them and at 2000m was on 8:12 pace, some 40m clear of 1986 champion Fell. The Canadian picked off Walker at the final water jump. The two Kenyans had been together at that point, with Kipkoech sprinting to victory in a Games record and pb to move to 8th on the Kenyan year list!

1. Johnstone Kipkoech KEN 8:14.72*
2. Gideon Chirchir KEN 8:15.25
3. Graeme Fell CAN 8:23.28
4. Colin Walker ENG 8:27.78
5. Tom Buckner ENG 8:29.84
6. Joel Bourgeois CAN 8:31.19
7. Justin Chaston WAL 8:32.20
8. Paul Chemase KEN 8:35.31

110 METRES HURDLES

(23rd, wind +1.6))

FOLLOWING an uncharacteristically ragged heat in 13.51, Jackson tied his own Games record of 13.08 in the final. Jarrett took silver again and Jackson's Welsh team-mate and training colleague Gray, who ran a pb 13.53 in his heat, was an unexpected third.

1. Colin Jackson WAL 13.08*
2. Tony Jarrett ENG 13.22
3. Paul Gray WAL 13.54
4. Andrey Tulloch ENG 13.69
5. Kyle Vander-Kuyp AUS 13.75
6. Ken Campbell SCO 13.86
7. Tim Kroeker CAN 13.93

dq. Robert Foster JAM (positive drugs test)(13.78)

400 METRES HURDLES (26th)

MATETE, who had threatened to boycott the Games because of a financial dispute with his national association, appeared after all, ran 49,13 for the one heat time under 50 sec, and was never troubled in breaking Alan Pascoe's 1974 Games record with a routine, for him, 48.67. It was Zambia's first ever Commonwealth gold since Edna Maskell's 80m hurdles win for Northern Rhodesia 40 years ago. Cadogan, second at the final hurdle, was overtaken on the run-in by the two Kenyans.

1. Samuel Matete ZAM 48.67*
2. Gideon Biwott KEN 49.43
3. Barnabas Kinyor KEN 49.50
4. Gary Cadogan ENG 49.71
5. Rohan Robinson AUS 49.76
6. Ken Harnden ZIM 50.02
7. Peter Crampton ENG 50.37
8. Ian Weakley JAM 51.25

HIGH JUMP (26th)

PARSONS caused a surprise, not so much by his third Commonwealth medal but, aged 30, and 11 years after setting his first UK record, he cleared 2.31 for a lifetime best. Forsyth and Smith succeeded at their second attempts at 2.31 as against Parsons' third and a jump-off

Tim Forsyth: high jump winner

was required. Both failed for a fourth time at 2.34, went clear at 2.32 and failed again at 2.34 (Smith, jumping first, going extremely close). With the bar set again at 2.32 Smith faltered but Forsyth went clear to clinch the gold.

1.	Tim Forsyth AUS	2.32
2.	Steve Smith ENG	2.32
3.	Geoff Parsons SCO	2.31
4.	Cory Siermachesky CAN	2.28
5.	Dalton Grant ENG	2.28
6.	Lochsley Thomson AUS	2.28
7=	Brendan Reilly ENG	2.25
7=	Rich Duncan CAN	2.25

POLE VAULT (27th)

OKKERT BRITS of South Africa, the most solid favourite of the Games, failed to clear his opening height of 5.50 in the tricky wind conditions and the gold went to the the only man still jumping when Brits started, English-born, Welsh-qualified Winter.

1.	Neil Winter WAL	5.40*
2.	Curtis Heywood CAN	5.30
3.	James Miller AUS	5.30
4.	Photis Stefani CYP	5.30
5.	Mike Edwards ENG	5.20
6.	Andrew Ashurst ENG	5.20
7.	Greg Halliday AUS	5.20
8.	Nick Buckfield ENG	5.20

LONG JUMP (26th)

HAVING registered a pb and the longest legal jump in Games history (8.22) in qualifying, Eregbu opened the final with 8.05w (+2.2) and that sufficed although Culbert, second also in 1990, came close with a fourth-round 8.00 (+2.0).

1.	Obinna Eregbu NGR	8.05w
2.	David Culbert AUS	8.00
3.	Ian James CAN	7.93w
4.	Ayo Aladefa NGR	7.93
5.	Fred Salle ENG	7.88
6.	Jai Taurima AUS	7.87
7.	Jerome Romain DMN	7.69w
8.	Craig Hepburn BAH	7.65

TRIPLE JUMP (28th)

ROMAIN of Dominica, a country which has never won a Games medal, had the galling experience of jumping 17.05w in the qualifying round but managing only 16.61 for fourth place in the final. The battle for medals could hardly have been closer. Golley led the way with a timely pb of 17.03 (+0.9, a "legal" Games record) in the first round, while Wellman (1st round) and Edwards (4th round) reached 17.00.

Neil Winter: a surprise pole vault winner

As both had a second best of 16.98 the medals were decided on the basis of their third best jumps: Edwards 16.81. Wellman 16.58.

1.	Julian Golley ENG	17.03
2.	Jon Edwards ENG	17.00
3.	Brian Wellman BER	17.00
4.	Jerome Romain DMN	16.61
5.	Edrick Floreal CAN	16.61
6.	Francis Agyepong ENG	16.33
7.	Nda. Mdhlongwa ZIM	16.02
8.	James Sabulei KEN	15.99

SHOT (28th)

SIMSON was in the form of his life, leading with 19.05 in the first round and setting pb's of 19.47 in the fourth and 19.49 in the fifth, and he needed to be to prevail against the rotational thrower Ireland, whose final put went 19.38. Ugwu in third place set a Nigerian record.

1.	Matt Simson ENG	19.49
2.	Courtney Ireland NZL	19.38
3.	Chima Ugwu NGR	19.26
4.	Carel Le Roux RSA	18.50
5.	Scott Cappos CAN	18.35
6.	Burger Lambrechts RSA	18.15
7.	Nigel Spratley ENG	17.96
8.	John Minns AUS	17.96

DISCUS (26th)

DEFENDING champion Olukoju led with his 61.98 opener until Austrian-born Reiterer – third in 1986 and second in 1990 – threw 62.76 in round 3. The Nigerian had a big foul in round 4 and came close with his two final throws. Weir, back in the Games after an absence of 12 years (he won the hammer in 1982 with 75.08) took the bronze.

1. Werner Reiterer AUS 62.76
2. Adewale Olukoju NGR 62.46
3. Robert Weir ENG 60.86
4. Martin Swart RSA 56.42
5. Frits Potgieter RSA 56.10
6. Glen Smith ENG 55.84
7. Ray Lazdins CAN 55.60
8. Darrin Morris SCO 54.98

HAMMER (22nd)

Head led the first round with 70.18. Then defending champion Carlin took over with 70.24 in round 2 despite the hammer clipping the cage and produced the winner of 73.48 in round 3. Two sets of brothers took part with the younger Carlin, Paul, having three no throws.

1. Sean Carlin AUS 73.48
2. Paul Head ENG 70.18
3. Peter Vivian ENG 69.80
4. Mike Jones ENG 68.42
5. Angus Cooper NZL 67.92
6. Boris Stoikos CAN 65.84
7. John Stoikos CAN 64.82
8. D. Dionisopoulos AUS 63.52

JAVELIN (28th)

THE FIRST four placings duplicated those of four years earlier as Backley became the first man to retain his javelin title. In round 1 Hill led with 81.84 to Backley's 80.46. Backley threw 80.56 in the second round and then the winning 82.74 in the third; he later fouled an 84m-plus effort. and became one of four Britons to gain a European/Commonwealth double, the others being Christie, Jackson and Gunnell.

1. Steve Backley ENG 82.74
2. Mick Hill ENG 81.84
3. Gavin Lovegrove NZL 80.42
4. Nigel Bevan WAL 80.38
5. Louis Fouche RSA 77.00
6. Andrew Currey AUS 74.88
7. Mark Roberson ENG 73.78
8. Phillip Spies RSA 72.70

DECATHLON (23rd/24th)

DEFENDING champion Michael Smith was in solid form. At the end of the first day he was second (4178) to Winter (4259) with the sprint/jump specialist Victor Houston on 4170 and Shirley on 4169. Smith took the lead after seven events (5891-5861) and eventually won by 252 points. Winter continued to excel with more pbs on the second day and took the Australian record from Shirley who – representing his native country – placed third in spite of an ankle injury which almost caused him to drop out before the javelin.

1. Michael Smith CAN 8326
2. Peter Winter AUS 8074
3. Simon Shirley ENG 7980
4. Dean Smith AUS 7926
5. Doug Pirini NZL 7840
6. Rafer Joseph ENG 7663
7. Alex Kruger ENG 7640
8. Jamie Quarry SCO 7610

30 KILOMETRES WALK (25th)

Berrett, the English-born Canadian, and Nelson fought it out (5k 22:25, 10k 43:45, 15k 64:33 - 64:34, 20k 85:16 - 85:19) before A'Hern (22:27, 44:07, 64:49, 85:32) moved ahead after 22k. The time of 2:07:53 was the second fastest in Games history.

1. Nick A'Hern AUS 2:07:53
2. Tim Berrett CAN 2:08:22
3. Scott Nelson NZL 2:09:10
4. Darrell Stone ENG 2:11:30
5. Martin St Pierre CAN 2:11:51
6. Simon Baker AUS 2:14:02
7. Steve Partington IOM 2:14:15
8. Craig Barrett NZL 2:14:19

4 X 100 METRES RELAY (28th)

WITH Christie (racing back in Europe), Jarrett and Regis unavailable, England had little chance of retaining the title. Canada - Donovan Bailey (controversially omitted from the 100m after failing to return for the Trials), Glenroy Gilbert, Carlton Chambers and Bruny Surin - broke the Games record in the heats with 38.63 and improved it to 38.39. Sierra Leone, with Horace Dove-Edwin, qualified for the final but were pulled out after the 100m disqualification was revealed.

1. Canada 38.39*
2. Australia 38.88
3. England 39.39
4. Jamaica 39.44
5. Scotland 39.56
6. Ghana 39.79
7. Gambia 41.54
8. Botswana 41.55

4X400 METRES RELAY (h 27th, F 28th)

ENGLAND'S splits were: David McKenzie 46.0, Peter Crampton 45.9, Adrian Patrick 46.1 and a stunning 44.2 by Du'aine Ladejo. Jamaica led from the start and looked to be heading for victory when Garth Robinson took over for the final leg well clear of Trinidad with Ladejo setting off the best part of 15m behind. But Ladejo, so keen to atone for his defeat in the 400m, judged his effort perfectly to win a thrilling race. The time of 3:02.14 was a Games record although still slightly inferior to Trinidad's 3:02.8 for 4x440y at the 1966 Games. Defending champions Kenya were never a factor and were disqualified for baulking the Welsh team (which had set a national record of 3:03.68 in the heats) at the final change.

1. England	3:02.14*
2. Jamaica	3:02.32
3. Trinidad & Tobago	3:02.78
4. Nigeria	3:03.06
5. Australia	3:03.46
6. South Africa	3:03.87
7. Wales	3:07.80
dq. Kenya	

WOMEN

100 METRES (23rd, with -0.2)

WITH Merlene Ottey chosing not defend her titles, Onyali was presented with a golden opportunity to land her first major title. She was never seriously threatened. The three medallists each ran their season's bests in the second semi: Onyali 11.03, Thomas, who as Dunn lost by an eyelash in the 1986 Games, 11.15, Opara-Thompson 11.19. Tombiri had won the first semi in 11.25 from Gainsford 11.28.

1. Mary Onyali NGR	11.06
2. Christy Opara-Thompson NGR	11.22
3. Paula Thomas ENG	11.23
4. Melinda Gainsford AUS	11.31
5. Dahlia Duhaney JAM	11.34
6. Hermine Joseph DMN	11.36
7. Mary Tombiri NGR	11.38
8. Stephanie Douglas ENG	11.48

200 METRES (26th, wind +1.3)

BOTH Onyali, fastest in heat and semi at 22.69w and 22.54w, and Freeman, 22.83 and 22.75, were seeking to complete a double. The Nigerian held a 2m lead into the straight but the Australian's superior endurance proved decisive for a unique Commonwealth Games double and the first in these events at this level since Valerie Brisco-Hooks in the 1984 Olympics. Freeman's time was an Australian record and broke the legal Games record of 22.50 although just short of Ottey's windy 22.19 in 1982.

1. Cathy Freeman AUS	22.25
2. Mary Onyali NGR	22.35
3. Melinda Gainsford AUS	22.68
4. Paula Thomas ENG	22.69
5. Pauline Davis BAH	22.77
6. Dahlia Duhaney JAM	22.85
7. Merlene Frazer JAM	23.18
8. Geraldine McLeod ENG	23.52

400 METRES (23rd)

THE OLDEST of all Games records – Marilyn Neufville's 51.02 in 1970 (a world record then) – fell at last as Freeman held off the strong finish of defending champion Yusuf in 50.38 with Richards a close third also inside the old figures. Freeman made history by becoming the first Aboriginal athlete to win a gold medal in any athletics event. Richards was fastest in the heats, 52.62, and semis, 51.23.

1. Cathy Freeman AUS	50.38*
2. Fatima Yusuf NGR	50.53
3. Sandie Richards JAM	50.69
4. Phylis Smith ENG	51.46
5. Renee Poetschka AUS	51.51
6. Melanie Neef SCO	52.09
7. Olabisi Afolabi NGR	52.21
8. Kylie Hanigan AUS	52.55

800 METRES (26th)

WITH Diane Modahl unable to defend and Kelly Holmes opting for the 1500m, the race was an open one but far removed from world class level. Crooks set off fast (27.47, 59.31), shadowed by Turner, but ran out of steam in the closing stages (600m 1:31.36), enabling Turner to win comfortably. Wamuyu became the first Kenyan to earn a medal in this event since 1978.

1. Inez Turner JAM	2:01.74
2. Charmaine Crooks CAN	2:02.35
3. Gladys Wamuyu KEN	2:03.12
4. Cathy Dawson WAL	2:03.17
5. Salina Kosgei KEN	2:03.78
6. Lisa Lightfoot AUS	2:03.82
7. Melanie Collins AUS	2:04.09
8. Sandra Dawson AUS	2:04.41

1500 METRES (28th)

SCHNURR ran Holmes surprisingly close, but

Yvonne Murray: Commonwealth gold at last

a 59.6 last lap which she led throughout carried the European silver medallist to her expected victory. Intermediate times were 67.65, 2:19.56 and 3:23.83. England's other medal hope, Ann Griffiths, was a non-starter due to a head cold.

1. Kelly Holmes ENG 4:08.86
2. Paula Schnurr CAN 4:09.65
3. Gwen Griffiths RSA 4:10.16
4. Leah Pells CAN 4:10.82
5. Margaret Leaney AUS 4:11.48
6. Jackline Maranga KEN 4:12.84
7. Robyn Meagher CAN 4:13.91
8. Julie Sakala ZIM 4:18.11

3000 METRES (23rd)

PRODUCING one of the finest performances of the meeting, Chalmers (the 1500m and 3000m champion of 1990) took 6 sec off her Games record with a Canadian record of 8:32.17. Chalmers, who hails from Victoria (as does runner-up Meagher), ignored the crazy start (62.66 first 400m) by the young Kenyans, Cheruiyot and Eunice Sagero (10th 9:18.15), but she alone set about closing the gap. By 1000m, reached by the Kenyans in 2:47.84, she was only 10m down and more than 30m clear of Wyeth and the rest. Ahead after 1200m Chalmers swiftly moved away from the spent Kenyans and by 2000m (5:44.94) was over 50m up. At one stage her lead was 100m.

1. Angela Chalmers CAN 8:32.17*
2. Robyn Meagher CAN 8:45.59
3. Alison Wyeth ENG 8:47.98
4. Sonia McGeorge ENG 8:54.91
5. Susie Power AUS 8:59.23
6. Rose Cheruiyot KEN 9:00.89
7. Leah Pells CAN 9:03.66
8. Laura Adam SCO 9:06.63

10,000 METRES (24th)

MURRAY, third in the 3000m in 1986 and second in 1990, finally struck gold. In her only previous 10,000m, at Oslo in 1985, she was tenth and last in 33:43.80, double lapped by Ingrid Kristiansen (setting a world record of 30:59.42). Murray was always in control as she stuck relentlessly to Meyer when the South African began to exert pressure ten laps from the finish. The first half had been pedestrian at 16:27.37, but the second 5000m was covered in 15:29.60. The time for the last 4000m was 12:10.24 – which is 15:13 5000 pace. The field was lapping at 80 sec when Meyer accelerated with a 70.36 followed by a 72.90. Murray struck 500m out and covered the last lap in 65.59 to win by 50m. Kilometre splits: 3:10.50, 3:12.52, 3:21.17, 3:21.04, 3:22.14, 3:19.36, 3:00.91. 3:06.02, 3:08.00, 2:55.31.

1. Yvonne Murray SCO 31:56.97
2. Elana Meyer RSA 32:06.02
3. Jane Omoro KEN 32:13.01
4. Suzanne Rigg ENG 33:01.40
5. Vikki McPherson SCO 33:02.74
6. Ulla Marquette CAN 33:16.29
7. Michelle Dillon AUS 33:19.01
8. Anne Hare NZL 33:19.66

MARATHON (27th)

JUST 16 runners and only two sub-2:30 performers in the field: Kanana, who faded to sixth after leading by 15 sec at halfway in 74:11. and Sally Eastall, who was 13th in 2:41:32. It was Canada's day as Bussières moved well clear with about 10k to go and Rouillard (34) caught and passed her some 2k from the finish to win in a pb. Liverpool-born Danson (35), who lives in Singapore, also ran her fastest time in third place.

1. Carole Rouillard CAN 2:30:41
2. Lizanne Bussières CAN 2:31:07
3. Yvonne Danson ENG 2:32:24
4. Karen Macleod SCO 2:33:16
5. Nyla Carroll NZL 2:34:03
6. Angeline Kanana KEN 2:35:02
7. Hayley Nash WAL 2:35:39
8. Sally Ellis ENG 2:37:14

100 METRES HURDLES (27th, wind -2.0)

Freeman was always ahead but Agyepong, off to a poor start, closed all the way and there was only 2/100ths between them at the finish. The luckless Court, who ran 13.07 in her abortive heptathlon, was a faller. The heats were run in more favourable conditions. In the first (+1.0) Freeman 12.97 won from Farquharson 13.09, and in the second (+2.1) Agyepong won in 12.98w from Rose 13.06w.

1.	Michelle Freeman JAM	13.12
2.	Jacqui Agyepong ENG	13.14
3.	Samantha Farquharson ENG	13.38
4.	Dionne Rose JAM	13.42
5.	Donalda Duprey CAN	13.75
6.	Lesley Tashlin CAN	13.85
7.	Jayne Flemming AUS	13.98
dnf.	Clova Court ENG	

400 METRES HURDLES (26th)

Gunnell, much the fastest in the heats in 55.25, retained her title and broke Debbie Flintoff's Games record of 54.94, but it was one of her shakiest performances. She entered the finishing straight way ahead of Duprey, but the latter drew perilously close before fading out of contention as Gunnell messed up the ninth hurdle. She recovered sufficiently, however, to win in 54.51 by 5m from the Jamaican pair of Hemmings and Parris.

1.	Sally Gunnell ENG	54.51*
2.	Deon Hemmings JAM	55.11
3.	Debbie Ann Parris JAM	55.25
4.	Donalda Duprey CAN	55.39
5.	Gowry Retchakan ENG	56.69
6.	Jackie Parker ENG	56.72
7.	Karlene Haughton JAM	57.00
8.	Maria Usifo NGR	59.20

HIGH JUMP (27th)

Inverarity was the clear favourite and ultimately won the title with a stylish 1.94 on her first attempt, but not before being pressurised by former world junior record holder Weavers, who also cleared a new Games record of 1.94 (second attempt) and came agonisingly close to 1.97 at the final attempt and thus becoming South Africa's first champion of the new era.

1.	Alison Inverarity AUS	1.94*
2.	Charmaine Weavers RSA	1.94*
3.	Debbie Marti ENG	1.91
4.	Tania Dixon NZL	1.91
5=	Lea Haggett ENG	1.88
5=	Andrea Hughes AUS	1.88
7.	Julia Bennett ENG	1.85
8.	Sara McGladdery CAN	1.85

LONG JUMP (27th)

A fractured left leg kept Boegman out of the 1990 Games but all went well this time. Idowu started with a pb equalling 6.73 (+1.6) and Opara-Thompson 6.72w/+2.5 as against Boegman's tentative 6.49, but in the second round the Australian took the lead with 6.76w and improved to 6.82w (+2.4) with her fifth jump.

1.	Nicole Boegman AUS	6.82w
2.	Yinka Idowu ENG	6.73
3.	Christy Opara-Thompson NGR	6.72w
4.	Jackie Edwards BAH	6.68w
5.	Joanne Henry NZL	6.65w
6.	Chantal Brunner NZL	6.63
7.	Dionne Rose JAM	6.47w
8.	Denise Lewis ENG	6.32w

SHOT (24th)

The 36 year-old Oakes won her fifth Commonwealth Games medal following bronze in 1978 (16.14), gold in 1982 (17.92), silver in 1986 (18.75) and 1990 (18.43). Augee took silver following bronze in 1986 and gold in 1990 with her best distance for two years despite a sore hand.

1.	Judy Oakes ENG	18.16
2.	Myrtle Augee ENG	17.64
3.	Lisa Vizaniari AUS	16.61
4.	Georgette Reed CAN	16.45
5.	Christine King NZL	16.27
6.	Maggie Lynes ENG	16.23
7.	Alison Grey SCO	15.25
8.	Shannon Kekula-Kristiansen CAN	14.98

DISCUS (23rd)

COSTIAN'S opener of 63.72 was never challenged. The surprise was the lowly placing of Jackie McKernan, the only other 60m thrower in the field.

1.	Daniela Costian AUS	63.72*
2.	Beatrice Faumuina NZL	57.12
3.	Lisette Etzebeth RSA	55.74
4.	Sharon Andrews ENG	55.34
5.	Jackie McKernan NIR	54.86
6.	Lisa-Marie Vizaniari AUS	53.88
7.	Debbie Callaway ENG	53.16
8.	Theresa Brick CAN	52.12

JAVELIN (26th)

No one threatened McPaul's opening throw of 63.76 although Hellier finished strongly with a final effort of 60.40 for the silver. Gibson, so long in the shadow of Sanderson and Whitbread, finally gained her first medal, a bronze.

1.	Louise McPaul AUS	63.76
2.	Kirsten Hellier NZL	60.40
3.	Sharon Gibson ENG	58.20
4.	Joanna Stone AUS	57.60
5.	Valerie Tulloch CAN	57.26
6.	Kate Farrow AUS	56.98
7.	Laverne Eve BAH	55.54
8.	Kaye Nordstrom NZL	54.90

HEPTATHLON (22nd/23rd)

LEWIS made a delightful breakthrough to obliterate her previous highest score of 6069. Clova Court was supposed to be the main English threat but after a brilliant 13.07 hurdles she had her usual dreadful high jump (1.53) and pulled out injured after being in fifth place overnight (3485) behind title holder Flemming (3794), Bond-Mills (3747), Lewis (3549) and Henry (3518). Lewis scored good points with 6.44 in her best event, the long jump, but it was the javelin which won her the title. With a previous best of 48.58 she couldn't believe it when the spear touched down at a colossal 53.68! As Flemming failed to reach 40m Lewis was suddenly in a commanding lead: 5469 to 5397. To win she needed to finish within 5.5 sec of Flemming in the 800m. That she did, running a pb of 2:17.60, although with a difference between them of 4.53 sec it was cutting it fine.

1.	Denise Lewis ENG	6325
2.	Jane Flemming AUS	6317
3.	Catherine Bond-Mills CAN	6193
4.	Joanne Henry NZL	6121
5.	Jenny Kelly ENG	5658
6.	Najuma Fletcher GUY	5611
7.	Kim Vanderhoek CAN	5467
8.	Caroline Ochola KEN	5407

10 KILOMETRES WALK (25th)

Saxby-Junna won the inaugural event four years ago by a two-minute margin in 45:03. This time she walked faster (21:59 at 5k), but the opposition was not outclassed, for Manning finished only 12 sec down.

1.	Kerry Saxby-Junna AUS	44:25*
2.	Anne Manning AUS	44:37
3.	Janice McCaffrey CAN	44:54
4.	Holly Gerke CAN	45:43
5.	Vicky Lupton ENG	45:48
6.	Lisa Langford ENG	46:01
7.	Verity Larby-Snook SCO	46:06
8.	Jane Saville AUS	47:14

4 X 100 METRES RELAY (28th)

FOR THE first time since the event entered the Games in 1954 someone other than England or Australia won the title. It was Nigeria (Faith Idehen, Mary Tombiri, Christy Opara-Thompson, Mary Onyali) who broke the duopoly, their time of 42.99 being a Games record.

1.	Nigeria	42.99*
2.	Australia	43.43
3.	England	43.46
4.	Jamaica	43.51
5.	Bahamas	44.89
6.	Canada	45.15
7.	Ghana	45.72

4 X 400 METRES RELAY (28th)

Phylis Smith 51.9, Tracy Goddard 52.1. Linda Keough 51.8 kept England in the lead for the first three legs, leaving Sally Gunnell (51.2) to stave off the assaults of Cathy Freeman (seeking her fourth medal of the Games), Sandie Richards and Fatima Yusuf, three of the very best 400m runners in the world. Gunnell managed to stay ahead until, in the last 25m, Freeman edged in front. She was, however, disqualified for baulking Yusuf on the final turn when striving to get on terms with Gunnell and Richards, and the race was awarded to England. Gunnell thus won her fifth Commonwealth Games gold medal.

1.	England	3:27.06*
2.	Jamaica	3:27.63
3.	Canada	3:32.52
4.	Ghana	3:47.49
dq	Australia	(3:26.84)
dq	Nigeria	(3:34.67)

Denise Lewis: a delightful breakthrough

AFRICAN GAMES AND CHAMPIONSHIPS

THE first All-African Games, at ten sports, were contested in Brazzaville, Congo on 18-25 July 1965. Subsequent Games were staged at Lagos, Nigeria in 1973, at Algiers in 1978, Nairobi, Kenya in 1987, Cairo, Egypt in 1991, and the 1995 Games are due to be held in Zimbabwe in September.

All-African Games records before 1995

MEN

100m	10.18	Frank Fredericks NAM	1991
	9.92w	Chidi Imo NGR (sf)	1987
200m	20.28	Frank Fredericks NAM	1991
400m	44.23	Innoc't Egbunike NGR	1987
800m	1:45.38	Cosmos Silei KEN	1973
1500m	3:36.21	Filbert Bayi TAN	1978
5000m	13:31.87	Jonn Ngugi KEN	1987
10000m	27:56.45	Thomas Osano KEN	1991
Mar	2:14:47	Bel. Dinsamo ETH	1987
3000mSt	8:15.82	Henry Rono KEN	1978
110mh	13.89	Fatwell Iimaiyo KEN	1978
400mh	48.03	Amadou Dia Bâ SEN	1987
HJ	2.19	Othmaa Belfaa ALG	1987
PV	5.20	S Si Mohamed ALG	1991
LJ	8.23	Paul Emordi NGR	1987
TJ	17.12	Francis Dodoo GHA	1987
SP	19.48	Nagi Assag EGY	1973
DT	59.22	Adewale Olukoju NGR	1991
HT	70.10	Hakim Toumi ALG	1987
JT	77.14	Chr. Okemefula NGR	1991
Dec	7431	M Mahour Bacha ALG	1991
4x100mR	39.06	Nigeria	1987
4x400mR	3:00.55	Nigeria	1987
20kmW	1:29:04	Shemsu Hassan ETH	1991

WOMEN

100m	11.12	Mary Onyali NGR	1991
200m	22.66	Mary Onyali NGR	1987
400m	50.71	Fatima Yusuf NGR	1991
800m	2:03.22	Selina Chirchir KEN	1987
1500m	4:10.68	Susan Sirma KEN	1991
3000m	8:49.33	Susan Sirma KEN	1991
10000m	33:40.37	Derartu Tulu ETH	1991
100mh	13.29	Maria Usifo NGR	1987
400mh	55.72	Maria Usifo NGR	1987
HJ	1.83	Lucienne N'Da CIV	1991
LJ	6.67	Chioma Ajunwa NGR	1991
SP	15.30	Elisabeth Olaba KEN	1987
DT	48.32	H Ahmed Khaled EGY	1991
JT	53.30	Samia Djémaa ALG	1987
Hept	5663	Yasmina Azzizi ALG	1987
4x100m	43.44	Nigeria	1987
4x400m	3:27.08	Nigeria	1987
5000mW	24:25.00	Agn Chelimo KEN	1991

Most gold medals at All-African Games - individual events

Men

3 Namakoro Naire MALI DT 1965-73-78

3 Adewale Olukoju NGR SP 1987, DT 1987-91

Women

5 Modupe Oshikoya NGR 100mh 1973, HJ 1973-78, LJ 1973-78

3 Alice Annum GHA LJ 1965, 100m & 200m 1973(& 4x100mR 1973)

3 Susan Sirma KEN 3000m 1987-91, 1500m 1991

Including relays - women

5 Mary Onyali NGR 200m 1987, 100m 1991, 4x100mR 1987-91, 4x400m 1987

African Championships, for athletics only, were first held at Dakar SEN in 1979, and have subsequently been held at Cairo EGY in 1982, Rabat MAR 1984, Cairo 1985, Annaba ALG 1988, Lagos NGR 1989, Cairo 1990 and 1991, Belle Vue Mauricia MRI 1992, Durban RSA 1993.

Frank Fredericks: African Games 100m & 200m record holder

ASIAN GAMES

THE first multi-sport Asian Games were held at New Delhi, India on 8-11 Mar 1951, when ten nations took part, and have been held at four-yearly intervals from 1954.

The 12th Games were staged at Hiroshima, Japan on 9-16 October 1994.

ASIAN GAMES 1994

Men

100m	1. Talal Mansoor QAT	10.18*
(-1.6)	2. Vitaliy Savin KZK	10.29
	3. Chen Wenzhong CHN	10.38
200m	1. Talal Mansoor QAT	20.41*
(+1.7)	2. Koji Ito JPN	20.70
	3. Ibrahim Ismail QAT	20.88
400m	1. Ibrahim Ismail QAT	45.48 (44.93* h)
	2. Son Ju-il KOR	45.87
	3. Aktawat Skoolchan THA	46.50
800m	1. Lee Jin-il KOR	1:45.72*
	2. Mu Weiguo CHN	1:46.44
	3. Kim Yong-hwan KOR	1:46.69
1500m	1. Mohamed Suleiman QAT	3:40.00*
	2. Mu Weiguo CHN	3:40.93
	3. Misuhiro Okuyama JPN	3:41.31
5000m	1. Toshinari Takaoka JPN	13:38.37*
	2. Ah Ibrahim Warsama QAT	13:39.59
	3. Sun Riping CHN	13:40.07
10,000m	1. Toshinari Takaoka JPN	28:15.48*
	2. Jun Hiratsuka JPN	28:18.10
	3. Sultan Al-Qahtani SAU	28:41.18
Mar	1. Hwang Young-cho KOR	2:11:13
	2. Toshiyuki Hayata JPN	2:11:57
	3. Kim Jae-ryong KOR	2:13:12
3000mSt	1. Sun Riping CHN	8:31.73*
	2. Saad Shadad Al-Asmari SAU	8:33.94
	3. Yasunori Uchitomi JPN	8:37.76
110mh	1. Li Tong CHN	13.30*
(+1.6)	2. Chen Yanhao CHN	13.39
	3. Nur Herman Majid MAL	13.73
400mh	1. Shunji Karube JPN	49.13*
	2. Yoshihiko Saito JPN	49.13*
	3. Ali Ismail Doka QAT	49.56
HJ	1. Takahisa Yoshida JPN	2.27
	2. Lee Jin-taek KOR	2.24
	3. Xu Yang CHN	2.24
PV	1. Igor Potapovich KZK	5.65
	2. Grigoriy Yegorov KZK	5.50
	3= Kim Chul-kyun KOR	5.40
	3= Teruyasu Yonekura JPN	5.40
LJ	1. Huang Geng CHN	8.34w
	2. Huang Baoting CHN	8.12*
	3. Konstantin Saravatskiy UZB	8.10
TJ	1. Oleg Sakirkin KZK	17.21
	2. Takashi Komatsu JPN	16.88
	3. Sergey Arzamasov KZK	16.57
SP	1. Liu Hao CHN	19.26*
	2. Sergey Rubtsov UZB	19.24
	3. Xie Shengying CHN	18.64
DT	1. Zhang Cunbiao CHN	58.78
	2. Ma Wei CHN	57.92
	3. Vadim Popov UZB	56.78
HT	1. Bi Zhong CHN	72.24*
	2. Koji Murofushi JPN	67.48
	3. Aquarab Abbas PAK	66.70

Oleg Sakirkin: triple jump winner

JT	1. Zhang Lianbiao CHN	83.38*
	2. Vladimir Parfyonov UZB	81.66
	3. Viktor Zaitsev UZB	78.64
Dec	1. Ramil Ganiyev UZB	8005*
	2. Oleg Veretelnikov UZB	7702
	3. Tomokazu Sugama JPN	7666
4x100mR	1. JPN	39.37
	2. CHN	39.45
	3. QAT	39.71
4x400mR	1. KOR	3:10.19
	2. THA	3:10.33
	3. QAT	3:10.49
20kmW	1. Chen Shaoguo CHN	1:21:15*
	2. Bu Lingtang CHN	1:21:56
	3. Valeriy Borisov KZK	1:25:31
50kmW	1. Sergey Korepanov KZK	3:54:37*
	2. Fumio Imamura JPN	3:56:16
	3. Tadahiro Kosaka JPN	4:05:00

WOMEN

100m	1. Liu Xiaomei CHN	11.27*
(+0.8)	2, Wang Heui-chen TPE	11.41
	3. Huang Xiaoyan CHN	11.43
200m	1. Wang Huei-chen TPE	23.34*
(-0.8)	2. Susanthika Jayasinghe SRI	23.57
	3. Damaryanthi Darsha SRI	23.61
400m	1. Ma Yuqin	51.17*
	2. Zhang Hengyun CHN	52.53
	3. Kalawati Saramma IND	52.57
800m	1. Qu Yunxia CHN	1:59.85*
	2. Liu Li CHN	2:00.66
	3. Shiny Wilson IND	2:02.22
1500m	1. Qu Yunxia CHN	4:12.48*
	2. Yan Wei CHN	4:13.32
	3. Khin Khin Htwe MYA	4:18.00
3000m	1. Zhang Linli CHN	8:52.97*
	2. Harumi Hiroyama	8:53.74
	3. Lu Ou (was Ma Liyan) CHN	8:58.68
10,000m	1. Wang Junxia CHN	30:50.34*
	2. Dong Li CHN	31:31.08
	3. Miki Igarashi JPN	31:45.82
Mar	1. Zhong Huandi CHN	2:29:32*
	2. Zhang Lirong CHN	2:36:27
	3. Nobuko Fujimura JPN	2:37:03
	4. Jung Young-im KOR	2:38:43
100mh	1. Olga Shishigina KZK	12.80
(-2.0)	2. Zhou Hongyang CHN	12.87
	3. Zhang Yu CHN	12.90
400mh	1. Leng Xueyan CHN	55.26*
	2. Hsu Pei-ching TPE	55.75
	3. Natalya Torshina KZK	55.81
	Han Qing CHN 1st 54.74 but drugs dq	
HJ	1. Svetlana Mounkova UZB	1.92
	2. Svetlana Zalevskaya KZK	1.89
	3. Rassamee Taemsri THA	1.83
LJ	1. Yao Weli CHN	6.91*
	2. Li Jing CHN	6.69
	3. Elma Muros PHI	6.41
SP	1. Sui Xinmei CHN	20.45
	2. Zhang Liuhong CHN	19.25
	3. Sunisa Yooyao THA	16.24
DT	1. Min Chunfeng CHN	62.52
	2. Ikuko Kitamori JPN	53.92
	3. Miyoko Nakanishi JPN	49.84
JT	1. Oksana Yarygina UZB	64.62
	2. Lee Young-sun KOR	62.30
	3. Ha Xiaoyan CHN	62.08
Hep	1. Ghada Shouaa SYR	6360*

Qu Junxia: a middle distance double

Medal table

Nation	gold	silver	bronze
CHN	22	17	8
JPN	5	9	10
KZK	4	4	3
QAT	4	1	4
KOR	3	3	3
UZB	3	2	3
TPE	1	2	1
SYR	1	-	-
THA	-	2	4
IND	-	1	2
SAU	-	1	1
SRI	-	1	1

One bronze for MAS, MYA, PAK, PHI

	2. Zhang Xiaohui CHN	5800
	3. Ma Chun-ping TPE	5786
4x100mR	1. CHN	43.85*
	2. THA	44.46
	3. JPN	44.57
4x400mR	1. CHN	3:29.11*
	2. IND	3:33.34
	3. THA	3:37.76
10kmW	1. Gao Hongmiao CHN	44:11*
	2. Gu Yan CHN	44:18
	3. Yuko Sato JPN	46:51

* Games record

ASIAN TRACK AND FIELD CHAMPIONSHIPS

THE first Asian Championships, as opposed to the multi-sport Games, were held at Marakina, near Manila, Philippines in 1973. The next edition will be at Jakarta, Indonesia, 20-24 Sep 1995.

Asian Championships records prior to 1995

Men

100m	10.22	Talal Mansoor QAT	1993
200m	20.41	Jang Jae-keun KOR	1985
400m	45.55	Ibrahim Ismail QAT	1993
800m	1:47.37	Batu Rajkumar MAL	1985
1500m	3:38.60	Kim Soon-hyung KOR	1993
5000m	13:41.70	Bahadur Prasad IND	1993
10000m	28:53.29	Kunimitsu Ito JPN	1981
Mar	2:20:29	Ling Jong-hyon PRK	1985
3000mSt	8:32.08	Sa'ad Shaddad Al-Asmari SAU	1993
110mh	13.82	Li Tong CHN	1993
400mh	49.10	Zaïd Abou Hamed SYR	1993
4x100mR	39.20	Qatar 1987, China	1991
4x400mR	3:05.22	Japan	1991
20kmW	1:26:29.69	Chen Shaoguo CHN	1993
HJ	2.31	Zhu Jianhua CHN	1983
PV	5.70	Grigoriy Yegorov KZK	1993
LJ	8.13	Nobuharu Asahara JPN	1993
TJ	17.22	Chen Yanping CHN	1991
SP	19.04	Liu Hao CHN	1993
DT	62.20	Yu Wenge CHN	1991
HT	70.54	Bi Zhong CHN	1993
JT	81.52	Zhang Lianbiao CHN	1991
Dec	7848	Gong Guohua CHN	1991

Women

100m	11.32	Tian Yumei CHN	1991 sf
200m	23.24	Chen Zhaojing CHN	1993
400m	51.23	Ma Yuqing CHN	1993
800m	2:03.16	Shiny Abraham IND	1985
1500m	4:17.78	Yan Wei CHN	1993
3000m	9:05.20	Zhong Huandi CHN	1989
10000m	32:25.27	Zhong Huandi CHN	1989
Mar	2:48:53	Asha Aggarwal IND	1985
100mh	13.07	Zhang Yu CHN	1993
400mh	56.14	P.T.Usha IND	1989
4x100mR	43.41	China	1991
4x400mR	3:32.95	India	1989
10km W	47:08.98	Gao Hongmiao CHN	1993
HJ	1.93	Hisayo Fukumitso JPN	1981
LJ	6.79	Li Yong-ae PRK	1991
TJ	14.05	Ren Ruiping CHN	1993
SP	19.69	Huang Zhihong CHN	1989
DT	61.92	Yu Houren CHN	1989
JT	62.14	Zhang Li CHN	1993
Hep	6259	Ghada Shouaa SYR	1993

Most individual gold medals: 10 P.T.Usha Women 400m 1983, 100m, 200m, 400m and 400mh 1985; 400m & 400mh 1987; 200m, 400m, 400mh 1989

4th ASIAN MARATHON CHAMPIONSHIPS

Men: 6 Feb, Oita City, Japan: Suzuki Yukio JPN 2:19:04

Women: 13 Mar, Nagoya, Japan: Eriko Asai JPN 2:30:30

P T Usha: most gold medals

EUROPEAN CHAMPIONSHIPS 1994

EUROPEAN STANDARDS may be down in many events compared to those shown in the heyday of Eastern European supremacy, but these were an exciting and fascinating championships. Held from 7th to 14th August in the Olympic Stadium, which was packed for most of the evening sessions and always enthusiastically supported by the Finnish fans and the many overseas visitors.

Russia, competing separately for the first time at these Championships, was the most successful nation, with 25 medal, including 10 gold. Their stars included Irina Privalova, who completed the women's sprint double, and Radion Gataullin, who matched the best ever pole vault achieved at a major championships, 6 metres to win a great competition. Linford Christie and Heike Drechsler won their third sucessive titles, a feat that just eluded Roger Black, pipped by his teammate Du'aine Ladejo at 400m although taking a third successive 4x400m gold, to equal Harald Schmid's record for the most gold medals, six, ever won by a man at these Championships.

The weather was warm and pleasant (24-28°C) for the first two days, but for the rest of the week there were several showers and temperatures 19-25°C. The humidity rose from c.40% at the start of the Championships to high during the final days especially for the men's marathon, when it was 80-84%. Dates given in brackets after the heading for each event are those of the final

MEN

100 METRES (8th, wind -0.5)

Christie won his third successive European 100m title to match the achievement of Valeriy Borzov in 1969, 1971 and 1974. He soon showed that he was over his recent hamstring injury with 10.08 in his quarter-final and was troubled only by the fact that he made the second of three false starts in the final. The highly impressive Geir Moen finished fastest of all.

1.	Linford Christie	GBR	10.14
2.	Geir Moen	NOR	10.20
3.	Aleks. Porkhomovskiy	RUS	10.31
4.	Oleg Kramarenko	UKR	10.38
5.	Daniel Cojocaru	ROM	10.39
6.	Marc Blume	GER	10.40
7.	Alexandros Terzian	GRE	10.42
8.	Jason John	GBR	10.46

200 METRES (11th, wind -0.1)

Once John Regis had pulled put to favour an Achilles injury, Moen was the clear favourite, and he took 0.1 off his national record in the final. Dologodin was an isolated second, and Stevens overcame a very slow start (reaction time (.292) to snatch bronze on the line. Trouabal had been well in contention but faded badly in the home straight.

Linford Christie: emulated Borzov

1.	Geir Moen	NOR	20.30
2.	Vladislav Dologodin	UKR	20.47
3.	Patrick Stevens	BEL	20.68
4.	Sergey Osovich	UKR	20.70
5.	Jean-Charles Trouabal	FRA	20.70
6.	Andrey Fedoriv	RUS	20.78
7.	Geor. Panagiotopoulos	GRE	20.92
8.	David Dollé	SUI	21.10

400 METRES (11th)

Ladejo (lane 5) was away steadily as Black (lane 3) chased Vdovin to 200m, but ran a great bend to draw up to a metre down on Black entering the home straight. The big two, who had each won their semis, pulled clear of the field and Ladejo was too strong in the finish. He thus prevented Black from winning a unique third successive 400m title. From lane 1 Rusterholz, who had run 45.88 in his semi, took bronze.

1.	Du'aine Ladejo	GBR	45.09
2.	Roger Black	GBR	45.20
3.	Matthias Rusterholz	SUI	45.96
4.	Dmitriy Golovastov	RUS	46.01
5.	Anton Ivanov	BUL	46.20
6.	Mikhail Vdovin	RUS	46.23
7.	Stefan Balosák	SVK	46.64
8.	Dmitriy Kosov	RUS	46.69

800 METRES (14th)

Benvenuti won the first semi-final in 1:47.01, and four men boke 1:46 in the second won by Motchebon in 1:45.75. Andrey Loginov RUS was 5th in 1:46.18. In the final Rodal was fastest away, reaching 200m in 25.53 with Douglas. The pace slowed to 400m 54.29, and Rodal still led at 600m 1:20.76, but lost to Benvenuti's kick. De Teresa came on the outside to pass Motechebon for the bronze.

1.	Andrea Benvenuti	ITA	1:46.12
2.	Vebjørn Rodal	NOR	1:46.53
3.	Tomás De Teresa	ESP	1:46.57
4.	Nico Motchebon	GER	1:46.65
5.	Giuseppe D'Urso	ITA	1:46.90
6.	Craig Winrow	GBR	1:47.09
7.	José Cerezo	ESP	1:47.58
8.	Atle Douglas	NOR	1:47.90

1500 METRES (9th)

Dubus had ensured a very fast pace in the first heat (1:58.78, 2:55.11), won by Cacho in 3:37.18, and the fastest losers all came from there as several fancied runners, including Jens-Peter Herold GER and Marcus O'Sullivan IRL, stupidly allowed the second heat to be run much more slowly. Di Napoli (9th 3:39.96) stretched the field in the final through laps of 58.12, 1:57.73 and 2:54.79 (bell 2:49.89). Cacho, who had stayed second to the Italian, then took over and was challenged only by his countryman Viciosa. Zorko produced his customary late charge to take the bronze.

1.	Fermin Cacho	ESP	3:35.27 CR
2.	Isaac Viciosa	ESP	3:36.01
3.	Branko Zorko	CRO	3:36.88
4.	Éric Dubus	FRA	3:37.44
5.	Andrey Bulkovskiy	UKR	3:37.81
6.	Manuel Pancorbo	ESP	3:38.16
7.	Rüdiger Stenzel	GER	3:38.36
8.	Abdelrader Chekhémani	FRA	3:38.42

5000 METRES (14th)

Runners in the second of the two heats ran intelligently by ensuring a much faster pace (8:09.54 at 3000m to 8:23.13 in heat 1), and were rewarded by all the fastest loser spots coming from that race. The winner was José Ramos POR in 13:30.33; he was 14th in 14:04.33 in the final which was a typical championship race in that nobody wanted to force the pace. Vener Kashayev RUS (12th 13:53.66) led at 1k 2:50.83 and 2k 5:40.16. Mohamed Ezzher FRA (15th 14:14.73) took over and led at 3k 8:24.56. Then

Andrea Benvenuti: kicked hardest

Domingos Castro POR (9th 13:42.09) made a surge and the pace picked up so that he led at 4k in 11:03.93. Baumann, the class of the field, bided his time and was always well placed. He kicked hard and the gold was assured. Denmark took a while to get around the others and was a clear second, before Antón added the bronze to his 10k gold. The fastest time of the Championships was the 13:30.33 by José Ramos of Portuga; who won heat two. He was 14th in the final.

1.	Dieter Baumann	GER	13:36.93
2.	Rob Denmark	GBR	13:37.50
3.	Abel Antón	ESP	13:38.04
4.	Abdellah Béhar	FRA	13:38.36
5.	John Nuttall	GBR	13:38.65
6.	José Carlos Adán	ESP	13:39.16
7.	Risto Ulmala	FIN	13:40.84
8.	Anacleto Jiménez	ESP	13:41.60

10,000 METRES (7th)

Although the winning time was the slowest for 20 years, this was a fascinating race. After laps of 72.5 and 70, Rousseau stretched the field, leading for a further three laps, but as the pace slowed to 68s and later back to the 70s, after a 65, the pack caught up. Rousseau, Panetta and Franke looked the dominant men for much of the race, but when Franke made a decisive move with a 62.5 lap after 8k, Panetta faded and ran off the track at 8400m. The surprising Pesava, who was to take 21.58 off his best and run a Czech record, took the lead, but just after the bell Rousseau kicked hard. He looked to have the race, until in the closing strides his form fell away and Antón ran smoothly through for a 56-second last lap and the gold medal.

Rousseau 1k 2:53.90, Junqueira 2k 5:42.55, Franke 3k 8:40.49, Panetta 4k 11:25.13, Franke 5k 14:12.84, Freigang 6k 17:04.86, 7k 19:54.79, Franke 8k 22:45.92, Castro 9k 25:34.69.

1.	Abel Antón	ESP	28:06.03
2.	Vincent Rousseau	BEL	28:06.63
3.	Stephane Franke	GER	28:07.95
4.	Róbert Stefko	SVK	28:08.02
5.	Paulo Guerra	POR	28:10.18
6.	João Junqueira	POR	28:10.55
7.	Jan Pesava	TCH	28:10.73
8.	Carlos de la Torre	ESP	28:10.77

MARATHON (14th)

A group of 25 were together at halfway 1:06:08. Soon afterwards Rodrigues went ahead and was joined was joined by Fiz. By 1hr 30 the three Spaniards were running together and stretching clear. Nerurkar who had been tracking the leaders throughout, passed António Pinto POR (9th 2:13:24) and Rodrigues but could not narrow the gap, with the Spaniards completing an unprecedented clean sweep of marathon medals. Times very good in humidity 80-84%. Temperature 20-22°C.

1.	Martin Fiz	ESP	2:10:31 CR
2.	Diego Garcia	ESP	2:10:46
3.	Alberto Juzdado	ESP	2:11:18
4.	Richard Nerurkar	GBR	2:11:56
5.	Luigi Di Lello	ITA	2:12:41
6.	António Rodrigues	POR	2:12:43
7.	Manuel Matias	POR	2:12:48
8.	Harri Hänninen	FIN	2:13:21

European Cup (run in conjunction. four of six to score): 1, ESP 8:49:54; 2, POR 8:54:59; 3, FRA 8:57:46; 4, GER 9:02:07; 5, POL 9:06:36; 6, GBR 9:10:09; 7, FIN 9:20:47, 8, SWE 9:25:57; 9, HOL 9:28:22.

3000 METRES STEEPLECHASE (12th)

Alessandro Lambruschini fell at a hurdle on the second lap, but Panetta helped him to his

Allessandro Lambruschini: so superior

feet, and such was his superiority that he recovered to win his first gold medal. Teammate Carosi took silver as van Dijck outkicked the brave Rowland for the bronze. Markus Hacksteiner SUI (12th 8:46.60) was the early leader, then Tom Hanlon GBR (10th 8:36.06) at 1k 2:50.44. Carosi led, then Kim Bauermeister GER (9th 8:32.58) 2k 5:41.25 before Panetta put in a burst with two laps to go to set his compatriots on their way.

1.	Aless Lambruschini	ITA	8:28.68
2.	Angelo Carosi	ITA	8:29.81
3.	William Van Dijck	BEL	8:30.93
4.	Mark Rowland	GBR	8:30.24
5.	Vladimir Pronin	RUS	8:29.35
6.	Martin Strege	GER	8:28.92
7.	Jim Svenøy	NOR	8:30.14
8.	Francesco Panetta	ITA	8:30.78

110 METRES HURDLES

(12th, wind +1.1)

Jackson won his heat in 13.16 and ran the world's fastest time of 1994 in his semi with a CR 13.04 (+1.0). He was only marginally slower as he won the final in handsome style. Schwarthoff's silver was his first since the 1987 European Juniors and he came through fast to beat Jarrett, who had beaten him back then. Edorh was ecstatic after improving his pb in both semi and final. The new Austrian citizen Mark McKoy won his heat in 13.50 but withdrew from the semis with an injury.

1.	Colin Jackson	GBR	13.08
2.	Florian Schwarthoff	GER	13.16
3.	Tony Jarrett	GBR	13.23
4.	Claude Edorh	GER	13.41
5.	Mike Fenner	GER	13.53
6.	Antti Haapakoski	FIN	13.54
7.	Dan Philibert	FRA	13.54
8.	George Boroi	ROM	13.61

400 METRES HURDLES (10th)

The favourite Diagana ran 48.47 in his semi and from lane 4 ran 48.23 in the final, yet had to settle for bronze behind the national records set by Tverdokhleb (lane 6) and Nylander (lane 5). The latter won his third successive European medal in his fourth final (7-3-2-2). Rodrigues ran Portuguese records in each round (49.05, 49.04, 48.77).

1.	Oleg Tverdokhleb	UKR	48.06
2.	Sven Nylander	SWE	48.22
3.	Stéphane Diagana	FRA	48.23
4.	Pedro Rodrigues	POR	48.77
5.	Edgar Itt	GER	49.11
6.	Peter Crampton	GBR	49.45
7.	Vadim Zadoynov	MOL	49.50
8.	Gary Cadogan	GBR	49.53

HIGH JUMP (9th)

Hoen (2.25/1, 2.31/2, 2.33/1, 2.35/3) became the first Norwegian man to win a European title since Sverre Strandli in the hammer in 1950. Smith, whose best outdoor jump this year was 2.28, once again showed his amazing big meet ability, and came ever so close to 2.35.

1.	Steinar Hoen	NOR	2.35 CR
2=	Artur Partyka	POL	2.33
2=	Steve Smith	GBR	2.33
4.	Håkan Sarnblom	NOR	2.31
5=	Dragutin Topic	IEP	2.31
5=	Jaroslaw Kotewicz	POL	2.31
7.	Leonid Pumalainen	RUS	2.28
8.	Lambros Papakostas	GRE	2.28

POLE VAULT (11th)

Gataullin (5.70/2, 5.85/2, 5.90/2, 6.00/2) won one of the greatest ever pole vault competitions. To retain his title he needed to clear 6 metres to beat Trandenkov, and he succeeded, to match Bubka's 1993 vault in Stuttgart, the best ever in a championship. Nine men went

Rodion Gataullin: one of the greatest vaults

over 5.70 or better and three achieved European Championship records from the previous mark held at 5.85 by Bubka and Gataullin. Galfione had been the first and was highly impressive to that height, while Collet returned to top form, although his 5.80 success was entirely due to brilliant 'Volzing'.

1.	Radion Gataullin	RUS	6.00 CR
2.	Igor Trandenkov	RUS	5.90
3.	Jean Galfione	FRA	5.85
4.	Philippe Collet	FRA	5.80
5.	Denis Petushinskiy	RUS	5.80
6.	Andrej Tiwontschik	GER	5.70
7.	Yevgeniy Krasnov	ISR	5.70
8=	Gianni Iapichino	ITA	5.70
8=	Valeriy Bukrejev	EST	5.70

LONG JUMP (10th)

Four men, headed by Kirilenko 8.11, jumped 8m or more in qualifying, but only three did so in the final. Mladenov did 8.02 in the 1st round, then Gombala 8.04 in the 2nd. After that only Koukodimos, whose 8.01 was his only valid jump, was over 8m until Mladenov, who had a big (8.20-8.30) no jump in the 2nd round, regained the lead with 8.09 in the final round. Tarasenko had a final no jump of c.8.40m. After 10 valid jumps out of 12 in the first round, there 23 no jumps and 25 valid jumps in the remaining five. It was fascinatingly close, but the winning performance was the worst since 1971.

1.	Ivailo Mladenov	BUL	8.09
2.	Milan Gombala	TCH	8.04
3.	Konstan Koukodimos	GRE	8.01
4.	Bogdan Tudor	ROM	7.99
5,	Dmitriy Bogryanov	RUS	7.96
6.	Stanislav Tarasenko	RUS	7.93
7.	Vitaliy Kirilenko	UKR	7.92
8.	Erik Nys	BEL	7.89

Ivailo Mladenov: took long jump lead in final round

TRIPLE JUMP (13th)

In cool, rainy condition nobody achieved the qualifying standard of 16.85, and a very modest of 16.24 was all that was needed to make the final. Bruziks, who had won the silver medal for the USSR in 1986, was the only man to exceed 17m in the first two rounds of the final, but Hélan, having taken the lead in the 4th round with 17.23, jumped a French record 17.55 in the 5th. Kapustin started slowly but got his rhythm together in the closing rounds and responded with a magnificent 17.62 in the final round.

1.	Denis Kapustin	RUS	17.62
2.	Serge Hélan	FRA	17.55
3.	Maris Bruziks	LAT	17.20
4.	Vasiliy Sokov	RUS	16.97
5.	Gennadiy Markov	RUS	16.89
6.	Jonathan Edwards	GBR	16.85
7.	Georges Sainte-Rose	FRA	16.59
8.	Audrius Raizgys	LIT	16.59

SHOT (13th)

No qualifier made the ridiculously high (out-of-date!) standard of 19.80, and only two achieved it in the final. Klimenko (20.54, 20.78, x, x, x, p) and Bagach were a class apart, and Virastyuk gave Ukraine the first of the two medal sweeps in Helsinki. Surprisingly no Russian made the final. As in the women's shot the standard was the lowest for 25 years

1.	Aleksandr Klimenko	UKR	20.78
2.	Aleksandr Bagach	UKR	20.34
3.	Roman Virastyuk	UKR	19.59
4.	Mika Halvari	FIN	19.52
5.	Markus Koistinen	FIN	19.51
6.	Dragan Peric	IEP	19.40
7.	Petur Gudmundsson	ISL	19.34
8.	Paolo Dal Soglio	ITA	19.15

Steve Backley: back on top

DISCUS (14th)

Dubrovshchik, the European Junior champion of 1991, brought Belarus their first gold medal, taking a decisive lead with 64.78 in the third round. He was disappointed to have a throw over 65m in the 5th round ruled a foul; a judges' error, he said. Shevchenko's best came immediately after Dubrovchik, as those two passed the 63.92 posted by Schult in the first round. Lars Riedel's bad back prevented him from competing in the final, after he had barely qualified with 58.66. Shevchenko led the qaulifeirs with 62.46, with Sergey Lyakhov RUS (9th in final 60.80) and Dubrovshchik also reaching 62m.

1.	Vladimir Dubrovshchik	BLS	64.78
2.	Dmitriy Shevchenko	RUS	64.56
3.	Jürgen Schult	GER	64.18
4.	Nick Sweeney	IRL	63.76
5.	Attila Horváth	HUN	63.60
6.	Vladimir Zinchenko	UKR	63.60
7.	Svein Inge Valvik	NOR	62.02
8.	Costel Grasu	ROM	61.40

HAMMER (11th)

Both Sidorenko (throwing 6th) and Astapkovich (9th) threw 79.54 in the first round of the final. In the second round both went over 80m, Astapkovich 80.40 and Sidorenko 80.50, but this effort was ruled out two rounds later after video replays had shown it to be a foul. Meanwhile he produced a decisive effort in the third round. Astapkovich, who had won the 1990 Europeans, thus gained his fourth successive major championship silver since then. Weis, who led the qualifiers at 79.56, just held off Nikulin, who added a 4th to 2-3-3 at previous European Championships.

1.	Vasiliy Sidorenko	RUS	81.10
2.	Igor Astapkovich	BLS	80.40
3.	Heinz Weis	GER	78.48
4.	Igor Nikulin	RUS	78.38
5.	Tibor Gécsek	HUN	77.62
6.	Aleksey Krykun	UKR	76.08
7.	Christoph Epalle	FRA	75.22
8.	Vadim Kolesnik	UKR	75.22

JAVELIN (8th)

Raty 84.76, Hill 84.44 and Zelezny 83.88 led the qualifiers. In the first round of final the lead was successively held by Hill 80.24, Zelezny 80.40, Backley 81.04 and, throwing last to huge encouragement by the packed crowd, Räty 81.80. In round two Zelezny regained the lead with 82.58, but was followed onto the runway by Backley, whose 85.20 proved decisive. The first four places went to men who had set world records, but strive as they might none could exceed 83m thereafter, although Räty passed Zelezny for the silver and Bodén moved to fourth. The big three stood on the podium in the reverse order to that they had in the 1992 Olympics.

1.	Steve Backley	GBR	85.20
2.	Seppo Räty	FIN	82.90
3.	Jan Zelezny	TCH	82.58
4.	Patrik Bodén	SWE	81.34
5.	Raymond Hecht	GER	81.18
6.	Mick Hill	GBR	80.66
7.	Terry McHugh	IRL	80.46
8.	Vladimir Sasimovich	BLS	78.88

DECATHLON (12th/13th)

Eduard Hämäläinen BLS, the favourite, took the lead after the shot and increased that lead after the high jump. At the end of day 1 he had 4512 points, with Dagård, who had closed with a pb 46.71 at 400m, 2nd at 4351, followed by Dvorák 4306, Nool 4285 and Lobodin 4255. At the start of the second day Hämäläinen, who has the world 110mh decathlon best of 13.57, fell at the first hurdle, which he reached too fast. That left Dagård leading by 58 from Dvorák, a lead he increased to 90 in the discus. At this stage Blondel was 197 points off the lead in 6th place, but he came through with a brilliant 5.40 in pouring rain in the pole vault to within 11 points of Dagård, and though he was 40 down after the javelin, the result was never in doubt in the 1500m, which Blondel went into with every confidence as his pb was some 16 secs better than Dagård, who set a Swedish record.

1.	Alain Blondel	FRA	8453
2.	Henrik Dagård	SWE	8362
3.	Lev Lobodin	UKR	8201
4.	Christian Plaziat	FRA	8127
5.	Stefan Schmid	GER	8109
6.	Sándor Munkacsi	HUN	8071
7.	Tomás Dvorák	TCH	8065
8.	Dezsö Szábo	HUN	7995

20 KILOMETRES WALK (8th)

Shchennikov won his major outdoor gold since the 1985 World Junior title to add to his six indoor titles (four World, two European). After a 20:33 first 5k, he speeded to share the lead with Massana at 10k (39:38) and was 25 secs ahead of Misyulya with 58:47 for 15k.

1.	Mikhail Shchennikov	RUS	1:18:45 CR
2.	Yevgeniy Misyulya	BLS	1:19:22
3.	Valentin Massana	ESP	1:20:33
4.	Giovanni De Benedictis	ITA	1:20:39
5.	Mikhail Orlov	RUS	1:21:01
6,	Giovanni Perricelli	ITA	1:21:51
7.	Igor Kollár	SVK	1:22:23
8.	Sándor Urbanik	HUN	1:22:49

50 KILOMETRES WALK (7th)

Kononen was heavily supported by the Finns for a home gold, and he was prominent early on with Garcia, who led at 5k in 22:56 and 10k 44:58 (22:02 second 5k). At 15k Toutain (1:07:21) was just ahead of Kononen and Spitsyn, but at 20k Garcia was out on his own for a while. Aleksandr Potashov BLS was ahead at 25k 1:51:25, but he was later disqualified and Skurygin led at 30k 2:13:34. Toutain forced the pace through 35k 2:35:04 with Garcia and Spitsyn, but Spitsyn proved strongest and powered away (45k 3:18:52) to win by nearly three minutes. Perricelli finished very fast and the medallists all set personal bests. Pavol Blazek SVK was 9th in 3:49:44, having placed 3-6-1 at the three previous Europeans at 20k.

1.	Valeriy Spitsyn	RUS	3:41:07
2.	Thierry Toutain	FRA	3:43:52
3.	Giovanni Perricelli	ITA	3:43:55
4.	Jesús Angel Garcia	ESP	3:45:25
5.	Robert Korzeniowki	POL	3:45:57
6.	German Skurygin	RUS	3:46:30
7.	Valentin Kononen	FIN	3:47:14
8.	Andrey Plotnikov	RUS	3:47:43

4 X 100 METRES RELAY (13th)

In heat 1 Tony Jarrett GBR passed the baton to Darren Braithwaite, who dropped it, and Liford Christie could but look on as the favourites went out. France won the second heat in 38.77 and the final clearly.

1.	FRA	38.57
2.	UKR	38.98
3.	ITA	38.99
4.	SWE	39.05
5.	GRE	39.25
6.	GER	39.36
7.	FIN	39.80
dq	RUS	2 fs

4 X 400 METRES RELAY (14th)

With just seven teams entered, no heats were necessary. David McKenzie 45.7 gave Britain a first leg lead and Whittle 45.3, Black 43.94 and Ladejo 44.23 each increased the margin. France and Russia were originally disqualified for passing too early on the first changeover, but were reinstated by the Jury of Appeal.

1.	GBR	2:59.13
2.	FRA	3:01.11
3.	RUS	3:03.10
4.	ITA	3:03.46
5.	GER	3:04.15
6.	POL	3:04.22
7.	FIN	3:04.55

Mikhail Shchennikov: first outdoor title

WOMEN

100 METRES (8th, wind +0.6)

Slowest away in the final, with a reaction time of .231, Privalova steamed through the field to win clearly, as Tarnopolskaya, very impressive on the first day when she won her heat in 11.13 and qf in 11.01, and Paschke filled, as expected, the other medal places.

1.	Irina Privalova	RUS	11.02
2.	Zhanna Tarnopolskaya	UKR	11.10
3.	Melanie Paschke	GER	11.28
4.	Anelia Nuneva	BUL	11.40
5.	Nelli Cooman	HOL	11.40
6.	Petya Pendareva	BUL	11.41
7.	Sanna Hernesniemi	FIN	11.43
8.	Marina Trandenkova	RUS	11.52

200 METRES (11th, wind 0.2)

Privalova was the fastest in each round, with 22.93 heat and 22.61 semi; a class apart, she became the eighth woman to complete the European 100m/200m sprint double. Tarnopolskaya, less well regarded at 200m than 100m, gained her second silver and confimed her improvement this year. Knoll had won the first semi in 22.75.

1.	Irina Privalova	RUS	22.32
2.	Zhanna Tarnopolskaya	UKR	22.77
3.	Galina Malchugina	RUS	22.90
4.	Silke Knoll	GER	22.99
5.	Maya Azarashvili	GEO	23.01
6.	Sanna Hernesniemi	FIN	23.24
7.	Lucrecia Jardim	POR	23.28
8.	Zlatka Georgieva	BUL	23.46

400 METRES (11th)

Pérec sprinted clear and was some five metres up by 200m, doubling that in the second half. Goncharenko was an expected second, but Smith was delighted to take the bronze, Britain's first medal at the event since 1962.

1.	Marie-José Pérec	FRA	50.33
2.	Svetlana Goncharenko	RUS	51.24
3.	Phylis Smith	GBR	51.30
4.	Yelena Andreyeva	RUS	51.65
5.	Anja Rücker	GER	51.85
6.	Melanie Neef	GBR	52.10
7.	Daniela Spasova	BUL	52.25
8.	Francine Landre	FRA	52.57

800 METRES (10th)

At the age of 37 Gurina at last won an outdoor gold to add to the two silver and two bronze medals that she has won at major championships. Griffiths was last in her heat and dejected by her 'failure'. However, aided by the fact that the other heats were slowly run, she went through to the semis as a fastest loser and then to the final, where she ran a pb, as did Rydz, Djaté and Brzezinska. 400m 58.17 Rogachova, 600m 1:28.43 Gurina. Dukhnova caught Gurina just before the finish, but the latter's desperate lunge for the line brought her victory by a millimetre or two. Irina Samorokhova RUS (9th 2:04.52) fell in trying to squeeze through a gap early in the race; she got to her feet quickly, but the effort of rejoining the pack was too much.

1.	Lyubov Gurina	RUS	1:58.55
2.	Natalya Dukhnova	BLS	1:58.55
3.	Lyudmila Rogachova	RUS	1:58.69
4.	Malgorzata Rydz	POL	1:59.12
5.	Ann Griffiths	GBR	1:59.81
6.	Carla Sacramento	POR	2:00.01
7.	Patricia Djaté	FRA	2:00.34
8.	Anna Brzezinska	POL	2:00.41

1500 METRES (14th)

Podkopayeva 4:08.72 and Kremlyova 4:08.80 won the heats. With a lot of runners fancying their big kick, the final started slowly and got

Lyubov Gurina: success at 37

slower with Blandine Bitzner FRA (11th 4:22.64) leading at 400m 1:13.38 and Geraldine Nolan IRL (12th 4:23.59) at 800m 2:31.33. There was an increase in tempo to 1200m 3:37.45 with Rogachova leading throughout the last lap, which she covered in a scintillating 56.5. Holmes, in her first season of 1500m running, split the formidable Russians.

1.	Lyudmila Rogachova	RUS	4:18.93
2.	Kelly Holmes	GBR	4:19.30
3.	Yekat Podkopayeva	RUS	4:19.37
4.	Lyubov Kremlyova	RUS	4:19.77
5.	Malgorzata Rydz	POL	4:19.80
6.	Carla Sacramento	POR	4:20.62
7.	Ellen Kiessling	GER	4:20.79
8.	Maite Zuñiga	ESP	4:20.83

3000 METRES (10th)

The top two were expected to be a class apart, and so it proved. As 400m was reached in 69.94, Murray burst into the lead and ran hard. She passed 1000m in 2:50.09 with O'Sullivan on her shoulder and by 1600m (4:31.78) and 2000m (5:41.57) these two had opened a gap over the rest. The first European gold by an Irish woman was ensured as O'Sullivan surged into the lead with 200m to go. Murray, not able to run fast enough to take the sting out her rival's kick, completed her set of 3000m medals (gold 1990, bronze 1986). There were five personal bests in the final, most notably from Szabo, who added a senior bronze to her European junior gold.

1.	Sonia O'Sullivan	IRL	8:31.84
2.	Yvonne Murray	GBR	8:36.48
3.	Gabriela Szabo	ROM	8:40.08
4.	Olga Churbanova	RUS	8:40.48
5.	Lyudmila Borisova	RUS	8:41.71
6.	Alison Wyeth	GBR	8:45.76
7.	Farida Fates	FRA	8:46.04
8.	Nadia Dandolo	ITA	8:49.42

10,000 METRES (13th)

Ribeiro, who had so impressed when winning the European Indoor 3000m, gave a magnificent display of distance running. She took the lead just before 5000m, reached in 15:49.39 with Ferreira and then strode away fluently, covering the second 5k in 15:18.98. Nicole Levèque FRA had dashed into an early lead to 1k 3:05.28, when she was caught by Catherina McKiernan IRL, who led at 2k 6:16.46 but later dropped out. Ferreira led at 3k 9:29.83 and 4k 12:39.41. Wessel was with the two Portuguese to 5k, but while Ribeiro sped on, Ferreira and Wessel were isolated in second

Fernanda Ribeiro: magnificent display

and third places. Guida led the chasing group for much of the time, but Nauer was the fastest finisher and passed Wessel for the bronze on the last lap. Ribeiro's splits: 6k 18:54.73, 7k 21:57.12, 8k 24:58.88, 9k 28:06.53.

1.	Fernanda Ribeiro	POR	31:08.75
2.	Conceição Ferreira	POR	31:32.82
3.	Daria Nauer	SUI	31:35.96
4.	Kathrin Wessel	GER	31:38.75
5.	Cristina Misaros	ROM	31:41.03
6.	Maria Guida	ITA	31:42.14
7.	Fernanda Marques	POR	31:53.12
8.	Klara Kashapova	RUS	31:55.99

MARATHON (7th)

The first three European marathons for women were won by Rosa Mota, and Machado maintained the national tradition. Always in the lead, she broke clear before half-way and was never seriously challenged. Katrin Dörre GER dropped out before 30k, having fallen back from the leading positions. Temperate was 28°C, but the humidity at 48% was much lower than in the rest of the week.

1.	Manuela Machado	POR	2:29:54
2.	Maria Curatolo	ITA	2:30:33
3.	Adriana Barbu	ROM	2:30:55
4.	Ornelia Ferrara	ITA	2:31:57
5.	Anuta Catuna	ROM	2:32:51

6. Ritva Lemettinen	FIN	2:33:05
7. Kirsi Rauta	FIN	2:33:32
8. Rosanna Munerotto	ITA	2:34:32

European Cup (held in conjunction, four of six to score): 1, ITA 10:11:48; 2, ROM 10:20:48; 3, FRA 10:39:39; 4, FIN 10:43:58; 5, POL 10:45:43; 6, GBR 10:47:38; 7, RUS 11:00:19.

100 METRES HURDLES

(9th, wind -1.7)

Dimitrova was fastest in each round. She won her heat in 12.72 and the first semi in 12.60. In the second semi Donkova and Kristin Patzwahl GER did not hear the recall gun after a false start, and Donkova ran the entire 100m. A few minutes grace was allowed and she managed to qualify. Dimitrova won the final by two metres with Graudyn just shading Donkova, who thus added bronze to her 1982 silver and 1986 gold.

1. Svetla Dimitrova	BUL	12.72
2. Yuliya Graudyn	RUS	12.93
3. Yordanka Donkova	BUL	12.93
4. Brigita Bukovec	SLO	13.01
5. Tatyana Reshetnikova	RUS	13.06
6. Julie Baumann	SUI	13.10
7. Jackie Agyepong	GBR	13.17
8. Anne Piquereau	FRA	13.25

400 METRES HURDLES (12th)

Gunnell was fastest in the heats, 55.17, and semis, 54.60, before completing her quartet of major titles, joining Daley Thompson and Linford Christie as the only holders of Olympic, World, European and Commonwealth titles. She did so majestically, running the fastest time of 1994. Rieger came through to gain some three metres on Knoroz in the last 30m and just make the line in time, taking .22 off her pb.

1. Sally Gunnell	GBR	53.33
2. Silvia Rieger	GER	54.68
3. Anna Knoroz	RUS	54.68
4. Heike Meissner	GER	54.79
5. Tatyana Kurochkina	BLS	55.18
5. Tatyana Tereshchuk	UKR	55.53
7. Olga Nazarova	RUS	55.98
8. Gowry Retchakan	GBR	56.05

HIGH JUMP (14th)

In anticipation this looked to be the most open of all events, with a dozen potential winners. Only two had clean sheets up to 1.93: Bilac and Zilinskiene. Gulyayeva cleared 1.96 on her first attempt and looked to have settled things until Bilac popped over on her third attempt. Bilac went on to clear 1.98, a national record, and to join the exclusive 2-metre club. Thus the ex-GDR woman brought Slovenia its first ever gold medal. Heike Henkel GER returned from the birth of her son in March to qualify with 1.92 but was 11th equal in the final at 1.85.

1. Britta Bilac	SLO	2.00
2. Yelena Gulyayeva	RUS	1.96
3. Nele Zilinskiene	LIT	1.93
4. Irina Babakova	UKR	1.93
5. Hanne Haugland	NOR	1.93
6. Heike Balck	GER	1.93
7= Svetlana Leseva	BUL	1.90
7= Yelena Topchina	RUS	1.90

LONG JUMP (12th)

Drechsler, 4th as an 18 year-old in 1982, won her third successive title by jumping over 7m twice ((7.14, 6.95, 6.76, 7.06, 6.94, 6.86). There was a close battle for the other medals, with Kravets taking silver and May, ex-GBR Britain now Italy, jumping well and consistently for the bronze

1. Heike Drechsler	GER	7.14
2. Inessa Kravets	UKR	6.99
3. Fiona May	ITA	6.90
4. Renata Nielsen	DEN	6.82
5. Ljudmila Ninova	AUT	6.80
6. Agata Karczmarek	POL	6.67
7. Irina Mushayilova	RUS	6.62
8. Iva Prandzheva	BUL	6.56

Svetlana Dimitrova: fastest in each round

TRIPLE JUMP (8th)

World champion Biryukova (14.89, x, 14.84, 14.49, x, 14.24) achieved her season's best in the first round, getting great height on her third phase. That stood up for the gold, although the favourite Lasovskaya (x, 13.61, 14.27, 14.24, 14.73w, 14.85w) finished well after a very slow start. Sofia Bozhanova BUL, originally 4th at 14.58, was disqualified due to a positive drugs test for metabolites of mesocarb.

1.	Anna Biryukova	RUS	14.89
2.	Inna Lasovskaya	RUS	14.85w
3.	Inessa Kravets	UKR	14.67w
4.	Yolanda Chen	RUS	14.48w
5.	Rodica Petrescu	ROM	14.42
6.	Sarka Kaspárková	TCH	13.98
7.	Ramona Molzan	GER	13.82
8.	Helga Radtke	GER	13.77

SHOT (7th)

With the second throw of the final Pavlysh missed her pb by just 5cm. That throw took the first ever European gold for the Ukraine in its own right. Defending champion Kumbernuss took silver as her final round 19.11 was better than Mitkova's 2nd best of 18.94; both having a best of 19.49. This was the first time since 1966 that there were no 20m puts in the Europeans, and 19.61 would not have won a medal in the last five finals. In 1982 behind the winning 21.59, seven were over 20m.

1.	Viktoriya Pavlysh	UKR	19.61
2.	Astrid Kumbernuss	GER	19.49
3.	Svetla Mitkova	BUL	19.49
4.	Stephanie Storp	GER	19.39
5.	Larisa Peleshenko	RUS	19.01
6.	Kathrin Neimke	GER	18.94
7.	Valentina Fedyushina	UKR	18.91
8.	Anna Romanova	RUS	18.40

DISCUS (10th)

Wyludda (qual 65.90; 65.40, 61.76, 63.60, 67.08, 68.72, 65.08) showed that she was over the effects of operations on both knees to dominate the event and produce the best throw in the world for two years. Bergmann became the first Norwegian woman to win a European throws medal.

1.	Ilke Wyludda	GER	68.72
2.	Ellina Zvereva	BLS	64.46
3.	Mette Bergmann	NOR	64.34
4.	Nicoleta Grasu	ROM	63.64
5.	Olga Chernyavskaya	RUS	62.54
6.	Jana Lauren	GER	60.44
7.	Marie-Paule Geldhof	BEL	59.48
8.	Lyudmila Filimonova	BLS	59.46

JAVELIN (12th)

Natalya Shikolenko turned her foot over on her first throw of the qualifying round, and could then manage only 55.08. Also going out was defending champion Päivi Alafrantti. In the absence of Shikolenko, Hattestad (65.18, 63.66, 66.42, 65.12, x, 68.00) had an easier win than expected, with only Forkel able to offer a challenge. Forkel led for two rounds, with the Norwegian going ahead in the third and adding gloss with her final throw.

1.	Trine Hattestad	NOR	68.00
2.	Karen Forkel	GER	66.10
3.	Felicia Tilea	ROM	64.34
4.	Silke Gast	GER	62.90
5.	Rita Ramanauskaite	LIT	61.54
6.	Tanja Damaske	GER	61.32
7.	Kinga Zsigmond	HUN	59.74
8.	Antoaneta Selenska	BUL	57.76

Viktoriya Pavlysh: won first gold for Ukraine

Sabine Braun: retained her heptathlon title despite being below her best

HEPTATHLON (8th/9th)

Wlodarczyk's 13.26 was fastest at 100mh, then Braun took the lead with the high jump and held on with the shot. Moskalets was easily best at 200m (23.77), and came through to take a first day lead at 3826 from Braun 3823, Turchinskaya 3790, Wlodarczyk 3785 and Ináncsi 3759. These five opened a gap on the rest after the long jump, with Moskalets increasing her lead to 42 over Braun. However the javelin proved decisive as Moskalets and Turchinskaya were well below their best That left Braun needing only to stay reasonably in touch in the 800m to retain her title and so she won despite being below par.

1.	Sabine Braun	GER	6419
2.	Rita Inánsci	HUN	6404
3.	Urszula Wlodarczyk	POL	6322
4.	Larisa Turchinskaya	RUS	6311
5.	Svetlana Moskalets	RUS	6308
6.	Peggy Beer	GER	6275
7.	Remigija Nazaroviene	LIT	6262
8.	Tina Rättyä	FIN	6241

10 KILOMETRES WALK (9th)

Gold for Finland, as the favourite Essayah was always prominent, going clear shortly before the finish. Standards have improved rapidly in the three stagings of this event - in 1986 the winning time was 46:09, in 1990 it was 44:00.

1.	Sari Essayah	FIN	42:37 CR
2.	Annarita Sidoti	ITA	42:43
3.	Yelena Nikolayeva	RUS	42:43
4.	Yelena Arshintseva	RUS	43:23
5.	Larisa Ramazanova	RUS	43:25
6.	Natalya Misyulya	BLS	43:39
7.	Elisabetta Perrone	ITA	43:47
8.	Susana Feitor	POR	43:47

4 X 100 METRES RELAY (13th)

A slick German team ran the fastest time in heat (42.94) and final. Irina Privalova gained several metres on the last leg, but her team had given her too much to do, and Silke Lichtenhagen just made the line in time.

1.	GER	42.90
2.	RUS	42.96
3.	BUL	43.00
4.	UKR	43.61
5.	GBR	43.63
6.	HOL	43.81
7.	FIN	43.96
8.	ITA	44.46

4 X 400 METRES RELAY

(h 13th, F 14th)

The French all ran brilliantly (Francine Landre 51.3, Viviane Dorsile 51.1, Evelyne Elien 50.54, M-J Pérec 49.36) and they smashed their national record.

The Russians were brought back into contention on the second leg by Yelena Andreyeva 50.22, but Linda Keough GBR ran into some congestion at the change-over to Phylis Smith and that probably cost Britain the silver medal. Sally Gunnell ran 49.45 on the final leg, but was held off by Anja Rücker's fine 49.80 and Goncharenko 50.08 was just ahead of both.

1.	FRA	3:22.34
2.	RUS	3:24.06
3.	GER	3:24.10
4.	GBR	3:24.14
5.	TCH	3:27.95
6.	SUI	3:28.78
7.	POL	3:29.75
8.	FIN	3:32.97

CR = Championships record

PLACING TABLE

Nation	*1st*	*2nd*	*3rd*	*4th*	*5th*	*6th*	*7th*	*8th*	*Points*
RUS	10	8	7	9	11	4	4	5	292
GER	5	4	5	7	6	9	3	1	191
GBR	6	5	2	3	3	6	1	3	145
UKR	3	6	3	4	1	3	2	1	122
FRA	4	3	2	4	1	3	2	1	102
ITA	2	3	3	3	2	2	1	6	92
ESP	3	2	4	1	-	2	1	3	78
NOR	3	2	1	1	1	-	2	1	58
BUL	2	-	3	1	1	1	2	3	53
POR	2	1	-	1	1	4	3	1	51
FIN	1	1	-	1	1	3	7	3	50
ROM	-	-	3	2	4	-	-	2	46
BLS	1	4	-	-	1	1	-	2	45
POL	-	1	1	1	3	2	1	1	39
SWE	-	2	-	2	-	-	-	-	24
TCH	-	1	1	-	1	1	2	-	24
BEL	-	1	2	-	-	-	1	1	22
HUN	-	1	-	-	2	1	1	2	22
SUI	-	-	2	-	-	2	-	1	19
GRE	-	-	1	-	1	-	2	1	15

Others (with medals in brackets): IRL (1G), LIT (1B) 13, SLO (1G) 13, SVK 9, HOL 7, IEP 7, CRO (1B) 6, LAT (1B) 6, DEN 5, UT 4, GEO 4, ISL 2, ISR 2, MOL 2, EST 1.

Du'aine Ladejo (left) prevents fellow Briton Roger Black (right) from becoming the first man to win the European 400m three times

EUROPEAN CUP

THE European Cup has been contested biennially by European nations, with each team entering one athlete per event and one team in each relay. From 1994 the event is staged annually. The Cup is dedicated to the memory of Dr Bruno Zauli, the former President of the European Committee of the IAAF, who died suddenly in 1963 soon after the decision had been made to start this competition.

From 1965 until 1981 the competition was staged with a qualifying round, semi-finals and final, but from 1983 the nations have been arranged into groups according to strength. Eight men's and eight women's teams were in A and B groups, with additional nations in C1 and C2 (and later C3) groups. In 1993 the competition became an annual one and the top group was renamed as the Super League, with a First League and three groups in the Second League. That changed further from 1995 with two groups in both First and Second Leagues.

Men's winners:
6 GDR 1970, 1975, 1977, 1979, 1981, 1983
6 USSR 1965, 1967, 1973, 1985, 1987, 1991
1 UK 1989, Russia 1993, Germany 1994
Women's winners:
9 GDR 1970, 1973, 1975, 1977, 1979, 1981, 1983, 1987, 1989
3 USSR 1965, 1967, 1985
2 Germany 1991, 1994
1 Russia 1993

Men's B Final (First League from 1993) winners: 1977 France, 1979 Yugoslavia, 1981 France, 1983 Czechoslovakia, 1985 Spain, 1987 France, 1989 Bulgaria, 1991 Spain, 1993 Sweden, 1994 Poland
Women's B Final (First League from 1993) winners: 1977 Bulgaria, 1979 Romania, 1981 Poland, 1983 Italy, 1985 France, 1987 Romania, 1989 France, 1991 Italy, 1993 Belarus, 1994 Poland

European Cup Best Performances
Achieved in final, A or Super League event, unless specified after year, SF in semi-final
Men

100m	10.12	Eugen Ray GDR	1977
200m	20.15	Pietro Mennea ITA	1977 SF
400m	44.75	David Grindley GBR	1993
800m	1:45.60	Tom McKean GBR	1991
1500m	3:33.63	José Man. Abascal ESP	1983 B
5000m	13:21.68	Salvatore Antibo ITA	1991
10000m	27:32.85	Fernando Mamede POR	1983 C
3000mSt	8:13.32	Mariano Scartezzini ITA	1981
110mh	13.10	Colin Jackson GBR	1993
400mh	47.85	Harald Schmid FRG	1979 & 1985
HJ	2.40	Patrik Sjöberg SWE	1989 B
PV	6.00	Rodion Gataullin RUS	1993
LJ	8.38	Robert Emmiyan URS	1987
TJ	17.77	Khristo Markov BUL	1985B
SP	22.05	Sergey Smirnov URS	1985

Harald Schmid: twice ran 47.85

DT	68.64	Wolfgang Schmidt GDR	1981 SF
HT	82.90	Jüri Tamm URS	1985
JT	89.84	Jan Zelezny TCH	1993
(old)	92.88	Uwe Hohn GDR	1985
4x100mR	38.28	USSR	1985
4x400mR	3:00.25	GBR	1993
Women			
100m	10.93w	Sonia Lannaman GBR	1977 SF
	10.95	Marlies Göhr GDR	1985 &1987
200m	21.99	Silke Gladisch GDR	1987
400m	48.60	Marita Koch GDR	1979
	48.60	Olga Vladykina URS	1985
800m	1:55.91	Jarmila Kratochvílová TCH	1985
1500m	3:58.40	Ravilya Agletdinova URS	1985
3000m	8:35.32	Zola Budd GBR	1985
3000m replaced by 5000m from 1995			
10000m	31:03.62	Kathrin Ullrich GER	1991
100mh	12.47	Cornelia Oschkenat GDR	1987
400mh	53.73	Sally Gunnell GBR	1993
HJ	2.06	Stefka Kostadinova BUL	1985
PV	to be included from 1997		
LJ	7.28	Galina Chistyakova URS	1985
TJ	14.71	Sofia Bozhanova BUL	1994 B2
SP	21.56	Natalya Lisovskaya URS	1987
DT	73.90	Diana Gansky GDR	1987
HT	to be included from 1997		
JT	73.20	Petra Felke GDR	1985
4x100mR	41.65	GDR	1985
4x400mR	3:18.58	USSR	1985

Most individual event wins in A/Super/ finals

Men: 7 Linford Christie GBR 100m 1987-89-91-93-94, 200m 1987-84

Women: 6 Marlies Göhr GDR 100m 1977-79-81-83-85-87

Most wins in A/Super/ finals including relays

Men: 10 Linford Christie GBR 7as above, 4x100mR 1989-93-94

Women: 12 Marlies Göhr GDR 6 as above, 4x100mR 1977-79-81-83-85-87

A record seven European Cup Finals have been contested by: Harald Schmid, Giovanni Evangelisti ITA (LJ), Judy Oakes GBR (SP).

1994 Competitions

Super League at **Birmingham, June 25/26**

Men: 1, GER 121; 2, GBR 106.5; 3, RUS 101; 4, UKR 87; 5, ITA 84.5; 6, SWE 81.5; 7, FRA 80; 8, ROM 55.

100m	1. Linford Christie GBR 10.21
(+0.9)	2. Marc Blume GER 10.37
	3. Pavel Galkin RUS 10.42
200m	1. Linford Christie GBR 20.67
(-0.1)	2. Sergey Osovich UKR 20.70
	3. Daniel Sangouma FRA 21.04
400m	1. Roger Black GBR 45.08
	2. Jean-Louis Rapnouil FRA 46.43
	3. Dmitriy Golovastov RUS 46.58
800m	1. Nico Motchebon GER 1:48.10
	2. Davide Cadoni ITA 1:48.42
	3. Craig Winrow GBR 1:48.76
1500m	1. Andrey Bulkovskiy UKR 3:49.33
	2. Rüdiger Stenzel GER 3:49.38
	3. Gary Lough GBR 3:49.57
5000m	1. Dieter Baumann GER 13:48.95
	2. Abdellah Béhar FRA 13:49.12
	3. Ovidiu Olteanu ROM 13:49.43
10,000m	1. Francesco Panetta ITA 28:38.45
	2. Stéphane Franke GER 28:38.99
	3. Oleg Strizhakov RUS 29:03.55

Oleg Tverdokhleb: beaten in European Cup but gained revenge at European Championships

3000mSt	1. Aless Lambruschini ITA 8:24.98
	2. Steffen Brand GER 8:27.83
	3. Justin Chaston GBR 8:29.99
110mh	1. Florian Schwarthoff GER 13.35
(+1.9)	2. Vladimir Belokon UKR 13.62
	3. Andrew Tulloch GBR 13.65
400mh	1. Sven Nylander SWE 49.36
	2. Oleg Tverdokhleb UKR 49.37
	3. Stéphane Diagana FRA 49.47
HJ	1. Hendrik Beyer GER 2.25
	2. Patrik Thavelin SWE 2.20
	3. Dalton Grant GBR 2.20
PV	1. Jean Galfione FRA 5.70
	2. Patrik Stenlund SWE 5.60
	3. Tim Lobinger GER 5.60
LJ	1. Oleg Tarasenko RUS 8.02
	2. Dietmar Haaf GER 7.84
	3. Bogdan Tudor ROM 7.78
TJ	1. Denis Kapustin RUS 17.30
	2. Tord Henriksson SWE 16.99
	3. Serge Hélan FRA 16.92
SP	1. Paulo Dal Soglio ITA 19.69
	2. Roman Virastyuk UKR 19.40
	3. Gheorghe Guset ROM 19.23
DT	1. Dmitriy Shevchenko RUS 64.74
	2. Jürgen Schult GER 64.42
	3. Vladimir Zinchenko UKR 62.80
HT	1. Vasiliy Sidorenko RUS 78.76
	2. Andrey Skvaruk UKR 78.20
	3. Christophe Epalle FRA 78.16
JT	1. Andrey Moruyev RUS 87.34
	2. Raymond Hecht GER 85.40
	3. Mick Hill GBR 85.28
4x100mR	1. GBR 38.72
	2. UKR 38.79
	3. GER 38.81
4x400mR	1. GBR 3:02.50
	2. RUS 3:03.57
	3. FRA 3:03.74

Zhanna Tarnopolskaya: short sprint winner

Women: 1. GER 99, 2. RUS 96, 3, GBR 89 4. UKR 87, 5. BLS 65, 6. FRA 61, 7. ROM 61, 8. ESP 51 (adjusted).

With news of Diane Modahl's disqualification through a positive test at an earlier meeting, Britain lost the eight points she gained from winning the 800 metres, having originally placed second with 97 points to GER 98 with RUS third with 95.

100m	1. Zha. Tarnopolskaya UKR 11.26
(+0.8)	2. Katharine Merry GBR 11.34
	3. Melanie Paschke GER 11.37
200m	1. Silke Knoll GER 23.04
(-2.9)	2. Katharine Merry 23.38
	3. Oksana Dyachenko 23.65
400m	1. Svet. Goncharenko RUS 52.08
	2. Melanie Neef GBR 52.43
	3. Francine Landre FRA 52.86
800m	1. Diane Modahl GBR 2:02.81 (later dq)
	2. Patricia Djaté FRA 2:02.95
	3. Yelena Zavadskaya UKR 2:04.43
1500m	1. Lyubov Kremlyova RUS 4:05.97
	2. Kelly Holmes GBR 4:06.48
	3. Violeta Beclea 4:09.26
3000m	1. Lyudmila Borisova RUS 8:52.21
	2. Farida Fates FRA 8:53.40
	3. Sonia McGeorge GBR 8:55.47
10,000m	1. Kathrin Wessel GER 32:26.85
	2. Rosario Murcia FRA 32:59.80
	3. Rocio Rios ESP 33:22.18
100mh	1. Jackie Agyepong GBR 13.00
(-1.4)	2. Yuliya Graudyn RUS 13.07
	3. Anne Piquereau FRA 13.21
400mh	1. Sally Gunnell GBR 54.62
	2. Tatyana Tereshchuk UKR 55.04
	3. Tatyana Kurochkina BLS 56.02

Helga Radtke: triple jump winner

HJ	1. Tatyana Shevchik BLS 1.94
	2. Monica Jagar ROM 1.91
	3. Yelena Gulyayeva RUS 1.88
LJ	1. Heike Drechsler GER 6.99
	2. Olga Rublyova RUS 6.65
	3. Larisa Kuchinskaya BLS 6.54
TJ	1. Helga Radtke GER 13.90
	2. Rodica Petrescu ROM 13.83
	3. Concepción Paredes ESP 13.81
SP	1. Astrid Kumbernuss GER 19.63
	2. Valentina Fedyushina UKR 19.30
	3. Larisa Peleshenko RUS 18.86
DT	1. Ilke Wyludda GER 68.36
	2. Olga Nikishina UKR 63.48
	3. Ellina Zvereva BLS 62.92
JT	1. Natalya Shikolenko BLS 69.00
	2. Karen Forkel GER 65.58
	3. Felicia Tilea ROM 63.88
4x100mR	1. UKR 43.38
	2. GBR 43.46
	3. GER 44.24
4x400mR	1. GBR 3:27.33
	2. GER 3:27.78
	3. RUS 3:28.85.

The bottom two teams were relegated

First League at Valencia, Spain 11/12 June
Men: 1. ESP 113, 2. POL 112.5 (after 7 points llost as Piotr Perzylo disqualified on positive drugs test), 3. BLS 102, 4. GRE 95.5, 5. HUN 89, 6. TCH 83, 7. BUL 71, 8. DEN 52.

Winners:

100m	Alexandros Terzian GRE 10.25
200m	Alexandros Terzian GRE 21.01
400m	Evgenios Papdopoulos GRE 47.00
800m	Luis-José González ESP 1:50.77
1500m	Fermin Cacho ESP 3:40.82
5000m	Antonio Serrano ESP 13:45.88
10000m	Carlos de la Torre ESP 28:28.45
3000mSt	Antonio Peula ESP 8:40.09
110mh	Levente Csillag HUN 13.85
400mh	Piotr Kotlarski POL 50.36
HJ	Jaroslaw Kotewicz POL 2.24
PV	Gennadiy Sidorov BLS 5.65
LJ	Bogdan Tudor ROM 7.78
TJ	Konst. Koukodimos GRE 8.40w
SP	Manuel Martínez ESP 20.09
DT	Attila Horváth HUN 62.50
HT	Vitaliy Alisevich BLS 77.58
JT	Konst. Gatsioudis GRE 82.02
4x100mR	ESP 39.91
4x400mR	POL 3:06.52

Women: 1. POL 106, 2. ITA 94, 3. POR 81, 4. TCH 80 (lost 8 points as Vladimira Malátová was disqualified due to a previous positive drugs test), 5. FIN 72, 6. SUI 68, 7. LIT 64, 8. AUT 43

100m	Lucrecia Jardim POR 11.36w
200m	Erika Suchovská TCH 23.14w
400m	Elzbieta Kilinska POL 52.98
800m	Malgorzata Rydz POL 2:00.40
1500m	Carla Sacramento POR 4:16.29
3000m	Anna Brzezinska POL 8:57.50
10000m	Conceição Ferreira POR 31:54.65
100mh	Carla Tuzzi ITA 12.97
400mh	Sylwia Pachut POL 57.45
HJ	Zuzana Kovacíková TCH 1.94
LJ	Agata Karczmarek POL 6.89
TJ	Sarka Kaspárková TCH 14.19w
SP	Dangouele Urbikiene LIT 18.68
DT	Vlad. Malátová TCH 62.76 (later dq)
JT	Genowefa Patla POL 61.60
4x100mR	ITA 44.42
4x400mR	TCH 3:30.17

The top two teams were promoted

Second League
Group 1 at Dublin, Ireland 12/13 June
Men: 1. BEL 102, 2. HOL 97, 3. POR 95, 4. IRL 90, 5. LIT 77, 6. ISL 63, 7. Small Nations 35
Women: 1. HOL 99, 2. BEL 88, 3. GRE 76, 4. DEN 74, 5. IRL 62, 6. ISL 55, 7. Small Nations 22
Group 2 at Istanbul, Turkey 12/13 June
Men: 1. NOR 107, 2. SUI 100, 3. SVK 89, 4. CYP 72, 5. ISR 70, 6. CRO 68, 7. TUR 54.
Women: 1. BUL 106, 2. NOR 97, 3. TUR 74, 4. SVK 65, 5. CRO 49, 6. CYP 48, 7. ISR 36
Group 3 at Ljubljana, Slovenia 12/13 June
Men: 1. FIN 127, 2. LAT 96, 3. SLO 90.5, 4. AUT 89.5, 5. EST 67, 6. MOL 56, 7. ALB 30
Women: 1. SWE 97, 2. HUN 95, 3. SLO 78 (after deducting 8 points lost due to Hedvika Korosák testing postive for drugs), 4. LAT 62, 5. EST 58, 6. MOL 53, 7. ALB 27
The first two in each group and the two best third placers as determined by the Hungarian tables (GRE and TUR women) were promoted to the First League in 1995.

1995 Matches
Super League Villeneuve d'Ascq, France 24/25 June
Men: GBR, GER, ITA, POL, RUS, ESP, SWE, UKR
Women: BLS, FRA, GBR, GER, ITA, POL, RUS, UKR
First League I Basel, Switzerland 10/11 June
Men: BEL, DEN, FRA, HOL, NOR, POR, SUI, TCH
Women: AUT, BEL, HOL, NOR, POR, ESP, SUI, TCH
First League 2 Turku, Finland 10/11 June
Men: BLS, BUL, FIN, GRE, HUN, LAT, ROM, SVK
Women: BUL, FIN, GRE, HUN, LIT, ROM, SWE, TUR
Second League 1 Tallinn, Estonia 10/11 June
Men: AUT, EST, IRL, ISL, LIT, Small nations
Women: DEN, EST, IRL, ISL,LAT Small nations
Second League 2 Ljubljana, SLO 10/11 June
Men: ALB, CRO, CYP, ISR, MOL, SLO, TUR
Women: ALB, CRO, CYP, ISR, MOL, SLO, SVK

EUROPEAN COMBINED EVENTS CUP

This competition has been held biennially since 1973. and now annually. Nations are now divided into a Super League, First League and two groups in the Second League for both men and women.

Winners

Men's decathlon 1973 Poland, 1975 USSR, 1977 USSR, 1979 GDR, 1981 FRG, 1983 FRG, 1985 USSR, 1987 GDR, 1989 GDR, 1991 GER, 1993 France, 1994 France
Women's pentathlon 1973 GDR, 1975 GDR, 1977 USSR, 1979 GDR
Women's heptathlon 1981 GDR, 1983 GDR, 1985 GDR, 1987 USSR, 1989 USSR, 1991 GER, 1993 Russia, 1994 Russia
Individual records
Decathlon: 8551 Uwe Freimuth GDR 1983;
Heptathlon: 6875 Larisa Nikitina USSR 1989.

1994 Results all on July 2/3
Super League Lyon, France

Men Dec: 1. FRA 24,864, 2. TCH 23,836, 3. ESP 23,723, 4. SWE 23,486, 5. HUN 22,565, 6. FIN 22,531, 7. HOL 22,170, 8. GER 22,087.
1. Christian Plaziat FRA 8505
2. Henrik Dagård SWE 8347
3. Tomás Dvorák TCH 8313
Women Hep: 1. RUS 18,876, 2. UKR 18,487, 3. FRA 18,474, 4. GER 18,462, 5. POL 18,150, 6. GBR 17,566, 7. FIN 17,354, 8. ROM 15,482.
1. Svetlana Moskalets RUS 6507
2. Nathalie Teppe FRA 6396
3. Peggy Beer 6362
The bottom two teams were relegated

First League: Bressanone, Italy

Men Dec: 1. UKR 24,204, 2. GBR 23,464, 3. RUS 23,136, 4. SUI 22,830, 5. BLS 21,464, 6. POL 21,447, 7. BEL 20,406, 8. ITA 19,353. *Individual:* Vitaliy Kolpakov UKR 8257.
Women Hep: 1. BLS 17,884, 2. HOL 17,537, 3. ITA 17,397, 4. TCH 16,577, 5. SWE 16,247, 6. ESP 16,204, 7. BEL 15,722, 8. SUI 15,571. *Individual:* Anzhela Atroshchenko BLS 6119.
The top two teams were promoted and the bottom three relegated

Second League Group 1 at Copenhagen, Denmark

Men Dec: 1. POR 20,846, 2. AUT 20,838, 3. DEN 20,702, 4. NOR 19,575, 5. IRL 15,339, 6. ISL 6929. *Individual:* Mario Ramos POR 7269.
Women Hep: 1. HUN 17,154, 2. DEN 15,004, 3. POR 14,854, 4. NOR 14,014, 5. ISL 13,775, 6. IRL 13,108. *Individual:* Rita Ináncsi HUN 6250.

Second League Group 2 at Tallinn. Estonia
Men Dec: 1. EST 23,262, 2. LAT 21,546, 3. GRE 21,398, 4. BUL 19,685. *Individual*: Erki Nool EST 8093.
Women Hep: 1. BUL 15,713, 2. LAT 14,567. *Individual*: Remijia Nazaroviené LIT 6091.
Winners of both C groups were promoted

1995 Matches on 1/2 July
Super League men at Valladolid, Spain; women at Helmond, Netherlands
Men: TCH, FIN, FRA, GBR, HUN, ESP, SWE, UKR
Women: BLS, FRA, GBR, GER, HOL, POL, RUS, UKR
First League men at Helmond, Netherlands; women at Valladolid, Spain
Men: BLS, EST, GER, HOL, POL, POR, RUS, SUI
Women: BUL, TCH, FIN, HUN, ITA, ROM, ESP, SWE
Second League 1 at Reykjavik, Iceland
Men: LAT, DEN, NOR, IRL, ISL
Women: LAT, DEN, NOR, IRL, ISL
Second League 2 at Dilbeek, Belgium
Men: GRE, AUT, BEL, BUL, ITA and individuals
Women: BEL, SUI, POR and individuals

EUROPEAN MARATHON CUP

This event was first held in 1981. Men's and women's races have been held on each occasion. but the latter did not incorporate a team competition until 1985. Not held in 1990, but reintroduced in 1994 when it was combined with the European Championships marathon.

Previous winners
Men's individual: 1981 Massimo Magnani ITA 2:13:29. 1983 Waldemar Cierpinski GDR 2:12:26. 1985 Michael Heilmann GDR 2:11:28. 1988 Ravil Kashapov URS 2:11:30
Men's team: 1981 Italy. 1983 GDR. 1985 GDR. 1988 USSR
Women's individual: 1981 Zoya Ivanova URS 2:38:58. 1983 Nadezhda Gumerova URS 2:38:36. 1985 Katrin Dörre GDR 2:30:11. 1988 Katrin Dörre GDR 2:28:28.
Women's team: 1985 GDR. 1988 USSR

EUROPEAN UNDER 23 CUP

This competition was held for the first time in 1992.
Winners: Men - GBR, Women - GER

1994 Results - on 30/31 July
Group A at Ostrava, TCH
Men: 1, GER 104, 2. ITA 100, 3. RUS 100, 4. FRA 91, 5. GBR 85, 6. GRE 75, 7. ESP 67, 8. TCH 55
Winners: 100m: (-2.7) Toby Box GBR 10.47, 200m: (-0.9) Evgenios Papadopoulos GRE 21.05, 400m: Andrey Boykov RUS 46.62, 800m: Jimmy Jean-Joseph FRA 1:50.34, 1500m: Salvatore Vincenti ITA 3:56.50, 5000m: Maurizio Leone ITA 14:03.89, 3000mSt: Stéphane Desaulty FRA 8:46.53, 110mh: (-0.4) Falk Balzer GER 13.82, 400mh: Ashraf Saber ITA 49.87, HJ: Dimitris Kokkotis GRE 2.24, PV: Gérald Baudouin FRA 5.70, LJ: Roman Orlik TCH 7.85, TJ: Tosi Fasinro GBR 16.74w (16.61), SP: Manuel Martinez ESP 19.93, DT: Nikolay Orekhov RUS 59.56, HT: Marcel Kunkel GER 71.88, JT: Konstantinos Gatsioudis GRE 83.82, 4x100m: GBR 39.23, 4x400m: GER 3:05.48.
Women: 1. RUS 108, 2. GER 91, 3. ROM 82, 4. TCH 65, 5. GBR 62, 6. ITA 61, 7. FIN 58, 8. BUL 47
Winners: 100m: (-3.4) Natalya Anisimova RUS 11.60, 200m: (-0.3) Yekaterina Lescheva RUS 23.52, 400m: Anja Rücker GER 51.42, 800m: Tatyana Grigoryeva RUS 2:01.56, 1500m: Yekaterina Dedkova RUS 4:17.16, 3000m: Gabriela Szabo ROM 9:12.42, 100mh: (-1.3) Erika Nicolae ROM 13.50, 400mh: IonelaTirlea 56.87, HJ: Zuzana Kovacíková TCH 1.94, LJ: Lyudmila Galkina RUS 6.48, TJ: Elena Dumitrascu ROM 13.79 (original winner Yelena Lysak RUS 13.88 disqualified on positive drugs test), SP: Irina Korzhanenko RUS 18.36, DT: Natalya Sadova RUS 60.56, JT: Dörthe Barby GER 57.56, 4x100m: RUS 44.22, 4x400m: GER 3:30.54.
Group B at Lillehammer, NOR
Men: 1. POL 100.5, 2. UKR 91, 3. FIN 86.5, 4. NOR 83, 5. HUN 80, 6. CYP 44, 7. AUT 40. BUL withdrew
Women: 1. UKR 105, 2. FRA 103, 3. POL 83, 4. HUN 68, 5. GRE 63, 6. ESP 61, 7. NOR 48, 8. HOL 45

EUROPEAN CUP FOR CHAMPION CLUBS

Contested annually since 1975 by the champion clubs of European nations. In the first year 12 clubs took part in Liège, Belgium, but the number increased to a peak of 21 clubs in 1987, and the teams were divided into two divisions from 1988, and then into three.

Men's winners (of Group A from 1988)

Year	*Venue*	*Winners*
1975	Liège	TV Wattenscheid, FRG
1976	Rieti	Alco Rieti, ITA
1977	W'hampton	TV Wattenscheid, FRG
1978	Bochum	TV Wattenscheid, FRG
1979	Lisboa	Fiat Iveco Torino, ITA
1980	Madrid	Fiat Iveco Torino, ITA
1981	Beograd	Dukla Praha, TCH
1982	Paris	Fiamme Oro Padova, ITA
1983	Verona	Fiamme Oro Padova, ITA
1984	Milano	Pro Patria Milano, ITA
1985	London	Pro Patria Milano, ITA
1986	Lisboa	R. Club de France, FRA
1987	Milano	R. Club de France, FRA
1988	Venice	R. Club de France, FRA
1989	Beograd	C. Zvezda Beograd, YUG
1990	Jérez de la Frontera	Larios, ESP
1991	Jérez de la Frontera	Larios, ESP
1992	Birmingham	Larios, ESP
1993	Budapest	Fiamme Oro Padova, ITA
1994	Malaga	Larios, ESP

1994 first eight (May 28-29)
1. Larios Madrid ESP 129, 2. Fiamme Azzurre Padova ITA 116, 3. Racing Cub FRA 97.5, 4. Ujpesti Torna Egylet HUN 90.5, 5. Dukla Praha TCH 90, 6. Haringey GBR 86, 7. CSKA Sofia BUL 66, 8. Fenerbahce SK TUR 63

Women's Winners

The women's competion has been staged annually from 1981. A record 22 clubs contested the 1990 meeting.

Year	*Venue*	*Winners*
1981	Napoli	Bayer Leverkusen, FRG
1982	Leverkusen	Bayer Leverkusen, FRG
1983	Paris	Bayer Leverkusen, FRG
1984	Madrid	Bayer Leverkusen, FRG
1985	Zürich	Bayer Leverkusen, FRG
1986	Amsterdam	Bayer Leverkusen, FRG
1987	Como	Bayer Leverkusen, FRG
1988	Lisboa	Bayer Leverkusen, FRG
1989	Zürich	Bayer Leverkusen, FRG
1990	Schwechat	SC Neubrandenburg, GDR
1991	L'Alfas del Pi	Stade Français, FRA
1992	Milano	Levski Spartak, BUL
1993	Limassol	Sisport Fiat, ITA
1994	Schwechat	Levski, Sofia BUL

1994 first eight of 19 clubs (May 29)
1. Levski, Sofia BUL 232, 2. Snam Gas Metano ITA 225.5, 3. LUCH Moskva RUS 222, 4. IBL Olimpija Ljubljana SLO 217.5, 5. Stade Français Paris FRA 207, 6. Budapesti Honved SC HUN 207, 7. PSK Olymp-Slavex Praha TCH 201.5, 8. Quelle Fürth/München GER 194.

Samuel Matete: competition record last year

European Champion Clubs Cup best performances

Men

100m	10.12	Ozmond Ezinwa NGR (Larios, ESP)	1993
hand timed	10.0	Pietro Mennea (Atletica Rieti, ITA)	1979
200m	20.51	Solomon Wariso (Haringey, GBR)	1994
	20.1m	Pietro Mennea (Atletica Rieti, ITA)	1979
400m	45.46	Cayetano Cornet (Larios, ESP)	1990
800m	1:46.60	Sebastian Coe (Haringey, GBR)	1989
1500m	3:38.44	Manuel Pancorbo (Larios, ESP)	1992
5000m	13:27.87	Gennaro Di Napoli (Fiamme Oro Padova, ITA)	1990
10000m	27:33.37	Fernando Mamede (Sporting Lisboa, POR)	1982
3000mSt	8:15.56	Francesco Panetta (Pro Patria Milano, ITA)	1987
110mh	13.53	Tony Jarrett (Haringey, GBR)	1994
400mh	48.84	Samuel Matete ZIM (Larios, ESP)	1994
High jump	2.33	Steinar Hoen (IK Tjalve, NOR) Div 2	1994
Pole vault	5.80	Pierre Quinon (Racing Club de France, FRA)	1985
Long jump	8.22	Giovanni Evangelisti (Pro Patria Osma, ITA)	1985
	8.33w	Jacques Rousseau (Racing Club de France)	1977
Triple jump	16.89	Milan Mikulás (Olympia Praha, TCH)	1993
Shot	21.13	Alessandro Andrei (Fiamme Oro Padova, ITA)	1984
Discus	66.60	Marco Bucci (Pro Patria Milano, ITA)	1984
Hammer	80.22	Heinz Weis (Bayer Leverkusen, FRG)	1989
Javelin	82.06	Radoman Scekic (Crvena Zvezda, YUG)	1991
(old)	86.10	Klaus Tafelmeier (Bayer Leverkusen, FRG)	1985
4x100mR	38.88	Pro Patria Milano, ITA	1991
4x400mR	3:04.21	Larios, ESP	1990

Women

100m	11.22	Katrin Krabbe (SC Neubrandenburg, GDR)	1990
200m	22.78	Marie-José Pérec (Stade Français, FRA)	1993
400m	50.53	Marie-José Pérec (Stade Français, FRA)	1991
800m	2:02.64	Vesna Bajer (Crvena Zvezda, YUG)	1988
1500m	4:12.51	Wendy Sly (Borough of Hounslow, GBR)	1983
3000m	8:57.93	Yvonne Mai (SC Neubrandenburg, GDR)	1990
100mh	12.90	Laurence Elloy (Stade Française, FRA)	1985
	12.86w	Sally Gunnell (Essex Ladies, GBR)	1988
400mh	57.39	Hélène Huart (Racing Club de France, FRA)	1987
High jump	1.97	Ulrike Meyfarth (Beyer Leverkusen, FRG)	1982
Long jump	6.90	Ludmila Ninova (SV Schwechat, AUT)	1992
Triple jump	13.66	Helga Radtke (Quelle Fürth/München, GER)	1994
Shot	19.95	Astrid Kumbernuss (SC Neubrandenburg, GDR)	1990
Discus	65.42	Astrid Kumbernuss (SC Neubrandenburg, GDR)	1990
Javelin	63.88	Ingrid Thyssen (Beyer Leverkusen, FRG)	1984
4x100mR	43.93	Trudovye Reservye Moskva, URS	1990
4x400mR	3:31.62	Essex Ladies, GBR	1992

SOUTH AMERICAN CHAMPIONSHIPS

THE first official South American Championships were held at Montevideo, Uruguay in 1919. Since then they have been held regularly, every two or three years. Of the 37 championships Santiago, Chile has staged the most, seven, as well as three unofficial ones (of which there were eight 1918-57). Women's events have been held at the last 27 championships, first in Lima, Peru in 1939.

Most gold medals - all individual events

Men

11 Manuel Plaza CHI 4 cross-country, 3 5000m & 10000m, 1 Mar

11 Osvaldo Suarez ARG 5 10000m, 4 5000m, 2 Mar 1956-67

9 Valerio Vallania ARG 4 HJ, 3 110mh, 1 LJ & Dec 1924-9

9 Robson da Silva BRA 5 100m, 4 200m 1985-93 (and 4 relay)

Women

9 Conceição Geremias BRA 3 Pen, 2 Hep, 2 400mh, 1 100m & LJ 1975-89

9 Alejandro Ramos CHI 4 800m & 1500m, 1 400m 1975-85

Most wins at one event: 7 Gert Weil CHI men's SP 1979-87

Championship best performances after 1993

Men

Event	Mark	Athlete	Year
100m	10.18	Robson C. da Silva BRA	1991
	10.1	Altevir Araujo BRA	1979
	10.1	Katsuiko Nakaia BRA ht	1981
200m	20.44	Robson C. da Silva BRA	1989
	20.2	Paulo Roberto Correa BRA	1981
400m	45.80	Hector Daley PAN	1987
800m	1:46.90	Luis Migueles ARG	1985
1500m	3:42.16	Ad. Domingues BRA	1985
5000m	13:53.69	Omar Aguilar CHI	1985
10000m	28:37.2	Antonio Silio ARG	1993
Mar	2:15:50	Juan Plagman CHI	1983
3000mSt	8:36.21	Ad. Domingues BRA	1991
110mh	13.87	Pedro Paulo Chiamulera BRA	1985
400mh	49.65	Eron.de Araujo BRA	1991
4x100mR	39.6A	Brazil	1981
4x400mR	3:05.60	Brazil	1991
HJ	2.22	Hugo Muñoz PER	1993
PV	5.25	Oscar Veit ARG	1987
LJ	7.95A	João de Oliveira BRA	1981
	7.99w	Paulo Sergio de Oliveira BRA	1993
TJ	17.21	Anisio Souza Silva BRA	1993
SP	20.14	Gert Weil CHI	1985
DT	59.46	Ramón Jiménez Gaona PAR	1993
HT	71.14	Andrés Charadia ARG	1993
JT	77.00	Luis Carlos Lucumi COL	1989
Dec	7491	Paulo A Martins Lima BRA	1987
20kmW	1:24:12	Héctor Moreno COL	1983

Women

Event	Mark	Athlete	Year
100m	11.56	Claudette Alves PinaARG ht	1991
	11.2	Carmela Bolivar PER	1981
200m	23.21	Ximena Restrepo COL	1991
400m	51.56	Maria M Figueiredo BRA	1991
800m	2:00.45	Maria M Figueiredo BRA	1991
1500m	4:19.18	Rita de Cassis BRA	1991
3000m	9:17.50	Carmen Souza Oliveira BRA	1991
10000m	33:27.85	Carmen Souza Oliveira BRA	1991
100mh	13.71	Nancy Vallecilla ECU	1985
	13.2	Beatriz Capotosto ARG	1983
400mh	57.16	Liliana Chalá ECU	1991
4x100mR	44.69	Brazil	1989
4x400mR	3:32.59	Brazil	1991
HJ	1.89	Orlane Lima dos Santos BRA	1991
LJ	6.26A	Conceição Geremias BRA	1981
	6.26	Maria Barbosa de Souza BRA	1993
	6.45w	Andrea Avila ARG	1993
TJ	13.91	Andrea Avila ARG	1993
SP	16.47	Elisangela Adriano BRA	1993
DT	55.14	Maria I Urrutia COL	1993
JT	57.40	Marieta Riera BRA	1991
Hept	5703	Conceição Geremias BRA	1983
10kmW	48:18.0	Miriam Ramon ECU	1993

GOODWILL GAMES

THE third Goodwill Games were staged at St Petersburg, Russia from 23 July to 7 August 1994, with the athletics events held between 24 and 29 July. The Games were founded as a result of the belief of Ted Turner, Chairman and President of Turner Broadcasting System Inc., that the world's top athletes should be able to compete in an environment free of political pressures. Previous Games were staged in Moscow in 1986 and Seattle in 1990.

The athletics events at previous Games featured principally competitors from the USA and USSR. In 1994 each event featured at least one US and one Russian or team, but invitations were issued to many of the world's top athletes. The 1998 Games will be held in New York.

1994 first three at each event. St Petersburg, Jul 24-29

MEN

100m	1. Dennis Mitchell USA	10.07
(-1.9)	2. Leroy Burrell USA	10.11
	3. Jon Drummond USA	10.12
200m	1. Michael Johnson USA	20.10
(+0.6)	2. Frank Fredericks NAM	20.17
	3. John Regis GBR	20.31
400m	1. Quincy Watts USA	45.21
	2. Du'aine Ladejo GBR	45.21
	3. Derek Mills USA	45.29
800m	1. Andrey Loginov RUS	1:46.65
	2. Stanley Redwine USA	1:46.84
	3. Paul Ruto KEN	1:47.01
Mile	1. Noureddine Morceli ALG	3:48.67
	2. Abdi Bile SOM	3:52.28
	3. Steve Holman USA	3:52.77
5000m	1. Moses Kiptanui KEN	13:10.76
	2. Paul Bitok KEN	13:24.41
	3. Jon Brown GBR	13:24.79
10,000m	1. Hammou Boutayeb MAR	28:10.89
	2. Oleg Strizhakov RUS	28:27.69
	3. Kipyego Kororia KEN	28:28.56
3000mSt	1. Marc Davis USA	8:14.30
	2. Mark Croghan USA	8:21.85
	3. Joseph Keter KEN	8:23.13
110mh	1. Colin Jackson GBR	13.29
(-1.9)	2. Tony Jarrett GBR	13.33
	3. Emilio Valle CUB	13.35
400mH	1. Derrick Adkins USA	47.86
	2. Samuel Matete ZAM	47.98
	3. Winston Graham JAM	49.13
HJ	1. Javier Sotomayor CUB	2.40
	2. Hollis Conway USA	2.28
	3. Leonid Pumalainen RUS	2.28
PV	1. Igor Trandenkov RUS	5.90
	2. Maksim Tarasov RUS	5.80
	3. Sergey Bubka UKR	5.70
LJ	1. Mike Powell USA	8.45w (8.33)
	2. Erick Walder USA	8.39
	3. Kar. Streete-Thompson USA	8.29
TJ	1. Kenny Harrison USA	17.43
	2. Mike Conley USA	17.25
	3. Oleg Sakirkin KZK	17.05
SP	1. C J Hunter USA	20.35
	2. Randy Barnes USA	20.22
	3. Sergey Nikolayev RUS	20.11
DT	1. Dmitriy Shevchenko RUS	64.68
	2. Sergey Lyakhov RUS	62.22
	3. Attila Horváth HUN	61.70
HT	1. Lance Deal USA	80.20
	2. Vasiliy Sidorenko RUS	80.12
	3. Yuriy Sedykh RUS	77.24

Dennis Mitchelll: beat Leroy Burrell in 100m

Event	Athlete	Result
JT	1. Andrey Shevchuk RUS	82.90
	2. Marcis Shtrobinders LAT	80.92
	3. Yuriy Rybin RUS	80.38
Dec	1. Dan O'Brien USA	8715
	2. Steve Fritz USA	8177
	3. Kip Janvrin USA	7908
20kmW tr	1. Bernardo Segura MEX	1:23:28.88
	2. Ruslan Shafikov RUS	1:23:28.90
	3. Jiao Baozong CHN	1:24:07.60
4x100mR	1. SMTC/USA	38.30
	2. CUB	38.76
	3. RUS	38.92
4x400mR	1. USA	2:59.42
	2. CUB	3:01.87
	3. RUS	3:02.70

WOMEN

Event	Athlete	Result
100m	1. Gwen Torrence USA	10.95
(-0.5)	2. Irina Privalova RUS	10.98
	3. Juliet Cuthbert JAM	11.12
200m	1. Gwen Torrence USA	22.09
(-0.7)	2. Irina Privalova RUS	22.23
	3. Carlette Guidry USA	22.42
400m	1. Jearl Miles USA	50.60
	2. Maicel Malone USA	50.60
	3. Natasha Kaiser-Brown USA	50.73
800m	1. Maria Mutola MOZ	1:57.63
	2. Lyudmila Rogachova RUS	1:58.43
	3. Irina Samorokova RUS	1:59.07
1500m	1. Yekat Podkopayeva RUS	4:04.92
	2. Sonia O'Sullivan IRL	4:04.97
	3. Lyudmila Rogachova RUS	4:05.00
3000m	1. Yelena Romanova RUS	8:41.06
	2. Fernanda Ribeiro POR	8:42.13
	3. Annette Peters USA	8:43.65
5000m	1. Yelena Romanova RUS	15:28.69
	2. Tatyana Pentukova RUS	15:30.15
	3. Gitta Karlshøj DEN	15:33.88
10,000m	1. Tecla Lorupe KEN	31:52.39
	2. Klara Kashapova RUS	32:05.42
	3. Gwen Coogan USA	32:08.77
2000mSt	1. Marina Pluzhnikova RUS	6:11.84
	2. Svetlana Pospelova RUS	6:25.19
	3. Lyud. Kuropatkina RUS	6:26.76
100mh	1. Brigitta Bukovec SLO	12.83w
(+3.8)	2. Aliuska López CUB	12.88
	3. Marina Azyabina RUS	12.99
400mH	1. Sally Gunnell GBR	53.51
	2. Kim Batten USA	54.22
	3. Anna Knoroz RUS	54.67
HJ	1. Silvia Costa CUB	1.95
	2. Yelena Topchina RUS	1.93
	3. Olga Bolshova RUS	1.93
PV	1. Sun Caiyun CHN	4.00
	2. Svetlana Abramova RUS	3.90
	3. Andrea Müller GER	3.90

Gwen Torrence: sprint double

Event	Athlete	Result
LJ	1. Heike Drechsler GER	7.12
	2. Svetlana Moskalets RUS	6.82
	3. Irina Mushailova RUS	6.77
TJ	1. Anna Biryukova RUS	14.57
	2. Lyudmila Dubkova RUS	13.99
	3. Sheila Hudson USA	13.97
SP	1. Sui Xinmei CHN	20.15
	2. Huang Zhihong CHN	20.08
	3. Svetla Mitkova BUL	19.74
DT	1. Barbara Echevarría CUB	64.84
	2. Olga Chernyavskaya RUS	63.82
	3. Daniela Costian AUS	63.72
JT	1. Trine Hattestad NOR	65.74
	2. Felicia Tilea ROM	59.48
	3. Oksana Yarygina UZB	59.30
Hep: (25/26):		
	1. Jackie Joyner-Kersee USA	6606
	2. Larisa Turchinskaya RUS	6492
	3. Ghada Shouaa SYR	6361
10,000W	1. Olympiada Ivanova RUS	42:30.31
	2. Yelena Saiko RUS	42:43.23
	3. Sari Essayah FIN	42:45.04
4x100mR	1. USA	42.98
	2. CUB	43.37
	3. UKR	43.86
4x400mR	1. USA	3:22.27
	2. RUS	3:25.00
	3. CUB	3:26.35

CONTINENTAL JUNIOR CHAMPIONSHIPS

1994 - Winners

AFRICAN JUNIOR CHAMPIONSHIPS

July 6-8, Algiers, Algeria. **Men:** 100m/200m (+3.5): Deji Aliu NGR 10.61/21.34w, 400m: Riaan Dempers RSA 46.92, 800m: Bekele Abaku ETH 1:48.43, 1500m: Philip Mosima KEN 3:44.52, 5000m: Daniel Komen KEN 13:31.10, 10,000m: Habte Regasa ETH 30:06.35, 3000mSt: Yarba Lakhal MAR 8:36.08, 110mh (+2.2)/400mh: Amine Harchouche ALG 14.73w/52.77, HJ: Younes Mounik MAR 2.12, PV: Rafik Mefti ALG 4.50, LJ: Francois Coetzee RSA 7.54, TJ: Nabil Amadou ALG 14.91, SP/DT: Frantz Kruger RSA 14.17/55.86, HT: Karim Horchani TUN 61.84, JT: Marius Corbett RSA 74.42, Dec: Donny Magnan SEY 6360, 4x100m/4x400m: RSA 41.12/3:09.66. **Women:** 100m: (-0.2) Philomena Mensah GHA 11.47, 200m: (+0.6) Heide Seyerling RSA 23.59, 400m: Bisi Afolabi NGR 53.59, 800m: Mari Louise Henning RSA 2:05.82, 1500m/3000m: Sally Barsosio KEN 4:16.61/8:53.40, 10,000m: Abate Birhan ETH 33:49.10, 100mh: (-0.7) Adri van der Merwe RSA 13.95, 400mh: Ronell Ullrich RSA 59.92, HJ: Orla Venter NAM 1.68, LJ: Endurance Ojokolo NGR 5.56, TJ: Baya Rahouli ALG 12.02, SP: Imene Hassan Mahrous EGY 11.99, DT: Saida Almoud MAR 43.46, JT: Malika Hamou ALG 39.78, Hep: Marie Antoinette Marchall BKF 4793, 4x100m: NGR 46.15, 4x400m: RSA 3:45.25, 5000mW: Amsale Yakobe ETH 24:11.45.

ASIAN JUNIOR CHAMPIONSHIPS

Sep 17-20, Jakarta, Indonesia. **Men:** 100m (+0.7)/200m (+1.0) Worasit Vechaput THA 10.43/21.07, 400m: S Basak IND 48.11, 800m: Abdul Rachman QAT 1:50.83, 1500m: Yin Changjia CHN 3:49.95, 5000m: Xia Fengyuan CHN 14:29.39, 10,000m: Junaedi Ferry IND 31:13.17, 3000mSt: Tadayuki Ojima JPN 8:55.51, 110mh: (-0.1) Khasif Mubarak QAT 14.28, 400mh: Sultan Mubarak QAT 51.21, HJ: Nori Yosu Arai JPN 2.17, PV: Tatsuya Sugaya JPN 4.80, LJ: Al-Nobi Rahman QAT 7.79w, TJ: Aleksandr Tumanov TKM 15.68, SP: Jabir Singh IND 16.89, DT: Rajiv Kumar IND 49.34, HT: Sigeru Hirao JPN 61.44, JT: Wang Weichun CHN 72.74, Dec: Chen Chien-hung TPE 6773, 4x100m: THA 39.66, 4x400m: JPN 3:11.22. **Women:** 100m: (+2.0) Damayanthi Darsha SRI 11.42, 200m: (+0.9) Susanthika Jayasinghe SRI 23.16, 400m: Jiang Lanying CHN 53.83, 800m: Huang Lixing CHN 2:05.11, 1500m: Zhang Jinqing CHN 4:30.51, 3000m: Wang Chunmei CHN 9:33.78, 5000m: Naomo Skashita JPN 16:19.58, 100mh: Fan Min-hua TPE 14.24, 400mh: Mayuko Niiji JPN 59.38, HJ: Lin Su-chi TPE 1.82, LJ: Feng Jie CHN 6.32, TJ: Luo Jun CHN 13.33, SP: Chen Huifen CHN 15.58, DT: Qin Lei CHN 52.72, JT: Ma Lina CHN 51.26, Hep: Lin Chao-hsiu TPE 5283, 4x100m/4x400m: CHN 44.75/3:42.38.

CENTRAL AMERICAN & CARIBBEAN JUNIOR CHAMPIONSHIPS

July 8-10, Port-of-Spain, Trinidad. **Men:** 100m (+0.3)/200m (-0.1): Obadele Thompson BAR 10.0/21.09, 400m: Michael McDonald JAM 46.2, 800m: Preston Campbell JAM 1:53.04, 1500m/5000m: Pablo Olmedo MEX 3:50.2/14:24.37, 10,000m: Juan Perea MEX 30:42.62, 3000mSt: Ismael Iglesias CUB 9:07.6, 110mh (+0.7): Gabriel Burnett BAR 14.27, 400mh: Edward Clarke JAM 51.05, HJ: Stephen Woodley BER 2.14, PV: Jorge Tienda MEX 4.55, LJ: Pedro Garcia CUB 7.63, SP: Christopher Merced PUR 14.52, DT: Guillermo Heredia MEX 48.04, HT: Aldo Bello VEN 54.68, Dec: Yonelvis Aguilla CUB 7046, 4x100m: JAM 41.08. **Women:** 100m: (+1.8) Debbie Ferguson BAH 11.1, 200m/100mh: Astia Walker JAM 23.42/13.44, 400m: Claudine Williams JAM 52.8, 800m: Michelle Ballantine JAM 2:08.42, 1500m: Laura Flores MEX 4:34.7, 3000m: Karla Betancourt MEX 9:53.2, 400mh: Tanja Jarrett JAM 59.48, HJ: Natalie Richardson JAM 1.79, LJ: Trecia-Kaye Smith JAM 6.40, TJ: Suzette Lee JAM 13.26, SP/JT: Nora Bicet CUB 12.50/50.50, DT: Fanny Garcia VEN 42.60, Hep: Yaquelin Martínez CUB 4944, 4x100m/4x400m: JAM 44.51/3:34.00, 5000mW: Maribel Rebollo MEX 22:11.5.

SOUTH AMERICAN JUNIOR CHAMPIONSHIPS

Sep 1-4, Santa Fé, Argentina. 100m/110mh: Emerson Perin BRA 10.89/14.26; 200m: Inacio Leao BRA 21.69, 400m: Victor Goulart BRA 48.18, 800m: Alcides Pinto COL 1:51.73, 1500m: António Horbach BRA 3:53.3, 5000m: André Santo BRA 14:39.6, 10,000m: Clodoaldo dos Santos BRA 31:59.9, 3000mSt: Gustavo de Paula BRA 9:03.81, 400mh: Carlos Zbinden COL 53.50, HJ: Ruimar Paulo BRA 2.04, PV: Leonidas Aguiar BRA 4.20, LJ: Jeremy Racey CHI 7.10, TJ: Sergio Santos BRA 15.50w, SP: Mauro Ordiales ARG 15.28, DT: Julio Piñero ARG 56.26; HT: Juan Cerra ARG 66.62, JT: Marcos Vieira BRA 60.90, Dec: Marcio Souza BRA 6530, 4x100m/4x400m: BRA 41.44/ 3:14.82, 10,000mW: Milton Uyaguari ECU 43:28.4. **Women:** 100m/200m: Felipa Palacios COL 11.84/24.19, 400m: Maricel Palmieri ARG 55.86, 800m/1500m: Clara Morales CHI 2:11.38/4:31.4, 3000m: Bertha Sánchez COL 9:41.36, 10,000m: Erika Olivera CHI 34:14.4; 100mh: Maureen Maggi BRA 14.13, 400mh: Kelly Oliveira BRA 60.69, HJ: Luciane Dambracher BRA 1.78, LJ: Helena Guerrero COL 5.60, TJ: Adriana Matoso BRA 12.40. SP: Josiani Soares BRA 13.63, DT: Fanny Garcia VEN 44.48, HT: Vanesa Valarella ARG 47.00, JT: Alessandra Resende BRA 52.52, Hep: Mariela Andrade ARG 4715, 4x100m/4x400m: BRA 47.00/3:48.49.

OTHER INTERNATIONAL CHAMPIONSHIPS 1994

Winners at other international meetings

BALKAN GAMES

Jul 9-10, Trikala, Greece: *Winners:* **Men:** 100m: (-1.1) Daniel Cojocaru ROM 10.44, 200: (-0.2) Evgenios Papadopoulos GRE 20.81, 400m/400mh: Mugur Mateescu ROM 47.24/50.33, 800m: Fotios Deligiannis GRE 1:48.91, 1500m/5000m: Zeki Öztürk TUR 3:43.87/13:58.57, 10,000m: Panagiotis Haramis GRE 29:31.36, 3000mSt: Florin Ionescu ROM 8:35.62, 110mh: Laszlo Sarucan ROM 14.18, HJ: Labros Papakostas GRE 2.30, PV: Christos Pallakis GRE 5.20, LJ: Dimitrios Hatzopoulos GRE 7.72, TJ: Kotzo Kostov BUL 16.53, SP: Radoslav Despotov BUL 18.09, DT: Christos Papadopoulos GRE 56.48, HT: Stavri Ivanov BUL 63.68, JT: Dimitrios Polymerou GRE 72.22, Dec: Alper Kasapoglou TUR 7282, 20kW: Aleksandar Rakovic YUG 1:25:05, 4x100m/4x400m: GRE 39.38/3:07.76. **Women** - 100m (-1.0): Ekaterini Koffa GRE 11.65, 200m: (-1.6) Ekaterina Toscheva BUL 23.94, 400m: Elena Vizitiou ROM 53.14, 800m: Evaggelia Tsouraki GRE 2:07.18, 1500m: Liliana Salageanu ROM 4:15.32, 3000m: Milka Mihailova BUL 9:15.29, 10,000m: Alina Tecuta ROM 33:06.07, 100mh: (-0.4) Erica Nicolae ROM 13.32, 400mh: Nicoleta Caratasu ROM 57.02, HJ: Niki Bakagianni GRE 1.87, LJ: Paraskevi Patoulidou GRE 6.49, TJ: Monica Toth ROM 12.98, SP: Mihaela Oana ROM 17.74, DT: Ekaterini Voggoli GRE 57.58, JT: Mirela Manjani ALB J 56.52, Hep: Yurka Khristova BUL 5710, 10,000mW: Norica Cîmpean ROM 45:10.4, 4x100m: GRE 44.73, 4x400m: ROM 3:36.42,

FRANCOPHONE GAMES

Jul 11-13, Bondoufle: *Winners:* **Men:** 100m: (+0.5) Bruny Surin CAN 10.08, 200m: (-1.7) Hermann Lomba FRA 20.90, 400m: Pierre-Marie Hilaire FRA 46.16, 800m: Mahjoub Haïda MAR 1:50.48m, 1500: Azzedine Sediki MAR 3:42.57, 5000m/10,000m,: Salah Hissou MAR 28:34.25, 3000mSt: Khalid Skah MAR 8:19.30, 110mh: (-1.1) Dan Philibert FRA 13.55, 400mh: Fadhel Khayati TUN 49.52, HJ: Cory Siermachesky CAN 2.20, PV: Gérald Baudouin FRA 5.60, LJ: Cheikh Tidiane Touré SEN 8.06w, TJ: Edrick Floreal CAN 16.83, SP: Gheorge Guset ROM 19.67, DT: Costel Grasu ROM 61.24, HT: Gilles Dupray FRA 74.94, JT: Grégory Wiesner SUI 75.12, Dec: Christian Mandrou FRA 7766, 20kmW: Jean-Olivier Brosseau FRA 1:25:48, 4x100m: CAN 39.16, 4x400m: SEN 3:05.73. **Women**: 100m: Patricia Girard FRA 11.46, 200m: (-0.6) Stacy Bowen CAN 23.19, 400m: Evelyne Elien FRA 52.58, 800m: Carmen Stanciu ROM 2:05.28, 1500m/3000m: Christina Misaros ROM 4:21.20/9:02.09, 100mh: (-0.7) Nicole Ramalalanirina MAD 13.17, 400mh: Donalda Duprey CAN 55.10, HJ: Monica Iagar ROM 1.89, LJ: Nadine Caster FRA 6.58w, TJ: Rodica Petrescu ROM 14.33, SP: Nathalie Ganguillet SUI 16.32, DT: Nicoleta Grasu ROM 60.84, JT: Nathalie Teppe FRA 57.44, Hep: Kimberley Vanderhoek CAN 5641, 10kmW: Janice McCaffrey CAN 45:38.06, 4x100m: FRA 43.61, 4x400m: CAN 3:38.12.

GULF CC CHAMPIONSHIPS

Apr 6-8, Doha, Qatar. 100m (+1.7)/200m (+1.9) Talal Mansour QAT 10.17/ 20.71, 400m: Ibrahim Ismail QAT 46.65, 800m: Abdulrahman Hassan QAT 1:49.37, 1500m: Mohamed Suleiman QAT 3:47.22, 5000m/3000mSt: Jamal Abdi QAT 14:58.86/8:47.15, 10,000m: Ahmad Ibrahim QAT 30:28.54, Half Mar: Ahmad Ibrahim QAT 1:13:02, 110mh: (+1.3) Rached Sheiban QAT 14.01, 400mh: Mohamed Al Bishi SAU 50.66, HJ: Abdallah Al Sheib QAT 2.10, PV: Walid Zaed QAT 5.01, LJ: Ahmed Hadil OMAN 7.57, TJ: Salem Al Ahmadi SAU 16.35, SP/DT: Khaled Al Khalidi SAU 17.29/51.18, HT: Walid Al Bikhit KUW 62.78, JT: Ali Saleh Al Jadami SAU 69.10, Dec: Ibrahim Nassir UAE 6596, 4x100m: QAT 39.70, 4x400m: SAU 3:14.64, 10kmW: Ibrahim Charif QAT 58:48.0.

Iberian 10,000 Champs. Apr 9, Braga. POR: Men: Paulo Guerra POR 27:52.44, Women – Conceição Ferreira POR 31:32.11,

IBERO-AMERICAN CHAMPIONSHIPS

Oct 27-30, Mar del Plata, Argentina. *Winners:* **Men**: 100m: Carlos Gats ARG 10.50w, 200m (+1.2)/400m Sebastián Keitel CHL 20.43/46.72, 800m: José de Oliveira BRA 1:49.49, 1500m: José López VEN 3:54.04, 5000m: Ronaldo da Costa BRA 13:47.99, 10,000m: Armando Quintanilla MEX 28:06.88, 3000mSt: Javier Rodriguez ESP 8:35.03, 110mh: Eric Batle CUB 14.31, 400mh: Everson Teixeira BRA 49.76, HJ: Gilmar Mayo COL 2.32, PV: Nuño Fernandes POR 5.15, LJ: Jaime Jefferson CUB 7.82w, TJ: Anisio Silva BRA 16.66, SP: Gert Weil COL 19.30, DT: Ramón Jiménez PAR 60.42, HT: Andrés Charadia ARG 70.80, JT: Luis Lucumi COL 75.40, Dec: Mario Anibal POR 7431, 4x100m: CUB 39.99, 4x400m: BRA 3:06.54, 20,000mW: Daniel Garcia MEX 1:21:19.92. **Women**: 100m: (+1.6) Cleide Amaral BRA 11.66, 200m (+4.9)/400m Ximena Restrepo COL 23.07w/52.69, 800m: Fatima dos Santos BRA 2:06.26, 1500m: Ana Souza BRA 4:28.50, 3000m/10,000m: Silvana Pereira BRA 9:14.53 /33:29.60, 100mh: Damarys Anderson CUB 13.81w, 400mh: Odalys Hernández CUB 57.89, HJ: Tania Fernández CUB 1.75, LJ/TJ: Andrea Avila ARG 6.58/13.18, SP: Herminia Fernández CUB 17.33, DT: Teresa Machado POR 61.20, HT: Maria Villamizar COL 55.70. JT: Sueli dos Santos BRA 65.96, Hep: Yolanda Pompa CUB 5370, 4x100m/4x400m: COL 44.87 /3:35.35, 10,000mW: Francesca Martinez MEX 47:01.80.

SOUTH AMERICAN (Odesur) GAMES

Nov 22-27, Valencia, Venezuela: 100m: (+0.4) Robinson Urrutia COL 10.29, 200m: (+0.4) Sebastián Keitel CHI 20.1, 400m: Wenceslao Ferrin COL 45.84, 800m/1500m: José Gregorio López VEN 1:50.53/3:47.56, 5000m: Jacinto Navarette COL 14:10.3, 10,000m: Rubén Maza VEN 29:49.1, Mar: Policarpio Calizaya BOL 2:32:06, 3000mSt: Jaime Valenzuela CHI 9:04.2, 110mh: Eliecer Pulgar VEN 14.33, 400mh: Llimy Rivas COL 51.14, HJ: Gilmar Mayo COL 2.25, PV: Oscar Veit ARG 5.10, LJ: Nelson Ferreira BRA 7.84, TJ: Sergio Saavedra VEN 16.26, SP: Gert Weil CHI 18.74, DT: Ramón Jimenez PAR 57.88, HT: Andrés Charadia ARG 70.80, JT: Nery Kennedy PAR 76.70, Dec: Iván Romero VEN -, 4x100m/ 4x400m: CHI 39.67/ 3:06.92, 20kmW: Querubin Moreno COL 1:29:10, 50kmW: Eloy Quispe BOL 4:36:08, **Women**: 100m/200m (+0.5): Felipa Palacios COL 11.51/23.6, 400m/ 400mh: Ximena Restrepo COL 51.31/56.05, 800m: Luciana Mendes BRA 2:01.99, 1500m: Marta Orellana ARG 4:22.33, 3000m/10,000m: Erika Olivera CHI 9:31.6/34:40.9, 100mh: Alejandra Martinez CHI 14.42, HJ: Alejandra Chomali CHI 1.73, LJ/TJ: Andrea Avila ARG 6.51/13.12, SP: Lila Morales VEN 13.02, DT: María Urrutia COL 58.08, JT: Zuleima Aramendiz COL 55.46, Hep: Zorababelia Cordoba COL 5448, 4x100m/4x400m: COL 44.98/3:40.33.

6th PAN-AM WALKS CUP

Atlanta, Georgia, USA 23-24 September.

Men team (20km and 50km): 1. MEX 889, 2. USA 834, 3. BRA 560. Winners: 20km: Bernardo Segura MEX1:24:15, 50km: Carlos Mercenario MEX 3:52:08.

Women team (10km): 1. MEX 442, 2. USA 431, 3. CAB 428. Winner: Graciella Mendoza MEZ 46:14.

10th ICMR MOUNTAIN RACING WORLD CUP

Berchtesgaden, Germany 4 September

Men: 13.7km, 1200m uphill: 1. Helmut Schmuck AUT 61:02, 2. Antonio Molinari ITA 61:36, 3. Ladislav Raim TCH 61:40; team: 1. ITA, 2. FRA, 3. GER.

Women: 7.5km, 685m uphill: 1. Gudrun Pflüger AUT 39:31, 2. Isabelle Guillot FRA 40:12, 3. Dita Hebelková TCH 41:18; team: 1. FRA, 2. AUT, 3. ITA.

Junior men: 7.5km, 685m uphill: 1. Martin Bajcicak SLO 35:59; team: 1. TCH, 2. ITA, 3. SUI.

IAAF/MOBIL GRAND PRIX

INTRODUCED in 1985, the Grand Prix links the world's leading invitational meetings, so that athletes earn points over the season, with a final contested by the leaders in the points tables. Half the standard events are held each year. There is an Individual Event Grand Prix for each event and an Overall Grand Prix for men and women. The number of meetings constituting the Grand Prix circuit was increased by three to 20 in 1990, but (including the final) decreased to 19 in 1991, 18 in 1992, 17 in 1993 and 16 in 1994 and 1995.

Qualified athletes for the Grand Prix are those who, in the current or preceding year have achieved a performance equal to or better than the 50th best in the world in the past year.

Scoring

For events prior to the Grand Prix Final: 9 points for 1st, then 7-6-5-4-3-2-1 for 2nd to 8th. Although an athlete may compete at any of the meetings, only his or her best five points scores count. Up to 1992 double points were then added in the final for the overall totals for each event and when athletes finished level on points at the end of the season, places were determined by their individual performances in the final.

From 1993 athletes qualified for the final as before, but their points earned during the year (up to 45) were then only included in the overall classification, to which treble points were awarded from the final itself. Individual events prize money was determined on the final only.

Award structure

For each event 1985-92: first $10,000, second $8000, third $6000, fourth $5000, fifth $4000, sixth $3000, seventh $2000, eight $1000.
Men's and women's overall Grand Prix awards (all events) 1985-92: first $25,000, second $15,000, third $10,000.
From 1993 these payments were substantially increased to:
For each event: first $30,000, second $20,000, third $14,000, fourth $10,000, fifth $8000, sixth $7000, seventh $6000, eight $5000.
Men's and women's overall Grand Prix awards (all events): first $100,000, second $50,000, third $30,000, fourth $20,000, fifth $15,000, sixth $13,000, seventh $12,000, eight $10,000.

Grand Prix meetings for 1994 and 1995

1994		*1995*
15 May	Mobil Banespa Meeting, São Paulo	14 May
22 May	New York Games	21 May
28 May	Bruce Jenner's Symantec Classic, San Jose	27 May
8 June	Golden Gala, Roma	7 June
8 July	BNP Meeting, Villeneuve d'Ascq 1993, Paris 1994	3 July
6 July	Athletissima, Lausanne	5 July
15 July	TSB Games, London	7 July
12 July	DN Galan, Stockholm	10 July
19 July	Nikaia Mobil Meeting, Nice	12 July
22 July	Mobil Bislett Games, Oslo	21 July
2 Aug	Herculis Vittel, Monte Carlo	25 July
17 Aug	Weltklasse, Zürich	16 Aug
21 Aug	ASV Sportfest der Weltklasse, Köln	18 Aug
19 Aug	Memorial Ivo van Damme, Bruxelles	25 Aug
30 Aug	ISTAF, Berlin	1 Sep
3 Sep	Grand Prix Final, Paris 1994, Monte Carlo 1995	9 Sep

IAAF/Mobil Grand Prix 1994 - Overall Individual Men

				Points	Award
1	Noureddine Morceli	ALG	1500/5000m	78	$100,000
2	Samuel Matete	ZAM	400mh	72 (1220)	$50,000
3	Mike Conley	USA	TJ	72 (1219)	$30,000
4	Dennis Mitchell	USA	100m	72 (1185)	$20,000
5	Javier Sotomayor	CUB	HJ	72 (1179)	$15,000
6	Andrey Abduvaliyev	TJK	HT	68	$13,000
7	Derrick Adkins	USA	400mh	66 (1219)	$12,000
8	Vénuste Niyongabo	BUR	1500m	66 (1082)	$10,000

Overall Individual Women

				Points	Award
1	Jackie Joyner-Kersee	USA	LJ	72 (1235)	$100,000
2	Svetlana Dimitrova	BUL	100mh	72 (1203)	$50,000
3	Sonia O'Sullivan	IRL	1500/5000m	72 (1184)	$30,000
4	Natalya Shikolenko	BLS	JT	70	$20,000
5	Gwen Torrence	USA	100/400m	66 (1229)	$15,000
6	Ilke Wyludda	GER	DT	66 (1109)	$13,000
7	Heike Drechsler	GER	LJ	63	$12,000
8	Angela Chalmers	CAN	1500m	62 (1188)	$10,000
9	Trine Hattestad	NOR	JT	62 (1130)	

Grand Prix II meetings - staging up to six Grand Prix events with points 5-4-3-2-1 adding to the main GP points:
1994 : Bratislava 1/6, Hengelo 4/6, Sevilla 5/6, St Denis 10/6, Indianapolis 25/6, Helsinki 29/6, Gateshead 1/7, Linz 29/7, Rieti 28/8.
1995: Bratislava 30/5, St Denis 1/6, Sevilla 3/6, Hengelo 5/6, Moscow 5/6, Helsinki 28/6, Gateshead 2/7, Linz 22/8, Rieti 5/9

IAAF International Invitation meetings at outdoor venues:
1994: Melbourne 24/2, Tokyo 3/5, Vancouver 29/5, Budapest 3/6, Moscow 5/6, Barcelona 25/7, Sestriere 31/7, Sheffield 4/9, Tokyo 17/9.
1995: Melbourne 23/2, Vancouver 28/5, Villeneuve d'Ascq 17/6, Madrid 20/6, Budapest 8/7, Barcelona 27/7, Sestriere 29/7, London (McDonald's) 27/8, New Delhi 13/9, Tokyo 15/9.

Grand Prix Final - at Stade Charléty, Paris
10 September 1994

Results, awards and scores prior to the final, with leading scorers who did not compete in Paris. * = Non-scorer at Grand Prix Final

Men

100 Metres (-0.6)

1	Dennis Mitchell	USA	10.12	$30,000	45
2	Linford Christie	GBR	10.13	$20,000	36
3	Jon Drummond	USA	10.18	$14,000	39
4	Frank Fredericks	NAM	10.21	$10,000	15
5	Donovan Bailey	CAN	10.24	$8000	28
6	Olapade Adeniken	NGR	10.25	$7000	30
7	Davidson Ezinwa	NGR	10.46	$6000	23
8	Osmond Ezinwa	NGR	11.33	$5000	14
Other leading scorers prior to GP Final:					
	Leroy Burrell	USA	44		
	Andre Cason	USA	32		
	Michael Green	JAM	17		

400 Metres

1	Derek Mills	USA	45.22	$30,000	31
2	Antonio Pettigrew	USA	45.26	$20,000	31
3	Samson Kitur	KEN	45.37	$14,000	34
4	Roger Black	GBR	45.39	$10,000	27
5	Andrew Valmon	USA	45.43	$8000	24
6	Darnell Hall	USA	45.79	$7000	21
7	Du'aine Ladejo	GBR	45.80	$6000	15
8	Jason Rouser	USA	46.33	$5000	29
Other leading scorer prior to GP Final:					
	Kennedy Ochieng	KEN	19		

1500 Metres

1	Noureddine Morceli	ALG	3:40.89	$30,000	27
2	Vénuste Niyongabo	BUR	3:41.72	$20,000	45
3	Abdi Bile	SOM	3:42.24	$14,000	30
4	Matthew Yates	GBR	3:42.79	$10,000	15
5	Benson Koech	KEN	3:42.95	$8000	20
6	Mohamed Suleiman	QAT	3:43.04	$7000	30
7	Andrey Bulkovskiy	UKR	3:43.14	$6000	13
8	Atoi Boru	KEN	3:43.25	$5000	19
9	Steve Holman	USA	3:43.47	$500	32
10	Terrance Herrington	USA	3:43.64	$500	14
11	Branko Zorko	CRO	3:44.32	$500	19
12	Azzeddine Sediki	MAR	3:44.41	$500	26
Other leading scorers prior to GP Final:					
	Simon Doyle	AUS	17		
	David Kibet	KEN	17		

5000 Metres

1	Khalid Skah	MAR	13:14.63	$30,000	37
2	Khalid Boulami	MAR	13:14.64	$20,000	13
3	Moses Kiptanui	KEN	13:14.93	$14,000	13
4	Salah Hissou	MAR	13:15.16	$10,000	20

5	Brahim Lahlafi	MAR	13:15.46	$8000	22
6	Aloÿs Nizigama	BUR	13:15.70	$7000	34
7	Bob Kennedy	USA	13:16.93	$6000	27
8	Worku Bikila	ETH	13:17.36	$5000	24
9	Fita Bayissa	ETH	13:23.24	$500	32
10	Ismael Kirui	KEN	13:24.45	$500	20
11	Simon Chemoiywo	KEN	13:58.32	$500	25
12	William Sigei	KEN	14:05.28	$500	33
Other leading scorers prior to GP Final:					
	Haile Gebresilassie	ETH	41		
	Noureddine Morceli	ALG	29		
	Paul Tergat	KEN	24		
	Paul Bitok	KEN	21		
	Dieter Baumann	GER	18		
	Smail Sghir	MAR	13		
	James Kariuki	KEN	13		
	Yobes Ondieki	KEN	13		

400 Metres Hurdles

1	Samuel Matete	ZAM	48.02	$30,000	45
2	Derrick Adkins	USA	48.05	$20,000	45
3	Stéphane Diagana	FRA	48.64	$14,000	22
4	Sven Nylander	SWE	48.75	$10,000	32
5	Winthrop Graham	JAM	48.76	$8000	29
6	Niklas Wallenlind	SWE	50.13	$7000	19
7	Torrance Zellner	USA	50.18	$6000	21
8	Oleg Tverdokhleb	UKR	50.23	$5000	33
Next leading scorers prior to GP Final:					
	Yoshihiko Saito	JPN	15		

High Jump

1	Javier Sotomayor	CUB	2.33	$30,000	45
2	Troy Kemp	BAH	2.33	$20,000	39
3	Dragutin Topic	YUG	2.30	$14,000	25
4	Jean-Charles Gicquel*	FRA	2.30	$2500	16.5
5	Steinar Hoen	NOR	2.25	$10,000	38
6	Håkon Särnblom	NOR	2.25	$8000	25
7=	Tony Barton	USA	2.25	$6000	27
	Hollis Conway	USA	2.25	$6000	27
	Tim Forsyth	AUS	2.25	$6000	20.5
Other leading scorers prior to GP Final:					
	Grigoriy Fedorkov	RUS	19.5		
	Steve Smith	GBR	19		

Triple Jump

1	Mike Conley	USA	17.68	$30,000	45
2	Oleg Sakirkin	KZK	17.17	$20,000	18
3	Vasiliy Sokov	RUS	16.87	$14,000	13
4	Brian Wellman	BER	16.86	$10,000	41
5	Maris Bruziks	LAT	16.64	$8000	21
6	Denis Kapustin	RUS	16.36	$7000	16
7	Edrick Floréal	CAN	16.22	$6000	23
8	Jonathan Edwards	GBR	15.81	$5000	21
Next leading scorers prior to GP Final:					
	Lofti Khaida	ALG	10		
	Reggie Jones	USA	10		

Shot

1	Randy Barnes	USA	20.60	$30,000	20
2	C. J. Hunter	USA	20.50	$20,000	21
3	Gregg Tafralis	USA	20.49	$14,000	20
4	Jim Doehring	USA	20.20	$10,000	21
5	Kevin Toth	USA	20.16	$8000	35
6	Dragan Peric	YUG	19.86	$7000	15
7	Paolo Dal Soglio	ITA	19.79	$6000	14
8	Aleksandr Klimenko	UKR	19.26	$5000	11
9	Kent Larsson	SWE	18.18	$2500	8
Other leading scorer prior to GP Final:					
	Pétur Gudmundsson	ISL	8		

Hammer

1	Andrey Abduvaliyev	TJK	81.46	$30,000	41
2	Igor Astapkovich	BLS	79.54	$20,000	38
3	Vasiliy Sidorenko	RUS	79.12	$14,000	19
4	Lance Deal	USA	79.06	$10,000	18
5	Heinz Weis	GER	77.42	$8000	14
6	Tibor Gécsek	HUN	76.24	$7000	14
7	Igor Nikulin	RUS	76.22	$6000	21
8	Christophe Epalle	FRA	76.14	$5000	12
Next leading scorers prior to GP Final:					
	Tore Gustafsson	SWE	7		
	Yuriy Sedykh	RUS	7		

WOMEN

100 Metres (+0.4)

1	Merlene Ottey	JAM	10.78	$30,000	18
2	Gwen Torrence	USA	10.82	$20,000	43
3	Irina Privalova	RUS	11.02	$14,000	41
4	Carlette Guidry-White	USA	11.12	$10,000	36
5	Zhanna Tarnopolskaya	UKR	11.16	$8000	30
6	Juliet Cuthbert	JAM	11.22	$7000	35
7	Liliana Allen	CUB	11.38	$6000	29
8	Petya Pendareva	BUL	11.61	$5000	20
Next leading scorer prior to GP Final:					
	Mary Onyali	NGR	15		

400 Metres

1	Marie-José Pérec	FRA	49.77	$30,000	27
2	Cathy Freeman	AUS	50.04	$20,000	34
3	Maicel Malone	USA	50.33	$14,000	33
4	Jearl Miles	USA	50.37	$10,000	33
5	Sandie Richards	JAM	51.04	$8000	22
6	Natasha Kaiser-Brown	USA	51.11	$7000	32
7	Pauline Davis	BAH	51.52	$6000	24
8	Deon Hemmings	JAM	52.45	$5000	12
Next leading scorer prior to GP Final:					
	Svetlana Goncharenko	RUS	10		

1500 Metres

1	Angela Chalmers	CAN	4:01.61	$30,000	35
2	Hassiba Boulmerka	ALG	4:01.85	$20,000	30
3	Yekaterina Podkopayeva	RUS	4:01.92	$14,000	43

4	Lyubov Kremlyova	RUS	4:05.52	$10,000	30
5	Lyubov Gurina	RUS	4:05.89	$8000	15
6	Carla Sacramento	POR	4:06.05	$7000	18
7	Lyudmila Rogachova	RUS	4:06.18	$6000	26
8	Anna Brzezinska	POL	4:08.40	$5000	16
9	Blandine Bitzner	FRA	4:11.67	$500	9
10	Regina Jacobs	USA	4:12.71	$500	19

Other leading scorers prior to GP Final:

Sonia O'Sullivan	IRL	40
Yvonne Graham	JAM	27
Gina Proccacio	USA	11

5000 Metres

1	Sonia O'Sullivan	IRL	15:12.94	$30,000	18
2	Lyudmila Borisova	RUS	15:14.61	$20,000	12
3	Alison Wyeth	GBR	15:15.45	$14,000	11
4	Yvonne Graham	JAM	15:18.25	$10,000	19
5	Catherina McKiernan	IRL	15:20.07	$8000	21
6	Kathrin Wessel	GER	15:23.17	$7000	16
7	Nadia Dandolo	ITA	15:25.02	$6000	9
8	Farida Fates	FRA	15:28.36	$5000	8
9	Gwen Griffiths	RSA	15:38.39	$500	8
10	Roberta Brunet	ITA	15:46.45	$500	9
11	Kathy Franey	USA	16:09.18	$500	6
12	Silvia Botticelli	ITA	16:10.34	$500	7

Other leading scorers prior to GP Final:

Annette Peters	USA	32
Yelena Romanova	RUS	18
Derartu Tulu	ETH	11
Carmen de Oliveira	BRA	9
Libby Johnson	USA	8
Margaret Kagiri	KEN	7
Claudia Lokar	GER	7
Yvonne Murray	GBR	7
Tecla Lorupe	KEN	7
Lynn Jennings	USA	7

100 Metres Hurdles (-0.5)

1	Svetlana Dimitrova	BUL	12.66	$30,000	45
2	Yuliya Graudyn	RUS	12.79	$20,000	39
3	Aliuska López	CUB	12.86	$14,000	29
4	Yordanka Donkova	BUL	12.88	$10,000	41
5	Tatyana Reshetnikova	RUS	12.89	$8000	33
6	Julie Baumann	SUI	12.89	$7000	22.5
7	Brigita Bukovec	SLO	12.97	$6000	27
8	Michelle Freeman	JAM	13.26	$5000	36

Other leading scorer prior to GP Final:

LaVonna Martin-Floreal	USA	24

Long Jump

1	Jackie Joyner-Kersee	USA	7.21	$30,000	45
2	Inessa Kravets	UKR	6.98	$20,000	37
3	Heike Drechsler	GER	6.83	$14,000	45
4	Ljudmila Ninova	AUT	6.78	$10,000	30
5	Renata Nielsen	DEN	6.70	$8000	28
6	Irina Mushayilova	RUS	6.70	$7000	18

7	Fiona May	ITA	6.52	$6000	27
8	Nicole Boegman	AUS	6.41	$5000	23
Next leading scorer prior to GP Final:					
	Yolanda Chen	RUS	10		

Discus

1	Ilke Wyludda	GER	65.84	$30,000	39
2	Mette Bergmann	NOR	64.72	$20,000	20
3	Ellina Zvereva	BLS	63.96	$14,000	36
4	Daniela Costian	AUS	63.72	$10,000	38
5	Barbara Echevarría	CUB	61.58	$8000	30
6	Olga Chernyavskaya	RUS	61.24	$7000	19
7	Nicoleta Grasu	ROM	59.70	$6000	22
8	Connie Price-Smith	USA	56.06	$5000	14
Next leading scorers prior to GP Final:					
	Franka Dietzsch	GER	12		
	Jana Lauren	GER	12		

Javelin

1	Natalya Shikolenko	BLS	68.26	$30,000	43
2	Trine Hattestad	NOR	67.04	$20,000	41
3	Claudia Isaila	ROM	66.56	$14,000	17
4	Felicia Tîlea	ROM	65.34	$10,000	23
5	Karen Forkel	GER	62.80	$8000	31
6	Louise McPaul	AUS	61.16	$7000	12
7	Yekaterina Ivakina	RUS	58.34	$6000	22
8	Tatyana Shikolenko	BLS	56.12	$5000	23
Next leading scorer prior to GP Final:					
	Jette Jeppesen	DEN	9		

Merlene Ottey: only 18 points but won $30,000 on the day

Mike Conley: 45 points not good enough to win overall title

MAJOR INTERNATIONAL EVENTS 1995-98

1995
Asian Cross-country Championships - Chiba, Japan (19 Feb)
Pan American Games - Mar del Plata, Argentina (3-18 Mar)
World Indoor Championships - Barcelona, Spain (10-12 Mar)
World Cross-Country Championships - Durham, GBR (25 Mar)
World Marathon Cup - Athens, Greece (9 Apr)
World Race Walking Cup - Beijing, China (29-30 Apr)
South American Championships - Manaus, Brazil (26-28 May)
European Cup -First and Second Leagues (10-11 Jun)
European Cup - Super League - Villeneuve d'Ascq, France (24-25 Jun)
European Cup Combined Events (1-2 Jul)
World Veterans Games - Buffalo, USA (13-23 Jul)
European Junior Championships - Nyiregyháza, Hungary (27-30 Jul)
World Student Games - Fukuoka, Japan (28 Aug - 3 Sep)
World Championships - Göteborg, Sweden (4-13 Aug)
IAAF Grand Prix Final - Monte Carlo, Monaco (9 Sep)
ICMR Mountain Race Cup, Edinburgh, GBR (10 Sep)
All-Africa Games - Zimbabwe (13-18 Sep)
IAU 100km World Cup, Winschoten, Netherlands (16 Sep)
Asian Championships - Jakarta, Indonesia (20-24 Sep)
World Half Marathon Championships - Montbéliard, France (1 Oct)
European Cross-country Championships
South East Asia Games - Chiangmai, Thailand (9-17 Dec)

1996
European Indoor Championships - Stockholm, Sweden (8-10 Mar)
World Cross-Country Championships - Cape Town, South Africa
World Road Relay Championships - Copenhagen, Denmark
European Cup -First and Second Leagues
European Cup - Super League - Madrid, Spain
European Cup Combined Events
European Under 23 Cup
Olympic Games - Atlanta, Georgia, USA (20 Jul - 4 Aug)
World Junior Championships - Sydney, Australia
World Half Marathon Championships - Palma de Mallorca, Spain
European Cross-country Championships

1997
World Indoor Championships - Athens, Greece
World Championships - to be announced after withdrawal of Mexico City, Mexico

1998
European Championships - Budapest, Hungary
World Cup - Johannesburg, South Africa
Goodwill Games - New York area (Jul 25 - Aug 9)

Notes from the Editor

Drugs
THE IAAF Council meeting in November determined to adopt the 'A' sample as the binding result after an athlete submits a urine sample, rather than wait for confirmation of the 'B' sample. The decision nonetheless leaves open all avenues of appeal, and will make little practical difference other than speed up procedures. Arne Ljungqvist, IAAF Doping Commission Chairman said that in his experience there had only been one case in 15 years where the B sample did not bear out the results of the A sample.

The Council further determined to increase the number of out-of-competition tests that it conducts from about 800 in 1994 to 1200 in 1995.

DANNY HARRIS, the 400m hurdler, competed in five major meetings in the USA and in Europe in May and June 1994, He had been reinstated by TAC following his drugs ban for cocaine usage, but he had not been reinstated by the IAAF, so when it was eventually realised that he was competing while still under a 4-year international ban, his results were annulled from Grand Prix standings.

At the end of the year, however, the IAAF reinstated Harris in the first-ever use of its "exceptional" circumstances rules. Harris had shown that he had beaten his drug addiction and IAAF President Primo Nebiolo backed Harris' case, stating that he had "showed as a man that he wanted to change his life. In this case we were able to help him both as an athlete and as a man."

IN OCTOBER 1994 the US Supreme Court recognised the jurisdictional rights of the IAAF and did not allowed Butch Reynolds to pursue his case against the IAAF, whose president Dr Primo Nebiolo declared:

"As I have had the opportunity to say in the past. I have always had complete confidence in the judicial system of the United States. Today's decision by the US Supreme Court, which ends our long march through this case, is not only of vital importance to the world athletics movement, but also takes on special significance for the entire Olympic movement and the sporting world in general."

THE four-year ban on John Ngugi was upheld by a three-man panel. They held that his failure to submit to an out-of-season doping control test on 13 Feb 1993 constituted a doping offence under IAAF rules. They added that Ngugi conceded his refusal to submit to testing even after the consequences of his refusal were explained to him. Any wish by Ngugi to seek reinstatement under the IAAF's 'exceptional circumstances' rule would be a matter for the IAAF Council, not the arbitration panel.

The Chinese phenomenon
THE biggest sensation and main talking point in athletics in 1993 was the string of amazing performances produced by Chinese women athletes, most particularly at the Chinese National Games.

Many in the West were quick to deride such achievements - and accused the Chinese of using drugs. Sure enough in 1994 several prominent Chinese sportswomen were caught for drug abuse, most notably two world record setting swimmers and two weightlifting world champions. In athletics the discus thrower Qiu Qiaoping tested positive and the 400m hurdler, Han Qing, was caught having finished first at the Asian Games.

However, it was Ma's army that had caught the headlines in 1993 - and most specifically two very special athletes Wang Junxia and Qu Yunxia. It must be pointed out that none of the athletes coached by Ma Junren tested positive either at competitions or in random tests conducted by the IAAF.
The controversial coach kept on hitting the headlines in 1994 as he capitalised on his successes. Early in the year he sold his secret potion to a health drinks company for a reported £900,000, and later his 'Ma's Family Army No. 1 high grade nutritious liquor' went on sale in Japan for £20 a small bottle. Apparently sales went well.

There were problems, however, with the runners. Liu Dong, the world champion at 1500m in 1993, left his squad, forced out as she refused to conform to Ma's party line on boyfriends and haircuts. Then came the news that Ma's star pupil Wang Junxia has vowed not to return to training under Ma's controversial regime. She was one of 16 athletes who left his training camp in December 1994, alleging that he kept too much of their earnings and protesting at his excessive discipline.

Wang told the *Beijing Youth News:* "If coach Ma had treated us better, we would have worked ourselves to death". Wang went on to say that she had been emotionally damaged by Ma's overly strict discipline. A month later, however, Wang went back to Ma!

In mid-February came a report in *China* Sports that Wang Junxia and a teammate had taken over coaching responsibilities of their team, with no mention of Ma Junren. In any case he was suffering from throat cancer and recuperating from injuries sustained in a car crash in late December 1994.

THEREIN, of course, lies the key reason. For all that drugs play their part in Chinese sport, as they do in Western sport, the success of the Chinese women has to be predominantly due to their enormous training loads. A policy, as I wrote last year, of 'killing off' the weak and the survival of the fittest'. Those that could manage the marathon-a- day regime could indeed produce amazing times. But would they be burnt out? Both Wang and Qu remained unbeaten in 1994, but they very sensibly undertook a far less intense racing programme. That could be ideal preparation for renewed vigour in 1995 or 1996. On the other hand many of the group might prove to have been like shooting stars.

We feel particularly sensitive to any possibility of state-sponsored drugs programmes - and many Westerners have been quick to allege that that is what is happening in China, as it was in the old GDR. However there is no evidence so far as I know of this, and it smacks of racialism to so label a whole nation. Cheating by the use of drugs is evil whosoever does this, but it is all to easy to throw around accusations about peoples and regimes about which we do not know enough.

IAAF Membership

WITH THE reinstatement of Cambodia to membership and with full rights being given to Yugoslavia the IAAF membership rose to 206 at the end of 1994.

New women's events

WORLD and European records for the women's pole vault and hammer were established at the end of December. Recognised were the best performances at that date which satisfied record conditions. The best ever pole vault mark, Sun Caiyun's 4.11 could not be recognised as there had been only two competitors at the event at Guangzhou on 21 Mar 1993. Also the best hammer mark, Svetlana Sudak's 67.34 was not submitted by the Belarus federation as there had not been any drug testing at that meeting at Minsk on 4 Jun 1994.

The Chinese lists for 1994 released in February 1995 showed that Sun Caiyun had twice vaulted 4.12 at Guangzhou late in 1994, but at the time of writing there was no news as to whether these were in meetings that conformed with record conditions, particularly for drug testing. Sun, however, looks like making such questions academic, as she set world indoor records at 4.10, 4.11, 4.12, 4.13 and 4.15 within three weeks in Germany in early 1995.

The first major championship to stage the pole vault will be the European Indoors of 1996 and the first to include the hammer the Worlds of 1997.

Agreed earlier in the year was the change from 3000m to 5000m for women at major championships, coming into force at World Championships 1995, Olympic Games 1996, World Cup 1998. The World Junior Championships will have women's events at 3000m and 5000m from 1996.

The IAAF Walking Committee determined that the women's walk should be at 20 kilometres rather than 10 kilometres at World Championships and World Cup events from 1997.

IAAF drop indoor walks

IN A move to encourage constructive changes in race walking, the IAAF Council voted to remove indoor race walking from its international calendar. Thus, walking events will no longer be contested at European and World Indoor Championships, although national federations are free to continue to stage such events at domestic level if they wish. Recent championship races on indoor circuits have tended to be farcical as the 'walkers' sped at ever increasing pace over the tight circuits.

The Council acted on the advice of the

IAAF Race Walking Working Group which recommended broad-based changes in all facets of race walking, including:

- Better training for judges, based on a standardised system of education.
- Modernisation of communication on course to speed up reports on warnings and disqualifications and to allow competitors to be aware of them.
- New rules for the judges to determine when the athletes have breached the "constant ground contact rule" that requires walkers to keep their feet in contact with the track.

THE IAAF Race Walking Working Group, appointed in November 1993, was chaired by César Moreno and comprised fellow Council members Alberto Juantorena, Lou Dapeng, Artur Takac and Igor Ter-Ovanesyan along with walkers Maurizio Damilano, Sari Essayah, Raul González, Bo Gustafsson and Jorge Llopart, and ex officio member Bob Bowman.

Grand Prix meetings rated

THE poll of the International Association of Athletes Representatives (IAAR) has resulted in Zürich once again being voted the best Grand Prix meeting.

Each of the GP I and II meetings were assessed in nine categories: communications, competition, food, hotel, organisation, reimbursements, services, technical and transport.

1. Zürich, 2. Oslo, 3. Monaco, 4. Stockholm, 5. Lausanne, 6. Brussels, 7. Cologne, 8. London, 9. Nice, 10. São Paulo, 11. Gateshead (top GP II meeting), 12. Hengelo, 13. Rieti, 14. St Denis, 15. Linz, 16. Rome, 17. Lille, 18. Seville, 19. Berlin, 20. New York, 21. San José, 22. Paris, 23. Bratislava.

EAA Meetings headed by Madrid

THE ANNUAL survey of European AA outdoor invitational meetings, scored on the Hungarian tables shows big changes from 1993. Reims drops from 1st to 10th and Madrid leaps up from 13th to 1st.

1. Madrid 42,413, 2. Edinburgh 41,957, 3. Dijon 41,788, 4. Jena 41.586, 5. Rhede 41,415, 6. Hechtel 41,342, 7. Padua 41,293, 8. Lisbon 41,144, 9. Cottbus 41,140, 10. Reims 41,090, 11. Lappeenranta 40,931, 12. Rovereto 40,887, 13. Granada 40,752, 14. Salamanca 40,716, 15. Tallinn 40,657, 16. Lublin 40,244, 17. Khania 40,038, 18. Moscow 39.730, 19. Kerkrade 39,559, 20. Tönsberg 39,424, 21. Århus 39,320, 22. Lapinlahti 39,167, 23. San Marino 39,125, 24. Zagreb 38,930, 25. Innsbruck 38,623, 26. Reykjavik 37,928.

Minimum age

THE IAAF Council determined during 1994 that athletes participating in the World Cross Country Championships, World Road Relay Championships, World Half Marathon Championships and World Marathon Cup should be at least 15 years of age.

Names

WE TRY to be consistent in our presentation of information in this Annual. One area where we encounter remarkable problems at times is over names.

Take for instance the Ethiopian world record holder for 5000m. When I first encountered him at the 1992 World Junior Championships he was entered as Haile Gsilase. On further investigation it appeared that the G was an abbreviation and could be expanded to Gebre. As presented by the Ethiopian team we settled on Haile Gebresilasie. In 1993 our African expert Yves Pinaud insisted that on information given to him the name should be Haile Guebre Selassie.

There was much debate on the name during 1994, at the end of which Bob Sparks, ATFS president, determined from Haile's agent, Jos Hermens, that the spelling should be Gebrselassie. So Gebre or Guebre or Gebr, one s or two in Selassie (or Silassie). There is no one right answer, much as statisticians might like there to be one. I shall settle for that given by Jos Hermens - and I do not want to change this again! Even so his name will be different in some sections of this Annual.

Other transliterations of African names which have caused problems include the 1993 and 1994 Boston Marathon winner. Cosmas or Cosmus Ndeti (or should it be N'deti?), and the 1994 New York women's winner Tecla Lorupe or Tegla Loroupe.

We have also agreed on Phillimon Hanneck (originally Harineki, and a variety of spellings for his first name). Again I want to try to standardise and if in determining one variation, just trust that this does not upset those who use others.

Of course if we are sure that an athlete wants to change - then we will. For example Rodion to Radion Gataullin.

ATHLETICS REFERENCE BOOKS 1994/5

Reviewed by Peter Matthews

Erfolge der deutschen Leichtathletik (Succesess in German Athletics). A5 174 pages, By Fritz Steinmetz and Dieter Huhn. All German finishers in the top eight of Olympic, World and European Championships are listed, with biographies of the top 50 stars and all the top eight from the World Championships 1983-93 and Europeans 1994. DM 29.80 from AGON-Sportverlag, Frankfurter Straße 92 A, 34121 Kassel, Germany.

Encyklopedia (Statystczna) Polskief Lekkiej Atletyki. 1919-1994. 310 pages, splendidly presented statistics covering the history of Polish athletics - placings in major championships, deep all-time lists, progressive records, Polish champions, indexes of athletes etc.. $25 from Tadeusz Wolejko, Sikorskiego 17, 62-020 Swardedz, Poland.

Helsinki '94 - Yleisurheilun EM-Kista. Text by a team of authors including ATFS member Matti Hannus (in Finnish), photographs by Mark Shearman. A4 208pp. A beautiful celebration of the European Championships, maintaining the outstanding quality of the series of books on major championships produced by the publishers, Juoksija, from whom the book can be bought at 285 Finnmarks plus postage - Box 50, 00441 Helsinki, Finland.

Kahden Kierroksen Tarina. A5 160 pages. By Matti Hannus. The history of the men's 800 metre running in Finland. The text is Finnish, but 32 pages of narrative the book is packed with statistics. Year lists, complete results of championship and international races, profiles etc. £10 in Europe, $20 overseas air mail from Matti Hannus, Ailakkitie 10 B 2, 90580 Oulu, Finland.

Moses Tanui - a Biography. A5 32p. Ottavio Castellini has produced an attractive profile of the Kenyan world champion who is now based in Italy, where he runs for the Fila Team of Brescia. $10 including postage from Ottavio at Via Giulia 171, 00186 Roma, Italy.

World all-time lists - men's 300m and 600m. Jean-Claude Patinaud is continuing his series of very deep world all-time lists. At the beginning of 1995 he added those for 300m and 600m. Details of these and other lists from him at 95 Cité Fort Creuse, Allée des Lauriers, Châteauneuf-la-Forêt, France

TAFWA All-Time Indoor List 1995 by Ed Gordon. A5 140pp. The annual compilation which includes deep all-time indoor lists of performers and performances for all events, men and women. From Ed Gordon, 180 Ardmore Road, Berkeley, CA 94707, USA.

ANNUALS

Annuals in varying sizes are produced for most major athletics nations. The following, containing year lists, records and in some cases results for the previous season, are amongst the most notable ones seen by this reviewer, and all give comprehensive details for their respective countries. Most should be obtainable from their national federations, whose addresses are given elsewhere. Some of those noted cover 1994, but at the time of writing most received cover 1993.

Annuario dell'Atletica 1993. A5 672p. Edited for FIDAL by Ottavio Castellini. The massive Italian annual was delayed at the printers last year, so that copies of this book, dealing with 1992 were not received until 1994. As usual there are detailed results, with annual and all-time lists, lists of previous champions, international athletes etc..

Asian athletics. A5 64 pages. DM 20 in Europe or US $15 for overseas airmail from the author, Heinrich Hubbeling, Haydnstrasse 8, 48691 Vreden, Germany. Top 30s for 1993 for athletes from Asian nations, together with continuation lists for countries other than China and Japan.

KNAU Atletiekstatistiek Aller Tijden. A5, 335 pages. Louis Weisscher and his team have produced deep Dutch all-times lists for seniors, junior age groups and veterans, with lists of all Dutch champions and leading performances at major international championships. From the KNAU, Postbus 567, 3430 An Nieuwegein, Netherlands - price 30 Dutch florins in Europe or Dfl. 35 airmail for cash (or Dfl. 45 and Dfl. 50 for cheques).

Suomen Yleisurheilu 1878-1899. A5 210 pages. The results of most diligent research is shown in this most impressive collection of results from a hundred years ago.

In addition to great detail on Finnish athletics, there are also world all-time lists rankings lists as at the end of 1899. FIM 90 in Europe or FIM 110 elsewhere (including postage) from the author, Risto Karasmaa, Otsonkallio 3 k 60, FIN 02110 Espoo, Finland.

Atletiekstatistiek Aller Tijden. 334pp, Dutch all-time lists for all events and age groups to the end of 1993 with lists of all Dutch champions and placings at major championships. From the KNAU, Postbus 567, 3430 An Nieuwegein, Netherlands. A5

Polskie lekkoatlecki na listach swiatowych 1929-1992. A5 93 pages. Janusz Wasko, Aleje Wyszynskiego 28/48, 22-400 Zamoso, Poland has produced a detailed analysis of Polish women's positions in world year lists.

L'Athlétisme Africain/African Athletics 1994 by Yves Pinaud with Walter Abmayr A5, 152p. The 13th edition of this definitive work. 100 deep men's and women's lists for Africa for 1993, with all-time lists, national championships and major meetings results. FF 92 from Editions Polymédias, 121 Avenue d'Italie, 75013 Paris, France.

Athlerama 93-94. The 32nd edition of the French Annual is edited by Yves Pinaud. A5, 428pp. As usual this splendid yearbook is packed with information on French athletics. 110 FF including postage from the Fédération Française d'Athlétisme, 10 rue du Faubourg Poissonnière, 75010 Paris. Maintaining the 60 years-ago series there are year lists for 1933.

Atletické Vykony 1993, the Czech Athletics Annual. 50 deep lists plus championships and international results. 30 DM or equivalent from Jirí Havlín, Pod skalkou 2737, 150 00 Praha, Czech Republic.

Atletismo '94. A5 192 pages the Argentina annual by Luis Vinker. From the Confederaciõn Argentina de Atletismo, 21 de Novembre 207, 3260 Concepción del Uruguay, Entre Rios, Argentina.

Athletics Australia Handbook of Records and Results 1993-94 A5 140p. Covering the Australian season to the end of April 1994, with lists records, results and ranking lists compiled by Paul Jenes.

British Athletics 1994 Compiled by the National Union of Track Statisticians, general editor Rob Whittingham. A5, 400p. Detailed results and statistics on 1993 for the UK, with 16 pages of colour photographs. £9.95 plus postage from Umbra Software Ltd, Unit 1, Bredbury Business Park, Bredbury Park Way, Stockport SK6 2SN, England.

1994 Canadian Athletics Annual 134pp. $15 plus $2 postage from its chief compiler Cecil Smith, 17 Drury Crescent, Brampton, Ontario, Canada L6T 1L1. Published by Athletics Magazine. 50-deep Canadian lists, records and results for 1993, as well as 25-deep all-time lists.

Caribbean Athletics Annual 1993 A5, 112pp. £10 or US $15 including postage from the compiler, Bernard Linley, Via Cassia 987, 00189 Roma, Italy. Results are given of major meetings and championships in the Caribbean in 1993, with 20-deep lists for 1993 and 35-deep all-time lists.

There is also a compilation of all medallists at the CAC Junior Championships 1974-92.

Laursen's Lille Lommebog 1994 by Erik Laursen. 90pp, includes Danish ranking lists for 1994 and all-time indoor lists. A6 size 30 Danish kroner, A5 size 40 D Kr plus postage 22 D Kr Europe or 36 kroner outside Europe from the author, Sandbakken 95, 8270 Høbjerg, Denmark. Giro 146 5333 or cash.

DAF 1993 i tal. A5 290pp. The Danish Annual. 95 Danish Kroner from the editor Erik Laursen, Sandbakken 95, 8270 Høbjerg, Denmark. Also available for the same price **Veteran Statistik 1993**, 330 pages of Danish veteran's statistics.

Deutsche Bestenliste 1993 A5 166 pp. 20 DM. Edited by Klaus Amrhein for the Deutschen Gesellschaft für Leichtathletik-Dokumentation e.V. Deep and detailed year lists for Germany for 1993. See DGLD details at the end of this review.

Deutsche Bestenliste 1994 A5 468 pp. price not given. Edited by Eberhard Vollmer. Basic lists for all age groups. DLV, Julius-Reiber-Strasse 19, 6100 Darmstadt, Germany.

DLV-Jahrbuch 1994/95. A5 354pp. Edited by Stefan Volknant & Eberhard Vollmer. 30 DM from Leichtathletik Fördergesellschaft mbH, Postfach 110463, 64219 Darmstadt, Germany. he official yearbook of the German Federation. Articles and review, with detailed results of 1994 meetings, records and top ten lists as well as illustrations, some in colour.

Eesti Kergejôustiku Aastraamat 1994. 142pp. Estonian ranking lists for 1993 are contained in this handbook published by the national federation: Eesti Kergejôustikuliit, Regati pst. 1, Tallinn EE0103.

El Atletismo Subamericano 1994. A5 128pp. By Luis Vinker for the IAAF regional delegation for South America. Results of major meetings in 1993 with 20 deep ranking lists.

Greek Athletics Annual. A5 314pp. From SEGAS. 50 deep year lists with best performances, also extensive biographical profiles of leading Greek athletes. In Greek characters.

Israeli Amateur Athletic Association 1994 Annual compiled by David Eiger and Arik Cooks. 28 pages. From David Eiger, 10 Ezra Hozsofer Str, Herzliya 46371, Israel. Records, championship results, 1994 top ten and all-time lists.

Japan Athletics Annual '94. A5 150pp. Compiled for the Japan AAF. 50 deep lists for senior and 20 deep for juniors for 1993 and all-time top 50s. Available from Yoshimasa Noguchi, Track & Field Magazine Sha Co, Ltd, 3-10-10 Misaki-cho, Chiyoda-ku, Tokyo 101, Japan.

KNAU Statistisch Jaarboek 1993, from the KNAU, Postbus 567, 3430 An Nieuwegein, Netherlands. A5, 272pp - price 45 Dutch florins (or Dfl. 35 if cash sent by registered letter). Edited by Louis Weisscher, it contains comprehensive ranking lists for 1993 for the Netherlands, all-time top tens, and an extensive chronology of the year plus championships and international match results and records.
The KNAU has also published a 52-page Junior Booklet and an 80-page booklet with indoor lists for 1993/4.

Latvijas Vieglatletikas Gadagramata '95. 176 pp. Most comprehensive coverage of Latvian athletics in 1994, lists and results, compiled by ATFS member Andris Stagis with Irma Jaunzeme. From the Latvia Track and Field Athletics Federation, Tërbatas iela 4, Riga LV-1723.

Norges Beste - Friidrettskalenderen 1994. A5 280pp. The Norwegian annual with deep national lists for 1993, Nordic top 20s, 30-deep Norwegian all-time lists and results of leading meetings. From Jo Nesse, Gjønnesskogen 2, 1340 Bekkestua, Norway.

Pacific Statistics. Issue no.9 (A5 size), including 1993 review and lists, is available for £2.50 (£3.50 for airmail outside Europe) from Tony Isaacs, 11 Manton Close, Trowbridge, Wilts BA14 0RZ, England.

Papua New Guinea Athletics - 1993 The Year in Review by Bob Snow. A5 98pp. From the author, Box 437, Rabaul, ENBP, Papua New Guinea. The seventh edition of this book contains 1993 and all-time lists for PNG athletes, with championships results.

SA Athletics 1994. A5, 216p. Surface mail £6 or $10 US, Air mail - Europe £7.50 or $12, USA and Far East $15 from SA Athletics Annual, Postbus 35209, Menlo Park, 0102 South Africa. The usual excellent assemblage of all-time lists, records, championship results and detailed 1993 lists for South Africa.

Schweizer Leichtathletik Jahrbuch 1994, the Swiss Athletics Annual, from the Swiss federation. A5 290pp. As usual most attractively produced with detailed championship results and comprehensive lists for all age groups for 1994, with records for all Swiss Cantons. A special feature details Swiss top tens and results for 1934, continuing the series in these annuals.

Scottish Athletics Yearbook 1994. A5 175p. Scottish lists compiled by Arnold Black, records and championship results for 1993. This and the 1995 edition (even bigger at 224 pages) available from Arnold Black, 19 Millrae Crescent, Glasgow, GL2 9UW Scotland. £4 including postage in the UK, £5 elsewhere.

Sverige Bästa 1993, edited by A.Lennart Julin. A5 288pp. 150 Swedish crowns including postage from Svenska Fri-Idrottsförbundet, Förlaget, Sofiatornet, Stadion, S-114 33, Stockholm, Sweden. As ever a model of precision, with deep 1993 lists for Sweden. Well illustrated including a colour cover of Erica Johansson.

FAST United States Track and Field Annual 1994, A5 480 pp. General editors Scott Davis, Dave Johnson and Howard Willman. 50 deep US year lists for 1993 and 60 plus deep US all-time lists, with 10-deep junior and collegiate lists. The extensive index of 265 pages includes all athletes ranked in the year lists, showing yearly progressions and championships records for each. From Scott Davis, 4432 Snowbird Circle, Cerritos, CA 90701, USA, $20 in USA, $28 overseas air mail, $22 sea mail.

Welsh Athletics Annual 1994 A5 232pp. Edited by Alan and Brenda Currie. Very comprehensive coverage of Welsh athletics, with lists, results and features. £7 including postage with cheques payable to 'Welsh Athletics Annual' from the Athletics Association of Wales, Morfa Stadium, Landore, Swansea SA1 7DF.

Yleisurheilu 1994. A5 640p. Once again the Finnish annual was the first to be produced and I received my copy, covering 1994, before the end of the year! There are very deep Finnish lists for all age groups - down to 9! - with an index of athletes and results of championships and international matches. It also contains indoor and outdoor world lists for 1994 - although these do suffer from the lack of information form the last part of the year or indeed from many countries from earlier. Edited by Jouko Nousiainen and Juhani Jalava for the Finnish Federation! From Juhani Jalava, Raaskinpolku 9 E 88, 20360 Turku, Finland - in Europe DM 40 or £13, Scandinavia SEK 120, rest of world DM 45 or £15, preferably in cash.

Who Is Who 1993 der Deutschen Leichtathletik. A5 288 p. The third edition of this most useful book by Klaus Amrhein, contains detailed biographical details for leading German athletes, together with championships and international match results for Germany in 1993 From the author at Lindenweg 3, 64846 Klein Zimmern, Germany for DM 30 (banknotes only).

L'Athlétisme Européen en Salle. A5 192pp. A European Indoor Handbook was produced in conjunction with the Championships at Paris (Bercy) in March 1994. Full results of previous championships, progressive European indoor records, 50 deep European indoor lists. 100 French francs from Polymédias, , 121 Avenue d'Italie, 75013 Paris, France.

IAAF Handbooks

From the IAAF, 17 rue Princesse Florestine, MC 98000, Monaco

IAAF Directory and Calendar 1995. Ring-bound, pocket-sized, compendium; 332 pages. The series of superb IAAF/ATFS Statistics Handbooks, edited by Mark Butler have continued in 1994 with those for:

5th IAAF World Junior Championships. A5 372pp. $15. Full results of previous World Juniors, medallists from Continental Junior Championships, continental and national junior records and junior all-time lists. Also complete results of IAAF World Series events earlier in 1994 - World CC and Road Relay.

7th IAAF World Cup in Athletics. A5 164pp. $15. Full results of previous World Cups, first three at IAAF World Series events and European Cups, world and continental records. top all-time top tens.

Statistical bulletins

The **DGLD - German** statistical group, the Deutschen Gessellschaft für Leichtathletik-Dokumentation, was founded in 1990. Its members produce annual national ranking lists for Germany and most impressive quarterly bulletins of up to 200 pages, packed with articles and statistical compilations. A major feature in each issue is detailed statistical profiles of athletes born in that quarter 70 years ago, 75, 80, 85, 90 etc. Membership normally costs DM 80 per year; details from Klaus Amrhein, Lindenweg 3, 64846 Klein Zimmern, Germany.

The **AEEA - Spanish** group the Asociacion Española de Estadisticos de Atletismo produce four bulletins each year packed with statistical items. Contact Manuel Villuendas, Sagusta 7, 28914 Leganes-Madrid, Spain.

Contents of 1994 issues:

No. 31 1/94. 188pp. Spanish merit rankings, leading athletes, top juniors 1993.

Performances by overseas athletes in Spain 1993.

No. 32 2/94. 246pp. Deep world performance lists for all events 1993.

No. 33 3/94. 278pp. Annual Spanish lists each year 1914-25, Spanish all-time lists as at end 1965. Current Spanish junior all-time lists.

No. 34 4/94. 202pp including World and Spanish Indoor Lists 1993/4, 60pp of the 1944 Spanish Annual and an index of previous bulletins.

The **NUTS - British** group publish **Track Stats** quarterly. Subscription £8 UK, £11 Europe, £14 USA and elsewhere from Bob Phillips, 15 Beech Hey Lane, Willaston, South Wirral, L64 1TS, England. Contents include articles, deep all-time lists, career profiles etc. - on British and world athletics. Publications in 1994 included a Track Stats Special - the third volume of the series:
Progressive British Records. Part 3 - Men's Track Events. A5 56pp. Full details of all men's track events from the earliest days of athletics to 1994. £5.
The previous volumes were:
Part 1 - Women's Records by Eric Cowe, John Brant and Peter Matthews. A5 64pp. 1992.
Part 2 -Men's Field Events by Ian Tempest and Peter Matthews. A5 32pp. 1993.
A final volume is planned - to include walks and an index of all men's record holders.

La Lettre de l'Athlétisme: For the most detailed French results and much else of interest to any statistician; edited by Yves Pinaud. Annual subscription (12 issues) 270 French Francs; payment by cheque drawn on a French bank or by international money order. La Lettre de l'Athlétisme, 121 Avenue d'Italie, 75013 Paris, France.

General

Idrottsboken 1994. 608 pp, A4. 788 Swedish kroner from Strömbergs/Brunnhages, Box 65, S-162 11 Vällingby, Sweden. The 50th edition of this magnificent book is as ever richly illustrated and packed with features and results for 1993 on more than 60 sports with special features for the half century of this publication. Coverage is international as well as Swedish. The editorial team headed by Ulf Pettersson includes ATFS member Ove Karlsson.

Magazines

Track Newsletter - 42 issues a year, including weekly mailings from March through September – deep results, with world or US performance lists each week, plus news briefs and other fast-breaking coverage. Annual subscription: $75 ($49 for USA, Mexico & Canada). Write c/o Track & Field News, 2570 El Camino Real # 606, Mountain View, CA 94040, USA.
Running Stats: the weekly chronicle of excellence in long distance running. Detailed coverage of the US and world scene; 44 issues a year. Annual airmail sub $80 (cheque drawn on US bank or International Postal Money Order) to Running Stats, 1085 14th, Suite 1260, Boulder, CO 80302, USA.
Leichtathletik. The weekly German athletics magazine, now in tabloid newspaper format, includes reports and detailed results of German and international results, background information, portraits, news and special pages about training and sports science. Subscription details from: Deutscher Sportverlag, Kurt Stoof GmbH & Co, Redaktion LEICHTATHLETIK, Eintrachtstrasse 110-118, 50668 Köln, Germany.

Second hand athletics books & magazines bought and sold. Free catalogue always available. No obligation booksearch service on any subject. For further details please ring any evening (01938 552023) or write to Len Lewis, 3 Aubet Drive, Guilsfield, Welshpool, Powys SY21 9LX, UK.

Books for review would be welcomed by the editor: Peter Matthews, 10 Madgeways Close, Great Amwell, Ware, Herts SG12 9RU, England.

My own books to be published in 1995:

Guinness Encyclopedia of Sports Records and Results - 4th edition by Peter Matthews. The authoritative reference source for the records, results and statistics of all important international sports and sports events. c. 432 pages. Price £14.99.
Guinness All-time Greats of British Sports by Peter Matthews and Ian Buchanan. Biographies for about 2000 of the top British and Irish sports men and women of all-time. 512 pages, price £12.99.
Still available:
Guinness International Who's Who in Sport by Peter Matthews with Ian Buchanan and Bill Mallon. Biographies for nearly 3000 of the top sports men and women of all-time (and leading horses and greyhounds). Athletics is very well represented with more than 450 entries. 730 pages, price £14.99.
These books can be obtained, postage extra (£1.50 per book), from Guinness Publishing, 33 London Road, Enfield, Middlesex EN2 6DJ, England.

WHERE HAVE ALL THE FLOWERS GONE?

by A. Lennart Julin

"THE STARS of the future" is a label regularly used to describe those teenagers being successful at the junior championships. To support that notion examples such as Javier Sotomayor, Heike Drechsler and Moses Kiptanui are given.

But is the case really proven? The truth is that we could easily find other examples among the superstars of today – Linford Christie, William Sigei and Marie-José Pérec – that lack championship success as juniors. And there is also ample supply of junior champions who never made it as seniors:

Do you even remember in which events the likes of Antje Avnann, Ţomasz Jedrusik, Diana Dietz and Reynaldo Quintero took world junior titles in 1988? Being around 25 years of age they ought to have been in their athletic prime now in 1994, instead they have more or less vanished out of sight.

There are really two questions to study in this context;

1) What have the junior stars of yesterday achieved as seniors?

2) What did the senior stars of today achieve as juniors?

A "complete" analysis would be a major scientific project but most likely a strategically made "probe" would give us a sufficiently representative idea about the situation.

I chose the 1989 European Juniors end the 1994 European Seniors for this purpose. The same geographical entity was concerned and the separation of five years would mean that the teenagers of Varazdin were in their mid-twenties for Helsinki. Therefore it was reasonable to assume that they should have established themselves in the senior ranks by now if they were ever going to.

In Table 1 you will find the individual medallists of the 1989 European Juniors. The names given in italics are those which competed also in the 1994 European Seniors. In parenthesis is listed what they achieved in Helsinki.

The list encompasses 35 events, i.e. there were 105 medals awarded. Those were distributed among 98 individual athletes. They could, based on their achievements in Helsinki, be divided into the following four groups (As the total number was almost exactly 100, the numbers given are also good approximations of the percentages.):

Medallists	Other Top-8	"Also ran"	Not competing
7	7	16	68

This shows more than two-thirds didn't even compete and only every 14th of the junior medallists managed to reach the medal

Diana Dietz: more or less vanished

podium as seniors. If one widens the scope by including all top-8 placers of 1989 only 61 of 280 started in Helsinki - thus 78% were lost! Among the "survivors" we found only two more senior medallists-to-be: Svetlana Doronina-Goncharenko (6th at 200m) and Rita Ináncsi (5th in Hep.).

Even sifting right through all the names of competitors in Varazdin only produces five more that would reach the rostrum in Helsinki: Matthias Rusterholz (semi), Steinar Hoen (12th), Jean Galfione (9th), Zhanna Tarnopolskaya (semi in 100m) and Melanie Paschke (semi).

If you study individual nations there are some other startling revelations: The UK and Italy had the medal figures 2-4-4 and 3-1-4 respectively in Varazdin, but only one each (Vincenzo Modica and Craig Winrow) of these ten and eight medallists started in Helsinki!

Now all these loss figures might seem quite alarming - or at least surprising - at first look. But are they really that unexpected?

TABLE 1: 1989 EUROPEAN JUNIOR MEDALLISTS

*- disqualified for doping or doping-related offence.

MEN

100m: 1) Aleksandr Shlychkov URS, 2) Marek Zalewski POL (heat), 3) *Jason Livingston GBR.
200m: 1) Marek Zalewski POL (100m heat), 2) Aleksandr Shlychkov URS, 3) Leif Jonsson SWE.
400m: 1) Wayne McDonald GBR, 2) Jan Lenzke CDR, 3) Dmitriy Golovastov URS (4th).
800m: 1) Craig Winrow GBR (6th), 2) Paul Burgess GBR, 3) Vaclav Hrich TCH
1500m; 1) Michael Kluwe FRG, 2) Marco Barbone ITA, 3) Morgan Tollofsén SWE
5000m: 1) Carsten Eich GDR (Mar 35th), 2) John Mayock GBR, 3) Jon Dennis GBR
10,000m: 1) Christian Leuprecht ITA, 2) Laurent Saudrais FRA, 3) Vincenzo Modica ITA (11th).
20 km Road; 1) Dirk Nürnberger GDR, 2) Dmitriy Solovyev URS, 3) Giacomo Leone ITA
3000mSt: 1) Angelo Giardiello ITA, 2) Spencer Duval GBR, 3) Kim Bauermeister FRG (9th).
110mh 1) Antti Haapakoski FIN (6th), 2) Sébastien Thibault FRA, 3) Dario Volturara ITA.
400mh: 1) Enzo Franciosi ITA, 2) Vyacheslav Orinchuk URS, 3) Radek Bartakovic TCH.
HJ: 1) Mats Kollbrink SWE, 2) Stevan Zoric YUG (11th), 3) Wolfgang Kreissig FRG (13th).
PV: 1) Maksim Tarasov URS, 2) Igor Zaitsev URS, 3) Olli-Pekka Mattila FIN.
LJ: 1) Peter Oldin WE. 2) Wayne Griffith GBR, 3) Rudi Van Lancker BEL
TJ: 1) Denis Kapustin URS (1st), 2) Sergey Bykov URS, 3) Mario Quintero ESP
SP: 1) Aleksandr Klimenko URS (1st), 2) Dirk Preuss GDR, 3) Matthew Simson GBR.
DT: 1) Andreas Seelig GDR (10th), 2) Ioan Oprea ROM, 3) Gennadiy Pronko URS
HT: 1) *Sergey Kirmasov URS, 2) Savvas Saritzoglou GRE, 3) Igor Fedorov URS
JT: 1) Vladimir Ovchinnikov URS, 2) Jarkko Kinnunen FIN, 3) Andrey Shevchuk (qual).
Dec: 1) Michael Kohnle FRG, 2) Norbert Lampe GDR, 3) David Bigham GBR.

WOMEN

100m: 1) Odiah Sidibé FRA (semi), 2) Zoya Taurin URS, 3) *Manuela Derr GDR
200m: 1) *Manuela Derr GDR, 2) Jana Schönenberger GDR, 3) Zoya Taurin URS
400m; 1) Anke Wöhlk GDR, 2) Elena Solcan ROM, 3) Julia Merino ESP.
800m: 1) Birthe Bruhns GDR, 2) Denisa Zavelca ROM, 3) Stella Jongmans HOL (semi).
1500m: 1) Snezana Pajkic YUG, 2) Anka Schäning GDR, 3) Olga Yegorova URS
3000m: 1) Olga Nazarkina URS, 2) Anke Schäning GDR, 3) Agate Balsamo ITA.
10,000m: 1) Olga Nazarkina URS, 2) Monica Cane POR, 3) Larisa Alekseyeva URS.
100mh: 1) Ilka Rönisch GDR, 2) Yulia Filippova-Graudyn URS (2nd), 3) Brigita Bukovec YUG (4th).
400mh: 1) Silvia Rieger FRG (2nd), 2) Anna Chuprina-Knoroz URS (3rd), 3) Heike Meissner GDR (4th).
HJ: 1) Yelena Yelesina URS, 2) Svetlana Lavrova URS, 3) Sarka Kaspárkova TCH (TJ 6th).
LJ: 1) Mirela Belu ROM, 2) Erica Johansson SWE (qual), 3) Lyudmila Galkiná URS (qual).
SP: 1) Astrid Kumbernuss GDR (2nd), 2) Gabi Völkl FRG, 3) Renata Bruková TCH
DT: 1) Astrid Kumbernuss GDR (SP 2nd), 2) Jana Lauren GDR (6th), 3) Jacqueline Goormachtigh HOL (qual)
JT: 1) Karen Forkel GDR (2nd), 2) Brita Heydrich GDR, 3) Nathalie Teppe FRA (9th).
Hep: 1) Tatyana Blokhina URS, 2) Beatrice Mau-Repnak (dnf), 3) Marcela Podracka TCH (11th).

TABLE 2: 1994 EUROPEAN CHAMPIONS MERITS AS JUNIORS

MEN

100m	Linford Christie	-
200m	Geir Moen	-
400mh:	Du'aine Ladejo	WJ90-7
800m	Andrea Benvenuti	WJ88-semi
1500m	Fermin Cacho	EJ87-12, WJ88-3
5000m	Dieter Baumann	-
10,000m	Abel Antón	EJ8l-5 (5OOOm)
Mar	Martin Fiz	WJCC82-16
3000mSt	A. Lambruschini	EJ83-4 (2000m St)
110mh	Colin Jackson	EJ85-2, WJ86-1
400mh:	Oleg Tverdokhleb	-
HJ	Steiner Hoen	EJ89-12, WJ9O-11
F;'	Radian Gataullin	EJ83-1
U	Ivaylo Mladenov	EJ91-5, WJ92-3
TJ	Denis Kapustin	EJ89-1
S?	Aleks. Klimenko	WJ88-1, EJ89-1
DV	Vlad. Dubrovshchik	EJ91-1
	Vasiliy Sidorenko	-
JT	Steve Backley	EJ87-1, WJ88-2
Dec	Alain Blondel	-

WOMEN

100m:	Irina Privalova	EJ85-heat, WJ86-semi
200m	Irina Privalova	see above
400m:	Marie-José Pérec	-
800m	Lyubov Gurina	-
1500m	Lyudmila Rogachova	
3000m	Sonia O'Sullivan	WJ88-heat
10,000m	Fernanda Ribeiro	EJ83-11, EJ85-4, WJ86-4, EJ87-1, WJ88-2 (all at 3000m)
Mar	Manuela Machado	-
100mh	Svetla Dimitrova	WJ88-1, WJ88-1 (both in Hep)
400mh:	Sally Gunnell	EJ83-semi/13 (100mh/Hep)
HJ	Britta Bilac	-
U	Heike Drechsler	EJ81-1
TJ	Anna Biryukova	-
SP	Viktoria Pavlysh	EJ87-6
	Ilke Wyludda	EJ85-1, WJ86-1, EJ87-1, WJ88-1
JT	Trine Hattestad	EJ81-5, EJ83-2
Hep	Sabine Braun	EJ83-2

First we must take into account that junior success basically means that you are among the very best in your year class, while the senior meets are open to the "créme de la créme" of 10-15 year classes.

Just remember how Al Oerter monopolised the major discus titles (only Olympics then) for almost two decades, or how Sergey Bubka has personified the pole vault ever since 19831

Therefore there will always be many more athletes getting medals as juniors than as seniors. This is therefore not synonymous with the juniors "failing" but just a recognition of the different premisses in age group competition vs open.

Secondly we all know that junior success quite often is the consequence of early physical maturity and/or doing "senior training" in the youth years. In both cases such athletes have already exhausted most of their potential while the talented "slow-starters" have more room left for improvement.

Thirdly, injuries! In a sport like athletics the stress and strain involved in propelling your body or an implement with maximum speed and force must be expected to take a sizeable toll of the talents.

Therefore the more revealing study to do concerns the second question listed above. In Table 2 the 36 winners of Helsinki are listed together with their previous achievements in World and European Junior Championships.

As you can see 24 out of the 36 (i.e. no less than two-thirds) had junior championship "experience". Fourteen of them (almost 40 %) can even claim junior medals!

These figures are in fact quite impressive if you take into consideration: that some left the junior ranks where there still was only one meet (the Europeans) every other year (World Juniors were introduced in 1986) that some come from "big powers" where you could have been an excellent junior but still unable to qualify for any of the only two spots available on the team, that untimely injuries quite easily could have deprived them of their often only chance to start at an international junior championship.

So based on this "mini study" the conclusion could be put something like this: The senior superstars were good – but not necessarily the best – as juniors. The majority of the junior superstars will, for a number of varying reasons, not reach the very top as seniors.

When will we ever learn?

A FEW STEPS FROM PARITY

by Mike Sheridan

"IN YOUR February issue Erik von Frenckell makes the following statement: 'We will therefore suggest that the 50km walk and certain events for women which, in the opinion of physicians, are dangerous, be omitted from the (Olympic) programme

"How much longer is this excuse going to be used when organisations wish to cut out women's events? Who are these physicians and where are the women who have suffered from any form of athletics? Do these people consider people like Mrs Fanny Blankers-Koen and myself as freaks? If this is so, I can give them ample proof in my own club (Mitcham AC) that we are not. Our members have competed in every type of athletics from track and field to cross-country and walking."

Thus wrote a determined Dorothy Tyler (Odam), twice a silver medallist in the Olympic high jump, to the leading British sports journal World Sports in March 1949. Nearly half a century has passed since Tyler put pen to paper on this subject. Much progress towards women's parity with men in athletics has been accomplished since 1949 but it has been a long struggle. On 12 August 1995 in Göteborg another landmark for the distaff athletes will be reached when the finalists in the first women's 5000m World Championship line up to contest the title. Following this in 1996, women will compete for the pole vault title at the European Indoor Championships; the 1997 World Championships in Mexico City introduces a women's hammer competition. Still awaited by Mrs Tyler's fin-de-siecle equivalents are a major championship steeple-chase event and a long walk to match the men's event.

The leading women distance runners have been experimenting with the 12 1/2 laps race since the late 1960's but not until 1981 did the IAAF recognise the event for world record purposes. The pace of improvement in the race has inevitably quickened since then but, interestingly, not dramatically. The world record of 14:37.33 was set nine years ago in 1986. An analysis of the top 100 performances at the event (as at 31 December 1994) reveals that the previous year, 1985, provides the largest contribution to these performances with 14. Next equal on 12 are 1993 and 1994, followed by 1985, 1991 and 1992 with 11 each. The most ancient of the top 100 times dates back to 1978 although this was achieved in a mixed race.

Looking at the top 100 performers, the leading country is the USA with 15 runners. 'Uncle Sam' is followed by Russia with 13 (but two of these could, in the aftermath of the break-up of the Soviet Union, be considered Ukranian). Africa features with Kenya's 8 contributors, the United Kingdom has 7, followed by united Germany's 6. At the date of this survey the feared Chinese occupied only four places of the 100.

While we do not know which of the above athletes who are still active will opt to run the 5000m at Göteborg, it is clear that the range of abilities are such that the possible medallists could emerge from either or both of the specialists at the 1500/3000 end of the range or, equally feasibly, the 10,000 exponents. Likewise, potentially outstanding at this new event could be athletes whose 5000 times are still modest.

A subjective list of these could include: Sally Barsosio KEN (8:53.40, 15:42.45, 31:15.38); Angela Chalmers CAN) (4:01.61, 8:32.17, 15:34.57); Yvonne Murray GBR (4:01.20, 8:29.02, 15:50.54, 31:56.97); Qu Yunxia CHN (3:50.46, 8:12.18, 15:28.91); Derartu Tulu ETH (4:12.08, 8:54.74, 15:21.29 ,31:06.02); Wang Xiuting CHN (8:50.68, 15:23.58, 31:27.0).

Then, if cross-country form can be taken as a guide and can be translated to track excellence, Barsosio's compatriot, Rose Cheruiyot could feature.

Historians will not hesitate to remind us that the men's 5000 was first contested at Olympic level in 1912. The winner was Finland's Hannes Kolehmainen in a time of 14:36.6 (being 24.6 seconds faster than the previous fastest recorded for the event). Remember that 14:37.33 women's world record has stood for nine years ?

The 100 best ever times are shared by forty-five athletes. The table below shows their bests over distances from 1500 metres to 10000 metres and the span of years in which the performances were achieved:

ATHLETE	1500	3000	5000	10,000	
Natalya Artyomova	3:59.16	8:31.67	14:54.08	31:56.33	RUS 1985 - 1991
Anne Audain	4:10.68	8:45.53	15:13.22	31:53.31	NZL 1976 - 1986
Irina Bondarchuk	8:42.84	15:12.62	33:10.7		RUS 1982 - 1984
Olga Bondarenko	4:05.99	8:33.99	14:55.76	30:57.21	RUS 1985 - 1986
Lyudmila Borisova	4:03.66	8:40.78	15:13.27		RUS 1992 - 1994
Cathy Branta-Easker	4:11.72	8:49.64	15:07.56		USA 1984 - 1985
Cindy Bremser	4:04.09	8:38.60	15:11.78		USA 1984 - 1986
Aurora Cunha	4:09.31	8:46.37	15:06.96	31:29.41	POR 1983 - 1986
Nadia Dandolo	4:20.20i	8:44.36	15:11.64	32:02.37	ITA 1983 - 1991
Albertina Dias	4:09.60	8:43.08	15:05.12	31:33.03	POR 1991 - 1993
Viorica Ghican	4:02.76	8:42.39	15:09.90	31:18.18	ROM 1988 - 1990
Yvonne Graham	4:02.69	8:45.87	15:13.67		JAM 1990 - 1995
Svetlana Guskova	3:57.05	8:42.04	15:02.12	31:42.43	MOL 1982 - 1986
Jill Hunter	4:17.28	8:47.36	15:09.98	31:07.88	GBR 1987 - 1992
Lynn Jennings	4:06.4	8:40.45i	15:07.92	31:19.89	USA 1990 - 1992
Esther Kiplagat	4:09.30	8:43.76	15:07.87	32:50.25	KEN 1984 - 1993
Ingrid Kristiansen	4:05.97	8:34.10	14:37.33	30:13.74	NOR - 1986
Tecla Lorupe	9:14.94	15:08.03	31:21.20		KEN 1992 - 1993
Liz McColgan	4:01.38	8:34.80i	15:01.08	30:57.07	GBR 1987 - 1991
Catherina McKiernan	4:21.30	8:51.33	15:09.10	31:19.11	IRL 1990 - 1994
Elana Meyer	4:02.15	8:32.00	14:44.15	30:52.51	RSA 1991 - 1994
Daria Nauer	4:16.56	8:54.53	15:13.93	31:35.96	SUI 1993 - 1994
Lynn Nelson	8:54.91	15:12.7	31:51.27		USA 1987 - 1988
Jane Ngotho	4:13.72	8:44.14	15:05.91	32:08.54	KEN 1991 - 1993
Loa Olafsson	4:10.7	8:42.3	15:08.8mx	31:45.4mx	DEN - 1978
Sonia O'Sullivan	3:59.10	8:21.64	14:45.92		IRL 1993 - 1994
Annette Peters	4:08.87	8:41.97	14:56.07	32:15.8	USA 1991 - 1994
Zola Pieterse	3:59.96	8:28.83	14:48.07		RSA - 1985
Uta Pippig	4:11:39i	8:40.99	15:04.87	31:21.36	GER 1991 - 1993
PattiSue Plumer	4:03.42	8:40.98	15:00.00		USA 1989 - 1992
Maricica Puica	3:57.22	8:27.83	15:06.04	33:32.97	ROM 1984 - 1987
Fernanda Ribeiro	4:10.30i	8:42.13	15:06.91	31:04.25	POR - 1994
Yelena Romanova	4:00.91	8:30.45	14:59.70	31:46.83	RUS 1988 - 1992
Susan Sirma	4:04.94	8:39.41	15:03.52	32:19.11	KEN 1990 - 1991
Mary Slaney	3:57.12	8:25.83	15:06.53	31:35.3	USA 1982 - 1985
Shelly Steely	4:05:07	8:41.28	15:08.67	32:41.14	USA 1990 - 1992
Angela Tooby	4:14.3	8:47.59	15:13.22	31:55.30	GBR 1985 - 1988
Christine Toonstra	4:10.00	8:45.96	15:07.68	31:43.55	HOL 1989 - 1992
Svetlana Ulmasova	3:58.76	8:26.78	15:05.50	32:14.83	UZB 1982 - 1986
Grete Waitz	4:00.55	8:31.75	15:08.80		NOR 1978 - 1982
Wang Junxia	3:51.92	8:06.11	15:05.8e	29:31.78	CHN - 1993
Kathrin Wessel	4:06.91i	8:41.79i	14:58.71	31:03 62	GER 1988 - 1991
Lynn Williams	4:00.27	8:37.30	15:01.30		CAN 1985 - 1989
Alison Wyeth	4:03.17	8:38.42	15:10.38		GBR 1993 - 1994
Zhong Huandi		8:41.67	15:05.69	30:13.37	CHN - 1993

AN ANSWER TO STATOPHOBIA

By Mark Butler

I UNDERSTAND how people can be alienated by the lists, scoring tables, evaluations and measurements which accompany athletics in greater amounts than any other sport. They may not care even who is second, let alone third. Worse, they may tend to devalue the importance of statistics and even to ridicule the role of a statistician. It is as if the "statophobes" feel there must be something wrong with those who follow statistics ... until they need to know a "stat" themselves.

Those who decide to overlook athletics statistics are missing out on a great deal if they wish to follow the sport. I am lucky enough to earn money for supplying statistical data, but even if it were not my business I would not wish to attend a track and field meeting without doing some sort of advance preparation. My own personal highlight of the 1988 Olympic Games was not the world record breaking performances of Griffith Joyner or the duels between DeLoach and Lewis or Barnes and Timmermann. It was the breakthrough of a British woman who set two national records and came within a few strides of a medal in the 400m hurdles – Sally Gunnell. If I had not done my homework, I would have been unable to appreciate her wonderfully unexpected achievement.

The more you know, the more you can enjoy. When Saïd Aouita lowered the world 5000m record to 12:58.39 in 1987, most knew that this was the first time 13 minutes had been bettered. A little more research would have yielded the fact that it had been 45 years since the first sub-14 run. We could then savour something which happens only once in a generation.

I am not saying that the only way to appreciate athletics is to carry with you an ATFS Annual or a year's supply of "Athletics International." You need no prior knowledge to relish the sight of Noureddine Morceli on the last lap opening up a yawning gap over world-class opposition, or Javier Sotomayor clearing a crossbar with inches to spare. Indeed, no statistics could adequately convey such magical moments.

In any case, statistics are not just figures. The term can apply to all sorts of data relating to athletes, including "human interest" information, for which there is a great thirst among the world's track and field media. Unfortunately, these are among the most difficult of "stats" to obtain. Many world class athletes need to devote most of their time to their sport. Would that more were like Mike Conley, who not only has a long string of major honours at long and triple jump, but is also an accomplished martial arts exponent and breeds both rottweilers and ostriches at his ranch in Arkansas!

The best statistics can be the most difficult to compile, such as win-loss records or win streaks. But should one include preliminaries? Personally I feel that Ed Moses' 122 race wins sounds better than 107 wins in finals. However, applying the principle to field event qualifying rounds would mean that Carl Lewis never had a 10-year win streak at the long jump.

Without statistics, what chance would we have in determining the relative merit of performances across time? Of course, we will never know how fast Nurmi, Zátopek or Hayes would have run with the advantages athletes have today. But the all-time and progressive records lists can at least tell us how far ahead of their time were Owens' 8.13 long jump (1935) or the late Wilma Rudolph's 11.18w 100m (1960).

Statistics are all-important to meeting organisers, for whom a world record performance can be the most powerful promotion. Which top athlete would not want to sprint in Zürich, run middle distance in Oslo or Rieti, or throw the javelin in Sheffield? The IAAF/Mobil Grand Prix Commission refer closely to the evaluation scores based on the best six events at each meeting.

The IAAF, keen to show the quality of their world championships, can point to the large number of personal bests, national and area records which regularly fall in these meetings. At both the Tokyo and Stuttgart World Championships, records were identified on the scoreboard immediately thanks to a team of statisticians who compiled and loaded all existing records into a database in advance.

As facts and figures play an increasingly purposeful role in athletics, so the role of a statistician gets more demanding. There are more meetings, more events, more competitors and more sophisticated technology available to measure their achievements. It is made all the more exciting, meaningful and fun thanks to statistics.

NATIONAL CHAMPIONS 1994 AND BIOGRAPHIES OF LEADING ATHLETES

By Peter Matthews

THIS SECTION incorporates biographies of 666 of the world's top athletes, 384 men and 282 women, listed by nation, with national champions at standard events in 1994 for the leading countries prominent in athletics.

The selection of athletes profiled has as ever changed considerably from last year's Annual, not only that all entries have been updated, but also that 126 newcomers (73 men and 53 women) have been introduced, with 25 others (12 men and 13 women) reinstated from previous Annuals, to replace those who have retired or faded a little from the spotlight.

The choice of who to include is always invidous, but I have concentrated on those who are currently in the world's top 10-12 per event, those who have the best championship records and those who I consider may make notable impact during the coming year.

Since this section was introduced in the 1985 Annual, biographies have been given for a total of 1919 athletes (1144 men and 775 women). There are now just 30 athletes (18 men, 12 women) who have been featured in all eleven editions of this Annual 1985-95. These are:

Men: Jaime Jefferson, Javier Sotomayor, Jüri Tamm, Jürgen Schult, Ronald Weigel, Julius Kariuki, Saïd Aouita, Radion Gataullin, Igor Nikulin, Yuriy Sedykh, Pavel Blazek, Patrik Sjöberg, Sergey Bubka, Mike Conley, Johnny Gray, Roger Kingdom, Carl Lewis, Jim Spivey.

Women: Lisa Ondeiki, Stefka Kostadinova, Silvia Costa, Katrin Dörre, Heike Drechsler, Helga Radtke, Merlene Ottey, Trine Hattestad, Galina Chistyakova, Lyubov Gurina, Margarita Ponomaryeva, Jackie Joyner-Kersee

Once again no doubt some of those dropped from this compilation will also again make their presence felt; the keen reader can look up their credentials in previous Annuals, and, of course, basic details may be in the athletes' index at the end of this book.

The biographical information includes:

a) Name; date and place of birth; height (in metres); weight (in kilograms).
b) Previous name(s) for married women; club or university; occupation.
c) Major championships record - all placings in such events as the Olympic Games, World Championships, European Championships, Commonwealth Games, World Cup and European Cup Final; leading placings in the World Indoor Championships, European or World Junior Championships, and other Continental Championships; and first three in European Indoors or World University Games.
d) National titles won or successes in other major events.
e) Records set: world, continental and national; indoor world bests (WIB).
f) Progression of best marks over the years at major event(s).
g) Personal best performances at other events.
h) Other comments.

See Introduction to this Annual for lists of abbreviations used for events and championships. Note that for comparison purposes decathlons and heptathlons made before the introduction of the current tables have been rescored using the 1984 IAAF Tables, except those marked *, for which event breakdowns were unavailable. Women's pentathlons (p) have not been rescored.

I am most grateful to various ATFS members who have helped check these details. Additional information or corrections would be welcomed for next year's Annual.

Peter Matthews

ALGERIA

Governing body: Fédération Algerienne d'Athlétisme, BP 88, El Biar, Alger. Founded 1963. **National Champions 1994**: **Men:** 100m/200m: Amar Hacini 10.4/21.1, 400m: Sadek Boumendil 46.4, 800m: Ryad Gatt 1:48.7, 1500m: Abdelhamid Slimani 3:44.2, 5000m/3000mSt: Mohamed Belabbès 13:55.7/8:37.2, 10000m: Azzeddine Sakhri 28:39.4, 110mh: Noureddine Tadjine 14.2, 400mh: Amine Harchouche 52.4, HJ: Othmane Belfaa 2.16, PV: Rafik Mefti 4.65, LJ/TJ: Lotfi Khaida 7.70/16.59, SP: Tahar Chachoua 14.65, DT: Yacine Louall 48.74, HT: Hakim Toumi 70.72, JT: Ryad Guellati 60.40, 10000mW: Younès Aouanouk 46:47.0. **Women**: 100m: Saliha Hamadi 11.7, 200m/400m: Nouria Mérah 24.3/55.6, 800m/1500m: Anissa Khali 2:13.8/4:32.5, 5000m/10000m: Nasria Baghdad 17:07.2/35:55.1, 100mh/SP/JT: Yasmina Azzizi 13.7/14.20/46.38, 400mh: Amel Baraket 61.8, HJ/LJ: Nacèra Zaaboub 1.66/5.97, TJ: Naïma Baraket 12.25, DT: Malika Hammou 36.66, HT: Samia Dahmani 36.30, 5000mW: Dounia Kara 24:14.7.

Noureddine MORCELI b.28 Feb 1970 Ténès 1.72m 62kg. Student, Riverside CC, USA 1989-90.
At 1500m: OG: '92- 7; WCh: '91- 1, '93- 1; WJ: '88- 2; WI: '91- 1; WCp: '94- 1; AfCh: '89- 4. Algerian champion 1989, GWG 1M 1994. Won overall GP 1994, 1500m 1990 (2nd overall), 1994. 9th World Jnr CC 1988.
World records 1500m 1992, mile 1993, 3000m 1994. WIR 1500m 3:34.16 '91. Algerian records 1990-3: 1500m (6), 1M (5), 3000m (2), 800m, 1000m, and 5000m. African indoor 1M records 3:53.50 and 3:50.81 '91.
Progression at 1500m, 1 mile, 5000m: 1986- 3:50.7, 1987- 3:53.1, 1988- 3:40.41, 1989- 3:37.87, 3:59.79, 13:56.3; 1990- 3:32.60, 3:53.06, 13:25.20; 1991- 3:31.00, 3:49.12; 1992- 3:28.86, 3:49.79; 1993- 3:29.20, 3:44.39; 1994- 3:30.61, 3:48.67, 13:03.85. pbs: 800m 1:44.79 '91, 1000m: 2:13.73 '93, 2000m 5:01.3 '94, 3000m 7:25.11 '94.
Unbeaten in 15 1500m/1M races in 1991, but lost four in 1992 including a poor run at the Olympics prior to getting the world record. Unbeaten again at 1500m/1M in 1993 and 1994. Coached by elder brother Abderahmane, 1500m: 3 WUG, 4 WCp and pb 3:36.26 in 1977.

Women

Hassiba BOULMERKA b.10 Jul 1968 Constantine 1.65m 57kg. CM Belcourt.
At (800m)/1500m: OG: '88- h/h; '92- 1; WCh: '91- 1, '93- 3; WCp: '94- 1; AfCh: '88- 1/1, '89- 1/1; WJ: '86- sf/h. At 800m: WCp: '89- 7; AfG: '87- 4. Won Algerian 800m 1987-9, 1500m 1987-90, Arab 800m 1987, 1989; 1500m 1992. GP: 3rd 1M 1991, 2nd 1500m 1994.

Hassiba Boulmerka

African records: 1500m (4), 1M (3) 1990-2; Algerian records at 800m & 1500m 1988-92, 3000m 1993.
Progression at 800m, 1500m: 1984- 2:25.4, 4:55.9; 1985- 2:18.6, 4:53.3; 1986- 2:06.86, 4:26.96; 1987- 2:04.33, 4:23.96; 1988- 2:02.09, 4:08.33; 1989- 2:00.21, 4:13.85; 1990- 2:00.44, 4:05.02; 1991- 1:58.72, 4:00.00; 1992- 2:01.51, 3:55.30; 1993- 4:04.29, 1994- 2:00.61, 4:01.05. pbs: 400m 56.7 '90, 1M 4:20.79 '91, 3000m 8:56.16 '93.
In 1991 she became the first African woman to win a world title and in 1992 the first athlete to win an Olympic gold medal for Algeria, with the fastest 1500m by a woman for four years.

ARGENTINA

Governing body: Confederación Argentina de Atletismo, 21 de Septiembre no. 207, 3260 Concepción del Uruguay, Entre Rios.
National Championships first held in 1920 (men), 1939 (women). **1994 Champions: Men**: 100m/200m: Carlos Gats 10.25/21.37, 400m: Guillermo Cacián 47.42, 800m: Carlos López 1:52.28, 1500m: Leonardo Malgor 3:55.07, 5000m:

Daniel Castro 14:16.5, 10000m: Antonio Silio 30:35.20, 3000mSt: Antonio Solis 8:58.1, 110mh: Oscar Ratto 14.34, 400mh: Gabriel Corradini 52.92, HJ: Erasmo Jara 2.05, PV: Oscar Veit 5.27, LJ: Néstor Madrid 7.25, TJ: Juan C Chávez 14.86, SP: Adrián Marzo 16.53, DT: Marcelo Pugliese 54.88, HT: Andrés Charadia 74.66, JT: Mauricio Silva 65.58, Dec: Diego Kerwitz 6329, 20kmW: José Aguilera 1:35:51. **Women**: 100m/200m: Danielle Lebreo 11.91/24.94, 400m: Ana Comaschi 55.44, 800m: Marta Orellana 2:06.9, 1500m: Mirian Rios 4:24.60, 5000m: Maria I Rodriguez 17:15.2, 10000m: Elisa Cobanea 34:24.7, 100mh: Veronica de Paoli 14.00, 400mh: Sandra Izquierdo 59.24, HJ: Mariela Andrade 1.74, PV: Mónica Falcioni 2.90, LJ/TJ: Andrea Avila 6.47/ 13.43, SP: Ana Carolina Vera 13.83, DT: Liliana Martinelli 52.62, HT: Zulma Lambert 51.40, JT: Silvina Medici 45.40, 10000mW: Lidia Carriego 51:53.3.

AUSTRALIA

Governing body: Athletics Australia, 21 O'Shanassy St, N.Melbourne, Victoria 3051. Founded 1897.

National Championships first held in 1893 (men) (Australasian until 1927), 1930 (women).

1994 Champions: **Men**: 100m: Damien Marsh 10.39, 200m: Stephen Brimacombe 20.84, 400m: Brett Callaghan 46.17, 800m: Brendan Hanigan 1:47.70, 1500m: Simon Doyle 3:40.22, 5000m: Julian Paynter 13:38.99, 10,000m: Jamie Harrison 29:30.84, Half Mar: Rod Higgins 64:22, Mar: Colin Dalton 2:16:17, 3000mSt: Shaun Creighton 8:41.49, 110mh: Kyle Vander-Kuyp 13.60, 400mh: Nick Ward 49.49, HJ: Tim Forsyth 2.33, PV: James Miler & Scott Huffman USA 5.45, LJ: Jai Taurima 8.00w, TJ: Andrew Murphy 16.76w, SP: John Minns 18.30, DT: Werner Reiterer 59.14, HT: Sean Carlin 74.72, JT: Andrew Currey 78.96, Dec: Dean Smith 7858, 5000mW: Nick A'Hern 19:11.99, 30kmW: Nick A'Hern 2:12:23, 50kmW: Michael Harvey 4:08:48. **Women**: 100m: Gwen Torrence USA 11.46, 200m: Cathy Freeman 22.75, 400m: Renee Poetschka 50.19, 800m: Sandra Dawson 2:02.93, 1500m: Margaret Leaney 4:12.7, 3000m: Elizabeth Miller 9:12.11, 10,000m: Susan Hobson 32:38.74, Half Mar: Heather Turland 74:58, Mar: Joanne Cowan 2:45:35, 100mh/Hep: Jane Flemming 13.61/6010, 400mh: Lauren Poetschka 56.06, HJ: Alison Inverarity 1.91, LJ: Nicole Boegman 6.48w, TJ: Yoko Morioka JPN 13.29w, SP/DT: Daniela Costian 16.08/65.38, HT: Debbie Sosimenko 60.84, JT: Joanna Stone 62.40, 5000mW: Kerry Junna-Saxby 20:45.03, 20kmW: Anne Manning 1:35:27.

Dean Capobianco

Dean CAPOBIANCO b.11 May 1970 1.82m 77kg. Curtin University.
At 200m: OG: '92- qf; WCh: '91- qf, '93- 5; WJ: '88- sf/2 4x400mR. Won AUS 100m 1991, 1993, 200m 1991-2.
Progression at 200m: 1987- 21.5, 1988- 21.46/ 21.0w, 1989- 21.28/20.6w, 1990- 20.60, 1991- 20.39, 1992- 20.57/20.53w, 1993- 20.18, 1994- 20.85. pbs: 100y 9.2 '93, 100m 10.25/10.17w/9.9w '93, 400m 45.47 '94, 110mh 14.15 '89, HJ 2.10 '88, LJ 7.21 '88.
Australian junior 110m hurdles record 1989. Missed most of 1994 season through a bursa on the ankle.

Sean CARLIN b.29 Nov 1967 Adelaide 1.98m 110kg. Salisbury. Teacher.
At HT: OG: '92- 8; WCh: '91- 9, CG: '90- 1, '94- 1; WJ: '86- 7. Australian champion 1987-8, 1990- 94, won AAA 1991.
Three Australian hammer records 1989-94, Commonwealth record 1994.
Progression at HT: 1984- 50.70, 1985- 66.10, 1986- 68.98, 1987- 70.36, 1988- 74.46, 1989- 76.32, 1990- 75.66, 1991- 74.90, 1992- 77.12, 1993- 75.36, 1994- 77.58. pbs: SP 15.57 '89, DT 52.42 '94.

Shaun CREIGHTON b.14 May 1967 1.80m 65kg. Ballarat H. Sport and recreation officer.
At 3000mSt: WCh: '91- h, '93- 9; CG: '90- 5; WUG: '91- 1; WCp: '92- 3. Won AUS 3000mSt 1991-4.
Australian records: 3000m steeplechase (2) 1992-3, 3000m 1994.

Progression at 3000mSt: 1988- 9:04.8, 1989- 8:39.8, 1990- 8:33.59, 1991- 8:27.20, 1992- 8:20.37, 1993- 8:16.22, 1994- 8:30.56. pbs: 1000m 2:23.1 '90, 1500m 3:38.59 '93, 1M 3:59.8 '90, 2000m 5:03.00 '92, 3000m 7:43.99 '94, 5000m 13:37.61 '91, 10000m 28:02.13 '94, 2000mSt 5:30.7 '92.
Broke Kerry O'Brien's 22 year-old Australian steeplechase record in December 1992.

Simon DOYLE b.9 Nov 1966 Queensland 1.84m 73kg. Degree in agriculture from University of Queensland.
At 1500m: WCh: '91- 12, '93- 9; CG: '90- 4 (8 800m), '94- sf. At 800m: WCp: '89- 5. Won AUS 800m 1989, 1991; 1500m 1991, 1993-4; 5000m 1990.
Australian records 1500m (2), 1M (2) 1991; 2000m 1992.
Progression at 1500m: 1987- 3:44.3, 1988- 3:41.6, 1989- 3:38.32, 1990- 3:34.27, 1991- 3:31.96, 1993- 3:33.39, 1994- 3:36.21. pbs: 400m 48.1 '91, 800m 1:45.38 '91, 1000m 2:18.22 '89, 1M 3:49.91 '91, 2000m 5:00.84 '92, 3000m 7:44.65 '94, 5000m 13:28.71 '92.
Made a great impression in 1990 with wins at 1500m in three Grand Prix meetings. Ill at 1991 World Championships and injured 1992.

Tim FORSYTH b.17 Aug 1973 1.99m 79kg. Glenhuntly.
At HJ: OG: '92- 3=; WCh: '91- dnq 21, '93- 9; CG: '94- 1; WI: '91- 8=; WJ: '90- 2; WCp: '94- 2. Won AUS HJ 1991-4.
Eight Australian high jump records 1990-3.
Progression at HJ: 1989- 2.16, 1990- 2.29, 1991- 2.31, 1992- 2.34, 1993- 2.35, 1994- 2.33.

Damien MARSH b.28 Mar 1971 1.88m 81kg. Southern Suburbs.
At 200m/4x100mR: WCh: '93- 8; CG: '94- 4/2R (sf 100m); WCp: '94- 6=;WI: '93- 2. At 100m: WJ: '90- 6. Won AUS 100m 1994, 200m 1993.
Australian 100m records 1993 and 1994.
Progression at 200m: 1988- 21.35, 1990- 21.61, 1991- 20.89/20.6, 1992- 20.70, 1993- 20.49/ 20.29w, 1994- 20.43/20.40w. pb 100m 10.16 '94.

Stephen MONEGHETTI b.26 Sep 1962 Ballarat 1.76m 60kg. Ballarat YCW Harriers. Education consultant.
At Mar: OG: '88- 5, '92- 48; WCh: '87- 4, '91- 11; CG: '86- 3 (5 at 10000m), '90- 2, '94- 1. At 10000m: WCh: '93- h; WCp: '89- 6. World CC: '87- 11, '89- 4, '92- 6. Won World Students CC 1986, AUS 10000m 1988. 2nd World Half Mar 1993.
World half marathon bests on certified courses: 60:34 to win Great North Run 1990, and in Tokyo (but 33m overall drop) 60:27 in 1992 and 60:06 in 1993.
Progression at 10000m, Mar: 1982- 30:41.7; 1983- 29:00.0; 1984- 28:56.50; 1985- 28:49.37; 1986- 28:20.95, 2:11:18; 1987- 28:07.37, 2:12:49; 1988- 28:18.98, 2:11:49; 1989- 27:55.05, 2:09:06; 1990- 28:01.76, 2:08:16; 1991- 27:57.45, 2:19:18; 1992- 27:47.69, 2:23:42; 1993- 28:03.65, 2:12:36; 1994- 28:03.48, 2:08:55. pbs: 3000m 8:01.53 '86, 5000m 13:30.84 '89.
Top class runner, but just one win in ten marathons, when he set his pb in Berlin 1990, before winning both at Tokyo and CG 1994. 2nd London 1989.

Werner REITERER b.27 Jan 1968 Austria 1.92m 110kg. Ringwood. Postal services officer.
At DT: OG: '88- dnq 15, '92- 10; WCh: '91- dnq; CG: '86- 3, '90- 2 (4 SP); '94- 1; WJ: '86- 2; WCp: '94- 4. AUS champion SP 1991, DT 1988-94, AAA DT 1991-2.
Unofficial Australian and world junior discus record 1987.
Progression at DT: 1984- 48.78, 1985- 60.10, 1986- 58.64, 1987- 65.62, 1988- 63.16, 1989- 63.02, 1990- 62.02, 1991- 64.06, 1992- 64.96, 1993- 62.98, 1994- 63.00, 1995- 64.52. pb SP 18.32 '89.

Kyle VANDER-KUYP b.30 May 1971 Paddington, NSW 1.84m 82kg. Administration officer.
At 110mh: WCh: '93-sf; CG: '90- 6, '94- 5; WJ: '90- 3; WCp: '92- 5, '94- 6. Won AUS 110mh 1992-4.
Four Australian 110mh records 1993-4.
Progression at 110mh: 1989- 14.23/14.04w, 1990- 13.85, 1991- 13.88, 1992- 13.74, 1993- 13.48, 1994- 13.45/13.2/13.27w. pbs: 100m 10.47/ 10.31w '94, 200m 21.57 '93, 400m 46.9 '91, 400mh 52.3 91.
First aboriginal to set an Australian record.

Women

Nicole BOEGMAN b.5 Mar 1967 Sydney 1.74m 62kg. née Boegman. Revesby, NSW and Hounslow, UK. Administrative assistant.
At LJ: OG: '88- 5, '92- dnq; WCh: '87- 8, '91- dnq 14, '93- 7; CG: '86- 8, '94- 1; WCp: '89- 3, '94- 7; WI: '85- 5, "91- 5. Won AUS LJ 1987-8, 1992-4; TJ 1993; WAAA LJ 1988-9.
Australian long jump record 1988, triple jump 1993 and 1995.
Progression at LJ: 1981- 5.72w, 1982- 6.45, 1983- 6.55/6.71w, 1984- 6.43, 1985- 6.50/6.67w, 1986- 6.55/6.63w, 1987- 6.67, 1988- 6.87, 1989- 6.74/ 6.82w, 1990- 6.60, 1991- 6.72, 1992- 6.63/6.73w, 1993- 6.75/6.81w, 1994- 6.67/6.82w. pbs: 100m 11.86 '88, 11.7w '93; 200m 24.27 '90, 23.9 '84; 400m 58.5 '90, 100mh 14.72 '84, TJ 13.28 '95, Hep 4966w '84.
Missed 1990 Commonwealth Games due to

Cathy Freeman

fractured left leg. Briefly married to Gary Staines, UK 5000m Olympian, from 1990.

Daniela COSTIAN b.30 Apr 1965 Braila, Romania 1.82m 87kg. Univ. of Queensland.
At DT: OG: '92- 3; WCh: '91- 5, '93- 2; EC: '86- 7dq; CG: '94-1; EJ: '83- 5; WUG: '85- 3; WCp: '94- 3. Balkan champion 1988. 3rd GP 1992. Won AUS SP 1991, 1993-4; DT 1989-94.
Five Australian discus records 1991-4.
Progression at DT: 1979- 32.30, 1980- 40.16, 1981- 40.60, 1982- 55.08, 1983- 60.50, 1984- 65.22, 1985- 67.54, 1986- 69.66, 1988- 73.84, 1989- 66.78, 1990- 68.96, 1991- 66.06, 1992- 66.24, 1993- 66.02, 1994- 68.72. pb SP 16.30 '93.
Suspended for contravening IAAF doping rules at the 1986 European Championships. Left Romania and sought political asylum in Turkey after winning 1988 Balkan title; then went to Australia, gaining citizenship in 1990.

Jane FLEMMING b.14 Apr 1965 Melbourne 1.68m 58kg. Knox-Sherbrooke. Promtions manager.
At Hep: OG: '88- 7, '92- dnf; WCh: '87- 10, '93- 7, CG: '86- 2 (6 at 100mh), '90- 1 (1 LJ, 4 100mh). '94-2 (9= LJ, 7 100mh); WUG: '89- 3. Won AUS 100m 1988, 1990; 100mh 1988, 1993-4; Hep 1985-8, 1993-4.
Four Australian heptathlon records 1987-90, Commonwealth record 1990.
Progression at Hep: 1982- 5232, 1983- 5472*, 1985- 5901, 1986- 6278w, 1987- 6390, 1988- 6492, 1989- 6286, 1990- 6695, 1992- 6046, 1993- 6343, 1994- 6317. pbs: 100m 11.50 '88, 11.4w '93; 200m 23.32 '93, 800m 2:11.75 '88, 100mh 12.98 '93, 12.9w '94; 400mh 57.88 '93, HJ 1.87 '87, LJ 6.78 '90, SP 14.18 '94, DT 45.04 '89, JT 49.28 '90.
Double gold medallist at the 1990 Commonwealth Games, when she was originally selected only for the long jump due to injury doubts.

Cathy FREEMAN b.16 Feb 1973 1.64m 52kg. Ringwood. Public relations adviser.
At 400m: OG: '92- qf; CG: '94- 1. At 200m/4x100mR: WCh: '93- sf; CG: '90- 1R, '94- 1/2R; WJ: '90- 5, '92- 2; WCp: '94- 3/3R. 2nd GP 400m 1994. Won AUS 200m 1990-1, 1994; AAA 200m 1993, 400m 1992.
AUS records: 200m (2), 400m 1994.
Progression at 200m, 400m: 1988- 24.50, 55.53; 1989- 23.86, 1990- 23.36; 1991- 23.50, 54.24; 1992- 23.09, 51.14; 1993- 22.37, 51.34; 1994- 22.25, 50.04. pbs: 100y 10.62 '93, 100m 11.24/11.15w '94.
The top athlete of the 1994 Commonwealth Games, when she won both 200m and 400m, took silver at 4 x 100m, and crossed the line in first place in the 4x400m relay, only to be disqualified for baulking Yusuf of Nigeria on the final turn.

Melinda GAINSFORD b.1 Oct 1971 1.73m 65kg. Cumberland Ryde Hornsby.
At 200m/4x100mR (100m): OG: '92- sf (qf); WCh: '93- (sf); CG: '94- 3/2R (4); WI: '93- 2; WCp '92- 4 (4), '94- (4)/3R. Won AUS 100m and 200m 1992-3, AAA 100m & 200m 1992.
Australian records 100m and 200m 1994.
Progression at 100m, 200m: 1988- 12.14, 1989- 11.89/11.59w, 24.02/23.89w; 1990- 11.77/11.72w, 23.89/23.50dq; 1991- 11.61, 23.62; 1992- 11.38, 22.68/22.26w; 1993- 11.22/11.15w, 22.49, 1994- 11.12A, 22.32. pb 400m 52.81 '92.

Alison INVERARITY b.12 Aug 1970 1.81m 61kg. University. Architecture student.
At HJ: OG: '92- 8; WCh: '91- 11; CG: '94- 1; WI: '93- 5; WUG: '91- 1; WCp: '94- 7. Australian champion 1991, 1993-4.
Australian high jump record 1994.
Progression at HJ: 1985- 1.72, 1986- 1.77, 1987- 1.83, 1989- 1.80, 1990- 1.90, 1991- 1.94, 1992- 1.96, 1993- 1.95, 1994- 1.98. pb TJ 12.37 '91.
Daughter of Australian Test cricketer John Inverarity.

Louise McPAUL b.24 Jan 1969 Wollongong, NSW 1.74m 65kg. Illawarra Blue Stars. Sales assistant.
At JT: OG: '92- 11; WCh: '91- 6; CG: '94- 1; WJ:

'88- dnq 15 (13 Hep); WCp: '94- 4; WUG: '91- 4. AUS champion 1990-1, 1993.
Progression at JT: 1984- 38.36, 1985- 38.50, 1986- 47.94, 1987- 51.30, 1988- 52.34, 1989- 50.50, 1990- 57.06, 1991- 63.34, 1992- 62.62, 1993- 60.86, 1994- 65.32, 1995- 65.80. pbs: 100mh 14.95 '93, HJ 1.80 '92, LJ 5.85 '93, SP 13.12 '92, Hep: 5709 '93.

Lisa ONDIEKI b.12 May 1960 Gawler, SA 1.66m 47kg. née O'Dea, formerly married to Kenny Martin (US steeplechaser/marathoner), married Yobes Ondieki on 10 Feb 1990. Nike TC, USA; was at University of Oregon.
At Mar: OG: '84- 7, '88- 2, '92- dnf; WCh: '87- dnf, '93- dnf; CG: '86- 1, '90- 1. Won AUS 10000m 1995, TAC Mar 1985. At 10000m: WCp: '85- dnf.
Commonwealth marathon bests 1986, 1988; Australian records: 5000m 1995, 10000m (5) 1983-92, Mar (4) 1983-6. World 10 miles road best 52:23 '87.
Progression at 10,000m, Mar: 1983- 33:12.1, 2:32:22; 1984- 32:50.6, 2:27:40; 1985- 32:17.86, 2:29:48; 1986- 2:26:07, 1987- 32:22.56, 2:30:59; 1988- 2:23:51, 1990- 2:25:28, 1991- 2:29:02, 1992- 31:11.72, 2:24:40; 1993- 2:27:27, 1994- 31:47.11, 2:31:01. pbs: 1500m 4:21.2 '83, 3000m 9:07.38 '90, 5000m 15:28.16 '95, 400mh 60.5 '79, Half Mar 1:08:33 '92.
Started as a 400m hurdler, switching to distance running in 1981. Has won 8 out of 20 marathons. Won at Osaka 1988, when she ran the world's fastest for a loop course, and at New York 1992 after 2nd 1985-6, 3rd 1991. Commonwealth half marathon best 1:09:39 to win Great North Run 1986, and had further wins in 1987 and 1989. Daughter Emma born 22 Oct 1990.

Renee POETSCHKA b.1 May 1971 Dampier, WA 1.74m 56kg. Was at University of Western Australia. Coach.
At 400m/4x400mR: OG: '92- sf; WCh: '91- sf; CG: '94- 5; WI: '93- 5; WJ: '90- h/1R; WUG: '91- 4. Won AUS 400m 1991, 1993-4, 400mh 1993.
Australian 400m record 1994.
Progression at 400mh: 1986- 55.72, 1987-, 1988- 53.85, 1989- 53.31, 1990- 52.80, 1991- 51.38, 1992- 51.41, 1993- 51.00, 1994- 50.19. pbs: 100m 11.6, 11.5w '91; 200m 23.44/23.1 '94, 800m 2:08.9 '91, 400mh 57.04 '93.
Younger sister Lauren (b.22 Oct 74) has 400mh pb 56.06 '94.

Kerry SAXBY-JUNNA b.2 Jun 1961 Ballina, NSW 1.65m 59kg. née Saxby. Ballina. Tour guide, Australian Institute of Sport.
At 10kmW: OG: '92- 15; WCh: '87- 2, '91- 5, '93- dnf; CG: '90- 1, '94- 1; WCp: '85- 10, '87- 4, '89- 2, '91- 5, '93- 5. Won GWG 1986. At 3000mW: WI: '89- 1, '91- 2, '93- 2. Won AUS 5000mW & 10kmW 1986-90, (5kW 1991-4), 3000mW 1987, 20kmW 1986-9.
World walking bests 1985-91 (no.): road: 5km (4) 20:34 '87, 10km (2) 1987-8, 15km 1:09:33 '85, 20km (3) 1:29:40 '88; track: 1500m(2) 5:50.51 '91; 3000m (5) 11:51.26 '91; 5000m (5) 20:17.19 '90; 10,000m (3) 42:14.2 '88 (mx) '89 & 42:25.2 '90. WIB 3000mW 12:01.65 '89. Four Commonwealth 10000mW track records.
Progression at 10kmW: 1983- 50:52, 1984- 48:22, 1985- 46:13, 1986- 44:53, 1987- 42:52, 1988- 41:30/42:14.2t, 1989- 42:46.45t, 1990- 41:57.22t, 1991- 42:30/43:53.41t, 1992- 42:23.9t, 1993- 42:22.6t, 1994- 43:09.
Her sister Sharon won the Australian schools under-17 800m in 2:10.1 in 1978.

Debbie SOSIMENKO b.5 Apr 1974. Asics West.
At HT: AUS champion 1993-4.
Six Commonwealth hammer records 1993-5. World junior hammer record 1993.
Progression at HT: 1989- 32.30, 1990- 44.30, 1991- 47.14, 1992- 51.48, 1993- 58.90, 1994- 62.38, 1995- 63.04. pb DT 45.00 '91.

AUSTRIA

Governing body: Österreichischer Leichtathletik Verband, A - 1040 Vienna, Prinz Eugenstrasse 12. Founded 1900.
National Championships first held in 1911 (men), 1918 (women). **1994 Champions**: **Men**: 100m: Martin Schützenauer 10.62, 200m: Thomas Griesser 21.33, 400m: Klaus Angerer 46.90, 800m: Thomas Ebner 1:49.11, 1500m: Werner Edler-Muhr 3:53.53, 5000m: Michael Buchleitner 14:20.68, 10000m: Robert Platzer 30:27.15, Half Mar/Mar: Max Wenisch 66:30/2:26:18, 3000mSt: Hans Funder 8:59.32, 110mh: Mark McKoy 13.52, 400mh: Peter Knoll 51.88, HJ: Pavel Vanicek 2.09, PV: Herman Fehringer 5.40, LJ: Manfred Auinger 7.35, TJ: Michael Mayrhofer 15.79, SP: Christian Nebl 18.40, DT: Erwin Pirklbauer 54.38, HT: Johann Lindner 63.00, JT: Gregor Högler 73.80, Dec: Leonhard Hudec 7402, 20kmW/50kmW: Stefan Wögerbauer 1:40:23/4:13:25, **Women**: 100m/200m: Sabine Tröger 11.39/23.55, 400m/400mh: Stefanie Zotter 54.69/58.22, 800m/1500m: Stephanie Graf 2:08.74/4:20.85, 3000m: Erika König-Zenz 9:48.00, 10000m: Carina Lilge-Leutner 36:30.69, Half Mar: Elisabeth Rust 1:19:22, Mar: Andrea Hofmann 2:51:30, 100mh: Elke Wölfling 13.86, HJ/Hep: Sigrid Kirchmann 1.91/5745, LJ: Ludmila Ninova 6.41, TJ: Christina Öppinger 12.85w, SP: Sonja Spendelhofer 14.29, DT: Maria

Schramseis 46.16, JT: Monika Brodschneider 49.20, 10000mW: Viera Toporek 51:32.76.

Mark McKOY b.10 Dec 1961 Georgetown, Guyana 1.81m 70kg. ATSV St Martin. PE graduate of Louisiana State University, USA.
At 110mh/R- 4x100m relay: OG: '84- 4, '88- 7, '92- 1; WCh: '83- 4, '87- 7, '91- 4; EC: '94- dns sf; CG: '82- 1/2R, '86- 1/1R; WUG: '83- 3; PAm: '83- 6. Won GP 1985, 3rd 1987, 1993. On 1980 Olympic team. At 60mh: WI: '87- fell, '91- 3, '93- 1. Won Canadian 110mh 1981-8, 1990-1; Austrian 1994.
Eleven Canadian and six Commonwealth 110mh records 1982-92, two Austrian 1994. WIB: 50mh 6.25 '86 (& European 6.39 '95), 60mh 7.47 '86. Commonwealth indoor record 50yh 5.95 '85.
Progression at 110mh: 1979- 14.19, 1980- 14.02, 1981- 13.97, 1982- 13.37, 1983- 13.53/13.51w, 1984- 13.27/13.16w, 1985- 13.27, 1986- 13.35/13.31w, 1987- 13.23, 1988- 13.17, 1990- 13.45, 1991- 13.27, 1992- 13.11/13.06w, 1993- 13.08, 1994- 13.14. pbs: 60m 6.49i '93, 100m 10.08 '93, 200m 20.96 '85, 60yh 6.89i '86, 60mh 7.44i '91, 7.41r '93; 400mh 53.75 '79.
Lived in England 1962-74. Suspended for two years after leaving 1988 Canadian team in Seoul prior to the sprint relay following the Johnson disqualification; admitted drug use to the Dubin enquiry, and was suspended from funding. Brought down by Greg Foster when leading 1987 World Indoor 60mh. Married Yvette Grabner, twin sister of Yvonne Mai, in 1991. After training with Colin Jackson made first improvement for four years with a Canadian record and then the 1992 Olympic title. In 1993 he won the World Indoor title, although lucky to get away with a second 'false' start., but lost his outdoor Worlds place when he refused to return for Canadian Championships. Became an Austrian citizen on 14 June 1994.

Women

Sigrid KIRCHMANN b.29 Mar 1966 Bad Ischl 1.81m 63kg. Union Ebensee. Teacher. PE graduate of University of Salzburg.
At HJ: OG: '92- 5; WCh: '87 & '91- dnq, '93- 3; EC: '86- 11, '90- 4, '94- 10; EI: '94- 3; EJ: '83- 7. Won Austrian HJ 1982-4, 1986-8, 1990-1, 1993-4; Hep 1986, 1994.
Austrian records HJ 1987 (2) and 1993, heptathlon 1987.
Progression at HJ: 1980- 1.67, 1981- 1.72, 1982- 1.85, 1983- 1.86, 1984- 1.87, 1985- 1.91, 1986- 1.90, 1987- 1.95, 1988- 1.90i/1.87, 1989- 1.88i/1.87, 1990- 1.93, 1991- 1.91, 1992- 1.94, 1993- 1.97, 1994- 1.96i/1.93. pbs: 100mh 13.87 '85, LJ 6.03 '85, SP 12.48 '94, JT 52.68 '86, Hep 5944 '85.

Ludmila NINOVA b.25 Jun 1960 Kula, Bulgaria 1.75m 61kg. SV Schwechat. Instructor. Former married name Rudoll.At LJ: OG: '92- dnq 13; WCh: '87- 9, '91- 7, '93- 6 (11 TJ); EC: '86- 5, '90- 5; WI: '93- 7; WUG: '87- 2; EI: '92- 3, '94- 2; WCp: '92- 3. Won Balkan LJ 1986, BUL 1987-8, AUT 1991-4. 2nd GP 1987.Three Bulgarian long jump records 1984-6. Austrian records LJ (3), TJ (2) 1991-4.Progression at LJ: 1979- 5.89, 1980- 5.80, 1982- 5.93, 1983- 6.23, 1984- 6.80, 1985- 6.64, 1986- 6.88, 1987- 6.87, 1988- 6.85, 1991- 6.95, 1992- 6.92/7.00w, 1993- 7.06, 1994- 7.09. pbs: HJ 1.72 '84, TJ 13.67i '92, 13.60 '93; Hep 5124 '84.
Left Bulgaria for Austria and returned to competition in 1991.

BAHAMAS

Governing body: Bahamas Amateur Athletic Association, P.O.Box SS 5517, Nassau.

Troy KEMP b.18 Jun 1966 1.87m 69kg. Was at Boise State University, USA.
At HJ: OG: '88- dnq 21=, '92- 7; WCh: '87- dnq 20=, '91- 5=, '93- 5; WI: '93- 4=; PAm: '87- 2, '91- 2; won TAC indoors 1989. 2nd GP 1992, 1994.
Commonwealth high jump record 1993.
Progression at HJ: 1984- 2.10, 1985- 2.13, 1986- 2.22, 1987- 2.28, 1988- 2.30i/2.27, 1989- 2.32, 1990- 2.31, 1991- 2.35, 1992- 2.34, 1993- 2.37, 1994- 2.36i/2.35.

Women

Pauline DAVIS b.9 Jul 1966 1.68m 57kg. University of Alabama, USA.
At 100m/200m/4x100mR: OG: '84, '88 & '92- sf/sf; WCh: '83- qf/qf, '87- qf/sf, '91- sf/7, '93- sf/sf; CG: '90- 3/3, '94- -/5; PAm: '87- 3/3; WCp: '89- 4R/1 4x400mR; CAG: '86- 1/1/2R. At 60m: WI: '91- 5. Won CAC 100m and NCAA 400m 1989. 3rd GP 100m 1989, 2nd 400m 1990.
National records 100m, 200m, 400m.
Progression at 100m, 200m, 400m: 1983- 11.56/11.3, 23.57, 1984- 11.51/11.1, 22.97, 1985- 11.47, 23.37/23.22w, 1986- 11.27/11.11w, 22.83, 1987- 11.19/11.16w, 22.49/22.1w; 1988- 11.17/11.12w, 22.67/51.11, 1989- 11.14/10.9, 22.50/50.18, 1990- 11.16, 22.55, 50.05; 1991- 11.18/11.08w, 22.73; 1992- 11.31/11.30w, 22.44, 51.30; 1993- 11.16, 22.89; 1994- 11.37/11.28w, 22.52, 50.46. pbs: 60m 7.16i '91, 300m 36.50 '93.

BELARUS

Governing body: Track & Field Athletics Federation of the Republic of Belarus, Scorina av. 49, Minsk 220005. Founded 1991.

National Champions 1994: **Men**: 100m: Aleksandr Shylchkov UKR 10.53, 200m: Leonid Safronnikov 21.30, 400m: Sergey Molchan 47.66, 800m/1500m: Ivan Komar 1:47.04/ 3:44.34, 5000m: Aleksey Tarasyuk 14:13.16, 10000m: Azat Rakipov 29:41.7, 3000mSt: Vasiliy Omelyusik 8:34.5, 110mh: Mikhail Ryabukhin 13.86, 400mh: Aleksey Fursa 52.16, HJ: Nikolay Moskalev 2.25, PV: Gennadiy Sidorov 5.50, LJ: Andrey Nikulin 7.56, TJ: Viktor Sazankov 16.28, SP: Dmitriy Goncharuk 19.88, DT: Vladimir Dubrovshchik 63.72, HT: Vitaliy Alisevich 77.92, JT: Oleg Gotsko 68.38, Dec: Yuriy Lekunovich 7299, 20kmW: Mikhail Khmelnitskiy 1:19:38. **Women**: 100m: Natalya Vinogradova 11.75, 200m: Margarita Molchan 23.71, 400m: Anna Kozak 53.52, 800m/ 1500m: Yelena Bychkovskaya 2:03.15/4:13.50, 3000m/10000m: Yelena Mazovka 9:26.4/ 33:45.2, 100mh: Lidiya Yurkova 13.14, 400mh: Natalya Ignatyuk 56.74, HJ: Tatyana Shevchik 1.96, LJ: Larisa Kuchinskaya 6.37, TJ: Natalya Klimovets 13.49, SP: Natalya Gurskaya 16.94, DT: Lyudmila Filimonova 63.84, HT: Svetlana Sudak 63.56, JT: Natalya Yermolovich 55.62, Hep: Anzhela Andrukevich 5419, 10kmW: Valentina Tsybulskaya 43:16.

Sergey ALAY b.11 Jun 1965 1.84m 98kg. Minsk TR.
At HT: WCh: '93- 4. BLS champion 1993.
Progression at HT: 1984- 71.26, 1985- 75.02, 1986- 79.64, 1987- 80.52, 1988- 81.52, 1989- 78.78, 1990- 79.92, 1991- 81.16, 1992- 82.00, 1993- 81.44, 1994- 76.70.

Vitaliy ALISEVICH b.15 Jun 1967 1.86m 112kg. Minsk SA.
At HT: EC: '94- 9; WJ: '86- 1; ECp: '94- 1B. BLS champion 1992, 1994.
Progression at HT: 1983- 61.46, 1984- 62.94, 1985- 70.20, 1986- 73.22, 1987- 78.60, 1988- 82.16, 1989- 77.70, 1990- 77.52, 1991- 79.16, 1992- 80.00, 1993- 81.32, 1994- 80.68.

Igor ASTAPKOVICH b.4 Jan 1963 Minsk 1.91m 118kg. Grodno Sp. Sports student.
At HT: OG: '92- 2; WCh: '91- 2, '93- 2; EC: '90- 1, '94- 2; WUG: '87- 1, '89- 1; ECp: '89- 2, '91- 1. Won GWG 1990. USSR champion 1989-90, CIS 1992. Won GP 1992 (2nd 1988, 1994).
BLS hammer record 1992.
Progression at HT: 1981- 66.56, 1982- 68.08, 1983- 75.02, 1984- 79.98, 1985- 80.16, 1986- 80.68, 1987- 82.96, 1988- 83.44, 1989- 82.52, 1990- 84.14, 1991- 84.26, 1992- 84.62, 1993- 82.28, 1994- 83.14.
World number one in 1990, when he lost just once, and won the Goodwill Games (84.12) and European titles with pbs. Since then he has won three major silver medals. Brother Konstantin (b.23 Oct 1970) has a best of 78.20 '93.

Vladimir DUBROVSHCHIK b.1 Jan 1972 1.93m 115kg.
At DT: EC: '94- 1; EJ: '91- 1; WCp: '94- 1; ECp: '94- 2B. BLS champion 1993-4.
Progression at DT: 1989- 53.04, 1990- 56.76, 1991- 61.40, 1992- 61.80, 1993- 63.26, 1994- 65.80. pb SP 16.57 '94.

Eduard HÄMÄLÄINEN b.21 Jan 1969 Grodno 1.92m 88kg. Minsk Dyn.
At Dec: OG: '92- dnf; WCh: '91- 7, '93- 2; EC: '94- dnf; WJ: '88- 3. CIS champion 1992. At Hep: WI inv: '93- 3.
BLS decathlon records 1993-4.
Progression at Dec: 1987- 7369, 1988- 7596, 1989- 7891, 1990- 7845, 1991- 8233, 1992- 8483w, 1993- 8724, 1994- 8735. pbs: 100m 10.69/10.50w '94; 400m 47.41 '93, 1500m 4:22.5 '87, 60mh 7.93i '93, 110mh 13.57 '93, HJ 2.11 '94, PV 5.30 '93, LJ 7.49/7.67w '93; SP 16.05 '94, DT 52.20 '94, JT 61.88 '93, Hep 6075i '93.
Won Götzis decathlon 1993 and 1994; in 1993 he ran 13.65 for 110mh, the fastest ever run in a decathlon, a record he improved to 13.57 in the World Championships. However, when favourite to win the 1994 European title and leading at the start of the second day he fell at the first hurdle.

Yevgeniy MISYULYA b.9 Mar 1964 1.77m 68kg. Minsk TR.
At 20kmW: OG: '88- 27; WCh: '91- 3, '93- 5; EC: '94- 2; WCp: '89- 3. USSR champion 1991, BLS 1993.
World road 20km walk best 1989.
Progression at 20kmW: 1985- 1:22:25, 1986- 1:20:41.6t, 1988- 1:19:16, 1989- 1:18:54, 1990- 1:20:15, 1991- 1:19:13, 1992- 1:19:03, 1993- 1:19:56, 1994- 1:19:22. Track pbs: 5000mW 18:39.2i '88, 10000mW 40:01.0 '85. Road 30kmW 2:02:45 '91.

Aleksandr POTASHOV b.12 Mar 1962 1.87m 80kg. Vitebsk Sp.
At 50kmW: OG: '88- 4, '92- dq; WCh: '91- 1; EC: '90- dq, '94- dq; WCp: '87- 7, '89- 5. USSR champion 1990. At 10000mW: EJ: '81- 2.
BLS 50km walk record 1993.
Progression at 50kmW: 1982- 4:10:44, 1983- 3:56:54, 1984- 4:00:46, 1985- 3:54:40, 1986- 3:51:17, 1987- 3:46:28, 1988- 3:41:00, 1989- 3:48:02, 1990- 3:40:02, 1991- 3:53:09, 1993- 4:03:20, 1994- 3:49:00. pbs: 10000mW 40:02.0 '85, 20kmW 1:20:12 '94, 30kmW 2:04:00 '93.

Disqualified after finishing second in the World Cup 50km 1991.

Vladimir SASIMOVICH b.14 Sep 1968 Minsk 1.78m 86kg. Minsk TR.
At JT: WCh: '91- 2, '93- 8; EC: '94- 8; WJ: '86- 1; EJ: '87- 2; WCp: '92- 3; ECp: '93- 1B3. USSR champion 1991, BLS 1993. 3rd GP 1991.
World junior javelin record 1986, BLS record 1993.
Progression at JT: 1984- 65.42, 1985- 77.60, new: 1986- 78.84, 1987- 77.12, 1988- 79.28, 1989- 81.06, 1990- 81.28, 1991- 87.08, 1992- 86.16, 1993- 86.48, 1994- 83.14.

Women

Svetlana BURAGA b.4 Sep 1965 1.68m 56kg. née Besprozvannaya. Minsk Sp. Instructor.
At Hep: OG: '88- 10; WCh: '87- 14, '93- 3; ECp: '87- 1, '93- 1C. Won BLS 100mh 1993.
BLS heptathlon record 1993.
Progression at Hep: 1983- 5352, 1985- 5743, 1986- 6073, 1987- 6585, 1988- 6597, 1990- 6174, 1991- 6104, 1992- 6075, 1993- 6635, 1994- 6284. pbs: 200m 23.18 '87, 800m 2:08.45 '88, 100mh 12.83/12.8 '88, HJ 1.84 '93, LJ 6.79i/6.63 '87, SP 14.55 '93, JT 42.80 '87.

Natalya DUKHNOVA b.16 Jul 1966 1.76m 64kg
At 800m: WCh: '93- h; EC: '94- 2; EI: '94- 1; WCp: '94- 3. BLS champion 1992-3.
Progression at 800m: 1989- 2:02.1, 1990- 2:01.26, 1991- 2:01.87, 1992- 2:00.59, 1993- 1:58.01, 1994- 1:57.87. pbs: 400m 52.1 '93, 1000m 2:36.56 '93, 1500m 4:11.19 '93.

Natalya Dukhnova: European Indoor champion

Tatyana LEDOVSKAYA b.21 May 1965 Shchekino, Tulsk region 1.71m 60kg. Minsk Sp.
At 400mh/R- 4x400m relay: OG: '88- 2/1R, '92- 4; WCh: '91- 1/1R, '93- sf; EC: '90- 1/2R; WCp: '89- 2; ECp: '89- 3. USSR champion 1988-9. At 400m: WI: '91- 3.
World record 4x400m relay 1988. BLS records 200m, 400m, 400mh.
Progression at 400mh: 1987- 56.92, 1988- 53.18, 1989- 54.68, 1990- 53.62, 1991- 53.11, 1992- 53.55, 1993- 54.60. pbs: 200m 23.32/22.7 '88, 400m 50.4/50.93 '88.
Made exceptionally rapid progress in 1988, taking 1.3 off her best in Seoul. Again showed her ability to peak for the big events by winning gold medals in Split and Tokyo, with indifferent form otherwise. Again with no form behind her ran well for fourth in Barcelona.

Natalya MISYULYA b.12 Apr 1966 1.57m 47kg. née Dmitrochenko.
At 10kmW: EC: '94- 6. At 3kW: EI: '87- 1.
pbs: 3000mW: 12:57.59i '87, 5000mW: 22:28.0 '86, 10000mW: 46:21.8 '86. Road 10kmW: 45:12 '85. 1990- 44:49, 1991- 45:45, 1993- 43:15, 1994- 43:29.

Tatyana SHEVCHIK b.11 Jun 1969 1.78m 59kg. Minsk Sp.
At HJ: OG: '92- 16; WCh: '93- dnq 15=; EC: '94- 9; ECp: '93- 1B. Won USSR indoor HJ 1990. BLS champion 1994.
BLS high jump record 1993.
Progression at HJ: 1985- 1.86, 1986- 1.83, 1987- 1.83, 1988- 1.86, 1989- 1.86, 1990- 1.92, 1991- 1.95, 1992- 1.96, 1993- 2.00, 1994- 1.96.

Natalya SHIKOLENKO b.1 Aug 1964 Andizhan, Uzbekistan 1.82m 79kg. Minsk Dyn. Student.
At JT: OG: '92- 2; WCh: '91- 11, '93- 3; EC: '90- nt, '94- dnq 14; ECp: '89- 4. Won USSR title 1990-1, CIS 1992, BLS 1993; GWG 1990. Won GP 1994 (2nd 1992).
BLS javelin records 1992-4.
Progression at JT: 1979-37.38, 1980- 49.94, 1981- 51.14, 1982- 55.06, 1983- 60.48, 1984- 63.64, 1985- 64.60, 1986- 63.56, 1987- 66.18, 1988- 66.48, 1989- 69.38, 1990- 65.76, 1991- 67.32, 1992- 70.36, 1993- 68.96, 1994- 71.40.
Injured on her first throw of the 1994 European qualifying.

Tatyana SHIKOLENKO b.10 May 1968 Krasnodar, Russia 1.75m 79kg.
At JT: WCh: '93- 4; WJ: '86- 4; EJ: '85- 5; WUG: '91- 1.
Progression at JT: 1984- 59.40, 1985- 59.90, 1986- 55.70, 1987- 59.74, 1988- 64.70, 1989- 60.74, 1990- 64.98, 1991- 63.56, 1992- 62.20, 1993- 65.18, 1994- 64.94.
Younger sister of Natalya.

Ellina ZVEREVA b.16 Nov 1960 Dolgoprudny 1.82m 90kg. formerly Kisheyeva. Minsk Dyn. Student.
At DT: OG: '88- 5; WCh: '91- 9; EC: '90- 6, '94- 2; WCp: '94- 2; ECp: '93- 1B. 3rd GP 1994. USSR champion 1986, BLS 1993.
BLS discus record 1988.
Progression at DT: 1979- 44.06, 1980- 51.38, 1981- 59.88, 1982- 62.52, 1983- 65.18, 1984- 68.56, 1985- 66.64, 1986- 68.96, 1987- 60.84, 1988- 71.58, 1990- 66.20, 1991- 63.80, 1992- 66.26/68.82dq, 1993- 66.32, 1994- 67.44.
Four year ban reported after positive steroids test when first at CIS Trials 1992, but back in 1993.

BELGIUM

Governing bodies: Ligue Royale Belge d'Athlétisme, Rue St.Laurent 14-26 (Bte 6), 1000 Bruxelles (KBAB). Vlaamse Atletiek Liga (VAL); Ligue Belge Francophone d'Athlétisme (LBFA). Original governing body founded 1889.
National Championships first held in 1889 (men), 1921 (women) **1994 Champions**: **Men**: 100m/200m: Patrick Stevens 10.48/20.64, 400m: Fredéric Masson 48.13, 800m: Patrick Grammens 1:50.11, 1500m: Christophe Impens 3:46.00, 5000m: Gino Van Geyte 14:01.51, 10000m: Ivo Claes 29:35.09, Mar: Vincent Rousseau 2:07:51, 3000mSt: William Van Dijck 8:37.66, 110mh: Jonathan Nsenga 13.72, 400mh: Jean-Pol Bruwier 50.14, HJ: Dominique Sandron 2.09, PV: Alan De Naeyer 5.30, LJ: Erik Nijs 7.97, TJ: ?, SP: Kurt Boffel 16.17, DT: Jo Vandaele 52.66, HT: Alex Malachenko 67.92, JT: Mark Van Mensel 66.86, Dec: Raf Coomans 7039, 20kmW (t): Benjamin Leroy 1:34:43.3, 50kmW: Luc Nicque 4:26:01. **Women**: 100: Sandrine Hennart 11.92, 200: Sylvia Dethier 24.25, 400m: Katrien Maenhout 55.21, 800m: Anneke Matthijs 2:04.66, 1500m: Anja Smolders 4:21.84, 3000m: Anne-Marie Danneels 9:12.89, 10000m/Half Mar: Marleen Renders 32:56.55/71:08, Mar: Françoise Maton 2:42:10, 100mh: Sylvia Dethier 13.37, 400mh: Melanie Moreels 58.06, HJ: Natalja Jonckheere 1.85, LJ: Sandrine Hennart 6.32, TJ: Sandra Swennen 12.44, SP: Greet Meulemeester 15.56, DT: Marie-Paule Geldhof 57.58, JT: Ingrid Didden 50.04, Hep: Annelies De Meester 5373, 5000mW: Christiane Ceulemans -.

Marc DOLLENDORF b.7 Feb 1966 Saint-Vith 1.91m 85kg. Exc. SC.
At 400mh: WCh: '93- sf; EC: '90- h, '94- sf; EJ: '85- 5. Won E Cp B 1993, BEL 400m 1993.
Four Belgian 400mh records 1994.
Progression at 400mh: 1984- 52.63, 1985- 51.30, 1986- 50.79, 1987- 51.83, 1988- 50.19, 1989- 50.41/50.2, 1990- 50.04, 1991- 49.94, 1992- 50.09, 1993- 49.82, 1994- 49.05. pbs: 200m 21.62 '90, 400m: 46.89 '94, 110mh 14.39 '94, HJ 1.93 '94.

Vincent ROUSSEAU b.29 Jul 1962 Mons 1.76m 60kg. RISC.
At 5000m: OG: '88- sf; WCh: '87- 5; EC: '86- 13, '90- h. 2nd GP 1986. At 10000m: OG: '92- h; WCh: '91- h; EC: '94- 2; WCp: '85- 5. Won World Half Mar 1993, Belgian 5000m 1984, 1989; 1500m 1985-6, 1988;Mar 1994, CC 1984, 1987-8, 1990-3.
Belgian 5000m and 10000m records 1993, marathon (3) 1993-4.
Progression at 5000m, 10000m, Mar: 1980- 14:30.5, 1981- 14:08.32, 1982- 13:40.21, 1983- 13:33.2, 1984- 13:24.81, 1985- 13:18.94, 28:40.63; 1986- 13:15.01, 1987- 13:28.56, 1988- 13:19.16, 28:47.78; 1989- 13:28.30, 1990- 13:25.61, 28:27.1; 1991- 13:38.95, 27:50.17; 1992- 13:17.28, 1993- 13:10.99, 27:23.18, 2:09:13; 1994- 13:32.06, 27:47.79, 2:07:51. pbs: 1500m 3:36.38 '85, 1M 3:54.69 '85, 2000m 4:58.97 '87, 3000m 7:39.41 '89, 2M 8:32.01 '93, Half Mar 61:06 '93, 60:23 (33m dh) '94.
Had a great year in 1993 when on the track he set Belgian records and achieved his best big race placing with fifth in the World 5000m. He then won his first major championship, the World Half Marathon, fittingly through the streets of Brussels. He had run 2:13:09 for fifth on his marathon début at Rotterdam in April, and improved to 2:09:13 to win at Reims in October 1993, 2:09:08 for 2nd at Tokyo in February 1994 and 2:07:51, the world's fastest for six years, to win at Rotterdam in April 1994. He also won the 1994 Brussels marathon.

William VAN DIJCK b.24 Jan 1961 Leuven 1.85m 65kg. Looise AV.
At 3km St: OG: '84- sf, '88- 5, '92- 9; WCh: '83- sf, '87- 3, '91- 9; EC: '86- 5, '90- 5, '94- 3; WCp: '92- 2. Belgian champion 1983, 1985-8, 1990-2, 1994. Won GP 1986.
Eight Belgian 3000m steeplechase records 1983-6.
Progression at 3kmSt: 1981- 8:44.92, 1982- 8:36.40, 1983- 8:21.73, 1984- 8:18.75, 1985- 8:13.77, 1986- 8:10.01, 1987- 8:12.18, 1988-

8:13.99, 1989- 8:22.5, 1990- 8:16.94, 1991- 8:19.29, 1992- 8:14.58, 1993- 8:24.03, 1994- 8:19.92. pbs: 800m 1:51.8 '83, 1500m 3:41.2 '85, 1M 3:57.59 '85, 2000m 5:06.84 '89, 3000m 7:45.40 '88, 5000m 13:23.40 '85, 10000m 28:58.75 '93, 2000mSt 5:22.24 '87.

BERMUDA

Governing body: Bermuda Track and Field Association, P.O.Box DV 397, Devonshire. Founded 1946.

Brian WELLMAN b.2 Aug 1967 1.75m 72kg. University of Arkansas, USA.
At TJ: OG: '88- dnq, '92- 5; WCh: '91- 6, '93- 8; WJ: '86- 8; WI: '93- 3; CG: '90- 11, '94- 3; PAm: '91- 5; WUG: '91- 1. 2nd PAm Jnr 1986; Won NCAA 1991. 3rd GP 1992.
Bermuda TJ records 1986-94.
Progression at TJ: 1986- 16.18, 1988- 16.38, 1989- 16.44w, 1990- 16.23, 1991- 17.07/17.41w, 1992- 17.24/17.30w, 1993- 17.27i/17.14, 1994- 17.41. pb LJ 7.61 '94.
Advanced to third in 1993 World Indoors after drugs disqualification of Nikolay Raev.

BRAZIL

Governing body: Confederação Brasileira de Atletismo (CBAT), AvenidaPedro Teixeira no 400, Planalto, 69.040-000 Manaus, Amazonas. Founded 1914 (Confederação 1977).
1994 National Champions: **Men**: 100m: Sidnei Telles Sousa 10.39, 200m: Robson C da Silva 20.81, 400m: Inaldo Sena 46.3, 800m: José Luiz Barbosa 1:47.00, 1500m: Edgar Martins de Oliveira 3:38.78, 5000m: Ronaldo da Costa 13:41.0, 10000m: Valdenor Pereira dos Santos 28:49.2, 3000mSt: Wander do Prado Moura 8:37.08, 110mh: Walmes de Souza 14.10, 400mh: Eronildes Araujo 49.89, HJ: Alcides Silva 2.10, PV: Marlon Borges 4.70, LJ: Douglas de Souza 8.20, TJ: Anisio Souza Silva 17.04, SP: Adilson Oliveira 18.72, DT: João Joaquim dos Santos 57.82, HT: Màrio Almeida Leme 58.80, JT: Luiz Fernando da Silva 71.64, Dec: José de Assis Nunes 7218, 20kmW: Sergio Galdino 1:29:17.4. **Women**: 100m: Cleide Amaral 11.66, 200m: Katia Santos 24.16, 400m: Maria Figueiredo 53.06, 800m: Fàtima dos Santos 2:03.8, 1500m: Soraya Vieira Telles 4:18.28, 5000m/10000m: Silvana Pereira 16:15.9/ 34:37.5, 100mh: Vânia dos Santos 14.11, 400mh: Marise Silva 59.4, HJ: Orlane dos Santos 1.82, LJ/TJ: Maria Aparecida de Sousa 6.28/13.40, SP: Alexandra Amaro 16.40, DT: Elisângela Adriano 53.76, HT: Maria Ines Pachêco 40.48, JT: Sueli Pereira dos Santos 60.20, Hep: Joelma de Sousa 5305, 10kmW: Rosemar Piazza 52:45.2.

José Luiz BARBOSA b.27 May 1961 Tres Lagoas 1.84m 68kg. Electropaulo.
At 800m: OG: '84- sf, '88- 6 (h 1500m), '92- 4; WCh: '83- sf, '87- 3, '91- 2, '93- sf; WI: '87- 1, '89- 2, '93- dnf; PAm: '83- 2 (2 4x400mR), '87- 2; SACh: '83- 1; WCp: '92- 4, '94- 7. Won AAA 1985.
Progression at 800m: 1978- 2:10, 1979- 1:53.20, 1980- 1:50.35, 1981- 1:48.3, 1982- 1:47.4, 1983- 1:44.3, 1984- 1:44.98, 1985- 1:44.79, 1986- 1:44.10, 1987- 1:43.76, 1988- 1:43.20, 1989- 1:44.20, 1990- 1:44.84, 1991- 1:43.08, 1992- 1:45.06, 1993- 1:44.18, 1994- 1:44.75. pbs: 400m 45.9 '83, 1000m 2:17.36 '85, 1500m 3:37.04 '91.
He had his best year at 800m in 1991, when he allied better tactics to his usual front-running style. He has run 37 sub-1:45 times to end 1993.

Robson Caetano **DA SILVA** b.4 Sep 1964 Rio de Janeiro 1.87m 74kg. ADCEP.
At 200m (100m, R- 4x100m relay): OG: '84- sf, '88- 3 (5), '92- 4 (sf); WCh: '83- (qf), '87- 4 (qf), '91- 4 (7), '93- dq sf; WI: '87- 3, '89- dq; WUG: '89- 1; WCp: '85- 1/2R, '89- 1, '92- 1/4R (4), '94- 4R; PAm: '83- sf/3R, '87- 2; SACh: '85- 1 (2/1R), '87- 1 (1/1R), '89- 1/1R, '91- 1 (1/1R), '93- 1 (1). Won GP 1989, 3rd 1987. Won PAm-J 100m 1982, SAm-J LJ 1981, 100m & 200m 1983.
S.American records: two 100m, five 200m 1985-9, 400m 1991. WIB 300m: 32.19 '89.
Progression at 100m, 200m: 1979- 11.4, 1980- 11.2, 1981- 11.0, 22.3; 1982- 10.34w/10.54/10.2; 21.46/21.4; 1983- 10.40/10.3, 20.95/20.8; 1984- 10.50/10.3, 20.71; 1985- 10.22/10.1, 20.44; 1986- 10.02, 20.28; 1987- 10.20/10.0, 20.20; 1988- 10.00, 20.04; 1989- 10.17, 19.96/19.7A; 1990- 10.12, 20.23; 1991- 10.08, 20.15; 1992- 10.17, 20.15; 1993- 10.20/ 10.19w, 20.16; 1994- 10.39, 20.66. pbs: 60m 6.63i '87, 400m 45.06 '91, 45.0 '90; LJ 7.40 '81.
In 1992 equalled record with three successive wins at one event in the World Cup.

Anisio Souza **SILVA** b.18 Jun 1969 1.85m 91kg. ADCEP.
At TJ: WCh: '91- dnq 26, '93- 7; WJ: '88- 8; PAm: '91- 2; SAm: '91- 1, '93- 1.
Progression at TJ: 1988- 16.21, 1989- 16.42, 1990- 17.00, 1991- 16.72, 1992- 16.97, 1993- 17.32, 1994- 17.04. pb LJ 7.36 '90.

Douglas de SOUZA b.6 Aug 1972 São Paulo 1.91m 81kg. SESI/SBC.
South American long jump record 1995.
At LJ: WCp: '94- 2. Brazilian champion 1994.
Progression at LJ: 1992- 7.57, 1993- 7.61, 1994-

8.20, 1995- 8.40.
A first-class basketball player who started long jumping only at the age off 20.

Women

Luciana de Paula **MENDES** b.26 Jul 1971 Rio de Janeiro 1.78m 58kg. SESI/SBC.
At 800m: WCp: '94- 2; SACh: '93- 2.
Brazilian 800m record 1994.
Progression at 800m: 1991- 2:03.2, 1992- 2:03.41, 1993- 2:00.37, 1994- 1:58.27. pbs: 400m 52.36 '93, 1000m 2:40.10 '94.

Sueli Pereira dos **SANTOS** b.8 Jan 1965 Cascavel 1.65m 63kg. ADCEP.
At JT: '91- dnq 28, '93- dnq 17; PAm: '87- 4, '91- 7; SACh: '85- 2, '87- 1, '89- 3, '91-2. Brazilian champion 1985-8, 1991, 1993-4.
Four South American javelin records 1987-94.
Progression at JT: 1983- 50.58, 1984- 50.94, 1985- 52.32, 1986- 55.40, 1987- 59.52, 1988- 60.34, 1989- 58.76, 1990- 57.48, 1991- 56.64, 1992- 56.40, 1993- 63.74, 1994- 65.96.

BULGARIA

Governing body: Bulgarian Athletics Federation, 75 bl. Vassil Levski, Sofia 1000. Founded 1924.
National Championships first held in 1926 (men), 1938 (women). **1994 Champions**: **Men**: 100m/200m: Stoyan Manolev 10.41/21.15, 400m: Anton Ivanov 46.67, 800m: Dian Petkov 1:52.39, 1500m: Svetlin Prodanov 3:44.54, 5000m/10000m: Khristo Stefanov 13:53.95/28:56.00, Mar: Petko Stefanov 2:25:31, 3000mSt: Venzislav Chavdarov 9:10.61, 110mh: Georgi Georgiev 14.19, 400mh: Plamen Nyagin 50.64, HJ: Dimitar Toichev 2.22, PV: Ilian Efremov 5.20, LJ: Ivaylo Mladenov 7.87, TJ: Kotzo Kostov 16.24, SP: Radoslav Despotov 18.20, DT: Ilia Iliev 53.94, HT: Plamen Minev 71.78, JT: Angel Mandshukov 70.46, Dec: Krasimir Petlichki 6537, 20kmW: Avni Bekir. **Women**: 100m: Desislava Dimitrova 11.25, 200m: Zlatka Georgieva 23.26, 400m/400mh: Daniela Spasova 52.73/58.86, 800m/1500m: Petya Strashilova 2:09.65/4:28.33, 3000m: Milka Mikhailova 9:19.98/33:21.10, Mar: Gergana Voynova 2:47:10, 100mh: Yordanka Donkova 12.56, HJ: Eleonora Milousheva 1.87, LJ: Shasmina Nikolova 6.36, TJ: Maria Dimitrova 12.95, SP: Svetla Mitkova 18.90, DT: Atanaska Angelova 59.54, JT: Antoaneta Selenska 56.38, Hep: Yurka Khristova 5562, 5000mW/10kmW: Nevena Mineva 23:18.6/55:03.

Ivaylo MLADENOV b.9 Oct 1973 Vratza 1.84m 68kg. Botev Vratza.
At LJ: WCh: '93- 5; EC: '94- 1; WI: '93- 6; EI: '94- 4; WJ: '92- 3; EJ: '91- 5. 2nd GP 1993. Bulgarian champion 1993-4.
Progression at LJ: 1990- 7.18, 1991- 7.94, 1992- 7.89, 1993- 8.27/8.35w, 1994- 8.30i/8.24. pb TJ 15.52 '94.

Women

Sofia BOZHANOVA b.4 Oct 1967 Purvomay 1.70m 58kg. Trakia Plovdiv. PE student.
At LJ: WCh: '87- 15; EC: '86- 10; EJ: '83- 6, '85- 1; ECp: '87- 3. At TJ: EC: '94- dq (4); EI: '92- 2, '94- 3. Won Balkan TJ 1992, Bulgarian LJ 1990-1, TJ 1990.
Three Bulgarian triple jump records 1990-4.
Progression at LJ, TJ: 1981- 5.95, 1982- 6.26, 1983- 6.40, 1984- 6.45, 1985- 6.68, 1986- 6.71, 1987- 6.80, 1988- 6.70/6.72w, 1989- 6.20i, 1990- 6.51, 14.06; 1991- 6.47, 14.08; 1992- 6.20, 13.98i/13.73/13.77w; 1993- 5.99, 13.66; 1994- 14.98.
Positive drugs test following 4th 1994 Europeans.

Svetla DIMITROVA b.27 Jan 1970 Botevgrad 1.72m 59kg. Spirala.
At 100mh: EC: '94- 1/3R; WCp: '94- 2. At Hep: OG: '88- 12, '92- 5; WCh: '93- 4; WJ: '86- 1, '88- 1; ECp: '89- 3dq. Won GP 100mh and 2nd overall 1994. Won Bulgarian Hep 1989, 100mh 1993.
Progression at 100mh, Hep: 1986- 6041; 1988- 12.9w, 6343; 1989- 6534 dq/6428; 1992- 13.22, 6658; 1993- 12.71, 6594; 1994- 12.53/12.50w. pbs: 200m 23.06w '92, 23.10 '93; 800m 2:07.90 '92, HJ 1.88 '86, LJ 6.64 '92, SP 15.50 '93, JT 48.18 '93.
Suspended following a positive drugs test when third in the 1989 European Cup heptathlon in what would have been a world junior record. Won Götzis heptathlon 1993 and concentrated on hurdling in 1994, when she was clearly the world's best. She has said that she will not compete again for Bulgaria; in November 1994 she left her husband and coach Ilian Pishtikov to seek Austrian citizenship.

Yordanka DONKOVA b.28 Sep 1961 Gorni Bogrov, Sofia 1.77m 67kg. Levski Spartak, Sofia. PE student.
At 100mh: OG: '80- sf, '88- 1, '92- 3; WCh: '87- 4; EC: '82- 2, '86- 1/2R, '94- 3; EJ: '79- 8; ECp: '81- 5, '87- 2/2R. At Hep: ECp: '83- 7. At 60mh: WI: '87- 2; EI: '82- 3, '84- 3, '87- 1, '89- 1, '92- 3, '94- 1. Won Balkan 100mh 1980, 1984, 1986; BUL 1984, 1986, 1994. Won GP 100mh and overall 1986, 2nd 1988.
Eleven Bulgarian 100mh records 1982-8, including five world records: four 1986, one 1988. WIB 60mh 7.74 '86.
Progression at 100mh: 1977- 14.84, 1978- 13.91, 1979- 13.57, 1980- 13.24, 1981- 13.39/12.9, 1982- 12.44, 1983- 12.65, 1984- 12.50, 1985- 13.24, 1986-

12.26/12.0w, 1987- 12.33, 1988- 12.21, 1992- 12.67, 1993- 12.81, 1994- 12.56/12.49w. pbs: 100m 11.27 '82, 200m 22.95 '82, 50mh 6.77i '93, 55mh 7.44i '87, HJ 1.78 '82, LJ 6.39 '82, Hep 6187 '83.
Displayed the finest ever sprint hurdling by a woman in 1986, with very sharp speed and technique, running ten sub-12.50 times. She ran a further four such times in 1987, and a record 12 in 1988 when she was unbeaten. She lost three fingers on her right hand in an accident on her fifth birthday. Son born February 1991. In 1994 she completed a full set of European medals.

Stefka KOSTADINOVA b.25 Mar 1965 Plovdiv 1.80m 60kg. Trakia Plovdiv. PE student. Married her coach Nikolai Petrov on 6 Nov 1989.
At HJ: OG: '88- 2, '92- 4; WCh: '87- 1, '91- 6, '93- dnq 15=; WI: '85- 1, '87- 1, '89- 1, '93- 1; EC: '86- 1; EJ: '81- 10; EI: '85- 1, '87- 1, '88- 1, '92- 2, '94- 1; WCp: '85- 1; ECp: '85- 1, '87- 1. Won GWG 1986, Balkan 1985-6, 1988; Bulgarian 1985-6, 1988, 1991. Won GP 1985, 1987 (3rd overall), 1993; 2nd 1991.
Three world records 1986-7. WIB: 2.04 & 2.05 '87, 2.06 '88.
Progression at HJ: 1977- 1.45, 1978- 1.66, 1979- 1.75, 1980- 1.84, 1981- 1.86, 1982- 1.90, 1983- 1.83i, 1984- 2.00, 1985- 2.06, 1986- 2.08, 1987- 2.09, 1988- 2.07, 1989- 2.04i/1.93, 1991- 2.03, 1992- 2.05, 1993- 2.05, 1994- 2.00i/1.96.
World number one high jumper 1985-8 and the winner of a record four World Indoor titles. After 34 successive wins 1984-6, lost once to Heike Redetzky before 19 further wins 1986-7. Had her 100th competition at 2 metres or more on 24 Jul 1993, with 106 in all and 20 of the 24 all-time performances at 2.05m or more to end 1994. A knee injury affected her form in 1989 and she broke a bone in her left foot when trying to return in 1990. Missed most of 1994 season through pregnancy and her son Nikolai was born in Januray 1995.

Svetlana LESEVA b.18 Mar 1967 Mikhaylovgrad 1.78m 63kg. née Isaeva. Trakia Plovdiv. PE student.
At HJ: OG: '92- dnq; WCh: '87- 7, '91- dnq 14=; EC: '86- 2, '90- 9, '94- 7=; WUG: '87- 1; EJ: '83- 4=, '85- 3; WI: '91- 8=; ECp: '91- 1. 3rd GP 1987. Bulgarian champion 1990.
Progression at HJ: 1981- 1.80, 1982- 1.79, 1983- 1.87, 1984- 1.84, 1985- 1.93, 1986- 1.97, 1987- 2.00, 1988- 1.93, 1989- 1.75i, 1990- 1.90, 1991- 1.98, 1992- 1.95, 1993- 1.80, 1994- 1.94i/1.93.
Married to Delko Lesev, pole vault 5.75i '92, 5.70 '91, 7th Worlds 1987, 2nd WJ 1986. Son, also named Delko, born 1989.

Svetla MITKOVA b.17 Jun 1964 Medovo 1.78m 96kg. Rozova Dolina, Kazanluk.
At SP(DT): OG: '88- 10/4, '92- 6; WCh: '83- (10), '87- 9/5, '91- 10, '93- 10 (dnq 13); EC: '86- 12 (5), '94- 3 (dnq 18); EJ: '81: 3 (2); ECp: '83- 5, '85- 5, '87- 4, '89- 6; EI: '92- 2, '94- 3. Bulgarian champion shot 1984-7, 1990-4; discus 1983, 1990, 1993; Balkan shot 1988. 2nd GP DT 1986.
Progression at SP, DT: 1979- 13.80, 44.30; 1980- 14.10, 50.70; 1981- 17.16, 59.84; 1982- 18.03, 60.58; 1983- 18.83, 66.80; 1984- 19.11, 64.84; 1985- 18.87, 54.34; 1986- 20.05, 68.90; 1987- 20.91, 69.72; 1988- 20.58, 69.14; 1989- 18.08, 58.80; 1990- 18.58, 61.88; 1991- 19.74, 62.52; 1992- 20.41, 64.10; 1993- 20.00, 61.18; 1994- 19.74, 59.78

Anelia NUNEVA b.30 Jun 1962 Byala, Ruse 1.69m 62kg. Levski Spartak, Sofia. PE student. Married name VECHERNIKOVA.
At 100m/R- 4x100m relay (200m): OG: '88- 8, '92- 6 (dns sf); WCh: '83- sf (6), '87- 6/4R; EC: '82- 4 (6), '86- 2/2R, '94- 4/3R; WCp: '85- 4; ECp: '83- 2 (4), '85- 3, '87- 2/2R; WUG: '85- 2/3R. At 60m: WI: '87- 2; EI: '84- 2, '87- 2, '92- 2. Won Balkan 100m 1984-6, 200m 1986. 2nd GP 100m 1987.
Bulgarian records 1982-8: six 100m, two 200m.
Progression at 100m, 200m: 1978- 12.23, 25.60; 1979- 12.10, 25.90; 1980- 12.50; 1981- 11.34/ 11.31w, 23.58; 1982- 11.14, 22.93; 1983- 11.07, 22.58; 1984- 11.10, 22.67; 1985- 11.14, 22.73; 1986- 11.04/10.9, 22.58; 1987- 10.86, 22.01; 1988- 10.85, 22.88; 1991- 11.43; 1992- 11.10, 22.62; 1993- 11.32, 23.18; 1994- 11.33/11.18w. pbs: 50m 6.12i '95, 55m 6.64i '87, 60m 7.03i '87
Ran seven sub-11.00 100m races in 1987 and five in 1988. Heading for a medal in the Olympic final when she pulled a hamstring. Gave birth to a son in October 1989. After illness returned to racing in summer 1991.

Iva PRANDZHEVA b.15 Feb 1972 Plovdiv 1.74m 57kg. Trakia Plovdiv. Student.
At TJ: WCh: '93- 3; EC: '94- nj (8 LJ). At LJ: WCh: '91- dnq; EJ: '91- 3, WJ: '90- 1. Won Bulgarian LJ 1992, TJ 1993.
Two Bulgarian triple jump records 1993.
Progression at LJ, TJ: 1987- 6.17, 1988- 6.27, 1989- 6.27, 1990- 6.53, 1991- 6.54, 1992- 6.62, 1993- 6.58, 14.23/14.32w; 1994- 6.77/6.95w, 14.38i/13.86. pb 100m 11.49 '94.

BURUNDI

Vénuste NIYONGABO b.9 Dec 1973 1.76m 60kg. Cus Parma. Tutsi.
At 1500m (800m): WCh: '93- sf; WJ: '92- 2 (4);

AfG: '91- 7. 2nd GP 1500m 1994.
Burundi records at 1000m, 1500m (4), 1M (2), 2000m 1993-4.
Progression at 1500m: 1991- 3:45.71, 1992- 3:38.59, 1993- 3:36.30, 1994- 3:30.66. pbs: 800m 1:45.13 '94, 1000m 2:15.91 '94, 1M 3:48.94 '94, 2000m 4:58.15 '93, 3000m 7:49.22i '94, 7:50.05 '93.
The world's fastest of 1993 at 2000m came through in 1994 to challenge Morceli as the world's best middle distance runner.

Aloÿs NIZIGAMA b.18 Jun1966. 1.72m 53kg. Tutsi.
At 10000m (5000m): WCh: '91- 6, '93- 5 (7). At 5000m: AfG: '91- 4; AfCh: '92-4.
Burundi record holder at 5000m and 10000m from 1990, 3000m from 1992.
Progression at 5000m, 10000m: 1990- 13:59.9, 29:27.7; 1991- 13:41.21, 28:03.03; 1992- 13:29.08, 27:54.69; 1993- 13:20.59, 27:47.77; 1994- 13:14.66, 27:20.51. pbs: 2000m 5:01.6 '94, 3000m 7:35.08 '94.

CANADA

Governing body: Athletics Canada, 1600 James Naismith Drive, Gloucester, Ontario K1B 5NA. Formed as the Canadian AAU in 1884.
National Championships first held in 1884 (men), 1925 (women). **1994 champions: Men**: 100m: Glenroy Gilbert 10.26, 200m: Robert Esmie 20.84, 400m: Byron Goodwin 46.15, 800m: Freddie Williams 1:49.78, 1500m: Kevin Sullivan 3:39.07, 5000m: Jeff Schiebler 13:52.36, 10000m: Brendan Matthias 29:10.91, 3000mSt: Zeba Crook 8:34.46; 110mh: Tim Kroeker 13.64, 400mh: Monte Raymond 51.46, HJ: Cory Siermachesky 2.27, PV: Owen Clements 5.30, LJ: Ian James 7.60, TJ: George Wright 15.94, SP: Scott Cappos 17.33, DT: Ray Lazdins 57.52, HT: Boris Stoikos 67.40, JT: Larry Steinke 71.18, Dec: Michael Smith 8128, 10kmW: Tim Berrett 40:52. **Women**: 100m: Simone Tomlinson 11.53w, 200m/400m: Stacey Bowen 23.40/53.25, 800m: Charmaine Crooks 2:03.83, 1500m/3000m: Angela Chalmers 4:06.56/ 8:38.42, 10000m: Ulla Marquette 33:16.83, 100mh/400mh: Donalda Duprey 13.22/55.73, HJ: Sara McGladdery 1.80, LJ/Hep: Catherine Bond-Mills 6.32/5842, TJ: Michelle Hastick 12.24, SP: Georgette Reed 16.40, DT: Anna Mosdell 50.04, HT: Theresa Brick 53.62, JT: Valerie Tulloch 55.78, 10kmW: Janice McCaffrey 45:17.

Donovan BAILEY b.16 Dec 1967 Manchester, Jamaica 1.82m 83kg. Phoenix TC. Marketing consultant.
At 100m/4x100mR: CG: '94- 1R; PAm: '92- 2R.
Progression at 100m: 1991- 10.42, 1992- 10.42/10.15w, 1993- 10.36, 1994- 10.03. pbs: 50m 5.78i '92, 60m 6.61i '92, 200m 20.76/20.39w '94.
Emigrated to Canada in 1981.

Tim BERRETT b.23 Jan 1965 Tunbridge Wells, England 1.78m 65kg. Brainsport Athletics Saskatoon. Graduate PE student, University of Alberta.
At 50kmW (20kmW): OG: '92- dq; WCh: '91- 15 (22), '93- 7 (20); WCp: '93- 5. At 3000mW: WI: '93- 4. At 30kmW: CG: '94- 2. Won Canadian 20kmW 1992-3.
Canadian track record 50,000m walk 1991.
Progression at 20kmW, 50kmW: 1984- 1:26:13, 1985- 1:34:55t, 1988- 1:25:09, 1989- 1:25:08, 1990- 1:24:25, 1991- 1:23:10, 3:56:14t; 1992- 1:22:38.1t, 3:50:55; 1993- 1:22:47, 3:50:23. pbs: 3000mW , 5000mW 18:47.56i '93, 10000mW 40:21.17 '91, 30kmW 2:08:22 '94.
A British junior international for four years 1981-4, he moved to Canada in 1987 to study at Queen's University, Kingston.

Michael SMITH b.16 Sep 1967 Kenora, Ontario 1.95m 98kg. Student at University of Toronto.
At Dec: OG: '88- 14, '92- dnf; WCh: '87- dnf, '91- 2, '93- dnf; CG: '86- 7, '90- 1, '94- 1; WJ: '86- 2. Won CAN Dec 1989-90, 1994. At Hep: WI inv: '93- 2.
Canadian decathlon records 1990 and 1991.
Progression at Dec: 1986- 7523, 1987- 8126, 1988- 8039, 1989- 8317, 1990- 8525, 1991- 8549, 1992- 8409, 1993- 8362, 1994- 8326. pbs: 100m 10.43 '85, 400m 47.05 '92, 1500m 4:20.04 '87, 60mh 7.94i '93, 110mh 14.34 '90, 14.24w '91; HJ 2.14 '89, PV 5.20 '94, LJ 7.76 '93, SP 16.38 '94, DT 52.00 '94, JT 69.38 '91, Hep 6279i '93.
Won the Commonwealth gold in 1990, when he added over 200 points to his best decathlon score and opened the second day with three personal bests. Won at Götzis 1991. Three no jumps in long jump at 1993 Worlds.

Bruny SURIN b.12 Jul 1967 Cap-Haïtien, Haiti 1.80m 81kg. Vidéotron, Montreal. Student.
At 100m/4x100m relay: OG: '92- 4; WCh: '91- 8, '93- 5/3R; CG: '90- 3 (7 LJ), '94- sf/1R. At LJ: OG: '88- dnq 15; PAm: '87- dnq 15. At TJ: WJ: '86- 11. At 60m: WI: '91- 8, '93- 1. Won Canadian 100m 1989-92.
Four Canadian 100m records 1989-92.
Progression at 100m, LJ: 1986- 10.95, 7.66, 1987- 10.62, 8.03; 1988- 10.71, 8.02/8.19w; 1989- 10.14/10.1, 8.00; 1990- 10.24/10.12w, 7.85w; 1991- 10.07/10.01w, 1992- 10.05/9.9, 1993- 10.02, 1994- 10.08. pbs: 50m 5.64i '95, 55m 6.17i '93, 60m 6.45i '93, 200m 20.48 '93, TJ 15.96 '86.
Moved to Canada in 1975.

Women

Angela CHALMERS b.6 Sep 1963 Brandon, Manitoba 1.72m 56kg. Adidas. Studied dietetics at Northern Arizona University, USA. Married Ed Espinoza in March 1989 and lives in Arizona.
At 3000m (1500m): OG: '88- 14 (h), '92- 3 (sf); WCh: '93- (5); CG: '90- 1 (1), '94- 1; WCp: '94- (2); PAm: '87- 2; WUG: '85- 3. Won GP 1500m 1994, Canadian 1500m 1989-90, 1993; NCAA CC 1986.
Canadian records 1000m, 2000m & 3000m 1994.
Progression at 1500m, 3000m: 1978- 4:27.3; 1979- 4:23.7; 1981- 4:21.37; 1983- 4:22.0i; 1984- 4:15.36, 9:33.58; 1985- 4:12.13, 9:00.02; 1986- 4:19.5i, 9:31.3; 1987- 4:06.43, 8:56.45; 1988- 4:05.78, 8:48.60; 1989- 4:03.18, 8:46.64; 1990- 4:06.91, 8:38.38; 1991- 4:07.02, 9:00.43; 1992- 4:02.11, 8:42.85; 1993- 4:07.95, 9:01.23; 1994- 4:01.61, 8:32.17. pbs: 800m 2:02.34 '88, 1000m 2:34.99 '94, 1M 4:24.91 '91, 2000m 5:34.49 '94, 5000m 15:34.57 '94.
In 1990 became the first to win the Commonwealth Games 1500m/3000m double. Has Sioux heritage from her mother.

Rosey EDEH b.13 Aug 1966 London, GBR 1.78m 54kg. Québec. Degree in art history from Rice University, USA.
At 400mh/4x400mR: OG: '88- h, '92- sf; WCh: '91- h, '93- 7; CG: '90- 7/3R; WUG: '89- 2; WCp: 1R. Canadian champion 1988-9, 1991, 1993.
Four Canadian 400mh records 1989-93.
Progression at 400mh: 1988- 56.26, 1989- 56.10, 1990- 56.25, 1991- 56.53, 1992- 55.26, 1993- 54.53, 1994- 55.15. pbs: 200m 23.98w '84, 400m 52.38 '92, 100mh 13.83 '89.
Her family moved to Canada when she was two.

Robyn MEAGHER b.17 Jun 1967 Antigonish, Nova Scotia 1.67m 54kg. Island Pacific. Social services research officer.
At 3000m (1500m): OG: '92- h; WCh: '91- h (h); CG: '90- (12), '94- 2; WCp: '94- 2. 2nd PAm Jnr 1500m 1984. Canadian champion 3000m 1991-2.
Progression at 1500m, 3000m: 1984- 4:21.8, 9:38.0; 1985- 4:21.16, 9:46.87; 1986- 4:20.4, 1987- 4:17.4, 1988- 4:09.37, 9:04.90; 1989- 4:08.98, 1990- 4:09.25, 8:52.18; 1991- 4:08.78, 8:58.92; 1992- 4:06.0, 8:43.71; 1993- 4:13.9, 9:22.53; 1994- 4:09.12, 8:45.59. pbs: 800m 2:04.61 '89, 1000m 2:43.82 '90, 1M 4:26.07 '92, 2000m 5:45.89 '94, 5000m 15:21.15 '92.

CHILE

Governing body: Federación Atlética de Chile, Calle Santo Toribio No 660, Nuñoa, Santiago de Chile. Founded 1917.

Gert WEIL b.3 Jan 1960 Puerto Montt 1.97m 124kg. Administrator. Larios, Spain.
At SP: OG: '84- 10, '88- 6, '92- dnq 13; WCh: '87- 10, '91- 9, '93- 6; WI: '89- 6, '91- 6; PAm: '83- 2, '87- 1, "91- 1; WCp: '85- 5, '89- 4, '92- 4. Won SACh 1979-81-83-85-87-89-91 and Jnr 1978.
Nine South American shot records 1984-6.
Progression at SP: 1978- 14.88, 1979- 16.42, 1980- 16.77, 1981- 17.48, 1982- 17.54, 1983- 18.29, 1984- 19.94, 1985- 20.47, 1986- 20.90, 1987- 20.68, 1988- 20.74, 1989- 20.73, 1990- 20.11, 1991- 19.68, 1992- 19.56, 1993- 19.95, 1994- 19.64. pb DT 55.98 '87.
Married Ximena Restrepo COL on 31 Jan 1992.

CHINA

Governing body: Athletic Association of the People's Republic of China, 9 Tiyuguan Road, Beijing 100061.
National Championships first held in 1910 (men), 1959 (women). **1994 Champions**. **Men**: 100m/200m: Chen Wenzhong 10.46/21.16, 400m: Lei Quan 46.66, 800m: Min Weiguo 1:48.21, 1500m: Song Pengyou 3:46.12, 5000m: Sun Reiping 14:04.63, 10000m: Zhang Fukui 29:03.72, Mar: Han Zongmin 2:18:27, 3000mSt: Gao Shuhai 8:31.56, 110mh: Chen Yanjie 13.71, 400mh: Yang Xianjun 50.94, HJ: Tao Xu 2.28, PV: Zhao Mingqiang 5.10, LJ: Huang Geng 8.15, TJ: Zou Sixin 16.47, SP: Lin Hao 19.14, DT: Ma Wei 58.98, HT: Bi Zhong 72.46, JT: Zhang Lianbiao 80.08, Dec: Cai Man 78.50, 20kmW: Pu Lingtang 1:18:04, 50kmW: Zhou Yonsheng 3:43:16. **Women**: 100m: Huang Xiaoyan 11.42, 200m: Chen Zhaojing 22.97, 400m: Ma Yuqin 50.45, 800m/1500m: Qu Yunxia 1:59.37/4:00.34, 3000m: Wang Xiaoxia 8:49.92, 10000m: Wang Junxia 31:38.17, Mar: Ren Xiujuan 2:38:23, 100mh: Zhang Yu 12.87, 400mh: Leng Xueyan 56.28, HJ: Guan Weihua 1.85, PV: Cai Weiyan 3.85, LJ: Li Jing 6.88, TJ: Ren Ruiping 14.36, SP: Zhang Liuhong 20.54, DT: Qiu Qiaoping 65.66, JT: Zhang Li 61.34, Hep: Zhang Xiaohui 6200, 10kmW: Gao Hongmiao 41:38.

HUANG Geng b.10 Jul 1970 Henan Province 1.79m 71kg.
At LJ: OG: '92- 8; WCh: '91- dnq 28; AsiC: '91- 1; AsiG: '90- 2, '94- 1. Chinese champion 1990, 1992, 1994.
Progression at LJ: 1989- 7.88, 1990- 8.18, 1991- 8.17, 1992- 8.22, 1993- 8.30, 1994- 8.15/8.34w.

LI Tong b.6 May 1967 Hangzhou, Zhejiang 1.90m 80kg. Computer science student at Washington State University.
At 110mh: OG: '92- sf; WCh: '91- 8, '93- sf;

AsiG: '94- 1; AsiC: '93- 1; WCp: '94- 5. Won NCAA indoor 55mh 1990-1. At LJ: WJ: '86- 7.
Nine Asian 110mh records 1989-94, Asian records at 50mh, 55mh, 60mh.
Progression at 110mh: 1988- 14.21, 1989- 13.68/13.49w, 1990- 13.62, 1991- 13.37/13.31w, 1992- 13.59/13.3, 1993- 13.26, 1994- 13.25. pbs: 100m 10.42 '92, 10.4 '87; 200m 21.01 '92, 50mh 6.54i '92, 55mh 7.08i '91, 60mh 7.69i '93, HJ: 2.10 '85, LJ 7.70 '86.
Started career at 400m and decathlon, then long jump, before high hurdles. Known in the USA as Tony Li. Fell when leading in 1990 Asian Games, 1991 NCAA and World Student Games.

Women

DONG Li b.9 Dec 1973. 1.64m 55kg.
At 10000m: AsiG: '94- 2.
Progression at 10000m: 1992- 33:09.50, 1993- 31:52.59, 1994- 31:31.08. pbs: 3000m 8:53.27 '94.

GAO Hongmiao b.8 Jul 1974 (or 1972) 1.62m 51kg.
At 10kmW: AsiG: '94- 1; AsiC: '93- 1. At 5000mW: WJ: '92- 1.
World junior 10,000m walk records track 1992, road 1993? Asian 10 km walk record 1994.
Progression at 10kmW: 1991- 42:56.09, 1992- 42:49.7, 1993- 41:57, 1994- 41:38. pb 5000mW 21:20.03 '92.
Date of birth now given as 1972, but in that case she would not have been a junior when she won the World Junior title in 1992.

HUANG Zhihong b.7 May 1965 Lanxi county, Zhejiang 1.74m 100kg. Student at Loughborough University, GBR.
At SP: OG: '88- 8, '92- 2; WCh: '87- 11, '91- 1, '93- 1; WUG: '89- 1; WCp: '89- 1, '94- 1; WI: '89- 2, '91- 2; AsiG: '86- 1, '90- 2; AsiC: '89- 1, '91- 1. Won GP 1991. Chinese champion 1988-92.
Asian shot record 1988.
Progression at SP: 1983- 16.12, 1984- 17.04, 1985- 18.01, 1986- 18.89, 1987- 20.22, 1988- 21.28, 1989- 20.73, 1990- 21.52, 1991- 20.85, 1992- 20.47, 1993- 20.57, 1994- 20.08.
The first Asian athlete to have won a World Cup event (1989) and the first to have won a Grand Prix series (1991).

LI Chunxiu b.13 Aug 1969 Qinghai Province. 1.70m 60kg.
At 10kmW: OG: '92- 3; WCp: '89- 14; won Asi-J 1986, EAG 1993.
Asian 10km road walk best 1993.
Progression at 10kmW: 1986- 46:45.0t, 1987- 46:41.5t, 1989- 46:00, 1990- 44:06, 1991- 44:41, 1992- 42:47.6t, 1993- 41:48, 1994- 43:01. pb 5000mW 21:54.9 '88, 21:03R '89.

LIU Dong b.27 Dec 1973 Liaoning 1.73m 55kg. Student at Shanghai University.
At 1500m: WCh: '93- 1; WJ: '92- 1, EAG: '93- 2.
Two Asian 800m records 1993.
Progression at 800m, 1500m: 1991- 2:02.4, 1992- 2:02.96, 4:05.14; 1993- 1:55.54, 4:00.50.
Did not compete in 1994 due to problems with her coach, but plans to return in 1995.

LIU Li b.12 Mar 1971 Liaoning 1.67m 47kg.
At 800m: WCh: '93- 6; WJ: '90- 5; AsiC: '93- 1. At 1500m: OG: '92- 5, WJ: '90- 5; won Asi J 800m 1990.
Progression at 800m, 1500m: 1989- 2:04.81, 1990- 2:02.38, 4:16.38; 1991- 2:01.6, 4:09.58; 1992- 4:00.20, 1993- 1:56.96, 3:59.34; 1994- 1:59.95, 4:14.54.

MA Yuqin b.11 Sep 1972 Zunhua, Hebei Prov.
At 400m/4x400mR: AsiG: '94- 1/1R; AsiC: '93- 1; won Asi J 1990. Chinese champion 1993-4.
Three Asian 400m records 1993, also Chinese record 1991.
Progression at 400m: 1989- 53.8, 1990- 52.97, 1991- 52.04, 1992- 52.95, 1993- 49.81, 1994- 50.45. pb 200m 22.95 '93.

MIN Chunfeng b.17 Mar 1969 Jiangxi Prov. 1.75m 79kg.
At DT (SP): OG: '92- 11; WCh: '91- 6, '93- 3; AsiG: '94- 1; AsiC: '91- 1 (2); WJ: '86- 3, '88- 4; WCp: '92- 3 (6). Chinese champion 1991, EAG 1993.
Progression at DT: 1984- 53.14, 1985- 54.70, 1986- 55.10, 1987- 62.50, 1988- 60.60, 1990- 63.50, 1991- 66.76, 1992- 63.92, 1993- 65.26, 1994- 66.26. pb SP 16.93 '88.

QU Yunxia b.25 Dec 1972 Liaoning 1.70m 58kg.
At 1500m (800m): OG: '92- 3; WUG: '91- 3; WJ: '90- 1 (6 800m); AsiG: '94- 1 (1); AsiC: '91- 1 (1); won Asi J 1990. At 3000m: Asi C: '93- 1. World CC: '92- 6. Chinese champion 800m 1994, 1500m 1992, 1994; 3000m 1992, EAG 1500m 1993. World 1500m record 1993, Four Asian 1500m records 1991-3.
Progression at 800m, 1500m, 3000m: 1989- 2:03.47, 4:11.36; 1990- 2:04.09, 4:11.89; 1991- 2:04.65, 4:07.71, 8:55.1; 1992- 3:57.08, 8:58.58; 1993- 1:56.24, 3:50.46, 8:12.18; 1994- 1:59.37, 4:00.34. pbs: 5000m 15:28.91 '91, Mar 2:24:32 '93.
Second in 2:24:32 on marathon début at Tianjin April 1993.Took 2.01 sec off the 13-year old world record for 1500m and was also ten seconds inside the previous world record for 3000m when second to Wang Junxia at the Chinese National Games 1993, a month after winning the World title at 3000m.

REN Ruiping b.1 Jan 1975 Shandong province.
At TJ: WJ: '94- 2; AsiC: '93- 1; WCp: '94- 3. Chinese champion 1994.
Three World junior triple jump records 1993-4.
Progression at TJ: 1991- 13.10, 1993- 14.29, 1994- 14.36.

SUI Xinmei b.29 Jan 1965 Shandong 1.72m 90kg. Student at Shanghai Institute of PE.
At SP: WCh: '93- 4; WI: '91- 1; AsiG: '90- 1, '94- 1; AsiC: '89- 2; WUG: '91- dq 1. Won GWG 1994.
Progression at SP: 1985- 16.24, 1986- 18.87, 1987- 18.87, 1988- 20.08, 1989- 19.81, 1990- 21.66, 1991- 20.54i/19.94 dq, 1993- 20.32, 1994- 20.74.
Disqualified on a positive drugs test, having won the 1991 World Student Games shot title, and was banned for two years.

SUN Caiyun b.21 Jul 1973.
Chinese pole vault champion 1992-3.
Four unofficial world pole vault records outdoors 1992-4; eight WIR 1993-5 (three unofficial 1993).
Progression at PV: 1991- 3.83, 1992- 4.05, 1993- 4.11, 1994- 4.12, 1995- 4.15i.
Lost world indoor pole vault record of 4.08 through positive drugs test for stimulants and three months ban from March 1994.

WANG Junxia b.9 Jan 1973 Jiahoe City, Jilin Province 1.60m 45kg.
At 10000m: WCh: '93- 1; WJ: '92- 1, AsiG: '94- 1; AsiC: '93- 1. At Mar: WCp: '93- 1. World CC: '92- 2 Jnr. Won Chinese 3000m 1993, 10,000m 1993-4, Mar 1993.
World records: 3000m (2), 10000m 1993. Asian records 3000m (3), 10000m (3), marathon 1993.
Progression at 1500m, 3000m, 10,000m, Mar: 1991- 4:17.18, 1992- 8:55.50, 32:29.90; 1993- 3:51.92, 8:06.11, 29:31.78, 2:24:07; 1994- 8:50.79, 30:53.04, 2:31:11. pb 5000m: none, but 14:50.34 for last 5000m in 10000m '94.
The star pupil of Ma Junren. Has won all three marathons that she has run, from 2:24:07 on début in Tianjin in April 1993. two weeks after running a world best Ekiden relay 5k split of 14:52. In 1993 she went on to double success at the Chinese Championships and to win the World 10000m title with a last 3k in 8:42.49. At the Chinese National Games in September 1993 she took 41.96 sec off the world record for 10,000m on the 8th, ran second to Qu Yunxia at 15000m in 3:51.92, inside the 13 year-old world record, on the 11th, and then set 3000m world records of 8:12.29 on the 12th and 8:06.11 on the 13th, compared to the 8:22.62 which had remained the world record since 1984. Moved to Liaoning province in 1986.

WANG Xiuting b.15 Jan 1965 Shandong Prov. 1.58m 48kg. PE student.
At 10000m (3000m): OG: '88- 7 (h), '92- 6; WCh: '87- 8 (h), '91- 3; AsiG: '86- 1, '90- 2. World 15km Rd: '88- 2, '89- 1. Won CHN 3000m 1989.
Asian records: 10000m (3), 5000m (2), 3000m (1) 1986-91.
Progression at 10000m: 1986- 32:47.77, 1987- 31:27.00, 1988- 31:40.23, 1990- 31:52.18, 1991- 31:35.99, 1992- 31:28.06, 1993- 31:32.23. pbs: 3000m 8:50.68 '87, 5000m 15:23.58 '91. Road: 15km 49:34 '89, Half Mar 1:10:14 '91, Mar 2:28:56 '92.
Fifth on marathon début Jan 1992 in Osaka, then second Beijing 1993.

WANG Yan b.3 May 1971 Liaoning 1.61m 46kg. Student.
At 10kmW: WCh: '93- dq; WCp: '93- 1. Chinese champion 1993.
World walk records 1986: 3km: 12:39.1, 5km: 21:33.8, with the latter at age 14 years 310 days, she is the youngest ever to set a world record. At 10km walk world junior record 1986, Asian record 1993.
Progression at 10kmW: 1984- 49:01, 1985- 46:09, 1986- 44:59.3t, 1987- 45:22.24t, 1992- 42:50, 1993- 42:26. pb 20kmW 1:37:24 '94.

ZHANG Linli b.6 Mar 1973 Liaoning 1.64m 48kg.
At 3000m: WCh: '93- 2; WJ: '92- 1; AsiG: '94- 1; AsiC: '93- 2; EAG: '93- 2. At Mar: WCp: '93- 2.
At 3000m: Asian record 1992 and World 1993.
Progression at 1500m, 3000m, 10000m: 1991- 4:15.96, 9:01.7; 1992- 8:46.86, 1993- 3:57.46, 8:16.50, 31:16.28; 1994- 4:13.97, 8:50.05, 32:19.33. pbs: 5000m 15:35.70 '91, Mar 2:24:42 '93.
Set a world 3000m record of 8:22.06 in first heat of Chinese National Games 1993, before third in the final in 8:16.50.

ZHANG Lirong b.3 Mar 1973 Liaoning 1.56m 48kg.
At 3000m: WCh: '93- 3; WJ: '92- 3; won EAG 1993. At 10000m: AsiC: '93- 2; At Mar: WCp: '93- 3; AsiG: '94- 2.
Asian 3000m record 1993.
Progression at 1500m, 3000m, 10000m, Mar: 1991- 4:19.17, 9:10.2, 2:33:59; 1992- 8:48.45, 33:37.1; 1993- 3:59.70, 8:21.84, 31:09.25, 2:24:52; 1994- 4:13.84, 8:50.51, 2:36:27.

ZHANG Liuhong b.16 Jan 1969 1.81m 86kg.
At SP: WI: '93- 3; AsiG: '94- 2; AsiC: '93- 1. Won EAG 1993. Chinese champion 1994.
Progression at SP: 1987- 16.74, 1988- 17.73, 1989- 17.93, 1990- 19.60, 1991- 19.74, 1993- 19.90, 1994- 20.54.

ZHANG Yu b.8 Apr 1971 Tianjin 1.76m 64kg.
At 100mh: OG: '92- sf; WCh: '91- sf; WCp: '92- 4; AsiG: '94- 3; AsiC: '91- 1, '93- 1. Chinese champion 1991-4, AsiJ 1990, EAG 1993.
Asian 100mh record 1993.
Progression at 100mh: 1989- 13.75, 1990- 13.38, 1991- 13.03/13.0, 1992- 12.92, 1993- 12.64, 1994- 12.86. pbs: 100m 11.5 '91, 200m 23.4 '92, 60mh 8.26i '93.

ZHONG Huandi b.28 Jun 1967 Yunnan Prov. 1.55m 43kg. Niko-Niko-Do, Japan.
At 10000m (3000m): OG: '92- 4; WCh: '91- 2, '93- 2; WUG: '87- 2; AsiG: '90- 1 (1); AsiC: '89- 1 (1), '91- 1 (1); WCp: '92- 3 (6). At Mar: OG: '88- 30; AsiG: '94- 1. World 15kmRd: ''88-4, '89- 2, '90- 3. Won Chinese 3000m 1989-90; 10000m 1989-92.
Asian 10000m record 1992.
Progression at 10000m, Mar: 1986- 33:31.58, 1987- 32:53.68, 2:32:13; 1989- 32:25.27, 1990- 31:50.98, 1991- 31:35.08, 1992- 31:21.08; 1993- 30:13.37, 2:25:36; 1994- 31:43.69, 2:29:32. pbs: 3000m 8:41.67 '93, 5000m 15:30.15 '89, 15kmRd 49:44 '89.

COLOMBIA

Governing body: Federación Colombiana de Atletismo, Calle 28 No. 25-18, Bogotá. Founded 1937.
National Champions 1994: **Men**: 100m: Robinson Urrutia 10.2, 200m: Wenceslao Ferrín 20.7, 400m: Wilson Cañizales 46.7, 800m: Diego Córdoba 1:50.0, 1500m/5000m: Jacinto Navarette 3:48.5/14:25.6, 10000m: Herder Vasquez 30:25.3, 3000mSt: Gonzao Vanegas 9:09.7, 110mh: José Rivas 14.4, 400mh: Llimi Rivas 51.1, HJ/TJ: Gilmar Mayo 2.28/16.04, PV: Juan Jaramillo 4.30, LJ: Lewis Asprilla 7.40, SP: Orlando Ibarra 15.91, DT: Isaac Vallecilla 49.10, HT: Fabián Vera 50.34, JT: Luis Lucumí 67.54, Dec: Cecilio Escobar 6102, 20kmW: Héctor Moreno 1:27:02, 35kmW: Rodrigo Moreno 2:57:31. **Women**: 100m: Mirtha Brack 11.5, 200m: Patricia Rodriguez 23.4, 400m/800m/400mh: Flor Robledo 54.9/2:14.4/60.1, 1500m: Julieth Mendoza 4:41.6, 3000m: Iglandini González 10:04.3, 10000m: Stella Castro 36:31.4, 100mh: Martha Dinas 14.0, HJ: Fernanda Mosquera 1.70, LJ: Elena Guerrero 5.80, TJ: Milli Figueroa 12.13, SP/DT: M Isabel Urrutia 14.01/53.04, HT: Maria Villamizar 51.18, JT: Zuleima Aramendiz 50.66, 10kmW: Cristina Bohorquez 51:48.

Gilmar MAYO b. 30 Sep 1969.
At HJ: SAmCh: '91- 1, '93- 4; PAm: '91- 11.
Four South American high jump records 1994, Colombian triple jump records 1989 & 1994.
Progression at HJ: 1990- 2.10, 1991- 2.20, 1992- 2.16, 1993- 2.20, 1994- 2.33. pb TJ: 16.04 '94.

Women

Ximena RESTREPO b.10 Mar 1969 Medellín 1.75m 58kg. Studied broadcasting at University of Nebraska. Married Gert Weil (nine SAm shot records to 20.90 '86, PAm champion 1987 & 1991) on 31 Jan 1992.
At 400m: OG: '92- 3; WCh: '91- 6, '93- 5; PAm: '91- 2 (2 200m); WJ: '88- sf (sf 100m, 200m); WCp: '92- 1R; won NCAA 1991. 2nd GP 1992. At 200m: OG: '88- h; SAm: '87- 1 (2 100m, 4x100m), '91- 1/2R/2R; CAG: '90- 2 4x100m, '93- 3 (2 4x100m).
South American records 200m 1991, 400m (3) 1991-2, 400mh 1994; Colombian 400m (8), 200m 1990-2, 400mh 1994.
Progression at 400m: 1988- 53.48, 1989- 55.55i, 1990- 51.64, 1991- 50.14, 1992- 49.64, 1993- 50.38, 1994- 51.31. pbs: 100m 11.54/11.3 '91, 11.30w '89; 200m 22.92/22.4A '91, 400mh 56.05 '94.
First Colombian to win an Olympic athletics medal. Won four gold medals: 200m, 400m and both relays at 1994 Ibero-American Champs.

CROATIA

Governing body: Hrvatski Atletski Savez, Tg Sportova 11, 41000 Zagreb. Founded 1912.
National Champions 1994: **Men**: 100m: Davor Pucevic 10.89, 200m: Tin Kaiser 22.19, 400m: Igor Marjanovic 48.20, 800m/1500m: Slobodan Mijolovic 1:50.81/3:47.32, 5000m: Nebojsa Pesic 14:28.00, 10000m: Mladen Krsek 30:54.4, 3000mSt: Sasa Ljubojevic 9:11.7, 110mh: Nedeljko Visnjic 14.40, 400mh: Franjo Pavlovic 53.16, HJ: Ivan Penavic 2.13, PV: Alen Simunkovic 4.60, LJ: Sinisa Ergotic 7.62, TJ: Djordje Kozul 15.85, SP: Mihovil Rendulic 17.17, DT: Dragan Mustapic 54.44, HT: Andrej Simunjak 60.56, JT: Ivan Mustapic 82.08. **Women**: 100m/200m: Rahela Markt 11.76/24.78, 400m/400mh: Sanja Happ 56.93/61.77, 800m/1500m: Mara Zuzul 2:08.46/4:29.76, 3000m: Tijana Stojcevic 10:09.10, 10000m: Slavica Brcic 39:41.0, 100mh: Dragana Ciganovic 14.42, HJ: Nevena Lendel 1.70, LJ/TJ: Silvija Babic 6.19/12.84, SP: Silvija Mogus 13.63, DT: Viktorija Florjan 47.84, JT: Valentina Belaic 53.54.

Branko ZORKO b.1 Jul 1967 Crskovec 1.80m 73kg.
At 1500m: OG: '88- h, '92- sf; WCh: '93- sf; EC: '90- h, '94- 3; WI: '93- 3; EI: '92- 3, '94- 2. At 3000m: WI: '89- 6; EI: '90- 3. Won Balkan 1500m 1989, YUG 1500m 1988-90.
Croatian records 1500m, 3000m, 5000m.

Progression at 1500m: 1985- 3:48.67, 1986- 3:45.00, 1987- 3:42.51, 1988- 3:37.33, 1989- 3:37.74, 1990- 3:40.22, 1991- 3:39.34, 1992- 3:36.88, 1993- 3:35.09. 1994- 3:34.84. pbs: 800m 1:47.67 '89, 1000m 2:18.62 '92, 1M 3:57.01 '93, 2000m 5:06.96 '90, 3000m 7:49.29i '90, 7:54.39 '89; 5000m 13:43.04 '89, 3000mSt 8:48.82 '90.
Had his spleen removed folllowing a serious traffic accident in October 1990, but has remained a fierce competitor.

CUBA

Governing body: Federación Cubana de Atletismo, 13 y C Vedado 601, Zone Postal 4, Habana 10400. Founded 1922.
National Champions 1994. **Men**: 100m: Leonardo Prevot 10.40, 200m: Jorge Aguilera 20.80, 400m: Norberto Tellez 45.93, 800m: Alain Miranda 1:48.77, 1500m: Amado Ramos 3:48.37, 5000m: Luis Cadet 14:28.03, 10000m: Ignacio Cuba 30:15.00, 3000mSt: Juan Ramon Conde 8:48.12, 110mh: Emilio Valle 13.41, 400mh: José Pérez 49.39, HJ: Javier Sotomayor 2.41, PV: Alberto Manzano 5.61, LJ: Jaime Jefferson 8.13, TJ: Yoelbi Quesada 17.22, SP: Carlos Fandino 18.27, DT: Roberto Moya 60.88, HT: Alberto Sánchez 74.24, JT: Emeterio González 74.96, Dec: Eugenio Balanque 8093, 20kmW: Ihosvany Diaz 1:29:06; 50kmW: Edel Oliva 4:07:06. **Women**: 100m/200m: Liliana Allen 11.18/22.72, 400m: Julia Duporty 51.01, 800m: Odalmis Limonta 2:06.56, 1500m: Liudmila Duboy 4:37.85, 3000m/10000m: Yesenia Centeno 9:41.49/ 35:16.88, 100mh: Aliuska López 13.15, 400mh: Lency Montelier 57.38, HJ: Silvia Costa 2.00, LJ/TJ: Niurka Montalvo 6.65/14.60, SP: Yumileidi Cumba 18.39, DT: Barbara Hechavarría 63.24, JT: Xiomara Rivero 60.80, Hep: Magalys García 6076, 10kmW: Oslaidis Cruz 51:31.

Alexis ELIZALDE b.19 Sep 1967 Ciudad Habana 1.92m 118kg.
At DT: WCh: '93- dnq 14; WCp: '94- 2; WUG: '91- 3, '93- 1. Won CAC 1993.
Progression at DT: 1985- 47.40, 1986- 50.88, 1987- 52.54, 1988- 53.04, 1989- 57.76, 1990- 59.62, 1991- 62.52, 1992- 60.92, 1993- 64.12, 1994- 62.74. pb SP 16.10 '88.

Roberto HERNANDEZ b.6 Mar 1967 Limonar, Matanzas 1.79m 74kg. Student.
At 400m/R- 4x400m relay: OG: '92- 8/2R; WCh: '87- 4/3R, '91- 4, '93- qf; PAm: '87- 3/2R, '91- 1; CAG: '90- 1 (1 200m); WJ: '86- 2/2R; WUG: '85- 2/1R, 89- 1; WCp: '89- 1/1R; WI: '87- 2. Won GWG 1990, CAC 1985, 1989; Cuban 1985, 1988, 1990-2 (200m 1988). Won PAm-J 200m & 400m 1986.
CAC & Cuban 400m records 1988 and 1990. Two world 300m bests 1990.
Progression at 400m: 1983- 48.0, 1984- 46.44, 1985- 45.14, 1986- 45.05, 1987- 44.61, 1988- 44.22, 1989- 44.58/44.3A, 1990- 44.14, 1991- 44.40, 1992- 44.52, 1993- 46.01. pbs: 200m 20.24 '88, 20.2 '85; 300m 31.48 '90.
Has run 53 times sub 45 secs, including a then season's record 17 in 1990 and 12 in 1991. Missed 1994 season through injury.

Jaime JEFFERSON b.17 Jan 1962 Guantanamo 1.89m 78kg.
At LJ: OG: '92- 5; WCh: '87- 6, '91- 9, '93- dnq 15; WI: '89- 5, '91- 2, '93- 3; PAm: '83- 1, '87- 3, '91- 1; CAG: '86- 1, '90- 2, '93- 3; WUG: '85- 1, '89- 1; WCp: '89- 8. CAC champion 1985, 1989; Cuban 1984-6, 1988-91, 1994.
Seven CAC & Cuban long jump records 1984-90.
Progression at LJ: 1981- 7.25, 1982- 7.50, 1983- 8.05, 1984- 8.37, 1985- 8.24/8.28w, 1986- 8.47, 1987- 8.51, 1988- 8.37, 1989- 8.29, 1990- 8.53, 1991- 8.26, 1992- 8.21/8.41w, 1993- 8.06, 1994- 8.13. pbs: 100m 10.2/10.35/10.33w '85, 200m 21.22 '92, TJ 16.28 '85.

Roberto MOYA b.11 Feb 1965 Ciudad Habana 1.93m 110kg.
At DT: OG: '92- 3; WCh: '91- 8, '93- dnq 17; PAm: '91- 2; CAG: '90- 1; WUG: '89- 3; WCp: '92- 2. Won CAC 1987 & 1989, Cuban 1989, 1992-4.
Progression at DT: 1984- 49.10, 1985- 56.48, 1986- 59.04, 1987- 62.92, 1988- 61.20, 1989- 63.78, 1990- 65.68, 1991- 63.92, 1992- 64.64, 1993- 64.08, 1994- 61.00. pb SP 15.79 '87.

Ivan PEDROSO b.17 Dec 1972 Ciudad Habana 1.77m 65kg. Larios, Spain.
At LJ: OG: '92- 4; WCh: '93- nj; WI: '93- 1; WJ: '90- 4; PAm: '91- 3; WCp: '92- 1. Won PAm J 1991, Cuban 1992-3.
Equalled CAC & Cuban long jump record 1992.
Progression at LJ: 1988- 7.43, 1989- 7.43, 1990- 8.06, 1991- 8.22, 1992- 8.53/8.79w, 1993- 8.49, 1994- 8.26i/8.16. pb TJ 16.05 '91.
Injured at 1993 World Championships.

Yoelbi Luis **QUESADA** b.4 Aug 1973 Sancti Spiritus 1.80m 73kg.
At TJ: OG: '92- 6; WCh: '91- 7, '93- 12; WI: '93- 5; WJ: '90- 2, '92- 1; WCp: '94- 1; PAm: '91- 1; CAG: '93- 1. Won CACJ 1990, PAmJ 1991, Cuban 1991-4.
Progression at TJ: 1989- 16.11, 1990- 16.68, 1991- 17.13, 1992- 17.23, 1993- 17.68, 1994- 17.61. pb LJ 7.88 '94.
World age-16 best 1990.

Javier SOTOMAYOR b.13 Oct 1967 Limonar, Matanzas 1.95m 82kg. PE teacher, graduate of Habana Institute of PE. Larios, Spain.
At HJ: OG: '92- 1; WCh: '87- 9, '91- 2, '93- 1; PAm: '87- 1, '91- 1; CAG: '90- 1, '93- 1; WJ: '86- 1; WCp: '85- 3, '89- 3, '92- 2, '94- 1; WUG: '89- 1; WI: '85- 2, '87- 4, '89- 1, '91- 3=, '93- 1. Cuban champion 1984, 1986-9, 1991-4; CAC 1985, 1989; PAm-J 1986; GWG 1994. Won GP 1988 (third overall), 1994.
World high jump records 1988, 1989 the first 8-foot jump, and 1993. WIR 2.43m 1989. World junior record 1986, nine CAC & Cuban records 1984-93.
Progression at HJ: 1980- 1.65, 1981- 1.84, 1982- 2.00, 1983- 2.17, 1984- 2.33, 1985- 2.34, 1986- 2.36, 1987- 2.37, 1988- 2.43, 1989- 2.44, 1990- 2.36, 1991- 2.40, 1992- 2.36, 1993- 2.45, 1994- 2.42.
Master technician, with very fast, head-on approach. Set world age bests each year from 15 to 19 in 1983-7. Married high jumper (1.90 '90) Maria del Carmen Garcia in Sept. 1989.
Has cleared 2.30m or better in 168 meetings (68 at 2.35 or more and 20 at 2.40 or more) 1984-94.

Emilio VALLE b.21 Apr 1967 Sancti Spiritus 1.82m 70kg. Larios, Spain.
At 110mh: OG: '92- 6; WCh: '93- 4; WJ: '86- 3 (1 400mh); WCp: '94- 3; PAm: '91- 4; CAG: '90- 1 (1 4x400mR), '93- 1; WUG: '89- 2; WCp: '89- 3, '92- 3. Won CAC 110mh 1989, Cuban 110mh 1988-9, 1992-4; 400mh 1987. At 60mh: WI: '89- 5, '91- 4, '93- 7.
CAC & Cuban 110mh record 1993.
Progression at 110mh: 1984- 14.4, 1985- 14.46, 1986- 13.97, 1987- 13.76, 1988- 13.60, 1989- 13.30/13.21w, 1990- 13.64, 1991- 13.74, 1992- 13.39, 1993- 13.19, 1994- 13.33. pbs: 100m 10.54 '94, 200m 21.70 '93, 60mh 7.59i '89, 400mh 50.02 '86.

Women

Liliana ALLEN b.24 May 1970 Holguín 1.70m 62kg. Married to 400m runner Agustin Pavo.
At 100m/4x100mR (200m): OG: '92- 8; WCh: '91- sf/6R, '93- 8; WJ: '88- 3/2R (3); PAm: '87- 4, '91- 1/2R (1); CAG: '90 & '93- 1/1R (1); WCp: '89- 5/4R, '92- 2, '94- 2; WUG: '89- 1 (2), '93- 2 (5). At 60m: WI: '89- 4, '91- 3, '93- 4. Won CACJ 100m 1986, PAmJ 100m/200m 1989, Cuban 100m 1988-94, 200m 1988, 1990-4.
Cuban 100m records 1989 and 1992, 200m 1994.
Progression at 100m, 200m: 1985- 12.20; 1986- 11.83, 24.81; 1987- 11.42/11.19w, 23.83; 1988- 11.18, 23.13/22.97w; 1989- 11.14/10.9, 23.00/22.7; 1990- 11.22/11.19w, 23.22; 1991- 11.21, 23.11; 1992- 11.10, 22.98; 1993- 11.19, 23.12/22.90w; 1994- 11.14, 22.72. pb 60m 7.12i '91.

Silvia COSTA b.4 May 1964 Pinar del Rio 1.79m 60kg. Larios, Spain.
At HJ: OG: '92- 6; WCh: '83- 10=, '87- 4, '93- 2; WI: '85- 3=, '93- 7=; PAm: '79- 8, '83- 2, '87- 2; WUG: '83- 2, '85- 1, '89- 2; WCp: '85- 4, '89- 1, '94- 3; CAG: '82- 1, '86- 1, '90- 2. Won CAC 1985, 1989, Cuban 1981-8, 1994; GWG 1994. 2nd GP 1989.
Two world junior high jump records 1982. 15 Cuban records 1980-9.
Progression at HJ: 1977- 1.57, 1978- 1.64, 1979- 1.82, 1980- 1.90, 1981- 1.88, 1982- 1.95, 1983- 1.98, 1984- 1.99, 1985- 2.01, 1986- 1.99, 1987- 1.96, 1988- 2.02, 1989- 2.04, 1990- 1.82, 1991- 1.96i, 1992- 1.97, 1993- 1.98, 1994- 2.00. pb 100mh 13.73 '88.
Married to Lázaro Martinez (1992 Olympic 4x400m silver medallist, pb 45.37 '83, 45.1 '89). Daughter born 1990. She returned to competition but then suffered a ruptured Achilles.

Julia DUPORTY b.9 Feb 1971 Guantánamo 1.71m 63kg.
At 400m/4x400mR: WCp: '94- 5/3R; PAm: '91- 2R; CAG: '90- 1R, '94- 1/1R. At 200m: WJ: '90- 8/3R. Won Cuban 400m 1994.
Progression at 400m: 1987- 57.08, 1988- 56.9, 1990- 55.18, 1991- 53.27, 1992- 52.75, 1993- 51.81, 1994- 50.61. pbs: 100m 11.81 '90, 200m 23.15 '94.

Silvia Costa:

Bárbara HECHAVARRIA b.6 Aug 1966 Holguin 1.70m 94kg.
At DT: OG: '92- dnq 15; WCh: '91- 12, '93- 6; WCp: '94- 4; PAm: '91- 1; CAG: '90- 1, '93- 1. Won CAC 1987, Cuban 1991, 1994; GWG 1994.
Progression at DT: 1983- 45.90, 1984- 49.52, 1985- 50.42, 1986- 54.70, 1987- 57.64, 1988- 60.26, 1989- 68.18, 1990- 64.14, 1991- 67.42, 1992- 64.66, 1993- 62.52, 1994- 65.62.

Belsy LAZA b.5 Jun 1967 Ciudad Habana 1.74m 96kg.
At SP: OG: '92- 4; WCh: '91- 9, '93- 8; WI: '89- 6, '91- 5, '93- 7; WUG: '89- 2; PAm: '87- 3, '91- 1; WCp: '89- 6, '92- 1, '94- 2; CAG: '90- 1; Cuban champion 1987-93. Cuban & CAC shot record 1992.
Progression at SP: 1982- 12.66, 1983- 13.82, 1984- 16.09, 1985- 16.90, 1986- 17.85, 1987- 18.49, 1988- 19.34, 1989- 19.98, 1990- 19.16, 1991- 19.54, 1992- 20.96, 1993- 19.33, 1994- 19.07.

Aliuska LOPEZ b.29 Aug 1969 Ciudad Habana 1.69m 53kg. Larios, Spain.
At 100mh: OG: '92- 6; WCh: '87- sf, '91- 7/6R, '93- 4; PAm: '87- 3 (2R), '91- 1; CAG: '90 & '93- 1/1R; WJ: '86- 2, '88- 1; WUG: '87- 2; WCp: '92- 1, '94- 1. 3rd GP 1994. At 60mh: WI: '91- 3, '93- 5. Won Cuban 100mh 1986-9, 1993-4.
Two world junior 100mh records 1987; six Cuban records 1986-93.
Progression at 100mh: 1984- 14.4, 1985- 13.5/13.97, 1986- 13.14, 1987- 12.84, 1988- 12.96, 1989- 12.87, 1990- 12.73, 1991- 12.91, 1992- 12.87, 1993- 12.73, 1994-12.74. pbs: 100m 11.53 '87, 200m 24.22 '87, 60mh 8.02i '90, 400mh 64.32 '86.

Isel LOPEZ b.11 Jul 1970 Santiago de Cuba 1.74m 74kg.
At JT: OG: '92- dnq 13; WCh: '91- nt; WJ: '86- 7, '88- 2; WUG: '91- 2; WCp: '94- 3; CAG: '93- 1. Cuban champion 1990, 1992, CAC 1993.
Progression at JT: 1985- 45.50, 1986- 57.44, 1987- 58.78, 1988- 60.52, 1989- 63.54, 1990- 66.16, 1991- 62.32, 1992- 65.62, 1993- 61.48, 1994- 62.74.

Maritza MARTEN b.17 Aug 1963 Ciudad Habana 1.77m 83kg.
At DT: OG: '92- 1; WCh: '87- 9, '91- 10, '93- 4; PAm: '83- 2, '87- 1; CAG: '86- 2; WCp: '85- 3, '89- 3, '92- 1; WUG: '85- 1, '89- 3. Won PAm-J 1982, CAC 1985, Cuban champion 1982-7, 1989-90, 1993. 2nd GP 1988.
CAC & Cuban discus records 1985 & 1989.
Progression at DT: 1977- 41.34, 1978- 47.46, 1979- 53.30, 1980- 54.94, 1981- 53.70, 1982- 59.54, 1983- 63.94, 1984- 67.76, 1985- 70.50, 1986- 66.86, 1987- 66.98, 1988- 67.02, 1989- 70.50, 1990- 65.48, 1991- 66.26, 1992- 70.68, 1993- 65.96. pb SP 16.04 '89.
Had a baby in 1994.

Niurka MONTALVO b.4 Jun 1968 Ciudad Habana 1.70m 53kg.
At TJ (LJ): WCh: '93- 4; WI: '91- 5; WUG: '93- 1; WCp: '94- 5 (2); CAG: '93- 1 (1). Won CAC LJ 1987, 1990, 1993; TJ 1993, Cuban LJ 1988, 1990, 1993-4, TJ 1993-4.
Cuban records: long jump 1990 & 1992, six (also CAC) triple jump 1992-4.
Progression at LJ, TJ: 1984- 5.83, 1985- 6.18, 1986- 6.29, 1987- 6.32/6.52w, 1988- 6.62, 1989- 6.53, 1990- 6.87. 1991- 6.69, 12.51; 1992- 6.88, 13.92; 1993- 6.64/6.75w, 14.51; 1994- 6.71/6.78w, 14.60. pb 100mh 13.57 '90.

Ioamnet QUINTERO b.18 Sep 1972 Ciudad Habana 1.89m 70kg. Larios, Spain.
At HJ: OG: '92- 3; WCh: '93- 1; WI: '93- 6; PAm: '91- 1; WJ: '90- 4; WCp: '92- 1. Won PAmJ 1987, Cuban 1990-3.
Progression at HJ: 1987- 1.72, 1988- 1.80, 1989- 1.89, 1990- 1.95, 1991- 1.93, 1992- 1.98, 1993- 2.01i/2.00, 1994- 1.97.
Snapped Achilles tendon at Brussels 1993, just two weeks after winning the world title.

CZECH REPUBLIC

Governing body : Cesky atléticky svaz, Mezi stadiony PS 40, 16017 Praha 6 Strahov. AAU of Bohemia founded in 1897.
National Championships first held in 1907 (Bohemia), 1919 (Czechoslovakia).
1994 Champions: **Men**: 100m/200m: Jirí Valík 10.52/21.35, 400m: Jirí Benda 47.25, 800m: Pavel Soukup 1:52.35, 1500m: Milan Drahonovsky 3:49.8, 5000m: Radim Kuncicky 14:11.49, 10000m: Jan Pesava 29:25.75, Half Mar: Jan Bláha 64:45, Mar: Petr Klimes 2:18:28, 3000mSt: Jirí Soptenko 8:54.06, 110mh: Tomás Dvorák 14.04, 400mh: Václav Novotny 51.91, HJ: Tomás Janku 2.20, PV: Martin Kysela 5.25, LJ: Milan Gombala 7.77, TJ: Michal Coubal 16.15, SP: Miroslav Menc 18.60, DT: Imrich Bugár 59.52, HT: Pavel Sedlácek 73.64, JT: Jan Zelezny 77.28, Dec: Kamil Damasek 7570, 20kmW: Hubert Sonnel 1:23:02, 50kmW: Roman Bílek 4:01:46. **Women**: 100m/200m: Erika Suchovská 11.80w/23.30, 400m: Nada Kostovalová 52.80, 800m: Ludmila Formanová 2:02.60, 1500m/3000m: Vera Kuncická 4:29.0/9:36.20, 10000m/Mar: Alena Peterková 33:58.98/2:31:43, Half Mar: Radka Pátková 77:43, 100mh: Iveta Rudová 13.62, 400mh: Ivana Sekyrová 58.59, HJ: Zuzana Kovácíková 1.91, PV: Daniela Bártová 3.55, LJ: Gabrila Vánová 6.02, TJ: Sárka Kaspárková 13.09, SP/DT: Alice Matejková 15.67/61.12, JT: Nikola Tomecková 54.74, Hep: Dana Jandová 5157, 10kmW: Kamila Holpuchová 49:46.2.

Tomás DVORÁK b.11 May 1972 1.86m 80kg. Dukla Praha.
At Dec: WCh: '93- 10; ECp: '94- 3; WJ: '90- 17; EJ: '91- 2.
Won Czech 110mh 1994.
Progession at Dec: 1989- 6999, 1990- 7251w, 1991- 7748, 1993- 8054, 1994- 8313. pbs: 100m 10.83 '93, 10.76w '94; 200m 21.71 '94, 400m 48.36 '94, 1500m 4:31.86 '90, 110mh 13.99/13.93w '94, HJ 2.04 '94, PV 4.65i/4.60 '93, LJ 7.75 '94, SP 15.52 '94, DT 43.00 '94, JT 66.16 '94.

Jan ZELEZNY b.16 Jun 1966 Mlada Boleslav 1.86m 77kg. LIAZ Jablonec nad Nisou.
At JT: OG: '88- 2, '92- 1; WCh: '87- 3, '91- dnq 18, '93- 1; EC: '86- dnq 18, '90- dnq 13, '94- 3; EJ: '83- 6, '85- 4; WCp: '92- 1; ECp: '87- 3, '89- 2, '91- 1. Won GP JT and 2nd overall 1991 and 1993. CS champion 1986, 1990, Czech 1994.
Four world javelin records 1987-93, eight CS records 1986-93.
Progression at JT: 1979- 44.44, 1982- 57.22, 1983- 74.34, 1984- 80.32, 1985- 84.68, new: 1986- 82.48, 1987- 87.66, 1988- 86.88, 1989- 84.74, 1990- 89.66, 1991- 90.72, 1992- 94.74, 1993- 95.66, 1994- 91.82.
Lost just once to Seppo Räty in both 1992 and 1993 and at three meetings in 1994. His 94.74 throw in 1992 was made with a new 'Németh' javelin, later ruled illegal by the IAAF. In 1993 he added 4.08m to Backley's world record when he threw 95.44 at Pietersburg, South Africa in April, and he added a further 12 cm at Sheffield in August. Entered hospital at the end of the 1989 season due to a fractured vertebra, but recovered to regain the world record in 1990. In 1991 he was most unlucky not to qualify for the World final, when he fell, perhaps over the line, on a long throw; otherwise lost only once, to Steve Backley. His father, Jaroslav, threw the javelin 68.46m in 1969.

Robert ZMELIK b.18 Apr 1969 Prostejov 1.85m 81kg. Dukla Praha. Soldier.
At Dec: WCh: '91- 4; EC: '90- 4; WJ: '86- 10, '88- 2; EJ: '87- dnf. At Hep: EI: '92- 2. At LJ: WI: '91- 6.
Five CS decathlon records 1990-2. World best for 1 hour decathlon 7897 '92.
Progression at Dec: 1986- 7108, 1987- 7329, 1988- 7659, 1989- 7847, 1990- 8249, 1991- 8379, 1992- 8627, 1993- 8188. pbs: 100m 10.75 '93, 10.55w '92; 200m 21.71 '91, 21.4 '88; 400m 48.20 '91, 1500m 4:21.24 '91, 50mh 6.54i '91, 110mh 13.75 '90, 13.4dt '92; HJ 2.11 '91, PV 5.20ex/5.15 '92, LJ 8.09i/8.06 '92, TJ 14.73 '85, SP 14.65i/14.53 '92, DT 45.40 '92, JT 62.84 '91, Hep 6118i '92.
Added 260 points to CS decathlon record when fourth in Split, and a further 130 points when fourth in Tokyo. Injured in 1994.

Robert Zmelik

Women

Sárka KASPARKOVA b.20 May 1971 Karviná 1.85m 66kg. AAC Brno. Teacher.
At TJ: WCh: '93- 7; EC: '94- 6; WI: '93- 7; EI: '92- 4. At HJ: OG: '92- dnq; WJ: '88- 6; EJ: '89- 3. Won CS HJ 1988, CZE TJ 1993-4, Eur U23Cp TJ 1992, ECp I TJ 1994.
Four Czech triple jump records 1992-3.
Progression at HJ, TJ: 1983- 1.42, 1984- 1.59, 1985- 1.71, 1986- 1.77, 1987- 1.80, 1988- 1.89, 1989- 1.91, 1990- 1.81, 1991- 1.78, 1992- 1.92, 14.00; 1993- 1.95i, 14.16; 1994- 1.82, 14.46i/14.14/ 14.20w. pbs: 100mh 14.72 '94, LJ 6.27/6.29w '93.

DENMARK

Governing body: Dansk Athletik Forbund, Idraettens Hus, Brøndby Stadion 20, DK-2605 Brøndby.
National Championships first held in 1894.
1994 Champions: **Men**: 100m/200m: Lars Pedersen 10.59w/21.73, 400m: Oral Shaw 47.73, 800m: Wilson Kipketer KEN 1:48.00, 1500m: Robert Kiplagat 3:50.64, 5000m/10000m: Klaus Hansen 14:30.85/29:08.0, Mar: Palle Redder Madsen 2:20:25, 3000mSt: Kåre Sørensen 8:52.24, 110mh: Bogdan Deoniziak 14.34w, 400mh: Poul Gundersen 52.64, HJ: Michael Mikkelsen 2.09,

PV: Martin Voss 5.30, LJ: Bent Jakobsen 7.52w, TJ: Gjerlev Laursen 15.82w, SP: Jan A Sørensen 16.12, DT: Brian Møller 53.14, HT: Jan Bielecki 68,46, JT: Kenneth Petersen 69.18, Dec: Carsten Bomme 7103, 10kmW/20kmW: Claus Jørgensen 43:35/1:30:56, 50kmW: Torben Kristiansen 4:45:49. **Women**: 100m/200m: Camilla Voigt 12.09w/25.43, 400m: Karen Gydesen 55.27, 800m: Sandra Gairy 2:12.48, 1500m: Lene Tingleff 4:44.49, 3000m: Anja Jørgensen 9:38.48, 10000m: Nina Christiansen 33:49.53, Mar: Inger Plum 2:56:54, 100mh/SP: Maria Novak 13.32/15.47, 400mh: Ane Skak 61.95, HJ: Pia Zinck 1.80, LJ: Renata Nielsen 6.61w, TJ: Dorthe Jensen 12.40w, DT: Annette Bøgh 50.00, HT: Malene Kjærsgaard 47.98, JT: Jette Ø.Jeppesen 54.16, Hep: Charlotte Beiter 5162, 5kmW: Gunhild Klarskov-Kristiansen 27:16.

Women

Renata NIELSEN b.18 May 1966 1.76m 63kg. née Pytelewska POL, married to Lars Nielsen.
At LJ: OG: '92- 11; WCh: '93- 3 (dnq 20 TJ); EC: '94- 4; WI: '91- 10, '93- 9. Polish champion 1990, Danish 1990, 1992-4.
Danish records 1993-4: 5 LJ, 3 TJ.
Progression at LJ: 1982- 6.12/6.13w, 1983- 6.23/6.37w, 1984- 5.89/5.91w, 1985- 6.24/6.27w, 1986- 6.14/6.34w, 1987- 6.23i/6.11, 1989- 6.05, 1990- 6.53, 1991- 6.86, 1992- 6.65, 1993- 6.84, 1994- 6.96/7.09w. pbs: 100m 12.02 '93, 200m 25.42 '90, TJ 13.71 '93.
Has two children - twin boys.

ESTONIA

Governing body: Eesti Kergejôustikuliit, Regati pst. 1, Tallinn EE0 103. Founded 1920.
National Championships first held in 1917.
1994 Champions: **Men**: 100m: Andrei Morozov 10.63, 200m: Andrus Hämelane 21.95, 400m: Rainis Jaansoo 48.38, 800m: Oleg Holdai 1:53.17, 1500m: Indrek Mänd 3:55.47, 5000m/3000mSt: Pavel Loskutov 14:19.96/8:49.72, 10000m: Toomas Tarm 30:331.80, Mar: Henno Haava 2:22:45, 110mh/400mh: Indrek Kaseorg 14.37/51.51, HJ: Ain Evard 2.21, PV: Erki Nool 5.30, LJ/TJ: Sergei Tanaga 7.40/16.15, SP: Ants Kiisa 17.62, DT: Aleksander Tammert 52.66, HT: Jüri Tamm 76.78, JT: Donald Sild 79.26, Dec: Valter Külvet 7369, 20000mW: Mart Järviste 1:41:16. **Women**: 100m/200m: Milena Alver 12.09/24.90, 400m/400mh: Tiia Eeskivi 56.13/59.12, 800m: Agneta Land 2:14.48, 1500m/3000m: Jane Salumäe 4:29.54/9:33.67, Mar: Galina Bernat 2:57:09, 100mh: Kertu Tiitso 13.95, HJ/LJ: Virge Naeris 1.80/6.32, TJ: Renna Tôniste 12.15, SP/DT: Eha Rünne 16.15/54.44, JT: Maret Kelviste 48.90, Hep: Virge Treiel 4942, 5000mW: Natalia Ivanova 29:22.60.

Valeri BUKREJEV b.15 Jun 1964 Tallinn 1.86m 82kg. Tallinna KJK Kalev.
At PV: OG: '92- dnq; WCh: '93- 7; EC: '94- 8=. Estonian champion 1984, 1986-7, 1991-3.
Ten Estonian pole vault records 1986-94.
Progression at PV: 1977- 3.00, 1978- 3.40, 1979- 4.00, 1980- 4.40, 1981- 4.70, 1982- 5.02, 1983- 5.25, 1984- 5.39, 1985- 5.20, 1986- 5.45, 1987- 5.61, 1988- 5.66, 1989- 5.60, 1990- 5.60, 1991- 5.65, 1992- 5.70, 1993- 5.81/5.86ex, 1994- 5.86. pb HJ 2.05 '84.

Donald-Aik SILD b.3 Oct 1968 Tallinn 2.00m 107kg.
At JT: EC: '94- 12. Estonian champion 1993-4.
Estonian javelin record 1994.
Progression at JT: 1986- 60.78, 1987- 67.84, 1988- 74.06, 1989- 78.28, 1990- 72.46, 1991- 74.34, 1992- 76.40, 1993- 80.90, 1994- 85.28.
His father Heino set an Estonian shot record of 20.53 in 1979.

Jüri TAMM b.5 Feb 1957 Pärnu 1.91m 120kg. Tallinna KJK Kalev. Teacher.
At HT: OG: '80- 3, '88- 3, '92- 5; WCh: '87- 2; EC: '94- dnq 23; WCp: '85- 1; ECp: '85- 1; WUG: '81- 2, '83- 1. USSR champion 1987-8, Estonian 1991, 1993-4. 3rd GP 1990.
World hammer record in 1980, only to be overtaken by Yuriy Sedykh in same competition.
World bests 35lb weight 1991 (24.33) and 1992.
Progression at HT: 1973- 36.52, 1974- 49.16, 1975- 54.76, 1976- 66.86, 1977- 72.44, 1978- 74.58, 1979- 75.18, 1980- 80.46, 1981- 77.26, 1982- 74.82, 1983- 79.18, 1984- 84.40, 1985- 84.08, 1986- 80.88, 1987- 82.02, 1988- 84.16, 1989- 78.58, 1990- 79.94, 1991- 80.56, 1992- 81.86, 1993- 76.94, 1994- 78.06. pb 35lbWt 25.17 '92.

ETHIOPIA

Governing body: Ethiopian Athletic Federation, Addis Ababa Stadium, PO Box 3241, Addis Ababa.

ADDIS Abebe b.1970 or 14 Sep 1972? 1.60m 50kg. Soldier.
At 10000m (5000m): OG: '92- 3 (h); WCh: '91- 13; WJ: '88- 1 (3); WCp: '89- 2, '92- 1; AfCh: '89- 1 (2), '90- 3. World CC: '89- 1J, '91- 9, '93- 8, '94- 7. World Half Mar: '94- 17.
World junior records in 1988 and 1989 at both 5000m and 10000m.
Progression at 5000m, 10000m: 1988- 13:23.27, 27:50.24; 1989- 13:23.17, 27:17.82; 1990- 13:35.67,

27:42.65; 1991- 13:21.27, 27:47.70; 1992- 13:17.61, 27:38.37. pb 3000m 8:00.4 '89, Half Mar 62:14 '94. Collected the biggest ever prize in athletics history, $500,000, for his world road record 27:40 for 10 km in Jakarta 24 Jan 1993. A year later won the same race in 27:43 and has concentrated solely on road racing for the last two years. Was surely older than his official age of 15 when he ran world junior records in 1988.

FITA Bayissa b.15 Dec 1972 1.75m 52kg. Policeman.
At 5000m (10000m): OG: '92- 3 (9); WCh: '91- 2, '93-3 (dnf); WJ: '90- 1; AfG: '91- 1, '93- (2); WCp: '92- 1. World CC: '90- 3 Jnr, '91- 3 Jnr, '92- 3. 2nd World Road Relay 1994.
World junior 5000m record 1991.
Progression at 5000m, 10000m: 1990- 13:42.59, 1991- 13:16.64, 1992- 13:13.03, 27:14.26; 1993- 13:05.40, 27:26.90; 1994- 13:07.70, 27:51.56. pbs: 1500m 3:41.37 '94, 3000m 7:40.06 '94.
Won IAAF World Cross Challenge 1991/2. Won at Bislett Games in 10,000m début in 27:14.26 in 1992.

HAILE Gebrselassie b.18 Apr 1973 Arssi 1.60m 64kg.
At 5000m/10000m: WCh: '93- 2/1; WJ: '92- 1/1; AfG: '93 - 2/3. World CC: '91- 8J, '92- 2J, '93- 7, '94- 3. 2nd World Road Relay 1994.
World 5000m record 1994, Ethiopian records 1993-4: 1500m, 3000m, 5000m (2).
Progression at 5000m, 10000m: 1992- 13:36.06, 28:31.62; 1993- 13:03.17, 27:30.17; 1994- 12:56.96, 27:15.00. pbs: 1500m 3:37.04 '94, 2000m 5:01.6 '94, 3000m 7:37.49 '94.
After finishing a place behind Ismael Kirui at two successive World Junior cross-country championships, he outkicked his rival to complete a brilliant double at the 1992 World Juniors. Set the world record for the 5000m in Rome in 1994. Lives during the summer in a house in the Netherlands owned by his manager, Jos Hermens. His brother Tekeye was 13th in the 1991 London Marathon (World Cup) in 2:12:05 and improved his pb to 2:11:45 in 1994.

Abebe MEKONNEN b.9 Jan 1964 1.58m 59kg. Police lieutenant.
At Mar: OG: '92- dnf; WCh: '87- dnf, '91- dnf; WCp: '85-5; AfCh: '85- 5. At 10000m: AfG: '87- 2. World CC: '86- 2, '87- 4, '88- 5, '90- 8.
Progression at Mar: 1984- 2:11:30, 1985- 2:09:05, 1986- 2:08:39, 1987- 2:11:10, 1988- 2:07:35, 1989- 2:09:06, 1990- 2:11:52, 1991- 2:10:26, 1992- 2:13:09, 1993- 2:12:00, 1994- 2:09:17. pb 10000m 28:58.70 '87.
Of his 31 marathons has won nine: Rotterdam, Addis Ababa and Montreal 1986, Paris 1987, Tokyo 1988-9, 1993; Beijing 1988, Boston 1989. 2nd in London and Beijing in 1994.

WORKU Bikila b.1970 1.76m 60kg. Policeman.
At 5000m: WCh: '93- 6; OG: '92- 6; AfrG: '93- 3. World CC: '93- 9. 2nd World Road Relay 1994.
Progression at 5000m: 1992- 13:23.52, 1993- 13:06.64, 1994- 13:08.62. pb 3000m 7:47.6 '93.

Women

DERARTU Tulu b. 21 Mar 1972 Arusi province 1.55m 44kg. Prison administrator.
At 10000m (3000m): OG: '92- 1; WCh: '91- 8; WJ: '90- 1; AfG: '91- 1; AfCh: '90- 1 (1), '92 - 1 (1); WCp: '92- 1 (1). World CC: '89- 23, '90- 15, '91- 2.
Two African 10000m records 1992. World junior 10000m record 1991 (32:08.74), Ethiopian records 1500m, 5000m (2), 10000m (4) 1991-2.
Progression at 3000m, 10000m: 1990- 9:11.21, 32:56.26; 1991- 9:01.04, 31:45.95; 1992- 9:01.12, 31:06.02; 1994- 8:54.74, 31:48.93. pbs: 1500m 4:12.08 '92, 5000m 15:21.29 '91.
Undefeated on the track in 1992, but missed most of 1993 season through injury.

FINLAND

Governing body: Suomen Urheiluliitto, Radiokatu 20, SF-00240 Helsinki. Founded 1906.
National Championships first held in 1907 (men), 1913 (women). **1994 Champions**: **Men**: 100m: Ari Pakarinen 10.42, 200m: Kai Kyllönen 21.00, 400m: Ari Pinomäki 47.07, 800m: Mikael Söderman 1:47.49, 1500m: Sami Alanen 3:47.68, 5000m/10,000m: Pasi Mattila 14:01.99/29:35.55, Mar: Yrjö Pesonen 2:20:30, 3000mSt: Ville Hautala 8:52.39, 110mh: Antti Haapakoski 13.68, 400mh: Vesa-Pekka Pihlavisto 49.75, HJ: Juha Isolehto 2.22, PV: Jani Lehtonen 5.60, LJ: Olli Kärki 7.91w, TJ: Heikki Herva 16.54, SP: Mika Halvari 19.79, DT: Harri Uurainen 57.68, HT: Mika Laaksonen 75.22, JT: Juha Laukkanen 81.92, Dec: Jarkko Finni 7643, 20kmW/50kmW: Valentin Kononen 1:22:05/3:54:50. **Women**: 100m/200m: Sanna Hernesniemi 11.36/23.14, 400m: Heidi Suomi 53.36, 800m: Satu Jääskeläinen 2:05.23, 1500m: Marjo Piipponen 4:24.17, 3000m: Päivi Tikkanen 9:19.20, 10000m: Annemari Sandell 32:55.24, Mar: Anne Jääskeläinen 2:46:18, 100mh: Jutta Kemilä 13.58, 400mh: Petra Stenman 58.16, HJ: Kaisa Lehtonen 1.81, LJ: Ringa Ropo 6.42w, TJ: Marika Salminen 13.61, SP: Karolina Lundahl 17.64, DT: Kirsi Lindfors 54.78, JT: Mikaela Ingberg 58.54, Hep: Tiia Hautala 5763, 5000mW/10kmW: Sari Essayah 20:28.62/43:52.

Antti HAAPAKOSKI b.6 Feb 1971 1.87m 74kg. Kalajoen Junkkarit.
At 110mh: OG: '92- qf; WCh: '91- h; '93- sf; EC: '90- sf, '94- 6; WJ: '88- h, '90- 1; EJ: '89- 1; WCp: '94- 8. Finnish champion 1990, 1993-4.
Progression at 110mh: 1987- 15.23w, 1988- 14.53, 1989- 13.97, 1990- 13.65/13.6, 1991- 13.69, 1992- 13.55, 1993- 13.67, 1994- 13.45/13.26w. pbs: 100m 11.00 '93, 400m 48.74 '92, LJ 7.22 '92, TJ 14.13 '87, Dec 7167 '92.

Harri HAKKARAINEN b.16 Oct 1969 Kaavi 1.94m 110kg. Kaavin Kaiku.
At JT: EC: '94- dnq 13.
Progression at JT: 1986- 60.38, 1987- 63.88, 1988- 65.78, 1989- 70.06, 1990- 71.52, 1991- 83.16, 1992- 83.46, 1993- 84.36, 1994- 85.46.

Kimmo KINNUNEN b.31 Mar 1968 Äänekoski 1.87m 98kg. Forest foreman. Äänekosken Urheilijat.
At JT: OG: '88- 10, '92- 4; WCh: '91- 1, '93- 2; EC: '90- 8; WJ: '86- 5; EJ: '85- 9, '87- 5. 2nd GP 1991.
Progression at JT: 1984- 60.74, 1985- 78.40, new: 1986- 71.72, 1987- 72.94, 1988- 80.24, 1989- 83.10, 1990- 81.46, 1991- 90.82, 1992- 83.42, 1993- 84.78, 1994- 79.34.
Improved his pb from 85.46 to 88.48 in qualifying, and to 90.82 with his first throw in the final to take the gold medal in Tokyo 1991. Threw a 16-year-old world best with 600g javelin, 82.36 in 1984. Coached by his father Jorma, who set a world record of 92.70m in 1969 and competed at three Olympic Games, with the silver medal in 1968. His brother Jarkko (b.21 Apr 1970) was second in 1989 European Juniors, pb 79.70 '90.

Valentin KONONEN b.7 Mar 1969 Helsinki 1.81m 68kg. Korson Kaiku. Marketing student.
At 50kmW: OG: '92- 7; WCh: '91- 5, '93- 2; EC: '90- 6, '94- 7; WCp: '93- 6. Won Finnish 20kmW 1991-2, 1994; 50kmW 1994.
Finnish walks records: track 10,000m (2) 1992-3, 20,000m 1993, road 50km 1993.
Progression at 50kmW: 1989- 4:02:34, 1990- 3:56:40, 1991- 3:48:54, 1992- 3:52:27, 1993- 3:42:02, 1994- 3:47:14. pbs: 5000mW 20:09.2 '92, 10000mW 39:30.95 '93, 20kmW 1:22:05 '94, 1:22:22.6t '93.
Brother and sisters are performers with the Finnish National Ballet.

Juha LAUKKANEN b.6 Jan 1969 Pielavesi 1.86m 90kg. Laukkalan Luja. Marketing student.
At JT: OG: '92- 6; EC: '94- dnq 18; WJ: '88- 10; EJ: '87- 6. Finnish champion 1992, 1994.
World junior javelin record 1987.
Progression at JT: 1986- 74.40, 1987- 79.46, 1988- 77.08, 1989- 78.68, 1990- 83.36, 1991- 87.06, 1992- 88.22, 1993- 84.58, 1994- 85.54.

Ari PAKARINEN b.14 May 1969 1.82m 98kg, Pyhäselän Urheilljat.
At JT: WCh: '91- dnq 19, '93- 5
Progression at JT: 1987- 64.04, 1988- 71.46, 1989- 79.30, 1990- 80.76, 1991- 82.52, 1992- 84.00, 1993- 83.06, 1994- 83.38.

Seppo RÄTY b.27 Apr 1962 Helsinki 1.89m 110kg. Tohmajärven Urheilijat. Customs officer.
At JT: OG: '88- 3, '92- 2; WCh: '87- 1, '91- 2, '93- dnq 28; EC: '86- dnq 17, '90- 5, '94- 2. Won ECp B 1993. Finnish champion 1985-6, 1989-91, 1993. Two world javelin records 1991 and six Finnish records 1986-92. WIB 81.48 in 1990.
Progression at JT: 1978- 59.04, 1979- 63.20, 1980- 71.14, 1981- 75.44, 1982- 72.74, 1983- 74.38, 1984- 82.60, 1985- 85.72, new: 1986- 81.72, 1987- 83.54, 1988- 83.26, 1989- 83.92, 1990- 86.92, 1991- 96.96R, 1992- 90.60, 1993- 85.68, 1994- 85.22.
One of the most surprising world champions of 1987, when he twice improved his national record in Rome. In 1991 he sensationally twice improved his best by five metres with world records at 91.98 and 96.96.

Women

Sari ESSAYAH b.21 Feb 1967 Haukivuori 1.62m 50kg. Lapinlahden Veto. Economics student.
At 10kmW: OG: '92-4; WCh: '87- 19, '91- 3, '93- 1; EC: '90- 5, '94- 1; WUG: '91- 1; WCp: '89- 37, '93- 2. At 5000mW: EJ: '85- 11; WUG: '89- 3. At 3000mW: WI: '93- 7. Won FIN 5000mW 1987-94, 10kmW 1989-91, 1993-4.
Two European 5000m walk records 1994, Finnish records 1987-94: track 3000m (7), 5000m (8), 10,000m; 10km road (4).
Progression at 10kmW: 1983- 53:54, 1984- 52.08, 1985- 48:51.3t, 1987- 47:30, 1988- 44:26, 1989- 45:22, 1990- 43:47, 1991- 43:13, 1992- 43:37/ 44:15.8t, 1993- 42:37.0t, 1994- 42:37. pbs: 3000m 11:59.60 '93, 5000m 20:28.62 '94, 20kmW 1:39:59 '89, Mar (running) 3:02:37 '88.
Finnish mother and Moroccan father. Married to triathlete Robert Knapp.

FRANCE

Governing body: Fédération Française d'Athlétisme, 33 avenue Pierre-de-Coubertin, 75013 Paris. Founded 1920.
National Championships first held in 1888 (men), 1918 (women). **1994 Champions**: **Men**: (in brackets non-FRA winners) 100m/200m: Jean-Charles Trouabal 10.38/20.40, 400m: Stéphane Diagana 45.49, 800m: Ousmane Diarra 1:45.93 (Arthémon Hatungimana BUR

1:45.02), 1500m: Samir Benfarès 3:36.54, 5000m/ 10000m: Mohamed Ezzher 13:51.03/28:25.08 (M'Hamed Choumassi MAR 13:47.16), Half Mar: Bertrand Fréchard 1:04:25, Mar: Philippe Rémond 2:13:22, 3000mSt: Ali Belghazi 8:31.24, 110mh: Dan Philibert 13.53, 400mh: Stéphane Caristan 50.45 (Hamadou Mbaye SEN 49.92), HJ: Jean-Claude Gicquel 2.30, PV: Jean Galfione 5.85, LJ/TJ: Serge Hélan 7.88w/16.99 (LJ Robert Emmiyan ARM 8.00), SP: Jean-Louis Lebon 17.64, DT: Frédéric Selle 54.14 (Mickael Conjungo CAF 58.00), HT: Gilles Dupray 75.58 JT: Pascal Lefèvre 75.48, Dec: Sébastien Levicq 8043, 20kmW: Thierry Toutain 1:24:59, 50kmW: René Piller 3:52:48. **Women**: 100m: Odiah Sidibé 11.50, 200m: Odile Singa 23.46, 400m: Francine Landre 51.21, 800m: Patricia Djaté-Taillard 2:00.38, 1500m: Blandine Bitzner-Ducret 4:11.82, 3000m: Farida Fates 9:07.90, 10000m/Half Mar: Nicole Lévêque 32:14.48/1:12:55, Mar: Maria Rebelo 2:35:07, 100mh: Anne Piquereau 12.76, 400mh: Carole Nelson 56.61, HJ: Sandrine Fricot 1.92, LJ: Nadine Castor 6.50, TJ: Betty Lise 13.92, SP: Annick Lefebvre 15.57, DT: Agnès Teppe 55.40, HT: Cécile Lignot 53.42, JT: Nadine Auzeil 61.00, 10kmW: Nora Leksir 49:32.

Gérald BAUDOUIN b.15 Nov 1972 Grenoble 1.83m 79kg. Dôle AC.
At PV: WCh: '93- dnq; EC: '94- 10=; WJ: '90- 4; EJ: '91- 1.
Progression at PV: 1986- 4.10, 1987- 4.71, 1988- 5.00, 1989- 5.40, 1990- 5.40, 1991- 5.62, 1992- 5.70, 1993- 5.65, 1994- 5.80.
Had an operation on his right Achilles in January 1995.

Alain BLONDEL b.7 Dec 1962 Petit-Quevilly 1.86m 80kg. Stade Sotteville. Computer scientist.
At Dec: OG: '88- 6, '92- 15; WCh: '87- 7, '91- 13, '93- 5; EC: '86- 8, '90- 5, '94- 1; ECp: '91- 3, '93- 3, '94- 4. French champion 1986, 1992. At Hep: EI: '94- 3.
Progression at Dec: 1981- 5873, 1982- 6494*, 1983- 6959, 1984- 7668, 1985- 7763, 1986- 8185, 1987- 8228, 1988- 8387, 1989- 8182, 1990- 8216, 1991- 8211, 1992- 8285, 1993- 8444, 1994- 8453. pbs: 100m 10.74w '86, 10.89 '90; 200m 21.78 '88, 21.73w '89; 400m 47.44 '88, 1500m 4:04.76 '94, 110mh 14.07 '86, 14.0w '90; 400mh 51.07 '94, HJ 2.04 '84, PV 5.40 '93, LJ 7.53 '94, 7.56i '87, 7.59w '86; SP 14.06 '93, DT 47.28 '90, JT 66.52 '94, 1Hr Dec: 7715 '90, Hep 6087i '91.
Elected a vice-president of French Federation in March 1993.

Pierre CAMARA b.10 Sep 1965 Castres 1.81m 74kg. Neuilly-Plaisance.
At TJ: OG: '92- 11; WCh: '91- dnq 22, '93- 5; WI: '93- 1; EC: '90- dnq 15; ECp: '89- 5, '93- 1. French champion 1988, 1990, 1992-3.
Progression at TJ: 1983- 15.35, 1984- 16.40, 1986- 16.52i/16.29, 1986- 16.28i/16.02, 1987- 16.82, 1988- 16.79, 1989- 16.87, 1990- 16.87, 1991- 17.08, 1992- 17.34, 1993- 17.59i/17.30/17.46w, 1994- 17.35i/16.88/16.93w. pbs: LJ 7.54 '84.
Injured in June 1994 and missed rest of season. Lives with Laurence Bily (French 100m rec 11.04 '90, 2nd EI 60m 1989 and 1990); their son Nathy born 28 Nov 1993. Pierre's father came from Guinea.

Philippe COLLET b.13 Dec 1963 Nancy 1.77m 76kg. ASPTT Grenoble. Company manager.
At PV: OG: '88- 5=, '92- 7; WCh: '87- dnq, '91- nh; EC: '86- 3, '90- 4, '94- 4; EI: '86- 3; WCp: '85- 2, '89- 1, '92- 2; EJ: '81- 11; ECp: '85- 2, '89- 4, '91- 4=; WUG: '85- 2. Won FRA PV 1985, 1988-9, 1991-2.
French indoor pole vault records 1989 (2nd) & 1990 in Masters at Grenoble.
Progression at PV: 1978- 3.30, 1979- 4.10, 1980- 4.90, 1981- 5.10, 1982- 5.20, 1983- 5.60, 1984- 5.60, 1985- 5.80, 1986- 5.85, 1987- 5.80i/5.75, 1988- 5.80, 1989- 5.92i/5.75, 1990- 5.94i/5.80, 1991- 5.80, 1992- 5.80, 1993- 5.20, 1994- 5.80. pbs: 100m 10.81w '85, Dec 7011 '86.

Stéphane DIAGANA b.23 Jul 1969 Saint-Affrique 1.86m 75kg. EA Franconville. Biology student.
At 400mh/4x400mR: OG: '92- 4; WCh: '93- 4; EC: '90- 5, '94- 3/2R; WCp: '92- 3, '94- 3R; ECp: '93- 1, '94- 3. 3rd GP 1994. Won French 400m 1992-4, 400mh 1990.
Seven French 400mh records 1990-3.
Progression at 400mh: 1987- 54.1, 1989- 51.60, 1990- 48.92, 1991- 51.90, 1992- 48.13, 1993- 47.64, 1994- 48.22. pbs: 200m 20.81i '92, 20.95 '93; 400m 45.18 '92, 60mh 8.10i '88, 110mh 14.56 '87, 200mh 22.94 '94.
His father came from the Congo, of Sénégalese origin. From a best of 51.60 pre 1990, he ran 50.11 to win the French title, then 49.26 and 48.92 in Split. In 1992 he ran 48.55 prior to the Olympics where he ran French records in each round.

Éric DUBUS b.28 Feb 1966 Pézenas 1.86m 70kg. Stade Bordeaux UC.
At 1500m: EC: '90- h, '94- 4; At 3000m: WI: '93- 2; EI: '90- 1. At 5000m: WCh: '91- h.
Porogression at 1500m: 1984- 3:57.6, 1985- 3:50.20, 1986- 3:48.87, 1987- 3:43.2, 1988- 3:43.58, 1989- 3:40.49, 1990- 3:37.36, 1991- 3:38.5, 1992- 3:38.08, 1993- 3:37.03, 1994- 3:34.75. pbs: 800m 1:49.30 '89, 1000m 2:24.66 '88, 1M 3:54.16i '94, 3:58.63 '90; 2000m 5:02.05 '92, 3000m 7:43.44i '95, 7:48.37 '91; 5000m 13:45.89 '91.

Christophe ÉPALLE b.23 Jan 1969 St Etienne 1.94m 109kg. Neuilly-Plaisance.
At HT: OG: '92- 10; WCh: '93- 8; EC: '94- 7; WJ: '88- 8; WUG: '91- 5, '93- 3; ECp: '93- 2, '94- 3. Won NCAA HT & 35lbWt indoors 1991.
French hammer record 1993.
Progression at HT: 1985- 49.76, 1986- 56.76, 1987- 60.54, 1988- 63.52, 1989- 67.00, 1990- 68.90, 1991- 73.52, 1992- 76.86, 1993- 79.98, 1994- 79.20. pbs: SP 17.48 '91, DT 54.98 '92, 35lbWt 22.73i '91.

Jean GALFIONE b.9 Jun 1971 Paris 1.84m 82kg. Stade Français.
At PV: OG: '92- dnq 13; WCh: '91- 10, '93- 8; EC: '94- 3; WI: '93- 3; WJ: '90- 1; EJ: 89- 9; EI: '92- 4, '94- 2; WUG: '93- 3; WCp: '94- 2; ECp: '93- 4, '94- 1. French champion 1993-4.
Three French pole vault records 1993-4.
Progression at PV: 1987- 4.15, 1988- 5.16, 1989- 5.50, 1990- 5.60i/5.45, 1991- 5.80, 1992- 5.90, 1993- 5.93, 1994- 5.94. pbs: 100m 10.7 '92, 10.90 '94; 110mh 15.2 '92, HJ 2.01 '92, Dec 7068 '92.

Jean-Charles GICQUEL b.24 Feb 1967 Ploërmel 2.00m 81kg. ACR Locminé. Student in communication.
At HJ: WCh: '93- 11=; EC: '90- dnq 14, '94- 9=; EI: '94- 2; ECp: '89- 8, '93- 2. French champion 1987, 1990, 1994.
French high jump record indoors and out 1994.
Progression at HJ: 1981- 1.89, 1982- 1.97, 1983- 2.07, 1984- 2.09, 1985- 2.23, 1986- 2.21i/2.18, 1987- 2.27, 1988- 2.28, 1989- 2.27, 1990- 2.30, 1991- 2.25i/2.24, 1992- 2.23, 1993- 2.30, 1994- 2.35i/2.33.
French indoor records at 2.33 and 2.35 for European Indoor silver 1994.

Serge HÉLAN b.24 Feb 1964 Pointe-à-Pitre, Guadeloupe 1.76m 70kg. CA Montreuil
At TJ: OG: '84- 8, '92- dnq 20; WCh: '87- dnq 17, '91- dnq 21, '93- 9; EC: '86- 9, '90- dnq, '94- 2; EJ: '83- 6; WI: '89- 6; EI: '87- 1, '92- 2; WCp: '94- 5; ECp: '94- 3. At LJ: WI: '85- 6. Won French LJ 1993, TJ 1986-7, 1989, 1991, 1994.
French triple jump records 1986, 1991 and 1994.
Progression at TJ: 1981- 13.98, 1982- 15.83, 1983- 16.12, 1984- 16.66, 1985- 16.69, 1986- 17.13, 1987- 17.15i/16.84, 1988- 17.01, 1989- 17.12i/16.78, 1990- 17.10, 1991- 17.45, 1992- 17.18, 1993- 17.25, 1994- 17.55. pb LJ 8.12 '92.

William MOTTI b.25 Jul 1964 Bondy 1.98m 95kg. Paillon AC Nice. Was at Mt.St Mary's College, USA.
At Dec: OG: '84- 5, '92- 7; WCh: '87- 10; EC: '86- dnf, '94- dnf; ECp: '93- 10, '94- 5; EJ: '81- 2 at HJ, '83- dnf. French champion 1985, 1991. At Hep: WI: '93- 6.
Two French decathlon records 1984-5. US collegiate record 1984.
Progression at Dec: 1982- 7739, 1983- 7315, 1984- 8278, 1985- 8306, 1986- 8006, 1987- 8327w, 1988- 6406, 1989- 7926, 1991- 8224, 1992- 8164, 1993- 7829, 1994- 8224. pbs: 100m 11.03/10.96w '85, 400m 48.01 '84, 1500m 4:23.59 '87, 110mh 14.67/14.5 '84, 14.57w '87, HJ 2.22i/2.20 '82, PV 5.00 '91, LJ 7.63 '85, SP 16.96 '91, DT 52.70 '89, JT 71.92 '92.
Received a two-year ban for drugs abuse in 1989.

Dan PHILIBERT b.6 Aug 1970 Paris 1.83m 77kg. Stade Français. Student.
At 110mh: OG: '92- sf; WCh: '91- 5, '93- sf; EC: '94- 7; WJ: '88- 7; EJ: 89- h; ECp: '94- 7. French champion 1991-4. At 60mh: '94- 4
Progression at 110mh: 1987- 14.08/13.92w, 1989- 13.84/13.65w/13.6, 1990- 13.66, 1991- 13.33, 1992- 13.35, 1993- 13.42, 1994- 13.43. pbs: 50mh 6.66i '91, 60mh 7.58i '94.
Martiniquean father. Won the Mediterranean Games 110mh 1991 and 1993.

René PILLER b.23 Apr 1965 Héricourt 1.68m 56kg. GA Haut-Saônois. Railways employee.
At 50kmW: OG: '92- 15; WCh: '91- 8, '93- 6; EC: '90- 15, '94- dq; WCp: '93- 12. Won French 50km 1989, 1990, 1992, 1994; 100kmW 1988, 1991.
World 50km track walk record 1994.
Progression at 50kmW: 1986- 4:18:01, 1987- 4:06:52, 1988- 3:54:06.5t, 1989- 3:51.17, 1990- 3:56:36.1t, 1991- 3:55:48, 1992- 4:02:12, 1993- 3:48:57, 1994-3:41:28.2t. pbs: 5000mW 20:09.03 '93, 20kmW 1:22:16 '92, 1HrW 14715m '92, 100kmW 9:14:12 '88.

Christian PLAZIAT b.28 Oct 1963 Lyon 1.91m 87kg. PS Besançon.
At Dec: OG: '88- 5, '92- dnf; WCh: '87- 4, '91- 9, '93- 6; EC: '86- 7, '90- 1, '94- 4; ECp: '89- 1, '91- 1, '93- 2, '94- 1. French champion 1987-90. At Hep: EI: '92- 1, '94- 1. At HJ: EJ: '81- 12.
Six French decathlon records 1987-90. WIB octathlon 7084 '89, heptathlon 6273 '90, 6277 '91, 6289 & 6418 '92.
Progression at Dec: 1981- 6489, 1982- 7221, 1983- 7770, 1985- 8211w/8018, 1986- 8196, 1987- 8315, 1988- 8512, 1989- 8485, 1990- 8574, 1991- 8518, 1992- dnf, 1993- 8398, 1994- 8505. pbs: 60m 6.83i '92, 100m 10.55/10.44w '90, 10.3w '88, 10.4 '86; 200m 21.52/21.5 '90, 400m 47.10 '90, 1500m 4:23.49 '88, 50mh 6.69i '92, 60mh 7.87i '94, 110mh 13.92/13.86w '92, 13.9 '91, 400mh 51.03 '91, HJ 2.20 '83, PV 5.20i '92, 5.10 '88, LJ 7.90 '90, TJ 14.94i '90, 14.93 '89, SP 15.86 '86, DT 49.08 '86, JT 63.02 '85, new 58.22 '87.

Won Götzis decathlon1989 and Talence each year 1988-91.

Thierry TOUTAIN b.14 Feb 1962 Toul 1.82m 75kg. GA Haut-Saônois. Policeman.
At 20kmW: OG: '88- 18, '92- dq WCh: '91- 9; EC: '90- 3; WCp: '89- 10, '91- 3. At 50kmW: WCh: '87- 14; EC: '94- 2; WCp: '87- 15, '93- 18. Won French 20kmW 1989-91, 1994; 50kmW 1988, 1993.
At 30km and 2 hours track walk: French records 2:09:15.3 and 27,894m 1989, World 1991. French road and track walk records 20km 1990, 1 hour track and 50km 1993. European record track 50,000m walk 1994.
Progression at 20kmW, 50kmW: 1982- 1:33:25.5, 1983- 1:40:18.41t, 1984- 1:29:50.4, 1985- 1:33:05.0t, 1986- 1:30:25.3, 1987- 1:28:58.97t, 3:55:58; 1988- 1:22:55, 1989- 1:22:06, 1990- 1:21:25, 1991- 1:20:56, 1992- 1:21:14.9t, 4:05:09; 1993- 1:22:51, 3:47:40; 1994- 1:21:20, 3:43:52. pbs: track 5000mW 19:49.1 '93, 20kmW 1:21:14.9 '92, 30kmW 2:03:56.5 '91, 50km W 3:45:24.2t '94. 1HrW 15167m '93, 2HrW 29,090m '91.

Jean-Charles TROUABAL b.20 May 1965 Paris 1.87m 77kg. Essonne Athlétic. PE teacher.
At 200m/R- 4x100m relay: OG: '92- h; WCh: '91- 6/2R, '93- 6; EC: '90- 2/1R, '94- 5/1R; WCp: '94- 5R, ECp: '91- 1/1R, '93- 2R. At 100m: OG: '88- qf. Won French 100m 1992-4, 200m 1988, 1990-4.
World 4x100m record 1990.
Progression at 200m: 1984- 21.7, 1985- 21.38, 1986- 21.54, 1987- 20.94/20.88w, 1988- 20.55, 1989- 20.71/20.68w, 1990- 20.31, 1991- 20.30, 1992- 20.40, 1993- 20.20, 1994- 20.39/20.35w. pbs: 60m 6.65i '92, 100m 10.19 '93, 400m 46.92 '90.
Martiniquean origin.

Jean-Charles Trouabal: relay gold in Helsinki

Women

Patricia DJATÉ b.3 Jan1971 Paris 1.73m 59kg. Married name Taillard. SAPamiers Base Ariège. PE student.
At 800m: EC: '94- 7; ECp: '94- 2; WJ: '90- 8. Won FRA 800m 1994.
French 800m record 1994.
Progression at 800m: 1988- 2:09.52, 1989- 2:08.55, 1990- 2:05.05, 1991- 2:04.95, 1992- 2:03.25, 1993- 2:00.75, 1994- 1:58.07. pbs: 400m 52.99 '94, 1000m 2:37.47 '94, 1500m 4:24.46 '92.
Married to Frédéric Taillard (800m 1:48.42 '94). Her father came from the Ivory Coast.

Patricia GIRARD b.8 Apr 1968 Pointe-à-Pitre, Guadeloupe 1.62m 48kg. Neuilly Plaisance Sports.
At 100mh/4x100mR: OG: '88- 7R, '92- 4R (sf 100m); WCh: '93- sf/R; ECp: '93- 2R. At 60mh: WI: '93- 3; EI: '90- 4. At 60m: EI: '94- 3. At 100m: EC: '94- sf. Won FRA 100mh 1993.
Progression at 100mh: 1985- 14.4, 1986- 13.82w, 1987- 13.45, 1988- 13.42, 1989- 13.53, 1992- 12.91, 1993- 12.91, 1994- 12.93. pbs: 50m 6.28i '93, 60m 7.16i '94, 100m 11.11 '94, 200m 23.49 '92, 60mh 7.93i '94.
Two year drugs ban from 17 Mar 1990.

Marie-José PÉREC b.9 May 1968 Basse Terre, Guadeloupe 1.80m 60kg. Stade Français.
At 400m/4x100mR (4x400mR): OG: '92- 1; WCh: '91- 1/5R; EC: '90- 3, '94- 1 (1R); WCp: '89- dq, '94- (4R); won E.Cup B 1989. At 200m: OG: '88- qf; WCh: '93- 4/4R; EI: '89- 1; WI: '89- 6; WCp: '92- 1/2R; ECp: '93- 2/2R (2 100m). Won GP 400m 1994, French 100m 1991, 200m 1992, 400m 1988, 400mh 1989.
French records: 100m 1991, three 200m 1991-3, seven 400m 1988-92.
Progression at 200m/400m: 1984- 25.44/25.0; 1985- 24.14; 1986- 24.33/24.00w; 1987- 24.52; 1988- 22.72, 51.35; 1989- 22.36, 51.05; 1990- 22.92, 50.84; 1991- 22.26, 49.13; 1992- 22.20, 48.83; 1993- 21.99; 1994- 22.61, 49.77. pbs: 60m 7.29i '92,

100m 10.96 '91, 300m 36.81 '88, 400mh 55.76 '89. Disqualified for breaking lane after winning the 1989 World Cup 400m in 50.30. Ran French records of 50.53 and 49.32 in her first two races at 400m in 1991, then 49.76 to win in Nice and then improved to 49.13 to win the world title. Now coached by John Smith.

Anne PIQUEREAU b.15 Jun 1964 Poitiers 1.71m 63kg. Stade Clermont-Ferrand. Studied Physiotherapy.
At 100mh: OG: '88- qf, '92- sf; WCh: '87- 5, '91- sf; EC: '86- sf, '90- sf, '94- 8; EJ: '81- 3; WUG: '85- 3; WCp: '92- 2; ECp: '87- 5, '94- 3. Won FRA 100mh 1988, 1992, 1994. At 60mh: WI: '91- 5; EI: '85- 3, '86- 2, '94- 3; WIG: '85- 3.
Progression at 100mh: 1980- 14.54/13.86w, 1981- 13.76/13.67w, 1982- 13.64/13.5w, 1983- 13.22/ 13.0, 1984- 13.39/13.30w, 1985- 12.89, 1986- 12.95, 1987- 12.82, 1988- 12.94/12.83w, 1989- 12.87, 1990- 12.82, 1991- 12.74, 1992- 12.85/12.70w, 1993- 13.13, 1994- 12.76/12.64w. pbs: 100m: 11.87/11.5 '87, 200m 24.1 '89, 50mh 6.83i '91, 60mh 7.88i '90, LJ 6.52 '91.

Nathalie TEPPE b. 22 May 1972 Bourg-en-Bresse 1.83m 63kg. Stade Français.
At Hep: WCh: '93- 14; EC: '94- 9 (9 JT); EJ: '91- 2; ECp: '94- 2. At JT: EJ: '89- 3.
Progression at JT, Hep: 1987- 51.66, 4038; 1988- 56.16, 5289, 1989- 61.36, 5789; 1990- 55.80, 6113; 1991- 53.32, 5868; 1992- 58.02, 6145; 1993- 60.90, 6256; 1994- 61.60, 6396. pbs: 200m 25.29, 800m 2:15.90 '94, 100mh 13.76 '94, HJ 1.85 '93, LJ 6.18 '94, SP 13.77 '94.

Monique TOURRET b.11 Jul 1967 Poitiers 1.73m 62kg. née Éwanjé-Epée. US Créteil.
At 100mh: OG: '88- 7, '92- h; WCh: '91- 4; EC: '86- sf, '90- 1, '94- h; EJ: '85- 1 (6 Hep); WUG: '89- 1; ECp: '89- 1B, '91- 2. French champion 1989-91. At 60mh: WI: '91- 2; EI: '90- 2, '92- 2. Won GP 100mh 1990.
European junior record 1985, two French 100mh records 1989-90.
Progression at 100mh: 1983- 14.6, 1984- 13.78, 1985- 13.10, 1986- 13.07, 1987- 12.98, 1988- 12.87/ 12.86w, 1989- 12.65, 1990- 12.56, 1991- 12.67, 1992- 13.01, 1994- 13.08/12.96w. pbs: 100m 11.86/11.6 '86, 200m 24.83 '85, 50mh 6.81 '91, 60mh 7.82i '91, HJ 1.74 '85, LJ 6.23 '85, SP 12.32 '85, Hep 5493 '85.
Married Christophe Tourret (5.20 PV '90) on 13 Dec 1991; daughter Mary-Lou born on 23 Sep 1993. Her father was from Cameroon; her sister Maryse (b.4 Sep 1964), now Maury, set four French high jump records 1983-5, best 1.96 '85, was fourth at the 1984 Olympics, and at the European Indoors: '83- 3, '84- 2, '89- 3.

GERMANY

Governing body: Deutscher Leichtathletik Verband (DLV), Julius-Reiber-Strasse 19, PO Box 110463, D-6100 Darmstadt. Founded 1898.
National Championships first held in 1891.
1994 Champions: **Men**: 100m: Marc Blume 10.28, 200m: Michael Huke 20.60, 400m: Kai Karsten 46.10, 800m: Nico Motchebon 1:46.64, 1500m: Rüdiger Stenzel 3:49.91, 5000m/ 10000m: Dieter Baumann 13:46.67/ 28:20.66, Half Mar: Klaus-Peter Nabein 64:11, Mar: Stephan Freigang 2:16:35, 3000mSt: Martin Strege 8:30.30, 110mh: Florian Schwarthoff 13.34, 400mh: Edgar Itt 48.48, HJ: Hendrik Beyer 2.30, PV: Tim Lobinger 5.55, LJ: Dietmar Haaf 8.24, TJ: Volker Mai 16.58, SP: Sven Buder 20.44, DT: Lars Riedel 65.50, HT: Heinz Weis 79.68, JT: Raymund Hecht 85.88, Dec: Norbert Demmel 7919, 20kmW: Axel Noack 1:24:25, 50kmW: Ronald Weigel 3:52:56. **Women**: 100m/200m: Melanie Paschke 11.20/ 22.45, 400m: Anja Rücker 52.05, 800m: Christine Wachtel 2:02.70, 1500m: Ellen Kiessling 4:15.26, 3000m: Andrea Karhoff 9:10.42, 10000m/Mar: Kathrin Wessel 32:44.11/2:36:29, Half Mar: Monika Schäfer 74:00; Mar: , 100mh: Kristin Patzwahl 13.12, 400mh: Heike Meissner 54.52, HJ: Heike Balck 1.90, PV: Andrea Müller 3.95, LJ: Heike Drechsler 7.13w, TJ: Helga Radtke 14.49, SP: Stephanie Storp 19.79, DT: Ilke Wyludda 63.76, HT: Simone Mathes 58.34, JT: Karen Forkel 67.72, Hep: Birgit Clarius 6109, 5kmW/10kmW: Beate Gummelt 21:19.00/ 43:58. In championships won below, note FRG and GDR to 1990, GER from 1991.

Dieter BAUMANN b.9 Feb 1965 Blaustein 1.78m 64kg. LG Bayer Leverkusen. Photographic worker.
At 5000m: OG: '88- 2, '92- 1; WCh: '91- 4; EC: '86- h, '94- 1; ECp: '94- 1. At 3000m: WI: '89- 3; EI: '87- 2, '89- 1. At 1500m: WCh: '87- sf; WI: '87- 7; ECp: '87- 5, '89- dq. Won FRG 1500m 1987-9, 5000m 1986, 1988, 1991-2; GER 10000m 1994.
German records 3000m 1991, 5000m 1992. European indoor 3000m record (7:37.51) 1995.
Progression at 1500m, 5000m: 1982- 4:03.75, 15:42.96; 1983- 3:52.99, 14:40.4; 1984- 3:50.37, 14:21.59; 1985- 3:40.48, 13:48.0; 1986- 3:36.40, 13:35.04; 1987- 3:33.54, 13:30.85; 1988- 3:34.82, 13:15.52; 1989- 3:34.25, 13:18.58; 1990- 3:40.38; 1991- 3:34.93, 13:24.58; 1992- 3:33.91, 13:09.03; 1994- 3:38.49, 13:12.47. pbs: 800m: 1:48.40 '90, 1000m 2:18.79i '89, 2:22.4 '86, 1M 3:51.12 '92, 2000m 4:59.88 '87, 3000m 7:33.91 '91, 10000m 28:20.66 '94.

Missed most of 1990 season through injury. Undefeated in 5000m finals in 1992, when he added Olympic gold to the silver he had won in 1988. Missed 1993 season through injury. Married to his coach Isabell (née Hozang) who ran at 1500m in the 1981 European Juniors.

Wolf-Hendrik BEYER b.14 Feb 1972 Düsseldorf 2.00m 82kg. LG Bayer Leverkusen.
At HJ: OG: '92- dnq; WCh: '93- dnq 18; WI: '93- 7; EI: '94- 3; WJ: '90- 4; ECp: '93- 4, '94- 1. GER champion 1993-4.
Progression at HJ: 1988- 2.00, 1989- 2.17, 1990- 2.23, 1991- 2.25i/2.20, 1992- 2.32, 1993- 2.36i/ 2.33, 1994- 2.31/2.38i.

Steffen BRAND b.10 Mar 1965 Recklinghausen 1.76m 66kg. Bayer Leverkusen. Medical student.
At 3000mSt: OG: '92- 5; WCh: '93- 6; ECp: '93- 1, '94- 2. At 5000m: ECp: '87- 5, '89- 6. At 1500m: EI: '90- 4. Won FRG 5000m 1990, GER 3000mSt 1992-3.
Progression at 5000m, 3000mSt: 1983- 14:47.30, 1984- 14:19.17, 1985- 14:04.37, 1986- 14:17.90, 1987- 13:41.37, 1988- 13:38.99, 1989- 13:48.0, 1990- 13:29.25, 1992- 13:37.38, 8:16.60; 1993- 13:37.92, 8:15.33; 1994- 8:23.75. pbs: 800m 1:50.0 '88, 1000m 2:21.22 '90, 1500m 3:37.85 '87, 3000m 7:50.85i/7:51.64 '94.
Started at steeplechase as a junior (2000m 5:56.22 in 1983), and after missing 1991 through injury, returned with great success in 1992.

Oliver-**Sven BUDER** b.23 Jun 1966 Erlabrunn 2.00m 130kg. TV Wattenscheid. Student.
At SP: WCh: '91- 4, '93- 7; EC: '90- 2, '94- dnq 16; EJ: '85- 1; WCp: '94- 4; ECp: '93- 4, '94- 4; WI: '91- 7, '93- 8; EI: '90- 3. Won GER 1991, 1993-4.
Progression at SP: 1984- 16.58, 1985- 19.34, 1986- 19.29, 1987- 20.14, 1988- 19.05, 1989- 20.22, 1990- 21.06, 1991- 20.20, 1992- 19.76i/19.70, 1993- 20.15, 1994- 20.44. pb DT 54.14 '91.

Claude EDORH b.27 Feb 1972 Dabou, Ivory Coast 1.81m 82kg. ASV Köln.
At 110mh: EC: '94- 4; WJ: '90- sf; EJ: '91- 3.
Progression at 110mh: 1990- 14.15, 1991- 13.98, 1992- 13.82, 1993- 13.69, 1994- 13.41. pbs: 100m 10.70 '92, 200m 21.68 '92.

Mike FENNER b.24 Apr 1971 Berlin 1.87m 90kg. SCC Berlin.
At 110mh: WCh: '91- h; EC: '94- 5; WJ: '90- 6; EJ: '89- sf. Won EU23 Cp 1992. At 60mh: EJ: '94- 3.
Progression at 110mh: 1988- 15.24, 1989- 14.26, 1990- 13.85, 1991- 13.79, 1992- 13.75, 1993- 13.64, 1994- 13.42. pbs: 100m 10.80 '91, 50mh 6.47i '94, 60mh 7.54i '94.
Was a good footballer.

Stéphane FRANKE b.12 Feb 1964 Versailles, France 1.76m 60kg. Salamander Kornwestheim. Sports marketing officer for Mercedes.
At 10000m: OG: '92- h; WCh: '91- 12, '93- 4; EC: '94- 3 (10 5000m); WCp: '94- 4; ECp: '91- 3, '94- 2. Won GER 10000m 1993. 3rd GP 5000m 1993
Progression at 5000m, 10,000m: 1988- 14:14.43, 1989- 14:04.3, 1990- 13:50.90, 1991- 28:04.41, 1992- 13:48.12, 28:11.99; 1993- 13:13.17, 27:57.98; 1994- 13:14.68, 28:07.95. pbs: 800m 1:50.81 '88, 1000m 2:24.03 '85, 1500m 3:42.69 '85, 3000m 7:40.11 '93, Mar 2:19:18 '93.
Studied at George Mason and Cal State Pomona Universities, USA.

Stephan FREIGANG b.27 Sep 1967 Löbau 1.77m 64kg. SC Cottbus. Sports student.
At Mar: OG: '92- 3; WCh: '91- 18. At 10000m: EC: '94-10; WJ: '86- 4 (4 at 20km Rd); WUG: '91- 1; ECp: '89- 5. At 5000m: ECp: '93- 7. Won GDR 5000m 1989, GER Half Mar 1993, Mar 1994.
Progression at 10,000m, Mar: 1986- 29:02.43, 1987- 29:32.70, 2:14:34; 1988- 29:14.36, 2:12:28; 1989- 28:51.01, 1990- 28:05.22, 2:09:45; 1991- 28:05.47, 2:12:00; 1992- 28:33.45, 2:14:00; 1993- 27:59.72, 2:11:53; 1994- 28:06.32, 2:16:35; 1995- 2:10:12. pbs: 1500m 3:48.88 '93, 3000m 8:13.33 '88, 5000m 13:30.40 '93, Half Mar 61:14 '92 (GER rec).
At the marathon broke 2:10 when fourth in Berlin 1990; won at Budapest 1987, Palermo 1991, Frankfurt 1993. 2nd Beppu 1995.

Dietmar HAAF b.6 Mar 1967 Bad Cannstatt 1.73m 64kg. Salamander Kornwestheim. Electronics student at Stuttgart University, formerly USC, USA.
At LJ: OG: '92- dnq 14; WCh: '87- dnq, '91- 4; EC: '86- 10, '90- 1, '94- dnq 24; WI: '89- 2, '91- 1; EI: '90- 1, '94- 1; WJ: '86- 1; EJ: '85- 5; ECp: '91- 1, '94-2. FRG champion 1986-92, 1994.
Progression at LJ: 1981- 5.83, 1982- 6.48, 1983- 7.07, 1984- 7.54/7.66w, 1985- 7.78, 1986- 7.97, 1987- 8.05/8.10w, 1988- 8.04, 1989- 8.25i/ 7.99/8.22w, 1990- 8.25, 1991- 8.23/8.30w, 1992- 8.16, 1993- 8.09, 1994- 8.24. pbs: 100m 10.5 '87, 10.82 '85; 200m 21.62 '86.
The smallest world class long jumper, he has a fine major meeting record.

Raymond HECHT b.11 Nov 68 Gardelegen 1.91m 93kg. TV Wattenscheid. Mechanical engineer.
At JT: WCh: '91- 12, '93- dnq 23; EC: '90- 10, '94- 5; WCp: '94- 2; ECp: '93- 4, '94- 2; EJ: '87- 3. GER champion 1993-4. 2nd GP 1993.

Four German javelin records 1991-4.
Progression at JT: 1984- 66.20, 1985- 69.32; new: 1986- 71.08 (71.14 old), 1987- 75.90, 1990- 83.24, 1991- 90.84, 1992- 79.58, 1993- 88.90, 1994- 90.06. As a junior was ranked fourth in the world in 1987. Missed 1988-9 and re-emerged in 1990.

Jens-Peter HEROLD b.2 Jun 1965 Neuruppin 1.76m 66kg. SCC Berlin. Mechanic.
At 1500m: OG: '88- 3, '92- 6; WCh: '87- 6, '91- 4, '93- h; EC: '90- 1, '94- h; EI: '87- 2, '90- 1; WCp: '89- 3 (2 800m); ECp: '87- 3, '89- 4, '91- 2, '93- 6 (4 800m). Won GDR 800m 1987, 1989; 1500m 1987-90, GER 1500m 1991-3. 2nd GP 1M 1990, 2nd= 1500m 1991.
GDR records 1500m 1987, 1M (now GER) 1988. German indoor records 1000m 2:17.09'93, 1500m 3:36.23 '93, 1M 3:53.74 '94, 2000m 4:56.23i 93.
Progression at 1500m: 1979- 4:23.5, 1981- 4:12.8, 1983- 3:48.87, 1984- 3:49.67, 1985- 3:43.9, 1986- 3:37.92, 1987- 3:33.28, 1988- 3:33.33, 1989- 3:34.00, 1990- 3:33.2, 1991- 3:34.3, 1992- 3:32.77, 1993- 3:34.42, 1994- 3:35.44. pbs: 400m 49.5 '85, 800m 1:44.88 '90, 1000m 2:16.52 '93, 1M 3:49.22 '88, 2000m 4:56.23i '93, 3000m 8:00.60i '91, 5000m 14:14.5 '86.
Employed his finishing kick to best effect when he won gold in Split to complete the European double, indoors and out; his first major titles.

Robert IHLY b.5 May 1963 Asbest, USSR 1.74m 64kg. LG Offenburg. Engineer
At 20kmW: OG: '92- 11; WCh: '91- 6, '93- 7; EC: '90- 9; WCp: '93- 8. At 50kmW: EC: '94- dnf. Won FRG/GER 20kmW 1990-3, 50kmW 1989-90. Three FRG 20km walk records 1990, two road, one track.
Progression at 20kmW, 50kmW: 1983- 1:30:00, 1984- 1:27:30, 1985- 1:25:47, 1986- 1:25:40?, 1987- 1:27:40, 4:02:08; 1988- 1:26:46, 4:01:44; 1989- 1:23:45, 4:05:45; 1990- 1:20:28, 4:00:23; 1991- 1:20:52, 1992- 1:19:59, 1993- 1:21:26, 1994- 1:21:14, 3:58:10. pbs: 3000mW 19:04.52i '92, 1HrW 14605m '90, 30kmW 2:11:52.8 '92; road 10kmW 39:31 '90.

Edgar ITT b.8 Jun 1967 Gedern 1.86m 75kg. TV Gelnhausen. Student.
At 400mh/R- 4x400m relay: OG: '88- 8/3R; WCh: '87- h/4R; EC: '90- 8/2R, '94- 5. At 400m: EC: '86- 2R; WJ: '86- 3; EJ: '85- 2R; WUG: '89- 3R; WCp: '89- 7; ECp: '87- 3/3R, '89- 1, '94- 5. GER champion 400mh 1994.
Progression at 400m/400mh: 1983- -/58.1, 1984- 47.49/54.3, 1985- 47.34/55.1, 1986- 45.72/49.68, 1987- 45.38/49.14, 1988- 45.43/48.65, 1989- 45.41/48.95, 1990- 46.31/49.00, 1991- 51.29, 1992- 47.24/49.74, 1993- 47.24/49.75, 1994- 46.77/48.48. pbs: 100m 10.64 '89, 200m 20.81 '89, 800m 1:45.70 '88, 110mh 14.3 '85.
On 19 June 1988 was the first FRG athlete to defeat Harald Schmid at 400mh for eight years. After some four years away from major events returned to top form in 1994.

Ralf JAROS b.13 Dec 1965 Düsseldorf 1.93m 85kg. Bayer Leverkusen. Businessman.
At TJ: OG: '84- dnq 17, '92- dnq 13; WCh: '91- 9, '93- 4; EC: '90- 12; WI: '85- 6; EJ: '83- 7; ECp: '85- 6, '91- 1, '93- 3. FRG/GER champ 1984-5, 1990-3. German TJ record 1991.
Progression at TJ: 1980- 13.86, 1981- 14.91, 1982- 15.92/16.27w, 1983- 16.51i/16.14, 1984- 16.81, 1985- 17.29, 1986- 16.94, 1987- 16.68, 1989- 16.65, 1990- 17.08, 1991- 17.66, 1992- 17.28, 1993- 17.34, 1994- 16.89/17.10i. pbs: 10.94 '93, LJ 7.93i '88, 7.78 '92.
After five years of having problems with his knees, had a marvellous year in 1991, but disappointed in 1992 when he just missed the Olympic final.

Paul MEIER b.27 Jul 1971 Velbert 1.96m 90kg. Bayer Leverkusen. Mechanical engineering student.
At Dec: OG: '92- 6; WCh: '93- 3; WJ: '90- 8; ECp:

Nico Motchebon: European indoor record holder at 800m

'93- 1. EI Pen: '92- 5.
Progression at Dec: 1990- 7233, 1991- 7797, 1992- 8192, 1993- 8548. pbs: 100m 10.53 '93, 200m 21.46 '93, 400m 47.36 '93, 1500m 4:32.05 '93, 110mh 14.39 '93, HJ 2.15 '92, PV 4.90 '92, LJ 7.86/7.95w '93; SP 16.02 '92, DT 49.00 '92, JT 62.74 '92, Hep: 6067i '93.
Set pbs at all ten decathlon events in 1992, including three at the Olympics. Missed 1994 season through injury.

Nico MOTCHEBON b.13 Nov 1969 Berlin 1.86m 81kg. SCC Berlin. Student.
At 800m: WCh: '93- sf; EC: 94- 4; WCp: '94- 5; WUG: '93- 3; ECp: '94- 1; WI: '93- 3; EI: '94- 4. Won GER 800m 1993-4.
Progression at 800m: 193- 1994- 1:44.61, 1995- 1:44.88i. pbs: 400m 47.12 '94. 1000m 2:20.67 '94.
German mother, Cameroon father. At modern pentathlon he was German champion 1989 and 1991, with a world team bronze (5th individual) and European team silver in 1991. Taking up athletics only in 1993 he rapidly reached international class with the World Indoor bronze in his first important meeting and only his ninth race. In February 1995 he broke Seb Coe's European indoor record for 800m.

Axel NOACK b.23 Sep 1961 Görlitz 1.81m 68kg. Berliner TSC. Building worker.
At 20kmW: OG: '88- 8, '92- 20; WCh: '87- dnf, '91- 11; EC: '86- dq, '90- dnf; WCp: '87- 6, '91- 9. At 50kmW: WCh: '93- 4; EC: '94- 10; WCp: '85- 3. At 5kmW: EI: '90- 3. GDR champion 20kmW 1987, 50kmW 1984, GER 20kmW 1994.
World 20km road walk best 1987.
Progression at 20kmW, 50kmW: 1981- 1:35:23; 1982- 1:33:23; 1983- 1:24:19, 4:22:41; 1984- 1:26:20, 4:00.41; 1985- 1:26:54, 3:56.22; 1986- 1:21:55; 1987- 1:19:12; 1988- 1:20:39; 1989- 1:33:16, 4:10:51; 1990- 1:21:12, 4:13:42; 1991- 1:21:24, 1992- 1:21:25, 1993- 1:26:41, 3:43:50; 1994- 1:24:25, 3:50:32. track pbs: 3000mW 11:04.03i '95, 11:36.11 '87; 5000mW 18:38.8i '90, 19:28.09 '87; 10000mW 39:29.72 '87, 20000mW 1:22:26.1 '90; road 10kmW 39:08 '88.

Lars RIEDEL b.28 Jun 1967 Zwickau 1.99m 110kg. USC Mainz. Computer salesman.
At DT: OG: '92- dnq 14; WCh: '91- 1, '93- 1; EC: '90- dnq 15, '94- dns; WJ: '86- 4; ECp: '91- 2, '93- 1. GER champion 1992-4. Won GP 1993, 2nd 1991.
Progression at DT: 1985- 52.02, 1986- 58.66, 1988- 62.26, 1989- 60.84, 1990- 64.86, 1991- 67.78, 1992- 68.66, 1993- 68.42, 1994- 66.08. pbs: SP 15.93 '91, JT 61.14 '93, Dec 6087 '93.
Second GDR Champs 1990, then threw consistently far in 1991, when he was world champion. In 1992 improved to 67.90, but failed at the Olympics before making a fine comeback with four throws over 68m at the ISTAF meeting. Was clearly world number one in 1993. In 1994 a bad back caused his withdrawal from European final.

Stefan SCHMID b.6 May 1970 Würzburg. LG Karlstadt.
At Dec: EC: '94- 5; ECp: '93- 6. German champion 992.
Progression at Dec: 1990- 7532, 1991- 7866, 1992- 8012, 1993- 8061, 1994- 8309. pbs: 100m 10.90 '91, 10.76w '94; 200m 21.68'91, 400m 48.32 '93, 1500m 4:26.51 '94, 110mh 14.20 '90, HJ 2.00 '94, PV 5.00 '92, LJ 7.83 '94, SP 14.31 '94, DT 43.38 '94, JT 71.68 '94.
After a season in which he broke into the world's top ten he had a cartilege operation at the end of 1994.

Jürgen SCHULT b.11 May 1960 Neuhaus/ Kreis Hagenow 1.93m 110kg. Schweriner SC. Trainee journalist.
At DT: OG: '88- 1, '92- 2; WCh: '83- 5, '87- 1, '91- 6, '93- 3; EC: '86- 7, '90- 1, '94- 3; EJ: '79- 1; WCp: '85- 2, '89- 1, '94- 5; ECp: '83- 1, '85- 4, '87- 2, '89- 1, '91- 2, '94- 2. GDR champion 1983-90. 3rd GP 1993.
World discus record 1986.
Progression at DT: 1978- 51.82, 1979- 57.22, 1980- 61.26, 1981- 61.56, 1982- 63.18, 1983- 66.78, 1984- 68.82, 1985- 69.74, 1986- 74.08, 1987- 69.52, 1988- 70.46, 1989- 68.12, 1990- 67.08, 1991- 67.20, 1992- 69.04, 1993- 66.12, 1994- 66.08. pb SP 17.45 '82.
Although he has not got near his world record distance he has been most consistent, winning World, Olympic and European titles, and being undefeated in 1988 and 1989.

Florian SCHWARTHOFF b.7 May 1968 Dortmund 2.01m 76kg. TV Heppenheim. Architectural student.
At 110mh: OG: '88- qf, '92- 5; WCh: '87- sf, '91- 7, '93- 5; EC: '90- sf, '94- 2; WCp: '94- 4; ECp: '89- 3, '91- 2 (5 200m), '93- 2, '94- 1; EJ: '87- 2; WUG: '89- 3. FRG/GER champion 1987-8, 1990-2, 1994. At 60mh: WI: '93- 4; EI: '90- 3.
Four FRG 110mh records 1988-92 and three at 60mh indoors in 1990.
Progression at 110mh: 1986- 14.13, 1987- 13.69, 1988- 13.50, 1989- 13.37, 1990- 13.37, 1991- 13.38, 1992- 13.13, 1993- 13.27. 1994- 13.16. pbs: 100m 10.68 '92, 10.46w '90; 200m 20.86 '91, 60mh 7.52i '90, LJ 7.69 '86.
Perhaps the tallest ever top-class high hurdler. His European silver in 1994, one place ahead of Tony Jarrett, was his first medal since the 1987 European Juniors when he was second to Jarrett.

Ralf SONN b.17 Jan 1967 Weinheim 1.97m 85kg. MTG Mannheim. Medical student.
At HJ OG: '92- 6; WCh: '93- 4; EC: '90- 7, '94- 12; EI: '89- 4, '92- 3=; ECp: '89- 6, '91- 7. Won GER title 1992.
Progression at HJ: 1980- 1.65, 1981- 1.76, 1982- 1.75, 1983- 2.00, 1984- 2.06, 1985- 2.11, 1986- 2.16, 1987- 2.23, 1988- 2.25, 1989- 2.32, 1990- 2.36i/2.31, 1991- 2.39i/2.20, 1992- 2.36i/2.32, 1993- 2.36i/2.34, 1994- 2.34i/2.28. pb LJ 7.15 '87.

Ronald WEIGEL b.8 Aug 1959 Hildburghausen 1.77m 62kg. LAC Halensee Berlin. Trainee journalist, former soldier.
At 50kmW (20kmW): OG: '88- 2 (2), '92- 3; WCh: '83- 1, '87- 2, '91- dnf (16), '93- dnf; EC: '86- dq, '90- 9; WCp: '87- 1, '91- 3. At 10kmW: EJ: '77- 2. At 5000mW: WI: '91- 9, '93- 5; EI: '87- 2, '94- . Won GDR 20kmW 1984, 1988-9; 50kmW 1983, 1985, 1988. GER 50kmW 1991-2, 1994.
At 20km walk: European track records 1:20:54.9 1983 and 1:19:18.3 1990. WIB: 5000mW: 18:44.97 '87 & 18:11.41 '88, 20kmW: 1:20:40 '80. World fastest 50km road walk 1984 and 1986; GDR record 10000mW 1980, road bests at 20kmW (2) 1984; 30kmW (4) 1983-8, best 2:11:44 '88; 50kmW (4) 1982-6. 
Progression at 20kmW, 50kmW: 1975- 1:40:56; 1976- 1:30:49; 1977- 1:27:51; 1978- 1:27:00; 1979- 1:25:00; 1980- 1:20:40i, 1:22:50; 1981- 1:22:40, 3:49:53; 1982- 1:25:12t, 3:44:20; 1983- 1:20:54.9t, 3:41:31; 1984- 1:19:56, 3:38:31; 1985- 1:22:12, 3:47.15; 1986- 1:20:39, 3:38:17; 1987- 1:20:40, 3:41:30; 1988- 1:20:00, 3:38:56; 1989- 1:21:36; 1990- 1:19:18.3t, 3:44:50; 1991- 1:21:04, 3:45:57; 1992- 1:22:51, 3:51:37; 1993- 1:23:51; 1994- 1:23:11, 3:52:56. Track pbs: 3000mW 11:18.0 '84, 5000mW 18:53.38 '84, 18:11.41i '88; 10000mW 38:12.13 '80, 1hrW 14750mi '84.

Heinz WEIS b.14 Jul 1963 Trier 1.93m 110kg. LG Bayer Leverkusen. Businessman.
At HT OG: '88- 5, '92- 6; WCh: '87- 6, '91- 3; EC: '90- 8, '94- 3; WUG: '85- 1, '87- 2, '89- 2, '91- 3; WCp: '89- 1, '94- 3; ECp: '89- 1, '91- 4, '94- 4. FRG/GER champion 1988-92, 1994. 3rd GP 1990.
Three FRG hammer records 1988-9.
Progression at HT: 1980- 53.34, 1981- 60.86, 1982- 61.56, 1983- 65.30, 1984- 68.98, 1985- 78.18, 1986- 76.08, 1987- 80.18, 1988- 82.52, 1989- 82.84, 1990- 81.36, 1991- 80.44, 1992- 80.46, 1993- 75.56, 1994- 81.20. pb SP 14.30 '87.
Threw brilliantly in the 1987 World Chams, being in a medal place up to his pb in the fifth round, only to end up sixth. Since then has compiled a fine competitive record, world number one 1989.

Women

Alina ASTAFEI b.7 Jun 1969 Bucuresti 1.81m 60kg. Student. USC Mainz. Married to volleyball international Alin Stavariu.
At HJ: OG: '88- 5, '92- 2; WCh: '87- dnq 17=, '93- 4=; WI: '93- 4; EC: '90- dnq 17; EI: '89- 1, '90- 3; WJ: '86- 2, '88- 1; EJ: '87- 2; WUG: '89- 1; WCp: '89- 3, '92- 2; ECp: '89- 1, '93- 1. Romanian champion 1986, 1988-9, 1992. 2nd GP 1993.
Three world junior and three Romanian high jump records 1988.
Progression at HJ: 1984- 1.80, 1985- 1.89, 1986- 1.93, 1987- 1.93i/1.88, 1988- 2.00, 1989- 2.00, 1990- 1.98, 1992- 2.00, 1993- 2.00, 1994- 2.02i, 1995- 2.03i.
Given three year suspension by Romanian Federation for refusing to compete at the 1994 European Indoor Championships, but now living in Germany. She gained German citizenship in 1995 and made an impressive return to competition.

Heike BALCK b.19 Aug 1970 Schwerin 1.80m 54kg. Schweriner SC. Social worker.
At HJ: WCh: '91- 12, '93- dnq 20; EC: '90- 5=,

Alina Astafei: a 'new' German

'94- 6; WCp: '89- 4, '94- 4; ECp: '89- 3; WJ: '88- 7; EJ: '87- 3; WI: '91- 3. GDR champion 1989-90, GER 1994.
World junior high jump record 1989.
Progression at HJ: 1983- 1.50, 1984- 1.63, 1985- 1.75, 1986- 1.85, 1987- 1.93, 1988- 1.94, 1989- 2.01, 1990- 1.97, 1991- 1.96i/1.95, 1992- 1.92, 1993- 1.95, 1994- 1.95.

Peggy BEER b.15 Sep 1969 Berlin 1.76m 66kg. LAC Halensee Berlin. Student.
At Hep: OG: '92- 6; WCh: '91- 7; EC: '90- 3, '94- 6; WJ: '86- 4, '88- 3; EJ: '87- 1; ECp: '91- 1, '94- 3. GER champion 1991.
Progression at Hep: 1984- 5479, 1985- 5459, 1986- 5900, 1987- 6068, 1988- 6067w, 1989- 6241, 1990- 6531, 1991- 6494, 1992- 6460. 1993- dnf, 1994- 6362. pbs: 200m 23.59 '91, 800m 2:05.79 '90, 60mh 8.14i '91, 100mh 13.25 '92, HJ 1.88 '86, LJ 6.41/6.48w '91, SP 13.94 '92, JT 51.26 '94, Pen 4627i '93.
Her father Klaus won seven GDR title and did his pb of 8.19 to win the 1968 Olympic long jump silver medal and her mother Sigrun Albert ran 100m in 11.8 in 1963.. Her brother Ron had a LJ best of 8.23 '88, was the 1983 European Junior champion and GDR champion 1986 and 1988.

Sabine BRAUN b.19 Jun 1965 Essen 1.74m 62kg. TV Wattenscheid. Student of sport and biology.
At Hep: OG: '84- 6, '88- 14, '92- 3; WCh: '87- 18, '91- 1, '93- 2; EC: '90- 1, '94- 1; EJ: '83- 2; WUG: '89- 2; ECp: '85- 4, '89- 5. At LJ: EJ: '83- 8; WCp: '85- 5, '94- 5; ECp: '85- 3, '89- 6. Won FRG LJ 1985, Hep 1989, GER 100mh 1992.
Three FRG heptathlon records 1989-90, GER record 1992.
Progression at Hep: 1982- 5477, 1983- 6254, 1984- 6436, 1985- 6323, 1986- 6418, 1987- 5621, 1988- 6432, 1989- 6575, 1990- 6688, 1991- 6672, 1992- 6985, 1993- 6797, 1994- 6665. pbs: 100m 11.59 '85, 200m 23.60 '85, 400m 55.03 '83, 800m 2:09.41 '84, 100mh 13.05 '92, HJ 1.94 '92, LJ 6.73 '85, SP 14.84 '92, JT 54.10 '86.
Missed major events in 1986-7 through injury. Won at Götzis 1990-2, 1994. World best 6214 for 45-minute heptathlon 1993.

Grit BREUER b.16 Feb 1972 Röbel 1.66m 61kg. SC Neubrandenburg.
At 400m (R- 4x400m relay): OG: '88- resR; WCh: '91- 2/3R (3 4x100mR); EC: '90- 1/1R; WJ: '88- 1 (1R & 1 4x100mR); WI: '91- 1R (3 200m); WCp: '89- 2/2R; ECp: '89- 1/1R, '91- 2/1R. GDR champion 1989-90.
World junior records 400m 1990 and 1991, 4x100mR and 4x400mR 1988, indoor 200m 1991. WIR 4x400mR 1991.
Progression at 200m, 400m: 1985- 56.21, 1986- 55.7, 1987- 24.03, 52.59; 1988- 23.04, 51.14; 1989- 22.82, 50.48; 1990- 22.49, 49.50; 1991- 22.45, 49.42; 1992- 22.71i. pb 100m 11.13 '90.
Olympic bronze medal at age 16 as she ran in heats of 4x400m relay. Although a junior until 1991, she did not contest the 1989 or 1991 European or 1990 World Juniors, but concentrated with great success on senior competition. Drugs ban in 1992, first for allegedly tampering with sample. That ban was lifted by the DLV, but then caught again for use of Clenbuterol. She is expected to return to competition when her three-year ban ends in August 1995.

Birgit CLARIUS b.18 Mar 1965 Giessen 1.76m 65kg, LAC Quelle Fürth/München 1860. Student of dietetics.
At Hep: OG: '92- 7; WCh: '93- 8; EC: '86- dnf, '90- 7; WUG: '89- 4, '91- 1; ECp: '89- 8. At Pen: WI inv: '93- 3; EI: '92- 4. Won FRG Hep 1990, GER 1992-4.
Progression at Hep: 1982- 5535, 1983- 5347, 1984- 5961, 1986- 6179, 1988- 6204, 1989- 6247w, 1990- 6359, 1991- 6419, 1992- 6478, 1993- 6500, 1994- 6109. pbs: 200m 24.72/24.69w '93, 800m 2:08.33 '93, 100mh 13.61 '93; 400mh 58.65 '91, HJ 1.84 '92, LJ 6.28 '92, 6.34w '91; SP 15.60 '92, JT 51.60 '90, Pen: 4641i '93.
Overcame a long series of injuries and illness in 1984-8, with no competition in 1985 and 1987. On 15 Oct 1993 married Michael Hess (TJ 15.13 and Dec 7358 '84).

Tanja DAMASKE b.16 Nov 1971 Berlin 1.77m 69kg. OSC Berlin.
At JT: EC: '94- 6; WJ: '90- 1; WUG: '93- 2.
Progression at JT: 1986- 44.38, 1988- 52.50, 1989- 51.20, 1990- 61.06, 1991- 59.84, 1992- 55.86, 1993- 60.96, 1994- 64.24. pb SP 14.47 '94.

Franka DIETZSCH b.22 Jan 1968 Wolgast 1.83m 95kg. SC Neubrandenburg. Student.
At DT: OG: '92- 12; WCh: '91- dnq 13, '93- 8; EC: '94- 9; WJ: '86- 2; WUG: '89- 4.
Progression at DT: 1982- 43.80, 1983- 50.04, 1984- 51.16, 1985- 56.94, 1986- 64.34, 1987- 66.34, 1988- 65.56, 1989- 68.26, 1990- 67.42, 1991- 61.22, 1992- 64.64, 1993- 62.06, 1994- 62.76. pb SP 15.02 '85.

Katrin DÖRRE b.6 Oct 1961 Leipzig 1.70m 56kg. LG Odenwald. Studied medicine at University of Leipzig. Married to her coach Wolfgang Heinig.
At Mar: OG: '88- 3, '92- 5; WCh: '91- 3, '93- 6; EC: '86- dnf. '94- dnf; WCp: '85- 1, '87- 3, '91- 4; ECp: '85- 1, '88- 1. World 15km Rd: '90- 6. Won GDR 3000m 1980.
Six GDR marathon records 1982-7.
Progression at Mar: 1982- 2:43:19, 1983- 2:37:41,

1984- 2:26:52, 1985- 2:30:11, 1986- 2:29:33, 1987- 2:25:24, 1988- 2:26:21, 1990- 2:33:21, 1991- 2:27:43, 1992- 2:27:34, 1993- 2:27:09, 1994- 2:25:15. pbs: 800m 2:05.4 '80, 1000m 2:44.8 '80, 1500m 4:18.7 '79, 3000m 9:04.01 '84, 10000m 33:00.0 '84, 1Hr 17709m '88 (GDR rec). Road: 10km 32:14 '92, Half Mar 70:04 '93 (GER rec).
Has won 18 of her 31 marathons, including her first 11 1982-6, with major wins Osaka 1984 and 1991, Tokyo 1984-5, 1987, Nagoya 1986, London 1992-4, Berlin 1994. Second Tokyo 1992, third New York 1990, Tokyo 1991 & 1993, Osaka 1992. Daughter Katharina born August 1989.

Heike DRECHSLER b.16 Dec 1964 Gera 1.81m 68kg. née Daute. TuS Jena (to Chemnitz 1995).
At LJ/R - 4x100m relay: OG: '88- 2 (3 100m & 200m), '92- 1; WCh: '83- 1, '87- 3 (2 100m), '91- 2/3R, '93- 1; WI: '87- 1 (1 200m), '91- 2; EC: '82- 4, '86- 1 (1 200m), '90- 1 (2 200m), '94- 1; EI: '83- 3, '85- 3, '86- 1, '87- 1, '88- 1, '94- 1; EJ: '81- 1; WCp: '85- 1, '92- 1; ECp: '83- 1, '85- 2, '87- 1/1R (2 4x400mR), '91- 1/2R, '93- 1, '94- 1. Won GDR LJ 1981, 1983-8, 1990; 200m 1986, 1988; GER LJ 1992, 1994; 100m 1992; GWG LJ 1994. Won GP LJ and 2nd overall 1990, won both 1992, 3rd LJ 1994.
World records: three LJ 1985-6, two 200m 1986. WIB: LJ (6): 6.88 '83, 6.99 '84 & '85, 7.25 & 7.29 '86, 7.37 '88; 100y: 10.24 '86, 10.24 & 10.15 '87; 200m: 22.27 '87. World junior LJ records 1981 and 1982, heptathlon 1981. Eight GDR LJ records 1983-8, GER record 1992.
Progression at 100m, 200m, LJ: 1977- 4.40, 1978- 5.69, 1979- 12.3, 6.07; 1980- 6.64/6.70w, 1981- 11.75, 24.16, 6.91/7.01w; 1982- 6.98, 1983- 7.14/ 7.27w, 1984- 7.40, 1985- 23.19, 7.44; 1986-10.91/ 10.80w, 21.71, 7.45; 1987-10.95, 22.18, 7.40; 1988- 10.91/10.85w, 21.84, 7.48; 1990- 11.14, 22.19, 7.30; 1991- 11.09, 22.58/22.4, 7.37/7.39w; 1992- 11.24, 7.48/7.63w; 1993- 11.36, 23.16, 7.21; 1994- 11.38, 22.84, 7.29/7.39Aw. pbs: 800m 2:11.53 '94, 100mh 13.34 '94, HJ 1.88i '92, TJ 13.35 '93, SP 13.58 '94, JT 40.64 '94, Hep 6741 '94.
The youngest gold medallist of the 1983 world championships, she has jumped consistently over 7 metres ever since - her 100th competition at this level coming at the 1992 Olympics and to the end of 1994 she has 152 competitions at 7m or more. Her 7.63w at the high altitude of Sestriere in 1992 was the first 25 ft long jump by a woman; the wind just over the legal limit at +2.1. Made a sensational breakthrough in 1986 into a great sprinter, winning the GDR indoor 100y title in 10.24, and equalling Marita Koch's world 200m record. Showed further versatility with 50.0 400m relay leg in the 1987 European Cup. Had 27 successive LJ wins until injured at the 1987 World Champs; where she had to withdraw from the relay and from 1982 to September 1994 won 182 of 211 LJ competitions. Son, Toni, born 1 Nov 1989.
In her first heptathlon since her world junior record in 1981, she scored a marvellous 6741 points to win at Talence in 1994.

Karen FORKEL b.24 Sep 1970 Wolfen 1.72m 63kg. SV Halle. Student of computer technology at Halle University.
At JT: OG: '92- 3; WCh: '91- 12, '93- 2; EC: '90- 2, '94- 2; WJ: '88- 1; EJ: '87- 3; '89- 1; WCp: '94- 3; ECp: '93- 2, '94- 2. Won GDR JT 1990, GER 1991, 1994. 3rd GP 1990.
Progression at JT: 1983- 34.20, 1984- 40.96, 1985- 44.64, 1986- 51.42, 1987- 59.78, 1988- 64.68, 1989- 70.12, 1990- 69.38, 1991- 70.20, 1992- 69.58, 1993- 67.94, 1994- 69.20.
Threw 68.14 in qualifying but only 57.90 for last place in final of 1991 World Champs when she was the favourite for gold.

Beate GUMMELT b.4 Feb 1968 Leipzig 1.69m 54kg. née Anders. LAC Halensee Berlin. Student teacher.
At 10kmW: OG: '92- 16; WCh: '87- 16, '91- 10, '93- 5; EC: '90- 6, '94- 9; WCp: '89- 1, '91- 7, '93- 13. At 3000mW: WI: '89- 2, '91- 1, '93- 4; EI: '89- 1, '90- 1, '92- 3, '94- 2. Won GDR 5000mW 1988, 1990; 10kmW: 1987-90. GER 5000mW 1991-4, 10kmW 1991-4.
World record 3000m and 5000m walks 1990. WIR 3000mW 12:02.2 '89, 11:59.36 '90. 11:56.0 '91. European records 10,000mW 1990, 3000mW 1993. GDR records: track 5000mW (2) 1988-90, road 10kmW (5) 1987-90; GER 10,000m 1993.
Progression at 10kmW: 1987- 46:08, 1988- 44:33, 1989- 43:08, 1990- 42:29.4t, 1991- 43:53, 1992- 42:11.5t, 1993- 43:09, 1994- 42:36. pbs: 3000mW 11:52.01 '93, 5000mW 20:07.52 '90, 20kmW 1:36:55 '89. Married Bernd Gummelt (2nd 1990 EC 50km walk) in 1993.

Anja GÜNDLER b.18 Mar 1972 Frankenberg 1.84m 85kg. OSC Berlin.
At DT: WCh: '93- 5; WJ: '90- 3; EJ: '91- 1; WUG: '93- 3. German champion 1993.
Progression at DT: 1986- 40.04, 1987- 48.68, 1988- 53.96, 1989- 55.42, 1990- 59.52, 1991- 60.66, 1992- 60.34, 1993- 62.92, 1994- 61.20. pb SP 17.44 '90.

Heike HENKEL b.5 May 1964 Kiel 1.82m 63kg. née Redetzky. LG Bayer Leverkusen.
At HJ: OG: '84- 11=, '88- dnq 13, '92- 1; WCh: '87- 6, '91- 1, '93- ns; EC: '86- 6, '90- 1, '94- 11=; EJ: '81- 5; ECp: '85- 6, '87- 3, '89- 4=, '91- 3, '93- 2; WI: '87- 6, '89- 3, '91- 1, '93- 2; EI: '88- 2=, '90- 1, '92- 1. Won overall & HJ GP 1991, FRG/GER HJ 1984-8, 1990-3.
Two German HJ records 1991. WIR 2.07 '92.

Progression at HJ: 1978- 1.58, 1979- 1.68, 1980- 1.85, 1981- 1.87i/1.85, 1982- 1.89, 1983- 1.87i/1.80, 1984- 1.91, 1985- 1.92, 1986- 1.93, 1987- 1.96, 1988- 1.98, 1989- 2.00, 1990- 2.01i/2.00, 1991- 2.05, 1992- 2.04/2.07i, 1993- 2.02i/2.01, 1994- 1.95. pbs: 100m 12.3 '80, 100mh 14.04/14.0 '81, LJ 6.13 '81. Married Rainer Henkel, world swimming champion in 1986 at 400m and 1500m freestyle, in May 1989. In 1990 she twice improved the FRG indoor high jump record, previously set in 1982 by Ulrike Meyfarth, and in 1991 she took Meyfarth's outdoor record. World's best 1991-2. In all she has won 26 national titles. Had to withdraw from the World final in 1993 due to injury. Son, Ravn, born on 27 Feb 1994.

Silke-Beate **KNOLL** b.21 Feb 1967 Rottweil 1.63m 52kg. LG Olympia Dortmund. Student of Slavic languages.
At 200m/R- 4x100m relay: OG: '88- qf, '92- sf/5R; WCh: '87- h/5R, '91- sf, '93- sf; EC: '90- 5/2R (4 4x400mR), '94- 4/1R; EJ: '85- 1 4x400mR; WI: '89- 4; EI: '88- 3, '94- 2; WUG: '89- 3R; WCp: '94- 2R; ECp: '87- 3R, '93- 3/3R, '94- 1/3R. Won FRG 200m 1990. GER 1992-3.
WIR 4x200mR 1988.
Progression at 200m: 1982- 25.8, 1983- 26.1, 1984- 25.7, 1985- 23.8, 1986- 23.67, 1987- 23.07, 1988- 22.97i/23.06, 1989- 22.96i/23.34, 1990- 22.40, 1991- 22.81, 1992- 22.29, 1993- 22.75/22.74w, 1994- 22.55. pbs: 60m 7.35i '94, 100m 11.17 '92, 300m 36.33 '90, 400m 51.90 '94, LJ 5.76 '85.

Astrid KUMBERNUSS b.5 Feb 1970 Grevesmühlen 1.86m 90kg. SC Neubrandenburg. Sports student.
At SP: WCh: '93- 6; EC: '90- 1, '94- 2; EI: '92- 3, '94- 1; EJ: '89- 1; WCp: '94- 3; ECp: '91- 2, '94- 1. 3rd GP 1991, 2nd 1993. At DT: WJ: '88- 2; EJ: '87- 2, '89- 1.
World junior shot record 1989.
Progression at SP, DT: 1983- 11.16, 33.48; 1984- 13.44, 44.00; 1985- 14.23, 46.96; 1986- 15.39, 53.92; 1987- 18.20, 63.88; 1988- 18.73, 66.60; 1989- 20.54, 64.74; 1990- 20.77, 65.42; 1991- 19.67, 60.88; 1992- 20.03i/19.69, 1993- 19.92, 59.64; 1994- 20.06.

Jana LAUREN b. 28 Jun 1970 Berlin 1.82m 82kg. Berliner TSC.
At DT: EC: '94- 6; EJ: '89- 2; ECp: '93- 5.
Progression at DT: 1983- 37.50, 1984- 38.50, 1985- 44.40, 1986- 51.40, 1987- 55.72, 1988- 60.94, 1989- 66.30, 1990- 60.70, 1991- 61.42, 1992- 60.94, 1993- 62.80, 1994- 62.70.

Heike MEISSNER b.29 Jan 1970 Dresden 1.72m 56kg. Dresdner SC. Student.
At 400mh/4x400mR: OG: '92- sf/6R; WCh: '91- 7, '93- sf; EC: '94- 4/3R; WUG: '93- 1; EJ: '89- 3; WCp: '94- 2R; ECp: '91- 3, '94- 5/2R. GDR champion 1990, GER 1991-2, 1994.
Progression at 400mh: 1986- 59.61, 1987- 60.99, 1989- 56.77, 1990- 56.78, 1991- 54.77, 1992- 55.09, 1993- 54.64, 1994- 54.52. pbs: 100m 12.0 '91, 200m 24.28 '93, 400m 52.36 '94, 800m 2:03.80i '95, 2:12.1 '90.

Kathrin NEIMKE b.18 Jul 1966 Magdeburg 1.80m 91kg. SC Magdeburg. Repro photographer.
At SP: OG: '88- 2, '92- 3; WCh: '87- 2, '91- 8, '93- 3; EC: '90- 3, '94- 6; WI: '91- 6, '93- 8; EI: '88- 3; WUG: '87- 2; WCp: '92- 3. GDR champion 1988, GER 1992-3.
Progression at SP: 1981- 11.92, 1982- 12.98, 1983- 15.76, 1984- 16.09, 1985- 18.09, 1986- 19.68, 1987- 21.21, 1988- 21.11, 1990- 20.51, 1991- 19.57i/18.92, 1992- 19.78, 1993- 19.78, 1994- 19.89. pb DT 58.82 '86.

Melanie PASCHKE b.29 Jun 1970 Braunschweig 1.68m 54kg, LG Braunschweig.
At 100m/4x100mR: WCh: '93- 5R; EC: '94- 3/1R; EJ: '87- sf/4R, '89- sf/2R; WCp: '94- 5/2R (7 200m); ECp: '93- 4, '94-3/3R. At 60m: EI: '94- 2. Won GER 100m 1993-4, 200m 1994.
Progression at 100m, 200m: 1984- 12.3, 1985- 12.1, 25.5; 1986- 12.17, 25.20; 1987- 11.68, 24.57; 1988- 11.85, 24.67; 1989- 11.69, 24.39; 1991- 11.59, 24.36; 1992- 11.56, 24.36; 1993- 11.23, 23.43/22.97w; 1994- 11.12, 22.45. pb 60m 7.17i '94.

Kristin PATZWAHL b.16 Jul 1965 Leipzig 1.69m 60kg. LAC Halensee Berlin. Student.
At 100mh OG: '92- sf; WCh: '91- 8, '93- sf; EC: '90- 7, '94- sf; WCp: '94- 5; ECp: '91- 3. GER champion 1991, 1993-4.
Progression at 100mh: 1982- 14.62, 1983- 14.03, 1984- 14.11, 1985- 13.49, 1986- 13.23, 1987- 13.11/13.01w, 1988- 12.94, 1989- 12.88, 1990- 12.80, 1991- 13.07, 1992- 13.00, 1993- 12.98, 1994- 12.94. pbs: 100m 11.69 '89, 50mh 6.75i '89, 60mh 7.98i '91.

Uta PIPPIG b.7 Sep 1965 Leipzig 1.70m 49kg. SC Charlottenburg Berlin. Medical student.
At 10000m: OG: '92- 7; WCh: '91- 6, '93- 9. At Mar: WCh: '87- 14; WCp: '87- 8, '89- 3. At 3000m: ECp: '91- 2. World 15k road: '91- 3. Won GDR Mar 1986-7, FRG CC 1990.
FRG records 5000m and 10000m 1990, marathon 1990 and 1991, German marathon record 1994. WIB 5000m 1991.
Progression at 10000m, Mar: 1984- 36:54.8, 2:47:42; 1985- 34:42.62, 2:36:45; 1986- 34:04.63, 2:37:56; 1987- 2:30:50; 1988- 2:32:20; 1989- 32:42.55, 2:35:17; 1990- 31:40.92, 2:28:03; 1991-

31:51.36, 2:26:52; 1992- 31:21.36, 2:27:12; 1993- 31:29.70, 2:26:24; 1994- 2:21:45. pbs: 1500m 4:11.39i '91, 4:14.80 '92; 3000m 8:40.99 '93, 5000m 15:04.87 '91; road: 15km 48:44 '91 (GER rec), Half Mar 67:59 '94.
Left Potsdam, GDR for the FRG in January 1990. Won Berlin Marathon 1990, 1992. Boston 2nd 1990, 3rd 1991-2. After a series of track pbs in 1993 she won the New York marathon and ran the third fastest ever marathon by a woman to win Boston 1994. After completing important exam in the late summer of 1994, she is delaying medical studies for two years.

Helga RADTKE b.16 May 1962 Sassnitz 1.71m 64kg. LAC Quelle Fürth/München.
At LJ (TJ): OG: '92- dnq 20; WCh: '83- 12, '87- 4, '91- dnq 13, '93- dnq 13 (5); WI: '85- 1, '87- 2; EC: '86- 3, '90- 3, '94- dnq 18 (8); EI: '83- 2, '86- 2, '90- 3; EJ: '79- 1; WCp: '89- 4; ECp: '89- 2. At TJ: WI: '93- 5; EI: '92- 3; WCp: '92- 6, '94- 6; ECp: '93- 2, '94- 1. Won GDR LJ 1989, GER TJ 1993-4.
Nine German triple jump records 1991-4.
Progression at LJ, TJ: 1976- 5.32, 1977- 5.68, 1978- 5.74, 1979- 6.63, 1980- 6.71, 1982- 6.83, 1983- 6.83, 1984- 7.21, 1985- 7.19, 1986- 7.17, 1987- 7.16/7.17w, 1988- 6.76i/6.73, 1989- 7.15, 1990- 6.97, 13.63i; 1991- 6.74, 13.83; 1992- 6.79, 6.83w, 14.30/14.44w; 1993- 6.66, 14.19; 1994- 6.60/6.72w, 14.46. pbs: 100m 11.6 '85, 100mh 14.67 '79, HJ 1.75 '82.

Silke Renk: Olympic champion

Silke RENK b.30 Jun 1967 Querfurt 1.73m 75kg. SV Halle. Sports science student at Leipzig University.
At JT: OG: '88- 5, '92- 1; WCh: '91- 3, '93- 6; EC: '90- 4; WUG: '89- 1. GER champion 1992-3. 3rd GP 1992.
Progression at JT: 1981- 42.62, 1982- 45.28, 1983- 51.16, 1984- 51.36, 1985- 59.08, 1986- 62.06, 1987- 64.74, 1988- 71.00, 1989- 66.16, 1990- 66.50, 1991- 68.34, 1992- 68.34, 1993- 65.80, 1994- 56.88.
Successively 5-4-3 at major championships 1988-91, and then won Olympic title.

Nicole RIEGER b.5 Feb 1972 Landau/Pfalz 1.68m 53kg. ASV Landau.
Seven European and 14 German pole vault records outdoors, one world and ten European indoor records.
Progression at PV: 1988- 2.90, 1989- 3.50, 1990- 3.45, 1991- 3.90, 1992- 3.92, 1993- 3.80, 1994- 4.08i/4.00. pbs: HJ 1.57 '91, LJ 5.43 '89.

Silvia RIEGER b.14 Nov 1970 Emden 1.75m 55kg. TuS Eintracht Hinte. Bank clerk.
At 400mh/4x400mR: OG: '92- h; WCh: '93- sf; EC: '90- sf, '94- 2; WJ: '88- 3; EJ: '87- 1/2R, '89- 1/3R; WCp: '94- 2/2R; ECp: '93- 4. FRG champion 1990, GER 1993.
Progression at 400mh: 1985- 64.7, 1986- 60.9, 1987- 57.44, 1988- 57.88, 1989- 56.33, 1990- 55.18, 1991- 55.15, 1992- 55.10, 1993- 54.90, 1994- 54.68. pbs: 100m 11.8 '87, 12.02 '92; 200m 24.04 '94, 24.0 '90; 400m 52.92 '94, 800m 2:07.21 '92, 100mh 13.7 '93, 13.86 '94; LJ 5.92 '87.
Improved pb from 56.33 to 55.18 to win 1990 FRG 400mh.

Stephanie STORP b.28 Nov 1968 Braunschweig 1.94m 95kg. VfL Wolfsburg. Works for Volkswagen.
At SP: OG: '92- 7; WCh: '87- 10, '91- 6, '93- 11; WI: '89- 4; EC: '86- 11 (10 DT), '90- 7, '94- 4; WI: '91- 4, '93- 2; EI: '89- 1; WJ: '86- 2 (4 DT); EJ: '85- 3 (6 DT); ECp: '93- 3. 3rd GP 1989. GER champion 1994.
Progression at SP: 1983- 12.88, 1984- 15.18, 1985- 17.72, 1986- 19.11, 1987- 19.90, 1988- 19.73, 1989- 20.30i/20.08, 1990- 20.34, 1991- 19.80, 1992- 19.59, 1993- 19.71, 1994- 19.85. pb DT 58.88 '89, JT 47.92 '89.

Susen TIEDTKE b.23 Jan 1969 Berlin 1.74m 56kg. SC Charlottenburg Berlin. Clerk. Married US long jumper Joe Greene 4 Dec 1993.
At LJ: OG: '92- 8; WCh: '91- 5, '93- 9; WI: '93- 2; EJ: '87- 3. GER champion 1993.

Progression at LJ: 1986- 6.22, 1987- 6.44, 1988- 6.08, 1989- 6.53, 1990- 6.58, 1991- 7.00, 1992- 6.74/ 7.02w, 1993- 6.85/7.19w, 1994- 6.54/6.65i/6.81w.
Was GDR youth champion gymnast at 13, and a candidate for the 1984 Olympics, which the GDR boycotted. Jumped 6.03 in her first ever LJ in May 1986. Coached by her father Jürgen Tiedtke (PV 4.50 in 1964). In 1966 her mother Ingrid was 5th in the European 200m and ran a pb of 23.5. Her uncle Manfred Tiedtke was 10th in 1968 OG decathlon.

Kathrin WESSEL b.14 Aug 1967 Annaberg 1.72m 52kg. SC Berlin. Student teacher. née Ullrich, married Andre Weßel (5000m 13:51.61 '89, 10000m 28:32.47 '88) in 1992.
At 10000m: OG: '88- 4, '92- h; WCh: '87- 3, '91- 4, '93- 13; EC: '90- 2, '94- 4; WCp: '89- 1; ECp: '87- 1, '89- 1, '91- 1, '94- 1. At 3000m: EJ: '85- 8. Won GDR 3000m & 10000m 1987-90, CC 1987, 1989-90; GER 10000m 1991-4, Mar 1994.
GDR records 1987-9: 10000m and 5000m (2); GER records 5000m and 10000m 1991.
Progression at 3000m, 10000m: 1982- 9:36.37, 1983- 9:23.78. 1984- 9:17.04, 1985- 9:14.47, 1986- 9:09.92, 1987- 8:50.51, 31:11.34; 1988- 8:41.79i/ 8:44.81, 31:26.79; 1989- 8:45.43, 31:33.92; 1990- 9:00.37, 31:47.70; 1991- 8:47.11, 31:03.62; 1992- 8:49.08i/8:51.14, 31:20.62; 1993- 8:53.45, 32:00.52; 1994- 8:50.1, 31:38.75. pbs: 800m 2:09.54 '83, 1000m 2:44.1 '86, 1500m 4:06.91i '88, 2000m 5:49.38 '91, 5000m 14:58.71 '91, Half Mar 70:47 '94, Mar 2:36:29 '94.
Has compiled a good record in major races, with a fine finishing kick.

Ilke WYLUDDA b.28 Mar 1969 Leipzig 1.85m 97kg. SV Halle. PE student.
At DT: OG: '92- 9; WCh: '87- 4, '91- 2, '93- 11; EC: '90- 1, '94- 1; WJ: '86- 1, '88- 1; EJ: '85- 1 (2 SP), '87- 1 (1 SP); WCp: '89- 1, '92- 2, '94- 1; ECp: '89- 1, '91- 1, '94- 1. Won GDR DT 1989-90, GER 1991-2, 1994. Won GWG 1990, GP 1990, 1992, 1994.
Eleven world junior records at discus 1986-8 and two at shot 1987-8.
Progression at SP, DT: 1982- 13.72, 46.54; 1983- 15.18, 51.12; 1984- 16.42, 57.74; 1985- 18.27, 62.36; 1986- 19.08, 65.86; 1987- 20.11, 71.64; 1988- 20.23, 74.40; 1989- 19.18, 74.56; 1990- 18.42, 71.10; 1991- 18.96, 69.12; 1992- 70.96, 1993- 64.06, 1994- 68.72.
Holds GDR age records for DT age 13-15, SP 14-15 as well as world bests at junior level, where she was dominant 1986-8. Unbeaten in her senior career, 1989 to World championships 1991, where she was beaten by Tsvetanka Khristova after 41 successive discus victories. Operation on right knee March 1993 and left knee September 1993.

GREECE

Governing body: Hellenic Amateur Athletic Association (SEGAS), 137 Syngrou Avenue, Athens 171 21. Founded 1896.
National Championships first held in 1896 (men), 1930 (women). **1994 Champions**: **Men**: 100m: Alexandros Terzian 10.27, 200m: Georgios Panagiotopoulos 20.92, 400m: Andreas Linardatos 47.63 (Evripidis Demosthenous CYP 47.00), 800m: Michalis Anagnostou 1:51.10, 1500m: Dimitrios Katsoulis 3:46.89, 5000m: Panagiotis Papoulias 14:22.54, 10000m: Panagiotis Haramis 29:37.51, 3000mSt: Antonios Vouzis 8:59.42, 110mh: Dimitrios Siatounis 14.53, 400mh: Panagiotis Mandelidis 52.54, HJ: Dimitrios Kokotis 2.25, PV: Christos Pallakis 5.30, LJ: Konstantinos Koukodimos 8.35, TJ: Christos Meletoglou 16.45, SP: Konstantinos Kollias 17.04, DT: Christos Papadopoulos 57.16, HT: Alexandros Papadimitriou 73.14, JT: Dimitrios Polymerou 73.80, Dec: Michalis Simitzis 7464, 20kmtW/ 50kmW: Spyros Kastanis 1:27:26.1/ 3:55:34. **Women**: 100m: Katerina Kofa 11.46, 200m: Eufrosyni Patsou 24.8, 400m: Aikaterini Galiti 55.61, 800m/1500m: Irini Akrivou 2:08.10 /4:24.53, 3000m: Chrisostomia Iakovou 9:37.23, 10000m: Georgia Abatzidou 34:47.98, 100mh: Gabriela Zaharia 14.10, 400mh: Marina Vasarmidou 60.47, HJ: Vassiliki Xenou 1.86, LJ: Paraskevi Patoulidou 6.51, TJ: Efi Hatzi 12.85, SP: Kaliopi Ouzouni 16.26, DT: Anastasia Kelesidou 58.44, JT: Dimitra Sargioti 52.78, Hep: Athina Papasotiriou 5393, 10000mW: Christina Kokotou 49:59.88.

Konstantinos KOUKODIMOS b.14 Sep 1969 Melbourne, Australia 1.86m 80kg. GAS Archelaos, Katerini.
At LJ: OG: '92- 6; WCh: '91- 12, '93- dnq 13; EC: '90- 10, '94- 3; WI: '91- 4; EI: '94- 2; WJ: '86- 8, '88- 8; EJ: '87- 6; WCp: '92- 5. Won Greek LJ 1990-2, 1994; Balkan 1988, 1991-2. Won Med Games 1991.
Four Greek long jump records 1990-4.
Progression at LJ: 1985- 7.26, 1986- 7.69, 1987- 7.78, 1988- 7.91i/7.87, 1989- 7.74, 1990- 7.97i/7.96, 1991- 8.26, 1992- 8.22, 1993- 7.90, 1994- 8.36/ 8.40w. pb 100m 10.5 '88.
Born in Australia to Greek immigrants who returned to Greece when he was aged three. Owns the biggest fast food restaurant in his home town of Katerini at the foot of Mount Olympus.

HUNGARY

Governing body: Magyar Atlétikai Szövetség, 1143 Budapest, Dózsa György utca 1-3. Founded 1897.F

National Championships first held in 1896 (men), 1932 (women). **1994 Champions. Men**: 100m: Attila Kovács 10.66, 200m: Pál Rezák 20.8, 400m: Gábor Kiss 47.22, 800m: Miklós Árpási 1:50.74, 1500m: Róbert Banai 3:49.50, 5000m: Imre Berkovics 14:01.5, 10000m: Tamás Kliszek 29:25.34, Half Mar: Péter Jáger 64:30, Mar: Zoltán Holba 2:20:02, 3000mSt: Béla Vágó 8:49.70, 110mh: Levente Csillag 13.90, 400mh: Dusán Kovács 50.58, HJ: Zoltán Bakler 2.22, PV: István Bagyula 5.20, LJ: János Uzsoki 7.88, TJ: Gyula Pálóczi 16.61w, SP: Jenö Kóczián 19.50, DT: Attila Horváth 63.06, HT: Tibor Gécsek 78.18, JT: József Belák 69.90, Dec: Zsolt Kürtösi 7604, 20kmW: Sándor Urbanik 1:22:55, 50kmW: Gyula Dudás 3:55:23. **Women**: 100m/200m: Éva Barati 11.89/23.6, 400m Mónika Mádai 54.08, 800m: Szilvia Csoszánszky 2:05.69, 1500m/3000m: Anikó Javos 4:16.11/9:07.13, 10000m: Éva Dóczi 33:58.31, Half Mar: Kornélia Pásztor 73:31, Mar: Gizella Molnár 2:50:29, 100mh: Zita Bálint 13.60, 400mh: Judit Szekeres 57.75, HJ: Erzsébet Fazekas 1.89, LJ: Rita Ináncsi 6.51w, TJ: Éva Medovárszky 12.79, SP: Hajnal Herth-Vörös 14.57, DT: Katalin Csöke-Tóth 55.44, JT: Kinga Zsigmond 62.42, Hep: Enikö Kiss 5020, 10kmW: Mária Rosza-Urbanik 44:55.

István BAGYULA b.2 Jan 1969 Budapest 1.85m 76kg. Csepel SC. Former student at George Mason University, USA.
At PV: OG: '88- 7, '92- 9; WCh: '87- dnq, '91- 2, '93- 10; EC: '90- 10, '94- 10=; WI: '89- 6; EI: '92- 2; WJ: '86- dnq, '88- 1; EJ: '87- 3; WSG: '91- 1, '93- 1; ECp: '91- 3. Won Hungarian PV 1988-9, 1994; NCAA 1990-2 (and 1990-1 indoors).
World junior pole vault record 1988; seven Hungarian records 1988-91.
Progression at PV: 1982- 4.30, 1983- 4.63, 1984- 4.90, 1985- 5.10, 1986- 5.50, 1987- 5.50, 1988- 5.65, 1989- 5.60i/5.51, 1990- 5.70i/5.60, 1991- 5.92, 1992- 5.82i/5.80, 1993- 5.70, 1994- 5.70.
Excellent season in 1991, when it took Bubka's last chance clearance at 5.95 to beat him at the World Championships.

Tibor GÉCSEK b.22 Sep 1964 Szentgotthard 1.84m 100kg. Szombathelyi AC '93. Entrepreneur, formerly diesel engine mechanic.
At HT: OG: '88- 6, '92- 4; WCh: '87- 7, '91- 4, '93- 3; EC: '90- 2, '94- 5; EJ: '83- 6; ECp: '91- 2. Hungarian champion 1986-94. Won GP 1988, 2nd 1990.
Four Hungarian hammer records 1987-8.
Progression at HT: 1980- 34.26, 1981- 50.62, 1982- 60.60, 1983- 67.90, 1984- 73.66, 1985- 77.62, 1986- 77.66, 1987- 79.14, 1988- 81.68, 1989- 77.30, 1990- 80.92, 1991- 80.72, 1992- 81.02, 1993- 81.00, 1994- 80.22. pbs: SP 14.65 '85, DT 48.72 '85.

Attila HORVATH b.28 Jul 1967 Köszeg 1.94m 117kg. Haladás VSE.
At DT: OG: '92- 5; WCh: '91- 3; EC: '90- 8, '94- 5; WJ: '86- 5; EJ: '85- 1; ECp: '91- 1. 3rd GP 1991. Hungarian champion 1987, 1990-4.
Hungarian discus record 1994.
Progression at DT: 1982- 44.06, 1983- 52.44, 1984- 56.28, 1985- 61.84, 1986- 60.76, 1987-62.94, 1988- 64.18, 1989- 63.44, 1990- 65.46, 1991- 67.06, 1992- 65.24, 1993- 64.52, 1994- 68.58. pbs: SP 17.55 '92, HT 65.64 '85.
World age 17 best discus 1985.

Dezsö SZABÓ b.4 Sep 1967 Budapest 1.84m 82kg. Újpesti TE-SAAB.
At Dec: OG: '88- 13, '92- 4; WCh: '91 & '93- dnf; EC: '90- 2, '94- 8; WSG: '89- 3. At Hep: WI: '93- 5. Won Hungarian Dec 1987-91, PV 1987, 1990, 1992.
Four Hungarian decathlon records 1988-90.
Progression at Dec: 1984- 6529, 1985- 6981, 1986- 7330, 1987- 7918, 1988- 8209, 1989- 8080, 1990- 8436, 1991- 8141, 1992- 8199, 1993- 8101, 1994- 7995. pbs: 100m 10.88 '90, 10.86w '88; 200m 22.17 '91, 21.83w '90; 400m 47.17 '90, 1500m 4:11.07 '90, 110mh 14.52 '90, HJ 2.06 '88, PV 5.40 '90, LJ 7.58 '89, 7.65w '88, SP 13.73 '92, DT 43.74 '91, JT 62.48 '91, Hep 6130i '90.
Five pbs when he won European silver medal.

Sándor URBANIK b.15 Dec 1964 Esztergom 1.72m 56kg. Békéscsabai. Electrician.
At 20kmW: OG: '88- 21, '92- 8; WCh: '91- 14, '93- 10; EC: '86- 15, '90- 15, '94- 8. At 5000mW: WI: '87- 6, '89- 4, '91- 6; EI: '88- 3. Won Hungarian 20kmW 1986-94.
Six Hungarian records 20kmW 1985-92.
Progression at 20kW: 1985- 1:23:47, 1986- 1:22:11, 1987- 1:23:37, 1988- 1:21:34, 1989- 1:24:47, 1990- 1:22:12, 1991- 1:21:05, 1992- 1:20:55, 1993- 1:23:31, 1994- 1:21:55. pbs: 3000mW 11:11.4?i '89, 5000mW 18:34.77i '89, 19:09.83 '93; 10000mW 40:00.43 '85.
His wife **Mária Rosza** (b.12 Feb 1967) is Hungarian record holder at 10km walk, 42:53 '94, and at this event was 12th in the 1992 Olympics, 10th 1993 Worlds, and 14th 1994 Europeans.

Women

Rita INÁNCSI b.6 Jan 1971 Budapest 1.90m 70kg. Budapesti Honvéd SE. Sports instructor.
At Hep: OG: '92- dnf; WCh: '91-11, '93- 11; EC:

'90- 10, '94- 2; WJ: '88- 7, '90- 2; EJ: '89- 5; Won ECp B '94. At Pen: EI: '94- 2. Won Hungarian LJ 1993-4, Hep 1989, 1991-3.
Three Hungarian heptathlon records 1991-4.
Progression at Hep: 1986- 5202, 1987- 5487, 1988- 5767, 1989- 5838, 1990- 6076, 1991- 6198, 1992- 6046, 1993- 6263, 1994- 6573. pbs: 100m 11.94 '94, 200m 24.20w '94, 24.67 '93; 800m 2:16.02 '94, 60mh 8.39i '94, 100mh 13.66 '94, HJ 1.87 '94, LJ 6.78 '94, TJ 13.05i '94, SP 14.72 '91, JT 48.80 '94, Pen 4775i '94.
Sister Vera (b. 21 Jul 1975) was sixth in 1994 European Junior heptathlon and has a javelin best of 56.52 '94.

ICELAND

Governing body: Frjálsíþróttasamband Islands, P.O.Box 1099, Iþróttamidstödinni Laugardal, 121 Reykjavik. Founded in 1947.
National Championships first held in 1927.
1994 Champions: **Men:** 100m/110mh: Jón Arnar Magnússon 10.68/14.75, 200m: Fridik Arnarson 22.33, 400m/400mh: Egill Eidsson 49.58/54.21, 800m/1500m: Finbogi Gylfsson 1:54.36/4:06.15, 5000m/10000m: Sigmar Gunnarsson 15:20.73/ 31:24.60, Mar: Daniel Smári Gudmundsson 2:36:20, 3000mSt: Rögnvaldur G Ingbórsson 9:33.48, HJ/TJ: Einar Kristjánsson 2.03/13.65w, PV: Sigurdur T Sigurdsson 4.70, LJ: Bjarni Þór Traustason 7.10w, SP: Pétur Gudmundsson 19.99, DT: Vésteinn Hafsteinsson 62.34, HT: Gudmundur Karlsson 66.28, JT: Unnar Gardarsson 70.98, Dec: Ólafur Gudmundsson 7225. **Women**: 100m/ 200m/100mh: Gudrun Arnardóttir 11.85w/ 24.18/13.68w, 400m: Snjólaug Vilhlemsdóttir 57.98, 800m/1500m: Frida Rún Þórdardóttir 2:16.01/4:28.06, 5000m/Mar: Anna Cosser 17:51.73/2:58:02, HJ: Þórdis Lilja Gisladóttir 1.80, LJ/TJ: Sigridur Anna Gudjónsdóttir 5.55w/ 12.13w, SP: Sigrún Hreidarsdóttir 10.38, DT: Gudbjörg Vidarsdóttir 40.80, JT: Birgitta Gudjónsdóttir 49.64, Hep: Þuridur Ingvarsdóttir 4803.

Péter GUDMUNDSSON b.9 Mar 1962 1.93m 124kg.
At SP: OG: '88 & '92- dnq 14; WCh: '91- dnq 15, '93- dnq; EC: '90- 11, '94- 7; WI: '91- 4; EI: '94- 3. Won ECp B2 1993.
Icelandic shot record 1990.
Progression at SP: 1983- 16.89, 1985- 15.58, 1986- 18.28, 1987- 19.31, 1988- 20.03, 1989- 19.79, 1990- 21.26, 1991- 20.05i/19.95, 1992- 20.10, 1993- 20.53, 1994- 20.44. pb DT 55.98 '93, HT 46.74 '87.

Vesteinn HAFSTEINSSON b.12 Dec 1960 Selfoss 1.90m 112kg. Graduate of Alabama University, USA.
At DT: OG: '84- dnq 14, '88- dnq 18=, '92- 11; WCh: '83, '87, '91 & '93- dnq; EC: '90- 12, '94- dnq 14.
Icelandic discus records 1983-9.
Progression at DT: 1980- 54.60, 1981- 58.20, 1982- 59.48, 1983- 65.60, 1984- 63.60, 1986- 63.98, 1987- 64.86, 1988- 65.60, 1989- 67.64, 1990- 64.30, 1991- 66.68, 1992- 67.16, 1993- 63.52, 1994- 64.80. pbs: SP 16.90 '91, HT 48.06 '91.
Suspended following positive drugs test 1984.

INDIA

Governing body: Amateur Athletic Federation of India, Room No.1148A, Gate No 28, East Block, Jawaharlal Nehru Stadium, Lodi Complex, New Delhi 110003. Founded 1946.
National Championships first held as Indian Games in 1924. **1994 Champions not known**

IRELAND

Governing Body: Bórd Lúthchleas na h'Eireann (BLE), 11 Prospect Road, Glasnevin, Dublin 9. Founded in 1967. Original Irish AAA founded in 1885.
National Championships first held in 1873.
1994 BLE champions: **Men**: 100m: Jeff Pamplin 10.94, 200m/400mh: Tom McGuirk 21.58/51.31, 400m: Sean McAteer 47.17, 800m: David Matthews 1:49.81, 1500m: Niall Bruton 3:42.27, 5000m: Cormac Finnerty 13:50.66, 10000m: Noel Berkeley 29:22.52, Half Mar: John Griffin 65:06, Mar: Eamonn Tierney 2:27:30, 3000mSt: Liam O'Brien 8:56.43, 110mh: T J Kearns 13.92, HJ: Kevin Keane 2.11, PV: Neill Young GBR 4.60, LJ: Jonathan Kron 7.12, TJ: Michael McDonald GBR 15.45, SP/DT: Nick Sweeney 17.37/60.36, HT: Ronald Quinlan 57.10, JT: Terry McHugh 72.32, Dec: John Naughton 5964, 10kmW: Michael Casey 44:09.82, 20kmW: Pat Murphy 1:26:28. **Women**: 100m: Terrie Horgan 12.18, 200m: Marisa Smith 24.36, 400m: Stephanie McCann GBR 54.81, 800m: Aisling Molloy 2:04.50, 1500m: Sinead Delahunty 4:14.63, 3000m: Geraldine Hendricken 9:35.62, Half Mar: Cathy Shum 72:48, Mar: Eleanor Hill 2:57:42, 100mh: Patricia Naughton 14.47, 400mh: Mandy Bloomer 60.77, HJ: Laura Sharpe 1.85, LJ: Jacqui Stokes 6.00, TJ: Siobhan Hoey 12.10, SP: Kelly Kane 13.68, DT: Ailish O'Brien 42.46, HT: Brenda Thompson 39.98, JT: Dara Shakespeare 50.26, Hep: Brid Hallissey 5148, 5000mW/10kmW: Deirde Gallagher 23:34.0/49:03.

Marcus O'SULLIVAN b.22 Dec 1961 Cork City

1.75m 60kg. Leevale and New Balance TC, USA. Degree in accountancy from Villanova University.
At 1500m: OG: '84- sf, '88- 8, '92- sf; WCh: '87- sf; WI: '87- 1, '89- 1, '91- 4, '93- 1; EC: '86- 6, '94- h; EI: '85- 2. At 5000m: 1990- dnf. Won AAA 1500m 1985, Irish 1500m 1984, 800m 1986, 1989, 1992.
WIB 1500m 3:35.6 1989, and 3:35.4 unofficial 1988. Ran on Ireland's 4x1M world best 1985. Three Irish 800m records 1984-5.
Progression at 1500m, 1M: 1980- 3:47.7; 1981- 3:48.5, 4:03.0i; 1982- 3:42.7, 4:00.1; 1983- 3:43.2, 3:56.65; 1984- 3:37.40, 3:55.82; 1985- 3:37.20, 3:52.64; 1986- 3:35.76, 3:53.55; 1987- 3:36.7, 3:52.76; 1988- 3:35.4i/3:36.04, 3:50.94i; 1989- 3:35.36, 3:51.64; 1990- 3:35.23, 3:55.51; 1991- 3:36.44, 3:55.17i/3:56.23; 1992- 3:34.57, 3:57.38i/ 3:57.68; 1993- 3:34.69, 3:52.76; 1994- 3:34.96, 3:53.86. pbs: 800m 1:45.87 '85, 1000m 2:19.15 '87, 2000m 4:58.08 '88, 3000m 7:42.53 '89, 5000m 13:27.32 '90.

Nick SWEENEY b.26 Mar 1968 1.95m 121kg, DSD. Was at Harvard University.
At DT: OG: '92- dnq 23; WCh: '93- 6; EC: '94- 4; WSG: '93- 3; EJ: '87- 7. Won Irish SP 1994, DT 1987, 1991-4.
Six Irish discus records 1991-4.
Progression at DT: 1986- 45.74, 1987- 50.42, 1988- 54.10, 1989- 54.70, 1991- 58.46, 1992- 62.48, 1993- 63.26, 1994- 66.00. pb SP 17.37 '94.

Nick Sweeney: just missed a medal in Helsinki

Women

Catherina McKIERNAN b. 30 Nov 1969 Cornafean 1.65m 48kg. Cavan.
At 3000m: OG: '92- h; WCh: '91- h. At 10000m: WCh: '93- dnf; EC: '94- '94- dnf. World CC: '92- 2, '93- 2, '94- 2; Eur CC: '94- 1. Won Irish 3000m & CC 1990-3.
Two Irish 10000m records 1993-4.
Progression at 3000m, 10000m: 1988- 9:52.0, 1990- 9:16.60, 1991- 8:54.61, 1992- 8:51.33, 1993- 8:58.04, 32:14.74; 1994- 8:51.67, 31:19.11. pbs: 1500m 4:21.30 '90, 1M 4:37.74 '92, 5000m 15:09.10 '94.
Won IAAF cross-country challenge 1991/2, 1992/3 and 1993/4 after 5th place 1990/1.

Sonia O'SULLIVAN b.28 Nov 1969 Cobh 1.73m 53kg. Reebok RC. Studied accountancy at Villanova University, USA.
At 3000m (1500m): OG: '92- 4 (sf); WCh: '93- 4 (2); EC: '90- 11, '94- 1; WJ: '88- h; WSG: '91- 2 (1); WCp: '94- (5). World CC: '92- 7. Won overall and 3000m GP 1993, 5000m 1992 & 1994 (3rd overall); NCAA 3000m 1990-1, CC 1990; Irish CC 1987, 800m 1992, 1500m 1987, 1990; 5000m 1990.
WIB 5000m 15:17.28 '91, World 2000m & European 3000m record 1994, Irish records 1990-4: 800m, 1000m, 1500m (5), 1M (2), 2000m (3), 3000m (6), 5000m (3).
Progression at 1500m, 3000m: 1986- 10:02.7, 1987- 9:01.52, 1988- 9:13.6, 1989- 9:10.62, 1990- 4:08.49, 8:52.65; 1991- 4:05.81, 8:54.16; 1992- 4:01.23, 8:39.67; 1993- 3:59.60, 8:28.74; 1994- 3:59.10, 8:21.64. pbs: 800m 2:00.69 '94, 1000m 2:34.66 '93, 1500m 4:01.23 '92, 1M 4:17.25 '94, 2000m 5:25.36 '94, 5000m 14:45.92 '93.
Brilliant form in 1992, when she set six Irish records from 1500m to 5000m, including five in eleven days in August, and improved further in 1993, although she was disappointed to lose to Chinese women at the Worlds. Records tumbled in 1994, when she also won the European 3000m title, the first ever for an Irish woman. Now lives in Teddington, England.

ISRAEL

Governing body: Israeli Athletic Association, 4 Marmorek Street, PO Box 4575, Tel Aviv 61044. Founded as Federation for Amateur Sport in Palestine 1931.
National Championships first held in 1935. **1994 Champions**: **Men**: 100m/200m: Kfir Golan 10.69/21.41, 400m/400mh: Aleksey Bazarov 47.29/51.08, 800m: Yaniv Vaknin 1:52.62, 1500m/ 5000m/10000m/Mar: Dov Kremer 3:53.09/ 14:40.60/29:59.98/2:18:08, Half Mar: Amit Ne'eman 69:15, 110mh/Dec: Erez Meltzer 14.98/

7003, HJ: Itai Margalit 2.16, PV: Yevgeniy Krasnov 5.66, LJ: Mark Malisov 7.45, TJ: Avi Thierry 16.09, SP: Yoav Sharf 18.04, DT: Sergey Lukashok 59.12, HT: Igor Giller 62.42, JT: Aleksandr Fingert 75.68, 20kW: Vladimir Ostrovskiy 1:33:40, 50kmW: Shaul Ladany 5:46:25. **Women**: 100m/200m: Galit Maretzki 12.45/25.36,400m: Tamar Levav 57.87, 800m/1500m: Duha Suliman 2:14.96/4:56.39, 3000m/10000m: Nili Avramaki 10:38.44/37:17.92, Half Mar/Mar: Loli Leibowitz 1:22:09/2:51:36, 100mh: Olga Dugadetsko 15.09, HJ: Ada Nwadike 1.77, LJ/TJ: Sarah Rosenberg 5.70/12.35, SP: Tzila Asher 13.11, DT: Ilana Goldberg 40.34, JT: Dorit Ashkenazi 43.24, Hep: Anat Morad 3897, 10kmW: Yulia Kotler 55:59.

Yevgeniy **'Danny' KRASNOV** b.25 May 1970 1.83m 77kg. Emigrated from USSR in 1991.
At PV: OG: '92- 8; WCh: '93- dnq; EC: '94- 7. ISR champion 1991-4.
Nine Israeli pole vault records 1991-4.
Progression at PV: 1989- 5.40, 1990- 5.40i, 1991- 5.30, 1992- 5.60, 1993- 5.65, 1994- 5.75. pb LJ 7.07 '94.

ITALY

Governing Body: Federazione Italiana di Atletica Leggera (FIDAL), Via della Camilluccia n.701-703, 00135 Roma. Constituted 1926. First governing body formed 1896.
National Championships first held in 1906 (men), 1927 (women). **1994 champions**: **Men**: 100m: Sandro Floris 10.41, 200m: Giorgio Marras 20.49, 400m: Marco Vaccari 46.50, 800m: Giuseppe D'Urso 1:48.61, 1500m: Tonino Viali 3:45.67, 5000m: Angelo Carosi 13:50.22, 10000m: Stefano Baldini 28:46.59, Half Mar: Vincenzo Modica 62:20, Mar: Salvatore Nicosia 2:16:22, 3000mSt: Alessandro Lambruschini 8:28.89, 110mh: Laurent Ottoz 13.50, 400mh: Georgio Frinolli 49.51, HJ: Roberto Ferrari 2.22, PV: Andrea Pegoraro 5.50, LJ: Milko Campus 7.93, TJ: Maurizio Gifaldi 16.29, SP: Paulo Dal Soglio 19.7, DT: Diego Fortuna 58.22, HT: Enrico Sgrulletti 72.44, JT: Carlo Sonego 73.04, Dec: Beniamino Poserina 7595, 10000mW: Michele Didoni 41:18.73, 20km: Giuseppe De Gaetano 1:24:16, 50kmW: Giovanni Di Benedictis 3:50:16. **Women**: 100m/200m: Giada Gallina 11.65/23.67, 400m: Patrizia Spuri 53.74, 800m/1500m: Seremella Sbrissa 2:07.92/4:14.84, 3000m: Roberta Brunet 9:12.24, 10000m/Half Mar: Maria Guida 32:57.28/70:19, Mar: Maura Viceconte 2:35:15, 100mh: Carla Tuzzi 13.29, 400mh: Virna De Angeli 56.79, HJ: Antonella Bevilacqua 1.90, LJ: Fiona May 6.70, TJ: Barbara Lah 13.80, SP/DT: Mara Rosolen 16.46/52.80, JT: Claudia Coslovich 60.32, Hep: Karin Periginelli 5934, 5000mtW/10kmRW: Elisabetta Perrone 20:49.39/44:03.

Andrea BENVENUTI b.13.12.69 Negrar, Venezia 1.85m 75kg. Fiamme Azzure Roma.
At 800m: OG: '92- 5; WCh: '93- h; EC: '94- 1; WJ: '88- sf; WCp: '92- 3; ECp: '93- 2. Italian champion 1992. 2nd GP 1992.
Italian 1000m record 1992.
Progression at 800m: 1985- 1:56.5, 1986- 1:52.1, 1987- 1:51.77i/1:52.1, 1988- 1:49.6, 1989- 1:48.83, 1990- 1:48.33, 1991- 1:46.76, 1992- 1:43.92, 1993- 1:44.55, 1994- 1:44.08. pbs: 400m 47.32 '92, 600m 1:15.13 '93, 1000m 2:15.76 '92, 1500m 3:41.60 '92.

Salvatore BETTIOL b.28 Nov 1961 Volpago del Montello 1.70m 57kg. Paf Verona.
At Mar: OG: '92- 5; WCh: '87- 13, '91- 6, '93- dnf; EC: '90- 4; WCp: '87- 3, '89- 7, '91- 10. Italian champion 1987, 1991. World CC best: '89- 17.
Progression at Mar: 1984- 2:17:16, 1985- 2:14:17, 1986- 2:13:27, 1987- 2:11:28/2:10:01 sh; 1988- 2:11:41; 1989- 2:10:08, 1990- 2:10:40, 1991- 2:11:48, 1992- 2:14:15, 1993- 2:11:44, 1994- 2:09:40. pbs: 1500m 3:57.5 '86, 3000m 8:03.31 '89, 5000m 13:56.21 '89, 10000m 29:04.4 '88, Half Mar 62:21 '92.
Consistent marathon runner, but only two wins in 21 races: Venice 1986-7; at New York: 6th 1986, 2nd 1988, 4th 1989, 9th 1994. Second London 1990, 4th 1994 (his first sub 2:10).

Angelo CAROSI b.20 Jan 1964 Priverno 1.82m 66kg. Forestale. Forest warden.
At 3000mSt: WCh: '91- 7, '93- 8; EC: '90- 4, '94- 2. Won Italian 5000m 1994, 3000mSt 1989, 1991.
Progression at 3000mSt: 1984- 8:56.46, 1985- 8:51.62, 1986- 8:37.23, 1987- 8:27.38, 1989- 8:23.83, 1990- 8:17.48, 1991- 8:20.28, 1992- 8:39.81, 1993- 8:19.66, 1994- 8:14.02. pbs: 1500m 3:42.43 '87, 3000m 7:49.91 '93, 2M 8:35.41 '90, 5000m 13:25.38 '93, 10000m 28:59.4 '90, 2000mSt 5:21.23 '90.

Paulo DAL SOGLIO b.29 Jul 1970 Schio, Vicenza 1.89m 110kg. Carabinieri Bologna.
At SP: WCh: '93- dnq; EC: '94-8; WI: '93- 5; WJ: '88- dnq; EJ: '89- 6; WSG: '93- 2; ECp: '93- 2, '94- 1. Italian champion 1994.
Progression at SP: 1988- 17.69, 1989- 18.23, 1990- 18.48, 1991- 18.60, 1992- 19.76, 1993- 20.43/20.65i, 1994- 20.68. pb DT 52.90 '92.

Giovanni DE BENEDICTIS b.8 Jan 1968 Pescara 1.80m 55kg. Carabinieri Bologna. Soldier.
At 20kmW: OG: '88- 9, '92- 3; WCh: '91- 4, '93- 2; EC: '90- 8, '94- 4; WCp: '89- 14, '91- 5, '93- 7. At 10000mW: WJ: '86- 4; EJ: '85- 3, '87- 1. Won

Italian 10000mW 1988-91, 20kmW 1989-91, 50kmW 1994. At 5000mW: WI: '89- 5, '91- 2; EI: '89- 3, '90- 2, '92- 1.
World best 2 miles walk 11:47.02 in 1989 and at 3000m 1990.
Progression at 20kmW: 1986- 1:30:41, 1987- 1:26:47, 1988- 1:21:18, 1989- 1:22:01, 1990- 1:22:14, 1991- 1:20:29, 1992- 1:22:17.0t, 1993- 1:21:16, 1994- 1:20:39. pbs: 3000mW 10:47.11 '90, 5000mW 18:19.97i '92, 18:42.50 '91; 10000mW 39:10.35 '90, 1HrW 14680 '90, 50kmW 3:50:16 '94.
Inside world record for 5000m walk but pipped by Shchennikov for world indoor title in 1991.

Gennaro DI NAPOLI b.5 Mar 1968 Napoli 1.85m 61kg. Snam Gas Metano.
At 1500m: OG: '88- sf, '92- sf; WCh: '91- 8, '93- 12; EC: '90- 2, '94- 9; EJ: '87- 1; WCp: '89- 4; ECp: '89- 3, '91- 3. At 3000m: WI: '93- 1; EI: '92-1; Won Italian 1500m 1990-2.
Italian records: 1500m 1989 & 1990, 2000m 1991.
Progression at 1500m: 1985- 3:57.09, 1986- 3:49.4, 1987- 3:41.2, 1988- 3:34.72, 1989- 3:32.98, 1990- 3:32.78, 1991- 3:33.74, 1992- 3:33.80, 1993- 3:36.01, 1994-3:34.42. pbs: 800m 1:45.84 '90, 1000m 2:17.28 '91, 1M 3:53.48 '92, 2000m 4:55.0 '91, 3000m 7:42.68 '93, 5000m 13:27.87 '90.

Giuseppe D'URSO b.15 Sep 1969 Catania 1.78m 56kg. Fiamme Azzurre.
At 800m: WCh: '91- h; '93- 2; EC: '90- 7, '94- 5; WJ: '88- 5; WSG: '91- 1. Italian champion 1993-4. At 1500m: ECp: '94- 5.
Progression at 800m, 1500m: 1985- 1:56.1, 1986- 1:51.97, 1988- 1:47.61, 1989- 1:46.9, 3:48.6; 1990- 1:46.41, 3:46.31; 1991- 1:45.94, 1992- 1:45.31, 3:43.15; 1993- 1:44.83, 1994- 1:44.20, 3:36.03. pbs: 400m 48.9 '88, 1000m 2:16.19 '93, 1M 4:00.01 '93.

Alessandro LAMBRUSCHINI b.7 Jan 1965 Fucecchio, Firenze 1.78m 63kg. Fiamme Oro Padova.
At 3000mSt: OG: '88- 4, '92- 4; WCh: '87- 9, '93- 3; EC: '86- h, '90- 3, '94- 1; WCp: '89- 2, '94- 3; ECp: '89- 1, '91- 1, '94- 1. At 2000mSt: EJ: '83- 4. At 5000m: ECp: '93- 2 (4 1500m). Won Italian 1500m 1986, 1993; 3000mSt 1986-7, 1990, 1992, 1994.
World best 2000m steeplechase 1989.
Progression at 3000mSt: 1983- 9:06.0, 1984- 8:55.43, 1985- 8:36.09, 1986- 8:18.39, 1987- 8:19.17, 1988- 8:12.17, 1989- 8:21.21, 1990- 8:15.82, 1991- 8:19.33, 1992- 8:13.38, 1993- 8:08.78, 1994- 8:17.62. pbs: 800m: 1:47.81 '86, 1000m 2:18.12 '88, 1500m 3:35.27 '87, 1M 3:59.46 '92, 2000m 5:03.83 '92, 3000m 7:48.59 '93, 5000m 13:30.96 '93, 10,000m: 29:56.5, 2000mSt 5:18.36 '89, 400mh 55.7.

Francesco PANETTA b.10 Jan 1963 Siderno 1.75m 64kg. Paf Verona. Student.
At 3000mSt (10000m): OG: '84- sf (h), '88- 9; WCh: '87- 1 (2), '91- 8, '93- (6); EC: '86- 2, '90- 1, '94- 8 (dnf); ECp: '85- 7, '87- 1, '89- (1), '91- (2), '93- 2 (2), '94- (1). At 2000mSt: EJ: '81- 7. World CC: '81- 9 Jnr, '84- 10, '89- 12. Won Italian 3000mSt 1985, 1988; 5000m 1988, 10000m 1986, CC 1987-90.
Italian 3000m, 10000m and 3000mSt records 1987.
Progression at 3000mSt, 10000m: 1981- 9:09.3; 1982- 8:33.24, 29:31.6; 1983- 8:35.39, 28:41.2; 1984- 8:26.90, 28:03.99; 1985- 8:21.60, 27:44.65; 1986- 8:16.85, 27:51.05; 1987- 8:08.57, 27:26.95; 1988- 8:16.04, 27:33.14; 1989- 8:21.19, 27:24.16; 1990- 8:12.66, 28:10.73; 1991- 8:14.41, 28:03.10; 1992- 27:45.46; 1993- 8:22.95, 28:13.99; 1994- 28:38.45, 8:23.55. pbs: 1500m 3:39.88 '87, 2000m 5:04.1 '88, 3000m 7:42.73 '87, 2M 8:30.7 '86, 5000m 13:06.76 '93, Half Mar 61:48 '87.
Followed his valiant silver (when he had led by some 40m at 2000m) in the 1986 European steeplechase with gold and silver in Rome 1987, and outkicked Mark Rowland for the gold in Split 1990.

Giovanni PERRICELLI b.25 Aug 1967 Milano 1.70m 57kg. Fiamme Azzurre. Customs officer.
At 50kmW: OG: '88- 11, '92- dnf; WCh: '91- dnf, '93- 13; EC: '90- 7, '94- 3; WCp: '91- 5. At 20kmW: WCp: '93- 10. Won Italian 50kmW 1987, 1989, 1991-2.
Italian 50km walk record 1994.
Progression at 50kmW: 1987- 3:47:50 (49.3km),

Gennaro Di Napoli: retained World Indoor title

1988- 3:47:14, 1989- 3:58:10, 1990- 4:03:36, 1991- 3:49:40, 1992- 3:55:01, 1993- 3:54:30, 1994- 3:43:55. pbs: 3000mW 11:55.43 '94, 5000mW 19:17.88i/19:43.83 '93, 10000mW 39:33.12 '94, 20kmW 1:21:37 '91, 30kmW 2:08:22 '94.

Women

Antonella BEVILACQUA b.15 Oct 1971 Foggia 1.71m 56kg. Snam Gas Metano.
At HJ: OG: '92- dnq 22; WCh: '93- 6; EC: '94- dnq 19=; WJ: '90- 8; EJ: '89- 5=; ECp: '93- 4=. Won EU23 Cp 1992, Italian champion 1991-4.
Progression at HJ: 1985- 1.67, 1986- 1.79, 1987- 1.82, 1988- 1.82, 1989- 1.83, 1990- 1.89, 1991- 1.89i/ 1.86, 1992- 1.95, 1993- 1.94/1.95i, 1994- 1.98i/1.92.

Maria CURATOLO b.10 Oct 1963 Torino 1.47m 39kg. Fiat Sud Formia.
At Mar: OG: '88- 8; EC: '94- 2. At 10000m: WCh: '87- dnf h; EC: '86- 10. World 15km road: '86- 7, '87- 3. Won Italian 10000m 1985, 1987, 1989; CC 1987-8.
Italian 10000m record 1986.
Prgression at Mar: 1984- 2:36:05, 1985- 2:40:10, 1987- 2:38:30/2:30:15sh, 1988- 2:30:14, 1994- 2:30:33. pbs: 1500m 4:18.56 '87, 3000m 8:53.55 '87, 5000m 15:45.54 '87, 10000m 32:06.38 '86, Half Mar 71:08 '94.
Must be the world's smallest top-class athlete. Has won five of her ten marathons, returning to the event after six years to take the 1994 European silver.

Fiona MAY (ex GBR) b.12 Dec 1969 Slough 1.81m 60kg. Snam Gas Metano. Married to Gianni Iapichino (PV 5.70 ITA rec '94).
At LJ: OG: '88- 6, '92- dnq; WCh: '91- dnq 19, '93- dnq 14; EC: '90- 7, '94- 3; CG: '90- 3; WJ: '86- 8, '88- 1; EJ: '87- 1; WSG: '91- 2; ECp: '89- 3, '91- 3, '93- 3. Won UK 1989, 1991, 1993; AAA 1989-92, Italian 1994.
Three Italian long jump records 1994.
Progression at LJ: 1982- 5.34, 1983- 5.91, 1984- 6.30, 1985- 6.22/6.23w, 1986- 6.27/6.47w, 1987- 6.53/6.64w, 1988- 6.82/6.88w, 1989- 6.98w/6.80, 1990- 6.88, 1991- 6.77/6.91w, 1992- 6.73/6.76w, 1993- 6.86, 1994- 6.95A/6.90/7.00wA. pbs: 60m 7.7i '92, 100m 12.16 '88, 11.88w/12.1 '89; 200m 25.4 '89, HJ 1.72 '83.
Competed for Britain to 1993, Italy from 1994.

Elisabetta PERRONE b.9 Jul 1968 Camburzano, Vercelli 1.68m 60kg. Snam Gas Metano.
At 10kmW: OG: '92- 19; WCh: '93- 4; EC: '94- 7; WCp: '93- 11. Won Italian 5000mW 1994.
Progression at 10kmW: 1988- 53:08, 1989- 51:18, 1990- 48:23, 1991- 46:19, 1992- 44:19, 1993- 41:56/44:01.6t, 1994- 42:15/43:27.6t. pbs: 3000mW 11:56.40 '93, 5000mW 20:49.39 '94, 20kmW: 1:33:37 '93.

Ileana SALVADOR b.16 Jan 1962 Noale 1.63m 52kg. Sisport Fiat. Teacher. Married to Maurizio Facchin.
At 10kmW: OG: '92- dq; WCh: '91- 7, '93- 2; EC: '90- 3, '94- 11; WCp: '87- 45, '89- 3, '91- 6., '93- 6 At 5kmW: WSG: '89- 1. At 3000mW: WI: '89- 3, '91- 3, '93- 3; EI: '89- 2, '90- 2, '92- 2. Won Italian 5000mW 1989-93, 10kmW 1987, 1989-90, 1992.
World bests 3000m track and 10km road walk 1993. Unratified world records at 5000m and 10000m track walks and a further European 5000m walk record 1989. Five Italian 10000m track records 1988-93, three road 1989-93.
Progression at 10kmW: 1987- 49:36, 1988- 45:58.1t, 1989- 42:39.2t, 1990- 43:27/42:40Sh, 1991- 43:36, 1992- 42:07, 1993- 41:30/42:23.7t, 1994- 44:51. Track pbs: 1MW 6:19.39 '91, 3000mW 11:48.24 '93; 2MW 13:11.00i '90 & 13:23.04 '89 (world bests), 5000mW 20:25.2 '92; road 20kmW 1:31:53 '93.
Disqualified at the 1992 Olympics having originally been listed as bronze medallist.

Annarita SIDOTI b.25 Jul 1969 Gioiosa Marea, Sicily 1.50m 42kg. Tyndaris Caleca Patti. Natural sciences student.
At 10kmW OG: '92- 7; WCh: '91- 9, '93- 9; EC: '90- 1, '94- 2; WCp: '89- 8, '91- 9, '93- 7; WSG: '91- 3. At 5000mW: WJ: '88- 4; EJ: '87- 7. At 3000mW: WI: '93- 6; EI: '90- 3, '92- 4, '94- 1. Won Italian 10kmW 1991, 20kmW 1992.
Progression at 10kmW: 1987- 49:37, 1988- 47:57.9t, 1989- 44:59, 1990- 44:00, 1991- 43:37, 1992- 43:03, 1993- 42:41, 1994- 41:46. Track pbs: 1MW 6:46.53 '90, 3000mW 11:54.32i '94, 12:34.52 '93; 5000mW 20:46.9 '95, 10000mW 43:33.7 '93; road 20kmW 1:36:54 '92.
Perhaps the smallest ever major champion when she won the 1990 European title.

JAMAICA

Governing body: Jamaica Amateur Athletic Association, PO Box 272, Kingston 5. Founded 1932. **1994 Champions**: **Men**: 100m: Michael Green 10.38, 200m: Garth Robison 21.02, 400m: Gregory Haughton 45.32, 800m: Mario Watson 1:47.20, 1500m: Stephen Green 3:44.10, Mar: Basil Brown 2:32:50, 110mh: Robert Foster 13.94, 400mh: Mitchell Francis 50.62, HJ: Dennis Fearon 2.14, PV: Clinton Gordon 3.70, LJ: Ronald Chambers 7.97, TJ: Anthony Williams 15.45, DT: Linval Swaby 47.44, HT: John Paul Clarke 52.20, JT: Victor Houston BAR 53.24. **Women**: 100m: Dahlia Duhaney 11.32, 200m: Marlene Frazer 23.21, 400m: Sandie Richards 51.17, 800m:

Michelle Freeman: won Commonwealth gold

Charmaine Howell 2:11.82, 1500m: Janice Turner 4:39.87, 100mh: Michelle Freeman 13.17, 400mh: Deon Hemmings 55.48, HJ: Natalie Richardson 1.72, LJ: Lacena Golding 6.47, TJ: Suzette Lee 13.22, DT: Grettel Miller 40.20.

Winthrop GRAHAM b.17 Nov 1965 St.Elizabeth 1.78m 72kg. Was at University of Texas. Married Yvonne Mai GER 18 Jan 1992.
At 400mh/4x400m R: OG: '88- 5/2R, '92- 2; WCh: '87- sf, '91- 2/3R, '93- 3; PAm: '87- 1/3R. Won CAC 1987, NCAA 1989, GWG 1990. 3rd GP 1990, 1992.
Seven CAC & Jamaican 400mh records 1987-93.
Progression at 400mh: 1984- 53.1, 1985- 51.64, 1986- 50.03, 1987- 48.49, 1988- 48.04, 1989- 48.20, 1990- 48.03, 1991- 47.74, 1992- 47.62, 1993- 47.60, 1994- 48.06. pb 400m 45.59 '88, 45.5 '89.
Steady improvement to silver medals in both Tokyo and Barcelona.

Michael GREEN b.7 Nov 1970 1.76m 73kg. Was at Clemson University.
At 100m: WCh: '91- sf; CG: '94- 2; PAm: '91- 6; NCAA champion 1993, Jamaican 1993-4. Won NCAA indoor 55m 1992-3.
Progression at 100m: 1990- 10.34w, 1991- 10.21/10.02w, 1992- 10.14/10.08w, 1993- 10.09/10.03w, 1994- 10.05/10.04w. pbs: 55m 6.08i '92, 60m 6.55i '93, 200m 20.72i '92, 20.86 '91, 20.73w '93.

Gregory HAUGHTON b. 10 Nov 1973 1.85m 79kg. Student at Central Arizona University.
At 400m/4x400mR: WCh: '93- 6; WJ: '92- sf/2R. Won CAC 400m 1993, Jamaican 1994.
Progression at 400m: 1991- 47.30, 1992- 46.88, 1993- 44.78, 1994- 44.93. pbs: 200m 20.99 '93, 300m 33.00 '93.

Ray STEWART b.18 Mar 1965 Kingston 1.78m 73kg. Degree in radio and television from Texas Christian University, USA.
At 100m/4x100mR: OG: '84- 6/2R, '88- 7, '92- 7; WCh: '83- sf, '87- 2/3R, '91- 6, '93- 8 (qf 200m); CG: '90- sf/3R; PAm: '83- 5, '87- 2/3R; CAG: '86- 3/2R. Won Jamaican 100m 1984, 1986, 1988-9, 1991; NCAA 1987, 1989.
CAC & Jamaican 100m records 1989 and 1991.
Progression at 100m: 1982- 10.73, 1983- 10.22, 1984- 10.19, 1986- 10.29/10.21w, 1987- 10.08/9.89w/9.8w, 1988- 10.08/10.01w, 1989- 9.97, 1990- 10.17, 1991- 9.96, 1992- 10.06, 1993- 10.11, 1994- 10.21/10.09w. pbs: 55m 6.07i '89, 60m 6.41 '91, 200m 20.41 '88, 20.31w '87.
Youngest man in the 1984 Olympic 100m final. After World silver and bronze medals in 1987 he was the world's best 100m man in 1989.

Women

Juliet CAMPBELL b.17 Mar 1970 1.75m 62kg. Student at Auburn University, USA.
At 400mh: OG: '92- qf; WCh: '93- 7/4R. Won Jamaican and NCAA 400m 1993.
Jamaican 400m record 1993.
Progression at 400m: 1989- 53.1, 1990- 53.01, 1991- 53.59, 1992- 51.11, 1993- 50.11, 1994- 51.65. pbs: 60y 6.72i '90. 100m 11.15w '93, 11.49 '90; 200m 22.80/22.66w '93.

Juliet CUTHBERT b.4 Sep 1964 1.60m 52kg. Was at University of Texas.
At 100m/4x100mR (200m): OG: '84- sf; '88- 7, '92- 2 (2); WCh: '83- qf/3R, '91- 6/1R. Won NCAA 100m 1986, 200m 1985-6; Jamaican 100m 1992. 3rd GP 100m 1993.
Progression at 100m, 200m: 1979- 11.6w, 1980- 12.25/12.0, 24.3/24.66; 1983- 11.39w/11.63, 23.29; 1984- 11.42, 24.26; 1985- 11.18, 22.78/22.39w; 1986- 11.24/10.97w, 22.71/22.35w; 1987- 11.07/10.95w, 22.59/22.25w/21.8w; 1988- 11.03/10.96w, 22.59; 1990- 11.16, 22.90; 1991- 11.12, 22.71; 1992- 10.83/10.7, 21.75; 1993- 11.16, 22.93; 1994- 11.01, 22.85/22.74w. pbs: 50m 6.15i '95, 60y 6.71i '85, 60m 7.09i '92, 400m 53.1 '86.
Member of 1980 Jamaican Olympic relay squad.

Michelle FREEMAN b.5 May 1969 1.70m 61kg. Student at University of Florida.
At 100mh/4x100mR: OG: '92- qf; WCh: '91- sf, '93- 7/3R; CG: '94- 1; WJ: '88- h (sf 100m); PAm:

'91- 5. At 100m: CG: '90- h. At 60mh: WI: '93- dnf. Won Jamaican 100mh 1991-4, NCAA 1992. 3rd GP 1992.
WIR 55mh 1992. Four Jamaican 100mh records 1990-2.
Progression at 100mh: 1988- 13.70, 1989- 13.61/ 13.4, 1990- 13.18/13.09w, 1991- 12.98, 1992- 12.75, 1993- 12.77, 1994- 12.93/12.74w. pbs: 55m 6.66i '93, 60m 7.15i '93, 100m 11.16 '93, 11.13w '92; 200m 22.87 '92, 55mh 7.34i '92, 60mh 7.90i '93.
Had to withdraw from 1988 Olympic team through injury.

Yvonne GRAHAM b.22 Aug 1965 Annaberg - Buchholz 1.68m 54kg. née Grabner, then Mai (GDR). Married Winthrop Graham 18 Jan 1992.
At 1500m: WCh: '91- 13; EC: '90- 7; WCp: '89- 3; ECp: '89- 2; WI: '89- 3, '91- 6.
CAC & Jamaican records 1994: 5 at 1500m, 1M (4:24.64), 3 at 3000m, 5000m. Jamaican 800m record 1994.
Progression at 1500m, 3000m: 1982- 4:27.6, 1983- 4:13.06, 1985- 4:10.48, 1987- 4:04.4, 1988- 4:08.86, 8:58.19; 1989- 4:03.15, 8:49.97; 1990- 4:02.69, 8:57.93; 1991- 4:06.09, 8:52.78; 1992- 4:08.34, 1994- 4:04.35, 8:45.87. pbs: 400m 54.5 '85, 800m 1:58.32 '90, 1000m 2:32.77 '90, 1M 4:22.97 '90, 2000m 5:45.07 '91, 5000m 15:13.67 '94.
A law student in the GDR she competed for SC Empor Rostock. Previously married to Volker Mai, European Junior LJ and TJ champion from 1985. Her twin sister Yvette is married to Mark McKoy.

Deon HEMMINGS b.9 Oct 1968 1.76m 61kg. Student at Central State University, Ohio.
At 400mh/4x400mR: OG: '92- 7; WCh: '91- h, '93- 6; CG: '94- 2/2R; PAm: '91- 2. WI '93- 1R. Won JAM 400mh 1994.
CAC & Jamaican 400mh record 1993.
Progression at 400mh: 1990- 61.72, 1991- 56.5, 1992- 54.70, 1993- 54.12, 1994- 54.48. pbs: 100m 11.74 '91, 300m 37.71 '93, 400m 51.45 '94.

Merlene OTTEY b.10 May 1960 Cold Spring 1.74m 57kg. Larios, Spain. Graduate of Nebraska University. Now lives in Italy. Formerly married to Nat Page (USA).
At 100m/200m/4x100mR: OG: '80- -/3, '84- 3/3, '88- sf/4, '92- 5/3; WCh: '83- 4/2/3R, '87- 3/3, '91- 3/3/1R, '93- 2/1/3R; WI 200m (60m): '87- 2 (4), '89- 1 (3), '91- 1 (2); CG: '82: 2/1/3R, '90- 1/1/3R; PAm: '79- -/3; WCp: '94- -/2. Won NCAA 100m 1982-3, 200m 1983; TAC 100m 1984-5, 200m 1982 and 1984-5; CAC 100m & 200m 1985. Won overall GP 1987 & 1990 (2nd 1991-2); 100m 1987, 1989, 1991, 1994; 200m 1990, 1992.
Commonwealth records: 200m (7), 100m (6) 1980-94, CAC 100m (7), 200m (9). WIR: 50m 6.00 '94, 60m 6.96 '92, 200m (3) 22.24 twice '91, 21.87 '93; 300y (8) 1980-2 best 32.63 '82, 300m (3), best 35.83 '81.
Progression at 100m, 200m: 1975- 25.9; 1976- 12.0, 24.7; 1977- 12.2, 25.1; 1978- 12.6, 24.5; 1979- 11.59/ 11.4, 23.10/22.79w; 1980- 11.36/11.0, 22.20; 1981- 11.07/10.97w, 22.35; 1982- 11.03/10.97w, 22.17; 1983- 11.07/10.98w, 22.19/22.11w/21.9w; 1984- 11.01, 22.09; 1985- 10.92, 21.93; 1986- 11.06/10.7w, 22.43; 1987- 10.87/10.8, 22.06; 1988- 11.00/10.7, 21.99; 1989- 10.95, 22.21; 1990- 10.78, 21.66; 1991- 10.79/10.78w, 21.64; 1992- 10.80, 21.94; 1993- 10.93, 21.87i/22.27; 1994- 10.78, 22.07. pbs: 150m 16.46 (world best) '89, 400m 51.12 '83.
In 1993 she at last won the World title outdoors at 200m, having lost the 100m by just 0.001 - on both occasions she received an overwhelming reception from the crowd on the victory rostrum. Previously she had won four Olympic and five World bronze medals and the 1983 World 200m silver, but also anchored the Jamaican team to World gold in the sprint relay in 1991. Ranked in the world's top ten each year 1980-93. Won 73 successive finals (and 15 heats) 21 May 1989 to 8 Mar 1991, when beaten by Irina Privalova in World Indoor 60m. Her unbeaten runs at 100m: 57 finals from 3rd in 1987 World Champs, and 36 finals at 200m from 6 May 1989, were ended in Tokyo 1991. In 1990 she won all 36 finals, with a one-day 10.93 and 21.66 double at Zürich, both into the wind, and a one year record of seven sub-22.00 200m times. Has a record 37 legal times sub 11.00 for 100m (previous best 33 by Marlies Göhr). Appointed a roving ambassador for Jamaica in 1993.

Debbie Ann PARRIS b.24 Mar 1973 1.62m 48kg. Student at Louisiana State University.
At 400mh: WCh: '93- sf; CG: '94- 3; WJ: '92- 8 (2 4x400m); WSG: '93- 2. NCAA champion 1993-4, CAC 1993.
Progression at 400mh: 1992- 57.34, 1993- 55.80, 1994- 55.17. pbs: 200m 23.53 '93, 400m 52.14 '94, 100mh 13.51 '93.

Sandie RICHARDS b.6 Nov 1968 1.70m 61kg. Was at University of Texas.
At 400m/R- 4x400m relay: OG: '88- qf/5R, '92- 7/5R; WCh: '87- sf/6R, '93- 3/4R; CG: '94- 3/2R; WI: '93- 1/2R; WJ: '86- 3; WSG: '87- 3; PAm: '87- 8/3R, '91- 6/3R; WCp: '94- 3R. Won JAM 400m 1991-2, 1994, PAm Jnr 1986, GP 1992.
Jamaican 400m record 1987.
Progression at 400m: 1986- 52.18, 1987- 50.92, 1988- 51.62, 1989- 51.46, 1990- 51.94, 1991- 51.06, 1992- 50.19, 1993- 50.44, 1994- 50.69. pbs: 200m 23.66 '86, 23.15w '87; 800m 2:04.79 '93.

Gillian RUSSELL b.28 Sep 1973 1.66m 48kg. Student at University of Miami.
At 100mh/R- 4x100m relay: OG: '92- sf; WCh: '93- sf; WJ: '88- sf, '90- 1/1R, '92- 1/1R. NCAA champion 1993-4, Jamaican 1988.
Progression at 100mh: 1988- 13.79, 1989- 13.90, 1990- 13.31, 1991- 13.73, 1992- 13.07, 1993- 13.00, 1994- 12.97. pbs: 100m 11.41 '93, 11.3/11.53w '92; 55mh 7.51i '94, 60mh 8.17i '94.
Has a record four World Junior gold medals.

JAPAN

Governing body: Nippon Rikujo-Kyogi Renmei, 1-1-1 Jinnan, Shibuya-Ku, Tokyo 150. Founded 1911.
National Championships first held in 1914 (men), 1925 (women). **1994 Champions**: **Men**: 100m: Satoru Inoue 10.47, 200m: Kazuhiro Takahashi 20.90, 400m: Shigekazu Omori 46.36, 800m:Tomonari Ono 1:46.73, 1500m: Mitsuhiro Okuyama 3:41.77, 5000m: Katsuhiko Hanada 13:34.35 10000m: Aloÿs Nizigama BUR 27:51.85, Mar: Kenichi Suzuki 2:11:05, 3kmSt: Daniel Njenga KEN 8:19.21, 110mh: Nobuaki Hoki 14.16, 400mh: Shunji Karube 49.19, HJ: Takahisa Yoshida 2.24, PV: Toshiyuki Hashioka 5.40, LJ: Nobuharu Asahara 8.06, TJ: Takashi Komatsu 16.31, SP: Yuji Okano 17.13, DT: Yuji Yamasaki 50.48, HT: Nobuhiro Todoroki 66.08, JT: Kazuhiro Mizoguchi 75.62, Dec: Munehiro Kaneko 7703, 20kmW: Tsutomu Takushima 1:25:47, 50kmW: Fumio Imamura 3:53:29. **Women**: 100m/200m: Toshie Kitada 11.90/24.06, 400m: Keiko Amano 54.94, 800m/1500m: Lyudmila Vasilyeva RUS 2:04.06/4:14.53, 3000m: Wang Xiuting CHN 8:50.68, 10000m: Zhong Huandi CHN 31:59.45, Mar: Tomoe Abe 2:26:09, 100mh: Naoko Kobayashi 13.60, 400mh: Sahoko Jodo 58.83, HJ: Chinami Sadahiro 1.84, LJ: Maho Hanaoka 6.29, TJ: Seiko Nishiuchi 12.91, SP: Aya Suzuki 15.44, DT: Miyoko Nakanishi 47.90, JT: Akiko Miyajima 57.48, Hep: Akiko Kurabe 5295, 10kmW: Yuko Sato 44:44.

Yoshihiko SAITO b.12 Feb 1972 Tomioka City, Gunma Pref. 1.77m 63kg. Student at Hosei University.
At 400mh: OG: '92- h; WCh: '91- h, '93- sf; WJ: '90- 2; WSG: '91- 2, '93- 2; AsG: '94- 2; AsCh: '91- 1. Won Asian Jnr 1990, Japan champion 1992-3. At 4x400mR: WI: '93- 3R.
Four Asian (and two Asian junior) 400mh records 1991-3.
Progression at 400mh: 1987- 57.65, 1988- 53.37, 1989- 51.44, 1990- 49.87, 1991- 49.10, 1992- 49.01, 1993- 48.68, 1994- 49.13. pbs: 400m 46.43/46.3 '93, 110mh 14.59 '89, 14.4 '90.

Hiromi TANIGUCHI b.4 Apr 1960 Nango Town, Miyazaki Pref. 1.76m 56kg. Graduate of Nihon College of PE, employee of Asahi Kasei Chemical.
At Mar: OG: '92- 8; WCh: '91- 1; AsG: '86- 2.
Progression at Mar: 1985- 2:10:01, 1986- 2:10:08, 1987- 2:09:50, 1988- 2:07:40, 1989- 2:09:34, 1990- 2:10:56, 1991- 2:11:55, 1992- 2:14:42, 1993- 2:11:02, 1994- 2:10;46. pbs: 1500m 3:54.0 '82, 5000m 13:49.17 '89, 10000m 28:34.18 '89.
Has won 7 of 18 marathons including Beppu 1985, Tokyo and London 1987, Tokyo and Sapporo 1989, Rotterdam 1990. Fastest time when second in Beijing 1988.

Women

Tomoe ABE b.13 Aug 1971 Oita pref. 1.50m 38kg. Employee of Asahi Kasei Chemical.
At Mar: WCh: '93- 3. Japanese champion 1994. Japanese marathon record 1994.
Progression at Mar: 1993- 2:26:27, 1994- 2:26:09. pbs: 3000m 9:22.15 '89, 5000m 15:53.46 '93, 10000m 32:55.78 '93, 20km Rd 67:39 '93.
Second in Osaka 1993 on marathon début in 2:26:27 and then third in Stuttgart. Won 1994 Osaka marathon in national record time.

Junko ASARI b.22 Sep 1969 Akita pref. 1.64m 42kg. Daihatsu motors employee.
At Mar: WCh: '93- 1.
Progression at Mar: 1991- 2:37:01, 1992- 2:28:57, 1993- 2:26:26, 1994- 2:26:10. pbs: 3000m 9:22.1 '89, 5000m 16:06.04 '93, 10000m 32:25.45 '92, 20km 68:51.9/67:54Rd '92.
Her wins at Osaka and Stuttgart in 1993 came in her fourth and fifth marathons. Then third in Osaka 1994.

Nobuko FUJIMURA b.18 Dec 1965 Kameoka City, Kyoto pref. 1.63m 48kg. Graduate of Osaka College of PE. Daihatsu motors employee.
At Mar: AsG: '94- 3.
Progression at Mar: 1993- 2:30:02, 1994- 2:26:09. pb Half Mar 72:38.
Second at Osaka 1994, when sharing national record with the winner Tomoe Abe.

Miyoko TAKAHASHI b.24 Sep 1969 Kawasaki City, Kanagawa pref. 1.71m 53kg. née Asahina. Employee of Asahi Kasei Chemical
World Half Mar: '93- 4. Won Japanese 10,000m 1989.
Japanese marathon record 1994.
Progression at Mar: 1992- 2:30:48, 1993- 2:30:58, 1994- 2:25:52. pbs: 1500m 4:20.74 '88, 3000 9:05.53 '88, 5000m 15:44.74 '91, 10000m 32:14.65 '89; Road pbs: 20km 67:42 '94, Half Mar 70:15 '93.
Won Rotterdam marathon 1994. In July 1994

she married Koichi Takahashi, who has a marathon best of 2:10:55 '93.

Mari TANIGAWA b.27 Oct 1962 Fukuoka 1.60m 44kg.
World Half Mar: '93- 2, '94- 10. At Mar: WCp: '91- 14; Japanese champion 1991.
Progression at Mar: 1988- 3:00:58, 1989- 2:43:04, 1990- 2:34:10, 1991- 2:31:27, 1992- 2:31:09, 1993- 2:28:22, 1994- 2:27:55. pbs: Half Mar 70:09 '93.
Has won 3 of 14 marathons: Tokyo 1991, Gold Coast 1992, Paris 1994; second at Nagoya 1992 and Tokyo 1993.

Yoshiko YAMAMOTO b.6 Jun 1970 Kobe City 1.59m 44kg. Daiei Store employee.
Progression at Mar: 1989- 2:38:10, 1990- 2:35:11, 1991- 2:36:22, 1992- 2:26:26, 1993- 2:29:12. pbs: 5000m 15:53.2 '91, 10000m 32:51.78 '91, 20k Rd 66:30 '93, Half Mar 1:11:50 '93.
Won Paris marathon 1990. Great improvement in 1992 to run 2:27:58 for 4th in Osaka, second in Boston Marathon, when she equalled the Asian record, and third in New York. Fourth and fifth successive sub-2:30 runs when 3rd Osaka and 1st Amsterdam 1993.

KAZAKHSTAN

Governing body: Athletic Federation of the Republic of Kazakhstan, Abai Street 48, 480072 Alma-Ata. Founded 1959.
National Champions 1994: Men: 100m: Vitaliy Savin 10.43, 200m: Aleksey Martynenko 21.49, 400m: Andrey Kondratyuk 48.37, 800m: B Kaveshnikov KGZ 1:51.94, 1500m/5000m: Aleksandr Mikitenko 3:54.73/14:20.84, 10000m: Vladimir Gusev 30:48.0, 3000mSt: Aleksandr Saprykin RUS 8:55.03, 110mh: K Bagmetov 15.55, 400mh: Sergey Pankov 53.20, HJ: Stanislav Mingazov KGZ 2.18, PV: Aleksandr Korchagin 5.60, LJ: Andrey Shalagayev 7.09, TJ: Meiram Beyspekov 16.44, SP: Sergey Rubtsov 19.50, DT: Yevgeniy Buchatskiy 44.50, HT: T Khayirov 47.10, JT: Viktor Yevsyukov 60.04, Dec: Ivan Yarkin 6944, 10kmW: Sergey Korepanov 41:50.4. **Women**: 100m/200m: Natalya Gridasova 11.82/ 24.01, 400m: Marina Strakova 56.35, 800m: O Ivashchenko 2:10.51, 1500m: Yelena Rezvanova 4:36.04, 5000m: Garifa Kuku 16:22.53, 10000m: Lidiya Shutova 36:18.0, 100mh: Olga Shishigina 13.11, 400mh: Natalya Torshina 57.53, HJ: Svetlana Zalevskaya 1.84, LJ: Yelina Selina 6.36, TJ: Yelena Parfenova 12.91, SP: Olga Rudoy 13.93, DT: Olga Silifonova 37.10, JT: Natalya Sirotina 46.48, Hep: Svetlana Kazanina 5770.

Igor POTAPOVICH b.6 Sep 1967 Alma-Ata 1.85m 75kg. Alma-Ata Dyn.
At PV: WCh: '93- dnq 14=; EI: '89- 2; WJ: '86- 1; WCp: '92- 1; AsG: '94- 1; AsC: '93- 2.
Progression at PV: 1981- 3.10, 1982- 4.20, 1983- 4.80, 1984- 5.10, 1985- 5.20, 1986- 5.50, 1987- 5.60, 1988- 5.65, 1989- 5.75i/5.70, 1990- 5.85, 1991- 5.90, 1992- 5.92, 1993- 5.80, 1994- 5.81.

Oleg SAKIRKIN b.23 Jan 1966 Chimkent 1.82m 72kg. Chimkent TR, Kazakh SSR.
At TJ: WCh: '87- 3, '93- dnq; WSG: '89- 3, '93- 2; WCp: '94- 3; ECp: '89- 1, '91- 7; EI: '88- 1, '90- 2; AsC: '93- 2. 2nd GP 1994.
Asian triple jump record 1994.
Progression at TJ: 1978- 12.20, 1979- 13.30, 1980- 13.87, 1981- 14.12, 1982- 14.80, 1983- 15.50, 1984- 15.93, 1985- 16.39, 1986- 17.12, 1987- 17.43, 1988- 17.50, 1989- 17.58, 1990- 17.36i/16.92, 1991- 17.43, 1992- 17.20, 1993- 17.17?w/17.09i/16.89, 1994- 17.35/17.49w. pbs: 100m 10.7, LJ 7.76 '87.

Grigoriy YEGOROV b.12 Jan 1967 Chimkent 1.85m 75kg. Alma-Ata Dyn. Sports student.
At PV: OG: '88- 3; WCh: '93- 2; EC: '90- 2; WI: '89- 2, '93- 2; WCp: '94- 6; ECp: '87- 1, '91- 1; EI: '89- 1, '90- 2; WJ: '86- 5; EJ: '85- 2; AsG: '94- 2; AsC: '93- 1. 2nd GP 1993.
Asian pole vault record holder.
Progression at PV: 1981- 3.00, 1982- 4.10, 1983- 5.00, 1984- 5.45, 1985- 5.55, 1986- 5.61i/5.50, 1987- 5.70, 1988- 5.85, 1989- 5.81, 1990- 5.90i/5.87, 1991- 5.85, 1992- 5.85, 1993- 5.90, 1994- 5.70. pb 100m 10.7.
Has a great record with medals at each of the major events that he has contested as a senior.

Women

Olga SHISHIGINA b. 23 Dec 1968 1.62m 54kg.
At 100mh: AsG '94- 1.
Three Asian 60mh records indoors 1995.
Progression at 100mh: 1990- 14.04, 1991- 13.47, 1993- 13.29, 1994- 12.78. pbs: 200m 23.6 94, 50mh 6.77i '95, 60mh 7.85i '95 (both Asian indoor recs).

KENYA

Governing body: Kenya Amateur Athletic Association, Nyayo National Stadium, PO Box 46722, Uhuru-High-Way, Nairobi. Founded 1951.
1994 National Champions: **Men**: 100m/200m: Joseph Gikonyo 10.37/20.6, 400m: Charles Gitonga 45.2, 800m: Patrick Konchellah 1:47.44, 1500m: Reuben Chesang 3:42.12, 5000m: Simon Chemoiywo 13:36.01, 10000m: William Sigei 28:04.5, 3000mSt: Joseph Keter 8:28.31, 110mh/ 400mh: Barnabas Kinyor 14.2/49.07, HJ: Justus Musembi 2.15, PV: Kenneth Kirui 4.40, LJ: James Sabulei, TJ: Jacob Katonen 16.50, SP/DT:

James Nyambureti 16.11/54.48, HT: Morri Omoro 54.70, JT: Paul Langat 71.60, 20kmW: Justus Kavulanya 1:24:02. **Women**: 100m/200m: Joyce Odhiambo 11.93/24.2, 400m/800m: Gladys Wamuyu 54.02/ 2:05.02, 1500m: Nancy Kiprop 4:25.29, 3000m: Eunice Segero 9:11.58, 10000m: Hellen Kimaiyo 33:28.35, 100mh: Caroline Kola 14.60, 400mh: Sarah Imbayi 59.2, HJ: Fridah Mwirichia 1.63, LJ: Joyce Odhiambo 6.05, TJ: Eunice Basweti 12.39, SP: ?, DT: Elizabeth Olaba 42.96, JT: Milka Johnson 46.12, 10kmW: Alusia Kimweno 51:15.

Lameck AGUTA b.10 Oct 1971.
At 10000m: CG: '94- 1. World Half Mar: '92- 4, '93- 4.
Progression at 10000m, Mar: 1991- 28:14.77, 1992- 27:56.21, 1993- 28:34.22, 2:17:36; 1994- 28:38.22, 2:10:41. pbs: 5000m 13:31.61 '92, Road: 15km 43:41 '92, Half Mar 60:55dh '92.
His twin brother Zakaria Nyambeso won the 1994 Mombasa Marathon in 2:12:12.

Eliud BARNGETUNY b.20 May 1973 1.75m 58kg.
Progression at 3000mSt: 1992- 8:31.32, 1993- 8:28.85, 1994- 8:10.84. pbs: 1500m 3:41.24 '92, 3000m 7:49.74 '92, 5000m 13:35.5 '92, 2000mSt 5:25.31 '93

Jonah Kipchirchir **BIRIR** b.27 Dec 1971 Eldama Ravine, Baringo 1.68m 61kg. Tugen. K-Way Club, Italy,
At 800m: WJ: '88- 1, '90- 2. At 1500m: OG: '92- 5; WCh: '93- sf; WCp: '92- 2. World CC: '89- 13 Jnr.
African junior 800m record 1990.
Progression at 1500m: 1989- 3:41.1, 1990- 3:43.4, 1991- 3:39.10, 1992- 3:33.36, 1993- 3:33.86, 1994- 3:35.65. pbs: 800m 1:45.95 '91, 1000m 2:18.06 '92, 1M 3:52.54 '92, 3000m 7:49.33i '92.
Elder brother of Matthew Birir, although reportedly born only six months earlier!

Matthew Kiprotich **BIRIR** b.5 Jul 1972 Eldama Ravine, Baringo 1.72m 62kg. Tugen.
At 3000mSt: OG: '92- 1; WCh: '93- 4; WJ: '88- 2, '90- 1. World Jnr CC: '90- 6.
World junior 3000m steeplechase records 1990 and 1991.
Progression at 3000mSt: 1987- 8:56.8, 1988- 8:43.4, 1989- 8:56.77, 1990- 8:28.43, 1991- 8:24.47, 1992- 8:08.84, 1993- 8:09.42, 1994- 8:14.68. pbs: 1500m 3:38.84 '94, 5000m 13:49.61 '90, 2000mSt 5:23.49 '92.

Paul BITOK b.26 Jun 1970 Kilibwoni 1.73m 58kg. Nandi. Airman (SPTE).
At 5000m: OG: '92- 2; WCh: '93- 8; WJ: '88- 9; AfrG: '93- 4. Won GP 1992.
Progression at 5000m: 1988- 14:08.8, 1992- 13:08.89, 1993- 13:08.68, 1994- 13:07.30. pbs: 2000m 5:02.0 '94, 3000m 7:33.28 '92.
Member of the winning World Road Relay team 1992. No relation to the other notable Bitoks.

Atoi BORU 25 Oct 1973 1.60m 55kg.
At 1500m: WJ: '88- 6, '92- 1.
Progression at 1500m: 1988- 3:41.8, 1989- 3:40.2, 1991- 3:43.5, 1992- 3:36.4, 1993- 3:34.61, 1994- 3:34.12. pbs: 1000m 2:19.06 '93, 1M 3:57.69 '92, 5000m 14:20.4 '87,
If his date of birth is correct he has been an astonishing prodigy, running 1500m in 3:41.8 at altitude in 1988 at the age of 14 - and 14:20.4 for 5000m at 13 in 1987 (but then he was given as born in 1971!).

Richard CHELIMO b.21 Apr 1972 Chesubet 1.65m 55kg. Elgeyo Marakwet. Civil servant with Kenyan Army (private).
At 10000m: OG: '92- 2; WCh: '91- 2, '93- 3; WJ: '90- 1. World CC: '90- 2 Jnr, '91- 4, '92- 5. 2nd GP 5000m 1991-3. Won Kenyan 10000m 1992.
World 10000m record 1993. World junior records: 5000m (3) and 10000m 1991. African and Commonwealth 10000m record 1991.
Progression at 5000m, 10000m: 1987- 14:31.4, 1989- 14:16.2, 1990- 13:59.49, 28:18.57; 1991- 13:11.76, 27:11.18; 1992- 13:10.46, 27:15.53; 1993- 13:05.14, 27:07.91. pbs: 3000m 7:41.63 '93, 2M 8:26.29 '91.
He won the 1990 World Juniors by 22 seconds from his brother Ismael Kirui. Since then has run many fast times, with two silvers and a bronze in major 10000m races.

Simon CHEMOIYWO b.20 Apr 1968 1.70m 60kg. Elgeiyo. Air Force corporal.
At 5000m: Afr G: '93- 1. World CC: '94- 2. Won Kenyan 5000m 1994.
Progression at 5000m: 1992- 13:18.95, 1993- 13:09.68, 1994- 13:07.57. pbs: 3000m 7:49.51 '92, 10000m: 28:11.0 '93. Road 10km 28:10 '93, 10M 46:27 '93.

Reuben CHESANG b.1966 1.70m 55kg.
At 1500m: CG: '94- 1. Won KEN 1500m 1994.
Progression at 1500m: 1989- 3:41.5, 1991- 3:42.8, 1992- 3:40.02, 1993- 3:39.88, 1994- 3:36.70. pbs: 800m 1:46.91 '92, 1000m 2:18.59 '92, 1M 4:00.10 '92, 2000m 5:02.43i '93, 3000m 7:52.05i '92, 7:53.00 '93; 5000m 13:31.80 '93, 3000mSt 8:31.28 '93.

Charles GITONGA b.5 Oct 1971 Nyeri 1.75m 65kg.
At 400m/4x400mR: WCh: '91- h/5R; CG: '94- 1,
Progression at 400m: 1987- 47.5, 1991- 45.7A,

1992- 46.2A, 1993- 45.1A, 1994- 45.00. pb 200m 20.8 '92.

Julius KARIUKI b.12 Jun 1961 Nyahururu 1.81m 62kg. Mission Viejo club, formerly biochemistry student at Riverside CC, California. Kikuyu.
At 3000mSt: OG: '84- 7, '88- 1; WCh: '91- 4; CG: '90- 1; AfCh: '85- 1; WCp: '85- 1, '89- 1. Won GP 1988 & 1990, 3rd 1993. At 3000m: WI: '87- 6. At 10000m: WSG: '89- 1.
World best 2000m steeplechase 1990.
Progression at 3000mSt: 1981- 9:34.5, 1984- 8:17.47, 1985- 8:20.74, 1986- 8:15.92, 1988- 8:05.51, 1989- 8:12.18, 1990- 8:13.28, 1991- 8:11.28, 1992- 8:16.77, 1993- 8:13.38, 1994- 8:22.64. pbs: 1000m 2:20.98 '90, 1500m 3:37.79 '86, 1M 4:00.43 '86, 2000m 5:04.71 '86, 3000m 7:47.35 '86, 5000m 13:35.72 '89, 10000m 28:35.46 '89, 2000mSt 5:14.43 '90.
Ran the second fastest time ever, and the fastest on auto timing to win at 1988 Olympics.

Erick KETER b.22 Ju 1966 Kabaruso, Kericho 1.70m 60kg. Kenya Ports Authority. Kipsigis.
At 400mh/4x400mR: OG: '92- sf; WCh: '91- 7, '93- 5; AfG: '91- 1/1R, '93- 1/1R?.
Four Kenyan 400mh records 1991-3.
Progression at 400mh: 1989- 53.9, 1990- 53.2, 1991- 48.47, 1992- 48.28, 1993- 48.24, 1994- 51.29. pbs: 400m 46.16 '93, 110mh 14.7 '86.
Made a startling breakthrough in 1991, improving from 53.2 in 1990 to 49.6 in May and to Kenyan records of 48.62 and 48.47 in the preliminary rounds in the World Championships.

Joseph KETER b. 13 Jun 1969 1.78m 64kg. Nandi.
At 3000mSt: AfG: '93- 1. Kenyan champion 1993.
Progression at 3000mSt: 1991- 8:44.0, 1992- 8:21.74, 1993- 8:21.04, 1994- 8:15.86. pb 3000m 7:56.39 '93.

David Ruto **KIBET** b. 24 Nov 1963 Burnt Forest, Uasin Gishu 1.89m 68kg. Parachutist in Kenyan Air Force (lance corporal). Nandi.
At 1500m: OG: '92- 10; WCh: '91- 7, '93- sf; AfCh: '90-3; AfrG: '93- 1. Kenyan champion 1990-1, 1993.
Kenyan 1500m record 1992.
Progression at 1500m: 1988- 3:41.6, 1989- 3:39.9, 1990- 3:34.96, 1991- 3:33.51, 1992- 3:32.13, 1993- 3:33.88, 1994- 3:35.35. pbs: 1000m 2:18.47 '91, 1M 3:51.80 '91, 2000m 4:55.31 '92, 3000m 7:49.9i '91, 2M 8:22.34i '92.
Started as a high jumper. Won Dream Mile 1992.

Wilson KIPKETER b.12 Dec 1970 1.72m 62kg.
At 800m: WJ: '88- dq, '90- 4. Danish champion 1993-4.
Progression at 800m: 1985- 1:49.6, 1986- 1:50.3, 1987-c.1:52 , 1988- 1:47.0, 1989- 1:47.2, 1990- 1:45.7, 1991- 1:46.19, 1992- 1:45.62, 1993- 1:45.46, 1994- 1:43.29. pbs: 400m 46.85 '94, 1000m 2:18.56i '92, 1500m 3:42.80 '93, 1M 3:59.57 '93.
Went to live in Denmark in 1990. Competed in World Juniors with year of birth 1972. But back in 1985 he was shown as second fastest African junior at 1:49.6 with year of birth 1968!

Johnstone KIPKOECH b.20 Dec 1968 1.73m 65kg.
At 3000mSt: CG: '94- 1; AfCh: '91- 3. At 2000mSt: WJ: '86- 2.
Progression at 3000mSt: 1983- 9:08.6, 1984- 9:05.3, 1985- 8:57.8, 1986- 8:48.8, 1989- 8:33.3, 1990- 8:26.42, 1991- 8:18.59, 1993- 8:23.82, 1994- 8:14.72. pbs: 1M 4::04.07 '93, 2000m 5:07.22i '92, 3000m 7:45.60 '91, 2000mSt 5:29.56 '86.
World age-17 best when he was second at the 1986 World Junior 2000m steeplechase. Third in 1991 Kenyan Championships, but deselected for World Championships in favour of Julius Kariuki.

Nixon KIPROTICH b.4 Dec 1962 Baringo 1.85m 68kg. Tugen.
At 800m: OG: '88- 8, '92- 2; CG: '90- 2; WCp: '89- 3; AfCh: '89- 1 (3 1500m). East African champion 1988. Won GP 1990 & 1992.
Progression at 800m: 1986- 1:47.58, 1987- 1:46.8, 1988- 1:44.5, 1989- 1:43.38, 1990- 1:44.43, 1991- 1:47.98, 1992- 1:43.31, 1993- 1:43.54, 1994- 1:44.48. pbs: 400m 45.8 '89, 1000m 2:16.45 '89, 1500m 3:38.76 '89, 1M 4:01.79 '89, TJ 14.78 '85.

Moses KIPTANUI b.1 Oct 1971 (but age 22 in 1992 he said!) Elgeyo Marakwet area 1.79m 69kg. Marakwet. Soldier (corporal).
At 3000mSt: WCh: '91- 1, '93- 1; AfG: '91- 1; WCp: '94- 1; won GP 1991, 2nd 1993. At 1500m: WJ: '90- 1; AfCh: '90- 1. 3rd GP 5000m 1994. Won Kenyan 3000mSt 1991, 1500m 1992; GWG 5000m 1994.
World records at 3000m and 3000m steeplechase, Kenyan records 2000m and 5000m and WIRs 3000m (7:37.31 '92, 7:35.13 '95).
Progression at 1500m, 3000mSt, 5000m: 1989- 8:46.6, 1990- 3:36.73; 1991- 3:35.40, 8:06.46; 1992- 3:34.00, 8:02.08, 13:00.93; 1993- 3:35.44, 8:06.36, 13:14.62; 1994- 3:34.44, 13:10.76, 8:08.80. pbs: 1M 3:52.06 '91, 2000m 4:52.53 '92, 3000m 7:28.96 '92, 2M 8:16.18i '92.
Made an astonishing (even by Kenyan standards) breakthrough into top-class. In 1990, with no known form the previous year he won the World Junior and African senior titles at 1500m. In 1991 he turned to the steeplechase,

Patrick Konchellah: Commonwealth 800 gold

threatening the world record with 8:07.89 in Stockholm. He went on to win the world title easily and to run 8:06.46. In 1992 he did not make the Kenyan Olympic team as he was 4th at 3000mSt in the Kenyan Trials, slowed by injury. However he showed sensational form in August when he set world records for 3000m in Köln and three days later for the steeplechase in Zürich, followed by close attempts at world records for 2000m and on his début at 5000m.

David Singeoi KIPTOO b.26 Jun 1965 1.75m 68kg.
At 400m: CG: '94- 1,
Progression at 800m: 1990- 1:49.60, 1991- 1:46.89, 1992- 1:48.10, 1993- 1:45.64, 1994- 1:44.07. pb 400m 46.5 '88, 47.15 '90, 400mh 50.86 '91.

William KIPTUM b.1971. Nandi. Soldier. 1.68m 55kg.
Progression at 10000m: 1994- 27:17.20. pb 5000m 13:29.66 '94
Only began serious running in 1993. In 1994 he was second in the Kenyan cross-country but only 30th in the Worlds, at 10,000m he ran 28:20.0 for second in the Kenyan Champs and then improved to 27:17.20 behind Sigei's world record in Oslo.

Ismael KIRUI b.20 Feb 1975 Marakwet 1.60m 54kg. Marakwet.
At 5000m: WCh: '93- 1; WJ: '92- 2. Won GP 1993. At 10000m: WJ: '90- 2. World CC: Jnr '90- 4, '91- 7, '92- 1; Snr: '93- 3. Won Kenyan 10000m 1993. World junior records 3000m, 5000m (3) 1993.
Progression at 5000m: 1990- 13:59.6, 28:40.77; 1992- 13:15.67, 29:35.0; 1993- 13:02.75, 28:07.1; 1994- 13:14.46. pbs: 2000m 5:04.4 '93, 3000m 7:39.82 '93. Road 12k 33:42 '94 (world best).
Won IAAF Cross Challenge 1992/3. Younger brother of Richard Chelimo to whom he was runner-up at the 1990 World Juniors. Their sister Catherine was 6th in the 1993 World Junior CC.

Samson KITUR b.25 Feb 1966 Moiben, Eldoret 1.82m 75kg. Nandi. K-Way club, Italy.
At 400m/4x400mR: OG: '92- 3; WCh: '91- sf/5R, '93- 3/2R; CG: '90- 2/1R; AfG: '91- 1/1R; AfCh: '90- 1; WI: '91- 2; WCp: '94- 6/2R. 3rd GP 1994. Kenyan champion 1989, 1991.
Progression at 400m: 1989- 45.2, 1990- 44.88, 1991- 45.23, 1992- 44.18, 1993- 44.34, 1994- 44.32. pbs: 100m 10.3 '89, 200m 21.14/20.7 '90, 800m 1:47.53 '90.
Younger brother of Simeon (49.70 for 400mh 1984) and David (Kenyan record 44.73 for 400m 1987, 6th WCh).

Benson KOECH b.10 Nov 1974 1.73m 65kg. Student. Elgeiyo.
At 800m: WJ: '92- 1.
Progression at 800m, 1500m: 1991- 3:43.4, 1992- 1:44.77, 3:42.7; 1993- 1:46.00, 3:36.47; 1994- 1:43.17, 3:34.72. pb 1000m 2:18.46 '93.
A student from the renowned St Patrick's School in Iten, he made an astonishing breakthrough at the 1992 World Juniors when, with a pre Games best of 1:49.6 he ran successively 1:48.46, 1:47.57 and 1:44.77, the third best of all-time by a junior. Ran 3:58.3 road mile in Denmark in 1991.

Patrick KONCHELLAH b.1963. Masai. 1.85m 70kg.
At 800m: CG: '94- 1. Kenyan champion 1994.
Progression at 800m: 1989- 1:49.8, 1990- 1:47.3, 1991- 1:48.0, 1992- 1:46.6, 1993- 1:45.71, 1994- 1:44.24. pb 1000m 2:18.68 '92.

Kibiego KORORIA b.25 Dec 1971 1.80m 64kg. Sabaot.
World Junior CC: '89- 2, '90- 1.
Progression at 5000m, 10000m: 1989- 13:53.7, 29:48.5; 1990- 13:29.91, 28:03.79; 1993- 13:11.89, 28:10.20; 1994- 13:16.17, 28:28.56. pb 3000m 7:44.98 '93.

Richard (John) KOSGEI b.29 Dec 1970 1.70m 52kg. Student at Barton County CC, USA.

Progression at 3000mSt: 1989- 8:51.67, 1990- 9:12.0, 1991- 8:33.84, 1992- 8:28.64, 1993- 8:12.68, 1994- 8:10.20. pbs: 1000m 2:20.10 '94, 1500m 3:42.24 '93, 3000m 7:50.88 '94, 5000m 13:41.34 '92, 2000mSt 5:24.75 '94.

Sammy Kibet LANGAT b. 24 Jan 1970. 1.68m 57kg. Kipsigis.
At 800m: AfCh: '92- 4, '93- 1.
Progression at 800m: 1992- 1:46.84, 1993- 1:44.06, 1994- 1:44.46. pb 1000m 2:19.58 '93.

Benson MASYA b.14 May 1970 Kitui region. 1.67m 60kg Kamba tribe.
Won World Half Mar 1992.
Progression at Mar: 1991- 2:18:24, 1992- 2:14:19, 1994- 2:12:35. pbs: 10,000m 28:45.5 '91, 3000mSt 9:13.0 '91. Road: 10km 28:08 '92, 15km 42:57 94, Half Mar 60:02 '94.
Won Great North Run in 61:28 in 1991, and repeated on the course to win the first World half marathon title 1992 in 60:24, a world best time on a certified course, and had a further victory in 1994 in 60:02. Won Honolulu Marathon 1991, 1992 and 1994. Formerly a bantamweight boxer.

William MUTWOL b.10 Oct 1967 Kapsowar, Elgeyo Marakwet 1.67m 56kg. Civil servant working for Kenyan Army (private). Marakwet.
At 3000mSt: OG: '92- 3; AfG: '91- 2; AfCh: '90- 2. Won Kenyan 3000mSt 1992. World CC: '86- 9 Jnr, '90- 5, '91- 12, '92- 2.
Progression at 3000mSt: 1984- 9:00.7, 1985- 8:46.4, 1986- 8:49.4, 1987- 8:39.1, 1988- 8:34.6, 1989- 8:39.0, 1990- 8:12.75, 1991- 8:11.85, 1992- 8:10.74, 1994- 8:11.52. pbs: 1500m 3:46.0 '90, 3000m 7:49.71 '92, 5000m 13:22.15 '92, 2000mSt 5:24.11 '90.
Member of the winning World Road Relay team 1992. Ran world road best for 5km of 13:12 in 1992.

Cosmas NDETI b.24 Nov 1971 1.68m 57kg.
At Mar: WCh: '93- dnf. World Half Mar: '92- 10. Kenyan marathon record 1994.
Progression at Mar: 1992- 2:14:28, 1993- 2:09:33, 1994- 2:07:15. pbs: 5000m 14:03.5 '90, 10000m 28:31.48 '91, Half Mar 61:04 '92.
Boston marathon winner 1993-4.

Kennedy OCHIENG b.30 Dec 1971 Kogutu 1.68m 64kg. Luo. Works for Kenyan Ports Authority.
At 400m/4x400mR: WCh: '93- 8/2R; AfCh: '92- 2/3R, '93- 1/1R; WJ: '90- sf. Won Kenyan and AAA 400m 1993.
Progression at 400m: 1990- 46.6, 1991- 46.85, 1992- 45.2, 1993- 44.5/44.82, 1994- 45.20.

Yobes ONDIEKI b.21 Feb 1961 Kisii 1.70m 55kg. Kisii. Business administration student in Albuquerque, formerly at Iowa State University.
At 5000m: OG: '88- 12, '92- 5; WCh: '91- 1; CG: '90- 9. 3rd GP 1990.
World 10000m record 1993, Kenyan 5000m records 1989 and 1991.
Progression at 5000m, 10000m: 1980- 15:01.0, 1981- 14:36.51, 1982- 13:49.5, 1983- 13:35.5, 28:25.44; 1984- 13:51.95, 1985- 14:14.26, 1988- 13:17.06, 1989- 13:04.24, 1990- 13:05.60, 1991- 13:01.82, 1992- 13:03.58, 1993- 13:05.09, 26:58.38; 1994- 13:13.80. pbs: 1500m 3:34.36 '90, 1M 3:55.32 '91, 2000m 5:01.6 '89, 3000m 7:34.18 '92, Half Mar 61:41 '94.
On 10 July 1993 in Oslo, in only his second track 10km, he became the first man to run 10,000m in under 27 minutes, taking nearly ten seconds off the five-day-old world record set by compatriot Richard Chelimo.
His best result while at Iowa State was second in 1985 NCAA cross-country. Emerged into world class in 1988, and then had a magnificent season in 1989, when he became the first man to beat Saïd Aouita at 5000m for ten years. Fell in Commonwealth Games final 1990, but overcame his bad luck in major events by a decisive win in Tokyo 1991, after running away from the field on the second lap. Married Australian marathon runner Lisa Martin in February 1990.

Thomas OSANO b. 4 Jun 1970 Kisii 1.64m 54kg. Oki Electric Co, Japan.
At 10000m: WCh: '91- 4; AfG: '91- 1; Won Japanese 10000m 1991. World CC: '87- 10 Jnr, '89- 4 Jnr.
Progression at 10,000m: 1990- 28:02.28, 1991- 27:28.87, 1992- 27:55.34. pb 5000m 13:28.8 '91, road 10M 46:05 '94, Half Mar 61:32 '94, Mar 2:18:43 '94.
Training in mechanics in Japan.

Ondoro OSORO b.3 Dec 1967 Kisii 1.68m 63kg. Civil servant working for Kenyan Armed Forces (private). Kisii.
At 5000m: WCh: '91- h; AfG: '91- 3. World CC: '91- 5.
Progression at 5000m, 10000m: 1985- 14:05.4, 29:10.3; 1986- 30:03.2, 1987- 29:56.2, 1989- 13:36.2, 28:44.4; 1990- 14:02.1, 29:08.6; 1991- 13:11.77, 1992- 13:49.3, 1993- 13:15.21, 27:24.24; 1994- 13:16.39, 27:28.36. pbs: 3000m 7:43.20 '93, 2M 8:29.67 '91, Half Mar 62:10 '93.
Won IAAF World Cross Challenge 1991 (2nd 1992).

Paul RUTO b. 3 Nov 1960 1.84m 68kg. Nandi. Soldier.
At 800m: WCh: '93- 1; AfG: '93- 2.

Progression at 800m: 1985- 1:51.9, 1987- 1:48.2, 1988- 1:47.4, 1990- 1:47.0, 1991- 1:44.92, 1992- 1:44.33, 1993- 1:44.65, 1994- 1:45.41. pb 1M 4:05.19 '93.

Patrick Kiprop **SANG** b.11 Apr 1964 Kapsisiywa, Nandi 1.80m 65kg. Was at the University of Texas 1983-6. LC Zürich.
At 3000mSt: OG: '88- 7, '92- 2; WCh: '87- 8, '91- 2, '93- 2; WSG: '89- 1; AfG: '87- 1. Won GP 1993, 2nd 1990-1, 3rd 1988.
Progression at 3000mSt: 1982- 9:13.2, 1983- 8:41.00, 1984- 8:22.45, 1985- 8:23.68, 1986- 8:31.1, 1987- 8:14.75, 1988- 8:12.00, 1989- 8:06.03, 1990- 8:15.50, 1991- 8:13.44, 1992- 8:09.55, 1993- 8:07.53, 1994- 8:12.16. pbs: 1500m 3:44.17 '86, 2000m 5:03.46 '88, 3000m 7:49.05 '89, 5000m 13:34.95 '92.
Won the silver medal in each major steeplechase 1991-3.

William SIGEI b.14 Oct 1969 Kericho 1.78m 57kg. Kipsigis. Air Force corporal.
At 10000m: WCh: '93- 10; Afr G: '93- 1. Won Kenyan 5000m 1989, 1992; CC 1993-4. World CC: '92- 8, '93- 1, '94- 1.
World 10000m record 1994.
Progression at 5000m, 10000m: 1989- 13:44.6, 1991- 13:56.3, 1992- 13:15.01, 28:35.0/27:45Rd; 1993- 13:07.35, 27:16.81; 1994- 13:06.72, 26:52.23. pbs: 800m 1:52.8 '86, 1500m 3:49.0 '87, 3000m 7:39.51 '92, road world bests on certified courses: 10km 27:24 '94, 10M 46:01 '94.
Member of the winning World Road Relay team 1992 and now the world's top cross-country runner. Older brother Paul Sigei was a leading 10,000m runner.

Moses TANUI b.20 Aug 1965 Nandi district 1.65m 65kg. K-Way Club, Italy.
At 10000m (5000m): OG: '88- 8, '92- 8; WCh: '91- 1, '93- 2; CG: '90- 2 (5); AfCh: '89- 2 (3). Won Kenyan 10000m 1988-91. World CC: '87- 18, '88- 6, '89- 9, '90- 2, '91- 2, '93- 4. 9th World Half Mar 1994.
Progression at 5000m, 10000m, Mar: 1986- 14:45.0, 1987- 13:54.0, 28:53.1; 1988- 13:36.74, 27:40.59; 1989- 13:24.85, 28:14.67; 1990- 13:28.31, 27:43.62; 1991- 13:21.75, 27:35.89; 1992- 13:17.80, 28:12.71; 1993- 13:22.82, 27:18.32, 2:15:36; 1994- 13:29.30, 28:06.76, 2:09:40. pbs: 1500m 3:41.8 '89, 3000m 7:41.87 '93, 2M 8:33.47 '88.
Won the Stramilano half marathon each year 1990-3, setting a world best 59:47 in 1993, and Great North Run 1993. Ninth in New York on his marathon début 1993 and sub-2:10 for 10th in Boston 1994.

William Kiptarus **TANUI** b.22 Feb 1964 Kemeloi, Nandi 1.83m 70kg. Clerk in Kenyan Air Force (corporal).
At 800m: OG: '92- 1; WCh: '93- 7; AfG: '91- 1; AfCh: '90- 1; WCp: '92- 2, '94- 2. At 1500m: CG: '90- 6. Won Kenyan 800m 1990, 1992-3; AAA 1990. 3rd GP 800m 1990, 1992.
Progression at 800m, 1500m: 1986- 1:48.2; 1987- 1:47.6; 1988- 1:47.3; 1989- 1:47.5, 3:36.6; 1990- 1:43.39, 3:34.25; 1991- 1:43.30, 3:36.53; 1992- 1:43.37, 3:36.2; 1993- 1:44.30, 3:37.8; 1994- 1:44.18, 3:36.56. pbs: 1000m 2:15.83 '90, 1M 3:53.80 '93.
Emerged in 1989 to win Commonwealth Games trial 1500m, and was world number one at 800m in 1990. Finished first in the 1991 World Indoor 800m, but disqualified for breaking early from his lane. A vegetarian.

Paul TERGAT b.17 Jun 1969 Baringo 1.82m 62kg. Air Force sergeant (SPTE). Turgen.
World Half Mar: '92- 5. World CC: '93- 10, '94- 4. 11th World Half Mar 1994. Won Kenyan CC 1992.
Progression at 5000m, 10000m: 1991- 29:46.8, 1992- 13:48.64, 1993- 13:20.16, 27:18.43; 1994- 13:15.07, 27:23.89. pbs: 1500m 3:45 '91, 15km 42:13 '94 (world best), Half Mar 60:13 '94.
A former basketball player, he made a sensational impact when he emerged for third in the Kenyan Armed Forces CC, followed closely by wins in the Kenyan CC Championships and the Nairobi CC in 1992; he had however to miss his first run outside Kenya at the World CC Championships through injury. At half marathon in 1994 won the Stramilano and was 3rd in the Great North Run.

Women

Delilah ASIAGO b.24 Feb 1972 1.64m 50kg. Oki Electronics, Japan. Kisii.
At 10000m: WCh: '91- 12. At 3000m: AfG: '91- 3. World junior 10000m record 1991.
Progression at 10000m: 1987- 34:50.6, 1988- 36:08.3, 1989- 36:01.4, 1990- 32:49.48, 1991- 31:40.56, 1992- 31:57.24. pbs: 3000m 8:55.53 '91, 5000m 15:32.4 '91. Road: 15km 48:59 '94, Half Mar 69:05 '91.
Trained in Japan from 1989 to 1992 and now lives in Boulder, Colorado, racing onthe US road running circuit.

Selina (Sally) BARSOSIO b.21 Mar 1978 1.65m 43kg. Schoolgirl. Elgeyo Marakwet.
At 10000m: WCh: '93- 3; WJ: '92- 3; AfCh: '92- 5 (5 3000m). Won Kenyan 10000m 1993, African Junior 3000m 1994. World CC: '93- 3J, '94- 1J.
World Junior (not ratified as no drugs test) and Kenyan 10000m record 1993.
Progression at 10000m: 1992- 32:41.76, 1993- 31:15.38. pbs: 1500m 4:24.7 '94, 3000m 8:53.40 '94, 5000m 15:42.45 '94.

Sally Barsosio: World Junior CC champion

A prodigious talent at 15 (18 according to some sources), but remarkably fortunate to be reinstated after disqualification in the 1993 World 10,000m. She had caused havoc during the race by continually baulking Elana Meyer and running across several other runners. Her elder sister Chepkemoi Barsosio was the national secondary schools cross-country in 1994.

Hellen CHEPNGENO b.2 Aug 1967 Kericho District. Corporal in Prisons Service.
At 3000m: AfCh: '93- 3 (4 1500m). World CC: '92- 15, '94- 1. Won Kenyan 1500m 1992.
Progression at 3000m: 1991- 9:47.5, 1992- 9:20.0, 1993- 8:44.04. pbs: 800m 2:06.6 '92, 1500m 4:07.35 '93, 5000m 15:21.98 '93, road 10M 54:05 '84, JT 41.07 '85.
Son born 1989. A high jumper and javelin thrower until injury made her turn to running.

Hellen Chepchirchir **KIMAIYO** b.8 Sep 1968 Moiben 1.63m 50kg. Uasin Gishu. Clerk with Kenyan Post & Telecoms. Married to Charles Kipkorir.
At 10000m: OG: '92- 9. At 3000m (1500m): OG: '84- h; WCp: '89- 5; Af Ch: '85- 1 (3), '87- 2, '89- 1 (2). World CC: '92- 11, '93- 12. Won Kenyan 1500m 1989, 3000m 1984-5, 1989, 1992; 10000m 1994, CC 1992.
Kenyan records: 3000m 1984, 10000m 1992.
Progression at 10000m: 1985- 34:18.23, 1992- 31:38.91, 1993- 32:43.4, 1994- 32:16.72. pbs: 800m 2:07.83 '84, 1500m 4:15.2 '91, 3000m 8:55.05 '92, 5000m 15:19.20 '92; Road 10M 52:10 '92, Half Mar 72:02 '94.
Has two children.

Tecla LORUPE Chepkite b.9 May 1973 Kapsoit, West Pokot 1.53m 40kg. Pokot. Works for Kenyan Post & Telecommunication Corporation.
At 10000m: OG: '92- 17; WCh: '93- 4. World Half Mar: '93- 3. World CC: '89- 28J, '90- 16J. Won GWG 10000m 1994.
Kenyan records 10000m 1993, Marathon 1994.
Progression at 10000m, Mar: 1992- 31:34.30mx/ 32:34.07, 1993- 31:21.20, 1994- 31:52.39, 2:27:37. pbs: 5000m 15:08.03 '93, Half Mar 69:27 '94.
Made a brilliant début at the marathon to win in New York in 1994.

KOREA

Governing body: Korea Amateur Athletic Federation, 10 Chamshil Dong, Songpa-Gu, Seoul. Founded 1945.
1994 National Champions: Men: 100m: Chin Sun-kuk 10.46, 200m: Lee Sung-woo 21.25, 400m: Shon Joo-il 45.37, 800m: Lee Jin-il 1:44.14, 1500m: Kim Soon-hyung 3:40.59, 5000m: Ko Jung-won 14:08.3, 10000m: Yu Young-hun 29:18.18, 3000mSt: Yun Sun-ho 8:52.60, 110mh/400mh: Lee Jung-ho 14.16/51.58, HJ: Lee Jin-taek 2.32, PV: Kim Chul-kyun 5.40, LJ: Sung Hee-joon 7.68, TJ: Park Min-soo 16.73, SP: Lee Seung-hoon 17.34, DT: Chae Joon-ki 54.04, HT: Lee Joo-yung 61.34, JT: Kim Ki-hoon 75.04, Dec: Kim Tae-keun 7611, 20kmW: Han Ki-yeon 1:35:54. **Women**: 100m/ 200m: Lee Young-sook 11.49/23.98, 400m: Li Ji-yeon 56.01, 800m/ 1500m: Kim Hye-young 2:08.27/4:29.02, 3000m: Park Hyun-hei 9:30.09, 10000m: Lee Mi-kyung 33:26.43, 100mh: Kim Sun-jin 14.14, 400mh: Kim Mi-young 64.00, HJ: Yun Myong-ja 1.75, LJ/TJ: Lim Sook-hyun 6.17/ 13.09, SP: Lee Myung-sun 16.41, DT: Chung Ha-young 48.72, JT: Lee Young-sun 60.90, Hep: Kim Nan-Young 5348, 10kmW: Kang Ok-hei 54:12.

HWANG Young-cho b.22 Mar 1970 Samchok 1.68m 57kg. Kyugju University.
At Mar: OG: '92- 1; WSG: '91- 1; AsG: '94- 1. Won Asian 10000m 1991.
Korean marathon records 1992 and 1994.
Progression at Mar: 1991- 2:12:35, 1992- 2:08:47, 1994- 2:08:09. pbs: 5000m 13:59.70 '90, 10000m 29:32.01 '91.
Won Seoul marathon 1991 and 1992. The first

athlete to win an Olympic medal while representing Korea, although Sohn Kee-chung had won the 1936 marathon in Japanese colours. 4th Boston 1994.

KIM Jae-ryong b.25 Apr 1966 1.72m 60kg.
At Mar: OG: '92- 10; WCh: '93- 4; AsG: '94- 3. At 5000m/10000m: AsG: '90- 5/2, AsCh: '91- 4/3.
Progression at Mar: 1987- 2:13:25, 1988- 2:20:11, 1989- 2:19:01, 1991- 2:11:51, 1992- 2:09:30, 1993- 2:09:43, 1994- 2:09:42. pbs: 5000m 13:51.89 '87, 10000m 28:49.61 '90.
Won Seoul marathon 1992 and Boston 1993

KIM Wan-ki b.8 Jul 1968 1.70m 57kg.
At Mar: OG: '92- 28; WCh: '91- dnf; AsG: '90- 5; WSG: '93- 2.
Korean marathon records 1990 and 1994.
Progression at Mar: 1990- 2:11:34, 1991- 2:11:02, 1992- 2:09:31, 1993- 2:09:25, 1994- 2:08:34. pbs: 5000m 14:03.70 '91, 10000m 29:43.7 '92.
Won Seoul marathon 1990 and second in 1992. Third in New York in 1992.

LEE Jin-il b.2 Nov 1973 1.83m 68kg.
At 800m: WCh: '93- h; WJ: '92- 2; WCp: '92- 5; AsG: '94- 1; AsiC: '91- 1, '93- 1.
Two Asian 800m records 1994, three Korean records 1992-4.
Progression at 800m: 1990- 1:50.50, 1991- 1:47.88, 1992- 1:46.34, 1993- 1:47.13, 1994- 1:44.14. pbs: 1500m 3:40.67 '94.

LATVIA

Governing body: Latvia Track and Field Athletics Federation, Tërbatas iela 4, Riga LV-1723. Founded 1921. Athletes competed for USSR prior to 1992.
National Championships first held in 1920 (men), 1922 (women) **1994 Champions**: **Men**: 100m: Albert Baturin 10.4, 200m: Sergej Inshakov 21.46, 400m/800m: Inguns Sviklinsh 48.1/1:53.4, 1500m: Aleksandr Proshchenko 3:57.1, 5000m/ 3000mSt: Girts Fogels 14:48.1/9:06.3, 10000m: Uldis Pastars 30:59.1, Half Mar: Aleksandr Prokopchuk 66:35, Mar: Normunds Ivzans 2:43:09, 110mh: Guntis Peders 13.99, 400mh: Egils Tebelis 52.0, HJ: Normunds Sietinsh 2.20 PV: Aleksandr Matusevich 5.30, LJ: Andris Strikis 7.75, TJ: Maris Bruziks 16.73, SP/HT: Aleksej Lukashenko 17.50/57.48, DT: Andris Smochs 51.60, JT: Martsis Shtrobinders 80.78, Dec: Gvido Einbergs 7592, 20000mW/50kmW: Modris Liepinsh 1:23:33.8/3:58:46. **Women**: 100m/100mh: Ludmila Olijare 12.16/13.49, 200m: Ludmila Nefjodova 25.1, 400m/400mh: Lana Yekabsone 54.7/58.1, 800m: Inese Redlikha 2:20.3, 1500m: Yelena Chelnova 4:33.5, 3000m/ 5000m: Tatjana Ribakova 10:04.7/17:51.1, Half Mar: Anita Klapote 1:22:16, Mar: Laila Tseika 3:19:56, HJ/Hep: Valentina Gotovska 1.92/5095, LJ/TJ: Yelena Blazhevica 5.95/13.36, SP: Yevgenija Uchaikina 10.76, DT: Iveta Garancha 45.04, JT: Iveta Lochmele 51.58, 10kmW: Ilse Apse 52:48, 20kmW: Vineta Matulena 1:54:21.

Maris BRUZIKS b.25 Aug 1962 Plavinas 1.87m 73kg.
At TJ: OG: '92- 10; WCh: '93 dnq 16; EC: '86- 2, '94- 3; EI: '86- 1, '92- 4; WI: '87- 7, '93- 2; WSG: '87- 3; WCp: '92- 4. Won ECp II 1994. Latvian champion 1983-4, 1988-9, 1992-4.
WIB triple jump 17.54 '86, Latvian record 1988.
Progression at TJ: 1977- 11.60, 1978- 13.57, 1979- 14.60, 1980- 15.43, 1981- 15.48i, 1982- 15.55, 1983- 16.47, 1984- 17.15, 1985- 17.38, 1986- 17.54i/17.33, 1987- 16.97i/16.90, 1988- 17.56, 1989- 17.19/ 17.42w, 1990- 16.98, 1991- 17.38, 1992- 17.29i/ 17.01, 1993- 17.36i/17.28, 1994- 17.30. pbs: HJ 2.15i '85, LJ 7.91 '84.

LITHUANIA

Governing body: Athletic Federation of Lithuania, Zemaitas 6, Vilnius 232675. Founded 1921. Athletes competed for USSR prior to 1992.

Vaclavas KIDYKAS b.17 Oct 1961 Vytenai, Klaipeda 1.97m 118kg. Kaunas. Veterinary student.
At DT: OG: '88- dnq 13, '92- dnq 15; WCh: '87- 8, '93- 11; EC: '86- 3; WSG: '85- 2, '87- 2; ECp: '87- 1. Lithuanian champion 1989-90, 1993.
Lithuanian discus record 1985.
Progression at DT: 1978- 33.24, 1979- 41.42, 1980- 47.86, 1981- 55.42, 1982- 59.80, 1983- 61.42, 1984- 62.60, 1985- 67.34, 1986- 67.00, 1987- 66.80, 1988- 68.44, 1989- 64.32, 1990- 67.04, 1991- 65.98, 1992- 66.12, 1993- 65.26. pb SP 18.33 '91.

Women

Remigija NAZAROVIENE b.2 Jun 1967 Ashkhabad, Turkmenistan 1.79m 70kg. Vilnius. née Sablovskaite. Teacher. Married Andrey Nazarov, Estonian decathlete (pb 8322 '87), in 1988.
At Hep: OG: '88- 5, '92- 14; EC: '90- 6, '94- 7; EJ: '85- 4; ECp: '89- 2, '94- 1C. Won USSR title 1988, Lithuanian 1986-7, 1990.
Lithuanian records: 100mh (2) 1989, Hep (3) 1987-9.
Progression at Hep: 1985- 5693, 1986- 5875,

1987- 6241, 1988- 6566, 1989- 6604, 1990- 6380, 1992- 6513, 1994- 6262. pbs: 100m 12.28 '86, 200m 23.92 '88, 23.7 '89; 800m 2:09.26 '89, 100mh 13.18/12.9 '89, HJ 1.86 '89, LJ 6.58 '89, SP 16.22 '88, JT 47.40 '88.
Son Deividas born 1991.

LUXEMBOURG

Governing body: Fédération Luxembourgeoise d'Athlétisme, 14 avenue de la Gare, 1610 Luxembourg. Founded 1928.
1994 National Champions: **Men**: 100m/200m: Serge Muller 10.88/22.25, 400m: Paul Cens 50.18, 800m/1500m: Pascal Wenzel 1:54.80/4:01.70, 5000m: Jean-Pierre Ernzen 15:26.80, 10000m: José Ribeiro 32:2055, Mar: Romain Possing 2:31:33, 3000mSt: Marc Urwald 9:49.18, 110mh: Thierry Eischen 14.67, 400mh: Romain Bartringer 57.15, HJ: Raymond Conzemius 2.11, PV/LJ: Bernard Felten 4.60/7.02, TJ: Richard Czerwonka 13.77, SP: Marcel Weber 14.55, DT: Carlo Bartolucci 48.56, HT: Charles De Ridder 62.14, JT: Marc Goedert 61.90, Dec: Frank Krier 6217. **Women**: 100m/200m/100mh: Véronique Linster 12.25/25.36/14.13, 400m/SP: Sandra Felten 58.75/11.29, 800m: Henrietta Van Cruchten 2:25.07, 1500m: Tiziana Finzi 5:04.10, 3000m/10000m/Mar: Danièle Kaber 10:03.44/36:45.91/2:39:39, 400mh: Marielse Van Cruchten 64.65, HJ: Sheila Martin 1.62, LJ/Hep: Claudia Czerwonka 5.63/4586, DT: Anne-Marie Wirtz 36.94, JT: Nathalie Thill 36.04.

MEXICO

Governing body: Federación Mexicana de Atletismo, Anillo Periférico y Av. del Conscripto, 11200 M.Hidalgo D.F. Founded 1933.

Dionicio CERON b.8 Oct 1965 1.70m 58kg. Studied civil engineering at Mexico City University.
At Mar: OG: '92- dnf. At 10000m: won CAG 1990 & 1993, CAC 1991.
CAC marathon record to win Beppu 1992.
Progression at Mar: 1990- 2:12:18, 1991- 2:10:02, 1992- 2:08:36, 1993- 2:08:51, 1994- 2:08:53. pbs: 10000m 28:14.48 '91. Road: 15km 42:42 '90, Half Mar 60:46 '90, 60:17 dh '93.
Emerged on US road running circuit in 1990, setting a world half marathon best on a loop course. Second Rotterdam marathon 1991. Won Beppu marathon in 1992, and four in succession: Rotterdam, Mexico City and Fukuoka in 1993, London in 1994, before being 16th at Fukuoka in 1994 when he suffered from back pain.

Andrés ESPINOSA b.4 Feb 1963 1.67m 55kg. Soldier.
At Mar: WCp: '91- 57.
CAC marathon record 1994.
Progression at Mar: 1990- 2:14:10, 1991- 2:10:00, 1992- 2:10:44, 1993- 2:10:04, 1994- 2:07:19. pbs: 10000m 27:59.86 '92, road 15km 43:41 '92, Half Mar 61:34 '94.
Has compiled a most consistent record in US marathons: 2nd in San Francisco 1990, and New York 1991 and 1992, 3rd Boston 1992, 1st New York 1993, 2nd Boston 1994.

Daniel GARCIA b.28 Oct 1971 1.64m 55kg.
At 20kmW: OG: '92-7; WCh: '93- dq; WCp: '93- 1; WSG: '93- 2; CAG: '93- 1.
Progression at 20kmW, 50kmW: 1991- 4:04:51, 1992- 1:22:16.1t, 3:57:38; 1993- 1:19:42, 3:52:23; 1994- 1:20:33, 4:00:17.

Carlos MERCENARIO b.3 May 1967 1.75m 63kg.
At 20kmW: OG: '88- 7; WCh: '87- dq, '91- 12; WCp: '87- 1; PAm: '87- 1; CAG: '90- 2. At 50kmW: OG: '92- 2; WCH: '93- 8; WCp: '91- 1, '93- 1; PAm: '91- 1. Won PAm-J 10kmW 1984 & 1986.
At 20km road walk: world junior best when second America's Cup 1986, world best 1987.
Progression at 20kmW, 50kmW: 1985- 1:24:07, 1986- 1:21:33, 1987- 1:19:24, 1988- 1:20:53, 1989- 1:21:53, 1990- 1:19:30, 3:50:10; 1991- 1:21:37, 3:42:03; 1992- 1:25:52, 3:48:05.9t; 1993- 1:21:39, 3:50:28; 1994- 1:21:40, 3:52:06.
In 1993 he became the first man to win World Cup races at both 20km and 50km, and tied the record with three individual wins.

Armando QUINTANILLA b.19 Apr 1968 1.75m 56kg.
At 10000m: OG: '92- 16; WCh: '93- 14; WCp: '92- 5. Won Ibero-American 1994. Won CAC 5000m 1991.
Progression at 10,000m: 1992- 27:49.24, 1993- 27:51.41, 1994- 27:18.59. pbs: 5000m 13:30.66 '92.

German SÁNCHEZ b.15 Sep 1966 1.73m 65kg.
At 50kmW: OG: '92- dq; WCh: '93- 12, WCp: '93- 3; CAG: '93- 2. Won America's Cup 1992.
Progression at 50kmW: 1991- 4:03:40, 1992- 3:51:02, 1993- 3:54:07, 1994- 3:56:00. Pb 20kmW ?.

Bernardo SEGURA b.11 Feb 1970 1.79m 61kg.
At 20kmW: WCh: '93- dq; WSG: '93- 3. Won America's Cup 1992, GWG 1994.
World record 20,000m track walk 1994.
Progression at 20kmW: 1991- 1:22:01, 1992- 1:24:09, 1993- 1:19:39, 1994- 1:17:25.6t. pbs: 10,000mW 38:24 '94, 1HrW: 15,577.3m '94, 50kmW 4:03:51 '94.

His brother Jorge won the world junior 10,000m walk title in 1994.

German SILVA b.9 Jan 1968 Vera Cruz province 1.60m 50kg.
At 10000m: OG: '92- 6; WCh: '93- 9. At 3000mSt: PAm: '91- 6; won CAG 1990. 2nd World Half Mar 1994.
Progression at 10000m: 1990- 28:02.03, 1991- 28:19.48, 1992- 27:46.52, 1993- 28:03.64, 1994- 28:33.49. pbs: 5000m 13:26.11 '93, Half Mar 60:28 '94, Mar 2:09:18 '94, 3000mSt 8:33.52 '89.
At the marathon did not finish Rotterdam 1992, 3rd London and 1st New York 1994.

MOROCCO

Governing Body: Fédération Royale Marocaine d'Athlétisme, Complex Sportif Prince Moulay Abdellah, PO Box 1778 R/P, Rabat. Founded 1957.
1994 champions: Men: 100m/200m: Mohamed Moudamane 10.3/21.3, 400m: Benyounès Lahlou 47.2, 800m: Saïd Ouaboudou 1:50.8, 1500m: Mohamed Ramdi 3:47.1, 5000m: Abdelkrim Mouni 14:01.4, 10000m Mohamed Riad 29:10.5, 3000mSt: Yarba Lakhal 8:38.4, 110mh: Zouhair Khazine 14.2, 400mh: Mohamed Debbab 50.4, HJ: Tarek Koraïchi 2.05, PV: Adil Belhadj 3.20, LJ: Younès Moudrik 7.27, TJ: Hassan Ghazala 16.01, SP: Mustapha Moutachakir 14.34, DT: Rédouane Jaouhari 45.42, HT: Abdellah Chahine 58.02, JT: Ahmed Roudane 65.94, 20kmW: Hassan Kouchaoui 1:5409. **Women**: 100m/200m: Laifa Lahcen 11.7/24.18, 400m: Nezha Bidouane 54.7, 800m: Samira Raif 2:09.6, 1500m: Zoubida Ould Lidam 4:42.0, 3000m: Fatima Maama 9:32.4, 5000m: Zahra Ouaziz 15:50.1, 10000m: Halima Alaoui Nabaoui 37:23.4, 100mh: Nawal Ettoumi 15.25, 400mh: Nadia Zétouani 57.1, HJ: Toura Aboudi 1.60, LJ: Fatma Zohra Dkouk 5.09, TJ: Hasna Attiallah 12.86, SP: Fouzia Fatihi 15.42, DT: Latifa Allam 53.78, HT: Touria Antar 39.10, JT: Rkia Ramoudi 47.48, 5000mW: Mériem Kouch 26:26.6.

Saïd AOUITA b.2 Nov 1959 Kenitra 1.75m 58kg.
At 5000m: OG: '84- 1; WCh: '87- 1; WCp: '89- 1. At 3000m: WI: '89- 1; At 1500m: OG: '88- sf; WCh: '83- 3, '91- 11; WSG: '81- 1; AfCh: '79- 9, '82- 2, '84- 1. At 800m: OG: '88- 3; AfCh: '82- 3. Pan-Arab 1500m champion 1985. Won GP 5000m 1986 (2nd 1989), 1M 1988, overall 1986 & 1988-9, 2nd= 1500m 1991.
World records: 1500m & 5000m 1985; 2000m & 5000m (and 2 miles world best) 1987, 3000m 1989. African records (1984-9): 1500m- 3, 1M- 2, 2000m- 4, 3000m- 1, 5000m- 4. Disallowed indoor world best 7:36.66 for 3000m 1992.
Progression at 800m, 1500m, 5000m: 1978- 14:10.0; 1979- 3:42.3, 13:48.5; 1980- 1:47.8, 3:37.08, 14:00.7; 1981- 1:48.26, 3:37.69, 14:14.2; 1982- 1:47.4, 3:37.37, 14:05.7; 1983- 1:44.83, 3:32.54; 1984- 1:46.81, 3:31.54, 13:04.78; 1985- 1:45.81, 3:29.46, 13:00.40; 1986- 3:36.1, 13:00.86; 1987- 1:44.74, 3:30.69, 12:58.39; 1988- 1:43.86, 3:32.69; 1989- 3:30.63, 13:06.36; 1990- 3:45.58i, 1991- 3:33.28, 13:37.95; 1992- 3:37.88; 1993- 3:37.60, 13:39.75. pbs: 1000m 2:15.16 '88, 1M 3:46.76 '87, 2000m 4:50.81 '87, 3000m 7:29.45 '89, 2M 8:13.45 '87, 10000m 27:26.11 '86, 3000mSt 8:21.92 '87.
37th world junior CC 1978. Unbeaten at 5000m from 1979 to defeat by Yobes Ondieki in Sevilla on 20 Jun 1989. Lost to Steve Cram in his WR 1500m at Nice in 1985, but from then won 44 consecutive races at all distances until beaten by Alessandro Lambruschini in the 1987 Mediterranean Games 3000m steeple, his first run at that event since his African junior record 8:40.2 in 1979. At 1500m/1M he won 39 successive races from that Nice loss to his first race in 1991, although, through injury, he did not run the 1988 Olympic semis. His Olympic bronze medal at 800m was an unprecedented feat for a 5000m champion. Missed 1992 Olympics through injury. He was technical director of the Moroccan Federation, but left that post and returned to competition in January 1995.

Khalid BOULAMI b. 7 Aug 1969.
At 5000m: 2nd GP 1994. World CC: '94- 15. Won Moroccan 5000m 1990, 10000m 1991.
Progression at 5000m: 1990- 13:52.74, 1991- 13:53.36, 1992- 13:46.15, 1993- 13:33.77, 1994- 13:12.95. pb 10000m 28:48.43 '94.

Rachid EL BASIR (or **LABSIR**) b.4 Oct 1968 1.80m 61kg.
At 1500m: OG: '92- 2; WCh: '91- sf, '93- 7; WI: '93- 9.
Progression at 1500m: 1989- 3:41.23, 1990- 3:37.52, 1991- 3:36.57, 1992- 3:34.40, 1993- 3:35.51, 1994- 3:35.84. pbs: 800m: 1:46.53 '92, 1000m: 2:20.8 '91, 1M: 3:54.84 '92, 3000m: 7:51.89 '91.

Larbi EL KHATTABI b.16 May 1967 1.74m 68kg.
At 3000mSt: OG: '92- 10; WCh: '93- 7. World CC: '94- 14. Winning World Road Relay team 1994.
Progression at 3000mSt: 1986- 9:28.1, 1987- 9:00.2, 1988- 8:52.55, 1989- 8:30.87, 1990- 8:40.0, 1991- 8:42.39, 1992- 8:23.82, 1993- 8:16.60, 1994- 8:16.18. pbs: 3000m 8:04.05 '89, 5000m 13:47.49 '89, Half Mar 62:43 '93.

Salah HISSOU b.1972. 1.76m 62kg.
At 5000m: WJ: '90: dnf h. Won Pan-Arab

10000m & CC, 2nd 5000m 1992, Moroccan 5000m 1991. World CC: '91- 14J, '94- 11. Winning World Road Relay team 1994.
Progession at 5000m, 10000m: 1989- 14:15.0, 1990- 14:05.9, 1991- 13:37.40, 1992- 13:41.55, 28:31.62; 1993- 13:49.5, 1994- 13:04.93, 27:21.75. pbs: 1500m 3:42.5 '90, 3000m 7:38.14 '94. Road: 20km 58:20 '94 (world best), Half Mar 62:20 '94.
Great breakthrough in 1994.

Mohamed ISSANGAR b.12 Dec 1964 1.80m 62kg.
At 5000m: OG: '92- 9; WCh: '91- h; AfCh: '88- 3, '90- 3.
Progression at 5000m: 1988- 13:40.9, 1989- 13:19.54, 1990- 13:08.51, 1991- 13:18.03, 1992- 13:18.94, 1993- 13:14.23, 1994- 13:12.13. pbs: 1500m 3:39.51 '91, 1M 3:57.03 '90, 3000m 7:39.30 '93.
Burst onto the Grand Prix scene in 1989 and in 1990 showed further improvement by winning at Lausanne, Oslo and London.

Brahim JABBOUR b.1 Jan 1970 1.78m 56kg.
At 5000m: WCh: '93- 6. Winning World Road Relay team 1994.
Progession at 5000m: 1992- 13:36.44, 1993- 13:08.86, 1994- 13:17.55. pbs: 3000m 7:36.54 '93. pbs: 1500m 3:40.44 '92, 2000m 5:17.03 '92, 3000m 7:36.54 '93, Half Mar 63:07 '93.
Enormous improvement in 1993.

Brahim LAHLAFI b.15 Apr 1968 1.72m 62kg.
At 5000m: WCp: '94- 1. World CC: '93- 11.
Progession at 5000m: 1988- 14:02.2, 1989- 14:13.0, 1990- 13:21.11, 1991- 13:23.79, 1993- 13:15.85, 1994- 13:03.36. pbs: 1500m 3:43.24 '93, 3000m 7:40.31 '94, 2M 8:16.11 '94, 10000m 29:15.1 '88, Half Mar 61:39 '94.

Abdelaziz SAHERE b.18 Sep 1967 1.83m 63kg. Olympique Marocain, Rabat.
At 3000mSt: OG: '88- h; WCh: '91- 6, '93- 13; AfCh: '88- 2, '90- 1 (2 1500m); 3rd GP 1991. At 1500m: WI: '90- 8.
Five Moroccan 3000m steeple records 1991-4.
Progression at 3000mSt: 1986- 9:03.6, 1987- 8:39.0, 1988- 8:22.45, 1990- 8:28.53, 1991- 8:12.21, 1992- 8:19.65, 1993- 8:15.25, 1994- 8:11.11. pbs: 800m 1:49.9 dq '90, 1000m 2:23.59 '89, 1500m 3:36.13 '90, 1M 3:56.14 '90, 3000m 7:53.21 '88.
Married to Nezha Bidouane (400mh pb 55.08 '92, African champion 1990).

Azzedine SEDIKI b.21 May 1970 Rabat. Soldier
At 1500m: Moroccan champion 1993.
Progression at 1500m: 1993- 3:41.01, 1994- 3:32.71. pbs: 1M 3:55.67 '94.
Improved over 8 seconds at 1500m when he ran 3:32.71 for 2nd at Nice in 1994.

Khalid SKAH b.29 Jan 1967 Midelt 1.72m 60kg. Based in the summer in Norway. IL i BUL, Oslo.
At 10000m (5000m): OG: '92- 1; WCh: '91- 3 (6), '93- (5); WCp: '94- 1; AfCh: '89- (5). Won GP 5000m 1990, 1994. World CC '90- 1, '91- 1, '92- 4, '93- 6, '94- 5. Won World Half Mar and on winning World Road Relay team 1994.
World 2 miles best 1993. Moroccan 10000m record 1993.
Progression at 5000m, 10000m: 1986- 14:28.4, 1987- 14:26.11, 1988- 13:56.1, 1989- 13:17.30, 1990- 13:09.55, 27:29.27; 1991- 13:17.72, 27:23.29; 1992- 13:09.10, 27:46.70; 1993- 13:06.82, 27:17.74; 1994- 13:00.54, 27:38.74. pbs: 1000m 2:26.0 '90, 1500m 3:42.06 '90, 2000m 5:03.9 '90, 3000m 7:36.76 '94, 2M 8:12.17 '93, 3000mSt 8:19.30 '94, Half Mar 60:27 '94.
Second in the Arab junior and 68th in the World Junior CC in 1986. After winning the World CC he ran 27:29.27 in his track début at 10000m in Brussels 1990. At first disqualified after Olympic 10000m in 1992 due to the alleged help rendered by lapped teammate Hammou Boutayeb, he was reinstated and awarded gold medal.

MOZAMBIQUE

Governing body: Federaçao Mocambicana de Atletismo, CP 1094, Maputo. Founded 1978.

Maria Lurdes **MUTOLA** b. 27 Oct 1972 Maputo 1.62m 61kg. Student in Eugene, USA.
At 800m (1500m): OG: '88- h, '92- 5 (9); WCh: '91- 4, '93- 1; WI: '93- 1; AfCh: '88- 2, '90- 1 (1); AfG: '91- 1, '93- 1; WCp: '92- 1/3R, '94- 1. Won GWG 1994, GP 1993.
African records: eight 800m 1991-4, 1000m 1993.
African junior records 800m (3) and 1500m 1991.
Mozambique records at all distances 200-3000m.
Progression at 800m, 1500m: 1988- 2:04.36, 1989- 2:05.7, 4:31.5; 1990- 2:13.54, 4:25.27; 1991- 1:57.63, 4:12.72; 1992- 1:57.49, 4:02.60; 1993- 1:55.43, 4:04.97; 1994- 1:55.19, 4:13.93. pbs: 200m 23.86 '94, 300m 37.16 '94, 400m 51.37 '94, 1000m 2:32.57 '93, 1M 4:36.09 '91, 3000m 10:04.4 '90.
Star soccer player at school in Maputo; enabled to attend school in the USA by a grant from the Olympic Solidarity Committee. 30 successive wins in 800m finals 1992-4.

Argentina da Gloria **PAULINO** b.7 Jul 1973 1.66m 59kg.
At 800m: WCh: '93- 7 (fell). At 400m: AfG: '93- 1.
Progression at 400m, 800m: 1992- 52.34, 2:03.81;

1993- 51.82, 1:56.62; 1994- 2:00.71.
Distant relative of Maria Mutola; only started running in 1992, with 2:03.82 for 800m in her first ever track race.

NAMIBIA

Governing body: Namibia AAU, PO Box 11086, Windhoek.

Frank FREDERICKS b.2 Oct 1967 Windhoek 1.80m 70kg. Doing a masters course in business administration at Brigham Young University, USA.
At 100m/200m: OG: '92- 2/2; WCh: '91- 5/2, '93- 6/1; CG: '94- 3/1; AfG: '91- 1/1; WCp: '94- -/1. At 60m: WI: '93- 2. Won NCAA 100m & 200m 1991, South African 200m 1987. Won GP 200m 1993 (2nd 1991).
African records: 100m 1991, 200m (7) 1989-93.
Progression at 100m, 200m: 1985- 10.73, 21.68; 1986- 10.1, 20.6; 1987- 10.36, 20.58/20.41w; 1988- 10.32, 20.57; 1989- 10.02, 20.31/20.09w; 1990- 10.16/10.14w, 20.32/20.20w; 1991- 9.95/ 9.89w; 20.08/20.0/19.90w; 1992- 10.02/9.91w, 19.97; 1993- 10.03, 19.85; 1994- 10.04/10.00w, 19.97. pbs: 50m 5.71i '95, 55m 6.13i '93, 60m 6.47 '91, 400m 46.28 '89, LJ 7.57i '91.
After three major silver medals, including the first Olympic medal ever won by a Namibian, he became their first world champion with his very strong finish in the 200m in 1993. A former soccer player, Fredericks was sent to the USA by the Rossing Uranium Mine to study computer science and became the first non US sprinter to win the NCAA double. Able to compete internationally once Namibia gained independence in 1990 and IAAF affiliation 1991.

Luchetz SWARTBOOI b.7 Feb 1966. Librarian's assistant.
At Mar: OG: '92- dnf; WCh: '93- 2.
Four Namibian marathon records 1992-4, 5000m 1994.
Progression at Mar: 1992- 2:10:01, 1993- 2:09:57, 1994- 2:09:08. pb 5000m 13:46.91 '94. road pbs: 10k 28:24 '93, Half Mar 61:26 '93.
Won two fast marathons in Namibia in 1992 and led early on in the Olympics. Third Boston Marathon 1993.

NETHERLANDS

Governing body: Koninklijke Nederlandse Atletiek-Unie (KNAU), PO Box 567, 3430 AN Nieuwegein. Founded 1901.
National Championships first held in 1910 (men), 1921 (women). **1994 Champions**: **Men**: 100m: Regillio v d Vloot 10.41, 200m: Miquel Jansson 20.59, 400m: Patrick Snoek 47.49, 800m: Marko Koers 1:50.03, 1500m: Simon Vroemen 3:46.59, 5000m: Marcel Versteeg 13:56.14, 10000m: Luc Krotwaar 28:46.71, Half Mar: John Vermeule 66:22, Mar: Aart Stigter 2:15:38, 3000mSt: Ron van Diepen 8:48.32, 110mh: Robin Korving 14.01, 400mh: Marco Beukenkamp 50.51, HJ: Sven Ootjers 2.20, PV: Laurens Looije 5.25 5.25, LJ: Frans Maas 7.70, TJ: Paul Lucassen 15.43, SP/DT: Ben Vet 16.73/52.56, HT: Frank v dVool 59.74, JT: Johan van Lieshout 73.70, Dec: Marcel Dost 7896w, 20kmW/50kmW: Harold van Beek 1:40:46/4:12:30. **Women**: 100m/200m: Jacqueline Poelman 11.33/23.44, 400m: Gretha Tromp 53.26, 800m/1500m: Stella Jongmans 2:04.82/4:15.69, 3000m: Grete Koens 9:09.84, 10000m: Christine Toonstra 33:46.31, Half Mar: Irma Heeren 1:15:23, Mar: Carla Beurskens 2:29:43, 100mh/ LJ/Hep: Sharon Jaklofsky 13.39w/6.60w/ 5895w, 400mh: Ester Goossens 57.13, HJ: Anoek van Diessen 1.79, TJ: Ingrid vaan Lingen 12.41, SP: Corrie de Bruin 17.24, DT: Jacqueline Goormachtigh 57.10, JT: Marjo Bus 52.00.

Women

Ellen VAN LANGEN b.9 Feb 1966 Oldenzaal 1.72m 56kg. ADA. Economics graduate of Amsterdam University.
At 800m: OG: '92- 1; WCh: '91- h; EC: '90- 4; WUG: '89- 2. Won Dutch 800m 1989-90, 1992; 1500m 1990; ECp B3 800m 1993.
Three Dutch 800m records 1990-2.
Progression at 800m: 1986- 2:14.2, 1987- 2:09.89, 1988- 2:06.30, 1989- 1:59.82, 1990- 1:57.57, 1991- 1:58.86, 1992- 1:55.54, 1993- 1:59.23, 1994- 1:59.89. pbs: 400m 53.66 '89, 1500m 4:06.92 '92, 1M 4:31.88 '92.
Played soccer until 1986. Achilles injury in 1991 but came back with a brilliant season at 800m in 1992. Injuries cost her most of the 1993 season and also to withdraw from the 1994 Europeans.

NEW ZEALAND

Governing body: Athletics New Zealand, PO Box 741, Wellington.
National Championships first held in 1887 (men), 1926 (women). **1994 Champions: Men**: 100m: Gus Nketia 10.40w, 200m: Todd Blythe 21.02, 400m: Nick Cowan 46.64, 800m: Mark Tonks 1:48.51, 1500m: Richard Potts 3:42.10, 3000m/5000m: Phil Clode 8:13.85/14:25.31, 10000m: Jeff Spillane 30:02.20, Mar: Paul Smith 2:19:12, 3000mSt: Phil Costley 8:39.96, 110mh: Simon Poelman 14.60, 400mh: Johnathan Schmidt 51.85, HJ: Roger Te Puni 2.20, PV: Paul

Gibbons 5.20, LJ: Jonathon Moyle 7.59w, TJ: Jari Lamsa AUS 16.30, SP: Patrick Hellier 15.99, DT: Chris Mene 53.90, HT: Angus Cooper 67.78, JT: Gavin Lovegrove 78.56, Dec: Grant Chapman 6485, 5000mW/20kmW: Scott Nelson 20:39:06/1:25:19. **Women**: 100m/200m: Michelle Seymour 11.42w/23.68, 400m: Kirstin Gill 54.49, 800m: Toni Hodgkinson 2:08.47, 1500m: Geraldine MacDonald 4:18.75, 3000m/5000m: Anne Hare 9:17.34/15:59.30, 10000m: Raewyn Rodger 33:16.01, Mar: Nyla Caroll 2:37:37, 100mh: Vanessa Jack 13.75, 400mh: Lynn Massey 58.66, HJ: Tracy Phillips 1.85, PV: Melina Hamilton 3.20, LJ/Hep: Joanne Henry 6.48w/5970, TJ: Tania Murray 13.14, SP/DT: Beatrice Faumuina 15.37/54.98 (Christina King disqualified after 15.46 in shot due to positive drugs test), HT: Raylene Bates 45.34, JT: Kirsten Hellier 57.58, 3000mW/10kmW: Lin Murphy 13:54.90/50:00.

Gavin LOVEGROVE b.21 Oct 1967 Hamilton 1.87m 90kg.
At JT: OG: '92- 9; WCh: '87- dnq 23, '91- 4, '93- dnq 15; CG: '86- 3, '90- 3, '94- 3; WJ: '86- 3; WCp: '94- 3. Won NZ title 1987, 1990-4; Australian 1987, 1989.
Eight NZ javelin records 1986-92, world junior record 1986.
Progression at JT: 1984- 74.70, 1985- 79.12, new: 1986- 79.58, 1987- 80.20, 1988- 80.70, 1989- 83.90, 1990- 82.64, 1991- 85.18, 1992- 86.14, 1993- 84.54, 1994- 85.46. pb SP 14.52 '86.

NIGERIA

Governing body: The Athletic Federation of Nigeria, P.O.Box 211, Lagos. Founded 1944.
1994 National Champions: **Men**: 100m: Olapade Adeniken 10.33, 200m: Oluyemi Kayode 20.93, 400m: Sunday Bada 45.75, 800m: Michael Egbeasor 1:49.00, 1500m: ?, 5000m/10000m: Abba Mustapha 14:37.33/30:30.82, 3000mSt: Zakaria Fwangfur 9:01.40, 110mh: William Erese 14.18, 400mh: Ibrahim Rilwan 51.61, HJ: Anthony Idiatu 2.10, PV: Saliu Festus 4.10, LJ: Obinnah Eregbu 7.91, TJ: Olu Sule 15.72, SP: Chima Ugwu 18.05, DT: Adewale Olukoju 62.16, HT: Chris Majuk 46.64, JT: Pius Bazighe 72..96, Dec: Tommy Ozono 6813 **Women**: 100m/200m: Mary Onyali 11.35/23.16, 400m: Fatima Yusuf 51.52, 800m: ?, 1500m: Mercy Emmanuel 4:36.67, 5000m: Grace Ishaku 17:44.44, 10000m: Angela Agboogu 38:04.76, 100mh: Gloria Oguruogu 14.29, 400mh: Mari Usifo 57.09, HJ: N Nkechi 1.70, LJ: Endurance Ojokolo 5.77, TJ: Willim Abiola 12.58, SP: Vivian Chukwuemeka 14.12, DT: Grace Apiafi 49.64, JT: Ojiego Nkiru 47.02, Hep: Rita Izoje Egbuson 4375.

Olapade ADENIKEN b.19 Aug 1969 1.86m 78kg. Was at University of Texas at El Paso, USA.
At 100m/4x100m relay (200m): OG: '88- sf (sf), '92- 6/2R (5); WCh: '91- sf/4R (5); CG: '94- 6; WJ: '88- 4/2R (2); WUG: '89- 2; AfCh: '88- 4/1R, '89- 1/1R; WCp: '89- 4/4R (3), '92- 2/3R, '94- 2/2R. Won NCAA 100m/200m 1992. 2nd GP 100m 1992.
African junior records 100m and 200m 1988. Nigerian records 100m 1992, 200m (2) 1991-2. WIR 100m 10.13 '95.
Progression at 100m, 200m: 1986- 10.65/10.5, 21.86; 1987- 10.3, 21.1; 1988- 10.29/9.9, 20.67; 1989- 10.16/10.05w, 20.38/20.22w; 1990- 10.10, 20.37/20.18w; 1991- 10.10/10.00w, 20.30/20.09w; 1992- 9.97, 20.11/20.00w; 1993- 10.15/10.00w, 20.12; 1994- 9.95A, 20.28/20.23w. pbs: 55m 6.17i '90, 60m 6.61i '95, 400m 46.34 '90.

Sunday BADA b.22 Jun 1969. 1.88m 79kg.
At 400m/4x400mR: OG: '92- sf/5R; WCh: '93- 5; CG: '94- 3/4R; WI: '93- 2; AfCh: '90- 3/1R (3 200m); '91-2/2R; WCp: '92- 1/1R, '94- 2R. Nigerian champion 1990-4.
Progression at 400m: 1990- 46.19, 1991- 45.81, 1992- 44.99, 1993- 44.63, 1994- 44.96. pbs: 200m 20.80 '92, 300m 32.66 '92.

Daniel Philip EFFIONG b. 17 Jun 1972. 1.87m 79kg. Student at Azusa Pacific Universty, USA.
At 100m/4x100mR (200m): WCh: '93- 7 (qf); CG: '94- (3); WUG: '91- (2), '93- 1; AfCh: '90- 4; '93- 1/2R; AfG: '91- (3). Won Nigerian 100m 1993, 200m 1992.
Nigerian 200m record 1994.
Progression at 100m, 200m: 1990- 10.29/10.1, 21.4; 1991- 10.18, 20.56/20.5; 1992- 10.11, 20.45/20.38w; 1993- 9.98/9.97w, 20.15; 1994- 10.08/9.94w (9.98w? at 99.96m), 20.10.

Obinna EREGBU b.9 Nov 1969. 1.83m 75kg. Student at Central Arizona University, USA, formerly at Iowa State.
At LJ: WCh: '93- dnq 18; CG: '94- 1; WUG: '93- 2; AfG: '93- 1; WCp: '94- 4. Nigerian champion 1993-4. At 100m: WJ: '86- 6.
Progression at LJ: 1986- 7.54, 1988- 7.88, 1989- 7.83, 1990- 7.82i/7.95w, 1991- 8.04/8.06w, 1992- 8.09/8.18w, 1993- 8.18/8.32w, 1994- 8.22. pbs: 55m 5.9/6.13i '93, 60m 6.63i '93, 100m 10.37 '91, 10.25w '92, 10.3 '90.

Davidson EZINWA b.22 Nov 1971 1.82m 80kg. Student at Azusa Pacific College, California.
At 100m/4x100m relay: OG: 92- 8/2R; CG: '90- 2/2R (5 200m); WJ: '88- 2R, '90- 1/3R (2 200m); WCp: '89- 4R; AfG: '91- 2/1R; At 200m: AfCh: '89- 2/1R. Won Nigerian 100m 1992, 200m 1989.

Mary Onyali: gold and silver at the Commonwealth Games

African 200m record 1990. Nigerian records: 100m (2) 1992-4, 200m (2) 1991-2.
Progression at 100m, 200m: 1988- 10.44/10.3, 20.92; 1989- 10.33/10.1, 19.9/20.82, 1990- 10.05, 20.30/20.0w; 1991- 10.04, 20.55/20.51w; 1992- 9.96/9.91w, 20.25; 1993- 10.14, 21.26; 1994- 9.94, 20.43. pbs: 50m 5.64i '92, 60y 6.12i '92, 400m 46.9 '94.
World age bests at 17 200m 1989 and 18 , 10.05 for 100m in January 1990 at the Nigerian trials, followed by two silver medals in Auckland. His twin brother Osmond also ran on the Nigerian 4x100m silver medal teams at the 1988 World Juniors and in Auckland, where he was 8th equal at 100m.

Adewale OLUKOJU b.27 Jul 1968 Zaria 1.88m 110kg. Student at Azusa Pacific University, USA.
At (SP/)DT: OG: '88- dnq 23; WCh: '91- 11; CG: '90- 2/1, '94- 2; WJ: '86- 6/7; WUG: '91- 1, '93- 2; AfG: '91- 2/1; AfCh: '87- 1/1, '88- 3/1 '92- 3/1; WCp: '92- 5, '94- 3.
Three African discus records 1989-91. African junior records for shot (18.13) and discus 1987.
Progression at DT: 1984- 56.88?, 1985- 50.88, 1986- 54.00, 1987- 56.92, 1988- 63.60/64.12u, 1989- 65.54, 1990- 64.56, 1991- 67.80, 1992- 64.40, 1993- 66.48, 1994- 62.46. pbs: SP 19.44i '90, 18.75 '89; HT 58.40 '90.

Women

Mary ONYALI b.3 Feb 1968 Gongola 1.65m 52kg. Graduated in telecommunications from Texas Southern University, USA,
At 200m/R- 4x100m relay (100m): OG: '88- sf, '92- sf/3R (7); WCh: '87- 6, '91- 7/4R (5 4x400mR), '93- 5/5; CG: '94- 2/1R (1); AfG: '87- 1/1R (3, 1 4x400mR), '91- (1)/1R, '93- 1/1R; AfCh: '85- 2, '89- 1 (1), '93- 1/1R (1 4x400mR); WUG: '87- 2/3R; WI: '87- 5; WJ: '86- 2/3R (dq); WCp: '89- 2 (2); '94- 4/1R (3). Won NCAA 1988. 3rd GP 1988. At 100m: AfCh: '88- 1; 3rd GP 1991. Won Nigerian 100m 1985-8, 1991-4; 200m 1985-8, 1990, 1992, 1994.
African records: seven 100m 1986-93, seven 200m 1986-90; junior 100m 1986, 200m 1986-7.
Progression at 100m, 200m: 1984- 12.2, 25.3; 1985- 11.91/11.8, 23.85, 1986- 11.28, 22.90/22.77w, 1987- 11.31/11.24w/11.2, 22.52; 1988- 11.09, 22.43; 1989- 11.14, 22.45; 1990- 11.09/10.9w, 22.31; 1991- 11.04, 22.72; 1992- 11.15/11.08w, 22.60/22.45w; 1993- 10.97, 22.32; 1994- 11.03, 22.35/22.33w. pbs: 60m 7.24i '93, 400m 52.50 '87.
Concentrating on 100m in 1991 she ran African records of 11.07 and 11.04 before a sensational 10.81 in semi-final of Nigerian Championships, which was later declared faulty.

Fatima YUSUF b.2 May 1971 Owo, Ondo State 1.80m 64kg. Student at Azusa Pacific University.
At 400m/4x400mR: WCh: '91- sf/5R; CG: '90- 1 (3 4x100mR), '94- 2; WJ: '88- h, '90- 1 (dq sf 200m); AfG: '91- 1/1R (2 200m); AfCh: '89- 2/1R. 90- 1/1R (1 200m, 4x100mR); WCp: '89- 5R, '94- 2. 3rd GP 400m 1990. Nigerian champion 1994.
Three African 400m records 1990-1.
Progression at 400m: 1987- 54.23, 1988- 54.23, 1989- 51.99, 1990- 50.59/50.5, 1991- 50.41, 1992- 51.83, 1993- 52.59, 1994- 50.53. pbs: 100m 11.69 '94, 200m 22.84 '91, 300m 36.25 '90, 800m 2:14.56 '91.
In 1990 she broke the African record to win the Commonwealth title while still a junior, and went on to win the World Junior title and four gold medals at the African Championships.

NORWAY

Governing body: Norges Fri-Idrettsforbund, Karl Johansgaten 2, 0154 Oslo 1. Founded 1896.
National Championships first held in 1897

(men), 1947 (women). **1994 Champions**: **Men**: 100m: Geir Moen 10.45, 200m: Kennet Kjensli 21.35, 400m: Atle Douglas 46.66, 800m/1500m: Tor Øyvind Ødegård 1:51.02/3:44.90, 5000m/10000m: Bjørn Nordheggen 14:02.89/28:55.87, Half Mar: Frank Bjørkli 64:50, Mar: Terje Hole 2:23:49, 3000mSt: Jim Svenøy 8:47.83, 110mh: Gaute Gundersen 14.06, 400mh: Atle Lunn 51.41, HJ: Steinar Hoen 2.30, PV: Trond Barthel 5.52, LJ: Pål Sæther 7.40, TJ: Ketill Hanstveit 16.44, SP: Kjell Ove Hauge 18.82, DT: Svein Inge Valvik 60.00, HT: Anders Halvorsen 62.52, JT: Havard Johansen 74.26, Dec: Trond Høiby 6682, 10kmW: Martin Engelsviken 42:35.42, 20kmW: Sverre Jensen 1:29:08. **Women**: 100m: Ingvild Larsen 11.73, 200m/400m: Sølvi Meinseth 23.57/52.61, 800m: Toril Hatling 2:05.96, 1500m/3000m: Hilde Stavik 4:18.18/8:57.40, 10000m: Grete Kirkeberg 33:46.01, Half Mar: Ingrid Kristiansen 73:14, Mar: Anita Bergdal 2:54:55, 100mh: Monica Grefstad 13.45, 400mh: Ellen Bergin 60.07, HJ/TJ: Hanne Haugland 1.90/13.56, LJ: Ingvild Larsen 6.38, SP: Janne Antonsen 14.52, DT: Mette Bergmann 63.70, JT: Trine Hattestad 64.62, Hep: Monica Penne 4871, 5000mW/10kmW: Kjersti Tysse 22:22.64/46:44.

Atle DOUGLAS b.9 Jun 1968 Oxford, England 1.88m 78kg. SK Vidar.
At 800m: OG: '92- sf; WCh: '93- sf; EC: '90- sf, '94- 8. Won ECp A 1993. NOR champion 400m 1992-4, 800m 1987-90, 1993.
Three Norwegian records 1992-3.
Progression at 800m: 1987- 1:47.08, 1988- 1:46.70, 1989- 1:49.89, 1990- 1:46.06, 1991- 1:52.72, 1992- 1:45.15, 1993- 1:44.74, 1994- 1:44.16. pbs: 200m 22.84 '90, 400m 46.66 '94, 1000m 2:21.98 '93, 1500m 3:57.04 '87.
Half Norwegian and half Jamaican, his father lives in England, but Atle moved with his mother and his two brothers and two sisters to Bergen, and he gained Norwegian citizenship. In 1992, with 1:45.15 at the Bislett Games, he broke the 37 year-old Norwegian 800m record of Auden Boysen (1:45.9).

Steinar HOEN b.8 Feb1971 Oslo 1.92m 80kg. IK Tjalve. Business economics student.
At HJ: OG: '92- dnq; WCh: '91- 14, '93- dnq; EC: '94- 1; EI: '94- 4; WJ: '90- 11; EJ: '89- 12; WCp: '94- 4. Norwegian champion 1991, 1993-4.
Seven Norwegian high jump records 1991-4.
Progression at HJ: 1987- 1.96, 1988- 2.07, 1989- 2.17, 1990- 2.17, 1991- 2.29, 1992- 2.30, 1993- 2.32, 1994- 2.36i/2.35. pbs: LJ 7.35 '93, TJ 14.46 '89.

Geir MOEN b.26 Jun 1969 Oslo 1.90m 85kg. Moss. Teacher.
At 200m (100m): WCh: '93- qf; EC: '90- (h); '94- 1 (2); WCp: '94- 3. Won NOR 100m 1989, 1993-4; 200m 1988, 1991, 1993.
Norwegian records 100m, 200m (3) 1994.
Progression at 100m, 200m: 1985- 11.66, 23.2; 1986- 11.14, 22.5; 1987- 10.80, 21.93; 1988- 10.64, 21.42; 1989- 10.66, 21.15; 1990- 10.57, 21.36; 1991- 10.56, 21.11; 1992- 10.48, 21.20; 1993- 10.50, 20.80; 1994- 10.17, 20.30. pbs: 60m 6.66i '95, 400m 49.07 '93, LJ 7.37 '89.
Dramatic improvement in 1994.

Vebjørn RODAL b.16 Sep 1972 Berkåk 1.86m 78kg. Oppdal FIK. Marketing student.
At 800m: OG: '92- sf; WCh: '93- sf; EC: '94- 2; WJ: '90- sf; EJ: '91- 7. NOR champion 1992.
Norwegian records 400m and 800m (2) 1994.
Progression at 800m: 1986- 2:05.6, 1987- 2:06.5, 1988- 1:55.05, 1989- 1:52.34, 1990- 1:49.15, 1991- 1:47.08, 1992- 1:45.33, 1993- 1:45.83, 1994- 1:43.50. pbs: 400m 46.56 '94, 1000m 2:18.90 '92.

Håkon SÄRNBLOM b.3 Mar 1966 Oslo 1.95m 84kg. Minerva.
At HJ: OG: '92- dnq 19; WCh: '91- dnq 19; EC: '90- dnq 22, '94- 4. NOR champion 1986-7, 1989-90, 1992.
Four Norwegian high jump records 1987-91.
Progression at HJ: 1983- 1.96, 1984- 2.03, 1985- 2.11, 1986- 2.18, 1987- 2.23, 1988- 2.19, 1989- 2.21, 1990- 2.25, 1991- 2.28, 1992- 2.28, 1993- 2.20, 1994- 2.31.
Has played basketball for Norway. Lives with Hanne Haugland.

Women

Mette BERGMANN b.9 Nov 1962 Fredrikstad 1.74m 78kg. SK Vidar. Nurse.
At DT: OG: '92- dnq; WCh: '91- dnq, '93- dnq; EC: '86- dnq, '90- 12, '94- 3. 2nd GP 1994. NOR champion 1984-94.
Three Norwegian discus records 1994.
Progression at DT: 1982- 42.40, 1983- 47.56, 1984- 56.18, 1985- 59.40, 1986- 58.20, 1987- 57.58, 1988- 62.30, 1989- 63.12, 1990- 59.28, 1991- 60.92, 1992- 61.70, 1993- 61.80, 1994- 66.46. pbs: SP 12.67 '85, HT 49.16 '94.
In 1994 she won her 11th successive Norwegian title and surged into the world élite.

Else Katrine **Trine HATTESTAD** b.18 Apr 1966 Lørenskog 1.72m 70kg. née Solberg. IF Minerva. Fitness instructor.
At JT: OG: '84- 5, '88- dnq 18, '92- 5; WCh: '87- dnq 24, '91- 5;, '93- 1; EC: '82- dnq, '86- 9, '94- 1; EJ: '81- 5, '83- 2; WCp: '94- 1. Won Norwegian JT 1983-6, 1988-9, 1991-4. Won GP 1992 (2nd 1994, 3rd 1986).
Eleven Norwegian javelin records 1981-93.
Progression at JT: 1978- 31.04, 1979- 44.08, 1980-

49.54, 1981- 56.06, 1982- 58.02, 1983- 61.58, 1984- 65.02, 1985- 68.94, 1986- 67.80, 1987- 68.20, 1988- 67.50, 1989- 71.12, 1991- 71.44, 1992- 69.50, 1993- 72.12, 1994- 71.32.
After disappointing at previous major events she came through in 1993 to win the World title. Received a 2-year ban after a drugs test when she won the European Cup C1 javelin in Brussels in 1989. However, after discoveries of variances in the results of tests, she was reinstated and successfully sued her federation for $50,000 loss of earnings. Son, Joachim, born in 1991. She was the top goalscorer at handball in Norwegian second division in 1984, and but for her interest in the javelin would have been a candidate for the national team.

Hanne HAUGLAND b.14 Dec 1967 Haugesund 1.83m 65kg. SK Vidar.
At HJ: WCh: '87- dnq 20=, '93- 9=; EC: '90- 8, '94- 5; EI: '89- 2; EJ: '85- 12. Won Norwegian HJ 1986-7, 1989-90, 1992-4; LJ 1989-90, TJ 1994. 3rd GP 1993.
Five Norwegian HJ records 1987-94, triple jump 1994.
Progression at HJ: 1981- 1.61, 1982- 1.70, 1983- 1.80, 1984- 1.84, 1985- 1.87, 1986- 1.89, 1987- 1.93, 1988- 1.91, 1989- 1.96i/1.94, 1990- 1.92, 1991- 1.96i/1.86, 1992- 1.92i/1.90, 1993- 1.93, 1994- 1.98i/1.97, 1995- 2.00i. pbs: 100m 12.21 '90, 100mh 14.07 '91, LJ 6.34 '91, TJ 13.56 '94, Hep 4756 '88.
Her grandfather Eugen Haugland won seven Norwegian TJ titles between 1931 and 1948 and was fourth in European TJ 1946, and her father Terje had a long jump pb of 7.87 '70 (EC: '69- 11, '71- 13). Three generations as European finalists were completed by Hanne in Split.
Lives with Håkon Särnblom.

POLAND

Governing body: Polski Zwiazek Lekkiej Atletyki (PZLA), 02 034 Warszawa, ul.Wawelska 5. Founded 1919.
National Championships first held in 1920 (men), 1922 (women). **1994 Champions**: **Men**: 100/200: Marek Zalewski 10.36/21.42, 400: Tomasz Czubak 45.89, 800: Piotr Piekarski 1:49.45, 1500: Piotr Kitlinski 3:48.20, 5000: Slawomir Kapinski 13:59.07, 10000: Grzegorz Gajdus 29:06.84, Half Mar: Miroslaw Plawgo 63:56, Mar: Janusz Wójcik 2:13:55, 3000St: Rafal Wojcik 8:45.98, 110mh: Ronald Mehlich 13.91, 400mh: Piotr Kotlarski 49.75, HJ: Artur Partyka 2.26, PV: Krzysztof Kusiak 5.20, LJ: Roman Golanowski 7.79, TJ: Piotr Weremczuk 16.43, SP: Helmut Krieger 19.10, DT: Marek Majkrzak 56.06, HT: Lech Kowalski 72.74, JT: Miroslaw Witek 80.74, Dec: Sebastian Chmara 7407, 20kmW: Robert Korzeniowski 1:22:33, 50kmW: Slawomir Cielica 4:05:52. **Women**: 100/200: Izabela Czajko 11.79/24.07, 400: Elzbieta Kilinska 52.86, 800: Anna Jakubczak 2:03.73, 1500: Malgorzata Rydz 4:14.46, 3000/10000/Mar: Aniela Nikiel 9:14.53/34:11.28/2:37:07, Half Mar: Isabela Zatorska 73:59, 100mh: Maria Kamrowska 13.54, 400mh: Monika Warnicka 55.93, HJ: Iwona Kielan 1.88, LJ: Agata Karczmarek 6.87, TJ: Urszula Wlodarczyk 13.44w, SP: Krystyna Danilczyk 18.18, DT: Renata Katewicz 63.78, JT: Genowefa Patla 58.06, Hep: Elzbieta Raczka 5133, 5000mW/ 10kmW/ 20kmW: Katarzyna Radtke 21:05.53/ 45:16/ 1:33:36.

Jan HURUK b.27 Jan 1960 Orsk 1.78m 65kg. GRYF Slupsk.
At Mar: OG: '92- 7; WCh: '91- 4; EC: '90- dnf, '94- 13; WCp; '91- 3. Won Polish 10000m 1987.
Polish marathon record 1990.
Progression at Mar: 1988- 2:17:11, 1989- 2:13:12, 1990- 2:10:16, 1991- 2:10:21, 1992- 2:10:07, 1993- 2:11:57, 1994- 2:14:27, 1995- 2:11:25. pbs: 3000m 7:55.05 '89, 5000m 13:34.63 '88, 10000m 28:18.42 '89, 3000mSt 8:38.63 '85.
Won Marrakech marathon 1990, second London 1992. Operations on both Achilles in late 1993.

Robert KORZENIOWSKI b.30 Jul 68 Lubaczów 1.70m 63kg. AZS AWF Katowice and US Tourcoing, France.
At 20kmW (50kmW): OG: '92- dnf (dq); WCh: '91- 10; EC: '90- 4, '94- dq (5); WCp: '89- 40, '91- 7, '93- 4; WUG: '91- 1, '93- 1. At 10kmW: EJ: '87- dq. At 5000mW: WI: '93- 2. Won Polish 20kmW 1990-4, 50kmW 1993.
World best 5km road walk: 18:21 '90. Polish records 1990-3: 3000mW (5), 10kmW (3), 20kmW (2), 50km W (2).
Progression at 20kmW, 50kmW: 1987- 1:29:40, 1988- 1:26:04, 1989- 1:23:19, 1990- 1:19.32, 1991- 1:21:19, 1992- 1:19:14, 3:46:42; 1993- 1:20:55, 3:44:24; 1994- 1:20:55, 3:45:57. pbs: 3000mW 12:22.0 '88, 5000mW 18:17.22 '92, 10000mW 39:00.11 '94, 1 Hr 14,794m '92; road 10kmW 39:19 '92, 35kmW 2:28:30 (world best) '93.
Disqualified in 2nd place in the stadium just before finish of the 1992 Olympic 50km walk.

Artur PARTYKA b.25 Jul 1969 Stalowa Wola 1.92m 69kg. LKS Lódz. Student.
At HJ: OG: '88- dnq 20, '92- 3=; WCh: '91- 12, '93- 2; EC: '90- 11, '94- 2=; WJ: '88- 1; EJ: '87- 1; WI: '91- 2; EI: '90- 1; ECp: '93- 1. Won POL HJ 1989-94.

Two Polish high jump records 1993.
Progression at HJ: 1984- 1.94, 1985- 2.04, 1986- 2.18, 1987- 2.23, 1988- 2.28, 1989- 2.32, 1990- 2.34i/ 2.33, 1991- 2.37i/2.32, 1992- 2.34, 1993- 2.37, 1994- 2.33, 1995- 2.37i.
Is compiling a great competitive record, with medals at all major championships.

Women

Renata KATEWICZ b.2 May 1965 1.80m 90kg. Zaglebie Lubin. Cook.
At DT: OG: '88- dnq 13; WCh: '87- 11, '93- dnq 15; EC: '86- 8, '94- dnq 16; EJ: '83- 6; WUG: '93- 1; ECp: '85- 4, '87- 6, '89- 6, '91- 4, '93- 3. Polish champion 1985-7, 1992, 1994.
Four Polish discus records 1985-8.
Progression at DT: 1982- 50.38, 1983- 58.52, 1984- 60.60, 1985- 63.26, 1986- 64.34, 1987- 64.56; 1988- 66.18, 1989- 63.80, 1990- 59.28, 1991- 60.42, 1992- 63.80, 1993- 65.94, 1994- 65.72. pb SP 17.27 '87.

Renata KOKOWSKA b.4 Dec 1958 Glubczyn 1.70m 57kg. née Pyrr. Bukowina Walcz. Agricultural technician.
At Mar: WCh: '87- dnf; WCp: '91- 6. At 10000m: ECp: '85-7, '87- 8. At 1500m: ECp: '83- 7. Won Polish 3000m 1985-6, 5000m 1984, 1986; 10000m 1984-8.
Four Polish 10000m records 1984-7.
Progression at 10000m, Mar: 1984- 34:04.66, 1985- 34:03.28, 1986- 33:27.95, 2:36.11; 1987- 33:00.60, 2:33:07; 1988- 33:07.08, 2:29:16; 1989- 2:31:19, 1990- 2:28:50, 1991- 2:27:36, 1992- 2:29:59, 1993- 2:26:20. pbs: 800m 2:06.5 '78, 1500m 4:13.91 '84, 3000m 9:00.24 '86, 5000m 15:56.19 '86, 10000m 33:14.87 '91.
Won Amsterdam marathon 1990, Berlin 1988, 1991, 1993; 2nd 1990, 1992. 2nd London 1992.

Wanda PANFIL b.26 Jan 1959 Ropoczno 1.67m 54kg. Lechia Tomaszów. Married to Mauricio Gonzalez (Mex, 10000m pb 27:43.64 '88) and now lives in Mexico.
At Mar: WCh: '91- 1; OG: '88- 22, '92- 22. At 10000m: EC: '90- 7; ECp: '89- 5; won GWG 1990. At 3000m: ECp: '83- 6, '85- 4, '87- 8. Won Polish 3000m 1984, 1987; 5000m 1985, 1987-8; Mar 1988. Polish records: four marathon 1987-91, six 5000m 1984-9, 2000m & 3000m 1990.
Progression at 10000m, Mar: 1987- 33:06.31, 2:32:01; 1988- 2:32:23; 1989- 33:18.57, 2:27:05; 1990- 32:01.17, 2:26:31; 1991- 31:53.83, 2:24:18; 1992- 2:29:29. pbs: 800m 2:04.62 '82, 1500m 4:13.94 '85, 2000m 5:45.36 '90, 3000m 8:52.07 '90, 5000m 15:41.29 '89.
Has won six of her 12 marathons: Debno 1988, Nagoya, London and New York 1990; Boston 1991; including five in succession to her world title in 1991. 2nd Berlin 1987, London 1989.

Malgorzata RYDZ b.18 Jan 1967 Klobuck 1.62m 52kg. née Kapkowska. Budowlani Czestochowa.
At 1500m (800m): OG: '92- 7; WCh: '91- 8, '93- h; EC: '94- 5 (4); WI: '89- 8; EI: '94- 3; WCp: '92- 2; ECp: '89- 4, '91- 5 (5), '93- 4 (7). Won Polish 800m 1988, 1991-3, 1500m 1988-94.
Progression at 1500m: 1985- 4:28.8, 1988- 4:14.00, 1989- 4:08.40, 1990- 4:12.45, 1991- 4:05.52, 1992- 4:01.91, 1993- 4:02.29, 1994- 4:03.78. pbs: 400m 54.87 '93, 800m 1:59.12 '94, 1M 4:28.39 '94, 2000m 5:48.39 '90, 3000m 8:58.64 '93.

Urszula WLODARCZYK b.22 Dec 1965 Walbrzych 1.80m 66kg. AZS-AWF Wroclaw.
At Hep: OG: '92- 8; WCh: '91- 6, '93- 5; EC: '94- 3; WUG: 91- 2 (4 TJ), '93- 1; ECp: '91- 4, '93- 3, '94- 5. At Pen: WI inv: '93- 2; EI: '92- 3, '93- 3. Won Polish 100mh 1991, TJ 1990-2, 1994; Hep 1990-2.
Two Polish triple jump records 1991.
Progression at Hep: 1982- 4779*, 1983- 4914, 1984- 5173, 1985- 5504, 1986- 5721, 1987- 5831, 1988- 5825, 1989- 5898, 1990- 6021, 1991- 6425, 1992- 6407, 1993- 6394, 1994- 6322. pbs: 100m 11.94 '91, 200m 24.03/23.89w '92, 800m 2:10.92 '91, 60mh 8.26i '94, 100mh 13.19 '94, HJ 1.84 '91, LJ 6.59/6.67w '93, TJ 13.98 '93, SP 14.62 '91, JT 46.22 '91, Pen 4668i '94.

PORTUGAL

Governing body: Federação Portuguesa de Atletismo, Av.Infante Santo, 68-7°, E/F 1, 1300 Lisboa. Founded 1921.
National Championships first held in 1910 (men), 1937 (women). **1994 Champions**: **Men**: 100m: Luís Cunha 10.36w, 200m: Vitor Jorge 21.1, 400m: Carlos Silva 47.54, 800m: António Abrantes 1:50.24, 1500m: João Junquira 3:42.96, 5000m: António Pinto 13:23.09, 10000m: Paulo Guerra 27:52.44, Mar: Galhardo Pires 2:15:24, 3000mSt: Luís Jesus 8:29.76, 110mh: João Lima 14.36, 400mh: Pedro Rodrigues 50.60, HJ: Esteves Costa 2.07, PV: F Nuno Fernandes 5.40, LJ/TJ: Carlos Calado 7.78w/16.07, SP: Fernando Alves 17.25, DT: Paulo Santos 48.98, HT: Vitor Costa 66.26, JT: João Reis 69.02, Dec: Mario Anibal Ramos 7309, 20kmW/50kmW: José Magalhães 1:31:51/4:17:39. **Women**: 100m: M Carmo Tavares 11.94, 200m: Lucrécia Jardim 23.15, 400m: Cristina Regalo 54.95, 800m: Carla Sacramento 2:02.87, 1500m: Marina Bastos 4:09.59, 3000m: Ana Dias 9:16.05, 10000m: Conceição Ferreira 31:32.11, Mar: Fátima Neves 2:35:54, 100mh/LJ/TJ: Isabel Pereira 13.45/6.26/ 12.76, 400mh: M José Valamatos 60.79, HJ: Sandra Turpin 1.70, PV: Ana Morais 2.50, SP: Sónia Grácio 13.70, DT: Elisa Costa 45.30, HT: Cláudia Ferreira 35.68, JT: Helena Gouveia 52.38, Hep:

Paulo Guerra: European CC champion

Sónia Machado 7061, 10kmW: Susana Feitor 45:50.

Domingos CASTRO b.22 Nov 1963 Guimarães 1.67m 56kg. Sporting Club de Portugal.
At 5000m (10000m): OG: '88- 4, '92- 11 (h); WCh: '87- 2, '91- 5, '93 (h); EC: '86- (5), '94- 9 (17). Won GWG 10000m 1986. World CC: '90- 7, '92- 11, '93- 12. Eur CC: '94- 2. Won Portuguese 5000m 1986-7, 1989; 10000m 1986-7, 1992-3; CC 1990, 1993-4.
Progression at 5000m, 10000m: 1982- 14:59.3; 1983- 13:48.52, 30:29.1; 1984- 13:52.54, 30:39.6; 1985- 13:38.60; 1986- 13:19.03, 28:01.62; 1987- 13:18.59, 28:09.54; 1988- 13:16.09, 27:43.30; 1989- 13:14.41, 27:36.00; 1991- 13:24.71; 1992- 13:19.98, 27:39.03; 1993- 13:14.65, 27:34.53; 1994- 13:17.33, 28:27.14. pbs: 1500m 3:39.2 '86, 3000m 7:43.32 '89, Mar 2:12:49 '94.
In 1987 he was a surprise silver medallist at 5000m in Rome. Desperately unlucky to miss a medal at 5000m in Seoul.
Twin brother of Dionisio, who at 5000m was 4th at EC 1990 and 8th WCh 1987 and 1991, pbs: 5000m 13:13.59 '90, 10000m 27:42.84 '88, 20000m 57:18.4 '90; world record 20,000m 57:18.4 '90.

Paulo GUERRA b.21 Aug 1970 Barrancos 1.74m 64kg. Maratona CP.
At 10000m: EC: '94- 1. World CC: '93- 21, '94- 13. Eur CC '94- 1. Won POR 10000m 1994.
Progression at 5000m, 10000m: 1990- 14:00.90, 1991- 14:12.02, 1992- 14:07.11, 1993- 13:42.35, 28:11.14; 1994- 13:25.13, 27:52.44. pbs: 1500m 3:45.22 '94, 1M 4:09.7 '91, 3000m 8:03.99 '91, 3000mSt 8:43.86 '91, Half Mar 62:29 '94.
In a breakthrough 1994 season he was the top European placer in the World cross-country, won the Iberian 10,000m and was 5th in the Europeans, and then ran away with the inaugural European cross-country.

Manuel MATIAS b.30 Mar 1962 Ferreira do Alentejo 1.72m 58kg. Maratona C.Portugal.
At Mar: WCh: '91- dnf; EC: '90- 8, '94- 7; WCp: '91- 2, '93- 36.
Progression at Mar: 1988- 2:10:19, 1989- 2:09.43, 1990- 2:14.27, 1991- 2:10:21, 1992- 2:08:38, 1993- 2:15:25, 1994- 2:08:33. pbs: 1500m 3:44.15 '87, 3000m 7:59.26 '89, 5000m 13:46.37 '90, 10000m 28:21.67 '94, 3000mSt 8:37.5 '86.
Has won three of his 16 marathons, his début at Paris 1988, Fukuoka 1989 and Gyeongju 1994. Second Berlin 1992 and Fukuoka 1994. Fourth at Chicago 1988, London 1989.

António PINTO b.22 Mar 1966 Amarante 1.66m 58kg. Maratona CP
At 10000m: OG: '88- 13, '92- dnf; EC: '90- 14, '94- 9; Won ECp C2 1991. Portuguese CC 1992, 5000m 1994.
Progression at 10000m, Mar: 1986- 31:13.3, 1987- 28:28.73, 1988- 28:01.00, 1989- 28:30.11, 1990- 28:14.32; 1991- 28:30.3, 2:12:39; 1992- 28:59.02, 2:10:02; 1994- 27:48.1, 2:08:31. pbs: 1500m 3:42.4 '90, 3000m 7:52.53 '90, 5000m 13:21.1 '94, Half Mar 61:55 '94.
Previously a cyclist, started running in 1986. Has run six marathons, 7th at Carpi 1991 on his début and wins at London 1992 and Berlin1994, 2nd Paris 1994.

Pedro RODRIGUES b.8 Jul 1971 Lisboa 1.82m 77kg. Engineering student at Lisbon, then University of Southern California, USA. Benfica.
At 400mh: OG: '92- h; WCh: '91- h, '93- h; EC: '90- h, '94- 4; WJ: '90- 4; EJ: '89- 5. Won POR 400mh 1990-4.
Four Portuguese records at 400mh 1992-4.
Progression at 400mh: 1988- 54.41, 1989- 51.58, 1990- 50.33, 1991- 50.04, 1992- 49.46, 1993- 50.07, 1994- 48.77. pbs: 200m 21.82 '91, 400m 46.80 '94, 800m 1:52.98 '94, 110mh 14.12 '92.
Set national records in each of the three rounds of the 1994 Europeans

Women

Maria Albertina DIAS b.26 Apr 1965 Porto 1.63m 48kg. Maratona Cube da Maia.

At 10000m: OG: '88- 10, '92- 13; WCh: '91- dnf, '93- 7. At 3000m: WI: '91- 4. World CC: '89- 18, '90- 2, '91- 6, '92- 3, '93- 1, '94- 5. World road 15km: '89- 8, '91- 12; Half Mar: '94- 4. Won Portuguese 1500m 1992, 3000m 1986, 1989, 1991; 10000m 1993, CC 1992-3.
Portuguese records 1M 1991, 3000m 1991 & 1992, 5000m 1993.
Progression at 3000m, 10000m, Mar: 1984- 9:41.33, 1985- 9:18.2, 1986- 9:17.96, 34:12.81; 1987- 9:08.17, 32:41.5; 1988- 9:00.40, 32:07.13; 1989- 8:48.87, 32:07.95; 1990- 8:57.17, 32:27.84; 1991- 8:43.50, 32:03.76; 1992- 8:43.08, 31:42.70; 1993- 8:43.76, 31:33.03, 2:26:49; 1994- 2:33:21. pbs: 800m 2:07.9 '88, 1500m 4:09.60 '91, 1M 4:29.97 '91, 5000m 15:05.12 '93, Half Mar 69:57 '94.
Second IAAF World Cross Challenge 1992. Brilliant marathon début for 2nd in Berlin 1993. Injured most of 1994.

Susana FEITOR b.20 Jan 1975 Rio Maior 1.60m 54kg. C Natação Rio Maior.
At 10km walk: WCh: '93- 11; EC: '94- 8. At 5000mW: WJ: '90- 1, '92- dq, 94- 2; EJ: '89- 6, '91- 2, '93- 1. Won POR 10kmW 1992, 1994
National walks records 1989-94: 3000m (8), 5000m (7), 10km (7).
Progression at 10kmW: 1991- 45:37, 1992- 45:24, 1993- 43:44, 1994- 43:30. Track pbs: 3000m 12:21.7i '94, 5000m 21:01.8 '93.
Had a hugely successful junior career to her world silver medal in front of her home crowd in 1994, four years after she had won this title.

Maria Conceição FERREIRA b.13 Mar 1962 Aveleda 1.48m 40kg. SC Braga.
At 10000m: OG: '92- dnf; WCh: '87- h, '91- 11, '93- 6; EC: '86- 26, '94- 2. At Mar: OG: '84- 39, '88- 20; EC: '90- dnf. World CC '94- 3; road 15km: '88- 8, '90- 9, '91- 9; Half Mar: '93- 1. Won Portuguese 3000m 1990, 10000m 1986, 1988, 1994; CC 1989-91, 1994.
Portuguese 10000m record 1992.
Progression at 10000m, Mar: 1984- 34:13.89, 2:43:58; 1985- 33:17.41, 1986- 33:21.25, 1987- 32:25.7, 1988- 32:28.8, 2:34:23; 1989- 32:06.51, 2:32:50; 1990- 31:45.75, 2:30:34; 1991- 31:51.47, 2:30:18; 1992- 31:16.42; 1993- 31:30.60, 1994- 31:32.11. pbs: 1500m 4:19.8 '93, 3000m 8:53.27 '91, 5000m 15:28.70 '94, Half Mar 70:07 '93.
Ran on winning World Road Relay team 1992.

M Manuela MACHADO b.9 Aug 1963 Viana do Castelo 1.61m 52kg. Sporting Club de Braga.
At Mar: OG: '92- 7; WCh: '91- 7, '93- 2; EC: '90- 10, '94- 1. Won POR Mar 1993.
Progression at Mar: 1988- 2:45:37, 1989- 2:38:45, 1990- 2:33:46, 1991- 2:32:33, 1992- 2:27:42, 1993- 2:30:54, 1994- 2:29.54. pbs: 800m 2:14.8i '87, 1500m 4:24.0 '91, 3000m 9:09.28 '92, 10000m 32:09.1 '94, Half Mar 71:48 '94.
Her World silver in 1993 was her best placing in 12 marathons, but in December 1993 she won at Lisbon and after 7th in Nagoya went on to win the 1994 European title.

Fernanda RIBEIRO b,23 Jun 1969 Penafiel 1.61m 48kg. Maratona C.Maia,
At 10000m: WCh: '93- 11; EC: '94- 1; WCp: '94- 2. At 3000m: OG: '88- h, '92- h; WCh: '87- h; EC: '86- h, '90- dnf; WJ: '86- 4, '88- 2; EJ: '83- 11, '85- 4, '87- 1; EI: '94- 1. World CC: '94- 10; Eur CC: '94- 6. Won POR 1500m 1989-90, 3000m 1985, 1993; 10000m 1992.
Portuguese 3000m and 10000m (2) records 1994.
Progression at 3000m, 10000m: 1982- 9:53.7, 1983- 9:21.71, 1984- 9:11.62, 1985- 9:14.19, 1986- 9:09.39, 1987- 8:56.33, 1988- 9:00.38, 1989- 9:04.33, 32:38.07; 1990- 9:03.35, 32:39.34; 1991- 8:57.64, 33:45.45; 1992- 8:56.10, 32:22.70; 1993- 8:51.91, 31:50.51; 1994- 8:42.13, 31:04.25. pbs: 800m 2:05.83 '94, 1500m 4:10.30i/4:10.54 '94, 5000m 15:06.91 '94, Half Mar 71:11 '93.
Set national age records each age 13-22 at 3000m and 14-18 and 20 at 1500m, and fulfilled long-time promise in 1994 with brilliant performances to win European titles indoors and out.

Carla SACRAMENTO b.10 Dec 1971 Lisboa 1.68m 53kg. Maratona Clube de Maia.
At 800m (1500m): OG: '92- sf (sf 1500m); WCh: '93- h (11); EC: '94- 6 (6); WI: '93- (7); EI: '92- 4, '94- 3. Eur CC: '94- 11. Won Portuguese 800m 1986-7, 1993-4; 1500m 1991.
Portuguese records 1989-94: 800m (6), 1500m (3), 1000m (2), 1M and 2000m.
Progression at 800m, 1500m: 1985- 2:15.15/ 2:13.56dq, 1986- 2:10.48, 1987- 2:09.3, 4:35.96; 1988- 2::04.27, 4:29.41; 1989- 2:03.89, 4:21.92; 1990- 2:04.83, 4:15.06; 1991- 2:04.94, 4:20.43; 1992- 2:00.57, 4:04.10; 1993- 1:59.42, 4:06.33; 1994- 1:59.39, 4:06.05. pbs: 200m 25.49 '92, 400m 55.21 '89, 1000m 2:39.2 '93, 1M 4:29.65 '94, 2000m 5:47.14 '94, 3000m 9:32.7 '90.

QATAR

Governing body: Qatar Amateur Athletic Federation, PO Box 8139, Doha. Founded 1963.

Ibrahim ISMAIL Muftah b.10 May 1972 1.85m 75kg.
At 400m (200m: OG: '92- 7; WCh: '91- sf, '93- sf; WJ: '90- 6; AsiG: 90- 2, '94- 1/3R (3); AsiC: '89- 1; '91- 1 (2), '93- 1; WCp: '92- 4, '94- 4. Won Asian J 1988, 1990 (2nd 200m).
Asian junior records 400m 1989-91. Qatar 400m

records 1986-93.
Progression at 400m: 1988- 46.59, 1989- 45.60, 1990- 45.57, 1991- 45.37, 1992- 44.89, 1993- 44.85, 1994- 44.93. pbs: 100m 10.66 '91, 10.3 '88; 200m 20.85 '92.

Talal MANSOOR Al-Rahim b. 8 May 1964 1.80m 73kg.
At 100m (200m): OG: '84- hR, '88- qf, '92- sf; AsiG: '86- 1, '90- 1, "94 1/3R (1); AsiC: '87- 1 (1), '91- 1, '93- 1; WCp: '92- 5, '94- 3. At 60m: WI: '93- 3.
Asian records 100m 1990 and 1992, 200m 1994.
Progression at 100m: 1985- 10.36, 1986- 10.30, 1987- 10.29, 1988- 10.33, 1990- 10.18, 1991- 10.24, 1992- 10.14, 1993- 10.22/10.20w, 1994- 10.17. pbs: 60m 6.51i '93, 200m 20.41 '94, 400m 48.80 '87.

Mohamed SULEIMAN b. 23 Nov 1969 Somalia 1.69m 66kg.
At 1500m (5000m): OG: '88- h, '92- 3; WCh: '91- 9, '93- 4; WJ: '88- 7; AsiG: '86- 3, 90- 1 (1), '94- 1 (4 800m); AsiC: '87- 5, '89- 3, '91- 1 (1); WCp: '92- 1, '94- 3; Asi J: '86- 2 (3 2000mSt), '88- 1.
Asian records: 1500m (7), 1M (4), 3000m 1991-4.
Progression at 1500m: 1986- 3:44.68, 1987- 3:44.51, 1988- 3:41.95, 1989- 3:41.38, 1990- 3:40.57, 1991- 3:34.57, 1992- 3:34.12, 1993- 3:33.29, 1994- 3:32.73. pbs: 800m 1:46.82 '94, 1M 3:51.32 '94, 2000m 5:06.08 '92, 3000m 7:38.20 '93, 5000m 13:25.15 '92, 2000mSt 5:47.25 '88, 3000mSt 8:43.8 '89.
The first ever Olympic medallist from Qatar. He ran the fastest ever 1500m in qualifying, 3:34.77 in Barcelona. All Qatar records from 1500m to 5000m.

ROMANIA

Governing body: Federatia Romana de Atletism, Str. Vasile Conta 16, 70139 Bucuresti. Founded 1912.
National Championships first held in 1921 (men), 1925 (women). **1994 Champions: Men:** 100m/200m: Daniel Cojocaru 10.21/20.75, 400m: Ionics Carabas 47.25, 800m: Ion Bogde 1:47.80, 1500m/5000m: Ovidiu Olteanu 3:40.61/13:58.41, 10000m: Ion Avramescu 13:58.74/29:16.45, Half Mar: Laurentiu Staicu 64:01, Mar: Marian Gigea 2:21:48, 3000mSt: Florin Ionescu 8:40.32, 110mh: George Boroi 13.46, 400mh: Mugur Mateescu 49.76, HJ: Cristian Popescu 2.15, PV: Razvan Enescu 4.60, LJ: Bogdan Tudor 7.86, TJ: Lucian Sfia 16.23, SP: Gheorghe Guset 19.97, DT: Costel Grasu 63.68, HT: Cosmin Sorescu 63.46, JT: Valentin Jula 69.98, Dec: Romeo Hurduc 6901, 20kmW: Gheorghe Frecateanu 1:26:10, 50kmW: Radu Mihalescu 4:20:52. **Women:** 100m/100mh: Erica Niculae 11.71, 13.38, 200m: Liliana Bara 24.44, 400m: Elena Vizitiu 52.99, 800m/1500m: Violeta Beclea 2:00.47/4:10.58, 3000m/10000m: Cristina Misaros 8:50.20/32:38.04, 5000m: Daniela Bran 16:16.9, Half Mar: Elena Fidatov 71:20, Mar: Cristina Pomacu 2:38:04, 2000mSt: Olimpia Pop 6:41.74, 400mh: Ionela Tirlea 56.98, HJ: Adriana Solcanu 1.84, PV: Gabriela Mihalcea 3.82, LJ: Marieta Ilcu 6.42, TJ: Rodica Petrescu 14.47, SP: Mihaela Oana 17.77, DT: Manuela Tirneci 63.90, HT: Mihaela Melinte 63.44, JT: Felicia Tilea 63.38, Hep: Mihaela Gheorghiu 5426, 10000mW: Norica Cîmpeanu 46:31.

George BOROI b. 26 Aug 1964 Berislavesti 1.82m 71kg. Steaua Bucuresti.
At 110mh: OG: '92- qf; WCh: '93- sf; EC: '90- h, '94- 8. At 60mh: WI: '91- 7, '93- 6; EI: '94- 2.
Won ROM 100m 1989, 110mh 1989-90, 1993.
ROM 110mh record 1993.
Progression at 110mh: 1983- 14.67, 1984- 14.50, 1985- 14.57, 1986- 14.03, 1987- 13.94, 1988- 13.74, 1989- 13.67, 1990- 13.73, 1991- 13.61, 1992- 13.53, 1993- 13.34, 1994- 13.46. pbs: 100m 10.54 '93, 200m 21.55 '90, 60mh 7.50i '94.

Costel GRASU b.5 Jul 1967 Fetesti 1.93m 114kg. Mining worker. Dinamo Bucuresti.
At DT: OG: '92- 4; WCh: '91- dnq 21, '93- 4; EC: '94- 8; Won ECp DT C1 '91, B '93; Balkan DT 1992, ROM SP 1989, 1991, DT 1989, 1991-3.
Progression at DT: 1983- 45.76, 1984- 54.52, 1985- 55.22, 1986- 55.54, 1987- 54.86, 1988- 60.82, 1989- 60.72, 1990- 59.46, 1991- 64.18, 1992- 67.08, 1993- 66.90, 1994- 63.68. pb SP 19.42 '89.
Married to Nicoleta (née Gradinaru) (qv).

Sorin MATEI b.6 Jul 1963 Bucuresti 1.84m 71kg. Teacher. Universitatea Craieva.
At HJ: OG: '80- 13, '88- dnq 20=, '92- 13; WCh: '83- 17, '87- 6, '91- dnq 17=; EC: '82- dnq, '86- 14, '94- dnq 20=; WI: '87- 5=, '91- 6=; EI: '88- 3, '92- 2; EJ: '81- 5; WUG: '87- 3. 3rd GP 1988.
Ten Romanian high jump records 1980-90.
Progression at HJ: 1977- 1.88, 1978- 2.03, 1979- 2.12i, 1980- 2.27, 1981- 2.22, 1982- 2.28, 1983- 2.30, 1984- 2.34, 1985- 2.35, 1986- 2.32, 1987- 2.32, 1988- 2.37, 1989- 2.30, 1990- 2.40, 1991- 2.35, 1992- 2.36i/2.30, 1993- 2.35i/2.30, 1994- 2.30?/2.25, 1995- 2.38i.
One of the smallest top-class high jumpers, his 2.40m record in 1990 gives him a differential of 56cm over his own height, equal third best ever.

Women

Adriana BARBU b.17 Jan 1961 1.61m 53kg. née Mustata, then Andreescu.
At Mar: EC: '94- 3. World Half Mar: '93- 9, '94- 9.
Romanian marathon records 1983 and 1994.

Progression at Mar: 1983- 2:45:27, 1984- 2:53:37, 1985- 2:46:21, 1986- 2:40:19, 1987- 2:36:21, 1988- 2:39:45, 1989- 2:37:01, 1992- 2:37:19, 1993- 2:34:38, 1994- 2:29:21. pbs: 3000m 9:30.25 '82, 10000m 33:21.06 '89, Half Mar 70:38 '94.
Won Marrakech marathon 1994.

Violeta BECLEA b.26 Mar 1965 Dolhesti Mari 1.66m 50kg. Technician. Rapid Bucuresti.
At 800m: WI: '89- 4, '91- 2; EI: '90- 3. At 1500m: OG: '92- sf; WCh: '91- 10, '93- 9; EC: '94- h; WI: '93- 2; ECp: '93- 2. Won ROM 800m 1993, 1500m 1990-1, 1993. 3rd GP 1M 1993.
Progression at 800m, 1500m: 1982- 2:05.07, 4:23.85, 1983- 2:03.63, 1985- 2:00.75, 4:11.01; 1986- 1:58.7, 4:04.56; 1987- 1:59.53, 4:07.56; 1988- 1:59.35, 4:07.94; 1989- 1:58.94, 4:07.24; 1990- 2:01.05, 4:03.14; 1991- 2:00.19, 4:02.21; 1992- 4:03.29; 1993- 1:59.13, 3:59.35; 1994- 1:59.30i/ 2:00.47, 4:03.76. pbs: 1000m 2:34.89i '95, 2:36.74 '89; 1M 4:21.69 '93, 3000m 8:57.00 '91.

Anuta CATUNA b.1 Oct 1968 1.52m 48kg.
At Mar: EC: '94- 5. World Half Mar: '92- 4, '93- 6, '94- 3. Won ROM 10000m 1992, Half Mar 1993.
Progression at 10,000m, Mar: 1985- 34:57.34, 1986- 34:07.13, 1987- 34:26.68, 2:52:51; 1988- 33:11.58, 3:04:23; 1989- 33:48.24, 1990- 34:05.2, 1991- 32:36.54, 1992- 32:32.66, 1993- 32:18.40, 1994- 2:29:39. pbs: 1500m 4:12.86u '93, 3000m 9:07.08 '90, Half Mar 69:35 '94.
4th New York Marathon 1994.

Mirela DULGHERU b.5 Oct 1966 Ploiesti 1.70m 65kg. Teacher. Prahova Ploiesti
At 1500m: OG: '92- 4; WCh: '93- 11; WUG: '93- 1; WI: '91- 9, '93- 8; EI: '90- 4. Balkan champion 1989, 1992, Romanian 1992.
Progression at LJ: 1984- 6.34, 1985- 6.31, 1986- 6.60, 1987- 6.74, 1988- 6.51, 1989- 6.76i/6.67, 1990- 6.84, 1991- 6.88i/6.61, 1992- 7.14, 1993- 6.99i/6.77/6.83w, 1994- 6.69i/6.62. pbs: 60m 7.21i '92, 100m 11.39 '89.

Elena FIDATOV b.24 Jul 1960 Tulcea 1.68m 52kg. Coach. CSU Bacau.
At 1500m: OG: '92- 11; WCh: '91- 14, '93- h (h 3000m); EC: '90- 5. World Half Mar: '94- 5. Eur CC: '94- 3. Won Balkan 1500m 1992, ROM 1500m 1988, 3000m 1986-7, 1990.
Progression at 1500m, 3000m: 1978- 9:42.4, 1980- 9:31.2, 1981- 4:18.97, 9:28.10; 1982- 9:29.29, 1984- 4:11.6, 8:54.32; 1985- 4:10.05, 8:47.60; 1986- 4:03.92, 8:50.26; 1987- 4:05.88, 8:42.16; 1988- 4:07.72, 8:50.24; 1989- 4:10.26, 8:59.43; 1990- 4:05.8, 9:02.62; 1991- 4:06.99, 9:09.88; 1992- 4:04.55, 8:50.25; 1993- 4:05.61, 8:44.93. pbs: 1M 4:31.69 '91, 5000m 15:41.83 '86, 10000m 33:49.99 '85, Half Mar 70:13 '94.

Nicoleta GRASU b.11 Sep 1971 Secuieni 1.76m 88kg. Administration officer. Dinamo Bucuresti.
At DT: OG: '92- dnq 13; WCh: '93- 7; EC: '94- 4; WJ: '90- 6. Won Balkan 1992, ROM 1993.
Progression at DT: 1987- 50.82, 1988- 51.06, 1989- 52.54, 1990- 56.02, 1991- 59.90, 1992- 65.66, 1993- 65.16, 1994- 63.78/64.40?. pb SP 15.00 '92.
Married to Costel Grasu (qv).

Marieta ILCU b.16 Oct 1962 Darabani, Botosani 1.72m 64kg. Student. Metalul Hunedoara.
At LJ: OG: '92- dnq 16; WCh: '87- dnq 14, '91- 6; EC: '90- 2; WI: '89- 2, '91- 3, '93- 1; EI: '92- 2; WUG: '85- 3, '87- 1, '89- 2; WCp: '89- 2; ECp: '89- 4, '93- 6. 2nd GP 1989, 3rd 1990. Won ROM LJ 1985, 1990-1, 1993; 100m 1988-90.
Progression at LJ: 1979- 6.09, 1980- 6.34, 1981- 6.32, 1982- 6.34, 1983- 6.30, 1984- 6.69, 1985- 6.87, 1986- 6.80, 1987- 6.93, 1988- 6.98, 1989- 7.08, 1990- 7.06, 1991- 6.77/6.89i, 1992- 6.98, 1993- 6.94i/6.50, 1994- 6.60i/6.42. pbs: 60m 7.1i '91, 100m 11.36/11.3 '88, 200m 23.40 '88.

Claudia ISAILA b.17 Jul 1973 Sibiu 1.67m 62kg. CSS Soimii Sibiu.
At JT: WCh: '93- 7; EC: '94- 11; WJ: '90- 5, '92- 1; EJ: '91- 5. 3rd GP 1994.
Progression at JT: 1989- 53.12, 1990- 55.74. 1991- 56.10, 1992- 63.04, 1993- 61.54, 1994- 66.56.

Margareta KESZEG b.31 Aug 1965 Medias 1.65m 51kg. Married name Elena. Universitatea Craieva.
At 3000m: OG: '92- 11; WCh: '91- 5; EC: '90- 5; WI: '89- 3; WI: '91- 2, '93- 2; EI: '90- 2, '92- 1, '94- 2; WCp: '92- 3; ECp: '91- 1, '93- 1. World CC: '94- 11. Won ROM 3000m 1989, 1992. At 1500m: EJ: '83- 1; WI: '85- 5; WUG: '85- 2. 3rd 1500m GP 1990, 2nd 3000m 1991.
Progression at 3000m: 1985- 8:46.44, 1986- 8:51.54, 1987- 8:52.81, 1988- 8:51.96, 1989- 8:44.33, 1990- 8:47.81, 1991- 8:42.02, 1992- 8:39.94, 1993- 8:45.86, 1994- 8:55.61i. pbs: 800m 2:03.37 '83, 1500m 4:04.49 '86, 1M 4:24.02 '91.

Ella KOVACS b.11 Dec 1964 Ludus, Mures 1.70m 55kg. Student. Steaua Bucuresti.
At 800m: OG: '92- 6; WCh: '91- 3, '93- 3; EC: '90- 5; WI: '91- 3, '93- 5; EI: '85- 1, '92- 1, '94- 2; WCp: '92- 4; ECp: '91- 1, '93- 1. Won Balkan 1989, ROM 1991-2.
Progression at 800m: 1982- 2:04.55, 1984- 1:58.42, 1985- 1:55.68, 1986- 1:59.91, 1987- 1:56.76, 1988- 1:58.10, 1989- 1:58.60, 1990- 1:58.33, 1991- 1:57.58, 1992- 1:57.19, 1993- 1:56.58, 1994- 1:59.43i/2:00.52dq. pbs: 400m 53.22 '90, 1000m 2:32.40 '93, 1500m 4:06.38 '84.
3-month drugs ban for ephedrine June 1994.

Mihaela MELINTE b.27 Mar 1975 1.70m 78kg.
At HT: ROM champion 1993-4.
Three Romanian and world junior hammer records 1992-4.
Progression at HT: 1992- 58.70, 1993- 62.52, 1994- 65.48.

Liliana NASTASE b.1 Aug 1962 Vinju Mare, Mehedinti 1.69m 67kg. née Alexandru. Teacher. Steaua Bucuresti.
At Hep: OG: '92- 4 (qf 100mh); WCh: '87- 5, '91- 2; EC: '90- dnf; WUG: '85- 2, '87- 1; ECp: '91- 1B. At Pen: WI inv: '93- 1; EI: '92- 1. At 100m: ECp: '89- 8. Won Balkan Hep 1985, 100mh 1983; ROM 100mh 1984, 1991-2; Hep 1984-8, 1991.
Eight Romanian heptathlon records 1984-9. WIB pentathlon 4705u '90, 4655 '91, 4726 '92.
Progression at Hep: 1980- 4652*, 1982- 5378*, 1983- 5753, 1984- 6086, 1985- 6313, 1986- 6172, 1987- 6364, 1988- 6352. 1989- 6602, 1990- 6435, 1991- 6493, 1992- 6619, 1993- 6260, 1994- 6093. pbs: 100m 11.85 '89, 200m 23.35 '92, 800m 2:07.6 '91, 60mh 8.08i '91, 100mh 12.81 '91, 12.8w '84, 400mh 59.41 '83, HJ 1.82 '92, LJ 6.78 '89, SP 14.44i/14.36 '92, JT 47.72 '89, Hep: 4737i '93.

Iulia NEGURA b.26 Jan 1967 Vacu 1.65m 57kg. PE student. CSU Bacau.
At 10000m: WCh: '91- 17, '93- 16; EC: '94- 13; WUG: '93- 1; ECp: '91- 3, '93- 3. World road 15km: 90- 1, '91- 1, Half Mar: '92- 10, '93- 7, '94- 2. World CC: '90- 12. Won ROM 10000m 1990-1.
Progression at 10000m: 1987- 34:43.10, 1988- 33:25.2, 1989- 32:58.04, 1990- 33:14.74, 1991- 31:52.58, 1993- 32:11.58, 1994- 32:26.58. pbs: 1500m 4:13.25 '89, 3000m 8:53.19 '91, 5000m 15:34.30 '89. Road 15km 48:42 '91, Half Mar 69:15 '94.
Retained her World 15km road title in 1991, 1:30 faster than she ran in 1990 and improved each year at half marathon to second 1994.

Gabriela SZABO b. 14 Nov 1975 1.60m 42kg.
At 3000m: EC: '94- 3; WJ: '92- 2, '94- 1; EJ: '91- 1, '93-1; WCp: '94- 3. World CC: '94- 4J.
Progression at 3000m: 1991- 9:19.28, 1992- 8:48.28, 1993- 8:50.97, 1994- 8:40.08. pb 1500m 4:10.32 '93.

Felicea TILEA b.29 Sep 1967 Nagura Ilvei 1.67m 74kg. CSM Zalau.
At JT: WCh: '93- 8; EC: '90- dq (9), '94- 3; ECp: '93- 1. ROM champion 1990.
Progression at JT: 1986- 51.42, 1987- 51.44, 1989- 59.54, 1990- 64.02, 1993- 65.62, 1994- 66.40.
Two-year drugs ban after positive test for steroids when 9th at 1990 European Champs.

RUSSIA

Governing body: All-Russia Athletic Federation, Luzhnetskaya Naberezhnaya 8, Moscow 119871. Founded 1911.
National Championships First held in 1911, USSR women's from 1922. **1994 Champions**: **Men**: 100m: Aleksandr Porkhomovskiy 10.17, 200m: Andrey Fedoriv 20.56, 400m: Dmitriy Kosov 45.55, 800m: Andrey Loginov 1:51.10, 1500m: Vyacheslav Shabunin 3:41.55, 5000m: Andrey Tikhonov 13:41.68, 10000m: Sergey Fedotov 28:50.73, Mar: Anatoliy Archakov 2:14:08, 3000mSt: Vladimir Pronin 8:42.68, 110mh: Dmitriy Buldov 13.49w, 400mh: Sergey Vodryekh 49.90, HJ: Leonid Pumalainen 2.28, PV: Igor Trandenkov 5.85, LJ: Dmitriy Bagryanov 8.21, TJ: Vasiliy Sokov 17.42, SP: Sergey Nikolayev 20.14, DT: Sergey Lyakhov 61.58, HT: Igor Nikulin 78.94, JT: Yuriy Rybin 82.96, Dec: Valeriy Belousov 7992, 20kmW: Vladimir Andreyev 1:21:53, 50kmW: German Skurygin 3:48:10. **Women**: 100m: Natalya Voronova 11.20, 200m: Galina Malchugina 22.29, 400m: Yelena Andreyeva 51.61, 800m: Irina Samorukova 1:59.23, 1500m: Lyudmila Rogachova 4:02.40, 3000m: Olga Churbanova 8:51.61, 5000m: Klara Kashapova 15:27.55, 10000m: Tatyana Pentukova 32:19.96, Mar: Larisa Zyusko 2:39:31, 2000mSt: Marina Pluzhnikova 6:21.71, 100mh: Marina Azyabina 12.69, 400mh: Anna Knoroz 54,67, HJ: Yelena Topchina 1.97, PV: Svetlana Abramova 3.80, LJ: Irina Mushailova 7.20, TJ: Inna Lasovskaya 14.74, SP: Irina Khudorozhkina 19.81, DT: Olga Chernyavskaya 63.20, HT: Olga Kuzenkova 64.40, JT: Lada Chernova 58.16, Hep: Svetlana Moskalets 6598, 10kmW: Yelena Arshintseva 43:01.

Note: Clubs are shown in the biographies after height and weight. Based on the major cities, they have affiliations, abbreviated as follows: Dyn - Dynamo, Sp - Spartak, VS - Army.

Dmitriy BAGRYANOV b.18 Dec 1967 Moskva 1.88m 81kg. MoskvaSp. Serviceman.
At LJ: OG: '92- 7; WCh: '91- dnq; EC: '94- 5; WI: '91- 7; EI: '92- 1. Won USSR LJ 1991, CIS 1992, RUS 1994.
Progression at LJ: 1990- 7.61, 1991- 8.20, 1992- 8.35, 1993- 8.07, 1994- 8.23i/8.21. pb 400mh 50.19 '89.
Switched from 400m hurdles to long jump.

Pyotr BOCHKARYOV b.3 Nov 1967 Moskva 1.86m 82kg. Moskva Sp. Student.
At PV: WUG: '91- 3; EI: '92- 1, '94- 1.
Progression at PV: 1982- 3.80, 1983- 4.50, 1984-

5.00, 1985- 5.20, 1986- 5.30, 1987- 5.30i, 1988- 5.60, 1989- 5.50, 1990- 5.70, 1991- 5.75, 1992- 5.85, 1993- 5.80, 1994- 5.90i/5.70.
His mother Irina Turova won European gold at 100m and 4x100m and was 2nd at 200m in 1954, with bests of 100m 11.6 (1954) and 200m 24.2 (1956) and the USSR 100m title 1954. His grandmother Galina Turova was USSR champion at 80mh 1934, LJ 1934, 1943 and 1945 and DT 1934 and 1937.

Radion GATAULLIN b.23 Nov 1965 Tashkent. St Petersburg VS. Doctor.
At PV: OG: '88- 2; WCh: '87- 3, '91- 4; WI: '89- 1, '93- 1; EC: '86- nh, '90- 1, '94- 1; EI: '88- 1, '90- 1; EJ: '83- 1; WUG: '85- 1, '87- 2; ECp: '89- 1, '93- 1, '94- nh. USSR champion 1985, 1989, 1991. Won GWG 1990, GP 1989.
World junior pole vault record 1984. WIB 6.00 and 6.02 '89, Russian records 1992 and 1993.
Progression at PV: 1977- 2.80, 1978 - 3.10, 1979- 3.80, 1980- 4.20, 1981- 4.80, 1982- 5.20, 1983- 5.55, 1984- 5.65, 1985- 5.75, 1986- 5.85, 1987- 5.90, 1988- 5.95, 1989- 6.02i/6.00, 1990- 5.92, 1991- 5.90, 1992- 5.95, 1993- 6.00, 1994- 6.00. pbs: 110mh 14.4, LJ 7.27 '90.
The world's second six-metre vaulter, a height he matched in retaining his European title in 1994, and thus equalling the world best in a championship. Moved from Tashkent (UZB) to St Petersburg in order to compete for Russia. Married to Tatyana Reshetnikova (qv).

Denis KAPUSTIN b.5 Oct 1970 Kazan 1.89m 86kg. Kazan Sp. Student.
At TJ: WCh: '93- 6; EC: '94- 1; EI: '94- 2; EJ: '89- 1; WUG: '91- 4; ECp: '94- 1.
Progression at TJ: 1989- 16.37/16.63w, 1990- 16.68, 1991- 17.34, 1992- 17.48, 1993- 17.54, 1994- 17.62/17.86w. pb LJ: 7.68i '91.

Sergey LYAKHOV b.1 May 1968 1.95m 105kg. Moskva Dyn.
At DT: WCh: '91- 9; EC: '94- 9. USSR champion 1990, RUS 1994.
Progression at DT: 1985- 46.94, 1986- 52.54, 1987- 60.06, 1988- 62.64, 1989- 63.64, 1990- 64.36, 1991- 63.88, 1992- 66.64, 1993- 66.12, 1994- 65.64.

Vyacheslav LYKHO b.16 Jan 1967 1.96m 120kg. Moskva Dyn.
At SP: OG: '92- 3; WCh: '87- 9; EC: '90- 3 dq; WJ: '86- 2. USSR champion 1990.
Progression at SP: 1985- 16.40i/15.83, 1986- 19.53i/19.34, 1987- 21.20, 1988- 20.96, 1989- 20.88, 1990- 21.16i/21.00, 1991- 20.77, 1992- 20.94, 1993- 20.31i, 1994- 19.60i. pb DT 53.54 '86.
Lost 1990 European bronze when test for stimulants proved positive; three month ban.

Gennadiy MARKOV b.15 Jun 1967 Stavropol 1.82m 75kg. Stavropol VS. Teacher.
At TJ: EC: '94- 5.
Progression at TJ: 1989- 16.55, 1990- 16.66, 1991- 16.57, 1992- 16.71, 1993- 17.06, 1994- 17.38

Vladimir MELIKHOV b.30 Mar 1969 Volgograd 1.86m 76kg. Volgograd VS.
At TJ: WJ: '88-1; WI: '93- 4.
Progression at TJ: 1988- 16.76, 1989- 16.56, 1990- 17.03, 1991- 17.13, 1993- 17.28, 1994- 17.21/17.49w.

Andrey MORUYEV b.6 May 1970 Petrozavodsk 1.85m 90kg. Moskva VS. Soldier.
At JT: EC: '94- 9; ECp: '94- 1.
Two Russian javelin records 1993-4.
Progression at JT: 1990- 77.62, 1991- 80.50, 1992- 79.60, 1993- 86.20, 1994- 87.34.

Sergey NIKOLAYEV b.12 Nov 1966 Fedykovo, Pskov region 1.89m 122kg. St Petersburg Sp.
At SP: WCh: '91- 5; EC: '90- 7, '94- dnq; WCp: '92- 2; ECp: '94- 5. Russian champion 1994.
European junior LJ record 1987.
Progression at SP: 1985- 17.12, 1987- 19.21, 1988- 19.97, 1989- 21.35, 1990- 20.41, 1991- 20.40i/20.34, 1992- 20.93, 1993- 19.74/20.44i, 1994- 20.24.

Igor NIKULIN b.14 Aug 1960 Moscow 1.91m 106kg. St Petersburg VS. Teacher.
At HT: OG: '92- 3; WCh: '83- 4, '87- 5; EC: '82- 2, '86- 3, '90- 3, '94- 4; EJ: '79- 1; WUG: '81- 3, '85- 3; WCp: '92- 1. USSR champion 1981 and 1984, RUS 1994. 3rd GP 1988, 2nd 1992.
Progression at HT: 1975- 48.50, 1976- 58.14, 1977- 63.40, 1978- 71.60, 1979- 75.20, 1980- 80.34, 1981- 77.50, 1982- 83.54, 1983- 82.92, 1984- 82.56, 1985- 78.88, 1986- 82.34, 1987- 82.00, 1988- 83.78, 1989- 78.40, 1990- 84.48, 1991- 80.62, 1992- 83.44, 1993- 78.98, 1994- 79.20.
One of the world's most consistent throwers since he became the youngest ever 80m hammer thrower in 1980. His father Yuriy was fourth in the 1964 Olympic hammer.

Mikhail ORLOV b.25 Jun 1967 Yaroslavl 1.68m 68kg. Yaroslav VS. Soldier.
At 20kmW: EC: '94-5. At 5000mW: WI: '93- 3. At 10000mW: WJ: '86- 10; EJ: '85- 6.
Progression at 20kmW: 1989- 1:22:09, 1990- 1:20:07, 1991- 1:21:51, 1993- 1:23:01, 1994- 1:21:01. pbs: 5000mW 18:32.32i '92, 18:43.48 '93.

Yevgeniy PALCHIKOV b.12 Oct 1968 Irkutsk 1.98m 118kg. Irkutsk VS. Student.
At SP: WCh: '93- 4; EJ: '87- 2; ECp: '93- 3. Russian champion 1993.
Progression at SP: 1986- 16.40, 1987- 18.63, 1988-

19.09, 1989- 19.56, 1990- 18.57i, 1991- 19.64, 1992- 19.75, 1993- 20.86, 1994- 20.94.

Denis PETUSHINSKY b.28 Jun 1967 Irkutsk 1.88m 81kg. Moskva Sp. Student.
At PV: WCh: '93- 6; EC: '94- 5; EI: '94- 4. RUS champion 1993.
Progression at PV: 1985- 5.10, 1986- 5.40, 1987- 5.50, 1988- 5.65, 1989- 5.65i/5.60, 1990- 5.71, 1991- 5.72, 1992- 5.72i/5.70, 1993- 5.90, 1994- 5.86.

Aleksandr PORKHOMOVSKIY b.12 Aug 1972 Moskva 1.74m 68kg. Moskva FSO. Jeweller.
At 100m/4x100mR: WCh: '93- sf; EC: '94- 3; WCp: '94- 4; ECp: '93- 2/3R; EJ: '91- 6/1R. At 60m: EI: '94- 4. Won RUS 100m 1992-4.
Russian 100m record 1994.
Progression at 100m: 1989- 10.82, 1990- 10.81, 1991- 10.52, 1992- 10.43, 1993- 10.16, 1994- 10.12. pbs: 50m 5.64i '94, 60m 6.59i '94, 200m 20.35 '94.

Yuriy SEDYKH b.11 Jun 1955 Novocherkassk 1.85m 110kg. Moskva VS. Graduate of the Kiev Institute of Physical Culture.
At HT: OG: '76- 1, '80- 1, '88- 2; WCh: '83- 2, '91- 1; EC: '78- 1, '82- 1, '86- 1; EJ: '73- 1; WUG: '75- 3, '77- 2, '79- 3; WCp: '77- 4, '81- 1; ECp: '77- 3, '81- 1. USSR champion 1976, 1978, 1980. Won GWG 1986. GP 1986 & 1990 (3rd 1992).
World junior records 1973 and 1974, and eight Soviet records, including six world records: 80.38, 80.64 and 81.80 in 1980, 86.34 in 1984, 86.66 and 86.74 in 1986.
Progression at HT: 1971- 57.02, 1972- 62.96, 1973- 69.04, 1974- 70.86, 1975- 75.00, 1976- 78.86, 1977- 76.60, 1978- 79.76, 1979- 77.58, 1980- 81.80, 1981- 80.18, 1982- 81.66, 1983- 80.94, 1984- 86.34, 1985- 82.70, 1986- 86.74, 1987- 80.34, 1988- 85.14, 1989- 81.92, 1990- 82.80, 1991- 82.62, 1992- 82.18, 1993- 76.92, 1994- 80.14. pb 35lb Wt 23.46 '79 (three WIB).
The greatest ever hammer thrower reached his peak at the 1986 Europeans when he responded to Litvinov's opening 85.74 with five throws averaging 86.16 including his 6th world record. In 1991 he became, at 36, the oldest ever world champion.

Aleksandr SELEZNYOV b.25 Jan 1963 Smolensk 1.82m 100kg. Smolensk VS. Teacher.
At HT: WCh: '93- 6; WUG: '91-4; EJ: '83- 2.
Progression at DT: 1981- 64.70, 1982- 68.08, 1983- 74.28, 1984- 75.80, 1985- 76.96, 1986- 75.90, 1987- 76.50, 1988- 78.80, 1989- 79.02, 1990- 80.50, 1991- 80.62, 1992- 77.58, 1993- 81.70, 1994- 80.96.

Mikhail SHCHENNIKOV b.24 Dec 1967 Sverdlovsk 1.82m 70kg. Moskva VS. Serviceman.
At 20kmW: OG: '88- 6, '92- 12; WCh: '91- 2, '93- dq; EC: '90- dnf, '94- 1; WCp: '89- 2, '91- 1, '93- 5. USSR champion 1988. At 10000mW: WJ: '85- 1; EJ: '86- 1. At 5000mW: WI: 1st '87, '89, '91, '93; EI: 1st '89-90, '94.
World road best 20km walk 1988. At 5000mW WJR 19:19.3 '86, WIR 18:27.79 '87, 18:27.10 '89, 18:23.55 '91 (all when winning WI titles).
Progression at 20kmW: 1986- 1:33:56, 1987- 1:23:08, 1988- 1:19:08, 1989- 1:20:34, 1990- 1:19:07, 1991- 1:19:46, 1992- 1:19:53, 1993- 1:18:33, 1994- 1:18:45. pbs: 3000mW 11:05.14i '87, 5000mW 18:15.91i '89, 18:52.01 '91; 10000mW 39:27.59 '88.
Won a record four World Indoor titles. Disqualified outside stadium at finish of 20km walk in 1993 World Champs when in third place.

Dmitriy SHEVCHENKO b.13 May 1968 Taganrog, Rostov-na-Donu 2.00m 120kg. Krasnodar Dyn. Serviceman.
At DT: OG: '92- 8; WCh: '91- 7, '93- 2; EC: '94- 2; ECp '93- 2, '94- 1. USSR champion 1991, CIS 1992, Russian 1992-3, GWG 1994.
Progression at DT: 1986- 57.30, 1987- 60.34, 1988- 59.68, 1989- 59.38/61.62?, 1990- 64.10, 1991- 63.70, 1992- 67.30, 1993- 66.90, 1994- 64.74.

Vasiliy SIDORENKO b.1 May 1961 Volgograd 1.87m 106kg. Volgograd Dyn. Welder
At HT: WCh: '93- 5; EC: '94- 1; WCp: '94- 4; ECp: '94- 1. 3rd GP 1994. Russian champion 1992.
Progression at HT: 1979- 59.98, 1980- 68.78, 1981- 69.30, 1983- 74.10, 1984- 76.80, 1985- 80.40, 1986- 80.70, 1987- 80.02, 1988- 80.52, 1989- 82.30, 1990- 80.98, 1991- 79.76, 1992- 82.54, 1993- 80.04, 1994- 82.02.

German SKURYGIN b.23 Dec 1963 Vutno Udmurtiya 1.64m 61kg. Izhevsk TU. Teacher.
At 50kW: EC: '94- 6. RUS champion 1994.
Progression at 50kmW: 1989- 3:50:25, 1990- 3:51:04, 1991- 3:53:33, 1992- 3:59:42, 1993- 3:56:19, 1994- 3:46:30. pb 20kmW 1:22:12 '88.

Sergey SMIRNOV b.17 Sep 1960 Leningrad 1.92m 126kg. St Petersburg VS. Engineer.
At SP: OG: '88- 8; WCh: '83- dnq; EC: '86- dnc, '90- 4; WI: '87- 3, '93- 7; EI: '86- 2, '87- 3; WUG: '83- 3; WCp: '85- 2; ECp: '85- 1, '87- 5, '91- 2. Won GWG 1986. USSR champion 1985-7.
Two USSR shot records 1985-6.
Progression at SP: 1980- 16.31, 1981- 18.86, 1982- 20.42, 1983- 21.00, 1984- 21.63, 1985- 22.05, 1986- 22.24, 1987- 21.74, 1988- 21.88, 1989- 20.80, 1990- 21.34i/21.01, 1991- 20.55i/20.33, 1992- 21.01i/20.87, 1993- 20.94i/19.66, 1994- 20.01.

Vasiliy SOKOV b.7 Apr 1968 Dushanbe 1.86m 73kg. Moskva VS. Serviceman.

At TJ: OG: '92- 9; WCh: '91- 4, '93- dnq 15 (dnq LJ); EC: '94- 4; EI: '92- 3, '94- 3; ECp: '93- 4. 3rd GP 1994. At LJ: EJ: '87- 9. Won RUS TJ 1993-4.
Progression at LJ, TJ: 1985- 15.75, 1986- 7.34, 16.35; 1987- 7.77, 16.61; 1988- 8.18; 1989- 8.06, 17.37/17.73w; 1990- 17.47; 1991- 7,87, 17.52; 1992- 7.67, 17.30i/17.06; 1993- 8.00i, 17.59; 1994- 17.43.
Concentrated on triple jumping rather than long jumping with immediate success in 1989.

Valeriy SPITSYN b.5 Dec 1965 Magnitogorsk 1.78m 67kg. Magnitogorsk Sp.
At 50kmW: OG: '92- 4; WCh: '93- 3; EC: '94- 1; WCp: '91- 8. CIS champion 1992, RUS 1988.
Progression at 50kmW: 1988- 4:06:02, 1989- 3:48:38, 1990- 3:54:26, 1991- 3:50:18, 1992- 3:54:39/ 3:33:32 short, 1993- 3:42:50, 1994- 3:41:07. pbs: 20kmW 1:22:15 '91, 30kmW 2:04:24 '92.

Stanislav TARASENKO b.23 Jul 1966 Zhukovka, Rostov/Don region 1.88m 82kg. Taganrog VS. Soldier.
At LJ: WCh: '93- 2; EC: '94- 6; ECp: '93- 3, '94- 1. Russian champion 1991-3.
Russian indoor long jump record 1994.
Progression at LJ: 1989- 7.96, 1990- 7.94, 1991- 8.01, 1992- 8.08, 1993- 8.23/8.28w, 1994- 8.43i/ 8.25/8.31w.

Maksim TARASOV b.2 Dec 1970 Yaroslavl 1.94m 80kg. Yaroslavl Sp. Soldier.
At PV: OG: '92- 1; WCh: '91- 3, '93- 3=; WJ: '88- 2; EJ: '89- 1. Won CIS PV 1992. 3rd GP 1993.
Three world junior records 1989.
Progression at PV: 1982- 2.90, 1983- 3.30, 1984- 3.80, 1985- 4.50, 1986- 5.00, 1987- 5.40, 1988- 5.60, 1989- 5.80, 1990- 5.85, 1991- 5.85/5.90ex, 1992- 5.90, 1993- 5.90, 1994- 5.90. pbs: 100m 10.8 '89, HJ 1.95, LJ 7.40.
All world age bests from 16 to 19, 1987-90.

Igor TRANDENKOV b.17 Aug 1966 Leningrad 1.91m 80kg. St Petersburg Dyn. Teacher.
At PV: OG: '92- 2; WCh: '93- 3=; EC: '94- 2; WI: '93- 4; EI: '94- 3; EJ: '85- 1. Russian champion 1994, won GWG 1994.
Progression at PV: 1979- 2.80, 1980- 3.30, 1981- 3.60, 1982- 3.90, 1983- 5.10, 1984- 5.30, 1985- 5.45, 1986- 5.50i/5.40, 1987- 5.60, 1988- 5.60, 1989- 5.70, 1990- 5.75, 1991- 5.60, 1992- 5.90, 1993- 5.90i/5.80, 1994- 5.90.
Married to Marina Trandenkova (b. 7 Jan 1967) OG 92: qf 200m/2R; ECp '93 1R; pbs: 100m 11.08 '92, 200m 22.50 '92.

Leonid VOLOSHIN b.30 Mar 1966 Ordzhonikidze 1.80m 72kg. Krasnodar Dyn. Serviceman.
At TJ: OG: '92- 4; WCh: '91- 2, '93- 2; EC: '90- 1; WI: '91- 2; EI: '92- 1, '94- 1. At LJ: OG: '88- 8; EJ: '85- 4. Won USSR LJ 1988, TJ 1991. 2nd GP 1992.
WIR triple jump 1994.
Progression at LJ, TJ: 1982- 6.92; 1983- 7.22, 14.90; 1984- 7.59i, 15.72i; 1985- 7.79; 1986- 8.06; 1987- 8.09; 1988- 8.46, 15.72; 1989- 8.15, 16.68; 1990- 8.09, 17.74; 1991- 7.93/7.94i/8.09w, 17.75; 1992- 17.53i/17.36/17.64w, 1993- 7.85, 17.65; 1994- 7.82i, 17.77i.
Made a spectacular conversion from long jump to triple jump in 1990, when he jumped 17.40 in Bryansk, followed by two pbs in Split and a further win at the Grand Prix final. Improved his pb again when second in Tokyo 1991.

Women

Tatyana ALEKSEYEVA b.7 Oct 1963 Novosibirsk 1.70m 60kg. Novosibirsk Dyn. Teacher.
At 400m/4x400mR: WCh: '91- gold ran ht, '93- 4/2R; WI: '93- 2; EI: '94- 2; WUG: '85- 1/1R; ECp: '93- 1R.
Progression at 400m: 1982- 52.81, 1983- 52.6, 1984- 51.39, 1985- 51.39, 1987- 52.72, 1988- 52.08, 1989- 50.74, 1990- 51.50, 1991- 50.83, 1992- 51.04, 1993- 50.49. pbs: 100m 11.16 '84, 200m 22.77 '84, 22.71w '91, 300m 36.10+ '93.

Yelena ARSHINTSEVA b.5 Apr 1971 Saransk 1.64m 54kg. Saransk Sp. Student
At 10kmW: WCh: '93- 12; EC: '94- 4. At 3000mW: WI: '93- 5; EI: '94- 3. Won RUS 10kmW 1993-4.
Progression at 10kmW: 1990- 47:59, 1991- 43:52, 1992- 42:52, 1993- 42:03, 1994- 43:01. pbs: 3000mW 11:57.48i '94, 5000mW 21:18.39 '92.

Marina AZYABINA b.15 Jun 1963 Izhevsk 1.74m 62kg. Izhevsk Sp. Biologist.
At 100mh: OG: '92- sf; WCh: '93- 2; EC: '94- sf; WUG: '91- 1; ECp: '93- 1. CIS Champion 1992, Russian 1993.
Progression at 100mh: 1983- 13.6, 1984- 13.5, 1985- 13.4, 1987- 13.34/13.1, 1988- 13.00, 1989- 12.98, 1990- 12.86, 1991- 12.89, 1992- 12.76, 1993- 12.47, 1994- 12.94/12.74w. pbs: 100m 11.78 '93, 60mh 8.02i '93.

Anna BIRYUKOVA b. 27 Sep 1967 Sverdlovsk 1.74m 58kg. née Derevyankina. Moskva VS. Teacher.
At TJ: WCh: '93- 1; EC: '94- 1; EI: '94- 2; WCp: '94- 1. Won GWG 1994.
World triple jump record 1993.
Progression at LJ, TJ: 1983- 6.20; 1984- 6.47, 1985- 6.22, 1986- 6.38, 1988- 6.55, 1989- 6.86i/6.87, 13.30i; 1990- 6.89, 1991- 6.54i, 1993- 6.73, 15.09; 1994- 6.69i/6.64, 14.89.

Yolanda Chen: triple jump gold and record

3rd 1989 and 2nd 1990 in USSR long jump. She retired in 1991 though injury, but after her son Aleksandr was born in March 1992 she returned to competition in 1993, and at the triple jump made rapid progress to 14.74w in Bratislava on 1 June and a world record to win the first world title at the event in August.

Tatyana BLOKHINA b. 12 Mar 1970 Kuybyshev 1.86m 70kg. St Petersburg Sp.
At Hep: WCh: '93- dnf; EJ: '87- 4, '89- 1. Russian champion 1993.
Progression at Hep: 1987- 5833, 1988- 5864, 1989- 6032, 1991- 5990, 1992- 6484, 1993- 6703. pbs: 200m 23.71 '92, 800m 2:09.27 '92, 60mh 8.36i '93, 100mh 13.40 '93, HJ: 1.95 '92, LJ 6.21w '93, 5.99 '93; SP 14.94 '93, JT 52.16 '93, Pen 4669i '93.
Won Talence heptathlon 1993.

Lyudmila BORISOVA b.3 Aug 1966 Leningrad 1.72m 57kg. St Petersburg Sp. Student.
At 3000m: WCh: '91- 13, '93- 8; EC: '94- 5; WI: '89- 6; WUG: '91- 4; ECp: '94- 1. USSR champion 1991. 2nd GP 5000m 1994.
Progression at 1500m, 3000m: 1986- 4:14.88, 9:12.0; 1987- 4:09.42, 9:05.91; 1988- 4:06.94, 1989- 4:13.65, 9:04.75i/9:08.31; 1990- 4:04.56, 9:04.39; 1991- 4:08.75, 8:51.49; 1992- 4:03.66, 8:49.87; 1993- 8:40.78; 1994- 4:05.66, 8:41.71. pbs: 800m: 2:01.30 '88, 1M 4:36.38i '94, 200m 5:46.59 '94, 5000m 15:13.27 '94.

Yolanda CHEN b.26 Jul 61 Moskva 1.69m 55kg. Moskva Sp.
At LJ: EC: '90- 5; WUG: '89- 1; EI: '89- 2. At TJ: WCh: '93- 2; EC: '94- 4; WI: '93- 2; ECp: '93- 1. Won RUS TJ 1993, GP TJ 1993.
World triple jump record and WIR 14.46 1993.
Progression at LJ, TJ: 1974- 4.97, 1975- 5.30, 1976- 5.55, 1977- 5.74, 1978- 6.16, 1979- 6.14, 1980- 6.44, 1981- 6.60, 1982- 6.75, 1983- 6.77, 1984- 6.83, 1985- 6.51i, 1986- 6.80, 1987- 6.50, 1988- 7.16, 1989- 7.05i/6.74/6.87w, 1990- 7.03i/ 6.97/7.11w, 1991- 6.82i/6.67, 12.82; 1992- 6.68, 13.72; 1993- 6.90i/ 6.65, 14.97; 1994- 6.61, 14.58. pbs: 100m 11.8, HJ 1.71.
Father, Yevgeniy Chen, was world ranked triple jumper 1954-8, pb 16.00 '58.

Olga CHERNYAVSKAYA b.17 Sep 1963 Irbit Severdlovsk region 1.80m 80kg. née Davydova, then Burova. Stavropol VS. Servicewoman.
At DT: OG: '92- 5; WCh: '93- 1; EC: '90- 2, '94- 5; WCp: '89- 5; ECp: '89- 4. USSR champion 1989-90, RUS 1994.
Progression at DT: 1981- 54.72, 1982- 47.90, 1983- 58.30, 1984- 56.88, 1985- 59.20, 1986- 58.28, 1987- 60.20, 1988- 65.34, 1989- 68.10, 1990- 68.32, 1991- 63.68, 1992- 68.38, 1993- 67.40, 1994- 65.60.

Galina CHISTYAKOVA b.26 Jul 1962 Izmail, Ukraine 1.69m 54kg. Moskva Sp. Teacher. Married to Aleksandr Beskrovniy (TJ: 17.53m '84, 1 EJ '79, 5 EC '82).
At LJ: OG: '88- 3; WCh: '87- 5; WI: '87- 4, '89- 1; EC: '86- 2; EI: '85- 1, '87- 2, '88- 2, '89- 1, '90- 1; WCp: '85- 2, '89- 1; ECp: '85- 1, '87- 2, '89- 1. Won GWG 1986, GP 1985 & 1989 (2nd overall). At TJ: WCp: '92- 2; won CIS 1992, 2nd GP 1993.
World LJ record 1988, four USSR records 1984-8. World TJ record 1989. WIB: LJ 7.25 '85, five TJ 13.58 '86; 13.86, 13.96, 13.98 '87, 14.45 '89.
Progression at LJ, TJ: 1973- 3.75, 1974- 4.20, 1975- 4.96, 1976- 5.25, 1977- 5.80, 1978- 6.04, 1979- 6.43, 1980- 6.43, 1981- 6.36/6.54w, 1982- 6.43, 1984- 7.29, 1985- 7.28, 1986- 7.34, 13.58i; 1987- 7.27, 13.98i; 1988- 7.52, 1989- 7.30i/7.24/7.36w, 14.52; 1990- 7.35, 14.15i; 1991- 6.69, 14.04; 1992- 6.60/ 6.66w, 14.62; 1993- 6.33, 14.40; 1994- 6.67, 14.21i/ 14.12. pb 100m 11.6 '84.
Gave birth to a daughter in 1983. Injured her knee after jumping 7.35 in Bratislava 1990, and on return to competiton has concentrated on triple jumping.

Olga CHURBANOVA b.16 Jul 1964

Sverdlovsk 1.70m 53kg. née Sinitsina. Yekaterinburg VS. Teacher.
At 3000m: EC: '94- 4. World CC: '93- 11, '94- 9. Won CIS 3000m 1992, Russian 3000m 1994, CC 1993-4. Winning World Road Relay team 1994.
Progression at 1500m, 3000m: 1988- 4:11.9, 9:03.51; 1990- 9:09.9, 1991- 4:15.08; 1992- 8:58.03; 1993- 4:10.71, 8:53.63; 1994- 4:02.10, 8:40.48. pb 800m 2:01.47 '93.

Lyudmila GALKINA b. 20 Jan 1972 Saratov 1.72m 57kg. Saratov Sp. Student.
AT LJ (TJ): WCh: '93- 5; EC: '94- dnq 16; EJ: '89- 3, '91- 2 (1); ECp: '93- 6.
Progression at LJ: 1988- 6.34, 1989- 6.52/6,62w, 1990- 6.63, 1991- 6.62, 1992- 6.60, 1993- 6.75, 1994- 6.78, 1995- 6.92i. pb TJ 13.67 '91.

Svetlana GONCHARENKO b.28 May 1971 Rostov na Donu 1.76m 61kg. née Doronina. Novocherkassk Sp. Student.
At 400m: EC: '94- 2/2R; EI: '94- 1, ECp: '94- 1/3R. At 200m: EJ: '87- 5 (2 4x100mR).
Progression at 400m: 1988- 54.22, 1992- 53.69, 1993- 54.00, 1994- 51.00. pbs: 100m 11.48 '92, 10.8 '94; 200m 23.40 '93, 22.6 '94; 300m 36.81i '94.

Yuliya GRAUDYN b.13 Nov 1970 Moscow 1.71m 60kg. née Filippova. Moskva VS.
At 100mh: EC: '94- 2; WJ: '88- 4; EJ: '87- 6, '89- 2; 2nd GP 1994. At 60mh: WI: '93- 4.
Progression at 100mh: 1988- 13.21, 1989- 13.36, 1991- 13.18, 1992- 12.82, 1993- 12.85, 1994- 12.62/ 12.51Aw. pbs: 50mh 6.73i '95, 60mh 7.93i '94, 7.6i '93.
Won original 60m final at World Indoors 1993, but only 4th in the re-run. Her husband Vladimir was second in World and European Indoors at 800m in 1987 and had a pb of 1:44.10 (1988).

Yelena GULYAYEVA b.14 Aug 1967 Moskva 1.82m 61kg. née Rodina. Moskva VS. Teacher.
At HJ: WCh: '93- 4=; EC: '94- 2; ECp: '91- 1dq, '94- 3; WI: '91- 6=. USSR champion 1988, 1991.
Progression at HJ: 1981- 1.70, 1982- 1.70, 1983- 1.80, 1984- 1.84, 1985- 1.80, 1987- 1.80, 1988- 1.94, 1989- 1.89i/1.88, 1990- 1.92i/1.91, 1991- 1.99, 1993- 1.98, 1994- 2.00i/1.98.
Two years suspension after being disqualified on positive drugs test when winning the 1991 European Cup high jump.

Lyubov GURINA b.6 Aug 1957 Matushkino, Kirov region 1.67m 57kg. Kirov Sp. Decorator.
At 800m: OG: '92- 8; WCh: '83- 2, '87- 3, '93- 2; EC: '86- 3, '90- 7, '94- 1; WI: '91- 4; EI: '90- 1. Won GWG 1986. USSR champion 1987, Russian 1993. 2nd GP 1991, 1993. At 1500m: OG: '88- h. World record 4x800m relay 1984.
Progression at 800m, 1500m: 1976- 2:15.7, 1977- 2:08.0, 1978- 2:04.6, 1979- 2:00.2, 4:13.3; 1980- 1:59.9, 1981- 1:58.72, 4:09.40; 1982- 1:57.3, 1983- 1:56.11, 1984- 1:56.26, 1986- 1:57.52, 4:06.34; 1987- 1:55.56, 4:09.82; 1988- 1:56.56, 4:08.59; 1989- 1:59.74, 1990- 1:58.56, 1991- 1:58.50, 1992- 1:57.39, 4:03.32; 1993- 1:57.10, 4:03.32; 1994- 1:56.53, 4:02.47. pbs: 400m 51.38 '83, 1000m 2:32.97 '93, 1M 4:34.07i '92.
Became, in 1994, at the age of 37, the oldest ever female European champion; thus gaining her first outdoor gold medal, at the same stadium at which she won the 1983 World silver.

Yekaterina IVAKINA b.4 Dec 1964 Stavropol 1.68m 67kg. née Slyadneva. Stavropol VS. Servicewoman.
At JT: WCh: '93- 5; EC: '94- dnq 15; ECp: '93- 3, '94- 4. Russian champion 1993.
Progression at DT: 1985- 53.02, 1986- 57.92, 1987- 60.42, 1988- 64.04, 1989- 63.08, 1990- 61.90, 1992- 64.10, 1993- 65.36, 1994- 64.04.

Olympiada IVANOVA b.5 May 1970. Cheboksary Dyn.

Yuliya Graudyn: European hurdles silver

At 10kmW: WCp: '93- 12; won GWG 1994.
Progression at 10kmW: 1987- 45:15, 1992- 45:18, 1993- 42:24, 1994- 42:30.31t. pbs: 3000mW 12:16.83i '94, 5000mW 20:56.10 '94.

Anna KNOROZ b.30 Jul 1970 Moskva 1.62m 50kg. née Chuprina. St Petersburg VS. Student
At 400mh/4x400mR: WCh: '93- sf; EC: '94- 3; WUG: '91- 3/2R; EJ: '89- 2R; WCp: '94- 3; ECp: '93- 2. USSR champion 1991, RUS 1992-4.
Progression at 400mh: 1987- 59.6, 1988- 57.66, 1989- 56.70, 1991- 55.12, 1992- 55.15, 1993- 54.42, 1994- 54.11. pb 400m 52.78 '93.

Larisa KOROTKEVICH b.3 Jan 1967 Krivye Vitebsk region 1.80m 86kg. Krasnodar Dyn. Teacher.
At DT: OG: '92- 4; WCh: '87- 10, '93- dnq 14; EJ: '85- 3; WCp: '92- 4; ECp: '93- 1, '94- 4. Russian champion 1993.
Progression at DT: 1983- 52.74, 1984- 56.70, 1985- 59.02, 1986- 64.42, 1987- 64.94, 1988- 66.08, 1989- 60.74, 1990- 67.50, 1991- 63.44, 1992- 71.30, 1993- 68.14, 1994- 62.08.

Lyubov KREMLYOVA b.21 Dec 1962 Maykop 1.66m 52kg. Moskva VS. Teacher
At 3000m: EC: '90- 4; ECp: '91- 3; WI: 91- 3. At 1500m: EC: '94- 4; EI: '92- 2; ECp: '93- 1. At 800m: ECp: '93- 2. Won GP 1M 1993, 2nd 1500m 1992. WIR 1000m (2:34.1) 1995.
Progression at 800m, 1500m, 3000m: 1981- 4:21.2; 1983- 2:00.05, 4:05.67; 1984- 1:58.95, 4:02.04; 1985- 4:12.3; 1986- 1:59.1, 4:01.57; 1987- 2:00.9, 4:07.1; 1988- 1:59.7, 4:02.41, 8:52.09; 1989- 2:01.70, 4:05.53, 8:52.99; 1990- 4:03.20, 8:46.94; 1991- 2:00.08, 4:05.54, 8:49.72; 1992- 1:59.71, 3:58.71, 8:46.99; 1993- 1:59.8, 4:04.88; 1994- 1:59.47, 4:01.05. pbs: 1000m 2:33.55 '93, 1M 4:22.46 '93, 2000m 5:41.26 '92.

Svetlana KRIVELYOVA b.13 Jun 1969 Bryansk 1.84m 91kg. Moskva Dyn. Teacher.
At SP: OG: '92- 1; WCh: '91- 3, '93- 2; WJ: '88- 4; WI: '91- 8, '93- 1; WUG: '91- 1. USSR champion 1991, Russian 1992. Won GP 1993.
Progression at SP: 1985- 15.18, 1986- 16.76, 1987- 17.51, 1988- 18.35, 1989- 18.36, 1990- 19.70, 1991- 20.36, 1992- 21.06, 1993- 20.84.
Took World Student Games gold medal in 1991 after Sui Xinmei disqualified.

Olga KUZENKOVA b.4 Oct 1970.
At HT: Russian champion 1992-4, CIS 1992.
Three world hammer records 1993-4, and her 66.84 in 1994 was the first record for the event accepted by the IAAF.
Progression at HT: 1990- 59.50, 1991- 61.52, 1992- 65.40, 1993- 64.64, 1994- 66.84.

Inna LASOVSKAYA b.17 Dec 1969 Moskva 1.77m 68kg. Moskva VS. Servicewoman.
At TJ: WCh: '93- nj; EC: '94- 2; WI: '93- 3; EI: '94- 1. Russian champion 1994.
Russian triple jump record 1993. Four WIR 14.16 '89, 14.61, 14.78 and 14.90 '94.
Progression at TJ: 1989- 14.40i, 1990- 14.09i/13.65, 1991- 14.05, 1992- 14.13i/14.07, 1993- 14.70, 1994- 14.94. pb LJ 6.68 '88.

Yelena LYSAK b.19 Oct 1975 Tashkent 1.75m 55kg. Bryansk Dyn. Student.
At TJ (LJ): WJ: '94- 1 (1); EJ: '93- 1 (4).
European junior triple jump records (3) 1993-4.
Progression at LJ, TJ: 1988- 5.79, 1989- 5.83, 1990- 5.97, 1991- 6.21, 13.22; 1992- 6.20/6.53w, 13.43; 1993- 6.40, 13.86; 1994- 6.45/6.72w, 14.32/14.43w.
Drugs ban after winning European Under-23 Cup TJ 1994.

Galina MALCHUGINA b.17 Dec 1962 Bryansk 1.68m 65kg. née Mikheyeva. Moskva VS. Teacher.
At 200m/4x100mR: OG: '88- 8/3R, '92- 8/2R; WCh: '91- 5/2R, '93- 7/1R; EC: '90- 3, '94- 3/2R; EJ: '79- 7/2R; WUG: '89- 1/2R; WCp: '89- 5/2R; ECp: '91- 1R: WI: '91- 5; EI: '90- 3, '94- 1. 3rd GP 200m 1990, 1992. Won USSR 100m 1991, RUS 200m 1994.
Progression at 100m, 200m: 1978- 24.76, 1979- 11.72, 23.70; 1980- 24.21/24.0; 1981- 11.58, 23.16; 1982- 11.62, 23.28/23.2; 1984- 11.51, 22.74; 1985- 11.42, 23.06; 1987- 11.56, 23.15/22.2w; 1988- 11.07/10.8, 22.42; 1989- 11.47/10.99w, 22.68; 1990- 11.10, 22.23; 1991- 11.20, 22.49; 1992- 10.96, 22.22; 1993- 11.25, 22.22; 1994- 11.42, 22.29. pb 60m 7.16i '90.

Olga MARKOVA b.6 Aug 1968 St Petersburg 1.63m 47kg. St Petersburg VS.
Russian marathon record 1992.
Progression at Mar: 1988- 2:42:12, 1989- 2:40:00, 1990- 2:37:06, 1991- 2:28:27, 1992- 2:23:43, 1993- 2:25:27, 1994- 2:32:22. pbs: 1500m 4:24.0 '88, 3000m 9:15.0 '90, 10000m 33:51.83 '91. Road: 15km 49:30 '92, Half Mar 1:11:42 '90.
Lives in Gainesville, Florida. At the marathon has three wins in 12 races. to failure to finish at Boston 1994. In 1991 she was 3rd in Los Angeles and 2nd in New York, and in 1992 won Boston to go to 4th on the world all-time list and was 2nd in New York.

Svetlana MASTERKOVA b.17 Jan 1968 Moskva 1.72m 59kg. Moskva TR. Student.
At 800m: WCh: '91- 8; WI: '93- 2; EJ: '85- 6; ECp:

'91- 3. Won USSR 800m 1991. 3rd GP 1993.
Progression at 800m: 1982- 2:11.7, 1983- 2:04.3, 1984- 2:04.59, 1985- 2:02.69, 1986- 2:03.34, 1989- 2:02.70, 1990- 1:59.83, 1991- 1:57.23, 1992- 1:57.63, 1993- 1:57.48. pb 400m 53.12 '92, 1000m 2:41.86i '92.

Svetlana MOSKALETS b.22 Jan 1969 Mytishchi, Moskva region 1.72m 62kg. née Akimova. Moskva VS.
At Hep: EC: '94- 5; ECp: '94- 1. Won USSR LJ 1987, RUS Hep 1994.
Progression at Hep: 1984- 5398, 1985- 5680, 1986- 5921, 1988- 6129, 1989- 6230, 1990- 5947, 1991- 6063, 1993- 6510, 1994- 6598. pbs: 200m 23.55 '93, 800m 2:14.54 '94, 100mh 13.20 '94, HJ 1.89, LJ 6.82 '94, SP 13.78 '94, JT 42.48 '94.
Daughter born June 1992.

Irina MUSHAYILOVA b.6 Jan 1967 Krasnodar 1.69m 64kg. Krasnodar Dyn. Student.
At LJ: OG: '92- 5; EC: '94- 7; WI: '93- 4. Russian champion 1994.
Progression at LJ, TJ: 1988- 6.39w, 1989- 6.61, 1990- 6.75, 1991- 6.76, 13.81; 1992- 6.89, 13.47i; 1993- 7.02, 14.79; 1994- 7.20, 13.94/13.98w.

Olga NAZAROVA b.28 Feb 1962 Leningrad 1.77m 63kg. née Grigoryeva. St Petersburg TU. Teacher.
At 400mh: WCh: '93- sf; EC: '94- 7; WUG: '89- 6.
Progression at 400mh: 1981- 58.5, 1982- 56.08, 1985- 56.04, 1986- 55.62, 1987- 56.02, 1988- 55.47, 1989- 55.56, 1990- 55.80, 1991- 55.80, 1992- 55.57, 1993- 55.08, 1994- 54.82. pb 400m 51.44 '86.

Yelena NIKOLAYEVA b.1 Feb 1966 Akshiki Chuvashskaya 1.68m 58kg. née Kuznetsova. Cheboksary Dyn. Student.
At 10kmW: OG: '92- 2; WCh: '87- 5, '93- 7; EC: '94- 3; WCp: '87- 5, '93- 3. USSR champion 1987-8, CIS 1992. At 3000mW: WI: '91- 5, '93- 1; EI: '94- 4.
Three world 10km track walk records 1986-8, European records 3000m 1992, 5000m: 21:32.4 '87, 21:08.65 '88.
Progression at 10kmW: 1984- 48:29.1, 1985- 46:37, 1986- 44:32.50t, 1987- 43:57, 1988- 43:36.41t, 1991- 43:25, 1992- 42:40, 1993- 43:11, 1994- 42:43. pbs: 3000mW 11:49.73i '93, 11:54.8 '92; 5000mW 21:00.80 '91. Road 5kmW 20:48 '94.

Vera ORDINA b.4 Jun 1968 1.72m 56kg. St Petersburg VS.
At 400mh: OG: '92- 5; EC: '94- sf; ECp: '93- 4.
Progression at 400mh: 1985- 59.28, 1986- 59.30, 1987- 56.2/56.77, 1988- 57.50, 1989- 55.42, 1990- 55.86, 1991- 55.31, 1992- 54.37, 1993- 55.33, 1994- 54.92. pb 100mh 13.35/13.0 '88.

Larisa PELESHENKO b.29 Feb 1964 Slantsy Leningrad region 1.87m 95kg. née Agapova. St Petersburg Sp. Teacher.
At SP: WCh: '93- 9; EC: '94- 5; EI: '88- 2, '94- 2; WUG: '87- 3, '89- 4; ECp: '89- 3, '94- 3.
Progression at SP: 1981- 14.60, 1982- 15.95, 1983- 18.23, 1984- 19.30, 1985- 18.78i, 1986- 19.26, 1987- 20.99, 1988- 20.89, 1989- 19.68, 1990- 19.56, 1992- 19.65, 1993- 19.90i/19.23, 1994- 20.00i/19.81.

Yekaterina PODKOPAYEVA b.11 Jun 1952 Ulyanovsk, nr Kaluga 1.64m 54kg. née Poryvkina. Moskva VS. Teacher.
At 800m/1500m: WCh: '83- 3/3; At 1500m: OG: '92- 8; EC: '94- 5; WI: '93- 1; WCp: '89- 2, '92- 1; EI: '92- 1, '94- 1. At 800m: ECp: '79- 2. Won GWG 1500m 1994, USSR 800m 1979, 1984; 1500m 1989. 3rd GP 1500m 1994.
WIB 2000m 5:43.30 '83.
Progression at 800m/1500m: 1970- 2:20.2, 1971- 2:15.3, 1972- 2:08.6, 1973- 2:06.8, 1974- 2:09.0, 1975- 2:05.6, 1976- 2:05.2/4:15.7, 1977- 2:06.6/ 4:13.7, 1978- 2:00.6/4:11.7, 1979- 1:57.2, 1980- 1:58.9/3:57.4, 1982- 4:10.07, 1983- 1:55.96/4:00.3, 1984- 1:57.07/3:56.65, 1985- 1:56.65/4:01.96, 1988- 2:01.37/4:04.57, 1989- 2:00.16/4:05.26 1990- 1:59.7/4:03.62, 1991- 2:06.9, 4:08.59; 1992- 2:00.52, 4:02.03; 1993- 4:02.48, 1994- 1:59.25, 3:59.78. pbs: 400m 52.74 '85, 1000m 2:36.08i '93, 2:36.16 '94; 1M 4:23.78 '93, 2000m 5:40.96 '92, 3000m 8:56.02 '89.
Has had an astonishingly long career, with her great record in 1994 making her the leading candidate for world top ranking at 1500m. The oldest ever European Indoor champion at 39 and again at 41, oldest World Cup winner at 40, and oldest World Indoor champion at 40. Sons Andrey born 1981, Fyodor 1986.

Margarita PONOMARYEVA b.19 Jun 1963 Balkhash, Kazakhstan 1.78m 58kg. Married name was Khromova. St Petersburg Sp. Economist.
At 400mh/4x400mR: OG: '92- 6; WCh: '87- sf, '91- 8, '93- 3/2R; EC: '86- 8, '90- 5; EJ: '81- 3/2R; WUG: '89- 1/3R; WCp: '85- 6, '92- 3/2R; ECp: '91- 1/1R. 3rd GP 1991. At 4x400mR: WI: '91- 2. Won CIS 400mh 1992.
World 400mh record 1984. WIR 4x400mR 1991.
Progression at 400mh: 1981- 57.45, 1983- 56.9, 1984- 53.58, 1985- 55.48, 1986- 54.57, 1987- 54.58, 1988- 54.95, 1989- 54.98, 1990- 55.22, 1991- 54.08, 1992- 53.66, 1993- 53.48. pb 400m 51.10 '91.

Irina PRIVALOVA b.22 Nov 1968 Malakhovka, near Moskva 1.74m 63kg. Married name was Sergeyeva. Moskva Sp. Degree in journalism from Moscow State University.
At 100m (/200m, 4x100mR): OG: '92- 3/4/2R;

WCh: '91- 4/4/2R, '93- 4/3/1R (2 4x400mR); EC: '90- 6, '94- 1/1/2R; WJ: '86- sf/5R; EJ: '85- h; WCp: '94- 1/2 (1 400m); ECp: '89- 3/5; '91- 1/1/1R, '93- 1/1/1R. At 60m/200m: WI: '91- 1/2, '93- 2/1. Won USSR 100m 1989-90, CIS 100m/200m 1992, RUS 200m 1993. GP 100m: 2nd 1993, 3rd 1994.
European 100m record 1994. Two USSR/CIS 100m records 1991-2, three 200m 1992, Russian 200m 1993, 100m 1994; WIR: 50m 6.05 and 6.00 (not ratified due to inaccurate camera alignment) '93, 6.03 '94, 5.96 '95; 60m 6.92 '93 & '95, 300m 1993. European IR 60m 6.97 '92, 200m 22.26 '92, 22.10 '95.
Progression at 100m, 200m, 400m: 1982- 11.9, 1983- 11.7, 1984- 11.79; 1985- 11.59, 24.54; 1986- 11.3i/11.52/11.37w, 24.10; 1987- 11.44/11.2, 23.3; 1989- 11.26, 23.00; 1990- 11.21, 23.01; 1991- 10.98, 22.21; 1992- 10.82/10.81w, 21.93; 1993- 10.94, 21.88, 49.89; 1994- 10.77, 22.02/21.82w, 50.62. pbs 50m 6.01i '94, 300m 35.45i '93, 100mh 13.4 '87, HJ 1.72 '82, LJ 6.48i '85, 6.45 '84, TJ 13.72i '89.
Son born 1988. Formerly a skater, she long jumped 6.45 at age 15 in 1984. Won CIS title in 1992 with 10.81 for 100m to equal European record, but time later adjusted to 10.82. Ran 49.89 on 400m début July 1993. At the 1994 World Cup she won the 100m, was 2nd at 200m and won the 400m, in just her second 400m.

Tatyana RESHETNIKOVA b.14 Oct 1966 Leningrad 1.70m 63kg. St Peterburg Sp. Married to Radion Gataullin.
At 100mh: EC: '94- 5. Russian champion 1994.
Progresion at 100mh: 1985- 13.78/13.5, 1986- 13.38, 1987- 12.80, 1990- 12.92, 1991- 12.92, 1992- 12.73, 1993- 13.00, 1994- 12.53. pbs: 50mh 6.87i '93, 60mh 7.96i '93.

Lyudmila ROGACHOVA b.30 Oct 1966 Lad Balka Stavropol region 1.66m 57kg. Stavropol Sp. Teacher.
At 1500m: OG: '92- 2; WCh: '91- 3, '93- 13; EC: '94- 1 (3 800m); WI: '91- 1; EI: '94- 2; EC: '90- 4; WUG: '89- 3. Won USSR 1500m 1990, CIS 800m 1992, RUS 1500m 1993-4, GP 1500m 1992.
Progression at 800m, 1500m: 1980- 2:14.4, 4:44.6; 1981- 2:10.2, 4:32.4; 1982- 2:09.2, 4:30.6; 1983- 2:06.46, 4:26.6; 1984- 2:03.7, 4:15.8; 1985- 2:05.84, 4:19.2; 1986- 2:05.6, 4:17.6; 1987- 2:00.54, 4:08.10; 1988- 1:56.82, 4:04.29; 1989- 1:59.08, 4:07.5; 1990- 1:57.1, 4:02.3i/4:03.07; 1991- 1:58.67, 4:02.72; 1992- 1:57.93, 3:56.91; 1993- 1:58.13, 4:05.77; 1994- 1:58.43, 4:02.40. pbs: 1000m 2:33.96 '93, 1M 4:21.30 '92.
Front ran Olympic 1500m 1992, and held on to smash through 4 minutes for the first time, but run down by Hassiba Boulmerka.

Anna ROMANOVA b.9 Mar 1968 Bryansk 1.81m 88kg. Bryansk Sp. Teacher.
At SP: WCh: '93- dnq 13; EC: '94- 8; WI: '93- 5; WJ: '86- 4; EI: '92- 5, '94- 4; ECp: '93- 1. Russian champion 1993.
Progression at SP: 1984- 15.67, 1985- 17.32, 1986- 17.50i/17.43, 1987- 18.23, 1988- 19.06, 1989- 19.02i/17.89, 1990- 19.06, 1991- 18.95i/18.69, 1992- 20.01i/19.58, 1993- 20.24, 1994- 19.75.

Yelena ROMANOVA b.20 Mar 63 Nezhenskoye Voronezh region 1.60m 51kg. née Malykhina. Volgograd VS. Student.
At 3000m (10000m): OG: '88- 4, '92- 1; WCh: '87- 5 (h), '91- 2 (dnf), '93- 6; EC: '90- 2 (1); WUG: '83- 2. At 1500m: EJ: '81- 2. Won GWG 5000m 1990, 3000m & 5000m 1994. World CC: '88- 6, '89- 9, '90- 2, '91- 8. Winning World Road Relay team 1994. Won RUS 3000m 1993.
Progression at 1500m, 3000m, 10000m: 1976- 5:13.2, 1977- 4:46.7, 1978- 4:32.2, 1979- 4:25.9, 1980- 4:22.5, 1981- 4:16.09, 8:56.03; 1982- 4:10.72, 8:59.18; 1983- 4:09.0, 8:59.79; 1985- 4:18.0, 9:11.03; 1986- 4:04.60, 8:47.79i/8:56.34; 1987- 4:07.4, 8:41.15; 1988- 4:04.96, 8:30.45; 1989- 8:55.80, 1990- 8:43.68, 31:46.83; 1991- 8:36.06, 32:06.73; 1992- 4:00.91, 8:33.72; 1993- 8:35.48, 1994- 4:07.92, 8:41.06. pbs: 800m 2:04.0, 5000m 14:59.70 '91.
Son born 1984. In 1990 after silver at 3000m was an unexpected entrant in the European 10000m, at which she won the gold medal and took her pb from 32:25.08 to 31:46.83.

Yelena SAYKO b. 15 May 1966 Chelyabinsk 1.64m 50kg. Chelyabinsk Dyn. Student.
At 10kmW: OG: '92- 8; WCh: '91- dq, '93- 8; WCp: '91- 3.
Progression at 10kmW: 1988- 45:19, 1989- 44:45, 1990- 44:04, 1991- 42:22, 1992- 43:13, 1993- 42:04, 1994- 42:43.23t. track pbs: 3000mW 12:34.61i '89, 5000mW 20:59.82 '94.

Yelena SINCHUKOVA b.23 Jan 1961 Kemerovo 1.74m 66kg. née Ivanova. Moskva VS. Servicewoman.
At LJ: WCh: '91- 4, '93- 10; EC: '82- 3; WCp: '92- 2; ECp: '93- 2. At Pen: EJ: '79- 6. Won USSR LJ 1991, Russian 1993.
Progression at LJ: 1978- 6.19, 1979- 6.36, 1981- 6.17, 1982- 6.81, 1983- 6.53i, 1984- 7.01, 1985- 6.84i/6.81, 1986- 6.88, 1987- 7.05, 1991- 7.20, 1992- 7.04, 1993- 6.85/6.94w, 1994- 6.77. pbs: TJ 14.09 '92, Pen 4144* '79.

Yelena TOPCHINA b.28 Oct 1966 Leningrad 1.79m 58kg. St Petersburg VS. Student.
At HJ: WCh: '93- 11=; EC: '94- 9=; EJ: '83- 1; EI: '90- 5; Russian champion 1993-4.

Progression at HJ: 1981- 1.80, 1982- 1.88, 1983- 1.94, 1984- 1.88, 1985- 1.90, 1986- 1.92, 1987- 1.86i, 1989- 1.91, 1990- 1.96i/1.95, 1991- 1.93i/1.89, 1993- 1.99, 1994- 1.97.
Served two year drugs disqualification 1991-3.

Larisa TURCHINSKAYA b.29 Apr 1965 Kostroma 1.77m 70kg. née Nikitina. Moskva VS. Teacher.
At Hep: WCh: '87- 2, '93- dnf; EC: '94- 4; EJ: '83- 7; WUG: '89- 1; ECp: '89- 1. USSR champion 1987, 1989. At Pen: EI: '94- 1.
European heptathlon record 1989.
Progression at Hep: 1981- 5263, 1982- 5520*, 1983- 5674, 1984- 6276, 1985- 6171, 1986- 6316, 1987- 6564, 1988- 6506, 1989- 7007, 1990- 6320, 1993- 6415, 1994- 6596. pbs: 200m 23.97 '89, 800m 2:14.32 '.., 100mh 13.40 '89, HJ 1.89 '89, LJ 6.75 '89, SP 16.45 '89, JT 59.28 '89, Hep 4801i '93.
Drugs ban 1990-2.

Irina TYUKHAY b.14 Jan 1967 Krasnoyarsk 1.71m 64kg. Krasnoyarsk Sp.
At Hep: EC: '94- 10; ECp: '94- 6. At Pen: WI Inv: '93- 4.
Progression at Hep: 1984- 5226*, 1985- 5863, 1986- 5922, 1987- 5844, 1988- 6129, 1989- 6230, 1990- 5947, 1991- 6063, 1992- 6478, 1993- 6406, 1994- 6412. pbs: 200m 24.29 '92, 800m 2:15.92 '92, 60mh 8.20i '93, 100mh 13.30 '94, 13.0 '88; HJ 1.89 '92, LJ 6.73 '92, SP 14.67 '94, JT 43.20 '89, Pen 4686i '93.

Natalya VORONOVA b.9 Jul 1965 Moskva 1.69m 61kg. née Pomoshnikova. Moskva VS. Student of journalism.
At 100m (200m)/4x100mR: OG: '88- 6/3R; WCh: '87- sf/3R, '93- 6/6/1R; WI: '93- (3); EJ: '83- 1 (4, 2R); WUG: '89- 3/2R; WCp: '89- 7/2R, '92- 2 (1); ECp: '85- 2R, '93- 1R. Won USSR 100m 1984 (tie), Russian 100m 1992-4, 200m 1992.
Progression at 100m, 200m: 1980- 12.5, 25.9; 1981- 11.9, 25.1; 1982- 11.8, 24.8; 1983- 11.48, 23.34; 1984- 11.42/11.2, 23.1; 1985- 11.27, 23.25/22.6; 1986- 11.20/11.0, 23.02; 1987- 11.07, 23.0; 1988- 10.98, 23.1; 1989- 11.36/11.05w, 1992- 11.11, 22.98; 1993- 11.17/11.16w, 22.35; 1994- 11.37/11.13dq, 22.84i/22.8i/22.82dq. pb 60m 7.06i '93.
3-month drugs ban for ephedrine 1 June 1994.

Valentina YEGOROVA b.16 Feb 1964 Chuvash ASSR 1.56m 52kg. Cheboksary Sp. née Vasilyeva.
At Mar: OG: '92- 1; EC: '90- 2; WCp: '91- 3.
Russian marathon record 1994.
Progression at Mar: 1988- 2:30:59, 1989- 2:40:14, 1990- 2:29:47, 1991- 2:28:18, 1992- 2:29:41, 1993- 2:26:40, 1994- 2:23:33. pbs: 3000m 9:11.2 '85, 5000m 15:40.49 '86, 10000m 32:56.13 '89.
Fourth in Los Angeles and Tokyo marathons in 1992 on either side of Olympic triumph, that was the second marathon win of her career (now 17 races); previously at Ufa 1988, and she won theTokyo marathon in 1993 and 1994. 2nd Boston 1994.

Yelena YELESINA b.4 Apr 1970 Chelyabinsk 1.84m 57kg. Chelyabinsk VS.
At HJ: WCh: '91- 2; EC: '90- 3; WJ: '88- 2; EJ: '87- 3=, '89- 1; WUG: '91- 4; EI: '92- 3. Won GWG 1990. USSR champion 1990.
Progression at HJ: 1983- 1.55, 1984- 1.65, 1985- 1.70, 1986- 1.83, 1987- 1.89, 1988- 1.98, 1989- 1.95, 1990- 2.02, 1991- 1.98, 1992- 1.94i/1.93, 1993- 1.91, 1994- 1.95.

Yevgeniya ZHDANOVA b.21 Jul 1966 Sverdlovsk 1.74m 53kg. Yekaterinburg VS. Student.
At HJ: EC: '94- dnq 15; ECp: '93- 7. Russian champion 1991-2.
Progression at HJ: 1989- 1.86, 1990- 1.92i/1.88, 1991- 1.92, 1992- 1.91i, 1993- 1.95, 1994- 1.98.

Tatyana ZHURAVLYOVA b.19 Dec 1967 Saratov 1.83m 74kg. Stavropol Dyn. Student.
At Hep: WCh: '91- 8, '93- 10; WUG: '91- 4; ECp: '93- 1. Russian champion 1993.
Progression at Hep: 1987- 5670, 1988- 6156, 1989- 6158, 1990- 6292, 1991- 6370, 1993- 6369, 1994- 6290. pbs: 200m 24.18 '91, 800m 2:08.21 '93, 100mh 13.70 ', HJ 1.83 ', LJ 6.60 '93, SP 16.45 ', JT 44.80 '93.

RWANDA

Governing body: Fédération Rwandaise d'Athlétisme, BP 1044, Kigali. Founded 1973.

NTAWULIKURA, Mathias b. 14 Jul 1964 1.71m 66kg. Pro Patria Milano, Italy. A Tutsi.
At 5000m: WCh: '93- 10. At 10000m: OG: '92- h; WCh: '91- 7; AfG: '91- 5/5; AfCh: '88- 5/5. World CC: '91- 18, '92- 13, '94- 10.
Rwanda records 3000m, 5000m, 10000m 1990-4.
Progression at 5000m, 10000m: 1988- 13:48.2, 29:51.79; 1989- 13:52.37, 1990- 13:34.76, 28:41.10; 1991- 13:19.88, 27:49.32; 1992- 13:11.29, 27:52.51; 1993- 13:14.82, 27:47.59; 1994- 13:25.27. 27:36.15. pbs: 3000m 7:41.64 '92, Half Mar 61:48 '91.
First came to world notice with in 1991 with 12th in World CC challenge and with many national records, from two at 3000m in the World Indoor championships (8th).

SAUDI ARABIA

AL-ASMARI, Sa'ed Shaddad b.24 Sep 1968. 1.85m 72kg.
At 3000mSt: WCp: '94- 2; AsiG: '94- 2; AsiCh: '93- 1. Arab champion 1993.
Asian 3000m steeplechase record 1994. Saudi 1500m records 1992-4.
Progression at 3000mSt: 1992- 9:08.86, 1993- 8:29.38, 1994- 8:15.95. pb 1500m 3:41.1 '94.

SLOVAKIA

Governing body: Slovak Athletic Federation, Junacka 6, 83280 Bratislava. Founded 1939.
National Championships first held in 1939.
1994 Champions: Men: 100m: Martin Brinarsky 10.92, 200m: Marián Vanderka 21.28, 400m: Stefan Balosák 46.36, 800m: Jozef Pribula 1:52.61, 1500m: Michal Kucera 3:53.24, 5000m/10000m: Rupert Sadek 15:24.25/ 31:38.21, Half Mar: Peter Hritz 68:20, Mar: Petr Pipa 2:15:03, 3000mSt: Milos Kovacech 8:48.28, 110mh: Igor Kovác 13.75, 400mh: Jozef Kucej 49.84, HJ: Lubos Benko 2.14, PV: Michal Senkovic 4.60, LJ: Andrej Benda 7.55, TJ: Marek Samsely 15.43, SP/DT: Jaroslav Zitnansky 17.63/53.26, HT: Miroslav Vrican 63.00, JT: Pavol Florek 67.96, 20kmW: Igor Kollár 1:24:48.
Women: 100m/200m: Jarmila Zifcáková 12.31/ 24.78, 400m: Eva Labudová 55.78, 800m: Renata Polanská 2:12.45, 1500m: Andrea Sollárová 4:37.72, 3000m: Lenka Stancelová 10:08.20, 10,000m: Danira Bulová 44:02.75, Half Mar: Beresová 83:31, Mar: Ludmila Melicherová 2:40:27, 100mh: Marcela Podracká 14.50, 400mh: Pavla Jelínková 61.15, HJ: Lenka Riháková 1.90, LJ/TJ: Katarin Horniaková 5.48/12.07, SP: Radka Charfreitagová 13.71, DT: Ivona Holubová 51.36, JT: Beáta Buchalová 47.34, 10kmW: Iveta Brozmanová 49:34.

Pavol BLAZEK b.9 Jul 1958 Trnava 1.68m 58kg. Dukla B.Bystrica. Soldier.
At 20kmW (50kmW): OG: '80- 14 (10), '88- 15 (12), '92- 17; WCh: '83- 6 (17), '87- 11 (18), '91- 17, '93- 15; EC: '78- 14, '82- 3 (dnf), '86- 6, '90- 1, '94- (9); WCp: '79- 18, '81- 11, '83- 9, '85- 10, '87- 21, '89- 8, '91- 30, '93- 27 (equal record no. of appearances). At 5000mW: WI: '89- 6. Won CS 20kmW 1981, 1990-1. World best 20km road walk 1990.
Progression at 20kmW: 1977- 1:33:34, 1978- 1:27:50, 1979- 1:25:14, 1980- 1:25:00t, 1981- 1:24:07, 1982- 1:23:59, 1983- 1:21:37, 1984- 1:21:24t, 1985- 1:22:30, 1986- 1:21:21, 1987- 1:21:36, 1988- 1:20:17, 1989- 1:21:53, 1990- 1:18:13, 1991- 1:21:43, 1992- 1:21:55.6t, 1993- 1:21:15.4t, 1994- 1:22:57. Track pbs: 3000mW: 11:12.1i '88, 5000mW 18:41.34i '89, 19:09.73 '90, 10000mW 39:31.83i '86, 20kmW 1:19:54.0 '90, Road 50kmW 3:47:31 '88.
At his fourth European Championships took the gold medal, although after he had finished was first listed as disqualified.

SLOVENIA

Governing body: Atletska zveza Slovenije, Aljazeva ul.32, 61007 Ljubljana. Current organisation founded 1945. Athletes competed for Yugoslavia to 1991.

Women

Britta BILAC b.4 Dec 1968 1.81m 61kg. née Vörös. Ex GDR.
At HJ: OG: '92- 15; WCh: '93- 11=; EC: '94- 1; EI: '90- 2, '92- 4; WCp: '94- 1. SLO champion 1992-3.
Nine Slovenian high jump records 1992-4.
Progression at HJ: 1983- 1.72, 1984- 1.77, 1985- 1.79, 1986- 1.85, 1987- 1.84, 1988- 1.88, 1989- 1.91, 1990- 1.94i, 1991- 1.92, 1992- 1.94, 1993- 1.97i/1.94, 1994- 2.00.
Married to Borut Bilac (b. 14 Apr 1965) 3rd 1990 European LJ, pb. 8.24 '90. Having cleared 2.00 indoors, she improved her outdoor best to 1.98 and 2.00 in taking 1994 European gold, the first ever for her new country.

Brigita BUKOVEC b.21 May 1970 Ljubljana 1.68m 57kg.
At 100mh: OG: '92- sf; WCh: '91- h, '93- sf; EC: '90- sf, '94- 4; WJ: '88- sf; EJ: '87- h, '89- 3. GWG 100mh champion 1994, SLO 1992-3, YUG 1989-91. At 60mh: WI: '93- 7; EI: '94- 4.
Seven Slovenian 100mh records 1993-4, two Yugoslav 1990-1.
Progression at 100mh: 1986- 14.08, 1987- 13.78, 1988- 13.77/13.56w, 1989- 13.40, 1990- 13.23/ 13.14w, 1991- 13.16, 1992- 13.12/13.02w, 1993- 12.98/12.89w, 1994- 12.77/12.59w. pbs: 100m 11.91 '92, 11.80w '93; 200m 24.52 '89, 50mh 6.80i '95, 60mh 7.90i '95.

SOMALIA

Governing body: Somali Amateur Athletic Association, PO Box 3792, Mogadishu. Founded 1959.

Abdi BILE Abdi b. 28 Dec 1962 Las Anod 1.85m 75kg. Studied marketing at George Mason University, USA.
At 1500m: OG: '84- sf (qf 800m); WCh: '87- 1, '93- 3; AfCh: '82- 8, '85- 2; WCp: '89- 1. NCAA champion 1985, 1987. 1st GP 1987 & 1989, 2nd 1993, 3rd 1994.
Two African 1000m records 1989. SOM records all distances 800m to 3000m.
Progression at 800m, 1500m: 1981- 1:50.0; 1982-

1:52.8, 3:51.6; 1984- 1:46.1, 3:35.89dq; 1985- 1:47.24, 3:34.24; 1986- 1:51.2, 3:34.01; 1987- 1:44.47, 3:31.71; 1988- 1:44.42, 3:33.6; 1989- 1:43.60, 3:30.55; 1990- 1:46.64, 3:34.28; 1991- 1:46.39, 3:34.6; 1993- 1:45.17, 3:32.83; 1994- 1:46.01, 3:33.63. pbs: 1000m 2:14.50 '89, 1M 3:49.40 '88, 2000m 4:59.77 '87, 3000m 7:42.18 '94.
The first Somali world champion at any sport. Missed the 1988 Olympics due to a stress fracture in his left foot, but in 1989 he won the Oslo Dream Mile and World Cup 1500m, with national records at 800m, 1000m, 1500m and 3000m. Made a fine comeback in 1993 to win the World bronze medal.

SOUTH AFRICA

Governing body: Athletics South Africa, P.O. Box 1261, Pretoria 0001. Original body founded 1894. IAAF Membership terminated in 1976 and provisionally reinstated in 1992.
National Championships first held in 1894 (men), 1929 (women). **1994 Champions**: **Men**: 100m/200m: Johan Venter 10.33/20.87, 400m: Riaan Dempers 45.15, 800m: Hezekiel Sepeng 1:47.72, 1500m: Whaddon Niewoudt 3:49.86, 5000m/3000mSt: Shadrack 14:07.97/8:54.22, 10000m: Xolile Yawa 29:01.59, Half Mar: Meshack Mogotsi 62:03, Mar: Isaac Radebe 2:15:06, 110mh: Shaun Bownes 14.22, 400mh: Ferrins Pieterse 49.70, HJ: Gidius Botha 2.15, PV: Okkert Brits 5.80, LJ: Ampie de Beer 7.80w, TJ: Wikus Olivier 16.91w, SP: Burger Lambrechts 18.85, DT: Frits Potgieter 58.40, HT: Rumen Koprivchin 65.64, JT: Louis Fouche 78.70, Dec: Danie van Wyk 7520, 20kW: Chris Britz 1:27:29, 50kW: Johan Moerdyk 4:11:22. **Women**: 100m/200m: Yolanda Steyn 11.80/23.03, 400: Adri de Jongh 53.05, 800/1500: Camilla Spires 2:05.66/4:21.45, 3000: Alta Lohann 9:28.87, 10,000: Zola Pieterse 34:57.1, Half Mar: Nora Maraga KEN 73:37, Mar: Grace de Oliveira 2:46:00, 100mh: Adri van der Merwe 13.70, 400H: Lana Uys 57.59, HJ: Charmaine Weavers 1.90, LJ: Karen Botha 6.41, TJ: Petrusa Swart 12.52, SP: Veronica Abrahamse 14.67, DT: Lizette Etsebeth 52.30, HT: Louise Meintjes 42.16, JT: Ansie Rogers 55.22, Hep: Chrisna Oosthuizen 5693, 10kW: Felicita Falconer 54:13.2, 20kW: D Beckley 1:57:05.

Okkert BRITS b. 2 Aug 1973 1.98m 82kg.
At PV: CG: '94- nh; WJ: '92- 3; AfCh: '92- 1, '93- 1; WCp: '92- 3, '94- 1. SA champion 1993-4.
14 African pole vault records 1993-4 (5.50-5.90).
Progression at PV: 1989- 4.50, 1990- 4.80, 1991- 5.25, 1992- 5.46, 1993- 5.71, 1994- 5.90.

Hezekiel SEPENG b. 30 Jun 1974 1.78m 58kg.
At 800m: WCh: '93- 5; CG: '94- 2; WJ: '92- 5; AfCh: '93- 4. SA champion 1993-4.
Progression at 800m: 1992- 1:47.51, 1993- 1:45.46, 1994- 1:45.32. pbs: 400m 46.75 '93, 1000m 2:21.56 '94, 1500m 3:43.08 '93.

Women

Elana MEYER b.10 Oct 1966 Albertina 1.58m 45kg. née van Zyl.
At 10000m: OG: '92- 2; WCh: '93- dnf; CG: '94- 2; WCp: '94- 1. At 1500m: AfCh: '92- 1, '93- 1. World CC: '93- 6, 94- 6. Won World Half Mar 1994. Won SA 1500m 1992; 3000m 1987-9, 1992-3; 10000m 1991.
World road bests half marathon & 15km 1991. African marathon & 10000m records 1994.
SA records 2000m 1987, 3000m 1991, 5000m (2) 1991-2, 10000m (5) 1989-94, Mar 1994.
Progression at 3000m, 10000m: 1981- 10:00.2, 1982- 9:24.9, 1983- 9:09.32, 1984- 9:12.20, 1985- 8:58.73; 1986- 9:17.16, 1987-8:52.39, 1988- 8:54.84, 1989- 8:55.78, 32:28.9; 1990- 8:54.83, 1991- 8:32.00, 31:33.46; 1992- 8:38.45, 31:11.75; 1993- 8:32.81, 32:28.02; 1994- 9:02.43, 30:52.51. pbs: 800m 2:06.23 '85, 1000m 2:43.63 '87, 1500m 4:02.15 '92, 1M 4:30.21 '89, 2000m 5:40.7 '92, 5000m 14:44.15 '92.
Road (all RSA records): 10km 31:33 '91, 15km 46:57 '91, Half Mar 67:59 '91, 67:22 (33m dh) '93, Mar 2:25:15 '94.
Gave up in World 10000m final in 1993 after being repeatedly baulked by Sally Barsosio. 3rd Boston 1994 on marathon début.

Charmaine WEAVERS b.27 Feb 1964 Estcourt 1.78m 65kg. née Gale. Gymnasium attendant.
At HJ: OG: '92- dnq; WCh: '93- dnq; CG: '94- 2; AfCh: '92- 2, '93- 1; WCp: '94- 2. Won SA HJ 1980, 1988-92, 1994.
Two world junior high jump bests 1981; seven SA records 1980-5.
Progression at HJ: 1977- 1.72, 1978- 1.77, 1979- 1.83, 1980- 1.92, 1981- 1.96, 1982- 1.90, 1983- 1.90, 1984- 1.88, 1985- 2.00, 1986- 1.99, 1987- 1.96, 1988- 1.97, 1989- 1.96, 1990- 1.90, 1991- 1.93, 1992- 1.95, 1993- 1.92, 1994- 1.94.

SPAIN

Governing body: Real Federación Española de Atletismo, Calle Miguel Angel 16, Madrid 28010. Founded 1920.
National Championships first held in 1917 (men), 1931 (women). **1994 Champions**: 100m: Pedro Nolet 10.61, 200m: Frutos Feo 21.24, 400m: Cayetano Cornet 47.08, 800m: Tomás De Teresa 1:48.55, 1500m: Isaac Viciosa 3:42.25, 5000m: Anacleto Jiménez 13:36.40, 10000m: Abel Antón 28:36.97, Half Mar: Francisco Cortés 64:28, Mar: José Apalanza 2:16:09, 3000mSt: Antonio Peula 8:28.28, 110mh: Antonio Lanau 14.12, 400mh:

Iñigo Monreal 50.46, HJ: Gustavo Becker 2.21, PV: Isaac Molinero 5.45, LJ: Angel Hernández 7.86, TJ: Julio López 16.41, SP: Manuel Martínez 19.37, DT: David Martinez 54.00, HT: Francisco Fuentes 65.62, JT: Julián Sotelo 75.08, Dec: Antonio Peñalver 8160w, 20kmW/50kmW: Valentín Massana 1:21:49/3:38:43. **Women**: 100m: Cristina Castro 11.77, 200m: Cristina Pérez 24.16, 400m: Sandra Myers 51.83, 800m: Sonia Alvarez 2:07.65, 1500m: M Teresa Zuñiga 4:26.72, 3000m: Estela Estévez 9:00.54, 10000m: Ana I Alonso 32:44.00, Half Mar: Rocio Rios 71:23, Mar: Ana Isabel Alonso 2:33:18, 100mh: M José Mardomingo 13.23, 400mh: Miriam Alonso 58.58, HJ: M Mar Martinez 1.81, LJ: Yolanda Rodriguez 6.28, TJ: Concepción Paredes 14.01, SP: Margarita Ramos 16.79, DT: Ángeles Barreiro 56.12, JT: Cristina Larrea 53.78, Hep: Inmaculada Clopes 5543w, 10000mW/10kmW: Encarna Granados 47:02.65/46:19.

Abel ANTON b.24 Oct 1962 Ojoel, Soria 1.79m 63kg. Reebok.
At 5000m (10000m): OG: '88- sf, '92- 8; WCh: '87- 14, '91- 11, '93- 11; EC: '86- h, '90- 11, '94- 3 (1); EJ: '81- 5; WCp: '92- 4; ECp: '87- (1), '93- 3. At 3000m: EI: '89- 2. Won Spanish 5000m 1992-3, 10000m 1994.
Progression at 5000m, 10000m: 1981- 14:18.29, 1982- 14:13.94, 1983- 14:06.04, 1984- 13:27.95, 1985- 13:25.81, 1986- 13:32.61, 1987- 13:21.44, 28:46.65; 1988- 13:20.67, 1990- 13:29.81, 1991- 13:26.52, 28:38.27; 1992- 13:21.86, 1993- 13:17.48, 28:09.04; 1994- 13:15.17, 28:06.03. pbs: 1000m 2:20.44 '86, 1500m 3:37.5 '85, 2000m 5:01.35 '87, 3000m 7:46.08 '87.

Fermin CACHO b.16 Feb 1969 Agreda, Soria 1.75m 63kg. Rumancia.
At 1500m: OG: '92- 1; WCh: '91- 5, '93- 2; EC: '90- 11, '94- 1; WJ: '88- 3; EJ: '87- 12; WCp: '89- 6, '92- 4; ECp: '93- 2; WI: '91- 2; EI: '90- 2. Won Spanish 1500m 1989-93.
Spanish 1000m record 1993.
Progression at 1500m: 1986- 3:58.17, 1987- 3:45.9, 1988- 3:42.56, 1989- 3:36.23, 1990- 3:37.04, 1991- 3:32.03, 1992- 3:32.69, 1993- 3:32.01, 1994- 3:35.27. pbs: 800m 1:45.37 '91, 1000m 2:16.13 '93, 1M 3:50.74 '91, 3000m 7:46.11i '92.
Good footballer at school, concentrated on athletics from age 17.

Tomás DE TERESA b.5 Sep 1968 Santoña, Cantabria 1.83kg 69kg.Numancia.
At 800m: WCh: '91- sf; EC: '94- 3; WI: '91- 2; EI: '90- 2; EJ: '97- 1; WCp: '89- 8; ECp: '89- 6, '91- 4. Won Spanish 800m 1989, 1991, 1994.
Spanish 800m record 1990.
Progression at 800m: 1984- 1:56.1, 1985- 1:52.6, 1986- 1:51.36, 1987- 1:48.67, 1988- 1:46.80, 1989- 1:46.26, 1990- 1:44.99, 1991- 1:45.44, 1992- 1:45.39, 1993- 1:46.23, 1994- 1:45.89. pbs: 400m 47.24 '89, 1000m 2:19.99 '94.

Martin FIZ b.3 Mar 1963 Vitoria 1.69m 56kg. Reebok RC.
At Mar: EC: '94- 1. At 5000m: OG: '92- h; WC: '91- h; EC: '90- h. World CC: '90- 15, '91- 20, '93- 14. Won Spanish CC 1990, 1992.
Spanish marathon record 1994.
Progression at 10000m, Mar: 1987- 29:17.2, 1990- 28:40.81, 1991- 28:00.19, 1992- 28:12.07, 1993- 28:00.97, 2:12:47; 1994- 28:37.71, 2:10:21. pbs: 1500m 3:44.0 '88, 3000m 7:50.17 '90, 5000m 13:20.01 '91, 3000mSt 8:28.9 '88.
In 1982 he was 16th in the World Junior cross-country and was Spanish junior champion at 5000m. Won Helsinki marathon on début at the event in 1993, and after 12th at Boston returned to Finland to win the 1994 European title.

Diego GARCIA b.12 Oct 1961 1.72m 62kg. Iraurgi.
At Mar: OG: '92- 9; WCh: '91- 14; EC: '94- 2; WCp: '91- 23, '93- 10.
Progression at Mar: 1991- 2:12:54, 1992- 2:10:30, 1993- 2:10:38, 1994- 2:10:46. pbs: 10000m 28:48.5 '92.

Martin Fiz: lead Spanish triumph in European Championships marathon

Third at Fukuoka 1992 was his best marathon placing until the European silver in 1994.

Jesús Angel GARCIA b.17 Oct 1969 Madrid 1.71m 62kg. Valencia CF.
At 50kmW: OG: '92- 10; WCh: '93- 1; EC: '94- 4; WCp: '92- 2.
Progression at 50kmW: 1991- 4:05:10, 1992- 3:48:24, 1993- 3:41:41, 1994- 3:41:28. pbs: 10000mW 42:27.52 '90, road: 10kmW 40:38 '91, 20kmW 1:24:11 '91.

Basilio LABRADOR b.29 Mar 1967 Los Realejos, Tenerife 1.65m 62kg. CEAT.
At 50kmW: WCh: '91- dnf, '93- 5; EC: '90- 4, '94- 17; WCp: '89- 19, '91- 23, '93- 15.
Progression at 50kmW: 1989- 3:59:51, 1990- 3:54:45, 1991- 4:03:42, 1992- 4:04:14, 1993- 3:46:46, 1994- 3:55:38. pbs: 10000mW 42:24.2 '90, 20kmW 1:23:44 '93; road 10kmW 41:27 '90.

Valentin MASSANA b.5 Jul 1970 Barcelona 1.62m 50kg. CN Barcelona.
At 20kmW: OG: '92- dq; WCh: '91- 5, '93- 1; EC: '90- 5, '94- 3; WCp: '91- 10, '93- 2. At 10kmW: WJ: '88- 2: EJ: '87- 2, '89- 1. At 5000mW: WI:.'91- 5. Won Spanish 20kmW 1991-4, 50kmW 1993-4. Spanish walks records 20km 1992, 50km 1994.
Progression at 20kmW, 50kmW: 1987- 1:31:50, 1990- 1:22:33, 1991- 1:20:29, 1992- 1:19:25, 1993- 1:20:50, 3:46:11; 1994- 1:20:33, 3:38:43. pbs: 5000mW 18:59.60i '91, 19:36.5 '89; 10000mW 40:14.17 '89, 1HrW 14,367m '90; road 10kmW 39:27 '92.

Antonio PEÑALVER b.1 Dec 1968 Alhama, Murcia 1.91m 77kg. Alfil. Student.
At Dec: OG: '88- 23, '92- 2; WCh: '91- 8; EC: '90- 6, '94-dnf; WJ: '86- 7; EJ: '87- 8; ECp: '91- 1B, '93- 9, '94- 6. Spanish champion 1989. At Hep: EI: '92- 3. Nine Spanish decathlon records 1988-92.
Progression at Dec: 1986- 7229, 1987- 7044, 1988- 7891, 1989- 8050, 1990- 8214, 1991- 8306, 1992- 8534w/8478, 1993- 7738, 1994- 8160w/8084. pbs: 100m 11.01 '90, 10.76w '92; 200m 22.0 '90, 400m 48.88 '88, 1500m 4:28.84 '90, 110mh 14.09/ 13.92w '92; HJ 2.12 '92, PV 5.00 '92, LJ 7.55 '90, TJ 15.00 '85, SP 17.32 '91, DT 50.66 '91, JT 63.08 '91, Hep 6062i '92.
Missed 1993 World Championships due to a broken finger.

Daniel PLAZA b.3 Jul 1966 Barcelona 1.81m 63kg. AAC.
At 20kmW: OG: '88- 12, '92- 1; WCh: '91- dq, '93- 3; EC: '90- 2, '94- dq; WCp: '87- 22, '89- 11, '91- 4, '93- 6. At 10kmW: EJ: '85- 2. Won Spanish 20kmW 1986, 1989.
Progression at 20kmW: 1984- 1:29:27t, 1985- 1:28:30, 1986- 1:26:50.5t, 1987- 1:24:01, 1988- 1:21:53, 1989- 1:22:09, 1990- 1:21:56, 1991- 1:20:47, 1992- 1:20:42, 1993- 1:21:11, 1994- 1:21:54. Track pbs: 5000mW 19:07.24 '90, 10000mW 40:34.3 '90, 20000mW 1:26:50.5 '86, 1HrW 14,842m '90; road: 10kmW 39:38 '90, 50kmW 3:49:31 '92.
In 1992 he became Spain's first ever Olympic champion in athletics. Disqualified in Tokyo 1991 after finishing third.

Isaac VICIOSA b.26 Dec 1969 1.75m 68kg. At. Melgar.
At 1500m: WCh: '93- h; EC: '94- 2; WCp: '94- 7. Spanish champion 1994.
Progression at 1500m: 1990- 3:45.3, 1991- 3:37.13, 1992- 3:40.2, 1993- 3:34.75, 1994- 3:36.01. pbs: 800m 1:47.65 '94, 1000m 2:19.56 '94, 1M 3:52.72 '94, 2000m 5:06.03 '93, 3000m 7:41.46i '94.

Women

Encarnación GRANADOS b.30 Jan 1972 Gerona 1.73m 53kg. GEiEG.
At 10kmW: WCh: '93- 3; EC: '94- 15. Spanish champion 1992, 1994 (road), 1993 (track).
Progression at 10kmW: 1991- 48:38, 1992- 44:51, 1993- 43:21, 1994- 44:35. pbs: track 3000mW 12:59.51i '94, 5000mW 22:12.7 '93, road 5kmW 21:38 '93.

Sandra MYERS b. 9 Jan 1961 Little River, Kansas 1.68m 58kg. Bikila Madrid. Music graduate of UCLA. Piano teacher.
At 400m: WCh: '91- 3, '93- 6; EC: '94- sf; WI: '91- 2, '93- 4; EI: '92- 1. At 400mh: WCp: '81- 7. At 100m: OG: '88- h; WCp: '89- 6. At 200m: EC: '90- 4; EI: '90- 4. Won TAC 400mh 1981, ECup B 100m & 200m 1991, 200m 1993; Spanish 100m 1988, 200m 1988-9, 400m 1990, 1993-4; LJ 1989. Spanish records 1988-91: 100m (4), 200m (3), 400m (4), LJ. US 400mh record 1980.
Progression at 400mh: 1980- 56.40, 1981- 56.38, 1983- 58.40, 1984- 61.53, 1987- 58.0; at 200m, 400m: 1987- 23.4, 52.7; 1988- 23.34, 53.76; 1989- 23.54i, 23.77; 1990- 22.38, 51.01; 1991- 22.62, 49.67, 1992- 23.00i, 51.21i/51.91; 1993- 23.28, 50.83; 1994- 23.54/23.30w, 50.33. pbs: 50m 6.28i '95, 60m 7.23i '90, 100m 11.06 '91, 600m 1:26.99 '93, 800m 2:10.18 '93, 100mh 13.48 '89, LJ 6.68i/6.60 '88.
As a teenager was principally a long jumper, taking up the 400mh with immediate success in 1980 winning AIAW titles at that event and LJ when at Cal State Northridge. Moved to Spain and took up Spanish citizenship, married to coach Javier Echarri. Breakthrough at 400m in May 1990 with Spanish records 51.22 and 51.18, and improved massively at 200m to place fourth in Split. In 1991 became the first Spanish women to win a World Championships medal. Missed 1992 Olympics through injury.

Maria Teresa ZUÑIGA b.28 Dec 1964 Eibar, Guipuzcoa 1.67m 56kg. Aurrerá. Police officer.
At 800m: OG: '88- 7; WCh: '91- h; EC: '90- sf; WCp: '89- 5. At 1500m: OG: '92- 6; WCh: '93- 12; EC: '94- 8; WI: '93- 5. Won Spanish 400m 1988, 800m 1982-3, 1990-2; 1500m 1989, 1993-4.
Spanish records: 800m (2) 1988, 1500m (2) 1988-92, 1000m 1989.
Progression at 800m, 1500m: 1979- 2:18.8i/2:19.02, 1980- 2:11.5, 1981- 2:10.4, 1982- 2:07.38, 4:21.8; 1983- 2:05.36, 1984- 2:06.59, 1985- 2:05.50i/2:08.54, 1986- 2:06.83, 1987- 2:02.61, 4:12.99; 1988- 1:57.45, 4:06.44; 1989- 1:58.49, 4:14.45; 1990- 2:00.11, 4:13.17i/4:22.67; 1991- 2:02.16, 1992- 2:01.28, 4:00.59; 1993- 2:03.52, 4:07.46, 1994- 2:03.96, 4:08.63. pbs: 200m 24.3 '88, 400m 52.71 '88, 1000m 2:34.66 '89, 1M 4:28.56 '92.

SWEDEN

Governing body: Svenska Friidrottsförbundet, Box 5628, S-114 86 Stockholm. Founded 1895.
National Championships first held in 1896 (men), 1927 (women). **1994 Champions**: **Men**: 100m: Peter Karlsson 10.32, 200m: Lars Hedner 20.82, 400m/400mh: Marko Granat 47.03/50.22, 800m: Torbjörn Johansson 1:48.08, 1500m: Peter Koskenkorva 3:46.54, 5000m: Claes Nyberg 14:14.55, 10000m: Kari Niemelä 29:36.99, Half Mar: Magnus Bergman 1:04:56, Mar: Anders Szalkai 2:16:02, 3000mSt: Magnus Bengtsson 8:46.22, 110mh: Niklas Eriksson 13.81, HJ: Patrick Thavelin 2.17, PV: Peter Widén 5.52, LJ: Mattias Sunneborn 7.94w, TJ: Arne Holm 16.90, SP: Sören Tallhem 18.88, DT: Kristian Pettersson 59.60, HT: Tore Gustafsson 73.52, JT: Patrik Bodén 86.24, Dec: Einar Cronstedt 7267, 10000mW/20kmW: Stefan Johansson 40:39.2/1:27:50, 50kmW: ?. **Women**: 100m: Therese Olofsson 11.72, 200m: Marika Johansson 23.84, 400m: Charlotta Johansson 52.67, 800m/1500m: Maria Akraka 2:02.75/4:12.28, 3000m: Pia Westin 9:29.68, 10000m/Mar: Midde Hamrin 33:46.89/2:46:58, Half Mar: Ingmaria Nilsson 1:14:08, 100mh: Ulrika Jeppsson 13.69, 400mh: Monica Westén 55.92, HJ: Emalie Färdigh 1.86, LJ: Annica Sandström 6.31, TJ: Nancy Mases 12.73, SP: Linda-Marie Mårtensson 16.03, DT: Anna Söderberg 58.74, JT: Elisabet Wahlander 53.40, Hep: Elisabet Hallerbåck 5374, 5000mW/10000mW: Veronica Öqvist 24:18.1/49:31.1.

Patrik BODÉN b.30 Jun 1967 Fryksände 1.87m 106kg. IF Göta. Studied engineering at University of Texas.
At JT: OG: '92- dnq 16; WCh: '91- 8, '93- 9; EC: '90- 3, '94- 4; WJ: '86- 8; WCp: '94- 4; ECp: '94- 4. Swedish champion 1992-4, won NCAA 1989-91. World javelin record 1990.
Progression at JT: 1983- 58.14, 1984- 63.58, 1985- 74.26; new: 1986- 74.66, 1987- 78.10, 1988- 76.52, 1989- 82.28, 1990- 89.10, 1991- 85.58R, 1992- 84.20, 1993- 88.26, 1994- 86.76. pbs: SP 15.76 '93, DT 49.28 '89, HT 53.44 '92.
Was fourth at LJ in National age 12 championships in 1979. Operations on right shoulder in 1990 and October 1991, on knees in 1990 and June 1991.

Henrik DAGÅRD b.7 Aug 1969 Halmstad 1.84m 81kg. Hässelby SK.
At Dec: WCh: '91- dnf, '93- 13; EC: '90- 9, '94- 2; WJ: '88- 4; EJ: '87- 7; ECp: '94- 2.
Three Swedish decathlon records 1994.
Progression at Dec: 1986- 6370, 1987- 7070, 1988- 7529, 1989- 8030, 1990- 8052, 1991- 7912, 1992- 7744, 1993- 7965, 1994- 8403. pbs: 100m 10.58 '89, 10.45w '94; 200m 21.25 '88, 400m 46.71 '94, 1500m 4:34.46 '90, 110mh 13.97 '94, HJ 2.07 '89, PV 5.00 '94, LJ 7.48 '89, TJ 14.08 '86, SP 15.52 '94, DT 45.64 '94, JT 69.26 '93.
Scored 8347 or higher in each of his four decathlons in 1994.

Sven NYLANDER b.1 Jan 1962 Varberg 1.94m 85kg. Malmö AI. Was at Southern Methodist University, USA.
At 400mh: OG: '84- 4, '92- sf; WCh: '83- 4, '87- 4, '91- sf, '93- sf; EC: '82- 7, '86- 3, '90- 2, '94- 2; ECp: '94- 1. Won NCAA 1983. At 110mh: EJ: 79- 6. Won Swedish 400mh 1982, 1987, 1990, 1992; 110mh 1979, 1983.
Six Swedish 400mh records 1982-94.
Progression at 400mh: 1978- 54.8, 1979- 52.62, 1981- 51.58, 1982- 49.64, 1983- 48.88, 1984- 48.97, 1985- 50.39, 1986- 48.83, 1987- 48.37, 1988- 49.35, 1990- 48.43, 1991- 49.39, 1992- 48.75, 1993- 49.21, 1994- 48.22. pbs: 100m 10.63 '87, 200m 21.18 '86, 400m 47.8i '81, 48.10 '82; 110mh 13.98/13.73w/ 13.7 '86, LJ 6.82i '79.
Had a remarkable record of making all major championships finals 1982-7, setting national records three times in these races. Returned in 1990 and again ran brilliantly for the European silver, but in 1991 went out in the semis in Tokyo; the first time that he did not make a major final. In 1994 he set his first Swedish record for seven years to take another European silver.

Patrik SJÖBERG b.5 Jan 1965 Göteborg 2.00m 82kg. Örgryte IS.
At HJ: OG: '84- 2, '88- 3=, '92- 2; WCh: '83- 11, '87- 1, '91- 7; EC: '82- 10=, '86- 6; EI: 1st 1985, 1987-8, 1992; EJ: '81- 8, '83- 3; WCp: '85- 1, '89- 1; WI: '85- 1, '87- dnq, '89- 3, '91- 13, '92- 2. Won GP 1992 (2nd 1988). Won SWE HJ 1981-7, 1989.
Twelve Swedish high jump records 1982-7,

European record 1985, World record 1987. WIB: 2.38 '85, 2.41 '87.
Progression at HJ: 1975- 1.30, 1976- 1.40, 1977- 1.59, 1978- 1.80, 1979- 1.91, 1980- 2.07, 1981- 2.21, 1982- 2.26, 1983- 2.33, 1984- 2.33, 1985- 2.38, 1986- 2.34, 1987- 2.42, 1988- 2.39i/2.37, 1989- 2.40, 1990- 2.34, 1991- 2.34, 1992- 2.38i/2.34, 1993- 2.39i/2.32. pbs: LJ 7.72 '87, TJ 15.87 '83.
Extraordinary record for the Swedish team from début at the age of 16, having never lost in 21 appearances, including five European Cup (C/B) wins. He missed the 1993 World Champs and the 1994 season through injury, but returned to competition in February 1995. He has jumped 2.30 or higher in 110 competitions.

Niklas WALLENLIND b.21 Nov 1968 Göteborg 1.85m 75kg. Mölndals AIK.
At 400mh: OG: '92- 5; WCh: '91- 8, '93- sf; EC: '90- 3, '94- sf; EJ: 87- 1. Swedish champion 400mh 1989, 1993; 400m 1989-92.
Swedish 400mh record 1992.
Progression at 400mh: 1985- 55.3, 1986- 54.26, 1987- 50.65, 1988- 50.95, 1989- 50.28, 1990- 48.52, 1991- 49.77, 1992- 48.35, 1993- 49.45, 1994- 49.31. pbs: 100m 11.06 '90, 200m 21.44 '92, 400m 46.37 '92, 800m 1:53.41 '87, TJ 12.10 '92.
Won the European Junior gold in 1987 in 50.65, having entered the meeting with a pb of 52.28. In 1990 he made similar improvement to take the European bronze in 48.52, after 48.80 in the semis and a pre-meet best of 49.74.

Dag WENNLUND b.9 Oct 1963 Mariestad 1.88m 97kg. Mariestads AIF. Was at University of Texas, USA.
At JT: OG: '88- 8, '92- dnq 15; WCh: '87- 8, '91- 7, '93- 7; EC: '86- dnq 15, '90- dnq 16, '94- 10; EJ: '81- 12. Swedish champion 1985-6, 1991. Won NCAA 1986-7.
Three Swedish javelin records 1985-7.
Progression at JT: 1980- 65.06, 1981- 70.50, 1982- 78.20, 1983- 81.06, 1984- 82.34, 1985- 92.20. new: 1986- 81.86, 1987- 82.64, 1988- 81.30, 1989- 82.52, 1990- 79.62, 1991- 85.52R, 1992- 80.80, 1993- 82.58, 1994- 84.36. pbs: SP 13.09 '82, DT 40.74 '84, HT 41.70 '84.

SWITZERLAND

Governing body: Schweizerischer Leichtathletikverband (SLV), Postfach 8222, CH 3001, Bern. Formed 1905 as Athletischer Ausschuss des Schweizerischen Fussball-Verbandes.
National Championships first held in 1906 (men), 1934 (women). **1994 Champions**: **Men**: 100m: David Dollé 10.48, 200m: Alain Reimann 21.03, 400m: Matthias Rusterholz 45.94, 800m: Enrico Cariboni 1:50.70, 1500m: André Bucher 3:45.32, 5000m: Markus Graf 14:07.16, 10000m: Arnold Mächler 28:57.11, Half Mar: Hansjörg Brücker 63:40, Mar: Peter Schneider 2:18:58, 3000mSt: Markus Hacksteiner 8:48.33, 110mh: Gunnar Schrör 14.13, 400mh: Daniel Ritter 49.95, HJ: Jan Berrada FRA 2.15, PV: Raynald Mury 5.30, LJ: Simon Schranz 7.57, TJ: Carlos Lima 15.29, SP: Hansruedi Meyer 17.43, DT: Patrick Buchs 51.88, HT: Oliver Sack 68.48, JT: Gregory Wiesner 71.40, Dec: Mirko Spada 7933w, 10000mW: Pascal Charrière 42:14.81. **Women**: 100m: Margret Haug 11.68, 200m: Regula Anliker-Aebi 23.08, 400m: Kathrin Lüthi 53.36, 800m: Anita Brägger 2:07.46, 1500m/3000m: Daria Nauer 4:16.56/9:22.50, 10000m/Half Mar: Isabella Moretti 35:16.22/75:49, Mar: Anne-Lise Blaser 2:55:12, 100mh: Julia Baumann 12.91, 400mh: Anita Protti 55.96, HJ: Sieglinde Cadusch 1.84, LJ: Rita Schönenberger 6.23, TJ: Doris Stelzmüller 12.64, SP/DT: Nathalie Ganguillet 15.87/50.28, JT: Michaela Dunkel 50.30, Hep: Manuela Marxer LIE 5976, 5000mW: Heidi Mäder 25:54.74.

Matthias RUSTERHOLZ b.16 Aug 1971 Herisau 1.83m 70kg. TV Herisau (Appenzell). Primary school teacher.
At 400m: EC: '94- 3. Swiss champion 1993-4.
Progression at 400m: 1987- 50.64, 1988- 48.37, 1989- 47.74, 1990- 47.04, 1991- 46.69, 1992- 46.57, 1993- 46.20, 1994- 45.43. pbs: 100m 10.68 '94, 200m 21.42 '93.

Women

Julie BAUMANN b.17 June 1964 St.Jerome, Québec, Canada 1.64m 54kg. LC Zürich. Psychology graduate of Concordia University, Canada. née Rocheleau.
At 100mh: OG: '88- 6 (qf 100m); WCh: '91- 5, '93- sf; EC: '94- 6; CG: '86- 4. At 60mh: WI: '93- 1. Won Swiss 100mh 1991, 1993-4.
Commonwealth 100mh record 1988, Swiss 1991.
Progression at 100mh: 1981- 14.32, 1982- 14.19, 1983- 13.93, 1984- 13.81, 1985- 13.8, 1986- 13.46/13.32w, 1987- 13.38, 1988- 12.78, 1991- 12.76, 1992- 12.93/12.87w, 1993- 12.99, 1994- 12.82. pbs: 50m 6.30i '89, 60m 7.34i '88, 50mh 6.73i '93, 60mh 7.95i '92, 100m 11.13 '88, 200m 24.00 '91.
Won the Mobil Grand Prix series at sprint hurdles, and was third overall, in 1988 when she set seven Canadian indoor records. Banned for two year following a positive drugs test in 1989. Swiss citizenship following her marriage.

Daria NAUER b.21 May 1966 1.68m 48kg. TV Längasse Bern. Infant teacher.
At 10000m: EC: '94- 3. At 3000m: WCh: '91- h, '93- h. World CC: '92- 21, '93- 24, '94- 12. Won Swiss 1500m 1994, 3000m 1990, 1992, 1994; CC 1992-4.

Swiss records 5000m 1993 & 1994, 10000m 1994.
Progression at 3000m, 10000m: 1980- 10:23.99, 1981- 10:20.48, 1982- 10:09.79, 1983- 9:57.46, 1984- 9:56.16, 1985- 9:46.37, 1986- 9:29.99, 1987- 9:19.13, 1988- 9:17.73, 1989- 9:28.69, 1990- 9:09.12, 1991- 8:57.50, 1992- 9:01.41, 1993- 8:54.53, 32:38.02; 1994- 8:57.13, 31:35.96. pbs 800m 2:08.66 '91, 1000m 2:49.04 '92, 1500m 4:16.56 '94, 5000m 15:13.93 '94.
After her track début at 10,000m in a mixed race in 1993, improved in May 1994 to 32:22.67, and then to 31:35.96 to take the European bronze.

Anita PROTTI b. 4 Aug 1964 1.70m 64kg. Lausanne-Sports.
At 400mh: OG: '88- sf; WCh: '91- 6; EC: '90- 2, '94- sf. At 400m: WI: '91- 3; EI: '89- 3. Won Swiss 400m 1988, 1991; 800m 1990, 400mh 1994.
Swiss records 400m, 400mh 1987-91
Progression at 400mh: 1980- 67.28, 1981- 62.75, 1982- 62.06, 1983- 61.34, 1984- 59.98, 1985- 58.72, 1986- 59.58, 1987- 56.69, 1988- 54.56, 1989- 54.71, 1990- 54.36, 1991- 54.25, 1994- 55.96. pbs: 400m 51.32 '90, 800m 1:59.98 '90.

SYRIA

Ghada SHOUAA. b.9 Oct 1973 1.78m 65kg.
At Hep: AsiG: '94- 1; AsiC: '91- 2, '93- 1.
Syrian records from 1991.
Progression at Hep: 1991- 5425, 1992- 5508, 1993- 6259, 1994- 6361. Syrian records: 200m 24.48 '94, 100mh 14.08 '93, HJ 1.81 '94, LJ 6.31 '93, SP 14.36 '94, JT 53.90'94.

TAJIKISTAN

Governing body: Light Athletic Federation of Republic of Tajikistan, Firdavsi Street 63, app. 54, Dushanbe 734061. Founded 1932.

Andrey ABDUVALIYEV b.30 Jun 1966 Leningrad 1.86m 112kg. Dushanbe Dyn.
At HT: OG: '92- 1; WCh: '91- 5, '93- 1; EJ: '85- 1; WCp: '94- 1. Won GP 1994, USSR HT 1991.
Three Asian hammer records 1993-4.
Progression at HT: 1981- 52.40, 1982- 59.70, 1983- 65.20, 1984- 71.54, 1985- 73.20, 1986- 74.76, 1987- 74.06, 1988- 80.38, 1989- 81.00, 1990- 83.46, 1991- 82.80, 1992- 82.54, 1993- 82.78, 1994- 83.36.
Trains under Anatoliy Bondarchuk at the Kiev Hammer School. In 1990 he withdrew from the Europeans at the warm-up, and in 1991 disappointed by failing to complete the USSR clean sweep in the hammer in the Worlds. He won the Olympic gold, although that was one of only two wins in ten competitions during 1992. After Tajikistan became a member of the Asian AA in May 1993, he won the World title with his second Asian record of the year. In 1994 he confirmed his position as world number one with 12 wins in 16 competitions.

TANZANIA

Governing body: Tanzania Amateur Athletic Association, PO Box 2172, Dar es Salaam. Founded 1954.

Bóay AKONAY b.3 Jan 1970 1.68m 62kg.
At 10000m: WCh: '93- 13; WJ: '88- 6 (5000m 5, 20kmRd 7); AfG: '91- 6. World Half Mar: '92- 3.
Progression at 10000m, Mar: 1988- 29:02.7, 1989- 30:01.4, 1990- 28:51.6, 1991- 28:27.47, 1992- 27:50.27, 1993- 28:18.97, 2:13:52; 1994- 2:08:35. pbs: 5000m 13:35.79 '92, 10000m: 28:49.0 '94, Road 10M 45:42 '92, Half Mar 60:45 '92.
Won Palermo marathon on début in 1993 and Fukuoka in 1994 after 6th at Boston.

TRINIDAD & TOBAGO

Governing body: National Amateur Athletic Association of Trinidad & Tobago, 1 Second Street, St Joseph, Trinidad. Founded 1945, reformed 1971.
1994 Champions Men: 100m: Ato Boldon 10.1, 200m/ 400m: Neil de Silva 20.8/45.9, 1500m: Nigel Sinaswee 4:01.9, 10000m: Adesh Seenath 32:26.2, 110mh: Karl Chaihong 14.5, 400mh: Anthony Julien 53.7, HJ: Kerry Edwards 2.05, PV: Kevin Stephens 3.15, LJ: Brent Yorke 7.92, TJ: Sherwin Elcock 14.00, SP: Hubert Maingot 14.79, DT: Anthony Alexander 41.06, JT: Ric Francis 57.56. **Women**: 100m/200m: Heidiann Harper 11.1/24.2, 400m: Angela Joseph 53.9, 1500m: Charleen Neptune 4:41.2, 100mh/400mh: Victoria Pacifique 15.8/62.5, HJ: Michelle Alleyne 1.60, LJ: Anne Walcott 5.18, SP: Marissa Duke 12.39, DT: Jocelyn Huggins 38.74, JT: Gwendolyn George 41.84.

Ato BOLDON b.30 Dec 1973 1.76m 75kg. Engineering student at San Jose CC, USA
At 100m/200m: OG: '92- h/h; WCh: '93- qf/-; CG: '94- 4/sf; WJ: '92- 1/1.
Progression at 100m, 200m: 1991- 10.54/10.44w, 21.07; 1992- 10.22, 20.63/20.6; 1993- 10.23, 20.59; 1994- 10.07, 20.53.
Only started athletics when a USA student.

UKRAINE

Governing body: Ukrainian Athletic Federation, Esplanadnaya Str. 42, Kiev 23. Founded 1991.
National Champions 1994: **Men**: 100m: Vladislav Dologodin 10.21, 200m: Aleksey Chikhachov 20.76, 400m: Vadim Ogiy 46.08, 800m: Andrey

Buzhenko 1:52.50, 1500m: Igor Lishinskiy 3:46.16, 5000m/10000m: Valeriy Chesak 13:59.00/ 29:25.27, Mar: Pavel Vasilenko 2:17:53, 3000mSt: Aleksey Patserin 8:43.02, 110mh: Vladimir Belokon 13.40, 400mh: Gennadiy Gorbenko 51.10, HJ: Yuriy Sergiyenko 2.24, PV: Vasiliy Bubka 5.40, LJ: Vitaliy Kirilenko 7.94, TJ: Vladimir Kravchenko 16.97, SP: Aleksandr Bagach 20.64, DT: Vladimir Zinchenko 63.26, HT: Andrey Skvaruk 81.72, JT: Andrey Maznichenko 78.00, Dec: Sergey Blonskiy 7400, 20kmW: Anatoliy Kozlov 1:23:55. **Women**: 100m: Zhanna Tarnopolskaya 11.00, 200m: Viktoriya Fomenko 22.81, 400m: Lyudmila Koshchey 52.32, 800m: Yelena Zavadskaya 1:58.81, 1500m: Yelena Storchovaya 4:13.26, 3000m: Tatyana Belovol 9:18.65, 10000m: Natalya Vorobyova 34:05.68, 2000mSt: Olga Kozel 6:25.12, 100mh: Nadyezhda Bodrova 12.98, 400mh: Tatyana Tereshchuk 54.96, HJ: Irina Mikhalchenko 1.88, LJ: Yelena Semiraz 6.79, TJ: Viktoriya Vershinina 13.77, SP: Valentina Fedyushina 20.56, DT: Olga Nikishina 59.44, HT: Marina Pirog 60.36, JT: Irina Kostyuchenkova 60.94, Hep: Irina Matyusheva 6122, 10kmW: Taytana Ragozina 44:36.

Aleksandr BAGACH b.21 Nov 1966 1.94m 125kg. Brovary TR.
At SP: WCh: '93- 3; EC: '94- 2; WI: '93- 3; EI: '92- 1, '94- 1; ECp: '89- dq3, '93- 1. USSR champion 1989, UKR 1994.
Progression at SP: 1984- 18.44, 1985- 18.79, 1986- 19.36, 1987- 20.01, 1988- 20.65i/20.21, 1989- 21.42 dq, 1991- 20.41, 1992- 21.19, 1993- 21.32i/20.85, 1994- 21.05i/20.64.
Disqualified for a positive drugs test after placing third at the 1989 European Cup, but stepped up to third after Mike Stulce caught for drugs use at 1993 World Championships.

Sergey BUBKA b.4 Dec 1963 Voroshilovgrad (now Lugansk) 1.83m 80kg. OSC Berlin and Donetsk U.
At PV: OG: '88- 1, '92- nh; WCh: '83- 1, '87- 1, '91- 1, '93- 1; WI: '85- 1, '87- 1, '91- 1; EC: '86- 1, '90- 6; EJ: '81- 7=; EI: '85- 1; WCp: '85- 1; ECp: '85- 1, '93- 2. USSR champion 1984. Won GWG 1986. Won overall GP 1991, 1993, 3rd 1987; won PV 1985, 1987, 1991, 1993; 2nd 1989.
17 world pole vault records 1984-94, including the world's first six-metre jump. 18 WIB from 5.81 '84 to 6.15 '93.
Progression at PV: 1975- 2.70, 1976- 3.50, 1977- 3.60, 1978- 4.40, 1979- 4.80, 1980- 5.10, 1981- 5.40, 1982- 5.55, 1983- 5.72, 1984- 5.94, 1985- 6.00, 1986- 6.01, 1987- 6.03, 1988- 6.06, 1989- 6.03i/6.00, 1990- 6.05i/5.90, 1991- 6.10/6.12i, 1992- 6.13, 1993- 6.15i/6.05, 1994- 6.14.
The surprise world champion in 1983 has gone on to dominate the world of pole vaulting, and was not beaten in a championship from then until sixth in Split in 1990. Won his fourth successive World title in 1993 and by the end of 1994 had jumped 6.00m or higher in 37 competitions, and 5.90m plus in 87. On 15 Mar 1991 he became the first vaulter to clear 20 feet when he set his 13th world indoor record at 6.10m.

Vasiliy BUBKA b.26 Nov 1960 Voroshilovgrad 1.84m 76kg. Donetsk U. Teacher. Elder brother of Sergey.
At PV: WCh: '93- 9; EC: '86- 2; WI: '85- 3. USSR champion 1985, UKR 1994.
Progression at PV: 1975- 3.25, 1976- 4.20, 1977- 4.90, 1978- 5.05, 1979- 5.20i, 1980- 5.20, 1981- 5.30, 1982- 5.50, 1983- 5.60i, 1984- 5.70i, 1985- 5.85, 1986- 5.80, 1987- 5.75, 1988- 5.86, 1989- 5.80, 1990- 5.81, 1991- 5.82, 1992- 5.80, 1993- 5.70, 1994- 5.75i/5.74.

Andrey BULKOVSKIY b.22 Jul 1972 Lvov 1.84m 64kg.
At 1500m (800m): WCh: '93- h; EC: '94- 5; EJ: '91- 2; ECp: '93- 1 (1), '94- 1.
Progression at 1500m: 1986- 4:09.0, 1987- 4:02.0, 1988- 3:56.98, 1989- 3:51.8, 1990- 3:49.40, 1991- 3:45.52, 1992- 3:44.52, 1993- 3:37.51, 1994- 3:36.99. pbs: 800m 1:47.32 '93, 1M 3:55.28 '94, 2000m 5:08.22i '94, 3000m 8:30.68 '93.
Ethnically Polish. He caused a sensation with sprint finishes to win the European Cup Superleague double in 1993.

Vladislav DOLOGODIN b.23 Feb 1972 1.88m 83kg. Kharkov Dyn.
At 200m/4x100mR: EC: '94- 2/2R; EI: '94- 2. At 100m: ECp: '94- 5. Won UKR 100m 1994.
Progression at 100m, 200m: 1991- 21.43/21.2; 1992- 10.3, 21.3; 1993- 10.32, 20.38; 1994- 10.18, 20.36. pb 60m 6.60i '94.

Vitaliy KIRILENKO b.25 Apr 1968 1.92m 80kg. Kharkov Dyn.
At LJ: WCh: '93- 3; EC: '94- 7; WSG: '93- 3. UKR champion 1993-4.
Progression at LJ: 1989- 7.88, 1991- 7.90, 1992- 8.05, 1993- 8.21, 1994- 8.21.

Aleksandr KLIMENKO b.27 Mar 1970 Kiev 1.95m 115kg. Kiev U.
At SP: OG: '92- 8; WCh: '91- 3, '93- dnq 13; EC: '94- 1; WI: '93- 4; WSG: '91- 1, '93- 1; WJ: '88- 1; EJ: '89- 1; EI: '92- 2; WCp: '94- 2. USSR champion 1991, UKR 1992. 2nd GP 1992.
Progression at SP: 1987- 16.69, 1988- 19.18, 1989- 19.38, 1990- 19.63i/19.54, 1991- 20.37, 1992- 20.84, 1993- 20.84i/20.78, 1994- 20.78.
Coached by his father Anatoliy (pb 18.86 '77).

Vitaliy KOLPAKOV b.2 Feb 1972 1.95m 92kg. At Dec: EC: '94- 9; WJ: '90- 4; EJ: '91- 1; ECp: '93- 5, '94- 1B. UKR champion 1992-3.
Progression at Dec: 1989- 6927, 1990- 7384, 1991- 7813, 1992- 7902, 1993- 8297, 1994- 8257. pbs: 100m 10.93 '94, 400m 47.83 '93, 1500m 4:32.20 '93, 110mh 14.33 '93, HJ 2.16 '94, PV 4.80 '93, LJ 7.80 '93, SP 15.32 '93, DT 47.14 '94, JT 60.02 '93, 1 Hr Dec 7652 '93.

Lev LOBODIN b.1 Apr 1969 1.88m 84kg.
At Dec: EC: '94- 3; ECp: '94- 2. UKR champion 1991.
Progression at Dec: 1988- 7019, 1991- 8018, 1992- 7998, 1993- 8156, 1994- 8201. pbs: 100m 10.82 '93, 10.65w '94; 400m 48.63 '93, 1500m 4:30.00 '91, 110mh 14.05 '93, HJ 2.10 '91, PV 5.00 '94, LJ 7.48i/7.45 '94, SP 15.40 '92, DT 45.50 '94, JT 55.34 '92.

Andrey SKVARUK b.9 Mar 1967 1.87m 102kg. Kharkov Dyn.
At HT: WCh: '93- nt; EC: '94- 1. UKR champion 1992, 1994.
Progression at LJ: 1985- 65.42, 1986- 72.54, 1989- 73.60, 1990- 77.24, 1991- 71.60, 1992- 82.92, 1993- 80.80, 1994- 81.72.

Oleg TVERDOKHLEB b.3 Nov 1969 Dnepropetrovsk 1.84m 73kg. Dnepropetrovsk U.
At 400mh: OG: '92- 6; WCh: '93- 6; EC: '94- 1; WSG: '91- 3; WCp: '92- 5, '94- 2; ECp: '93- 3, '94- 2. Ukrainian 400mh record 1994.
Progression at 400mh: 1986- 53.31, 1987- 51.68, 1988- 50.90; 1989- 50.07, 1990- 50.32, 1991- 49.80, 1992- 48.63, 1993- 48.62, 1994- 48.06. pbs: 200m 21.00 '93, 400m 46.18 '94.

Vladimir ZINCHENKO b.25 Jul 1959 1.92m 115kg. Zaporozhye SA.
At DT: OG: '92- dnq; WCh: '87- 5, '93- 5; EC: '94- 6; ECp: '93- 3, '94- 3. USSR champion 1987, CIS 1992, UKR 1992-4.
Progression at DT: 1977- 60.60, 1978- 59.96, 1979- 62.02, 1980- 66.14, 1981- 60.74, 1983- 66.70, 1984- 66.16, 1985- 66.46, 1986- 63.26, 1987- 67.58, 1988- 68.88, 1989- 63.20, 1990- 61.14, 1991- 64.64, 1992- 65.90, 1993- 65.28, 1994- 64.90. pb SP 19.37i '83.

Women

Inga BABAKOVA b.27 Jun 1967 Ashkabad 1.81m 55kg. née Butkus. Nikopol U.
At HJ: WCh: '91- 3; EC: '94- 4; WI: '93- 3; ECp: '93- 4=. 3rd GP 1991. UKR champion 1991-2.
Progression at HJ: 1987- 1.89, 1988- 1.92, 1989- 1.89i, 1991- 2.02, 1992- 2.00, 1993- 2.00i/1.96, 1994- 2.00.
Improved ten centimetres in 1991, having had no previous international experience.

Larisa BEREZHNAYA b.28 Feb 1961 Kiev 1.78m 66kg. Kiev SA. PE student.
At LJ: WCh: '91- 3, '93- 2; EC: '90- 4; ECp: '91- 2, '93- 5; WI: '89- 3, '91- 1, '93- 5; EI: '92- 1. Won USSR LJ 1989, UKR 1993.
Progression at LJ: 1980- 6.24, 1983- 6.68, 1984- 6.63, 1985- 6.65i, 1986- 7.19, 1987- 6.90, 1988- 7.07, 1989- 7.20i/7.18w/7.12, 1990- 7.10/7.13w, 1991- 7.24, 1992- 7.08i/7.01/7.15w, 1993- 6.99, 1994- 6.89i/6.66. pb 100mh 13.6 '79.

Valentina FEDYUSHINA b.18 Feb 1965 Feodosiya 1.90m 92kg. Simferopol SA.
At SP: OG: '88- dnq 13; WCh: '93- 7; EC: '94- 7; WI: '93- 4; EI: '92- 4; ECp: '93- 2, "94- 2. UKR champion 1994.
Progression at SP: 1982- 15.69, 1983- 17.31, 1984- 18.15, 1985- 19.01, 1986- 19.19/18.88, 1987- 20.28, 1988- 21.08, 1989- 17.56i, 1990- 19.90, 1991- 21.60i/ 19.04, 1992- 20.51i/20.30, 1993- 20.16, 1994- 20.82i/20.56.

Yelena KHLOPOTNOVA b.4 Aug 1963 Ust-Kamenogorsk 1.72m 64kg. formerly Kokonova, née Stetsura. Kharkov U. Student.
At LJ: WCh: '93- 4; EC: '94- 12; EI: '86- 3, '90- 2; WSG: '91- 3. USSR champion 1984-5, UKR 1992. USSR long jump record 1985.
Progression at LJ: 1981- 6.20, 1982- 6.50, 1983- 6.83, 1984- 7.09, 1985- 7.31, 1986- 7.00i, 1987- 6.95, 1988- 7.29, 1989- 6.89i, 1990- 7.06i, 1991- 6.94, 1992- 6.95, 1993- 6.83/7.01w, 1994- 7.03.

Inessa KRAVETS b.5 Oct 1966 Dnepropetrovsk 1.78m 58kg. née Shulyak. Kiev U. Married to Sergey Izvachuk.
At LJ (TJ): OG: '88- 10. '92- 2; EC: '90- 6, '94- 2 (3); EI: '94- 3; WSG: '91- 1; WCp: '94- 1. At TJ: WI: '93- 1; EI: '92- 1; ECp: '93- 3. Won GWG 1990. Won USSR LJ 1988, 1990; TJ 1991; CIS LJ 1992. 2nd GP LJ 1990, 1992, 1994.
World triple jump record 1991, three WIR 1991-3.
Progression at LJ, TJ: 1982- 6.19, 1983- 6.27, 1984- 6.44, 1985- 6.45i/6.39, 1986- 6.61, 1987- 6.72, 1988- 7.27, 1989- 6.88i/6.86, 1990- 7.10, 14.08; 1991- 6.95, 14.95; 1992- 7.37, 14.41; 1993- 6.87/7.02w, 14.70; 1994- 7.09, 14.91. pbs: 200m 24.0 '90, HJ 1.75 '83.
Three month drugs ban for stimulants 1993. Reported to be complemplating emigrating to Israel.

Larisa MIKHALCHENKO b.16 May 1963 Lvov 1.80m 93kg. Kharkov Dyn. Teacher.
At DT: OG: '88- 10; WCh: '87- 7, '91- 3, '93- 10; EJ: '81- 3; ECp: '91- 2, '93- 2. Won USSR DT 1991.
Progression at DT: 1979- 47.96, 1980- 52.14,

Inna Yevseyeva

1981- 54.74, 1982- 56.28, 1983- 62.00, 1984- 58.22, 1985- 64.92, 1986- 64.48, 1987- 64.88, 1988- 70.80, 1989- 63.22, 1990- 65.02, 1991- 69.20, 1982- 67.08, 1993- 63.90.

Olga NIKISHINA b.29 Apr 1966 1.72m 86kg.
At DT: EC: '94- 10, ECp: '94- 1. UKR champion 1990, 1993-4.
Progression at DT: 1984- 51.26, 1985- 59.72, 1986- 62.24, 1987- 60.78, 1988- 61.62, 1989- 60.32, 1990- 63.54, 1991- 59.36, 1992- 61.82, 1993- 62.32, 1994- 66.00.

Viktoria PAVLYSH b.15 Jan 1969 1.74m 80kg. Kharkov Dyn.
At SP: OG: '92- 8; EC: '94- 1; EJ: '87- 6; WCp: '94- 4. 3rd GP 1993. Ukrainian champion 1993.
Progression at SP: 1986- 15.73, 1987- 16.48, 1988- 16.28, 1989- 17.28, 1990- 17.86, 1991- 18.76, 1992- 19.66, 1993- 19.22, 1994- 19.61.

Zhanna TARNOPOLSKAYA b.6 Jul 1972 Nezhina, nr Chernigov 1.66m 52kg. Kiev Sp to Maccabi Tel Aviv. Married to Igor Pintsuvich (2nd WJ 110mh 1992).
At 100m (200m): WCh: '93- sf; EC: 2/4R (2); EJ: '91- 1/4R (1); ECp: '93- 3 (4), '94- 1/1R. At 60m: WI: '93- 3; EI: '92- 1. Won UKR 100m 1994.
WIR 50m at 6.09 for a few minutes in 1993. Two Ukrainian 100m records 1994.
Progression at 100m, 200m: 1987- 11.8, 1988- 11.75/11.5, 23.75; 1989- 11.64/11.5, 24.03; 1990- 11.99, 1991- 11.29/11.0, 23.56; 1992- 11.17, 1993- 11.08, 22.79; 1994- 10.99, 22.66. pbs: 50m 6.09i '93, 60m 7.07i '93.
Reported in 1994 as having signed a two-year contract committing her to emigrate to Israel.

Tatyana TERESHCHUK b.11 Oct 1969. Lugansk.
At 400mh: EC: '94- 6; ECp: '94- 2. UKR champion 1994.
Progession at 400mh: 1989- 57.58, 1990- 57.98, 1991- 57.19, 1993- 58.20/57.9, 1994- 54.96

Inna YEVSEYEVA b.14 Aug 1964 1.82m 62kg. Zhitomir U. Student.
At 800m: OG: '88- 6, '92- 4; WCh: '91- h; WSG: '89- 3, '91- 1; EI: '92- 2.
WIR 1000m 1992.
Progression at 800m: 1983- 2:02.7, 1985- 2:02.7, 1986- 2:00.6, 1988- 1:56.0, 1989- 1:59.75, 1990- 2:01.49, 1991- 1:58.30, 1992- 1:57.20, 1993- 1:59.03, 1994- 2:03.23. pbs: 400m 50.80/50.6 '86, 600m 1:25.87i '88, 1000m 2:33.93i '92, 1500m 4:12.6 '88, 400mh 55.85 '86.

UNITED KINGDOM

Governing body: British Athletics Federation, 225a Bristol Road, Edgbaston, Birmingham, B5 7UB. Founded 1991 (replacing BAAB, founded 1932). The Amateur Athletic Association was founded in 1880 and the Women's Amateur Athletic Association in 1922.
National Championships (first were English Championships 1863-79): **UK Nationals** first held in 1977, not held in 1994, except for walks and road runs: men Half Mar: Paul Evans 61:30, 20kmW: Darrell Stone 1:27:24, 50kmW: Ed Shillabeer 4:54:32, women - Half Mar: Andrea Wallace 71:34, 10km: Lisa Longford 47:07.
AAA Championships first held in 1880 (women 1922). **1994 Champions: Men**: 100m: Linford Christie 9.91w, 200m: Solomon Wariso 20.67w, 400m: Roger Black 44.94, 800m: Craig Winrow 1:48.45, 1500m: Kevin McKay 3:40.59, 5000m: Dermot Donnelly 13:52.63, 10000m: Rob Denmark 28:03.34, Half Mar: Mark Hudspith 63:37, Mar: Dionicio Ceron MEX 2:08:53, 3000mSt: Justin Chaston 8:28.28, 110mh: Andrew Tulloch 13.70, 400mh: Peter Crampton 49.82, HJ: Brendan Reilly 2.24, PV: Andrew Ashurst 5.30, LJ: Barrington Williams 7.77, TJ: Jonathan Edwards 17.39, SP: Paul Edwards 18.32, DT: Kevin Brown 58.60, HT: Peter Vivian 70.80, JT: Mick Hill 84.60, Dec: Brian Thomas 7458, 10000mW: Darrell Stone 43:09.28. **Women**: 100m/200m: Katharine Merry

11.27w/22.85, 400m: Melanie Neef 52.56, 800m: Diane Modahl 2:01.35, 1500m: Kelly Holmes 4:01.41, 3000m: Sonia McGeorge 9:03.80, 10000m: Zara Hyde 33:23.25, Half Mar: Linda Rushmere 74:31, Mar: Katrin Dörre GER 2:32:34, 100mh: Clova Court 13.06, 400mh: Gowry Retchakan 57.08, HJ: Julia Bennett 1.89, PV: Kate Staples 3.65, LJ: Yinka Idowu 6.58w, TJ: Michelle Griffith 14.08, SP: Judy Oakes 18.38, DT: Jacqueline McKernan 56.94, HT: Lorraine Shaw 59.58, JT: Shelley Holroyd 57.08, Hep: Vicki Schofield 5587, 5000mW/10kmW: Verity Snook 23:22.52/48:05.
National Road Walk Champions: **Men**: 20km: Chris Cheeseman 1:29:11, 50km: Les Morton 4:32:25. **Women**: 5km: Melanie Wright 24:27, 10kmW: Perry Williams IRL 48:13, 20km: Vikki Lupton 1:44:48.

Stephen BACKLEY b.12 Feb 1969 Sidcup 1.96m 95kg. Cambridge H.
At JT: OG: '92- 3; WCh: '91- dnq 15, '93- 4; EC: '90- 1, '94- 1; CG: '90- 1, '94- 1; WJ: '88- 2; EJ: '87- 1; WCp: '89- 1, '94- 1; ECp: '89- 1; WSG: '89- 1, '91- 1. Won GP 1989 (3rd overall), UK 1988-90; AAA 1989, 1992.
Three world javelin records 1990-2, world junior record 1988. Eight UK and Commonwealth records 1989-92.
Progression at JT (old): 1985- 64.34, new: 1986- 64.98 (69.74), 1987- 78.16, 1988- 79.50, 1989- 85.90, 1990- 90.98, 1991- 91.36, 1992- 91.46, 1993- 85.10, 1994- 85.20.
The first British male thrower to set a world record: 89.58 in Stockholm with a Sandvik javelin, and 90.98 at Crystal Palace on his second throw with a Németh model, both 1990. When these were banned at the end of 1991 his 89.58 was reinstated as the world record and in New Zealand in 1992 he achieved the first 90m throw with the revised javelin specification.

Roger BLACK b.31 Mar 1966 Portsmouth 1.90m 79kg. Team Solent.
At 400m/4x400mR: OG: '92- sf/3R; WCh: '87- 2R, '91- 2/1R; EC: '86- 1/1R, '90- 1/1R, '94- 2/1R; CG: '86- 1/1R; EJ: '85- 1/1R; WCp: '94- 1R; ECp: '87- 2/2R, '91- 1/1R, '94- 1/1R. Won UK 200m 1987, 400m 1990, 1992; AAA 400m 1994. Won 400m GP 1991.
UK 400m record and European 300m best 1986, Three European & Commonwealth 4x400mR records 1987-91.
Progression at 400m: 1984- 47.7, 1985- 45.36, 1986- 44.59, 1987- 44.99, 1989- 46.2, 1990- 44.91, 1991- 44.62, 1992- 44.72, 1993- 45.86, 1994- 44.78.
pbs: 100m 10.57 '91, 10.4 '87; 200m 20.60 '90, 300m 32.08 '86, 600m 1:16.2 '91, 800m 1:52.1 '90.
Started his international career with six gold medals in three international championships in 1985-6. Missed the 1987 World 400m (though he ran in the relay), 1988 and most of 1989 through injury, but returned to another European double. In 1992 more surgery was required on a badly aligned hip, and then in 1993 his season was brought to an early close by a debilitating virus illness. Despite so much adversity he fought back to fitness in 1994 and won a men's record 5th gold medal at relay as well as individual silver.

Linford CHRISTIE b.2 Apr 1960 St.Andrews, Jamaica 1.89m 77kg. Thames Valley Harriers.
At 100m/4x100mR (200m): OG: '88- 2/2R (4), '92- 1/4R (sf); WCh: '87- 3, '91- 4/3R, '93- 1/2R; EC: '86- 1/3R (sf), '90- 1/2R (3), '94- 1; CG: '86- 2, '90- 1/1R, '94- 1; WCp: '89- 1/2R, '92- 1 (2), '94- 1/1R; ECp: '87- 1 (1), '89- 1/1R, '91- 1, '93- 1/1R, '94- 1/1R (1). At 200m: WI: '91- 2; EI: '86- 1, '88- 3. At 60m: WI: '91- 2; EI: '88- 1, '90- 1. Won UK 100m 1985, 1987, 1990-3; 200m 1985 (tie), 1988; AAA 100m 1986, 1988-9, 1991-4; 200m 1988. GP 100m: 2nd 1994, 3rd 1992.
WIR 200m (20.25) 1995. European records: 100m (3) 1988-93, 4x100m 1993, indoor 60m (3) 1990 (6.51), 1994 (6.48), 1995 (6.47). Commonwealth records: 100m (2) 1991-3, 4x100m (4) 1989-93. UK records: five 100m 1986-93, one 200m 1988. WIR 4x200mR 1991.
Progression at 100m, 200m: 1977- 10.9, 23.2; 1978- 22.5; 1979- 10.7/10.6w, 21.89/21.8; 1980- 10.73/10.6/10.5w, 22.0/21.4w; 1981- 10.85/10.7, 21.6/21.70i; 1982- 10.50, 21.38/21.2; 1983- 10.46/10.4, 21.71i/21.31w; 1984- 10.44/10.31w, 21.0/21.44; 1985- 10.42/10.20w, 21.37i; 1986- 10.04, 20.51; 1987- 10.03, 20.48; 1988- 9.97, 20.09; 1989- 10.10/10.08w, 20.51; 1990- 10.02/9.93w, 20.33; 1991- 9.92/9.90w, 20.43; 1992- 9.96, 20.25; 1993- 9.87, 20.39/20.19w; 1994- 9.91, 20.67/20.56i.
pbs: 60m 6.43+ '91, 6.47i '95; 150m 14.97 '94, 300m 33.80 '88, 400m 47.75 '91.
After a late start to an international sprinting career, become established as Europe's fastest man and reached the pinnacle of sprinting fame with gold medals at the 1992 Olympics and 1993 World Championships, where he missed tying the world record for 100m by a tiny margin. His 23 major championships medals (ten gold) is a British male record as is his total of 25 national titles; elevated a place at 1987 Worlds and 1988 Olympics following the disqualification of Ben Johnson. With a triple in 1994 he has won a record 7 individual (unbeaten) and 3 relay races in the European Cup. Unbeaten by a European at 100m since 17 Jul 1989.

In October 1993 his home track, the West London Stadium was renamed as the Linford Christie Stadium.

Robert DENMARK b.23 Nov 1968 Billericay 1.74m 60kg. Basildon. Sports sciences graduate of Newcastle Polytechnic.
At 5000m: OG: '92- 7; WCh: '91- 9, '93- 9; EC: '94- 2; CG: '94- 1; ECp: '93- 1. At 10000m: WCp: '94- 3. At 3000m: WI: '91- 3. Won AAA 10000m 1994, Indoor 3000m 1990-91, rd 10km 1992.
Progression at 5000m, 10000m: 1990- 14:08.02, 1991- 13:13.01, 1992- 13:10.24, 1993- 13:16.48, 1994- 13:22.40, 28:03.34. pbs: 800m 1:48.84 '90, 1500m 3:38.34 '92, 1M 3:55.38 '90, 3000m 7:39.55 '93, 2M 8:21.97 '91.

Jonathan EDWARDS b.10 May 1966 London 1.81m 70kg. Gateshead. Physics graduate from Durham University.
At TJ: OG: '88- dnq 23, '92- dnq; WCh: '93- 3; EC: '94- 6; CG: '90- 2, '94- 2; WI: '93- 6; WCp: '89- 3, '92- 1; ECp: '93- 2, '94- 4. Won UK 1989, 1992; AAA 1989, 1994.
Progression at TJ: 1983- 13.84, 1984- 14.87/ 15.01w, 1985- 15.09, 1986- 16.05, 1987- 16.35, 1988- 16.74, 1989- 17.28, 1990- 16.51/16.93w, 1991- 17.43, 1992- 17.34, 1993- 17.44/17.70w, 1994- 17.39. pbs: 60m 6.77i '93, 100m 10.7/10.80 '92, 10.63w '90, 10.6w '89; LJ 7.41/7.45w '92.
A committed Christian previously refused to compete on Sundays, thus passing the 1991 World Championships, but did so in 1993.

Julian GOLLEY b.12 Sep 1971 Hammersmith, London 1.85m 80kg. Belgrave H. Student.
At TJ: OG: '92- dnq 26; EC: '94- 9; CG: '94- 1; WJ: '90- 11; WSG: '93- 3; WCp: '94- 2. Won AAA 1992.
Progression at TJ: 1988- 14.36, 1989- 15.55/ 15.64w, 1990- 15.88/16.01w, 1991- 16.06i/16.01/ 16.15w, 1992- 16.95, 1993- 16.87/16.88w, 1994- 17.06.

Dalton GRANT b.8 Apr 1966 London 1.86m 74kg. Haringey. Part-time social worker.
At HJ: OG: '88- 7=, '92- dnq; WCh: '91- 4, '93- dnq 14=; EC: '90- 4=, '94- 9=; WI: '87- 8=, '89- 4, '93- 4=; EI: '89- 2, '94- 1; CG: '86- 7, '90- 2, '94- 5; EJ: '85- 6; WCp: '89- 2; ECp: '89- 1, '91- 1, '94- 3. Won AAA 1989-90, UK 1990-1, 1993.
Nine UK high jump records 1988-91, three Commonwealth records 1989-91. Four UK indoor records 1989 to 2.35, equalling the Commonwealth record.
Progression at HJ: 1981- 1.90, 1982- 2.10, 1983- 2.10, 1984- 2.16, 1985- 2.22, 1986- 2.20, 1987- 2.28i/2.25, 1988- 2.31, 1989- 2.35i/2.34, 1990- 2.34, 1991- 2.36, 1992- 2.28, 1993- 2.34, 1994- 2.37i/2.34. pbs: 60mh 8.4i '92, 110mh 15.38 '91, LJ 7.00/7.14w '93, TJ 14.93 '86.
In 1991 from a season's best of 2.20 he won the European Cup with 2.30. Then further moderate form until Tokyo, where he entered at 2.31, 1 cm above his year's best, cleared that, passed 2.34 and then cleared 2.36!

Rob Denmark: European silver, Commonwealth gold

David GRINDLEY b.29 Oct 1972 1.88m 79kg. Wigan H. Accountancy student at Manchester Metropolitan University.
At 400m/4x400mR: OG: '92- 6/3R; WJ: '90- 2R; EJ: '91- 1/1R; EI: '92- 3; ECp: '93- 1/1R. Won GP 1993.
UK 400m record 1992.
Progression at 400m: 1988- 49.6, 1989- 50.1, 1990- 46.39, 1991- 45.41, 1992- 44.47, 1993- 44.53. pbs: 200m 21.50 '92, 20.89w '93; 300m 32.45 '93, 600m 1:17.1 '91, 800m 1:52.7 '91.
Dramatic improvement in 1990, starting with nearly two seconds off his 400m pb with 48.0 and further with international wins in 47.52, 47.26 and 46.39. In 1991 he won double European Junior gold and in 1992 broke the British record to make the Olympic final. Had to miss 1993 Worlds through injury. Missed whole of 1994 season through ligament damage to his left foot.

Michael HILL b.22 Oct 1964 Leeds 1.90m 98kg. Leeds City. Student.
At JT: OG: '88- dnq 20, '92- 11; WCh: '87- 7, '91- 5, '93- 3; EC: '86- 8, '90- 4, '94- 6; CG: '86- 2, '90- 2, '94- 2; EJ: '83- 11; WCp: '92- 5; ECp: '87- 4,

'91- 6, '93- 2, '94- 3. Won UK 1985-7, 1992-3; AAA 1987, 1990-1, 1994. 2nd GP 1987, 3rd 1993. UK and Commonwealth javelin record 1987.
Progression at JT: 1980- 56.32, 1981- 59.14, 1982- 64.72, 1983- 74.36, 1984- 71.08, 1985- 82.30, 1986- 82.04; new: 1986- 78.56, 1987- 85.24, 1988- 81.30, 1989- 82.56, 1990- 85.88, 1991- 86.32, 1992- 85.32, 1993- 86.94, 1994- 86.36.
Earned World bronze 1993 after disqualification of Dmitriy Polyunin. Operations on left knee in 1989 and March 1990. A seven handicap golfer.

Colin JACKSON b.18 Feb 1967 Cardiff 1.82m 73kg. Brecon.
At 110mh: OG: '88- 2, '92- 7; WCh: '87- 3, '91- sf, '93- 1/2 4x100mR; EC: '90- 1, '94- 1; CG: '86- 2, '90- 1, '94- 1; WJ: '86- 1; EJ: '85- 2; WCp: '89- 2, '92- 1; ECp: '87- 2, '89- 1, '91- 1, '93- 1. Won UK 1986, 1989-90, 1992; AAA 1986, 1988-90, 1992-3; GWG 1994. Won GP 1993, 3rd 1989. At 60mh: WI: '87- 4, '89- 2, '93- 2; EI: '87- 2, '89- 1, '94- 1 (1 60m).
World records for 110mh 1993, 60mh indoors 1994; 7 European 8 Commonwealth and 9 UK records at 110mh 1988-93; 9 UK, 4 Commonwealth & European records at 60mh toW IRs 7.36 & 7.30 '94. European junior 110mh record 1986. World best 200mh 1991.
Progression at 110mh: 1984- 13.92, 1985- 13.69, 1986- 13.44/13.42w, 1987- 13.37, 1988- 13.11, 1989- 13.11/12.95w, 1990- 13.08/12.8w, 1991- 13.09, 1992- 13.04, 1993- 12.91, 1994- 12.98/ 12.94Aw. pbs: 60m 6.49i '94, 100m 10.29 '90, 200m 21.19/21.0 '88, 21.18w '89; 200mh 22.63 '91, HJ 1.81 '82, LJ 7.96w '86, 7.56 '85; JT 52.86 '84.
World number one in 1992 with record 15 sub-13.20 times although a second round injury held him back to 7th in the Olympic final. Had majestic seasons in 1993 and 1994, each with 13 times under 13.20. In 1993 he set the world record to win his first World title and in 1994 he was undefeated. A run of 44 successive sprint hurdles victories from 29 Aug 1993 was ended at Madrid on 9 Feb 1995 by Allen Johnson at 60mh, when both men ran 7.42. Injury cost him the chance of medal at the 1986 Europeans, and he had operations on right knee 1990 and on left in 1991, after he had to withdraw from World Championships semis following a warm-up accident. Achieved a unique double with European Indoor titles at 60m and 60mh 1994.

Anthony JARRETT b.13 Aug 1968 Enfield, London 1.88m 80kg. Haringey. Part-time community worker.
At 110mh/4x100mR: OG: '88- 6, '92- 4/4R; WCh: '91- 3/3R, '93- 2/2R; EC: '90- 2, '94- 3; CG: '90- 2 (resR), '94- 2; EJ: '87- 1/1R; WCp: '94- 1/1R; ECp: '89- 1R, '93- 1R. UK champion 1987-8. 2nd GP 1993. At 60mh: EI: '90- 2.
Progression at 110mh: 1985- 15.1, 1986- 14.14/14.06w, 1987- 13.72, 1988- 13.45/13.35w, 1989- 13.31, 1990- 13.21, 1991- 13.13, 1992- 13.17/13.04w, 1993- 13.00, 1994- 13.22/13.1. pbs: 100m 10.55 '93, 10.42w '87, 200m 20.67 '90, 60mh 7.42i '95, 200mh 22.77w '91, 23.8 '88.

Du'aine LADEJO b.14 Feb 1971 Paddington, London 1.86m 83kg. Belgrave H. Graduate of University of Texas.
At 400m/4x400mR: OG: '92- resR; WCh: '93- qf/hR; EC: '94- 1/1R; CG: '94- 2/1R; WJ: '90- 7; WCp: '92- 3R, '94- 2/1R; ECp: '93- 1R, '94- 1R. UK champion 1993.
Progression at 400m: 1990- 46.66, 1991- 46.97, 1992- 45.25, 1993- 45.92/45.2, 1994- 44.94. pbs: 200m 20.96 '93, 300m 32.73 '94.
Spent eight years in the USA, where he played American Football in high school and having originally gone for basketball coaching turned to track at university. Olympic bronze medal as he ran in heats of the 4x400m in 1992. Clearly benefitting from Tony Hadley's coaching he leapt into world class in 1994.

Richard NERURKAR b.6 Jan 1964 Wolverhampton 1.77m 61kg. Bingley H. Masters degree at Harvard University, USA, formerly at Oxford University. Formerly a language teacher.
At 10000m: OG: '92- 17; WCh: '91- 5; EC: '90- 5. At Mar: EC: '94- 4; WCp: '93- 1. Won AAA 10000m 1990, English CC 1990-1, 1993.
Progression at 5000m, 10000m, Mar: 1987- 13:45.45, 28:57.40; 1988- 13:37.3i, 28:29.0; 1989- 13:27.86i/13:29.11, 28:37.14; 1990- 13:23.36, 28:05.16; 1991- 13:31.88, 27:57.14; 1992- 13:28.94, 28:07.44; 1993- 13:30.06, 27:40.03, 2:10:03; 1994- 13:36.89, 28:53.03, 2:11:56. pbs: 1500m 3:48.7 '90, 1M 4:05.1 '90, 3000m 7:48.00 '92, 2M 8:32.1 '90, Half Mar 61:33 '92.
He was a useful runner while at school (won Northern Schools at age 14) but did not make a major impression until after graduation. Excelled for fifth places in European and World Championships. In 1993 he won his first two marathons, at Hamburg (2:10:57 on his début) and the World Cup.

John REGIS b.13 Oct 1966 Lewisham, London 1.81m 88kg. Belgrave H.
At 200m/4x100mR (/4x400mR) (100m): OG: '88- sf/2R (h), '92: 6/4R/3R; WCh: '87- 3, '91- sf/3R/1R, '93- 2/2R; EC: '90- 1/2R/1R (3); CG: '86- 8, 90- 2/1R (7), '94- 2; WCp: '89- 2R, '94- 1R; ECp: '89- 1/1R, '91- 2, '93- 1/1R/1R, '94- 1R; WI: '89- 1; EI: '87- 3, '89- 2. At 100m: EJ: '85- 3/1R.

Won UK 200m 1985 (=), 1986, 1991, 1993; 100m 1988; AAA 200m 1986-7, 1990, 1992. 3rd GP 200m 1991, 2nd 1993.
Four UK 200m records 1987-94. European & Commonwealth 4x400m record 1990, Commonwealth 4x100m records 1989 and 1990. WIR 4x200m 1991. European 300m bests 1991, 1992.
Progression at 100m, 200m: 1982- 11.3, 22.6; 1983- 11.1, 22.0; 1984- 10.8, 21.31; 1985- 10.51/ 10.45w, 20.78; 1986- 10.43, 20.41; 1987- 10.37, 20.18; 1988- 10.31, 20.32; 1989- 10.39, 20.35; 1990- 10.20/10.07w, 20.11; 1991- 10.22, 20.12; 1992- 10.32, 20.09; 1993- 10.15, 19.94; 1994- 10.38/ 10.10w, 19.87. pbs: 60m 6.71i '91, 300m 31.67 '92, 400m 45.48 '93, 200mh 22.79 '91, TJ 14.28 '82.
In 1987 he very nearly won the World title, as he led at 195m. At the 1990 Europeans he won a men's record four medals, including a 43.93 third leg to ensure Britain's 4x400m gold. Withdrew from 1994 European through Achilles injury, but came back for Commonwealth silver. Cousin of soccer international Cyrille Regis.

Curtis ROBB b.7 Jun 1972 Liverpool 1.86m 66kg. Liverpool H. Medical student at Sheffield University.
At 800m: OG: '92- 6; WCh: '93- 4; WSG: '91- 2=; EJ: '91- 1. At 1500m: ECp: '93- 5. Won UK and AAA 800m 1992, UK 1500m 1993.
Progression at 800m, 1500m: 1988- 4:00.3, 1989- 3:50.4; 1990- 1:48.36, 3:46.9; 1991- 1:46.63, 3:49.69; 1992- 1:45.16, 1993- 1:44.92, 3:38.56; 1994- 1:48.07. pbs: 400m 48.9 '93, 1000m 2:18.99 '92
AAA junior champion at 1500m 1990-1.

Mark ROWLAND b.7 Mar 1963 Watersfield, W.Sussex. 1.83m 68kg. Phoenix.
At 3000mSt: OG: '88- 3; EC: '90- 2, '94- 4. At 5000m: CG: '90- 7. At 3000m: EI: '87- 4; WI: '87- 4. Won UK 1500m 1985, AAA 3000mSt 1988, 5000m 1989.
European best 2000m steeple 5:19.86 in 1988. UK 3000mSt record 1988.
Progression at 1500m, 3000mSt: 1980- 3:57.5; 1983- 3:47.9; 1984- 3:42.6; 1985- 3:42.6; 1986- 3:37.2; 1987- 3:39.24, 8:21.03; 1988- 3:34.53, 8:07.96; 1989- 3:40.63, 8:17.22; 1990- 3:37.15, 8:13.27; 1992- 8:20.32, 1994- 8:22.20. pbs: 800m 1:49.8 '84, 1M 3:52.99 '86, 2000m 5:08.07 '85, 3000m 7:49.82 '89, 2M 8:26.19 '87, 5000m 13:21.83 '88.
Second in English Schools 800m 1979, but gave up athletics for soccer 1981-2. Took up the steeplechase in 1987, running 8:26.76 on début. Took 8.38 sec off his best in 1988 Olympic final. Missed 1991 season outdoors and all of 1993 through injury.

Steve SMITH b.29 Mar 1973 Liverpool 1.86m 70kg. Liverpool H.
At HJ: OG: '92- 12; WCh: '91- dnq 29, '93- 3; EC: '94- 2; CG: '94- 2; WI: '93- 3; WJ: '90- dnq, '92- 1; EJ: '91- 1; WCp: '94- 3; ECp: '93- 6. Won AAA 1992.
World junior record 1992, two British & Commonwealth records 1992-3.
Progression at HJ: 1987- 1.84, 1988- 1.99, 1989- 2.09, 1990- 2.25, 1991- 2.29, 1992- 2.37, 1993- 2.37, 1994- 2.38i/2.33. pbs: 100m 11.2 '93, LJ 7.51 '92, 7.65w '93; TJ 13.61 '90.
Improved UK junior record from 2.31 to 2.33, 2.35 and 2.37 in taking the 1992 World Junior ttitle. Cleared 2.37 again for bronze at World indoors and out 1993. Gambled at Olympics, when he very nearly won a medal, narrowly failing at 2.34, but actually clearing only 2.24.

Matthew YATES b.4 Feb 1969 Rochford 1.90m 76kg. Newham & Essex Beagles.
At 1500m: OG: '92- sf; WCh: '91- 10, '93- 6; EI: '92- 1. At 800m: EC: '90-8; CG: '90- 3. Won AAA 1500m 1991, 1993. 3rd GP 1993.
Progression at 800m, 1500m: 1985- 4:01.73; 1986- 1:53.1; 1987- 1:51.2, 3:51.3; 1988- 1:50.69, 3:51.2; 1989- 1:47.58, 3:44.17; 1990- 1:46.25, 3:35.15; 1991- 1:47.18, 3:34.00; 1992- 1:45.05, 3:38.55; 1993- 1:46.00, 3:35.04; 1994- 1:48.42, 3:35.32. pbs: 1000m 2:16.34 '90, 1M 3:52.75 '93, 3000m 7:50.82i '93.
Won the 5th Avenue Mile 1991.

Women

Jackie AGYEPONG b.5 Jan 1969 London 1.72m 63kg. Shaftesbury Barnet H. Catering manager.
At 100mh: OG: '92- qf; WCh: '93- sf; EC: '90- h, '94- 7; CG: '94- 2; WJ: '88- sf (5 4x100mR); EJ: '87- fell; WCp: '94- 3/8R; ECp: '93- 2, '94- 1. Won UK 1993.
Progression at 100mh: 1985- 15.1, 1986- 14.8/ 14.6w, 1987- 13.68, 1988- 13.72, 1989- 13.50, 1990- 13.17, 1991- 13.23, 1992- 13.19/13.11w, 1993- 13.03/13.01w, 1994- 12.93. pbs: 60m 7.41i '89, 100m 11.81 '93, 11.72w '88, 200m 24.18 '90, 24.1w '93; 60mh 8.05i '95 (UK record).
Her brother Francis Agyepong (b. 16 Jun 1965) was 6th in the 1994 CG at triple jump, won the UK title 1990 and AAA 1993, with pb 16.95 '94, 17.00w '92. Jackie fell in several major races early in her career, but came through to world class in 1993-4.

Sally GUNNELL b.29 Jul 1966 Chigwell 1.67m 56kg. Essex Ladies. Solicitor's clerk. Married Jon Bigg (800m: 1:48.40 '85) 19 Oct 1992.
At 400mh/4x400mR: OG: '88- 5, '92- 1/3R; WCh: '91- 2/4R, '93- 1/3R; EC: '90- 6/3R, '94- 1/4R;

CG: '90- 1/1R, '94- 1/1R; WCp: '89- 3, '94- 1/1R; ECp: '89- 2/3R, '91- 2/3R, '93- 1/5R, '94- 1/1R. 2nd GP 1989 & 1991. At 100mh: OG: '88- sf; WCh: '87- sf; EC: '86- ht; CG: '86- 1, '90- 2; EJ: '83- sf (13 Hep). At 400m: WI: '89- 6; EI: '88- 4, '89- 1, '90- 4. Won UK 100mh 1986, AAA 100mh 1986-9, 1991-3; 400mh 1988; GWG 400mh 1994.
World 400mh record 1993, Commonwealth 1991. UK records: eight at 400mh 1988-93, one 100mh 1988, four 4x400mR 1990-1.
Progression at 100mh, 400mh: 1982- 15.0; 1983- 13.71; 1984- 13.30; 1985- 13.48/13.46w; 1986- 13.11; 1987- 13.01, 59.9; 1988- 12.82/12.80w, 54.03; 1989- 13.26, 54.64; 1990- 13.12, 55.38; 1991- 13.02, 53.16; 1992- 13.13, 53.23; 1993- 13.08, 52.74; 1994- 13.09, 53.33. pbs: 100m 11.83 '90, 11.8 '87, 11.79w '86; 200m 23.30 '93; 300m 36.44 '93, 400m 51.04 '94, 800m 2:08.36i '91, 2:13.22 '84; 60mh 8.27i '90, HJ 1.67 '83, LJ 6.08 '83, SP 11.18 '84, Hep 5493 '84.
First national title was 1980 WAAA junior LJ. Switched to 400mh from 100mh in 1988, and from her début of 59.9 in 1987 improved rapidly to 54.03 in Seoul.

Kelly HOLMES b.19 Apr 1970 Pembury, Kent 1.63m 54kg. Middlesex Ladies. Army corporal.
At 1500m: EC: '94- 2; CG: '94- 1; WCp: '94- 3; ECp: '94- 2. At 800m: WCh: '93- sf. Won UK and AAA 800m 1993, AAA 1500m 1994.
English 800m record 1993.
Progression at 800m, 1500m: 1984- 2:15.1, 4:35.3; 1985- 2:13.1, 4:41.4; 1986- 2:11.0, 4:26.9; 1987- 2:09.45, 4:26.10; 1989- 2:12.1, 1991- 2:11.8, 1992- 2:03.94, 4:27.7; 1993- 1:58.64, 4:17.3; 1994- 1:59.43, 4:01.41. pbs: 400m 54.7 '94, 1000m 2:37.29 '93.
The winner of the English Schools Junior 1500m in 1984, she hardly competed for four years after being a Junior International in 1987, and joining the Army at 18. Came back in 1992 to win the Southern 800m and compete in an Under 23 international. Made a great breakthrough in 1993, which she consolidated in 1994. She has played for the Army at volleyball and been Army judo champion.

Elizabeth McCOLGAN b.24 May 1964 Dundee 1.68m 45kg. née Lynch. Dundee Hawkhill H. Married steeplechaser Peter McColgan (pb 8:29.35 and 7 CG 1986 for 3000mSt) in 1987.
At 10000m (3000m): OG: '88- 2, '92- 5; WCh: '87- 5, '91- 1; CG: '86- 1, '90- 1 (3); EC: '86- 7 (12); WSG: '86- 3. At 3000m: WI: '89- 2 (6 1500m). Won World Half Mar 1992. Won UK 3000m 1989, 1991-2; 5000m 1988, 10000m 1986. World CC: '87- 2, '91- 3. GP: 3rd 3000m 1987, won 5000m 1988.
Four Commonwealth 10000m records 1986-91. UK half marathon best 1991. WIR 5000m 15:03.17 '92. Fastest ever half marathon on a certified course at Tokyo in January 1992.
Progression at 3000m, 10000m, Mar: 1979- 11:15.1; 1980- 10:41.8; 1982- 9:42.3; 1983- 9:34.5; 1984- 9:49.2; 1985- 9:03.80, 33:19.14; 1986- 8:46.53, 31:41.42; 1987- 8:39.85, 31:19.82; 1988- 8:42.50, 31:06.99; 1989- 8:34.80i, 8:44.93; 1990- 8:43.14, 32:23.56; 1991- 8:38.23, 30:57.07, 2:27:32; 1992- 8:41.07, 31:26.11, 2:27:38; 1993- 2:29:37. pbs: 800m 2:05.9 '87, 1000m 2:41.8 '87, 1500m 4:01.38 '87, 1M 4:26.11 '87, 2000m 5:40.24 '87, 5000m 15:01.08 '87, Half Mar 67:11 '92.
NCAA indoor mile champion 1986, while at University of Alabama. World road 10km bests on a loop course 31:07 '87, 30:59 '88 and 30:38 '89 a week after her World indoor silver at 3000m (and 6th at 1500m just 13 minutes later). Made an very fast return after daughter Eilish born 25 Nov 1990 to place third in World CC in March 1991, prior to her gold medal in Tokyo. Won her first two marathon races, the then fastest ever début marathon 2:27:32 at New York 1991 and Tokyo 1992, then third in London 1993. Returned from injury to road race competition in October 1994.

Katharine MERRY b.21 Sep 1974 Dunchurch 1.71m 58kg Birchfield H.
At 200m/4x100mR (100m): WCh: '93- qf; EC: '94- sf/5R; WJ: '90- (8)/2R; '92- 5/4R (6); EJ: '89- 5 (7 100m), '91- 3/2R, '93- 1/1R (2); ECp: '93- 6/6R, '94- 2/2R (2). Won UK 200m 1993, AAA 100m & 200m 1994.
UK indoor 200m record 1994.
Progression at 100m, 200m: 1986- 12.9; 1987- 12.1, 25.4; 1988- 11.85/11.79w, 24.9; 1989- 11.67/ 11.47w, 23.94/23.54w/23.9; 1990- 11.60, 23.65; 1991- 11.67, 23.50/23.41w; 1992- 11.52, 23.38; 1993- 11.58/11.40w, 23.20; 1994- 11.34/11.27w, 22.85. pbs: 60m 7.34i '94, 300m 38.7 '91, 400m 54.0 '94, HJ 1.74 '88, LJ 5.55 '87, 6.05w '88.
UK girls records for 100m and pentathlon (3518) 1989. Ran UK age records at 13 for 100m and at 14 for 100m and 200m. Won the WAAA girls indoor 60m in 1989 with a stunning 7.35. Six years as a British junior international, with 11 national age-group titles. After two second places at the 1994 European Cup, injury caused a below-par performance at the Europeans and her withdrawal from the Commonwealth Games.

Yvonne MURRAY b.4 Oct 1964 Musselburgh. 1.70m 50kg. Motherwell. Clerk.
At 3000m (1500m): OG: '88- 3, '92- 8; WCh: '87- 7 (h), '93- 9; EC: '86- 3, '90- 1, '94- 2; CG: '82- 10 (10), '86- 3 (5), '90- 2 (4); EJ: '81- 6; WCp: '89- 1, '94- 1; ECp: '87- 2, '89- 2, '91- 5, '93- (3); WI: '87- 5, '93- 1; EI: '85- 3, '86- 2, '87- 1. At 10000m: CG:

'94- 1. Won UK 3000m 1985, 1987, 1993; 5000m 1983; AAA 1500m 1992, 3000m 1988, 1990-1. 2nd GP 1993.
Commonwealth 2000m records 1986 (5:29.58) and 1994. UK junior 3000m record 1982.
Progression at 1500m, 3000m, 10000m: 1979- 4:49.6; 1980- 4:30.0, 10:11.8; 1981- 4:29.23, 9:30.0; 1982- 4:15.1, 9:07.77; 1983- 4:15.94, 9:04.14; 1984- 4:11.5, 8:58.54; 1985- 4:08.9, 9:00.97/9:00.94i, 33:43.80; 1986- 4:05.76, 8:37.15; 1987- 4:01.20, 8:42.07; 1988- 4:06.34, 8:29.02; 1989- 4:03.13, 8:38.51; 1990- 4:07.68, 8:39.46; 1991- 4:14.0, 8:36.05; 1992- 4:05.87, 8:36.63; 1993- 4:08.63, 8:30.30; 1994- 4:01.44, 8:29.60, 31:56.97. pbs: 800m 2:00.80 '87, 1000m 2:37.29 '89, 1M 4:22.64 '94, 2000m 5:26.93 '94, 5000m 15:50.54 '84, road 5km 15:20 '93.
At the 1986 Europeans she improved her 3000m pb by 5.76 sec. in the heat and a further 12.41 sec. in the final. Improved by 8.13 in the 1988 Olympics. In 1989 she became the first British woman to win a World Cup event and in 1990 won the European title with a devastating kick from 600m to go.

Paula RADCLIFFE b.17 Dec 1973 Northwich 1.72m 51kg. Bedford & County. Student at Loughborough University.
At 3000m: WCh: '93- 7; WJ: '92- 4; EJ: '91- 4. World CC: '91- 15J, '92- 1J, '93- 18.
Progression at 1500m, 3000m: 1988- 4:41.0, 1989- 4:34.9, 1990- 4:31.3, 9:41.4; 1991- 4:23.68, 9:23.29; 1992- 4:16.82, 8:51.78; 1993- 4:11.6, 8:40.40; 1994- 4:23.84. pbs: 400m 58.9 '92, 800m 2:05.97 '93, 1000m 2:47.17 '93, 1M 4:36.4 est '93, 2000m 5:39.20 '93, 5000m 16:16.77i '92.
Injured in 1994. Her great aunt won an Olympic swimming silver medal in 1924.

Gowry RETCHAKAN b.21 Jun 1960 Paddington, London 1.57m 46kg. Thurrock H. Married ITV statistician Ian Hodge in September 1990; former married name Varadakumar. Worked for the IAAF development department.
At 400mh: OG: '92- sf; WCh: '91- sf, '93- sf; EC: '90- h, '94- 8; CG: '94- 5; WCp: '92- 2; won AAA 1990-2, 1994; UK 1992-3. At 100mh: AsiG (for Sri Lanka): '82- 6.
Progression at 400mh: 1984- 64.7, 1985- 59.9, 1988- 61.04, 1989- 57.17, 1990- 56.73, 1991- 54.88, 1992- 54.63, 1993- 55.84, 1994- 55.78. pbs: 100m 12.3 '91, 200m 24.9/24.7w '92, 400m 55.1 '91!, 800m 2:07.37i '93, 2:11.8 '91; 60mh 8.7i '92, 100mh 14.0 '92, 14.52w '89, 14.65 '82; 200mh 28.1 '89, TJ 10.75 '89.
First national title as a junior in Sri Lanka in 1977. Son Sunni born 1987.

Phylis SMITH b.29 Sep 1965 Birmingham 1.69m 62kg. née Watt. Wigan & District H.
At 400m/4x400mR: OG: '92- 8/3R; WCh: '91- 4R, '93- 3R; EC: '94-3/4R; CG: '94- 4/1R; WCp: '94- 4/1R; ECp: '94- 1R. Won UK 200m 1990, 400m 1993, AAA 400m 1993.
Two UK records 4x400mR 1991.
Progression at 400m: 1984- 55.9, 1985- 56.2i, 1986- 53.52, 1987- 55.8, 1990- 53.1, 1991- 52.26, 1992- 50.40, 1993- 51.70, 1994- 51.30. pbs: 60m 7.39i '90, 100m 11.60 '87, 11.40w '90; 200m 23.40 '92, 300m 37.37 '91, 400mh 64.9 '85.
Made international début indoors in 1986, son born in 1988. Had to miss individual 400m at 1993 World Championships through illness, but recovered in time to contribute a 50.0 leg and gain a bronze medal in the relay.

Alison WYETH b.26 May 1964 Southampton 1.78m 58kg. Parkside. Formerly IAAF Development officer.
At 3000m: OG: '92- 9; WCh: '91- 11, '93- 5; EC: '90- 10, '94- 6; CG: '90- 11, '94- 3; ECp: '93- 3; 3rd GP 3000m 1993, 5000m 1994. At 1500m: WSG: '87- h. Won UK 1500m 1990-1; AAA 1500m 1993, 3000m 1989.
Progression at 1500m, 3000m: 1984- 4:28.7, 9:59.5; 1985- 4:27.3, 1986- 4:33.0, 9:51.65; 1987- 4:12.02, 9:31.11; 1988- 4:11.16, 9:23.17 (9:11.3 mx); 1989- 4:10.83, 8:48.96; 1990- 4:10.77, 8:52.26; 1991- 4:07.5, 8:44.73; 1992- 4:05.52, 8:43.93; 1993- 4:03.17, 8:38.42; 1994- 4:04.19, 8:45.76. pbs: 800m 2:04.8 '89, 1M 4:24.87 '91, 2000m 5:38.50 '93. 5000m 15:10.38 '94.

USA

Governing body: USA Track and Field (formerly TAC - The Athletics Congress of the USA), P.O.Box 120, Indianapolis, Indiana 46206. Founded 1979, when it replaced the AAU (founded 1888) as the governing body.
National Championships first held in 1876 (men), 1923 (women). **1994 Champions**: **Men**: 100m: Dennis Mitchell 10.14, 200m: Ron Clark 20.77, 400m: Antonio Pettigrew 44.43, 800m: Mark Everett 1:46.08, 1500m: Terrance Herrington 3:37.77, 5000m: Matt Giusto 14:04.30, 10000m: Tom Ansberry 29:01.84, Half Mar: Rod DeHaven 63:38, Mar: Paul Pilkington 2:12:13, 3000mSt: Mark Croghan 8:23.47, 110mh: Mark Crear 13.36, 400mh: Derrick Adkins 48.41, HJ: Hollis Conway 2.28, PV: Scott Huffman 5.97, LJ: Mike Powell 8.68w, TJ: Mike Conley 17.51, SP: C J Hunter 20.82, DT: Mike Gravelle 61.38, HT: Lance Deal 82.50, JT: Todd Riech 77.86, Dec: Dan O'Brien 8707, 20kmW/50kmW: Allen James 1:28:35.9/3:55.39. **Women**: 100m: Gail Devers 11.12, 200m: Carlette Guidry 22.71, 400m: Natasha Kaiser-Brown 50.73, 800m: Joetta Clark

2:00.41, 1500m: Regina Jacobs 4:07.71, 3000m: Annette Peters 9:01.69, 5000m: Ceci St Geme 16:57.71 10000m: Olga Appell 32:23.76, Mar: Linda Somers 2:33:42, 100mh/LJ: Jackie Joyner-Kersee 12.88/7.14w, 400mh: Kim Batten 54.51, HJ: Angela Bradburn 1.92, TJ: Sheila Hudson-Strudwick 14.23, SP/DT: Connie Price-Smith 19.60/59.46, HT (non-champs): Sonja Fitts 58.06, JT: Donna Mayhew 58.94, Hep: Kym Carter 6371, 10kmW: Teresa Vaill 45:01.46.

NCAA Championships first held in 1921 (men), 1982 (women). **1994 champions**: **Men**: 100m: Sam Jefferson 10.12w, 200m: Andrew Tynes BAH 20.20w, 400m: Derek Mills 45.06, 800m: Jose Parrilla 1:46.01, 1500m: Graham Hood CAN 3:42.10, 5000m: Brian Baker 14:22.09, 10000m: Teddy Mitchell 29:39.54, 3000mSt: Jim Svenøy NOR 8:41.22, 110mh: Robert Foster JAM 13.53, 400mh: Octavius Terry 49.85, HJ: Randy Jenkins 2.31, PV: Nick Hysong 5.70, LJ/TJ: Erick Walder 8.34/16.91, SP: Brent Noon 20.67, DT: John Godina 60.48, HT: Balázs Kiss HUN 74.84, JT: Todd Reich 81.30, Dec: Enoch Borozinski 7870. **Women**: 100m: Holli Hyche 11.23, 200m: Merlene Frazer JAM 22.49w, 400m: Flirtisha Harris 51.65, 800m: Inez Turner JAM 2:01.50, 1500m: Amy Rudolph 4:17.99, 3000m: Karen Hecox 9:22.63, 5000m: Jen Rhines 16:21.60, 10000m: Carole Zajac 33:32.36, 100mh: Gillian Russell JAM 12.97, 400mh: Debbie Ann Parris JAM 55.54, HJ: Gai Kapernick AUS 1.89, LJ: Dedra Davis BAH 6.85w, TJ: Nicola Martial GUY 13.71, SP: Eileen Vanisi 17.74, DT: Danyel Mitchell 59.08, JT: Valerie Tulloch CAN 57.18, Hep: Diane Guthrie JAM 6032.

Derrick ADKINS b.2 Jul 1970 Brooklyn, New York 1.88m 80kg. Reebok. Studied engineering at Georgia Tech.
At 400mh: WCh: '91- 6, '93- 7; WUG: '91- 1, '93- 1. Won GWG 1994, US 1994, PAm-J 1989. 2nd GP 1994.
Progression at 400mh: 1987- 52.65, 1988- 50.71, 1989- 50.25, 1990- 49.53, 1991- 48.60, 1992- 48.64, 1993- 48.39, 1994- 47.70. pbs: 100m 10.48, 400m 46.37i '94, 55mh 7.23i '94, 110mh 13.69 '92.

Charles AUSTIN b.19 Jun 1967 Bay City, Texas 1.84m 77kg. Mazda TC. Was at Southwest Texas State University.
At HJ: OG: '92- 8=; WCh: '91- 1; WI: '91- 6=. Won NCAA 1990, 2= TAC 1991.
US high jump record 1991.
Progression at HJ: 1986- 2.11, 1987- 2.16, 1988- 2.19, 1989- 2.27, 1990- 2.35, 1991- 2.40, 1992- 2.33i/ 2.32, 1993- 2.35i, 1994- 2.32. pb TJ 14.91i '90.

Randy BARNES b.16 Jun 1966 Charleston, W.Virginia 1.94m 137kg. Goldwin TC. Was at Texas A&M University.
At SP: OG: '88- 2; WCh: '93- 2; WCp: '89- 3; WI: '89- 2. Won GP 1994, US Oly Trials 1988, US 1989, 1993; GWG 1990.
World shot record 1990. WIB 22.66 '89.
Progression at SP: 1984- 15.77, 1985- 18.56, 1986- 21.88, 1987- 20.94, 1988- 22.42, 1989- 22.66i/22.18, 1990- 23.12, 1993- 21.80, 1994- 20.82. pb DT 61.18 '86.
A spinner, from a 1985 best of 20.36 with the 12lb shot, he made a sensational start to his senior career, from 19.83 indoors to 21.08 and 21.88 in April 1986, the latter improving Randy Matson's university record (WR 21.78 '67). Returned to competition February 1993 after two years ban for positive drugs test for methyltestosterone at Malmö August 1990.

Arturo BARRIOS b.12 Dec 1963 Mexico City 1.74m 60kg. Reebok RT, USA. Mechanical engineering graduate of Texas A&M University, USA. Became naturalised US citizen in September 1994.
At 10000m: OG: '88- 5 (h 5000m), '92- 5; WCh: '87- 4. At 5000m: PAm: '87- 1, '91- 1; CAmG: '90- 1 (1 1500m); WCp: '92- 2. Won PAm-J 1980 (3 at 3000mSt), GP 1987 & 1989.
World records: 10000m 1989, 20000m and 1 hour 1991; also CAC records: 1500m & 2000m 1989, 3000m 1987, 5000m 1987 & 1989, 10000m (3) 1988-9.

Arturo Barrios: naturalised in September 1994

Progression at 5000m, 10000m, Mar: 1980- 14:26.4, 31:20.4; 1982- 14:49.6, 31:50.6; 1983- 14:14.9; 1984- 14:03.46, 29:23.9; 1985- 13:46.37, 28:42.77; 1986- 13.25.83, 27:50.28, 2:14:09; 1987- 13:13.52, 27:56.1; 1988- 13:17.82, 27:25.07; 1989- 13:07.79, 27:08.23; 1990- 13:08.52, 27:18.22; 1991- 13:24.17, 27:37.36; 1992- 13:10.52, 27:34.60; 1993- 13:09.58, 27:34.27, 2:12:21; 1994- 2:08:28. pbs: 1500m: 3:37.61 '89, 2000m 5:03.4 '89, 3000m 7:35.71 '89, 2M 8:24.99 '86, 20000m 56:54.03 '91, 1Hr 21101m '91, Half Mar 60:42 '92, 2000mSt 5:46.0 '80, 3000mSt 8:46.9 '83.
First came to the fore as a road runner; in 1986 he set a world 10km best for a loop course of 27:41 at Phoenix. Concentrated on track racing with much success from 1987, but completed four successive wins in the San Francisco Bay to Breakers 12km 1987-90. Third New York marathon 1993 and 1994.

Tony BARTON b.17 Oct 1969 Washington DC 1.90m 74kg. Adidas. Was at George Mason University.
At HJ: WCh: '93- 8; WCp: '92- 5; WJ: '88- dnq; WUG: '93- 1=. At LJ: 3rd GP 1993.
Progression at HJ: 1987- 2.10, 1988- 2.18, 1989- 2.22i/2.21, 1990- 2.31, 1991- 2.30i/2.27, 1992- 2.32, 1993- 2.31, 1994- 2.30. pbs: LJ 8.12 '93, TJ 15.96 '90.

Dion BENTLEY b.26 Aug 1971 Pittsburgh 1.93m 87kg. Was at University of Florida.
At LJ: WJ: '90- 2; WCp: '94- 3. Won PAm-J 1989.
Progression at LJ: 1988- 7.80, 1989- 8.16, 1990- 8.05/8.07w, 1991- 7.98i, 1992- 7.98i/7.96, 1993- 8.39, 1994- 8.28.
Three month drugs ban from June 1993.

Kevin BRAUNSKILL b.31 Mar 1969 Dover, Delaware 1.75m 70kg. Goldwin TC. Was at North Carolina State.
At 200m/4x100mR: WJ: '88- 1/1R; WUG: '89- 3; PAm: '91- dnf; WCp: '92- 1R.
Progression at 100m, 200m: 1987- 21.4, 1988- 10.39, 20.63; 1989- 10.34, 20.50; 1990- 10.29, 20.45/19.9; 1991- 10.34, 20.53/20.21w; 1992- 10.29, 20.57/20.4; 1993- 10.36/10.11w, 20.49; 1994- 10.24/10.13w, 20.22. pbs: 55m 6.17i '91, 300m 32.48 '93, 400m 45.99 '91.

Tim BRIGHT b.28 Jul 1960 Taft, California 1.88m 79kg. Mizuno TC. Was at Abilene Christian University.
At Dec: OG: '84- 12, '88- 7; WCh: '87- dnf; At PV: OG: '92- nh; WCh: '91- 6; WCp: '85- 3, '89- 2; won TAC 1991-2.
Progression at PV, Dec: 1978- 4.37; 1979- 4.90; 1980- 5.03; 1981- 5.33; 1982- 5.51, 7445w; 1983- 5.35i, 7737; 1984- 5.50i/5.40, 8106; 1985- 5.52, 8221; 1986- 5.70, 8302; 1987- 5.75, 8340; 1988- 5.75, 8287; 1989- 5.81, 7087; 1990- 5.82, 1991- 5.75, 1992- 5.80, 1993- 5.73, 1994- 5.65/5.70ex. pbs: 100m: 10.90 '87, 10.73w/10.7 '85, 400m 48.72 '86, 1500m 4:39.35 '86, 110mh 14.16 '87, 14.09w '85, 13.9 '83, 13.8w '90; HJ 2.11 '86, LJ 7.38 '88, 7.49w '85, SP 14.38 '86 (14.41?), DT 44.80 '84, JT 61.60 '88.
Has concentrated on the pole vault since 1988, when his 5.70 at the 1988 Olympics was the best ever in a decathlon. Was fourth in the 1988 US Trials at pole vault on the same day that he was second in the decathlon. Married Julie Goodrich (LJ 6.40 '88, 3rd PanAm '91 in 6.53w) in 1989.

Mike BUNCIC b.25 Jul 1962 Fair Lawn, New Jersey 1.93m 111kg. Nike. Degree in education from University of Kentucky.
At DT: OG: '88- 10, '92- dnq 18; WCh: '91- 5, '93- 9; WUG: '85- 6, '87- 5.
Progression at DT: 1981- 53.04, 1982- 58.78, 1983- 59.68, 1984- 64.74, 1985- 66.42, 1986- 65.10, 1987- 68.98, 1988- 68.92, 1989- 68.88, 1990- 67.72, 1991- 69.36, 1992- 64.60, 1993- 67.12, 1994- 60.90. pb SP 19.53 '89.
Yugoslav parents. US junior discus champion 1981, USA Champs second 1989-91 and 1993, third 1986, 1988.

Leroy BURRELL b.21 Feb 1967 Philadelphia 1.83m 82kg. Santa Monica TC. Studied communications at University of Houston.
At 100m/4x100m relay: OG: '92- 5/1R; WCh: '91- 2/1R (qf 200m), '93- 1R; WCp: '89- 2. Won overall and 100m GP 1990, GWG 1990. Won TAC 100m 1989, 1991, NCAA: 55m indoors and 100m 1990, indoor LJ 1989-90.
World records: 100m 1991 & 1994, 4x100mR (4) 1991-3, 4x200mR 1989 & 1992. WIR 60m 6.48 in 1991.
Progression at 100m, 200m: 1985- 10.43, 21.51; 1986- 10.46/10.32w/10.1w, 20.94/20.71w; 1988- 10.31/10.09w, 1989- 9.94, 20.40; 1990- 9.96/9.94w, 20.14/19.61w; 1991- 9.88, 20.31/20.02w; 1992- 9.97/9.96w, 20.12; 1993- 10.02/9.85w, 20.35; 1994- 9.85, 20.94/20.05w. pbs: 55m 6.09i '89, 60m 6.41 '92, LJ: 8.37 '89, TJ 15.04 '85.
World's fastest man of 1990, when he won 19 of 22 finals at 100m; and the fastest ever 200m, with wind assistance. In 1991 he went into the World Championships unbeaten at 100m, having won all eight finals, with a world record 9.90 at TAC, but despite improving to 9.88 he lost to Carl Lewis. Younger sister Dawn was top US high school long jumper at 6.16i in 1991.

Andre CASON b.20 Jan 1969 Virginia Beach 1.70m 70kg. Nike International. Student at

Texas A&M University.
At 100m/4x100mR: WCh: '91- 1R, '93- 2/1R; WJ: '88- 1/1R; WUG: '89- 1/1R; PAm: '91- 2; WCp: '89- 1R. 3rd TAC 1989. At 60m: WI: '91- 1.
Two world records 4x100m relay 1991-3, world indoor records 60m 6.45 and 6.41 in 1992.
Progression at 100m: 1985- 10.83, 1986- 10.38, 1987- 10.49/10.2, 1988- 10.08, 1989- 10.04, 1990- 10.12/10.08w, 1991- 9.99, 1992- 10.08/9.88w, 1993- 9.79w/9.92, 1994- 9.98. pbs: 50m 5.62i '92, 55m 6.04i '90, 60m 6.41i '92, 100y 9.36 '94, 200m 20.70 '89, 20.11w '90; LJ 7.58i '87.
Fourth in the TAC 100m in 1991, he followed his relay gold in Tokyo by becoming the 12th sub 10.00 runner in history. His 1992 season ended with a torn left Achilles in the US Trials 100m heats. In a marvellous season in 1993 he twice ran 9.79w at the US Trials before 9.85w in the final and then improved his pb three times at the World Champs, although second to Linford Christie.

Mike CONLEY b.5 Oct 1962 Chicago 1.85m 77kg. Foot Locker AC. Was at University of Arkansas. Coach, dog trainer and deputy sherriff.
At TJ: OG: '84- 2, '92- 1; WCh: '83- 4, '87- 2, '91- 3, '93- 1; PAm: '87- 1; WI: '87- 1, '89- 1; WCp: '89- 1; WUG: '83- 2. At LJ: WCh: '83- 3, '87- 8; WI: '89- 3; WCp: '85- 1. Won US Trials TJ 1984, NCAA LJ/TJ 1984-5 (2nd 200m 1985). Won US LJ 1985, TJ 1984, 1987-9, 1993-4; GWG TJ 1986, AAA TJ 1983. Won GP LJ 1985 (3rd 1989), TJ 1986, 1988 (2nd overall), 1990, 1992, 1994 (3rd overall).
WIB triple jump 17.76 '87.
Progression at LJ, TJ: 1978- 5.84, 13.00; 1979- 7.14, 13.99; 1980- 6.84, 15.13; 1981- 7.46/7.56w, 15.80/15.83w; 1982- 8.19, 17.01; 1983- 8.38w/8.28, 17.23i/17.37w; 1984- 8.21/8.23w, 17.50; 1985- 8.43/8.53w, 17.71/17.72w; 1986- 8.33/8.63w, 17.69/17.84w; 1987- 8.32/8.55w, 17.87; 1988- 8.23, 17.59/17.62w; 1989- 8.15, 17.65i/17.57; 1990- 17.56; 1991- 7.98, 17.62; 1992- 8.34, 17.72/18.17w; 1993- 8.16, 17.86; 1994- 17.68. pbs: 100m 10.36 '86, 200m 20.21/20.12w '85, 20.0 '84.
The greatest ever LJ/TJ combined exponent and the only athlete to win the IAAF Grand Prix at any event on each occasion contested; triple jump 1986-94. Won the NCAA double indoors and out 1984-5. First or second in TAC triple jump each year 1983-94. Unbeaten at triple jump in 1989. After the Olympic title in 1992, he took gold at his fourth World Championships in 1993. Had been an outstanding high school basketball player and is a black belt at taekwondo.

Hollis CONWAY b.8 Jan 1967 Chicago, Illinois 1.83m 68kg. Reebok. Business graduate of Southwestern Louisiana University.
At HJ: OG: '88- 2, '92- 3=; WCh: '91- 3, '93- 6; WJ: '86- 2; WUG: '89- 2, '91- 1; PAm: '91- 3; WI: '91- 1, '93- 8. Won NCAA 1989, US 1990-4, GWG 1990. Won GP 1990 (3rd 1992).
Two US HJ records 1989, also indoors 2.37 for 1989 NCAA and 2.40 for 1991 World Indoors.
Progression at HJ: 1981- 1.72, 1982- 1.88, 1983- 2.03, 1984- 2.08, 1985- 2.18, 1986- 2.29, 1987- 2.34, 1988- 2.36, 1989- 2.39, 1990- 2.38, 1991- 2.40i/2.37, 1992- 2.35, 1993- 2.38, 1994- 2.32i/2.30. pbs: LJ 7.64 '88, TJ 16.17 '87.
Has jumped 56cm over his own height, close to the record of 59cm by Franklin Jacobs.

Mark CREAR b. 2 Oct 1968 San Francisco 1.86m 82kg. Reebok. Was at the University of Southern California.
At 110mh: WCh: '93- sf. NCAA champion 1992, US 1994.
Progression at 110mh: 1990- 13.65/13.51w, 1992- 13.33, 1993- 13.26/13.22w/12.9w, 1994- 13.07. pbs: 50mh 6.41i '95, 55mh 7.18i '94, 60mh 7.57i '94.

Mark CROGHAN b.8 Jan 1968 Akron, Ohio 1.75m 60kg. Nike International. Was at Ohio State University.
At 3000mSt: OG: '92- sf; WCh: '91- h, '93- 5; US champion 1991, 1994; NCAA 1990-1.
Progression at 3000mSt: 1989- 8:46.07, 1990- 8:25.99, 1991- 8:10.69, 1992- 8:14.11, 1993- 8:09.76, 1994- 8:10.56. pbs: 1500m 3:39.05 '94, 1M 4:08.81i '91, 3000m 7:52.19 '91, 2M 8:33.70 '92, 5000m 13:44.22 '92.
Took up steeplechase as a college junior.

Marc DAVIS b. 17 Dec 1969 Oceanside, San Diego 1.83m 65kg. Nike International. Was at University of Arizona.
At 3000mSt: WCh: '93- 11. US champion 1993. Won GWG 3000mSt 1994, NCAA 5000m 1989, 3000mSt 1992.
US 2 miles record 1994.
Progression at 3000mSt: 1986- 9:24.5, 1987- 9:31.26, 1988- 9:12.6, 1991- 8:43.79, 1992- 8:33.93, 1993- 8:14.26, 1994- 8:14.30. pbs: 1500m 3:36.31 '94, 1M 4:01.45 '94, 3000m 7:38.03 '93, 2M 8:12.74 '94, 5000m 13:32.58 '89.

Lance DEAL b.21 Aug 1961 Riverton, Wyoming 1.83m 116kg. New York AC. Was at Montana State University. Wood and metal worker.
At HT: OG: '88- dnq 17, '92- 7; WCh: '91- dnq 13, '93- 9; WCp: '89- 2, '92- 3, '94- 2. US champion 1989, 1993-4, GWG 1994. Won PAm-J discus 1980.
World bests 35lb weight: outdoors 24.05 '90, 25.41 '93; indoors: 24.17 '91, 24.54, 24.65, 24.67

'92, 24.82 '93, 24.90 '95. US hammer record 1994.
Progression at HT: 1984- 62.52, 1985- 68.48, 1986- 74.66, 1987- 75.94, 1988- 75.64, 1989- 78.34, 1990- 77.66, 1991- 78.44, 1992- 81.08, 1993- 80.80, 1994- 82.50. pbs: SP 18.35i '81, 18.22 '84, DT 61.62 '84.
An all-American linebaacker at American football in high school, he switched from discus (left-handed) to hammer in 1984. US indoor Grand Prix overall champion 1993.

Tony DEES 6 Aug 1963 Pascagoula, Mississippi 1.93m 95kg. Nike International. Was at University of Mississippi, now finishing degree at University of Tampa.
At 110mh: OG: '92- 2; WCh: '93- 8. Won GP 1991. At 60mh: WI: '93- 3.
Progression at 110mh: 1982- 13.98, 1983- 13.68/13.6, 1984- 13.65, 1985- 13.86, 1986- 13.65, 1987- 13.86, 1988- 13.54/13.51w, 1989- 13.61, 1990- 13.24/13.09w, 1991- 13.05, 1992- 13.08, 1993- 13.12 1994- 13.40. pbs: 55m 6.12i '90, 100m 10.15/10.03w '91, 200m 20.54 '84, 20.37w/20.2w '83; 50mh 6.43i '91, 55mh 6.98i '90, 60mh 7.43i '93.
After several years as a useful sprinter/hurdler, broke through to top class in 1990, when he won the TAC indoor 55mh. Previous championships bests were fourth places NCAA 60yh 1983, TAC 55mh 1988. In 1991 he ran the year's fastest time and took the Grand Prix title but was only sixth at TAC and missed Tokyo.

Brian DIEMER b.10 Oct 1961 Grand Rapids, Michigan 1.76m 64kg. Nike International. Graduate of University of Michigan. Landscape designer.
At 3000mSt: OG: '84- 3, '88- sf, '92- 7; WCh: '83- sf, '87- 4, '91- 5, '93- h; WCp: '89- 4. Won NCAA 1983, US 1988-90, 1992-3; GWG 1990.
Progression at 3000mSt: 1981- 8:45.48, 1982- 8:37.96, 1983- 8:22.13, 1984- 8:13.16, 1985- 8:20.64, 1986- 9:09.4, 1987- 8:14.46, 1988- 8:20.44, 1989- 8:16.92, 1990- 8:20.61, 1991- 8:16.57, 1992- 8:16.51, 1993- 8:22.41, 1994- 8:33.07. pbs: 1500m 3:42.48 '89, 1M 3:59.93i '83, 2000m 5:07.89i '87, 3000m 7:47.31 '92, 2M 8:30.49i '83, 3M 13:14.60i '84, 5000m 13:47.15 '82, 10000m 30:08.8 '80.
Splendidly consistent record at major meetings from his Olympic bronze in 1984 to his first failure in 1993.

Jim DOEHRING b.27 Jan 1962 Santa Barbara, California 1.83m 118kg. Reebok RT. Was at San Jose State University.
At SP: OG: '88- 11, '92- 2; WI: '93- 2. Won TAC 1990.
Progression at SP: 1981- 18.34, 1983- 18.31, 1984- 19.97, 1985- 20.62, 1986- 21.29, 1987- 20.45i/19.67, 1988- 21.04, 1989- 21.57, 1990- 21.20, 1991- 20.75i dq, 1992- 21.60, 1993- 21.56i/21.15, 1994- 21.09.
Two year drugs ban from random test December 1990 was lifted in 1992.

Jon DRUMMOND b.9 Sep 1968 Philadelphia 1.75m 72kg. Nike LA. Was at Texas Christian University.
At 200m/4x100m relay: WCh: '93- 1R; WUG: '91- 1/1R. 3rd GP 100m 1994. At 60m: WI: '93- 4. Won AAA 200m 1991.
World record 4x100m relay 1993.
Progression at 100m, 200m: 1986- 10.5; 1987- 10.28/10.23w, 20.64; 1988- 10.25/10.0w, 20.79i; 1989- 10.21, 20.82; 1990- 10.10, 1991- 10.19/10.03w, 20.58; 1992- 10.12, 20.37; 1993- 10.03/9.92w, 21.05i; 1994- 9.99. pbs: 50m 5.67i '92, 60m 6.54i '93, 100y 9.33 '94.

Mark EVERETT b.2 Sep 1968 Milton, Florida 1.83m 70kg. JD?. Finishing sports administration degree at University of Florida.
At 800m: OG: '88- h, '92- dnf; WCh: '91- 3/res R, '93- sf; WI: '93- 1R; WCp: '94- 1. US champion 1988, 1990-1, 1993-4; NCAA 1990.
WIB 600y 1:07.53 in 1992, beating the 22-year-old mark by Martin McGrady.
Progression at 400m, 800m: 1986- 47.55y, 1987- 46.37, 1:47.36; 1988- 45.91, 1:44.46; 1989- 46.09i, 1:47.86; 1990- 45.46, 1:44.70; 1991- 44.59, 1:43.93; 1992- 45.47, 1:43.40; 1993- 1:44.43, 1994- 45.81, 1:44.36. pbs: 100m 10.9 '86, 200m 21.9 '86, 500m 1:00.19i '92, 600y 1:07.53i '92.
An ungainly looking but effective runner. Silver medal as he ran in the heats of the 4x400m relay at the 1991 World Championships.

Greg FOSTER b.4 Aug 1958 Chicago 1.90m 88kg. World Class AC. Graduate of UCLA.
At 110mh: OG: '84- 2; WCh: '83- 1, '87- 1, '91- 1; PAm: '87- dnf; WCp: '81- 1. Won TAC 110mh 1981, 1983, 1986-7, 1991; NCAA 110mh 1978, 1980; 200m 1979; US Olympic Trials 1984, GWG 1986. 2nd GP 110mh and overall 1987. At 60mh: WI: '87- fell, '91- 1. Won overall Mobil indoor GP 1987.
US 110mh record 1978; WIB: 50yh: 5.88 '86, 50mh: 6.35 '85, 60mh: 7.36 '87.
Progression at 110mh: 1977- 13.54 (120yh), 1978- 13.22, 1979- 13.28/13.0, 1980- 13.27, 1981- 13.03, 1982- 13.22, 1983- 13.11, 1984- 13.15, 1985- 13.24, 1986- 13.25, 1987- 13.17/13.15w, 1988- 13.39, 1989- 13.19, 1990- 13.15, 1991- 13.06, 1992- 13.32, 1993- 13.27, 1994- 13.26/13.22w. pbs: 100m 10.28 '79, 200m 20.20 '79.
Three times world champion outdoors and once indoors and ranked 15 years in the world top ten (a record for any running event) for 110mh,

1977-87 and 1989-92, including ten years in top two. Has run a record 56 (and 4 wa) sub 13.30 times, including 20 sub 13.20. His 7.36 for 60mh indoors in January 1987 was adjudged to have been with a flying start. Competed at 1988 Olympic Trials wearing a plaster cast for a compound fracture of his left forearm three weeks earlier. Broke arm again in two places playing basketball on 30 Jan 1989. Three month ban after positive drugs test 19 Jan 1990.

Steve FRITZ b. 1 Nov 1967 Salina, Kansas 1.90m 89kg. Accusplit. Was at Kansas State University.
At Dec: WCh: '93- 7; WUG: '91- 1.
Indoor world best pentathlon 4478 '95.
Progression at Dec: 1988- 7015, 1989- 7707, 1990- 7924, 1991- 8079, 1992- 8073, 1993- 8324, 1994- 8548. pbs: 100m 10.80 '93, 10.63w '94; 400m 48.40 '93, 1500m 4:28.11 '92, 110mh 13.99 '93, HJ 2.15 '91, PV 5.10 '91, LJ 7.82 '92, 7.84w '94; SP 16.13i '95, 14.54 '94; DT 47.38 '94, JT 67.46 '94.

Johnny GRAY b.19 Jun 1960 Los Angeles 1.90m 75kg. Santa Monica TC. Studied civil engineering at Cal State, Los Angeles.
At 800m: OG: '84- 7, '88- 5, '92- 3; WCh: '87- qf, '91- 6, '93- sf; PAm: '87- 1. Won US Olympic Trials 1988, TAC 1985-7, 1989, 1992; GWG 1986. Five US 800m records 1984-5. Two 600m world bests 1984-6. WIB 1000y 2:04.39 '86.
Progression at 800m: 1977- 2:06.0y, 1978- 1:51.1, 1979- 1:49.39, 1980- 1:47.06, 1982- 1:45.41, 1983- 1:45.50, 1984- 1:42.96, 1985- 1:42.60, 1986- 1:43.46, 1987- 1:44.09, 1988- 1:42.65, 1989- 1:43.39, 1990- 1:43.72, 1991- 1:43.84, 1992- 1:42.80, 1993- 1:44.03, 1994- 1:43.73. pbs: 400m 46.3 '83, 600m 1:12.81 '86, 1000m 2:17.27 '84, 1500m 3:42.43 '90, 1M 4:07.64 '84.
His Olympics progression: 7th, 5th, 3rd! Ran fastest ever 800m relay leg, 1:43.3, on 6 Apr 1985 at Tempe. Has a record 24 sub 1:44 times for 800m. His many fast runs and big wins in invitational meetings have been regularly interspersed with very bad runs.

Joe GREENE b.17 Feb 1967 Wright-Patterson AF Base, Dayton, Ohio. 1.83m 68kg. Mazda TC. Was at Ohio State University.
At LJ: OG: '92- 3; WCh: '93- dnq 17; WI: '93- 2; won NCAA 1989.
Progression at LJ: 1986- 7.34w, 1987- 7.80/7,81w, 1988- 7.88, 1989- 8.10/8.41w, 1990- 8.11i/8.02/8.28w, 1991- 8.24/8.34w, 1992- 8.38/8.66w, 1993- 8.33/8.35w, 1994- 8.07. pb TJ 16.88 '89, 16.93w '90.
Married German long jumper Susen Tiedtke on 4 Dec 1993.

Danny HARRIS b.7 Sep 1965 Torrance, Cal. 1.83m 77kg. Nike International. Was at Iowa State University.
At 400mh: OG: '84- 2; WCh: '87- 2, '91- 5. Won NCAA 1984-6, TAC 1986, 1991. Won GP 1988 & 1990 (third overall), 2nd 1986.
Progression at 400mh: 1984- 48.02, 1985- 47.63, 1986- 47.82, 1987- 47.48, 1988- 47.74, 1989- 48.27, 1990- 47.49, 1991- 47.38, 1994- 48.18. pbs: 100m 10.5 '84, 9.9w '85; 200m 20.91 '84; 400m 45.19 '86, 800m 1:49.48 '92, 110mh 14.00 '86.
US high school record at 35.52 for 300mh in 1983. Made his debut at 400mh on 24 Mar 1984, set world junior records in 5 of first 11 races at the event, taking the record from 49.55 to 48.02! Good footballer in college. On 4 Jun 1987 ran a pb 47.56 to end the long win streak of Edwin Moses, but as in LA had to settle for silver in Rome when he again ran a pb. He ran nine sub 48.00 times, a record for one year, in 1990 when he was unbeaten in 14 races at 400mh until by 0.02 to Samuel Matete in the Grand Prix final. Four year ban after positive test for cocaine at 1992 TAC Indoors. This was reduced to two years by USA Track & Field in 1994 and he ran in five Grand Prix meetings in the summer of 1994 before the IAAF realised that he was competing while still banned from international events as they did not endorse the USATF decision. However, in November the IAAF Council reinstated him.

Kerry '**Kenny**' **HARRISON** b.13 Feb 1965 Milwaukee 1.78m 75kg. Mizuno TC. Was at Kansas State University.
At TJ: WCh: '91- 1, '93- 10; WUG: '87- 2. Won NCAA 1986, TAC 1990-1, GWG 1990, 1994. 2nd PAm-J 1984.
Progression at TJ: 1982- 14.84, 1983- 15.96, 1984- 16.50, 1985- 16.29i, 1986- 17.07/17.41w, 1987- 17.07/17.42w, 1988- 17.15/17.56w, 1989- 17.47/17.74w, 1990- 17.93, 1991- 17.78, 1992- 17.06/17.58w, 1993- 17.27, 1994- 17.43. pb LJ 8.17i '86, 8.14 '87, 8.23w '88.
Second on the all-time list with 17.93 at Helsinki, and lost only once in 1990. Won all eight competions in 1991, culminating in the world title.

Courtney HAWKINS b.11 Jul 1967 West Palm Beach, Florida 1.87m 75kg. Adidas. Was at University of Kansas.
At 110mh: 3rd TAC 1989.
Progression at 110mh: 1986- 13.95, 1987- 13.80, 1989- 13.41/13.3, 1990- 13.28, 1991- 13.30, 1992- 13.66, 1993- 13.25, 1994- 13.27. pbs: 55mh 7.10i '91, 60mh 7.47i '92.

Steve HOLMAN b.2 Mar 1970 Indianapolis

1.86m 66kg. Nike. Graduate of Georgetown University.
At 1500m: OG: '92- sf; WI: '93- 4. Won NCAA 1992.
Progression at 1500m: 1988- 3:52.8, 1989- 3:45.41, 1990- 3:39.60, 1991- 3:38.37, 1992- 3:34.95, 1993- 3:35.29, 1994- 3:34.96. pbs: 800m 1:46.13 '94, 1000m 2:19.96i '93, 1M 3:50.91 '94, 2000m 5:07.72 '92, 3000m 7:46.27i '93, 5000m 13:47.63i '92.
Actual Christian names are Clyfton Orlando.

Scott HUFFMAN b.30 Nov 1964 Quinter, Kansas 1.75m 75kg. Foot Locker AC. Was at University of Kansas.
At PV: WCh: '93- 5; WI: '91- 9; WCp: '94- 5. 3rd GP 1991. US champion 1993-4.
US pole vault record 1994.
Progression at PV: 1980- 3.43, 1981- 3.66, 1982- 3.96, 1983- 5.00, 1984- 5.03, 1985- 5.62, 1986- 5.60, 1987- 5.59, 1988- 5.65, 1989- 5.56, 1990- 5.80/5.85ex, 1991- 5.80, 1992- 5.85, 1993- 5.85, 1994- 5.97.
Has developed an interesting 'Huffman Roll' technique in spinning around the PV bar. His father Galen vaulted 14 ft inthe 1960s.

C J (Cottrell J) **HUNTER** b.14 Dec 1968 Washington DC 1.86m 135kg. US West TC. Was at Penn State University.
At SP: WCh: '91- dnq 19; PAm: '91- 3; WUG: '91- 6; WCp: '94- 1. US & GWG champion 1994. 2nd GP 1994.
Progression at SP: 1986- 15.56, 1987- 18.44i/ 17.86, 1988- 18.29, 1989- 19.47, 1990- 19.99i/ 19.94, 1991- 19.89i/19.55, 1992- 20.34/20.62i, 1993- 20.82, 1994- 20.94. pb DT 53.08 '88.

Sam JEFFERSON b.19 Apr 1971 Waco, Texas 1.69m 69kg. Student at University of Houston.
At 100m/4x100m: WUG: '93- 2/1R; WCp: '94- 3R. Won NCAA 100m 1994.
Progression at 100m, 200m: 1988- 10.3w, 1989- 10.53/10.31w, 1990- 10.53.10.50w, 1991- 10.31/10.22w, 21.42; 1992- 10.27/10.24w, 20.74w; 1993- 10.13/10.05w, 20.32; 1994- 10.12/10.08wA, 20.67.

Allen JOHNSON b.1 Mar 1971 Washington DC 1.78m 70kg. Nike Atlantic Coast. Was at University of North Carolina.
At 110mh: WCp: '94- 2.
Progression at 110mh: 1991- 14.11, 1992- 13.63, 1993- 13.47/13.34w, 1994- 13.25/13.23wA. pbs: 200m 20.77 '94, 50mh 6.47i '95, 55mh 7.03i '94, 60mh 7.38i'95, LJ 8.14i/7.91 '93.
Having leapt into world class in 1994, on 8 Feb 1995 in Madrid he ended Colin Jackson string of 44 sprint hurdles victories.

Dave JOHNSON b.7 Apr 1963 Missoula, Montana 1.90m 91kg. Reebok. Was at Azusa Pacific University.
At Dec: OG: '88- 9, '92- 3; WCh: '91- dnf; WUG: '89- 1. Won TAC 1986, 1989-90, 1992; GWG 1990.
Progression at Dec: 1982- 6297*, 1983- 7225*, 1984- 7933, 1985- 7948, 1986- 8203w, 1987- 8045, 1988- 8245, 1989- 8549, 1990- 8600w, 1991- 8467, 1992- 8727w/8705, 1994- 8219. pbs: 100m 10.79 '89, 10.77w '85; 400m 48.19 '91, 1500m 4:23.00 '91, 110mh 14.17 '91, HJ 2.10 '90, PV 5.28 '91, LJ 7.59 '89, SP 15.05 '92, DT 49.88 '91, JT 74.58 '92.
Started in college as a footballer. Topped decathlon world lists in 1989 and 1990. After failing to finish three times he came back in April 1992 with 8727w for sixth all-time, including the best ever second day score of 4411. He improved that record to 4455 later that year at the US Trials.

Michael JOHNSON b.13 Sep 1967 Dallas 1.85m 78kg. Nike International. Degree in marketing from Baylor University.
At 400m/4x400mR: WCh: '93- 1/1R; WUG: '89- 2R. At 200m: OG: '92- sf/1R; WCh: '91- 1; Won NCAA 200m 1990, GWG 200m 1990, 1994; US 200m 1990-2, 400m 1993. Won GP 1991 (third overall), 3rd 1993.
World records 4x400m relay 1992 and 1993. WIR 44.97 in 1994. US indoor 200m records 20.59 to win 1989 NCAA and 20.55 in Jan 1991.
Progression at 200m, 400m: 1986- 21.30, 1987- 20.41, 46.29; 1988- 20.07, 45.23; 1989- 20.47/ 20.06w, 46.49; 1990- 19.85, 44.21; 1991- 19.88, 44.17; 1992- 19.79, 43.98; 1993- 20.06, 43.65; 1994- 19.94, 43.90. pbs: 100m 10.09 '94, 300m 31.56 '94.
His upright style, with little knee lift and rapid, short strides made a considerable impact when he burst onto the international scene and was the best in the world at both 200m and 400m in 1990. He ran a 43.5 400m relay split in April 1988 before a broken leg curtailed his season. Has a record 11 sub-20 sec. times. His run of 32 successive wins at 200m from May 1990 was ended by Frank Fredericks in Rome on 9 Jun 1992 and he was ill at the 1992 Olympics, but at 400m he has won 38 successive finals from 1990 to his world indoor record in February 1995. His 42.93 anchor on the 1993 US gold medal team is the fastest 400m relay leg ever run.

Bob KENNEDY b.18 Aug 1970 Bloomington, Indiana 1.83m 66kg. NI TC. Student at University of Mississippi.
At 5000m: OG: '92- 12; WCh: '91- 12, '93- h. At 3000m: WI: '93- 4. Won US CC 1992, PAm-J 1500m 1989, NCAA 1500m 1990.
US 3000m record 1994.

Progression at 5000m: 1989- 14:21.40, 1990- 13:42.80, 1991- 13:22.17, 1992- 13:28.18, 1993- 13:14.91, 1994- 13:02.93. pbs: 1500m 3:38.32 '91, 1M 3:56.21 '94, 2000m 5:02.6+ '94, 3000m 7:35.33 '94, 2M 8:28.05 '94.

Roger KINGDOM b.26 Aug 1962 Vienna, Georgia 1.85m 91kg. Foot Locker AC. Was at University of Pittsburgh.
At 110mh: OG: '84- 1, '88- 1; PAm: '83- 1; WUG: '89- 1; WCp: '89- 1. Won NCAA 1983, US Olympic Trials 1988, TAC 1985, 1988-90; GWG 1990. At 60mh: WI: '89- 1. Won GP 110mh and second overall 1989.
World 110m hurdles record 1989.
Progression at 110mh: 1982- 14.07, 1983- 13.44, 1984- 13.16/13.1/13.00w, 1985- 13.14, 1986- 13.40/13.39w, 1987- 13.51/13.3/13.44w, 1988- 12.97, 1989- 12.92/12.87w, 1990- 13.21/13.11w, 1992- 13.29, 1993- 13.40/13.38w, 1994- 13.39. pbs: 200m 21.08w '84, 50mh 6.47i '89, 55mh 6.98i '89, 60mh 7.37i '89, HJ 2.14i '84.
Became the second man to run 110m hurdles in sub-13.00, at high altitude in 1988, when he won all 25 races at 110mh. Ran the third fastest ever time, 12.98, to take the Olympic title. Improved in 1989 with the world record in Zürich and the fastest ever wind-aided time at the World Cup. Has run 44 (and 9 wa) sub 13.30 times, including a then record 18 (and 3w) in 1989. He ran 60m hurdles indoors in 1989 in a time of 7.37, corrected from the originally announced 7.36, which equalled the world record. Missed 1991 outdoor season following two operations on his right knee. Now a keen golfer.

Carl LEWIS b.1 Jul 1961 Birmingham, Alabama 1.88m 80kg. Santa Monica TC. Was at University of Houston.
At 100m/LJ/4 x100mR: OG: '84- 1/1/1R (1 200m), '88- 1/1 (2 200m); '92- 1 LJ/1R; WCh: '83- 1/1/1R, '87- 1/1/1R; '91- 1/2/1R, '93- 4/- (3 200m); PAm: LJ '79- 3, '87- 1/1R; WCp: '81- 9/1. Won TAC 100m 1981-3, 1986, 1990; 200m 1983, 1987; LJ 1981-3, 1986-7, 1991. Won PAm-J 100m & 200m 1980; NCAA 100m, LJ 1981; 100m/200m/LJ at US Olympic Trials 1984, 100m/LJ (2nd 200m) 1988; GWG LJ 1990.
World records: 4x100mR (5) 1983-92, 4x200mR 1989, 1992; 100m 1988 (with the disallowance of Ben Johnson's 9.83) and 1991. Low altitude world bests at 100m (3), 200m, LJ (4). WIB: 60y: 6.02 '83, LJ: 8.49 '81, 8.56 '82, 8.79 '84. US records 100m 1987 and 1988, 200m 1983.
Progression at LJ, 100m, 200m: 1974- 5.51, 1975- 6.07; 1976- 6.93, 11.1y; 1977- 7.26, 10.6y; 1978- 7.85, 10.5/9.3y; 1979- 8.13, 10.3/10.67, 20.9; 1980- 8.11/8.35w, 10.21/ 10.16w, 20.66; 1981- 8.62/ 8.73w, 10.00/9.99w, 20.73; 1982- 8.76, 10.00, 20.27; 1983- 8.79, 9.97/9.93w, 19.75; 1984- 8.79i/ 8.71, 9.99, 19.80; 1985- 8.62/8.77w, 9.98/9.90w, 20.69/20.3w; 1986- 8.67w/8.37i/8.35, 10.06/ 9.91w, 20.41/20.23w/20.1; 1987- 8.75/8.77w, 9.93, 19.92; 1988- 8.76, 9.92/9.78w, 19.79; 1989- 8.54, 10.05, 20.47; 1990- 8.51, 10.05; 1991- 8.87/ 8.91w, 9.86/9.80w, 20.46; 1992- 8.68/8.72w, 10.07/9.95w, 20.15; 1993- 10.02/9.90w, 19.99; 1994- 10.04, 8.66A/8.72wA. pbs: 50m 5.72i '87, 60m 6.46 '92, 300m 32.18 '84, 400m 47.01 '93.
Won 65 successive long jumps from a defeat by Larry Myricks at the US Indoors on 28 Feb 1981 until his epic clash with Mike Powell on 31 Aug 1991. He has 71 long jumps over 28ft (8.53m), and the most legal times: 15 sub-10.00 100m and 9 sub-20.00 200m. Anchored 11 of the 15 sub-38 sec times run at 4x100m relay pre 1993. Emulated Jesse Owens in winning four Olympic gold medals and has added four more. He has a record eight World Championships gold medals and nine medals in all. Sullivan Award winner 1981. Sister Carol was World long jump bronze medallist in 1983 and made the US Olympic teams of 1980, 1984 and 1988.

Steve LEWIS b.16 May 1969 Los Angeles 1.88m 84kg. Santa Monica TC. Was at UCLA.
At 400m/R- 4x400m relay: OG: '88- 1/1R, '92- 2/1R. Won NCAA & TAC 1990.
Five world junior 400m records 1988. World 4x400m relay records 1988 and 1992.
Progression at 400m: 1982- 54.2, 1983- 51.9, 1984- 50.8, 1985- 47.93, 1986- 46.50, 1987- 45.76, 1988- 43.87, 1989- 44.47, 1990- 44.75, 1991- 44.52, 1992- 44.08, 1993- 44.54, 1994- 44.68A. pbs: 100m 10.41 '92, 200m 20.58 '92, 300m 31.82 '92.
Had a sensational 1988 season when he ran the nine fastest ever 400m times by a junior, and won two Olympic gold medals.

Roland McGHEE b.15 Oct 1971 1.80m 70kg. Middle Tennessee State University.
At LJ/4x100mR: WCp: '94- 3R.
Progression at LJ: 1988- c.6.99, 1989- 7.32, 1990- 7.32i, 1991- 8.05i, 1992- 8.06/8.23w, 1993- 8.38, 1994- 8.47. pbs: 100m 10.0/10.41 '94, 200m 20.4 '94, TJ 16.56i '93.

Pat MANSON b.29 Nov 1967 West Point, New York 1.78m 72kg. Goldwin TC. Was at University of Kansas.
At PV: WJ: '86- nh; PAm: '91- 1.
Progression at PV: 1983- 3.58, 1984- 4.62, 1985- 5.10, 1986- 5.49, 1987- 5.50, 1988- 5.65, 1989- 5.69i/5.65, 1990- 5.60i, 1991- 5.70, 1992- 5.71, 1993- 5.75, 1994- 5.85.

Michael MARSH b.4 Aug 1967 Los Angeles 1.78m 68kg. Santa Monica TC. Was at UCLA.

At 200m/4x100mR: OG: '92- 1/1R; WCh: '91- resR, '93- 4; WJ: '86- dq R; WUG: '89- 1R. US champion 1993.
World records three 4x100mR 1991-2, 4x200mR 1992. US and world low-altitude 200m record 1992.
Progression at 100m, 200m: 1985- 10.6, 20.82; 1986- 10.22, 20.69; 1987- 10.26/10.16w, 20.59/20.52w/20.5; 1988- 10.12/9.94w, 20.35; 1989- 10.07, 20.42; 1990- 10.08/10.07w, 20.47/20.44w; 1991- 10.15/10.00w, 20.44; 1992- 9.93, 19.73; 1993- 10.20/9.97w, 20.04/19.97w; 1994- 10.00, 20.48. pbs: 50m 5.73i '90, 60m 6.57i '92, 300m 32.10 '93, 400m 45.46 '94.
Gold medal as he ran in the heats of the 4x100m relay. at the 1991 Worlds. After three major championships appearances at the sprint relay, made individual event début with the Olympic gold at 200m in 1992, running a world low-altitude best for 200m in the semi-final.

Anthuan MAYBANK b.30 Dec 1969 Georgetown, South Carolina 1.85m 75kg. Was at University of Iowa.
Progression at 400m, LJ: 1988- 46.82, 1989- 46.39, 7.83; 1990- 47.25, 1991- 45.76, 7.81i; 1992- 45.04, 8.06i/7.81; 1993- 44.99, 8.25/8.40w; 1994- 45.76, 7.84w; 1995- 8.25i. pb 200m 20.59/20.55w '94.

Derek MILLS b.9 Jul 1972 Washington DC 1.75m 68kg. Studied electrical engineering at GeorgiaTech University.
At 400m: WCh: '93- res R (gold); WJ: '90- 5/1R. Won GP & NCAA 1994.
Progression at 400m: 1989- 47.37, 1990- 46.43, 1991- 46.09, 1992- 44.86, 1993- 44.62, 1994- 44.59. pb 200m 20.94w '92.

Dennis MITCHELL b.20 Feb 1966 Havelock, North Carolina 1.74m 69kg. Mazda TC. Was at University of Florida.
At 100m/4x100mR OG: '88- 4, '92- 3/1R; WCh: '91- 3/1R, '93- 3/1R. At 200m: WI: '85- 6. At 60m: WI: '93- 6. Won GP & GWG 100m 1994, US 100m 1992, 1994; NCAA 200m 1989, PAm Jnr 400m 1984, GP 100m 1992.
At 4x100m relay: four world records 1991-3, world junior record 1983.
Progression at 100m, 200m: 1982- 10.50w, 1983- 10.47/10.2, 20.7/21.09/20.73w; 1984- 10.56/10.3, 21.06; 1985- 10.21, 20.49/20.47w; 1986- 10.33/10.23w, 20.52; 1987- 10.12/10.11w, 20.36/20.21w; 1988- 10.03/9.86w, 20.29; 1989- 10.03/10.00w, 20.09; 1990- 10.16/10.05w, 20.33; 1991- 9.91, 20.63; 1992- 10.04/9.94w/9.92rw, 20.20/20.18w; 1993- 9.99/9.85w, 20.25; 1994- 9.94, 20.63. pbs: 60m 6.42 '91, 300m 32.22 '88, 400m 45.26 '86.
Had his best ever season in 1994 when he ran five times under 10.00 in six weeks. Twin sister Denise was 3rd NCAA and 6th TAC in pb 51.72 at 400m in 1987.

Chris NELLOMS b.14 Aug 71 Dayton, Ohio 1.75m 74kg. Accusplit SC. Student at Ohio State University.
At 400m/4x400mR: WJ: '88- 1R, '90- 1/1R (1 4x100mR). Won PAm-J 400m 1989. At 200m: WUG: '93- 2.
Progression at 200m, 400m: 1987- 21.55, 47.53; 1988- 21.04, 45.80; 1989- 20.4/20.90/20.73w, 46.19; 1990- 20.47/20.36w, 45.36; 1991- 20.62/20.55w, 46.24; 1992- 20.27/19.94w, 45.84; 1993- 20.23/20.17w, 1994- 20.57i/20.70. pbs: 100m 10.33/10.03w '92, 300m 32.38 '93.
He has a record four World Junior gold medals, with a unique triple in 1990 and a relay gold from 1988. Set US high school record of 13.30 for the junior 110mh in 1990. US high school athlete of the year 1990, unbeaten at 400m from 1980 until 18 Jan 1991 when he lost indoors to Antonio Mackay. His second at 1989 TAC juniors was his only 200m loss in 1989-90. He was shot and almost killed in August 1992, but has since made a determined recovery and returned to top-class form.

Brent NOON b.29 Aug 1971 1.88m 123kg. Student at University of Georgia.
NCAA shot champion 1992-4.
Progression at SP: 1992- 20.26, 1993- 20.48, 1994- 20.67.

Chris Nelloms: recovered from shooting

With 23.21 with the 6.25kg shot Noon became the second best ever in US high school history, but took a year out in 1991.

Dan O'BRIEN b.18 Jul 1966 Portland 1.89m 84kg. Foot Locker AC. Was at University of Idaho.
At Dec: WCh: '91- 1, '93- 1; US champion 1991, 1993-4. Won GWG 1994. At Hep: WI inv '93- 1. World decathlon record 1992. US decathlon record in Tokyo and best at TAC (not a record due to wind assistance) in 1991. WIR Pentathlon 4497 '92, Heptathlon 6476 '93.
Progression at Dec: 1982-5583*, 1983- 6438*, 1984- 6873*, 1988- 7891, 1989- 7987, 1990- 8483w, 1991- 8844w/8812, 1992- 8891, 1993- 8817, 1994- 8715. pbs: 50m 5.84i '93, 60m 6.67i '93, 100m 10.41/ 10.23w '91; 400m 46.53 '91, 1500m 4:33.19 '89, 50mh 6.65i '93, 55mh 7.18i '91, 60mh 7.85i '93, 110mh 13.81 '94, HJ 2.20 '94, PV 5.25 '91, LJ 8.08 '92, 8.11w '91; SP 16.69 '92, DT 52.86 '90, JT 62.58 '92.
The successor of Daley Thompson as the world's best decathlete, he has amassed all the best first-day totals. In his 8844 in 1991 he scored 4747 points, but there was no wind gauge for the 100m at which he ran 10.23, the fastest ever run in a decathlon, and the wind was over the limit for the 110mh. He excelled in Tokyo, where he would surely have smashed the world record but for a near disaster in the high jump, clearing only his opening height 1.91m and losing up to 200 points; he improved at 400m from 47.70 to 46.53. After a legal wind first day record 4698 at the 1992 US Olympic Trials, he failed his opening height of 4.90 in the vault, and thus missed the Olympics. Came back in September with 4720 first day and a total of 8896 in Talence. Won all three decathlons in 1994, with 8707, 8715 and 8710, and first day scores of 4738w at the US Champs and 4736 at the Goodwill Games).
Finnish mother, black father, adopted at the age of two by an Oregon couple.

Antonio PETTIGREW b.3 Nov 1967 Macon, Georgia 1.80m 70kg. Reebok TC. Was at St Augustine's College.
At 400m/4x400m relay: WCh: '91- 1/2R, '93- res (1)R; WCp: '89- 5/2R, '92- 4R, '94- 1. 2nd GP 1994. US champion 1989, 1991, 1994.
Progression at 400m: 1986- 47.19, 1987- 46.31, 1988- 45.36, 1989- 44.27, 1990- 45.26, 1991- 44.36, 1992- 44.71, 1993- 44.45, 1994- 44.43. pbs: 100m 10.42 '94, 200m 20.38 '94, 300m 32.33 '89.

Jack PIERCE b.23 Sep 1962 Cherry Hill, New Jersey 1.85m 84kg. Mizuno TC. Was at Morgan State University.
At 110mh: OG: '92- 3; WCh: '87- 4, '91- 2, '93- 3. US champion 1992-3. At 60mh: WI: '91- 8.
Progression at 110mh: 1981- 14.18/14.09w, 1982- 13.77/13.7w, 1983- 13.61/13.6/13.44w, 1984- 13.60, 1985- 13.36, 1986- 13.55/13.4/13.53w, 1987- 13.41, 1988- 13.41, 1989- 13.24/13.16w, 1990- 13.43, 1991- 13.06, 1992- 13.13, 1993- 13.06, 1994- 13.48/13.41w. pbs: 200m 20.90 '84, 50mh 6.56i '89, 55mh 7.04i '89, 60mh 7.54i '89.
In 1991 he very nearly won the gold in Tokyo, when he took 0.17 off his pb and lost by just a millimetre or two to Greg Foster.

Mike POWELL b.10 Nov 1963 Philadelphia 1.88m 77kg. Foot Locker AC. Sociology degree from UCLA, formerly at UC/Irvine.
At LJ: OG: '88- 2, '92- 2; WCh: '91- 1, '93- 1; WUG: '87- 1. Won GP 1991, 2nd 1989, 3rd 1987 & 1991. US champion 1990, 1992-4; GWG 1994. World long jump record 1991.
Progression at LJ: 1982- 7.48, 1983- 8.06, 1984- 7.98/8.14w, 1985- 8.17/8.28w, 1986- 8.04/ 8.22w, 1987- 8.27, 1988- 8.49, 1989- 8.49/8.55w, 1990- 8.66, 1991- 8.95, 1992- 8.64/8.99w, 1993- 8.70, 1994- 8.58/8.95wA. pbs: 100m 10.45 '85, 200m 21.21/20.99w '85, HJ 2.16 '84, TJ 15.75 '84.
Played point guard at basketball on his high school team. Topped the world long jump rankings in 1990, and after losing 15 times to Carl Lewis from 1983 to 1991 won that epic contest in Tokyo to end the latter's winning streak and to take the world record that Bob Beamon had set back in 1968. 1991 Sullivan Award winner. Long jump win streak of 34 from 1992 ended by Kareem Streete-Thompson at Innsbruck 7 June 1994.

Tom PUKSTYS b.28 May 1968 Glen Ellyn, Illinois 1.88m 91kg. Adidas. Was at University of Florida.
At JT: OG: '92- 10; WCh: '91- dnq 26, '93- 10; WCp: '92- 4. US champion 1992-3.
US javelin record 1993.
Progression at JT: 1987- 71.34, 1988- 75.72, 1989- 74.82, 1990- 83.30, 1991- 81.68, 1992- 83.20, 1993- 85.70, 1994- 82.32. Races motorcycles.

Robert READING b.9 Jun 1967 Buffalo 1.93m 82kg. Accusplit SC. Was at University of Southern California.
At 110mh: WUG: '89- 6. Won NCAA 1989.
Progression at 110mh: 1986- 13.83, 1987- 13.64, 1988- 13.70/13.4, 1989- 13.42/13.19w, 1990- 13.59/13.38w, 1991- 13.56/13.53w, 1992- 13.68/ 13.3, 1993- 13.69/13.5, 1994- 13.34/13.18w. pbs: 50mh 6.56i '90, 55mh 7.10i '90, 60mh 7.75i '89.

Harry 'Butch' REYNOLDS Jr b.8 Jun 1964 Akron, Ohio 1.90m 80kg. Foot Locker AC. Ohio

State University.
At 400m/4x400mR: OG: '88- 2/1R; WCh: '87- 3/1R, '93- 2/1R; WI: '93- 1. Won NCAA and TAC 1987, Olympic Trials 1988. 2nd GP 1993. World records 400m 1988, 4x400mR 1988 and 1993. WIB 500m 1:00.86 '86, 600y 1:06.87 '87 (o/s track).
Progression at 400m: 1983- 48.1, 1984- 45.47, 1986- 45.36, 1987- 44.10, 1988- 43.29, 1989- 44.30, 1990- 44.22, 1991- 47.40, 1992- 44.14, 1993- 44.12, 1994- 45.18. pbs: 200m 20.46 '87, 300m 32.05 '87.
In 1987 ran 12 sub 45.00 times and the three fastest ever low-altitude times, 44.10, 44.13 and 44.15. In 1988 ran a low-altitude record of 43.93 to win the US Trials, smashed Lee Evans's 20-year-old world record in Zürich, but was surprisingly defeated at the Olympics. Two year ban after positive drugs test in 1990 for Nandrolene at Monaco; reinstated by TAC in 1991 due to alleged irregularities in testing procedure, but the IAAF resisted his vigorous claims to run again internationally. Court rulings in the USA allowed him to run inthe 1992 US Trials, at which he was 5th in the 400m, but the IAAF extended his ban to the end of 1992 for bringing the sport into disrepute. On 14 Dec 1992 the US District Court in Columbus, Ohio awarded for him against the IAAF: $6,839,902 for loss of earnings during his two-year suspension, and $20,356,008 punitive damages. Brother Jeff has 400m pb 44.98 '88.

Jim SPIVEY b.7 Mar 1960 Schiller Park, Illinois 1.80m 63kg. Asics TC. Graduate of Indiana University.
At 1500m: OG: '84- 5, '92- 8; WCh: '87- 3, '93- 5; PAm: '87- 2; WI: '87- 4; WUG: '81- 4. Won NCAA 1982, TAC 1984-5, 1987, 1992. GP 1M/1500m: 3rd 1986, 2nd 1987-8. At 5000m: WCh: '83- sf. US 2000m record 1987.
Progression at 1500m, 1M: 1976- 4:35.5M; 1977- 4:18.3M; 1978- 4:06.2 (1600m); 1979- 3:44.66; 1980- 3:38.56, 3:58.9i; 1981- 3:37.24, 3:57.0; 1982- 3:37.34, 3:55.56; 1983- 3:36.4, 3:50.59; 1984- 3:34.19, 3:53.88; 1985- 3:35.15, 3:52.95; 1986- 3:34.4, 3:49.80; 1987- 3:34.37, 3:51.91; 1988- 3:31.01, 3:50.57; 1989- 3:36.85, 3:57.17; 1990- 3:34.47, 3:56.44; 1991- 3:33.81, 3:49.83; 1992- 3:32.94, 3:52.69; 1993- 3:34.67, 3:52.37; 1994- 3:36.80. pbs: 800m 1:46.5 '82, 1000m 2:16.54 '84, 2000m 4:52.44 '87, 3000m 7:37.04 '93, 2M 8:24.14 '86, 5000m 13:15.86 '94.
Has a renowned finishing kick. Missed Olympic selection in 1988 as he was 4th in the US Trials, but showed that he would have been a prime contender with his 3:31.01 in Koblenz.

Dean STARKEY b.27 Mar 1967 Park Ridge, Illinois 1.88m 77kg. Reebok TC. Was at University of Illinois.
At PV: WCh: '93- dnq 18; WUG: '89- 2.
Progression at PV: 1984- 4.62, 1985- 4.95, 1986- 5.38, 1987- 5.50, 1988- 5.57, 1989- 5.69, 1990- 5.70, 1991- 5.81, 1992- 5.91, 1993- 5.70, 1994- 5.92.

Kareem STREETE-THOMPSON b.30 Mar 1973 Ithaca, New York 1.83m 82kg. Reebok. Student at Rice University.
At LJ: OG: '92- dnq (h 100m); WCh: '91- dnq; CG: '90- 11 (qf 100m); WJ: '88- dnq; '90- 3; WUG: '93- 1. Won CAC Jnr 1990 and 1992.
Progression at LJ: 1988- 6.84, 1989- 7.83, 1990- 7.95, 1991- 8.09/8.40w, 1992- 8.12/8.39w, 1993- 8.36, 1994- 8.63/8.64w. pbs: 55m 6.16i '94, 60m 6.61i '94, 100m 10.21 '94, 10.19w '93; 200m 21.68 '92.
Originally representing the Cayman Islands, he has become a US citizen.

Eugene SWIFT b. 14 Sep 1964 Oakland, California. 1.80m 75kg.
Progression at 110mh: 1987- 14.14?, 1988- 13.99, 1989- 13.87/13.72w, 1990- 13.76, 1991- 13.49, 1992- 13.86/13.72w, 1993- 13.56/13.52w, 1994- 13.23. pb 400mh 51.06 '91.

Gregg TAFRALIS b.9 Apr 1958 San Francisco 1.83m 129kg. Health instructor.
At SP: OG: '88- 9; WCh: '87- dnq 13; PAm: '87- 2; WI: '87- 4. 3rd GP 1992, 1994.
Progression at SP: 1979- 17.63, 1980- 17.91, 1981- 18.24, 1982- 20.12, 1983- 20.20, 1984- 21.25, 1985- 21.32, 1986- 21.45, 1987- 21.32, 1988- 21.36, 1989- 21.32, 1990- 19.57i, 1991- 19.43, 1992- 21.98, 1993- 19.93i/19.77, 1994- 20.89. pb DT 62.38 '86.

Kory TARPENNING b.27 Feb 1962 Portland 1.80m 75kg. Nike International. PE graduate of University of Oregon.
At PV: OG: '88- 10, '92- 4; WI: '91- 4; WCp: '92- nh. Won Olympic Trials 1988, TAC 1988-9. 2nd GP 1991.
Progression at PV: 1980- 4.52, 1981- 5.03, 1982- 5.10i, 1983- 5.28, 1984- 5.50, 1985- 5.65, 1986- 5.70, 1987- 5.80, 1988- 5.89, 1989- 5.80, 1990- 5.83, 1991- 5.75, 1992- 5.86, 1993- 5.75, 1994- 5.85. pb LJ 7.69w/7.68 '91.
Currently living in Paris, training with Jean-Claude Perrin.

Glenn TERRY b.10 Feb 1971 Cleveland 1.93m 82kg. Asics. Student at University of Indiana.
At 110mh: WUG: '93- 2; WJ: '90- sf. Won PAm-J 1989, NCAA 110mh and indoor 55mh 1993.
Progression at 110mh: 1989- 13.83, 1990- 13.64/13.4w, 1991- 13.75, 1992- 13.64, 1993- 13.35/13.24w, 1994- 13.55/13.46w. pbs: 50mh 6.59i '94, 55mh 7.09i '93.

Octavius TERRY b.7 Nov 1972 Atlanta 1.89m

74kg. Student at Georgia Tech.
At 400mh: Won NCAA 400mh 1994.
Progression at 400mh: 1991- 52.70, 1992- 49.71, 1993- 51.36, 1994- 49.03. pb 400m 46.53 '94.

Kevin TOTH b.27 Feb 1962 Cleveland 1.93m 141kg. Nike International. Was at McNeese State University.
At SP: WCh: '93- 9.
Progression at SP: 1990- 18.06, 1991- 18.78, 1992- 20.99, 1993- 21.29, 1994- 21.25i/21.07.

Andrew VALMON b.1 Jan 1965 Brooklyn, New York 1.86m 78kg. Mazda TC. Was at Seton Hall University. Eastman Kodak sales rep.
At 400m/4x400mR: OG: '88- resR, '92- 1R; WCh: '91- 5/2R, '93- 1R; WI: '91- 2. 2nd PAm Jnr 1984, 2nd GP 1991.
World records 4x400m relay 1992 and 1993.
Progression at 400m: 1983- 46.81, 1984- 45.92, 1985- 45.13, 1986- 45.61, 1987- 44.89, 1988- 44.55, 1989- 45.21, 1990- 44.35, 1991- 44.65, 1992- 44.51, 1993- 44.28, 1994- 44.97. pbs: 200m 21.14 '91, 21.0 '86, 300m 32.04 '90, 800m 1:50.58 '93.
Gold medal as he ran in preliminary rounds for the US 4x400mR team at the 1988 Olympics. Ran pb 44.28 in US Trials 1993 yet only 4th.

Erick WALDER b.5 Nov 1971 Mobile, Alabama 1.86m 77kg. Student at University of Arkansas.
At LJ: WCh: '93- 4. At TJ: WJ: '90- 15. Won NCAA LJ 1992-4, TJ 1994, indoor LJ & TJ 1992-4.
Progression at LJ, TJ: 1989- 7.36, 15.56; 1990- 16.25/16.31w, 1991- 7.79/7.84w, 16.05i; 1992- 8.47/8.58w, 16.88i/16.58/16.66w; 1993- 8.53, 16.86i/16.67/16.87w, 1994- 8.74, 17.24i/17.12. pbs: 200m 21.34 '92, HJ 2.11 '90.
His ten NCAA titles is a record for field events.

Anthony WASHINGTON b.16 Jan 1966 Glasgow, Montana 1.86m 107kg. Graphic artist. Graduate of Syracuse University.
At DT: OG: '92- 12; WCh: '91- dnq 28, '93- 11; PAm: '91- 1; WUG: '91- 2; WCp: '92- 1. US champion 1991, 1993. 2nd GP 1993.
Progression at DT: 1985- 52.88, 1986- 56.46, 1987- 60.16, 1988- 61.86, 1989- 64.18, 1990- 61.34, 1991- 65.04, 1992- 67.88, 1993- 66.86, 1994- 64.18. pb HT 59.58 '89.
Set pbs when fourth at 1989 TAC and when winning TAC and Pan-Am Games in 1991.

Quincy WATTS b.19 Jun 1970 Detroit 1.90m 88kg. Nike International. Student at University of Southern California.
At 400m/4x400mR: OG: '92- 1/1R; WCh: '91- 2R, '93- 4/1R; PAm: '91- 4/2R. Won GWG 1994, NCAA 1992, 3rd GP 1993. At 4x100mR: WJ: '88- 1.
World records 4x400m relay 1992 and 1993.
Progression at 400m: 1987- 47.56, 1988- 46.67, 1990- 47.02, 1991- 44.98, 1992- 43.50, 1993- 44.13, 1994- 45.03. pbs 100m 10.30/10.17w '87, 200m 20.50 '87, 300m 32.07 '93.
A surprise third in TAC 400m 1991, but gave up his World place to Danny Everett, before producing the fastest legs, 43.6 and 43.4 (third best of all-time), in the relay. Double gold in 1992 Olympics, including fastest ever, 43.1 on second leg of 4x400m relay. A fine basketball player in high school, he also played as a wide receiver at football for USC.

Tony WHEEELER b. 19 Jan 1975 1.80m 70kg. Student at Clemson University.
At 200m: WJ: '94- 1 (1 4x400m, 2 4x100m).
Progression at 200m: 1993- 21.29i/21.48, 1994- 20.47.

Jeff WILLIAMS b.31 Dec 1964 Los Angeles 1.83m 68kg. Was at Prairie View A&M.
At 200m/4x100mR: WCp: '92- 3/1R. At 100m: PAm: '91- 3.
Progression at 100m 200m: 1986- 20.85w, 1987- 10.3, 20.60; 1989- 10.28/10.24w, 20.51; 1990- 10.23, 20.49/20.3; 1991- 10.21/10.16w, 20.66/20.25w; 1992- 10.28/10.20w?, 20.27/20.25w; 1993- 10.23, 20.47; 1994- 10.19, 20.19. pbs: 50m 5.78i '92, 100y 9.42y '94, 300m 32.47 '90.

Todd WILLIAMS b.7 Mar 1969 Detroit 1.78m 66kg. Team Adidas. Was at University of Tennessee.
At 10000m: OG: '92- 10; WCh: '93- 7. Won US 10000m 1993, CC 1991, 1993.
Progression at 5000m, 10000m: 1988- 14:24.29i, 29:46.5; 1989- 14:14.08, 28:57.7; 1990- 13:48.16i/13:55.26, 28:41.97; 1991- 13:41.50i/13:49.27, 28:18.4; 1992- 13:36.99, 28:05.9; 1993- 13:20.13, 27:40.37; 1994- 13:47.0. pbs: 1M 4:05.39i '94, 3000m 7:47.69 '93, 2M 8:24.54 '92, Half Mar 61:52 '91, 60:11 (33m dh) '93.

Kevin YOUNG b.16 Sep 1966 Los Angeles 1.93m 82kg. Nike International. Sociology graduate of UCLA.
At 400mh: OG: '88- 4, '92- 1; WCh: '91- 4, '93- 1; PAm: '87- 2. US champion 1992-3, NCAA 1987-8. Won 400mh and overall GP 1992.
World 400mh record 1992.
Progression at 400mh: 1985- 51.09, 1986- 48.77, 1987- 48.15, 1988- 47.72, 1989- 47.86, 1990- 48.45, 1991- 47.83, 1992- 46.78, 1993- 47.18, 1994- 49.70. pbs: 400m 45.11 '92, 800m 1:51.42 '88, 110mh 13.65 '92, 200mh 22.74 '92, LJ 7.73 '86, TJ 14.91 '85.
Reached world no. one ranking in 1989, after 10-5-3 in 1986-8. From 1989 has run 13 strides all the way. as opposed to previous practice of 12 strides between the first 4-5 hurdles of

400mh. World athlete of the year in 1992, when he ran a record ten times sub-48 seconds, won all his 17 finals at 400mh and took 0.24 off the world record set by Ed Moses in 1983 to win the Olympic title. He stretched his win streak to 25 finals until his loss 48.85 to 48.86 to Samuel Matete at London on 23 Jul 1993.

Women

Olga APPELL b.2 Aug 1963 Durango 1.75m 59kg. née Avalos.
At Mar: OG: '92- dnf; PAm: '91- 1. Won US 10000m and CC 1994.
Mexican records: 10000m and Marathon (3).
Progression at Mar: 1990- 2:40:04, 1991- 2:33:18, 1992- 2:30:22, 1993- 2:28:56, 1994- 2:28:12. pbs: 3000m 9:13.84 '94, 10000m 32:03.42 '94, Half Mar 68:34 '93 (33m dh).
Won Long Beach and Sapporo marathons in 1992, Los Angeles 1994; second New York 1993. Formerly Mexican, became US citizen on 25 Feb 1994.

Kim BATTEN b.29 Mar 1969 McRae, Georgia 1.70m 57kg. Reebok RC. Was at Florida State University.
At 400mh: WCh: '91- 5, '93- 4; 3rd GP 1993. At 400m: WI: '93 -6. Won US 400mh 1994.
Progression at 400mh: 1986- 61.1, 1987- 60.94, 1988- 58.31, 1989- 58.60, 1990- 55.45, 1991- 53.98, 1992- 54.35, 1993- 53.84, 1994- 53.72. pbs: 200m 23.54 '90, 400m 52.20 '92, 50mh 7.01i '92, 55mh 7.55i '92, 100mh 13.14/13.06w '91, 13.0 '90; LJ 6.21i '91, 6.15/6.34w '90, TJ 12.95i '91, 12.92 '90.
Collegiate 400m hurdles record 1991.

Dawn BOWLES b.12 Nov 1968 Neptune, New Jersey. 1.63m 48kg. Foot Locker AC. Sociology student at Louisiana State University.
At 100mh: WCh: '93- 6; PAm: '91- 4; WUG: '93- 2. Won NCAA 1991.
Progession at 100mh: 1985- 14.51/14.2, 1986- 14.04, 1987- 13.63/13.48w, 1988- 13.30/13.10w, 1990- 13.17, 1991- 12.82/12.70w, 1992- 12.84/12.70w, 1993- 12.84/12.74w, 1994- 12.88. pbs: 55m 6.92i '94, 100m 11.53/11.47w '94; 200m 23.96/23.80w '92, 55mh 7.51i '92, 60mh 8.10i '94.

Tonja BUFORD b.13 Nov 1970 Dayton, Ohio 1.76m 62kg. Mizuno TC. Student at University of Illinois.
At 400mh: OG: '92- sf; WCh: '93- 5; PAmG: '91- 3. Won NCAA 1992.
Progression at 400mh: 1987- 62.5, 1988- 61.86, 1989- 60.93, 1990- 59.46, 1991- 56.45, 1992- 54.75, 1993- 54.38, 1994- 55.26. pbs: 100m 11.50 '92, 200m 23.42 '92, 400m 53.10 '94, 55mh 7.60i '93, 100mh 13.07/12.94w '92.

Kym CARTER b.12 Mar 1964 Inglewood, California 1.88m 80kg. Was at Louisiana State University.
At Hep: OG: '92- 11; WCh: '91- 20, '93- 7. At Pen: WI inv: '93- 5. Won US Hep1994.
Progression at Hep: 1987- 5549, 1990- 6003w, 1991- 6183, 1992- 6256, 1993- 6357, 1994- 6371. pbs: 200m 24.00 '93, 23.94w '94; 800m 2:06.80 '92, 100mh 13.53 '93, HJ 1.89 '82, LJ 6.21 '94, 6.25w '93; SP 16.07 '94, JT 40.68 '92, Pen 4566i '93.
Fifth ranked US high jumper in 1982.

Joetta CLARK b.1 Aug 1962 East Orange, New Jersey 1.72m 52kg. Foot Locker AC. Graduate of University of Tennessee. Legal investigator.
At 800m: OG: '88- sf, '92- 7; WCh: '87- sf, '91- sf, '93- h; WCp: '85- 5, '89- 9, '92- 2, '94- 5; WUG: '85- 6 (3 4x400mR), '87- 3; WI: '87- 6, '93- 3. US champion 1988-9, 1992-4; NCAA 1983-4.
Progression at 800m: 1976- 2:20.0, 1977- 2:11.3y, 1978- 2:05.29, 1979- 2:03.54, 1980- 2:03.83, 1981- 2:03.45, 1982- 2:01.32, 1983- 2:01.34, 1984- 2:00.15, 1985- 1:58.98, 1986- 2:00.2, 1987- 1:59.45, 1988- 1:59.79, 1989- 1:59.83, 1990- 1:59.69, 1991- 1:58.95, 1992- 1:58.06, 1993- 1:58.17, 1994- 1:58.39. pbs: 400m 52.20 '92, 1000m 2:37.9i '86, 2:39.13 '91; 1500m 4:12.82 '94, 1M 4:35.17 '92, 400mh 57.11 '85.
Daughter of the celebrated school principal, Joe Clark. Her brother (and coach) J.J.Clark has a 1500m pb of 3:41.5.

Kim Batten: only woman to defeat Sally Gunnell over 400m hurdles in 1994

Gail DEVERS b.19 Nov 1966 Seattle 1.62m 52kg. Nike International. Studying sociology and assistant coach at UCLA. Married Ron Roberts in June 1988.
At 100m/4x100mR (100mh): OG: '88- (sf); '92- 1/1R (5); WCh: '93- 1/2R (1); PAm: '87- 1/1R. At 60m: WI: '93- 1. Won NCAA 100m 1988, US 100m 1993-4, 100mh 1991-2. 2nd GP 100mh 1992. US records 100mh (4) 1988-93, indoor 60m 1993.
Progression at 100m, 100mh: 1983- 11.69; 1984- 11.51/11.34w, 14.32; 1985- 11.19, 13.16/13.15w; 1986- 11.12/10.96w, 13.08; 1987- 10.98/10.85w, 13.28/13.1w; 1988- 10.97/10.86w, 12.61; 1991- 11.29, 12.48; 1992- 10.82, 12.55; 1993- 10.82, 12.46; 1994- 11.12/10.77w. pbs: 50m 6.10i '93, 60m 6.95i '93, 200m 22.71/22.55w '87, 400m 52.66 '87, 800m 2:11.07 '82, 55mh 7.58i '92, 60mh 7.85i '94, 400mh 59.26 '85, LJ 6.77 '88, TJ 12.97/13.31w '86.
The fastest ever woman sprinter-hurdler. A serious thyroid disorder (Graves's Disease) caused her to miss competition in 1989-90, but after being close to having to have a foot amputated she made an astonishingly speedy return to the top to win the TAC 100mh in 1991, and on to world silver and the US record in Berlin. In 1992 she was a surprise winner of the Olympic 100m but tripped over the last hurdle when well clear of the field in the 100mh.

Sandra FARMER-PATRICK b.18 Aug 1962 Kingston, Jamaica 1.73m 63kg. Flo-Jo International. Degree in industrial psychology from Cal.State University, Los Angeles.

At 400mh: OG: '84- 8, '92- 2; WCh: '83- h, '87- 4, '91- 4, '93- 2; CG: '82- 9; PAm: '83- 4, '87- 2; WCp: '89- 1, '92- 1; CAmG: '82- 1/3R. US champion 1989, 1992-3. Won overall GP 1993 (3rd 1989), individual 1989, 1991 & 1993; 2nd 1987.
Jamaican 400mh record holder from 1977, three US records 1989-93.
Progression at 400mh: 1977- 58.90, 1978- 59.8, 1979- 58.31, 1980- 58.62, 1981- 57.54, 1982- 57.4, 1983- 56.43, 1984- 56.05, 1985- 55.75, 1986- 55.89, 1987- 54.38, 1988- 54.49, 1989- 53.37, 1990- 54.46, 1991- 53.54, 1992- 53.59, 1993- 52.79. pbs: 200m 23.32 '89, 400m 51.35 '92, 800m 2:10.94 '84, 100mh 13.58/13.0w '89.
Born Sandra Miller, she took her grandmother's name of Farmer, when she moved from Kingston, Jamaica to Brooklyn, NY at the age of nine. She competed for the US as a junior, but then internationally for Jamaica. Married Dave Patrick (400mh) 2 Jan 1988 and changed nationality to US, but disqualified after winning semi at US Olympic Trials 1988. Unbeaten in 15 finals at 400mh in 1989, but second in TAC 1990. She ran the race of her life to take 0.58 off her 4-year old US record and run under the old world record, but second to Sally Gunnell at the 1993 Worlds.

Carlette GUIDRY-WHITE b.4 Sep 1968 Houston 1.68m 50kg. Nike International. Studied speech communication at Texas University. Married Mon White (400m 46.37 '90) in November 1991.
At 100m: WCh: '91- 8; At 200m/4x100mR: OG: '92- 5/1R; WJ: '86- 4/1R (7 LJ). Won US 100m 1991, 200m 1994; PAm-J 200m & LJ 1986, GWG 100m 1990, NCAA 60m & 200m indoors 1990.
Progression at 100m, 200m: 1983- 11.6; 1984- 24.45/24.28w; 1985- 11.61, 23.84; 1986- 11.59/ 11.48w, 23.46/22.9; 1987- 11.56/11.52w, 23.35; 1988- 11.11, 22.99/22.96w/22.7; 1989- 11.30/ 11.29w, 22.90; 1990- 11.03, 22.62; 1991- 10.94/ 10.91w, 22.78/22.44w; 1992- 11.09/11.07w, 22.24; 1993- 11.35/11.24w, 22.98/22.76w; 1994- 11.12/ 10.97w, 22.38. pbs: 55m 6.66i '90, 60m 7.12i '93, 400m 51.51 '94, LJ 6.42 '86, 6.47w '87; TJ 12.99 '86.
Including four at relays won eight NCAA titles indoors and out.

Suzy HAMILTON b.8 Aug 1968 Stevens Point, Wisconsin 1.60m 48kg. née Favor. Reebok RC. Graphic design graduate of University of Wisconsin. Married 1991.
At 1500m: OG: '92- h; WCh: '91- h; WUG: '89- 2; WJ: '86- 9. Won PAm-J 1984 & 1986. Won TAC 1990-1, and record nine NCAA titles: 800m 1990, 1500m 1987-90, indoor 1M 1987,

Susy Hamilton: won a record 9 NCAA titles

1989-90; 3000m 1990.
Progression at 1500m: 1983- 4:55.23 1M, 1984- 4:19.46, 1985- 4:19.43, 1986- 4:18.62, 1987- 4:09.20, 1988-4:13.91, 1989- 4:09.7, 1990- 4:08.00, 1991- 4:06.13, 1992- 4:04.53, 1993- 4:10.69, 1994- 4:04.57. pbs: 800m 1:59.02 '94, 1M 4:27.31 '89, 2000m 5:42.86 '94, 3000m 9:02.30i '90.
Won 21 individual and two relay Big 10 conference titles.

Sheila HUDSON-STRUDWICK b.30 Jun 1967 Kitzengen, FRG 1.65m 50kg. née Hudson. Mizuno TC. Degree in architecture from University of California.
At TJ: WCh: '93- dnq 17; WCp: '92- 4, '94- 2. US champion 1987, 1989-90, 1992, 1994; NCAA 1987-8, 1990 (and LJ 1990).
Two world triple jump bests 1987, six US records 1987-94.
Progression at TJ: 1984- 12.29, 1985- 12.47, 1986- 13.50, 1987- 13.85/13.92w, 1988- 13.79, 1989- 13.90/14.01w, 1990- 14.04/14.07w, 1991- 13.23/ 13.75w, 1992- 14.23, 1993- 13.86, 1994- 14.23. pbs: 100m 12.19 '88, 200m 24.89 '88. LJ 6.73 '90.
Won NCAA LJ/TJ double indoors and out in 1990. Daughter of a US serviceman and Korean mother. Married swimmer Warren Strudwick 1994.

Holli HYCHE b.6 Sep 1971 Indianapolis 1,65m 52kg Student at Indiana State University.
Won NCAA 100m 1993-4, 200m 1994.
Progression at 100m, 200m: 1990- 11.74, 23.92; 1992- 11.45/11.42w, 23.28; 1993- 11.12/10.93w /10.9w, 22.34; 1994- 11.03, 22.41. pbs: 55m 6.70i '94, 60m 7.21i '94, 400m 53.29 '94.

Regina JACOBS b.28 Aug 1963 Los Angeles 1.63m 53kg. Mizuno TC. Graduate of Stanford University.
At 1500m: OG: '88- h, '92- sf; WCh: '87- h; WCp: '89- 9. US champion 1987, 1989, 1994.
Progression at 150m: 1980- 4:32.6, 1981- 4:25.0, 1983- 4:13.09, 1984- 4:11.33, 1985- 4:15.41, 1986- 4:02.6, 1987- 4:03.70, 1988- 4:00.46, 1989- 4:10.91, 1992- 4:03.72, 1993- 4:15.71, 1994- 4:02.15. pbs: 800m 1:59.36 '87, 1000m 2:35.03 '94, 1M 4:27.28 '94, 2000m 5:38.52 '94, 3000m 9:01.2 '87.

Lynn JENNINGS b.1 Jul 1960 Princeton, New Jersey 1.65m 52kg. Nike International. History graduate of Princeton University. Freelance writer.
At 10000m: OG: '88- 6, '92- 3; WCh: '87- 6, '91- 5, '93- 5. At 3000m: '93- 3. World CC: '86- 2, '87- 4, '88- 4, '89- 6, '90- 1, '91- 1, '92- 1, '93- 3. Won US 3000m 1988, 1990; 10000m 1987, 1991-3, record seven CC titles, 1985, 1987-91, 1993.
WIB: 2 miles 9:28.15 TAC '86, 5000m 15:22.64 '90. US 10000m record 1992. US road 10km record 31:06 '90.
Progression at 3000m, 10000m: 1979- 9:51.2, 1982- 9:35.6, 1983- 9:01.44, 1984- 9:45.4, 1985- 8:49.86, 32:03.37; 1986- 8:53.19i, 1987- 8:49.23, 31:45.43;, 1988- 8:48.19, 31:39.93; 1989- 9:15.74, 1990- 8:40.45i/8:46.08, 1991- 8:53.0, 31:54.44; 1992- 8:44.60, 31:19.89; 1993- 8:52.55, 31:30.53; 1994- 8:59.2. pbs: 800m 2:06.26i '92, 2:06.54 '86; 1500m 4:06.4 '90, 1M 4:24.14 '90, 2000m 5:49.8i '90, 5:52.62 '86; 2M 9:28.15i '86, 5000m 15:07.92 '90.
TAC junior 1500m and CC champion 1977. As an unofficial entrant ran 2:46+ for third woman at age 17 in 1978 Boston marathon. After reuniting with her high school coach John Babington, she won three successive World CC titles 1990-2. In 1990 she become the first runner to win TAC titles in outdoor and indoor track, road racing and cross-country in one year.

Jackie JOYNER-KERSEE b.3 Mar 1962 East St.Louis, Illinois 1.78m 70kg. McDonald's TC. Was at UCLA, where she is now assistant basketball coach. Sister of triple jumper Al Joyner. Married coach Bobby Kersee on 11 Jan 1986.
At Hep/LJ: OG: '84- 2/5, '88- 1/1, '92- 1/3; WCh: '83- dnf/-, '87- 1/1, '91- dnf/1, '93- 1/-. Won US Hep 1982, 1987, 1991-3; LJ 1987, 1990-4, 100mh 1994; NCAA Hep 1982-3, GWG Hep 1986, 1990, 1994; PAm-J LJ 1980. Won overall and LJ GP 1994, 3rd LJ 1985, 1992. Won Mobil Indoor GP 1987 & 1989.
Four world heptathlon records 1986-8, world long jump record 1987. US records: 100mh (2) 1988, LJ (5) 1985-94, heptathlon (6) 1984-8. Two WIB 55mh 7.37 '89.
Progression at LJ, Hep: 1974- 5.10, 1975- 5.22, 1976- 5.31, 1977- 5.69, 1978- 5.55/6.06w; 1979- 6.28/6.30w; 1980- 6.34/6.42w; 1981- 6.39/ 6.47w, 5754w; 1982- 6.44/6.61w, 6066; 1983- 6.74/6.77w, 6390; 1984- 6.81, 6579; 1985- 7.24, 6718; 1986- 7.12/7.15w, 7158; 1987- 7.45, 7128; 1988- 7.40/7.45w, 7291; 1990- 7.12, 6783; 1991- 7.32, 6878; 1992- 7.17, 7044; 1993- 7.08/7.09w, 6837; 1994- 7.49, 6606. pbs: 100m 11.71 '86, 200m 22.30 '87, 400m 53.64 '90, 800m 2:08.51 '88, 50mh 6.84i '93, 60mh 7.81i '89, 100mh 12.61 '88, 400mh 55.05 '85, HJ 1.93 '88, TJ 13.20 '85, SP 16.84 '88, JT 50.12 '86.
Sullivan Award winner 1986. Won both long jump and heptathlon by huge margins at the 1987 World Championships and went on to the Olympic double in 1988. Won 12 successive heptathlons 1985-91, before she pulled up with a hamstring injury at the 1991 Worlds. The previous day she had retained her long jump title, but had suffered a severe ankle injury. In her

career has won 23/33 heptathlons to the end of 1994 and has the five highest ever scores, the first five over 7000. Won at Götzis 1986.

Natasha KAISER-BROWN. b.14 May 1967 Des Moines, Iowa 1.75m 59kg. née Kaiser. Cheetahs Was at University of Missouri, where she now coaches. Married Brian Brown (HJ 2.34i '90, US champion 1989) in 1992.
At 400m/4x400mR: OG: '92- silver R; WCh: '93- 2/1R; PAm: '91- 4/1R. Won US 400m 1994.
Progression at 400m: 1984- 54.09, 1985- 55.0, 1986- 51.48, 1987- 52,57, 1988- 51.73, 1989- 50.86, 1990- 51.55, 1991- 51.20, 1992- 50.42, 1993- 50.17, 1994- 50.38. pbs: 100m 11.83 '93, 11.60w '89; 200m 23.36 '92

Anne Marie LETKO b.7 Mar 1969 Rochester, NY 1.70m 52kg. Nike. Was at Wake Forest University. At 10000m: WCh: '91- dnf; '93- 8; WUG: '91- 1; WCp: '92- 5.
Progression at 10000m: 1988- 35:51.75, 1990- 33:06.21, 1991- 32:26.65, 1992- 33:47.20, 1993- 31:37.26, 1994- 32:41.67. pbs: 1500m 4:26.29 '94, 3000m 9:15.03i '90, 5000m 15:43.37 '94, Half Mar: 70:03 '94, Mar 2:30:19 '94.
In the New York Marathon she was prominent for much of the 1993 race (her début), but dropped out at 23 miles; she was 3rd in 1994.

Maicel MALONE b.12 Jun 1969 Indianapolis 1.78m 62kg. Was at Arizona State University. Married James Trapp (100m 10.16/10.04w '91, 200m: 20.49 '91) 16 Aug 1991 and pro-footballer Aaron Wallace Jr in November 1994.
At 400m/R- 4x100m relay: WCh: '93- 1R; WUG: '91- 1/1R, '93- 1R; WJ: '86- 3/1R (sf 200m), '88- 2/2R; PAm: '91- 1R; 3rd GP 1994, Won NCAA 1988, 1990, indoors 1990. 2nd Pan-American Junior 100m and 200m 1986.
Progression at 400m: 1984- 55.22, 1985- 53.7, 1986- 52.42, 1987- 52.7, 1988- 50.96, 1989- 52.09, 1990- 51.13, 1991- 50.33, 1992- 52.16i, 1993- 51.37, 1994- 50.05. pbs: 100m 11.47 '91, 11.18w '86, 200m 22.91 '91, 300m 36.9i '91.
Olympic relay reserve 1988. Won NCAA indoor 400m 1990-2 (US indoor record 51.05 '91). Son born 3 Nov 1992.

LaVonna MARTIN b.18 Nov 1966 Dayton, Ohio 1.70m 66kg. Reebok RC. Graduate of University of Tennessee. Married to Edrick Floreal CAN LJ 8.20 '91, 8.39w '89; TJ 17.29 '89.
At 100mh: OG: '88- sf, '92- 2; WCh: '87- 8; PAm: '87- 1. At 60mh: '93- 2. Won PAm-J 1984, NCAA 1987, TAC 1987, 1990. Won Mobil Indoor GP 1990.
Progression at 100mh: 1983- 13.63, 1984- 13.55, 1985- 13.10/13.02w, 1986- 12.95, 1987- 12.80, 1988- 12.85, 1989- 13.01, 1990- 12.74, 1992- 12.69, 1993- 12.78, 1994- 12.86. pbs: 100m 11.46 '86, 11.44w '88; 200m 23.24 '87, 22.94w '85; 400m 52.6 '85, 55mh 7.41i '90, 60mh 7.93i '93, 400mh 57.84 '85.
Received two-year ban after positive steroids test 1990; claimed she was given furosenide unknowingly by her coach Tatyana Zelentsova.

Jearl MILES b.4 Sep 1966 Gainesville 1.70m 60kg. Reebok RC. Was at Alabama A&M University .
At 400m: OG: '92- sf/2R; WCh: '91- 5/2R, '93- 1/1R; WI: '93- 3; PAm: '91- 3; WUG: '89- 2/1R; WCp: '92- 1, '94- 3. US champion 1993, GWG 1994.
Progression at 400m: 1986- 52.41, 1987- 52.36, 1988- 51.28, 1989- 51.52, 1990- 51.76, 1991- 50.19, 1992- 50.30, 1993- 49.82, 1994- 50.11. pbs: 200m 23.29 '93, 800m 2:04.78 '92, LJ 6.36/6.47w '88.

Annette PETERS b. 31 May 1965 Reno, Nevada 1.65m 49kg. née Hand. Nike West. Was at the University of Oregon. Elementary school teacher
At 3000m: OG: '92- h; WCh: '91- 8, '93- 10; WUG: '87- 4. Won US 1500m 1993, 3000m 1993-4, NCAA 5000m 1988.
US 5000m record 1993.
Progression at 3000m: 1985- 9:19.23, 1986- 9:04.45, 1987- 8:59.90, 1988- 8:59.15, 1989- 9:00.61, 1990- 8:54.64, 1991- 8:44.02, 1992- 8:42.09, 1993- 8:43.59, 1994- 8:41.97. pbs: 800m 2:13.2 '86, 1500m 4:08.87 '93, 1M 4:38.19 '88, 2000m 5:38.08 '92, 5000m 14:56.07 '93, 10000m 32:15.8 '91.

Connie PRICE-SMITH b.3 Jun 1962 St. Charles, Missouri 1.92m 93kg. née Price, married John Smith 1991. Nike North. Was at Southern Illinois University on a basketball scholarship.
At DT (SP): OG: '88-dnq 16 (dnq 18), '92- dnq; WCh: '87- nt, '91- 11, '93- dnq 19 (dnq 14); PAm: '87- 3, '91- 2; WCp: '89- 7, '94- 6. AT SP: WI: '91- 7. Won US SP 1988, 1990, 1992-4; DT 1987, 1989-90, 1992-4; US Olympic Trials DT 1988.
Progression at SP/DT: 1985- 15.24i/50.32, 1986- 17.28/53.52, 1987- 18.29/64.82, 1988- 19.15/62.54, 1989- 18.55i/62.86, 1990- 18.92/59.00, 1991- 19.34/59.24, 1992- 19.06/64.00, 1993- 19.25/63.52, 1994- 19.60/62.32.

Meredith RAINEY b.15 Oct 1968 New York 1.67m 54kg. Foot Locker AC. Social studies graduate of Harvard University, now studying for an MBA.
At 800m: OG: '92- h; WCh: '91- h, '93- 5. US champion 1990, NCAA 1989.
Progression at 800m: 1989- 2:02.67, 1990- 1:59.73,

1991- 1:59.30, 1992- 1:59.18, 1993- 1:57.63, 1994- 1:59.90. pbs: 400m 51.56 '90, 1000m 2:40.80 '90.
Starred at track as a girl but played other sports including basketball and volleyball from the age of 12 until she took up the sport again after she went to Harvard in 1986. Engaged to Andrew Valmon.

Rochelle STEVENS b.8 Sep 1966 Memphis 1.70m 55kg. Maybelline TC. Graduate of Morgan State University. Teacher.
At 400m/4x400mR: OG: '92- 6/2R; WCh: '91- 2R; PAm: '87- 1R; WUG: '87- 1R; WCp: '89- 4/4R, '94- 5R. Won NCAA 1988, TAC 1989, 1992.
Progression at 400m: 1985- 53.31, 1986- 51.90, 1987- 51.23, 1988- 51.23, 1989- 50.75, 1990- 50.39, 1991- 50.71, 1992- 50.06, 1993- 52.39, 1994- 51.45. pbs: 100m 11.37 '88, 11.1 '87, 200m 22.84 '87, 300m 37.25 '93, 800m 2:11.01 '83.
Olympic relay reserve 1988.

Cheryl TAPLIN b.2 Sep 1972 Seattle 1.65m 56kg. Was at Louisiana State University.
At 100m/4x100mR: WUG: '93- 1R.
Progression at 100m: 1988- 11.96, 1989- 11.72w, 1990- 11.94, 1991- 11.41/11.28w, 1992- 11.39/ 11.19w, 1993- 11.23/11.08w, 1994- 11.07/10.99w. pbs: 55m 6.72i '94, 200m: 22.88/22.80w '94.

Lynda TOLBERT-GOODE b.3 Oct 1967 Washington, DC 1.63m 52kg. née Tolbert. Nike Central. Was at Arizona State University
At 100mh OG: '92- 7; WCh: '93- 3; WCp: '89- 3=. Won NCAA 1988, 1990; US 1989, 1993; GP 1992.
Progression at 100mh: 1984- 14.12, 1985- 13.72, 1986- 13.61/13.50w, 1987- 13.06, 1988- 12.76/ 12.75w, 1989- 12.75, 1990- 12.82, 1991- 13.40/ 13.00w, 1992- 12.71/12.66w, 1993- 12.67, 1994- 13.00/12.90w. pbs: 100m 11.49/11.41w '88, 55mh 7.44i '90, 60mh 8.06i '88, LJ 6.10 '87.

Gwen TORRENCE b.12 Jun 1965 Atlanta 1.70m 57kg. Mazda TC. Was at University of Georgia, studying family and child development.
At 100m/200m/4x100mR (4x400mR): OG: '88- 5/6, '92- 4/1/1R (2R); WCh: '87- 5, '91- 2/2, '93- 3/2/2R (1R); PAm: '87- 1/1R; WUG: '85- 1R, '87- 1/1/1R. Won US 100m 1992, 200m 1988, 1991-3; NCAA 100m & 200m 1987; GWG 100m & 200m 1994. Won GP 100m 1993, 2nd 100m 1991 & 1994, 200m 1992. At 60m: WI: '89- 2, '91- 4. Won NCAA indoor 55m 1986-7 (6.56 WIB '87), TAC 1988 (tie), 1989.
Progression at 100m, 200m, 400m: 1982- 24.2; 1983- 11.92, 24.34/23.9y; 1984- 11.41/11.37w, 23.54; 1985- 11.40/11.11w, 22.96; 1986- 11.30 /11.01w, 22.53; 1987- 11.09/11.08w, 22.40/ 22.33w/22.2w; 1988- 10.91/10.78w, 22.02; 1989- 11.12, 1990- 11.28, 22.82; 1991- 10.96/10.85w, 22.07; 1992- 10.86/10.82w, 21.72, 49.64; 1993- 10.87, 22.00, 49.83; 1994- 10.82, 21.85, 50.20. pb 60m 7.07i '89.
Won 49 successive races at indoor short sprints from 31 Jan 1986 to defeat by Dawn Sowell on 17 Feb 1989, including tie with Evelyn Ashford in 1988. Married to Manley Waller (100m 10.26 '86); son born 1989. Ran 49.1 lead-off 400m relay leg at 1993 World Championships, at which she won four medals.

Janeene VICKERS b.3 Dec 1968 Torrance, California 1.70m 62kg. World Class AC. Was at UCLA.
At 400m/4x400mR: OG: '92- 3; WCh: '91- 3; WJ: '86- 4/1R. 2nd PAm-J 400m 1986. Won NCAA 1989-90, TAC 1990.
Progression at 400mh: 1987- 57.80, 1988- 56.10, 1989- 55.27, 1990- 54.80, 1991- 53.47, 1992- 54.31, 1993- 56.21. pbs: 100m 11.56/11.41w '91, 200m 23.20 '91, 400m 51.57 '91, 100mh 13.16 '91, 13.05w '90.
US high school athlete of the year 1987, when she first tried the 400m hurdles. The previous year she had a 400m best of 52.25.

Dannette YOUNG b.6 Oct 1964 Jacksonville 1.70m 55kg. Reebok RC. Was at Alabama A&M. Sales clerk.
At 200m/4x100mR: OG: '88- resR; WCh: '91- 6, '93- 8; WCp: '89- 4; WUG: '87- 3/1R. 2nd GP 1988. Won TAC 1989, GWG 1990.
Progression at 200m, 400m: 1982- 24.0y, 1983- 23.76, 1984- 23.38/23.32w, 1985- 22.92/22.85w, 1986- 23.12/22.84w, 1987- 22.72, 1988- 22.23/ 22.21w, 52.46; 1989- 22.29, 1990- 22.40/22.19w, 1991- 22.24, 53.07; 1992- 22.55, 50.46; 1993- 22.51/22.44w, 51.59; 1994- 22.29/22.16w, 51.29. pbs: 60m 7.29i '94, 100m 11.10 '88.
Has won two Olympic relay medals after running in heats only: gold at 4x100m 1988, silver 4x400m 1992. Son born 1980.

YUGOSLAVIA

Governing body: Atletski Savez Jugoslavije, Strahinjica Bana 73a, 11000 Beograd. Founded in 1921.
National Championships first held in 1920 (men) and 1923 (women). **1994 champions**: **Men**: 100m: Aleksandar Tomic 10.73, 200m/ 400m: Nenad Djurovic 21.52/46.84, 800m: Slobodan Popovic 1:47.89, 1500m: Dejan Pajkic 3:50.07, 5000m: Ljubisa Djokic 14:17.80, 10000m/ Mar: Borislav Devic 29:50.20/2:23:24, Half Mar: Aleksandar Milovanovic 1:14:53, 3000mSt: Vule Maksimovic 8:41.32, 110mh: Dragisa Jovanovic 14.67, 400mh: Sinisa Pesa 52.40, HJ: Stevan

Zoric 2.25, PV: Aca Stankovic 4.70, LJ: Danijel Misic 7.58, TJ: Zeljko Obradovic 15.63, SP/DT: Dragan Peric 20.41/56.94, HT: Dragan Majstorovic 56.16, JT: Jovan Djukic 69.28, Dec: Slavoljub Nikolic 6440, 10000mW: Aleksandar Rakovic 43:53.4. **Women**: 100m/200m: Marina Zivkovic 11.73/23.82, 400m: Andjelka Vukadinovic 55.32, 800m: Jelena Stanisavljevic 2:11.19, 1500m: Olivera Jevtic 4:28.73, 3000m: Natasa Zrnic 10:06.05, 10000m: Ljiljana Jovanovic 37:00.3, Half Mar: Radislavka Racic 1:31:42, Mar: Ilona Kalmar 3:04:55, 100mh: Irena Vidojevic 13.97, 400mh: Dusica Dejanov 62.68, HJ: Tatjana Mitrovic 1.71, LJ: Maja Radmanovic 5.57, TJ: Dejana Rakita 12.31, SP: Monika Balog 12.93, DT: Tatjana Majhenic 41.52, JT: Ilinka Kuljanin 46.20, Hep: Danijela Srdanovic 3946, 5000mW: Ivana Jovanovic 29:46.4.

Dragan PERIC b.8 May 1964 Zivinice 1.86m 107kg. AK Partizan.
At SP: OG: '92- 7; WCh: '91- 7, '93- 5; EC: '90- 13, '94- 6; EI: '94- 2. Yugoslav champion SP 1990-4, DT 1992-4.
Yugoslav shot record 1993, discus 1991.
Progression at SP: 1980- 11.35, 1981- 12.23, 1982- 14.88, 1983- 17.24, 1985- 16.89, 1986- 17.70, 1987- 18.86, 1988- 19.92, 1989- 20.42, 1990- 20.06, 1991- 20.47, 1992- 20.91, 1993- 21.26, 1994- 20.64i/20.57. pb DT 61.94 '91.

Dragutin TOPIC b.12 Mar 1971 Belgrade 1.97m 77kg. Crvena Zvezda. Student at Belgrade University of PE.
At HJ: OG: '92- 8=; WCh: '91- 9, '93- dnq; EC: '90- 1, '94- 5=; WJ: '90- 1; EJ: '89- 4; EI: '92- 3=. 3rd GP 1994. Yugoslav champion 1993.
World junior high jump record 1990, five Yugoslav records 1990-3.
Progression at HJ: 1985- 1.85, 1986- 1.95, 1987- 1.95, 1988- 2.06, 1989- 2.23, 1990- 2.37, 1991- 2.32/2.34i, 1992- 2.35, 1993- 2.38, 1994- 2.32. pbs: LJ 7.48i '93, TJ 15.66 '92, Dec 6155h '93.
Completed a marvellous major championships double in Split. Was at high school in Illinois, USA for a year in 1987/8, but played basketball while there and did not compete as a high jumper.

ZAMBIA

Governing body: Zambia Amateur Athletic Association, PO Box 22693, Kitwe.

Samuel MATETEb.7 Jul 1968 Chingola 1.83m 77kg. Student at Auburn University, formerly at Blinn CC, USA 1988-90.
At 400mh: OG: '88- h, '92- dq sf; WCh: '91- 1. '93- 2; CG: '90- 5, '94- 1; AfG: '87- sf; AfCh: '88- 5 (4.400m); WJ: '88- 5; WCp: '92- 1/1R, '94- 1/2R. Won GP 1994 (2nd overall), 2nd 1990, 1992. Won NCAA 1991.
African 400mh record 1991. Zambian records 1989-91: 11 at 400mh, 2 at 400m.
Progression at 400mh: 1987- 51.48, 1988- 50.5, 1989- 48.67, 1990- 47.91, 1991- 47.10, 1992- 47.91, 1993- 47.60, 1994- 47.90. pbs: 100m 10.77 '89, 200m 21.04 '89, 400m 44.88 '91.
Five national records in a month in 1989 from 49.94 to 48.67. He moved up to world number two in 1990. In 1991 he was unbeaten in 23 races at 400mh, improving to 47.80 and then to 47.10 (the second fastest ever run) in Zürich prior to becoming the first Zambian world champion. In 1992 he was disqualified after finishing third in his Olympic semi for trailing leg knocking down hurdle in another lane. In 1994 he won Zambia's first Commonwealth athletics gold medal. Apparently over age when he competed in the 1988 World Juniors.

ZIMBABWE

Governing body: Amateur Athletic Association of Zimbabwe, PO Box MP 187, Mount Pleasant, Harare, Zimbabwe. Founded in 1912.

Phillimon HARINEKI (Hanneck) b.12 May 1971 1.70m 59kg.
At 5000m: WCh: '93- h; CG: '94- 2. At 1500m: OG: '92- sf; AfCh: '89- 7.
Zimbabwe records 1500m, 3000m, 5000m.
Progression at 1500m, 5000m: 1988- 3:48.7, 1989- 3:43.19, 1990- 3:47.66, 1991- 3:35.76, 1992- 3:37.20, 1993- 3:37.46, 13:14.76; 1994- 13:14.50. pbs: 800m 1:47.28 '91, 1M 3:53.13 '92, 3000m 7:42.06 '92, road 10km 27:45 '93, Half Mar 64:04 '93.

Phillimon Harineki: second in Commonwealth Games 5000

AMENDMENTS TO ATHLETICS 1994

P.50. It was Addis Abebe and not Mekonnen who won the Bob Hasan 10k in Jakarta.
P.89 European Junior Championships
The disqualification of Mariana Florea for a positive drugs test meant that not only did she lose the 400m gold, but ROM lost the 4x400m gold. Revised result: 1. GER 3:33.91, 2. RUS 3:39.76, 3. FRA 3:41.53
P.95 S.American Championships: 10,000m: Silio 28:37.2, LJ: Oliveira 7.99w, Valiente 7.38w, 20kmW: Jefferson Pérez ECU 1:24:31, W LJ: Avila 6.45w, Massa 6.00w; TJ: Barbosa 12.77w; SP: Adriano 16.47.
P.99 Central American & Caribbean Championships: TJ: Saavedra 16.49.
World record etc: Having corrected the time successfully in the 1993 Annual for some reason confusion continued to reign and Morceli's 1500m time in 1992 was shown as 3:28.82 and not, as it should have been, 3:28.86.
UK: AAA Champions 1993: LJ: Nicole Boegman AUS 6.50w, TJ: Lene Espegren.

Men 1993
100m: 10.05 Effiong & 10.25 Barron 21 May, 10.16 1.2 Gilbert, 10.18 Savin - not in KZK list, so may be wa, next 10.34 +1.0 13 Jun; 10.32 +1.8 Plamen Stoyanov BUL 16.5.72 5rA ECP Budapest 29 May (not 10.3, 10.32 1.1 Andre Domingos da Silva BRA 26.11.72 1s Curitaba 29 May, 10.34 Sidnei Souza (and 200m, 400m), 10.36 Miranda (not wa - MEX rec?), 10.37 1.0 Zhang; delete 10.37A Cardenas (hand time); 10.14w Zisimides, 10.23w Jin Sun-kuk, 10.27Aw Nico Schutte RSA 25.6.64 1 Colorado 2 Aug, 10.38w 3.1 Talavera, delete 10.19w Phillips, 10.29w Dollé & 10.35Aw Bailey. Doubtful: 10.30 0.9 Joe Rogers USA 3 Houston 21 May, also wa times at Artemisa 22 Apr (Fuentes 10.12 etc) doubtful as auto, doubful 10.32w +2.5 Patrick Amarteifio GER 73 28 Aug. Hand: 9.9 Ondiek & 10.1 Gikonyo on 29 Jul, 10.1 Arnaldo Silva, 10.2 Ferrin 22 May, 10.2 0.2 Ceselin, 10.2A 0.4 Johan Rossouw RSA 65 6 Apr, 10.2 Hyacinthe Kamelan CIV 66 10 Apr, 10.2 Saad Marzouk Al-Mutary KUW 70 21 Apr, 10.2 Tihomir Buinjac CRO 74 19 May, 10.2 1.7 Bradley Rose CAN 71 20 Jun, 10.2 Benjamin Sirimou CAM 69 7 Aug, 10.2A John Jairo Mena COL 67 2 Oct
200m: 20.02 Telles and 20.58 Domingos da Silva - in May 1994 the Brazilian Federation announced that it was withdrawing recognition (also from 20.27 at Americana 27 Feb) so best auto for Telles: 20.75 -0.8 2 São Paulo 16 May, da Silva: 20.76 0.2 2 Rio de Janeiro 27 Jun, 20.65 Hervey 4.5.73, 20.67 -0.5 Georgiev, delete 20.78A Walton (hand timed), 20.79 Cojocaru -0.3, 20.85 1.7 Napier 17 Jun (not 20.80 18 Jun), 20.86 Ferguson (not 20.85), 20.91w 3.2 Miles, 20.92 1.0 Delavantie Brown 71 (not 20.94), 20.93 Barbulescu 0.5, 20.94 Masai Troutman USA 71 29 May, 20.95 Diagana 26 Apr, Lewis MNT, 20.95 1.2 Gamper, 20.96 Matt Hemmingway USA 72 17 Apr, 20.96 Keitel 93. Best low altitude: 20.79 Miller 1h2 Pac10 Berkeley 21 May. wa: 20.81 2.2 Zhang, 20.82 5.2 Earl Jenkins USA 70 14 May. Hand: 20.5 3.0 Gats, 20.7 Leonid Yashinskiy UKR 66 2 Aug
400m: Calvin Harrison tested positive for pseudoephedrine at the US Junior Championships, so replace his 45.07 by 45.25 1 Norwalk 19 Jun. 46.06 Bosso 10.9.69, 46.29 Pryce 69, 46.30 Louis Sales USA 71 21 May, 46.30 Ekyepong 73, 46.32 Sinclair 71, 46.35 Hagan b.69, Ramsey b. 74, 46.40 Hugh Powell JAM 70, 46.43A Canizales 30 Jul (46.30 was manual), 46.47 Shon Joo-il, 46.48 Tyson Spears USA 71 29 May, delete 46.35 Chase. Hand timed: 44.9A Matilu 2h1 Nairobi 2 Jul (from 45.0A), 45.1 Solomon Amagatcher GHA 20.12.70 1 NC Kumasi 3 Jul, 45.4 Ibrahim Hassan GHA .71 2 NC Kumasi 3 Jul, 45.5A Elkana Nyangau KEN 62 4 NC Nairobi 3 Jul, 45.8A Kennedy Oyunge 2h2 NC Nairobi 2 Jul (from 46.2A), 46.3A Bekele Ergego ETH 73 28 May, 46.3A Godwin Kikete KEN & Stephen Mwanzia KEN 62 2 Jul
800m: 1:45.46 Kipketer KEN, 1:46.49 Lee Jin-il 1 Kwangju 12 Oct (from 1:47.13), 1:47.43 Smiljanic CAN, 1:47.64A Kotze & 1:47.87A Mouton on 3 May, 1:47.70 Rhymer 72, 1:47.79A Vernon-Watson, 1:47.81 Kim Yong-hwan KOR 71 12 Oct (not 1:47.67), 1:47.89 Kim Soo-hyung KOR 73 12 Oct, delete 1:47.57 Korir (was Kinyor)
1500m: 3:37.8 Mohamed Moughit MAR 70 1 Rabat 26 May, 3:38.35 Kiplagat KEN, 3:38.85 Terrier 2, 3:39.2A Cleophas Bitok KEN 73 Nairobi 12 Jun, 3:39.48 Siba 15.2.73 (& 1M 3:59.33), 3:39.55 Sammy Koskei, 3:39.95 Silva, 3:40.23 Cuenca SUI, 3:40.9 Mohamed Belasri MAR 73 26 May, 3:41.01 Azzeddine Sediki

MAR 70 6 Jul, 3:41.06 Bart Meganck 13 Aug (from 3:41.42). 100th best 3:39.62.
1M: 3:58.70 Fourie, 3:58.89 Bahtiri SLO 72 (not Boushra), 3:59.57 Kipketer 70
2000m: 5:05.0+ El Basir 31 Jul
3000m: 7:49.80 Barngetuny 20.5.73, 7:52.58 Joel (not Joseph) Keter, 7:53.3+ Charles Cheruiyot KEN 64 2 Jul; indoor OK 7:53.96 Chesire 7 Feb
5000m: 13:30.98 Kaldy 31 Jul, 13:32.51 Katsuhiro Kawauchi, 13:34.19 Barnabas Korir KEN 65 11 Hechtel 31 Jul, 13:36.70 El Ghazali 9 Maia 10 Jul, 13:36.98 Joseph Kariuki KEN 70, 13:37.45 Kiprobon 1 May, 13:40.5A Joseph Kibor 12 Jun (not Keter, delete 13:40.6 mark), 13:41.81 Randich 67 (& 10k 28:16.95), 13:43.77 Mosima 77
10000m: 27:25.23 Sigei and next two at Durban 24 Jun, 27:42.3 Tanui 3 Aug, 27:55.9 Keino at Nairobi, 28:07.1A Kirui & 28:29.8A Ondieki 2 Jul, 28:18.02 Joseph Kariuki KEN 70, delete 27:58.59 Belhadj (one lap short, so Ulmala to 12th, Cishahayo to 13th), 28:26.63 Toyi, 28:28.1 Takaoka 1, 28:33.12 Ibata & 28:34.61 Sakhri 69 on 31 May, 28:38.8A Kirui 11 Jun, 28:43.63 Smith 65, 28:47.9A Cherusei, 28:48.2 Sambu
15km: 43:43 Juan José Castillo PER 68 5 Portland 27 Jun, 43:54 Kimeli 7
Half Mar: 60:50 Maino 68, 61:17 Essebani 63, 61:49 Tadesse Gebre 68 (Delete at 62:21), Sakhri 20.11.61, 61:55 Tessema 28.1.68, 62:08 João Lopes 4.3.67, 62:11 Thlobo 11 NC Durban 28 Aug (from 62:38), 62:23A Tegnu Abebe ETH 74 2 Addis Ababa 24 Apr, 62:30 Ngatia 59, 62:30 Boniface Merande KEN 13.2.62 6 Berlin 4 Apr, 62:31 Gebre Medihin 71, 62:34 Kingstone Maringe ZIM 1 Aug, 62:35A Gemechu Kebede ETH 73 24 Apr, 62:40 Ngunzu 59, 62:43 Larbi Khattabi MAR 67 4 Apr, 62:45 Bernard Mvuyékuré BUR 9 May. Short course - Lisbon: 62:01 António Salvador POR 6.4.67 16, 62:04 Diego Garcia ESP 12.10.61 18, 62:08 Joaquim Cardoso POR 27.7.69 22
Mar: 2:10:38 Gurny, 2:10:44 Zhelonkin 21.1.66, 2:10:57 Nerurkar 1 Hamburg 23 May, 2:11:00 Patricio 9.10.64, 2:13:16 Nicholas Kioko .71, 2:13:03 Yu Young-hun .72 and 2:13:07 Lee Sun-chun both KOR at Chuncheon 29 Oct, 2:13:06 Achour, 2:13:10 Huh Ui-ku, 2:13:25 Herbritsch, 2:13:27 Wu Yiwen, 2:13:52 Gebrselassie, 2:14:27 Hussein 67, 2:14:37 Oe 63
100km: 6:47:14 Oleg Bykov BLS 3 Kalisz 9 Oct
24 Hr: 243.200t Maksim Vorobyev, 252.420 de Sousa .41, 244.742 Klement 22.10.57
3000mSt: 8:28.85 Barngetuny 20.5.73, 8:29.38 (not 8:24.80) Al-Asmari 5 Jun, 8:34.0A Peter Kipkasi 2h1 Nairobi 2 Jul, 8:36.8A Henry Bitok KEN 12 Jun, 8:37.4 Rono 72, 8:37.8A William Kiprono KEN 12 Jun, 8:38.0A Barmao 63, 8:38.9 Bouldadj 21 Jul, 8:39.0A Wilson Boit KEN 2 Jul. 100th best 8:36.20.
110mh: 13.73 0.0 Edorh, 13.74 Delavantie Brown JAM 10.10.71 2 Indianapolis 8 May, 13.86 (not 13.85) Black, 13.87 Mabry 70, 13.88 -0.4 Mattern, 13.92 Soto 67, 13.94 Wan Wenyuan, 13.96 Avery Anderson 73, 13.97 Westbrook 70, 13.98 Ledoux (not 13.96); Renumber from 90th, 100th best 13.84. Unconfirmed 13.85 Smith was hand 13.9. wa: 13.81 Mabry 3.8.70, 13.86 Lewis 72. Delete 13.96w Balzer. Hand timed: delete 13.8 Razzaq (was in 1991), 13.7w Jeff Jackson USA 14.3.74 2 College Station 20 Mar.
400mh: 49.27/49.2A Biwott 16.6.67, 50.04 Lahlali 19.1.71, 50.05 Mbaye 21.4.64, 50.36 McCullough 29.11.69, 50.37 Kobayashi 12 Jun, 50.38 Ritter 1 Aug, 50.40 Beukenkamp 24 Jul, 50.43 El Hafni A, 50.52 Ouakof, 50.76 Sinclair 15 May (from 50.78), 50.76 Woody 73, 50.90 Schott 73, 50.99A Jonker 22 Feb
HJ: 2.37 Kemp 2, 2.34 Sankovich and 2.31 Zhukovskiy on 14 May, 2.31i Ortiz 14 Feb, 2.30 Lee Jin-taek at Kwangju 15 Oct, 2.28i Buglakov 27 Jan, 2.28 Bi and Zhou on 11 Sep, 2.25i Pchelintsev 30.11.70, 2.24 Fujishima Tokyo 17 Oct (his reported 2.25 was 2.20)2.23 Kim Tae-hee KOR 16 Jun, 2.23 Mingazov 65, 2.23 Cho Hyun-wook KOR 70 15 Oct. 2.24 exh: Detchenique FRA
PV: 5.94 Bubka 7 Aug, 5.90I Trandenkov 2, 5.70i Ishutin RUS, 5.65 Tivonchik 12.7.70, 5.60 Aleksandr Zhukov MOL 1 Kishinev 20 Jun (from 5.55i), 5.55 Yeliseyev 1 Naimette 19 Sep, 5.50i Gracia 4, 5.50 Stepanov 18 Jun, 5.45 Mury 1 Aug, 5.40 Isakov 14 May. Best out: 5.60 Holl 20 Jun, 5.50 Yanchevskiy 22 May
LJ: 8.43 Powell 4 Aug and 8.39 1 Aug; 8.09 Chao 9.12.72, 8.04 Georgiev delete wind reading (no gauge in stadium!), 7.96 Digno 28.8.65, Zaozerskiy on 25 Jul, 7.91i Ivanov ¶, 7.91 Giorgios Zambetakis 18 Jun, 7.89 Andrey Nikulin (and delete in best outdoors), 7.89 Sarvatskiy 71, 7.85A Jacob Katonen KEN 3 Jul, 7.85 Voloshin 27 Aug, 7.84 Taurima, delete 7.84 Carter (wa), 7.80 Szabó 5 Aug; wa: 7.88 4.9 Francisco J García ESP 70 20 Jun, delete 7.83w Savinok. low alitude best: Reggie Jones did not do 8.05 at Innsbruck
TJ: 17.32 Silva 8 Aug, Not in KZK lists - may

be wa: 17.28 Arzamasov - next 16.90 1.7 2 Almaty 15 May, 17.17 Sakirkin - next 17.09i 3 RUS Ch Moskva 27 Feb, 17.06 Markov 12.3.66, 16.89 1.6 2 WUG Buffalo 15 Jul, 16.82 Dimitrov delete wind reading (no gauge in stadium!), 16.59 Dodoo 1 Kumasi 3 Jul (from 16.52), 16.50 Aleksandr Bashkatov KZK 72 29 Apr, 16.48 Meyram Beispekov 74, 16.41 Owusu 16 May (from 16.31), 16.37A Carlos Atencio PER 72 11 Jun, 16.31 1.7 Dorel Eftene ROM 69 28 Aug. Delete unconfirmed 16.86 Chen. Best out: 16.44 0.3 Glushenko 4 Jul. wa: 17.21 2.1 Rabenala, 16.65 3.9 Julio López ESP 8.3.72 1 Salamanca 23 May, 16.42 Christos Meletoglou GRE 72 27 Jun, 16.38 3.0 Aleksey Dzhashitov RUS 70 23 May,16.30 Moskalenko 70

SP: 21.98, 21.49, 21.21 Günthör and 21.47, 21.46 Barnes all in Aug not Oct, 21.78 Barnes 25 Jul, 21.23 Günthör at Bern. delete unconfirmed 19.00 Al Khalili. Ancillary marks: add 21.51 Günthör 29 Jun

DT: 67.02, 66.76 and 66.00 Riedel Aug not Oct, 66.86 Washington, 66.56 Riedel & 65.74 de Bruin (drugs dq) 1 Aug; 66.18 Kaptyukh and 65.66 de Bruin 12 Jun, 65.92 Ubartas drugs dq that meeting - previous best 64.24 2 WK Zürich 4 Aug; 63.26 Dubrovshchik 24 Jul, 61.82 Lukashok 31 Jul, 60.46 Sidorov 15 May, 59.44 Han 2 10 Jun. Delete 60.56 Godina (see 60.48). Delete 58.56 Ghourbani and questionable 65.42 Möllenbeck, 62.86 Többen, 59.52 Schmitz (58.98 was 1st), 58.88 Buder

HT: 80.16 Abduvaliyev 29 Aug, 75.24 Chmyr 3, 74.06 Varich 7

JT: 89.84 (not 89.64) Zelezny, 85.68 Räty 1 Aug, 86.20 Moruyev 28 Aug, 81.40 Yevsyukov 1 Almaty 26 May (from 78.60), 77.98 Sjepovic, 76.46 Tihomir Mustapic CRO 68 2 Zagreb 7 Jun, 75.90 Arunas Jursas LIT 72 1 Kaunas 22 May, 75.80 Lee Wook-jong KOR 66 Daegu 6 May, 75.12 Kenneth Petersen, 75.08 Jorma Markus FIN 52 - Oct, 74.90 Ambrosi Matiashvili GEO 71 -, 74.82 Wilhelm Pauer RSA 67 1 Mar. 50th best 79.02. 86.18exh Zelezny 1 Agordo 18 Jul

One Hour Dec: 7590 Fritz

Dec: 8317 Fritz etc Talence 12 Sep, 7982w Steele (11.06w/2.5, 7.16W/8.8, 13.19, 2.02, 48.61, 14.85W/8.2, 47.98, 4.65, 62.10, 4:47.63), 7935w Fucci (11.06/-0.9, 7.29w/2.5...14.09W/5.1, 41.28, 5.15, 56.62, 4:48.54), 7907 Zhdanovich, 7902 Dudakov (11.50, 7.21, 13.97, 2.12, 50.26, 14.90, 45.30, 4.80, 52.62, 4:32.35), 7888 Balanque, 7831 Huff (11.03/1.3, 7.15/0.3...15.22/1.1, 46.04, 4.75, 59.46, 4:58.65), 7824 Cai (PV 4.40), 7821 Matsanov 25 Jul (1.0/-0.8, 7.04/-1.0, 14.83, 2.03, 51.3, 14.2/1.4, 43.??, 4.80, 53.54, 4:38.7), 7809w Barker (10.88W/6.2, 7.06/-0.7, 13.22, 2.07, 49.91, 14.47W/4.4, 41.54, 4.70 58.68, 4:57.10), Duany - 7749 was 7631, 7715 best (see Junior list for details), 7748 Chernyavskiy 2.8.68, 7733 Pendergist (11.24/-0.4, 7.11/-0.9, 13.37, 2.11, 50.77, 15.03/1.4, 37.62, 4.50, 60.94, 4:31.34), 7702w Richards (11.35/0.6, 7.07W/4.5, 13.12 2.04, 50.45, 15.01w/2.2, 40.56, 5.10, 54.72, 4:44.07), 7686 Zuber (11.37, 7.66, 12.87 2.03, 50.86, 14.52, 35.36, 4.80, 53.92, 4:38.36), 7678 Lee (11.05, 7.37w, 13.43, 2.11, 50.31, 14.64, 38.26, 4.80, 50.96, 5:01.59), 7671 Borozinski 2.7.71 (11.06, 6.84, 14.28, 1.97, 50.36, 15.04, 43.54, 4.40, 57.88, 4:35.36), 7641 Zhao (4:43.11), 7633 Valle 29.8.68, 7621 Foxson (11.25/0.8, 7.24/1.9, 14.14, 1.93, 49.40, 15.81/0.3, 42.56, 4.50, 58.00, 4:39.06), 7617w Wilcox (10.75/1.7, 6.98/-0.3...14.98W/5.1, 41.20, 4.45, 48.42 4:48.36), 7601 Veretelnikov (PV 4.30), 7517 Schwieger (0.91, 7.00, 13.33, 2.11, 49.58, 14.88, 39.40, 4.30, 49.38, 4:44.46), 7531 Petlichki (delete 2nd listing between 7428 & 7425), delete 7585 Kim Tae-keun - see 7535 KimTae-gun. Best non wa: 7813 Pirini - delete marks, 7754 Long (11.36/-0.3, 698/-0.5, 14.58, 2.00, 49.58, 14.67/0.4, 45.68, 4.90, 55.56, 5:00.92).

Wind speeds: 100m. LJ, 110mh: 8366 Meier -2.3, 3.1, -1.3; 8331 O'Brien 1.3, -0.1, 1.1; 8277 Plaziat -2.3, 2.6, -1.4; 8204 Blondel -1.4, 1.9, -1.3; 8176w Fritz 1.7, -0.6, 5.1; 8076 Keskitalo -2.3, 1.6, -1.4; 8061 Schmid -0.2, -0.2, -1.3; 8052 Janvrin 0.5, -0.3, 0.4; 8013w Long 1.3, 1.8, 5.1; 8007 Huffins 3.0, 2.1, 3.0; 7918w Blums 2.7, 4.9, 2.9; 7886 Kotsyubenko 0.9, 0.4, -1.1; 7871w Ranzi 0.4, 5.5, 0.7;7736w Shelton 0.6, 4.3, 2.4; 7588 Burrell -2.3, 1.3, -2.2; 7576 Johnson 0.1, 0.1, 1.4

4x100m: 37.99 and 38.19 at Zürich 4 Aug, delete 39.32A MEX (1992 mark) add 39.79 (López, Cardeñas, Adam, Miranda) 4h4 WC Stuttgart 21 Aug, 39.16 CHN (Liang M, Zheng Y, Huand D, Luo X) 13 Sep, 39.38 SUI (Widmer, Bettex, Reimann, Dollé) 1 Luzern 29 Jun, 39.96A COL 26 Apr (from 40.04A), 40.12A VEN, 40.13A SEN 23 Jun, 40.2A CHI 2 Jul

4x400m: 3:06.3 GHA 1 Kumasi 2 Jul, 3:07.76 RSA/Western Transvaal 1 Bellville 24 Apr, 3:09.07 MRI 27 Aug, 3:09.20 MAD 27 Aug

5000mW: cut at 19:35.0

10,000mW: 40:56,0 Abdelwahab Ferguène ALG 58 21 Jul

20kmW: note numbers from 11th incorrectly omit some CHN walkers, so 100th = 1:23:37. 1:23:41 Claudio Luiz Bertolino BRA 31.3.63 1 São Caetano 31 Jul, 1:24:31 Pérez (not 1:24:03), 1:24:42 (not 24) Yamigasawa. Track: 1:23:18.0 Dudás.

Junior Men 1993

100m: 10.45w 2.2 Frempong, 10.37w López 10.5.74, 10.42w Volsan 1.10.74. Hand: 10.2 Tihomir Buinjac CRO 28.2.74 1 Zalaegerszeg 19 May,

200m: delete 20.65 Hervey and 20.93 Barron - not J; 20.93 Page 21.6.74, delete 21.06w, 21.08w. Hand: 20.6 Cardeñas.

400m: Calvin Harrison tested positive for pseudoephedrine at the US Junior Championships, so his 45.07, 45.10, 45.65 and 45.79 marks are relegated to a footnote, while his best mark for the lists is his 45.25. 46.35 Ramsey 11.9.74, 46.53 Page 21.6.74, 46.61 Johnson 6.4.77

800m: 1:47.5 Hailu Zewde 13.9.74, 1:48.61 Sammy Biwott KEN 23.7.74 Stockholm 3 Aug, 1:48.8 Gorelyov 1.6.74, 1:48.8 Kassim Hamisi TUN 15.6.74 Dar es Salaam 29 Oct, 1:49.07 Brian Woodward USA .74 1 Chapel Hill 4 Apr

1000m: 2:23.4 Swift-Smith (& 1500m), 2:23.75 Seth Wetzel USA 74 6 Mar, 2:23.9 Ali Hakimi (& 3:44.5) 1500m

1500m: 3:42.7 Yarba Lakhal MAR 74 Rabat 26 May, 3:42.7A Vincent Malakwen KEN 19.7.74 Nairobi 29 Jul, 3:43.3 Sammy Rono KEN Nairobi 2 Jul, 3:43.4 Kassim Hamisi TAN 15.6.74 Dar es Saleem 30 Oct, 3:45.3 Mark Olivo VEN 2.8.74 2 Caracas 9 Oct, 3:45.50 Eric O'Brien USA 74 3 Chapel Hill 8 May, 3:45.73 Seth Wetzel USA 74 10 Chapel Hill 15 May, 3:45.95 Ulymov 30.7.74

3000m: 7:56.3 Hicham El Guerrouj MAR 14.9.74 Casablanca 14 Feb, 8:06.8 Socha = Maciej, 8:08.8 Ali Hakimi TUN 24.4.76 St Maur 21 Jul, 8:09.3 Yarba Lakhal MAR 74 Casablanca 14 Feb

5000m: 13:54.34 Mark Too KEN 74 Conegliano 10 Jul

10000m: 29:18.26 Mark Too KEN 74 S.Giovanni Valdarno 15 May, 29:27.7 Sosaku Mizutani JPN 2 Hiroshima16 Oct, 29:36.8A Charles Tangus KEN 74 Nairobi 19 May

Mar: delete 2:14:54 da Silva (b.69), 2:16:40 Tolosa Guebre ETH 75 Arusha 1 Aug, 2:17:51 John Tsotsetsi RSA 13 Cape Town 20 Mar, 2:18:08 Beruhe Bekele ETH 76 Addis Ababa 4 Jul, 2:18:59 Gezahegu Bira ETH 75 Addis Ababa 4 Jul

3000mSt: 8:48.8A Stephen Chepseba KEN 24.4.74 Nairobi 19 May, 8:53.1 Yarba Lakhal MAR 74 Nairobi 2 Jul, 8:59.70 Yilmaz 2 Istanbul 4 Jul

110mh: 14.12 Perin 2 Pres. Pudente 5 Jun, 14.21 Sarucan 10.8.74. Hand 13.7w Jeff Jackson USA 14.3.74 2 College Station 20 Mar

HJ: 2.18 Voronin 5.4.74

PV: 5.55 Yeliseyev 1 Naimette 19 Sep, 5.20 Derrick Prentice USA .74 4 SEC Knoxville 16 May, 5.20 Smiryagin 17.5.76, Smirnov 9.12.74

LJ: 7.87 2.0 Benda, 7.74 0.9 Vitaliy Sorokun KZK 30.4.74 1 NC Almaty 23 Jul, 7.72 Sung Hee-joon KOR 8.5.74 Seoul 15 Jun, 7.93w Trentin 20.6.74

TJ: 16.48 1.4 Meiram Beispekov KZK 29.4.74 2 Almaty 24 Jul, 16.23 Baró 16.1.74, 16.12 Ferrer 31.10.75, 16.10 0.8 Yevgeniy Inozemtsev KZK 14.4.74 1 Almaty 24 Jun, 16.03i Perveyev 17.4.74, 15.86 Taranov 20.3.75, 15.96w David Riggs USA .74 4 Monroe 16 May

SP: 18.39i Belonog - 17.74 4 EJ San Sebastián 1 Aug, 17.97 Ogden 5 Pac10 Berkeley 21 May, 17.84i Luvokin - 16.76 2 Stavropol 29 May, 16.98i Michael Natho GER 24.2.74 2 Minsk 27 Feb, 16.80 Gurpreet Singh IND 74 1 New Delhi 23 Nov, 16.70 Onder 30.1.74 1

DT: 55.74 Cherevko Grodno 20 Jun, 53.52 Pvel Pirozhkov UKR 10.3.74 3 Rovno 25 May, 53.02 Ignatyev 11.5.74, 53.00 Kononchik 5.4.74, 52.80 Vitkovsky 24.5.76, 52.64 Alex Kolovyansky USA .74 1 Washington DC 17 Apr, 52.56 Jonathan Ogden USA 31.7.74 7 Modesto 8 May, delete 54.38 Gomez

HT: 69.26 Annus b.1973 or 1974? 68.50 Horváth - Szombathely 17 Sep, 67.02 Tugay 22.3.75, 66.92 Mokrov 4.1.74, 66.60 Aleksandr Kukharenko BLS 75 Gomel 15 Jul, 66.36 Shevchenko 12.5.76, 65.48 Vasilyev 23.6.75, 65.40 A Kuprenya UKR 6 Rovno 25 May, 64.98 Andrey Skonnikov UKR 20.2.75 3 Kiev 2 May, 64.00 Aleksandr Baburkhin, 63.60 Lobzov 14.2.74, delete 65.34 Sergeyev

JT: 70.98 Petr Kivako BLS 17.6.74 Grodno 12 Sep, 69.90 Sokolov 5.5.74

Dec: Duany - change 7749 to 7631, 7715 was best, 7433w Jeffrey - 7322 Canberra 31 Jan, 7417 Theriault JT 53.70

4 x 100m: 40.95 IND New Delhi 16 Nov

4 x 400m: 3:12.89 SAU, 3:12.98 FRA (Dufourt, Zami, Maria, Thévenin) 1 Tarbes 17 Jul

Women 1993

100m: 11.22 Vorster 11.9.65 (and 22.83 200m), 11.38 Opara-Thompson (& 23.36), 11.44 Yue Lin at Changsha 13 May, 11.52 Kate

Iheagwan, 11.58 +0.7 G Rockmeier (add 11.57w 2.1 20 May); 11.37w Olga Voronova 23.2.68. Hand: 11.2 Hanitriniaina Rakotondrabe MAD .67 1 Antanarivo 16 May, 11.3 Philomena Mensah GHA 75 3 Jul, 11.3A -1.8 Patricia Rodriguez COL 70 17 Jul
200m: 23.57 Chen 12 Sep, 23.66 de Jesus Santos, 23.67 Ravaonirina 25 Jun, 23.44w Mary Tombiri NIG 72 8 May, 23.61w? Böhme, delete 23.51w Hagenmüller. Hand: 23.3A Ximena Restrepo COL 69 - May, 23.4 1.8 Conte, 23.4 1.0 Amaral, 23.5 Philomena Mensah GHA 75 2 Jul
300m: 37.19 Yelena Ruzina RUS3.4.64 1 & 37.41 Yelena Dubtsova RUS 71 2 both Bryansk 18 Jul; 37.82 Doreen Fahrendorff GER 68 1 Sindelfingen 29 May, 37.96 Sølvi Meinseth GER 67 9 May
400m: 52.36 Mendes was OK, 52.46 Odoemenam & 53.26 Awora 24 Jun, 53.42 Alolabi 75. Hand: 53.0 Grace Birungi UGA 73 & 53.1 Mary Awora UGA on 12 Jun
800m: 1:55.54 Liu Dong, 2:01.36 Liu 5 Jun, 2:02.03 Naude 3 May, 2:02.70 Liu Shufang, 2:02.76 Samorokhova 15.4.64, 2:03.10 Gabbasova UZB
1500m:4:00.50 Liu Dong, 4:11.5A Chesire & 4:13.0A Ngotho 23 Jul, 4:14.2 Ulla Marquette CAN 58 (not Meagher)
2000m: 5:49.00 Zola Pieterse RSA 66 6 Nov
3000m: 9:06.36Saito, 9:08.52 Shimizu (not 9:09.52), 9:08.72 Irina Volynskaya KZK 72 18 Jun
5000m: 15:43.6+ Sally Barsosio KEN 21.3.78 4k WC Stuttgart 21 Aug, 15:46.64 Kiyomiya, 15:57.1 Wang Mingxia CHN 71 18 Dec, 15:59.8 Ando 27 Jun
10000m: 32:38.02 mx Daria Nauer SUI Liestal 1 Sep, 32:59.03 Hong Tuo 72
15km road: 49:23 Elana Meyer RSA 10.10.66 1 Milnerton 2 Oct
Half Mar: 72:11 Van Blunk 1 NC Fairfield 27 Jun (from 72:18). move to uncertain distance list: 71:23 Dias
Mar: 2:29:42 Zhang Linli 2 & 2:29:45 Zhag Lirong 3 WCp San Sebastián 31 Oct, 2:30:36 Li 25.5.66, 2:32:33 Chen 67; note numbers from 60th to 150th should be one lower.
100km: 7:44:29 Maskina 14.4.64, 7:57:45 Petrova 1 Santa Cruz de Bezana 2 Oct (from 8:02:50), 8:08:22 Anni Lønstad DEN 19.8.53 1 Neuwittenbek 16 Oct, 8:24:00 Maton Chantal FRA 49 1 St Anand 27 Mar
100mh: 13.16 1.6 Ime Akpan ¶ 1s1 NCAA New Orleans 4 Jun (pre drugs dq), 13.29 Shishigina 23.12.68 UKR Ch (not NC), 13.42 1.5 Zhang Xiaohui CHN 71 11 Sep, 13.45A Le Roux 3 May, 13.46 Kobayashi 12 Jun; 13.43w Marxer - best legal 13.53 1.2 1 Aug
400mh: 56.09 Bidouane 20 Jun, 56.66 Zhu 8 Sep, 57.98 Taiye Akinremi NGR 72 1 Tucson 26 May, 58.07 Xu 4 Jun, 58.44A Liliana Chala ECU 65 27 Apr, 58.58 (& 58.2) Pais 69
HJ: 1.91 Yelesina 18 Jun, 1.91 Blokhina 10 Sep, 1.88 Ge Ping 5 Jun, 1.88 Bogomaz 5 Sep, 1.87 Natalya Moiseyenko KZK 67 15 May, 1.86 Iva Vasileva BUL 72 22 May, 1.86 Liu Bo 1 Jun, 1.86 Voveryte 2 Jul, 1.84 Raina Turner USA 25.9.74 2 Atlanta 22 May; delete 1.88 Volf. Best out: 1.88 Ivanova 18 Jun
PV: 11 perfs by 6 - renumber.
LJ: 7.01 Yao Weili 5 Jun, 6.85 1.9 Tiedtke 8 Jun, 6.74 Rubleva NJ, 6.60 Wu Lingmei 1.2.73, 6.58 Zhang Hongling (& 13.43 TJ), 6.57 Yu Huaxiu, 6.49 Selina 11.7.64, 7.07w +3.4 Joyner-Kersee 16 Jun (&6770 Hep); best outdoor: 6.66 Radtke 26 May (delete 6.61w), 6.58 Chen 18 Sep
TJ: 13.48 Zhou & 13.20 Li Jing 3 Jun, 13.48 Boyko, 13.40 Baranova, 13.20 Shekhovtsova 5 Sep, 13.10 Chen 74, 13.08 Xiang 21 Mar. Best low altitude: 13.73 -1.5 Avila 1 NC Buenos Aires 24 Oct
SP: 18.10 Yelena Baltabayeva 1 Almaty 14 May (from 17.28). Delete 15.80 Andrews (after 16.10). 50th best 17.78.
DT: 59.86 Cheng Q 23 Apr, 58.90 Li at Taiyun, 56.70 Maria Isabel Urrutia COL 25.3.65 1 Pereira 22 May (from 55.14), 55.34 Elisangela Adriano BRA 72 13 Jun, delete 58.52 Wan Dong
HT: Add perfs: Melinte 60.02 1 NC Bucuresti 5 Sep, 59.74 1 Bucuresti 6 Jun, 58.44 1 Bucuresti 30 May; Sudak 59.60 2 Krasnodar 20 Feb. 53.58 Legault was 1 Princeton 16 May
JT 64.68 Han & 62.12 Song Q 25 Apr, 63.46 Zhang 1 26 Apr, 59.64 Liu ui 4 Jun; delete 54.72 Han
Hep: 6249 Wu Shuling (HJ 1.77), 5902 Podracká 16, 5840 Cardenas - note also best auto timed 5838 2 CAG Ponce 28 Nov (13.88, 1.76, 13.21 24.67, 6.10, 36.62, 2:23.68), 5819 Alena Vlasova KZK 2.12.69 1 Almaty 15 May (14.35 1.72 14.14 24.86 5.98 35.96 2:16.24) (from 5578), 5773 and others 2 Jun, 5759 Kazanina 31.10.71 (800m 2:14.87), 5670 Look-Jaeger (14.20, 1.76, 11.79, 25.74, 5.74, 39.04, 2:14.16), 5644 Roy (14.95, 1.75, 13.26, 25.97, 5.68, 42.68, 2:17.15), 5642 Madden (13.51w, 1.79, 11.54, 25.02w, 5.72, 39.44, 2:30.29), 5578 Alena Vlasova 69, 5549 Geremias. 100th best 5636.

4x100m: 44.65 THA 1struner Srichurat, 45.11 Almaty (KZK) (Kopylova, Chernova, Serdyuk, Vyazova) 1 Almaty 24 Jul (from 45.87), 45.99 ARG 5 Jun, Hand: 46.1 GHA 29 May, 46.3A Kecoso (KEN) 3 Jul
4x400m: 3:35.83 MAS (R Shanti, J Mary, G Shanti, R Abdul Salam) (delete 3:41.66), 3:45.04 TPE-Jnrs 13 Nov, 3:45.4 MAR 13 Jun, delete 3:41.66 MAS
5000mW: marks from 21:04.48 to 22:37.68 missed - see list at end
10kmW: 42:47 Ramazanova 27.9.71, 45:00 Sazonova 28.5.68, 45:18 Kozhomina RUS, 46:55.74t Galina Arutyunova KZK 67 14 Feb
Junior Women
100m: 11.59A Richards, Hand: 11.3 Philomena Mensah GHA 75 1 NC Kumasi 3 Jul
200m: 23.54 -0.2 Combe
400m: 53.42 Bisi Afolabi NGR 75 Lagos 18 Jun
800m: 2:05.35 Voronicheva 5.10.77, 2:05.93 Janice Nichols USA 31.8.74 2 Tucson 26 May, 2:06.18 Kushnir 16.8.75
3000m: 9:00.27 Costescu 5
5000m: 16:01.21 Okamoto 29.11.74, 16:07.3 Tomoko Morigaki 4.9.76 28 Nov, 16:10.0 Chizuko Ishikawa JPN 14.2.74 Mito 4 Dec, 16:11.30 Tobise 20.6.74, 16:11.3 Ueno 11.6.76, 16:11.8 Morigaki 4.9.76, 16:13.4 Kawakami 1.8.75
400mh: 57.68 Blunt 21.4.74, 58.83 Amina Belkrouchi MAR 76 Rabat 26 May, 59.10 Cui Xiuzhong CHN .75 NC Jinan 4 Jun, 59.10 Kardash 15.11.74, Klimova 21.5.74
HJ: 1.86 Voveryte Kaunas 2 Jul, 1.84 Liu Yan at Taiyuan
PV: 3.50i Bártová 6.5.74
LJ: 6.36 Shehu 22.5.74
TJ: 13.10 -0.2 Chen Huoqiang CHN .74 5 Beijing 4 May
SP: 15.60i Racoltu - Bucuresti 6 Mar
DT: 58.90 Li Qiumei at Taiyuan
JT: 54.86 Manjani 21.12.76
Hep: 5391 Birina 18.3.76
5000mW: Feitor - delete 22:01.8 replace by 22:03.0 on 10 Jul, 22:26 Maribel Rebollo
Men Index: Urbano, José b. 1 Mar 66

World Indoors 1994
60m: 6.60 Vladislav Dologodin UKR 1h Kiev 12 Feb
1500m: 3:38.2+ Eric Dubus and 3:38.4+ Michaël Damian at Karlsuhe 1 Mar
3000m: 7:51.20 Mohamed Choumassi MAR 6 Liévin 13 Feb
60mh: 7.53 Belokon 1s and 7.62 Andrey Karatayev s Kiev 12 Feb, 7.63 Sergey Usov BLS 1 Minsk 29 Jan
HJ: 2.30 Papakostas 20 Feb; **PV**: 5.80 Korchagin KZK 1 Almaty 18 Feb; **LJ**: 8.05 Hernández 19 Feb; **TJ**: 16.81 Romain; **SP:** 20.02 Martínez 13 Feb, 19.93 Virastyuk 1 Lvov 29 Jan, 19.84 Nikolayev 1 S Peterburg 12 Feb, 19.78 Sergey Smirnov RUS 1 S Peterburg 19 Feb, 19.65 Jonny Reinhsrdt GER 2 Sassnitz 5 Feb; **5000mW**: 18:32.0 and 18:40.0 on 5 Feb, 19:03.2 Mikhail Khmelnitskiy BLS 4 Feb, 19:11.37 Kozlov
Women:
60m: 7.20 Anzhelika Shevchuk UKR 1s Kiev 12 Feb; **400m**: 52.75 Zürcher-Scalabrin; **1M**: 4:32.69 Rogachova; **3000m**: 8:55.58 Yelena Lipsnis 1 & 8:58.30 Svetlana Bulbanyovich RUS 2 Sankt Peterburg 20 Feb, 9:07.0 Elisa Rea ITA 1 Genova 26 Feb
55mh: 7.55 Dawn Bowles USA 1 Baton Rouge 29 Jan
60mh: 8.01 López 2 Piraeus 28 Feb, 8.06 Natalya Yudakova RUS 1s1 Lipetsk 27 Feb
LJ: 6.78 Ninova 2 Paris 11 Mar
TJ: 13.82 Concepcion Paredes ESP 2 San Sebastián 3 Mar, 13.78 Matyashova 1 S Peterburg 6 Mar, 13.76 Vershinina
SP: 20.00 Peleshenko 1 Sankt Peterburg 19 Feb, 18.58 Irina Zhuk 1 & 18.07 Viktoriya Pavlysh UKR 2 Kiev 13 Feb
5000mW: 12:21.7 Susana Feitor POR 1 Braga 19 Feb, 12:24.3 Valentina Tsbulskaya BLS 2 Minsk 5 Feb

Previous Annuals

1992 World Lists
Women: 3000m: 9:08.9 Lisa Harvey; **Junior Men**: 800m: Cadoni- 1:46.67 dq
1991 World Lists
Men:110m: Hand 13.8 Abdul Razzaq PAK 70 29 Sep, **SP**: delete 18.30 Terzer (was 13.80!); **35lb Wt**: 22.08 Donatas Plunge LIT 11.11.60 1 Espoo 29 Sep

With acknowledgements to Francisco Ascorbe, Patrice Bertignon, Roger Cass, José Maria García, Fernando Grandio, Heinrich Hubbeling, Vaclav Klvana, Winfried Kramer, Stuart Mazdon, Yves Pinaud, KZK lists, European Athletics Yearbook, FAST Annual and others.

Obituaries 1993:
Reino SEPP (Estonia)

MISSING WOMEN'S 5000M WALK 1993

21:04.48	Essayah				1		Jyväskylä	12 Jun
21:15.4	Maria Grazia	Orsani	ITA	11.6.69	1		Avellino	8 May
21:19.91		Essayah			1	vSWE	Stockholm	28 Aug
21:20.57		Essayah			1		Kangasniemi	6 Jun
21:21.80		Feitor			1	EJ	San Sebastián	29 Jul
21:22.6	Tatyana	Ragozina	UKR	3.9.64	1		Alushta	21 Feb
21:28.17	Teresa	Vaill (10)	USA	20.11.62	1	PennR	Philadelphia	24 Apr
21:34.0		Orsani			1		Fisciano	18 Apr
21:34.1	Madelein	Svensson	SWE	20.7.69	1	NC	Arboga	22 Jul
21:39.3	Olimpiada	Ivanova	RUS	5.5.70	1		Vladimir	15 Aug
21:39.75	Natalya	Trofimova	RUS	17.1.75	2	EJ	San Sebastián	29 Jul
	(22/13)							
21:42.5	Zinaida	Sviridenko	RUS	24.12.68	1		Moskva	25 Jul
21:45.52	Rossella	Giordano	ITA	1.12.72	3	NC	Bologna	2 Aug
21:47.5	Jane	Saville	AUS	5.11.74	2	NC	Brisbane	6 Mar
21:47.6 mx	Gabrielle	Blythe	AUS	9.3.69	mx		Canberra	12 Mar
	21:55.52				1		Melbourne	20 Feb
21:49.33	Kathrin	Born	GER	4.12.70	2	NC	Duisburg	10 Jul
21:49.65	Irina	Stankina	RUS	25.3.77	3	EJ	San Sebastián	29 Jul
21:50.10	Emi	Hayashi	JPN	9.7.72	1		Otsu	19 Dec
21:54.0		Svensson			1		Ornskoldsvik	10 Jul
21:55.5	Anne	Manning	AUS	13.11.59	3	NC	Brisbane	6 Mar
21:57.38	Mária	Rosza-Urbanik	HUN	12.2.67	1		Wien	30 May
22:08.5	Jenny	Jones	AUS	20.4.67	4	NC	Brisbane	6 Mar
22:09.19	Yuko	Sato	JPN	23.1.68	2		Otsu	19 Dec
22:12.7	Encarnacion	Granados	ESP	30.1.72	1		Vic	23 May
22:15.05	Alison	Baker	CAN	6.8.64	1		Ottawa	3 Jul
22:15.48	Andrea	Alföldi	HUN	22.9.64	2		Wien	30 May
22:20.0	Olga	Leonenko	UKR	13.2.70	2		Alushta	21 Feb
22:22.33	Natalya	Serbinenko	UKR	27.1.59	1		Kiev	15 May
22:26.8	Zuzana	Zemková	SVK	17.7.67	2		Banská Bystrica4 Sep	
22:27.17	Cristiana	Pellino	ITA	21.9.70	1		Rieti	8 May
22:29.68	Yuka	Mitsumori	JPN	8.1.72	1		Tokyo	22 May
22:31.16	Michaela	Hafner	ITA	2.8.73	4	NC	Bologna	2 Aug
22:32.56	Sandy	Leddin	GER	1.11.70	3	NC	Duisburg	10 Jul
22:33.00	Nevena	Mineva	BUL	17.6.72	1	NC	Sofia	1 Aug
22:33.02	Rie	Mitsumori	JPN	26.10.74	3		Otsu	19 Dec
22:34.50	Vicky	Lupton	GBR	17.4.72	1	AAA	Birmingham	17 Jul
22:35.8 mx	Simone	Wolowiec	AUS	12.2.74	mx		Melbourne	25
Nov 22:36.7	Yuliya	Odzilyayeva	RUS	.70	1		Valdimir	15 Aug
22:37.30	Norica	Cimpan	ROM	22.3.72	1		Bucuresti	31 Jul
22:37.47	Julie	Drake	GBR	21.5.69	2	AAA	Birmingham	17 Jul
22:37.68	Olga	Panferova	RUS	21.8.77	3		Cheboksary	5 Jun

INTRODUCTION TO WORLD LISTS AND INDEX

Records
WORLD, World Junior, Olympic, Continental and Area records are listed. In running events up to and including 400 metres, only fully automatic times are shown.

Marks listed are those which are considered statistically acceptable by the ATFS, and thus may differ from official records where, for instance the performance was set indoors.

World All-time and Year Lists
THESE lists are presented in the following format: Mark, Wind reading (where appropriate), Name, Nationality (abbreviated), Date of birth, Position in competition, Meeting name (if significant), Venue, Date of performance.

In standard events the best 30 or so performances are listed followed by the best marks for other athletes. Position, meet and venue details have been omitted for reasons of space beyond 100th in year lists.

Indexes
THESE lists contain the names of all athletes ranked with full details in the world year lists. The format of the index is as follows:

Family name, First name, Nationality, Birthdate, Height (cm) and Weight (kg), 1994 best mark, Lifetime best as at the end of 1993 and the relevant year.

An asterisk before the name indicates an athlete who is profiled in the Biographies section.

General Notes
Altitude aid
MARKS set at an altitude of 1000m or higher have been suffixed by the letter "A".

Although there are not separate world records for altitude assisted events, it is understood by experts that in all events up to 400m in length (with the possible exclusion of the 110m hurdles), and in the horizontal jumps, altitude gives a material benefit to performances. For events beyond 800m, however, the thinner air of high altitude has a detrimental effect.

Supplementary lists are included in relevant events for athletes with seasonal bests at altitude who have low altitude marks qualifying for the main list.

Some leading venues over 1000m

Addis Ababa ETH	2365m
Air Force Academy USA	2194
Albuquerque USA	1555
Bloemfontein RSA	1392
Bogotá COL	2600
Boksburg RSA	1600
Boulder USA	1655
Calgary CAN	1045
Cali COL	1046
Ciudad México MEX	2247
Colorado Springs USA	1823
Denver USA	1609
Echo Summit USA	2250
El Paso USA	1126
Flagstaff USA	2105
Font-Romeu FRA	1850
Fort Collins USA	1521
Germiston RSA	1661
Guadalajara MEX	1567
Harare ZIM	1473
Johannesburg RSA	1748
Krugersdorp RSA	1740
Leninaken ARM	1556
Nairobi KEN	1675
Pietersberg RSA	1230
Pocatello USA	1361
Potchefstroom RSA	1351
Pereira COL	1470
Pretoria RSA	1400
Provo USA	1380
Reno USA	1369
Rustenburg RSA	1157
Secunda RSA	1628
Sestriere ITA	2050
Soria ESP	1056
South Lake Tahoe USA	1909
Tsakhkadzor GEO	1980
Windhoek NAM	1725

Some others over 500m

Alma-Ata (Almaty) KZK	847
Bern SUI	555
Boise USA	818
Canberra AUS	581
La Chaux de Fonds SUI	997
Caracas VEN	922
Edmonton CAN	667
Lubbock USA	988
Madrid ESP	640
München GER	520
Salamanca ESP	806
São Paulo BRA	725
Sofia BUL	564
Spokane USA	576
Tucson USA	728

Automatic timing
IN the main lists for sprints and hurdles, only times recorded by fully automatic timing devices are included.

Hand timing
IN the sprints and hurdles supplementary lists are included for races which are hand timed. Any athlete with a hand timed best 0.01 seconds or more better than his or her automatically timed best has been included, but hand timed lists have been terminated close to the differential levels considered by the IAAF to be equivalent to automatic times, i.e. 0.24 sec. for 100m, 200m, 100mh, 110mh, and 0.14 sec. for 400m and 400mh.

This effectively recognises bad hand timekeeping, for there should be no material difference between hand and auto times, but what often happens is that badly trained timekeepers anticipate the finish, as opposed to reacting to the flash at the start.

In events beyond 400m, automatically timed marks are integrated with hand timed marks, the latter identifiable by times being shown to tenths. All-time lists also include some auto times in tenths of a second, where the 1/100th time is not known, but the reader can differentiate these from hand timed marks as they are identified with the symbol '.

Indoor marks
INDOOR marks are included in the main lists for field events and straightway track events, but not for other track events. This is because track sizes vary in circumference (200m is the international standard) and banking, while outdoor tracks are standardised at 400m. Athletes whose seasonal bests were set indoors are shown in a supplemental list if they also have outdoor marks qualifying for the world list.

Mixed races
FOR record purposes athletes may not, except in road races, compete in mixed sex races. Statistically there would not appear to be any particular logic in this, and women's marks set in such races, permitted and fairly common in a few nations such as Australia and Canada, are shown in our lists - annotated with mx. In such cases the athlete's best mark in single sex competition is appended.

Supplementary marks
Non-winning marks in a field event series which, had they been winning marks, would have qualified for the top 30 performances list are included in a supplement at the end of the relevant events. Full information on series has not been avaialble for all leading marks, so this data is limited.

Tracks
As with climatic conditions it should be borne in mind that the type and composition of tracks and runways will affect standards of performance.

Wind assistance
In the lists for 100m, 200m, 100mh, 110mh, long jump and triple jump, anemometer readings have been shown where available. The readings are given in metres per second to one decimal place. Where the figure was given originally to two decimal places, it has been rounded to the next tenth upwards, e.g. a wind reading of +2.01 m/s, beyond the IAAF legal limit of 2.0, is rounded to +2.1; or -1.22 m/s is rounded up to -1.2.

For multi-events a wind-assisted mark in one in which any of these events is aided by a wind over 4.0 m/s; such assisted marks are shown with a capital W.

Drugs bans
The IAAF have determined that the IAAF Executive Council may decertify an athlete's records, titles and results if he or she later admits to having used a banned substance before those performances. We have not removed any such athletes from all-time lists, but for information have shown ¶ after the name of any athlete who has at any stage in his or her career undergone a drugs suspension of a year or more (thus not including the 3 month bans for ephedrine etc.). This should not be taken as implying that the athlete was using drugs at that time. Nor have those athletes who have subsequently unofficially admitted to using banned substances been indicated; the ¶ is used only for those who have been caught.

Venues
From time to time place names are changed. Our policy is to use names in force at the time that the performance was set. Thus Leningrad prior to 1991, St Petersburg from its re-naming.

Amendments
Keen observers may spot errors in the lists. They are invited to send corrections to the editor, who will also welcome news and results for 1995.

Peter Matthews, 10 Madgeways Close, Great Amwell, Ware, Herts SG12 9RU, England
Fax 44 1920 877392

Event	Record	Name	Nat	Venue	Date

WORLD & CONTINENTAL RECORDS

(as at February 1995)

Key W = World, Afr = Africa, Asi = Asia, CAC = C.America & Caribbean, E = Europe, NAm = N.America, Oce = Oceania, SAm = S.America, WJ = World Junior

A = altitude over 1000m
* = awaiting ratification
+ = timing by photo-electric-cell
§ = not officially ratified

100 METRES

Event	Record	Name	Nat	Venue	Date
W,NAm	9.85¶	Leroy BURRELL	USA	Lausanne	6 Jul 94
E	9.87	Linford CHRISTIE	GBR	Stuttgart	15 Aug 93
Afr	9.94	Davidson EZINWA	NGR	Linz	4 Jul 94
CAC	9.96	Ray STEWART	JAM	Tokyo	25 Aug 91
SAm	10.00A	Róbson da SILVA	BRA	Ciudad de México	22 Jul 88
Asi	10.14	Talal MANSOOR	QAT	Budapest	18 Jun 92
Oce	10.11	Gus NKETIA	NZL	Victoria	22 Aug 94
WJ	10.05 §	Davidson EZINWA	NGR	Bauchi	3 Jan 90
	10.08A	Obadele THOMPSON	BAR	El Paso	16 Apr 94

¶ Performances of 9.79 & 9.83 by Ben Johnson (CAN) have been disallowed following disqualification for drug abuse

200 METRES

Event	Record	Name	Nat	Venue	Date
W,E	19.72A	Pietro MENNEA	ITA	Ciudad de México	12 Sep 79
NAm	19.73	Michael MARSH	USA	Barcelona	5 Aug 92
Afr	19.85	Frank FREDERICKS	NAM	Stuttgart	20 Aug 93
CAC	19.86A	Donald QUARRIE	JAM	Cali	3 Aug 71
SAm	19.96	Róbson da SILVA	BRA	Bruxelles	25 Aug 89
Oce	20.06A	Peter NORMAN	AUS	Ciudad de México	16 Oct 68
Asi	20.41	CHANG Jae-keun	KOR	Jakarta	27 Sep 85
	20.41	Talal MANSOOR	QAT	Hiroshima	15 Oct 94
WJ	20.07 §	Lorenzo DANIEL	USA	Starkville	18 May 85
	20.13	Roy MARTIN	USA	Indianapolis	16 Jun 85

400 METRES

Event	Record	Name	Nat	Venue	Date
W,NAm	43.29	Butch REYNOLDS	USA	Zürich	17 Aug 88
CAC	44.14	Roberto HERNANDEZ	CUB	Sevilla	30 May 90
Afr	44.17	Innocent EGBUNIKE	NGR	Zürich	19 Aug 87
E	44.33	Thomas SCHÖNLEBE	GER	Roma	3 Sep 87
Oce	44.38	Darren CLARK	AUS	Seoul	26 Sep 88
Asi	44.56	Mohamed AL MALKY	OMN	Budapest	12 Aug 88
SAm	45.02	Inaldo SENA	BRA	Madrid	6 Sep 94
	45.0 m	Róbson da SILVA	BRA	Rio de Janeiro	31 Aug 90
WJ	43.87	Steve LEWIS	USA	Seoul	28 Sep 88

800 METRES

Event	Record	Name	Nat	Venue	Date
W,E,C	1:41.73+	Sebastian COE	GBR	Firenze	10 Jun 81
SAm	1:41.77	Joaquim CRUZ	BRA	Koln	26 Aug 84
Afr	1:42.28	Sammy KOSKEI	KEN	Koln	26 Aug 84
NAm	1:42.60	Johnny GRAY	USA	Koblenz	28 Aug 85
CAC	1:43.44	Alberto JUANTORENA	CUB	Sofia	21 Aug 77
Asi	1:44.14	LEE Jin-Il	KOR	Seoul	17 Jun 94
Oce	1:44.3 m	Peter SNELL	NZL	Christchurch	3 Feb 62
WJ	1:44.9 my§	Jim RYUN	USA	Terre Haute	10 Jun 66
	1:44.3 m	Joaquim CRUZ	BRA	Rio de Janeiro	27 Jun 81

World Records at other events recognised by the IAAF

Event	Record	Name	Nat	Venue	Date
1000m	2:12.18	Sebastian COE	GBR	Oslo	11 Jul 81
2000m	4:50.81	Saïd AOUITA	MAR	Paris	16 Jul 87

1500 METRES

W,Afr	3:28.86	Noureddine MORCELI	ALG	Rieti	6 Sep 92
E	3:29.67	Steve CRAM	GBR	Nice	16 Jul 85
NAm	3:29.77	Sydney MAREE	USA	Koln	25 Aug 85
Oce	3:31.96	Simon DOYLE	AUS	Stockholm	3 Jul 91
Asi	3:32.73	Mohamed SULEIMAN	QAT	Köln	21 Aug 94
SAm	3:34.63	Joaquim CRUZ	BRA	Hengelo	14 Aug 88
CAC	3:37.61	Arturo BARRIOS	MEX	Hengelo	13 Aug 89
WJ	3:34.92	Kipkoech CHERUIYOT	KEN	München	26 Jul 83

1 MILE

W, Afr	3:44.39	Noureddine MORCELI	ALG	Rieti	5 Sep 93
E	3:46.32	Steve CRAM	GBR	Oslo	27 Jul 85
NAm	3:47.69	Steve SCOTT	USA	Oslo	7 Jul 82
Oce	3:49.08	John WALKER	NZL	Oslo	7 Jul 82
Asi	3:51.32	Mohamed SULEIMAN	QAT	Oslo	22 Jul 94
SAm	3:53.00	Joaquim CRUZ	BRA	Los Angeles	13 May 84
CAC	3:57.34	Byron DYCE	JAM	Stockholm	1 Jul 74
WJ	3:51.3 m§	Jim RYUN	USA	Berkeley	17 Jul 66

3000 METRES

W,Afr	7:25.11	Noureddine MORCELI	ALG	Monaco	2 Aug 94
E	7:32.79	Dave MOORCROFT	GBR	London	17 Jul 82
NAm	7:33.37 §	Sydney MAREE	USA	London	17 Jul 82
	7:35.33 *	Bob KENNEDY	USA	Nice	18 Jul 94
	7:36.69	Steve SCOTT	USA	Ingelheim	1 Sep 81
CAC	7:35.71	Arturo BARRIOS	MEX	Nice	I0 Jul 89
Oce	7:37.49	John WALKER	NZL	London	17 Jul 82
Asi	7:38.20	Mohamed SULEIMAN	QAT	Berlin	27 Aug 93
SAm	7:45.34	Clodoaldo DO CARMO	BRA	Koblenz	26 Aug 92
WJ	7:39.82	Ismael KIRUI	KEN	Berlin	27 Aug 93

5000 METRES

W,Afr	12:56.96	Haile GEBRSELASSIE	ETH	Hengelo	4 Jun 94
E	13:00.41	Dave MOORCROFT	GBR	Oslo	7 Jul 82
NAm	13:01.15	Sydney MAREE	USA	Oslo	27 Jul 85
CAC	13:07.79	Arturo BARRIOS	MEX	London	14 Jul 89
Oce	13:12.87	Dick QUAX	NZL	Stockholm	5 Jul 77
SAm	13:19.64	Antonio SILIO	ARG	Roma	17 Jul 91
Asi	13:20.43	Toshinari TAKAOKA	JPN	Stockholm	2 Jul 92
WJ	13:02.75	Ismael KIRUI	KEN	Stuttgart	16 Aug 93

10,000 METRES

W, Afr	26:52.23	William SIGEI	KEN	Oslo	22 Jul 94
CAC	27:08.23	Arturo BARRIOS	MEX	Berlin	18 Aug 89
E	27:13.81	Fernando MAMEDE	POR	Stockholm	2 Jul 84
NAm	27:20.56	Mark NENOW	USA	Bruxelles	5 Sep 86
Asi	27:35.33	Takeyuki NAKAYAMA	JPN	Helsinki	2 Jul 87
SAm	27:38.72	Antonio SILIO	ARG	Bruxelles	3 Sep 93
Oce	27:39.89	Ron CLARKE	AUS	Oslo	14 Jul 65
WJ	27:11.18	Richard CHELIMO	KEN	Hengelo	25 Jun 91

World Records at other events recognised by the IAAF

20km	56:55.6	Arturo BARRIOS (now USA)	MEX	La Flèche	30 Mar 91
1 Hour	21,101 m	Arturo BARRIOS (now USA)	MEX	La Flèche	30 Mar 91
25km	1:13:55.8	Toshihiko SEKO	JPN	Christchurch	22 Mar 81
30km	1:29:18.8	Toshihiko SEKO	JPN	Christchurch	22 Mar 81

MARATHON

W,Afr	2:06:50	Belayneh DINSAMO	ETH	Rotterdam	17 Apr 88
E	2:07:12	Carlos LOPES	POR	Rotterdam	20 Apr 85
CAC	2:07:19	Andrés ESPINOSA	MEX	Boston	18 Apr 94
Asi	2:07:35	Taisuke KODAMA	JPN	Beijing	19 Oct 86
Oce	2:07:51	Rob DE CASTELLA	AUS	Boston	21 Apr 86
NAm	2:08:47	Bob KEMPAINEN	USA	Boston	18 Apr 94
SAm	2:09:55	Osmiro SILVA	BRA	Marrakesh	13 Jan 91
WJ	2:12:49	Negash DUBE	ETH	Beijing	18 Oct 87
	2:12:49	Tesfaye DADI	ETH	Berlin	9 Oct 88

Boston course has an overall net drop of 139m (0.33%), and in 1994 there was a strong following wind.

110 METRES HURDLES

W, E	12.91	Colin JACKSON	GBR	Stuttgart	20 Aug 93
NAm	12.92	Roger KINGDOM	USA	Zürich	16 Aug 89
CAC	13.19	Emilio VALLE	CUB	Stuttgart	19 Aug 93
Asi	13.25	LI Tong	CHN	Linz	4 Jul 94
Oce	13.45	Kyle VANDER-KUYP	AUS	Melbourne	24 Feb 94
	13.45	Kyle VANDER-KUYP	AUS	Helsinki	29 Jun 94
SAm	13.62 A	Elvis CEDEÑO	VEN	Ciudad de México	22 Jul 88
Afr	13.63 A§	Wessel BOSMAN	RSA	Johannesburg	23 Apr 88
	13.64A	Kobus SCHOEMAN	RSA	Pretoria	15 May 93
WJ	13.23	Renaldo NEHEMIAH	USA	Zürich	16 Aug 78

400 METRES HURDLES

W,NAm	46.78	Kevin YOUNG	USA	Barcelona	6 Aug 92
Afr	47.10	Samuel MATETE	ZAM	Zürich	7 Aug 91
E	47.48	Harald SCHMID	GER	Athinai	8 Sep 82
	47.48 §	Harald SCHMID	GER	Roma	1 Sep 87
CAC	47.60	Winthrop GRAHAM	JAM	Zürich	4 Aug 93
Asi	48.68	Yoshihiko SAITO	JPN	Tokyo	12 Jun 93
SAm	48.88	Eronildes de ARAUJO	BRA	Madrid	6 Sep 94
Oce	49.32	Bruce FIELD	AUS	Christchurch	29 Jan 74
WJ	48.02	Danny HARRIS	USA	Los Angeles	17 Jun 84

3000 METRES STEEPLECHASE

W,Afr	8:02.08	Moses KIPTANUI	KEN	Zürich	19 Aug 92
E	8:07.62	Joseph MAHMOUD	FRA	Bruxelles	24 Aug 84
NAm	8:09.17	Henry MARSH	USA	Koblenz	28 Aug 85
Oce	8:14.05	Peter RENNER	NZL	Koblenz	29 Aug 84
Asi	8:15.95	Sa'ad Shaddad AL-ASMARI	SAU	Monaco	2 Aug 94
SAm	8:19.80	Clodoaldo do CARMO	BRA	Bruxelles	28 Aug 92
CAC	8:27.55	Juan Ramón CONDE	CUB	Habana	5 Jul 91
WJ	8:19.21	Daniel NJENGA	KEN	Tokyo	11 Jun 94

HIGH JUMP

W,CAC	2.45	Javier SOTOMAYOR	CUB	Salamanca	27 Jul 93
E	2.42	Patrik SJÖBERG	SWE	Stockholm	30 Jun 87
	2.42 i§	Carlos THRÄNHARDT	GER	Berlin	26 Feb 88
NAm	2.40 i§	Hollis CONWAY	USA	Sevilla	10 Mar 91
		Charles AUSTIN	USA	Zürich	7 Aug 91
Asi	2.39	ZHU Jianhua	CHN	Eberstadt	10 Jun 84
Oce	2.35	Tim FORSYTH	AUS	Canberra	25 Jan 93
SAm	2.33	Gilmar MAYO	COL	Pereira	17 Oct 94
Afr	2.28	Othmane BELFAA	ALG	Amman	20 Aug 83
		Othmane BELFAA	ALG	Athinai	11 Jul 91
WJ	2.37	Dragutin TOPIC	YUG	Plovdiv	12 Aug 90
		Steve SMITH	GBR	Seoul	20 Sep 92

POLE VAULT

W,E	6.15 i§	Sergiy BUBKA	UKR	Donetsk	21 Feb 93
	6.14 A	Sergiy BUBKA	UKR	Sestriere	31 Jul 94
NAm	5.97	Scott HUFFMAN	USA	Knoxville	18 Jun 94
Asi	5.90i	Grigoriy YEGOROV	KZK	Moskva	2 Feb 93
	5.90	Grigoriy YEGOROV	KZK	Stuttgart	19 Aug 93
	5.90	Grigoriy YEGOROV	KZK	London	10 Sep 93
Afr	5.90	Okkert BRITS	RSA	London	10 Sep 94
SAm	5.76	Tom HINTNAUS	BRA	Zürich	21 Aug 85
Oce	5.72	Simon ARKELL	AUS	Adelaide	14 Feb 93
CAC	5.65	Angel GARCIA	CUB	Habana	12 Jun 92
	5.72 *	Paul BENAVIDES	MEX	El Paso	18 Jun 94
WJ	5.80	Maksim TARASOV	RUS	Bryansk	14 Jul 89

LONG JUMP

W,NAm	8.95	Mike POWELL	USA	Tokyo	30 Aug 91
E	8.86 A	Robert EMMIYAN	ARM	Tsakhkadzor	22 May 87
CAC	8.53	Jaime JEFFERSON	CUB	Habana	12 May 90
		Ivan PEDROSO	CUB	Sevilla	17 Jul 92
SAm	8.36	João Carlos de OLIVEIRA	BRA	Rieti	21 Jul 79
Asi	8.36	CHEN Zunrong	CHN	Shizuoka	5 May 92
Oce	8.27	Gary HONEY	AUS	Budapest	20 Aug 84
Afr	8.27	Yusuf ALLI	NGR	Lagos	8 Aug 89
WJ	8.34	Randy WILLIAMS	USA	München	8 Sep 72

TRIPLE JUMP

W,NAm	17.97	Willie BANKS	USA	Indianapolis	16 Jun 85
E	17.92	Khristo MARKOV	BUL	Roma	31 Aug 87
SAm	17.89 A	João Carlos de OLIVEIRA	BRA	Ciudad de México	15 Oct 75
CAC	17.78	Lázaro BETANCOURT	CUB	Habana	15 Jun 86
Oce	17.46	Ken LORRAWAY	AUS	London	7 Aug 82
Asi	17.35	Oleg SAKIRKIN	KZK	Moskva	5 Jun 94
Afr	17.26	Ajayi AGBEBAKU	NGR	Edmonton	8 Jul 83
WJ	17.50	Volker MAI	GER	Erfurt	23 Jun 85

SHOT

W,NAm	23.12	Randy BARNES	USA	Westwood	20 May 90
E	23.06	Ulf TIMMERMANN	GER	Khania	22 May 88
SAm	20.90	Gert WEIL	CHL	Wirges	17 Aug 86
Afr	20.76	Ahmed Kamel SHATTA	EGY	Al Qâhira	24 Mar 88
CAC	20.28	Paúl RUIZ	CUB	Rostock	29 May 88
Oce	19.80	Les MILLS	NZL	Honolulu	3 Jul 67
Asi	19.78	MA Yongfeng	CHN	Beijing	9 Jun 90
WJ	21.05 i§	Terry ALBRITTON	USA	New York	22 Feb 74
	20.65 §	Mike CARTER	USA	Boston	4 Jul 79
	20.38	Terry ALBRITTON	USA	Walnut	27 Apr 74

DISCUS

W,E	74.08	Jürgen SCHULT	GER	Neubrandenburg	6 Jun 86
NAm	72.34 ¶	Ben PLUCKNETT	USA	Stockholm	7 Jul 81
	71.32 §	Ben PLUCKNETT	USA	Eugene	4 Jun 83
CAC	71.06	Luis DELIS	CUB	Habana	21 May 83
Afr	68.48 §	John VAN REENEN	RSA	Stellenbosch	14 Mar 75
	67.80	Adewale OLUKOJU	NGR	Modesto	11 May 91
Oce	65.62 §	Werner REITERER	AUS	Melbourne	15 Dec 87
	65.08	Wayne MARTIN	AUS	Newcastle	3 Jan 79
Asi	65.02	YU Wenge	CHN	Nanjing	20 May 92
SAm	64.30	Ramón JIMÉNEZ-GAONA	PAR	Eugene	23 May 92
WJ	65.62 §	Werner REITERER	AUS	Melbourne	15 Dec 87
	63.64	Werner HARTMANN	GER	Strasbourg	25 Jun 78

¶ Disallowed by the IAAF following retrospective disqualification for drug abuse, but ratified by the AAU/TAC

HAMMER

W,E	86.74	Yuriy SEDYKH	UKR/RUS	Stuttgart	30 Aug 86
Asi	83.36	Andrey ABDUVALIYEV	TJK	Budapest	3 Jun 94
NAm	82.50	Lance DEAL	USA	Knoxville	17 Jun 94
Oce	77.58	Sean CARLIN	AUS	Canberra	11 Feb 94
CAC	76.14	Alberto SANCHEZ	CUB	Habana	26 May 94
SAm	74.66	Andrés CHARADIA	ARG	Córdoba	9 Oct 94
Afr	74.02	Hakim TOUMI	ALG	El Djezair	24 May 93
WJ	78.14	Roland STEUK	GER	Leipzig	30 Jun 78

JAVELIN

W,E	95.66	Jan ZELEZNY	TCH	Sheffield	29 Aug 93
NAm	89.16 §	Tom PETRANOFF	USA	Potchefstroom	1 Mar 91
	85.70	Tom PUKSTYS	USA	Kuortane	26 Jun 93
Asi	87.60	Kazuhiro MIZOGUCHI	JPN	San José	27 May 89
Afr	87.26 @	Tom PETRANOFF	RSA	Belle Vue Mauricia	28 Jun 92
Oce	86.14	Gavin LOVEGROVE	NZL	Wellington	18 Jan 92
CAC	79.24	Ramón GONZALEZ	CUB	Athinai	20 Jun 87
SAm	77.80	Luís LUCUMI	COL	Medellin	7 Aug 89
WJ	80.94	Aki PARVIAINEN	FIN	Jyväskylä	5 Jul 92
Invalid implement - no longer accepted					
W,E	96.96	Seppo RÄTY	FIN	Punkalaidun	2 Jun 91
CAC	84.86	Ramón GONZALEZ	CUB	Potsdam	3 Jul 90

@ Tom Petranoff a South African citizen from September 1991

DECATHLON (1984 Tables)

W,NAm	8891	Dan O'BRIEN	USA	Talence	5 Sep 92
E	8847	Daley THOMPSON	GBR	Los Angeles	9 Aug 84
Oce	8366 m	Simon POELMAN	NZL	Christchurch	22 Mar 87
	8207	Simon POELMAN	NZL	Auckland	29 Jan 90
SAm	8291 m	Tito STEINER	ARG	Provo	23 Jun 83
	8266	Pedro da SILVA	BRA	Walnut	24 Apr 87
Asi	8106	Ramil GANIYEV	UZB	Wien	26 Jun 94
CAC	8093	Eugenio BALANQUE	CUB	Habana	24 Jun 94
Afr	7934 m	Ahmed MAHOUR BACHA	ALG	El Djezair (Alger)	9 Jul 85
	7625	Danie VAN WYK	RSA	Pretoria	13 Apr 94
WJ	8397	Torsten VOSS	GER	Erfurt	7 Jul 82

20 000M WALK (Track)

W, CAC	1:17:25.6	Bernardo SEGURA	MEX	Fana	7 May 94
E	1:18:35.2	Stefan JOHANSSON	SUE	Fana	15 May 92
Oce	1:20:12.3	Nick A'HERN	AUS	Fana	8 May 93
Asi	1:20:24.4	LI Mingcai	CHN	Jinan	15 Mar 92
SAm	1:21:30.8	Marcelo PALMA	BRA	São Paulo	15 Jun 91
NAm	1:22:38.1	Tim BERRETT	CAN	Fana	15 May 92
Afr	1:22:51.84*	Hatem GHOULA	TUN	Leutkirch	8 Sep 94
	1:24:56.6	Abdelwahab FERGUÈNE	ALG	Neuilly-Plaisance	3 May 92
WJ	1:22:42	Andrey PERLOV	RUS	Donetsk	6 Sep 80

20 KM WALK (ROAD)

W, Asi	1:18:04	BO Lingtang	CHN	Beijing	7 Apr 94
E	1:18:13	Pavol BLAZEK	SVK	Hildesheim	16 Sep 90
Oce	1:19:22	Dave SMITH	AUS	Hobart	19 Jul 87
CAC	1:19:24	Carlos MERCENARIO	MEX	New York	3 May 87
SAm	1:20:19	Querubín MORENO	COL	New York	3 May 87
NAm	1:21:13	Guillaume LEBLANC	CAN	St. Léonard	5 Oct 86
Afr	1:22:51	Abdelwahab FERGUENE	ALG	Hildesheim	23 Aug 92
WJ	1:21:27	GAO Yunbing	CHN	Beijing	7 Apr 94

50,000M WALK (Track)

W,E	3:41:28.2	René PILLER	FRA	Fana	7 May 94
CAC	3:41:38.4	Raúl GONZALEZ	MEX	Fana	25 May 79
Oce	3:43:50.0	Simon BAKER	AUS	Melbourne	9 Sep 90
Asi	3:48:13.7	ZHAO Yongsheng	CHN	Fana	7 May 94
NAm	3:56:13.0	Tim BERRETT	CAN	Saskatoon	21 Jul 91
SAm	4:17:11.0	Mauricio CORTEZ	COL	Caracas	16 Nov 86
Afr	4:21:44.5	Abdelwahab FERGUÈNE	ALG	Toulouse	25 Mar 84

50 KM WALK (Road)

W,E	3:37:41	Andrey PERLOV	RUS	Sankt Peterburg	5 Aug 89
CAC	3:41:20	Raúl GONZALEZ	MEX	Praha-Podebrady	11 Jun 78
Oce	3:43:13	Simon BAKER	AUS	L'Hospitalet	28 May 89
Asi	3:43:16	ZHOU Yongsheng	CHN	Beijing	10 Apr 94
NAm	3:47:48	Marcel JOBIN	CAN	Québec	20 Jun 81
SAm	4:01:31	Héctor MORENO	COL	Seoul	30 Sep 88
Afr	4:09:37	Johan MOERDYK	RSA	Cape Town	30 Oct 93

4 x 100 METRES RELAY

W, NAm	37.40	USA (Marsh, Burrell, Mitchell, C.Lewis)	Barcelona	8 Aug 92
	37.40	USA (Drummond, Cason, Mitchell, Burrell)	Stuttgart	21 Aug 93
E	37.77	GBR (Jackson, Jarrett, Regis, Christie)	Stuttgart	22 Aug 93
Afr	37.98	NGR (Kayode, Imoh, Adeniken, D.Ezinwa)	Barcelona	8 Aug 92
CAC	38.00	CUB (Simon, Lamela, Isasi, Aguilera)	Barcelona	8 Aug 92
Oce	38.46	AUS (Henderson, Marsh, Capobianco, Jackson)	Stuttgart	21 Aug 93
Asi	38.77	JPN (Aoto, Susuki, Inoue, Sugimoto)	Barcelona	8 Aug 92
SAm	38.8 m	BRA (Oliveira, da Silva, Nakaya, Correia)	São Paulo	1 May 84
	39.02A	BRA (de Castro, dos Santos, Pegado, A Araujo)	Ciudad de México	4 Sep 79
WJ	39.00A	USA (Jessie, Franklin, Blalock, Mitchell)	Air Force Academy	18 Jul 83

4 x 400 METRES RELAY

W,NAm	2:54.29	USA (Valmon, Watts, Reynolds, Johnson)	Stuttgart	22 Aug 93
E	2:57.53	GBR (Black, Redmond, Regis, Akabusi)	Tokyo	1 Sep 91
CAC	2:59.13	CUB (Martínez, Herrera, N Téllez, Hernández)	Barcelona	7 Aug 92
Afr	2:59.32	NGR (Uti, Ugbisie, Peters, Egbunike)	Los Angeles	11 Aug 84
Oce	2:59.70	AUS (Frayne, Clark, Minihan, Mitchell)	Los Angeles	11 Aug 84
Asi	3:01.26	JPN (Konakatomi, Takano, Watanabe, Ito)	Tokyo	31 Aug 91
SAm	3:01.38	BRA (E Araujo, Tenorio, de Menezes, de Souza)	Barcelona	7 Aug 92
WJ	3:01.90	USA (Campbell, Rish, Waddle, Reed)	Athinai	20 Jul 86

WORLD RECORDS AT OTHER EVENTS RECOGNISED BY THE I.A.A.F.

4 x 200m	1:18.68	Santa Monica Track Club (Marsh, Burrell, Heard, C Lewis)	USA	Walnut	17 Apr 94
4 x 800m	7:03.89	United Kingdom Team (Elliott, Cook, Cram, Coe)	GBR	London	30 Aug 82
4 x l500m	14:38.8 m	F.R.Germany Team (Wessinghage, Hudak, Lederer, Fleschen)	GER	Köln	17 Aug 77

Track Walking

2 Hours	29,572m	Maurizio DAMILANO	ITA	Cuneo	4 Oct 92
30km	2:01:44.1	Maurizio DAMILANO	ITA	Cuneo	4 Oct 92

WOMEN

100 METRES

W,NAm	10.49	Florence GRIFFITH JOYNER	USA	Indianapolis	16 Jul 88
E	10.77	Irina PRIVALOVA	RUS	Lausanne	6 Jul 94
CAC	10.78	Merlene OTTEY	JAM	Sevilla	30 May 90
	10.78	Merlene OTTEY	JAM	Paris	3 Sep 94
Afr	10.97	Mary ONYALI	NGR	Stuttgart	15 Aug 93
Asi	11.02	LIU Xiaomei	CHN	Beijing	8 Sep 93
Oce	11.12A	Melinda GAINSFORD	AUS	Sestriere	31 Jul 94
SAm	11.26	Jennifer INNIS	GUY	Walnut	15 Jul 84
WJ	10.88 §	Marlies OELSNER/GÖHR	GER	Dresden	1 Jul 77
	10.89	Kathrin KRABBE	GER	Berlin	20 Jul 88

200 METRES

W,NAm	21.34	Florence GRIFFITH JOYNER	USA	Seoul	29 Sep 88
CAC	21.64	Merlene OTTEY	JAM	Bruxelles	13 Sep 91
E	21.71	Marita KOCH	GER	Chemnitz	10 Jun 79
	21.71 §	Marita KOCH	GER	Potsdam	21 Jul 84
	21.71	Heike DRECHSLER	GER	Jena	29 Jun 86
	21.71 §	Heike DRECHSLER	GER	Stuttgart	29 Aug 86
Afr	22.06 A§	Evette DE KLERK	RSA	Pietersburg	8 Apr 89
	22.31	Mary ONYALI	NGR	Villeneuve d'Ascq	29 Jun 90
Oce	22.25	Cathy FREEMAN	AUS	Victoria	26 Aug 94
Asi	22.56	WANG Huei-Chen	TPE	Yilian	30 Oct 92
	22.56	CHEN Zhaojing	CHN	Beijing	13 Sep 93
SAm	22.92	Ximena RESTREPO	COL	Lincoln	20 May 91
WJ	22.19	Natalya BOCHINA	RUS	Moskva	30 Jul 80

400 METRES

W,E	47.60	Marita KOCH	GER	Canberra	6 Oct 85
NAm	48.83	Valerie BRISCO	USA	Los Angeles	6 Aug 84
CAC	49.57	Grace JACKSON	JAM	Nice	10 Jul 88
	49.2 mA	Ana QUIROT	CUB	Bogotá	13 Aug 89
SAm	49.64	Ximena RESTREPO	COL	Barcelona	5 Aug 92
Asi	49.81	MA Yuqin	CHN	Beijing	11 Sep 93
Oce	50.04	Cathy FREEMAN	AUS	Paris	3 Sep 94
Afr	50.12 A§	Myrtle BOTHMA	RSA	Germiston	11 Apr 86
	50.41	Fatima YUSUF	NGR	Lausanne	10 Jul 91
WJ	49.42	Grit BREUER	GER	Tokyo	27 Aug 91

800 METRES

W,E	1:53.28	Jarmila KRATOCHVÍLOVÁ	TCH	München	26 Jul 83
CAC	1:54.44	Ana QUIROT	CUB	Barcelona	9 Sep 89
Afr	1:55.19	Maria Lurdes MUTOLA	MOZ	Zürich	17 Aug 94
Asi	1:55.54	LIU Dong	CHN	Beijing	9 Sep 93
NAm	1:56.90	Mary SLANEY	USA	Bern	16 Aug 85
SAm	1:57.96	Letitia VRIESDE	SUR	Hengelo	28 Jun 92
Oce	1:59.0 m	Charlene RENDINA	AUS	Melbourne	28 Feb 76
WJ	1:57.18	WANG Yuan	CHN	Beijing	8 Sep 93

World Records at other events recognised by the IAAF

l000m	2:30.6 m§	Tatyana PROVIDOKHINA	RUS	Podolsk	20 Aug 78
	2:30.67	Christine WACHTEL	GER	Berlin	17 Aug 90
2000m	5:25.36	Sonia O'SULLIVAN	IRL	Edinburgh	8 Jul 94

1500 METRES

W, Asi	3:50.46	QU Yunxia	CHN	Beijing	11 Sep 93
E	3:52.47	Tatyana KAZANKINA	RUS	Zürich	13 Aug 80
Afr	3:55.30	Hassiba BOULMERKA	ALG	Barcelona	8 Aug 92
NAm	3:57.12	Mary DECKER/SLANEY	USA	Stockholm	26 Jul 83
CAC	4:04.35	Yvonne GRAHAM	JAM	Bruxelles	19 Aug 94
SAm	4:05.67	Letitia VRIESDE	SUR	Tokyo	31 Aug 91
Oce	4:06.47	Christine PFITZINGER	NZL	San José	27 Jun 87
WJ	3:59.81	WANG Yuan	CHN	Beijing	11 Sep 93

1 MILE

W,E	4:15.61	Paula IVAN	ROM	Nice	10 Jul 89
NAm	4:16.71	Mary SLANEY	USA	Zürich	21 Aug 85
Afr	4:20.79	Hassiba BOULMERKA	ALG	Oslo	6 Jul 91
CAC	4:24.64	Yvonne GRAHAM	JAM	Zürich	`17 Aug 94
Oce	4:29.28	Penny JUST	AUS	Oslo	27 Jul 85
SAm	4:30.05	Soraya TELLES	BRA	Praha	9 Jun 88
WJ	4:17.57§	Zola BUDD	GBR	Zürich	21 Aug 85

3000 METRES

W, Asi	8:06.11	WANG Junxia	CHN	Beijing	13 Sep 93
E	8:21.64	Sonia O'SULLIVAN	IRL	London	15 Jul 94
NAm	8:25.83	Mary SLANEY	USA	Roma	7 Sep 85
Afr	8:32.00 §	Elana MEYER	RSA	Durban	29 Apr 91
	8:32.81	Elana MEYER	RSA	Oslo	10 Jul 93
Oce	8:44.1 m	Donna GOULD (in mixed race)	AUS	Eugene	13 Jul 84
	8:45.53	Anne AUDAIN	NZL	Brisbane	4 Oct 82
CAC	8:45.87	Yvonne GRAHAM	JAM	Nice	18 Jul 94
SAm	9:02.37	Delirde BERNARDI	BRA	Linz	4 Jul 94
WJ	8:28.83 §	Zola BUDD	GBR	Roma	7 Sep 85
	8:36.45	MA Ningning	CHN	Jinan	6 Jun 93

5000 METRES

W,E	14:37.33	Ingrid KRISTIANSEN	NOR	Stockholm	5 Aug 86
Afr	14:44.15 §	Elana MEYER	RSA	Bellville	6 Mar 92
	14:46.41	Elana MEYER	RSA	Hechtel	31 Jul 93
NAm	14:56.07 *	Annette PETERS	USA	Berlin	27 Aug 93
	15:00.00	PattiSue PLUMER	USA	Stockholm	3 Jul 89
Asi	15:05.69+ §	ZHONG Huandi	CHN	Beijing	8 Sep 93
Oce	15:13.23	Anne AUDAIN	NZL	Auckland	17 Mar 82
CAC	15:13.67	Yvonne GRAHAM	JAM	Köln	21 Aug 94
SAm	15:22.01	Carmen de OLIVEIRA	BRA	Hechtel	31 Jul 93
WJ	14:48.07 §	Zola BUDD	GBR	London	26 Aug 85

10,000 METRES

W, Asi	29:31.78	WANG Junxia	CHN	Beijing	8 Sep 93
E	30:13.74	Ingrid KRISTIANSEN	NOR	Oslo	5 Jul 86
Af r	30:52.51	Elana MEYER	RSA	London	10 Sep 94
Oce	31:11.72	Lisa ONDIEKI	AUS	Helsinki	30 Jun 92
NAm	31:19.89	Lynn JENNINGS	USA	Barcelona	7 Aug 92
SAm	31:47.76	Carmen de OLIVEIRA	BRA	Stuttgart	21 Aug 93
CAC	32:09.6 m	Olga APPELL (now USA)	MEX	Walnut	17 Apr 92
WJ	31:15.38 §	Selina BARSOSIO	KEN	Stuttgart	21 Aug 93
	31:40.56	Delilah ASIAGO	KEN	Tokyo	16 Jun 91

World Records at other events recognised by the IAAF

1 Hour	18,084 m	Silvana CRUCIATA	ITA	Roma	4 May 81
20km	1:06:48.8	Izumi MAKI	JPN	Amagasaki	20 Sep 93
25km	1:29:29.2	Karolina SZABÓ	HUN	Budapest	22 Apr 88
30km	1:47:05.6	Karolina SZABÓ	HUN	Budapest	22 Apr 88

MARATHON

W,E	2:21:06	Ingrid KRISTIANSEN	NOR	London	21 Apr 85
NAm	2:21:21	Joan BENOIT/SAMUELSON	USA	Chicago	20 Oct 85
Oce	2:23:51	Lisa MARTIN/ONDIEKI	AUS	Osaka	31 Jan 88
Asi	2:24:07	WANG Junxia	CHN	Tianjin	4 Apr 93
Afr	2:25:15	Elana MEYER	RSA	Boston	18 Apr 94
SAm	2:27:41	Carmen de OLIVEIRA	BRA	Boston	18 Apr 94
CAC	2:28:56	Olga APPELL	MEX	New York	14 Nov 93
WJ	2:30:15	GU Dongmei	CHN	Tianjin	4 Apr 93

Boston course has an overall net drop of 139m (0.33%), and in 1994 there was a strong following wind.

100 METRES HURDLES

W,E	12.21	Yordanka DONKOVA	BUL	Stara Zagora	20 Aug 88
NAm	12.46	Gail DEVERS	USA	Stuttgart	20 Aug 93
Asi	12.64	ZHANG Yu	CHN	Beijing	9 Sep 93
CAC	12.73	Aliuska LÓPEZ	CUB	Dijon	24 Jun 90
	12.73	Aliuska LÓPEZ	CUB	Stuttgart	20 Aug 93
Oce	12.93	Pam RYAN	AUS	München	4 Sep 72
Afr	13.02	Yasmina AZZIZI	ALG	Brescia	16 May 92
SAm	13.16	Nancy VALLECILLA	ECU	Indianapolis	13 Aug 87
WJ	12.84	Aliuska LÓPEZ	CUB	Zagreb	16 Jul 87

400 METRES HURDLES

W, E	52.74	Sally GUNNELL	GBR	Stuttgart	19 Aug 93
NAm	52.79	Sandra FARMER-PATRICK	USA	Stuttgart	19 Aug 93
Oce	53.17	Debbie FLINTOFF-KING	AUS	Seoul	28 Sep 88
Afr	53.74 A §	Myrtle BOTHMA	RSA	Johannesburg	18 Apr 86
	54.53	Myrtle BOTHMA	RSA	Barcelona	3 Aug 92
Asi	53.96	HAN Qing	CHN	Beijing	9 Sep 93
CAC	54.12	Deon HEMMINGS	JAM	Stuttgart	17 Aug 93
SAm	56.05	Ximena RESTREPO	ECU	Valencia, VEN	26 Nov 94
WJ	55.20	Leslie MAXIE	USA	San Jose	9 Jun 84

HIGH JUMP

W,E	2.09	Stefka KOSTADINOVA	BUL	Roma	30 Aug 87
CAC	2.04	Silvia COSTA	CUB	Barcelona	9 Sep 89
NAm	2.03	Louise RITTER	USA	Austin	8 Jul 88
		Louise RITTER	USA	Seoul	30 Sep 88
Afr	2.01 §	Desiré DU PLESSIS	RSA	Johannesburg	16 Sep 86
	1 95	Lucienne N'DA	CIV	Belle Vue Mauricia	28 Jun 92
Oce	1 98	Vanessa WARD	AUS	Perth	12 Feb 89
	1.98	Alison INVERARITY	AUS	Ingolstadt	17 Jul 94
Asi	1.97	JIN Ling	CHN	Hamamatsu	7 May 89
SAm	1.92	Orlane dos SANTOS	BRA	Bogotá	11 Aug 89
WJ	2.01 §	Olga TURCHAK	KZK	Moskva	7 Jul 86
	2.01	Heike BALCK	GER	Chemnitz	18 Jun 89

POLE VAULT

W,Asi	4.12 §	SUN Caiyun	CHN	Guangzhou	22 Oct 94
	4.12 §	SUN Caiyun	CHN	Guangzhou	25 Nov 94
	4.15i	SUN Caiyun	CHN	Erfurt	15 Feb 95
W,Asi,WJ	4.05	SUN Caiyun	CHN	Nanjing	21 May 92
Eur	4.08 i	Nicole RIEGER	GER	Karlsruhe	1 Mar 94
	4.01	Marina ANDREYEVA	RUS	Voronezh	18 Jun 94
Oce	3.56	Sarelle VERKADE	NZL	Auckland	28 Jan 95
NAm	3.51 *	Melissa PRICE	USA	Fresno	13 Jul 94
SAm	2.90 ++	Mónica FALCION	ARG	Buenos Aires	2 Oct 94
Afr	?				

LONG JUMP

W,E	7.52	Galina CHISTYAKOVA	RUS	Sankt Peterburg	11 Jun 88
NAm	7.49	Jackie JOYNER-KERSEE	USA	New York	22 May 94
	7.49A *	Jackie JOYNER-KERSEE	USA	Sestriere	31 Jul 94
Asi	7.01	YAO Weili	CHN	Jinan	6 Jun 93
CAC	6.96 A	Madeline de JESUS	PUR	Ciudad de México	24 Jul 88
Oce	6.87	Nicole BOEGMAN	AUS	Gateshead	14 Aug 88
Afr	6.85 A§	Karen KRUGER/BOTHA	RSA	Johannesburg	23 Mar 90
	6.78	Karen BOTHA	RSA	Belle Vue Mauricia	25 Jun 92
SAm	6.82	Jennifer INNIS (now USA)	GUY	Nice	14 Aug 82
WJ	7.14 §	Heike DAUTE/DRECHSLER	GER	Bratislava	4 Jun 83
	6.98	Heike DAUTE/DRECHSLER	GER	Potsdam	18 Aug 82

TRIPLE JUMP

W,E	15.09	Anna BIRYUKOVA	RUS	Stuttgart	21 Aug 93
CAC	14.60	Niurka MONTALVO	CUB	Habana	24 Jun 94
Asi	14.55	LI Huirong	CHN	Sapporo	19 Jul 92
NAm	14.23	Sheila HUDSON	USA	New Orleans	20 Jun 92
	14.23	Sheila HUDSON-STRUDWICK	USA	Knoxville	16 Jun 94
SAm	13.91A	Andrea AVILA	ARG	Lima	4 Jul 93
Afr	13.46A §	Charmaine BARNARD	RSA	Bloemfontein	12 Apr 92
	13.00	Stéphanie BETGA	CMR	Meknès	28 Mayl 94
Oce	13.27	Nicole BOEGMAN	AUS	Brisbane	6 Mar 93
WJ	14.36	REN Ruiping	CHN	Beijing	1 Jun 94

SHOT

W,E	22.63	Natalya LISOVSKAYA	RUS	Moskva	7 Jun 87
Asi	21.76	LI Meisu	CHN	Shijiazhuang	23 Apr 88
CAC	20.96	Belsy LAZA	CUB	Ciudad de México	2 May 92
NAm	20.18	Ramona PAGEL	USA	San Diego	25 Jun 88
Oce	19.74	Gael MARTIN	AUS	Berkeley	14 Jul 84
SAm	17.36	Elisangela ADRIANO	BRA	Austin	9 May 92
Afr	17.32 §	Mariette VAN HEERDEN	RSA	Germiston	29 Nov 80
	16.86	Grace APIAFI	NGR	Santa Barbara	19 May 90
WJ	20.54	Astrid KUMBERNUSS	GER	Orimattila	1 Jul 89

DISCUS

W, E	76.80	Gabriele REINSCH	GER	Neubrandenburg	9 Jul 88
Asi	71.68	XIAO Yanling	CHN	Beijing	14 Mar 92
CAC	70.88	Hilda RAMOS	CUB	Habana	8 May 92
Oce	68.72	Daniela COSTIAN	AUS	Auckland	22 Jan 94
NAm	66.10	Carol CADY	USA	San José	31 May 86
Afr	58.80 §	Nanette VAN DER WALT	RSA	Port Elizabeth	15 Feb 86
	57.58	Nanette VAN DER WALT	RSA	Germiston	25 Apr 92
SAm	58.50	Maria URRUTIA	COL	Valencia	26 Jun 92
WJ	74.40	Ilke WYLUDDA	GER	Berlin	13 Sep 88

HAMMER

W, E	67.34 §	Svetlana SUDAK	BLS	Minsk	4 Jun 94
	66.84	Olga KUZNETSOVA	RUS	Adler	23 Feb 94
Oce	63.04	Debbie SOSIMENKO	AUS	Sydney	12 Feb 95
Asi	61.20	Aya SUZUKI	JPN	Wakayama	30 Apr 89
NAm	58.68	Sonja FITTS	USA	Jamaica, New York	14 May 94
SAm	55.70	María VILLAMIZAR	COL	Mar del Plata	30 Oct 94
Afr	53.70	Caroline FOURNIER	MRI	Montreul-sous-Bois	21 Jun 94
CAC	49.68	Lydia DE LA CRUZ	MEX	Ciudad México	14 May 94
WJ	65.48	Mihaela MELIINTE	ROM	Bucuresti	26 Feb 94

JAVELIN

W,E	80.00	Petra FELKE/MEIER	GER	Potsdam	9 Sep 88
CAC	71.82	Ivonne LEAL	CUB	Kobe	30 Aug 85
Asi	70.42	ZHANG Li	CHN	Tianjin	6 Aug 90
Oce	69.80	Sue HOWLAND	AUS	Belfast	30 Jun 86
NAm	69.32	Kate SCHMIDT	USA	Fürth	11 Sep 77
SAm	65.96	Sueli dos SANTOS	BRA	Mar del Plata	28 Oct 94
Afr	62.34 §	Susan LION-CACHET	RSA	Pretoria	7 Nov 87
	62.16	Samia DJEMAA	ALG	El Djezair (Alger)	19 Jun 87
WJ	71.88	Antoaneta TODOROVA	BUL	Zagreb	15 Aug 81

HEPTATHLON (1984 Tables)

W,NAm	7291	Jackie JOYNER-KERSEE	USA	Seoul	24 Sep 88
E	7007	Larisa NIKITINA	RUS	Bryansk	11 Jun 89
Asi	6750	MA Miaolan	CHN	Beijing	12 Sep 93
Oce	6695	Jane FLEMMING	AUS	Auckland	28 Jan 90
Afr	6392	Yasmina AZZIZI	ALG	Tokyo	27 Aug 91
CAC	6076	Magalys GARCIA	CUB	Habana	24 Jun 94
SAm	6017	Conceição GEREMIAS	BRA	Caracas	25 Aug 83
WJ	6465	Sybille THIELE	GER	Schwechat	28 Aug 83

5000 METRES WALK (Track)

W	20:07.52 §	Beate ANDERS	GER	Rostock	23 Jun 90
	20:17.19	Kerry SAXBY-JUNNA	AUS	Sydney	14 Jan 90
E	20:07.52 §	Beate ANDERS	GER	Rostock	23 Jun 90
	20:28.62 *	Sari ESSAYAH	FIN	Tuusula	9 Jul 94
	20:50.03	Ileana SALVADOR	ITA	Macerata	6 Sep 89
Oce	20:17.19	Kerry SAXBY-JUNNA	AUS	Sydney	14 Jan 90
Asi	20:37.7 m	JIN Bingjie	CHN	Hefei	3 Mar 90
NAm	21:28.17 *	Teresa VAILL	USA	Philadelphia	24 Apr 93
	21:32.87	Debbie LAWRENCE	USA	Philadelphia	25 Apr 92
SAm	22:30.45	Bertha VERA	ECU	Seoul	20 Sep 92
CAC	23:38.25	Maria COLIN	MEX	Monterrey	9 Apr 86
Afr	23:10.88	Amsale YAKOBE	ETH	Seoul	20 Sep 92
WJ	20:37.7 m	JIN Bingjie	CHN	Hefei	3 Mar 90

10,000 METRES WALK (Track)

W,E	41:56.23	Nadyezhda RYASHKINA	RUS	Seattle	24 Jul 90
Oce	41:57.22	Kerry SAXBY-JUNNA	AUS	Seattle	24 Jul 90
Asi	42:46.7 m	CUI Yingzi	CHN	Jinan	15 Mar 92
		CHEN Yueling	CHN	Jinan	15 Mar 92
NAm	44:30.1 m	Alison BAKER	CAN	Fana	15 May 92
CAC	47:01.80	Francesca MARTINEZ	MEX	Mar del Plata	28 Oct 94
SAm	47:01.83	Miriam RAMON	ECU	Mar del Plata	28 Oct 94
Afr	51:24.6 m	Sabeha MANSOURI	ALG	Boumerdes	6 Apr 89
WJ	42:55.38	CUI Yingzi	CHN	Tangshan	27 Sep 91

10 KM WALK (Road)

W,Oce	41:30	Kerry SAXBY-JUNNA	AUS	Canberra	27 Aug 88
W.Eur	41:30	Ileana SALVADOR	ITA	Livorno	10 Jul 93
Asi	41:38	GAO Hongmiao	CHN	Beijing	7 Apr 94
CAC	43:27	Graciella MENDOZA	MEX	Hull	8 Oct 89
NAm	45:06	Ann PEEL	CAN	New York	3 May 87
		Janice McCAFFREY	CAN	Washington	29 Mar 92
SAm	46:13	Miriam RAMON	ECU	Stuttgart	14 Aug 93
Afr	47:23	Dounia KARA	ALG	Hildesheim	28 Aug 94
WJ	41:57	GAO Hongmiao	CHN	Beijing	8 Sep 93

4x100 METRES RELAY

W,E	41.37	GDR (Gladisch, Rieger, Auerswald, Göhr)	Canberra	6 Oct 85
NAm	41.49	USA (Finn, Torrence, Vereen, Devers)	Stuttgart	22 Aug 93
CAC	41.94	JAM (Duhaney, Cuthbert, McDonald, Ottey)	Tokyo	1 Sep 91
	41.94	JAM (Freeman, Campbell, Mitchell, Ottey)	Stuttgart	22 Aug 93
Afr	42.39	NGR (Utondu, Idehen, Opara-Thompson, Onyali)	Barcelona	7 Aug 92
Asi	43.16	CHN/Guangxi (Xiao, Tian, Huang, Qu)	Beijing	11 Sep 93
Oce	43.18	AUS (Wilson, Wells, Boyd, Boyle)	Montréal	31 Jul 76
SAm	44.60	BRA (Amaral, Gomes, C.Santos, V.Santos)	Manaus	15 Sep 90
WJ	43.33 §	GDR (Breuer, Krabbe, Dietz, Henke)	Berlin	20 Jul 88
	43.48	GDR (Breuer, Krabbe, Dietz, Henke)	Sudbury	31 Jul 88

4x400 METRES RELAY

W,E	3:15.17	URS (Ledovskaya, Nazarova, Pinigina, Bryzgina)	Seoul	1 Oct 88
NAm	3:15.51	USA (D.Howard, Dixon, Brisco, Griffith Joyner)	Seoul	1 Oct 88
CAC	3:23.13	JAM (Richards, Thomas, Rattray, Powell)	Seoul	1 Oct 88
Asi	3:24.28	CHN / Hebei (An, Bai, Cao, Ma)	Beijing	13 Sep 93
Afr	3:24.45	NGR (Yusuf, Onyali, Bakare, Opara)	Tokyo	1 Sep 91
Oce	3:25.56	AUS (Canty, Burnard, Rendina, Nail)	Montréal	31 Jul 76
SAm	3:29.22A	BRA (Oliveira, García, Telles, Souza)	Ciudad de México	24 Jul 88
WJ	3:28.39	GDR (Derr, Fabert, Wöhlk, Breuer)	Sudbury	31 Jul 88

Other Relay World Records recognised by the IAAF

4x200m	1:28.15	GDR (Göhr,R Müller, Wöckel, Koch)	Jena	9 Aug 80
4x800m	7:50.17	USSR (Olizarenko, Gurina, Borisova, Podyalovskaya)	Moskva	5 Aug 84

WORLD BESTS - NON-STANDARD EVENTS

Men

60m	6.38	Ben Johnson ¶	CAN	Rome (in 100m)	30 Aug 87
drugs dq	6.37	Ben Johnson		Seoul (in 100m)	24 Sep 88
150m	14.8	Pietro Mennea	ITA	Cassino	22 May 83
	14.97	Linford Christie	GBR	Sheffield	4 Sep 94
300m	31.48	Danny Everett	USA	Jerez de la Frontera	3 Sep 90
	31.48	Roberto Hernández	CUB	Jerez de la Frontera	3 Sep 90
500m	1:00.08	Donato Sabia	ITA	Busto Arsizio	26 May 84
600m	1:12.81	Johnny Gray	USA	Santa Monica	24 May 86
2000m Steeple	5:14.43	Julius Kariuki	KEN	Rovereto	21 Aug 90
200mh	22.63	Colin Jackson	GBR	Cardiff	1 Jun 91
(hand time)	22.5	Martin Lauer	FRG	Zürich	7 Jul 59
220yh straight	21.9	Don Styron	USA	Baton Rouge	2 Apr 60
300mh	34.6	David Hemery	GBR	London (CP)	15 Sep 72
35lb weight	25.41	Lance Deal	USA	Azusa	20 Feb 93
Pentathlon	4282	Bill Toomey	USA	London (CP)	16 Aug 69
(1985 tables)		(7.58, 66.18, 21.3, 44.52, 4:20.3)			
Double decathlon	14274	Indrek Kaseorg	EST	Punkalaidun	12/13 Sep 92

11.75, 7.00, 200mh 25.01, 12.13, 5k 17:36.07, 2:04.84, 1.99, 400m 50.72, HT 32.26, 3kSt 10:50.14
15.11, DT 37.04, 200m 23.30, 4.30, 10:18.50, 400mh 54.00, 57.78, 4:47.36, TJ 14.05, 10k 45:35.95

Women

60m	6.9	Alice Annum	GHA	Mainz	17 Jun 75
150m	16.10	Florence Griffith-Joyner	USA	Seoul (in 200m)	29 Sep 88
300m	34.1	Marita Koch	GDR	Canberra (in 400m)	6 Oct 85
500m	1:05.9	Tatana Kocembová	TCH	Ostrava	2 Aug 84
600m	1:23.5	Doina Melinte	ROM	Poiana Brasov	27 Jul 86
2000m Steeple	6:11.84	Marina Pluzhnikova	RUS	Sankt Peterburg	25 Jul 94
200mh	25.7	Pamela Ryan	AUS	Melbourne	25 Nov 71
Double heptathlon	10824	Irina Stasenko	RUS	Punkalaidun	12/13 Sep 92

100mh 14.95, HJ 1.57, 1500m 4:44.41, 400mh 61.82, SP 12.71, 200m 25.58, 100m 12.86
LJ 5.56, 400m 59.09, JT 37.52, 800m 2:17.88, 200mh 28.98, DT 30.32, 3000m 10:46.93

WORLD INDOOR RECORDS

Men	to 17 Mar 1995				
50 metres	5.61	Manfred Kokot	GDR	E.Berlin	4 Feb 73
	5.61	James Sanford	USA	San Diego	20 Feb 81
	5.55 #	Ben Johnson ¶	CAN	Ottawa	31 Jan 87
60 metres	6.41	Andre Cason	USA	Madrid	14 Feb 92
	6.41 #	Ben Johnson	CAN	Indianapolis	7 Mar 87
200 metres	20.25	Linford Christie	GBR	Liévin	19 Feb 95
400 metres	44.63	Michael Johnson	USA	Atlanta	4 Mar 95
800 metres	1:44.84	Paul Ereng	KEN	Budapest	4 Mar 89
1000 metres	2:15.26	Noureddine Morceli	ALG	Birmingham	22 Feb 92
1500 metres	3:34.16	Noureddine Morceli	ALG	Sevilla	28 Feb 91
1 mile	3:49.78	Eamonn Coghlan	IRL	East Rutherford	27 Feb 83
3000 metres	7:37.31	Moses Kiptanui	KEN	Sevilla	20 Feb 92
5000 metres	13:20.4	Suleiman Nyambui	TAN	New York	6 Feb 81
50 m hurdles	6.25	Mark McKoy	CAN	Kobe	5 Mar 86
60 m hurdles	7.30	Colin Jackson	GBR	Sindelfingen	6 Mar 94
High jump	2.43	Javier Sotomayor	CUB	Budapest	4 Mar 89
Pole vault	6.15	Sergey Bubka	UKR	Donyetsk	21 Feb 93
Long jump	8.79	Carl Lewis	USA	New York	27 Jan 84
Triple jump	17.77	Leonid Voloshin	UKR	Grenoble	6 Feb 94
Shot	22.66	Randy Barnes	USA	Los Angeles	20 Jan 89
5000m walk	18:07.08	Mikhail Shchennikov	RUS	Moskva	14 Feb 95
4 x 200m	1:22.11	United Kingdom		Glasgow	3 Mar 91
		(Linford Christie, Darren Braithwaite, Ade Mafe, John Regis)			
4 x 400m	3:03.05	Germany		Sevilla	10 Mar 91
		(Rico Lieder, Jens Carlowitz, Karsten Just, Thomas Schönlebe)			
4 x 800m	7:17.8	USSR		Sofia	14 Mar 71
		(Valeriy Taratynov, Stanislav Meshcherskikh, Aleksey Taranov, Viktor Semyashkin)			
Heptathlon	6476	Dan O'Brien	USA	Toronto	13/14 Mar 93
	(6.67 60m, 7.84 LJ, 16.02 SP, 2.13 HJ, 7.85 60mh, 5.20 PV, 2:57.96 1000m)				
Women					
50 metres	5.96	Irina Privalova	RUS	Madrid	9 Feb 95
60 metres	6.92	Irina Privalova	RUS	Madrid	11 Feb 93
	6.92	Irina Privalova	RUS	Madrid	9 Feb 95
200 metres	21.87	Merlene Ottey	JAM	Liévin	13 Feb 93
400 metres	49.59	Jarmila Kratochvílová	TCH	Milano	7 Mar 82
800 metres	1:56.40	Christine Wachtel	GDR	Wien	13 Feb 88
1000 metres	2:33.93 §	Inna Yevseyeva	UKR	Moskva	7 Feb 92
	2:34.41	Lyubov Kremlyova	RUS	Erfurt	15 Feb 95
1500 metres	4:00.27 +	Doina Melinte	ROM	East Rutherford	9 Feb 90
1 mile	4:17.14	Doina Melinte	ROM	East Rutherford	9 Feb 90
3000 metres	8:33.82	Elly van Hulst	HOL	Budapest	4 Mar 89
5000 metres	15:03.17	Elizabeth McColgan	GBR	Birmingham	22 Feb 92
50 m hurdles	6.58	Cornelia Oschkenat	GDR	Berlin	20 Feb 88
60 m hurdles	7.69	Lyudmila Narozhilenko	URS	Chelyabinsk	4 Feb 90
High jump	2.07	Heike Henkel	GER	Karlsruhe	9 Feb 92
Pole vault	4.15	Sun Caiyun	CHN	Erfurt	15 Feb 95
Long jump	7.37	Heike Drechsler	GDR	Wien	13 Feb 88
Triple jump	15.03	Yolanda Chen	RUS	Barcelona	11 Mar 95
Shot	22.50	Helena Fibingerová	TCH	Jablonec	19 Feb 77
3000m walk	11:44.00	Alina Ivanova	UKR	Moskva	7 Feb 92
4 x 200m	1:32.55	SC Eintracht Hamm	FRG	Dortmund	20 Feb 88
		(Helga Arendt, Silke-Beate Knoll, Mechthild Kluth, Gisela Kinzel)			
4 x 400m	3:27.22	Germany		Sevilla	10 Mar 91
		(Sandra Seuser, Annett Hesselbarth, Katrin Schreiter, Grit Breuer)			
4 x 800m	8:18.71	Russia		Moskva	4 Feb 94
		(Olga Kuznetsova, Yelena Afanasyeva, Yelena Zaitseva, Yekaterina Podkopayeva)			
Pentathlon	4991	Irina Belova	RUS	Berlin	14/15 Feb 92
		(8.22 60mh, 1.93 HJ, 13.25 SP, 6.67 LJ, 2:10.26 800m)			

mx unratified, in mixed sex race
¶ The IAAF stripped Johnson of his records in January 1990, after he had admitted long-term steroid use.

LONG DISTANCE WORLD BESTS - MEN TRACK

	hr:min:sec	Name	Nat	Venue	Date
15 km	0:42:34.0	Arturo Barrios	MEX	La Flèche	30 Mar 91
10 miles	0:45:57.6	Jos Hermens	HOL	Papendal	14 Sep 75
15 miles	1:11:43.1	Bill Rodgers	USA	Saratoga, Cal.	21 Feb 79
20 miles	1:39:14.4	Jack Foster	NZL	Hamilton, NZ	15 Aug 71
30 miles	2:42:00	Jeff Norman	GBR	Timperley, Cheshire	7 Jun 80
50 km	2:48:06	Jeff Norman	GBR	Timperley, Cheshire	7 Jun 80
40 miles	3:48:35	Don Ritchie	GBR	Hendon, London	16 Oct 82
50 miles	4:51:49	Don Ritchie	GBR	Hendon, London	12 Mar 83
100 km	6:10:20	Don Ritchie	GBR	Crystal Palace	28 Oct 78
150 km	10:36:42	Don Ritchie	GBR	Crystal Palace	15 Oct 77
100 miles	11:30:51	Don Ritchie	GBR	Crystal Palace	15 Oct 77
200 km	15:11:10#	Yiannis Kouros	GRE	Montauban, Fra	15-16 Mar 85
200 miles	27:48:35	Yiannis Kouros	GRE	Montauban, Fra	15-16 Mar 85
500 km	60:23.00	Yiannis Kouros	GRE	Colac, Aus	26-29 Nov 84
500 miles	105:42:09	Yiannis Kouros	GRE	Colac, Aus	26-30 Nov 84
1000 km	136:17:00	Yiannis Kouros	GRE	Colac, Aus	26-31 Nov 84
1500 km	12d 21:10:34	Gary Parsons	AUS	Nanango, Qld	10-23 Mar 1994
1000 mile	13d 17:41:44	Gary Parsons	AUS	Nanango, Qld	10-24 Mar 1994
	kilometres				
2 hrs	37.994	Jim Alder	GBR	Walton-on-Thames	17 Oct 64
12 hrs	162.400	Yiannis Kouros	GRE	Montauban, Fra	15 Mar 85
24 hrs	283.600	Yiannis Kouros	GRE	Montauban, Fra	15-16 Mar 85
48 hrs	452.270	Yiannis Kouros	GRE	Montauban, Fra	15-17 Mar 85
6 days	1030.000 indoors	Jean-Gilles Bousiquet	FRA	La Rochelle	16-23 Nov 92
Outdoors	1023.200	Yiannis Kouros	GRE	Colac, Aus	26 Nov-1 Dec 84

 # Running watch time, no stopped times known.

LONG DISTANCE ROAD BESTS

Where superior to track bests and run on properly measured road courses.

	hr:min:sec	Name	Nat	Venue	Date
15 km	0:42:28	Mike Musyoki	KEN	Portland, Oregon	26 Jun 83
Half mar	0:59:47	Moses Tanui	KEN	Milan	3 Apr 93
30 km	1:28:40	Steve Jones	GBR	Chicago	10 Oct 85
20 miles	1:35:22	Steve Jones	GBR	Chicago	10 Oct 85
30 miles	2:37:31	Thompson Magawana	RSA	Claremont-Kirstenbosch	12 Apr 88
50km	2:43:38	Thompson Magawana	RSA	Claremont-Kirstenbosch	12 Apr 88
40 miles	3:45:39	Andy Jones	CAN	Houston	23 Feb 91
50 miles	4:50:21	Bruce Fordyce	RSA	London-Brighton	25 Sep 83
1000 miles	10d:10:30:35	Yiannis Kouros	GRE	New York	21-30 May 88
	kilometres				
12 hrs	162.543	Yiannis Kouros	GRE	Queen's, New York	7 Nov 84
24 hours	286.463	Yiannis Kouros	GRE	New York	28-29 Sep 85
6 days	1028.370	Yiannis Kouros	GRE	New York	21-26 May 88
Uncertain measurement					
10 miles	0:45:13	Ian Stewart	GBR	Stoke-on-Trent	8 May 77

LONG DISTANCE TRACK EVENTS - WOMEN

	hr:min:sec	Name	Nat	Venue	Date
15 km	0:49:44.0	Silvana Cruciata	ITA	Rome	4 May 81
10 miles	0:54:21.8	Lorraine Moller	NZL	Auckland	9 Jan 93
20 miles	1:59:09 !	Chantal Langlacé	FRA	Amiens	3 Sep 83
30 miles	3:19:41	Carolyn Hunter-Rowe	GBR	Barry, Wales	7 Mar 93
50 km	3:26:45	Carolyn Hunter-Rowe	GBR	Barry, Wales	7 Mar 93
40 miles	4:26:43	Carolyn Hunter-Rowe	GBR	Barry, Wales	7 Mar 93
50 miles	6:07:58	Linda Meadows	AUS	Burwood, Vic	18 Jun 1994
100 km	7:50:09 *	Ann Trason	USA	Hayward, Cal.	3-4 Aug 91
100 miles	14:29:44	Ann Trason	USA	Santa Rosa, USA	18-19 Mar 89
200 km	19:28:48	Eleanor Adams	GBR	Melbourne	19-20 Aug 89
200 miles	39:09:03	Hilary Walker	GBR	Blackpool	5-7 Nov 88
500 km	77:53:46	Eleanor Adams	GBR	Colac, Aus.	13-15 Nov 89
500 miles	130:59:58	Sandra Barwick	NZL	Campbelltown, Aus	18-23 Nov 90
	kilometres				
2 hrs	32.652	Chantal Langlacé	FRA	Amiens	3 Sep 83
12 hrs	147.600	Ann Trason	USA	Hayward, Cal	3-4 Aug 91

24 hrs	240.169	Eleanor Adams	GBR	Melbourne	19-20 Aug 89
48 hrs	366.512	Hilary Walker	GBR	Blackpool	5-7 Nov 88
6 days	883.631	Sandra Barwick	NZL	Campbelltown, NSW	18-24 Nov 90
Indoors where superior to track best					
200 km	19:00:31	Eleanor Adams	GBR	Milton Keynes	3/4 Feb 90

*Timed on one running watch only, * lap recirded by computer*

LONG DISTANCE ROAD BESTS - WOMEN

Run on properly measured road courses.

	hr:min:sec	*Name*	*Nat*	*Venue*	*Date*
15 km	0:46:57	Elana Meyer	RSA	Cape Town	2 Nov 91
10 miles	0:51:41	Jill Hunter	GBR	New York	20 Apr 91
	0:50:31 u	Ingrid Kristiansen	NOR	Amsterdam	11 Oct 89
Half mar	1:06:40 ?	Ingrid Kristiansen	NOR	Sandnes	5 Apr 87
	1:07:11	Liz McColgan	GBR	Tokyo - 33m drop	26 Jan 92
25 km	1:21:21	Ingrid Kristiansen	NOR	London	10 May 87
30 km	1:38:27	Ingrid Kristiansen	NOR	London	10 May 87
20 miles	1:46:04	Ingrid Kristiansen	NOR	London	10 May 87
30 miles	3:01:16	Frith van der Merwe	RSA	Claremont - Kirstenbosch	25 Mar 89
50 km	3:08:13	Frith van der Merwe	RSA	Claremont - Kirstenbosch	25 Mar 89
40 miles	4:26:13	Ann Trason	USA	Houston	23 Feb 91
50 miles	5:40:18	Ann Trason	USA	Houston	23 Feb 91
100 km	7:09:44	Ann Trason	USA	Amiens	27 Sep 93
100 miles	13:47:41	Ann Trason	USA	Queen's New York	4 May 91
200 km	19:08:21 +	Sigrid Lomsky	GER	Basel	1-2 May 93
1000 km	7d 01:11:00	Sandra Barwick	NZL	New York	16-23Sep 91
1000 miles	12d 14:38:40	Sandra Barwick	NZL	New York	16-29 Sep 91
	kilometres				
24 hours	243.657	Sigrid Lomsky	GER	Basel	1-2 May 93

+ time at 201 km on one running watch

WORLD MEN'S ALL-TIME LISTS

100 METRES

Mark	Wind	Name		Nat	Born	Pos	Meet	Venue	Date
9.83	1.0	Ben	Johnson ¶	CAN	30.12.61	1	WCh	Roma	30 Aug 87
9.85	1.2	Leroy	Burrell	USA	21.2.67	1rA	Athl	Lausanne	6 Jul 94
9.86	1.2	Carl	Lewis	USA	1.7.61	1	WCh	Tokyo	25 Aug 91
9.87	0.3	Linford	Christie	GBR	2.4.60	1	WCh	Stuttgart	15 Aug 93
9.88	1.2		Burrell			2	WCh	Tokyo	25 Aug 91
9.90	1.9		Burrell			1	TAC	New York	14 Jun 91
9.91	1.2	Dennis	Mitchell	USA	20.2.66	3	WCh	Tokyo	25 Aug 91
9.91	1.9		Christie			1	CG	Victoria	23 Aug 94
9.92	1.1		Lewis			1	OG	Seoul	24 Sep 88
9.92	1.2		Christie			4	WCh	Tokyo	25 Aug 91
9.92	0.3	Andre	Cason	USA	20.1.69	2	WCh	Stuttgart	15 Aug 93
9.93A	1.4	Calvin	Smith	USA	8.1.61	1	USOF	Air Force Academy	3 Jul 83
9.93	1.0		Lewis			2	WCh	Roma	30 Aug 87
9.93	1.1		Lewis			1	WK	Zürich	17 Aug 88
9.93	1.9		Lewis			2	TAC	New York	14 Jun 91
9.93	1.3		Lewis			1s1	WCh	Tokyo	25 Aug 91
9.93	-0.6	Michael	Marsh	USA	4.8.67	1	MSR	Walnut	18 Apr 92
9.94	0.8		Burrell			1	TAC	Houston	16 Jun 89
9.94	1.1		Burrell			1s2	WCh	Tokyo	25 Aug 91
9.94	0.3		Cason			1s1	WCh	Stuttgart	15 Aug 93
9.94	0.2	Davidson	Ezinwa	NGR	22.11.71	1	GP II	Linz	4 Jul 94
9.94	1.9		Mitchell			1	Bisl	Oslo	22 Jul 94
9.94	0.5		Mitchell			1	v Afr	Durham	13 Aug 94
9.95A	0.3	Jim	Hines (10)	USA	10.9.46	1	OG	Ciudad México	14 Oct 68
9.95	1.2	Frank	Fredericks	NAM	2.10.67	5	WCh	Tokyo	25 Aug 91
9.95A	1.9	Olapade	Adeniken	NGR	19.8.69	1A		El Paso	16 Apr 94
		(28 performances by 12 athletes)							
Most 'legal' sub 10.00 times: 15 Lewis, 8 Mitchell, 7 Burrell, Christie; 6 Johnson, 5 Cason, 4 Smith, Ezinwa									
9.96	0.1	Mel	Lattany	USA	10.8.59	1r1		Athens, Ga.	5 May 84
9.96	1.2	Ray	Stewart	JAM	18.3.65	6	WCh	Tokyo	25 Aug 91
9.98A	0.6	Silvio	Leonard	CUB	20.9.55	1	WPT	Guadalajara	11 Aug 77
9.98	0.3	Daniel	Effiong	NGR	17.6.72	2s1	WCh	Stuttgart	15 Aug 93
9.99	1.9	Jon	Drummond	USA	9.9.68	2	Bisl	Oslo	22 Jul 94
10.00	2.0	Marian	Woronin	POL	13.8.56	1	Kuso	Warszawa	9 Jun 84
10.00	1.0	Chidi	Imo	NGR	27.8.63	1	ISTAF	Berlin	15 Aug 86
10.00#A	1.6	Robson	da Silva	BRA	4.9.64	1	IbAm	Ciudad México	22 Jul 88
		10.02 1.8				1	IbAmC	Habana	27 Sep 86
		(20)							
10.01A	0.9	Pietro	Mennea	ITA	28.6.52	1		Ciudad México	4 Sep 79
10.01A	1.9	Bode	Osagiobare	NGR	1.12.70	2A		El Paso	16 Apr 94
10.02A	2.0	Charles	Greene	USA	21.7.44	1q4	OG	Ciudad México	13 Oct 68
10.02	1.0	James	Sanford	USA	27.12.57	1	Pepsi	Westwood	11 May 80
10.02	0.7	Daniel	Sangouma	FRA	7.2.65	2	BNP	Villeneuve d'Ascq	29 Jun 90
Some observers felt that this was run with the benefit of a flying start, but it was artified as a French record									
10.02	0.3	Bruny	Surin	CAN	12.7.67	5	WCh	Stuttgart	15 Aug 93
10.03A	1.9	Stanley	Floyd	USA	23.6.61	1r1	NCAA	Provo	5 Jun 82
10.03	-2.5&	Viktor	Bryzgin	UKR	22.8.62	1rA	Znam	Leningrad	7 Jun 86
		wind reading of -2.5 almost certainly incorrect, but mark accepted as a national record.							
10.03	0.4	Joe	DeLoach	USA	5.6.67	1	NCAA	Eugene	4 Jun 88
10.03	1.8	Donovan	Bailey	CAN	16.12.67	1		Duisburg	12 Jun 94
		(30)							
10.04A	0.3	Lennox	Miller	JAM	8.10.46	2	OG	Ciudad México	14 Oct 68
10.04	1.8	Mark	Witherspoon	USA	3.9.63	1	TAC	San José	27 Jun 87
10.04	0.5	Emmit	King	USA	24.3.59	1	TAC	Tampa	17 Jun 88
10.05	-1.1	Steve	Riddick	USA	18.9.51	1	WK	Zürich	20 Aug 75
10.05	1.8	Harvey	Glance	USA	28.3.57	1r1	FlaR	Tampa	30 Mar 85
10.05	1.9	Michael	Green	JAM	7.11.70	2	CG	Victoria	23 Aug 94
10.06	1.1	Bob	Hayes	USA	20.12.42	1	OG	Tokyo	15 Oct 64
10.06	0.0	Hasely	Crawford	TRI	16.8.50	1	OG	Montreal	24 Jul 76
10.06	1.6	Ron	Brown	USA	31.3.61	3	WK	Zürich	24 Aug 83
10.06	2.0	Leandro	Peñalver	CUB	23.5.61	1	PAm	Caracas	24 Aug 83
		(40)							
10.06	1.9	Frank	Emmelmann	GDR	15.9.61	1		Berlin	22 Sep 85

Mark	Wind	Name		Nat	Born	Pos	Meet	Venue	Date
10.06	0.3	Andrés	Simon	CUB	15.9.61	1		Habana	1 Aug 87
10.06A	2.0	Johan	Rossouw	RSA	20.10.65	1		Johannesburg	23 Apr 88
10.06	1.3	Patrick	Williams	JAM	11.11.65	1	S&W	Modesto	5 May 90
10.06	2.0	Rodney	Lewis	USA	17.7.66	1h3	NC	Knoxville	15 Jun 94
10.07	0.0	Valeriy	Borzov	UKR	20.10.49	1q3	OG	München	31 Aug 72
10.07	0.0	Don	Quarrie	JAM	25.2.51	2	OG	Montreal	24 Jul 76
10.07	1.7	Clancy	Edwards	USA	9.8.55	1	NCAA	Eugene	2 Jun 78
10.07A	1.8	Eddie	Hart	USA	24.4.49	1	USOF	Air Force Academy	30 Jul 78
10.07	-0.1	Steve	Williams	USA	13.11.53	1	WK	Zürich	16 Aug 78
		(50)							
10.07A	0.6	Mike	Roberson	USA	25.3.56	1s1	WUG	Ciudad México	8 Sep 79
10.07	0.5	Lee	McRae	USA	23.1.66	1	WUG	Zagreb	14 Jul 87
10.07	0.5	Brian	Cooper	USA	21.8.65	2	TAC	Tampa	17 Jun 88
10.07	1.1	Emmanuel	Tuffour	GHA	2.12.66	1		Schriesheim	18 Jun 94
10.07	1.9	Ato	Boldon	TRI	30.12.73	4	CG	Victoria	23 Aug 94

Times recorded in the 1988 Ibero-American Championships may not have been automatically recorded.

Disqualified for drug abuse

Mark	Wind	Name		Nat	Born	Pos	Meet	Venue	Date
9.79	1.1	Ben	Johnson ¶	CAN	30.12.61	-	OG	Seoul	24 Sep 88
10.02	1.9	Horace	Dove-Edwin ¶	SLE	10.2.67	(2)	CG	Victoria	23 Aug 94

Wind gauge illegally placed (on outside of track) and track 99.96m

Mark	Wind	Name		Nat	Born	Pos	Meet	Venue	Date
9.96	1.7	Tim	Montgomery	USA	28.1.75	1	JUCO	Odessa, TX	21 May 94
9.98	1.7	Daniel	Effiong	NGR	17.6.72	2	JUCO	Odessa, TX	21 May 94
10.03	1.7	Warren	Johnson	JAM	7.11.73	3	JUCO	Odessa, TX	21 May 94

Doubtful wind readings

Mark	Wind	Name		Nat	Born	Pos	Meet	Venue	Date
9.91	-2.3	Davidson	Ezinwa	NGR	22.11.71	1		Azusa	11 Apr 92
10.02	1.2	Ronald	Desruelles ¶	BEL	14.2.55	1		Naimette	11 May 85

Low altitude marks for athletes with lifetime bests at high altitude

10.03 0.8 Hines 1s1 AAU Sacramento 20 Jun 68 10.07 2.0 Floyd 1 Austin 24 May 80

10.03 1.7 Leonard 1 Habana 13 Sep 77

Wind-assisted marks

Mark	Wind	Name		Nat	Born	Pos	Meet	Venue	Date
9.78	5.2	Carl	Lewis	USA	1.7.61	1	OT	Indianapolis	16 Jul 88
9.79	5.3	Andre	Cason	USA	20.1.69	1h4	NC	Eugene	16 Jun 93
9.79	4.5		Cason			1s1	NC	Eugene	16 Jun 93
9.80	4.3		Lewis			1q2	WCh	Tokyo	24 Aug 91
9.85	5.3		Burrell			2h4	NC	Eugene	16 Jun 93
9.85	4.8		Cason			1	NC	Eugene	17 Jun 93
9.85	4.8	Dennis	Mitchell	USA	20.2.66	2	NC	Eugene	17 Jun 93
9.86	5.2		Mitchell			2	OT	Indianapolis	16 Jul 88
9.86	2.5		Burrell			1	TexR	Austin	9 Apr 94
9.87	11.2	William	Snoddy	USA	6.12.57	1		Dallas	1 Apr 78
9.87	4.9	Calvin	Smith	USA	8.1.61	1s2	OT	Indianapolis	16 Jul 88
9.87	5.2		C.Smith			3	OT	Indianapolis	16 Jul 88
9.88	2.3	James	Sanford	USA	27.12.57	1		Westwood	3 May 80
9.88	5.2	Albert	Robinson	USA	28.11.64	4	OT	Indianapolis	16 Jul 88
9.88	3.1		Cason			1rA	S&W	Modesto	16 May 92
9.89	4.2	Ray	Stewart	JAM	18.3.65	1s1	PAm	Indianapolis	9 Aug 87
9.89	4.1	Frank	Fredericks	NAM	2.10.67	1q4	WCh	Tokyo	24 Aug 91
9.90	2.5		Lewis			1	MSR	Walnut	28 Apr 85
9.90	5.2	Joe	DeLoach	USA	5.6.67	5	OT	Indianapolis	16 Jul 88
9.90	3.7		Johnson			1	NC	Ottawa	6 Aug 88
9.90	3.0		Stewart			1		Vigo	30 Jun 89
9.90	4.3		Christie			2q2	WCh	Tokyo	24 Aug 91
9.90	4.8		Lewis			3	NC	Eugene	17 Jun 93
		23 wind assisted marks to 9.90							
9.91	5.3	Bob	Hayes	USA	20.12.42	1s1	OG	Tokyo	15 Oct 64
9.91	4.2	Mark	Witherspoon	USA	3.9.63	2s1	PAm	Indianapolis	9 Aug 87
9.92A	4.4	Chidi	Imo	NGR	27.8.63	1s1	AfrG	Nairobi	8 Aug 87
9.92	5.3	Jon	Drummond	USA	9.9.68	3h4	NC	Eugene	16 Jun 93
9.93	7.5	Pablo	Montes	CUB	23.11.45	1s	CAC	Panama City	1 Mar 70
9.94	2.7	Vitaliy	Savin	KZK	23.1.66	1	CIS Ch	Moskva	22 Jun 92
9.94	2.5	Daniel	Effiong	NGR	17.6.72	2	TexR	Austin	9 Apr 94
9.95	8.9	Willie	Gault	USA	5.9.60	1		Knoxville	2 Apr 83
9.95	2.4	Mel	Lattany	USA	10.8.59	1		Athens, Ga	7 May 83
9.97	7.7	Andrés	Simon	CUB	15.9.61	1s1	WUG	Kobe	30 Aug 85
9.97	3.4	Roy	Martin	USA	25.12.66	1	SWC	Houston	18 May 86
9.98	11.2	Cole	Doty	CAN	6.6.55	2		Dallas	1 Apr 78
9.98	5.2	Emmit	King	USA	24.3.59	7	OT	Indianapolis	16 Jul 88
9.98	5.2	Daron	Council	USA	26.12.64	1h4	TAC	Houston	15 Jun 89

Mark	Wind	Name		Nat	Born	Pos	Meet	Venue	Date
9.99	7.2	Pietro	Mennea	ITA	28.6.52	1	vGRE	Bari	13 Sep 78
9.99#A	2.7	Leandro	Peñalver	CUB	23.5.61	1h2	IbAmC	Ciudad México	22 Jul 88
10.00	6.0					1s2	PAm	Indianapolis	9 Aug 87
10.00	2.6	Jeff	Phillips	USA	16.5.57	2	NCAA	Baton Rouge	5 Jun 81
10.00	2.6	Lorenzo	Daniel	USA	23.3.66	1	SEC	Knoxville	18 May 86
10.00	3.7	Desai	Williams	CAN	12.6.59	2	NC	Ottawa	6 Aug 88
10.00	4.3	Tim	Jackson	AUS	4.7.69	1	CGT	Sydney	2 Dec 89
10.00	2.7	Frank	Fredericks	NAM	2.10.67	1		Cottbus	15 Jun 94
10.01	2.3	Ron	Brown	USA	31.3.61	2	MSR	Walnut	24 Apr 83
10.01#A	2.7	José	Arqués	ESP	16.5.60	2h2	IbAmC	Ciudad México	22 Jul 88
10.01	4.3	Bruny	Surin	CAN	12.7.67	3q2	WCh	Tokyo	24 Aug 91
10.01	4.1	Atlee	Mahorn	CAN	27.10.65	3q4	WCh	Tokyo	24 Aug 91
10.01	2.8	Glenroy	Gilbert	CAN	31.8.68	1h1	SEC	Knoxville	15 May 93
10.01	2.8	Michael	Green	JAM	7.11.70	1		Clemson	16 May 93
10.02	5.9	Allan	Wells	GBR	3.5.52	1	CG	Brisbane	4 Oct 82
10.02	2.9	Terry	Scott	USA	23.6.64	1	NCAA	Austin	1 Jun 85
10.02A	6.2	Aaron	Thigpen	USA	18.9.64	1	WAC	Provo	10 May 86
10.02	4.5	Lee	McRae	USA	23.1.66	2	TAC	Eugene	20 Jun 86
10.02	3.1	Michael	Green	JAM	7.11.70	1s2	NCAA	Eugene	31 May 91
10.03	3.5	Harvey	Glance	USA	28.3.57	1rA	CalR	Modesto	9 May 87
10.03	2.6	Tony	Dees	USA	6.8.63	2		Luzern	6 Jul 91
10.03	2.4	James	Trapp	USA	28.12.70	1rA		Austin	9 May 92
10.03	5.1	Chris	Nelloms	USA	14.8.71	1	Big 10	Minneapolis	23 May 92
10.03	3.0	Tim	Harden	USA	27.1.74	1	SEC	Fayetteville	15 May 94
10.04	11.2	Ray	Brooks	USA	24.1.56	3		Dallas	1 Apr 78
10.04	2.2	Floyd	Heard	USA	24.3.66	1s2	TAC	New York	13 Jun 91
10.04	2.8	Devlon	Dunn	USA	1.4.67	1		Pieksamäki	3 Jul 91
10.04		Anthony	Phillips	USA	5.10.70	1		Abilene	8 May 93
10.04	4.8	David	Oaks	USA	12.5.72	1	Big8	Lawrence	21 May 94

Hand timing

Mark	Wind	Name		Nat	Born	Pos	Meet	Venue	Date
9.8		Harvey	Glance	USA	28.3.57	1		Auburn	9 Apr 77
9.8	0.4	Jeff	Phillips	USA	16.5.57	1		Knoxville	22 May 82

Wind-assisted

Mark	Wind	Name		Nat	Born	Pos	Meet	Venue	Date
9.7	3.8	Osvaldo	Lara	CUB	13.7.55	1		Santiago de Cuba	24 Feb 82
9.7	3.5	Ben	Johnson ¶	CAN	30.12.61	1		Perth	24 Jan 87

200 METRES

Mark	Wind	Name		Nat	Born	Pos	Meet	Venue	Date
19.72A	1.8	Pietro	Mennea	ITA	28.6.52	1	WUG	Ciudad México	12 Sep 79
19.73	-0.2	Michael	Marsh	USA	4.8.67	1s1	OG	Barcelona	5 Aug 92
19.75	1.5	Carl	Lewis	USA	1.7.61	1	TAC	Indianapolis	19 Jun 83
19.75	1.7	Joe	DeLoach	USA	5.6.67	1	OG	Seoul	28 Sep 88
19.79	1.7		Lewis			2	OG	Seoul	28 Sep 88
19.79	1.0	Michael	Johnson	USA	13.9.67	1	OT	New Orleans	28 Jun 92
19.80	-0.9		Lewis			1	OG	Los Angeles	8 Aug 84
19.82A	2.0		Lewis			1		Sestriere	11 Aug 88
19.83A	0.9	Tommie	Smith	USA	12.6.44	1	OG	Ciudad México	16 Oct 68
19.84	0.2		Lewis			1q3	OT	Los Angeles	19 Jun 84
19.85	0.4		Johnson			1	IAC	Edinburgh	6 Jul 90
19.85	0.3	Frank	Fredericks	NAM	2.10.67	1	WCh	Stuttgart	20 Aug 93
19.86A	1.0	Don	Quarrie	JAM	25.2.51	1	PAm	Cali	3 Aug 71
19.86	-0.2		Lewis			1	OT	Los Angeles	21 Jun 84
19.86	1.0		Marsh			2	OT	New Orleans	28 Jun 92
19.87	0.8	Lorenzo	Daniel	USA	23.3.66	1	NCAA	Eugene	3 Jun 88
19.87A	1.8	John	Regis (10)	GBR	13.10.66	1		Sestriere	31 Jul 94
19.88A	1.5		Johnson			1		Sestriere	8 Aug 90
19.88	-0.9		Johnson			1	GPF	Barcelona	20 Sep 91
19.89	1.0		Johnson			1	VD	Bruxelles	13 Sep 91
19.90	0.3		Johnson			1	TAC	Norwalk	16 Jun 90
19.91	1.9		Johnson			1		Salamanca	13 Jul 92
19.92A	1.9	John	Carlos	USA	5.6.45	1	FOT	Echo Summit	12 Sep 68
19.92	1.3		Lewis			1		Madrid	4 Jun 87
19.93	-1.5		Daniel			1	SEC	Auburn	15 May 88
19.94	1.4		Johnson			1	McV	Sheffield	15 Sep 91
19.94	1.1		Marsh			1rA		Austin	9 May 92
19.94	0.3		Regis			2	WCh	Stuttgart	20 Aug 93
19.94	0.0		Johnson			1	Herc	Monaco	2 Aug 94

Mark	Wind	Name		Nat	Born	Pos	Meet	Venue	Date
19.95	1.9	Floyd	Heard	USA	24.3.66	1	SWC	Lubbock	17 May 87
19.95	-1.0		Marsh			1rA	WK	Zürich	19 Aug 92
		(31/12)							
19.96	-0.9	Kirk	Baptiste	USA	20.6.63	2	OG	Los Angeles	8 Aug 84
19.96	0.4	Robson Caetano	da Silva	BRA	4.9.64	1	VD	Bruxelles	25 Aug 89
19.99	0.6	Calvin	Smith	USA	8.1.61	1	WK	Zürich	24 Aug 83
20.00	0.0	Valeriy	Borzov	UKR	20.10.49	1	OG	München	4 Sep 72
20.01	-1.0	Michael	Bates	USA	19.12.69	3rA	WK	Zürich	19 Aug 92
20.03	1.6	Clancy	Edwards	USA	9.8.55	1		Westwood	29 Apr 78
20.03	1.5	Larry	Myricks	USA	10.3.56	2	TAC	Indianapolis	19 Jun 83
20.05	1.0	Roy	Martin	USA	25.12.66	3	OT	Indianapolis	20 Jul 88
		(20)							
20.05	1.0	Albert	Robinson	USA	28.11.64	4	OT	Indianapolis	20 Jul 88
20.06A	0.9	Peter	Norman	AUS	15.6.42	2	OG	Ciudad México	16 Oct 68
20.06	1.7	Silvio	Leonard	CUB	20.9.55	1	Kuso	Warszawa	19 Jun 78
20.07		James	Mallard	USA	29.11.57	1		Tuscaloosa	20 Apr 79
20.08	0.9	LaMonte	King	USA	18.12.59	1	TAC	Walnut	15 Jun 80
20.08A	1.6	Dwayne	Evans	USA	13.10.58	1		Albuquerque	13 Jun 87
20.08	0.3	Danny	Everett	USA	1.11.66	2	TAC	Norwalk	16 Jun 90
20.09	1.7	Linford	Christie	GBR	2.4.60	4	OG	Seoul	28 Sep 88
20.09A	1.9	Dennis	Mitchell	USA	20.2.66	1	NCAA	Provo	2 Jun 89
20.10	1.7	Millard	Hampton	USA	8.7.56	1	OT	Eugene	22 Jun 76
		(30)							
20.10	-0.2	Daniel	Effiong	NGR	17.6.72	1	Jen	San José	28 May 94
20.11	0.7	Attila	Kovács	HUN	2.9.60	1	NC	Miskolc	21 Aug 87
20.11	0.2	Olapade	Adeniken	NGR	19.8.69	1	NCAA	Austin	6 Jun 92
20.11	1.2	Bryan	Bridgewater	USA	7.9.70	1	NCAA II	Abilene	29 May 93
20.12	1.0	Mark	Witherspoon	USA	3.9.63	2	TAC	Houston	17 Jun 89
20.12	-0.8	Leroy	Burrell	USA	21.2.67	1s1	OT	New Orleans	27 Jun 92
20.14	1.8	James	Gilkes	GUY	21.9.52	1		Ingelheim	12 Sep 78
20.15A	0.3	Mike	Miller	USA	29.12.59	1h2	NCAA	Provo	2 Jun 82
20.16	-0.1	Steve	Williams	USA	13.11.53	1		Stuttgart	26 Aug 75
20.16	1.5	Elliott	Quow	USA	3.3.62	3	TAC	Indianapolis	19 Jun 83
		(40)							
20.16	-0.4	Gilles	Quénéhervé	FRA	17.5.66	2	WCh	Roma	3 Sep 87
20.17	0.4	Atlee	Mahorn	CAN	27.10.65	1q1	WCh	Tokyo	26 Aug 91
20.17	1.0	James	Trapp	USA	28.12.70	6	OT	New Orleans	28 Jun 92
20.18	0.2	Henry	Thomas	USA	10.7.67	1		Eagle Rock	14 May 88
20.18	0.3	Dean	Capobianco	AUS	11.5.70	5	WCh	Stuttgart	20 Aug 93
20.19	0.0	Larry	Black	USA	20.7.51	2	OG	München	4 Sep 72
20.19	0.7	James	Sanford	USA	27.12.57	1		Westwood	28 Apr 79
20.19	1.9	Phil	Epps	USA	11.11.59	1		College Station	20 Mar 82
20.19	0.6	John	Dinan	AUS	18.11.59	1		Canberra	6 Mar 86
20.19	0.0	Jeff	Williams	USA	31.12.64	2A	MSR	Walnut	17 Apr 94
		(50)							

Low altitude best: 20.06 0.4 Quarrie 1 WK Zürich 16 Aug 74

Wind-assisted marks

Mark	Wind	Name		Nat	Born	Pos	Meet	Venue	Date
19.61	>4.0	Leroy	Burrell	USA	21.2.67	1	SWC	College Station	19 May 90
19.79A	4.0		Marsh			1		Sestriere	21 Jul 92
19.86	4.6	Roy	Martin	USA	25.12.66	1	SWC	Houston	18 May 86
19.88	3.4	Lorenzo	Daniel	USA	23.3.66	1	SEC	Tuscaloosa	17 May 87
19.90	3.6	Frank	Fredericks	NAM	2.10.67	1	NCAA	Eugene	1 Jun 91
19.91	>4.0		Johnson			2	SWC	College Station	19 May 90
19.91		James	Jett	USA	28.12.70	1		Morgantown	18 Apr 92
19.94	4.0	James	Sanford	USA	27.12.57	1s1	NCAA	Austin	7 Jun 80
19.94	3.7	Chris	Nelloms	USA	14.8.71	1	Big 10	Minneapolis	23 May 92
19.95	3.4	Mike	Roberson	USA	25.3.56	1h3	NCAA	Austin	5 Jun 80
20.00A	3.4	Olapade	Adeniken	NGR	19.8.69	1		Air Force Academy	23 May 92
20.01	2.5	Derald	Harris	USA	5.4.58	1		San José	9 Apr 77
20.05A	3.8	Cyprean	Enweani	CAN	19.3.64	1		Calgary	3 Jul 88
20.07A	2.1	James	Butler	USA	21.6.60	1r1	NCAA	Provo	4 Jun 82
20.06		Renward	Wells	BAH	23.2.70	1		Stillwater	2 Apr 94
20.09	3.7	Brady	Crain	USA	8.8.56	1	TAC	San José	9 Jun 80
20.09	2.2	Dwayne	Evans	USA	13.10.58	1		Walnut	1 Jun 86
20.10	4.6	Stanley	Kerr	USA	19.6.67	2	SWC	Houston	18 May 86
20.10	2.4	Marcus	Adam	GBR	28.2.68	1	CG	Auckland	1 Feb 90
20.11	3.7	Allan	Wells	GBR	3.5.52	1		Edinburgh	20 Jun 80
20.11	>4.0	Andre	Cason	USA	20.1.69	3	SWC	College Station	19 May 90

Mark	Wind	Name		Nat	Born	Pos	Meet	Venue	Date
20.12	3.6	Mike	Conley	USA	5.10.62	1h3	NCAA	Austin	30 May 85
20.14	3.4	Daron	Council	USA	26.12.64	2	SEC	Tuscaloosa	17 May 87
20.14A	2.5	Tshakile	Nzimande	RSA	19.11.61	1		Pietersburg	15 Feb 92
20.15	3.6	Jimmy	French	USA	2.4.70	3	NCAA	Eugene	1 Jun 91
20.15 ?	2.4	Sidney	Telles Sousa	BRA	26.7.66	1		Americana	13 Feb 93
20.16	3.9?	Danny	Peebles	USA	30.5.66	2	NCAA	Baton Rouge	5 Jun 87
20.17	2.4	Chris	Nelloms	USA	14.8.71	2	WUG	Buffalo	17 Jul 93
20.18A	2.6	Oluyemi	Kayode	NGR	7.7.68	1		El Paso	22 May 93
Low altitude best: 20.09	3.6		Adeniken			2	NCAA	Eugene	1 Jun 91

* 220 yards less 0.12 seconds

Hand timing

Mark	Wind	Name		Nat	Born	Pos	Meet	Venue	Date
19.7A		James	Sanford	USA	27.12.57	1		El Paso	19 Apr 80
19.7A	0.2	Robson C.	da Silva	BRA	4.9.64	1	AmCp	Bogotá	13 Aug 89
19.8"	1.3	Don	Quarrie	JAM	25.2.51	1	Pre	Eugene	7 Jun 75
19.8*	1.3	Steve	Williams	USA	13.11.53	2	Pre	Eugene	7 Jun 75
19.8		James	Mallard	USA	29.11.57	1	SEC	Tuscaloosa	13 May 79
19.9		Mel	Lattany	USA	10.8.59	2		Tuscaloosa	13 May 79
19.9		Davidson	Ezinwa	NGR	22.11.71	1		Bauchi	18 Mar 89

Wind-assisted

Mark	Wind	Name		Nat	Born	Pos	Meet	Venue	Date
19.8*		Carl	Lawson	JAM	27.10.47	1		Moscow	19 May 73
19.8*	3.4	James	Gilkes	GUY	21.9.52	1	NCAA	Austin	8 Jun 74
19.8	4.4	Desmond	Ross	USA	30.12.61	1	Big8	Manhattan	11 May 85
19.9*		Gerald	Tinker	USA	19.1.51	1		Kent	5 May 73
19.9*	3.4	Reggie	Jones	USA	30.12.53	2	NCAA	Austin	8 Jun 74
19.9		Silvio	Leonard	CUB	20.9.55	1		Habana	22 May 77
19.9	4.4	Chidi	Imo	NGR	27.8.63	2	Big8	Manhattan	11 May 85

*" during 220 yards race, * 220 yards less 0.1 seconds*

300 METRES

In 300m races only, not including intermediate times in 400m races

Mark	Name		Nat	Born	Pos	Meet	Venue	Date
31.48	Danny	Everett	USA	1.11.66	1		Jerez de la Frontera	3 Sep 90
31.48	Roberto	Hernández	CUB	6.3.67	2		Jerez de la Frontera	3 Sep 90
31.56	Michael	Johnson	USA	13.9.67	1		Salamanca	22 Jul 94
31.67	John	Regis	GBR	13.10.66	1	Vaux	Gateshead	17 Jul 92
31.69		Hernández			1	PTS	Bratislava	20 Jun 90
31.70	Kirk	Baptiste	USA	20.6.63	1	Nike	London	18 Aug 84
31.72		Johnson			1	Vaux	Gateshead	30 Jul 93
31.73	Thomas	Jefferson	USA	8.6.62	1	DCG	London	22 Aug 87
31.74	Gabriel	Tiacoh	CIV	10.9.63	1		La Coruña	6 Aug 86
31.82	Steve	Lewis	USA	16.5.69	2	Vaux	Gateshead	17 Jul 92
	(10/8)							
31.88	Darren	Clark	AUS	6.9.65	1	UlstG	Belfast	30 Jun 86
31.97	Innocent	Egbunike	NGR	30.11.61	1	IAC	London	8 Aug 86
32.04	Andrew	Valmon	USA	1.1.65	3		Jerez de la Frontera	3 Sep 90
32.05	Butch	Reynolds ¶	USA	8.6.64	1	Giro	Belfast	20 Jul 87
32.05	Robson Caetano	da Silva	BRA	4.9.64	1		Jerez de la Frontera	17 Sep 91
32.07	Quincy	Watts	USA	19.6.70	2	Vaux	Gateshead	30 Jul 93
32.08	Roger	Black	GBR	31.3.66	4	IAC	London	8 Aug 86
32.10	Michael	Marsh	USA	4.8.67	3	Vaux	Gateshead	30 Jul 93
32.14	Todd	Bennett	GBR	6.7.62	2	Nike	London	18 Aug 84
32.16	Mel	Lattany	USA	10.8.59	1		Gateshead	31 Jul 83
32.16	Walter	McCoy	USA	15.11.58	3	Nike	London	18 Aug 84
32.17	Darrell	Robinson	USA	23.12.63	1	DCG	Birmingham	19 Aug 86
	(20)							

400 METRES

Mark	Name		Nat	Born	Pos	Meet	Venue	Date
43.29	Butch	Reynolds ¶	USA	8.6.64	1	WK	Zürich	17 Aug 88
43.50	Quincy	Watts	USA	19.6.70	1	OG	Barcelona	5 Aug 92
43.65	Michael	Johnson	USA	13.9.67	1	WCh	Stuttgart	17 Aug 93
43.71		Watts			1s2	OG	Barcelona	3 Aug 92
43.74		Johnson			1	NC	Eugene	19 Jun 93
43.81	Danny	Everett	USA	1.11.66	1	OT	New Orleans	26 Jun 92
43.83		Watts			1	WK	Zürich	19 Aug 92
43.86A	Lee	Evans	USA	25.2.47	1	OG	Ciudad México	18 Oct 68
43.87	Steve	Lewis	USA	16.5.69	1	OG	Seoul	28 Sep 88
43.90		Johnson			1		Madrid	6 Sep 94
43.93		Reynolds			1	OT	Indianapolis	20 Jul 88
43.93		Reynolds			2	OG	Seoul	28 Sep 88
43.94		Johnson			1	ISTAF	Berlin	27 Aug 93

Mark	Wind	Name		Nat	Born	Pos	Meet	Venue	Date
43.97A		Larry	James	USA	6.11.47	2	OG	Ciudad México	18 Oct 68
43.97			Watts			1s1	OT	New Orleans	24 Jun 92
43.98			Everett			2	OT	Indianapolis	20 Jul 88
43.98			Johnson			1rA	TSB	London	10 Jul 92
44.00			Watts			1	NCAA	Austin	6 Jun 92
44.04			Johnson			1	ISTAF	Berlin	30 Aug 94
44.06A			Evans			1	FOT	Echo Summit	14 Sep 68
44.06			Everett			1		Sevilla	30 May 90
44.08			Lewis			2	OT	New Orleans	26 Jun 92
44.09			Everett			3	OG	Seoul	28 Sep 88
44.10			Reynolds			1	JO	Columbus	3 May 87
44.11			Lewis			1s2	OT	Indianapolis	18 Jul 88
44.12			Reynolds			2	NC	Eugene	19 Jun 93
44.13			Reynolds			1	NCAA	Baton Rouge	6 Jun 87
44.13A			Watts			1		Sestriere	28 Jul 93
44.13			Reynolds			2	WCh	Stuttgart	17 Aug 93
44.14		Roberto	Hernández	CUB	6.3.67	2		Sevilla	30 May 90
44.14			Reynolds ¶			2s1	OT	New Orleans	24 Jun 92
		(31/8)							
44.17		Innocent	Egbunike	NGR	30.11.61	1rA	WK	Zürich	19 Aug 87
44.18		Samson	Kitur (10)	KEN	25.2.66	2s2	OG	Barcelona	3 Aug 92
44.21		Ian	Morris	TRI	30.11.61	3s2	OG	Barcelona	3 Aug 92
44.26		Alberto	Juantorena	CUB	21.11.50	1	OG	Montreal	29 Jul 76
44.27		Alonzo	Babers	USA	31.10.61	1	OG	Los Angeles	8 Aug 84
44.27		Antonio	Pettigrew	USA	7.11.67	1	TAC	Houston	17 Jun 89
44.28		Andrew	Valmon	USA	1.1.65	4	NC	Eugene	19 Jun 93
44.30		Gabriel	Tiacoh	CIV	10.9.63	1	NCAA	Indianapolis	7 Jun 86
44.33		Thomas	Schönlebe	GDR	6.8.65	1	WCh	Roma	3 Sep 87
44.38		Darren	Clark	AUS	6.9.65	3s1	OG	Seoul	26 Sep 88
44.40		Fred	Newhouse	USA	8.11.48	2	OG	Montreal	29 Jul 76
44.41A		Ron	Freeman	USA	12.6.47	3	OG	Ciudad México	18 Oct 68
		(20)							
44.45A		Ronnie	Ray	USA	2.1.54	1	PAm	Ciudad México	18 Oct 75
44.45		Darrell	Robinson	USA	23.12.63	2	Pepsi	Westwood	17 May 86
44.47		Michael	Franks	USA	23.9.63	1	WCp	Canberra	5 Oct 85
44.47		David	Grindley	GBR	29.10.72	4s2	OG	Barcelona	3 Aug 92
44.48		Roddie	Haley	USA	6.12.65	1	SWC	Houston	18 May 86
44.50		Erwin	Skamrahl	FRG	8.3.58	1r1		München	26 Jul 83
44.50		Derek	Redmond	GBR	3.9.65	1s2	WCh	Roma	1 Sep 87
44.50		Bert	Cameron	JAM	16.11.59	4s1	OG	Seoul	26 Sep 88
44.56		Mohamed	Al Malky	OMA	1.12.62	1	HGP	Budapest	12 Aug 88
44.58		Patrick	Delice	TRI	12.11.67	1	NCAA II	Abilene	29 May 93
		(30)							
44.59		Roger	Black	GBR	31.3.66	1	EC	Stuttgart	29 Aug 86
44.59A		Raymond	Pierre	USA	19.9.67	1	NCAA	Provo	3 Jun 89
44.59		Mark	Everett	USA	2.9.68	1	WG	Helsinki	27 Jun 91
44.59A		Derek	Mills	USA	9.7.72	1		Sestriere	31 Jul 94
44.60A		John	Smith	USA	5.8.50	1	PAm	Cali	1 Aug 71
44.60		Viktor	Markin	URS	23.2.57	1	OG	Moskva	30 Jul 80
44.61		Kevin	Robinzine	USA	12.4.66	4	OT	Indianapolis	20 Jul 88
44.63		Sunday	Bada	NGR	22.6.69	3s2	WCh	Stuttgart	16 Aug 93
44.66		Vince	Matthews	USA	16.12.47	1	OG	München	7 Sep 72
44.66		Tyrone	Kemp	USA	4.4.69	1	Gator	Gainesville	8 Apr 89
		(40)							
44.67*		Curtis	Mills	USA	6.10.48	1	NCAA	Knoxville	21 Jun 69
44.68		Sunder	Nix	USA	2.12.61	1	USOF	Indianapolis	24 Jul 82
44.69		Antonio	McKay	USA	9.2.64	4=	WK	Zürich	13 Aug 86
44.70		Karl	Honz	FRG	28.1.51	1	NC	München	21 Jul 72
44.70		Cliff	Wiley	USA	21.5.55	1	TAC	Sacramento	21 Jun 81
44.70		Tim	Simon	USA	11.9.66	1h2	TAC	Norwalk	15 Jun 90
44.71		Andre	Phillips	USA	5.9.59	3	Pepsi	Westwood	17 May 86
44.71		Miles	Murphy	AUS	19.5.67	1	NC	Perth	26 Mar 88
44.72		Hartmut	Weber	FRG	17.10.60	1	EC	Athinai	9 Sep 82
44.73		Willie	Smith	USA	28.2.56	1		Tuscaloosa	15 Apr 78
44.73A		James	Rolle	USA	2.2.64	1	USOF	Air Force Academy	2 Jul 83
44.73		David	Kitur	KEN	12.10.62	3s2	WCh	Roma	1 Sep 87
		(52)							

Mark Wind	Name		Nat	Born	Pos	Meet	Venue	Date
Performance made after positive drugs test and subsequent disqualification								
44.71	Mark	Rowe	USA	28.7.60	2	TAC	Houston	17 Jun 89
Low altitude marks for athletes with bests at high altitude								
44.60	Pierre 1 PAm	Indianapolis 13 Aug 87		44.62	Mills	6	NC Eugene	19 Jun 93
Hand timing								
44.1	Wayne	Collett	USA	20.10.49	1	OT	Eugene	9 Jul 72
44.2*	John	Smith	USA	5.8.50	1	AAU	Eugene	26 Jun 71
44.2	Fred	Newhouse	USA	8.11.48	1s1	OT	Eugene	7 Jul 72
44.4A	Vince	Matthews	USA	16.12.47	1		Echo Summit	31 Aug 68
44.5"	Tommie	Smith	USA	12.6.44	1		San José	20 May 67
44.5A	Kennedy	Ochieng	KEN	30.12.71	1	NC	Nairobi	3 Jul 93
44.6	Adolph	Plummer	USA	3.1.38	1	WAC	Tempe	25 May 63

- 440 yards less 0.3 seconds, " during 440 yards race*

MEN All-time

600 METRES

Mark	Name		Nat	Born	Pos	Meet	Venue	Date
1:12.81	Johnny	Gray	USA	19.6.60	1		Santa Monica	24 May 86
1:13.2+	John	Kipkurgat	KEN	16.3.44	1		Pointe-à-Pierre	23 Mar 74
1:13.80	Earl	Jones	USA	17.7.64	2		Santa Monica	24 May 86
1:14.15	David	Mack	USA	30.5.61	3		Santa Monica	24 May 86
1:14.3 A	Lee	Evans	USA	25.2.47	1		Echo Summit	31 Aug 68
1:14.6 A	Larry	James	USA	6.11.47	2		Echo Summit	31 Aug 68
1:14.8 A	Mark	Winzenried	USA	13.10.49	3		Echo Summit	31 Aug 68
1:14.84	James	Robinson	USA	27.8.54	2		Sacramento	21 Jul 84
1:14.9	Martin	McGrady	USA	20.4.46	1		Melbourne	17 Mar 70
1:14.95	Steve	Heard	GBR	29.4.62	1		London	14 Jul 91
	(10)	*+ during 800 metres race*						

800 METRES

Mark	Name		Nat	Born	Pos	Meet	Venue	Date
1:41.73!	Sebastian	Coe	GBR	29.9.56	1		Firenze	10 Jun 81
1:41.77	Joaquim	Cruz	BRA	12.3.63	1	ASV	Köln	26 Aug 84
1:42.28	Sammy	Koskei	KEN	14.5.61	2	ASV	Köln	26 Aug 84
1:42.33		Coe			1	Bisl	Oslo	5 Jul 79
1:42.34		Cruz			1r1	WK	Zürich	22 Aug 84
1:42.41		Cruz			1	VD	Bruxelles	24 Aug 84
1:42.49		Cruz			1		Koblenz	28 Aug 85
1:42.54		Cruz			1	ASV	Köln	25 Aug 85
1:42.60	Johnny	Gray	USA	19.6.60	2r1		Koblenz	28 Aug 85
1:42.65		Gray			1	WK	Zürich	17 Aug 88
1:42.80		Gray			1	OT	New Orleans	24 Jun 92
1:42.88	Steve	Cram	GBR	14.10.60	1rA	WK	Zürich	21 Aug 85
1:42.96		Gray			1		Koblenz	29 Aug 84
1:42.97	Peter	Elliott	GBR	9.10.62	1		Sevilla	30 May 90
1:42.98		Cruz			1r1	ISTAF	Berlin	23 Aug 85
1:43.00		Cruz			1	OG	Los Angeles	6 Aug 84
1:43.06	Billy	Konchellah	KEN	20.10.61	1	WCh	Roma	1 Sep 87
1:43.07		Coe			2	ASV	Köln	25 Aug 85
1:43.08	José Luiz	Barbosa	BRA	27.5.61	1		Rieti	6 Sep 91
1:43.10		Gray			1	APM	Hengelo	14 Aug 88
1:43.16	Paul	Ereng	KEN	22.8.67	1	WK	Zürich	16 Aug 89
1:43.17	Benson	Koech	KEN	10.11.74	1		Rieti	28 Aug 94
1:43.19		Cram			1		Rieti	7 Sep 86
1:43.20		Barbosa			2	WK	Zürich	17 Aug 88
1:43.22		Cram			1	CG	Edinburgh	31 Jul 86
1:43.22		Ereng			1	Nik	Nice	10 Jul 89
1:43.23		Cruz			2r1	WK	Zürich	21 Aug 85
1:43.28		Gray			2	VD	Bruxelles	24 Aug 84
1:43.28		Gray			3	ASV	Köln	26 Aug 84
1:43.28		Koskei			2		Koblenz	29 Aug 84
	(30/10)							
1:43.29	Wilson	Kipketer	KEN	12.12.70	1	Bisl	Oslo	22 Jul 94
1:43.30	William	Tanui	KEN	22.2.64	2		Rieti	6 Sep 91
1:43.31	Nixon	Kiprotich	KEN	4.12.62	1		Rieti	6 Sep 92
1:43.35	David	Mack	USA	30.5.61	3r1		Koblenz	28 Aug 85
1:43.40	Mark	Everett	USA	2.9.68	1	Bisl	Oslo	4 Jul 92
1:43.44	Alberto	Juantorena	CUB	21.11.50	1	WUG	Sofia	21 Aug 77
1:43.50	Vebjørn	Rodal	NOR	16.9.72	2	Bisl	Oslo	22 Jul 94
1:43.5*	Rick	Wohlhuter	USA	23.12.48	1		Eugene	8 Jun 74

Mark	Wind	Name		Nat	Born	Pos	Meet	Venue	Date
1:43.54		William	Wuycke	VEN	21.5.58	2		Rieti	7 Sep 86
1:43.56		Rob	Druppers	NED	29.4.62	4	ASV	Köln	25 Aug 85
		(20)							
1:43.57		Mike	Boit	KEN	6.1.49	1	ISTAF	Berlin	20 Aug 76
1:43.60		Abdi	Bile	SOM	28.12.62	3	WK	Zürich	16 Aug 89
1:43.62		Earl	Jones	USA	17.7.64	2r1	WK	Zürich	13 Aug 86
1:43.63		Agberto	Guimarães	BRA	18.8.57	3		Koblenz	29 Aug 84
1:43.65		Willi	Wülbeck	FRG	18.12.54	1	WCh	Helsinki	9 Aug 83
1:43.70		Robert	Kibet	KEN	15.12.65	2	Bisl	Oslo	1 Jul 89
1:43.7		Marcello	Fiasconaro	ITA	19.7.49	1	vCS	Milano	27 Jun 73
1:43.84		Olaf	Beyer	GDR	4.8.57	1	EC	Praha	31 Aug 78
1:43.84		Martin	Steele	GBR	20.9.62	1rA	Bisl	Oslo	10 Jul 93
1:43.86		Ivo	Van Damme	BEL	21.2.54	2	OG	Montreal	25 Jul 76
		(30)							
1:43.86		Saïd	Aouita	MAR	2.11.59	1	ASV	Köln	21 Aug 88
1:43.88		Donato	Sabia	ITA	11.9.63	1		Firenze	13 Jun 84
1:43.88		Tom	McKean	GBR	27.10.63	1	vKEN	London	28 Jul 89
1:43.9		José	Marajo	FRA	10.8.54	1		Saint Maur	12 Sep 79
1:43.91		John	Kipkurgat	KEN	16.3.44	1	CG	Christchurch	29 Jan 74
1:43.92		John	Marshall	USA	5.11.63	3	OT	Los Angeles	19 Jun 84
1:43.92		James	Robinson	USA	27.8.54	4	OT	Los Angeles	19 Jun 84
1:43.92		Andrea	Benvenuti	ITA	13.12.69	1	Herc	Monaco	11 Aug 92
1:43.92		Paul	Ruto	KEN	3.11.60	2rA		Rieti	5 Sep 93
1:43.95		Philippe	Collard	FRA	26.2.60	1	Nik	Nice	13 Jul 87
		(40)							
1:43.97		José	Parrilla	USA	31.3.72	3	OT	New Orleans	24 Jun 92
1:43.98		David	Sharpe	GBR	8.7.67	1rB	WK	Zürich	19 Aug 92
1:44.00		George	Kersh	USA	3.7.68	4	OT	New Orleans	24 Jun 92
1:44.03		Peter	Braun	FRG	1.8.62	1r1		Koblenz	6 Aug 86
1:44.06		Moussa	Fall	SEN	28.8.63	4	WK	Zürich	17 Aug 88
1:44.06		Sammy	Langat (Kibet)	KEN	70	3rA		Rieti	5 Sep 93
1:44.07		Luciano	Susanj	YUG	10.11.48	1	EC	Roma	4 Sep 74
1:44.07		David	Kiptoo Singoei	KEN	26.6.65	1		Lappeenranta	26 Jul 94
1:44.09		Steve	Ovett	GBR	9.10.55	2	EC	Praha	31 Aug 78
1:44.10		Vladimir	Graudyn	RUS	26.8.63	1	Bisl	Oslo	2 Jul 88
1:44.10		Ari	Suhonen	FIN	19.12.65	4	WK	Zürich	16 Aug 89
		(51)	*! photo-electric cell time,*	** 880 yards less 0.6 seconds*					

1000 METRES

Mark	Wind	Name		Nat	Born	Pos	Meet	Venue	Date
2:12.18		Sebastian	Coe	GBR	29.9.56	1	OsloG	Oslo	11 Jul 81
2:12.88		Steve	Cram	GBR	14.10.60	1		Gateshead	9 Aug 85
2:13.40			Coe			1	Bisl	Oslo	1 Jul 80
2:13.73		Noureddine	Morceli	ALG	28.2.70	1	BNP	Villeneuve d'Ascq	2 Jul 93
2:13.9		Rick	Wohlhuter	USA	23.12.48	1	King	Oslo	30 Jul 74
2:14.09		Joaquim	Cruz	BRA	12.3.63	1	Nik	Nice	20 Aug 84
2:14.50		Abdi	Bile	SOM	28.12.62	1		Jerez de la Frontera	13 Sep 89
2:14.51			Bile			1	RMPG	London	14 Jul 89
2:14.53		Willi	Wülbeck	FRG	18.12.54	2	Bisl	Oslo	1 Jul 80
2:14.54			Cruz			1	Pre	Eugene	21 Jul 84
		(10/7)							
2:14.95		Sammy	Koskei	KEN	14.5.61	1	VD	Bruxelles	30 Aug 85
2:15.16		Said	Aouita	MAR	2.11.59	1	McV	London	28 Aug 88
2:15.23		Rob	Druppers (10)	NED	29.4.62	1		Utrecht	17 Aug 85
2:15.25		Andreas	Busse	GDR	6.5.59	1		Berlin	31 Jul 83
2:15.3 '		Mike	Boit	KEN	6.1.49	1		Wattenscheid	23 Sep 77
2:15.5		Ivo	Van Damme	BEL	21.2.54	1		Namur	14 Jul 76
2:15.76		Andrea	Benvenuti	ITA	13.12.69	1		Nuoro	12 Sep 92
2:15.81		Agberto	Guimarães	BRA	18.8.57	2		Bern	29 Jul 83
2:15.83		William	Tanui	KEN	22.2.64	1		Auckland	20 Jan 90
2:15.89		Juma	N'diwa	KEN	28.11.60	3	VD	Bruxelles	30 Aug 85
2:15.91		Steve	Ovett	GBR	9.10.55	1		Koblenz	6 Sep 79
2:15.91		Vénuste	Niyongabo	BUR	9.12.73	1		Madrid	6 Sep 94
2:16.0 '		Danie	Malan	RSA	26.6.49	1	HB	München	24 Jun 73
2:16.0		Vladimir	Malozemlin	RUS	26.1.56	1		Kiev	11 Jun 81
		(20)							
2:16.1		Tom	Byers	USA	12.5.55	1		København	6 Aug 81
2:16.13		Fermin	Cacho	ESP	16.2.69	1		Andújar	6 Sep 93
2:16.19		Giuseppe	D'Urso	ITA	15.9.69	1		Parma	15 Sep 93

Mark Wind	Name		Nat	Born	Pos	Meet	Venue	Date
2:16.2	Jürgen	May	GDR	18.6.42	1		Erfurt	20 Jul 65
2:16.2	Franz-Josef	Kemper	FRG	30.9.45	1		Hannover	21 Sep 66
2:16.25	James	Maina Boi	KEN	4.4.54	3	R-W	Koblenz	6 Sep 79
2:16.30	Peter	Elliott	GBR	9.10.62	1		Hamilton	17 Jan 90
2:16.3	James	Robinson	USA	27.8.54	2		København	6 Aug 81
2:16.3	Andreas	Hauck	GDR	19.6.60	1		Potsdam	12 Jul 84
2:16.32	Samuel	Tirop	KEN	13.1.59	2		Auckland	20 Jan 90
	(30)							

MEN All-time

1500 METRES

Mark	Name		Nat	Born	Pos	Meet	Venue	Date
3:28.86	Noureddine	Morceli	ALG	28.2.70	1		Rieti	6 Sep 92
3:29.20		Morceli			1	MedG	Narbonne	20 Jun 93
3:29.46	Saïd	Aouita	MAR	2.11.59	1	ISTAF	Berlin	23 Aug 85
3:29.57+		Morceli			1M		Rieti	5 Sep 93
3:29.67	Steve	Cram	GBR	14.10.60	1	Nik	Nice	16 Jul 85
3:29.71		Aouita			2	Nik	Nice	16 Jul 85
3:29.77	Sebastian	Coe	GBR	29.9.56	1		Rieti	7 Sep 86
3:29.77	Sydney	Maree	USA	9.9.56	1	ASV	Köln	25 Aug 85
3:30.06		Morceli			1A	WK	Zürich	4 Aug 93
3:30.15		Cram			1	VD	Bruxelles	5 Sep 86
3:30.55	Abdi	Bile	SOM	28.12.62	1		Rieti	3 Sep 89
3:30.61		Morceli			1	BNP	Villeneuve d'Ascq	8 Jul 94
3:30.63		Aouita			1	APM	Hengelo	13 Aug 89
3:30.66	Vénuste	Niyongabo	BUR	9.12.73	2	BNP	Villeneuve d'Ascq	8 Jul 94
3:30.69		Aouita			1	Bisl	Oslo	4 Jul 87
3:30.72		Morceli			1	TSB	London	15 Jul 94
3:30.75		Morceli			1rA	WK	Zürich	19 Aug 92
3:30.77	Steve	Ovett	GBR	9.10.55	1		Rieti	4 Sep 83
3:30.92	José Luis	González	ESP	8.12.57	3	Nik	Nice	16 Jul 85
3:30.95		Cram			1	VD	Bruxelles	19 Aug 88
3:30.95		Niyongabo			1	Nik	Nice	18 Jul 94
3:31.00		Morceli			1	WG	Helsinki	27 Jun 91
3:31.00		Morceli			1rA	WK	Zürich	7 Aug 91
3:31.01	Jim	Spivey (10)	USA	7.3.60	1	R-W	Koblenz	28 Aug 88
3:31.01		Morceli			1	DNG	Stockholm	3 Jul 91
3:31.13	José Manuel	Abascal	ESP	17.3.58	1		Barcelona	16 Aug 86
3:31.16		Niyongabo			1	ISTAF	Berlin	30 Aug 94
3:31.20		Bile			1	GG	Pescara	19 Jul 89
3:31.24		Maree			1	ASV	Köln	28 Aug 83
3:31.34		Cram			1	OsloG	Oslo	27 Jun 85
	(30/11)							
3:31.58	Thomas	Wessinghage	FRG	22.2.52	2		Koblenz	27 Aug 80
3:31.75	Pierre	Délèze	SUI	25.9.58	1	WK	Zürich	21 Aug 85
3:31.76	Steve	Scott	USA	5.5.56	4	Nik	Nice	16 Jul 85
3:31.96	Harald	Hudak	FRG	28.1.57	3		Koblenz	27 Aug 80
3:31.96	Simon	Doyle	AUS	9.11.66	2	DNG	Stockholm	3 Jul 91
3:32.01	Fermin	Cacho	ESP	16.2.69	2	WK	Zürich	4 Aug 93
3:32.13	David	Kibet	KEN	24.11.63	2		Rieti	6 Sep 92
3:32.16	Filbert	Bayi	TAN	23.6.53	1	CG	Christchurch	2 Feb 74
3:32.4	John	Walker	NZL	12.1.52	1	OsloG	Oslo	30 Jul 75
	(20)							
3:32.41	William	Kemei	KEN	22.2.69	2rA	WK	Zürich	19 Aug 92
3:32.49	Wilfred	Kirochi	KEN	12.12.66	1	VD	Bruxelles	28 Aug 92
3:32.69	Peter	Elliott	GBR	9.10.62	1	McV	Sheffield	16 Sep 90
3:32.71	Azzeddine	Sediki	MAR	21.5.70	2	Nik	Nice	18 Jul 94
3:32.73	Mohamed	Suleiman	QAT	23.11.69	2	ASV	Köln	21 Aug 94
3:32.77	Jens-Peter	Herold	GER	2.6.65	4		Rieti	6 Sep 92
3:32.78	Gennaro	Di Napoli	ITA	5.3.68	1		Rieti	9 Sep 90
3:33.07	Kipkoech	Cheruiyot	KEN	2.12.64	1		Grosseto	10 Aug 86
3:33.1	Jim	Ryun	USA	29.4.47	1	vComm	Los Angeles	8 Jul 67
3:33.12	Joseph	Chesire	KEN	12.11.57	2	Nik	Nice	15 Jul 92
	(30)							
3:33.16	Ben	Jipcho	KEN	1.3.43	3	CG	Christchurch	2 Feb 74
3:33.28	Omer	Khalifa	SUD	18.12.56	2		Grosseto	10 Aug 86
3:33.34	Steve	Crabb	GBR	30.11.63	3	Bisl	Oslo	4 Jul 87
3:33.36	Jonah	Birir	KEN	12.12.71	5	VD	Bruxelles	28 Aug 92
3:33.39	Mike	Hillardt	AUS	22.1.61	4	ISTAF	Berlin	23 Aug 85

Mark	Wind	Name		Nat	Born	Pos	Meet	Venue	Date
3:33.5+		Ray	Flynn	IRL	22.1.57	2	OsloG	Oslo	7 Jul 82
3:33.54		Dieter	Baumann	FRG	9.2.65	2rA	R-W	Koblenz	13 Aug 87
3:33.54		Hervé	Phélippeau	FRA	16.9.62	2	GG	Bologna	18 Jul 90
3:33.56		Johan	Landsman	RSA	12.5.64	6	WK	Zürich	4 Aug 93
3:33.6+		Joe	Falcon	USA	23.6.66	3	Bisl	Oslo	14 Jul 90
		(40)							
3:33.61		Hicham	El Guerrouj	MAR	14.9.74	3	Nik	Nice	18 Jul 94
3:33.67+		Mike	Boit	KEN	6.1.49	2	VD	Bruxelles	28 Aug 81
3:33.68		Jürgen	Straub	GDR	3.11.53	1		Potsdam	31 Aug 79
3:33.74		Willi	Wülbeck	FRG	18.12.54	4		Koblenz	27 Aug 80
3:33.79		David	Moorcroft	GBR	10.4.53	1	FBK	Hengelo	27 Jul 82
3:33.83		John	Robson	GBR	31.1.57	2	VD	Bruxelles	4 Sep 79
3:33.87		Johan	Fourie	RSA	2.12.59	1	NC	Stellenbosch	10 Apr 87
3:33.89		Rod	Dixon	NZL	13.7.50	4	CG	Christchurch	2 Feb 74
3:33.99		Steve	Lacy	USA	17.1.56	4	OsloG	Oslo	15 Jul 80
3:33.99		Todd	Harbour	USA	24.3.59	2	WK	Zürich	18 Aug 82
		(50)	*+ during mile race*						

1 MILE

Mark	Wind	Name		Nat	Born	Pos	Meet	Venue	Date
3:44.39		Noureddine	Morceli	ALG	28.2.70	1		Rieti	5 Sep 93
3:46.32		Steve	Cram	GBR	14.10.60	1	Bisl	Oslo	27 Jul 85
3:46.76		Saïd	Aouita	MAR	2.11.59	1	WG	Helsinki	2 Jul 87
3:46.78			Morceli			1	ISTAF	Berlin	27 Aug 93
3:46.92			Aouita			1	WK	Zürich	21 Aug 85
3:47.30			Morceli			1	VD	Bruxelles	3 Sep 93
3:47.33		Sebastian	Coe	GBR	29.9.56	1	VD	Bruxelles	28 Aug 81
3:47.69		Steve	Scott	USA	5.5.56	1	OsloG	Oslo	7 Jul 82
3:47.78			Morceli			1	Bisl	Oslo	10 Jul 93
3:47.79		José Luis	González	ESP	8.12.57	2	Bisl	Oslo	27 Jul 85
3:48.31			Cram			1	Bisl	Oslo	5 Jul 86
3:48.40		Steve	Ovett	GBR	9.10.55	1	R-W	Koblenz	26 Aug 81
3:48.53			Coe			1	WK	Zürich	19 Aug 81
3:48.53			Scott			1	Bisl	Oslo	26 Jun 82
3:48.67			Morceli			1	GWG	St Peterburg	26 Jul 94
3:48.73			Scott			2	Bisl	Oslo	5 Jul 86
3:48.8			Ovett			1	Bisl	Oslo	1 Jul 80
3:48.80		William	Kemei	KEN	22.2.69	1	ISTAF	Berlin	21 Aug 92
3:48.83		Sydney	Maree	USA	9.9.56	1		Rieti	9 Sep 81
3:48.85			Maree			2	Bisl	Oslo	26 Jun 82
3:48.85			Cram			1	Bisl	Oslo	2 Jul 88
3:48.94		Vénuste	Niyongabo	BUR	9.12.73	1	Bisl	Oslo	22 Jul 94
3:48.95			Coe			1	OsloG	Oslo	17 Jul 79
		(23/10)							
3:49.08		John	Walker	NZL	12.1.52	2	OsloG	Oslo	7 Jul 82
3:49.20		Peter	Elliott	GBR	9.10.62	2	Bisl	Oslo	2 Jul 88
3:49.22		Jens-Peter	Herold	GDR	2.6.65	3	Bisl	Oslo	2 Jul 88
3:49.31		Joe	Falcon	USA	23.6.66	1	Bisl	Oslo	14 Jul 90
3:49.34		David	Moorcroft	GBR	10.4.53	3	Bisl	Oslo	26 Jun 82
3:49.40		Abdi	Bile	SOM	28.12.62	4	Bisl	Oslo	2 Jul 88
3:49.45		Mike	Boit	KEN	6.1.49	2	VD	Bruxelles	28 Aug 81
3:49.77		Ray	Flynn	IRL	22.1.57	3	OsloG	Oslo	7 Jul 82
3:49.77		Wilfred	Kirochi	KEN	12.12.69	2	Bisl	Oslo	6 Jul 91
3:49.80		Jim	Spivey	USA	7.3.60	3	Bisl	Oslo	5 Jul 86
		(20)							
3:49.91		Simon	Doyle	AUS	9.11.66	4	Bisl	Oslo	6 Jul 91
3:49.98		Thomas	Wessinghage	FRG	22.2.52	3	ISTAF	Berlin	17 Aug 83
3:50.34		Todd	Harbour	USA	24.3.59	5	OsloG	Oslo	11 Jul 81
3:50.38		Pierre	Délèze	SUI	25.9.58	4	R-W	Koblenz	25 Aug 82
3:50.52		Hauke	Fuhlbrügge	GER	21.3.66	6	Bisl	Oslo	6 Jul 91
3:50.54		José Manuel	Abascal	ESP	17.3.58	2	GP-GG	Roma	10 Sep 86
3:50.64		Graham	Williamson	GBR	15.6.60	4		Cork	13 Jul 82
3:50.73		Wilson	Waigwa	KEN	15.2.49	2	R-W	Koblenz	31 Aug 83
3:50.74		Fermin	Cacho	ESP	16.2.69	7	Bisl	Oslo	6 Jul 91
3:50.82		Johan	Fourie	RSA	2.12.59	1		Port Elizabeth	11 Mar 87
		(30)							
3:50.84		Tom	Byers	USA	12.5.55	6	R-W	Koblenz	25 Aug 82
3:50.91		Steve	Holman	USA	2.3.70	3	Bisl	Oslo	22 Jul 94

Mark Wind	Name		Nat	Born	Pos	Meet	Venue	Date
3:50.98	José	Marajo	FRA	10.8.54	4	OsloG	Oslo	9 Jul 83
3:51.0	Filbert	Bayi	TAN	23.6.53	1	King	Kingston	17 May 75
3:51.02	John	Gladwin	GBR	7.5.63	2	WK	Zürich	19 Aug 87
3:51.06	Frank	O'Mara	IRL	17.7.60	4	GP-GG	Roma	10 Sep 86
3:51.1	Jim	Ryun	USA	29.4.47	1	AAU	Bakersfield	23 Jun 67
3:51.12	Dieter	Baumann	GER	9.2.65	3	ISTAF	Berlin	21 Aug 92
3:51.31	Tony	Morrell	GBR	3.5.62	4	Bisl	Oslo	14 Jul 90
3:51.32	Mohamed	Suleiman	QAT	23.11.69	4	Bisl	Oslo	22 Jul 94
	(40)							
Indoor marks								
3:49.78	Eamonn	Coghlan	IRL	24.11.52	1		East Rutherford	27 Feb 83
3:50.94	Marcus	O'Sullivan	IRL	22.12.61	1		East Rutherford	13 Feb 88

2000 METRES

Mark	Name		Nat	Born	Pos	Meet	Venue	Date
4:50.81	Saïd	Aouita	MAR	2.11.59	1	BNP	Paris	16 Jul 87
4:51.39	Steve	Cram	GBR	14.10.60	1	BGP	Budapest	4 Aug 85
4:51.52	John	Walker	NZL	12.1.52	1	Bisl	Oslo	30 Jun 76
4:51.98		Aouita			1	VD	Bruxelles	5 Sep 86
4:52.20	Thomas	Wessinghage	FRG	22.2.52	1		Ingelheim	31 Aug 82
4:52.40	José Manuel	Abascal	ESP	17.3.58	1		Santander	7 Sep 86
4:52.44	Jim	Spivey	USA	7.3.60	1	Athl	Lausanne	15 Sep 87
4:52.53	Moses	Kiptanui	KEN	1.10.71	1	ISTAF	Berlin	21 Aug 92
4:52.82	Peter	Elliott	GBR	9.10.62	2	Athl	Lausanne	15 Sep 87
4:53.06	Jack	Buckner	GBR	22.9.61	3	Athl	Lausanne	15 Sep 87
4:53.69	Gary	Staines (10)	GBR	3.7.63	4	Athl	Lausanne	15 Sep 87
4:54.02		Aouita			1		Rieti	4 Sep 85
4:54.20	Sydney	Maree	USA	9.9.56	2		Rieti	4 Sep 85
4:54.46	Pierre	Délèze	SUI	25.9.58	5	Athl	Lausanne	15 Sep 87
4:54.71	Steve	Scott	USA	5.5.56	2		Ingelheim	31 Aug 82
4:54.88		Abascal			1		Santander	3 Sep 85
4:54.98		Aouita			1		Madrid	4 Jun 85
	(17/13)							
4:55.0	Gennaro	Di Napoli	ITA	5.3.68			Torino	26 May 91
4:55.31	David	Kibet	KEN	24.11.63	2	ISTAF	Berlin	21 Aug 92
4:56.1	Michel	Jazy	FRA	13.6.36	1		Saint Maur	12 Oct 66
4:56.41	Johan	Fourie	RSA	2.12.59	1		Stellenbosch	22 Apr 85
4:56.70	Pascal	Thiébaut	FRA	6.6.59	2	BNP	Paris	16 Jul 87
4:57.1	Willy	Polleunis	BEL	27.12.47	1		Louvain	21 Sep 78
4:57.53	José Luis	Carreira	ESP	30.3.62	2		Santander	7 Sep 86
	(20)							
4:57.66	Eamonn	Coghlan	IRL	24.11.52	1		London	29 Aug 83
4:57.71	Steve	Ovett	GBR	9.10.55	1	OsloG	Oslo	7 Jul 82
4:57.8	Harald	Norpoth	FRG	22.8.42	1		Hagen	10 Sep 66
4:57.83	Jens-Peter	Herold	GER	2.6.65	3	ISTAF	Berlin	21 Aug 92
4:58.08	Marcus	O'Sullivan	IRL	22.12.61	3	McV	London	28 Aug 88
4:58.1	Francis	González	FRA	6.2.52	1		Rennes	22 Jun 79
4:58.15	Vénuste	Niyongabo	BUR	9.12.73	1		Noisy le Grand	3 Jul 93
4:58.21	Noureddine	Morceli	ALG	28.2.70	1		St Denis	4 Jun 92
4:58.29	Peter	Wirz	SUI	29.7.60	2		Langenthal	27 Jul 84
4:58.38	Graham	Williamson	GBR	15.6.60	2		London	29 Aug 83
	(30)							
Indoor marks								
4:54.07	Eamonn	Coghlan	IRL	24.11.52	1		Inglewood	20 Feb 87
4:56.23	Jens-Peter	Herold	GER	2.6.65	1		Karlsruhe	6 Mar 93

3000 METRES

Mark	Name		Nat	Born	Pos	Meet	Venue	Date
7:25.11	Noureddine	Morceli	ALG	28.2.70	1	Herc	Monaco	2 Aug 94
7:28.96	Moses	Kiptanui	KEN	1.10.71	1	ASV	Köln	16 Aug 92
7:29.24		Morceli			1	Herc	Monaco	7 Aug 93
7:29.45	Saïd	Aouita	MAR	2.11.59	1	ASV	Köln	20 Aug 89
7:32.1	Henry	Rono	KEN	12.2.52	1	Bisl	Oslo	27 Jun 78
7:32.23		Aouita			1	ASV	Köln	17 Aug 86
7:32.54		Aouita			1	WK	Zürich	13 Aug 86
7:32.79	David	Moorcroft	GBR	10.4.53	1		London	17 Jul 82
7:32.94		Aouita			1	VD	Bruxelles	30 Aug 85
7:33.28	Paul	Bitok	KEN	26.6.70	2	ASV	Köln	16 Aug 92
7:33.3		Aouita			1	VD	Bruxelles	24 Aug 84

Mark	Wind	Name		Nat	Born	Pos	Meet	Venue	Date
7:33.37		Sydney	Maree	USA	9.9.56	2		London	17 Jul 82
7:33.91		Dieter	Baumann	GER	9.2.65	1	ASV	Köln	8 Sep 91
7:34.18		Yobes	Ondieki	KEN	21.2.61	3	ASV	Köln	16 Aug 92
7:34.36			Bitok			1	Nik	Nice	18 Jul 94
7:34.69			Baumann			1	ASV	Köln	21 Aug 94
7:34.74			Ondieki			2	ASV	Köln	8 Sep 91
7:34.74			Morceli			1		Narbonne	19 Jun 94
7:34.79			Aouita			1	Bisl	Oslo	1 Jul 89
7:34.98			Bitok			1	ASV	Köln	1 Aug 93
7:35.00			Bitok			1	Nik	Nice	15 Jul 92
7:35.01			Ondieki			1	Nik	Nice	10 Jul 89
7:35.08		Aloÿs	Nizigama (10)	BUR	18.6.66	2	Nik	Nice	18 Jul 94
7:35.1		Brendan	Foster	GBR	12.1.48	1		Gateshead	3 Aug 74
7:35.23			Kiptanui			3	Nik	Nice	18 Jul 94
7:35.33		Bob	Kennedy	USA	18.8.70	4	Nik	Nice	18 Jul 94
7:35.43			Ondieki			1	BNP	Villeneuve d'Ascq	25 Jun 89
7:35.47			Kiptanui			2	Nik	Nice	15 Jul 92
7:35.71		Arturo	Barrios	MEX	12.12.63	2	Nik	Nice	10 Jul 89
7:35.79			Kiptanui			2	ASV	Köln	1 Aug 93
		(30/13)							
7:35.84		Doug	Padilla	USA	4.10.56	1	OsloG	Oslo	9 Jul 83
7:36.54		Brahim	Jabbour	MAR	1.1.70	2	Herc	Monaco	7 Aug 93
7:36.69		Steve	Scott	USA	5.5.56	1		Ingelheim	1 Sep 81
7:36.75		Thomas	Wessinghage	FRG	22.2.52	2		Ingelheim	1 Sep 81
7:36.76		Khalid	Skah	MAR	29.1.67	3	ASV	Köln	21 Aug 94
7:37.04		Jim	Spivey	USA	7.3.60	3	ASV	Köln	1 Aug 93
7:37.49		John	Walker	NZL	12.1.52	3		London	17 Jul 82
		(20)							
7:37.49		Haile	Gebrselassie	ETH	18.4.73	2	Herc	Monaco	2 Aug 94
7:37.6		Emiel	Puttemans	BEL	8.10.47	1		Århus	14 Sep 72
7:37.60		Eamonn	Coghlan	IRL	24.11.52	1	Bisl	Oslo	1 Jul 80
7:37.70		Rudy	Chapa	USA	7.11.57	1		Eugene	10 May 79
7:37.73		William	Sigei	KEN	14.10.69	3	Herc	Monaco	7 Aug 93
7:37.74		Cyrille	Laventure	FRA	29.3.64	2	ASV	Köln	19 Aug 90
7:38.03		Marc	Davis	USA	17.12.69	4	Herc	Monaco	7 Aug 93
7:38.14		Salah	Hissou	MAR	72	4	ASV	Köln	21 Aug 94
7:38.20		Mohamed	Suleiman	QAT	23.11.69	1	ISTAF	Berlin	27 Aug 93
7:38.39		M. Brahim	Boutayeb	MAR	15.8.67	2	Nik	Nice	15 Jul 91
		(30)							
7:38.70		Aïssa	Belaout	ALG	12.8.68	5	Herc	Monaco	7 Aug 93
7:39.09		Peter	Koech	KEN	18.2.58	4		London	17 Jul 82
7:39.12		Atiq	Naaji	FRA	21.11.66	2		Narbonne	19 Jun 94
7:39.27		Filbert	Bayi	TAN	23.6.53	3	Bisl	Oslo	1 Jul 80
7:39.29		Abdellah	Béhar	FRA	5.7.63	3	Herc	Monaco	2 Aug 94
7:39.30		Mohamed	Issangar	MAR	12.12.64	5	ASV	Köln	1 Aug 93
7:39.38		Paul	Kipkoech	KEN	6.1.63	2	ASV	Köln	17 Aug 86
7:39.41		Vincent	Rousseau	BEL	29.7.62	4	Nik	Nice	10 Jul 89
7:39.5		Kipchoge	Keino	KEN	17.1.40	1		Hälsingborg	27 Aug 65
7:39.55		Robert	Denmark	GBR	23.11.68	6	ASV	Köln	1 Aug 93
		(40)							
7:39.69		António	Leitão	POR	22.7.60	2	VD	Bruxelles	26 Aug 83
7:39.82		Ismael	Kirui	KEN	20.2.75	4	ISTAF	Berlin	27 Aug 93
7:40.06		Fita	Bayissa	ETH	15.12.72	6	ASV	Köln	21 Aug 94
7:40.11		Stephane	Franke	GER	12.2.64	5	ISTAF	Berlin	27 Aug 93
7:40.19		Bill	McChesney	USA	8.1.59	2	ASV	Köln	22 Aug 82
7:40.3		Suleiman	Nyambui	TAN	13.2.53	2	Bisl	Oslo	27 Jun 78
7:40.31		Brahim	Lahlafi	MAR	15.4.68	3		Narbonne	19 Jun 94
7:40.4		Nick	Rose	GBR	30.12.51	3	Bisl	Oslo	27 Jun 78
7:40.41		Frank	O'Mara	IRL	17.7.60	5	Nik	Nice	10 Jul 89
7:40.43		Jack	Buckner	GBR	22.9.61	1	Bisl	Oslo	5 Jul 86
		(50)							

2 MILES

Mark	Wind	Name		Nat	Born	Pos	Meet	Venue	Date
8:09.01		Moses	Kiptanui	KEN	10.10.71	1		Hechtel	30 Jul 94
8:12.17		Khalid	Skah	MAR	29.1.67	1		Hechtel	31 Jul 93
8:12.74		Marc	Davis	USA	17.12.69	1		Göteborg	24 Aug 94
8:13.45		Saïd	Aouita	MAR	2.11.59	1		Torino	28 May 87
8:13.51		Steve	Ovett	GBR	9.10.55	1	IAC	London	15 Sep 78

Mark	Wind	Name		Nat	Born	Pos	Meet	Venue	Date

5000 METRES

Mark	Name		Nat	Born	Pos	Meet	Venue	Date
12:56.96	Haile	Gebrselassie	ETH	18.4.73	1	APM	Hengelo	4 Jun 94
12:58.39	Saïd	Aouita	MAR	2.11.59	1	GG	Roma	22 Jul 87
13:00.40		Aouita			1	Bisl	Oslo	27 Jul 85
13:00.41	David	Moorcroft	GBR	10.4.53	1	OsloG	Oslo	7 Jul 82
13:00.54	Khalid	Skah	MAR	29.1.67	1	BNP	Villeneuve d'Ascq	8 Jul 94
13:00.86		Aouita			1		La Coruña	6 Aug 86
13:00.93	Moses	Kiptanui	KEN	1.10.71	1	VD	Bruxelles	28 Aug 92
13:01.15	Sydney	Maree	USA	9.9.56	2	Bisl	Oslo	27 Jul 85
13:01.82	Yobes	Ondieki	KEN	21.2.61	1	WK	Zürich	7 Aug 91
13:01.89		Skah			1	Bisl	Oslo	22 Jul 94
13:02.75	Ismael	Kirui	KEN	20.2.75	1	WCh	Stuttgart	16 Aug 93
13:02.93	Bob	Kennedy	USA	18.8.70	2	Bisl	Oslo	22 Jul 94
13:03.17		Gebrselassie			2	WCh	Stuttgart	16 Aug 93
13:03.36	Brahim	Lahlafi (10)	MAR	15.4.68	3	Bisl	Oslo	22 Jul 94
13:03.58		Ondieki			1	Athl	Lausanne	8 Jul 92
13:03.85	Noureddine	Morceli	ALG	28.2.70	1	WK	Zürich	17 Aug 94
13:04.24		Ondieki			1	Bisl	Oslo	1 Jul 89
13:04.52		Aouita			1	OsloG	Oslo	27 Jun 85
13:04.67		Skah			1	WK	Zürich	4 Aug 93
13:04.78		Aouita			1		Firenze	13 Jun 84
13:04.93	Salah	Hissou	MAR	72	4	Bisl	Oslo	22 Jul 94
13:05.09		Ondieki			2	WK	Zürich	4 Aug 93
13:05.14	Richard	Chelimo	KEN	21.4.72	3	WK	Zürich	4 Aug 93
13:05.39		Gebrselassie			4	WK	Zürich	4 Aug 93
13:05.40	Fita	Bayissa	ETH	15.12.72	3	WCh	Stuttgart	16 Aug 93
13:05.59		Aouita			1	OG	Los Angeles	11 Aug 84
13:05.59	Salvatore	Antibo	ITA	7.2.62	1	GG	Bologna	18 Jul 90
13:05.60		Ondieki			1	VD	Bruxelles	10 Aug 90
13:05.93		Kennedy			2	BNP	Villeneuve d'Ascq	8 Jul 94
13:06.20	Henry	Rono	KEN	12.2.52	1		Knarvik	13 Sep 81
	(30/16)							
13:06.64	Worku	Bikila	ETH	70	4	WCh	Stuttgart	16 Aug 93
13:06.72	William	Sigei	KEN	11.10.69	1	TSB	London	15 Jul 94
13:06.76	Francesco	Panetta	ITA	10.1.63	6	WK	Zürich	4 Aug 93
13:07.29	Wodajo	Bulti	ETH	11.3.57	1		Rieti	16 Sep 82
	(20)							
13:07.30	Paul	Bitok	KEN	26.6.70	2	TSB	London	15 Jul 94
13:07.54	Markus	Ryffel	SUI	5.2.55	2	OG	Los Angeles	11 Aug 84
13:07.57	Simon	Chemoiywo	KEN	2.5.69	1	Herc	Monaco	2 Aug 94
13:07.70	António	Leitão	POR	22.7.60	2		Rieti	16 Sep 82
13:07.79	Arturo	Barrios	MEX	12.12.63	1	RMPG	London	14 Jul 89
13:08.03	Aïssa	Belaout	ALG	12.8.68	2	BNP	Villeneuve d'Ascq	2 Jul 93
13:08.51	Mohamed	Issangar	MAR	12.12.64	1	PG	London	20 Jul 90
13:08.54	Fernando	Mamede	POR	1.11.51	1		Tokyo	17 Sep 83
13:08.86	Brahim	Jabbour	MAR	1.1.70	3	BNP	Villeneuve d'Ascq	2 Jul 93
13:09.03	Dieter	Baumann	GER	9.2.65	1	Expo	Sevilla	6 Jun 92
	(30)							
13:09.50	Peter	Koech	KEN	18.2.58	2	DNG	Stockholm	6 Jul 82
13:09.76	Ibrahim	Kinuthia	KEN	22.5.63	1	GGala	Roma	17 Jul 91
13:09.80	Ian	Hamer	GBR	18.4.65	1	GGala	Roma	9 Jun 92
13:10.06	Alberto	Cova	ITA	1.12.58	3	Bisl	Oslo	27 Jul 85
13:10.15	Jack	Buckner	GBR	22.9.61	1	EC	Stuttgart	31 Aug 86
13:10.24	Robert	Denmark	GBR	23.11.68	3	GGala	Roma	9 Jun 92
13:10.40	Hansjörg	Kunze	GDR	28.12.59	1		Rieti	9 Sep 81
13:10.44	M Brahim	Boutayeb	MAR	15.8.67	3	GGala	Roma	17 Jul 91
13:10.66	Ezekel	Bitok	KEN	15.2.66	1	GGala	Roma	9 Jun 93
13:10.88	Jonah	Koech	KEN	2.2.68	6	GGala	Roma	9 Jun 92
	(40)							
13:10.99	Vincent	Rousseau	BEL	29.7.62	3	Bisl	Oslo	10 Jul 93
13:11.14	John	Ngugi	KEN	10.5.62	2	VD	Bruxelles	10 Aug 90
13:11.29	Mathias	Ntawulikura	RWA	14.7.64	7	GGala	Roma	9 Jun 92
13:11.50	Tim	Hutchings	GBR	4.12.58	4	OG	Los Angeles	11 Aug 84
13:11.57	Stefano	Mei	ITA	3.2.63	2	EC	Stuttgart	31 Aug 86
13:11.69	Hammou	Boutayeb	MAR	.56	2	DNG	Stockholm	2 Jul 90
13:11.77	Ondoro	Osoro	KEN	3.12.67	5	GGala	Roma	17 Jul 91

Mark	Wind	Name		Nat	Born	Pos	Meet	Venue	Date
13:11.89		Kibiego	Kororia	KEN	25.12.71	3	GGala	Roma	9 Jun 93
13:11.93		Alberto	Salazar	USA	7.8.58	3	DNG	Stockholm	6 Jul 82
13:11.99		Valeriy	Abramov	RUS	22.8.56	2		Rieti	9 Sep 81
		(50)							

10000 METRES

Mark	Wind	Name		Nat	Born	Pos	Meet	Venue	Date
26:52.23		William	Sigei	KEN	11.10.69	1	Bisl	Oslo	22 Jul 94
26:58.38		Yobes	Ondieki	KEN	21.2.61	1	Bisl	Oslo	10 Jul 93
27:07.91		Richard	Chelimo	KEN	21.4.72	1	DNG	Stockholm	5 Jul 93
27:08.23		Arturo	Barrios	MEX	12.12.63	1	ISTAF	Berlin	18 Aug 89
27:11.18			Chelimo			1	APM	Hengelo	25 Jun 91
27:11.62		John	Ngugi	KEN	10.5.62	1	VD	Bruxelles	13 Sep 91
27:13.81		Fernando	Mamede	POR	1.11.51	1	DNG	Stockholm	2 Jul 84
27:14.26		Fita	Bayissa	ETH	15.12.72	1	Bisl	Oslo	4 Jul 92
27:15.00		Haile	Gebrselassie	ETH	18.4.73	1	Athl	Lausanne	6 Jul 94
27:15.53			Chelimo			2	Bisl	Oslo	4 Jul 92
27:16.50		Salvatore	Antibo	ITA	7.2.62	1	WG	Helsinki	29 Jun 89
27:16.81			Sigei			2	Bisl	Oslo	10 Jul 93
27:17.20		William	Kiptum (10)	KEN	71	2	Bisl	Oslo	22 Jul 94
27:17.48		Carlos	Lopes	POR	18.2.47	2	DNG	Stockholm	2 Jul 84
27:17.74		Khalid	Skah	MAR	29.1.67	1	VD	Bruxelles	3 Sep 93
27:17.82		Addis	Abebe	ETH	.70	2	WG	Helsinki	29 Jun 89
27:18.22			Barrios			1	ISTAF	Berlin	17 Aug 90
27:18.32		Moses	Tanui	KEN	20.8.65	2	VD	Bruxelles	3 Sep 93
27:18.43		Paul	Tergat	KEN	17.6.69	3	VD	Bruxelles	3 Sep 93
27:18.45			Barrios			1	DNG	Stockholm	3 Jul 89
27:18.59		Armando	Quintanilla	MEX	19.4.68	3	Bisl	Oslo	22 Jul 94
27:19.15			Ngugi			1		Koblenz	4 Sep 90
27:20.39			Gebrsilassie			1	VD	Bruxelles	19 Aug 94
27:20.51		Aloÿs	Nizigama	BUR	18.6.66	4	Bisl	Oslo	22 Jul 94
27:20.56		Mark	Nenow	USA	16.11.57	1	VD	Bruxelles	5 Sep 86
27:21.22			Chelimo			4	VD	Bruxelles	3 Sep 93
27:21.46		M.Brahim	Boutayeb	MAR	15.8.67	1	OG	Seoul	26 Sep 88
27:21.75		Salah	Hissou	MAR	72	2	VD	Bruxelles	19 Aug 94
27:22.06			Nizigama			3	VD	Bruxelles	19 Aug 94
27:22.47#		Henry	Rono	KEN	12.2.52	1		Wien	11 Jun 78
		(30/21)							
27:22.78		Antonio	Martins	FRA	23.8.63	3	Bisl	Oslo	4 Jul 92
27:23.06		Eamonn	Martin	GBR	9.10.58	1	Bisl	Oslo	2 Jul 88
27:23.18		Vincent	Rousseau	BEL	29.7.62	5	VD	Bruxelles	3 Sep 93
27:24.16		Francesco	Panetta	ITA	10.1.63	3	WG	Helsinki	29 Jun 89
27:24.24		Ondoro	Osoro	KEN	3.12.67	6	VD	Bruxelles	3 Sep 93
27:24.95		Werner	Schildhauer	GDR	5.6.59	1	NC	Jena	28 May 83
27:25.16		Kipkemboi	Kimeli	KEN	30.11.66	3	OG	Seoul	26 Sep 88
27:25.48		Hammou	Boutayeb	MAR	.56	2	Bisl	Oslo	14 Jul 90
		(30)							
27:25.61		Alberto	Salazar	USA	7.8.58	2	Bisl	Oslo	26 Jun 82
27:26.00		Hansjörg	Kunze	GDR	28.12.59	4	Bisl	Oslo	2 Jul 88
27:26.11		Saïd	Aouita	MAR	2.11.59	1	Bisl	Oslo	5 Jul 86
27:26.95		Alex	Hagelsteens	BEL	15.7.56	3	Bisl	Oslo	26 Jun 82
27:28.87		Thomas	Osano	KEN	4.6.70	3	Bisl	Oslo	6 Jul 91
27:29.16		Craig	Virgin	USA	2.8.55	1		Paris	17 Jul 80
27:29.41		Wodajo	Bulti	ETH	11.3.57	1	WG	Helsinki	2 Jul 87
27:30.3 '		Brendan	Foster	GBR	12.1.48	1	AAA	London	23 Jun 78
27:30.47		Samson	Kimobwa	KEN	15.9.55	1	WG	Helsinki	30 Jun 77
27:30.80		David	Bedford	GBR	30.12.49	1	AAA	London	13 Jul 73
		(40)							
27:30.99		Martti	Vainio ¶	FIN	30.12.50	1	EC	Praha	29 Aug 78
27:31.16		Thierry	Pantel	FRA	6.7.64	3	Bisl	Oslo	14 Jul 90
27:31.19		Nick	Rose	GBR	30.12.51	3	OsloG	Oslo	9 Jul 83
27:31.48		Venanzio	Ortis	ITA	29.1.55	2	EC	Praha	29 Aug 78
27:31.52		Aleksandr	Antipov	LIT	9.3.55	3	EC	Praha	29 Aug 78
27:32.52		Are	Nakkim	NOR	13.2.64	4	Bisl	Oslo	14 Jul 90
27:34.38		Jean-Louis	Prianon	FRA	22.2.60	2	WG	Helsinki	2 Jul 87
27:34.53		Domingos	Castro	POR	22.11.63	3	DNG	Stockholm	5 Jul 93
27:34.58		Julian	Goater	GBR	12.1.53	5	Bisl	Oslo	26 Jun 82
27:34.96		Julius	Korir -2	KEN	12.5.58	1	ISTAF	Berlin	10 Sep 91
		(50)							

Mark Wind	Name		Nat	Born	Pos	Meet	Venue	Date

HALF MARATHON

Included in these lists are the slightly downhill courses: Newcastle to South Shields 30.5m, Tokyo 33m. Lisboa 40m

Mark	Name		Nat	Born	Pos	Meet	Venue	Date
59:47	Moses	Tanui	KEN	20.8.65	1		Milano	3 Apr 93
60:02	Benson	Masya	KEN	14.5.70	1	GNR	South Shields	18 Sep 94
60:03		Tanui			2	GNR	South Shields	18 Sep 94
60:06	Steve	Moneghetti	AUS	26.9.62	1		Tokyo	24 Jan 93
60:11	Matthews	Temane	RSA	14.12.60	1	NC	East London	25 Jul 87
60:11	Zithulele	Singe	RSA	9.6.63	2	NC	East London	25 Jul 87
60:11	Todd	Williams	USA	7.3.69	2		Tokyo	24 Jan 93
60:13	Paul	Tergat	KEN	17.6.69	1	Stra	Milano	16 Apr 94
60:15		Tanui			1		South Shields	19 Sep 93
60:17	Dionicio	Ceron	MEX	9.10.65	3		Tokyo	24 Jan 93
60:23	Vincent	Rousseau	BEL	29.7.62	1		Tokyo	23 Jan 94
60:24		Masya			1	WCh	South Shields	20 Sep 92
60:24		Masya			1		Den Haag	3 Apr 93
60:27		Moneghetti			1		Tokyo	26 Jan 92
60:27	Khalid	Skah (10)	MAR	29.1.67	1	WCh	Oslo	24 Sep 94
60:28		Ceron			2		Tokyo	23 Jan 94
60:28	German	Silva	MEX	9.1.68	2	WCh	Oslo	24 Sep 94
60:31*	Julius	Korir	KEN	12.5.58	1		Remich	22 Sep 91
60:33*	Joseph	Keino	KEN	.63	2		Remich	22 Sep 91
60:34		Moneghetti			1	GNR	South Shields	16 Sep 90
	(20/13)							
60:34	Carsten	Eich	GER	9.1.70	1		Berlin	4 Apr 93
60:40	Antonio	Silio	ARG	9.5.66	2	WCh	South Shields	20 Sep 92
60:42	Arturo	Barrios	MEX	12.12.62	2		Tokyo	26 Jan 92
60:42	Andrew	Masai	KEN	13.12.60	2		Milano	3 Apr 93
60:42	Sammy	Lelei	KEN	14.8.64	2		Berlin	4 Apr 93
60:43	Mike	Musyoki	KEN	28.5.56	1	GNR	South Shields	8 Jun 86
60:45	Boay	Akonay	TAN	3.1.70	3	WCh	South Shields	20 Sep 92
	(20)							
60:47	Carlos	Monteiro	POR	14.12.65	1		Setúbal	4 Apr 93
60:50	Zablon	Miano	KEN		2		Den Haag	3 Apr 93
60:51	Domingos	Castro	POR	22.11.63	2		Setúbal	4 Apr 93
60:54	Carlos	Patricio	POR	9.1.64	3		Setúbal	4 Apr 93
60:54	Ronaldo	da Costa	BRA	7.6.70	3	WCh	Oslo	24 Sep 94
60:55	Mark	Curp	USA	5.1.59	1		Philadelphia	18 Sep 85
60:55	Lameck	Aguta	KEN	10.10.71	4	WCh	South Shields	20 Sep 92
60:56	Xolile	Yawa	RSA	29.9.62	3	NC	East London	25 Jul 87
60:58	Lawrence	Peu	RSA	13.2.66	1	NC	East London	18 May 91
60:59	Steve	Jones	GBR	4.8.55	2	GNR	South Shields	8 Jun 86
	(30)							
61:00	John	Treacy	IRE	4.6.57	1	GNR	South Shields	24 Jul 88
61:01	Godfrey	Kiprotich	KEN	23.11.64	4	WCh	Oslo	24 Sep 94
61:02*#	Mohamed	Kedir	ETH	18.9.54	1	Stra	Milano	4 Apr 82
61:03	Nick	Rose	GBR	30.12.53	3		Philadelphia	15 Sep 85
61:03	David	Tsebe	RSA	9.11.66	1	NC	Durban	22 Jul 90
61:03	Rammy	Tsebe	RSA	7.10.64	2	NC	Durban	22 Jul 90
61:03	Vicenzo	Modica	ITA	2.3.71	4		Milano	3 Apr 93
61:04	Carl	Thackery	GBR	14.10.62	1		Barnsley	12 Apr 87
61:04	Cosmas	N'Deti	KEN	24.11.71	3		Tokyo 33m dh	26 Jan 92
61:04		Lee Bong-ju	KOR	69	4		Tokyo 33m dh	26 Jan 92
	(40)							

MARATHON

Note Boston marathon is downhill overall (139m) and, as a point-to-point course, in some years, such as 1994, has been strongly wind-aided - next bests are shown if to standard as a supplement.

Mark	Name		Nat	Born	Pos	Meet	Venue	Date
2:06:50	Belayneh	Dinsamo	ETH	28.6.65	1		Rotterdam	17 Apr 88
2:07:07	Ahmed	Salah	DJI	.56	2		Rotterdam	17 Apr 88
2:07:12	Carlos	Lopes	POR	18.2.47	1		Rotterdam	20 Apr 85
2:07:13	Steve	Jones	GBR	4.8.55	1		Chicago	20 Oct 85
2:07:15	Cosmus	N'Deti	KEN	24.11.71	1		Boston	18 Apr 94
2:07:19	Andrés	Espinosa	MEX	4.2.63	2		Boston	18 Apr 94
2:07:35	Taisuke	Kodama	JPN	26.7.58	1		Beijing	19 Oct 86
2:07:35	Abebe	Mekonnen	ETH	9.1.64	1		Beijing	16 Oct 88
2:07:40	Hiromi	Taniguchi	JPN	4.4.60	2		Beijing	16 Oct 88
2:07:51	Robert	de Castella	AUS	27.2.57	1		Boston	21 Apr 86

MEN All-time

Mark	Wind	Name		Nat	Born	Pos	Meet	Venue	Date
2:07:51		Vincent	Rousseau	BEL	29.7.62	1		Rotterdam	17 Apr 94
2:07:57		Kunimitsu	Ito	JPN	6.1.55	2		Beijing	19 Oct 86
2:08:01		Juma	Ikangaa	TAN	19.7.60	1		New York	5 Nov 89
2:08:04		Zithulele	Sinqe	RSA	9.6.63	1	NC	Port Elizabeth	3 May 86
2:08:05			Jones			1		Chicago	21 Oct 84
2:08:07		David	Tsebe	RSA	9.11.66	1		Berlin	27 Sep 92
2:08:08		Djama	Robleh	DJI	.58	2		Chicago	20 Oct 85
2:08:08		Jackson	Kipngok	KEN	16.8.66	3		Boston	18 Apr 94
2:08:09			Salah			1	WCp	Hiroshima	14 Apr 85
2:08:09			Hwang Young-cho	KOR	22.3.70	4		Boston	18 Apr 94
		2:08:47				2	Beppu	Oita	2 Feb 92
2:08:10			Ikangaa			1		Tokyo	9 Feb 86
2:08:14		Ibrahim	Hussein	KEN	3.6.58	1		Boston	20 Apr 92
2:08:15		Takeyuki	Nakayama	JPN	20.12.59	2	WCp	Hiroshima	14 Apr 85
2:08:15		Willie	Mtolo	RSA	5.5.64	2	NC	Port Elizabeth	3 May 86
2:08:16			Jones			1		London	21 Apr 85
2:08:16		Steve	Moneghetti	AUS	26.9.62	1		Berlin	30 Sep 90
2:08:18			de Castella			1		Fukuoka	6 Dec 81
2:08:18			Nakayama			1	NC	Fukuoka	6 Dec 87
2:08:19		Gelindo	Bordin	ITA	2.4.59	1		Boston	16 Apr 90
		(30/22)							
2:08:27		Toshihiko	Seko	JPN	15.7.56	1		Chicago	26 Oct 86
2:08:28		Arturo	Barrios	USA	12.12.62	5		Boston	18 Apr 94
2:08:31		António	Pinto	POR	22.3.66	1		Berlin	25 Sep 94
2:08:32		Gidamis	Shahanga	TAN	4.9.57	2		Berlin	30 Sep 90
2:08:33		Charles	Spedding	GBR	9.5.52	2		London	21 Apr 85
2:08:33		Manuel	Matias	POR	30.3.62	1		Kyongju	20 Mar 94
2:08:34		Derek	Clayton	AUS	17.11.42	1		Antwerpen	30 May 69
2:08:34			Kim Wan-ki	KOR	8.7.68	2		Kyongju	20 Mar 94
2:08:35		Boay	Akonay	TAN	3.1.70	6		Boston	18 Apr 94
		(30)							
2:08:36		Dionisio	Ceron	MEX	9.10.65	1	Beppu	Oita	2 Feb 92
2:08:44		Wodajo	Bulti	ETH	11.3.57	3		Rotterdam	17 Apr 88
2:08:47		Jörg	Peter	GDR	23.10.55	3		Tokyo	14 Feb 88
2:08:47		Bob	Kempainen	USA	18.6.66	7		Boston	18 Apr 94
2:08:50		Sammy	Nyangincha	KEN	10.11.62	2		Berlin	25 Sep 94
2:08:52		Alberto	Salazar	USA	7.8.58	1		Boston	19 Apr 82
2:08:53		Koichi	Morishita	JPN	5.9.67	1	Beppu	Oita	3 Feb 91
2:08:54		Dick	Beardsley	USA	21.3.56	2		Boston	19 Apr 82
2:08:55		Takeshi	Soh	JPN	9.1.53	2		Tokyo	13 Feb 83
2:08:57		Alejandro	Cruz	MEX	10.2.68	1		Chicago	30 Oct 88
		(40)							
2:08:58		Mark	Plaatjes	RSA	2.6.62	1	NC	Port Elizabeth	4 May 85
2:08:59		Rod	Dixon	NZL	13.7.50	1		New York	23 Oct 83
2:09:00		Greg	Meyer	USA	18.9.55	1		Boston	18 Apr 83
2:09:01		Gerard	Nijboer	NED	18.8.55	1		Amsterdam	26 Apr 80
2:09:03		Michael	Heilmann	GDR	26.10.61	4	WCp	Hiroshima	14 Apr 85
2:09:03		Douglas	Wakiihuri	KEN	26.9.63	1		London	23 Apr 89
2:09:04		Tena	Negere	ETH	72	1		Fukuoka	6 Dec 92
2:09:06		Shigeru	Soh	JPN	9.1.53	1	Beppu	Oita	5 Feb 78
2:09:08		Geoff	Smith	GBR	24.10.53	2		New York	23 Oct 83
2:09:08		Lucketz	Swartbooi	NAM	7.2.66	8		Boston	18 Apr 94
		(50)							

Short course

Mark	Name		Nat	Born	Pos	Meet	Venue	Date
2:08:13	Alberto	Salazar	USA	7.8.58	1		New York (-148m)	25 Oct 81

2000 METRES STEEPLECHASE

Mark	Name		Nat	Born	Pos	Meet	Venue	Date
5:14.43	Julius	Kariuki	KEN	12.6.61	1		Rovereto	21 Aug 90
5:16.22	Phillip	Barkutwo	KEN	6.10.66	2		Rovereto	21 Aug 90
5:18.36	Alessandro	Lambruschini	ITA	7.1.65	1		Verona	12 Sep 89
5:18.38	Azzedine	Brahmi	ALG	13.9.66	1		Verona	17 Jun 92
5:19.68	Samson	Obwocha	KEN	7.10.54	1		Birmingham	19 Jul 86
5:19.86	Mark	Rowland	GBR	7.3.63	1	McV	London	28 Aug 88
5:20.00	Krzysztof	Wesolowski	POL	9.12.56	1	Bisl	Oslo	28 Jun 84
5:20.25	Julius	Korir	KEN	21.4.60	2		Birmingham	19 Jul 86
5:20.81	Boguslaw	Maminski	POL	18.12.55	2	Bisl	Oslo	28 Jun 84
5:21.2	Eshetu	Tura	ETH	19.1.50	1		Montreal	14 Jul 76

3000 METRES STEEPLECHASE

Mark	Wind	Name		Nat	Born	Pos	Meet	Venue	Date
8:02.08		Moses	Kiptanui	KEN	1.10.71	1	WK	Zürich	19 Aug 92
8:05.25			Kiptanui			1		Rieti	6 Sep 92
8:05.35		Peter	Koech	KEN	18.2.58	1	DNG	Stockholm	3 Jul 89
8:05.37		Philip	Barkutwo	KEN	6.10.66	2		Rieti	6 Sep 92
8:05.4		Henry	Rono	KEN	12.2.52	1		Seattle	13 May 78
8:05.51		Julius	Kariuki	KEN	12.6.61	1	OG	Seoul	30 Sep 88
8:06.03		Patrick	Sang	KEN	11.4.64	2	DNG	Stockholm	3 Jul 89
8:06.36			Kiptanui			1	WCh	Stuttgart	21 Aug 93
8:06.46			Kiptanui			1	VD	Bruxelles	13 Sep 91
8:06.79			Koech			2	OG	Seoul	30 Sep 88
8:07.53			Sang			2	WCh	Stuttgart	21 Aug 93
8:07.62		Joseph	Mahmoud	FRA	13.12.55	1	VD	Bruxelles	24 Aug 84
8:07.89			Kiptanui			1	DNG	Stockholm	3 Jul 91
8:07.96		Mark	Rowland	GBR	7.3.63	3	OG	Seoul	30 Sep 88
8:08.02		Anders	Gärderud	SWE	28.8.46	1	OG	Montreal	28 Jul 76
8:08.39			Barkutwo			1	GGala	Roma	17 Jul 91
8:08.53			Kiptanui			2	GGala	Roma	17 Jul 91
8:08.57		Francesco	Panetta (10)	ITA	10.1.63	1	WCh	Roma	5 Sep 87
8:08.78		Alessandro	Lambruschini	ITA	7.1.65	3	WCh	Stuttgart	21 Aug 93
8:08.80			Kiptanui			1	WK	Zürich	17 Aug 94
8:08.84		Matthew	Birir	KEN	25.11.69	1	OG	Barcelona	7 Aug 92
8:09.11		Bronislaw	Malinowski	POL	4.6.51	2	OG	Montreal	28 Jul 76
8:09.16			Kiptanui			1	DNG	Stockholm	12 Jul 94
8:09.16			Kiptanui			1	ISTAF	Berlin	30 Aug 94
8:09.17		Henry	Marsh	USA	15.3.54	1	R-W	Koblenz	28 Aug 85
8:09.18		Boguslaw	Maminski	POL	18.12.55	2	VD	Bruxelles	24 Aug 84
8:09.42			Birir			4	WCh	Stuttgart	21 Aug 93
8:09.55			Sang			2	OG	Barcelona	7 Aug 92
8:09.70			Gärderud			1	DNG	Stockholm	1 Jul 75
8:09.70			Malinowski			1	OG	Moskva	31 Jul 80
8:09.76		Mark	Croghan	USA	8.1.68	5	WCh	Stuttgart	21 Aug 93
		(31/16)							
8:10.01		William	van Dijck	BEL	24.1.61	1	VD	Bruxelles	5 Sep 86
8:10.20		Richard	Kosgei	KEN	29.12.70	2	ISTAF	Berlin	30 Aug 94
8:10.32		Hagen	Melzer	GDR	16.6.59	2	WCh	Roma	5 Sep 87
8:10.36		Frank	Baumgartl	GDR	29.5.55	3	OG	Montreal	28 Jul 76
		(20)							
8:10.74		William	Mutwol	KEN	10.10.67	3	OG	Barcelona	7 Aug 92
8:10.84		Eliud	Barngetuny	KEN	20.5.73	1	Herc	Monaco	2 Aug 94
8:11.04		Krzysztof	Wesolowski	POL	9.12.56	1	VD	Bruxelles	30 Aug 85
8:11.11		Abdelaziz	Sahere	MAR	18.9.67	4	ISTAF	Berlin	30 Aug 94
8:11.27		Azzedine	Brahmi	ALG	13.9.66	1	Bisl	Oslo	4 Jul 92
8:11.80		Julius	Korir	KEN	21.4.60	1	OG	Los Angeles	10 Aug 84
8:11.93		Rainer	Schwarz	FRG	5.6.59	2	R-W	Koblenz	28 Aug 85
8:12.0 '		George Kip	Rono	KEN	4.1.58	1	GGala	Roma	5 Aug 80
8:12.11		Colin	Reitz	GBR	6.4.60	2	VD	Bruxelles	5 Sep 86
8:12.48		Filbert	Bayi	TAN	23.6.53	2	OG	Moskva	31 Jul 80
		(30)							
8:12.5 '		Mariano	Scartezzini	ITA	7.11.54	2	GGala	Roma	5 Aug 80
8:12.58		Graeme	Fell	CAN	19.3.59	3	R-W	Koblenz	28 Aug 85
8:12.58		Tom	Hanlon	GBR	20.5.67	3	Herc	Monaco	3 Aug 91
8:12.60		Tapio	Kantanen	FIN	31.5.49	4	OG	Montreal	28 Jul 76
8:12.69		Micah	Boinett	KEN	19.12.65	1	Nik	Nice	15 Jul 92
8:13.16		Brian	Diemer	USA	10.10.61	2	R-W	Koblenz	29 Aug 84
8:13.57		Eshetu	Tura	ETH	19.1.50	3	OG	Moskva	31 Jul 80
8:13.75		Uwe	Pflügner	GDR	24.11.66	2	APM	Hengelo	12 Aug 90
8:13.88		Raymond	Pannier	FRA	12.2.61	1	Nik	Nice	13 Jul 87
8:13.91		Ben	Jipcho	KEN	1.3.43	1	WG	Helsinki	27 Jun 73
		(40)							
8:14.02		Angelo	Carosi	ITA	20.1.64	4	Herc	Monaco	2 Aug 94
8:14.05		Michael	Karst	FRG	28.1.52	1	DNG	Stockholm	5 Jul 77
8:14.05		Peter	Renner	NZL	27.10.59	3	R-W	Koblenz	29 Aug 84
8:14.13		Joshua	Kipkemboi	KEN	22.2.59	1	R-W	Koblenz	6 Aug 86
8:14.17		Samson	Obwocha	KEN	7.10.54	2	R-W	Koblenz	6 Aug 86
8:14.18		Bernard	Barmasai	KEN		5	Herc	Monaco	2 Aug 94

Mark	Wind	Name		Nat	Born	Pos	Meet	Venue	Date
8:14.26		Marc	Davis	USA	17.12.69	4	WK	Zürich	4 Aug 93
8:14.72		Johnstone	Kipkoech	KEN	20.12.68	1	CG	Victoria	23 Aug 94
8:15.06		Patriz	Ilg	FRG	5.12.57	1	WCh	Helsinki	12 Aug 83
8:15.07		Féthi	Baccouche	TUN	16.11.60	1	WG	Helsinki	2 Jul 87
		(50)							

110 METRES HURDLES

Mark	Wind	Name		Nat	Born	Pos	Meet	Venue	Date
12.91	0.5	Colin	Jackson	GBR	18.2.67	1	WCh	Stuttgart	20 Aug 93
12.92	-0.1	Roger	Kingdom	USA	26.8.62	1	WK	Zürich	16 Aug 89
12.93	-0.2	Renaldo	Nehemiah	USA	24.3.59	1	WK	Zürich	19 Aug 81
12.97A	2.0		Kingdom			1		Sestriere	11 Aug 88
12.97A	-1.6		Jackson			1A		Sestriere	28 Jul 93
12.98	1.5		Kingdom			1	OG	Seoul	26 Sep 88
12.98	0.2		Jackson			1	TOTO	Tokyo	15 Sep 94
12.99	1.2		Jackson			1	VD	Bruxelles	3 Sep 93
12.99	-0.3		Jackson			1		Madrid	6 Sep 94
13.00	0.9		Nehemiah			1	Pepsi	Westwood	6 May 79
13.00	0.5	Tony	Jarrett	GBR	13.8.68	2	WCh	Stuttgart	20 Aug 93
13.02	0.6		Kingdom			1	ISTAF	Berlin	18 Aug 89
13.02	0.9		Jackson			1A	ISTAF	Berlin	30 Aug 94
13.03	-0.2	Greg	Foster	USA	4.8.58	2	WK	Zürich	19 Aug 81
13.03	0.3		Kingdom			1		Athinai	3 Sep 88
13.03	1.3		Jackson			1	McD	Sheffield	4 Sep 94
13.04	0.0		Nehemiah			1		Koblenz	26 Aug 81
13.04	1.6		Kingdom			1	ISTAF	Berlin	26 Aug 88
13.04	-0.5		Jackson			1	ASV	Köln	16 Aug 92
13.04	1.0		Jackson			1s1	EC	Helsinki	12 Aug 94
13.05	1.4	Tony	Dees	USA	6.8.63	1		Vigo	23 Jul 91
13.05	1.8		Jackson			1	ISTAF	Berlin	21 Aug 92
13.06	1.4		Foster			2		Vigo	23 Jul 91
13.06	0.7		Foster			1	WCh	Tokyo	29 Aug 91
13.06	0.7	Jack	Pierce	USA	23.9.62	2	WCh	Tokyo	29 Aug 91
13.06	-0.6		Jackson			1	TSB	London	10 Jul 92
13.06	-0.5		Jackson			1rA	WK	Zürich	19 Aug 92
13.06	0.5		Pierce			3	WCh	Stuttgart	20 Aug 93
		(28/7)							
13.07	0.9	Mark	Crear	USA	2.10.68	2rA	ISTAF	Berlin	30 Aug 94
13.08	1.2	Mark	McKoy	CAN	10.12.61	1	BNP	Villeneuve d'Ascq	2 Jul 93
13.13	1.4	Florian	Schwarthoff	GER	7.5.68	2		Bad Homburg	24 May 92
		(10)							
13.17	-0.4	Sam	Turner	USA	17.6.57	2	Pepsi	Westwood	15 May 83
13.17	0.0	Tonie	Campbell	USA	14.6.60	3	WK	Zürich	17 Aug 88
13.19	-0.3	Emilio	Valle	CUB	21.4.67	3s3	WCh	Stuttgart	19 Aug 93
13.20	2.0	Stéphane	Caristan	FRA	31.5.64	1	EC	Stuttgart	30 Aug 86
13.20	1.8	Aleksandr	Markin	RUS	8.9.62	1	Znam	Leningrad	11 Jun 88
13.21	0.6	Alejandro	Casañas	CUB	29.1.54	1	WUG	Sofia	21 Aug 77
13.21	1.8	Vladimir	Shishkin	RUS	12.1.64	2	Znam	Leningrad	11 Jun 88
13.23	0.7	Eugene	Swift	USA	14.9.64	1		Fresno	9 Apr 94
13.24	0.3	Rod	Milburn	USA	18.5.50	1	OG	München	7 Sep 72
13.24	2.0	Arthur	Blake	USA	19.8.66	2	Athl	Lausanne	24 Jun 88
		(20)							
13.25	0.1	Andre	Phillips	USA	5.9.59	1	USOF	Baton Rouge	28 Jul 85
13.25	1.3	Courtney	Hawkins	USA	11.7.67	1	Indy	Indianapolis	25 Jun 93
13.25	-0.1		Li Tong	CHN	6.5.67	2rA	GP II	Linz	4 Jul 94
13.25	1.3	Allen	Johnson	USA	1.3.71	3	McD	Sheffield	4 Sep 94
13.26	1.6	Willie	Gault	USA	5.9.60	1	USOF	Indianapolis	25 Jul 82
13.26	0.0	Igor	Kazanov	LAT	24.9.63	2s1	WCh	Stuttgart	19 Aug 93
13.27	1.8	Sergey	Usov	BLR	16.1.64	3	Znam	Leningrad	11 Jun 88
13.28	1.1	Guy	Drut	FRA	6.12.50	1	NC	St. Etienne	29 Jun 75
13.28	1.0	Andrey	Prokofyev	RUS	6.6.59	1r2	GWG	Moskva	6 Jul 86
13.28	-1.0	Philippe	Tourret	FRA	8.7.67	1	Herc	Monaco	12 Aug 90
		(30)							
13.29	1.9	Rod	Woodson	USA	10.3.65	1		Irvine	14 Jun 87
13.29	-0.1	Jonathan	Ridgeon	GBR	14.2.67	1	WUG	Zagreb	15 Jul 87
13.30	2.0	Cletus	Clark	USA	20.1.62	3	Athl	Lausanne	24 Jun 88
13.31		Keith	Talley	USA	28.1.64	2r1	GWG	Moskva	6 Jul 86
13.33A	0.0	Willie	Davenport	USA	8.6.43	1	OG	Ciudad México	17 Oct 68
13.33	0.7	Dan	Philibert	FRA	6.8.70	5	WCh	Tokyo	29 Aug 91

Mark	Wind	Name		Nat	Born	Pos	Meet	Venue	Date
13.34	1.8	Dedy	Cooper	USA	22.5.56	2		Houston	3 May 80
13.34	1.0	George	Boroi	ROM	26.8.64	1	RomIC	Bucuresti	18 Jun 93
13.34	0.7	Robert	Reading	USA	9.6.67	2		Fresno	9 Apr 94
13.35	2.0	Arto	Bryggare	FIN	26.5.58	1h1	OG	Los Angeles	5 Aug 84
		(40)							
13.35	0.1	Tomasz	Nagorka	POL	2.10.67	1	NC	Pila	15 Jul 90
13.35	1.9	Glenn	Terry	USA	10.2.71	1h1	WUG	Buffalo	16 Jul 93
13.37	2.0	Thomas	Munkelt	GDR	3.8.52	1	ECp	Helsinki	14 Aug 77
13.37	0.2	Milan	Stewart	USA	31.10.60	2		Paris	22 Jul 86
13.38A	1.8	Ervin	Hall	USA	5.3.47	1s1	OG	Ciudad México	17 Oct 68
13.38	1.6	Jerry	Wilson	USA	4.11.50	1	AAU	Eugene	20 Jun 75
13.39	1.9	Larry	Cowling	USA	6.7.60	1	vGDR	Karl-Marx-Stadt	10 Jul 82
13.39	1.6		Chen Yanjie	CHN	2.1.72	2	AsiG	Hiroshima	15 Oct 94
13.40	2.0	Holger	Pohland	GDR	5.4.63	1	vURS	Tallinn	21 Jun 86
13.40	0.3	Vladimir	Belokon	UKR	13.2.69	1	NC	Kiev	27 May 94
		(50)							
Low altitude best: 13.38	0.0		Davenport			3	OG	Montreal	28 Jul 76
Wind-assisted marks									
12.87	2.6	Roger	Kingdom	USA	26.8.62	1	WCp	Barcelona	10 Sep 89
12.91	3.5	Renaldo	Nehemiah	USA	24.3.59	1	NCAA	Champaign	1 Jun 79
12.94A	2.8		Jackson			1rA		Sestriere	31 Jul 94
12.95	2.6		Jackson			2	WCp	Barcelona	10 Sep 89
12.99	2.7		Jackson			1	v3N	Birmingham	23 Jun 89
13.00	3.5		Nehemiah			1	USOF	Syracuse	26 Jul 81
13.00	2.7		Kingdom			1		Sacramento	21 Jul 84
13.01	3.6		Jackson			1	v USA	Edinburgh	2 Jul 93
13.04	4.0		Jarrett			1	BNP	Villeneuve d'Ascq	6 Jul 92
13.05	2.5		Jackson			1	TSB	Edinburgh	8 Jul 94
13.06	2.1	Mark	McKoy	CAN	10.12.61	1	Gugl	Linz	13 Aug 92
13.14	2.9	Igor	Kazanov	LAT	24.9.63	1r1	Znam	Leningrad	8 Jun 86
13.18	4.7	Robert	Reading	USA	9.6.67	1		Azusa	23 Apr 94
13.20	2.4	Arthur	Blake	USA	19.8.66	2	IAC	Edinburgh	6 Jul 90
13.21A	2.5	Eric	Cannon	USA	2.3.67	2	NCAA	Provo	3 Jun 89
13.23A	2.8	Allen	Johnson	USA	1.3.71	2rA		Sestriere	31 Jul 94
13.24	2.4	Glenn	Terry	USA	10.2.71	1s2	WUG	Buffalo	18 Jul 93
13.26A	2.6	Antti	Haapakoski	FIN	6.2.71	1rB		Sestriere	31 Jul 94
13.27A	2.6	Kyle	Vander-Kuyp	AUS	30.5.71	2rB		Sestriere	31 Jul 94
13.28	2.7	Henry	Andrade	USA	17.4.62	3		Sacramento	21 Jul 84
13.32A	2.8	Laurent	Ottoz	ITA	10.4.70	3rA		Sestriere	31 Jul 94
13.33	2.9	Gennadiy	Chugunov	AZE	26.11.63	3r1	Znam	Leningrad	8 Jun 86
13.36*	3.5	Ricky	Stubbs	USA	18.12.51	1	TexR	Austin	13 Apr 74
13.37		Brian	Amos	USA	26.12.71	1		Abilene	12 May 94
13.38*	2.3	Charles	Foster	USA	2.7.53	1	NCAA	Austin	7 Jun 74
13.38	3.4	Al	Lane	USA	27.4.62	1h3	NCAA	Eugene	31 May 84
13.38	4.0	Eric	Reid	USA	17.2.65	2	SEC	Tuscaloosa	17 May 87
13.39		Colin	Williams	USA		1		Dallas	1 Apr 78
13.39		Dietmar	Koszewski	FRG	26.7.67	1		Berlin	14 Jul 90
Hand timing									
12.8	1.0	Renaldo	Nehemiah	USA	24.3.59	1		Kingston	11 May 79
13.0	1.8	Guy	Drut	FRA	6.12.50	1	ISTAF	Berlin	22 Aug 75
13.0	1.0	Greg	Foster	USA	4.8.58	2		Kingston	11 May 79
13.0*	2.0	Rod	Milburn	USA	18.5.50	1s1	AAU	Eugene	25 Jun 71
13.0	0.8	Mark	McKoy	CAN	10.12.61	1	Nik	Nice	16 Jul 85
13.0		Stéphane	Caristan	FRA	25.1.64	1		Creteil	3 May 86
13.0		Vladimir	Shishkin	RUS	12.1.64	1		Staiki	7 May 88
13.1		Tonie	Campbell	USA	14.6.60	1		Nassau	7 May 83
13.1A*	0.9	Lance	Babb	USA	8.11.50	2	ITA	El Paso	10 May 75
13.1		Igor	Kazanov	LAT	24.9.63	2		Staiki	7 May 88
13.1	1.9	Philippe	Tourret	FRA	8.7.67	1		Pau	10 Jun 89
Wind-assisted				** 120 yards time*					
12.8	2.4	Colin	Jackson	GBR	18.2.67	1		Sydney	10 Jan 90
12.9	4.1	Mark	Crear	USA	2.10.68	1rA	S&W	Modesto	8 May 93
13.0		Alejandro	Casañas	CUB	29.1.54	1	Barr	Habana	22 May 77
13.0		Tonie	Campbell	USA	14.6.60	1		Los Angeles	16 Jul 86
13.0		Keith	Talley	USA	28.1.64	1		Tuscaloosa	26 Mar 88
13.0	4.1	Li Tong		CHN	6.5.67	2rA	S&W	Modesto	8 May 93
13.1*	3.2	Tom	Hill	USA	17.11.49	1s1	USTFF	Wichita	13 Jun 70
13.1*	4.5	Larry	Shipp	USA	15.5.54	1	KansR	Lawrence	20 Apr 74
13.1		Ronnie	McCoy	USA	20.5.63	1		Naperville	10 May 85

200 METRES HURDLES

Mark	Wind	Name		Nat	Born	Pos	Meet	Venue	Date
22.63	-0.3	Colin	Jackson	GBR	18.2.67	1		Cardiff	1 Jun 91
22.69		Glenn	Davis	USA	12.9.34	1		Bern	20 Aug 60
22.72	1.6	Laurent	Ottoz	ITA	10.4.70	1		Milano	25 May 94
22.74	-0.8	Kevin	Young	USA	16.9.66	1		Belfast	31 Aug 92
22.5	hand	Martin	Lauer	FRG	2.1.37	1		Zürich	7 Jul 59
22.6*	hand	Charles	Tidwell	USA	20.3.37	1		Berkeley	14 Jun 58

** 220 yards less 0.1 sec..*

400 METRES HURDLES

Mark	Name		Nat	Born	Pos	Meet	Venue	Date
46.78	Kevin	Young	USA	16.9.66	1	OG	Barcelona	6 Aug 92
47.02	Edwin	Moses	USA	31.8.55	1		Koblenz	31 Aug 83
47.10	Samuel	Matete	ZAM	27.7.68	1rA	WK	Zürich	7 Aug 91
47.13		Moses			1		Milano	3 Jul 80
47.14		Moses			1	Athl	Lausanne	14 Jul 81
47.17		Moses			1	ISTAF	Berlin	8 Aug 80
47.18		Young			1	WCh	Stuttgart	19 Aug 93
47.19	Andre	Phillips	USA	5.9.59	1	OG	Seoul	25 Sep 88
47.23	Amadou	Dia Bâ	SEN	22.9.58	2	OG	Seoul	25 Sep 88
47.27		Moses			1	ISTAF	Berlin	21 Aug 81
47.32		Moses			1		Koblenz	29 Aug 84
47.37		Moses			1	WCp	Roma	4 Sep 81
47.37		Moses			1	WK	Zürich	24 Aug 83
47.37		Moses			1	OT	Indianapolis	17 Jul 88
47.37		Young			1	Athl	Lausanne	7 Jul 93
47.38		Moses			1	Athl	Lausanne	2 Sep 86
47.38	Danny	Harris	USA	7.9.65	1	Athl	Lausanne	10 Jul 91
47.40		Young			1	WK	Zürich	19 Aug 92
47.42		Young			1	ASV	Köln	16 Aug 92
47.43		Moses			1	ASV	Köln	28 Aug 83
47.45		Moses			1	AAU	Westwood	11 Jun 77
47.46		Moses			1	WCh	Roma	1 Sep 87
47.48	Harald	Schmid	FRG	29.9.57	1	EC	Athinai	8 Sep 82
47.48		Harris			2	WCh	Roma	1 Sep 87
47.48		Schmid			3	WCh	Roma	1 Sep 87
47.49		Harris			1	Athl	Lausanne	12 Jul 90
47.50		Moses			1	WCh	Helsinki	9 Aug 83
47.51		Phillips			1	VD	Bruxelles	5 Sep 86
47.53		Moses			1	WCp	Montreal	24 Aug 79
47.53		Moses			1	ISTAF	Berlin	15 Aug 86
	(30/7)							
47.60	Winthrop	Graham	JAM	17.11.65	1	WK	Zürich	4 Aug 93
47.64	Stéphane	Diagana	FRA	23.7.69	4	WCh	Stuttgart	19 Aug 93
47.70	Derrick	Adkins	USA	2.7.70	1	GP II	Linz	4 Jul 94
	(10)							
47.75	David	Patrick	USA	12.6.60	4	OT	Indianapolis	17 Jul 88
47.82	John	Akii-Bua	UGA	3.12.49	1	OG	München	2 Sep 72
47.82	Kriss	Akabusi	GBR	28.11.58	3	OG	Barcelona	6 Aug 92
47.92	Aleksandr	Vasilyev	BLR	26.7.61	2	ECp	Moskva	17 Aug 85
48.06	Oleg	Tverdokhleb	UKR	3.11.69	1	EC	Helsinki	10 Aug 94
48.12A	David	Hemery	GBR	18.7.44	1	OG	Ciudad México	15 Oct 68
48.16	Tony	Rambo	USA	30.5.60	3s1	OT	Los Angeles	17 Jun 84
48.22	Sven	Nylander	SWE	1.1.62	2	EC	Helsinki	10 Aug 94
48.24	Eric	Keter	KEN	22.7.66	2s2	WCh	Stuttgart	17 Aug 93
48.28	Tranel	Hawkins	USA	17.9.62	3	OT	Los Angeles	18 Jun 84
	(20)							
48.34	Vasiliy	Arkhipenko	UKR	28.1.57	2	ECp	Torino	4 Aug 79
48.34	McClinton	Neal	USA	11.7.68	4rA	Athl	Lausanne	8 Jul 92
48.35	Niklas	Wallenlind	SWE	21.11.68	3s1	OG	Barcelona	5 Aug 92
48.39	Quentin	Wheeler	USA	27.4.55	2	AAU	Walnut	17 Jun 79
48.39	Derrick	Adkins	USA	2.7.70	3	ASV	Köln	1 Aug 93
48.42	David	Lee	USA	23.4.59	4	WK	Zürich	24 Aug 83
48.44A	Harry	Schulting	NED	11.2.56	1	WUG	Ciudad México	12 Sep 79
48.46A	Larry	Cowling	USA	6.7.60	2	NCAA	Provo	4 Jun 82
48.46A	Dries	Vorster	RSA	25.10.62	1		Pretoria	11 Apr 89
48.48	James	Walker	USA	25.10.57	1	SEC	Tuscaloosa	13 May 79
	(30)							

Mark	Wind	Name		Nat	Born	Pos	Meet	Venue	Date
48.48		Toma	Tomov	BUL	6.5.58	2	BGP	Budapest	11 Aug 86
48.48		Olaf	Hense	GER	19.11.67	2	ECp	Roma	26 Jun 93
48.48		Edgar	Itt	GER	8.6.67	1	NC	Erfurt	3 Jul 94
48.50		Uwe	Ackermann	GDR	12.9.60	1	vUSA	Karl-Marx-Stadt	9 Jul 82
48.50		Henry	Amike	NGR	4.10.61	4s1	WCh	Roma	31 Aug 87
48.51		Ralph	Mann	USA	16.6.49	2	OG	München	2 Sep 72
48.52		Reggie	Davis	USA	17.1.64	2	Gator	Knoxville	23 May 87
48.55		Jim	Bolding	USA	24.3.49	1		Paris	8 Jul 75
48.55		Tom	Andrews	USA	15.6.54	1	AAU	Westwood	12 Jun 76
48.58		Volker	Beck	GDR	30.6.56	3	ECp	Torino	4 Aug 79
		(40)							
48.59		Alan	Pascoe	GBR	1.10.47	1	DNG	Stockholm	30 Jun 75
48.60		Aleksandr	Yatsevich	RUS	8.9.56	2	EC	Athinai	8 Sep 82
48.61		Vadim	Zadoinov	MOL	24.5.69	4	EC	Split	29 Aug 90
48.63		Bart	Williams	USA	20.9.56	2	Athl	Lausanne	10 Jul 84
48.64		Jim	Seymour	USA	27.7.49	4	OG	München	2 Sep 72
48.68		Kevin	Henderson	USA	4.2.65	1	TAC	Tampa	18 Jun 88
48.68		Yoshihiko	Saito	JPN	12.2.72	1	NC	Tokyo	12 Jun 93
48.69		Mike	Shine	USA	19.9.53	2	OG	Montreal	25 Jul 76
48.71		Vladimir	Budko	BLR	4.2.65	1	Spart	Tashkent	18 Sep 86
48.72A		Dale	Laverty	USA	30.4.65	2		El Paso	20 Apr 86
		(50)							

Low altitude bests

48.52 Hemery 3 OG München 2 Sep 72 | 48.71 Schulting 2 WK Zürich 15 Aug 79

48.59 Vorster 1 Durban 29 Apr 91

Hand timing

Mark	Wind	Name		Nat	Born	Pos	Meet	Venue	Date
48.1		Jim	Bolding	USA	24.3.49	1		Milano	2 Jul 74
48.4		Ralph	Mann	USA	16.6.49	1	OT	Eugene	2 Jul 72
48.5		Aleksandr	Yatsevich	RUS	8.9.56	1		Kiev	9 Aug 82

HIGH JUMP

Mark	Wind	Name		Nat	Born	Pos	Meet	Venue	Date
2.45		Javier	Sotomayor	CUB	13.10.67	1		Salamanca	27 Jul 93
2.44			Sotomayor			1	CAC	San Juan	29 Jul 89
2.43			Sotomayor			1		Salamanca	8 Sep 88
2.43i			Sotomayor			1	WI	Budapest	4 Mar 89
2.42		Patrik	Sjöberg	SWE	5.1.65	1	DNG	Stockholm	30 Jun 87
2.42i		Carlo	Thränhardt	FRG	5.7.57	1		Berlin	26 Feb 88
2.42			Sotomayor			1		Sevilla	5 Jun 94
2.41		Igor	Paklin	KGZ	15.7.63	1	WUG	Kobe	4 Sep 85
2.41i			Sjöberg			1		Piraeus	1 Feb 87
2.41i			Sotomayor			1	WI	Toronto	14 Mar 93
2.41			Sotomayor			1	TSB	London	15 Jul 94
2.40		Rudolf	Povarnitsyn	UKR	13.6.62	1		Donyetsk	11 Aug 85
2.40i			Thränhardt			1		Simmerath	16 Jan 87
2.40i			Sjöberg			1		Berlin	27 Feb 87
2.40			Sotomayor			1	NC	Habana	12 Mar 89
2.40			Sjöberg			1	ECp-B	Bruxelles	5 Aug 89
2.40			Sotomayor			1	AmCp	Bogota	13 Aug 89
2.40		Sorin	Matei	ROM	6.7.63	1	PTS	Bratislava	20 Jun 90
2.40i		Hollis	Conway	USA	8.1.67	1	WI	Sevilla	10 Mar 91
2.40			Sotomayor			1		Saint Denis	19 Jul 91
2.40		Charles	Austin	USA	19.12.67	1	WK	Zürich	7 Aug 91
2.40			Sotomayor			1	Barr	Habana	22 May 93
2.40			Sotomayor			1	TSB	London	23 Jul 93
2.40			Sotomayor			1	WCh	Stuttgart	22 Aug 93
2.40i			Sotomayor			1		Wuppertal	4 Feb 94
2.40i			Sotomayor			1	TSB	Birmingham	26 Feb 94
2.40			Sotomayor			1		Eberstadt	10 Jul 94
2.40			Sotomayor			1	Nik	Nice	18 Jul 94
2.40			Sotomayor			1	GWG	St Peterburg	29 Jul 94
2.40			Sotomayor			1	WCp	London	11 Sep 94
		(30/8)							
2.39			Zhu Jianhua	CHN	29.5.63	1		Eberstadt	10 Jun 84
2.39i		Dietmar	Mögenburg	FRG	15.8.61	1		Köln	24 Feb 85
		(10)							
2.39i		Ralf	Sonn	GER	17.1.67	1		Berlin	1 Mar 91

Mark	Wind	Name		Nat	Born	Pos	Meet	Venue	Date
2.38i		Gennadiy	Avdeyenko	UKR	4.11.63	2	WI	Indianapolis	7 Mar 87
2.38		Sergey	Malchenko	RUS	2.11.63	1		Banská Bystrica	4 Sep 88
2.38		Dragutin	Topic	YUG	12.3.71	1		Beograd	1 Aug 93
2.38i		Steve	Smith	GBR	29.3.73	2		Wuppertal	4 Feb 94
2.38i		Wolf-Hendrik	Beyer	GER	14.2.72	1		Weinheim	18 Mar 94
2.37		Valeriy	Sereda	RUS	30.6.59	1		Rieti	2 Sep 84
2.37		Tom	McCants	USA	27.11.62	1	JO	Columbus	8 May 88
2.37		Jerome	Carter	USA	25.3.63	2	JO	Columbus	8 May 88
2.37		Sergey	Dymchenko	UKR	23.8.67	1		Kiev	16 Sep 90
		(20)							
2.37i		Artur	Partyka	POL	25.7.69	1		Sulingen	3 Feb 91
2.37		Troy	Kemp	BAH	18.6.66	1		Pau	26 Jun 93
2.37i		Dalton	Grant	GBR	8.4.66	1	EI	Paris	13 Mar 94
2.36		Gerd	Wessig	GDR	16.7.59	1	OG	Moskva	1 Aug 80
2.36		Sergey	Zasimovich	KZK	6.9.62	1		Tashkent	5 May 84
2.36		Eddy	Annys	BEL	15.12.58	1		Ghent	26 May 85
2.36i		Jim	Howard	USA	11.9.59	1		Albuquerque	25 Jan 86
2.36i		Jan	Zvara	TCH	12.2.63	1	vGDR	Jablonec	14 Feb 87
2.36i		Gerd	Nagel	FRG	22.10.57	1		Sulingen	17 Mar 89
2.36		Nick	Saunders	BER	14.9.63	1	CG	Auckland	1 Feb 90
		(30)							
2.36		Doug	Nordquist	USA	20.12.58	2	TAC	Norwalk	15 Jun 90
2.36		Georgi	Dakov	BUL	21.10.67	2	VD	Bruxelles	10 Aug 90
2.36		Lambros	Papakostas	GRE	20.10.69	1	NC	Athinai	21 Jun 92
2.36i		Steinar	Hoen	NOR	8.2.71	1		Balingen	12 Feb 94
2.35i		Vladimir	Yashchenko	UKR	12.1.59	1	EI	Milano	12 Mar 78
2.35		Jacek	Wszola	POL	30.12.56	1		Eberstadt	25 May 80
2.35i		Aleksandr	Kotovich	UKR	6.11.61	1		Vilnius	13 Jan 85
2.35i		Brent	Harken	USA	1.12.61	1		Moscow	15 Feb 91
2.35		Darrin	Plab	USA	26.9.70	2	OT/NC	New Orleans	28 Jun 92
2.35		Tim	Forsyth	AUS	17.8.73	1		Canberra	25 Jan 93
		(40)							
2.35i		Jean-Charles	Gicquel	FRA	24.2.67	2	EI	Paris	13 Feb 94
2.34		Paul	Frommeyer	FRG	28.6.57	1		Recke	17 Jun 83
2.34		Dwight	Stones	USA	6.12.53	1	OT	Los Angeles	24 Jun 84
2.34i		Yuriy	Sergiyenko	UKR	19.3.65	1	UkrCh	Kiev	2 Feb 85
2.34		Dennis	Lewis	USA	20.3.59	1		Los Angeles	30 Mar 85
2.34		Róbert	Ruffíni	TCH	26.1.67	1	v2-N	Praha	3 Jul 88
2.34i		Aleksey	Yemelin	RUS	16.10.68	1	NC	Chelyabinsk	4 Feb 90
2.34i		Brian	Brown	USA	6.6.67	1	NCAA	Indianapolis	9 Mar 90
2.34		Rolandas	Verkys	LIT	17.3.67	1	Kuso	Warszawa	16 Jun 91
2.34		Arturo	Ortiz	ESP	18.9.66	2	ECp/B	Barcelona	22 Jun 91
		(50)							
2.34		Marino	Drake	CUB	13.6.67	2		Saint Denis	19 Jul 91
2.34		Andrey	Sankovich	BLR	15.7.65	1		Gomel	14 May 93

Best outdoor marks for athletes with indoor bests

Name	Mark	Pos	Meet	Venue	Date
Thranhärdt	2.37	2		Rieti	2 Sep 84
Smith	2.37	1	WJ	Seoul	20 Sep 92
Partyka	2.37	2	WCh	Stuttgart	22 Aug 93
Mögenburg	2.36	3		Eberstadt	10 Jun 84
Zvara	2.36	1		Praha	23 Aug 87
Howard	2.36	1		Rehlingen	8 Jun 87
Grant	2.36	4	WCh	Tokyo	1 Sep 91
Nagel	2.35	1		Forbach	7 Aug 88
Hoen	2.35	1	Bisl	Oslo	22 Jul 94
Yashchenko	2.34	1	Prav	Tbilisi	16 Jun 78
Yemelin	2.34	2	EC	Split	1 Sep 90
Sonn	2.34	4	WCh	Stuttgart	22 Aug 93

POLE VAULT

Mark	Name		Nat	Born	Pos	Meet	Venue	Date
6.15i	Sergey	Bubka	UKR	4.12.63	1		Donyetsk	21 Feb 93
6.14i		S Bubka			1		Liévin	13 Feb 93
6.14A		S Bubka			1		Sestriere	31 Jul 94
6.13i		S Bubka			1		Berlin	21 Feb 92
6.13		S Bubka			1	TOTO	Tokyo	19 Sep 92
6.12i		S Bubka			1	Mast	Grenoble	23 Mar 91
6.12		S Bubka			1		Padova	30 Aug 92
6.11i		S.Bubka			1		Donyetsk	19 Mar 91
6.11		S Bubka			1		Dijon	13 Jun 92
6.10i		S.Bubka			1		San Sebastian	15 Mar 91
6.10		S Bubka			1	MAI	Malmö	5 Aug 91
6.09		S Bubka			1		Formia	8 Jul 91
6.08i		S.Bubka			1	NC	Volgograd	9 Feb 91
6.08		S Bubka			1	Znam	Moskva	9 Jun 91

Mark	Wind	Name		Nat	Born	Pos	Meet	Venue	Date
6.07			S.Bubka			1	Super	Shizuoka	6 May 91
6.06			S.Bubka			1	Nik	Nice	10 Jul 88
6.05			S.Bubka			1	PTS	Bratislava	9 Jun 88
6.05i			S.Bubka			1		Donyetsk	17 Mar 90
6.05i			S Bubka			1		Berlin	5 Mar 93
6.05			S Bubka			1	GPF	London	10 Sep 93
6.05i			S Bubka			1	Mast	Grenoble	6 Feb 94
6.05			S Bubka			1	ISTAF	Berlin	30 Aug 94
6.03			S.Bubka			1	Ros	Praha	23 Jun 87
6.03i			S.Bubka			1		Osaka	11 Feb 89
6.02i		Radion	Gataullin	RUS	23.11.65	1	NC	Gomel	4 Feb 89
6.01			S.Bubka			1	GWG	Moskva	8 Jul 86
6.01i			S Bubka			1		Grenoble	7 Feb 93
		(27/2).. At 6.00: Bubka 12 performances, Gataullin 6							
5.97		Scott	Huffman	USA	30.11.64	1	NC	Knoxville	18 Jun 94
5.96		Joe	Dial	USA	26.10.62	1		Norman	18 Jun 87
5.94i		Philippe	Collet	FRA	13.12.63	1	Mast	Grenoble	10 Mar 90
5.94		Jean	Galfione	FRA	9.6.71	1		Dijon	12 Jun 94
5.93i		Billy	Olson	USA	19.7.58	1		East Rutherford	8 Feb 86
5.92		István	Bagyula	HUN	2.1.69	1	Gugl	Linz	5 Jul 91
5.92		Igor	Potapovich	KZK	6.9.67	2		Dijon	13 Jun 92
5.92		Dean	Starkey	USA	27.3.67	1	Banes	São Paulo	21 May 94
		(10)							
5.91		Thierry	Vigneron	FRA	9.3.60	2	GGala	Roma	31 Aug 84
5.91i		Viktor	Ryzhenkov	UZB	25.8.66	2		San Sebastian	15 Mar 91
5.90		Pierre	Quinon	FRA	20.2.62	2	Nik	Nice	16 Jul 85
5.90i		Ferenc	Salbert	FRA	5.8.60	1	Mast	Grenoble	14 Mar 87
5.90		Miroslaw	Chmara	POL	9.5.64	1	BNP	Villeneuve d'Ascq	27 Jun 88
5.90i		Grigoriy	Yegorov	KZK	12.1.67	1		Yokohama	11 Mar 90
5.90		Maksim	Tarasov	RUS	2.12.70	2		St Denis	4 Jun 92
5.90		Igor	Trandenkov	RUS	17.8.66	2	ASV	Köln	16 Aug 92
5.90		Denis	Petushinskiy	RUS	29.1.67	1	Znam	Moskva	13 Jun 93
5.90i		Pyotr	Bochkaryov	RUS	3.11.67	1	EI	Paris	12 Mar 94
		(20)							
5.90		Okkert	Brits	RSA	22.8.73	1	WCp	London	10 Sep 94
5.89		Kory	Tarpenning	USA	27.2.62	1	OT	Indianapolis	21 Jul 88
5.87		Earl	Bell	USA	25.8.55	1		Jonesboro	14 May 88
5.86		Vasiliy	Bubka	UKR	26.11.60	1		Chelyabinsk	16 Jul 88
5.86		Bill	Payne	USA	21.12.67	1	SWC	Houston	19 May 91
5.86		Valeri	Bukrejev	EST	15.6.64	1		Somero	3 Jul 94
5.85		Konstantin	Volkov	RUS	28.2.60	1	Izv	Kiev	22 Jun 84
5.85		Pat	Manson	USA	29.11.67	2	TOTO	Tokyo	15 Sep 94
5.84		Mike	Tully	USA	21.10.56	1		Irvine	1 May 88
5.83i		Jani	Lehtonen	FIN	11.8.68	1	DNG	Stockholm	8 Mar 94
		(30)							
5.83i		Lawrence	Johnson	USA	7.5.74	1	NCAA	Indianapolis	12 Mar 94
5.82		Aleksandr	Krupskiy	RUS	4.1.60	1	BGP	Budapest	20 Aug 84
5.82		Aleksandr	Parnov	UZB	10.5.59	1		Sumgait	21 Aug 85
5.82		Tim	Bright	USA	28.7.60	1	Nik	Nice	10 Jul 90
5.81		Vladimir	Polyakov	RUS	17.4.60	1	vGDR	Tbilisi	26 Jun 81
5.81i		Marian	Kolasa	POL	12.8.59	1		Praha	13 Feb 86
5.80		Pavel	Bogatyryov	RUS	19.3.61	1		Schwechat	19 Jun 85
5.80i		Dave	Volz	USA	2.5.62	2		New York	14 Feb 86
5.80		Atanas	Tarev	BUL	31.1.58	2	Athl	Lausanne	2 Sep 86
5.80		Aleksandr	Obizhajevs	LAT	16.9.59	2	URS Ch	Bryansk	17 Jul 87
		(40)							
5.80A		Doug	Fraley	USA	7.3.65	2		Sestriere	21 Jul 92
5.80i		Werner	Holl	GER	28.1.70	1		Nordlingen	7 Mar 93
5.80		Greg	Duplantis	USA	22.1.62	2		Århus	1 Jul 93
5.80i		Aleksandr	Korchagin	KZK	25.1.72	1		Almaty	18 Feb 94
5.80		Gérald	Baudouin	FRA	15.11.72	4	BNP	Villeneuve d'Ascq	8 Jul 94
5.78		Wladyslaw	Kozakiewicz	POL	8.12.53	1	OG	Moskva	30 Jul 80
5.77		Philippe	Houvion	FRA	5.1.57	1		Paris	17 Jul 80
5.77i		Hermann	Fehringer	AUT	8.12.62	1	NC	Wien	24 Feb 91
5.77i		Javier	Garcia	ESP	22.7.66	3	Mast	Grenoble	14 Mar 92
5.76		Jeff	Buckingham	USA	14.6.60	1		Lawrence	16 Jul 83
5.76		Tom	Hintnaus	BRA	15.2.58	1	WK	Zürich	21 Aug 85
		(51)							

Best outdoor marks for athletes with lifetime bests indoors

Name	Mark	Pos	Meet	Venue	Date
Yegorov	5.90	2	WCh	Stuttgart	19 Aug 93
Collet	5.85	2		Paris	22 Jul 86
Lehtonen	5.82	1		Kuortane	26 Jun 93
Kolasa	5.80	1		Kamp-Lintfort	1 Sep 86
Olson	5.80	1		Dallas	11 Apr 87
Salbert	5.80	1		Dreux	4 Jun 87
Ryzhenkov	5.80	1	vGDR	Rostock	24 Jun 90
Volz	5.80	2	OT	New Orleans	21 Jun 92
Johnson	5.80	1	SEC	Fayetteville	15 May 94
Fehringer	5.77	2	Gugl	Linz	5 Jul 91

Unsanctiond meeting

Name	Mark	Pos	Meet	Venue	Date
Volkov	5.84	1		Irkutsk	2 Aug 81

Exhibition

Mark	Wind	Name		Nat	Born	Pos	Meet	Venue	Date
5.86i		Larry	Jessee	USA	31.3.52	1		Newcastle	16 Oct 85
5.80		Gianni	Iapichino	ITA	2.3.69	1		Iglesias	11 Sep 94

LONG JUMP

Mark	Wind	Name		Nat	Born	Pos	Meet	Venue	Date
8.95	0.3	Mike	Powell	USA	10.11.63	1	WCh	Tokyo	30 Aug 91
8.90A	2.0	Bob	Beamon	USA	29.8.46	1	OG	Ciudad México	18 Oct 68
8.87	-0.2	Carl	Lewis	USA	1.7.61	*	WCh	Tokyo	30 Aug 91
8.86A	1.9	Robert	Emmiyan	ARM	16.2.65	1		Tsakhkadzor	22 May 87
8.79	1.9		Lewis			1	TAC	Indianapolis	19 Jun 83
8.79i	-		Lewis			1		New York	27 Jan 84
8.76	1.0		Lewis			1	USOF	Indianapolis	24 Jul 82
8.76	0.8		Lewis			1	OT	Indianapolis	18 Jul 88
8.75	1.7		Lewis			1	PAm	Indianapolis	16 Aug 87
8.74	1.4	Larry	Myricks	USA	10.3.56	2	OT	Indianapolis	18 Jul 88
8.74A	2.0	Erick	Walder	USA	5.11.71	1		El Paso	2 Apr 94
8.72	-0.2		Lewis			1	OG	Seoul	26 Sep 88
8.71	-0.4		Lewis			1	Pepsi	Westwood	13 May 84
8.71	0.1		Lewis			1	OT	Los Angeles	19 Jun 84
8.70	0.8		Myricks			1	TAC	Houston	17 Jun 89
8.70	0.7		Powell			1		Salamanca	27 Jul 93
8.68	1.0		Lewis			Q	OG	Barcelona	5 Aug 92
8.67	0.4		Lewis			1	WCh	Roma	5 Sep 87
8.67	-0.7		Lewis			1	OG	Barcelona	6 Aug 92
8.66	0.8		Lewis			-	MSR	Walnut	26 Apr 87
8.66	1.0		Myricks			1		Tokyo	23 Sep 87
8.66	0.9		Powell			1	BNP	Villeneuve d'Ascq	29 Jun 90
8.66A	1.4		Lewis			*		Sestriere	31 Jul 94
8.65	0.2		Lewis			1	VD	Bruxelles	24 Aug 84
8.65	0.7		Lewis			1	TAC	San José	26 Jun 87
8.64	1.7		Lewis			1	TAC	New York	15 Jun 91
8.64	-0.5		Powell			2	OG	Barcelona	6 Aug 92
8.63	2.0		Myricks			2	TAC	San José	26 Jun 87
8.63	0.6		Powell			2	TAC	New York	15 Jun 91
8.63	0.5	Kareem	Streete-Thompson	USA	30.3.73	1	GP II	Linz	4 Jul 94
		(30/7)							
8.54	0.9	Lutz	Dombrowski	GDR	25.6.59	1	OG	Moskva	28 Jul 80
8.53	1.2	Jaime	Jefferson	CUB	17.1.62	1	Barr	Habana	12 May 90
8.53	1.6	Ivan	Pedroso	CUB	17.12.72	1	Ib Am	Sevilla	17 Jul 92
		(10)							
8.50	0.2	Llewellyn	Starks	USA	10.2.67	2		Rhede	7 Jul 91
8.47	0.8	Roland	McGhee	USA	15.10.71	1		Rhede	29 Jul 94
8.46	1.2	Leonid	Voloshin	RUS	30.3.66	1	NC	Tallinn	5 Jul 88
8.45	2.0	Nenad	Stekic	YUG	7.3.51	1	PO	Montreal	25 Jul 75
8.44	1.7	Eric	Metcalf	USA	23.1.68	1	TAC	Tampa	17 Jun 88
8.43	0.8	Jason	Grimes	USA	10.9.59	-	TAC	Indianapolis	16 Jun 85
8.43	1.6	Mike	Conley	USA	5.10.62	1		Lausanne	10 Jul 85
8.43	1.8	Giovanni	Evangelisti	ITA	11.9.61	1		San Gio.Valdarno	16 May 87
8.43i	-	Stanislav	Tarasenko	RUS	23.7.66	1		Moskva	26 Jan 94
8.41	1.5	Craig	Hepburn	BAH	10.12.69	1	NC	Nassau	17 Jun 93
		(20)							
8.39	0.8	Dion	Bentley	USA	26.8.71	2	NCAA	New Orleans	3 Jun 93
8.38	0.4	Konstantin	Semykin	RUS	26.5.60	1	Drz	Moskva	17 Aug 84
8.38	-0.1	Joe	Greene	USA	17.2.67	1	Pre	Eugene	6 Jun 92
8.37A	0.4	Leroy	Burrell	USA	21.2.67	2	NCAA	Provo	2 Jun 89
8.36	1.0	João Carlos	de Oliveira	BRA	28.5.54	1		Rieti	21 Jul 79
8.36	1.6	Frank	Paschek	GDR	25.6.56	1	OD	Berlin	28 May 80
8.36	1.5		Chen Zunrong	CHN	20.10.62	*		Shizuoka	5 May 92
8.36	1.6	Konstandinos	Koukodimos	GRE	14.9.69	1		Khania	5 Jun 94
8.35	0.0	Ralph	Boston	USA	9.5.39	1	CalR	Modesto	29 May 65

Mark	Wind	Name		Nat	Born	Pos	Meet	Venue	Date
8.35A	0.0	Igor	Ter-Ovanesyan	RUS	19.5.38	1	PO	Ciudad México	19 Oct 67
		(30)							
8.35	0.8	Josef	Schwarz	FRG	20.5.41	1	vUSA	Stuttgart	15 Jul 70
8.35	-0.6	Arnie	Robinson	USA	7.4.48	1	OG	Montreal	29 Jul 76
8.35	2.0	Henry	Lauterbach	GDR	22.10.57	1		Erfurt	2 Aug 81
8.35	2.0	Sergey	Layevskiy	UKR	3.3.59	1		Dnepropetrovsk	16 Jul 88
8.35	1.4	Dmitriy	Bagryanov	RUS	18.12.67	1		Granada	30 May 92
8.34	0.0	Randy	Williams	USA	23.8.53	Q	OG	München	8 Sep 72
8.34	0.0	Vladimir	Ochkan ¶	UKR	13.1.68	1	RigC	Riga	5 Jun 88
8.34	1.1		Nai Hui-Fang	TPE	26.2.69	1	EAsiG	Shanghai	15 May 93
8.33	1.0	Sergey	Rodin	RUS	28.5.63	1		Leningrad	27 Jul 83
8.33i	-	Reggie	Kelly	USA	30.9.62	1		Jackson	3 Dec 83
		(40)							
8.33	2.0	Vladimir	Ratushkov	RUS	1.1.65	1	Znam	Volgograd	11 Jun 89
8.32		Ubaldo	Duany	CUB	16.5.60	2	NC	Santiago de Cuba	22 Feb 86
8.32A		Ralph	Spry	USA	16.6.60	1		Albuquerque	9 Jun 88
8.31	0.7	Atanas	Atanasov	BUL	7.10.56	1		Sofia	4 Jul 84
8.31	1.2	Igor	Streltsov	UKR	1.5.65	2		Dnepropetrovsk	16 Jul 88
8.30	1.8	László	Szálma	HUN	21.10.57	1		Budapest	7 Jul 85
8.30	2.0	Andreas	Steiner	AUT	21.2.64	1		Innsbruck	5 Jun 88
8.30	0.0		Huang Geng	CHN	10.7.70	1	NG	Beijing	9 Sep 93
8.30i	-	Ivailo	Mladenov	BUL	6.10.73	1		Pireas	28 Feb 94
8.29A		Grigoriy	Petrosyan	ARM	21.2.58	1		Yerevan	20 Oct 86
8.29	0.1	Yevgeniy	Tretyak	RUS	18.7.71	1		Stavropol	28 May 94
		(51)							
Low altitude marks for athletes with high altitude bests									
8.53	0.9		Walder			1	NCAA	New Orleans	3 Jun 93
8.33	1.3		Beamon			1	AAU	Sacramento	20 Jun 68
8.31	-0.1		Ter-Ovanesyan			1		Yerevan	10 Jun 62
Wind-assisted marks									
8.99A	4.4	Mike	Powell	USA	10.11.63	1		Sestriere	21 Jul 92
8.95A	3.9		Powell			1		Sestriere	31 Jul 94
8.91	2.9	Carl	Lewis	USA	1.7.61	2	WCh	Tokyo	30 Aug 91
8.90	3.7		Powell			1	S&W	Modesto	16 May 92
8.79	3.0	Ivan	Pedroso	CUB	17.12.72	1	Barr	Habana	21 May 92
8.77	3.9		Lewis			1	Pepsi	Westwood	18 May 85
8.77	3.4		Lewis			1	MSR	Walnut	26 Apr 87
8.73	4.6		Lewis			Q	TAC	Sacramento	19 Jun 81
8.73	3.2		Lewis			Q	TAC	Indianapolis	17 Jun 83
8.73A	2.6		Powell			1		Sestriere	31 Jul 91
8.72	2.2		Lewis			1	NYG	New York	24 May 92
8.72A	3.9		Lewis			2		Sestriere	31 Jul 94
8.68	4.1		Powell			1	NC	Knoxville	18 Jun 94
8.67	3.3		Lewis			1	TAC	Eugene	20 Jun 86
8.66	2.4		Myricks			1	MSR	Walnut	22 Apr 89
8.66A	4.0	Joe	Greene	USA	17.2.67	2		Sestriere	21 Jul 92
8.64A	3.1		Myricks			1	USOF	Air Force Academy	2 Jul 83
8.64	3.5		Powell			1		Modesto	14 May 94
8.64	3.5	Kareem	Streete-Thompson	USA	30.3.73	2	NC	Knoxville	18 Jun 94
8.63	3.9	Mike	Conley	USA	5.10.62	2	TAC	Eugene	20 Jun 86
8.57	5.2	Jason	Grimes	USA	10.9.59	1	vFRG,AFR	Durham	27 Jun 82
8.49	2.6	Ralph	Boston	USA	9.5.39	1	FOT	Los Angeles	12 Sep 64
8.46	3.4	Randy	Williams	USA	23.8.53	1		Eugene	18 May 73
8.46		Vernon	George	USA	6.10.64	1		Houston	21 May 89
8.44		Keith	Talley	USA	28.1.64	Q		Odessa	16 May 85
8.42		Anthony	Bailous	USA	6.4.65	Q		Odessa	16 May 85
8.42A	4.5	Milan	Gombala	TCH	29.1.68	3		Sestriere	21 Jul 92
8.41	4.3	Shamil	Abbyasov	KGZ	16.4.57	2	vUSA	Indianapolis	3 Jul 82
8.41	3.3	Andre	Ester	USA	27.4.65	1	TexR	Austin	4 Apr 87
8.40	4.3	Henry	Hines	USA	12.2.49	1	CalR	Modesto	27 May 72
8.40	2.1	Anthuan	Maybank	USA	30.12.69	1	DrakeR	Des Moines	24 Apr 93
8.40	3.4	Konstandinos	Koukodimos	GRE	14.9.69	1	ECp I	Valencia	11 Jun 94
8.39	6.2	Gary	Honey	AUS	26.7.59	2		Sacramento	21 Jul 84
8.39	3.5	Edrick	Floreal	CAN	5.10.66	1		Fayetteville	22 Apr 89
8.39	5.7	Yusuf	Alli	NGR	28.7.60	1	CG	Auckland	1 Feb 90
8.39	2.4		Chen Zunrong	CHN	20.10.62	1		Shizuoka	5 May 92
8.37	3.5	Arnie	Robinson	USA	7.4.48	1	OT	Eugene	25 Jun 76

Mark	Wind	Name		Nat	Born	Pos	Meet	Venue	Date
8.37	2.8	Jacques	Rousseau	FRA	10.3.51	1	NC	Lille	26 Jun 76
8.37		Sergey	Rodin	RUS	28.5.63	1		Moskva	6 Jul 84
8.36	5.2	Ralph	Spry	USA	16.6.60	1	NCAA	Houston	3 Jun 83
8.35A	5.5	Reggie	Jones	USA	8.5.71	2		Sestriere	28 Jul 93
8.35	2.2	Ivaylo	Mladenov	BUL	6.10.73	1	NC	Sofia	1 Aug 93
8.34		Mike	McRae	USA	9.7.55	1	SW	Modesto	12 May 84
8.34	2.7	Jarmo	Kärnä	FIN	4.8.58	1		Riga	4 Jun 89
8.34	2.4		Huang Geng	CHN	10.7.70	1	AsiG	Hiroshima	11 Oct 94
8.33		Phil	Shinnick	USA	21.4.43	1	CalR	Modesto	25 May 63
8.33	2.1	Charlton	Ehizuelen	NGR	30.11.53	1	KansR	Lawrence	19 Apr 75
8.33	3.7	Andrzej	Klimaszewski	POL	14.5.60	1	Kuso	Warszawa	13 Jun 80
8.33	3.6	Sergey	Vasilenko	KZK	27.9.65	1B	Znam	Leningrad	11 Jun 88
8.33	5.6	David	Culbert	AUS	17.3.67	1		Melbourne	11 Nov 89
8.32	3.8	David	Giralt	CUB	28.6.59	1	WPT	Québec City	11 Aug 79
8.32A	3.1	Francois	Fouché	RSA	5.6.63	1		Johannesburg	13 May 89
8.32	2.7	Obinna	Eregbu	NGR	9.11.69	1	AfCh	Durban	27 Jun 93
8.31		Mike	Davis	USA	5.1.64	1		Houston	18 May 86
8.31	3.1	Gordon	Laine	USA	24.2.58	4	OT	Indianapolis	18 Jul 88
8.31	5.9	Gordon	McKee	USA	12.10.66	1		San Angelo	12 Apr 90
8.31A	3.0	Milko	Campus	ITA	2.4.69	3		Sestriere	31 Jul 94
Best low altitude wa			8.58 3.7	Walder		1	SEC	Starkville	16 May 92

TRIPLE JUMP

Mark	Wind	Name		Nat	Born	Pos	Meet	Venue	Date
17.97	1.5	Willie	Banks	USA	11.3.56	1	TAC	Indianapolis	16 Jun 85
17.93	1.6	Kenny	Harrison	USA	13.2.65	1	DNG	Stockholm	2 Jul 90
17.92	1.6	Khristo	Markov	BUL	27.1.65	1	WCh	Roma	31 Aug 87
17.90	1.0	Vladimir	Inozemtsev	UKR	25.5.64	1	GPB	Bratislava	20 Jun 90
17.89A	0.0	João Carlos	de Oliveira	BRA	28.5.54	1	PAm	Ciudad México	15 Oct 75
17.87	1.7	Mike	Conley	USA	5.10.62	1	TAC	San José	27 Jun 87
17.86	1.3	Charles	Simpkins	USA	19.10.63	1	WUG	Kobe	2 Sep 85
17.86	0.3		Conley			1	WCh	Stuttgart	16 Aug 93
17.84	0.7		Conley			1		Bad Cannstatt	4 Jul 93
17.81	2.0		Markov			1	Nar	Sofia	31 May 87
17.80	0.6		Markov			1	BGP	Budapest	11 Aug 86
17.79	-0.8		Harrison			1	OD	Berlin	4 Jul 90
17.78	1.0	Nikolay	Musiyenko	UKR	16.12.59	1	Znam	Leningrad	7 Jun 86
17.78	0.6	Lázaro	Betancourt ¶	CUB	18.3.63	1	Barr	Habana	15 Jun 86
17.78	-0.8		Harrison			1	WCh	Tokyo	26 Aug 91
17.77	1.9		Markov			1	ECp-B	Budapest	11 Aug 85
17.77	1.0	Aleksandr	Kovalenko (10)	RUS	8.5.63	1	NC	Bryansk	18 Jul 87
17.77	1.4		Markov			1	NC	Sofia	3 Sep 88
17.77i	-	Leonid	Voloshin	RUS	30.3.66	1		Grenoble	6 Feb 94
17.76i	-		Conley			1	TAC	New York	27 Feb 87
17.75	0.3	Oleg	Protsenko	RUS	11.8.63	1	Znam	Moskva	10 Jun 90
17.75	1.0		Voloshin			2	WCh	Tokyo	26 Aug 91
17.74	0.0		Harrison			1		Grossetto	13 Aug 90
17.74	0.8		Voloshin			1	EC	Split	31 Aug 90
17.72	0.9		Harrison			1	GWG	Seattle	26 Jul 90
17.72	0.1		Conley			1	WK	Zürich	19 Aug 92
17.71	1.9		Conley			2	TAC	Indianapolis	16 Jun 85
17.71	2.0		Banks			1		Barcelona	8 Jul 85
17.69	1.0		Protsenko			1	NC	Leningrad	4 Aug 85
17.69	0.2		Conley			1	GWG	Moskva	9 Jul 86
17.69	1.5	Igor	Lapshin	BLR	8.8.63	1		Staiki	31 Jul 88
		(31/13)							
17.68	-0.5	Yoelbi	Quesada	CUB	4.8.73	1	Barr	Habana	23 May 93
17.66	1.7	Ralf	Jaros	GER	13.12.65	1	ECp	Frankfurt-am-Main	30 Jun 91
17.65	1.0	Aleksandr	Yakovlev	UKR	8.9.57	1	Znam	Moskva	6 Jun 87
17.62	0.4	Denis	Kapustin	RUS	5.10.70	1	EC	Helsinki	13 Aug 94
17.60	0.6	Vladimir	Plekhanov	RUS	11.4.58	2	NC	Leningrad	4 Aug 85
17.59i	-	Pierre	Camara	FRA	10.9.65	1	WI	Toronto	13 Mar 93
17.59	0.3	Vasiliy	Sokov	RUS	7.4.68	1	NC	Moskva	19 Jun 93
		(20)							
17.58	1.5	Oleg	Sakirkin	KZK	23.1.66	2	NC	Gorkiy	23 Jul 89
17.57A	0.0	Keith	Connor	GBR	16.9.57	1	NCAA	Provo	5 Jun 82
17.56	1.9	Maris	Bruziks	LAT	25.8.62	1		Riga	3 Sep 88
17.55	0.3	Vasiliy	Grishchenkov	RUS	23.1.58	1	Spa	Moskva	19 Jun 83

Mark	Wind	Name		Nat	Born	Pos	Meet	Venue	Date
17.55	0.9	Serge	Hélan	FRA	24.2.64	2	EC	Helsinki	13 Aug 94
17.53	1.0	Aleksandr	Beskrovniy	RUS	5.4.60	2	Spa	Moskva	19 Jun 83
17.53	1.6	Zdzislaw	Hoffmann	POL	27.8.59	1		Madrid	4 Jun 85
17.53	1.0	Gennadiy	Valyukevich	BLR	1.6.58	1		Erfurt	1 Jun 86
17.53	1.6	Al	Joyner	USA	19.1.60	Q	TAC	San José	26 Jun 87
17.53	0.9	Milán	Mikulás	TCH	1.4.63	1	NC	Praha	17 Jul 88
		(30)							
17.53	1.9	Oleg	Denishchik	BLR	10.11.69	2	NC	Kiev	12 Jul 91
17.50	0.4	Volker	Mai	GDR	3.5.66	1	vURS	Erfurt	23 Jun 85
17.48	1.9	Jorge	Reyna	CUB	10.1.63	1		Santiago de Cuba	27 Feb 87
17.46	1.7	Ken	Lorraway	AUS	6.2.56	1		London	7 Aug 82
17.45	1.9	Aleksandr	Leonov ¶	BLR	7.2.62	1		Sochi	24 May 87
17.44	-0.?	Viktor	Saneyev	GEO	3.10.45	1		Sukhumi	17 Oct 72
17.44	2.0	Dirk	Gamlin	GDR	26.10.63	1		Dresden	7 Jul 85
17.44	0.1	Jonathan	Edwards	GBR	10.5.66	3	WCh	Stuttgart	16 Aug 93
17.43	0.0	Peter	Bouschen	FRG	16.5.60	1		Düsseldorf	2 Jun 88
17.41	0.0	John	Herbert	GBR	20.4.62	3	WUG	Kobe	2 Sep 85
		(40)							
17.41	-0.8	Frank	Rutherford	BAH	23.11.64	2	GP	São Paulo	17 May 92
17.41A		Brian	Wellman	BER	8.9.67	1		El Paso	16 Apr 94
17.40A	0.4	Pedro	Pérez Dueñas	CUB	23.2.52	1	PAm	Cali	5 Aug 71
17.40	1.9	Oleg	Grokhovskiy	KZK	3.5.68	2	NP	Alma-Ata	8 Sep 91
17.38	1.0	Gennadiy	Markov	RUS	12.3.66	1		Stavropol	29 May 94
17.37	0.7	Vyacheslav	Bordukov	RUS	1.1.59	2	Nar	Sofia	19 May 84
17.37i	-	Vasif	Asadov	AZE	27.8.65	2	NC	Volgograd	12 Feb 88
17.36	1.3	Ray	Kimble	USA	19.4.53	1	S&W	Modesto	9 May 87
17.36	1.8	Vladimir	Chernikov	UZB	3.8.59	1		Odessa	21 Aug 88
17.35	-0.3	Jaak	Uudmäe	EST	3.9.54	1	OG	Moskva	25 Jul 80
17.35	1.7	Jacek	Pastusinski	POL	8.9.64	5	WCh	Roma	31 Aug 87
		(51)							
Low altitude best		17.36 -0.1	Wellman			1	BNP	Villeneuve dAscq	8 Jul 94
Best outdoors:		17.46w 2.4	Camara			1	ECp	Roma	27 Jun 93
Wind-assisted marks									
18.20	5.2	Willie	Banks	USA	11.3.56	1	OT	Indianapolis	16 Jul 88
18.17	2.1	Mike	Conley	USA	5.10.62	1	OG	Barcelona	3 Aug 92
17.93	5.2	Charles	Simpkins	USA	19.10.63	2	OT	Indianapolis	16 Jul 88
17.91	3.2		Simpkins			1	TAC	Eugene	21 Jun 86
17.86	3.9		Simpkins			1	OT	New Orleans	21 Jun 92
17.84	2.3		Conley			2	TAC	Eugene	21 Jun 86
17.82	3.6		Banks			1	Jen	San José	31 May 86
17.81	4.6	Keith	Connor	GBR	16.9.57	1	CG	Brisbane	9 Oct 82
17.75		Gennadiy	Valyukevich	BLR	1.6.58	1		Uzhgorod	27 Apr 86
17.74	3.5		Harrison			1	Oda	Hiroshima	3 May 89
17.73	4.1	Vasiliy	Sokov	RUS	7.4.68	1		Riga	3 Jun 89
17.72	3.2		Conley			1	NCAA	Austin	1 Jun 85
17.70	2.9	Jonathan	Edwards	GBR	10.5.66	1	v USA	Edinburgh	2 Jul 93
17.63	4.3	Robert	Cannon	USA	9.7.58	3	OT	Indianapolis	16 Jul 88
17.58	5.2	Al	Joyner	USA	19.1.60	5	OT	Indianapolis	16 Jul 88
17.56	3.7	Ron	Livers	USA	20.7.55	1	AAU	Walnut	17 Jun 79
17.55	3.6	Zdzislaw	Hoffmann	POL	27.8.59	1	Kuso	Warszawa	9 Jun 84
17.54	3.2	Ken	Lorraway	AUS	6.2.56	2	CG	Brisbane	9 Oct 82
17.53	4.8	Ray	Kimble	USA	19.4.53	7	OT	Indianapolis	16 Jul 88
17.51	3.0		Chen Yanping	CHN	17.1.66	1	AsiG	Beijing	3 Oct 90
17.49	4.5	Vladimir	Melikhov	RUS	30.3.69	2		Sevilla	5 Jun 94
17.48	2.9	Georges	Sainte-Rose	FRA	3.9.69	1		Montgeron	23 Jun 91
17.47	3.7	Joseph	Taiwo	NGR	24.8.59	1	GP	São Paulo	17 May 92
17.41	4.7	Brian	Wellman	BER	8.9.67	1	SWC	Houston	19 May 91
17.38	4.2	Milan	Tiff	USA	5.7.49	1	AAU	Westwood	11 Jun 77
17.38	2.8	Vyacheslav	Bordukov	RUS	1.1.59	1		Moskva	16 Aug 87
17.35	4.8	Andrey	Kayukov	RUS	12.4.64	4		Sevilla	5 Jun 94

SHOT

Mark	Wind	Name		Nat	Born	Pos	Meet	Venue	Date
23.12		Randy	Barnes ¶	USA	16.6.66	1		Westwood	20 May 90
23.10			Barnes			1	Jen	San José	26 May 90
23.06		Ulf	Timmermann	GDR	1.11.62	1		Khania	22 May 88
22.91		Alessandro	Andrei	ITA	3.1.59	1		Viareggio	12 Aug 87
22.86		Brian	Oldfield	USA	1.6.45	1	ITA	El Paso	10 May 75

Mark	Wind	Name		Nat	Born	Pos	Meet	Venue	Date
22.75		Werner	Günthör	SUI	1.6.61	1		Bern	23 Aug 88
22.66i			Barnes			1	Sunkist	Los Angeles	20 Jan 89
22.64		Udo	Beyer	GDR	9.8.55	1		Berlin	20 Aug 86
22.62			Timmermann			1		Berlin	22 Sep 85
22.61			Timmermann			1		Potsdam	8 Sep 88
22.60			Timmermann			1	vURS	Tallinn	21 Jun 86
22.56			Timmermann			1		Berlin	13 Sep 88
22.55i			Timmermann			1	NC	Senftenberg	11 Feb 89
22.52		John	Brenner	USA	4.1.61	1	MSR	Walnut	26 Apr 87
22.51			Timmermann			1		Erfurt	1 Jun 86
22.47			Timmermann			1		Dresden	17 Aug 86
22.47			Günthör			1	WG	Helsinki	2 Jul 87
22.47			Timmermann			1	OG	Seoul	23 Sep 88
22.45			Oldfield			1	ITA	El Paso	22 May 76
22.43			Günthör			1	v3-N	Lüdenscheid	18 Jun 87
22.42			Barnes			1	WK	Zürich	17 Aug 88
22.39			Barnes			2	OG	Seoul	23 Sep 88
22.36+			Timmermann			1		Athinai	16 May 88
22.31			Beyer			1	NC	Potsdam	20 Aug 87
22.28			Oldfield			1	ITA	Edinburgh	18 Jun 75
22.28			Barnes			1	MSR	Walnut	22 Apr 90
22.26i			Günthör			1	NC	Magglingen	8 Feb 87
22.26			Brenner			1		Westwood	18 Apr 87
22.25			Günthör			1	WK	Zürich	19 Aug 87
22.24		Sergey	Smirnov	RUS	17.9.60	2	vGDR	Tallinn	21 Jun 86
22.24i			Timmermann			1	WCh	Indianapolis	7 Mar 87
		(31/8)							
22.10		Sergey	Gavryushin	RUS	27.6.59	1		Tbilisi	31 Aug 86
22.09		Sergey	Kasnauskas	BLR	20.4.61	1		Staiki	23 Aug 84
		(10)							
22.02i		George	Woods	USA	11.2.43	1	LAT	Inglewood	8 Feb 74
22.02		Dave	Laut	USA	21.12.56	1		Koblenz	25 Aug 82
22.00		Aleksandr	Baryshnikov	RUS	11.11.48	1	vFRA	Colombes	10 Jul 76
21.98		Gregg	Tafralis	USA	9.4.58	1		Los Gatos	13 Jun 92
21.96		Mikhail	Kostin	RUS	10.5.59	1		Vitebsk	20 Jul 86
21.93		Remigius	Machura ¶	TCH	3.7.60	1		Praha	23 Aug 87
21.85		Terry	Albritton	USA	14.1.55	1		Honolulu	21 Feb 76
21.82		Al	Feuerbach	USA	14.1.48	1		San José	5 May 73
21.78		Randy	Matson	USA	5.3.45	1		College Station	22 Apr 67
21.77i		Mike	Stulce ¶	USA	21.7.69	1	v GBR	Birmingham	13 Feb 93
		(20)							
21.76		Mike	Carter	USA	29.10.60	2	NCAA	Eugene	2 Jun 84
21.74		Janis	Bojars	LAT	12.5.56	1		Riga	14 Jul 84
21.73		Augie	Wolf ¶	USA	3.9.61	1		Leverkusen	12 Apr 84
21.69		Reijo	Ståhlberg	FIN	21.9.52	1	WCR	Fresno	5 May 79
21.68		Geoff	Capes	GBR	23.8.49	1	4-N	Cwmbran	18 May 80
21.68		Edward	Sarul	POL	16.11.58	1		Sopot	31 Jul 83
21.67		Hartmut	Briesenick	GDR	17.3.49	1		Potsdam	1 Sep 73
21.61		Kevin	Akins	USA	27.1.60	1	S&W	Modesto	14 May 83
21.60		Jim	Doehring	USA	27.1.62	2		Los Gatos	13 Jun 92
21.58		Vladimir	Kiselyov	UKR	1.1.57	3	Drz	Moskva	17 Aug 84
		(30)							
21.53		Yevgeniy	Mironov ¶	RUS	1.11.49	1	NC	Kiev	24 Jun 76
21.51		Ralf	Reichenbach	FRG	31.7.50	1	ISTAF	Berlin	8 Aug 80
21.44		Mikhail	Domorosov	BLR	5.3.55	2		Staiki	23 Aug 84
21.43		Mike	Lehmann	USA	11.3.60	2	Jen	San José	28 May 83
21.42i		Fred	DeBernardi	USA	2.3.49	1	ITA	Portland	20 Apr 74
21.42		Aleksandr	Bagach ¶	UKR	21.11.66	1	NC	Gorkiy	22 Jul 89
21.35		Ron	Semkiw	USA	28.3.54	1		Mesa	5 Mar 74
21.35		Sergey	Nikolayev	RUS	12.11.66	1		Voronezh	5 Aug 89
21.33		Hans	Höglund	SWE	23.7.52	1	NCAA	Provo	6 Jun 75
21.32		Heinz-Joachim	Rothenburg	GDR	9.4.44	1		Potsdam	3 Jun 72
		(40)							
21.31		Hans-Peter	Gies	GDR	9.5.47	2		Potsdam	25 Aug 72
21.30		Helmut	Krieger	POL	17.7.58	1	NC	Grudziadz	27 Jun 86
21.29		Kevin	Toth	USA	29.12.67	1		Hechtel	31 Jul 93
21.26		Pétur	Gudmundsson	ISL	9.3.62	1		Mosfellsbaer	10 Nov 90

Mark	Wind	Name		Nat	Born	Pos	Meet	Venue	Date
21.26		Dragan	Peric	YUG	8.5.64	1	NC	Beograd	24 Jul 93
21.25		Hans-Jürgen	Jacobi	GDR	26.7.50	2	NC	Cottbus	16 Jul 80
21.25i		Maris	Petrashko	LAT	6.3.61	1		Vilnius	6 Jan 89
21.24i		Sören	Tallhem	SWE	16.2.64	1	NCAA	Syracuse	9 Mar 85
21.22		Lars Arvid	Nilsen ¶	NOR	15.4.65	1	NCAA	Indianapolis	6 Jun 86
21.22		Klaus	Görmer	GDR	5.7.63	3	NC	Potsdam	20 Aug 87
		(50) No changes to top 50 in 1994							

Not recognised by GDR authorities

Mark	Wind	Name		Nat	Born	Pos	Meet	Venue	Date
22.11		Rolf	Oesterreich	GDR	24.8.49	1		Zschopau	12 Sep 76

Subsequent to drugs disqualification

Mark	Wind	Name		Nat	Born	Pos	Meet	Venue	Date
22.84			Barnes			1		Malmö	7 Aug 90
21.82		Mike	Stulce	USA	14.7.69	1		Brenham	9 May 90

Best outdoor marks for athletes with lifetime bests indoors

Mark	Name	Pos	Meet	Venue	Date
21.70	Stulce ¶	1	OG	Barcelona	31 Jul 92
21.63	Woods	2	CalR	Modesto	22 May 76
21.41	DeBernardi	1	ITA	El Paso	27 Apr 74

DISCUS

Mark	Wind	Name		Nat	Born	Pos	Meet	Venue	Date
74.08		Jürgen	Schult	GDR	11.5.60	1		Neubrandenburg	6 Jun 86
71.86		Yuriy	Dumchev	RUS	5.8.58	1		Moskva	29 May 83
71.32		Ben	Plucknett ¶	USA	13.4.54	1	Pre	Eugene	4 Jun 83
71.26		John	Powell	USA	25.6.47	1	TAC	San José	9 Jun 84
71.26		Rickard	Bruch	SWE	2.7.46	1		Malmö	15 Nov 84
71.26		Imrich	Bugár	TCH	14.4.55	1	Jen	San José	25 May 85
71.18		Art	Burns	USA	19.7.54	1		San José	19 Jul 83
71.16		Wolfgang	Schmidt	GDR	16.1.54	1		Berlin	9 Aug 78
71.14			Plucknett			1		Berkeley	12 Jun 83
71.06		Luis M.	Delís ¶	CUB	6.12.57	1	Barr	Habana	21 May 83
71.00			Bruch			1		Malmö	14 Oct 84
70.98		Mac	Wilkins (10)	USA	15.11.50	1	WG	Helsinki	9 Jul 80
70.98			Burns			1	Pre	Eugene	21 Jul 84
70.92			Schmidt	FRG		1		Norden	9 Sep 89
70.86			Wilkins			1		San José	1 May 76
70.82			Plucknett			1		Salinas	1 Jun 83
70.72			Bugár			1	vHUN,AUT	Schwechat	18 Jun 83
70.66			Wilkins			1	AAU	Walnut	16 Jun 79
70.58			Delís			1		Salinas	19 May 82
70.48			Wilkins			1		San José	29 Apr 78
70.48			Wilkins			1	Pre	Eugene	31 May 78
70.48			Bruch			1		Malmö	12 Sep 84
70.46			Schult			1		Berlin	13 Sep 88
70.44			Wilkins			2	TAC	San José	9 Jun 84
70.38		Jay	Silvester	USA	27.8.37	1		Lancaster	16 May 71
70.36			Wilkins			1	SW	Modesto	14 May 83
70.30			Dumchev			1		Bryansk	31 Jul 88
70.26			Bugár			1	vITA	Cagliari	8 Sep 84
70.24			Schmidt			1		Potsdam	18 Aug 78
70.24			Bugár			1		Nitra	26 Aug 84
		(30/11)							
70.06		Romas	Ubartas ¶	LIT	26.5.60	1		Smolininkay	8 May 88
70.00		Juan	Martínez ¶	CUB	17.5.58	2	Barr	Habana	21 May 83
69.70		Gejza	Valent	TCH	3.10.53	2		Nitra	26 Aug 84
69.62		Knut	Hjeltnes ¶	NOR	8.12.51	2	Jen	San José	25 May 85
69.46		Al	Oerter	USA	19.9.36	1	TFA	Wichita	31 May 80
69.44		Georgiy	Kolnootchenko	BLR	7.5.59	1	vUSA	Indianapolis	3 Jul 82
69.40		Art	Swarts ¶	USA	14.2.45	1		Scotch Plains	8 Dec 79
69.36		Mike	Buncic	USA	25.7.62	1		Fresno	6 Apr 91
69.26		Ken	Stadel	USA	19.2.52	2	AAU	Walnut	16 Jun 79
		(20)							
68.88		Vladimir	Zinchenko	UKR	25.7.59	1		Dnepropetrovsk	16 Jul 88
68.66		Lars	Riedel	GER	28.6.67	1	ISTAF	Berlin	21 Aug 92
68.64		Dmitriy	Kovtsun ¶	UKR	29.9.55	1		Riga	6 Jul 84
68.58		Attila	Horváth	HUN	28.7.67	1		Budapest	24 Jun 94
68.52		Igor	Duginyets	UKR	20.5.56	1	NC	Kiev	21 Aug 82
68.50		Armin	Lemme	GDR	28.10.55	1	vUSA	Karl-Marx-Stadt	10 Jul 82
68.48		John	van Reenen	RSA	26.3.47	1		Stellenbosch	14 Mar 75
68.44		Vaclavas	Kidikas	LIT	17.10.61	1		Sochi	1 Jun 88

Mark	Wind	Name		Nat	Born	Pos	Meet	Venue	Date
68.30		Stefan	Fernholm	SWE	2.7.59	1		Västerås	15 Jul 87
68.12		Markku	Tuokko ¶	FIN	24.6.51	1	WCR	Fresno	5 May 79
		(30)							
68.12		Iosif	Nagy	ROM	20.11.46	2		Zaragoza	22 May 83
68.12		Erik	de Bruin ¶	NED	25.5.63	1		Sneek	1 Apr 91
68.08		Hein-Direck	Neu ¶	FRG	13.2.44	1		Bremerhaven	27 May 77
68.00		Svein Inge	Valvik	NOR	20.9.56	1		Juarez	31 May 82
67.88		Tony	Washington	USA	16.1.66	1	S&W	Modesto	16 May 92
67.82		Velko	Velev ¶	BUL	4.1.48	1		Riga	13 Aug 78
67.80		Alwin	Wagner	FRG	11.8.50	1		Melsungen	1 Jul 87
67.80		Adewale	Olukoju	NGR	27.7.68	1	S&W	Modesto	11 May 91
67.76		Vitaliy	Pishchalnikov	RUS	1.4.58	1		Stavropol	9 May 84
67.64		Vésteinn	Hafsteinsson ¶	ISL	12.12.60	1		Selfoss	31 May 89
		(40)							
67.62		Randy	Heisler	USA	7.8.61	1		Bloomington	29 Jun 87
67.62		Marco	Martino	ITA	21.2.60	1	v4N	Spoleto	28 May 89
67.60		Rolf	Danneberg	FRG	1.3.53	1		Berlin	30 May 87
67.56		Wolfgang	Warnemünde	GDR	8.5.53	1		Rostock	2 Jun 80
67.54		Siegfried	Pachale	GDR	24.10.49	1		Karl-Marx-Stadt	29 May 76
67.54		Hilmar	Hossfeld	GDR	18.1.54	2	OT	Jena	17 May 80
67.54		Werner	Hartmann	FRG	20.4.59	1		Georgsheil	29 Apr 82
67.38		Tim	Vollmer	USA	13.9.46	2		Lancaster	16 May 71
67.38		Ferenc	Tégla	HUN	15.7.47	1		Szentes	12 Oct 77
67.32		Rob	Gray ¶	CAN	5.10.56	1		Etobicoke	30 Apr 84
		(50)							
Subsequent to drugs disqualification				*! recognised as US record*					
72.34!		Ben	Plucknett	USA	13.4.54	1	DNG	Stockholm	7 Jul 81
71.20			Plucknett			1	CalR	Modesto	16 May 81
70.84		Kamy	Keshmiri ¶	USA	23.1.69	1		Salinas	27 May 92
Sloping ground									
72.08		John	Powell	USA	25.6.47	1		Klagshamn	11 Sep 87
69.80		Stefan	Fernholm	SWE	2.7.59	1		Klagshamn	13 Aug 87

HAMMER

Mark	Wind	Name		Nat	Born	Pos	Meet	Venue	Date
86.74		Yuriy	Sedykh	RUS	11.6.55	1	EC	Stuttgart	30 Aug 86
86.34			Sedykh			1		Cork	3 Jul 84
86.04		Sergey	Litvinov	RUS	23.1.58	1	OD	Dresden	3 Jul 86
85.74			Litvinov			2	EC	Stuttgart	30 Aug 86
85.68			Sedykh			1	BGP	Budapest	11 Aug 86
85.60			Sedykh			1	PTG	London	13 Jul 84
85.60			Sedykh			1	Drz	Moskva	17 Aug 84
85.20			Litvinov			2		Cork	3 Jul 84
85.14			Litvinov			1	PTG	London	11 Jul 86
85.14			Sedykh			1	Kuts	Moskva	4 Sep 88
85.02			Sedykh			1	BGP	Budapest	20 Aug 84
84.92			Sedykh			2	OD	Dresden	3 Jul 86
84.88			Litvinov			1	GP-GG	Roma	10 Sep 86
84.80			Litvinov			1	OG	Seoul	26 Sep 88
84.72			Sedykh			1	GWG	Moskva	9 Jul 86
84.64			Litvinov			2	GWG	Moskva	9 Jul 86
84.62		Igor	Astapkovich	BLR	4.1.63	1	Expo	Sevilla	6 Jun 92
84.60			Sedykh			1	8-N	Tokyo	14 Sep 84
84.58			Sedykh			1	Znam	Leningrad	8 Jun 86
84.48		Igor	Nikulin	RUS	14.8.60	1	Athl	Lausanne	12 Jul 90
84.46			Sedykh			1		Vladivostok	14 Sep 88
84.40		Jüri	Tamm	EST	5.2.57	1		Banská Bystrica	9 Sep 84
84.36			Litvinov			2	vGDR	Tallinn	22 Jun 86
84.26			Sedykh			1	Nik	Nice	15 Jul 86
84.26			Astapkovich			1		Reims	3 Jul 91
84.16			Tamm			1		Kharkov	19 Jun 88
84.14			Litvinov			1	Spart	Moskva	21 Jun 83
84.14			Sedykh			1	WG	Helsinki	7 Jul 86
84.14			Astapkovich			1	EC	Split	31 Aug 90
		(30/5)							
83.46		Andrey	Abduvaliyev	TJK	30.6.66	1		Adler	26 May 90
83.40		Ralf	Haber	GDR	18.8.62	1		Athinai	16 May 88
82.84		Heinz	Weis	FRG	14.7.63	1	ISTAF	Berlin	18 Aug 89

Mark Wind	Name		Nat	Born	Pos	Meet	Venue	Date
82.64	Günther	Rodehau	GDR	6.7.59	1		Dresden	3 Aug 85
82.54	Vasiliy	Sidorenko	RUS	1.5.61	1		Krasnodar	24 May 92
	(10)							
82.54	Sergey	Kirmasov	RUS	25.3.70	1		Sochi	22 May 93
82.50	Lance	Deal	USA	21.8.61	1	NC	Knoxville	17 Jun 94
82.40	Plamen	Minev	BUL	28.4.65	1	NM	Plovdiv	1 Jun 91
82.24	Benjaminas	Viluckis	LIT	20.3.61	1		Klaipeda	24 Aug 86
82.24	Vyacheslav	Korovin	RUS	8.9.62	1		Chelyabinsk	20 Jun 87
82.16	Vitaliy	Alisevich	BLR	15.6.67	1		Parnu	13 Jul 88
82.08	Ivan	Tanev	BUL	1.5.57	1	NC	Sofia	3 Sep 88
82.00	Sergey	Alay	BLR	11.6.65	1		Staiki	12 May 92
81.88	Jud	Logan ¶	USA	19.7.59	1		University Park	22 Apr 88
81.78	Christoph	Sahner	FRG	23.9.63	1		Wemmetsweiler	11 Sep 88
	(20)							
81.72	Andrey	Skvaryuk	UKR	9.3.67	1	NC	Kiev	27 May 94
81.70	Aleksandr	Seleznyov	RUS	25.1.63	2		Sochi	22 May 93
81.68	Tibor	Gécsek	HUN	22.9.64	1		Szombathely	13 Sep 88
81.52	Juha	Tiainen	FIN	5.12.55	1		Tampere	11 Jun 84
81.44	Yuriy	Tarasyuk	BLR	11.4.57	1		Minsk	10 Aug 84
81.32	Klaus	Ploghaus	FRG	31.1.56	1		Paderborn	25 May 86
81.20	Igor	Grigorash	RUS	18.8.59	1		Kiev	23 Aug 84
81.18	Albert	Sinka	HUN	22.11.62	1		Székesfehérvár	7 Aug 88
81.10	Sergey	Ivanov	RUS	3.1.62	1		Chelyabinsk	27 Jun 87
80.92	Matthias	Moder	GDR	17.6.63	1		Halle	11 Jun 85
	(30)							
80.90	Yaroslav	Chmyr	UKR	29.11.67	1		Chernigov	2 Jun 90
80.80	Karl-Hans	Riehm	FRG	31.5.51	1		Rhede	30 Jul 80
80.78	Donatas	Plunge	LIT	11.11.60	1		Volgograd	22 Sep 89
80.78	Aleksandr	Krasko	BLR	18.9.72	1		Minsk	22 Jul 94
80.68	Viktor	Litvinenko	UKR	22.12.57	2		Kiev	23 Aug 84
80.64	Emanuil	Dyulgherov	BUL	7.2.55	1		Sofia	25 Aug 84
80.62	Viktor	Apostolov ¶	BUL	1.10.62	1		Sofia	28 Jul 90
80.60	Imre	Szitás	HUN	4.9.61	1		Szombathely	11 Jul 88
80.50	Detlef	Gerstenberg	GDR	5.3.57	1		Berlin	15 Jul 84
80.48	Boris	Zaychuk	RUS	28.8.47	2		Sochi	24 May 80
	(40)							
80.38	Frantisek	Vrbka	TCH	23.7.58	2	ECp	Moskva	18 Aug 85
80.36	Aleksey	Krykun	UKR	12.12.68	1		Donetsk	29 May 93
80.32	Nikolay	Lysenko	RUS	14.7.66	1		Ordzhonikidze	24 Sep 88
80.24	Grigoriy	Shevtsov	RUS	16.8.58	1		Volgograd	9 May 83
80.20	Igor	Shchegolev	RIS	26.10.60	1		Volgograd	6 Sep 86
80.18	Zdzislaw	Kwasny	POL	6.11.60	2	ECp	London	21 Aug 83
80.16	Anatoliy	Chyuzhas	BLR	18.4.56	2		Klaipeda	27 May 84
80.14	Tore	Gustafsson	SWE	11.2.62	1		Lappeenranta	4 Jul 89
80.02	Ken	Flax	USA	20.4.63	1	S&W	Modesto	7 May 88
79.98	Christophe	Epalle	FRA	23.1.69	1		Clermont-Ferrand	20 May 93
	(50)							

Extra trial: 81.04 Mariusz Tomaszewski POL 23.4.56 Zabrze 1 Jul 84
Chain exceeding legal length: 81.12 Grigoriy Shevtsov RUS 16.8.58 1 Sochi 12 May 83
Questionable measurement: 82.40 Plamen Minev BUL 28.4.65 1 Sofia 8 Aug 87

JAVELIN

Mark Wind	Name		Nat	Born	Pos	Meet	Venue	Date
95.66	Jan	Zelezny	TCH	16.6.66	1	McD	Sheffield	29 Aug 93
95.54A		Zelezny			1		Pietersburg	6 Apr 93
94.74 Irreg		Zelezny			1	Bisl	Oslo	4 Jul 92
91.82		Zelezny			1	McD	Sheffield	4 Sep 94
91.68		Zelezny			1	GP	Gateshead	1 Jul 94
91.50		Zelezny			1	Kuso	Lublin	4 Jun 94
91.46	Steve	Backley	GBR	12.2.69	1		Auckland	25 Jan 92
91.40		Zelezny			1	BNP	Villeneuve d'Ascq	2 Jul 93
91.28		Zelezny			1	BNP	Villeneuve d'Ascq	8 Jul 94
90.68		Zelezny			1	Nik	Nice	21 Jul 93
90.60		Zelezny			1		Stellenbosch	13 Apr 93
90.60	Seppo	Räty	FIN	27.4.62	1		Nurmijärvi	20 Jul 92
90.18		Zelezny			1	TOTO	Tokyo	19 Sep 92
90.06	Raymond	Hecht	GER	11.11.68	1		Eschenbach	12 Feb 94
90.02		Zelezny			1	GS	Ostrava	24 Jun 92

Mark	Wind	Name		Nat	Born	Pos	Meet	Venue	Date
89.98			Zelezny			1		Auckland	29 Mar 94
89.92			Zelezny			1		Göteborg	24 Aug 94
89.84			Zelezny			1	ECp	Roma	27 Jun 93
89.66			Zelezny			1	OG	Barcelona	8 Aug 92
89.58			Backley			1	DNG	Stockholm	2 Jul 90
89.16A		Tom	Petranoff	USA	8.4.58	1		Potchefstroom	1 Mar 91
89.10		Patrik	Bodén	SWE	30.6.67	1		Austin	24 Mar 90
89.06			Hecht			1		St Denis	10 Jun 94
89.00			Räty			1	vSWE	Heslinki	29 Aug 92
88.90			Hecht			2	BNP	Villeneuve d'Ascq	2 Jul 93
88.54			Hecht			1		Luzern	29 Jun 94
88.46			Backley			1	NC	Cardiff	3 Jun90
88.36			Räty			2	TOTO	Tokyo	19 Sep 92
88.36			Zelezny			1	Athl	Lausanne	7 Jul 93
88.34			Zelezny			1		Lahti	25 Aug 92
88.34			Zelezny			1	VD	Bruxelles	19 Aug 94
		(31/6)							
88.22		Juha	Laukkanen	FIN	6.1.69	1		Kuortane	20 Jun 92
87.60		Kazuhiro	Mizoguchi	JPN	18.3.62	1	Jen	San José	27 May 89
87.34		Andrey	Moruyev	RUS	6.5.70	1	ECp	Birmingham	25 Jun 94
87.20		Viktor	Zaitsev	UZB	6.6.66	1	OT	Moskva	23 Jun 92
		(10)							
87.08		Vladimir	Sasimovich	BLR	14.9.68	3	WCh	Tokyo	26 Aug 91
86.94		Mike	Hill	GBR	22.10.64	1	NC	London	13 Jun 93
86.80		Einar	Vihljálmsson	ISL	1.6.60	1		Reykjavik	29 Aug 92
86.64		Klaus	Tafelmeier	FRG	12.4.58	1	NC	Gelsenkirchen	12 Jul 87
86.50		Tapio	Korjus	FIN	10.2.61	1		Lahti	25 Aug 88
86.14		Gavin	Lovegrove	NZL	21.10.67	1		Wellington	18 Jan 92
85.74		Dmitriy	Polyunin ¶	UZB	6.4.69	2	OT	Moskva	23 Jun 92
85.70		Andrey	Shevchuk	RUS	8.3.70	2	Slovn	Bratislava	1 Jun 93
85.70		Tom	Pukstys	USA	28.5.68	2		Kuortane	26 Jun 93
85.46		Harri	Hakkarainen	FIN	16.10.69	1		Leppävirta	7 Jun 94
		(20)							
85.28		Donald	Sild	EST	3.10.68	2		St Denis	10 Jun 94
85.16		Viktor	Yevsyukov	KZK	6.10.56	1	vGDR	Karl-Marx-Stadt	21 Jun 87
84.86		Ramón	González	CUB	24.8.65	1		Potsdam	3 Jul 90
84.84		Volker	Hadwich	GDR	23.9.64	1	vITA,TCH	Macerata	5 Sep 89
84.80		Pascal	Lefévre	FRA	25.1.65	2	Nik	Nice	10 Jul 90
84.78		Kimmo	Kinnunen	FIN	31.3.68	2	WCh	Stuttgart	16 Aug 93
84.76		Peter	Borglund	SWE	29.1.64	1	vFIN	Stockholm	19 Aug 89
84.56		Klaus-Peter	Schneider	FRG	7.4.58	1	NC	Hamburg	13 Aug 89
84.54		Yuriy	Rybin	RUS	5.3.63	1	NC-w	Adler	24 Feb 91
84.36		Dag	Wennlund	SWE	9.10.63	1	Herc	Monaco	2 Aug 94
		(30)							
84.30	S	Lev	Shatilo	RUS	21.10.62	1	Znam	Moskva	7 Jun 87
84.14		Silvio	Warsönke	GDR	2.8.67	1		Rostock	29 May 88
84.12		Boris	Henry	GER	14.12.73	1		Gengenbach	29 Aug 93
84.06		Detlef	Michel	GDR	13.10.55	1		Berlin	13 Sep 88
84.00		Ari	Pakarinen	FIN	14.5.69	2		Pyhäselkä	5 Sep 92
84.00		Vladimir	Parfyonov	UZB	17.6.70	1		Tashkent	16 Sep 94
83.88		Dave	Stephens	USA	8.2.62	1		Knoxville	3 May 91
83.84		Roald	Bradstock	GBR	24.4.62	1		Tucson	2 May 87
83.82		Kostas	Gatsioudis	GRE	17.12.73	1	ECp 23	Ostrava	30 Jul 94
83.44		Oleg	Pakhol	RUS	12.5.64	1		Nizhniy Novgorod	18 Jul 90
83.40		Marko	Hyytiäinen	FIN	27.11.66	1		Heinola	11 Jun 90
		(40)							
83.38			Zhang Lianbiao	CHN	25.1.69	1	AsiG	Hiroshima	16 Oct 94
83.34		Sejad	Krdzalic	YUG	5.1.60	1		Beograd	30 May 87
83.32		Sigurdur	Einarsson	ISL	28.9.62	1		Mosfellsbær	5 Jul 92
83.30		Gerald	Weiss	GDR	8.1.60	1		Jena	3 Jun 88
83.30		Marek	Kaleta	EST	17.12.61	1		Pieksämäki	12 Aug 90
83.28		Peter	Schreiber	FRG	9.8.64	1		Wattenscheid	6 Jul 90
83.20		Heino	Puuste	EST	7.9.55	2	vGDR	Tallinn	22 Jun 86
83.00		Brian	Crouser ¶	USA	9.7.62	1		Corvallis	16 May 87
82.74		Duncan	Atwood ¶	USA	11.10.55	1	TAC	San José	26 Jun 87
82.70		Ivan	Mustapic	CRO	9.7.66	1		Zagreb	25 Jul 92
		(50)							

Mark	Wind	Name		Nat	Born	Pos	Meet	Venue	Date
Javelins with roughened tails, now banned by the IAAF									
96.96		Seppo	Räty	FIN	27.4.62	1		Punkalaidun	2 Jun 91
91.98			Räty			1	Super	Shizuoka	6 May 91
91.36			Backley			1	McV	Sheffield	15 Sep 91
90.98			Backley			1	PG	London	20 Jul 90
90.84		Raymond	Hecht	GER	11.11.68	1		Gengenbach	8 Sep 91
90.82		Kimmo	Kinnunen	FIN	31.3.68	1	WCh	Tokyo	26 Aug 91
90.72			Zelezny			1	Athl	Lausanne	10 Jul 91
90.40			Zelezny			1	GPB	Bratislava	4 Jun 91
89.86			Zelezny			1	PG	London	12 Jul 91
89.66			Zelezny			1	Bisl	Oslo	14 Jul 90
89.64			Räty			1		Elimäki	9 Jun 91
7.00		Peter	Borglund	SWE	29.1.64	1		Stockholm	13 Aug 91
85.52		Dag	Wennlund	SWE	9.10.63	1	NC	Helsingborg	27 Jul 91
85.08		Radoman	Scekic	YUG	1.10.67	1		Zagreb	12 Jun 91
84.94		Sigurdur	Einarsson	ISL	28.9.62	2	Super	Shizuoka	6 May 91
84.54		Terry	McHugh	IRL	22.8.63	1	vE,RUS	Limerick	14 Jun 91
84.46	R?	Andreas	Linden	GER	20.2.65	1		Gersthofen	9 Jun 91
84.20		Mike	Barnett	USA	21.5.61	1		Santa Barbara	11 Jul 91
83.92		Andrey	Maznichenko	UKR	29.9.66	3	NC-w	Adler	24 Feb 91
83.88		Dave	Stephens	USA	8.2.62	1		Knoxville	3 May 91
82.82		Peter	Blank	FRG	10.4.62	1	NC	Düsseldorf	12 Aug 90

DECATHLON

Mark	Wind	Name		Nat	Born	Pos	Meet	Venue	Date
8891		Dan	O'Brien	USA	18.7.66	1		Talence	5 Sep 92
			10.43w 8.08 16.69 2.07 48.51 13.98 48.56 5.00 62.58 4:42.10						
8847		Daley	Thompson	GBR	30.7.58	1	OG	Los Angeles	9 Aug 84
			10.44 8.01 15.72 2.03 46.97 14.33 46.56 5.00 65.24 4:35.00						
8844w			O'Brien			1	TAC	New York	13 Jun 91
			10.23 7.96 16.06 2.08 47.70 13.95W 48.08 5.10 57.40 4:45.54						
8832		Jürgen	Hingsen	FRG	25.1.58	1	OT	Mannheim	9 Jun 84
			10.70w 7.76 16.42 2.07 48.05 14.07 49.36 4.90 59.86 4:19.75						
8825			Hingsen			1		Filderstadt	5 Jun 83
			10.92 7.74 15.94 2.15 47.89 14.10 46.80 4.70 67.26 4:19.74						
8817			O'Brien			1	WCh	Stuttgart	20 Aug 93
			10.57 7.99 15.41 2.03 47.46 14.08 47.92 5.20 62.56 4:40.08						
8812			O'Brien			1	WCh	Tokyo	30 Aug 91
			10.41 7.90 16.24 1.91 46.53 13.94 47.20 5.20 60.66 4:37.50						
8811			Thompson			1	EC	Stuttgart	28 Aug 86
			10.26 7.72 15.73 2.00 47.02 14.04 43.38 5.10 62.78 4:26.16						
8792		Uwe	Freimuth	GDR	10.9.61	1	OD	Potsdam	21 Jul 84
			11.06 7.79 16.30 2.03 48.43 14.66 46.58 5.15 72.42 4:25.19						
8774			Thompson			1	EC	Athinai	8 Sep 82
			10.51 7.80 15.44 2.03 47.11 14.39 45.48 5.00 63.56 4:23.71						
8762		Siegfried	Wentz	FRG	7.3.60	2		Filderstadt	5 Jun 83
			10.89 7.49 15.35 2.09 47.38 14.00 46.90 4.80 70.68 4:24.90						
8741			Hingsen			1	NC	Ulm	15 Aug 82
			10.74w 7.85 16.00 2.15 47.65 14.64 44.92 4.60 63.10 4:15.13						
8735		Eduard	Hämäläinen	BLR	21.1.69	1		Götzis	29 May 94
			10.50 7.26 16.05 2.11 47.63 13.82 49.70 4.90 60.32 4:35.09						
8730			Thompson			1		Götzis	23 May 82
			10.50w 7.95 15.31 2.08 46.86 14.31 44.34 4.90 60.52 4:30.55						
8730			Hingsen			2	EC	Stuttgart	28 Aug 86
			10.87w 7.89w 16.46 2.12 48.79 14.52 48.42 4.60 64.38 4:21.61						
8727w/8705		Dave	Johnson	USA	7.4.63	1		Azusa	24 Apr 92
			10.96 7.52w/7.43 14.61 2.04 48.19 14.17 49.88 5.28 66.96 4:29.38						
8724			Hämäläinen			2	WCh	Stuttgart	20 Aug 93
			10.72 7.05 15.49 2.09 47.64 13.57 49.26 5.30 61.88 4:39.34						
8715			O'Brien			1	GWG	St Peterburg	29 Jul 94
			10.49 7.81 15.70 2.20 47.73 13.81 48.10 4.90 62.20 5:10.9						
8714			Thompson			1	WCh	Helsinki	13 Aug 83
			10.60 7.88 15.35 2.03 48.12 14.37w 44.46 5.10 65.24 4:29.72						
8710			O'Brien			1		Talence	11 Sep 94
			10.43 7.75 15.81 2.06 48.06 13.91 48.88 5.20 59.56 4:56.58						
8707			O'Brien			1	NC	Knoxville	15 Jun 94
			10.31 7.81 15.87 2.17 48.19 13.98 46.34 5.15 62.28 5:16.42						
8709		Aleksandr	Apaychev	UKR	6.5.61	1	vGDR	Neubrandenburg	3 Jun 84
			10.96 7.57 16.00 1.97 48.72 13.93 48.00 4.90 72.24 4:26.51						

Mark	Wind	Name		Nat	Born	Pos	Meet	Venue	Date
8698		Grigoriy	Degtyaryov	RUS	16.8.58	1	NC	Kiev	22 Jun 84
			10.87 7.42 16.03 2.10 49.75 14.53 51.20 4.90 67.08 4:23.09						
8695			Hingsen			2	OG	Los Angeles	9 Aug 84
			10.91 7.80 15.87 2.12 47.69 14.29 50.82 4.50 60.44 4:22.60						
8680		Torsten	Voss (10)	GDR	24.3.63	1	WCh	Roma	4 Sep 87
			10.69 7.88 14.98 2.10 47.96 14.13 43.96 5.10 58.02 4:25.93						
8676			Wentz			3	EC	Stuttgart	28 Aug 86
			10.83 7.60 15.45 2.12 47.57 14.07 45.66 4.90 65.34 4:35.00						
8667		Guido	Kratschmer	FRG	10.1.53	1		Filderstadt	14 Jun 80
			10.58w 7.80 15.47 2.00 48.04 13.92 45.52 4.60 66.50 4:24.15						
8667			Thompson			1	vFRA	Arles	18 May 86
			10.56 7.81 15.39 1.98 47.52 14.35 47.62 4.90 63.28 4:30.04						
8663			Thompson			1	CG	Edinburgh	28 Jul 86
			10.37 7.70w 15.01 2.08 47.30 14.22 43.72 5.10 60.82 4:39.63						
8649			Johnson			1	OT	New Orleans	27 Jun 92
			11.18 7.27 15.05 2.00 48.21 14.44 48.70 5.20 74.58 4:27.17						
		(30/11)							
8634		Bruce	Jenner	USA	28.12.49	1	OG	Montreal	30 Jul 76
			10.94 7.22w 15.35 2.03 47.51 14.84 50.04 4.80 68.52 4:12.61						
8627		Robert	Zmelík	TCH	18.4.69	1		Götzis	31 May 92
			10.62w 8.02 13.93 2.05 48.73 13.84 44.44 4.90 61.26 4:24.83						
8574		Christian	Plaziat	FRA	28.10.63	1	EC	Split	29 Aug 90
			10.72 7.77 14.19 2.10 47.10 13.98 44.36 5.00 54.72 4:27.83						
8549		Michael	Smith	CAN	16.9.67	2	WCh	Tokyo	30 Aug 91
			10.81 7.68 15.69 2.09 47.53 14.78 48.42 4.40 65.46 4:29.14						
8548		Paul	Meier	GER	27.7.71	3	WCh	Stuttgart	20 Aug 93
			10.57 7.57 15.45 2.15 47.73 14.63 45.72 4.60 61.22 4:32.05						
8548		Steve	Fritz	USA	1.11.67	2	NC	Knoxville	15 Jun 94
			10.63 7.84 14.37 2.05 48.70 14.27 46.76 4.95 64.58 4:43.09						
8547		Igor	Sobolevskiy	UKR	4.5.62	2	NC	Kiev	22 Jun 84
			10.64 7.71 15.93 2.01 48.24 14.82 50.54 4.40 67.40 4:32.84						
8534		Siegfried	Stark	GDR	12.6.55	1		Halle	4 May 80
			11.10w 7.64 15.81 2.03 49.53 14.86w 47.20 5.00 68.70 4:27.70						
8534w/8478		Antonio	Peñalver	ESP	1.12.68	1		Alhama	24 May 92
			10.76w 7.42w/7.19 16.50 2.12 49.50 14.32 47.38 5.00 59.32 4:39.94						
		(20)							
8519		Yuriy	Kutsenko	RUS	5.3.52	3	NC	Kiev	22 Jun 84
			11.07 7.54 15.11 2.13 49.07 14.94 50.38 4.60 61.70 4:12.68						
8506		Valter	Külvet	EST	19.2.64	1		Staiki	3 Jul 88
			11.05 7.35 15.78 2.00 48.08 14.55 52.04 4.60 61.72 4:15.93						
8500		Christian	Schenk	GER	9.2.65	4	WCh	Stuttgart	20 Aug 93
			11.22 7.63 15.72 2.15 48.78 15.29 46.94 4.80 65.32 4:24.44						
8491		Aleksandr	Nevskiy	UKR	21.2.58	2		Götzis	20 May 84
			10.97 7.24 15.04 2.08 48.44 14.67 46.06 4.70 69.56 4:19.62						
8485		Konstantin	Akhapkin	RUS	19.1.56	1	NC	Moskva	2 Aug 82
			11.10 7.72 15.25 2.02 49.14 14.38 45.68 4.90 62.42 4:19.60						
8466		Nikolay	Avilov	UKR	6.8.48	1	OG	München	8 Sep 72
			11.00 7.68 14.36 2.12 48.45 14.31 46.98 4.55 61.66 4:22.82						
8453		Alain	Blondel	FRA	7.12.62	1	EC	Helsinki	13 Aug 94
			11.12 7.50 13.78 1.99 48.91 14.18 45.08 5.40 60.64 4:20.48						
8447		Robert	de Wit	NED	7.8.62	1	NC	Eindhoven	22 May 88
			11.07 6.98 15.88 2.04 48.80 14.32 46.20 5.00 63.94 4:20.98						
8437		Richardas	Malakhovskis	LIT	28.4.65	2		Staiki	3 Jul 88
			10.93 7.04 14.94 2.09 47.77 14.34 44.04 4.90 59.58 4:13.67						
8436		Dezsö	Szabó	HUN	4.9.67	2	EC	Split	29 Aug 90
			11.06 7.49 13.65 1.98 47.17 14.67 40.78 5.30 61.94 4:11.07						
		(30)							
8417		Sergey	Zhelanov	RUS	14.6.57	4	NC	Kiev	22 Jun 84
			11.04 7.50 14.31 2.13 48.94 14.40 43.44 5.00 65.90 4:37.24						
8415		Dave	Steen	CAN	14.11.59	3		Talence	17 Jul 88
			11.02 7.56 13.99 1.98 48.22 14.95 44.08 5.20 65.36 4:21.46						
8403		Henrik	Dagård	SWE	7.8.69	4		Talence	11 Sep 94
			10.82 7.37 14.80 1.97 47.25 14.24 43.24 5.00 66.34 4:39.91						
8400h		Aleksandr	Grebenyuk	RUS	22.5.51	1	NC	Riga	3 Jul 77
			10.7 7.12 15.50 2.02 48.8 14.3 45.52 4.70 71.52 4:27.3						
8397		Fred	Dixon	USA	5.11.49	1	vURS	Bloomington	14 Aug 77
			10.85 7.44 15.20 2.04 48.54 14.94 47.14 4.60 67.88 4:30.21						
8381w		John	Sayre	USA	25.3.61	1	TAC	Indianapolis	18 Jun 85
			10.86W 7.41w 14.22 2.00 49.98 14.84W 46.08 5.30 67.68 4:37.07						

Mark	Wind	Name		Nat	Born	Pos	Meet	Venue	Date
8375		Pavel	Tarnavetskiy	UKR	22.2.61	3	WCh	Roma	4 Sep 87
			11.01 7.43 15.32 2.07 49.22 14.86 47.66 4.90 58.60 4:23.96						
8366		Vadim	Podmaryov	UZB	4.9.58	1		Tashkent	26 May 85
			11.09 7.56 15.28 2.08 50.00 14.89 48.58 4.60 67.46 4:32.31						
8366h		Simon	Poelman	NZL	27.5.63	1	NC	Christchurch	22 Mar 87
			10.6 7.34 15.11 2.06 49.4 14.1 46.66 4.95 56.94 4:27.2						
8364		Igor	Maryin	RUS	28.4.65	2	NC	Kiev	31 Jul 88
			10.91 7.79 15.10 2.04 49.22 15.71 43.16 5.00 67.70 4:32.19						
		(40)							
8362		Thomas	Fahner	GDR	18.7.66	3		Götzis	19 Jun 88
			11.04 7.55w 15.01 1.93 47.94 14.54 46.66 4.60 68.40 4:27.77						
8356		Viktor	Gruzenkin	RUS	19.12.51	5	NC	Kiev	22 Jun 84
			10.92 7.67 15.98 2.07 50.06 14.65 46.70 4.60 65.74 4:43.00						
8340		Tim	Bright	USA	28.7.60	1	TAC	San Jose	24 Jun 87
			10.90w 7.31 14.35 2.11 49.24 14.16 41.12 5.50 57.68 4:44.49						
8334		Rainer	Pottel	GDR	29.8.53	1	ECp	Birmingham	30 Aug 81
			11.06 7.68 14.38 2.01 48.35 14.57 39.52 4.80 67.46 4:22.67						
8334		Stefan	Niklaus	SUI	17.4.58	1	NC	Lausanne	3 Jul 83
			10.82 7.32 15.44 2.01 47.47 14.79 48.68 4.40 67.84 4:41.29						
8330		Mikhail	Medved	UKR	30.1.64	3	NC	Kiev	31 Jul 88
			11.24 7.46 15.73 2.07 50.13 14.40 45.32 5.00 64.50 4:41.26						
8327w		William	Motti ¶	FRA	25.7.64	1	ECp-B	Arles	5 Jul 87
			10.98W 7.39 15.13 2.13 48.83 14.57w 47.66 4.40 61.82 4:30.39						
8326		Andreas	Rizzi	FRG	6.5.59	4		Filderstadt	5 Jun 83
			10.52 7.71 14.78 2.00 46.82 14.91w 43.62 4.70 50.92 4:21.04						
8322		Mike	Ramos	USA	1.11.62	1	Pac10	Los Angeles	20 May 86
			10.77 7.39 14.67 2.16 50.16 14.98 49.06 4.80 63.52 4:48.06						
8322		Andrey	Nazarov	EST	9.1.65	1		Sochi	17 May 87
			10.71 7.69 13.73 2.16 49.21 13.88 41.68 4.70 56.60 4:36.36						
		(50)							
Best non wind-aided									
8306		William	Motti	FRA	25.7.64	1	NC	Athis-Mons	7 Jul 85
			11.03 7.63 15.11 2.16 48.43 14.75 45.98 4.40 63.38 4:43.06						
8296		Sheldon	Blockburger	USA	19.9.64	1		Brescia	16 May 93
			10.80 7.48 14.98 2.12 49.12 14.34 42.74 4.70 60.90 4:40.08						
8291Ah		Tito	Steiner	ARG	1.3.52	1		Provo	23 Jun 83
			10.8 7.45 16.35 2.04 49.0 14.1 50.02 4.56 61.50 4:51.6						
8126h		Derek	Huff	USA	26.11.66	1		Tucson	19 Mar 92
			11.08 7.42 15.25 2.08 49.97 15.1h 46.72 4.95 62.02 4:53.97						
8111		Herbert	Peter	FRG	24.6.57	7		Filderstadt	5 Jun 83
			11.29 7.11 12.97 2.06 48.55 14.95 44.02 4.40 66.80 4:08.42						
8076		John	Sayre	USA	25.3.61	2	MSR	Walnut	25 Apr 86
			11.23w 6.93w 14.53 1.99 49.32 14.82 48.52 5.00 64.90 4:47.29						
8052		Kip	Janvrin	USA	8.7.65	2		Aachen	8 Aug 93
			11.31 6.78 14.22 1.91 48.90 14.79 45.70 5.00 61.54 4:16.00						

4 x 100 METRES RELAY

Mark	Team		Pos	Meet	Venue	Date
37.40	USA	Marsh, Burrell, Mitchell, Lewis	1	OG	Barcelona	8 Aug 92
37.40	USA	Drummond, Cason, D.Mitchell, L.Burrell	1s1	WCh	Stuttgart	21 Aug 93
37.48	USA	Drummond, Cason, D.Mitchell, L.Burrell	1	WCh	Stuttgart	22 Aug 93
37.50	USA	Cason, Burrell, Mitchell, Lewis	1	WCh	Tokyo	1 Sep 91
37.67	USA	Marsh, Burrell, Mitchell, Lewis	1	WK	Zürich	7 Aug 91
37.75	USA	Cason, Burrell, Mitchell, Marsh	1h2	WCh	Tokyo	31 Aug 91
37.77	GBR	C.Jackson, Jarrett, Regis, L.Christie	2	WCh	Stuttgart	22 Aug 93
37.79	FRA	Morinière, Sangouma, Trouabal, Marie-Rose	1	EC	Split	1 Sep 90
37.79	Santa Monica TC/USA	Marsh, Burrell, Heard, Lewis	1	Herc	Monte Carlo	3 Aug 91
37.79	USA - Santa Monica TC	Marsh, Burrell, Heard, Lewis	1	MSR	Walnut	17 Apr 94
37.82	World All-Stars	Drummond/USA, Jarrett/GBR, Regis/GBR, Mitchell/USA	2	MSR	Walnut	17 Apr 94
37.83	USA	Graddy, R.Brown, C.Smith, Lewis	1	OG	Los Angeles	11 Aug 84
37.83	CAN	Esmie, Gilbert, Surin, Mahorn	3	WCh	Stuttgart	22 Aug 93
37.86	USA	E.King, Gault, C.Smith, Lewis	1	WCh	Helsinki	10 Aug 83
37.87	FRA	Morinière, Sangouma, Trouabal, Marie-Rose	2	WCh	Tokyo	1 Sep 91
37.89	Santa Monica TC (USA)	Marsh, Burrell, Heard, Lewis	1	TexR	Austin	9 Apr 94
37.90	USA	McRae, L.McNeill, Glance, Lewis	1	WCh	Roma	6 Sep 87
37.93	Santa Monica TC/USA	Witherspoon, Burrell, Heard, Lewis	1		Barcelona	16 Jul 90
37.97	Santa Monica TC/USA	Marsh, Burrell, Heard, Lewis	1	MSR	Walnut	18 Apr 92
37.98	USA	McRae, Heard, Glance, Lewis	1	GWG	Moskva	9 Jul 86

Mark	Wind	Name	Nat	Born	Pos	Meet	Venue	Date
37.98	GBR	Braithwaite, Regis, Adam, Christie			2	EC	Split	1 Sep 90
37.98	NGR	Kayode, Imoh, Adeniken, D.Ezinwa			2	OG	Barcelona	8 Aug 92
37.99	USA	Drummond, Cason, C.Smith, Dees			1	WK	Zürich	4 Oct 93
37.99	CAN	Esmie, Gilbert, Surin, Mahorn			2s1	WCh	Stuttgart	21 Aug 93
	(24 by 5 nations)							
38.00	CUB	Simon, Lamela, Isasi, Aguilera			3	OG	Barcelona	8 Aug 92
38.02	URS	Yevgenyev, Bryzgin, Muravyov, Krylov			2	WCh	Roma	6 Sep 87
38.29	GDR	Schröder, Kübeck, Prenzler, Emmelmann			2	vUSA	Karl-Marx-Stadt	9 Jul 82
38.33	POL	Zwolinski, Licznerski, Dunecki, Woronin			2	OG	Moskva	1 Aug 80
38.37	ITA	Tilli, Simionato, Pavoni, Mennea			2	WCh	Helsinki	10 Aug 83
	(10)							
38.39A	JAM	Stewart, Fray, Forbes, L.Miller			1s1	OG	Ciudad México	19 Oct 68
38.46	U/RUS	Zharov, Krylov, Fatun, Goremykin			4	EC	Split	1 Sep 90
38.46	AUS	Henderson, Marsh, Capobianco, Jackson			4s1	WCh	Stuttgart	21 Aug 93
38.54	FRG	Heer, Haas, Klein, Schweisfurth			1	R-W	Koblenz	28 Aug 88
38.61	GHA	Gariba, Boateng, Amegatcher, Tuffour			5s1	WCh	Stuttgart	21 Aug 93
38.67	HUN	Karaffa, Nagy, Tatár, Kovács			1	BGP	Budapest	11 Aug 86
38.73A	CIV	Ouré, Meité, Nogboum, Kablan			2	WUG	Ciudad México	13 Sep 79
38.77	JPN	Aoto, Suzuki, Inoue, Sugimoto			6	OG	Barcelona	8 Aug 92
38.79	UKR	Osovich, Vanyaykin, Kramarenko, Dologodin			2	ECp	Birmingham	25 Jun 94
38.82	TCH	Matousek, Demec, Kynos, Bohman			4	OG	München	10 Sep 72
	(20)							
Best low altitude marks								
38.41	JAM	Mair, Smith, Wright, Stewart			3	WCh	Roma	6 Sep 87
38.77	CIV	Lagazane, Zirignon, Waota, Meité			1h1	WCh	Stuttgart	21 Aug 93

4 x 400 METRES RELAY

Mark	Nat	Name	Pos	Meet	Venue	Date
2:54.29	USA	Valmon 44.5, Watts 43.6, Reynolds 43.23, Johnson 42.94	1	WCh	Stuttgart	22 Aug 93
2:55.74	USA	Valmon 44.6, Watts 43.00, M.Johnson 44.73, S.Lewis 43.41	1	OG	Barcelona	8 Aug 92
2:56.16A	USA	Matthews 45.0, Freeman 43.2, James 43.9, Evans 44.1	1	OG	Ciu. México	20 Oct 68
2:56.16	USA	Everett 44.0, S.Lewis 43.6, Robinzine 44.7, Reynolds 43.9	1	OG	Seoul	1 Oct 88
2:57.29	USA	Everett 45.1, Haley 44.0, McKay 44.20, Reynolds 44.00	1	WCh	Roma	6 Sep 87
2:57.53	GBR	Black 44.7, Redmond 44.0, Regis 44.22, Akabusi 44.59	1	WCh	Tokyo	1 Sep 91
2:57.57	USA	Valmon 44.9, Watts 43.4, D.Everett 44.31, Pettigrew 44.93	2	WCh	Tokyo	1 Sep 91
2:57.91	USA	Nix 45.59, Armstead 43.97, Babers 43.75, McKay 44.60	1	OG	Los Angeles	11 Aug 84
2:58.22	GBR	Sanders 45.85, Akabusi 44.48, Regis 43.93, Black 43.96	1	EC	Split	1 Sep 90
2:58.65	USA	Frazier 45.3, B.Brown 44.62, Newhouse 43.8, Parks 45.00	1	OG	Montreal	31 Jul 76
2:58.72	USA	Valmon 45.1, Pettigrew 44.0, Mills 44.65, Johnson 44.96	1h2	WCh	Stuttgart	21 Aug 93
2:58.86	GBR	Redmond 45.2, Akabusi 44.5, Black 44.81, Brown 44.34	2	WCh	Roma	6 Sep 87
2:59.06	USA	Everett 45.3, Franks 44.6, Pierre 44.7, McKay 44.5	1s2	WCh	Roma	5 Sep 87
2:59.12	USA	McCoy 45.20, Wiley 44.41, W.Smith 44.58, Darden 44.93	1	WCp	Roma	6 Sep 81
2:59.13	GBR	Akabusi 45.87, Cook 44.74, T.Bennett 44.17, P.Brown 44.35	2	OG	Los Angeles	11 Aug 84
2:59.13	CUB	Martínez 45.6, Herrera 44.38, Tellez 44.81, Hernández 44.34	1h2	OG	Barcelona	7 Aug 92
2:59.13	GBR	McKenzie 45.7, Whittle 45.3, Black 43.96, Ladejo 44.19	1	EC	Helsinki	14 Aug 94
2:59.14	USA	Hall 45.6, M.Johnson 44.46, C.Jenkins 44.59, Watts 44.49	2h2	OG	Barcelona	7 Aug 92
2:59.16	CUB	Peñalver 45.2, Pavó 45.2, Martínez 44.90, Hernández 43.88	3	WCh	Roma	6 Sep 87
2:59.32	NGR	Uti 45.34, Ugbisie 44.48, Peters 44.94, Egbunike 44.56	3	OG	Los Angeles	11 Aug 84
	(20/4)					
2:59.63	KEN	D.Kitur 45.4, S.Kitur 45.13, Kipkemboi 44.76, Kemboi 44.34	3h2	OG	Barcelona	7 Aug 92
2:59.70	AUS	Frayne 45.38, Clark 43.86, Minihan 45.07, Mitchell 45.39	4	OG	Los Angeles	11 Aug 84
2:59.86	GDR	Möller 45.8, Schersing 44.8, Carlowitz 45.3, Schönlebe 44.1	1	vSU	Erfurt	23 Jun 85
2:59.95	YUG	Jovkovic, Djurovic, Macev, Brankovic 44.3	2h3	WCh	Tokyo	31 Aug 91
2:59.96	FRG	Dobeleit 45.7, Henrich 44.3, Itt 45.12, Schmid 44.93	4	WCh	Roma	6 Sep 87
	(10)					
3:00.09	FRA	Rapnouil 45.5, Hilaire 45.5, Farraudière 44.86, Diagana 44.19	4	WCh	Stuttgart	22 Aug 93
3:00.16	URS	Lovachov, Lomtyev, Kurochkin, Markin 43.9	1	Drz	Moskva	18 Aug 84
3:00.44	RUS	Kliger 45.72, Kosov 45.09, Vdovin 44.73, Golovastov 44.90	5	WCh	Stuttgart	22 Aug 93
3:00.58A	POL	Gredzinski 46.8, Balachowski 44.7, Werner 44.5, Badenski 44.5	4	OG	Ciu. México	20 Oct 68
3:01.05	TRI	Delice, A Daniel, De Silva, Morris	1h1	OG	Barcelona	7 Aug 92
3:01.12	FIN	Lönnqvist 46.7, Salin 45.1, Karttunen 44.8, Kukkoaho 44.5	6	OG	München	10 Sep 72
3:01.26	JPN	Konakatomi, Takano 44.0, Watanabe, Ito	4h1	WCh	Tokyo	31 Aug 91
3:01.37	ITA	Bongiorni 46.2, Zuliani 45.0, Petrella 45.3, Ribaud 44.9	4	EC	Stuttgart	31 Aug 86
3:01.38	BRA	Nunes 46.5, Rocha 45.30, Menezes 44.81, S.Telles 44.76	1h3	OG	Barcelona	7 Aug 92
3:01.60	BAR	Louis 46.67, Peltier 44.97, Edwards 45.04, Forde 44.92	6	OG	Los Angeles	11 Aug 84
3:01.61	BUL	Georgiev 45.9, Stankulov 46.0, Raykov 45.07, Ivanov 44.66	2h1	WCh	Stuttgart	21 Aug 93
	(20)					

20,000 METRES WALK t = track walk

Mark	First name	Name	Nat	Born	Pos	Meet	Venue	Date
1:17:25.6t	Bernardo	Segura	MEX	11.2.70	1	SGP	Fana	7 May 94

Mark	Wind	Name	Nat	Born	Pos	Meet	Venue	Date
1:18:04		Bo Lingtang	CHN	12.8.70	1	NC	Beijing	7 Apr 94
1:18:13		Pavol Blazek	TCH	9.7.58	1		Hildesheim	16 Sep 90
1:18:20		Andrey Perlov	RUS	12.12.61	1	NC	Moskva	26 May 90
1:18:33		Mikhail Shchennikov	RUS	24.12.67	1	4-N	Livorno	10 Jul 93
1:18:35.2t		Stefan Johansson	SWE	11.4.67	1	SGP	Fana	15 May 92
1:18:37		Aleksandr Pershin	RUS	4.9.68	2	NC	Moskva	26 May 90
1:18:40.0t		Ernesto Canto	MEX	18.10.59	1	SGP	Fana	5 May 84
1:18:45		Shchennikov			1	EC	Helsinki	8 Aug 94
1:18:46		Tan Mingjun	CHN	17.7.70	2	NC	Beijing	7 Apr 94
1:18:51		Frants Kostyukevich	BLR	4.4.63	3	NC	Moskva	26 May 90
1:18:54		Yevgeniy Misyulya	BLR	13.3.64	1	NC-w	Sochi	19 Feb 89
1:18:54		Maurizio Damilano	ITA	6.4.57	1	7N	La Coruña	6 Jun 92
1:18:56		Grigoriy Kornev	RUS	14.3.61	4	NC	Moskva	26 May 90
1:18:58		Ar Pershin			1	NC-w	Sochi	17 Feb 91
1:19:03		Misyulya			1	NC-w	Sochi	22 Feb 92
1:19:05		Kostyukevich			2	NC-w	Sochi	17 Feb 91
1:19:07		Shchennikov			5	NC	Moskva	26 May 90
1:19:08		Shchennikov			1	NC	Kiev	30 Jul 88
1:19:08		Yuriy Kuko	BLR	23.1.68	2	4-N	Livorno	10 Jul 93
1:19:12		Axel Noack	GDR	23.9.61	1	vSU	Karl-Marx-Stadt	21 Jun 87
1:19:13		Misyulya			1	NC	Kiev	11 Jul 91
1:19:14		Robert Korzeniowski	POL	30.7.68	1	NC	Warszawa	20 Jun 92
1:19:16		Chen Shaoguo	CHN	20.1.71	3	NC	Beijing	7 Apr 94
1:19:17		Vladimir Andreyev	RUS	7.9.66	3	NC-w	Sochi	17 Feb 91
1:19:18.3t		Ronald Weigel	GDR	8.8.59	1	SGP	Fana	26 May 90
1:19:21		Andreyev			6	NC	Moskva	26 May 90
1:19:22		David Smith	AUS	24.7.55	1		Hobart	19 Jul 87
1:19:22		Misyulya			2	EC	Helsinki	8 Aug 94
1:19:22.5t		Aleksey Pershin	RUS	23.9.62	1	SGP	Fana	7 May 88
		(30/21)						
1:19:24		Carlos Mercenário	MEX	23.5.67	1	LT	New York	3 May 87
1:19:24.1t		Walter Arena	ITA	30.5.64	2	SGP	Fana	26 May 90
1:19:25		Valentin Massana	ESP	5.7.70	2	7N	La Coruña	6 Jun 92
1:19:29		Valdas Kazlauskas	LIT	7.8.58	2	NC-w	Sochi	19 Feb 89
1:19:30		Jozef Pribilinec	TCH	6.7.60	1	LT	Bergen	24 Sep 83
1:19:32		Viktor Mostovik	MOL	7.1.63	2	LT	New York	3 May 87
1:19:33		Nick A'Hern	AUS	6.1.69	1		Melbourne	15 Dec 90
1:19:35		Domingo Colin	MEX	4.8.52	1		Cherkassy	27 Apr 80
1:19:38		Mikhail Khmelnitskiy	BLR	24.6.69	1		Novopolotsk	21 May 94
		(30)						
1:19:41		Igor Plotnikov	RUS	12.7.64	4	NC-w	Sochi	17 Feb 91
1:19:41		Dmitriy Dolnikov	RUS	19.11.72	1		Adler	14 Feb 93
1:19:42		Daniel Garcia	MEX	28.10.71	2		Eschborn	12 Jun 93
1:19:43		Anatoliy Solomin	UKR	2.7.52	3	LT	Bergen	24 Sep 83
1:19:43		Nikolay Matyukhin	RUS	13.12.68	2		Adler	14 Feb 93
1:19:48		Yevgeniy Zaikin	RUS	19.6.57	5	NC-w	Sochi	17 Feb 91
1:19:52		Reima Salonen	FIN	23.12.55	1	IM	Pihtipudas	21 Jun 86
1:19:52		Vyacheslav Cherepanov	RUS	2.11.64	4		Adler	14 Feb 93
1:19:53		Yevgeniy Yevsyukov	RUS	2.1.50	2		Cherkassy	27 Apr 80
1:19:53		Yuriy Gordeyev	RUS	64	3	4-N	Livorno	10 Jul 93
		(40)						
1:19:54.0t		Pavol Blazek	TCH	9.7.58	3	SGP	Fana	26 May 90
1:19:58		Oleg Troshin	RUS	1.8.64	1		Moskva	22 Apr 90
1:19:59		Robert Ihly	GER	5.5.63	3	7N	La Coruña	6 Jun 92
1:20:00		José Marin	ESP	20.1.50	2		Barcelona	17 Apr 83
1:20:00		Li Mingcai	CHN	22.8.71	3	NG	Beijing	8 Sep 93
1:20:03		Viktor Ginko	BLR	7.12.65	5	4-N	Livorno	10 Jul 93
1:20:04		Anatoliy Gorshkov	UKR	4.8.58	3	LT	New York	3 May 87
1:20:06		Sergey Protsyshin	UKR	26.2.59	4	NC	Kiev	30 Jul 88
1:20:06		Zhou Yongshen	CHN	15.10.72	5	NC	Beijing	7 Apr 94
1:20:06.8t		Daniel Bautista	MEX	4.8.52	1		Montreal	17 Oct 79
		(50)						

50 KILOMETRES WALK

t = track

Mark	Wind	Name	Nat	Born	Pos	Meet	Venue	Date
3:37:41		Andrey Perlov	RUS	12.12.61	1	NC	Leningrad	5 Aug 89
3:38:17		Ronald Weigel	GDR	8.8.59	1	IM	Potsdam	25 May 86
3:38:29		Vyacheslav Ivanenko	RUS	1.3.61	1	OG	Seoul	30 Sep 88

Mark	Wind	Name		Nat	Born	Pos	Meet	Venue	Date
3:38:31			Weigel			1		Berlin	20 Jul 84
3:38:43		Valentin	Massana	ESP	5.7.70	1	NC	Orense	20 Mar 94
3:38:56			Weigel			2	OG	Seoul	30 Sep 88
3:39:45		Hartwig	Gauder	GDR	10.11.54	3	OG	Seoul	30 Sep 88
3:39:47			Perlov			1		Leningrad	3 Aug 85
3:40:02		Aleksandr	Potashov	BLR	12.3.62	1	NC	Moskva	27 May 90
3:40:07			Perlov			1		Kharkov	5 Sep 87
3:40:07		Andrey	Plotnikov	RUS	12.8.67	2	NC	Moskva	27 May 90
3:40:46		José	Marin	ESP	21.1.50	1		Valencia	13 Mar 83
3:40:53			Gauder			1	WCh	Roma	5 Sep 87
3:40:55			Gauder			1	EC	Stuttgart	31 Aug 86
3:41:00			Potashov			4	OG	Seoul	30 Sep 88
3:41:07		Valeriy	Spitsyn	RUS	5.12.65	1	EC	Helsinki	13 Aug 94
3:41:20		Raul	González (10)	MEX	29.2.52	1		Podebrady	11 Jun 78
3:41:24			Gauder			2		Berlin	20 Jul 84
3:41:28		Jesús Angel	Garcia	ESP	17.10.69	2	NC	Orense	20 Mar 94
3:41:28.2t		René	Piller	FRA	23.4.65	1	SGP	Fana	7 May 94
3:41:30			Weigel			2	WCh	Roma	5 Sep 87
3:41:31			Weigel			1		Naumberg	1 May 83
3:41:38.4t			González			1	SGP	Fana	25 May 79
3:41:41			Garcia			1	WCh	Stuttgart	21 Aug 93
3:41:51		Venyamin	Nikolayev	RUS	7.10.58	2		Leningrad	3 Aug 85
3:41:54			Ivanenko			2	EC	Stuttgart	31 Aug 86
3:42:00		Stanislav	Vezhel	BLR	11.10.58	3	NC	Moskva	27 May 90
3:42:02		Valentin	Kononen	FIN	7.3.69	2	WCh	Stuttgart	21 Aug 93
3:42:03		Carlos	Mercenario	MEX	23.5.67	1	WCp	San José	2 Jun 91
3:42:04		Yevgeniy	Yevsyukov	RUS	2.1.50	3		Leningrad	3 Aug 85
		(30/17)							
3:42:20		Pavel	Szikora	TCH	26.3.52	1		Dudince	4 Apr 87
3:42:36		Reima	Salonen	FIN	19.10.55	1	NC	Vantaa	24 May 86
3:42:37		Valeriy	Suntsov	RUS	10.7.55	4		Leningrad	3 Aug 85
		(20)							
3:43:13		Simon	Baker	AUS	6.2.58	1	LT	L'Hospitalet	28 May 89
3:43:14		Dietmar	Meisch	GDR	10.2.59	3	LT	New York	2 May 87
3:43:16			Zhou Yongshen	CHN	15.10.72	1	NC	Beijing	10 Apr 94
3:43:36		Martín	Bermúdez	MEX	19.7.58	1	LT	Eschborn	30 Sep 79
3:43:50		Axel	Noack	GER	23.9.61	4	WCh	Stuttgart	21 Aug 93
3:43:52		Thierry	Toutain	FRA	14.2.62	2	EC	Helsinki	13 Aug 94
3:43:55		Giovanni	Perricelli	ITA	25.8.67	3	EC	Helsinki	13 Aug 94
3:43:57		Vitaliy	Matsko	RUS	8.6.60	2	NC	Leningrad	5 Aug 89
3:43:57		Vitaliy	Popovich	UKR	22.10.62	3	NC	Leningrad	5 Aug 89
3:43:59		Enrique	Vera-Ybánez	MEX	31.5.54	2	LT	Eschborn	30 Sep 79
3:44:08		Viktor	Dorovskikh	RUS	19.10.50	5		Leningrad	3 Aug 85
		(30)							
3:44.12		Anatoliy	Grigoryev	RUS	.61	1		Yevpatoriya	1 Oct 89
3:44:24		Erling	Andersen	NOR	22.9.60	2	WCp-s	Borås	15 Jun 85
3:44:24		Robert	Korzeniowski	POL	30.7.68	1	NC	Zamosc	26 Sep 93
3:44:33		Jorge	Llopart	ESP	5.5.52	1		Reus	26 Aug 79
3:44:45		Aleksey	Volgin	RUS	.68	1		Novopolotsk	16 Sep 90
3:44:49		Bo	Gustafsson	SWE	29.9.54	7	OG	Seoul	30 Sep 88
3:45:34		Viktor	Ginko	BLR	7.12.65	1		Podrebrady	23 Apr 94
3:45:35		Nikolay	Matyukhin	RUS	13.12.68	1		Izhevsk	27 Aug 94
3:45:43		Raffaello	Ducceschi	ITA	25.2.62	8	OG	Seoul	30 Sep 88
3:45:51		Uwe	Dünkel	GDR	3.11.60	1		Berlin	18 Jul 81
		(40)							
3:45:51		Sergey	Protsyshin	UKR	17.4.59	4	EC	Stuttgart	31 Aug 86
3:46:08		Vyacheslav	Smirnov	RUS	.57	4	NC	Leningrad	5 Aug 89
3:46:11.0t		Nikolay	Udovenko	UKR	6.10.56	1		Uzhgorod	3 Oct 80
3:46:28		Valeriy	Yarets	RUS	.56	6		Leningrad	3 Aug 85
3:46:30		German	Skurygin	RUS	23.12.63	6	EC	Helsinki	13 Aug 94
3:46:34		Willi	Sawall	AUS	7.11.41	1		Adelaide	6 Apr 80
3:46:41			Sun Xiaoguang	CHN	15.1.65	1		Zhengzhou	5 Mar 91
3:46:43		Bernd	Gummelt	GDR	21.12.63	2		Berlin	20 May 90
3:46:46		Basilio	Labrador	ESP	29.3.67	5	WCh	Stuttgart	21 Aug 93
3:46:51		Maurizio	Damilano	ITA	6.4.57	1	NC	Pomigliano	25 Mar 90
		(50)							

Mark	Wind	Name		Nat	Born	Pos	Meet	Venue	Date

JUNIOR MEN'S ALL-TIME LISTS

Note that care should be taken with junior lists as some athletes may be over age.

100 METRES

Mark	Wind	Name		Nat	Born	Pos	Meet	Venue	Date
10.05		Davidson	Ezinwa	NGR	22.11.71	1		Bauchi	4 Jan 90
10.07	2.0	Stanley	Floyd	USA	23.6.61	1		Austin	24 May 80
10.08	0.0	Andre	Cason	USA	13.1.69	1	TAC-j	Tallahassee	24 Jun 88
10.08A	1.9	Obadele	Thompson	BAR	30.3.76	3		El Paso	16 Apr 94
10.09A	1.8	Mel	Lattany	USA	10.8.59	2r2	USOF	Air Force Academy	30 Jul 78
10.10	1.9	Stanley	Kerr	USA	19.6.67	1	TAC-j	Towson	28 Jun 86
10.11	1.9	Harvey	Glance	USA	28.3.57	1	FOT	Eugene	20 Jun 76
10.11	2.0	Tim	Montgomery	USA	28.1.75	3h3	NC	Knoxville	15 Jun 94
10.13	1.9	Derrick	Florence	USA	19.6.68	2	TAC-j	Towson	28 Jun 86
10.14	0.8	Ronnie Ray	Smith	USA	28.3.49	2s1	AAU	Sacramento	20 Jun 68
10.14	2.0	Sven	Matthes	GDR	23.8.69	1		Berlin	13 Sep 88
Wind-assisted									
10.07	2.9	Lee	McRae	USA	23.1.66	2h5	NCAA	Austin	30 May 85
10.08	4.0	Johnny	Jones	USA	4.4.58	1		Austin	20 May 77
10.09	4.1	Stanley	Blalock	USA	18.3.64	1		Athens, Ga	19 Mar 83
10.09	3.1	Innocent	Asunze	NGR	30.12.72	1r1		Lagos	10 Jun 90
10.10		Rodney	Bridges	USA	31.5.71	1s1	JUCO	Odessa, Tx	18 May 90
10.11	4.0	Rod	Richardson	USA	17.9.62	1		Austin	22 May 81
10.12	3.7	Calvin	Smith	USA	8.1.61	1h5	NCAA	Austin	5 Jun 80
10.12A		Jerome	Harrison	USA	17.2.62	1		Colorado Springs	25 Jul 81
10.12		Héctor	Fuentes	CUB	27.7.74	1		Artemisa	22 Apr 93
Hand timing									
9.9	1.8	Johnny	Jones	USA	4.4.58	1	TexR	Austin	2 Apr 77
9.9		Oladape	Adeniken	NGR	19.8.69	2	NC	Bauchi	2 Jul 88
9.8w		Michael	Taylor	USA	4.8.65	1		Shreveport	11 Apr 83
Doubful timing: 9.8		Osmond	Ezinwa	NGR	22.11.71	1h2		Bauchi	3 Jan 90

200 METRES

Mark	Wind	Name		Nat	Born	Pos	Meet	Venue	Date
20.07	1.5	Lorenzo	Daniel	USA	23.3.66	1	SEC	Starkville	18 May 85
20.13	1.7	Roy	Martin	USA	25.12.66	1		Austin	11 May 85
20.22	1.7	Dwayne	Evans	USA	13.10.58	2	FOT	Eugene	22 Jun 76
20.23	0.5	Michael	Timpson	USA	6.6.67	1		University Park	16 May 86
20.24	0.2	Joe	DeLoach	USA	5.6.67	3		Los Angeles	8 Jun 85
20.29	1.5	Clinton	Davis	USA	17.8.65	1	TAC-j	University Park	26 Jun 83
20.30		Davidson	Ezinwa	NGR	22.11.71	1h1		Bauchi	3 Jan 90
20.37	1.0	Jürgen	Evers	FRG	29.4.65	1	EJ	Schwechat	28 Aug 83
20.37	0.2	Roberto	Hernández	CUB	6.3.67	1		Sevilla	24 May 86
20.39A	1.0	Marshall	Dill	USA	9.8.52	2	PAm	Cali	3 Aug 71
20.39	0.9	Stanley	Kerr	USA	19.6.67	1	TAC-j	Towson	29 Jun 86
20.42	1.8	Silvio	Leonard	CUB	20.9.55	2		Potsdam	13 Jun 74
Wind-assisted									
20.01	2.5	Derald	Harris	USA	5.4.58	1		San José	9 Apr 77
20.10	4.6	Stanley	Kerr	USA	19.6.67	2r2	SWC	Houston	18 May 86
20.30	2.6	Tony	Wheeler	USA	19.1.75	3	NCAA	Boise	4 Jun 94
20.34A	2.2	Marshall	Dill	USA	9.8.52	1s2	PAm	Cali	3 Aug 71
20.36	4.8	Chris	Nelloms	USA	14.8.71	1		Indianapolis	9 Jun 90
20.39	3.3	Stanley	Floyd	USA	23.6.61	1h4	NCAA	Austin	5 Jun 80
Hand timing									
19.9		Davidson	Ezinwa	NGR	22.11.71	1		Bauchi	18 Mar 89
20.1		Marshall	Dill	USA	9.8.52	1		Windsor	1 Jul 71
20.1		Harvey	Glance	USA	28.3.57	1		Auburn	17 Apr 76
20.1*	1.8	Willie	Turner	USA	14.10.68	2		Sacramento	10 Jun 67

* 220 yards less 0.1 secs

400 METRES

Mark	Wind	Name		Nat	Born	Pos	Meet	Venue	Date
43.87		Steve	Lewis	USA	16.5.69	1	OG	Seoul	28 Sep 88
44.69		Darrell	Robinson	USA	23.12.63	2	USOF	Indianapolis	24 Jul 82
44.73A		James	Rolle	USA	2.2.64	1	USOF	Air Force Academy	2 Jul 83
44.75		Darren	Clark	AUS	6.9.65	4	OG	Los Angeles	8 Aug 84
44.75		Deon	Minor	USA	22.1.73	1s1	NCAA	Austin	5 Jun 92
45.01		Thomas	Schönlebe	GDR	6.8.65	1		Berlin	15 Jul 84
45.04A		Wayne	Collett	USA	20.10.49	1q2	FOT	Echo Summit	13 Sep 68
45.05		Roberto	Hernández	CUB	6.3.67	2		Santiago de Cuba	21 Feb86

Mark	Wind	Name		Nat	Born	Pos	Meet	Venue	Date
45.09		Kevin	Robinzine	USA	12.4.66	4	TAC	Indianapolis	16 Jun 85
45.09		Henry	Thomas	USA	10.7.67	2r2	ISTAF	Berlin	23 Aug 85
45.15A		Riaan	Dempers	RSA	4.3.77	1	NC	Secunda	6 May 94
45.17		William	Reed	USA	1.4.70	1	TAC-j	Tucson	20 Jul 87
44.9+A	hand	Steve	Williams	USA	13.11.53	1	WAC	El Paso	13 May 72

Positive drugs test for pseudoephedrine

Mark	Wind	Name		Nat	Born	Pos	Meet	Venue	Date
45.07		Calvin	Harrison	USA	20.1.74	1	NC-j	Spokane	27 Jun 93

800 METRES

* 880 yards less 0.6 seconds

Mark	Wind	Name		Nat	Born	Pos	Meet	Venue	Date
1:44.3*		Jim	Ryun	USA	29.4.47	1	USTFF	Terre Haute	10 Jun 66
1:44.3		Joaquim	Cruz	BRA	12.3.63	1		Rio de Janeiro	27 Jun 81
1:44.77		Benson	Koech	KEN	10.11.74	1	WJ	Seoul	19 Sep 92
1:45.34		José	Parrilla	USA	31.3.72	1	SEC	Baton Rouge	19 May 91
1:45.45		Andreas	Busse	GDR	6.5.59	1	GS	Ostrava	7 Jun 78
1:45.46		Hezekiel	Sepeng	RSA	30.6.74	3s1	WCh	Stuttgart	15 Aug 93
1:45.64		David	Sharpe	GBR	8.7.67	5	VD	Bruxelles	5 Sep 86
1:45.77		Steve	Ovett	GBR	9.10.55	2	EC	Roma	4 Sep 74
1:45.84		Detlef	Wagenknecht	GDR	3.1.59	1	NC	Leipzig	2 Jul 78
1:45.96A		Jozef	Plachy	TCH	28.2.49	3s2	OG	Ciudad México	14 Oct 68
1:46.06		Vincent	Malakwen	KEN	19.7.74	2B		Rieti	5 Sep 93
1:46.16		Jonah	Birir	KEN	12.12.71	3		Rovereto	21 Aug 90

1000 METRES

Mark	Wind	Name		Nat	Born	Pos	Meet	Venue	Date
2:18.31		Andreas	Busse	GDR	6.5.59	1		Dresden	7 Aug 77
2:18.37		Vincent	Malakwen	KEN	19.7.74	1	ISTAF	Berlin	27 Aug 93
2:18.46		Benson	Koech	KEN	10.11.74	4	Pre	Eugene	5 Jun 93
2:18.70		Steffan	Oehme	GDR	30.8.63	5		Cottbus	30 May 81

1500 METRES

Mark	Wind	Name		Nat	Born	Pos	Meet	Venue	Date
3:34.92		Kipkoech	Cheruiyot	KEN	2.12.64	1		München	26 Jul 83
3:36.07		Wilfred Oanda	Kirochi	KEN	12.12.69	4		Rieti	31 Aug 88
3:36.1+		Jim	Ryun	USA	29.4.47	1		Berkeley	17 Jul 66
3:36.4A		Atoi	Boru	KEN	25.10.73	1	NC	Nairobi	13 Jun 92
3:36.47		Benson	Koech	KEN	10.11.74	4	Herc	Monte Carlo	7 Aug 93
3:36.73		Moses	Kiptanui	KEN	1.10.71	6		Rovereto	21 Aug 90
3:36.6+		Graham	Williamson	GBR	15.6.60	3	OsloG	Oslo	17 Jul 79
3:37.5		Tom	Byers	USA	12.4.55	3		Torino	24 Jul 74
3:37.83		Noureddine	Morceli	ALG	20.2.70	1		Verona	12Sep 89
3:37.95		William	Koila	KEN	4.8.74	1		New Delhi	4 Sep 91
3:38.07		Ari	Paunonen	FIN	10.3.58	1	NC	Tampere	31 Jul 77
3:38.2		José M	Abascal	ESP	17.3.58	1		Barcelona	10 Sep 77

1 MILE

Mark	Wind	Name		Nat	Born	Pos	Meet	Venue	Date
3:51.3		Jim	Ryun	USA	29.4.47	1		Berkeley	17 Jul 66
3:53.15		Graham	Williamson	GBR	15.6.60	3	OsloG	Oslo	17 Jul 79
3:53.92		Kipkoech	Cheruiyot	KEN	2.12.64	8	ISTAF	Berlin	17 Aug 83
3:55.63		Ari	Paunonen	FIN	10.3.58	3		London	26 Jun 77
3:56.87		Mike	Hillardt	AUS	22.1.61	5	ISTAF	Berlin	8 Aug 80

2000 METRES

Mark	Wind	Name		Nat	Born	Pos	Meet	Venue	Date
5:04.4		Harald	Hudak	FRG	28.1.57	4	Bis	Oslo	30 Jun 76
5:04.4+		Ismael	Kirui	KEN	20.2.75	3	ISTAF	Berlin	27 Aug 93
5:04.5		Christian	Leuprecht	ITA	28.5.71	1		Lana	11 Oct 90

3000 METRES

Mark	Wind	Name		Nat	Born	Pos	Meet	Venue	Date
7:39.82		Ismael	Kirui	KEN	20.2.75	3	ISTAF	Berlin	27 Aug 93
7:42.93		Andrew	Sambu	TAN	5.10.72	1		Grossetto	11 Aug 91
7:43.20		Ari	Paunonen	FIN	10.3.58	3		Köln	22 Jun 77
7:47.47		Charles	Cheruiyot	KEN	2.12.64	3	ISTAF	Berlin	17 Aug 83
7:48.28		Jon	Richards	GBR	19.5.64	9	OsloG	Oslo	9 Jul 83
7:49.74		Eliud	Barngetuny	KEN	.73	1		Nuoro	12 Sep 92
7:50.22+		Richard	Chelimo	KEN	21.4.72	1	GG	Roma	17 Jul 91
7:51.53		Christian	Leuprecht	ITA	28.5.71	5		Padova	16 Sep 90
7:51.84		Steve	Binns	GBR	25.8.60	2		Gateshead	8 Sep 79
7:53.4		Eddy	De Pauw	BEL	8.6.60	2		Bornem	3 Aug 79
7:54.2		Raf	Wijns	BEL	7.1.64	4		Bosvoorde	4 Aug 83
7:54.7		Mohamed	Choumassi	MAR	2.12.69	1		Västerås	30 Jun 88

5000 METRES

Mark	Wind	Name		Nat	Born	Pos	Meet	Venue	Date
13:02.75		Ismael	Kirui	KEN	20.2.75	1	WCh	Stuttgart	16 Aug 93
13:11.76		Richard	Chelimo	KEN	21.4.72	4	GG	Roma	17 Jul 91
13:16.64		Fita	Bayissa	ETH	15.12.72	2	WCh	Tokyo	1 Sep 91
13:20.12		Andrew	Sambu	TAN	5.10.72	3	MAI	Malmö	5 Aug 91
13:23.17		Addis	Abebe	ETH	5.9.70	1	Znam	Volgograd	11 Jun 89
13:24.07		Philip	Mosima	KEN	2.1.76	5	CG	Victoria	24 Aug 94
13:25.33		Charles	Cheruiyot	KEN	2.12.64	1		München	26 Jul 83
13:26.88		Terry	Thornton	RSA	23.9.67	1		Stellenbosch	8 Nov 86
13:27.04		Steve	Binns	GBR	25.8.60	3	IAC	London	14 Sep 79
13:28.85		Josphat	Machuka	KEN	12.12.73	3	AfrCh	Belle Vue Mauricia	27 Jun 92
13:29.91		Kibiego	Kororia	KEN	25.12.71	2		Vigo	5 Jul 90
13:31.10		Daniel	Komen	KEN	17.5.76	1		Alger	8 Jul 94

10000 METRES

Mark	Wind	Name		Nat	Born	Pos	Meet	Venue	Date
27:11.18		Richard	Chelimo	KEN	21.4.72	1	APM	Hengelo	25 Jun 91
27:17.82		Addis	Abebe	ETH	5.9.70	2	WG	Helsinki	29 Jun 89
27:57.68		Josphat	Machuka	KEN	12.12.73	3	VD	Bruxelles	25 Aug 92
28:03.79		Kibiego	Kororia	KEN	25.12.71	2		Kobe	29 Apr 90
28:03.99		Haile	Gebrselassie	ETH	18.4.73	1	WJ	Seoul	18 Sep 92
28:07.1A		Ismael	Kirui	KEN	20.2.75	1	NC	Nairobi	3 Jul 93
28:07.70		Petro	Metta	TAN	18.12.73	1		Formia	8 Jul 91
28:12.78		Bidelu	Kibret	ETH	.69	11	VD	Bruxelles	19 Aug 88
28:20.78		Kenji	Takao	JPN	22.3.75	6rA		Kobe	24 Apr 94
28:22.48		Christian	Leuprecht	ITA	28.5.71	3		Koblenz	4 Sep 90
28:25.77		Mohamed	Choumassi	MAR	2.12.69	21	Bis	Oslo	2 Jul 88
28:27.56		Joseph	Kibor	KEN	22.12.72	5	CG	Auckland	27 Jan 90
6 miles: 27:11.6		Gerry	Lindgren	USA	9.3.46	2	AAU	San Diego	27 Jun 65

MARATHON

Mark	Wind	Name		Nat	Born	Pos	Meet	Venue	Date
2:12:49		Negash	Dube	ETH	20.5.68	2		Beijing	18 Oct 87
2:12:49		Tesfayi	Dadi	ETH	19.5.69	5		Berlin	9 Oct 88

3000 METRES STEEPLECHASE

Mark	Wind	Name		Nat	Born	Pos	Meet	Venue	Date
8:19.21		Daniel	Njenga	KEN	7.5.76	1	JPN Ch	Tokyo	12 Jun 94
8:24.47		Matthew	Birir	KEN	5.7.72*	3		Getxo	29 Jun 91
8:24.58		Christopher	Koskei	KEN	14.8.74	2	AfCh	Durban	25 Jun 93
8:24.87			Sun Ripeng	CHN	25.1.74	1	NG	Beijing	11 Sep 93
8:29.50		Ralf	Pönitzsch	GDR	20.10.57	4	vPOL,URS	Warszawa	19 Aug 76
8:29.85		Paul	Davies-Hale	GBR	21.6.62	3	vPOL,SUI	London	31 Aug 81
8:30.29		Anton	Nicolaisen	RSA	25.1.68	1		Durban	7 Dec 87
8:31.27		Shigeyuki	Aikyo	JPN	29.1.64	9h1	WCh	Helsinki	9 Aug 83
8:31.32		Eliud	Barngetuny	KEN	20.5.73	2		Bologna	9 Sep 92
8:31.51		Paul	Chemase	KEN	24.8.76	1	WJ	Lisboa	23 Jul 94
8:31.62		Mwangangi	Muindi	KEN	14.8.73	1	WJ	Seoul	20 Sep 92
8:31.85		Arsenios	Tsiminos	GRE	19.1.61	3	vSPA,BEL-j	Barcelona	31 Aug 80

* Birir's birthdate previously reported as 25.11.69

110 METRES HURDLES

Mark	Wind	Name		Nat	Born	Pos	Meet	Venue	Date
13.23	0.0	Renaldo	Nehemiah	USA	24.3.59	1r2	WK	Zürich	16 Aug 78
13.44	-0.8	Colin	Jackson	GBR	18.2.67	1	WJ	Athinai	19 Jul 86
13.46	1.8	Jon	Ridgeon	GBR	14.2.67	1	EJ	Cottbus	23 Aug 85
13.47	1.9	Holger	Pohland	GDR	5.4.63	2	vUSA	Karl-Marx-Stadt	10 Jul 82
13.52	2.0	Alejandro	Casañas	CUB	29.1.54	1		Warszawa	28 Jun 72
13.52	0.6	Ubeja	Anderson	USA	30.3.74	1		Knoxville	16 May 93
13.56	0.5	Frank	Busemann	GER	26.2.75	1h2		Mannheim	4 Jun 94
13.57	1.4	Robert	Gaines	USA	14.4.57	2s1	FOT	Eugene	24 Jun 76
13.57*	0.5	Greg	Foster	USA	4.8.58	1	WCR	Fresno	7 May 77
13.64	2.0	Glenn	Terry	USA	10.2.71	1		Indianapolis	23 May 90
13.65	0.9	Antti	Haapakoski	FIN	6.2.71	1		Jamsankoski	26 Jul 90
13.66	2.0	Arto	Bryggare	FIN	26.5.58	4	ECp	Helsinki	14 Aug 77
Wind-assisted									
13.42	4.5	Colin	Jackson	GBR	18.2.67	2	CG	Edinburgh	27 Jul 86
13.47	2.1	Frank	Busemann	GER	26.2.75	1	WJ	Lisboa	22 Jul 94
13.54	4.1	Rod	Wilson	USA	24.9.61	1h2	NCAA	Austin	6 Jun 80
13.55	3.1	Arto	Bryggare	FIN	26.5.58	1	vGBR	Oulu	10 Jul 77
13.65	3.2	Dan	Philibert	FRA	6.8.70	1		Créteil	9 Jul 89
13.65	2.1	Dudley	Dorival	USA	1.9.75	2	WJ	Lisboa	22 Jul 94

Mark	Wind	Name		Nat	Born	Pos	Meet	Venue	Date

400 METRES HURDLES

Mark	Wind	Name		Nat	Born	Pos	Meet	Venue	Date
48.02		Danny	Harris	USA	7.9.65	2s1	FOT	Los Angeles	17 Jun 84
48.74		Vladimir	Budko	BLR	4.2.65	2	DRZ	Moskva	18 Aug 84
49.10		Yoshihiko	Saito	JPN	12.2.72	1		Kanazawa	17 Oct 91
49.33A		Joseph	Maritim	KEN	22.10.68	4	AfrG	Nairobi	9 Aug 87
49.45		Belfred	Clark	USA	19.8.65	1	TAC-j	Los Angeles	24 Jun 84
49.50		Kelly	Carter	USA	15.2.69	1	WJ	Sudbury	29 Jul 88
49.61		Harald	Schmid	FRG	29.9.57	1	vUSA-j	Lüdenscheid	7 Jul 76
49.62		Dennis	Otono	NGR	16.4.58	2	NCAA	Champaign	4 Jun 77
49.64		József	Szalai	HUN	8.3.61	3	BGP	Budapest	11 Aug 80
49.68		Edgar	Itt	FRG	8.6.67	1	NC-j	Wetzlar	7 Sep 86
49.71		Ruslan	Mishchenko	UKR	24.4.64	1	EJ	Schwechat	28 Aug 83
49.73		Rohan	Robinson	AUS	15.11.71	1	WJ	Plovdiv	10 Aug 90

HIGH JUMP

Mark	Wind	Name		Nat	Born	Pos	Meet	Venue	Date
2.37		Dragutin	Topic	YUG	12.3.71	1	WJ	Plovdiv	12 Aug 90
2.37		Steve	Smith	GBR	29.3.73	1	WJ	Seoul	20 Sep 92
2.36		Javier	Sotomayor	CUB	13.10.67	1		Santiago de Cuba	23 Feb 86
2.35i		Vladimir	Yashchenko	UKR	12.1.59	1	EI	Milano	12 Mar 78
		2.34				1	Prv	Tbilisi	16 Jun 78
2.35		Dietmar	Mögenburg	FRG	15.8.61	1		Rehlingen	26 May 80
2.34		Tim	Forsyth	AUS	17.8.73	1	Bisl	Oslo	4 Jul 92
2.33			Zhu Jianhua	CHN	29.5.63	1	AsiG	New Delhi	1 Dec 82
2.33		Patrik	Sjöberg	SWE	5.1.65	1	OsloG	Oslo	9 Jul 83
2.31		Jörg	Freimuth	GDR	10.9.61	3	OG	Moskva	1 Aug 80
2.31		Lochsley	Thomson	AUS	20.8.73	3	NC	Adelaide	8 Mar 92
2.30		Dothel	Edwards	USA	9.9.66	1	v3-N	Pullman	21 Jul 85
2.30		Jagan	Hames	AUS	31.10.75	2	NC	Sydney	13 Mar 94

POLE VAULT

Mark	Wind	Name		Nat	Born	Pos	Meet	Venue	Date
5.80		Maksim	Tarasov	RUS	2.12.70	1	vGDR-j	Bryansk	14 Jul 89
5.71		Lawrence	Johnson	USA	7.5.74	1		Knoxville	12 Jun 93
5.70		Viktor	Chistyakov	RUS	9.2.75	1		Leppävirta	7 Jun 94
5.65		Radion	Gataullin	UZB	23.11.65	2	NC	Donyetsk	8 Sep 84
5.65		István	Bagyula	HUN	2.1.69	1	WJ	Sudbury	28 Jul 88
5.62		Gérald	Baudouin	FRA	15.11.72	1	NC-j	Dreux	7 Jul 91
5.61		Thierry	Vigneron	FRA	9.3.60	1		Longwy	30 Sep 79
5.61i		Grigoriy	Yegorov	KZK	12.1.67	1	vGDR-j	Moskva	16 Feb 86
5.60		Konstantin	Volkov	RUS	28.2.60	1	ECp	Torino	5 Aug 79
5.60		Andrey	Grudinin	RUS	3.5.69	1		Simferopol	27 May 88
5.60i		Jean	Galfione	FRA	20.6.71	1		Miremas	24 Mar 90
5.60i		Yuriy	Yeliseyev	RUS	27.5.75	1		Malmö	2 Feb 94

LONG JUMP

Mark	Wind	Name		Nat	Born	Pos	Meet	Venue	Date
8.34	0.0	Randy	Williams	USA	23.8.53	Q	OG	München	8 Sep 72
8.28	0.8	Luis A	Bueno	CUB	22.5.69	1		La Habana	16 Jul 88
8.24	0.2	Eric	Metcalf	USA	23.1.68	1	NCAA	Indianapolis	6 Jun 86
8.24	1.8	Vladimir	Ochkan	UKR	13.1.68	1	vGDR-j	Leningrad	21 Jun 87
8.22		Larry	Doubley	USA	15.3.58	1	NCAA	Champaign	3 Jun 77
8.22		Ivan	Pedroso	CUB	17.12.72	1		Santiago de Cuba	3 May 91
8.21A	2.0	Vance	Johnson	USA	13.3.63	1	NCAA	Provo	4 Jun 82
8.20	1.5	James	Stallworth	USA	29.4.71	Q	WJ	Plovdiv	9 Aug 90
8.18		LaMonte	King	USA	18.12.59	2	CalR	Modesto	20 May 78
8.16	1.1	Dion	Bentley	USA	26.8.71	1	PAm-j	Santa Fé	23 Jun 89
8.15	1.2	Leroy	Burrell	USA	21.2.67	1		Los Angeles	19 Apr 86
8.14	1.5	Sheddric	Fields	USA	13.4.73	1	WelshG	Cwmbrân	14 Jul 91
Wind assisted									
8.40	3.2	Kareem	Streete-Thompson	CAY	30.3.73	1		Houston	5 May 91
8.35	2.2	Carl	Lewis	USA	1.7.61	1	NCAA	Austin	6 Jun 80
8.29	2.3	James	Beckford	JAM	9.1.75	1		Tempe	2 Apr 94
8.23	4.4	Peller	Phillips	USA	23.6.70	1		Sacramento	11 Jun 88
8.21	2.8	Masaki	Morinaga	JPN	27.3.72	1		Hamamatsu	7 Sep 91

TRIPLE JUMP

Mark	Wind	Name		Nat	Born	Pos	Meet	Venue	Date
17.50	0.4	Volker	Mai	GDR	3.5.66	1	vURS	Erfurt	23 Jun 85
17.42	1.3	Khristo	Markov	BUL	27.1.65	1	Nar	Sofia	19 May 84
17.40A	0.4	Pedro	Pérez	CUB	23.2.52	1	PAm	Cali	5 Aug 71

Mark	Wind	Name		Nat	Born	Pos	Meet	Venue	Date
17.29	1.3	James	Beckford	JAM	9.1.75	1		Tempe	2 Apr 94
17.27		Aliacer	Urrutia	CUB	22.9.74	1		Artemisa	23 Apr 93
17.23	0.2	Yoelvis	Quesada	CUB	4.8.73	1	NC	La Habana	13 May 92
17.03	0.6	Osiris	Mora	CUB	3.10.73	2	WJ	Seoul	19 Sep 92
17.00		Gustavo	Platt	CUB	29.7.54	1		La Habana	5 May 73
17.00		Yevgeniy	Timofeyev	RUS	22.2.74	1		Krasnodar	26 May 93
16.98	-0.2	Sergey	Bykov	UKR	11.5.71	1	WJ	Plovdiv	12 Aug 90
16.97	0.2	Igor	Parygin	RUS	3.2.67	1	WJ	Athinai	20 Jul 86
16.91		Héctor	Marquetti	CUB	7.4.68	1	CAC	Caracas	26 Jul 87
Drugs dq: 16.94	2.2		Juan M López	CUB	7.4.67	2	WJ	Athinai	20 Jul 86

SHOT

Mark	Wind	Name		Nat	Born	Pos	Meet	Venue	Date
21.05i		Terry	Albritton	USA	14.1.55	1	AAU	New York	22 Feb 74
20.65		Mike	Carter	USA	29.10.60	1	vSU-j	Boston	4 Jul 79
20.22			Carter			1		Abilene	5 May 79
20.20		Randy	Matson	USA	5.3.45	2	OG	Tokyo	17 Oct 64
20.20		Udo	Beyer	GDR	9.8.55	2	NC	Leipzig	6 Jul 74
19.99		Karl	Salb	USA	19.5.49	4	FOT	Echo Summit	10 Sep 68
19.74		Andreas	Horn	GDR	31.1.62	2	vSU-j	Cottbus	24 Jun 81
19.71		Vladimir	Kiselyov -1	UKR	1.1.57	1		Yalta	15 May 76
19.68		Ron	Semkiw	USA	28.3.54	1	vAFR	Dakar	4 Aug 73
19.53i		Vyacheslav	Lykho	RUS	16.1.67	1		Moskva	28 Dec 86
19.53		Manuel	Martinez	ESP	7.12.74	Q	WCh	Stuttgart	20 Aug 93
19.51		Viktor	Belyi	RUS	.64	6		Leningrad	26 Jul 83
19.48		Viktor	Bulat	RUS	1.4.71	1		Minsk	19 May 90

DISCUS

Mark	Wind	Name		Nat	Born	Pos	Meet	Venue	Date
65.62		Werner	Reiterer	AUS	27.1.68	1		Melbourne	15 Dec 87
63.64		Werner	Hartmann	FRG	20.4.59	1	vFRA	Strasbourg	25 Jun 78
63.26		Sergey	Pachin	UKR	24.5.68	2		Moskva	25 Jul 87
63.22		Brian	Milne	USA	7.1.73	1		University Park	28 Mar 92
62.52		John	Nichols	USA	23.8.69	1		Baton Rouge	23 Apr 88
62.04		Kenth	Gardenkrans	SWE	2.10.55	2		Helsingborg	11 Aug 74
61.84		Attila	Horváth	HUN	28.7.67	2		Budapest	18 May 85
61.84		Andreas	Seelig	GDR	6.7.70	1		Halle	15 May 88
61.54		Pedro	Acosta	CUB	15.1.70	1		La Habana	15 Jul 89
61.40		Vladimir	Dubrovshchik	BLR	7.1.72	1		Staiki	25 Jun 91
61.34			Li Shaojie	CHN	1.1.75	1		Jinan	1 Apr 93
61.30		Wolfgang	Schmidt	GDR	16.1.54	4	NC	Dresden	22 Jul 73

HAMMER

Mark	Wind	Name		Nat	Born	Pos	Meet	Venue	Date
78.14		Roland	Steuk	GDR	5.3.59	1	NC	Leipzig	30 Jun 78
78.00		Sergey	Dorozhon	UKR	17.2.64	1		Moskva	7 Aug 83
76.54		Valeriy	Gubkin	BLR	11.1.67	2		Minsk	27 Jun 86
76.42		Ruslan	Dikiy	TJK	18.1.72	1		Togliatti	7 Sep 91
75.52		Sergey	Kirmasov	RUS	25.3.70	1		Kharkov	4 Jun 89
75.24		Christoph	Sahner	FRG	23.9.63	1	vPOL-j	Göttingen	26 Jun 82
75.22		Yaroslav	Chmyr	UKR	29.11.66	1		Kiev	9 Sep 85
75.20		Igor	Nikulin	RUS	14.8.60	2		Leselidze	1 Jun 79
75.10		Eduard	Piskunov	UKR	26.9.67	1		Grodno	5 Jul 86
74.78		Matthias	Moder	GDR	17.6.63	1	NC-j	Cottbus	24 Jul 82
74.66		Ilya	Konovalov	RUS	14.3.71	1		Minsk	18 Jan 90
74.32		Sergey	Litvinov	RUS	23.1.58	1		Simferopol	7 Apr 77

JAVELIN

Mark	Wind	Name		Nat	Born	Pos	Meet	Venue	Date
80.94		Aki	Parviainen	FIN	26.10.74	4	NC	Jyväskylä	5 Jul 92
80.30		Kostas	Gatsioudis	GRE	17.12.73	1	NC	Athens	20 Jun 92
80.26		Vladimir	Ovchinnikov	RUS	2.8.70	Q	OG	Seoul	24 Sep 88
79.58		Gavin	Lovegrove	NZL	21.10.67	2		Nouméa	26 Oct 86
79.50		Steve	Backley	GBR	12.12.69	1	NC	Derby	5 Jun 88
79.46		Juha	Laukkanen	FIN	6.1.69	1		Joutsa	19 Jul 87
79.30			Li Rongxiang	CHN	.2.72			Beijing	25 Apr 91
78.84		Vladimir	Sasimovich	BLR	14.9.68	1	WJ	Athinai	18 Jul 86
78.62		Aleksey	Shchepin	RUS	3.4.72	1	v3N-j	Espoo	15 Jun 91
78.38		Jarkko	Kinnunen	FIN	21.4.70	2	vGDR-j	Orimattila	1 Jul 89
77.98		Marius	Corbett	RSA	26.9.75	1	WJ	Lisboa	24 Jul 94
77.96		Andrey	Shevchuk	RUS	8.3.70	1		Adler	24 Feb 89

Mark	Wind	Name	Nat	Born	Pos	Meet	Venue	Date

DECATHLON

Second day

Mark	Name		Nat	Born	Pos	Meet	Venue	Date
8397	Torsten	Voss	GDR	24.3.63	1	NC	Erfurt	7 Jul 82
	10.76 7.66	14.41 2.09 48.37			14.37 41.76 4.80 62.90 4:34.04			
8114	Michael	Kohnle	FRG	3.5.70	1	EJ	Varazdin	26 Aug 89
	10.95 7.09	15.27 2.02 49.91			14.40 45.82 4.90 60.82 4:49.43			
8104	Valter	Külvet	EST	19.2.64	1		Viimsi	23 Aug 81
	10.7w 7.26w	13.86 2.09 48.5			14.8 47.92 4.50 60.34 4:37.8			
8082	Daley	Thompson	GBR	30.7.58	1	ECp/s	Sittard	31 Jul 77
	10.70 7.54	13.84 2.01 47.31			15.26 41.70 4.70 54.48 4:30.4			
8036	Christian	Schenk	GDR	9.2.65	5		Potsdam	21 Jul 84
	11.54 7.18	14.26 2.16 49.23			15.06 44.74 4.20 65.98 4:24.11			
7938	Frank	Busemann	GER	26.2.75	1		Zeven	2 Oct 94
	10.68 7.37	13.08 2.03 50.41			14.34 39.84 4.40 63.00 4:37.31			
7913	Raul	Duany	CUB	4.1.75	2		La Habana	26 May 94
	11.50 7.13	13.99 2.10 49.70			14.77 37.76 4.50 65.58 4:24.03			
7906	Mikhail	Romanyuk	UKR	6.2.62	1	EJ	Utrecht	21 Aug 81
	11.26 7.11	13.50 1.98 49.98			14.72 42.94 4.90 59.74 4:30.63			
7827	Igor	Maryin	RUS	28.4.65	1		Frunze	9 Sep 84
	11.30 7.25	13.55 2.04 50.65			15.21 43.70 4.70 62.92 4:42.05			
7815	Thomas	Fahner	GDR	18.7.66	1	EJ	Cottbus	23 Aug 85
	11.13 7.17	13.33 2.00 49.31			15.18 42.02 4.90 62.02 4:51.46			
7813	Vitaliy	Kolpakov	UKR	2.2.72	1	EJ	Thesaloniki	9 Aug 91
	11.28 7.19	14.65 2.14 49.05			14.93 41.90 4.60 51.92 4:48.73			
7789	Pierre-Alexander	Vial	FRA	25.5.75	1		St Etienne	1 May 94
	10.82 7.29	12.90 1.86 48.98			14.61 42.98 4.80 54.04 4:30.41			

10,000 METRES WALK

Mark	Name		Nat	Born	Pos	Meet	Venue	Date
38:54.75	Ralf	Kowalsky	GDR	22.3.62	1		Cottbus	24 Jun 81
39:44.71	Giovanni	De Benedictis	ITA	8.1.68	1	EJ	Birmingham	7 Aug 87
39:50.73	Jefferson	Pérez	ECU	1.7.74	1	PAJ	Winnipeg	15 Jul 93
39:55.52	Ilya	Markov	RUS	19.6.72	1	WJ	Plovdiv	10 Aug 90
39:56.49	Alberto	Cruz	MEX	6.6.72	2	WJ	Plovdiv	10 Aug 90
39:59.58	Sergey	Tyulenyev	RUS	14.3.71	1		Kharkov	4 Jun 90
40:05.62	Michele	Didoni	ITA	7.3.74	1	EJ	San Sebastián	30 Jul 93
40:13.11	Yevgeniy	Shmalyuk	RUS	14.1.76	1		St Peterburg	28 May 94
40:14.17	Valentin	Massana	ESP	5.7.70	1	EJ	Varazdin	25 Aug 89
40:26.08	Dmitriy	Yesipchuk	RUS	17.11.74	2	EJ	San Sebastián	30 Jul 93
40:26.72	Dmitriy	Dolnikov	RUS	19.11.72	1		Krasnodar	1 Jun 91
40:26.93	Jorge	Segura	MEX	23.4.75	1	WJ	Lisboa	21 Jul 94

4 x 100 METRES RELAY

Mark	Nat	Team	Pos	Meet	Venue	Date
39.00A	USA	Jessie, Franklin, Blalock, Mitchell	1		Colorado Springs	18 Jul 83
39.13	USA	Nelloms, Bridges, Harris, Stallworth	1	WJ	Plovdiv	12 Aug 90
39.21	GBR	Condon, Campbell, Baulch, Fergus	1	WJ	Seoul	20 Sep 92
39.25	FRG	Dobeleit, Klameth, Evers, Lübke	1	EJ	Schwechat	28 Aug 83
39.53	URS	Inshakov, Gromadskiy, Semyonov, Goremykin	1h3	WJ	Plovdiv	11 Aug 90
39.54	NGR	Tetengi, D Ezinwa, Nwankwo, Adeniken	1h2	WJ	Sudbury	30 Jul 88
39.66	THA	Natanee, Seeharwang, Vechaprutti, Namwong	1	AsiC-j	Djakarta	20 Sep 94
39.69	GDR	Malke, Hoff, Thiele, Prenzler	1		Potsdam	10 Aug 77
39.69	FRA	Thessard, Patrick Barré, Panzo, Pascal Barré	1		Dôle	6 Aug 77
39.89	POL	Cywinski, Kusiowski, Zalewski, Mackowiak	1h1	EJ	Varazdin	26 Aug 89
39.90	CAN	Chambers, Tomlin, Robinson, Frempong-Manso	3	WJ	Lisboa	24 Jul 94

4 x 400 METRES RELAY

Mark	Nat	Team	Pos	Meet	Venue	Date
3:01.90	USA	Campbell, Rish, Waddle, Reed	1	WJ	Athinai	20 Jul 86
3:03.80	GBR	Grindley, Patrick, Winrow, Richardson	2	WJ	Plovdiv	12 Aug 90
3:04.12	JAM	R McDonald, D Clarke, Watts, M McDonald	2	WJ	Lisboa	24 Jul 94
3:04.22	CUB	Cadogan, Mordoche, González, Hernández	2	WJ	Athinai	20 Jul 86
3:04.58	GDR	Preusche, Löper, Trylus, Carlowitz	1	EJ	Utrecht	23 Aug 81
3:05.51	AUS	Burmeister, Hollingsworth, Greene, Robinson	3	WJ	Plovdiv	12 Aug 90
3:05.60	URS	Angelov, Oleynikov, Belikov, Golovastov	4	WJ	Plovdiv	12 Aug 90
3:05.77	FRG	Grüber, Seybold, Mikisch, Just	2	EJ	Schwechat	28 Aug 83
3:06.17A	RSA	- Transvaal	1	NC	Secunda	7 May 94
3:06.66	JPN	Hayashi, Nishihata, Ono, Sudo	3	WJ	Seoul	20 Sep 92
3:06.95	ITA	Campana, Petrella, Milocco, D'Amico	5	EJ	Schwechat	28 Aug 83

WOMEN'S ALL-TIME WORLD LISTS

100 METRES

Mark	Wind	Name		Nat	Born	Pos	Meet	Venue	Date
10.49	0.0	Florence	Griffith-Joyner	USA	21.12.59	1q1	OT	Indianapolis	16 Jul 88
10.61	1.2		Griffith-Joyner			1	OT	Indianapolis	17 Jul 88
10.62	1.0		Griffith-Joyner			1q3	OG	Seoul	24 Sep 88
10.70	1.6		Griffith-Joyner			1s1	OT	Indianapolis	17 Jul 88
10.76	1.7	Evelyn	Ashford	USA	15.4.57	1	WK	Zürich	22 Aug 84
10.77	0.9	Irina	Privalova	RUS	12.11.68	1rA	Athl	Lausanne	6 Jul 94
10.78A	1.0	Dawn	Sowell	USA	27.3.66	1	NCAA	Provo	3 Jun 89
10.78	1.7	Merlene	Ottey	JAM	10.5.60	1	Expo	Sevilla	30 May 90
10.78	0.4		Ottey			1	GPF	Paris	3 Sep 94
10.79A	0.6		Ashford			1	USOF	A.Force Academy	3 Jul 83
10.79	1.7		Ottey			1		Vigo	23 Jul 91
10.80	1.6		Ottey			1		Salamanca	13 Jul 92
10.81	1.7	Marlies	Göhr'	GDR	21.3.58	1	OD	Berlin	8 Jun 83
10.81	1.2		Ashford			2	OT	Indianapolis	17 Jul 88
10.82	1.4		Ottey			1	ISTAF	Berlin	17 Aug 90
10.82	2.0		Privalova			1	CIS Ch	Moskva	22 Jun 92
10.82	-1.0	Gail	Devers	USA	19.11.66	1	OG	Barcelona	1 Aug 92
10.82	1.5		Devers			1	Athl	Lausanne	7 Jul 93
10.82	-0.3		Devers			1	WCh	Stuttgart	16 Aug 93
10.82	-0.3		Ottey			2	WCh	Stuttgart	16 Aug 93
10.82	0.4	Gwen	Torrence	USA	12.6.65	2	GPF	Paris	3 Sep 94
10.83	1.7	Marita	Koch	GDR	18.2.57	2	OD	Berlin	8 Jun 83
10.83	0.0	Sheila	Echols	USA	2.10.64	1q2	OT	Indianapolis	16 Jul 88
10.83	-1.0	Juliet	Cuthbert (10)	JAM	9.4.64	2	OG	Barcelona	1 Aug 92
10.83	0.0		Torrence			1	VD	Bruxelles	19 Aug 94
10.84	1.7		Göhr			2	WK	Zürich	22 Aug 84
10.84	0.0		Ottey			1	Athl	Lausanne	10 Jul 91
10.84	0.2		Ottey			1	ISTAF	Berlin	10 Sep 91
10.84	1.3	Chioma	Ajunwa ¶	NGR	25.12.70	1		Lagos	11 Apr 92
10.84	-1.0		Privalova			3	OG	Barcelona	1 Aug 92
		(30 performances by 11 athletes)							
10.85	2.0	Anelia	Nuneva	BUL	30.6.62	1h1	NC	Sofia	2 Sep 88
10.86	0.6	Silke	Gladisch'	GDR	20.6.64	1	NC	Potsdam	20 Aug 87
10.86	0.0	Diane	Williams	USA	14.12.60	2q1	OT	Indianapolis	16 Jul 88
10.89	1.8	Katrin	Krabbe	GDR	22.11.69	1		Berlin	20 Jul 88
10.91	0.2	Heike	Drechsler'	GDR	16.12.64	2	GWG	Moskva	6 Jul 86
10.92	0.0	Alice	Brown	USA	20.9.60	2q2	OT	Indianapolis	16 Jul 88
10.93	1.8	Ewa	Kasprzyk	POL	7.9.57	1	NC	Grudziadz	27 Jun 86
10.94	1.0	Carlette	Guidry	USA	4.9.68	1	TAC	New York	14 Jun 91
10.95	1.0	Bärbel	Wöckel'	GDR	21.3.55	2	NC	Dresden	1 Jul 82
		(20)							
10.96	1.2	Marie-José	Pérec	FRA	9.5.68	1	NC	Dijon	27 Jul 91
10.96	2.0	Galina	Malchugina	RUS	17.12.62	2	CIS Ch	Moskva	22 Jun 92
10.97	0.0	Angella	Issajenko'	CAN	28.9.58	3	ASV	Köln	16 Aug 87
10.97	0.2	Mary	Onyali	NGR	3.2.68	1q2	WCh	Stuttgart	15 Aug 93
10.98	0.1	Marina	Zhirova	RUS	6.6.63	2	ECp	Moskva	17 Aug 85
10.98	0.8	Angela	Bailey	CAN	28.2.62	2	BGP	Budapest	6 Jul 87
10.98	1.6	Natalya	Pomoshchnikova'	RUS	9.7.65	2q2	OG	Seoul	24 Sep 88
10.99	1.3	Valerie	Brisco-Hooks	USA	6.7.60	1	Pepsi	Westwood	17 May 86
10.99	0.4	Zhanna	Tarnopolskaya	UKR	6.7.72	2A	GP II	Linz	4 Jul 94
11.01	0.6	Annegret	Richter	FRG	13.10.50	1s1	OG	Montreal	25 Jul 76
		(30)							
11.01	0.8	Pam	Marshall	USA	16.8.60	2	Athl	Lausanne	15 Sep 87
11.02	2.0	Romy	Müller'	GDR	26.7.58	3	OT	Dresden	24 May 80
11.02	-0.2	Lyudmila	Kondratyeva	RUS	11.4.58	2	Drz	Praha	16 Aug 84
11.02	0.0		Liu Xiaomei	CHN	11.1.72	1	NG	Beijing	8 Sep 93
11.03	2.0	Monika	Hamann'	GDR	8.6.54	2	NC	Dresden	1 Jul 77
11.03	2.0	Holli	Hyche	USA	6.9.71	1s1	NCAA	Boise	3 Jun 94
11.04	0.6	Inge	Helten	FRG	21.12.50	1h1		Fürth	13 Jun 76
11.04	1.7	Ingrid	Auerswald'	GDR	2.9.57	4	WK	Zürich	22 Aug 84
11.04	0.6	Laurence	Bily	FRA	5.5.63	1	NC	Tours	13 Aug 89
11.04	1.3	Lyudmila	Narozhilenko	RUS	21.4.64	1		Khania	31 May 92
		(40)							

Mark	Wind	Name		Nat	Born	Pos	Meet	Venue	Date
11.05	1.0	Kerstin	Behrendt	GDR	2.9.67	3	OT	Potsdam	8 Sep 88
11.05	0.0	Michelle	Finn	USA	8.5.65	3	GWG	Seattle	24 Jul 90
11.05	0.2	Irina	Slyusar	UKR	19.3.63	1		Kiev	15 Jul 92
11.06A	1.0	Evette	de Klerk'	RSA	21.8.65	1	NC	Germiston	20 Apr 90
11.06	1.7	Sandra	Myers	ESP	9.1.61	2		Vigo	23 Jul 91
11.07	-0.2	Renate	Stecher'	GDR	12.5.50	1	OG	München	2 Sep 72
11.07	2.0	Olga	Bogoslovskaya'	RUS	20.5.64	3	CIS Ch	Moskva	22 Jun 92
11.07	1.8	Cheryl	Taplin	USA	2.9.72	1		Baton Rouge	25 May 94
11.08A	1.2	Wyomia	Tyus	USA	29.8.45	1	OG	Ciudad México	15 Oct 68
11.08	2.0	Brenda	Morehead	USA	5.10.57	1	OT	Eugene	21 Jun 76
11.08	-0.1	Jeanette	Bolden	USA	26.1.60	2	WK	Zürich	13 Aug 86
11.08	0.8	Nelli (52)	Cooman	NED	6.6.64	3	EC	Stuttgart	27 Aug 86
Probably semi-automatic timing									
10.87	1.9	Lyudmila	Kondratyeva	RUS	11.4.58	1		Leningrad	3 Jun 80
10.99	1.9	Natalya	Bochina	RUS	4.1.62	2		Leningrad	3 Jun 80
Low altitude best: 10.91	1.6		Sowell			1	TAC	Houston	16 Jun 89
Wind-assisted marks									
10.54	3.0		Griffith-Joyner			1	OG	Seoul	25 Sep 88
10.60	3.2		Griffith-Joyner			1h1	OT	Indianapolis	16 Jul 88
10.70	2.6		Griffith-Joyner			1s2	OG	Seoul	25 Sep 88
10.77	2.3	Gail	Devers	USA	19.11.66	1	Jen	San José	28 May 94
10.78	3.1		Ashford			1		Modesto	12 May 84
10.78	5.0	Gwen	Torrence	USA	12.6.65	1q3	OT	Indianapolis	16 Jul 88
10.78	2.3		Ottey			1s2	WCh	Tokyo	27 Aug 91
10.79	3.3	Marlies	Göhr'	GDR	21.3.58	1	NC	Cottbus	16 Jul 80
10.80	2.9	Pam	Marshall	USA	16.8.60	1	TAC	Eugene	20 Jun 86
10.80	2.8	Heike	Drechsler'	GDR	16.12.64	1	Bisl	Oslo	5 Jul 86
10.81	2.4	Irina	Privalova	RUS	12.11.68	1		Rieti	26 Sep 92
10.81	3.8		Privalova			1		Rieti	5 Sep 93
10.82	2.2	Silke	Gladisch'	GDR	20.6.64	1s1	WCh	Roma	30 Aug 87
10.82A	2.8		Torrence			1		Sestriere	21 Jul 92
10.82	2.2		Devers			1	NC	Eugene	17 Jun 93
10.83	3.9		Echols			1h2	OT	Indianapolis	16 Jul 88
10.83	3.0		Ashford			2	OG	Seoul	25 Sep 88
10.84	2.9	Alice	Brown	USA	20.9.60	2	TAC	Eugene	20 Jun 86
10.89	3.1	Kerstin	Behrendt	GDR	2.9.67	2		Berlin	13 Sep 88
10.90	2.7	Chryste	Gaines	USA	14.9.70	2		Austin	9 May 92
10.91	4.6	Carlette	Guidry	USA	4.9.68	1s1	NCAA	Eugene	31 May 91
10.92	3.3	Bärbel	Wöckel'	GDR	21.3.55	2	NC	Cottbus	16 Jul 80
10.92	3.4	Angella	Taylor'	CAN	28.9.58	1s2	CG	Brisbane	4 Oct 82
10.93	3.8	Sonia	Lannaman	GBR	24.3.56	1	ECp/sf	Dublin	17 Jul 77
10.93	3.3	Ingrid	Auerswald'	GDR	2.9.57	3	NC	Cottbus	16 Jul 80
10.93	4.2	Holli	Hyche	USA	6.9.71	2h2	NC	Eugene	16 Jun 93
10.94	3.9	Jackie	Washington	USA	17.7.62	1		Houston	18 May 86
10.94A	3.0	Evette	de Klerk'	RSA	21.8.65	1h	NC	Germiston	20 Apr 90
10.96	2.9	Brenda	Morehead	USA	5.10.57	1s2	AAU	Walnut	16 Jun 79
10.96	4.2	Olga	Naumkina'	RUS	20.5.64	1	Znam	Volgograd	11 Jun 89
10.96A	2.5	Michelle	Finn	USA	8.5.65	1		Sestriere	8 Aug 90
10.97	3.3	Gesine	Walther	GDR	6.10.62	4	NC	Cottbus	16 Jul 80
10.97	3.0	Grace	Jackson	JAM	14.6.61	4	OG	Seoul	25 Sep 88
10.99	2.4	Chandra	Cheeseborough	USA	10.1.59	2		Modesto	14 May 83
10.99	5.1	Esther	Jones	USA	7.4.69	2	NCAA	Eugene	1 Jun 91
10.99	4.0	Cheryl	Taplin	USA	2.9.73	1	TexR	Austin	8 Apr 94
10.99	7.9	Inger	Miller	USA	12.6.72	1		Las Vegas	9 Apr 94
11.00	2.1	Laurence	Bily	FRA	5.6.63	1		Dijon	24 Jun 90
11.01	4.0	Heather	Hunte'	GBR	14.8.59	1		London	21 May 80
11.01	2.8	Kerry	Johnson	AUS	23.10.63	1h3	CGT	Sydney	2 Dec 89
11.01		Beatrice	Utondu	NGR	23.11.69	1		Springfield	1 May 93
11.02	5.0	Jennifer	Inniss	USA	21.11.59	3q3	OT	Indianapolis	16 Jul 88
11.02	2.1	Nicole	Mitchell	JAM	5.6.74	1	Mutual	Kingston	1 May 93
Hand timing									
10.7		Merlene	Ottey	JAM	10.5.60	1h		Kingston	15 Jul 88
10.7	1.1	Juliet	Cuthbert	JAM	9.4.64	1	NC	Kingston	4 Jul 92
10.8	1.8	Renate	Stecher'	GDR	12.5.50	1	NC	Dresden	20 Jul 83
10.8	-0.1	Annegret	Richter	FRG	13.10.50	1		Gelsenkirchen	27 Jun76

Mark	Wind	Name		Nat	Born	Pos	Meet	Venue	Date
10.8	0.5	Irina	Slyussar	UKR	19.3.63	1		Ordzhonik	13 Jul 85
10.8	0.6	Galina	Malchugina	RUS	17.12.62	1h	NP	Vladivostok	13 Sep 88
10.8	1.0	Marina	Molokova	RUS	24.8.62	1h	NP	Vladivostok	13 Sep 88
10.8		Svetlana	Goncharenko	RUS	28.5.71	1		Stavropol	28 May 94
10.7w	3.4	Merlene	Ottey	JAM	10.5.60	1h2		Shizuoka	27 Apr 86
10.8wA		Margaret	Bailes	USA	23.1.51	1		Flagstaff	29 Sep 68
10.8w	3.6	Sonia	Lannaman	GBR	24.3.56	1	vSU	Kiev	22 May 76
10.8w	3.8	Angella	Issajenko'	CAN	28.9.58	1		Perth	24 Jan 87

200 METRES

Mark	Wind	Name		Nat	Born	Pos	Meet	Venue	Date
21.34	1.3	Florence	Griffith-Joyner	USA	21.12.59	1	OG	Seoul	29 Sep 88
21.56	1.7		Griffith-Joyner			1s1	OG	Seoul	29 Sep 88
21.64	0.8	Merlene	Ottey	JAM	10.5.60	1	VD	Bruxelles	13 Sep 91
21.66	-1.0		Ottey			1	WK	Zürich	15 Aug 90
21.71	0.7	Marita	Koch	GDR	18.2.57	1	v Can	Karl-Marx-Stadt	10 Jun 79
21.71	0.3		Koch			1	OD	Potsdam	21 Jul 84
21.71	1.2	Heike	Drechsler'	GDR	16.12.64	1	NC	Jena	29 Jun 86
21.71	-0.8		Drechsler			1	EC	Stuttgart	29 Aug 86
21.72	1.3	Grace	Jackson	JAM	14.6.61	2	OG	Seoul	29 Sep 88
21.72	-0.1	Gwen	Torrence	USA	12.6.65	1s2	OG	Barcelona	5 Aug 92
21.74	0.4	Marlies	Göhr'	GDR	21.3.58	1	NC	Erfurt	3 Jun 84
21.74	1.2	Silke	Gladisch'	GDR	20.6.64	1	WCh	Roma	3 Sep 87
21.75	-0.1	Juliet	Cuthbert	JAM	9.4.64	2s2	OG	Barcelona	5 Aug 92
21.76	0.3		Koch			1	NC	Dresden	3 Jul 82
21.76	0.7		Griffith-Joyner			1q1	OG	Seoul	28 Sep 88
21.77	-0.1		Griffith-Joyner			1q2	OT	Indianapolis	22 Jul 88
21.78	-1.3		Koch			1	NC	Leipzig	11 Aug 85
21.77	1.0		Ottey			1	Herc	Monaco	7 Aug 93
21.79	1.7		Gladisch			1	NC	Potsdam	22 Aug 87
21.80	-1.1		Ottey			1	Nik	Nice	10 Jul 90
21.81	-0.1	Valerie	Brisco (10)	USA	6.7.60	1	OG	Los Angeles	9 Aug 84
21.81	0.4		Ottey			1	ASV	Köln	19 Aug 90
21.81	-0.6		Torrence			1	OG	Barcelona	6 Aug 92
21.82	1.3		Koch			1	NC	Karl-Marx-Stadt	18 Jun 83
21.83	-0.2	Evelyn	Ashford	USA	15.4.57	1	WCp	Montreal	24 Aug 79
21.83	0.5		Ottey			1	ASV	Köln	8 Sep 91
21.84	-1.1		Ashford			1	VD	Bruxelles	28 Aug 81
21.84	1.0		Drechsler			1	NC	Rostock	26 Jun 88
21.85	0.3	Bärbel	Wöckel'	GDR	21.3.55	2	OD	Potsdam	21 Jul 84
21.85	1.3		Griffith-Joyner			1	OT	Indianapolis	23 Jul 88
21.85	-0.8		Torrence			1	v Afr	Durham	12 Aug 94
		(31/12)							
21.88	2.0	Irina	Privalova	RUS	22.11.68	1		Rieti	5 Sep 93
21.93	1.3	Pam	Marshall	USA	16.8.60	2	OT	Indianapolis	23 Jul 88
21.95	0.3	Katrin	Krabbe	GDR	22.11.69	1	EC	Split	30 Aug 90
21.97	1.9	Jarmila	Kratochvílová	TCH	26.1.51	1	PTS	Bratislava	6 Jun 81
21.99	0.9	Chandra	Cheeseborough	USA	10.1.59	2	TAC	Indianapolis	19 Jun 83
21.99	1.1	Marie-José	Pérec	FRA	9.5.68	1	BNP	Villeneuve d'Ascq	2 Jul 93
22.01	-0.5	Anelia	Nuneva'	BUL	30.6.62	1	NC	Sofia	16 Aug 87
22.04A	0.7	Dawn	Sowell	USA	27.3.66	1	NCAA	Provo	2 Jun 89
		(20)							
22.06A	0.7	Evette	de Klerk'	RSA	21.8.65	1		Pietersburg	8 Apr 89
22.10	-0.1	Kathy	Cook'	GBR	3.5.60	4	OG	Los Angeles	9 Aug 84
22.13	1.2	Ewa	Kasprzyk	POL	7.9.57	2	GWG	Moskva	8 Jul 86
22.19	1.5	Natalya	Bochina	RUS	4.1.62	2	OG	Moskva	30 Jul 80
22.21	1.9	Irena	Szewinska'	POL	24.5.46	1		Potsdam	13 Jun 74
22.22	1.2	Galina	Malchugina	RUS	17.12.62	1q3	OG	Barcelona	3 Aug 92
22.23	-0.2	Dannette	Young	USA	6.10.64	1	Herc	Monaco	2 Aug 88
22.24	0.3	Gesine	Walther	GDR	6.10.62	2	NC	Dresden	3 Jul 82
22.24	0.1	Maya	Azarashvili	GEO	6.4.64	1		Kiev	16 Aug 88
22.24	0.8	Carlette	Guidry	USA	4.9.68	2	OT	New Orleans	28 Jun 92
		(30)							
22.25A	0.8	Angella	Taylor'	CAN	28.9.58	1		Colorado Springs	20 Jul 82
22.25	1.3	Cathy	Freeman	AUS	16.2.73	1	CG	Victoria	26 Aug 94
22.27	1.2	Elvira	Barbashina'	UZB	25.2.63	3	GWG	Moskva	8 Jul 86
22.29	0.7	Silke-Beate	Knoll	GER	21.2.67	1		Ingolstadt	19 Jul 92
22.30	0.0	Jackie	Joyner-Kersee	USA	3.3.62	1H	OT	Indianapolis	15 Jul 88

Mark	Wind	Name		Nat	Born	Pos	Meet	Venue	Date
22.31	0.1	Lyudmila	Kondratyeva	RUS	11.4.58	1		Moskva	12 Jun 80
22.31	0.9	Randy	Givens	USA	27.3.62	4	TAC	Indianapolis	19 Jun 83
22.31	1.1	Mary	Onyali	NGR	3.2.68	2	BNP	Villeneuve d'Ascq	29 Jun 90
22.32	-0.8	Marie-Christine	Cazier	FRA	23.8.63	2	EC	Stuttgart	29 Aug 86
22.32	-0.5	Melinda	Gainsford	AUS	1.10.71	1		Hobart	26 Feb 94
		(40)							
22.33	1.4	Inger	Miller	USA	12.12.72	1	MSR	Walnut	17 Apr 93
22.34	1.6	Holli	Hyche	USA	6.9.71	1	NCAA	New Orleans	5 Jun 93
22.35	1.8	Denise	Boyd'	AUS	15.12.52	1	NC	Sydney	23 Mar 80
22.35	-0.5	Natalya	Voronova	RUS	9.7.65	3s1	WCh	Stuttgart	19 Aug 93
22.36	1.7	Kerstin	Behrendt	GDR	2.9.67	3		Karl-Marx-Stadt	12 Jun 88
22.37	1.3	Sabine	Rieger/Günther	GDR	6.11.63	2	v URS	Cottbus	26 Jun 82
22.38	1.6	Renate	Stecher'	GDR	12.5.50	1	NC	Dresden	21 Jul 73
22.38	1.7	Brenda	Morehead	USA	5.10.57	1		Nashville	12 Apr 80
22.38	2.0	Lillie	Leatherwood	USA	6.7.64	1	SEC	Tuscaloosa	17 May 87
22.38	0.3	Sandra	Myers	ESP	9.1.61	4	EC	Split	30 Aug 90
		(50)							

Low altitude bests

22.37 1.4 Taylor' 1 NC Ottawa 1 Aug 82 22.46 Sowell 1 Kingston 6 May 89
22.45 -0.2 de Klerk' 1 NC Durban 22 Apr 89

Wind-assisted marks

Mark	Wind	Name		Nat	Born	Pos	Meet	Venue	Date
21.82	3.1	Irina	Privalova	RUS	12.11.68	1	Athl	Lausanne	6 Jul 94
21.84	2.3		Torrence			1		Austin	9 May 92
21.85	2.6		Koch			1		Karl-Marx-Stadt	27 May 79
21.85	2.6	Bärbel	Wöckel'	GDR	21.3.55	1	v USA	Karl-Marx-Stadt	10 Jul 82
22.16	3.1	Dannette	Young	USA	6.10.64	2	Athl	Lausanne	6 Jul 94
22.19A	3.1	Angella	Taylor'	CAN	28.9.58	1		Colorado Springs	21 Jul 82
22.26	4.2	Melinda	Gainsford	AUS	1.10.71	1		Sydney	22 Feb 92
22.33	3.7	Alice	Brown	USA	20.9.60	3s1	OT	Indianapolis	23 Jul 88
22.37	2.5	Esther	Jones	USA	7.4.69	1	NYG	New York	22 Jul 89

Hand timing

Mark	Wind	Name		Nat	Born	Pos	Meet	Venue	Date
21.9	0.0	Bärbel	Wöckel'	GDR	21.3.55	1		Tbilisi	27 Jun 81
22.0	-0.6	Marina	Molokova	RUS	24.8.62	1	Ros	Praha	23 Jun 87
22.1		Natalya	Bochina	RUS	4.1.62	1		Moskva	7 Jul 84
21.6w	2.5	Pam	Marshall	USA	16.8.60	1	TAC	San José	26 Jun 87

400 METRES

Mark	Name		Nat	Born	Pos	Meet	Venue	Date
47.60	Marita	Koch	GDR	18.2.57	1	WCp	Canberra	6 Oct 85
47.99	Jarmila	Kratochvílová	TCH	26.1.51	1	WCh	Helsinki	10 Aug 83
48.16		Koch			1	EC	Athinai	8 Sep 82
48.16		Koch			1	Drz	Praha	16 Aug 84
48.22		Koch			1	EC	Stuttgart	28 Aug 86
48.26		Koch			1	GO	Dresden	27 Jul 84
48.27	Olga	Vladykina'	UKR	30.6.63	2	WCp	Canberra	6 Oct 85
48.45		Kratochvílová			1	NC	Praha	23 Jul 83
48.59	Tatána	Kocembová'	TCH	2.5.62	2	WCh	Helsinki	10 Aug 83
48.60		Koch			1	ECp	Torino	4 Aug 79
48.60		Vladykina			1	ECp	Moskva	17 Aug 85
48.61		Kratochvílová			1	WCp	Roma	6 Sep 81
48.65		Bryzgina'			1	OG	Seoul	26 Sep 88
48.73		Kocembová			2	Drz	Praha	16 Aug 84
48.77		Koch			1	v USA	Karl-Marx-Stadt	9 Jul 82
48.82		Kratochvílová			1	Ros	Praha	23 Jun 83
48.83	Valerie	Brisco	USA	6.7.60	1	OG	Los Angeles	6 Aug 84
48.83	Marie-José	Pérec	FRA	9.5.68	1	OG	Barcelona	5 Aug 92
48.85		Kratochvílová			2	EC	Athinai	8 Sep 82
48.86		Kratochvílová			1	WK	Zürich	18 Aug 82
48.86		Koch			1	NC	Erfurt	2 Jun 84
48.87		Koch			1	VD	Bruxelles	27 Aug 82
48.88		Koch			1	OG	Moskva	28 Jul 80
48.89		Koch			1		Potsdam	29 Jul 79
48.89		Koch			1		Berlin	15 Jul 84
48.94		Koch			1	EC	Praha	31 Aug 78
48.96		Vladykina			1	NC	Leningrad	3 Aug 85
48.97		Koch			1	WCp	Montreal	26 Aug 79
48.97		Koch			1		Berlin	22 Sep 85
48.98		Vladykina			1	Izv	Kiev	22 Jun 84
	(30/6)							

Mark Wind	Name		Nat	Born	Pos	Meet	Venue	Date
49.05	Chandra	Cheeseborough	USA	10.1.59	2	OG	Los Angeles	6 Aug 84
49.11	Olga	Nazarova	RUS	1.6.65	1s1	OG	Seoul	25 Sep 88
49.19	Mariya	Pinigina'	UKR	9.2.58	3	WCh	Helsinki	10 Aug 83
49.24	Sabine	Busch	GDR	21.11.62	2	NC	Erfurt	2 Jun 84
	(10)							
49.28	Irena	Szewinska'	POL	24.5.46	1	OG	Montreal	29 Jul 76
49.30	Petra	Müller'	GDR	18.7.65	1		Jena	3 Jun 88
49.42	Grit	Breuer	GER	16.2.72	2	WCh	Tokyo	27 Aug 91
49.43	Kathy	Cook'	GBR	3.5.60	3	OG	Los Angeles	6 Aug 84
49.47	Aelita	Yurchenko	UKR	1.1.65	2	Kuts	Moskva	4 Sep 88
49.56	Bärbel	Wöckel'	GDR	21.3.55	1		Erfurt	30 May 82
49.57	Grace	Jackson	JAM	14.6.61	1	Nik	Nice	10 Jul 88
49.58	Dagmar	Rübsam'	GDR	3.6.62	3	NC	Erfurt	2 Jun 84
49.61	Ana Fidelia	Quirot	CUB	23.3.63	1	PAm	Habana	5 Aug 91
49.64	Gwen	Torrence	USA	12.6.65	2	Nik	Nice	15 Jul 92
	(20)							
49.64	Ximena	Restrepo	COL	10.3.69	3	OG	Barcelona	5 Aug 92
49.66	Christina	Lathan'	GDR	28.2.58	3	OG	Moskva	28 Jul 80
49.66	Lillie	Leatherwood	USA	6.7.64	1	TAC	New York	15 Jun 91
49.67	Sandra	Myers	ESP	9.1.61	1	Bisl	Oslo	6 Jul 91
49.75	Gaby	Bussmann	FRG	8.10.59	4	WCh	Helsinki	10 Aug 83
49.81		Ma Yuqin	CHN	11.9.72	1	NG	Beijing	11 Sep 93
49.82	Jearl	Miles	USA	4.9.66	1	WCh	Stuttgart	17 Aug 93
49.84	Diane	Dixon	USA	23.9.64	3s1	OG	Seoul	25 Sep 88
49.86	Charity	Opara ¶	NGR	20.5.72	1	Slov	Bratislava	1 Jun 92
49.87	Denean	Howard/Hill	USA	5.10.64	4s1	OG	Seoul	25 Sep 88
	(30)							
49.89	Irina	Privalova	RUS	12.11.68	1	Kuts	Moskva	30 Jul 93
49.91	Marita	Payne'	CAN	7.10.60	4	OG	Los Angeles	6 Aug 84
49.91	Jillian	Richardson	CAN	10.3.65	5s1	OG	Seoul	25 Sep 88
49.99	Pam	Marshall	USA	16.8.60	1	Pepsi	Westwood	17 May 86
50.03	Gesine	Walther	GDR	6.10.62	2		Jena	13 May 84
50.04	Cathy	Freeman	AUS	16.2.73	2	GPF	Paris	3 Sep 94
50.05	Pauline	Davis	BAH	9.7.66	2	ASV	Köln	19 Aug 90
50.05	Maicel	Malone	USA	12.6.69	1	Athl	Lausanne	6 Jul 94
50.06	Rochelle	Stevens	USA	8.9.66	1s2	OT	New Orleans	22 Jun 92
50.07	Irina	Nazarova'	RUS	31.7.57	4	OG	Moskva	28 Jul 80
	(40)							
50.07	Kirsten	Emmelmann'	GDR	19.4.61	2	ISTAF	Berlin	23 Aug 85
50.11	Juliet	Campbell	JAM	17.3.70	1		Kingston	3 Jul 93
50.12A	Myrtle	Bothma'	RSA	18.2.64	1	NC	Germiston	11 Apr 86
50.14	Riita	Salin	FIN	16.10.50	1	EC	Roma	4 Sep 74
50.15	Ellen	Streidt'	GDR	27.7.52	2	OD	Berlin	10 Jul 76
50.17	Nina	Zyuskova	UKR	15.5.52	5	OG	Moskva	28 Jul 80
50.17	Natasha	Kaiser-Brown	USA	14.5.67	2	WCh	Stuttgart	17 Aug 93
50.19	Irina	Baskakova	RUS	25.8.56	2	Spa	Moskva	21 Jun 83
50.19	Sandie	Richards	JAM	6.11.68	7	OG	Barcelona	5 Aug 92
50.19	Renee	Poetschka	AUS	1.5.71	1	NC	Sydney	12 Mar 94
	(50)							
Hand timing								
48.9	Olga	Nazarova	RUS	1.6.65	1	NP	Vladivostok	13 Sep 88
49.2A	Ana Fidelia	Quirot	CUB	23.3.63	1	AmCp	Bogotá	13 Aug 89
49.9	Lyudmila	Dzhigalova ¶	UKR	22.10.62	1		Kiev	24 Jun 88

800 METRES

Mark	Name		Nat	Born	Pos	Meet	Venue	Date
1:53.28	Jarmila	Kratochvílová	TCH	26.1.51	1		München	26 Jul 83
1:53.43	Nadezhda	Olizarenko'	UKR	28.11.53	1	OG	Moskva	27 Jul 80
1:54.44	Ana Fidelia	Quirot	CUB	23.3.63	1	WCp	Barcelona	9 Sep 89
1:54.68		Kratochvílová			1	WCh	Helsinki	9 Aug 83
1:54.81	Olga	Mineyeva	RUS	1.9.52	2	OG	Moskva	27 Jul 80
1:54.85		Olizarenko			1	Prav	Moskva	12 Jun 80
1:54.94	Tatyana	Kazankina ¶	RUS	17.12.51	1	OG	Montreal	26 Jul 76
1:55.04		Kratochvílová			1	OsloG	Oslo	23 Aug 83
1:55.05	Doina	Melinte	ROM	27.12.56	1	NC	Bucuresti	1 Aug 82
1:55.1 ‘		Mineyeva			1	Znam	Moskva	6 Jul 80
1:55.19	Maria	Mutola	MOZ	27.10.72	1	WK	Zürich	17 Aug 94
1:55.26	Sigrun	Wodars/Grau	GDR	7.11.65	1	WCh	Roma	31 Aug 87

Mark	Wind	Name		Nat	Born	Pos	Meet	Venue	Date
1:55.32		Christine	Wachtel	GDR	6.1.65	2	WCh	Roma	31 Aug 87
1:55.41			Mineyeva			1	EC	Athinai	8 Sep 82
1:55.42		Nikolina	Shtereva (10)	BUL	25.1.55	2	OG	Montreal	26 Jul 76
1:55.43			Mutola			1	WCh	Stuttgart	17 Aug 93
1:55.46		Tatyana	Providokhina	RUS	26.3.53	3	OG	Moskva	27 Jul 80
1:55.5			Mineyeva			1	Kuts	Podolsk	21 Aug 82
1:55.54		Ellen	van Langen	NED	9.2.66	1	OG	Barcelona	3 Aug 92
1:55.54			Liu Dong	CHN	27.12.73	1	NG	Beijing	9 Sep 93
1:55.56		Lyubov	Gurina	RUS	6.8.57	3	WCh	Roma	31 Aug 87
1:55.60		Elfi	Zinn	GDR	24.8.53	3	OG	Montreal	26 Jul 76
1:55.62			Mutola			1A	WK	Zürich	4 Aug 93
1:55.68		Ella	Kovacs	ROM	11.12.64	1	RomIC	Bucuresti	2 Jun 85
1:55.69		Irina	Podyalovskaya	BLR	19.10.59	1	Izv	Kiev	22 Jun 84
1:55.70			Wodars			2	WCp	Barcelona	9 Sep 89
1:55.74		Anita	Weiss'	GDR	16.7.55	4	OG	Montreal	26 Jul 76
1:55.80			Providokhina			1	EC	Praha	31 Aug 78
1:55.82			Mushta'			2	EC	Praha	31 Aug 78
1:55.84			Quirot			4	WCh	Roma	31 Aug 87
		(30/18)							
1:55.96		Lyudmila	Veselkova	RUS	25.10.50	2	EC	Athinai	8 Sep 82
1:55.96		Yekaterina	Podkopayeva' ¶	RUS	11.6.52	1		Leningrad	27 Jul 83
		(20)							
1:55.99		Lilia	Nurutdinova ¶	RUS	15.12.63	2	OG	Barcelona	3 Aug 92
1:56.0		Valentina	Gerasimova	KZK	15.5.48	1	NC	Kiev	12 Jun 76
1:56.0		Inna	Yevseyeva	UKR	14.8.64	1		Kiev	25 Jun 88
1:56.1		Ravilya	Agletdinova'	BLR	10.2.60	2	Kuts	Podolsk	21 Aug 82
1:56.2 '		Totka	Petrova ¶	BUL	17.12.56	1		Paris	6 Jul 79
1:56.2		Tatyana	Mishkel	UKR	10.6.52	3	Kuts	Podolsk	21 Aug 82
1:56.21		Martina	Kämpfert'	GDR	11.11.59	4	OG	Moskva	27 Jul 80
1:56.21		Zamira	Zaytseva	UZB	16.2.53	2		Leningrad	27 Jul 83
1:56.24			Qu Yunxia	CHN	25.12.72	2	NG	Beijing	9 Sep 93
1:56.42		Paula	Ivan	ROM	20.7.63	1	Balk	Ankara	16 Jul 88
1:56.44		Svetlana	Styrkina	RUS	1.1.49	5	OG	Montreal	26 Jul 76
		(30)							
1:56.51		Slobodanka	Colovic	YUG	10.1.65	1		Beograd	17 Jun 87
1:56.57		Zoya	Rigel	RUS	15.10.52	3	EC	Praha	31 Aug 78
1:56.6		Tamara	Sorokina'	RUS	15.8.50	5	Kuts	Podolsk	21 Aug 82
1:56.62		Tina	Paulino	MOZ	7.7.73	2	NYG	New York	22 May 93
1:56.64		Nadezhda	Loboyko	KZK	30.6.61	1	NC	Kiev	7 Jul 90
1:56.67		Fita	Lovin'	ROM	14.1.51	2	Prav	Moskva	12 Jun 80
1:56.7		Dalia	Matuseviciene	LIT	12.11.62	2		Kiev	25 Jun 88
1:56.76		Svetlana	Masterkova	RUS	17.1.68	2rA		Zürich	4 Aug 93
1:56.78		Lyudmila	Borisova	RUS	30.7.59	3	Izv	Kiev	22 Jun 84
1:56.82		Lyudmila	Rogachova	RUS	10.10.66	1		Parnu	13 Jul 88
		(40)							
1:56.84		Nina	Ruchayeva	RUS	17.4.56	2r1	NP/s	Moskva	19 Jul 84
1:56.90		Mary	Slaney	USA	4.8.58	1		Bern	16 Aug 85
1:56.9		Olga	Dvirna	RUS	11.2.53	6	Kuts	Podolsk	21 Aug 82
1:56.91		Kim	Gallagher	USA	11.6.64	3	OG	Seoul	26 Sep 88
1:56.95		Jolanta	Januchta	POL	16.1.55	1	BGP	Budapest	11 Aug 80
1:56.96		Zuzana	Moravcíková	TCH	30.12.56	1		Leipzig	27 Jul 83
1:56.96			Liu Li	CHN	12.3.71	1h2	NG	Beijing	8 Sep 93
1:56.97		Valentina	Zhukova'	BLR	26.10.59	5	Izv	Kiev	22 Jun 84
1:57.0 '		Olga	Vakhrusheva	UKR	26.11.47	3	Prav	Moskva	12 Jun 80
1:57.06		Ulrike	Klapezynski'	GDR	17.11.53	1	OT	Berlin	10 Jul 76
		(50)							

1000 METRES

Mark	Name		Nat	Born	Pos	Meet	Venue	Date
2:30.6	Tatyana	Providokhina	RUS	26.3.53	1		Podolsk	20 Aug 78
2:30.67	Christine	Wachtel	GDR	6.1.65	1	ISTAF	Berlin	17 Aug 90
2:30.85	Martina	Kämpfert'	GDR	11.11.59	1		Berlin	9 Jul 80
2:31.50	Natalya	Artyomova ¶	RUS	5.1.63	1	ISTAF	Berlin	10 Sep 91
2:31.5	Maricica	Puica	ROM	29.7.50	1		Poiana Brasov	1 Jun 86
2:31.51	Sandra	Gasser ¶	SUI	27.7.62	1		Jerez de la Frontera	13 Sep 89
2:31.6 '	Beate	Liebich	GDR	21.2.58	2		Berlin	9 Jul 80
2:31.65	Olga	Dvirna	RUS	11.2.53	1		Athinai	1 Sep 82
2:31.74	Anita	Weiss'	GDR	16.7.55	1		Potsdam	13 Jul 80

Mark Wind	Name		Nat	Born	Pos	Meet	Venue	Date
2:31.77	Sigrun	Wodars/Grau	GDR	7.11.65	2	ISTAF	Berlin	17 Aug 90
	(10)							
2:31.85	Doina	Melinte	ROM	27.12.56	3	ISTAF	Berlin	17 Aug 90
2:31.95	Ulrike	Bruns'	GDR	17.11.53	1	ISTAF	Berlin	18 Aug 78
2:32.25	Letitia	Vriesde	SUR	5.10.64	2	ISTAF	Berlin	10 Sep 91
2:32.29	Christiane	Wartenberg'	GDR	27.10.56	2		Potsdam	13 Jul 80
2:32.40	Ella	Kovacs	ROM	11.12.64	1	BNP	Villeneuve d'Ascq	2 Jul 93
2:32.57	Maria	Mutola	MOZ	27.10.72	1	Pre	Eugene	5 Jun 93
2:32.6	Raisa	Belousova	RUS	29.2.52	2	Kuts	Podolsk	5 Aug 79
2:32.70	Jolanta	Januchta	POL	16.1.55	1	WK	Zürich	19 Aug 81
2:32.77	Yvonne	Mai	GDR	22.8.65	5	ISTAF	Berlin	17 Aug 90
2:32.8	Tamara	Sorokina'	RUS	15.8.50	1		Podolsk	24 Jul 76
	(20)							

1500 METRES

Mark Wind	Name		Nat	Born	Pos	Meet	Venue	Date
3:50.46		Qu Yunxia	CHN	25.12.72	1	NG	Beijing	11 Sep 93
3:51.92		Wang Junxia	CHN	9.1.73	2	NG	Beijing	11 Sep 93
3:52.47	Tatyana	Kazankina ¶	RUS	17.12.51	1	WK	Zürich	13 Aug 80
3:53.96	Paula	Ivan'	ROM	20.7.63	1	OG	Seoul	1 Oct 88
3:54.23	Olga	Dvirna	RUS	11.2.53	1	NC	Kiev	27 Jul 82
3:55.0 '		Kazankina ¶			1	Znam	Moskva	6 Jul 80
3:55.30	Hassiba	Boulmerka	ALG	10.7.68	1	OG	Barcelona	8 Aug 92
3:56.0		Kazankina ¶			1		Podolsk	28 Jun 76
3:56.14	Zamira	Zaytseva	UZB	16.2.53	2	NC	Kiev	27 Jul 82
3:56.22		Ivan			1	WK	Zürich	17 Aug 88
3:56.50	Tatyana	Pozdnyakova	RUS	4.3.56	3	NC	Kiev	27 Jul 82
3:56.56		Kazankina ¶			1	OG	Moskva	1 Aug 80
3:56.63	Nadezhda	Ralldugina	RUS	15.11.57	1	Drz	Praha	18 Aug 84
3:56.65	Yekaterina	Podkopayeva' ¶	RUS	11.6.52	1		Rieti	2 Sep 84
	(10)							
3:56.7 '	Lyubov	Smolka	UKR	29.11.52	2	Znam	Moskva	6 Jul 80
3:56.7	Doina	Melinte	ROM	27.12.56	1		Bucuresti	12 Jul 86
3:56.8 '	Nadezhda	Olizarenko'	UKR	28.11.53	3	Znam	Moskva	6 Jul 80
3:56.9 '		Zaytseva			4	Znam	Moskva	6 Jul 80
3:56.91	Lyudmila	Rogachova	RUS	10.10.66	2	OG	Barcelona	8 Aug 92
3:57.05	Svetlana	Guskova	MOL	19.8.59	4	NC	Kiev	27 Jul 82
3:57.08		Qu Yunxia			3	OG	Barcelona	8 Aug 92
3:57.12	Mary	Slaney	USA	4.8.58	1	vNord	Stockholm	26 Jul 83
3:57.22	Maricica	Puica	ROM	29.7.50	1		Bucuresti	1 Jul 84
3:57.24		Decker			1	VD	Bruxelles	30 Aug 85
3:57.4 '	Totka	Petrova ¶	BUL	17.12.56	1	Balk	Athinai	11 Aug 79
3:57.4 '		Podkopayeva			5	Znam	Moskva	6 Jul 80
3:57.46		Zhang Linli	CHN	6.3.73	3	NG	Beijing	11 Sep 93
3:57.48		Puica			1	NC	Bucuresti	31 Jul 82
3:57.70		Pozdnyakova			2		Rieti	2 Sep 84
3:57.71	Christiane	Wartenberg'	GDR	27.10.56	2	OG	Moskva	1 Aug 80
	(30/20)							
3:57.72	Galina	Zakharova	RUS	7.9.56	1	NP	Baku	14 Sep 84
3:57.92	Tatyana	Dorovskikh ¶	UKR	12.8.61	4	OG	Barcelona	8 Aug 92
3:58.2 '	Natalia	Marasescu' ¶	ROM	3.10.52	1	NC	Bucuresti	13 Jul 79
3:58.37	Tatyana	Providokhina	RUS	26.3.53	1	Kuts	Podolsk	22 Aug 82
3:58.40	Ravilya	Agletdinova '	BLR	10.2.60	1	ECp	Moskva	18 Aug 85
3:58.5 '	Ileana	Silai ¶	ROM	14.10.41	2	NC	Bucuresti	13 Jul 79
3:58.64		Wang Renmei	CHN	5.7.70	4	NG	Beijing	11 Sep 93
3:58.65	Gabriella	Dorio	ITA	26.6.57	2		Tirrenia	25 Aug 82
3:58.67	Hildegard	Körner'	GDR	20.12.59	2	WCh	Roma	5 Sep 87
3:58.71	Lyubov	Kremlyova	RUS	21.12.62	1	WK	Zürich	19 Aug 92
	(30)							
3:58.76	Svetlana	Ulmasova	UZB	4.2.53	2	Kuts	Podolsk	22 Aug 82
3:58.89	Tamara	Sorokina'	RUS	15.8.50	1	Znam	Leningrad	26 Jul 81
3:59.01	Giana	Romanova	RUS	10.3.55	1	EC	Praha	3 Sep 78
3:59.10	Sonia	O'Sullivan	IRL	28.11.69	1	Nik	Nice	18 Jul 94
3:59.16	Natalya	Artyomova ¶	RUS	5.1.63	1	WK	Zürich	7 Aug 91
3:59.34		Liu Li	CHN	12.3.71	5	NG	Beijing	11 Sep 93
3:59.35	Violeta	Beclea	ROM	26.3.65	1	Herc	Monaco	7 Aug 93
3:59.48	Yelena	Sipatova	RUS	7.6.55	4	Kuts	Podolsk	22 Aug 82
3:59.67	Anna	Bukis	POL	8.9.53	3	BGP	Budapest	29 Jul 81

Mark	Wind	Name		Nat	Born	Pos	Meet	Venue	Date
3:59.70			Zhang Lirong	CHN	3.3.73	6	NG	Beijing	11 Sep 93
		(40)							
3:59.8		Raisa	Katyukova'	BLR	16.9.50	2		Podolsk	28 Jun 76
3:59.81			Wang Yuan	CHN	8.4.76	7	NG	Beijing	11 Sep 93
3:59.90		Angelika	Zauber	GDR	5.11.58	1	NC	Jena	9 Aug 81
3:59.90		Cornelia	Bürki	SUI	3.10.53	5	WCh	Roma	5 Sep 87
3:59.9		Ulrike	Klapezynski'	GDR	17.11.53	1		Potsdam	14 Jul 76
3:59.9		Beate	Liebich	GDR	21.2.58	1	OT	Potsdam	5 Jul 80
3:59.96		Zola	Budd'	GBR	26.5.66	3	VD	Bruxelles	30 Aug 85
4:00.05			Lu Yi	CHN	10.4.74	8	NG	Beijing	11 Sep 93
4:00.07		Andrea	Lange'	GDR	3.6.66	2	NC	Potsdam	22 Aug 87
4:00.12		Fita	Lovin'	ROM	14.1.51	1	RomIC	Bucuresti	4 Jun 83
		(50)							
Drugs disqualification									
3:59.06		Sandra	Gasser ¶	SUI	27.7.62	3	WCh	Roma	5 Sep 87

1 MILE

Mark	Name		Nat	Born	Pos	Meet	Venue	Date
4:15.61	Paula	Ivan'	ROM	20.7.63	1	Nik	Nice	10 Jul 89
4:15.8	Natalya	Artyomova ¶	RUS	5.1.63	1		Leningrad	5 Aug 84
4:16.71	Mary	Slaney	USA	4.8.58	1	WK	Zürich	21 Aug 85
4:17.00		Artyomova			1	GPF	Barcelona	20 Sep 91
4:17.25	Sonia	O'Sullivan	IRL	28.11.69	1	Bisl	Oslo	22 Jul 94
	(5/4)							
4:17.33	Maricica	Puica	ROM	29.7.50	2	WK	Zürich	21 Aug 85
4:17.57	Zola	Budd'	GBR	26.5.66	3	WK	Zürich	21 Aug 85
4:18.13	Doina	Melinte	ROM	27.12.56	1	Bisl	Oslo	14 Jul 90
4:19.41	Kirsty	McDermott/Wade	GBR	6.8.62	2	Bisl	Oslo	27 Jul 85
4:20.79	Hassiba	Boulmerka	ALG	10.7.68	1	Bisl	Oslo	6 Jul 91
4:20.89	Lyudmila	Veselkova	RUS	25.10.50	1		Bologna	12 Sep 81
	(10)							
Indoors								
4:17.14	Doina	Melinte	ROM	27.12.56	1		East Rutherford	9 Feb 90

2000 METRES

Mark	Name		Nat	Born	Pos	Meet	Venue	Date
5:25.36	Sonia	O'Sullivan	IRL	28.11.69	1	TSB	Edinburgh	8 Jul 94
5:26.93	Yvonne	Murray	GBR	4.10.64	2	TSB	Edinburgh	8 Jul 94
5:28.69	Maricica	Puica	ROM	29.7.50	1	PTG	London	11 Jul 86
5:28.72	Tatyana	Kazankina ¶	RUS	17.12.51	1		Moskva	4 Aug 84
5:29.41+		Wang Junxia	CHN	9.1.73	1h2	NG	Beijing	12 Sep 93
5:29.58		Murray			2	PTG	London	11 Jul 86
5:29.64	Tatyana	Pozdnyakova	UKR	4.3.56	2		Moskva	4 Aug 84
5:29.65		Wang Junxia			1+	NG	Beijing	13 Sep 93
5:30.19	Zola	Budd'	GBR	26.5.66	3	PTG	London	11 Jul 86
5:30.92	Galina	Zakharova	RUS	7.9.56	3		Moskva	4 Aug 84
	(10/8)							
5:32.7 '	Mary	Slaney	USA	4.8.58	1		Eugene	3 Aug 84
5:33.85	Christina	Boxer'	GBR	25.3.57	2	PTG	London	13 Jul 84
5:34.49	Angela	Chalmers	CAN	6.9.63	1	McD	Sheffield	4 Sep 94
5:35.16+		Zhang Linli	CHN	6.3.73	1h1	NG	Beijing	12 Sep 93
5:35.2+		Zhang Lirong	CHN	4.6.73	1h1	NG	Beijing	12 Sep 93

3000 METRES

Mark	Name		Nat	Born	Pos	Meet	Venue	Date
8:06.11		Wang Junxia	CHN	9.1.73	1	NG	Beijing	13 Sep 93
8:12.18		Qu Yunxia	CHN	25.12.72	2	NG	Beijing	13 Sep 93
8:12.19		Wang Junxia			1h2	NG	Beijing	12 Sep 93
8:12.27		Qu Yunxia			2h2	NG	Beijing	12 Sep 93
8:16.50		Zhang Linli	CHN	6.3.73	3	NG	Beijing	13 Sep 93
8:19.78		Ma Liyan	CHN	3.11.68	3h2	NG	Beijing	12 Sep 93
8:21.26		Ma Liyan			4	NG	Beijing	13 Sep 93
8:21.64	Sonia	O'Sullivan	IRL	28.11.69	1	TSB	London	15 Jul 94
8:21.84		Zhang Lirong	CHN	3.3.73	5	NG	Beijing	13 Sep 93
8:22.06		Zhang Linli			1h1	NG	Beijing	12 Sep 93
8:22.44		Zhang Lirong			2h1	NG	Beijing	12 Sep 93
8:22.62	Tatyana	Kazankina ¶	RUS	17.12.51	1		Leningrad	26 Aug 84
8:25.83	Mary	Slaney	USA	4.8.58	1	GG-GP	Roma	7 Sep 85
8:26.53	Tatyana	Samolenko' ¶	UKR	12.8.61	1	OG	Seoul	25 Sep 88
8:26.78	Svetlana	Ulmasova (10)	UZB	4.2.53	1	NC	Kiev	25 Jul 82
8:27.12	Lyudmila	Bragina	RUS	24.7.43	1	v USA	College Park	7 Aug 76

Mark Wind	Name		Nat	Born	Pos	Meet	Venue	Date
8:27.15	Paula	Ivan'	ROM	20.7.63	2	OG	Seoul	25 Sep 88
8:27.68		Wang Junxia			1	NC	Jinan	6 Jun 93
8:27.83	Maricica	Puica	ROM	29.7.50	2	GG-GP	Roma	7 Sep 85
8:28.71		Qu Yunxia			1	WCh	Stuttgart	16 Aug 93
8:28.74		O'Sullivan			1	Bisl	Oslo	10 Jul 93
8:28.83	Zola	Budd'	GBR	26.5.66	3	GG-GP	Roma	7 Sep 85
8:29.02	Yvonne	Murray	GBR	4.10.64	3	OG	Seoul	25 Sep 88
8:29.25		Zhang Linli			2	WCh	Stuttgart	16 Aug 93
8:29.30		Qu Yunxia			2	NC	Jinan	6 Jun 93
8:29.36	Svetlana	Guskova	MOL	19.8.59	2	NC	Kiev	25 Jul 82
8:29.59		Guskova			1		Moskva	6 Aug 84
8:29.60		Murray			2	TSB	London	15 Jul 94
8:29.69		Decker			1	ASV	Köln	25 Aug 85
8:29.71		Decker			1	Bisl	Oslo	7 Jul 82
	(30/16)							
8:30.45	Yelena	Romanova	RUS	20.3.63	4	OG	Seoul	25 Sep 88
8:31.67	Natalya	Artyomova ¶	RUS	5.1.63	5	OG	Seoul	25 Sep 88
8:31.75	Grete	Waitz'	NOR	1.10.53	1	OsloG	Oslo	17 Jul 79
8:32.00	Elana	Meyer'	RSA	10.10.66	1		Durban	29 Apr 91
	(20)							
8:32.0	Tatyana	Pozdnyakova	UKR	4.3.56	1		Ryazan	11 Aug 84
8:32.17	Angela	Chalmers	CAN	5.9.63	1	CG	Victoria	23 Aug 94
8:33.40	Galina	Zakharova	RUS	7.9.56	3	NC	Kiev	25 Jul 82
8:33.53	Natalia	Marasescu' ¶	ROM	3.10.52	2	EC	Praha	29 Aug 78
8:33.53	Yelena	Sipatova	RUS	7.6.55	1		Moskva	12 Jul 80
8:33.9 '	Tatyana	Sychova	RUS	29.11.57	2		Moskva	12 Jul 80
8:33.97	Elly	van Hulst	NED	9.6.59	1	WK	Zürich	17 Aug 88
8:33.99	Olga	Bondarenko'	RUS	2.6.60	1	EC	Stuttgart	28 Aug 86
8:34.0 '	Faina	Krasnova'	RUS	7.12.57	3		Moskva	12 Jul 80
8:34.02	Alla	Yushina	RUS	20.8.58	2		Leningrad	27 Jul 83
	(30)							
8:34.10	Ingrid	Kristiansen'	NOR	21.3.56	1	WK	Zürich	13 Aug 86
8:35.11	Brigitte	Kraus	FRG	12.8.56	2	WCh	Helsinki	10 Aug 83
8:35.74	Alla	Libutina	TJK	2.1.53	6	NC	Kiev	25 Jul 82
8:35.74	Zamira	Zaytseva	UZB	16.2.53	2	ECp	Moskva	17 Aug 85
8:36.0 '	Lyubov	Smolka	UKR	29.11.52	4		Moskva	12 Jul 80
8:36.38	Ulrike	Bruns'	GDR	17.11.53	1	OD	Berlin	20 Jul 84
8:36.40	Olga	Dvirna	RUS	11.2.53	1		Sochi	30 May 82
8:36.45		Ma Ningning	CHN	1.6.76	4	NC	Jinan	6 Jun 93
8:37.06	Wendy	Sly'	GBR	5.11.59	5	WCh	Helsinki	10 Aug 83
8:37.11	Doina	Melinte	ROM	27.12.56	1	v Eng,Rus	Bucuresti	15 Jun 86
	(40)							
8:37.25	Vicki	Huber	USA	29.5.67	6	OG	Seoul	25 Sep 88
8:37.30	Lynn	Williams	CAN	11.7.60	3	WK	Zürich	17 Aug 88
8:37.96	Agnese	Possamai	ITA	17.1.53	6	WCh	Helsinki	10 Aug 83
8:38.1	Yelena	Zhupiyova'	UKR	18.4.60	1		Kharkov	11 Aug 85
8:38.22	Olga	Kuzyukova	RUS	17.5.53	8		Leningrad	27 Jul 83
8:38.23	Liz	McColgan'	GBR	24.4.64	1	Nik	Nice	15 Jul 91
8:38.42	Alison	Wyeth	GBR	26.5.64	5	WCh	Stuttgart	16 Aug 93
8:38.60	Cindy	Bremser	USA	5.5.53	2	WK	Zürich	22 Aug 84
8:38.71	Cornelia	Bürki	SUI	3.10.53	2	PTG	London	20 Jul 85
8:38.83	Mariana	Stanescu	ROM	7.9.64	1	GWG	Moskva	6 Jul 86
	(50)							

Indoors

Mark	Name		Nat	Born	Pos	Meet	Venue	Date
8:33.82	Elly	van Hulst	NED	9.6.59	1	WI	Budapest	4 Mar 89
8:34.80	Liz	McColgan'	GBR	24.5.64	2	WI	Budapest	4 Mar 89

5000 METRES

Mark	Name		Nat	Born	Pos	Meet	Venue	Date
14:37.33	Ingrid	Kristiansen'	NOR	21.3.56	1		Stockholm	5 Aug 86
14:44.15	Elana	Meyer	RSA	10.10.66	1		Bellville	6 Mar 92
14:45.92	Sonia	O'Sullivan	IRL	28.11.69	1	ISTAF	Berlin	27 Aug 93
14:46.41		Meyer			1		Hechtel	31 Jul 93
14:48.07	Zola	Budd'	GBR	26.5.66	1	McV	London	26 Aug 85
14:49.35		Meyer'			1		Cape Town	8 Apr 91
14:50.29		Meyer			1	DNG	Stockholm	5 Jul 93
14:50.43		Meyer			1		Port Elizabeth	19 Dec 91

Mark Wind	Name		Nat	Born	Pos	Meet	Venue	Date
14:51.42		Meyer			1	DNG	Stockholm	2 Jul 92
14:51.45		Meyer			1	ISTAF	Berlin	21 Aug 92
14:54.08	Natalya	Artyomova ¶	RUS	5.1.63	1		Podolsk	9 Sep 85
14:55.76	Olga	Bondarenko'	RUS	2.6.60	2		Podolsk	9 Sep 85
14:56.07	Annette	Peters	USA	31.5.65	2	ISTAF	Berlin	27 Aug 93
14:57.43		Kristiansen			2	McV	London	26 Aug 85
14:58.70		Kristiansen			1	FBK	Hengelo	27 Jun 86
14:58.71	Kathrin	Ullrich	GER	14.8.67	1	ISTAF	Berlin	10 Sep 91
14:58.89		Kristiansen			1	Bisl	Oslo	28 Jun 84
14:59.01		Ullrich			1	DNG	Stockholm	3 Jul 89
14:59.11		O'Sullivan			2	ISTAF	Berlin	21 Aug 92
14:59.49		O'Sullivan			1	Toto	Fukuoka	18 Sep 93
14:59.70	Yelena	Romanova	RUS	20.3.63	2	ISTAF	Berlin	10 Sep 91
15:00.00	PattiSue	Plumer (10)	USA	27.4.62	2	DNG	Stockholm	3 Jul 89
15:01.08	Liz	Lynch/McColgan	GBR	24.5.64	1		Oslo	5 Aug 87
15:01.30	Lynn	Williams	CAN	11.7.60	3	DNG	Stockholm	3 Jul 89
15:01.83		Budd'	(RSA)		1		Stellenbosch	5 Jan 84
15:01.86		McColgan			1	Bisl	Oslo	4 Jul 92
15:02.12	Svetlana	Guskova	MOL	19.8.59	1	v GDR	Tallinn	21 Jun 86
15:02.23		Romanova			1	GWG	Seattle	24 Jul 90
15:03.29		McColgan'			1	ISTAF	Berlin	26 Aug 88
15:03.51		Bondarenko			1	GWG	Moskva	8 Jul 86
15:03.52	Susan	Sirma	KEN	26.5.66	3	ISTAF	Berlin	10 Sep 91
	(31/14)							
15:04.87	Uta	Pippig	GER	7.9.65	4	ISTAF	Berlin	10 Sep 91
15:05.12	Albertina	Dias	POR	26.4.65	2		Hechtel	31 Jul 93
15:05.50	Svetlana	Ulmasova	UZB	4.2.53	2	GWG	Moskva	8 Jul 86
15:05.69+		Zhong Huandi	CHN	28.6.67	1	NG	Beijing	8 Sep 93
15:05.8e+		Wang Junxia	CHN	9.1.73	2	NG	Beijing	8 Sep 93
15:05.91	Jane	Ngotho	KEN	29.11.69	5	ISTAF	Berlin	10 Sep 91
	(20)							
15:06.04	Maricica	Puica	ROM	29.7.50	1	WG	Helsinki	4 Jul 85
15:06.53	Mary	Slaney	USA	4.8.58	1	Pre	Eugene	1 Jun 85
15:06.91	Fernanda	Ribeiro	POR	23.6.69	1	TOTO	Tokyo	15 Sep 94
15:06.96	Aurora	Cunha	POR	31.5.59	2	WG	Helsinki	4 Jul 85
15:07.56	Cathy	Branta-Easker	USA	6.1.63	3	WG	Helsinki	4 Jul 85
15:07.68	Christine	Toonstra	NED	22.6.66	1		Hechtel	18 Jul 92
15:07.87	Esther	Kiplagat	KEN	8.12.66	3	ISTAF	Berlin	21 Aug 92
15:07.92	Lynn	Jennings	USA	1.7.60	1	DNG	Stockholm	2 Jul 90
15:08.03	Tecla	Lorupe	KEN	5.5.71	3	ISTAF	Berlin	27 Aug 93
15:08.67	Shelly	Steely	USA	23.10.62	4	ISTAF	Berlin	21 Aug 92
	(30)							
15:08.80	Grete	Waitz'	NOR	1.10.53	1	Bisl	Oslo	26 Jun 82
15:08.8 mx	Loa	Olafsson	DEN	29.1.58	1mx		Sollerød	30 May 78
15:09.10	Catherina	McKiernan	IRL	30.11.69	2	DNG	Stockholm	12 Jul 94
15:09.90	Viorica	Ghican	ROM	9.6.65	1	Expo	Sevilla	30 May 90
15:09.98	Jill	Hunter	GBR	14.10.66	2		Hechtel	18 Jul 92
15:10.38	Alison	Wyeth	GBR	26.5.64	1	ISTAF	Berlin	30 Aug 94
15:11.64	Nadia	Dandolo	ITA	11.9.62	1	GG	Bologna	18 Jul 90
15:11.78	Cindy	Bremser	USA	5.5.53	3	GWG	Moskva	8 Jul 86
15:12.62	Irina	Bondarchuk	RUS	17.9.52	1	Znam	Moskva	11 Jun 82
15:12.7	Lynn	Nelson	USA	8.1.62	1	Pre	Eugene	2 Jul 88
	(40)							
15:13.22	Anne	Audain'	NZL	1.11.55	1		Auckland	17 Mar 82
15:13.22	Angela	Tooby	GBR	24.10.60	2		Oslo	5 Aug 87
15:13.27	Lyudmila	Borisova	RUS	3.8.66	2	ASV	Köln	21 Aug 94
15:13.67	Yvonne	Graham	JAM	22.8.65	3	ASV	Köln	21 Aug 94
15:13.93	Daria	Nauer	SUI	21.5.66	4	ASV	Köln	21 Aug 94
15:14.23	Nadia	Dandolo	ITA	11.9.62	5	ASV	Köln	21 Aug 94
15:14.51	Paula	Fudge'	GBR	30.3.52	1		Knarvik	13 Sep 81
15:15.04	Uta	Pippig	GER	7.9.65	5	ISTAF	Berlin	27 Aug 93
15:15.2	Francie	Larrieu Smith	USA	23.11.52	2	Pre	Eugene	2 Jul 88
15:15.76	Päivi	Tikkanen	FIN	19.1.60	1		Lohja	27 Aug 89
	(50)							

Indoors

Mark Wind	Name		Nat	Born	Pos	Meet	Venue	Date
15:13.72	Uta	Pippig	FRG	7.9.65	1		Stuttgart	10 Feb 91

Mark	Wind	Name		Nat	Born	Pos	Meet	Venue	Date

10 000 METRES

Mark	Name		Nat	Born	Pos	Meet	Venue	Date
29:31.78		Wang Junxia	CHN	9.1.73	1	NG	Beijing	8 Sep 93
30:13.37		Zhong Huandi	CHN	28.6.67	2	NG	Beijing	8 Sep 93
30:13.74	Ingrid	Kristiansen'	NOR	21.3.56	1	Bisl	Oslo	5 Jul 86
30:23.25		Kristiansen			1	EC	Stuttgart	30 Aug 86
30:48.51		Kristiansen			1	Bisl	Oslo	1 Jul 89
30:49.30		Wang Junxia			1	WCh	Stuttgart	21 Aug 93
30:50.34		Wang Junxia			1	AsiG	Hiroshima	15 Oct 94
30:52.51	Elana	Meyer	RSA	10.10.66	1	WCp	London	10 Sep 94
30:57.07	Liz	McColgan	GBR	24.5.64	1	APM	Hengelo	25 Jun 91
30:57.21	Olga	Bondarenko'	RUS	2.6.60	2	EC	Stuttgart	30 Aug 86
30:59.42		Kristiansen			1	Bisl	Oslo	27 Jul 85
31:03.62	Kathrin	Ullrich	GER	14.8.67	1	ECp	Frankfurt-am-Main	30 Jun 91
31:04.25	Fernanda	Ribeiro	POR	23.6.69	2	WCp	London	10 Sep 94
31:05.21		Bondarenko			1	OG	Seoul	30 Sep 88
31:05.85		Kristiansen			1	WCh	Roma	4 Sep 87
31:06.02	Derartu	Tulu	ETH	21.3.72	1	OG	Barcelona	7 Aug 92
31:06.99		McColgan			1	Bisl	Oslo	2 Jul 88
31:07.88	Jill	Hunter (10)	GBR	14.10.66	2	ECp	Frankfurt-am-Main	30 Jun 91
31:08.42		Wang Junxia			1	NC	Jinan	2 Jun 93
31:08.44		McColgan			2	OG	Seoul	30 Sep 88
31:08.75		Ribeiro			1	EC	Helsinki	13 Aug 94
31:09.25		Zhang Lirong	CHN	3.3.73	3	NG	Beijing	8 Sep 93
31:09.40	Yelena	Zhupiyova'	UKR	18.4.60	2	WCh	Roma	4 Sep 87
31:10.46		Ma Liyan	CHN	6.9.68	4	NG	Beijing	8 Sep 93
31:11.34		Ullrich			3	WCh	Roma	4 Sep 87
31:11.72	Lisa	Ondieki'	AUS	12.5.60	1	WG	Helsinki	30 Jun 92
31:11.75		Meyer			2	OG	Barcelona	7 Aug 92
31:12.55		Zhong Huandi			2	WCh	Stuttgart	21 Aug 93
31:13.78		Bondarenko			1	Izv	Kiev	24 Jun 84
31:14.31		McColgan			1	WCh	Tokyo	30 Aug 91
	(30/15)							
31:15.00	Galina	Zakharova	RUS	7.9.56	2	Izv	Kiev	24 Jun 84
31:15.38	Sally	Barsosio	KEN	21.3.78	3	WCh	Stuttgart	21 Aug 93
31:16.28		Zhang Linli	CHN	6.3.73	5	NG	Beijing	8 Sep 93
31:16.42	M Conceição	Ferreira	POR	13.3.62	2	WG	Helsinki	30 Jun 92
31:18.18	Viorica	Ghican	ROM	9.6.65	1	WG	Helsinki	27 Jun 90
	(20)							
31:19.11	Catherina	McKiernan	IRL	30.11.69	1	ECp II	Dublin	12 Jun 94
31:19.76	Ulrike	Bruns'	GDR	17.11.53	3	EC	Stuttgart	30 Aug 86
31:19.89	Lynn	Jennings	USA	10.7.60	3	OG	Barcelona	7 Aug 92
31:21.20	Tecla	Lorupe	KEN	5.5.71	1		Warstein	6 Jul 93
31:21.36	Uta	Pippig	GER	7.9.65	2	OD	Jena	28 May 92
31:23.92		Liu Jianying	CHN	19.11.71	6	NG	Beijing	8 Sep 93
31:27.00		Wang Xiuting	CHN	11.5.65	1	NC	Guangzhou	29 Nov 87
31:27.58	Raisa	Sadreydinova	RUS	9.5.52	1	NC	Odessa	7 Sep 83
31:27.99		Hou Juhua	CHN	.67	2	NC	Guangzhou	29 Nov 87
31:28.83		Wei Li	CHN	.1.72	7	NG	Beijing	8 Sep 93
	(30)							
31:28.92	Francie	Larrieu Smith	USA	23.11.52	1	TexR	Austin	4 Apr 91
31:29.41	Aurora	Cunha	POR	31.5.59	2	Bisl	Oslo	5 Jul 86
31:31.08		Dong Li	CHN	9.12.73	2	AsiG	Hiroshima	15 Oct 94
31:31.54		Wang Yongmei	CHN	3.10.68	8	NG	Beijing	8 Sep 93
31:32.15		Feng Wenhui	CHN	21.1.74	9	NG	Beijing	8 Sep 93
31:32.50		Wang Yanfang	CHN	10.7.71	11	NG	Beijing	8 Sep 93
31:33.03	M Albertina	Dias	POR	26.4.65	7	WCh	Stuttgart	21 Aug 93
31:35.01	Lyudmila	Baranova	RUS	.50	1		Krasnodar	29 May 83
31:35.3	Mary	Slaney	USA	4.8.58	1		Eugene	16 Jul 82
31:35.96	Daria	Nauer	SUI	21.5.66	3	EC	Helsinki	13 Aug 94
	(40)							
31:37.26	Anne Marie	Letko	USA	7.3.69	8	WCh	Stuttgart	21 Aug 93
31:38.02	Lyudmila	Matveyeva	RUS	1.2.57	1	NC	Kiev	2 Aug 88
31:38.04	Judy	St Hilaire	USA	5.9.59	8	OG	Barcelona	7 Aug 92
31:38.91	Hellen	Kimaiyo	KEN	8.9.68	9	OG	Barcelona	7 Aug 92
31:40.38	Izumi	Maki	JPN	10.12.68	1		Kobe	3 May 92
31:40.56	Delilah	Asiago	KEN	24.2.72	1	JapC	Tokyo	16 Jun 91

Mark	Wind	Name		Nat	Born	Pos	Meet	Venue	Date
31:41.03		Cristina	Misaros	ROM	1.1.69	5	EC	Helsinki	13 Aug 94
31:41.09		Lydia	Cheromei	KEN	11.5.77	2	Afr Ch	Belle Vue Mauricia	27 Jun 92
31:42.02		Yekaterina	Khramenkova	BLR	16.6.56	4	NC	Kiev	2 Aug 88
31:42.14		Maria	Guida	ITA	23.1.66	6	EC	Helsinki	13 Aug 94
		(50)							

HALF MARATHON

Included in these lists are the slightly downhill courses: Newcastle to South Shields 30.5m, Tokyo 33m. Lisboa 40m

Mark	Name		Nat	Born	Pos	Meet	Venue	Date
66:40*	Ingrid	Kristiansen	NOR	21.3.56	1	NC	Sandnes	5 Apr 87
67:11	Liz	McColgan	GBR	24.5.64	1		Tokyo	26 Jan 92
67:22	Elana	Meyer	RSA	10.10.66	1		Tokyo	24 Jan 93
67:59		Meyer			1	NC	East London	18 May 91
67:59	Uta	Pippig	GER	7.9.65	1		Kyoto	20 Mar 94
68:32		Kristiansen			1		New Bedford	19 Mar 89
68:33	Lisa	Ondieki	AUS	12.5.60	2		Tokyo	26 Jan 92
68:34	Joan	Benoit	USA	16.5.57	1		Philadelphia	16 Sep 84
68:34	Olga	Appell	MEX	2.8.63	2		Tokyo	24 Jan 93
68:36		Meyer			1	WCh	Oslo	24 Sep 94
68:38	Colleen	de Reuck	RSA	13.4.64	1	NC	Durban	23 Jul 89
68:41	Junko	Kataoka	JPN	13.6.70	1		Tokyo	23 Jan 94
68:42		McColgan			1		Dundee	11 Oct 92
68:49	Grete	Waitz (10)	NOR	1.10.53	1	GNR	South Shields	24 Jul 88
68:53		McColgan			1	WCh	South Shields	20 Sep 92
68:58	Nadezhda	Ilyina	RUS	2.4.64	1		Chelyabinsk	18 Jun 94
69:03*		Kristiansen			1		Drammen	5 Oct 86
69:03*?		Martin (Ondieki)			1		Surfers Paradise	24 Jul 88
69:04		Meyer			2		Tokyo	23 Jan 94
69:05*		Kristiansen			1		Den Haag	23 Mar 91
	(20/11)							
69:05	Delilah	Asiago	KEN	24.2.72	1	GWR	Exeter	5 May 91
69:05	Nadia	Prasad/Bernard	FRA	6.10.67	1		Las Vegas	5 Feb 94
69:08	Firaya	Sultanova	RUS	29.4.61	2		Chelyabinsk	18 Jun 94
69:15	Iulia	Negura	ROM	26.1.67	2	WCh	Oslo	24 Sep 94
69:21	Megumi	Fujiwara	JPN	19.6.69	2	WCh	South Shields	20 Sep 92
69:22	Anuta	Catuna	ROM	1.10.68	1	NC	Bucuresti	21 Aug 93
69:27	Tecla	Lorupe	KEN	5.5.71	1		Lisboa	13 Mar 94
69:29	Marleen	Renders	BEL	24.12.68	1		Hasselt	2 Oct 94
69:31	Carmen	de Oliveira	BRA	17.8.65	2		Lisboa	13 Mar 94
	(20)							
69:32	Yelena	Paramanova	RUS		3		Chelyabinsk	18 Jun 94
69:33	Rosa	Mota	POR	29.6.58	1	GNR	South Shields	16 Sep 90
69:35	Valentina	Yegorova	RUS	16.2.64	1		Sankt Peterburg	12 Jun 93
69:37	Aurora	Cunha	POR	31.5.59	2		New Bedford	19 Mar 89
69:37	Midori	Fumoto	JPN	18.12.71	1		Gold Coast	12 Jul 92
69:38	Rosanna	Munerotto	ITA	3.12.62	3	WCh	South Shields	20 Sep 92
69:39	Cathy	O'Brien	USA	19.7.64	1		Philadelphia	16 Sep 90
69:39	Andrea	Wallace	GBR	22.11.66	1		Bath	21 Mar 93
69:48*	Dorthe	Rasmussen	DEN	27.1.60	2		Den Haag	23 Mar 91
69:56	Susan	Tooby	GBR	24.10.60	2	GNR	South Shields	24 Jul 88
	(30)							
69:57	Albertina	Dias	POR	26.4.65	4	WCh	Oslo	24 Sep 94
70:00	Angelina	Kanana	KEN	65	1		Remich	26 Sep 93
70:01	Heléna	Barócsi	HUN	9.7.66	1		Lisboa 40m dh	15 Mar 92
70:03	Anne Marie	Letko	USA	7.3.69	1		Philadelphia	18 Sep 94
70:04*	Carla	Beurskens	NED	10.2.52	1		Amsterdam	31 Mar 90
70:04	Katrin	Dörre	GER	6.10.61	3		Tokyo	24 Jan 93
70:04	Kaori	Kumura	JPN	22.8.70	1	AusC	Gold Coast	18 Jul 93
70:07	Conceição	Ferreira	POR	13.3.62	1	WCh	Bruxelles	3 Oct 93
70:09	Mari	Tanigawa	JPN	27.10.62	2	WCh	Bruxelles	3 Oct 93
70:10	Jane	Salumäe	EST	17.1.68	1		Den Haag	27 Mar 94
	(40)							
Downhill								
69:05	Nadia	Bernard-Prasad	FRA	6.10.67	1		Las Vegas	5 Feb 94
Uncertain distance								
68:37	Rosa	Mota	POR	29.6.58	1		Québec	11 Jun 89
68:56	Carla	Beurskens	NED	10.2.52	1		Grevenmacher	21 Sep 86
69:03	Carole	Rouillard	CAN	15.3.60	1		Québec	10 Jun 90

Mark Wind	Name		Nat	Born	Pos	Meet	Venue	Date
Short courses								
67:59		Kristiansen			1		Oslo (220m)	13 Sep 86
69:47	Nadezhda	Ilyina	RUS	2.4.64	1		Lisboa (97m)	13 Mar 93
70:02	Manuela	Dias	POR	19.6.63	2		Lisboa (97m)	13 Mar 93
70:04	Tatyana	Pozdnyakova	UKR	4.3.56	3		Lisboa 97m)	13 Mar 93
70:06	Maria	Rebelo	FRA	29.1.56	4		Lisboa (97m)	13 Mar 93

MARATHON

Note Boston times included in main list, but downhill overall (139m) and sometimes, as in 1994, strongly wind-aided - next bests are shown if to standard

Mark Wind	Name		Nat	Born	Pos	Meet	Venue	Date
2:21:06	Ingrid	Kristiansen	NOR	21.3.56	1		London	21 Apr 85
2:21:21	Joan	Benoit'	USA	16.5.57	1		Chicago	20 Oct 85
2:21:45	Uta	Pippig	GER	7.9.65	1		Boston	18 Apr 94
2:22:43		Benoit			1		Boston	18 Apr 83
2:22:48		Kristiansen			1		London	10 May 87
2:23:05		Kristiansen			2		Chicago	20 Oct 85
2:23:29	Rosa	Mota	POR	29.6.58	3		Chicago	20 Oct 85
2:23:33	Valentina	Yegorova	RUS	16.2.64	2		Boston	18 Apr 94
2:23:43	Olga	Markova	RUS	6.8.68	1		Boston	20 Apr 92
2:23:51	Lisa	Martin/Ondieki	AUS	12.5.60	1		Osaka	31 Jan 88
2:24:07		Wang Junxia	CHN	9.1.73	1		Tianjin	4 Apr 93
2:24:18	Wanda	Panfil	POL	26.1.59	1		Boston	15 Apr 91
2:24:26		Kristiansen			1		London	13 May 84
2:24:30		Mota			1		Boston	18 Apr 88
2:24:32		Qu Yunxia (10)	CHN	25.12.72	2		Tianjin	4 Apr 93
2:24:33		Kristiansen			1		Boston	17 Apr 89
2:24:40		Ondieki			1		New York	1 Nov 92
2:24:42		Zhang Linli	CHN	6.3.73	3		Tianjin	4 Apr 93
2:24:52		Benoit			1	OG	Los Angeles	5 Aug 84
2:24:52		Zhang Lirong	CHN	3.3.73	4		Tianjin	4 Apr 93
2:24:54	Grete	Waitz	NOR	1.10.53	1		London	20 Apr 86
2:24:55		Kristiansen			1		Boston	21 Apr 86
2:25:15	Elana	Meyer	RSA	10.10.66	3		Boston	18 Apr 94
2:25:15	Katrin	Dörre-Heinig	GER	6.10.61	1		Berlin	25 Sep 94
2:25:17		Mota			1	WCh	Roma	29 Aug 87
2:25:19	Alena	Peterková	TCH	13.11.60	4		Boston	18 Apr 94
2:25:21		Mota			1		Boston	20 Apr 87
2:25:24		Dörre			1		Tokyo	15 Nov 87
2:25:24		Mota			1		Boston	16 Apr 90
2:25:27		Markova			1		Boston	19 Apr 93
	(30/16)							
2:25:36		Zhong Huandi	CHN	28.6.67	5		Tianjin	4 Apr 93
2:25:46		Ma Liyan	CHN	3.11.68	6		Tianjin	4 Apr 93
2:25:52	Miyoko	Asahina	JPN	24.9.69	1		Rotterdam	17 Apr 94
2:25:56	Véronique	Marot	GBR	16.9.55	1		London	23 Apr 89
	(20)							
2:26:09	Tomoe	Abe	JPN	13.8.71	1		Osaka	30 Jan 94
2:26:09	Nobuko	Fujimura	JPN	18.12.65	2		Osaka	30 Jan 94
2:26:10	Junko	Asari	JPN	22.9.69	3		Osaka	30 Jan 94
2:26:20	Renata	Kokowska	POL	4.12.58	1		Berlin	26 Sep 93
2:26:23	Madina	Biktagirova ¶	BLR	20.9.64	1	OT	Los Angeles	1 Mar 92
2:26:26	Julie	Brown	USA	4.2.55	1		Los Angeles	5 Jun 83
2:26:26	Yumi	Kokamo	JPN	26.12.71	1		Osaka	26 Jan 92
2:26:26	Yoshiko	Yamamoto	JPN	6.6.70	2		Boston	20 Apr 92
2:26:26	Mitsuyo	Yoshida	JPN	29.10.66	4		Osaka	30 Jan 94
2:26:34	Carla	Beurskens	NED	10.2.52	2		Tokyo	15 Nov 87
	(30)							
2:26:36		Wang Yanfang	CHN	10.7.71	7		Tianjin	4 Apr 93
2:26:38		Xie Lihua	CHN	19.7.65	8		Tianjin	4 Apr 93
2:26:40	Kim	Jones	USA	2.5.58	2		Boston	15 Apr 91
2:26:46	Allison	Roe	NZL	30.5.56	1		Boston	20 Apr 81
2:26:49	M Albertina	Dias	POR	26.4.65	2		Berlin	26 Sep 93
2:26:51	Priscilla	Welch	GBR	22.11.44	2		London	10 May 87
2:26:55	Kamila	Gradus	POL	19.3.67	5		Boston	15 Apr 91
2:27:02	Akemi	Matsuno	JPN	27.4.68	2		Osaka	26 Jan 92
2:27:05	Tatyana	Polovinskaya	UKR	14.3.65	4	OG	Seoul	23 Sep 88

Mark	Wind	Name		Nat	Born	Pos	Meet	Venue	Date
2:27:06			Zhao Youfeng	CHN	5.5.65	5	OG	Seoul	23 Sep 88
		(40)							
2:27:16			Mun Gyong-ae	PRK	8.4.69	1		Beijing	15 Oct 89
2:27:32		Liz	McColgan	GBR	24.5.64	1		New York	3 Nov 91
2:27:35		Francie	Larrieu-Smith	USA	23.11.52	2	WCp	London	21 Apr 91
2:27:36		Frith	van der Merwe	RSA	26.5.64	1		Port Elizabeth	24 Feb 90
2:27:37		Tecla	Lorupe	KEN	5.5.71	1		New York	6 Nov 94
2:27:41		Carmen	de Oliveira	BRA	17.8.65	5		Boston	18 Apr 94
2:27:42		M Manuela	Machado	POR	9.8.63	4		Boston	20 Apr 92
2:27:44		Franziska	Moser	SUI	17.8.66	1		Frankfurt	23 Oct 94
2:27:49		Laura	Fogli	ITA	5.10.59	6	OG	Seoul	23 Sep 88
2:27:51		Patti	Catalano	USA	6.4.53	2		Boston	20 Apr 81
		(50)							

Best marks by women whose pbs were set at Boston (downhill 139m) or Port Elizabeth (downhill 149m)

Mark	Wind	Name		Nat	Born	Pos	Meet	Venue	Date
2:26:24		Uta	Pippig	GER	7.9.65	1		New York	14 Nov 93
2:26:31		Wanda	Panfil	POL	26.1.59	1		London	22 Apr 90
2:26:38		Olga	Markova	RUS	6.8.68	2		New York	1 Nov 92
2:26:40		Valentina	Yegorova	RUS	16.2.64	1		Tokyo	21 Nov 93
2:27:38		Kamila	Gradus	POL	19.3.67	1		Nagoya	7 Mar 93
2:27:50		Kim	Jones	USA	2.5.58	2		Berlin	29 Sep 91

2000 METRES STEEPLECHASE

Mark	Wind	Name		Nat	Born	Pos	Meet	Venue	Date
6:11.84		Marina	Pluzhnikova	RUS	25.2.63	1	GWG	St Peterburg	25 Jul 94
6:14.52		Svetlana	Rogova	RUS	4.8.67	1	Znam	Moskva	11 Jun 92
6:17.80		Irina	Mozharova	RUS	19.7.58	1	NC	Gorkiy	23 Jul 89
6:21.16		Lyudmila	Pushkina	UKR	2.10.65	2	CISCh	Moskva	24 Jun 92
6:21.42		Antonina	Grishayeva	MOL	59	2	Znam	Moskva	11 Jun 91
6:22.03		Stefania	Statkuviene	LIT	6.3.63	3	URSCh	Gorkiy	23 Jul 89
6:22.36		Svetlana	Lyegkodukh	UKR	24.11.69	1		Kiev	30 May 92
6:23.12		Anzhelika	Averkova	UKR	13.3.69	4	Znam	Moskva	11 Jun 91
6:24.18		Yelena	Krasnova	RUS		2	NC	Kiev	2 Aug 88
6:24.26		Irina	Matrosova	RUS	5.4.62	4	NC	Gorkiy	23 Jul 89

100 METRES HURDLES

Mark	Wind	Name		Nat	Born	Pos	Meet	Venue	Date
12.21	0.7	Yordanka	Donkova	BUL	28.9.61	1		Stara Zagora	20 Aug 88
12.24	0.9		Donkova			1h		Stara Zagora	28 Aug 88
12.25	1.4	Ginka	Zagorcheva	BUL	12.4.58	1	v TCH,Gre	Drama	8 Aug 87
12.26	1.5		Donkova			1	Balk	Ljubljana	7 Sep 86
12.26	1.7	Lyudmila	Narozhilenko ¶	RUS	21.4.64	1rB		Sevilla	6 Jun 92
12.27	-1.2		Donkova			1		Stara Zagora	28 Aug 88
12.28	1.8		Narozhilenko			1	NC	Kiev	11 Jul 91
12.28	0.9		Narozhilenko			1rA		Sevilla	6 Jun 92
12.29	-0.4		Donkova			1	ASV	Köln	17 Aug 86
12.32	1.6		Narozhilenko			1		St Denis	4 Jun 92
12.33	1.4		Donkova			1		Fürth	14 Jun 87
12.34	-0.5		Zagorcheva			1	WCh	Roma	4 Sep 87
12.35	0.1		Donkova			1h2	ASV	Köln	17 Aug 86
12.36	1.9	Grazyna	Rabsztyn	POL	20.9.52	1	Kuso	Warszawa	13 Jun 80
12.36	-0.6		Donkova			1	NC	Sofia	13 Aug 86
12.36	1.1		Donkova			1		Schwechat	15 Jun 88
12.37	1.4		Donkova			1	ISTAF	Berlin	15 Aug 86
12.38	0.0		Donkova			1	BGP	Budapest	11 Aug 86
12.38	-0.7		Donkova			1	EC	Stuttgart	29 Aug 86
12.38	0.2		Donkova			1	OG	Seoul	30 Sep 88
12.39	1.5	Vera	Komisova'	RUS	11.6.53	1	GG	Roma	5 Aug 80
12.39	1.5		Zagorcheva			2	Balk	Ljubljana	7 Sep 86
12.39	1.8	Natalya	Grigoryeva ¶	UKR	3.12.62	2	NC	Kiev	11 Jul 91
12.40	0.4		Donkova			1	GWG	Moskva	8 Jul 86
12.42	1.8	Bettine	Jahn	GDR	3.8.58	1	OD	Berlin	8 Jun 83
12.42	1.0		Zagorcheva			1		Sofia	14 Aug 85
12.42	-0.2		Donkova			1	VD	Bruxelles	5 Sep 86
12.42	0.2		Narozhilenko			1	GGala	Roma	9 Jun 92
12.43	-0.9	Lucyna	Kalek (Langer)	POL	9.1.56	1		Hannover	19 Aug 84
12.43	0.7		Zagorcheva			1	BGP	Budapest	6 Jul 87
		(30/8)							
12.44	-0.5	Gloria	Siebert'	GDR	13.1.64	2	WCh	Roma	4 Sep 87
12.45	1.3	Cornelia	Oschkenat'	GDR	29.10.61	1		Neubrandenburg	11 Jun 87
		(10)							

Mark	Wind	Name		Nat	Born	Pos	Meet	Venue	Date
12.46	0.2	Gail	Devers	USA	19.11.66	1	WCh	Stuttgart	20 Aug 93
12.47	1.1	Marina	Azyabina	RUS	15.6.63	1s2	NC	Moskva	19 Jun 93
12.50	0.0	Vera	Akimova'	RUS	5.6.59	1		Sochi	19 May 84
12.53	0.2	Tatyana	Reshetnikova	RUS	14.10.66	1rA	GP II	Linz	4 Jul 94
12.53	-0.4	Svetla	Dimitrova	BUL	27.1.70	1	Herc	Stara Zagora	16 Jul 94
12.54	0.4	Kerstin	Knabe	GDR	7.7.59	3	EC	Athinai	9 Sep 82
12.54	0.9	Sabine	Paetz/John'	GDR	16.10.57	1		Berlin	15 Jul 84
12.56	1.2	Johanna	Klier'	GDR	13.9.52	1	NC	Cottbus	17 Jul 80
12.56	1.2	Monique	Ewanje-Epée	FRA	11.7.67	1	BNP	Villeneuve d'Ascq	29 Jun 90
12.59	-0.6	Anneliese	Ehrhardt	GDR	18.6.50	1	OG	München	8 Sep 72
		(20)							
12.61	0.3	Svetlana	Gusarova	KZK	29.5.59	2	NC	Leningrad	3 Aug 85
12.61	0.2	Jackie	Joyner-Kersee	USA	3.3.62	1	Jenn	San José	28 May 88
12.62	1.2	Mihaela	Pogacian'	ROM	27.1.58	2	BNP	Villeneuve d'Ascq	29 Jun 90
12.62	1.1	Yulia	Graudyn	RUS	13.11.70	1A	ISTAF	Berlin	30 Aug 94
12.63	1.8	Zofia	Bielczyk	POL	22.9.58	1h1	Kuso	Warszawa	18 Jun 79
12.63	1.4	Heike	Theele'	GDR	4.10.64	2	NC	Jena	27 Jun 86
12.64	0.4	Paraskevi	Patoulidou	GRE	29.3.65	1	OG	Barcelona	6 Aug 92
12.64	0.1		Zhang Yu	CHN	8.4.71	1	NG	Beijing	9 Sep 93
12.65A	0.0	Danuta	Perka	POL	22.6.56	1h3	WUG	Ciudad México	9 Sep 79
12.65	0.0	Nadezhda	Korshunova	UKR	18.5.61	2		Sochi	19 May 84
		(30)							
12.66	0.0	Yelena	Biserova	RUS	24.3.62	3		Sochi	19 May 84
12.66	0.7	Lidiya	Yurkova '	BLR	15.1.67	1s2	NC	Kiev	5 Jul 90
12.67	0.6	Tatyana	Anisimova	RUS	19.10.49	2	EC	Praha	2 Sep 78
12.67	0.2	Lynda	Tolbert	USA	3.10.67	3	WCh	Stuttgart	20 Aug 93
12.68	1.1	Yelizaveta	Chernyshova	RUS	26.1.58	1h1	Znam	Volgograd	10 Jun 89
12.69	0.2	Laurence	Elloy	FRA	3.12.59	2h1	GWG	Moskva	8 Jul 86
12.69	0.4	LaVonna	Martin	USA	18.11.66	2	OG	Barcelona	6 Aug 92
12.70A	1.5	Tananjalyn	Stanley	USA	11.1.67	1	NCAA	Provo	3 Jun 89
12.70	0.0	Eva	Sokolova	RUS	25.3.62	1		Sevilla	20 Jun 89
12.71	-0.7	Yelena	Politika	UKR	24.8.64	2	NC	Kiev	15 Jul 86
		(40)							
12.73	0.6	Gudrun	Berend'	GDR	27.4.55	3	EC	Praha	2 Sep 78
12.73	1.9	Aliuska	López	CUB	29.8.69	2		Dijon	24 Jun 90
12.73	-0.8		Liu Huajin	CHN	7.2.60	1	AsiG	Beijing	2 Oct 90
12.73	-0.3	Florence	Colle	FRA	4.12.65	2	WK	Zürich	7 Aug 91
12.73	1.7	Nadezhda	Bodrova	UKR	13.7.61	1h1		Kiev	23 Jul 94
12.74	1.5	Anne	Piquereau	FRA	15.6.64	3		Saint Denis	19 Jul 91
12.75	0.4	Claudia	Zaczkiewicz'	FRG	4.7.62	2s2	OG	Seoul	30 Sep 88
12.75	-0.2	Michelle	Freeman	JAM	5.5.69	2	VD	Bruxelles	28 Aug 92
12.75	0.1		Xie Liuying	CHN	1.67	2	NG	Beijing	9 Sep 93
12.76		Nina	Derbina'	RUS	5.7.56	1		Leningrad	22 Jun 80
12.76	1.7	Xenia	Siska	HUN	3.11.57	3	BGP	Budapest	20 Aug 84
12.76	1.3	Julie	Baumann' ¶	SUI	17.6.64	1		Winthertur	7 Sep 91
		(52)							
Low altitude best: 12.69	1.9		Perka			4	Kuso	Warszawa	13 Jun 80
Wind assisted									
12.28	2.7	Cornelia	Oschkenat'	GDR	29.10.61	1		Berlin	25 Aug 87
12.29	3.5		Donkova			1	Athl	Lausanne	24 Jun 88
12.35	2.4	Bettine	Jahn	GDR	3.8.58	1	WCh	Helsinki	13 Aug 83
12.37	2.7	Gloria	Uibel/Siebert'	GDR	13.1.64	2		Berlin	25 Aug 87
12.39	2.8		Rabsztyn			1	4-N	Bremen	24 Jun 79
12.42	2.4	Kerstin	Knabe	GDR	7.7.59	2	WCh	Helsinki	13 Aug 83
12.50	2.7	Svetla	Dimitrova	BUL	27.1.70	1		St Denis	10 Jun 94
12.51	3.2	Johanna	Klier'	GDR	13.9.52	1	NC	Cottbus	17 Jul 80
12.51	3.6	Sabine	Paetz/John'	GDR	16.10.57	1		Dresden	27 Jul 84
12.51A	3.3	Yulia	Graudyn	RUS	13.11.70	1		Sestriere	31 Jul 94
12.53	2.2	Mihaela	Pogacian	ROM	27.1.58	1	IAC	Edinburgh	6 Jul 90
12.59A	3.3	Brigita	Bukovec	SLO	21.5.70	2		Sestriere	31 Jul 94
12.63	2.8	Eva	Sokolova	RUS	25.3.62	1s1	NC	Moskva	19 Jun 93
12.64	5.0	Anne	Piquereau	FRA	15.6.64	3		Dijon	12 Jun 94
12.66	2.6	Yelena	Politika	UKR	24.8.64	3	NC	Tallinn	5 Jul 88
12.66	4.7	Lynda	Tolbert	USA	3.10.67	1	BNP	Villeneuve d'Ascq	6 Jul 92
12.67	2.4	Natalya	Petrova	RUS	16.11.57	4	WCh	Helsinki	13 Aug 83
12.70	4.1	Rhonda	Blanford	USA	15.12.63	1	NCAA	Austin	1 Jun 85
12.70	5.0	Dawn	Bowles	USA	12.11.68	1	NCAA	Eugene	1 Jun 91
12.74	2.9	Michelle	Freeman	JAM	5.5.69	1	Jen	San José	28 May 94

Mark	Wind	Name		Nat	Born	Pos	Meet	Venue	Date
Unconfrmed timing									
12.66	3.0	Tatyana	Anisimova	RUS	19.10.49	2		Leningrad	4 Jun 80
12.71	3.0	Irina	Litovchenko	RUS	29.5.50	3		Leningrad	4 Jun 80
Hand timed									
12.3	1.5	Anneliese	Ehrhardt	GDR	18.6.50	1	NC	Dresden	22 Jul 73
12.3		Marina	Azyabina	RUS	15.6.63	1		Yekaterinburg	30 May 93
12.5	0.9	Pamela	Ryan'	AUS	12.8.39	1		Warszawa	28 Jun 72
12.5	0.0	Teresa	Nowak	POL	29.4.42	1		Warszawa	22 Jun 74
12.5	1.7	Lidia	Okolo-Kulak'	BLR	15.1.67	1		Staiki	28 May 88
12.5			Liu Huajin	CHN	7.2.60	1		Beijing	17 Sep 88
12.0w	2.1	Yordanka	Donkova	BUL	28.9.61	1		Sofia	3 Aug 86
12.1w	2.1	Ginka	Zagorcheva	BUL	12.4.58	2		Sofia	3Aug 86
12.5w	3.4	Maria	Merchuk'	MOL	28.12.59	1		Volgograd	25 Sep 81

400 METRES HURDLES

Mark	Name		Nat	Born	Pos	Meet	Venue	Date
52.74	Sally	Gunnell	GBR	29.7.66	1	WCh	Stuttgart	19 Aug 93
52.79	Sandra	Farmer-Patrick	USA	18.8.62	2	WCh	Stuttgart	19 Aug 93
52.94	Marina	Styepanova'	RUS	1.5.50	1s	Spart	Tashkent	17 Sep 86
53.11	Tatyana	Ledovskaya	BLR	21.5.66	1	WCh	Tokyo	29 Aug 91
53.16		Gunnell			2	WCh	Tokyo	29 Aug 91
53.17	Debbie	Flintoff-King	AUS	20.4.60	1	OG	Seoul	28 Sep 88
53.18		Ledovskaya			2	OG	Seoul	28 Sep 88
53.23		Gunnell			1	OG	Barcelona	5 Aug 92
53.24	Sabine	Busch	GDR	21.11.62	1	NC	Potsdam	21 Aug 87
53.32		Styepanova			1	EC	Stuttgart	30 Aug 86
53.33		Gunnell			1	EC	Helsinki	12 Aug 94
53.37		Farmer-Patrick			1	NYG	New York	22 Jul 89
53.47	Janeene	Vickers	USA	3.10.68	3	WCh	Tokyo	29 Aug 91
53.48	Margarita	Ponomaryova'	RUS	19.6.63	3	WCh	Stuttgart	19 Aug 93
53.51		Gunnell			1	GWG	St Peterburg	24 Jul 94
53.52		Gunnell			1	WK	Zürich	4 Aug 93
53.54		Farmer-Patrick			1	Nik	Nice	15 Jul 91
53.55		Busch			1		Berlin	22 Sep 85
53.55		Ledovskaya			1	Herc	Monaco	11 Aug 92
53.58		Ponomaryova			1	Izv	Kiev	22 Jun 84
53.58	Cornelia	Ullrich'	GDR	26.4.63	2	NC	Potsdam	21 Aug 87
53.59		Farmer-Patrick			1	ISTAF	Berlin	21 Aug 92
53.60		Busch			2	EC	Stuttgart	30 Aug 86
53.60		Farmer-Patrick			2	Herc	Monaco	11 Aug 92
53.61		Farmer-Patrick			1	Athl	Lausanne	10 Jul 91
53.62		Busch			1h2	NC	Jena	27 Jun 86
53.62		Busch			1	WCh	Roma	3 Sep 87
53.62		Ledovskaya			1	EC	Split	31 Aug 90
53.62		Farmer-Patrick			1	OT	New Orleans	21 Jun 92
53.62		Gunnell			1	WK	Zürich	7 Aug 91
53.63	Ellen	Fiedler'	GDR	26.11.58	3	OG	Seoul	28 Sep 88
	(31/10)							
53.65A	Myrtle	Bothma'	RSA	18.2.64	mx		Pretoria	12 Mar 90
53.72	Kim	Batten	USA	29.3.69	1	Nik	Nice	18 Jul 94
53.96		Han Qing	CHN	4.3.70	1	NG	Beijing	9 Sep 93
54.02	Anna	Ambraziené'	LIT	14.4.55	1	Znam	Moskva	11 Jun 83
54.04	Gudrun	Abt	FRG	3.8.62	6	OG	Seoul	28 Sep 88
54.11	Anna	Knoroz	RUS	30.7.70	3	Nik	Nice	18 Jul 94
54.12	Deon	Hemmings	JAM	9.10.68	2s3	WCh	Stuttgart	17 Aug 93
54.14	Yekaterina	Fesenko/Grun	RUS	10.8.58	1	WCh	Helsinki	10 Aug 83
54.15	Ann-Louise	Skoglund	SWE	28.6.62	4	EC	Stuttgart	30 Aug 86
54.23	Judi	Brown King	USA	14.7.61	1	PAm	Indianapolis	12 Aug 87
	(20)							
54.24	Susanne	Losch	GDR	12.2.66	1	v FRG	Düsseldorf	19 Jun 88
54.25	Anita	Protti	SUI	4.8.64	6	WCh	Tokyo	29 Aug 91
54.27	Genowefa	Blaszak'	POL	22.8.57	1	DNG	Stockholm	2 Jul 85
54.28	Karin	Rossley	GDR	5.4.57	1		Jena	17 May 80
54.34	Tatyana	Pavlova'	UZB	12.12.58	1h1	NC	Leningrad	2 Aug 85
54.35	Petra	Krug	GDR	9.11.63	1	vSU	Bryansk	14 Jul 89
54.36	LaTanya	Sheffield	USA	11.10.63	3s1	OG	Seoul	26 Sep 88
54.37	Vera	Ordina	RUS	4.6.68	2s1	OG	Barcelona	3 Aug 92
54.38	Tonja	Buford	USA	13.12.70	2s1	WCh	Stuttgart	17 Aug 93

Mark	Wind	Name		Nat	Born	Pos	Meet	Venue	Date
54.39		Tatyana	Kurochkina'	BLR	15.9.67	7	OG	Seoul	28 Sep 88
		(30)							
54.52		Heike	Meissner	GER	29.1.70	1	NC	Erfurt	3 Jul 94
54.52			Ling Xueyan	CHN	14.2.72	3	NG	Beijing	9 Sep 93
54.53		Natalya	Torshina	KZK	4.10.68	3s2	WCh	Stuttgart	17 Aug 93
54.53		Rosey	Edeh	CAN	13.8.66	4s2	WCh	Stuttgart	17 Aug 93
54.55		Bärbel	Broschat	GDR	2.11.57	1	WCh	Sittard	16 Aug 80
54.55		Cristieana	Matei'	ROM	2.1.62	2	GWG	Moskva	7 Jul 86
54.56		Yelena	Filipishina	RUS	18.6.62	2		Moskva	20 Jul 84
54.61		Nawal	El Moutawakil	MAR	15.4.62	1	OG	Los Angeles	8 Aug 84
54.62		Tuija	Helander-Kuusisto	FIN	23.5.61	5	WCh	Roma	3 Sep 87
54.63		Gowry	Retchakan	GBR	21.6.60	5s2	OG	Barcelona	3 Aug 92
		(40)							
54.64		Petra	Pfaff	GDR	16.10.60	4	WCh	Helsinki	10 Aug 83
54.68		Birgit	Uibel'	GDR	30.10.61	1		Dresden	19 May 84
54.68		Silvia	Rieger	GER	14.11.70	2	EC	Helsinki	12 Aug 94
54.69		Monica	Westén	SWE	15.3.66	1		Stockholm	13 Aug 90
54.78		Marina	Sereda'	UKR	12.4.64	2	Spart	Tashkent	18 Sep 86
54.80		Tatyana	Storozheva	RUS	22.3.54	1		Moskva	12 Jun 80
54.82		Schowonda	Williams	USA	3.12.66	4s1	WCh	Roma	1 Sep 87
54.82		Olga	Nazarova	RUS	28.2.62	4	Athl	Lausanne	6 Jul 94
54.86		Tonja	Brown	USA	5.9.60	3	GG-GP	Roma	7 Sep 85
54.89		Tatyana	Zelentsova	UZB	5.8.48	1	EC	Praha	2 Sep 78
		(50)							

Low altitude bests

Mark	Name	Pos	Meet	Venue	Date
54.44	Bothma	1	NC	Durban	22 Apr 89
55.55	Wilson	1	NCAA	Baton Rouge	5 Jun 87
56.03	Fick	1		Stellenbosch	25 Apr 83
55.85	van Rensburg	1	NC	Stellenbosch	17 Apr 82
56.18	Tata-Muya	4h1	OG	Seoul	25 Sep 88
56.40	Myers	1	AIAW	Eugene	24 May 80
56.55	van der Veen	2		Stellenbosch	18 Mar 91

Hand timing

Mark	Wind	Name		Nat	Born	Pos	Meet	Venue	Date
55.5		Olga	Veikshina	RUS	21.1.61	1		Leningrad	3 Jun 84
55.6		Malgorzata	Dunecka	POL	21.12.56	1	v TCH	Warszawa	27 Jul 85
55.7A		Rose	Tata-Muya	KEN	60	1		Nairobi	12 Aug 88
55.9		Yelena	Yefimova	BLR	.61	1		Kirov	15 Jul 84
56.0		Ann	Maenhout	BEL	8.2.69	1	NC	Bruxelles	16 Aug 92
56.0			Wang Lixia	CHN	.9.69	1		Guangzhou	26 Sep 92
56.0			Chen Qing	CHN	.12.71	1		Fuzhou	29 Oct 92
56.1		Nadezhda	Ryseva	RUS	7.12.55	2		Leningrad	21 Aug 80
56.2		Olga	Gerasimova	UZB	.56	2		Tashkent	22 Apr 84
56.2		Anfisa	Bikbulatova	RUS	1.3.65	1		Novosibirsk	15 Aug 87
56.3		Audrone	Aniuliené/Racaite	LIT	22.3.64	1	NC	Kaunas	3 Jul 85
56.3		Irina	Svetonosova	BLR	6.6.58	1		Lipetsk	19 Jul 86
56.3		Yelena	Stass	KZK	25.6.65	1		Alma-Ata	18 Jun 88
56.3		Elena	Zamperioli	ITA	29.10.67	1		Caorle	11 Jul 92
56.4		Lyubov	Shelomkova	RUS	14.6.56	2		Vilnius	5 Aug 84
56.4		Natalya	Ovsyannikova	KZK	.64	1		Alma-Ata	28 Aug 86

Drugs disqualification

Mark	Wind	Name		Nat	Born	Pos	Meet	Venue	Date
54.47			Guo Yue	CHN	23.1.69	2	NG	Beijing	9 Sep 93
54.6 hand		Chantal	Beaugeant	FRA	16.2.61	1		Tours	28 May 89

HIGH JUMP

Mark	Wind	Name		Nat	Born	Pos	Meet	Venue	Date
2.09		Stefka	Kostadinova	BUL	25.3.65	1	WCh	Roma	30 Aug 87
2.08			Kostadinova			1	NM	Sofia	31 May 86
2.07		Lyudmila	Andonova ¶	BUL	6.5.60	1	OD	Berlin	20 Jul 84
2.07			Kostadinova			1		Sofia	25 May 86
2.07			Kostadinova			1		Cagliari	16 Sep 87
2.07			Kostadinova			1	NC	Sofia	3 Sep 88
2.07i		Heike	Henkel'	GER	5.5.64	1	NC	Karlsruhe	8 Feb 92
2.06			Kostadinova			1	ECp	Moskva	18 Aug 85
2.06			Kostadinova			1		Fürth	15 Jun 86
2.06			Kostadinova			1		Cagliari	14 Sep 86
2.06			Kostadinova			1		Wörrstadt	6 Jun 87
2.06			Kostadinova			1		Rieti	8 Sep 87
2.06i			Kostadinova			1		Piraeus	20 Feb 88
2.05		Tamara	Bykova	RUS	21.12.58	1	Izv	Kiev	22 Jun 84
2.05			Kostadinova			1		Wörrstadt	14 Jun 86
2.05			Kostadinova			1		Rieti	7 Sep 86

Mark	Wind	Name		Nat	Born	Pos	Meet	Venue	Date
2.05i			Kostadinova			1	WI	Indianapolis	8 Mar 87
2.05			Kostadinova			1	Bisl	Oslo	4 Jul 87
2.05			Kostadinova			1		Padova	13 Sep 87
2.05			Kostadinova			1	BGP	Budapest	12 Aug 88
2.05			Henkel			1	WCh	Tokyo	31 Aug 91
2.05i			Kostadinova			1	NC	Sofia	1 Feb 92
2.05			Kostadinova			1		San Marino	4 Jul 92
2.05			Kostadinova			1	Toto	Fukuoka	18 Sep 93
		(24/4) 2.04 performances: 11 Kostadinova, 5 Henkel, 2 Bykova, 1 Costa							
2.04		Silvia	Costa	CUB	4.5.64	1	WCp	Barcelona	9 Sep 89
2.03		Ulrike	Meyfarth	FRG	4.5.56	1	ECp	London	21 Aug 83
2.03		Louise	Ritter	USA	18.2.58	1		Austin	8 Jul 88
2.02i		Susanne	Beyer'	GDR	24.6.61	2	WI	Indianapolis	8 Mar 87
2.02		Yelena	Yelesina	RUS	4.4.70	1	GWG	Seattle	23 Jul 90
2.02		Inga	Babakova'	UKR	27.6.67	2	ISTAF	Berlin	10 Sep 91
		(10)							
2.02i		Alina	Astafei	ROM	7.6.69	1		Berlin	4 Mar 94
2.01		Sara	Simeoni	ITA	19.4.53	1	v Pol	Brescia	4 Aug 78
2.01		Olga	Turchak	UKR	5.3.67	2	GWG	Moskva	7 Jul 86
2.01		Desiré	du Plessis	RSA	20.5.65	1		Johannesburg	16 Sep 86
2.01i		Gabriele	Günz	GDR	8.9.61	2		Stuttgart	31 Jan 88
2.01		Heike	Balck	GDR	19.8.70	1	vSU-j	Karl-Marx-Stadt	18 Jun 89
2.01i		Ioamnet	Quintero	CUB	8.9.72	1		Berlin	5 Mar 93
2.00		Rosemarie	Ackermann'	GDR	4.4.52	1	ISTAF	Berlin	26 Aug 77
2.00i		Coleen	Sommer'	USA	6l.6.60	1		Ottawa	14 Feb 82
2.00		Charmaine	Gale/Weavers	RSA	27.2.64	1		Pretoria	25 Mar 85
		(20)							
2.00i		Emilia	Dragieva'	BUL	11.1.65	3	WI	Indianapolis	8 Mar 87
2.00		Lyudmila	Avdyeyenko'	UKR	14.12.63	1	NC	Bryansk	17 Jul 87
2.00		Svetlana	Isaeva'	BUL	18.3.67	2	v TCH,Gre	Drama	8 Aug 87
2.00i		Larisa	Kositsyna	RUS	14.12.63	2	NC	Volgograd	11 Feb 88
2.00		Jan	Wohlschlag'	USA	14.7.58	1	Bisl	Oslo	1 Jul 89
2.00		Yolanda	Henry	USA	2.12.64	1	Expo	Sevilla	30 May 90
2.00		Biljana	Petrovic	YUG	28.2.61	1		St. Denis	22 Jun 90
2.00		Tatyana	Shevchik	BLR	11.6.69	1		Gomel	14 May 93
2.00i		Yelena	Gulyayeva ' ¶	RUS	14.8.67	1		Moskva	27 Jan 94
2.00i		Britta	Bilac'	SLO	4.12.68	1		Frankfurt	9 Feb 94
		(30)							
1.99i		Debbie	Brill	CAN	10.3.53	1		Edmonton	23 Jan 82
1.99i		Andrea	Bienias'	GDR	11.11.59	2	EI	Milano	7 Mar 82
1.99i		Katalin	Sterk	HUN	30.9.61	3	EI	Milano	7 Mar 82
1.99		Kerstin	Brandt'	GDR	9.12.61	3	ECp	London	21 Aug 83
1.99		Yelena	Topchina ¶	RUS	21.10.66	1		Rieti	5 Sep 93
1.98i		Andrea	Mátay	HUN	27.9.55	1	NC	Budapest	17 Feb 79
1.98		Valentina	Poluyko	BLR	15.7.55	1		Leningrad	26 Jul 83
1.98		Lyudmila	Butuzova	KZK	28.2.57	2	Znam	Sochi	10 Jun 84
1.98		Niculina	Vasile	ROM	13.2.58	1	RomIC	Bucuresti	2 Jun 85
1.98		Vanessa	Ward'	AUS	5.1.63	1		Perth	12 Feb 89
		(40)							
1.98		Andrea	Arens/Baumert	FRG	5.5.67	1	NC	Hamburg	12 Aug 89
1.98i		Yelena	Panikarovskikh'	RUS	4.12.59	1	NP	Moskva	25 Feb 90
1.98i		Antonella	Bevilacqua	ITA	15.10.71	1		Pireas	28 Feb 94
1.98i		Hanne	Haugland	NOR	14.12.67	2		Pireas	28 Feb 94
1.98i		Angie	Bradburn	USA	4.9.68	1	NC	Atlanta	5 Mar 94
1.98		Yevgenia	Zhdanova	RUS	21.7.66	2	Znam	Moskva	5 Jun 94
1.98		Alison	Inverarity	AUS	12.8.70	1		Ingolstadt	17 Jul 94
		(47) - 17 women on 1.97							

Best outdoor marks

2.00	Quintero	1	Herc	Monaco	7 Aug 93
2.00	Kositsyna	1		Chelyabinsk	16 Jul 88
2.00	Astafei	1	WJ	Sudbury	29 Jul 88
2.00	Bilac	1	EC	Helsinki	14 Aug 94
1.99	Beyer'	3	WCh	Roma	30 Aug 87
1.99	Gulyayeva	1	Znam	Moskva	9 Jun 91
1.98	Sommer	1	v FRG,Afr	Durham	26 Jun 82
1.98	Brill	2		Rieti	2 Sep 84
1.98	Sterk	1	NC	Budapest	17 Aug 86

POLE VAULT

Mark	Wind	Name		Nat	Born	Pos	Meet	Venue	Date
4.12			Sun Caiyun #	CHN	21.3.73	1		Guangzhou	22Oct 94
4.12			Sun Caiyun			1		Guangzhou	24Nov 94
4.11			Sun Caiyun			1		Guangzhou	21 Mar 93
4.08i		Nicole	Rieger	GER	5.2.72	1		Karlsruhe	1 Mar 94

Mark	Wind	Name		Nat	Born	Pos	Meet	Venue	Date
4.08i			Sun Caiyun			2		Karlsruhe	1 Mar 94
4.07i			Sun Caiyun			1		Landau	31 Jan 93
4.06i			Sun Caiyun			1		Zweibrücken	29 Jan 93
4.05			Zhang Chunzhen	CHN	.9.70	1		Guangzhou	10 Aug 91
4.05			Sun Caiyun			1	NC	Nanjing	21 May 92
4.03			Sun Caiyun			1		Guangzhou	11 Apr 92
4.02			Zhang Chunzhen			1	NC	Beijing	5 Jun 91
4.02i			Rieger			1	NC	Dortmund	26 Feb 94
4.01i			Rieger			1		Landau	20 Feb 94
4.01		Marina	Andreyeva	RUS	73	1	NC-23	Voronezh	18 Jun 94
4.01			Cai Weiyan	CHN	25.10.73	1		Hefei	3 Aug 94
4.00			Zhang Chunzhen			1		Guangzhou	24 Mar 91
4.00			Cai Weiyan			1		Wuhan	19 Oct 92
4.00i			Rieger			1		Clermont-Ferrand	28 Jan 94
4.00i		Andrea	Müller	GER	29.6.74	1		Sindelfingen	6 Mar 94
4.00i			Rieger			2		Sindelfingen	6 Mar 94
4.00			Rieger			1		Duisburg	12 Jun 94
4.00			Sun Caiyun			1	GWG	St Peterburg	24 Jul 94
4.00			Sun Caiyun			1		Tangshan	29 Aug 94
4.00			Cai Weiyan			2		Tangshan	29 Aug 94
		(24/6)							
3.96i		Gabriela	Mihalcea	ROM	27.1.64	1		Bucuresti	6 Feb 94
3.95i			Shao Jingwen	CHN	8.3.71	2		Landau	31 Jan 93
3.93		Tanja	Cors	GER	22.4.71	1		Bad Gendersheim	23 May 93
3.91		Caroline	Ammel	FRA	22.11.73	1		La Roche sur Yon	14 Jul 94
		(10)							
3.90		Carmen	Haage	GER	10.9.71	1		Spaichingen	15 Aug 92
3.90		Svetlana	Abramova	RUS	27.10.70	1		Schwechat	30 May 93
3.90		Christine	Adams	GER	28.2.74	2	NC	Erfurt	3 Jul 94
3.90		Daniela	Köpernick	GER	25.7.73	2		Ahlen	6 Aug 94
3.85		Janet	Zach	GER	19.6.75	3		Ahlen	6 Aug 94
3.80			Wu Weili	CHN	20.4.70	2	NC	Beijing	26 Jun 90
3.80			Zhu Rong	CHN	5.4.72			Beijing	15 Aug 92
3.80		Galina	Yenvarenko	RUS	70	2	NC	Moskva	18 Jun 93
3.80			Zhong Guiqing	CHN	75	1		Guangzhou	26 Mar 94
3.80		Natalya	Mekhanoshina	RUS	10.8.72	1		Moskva	11 Jun 94
		(20)							
Outdoor best: 3.89			Mihalcea			1		Iasi	19 Jul 94
Drugs disqualification:		4.08i	Sun Caiyun #	CHN		2		Karlsruhe	1 Mar 94

LONG JUMP

Mark	Wind	Name		Nat	Born	Pos	Meet	Venue	Date
7.52	1.4	Galina	Chistyakova	RUS	26.7.62	1	Znam	Leningrad	11 Jun 88
7.49	1.3	Jackie	Joyner-Kersee	USA	3.3.62	1	NYG	New York	22 May 94
7.49A	1.7		Joyner-Kersee			1		Sestriere	31 Jul 94
7.48	1.2	Heike	Drechsler	GER	16.12.64	1	v Ita	Neubrandenburg	9 Jul 88
7.48	0.4		Drechsler			1	Athl	Lausanne	8 Jul 92
7.45	0.9		Drechsler'			1	v URS	Tallinn	21 Jun 86
7.45	1.1		Drechsler			1	OD	Dresden	3 Jul 86
7.45	0.6		Joyner-Kersee			1	PAm	Indianapolis	13 Aug 87
7.45	1.6		Chistyakova			1	BGP	Budapest	12 Aug 88
7.44	2.0		Drechsler			1		Berlin	22 Sep 85
7.43	1.4	Anisoara	Cusmir'	ROM	28.6.62	1	RomIC	Bucuresti	4 Jun 83
7.40	1.8		Daute' (Drechsler)			1		Dresden	26 Jul 84
7.40	0.7		Drechsler			1	NC	Potsdam	21 Aug 87
7.40	0.9		Joyner-Kersee			1	OG	Seoul	29 Sep 88
7.39	0.3		Drechsler			1	WK	Zürich	21 Aug 85
7.39	0.5	Yelena	Byelevskaya'	BLR	11.10.63	1	NC	Bryansk	18 Jul 87
7.39			Joyner-Kersee			1		San Diego	25 Jun 88
7.37i	-		Drechsler			1	v Aut,Yug	Wien	13 Feb 88
7.37A	1.8		Drechsler			1		Sestriere	31 Jul 91
7.37		Inessa	Kravets	UKR	5.10.66	1		Kiev	13 Jun 92
7.36	0.4		Joyner			1	WCh	Roma	4 Sep 87
7.36	1.8		Byelevskaya			2	Znam	Leningrad	11 Jun 88
7.36	1.8		Drechsler			1		Jena	28 May 92
7.35	1.9		Chistyakova			1	GPB	Bratislava	20 Jun 90
7.34	1.6		Daute'			1		Dresden	19 May 84

Mark	Wind	Name		Nat	Born	Pos	Meet	Venue	Date
7.34	1.4		Chistyakova			2	v GDR	Tallinn	21 Jun 86
7.34			Byelevskaya			1		Sukhumi	17 May 87
7.34	0.7		Drechsler			1	v URS	Karl-Marx-Stadt	20 Jun 87
7.33	0.4		Drechsler			1	v URS	Erfurt	22 Jun 85
7.33	2.0		Drechsler			1		Dresden	2 Aug 85
7.33	-0.3		Drechsler			1	Herc	Monaco	11 Aug 92
		(31/6)							
7.31	1.5	Yelena	Kokonova'	UKR	4.8.63	1	NP	Alma-Ata	12 Sep 85
7.24	1.0	Larisa	Berezhnaya	UKR	28.2.61	1	Blanc	Granada	25 May 91
7.21	1.6	Helga	Radtke	GDR	16.5.62	2		Dresden	26 Jul 84
7.20	-0.5	Valy	Ionescu	ROM	31.8.60	1	NC	Bucuresti	1 Aug 82
		(10)							
7.20	2.0	Irena	Ozhenko'	LIT	13.11.62	1		Budapest	12 Sep 86
7.20	0.8	Yelena	Sinchukova'	RUS	23.1.61	1	HGP	Budapest	20 Jun 91
7.20	0.7	Irina	Mushayilova	RUS	6.1.67	1	NC	St Peterburg	14 Jul 94
7.17	1.8	Irina	Valyukevich	BLR	19.11.59	2	NC	Bryansk	18 Jul 87
7.16		Yolanda	Chen	RUS	26.7.61	1		Moskva	30 Jul 88
7.14	1.8	Niole	Medvedyeva	LIT	20.10.60	1		Riga	4 Jun 88
7.14	1.2	Mirela	Dulgheru	ROM	5.10.66	1	Balk G	Sofia	5 Jul 92
7.12	1.6	Sabine	Paetz/John'	GDR	16.10.57	2		Dresden	19 May 84
7.09	0.0	Vilma	Bardauskiene	LIT	15.6.53	Q	EC	Praha	29 Aug 78
7.09	1.5	Ljudmila	Ninova	AUT	25.6.60	1	GP II	Sevilla	5 Jun 94
		(20)							
7.08	0.5	Marieta	Ilcu	ROM	16.10.62	1	RumIC	Pitesti	25 Jun 89
7.07	0.0	Svetlana	Zorina	RUS	2.2.60	1		Krasnodar	15 Aug 87
7.06	0.4	Tatyana	Kolpakova	KGZ	18.10.59	1	OG	Moskva	31 Jul 80
7.06	-1.3	Chioma	Ajunwa ¶	NGR	25.12.70	1		Lagos	12 Jun 92
7.04	0.5	Brigitte	Wujak'	GDR	6.3.55	2	OG	Moskva	31 Jul 80
7.04	0.9	Tatyana	Proskuryakova'	RUS	13.1.56	1		Kiev	25 Aug 83
7.04	2.0	Yelena	Yatsuk	UKR	16.3.61	1	Znam	Moskva	8 Jun 85
7.04	0.3	Carol	Lewis	USA	8.8.63	5	WK	Zürich	21 Aug 85
7.01	-0.4	Tatyana	Skachko	UKR	18.8.54	3	OG	Moskva	31 Jul 80
7.01	-0.3	Eva	Murková	TCH	29.5.62	1	PTS	Bratislava	26 May 84
		(30)							
7.01	-1.0	Marina	Kibakina'	RUS	2.8.60	1		Krasnoyarsk	10 Aug 85
7.01	1.4		Yao Weili	CHN	6.5.68	1	NC	Jinan	5 Jun 93
7.00	2.0	Jodi	Anderson	USA	10.11.57	1	OT	Eugene	28 Jun 80
7.00		Margarita	Butkiene	LIT	19.8.49	1		Vilnius	25 May 83
7.00	-0.2	Birgit	Grosshennig	GDR	21.2.65	2		Berlin	9 Jun 84
7.00	0.6	Silvia	Khristova'	BUL	22.8.65	1		Sofia	3 Aug 86
7.00		Susen	Tiedtke	GER	23.1.69	2		Seoul	18 Aug 91
6.99	2.0	Sigrun	Siegl'	GDR	29.10.54	1	OD	Dresden	19 May 76
6.97	2.0	Agata	Karczmarek	POL	29.11.63	1		Lublin	6 Aug 88
		(40)							
6.97	1.3		Ma Miaolan	CHN	18.1.70	*	NG	Beijing	10 Sep 93
6.96	2.0	Anna	Wlodarczyk ¶	POL	24.3.51	1	NC	Lublin	22 Jun 84
6.96	1.8	Christine	Schima	GDR	6.9.62	3		Dresden	26 Jul 84
6.96A	0.0	Madeline	de Jesus	PUR	4.11.57	1	IbAC	Ciudad México	24 Jul 88
6.96	2.0	Renata	Nielsen	DEN	18.5.66	*	GP II	Sevilla	5 Jun 94
6.95A	1.5	Fiona	May	ITA	12.12.69	*		Sestriere	31 Jul 94
6.94	1.3	Yelena	Chicherova	RUS	9.8.58	2	Izv	Kiev	21 Jun 84
6.94	-1.0	Sheila	Echols	USA	2.10.64	1	NCAA	Baton Rouge	5 Jun 87
6.92	1.6	Angela	Voigt'	GDR	18.5.51	1		Dresden	9 May 76
6.92	0.8	Vera	Olenchenko	UZB	21.3.59	1		Baku	22 Sep 85
6.92	1.6	Heike	Grabe	GDR	11.3.62	2	PTS	Bratislava	13 Jun 87
6.92	1.7		Liu Shuzhen	CHN	7.5.66	1	NC	Beijing	24 Jun 90
		(52)							

Wind assisted

Mark	Wind	Name		Nat	Born	Pos	Meet	Venue	Date
7.63A	2.1	Heike	Drechsler	GER	16.12.64	1		Sestriere	21 Jul 92
7.45	2.6	Jackie	Joyner-Kersee	USA	3.3.62	1	OT	Indianapolis	23 Jul 88
7.39	2.6		Drechsler			1		Padova	15 Sep 91
7.39	2.9		Drechsler			1	Expo	Sevilla	6 Jun 92
7.39A	3.3		Drechsler			2		Sestriere	31 Jul 94
7.36	2.2		Chistyakova			1	Znam	Volgograd	11 Jun 89
7.35	3.4		Drechsler			1	NC	Jena	29 Jun 86
7.19A	3.7	Susen	Tiedtke	GER	23.1.69	1		Sestriere	28 Jul 93
7.17	3.6	Eva	Murková	TCH	29.5.62	1		Nitra	26 Aug 84
7.09	2.9	Renata	Nielsen	DEN	18.5.66	2		Sevilla	5 Jun 94

Mark	Wind	Name		Nat	Born	Pos	Meet	Venue	Date
7.06	3.4		Ma Miaolan	CHN	18.1.70	1	NG	Beijing	10 Sep 93
7.00	3.8	Ramona	Neubert'	GDR	26.7.58	1	v GBR	Dresden	14 Jun 81
7.00	4.2	Sue	Hearnshaw'	GBR	26.5.61	1	NC	Cwmbran	27 May 84
7.00A	2.1	Fiona	May	ITA	12.12.69	3		Sestriere	31 Jul 94
6.98	3.4	Ines	Schmidt	GDR	7.7.60	2		Nitra	26 Aug 84
6.97	2.7	Anna	Wlodarczyk ¶	POL	24.3.51	1	4-N	Warszawa	15 Jul 84
6.96		Tatyana	Shchelkanova	RUS	18.4.37	P	NC	Dnepropetrovsk	14 Aug 66
6.96A	3.0	Valentina	Uccheddu	ITA	26.10.66	4		Sestriere	31 Jul 94
6.95	3.0	Iva	Prandzheva	BUL	15.2.72	1		Sofia	15 May 94
6.93	4.6	Beverly	Kinch	GBR	14.1.64	5	WCh	Helsinki	14 Aug 83
6.93A	4.4	Ringa	Ropo	FIN	16.2.66	3		Sestriere	21 Jul 92
Best low altitude mark									
6.88	1.4		May	(GBR)		1	GG	Bologna	18 Jul 90
6.87	0.3		Montalvo			1	NC	Habana	18 Mar 90
6.78	0.7		Botha			1	Afr Ch	Belle Vue Mauricia	25 Jun 92
7.02wA	4.8		Tiedtke			2		Sestriere	21 Jul 92
6.98w	3.3		May	(GBR)		1	NC	Jarrow	4 Jun 89

TRIPLE JUMP

Mark	Wind	Name		Nat	Born	Pos	Meet	Venue	Date
15.09	0.5	Ana	Biryukova	RUS	27.9.67	1	WCh	Stuttgart	21 Aug 93
14.98	1.8	Sofia	Bozhanova ¶	BUL	4.10.67	1		Stara Zagora	16 Jul 94
14.97	0.9	Yolanda	Chen	RUS	26.7.61	1	NC	Moskva	18 Jun 93
14.95	-0.2	Inessa	Kravets	UKR	5.10.66	1	Znam	Moskva	10 Jun 91
14.94	0.2	Inna	Lasovskaya	RUS	17.12.69	1	Slov	Bratislava	1 Jun 94
14.91	1.4		Kravets			2	Slov	Bratislava	1 Jun 94
14.90i	-		Lasovskaya			1		Liévin	13 Feb 94
14.89	1.1		Biryukova			1	EC	Helsinki	8 Aug 94
14.88i			Lasovskaya			1	EI	Paris	13 Mar 94
14.81	0.4		Lasovskaya			1	GP II	Linz	4 Jul 94
14.79	1.7	Irina	Mushayilova	RUS	6.1.67	1	DNG	Stockholm	5 Jul 93
14.78i	-		Lasovskaya			1		Moskva	27 Jan 94
14.74	0.4		Biryukova			1	Gugl	Linz	25 Aug 93
14.74	0.6		Lasovskaya			1	NC	St Peterburg	16 Jul 94
14.72i	-		Biryukova			2	EI	Paris	13 Mar 94
14.71	1.6		Chen			1	BNP	Villeneuve d'Ascq	2 Jul 93
14.71	1.0		Bozhanova			1	ECp II	Istanbul	11 Jun 94
14.70	0.6		Lasovskaya			2	Slovn	Bratislava	1 Jun 93
14.70	0.1		Chen			2	WCh	Stuttgart	21 Aug 93
14.70	0.8		Kravets			1		Luzern	29 Jun 94
14.70	1.5		Biryukova			1		Sheffield	4 Sep 94
14.68	1.0		Biryukova			*	Slovn	Bratislava	1 Jun 93
14.68	0.2		Lasovskaya			2	NC	Moskva	18 Jun 93
14.67i	-		Lasovskaya			1		Grenoble	6 Feb 94
14.66	0.1		Biryukova			1	TOTO	Tokyo	15 Sep 94
14.65	1.8		Chen			2	DNG	Stockholm	5 Jul 93
14.65i	-		Lasovskaya			1		Madrid	11 Feb 94
14.64	-1.0		Lasovskaya			1	GGala	Roma	9 Jun 93
14.63	0.2		Lasovskaya			1	Banes	São Paulo	21 May 94
14.62	1.4	Galina	Chistyakova	RUS	26.7.62	1	vFra	Villeneuve d'Ascq	13 Sep 92
14.62	0.2		Biryukova			3	Slov	Bratislava	1 Jun 94
14.62	0.1		Kravets			2	TOTO	Tokyo	15 Sep 94
		(32/7)							
14.60	0.7	Niurka	Montalvo	CUB	4.6.68	1	NC	La Habana	24 Jun 94
14.55	0.9		Li Huirong	CHN	14.4.65	1	Nanbu	Sapporo	19 Jul 92
14.47	0.?	Rodica	Petrescu	ROM	13.3.71	1	NC	Bucuresti	18 Jun 94
		(10)							
14.47		Natalya	Kayukova	RUS	12.12.66	1		Sochi	10 Sep 94
14.46i	-	Sarka	Kaspárková	TCH	20.5.71	4	EI	Paris	13 Mar 94
14.46	1.0	Helga	Radtke	GER	16.5.62	1	NC	Erfurt	3 Jul 94
14.38i	-	Iva	Prandzheva	BUL	15.2.72	5	EI	Paris	13 Mar 94
14.36	0.0		Ren Ruiping	CHN	1.2.76	1	NC	Beijing	1 Jun 94
14.35	0.5	Yelena	Semiraz	UKR	21.11.65	2	NC	Kiev	13 Jul 91
14.32	-0.1	Yelena	Lysak ¶	RUS	19.10.75	1	NC-23	Voronezh	18 Jun 94
14.31	1.6	Lyudmila	Dubkova	RUS	27.2.68	3	NC	St Peterburg	16 Jul 94
14.30	1.8	Concepcion	Paredes	ESP	19.7.70	1		Segovia	28 Jun 94
14.28	0.9		Zhang Yan	CHN	.6.72	2	NG	Beijing	13 Sep 93
		(20)							

Mark	Wind	Name		Nat	Born	Pos	Meet	Venue	Date
14.23	1.8	Sheila	Hudson-Strudwick	USA	30.6.67	1	TAC	New Orleans	20 Jun 92
14.22	0.2	Eloina	Echevarria	CUB	23.8.61	2	NC	La Habana	24 Jun 94
14.22	0.4	Yelena	Govorova	UKR	18.9.73	1	ECp 23	Lillehammer	30 Jul 94
14.22		Ashia	Hansen	GBR	5.12.71	1		Welwyn	29 Aug 94
14.18	-0.1	Antonella	Capriotti	ITA	4.2.62	6	WCh	Stuttgart	21 Aug 93
14.17	-0.5	Zhanna	Gureyeva	BLR	10.6.70	3	GGala	Roma	9 Jun 93
14.16	1.4	Maria	Sokova	RUS	2.9.70	4	NC	St Peterburg	16 Jul 94
14.12	0.8		Ma Miaolan	CHN	18.1.70	3	NG	Beijing	13 Sep 93
14.10	0.8	Petra	Laux-Schneider	GER	24.1.67	2	NC	Erfurt	3 Jul 94
14.10	0.5	Natalya	Kuzina	RUS	19.7.70	5	NC	St Peterburg	16 Jul 94
		(30)							
14.09	0.7	Yelena	Sinchukova	RUS	23.1.61	2	vFra	Villeneuve d'Ascq	13 Sep 92
14.08	0.7	Michelle	Griffith	GBR	6.10.71	1	AAA	Sheffield	11 Jun 94
14.06	0.2		Liu Jingming	CHN	1.2.72	2	NC	Beijing	1 Jun 94
14.03i	-	Tanja	Bormann	GER	11.4.70	2	NC	Dortmund	26 Feb 94
14.03	0.9	Diana	Orrange	USA	9.8.67	2	NC	Knoxville	16 Jun 94
14.01		Ionela	Gogoase	ROM	4.2.71	1		Bucuresti	29 Jul 94
14.00	-0.6	Laiza	Carillo	CUB	27.11.68	3	NC	La Habana	24 Jun 94
13.98	1.0	Urszula	Wlodarczyk	POL	22.12.65	2	NC	Kielce	25 Jul 93
13.98	1.2		Li Jing	CHN	21.10.69	3	NC	Beijing	1 Jun 94
13.96	0.9	Ramona	Molzan	GER	1.8.71	Q	EC	Helsinki	7 Aug 94
		(40)							
13.95	1.8	Olga	Cepero	CUB	4.2.75	1		La Habana	11 Feb 94
13.94	0.0	Cynthea	Rhodes	USA	30.9.68	2	PennR	Philadelphia	30 Apr 94
13.93i	-	Valy	Ionescu	ROM	31.8.60	1	LAT	Inglewood	21 Feb 87
13.93i	-	Iolanda	Oanta	ROM	11.10.65	1		Bacau	23 Jan 93
13.93		Monica	Toth	ROM	7.3.70	1		Bucuresti	29 May 93
13.92	-	Irina	Babakova	UKR	5.11.65	1		Moskva	3 Jun 90
13.92i	-	Anja	Vokuhl	GER	17.8.73	2	NC	Sindelfingen	28 Feb 93
13.92	0.1		Zhang JIng	CHN	10.3.70	1		Guangzhou	21 Mar 93
13.92	0.7	Yamile	Aldama	CUB	14.8.72	4	NC	La Habana	24 Jun 94
13.92	1.6	Betty	Lise	FRA	5.9.72	1	NC	Annecy	22 Jul 94
		(50)							
Previously disqualified for drugs use									
14.70	0.5	Inessa	Kravets			1	Nik	Nice	21 Jul 93
14.61	0.2		Kravets			1	Athl	Lausanne	7 Jul 93
14.05	0.3	Agnieszka	Stanczyk	POL	20.1.71	1	NC	Kielce	25 Jul 93
Wind assisted									
14.85	2.4		Kravets			1	DNG	Stockholm	12 Jul 94
14.85	3.1		Lasovskaya			2	EC	Helsinki	8 Aug 94
14.74	2.7		Biryukova			1	Slovn	Bratislava	1 Jun 93
14.67	2.1		Kravets			3	EC	Helsinki	8 Aug 94
14.43	2.7	Yelena	Lysak ¶	RUS	15.3.75	1	EJ	Lisboa	21 Jul 94
14.07	2.8		Wang Xiangrong	CHN	.2.76	4	NG	Beijing	13 Sep 93
13.98	6.0	Monica	Toth	ROM	7.3.70	2		Gateshead	1 Jul 94

Best outdoor mark for athlete with all-time best indoors

Mark	Wind	Name	Pos	Meet	Venue	Date
14.23	-0.2	Prandzheva	3	WCh	Stuttgart	21 Aug 93
14.16	0.1	Kaspárková	7	WCh	Stuttgart	21 Aug 93
14.08	0.0	Bozhanova	1	NarM	Plovdiv	2 Jun 91
14.32w	4.9	Prandzheva	1		Sofia	3 Jul 93
14.20w	2.1	Kasparková	4	Slov	Bratislava	1 Jun 94

SHOT

Mark	Name		Nat	Born	Pos	Meet	Venue	Date
22.63	Natalya	Lisovskaya	RUS	16.7.62	1	Znam	Moskva	7 Jun 87
22.55		Lisovskaya			1	NC	Tallinn	5 Jul 88
22.53		Lisovskaya			1		Sochi	27 May 84
22.53		Lisovskaya			1		Kiev	14 Aug 88
22.50i	Helena	Fibingerová	TCH	13.7.49	1		Jablonec	19 Feb 77
22.45	Ilona	Slupianek' ¶	GDR	24.9.56	1		Potsdam	11 May 80
22.41		Slupianek			1	OG	Moskva	24 Jul 80
22.40		Slupianek			1		Berlin	3 Jun 83
22.38		Slupianek			1		Karl-Marx-Stadt	25 May 80
22.36		Slupianek			1		Celje	2 May 80
22.34		Slupianek			1		Berlin	7 May 80
22.34		Slupianek			1	NC	Cottbus	18 Jul 80
22.32		Fibingerová			1		Nitra	20 Aug 77
22.24		Lisovskaya			1	OG	Seoul	1 Oct 88
22.22		Slupianek			1		Potsdam	13 Jul 80

Mark	Wind	Name		Nat	Born	Pos	Meet	Venue	Date
22.19		Claudia	Losch	FRG	10.1.60	1		Hainfeld	23 Aug 87
22.14i			Lisovskaya			1	NC	Penza	7 Feb 87
22.13			Slupianek			1		Split	29 Apr 80
22.06			Slupianek			1		Berlin	15 Aug 78
22.06			Lisovskaya			1		Moskva	6 Aug 88
22.05			Slupianek			1	OD	Berlin	28 May 80
22.05			Slupianek			1		Potsdam	31 May 80
22.04			Slupianek			1		Potsdam	4 Jul 79
22.04			Slupianek			1		Potsdam	29 Jul 79
21.99			Fibingerová			1		Opava	26 Sep 76
21.98			Slupianek			1		Berlin	17 Jul 79
21.96			Fibingerová			1	GS	Ostrava	8 Jun 77
21.96			Lisovskaya			1	Drz	Praha	16 Aug 84
21.96			Lisovskaya			1		Vilnius	28 Aug 88
21.95			Lisovskaya			1	IAC	Edinburgh	29 Jul 88
		(30/4)							
21.89		Ivanka	Khristova	BUL	19.11.41	1		Belmeken	4 Jul 76
21.86		Marianne	Adam	GDR	19.9.51	1	v URS	Leipzig	23 Jun 79
21.76			Li Meisu	CHN	17.4.59	1		Shijiazhuang	23 Apr 88
21.73		Natalya	Akhrimenko	RUS	12.5.55	1		Leselidze	21 May 88
21.66			Sui Xinmei ¶	CHN	29.1.65	1		Beijing	9 Jun 90
21.61		Verzhinia	Veselinova	BUL	18.11.57	1		Sofia	21 Aug 82
		(10)							
21.60i		Valentina	Fedyushina	UKR	18.2.65	1		Simferopol	28 Dec 91
21.58		Margitta	Droese'	GDR	10.9.52	1		Erfurt	28 May 78
21.57	@	Ines	Müller'	GDR	2.1.59	1		Athinai	16 May 88
		21.45				1		Schwerin	4 Jun 86
21.53		Nunu	Abashidze ¶	UKR	27.3.55	2	Izv	Kiev	20 Jun 84
21.52			Huang Zhihong	CHN	7.5.65	1	NC	Beijing	27 Jun 90
21.45		Nadezhda	Chizhova	RUS	29.9.45	1		Varna	29 Sep 73
21.43		Eva	Wilms	FRG	28.7.52	2	HB	München	17 Jun 77
21.42		Svetlana	Krachevskaya'	RUS	23.11.44	2	OG	Moskva	24 Jul 80
21.31	@	Heike	Hartwig'	GDR	30.12.62	2		Athinai	16 May 88
		21.27				1		Khania	22 May 88
21.27		Liane	Schmuhl	GDR	29.6.61	1		Cottbus	26 Jun 82
21.21		Kathrin	Neimke	GDR	18.7.66	2	WCh	Roma	5 Sep 87
		(20)							
21.19		Helma	Knorscheidt	GDR	31.12.56	1		Berlin	24 May 84
21.10		Heidi	Krieger	GDR	20.7.65	1	EC	Stuttgart	26 Aug 86
21.06		Svetlana	Krivelyova	RUS	13.6.69	1	OG	Barcelona	7 Aug 92
21.05		Zdenka	Silhavá' ¶	TCH	15.6.54	2	NC	Praha	23 Jul 83
21.01		Ivanka	Petrova-Stoycheva	BUL	3.2.51	1	NC	Sofia	28 Jul 79
21.00		Mihaela	Loghin	ROM	1.6.52	1		Formia	30 Jun 84
21.00		Cordula	Schulze	GDR	11.9.59	4	OD	Potsdam	21 Jul 84
20.99		Larisa	Peleshenko'	RUS	29.2.64	1		Leselidze	13 May 87
20.96		Belsy	Laza	CUB	5.6.67	1		Ciudad México	2 May 92
		(30)							
20.95		Elena	Stoyanova ¶	BUL	23.1.52	2	Balk	Sofia	14 Jun 80
20.91		Svetla	Mitkova	BUL	17.6.64	1		Sofia	24 May 87
20.80		Sona	Vasícková	TCH	14.3.62	1		Praha	2 Jun 88
20.77		Astrid	Kumbernuss	GDR	5.2.70	1	vSU	Rostock	24 Jun 90
20.72		Grit	Haupt/Hammer	GDR	4.6.66	3		Neubrandenburg	11 Jun 87
20.61		María Elena	Sarría	CUB	14.9.54	1		Habana	22 Jul 82
20.60		Marina	Antonyuk	RUS	12.5.62	1		Chelyabinsk	10 Aug 86
20.54			Zhang Liuhong	CHN	16.1.69	1	NC	Beijing	5 Jun 94
20.53		Iris	Plotzitzka	FRG	7.1.66	1	ASV	Köln	21 Aug 88
20.50i		Christa	Wiese	GDR	25.12.67	2	NC	Senftenberg	12 Feb 89
		(40)							
20.47		Nina	Isayeva	RUS	6.7.50	1		Bryansk	28 Aug 82
20.47			Cong Yuzhen	CHN	22.1.63	2	IntC	Tianjin	3 Sep 88
20.44		Tatyana	Orlova	BLR	19.7.55	1		Staiki	28 May 83
20.40			Zhou Tianhua ¶	CHN	10.4.66	1		Beijing	5 Sep 91
20.34		Stephanie	Storp	FRG	28.11.68	1		Wolfsburg	1 Jul 90
20.27		Danguole	Bimbaite'	LIT	10.12.62	2		Leselidze	13 May 87
20.27		Lyudmila	Voyevudskaya	UKR	22.6.59	1		Nikolayev	7 Aug 87
20.24		Anna	Romanova	RUS	9.3.68	1		Bryansk	29 May 93

Mark	Wind	Name		Nat	Born	Pos	Meet	Venue	Date
20.23		Ilke	Wyludda	GDR	28.3.69	1	NC-j	Karl-Marx-Stadt	16 Jul 88
20.22		Margitta	Gummel'	GDR	29.6.41	2	OG	München	7 Sep 72
		(50)							

Best outdoor mark: 21.08 Fedyushina 1 Leselidze 15 May 88

@ meeting held under competitive conditions, but unsanctioned by GDR federation.

DISCUS

Mark	Wind	Name		Nat	Born	Pos	Meet	Venue	Date
76.80		Gabriele	Reinsch	GDR	23.9.63	1	v Ita	Neubrandenburg	9 Jul 88
74.56		Zdenka	Silhavá' ¶	TCH	15.6.54	1		Nitra	26 Aug 84
74.56		Ilke	Wyludda	GDR	28.3.69	1	NC	Neubrandenburg	23 Jul 89
74.44			Reinsch			1		Berlin	13 Sep 88
74.40			Wyludda			2		Berlin	13 Sep 88
74.08		Diana	Gansky'	GDR	14.12.63	1	v URS	Karl-Marx-Stadt	20 Jun 87
73.90			Gansky			1	ECp	Praha	27 Jun 87
73.84		Daniela	Costian ¶	ROM	30.4.65	1		Bucuresti	30 Apr 88
73.78			Costian			1		Bucuresti	24 Apr 88
73.42			Reinsch			1		Karl-Marx-Stadt	12 Jun 88
73.36		Irina	Meszynski	GDR	24.3.62	1	Drz	Praha	17 Aug 84
73.32			Gansky			1		Neubrandenburg	11 Jun 87
73.28		Galina	Savinkova'	RUS	15.7.53	1	NC	Donyetsk	8 Sep 84
73.26			Savinkova			1		Leselidze	21 May 83
73.26			Sachse/Gansky			1		Neubrandenburg	6 Jun 86
73.24			Gansky			1		Leipzig	29 May 87
73.22		Tsvetanka	Khristova ¶	BUL	14.3.62	1		Kazanlak	19 Apr 87
73.10		Gisela	Beyer	GDR	16.7.60	1	OD	Berlin	20 Jul 84
73.04			Gansky			1		Potsdam	6 Jun 87
73.04			Wyludda			1	ECp	Gateshead	5 Aug 89
72.96			Savinkova			1	v GDR	Erfurt	23 Jun 85
72.94			Gansky			2	v Ita	Neubrandenburg	9 Jul 88
72.92		Martina	Hellmann'	GDR	12.12.60	1	NC	Potsdam	20 Aug 87
72.90			Costian			1		Bucuresti	14 May 88
72.78			Hellmann			2		Neubrandenburg	11 Jun 87
72.78			Reinsch			1	OD	Berlin	29 Jun 88
72.72			Wyludda			1		Neubrandenburg	23 Jun 89
72.70			Wyludda			1	NC-j	Karl-Marx-Stadt	15 Jul 88
72.54			Gansky			1	NC	Rostock	25 Jun 88
72.52			Hellmann			1		Frohburg	15 Jun 86
72.52			Khristova			1	BGP	Budapest	11 Aug 86
		(31/10)							
72.14		Galina	Murashova	LIT	22.12.55	2	Drz	Praha	17 Aug 84
71.80		Maria	Vergova-Petkova	BUL	3.11.50	1	NC	Sofia	13 Jul 80
71.68			Xiao Yanling ¶	CHN	27.3.68	1		Beijing	14 Mar 92
71.58		Ellina	Zvereva' ¶	BLR	16.11.60	1	Znam	Leningrad	12 Jun 88
71.50		Evelin	Jahl'	GDR	28.3.56	1		Potsdam	10 May 80
71.30		Larisa	Korotkevich	RUS	3.1.67	1	RusCp	Sochi	29 May 92
71.22		Ria	Stalman	NED	11.12.51	1		Walnut	15 Jul 84
70.88		Hilda	Ramos	CUB	1.9.64	1		Habana	8 May 92
70.80		Larisa	Mikhalchenko	UKR	16.5.63	1		Kharkov	18 Jun 88
70.68		Maritza	Martén	CUB	16.8.63	1	Ib Am	Sevilla	18 Jul 92
		(20)							
70.50		Faina	Melnik	RUS	9.6.45	1	Znam	Sochi	24 Apr 76
70.34	@	Silvia	Madetzky	GDR	24.6.62	3		Athinai	16 May 88
		69.34				1		Halle	26 Jun 87
69.86		Valentina	Kharchenko	RUS	.49	1		Feodosiya	16 May 81
69.72		Svetla	Mitkova	BUL	17.6.64	2	NC	Sofia	15 Aug 87
69.50		Florenta	Craciunescu'	ROM	7.5.55	1	Balk	Stara Zagora	2 Aug 85
69.08		Carmen	Romero	CUB	6.10.50	1	NC	Habana	17 Apr 76
69.08		Mariana	Lengyel'	ROM	14.4.53	1		Constanta	19 Apr 86
68.94		Irina	Yatchenko	BLR	31.10.65	1	Nik	Nice	15 Jul 92
68.92		Sabine	Engel	GDR	21.4.54	1	v URS,Pol	Karl-Marx-Stadt	25 Jun 77
68.64		Margitta	Pufe'	GDR	10.9.52	1	ISTAF	Berlin	17 Aug 79
		(30)							
68.62			Yu Hourun	CHN	9.7.64	1		Beijing	6 May 88
68.62			Hou Xuemei	CHN	27.2.62	1	IntC	Tianjin	4 Sep 88
68.60		Nadezhda	Kugayevskikh	RUS	19.4.60	1		Oryol	30 Aug 83
68.58		Lyubov	Zverkova	RUS	14.6.55	1	Izv	Kiev	22 Jun 84

Mark	Wind	Name		Nat	Born	Pos	Meet	Venue	Date
68.38		Olga	Burova '	RUS	17.9.63	2	RusCp	Sochi	29 May 92
68.26		Franka	Dietzsch	GDR	22.1.68	3		Neubrandenburg	23 Jun 89
68.18		Tatyana	Lesovaya	KZK	24.4.56	1		Alma-Ata	23 Sep 82
68.18		Irina	Khval	RUS	17.5.62	1		Moskva	8 Jul 88
68.18		Barbara	Echevarría	CUB	6.8.66	2		Habana	17 Feb 89
67.96		Argentina	Menis	ROM	19.7.48	1	RomIC	Bucuresti	15 May 76
		(40)							
67.90		Petra	Sziegaud	GDR	17.10.58	1		Berlin	19 May 82
67.82		Tatyana	Belova	RUS	12.2.62	1		Irkutsk	10 Aug 87
67.80		Stefenia	Simova	BUL	5.6.63	1		Stara Zagora	27 Jun 92
67.54		Svetlana	Petrova	BLR	19.12.51	1		Brest-Litovsk	20 Sep 78
67.50			Li Qiumei	CHN	.9.74	1		Beijing	10 May 94
67.48		Meg	Ritchie	GBR	6.7.52	1	MSR	Walnut	26 Apr 81
67.40		Brigitte	Michel	GDR	19.8.56	2		Halle	14 Jun 79
67.34		Irina	Shabanova	RUS	2.8.64	1		Krasnodar	15 Aug 87
67.32		Natalya	Gorbachova	RUS	24.7.47	1		Leningrad	4 Jun 83
67.26		Svetla	Bozhkova	BUL	13.3.51	2		Sofia	5 Jul 80
		(50)							
Unofficial meeting									
78.14		Martina	Hellmann	GDR	12.12.60	1		Berlin	6 Sep 88
75.36		Ilke	Wyludda	GDR	28.3.69	2		Berlin	6 Sep 88

HAMMER

Mark	Wind	Name		Nat	Born	Pos	Meet	Venue	Date
67.34		Svetlana	Sudak	BLR	17.11.71	1		Minsk	5 Jun 94
66.84		Olga	Kuzenkova	RUS	4.10.70	1		Sochi	23 Feb 94
65.48		Mihaela	Melinte	ROM	27.3.75	1		Bucuresti	25 Feb 94
65.40			Kuzenkova			1		Bryansk	4 Jun 92
65.14			Kuzenkova			1		Rostov	26 Aug 94
65.04			Melinte			1		Bucuresti	10 Jun 94
64.64			Kuzenkova			1		Krasnodar	20 Feb 93
64.44		Alla	Fyodorova	RUS	66	1	NCw	Adler	24 Feb 91
64.44			Kuzenkova			1		Rostov na Donu	17 May 92
64.40			Kuzenkova			1	NC	St Peterburg	16 Jul 94
64.12			Kuzenkova			1		Rostov na Donu	17 Jul 93
63.86			Kuzenkova			1	CIS Ch	Moskva	22 Jun 92
63.70			Sudak			1		Grodno	4 May 93
63.56			Sudak			1		Gomel	9 Jul 94
63.44			Melinte			1	RomIC	Bucuresti	18 Jun 94
63.28			Kuzenkova			1		Moskva	26 Jan 94
63.20			Kuzenkova			1		Staiki	28 Apr 94
63.08		Larisa	Shtyrogrizhnaya	TJK	61	2	NCw	Adler	24 Feb 91
63.00			Kuzenkova			1		Sochi	18 Feb 94
62.98			Kuzenkova			1	NC	Moskva	19 Jul 92
62.98			Melinte			1	Balk-j	Ankara	2 Jul 94
62.70			Fyodorova			1		Adler	9 Feb 91
62.70			Sudak			1		Moskva	28 Feb 92
62.60			Kuzenkova			1		Cork	9 Jul 93
62.56			Fyodorova			1		Alma-Ata	11 May 91
62.52			Melinte			1	NC-j	Bucuresti	8 Aug 93
62.38			Fyodorova			1		Adler	26 May 91
62.38		Debbie	Sosimenko	AUS	5.4.74	1		Sydney	19 Feb 94
62.34			Kuzenkova			1		Moskva	27 Jan 93
62.22		Marina	Pirog	UKR	28.8.74	1		Kiev	23 Jul 94
		(30/7)							
61.96		Larisa	Baranova	RUS	29.6.61	1		Adler	11 Feb 90
61.80		Lyubov	Vasilyeva '	RUS	14.8.57	1		Moskva	18 Jun 91
61.66		Yulia	Styepanova	UKR	8.5.70	1		Kiev	1 Jun 91
		(10)							
61.68		Lyubov	Karpova	RUS	14.8.57	1		Moskva	4 Sep 94
61.50		Yelena	Pichugina	RUS	.64	1		Frunze	30 Sep 89
61.34		Viktoria	Polyanskaya	RUS	71	1		Krasnodar	19 Aug 94
61.20		Aya	Suzuki	JAP	18.11.67	1		Wakayama	30 Apr 89
60.36		Yelena	Rogachevskaya	UKR	12.12.63	2		Bryansk	19 Jun 90
59.92		Lorraine	Shaw	GBR	2.4.68	1		Colindale	1 Apr 94
59.86		Yelena	Lanina	RUS	.69	1	Kuts	Moskva	20 Aug 89
59.80		Natalya	Vasilenko	UKR	15.8.74	1		Chernigov	26 Jun 93

Mark	Wind	Name		Nat	Born	Pos	Meet	Venue	Date
59.62		Lyudmila	Gubkina	BLR	28.5.72	1		Pinsk	6 Jul 93
59.50		Tatyana	Konstantinova	RUS	.70	2		Moskva	26 Jan 94
		(20)							
59.06		Natalya	Panarina	RUS	6.5.75	1		Chelyabinsk	6 Jun 93
59.02		Simone	Mathes	GER	13.5.75	1		Rehlingen	23 May 94
58.92		Olga	Malakhova	UKR	25.8.71	2	NC	Kiev	27 May 94
58.68		Sonja	Fitts	USA	4.10.70	1		Jamaica, N.Y.	14 May 94
58.60		Yelena	Khrulyova	RUS	73	3		Adler	26 May 91
58.52		Carol	Cady	USA	6.6.62	1		Los Gatos	11 Jun 88
58.36		Oksana	Zatsepilova	RUS	20.4.74	2		Moskva	6 Aug 93
58.36		Livia	Mehes	ROM	6.3.65	2	NC	Bucuresti	17 Jun 94
58.20		Olga	Sokolova	RUS	.72	1		Adler	24 Feb 90
58.20		Lyudmila	Novikova	RUS	29.1.64	1		Leningrad	27 May 90
		(30)							
58.16		Viktoriya	Polyanskaya	RUS	71	1		Krasnodar	25 Apr 93
58.10		Natalya	Ignatova	RUS	3.1.74	2		Chelyabinsk	6 Jun 93
58.10		Oksana	Silchenko	BLR	10.8.70	1		Grodno	25 Jul 93
58.02		Olga	Malakhova	UKR	25.8.71	2	NC	Kiev	27 May 94
57.80		Irina	Lungu	ROM	5.4.75			Bucuresti	10 Jun 94
57.62		Kirsten	Münchow	GER	21.1.77	1		Dortmund	25 Jun 94
57.42		Alexandra	Earl-Givan	USA	25.4.70	2	NC	Knoxville	15 Jun 94
57.24		Diana	Bireva	URS	.63	4		Adler	25 Feb 90
56.82		Liz	Legault	USA	4.5.70	1	PennR	Philadelphia	30 Apr 94
56.78		Veronika	Ushakova	RUS	8.11.77	1	v3N-j	Warszawa	18 Jun 94
		(40)							

JAVELIN

Mark	Wind	Name		Nat	Born	Pos	Meet	Venue	Date
80.00		Petra	Felke	GDR	30.7.59	1		Potsdam	9 Sep 88
78.90			Felke			1		Leipzig	29 Jul 87
78.14			Felke			1	OT	Jena	3 Jun 88
77.52			Felke			1	Super	Tokyo	8 Oct 88
77.44		Fatima	Whitbread	GBR	3.3.61	Q	EC	Stuttgart	28 Aug 86
76.88			Felke			1	vIta,Cs	Macerata	5 Sep 89
76.82			Felke			1	v FRG	Düsseldorf	19 Jun 88
76.80			Felke			1		Khania	22 May 88
76.76			Felke			1		Berlin	27 Aug 88
76.64			Whitbread			1	WCh	Roma	6 Sep 87
76.50			Felke			1		Rostock	29 May 88
76.34			Whitbread			1	Bisl	Oslo	4 Jul 87
76.32			Whitbread			1	EC	Stuttgart	29 Aug 86
75.72			Felke			1		Granada	17 Jun 89
75.62			Whitbread			1	NC	Derby	25 May 87
75.40			Felke			1		Schwerin	4 Jun 85
75.16			Felke			1	Bisl	Oslo	2 Jul 88
75.04			Felke			1	GO	Dresden	17 Aug 86
74.94			Felke			1	v URS	Erfurt	22 Jun 85
74.92			Felke			1	OD	Berlin	29 Jun 88
74.90			Felke			1	OD	Berlin	27 Jun 85
74.76		Tiina	Lillak	FIN	15.4.61	1		Tampere	13 Jun 83
74.74			Whitbread			1		Crawley	26 Aug 87
74.72			Felke			1		Celje	5 May 84
74.70			Felke			1		Berlin	22 Sep 85
74.68			Felke			1	OG	Seoul	26 Sep 88
74.62			Felke			1		Berlin	13 Sep 88
74.56			Felke			1	ISTAF	Berlin	23 Aug 85
74.32			Felke			1		Neubrandenburg	11 Jun 87
74.24			Lillak			1		Fresno	7 Apr 84
74.24			Felke			1	OD	Potsdam	21 Jul 84
		(31/3)							
74.20		Sofia	Sakorafa	GRE	29.4.57	1	NC	Khania	26 Sep 82
73.58		Tessa	Sanderson	GBR	14.3.56	1		Edinburgh	26 Jun 83
72.70		Anna	Verouli ¶	GRE	13.11.56	1		Khania	20 May 84
72.16		Antje	Kempe-Zöllkau	GDR	23.6.63	2		Celje	5 May 84
72.12		Trine	Hattestad'	NOR	18.4.66	1	Bisl	Oslo	10 Jul 93
71.88		Antoaneta	Todorova'	BUL	8.6.63	1	ECp	Zagreb	15 Aug 81
71.82		Ivonne	Leal	CUB	27.2.66	1	WUG	Kobe	30 Aug 85
		(10)							

Mark	Wind	Name		Nat	Born	Pos	Meet	Venue	Date
71.40		Natalya	Shikolenko	BLR	1.8.64	1	GP II	Sevilla	5 Jun 94
71.00		Silke	Renk	GDR	30.6.67	2	NC	Rostock	25 Jun 88
70.76		Beate	Koch	GDR	18.8.67	1		Rostock	22 Jun 89
70.42			Zhang Li	CHN	26.6.61	1		Tianjin	6 Aug 90
70.20		Karen	Forkel	GER	24.9.70	1		Halle	9 May 91
70.14		Mayra	Vila ¶	CUB	5.6.60	2		Madrid	14 Jun 85
70.14		María Caridad	Colón	CUB	25.3.58	1	Barr	Habana	15 Jun 86
70.08		Tatyana	Biryulina	UZB	16.7.55	1		Podolsk	12 Jul 80
69.96		Ruth	Fuchs	GDR	14.12.46	1		Split	29 Apr 80
69.86		Natalya	Kolenchuková' ¶	BLR	29.4.64	1	NC	Leningrad	3 Aug 85
		(20)							
69.80		Sue	Howland ¶	AUS	4.9.60	2		Belfast	30 Jun 86
69.68		Ingrid	Thyssen	FRG	9.1.56	1	ISTAF	Berlin	21 Aug 87
69.60		Susanne	Jung	GDR	17.5.63	2	NC	Potsdam	22 Aug 87
69.56		Beate	Peters	FRG	12.10.59	1	NC	Berlin	12 Jul 86
69.32		Kate	Schmidt	USA	29.12.53	1		Fürth	11 Sep 77
69.28		Petra	Rivers	AUS	11.12.52	1	NC	Brisbane	20 Mar 82
68.80		Eva	Raduly-Zörgö	ROM	23.10.54	1	Znam	Moskva	5 Jul 80
68.78			Xu Demei	CHN	23.5.67	1	WCh	Tokyo	1 Sep 91
68.28		Saida	Gunba	GEO	30.8.59	2	Znam	Moskva	5 Jul 80
67.90		Dulce M.	García ¶	CUB	2.7.65	3	Barr	Habana	15 Jun 86
		(30)							
67.88		Natalya	Cherniyenko	UKR	1.10.65	1		Sochi	26 May 90
67.84		Jadviga	Putiniene	LIT	30.12.45	3	Znam	Moskva	5 Jul 80
67.68		Päivi	Alafrantti	FIN	8.5.64	1	EC	Split	30 Aug 90
67.64		Teresé	Nekrosaité	LIT	19.10.61	2		Duisburg	7 Jun 92
67.40		Tuula	Laaksalo	FIN	21.4.53	2		Pihtipudas	24 Jul 83
67.32		Regine	Kempter	GDR	4.4.67	2	NC	Jena	27 Jun 86
67.24		Ute	Hommola	GDR	20.1.52	1	v GBR	Dresden	13 Jun 81
67.24		Svetlana	Pestretsova	KZK	6.3.61	1	Kuts	Moskva	5 Sep 88
67.20		Fausta	Quintavalla	ITA	4.5.59	1		Milano	22 Jun 83
67.18		Zsuzsa	Malovecz	HUN	21.5.62	1	5-N	Forli	22 May 88
		(40)							
67.00		Corina	Girbea'	ROM	26.5.59	1	v Hun	Debrecen	13 Jun 82
67.00		Zinaida	Gavrilina	UKR	22.9.61	1	NC	Donyetsk	9 Sep 84
67.00		Irina	Kostyuchenkova	UKR	11.5.61	2	Znam	Leningrad	12 Jun 88
66.96		Ute	Richter	GDR	14.7.58	1		Neubrandenburg	21 May 83
66.80		Olga	Gavrilova	RUS	8.2.57	1	WCp	Canberra	4 Oct 85
66.80		Jana	Köpping	GDR	12.4.66	3	NC	Jena	27 Jun 86
66.56		Elena	Burgárová	TCH	13.11.52	2		Nitra	26 Aug 84
66.56		Claudia	Isaila	ROM	17.7.73	3	GPF	Paris	3 Sep 94
66.52		Alexandra	Beck	GDR	13.6.68	1		Khania	24 May 86
66.48		Eva	Helmschmidt	FRG	20.4.57	1	v Hol,Pol	Bielefeld	4 Jun 83
		(50)							

WOMEN All-time

HEPTATHLON

Mark	Wind	Name		Nat	Born	Pos	Meet	Venue	Date
7291		Jackie	Joyner-Kersee	USA	3.3.62	1	OG	Seoul	24 Sep 88
		12.69/+0.5	1.86 15.80	22.56/+1.6		7.27/+0.7		45.66 2:08.51	
7215			Joyner-Kersee			1	OT	Indianapolis	16 Jul 88
		12.71/-0.9	1.93 15.65	22.30/ 0.0		7.00/-1.3		50.08 2:20.70	
7158			Joyner-Kersee			1	USOF	Houston	2 Aug 86
		13.18/-0.5	1.88 15.20	22.85/+1.2		7.03/+2.9		50.12 2:09.69	
7148			Joyner			1	GWG	Moskva	7 Jul 86
		12.85/+0.2	1.88 14.76	23.00/+0.3		7.01/-0.5		49.86 2:10.02	
7128			Joyner-Kersee			1	WCh	Roma	1 Sep 87
		12.91/+0.2	1.90 16.00	22.95/+1.2		7.14/+0.9		45.68 2:16.29	
7044			Joyner-Kersee			1	OG	Barcelona	2 Aug 92
		12.85/-0.9	1.91 14.13	23.12/+0.7		7.10/+1.3		44.98 2:11.78	
7007		Larisa	Nikitina ¶	RUS	29.4.65	1	NC	Bryansk	11 Jun 89
		13.40/+1.4	1.89 16.45	23.97/+1.1		6.73/+4.0		53.94 2:15.31	
6985		Sabine	Braun	GER	19.6.65	1		Götzis	31 May 92
		13.11/-0.4	1.93 14.84	23.65/+2.0		6.63/+2.9		51.62 2:12.67	
6979			Joyner-Kersee			1	TAC	San José	24 Jun 87
		12.90/+2.0	1.85 15.17	23.02/+0.4		7.25/+2.3		40.24 2:13.07	
6946		Sabine	Paetz'	GDR	16.10.57	1	NC	Potsdam	6 May 84
		12.64/+0.3	1.80 15.37	23.37/+0.7		6.86/-0.2		44.62 2:08.93	
6935		Ramona	Neubert	GDR	26.7.58	1	v URS	Moskva	19 Jun 83
		13.42	1.82 15.25	23.49		6.79/+0.7		49.94 2:07.51	

Mark	Wind	Name	Nat	Born	Pos	Meet	Venue	Date
6910		Joyner			1	MSR	Walnut	25 Apr 86
	12.9/0.0	1.86 14.75	23.24/+2.8		6.85/+2.1		48.30 2:14.11	
6897		John'			2	OG	Seoul	24 Sep 88
	12.85/+0.5	1.80 16.23	23.65/+1.6		6.71/ 0.0		42.56 2:06.14	
6878		Joyner-Kersee			1	TAC	New York	13 Jun 91
	12.77	1.89 15.62	23.42		6.97/+0.4		43.28 2:22.12	
6875		Nikitina			1	ECp-A	Helmond	16 Jul 89
	13.55/-2.1	1.84 15.99	24.29/-2.1		6.75/-2.5		56.78 2:18.67	
6859	Natalya	Shubenkova	RUS	25.9.57	1	NC	Kiev	21 Jun 84
	12.93/+1.0	1.83 13.66	23.57/-0.3		6.73/+0.4		46.26 2:04.60	
6858	Anke	Behmer'	GDR	5.6.61	3	OG	Seoul	24 Sep 88
	13.20/+0.5	1.83 14.20	23.10/+1.6		6.68/+0.1		44.54 2:04.20	
6847		Nikitina			1	WUG	Duisburg	29 Aug 89
	13.47	1.81 16.12	24.12		6.66		59.28 2:22.07	
6845		Neubert			1	v URS	Halle	20 Jun 82
	13.58	1.83 15.10	23.14		6.84w		42.54 2:06.16	
6845	Irina	Belova ¶	RUS	17.2.68	2	OG	Barcelona	2 Aug 92
	13.25/-0.1	1.88 13.77	23.34/+0.2		6.82/0.0		41.90 2:05.08	
6841		Joyner			1	Int	Götzis	25 May 86
	13.09/-1.3	1.87 14.34	23.63/-0.8		6.76/-0.3		48.88 2:14.58	
6837		Joyner-Kersee			1	WCh	Stuttgart	17 Aug 93
	12.89/0.1	1.81 14.38	23.19/0.0		7.04/1.4		43.76 2:14.49	
6813		Paetz			1	OD	Potsdam	21 Jul 84
	12.71/+0.4	1.74 16.16	23.23w		6.58		41.94 2:07.03	
6805		Behmer			1	Int	Götzis	19 Jun 88
	13.28/+1.6	1.84 14.38	22.73/+4.0		6.62/+1.1		40.48 2:04.64	
6803	Jane	Frederick	USA	7.4.52	1	Int	Talence	16 Sep 84
	13.27/+1.2	1.87 15.49	24.15/+1.6		6.43/+0.2		51.74 2:13.55	
6797		Braun			2	WCh	Stuttgart	17 Aug 93
	13.25/0.1	1.90 14.62	24.12/0.0		6.54/1.0		53.44 2:17.82	
6789		Neubert			2	OD	Potsdam	21 Jul 84
	13.48/+0.4	1.74 15.03	23.47w		6.71		47.88 2:04.73	
6788		Neubert			1	v URS	Kiev	28 Jun 81
	13.70	1.86 15.41	23.58		6.82/+0.2		40.62 2:06.72	
6783		Joyner-Kersee			1	GWG	Seattle	23 Jul 90
	12.79	1.87 13.93	24.26/		6.91/		47.64 2:17.41	
6775		Vater'			3	OD	Potsdam	21 Jul 84
	13.30/+0.4	1.86 14.86	23.20w		6.84/+0.5		34.04 2:03.76	
	(30/9)							
6750		Ma Miaolan (10)	CHN	18.1.70	1	NG	Beijing	12 Sep 93
	13.28/1.5	1.89 14.98	23.86/		6.64/		45.82 2:15.33	
6741	Heike	Drechsler	GER	16.12.64	1		Talence	11 Sep 94
	13.34/-0.3	1.84 13.58	22.84/-1.1		6.95/+1.0		40.64 2:11.53	
6703	Tatyana	Blokhina	RUS	12.3.70	1	Decast	Talence	11 Sep 93
	13.69/-0.6	1.91 14.94	23.95/-0.4		5.99/-0.3		52.16 2:09.65	
6702	Chantal	Beaugeant ¶	FRA	16.2.61	2	Int	Götzis	19 Jun 88
	13.10/+1.6	1.78 13.74	23.96/+3.5		6.45/+0.2		50.96 2:07.09	
6695	Jane	Flemming	AUS	14.4.65	1	CG	Auckland	28 Jan 90
	13.21/+1.4	1.82 13.76	23.62/+2.4		6.57/+1.6		49.28 2:12.53	
6660	Ines	Schulz	GDR	10.7.65	3	Int	Götzis	19 Jun 88
	13.56/+0.4	1.84 13.95	23.93/+2.8		6.70/+0.7		42.82 2:06.31	
6658	Svetla	Dimitrova ¶	BUL	27.1.70	2		Götzis	31 May 92
	13.41/-0.7	1.75 14.72	23.06/+2.4		6.64/+1.9		43.84 2:09.60	
6646	Natalya	Grachova	UKR	21.2.52	1	NC	Moskva	2 Aug 82
	13.80	1.80 16.18	23.86		6.65/+3.5		39.42 2:06.59	
6635	Sibylle	Thiele	GDR	6.3.65	2	GWG	Moskva	7 Jul 86
	13.14/+0.6	1.76 16.00	24.18		6.62		45.74 2:15.30	
6635	Svetlana	Buraga	BLR	4.9.65	3	WCh	Stuttgart	17 Aug 93
	12.95/0.1	1.84 14.55	23.69/		6.58/-0.2		41.04 2:13.65	
6623	Judy	Simpson'	GBR	14.11.60	3	EC	Stuttgart	30 Aug 86
	13.05/+0.8	1.92 14.73	25.09/+0.0		6.56/+2.5		40.92 2:11.70	
	(20)							
6619	Liliana	Nastase	ROM	1.8.62	4	OG	Barcelona	2 Aug 92
	12.86/-0.9	1.82 14.34	23.70/+0.2		6.49/-0.3		41.30 2:11.22	
6616	Malgorzata	Nowak'	POL	9.2.59	1	WUG	Kobe	31 Aug 85
	13.27/+4.0	1.95 15.35	24.20/+0.0		6.37/+3.9		43.36 2:20.39	

Mark	Wind	Name		Nat	Born	Pos	Meet	Venue	Date
6604		Remigia	Nazaroviene'	LIT	2.6.67	2	URSCh	Bryansk	11 Jun 89
		13.26/+1.4	1.86 14.27	24.12/+0.7		6.58/+0.9		40.94 2:09.98	
6598		Svetlana	Moskalets	RUS	1.11.69	1	NC	Vladimir	17 Jun 94
		13.20/+0.8	1.82 13.78	23.56/+0.1		6.74/+0.8		42.48 2:14.54	
6573		Rita	Ináncsi	HUN	6.1.71	3		Götzis	29 May 94
		13.66/+2.0	1.84 13.94	24.20/+2.5		6.78/+1.4		46.28 2:16.02	
6572		Heike	Tischler	GDR	4.2.64	2	EC	Split	31 Aug 90
		14.08/-0.9	1.82 13.73	24.29/+0.9		6.22/-0.7		53.24 2:05.50	
6552		Nadezhda	Vinogradova'	RUS	1.5.58	2	NC	Kiev	21 Jun 84
		13.92/+1.0	1.80 15.19	23.84/+0.2		6.67/+0.1		38.60 2:06.80	
6551		Yelena	Martsenyuk	RUS	21.2.61	2		Staiki	2 Jul 88
		13.54/-0.4	1.82 15.32	24.25/+0.3		6.25/+0.7		47.56 2:12.72	
6541		Mila	Kolyadina	RUS	31.12.60	4	v GDR	Moskva	19 Jun 83
		14.05	1.82 16.28	24.81		6.48/+0.8		48.26 2:15.26	
6539		Tatyana	Shpak	UKR	17.11.60	3		Staiki	2 Jul 88
		13.57/-0.4	1.76 15.30	23.61/+0.5		6.52/-0.6		39.28 2:07.25	
		(30)							
6536		Yekaterina	Smirnova	RUS	22.10.56	3	v GDR	Moskva	19 Jun 83
		13.41	1.82 14.82	24.84		6.56/+1.1		45.66 2:13.38	
6531		Peggy	Beer	GDR	15.9.69	3	EC	Split	31 Aug 90
		13.27/-0.2	1.82 13.46	23.99/+0.4		6.38/+0.9		42.10 2:05.79	
6523		Sabine	Everts	FRG	4.3.61	1	v URS	Mannheim	10 Jun 82
		13.45	1.89 12.39	23.73		6.75		36.02 2:07.73	
6500		Birgit	Clarius	GER	18.3.65	1	NC	Vaterstetten	20 Jun 93
		13.61/1.3	1.81 15.22	24.69w/2.1		6.08/-0.6		50.20 2:11.29	
6493		Svetlana	Filatyeva '	RUS	3.4.64	1		Kiev	14 Aug 88
		13.77	1.89 13.89	24.94		6.30		48.44 2:11.89	
6487		Birgit	Dressel	FRG	4.5.60	4	EC	Stuttgart	30 Aug 86
		13.56/-1.6	1.92 14.12	24.68/+0.0		6.28/+1.1		45.70 2:15.78	
6478		Irina	Tyukhay	RUS	14.1.67	1		Yekaterinburg	3 Aug 92
		13.33/	1.89 14.60	24.53/		6.73/ 36.44 2:17.00			
6474		Marianna	Maslennikova	RUS	17.5.61	2	NC	Kiev	2 Aug 88
		13.37/+0.4	1.83 13.68	24.07/-0.0		6.28/+0.2		40.42 2:05.60	
6461		Valentina	Kurochkina	RUS	13.12.59	1		Tallinn	11 Aug 83
		13.89	1.85 14.40	24.51		6.63/+1.2		43.98 2:15.94	
6453		Valentina	Dimitrova	BUL	4.5.56	2	Int	Götzis	29 May 83
		14.31/+0.8	1.86 16.07	24.78/+1.0		6.26/+1.4		42.26 2:08.74	
		(40)							
6453		Cornelia	Heinrich'	FRG	2.6.60	2	Int	Götzis	18 Jun 89
		13.66/+1.9	1.90 15.33	24.58/+3.1		6.49/+2.2		41.26 2:20.56	
6442		Marion	Reichelt'	GDR	23.12.62	2	ECp	Arles	5 Jul 87
		13.47/+3.2	1.87 12.91	23.62/+1.9		6.68/+0.2		37.80 2:15.15	
6427m		Antonina	Sukhova	RUS	1.1.59	1		Tula	26 Aug 84
		13.0	1.82 13.79	24.8		6.41		45.88 2:13.5	
6425		Birgit	Gautzsch	GDR	14.12.67	2	vSU	Cottbus	20 Aug 89
		13.37/-1.2	1.80 13.78	23.84/-1.5		6.47/-0.1		43.92 2:17.13	
6425		Urszula	Wlodarczyk	POL	22.12.65	1		Talence	21 Sep 91
		13.62/-0.4	1.84 13.24	24.12/+0.2		6.29/+0.6		46.22 2:12.82	
6424		Jodi	Anderson	USA	11.10.57	2	OT	Los Angeles	17 Jun 84
		13.52	1.80 13.40	24.49		6.36		48.52 2:13.20	
6424		Irina	Matyusheva'	UKR	5.9.65	3	NC	Kiev	2 Aug 88
		13.40/+0.4	1.86 13.54	24.40/-0.0		6.28/+0.3		40.20 2:08.24	
6423m		Lyubov	Ratsu	MOL	6.2.61	1		Kisinau	28 Aug 83
		13.6	1.80 14.75	24.2		6.53		41.86 2:11.6	
6404		Satu	Ruotsalainen	FIN	21.10.66	4	WCh	Tokyo	27 Aug 91
		13.54/+1.1	1.88 12.46	24.20/+0.2		6.18/0.0		47.04 2:13.24	
6403		Emilia	Dimitrova ¶	BUL	13.11.67	6	GWG	Moskva	7 Jul 86
		13.73	1.76 13.46	23.17		6.29		43.30 2:09.85	
		(50)							

4 x 100 METRES RELAY

Mark	Nat	Team	Pos	Meet	Venue	Date
41.37	GDR	Gladisch, Rieger, Auerswald, Göhr	1	WCp	Canberra	6 Oct 85
41.49	RUS	Bogoslovskaya, Malchugina, Voronova, Privalova	1	WCh	Stuttgart	22 Aug 93
41.49	USA	Finn, Torrence, Vereen, Devers	2	WCh	Stuttgart	22 Aug 93
41.53	GDR	Gladisch, Koch, Auerswald, Göhr	1		Berlin	31 Jul 83
41.55	USA	Brown, Williams, Griffith, Marshall	1	ISTAF	Berlin	21 Aug 87
41.58	USA	Brown, Williams, Griffith, Marshall	1	WCh	Roma	6 Sep 87

Mark	Wind	Name	Nat	Born	Pos	Meet	Venue	Date
41.60	GDR	Müller, Wöckel, Auerswald, Göhr			1	OG	Moskva	1 Aug 80
41.61A	USA	Brown, Williams, Cheeseborough, Ashford			1	USOF	Air Force Academy	3 Jul 83
41.63	USA	Brown, Williams, Cheeseborough, Ashford			1	v GDR	Los Angeles	25 Jun 83
41.65	USA	Brown, Bolden, Cheeseborough, Ashford			1	OG	Los Angeles	11 Aug 84
41.65	GDR	Gladisch, Koch, Auerswald, Göhr			1	ECp	Moskva	17 Aug 85
41.68	GDR	Möller, Krabbe, Behrendt, Günther			1	EC	Split	1 Sep 90
41.69	GDR	Gladisch, Koch, Auerswald, Göhr			1	OD	Potsdam	21 Jul 84
41.73	GDR	Möller, Behrendt, Lange, Göhr			1		Berlin	13 Sep 88
41.76	GDR	Gladisch, Koch, Auerswald, Göhr			1	WCh	Helsinki	10 Aug 83
41.79	GDR	Gladisch, Drechsler, Auerswald, Göhr			1	v URS	Karl-Marx-Stadt	20 Jun 87
41.84	GDR	Gladisch, Gunther, Auerswald, Göhr			1	EC	Stuttgart	31 Aug 86
41.85	GDR	Müller, Wöckel, Auerswald, Göhr			1	OT	Potsdam	13 Jul 80
41.85	GDR	Gladisch, Koch, Auerswald, Göhr			1	WK	Zurich	22 Aug 84
41.87	GDR	Möller, Krabbe, Behrendt, Günther			1	ECp	Gateshead	5 Aug 89
	(20/3 nations)							
41.94	JAM	Duhaney, Cuthbert, McDonald, Ottey			1	WCh	Tokyo	1 Sep 91
42.08mx	BUL	Pavlova, Nuneva, Georgieva, Ivanova			mx		Sofia	8 Aug 84
	42.31	Zagorcheva, Nuneva, Georgieva, Donkova			2	ECp	Praha	27 Jun 87
42.39	NGR	Utondu, Idehen, Opara-Thompson, Onyali			2h2	OG	Barcelona	7 Aug 92
42.43	GBR	Hunte, Smallwood, Goddard, Lannaman			3	OG	Moskva	1 Aug 80
42.58	FRA	Girard, Sidibe, Bily, Pérec			3h2	OG	Barcelona	7 Aug 92
42.59	FRG	Possekel, Helten, Richter, Kroniger			2	OG	Montreal	31 Jul 76
42.71	POL	Tomczak, Pakula, Pisiewicz, Kasprzyk			3	ECp	Moskva	17 Aug 85
	(10)							
42.77	CAN	Bailey, Payne, Taylor, Gareau			2	OG	Los Angeles	11 Aug 84
42.89	CUB	Ferrer, López, Duporty, Allen			6	WCh	Stuttgart	22 Aug 93
42.97	UKR	Khristosenko, Kot, I Slyusar, German			1	SPA	Taskent	16 Sep 86
42.98	TCH	Sokolová, Soborová, Kocembová, Kratochvilová			1	WK	Zürich	18 Aug 82
43.16	Guangxi (CHN)	Xiao Y, Tian Y, Huang M, Ou Y			1	NG	Beijing	11 Sep 93
43.18	AUS	Wilson, Wells, Robertson, Boyle			5	OG	Montreal	31 Jul 76
43.35	KZK	Aleksandrova, Kvast, Miljauskiene, Sevalnikova			2	SPA	Taskent	16 Sep 86
43.37	FIN	Pirtimaa, Hanhijoki, Hernesniemi, Salmela			7	WCh	Stuttgart	22 Aug 93
43.44A	NED	van den Berg, Sterk, Hennipman, Bakker			4	OG	Ciudad México	20 Oct 68
43.67	ITA	Masullo, Dal Bianco, Ferrian, Tarolo			2	MedG	Athinai	11 Jul 91
	(20)							

Best at low altitude: 43.48 NED Cooman, Tromp, Olyslager, Vader 5s1 OG Seoul 1 Oct 88

4 x 400 METRES RELAY

Mark	Nat	Name	Pos	Meet	Venue	Date
3:15.17	URS	Ledovskaya 50.12, O.Nazarova 47.82, Pinigina 49.43, Bryzgina 47.80	1	OG	Seoul	1 Oct 88
3:15.51	USA	D.Howard 49.82, Dixon 49.17, Brisco 48.44, Griffith-Joyner 48.08	2	OG	Seoul	1 Oct 88
3:15.92	GDR	G.Walther 49.8, Busch 48.9, Rübsam 49.4, Koch 47.8	1	NC	Erfurt	3 Jun 84
3:16.71	USA	Torrence 49.0, Malone 49.4, Kaiser-Brown 49.48, Miles 48.78	1	WCh	Stuttgart	22 Aug 93
3:16.87	GDR	Emmelmann 50.9, Busch 48.8, Müller 48.9, Koch 48.3	1	EC	Stuttgart	31 Aug 86
3:18.29	USA		1	OG	Los Angeles	11 Aug 84
		Leatherwood 50.50, S.Howard 48.83, Brisco-Hooks 49.23, Cheeseborough 49.73				
3:18.29	GDR	Neubauer 50.58, Emmelmann 49.89, Busch 48.81, Müller 48.99	3	OG	Seoul	1 Oct 88
3:18.38	RUS	Ruzina 50.8, Alekseyeva 49.3, Ponomaryova 49.78, Privalova 48.47	2	WCh	Stuttgart	22 Aug 93
3:18.43	URS	Ledovskaya 51.7, Dzhigalova 49.2, Nazarova 48.87, Bryzgina 48.67	1	WCh	Tokyo	1 Sep 91
3:18.58	URS	I.Nazarova, Olizarenko, Pinigina, Vladykina	1	ECp	Moskva	18 Aug 85
3:18.63	GDR	Neubauer 51.4, Emmelmann 49.1, Müller 48.64, Busch 49.48	1	WCh	Roma	6 Sep 87
3:19.04	GDR	Siemon' 51.0, Busch 50.0, Rübsam 50.2, Koch 47.9	1	EC	Athinai	11 Sep 82
3:19.12	URS	Baskakova, I.Nazarova, Pinigina, Vladykina	1	Drz	Praha	18 Aug 84
3:19.23	GDR	Maletzki, Rohde, Streidt, Brehmer	1	OG	Montreal	31 Jul 76
3:19.49	GDR	Emmelmann, Busch, Neubauer, Koch	1	WCp	Canberra	4 Oct 85
3:19.50	URS	Yurchenko, O.Nazarova, Pinigina, Bryzgina	2	WCh	Roma	6 Sep 87
3:19.60	USA	Leatherwood, S.Howard, Brisco-Hooks, Cheeseborough	1		Walnut	25 Jul 84
3:19.62	GDR	Kotte, Brehmer, Köhn, Koch	1	ECp	Torino	5 Aug 79
3:19.66	GDR	Busch, Emmelmann, Neubauer, Müller	1	v FRG	Düsseldorf	20 Jun 88
3:19.73	GDR	K.Walther, Busch, Koch, Rübsam	1	WCh	Helsinki	14 Aug 83
	(20/3)					
3:20.32	TCH	Kocembová, Moravcíková, Matejkovicová, Kratochvílová	2	WCh	Helsinki	14 Aug 83
3:21.21	CAN	Crooks, Richardson, Killingbeck, Payne	2	OG	Los Angeles	11 Aug 84
3:21.94	UKR	Dzhigalova, Olizarenko, Pinigina, Vladykina	1	URSCh	Kiev	17 Jul 86
3:22.01	GBR	Hanson, Smith, Gunnell, Keough	4	WCh	Tokyo	1 Sep 91
3:22.34	FRA	Landre 51.3, Dorsile 51.1, Elien 50.54, Pérec 49.36	1	EC	Helsinki	14 Aug 94
3:22.49	FRG	Thimm, Arendt, Thomas, Abt	4	OG	Seoul	1 Oct 88
3:23.13	JAM	Richards, Thomas, Rattray-Williams, Powell	5	OG	Seoul	1 Oct 88
	(10)					

Mark	Wind	Name		Nat	Born	Pos	Meet	Venue	Date
3:24.28	Hebei (CHN)	An X, Bai X, Cao C, Ma Y				1	NG	Beijing	13 Sep 93
3:24.45	NGR	Yusuf, Onyali, Bakare, Opara				5	WCh	Tokyo	1 Sep 91
3:24.65	POL	Kasprzyk, Wojdecka, Kapusta, Blaszak				3	EC	Stuttgart	31 Aug 86
3:24.91	CUB	Duporte, Limonta, McLeon, Quirot				2	PAm	Habana	11 Aug 91
3:25.56	AUS	Canty, Burnard, Rendina, Nail				4	OG	Montreal	31 Jul 76
3:25.7a	FIN	Eklund, Pursiainen, Wilmi, Salin				2	EC	Roma	8 Sep 74
3:25.81	BUL	Ilieva, Stamenova, Penkova, Damyanova				1	v Hun,Pol	Sofia	24 Jul 83
3:27.54	LIT	Navickaite, Valiuliene, Mendzoryte, Ambraziene				3	SPA	Moskva	22 Jun 83
3:27.57	ESP	Merino, Lacambra, Myers, Ferrer				7	WCh	Tokyo	1 Sep 91
3:27.74	ROM	Korodi, Lazarciuc, Samungi, Tarita				4	OG	Moskva	1 Aug 80
	(20)								

5000 METRES WALK (TRACK)

Mark		Name		Nat	Born	Pos	Meet	Venue	Date
20:07.52		Beate	Anders	GDR	4.2.68	1	vSU	Rostock	23 Jun 90
20:17.19		Kerry	Junna-Saxby	AUS	2.6.61	1		Sydney	14 Jan 90
20:22.9	mx		Junna-Saxby			mx		Canberra	28 Feb 92
20:27.59		Ileana	Salvador	ITA	16.1.62	1		Trento	3 Jun 89
20:28.62		Sari	Essayah	FIN	21.2.67	1	NC	Tuusula	9 Jul 94
20:30.0			Junna-Saxby			1	NC	Brisbane	6 Mar 93
20:32.75			Saxby			1	NC	Brisbane	19 Mar 89
20:34.76			Essayah			1		Kokemäki	3 Jul 94
20:36.96			Saxby			1	CGT	Sydney	3 Dec 89
20:37.7			Jin Bingjie	CHN	1.4.71	1	NC	Hefei	3 Mar 90
20:38.0			Chen Yueling	CHN	1.4.68	2	NC	Hefei	3 Mar 90
20:38.14			Junna-Saxby			1		Sydney	20 Feb 93
20:38.65			Essayah			1	NC	Mikkeli	31 Jul 93
20:40.06			Junna-Saxby			1		Sydney	20 Feb 94
20:40.6		Olga	Kardopoltseva	BLR	11.9.66	1		Alushta	5 May 90
20:42.31			Salvador			1	NC	Bologna	23 Jun 92
20:44.02			Essayah			1	NC	Helsinki	28 Jul 91
20:45.03			Junna-Saxby			1	NC	Sydney	11 Mar 93
20:45.32			Saxby			1	NC	Perth	27 Mar 88
20:45.6			Salvador			1		Torino	23 May 92
		(20/7)							
20:46.9		Annarita	Sidoti	ITA	25.7.69	1		Messina	16 Apr 94
20:49.39		Elsabetta	Perrone	ITA	9.7.68	1	NC	Napoli	3 Jul 94
20:49.4+		Nadezhda	Ryashkina	RUS	22.1.67	1=	GWG	Seattle	24 Jul 90
		(10)							
20:50.3			Fan Xiaoling	CHN	29.3.71	2	NC	Zhengzhou	3 Mar 91
20:50.60		Alina	Ivanova	RUS	25.6.69	1	vGDR	Bryansk	15 Jul 89
20:51.96		Katarzyna	Radtke	POL	31.8.69	1		Sopot	20 Jun 93
20:52.24		Tamara	Surovtseva	BLR	12.6.60	2	vGDR	Rostock	23 Jun 90
20:56.10+		Olimpiada	Ivanova	RUS	5.5.70	1	GWG	St Peterburg	26 Jul 94
20:56.7			Zuo Xiaohui	CHN	.71	4	NC	Zhengzhou	3 Mar 91
20:59.7		Anne-Marie	Judkins	NZL	1.3.64	2		Brunflo	28 Jun 92
20:59.82+		Yelena	Sayko	RUS	24.12.67	2	GWG	St Peterburg	26 Jul 94
21:00.80		Yelena	Nikolayeva	RUS	17.3.66	1		Schwechat	12 Jun 91
21:01.8		Susana	Feitor	POR	28.1.75	1	SGP	Fana	8 May 93
		(20)							
Superior road performances									
20:25		Kerry	Junna-Saxby	AUS	2.6.61	1		Hildesheim	10 Jun 89
20:26		Ileana	Salvador	ITA	16.1.62	1		Barcelona	5 Apr 92
20:36		Alina	Ivanova	RUS	25.6.69	1		L'Hospitalet	21 Apr 91
20:37		Olga	Kardopoltseva	BLR	11.9.66	2		L'Hospitalet	21 Apr 91
20:38		Vera	Makolova	RUS	17.2.66	1	NC	Leningrad	5 Aug 89
20:48		Yelena	Nikolayeva	RUS	1.2.66	1		L'Hospitalet	29 May 94
20:53		Sada	Eidikite'	LIT	22.6.67	2		Hildesheim	10 Jun 89

t -= track

10,000 METRES WALK

Mark		Name		Nat	Born	Pos	Meet	Venue	Date
41:30		Kerry	Junna-Saxby	AUS	2.6.61	1	NC	Canberra	27 Aug 88
41:30		Ileana	Salvador	ITA	16.1.62	1	4-N	Livorno	10 Jul 93
41:38			Gao Hongmiao	CHN	8.7.72	1	NC	Beijing	7 Apr 94
41:46		Annarita	Sidoti	ITA	25.7.69	1		Livorno	12 Jun 94
41:48			Li Chunxiu	CHN	13.8.69	1	NG	Beijing	8 Sep 93
41:56		Elisabeta	Perrone	ITA	9.7.68	2	4-N	Livorno	10 Jul 93
41:56.23t		Nadezhda	Ryashkina	RUS	22.1.67	1	GWG	Seattle	24 Jul 90
41:57			Gao Hongmiao			2	NG	Beijing	8 Sep 93
41:57.22t			Junna-Saxby			2	GWG	Seattle	24 Jul 90

Mark Wind	Name		Nat	Born	Pos	Meet	Venue	Date
42:03	Yelena	Arshintseva	RUS	5.4.71	1		Adler	14 Feb 93
42:04	Yelena	Sayko	RUS	24.12.67	2		Adler	14 Feb 93
42:07		Salvador			1		Sesto San Giovanni	1 May 92
42:11.5t	Beate	Anders (10)	GER	4.2.68	1	SGP	Fana	15 May 92
42:13.7t	Madelein	Svensson	SWE	20.7.69	2	SGP	Fana	15 May 92
42:14.2t		Saxby			1mx		Canberra	26 Jan 88
42:15		Perrone			2		Livorno	12 Jun 94
42:16	Alina	Ivanova	RUS	25.6.69	1		Novopolotsk	27 May 89
42:17		A Ivanova			1		Sochi	17 Feb 91
42:20		Gu Yan	CHN	17.3.74	2	NC	Beijing	7 Apr 94
42:22		Sayko			1		Alitus	5 May 91
42:22.6t		Junna-Saxby			1	SGP	Fana	8 May 93
42:23.7t		Salvador			2	SGP	Fana	8 May 93
42:23.9t		Junna-Saxby			3	SGP	Fana	15 May 92
42:24	Olympiada	Ivanova	RUS	5.5.70	3	4-N	Livorno	10 Jul 93
42:25.2t		Saxby			1	SGP	Fana	26 May 90
42:26		Wang Yan	CHN	3.5.71	1		Shenzhen	18 Feb 93
42:26.29t		Junna-Saxby			1		Sydney	10 Jan 93
42:29		Sayko			2	NC-w	Sochi	16 Feb 91
42:29.4t		Anders			2	SGP	Fana	26 May 90
42:30 mx		Saxby			1 mx		Melbourne	4 May 91
	(30/15)							
42:31	Larisa	Ramazanova	RUS	27.9.71	3		Livorno	12 Jun 94
42:34	Yelena	Gruzinova	RUS	67	3		Adler	14 Feb 93
42:37.0t	Sari	Essayah	FIN	21.2.67	3	SGP	Fana	8 May 93
42:40	Yelena	Nikolayeva	RUS	17.3.66	1		Moskva	26 Apr 92
42:40	Yulia	Odzilyayeva	RUS	70	5		Livorno	12 Jun 94
	(20)							
42:44	Irina	Strakhova	RUS	4.3.59	3		Sochi	17 Feb 91
42:44	Olga	Kardopoltseva	BLR	11.9.66	2		Alitus	5 May 91
42:44		Long Yuwen	CHN	.8.75	3		Shenzhen	18 Feb 93
42:45	??	Li Yuxin	CHN	73	4		Shenzhen	18 Feb 93
42:46	Tamara	Kovalenko	RUS	25.4.64	1		Moskva	29 Jul 90
42:46.7t		Cui Yingzi	CHN	26.1.71	1	NC	Jinan	15 Mar 92
42:46.7t		Chen Yueling	CHN	1.4.68	2	NC	Jinan	15 Mar 92
42:47		Liu Hongyu	CHN	1.12.75	5		Shenzhen	18 Feb 93
42:47.4t	Katarzyna	Radtke	POL	31.8.69	4	SGP	Fana	8 May 93
42:50.0t		Guan Ping	CHN	1.2.66	5	NC	Jinan	15 Mar 92
	(30)							
42:52	Lidiya	Fesenko	RUS	5.10.62	4	NC-w	Sochi	16 Feb 91
42:53	Mária	Rosza	HUN	12.2.67	7		Livorno	12 Jun 94
42:53.9t		Tan Lihong	CHN	13.2.73	6	NC	Jinan	15 Mar 92
42:55	Cristina	Pellino	ITA	21.9.70	8		Livorno	12 Jun 94
42:57		Zhang Qinghua	CHN	.6.2.73	6		Shenzhen	18 Feb 93
42:58	Nina	Alyushenko	RUS	.68	5	NC-w	Sochi	16 Feb 91
43:01.6t	Anne-Marie	Judkins	NZL	1.3.64	2		Örnsköldsvik	4 Jul 92
43:03		Kong Yan	CHN	5.4.71	5	NC	Beijing	7 Apr 94
43:04	Vera	Makolova	RUS	17.2.66	1	NC	Leningrad	4 Aug 89
43:07		Song Lijuan	CHN	.2.76	6	NG	Beijing	8 Sep 93
	(40)							
43:09.4t		Fan Xiaoling	CHN	14.5.71	7	NC	Jinan	15 Mar 92
43:11	Olga	Krishtop'	RUS	8.10.57	3	NC	Moskva	26 May 90
43:11.4		Zhu Xiaolan	CHN	1.7.72	9	NC	Jinan	15 Mar 92
43:13	Natalya	Spiridonova	RUS	24.4.63	2		Moskva	29 Jul 90
43:15	Natalya	Misyulya	BLR	14.4.66	4	4-N	Livorno	10 Jul 93
43:15.6t		Jin Bingjie	CHN	1.4.71	1		Anshan	4 Sep 89
43:16	Katarzyna	Radtke	POL	31.8.69	2		Eisenhüttenstadt	15 May 94
43:16	Valentina	Tsybulskaya	BLR	17.3.68	1		Novopolotsk	21 May 94
43:21	Encarnacion	Granados	ESP	30.1.72	3	WCh	Stuttgart	14 Aug 93
43:22	Yevgeniya	Guryeva	RUS	12.6.69	4		Moskva	26 Apr 92
	(50)							

20 KILOMETRES WALK

Mark	Name		Nat	Born	Pos	Meet	Venue	Date
1:29:40	Kerry	Junna-Saxby	AUS	2.6.61	1		Värnamo	13 May 88
1:30:42	Olga	Kardopoltseva	BLR	11.9.66	1		Kaliningrad	29 Apr 90
1:31:53	Ileana	Salvador	ITA	16.1.62	1	NC	Baia Domizia	25 Sep 93
1:31:56	Yelena	Gruzinova	RUS	67	1		Izhevsk	27 Aug 94
1:31:58	Tamara	Romanova	RUS	2.7.67	1	CIS Ch	Moskva	25 Apr 92

Mark	Wind	Name		Nat	Born	Pos	Meet	Venue	Date

WORLD JUNIOR WOMEN'S ALL-TIME LISTS

Based on the age regulations introduced for 1988, that is under 20 in year of competition.

100 METRES

Mark	Wind	Name		Nat	Born	Pos	Meet	Venue	Date
10.88	2.0	Marlies	Oelsner	GDR	21.3.58	1	NC	Dresden	1 Jul 77
10.89	1.8	Katrin	Krabbe	GDR	22.11.69	1rB		Berlin	20 Jul 88
11.03	1.7	Silke	Gladisch	GDR	20.6.64	3	OD	Berlin	8 Jun 83
11.08	2.0	Brenda	Morehead	USA	5.10.57	1	OT	Eugene	21 Jun 76
11.13	2.0	Chandra	Cheeseborough	USA	10.1.59	2	OT	Eugene	21 Jun 76
11.13	-1.0	Grit	Breuer	GDR	16.2.72	1		Jena	6 Jun 90
11.14		Liliana	Allen	CUB	24.5.70	1		La Habana	1 Jun 89
11.14	1.7	Marion	Jones	USA	12.10.75	1		Norwalk	6 Jun 92
11.17A	0.6	Wenda	Vereen	USA	24.4.66	4	USOF	Air Force Academy	3 Jul 83
11.18	-0.8	Silvia	Chivas	CUB	10.9.54	1h1	OG	München	1 Sep 72
11.18	-0.4	Diana	Dietz	GDR	30.8.69	1	WJ	Sudbury	28 Jul 88
11.18	1.1	Nicole	Mitchell	JAM	5.6.74	3	NC	Kingston	2 Jul 93
Uncertain timing									
10.99	1.9	Natalya	Bochina	RUS	4.1.62	2		Leningrad	3 Jun 80
Wind assisted									
10.97	3.3	Gesine	Walther	GDR	6.10.62	4	NC	Cottbus	16 Jul 80
11.02	2.1	Nicole	Mitchell	JAM	5.6.74	1	Mutual	Kingston	1 May 93
11.06	2.2	Brenda	Morehead	USA	5.10.57	1s	OT	Eugene	21 Jun 76
11.09		Angela	Williams	TRI	15.5.65	1		Nashville	14 Apr 84
11.12	4.1	Marion	Jones	USA	12.10.75	1h		Cerritos	31 May 91
11.13	2.2	Beverly	Kinch	GBR	14.1.64	1	WUG	Edmonton	6 Jul 83
Hand timed									
10.9A	-0.8	Liliana	Allen	CUB	24.5.70	1	AmCp	Bogota	12 Aug 89
10.8wA		Margaret	Bailes	USA	23.1.51	1		Flagstaff	29 Sep 68

200 METRES

Mark	Wind	Name		Nat	Born	Pos	Meet	Venue	Date
22.19	1.5	Natalya	Bochina	RUS	4.1.62	2	OG	Moskva	30 Jul 80
22.37	1.3	Sabine	Rieger	GDR	6.11.63	2	vURS	Cottbus	26 Jun 82
22.42	0.4	Gesine	Walther	GDR	6.10.62	1		Potsdam	29 Aug 81
22.45	0.5	Grit	Breuer	GDR	16.2.72	2	ASV	Köln	8 Sep 91
22.51	2.0	Katrin	Krabbe	GDR	22.11.69	3		Berlin	13 Sep 88
22.52	1.2	Mary	Onyali	NGR	3.2.68	6	WCh	Roma	3 Sep 87
22.58	0.8	Marion	Jones	USA	12.10.75	4	TAC	New Orleans	28 Jun 92
22.70		Marita	Koch	GDR	18.2.57	1		Halle	16 May 76
22.70A	1.9	Kathy	Smallwood	GBR	3.5.60	2	WUG	Ciudad México	12 Sep 79
22.72	1.3	Silke	Gladisch	GDR	20.6.64	3	NC	Karl-Marx-Stadt	18 Jun 83
22.74A	2.0	Raelene	Boyle	AUS	24.6.51	2	OG	Ciudad México	18 Oct 68
22.76A		Evette	de Klerk	RSA	21.8.65	1		Sasolburg	21 Apr 84
Wind assisted									
22.34	2.3	Kathrin	Krabbe	GDR	22.11.69	1	WJ	Sudbury	30 Jul 88
22.49	2.3	Brenda	Morehead	USA	5.10.57	1	OT	Eugene	24 Jun 76
22.53	2.5	Valerie	Brisco	USA	6.7.60	2	AAU	Walnut	17 Jun 79
22.64	2.3	Chandra	Cheeseborough	USA	16.1.59	2	OT	Eugene	24 Jun 76
22.75	2.5	Wenda	Vereen	USA	24.4.66	1		Los Angeles	14 Apr 84

400 METRES

Mark	Wind	Name		Nat	Born	Pos	Meet	Venue	Date
49.42		Grit	Breuer	GDR	16.2.72	2	WCh	Tokyo	27 Aug 91
49.77		Christina	Brehmer	GDR	28.2.58	1		Dresden	9 May 76
50.19		Marita	Koch	GDR	18.2.57	3	OD	Berlin	10 Jul 76
50.59		Fatima	Yusuf	NGR	2.5.71	1	HGP	Budapest	5 Aug 90
50.86		Charity	Opara	NGR	20.5.72	2		Bologna	7 Sep 91
50.87		Denean	Howard	USA	5.10.64	1	TAC	Knoxville	20 Jun 82
50.87		Magdalena	Nedelcu	ROM	12.5.74	1	NC-j	Bucuresti	31 Jul 92
50.90		Sheila	Ingram	USA	23.3.57	3s1	OG	Montreal	28 Jul 76
50.92		Margit	Sinzel	GDR	17.6.58	5	OD	Berlin	10 Jul 76
50.92		Sandie	Richards	JAM	6.11.68	1		Odessa, Tx	16 May 87
50.96		Maicel	Malone	USA	12.6.69	1s1	OT	Indianapolis	17 Jul 88
50.98		Dagmar	Rübsam	GDR	3.6.62	2	NC	Jena	8 Aug 81
Hand timed									
50.5		Fatima	Yusuf	NGR	2.5.71	1	NC	Lagos	25 Aug 90

Mark Wind		Name	Nat	Born	Pos	Meet	Venue	Date

800 METRES

Mark Wind		Name	Nat	Born	Pos	Meet	Venue	Date
1:57.18		Wang Yuan	CHN	8.4.76	2h2	NG	Beijing	8 Sep 93
1:57.45	Hildegard	Ullrich	GDR	20.12.59	5	EC	Praha	31 Aug 78
1:57.63	Maria	Mutola	MOZ	27.10.72	4	WCh	Tokyo	26 Aug 91
1:57.77		Lu Yi	CHN	10.4.74	4	NG	Beijing	9 Sep 93
1:57.86	Katrin	Wühn	GDR	19.11.65	1		Celje	5 May 84
1:58.18	Marion	Hübner	GDR	29.9.62	2		Erfurt	2 Aug 81
1:58.24	Christine	Wachtel	GDR	6.1.65	3		Potsdam	25 May 84
1:58.37	Gabriela	Sedláková	TCH	2.3.68	4	ISTAF	Berlin	21 Aug 87
1:59.13	Maria	Pîntea	ROM	10.8.67	1		Bucuresti	15 Jun 86
1:59.17	Birte	Bruhns	GDR	4.11.70	1		Berlin	20 Jul 88
1:59.32	Martina	Kämpfert	GDR	11.11.59	2	NC	Leipzig	1 Jul 78
1:59.42	Rommy	Schmidt	GDR	20.6.59	3		Potsdam	19 Aug 78

1000 METRES

Mark Wind		Name	Nat	Born	Pos	Meet	Venue	Date
2:35.4	Irina	Nikitina	RUS	16.1.61	5	Kuts	Podolsk	5 Aug 79
2:35.4	Katrin	Wühn	GDR	19.11.65	3		Potsdam	12 Jul 84
2:36.36	Margrit	Klinger	FRG	22.6.60	2	ISTAF	Berlin	17 Aug 79
2:37.2	Véronique	Renties	FRA	3.7.60	2		Nice	19 Aug 79

1500 METRES

Mark Wind		Name	Nat	Born	Pos	Meet	Venue	Date
3:59.81		Wang Yuan	CHN	8.4.76	7	NG	Beijing	11 Sep 93
3:59.96	Zola	Budd	GBR	26.5.66	3	VD	Bruxelles	30 Aug 85
4:00.05		Lu Yi	CHN	10.4.74	8	NG	Beijing	11 Sep 93
4:01.71		Li Ying	CHN	24.6.75	4h2	NG	Beijing	10 Sep 93
4:03.5	Svetlana	Guskova	MOL	19.8.59	3	Kuts	Podolsk	13 Aug 78
4:04.42	Astrid	Pfeiffer	GDR	6.12.64	3	vUSA	Los Angeles	25 Jun 83
4:04.97	Ana	Padurean	ROM	5.9.69	1		Bucuresti	13 Jun 87
4:05.14		Liu Dong	CHN	27.12.73	1	WJ	Seoul	20 Sep 92
4:05.35	Dorina	Calenic	ROM	4.4.69	2		Bucuresti	13 Jun 87
4:05.96	Lynne	MacDougall	GBR	18.2.65	6	BGP	Budapest	20 Aug 84
4:06.02	Birgit	Friedmann	FRG	8.4.60	7		Dortmund	1 Jul 78
4:06.19	Maria	Pîntea	ROM	10.8.67	8		Pitesti	28 Jun 86

1 MILE

Mark Wind		Name	Nat	Born	Pos	Meet	Venue	Date
4:17.57	Zola	Budd	GBR	26.5.66	3	WK	Zürich	21 Aug 85
4:30.08	Lynne	MacDougall	GBR	18.2.65	4	IAC	London	7 Sep 84

2000 METRES

Mark Wind		Name	Nat	Born	Pos	Meet	Venue	Date
5:33.15	Zola	Budd	GBR	26.5.66	1		London	13 Jul 84

3000 METRES

Mark Wind		Name	Nat	Born	Pos	Meet	Venue	Date
8:28.83	Zola	Budd	GBR	26.5.66	3	GG	Roma	7 Sep 85
8:36.45		Ma Ningning	CHN	20.9.76	4	NC	Jinan	6 Jun 93
8:40.08	Gabriele	Szabo	ROM	14.11.75	3	EC	Helsinki	12 Aug 94
8:42.39		Li Ying	CHN	24.6.75	8	NG	Beijing	13 Sep 93
8:44.1mx	Donna	Gould	AUS	10.6.66	-		Eugene	13 Jul 84
8:46.86		Zhang Linli	CHN	6.3.73	1	WJ	Seoul	20 Sep 92
8:47.6	Svetlana	Guskova	MOL	19.8.59	4	Znam	Vilnius	18 Jul 78
8:48.45		Zhang Lirong	CHN	3.3.73	3	WJ	Seoul	20 Sep 92
8:49.92		Wang Xiaoxia	CHN	21.8.76	1	NC	Beijing	2 Jun 94
8:50.26	Rodica	Prescura	ROM	.70	2		Bucuresti	12 Jun 88
8:51.22	Annemari	Sandell	FIN	2.1.77	2	EJ	San Sebastián	1 Aug 93
8:51.59	Lydia	Cheromei	KEN	11.5.77	10	VD	Brussels	28 Aug 92

5000 METRES

Mark Wind		Name	Nat	Born	Pos	Meet	Venue	Date
14:48.07	Zola	Budd	GBR	26.5.66	1	McV	London	26 Aug 85
15:17.31	Lydia	Cheromei	KEN	11.5.77	7	ISTAF	Berlin	12 Aug 92
15:19.4	Yasuko	Kimura	JPN	6.1.76	1		Toyonaka	21 Dec 94
15:21.29	Derartu	Tulu	ETH	21.3.72	1	Super	Shizuoka	6 May 91
15:26.3	Atsumi	Yashima	JPN	28.6.75	2		Toyonaka	21 Dec 94
15:26.33	Annemari	Sandell	FIN	2.1.77	4	DNG	Stockholm	5 Jul 93
15:27.3 mx	Donna	Gould	AUS	10.6.66	-		Adelaide	6 Jun 84
15:28.91		Qu Yunxia	CHN	25.12.72	2		Tangshan	26 Sep 91
15:32.4+e	Delilah	Asiago	KEN	24.2.72	1'	Bisl	Oslo	6 Jul 91
15:35.70		Zhang Linli	CHN	6.3.73			Tangshan	26 Sep 91

Mark	Wind	Name		Nat	Born	Pos	Meet	Venue	Date
15:37.17			Hou Juhua	CHN	.67	1		Guangzhou	24 Oct 86
15:38.29		Akemi	Masuda	JPN	1.1.64	11	Bisl	Oslo	26 Jun 82

10000 METRES

Mark	Wind	Name		Nat	Born	Pos	Meet	Venue	Date
31:15.38		Sally	Barsosio	KEN	21.3.78	3	WCh	Stuttgart	21 Aug 93
31:32.15			Feng Wenhui	CHN	21.1.74	9	NG	Beijing	8 Sep 93
31:40.56		Delilah	Asiago	KEN	24.2.72	1	JPN Ch	Tokyo	15 Jun 91
31:41.09		Lydia	Cheromei	KEN	11.5.77	2	AfrCh	Belle Vue Mauricia	27 Jun 92
31:45.95		Derartu	Tulu	ETH	21.3.72	1h2	WCh	Tokyo	27 Aug 91
32:09.94			Ma Ningning	CHN	20.9.76	3	NC	Jinan	2 Jun 93
32:12.51		Marleen	Renders	BEL	24.12.68	12	WCh	Roma	4 Sep 87
32:16.24		Masami	Ishizaka	JPN	27.3.71	2	WUG	Duisburg	29 Aug 89
32:23.25		Esther	Wanjiru	KEN	27.3.77	2		Mito	8 May 94
32:25.74		Olga	Nazarkina	RUS	11.6.70	1	EJ	Varazdin	25 Aug 89
32:26.41		Mónica	Gama	POR	8.3.70	2	EJ	Varazdin	25 Aug 89
32:29.17		Yasuke	Kimura	JPN	6.1.76	1		Amagasaki	28 Oct 94

MARATHON

Mark	Wind	Name		Nat	Born	Pos	Meet	Venue	Date
2:30:15			Gu Dongmei	CHN	5.1.74	9		Tianjin	4 Apr 93
2:30:30		Akemi	Masuda	JPN	1.1.64	1		Eugene	11 Sep 83
2:31:03			Feng Wenhui	CHN	21.1.74	10		Tianjin	4 Apr 93
2:32:04			Zhen Guixia	CHN	26.4.73	2	NC	Tianjin	12 Apr 92
2:32:30			Ma Ningning	CHN	20.9.76	5		Beijing	30 Oct 94
2:33:59			Zhang Lirong	CHN	3.3.73			Dalian	27 Oct 91
2:35:44			Jung Young-im	KOR	5.1.75	1		Kyongju	20 Mar 94
2:36:24			Lee Mi-kyung	KOR	26.5.75	2		Kyongju	20 Mar 94
2:37:35			Wu Mei	CHN	9.11.73	3	NC	Tianjin	12 Apr 92

100 METRES HURDLES

Mark	Wind	Name		Nat	Born	Pos	Meet	Venue	Date
12.84	1.5	Aliuska	López	CUB	29.8.69	2	WUG	Zagreb	16 Jul 87
12.95	1.5	Candy	Young	USA	21.5.62	2	AAU	Walnut	16 Jun 79
12.95A	1.5	Cinnamon	Sheffield	USA	8.3.70	2	NCAA	Provo	3 Jun 89
13.00	0.7	Gloria	Kovarik	GDR	13.1.64	3h2	NC	Karl-Marx-Stadt	16 Jun 83
13.00	2.0	Lyudmila	Khristosenko	UKR	14.10.66	1	NC-j	Krasnodar	16 Jul 85
13.05	1.8	Heike	Terpe	GDR	4.10.64	4	OD	Berlin	8 Jun 83
13.07	0.2	Monique	Ewanje-Epée	FRA	11.7.67	2		Paris	22 Jul 86
13.07	1.1	Gillian	Russell	JAM	28.9.73	3	NC	Kingston	3 Jul 92
13.09	1.3	Ulrike	Denk	FRG	10.5.64	1		Rhede	29 Jul 83
13.10	0.7	LaVonna	Martin	USA	18.11.66	1	PennR	Philadelphia	27 Apr 85
13.10	-0.7	Heike	Tillack	GDR	6.1.68	1	WJ	Athinai	18 Jul 86
13.11	-0.1	Benita	Fitzgerald	USA	6.7.61	2	OT	Eugene	25 Jun 80
12.8	Hand	Lyudmila	Khristosenko	UKR	14.10.66	1		Krasnodar	29 Jun 85
Wind assisted									
13.02	4.1	LaVonna	Martin	USA	18.11.66	5	NCAA	Austin	1 Jun 85
13.10	4.5	Karen	Nelson	CAN	3.12.63	4	CG	Brisbane	8 Oct 82

400 METRES HURDLES

Mark	Wind	Name		Nat	Born	Pos	Meet	Venue	Date
55.20		Lesley	Maxie	USA	4.1.67	2	TAC	San Jose	9 Jun 84
55.53		Radostina	Dimitrova	BUL	1.6.66	3	OD	Potsdam	21 Jul 84
55.65		Schowonda	Williams	USA	3.12.66	3	NCAA	Austin	31 May 85
55.72			Zheng Liyuan	CHN	1.4.74	5	NG	Beijing	9 Sep 93
55.74A		Myrtle	Simpson	RSA	18.2.64	2	NC	Bloemfontein	16 Apr 83
55.84		Nelli	Voronkova	BLR	30.6.72	1	WJ	Plovdiv	10 Aug 90
55.93		Sofia	Sabeva	BUL	11.1.69	1	NC-j	Sofia	3 Jul 88
56.00		Ann-Louise	Skoglund	SWE	28.6.62	1		Göteborg	11 Aug 81
56.16		Esther	Mahr	USA	4.1.61	2s2	WCh	Sittard	15 Aug 80
56.22		Claudia	Bartl	GDR	2.5.68	1	EJ	Cottbus	25 Aug 85
56.25		Ionela	Tîrlea	ROM	9.2.76	1	WJ	Lisboa	22 Jul 94
56.28		Nadezhda	Asenova	BUL	28.3.62	1		Sofia	12 Jul 81

HIGH JUMP

Mark	Wind	Name		Nat	Born	Pos	Meet	Venue	Date
2.01		Olga	Turchak	KZK	5.3.67	2	GWG	Moskva	7 Jul 86
2.01		Heike	Balck	GDR	19.8.70	1	vURS-j	Karl-Marx-Stadt	18 Jun 89
2.00		Stefka	Kostadinova	BUL	25.3.65	1		Sofia	25 Aug 84
2.00		Alina	Astafei	ROM	7.6.69	1	WJ	Sudbury	29 Jul 88
1.98		Silvia	Costa	CUB	4.5.64	2	WUG	Edmonton	11 Jul 83

Mark	Wind	Name		Nat	Born	Pos	Meet	Venue	Date
1.98		Yelena	Yelesina	RUS	5.4.70	1	Druzh	Nyiregyháza	13 Aug 88
1.97		Svetlana	Isaeva	BUL	18.3.67	2		Sofia	25 May 86
1.96A		Charmaine	Gale	RSA	27.2.64	1	NC-j	Bloemfontein	4 Apr 81
1.96i		Desislava	Aleksandrova	BUL	27.10.75	2	EI	Paris	12 Mar 94
1.95		Larisa	Kositsyna	RUS	14.12.63	4	NC	Kiev	21 Aug 82
1.95		Maryse	Ewanje-Epée	FRA	4.9.64	3		Rieti	4 Sep 83
1.95		Ioamnet	Quintero	CUB	18.9.72	1		Columbus	28 Jul 90

POLE VAULT

Mark	Wind	Name		Nat	Born	Pos	Meet	Venue	Date
4.05			Sun Caiyun	CHN	21.7.73	1	NC	Nanjing	21 May 92
4.00			Cai Weiyan	CHN	25.10.73	1		Wuhan	19 Oct 92
3.90		Nicole	Rieger	GER	5.2.72	1	NC-j	Berlin	21 Jul 91
3.85		Janet	Zach	GER	19.6.75	3		Ahlen	6 Aug 94
3.80			Zhang Chunzhen	CHN	.70	1		Guangzhou	9 Sep 89
3.80		Daniela	Köpernick	GER	28.6.73	2		Zweibrücken	10 Jun 92
3.80		Christine	Adams	GER	28.2.74	1		Gladbeck	18 Jul 93
3.80			Zhong Guiqing	CHN	75	1		Guangzhou	26 Mar 94
3.75			Shao Jingwen	CHN	8.3.71	3	NC	Beijing	26 Jun 90
3.71		Nastja	Ryshich	GER	19.9.77	1		Jablonec	16 Jul 94
3.70		by eight junior women							

LONG JUMP

Mark	Wind	Name		Nat	Born	Pos	Meet	Venue	Date
7.14	1.1	Heike	Daute	GDR	16.12.64	1	PTS	Bratislava	4 Jun 83
7.00	-0.2	Birgit	Grosshennig	GDR	21.2.65	2		Berlin	9 Jun 84
6.91	0.0	Anisoara	Cusmir	ROM	29.6.62	1		Bucuresti	23 May 81
6.90	1.4	Beverly	Kinch	GBR	14.1.64	*	WCh	Helsinki	14 Aug 83
6.88	0.6	Natalya	Shevchenko	RUS	28.12.66	2		Sochi	26 May 84
6.84		Larisa	Baluta	UKR	13.8.65	2		Krasnodar	6 Aug 83
6.82	1.8	Fiona	May	GBR	12.12.69	*	WJ	Sudbury	30 Jul 88
6.81	1.6	Carol	Lewis	USA	8.8.63	1	TAC	Knoxville	20 Jun 82
6.81	1.4	Yelena	Davydova	KZK	16.11.67	1	NC-j	Krasnodar	17 Jul 85
6.79		Carmen	Sirbu	ROM	17.2.67	3	RomIC	Bucuresti	2 Jun 85
6.78		Kathy	McMillan	USA	7.11.57	1	AAU	Los Angeles	12 Jun 76
6.78i	-	Erica	Johansson	SWE	5.2.74	2	NC	Malmö	21 Feb 93
Wind assisted									
7.27	2.2	Heike	Daute	GDR	16.12.64	1	WCh	Helsinki	14 Aug 83
6.93	4.6	Beverly	Kinch	GBR	14.1.64	5	WCh	Helsinki	14 Aug 83
6.88	2.1	Fiona	May	GBR	12.12.69	1	WJ	Sudbury	30 Jul 88
6.84	2.8	Anu	Kaljurand	EST	16.4.69	2		Riga	4 Jun 88

TRIPLE JUMP

Mark	Wind	Name		Nat	Born	Pos	Meet	Venue	Date
14.36	0.0		Ren Ruiping	CHN	1.2.76	1	NC	Beijing	1 Jun 94
14.32	-0.1	Yelena	Lysak ¶	RUS	19.10.75	1		Voronezh	18 Jun 94
13.95	1.8	Olga Lidia	Cepero	CUB	4.2.75	1		La Habana	11 Feb 94
13.85	0.2	Tatyana	Matyashova	RUS	2.8.73	1	Prav	Sochi	25 May 91
13.80	1.3	Olga	Kontsevaya	RUS	.71	1		Sochi	13 May 90
13.79	0.0		Zhang Yan	CHN	.6.72			Hangzhou	12 Oct 91
13.78	1.5	Irina	Myelnikova II	RUS	14.5.75	1		Krasnodar	29 May 94
13.73			Liu Jinming	CHN	1.2.72			Dalian	7 May 91
13.73	1.6		Wang Xiangrong	CHN	.4.76	*	NG	Beijing	13 Sep 93
13.69	-0.1	Tatyana	Lebedyeva	RUS	21.7.76	3		Voronezh	18 Jun 94
13.68		Irina	Myelnikova I	RUS	9.1.74	1		Sverdlovsk	31 Jul 90
13.67	1.0	Lyudmila	Galkina	RUS	20.5.72	1	EJ	Thessaloniki	10 Aug 91
Wind assisted									
14.43	2.7	Yelena	Lysak ¶	RUS	19.10.75	1	WJ	Lisboa	21 Jul 94
14.07	2.8		Wang Xiangrong	CHN	.4.76	4	NG	Beijing	13 Sep 93

SHOT

Mark	Wind	Name		Nat	Born	Pos	Meet	Venue	Date
20.54		Astrid	Kumbernuss	GDR	5.2.70	1	vFin-j	Orimattila	1 Jul 89
20.51i		Heidi	Krieger	GDR	20.7.65	2		Budapest	8 Feb 84
		20.24				5		Spilt	30 Apr 84
20.23		Ilke	Wyludda	GDR	28.3.69	1	NC-j	Karl-Marx-Stadt	16 Jul 88
20.12		Ilona	Schoknecht	GDR	24.9.56	2	NC	Erfurt	23 Aug 75
20.02			Cheng Xiaoyan	CHN	20.11.75	3	NC	Beijing	5 Jun 94
19.90		Stephanie	Storp	FRG	28.11.68	1		Hamburg	16 Aug 87
19.63			Wang Yawen	CHN	23.8.73	1		Shijiazhuang	25 Apr 92
19.57		Grit	Haupt	GDR	4.6.66	1		Gera	7 Jul 84

Mark	Wind	Name		Nat	Born	Pos	Meet	Venue	Date
19.48		Ines	Wittich	GDR	14.11.69	5		Leipzig	29 Jul 87
19.42		Simone	Michel	GDR	18.12.60	3	vSU	Leipzig	23 Jun 79
19.23			Zhang Zhiying	CHN	19.7.73	1	NC-j	Hangzhou	8 May 92
19.05		Cordula	Schulze	GDR	11.9.59	3		Potsdam	6 Aug 78

DISCUS

Mark	Wind	Name		Nat	Born	Pos	Meet	Venue	Date
74.40		Ilke	Wyludda	GDR	28.3.69	2		Berlin	13 Sep 88
67.38		Irina	Meszynski	GDR	24.3.62	1		Berlin	14 Aug 81
67.00		Jana	Günther	GDR	7.1.68	6	NC	Potsdam	20 Aug 87
66.80		Svetla	Mitkova	BUL	17.6.64	1		Sofia	2 Aug 83
66.60		Astrid	Kumbernuss	GDR	5.2.70	1		Berlin	20 Jul 88
66.34		Franka	Dietzsch	GDR	22.1.68	2		St Denis	11 Jun 87
66.30		Jana	Lauren	GDR	28.6.70	1	vSU-j	Karl-Marx-Stadt	18 Jun 89
66.08			Cao Qi	CHN	1.1.74	1	NG	Beijing	12 Sep 93
65.96		Grit	Haupt	GDR	4.6.66	3		Leipzig	13 Jul 84
65.22		Daniela	Costian	ROM	30.4.65	3		Nitra	26 Aug 84
64.52		Martina	Opitz	GDR	12.12.60	3	NC	Karl-Marx-Stadt	12 Aug 79
64.42		Larisa	Korotkovich	BLR	23.1.67	1		Minsk	28 Apr 86

HAMMER

Mark	Wind	Name		Nat	Born	Pos	Meet	Venue	Date
65.48		Mihaela	Melinte	ROM	27.3.75	1		Bucuresti	26 Feb 94
59.80		Natalya	Vasilenko	UKR	15.8.74	1		Chernigov	27 Jun 93
59.06		Natalya	Panarina	RUS	6.5.75	1		Chelyabinsk	6 Jun 93
59.02		Simone	Mathes	GER	13.5.75	1		Rehlingen	23 May 94
58.90		Debbie	Sosimenko	AUS	5.4.74	1		Hobart	17 Jan 93
58.60		Yelena	Khrulyova	RUS	.73	3		Adler	26 May 91
58.36		Oksana	Zatsepilova	RUS	20.4.74	2		Moskva	6 Aug 93
58.24		Marina	Pirog	UKR	28.8.74	2		Chernigov	27 Jun 93
58.20		Olga	Sokolova	RUS	.72	1	NC-wj	Adler	24 Feb 90
58.10		Natalya	Ignatova	RUS	3.1.74	2		Chelyabinsk	6 Jun 93
57.80		Irina	Lungu	ROM	5.4.75			Bucuresti	10 Jun 94
57.62		Kirsten	Münchow	GER	21.1.77	1		Dortmund	25 Jun 94

JAVELIN

Mark	Wind	Name		Nat	Born	Pos	Meet	Venue	Date
71.88		Antoaneta	Todorova	BUL	8.6.63	1	ECp	Zagreb	15 Aug 81
71.82		Ivonne	Leal	CUB	27.2.66	1	WUG	Kobe	30 Aug 85
70.12		Karen	Forkel	GDR	24.9.70	1	EJ	Varazdin	26 Aug 89
68.94		Trine	Solberg	NOR	18.4.66	1	vSU	Oslo	16 Jul 85
68.38		Antje	Kempe	GDR	23.6.63	Q	EC	Athinai	8 Sep 82
67.32		Regina	Kempter	GDR	4.4.67	2	NC	Jena	27 Jun 86
66.52		Alexandra	Beck	GDR	13.6.68	1		Khaniá	24 May 86
64.88		Anja	Reiter	GDR	15.7.69	1	EJ	Birmingham	8 Aug 87
64.66			Sun Fei	CHN	16.3.73	1		Nanjing	21 May 91
64.56		Jana	Köpping	GDR	12.4.66	2	OD	Berlin	27 Jun 85
64.56		Xiomara	Rivera	CUB	24.12.68	1	CAC-j	Ciudad México	26 Jun 86
64.40		Heike	Galle	GDR	20.3.67	1	Znam	Leningrad	8 Jun 86

HEPTATHLON

Mark	Wind	Name		Nat	Born	Pos	Meet	Venue	Date
6465		Sibylle	Thiele	GDR	6.3.65	1	EJ	Schwechat	28 Aug 83
		13.49 1.90 14.63 24.07		6.65 36.22 2:18.36					
6436		Sabine	Braun	FRG	19.6.65	1	vBul	Mannheim	9 Jun 84
		13.68 1.78 13.09 23.88		6.03 52.14 2:09.41					
6428		Svetla	Dimitrova ¶	BUL	27.1.70	1	NC	Sofia	18 Jun 89
		13.49 1.77 13.98 23.59		6.49 40.10 2:11.10					
6403		Emilia	Dimitrova	BUL	13.11.67	6	GWG	Moskva	7 Jul 86
		13.73 1.76 13.46 23.17		6.29 43.30 2:09.85					
6276		Larisa	Nikitina	RUS	29.4.65	8	NC	Kiev	21 Jun 84
		13.87 1.86 14.04 25.26		6.31 48.62 2:22.76					
6218		Jana	Sobotka	GDR	3.10.65	6	OD	Potsdam	21 Jul 84
		14.40 1.74 13.28 24.19		6.27 43.64 2:06.83					
6198		Anke	Schmidt	GDR	5.2.68	7		Götzis	24 May 87
		13.80 1.72 13.32 23.82		6.63 35.78 2:12.44					
6194		Camelia	Cornateanu	ROM	23.1.67	2	NC	Pitesti	8 Aug 86
		14.35 1.86 14.70 24.97		6.15 38.94 2:11.93					
6187		Ionica	Domniteanu	ROM	8.1.69	1	Bal-j	Pitesti	26 Jul 87
		13.51 1.77 14.56 24.66		6.00 43.86 2:17.60					

Mark	Wind	Name		Nat	Born	Pos	Meet	Venue	Date
6179		Valentina	Savchenko	UKR	13.5.68	1	Drz	Plovdiv	5 Aug 84
		13.88 1.59 15.10 24.15		6.07 48.16 2:12.42					
6166		Beatrice	Mau	GDR	20.2.71	1	WJ	Plovdiv	11 Aug 90
		13.73 1.69 12.87 24.30		6.32 50.14 2:19.94					
6112		Nathalie	Teppe	FRA	22.5.72	1		Talence	1 Jul 90
		13.78 1.75 12.59 25.29w		5.89 55.44 2:18.34					
Disqualified for positive drugs test									
6534		Svetla	Dimitrova	BUL	27.1.70	H	ECp	Helmond	16 Jul 89
		13.30 1.84 14.35 23.33		6.47 39.20 2:13.56					

5000 METRES WALK

Mark	Name		Nat	Born	Pos	Meet	Venue	Date
20:37.7		Jin Bingjie	CHN	1.4.71	1	NC	Hefei	3 Mar 90
21:01.8	Susana	Feitor	POR	28.1.75	1	SGP	Fana	8 May 93
21:02.6		Li Jingxue	CHN	10.2.70	2		Anshan	2 Sep 89
21:05.41	Irina	Stankina	RUS	25.3.77	1	WJ	Lisboa	24 Jul 94
21:06.7		Sun Yan	CHN	4.5.73	5	NC	Zhengzhou	3 Mar 91
21:13.16		Cui Yingxi	CHN	26.1.71	1		Jinan	30 Oct 88
21:18.1		Wang Yili	CHN	4.4.71	3		Anshan	2 Sep 89
21:20.03		Gao Hongmiao	CHN	17.3.74	1	WJ	Seoul	20 Sep 92
21:22.8		Fan Xiaoling	CHN	29.3.71	4	NC	Hefei	3 Mar 90
21:24.71	Natalya	Trofimova	RUS	17.1.75	3	WJ	Lisboa	24 Jul 94
21:26.1		Kong Yan	CHN	5.4.71	5	NC	Hefei	3 Mar 90
21:27.9		Liu Caimei	CHN	1.3.71	7	NC	Hefei	3 Mar 90

4 x 100 METRES RELAY

Mark	Nat	Team	Pos	Meet	Venue	Date
43.44A	NGR	Utondu, Iheagwam, Onyali, Ogunkoya	1	AfrG	Nairobi	9 Aug 87
43.48	GDR	Breuer, Krabbe, Dietz, Henke	1	WJ	Sudbury	31 Jul 88
		Unsanctioned race 43.33 Breuer, Krabbe, Dietz, Henke	1		Berlin	20 Jul 88
43.73A	USA	Gilmore, Finn, Simmons, Vereen	2		Colorado Springs	19 Jul 83
43.82	JAM	Russell, R.Campbell, Frazer, Mitchell	1	WJ	Plovdiv	12 Aug 90
43.87	URS	Lapshina, Doronina, Bulatova, Kovalyova	1	vGDR-j	Leningrad	20 Jun 87
44.04	CUB	Riquelme, Allen, López, Valdivia	2	WJ	Sudbury	31 Jul 88
44.16	GBR	Soper, DSmith, Fraser, Merry	2	WJ	Plovdiv	12 Aug 90
44.23	FRA	Ropars, Simioneck, Declerk, Sidibé	1	EJ	Varazdin	27 Aug 89
44.63	FRG	Eichler, Rasch, Steger, Sommer	2	EJ	Donyetsk	21 Aug 77
44.75	CHN	Gao, Yen, Feng, Wang	1	AsiC-j	Djakarta	20 Sep 94
44.88	CAN	Amderson, Thomas, Taaffe, Garreau			Burnaby	26 Jul 85
44.90	JPN	Ito, Kakinuma, Shoji, Kaneko	6	WJ	Seoul	20 Sep 92
Hand timed						
43.9	FRA	Ropars, Simioneck, Declerk, Sidibé	1		Thaon	12 Aug 89

4 x 400 METRES RELAY

Mark	Nat	Team	Pos	Meet	Venue	Date
3:28.39	GDR	Derr, Fabert, Wöhlk, Breuer	1	WJ	Sudbury	31 Jul 88
3:30.38	AUS	Scamps, Poetschka, Hanigan, Andrews	1	WJ	Plovdiv	12 Aug 90
3:30.45	USA	Harris, Pritchett, Downing, Vickers	1	WJ	Athinai	20 Jul 86
3:30.72	BUL	Kireva, Angelova, Rashova, Dimitrova	3	v2N	Sofia	24 Jul 83
3:31.09	JAM	Williams, Cole, Turner, Scott	2	WJ	Plovdiv	12 Aug 90
3:31.41	URS	Zakharova, Kiryukhina, Ponomaryova, Zhdanova	2	EJ	Utrecht	23 Aug 81
3:31.57	ROM	Petrea, Florea, Tîrlea, Nedelcu	1	WJ	Seoul	20 Sep 92
3:31.81	CUB	Casanova, Duporty, Limonta, McLeon	3	WJ	Plovdiv	12 Aug 90
3:31.94	FRG	Wahl, Lix, Ley, Leistenschneider	3	EJ	Schwechat	28 Aug 83
3:33.56	NGR	Opara, Akinremi, Onyebuchi, Yusuf	1h2	WJ	Plovdiv	11 Aug 90
3:34.83	JPN	Amano, Kasajima, Yamagata, Kakinuma	5	WJ	Seoul	20 Sep 92
3:35.10	GBR	Honley, Robinson, Flockhart, Hall	3	EJ	Cottbus	25 Aug 85
Disqualified following positive drugs test on Nedelcu						
3:31.13	ROM	Tuta, Florea, Tîrlea, Nedelcu	1	EJ	San Sebastián	1 Aug 93

MEN'S WORLD LISTS 1994

100 YARDS

Mark	Wind	Name		Nat	Born	Pos	Meet	Venue	Date
9.30	1.6	Linford	Christie	GBR	2.4.60	1	TSB	Edinburgh	8 Jul
9.33	1.2	Jon	Drummond	USA	9.9.68	1	PennR	Philadelphia	30 Apr
9.36	1.2	Andre	Cason	USA	20.1.69	2	PennR	Philadelphia	30 Apr
9.36	1.6	Sam	Jefferson	USA	19.4.71	2	TSB	Edinburgh	8 Jul
9.40	1.6	Calvin	Smith	USA	8.1.61	3	TSB	Edinburgh	8 Jul
9.41	1.6	Slip	Watkins	USA	29.9.67	4	TSB	Edinburgh	8 Jul
9.42	2.0	Jeff	Laynes	USA	3.10.70	1h1		Fresno	9 Apr
9.42	0.5	Jeff	Williams	USA	31.12.64	1		Fresno	9 Apr
9.46	1.6	Jason	John	GBR	17.10.71	5	TSB	Edinburgh	8 Jul
9.47	2.0	Anthony	Barnes	USA	23.12.65	2h1		Fresno	9 Apr
9.48	2.0	Osmond	Ezinwa	NGR	22.11.71	3h1		Fresno	9 Apr
9.48	1.2	Rodney	Lewis	USA	17.7.66	3	PennR	Philadelphia	30 Apr

100 METRES

Mark	Wind	Name		Nat	Born	Pos	Meet	Venue	Date
9.85	1.2	Leroy	Burrell	USA	21.2.67	1rA	Athl	Lausanne	6 Jul
9.91	1.9	Linford	Christie	GBR	2.4.60	1	CG	Victoria	23 Aug
9.94	0.2	Davidson	Ezinwa	NGR	22.11.71	1	GP II	Linz	4 Jul
9.94	1.9	Dennis	Mitchell	USA	20.2.66	1	Bisl	Oslo	22 Jul
9.94	0.5		Mitchell			1	v Afr	Durham	13 Aug
9.95A	1.9	Olapade	Adeniken	NGR	19.8.69	1A		El Paso	16 Apr
9.97	0.2		Mitchell			2	GP II	Linz	4 Jul
9.97	0.9		Mitchell			1	DNG	Stockholm	12 Jul
9.98	1.6	Andre	Cason	USA	20.1.69	1h4	NC	Knoxville	15 Jun
9.98	0.2		Ezinwa			1h1	GP II	Linz	4 Jul
9.98	1.8		Christie			1s1	CG	Victoria	23 Aug
9.99	1.2		Ezinwa			2A	Athl	Lausanne	6 Jul
9.99	1.2		Mitchell			3A	Athl	Lausanne	6 Jul
9.99	1.9	Jon	Drummond	USA	9.9.68	2	Bisl	Oslo	22 Jul
9.99	0.5		Drummond			2	v Afr	Durham	13 Aug
9.99	1.5		Drummond			1		Rieti	28 Aug
10.00	1.0	Michael	Marsh	USA	4.8.67	1	MSR	Walnut	17 Apr
10.00	1.0		Mitchell			1A	ISTAF	Berlin	30 Aug
10.01A	1.9	Bode	Osagiobare	NGR	1.12.70	2A		El Paso	16 Apr
10.01	2.0		Cason			1	Jen	San José	28 May
10.01	0.2		Christie			1h2	GP II	Linz	4 Jul
10.01	1.0		Drummond			2A	ISTAF	Berlin	30 Aug
10.02	0.2		Christie			1q1	CG	Victoria	22 Aug
10.02	1.0		Christie			3A	ISTAF	Berlin	30 Aug
10.02	0.8		Christie			1A	TOTO	Tokyo	15 Sep
10.03	1.8	Donovan	Bailey	CAN	16.12.67	1		Duisburg	12 Jun
10.03	0.2		Christie			3	GP II	Linz	4 Jul
10.03	1.2		Drummond			4A	Athl	Lausanne	6 Jul
10.03	1.2		Drummond			1	GP	London	15 Jul
10.03	0.5		Adeniken			3	v USA	Durham	13 Aug
10.03	-0.1		Christie			1	VD	Bruxelles	19 Aug
10.03	1.7		Christie			1B	ISTAF	Berlin	30 Aug
		(32/10)							
10.04	1.2	Carl	Lewis	USA	1.7.61	1		Houston	7 May
10.04	1.8	Frank	Fredericks	NAM	2.10.67	1q3	CG	Victoria	22 Aug
10.05	1.9	Michael	Green	JAM	7.11.70	2	CG	Victoria	23 Aug
10.06	2.0	Rodney	Lewis	USA	17.7.66	1h3	NC	Knoxville	15 Jun
10.07	1.1	Emmanuel	Tuffour	GHA	2.12.66	1		Schriesheim	18 Jun
10.07	1.9	Ato	Boldon	TRI	30.12.73	4	CG	Victoria	23 Aug
10.08A	1.9	Obadele	Thompson	BAR	30.3.76	3A		El Paso	16 Apr
10.08	1.4	Daniel	Effiong	NGR	17.6.72	1	Slov	Bratislava	1 Jun
10.08	0.2	Bruny	Surin	CAN	12.7.67	4	GP II	Linz	4 Jul
10.09	2.0	Michael	Johnson	USA	13.9.67	2h3	NC	Knoxville	15 Jun
		(30)							
10.10	0.5	Anthony	Jones	USA	12.12.71	1	Big10	Madison	22 May
10.10	0.6	Osmond	Ezinwa	NGR	22.11.71	3h2	GP II	Linz	4 Jul
10.10	1.5	Glenroy	Gilbert	CAN	31.8.68	1h8	CG	Victoria	22 Aug
10.11	2.0	Tim	Montgomery	USA	28.1.75	3h3	NC	Knoxville	15 Jun
10.11	1.3	Augustine	Nketia	NZL	30.12.70	1h5	CG	Victoria	22 Aug

Mark	Wind	Name		Nat	Born	Pos	Meet	Venue	Date
10.12	0.2	Sam	Jefferson	USA	19.4.71	4h1	GP II	Linz	4 Jul
10.12	0.6	Aleksandr	Porkhomovskiy	RUS	12.8.72	1s1	NC	St Peterburg	14 Jul
10.13	1.3	Alvis	Whitted	USA	4.9.74	1		Knoxville	2 Apr
10.13	1.2	Vincent	Henderson	USA	20.10.72	1h5	NC	Knoxville	15 Jun
10.13	0.5	Randall	Evans	USA	26.10.70	4	vAFR	Durham	13 Aug
		(40)							
10.14	1.2	Tim	Harden	USA	27.1.74	2h5	NC	Knoxville	15 Jun
10.16		Terry	Bowen	USA	15.9.71	1h2	WAC	Fresno	20 May
10.16	1.9	Damien	Marsh	AUS	28.3.71	4	Bisl	Oslo	22 Jul
10.17		Nnamdi	Anusim	NGR	11.7.72	1B		Port Harcourt	18 Mar
10.17	1.7	Talal	Mansour	QAT	8.5.64	1		Doha	6 Apr
10.17		Deji	Aliu	NGR	22.11.75	1	NC-j	Benin City	28 May
10.17	1.3	Gilles	Quénéhervé	FRA	17.5.66	1h1		Genève	18 Jun
10.17	1.8	Geir	Moen	NOR	26.6.69	1		Tønsberg	20 Jul
10.18A	2.0	Robert	Esmie	CAN	5.7.72	1r1		Flagstaff	14 May
10.18	0.4	Vladislav	Dologodin	UKR	23.2.72	1s	NC	Kiev	26 May
		(50)							
10.18	1.9	Marcus	Reed	USA	17.7.72	2s1	NCAA	Boise	3 Jun
10.19	1.6	Omar	Loum	SEN	31.12.73	1		Noisy-le-Grand	2 Jul
10.19	0.8	Jeff	Williams	USA	31.12.64	1rC	Athl	Lausanne	6 Jul
10.19	0.9	Mark	Witherspoon	USA	3.9.63	5	DNG	Stockholm	12 Jul
10.20A	1.9	Fabian	Muyaba	ZIM	30.9.70	4		El Paso	16 Apr
10.20	2.0	Jacob	Swinton	USA	26.12.71	1h1	IC4A	Fairfax	21 May
10.20	0.2	Greg	Saddler	USA	29.6.74	1h1	NCAA	Boise	2 Jun
10.20	1.9	Tony	McCall	USA	16.6.74	3s1	NCAA	Boise	3 Jun
10.20	-0.2	Pavel	Galkin	RUS	9.10.68	1		Moskva	11 Jun
10.20	1.1	Marc	Blume	GER	28.12.73	3		Rhede	29 Jul
		(60)							
10.21	0.1	John	Mair	JAM	20.11.63	2		Clemson	16 Apr
10.21A	1.9	Kareem	Streete-Thompson	USA	30.3.73	5A		El Paso	16 Apr
10.21	1.6	Raymond	Stewart	JAM	18.3.65	4	Banes	São Paulo	21 May
10.21	-0.5	Andrew	Tynes	BAH	13.2.72	1		Fresno	21 May
10.21	2.0	Ron	Clark	USA	1.11.69	5h3	NC	Knoxville	15 Jun
10.21	0.2	Daniel	Cojocaru	ROM	27.5.69	1	NC	Bucuresti	17 Jun
10.22		Obadiah	Cooper	USA	8.3.70	1		Terre Haute	16 Apr
10.22	0.0	Donovan	Powell	JAM	13.6.71	1	PennR	Philadelphia	30 Apr
10.22	0.6	Calvin	Smith	USA	8.1.61	4h2	GP II	Linz	4 Jul
10.23	1.2	Jason	John	GBR	17.10.71	5	TSB	London	15 Jul
		(70)							
10.23	1.1	Terry	Williams	GBR	15.11.68	3q4	CG	Victoria	22 Aug
10.24	1.6	Ricky	Carrigan	USA	6.7.73	4h4	NC	Knoxville	15 Jun
10.24	1.8	Tim	Jackson	AUS	4.7.69	2		Tønsberg	20 Jul
10.24	2.0	Hermann	Lomba	FRA	11.10.60	1h4	NC	Annecy	23 Jul
10.24	0.5	Kevin	Braunskill	USA	31.3.69	1B		Lappeenranta	26 Jul
10.24	0.4	Kazuhiro	Takahashi	JPN	27.7.76	1	NC-j	Toyama	2 Aug
10.25	1.9	Henry	Neal	USA	18.10.70	1		College Station	16 Apr
10.25	1.0	Bryan	Bridgewater	USA	7.9.70	5	MSR	Walnut	17 Apr
10.25	1.9	Vitaliy	Savin	KZK	23.1.66	1		Almaty	21 May
10.25	0.2	Riley	Washington	USA	31.7.73	4h1	NCAA	Boise	2 Jun
		(80)							
10.25	1.8	Alexandros	Terzian	GRE	24.6.68	1	ECp I	Valencia	11 Jun
10.25	1.5	Ali	Stubbs	BAH	73			Nassau	17 Jun
10.25	1.8	Peter	Karlsson	SWE	23.11.70	3		Tønsberg	20 Jul
10.25	1.2	Jason	Gardener	GBR	17.9.75	2	WJ	Lisboa	21 Jul
10.25	1.2	Carlos	Gats	ARG	11.12.69	1	NC	Córdoba	8 Oct
10.25	1.6	Yoshitaka	Ito	JPN	23.6.70	1		Nagoya	31 Oct
10.26A	2.0	Travis	Grant	USA	31.8.72	3		El Paso	2 Apr
10.26	1.2	Aham	Okeke #	NOR	19.8.69	2		Fayetteville	23 Apr
10.26	1.9	Clinton	Bufuku	ZAM	6.2.72	2		Arlington	7 May
10.26	0.8	Sergey	Osovich	UKR	16.12.73	2	NC	Kiev	26 May
		(90)							
10.26	1.4	Darren	Braithwaite	GBR	20.1.69	4	Slov	Bratislava	1 Jun
10.26	1.3	Slip	Watkins	USA	29.9.67	2		Lapinlahti	26 Jun
10.26	1.6	Jean-Charles	Trouabal	FRA	20.5.65	2		Noisy le Grand	2 Jul
10.26	0.8	Andrey	Fedoriv	RUS	11.8.63	1s2	NC	St Peterburg	14 Jul
10.26	1.2	Deworski	Odom	USA	11.4.77	3	WJ	Lisboa	21 Jul
10.26	0.5	Kennet	Kjensli	NOR	12.3.69	2		Lappeenranta	26 Jul
10.27A	2.0	Salaam	Gariba	GHA	23.1.69	2		Flagstaff	14 May

Mark	Wind	Name		Nat	Born	Pos	Meet	Venue	Date
10.27	0.9	Sergey	Kornelyuk	BLR	1.5.69	1		Bialo-Podliaska	30 May
10.27	1.6	Brian	Lewis	USA	5.12.74	5h4	NC	Knoxville	15 Jun
10.27	1.2	Jeff	Laynes	USA	3.10.70	3h5	NC	Knoxville	15 Jun
10.27	1.5	Franklin	Nwankpa	NGR	26.5.73	2h2	CG	Victoria	22 Aug
		(101)							

Mark	Wind	Name		Nat	Born	Date
10.28	0.7	Aston	Morgan ¶	JAM	69	16 Jul
10.28	2.0	Sanusi	Turay	SLE	68	22 Aug
10.29	1.5	Steve	Brimacombe	AUS	71	20 Feb
10.29	1.1	Warren	Johnson	JAM	73	7 May
10.29	1.4	Michael	Rosswess	GBR	65	1 Jun
10.29	1.6	Ibrahim	Meité	CIV	76	2 Jul
10.29	0.8	Viktor	Malchugin	RUS	61	14 Jul
10.29	1.8	Max	Morinière	FRA	64	21 Aug
10.29		Patrick	Stevens	BEL	68	13 Sep
10.29	0.4	Robinson	Urrutia	COL	69	24 Nov
10.30	1.0	Chen Wenzhong		CHN	70	29 Apr
10.30	0.8	Andrey	Grigoryev	RUS	70	14 Jul
10.30	1.2	Carlton	Chambers	CAN	75	22 Jul
10.30	1.8	Konstantin	Rurak	UKR	74	23 Jul
10.30	0.9	André Domingos	Silva	BRA	72	13 Aug
10.31	1.7	Brian	Amos	USA	71	7 May
10.31	1.7	Anthony	Phillips	USA	70	7 May
10.31	0.8	Dmitriy	Vanyaykin	UKR	66	26 May
10.31	1.3	Aki	Bradley	USA	71	3 Jun
10.31	0.0	Bryan	Howard	USA	76	18 Jun
10.31	0.8	Oluyemi	Kayode	NGR	68	6 Jul
10.31	0.3	Vyacheslav	Kabanov	UKR	74	23 Jul
10.31		Anninos	Marcoulides	CYP	71	30 Jul
10.31		Oleg	Kramarenko	UKR	70	7 Aug
10.32	-0.5	Shane	Naylor	AUS	67	27 Jan
10.32		Tony	Ogbeta	NGR	74	18 Mar
10.32	1.0	Aaron	Thigpen	USA	64	14 May
10.32	0.3	Alexandr	Shlychkov	UKR	70	23 Jul
10.32	0.0	Marcel	Carter	USA	71	24 Jul
10.32	1.5	Domenico	Nettis	ITA	72	28 Aug
10.33	-0.5	Dean	Capobianco	AUS	70	28 Jan
10.33		Okechukwu	Ejiogu	NGR	76	18 Mar
10.33		Hashim	Ibrahim	NGR		18 Mar
10.33A	-0.2	Johann	Venter	RSA	71	6 May
10.33A	0.5	Peter	Ogilvie	CAN	72	14 May
10.33	1.7	Fred	Fields	USA	72	25 May
10.33	-2.3	Solomon	Wariso #	GBR	66	18 Jun
10.33	-1.3	Sylvanus	Hepburn	BAH	71	18 Jun
10.33	1.1	Björn	Sinnhuber	GER	68	18 Jun
10.33	1.4	Anthony	Dees	USA	63	29 Jun
10.33	1.1	Eric	Frempong	CAN	75	2 Jul
10.33	1.6	Eric	Perrot	FRA	69	2 Jul
10.33	1.3	Needy	Guims	FRA	74	2 Jul
10.33	2.0	Pascal	Théophile	FRA	70	23 Jul
10.34	1.7	Saad Muftah	Mubarak	QAT	64	6 Apr
10.34	1.6	Atlee	Mahorn	CAN	65	21 May
10.34		Sylvester	Omodiale	NGR	77	28 May
10.34	-1.3	Laurent	Leconte	FRA	68	18 Jun
10.34	0.9	Lars	Hedner	SWE	67	29 Jul
		(150)				
10.34	1.8	Elliot	Bunney	GBR	66	22 Aug
10.34	0.7	Steffen	Görmer	GER	68	24 Aug
10.34	0.8	Satoru	Inoue	JPN	71	15 Sep
10.34	0.4	Koji	Ito	JPN	70	24 Sep
10.35	0.5	Chris	Sanders	USA	72	22 May
10.35		Renward	Wells	BAH	70	17 Jun
10.35	1.1	Franck	Amegnigan	TOG	71	21 Jun
10.35	1.8	Torbjörn	Eriksson	SWE	71	20 Jul
10.35	0.2	David	Dollé	SUI	69	29 Jul
10.35	1.4	Toby	Box	GBR	72	7 Aug
10.35	1.4	Alexandros	Genovelis	GRE	68	7 Aug
10.36		Kerchavel	Patterson	USA	72	2 Apr
10.36	1.9	Dennis	Mowatt	JAM	69	7 May
10.36	1.8	Anthony	Barnes	USA	65	14 May
10.36	0.4	Colin	Jackson	GBR	67	21 May
10.36	-0.1	Arnaldo	Silva	BRA	64	28 May
10.36	0.5	Marek	Zalewski	POL	70	24 Jun
10.36	1.9	Sandro	Floris	ITA	65	8 Jul
10.36	1.7	Tetsuya	Nakamura	JPN	73	31 Oct
10.36	1.4	Leonardo	Prevot	CUB	71	5 Nov
10.37		Michael	Monye	NGR		18 Mar
10.37		Jonathan	Carter	USA	72	9 Apr
10.37A	1.3	Kevin	Franklin	USA	74	16 Apr
10.37	1.8	Claus	Hirsbro	DEN	68	11 Jun
10.37	0.0	Pat	Johnson	USA	76	18 Jun
10.37A		Joseph	Gikonyo	KEN	65	8 Jul
10.37	1.4	Ricardo	Greenidge	CAN	71	29 Jul
10.37			Jin Sun-kuk	KOR	70	28 Oct
10.37	0.6	Takahiro	Mazuka	JPN	76	30 Oct
10.38	1.1	Lorenzo	Hathorne	USA	72	26 Mar
10.38	0.8	Wayne	Watson	JAM	65	9 Apr
10.38	0.1	John	Regis	GBR	66	14 May
10.38	1.1	Juan	Jones	PUR	70	14 May
10.38	0.5	Tony	Simmons	USA	74	22 May
10.38		Cyril	Oriala	NGR	75	27 May
10.38	2.0	Pascal	Thurnherr	SUI	67	18 Jun
10.38	1.5	Michael	Huke	GER	69	1 Jul
10.38	0.8	Yuriy	Mizera	RUS	66	14 Jul
10.38	1.6	Sébastien	Carrat	FRA	74	16 Jul
10.38	-0.4	Mardi	Lestari	INA	68	10 Oct
10.39A	1.9	Bryant	Williams	USA	71	16 Apr
10.39	1.7	Kevin	Doss	USA	71	7 May
10.39	-0.7	Nobuharu	Asahara	JPN	72	19 May
10.39	1.6	Robson C	da Silva	BRA	64	21 May
10.39	0.8	Aleksey	Chikhachev	UKR	71	26 May
10.39	-0.2	Dmitriy	Mikhailovich	RUS	70	11 Jun
10.39	0.9	David	Tomlin	CAN	76	22 Jun
10.39	2.0	Matias	Ghansah	SWE	74	9 Jul
10.39	0.9	Marcelo	Silva	BRA	66	13 Aug
10.39	-0.1	Sidnei Telles	Sousa	BRA	66	17 Sep
		(200)				

Wind gauge illegally placed (on outside of track)

Mark	Wind	Name		Nat	Born	Pos	Meet	Venue	Date
9.96	1.7	Tim	Montgomery	USA	28.1.75	1	JUCO	Odessa, TX	21 May
9.98	1.7	Daniel	Effiong	NGR	17.6.72	2	JUCO	Odessa, TX	21 May
10.03	1.7	Warren	Johnson	JAM	7.11.73	3	JUCO	Odessa, TX	21 May
10.16	1.1	Aham	Okeke #	NOR	19.8.69	1s1	JUCO	Odessa, TX	20 May
10.16	1.7	Thaddeus	Shannon	USA	6.8.73	4	JUCO	Odessa, TX	21 May
10.24	1.7	Leon	Gordon	JAM	1.7.74	6	JUCO	Odessa, TX	21 May
10.25	1.3	Wendell	Gaskin	USA	7.1.73	4s2	JUCO	Odessa, TX	20 May
10.33		Rory	Gilpan	JAM	15.4.72	1h1	JUCO	Odessa, TX	19 May

Montgomery's time not recognised as a World Junior record. The track was reported to have been measured at 99.96m, but officials at Odessa JC insist that this was taken from the front edge of the start line and that the track measures 100m.

Wind-assisted

Mark	Wind	Name		Nat	Born	Pos	Meet	Venue	Date
9.86	2.5		Burrell			1	TexR	Austin	9 Apr
9.91	3.7		Christie			1	AAA	Sheffield	11 Jun
9.94	2.5	Daniel	Effiong	NGR	17.6.72	2	TexR	Austin	9 Apr
10.00	2.7	Frank	Fredericks	NAM	2.10.67	1		Cottbus	15 Jun
10.00A	3.5		Burrell			1		Sestriere	31 Jul

Mark	Wind	Name		Nat	Born	Pos	Meet	Venue	Date
10.01A	3.5		Drummond			2		Sestriere	31 Jul
10.01	2.3		Fredericks			1s2	CG	Victoria	23 Aug
10.02A	3.5		Adeniken			3		Sestriere	31 Jul
10.03	3.0	Tim	Harden	USA	27.1.74	1	SEC	Fayetteville	15 May
10.04	4.8	David	Oaks	USA	12.5.72	1	Big8	Lawrence	21 May
10.04	2.3	Michael	Green	JAM	7.11.70	2s2	CG	Victoria	23 Aug
10.07	3.7	Toby	Box	GBR	9.9.72	2	AAA	Sheffield	11 Jun
10.07	3.7	Michael	Rosswess	GBR	11.6.65	3	AAA	Sheffield	11 Jun
10.08	3.7	Jason	John	GBR	17.10.71	4	AAA	Sheffield	11 Jun
10.08A	3.1	Sam	Jefferson	USA	19.4.71	1rB		Sestriere	31 Jul
10.09	2.9	Raymond	Stewart	JAM	18.3.65	2		Austin	7 May
10.10A	3.5	John	Regis	GBR	13.10.66	4rA		Sestriere	31 Jul
10.11	4.5	Greg	Saddler	USA	29.6.74	1h2	SEC	Fayetteville	14 May
10.13A	3.1	Kevin	Braunskill	USA	31.3.69	2rB		Sestriere	31 Jul
10.14	4.5	Franklin	Nwankpa	NGR	26.5.73	1		Ames	23 Apr
10.14	4.3	Aston	Morgan ¶	JAM	18.2.69	1h1		Soria	8 Jul
10.16	4.8	Travis	Grant	USA	31.8.72	2	Big8	Lawrence	21 May
10.16A	3.5	Alexandros	Terzian	GRE	24.6.68	6rA		Sestriere	31 Jul
10.17	4.4	Aki	Bradley	USA	7.2.71	1h3	SEC	Fayetteville	14 May
10.17	2.3	Terry	Williams	GBR	15.11.68	5s2	CG	Victoria	23 Aug
10.19	5.1	Steve	Brimacombe	AUS	7.5.71	1		Perth	13 Feb
10.19		Dion	Miller	USA	26.2.75	1		Lubbock	26 Mar
10.19		Renward	Wells	BAH	23.2.70	1		Stillwater	2 Apr
10.19	3.3	Donovan	Powell	JAM	13.6.71	3	NCAA	Boise	4 Jun
10.19	2.6	Marc	Blume	GER	28.12.73	1s2	NC	Erfurt	1 Jul
10.20	3.5	Derrick	Thompson	USA	24.2.73	2h1	SEC	Fayetteville	14 May
10.20		Elliot	Bunney	GBR	11.12.66	1		Edinburgh	8 Jun
10.21	6.4	Kerry	Lawyer	USA	3.11.72	1B		Los Angeles	26 Mar
10.21	2.2	Clinton	Bufuku	ZAM	6.2.72	1	TexR	Austin	8 Apr
10.21	2.3	Lars	Hedner	SWE	27.5.67	1		Helsingborg	10 Jul
10.22	3.9	David	Dollé	SUI	30.5.69	1h		Bulle	3 Sep
10.22	3.3	Yoshitaka	Ito	JPN	23.6.70	1h		Nagoya	31 Oct
10.23	3.9	Arnaldo	Silva	BRA	26.3.64	1		Lisboa	21 Jun
10.24A	4.2	Sébastien	Carrat	FRA	20.5.74	1		Font Romeu	5 Jun
10.24	2.6	Steffen	Görmer	GER	28.7.68	2s2	NC	Erfurt	1 Jul
10.24	2.6	Slip	Watkins	USA	29.9.67	1		Serravalle	5 Jul
10.25	5.1	Dean	Capobianco	AUS	11.5.70	2		Perth	13 Feb
10.25	2.2	Bryant	Williams	USA	25.3.71	3	TexR	Austin	8 Apr
10.25	4.9	Aham	Okeke #	NOR	19.8.69	1r2	TexR	Austin	9 Apr
10.25	3.9	Luis	Cunha	POR	5.12.64	2		Lisboa	21 Jun
10.25	2.1	Marcel	Carter	USA	26.3.71	2		Caorle	16 Jul
10.26	2.2	Shane	Naylor	AUS	3.11.67	2		Auckland	22 Jan
10.26		Stacy	Mitchell	USA	16.10.75	1		Dallas	2 Apr
10.26A	3.1	Ezio	Madonia	ITA	7.8.66	3rB		Sestriere	31 Jul
10.27		Kevin	Lawson	TRI	4.3.70	1		Athens, Ga.	2 Apr
10.27	3.8	Carlton	Chambers	CAN	27.6.75	1		Victoria	29 Jul

Mark	Wind	Name		Nat	Born	Date
10.28		Sean	Robbins	USA	72	2 Apr
10.28	2.9	Aaron	Thigpen	USA	64	7 May
10.28	2.9	Anninos	Marcoulides	CYP	71	3 Jun
10.29	3.7	Trevor	Cameron	GBR	76	11 Jun
10.30	5.1	Ricky	Nalatu	AUS	72	13 Feb
10.30	3.0	David	Tomlin	CAN	76	22 Jun
10.30	3.3	Miquel	Janssen	ARU	70	12 Aug
10.31	6.5	Kyle	Vander-Kuyp	AUS	71	13 Feb
10.31	6.4	Anthuan	Maybank	USA	69	26 Mar
10.31	4.1	Peter	Hargraves	USA	72	14 May
10.31	4.5	Jason	Sanders	USA	71	14 May
10.31	2.6	Dan	O'Brien	USA	66	14 Jun
10.31A	3.1	Sandro	Floris	ITA	65	31 Jul
10.32	2.9	Dwayne	Miller	USA	69	7 May
10.32	3.0	Georgios	Panagiotopoulos	GRE	69	28 May
10.32	4.3	Janne	Haapasalo	FIN	65	2 Jul
10.33	4.9	Takayuki	Nakamichi	JPN	69	9 Apr
10.33	4.3	Franck	Amégnigan	TOG	71	11 Jun
10.34	3.5	Eddie	Kennison	USA	73	14 May
10.34	4.5	Kevin	Franklin	USA	73	14 May
10.34		Jason	Fergus	GBR	73	5 Jun
10.34	3.5	Julian	Golding	GBR	75	17 Sep
10.35	3.2	Marcus	Stokes	USA	74	13 Apr
10.35	4.1	Toya	Jones	USA	76	13 May
10.36	4.4	Clyde	Rudolph	USA	72	14 May
10.36	2.4	David	Bobb	USA	74	21 May
10.36		Ben	Singleton	USA	75	3 Jul
10.36	2.9	Michael	Huke	GER	69	12 Jun
10.36	4.1	Alexey	Knoroz	RUS	63	2 Jul
10.37A		Shaun	Powell	RSA	71	18 Mar
10.37	3.2	Grady	Labbe	USA	71	14 May
10.37		Ali	Evans	USA	75	27 May
10.37	3.3	Thomas	Leandersson	SWE	66	10 Jul
10.37	4.0	Steve	Gookey	GBR	71	11 Jun
10.38		.	Barragan	USA		12 Mar
10.38		Lawrence	Forbes	USA	73	2 Apr
10.38	2.3	Innokentiy	Zharov	RUS	68	29 May
10.38	2.9	Pál	Rezák	HUN	66	3 Jun
10.38	2.7	Nelson	Boateng	GHA	68	15 Jun
10.38A	3.4	Pedro	Nolet	ESP	70	8 Jul
10.39	2.9	Szabolcs	Alexa	HUN	69	3 Jun
10.39	2.2	Dmitriy	Mikhailovich	RUS	70	7 Jun
10.39	2.8	Andrew	Mensah	GBR	71	15 Jun

Rolling start: 10.29 2.7 Éric Perrot FRA 69 8 May

Mark	Wind	Name		Nat	Born	Pos	Meet	Venue	Date

Low altitude bests

Mark	Wind	Name	Date
10.27	1.1	Thompson	22 Aug
10.29	1.2	Streete-Thompson	15 Jun
10.31	-0.1	Osagiobare	9 Jun
10.32	0.9	Esmie	22 Jun
10.38	1.0	Muyaba	2 Jun
10.20w	2.4	Esmie	28 Jul
10.23w	2.9	Regis	7 May

Disqualified for positive drugs tests

Mark	Wind	Name		Nat	Born	Pos	Meet	Venue	Date
10.02	1.9	Horace	Dove-Edwin ¶	SLE	10.2.67	(2)	CG	Victoria	23 Aug
10.19	1.8	Aham	Okeke #	NOR	19.8.69	(2)		Tønsberg	20 Jul

Mark	Wind	Name		Nat	Born	Date
10.28	-0.1	Chidi	Imo ¶	NGR	63	9 Jun
10.26w	3.1	Tim	Williams ¶	USA	63	23 Apr

Doubtful timing

Mark	Wind	Name		Nat	Born	Date
10.20A		Robinson	Urrutia	COL	69	29 Jul
10.31A		John Jairo	Mena	COL	67	29 Jul
10.32A		Alexandre	Vallon-Haarau	RSA	70	15 Jan
10.36A		Luis	Vega	COL	63	29 Jul
10.20w		Chris	Allison	JAM	73	21 Apr
10.24w		Rory	Gilpan	JAM	72	21 Apr

Hand timing

Mark	Wind	Name		Nat	Born	Pos	Meet	Venue	Date
9.9		Anvar	Kuchmuradov	UZB	5.1.70	1		Tashkent	5 May
9.9		Vladislav	Dologodin	UKR	23.2.72	1		Kharkov	13 May
10.0		Deji	Aliu	NGR	22.11.75	1		Bauchi	15 Apr
10.0		Roland	McGhee	USA	15.10.71	1		Murray	23 Apr
10.0	0.2	Igor	Streltsov	UKR	1.5.65	h		Zaporozhe	14 May
10.0	0.3	Obadele	Thompson	BAR	30.3.76	1	CAC-j	Port of Spain	8 Jul

Mark	Wind	Name		Nat	Born	Date
10.1A		Joel	Isasi	CUB	67	9 Apr
10.1		Nnamdi	Anusim	NGR	72	15 Apr
10.1		Shavkat	Sharipov	UZB	72	5 May
10.1		Leonid	Safronnikov	BLR	71	28 Apr
10.1		Andrey	Fedoriv	RUS	63	12 May
10.1		Sergey	Osovich	UKR	73	14 May
10.1		Pavel	Galkin	RUS	68	28 May
10.1	-0.4	Arnaldo	Silva	BRA	64	3 Jun
10.1	1.7	Thierry	Lubin	FRA	70	4 Jun
10.1	1.2	Pavel	Kondratenko	RUS	68	6 Aug
10.1	1.3	Carlos	Gats	ARG	69	1 Oct
10.1	1.5	Luis	Cunha	POR	64	21 Oct

Wind assisted

Mark	Wind	Name		Nat	Born	Pos	Meet	Venue	Date
9.9	6.2	Rod	Mapstone	AUS	19.11.69	1		Perth	12 Nov
10.0	2.8	Sergey	Osovich	UKR	16.12.73	1h1		Uzhgorod	7 May
10.0		Renward	Wells	BAH	23.2.70	2		Fayetteville	25 May
10.0		Aston	Morgan ¶	JAM	18.2.69	2		Fayetteville	25 May
10.0	5.7	Fred	Martin	AUS	4.10.66	1		Sydney	5 Nov

Mark	Wind	Name		Nat	Born	Date
10.1	5.5	Paul	Henderson	AUS	71	19 Feb
10.1	5.5	Shaun	Mayne	AUS	70	19 Feb
10.1		Aham	Okeke ¶	NOR	69	25 Mar
10.1		Chad	Burnett	USA	75	13 Apr
10.1		John	George	USA	75	22 Apr
10.1	3.2	Vyacheslav	Kabanov	UKR	74	7 May
10.1		Claude	Toukene-Guébogo	CMR	75	21 Aug
10.1	6.2	Paul	Greene	AUS	72	12 Nov

200 METRES

Mark	Wind	Name		Nat	Born	Pos	Meet	Venue	Date
19.87A	1.8	John	Regis	GBR	13.10.66	1		Sestriere	31 Jul
19.94	0.0	Michael	Johnson	USA	13.9.67	1	Herc	Monaco	2 Aug
19.97A	1.8	Frank	Fredericks	NAM	2.10.67	2		Sestriere	31 Jul
19.97	1.5		Fredericks			1	CG	Victoria	26 Aug
20.01	0.0		Regis			2	Herc	Monaco	2 Aug
20.02	0.6		Johnson			1	VD	Bruxelles	19 Aug
20.09	0.1		Johnson			1	TOTO	Tokyo	15 Sep
20.10	-0.2	Daniel	Effiong	NGR	17.6.72	1	Jen	San José	28 May
20.10	1.6		Fredericks			1A	Athl	Lausanne	6 Jul
20.10	0.6		Johnson			1	GWG	St Peterburg	28 Jul
20.15	0.0		Effiong			1A		Tucson	7 May
20.15	0.1		Fredericks			2	TOTO	Tokyo	15 Sep
20.16	0.0		Effiong			1A	MSR	Walnut	17 Apr
20.17	1.6		Regis			2A	Athl	Lausanne	6 Jul
20.17	0.6		Fredericks			2	GWG	St Peterburg	28 Jul
20.18	0.3		Johnson			1	Banes	São Paulo	21 May
20.19	0.0	Jeff	Williams	USA	31.12.64	2A	MSR	Walnut	17 Apr
20.19	0.8		Williams			1	DNG	Stockholm	12 Jul
20.21	1.3		Effiong			1	Slov	Bratislava	1 Jun
20.21	0.6		Johnson			1		Kobenhavn	28 Aug
20.22A	1.8	Kevin	Braunskill	USA	31.3.69	3		Sestriere	31 Jul
20.23	1.2		Fredericks			1	v USA	Durham	12 Aug
20.24	1.6		Effiong			3A	Athl	Lausanne	6 Jul
20.25		Andrew	Tynes	BAH	13.2.72	1		Nassau	16 Jun
20.25	1.5		Regis			2	CG	Victoria	26 Aug
20.26	1.6		Johnson			4A	Athl	Lausanne	6 Jul
20.26	-0.1		Fredericks			1		Madrid	6 Sep
20.28	0.0	Olapade	Adeniken	NGR	19.8.69	3	Herc	Monaco	2 Aug
20.29	0.8		Fredericks			2	DNG	Stockholm	12 Jul
20.30	0.2		Fredericks			1	WG	Helsinki	29 Jun
20.30	0.2		Effiong			1A	GP II	Linz	4 Jul
20.30	-0.1	Geir	Moen	NOR	26.6.69	1	EC	Helsinki	11 Aug
		(32/9)							

Mark	Wind	Name		Nat	Born	Pos	Meet	Venue	Date
20.35	0.5	Aleksandr	Porkhomovskiy	RUS	12.8.72	1		Rieti	28 Aug
20.36	0.5	Vladislav	Dologodin	UKR	23.2.72	2		Rieti	28 Aug
20.38	1.7	Antonio	Pettigrew	USA	3.11.67	1		Durham	9 Apr
20.39	1.9	Jean-Charles	Trouabal	FRA	20.5.65	1		Noisy-le-Grand	2 Jul
20.39	1.6	Oluyemi	Kayode	NGR	7.7.68	1q3	CG	Victoria	24 Aug
20.41	-1.7	Talal	Mansour	QAT	8.4.64	1	AsiG	Hiroshima	15 Oct
20.42	1.6	Chris	Sanders	USA	8.5.72	1	Big10	Madison	22 May
20.42	0.4	Omar	Loum	SEN	31.12.73	1		Narbonne	19 Jun
20.43	0.7	Damien	Marsh	AUS	28.3.71	1		Brisbane	5 Feb
20.43		Davidson	Ezinwa	NGR	22.11.71	2		Eagle Rock	14 May
20.43	1.2	Sebastián	Keitel	CHI	14.2.73	1	IbAm	Mar del Plata	30 Oct
		(20)							
20.44A	1.0	Milton	Mallard	USA	24.11.73	1		El Paso	2 Apr
20.44	1.7	Aki	Bradley	USA	7.2.71	1	SEC	Fayetteville	15 May
20.44	1.9	Koji	Ito	JPN	29.1.70	1		Kumamoto	23 Oct
20.47		Jason	Rouser	USA	22.3.70	3		Eagle Rock	14 May
20.47	1.5	Tony	Wheeler	USA	19.1.75	1	USOF	Edwardsville	10 Jul
20.47	1.5	Ron	Clark	USA	1.11.69	2	vGBR	Gateshead	20 Jul
20.48		Brashant	Carter	USA	30.11.73	1		Denton	16 Apr
20.48	1.9	Dino	Napier	USA	24.11.69	1h2	NC	Knoxville	16 Jun
20.48	0.6	Michael	Marsh	USA	4.8.67	4	GWG	St Peterburg	28 Jul
20.48A	1.8	Giorgio	Marras	ITA	15.10.71	4		Sestriere	31 Jul
		(30)							
20.49A	1.3	Bode	Osagiobare	NGR	1.12.70	2rA		El Paso	16 Apr
20.50	1.5	Bryan	Bridgewater	USA	7.9.70	2	USOF	Edwardsville	10 Jul
20.50	1.6	Terry	Williams	GBR	15.11.68	2q3	CG	Victoria	24 Aug
20.51	0.6	Solomon	Wariso #	GBR	11.11.66	1A	ECCp	Malaga	29 May
20.51	1.2	Carlos	Gats	ARG	11.12.69	2	IbAm	Mar del Plata	30 Oct
20.52	0.0	Georgios	Panagiotopoulos	GRE	12.8.69	1		Rhede	29 Jul
20.53	-1.2	Bryan	Bronson	USA	9.9.72	1		Houston	24 Apr
20.53	1.6	Ato	Boldon	TRI	30.12.73	1q2	CG	Victoria	24 Aug
20.54	1.7	Clyde	Rudolph	USA	15.2.72	2	SEC	Fayetteville	15 May
20.54	1.7	Tim	Harden	USA	27.1.74	3	SEC	Fayetteville	15 May
		(40)							
20.55	1.1	Emmanuel	Tuffour	GHA	2.12.66	1		Schriesheim	19 Jun
20.55	1.5	Marcel	Carter	USA	26.3.71	3	vGBR	Gateshead	20 Jul
20.56	1.7	Greg	Saddler	USA	29.6.74	4	SEC	Fayetteville	15 May
20.56	0.3	Daniel	Sangouma	FRA	7.2.65	2rB	Athl	Lausanne	6 Jul
20.56	1.7	Andrey	Fedoriv	RUS	11.8.63	1	NC	St Peterburg	16 Jul
20.57	0.1	Marcus	Reed	USA	17.7.72	1		Pullman	21 May
20.57	0.5	Kazuhiro	Takahashi	JPN	27.7.76	1		Osaka	19 Jun
20.58	1.9	Roshaan	Griffin	USA	21.2.74	3h1	NC	Knoxville	16 Jun
20.58	0.6	Sergey	Osovich	UKR	16.12.73	6	GWG	St Peterburg	28 Jul
20.58A	1.8	Steve	Brimacombe	AUS	7.5.71	5		Sestriere	31 Jul
		(50)							
20.59	1.8	Ricky	Carrigan	USA	6.7.73	1rD	MSR	Walnut	17 Apr
20.59	1.6	Anthuan	Maybank	USA	30.12.69	2	Big10	Madison	22 May
20.59	-3.9	Miquel	Janssen	ARU	5.9.70	1	NED Ch	Assen	17 Jul
20.60		Renward	Wells	BAH	23.2.70			Nassaur	16 Jun
20.60	0.4	Michael	Huke	GER	30.3.69	1	NC	Erfurt	3 Jul
20.60	0.3	Troy	Douglas	BER	30.11.62	3rB	Athl	Lausanne	6 Jul
20.60	-0.1	Ivan	Garcia	CUB	29.2.72	3		Madrid	6 Sep
20.61		Deji	Aliu	NGR	22.11.75	1		Bauchi	16 Apr
20.61	0.3	Randall	Evans	USA	26.10.70	1	NCAA II	Raleigh	28 May
20.61	1.2	Leonardo	Prevot	CUB	13.6.71	3	IbAm	Mar del Plata	30 Oct
		(60)							
20.62A	1.3	Bryant	Williams	USA	25.3.71	3rA		El Paso	16 Apr
20.62	1.7	Vincent	Henderson	USA	20.10.72	5	SEC	Fayetteville	15 May
20.62	1.6	Anthony	Jones	USA	12.12.71	3	Big10	Madison	22 May
20.63	0.0	David	Oaks	USA	12.5.72	1		Norman	16 Apr
20.63	0.9	Dennis	Mitchell	USA	20.2.66	2		Hiroshima	30 Apr
20.63	0.1	Bruny	Surin	CAN	12.7.67	3	BNP	Villeneuve d'Ascq	8 Jul
20.64	1.9	Rod	Tolbert	USA	11.6.67	5h1	NC	Knoxville	16 Jun
20.64	0.4	Ibrahim	Meité	CIV	18.11.76	2		Narbonne	19 Jun
20.64	1.2	Gilles	Quénéhervé	FRA	17.5.66	1		Limoges	9 Jul
20.65	1.8	Eric	Frempong	CAN	1.10.75	1	NC-j	Ottawa	3 Jul
		(70)							
20.66A	-1.9	Robson	da Silva	BRA	4.9.64	1		Cochabamba	28 May
20.66	1.2	Rich	Wagner	USA	1.11.73	1		Pittsburgh	14 May

Mark	Wind	Name		Nat	Born	Pos	Meet	Venue	Date
20.66	1.1	Garth	Robinson	JAM	11.10.70	2h4	NCAA	Boise	1 Jun
20.66	0.4	Mark	Witherspoon	USA	3.9.63	1		Hechtel	30 Jul
20.67	0.1	Thomas	Jefferson	USA	8.6.62	1		Fairfax	14 May
20.67	-0.1	Linford	Christie	GBR	2.4.60	1	ECp	Birmingham	26 Jun
20.67	0.4	Patrick	Stevens	BEL	31.1.68	2		Hechtel	30 Jul
20.67	0.6	Floyd	Heard	USA	24.3.66	2		København	28 Aug
20.68		Jason	Hendrix	USA	24.10.72	1		Brenham	20 Apr
20.68	1.9	Terry	Bowen	USA	15.9.71	1		Los Angeles Ww	1 May
		(80)							
20.68A	0.2	Johann	Venter	RSA	30.12.71	1		Germiston	13 May
20.68	0.1	Jahshawn	St Julian	USA	8.8.68	1		Houston	20 May
20.68	1.7	Oleg	Fatun	RUS	23.3.59	2	NC	St Peterburg	16 Jul
20.69A	-1.0	Peter	Ogilvie	CAN	2.5.72	1		Flagstaff	14 May
20.69	0.8	Slip	Watkins	USA	29.9.67	5	DNG	Stockholm	12 Jul
20.69	0.5	David	Dollé	SUI	30.5.69	2s1	EC	Helsinki	11 Aug
20.69	1.2	Marcelo	Silva	BRA	19.2.66	4	IbAm	Mar del Plata	30 Oct
20.70		Brian	Lewis	USA	5.12.74	1r4		Fayetteville	23 Apr
20.70	1.6	Chris	Nelloms	USA	14.8.71	4	Big10	Madison	22 May
20.70	0.4	Alexander	Lack	GER	4.6.72	2	NC	Erfurt	3 Jul
		(90)							
20.70	1.4	Robert	Esmie	CAN	5.7.72	1s1	NC	Victoria	28 Jul
20.70	-1.6	Yoshitaka	Ito	JPN	23.6.70	2	AsiG	Hiroshima	15 Oct
20.71		Obadele	Thompson	BAR	30.3.76	1	Carif	Bridgetown	3 Apr
20.71	0.5	Brian	Irvin	USA	30.7.70	1		Portland	22 May
20.71A	-1.9	Arnaldo	Silva	BRA	26.3.64	2		Cochabamba	28 May
20.71	2.0	Doug	Walker	GBR	28.7.73	3q1	CG	Victoria	24 Aug
20.72A	1.0	Travis	Grant	USA	31.8.72	2		El Paso	2 Apr
20.72	2.0	Tim	Montgomery	USA	28.1.75	1		Austin	13 Apr
20.72	0.9	Aaron	Thigpen	USA	18.9.64	1rB		Austin	7 May
20.72	0.3	Atlee	Mahorn	CAN	27.10.65	4	Banes	São Paulo	21 May
20.72	1.3	Alexandros	Terzian	GRE	24.6.68	1	ECCp	Athina	28 May
20.72	1.6	Toby	Box	GBR	9.9.72	3q2	CG	Victoria	24 Aug
		(102)							

Mark	Wind	Name		Nat	Born	Date
20.74	1.7	Konstantin	Dyomin	RUS	74	16 Jul
20.75	-0.3	Aham	Okeke #	NOR	69	2 Jun
20.75	-0.3	Daniel	Cojocaru	ROM	69	18 Jun
20.75	0.0	Osmond	Ezinwa	NGR	71	24 Jul
20.76A	1.1	Eddie	Kennison	USA	73	16 Apr
20.76	1.7	Derrick	Thompson	USA	73	15 May
20.76	-2.7	Bryan	Howard	USA	76	21 May
20.76	0.7	Aleksey	Chikhachev	UKR	71	27 May
20.76	0.6	Donovan	Bailey	CAN	67	29 May
20.77	2.0	Shane	Lacey	USA	71	2 Apr
20.77	1.7	Allen	Johnson	USA	71	9 Apr
20.77	1.6	Kevin	Ansley	USA	72	23 Apr
20.77A		Clinton	Bufuku	ZAM	72	30 Apr
20.77	0.0	André Domingos	Silva	BRA	72	1 May
20.77	-1.4	Edward	Hervey	USA	73	7 May
20.77	0.5	Tony	McCall	USA	74	3 Jun
20.77	0.0	Robert	Kurnicki	GER	65	25 Jun
20.78	1.5	Calvin	Smith	USA	61	16 Jun
20.78	1.0	Hermann	Lomba	FRA	60	2 Jul
20.78	0.4	Björn	Sinnhuber	GER	68	3 Jul
20.78	1.7	Innokentiy	Zharov	RUS	68	16 Jul
20.78	0.5	Steve	Lewis	USA	69	24 Aug
20.79		Lorenzo	Hathorne	USA	72	25 May
20.79	-0.6	Phil	Goedluck	GBR	67	6 Aug
20.80		Alvis	Whitted	USA	74	4 Mar
20.80	0.1	Paul	Greene	AUS	72	21 May
20.80	0.7	Andrey	Gavrilenko	UKR	72	27 May
20.80	0.9	Jorge	Aguilera	CUB	66	24 Jun
20.80	2.0	Nelson	Boateng	GHA	68	24 Aug
20.81A	1.4	John	Lawson	RSA	66	7 May
20.81	1.1	Grady	Labbe	USA	71	15 May
20.81	0.4	Christian	Konieczny	GER	72	3 Jul
20.81	-0.2	Evgenios	Papadopoulos	GRE	73	10 Jul
20.81	1.6	Paul	McBurney	GBR	72	24 Aug
20.81	-0.9	Sidnei	Souza	BRA	66	18 Sep
20.82A	1.3	Shaun	Powell	RSA	71	7 May
20.82	1.1	Lars	Hedner	SWE	67	4 Jul
20.83		David	Coates	USA	70	20 May
20.83	0.4	Nobuharu	Asahara	JPN	72	21 May
20.83	0.5	Rodney	Lewis	USA	66	22 May
20.83	0.6	Sandro	Floris	ITA	65	29 May
20.83	0.3	Sylvanus	Hepburn	BAH	71	18 Jun
20.83	0.0	Pat	Johnson	USA	76	19 Jun
20.83	1.4	Ari	Pakarinen	FIN	68	20 Jul
20.83	-0.2	Torbjörn	Eriksson	SWE	71	31 Jul
20.84		Jeff	Laynes	USA	70	14 May
20.84	-1.6	Ioannis	Nafpliotis	GRE	70	22 May
20.84	2.0	Jamie	Baulch	GBR	73	24 Aug
		(150)				
20.85	-4.1	Dean	Capobianco	AUS	70	13 Mar
20.85		Emmanuel	Okoli	NGR	73	16 Apr
20.85		Frank	Nwankpa	NGR	73	23 Apr
20.85	1.7	Igor	Streltsov	UKR	65	19 Jun
20.85	1.7	Dmitriy	Bartenyev	RUS	69	16 Jul
20.85	1.5	Kevin	Widmer	SUI	70	21 Aug
20.85	0.5	Ibrahim	Ismail	QAT	72	14 Oct
20.86A	1.3	Riaan	Dempers	RSA	77	9 Mar
20.86	-1.4	Maurice	Greene	USA	75	26 Mar
20.87A	1.3	Nico	Schutte	RSA	64	9 Mar
20.87	1.2	Juan	Jones	PUR	70	14 May
20.88A	1.3	Fabian	Muyaba	ZIM	70	16 Apr
20.88	0.1	Chris	Jones	USA	73	20 May
20.88	1.2	Wenceslão	Ferrin	COL	69	30 Oct
20.89	1.3	Keith	Barker	USA	72	12 Mar
20.89A		Sean	Maye	USA	69	23 Apr
20.90	-1.4	Van	Smith	USA	73	26 Mar
20.90	2.0	Isaac	Carson	USA	73	12 May
20.90	0.4	Ron	Jones	USA	74	25 May
20.91	1.4	Marcus	Stokes	USA	74	1 Jun
20.91	0.0	Butch	Reynolds	USA	64	10 Jul
20.91	1.9	Ian	Mackie	GBR	75	23 Jul
20.92		Sean	Baksh	CAN	71	2 Apr
20.92	0.0	Greg	Foster	USA	58	17 Apr
20.92A	1.3	Chris	Neethling	RSA	68	7 May
20.92A	1.8	Carlo	Occhiena	ITA	72	31 Jul
20.93	0.4	David	Jackson	USA		25 May
20.93	1.3	Michael	Kutscher	GER	69	3 Jul
20.93	0.3	Alain	Reimann	SUI	67	6 Jul

Mark	Wind	Name		Nat	Yr	Date
20.93	-0.1	Mikhail	Vdovin	RUS	67	25 Aug
20.93	1.7		Tao Wu-Shium	TPE	73	15 Oct
20.94	0.3	Ricardo	Greenidge	CAN	71	22 Jun
20.94	1.8	Carlton	Chambers	CAN	75	3 Jul
20.94	-0.4	Leroy	Burrell	USA	67	17 Jul
20.94	0.5	Anninos	Markoulides	CYP	71	10 Aug
20.95		Joel	Isasi	CUB	67	11 Jun
20.95	1.7	Alexandr	Goremykin	RUS	71	16 Jul
20.95	0.5	Glenroy	Gilbert	CAN	68	30 Jul
		(188)				

Wind gauge illegally placed (on outside of track)

Mark	Wind	Name		Nat	Born	Pos	Meet	Venue	Date
20.19	0.8		Effiong			1	JUCO	Odessa	21 May
20.40	0.8	Roshaan	Griffin	USA	21.2.74	2	JUCO	Odessa, TX	21 May
20.49	0.8	Aham	Okeke #	NOR	19.8.69	3	JUCO	Odessa, TX	21 May
20.61	0.8	Ricardo	Greenidge	CAN	12.2.71	4	JUCO	Odessa, TX	21 May

Mark	Wind	Name		Nat	Yr	Date
20.85	0.8	Willie	Brown	USA		21 May
20.89	0.8	Andrew	Berry	USA	74	21 May

Wind-assisted

Mark	Wind	Name		Nat	Born	Pos	Meet	Venue	Date
20.05	2.2	Leroy	Burrell	USA	21.2.67	1		Houston	7 May
20.06		Renward	Wells	BAH	23.2.70	1		Stillwater	2 Apr
20.08	2.8		Johnson			1		Duisburg	12 Jun
20.20	2.6	Andrew	Tynes	BAH	13.2.72	1	NCAA	Boise	4 Jun
20.22	2.7	Steve	Brimacombe	AUS	7.5.71	1		Melbourne	19 Feb
20.23	2.2	Olapade	Adeniken	NGR	19.8.69	1rA		Austin	7 May
20.24	3.2	David	Oaks	USA	12.5.72	1	Big8	Lawrence	21 May
20.27	2.6	Aki	Bradley	USA	7.2.71	2	NCAA	Boise	4 Jun
20.30	2.6	Tony	Wheeler	USA	19.1.75	3	NCAA	Boise	4 Jun
20.35	4.3	Jean-Charles	Trouabal	FRA	20.5.65	1		Dijon	12 Jun
20.38	3.5	Tim	Harden	USA	27.1.74	2h2	SEC	Fayetteville	14 May
20.39	2.8	Donovan	Bailey	CAN	16.12.67	2		Duisburg	12 Jun
20.40	2.4	Damien	Marsh	AUS	28.3.71	1		Auckland	22 Jan
20.40	2.6	Clyde	Rudolph	USA	15.2.72	1h3	SEC	Fayetteville	14 May
20.41	3.5	Danny	McCray	USA	11.3.74	1		College Station	19 Mar
20.41	2.1	Marcel	Carter	USA	26.3.71	1h5	NC	Knoxville	16 Jun
20.46	3.4	Grady	Labbe	USA	4.1.71	1		Baton Rouge	25 May
20.50	4.5	Vincent	Henderson	USA	20.10.72	1h4	SEC	Fayetteville	14 May
20.55	4.0	Anthuan	Maybank	USA	30.12.69	1		Ames	23 Apr
20.55	2.2	Floyd	Heard	USA	24.3.66	2		Houston	7 May
20.55A	4.1	Thomas	Jefferson	USA	8.6.62	1		Soria	8 Jul
20.56	2.1	Marcus	Reed	USA	17.7.72	3h5	NC	Knoxville	16 Jun
20.59	3.2	Travis	Grant	USA	31.8.72	2	Big8	Lawrence	21 May
20.60	2.8	Derrick	Thompson	USA	24.2.73	3h1	SEC	Fayetteville	14 May
20.61		Garth	Robinson	JAM	11.10.70	1		Abilene	12 May
20.61	2.3	Nobuharu	Asahara	JPN	21.6.72	1s		Osaka	20 May
20.63	2.2	Raymond	Stewart	JAM	18.3.65	2rA		Austin	7 May
20.64	2.6	Patrick	Stevens	BEL	31.1.68	2		Bruxelles	17 Jul
20.69A		Tyler	Anderson	USA	27.4.70	1		Provo	23 Apr

Mark	Wind	Name		Nat	Yr	Date
20.73		Fabian	Muyaba	ZIM	70	14 May
20.73	2.6	Tony	McCall	USA	74	4 Jun
20.73	2.8	Julian	Golding	GBR	75	17 Sep
20.74		Marcus	Stokes	USA	74	26 Mar
20.74		Kevin	Lawson	TRI	70	2 Apr
20.75A	2.6	Chris	Neethling	RSA	68	7 May
20.78		Franklin	Nwankpa	NGR	73	9 Apr
20.78	2.6	Torbjörn	Eriksson	SWE	71	28 Aug
20.79		Sean	Adams	USA	71	12 May
20.80		Pat	Johnson	USA	76	9 Jul
20.80	2.3	Mark	Garner	AUS	69	26 Nov
20.81	2.1	Giovanni	Puggioni	ITA	66	14 Jul
20.82	4.1	Pedro Pablo	Nolet	ESP	70	8 Jul
20.83	6.1	Franck	Amégnigan	TOGO	71	11 Jun
20.83	3.3	Bruno	Marie-Rose	FRA	65	12 Jun
20.84	2.2	Tony	Miller	USA	69	7 May
20.86	2.4	Jason	John	GBR	71	22 Jan
20.86		Shane	Pratt	USA	73	26 Mar
20.87			Chen Wenzhong	CHN	70	5 Jun
20.88	3.2	Isaac	Harvin	USA	75	13 May
20.88	2.4	Augustine	Nketia	NZL	70	22 Jan
20.88	3.2	Trevor	Cameron	GBR	76	12 Jun
20.91	3.0	Fred	Fields	USA	72	25 May
20.94	3.9	Mark	Keddell	NZL	75	12 Nov

Drugs disqualification

Mark	Wind	Name		Nat	Born	Pos	Meet	Venue	Date
20.59	0.0	Tim	Williams ¶	USA	27.5.63	2rB	MSR	Walnut	17 Apr

Best low altitude

Mark	Wind	Name	Pos	Meet	Venue	Date
20.40	0.9	Braunskill	1	MSR	Walnut	17 Apr
20.62	-0.3	Marras	1s1	NC	Napoli	3 Jul
20.66	1.7	Osagiobare	6	SEC	Fayetteville	15 May
20.67	1.5	Brimacombe	7	CG	Victoria	26 Aug
20.73w	4.5	B Williams	2h4	SEC	Fayetteville	14 May
20.71	0.0	da Silva	3rA	MSR	Walnut	17 Apr
20.76	1.7	Kennison				1 Jun
20.83		Bryant Williams				27 Mar
20.93	0.9	Ogilvie				16 Apr
20.50w		Osagiobare	1h1	SEC	Fayetteville	14 May

Indoors

Mark	Wind	Name		Nat	Born	Pos	Meet	Venue	Date
20.56		Linford	Christie	GBR	2.4.60	1		Gent	9 Feb
20.57		Chris	Nelloms	USA	14.8.71	1	NC	Atlanta	5 Mar

Hand timing

Mark	Wind	Name		Nat	Born	Pos	Meet	Venue	Date
20.1	0.4	Sebastián	Keitel	CHI	14.2.73	1	Odesur	Valencia	23 Nov
20.3A		Joel	Lamela	CUB	29.1.71	1		Pereira	17 Oct
20.4		Ricky	Carrigan	USA	6.7.73	1		Sacramento	2 Apr
20.4A		Jorge	Aguilera	CUB	16.1.66	1		Pereira	17 Oct

Mark	Wind	Name		Nat	Born	Pos	Meet	Venue	Date
20.4A		Leonardo	Prevot	CUB	13.6.71	2		Pereira	17 Oct
20.5		Igor	Streltsov	UKR	1.5.65	1		Zaporozhe	30 Apr
20.5		Glenroy	Gilbert	CAN	31.8.68	2		Kingston	7 May
20.5		Oleg	Fatun	RUS	23.3.59	1		Stavropol	29 May
20.5		Pavel	Galkin	RUS	9.10.68	2		Stavropol	29 May

Mark	Wind	Name		Nat	Born	Date
20.6		André Domingos	Silva	BRA	72	26 Mar
20.6		Antoine	Boussombo	GAB		30 Apr
20.6		Aleksey	Chikhachev	UKR	65	30 Apr
20.6		Patrick	Delice	TRI	67	7 May
20.6	2.0	Leonid	Yazhinskiy	UKR	66	8 May
20.6A		Joseph	Gikonyo	KEN	65	8 Jul
20.6	0.4	Claudinei	Silva	BRA	70	23 Nov
20.7	0.6	Pat	Johnson	USA	76	26 Mar
20.7		Francis	Obikwelu	NGR	78	15 Apr
20.7		Amar	Hacini	ALG	71	3 Jun
20.7		Nelson	Boateng	GHA	68	25 Jun
20.7		Benjamin	Sirimou	CMR	69	21 Aug

Hand timing - wind-assisted

Mark	Wind	Name		Nat	Born	Pos	Meet	Venue	Date
20.4	5.5	Paul	Henderson	AUS	13.5.71	1		Perth	19 Feb
20.4		Roland	McGhee	USA	15.10.71	1		Murray	23 Apr
20.4	2.1	Carlos	Gats	ARG	11.12.69	1		Rieti	22 Jun
20.5	2.9	Eric	Frempong	CAN	1.10.75	2	vUSA-j	Buffalo	15 Jul

Mark	Wind	Name		Nat	Born	Date
20.6		Jerod	Douglas	USA		16 Apr
20.7		Greg	Turner	USA		2 Apr
20.7		Terrance	Branch	USA	71	23 Apr
20.7A		Wenceslao	Ferrin	COL	69	31 Jul

300 METRES

Mark	Wind	Name		Nat	Born	Pos	Meet	Venue	Date
31.56		Michael	Johnson	USA	13.9.67	1		Salamanca	22 Jul
32.19		Jason	Rouser	USA	22.3.70	1	Pre	Eugene	4 Jun
32.32		Quincy	Watts	USA	19.6.70	2	Pre	Eugene	4 Jun
32.42		Andrew	Valmon	USA	1.1.65	2		Salamanca	22 Jul
32.45		Roger	Black	GBR	31.3.66	1	McD	Sheffield	4 Sep
32.59			Valmon			2	McD	Sheffield	4 Sep
32.73		Du'aine	Ladejo	GBR	14.2.71	3	McD	Sheffield	4 Sep
32.76		Sunday	Bada	NGR	22.6.69	3		Salamanca	22 Jul
32.91		Kevin	Widmer	SUI	23.9.70	1		Geneve	23 Jul
33.06		Sean	Maye	USA	24.6.69	3	Pre	Eugene	4 Jun
33.10		Calvin	Davis	USA	2.4.72	4	McD	Sheffield	4 Sep

Hand timed

Mark	Wind	Name		Nat	Born	Pos	Meet	Venue	Date
32.9		Rohan	Robinson	AUS	15.11.71	1		Melbourne	6 Jan
32.9		Mark	Hylton	GBR	24.9.76	1		Basingstoke	21 Aug

400 METRES

Mark	Wind	Name		Nat	Born	Pos	Meet	Venue	Date
43.90		Michael	Johnson	USA	13.9.67	1		Madrid	6 Sep
44.04			Johnson			1	ISTAF	Berlin	30 Aug
44.32		Samson	Kitur	KEN	25.2.66	1	GGala	Roma	8 Jun
44.32			Johnson			1	v Afr	Durham	13 Aug
44.43		Antonio	Pettigrew	USA	3.11.67	1	NC	Knoxville	18 Jun
44.59A		Derek	Mills	USA	9.7.72	1		Sestriere	31 Jul
44.62			Mills			1		Luzern	29 Jun
44.68			Mills			1	TSB	London	15 Jul
44.68A		Steve	Lewis	USA	16.5.69	2		Sestriere	31 Jul
44.73			Mills			1	Herc	Monaco	2 Aug
44.73			Lewis			2	ISTAF	Berlin	30 Aug
44.78		Roger	Black	GBR	31.3.66	1		Rieti	28 Aug
44.78			Mills			2		Rieti	28 Aug
44.86			Mills			1		Padova	10 Jul
44.88			Pettigrew			2	v Afr	Durham	13 Aug
44.93		Greg	Haughton	JAM	10.11.73	1	JUCO	Odessa	21 May
44.93			Mills			1	WK	Zürich	17 Aug
44.93		Ibrahim	Ismail	QAT	22.6.72	1h1	AsiG	Hiroshima	11 Oct
44.94			Black			1	AAA	Sheffield	12 Jun
44.94			Kitur			2	Herc	Monaco	2 Aug
44.94		Du'aine	Ladejo	GBR	14.2.71	3	Herc	Monaco	2 Aug
44.96		Sunday	Bada	NGR	22.6.69	2		Madrid	6 Sep
44.97		Andrew	Valmon	USA	1.1.65	3		Rieti	28 Aug
45.00			Ladejo			2	TSB	London	15 Jul
45.00		Charles	Gitonga	KEN	5.10.71	1	CG	Victoria	23 Aug
45.02		Inaldo	Sena	BRA	18.6.71	3		Madrid	6 Sep
45.03A			Valmon			3		Sestriere	31 Jul
45.03		Quincy	Watts	USA	9.6.70	2	WK	Zürich	17 Aug
45.06			Mills			1	NCAA	Boise	4 Jun
45.06			Pettigrew			1s1	NC	Knoxville	17 Jun
45.06			Bada			3	vUSA	Durham	13 Aug
		(31/14)							

Mark	Name		Nat	Born	Pos	Meet	Venue	Date
45.09A	Abednigo	Matilu	KEN	21.11.68	1		Nairobi	18 Jun
45.11	Chris	Jones	USA	8.10.73	2	NCAA	Boise	4 Jun
45.14	Darnell	Hall	USA	26.9.71	1		Indianapolis	30 Jul
45.15A	Riaan	Dempers	RSA	4.3.77	1	NC	Secunda	6 May
45.18	Butch	Reynolds	USA	8.6.64	2	GGala	Roma	8 Jun
45.19	Jason	Rouser	USA	22.3.70	2	NC	Knoxville	18 Jun
	(20)							
45.20	Kennedy	Ochieng	KEN	30.12.71	1		Sevilla	5 Jun
45.20	Calvin	Davis	USA	2.4.72	3	NC	Knoxville	18 Jun
45.26A	Bobang	Phiri	RSA	5.5.68	2	NC	Secunda	6 May
45.26	Udeme	Ekpeyong	NGR	28.3.73	2	JUCO	Odessa, TX	21 May
45.27	Tony	Miller	USA	12.2.71	1h1	NCAA	Boise	2 Jun
45.27	Norberto	Tellez	CUB	23.12.72	4		Madrid	6 Sep
45.29	Brad	Pride	USA	7.6.74	1	SEC	Fayetteville	15 May
45.29	Wendell	Gaskin	USA	7.1.73	2s1	NC	Knoxville	17 Jun
45.35	Ed	Odom	USA	24.2.73	2		Atlanta	21 May
45.35	Deon	Minor	USA	22.1.73	1h3	NCAA	Boise	2 Jun
	(30)							
45.36	Marlon	Ramsey	USA	11.9.74	1		Austin	14 May
45.37		Shon Ju-il	KOR	6.10.69	1	NC	Seoul	17 Jun
45.41	Jude	Monye	NGR	16.11.73	2	SEC	Fayetteville	15 May
45.43	Matthias	Rusterholz	SUI	16.8.71	6	WK	Zürich	17 Aug
45.46A	Leonard	Byrd	USA	17.3.75	1		Albuquerque	30 Apr
45.46	Michael	Marsh	USA	4.8.67	1		Houston	7 May
45.46	Brian	Whittle	GBR	26.4.64	3	AAA	Sheffield	12 Jun
45.47	Dean	Capobianco	AUS	11.5.70	1		Sydney	30 Jan
45.47	David	McKenzie	GBR	3.9.70	4	AAA	Sheffield	12 Jun
45.47	Francis	Ogola	UGA	1.7.73	1		Nivelles	23 Jul
	(40)							
45.49	Darren	Clark	AUS	6.9.65	2		Sydney	30 Jan
45.49A	Hermanus	de Jager	RSA	16.3.71	1		Pretoria	12 Apr
45.49A	Arnaud	Malherbe	RSA	20.11.72	3	NC	Secunda	6 May
45.49	Stéphane	Diagana	FRA	23.7.69	1	NC	Annecy	24 Jul
45.50	Kevin	Lyles	USA	23.7.73	1	DogwR	Knoxville	8 Apr
45.50	Paul	Greene	AUS	9.12.72	4	CG	Victoria	23 Aug
45.52	Terrence	Branch	USA	11.3.71	2h1	NCAA	Boise	2 Jun
45.54	Eswort	Coombs	STV	26.11.72	4s2	CG	Victoria	23 Aug
45.55	Dmitriy	Kosov	RUS	28.9.68	1	NC	St Peterburg	15 Jul
45.62	Dmitriy	Golovastov	RUS	14.7.71	5	GWG	St Peterburg	24 Jul
	(50)							
45.63	Kempa	Busby	USA	9.10.73	3	JUCO	Odessa, TX	21 May
45.64	Wes	Russell	USA	3.3.71	1	Owens	Columbus	8 May
45.65A	Omokaro	Alohan	NGR	18.9.71	2		Nairobi	18 Jun
45.66	Ferdana	Johnson	USA	6.10.72	1r2		Houston	7 May
45.66	Mikhail	Vdovin	RUS	15.1.67	2	NC	St Peterburg	15 Jul
45.67	Devon	Edwards	USA	17.2.73	1	NCAA II	Raleigh	28 May
45.68	Kevin	Ansley	USA	23.10.72	4h3	NCAA	Boise	2 Jun
45.68	Patrick	Delice	TRI	12.11.67	1s1	CG	Victoria	23 Aug
45.69	Jonas	Motiejunas	USA	7.12.74	3		Atlanta	21 May
45.69	Danny	McCray	USA	11.3.74	2r2		Waco	25 May
	(60)							
45.71	Jacques	Farraudière	FRA	27.1.66	1		La Chaux de Fonds	21 Aug
45.74	Danny	McFarlane	JAM	14.2.72	2	NC	Kingston	2 Jul
45.75A	Milton	Mallard	USA	24.11.73	1		El Paso	16 Apr
45.76	Anthuan	Maybank	USA	30.12.69	2	Owens	Columbus	8 May
45.76	Jose	Parrilla	USA	31.3.72	4		Atlanta	21 May
45.77A	Julius	Chepkwony	KEN	69	3		Nairobi	18 Jun
45.77	Desmond	Johnson	USA	6.4.77	1	NC-j	Tallahassee	25 Jun
45.79	Duane	Hill	USA	9.1.73	4	JUCO	Odessa, TX	21 May
45.79A	Joseph	Magut	KEN	65	3		Nairobi	23 Jul
45.80	David	Oaks	USA	12.5.72	1		Arlington	1 Apr
	(70)							
45.80	Troy	Douglas	BER	30.11.62	1		Malles	20 Aug
45.81	Mark	Everett	USA	2.9.68	1		Gainesville	28 Apr
45.82	Ramon	Clay	USA	29.6.75	2	NC-j	Tallahassee	25 Jun
45.83	Sean	Maye	USA	24.6.69	2	DogwR	Knoxville	8 Apr
45.83	Michael	MacDonald	JAM	17.3.75	1	WJ	Lisboa	22 Jul
45.83	Hayden	Stephen	TRI	9.1.72	6s2	CG	Victoria	23 Aug
45.84	Seiji	Inagaki	JPN	28.4.73	2h1	AsiG	Hiroshima	11 Oct

Mark	Name		Nat	Born	Pos	Meet	Venue	Date
45.84	Wenceslao	Ferrin	COL	3.10.69	1	Odesur	Valencia	24 Nov
45.85	Rene	Rodriguez	USA	6.4.74	2		Los Angeles Ww	1 May
45.87	Robert	Guy	TRI	21.2.64	2	NCAA II	Raleigh	28 May
	(80)							
45.87	Ahmed	Ali Agabus	GHA	15.10.72	1		Aartselaar	21 Jul
45.89	Simon	Kemboi	KEN	1.3.67	2		Rehlingen	23 May
45.89	Tomas	Czubak	POL	16.12.73	1	NC	Pila	25 Jun
45.89A	Simeon	Kipkemboi	KEN	15.4.60	2h3		Kasarani	7 Jul
45.91	Raoul	Howard	USA	11.3.74	3		Houston	24 Apr
45.92	Emmanuel	Okoli	NGR	13.11.73	4	NC	Lagos	11 Jun
45.92	Pierre-Marie	Hilaire	FRA	19.11.65	2	NC	Annecy	24 Jul
45.92	Fabio	Grossi	ITA	3.9.67	2B		Bologna	2 Sep
45.93	Derrick	Thymes	USA	14.1.72	5	SEC	Fayetteville	15 May
45.94	Solomon	Amegatcher	GHA	20.12.70	1		Tuscaloosa	27 Mar
	(90)							
45.94	Clarence	Richards	JAM	15.4.71	3		Raleigh	23 Apr
45.94	Paul	Henry	JAM	15.10.72	1h3	IC4A	Fairfax	21 May
45.96	Neil	de Silva	TRI	15.11.69	4s1	CG	Victoria	23 Aug
45.98A	Alessandro	Aimar	ITA	5.6.67	5		Sestriere	31 Jul
45.98	Iwan	Thomas	GBR	5.1.74	7s2	CG	Victoria	23 Aug
45.99	Lamont	Smith	USA	11.12.72	1		Brenham	20 Apr
45.99A	Kisilu	Musyoka	KEN		5		Nairobi	23 Jul
46.00	Arnold	Payne	ZIM	17.10.72	5		Atlanta	21 May
46.00	David	Coates	USA	25.2.70	1		Naperville	28 May
46.01	Shante	Williams	USA	21.12.73	3		Los Angeles Ww	1 May
46.01	Lenval	Laird	JAM	69	3	NC	Kingston	2 Jul
46.01	Sebastián	Keitel	CHI	14.2.73	2	Odesur	Valencia	24 Nov
	(102)							

Mark	Name		Nat	Born	Date
46.04	Shane	Pratt	USA	73	13 Apr
46.04	Samuel	Matete	ZAM	68	6 May
46.04	Amar	Hacini	ALG	71	14 Jul
46.05A	Andrea	Nuti	ITA	67	31 Jul
46.05	Daniel	Bittner	GER	71	20 Aug
46.07	Otis	Scott	USA	71	27 May
46.07	Dennis	Blake	JAM	70	28 May
46.08	Vadim	Ogiy	UKR	72	27 May
46.09	Milton	Campbell	USA	76	28 May
46.10	Rich	Jones	USA	73	23 Apr
46.10	Louis	Sales	USA	71	21 May
46.10	Slobodan	Brankovic	YUG	67	22 May
46.10	Kai	Karsten	GER	68	2 Jul
46.10	Anton	Ivanov	BUL	71	9 Aug
46.11A	Cornelius	Cavijn	USA	74	30 Apr
46.11	Jean-Louis	Rapnouil	FRA	65	22 May
46.11	Adrian	Patrick	GBR	73	12 Jun
46.12	Beau	Lane	USA	73	26 Mar
46.13	Frankie	Atwater	USA	69	24 Jun
46.14	Ben	Beyers	USA	74	23 Apr
46.14A	Michael	Gichuhi	KEN		18 Jun
46.14	Michael	Joubert	AUS	70	13 Aug
46.15	Kendrick	Bullard	USA	72	15 May
46.15	Roxbert	Martin	JAM		2 Jul
46.15	Sadek	Boumendil	ALG	72	8 Jul
46.15	Byron	Goodwin	CAN	72	29 Jul
46.16	Mark	Graham	CAN	73	23 Apr
46.16A	Patrick	Ndururi	KEN	72	7 Jul
46.17	Brett	Callaghan	AUS	73	12 Mar
46.17	Rohan	McDonald	JAM	77	2 Jul
46.18	Désiré	Pierre-Louis	MRI	73	27 Mar
46.18A	Dorian	Green	USA	74	2 Apr
46.18	Vasiliy	Tverdokhleb	UKR	70	27 May
46.19	Maurice	Horton	USA	67	10 Jul
46.20	Sidnei	Sousa	BRA	66	3 Sep
46.20	Shigekazu	Omori	JPN	72	9 Sep
46.21A	Dirk	Pretorius	RSA	76	6 May
46.21	Hugh	Powell	JAM	70	28 May
46.22A	Juan	Vallin	MEX	69	5 Aug
46.23A	Riaan	Sullivan	RSA	71	6 May
46.23	Dmitriy	Bey	RUS	67	15 Jul
46.25	Barrington	Campbell	JAM		21 May
46.25	Antonio	McKay	USA	64	21 May
46.25	Eronilde	de Araújo	BRA	70	5 Nov
46.26	Calvin	Harrison	USA	74	2 Apr
46.26	Duane	Hill	USA	73	13 Apr
46.26	Ian	Morris	TRI	61	22 May
46.26	Hachim	Ndiaye	SEN	63	21 Aug
46.27	Lutz	Becker	GER	69	2 Jul
	(150)				
46.27A	Elkana	Nyangau	KEN	62	7 Jul
46.29	Marco	Vaccari	ITA	66	8 Jun
46.29	Omar	Mena	CUB	66	23 Jun
46.31	Jerome	Young	JAM	76	18 Jun
46.31	Rico	Lieder	GER	71	2 Jul
46.31	Shaun	Farrell	NZL	75	22 Jul
46.32	Stefan	Balosák	SVK	72	9 Aug
46.33	Bryan	Bronson	USA	72	24 Apr
46.34	George	Page	USA	74	16 Apr
46.34	Michael	Granville	USA	78	18 Jun
46.35A	Moses	Mabaso	RSA	77	8 Apr
46.35	Kevin	Widmer	SUI	70	31 Jul
46.36	Alvin	Harrison	USA	74	17 Apr
46.36	Sheldon	Edwards	JAM	73	21 May
46.36A	Raymundo	Escalante	MEX	64	18 Jun
46.36		Si Yandong	CHN	73	28 Jul
46.37	Craig	Taylor	JAM	68	2 Jul
46.37	Mark	Hylton	GBR	76	22 Jul
46.38	Valentin	Kulbatskiy	UKR	74	25 Jul
46.39	Evgenios	Papadopoulos	GRE	73	28 May
46.39	Thomas	Schönlebe	GER	65	7 Jun
46.39	Alex	Fugallo	GBR	70	12 Jun
46.39	Ade	Mafe	GBR	66	12 Jun
46.39	Roger	Franklin	USA	69	24 Jun
46.39	Wilson	Cañizales	COL	64	22 Jul
46.40	Hiroyuki	Hayashi	JPN	73	9 Apr
46.40	Bouchaïb	Belkaïd	MAR	67	11 Jul
46.40	R A Sugath	Tilakaratne	SRI	73	16 Jul
	(178)				

Mark	Name		Nat	Born	Pos	Meet	Venue	Date

Best at low altitude

45.38	Matilu	1		Rehlingen	23 May	45.86	Mallard	1			Fresno	21 May
45.45	Phiri	3s2	CG	Victoria	23 Aug	45.98	Dempers	1			Durban	23 Apr
45.67	Alohan	4	SEC	Fayetteville	15 May	46.04	de Jagar	23 Mar	46.20	Nuti		8 Jun
45.70	Byrd	3h2	NCAA	Boise	2 Jun	46.04	Malherbe	23 Apr	46.33	Aimar		21 May

Unconfirmed: 45.93 Henry Aguiar VEN 15.8.66 1 Barquisimeto 17 Jul

Indoors

46.11	Mark	Richardson	GBR	72	29 Jan	46.37	Derrick	Adkins	USA	70	5 Mar

Hand timing

Mark	Name		Nat	Born	Pos	Meet	Venue	Date
45.2	Udeme	Ekpeyong ¶	NGR	28.3.73	2s1	JUCO	Odessa, TX	20 May
45.4A	Patrick	Ndorori	KEN	72	1		Nairobi	11 Jun
45.5	Terrence	Branch	USA	11.3.71	1		Murray	23 Apr
45.5	Dmitriy	Kosov	RUS	28.9.68	1		Irkutsk	28 May
45.5A	Simon	Kemboi	KEN	1.3.67	2	NC	Nairobi	8 Jul
45.6	Michael	MacDonald	JAM	17.3.75	1		Kingston	12 Mar
45.6A	Kisilu	Musyoka	KEN				Nairobi	15 Jul
45.7	Duane	Hill	USA	9.1.73	1s2	JUCO	Odessa, TX	20 May
45.8A	Simeon	Kipkemboi	KEN	15.4.60	4	NC	Nairobi	8 Jul
45.8	Brett	Callaghan	AUS	5.10.73	1		Narrabeen	30 Jul

45.9	Omar	Mena	CUB	66	7 May	46.1A	Jacob	Omondi	KEN		10 Jun
46.1	Alvin	Daniel	TRI	68	14 May	46.1A	Kennedy	Oyunge	KEN		27 Aug
						46.2	Hezron	Maina	KEN	74	16 Apr

600 METRES

Mark	Name		Nat	Born	Pos	Meet	Venue	Date
1:15.1	Edgar	Itt	GER	8.6.67	1		Mayence	19 Apr
1:16.23	Kennedy	Osei	GHA	21.10.66	1		Pliezhausen	8 May

800 METRES

Mark	Name		Nat	Born	Pos	Meet	Venue	Date
1:43.17	Benson	Koech	KEN	10.11.74	1		Rieti	28 Aug
1:43.29	Wilson	Kipketer	KEN	12.12.70	1	Bisl	Oslo	22 Jul
1:43.50	Vebjørn	Rodal	NOR	16.9.72	2	Bisl	Oslo	22 Jul
1:43.64		Kipketer			1	iDAG	Göteborg	24 Aug
1:43.68		Kipketer			1	Herc	Monaco	2 Aug
1:43.73	Johnny	Gray	USA	19.6.60	1	GGala	Roma	8 Jun
1:43.89		Gray			3	Bisl	Oslo	22 Jul
1:43.95		Kipketer			1A	ISTAF	Berlin	30 Aug
1:44.07	David	Kiptoo Singoei	KEN	25.6.67	1		Lappeenranta	26 Jul
1:44.08	Andrea	Benvenuti	ITA	13.12.69	2	Herc	Monaco	2 Aug
1:44.14		Lee Jin-il	KOR	12.1.73	1	NC	Seoul	17 Jun
1:44.16	Atle	Douglas	NOR	9.6.68	2	iDAG	Göteborg	24 Aug
1:44.18	William	Tanui	KEN	22.2.64	2		Rieti	28 Aug
1:44.20	Giuseppe	D'Urso	ITA	15.9.69	3	Herc	Monaco	2 Aug
1:44.20		Koech			2A	ISTAF	Berlin	30 Aug
1:44.24	Patrick	Konchellah	KEN	63	1		Rhede	29 Jul
1:44.30		Rodal			1A	WG	Helsinki	29 Jun
1:44.35		Kipketer			2A	WG	Helsinki	29 Jun
1:44.36	Mark	Everett	USA	2.9.68	1	ASV	Köln	21 Aug
1:44.42		Konchellah			3A	ISTAF	Berlin	30 Aug
1:44.44	Joseph	Tengelei	KEN	8.12.72	3		Rieti	28 Aug
1:44.46		Douglas			4	Bisl	Oslo	22 Jul
1:44.46	Sammy	Langat	KEN	24.1.72	2		Lappeenranta	26 Jul
1:44.48	Nixon	Kiprotich	KEN	4.12.62	1		Hechtel	30 Jul
1:44.51		Kipketer			1		København	28 Aug
1:44.52		Tengelei			2rA	ASV	Köln	21 Aug
1:44.61	Nico	Motchebon	GER	13.11.69	5	Bisl	Oslo	22 Jul
1:44.63		Tengelei			1B	WK	Zürich	17 Aug
1:44.70		Konchellah			1	VD	Bruxelles	19 Aug
1:44.71		Douglas			1	TSB	Edinburgh	8 Jul
1:44.71		Rodal			2	TSB	Edinburgh	8 Jul
	(31/16)							
1:44.75	José Luiz	Barbosa	BRA	27.5.61	3	iDAG	Göteborg	24 Aug
1:44.89	Noureddine	Morceli	ALG	28.2.70	3rA	ASV	Köln	21 Aug
1:45.02	Arthémon	Hatungimana	BUR	21.1.74	1	FRA Ch	Annecy	24 Jul
1:45.02	Mahjoub	Haïda	MAR	1.7.70	5rA	ASV	Köln	21 Aug
	(20)							
1:45.03	Brendan	Hanigan	AUS	19.3.73	3		Lappeenranta	26 Jul
1:45.13	Vénuste	Niyongabo	BUR	9.12.73	1		Rovereto	24 Jul
1:45.13	Kennedy	Osei	GHA	21.10.66	2rB	WK	Zürich	17 Aug

Mark	Name		Nat	Born	Pos	Meet	Venue	Date
1:45.20	Mikael	Söderman	FIN	5.11.65	4		Lappeenranta	26 Jul
1:45.24	Davide	Cadoni	ITA	4.5.73	3	GGala	Roma	8 Jun
1:45.32	Ezekiel	Sepeng	RSA	30.6.74	1		Stellenbosch	23 Feb
1:45.41A	Paul	Ruto	KEN	3.11.60	1		Nairobi	18 Jun
1:45.43	Andrea	Giocondi	ITA	17.1.69	5	GGala	Roma	8 Jun
1:45.5A	Robert	Chirchir	KEN		1		Nairobi	15 Jul
1:45.51	Kipkemboi	Langat	KEN	25.3.68	1rA		Alcalá de Henares	2 Jul
	(30)							
1:45.55	Tor-Øyvind	Ødegård	NOR	28.2.69	7	Bisl	Oslo	22 Jul
1:45.57	David	Matthews	IRL	9.4.74	5		Rieti	28 Aug
1:45.60	Bruno	Konczylo	FRA	26.8.68	1		Noisy le Grand	2 Jul
1:45.67	William	Serem	KEN	71	3		Rhede	29 Jul
1:45.70	Graham	Hood	CAN	2.4.72	1		Cork	25 Jun
1:45.71	Andrey	Loginov	RUS	27.11.72	3rB	ISTAF	Berlin	30 Aug
1:45.79	Ari	Suhonen	FIN	19.12.65	3	WG	Helsinki	29 Jun
1:45.85	Charles	Nkazamyampi	BUR	1.11.64	8	Herc	Monaco	2 Aug
1:45.88	Tonny	Baltus	NED	28.12.65	3		Hechtel	30 Jul
1:45.89	Tomas	De Teresa	ESP	5.9.68	4s2	EC	Helsinki	12 Aug
	(40)							
1:45.91	Jarmo	Kokkola	FIN	31.5.68	5		Lappeenranta	26 Jul
1:45.93	Ousmane	Diarra	FRA	10.2.64	2	NC	Annecy	24 Jul
1:45.94	Samuel	Kipserem	KEN	68	1		Aartselaar	21 Jul
1:45.99	Esko	Parpala	FIN	2.7.65	2		Lapinlahti	26 Jun
1:45.99	Marko	Koers	NED	3.11.72	2	GP II	Linz	4 Jul
1:46.01	Jose	Parrilla	USA	31.3.72	1	NCAA	Boise	3 Jun
1:46.01	Abdi	Bile	SOM	28.12.62	1	Kuts	Moskva	31 Jul
1:46.02	José M	Cerezo	ESP	28.6.73	1		Baracaldo	18 Jun
1:46.03		Kim Soon-hyung	KOR	15.7.73	2		Seoul	14 May
1:46.06	Savieri	Nghidi	ZIM	3.2.68	3	CG	Victoria	26 Aug
	(50)							
1:46.07	Vincent	Malakwen	KEN	19.7.74	6		København	28 Aug
1:46.13	Martin	Steele	GBR	30.9.62	3		Cork	25 Jun
1:46.13	Steve	Holman	USA	2.3.70	7		København	28 Aug
1:46.18	Tomonari	Ono	JPN	7.2.74	3		Lapinlahti	26 Jun
1:46.18	Stanley	Redwine	USA	10.4.61	4	vAfr	Durham	13 Aug
1:46.20	Tom	McKean	GBR	27.10.63	9	Bisl	Oslo	22 Jul
1:46.2A	Billy	Konchellah	KEN	61	1h		Nairobi	29 Apr
1:46.22	Yoshito	Konno	JPN	7.4.71	1rB	WG	Helsinki	29 Jun
1:46.23	Jimmy	Jean-Joseph	FRA	15.10.72	1		Bron	17 Jun
1:46.25	Torbjörn	Johansson	SWE	23.1.70	6s2	EC	Helsinki	12 Aug
	(60)							
1:46.34	Arnaldo	Abrantes	POR	15.5.68	3		Alcalá	2 Jul
1:46.37	Johan	Botha	RSA	10.1.74	4		Rhede	29 Jul
1:46.41A	Barnabas	Samoei	KEN	65	3		Nairobi	23 Jul
1:46.44		Mu Weiguo	CHN	9.5.72	2	AsiG	Hiroshima	12 Oct
1:46.49	Alfredo	Laheurta	ESP	21.3.64	4		Alcalá	2 Jul
1:46.50		Kim Yong-hwan	KOR	20.6.71	2	NC	Seoul	17 Jun
1:46.52	Paul	Ereng	KEN	22.8.67	7	WG	Helsinki	29 Jun
1:46.53	Jurgens	Kotze	RSA	11.4.73	2		Port Elizabeth	15 Apr
1:46.53	Joachim	Dehmel	GER	27.6.69	3		Ingolstadt	17 Jul
1:46.54	Craig	Winrow	GBR	22.12.71	6	TSB	London	15 Jul
	(70)							
1:46.60	Luis Javier	González	ESP	17.6.69	2		Granada	1 Jun
1:46.6A	Henry	Ongeta	KEN	68	1		Nairobi	30 Apr
1:46.64	Stephen	Ole Marai	KEN	11.11.62	1	Barth	Luxemburg	30 Jun
1:46.65	Ahmed	Belkessam	ALG	27.3.62	7		Rieti	28 Aug
1:46.66	Ronald	Thorne	BAR	18.3.71	1		Gainesville	16 Apr
1:46.69	Frédéric	Cornette	FRA	29.6.67	3	NC	Annecy	24 Jul
1:46.69	Pavel	Dolgushev	RUS	11.7.68	1		Sochi	10 Sep
1:46.7A	Joel	Marwa	KEN		1h		Nairobi	10 Jun
1:46.73	Oliver	Münzer	AUT	16.2.70	4	GP II	Linz	4 Jul
1:46.75	Robert	Kibet	KEN	15.12.65	2rB	ASV	Köln	21 Aug
	(80)							
1:46.76	Alexander	Adam	GER	10.5.68	8		Lappeenranta	26 Jul
1:46.76	Terrance	Herrington	USA	31.7.66	5	vAfr	Durham	13 Aug
1:46.80	Andrés M	Díaz	ESP	12.7.69	5		Alcalá	2 Jul
1:46.82	Dean	Kenneally	AUS	8.3.67	1		Canberra	28 Jan
1:46.82	Vyacheslav	Shabunin	RUS	27.9.69	2		Sochi	10 Sep

Mark	Name		Nat	Born	Pos	Meet	Venue	Date
1:46.82	Mohamed	Suleiman	QAT	23.11.69	4	AsiG	Hiroshima	12 Oct
1:46.83	Jason	Pyrah	USA	6.4.69	6	vAfr	Durham	13 Aug
1:46.84	Terril	Davis	USA	21.4.68	1	USOF	Edwardsville	10 Jul
1:46.86	Sean	Abrahams	RSA	4.7.70	2		Stellenbosch	23 Feb
1:46.86A	Johannes	Makoena	RSA	25.9.69	3		Pretoria	18 Apr
	(90)							
1:46.87	Orlando	Castro	ESP	1.12.70	3		Baracaldo	18 Jun
1:46.90	Gilmar	Santos	BRA	16.12.70	4	Banes	São Paulo	21 May
1:46.90	Thomas	Ebner	AUT	17.11.71	5	GP II	Linz	4 Jul
1:46.92	Marius	van Heerden	RSA	8.9.74	1		Karlskrona	26 Jul
1:46.93	Tommy	Asinga	SUR	20.11.68	2	DogwR	Knoxville	8 Apr
1:46.94	Fermin	Cacho	ESP	16.2.69	4		Granada	1 Jun
1:46.94	José	Arconada	ESP	18.1.64	6		Alcalá	2 Jul
1:46.95	Alex	Morgan	JAM	27.12.72	3	NCAA	Boise	3 Jun
1:46.96	Joaquim	Cruz	BRA	12.3.63	4		Malmö	22 Aug
1:46.97	Erik	Nedeau	USA	30.8.71	1	IC4A	Fairfax	22 May
1:46.97	Alain	Miranda	CUB	19.10.75	2		Maia	16 Jul
1:46.98	George	Kersh	USA	3.7.68	4	NYG	New York	22 May
1:46.98	Greg	Rhymer	USA	22.2.72	1		Ypsilanti	25 May
	(103)							

Mark	Name		Nat	Born	Date
1:47.00	Andrew	Lill	GBR	71	15 Jul
1:47.0A	Simon	Langat	KEN		11 Jun
1:47.0A	Peter	Biwott	KEN	76	5 Jul
1:47.03	Mario	Vernon-Watson	JAM	71	6 May
1:47.04	Ivan	Komar	BLR	70	15 Jun
1:47.06	Barry	Acres	AUS	65	28 Jan
1:47.06	Edgar M	de Oliveira	BRA	67	17 Sep
1:47.09	Rich	Kenah	USA	70	4 Jun
1:47.10	Piotr	Piekarski	POL	64	23 Jul
1:47.14	Simon	Lewin	AUS	72	28 Jan
1:47.19	Simon	Bowen	JAM	70	22 May
1:47.21	Paul	Byrne	AUS	76	28 Jan
1:47.21	Barnabas	Kinyor	KEN	61	14 May
1:47.21	Jussi	Udelhoven	GER	66	10 Jun
1:47.23	Sammy	Koskei	KEN	61	29 Jul
1:47.24	Carsten	Otte	GER	71	15 Jun
1:47.27	Anthony	Abrahams	RSA	73	23 Feb
1:47.30	Peter	Philipp	SUI	72	17 Aug
1:47.3	Luis	Migueles	ARG	65	21 Jun
1:47.3A	Alfred	Sodia	KEN		15 Jul
1:47.31	Andrzej	Zahorski	POL	74	23 Jul
1:47.32	Julius	Achon	UGA	76	23 Aug
1:47.33	Lee	Byars	RSA	71	5 Apr
1:47.34	Jean-Christophe	Vialettes	FRA	67	17 Jun
1:47.34	Mark	Dailey	USA	68	12 Jul
1:47.35	Andréw	Beecher	JAM	70	2 Jul
1:47.35	Clive	Terrelonge	JAM	69	31 Jul
1:47.37	Conrad	Nichols	USA	73	3 Jun
1:47.39	Andrey	Butkovskiy	BLR	71	10 Jul
1:47.40	Andrey	Sudnik	BLR	67	4 Jul
1:47.40	Robin	Van Helden	NED	65	30 Jul
1:47.4A	Boniface	Kamaru	KEN		21 May
1:47.44	Brandon	Rock	USA	72	16 Jun
1:47.45	Imram	Sillah	GER	69	3 Jul
1:47.45	Robert	Kiplagat	KEN	70	22 Aug
1:47.48	William	Best	CAN	70	22 Aug
1:47.49	Ngumiso	Mdziniso	SWZ		22 Aug
1:47.50	Brad	Sumner	USA	70	17 Jul
1:47.5A	Geoffrey	Seurey	KEN	67	10 Jun
1:47.5A	Julius	Kipkoech	KEN	68	10 Jun
1:47.53	Elliott	Gaskins	USA	74	25 May
1:47.53	Patrick	Grammens	BEL	71	30 Jul
1:47.56	Jörgen	Zaki	SWE	72	22 Aug
1:47.57	David	Wilson	GBR	68	22 Aug
1:47.58	Tim	Cherry	AUS	67	24 Feb
1:47.58	Cliffie	Miller	RSA	64	12 Jun
1:47.58	Antonio	Franco	ESP	74	18 Jun
	(150)				
1:47.6	Benvenuto	Silva	BRA	72	15 May
1:47.6	Kader	Chékhémani	FRA	71	29 Jun
1:47.60	Carlos	Ward	USA	63	16 Jun
1:47.6A	Japhet	Kimutai	KEN	75	5 Jul
1:47.60	Carlos	Ward	USA	63	16 Jun
1:47.61	Alejandro	De Miguel	ESP	69	18 Jun
1:47.61	Javier	Soto	PUR	70	24 Jul
1:47.62	Shaun	Benefield	USA	72	3 Jun
1:47.62	Jens-Peter	Herold	GER	65	29 Jul
1:47.63	Abd. Hassan	Abdulrahman	QAT	77	4 Jul
1:47.64	Kevin	Sullivan	CAN	74	29 Jun
1:47.65	Isaac	Viciosa	ESP	69	25 Jun
1:47.66	Michael	Graham	USA	67	8 Jun
1:47.66	Reyes	Estévez	ESP	76	3 Aug
1:47.68	David	Krummenacker	USA	75	21 May
1:47.69	Pavel	Soukop	TCH	71	21 Jul
1:47.7	Valeriy	Starodubtsev	RUS	62	29 May
1:47.71	Joseph	Chepsorir	KEN	71	9 Apr
1:47.72	Michael	Joubert	AUS	70	28 Jan
1:47.74	Andrey	Bulkovskiy	UKR	72	29 Jun
1:47.75	Tony	Scott	AUS	71	5 Feb
1:47.76A	Henry	Lebo	KEN		18 Jun
1:47.76	Jamal Abdi	Hassan	QAT	72	21 Aug
1:47.78	Mike	Macinko	USA	67	4 Jun
1:47.79	Tomi	Kankare	FIN	72	29 Jun
1:47.80	Matthew	Landy	AUS	72	28 Jan
1:47.80	Ion	Bogde	ROM	72	18 Jun
1:47.80	Marco	Chiavarini	ITA	72	24 Jul
1:47.8A	Philip	Kibitok	KEN		11 Jun
1:47.81	Albert	Royster	USA	74	21 May
1:47.83	Dudley	Dawkins	JAM	72	28 May
1:47.85	Slobodan	Popovic	YUG	62	11 Aug
1:47.88	Frank	van Thiel	GER	69	23 May
1:47.89	Mark	Grey	JAM	71	25 May
1:47.89	Wieslaw	Paradowski	POL	73	23 Jul
1:47.9	Yevgeniy	Averbukh	RUS	69	29 May
1:47.90	Scott	Peters	USA	71	1 May
1:47.90	Fotis	Deligiannis	GRE	71	5 Jun
1:47.90	Joe	King	USA	72	16 Jun
	(189)				
1:47.91	Warren	Sherman	USA	72	25 May
1:47.92	Donnell	Johnson	USA	70	21 May
1:47.94	Khalifa	Kasmi	MAR		4 Jul
1:47.95	Thierry	Caquelard	FRA	66	17 Jun
1:47.96	Patrick	Schmitt	SUI	70	25 Jun
1:47.98A	Pieter	van Tonder	RSA	75	18 Apr
1:47.98	Simon	Doyle	AUS	66	25 Jun

Mark	Name		Nat	Born	Pos	Meet	Venue	Date
Indoors								
1:46.19	Paul	Ereng	KEN	22.8.67	1		Karlsruhe	1 Mar
1:46.35	Luis Javier	González	ESP	17.6.69	1		Sevilla	3 Feb
1:46.76	Ivan	Komar	BLR	18.3.70	1		Stuttgart	6 Feb
1:46.91	Rob	van Helden	NED	6.2.65	3		Karlsruhe	1 Mar
1:47.03	Michael	Wildner	AUT	70				1 Mar
1:47.24	Anatoliy	Makarevich	BLR	70				5 Feb
1:47.63	Gary	Brown	GBR	67				12 Feb
1:47.75	Marco	Runge	GER	71				6 Feb
1:47.82	Leon	Haan	NED	68				6 Feb

1000 METRES

Mark	Name		Nat	Born	Pos	Meet	Venue	Date
2:15.91	Vénuste	Niyongabo	BUR	9.12.73	1		Madrid	6 Sep
2:16.65		Niyongabo	BUR		1		Parma	12 Jun
2:18.71	Torbjörn	Johansson	SWE	23.1.70	1		Karlstad	7 Jul
2:18.73	José Luiz	Barbosa	BRA	27.5.61	1		San Diego	8 Jul
2:18.82	Rüdiger	Stenzel	GER	16.4.68	1		Hamburg	27 Jul
2:18.82	Joao	N'Tyamba	ANO	20.3.68	2		Hamburg	27 Jul
2:18.90	Edgar	de Oliveira	BRA	11.11.67	3		Hamburg	27 Jul
2:19.10	Gennaro	Di Napoli	ITA	5.3.68	1		Bolzano	10 Sep
2:19.23A	Fermin	Cacho	ESP	16.2.69	1		Soria	8 Jul
2:19.26	Jama Mohamed	Aden	SOM	62	4		Hamburg	27 Jul
2:19.40	Jonah	Birir	KEN	12.12.71	2		Bolzano	10 Sep
	(10)							
2:19.5	Guy	Nunige	FRA	66				7 Jul
2:19.54	Stephen	Ole Marai	KEN	62				6 Sep
2:19.55	Arthémon	Hatungimana	BUR	74				13 Sep
2:19.56	Isaac	Viciosa	ESP	69				6 Sep
2:19.68	José M	Cerezo	ESP	73				6 Sep
2:19.76	Kevin	Sullivan	CAN	74				19 Aug
2:19.82A	Brian	Treacy	GBR	71				8 Jul
2:19.99	Tomas	De Teresa	ESP	68				6 Sep
Indoors								
2:19.23	Jens-Peter	Herold	GER	2.6.65	1		Berlin	4 Feb
2:19.57	Mark	Eplinius	GER	70				4 Feb
2:19.95	Marco	Runge	GER	71				4 Feb

1500 METRES

Mark	Name		Nat	Born	Pos	Meet	Venue	Date
3:30.61	Noureddine	Morceli	ALG	28.2.70	1	BNP	Villeneuve d'Ascq	8 Jul
3:30.66	Vénuste	Niyongabo	BUR	9.12.73	2	BNP	Villeneuve d'Ascq	8 Jul
3:30.72		Morceli			1	TSB	London	15 Jul
3:30.95		Niyongabo			1	Nik	Nice	18 Jul
3:31.16		Niyongabo			1	ISTAF	Berlin	30 Aug
3:31.98		Niyongabo			1	ASV	Köln	21 Aug
3:32.25		Niyongabo			1	Herc	Monaco	2 Aug
3:32.71	Azzeddine	Sediki	MAR	21.5.70	2	Nik	Nice	18 Jul
3:32.73	Mohamed	Suleiman	QAT	23.11.69	2	ASV	Köln	21 Aug
3:33.61	Hicham	El Guerrouj	MAR	14.9.74	3	Nik	Nice	18 Jul
3:33.63	Abdi	Bile	SOM	28.12.62	2	Herc	Monaco	2 Aug
3:34.03		Sediki			3	ASV	Köln	21 Aug
3:34.09		Morceli			1	DNG	Stockholm	12 Jul
3:34.12	Atoi	Boru	KEN	25.10.73	1		Rieti	28 Aug
3:34.35		Niyongabo			1	VD	Bruxelles	19 Aug
3:34.42	Gennaro	Di Napoli	ITA	5.3.68	3	Herc	Monaco	2 Aug
3:34.43		Boru			4	ASV	Köln	21 Aug
3:34.43		Suleiman			2		Rieti	28 Aug
3:34.44	Moses	Kiptanui	KEN	10.10.71	3		Rieti	28 Aug
3:34.51		Bile			4		Rieti	28 Aug
3:34.54+		Niyongabo			1'	Bisl	Oslo	22 Jul
3:34.70		Morceli			1	WCp	London	10 Sep
3:34.72	Benson	Koech	KEN	10.11.74	5	ASV	Köln	21 Aug
3:34.75	Eric	Dubus	FRA	28.2.66	4	Nik	Nice	18 Jul
3:34.84	Branko	Zorko	CRO	1.7.67	4	Herc	Monaco	2 Aug
3:34.96	Steve	Holman	USA	2.3.70	2	DNG	Stockholm	12 Jul
3:34.96	Marcus	O'Sullivan	IRL	22.12.61	5		Rieti	28 Aug
3:35.02		O'Sullivan			5	Herc	Monaco	2 Aug
3:35.10		Niyongabo			1	GGala	Roma	8 Jun
3:35.13		Koech			6	Herc	Monaco	2 Aug
	(30/14)							
3:35.27	Fermin	Cacho	ESP	16.2.69	1	EC	Helsinki	9 Aug
3:35.32	Matthew	Yates	GBR	4.2.69	2	ISTAF	Berlin	30 Aug
3:35.35	David	Kibet	KEN	24.11.63	8	Herc	Monaco	2 Aug
3:35.38	Ahmed	Ibrahim Warsama	QAT	4.2.66	7		Rieti	28 Aug
3:35.44	Jens-Peter	Herold	GER	2.6.65	9	Herc	Monaco	2 Aug

Mark	Name		Nat	Born	Pos	Meet	Venue	Date
3:35.65	Jonah	Birir	KEN	12.12.71	5	Nik	Nice	18 Jul
	(20)							
3:35.83	Gary	Lough	GBR	6.7.70	3	TSB	London	15 Jul
3:35.84	Rachid	El Basir	MAR	4.10.68	7	ASV	Köln	21 Aug
3:35.99	Samir	Benfarès	FRA	6.6.68	9		Rieti	28 Aug
3:36.01	Isaac	Viciosa	ESP	26.12.69	2	EC	Helsinki	9 Aug
3:36.03	Giuseppe	D'Urso	ITA	15.9.69	2	GGala	Roma	8 Jun
3:36.12	Rüdiger	Stenzel	GER	16.4.68	6	ISTAF	Berlin	30 Aug
3:36.21	Simon	Doyle	AUS	9.11.66	3	GGala	Roma	8 Jun
3:36.23	Niall	Bruton	IRL	27.10.71	5	TSB	London	15 Jul
3:36.31	Marc	Davis	USA	17.12.69	1		Malmö	22 Aug
3:36.53	David	Strang	GBR	13.12.68	6	TSB	London	15 Jul
	(30)							
3:36.54	Graham	Hood	CAN	2.4.72	4	DNG	Stockholm	12 Jul
3:36.56	William	Tanui	KEN	22.2.64	8	Nik	Nice	18 Jul
3:36.62	Alessandro	Lambruschini	ITA	7.1.65	10	Herc	Monaco	2 Aug
3:36.70	Reuben	Chesang	KEN	66	1	CG	Victoria	28 Aug
3:36.73	Abdelkader	Chékhémani	FRA	18.7.71	5	BNP	Villeneuve d'Ascq	8 Jul
3:36.78	Kevin	Sullivan	CAN	20.3.74	2	CG	Victoria	28 Aug
3:36.80	Jim	Spivey	USA	7.3.60	1		Lappeenranta	26 Jul
3:36.82	Terrance	Herrington	USA	31.7.66	7	ISTAF	Berlin	30 Aug
3:36.99	Andrey	Bulkovskiy	UKR	22.7.72	2	Slov	Bratislava	1 Jun
3:37.04	Driss	Maazouzi	MAR	69	2	NC	Annecy	24 Jul
	(40)							
3:37.04	Haile	Gebrselassie	ETH	18.4.73	2		Hechtel	30 Jul
3:37.20	John	Mayock	GBR	26.10.70	8	TSB	London	15 Jul
3:37.21	Dominique	Löser	GER	21.1.73	12	ASV	Köln	21 Aug
3:37.22	Paul	Vandegrift	USA	16.5.69	9	TSB	London	15 Jul
3:37.24	Anacleto	Jiménez	ESP	24.2.67	1		Alcalá	2 Jul
3:37.60	Johan	Landsman	RSA	12.5.64	9	DNG	Stockholm	12 Jul
3:37.61	Edgar	de Oliveira	BRA	11.11.67	2		Malmö	22 Aug
3:37.74	Pat	Scammell	AUS	15.4.61	3		Hechtel	30 Jul
3:37.85	Davide	Tirelli	ITA	12.8.66	10	Nik	Nice	18 Jul
3:37.86	Kevin	McKay	GBR	9.2.69	3		Rhede	29 Jul
	(50)							
3:37.93	Whaddon	Niewoudt	RSA	6.1.70	1		La Celle St Cloud	4 Jul
3:37.99	Samuel	Kipserem	KEN	68	4		Rhede	29 Jul
3:38.01	Manuel	Pancorbo	ESP	7.7.66	6	GGala	Roma	8 Jun
3:38.03	Christian	Cushing-murray	USA	18.10.67	11	ISTAF	Berlin	30 Aug
3:38.07	José	Valente	BRA	1.7.69	5	Banes	São Paulo	21 May
3:38.10	Julius	Kipkoech	KEN	68	5	CG	Victoria	28 Aug
3:38.11	Mogens	Guldberg	DEN	2.8.63	10	TSB	London	15 Jul
3:38.12	Noureddine	Béhar	MAR	8.4.66	2		La Celle St Cloud	4 Jul
3:38.18	Moussa	Barkaoui	MAR	71	4	FRA Ch	Annecy	24 Jul
3:38.20	Jason	Pyrah	USA	6.4.69	2	NC	Knoxville	18 Jun
	(60)							
3:38.25	Richard	Potts	NZL	13.7.71	5		Rhede	29 Jul
3:38.28	Mustapha	El Ahmadi	MAR	68	3		La Celle St Cloud	4 Jul
3:38.31	Erik	Nedeau	USA	30.8.71	3	NC	Knoxville	18 Jun
3:38.37	Abdellah	Abdelhak	MAR	13.8.68	2		Alcalá	2 Jul
3:38.38	Phillip	Kandie	KEN		3		Alcalá	2 Jul
3:38.41	Christoph	Impens	BEL	9.12.69	10	BNP	Villeneuve d'Ascq	8 Jul
3:38.46	Werner	Edler-Muhr	AUT	4.2.69	6		Rhede	29 Jul
3:38.47	Cleophas	Bitok	KEN	73	4	Slov	Bratislava	1 Jun
3:38.49	Dieter	Baumann	GER	9.2.65	1		Duisburg	12 Jun
3:38.56	Dieudonné	Kwizera	BUR	6.6.67	2		Rovereto	24 Jul
	(70)							
3:38.61	Vyacheslav	Shabunin	RUS	27.9.69	4		St Denis	10 Jun
3:38.69	Alexandre	Billaudaz	FRA	3.3.72	4		La Celle St Cloud	4 Jul
3:38.71	M'Hamed	Choumassi	MAR	2.12.69	5		La Celle St Cloud	4 Jul
3:38.73	Ovidiu	Olteanu	ROM	6.8.70	6		La Celle St Cloud	4 Jul
3:38.74	Bob	Kennedy	USA	18.8.70	4	NC	Knoxville	18 Jun
3:38.76	Thomas	Lotik	KEN		3		Duisburg	12 Jun
3:38.78	Sergey	Melnikov	RUS	8.11.68	4	Barth	Luxemburg	30 Jun
3:38.80	Rod	Finch	GBR	5.8.67	2	APM	Hengelo	4 Jun
3:38.84	Matthew	Birir	KEN	5.7.72	1		Granada	1 Jun
3:38.85	Marko	Koers	NED	3.11.72	11	DNG	Stockholm	12 Jul
	(80)							
3:38.85	Antonio	Herrador	ESP	21.11.66	4		Hechtel	30 Jul

Mark	Name		Nat	Born	Pos	Meet	Venue	Date
3:38.86	Mark	Dailey	USA	11.12.68	2	PennR	Philadelphia	30 Apr
3:38.90	Andrea	Giocondi	ITA	17.1.69	11		Rieti	28 Aug
3:38.93	Brian	Treacy	GBR	29.7.71	6	CG	Victoria	28 Aug
3:38.99	Joaquim	Cruz	BRA	12.3.63	2	NC	Rio de Janeiro	18 Sep
3:39.05	Mark	Croghan	USA	8.1.68	6	iDAG	Göteborg	24 Aug
3:39.07	Nixon	Kiprotich	KEN	4.12.62	12	DNG	Stockholm	12 Jul
3:39.13	Torino	Viali	ITA	16.9.60	4		Padova	10 Jul
3:39.15	Mateo	Cañellas	ESP	27.4.72	4		Alcalá	2 Jul
3:39.19	Simon	Vroemen	NED	11.5.69	2		Nivelles	23 Jul
	(90)							
3:39.19	Stephen	Green	GBR	18.2.71	7	CG	Victoria	28 Aug
3:39.23	Tim	Pitcher	USA	11.10.70	3	PennR	Philadelphia	30 Apr
3:39.28	Reyes	Estévez	ESP	2.8.76	9	VD	Bruxelles	19 Aug
3:39.36	Matt	Giusto	USA	25.10.66	5	Barth	Luxemburg	30 Jun
3:39.41	Robert	Kiplagat	DEN/KEN	12.12.70	7	iDAG	Göteborg	24 Aug
3:39.43	Andrés	Martínez	ESP	8.2.68	5		Alcalá	2 Jul
3:39.44	Andy	Keith	GBR	25.12.71	6	TSB	Edinburgh	8 Jul
3:39.47	Lahoussine	Siba	MAR	15.2.73	8		Rhede	29 Jul
3:39.56	Guy	Nunige	FRA	11.2.66	3		Luzern	29 Jun
3:39.58	Abdelhamid	Slimani	ALG	.71	12		Rieti	28 Aug
	(100)							

Mark	Name		Nat	Born	Date
3:39.58	Peter	Philipp	SUI	72	30 Aug
3:39.78	Julius	Achon	UGA	76	24 Jul
3:39.86	Kim Soon-hyung		KOR	73	11 May
3:39.91	Milan	Drahonovsky	TCH	66	24 Aug
3:39.96	Johan	Botha	RSA	74	5 Apr
3:39.99	Massimo	Pegoretti	ITA	74	8 Jun
3:40.00	João	N'Tyamba	ANO	68	21 May
3:40.00	Michael	Busch	GER	66	12 Jun
3:40.01	Jason	Stewart	USA	72	30 Apr
3:40.06	Bahadur	Prasad	IND	65	3 Feb
3:40.06		Lee Jin-il	KOR	73	11 May
3:40.11	Shane	Healy	IRL	68	15 Jul
3:40.15	Darryl	Frerker	USA	63	18 Jun
3:40.17	Glen	Stewart	GBR	70	8 Jul
3:40.2	Simon	Lewin	AUS	72	17 Mar
3:40.22	Ali	Hakimi	TUN	76	4 Sep
3:40.23	Luis Miguel	Martin	ESP	72	6 Sep
3:40.24	Johan	Fourie	RSA	59	5 Apr
3:40.26	Réda	Abdenouz	ALG	68	10 Jun
3:40.34	Ajat	Rakipov	BLR	68	5 Jun
3:40.34	Carlton	Jones	USA	65	10 Jul
3:40.35	Iam	Grime	GBR	70	21 Aug
3:40.38	Philemon	Hanneck	ZIM	71	8 Jul
3:40.38	Michal	Bartoszak	POL	70	22 Aug
3:40.40	Cyrille	Laventure	FRA	64	30 Jun
3:40.41	Ronnie	Harris	USA	65	4 Jun
3:40.43	Martin	Johns	NZL	69	17 Apr
3:40.43	Dave	Wittman	USA	69	18 Jun
3:40.46	André	Bucher	SUI	76	24 Jul
3:40.47	Matthew	Barnes	GBR	68	8 Jul
3:40.57	Wander	Moura	BRA	69	18 Sep
	3:39.96				13 Aug
3:40.59	Esau	Faro	RSA	74	5 Apr
3:40.59	Alberto	Garcia	ESP	71	6 Sep
3:40.60	Michael	Buchleitner	AUT	69	10 Jun
3:40.61	Francois	Van Rensburg	RSA	70	23 Apr
3:40.62	Passmore	Furusa	ZIM	70	2 Apr
3:40.65	Mark	Sivieri	USA	73	18 Jun
3:40.69	Christoph	Meyer	GER	66	12 Jun
3:40.70	João Carlos	Leite	BRA	68	21 May
3:40.7	Bekim	Bahtiri	SLO	72	26 Jul
3:40.72	Javier	Rodriguez	ESP	74	5 Aug
3:40.72	Torsten	Kallweit	GER	68	29 Jul
3:40.76	Peter	O'Donoghue	AUS	61	30 Jan
3:40.77	Amos	Rota	ITA	70	8 Jun
3:40.81	Kobie van der Westhuizen		RSA	69	5 Apr
3:40.81	Stephan	Plätzer	GER	66	12 Jun
3:40.81	Shaun	Creighton	AUS	67	29 Jun
3:40.84	António	Travasos	POR	71	18 Jun
3:40.86	Jamey	Harris	USA	71	20 May
	(150)				
3:40.88	Scott	MacDonald	CAN	73	14 May
3:40.90	Youcef	Allem	FRA	69	10 Jul
3:40.91	Jim	Sorenson	USA	67	20 May
3:40.91	Jason	Casiano	USA	73	29 Jul
3:40.93		Mu Weiguo	CHN	72	16 Oct
3:41.02	Steffan	White	GBR	72	21 Aug
3:41.06	Brad	Jones	USA		1 Jun
3:41.07	Patrik	Johansson	SWE	72	22 Aug
3:41.09	Philip	Mosima	KEN	76	24 Jul
3:41.1	Sa'ad Shaddad	Al-Asmari	SAU	68	28 Feb
3:41.11	Igor	Leshchinskiy	UKR	73	23 Jul
3:41.17	Anatoliy	Butkovski	BLR	71	17 Jun
3:41.22A	Geoffrey	Seurey	KEN	67	23 Jul
3:41.25	Eliud	Barngetuny	KEN	73	25 Jun
3:41.28	David	Wilson	GBR	68	4 Jun
3:41.3	Nadir	Bosch	FRA	73	27 Jul
3:41.30	Jerry	Schumacher	USA	70	18 Jun
3:41.31	Bashir Ahmed	Boushra	QAT	77	21 Aug
3:41.31	Michael	Gottschalk	GER	72	21 Aug
3:41.31	Misuhiro	Okuyama	JPN	66	16 Oct
3:41.34	Christian	Vagner	FRA	65	4 Jul
3:41.35	Jim	Howarth	USA	66	25 May
3:41.37	Fita	Bayissa	ETH	72	28 May
3:41.37	Marcel	Laros	NED	71	4 Jun
3:41.39	Des	English	IRL	67	28 Aug
3:41.43	Mario	Silva	POR	61	18 Jun
3:41.45	Tendai	Chimusasa	ZIM	71	15 Jun
3:41.45	Kenneth	Tholén	SWE	69	22 Aug
3:41.48	Ian	Gillespie	GBR	70	10 Jun
3:41.49	Robert	Kibet	KEN	64	28 Aug

Indoors (+ during 1 mile)

Mark	Name		Nat	Born	Pos	Venue	Date
3:38.4+	Mickaël	Damian	FRA	9.11.69	-	Karlsruhe	1 Mar

Mark	Name		Nat	Born	Date
3:41.0	Robin	van Helden	NED	65	13 Feb
3:41.11	Rudy	Vlasselaer	BEL	65	29 Jan
3:41.36	Stephan	Kabat	GER	70	30 Jan

1 MILE

Mark	Name		Nat	Born	Pos	Meet	Venue	Date
3:48.67	Noureddine	Morceli	ALG	28.2.70	1	GWG	St Peterburg	26 Jul
3:48.94	Vénuste	Niyongabo	BUR	9.12.73	1	Bisl	Oslo	22 Jul
3:50.67	Abdi	Bile	SOM	28.12.62	2	Bisl	Oslo	22 Jul
3:50.91	Steve	Holman	USA	2.3.70	3	Bisl	Oslo	22 Jul
3:51.32	Mohamed	Suleiman	QAT	23.11.69	4	Bisl	Oslo	22 Jul
3:52.28		Bile			2	GWG	St Peterburg	26 Jul
3:52.48	David	Kibet	KEN	24.11.63	5	Bisl	Oslo	22 Jul
3:52.72	Isaac	Viciosa	ESP	26.12.69	6	Bisl	Oslo	22 Jul
3:52.77		Holman			3	GWG	St Peterburg	26 Jul
3:53.54	Vyacheslav	Shabunin	RUS	27.9.69	5	GWG	St Peterburg	26 Jul
3:53.64	Kevin	McKay	GBR	9.2.69	7	Bisl	Oslo	22 Jul
3:53.71	Hicham	El Guerrouj	MAR	14.9.74	8	Bisl	Oslo	22 Jul
3:53.86	Marcus	O'Sullivan	IRL	22.12.61	6	GWG	St Peterburg	26 Jul
3:54.30	David	Strang	GBR	13.12.68	9	Bisl	Oslo	22 Jul
3:54.82		Kibet			6	GWG	St Peterburg	26 Jul
3:55.10	Niall	Bruton	IRL	27.10.71	10	Bisl	Oslo	22 Jul
3:55.11	Simon	Doyle	AUS	9.11.66	1		Melbourne	24 Feb
3:55.28	Andrey	Bulkovskiy	UKR	22.7.72	1	WK	Zürich	17 Aug
3:55.38	Terrance	Herrington	USA	31.7.66	7	GWG	St Peterburg	26 Jul
3:55.50		Holman			2	WK	Zürich	17 Aug
	(20/16)							
3:55.67	Azzeddine	Sediki	MAR	21.5.70	3	WK	Zürich	17 Aug
3:55.83	Rüdiger	Stenzel	GER	16.4.68	4	WK	Zürich	17 Aug
3:55.85	Jens-Peter	Herold	GER	2.6.65	5	WK	Zürich	17 Aug
3:56.21	Bob	Kennedy	USA	18.8.70	1	Pre	Eugene	4 Jun
	(20)							
3:56.34	William	Tanui	KEN	22.2.64	8	GWG	St Peterburg	26 Jul
3:56.89	Pat	Scammell	AUS	15.4.61	2	NEC	Melbourne	24 Feb
3:57.05	Christian	Cushing-murray	USA	18.10.67	9	GWG	St Peterburg	26 Jul
3:57.21	Whaddon	Niewoudt	RSA	6.1.70	1		Port Elizabeth	15 Apr
3:57.35	Edgar	de Oliveira	BRA	11.11.67	2	Pre	Eugene	4 Jun
3:57.43	Carlton	Jones	USA	20.12.65	3	Pre	Eugene	4 Jun
3:57.47	Shannon	Lemora	USA	24.3.70	4	Pre	Eugene	4 Jun
3:57.88	Azat	Rakipov	BLR	25.11.68	10	GWG	St Peterburg	26 Jul
3:58.05	David	Wittman	USA	4.7.69	5	Pre	Eugene	4 Jun
3:58.18	Ovidiu	Olteanu	ROM	6.8.70	1		Bucuresti	29 May
	(30)							

Mark	Name		Nat	Born	Date
3:58.20	Francois	van Rensburg	RSA	70	25 Mar
3:58.25	Benny	McIntosh	USA	66	4 Jun
3:58.27	Atoi	Boru	KEN	73	24 Feb
3:58.34	John	Mayock	GBR	70	4 Sep
3:58.39	Matt	Barnes	GBR	68	25 Jun
3:58.71	Des	English	IRL	67	25 Jun
3:58.73	Martin	Keino	KEN	72	4 Jun
3:58.74	Jim	Svenøy	NOR	72	22 Jul
3:58.81	Gennaro	Di Napoli	ITA	68	4 Sep
3:58.89	Pavel	Dolgushev	RUS	68	25 Jun
3:58.94	Jonah	Birir	KEN	71	4 Sep
3:58.97	Andréw	Keith	GBR	71	25 Jun
3:58.99	Robert	Kibet	KEN	64	17 Aug
3:59.14A	Johan	Landsman	RSA	64	15 Apr
3:59.19	Chris	Katon	USA	70	4 Jun
3:59.20	Branko	Zorko	CRO	67	4 Sep
3:59.23	Shane	Healy	IRL	68	25 Jun
3:59.30	Jon	Warren	USA	65	4 Jun
3:59.36A	Johan	Fourie	RSA	59	15 Apr
3:59.48	Gary	Lough	GBR	70	4 Sep
	(50)				
3:59.57	Greg	Whiteley	USA	67	4 Jun
3:59.75	Jim	Howarth	USA	66	4 Jun
3:59.76A	Scott	Harris	RSA	68	15 Apr
3:59.96	Robbie	Johnston	NZL	67	19 Feb

Indoors

Mark	Name		Nat	Born	Pos	Venue	Date
3:53.74	Jens-Peter	Herold	GER	2.6.65	1	Karlsruhe	1 Mar
3:54.16	Éric	Dubus	FRA	28.2.66	2	Karlsruhe	1 Mar
3:54.28	Michael	Buchleitner	AUT	14.10.69	3	Karlsruhe	1 Mar
3:55.76	Mickaël	Damian	FRA	9.11.69	4	Karlsruhe	1 Mar
3:56.29	Andy	Keith	GBR	25.12.71	2	Boston	22 Jan
3:56.44	Mark	Carroll	IRL	15.1.72	3	Boston	28 Jan
3:57.50	Mirco	Döring	GER	21.7.71	5	Karlsruhe	1 Mar
3:57.71	Moses	Kiptanui	KEN	10.10.71	2	Fairfax	6 Feb
3:57.88	Paul	Vandegrift	USA	16.5.69	3	Fairfax	6 Feb
3:58.00o/s	Kevin	Sullivan	CAN	20.3.74	1	Notre Dame (o/s)	5 Feb
3:58.15	Eamonn	Coghlan	IRL	21.11.52	1	Allston	20 Feb

Mark	Name		Nat	Born	Date
3:58.39	Michal	Bartoszak	POL	70	6 Feb
3:58.67	Reuben	Reina	USA	67	28 Jan
3:59.40	o/sScott	MacDonald	CAN	73	5 Feb
3:59.42	Mark	Dailey	USA	68	6 Feb
3:59.6	Steve	Green	GBR	71	4 Mar
3:59.85	Mark	Sivieri	USA	72	28 Jan

2000 METRES

Mark	Name		Nat	Born	Pos	Meet	Venue	Date
5:00.61	Pascal	Thiébaut	FRA	6.6.59	1		Noisy le Grand	2 Jul
5:01.0+	Mohamed	Choumassi	MAR	2.12.69	1+	Herc	Monaco	2 Aug
5:01.2+	Marcus	O'Sullivan	IRL	22.12.61	1+	Nik	Nice	18 Jul
5:01.3+	Noureddine	Morceli	ALG	28.2.70	2+	Herc	Monaco	2 Aug
5:01.3+	Moses	Kiptanui	KEN	10.10.71	1+	ASV	Köln	21 Aug
5:01.36	Abdellah	Béhar	FRA	5.7.63	2		Noisy le Grand	2 Jul
5:01.6+	Aloÿs	Nizigama	BUR	18.6.66	3+	Nik	Nice	18 Jul
5:01.6+	Haile	Gebrselassie	ETH	18.4.73	3+	Herc	Monaco	2 Aug
5:02.0+	Paul	Bitok	KEN	26.6.70	4+	Nik	Nice	18 Jul
5:02.47	Ovidiu	Olteanu	ROM	6.8.70	3		Noisy le Grand	2 Jul
5:02.5+e	Joseph	Chesire	KEN	12.11.57	2+	ASV	Köln	21 Aug
5:02.6+	Bob	Kennedy	USA	18.8.70	5+	Nik	Nice	18 Jul
5:02.6+e	Brahim	Jabbour	MAR	1.1.70	4+	Herc	Monaco	2 Aug

Mark	Name		Nat	Born	Date
5:05.45A	Francois	van Rensburg	RSA	70	18 Apr
5:05.83	Robbie	Johnston	NZL	67	19 Aug
5:06.64+	Laban	Chege	KEN	67	6 Jul
5:06.8+	Yobes	Ondieki	KEN	61	6 Jul
5:06.93	Robert	Kiplagat	KEN/DEN	72	8 Aug
Indoors					
5:03.88	Éric	Dubus	FRA	66	6 Feb
5:05.18	Sergey	Melnikov	RUS	68	6 Feb

3000 METRES

Mark	Name		Nat	Born	Pos	Meet	Venue	Date
7:25.11	Noureddine	Morceli	ALG	28.2.70	1	Herc	Monaco	2 Aug
7:34.36	Paul	Bitok	KEN	26.6.70	1	Nik	Nice	18 Jul
7:34.69	Dieter	Baumann	GER	9.2.65	1	ASV	Köln	21 Aug
7:34.74		Morceli			1		Narbonne	19 Jun
7:35.08	Aloÿs	Nizigama	BUR	18.6.66	2	Nik	Nice	18 Jul
7:35.23	Moses	Kiptanui	KEN	10.10.71	3	Nik	Nice	18 Jul
7:35.33	Bob	Kennedy	USA	18.8.70	4	Nik	Nice	18 Jul
7:36.21		Kiptanui			2	ASV	Köln	21 Aug
7:36.76	Khalid	Skah	MAR	29.1.67	3	ASV	Köln	21 Aug
7:37.49	Haile	Gebrselassie	ETH	18.4.73	2	Herc	Monaco	2 Aug
7:38.14	Salah	Hissou	MAR	72	4	ASV	Köln	21 Aug
7:39.12	Atiq	Naaji	FRA	21.11.66	2		Narbonne	19 Jun
7:39.29	Abdellah	Béhar	FRA	5.7.63	3	Herc	Monaco	2 Aug
7:39.65	Jim	Spivey	USA	7.3.60	4	Herc	Monaco	2 Aug
7:40.06	Fita	Bayissa	ETH	15.12.72	6	ASV	Köln	21 Aug
7:40.31	Brahim	Lahlafi	MAR	15.4.68	3		Narbonne	19 Jun
7:40.73		Nizigama			1	Athl	Lausanne	6 Jul
7:40.75	Stephane	Franke	GER	12.2.64	5	Herc	Monaco	2 Aug
7:42.15	Smail	Sghir	MAR	16.3.72	6	Nik	Nice	18 Jul
7:42.18	Abdi	Bile	SOM	28.12.62	8	ASV	Köln	21 Aug
7:42.5+		Skah			1+	iDAG	Göteborg	24 Aug
7:42.62	Robert	Denmark	GBR	23.11.68	2	Athl	Lausanne	6 Jul
7:42.8+	Marc	Davis	USA	17.12.69	2+	iDAG	Göteborg	24 Aug
7:42.90		Nizigama			4		Narbonne	19 Jun
7:43.3+		Lahlafi			3+	iDAG	Göteborg	24 Aug
7:43.75	Yobes	Ondieki	KEN	21.2.61	3	Athl	Lausanne	6 Jul
7:43.76	M'Hamed	Choumassi	MAR	2.12.69	5		Narbonne	19 Jun
7:43.92	Brahim	Jabbour	MAR	1.1.70	6	Herc	Monaco	2 Aug
7:43.99	Shaun	Creighton	AUS	14.5.67	4	Athl	Lausanne	6 Jul
7:44.65	Simon	Doyle	AUS	9.11.66	1	OD	Jena	3 Jun
	(30/24)							
7:44.83	Mohamed	Suleiman	QAT	23.11.69	2	OD	Jena	3 Jun
7:44.87	Moses	Tanui	KEN	20.8.65	8	Herc	Monaco	2 Aug
7:45.27	Ismael	Kirui	KEN	20.2.75	7	Nik	Nice	18 Jul
7:45.74	Frank	O'Mara	IRL	17.7.60	5	Athl	Lausanne	6 Jul
7:46.48	Francesco	Panetta	ITA	10.1.63	6	Athl	Lausanne	6 Jul
7:46.71	Phillimon	Hanneck	ZIM	12.5.71	4	OD	Jena	3 Jun
	(30)							
7:46.96	Matt	Giusto	USA	25.10.66	7	Athl	Lausanne	6 Jul
7:47.26	João	Junqueira	POR	24.6.65	1		Lisboa	31 Jul
7:47.87	Domingos	Castro	POR	22.11.63	2		Lisboa	31 Jul
7:47.88	Anacleto	Jiménez	ESP	24.2.67	8	Athl	Lausanne	6 Jul
7:48.13	Brahim	Boutayeb	MAR	15.8.67	8	Nik	Nice	18 Jul
7:48.26	Johnstone	Kipkoech	KEN	20.12.68	1	Slov	Bratislava	1 Jun
7:48.35	Francois	van Rensburg	RSA	2.8.70	5	OD	Jena	3 Jun
7:48.45	Laban	Chege	KEN	67	2	Slov	Bratislava	1 Jun
7:48.69	Worku	Bikila	ETH	70	10	ASV	Köln	21 Aug

Mark	Name		Nat	Born	Pos	Meet	Venue	Date
7:48.73	Róbert	Stefko	SVK	28.5.68	4	Slov	Bratislava	1 Jun
	(40)							
7:49.50	Thomas	Lotik	KEN		1		Pliezhausen	8 May
7:49.56	Michal	Bartoszak	POL	21.6.70	3		Arnsberg	29 May
7:49.76	Risto	Ulmala	FIN	7.5.63	1		Lappeenranta	26 Jul
7:49.84	Hicham	El Guerrouj	MAR	14.9.74	1		Meklnès	19 Mar
7:49.84	Mogens	Guldberg	DEN	2.8.63	10	Athl	Lausanne	6 Jul
7:49.94	Reuben	Reina	USA	16.11.67	11	Athl	Lausanne	6 Jul
7:50.09	Mohamed	Issangar	MAR	12.12.64	10	Nik	Nice	18 Jul
7:50.17	Eliud	Barngetuny	KEN	20.5.73	1		Rovereto	24 Jul
7:50.30	Mark	Rowland	GBR	7.3.63	2		Lappeenranta	26 Jul
7:50.33	Gennaro	Di Napoli	ITA	5.3.68	1		Trento	25 Sep
	(50)							
7:50.47	Ondoro	Osoro	KEN	3.12.67	3		Lappeenranta	26 Jul
7:50.52	Angelo	Carosi	ITA	20.1.64	2		Rovereto	24 Jul
7:50.54	Julius	Korir	KEN	5.12.63	6	Slov	Bratislava	1 Jun
7:50.58	Simeon	Rono	KEN	9.4.72	1		Stockholm	2 Aug
7:50.81	Mohamed	Belabbès	ALG	11.3.66	12	ASV	Köln	21 Aug
7:50.88	Richard	Kosgei	KEN	29.12.70	2		Madrid	6 Sep
7:50.94	Vyacheslav	Shabunin	RUS	27.9.69	4	Slov	Bratislava	1 Jun
7:51.00	Abel	Antón	ESP	24.10.62	3		Madrid	6 Sep
7:51.04	Antonio	Serrano	ESP	8.3.65	4		Madrid	6 Sep
7:51.15	Réda	Benzine	ALG	19.4.71	13	ASV	Köln	21 Aug
	(60)							
7:51.2	Eduardo	Henriques	POR	24.3.68	2		Vila Real	28 May
7:51.26	Gary	Staines	GBR	3.7.63	5		Lappeenranta	26 Jul
7:51.3	Toshinari	Takaoka	JPN	24.9.70	1		Yamaguchi	3 Apr
7:51.64	Steffen	Brand	GER	10.3.65	4		Arnsberg	29 May

7:51.99	Wander	Moura	BRA	69	29 Jul	7:53.39	Alessandro	Lambruschini	ITA	65	12 Jun
7:52.02	Yuichi	Tajiri	JPN	71	26 Jun	7:53.52	Sami	Alanen	FIN	71	26 Jun
7:52.2	José	Regalo	POR	63	28 May	7:53.67	Jonah	Koech	KEN	68	25 Sep
7:52.20	James	Songok	KEN	70	8 May	7:54.03	Hosea	Kogo	KEN	68	26 Jul
7:52.22	James	Kariuki	KEN	69	24 Jul	7:54.1	José	Ramos	POR	68	28 May
7:52.33	José Carlos	Adán	ESP	67	6 Sep	7:54.1	Antonio	Silio	ARG	66	15 Aug
7:52.35	Andrés	Martínez	ESP	68	3 Aug	7:54.30	Johan	Fourie	RSA	59	3 Jun
7:52.55	Johan	Landsman	RSA	64	6 Jul	7:54.31	Ralf	Dahmen	GER	68	21 Aug
7:52.74	Vincenzo	Modica	ITA	71	24 Jul	7:54.50	Mohamed	Ezzher	FRA	60	19 Jun
7:52.81	Joseph	Kimani	KEN	72	3 Jul	7:54.53	John	Downes	GBR	67	21 Jun
7:53.22	Matthew	Birir	KEN	72	25 May	7:54.66	Thierry	Pantel	FRA	64	19 Jun
7:53.26	Maurizio	Leone	ITA	73	24 Jul	7:54.68	Pat	Carroll	AUS	61	28 Jan
							(88)				

Indoors

7:41.46	Isaac	Viciosa	ESP	26.12.69	1		Sevilla	3 Feb
7:41.90	Enrique	Molina	ESP	25.2.68	2		Liévin	13 Feb
7:42.54	Anacleto	Jiménez	ESP	24.2.67	1	NC	Sevilla	27 Feb
7:47.90	Aïssa	Belaout	ALG	12.8.68	4		Sevilla	27 Feb
7:49.22	Vénuste	Niyongabo	BUR	9.12.73	1		Gent	9 Feb
7:49.83	Andy	Keith	GBR	25.12.71	1		Fairfax	6 Feb
7:49.85	Christoph	Impens	BEL	9.12.69	2		Gent	9 Feb
7:49.91	Éric	Dubus	FRA	28.2.66	5		Liévin	13 Feb
7:50.77	Khalid	Kairouani	MAR	66	1		Boston	22 Jan
7:50.85	Steffen	Brand	GER	10.3.65	1		Berlin	4 Feb
7:50.90	Josephat	Kapkory	KEN	2.1.67	1	NCAA	Indianapolis	12 Mar
7:51.00	Brendan	Mathias	CAN	12.8.69	3		Fairfax	6 Feb
7:51.24	Jim	Svenøy	NOR	22.4.72	2	NCAA	Indianapolis	12 Mar
7:51.35	Mark	Carroll	IRL	15.1.72	2		Boston	22 Jan

7:51.72	Danny	Lopez	USA	68	9 Feb	7:53.99	Ron	Harris	USA	65	6 Feb
7:52.34	Kim	Bauermeister	GER	70	13 Mar	7:53.99	Rod	Finch	GBR	67	13 Mar
7:52.37	Ovidiu	Olteanu	ROM	70	13 Mar	7:54.02	Luc	Krotwaar	NED	68	19 Feb
7:52.97	Pascal	Thiébaut	FRA	59	26 Feb	7:54.08	Greg	Whiteley	USA	67	6 Feb
7:53.10	Victor	Rojas	ESP	68	13 Feb	7:54.30	Pete	Weilenmann	USA	66	6 Feb
7:53.30	Gino	Van Geyte	BEL	67	16 Jan	7:54.56	Marcel	Laros	NED	71	19 Feb

2 MILES

8:09.01	Moses	Kiptanui	KEN	10.10.71	1		Hechtel	30 Jul
8:12.74	Marc	Davis	USA	17.12.69	1	iDAG	Göteborg	24 Aug
8:12.92	Khalid	Skah	MAR	29.1.67	2	iDAG	Göteborg	24 Aug
8:16.11	Brahim	Lahlafi	MAR	15.4.68	3	iDAG	Göteborg	24 Aug
8:26.83	Matt	Giusto	USA	25.10.66	1		Portland	22 May

Mark		Name	Nat	Born	Pos	Meet	Venue	Date
8:27.00	John	Downes	GBR	21.7.67	2		Hechtel	30 Jul
8:28.05	Bob	Kennedy	USA	18.8.70	2		Portland	22 May
8:28.05	Michal	Bartoszak	POL	21.6.70	4	iDAG	Göteborg	24 Aug
8:28.19	Paul	Vandegrift	USA	16.5.69	3		Portland	22 May

Mark	Name		Nat	Born	Date	Mark	Name		Nat	Born	Date
8:28.34	Simon	Chemoiywo	KEN	68	24 Aug	8:30.27	Wander	Moura	BRA	69	24 Aug
8:29.11	John	Gregorek	USA	60	22 May	8:32.84	Peter	Sherry	USA	68	22 May
8:29.12	Gary	Staines	GBR	63	24 Aug	8:33.76	Claes	Nyberg	SWE	71	24 Aug

5000 METRES

Mark		Name	Nat	Born	Pos	Meet	Venue	Date
12:56.96	Haile	Gebrselassie	ETH	18.4.73	1	APM	Hengelo	4 Jun
13:00.54	Khalid	Skah	MAR	29.1.67	1	BNP	Villeneuve d'Ascq	8 Jul
13:01.89		Skah			1	Bisl	Oslo	22 Jul
13:02.93	Bob	Kennedy	USA	18.8.70	2	Bisl	Oslo	22 Jul
13:03.36	Brahim	Lahlafi	MAR	15.4.68	3	Bisl	Oslo	22 Jul
13:03.85	Noureddine	Morceli	ALG	28.2.70	1	WK	Zürich	17 Aug
13:04.93	Salah	Hissou	MAR	72	4	Bisl	Oslo	22 Jul
13:05.93		Kennedy			2	BNP	Villeneuve d'Ascq	8 Jul
13:06.72	William	Sigei	KEN	11.10.69	1	TSB	London	15 Jul
13:07.30	Paul	Bitok	KEN	26.6.70	2	TSB	London	15 Jul
13:07.57	Simon	Chemoiywo	KEN	28.4.68	1	Herc	Monaco	2 Aug
13:07.58		Chemoiywo			3	TSB	London	15 Jul
13:07.70	Fita	Bayissa	ETH	15.12.72	2	WK	Zürich	17 Aug
13:07.84		Skah			3	WK	Zürich	17 Aug
13:07.88		Morceli			1		Rieti	28 Aug
13:08.62	Worku	Bikila	ETH	70	3	BNP	Villeneuve d'Ascq	8 Jul
13:09.55		Lahlafi			4	BNP	Villeneuve d'Ascq	8 Jul
13:10.30		Bikila			4	WK	Zürich	17 Aug
13:10.33		Bikila			2	APM	Hengelo	4 Jun
13:10.49		Lahlafi			5	WK	Zürich	17 Aug
13:10.51		Skah			1		St Denis	10 Jun
13:10.76	Moses	Kiptanui	KEN	10.10.71	1	GWG	St Peterburg	26 Jul
13:10.79		Gebrselassie			2		St Denis	10 Jun
13:10.95		Hissou			2		Rieti	28 Aug
13:11.46		Sigei			2	Herc	Monaco	2 Aug
13:11.87		Gebrselassie			4	TSB	London	15 Jul
13:12.10		Bitok			5	Bisl	Oslo	22 Jul
13:12.13	Mohamed	Issangar	MAR	12.12.64	1	GGala	Roma	8 Jun
13:12.47	Dieter	Baumann	GER	9.2.65	1	ISTAF	Berlin	30 Aug
13:12.74		Skah			2	ISTAF	Berlin	30 Aug
13:12.95	Khalid	Boulami	MAR	7.8.69	3	ISTAF	Berlin	30 Aug
13:12.98		Kennedy			6	WK	Zürich	17 Aug
	(32/15)							
13:13.47	Smail	Sghir	MAR	16.3.72	4	ISTAF	Berlin	30 Aug
13:13.80	Yobes	Ondieki	KEN	21.2.61	5	BNP	Villeneuve d'Ascq	8 Jul
13:14.46	Ismael	Kirui	KEN	20.2.75	1	DNG	Stockholm	12 Jul
13:14.50	Phillimon	Hanneck	ZIM	12.5.71	2	GGala	Roma	8 Jun
13:14.66	Aloÿs	Nizigama	BUR	18.6.66	2	DNG	Stockholm	12 Jul
	(20)							
13:14.68	Stephane	Franke	GER	12.2.64	5	ISTAF	Berlin	30 Aug
13:15.07	Paul	Tergat	KEN	17.6.69	6	ISTAF	Berlin	30 Aug
13:15.17	Abel	Antón	ESP	24.10.62	7	ISTAF	Berlin	30 Aug
13:15.86	Jim	Spivey	USA	7.3.60	8	ISTAF	Berlin	30 Aug
13:16.17	Kibyego	Kororia	KEN	25.12.71	4	GGala	Roma	8 Jun
13:16.39	Ondoro	Osoro	KEN	3.12.67	5	TSB	London	15 Jul
13:16.70	Abdellah	Béhar	FRA	5.7.63	4		St Denis	10 Jun
13:17.33	Domingos	Castro	POR	22.11.63	5	DNG	Stockholm	12 Jul
13:17.55	Brahim	Jabbour	MAR	1.1.70	5		St Denis	10 Jun
13:17.78	James	Kariuki	KEN	72	10	ISTAF	Berlin	30 Aug
	(30)							
13:18.05	Anacleto	Jiménez	ESP	24.2.67	6		St Denis	10 Jun
13:18.32	Chala	Kelile	ETH	7.10.66	6	GGala	Roma	8 Jun
13:21.1	António	Pinto	POR	22.3.66	2		Maia	16 Jul
13:21.21	Ayele	Mezegbu	ETH	6.1.73	7	GGala	Roma	8 Jun
13:21.64	Brahim	Boutayeb	MAR	15.8.67	8	GGala	Roma	8 Jun
13:22.3	João	Junqueira	POR	24.6.65	3		Maia	16 Jul
13:22.34	Mustapha	Essaïd	FRA	20.1.70	11	BNP	Villeneuve d'Ascq	8 Jul
13:22.40	Robert	Denmark	GBR	23.11.68	7	TSB	London	15 Jul

Mark	Name		Nat	Born	Pos	Meet	Venue	Date
13:23.09	Atiq	Naaji	FRA	21.11.66	9		St Denis	10 Jun
13:23.54	John	Nuttall	GBR	11.1.67	3	CG	Victoria	24 Aug
	(40)							
13:23.82	Mohamed	Ezzher	FRA	26.4.60	10		St Denis	10 Jun
13:23.96	Jon	Brown	GBR	27.2.71	4	CG	Victoria	24 Aug
13:24.07	Philip	Mosima	KEN	2.1.76	5	CG	Victoria	24 Aug
13:24.09	Peter	O'Donoghue	AUS	1.10.61	1	NEC	Melbourne	24 Feb
13:24.39	William	Mutwol	KEN	10.10.67	8	TSB	London	15 Jul
13:24.46	Antonio	Martins	FRA	23.8.63	13	BNP	Villeneuve d'Ascq	8 Jul
13:24.50	José	Ramos	POR	28.7.68	2		Lisboa	9 Jul
13:24.68	Olayan Ali	Al-Qahtani	SAU	23.8.71	9	GGala	Roma	8 Jun
13:24.83	Pascal	Thiébaut	FRA	6.6.59	14	BNP	Villeneuve d'Ascq	8 Jul
13:25.13	Paulo	Guerra	POR	21.8.70	1		Lisboa	18 Jun
	(50)							
13:25.14	Jacky	Carlier	FRA	8.11.61	12		St Denis	10 Jun
13:25.17	M'Hamed	Choumassi	MAR	2.12.69	9	TSB	London	15 Jul
13:25.27	Mathias	Ntawulikura	RWA	14.7.64	1		Bologna	2 Sep
13:25.90	Aïssa	Belaout	ALG	12.8.68	4	GWG	St Peterburg	26 Jul
13:26.27	Jonah	Koech	KEN	2.2.68	3		Nürnberg	10 Jun
13:26.44	Joseph	Kimani	KEN	.9.72	2		Cork	25 Jun
13:26.53	Yasuyuki	Watanabe	JPN	8.6.73	11	TSB	London	15 Jul
13:26.6	Mohamed	Riad	MAR	71	2		Rabat	4 Jun
13:26.67	Frank	O'Mara	IRL	17.7.60	10	GGala	Roma	8 Jun
13:26.80	Jun	Hiratsuka	JPN	8.1.69	12	TSB	London	15 Jul
	(60)							
13:26.84	Julius	Korir	KEN	5.12.63	4		Nürnberg	10 Jun
13:26.94	Umberto	Pusterla	ITA	21.10.67	11	GGala	Roma	8 Jun
13:26.97	Paolo	Donati	ITA	22.1.62	12	GGala	Roma	8 Jun
13:27.00	Josephat	Kapkory	KEN	2.1.67	2		Bellinzona	25 Jun
13:27.58	Laban	Chege	KEN	67	5		Nürnberg	10 Jun
13:27.96	Shem	Kororia	KEN	27.8.72	2		Bologna	2 Sep
13:28.03	Róbert	Stefko	SVK	28.5.68	2		Cottbus	15 Jun
13:28.50	José Carlos	Adán	ESP	22.7.67	10	Bisl	Oslo	22 Jul
13:28.57	Mohamed	Belabbès	ALG	11.3.66	16	BNP	Villeneuve d'Ascq	8 Jul
13:28.80	Risto	Ulmala	FIN	7.5.63	7	VD	Bruxelles	19 Aug
	(70)							
13:28.97	Robbie	Johnston	NZL	21.8.67	2	NEC	Melbourne	24 Feb
13:29.30	Moses	Tanui	KEN	20.8.65	4		Hechtel	30 Jul
13:29.66	William	Kiptum	KEN	30.3.71	6	Herc	Monaco	2 Aug
13:29.91	John	Downes	GBR	21.7.67	1		Gävle	4 Jul
13:30.18	Julian	Paynter	AUS	15.7.70	3	NEC	Melbourne	24 Feb
13:30.31	Vincenzo	Modica	ITA	2.3.71	13	GGala	Roma	8 Jun
13:30.37	Carlos	Monteiro	POR	14.12.65	12	ISTAF	Berlin	30 Aug
13:30.67	Jonny	Danielson	SWE	4.9.64	2		Gävle	4 Jul
13:30.99	Simeon	Rono	KEN	9.4.72	3		Cork	25 Jun
13:31.10	Daniel	Komen	KEN	17.5.76	1	Afr-j	Alger	8 Jul
	(80)							
13:31.21	Antonio	Serrano	ESP	8.3.65	3		Sevilla	5 Jun
13:31.93	Vener	Kashayev	RUS	16.3.74	6h2	EC	Helsinki	11 Aug
13:32.06	Vincent	Rousseau	BEL	29.7.62	5		Hechtel	30 Jul
13:32.28		Hong Bo	CHN	.10.73	4	TOTO	Tokyo	15 Sep
13:32.31	Silvio	Guerra	ECU	18.9.68	3		Gävle	4 Jul
13:32.59	Noel	Berkeley	IRL	28.11.64	4		Gävle	4 Jul
13:32.68	Joseph	Kibor	KEN	22.12.72	1		Antony	30 Apr
13:33.31	Toshinari	Takaoka	JPN	24.9.70	1		Shizuoka	5 May
13:33.39	Abreham	Assefa	ETH	9.12.72	4		Cottbus	15 Jun
13:33.48	Armando	Quintanilla	MEX	19.4.68	1	MSR	Walnut	16 Apr
	(90)							
13:33.5	Francesco	Bennici	ITA	3.10.71	1		Palermo	10 Jul
13:33.56	Josephat	Machuka	KEN	12.12.73	2		Arnsberg	29 May
13:33.57	Martin	Bremer ¶	GER	19.3.70	3	WCp	London	11 Sep
13:33.72	Jonathan	Wyatt	NZL	20.12.72	3h2	CG	Victoria	22 Aug
13:33.76	Abderrahim	Zeitouna	MAR	70	4		Bologna	2 Sep
13:33.80	Ovidiu	Olteanu	ROM	6.8.70	1		Bucuresti	22 Jul
13:33.93	Marcel	Versteeg	NED	20.8.65	4	APM	Hengelo	4 Jun
13:34.0	Khalid	Kairouani	MAR	66	1		Dedham	4 Jun
13:34.02	Paul	Patrick	AUS	15.9.71	2		Melbourne	27 Jan
13:34.3	João	Lopes	POR	4.3.67	5		Maia	16 Jul
	(100)							

Mark	Name		Nat	Born	Date
13:34.35	Katsuhiko	Hanada	JPN	71	12 Jun
13:34.4	Yuichi	Tajiri	JPN	71	28 May
13:34.52	Réda	Benzine	ALG	71	2 Aug
13:34.81	Stefano	Baldini	ITA	71	8 Jun
13:34.9	Antonio	Silio	ARG	66	16 Jul
13:35.2	Kenji	Takao	JPN	75	28 May
13:35.2	Brahim	El Ghazali	FRA	68	16 Jul
13:35.21	Michal	Bartoszak	POL	70	28 Aug
13:35.40	Thomas	Lotik	KEN		9 Jul
13:35.54	Cormac	Finnerty	IRL	70	28 Aug
13:36.50	Piotr	Gladki	POL	72	29 May
13:36.75	Tendai	Chimusasa	ZIM	71	28 May
13:36.89	Richard	Nerurkar	GBR	64	23 May
13:37.08	Steffen	Brand	GER	65	8 Jun
13:37.20	Bahadur	Prasad	IND	65	11 Sep
13:37.59	Ricardo	Pintado	ESP	65	17 Jul
13:37.60	Enrique	Molina	ESP	68	17 Jul
13:38.51	Mike	Chesire	KEN	69	2 Sep
13:38.55	Getaneh	Tessema	ETH	68	28 May
13:38.61	Carlos	De La Torre	ESP	66	17 Jul
13:38.94	Shadrack	Mogotsi	RSA	62	5 Apr
13:39.10	Steve	Moneghetti	AUS	62	27 Jan
13:39.10	Ruben	Garcia	MEX	70	4 Jun
13:39.15	Pasi	Mattila	FIN	70	22 Jul
13:39.40	Krzysztof	Baldyga	POL	72	23 Jul
13:39.42	Jean	Verster	RSA	65	5 Apr
13:39.45	Andrey	Tikhonov	RUS	66	26 Jul
13:39.53	Paul	Kipsambu (Sum)	KEN	·	24 Aug
13:39.54	Jürg	Stalder	SUI	69	4 Jun
13:39.59	Ahmed Ibrahim	Warsama	QAT	66	16 Oct
13:39.68	Luc	Krotwaar	NED	68	9 Jul
13:39.80	Julius	Kariuki	KEN	61	8 Jul
13:39.8	Yuichiro	Fukushima	JPN	70	28 May
13:39.9	José	Dias	POR	68	16 Jul
13:39.95	Aleksandr	Mikitenko	KZK	70	26 Jul
13:40.07		Sun Riping	CHN	74	16 Oct
13:40.16	Francesco	Panetta	ITA	63	5 Jun
13:40.22	Hosea	Kogo	KEN	68	30 Jul
13:40.93	Wander	Moura	BRA	69	28 Aug
13:41.0	Ronaldo	da Costa	BRA	70	16 Sep
13:41.13	Thomas	Osano	KEN	70	4 Jun
13:41.21	Anton	Nicolaisen	RSA	68	5 Apr
13:41.57	Koichi	Fujita	JPN	66	30 Jul
13:42.07	Toshiyuki	Hayata	JPN	68	12 Jun
13:42.16	Wilson	Omwoyo	KEN	65	5 Jun
13:42.43	Pablo	Olmedo	MEX	75	16 Apr
13:42.52	Charles	Cheruiyot	KEN	64	8 Jul
13:42.92	Brian	Baker	USA	70	16 Apr
13:43.00	John	Kemboi	KEN	75	28 Aug
13:43.18	German	Silva	MEX	68	12 Jul
	(150)				
13:43.2A	.	Odene	KEN		10 Jun
13:43.2A	Samuel	Otieno	KEN	73	10 Jun
13:43.2	Bernard	Barmasai	KEN		29 Jun
13:43.38	Erick	Langat	KEN		28 Aug
13:43.39	Vyacheslav	Shabunin	RUS	69	2 Jul
13:43.5A	.	Mbiu	KEN		10 Jun
13:43.52	Sipho	Dlamini	SWZ	72	23 Apr
13:43.52	James	Songok	KEN	70	19 Aug
13:43.72	Mirco	Döring	GER	71	10 Jun
13:43.92A	Habte	Jifar	ETH	76	18 Jun
13:44.22	Ronnie	Harris	USA	65	28 Apr
13:44.30	David	Morris	USA	70	4 Jun
13:44.44	Masaki	Kido	JPN	70	15 Sep
13:44.63	John	Gregorek	USA	60	28 Apr
13:44.64	Ralf	Dahmen	GER	68	30 Aug
13:44.65	Hisayuki	Okawa	JPN	71	15 Sep
13:44.86	Brad	Barquist	USA	68	7 Jun
13:44.88	Kerry	Rodger	NZL	62	4 Jun
13:44.89	Larbi	Zeroual	MAR	71	10 Jun
13:44.91	Yuriy	Chizhov	RUS	72	26 Jul

Indoors

Mark	Name		Nat	Born	Pos	Meet	Venue	Date
13:33.51	Tendai	Chimusasa	ZIM	28.1.71	2		Stuttgart	6 Feb
13:41.71	Brendan	Mathias	CAN	69				19 Feb

10,000 METRES

Mark	Name		Nat	Born	Pos	Meet	Venue	Date
26:52.23	William	Sigei	KEN	11.10.69	1	Bisl	Oslo	22 Jul
27:15.00	Haile	Gebrselassie	ETH	18.4.73	1	Athl	Lausanne	6 Jul
27:17.20	William	Kiptum	KEN	30.3.71	2	Bisl	Oslo	22 Jul
27:18.59	Armando	Quintanilla	MEX	19.4.68	3	Bisl	Oslo	22 Jul
27:20.39		Gebrsilassie			1	VD	Bruxelles	19 Aug
27:20.51	Aloÿs	Nizigama	BUR	18.6.66	4	Bisl	Oslo	22 Jul
27:21.75	Salah	Hissou	MAR	72	2	VD	Bruxelles	19 Aug
27:22.06		Nizigama			3	VD	Bruxelles	19 Aug
27:23.89	Paul	Tergat	KEN	17.6.69	4	VD	Bruxelles	19 Aug
27:28.36	Ondoro	Osoro	KEN	3.12.67	5	VD	Bruxelles	19 Aug
27:29.45		Tergat			5	Bisl	Oslo	22 Jul
27:36.15	Mathias	Ntawulikura	RWA	14.7.64	6	VD	Bruxelles	19 Aug
27:38.74	Khalid	Skah	MAR	29.1.67	1	WCp	London	9 Sep
27:41.09		Ntawalikura			6	Bisl	Oslo	22 Jul
27:42.47		Osoro			7	Bisl	Oslo	22 Jul
27:47.79	Vincent	Rousseau	BEL	29.7.62	7	VD	Bruxelles	19 Aug
27:48.1	António	Pinto	POR	22.3.66	1		Maia	20 Jul
27:51.56	Fita	Bayissa	ETH	15.12.72	2	Athl	Lausanne	6 Jul
27:51.85		Nizigama			1	JPN Ch	Tokyo	11 Jun
27:52.44	Paulo	Guerra	POR	21.8.70	1	vESP	Braga	9 Apr
27:53.74	Joöo	Junqueira	POR	24.6.65	2	vESP	Braga	9 Apr
27:55.0	Joaquim	Pinheiro	POR	20.12.60	2		Maia	20 Jul
27:56.99	Antonio	Serrano	ESP	8.3.65	1	WG	Helsinki	29 Jun
27:57.01	Risto	Ulmala	FIN	7.5.63	2	WG	Helsinki	29 Jun
27:57.05	Hammou	Boutayeb	MAR	56	8	VD	Bruxelles	19 Aug
27:57.42	Róbert	Stefko	SVK	28.5.68	1		Praha	21 May
27:57.58		Kiptum			9	VD	Bruxelles	19 Aug
27:57.86	Stefano	Baldini	ITA	25.5.71	3	WG	Helsinki	29 Jun

Mark	Name		Nat	Born	Pos	Meet	Venue	Date
27:57.87	Mohamed	Ezzher	FRA	26.4.60	10	VD	Bruxelles	19 Aug
27:58.20	Carlos	De LaTorre	ESP	18.5.66	3	vPOR	Braga	9 Apr
	(30/23)							
27:58.51	Robbie	Johnston	NZL	21.8.67	1	Zat	Melbourne	15 Dec
27:59.72	Toshinari	Takaoka	JPN	24.9.70	1		Kobe	24 Apr
27:59.97	Yuichi	Tajiri	JPN	23.5.71	4	WG	Helsinki	29 Jun
28:01.65	Vincenzo	Modica	ITA	2.3.71	5	WG	Helsinki	29 Jun
28:02.13	Shaun	Creighton	AUS	14.5.67	2	Zat/NC	Melbourne	15 Dec
28:02.40	Antonio	Silio	ARG	9.5.66	12	VD	Bruxelles	19 Aug
	(30)							
28:03.34	Robert	Denmark	GBR	23.11.68	1	AAA	Sheffield	11 Jun
28:03.48	Steve	Moneghetti	AUS	26.9.62	3	Zat/NC	Melbourne	15 Dec
28:06.03	Abel	Antón	ESP	24.10.62	1	EC	Helsinki	7 Aug
28:06.32	Stephan	Freigang	GER	27.9.67	6	WG	Helsinki	29 Jun
28:06.36	Alberto	Juzdado	ESP	20.8.66	4	vPOR	Braga	9 Apr
28:06.70	Paolo	Donati	ITA	22.1.62	7	WG	Helsinki	29 Jun
28:06.76	Moses	Tanui	KEN	20.8.65	13	VD	Bruxelles	19 Aug
28:07.4	José	Dias	POR	4.2.68	3		Maia	20 Jul
28:07.94	Yasuyuki	Watanabe	JPN	8.6.73	4	Athl	Lausanne	6 Jul
28:07.95	Stephane	Franke	GER	12.2.64	3	EC	Helsinki	7 Aug
	(40)							
28:08.55	Umberto	Pusterla	ITA	21.10.67	8	WG	Helsinki	29 Jun
28:10.73	Jan	Pesava	TCH	14.1.72	7	EC	Helsinki	7 Aug
28:11.06	José Manuel	Garcia	ESP	24.1.66	5	vPOR	Braga	9 Apr
28:11.28	Toshiyuki	Hayata	JPN	2.5.68	2		Kobe	24 Apr
28:12.36	José Carlos	Adán	ESP	22.7.67	9	WG	Helsinki	29 Jun
28:12.50	Martin	Bremer ¶	GER	19.3.70	1		Troisdorf	26 Aug
28:12.88	Chala	Kelile	ETH	7.10.66	5	Athl	Lausanne	6 Jul
28:15.6	Juvenal	Ribeiro	POR	9.3.64	4		Maia	20 Jul
28:16.2	José	Santos	POR	20.12.70	5		Maia	20 Jul
28:16.27	José	Ramos	POR	28.7.68	6	vESP	Braga	9 Apr
	(50)							
28:17.00	Justin	Hobbs	GBR	12.3.69	10	WG	Helsinki	29 Jun
28:17.32	Nozomi	Saho	JPN	6.3.73	3		Kobe	24 Apr
28:17.63	Julius	Korir	KEN	5.12.63	6	Athl	Lausanne	6 Jul
28:17.81	Katsuhiko	Hanada	JPN	12.6.71	1		Kumamoto	23 Oct
28:18.10	Jun	Hiratsuka	JPN	8.1.69	2	AsiG	Hiroshima	10 Oct
28:18.26	Ronaldo	da Costa	BRA	7.6.70	2	IbAm	Mar del Plata	29 Oct
28:19.17	Seiichi	Miyajima	JPN	27.9.69	5		Kobe	24 Apr
28:20.1A	Samson	Tanui	KEN		3	NC	Nairobi	8 Jul
28:20.22	José Andrés	Pérez	ESP	27.11.69	10	vPOR	Braga	9 Apr
28:20.33	John	Scherer	USA	3.11.66	1	PennR	Philadelphia	28 Apr
	(60)							
28:20.38	Hisayuki	Osawa	JPN	.71	1		Fukushima	24 Sep
28:20.50	Alberto	Maravilha	POR	27.12.65	11	vESP	Braga	9 Apr
28:20.64	Josephat	Kapkory	KEN	2.1.67	1	MSR	Walnut	16 Apr
28:20.66	Dieter	Baumann	GER	9.2.65	1		Kappelrodeck	14 May
28:20.78	Kenji	Takao	JPN	23.3.75	6		Kobe	24 Apr
28:21.21	Shem	Kororia	KEN	27.8.72	14	VD	Bruxelles	19 Aug
28:21.67	Manuel	Matias	POR	30.3.62	12	vESP	Braga	9 Apr
28:22.00	Zoltán	Káldy	HUN	7.1.69	12	EC	Helsinki	7 Aug
28:22.16	Stephen	Mayaka	KEN	16.11.72	8		Kobe	24 Apr
28:22.29	Raimundo	Santos	POR	22.8.67	13	vESP	Braga	9 Apr
	(70)							
28:22.41	Noel	Berkeley	IRL	28.11.64	11	WG	Helsinki	29 Jun
28:22.48	Chris	Fox	USA	22.10.58	2	PennR	Philadelphia	28 Apr
28:22.82	Masayuki	Kobayashi	JPN	4.4.74	2		Tokyo	20 May
28:22.94	Katsuya	Natsume	JPN	1.12.66	3		Fukushima	24 Sep
28:23.12	Akira	Nakamura	JPN	26.6.67	9		Kobe	24 Apr
28:23.56	Yoshuke	Osawa	JPN	7.9.67	5	NC	Tokyo	11 Jun
28:23.87	António	Martins	FRA	23.8.63	13	EC	Helsinki	7 Aug
28:24.03	Jorge	Marquez	MEX	19.3.67	3	IbAm	Mar del Plata	29 Oct
28:24.07	Masaki	Kido	JPN	10.12.70	5		Fukushima	24 Sep
28:24.24	Junji	Haraguchi	JPN	22.6.67	6		Fukushima	24 Sep
	(80)							
28:24.47	Khristo	Stefanov	BUL	21.12.70	14	EC	Helsinki	7 Aug
28:25.35	Arnold	Mächler	SUI	11.5.64	2		Troisdorf	26 Aug
28:25.60	Gary	Staines	GBR	3.7.63	15	EC	Helsinki	7 Aug
28:26.36	António	Pérez	ESP	23.3.66	14	vPOR	Braga	9 Apr

Mark	Name		Nat	Born	Pos	Meet	Venue	Date
28:26.61	Francisco Javier	Cortés	ESP	26.10.71	1		Baracaldo	18 Jun
28:26.95	Cormac	Finnerty	IRL	14.1.70	12	WG	Helsinki	29 Jun
28:27.0	Takahiro	Sunada	JPN	19.1.73	1r2		Hachioji	27 Nov
28:27.14	Domingos	Castro	POR	22.11.63	3		Sevilla	5 Jun
28:27.4	João	Lopes	POR	4.3.67	6		Maia	20 Jul
28:27.69	Oleg	Strizhakov	RUS	18.7.63	2	GWG	St Peterburg	24 Jul
	(90)							
28:28.1	Kazumi	Honkawa	JPN	12.1.72	2r2		Hachioji	27 Nov
28:28.11	Sid-Ali	Sakhri	ALG	20.12.61	1		La Celle St Cloud	4 Jul
28:28.17	Seiji	Kushibe	JPN	11.11.71	7		Fukushima	24 Sep
28:28.56	Kibiego	Kororia	KEN	25.12.71	3	GWG	St Peterburg	24 Jul
28:28.83	Yayé	Aden	DJI	1.8.68	2		La Celle St Cloud	4 Jul
28:29.67	Greg	van Hest	NED	3.6.73	2	ECp II/1	Dublin	12 Jun
28:29.74	Daniel	Komen	KEN	17.5.76	1		Lisboa	20 Jul
28:29.75	Francisco	Guerra	ESP	13.12.57	15	vPOR	Braga	9 Apr
28:29.81	Paul	McCloy	CAN	6.11.63	1	Jer	Port Coquitlam	28 May'
28:30.15	Slawomir	Kapinski	POL	14.4.66	2	ECp I	Valencia	11 Jun
	(100)							

Mark	Name		Nat	Born	Date
28:30.17	Christian	Weber	CAN	66	28May'
28:30.69	Sean	Dollman	IRL	68	28May'
28:30.74	Joseph	Otwori	KEN	69	24 Apr
28:31.5A	Joseph	Kariuki	KEN	70	11 Jun
28:33.18	Martin	Jones	GBR	67	11 Jun
28:33.49	German	Silva	MEX	68	6 Jul
28:34.07	Jim	Westphal	USA	69	28 Apr
28:34.3	José Ramón	Rey	ESP	67	9 Apr
28:34.7	Tadashi	Fukushima	JPN	64	4 Dec
28:35.31	Brendan	Matthias	CAN	69	28May'
28:35.41	Juan Ramon	Muñoz	ESP	65	18 Jun
28:35.52	Masaki	Oya	JPN	66	24 Apr
28:35.58	Sergio	Jiménez	MEX		28 May
28:36.45	Yuji	Nakamura	JPN	70	28 May
28:36.6	Tetsuya	Kumagai	JPN	71	22 Oct
28:37.71	Martin	Fiz	ESP	63	16 Jul
28:37.90	Charles	Mulinga	ZAM	68	26 May
28:38.22	Lammeck	Aguta	KEN	71	27 Aug
28:38.45	Francesco	Panetta	ITA	63	25 Jun
28:38.5	Shinji	Kawashima	JPN	66	22 Oct
28:38.67	Sakae	Osaki	JPN	64	23 Oct
28:38.8	Mitsuhiro	Okuyama	JPN	66	27 Nov
28:38.95	Andrey	Zhulin	KZK	67	24 Jul
28:39.33	William	Koech	KEN	61	6 Jul
28:39.4	Azzeddine	Sakhri	ALG	68	30 Jul
28:39.64	Daniel	Njenga	KEN	76	1 Oct
28:39.74	Takeharu	Honda	JPN	67	20 May
28:39.83	Makoto	Otsu	JPN	69	20 May
28:39.92	Brad	Barquist	USA	68	16 Apr
28:40.16	Silvio	Guerra	ECU	68	29 Oct
28:40.41	Kenjiro	Jitsui	JPN	68	20 May
28:40.74	Tom	Ansberry	USA	63	24 Jul
28:40.8	Katsumi	Ikeda	JPN	67	27 Nov
28:41.18	Olayan Ali	Al-Qahtani	SAU	71	10 Oct
28:41.3	Mitsutoshi	Kawasaki	JPN	72	27 Nov
28:41.48	Paul	Aufdemberge	USA	64	28 Apr
28:41.9	Masaaki	Iijima	JPN	71	27 Nov
28:41.96	Dan	Middleman	USA	69	28 Apr
28:42.3	Minoru	Isono	JPN	73	27 Nov
28:42.6	Hiroyuki	Yamagishi	JPN	70	27 Nov
28:42.75	Petro	Meta	TAN	73	10 Sep
28:43.0A	Barnabas	Koskei	KEN		29 Apr
28:43.23	Oscar	Amaya	ARG	67	14 May
28:43.27	Michitane	Noda	JPN	75	20 May
28:43.68	Tim	Gannon	USA	65	28 Apr
28:43.7	Ryuji	Takei	JPN	71	27 Nov
28:43.82	Takayuki	Shimazaki	JPN	69	20 May
28:43.96	Julius	Gitahi	KEN	78	1 Oct
28:44.0	Yasushi	Watanabe	JPN	72	27 Nov
28:44.48	Jerry	Lawson	USA	66	28 Apr
	(150)				
28:44.5	Hideyuki	Suzuki	JPN	63	27 Nov
28:44.66	Akihiro	Shinoda	JPN	66	20 May
28:45.33	Katsuhiro	Kawauchi	JPN	73	20 May
28:45.87	Masayuki	Nishi	JPN	64	1 Oct
28:46.50	Eamonn	Martin	GBR	58	24 Jul
28:46.5	Juan	Puerta	ESP	71	9 Apr
28:46.53	Yuichiro	Fukushima	JPN	70	23 Oct
28:46.57	Jens	Karrass	GER	68	26 Aug
28:46.71	Luc	Krotwaar	NED	68	15 Jul
28:47.01	Daisuke	Isomatsu	JPN	73	20 May
28:47.10	Hiroyuki	Ito	JPN	71	20 May
28:47.17	Barry	Royden	GBR	66	11 Jun
28:47.57	Bob	Kempainen	USA	66	25 Mar
28:47.72	Tendai	Chimusasa	ZIM	71	27 Aug
28:48.4	Dan	Mayer	USA	72	9 Apr
28:48.43	Khalid	Boulami	MAR	69	11 Jul
28:48.6	Paul	Smith	NZL	65	22 Mar
28:48.61	Juan Antonio	Crespo	ESP	66	14 May
28:48.91	Ed	Eyestone	USA	61	24 Jul
28:49.0A	Boay	Akonay	KEN	70	25 Jul
28:49.02	Mohamed	Belabbès	ALG	66	6 Jul
28:49.05	Steve	Spence	USA	62	28 Apr
28:49.2	Valdenor	Pereira dos Santos	BRA	69	18 Sep
28:49.30	Markus	Graf	SUI	61	6 Jul
28:49.3	Kozo	Maehata	JPN	65	27 Nov
28:49.82	Antonio	Armuzzi	ITA	69	10 Sep
28:49.96	Carl	Udall	GBR	66	11 Jun

10 KILOMETRES ROAD

Mark	Name		Nat	Born	Pos	Meet	Venue	Date
27:24	William	Sigei	KEN	11.10.69	1	Cres	New Orleans	16 Apr
27:43	Addis	Abebe	ETH	5.9.70	1	Hasan	Jakarta	10 Apr
27:45	Phillimon	Hanneck	ZIM	12.5.71	2	Cres	New Orleans	16 Apr
27:46	Daniel	Komen	KEN	17.5.76	1		Vancouver	17 Apr
27:48	Simon	Chemoiywo	KEN	2.5.69	1		Manaus	9 Jan
27:50	Laban	Chege	KEN	67	1		Nürnberg	30 Apr
27:51	Lucketz	Swartbooi	NAM	7.2.66	1	Azalea	Mobile	26 Mar
27:51	Julius	Korir	KEN	5.2.63	2		Nürnberg	30 Apr
27:52		Chege			1		Zoetemeer	18 Sep

Mark	Name		Nat	Born	Pos	Meet	Venue	Date
27:54	Josephat	Machuka	KEN	12.12.73	3	Cres	New Orleans	16 Apr
27:56	Valdenor	dos Santos	BRA	21.2.69	2		Manaus	9 Jan
	28:03				1		San Diego	13 Jun
27:59		Hanneck			1		Chula Vista	16 Oct
	(12/10)							
28:01	Benson	Masya	KEN	14.5.70	1	Peach	Atlanta	4 Jul
28:03	Johnstone	Kipkoech	KEN	20.12.68	1		Naumberg	1 May
28:04	Gideon	Chirchir	KEN	24.2.66	3		Nürnberg	24 Apr
28:04	Philip	Mosima	KEN	2.1.76	3		Vancouver	17 Apr
28:04	Tendai	Chimusasa	ZIM	28.1.71	1		Leipzig	8 Oct
28:04	Godfrey	Kiprotich	KEN	23.11.64	2		Chula Vista	16 Oct
28:05	Peter	Kirwa	KEN		2		Naumburg	1 May
28:05	Lazarus	Nyakaraka	KEN	76	2	Peach	Atlanta	4 Jul
28:06	Ronaldo	da Costa	BRA	7.6.70	3		Manaus	9 Jan
28:06	John	Kipkoskei	KEN		3	Peach	Atlanta	4 Jul
	(20)							
28:06	Stephan	Freigang	GER	27.9.67	2		Leipzig	8 Oct
28:08	Carsten	Eich	GER	9.1.70	3		Leipzig	8 Oct
28:10	Charles	Omwoyo	KEN	62	4		Nürnberg	30 Apr
28:11	Paul	Tergat	KEN	17.6.69	1		Nojano	27 Aug
28:12	Thomas	Osano	KEN	4.6.70	2	Azalea	Mobile	26 Mar
28:12	Aloÿs	Nizigama	BUR	18.6.66	2		Nojano	27 Aug
28:14	Simon	Morolong	RSA	24.6.73	4	Peach	Atlanta	4 Jul
28:15	Lameck	Aguta	KEN	10.10.71	3		Mobile	26 Mar
28:15	Mbarak	Hussein	KEN	65	3		Chula Vista	16 Oct
28:15	Steve	Moneghetti	AUS	26.9.62	1		Melbourne	20 Nov
	(30)							
28:16	Rolando	Vera	ECU	27.4.65	1		Brunssum	10 Apr
28:17	Khalid	Skah	MAR	29.1.67	1		Ratingen	2 Jan
28:19	Pat	Carroll	AUS	17.8.61	2		Melbourne	20 Nov
28:20	Shadrack	Hoff	RSA	19.5.73	5	Peach	Atlanta	4 Jul
28:20	Moses	Tanui	KEN	20.8.65	1		Quartu	11 Sep
28:21	Marco	Gielen	NED	30.5.70	2		Brunssum	10 Apr
28:23	Arturo	Barrios	USA	12.12.63	1		Winter Haven	19 Mar
28:23	Jorge	Marquez	MEX	19.3.67	4	Azalea	Mobile	26 Mar
28:23	Dominic	Kirui	KEN	12.4.67	4	Cres	New Orleans	16 Apr
28:23	Paul	Evans	GBR	13.4.61	1	GWelsh	Cardiff	31 Jul
	(40)							
28:24	Martin	Jones	GB	21.4.67	4		Leipzig	8 Oct
28:25	Richard	Nerurkar	GBR	6.1.64	2	GWelsh	Cardiff	31 Jul
28:25	Mohamed	El Massoudi	MAR	69				May
28:25	Todd	Williams	USA	7.3.69	1		Mobile	5 Nov
28:27	Jon	Brown	GBR	27.2.71	5	Cres	New Orleans	16 Apr
28:28	Delmir	dos Santos	BRA	12.1.66	4		Manaus	9 Jan
28:28	Andrés	Espinosa	MEX	4.2.63	6	Azalea	Mobile	26 Mar
28:28	Eddy	Hellebuyck	BEL	22.1.61	1		Gent	23 May
28:28	William	Koech	KEN	2.12.61	4		Chula Vista	16 Oct
28:29	Stanley	Kimutai	KEN		2		San Diego	12 Jun
	(50)							
28:29	Benjamin	Paredes	MEX	30.4.62	7	Peach	Atlanta	4 Jul
28:29	Abderrahim	Zitouana	MAR	70	3		Quartu	11 Sep
28:30	Marc	Nenow	USA	16.11.57	2		Redondo Beach	30 Jan
28:30	Cormac	Finnerty	IRL	14.1.70	7	Azalea	Mobile	26 Mar
28:30	Yobes	Ondieki	KEN	21.2.61	1	Revco	Cleveland	15 May

Mark	Name		Nat	Born	Date	Mark	Name		Nat	Born	Date
28:31	Gilbert	Ruto	KEN		17 Apr	28:35	Pete	Weilenmann	USA	66	17 Apr
28:31	John	Kipngeno	KEN		17 Apr	28:35	Bo	Reed	USA	66	12 Jun
28:31	Jimmy	Muindi	KEN	73	17 Sep	28:35	Martin	Bremer ¶	GER	70	24 Sep
28:32	Brian	Abshire	USA	63	30 Jan	28:35	Francis	Nade	TAN	74	8 Oct
28:32	Richard	Rono	KEN		23 May	28:36	Anthony	Mwingereza	TAN	74	2 Jan
28:32	Paul	Taylor	GBR	66	17 Sep	28:36	Martin	ten Kate	NED	58	10 Apr
28:33	Pat	Porter	USA	59	17 Apr	28:36	Keith	Dowling	USA	69	4 Jul
28:33	Alejandro	Cruz	MEX	68	4 Jul	28:36	Julius	Koech	KEN		31 Jul
28:33	Jason	Mosigisi	KEN		18 Sep	28:36	Simon	Lopuyet	KEN		5 Nov
28:33	Silvio	Guerra	ECU	68	16 Oct	28:37	Adalberto	Velez	MEX		30 Jan
28:33	Shem	Kororia	KEN	72	31 Dec	28:37	Dieter	Baumann	GER	65	20 Mar
28:35	John	Treacy	IRL	57	26 Mar	28:37	Jackson	Kipngok	KEN	66	26 Mar
28:35	Simon	Karori	KEN	59	26 Mar	28:38	Mark	Flint	GBR	63	31 Jul
28:35	Michal	Bartoszak	POL	70	17 Apr	28:39	James	Sangok	KEN	70	24 Apr

Mark	Name		Nat	Born	Pos	Meet	Venue	Date
Downhill								
27:49	William	Koech	KEN	2.12.61	1		Pittsburgh	25 Sep
27:53	Stephen	Nyamu	KEN	71	2		Pittsburgh	25 Sep
27:56	Stanley	Kimutai	KEN		3		Pittsburgh	25 Sep
27:58	Mbarak	Hussein	KEN	65	4		Pittsburgh	25 Sep
28:13A	Mark	Coogan	USA	1.5.66	1		Salt Lake City	25 Jul
28:18A	Rod	DeHaven	USA	21.9.66	2		Salt Lake City	25 Jul
28:21	Silvio	Guerra	ECU	18.9.68	5		Pittsburgh	25 Sep
28:23	Brendan	Matthias	CAN	12.8.69	1		Toronto	1 May

Mark	Name		Nat	Born	Date	Mark	Name		Nat	Born	Date
28:35	Chris	Fox	USA	58	25 Aug	28:37	Gary	Westgate	CAN	66	1 May
28:37	Paul	McCloy	CAN	63	1 May						

"About 10k": Apr 4, Media Blenio: 1. Sigei 27:34, 2. Haile Gebrselassie ETH 27:34, 3. Tergat 27:40
Note Ekiden Relay legs: Litochoro 17 Apr: 27:57 Salah Hissou MAR, 28:19 Joseph Kibor KEN, 28:36 Badilu Kibret ETH

15 KILOMETRES ROAD

Mark	Name		Nat	Born	Pos	Meet	Venue	Date
42:13	Paul	Tergat	KEN	17.6.69	1		La Courneuve	29 May
42:33	Andrew	Masai	KEN	13.12.60	2		La Courneuve	29 May
42:35	Phillimon	Hanneck	ZIM	12.5.71	1	Gasp	Tampa	26 Feb
42:39	Jon	Brown	GBR	27.2.71	2	Gasp	Tampa	26 Feb
42:41	Ronaldo	da Costa	BRA	7.6.70	3	Gasp	Tampa	26 Feb
42:43	Alfornce	Muindi	KEN		4	Gasp	Tampa	26 Feb
42:44	Lucketz	Swartbooi	NAM	7.2.66	5	Gasp	Tampa	26 Feb
42:45	Benjamin	Paredes	MEX	30.4.62	7	Gasp	Tampa	26 Feb
42:45	Lazarus	Nyakaraka	KEN	76	6	Gasp	Tampa	26 Feb
42:51	José	Castillo	PER	68	8	Gasp	Tampa	26 Feb
	(10)							
42:51	Stephen	Nyamu	KEN	71	1		Tulsa	29 Oct
42:55	Mbarak	Hussein	KEN	65	2		Tulsa	29 Oct
42:56	Josephat	Machuka	KEN	12.12.73	9	Gasp	Tampa	26 Feb
42:57	Benson	Masya	KEN	14.5.70	1		Utica	15 Jul
42:58	Godfrey	Kiprotich	KEN	23.11.64	3		Tulsa	29 Oct
43:00	Haile	Gebrselasie	ETH	18.4.73	1		Nijmegen	20 Nov
43:03	Todd	Williams	USA	7.3.69	4		Tulsa	29 Oct
43:12	William	Koech	KEN	2.12.61	10	Gasp	Tampa	26 Feb
43:16	Dionicio	Cerón	MEX	9.10.65	11	Gasp	Tampa	26 Feb
43:21	Simon	Lopuyet	KEN		2		Nijmegen	20 Nov
	(20)							
43:22	Rolando	Vera	ECU	27.4.65	5		Tulsa	29 Oct
43:22	Thomas	Osano	KEN	4.6.70	13	Gasp	Tampa	26 Feb
43:24	Andrés	Espinosa	MEX	4.2.63	14	Gasp	Tampa	26 Feb
43:35	António	Pinto	POR	22.3.66	3		La Courneuve	29 May
43:47	Shadrack	Hoff	RSA	19.5.73	4		Utica	15 Jul
43:49	Addis	Abebe	ETH	5.9.70	3		Nijmegen	20 Nov
43:49	John	Kagwe	KEN	9.1.69	15	Gasp	Tampa	26 Feb
43:49	Smail	Sghir	MAR	16.3.72	4		La Courneuve	29 May
43:51	Mohammed	El Massoudi	MAR	69	5		La Courneuve	29 May
43:52	Ezael	Tlhobo	RSA	4.5.64	1		Port Elizabeth	11 Jun
	(30)							

Mark	Name		Nat	Born	Date	Mark	Name		Nat	Born	Date
43:53	Joaquim	Pinheiro	POR	60	29 May	44:02	Bertrand	Fréchard	FRA	69	29 May
43:53	Vincent	Rousseau	BEL	62	20 Nov	44:03	Simon	Morolong	RSA	73	15 Jul
43:54	Luiz	dos Santos	BRA	64	26 Feb	44:04	Jacques	van Rensburg	RSA	68	29 May
43:56	Khalid	Kairouani	MAR	66	15 Jul	44:04	Paul	Sigei	KEN		29 May
43:56	Keith	Brantly	USA	62	26 Feb	44:04	Tonnie	Dirks	NED	61	20 Nov
43:56	Valdenor	dos Santos	BRA	69	15 Jul	44:05	John	Treacy	IRL	57	29 May
43:58	Arturo	Barrios	USA	62	15 Jul	44:05	Elid	Kibet	KEN		29 Oct
43:59	Adugna	Atnafu	ETH	74	20 Nov						

10 MILES ROAD

Mark	Name		Nat	Born	Pos	Meet	Venue	Date
45:50	Charles	Omwoyo	KEN		1		Zaandam	18 Sep
45:52	Thomas	Osano	KEN	4.6.70	2		Zaandam	18 Sep
45:58	Simon	Lopuyet	KEN		3		Zaandam	18 Sep
46:01	William	Sigei	KEN	14.10.69	1		Washington	10 Apr
46:05		Osano			2		Washington	10 Apr
46:07	Josephat	Machuka	KEN	12.12.73	3		Washington	10 Apr
46:21		Lopuyet			1		Tilburg	29 May
46:22	Benson	Masya	KEN	14.5.70	1		Flint	27 Aug
46:35	Lazarus	Nykaraka	KEN		2		Flint	27 Aug
46:39	Kenji	Takao	JPN	23.3.75	1		Karatsu	13 Feb
46:43	Joseph	Kibor	KEN	22.12.72	1	NC	Erewash	4 Sep

Mark	Name		Nat	Born	Pos	Meet	Venue	Date
46:44	Arturo	Barrios	USA	12.12.63	3		Flint	27 Aug
	(12/10)							
46:52	Kazunori	Tachibana	JPN	.74	2		Kosa	11 Dec
46:56	Yasuyuki	Watanabe	JPN	8.6.73	1		Himayi	11 Feb
46:57	Masaki	Kido	JPN	10.12.70	2		Himayi	11 Feb
46:58	Simon	Chemoiywo	KEN	2.5.69	4		Washington	10 Apr
46:59	Osamu	Nara	JPN	9.1.71	3		Himayi	11 Feb
46:59	William	Mutwol	KEN	10.10.67	5		Washington	10 Apr
47:00	Gary	Staines	GBR	3.7.63	1	GSouth	Portsmouth	9 Oct
47:00	Nozomi	Saho	JPN	6.3.73	3		Kosa	11 Dec
47:06	Kozo	Maehata	JPN	10.6.75	4		Himayi	11 Feb
47:07	Tomonori	Watanabe	JPN	9.6.76	1	Jnr	Himayi	11 Feb
	(20)							
47:09	Masayuki	Nishi	JPN	25.1.64	4		Kosa	11 Dec
47:10		Naali	TAN		2		Tilburg	29 May
47:13	Bert	van Vlaanderen	NED	25.11.64	3		Tilburg	29 May
47:13	Jackson	Kipngok	KEN		5		Flint	27 Aug
47:14	Brian	Sheriff	ZIM	11.11.61	5		Kosa	11 Dec
47:08DH	Eric	Polonski	USA		1		River City	13 Feb

HALF-MARATHON

Mark	Name		Nat	Born	Pos	Meet	Venue	Date
60:02	Benson	Masya	KEN	14.5.70	1	GNR	South Shields	18 Sep
60:03	Moses	Tanui	KEN	20.8.65	2	GNR	South Shields	18 Sep
60:13	Paul	Tergat	KEN	17.6.69	1	Stra	Milano	16 Apr
60:23	Vincent	Rousseau	BEL	29.7.62	1		Tokyo	23 Jan
60:27	Khalid	Skah	MAR	29.1.67	1	WCh	Oslo	24 Sep
60:28	Dionicio	Ceron	MEX	9.10.65	2		Tokyo	23 Jan
60:28	German	Silva	MEX	9.1.68	2	WCh	Oslo	24 Sep
60:42		Tergat			3	GNR	South Shields	18 Sep
60:54	Ronaldo	da Costa	BRA	7.6.70	3	WCh	Oslo	24 Sep
61:01	Godfrey	Kiprotich	KEN	23.11.64	4	WCh	Oslo	24 Sep
61:05		da Costa			1		Buenos Aires	4 Sep
61:11	Pat	Carroll	AUS	17.8.61	1		Sydney	22 May
61:16	Shem	Kororia	KEN	27.8.72	5	WCh	Oslo	24 Sep
61:18	Andrew	Masai	KEN	13.12.60	1		Lyon	15 May
61:19		Masai			6	WCh	Oslo	24 Sep
61:26	Wanderley	Lima	BRA	11.8.69	3		Tokyo	23 Jan
61:26	Anthony	Kiprono	KEN	73	1		Gualtieri	4 Apr
61:26	Tendai	Chimusasa	ZIM	28.1.71	7	WCh	Oslo	24 Sep
61:28	Julius	Korir	KEN	5.12.63	1		Grevenmacher	25 Sep
61:30	Ezael	Tlhobo	RSA	4.5.64	1		Humansdorp	26 Mar
61:30	Wilson	Omwoyo	KEN	25.11.65	2		Gualtieri	4 Apr
61:30	Paul	Evans	GBR	13.4.61	4	GNR	Newcastle	18 Sep
61:30	Fackson	Nkandu	ZAM	71	8	WCh	Oslo	24 Sep
	(22/20)							
61:31	Julius	Ondieki	KEN	10.7.69	3		Gualtieri	4 Apr
61:32	Thomas	Osano	KEN	4.6.70	2		Grevenmacher	25 Sep
61:34	Andrés	Espinosa	MEX	4.2.63	1		Lisboa	13 Mar
61:34	Toshiyuki	Hayata	JPN	2.5.68	1		Yamaguchi	21 Mar
61:36	Barnabas	Katui	KEN	59	4		Gualtieri	4 Apr
61:36	Rolando	Vera	ECU	27.4.65	10	WCh	Oslo	24 Sep
61:37	Laban	Chege	KEN	67	3		Grevenmacher	25 Sep
61:38	Martin	Pitayo	MEX	10.11.60	12	WCh	Oslo	24 Sep
61:38	John	Kipkoskei	KEN		4		Grevenmacher	25 Sep
61:39	Brahim	Lahlafi	MAR	15.4.68	5	GNR	Newcastle	18 Sep
	(30)							
61:40	Bedilu	Kibret	ETH	69	13	WCh	Oslo	24 Sep
61:41	Yobes	Ondieki	KEN	21.2.61	4		Tokyo	23 Jan
61:41	Benjamin	Paredes	MEX	30.4.62	14	WCh	Oslo	24 Sep
61:43	William	Koech	KEN	2.12.61	5		Gualtieri	4 Apr
61:44	Carsten	Eich	GER	9.1.70	15	WCh	Oslo	24 Sep
61:45	Masayuki	Nishi	JPN	25.1.64	5		Tokyo	23 Jan
61:50	Kamel	Kohil	ALG	71	16	WCh	Oslo	24 Sep
61:52	Chouki	Achour	ALG	65			Siena	18 Apr
61:52	Charles	Omwoyo	KEN		1		Uster	17 Sep
61:53	Valdenor	dos Santos	BRA	21.12.69	1		Kyoto	20 Mar
	(40)							
61:53	Andrew	Eyapan	KEN		2		Uster	17 Sep

Mark	Name		Nat	Born	Pos	Meet	Venue	Date
61:54	Dmitriy	Kapitanov	RUS	15.5.68	5		Grevenmacher	25 Sep
61:55	António	Pinto	POR	22.3.66	2		Lisboa	13 Mar
61:57	Stephen	Mayaka	KEN	16.11.72	1		Surfers Paradise	17 Jul
61:57	Simon	Lopuyet	KEN		1		Griesheim	16 Nov
61:58	João	Lopes	POR	4.3.67	5		Lisboa	13 Mar
61:58	Saïd	Ermili	MAR	63	1		Paris	27 Mar
62:00	Stephan	Freigang	GER	27.9.67	3		Kyoto	20 Mar
62:02	Vladimir	Netreba	RUS	67	1		Chelyabinsk	18 Jun
62:03	Meshack	Mogotsi	RSA	12.12.62	1	NC	Durban	27 Aug
	(50)							
62:04	Joseph	Kibor	KEN	22.12.72	1		Oléron	24 Apr
62:05	Laurence	Peu	RSA	13.2.66	2	NC	Durban	27 Aug
62:06	Keita	Fujino	JPN	17.8.67	2		Yamaguchi	21 Mar
62:07	Simon	Meli	RSA	22.7.63	1		Bloemfontein	16 Jul
62:09	Meck	Mothuli	RSA	12.4.76	3	NC	Durban	27 Aug
62:10	Joseph	Kariuki	KEN	1.1.70	3		Canals	16 Apr
62:11	Seiichi	Miyajima	JPN	27.9.69	6		Tokyo	23 Jan
62:11	Róbert	Stefko	SVK	28.5.68	6		Gualtieri	4 Apr
62:11	Aleksandr	Gazizov	RUS	64	2		Chelyabinsk	18 Jun
62:12	Julius	Sumawe	TAN	65	3		Paris	27 Mar
	(60)							
62:13	Haruo	Urata	JPN	9.3.62	7		Tokyo	23 Jan
62:14	Francis	Nade	TAN	74	7		Gualtieri	4 Apr
62:14	Addis	Abebe	ETH	5.9.70	17	WCh	Oslo	24 Sep
62:15	Clair	Wathier	BRA	6.11.66	2		Buenos Aires	4 Sep
62:16	Francis	Robert Naali	TAN	72	4		Paris	27 Mar
62:17	Sammy	Lelei	KEN	14.8.64	5		Paris	27 Mar
62:18	Joaquim	Pinheiro	POR	20.12.70	1		Pombal	31 Jul
62:20	Vicenzo	Modica	ITA	2.3.71	2	Stra	Milano	16 Apr
62:20	Salah	Hissou	MAR	.72	18	WCh	Oslo	24 Sep
62:21	James	Kamau	KEN	17.6.69	1		Brusy-en-Artois	10 Apr
	(70)							
62:21	Luiz	dos Santos	BRA	6.9.64	3		Buenos Aires	4 Sep
62:21	Samson	Dhingani	ZIM	69	19	WCh	Oslo	24 Sep
62:22	Paulo	Catarino	POR	30.9.63	2		Porto	13 Feb
62:22	Xolile	Yawa	RSA	29.9.62	4	NC	Durban	27 Aug
62:22	Juan	Juárez	ARG	4.12.60	4		Buenos Aires	4 Sep
62:25	Abdelkadir	Mouaziz	MAR	69	1		Badajoz	7 May
62:25	Barry	Royden	GBR	66	6	GNR	South Shields	18 Sep
62:26	John	September	RSA	30.3.66	1		Milnerton	30 Apr
62:27	Teruo	Oga	JPN	25.8.67	4		Yamaguchi	21 Mar
62:27	Matthews	Motshwarateu	RSA	2.11.58	2		Philadelphia	18 Sep
	(80)							
62:27	Tahar	Mansouri	TUN	65	21	WCh	Oslo	24 Sep
62:28	Petro	Meta	TAN	73			Ostia	20 Mar
62:28	Simon Robert	Naali	TAN	66	1		St Peterburg	12 Jun
62:28	Fernando	Couto	POR	4.12.59	23	WCh	Oslo	24 Sep
62:29	William	Musyoki	KEN	25.11.66	1		Azpeitia	27 Mar
62:30	Ikaji	Salum	TAN		8		Gualtieri	4 Apr

Mark	Name		Nat	Born	Date
62:32	Winston	Muzuni	ZIM	67	6 Feb
62:32	Artur	Castro	BRA	67	20 Mar
62:32	Alberto	Juzdado	ESP	66	27 Mar
62:32	Francisco J	Cortes	ESP	71	24 Sep
62:33A	Frans	Motsamai	RSA		12 Nov
62:34	Sergey	Davidov	RUS		18 Jun
62:34	Daniel	Mutai	KEN		11 Sep
62:34	Samuel	Otieno	KEN	73	11 Sep
62:35	Hisayuki	Okawa	JPN	71	6 Feb
62:39	Simon	Morolong	RSA	73	27 Aug
62:40	Mohamed	El Massoudi	MAR	69	10 Apr
62:40	Paul	Yego	KEN		1 May
62:41	Moulay Ali	Ouadih	MAR	70	10 Apr
62:43	Adam	Motlagale	RSA	61	24 Sep
62:44	Paul	Arpin	FRA	60	24 Sep
62:45		Kim Jae-ryong	KOR	66	6 Feb
	(102)				

Positive drugs test

Mark	Name		Nat	Born	Pos	Meet	Venue	Date
61:59	Martin	Bremer ¶	GER	19.3.70	(2)		Griesheim	16 Nov

Uncertain course measurement

Mark	Name		Nat	Born	Pos	Meet	Venue	Date
61:46	James	Kamau	KEN	17.6.69	1		St Witz	26 Mar
61:57	Joaquim	Pinheiro	POR	20.12.70	1		Ovar	5 Oct
62:12	Henrique	Crisóstomo	POR	62	3		Ovar	5 Oct
62:29	Alcidio	Costa	POR	60	4		Ovar	5 Oct

Oct 9, Chihuahua (1400m A) "Half Mar", probably short: 1. Domingos Castro POR 60:46, 2. Rolando Vera ECU 60:53, 3. Jorge Marquez MEX 61:02, 4. Alejandro Cruz MEX 61:16, 6. Salvador Garcia 62:29.

MARATHON

Note Boston times both downhill overall (139m) and strongly wind-aided - next bests are shown if to standard. Hiroshima course 150m net drop.

Mark	Name		Nat	Born	Pos	Meet	Venue	Date
2:07:15 dh	Cosmus	N'Deti	KEN	24.11.71	1		Boston	18 Apr
2:07:19 dh	Andrés	Espinosa	MEX	4.2.63	2		Boston	18 Apr
	2:11:20				4		Fukuoka	4 Dec
2:07:51	Vincent	Rousseau	BEL	29.7.62	1		Rotterdam	17 Apr
2:08:08 dh	Jackson	Kipngok	KEN	16.8.66	3		Boston	18 Apr
	2:12:12				6		Berlin	25 Sep
2:08:09 dh		Hwang Young-cho	KOR	22.3.70	4		Boston	18 Apr
	2:11:13				1	AsiG	Hiroshima	9 Oct
2:08:28 dh	Arturo	Barrios	USA	12.12.62	5		Boston	18 Apr
	2:11:43				3		New York	6 Nov
2:08:31	António	Pinto	POR	22.3.66	1		Berlin	25 Sep
2:08:33	Manuel	Matias	POR	30.3.62	1		Kyongju	20 Mar
2:08:34		Kim Wan-ki	KOR	8.7.68	2		Kyongju	20 Mar
2:08:35 dh	Boay	Akonay	TAN	3.1.70	6		Boston	18 Apr
2:08:47 dh	Bob	Kempainen	USA	18.6.66	7		Boston	18 Apr
2:08:50	Sammy	Nyangincha	KEN	10.11.62	2		Berlin	25 Sep
2:08:53	Dionicio	Cerón	MEX	9.10.65	1		London	17 Apr
2:08:55	Steve	Moneghetti	AUS	26.9.62	1		Tokyo	13 Feb
2:09:08		Rousseau			2		Tokyo	13 Feb
2:09:08 dh	Lucketz	Swartbooi	NAM	7.2.66	8		Boston	18 Apr
2:09:13	Antonio	Serrano	ESP	8.3.65	3		Berlin	25 Sep
2:09:14	Isidro	Rico	MEX	15.5.61	3		Kyongju	20 Mar
2:09:15 dh		Nyangincha			9		Boston	18 Apr
2:09:17	Abebe	Mekonnen	ETH	9.1.64	2		London	17 Apr
2:09:18	German	Silva	MEX	9.1.68	3		London	17 Apr
2:09:40	Salvatore	Bettiol	ITA	28.11.61	4		London	17 Apr
2:09:40 dh	Moses	Tanui	KEN	20.8.65	10		Boston	18 Apr
2:09:42		Kim Jae-ryong	KOR	25.4.66	4		Kyongju	20 Mar
2:09:45		Akonay			1		Fukuoka	4 Dec
2:09:49	Grzegorz	Gajdus	POL	16.1.67	5		London	17 Apr
2:09:50		Matias			2		Fukuoka	4 Dec
2:09:57 dh		Lee Bong-ju	KOR	69	11		Boston	18 Apr
2:10:08	Michael	Kapkiai	KEN	27.12.68	1		Torino	24 Apr
2:10:12		Yu Young-hoon	KOR	27.2.72	5		Kyongju	20 Mar
	(30/26)							
2:10:15	Valdenor	dos Santos	BRA	21.12.69	3		Fukuoka	4 Dec
2:10:17	Willie	Mtolo	RSA	5.5.64	2		Rotterdam	17 Apr
2:10:19	Toshiyuki	Hayata	JPN	2.5.68	3		Tokyo	13 Feb
2:10:21 dh	Martin	Fiz	ESP	3.3.63	12		Boston	18 Apr
	2:10:31				1	EC	Helsinki	14 Aug
	(30)							
2:10:24	Turbo	Tumo	ETH	70	2		Torino	24 Apr
2:10:39 dh	Luiz	dos Santos	BRA	6.9.64	13		Boston	18 Apr
	2:11:16				1		Chicago	30 Oct
2:10:40	Benjamin	Paredes	MEX	30.4.62	4		Rotterdam	17 Apr
2:10:41		Cho Myong-hak	KOR	10.8.72	6		Kyongju	20 Mar
2:10:41	Lameck	Aguta	KEN	10.10.71	4		Berlin	25 Sep
2:10:42	Joaquim	Silva	POR	13.1.61	1		Wien	10 Apr
2:10:46	Hiromi	Taniguchi	JPN	5.4.60	5		Rotterdam	17 Apr
2:10:46	Diego	García	ESP	12.10.61	2	EC	Helsinki	14 Aug
2:10:49	Bert	van Vlaanderen	NED	25.11.64	5		Berlin	25 Sep
2:10:50	Tena	Negere	ETH	5.10.72	1		Venezia	9 Oct
	(40)							
2:10:56	Saïd	Ermili	MAR	63	1		Paris	24 Apr
2:10:56		Hu Gangjun #	CHN	4.12.70	1		Beijing	30 Oct
2:10:58	Martin	Pitayo	MEX	10.11.60	6		London	17 Apr
2:11:01	Andrew	Masai	KEN	13.12.60	3		Paris	24 Apr
2:11:05 dh	Kenichi	Suzuki	JPN	6.4.67	1		Hiroshima	6 Mar
2:11:05	Eamonn	Martin	GBR	9.10.58	8		London	17 Apr
2:11:06	Wanderley	Lima	BRA	11.8.69	1		Reims	23 Oct
2:11:10	Kenjiro	Jitsui	JPN	16.12.68	4		Tokyo	13 Feb
2:11:13	Maurilio	Castillo	MEX	1.12.62	3		Torino	24 Apr
2:11:15	Rolando	Vera	ECU	27.4.65	9		London	17 Apr
	(50)							

Mark	Name		Nat	Born	Pos	Meet	Venue	Date
2:11:18	Alberto	Juzdado	ESP	20.8.66	3	EC	Helsinki	14 Aug
2:11:19	Ahmed	Salah	DJI	31.12.56	4		Paris	24 Apr
2:11:21	Tadesse	Becho	ETH	68	4		Torino	24 Apr
2:11:28	Hajime	Nakatomi	JPN	24.8.68	1	Beppu	Oita	6 Feb
2:11:28	Toshiaki	Kurabayashi	JPN	29.4.66	5		Fukuoka	4 Dec
2:11:30	Tadesse	Belayneh	ETH	24.4.66	2		Venezia	9 Oct
2:11:31	Kozo	Akutsu	JPN	11.11.60	6		Fukuoka	4 Dec
2:11:34	Rodrigo	Gavela	ESP	5.1.66	3		Venezia	9 Oct
2:11:35 dh	Hiroshi	Tako	JPN	10.9.68	2		Hiroshima	6 Mar
2:11:35	Pablo	Sierra	ESP	13.5.69	1		St Paul	2 Oct
	(60)							
2:11:35	Mukhamet	Nazhipov	RUS	10.9.64	3		Beijing	30 Oct
2:11:37	Aiduna	Aitnafa	ETH	28.10.74	1		Eindhoven	9 Oct
2:11:39	Kenichiro	Takeuchi	JPN	12.2.64	2	Beppu	Oita	6 Feb
2:11:40 dh	Thabiso	Moqhali	LES	7.12.67	15		Boston	18 Apr
2:11:41	Girma	Urge	ETH	65	3	Beppu	Oita	6 Feb
2:11:42	Carlos	Patricio	POR	9.1.64	10		London	17 Apr
2:11:43	Vladimir	Kotov	BLR	21.2.58	2		Eindhoven	9 Oct
2:11:44	Sid-Ali	Sakhri	ALG	20.12.61	4		Venezia	9 Oct
2:11:45	Tekeye	Gebrselassie	ETH	16.10.70	3		Eindhoven	9 Oct
2:11:50	Eddy	Hellebuyck	BEL	22.1.61	1		Antwerp	10 Apr
	(70)							
2:11:51	Pat	Carroll	AUS	17.8.61	4	Beppu	Oita	6 Feb
2:11:51	Chawki	Achour	ALG	8.4.65	5		Venezia	9 Oct
2:11:51	Ed	Eyestone	USA	15.6.61	2		Chicago	30 Oct
2:11:52 dh	Wieslaw	Perszke	POL	18.2.60	3		Hiroshima	6 Mar
2:11:52 dh	John	Kagwe	KEN	9.1.69	16		Boston	18 Apr
2:11:52	Jacek	Kasprzyk	POL	27.8.70	4		Beijing	30 Oct
2:11:53 dh	Shinji	Kawashima	JPN	4.6.66	4		Hiroshima	6 Mar
2:11:54	Xolile	Yawa	RSA	29.9.62	7		Kyongju	20 Mar
2:11:54		Kim Ei-yong	KOR		8		Kyongju	20 Mar
2:11:56	Richard	Nerurkar	GBR	6.1.64	4		Helsinki	14 Aug
	(80)							
2:11:56		Zhang Fukui	CHN	27.1.70	5		Beijing	30 Oct
2:11:57	Zbigniew	Nadolski	POL	14.1.67	1		Lisboa	27 Nov
2:12:01	Zithulele	Singe	RSA	9.6.63	9		Kyongju	20 Mar
2:12:04	Roberto	Crosio	ITA	15.6.66	1		Carpi	23 Oct
2:12:07	Mark	Flint	GBR	19.2.63	11		London	17 Apr
2:12:07	Girma	Daba	ETH	71	6		Venezia	9 Oct
2:12:10	Johannes	Maremane	RSA	65	5		Hiroshima	6 Mar
2:12:12	Zacharia	Nyambaso	KEN	71	1		Mombasa	19 Jun
2:12:12	Mario	Sousa	POR	3.11.61	7		Venezia	9 Oct
2:12:13	Paul	Pilkington	USA	12.10.58	1		Los Angeles	6 Mar
	(90)							
2:12:13	Sergey	Struganov	RUS	5.4.66	5		Paris	24 Apr
2:12:14	Peter	Fonseca	CAN	5.10.66	2		Reims	23 Oct
2:12:15	Fernando	Couto	POR	4.12.59	12		London	17 Apr
2:12:15	Shingo	Nakamura	JPN	4.8.63	7		Fukuoka	4 Dec
2:12:20	Frank	Bjørkli	NOR	30.1.65	6		Rotterdam	17 Apr
2:12:21	Leonid	Shvetsov	RUS	28.3.69	2		St Paul	2 Oct
2:12:22	Aleksey	Zhelonkin	RUS	1.1.66	6		Beijing	30 Oct
2:12:23	Steve	Brace	GBR	7.7.61	13		London	17 Apr
2:12:24	Tesfaye	Bekele	ETH	5.2.71	14		London	17 Apr
2:12:24	Oleg	Strizhakov	RUS	18.7.63	6		Paris	24 Apr
	(100)							
2:12:24	Sammy	Lelei	KEN	14.8.62	4		New York	6 Nov
2:12:27	Vladimir	Bukhanov	UKR	1.10.61	1		Beograd	23 Apr
2:12:28	Yared	Kebede	ETH	73	7		Beijing	30 Oct
2:12:29	Jean-Luc	Assemat	FRA	23.4.63	7		Rotterdam	17 Apr
2:12:31	Slawomir	Gurny	POL	2.9.64	8		Rotterdam	17 Apr
2:12:34	Gemechu	Kebede	ETH	.73	8		Beijing	30 Oct
2:12:35 dh	Benson	Masya	KEN	14.5.70	17		Boston	18 Apr
2:12:36	Gilbert	Ruto	KEN	3.3.66	7		Berlin	25 Sep
2:12:41	Luigi	Di Lello	ITA	31.5.68	5		Helsinki	14 Aug
2:12:43	António	Rodrigues	POR	14.6.63	6		Helsinki	14 Aug
	(110)							
2:12:44	Davide	Milesi	ITA	27.12.64	2		Wien	10 Apr
2:12:44	Artur	de Castro	BRA	12.11.67	15		London	17 Apr
2:12:45 dh	Ezekiel	Bitok	KEN	15.2.66	18		Boston	18 Apr

Mark	Name		Nat	Born	Pos Meet	Venue	Date
2:12:48	José Esteban	Montiel	ESP	20.9.62	16	London	17 Apr
2:12:49 dh	Carlos	Tarazona	VEN	14.8.65	19	Boston	18 Apr
2:12:49	Domingos	Castro	POR	22.11.63	5	New York	6 Nov
2:12:51	Steve	Plasencia	USA	28.10.56	4	St Paul	2 Oct
2:12:52	Luca	Barzaghi	ITA	1.6.68	2	Los Angeles	6 Mar
2:12:52	Tadao	Uchikoshi	JPN	30.10.65	9	Rotterdam	17 Apr
2:12:52	Mark	Hudspith	GBR	19.1.69	17	London	17 Apr
	(120)						
2:12:52	Juvenal	Ribeiro	POR	9.3.64	8	Berlin	25 Sep
2:12:54		Baek Seung-do	KOR	16.6.68	6	Tokyo	13 Feb
2:12:54		Ning Limin	CHN	9.4.73	9	Beijing	30 Oct
2:12:55	Yakov	Tolstikov	RUS	20.5.59	3	Wien	10 Apr
2:12:55	Jorge	Marquez	MEX	19.3.67	10	Rotterdam	17 Apr
2:12:55	Andrey	Kuznetsov	RUS	27.1.57	2	Beograd	23 Apr
2:12:56	Patrick	Moturi	KEN		3	Chicago	30 Oct
2:12:57	Konrad	Dobler	GER	27.4.57	7	Tokyo	13 Feb
2:12:58	Eduard	Tukhbatullin	RUS	13.10.71	1	Hamburg	24 Apr
2:12:59	Luiz	da Silva	BRA	23.1.69	1	Porto Alegre	29 May
2:12:59	Samwel	Maritim	KEN	65	9	Berlin	25 Sep
	(131)						

Mark	Name		Nat	Born	Date
2:13:00dh	Keith	Brantly	USA	62	18 Apr
2:13:01	Piotr	Poblocki	POL	65	5 Jun
2:13:01	Diamantino	dos Santos	BRA	61	23 Oct
2:13:02	Barnabas	Qamunga	TAN	67	24 Apr
2:13:05	Miroslaw	Plawgo	POL	70	25 Sep
2:13:09	Ovidio	Castilla	MEX		30 Oct
2:13:11	Takeyuki	Nakayama	JPN	59	24 Apr
2:13:12dh	Joaquim	Pinheiro	POR	60	18 Apr
2:13:12	Leszek	Beblo	POL	66	6 Nov
2:13:15	Juan F	Romera	ESP	60	17 Apr
2:13:16		SongJae-phil	KOR	65	20 Mar
2:13:16	Driss	Dacha	MAR	62	20 Mar
2:13:18	Geraldo	de Assis	BRA	65	29 May
2:13:19	Terje	Næss	NOR	61	23 Oct
2:13:20	Abel	Mokibe	RSA	62	23 Oct
2:13:21	Andrzej	Krzyscin	POL	67	6 Mar
2:13:21	Heinz-Bernd	Bürger	GER	66	10 Apr
2:13:21	Harri	Hänninen	FIN	63	14 Aug
2:13:21	Piotr	Sarafenyuk	UKR	66	25 Sep
	(150)				
2:13:21	William	Musyoki	KEN	66	23 Oct
2:13:21	Don	Janicki	USA	60	30 Oct
2:13:22	Philippe	Rémond	FRA	63	24 Apr
2:13:23	Marnix	Goegebeur	BEL	62	6 Mar
2:13:23		Chang Ki-shik	KOR	70	24 Sep
2:13:23	Juan	Torres	ESP	59	23 Oct
2:13:24dh	Mark	Coogan	USA	66	18 Apr
2:13:25	Julius	Sumawe	TAN	65	24 Apr
2:13:27	Naoto	Suzuki	JPN	65	13 Feb
2:13:29	Antoni	Niemczak	POL	55	23 Apr
2:13:30	Dominique	Chauvelier	FRA	56	14 Aug
2:13:31	Volmirde	Carvalho	BRA	59	29 May
2:13:31	Bartolomé	Serrano	ESP	69	23 Oct
2:13:33	Gumersindo	Olmedo	MEX	63	6 Mar
2:13:34	Colin	Moore	GBR	60	16 Jan
2:13:34	Masahi	Oya	JPN	66	4 Dec
2:13:35	Bruce	Deacon	CAN	66	17 Apr
2:13:35	Carsten	Eich	GER	70	24 Apr
2:13:35	Abdellah	Sbaïti	MAR	67	9 Oct
2:13:35	Héctor	Martin	MEX		30 Oct
2:13:37	Ignacio Alberto	Cuba	CUB	62	20 Nov
2:13:37	Alexis	Cuba	CUB	64	20 Nov
2:13:38	Marcelino	Crisanto	MEX	65	6 Mar
2:13:40	Peter	Whitehead	GBR	64	17 Apr
2:13:42	Marco	Gozzano	ITA	63	9 Oct
2:13:43	Noureddine	Sobhi	FRA	62	14 Aug
2:13:44	Jeff	Jacobs	USA	64	30 Oct
2:13:48	Cephas	Matafi	ZIM	71	23 Apr
2:13:50	Kazuo	Matsumoto	JPN	67	6 Feb
2:13:50	dhDan	Held	USA	65	18 Apr
2:13:50	Juan	Juárez	ARG	60	24 Apr
2:13:51	Abel	Gisemba	KEN	71	1 May
2:13:53	Benedict	Ako	TAN	68	24 Apr
2:13:55	Janusz	Wojcik	POL	64	1 May
2:13:57	Petro	Meta	TAN	73	9 Oct
2:13:57	Omar	Moussa	DJI	61	23 Oct
2:13:57	Daniel	Böltz	SUI	62	27 Nov
2:13:57	Juma	Ikangaa	TAN	60	4 Dec
2:13:58	Ronny	Ligneel	BEL	64	9 Oct
2:13:59	Samuel	Okemya	KEN	68	4 Dec
	(190)				
2:14:02	Clair	Wathier	BRA	66	25 Sep
2:14:03	Peter	Fleming	GBR	61	19 Mar
2:14:03		Kim Ki-book	KOR		20 Mar
2:14:08	Anatoliy	Archakov	RUS	66	24 Apr
2:14:08	Simon	Karori	KEN	59	24 Apr
2:14:09	Gino	Deleu	BEL	66	9 Oct
2:14:11	Bedaso	Turube	ETH	69	25 Sep
2:14:11	Sergio	Jiménez	MEX		3 Apr
2:14:12	Simon	Qamunga	TAN	67	9 Oct
2:14:14	Tomasz	Kozlowski	POL	60	23 Apr
	(200)				
2:14:14	Mirko	Vindis	SLO	63	24 Apr
2:14:14	Yahé	Aden	DJI	67	23 Oct
2:14:15	Daniel	Ondieki	KEN		19 Jun
2:14:16dh	Zablon	Miano	KEN	68	18 Apr
2:14:18	Chris	Verbeeck	BEL	59	5 Jun
2:14:18	Timothy Ndonye	Moni	KEN		19 Jun
2:14:19	Katsuya	Natsume	JPN	66	6 Mar
2:14:21	Vladimir	Yepanov	RUS	68	24 Apr
2:14:25	Minoni	Takeishi	JPN	68	4 Dec
2:14:25	Ken	Abe	JPN	68	18 Dec
2:14:26dh	Josphat	Ndeti	KEN	73	18 Apr
2:14:26	Francis Robert	Naali	TAN	72	25 Sep
2:14:26	Akira	Zayasu	JPN	73	18 Dec
2:14:27	James	Gombetza	ZIM	62	23 Apr
2:14:27	Jan	Huruk	POL	60	14 Aug
2:14:29	Jesús	Herrera	MEX	62	14 Apr
2:14:29	Aleksandr	Pershin	RUS	68	24 Apr
2:14:30dh	Masaki	Higa	JPN	69	8 Mar
2:14:30	György	Markó	HUN	60	24 Apr
2:14:30	Jean-Marie	Gehin	FRA	61	12 Jun

Uncertain distance: Poitiers 30 Oct: 1. Yermashev RUS 2:13:19, 2. Yuriy Mikhailov RUS 53 2:14:26

Drugs disqualification: 2:10:28 Hu Gangjun # CHN 4.12.70 3 Rotterdam 17 Apr

100 KILOMETRES

Mark	Name		Nat	Born	Pos	Meet	Venue	Date
6:22:43	Aleksey	Volgin	RUS	21.1.68	1	IAU WC	Saroma	26 Jun
6:23:34	Jaroslav	Janicki	POL	6.7.66	2	IAU WC	Saroma	26 Jun
6:24:29	Kazimierz	Bak	GER	31.8.56	3	IAU WC	Saroma	26 Jun
6:26:58	Shaun	Meiklejohn	RSA	30.11.61	4	IAU WC	Saroma	26 Jun
6:27:43		Volgin			1	IAU	Santa Cruz de Bezana	1 Oct
6:27:59		Bak			1	IAU	Rodenbach	16 Apr
6:29:42	Jean-Paul	Praet	BEL	8.11.55	1	IAU	Torhout	17 Jun
6:32:19	Andrzej	Magier	POL	23.1.62	5	IAU WC	Saroma	26 Jun
6:33:38	Eiji	Nakagawa	JPN		6	IAU WC	Saroma	26 Jun
6:33:43		Janicki			1	IAU EC	Winschoten	3 Sep
6:33:43		Magier			2	IAU EC	Winschoten	3 Sep
6:35:37		Magier			1	IAU	Kalisz	8 Oct
6:36:26	Kiminari	Kondo	JPN		7	IAU WC	Saroma	26 Jun
6:36:38	Konstantin	Santalov	RUS	3.1.66	1	IAU	Rognonas	3 Apr
6:36:43		Praet			2	IAU	Rognonas	3 Apr
6:37:27	Narisha	Kojima	JPN	16.8.64	8	IAU WC	Saroma	26 Jun
6:37:29	Mikhail	Kokorev	RUS	.65	3	IAU EC	Rognonas	3 Apr
6:37:47	Denis	Gack	FRA	24.2.59	3	IAU WC	Winschoten	3 Sep
6:38:21	Sergey	Soldatov	RUS	.60	1	IAU	Amiens	24 Sep
6:38:55		Magier			2	IAU	Rodenbach	16 Apr
6:39:32	Leonid	Krupskiy	RUS	.52	2	IAU	Amiens	24 Sep
6:39:51	Nikolay (22/14)	Gromov	RUS	.59	3	IAU	Amiens	24 Sep
6:41:40	Tom	Johnson	USA		9	IAU WC	Saroma	26 Jun
6:41:49	Yuriy	Starikov	RUS	7.11.57	2	IAU	Torhout	17 Jun
6:42:50	Bernard	Curton	FRA	.52	4	IAU	Rognonas	3 Apr
6:43:02	Tim	Sloan	AUS		10	IAU WC	Saroma	26 Jun
6:43:58	Mikhail	Soumoshchkin	RUS		4	IAU	Amiens	24 Sep
6:44:18	Don (30)	Wallace	AUS	19.7.61	1	IAU	Kurow	31 Jan
6:44:19	Roland	Vuillemenot	FRA	21.8.46	11	IAU WC	Saroma	26 Jun
6:44:51	Igor	Ryabov	RUS	.67	5	IAU	Amiens	24 Sep
6:45:55	Rich	Hanna	USA		12	IAU WC	Saroma	26 Jun
6:46:03	Lutz	Aderhold	GER	31.7.52	3	IAU	Rodenbach	17 Apr
6:46:13	Jesús	Corredor	ESP		2		Madrid	15 May
6:46:57	Aleksandr	Motorin	RUS	.55	5	IAU EC	Winschoten	3 Sep
6:47:26	Sergey	Kovel	BLS	29.7.61	13	IAU WC	Saroma	26 Jun
6:48:03	Aleksandr	Masarygin	RUS	18.10.60	3		Madrid	15 May
6:48:30	Michael	Sommer	GER	2.3.64	2	IAU NC	Kiel	24 Sep
6:49:11	Aleksey (30)	Kononov	RUS	6.6.60	1	IAU	Faenza	28 May

Marks made on courses not checked by calibrated bicycle

Mark	Name		Nat	Born	Pos	Meet	Venue	Date
6:16:21	Konstantin	Santalov	RUS	3.1.66	1		Kalingrad	9 Apr
6:18:49	Aleksey	Volgin	RUS	21.1.66	2		Kalingrad	9 Apr
6:22:20	Aleksey	Kononov	RUS	6.6.60	3		Kalingrad	9 Apr
6:23:50	Igor	Riabov	RUS	.67	4		Kalingrad	9 Apr
6:26:59	Sergey	Koval	BLS	29.7.61	5		Kalingrad	9 Apr
6:31:38	Leonid	Krupskiy	RUS	.52	6		Kalingrad	9 Apr
6:33:02	José	Carreira	BRA	.64	1		São Paulo	13 Nov
6:43:55	Anatoliy	Kruglikov	RUS	.57	7		Kalingrad	9 Apr
6:47:04	Luiz Carlos	Matos	BRA		2		São Paulo	13 Nov
6:48:28	Sergey	Baluk	RUS	.58	8		Kalingrad	9 Apr

24 HOURS

Track races

Mark	Name		Nat	Born	Pos	Meet	Venue	Date
271.200 km	Anatoliy	Kruglikov	RUS	.57	1		Podolsk	27 Aug
268.975	Eduard	Khirov	RUS	.61	2		Podolsk	27 Aug
264.400	Mikhail	Yeremisov	RUS	.61	3		Podolsk	27 Aug
262.238	Seigi	Arita	JPN		1	IAU	Arcueil	9 Oct
258.101	Vasiliy	Amelin	RUS	.57	4		Podolsk	27 Aug
254.926	Aleksandr	Kostin	RUS	.52	5		Podolsk	27 Aug
252.950		Khirov			1	NC	Moskva	21/22 May
252.667	Ivan	Lubutiin	RUS	.59	6		Podolsk	27 Aug
244.534	Max	Granier	FRA	51	2	IAU	Arcueil	9 Oct
240.146	Aleksey	Barskov	RUS	.60	7		Podolsk	27 Aug

Road races

Mark	Name		Nat	Born	Pos	Meet	Venue	Date
262.758	Paul	Beckers	BEL	22.8.62	1	IAU	Torhout	13/14 Aug

Mark	Name		Nat	Born	Pos	Meet	Venue	Date
261.122	Janos	Bogár	HUN	23.6.64	1	IAU EC	Szeged	21 May
254.013	Jean-Pierre	Guyomarc'h	FRA	.54	2	IAU EC	Szeged	21 May
252.110	Valery	Klement	GER	22.10.57	3	IAU EC	Szeged	21 May
250.068	Marcel	Foucat	FRA	.50	1	NC	Courcon	17/18 Sep
249.283	Vladimir	Tivikov	RUS	.51	4	IAU EC	Szeged	21 May
247.471	Maksim	Vorobyev	RUS		5	IAU EC	Szeged	21 May
245.358	René	de Sousa	FRA	.41	2	NC	Courcon	17/18 Sep
243.594	Paul	Dessalle	FRA	.50	3	NC	Courcon	17/18 Sep
243.340	James	Zarei	GBR	13.1.44	6	IAU EC	Szeged	21 May
242.297	András	Low	HUN	.67	1	IAU	Basel	1 May
242.055	Joseph	Grall	FRA		1	IAU	Niort	6/7 Nov
Indoor								
270.296 km	Anatoliy	Kruglikov	RUS	.57	1		Podolsk	26/27 Feb
269.560	Nasibula	Khusnulin	RUS	.55	2		Podolsk	26/27 Feb
258.302	Eduard	Khirov	RUS	.61	3		Podolsk	26/27 Feb
252.434	Maksim	Vorobyev	RUS		4		Podolsk	26/27 Feb
252.412	Anatoliy	Laput	BLS	.59	5		Podolsk	26/27 Feb
245.713	Vasiliy	Amelin	RUS	.57	6		Podolsk	26/27 Feb

2000 METRES STEEPLECHASE

Mark	Name		Nat	Born	Pos	Meet	Venue	Date
5:24.75	Richard	Kosgei	KEN	29.12.70	1		Rovereto	24 Jul
5:25.50	Alessandro	Lambruschini	ITA	7.1.65	2		Rovereto	24 Jul
5:26.75	Bernard	Barmasai	KEN		3		Rovereto	24 Jul
5:29.93	Alessandro	Briana	ITA	21.3.73	4		Rovereto	24 Jul
5:30.44	Josephat	Kapkory	KEN	2.1.67	5		Rovereto	24 Jul
5:31.62	Giuseppe	Maffei	ITA	28.1.74	6		Rovereto	24 Jul
5:31.82	Gianni	Crepaldi	ITA	19.10.68	7		Rovereto	24 Jul
5:32.34	Johnstone	Kipkoech	KEN	20.12.68	1		Pliezhausen	8 May
During 3000m races								
5:22.97+	Moses	Kiptanui	KEN	1.10.71	1+	WK	Zürich	17 Aug
5:30.36+	Josephat	Kapkory	KEN	2.1.67	1+	Nik	Nice	18 Jul
5:30.72+	Marc	Davis	USA	17.12.69	1+	GWG	St Peterburg	25 Jul

3000 METRES STEEPLECHASE

Mark	Name		Nat	Born	Pos	Meet	Venue	Date
8:08.80	Moses	Kiptanui	KEN	10.10.71	1	WK	Zürich	17 Aug
8:09.16		Kiptanui			1	DNG	Stockholm	12 Jul
8:09.16		Kiptanui			1	ISTAF	Berlin	30 Aug
8:10.20	Richard	Kosgei	KEN	29.12.70	2	ISTAF	Berlin	30 Aug
8:10.56	Mark	Croghan	USA	8.1.68	3	ISTAF	Berlin	30 Aug
8:10.84	Eliud	Barngetuny	KEN	20.5.73	1	Herc	Monaco	2 Aug
8:11.11	Abdelaziz	Sahere	MAR	18.9.67	4	ISTAF	Berlin	30 Aug
8:11.52	William	Mutwol	KEN	10.10.67	2	DNG	Stockholm	12 Jul
8:11.63		Kosgei			1	Nik	Nice	18 Jul
8:12.07		Barngetuny			3	DNG	Stockholm	12 Jul
8:12.16	Patrick	Sang	KEN	11.4.64	2	Herc	Monaco	2 Aug
8:12.16		Sang			5	ISTAF	Berlin	30 Aug
8:13.26		Mutwol			3	Herc	Monaco	2 Aug
8:13.27		Croghan			2	Nik	Nice	18 Jul
8:13.61		Croghan			4	DNG	Stockholm	12 Jul
8:13.77		Kosgei			1	BNP	Villeneuve d'Ascq	8 Jul
8:14.02	Angelo	Carosi	ITA	20.1.64	4	Herc	Monaco	2 Aug
8:14.18	Bernard	Barmasai	KEN		5	Herc	Monaco	2 Aug
8:14.30	Marc	Davis	USA	17.12.69	1	GWG	St Peterburg	25 Jul
8:14.37		Barngetuny			3	Nik	Nice	18 Jul
8:14.68	Matthew	Birir	KEN	5.7.72	6	Herc	Monaco	2 Aug
8:14.72	Johnstone	Kipkoech	KEN	20.12.68	1	CG	Victoria	23 Aug
8:15.25	Gideon	Chirchir	KEN	24.2.66	2	CG	Victoria	23 Aug
8:15.33		Mutwol			4	Nik	Nice	18 Jul
8:15.86	Joseph	Keter	KEN	13.6.69	7	Herc	Monaco	2 Aug
8:15.95	Sa'ad Shaddad	Al-Asmari	SAU	24.9.68	8	Herc	Monaco	2 Aug
8:16.18	Larbi	El Khattabi	MAR	16.5.67	5	Nik	Nice	18 Jul
8:16.74		Barngetuny			2	WK	Zürich	17 Aug
8:17.03		Barngetuny			1	VD	Bruxelles	19 Aug
8:17.03		Birir			6	ISTAF	Berlin	30 Aug
	(30/17)							
8:17.62	Alessandro	Lambruschini	ITA	7.1.65	3	BNP	Villeneuve d'Ascq	8 Jul
8:19.21	Daniel	Njenga	KEN	7.5.76	1	JPN Ch	Tokyo	12 Jun

Mark	Name		Nat	Born	Pos	Meet	Venue	Date
8:19.30	Khalid	Skah	MAR	29.1.67	1	FrancG	Bondoufle	12 Jul
	(20)							
8:19.92	William	van Dijck	BEL	24.1.61	7	VD	Bruxelles	19 Aug
8:20.04	Tom	Hanlon	GBR	20.5.67	9	Herc	Monaco	2 Aug
8:20.98	Simeon	Rono	KEN	9.4.72	2		Hechtel	30 Jul
8:22.20	Mark	Rowland	GBR	7.3.63	8	ISTAF	Berlin	30 Aug
8:22.64	Julius	Kariuki	KEN	12.6.61	4		St Denis	10 Jun
8:23.19	Kim-Lars	Bauermeister	GER	20.11.70	9	ISTAF	Berlin	30 Aug
8:23.28	Graeme	Fell	CAN	19.3.59	3	CG	Victoria	23 Aug
8:23.55	Francesco	Panetta	ITA	10.1.63	5	GGala	Roma	8 Jun
8:23.75	Steffen	Brand	GER	10.3.65	3		Duisburg	12 Jun
8:23.90	Justin	Chaston	GBR	4.11.68	9	Nik	Nice	18 Jul
	(30)							
8:25.33	Markus	Hacksteiner	SUI	18.11.64	4		Luzern	29 Jun
8:25.53	Ricardo	Vera	URU	16.9.62	4		Hechtel	30 Jul
8:25.63	Josephat	Kapkory	KEN	2.1.67	10	Herc	Monaco	2 Aug
8:25.87	Martin	Strege	GER	21.2.66	7	GGala	Roma	8 Jun
8:26.33	Vladimir	Pronin	RUS	27.5.69	5	EC	Helsinki	12 Aug
8:26.99	David	Kemei	KEN	70	1		Maia	16 Jul
8:27.66	Wander do Prado	Moura	BRA	22.2.69	2	NC	Tokyo	12 Jun
8:27.78	Colin	Walker	GBR	29.10.62	4	CG	Victoria	23 Aug
8:27.90A	Wilson	Boit	KEN	72	1		Nairobi	18 Jun
8:27.98	Thierry	Brusseau	FRA	22.7.64	10	Nik	Nice	18 Jul
	(40)							
8:28.12	Barnabas	Barmao	KEN	10.12.69	2		Narbonne	19 Jun
8:28.12	Jim	Svenøy	NOR	22.4.72	7	EC	Helsinki	12 Aug
8:28.18	Elisardo	De La Torre	ESP	10.10.71	1		Pontevedra	9 Jun
8:28.28	Antonio	Peula	ESP	21.3.66	1	NC	San Sebastián	17 Jul
8:28.33	Spencer	Duval	GBR	5.1.70	2	AAA	Sheffield	12 Jun
8:29.12	Marcel	Laros	NED	10.10.71	2		Århus	7 Jul
8:29.45	Michael	Buchleitner	AUT	14.10.69	4	GP II	Linz	4 Jul
8:29.54	Akira	Nakamura	JPN	26.6.67	3	NC	Tokyo	12 Jun
8:29.59	Laban	Chege	KEN	67	5		Duisburg	12 Jun
8:29.76	Luis	Jesus	POR	19.11.68	1	NC	Lisboa	10 Jul
	(50)							
8:29.84	Tom	Buckner	GBR	16.4.63	5	CG	Victoria	23 Aug
8:30.18	Gianni	Crepaldi	ITA	19.10.68	2	NC	Napoli	3 Jul
8:30.29	Wolfgang	Fritz	AUT	3.4.68	11	ISTAF	Berlin	30 Aug
8:30.30	Benjamin	Simatei	KEN	68	3		Århus	7 Jul
8:30.30	Jon	Azkueta	ESP	2.7.67	2	NC	San Sebastián	17 Jul
8:30.49	Vitor	Almeida	POR	6.3.70	2		Maia	16 Jul
8:30.56	Shaun	Creighton	AUS	14.5.67	1		Sydney	30 Jan
8:30.59	Ali	Belghazi	FRA	22.9.62	12	BNP	Villeneuve d'Ascq	8 Jul
8:31.19	Joël	Bourgeois	CAN	25.4.71	6	CG	Victoria	23 Aug
8:31.4	Dan	Reese	USA	15.10.63	2	MSR	Walnut	16 Apr
	(60)							
8:31.51	Paul	Chemase	KEN	24.8.76	1	WJ	Lisboa	23 Jul
8:31.56		Gao Shuhai	CHN	18.10.68	1	NC	Beijing	2 Jun
8:31.73		Sun Ripeng	CHN	25.1.74	1	AsiG	Hiroshima	14 Oct
8:31.86	Danny	Lopez	USA	25.9.68	3	NC	Knoxville	17 Jun
8:32.16	Marcelo	Cascabelo	ARG	6.2.64	5		Maia	16 Jul
8:32.31	Yann	Millon	FRA	26.3.70	2	NC	Annecy	23 Jul
8:32.34	Giuseppe	Maffei	ITA	28.1.74	4		Bologna	2 Sep
8:32.45	Gabriel	Garín	ESP	13.8.69	4	NC	San Sebastián	17 Jul
8:32.89	Eliseo	Martín	ESP	5.11.73	5	NC	San Sebastián	17 Jul
8:32.97	Vladimir	Golyas	RUS	25.1.71	4	ECp	Birmingham	26 Jun
	(70)							
8:33.04	Yasunori	Uchitomi	JPN	29.10.72	4	NC	Tokyo	12 Jun
8:33.07	Brian	Diemer	USA	10.10.61	4	NC	Knoxville	17 Jun
8:33.2A	Christopher	Koskei	KEN	14.8.74	4		Nairobi	11 Jun
8:33.30	Benito	Nogales	ESP	1.8.65	3		Baracaldo	18 Jun
8:33.64	Julius	Chelule	KEN	25.12.78	2	WJ	Lisboa	23 Jul
8:33.73	Vasiliy	Omelyusik	BLR	17.3.65	1	Mal	Grudziadz	1 Jun
8:33.78	Aleksey	Patserin	UKR	16.5.67	5	ECp	Birmingham	26 Jun
8:33.79	Hassan	Ouhrouch	MAR	2.6.64	1		Ciudad Real	24 Jun
8:33.88	Pau	Bundo	ESP	13.10.70	2		Barcelona	26 Jul
8:33.96	Rezki	Chaïb	ALG	23.6.72	3	FRA Ch	Annecy	23 Jul
	(80)							
8:34.42	Irba	Lakhal	MAR	12.2.75	3	WJ	Lisboa	23 Jul

Mark	Name		Nat	Born	Pos	Meet	Venue	Date
8:34.42	Michal	Bartoszak	POL	21.6.70	1		Bialogard	24 Sep
8:34.46	Zeba	Crook	CAN	28.12.66	1	NC	Victoria	29 Jul
8:34.49	Henri	Belkacem	FRA	16.3.64	6		Maia	16 Jul
8:34.51	Mariusz	Staniszewski	POL	17.10.70	2		Bialogard	24 Sep
8:35.03	Javier	Rodriguez	ESP	22.2.74	1	IbAm	Mar del Plata	30 Oct
8:35.13	Marc	Ruiz	ESP	5.2.74	3		Barcelona	26 Jul
8:35.20	Kåre	Sørensen	DEN	4.4.67	9h2	EC	Helsinki	9 Aug
8:35.62	Florian	Ionescu	ROM	3.2.71	1	Balk	Trikala	9 Jul
8:35.71	Torsten	Herwig	GER	19.10.68	4		Cottbus	15 Jun
	(90)							
8:35.87	Ville	Hautala	FIN	19.11.68	7h1	EC	Helsinki	9 Aug
8:35.88	Andre	Green	GER	21.4.73	6		Duisburg	12 Jun
8:36.18	Azzedine	Brahmi	ALG	13.9.66	13	Herc	Monaco	2 Aug
8:36.19	Hilaire	Ntirampéba	BUR		3	FrancG	Bondoufle	12 Jul
8:36.20	Andreas	Fischer	GER	11.4.68	7		Duisburg	12 Jun
8:36.4A	Kirwa	Tanui	KEN		1h		Nairobi	10 Jun
8:36.53	Jan	Zakrzewski	POL	70	3		Bialogard	24 Sep
8:36.54	Matt	McGuirk	USA	15.8.64	7	Pre	Eugene	4 Jun
8:36.55	Sumito	Ogino	JPN	2.4.73	5	NC	Tokyo	12 Jun
8:36.61	Simon	Vroemen	NED	11.5.69	1		Utrecht	12 Aug
	(100)							

Mark	Name		Nat	Born	Date
8:36.63	Greg	Metcalf	USA	69	4 Jun
8:36.7	Eugenio	Frangi	ITA	71	15 Sep
8:36.81	Rubén	García	MEX	70	30 Oct
8:37.18	José Ramon	Rey	ESP	67	31 Jul
8:37.2	Mohamed	Belabbès	ALG	66	26 Jul
8:37.33	Eduardo	Henriques	POR	68	10 Jul
8:37.4	Dmitriy	Drozdov	RUS	72	16 Apr
8:37.46	Antonios	Vouzis	GRE	66	9 Jul
8:37.5	Francis	O'Neill	USA	70	8 Jul
8:37.52	Mohamed	Driouche	ALG	67	8 Jul
8:37.59	Ramiro	Morán	ESP	69	17 Jul
8:37.87	Seyed Hamid	Sadjadi	IRN	69	14 Oct
8:37.92	Gavin	Gaynor	USA	65	14 May
8:38.24A	Philip	Chirchir	KEN		8 Jul
8:38.39	Mick	Hawkins	GBR	61	12 Jun
8:38.42	Christian	Stang	GER	69	12 Jun
8:38.50	Hamadi	Chabouh	TUN	62	12 Jul
8:38.68	Godfrey	Siamusiye	ZAM	72	26 Mar
8:38.7A	Henry	Kimeli	KEN	66	11 Jun
8:38.80	Robert	Hough	GBR	72	15 Jul
8:38.94	Angelo	Giardello	ITA	70	3 Jul
8:39.22A	Christopher	Kipsang	KEN		18 Jun
8:39.24	Harald	Graham	USA	66	4 Jun
8:39.30	Bizuneh	Yae Tura	ETH	70	29 Apr
8:39.34	Richard	Russell	AUS	70	19 Feb
8:39.36	Robert	Cook	USA	71	22 May
8:39.48	Juan Maria	Artola	ESP	70	9 Jun
8:39.54	Jean-Pierre	Poulin	CAN	70	12 Jul
8:39.71	Keith	Cullen	GBR	72	15 Jul
8:39.88	Inocencio	López	ESP	66	8 Oct
8:39.96	Phil	Costley	NZL	70	5 Mar
	(131)				

110 METRES HURDLES

Mark	Wind	Name		Nat	Born	Pos	Meet	Venue	Date
12.98	0.2	Colin	Jackson	GBR	18.2.67	1	TOTO	Tokyo	15 Sep
12.99	-0.3		Jackson			1		Madrid	6 Sep
13.02	0.9		Jackson			1A	ISTAF	Berlin	30 Aug
13.03	1.3		Jackson			1	McD	Sheffield	4 Sep
13.04	1.0		Jackson			1s1	EC	Helsinki	12 Aug
13.07	1.2		Jackson			1		Rieti	28 Aug
13.07	0.9	Mark	Crear	USA	2.10.68	2rA	ISTAF	Berlin	30 Aug
13.08	1.1		Jackson			1	EC	Helsinki	12 Aug
13.08	1.6		Jackson			1	CG	Victoria	23 Aug
13.08	-0.8		Jackson			1	GPF	Paris	3 Sep
13.13	0.4		Crear			1	ASV	Köln	21 Aug
13.14	-0.8	Mark	McKoy	AUT	10.12.61	2	GPF	Paris	3 Sep
13.15	-0.1		McKoy			1A	GP II	Linz	4 Jul
13.16	1.5		Jackson			1h2	EC	Helsinki	11 Aug
13.16	1.1	Florian	Schwarthoff	GER	7.5.68	2	EC	Helsinki	12 Aug
13.16	1.3		McKoy			2	McD	Sheffield	4 Sep
13.19	-0.7		Jackson			1A	WK	Zürich	17 Aug
13.20	1.3		Jackson			1h1	Bisl	Oslo	22 Jul
13.20	1.5		Crear			1	v Afr	Durham	13 Aug
13.22	-0.3		Jackson			1	Bisl	Oslo	22 Jul
13.22	0.0		Jackson			1	VD	Bruxelles	19 Aug
13.22	1.6	Tony	Jarrett	GBR	13.8.68	2	CG	Victoria	23 Aug
13.22	-0.3		McKoy			2		Madrid	6 Sep
13.23	0.7	Eugene	Swift	USA	14.9.64	1		Fresno	9 Apr
13.23	0.6		Jackson			1	v3N	Istanbul	22 May
13.23	1.1		Jarrett			3	EC	Helsinki	12 Aug
13.23	-0.3		Jarrett			3		Madrid	6 Sep
13.23	-1.6		Jarrett			1	WCp	London	11 Sep
13.25	-0.1		Li Tong	CHN	6.5.67	2rA	GP II	Linz	4 Jul

Mark	Wind	Name		Nat	Born	Pos	Meet	Venue	Date
13.25	-0.1		Li Tong	CHN	6.5.67	2rA	GP II	Linz	4 Jul
13.25	1.3	Allen	Johnson	USA	1.3.71	3	McD	Sheffield	4 Sep
		(30/7)							
13.26	-0.3	Greg	Foster	USA	4.8.58	1h3	Bisl	Oslo	22 Jul
13.27	-0.3	Courtney	Hawkins	USA	11.7.67	2h3	Bisl	Oslo	22 Jul
13.33	1.2	Emilio	Valle	CUB	21.4.67	1rB	ISTAF	Berlin	30 Aug
		(10)							
13.34	0.7	Robert	Reading	USA	9.6.67	2		Fresno	9 Apr
13.39	-0.1	Roger	Kingdom	USA	26.8.62	6rA	GP II	Linz	4 Jul
13.39	1.6		Chen Yanhao	CHN	2.1.72	2	AsiG	Hiroshima	15 Oct
13.40	0.3	Vladimir	Belokon	UKR	13.2.69	1	NC	Kiev	27 May
13.40	0.8	Anthony	Dees	USA	6.8.63	3	Nik	Nice	18 Jul
13.41	0.5	Brian	Amos	USA	26.12.71	2	USOF	Edwardsville	9 Jul
13.41	1.1	Claude	Edorh	GER	27.2.72	4	EC	Helsinki	12 Aug
13.42	0.4	Mike	Fenner	GER	24.4.71	1		Berlin	11 Jun
13.42	1.2	Laurent	Ottoz	ITA	10.4.70	2rB	ISTAF	Berlin	30 Aug
13.43	1.5	Dan	Philibert	FRA	6.8.70	2h2	EC	Helsinki	11 Aug
		(20)							
13.45	1.0	Kyle	Vander-Kuyp	AUS	30.5.71	1	NEC	Melbourne	24 Feb
13.45	1.6	Antti	Haapakoski	FIN	6.2.71	2		Lappeenranta	26 Jul
13.46	-0.1	Georg	Boroi	ROM	26.8.64	1	NC	Bucuresti	17 Jun
13.48	0.0	Duane	Ross	USA	5.12.72	1	PennR	Philadelphia	30 Apr
13.48	0.5	Jack	Pierce	USA	23.9.62	6	Herc	Monaco	2 Aug
13.49	0.0	Ubeja	Anderson	USA	30.3.74	2	MSR	Walnut	17 Apr
13.50	0.2	Igor	Kovác	SVK	12.5.69	4=	WG	Helsinki	29 Jun
13.52	1.0	Kevin	White	USA	16.8.74	1		Tempe	2 Apr
13.52	0.9	Kai	Kyllönen	FIN	30.1.65	1		Jyväskylä	2 Aug
13.52	1.3	Andrew	Tulloch	GBR	1.4.67	2h3	EC	Helsinki	11 Aug
		(30)							
13.53	1.5	Robert	Foster #	JAM	12.7.70	1	NCAA	Boise	4 Jun
13.53	1.8	Paul	Gray	GBR	25.5.69	2h2	CG	Victoria	22 Aug
13.54	1.6	Igor	Kazanov	LAT	24.9.63	2		Cottbus	15 Jun
13.55	0.7	Richard	Benoy	USA	14.7.68	4		Fresno	9 Apr
13.55	0.5	Glenn	Terry	USA	10.2.71	4	USOF	Edwardsville	9 Jul
13.56	-0.3	Dietmar	Koszewski	GER	26.7.67	1		Zeven	21 May
13.56	0.5	Frank	Busemann	GER	26.2.75	1h2		Mannheim	4 Jun
13.56	1.5	Jeff	Jackson	USA	14.3.74	2	NCAA	Boise	4 Jun
13.56	-1.1	Jonathan	N'senga	BEL	21.4.73	2	FrancG	Bondoufle	12 Jul
13.57A	1.2	Tim	Kroeker	CAN	25.5.71	1		Flagstaff	14 May
		(40)							
13.58	1.2	Rob	Jones	USA	11.11.70	1		Pittsburgh	14 May
13.58	0.2	Eric	Kaiser	GER	7.3.71	1		Konstanz	23 Jul
13.59	0.9	Jerry	Roney	USA	5.1.70	2rB		Austin	7 May
13.59		Timur	Yudakov	RUS	12.7.66	1		Moskva	29 May
13.60	1.2	Brett	Shields	USA	24.8.70	2		Pittsburgh	14 May
13.60	0.0	Vincent	Clarico	FRA	8.1.66	1		Vanves	17 Jun
13.60	0.8	Andrey	Karatayev	UKR	6.3.66	1h		Kiev	23 Jul
13.60	0.7	T J (Thomas)	Kearns	IRL	2.6.66	3h1	EC	Helsinki	11 Aug
13.61	0.9	Chris	Phillips	USA	24.7.72	1s2	NCAA	Boise	3 Jun
13.62	0.6	Niklas	Eriksson	SWE	22.2.69	1		Gävle	4 Jul
		(50)							
13.65		Larry	Harrington	USA	24.11.70	2h3		Atlanta	22 May
13.65	1.3	Jyrki	Kähkönen	FIN	5.6.67	5h3	EC	Helsinki	11 Aug
13.65	0.4	Aleksandr	Markin	RUS	8.9.62	1	Army	Rostov	25 Aug
13.66	0.5	Sébastien	Thibault	FRA	25.7.70	2s1	NC	Annecy	24 Jul
13.66	1.3	Sven	Göhler	GER	25.2.74	1rB		Rhede	29 Jul
13.67	0.2	Tiberia	Patterson	USA	26.1.71	1		Athens, Oh.	21 May
13.67	1.6	Dmitriy	Kolesnichenko	UKR	28.2.72	1	ECp23	Lillehammer	31 Jul
13.67	1.3	Hubert	Grossard	BEL	28.3.68	6h3	EC	Helsinki	11 Aug
13.68	0.4	Vladislav	Guba	UKR	17.12.71	2	NC	Kiev	27 May
13.68	-0.1	Mircea	Oiada	ROM	20.2.69	2	NC	Bucuresti	17 Jun
		(60)							
13.68	1.9	Claes	Albihn	SWE	12.5.71	5=	ECp	Birmingham	26 Jun
13.68	1.6	Gaute	Gundersen	NOR	13.6.72	2	ECp23	Lillehammer	31 Jul
13.68	0.4	Sergey	Vetrov	RUS	8.5.68	2	Army	Rostov	25 Aug
13.69	0.2	Scott	Thompson	USA	24.7.73	2		Athens, Oh.	21 May
13.70	1.9	Ronald	Mehlich	POL	26.9.69	1h1	v3N	Mielec	1 Jul
13.70	-2.0	Aleksandr	Gorshenin	RUS	11.5.69	2s3	NC	St Peterburg	14 Jul
13.71	1.1	Phil	Riley	USA	24.9.72	1		Raleigh	23 Apr

Mark	Wind	Name		Nat	Born	Pos	Meet	Venue	Date
13.71	1.2	Alexis	Sánchez	CUB	3.3.71	1	NC	La Habana	23 Jun
13.71A	0.0	Thierry	Richard	FRA	22.9.61	1		Font-Romeu	14 Jul
13.72	0.9	Terry	Reese	USA	20.6.67	1	PennR	Philadelphia	30 Apr
		(70)							
13.72	0.7	Andrey	Dydalin	RUS	7.6.66	3		Gladbeck	25 Jun
13.72	0.4	Gennadiy	Dakshevich	RUS	15.3.66	3	Army	Rostov	25 Aug
13.73	1.6	Nur Herman	Majid	MAL	2.8.69	3	AsiG	Hiroshima	16 Oct
13.74	0.2	Arthur	Blake	USA	19.8.66	1		Gainesville	1 May
13.74	0.3	Rod	Jett	USA	28.10.66	6	Jen	San José	28 May
13.75		Reinaldo	Quintero	CUB	7.10.69	1		La Habana	24 Feb
13.75		Marcus	Dixon	USA	6.7.70	1h2		Raleigh	23 Apr
13.75	0.1	Mikhail	Ryabukhin	RUS	25.3.67	1h2	Kuso	Lublin	4 Jun
13.75	1.8	Levente	Csillag	HUN	22.3.73	1		Budapest	19 Jun
13.75	0.5	Lloyd	Cowan	GBR	8.7.62	2h3	BELCh	Bruxelles	17 Jul
		(80)							
13.76	1.0	Andrew	Parker	JAM	11.1.65	3		Tempe	2 Apr
13.76	-0.8	Hugh	Teape	GBR	26.12.63	1		Birmingham	21 May
13.76	1.2	Falk	Balzer	GER	14.12.73	4r2	ISTAF	Berlin	30 Aug
13.76	1.6	Nobuaki	Hoki	JPN	29.10.70	4	AsiG	Hiroshima	16 Oct
13.76	1.6	Takahiro	Matsuhisa	JPN	10.4.68	5	AsiG	Hiroshima	16 Oct
13.77		Omar	Portuondo	CUB	1.5.70	2		La Habana	24 Feb
13.77	1.2	Mathieu	Jouÿs	FRA	13.2.72	2h2	NC	Annecy	24 Jul
13.78		Erik	Batte	CUB	10.12.74	3		La Habana	24 Feb
13.79		William	Erese	NGR	73	1	NC-j	Benin City	28 May
13.79	1.8	Viktor	Bolkun	UKR	2.7.70	1		Barcelona	21 Jun
		(90)							
13.79	0.4	Dudley	Dorival	USA	1.9.75	1	NC-j	Tallahassee	25 Jun
13.80	0.9-	David	Cooper	AUS	10.8.72	3		Brisbane	5 Feb
13.80		Neil	Owen	GBR	18.10.73	1		London (He)	5 Jun
13.81	1.1	Larry	Ryans	USA	28.7.71	2		Raleigh	23 Apr
13.81	0.5	Ross	Flowers	USA	10.8.71	6s1	NC	Knoxville	16 Jun
13.81	0.6	Dan	O'Brien	USA	18.7.66	D	GWG	St Peterburg	29 Jul
13.81	1.5	Kehinde	Aladefa	NGR	19.9.71	4	vUSA	Durham	13 Aug
13.82	0.9	Wagner	Marseille	HAI	13.9.70	4	PennR	Philadelphia	30 Apr
13.82	-3.0	Eduard	Hämäläinen	BLR	21.1.69	D		Götzis	29 May
13.83	2.0	Keevan	Mills	USA	10.7.72	1		San Angelo	16 Apr
		(100)							
13.83	-2.3	Dmitriy	Buldov	RUS	2.7.68	3h1	NC	St Peterburg	15 Jul
13.83	0.7	Robin	Korving	NED	29.7.74	1		Aartselaar	21 Jul
13.83	1.2	Patrik	Torkelson	SWE	24.4.73	1r2		Karlskrona	26 Jul
13.83	1.0	Miguel	Soto	PUR	8.12.67	7		Rhede	29 Jul
		(104)							

Mark	Wind	Name		Nat	Born	Date
13.84	1.8	Thierry	Herbe	FRA	71	21 Jun
13.84	0.8	Tibor	Bédi	HUN	74	23 Jul
13.84	1.8	Emerson	Perin	BRA	75	27 Aug
13.85	1.5	Demetrius	Powell	USA	73	2 Apr
13.85	-0.3	Fumihiro	Kawata	JPN	71	29 Apr
13.85	0.0	David	Kafka	FRA	72	17 Jun
13.85	1.8	Jiri	Hudec	TCH	64	19 Jun
13.86	1.1	Terry	Winston	USA	72	15 May
13.86		Eric	Cannon	USA	67	22 May
13.86	-0.1	Frank	Mensah	USA	74	2 Jun
13.86	0.1	Vladimir	Shishkin	RUS	64	11 Jun
13.86	0.0	Luigi	Bertocchi	ITA	65	25 Jun
13.86	0.8	Alexandre	Yenko	MOL	72	23 Jul
13.86	1.6	Kenneth	Campbell	GBR	72	23 Aug
13.87	1.7	Antonio	Lanau	ESP	66	19 Jun
13.87	-1.0	Krzysztof	Mehlich	POL	74	10 Sep
13.88		Shannon	Flowers	USA	71	4 Jun
13.88		Mustapha	Sdad	MAR	70	4 Jun
13.89		Moses	Oyiki Orode	NGR		26 May
13.90	-0.7	Brandon	Gantt	USA	72	8 Apr
13.90	-0.4	Marcus	Stokes	USA	74	23 Apr
13.90		Khary	Burnley	USA	75	25 May
13.90	0.0	Olivier	Vallaeys	FRA	66	17 Jun
13.90	2.0	Gunnar	Schrör	SUI	67	6 Jul
13.91		Anier Octavio	Garcia	CUB	76	18 Feb
13.91		Steve	Adegbite	NGR	72	24 Apr
13.91	1.8	Jean Marc	Grava	FRA	71	9 Jul
13.91	2.0	Gabriele	Maccarone	ITA	69	24 Sep
13.91	-0.3	Steve	Adegbite	NGR	72	24 Apr
13.91	0.9	Viktor	Zbozínek	TCH	72	21 May
13.91	0.2	William	Adams	USA	73	21 May
13.91	0.9	Kevin	Ellis	USA	73	3 Jun
13.91	1.8	Jean-Marc	Grava	FRA	71	9 Jul
13.92	1.1	Marco	Morgan	USA	71	28 May
13.92	0.3	Pat	Duffy	USA	65	28 May
13.92	-1.3		Zhou Zhong	CHN	66	5 Jun
		(150)				
13.92	-0.1	Tomasz	Nagorka	POL	67	2 Jul
13.92	0.2		Zheng Jinsuo	CHN	70	31 Aug
13.93	1.1	Darius	Pemberton	USA	75	15 May
13.93		Steve	Brown	USA	64	22 May
13.93	1.6	Andrea	Bergna	ITA	68	16 Jul
13.93	0.6	Helge	Bormann	GER	67	20 Aug
13.94A	2.0	Richard	Price	USA	69	2 Apr
13.94	1.0	Stéphane	Remion	FRA	70	19 Jun
13.94	0.2		Zhang Feng	CHN	72	31 Aug
13.95A	1.8	Kobus	Schoeman	RSA	65	18 Mar
13.95	0.0	Keith	Talley	USA	64	27 Mar
13.95	0.0	Derek	Spears	USA	74	30 Apr
13.95			Lee Jung-ho	KOR	73	14 May
13.95	0.0	Emmanuel	Romary	FRA	68	17 Jun
13.95	-2.3	Yevgeniy	Pechonkin	RUS	73	15 Jul
13.95	0.5	Hubert	Rochard	FRA	68	24 Jul
13.97	1.0	Avory	Anderson	USA	73	2 Apr
13.97	1.0	James	Armstrong	USA	67	2 Apr
13.97	-0.3	Toshihiko	Iwasaki	JPN	67	29 Apr
13.97	0.4	Hisanobu	Konae	JPN	72	10 Jun
13.97	1.5	Jerome	Millet	FRA	69	2 Jul
13.97	0.3	Henrik	Dagård	SWE	69	29 Jul
13.97	0.2		Bai Yong	CHN	72	31 Aug

Mark	Wind	Name		Nat	Born	Pos	Meet	Venue	Date

Mark	Wind	Name		Nat	Born	Date
13.98A	1.8	Shaun	Bownes	RSA	70	18 Mar
13.98	0.8	Fausto	Frigerio	ITA	66	21 May
13.98	0.3	Vladimir	Dobridnyev	UKR	70	28 May
13.98	1.9	Tomasz	Krawczyk	POL	74	1 Jul
13.98	1.6	Rasheed	Sheban Marzook	QAT	67	15 Oct
13.99		Prodromos	Katsantonis	CYP	75	13 May
13.99	0.3	Chad	Black	USA	72	25 May
13.99	1.7	Wojciech	Sitek	POL	74	29 May
13.99	1.4	Ryoji	Yukishita	JPN	69	16 Jul
13.99		Guntis	Peders	LAT	76	17 Jul
13.99	0.5	Tomás	Dvorák	TCH	72	3 Sep
(184)						

Best at low altitude: 13.62 1.6 Kroeker 5 Cottbus 15 Jun

Wind-assisted

Mark	Wind	Name		Nat	Born	Pos	Meet	Venue	Date
12.94A	2.8	Colin	Jackson	GBR	18.2.67	1rA		Sestriere	31 Jul
13.05	2.5		Jackson			1	TSB	Edinburgh	8 Jul
13.18	4.7	Robert	Reading	USA	9.6.67	1		Azusa	23 Apr
13.19	2.3		McKoy			1A	Athl	Lausanne	6 Jul
13.22	2.3	Greg	Foster	USA	4.8.58	2	Athl	Lausanne	6 Jul
13.23A	2.8	Allen	Johnson	USA	1.3.71	2rA		Sestriere	31 Jul
13.26A	2.6	Antti	Haapakoski	FIN	6.2.71	1rB		Sestriere	31 Jul
13.27A	2.6	Kyle	Vander-Kuyp	AUS	30.5.71	2rB		Sestriere	31 Jul
13.32A	2.8	Laurent	Ottoz	ITA	10.4.70	3rA		Sestriere	31 Jul
13.37		Brian	Amos	USA	26.12.71	1		Abilene	12 May
13.41A	2.8	Jack	Pierce	USA	23.9.62	4rA		Sestriere	31 Jul
13.42	2.1	Vladislav	Guba	UKR	17.12.71	1		Kiev	23 Jul
13.46	4.8	Glenn	Terry	USA	10.2.71	2		Azusa	23 Apr
13.46	2.9	Arthur	Blake	USA	19.8.66	3		Modesto	14 May
13.47	2.1	Frank	Busemann	GER	26.2.75	1	WJ	Lisboa	22 Jul
13.48	2.6	Igor	Kovác	SVK	12.5.69	1		Praha	14 May
13.48	2.1	Andrey	Karatayev	UKR	6.3.66	2		Kiev	23 Jul
13.49	2.8	Aleksandr	Gorshenin	RUS	11.5.69	1s1	NC	St Peterburg	15 Jul
13.49	2.6	Dmitriy	Buldov	RUS	2.7.68	1	NC	St Peterburg	15 Jul
13.49	2.1	Dmitriy	Kolesnichenko	UKR	28.2.72	3		Kiev	23 Jul
13.52	2.9	Jerry	Roney	USA	5.1.70	3	TexR	Austin	9 Apr
13.52	3.6	Igor	Kazanov	LAT	24.9.63	1		Dijon	12 Jun
13.53		Jeff	Jackson	USA	14.3.74	2		Arlington	1 Apr
13.54	2.8	Mikhail	Ryabukhin	BLR	25.3.67	2s1	RUS Ch	St Peterburg	15 Jul
13.54	2.2	Gennadiy	Dakshevich	RUS	15.3.66	1s2	NC	St Peterburg	15 Jul
13.55	2.2	Aleksandr	Markin	RUS	8.9.62	2s2	NC	St Peterburg	15 Jul
13.56	2.2	Derek	Knight	USA	11.10.67	1		Eagle Rock	14 May
13.58	3.4	Cletus	Clark	USA	20.1.62	2		Houston	7 May
13.62	2.6	Vladimir	Shishkin	RUS	12.1.64	5	NC	St Peterburg	15 Jul
13.64	3.7	Sergey	Vetrov	RUS	8.5.68	4		Nurmijärvi	2 Jul
13.65	2.1	Dudley	Dorival	USA	1.9.75	2	WJ	Lisboa	22 Jul
13.69	3.1	Ross	Flowers	USA	10.8.71	1rB		Modesto	14 May
13.71	2.4	Terry	Reese	USA	20.6.67	2		Durham	9 Apr
13.74	2.3	Pat	McGhee	USA	24.6.66	2h2		Modesto	14 May
13.74	6.1	Larry	Wade	USA	22.11.74	2		Waco	25 May
13.74	2.5	Patrik	Torkelson	SWE	24.4.73	2h3	NC22	Luleå	5 Aug
13.77	2.2	Frank	Mensah	USA	11.5.74	1h2	SEC	Fayetteville	14 May
13.78	3.5	Steve	Adegbite	NGR	23.5.72	3		Houston	7 May
13.81	2.9	Kevin	Ellis	USA	29.6.73	3	TexR	Austin	9 Apr
13.81		Curt	Young	USA	18.1.74	3		Abilene	12 May
13.81	6.1	Derek	Spears	USA	11.4.74	3		Waco	25 May
13.81	3.1	Jean-Marc	Grava	FRA	2.12.71	1		Amiens	29 Jun
13.81	2.2	Yevgeniy	Pechenkin	RUS	9.10.73	5s2	NC	St Peterburg	15 Jul
13.81A	2.6	Andrea	Bergna	ITA	20.8.68	4rB		Sestriere	31 Jul

Mark	Wind	Name		Nat	Born	Date
13.83	6.1	Marcus	Stokes	USA	74	25 May
13.83	3.4	David	Ashford	USA	64	11 Jun
13.83	3.7	Guntis	Peders	LAT	73	2 Jul
13.83	2.4	Sylvers	Bianay Balcot	FRA	73	17 Jul
13.83A	2.6	Gabriele	Maccarone	ITA	69	31 Jul
13.84	2.6	Jiri	Hudec	TCH	64	14 May
13.87	4.1	Emmanuel	Romary	FRA	68	4 Jun
13.88	2.6	Viktor	Zbozínek	TCH	72	14 May
13.90	3.6	Gunnar	Schrör	SUI	67	18 Jun
13.91	3.2	Gary	Gatlin	USA		27 May
13.93		Art	Smith	USA	69	12 May
13.93	2.6	Tomás	Dvorák	TCH	72	14 May
13.94		Isaac	Carson	USA	73	20 May
13.94	2.1	Hubert	Rochard	FRA	68	9 Jul
13.95	3.7	Vadim	Kurach	RUS	70	2 Jul
13.97	4.0	Miguel	De Los Santos	ESP	73	4 Jun
13.97	2.4	Sébastien	Denis	FRA	71	17 Jul

Hand timing

Mark	Wind	Name		Nat	Born	Pos	Meet	Venue	Date
13.1	0.1	Tony	Jarrett	GBR	13.8.68	1rA		Austin	7 May
13.2		Kyle	Vander-Kuyp	AUS	30.5.71	1		Melbourne	3 Feb
13.2	0.1	Kevin	White	USA	16.8.74	2rA		Austin	7 May
13.2	0.1	Jerry	Roney	USA	5.1.70	3rA		Austin	7 May
13.4A	-0.5	Omar	Portuondo	CUB	1.5.70	1		Ciudad México	13 May
13.4		Chris	Phillips	USA	24.7.72	1		Fayetteville	25 May
13.5		Arthur	Smith	USA	16.5.69	2		Abilene	21 Apr

Mark	Wind	Name		Nat	Born	Pos	Meet	Venue	Date
13.5		Vladislav	Guba	UKR	17.12.71	1		Dnepropetrovsk	13 May
13.5A	-0.5	Miguel	Soto	PUR	8.12.67	2		Ciudad México	13 May
13.5	0.2	Andrey	Karatayev	UKR	6.3.66	1		Belaya Tserkov	9 Jul
13.6		Vladimir	Dobridnev	UKR	14.1.70	h		Dnepropetrovsk	13 May
13.6		Gabriele	Maccarone	ITA	10.4.69	1		Rieti	21 Jun
13.6		Guntis	Peders	LAT	15.8.73	1		Valmiera	19 Aug
13.7		Mikhail	Ryabukhin	BLR	67				28 Apr
13.7	0.1	Philip	Riley	USA	71				7 May
13.7	0.1	Marcus	Stokes	USA	74				7 May
13.7A	-0.5	Eugenio	Balanque	CUB	68				13 May

Wind assisted

Mark	Wind	Name		Nat	Born	Pos	Meet	Venue	Date
13.6		Mustahpa	Sdad	MAR	70	1		Meknès	23 Apr
13.7	3.2	Miguel	De Los Santos	ESP	73				19 Jul
13.8		Zouhaïr	Khazine	MAR	66				23 Apr

200 METRES HURDLES

Mark	Wind	Name		Nat	Born	Pos	Meet	Venue	Date
22.72	1.6	Laurent	Ottoz	ITA	10.4.70	1		Milano	25 May
22.94		Stéphane	Diagana	FRA	23.7.69	1		St Paul de la Réunion	29 Oct
23.12		Stéphane	Caristan	FRA	31.5.64	2		St Paul de la Réunion	29 Oct
23.17	1.6	Mario	Gorlani	ITA	30.10.69	2		Milano	25 May

400 METRES HURDLES

Mark	Name		Nat	Born	Pos	Meet	Venue	Date
47.70	Derrick	Adkins	USA	2.7.70	1	GP II	Linz	4 Jul
47.84		Adkins			1	Nik	Nice	18 Jul
47.86		Adkins			1	GWG	St Peterburg	26 Jul
47.90	Samuel	Matete	ZAM	27.7.68	1	Herc	Monaco	2 Aug
47.90		Matete			1	v USA	Durham	13 Aug
47.90		Adkins			1	WK	Zürich	17 Aug
47.93		Adkins			1	Bisl	Oslo	22 Jul
47.94		Adkins			1	Athl	Lausanne	6 Jul
47.94		Adkins			2	Herc	Monaco	2 Aug
47.94		Matete			2	WK	Zürich	17 Aug
47.97		Adkins			1	BNP	Villeneuve d'Ascq	8 Jul
47.98		Matete			2	GWG	St Peterburg	26 Jul
47.99		Matete			2	Athl	Lausanne	6 Jul
48.02		Matete			1	GPF	Paris	3 Sep
48.03		Matete			1		Madrid	6 Sep
48.05	Winthrop	Graham	JAM	17.11.65	2	GP II	Linz	4 Jul
48.05		Adkins			2	GPF	Paris	3 Sep
48.06		Adkins			1		Luzern	29 Jun
48.06	Oleg	Tverdokhleb	UKR	3.11.69	1	EC	Helsinki	10 Aug
48.09		Matete			2	Nik	Nice	18 Jul
48.11		Matete			1	GGala	Roma	8 Jun
48.13		Graham			3	Athl	Lausanne	6 Jul
48.15		Matete			1	VD	Bruxelles	19 Aug
48.18	Danny	Harris	USA	7.9.65	4	Athl	Lausanne	6 Jul
	Before cleared to compete from IAAF suspension							
48.20A		Adkins			1		Sestriere	31 Jul
48.20		Matete			1	ASV	Köln	21 Aug
48.22		Matete			1	TSB	London	15 Jul
48.22	Sven	Nylander	SWE	1.1.62	2	EC	Helsinki	10 Aug
48.22		Matete			1	ISTAF	Berlin	30 Aug
48.22	Stéphane	Diagana	FRA	23.7.69	2		Madrid	6 Sep
48.22		Graham			3		Madrid	6 Sep
48.23		Diagana			3	EC	Helsinki	10 Aug
48.24		Matete			1	Slov	Bratislava	1 Jun
	(33/7)							
48.48	Edgar	Itt	GER	8.6.67	1	NC	Erfurt	3 Jul
48.77	Pedro	Rodrigues	POR	8.7.71	4	EC	Helsinki	10 Aug
48.88	Eronildo	de Araújo	BRA	31.12.70	4		Madrid	6 Sep
	(10)							
49.03	Octavius	Terry	USA	7.11.72	2	NC	Knoxville	17 Jun
49.05	Marc	Dollendorf	BEL	7.2.66	5	ASV	Köln	21 Aug
49.07	Torrance	Zellner	USA	6.1.70	3	NC	Knoxville	17 Jun
49.07A	Barnabas	Kinyor	KEN	3.8.61	1	NC	Nairobi	8 Jul
49.07	Gary	Cadogan	GBR	8.10.66	3	Bisl	Oslo	22 Jul
49.13	Shunji	Karube	JPN	8.5.69	1	AsiG	Hiroshima	11 Oct
49.13	Yoshihiko	Saito	JPN	12.2.72	2	AsiG	Hiroshima	11 Oct
49.19	Olaf	Hense	GER	19.11.67	6	ASV	Köln	21 Aug
49.24	Fabrizio	Mori	ITA	28.6.69	4	GGala	Roma	8 Jun
49.26	Peter	Crampton	GBR	4.6.69	3s2	EC	Helsinki	8 Aug

Mark	Name		Nat	Born	Pos	Meet	Venue	Date
49.29	Eric	Thomas	USA	1.12.73	1	JUCO	Odessa, TX	21 May
49.29	Kazuhiko	Yamazaki	JPN	10.5.71	3	TOTO	Tokyo	15 Sep
49.30	Vadim	Zadoinov	MOL	24.5.69	4s2	EC	Helsinki	8 Aug
49.31	Niklas	Wallenlind	SWE	21.11.68	5s2	EC	Helsinki	8 Aug
49.33	Domingo	Cordero	PUR	17.10.65	2	Banes	São Paulo	21 May
49.39	José	Pérez	CUB	19.3.71	1	NC	La Habana	25 Jun
49.43	Giorgio	Frinolli	ITA	12.7.70	1		Formia	5 Jun
49.43	Ruslan	Mashchenko	RUS	11.11.71	1		Moskva	11 Jun
49.43	Gideon	Biwott	KEN	26.6.66	2	CG	Victoria	26 Aug
49.49	Nick	Ward	AUS	18.1.70	1	NC	Sydney	13 Mar
	(30)							
49.52	Kevin	Henderson	USA	4.2.65	1	USOF	Edwardsville	10 Jul
49.52	Fadhel	Khayatti	TUN	18.1.65	1	FranG	Bondoufle	12 Jul
49.53	Marty	Beck	USA	2.3.70	1h1	NC	Knoxville	15 Jun
49.53	Rohan	Robinson	AUS	15.11.71	5	Bisl	Oslo	22 Jul
49.55	Michael	Kaul	GER	25.7.67	2	NC	Erfurt	3 Jul
49.56	Ali Ismail	Doka	QAT	2.8.73	3	AsiG	Hiroshima	11 Oct
49.63	Helge	Bormann	GER	21.8.67	3	NC	Erfurt	3 Jul
49.65A	Paolo	Bellino	ITA	19.8.69	4		Sestriere	31 Jul
49.68	Simon	Hollingsworth	AUS	9.5.72	3	NC	Sydney	13 Mar
49.68	Jozef	Kucej	SVK	23.3.65	3	Slov	Bratislava	1 Jun
	(40)							
49.69	Vesa-Pekka	Pihlavisto	FIN	15.4.65	1		Lappeenranta	26 Jul
49.70A	Ferrins	Pieterse	RSA	22.3.67	1	NC	Secunda	7 May
49.70	Ashraf	Saber	ITA	2.4.73	1		Rieti	22 May
49.70	Kevin	Young	USA	16.9.66	2	NYG	New York	22 May
49.70	Jean-Paul	Bruwier	BEL	18.2.71	1		Nivelles	23 Jul
49.72	Bryan	Bronson	USA	9.9.72	2r2		Austin	7 May
49.72	Marco	Morgan	USA	14.4.71	4	NC	Knoxville	17 Jun
49.72	Maurice	Horton	USA	10.11.69	1		Lindau	31 Jul
49.73	Ian	Weakley	JAM	24.2.74	2	JUCO	Odessa, TX	21 May
49.74	Alejandro	Argudin	CUB	10.3.74	2s		La Habana	9 Jun
	(50)							
49.75	Piotr	Kotlarski	POL	5.4.69	2	NC	Pila	26 Jun
49.75A	Rere	Sang	KEN	72	3		Nairobi	23 Jul
49.76	Mugur	Mateescu	ROM	13.6.69	1	NC	Bucuresti	18 Jun
49.76	Everson	Teixeira	BRA	23.11.74	1	IbAm	Mar del Plata	30 Oct
49.77	Winston	Sinclair	JAM	11.10.71	1		Lafayette	15 May
49.81	John	Rothell	USA	29.3.72	2	WG	Helsinki	29 Jun
49.84	Maurice	Mitchell	USA	14.5.71	2s2	NC	Knoxville	16 Jun
49.86	Mitchell	Francis	JAM	13.6.72	3	NCAA	Boise	4 Jun
49.87	Mark	Thompson	JAM	2.8.67	1		Fairfax	14 May
49.89	Ken	Harnden	ZIM	31.3.73	2	Owens	Columbus	8 May
	(60)							
49.89	Giampiero	Idda	ITA	27.6.69	1h4		Napoli	2 Jul
49.89	Chanond	Keanchan	THA	24.1.70	4	AsiG	Hiroshima	11 Oct
49.90	Sergey	Podrez	RUS	26.2.71	1	NC	St Peterburg	15 Jul
49.90A	Joseph	Maritim	KEN	22.10.68	4		Nairobi	23 Jul
49.90	Mohammed	Amin	PAK	69	5	AsiG	Hiroshima	11 Oct
49.91	German	Petrov	RUS	26.3.67	2		Århus	7 Jul
49.92	David	Patrick	USA	12.6.60	7	NC	Knoxville	17 Jun
49.92	Tony	McKennie	USA	26.10.67	2	USOF	Edwardsville	10 Jul
49.92	Hamadou	Mbaye	SEN	21.4.60	1	FRA Ch	Annecy	24 Jul
49.93	Wayne	Whyte	JAM	4.5.74	3	JUCO	Odessa, TX	21 May
	(70)							
49.94	Ismo	Hämeenniemi	FIN	1.6.70	2		Lappeenranta	26 Jul
49.95	Daniel	Ritter	SUI	28.12.65	1	NC	Lausanne	31 Jul
49.95	Pawel	Januszewski	POL	2.1.72	6s1	EC	Helsinki	8 Aug
49.97	Aleksandr	Belikhov	RUS	27.12.72	2		Moskva	11 Jun
49.98	Zaid Abou	Hamed	SYR	22.4.70	1	NEC	Melbourne	24 Feb
49.98A	Johan	Steynberg	RSA	6.6.72	2	NC	Secunda	7 May
49.99	Larry	Sanders	USA	26.4.70	5	Banes	São Paulo	21 May
50.01	Sammy	Biwott	KEN	23.7.74	2		Granada	1 Jun
50.01A	Charles	Kamau	KEN		3		Nairobi	18 Jun
50.01	Dusan	Kovács	HUN	31.7.71	4h3	EC	Helsinki	7 Aug
	(80)							
50.02	Kenny	Hall	USA	25.1.67	1		Los Angeles Ww	1 May
50.04	Ryan	Hayden	USA	13.3.71	2		Indianapolis	30 Jul
50.05	Pat	Mann	USA	24.4.66	1		Fairfax	25 May

Mark	Name		Nat	Born	Pos	Meet	Venue	Date
50.05	Hideaki	Kawamura	JPN	15.9.74	3	NC	Tokyo	11 Jun
50.06	Niklas	Eriksson	SWE	22.2.69	1		Byrkjelo	24 Jul
50.06	Judex	Lefou	MRI	24.6.66	2	FRA Ch	Annecy	24 Jul
50.08	Juan	Vallin	MEX	7.9.69	1	NC	Jalapa	7 Aug
50.10	Carsten	Köhrbrück	GER	26.6.66	4	NC	Erfurt	3 Jul
50.12	Marko	Granat	SWE	7.1.66	2		Karlskrona	26 Jul
50.18	Derek	Spears	USA	11.4.74	1		Houston	24 Apr
	(90)							
50.19	Steve	Coupland	GBR	15.6.65	2	AAA	Sheffield	12 Jun
50.19	Pedro	Piñera	CUB	20.12.71	3	NC	La Habana	25 Jun
50.22A	Grant	Roberts	RSA	22.5.71	3	NC	Secunda	7 May
50.24	Lawrence	Lynch	GBR	1.11.67	5h3	EC	Helsinki	7 Aug
50.24	Noriaki	Matsue	JPN	15.7.71	2		Fukushima	25 Sep
50.25A	Johan	Jonker	RSA	19.3.70	4	NC	Secunda	7 May
50.25	Ibou	Faye	SEN	69	3	FrancG	Bondoufle	12 Jul
50.26	Oscar	Pitillas	ESP	16.10.71	3		Granada	1 Jun
50.29	Pat	McGhee	USA	24.6.66	1r2	MSR	Walnut	17 Apr
50.30	Miro	Kocuvan	SLO	15.6.71	6h3	EC	Helsinki	7 Aug
	(100)							

Mark	Name		Nat	Born	Date
50.31A	Mario	Toerien	RSA	72	7 May
50.34	Juan	Hernández	CUB	68	25 Jun
50.34	Mauro	Maurizi	ITA	68	3 Jul
50.35	Curt	Young	USA	74	24 Apr
50.36	Jose	Lopez	USA	72	21 May
50.38	Iñigo	Monreal	ESP	74	10 Jul
50.38	Aleksey	Bazarov ¶	ISR	63	16 Jul
50.42	Joey	Woody	USA	73	1 Jun
50.42	Salvador	Vila	ESP	69	4 Jun
50.43	Atsushi	Yamamoto	JPN	70	25 Sep
50.45	Stéphane	Caristan	FRA	64	24 Jul
50.46	Akira	Michishita	JPN	65	11 Jun
50.46	Hidekazu	Katsuki	JPN	69	25 Sep
50.49	Hubert	Rakotombélontsoa	MAD	68	25 Jun
50.49	Vyacheslav	Orinchuk	UKR	70	4 Jul
50.50A	Cornelius	du Rand	RSA	72	18 Apr
50.50	Kostas	Pochanis	CYP	73	27 May
50.51	Marco	Beukenkamp	NED	63	16 Jul
50.52	Jerry	Roney	USA	70	7 May
50.54	Steffen	Kolb	GER	73	7 Aug
50.56	Tom	McGuirk	IRL	71	1 May
50.56	Gennadiy	Gorbenko	UKR	75	21 Jul
50.57	Petteri	Pulkkinen	FIN	73	29 Jun
50.58	Vincenzo	Cox	USA	73	24 Apr
50.58	Quinton	Milner	USA	74	24 Apr
50.58	Massimo	Redaelli	ITA	71	2 Jul
50.58	Hadi Soua'an	Al-Somaily	SAU	76	11 Oct
50.59	Rod	Zuyderwyk	AUS	71	13 Mar
50.60	Mamoru	Teramoto	JPN	72	22 May
50.60	Mohamed	Debbab	MAR	68	12 Jul
50.60	Gary	Jennings	GBR	72	21 Jul
50.61	Ben	Beyers	USA	74	22 May
50.62	Tomonori	Takane	JPN	73	11 Jun
50.64	Darren	Wright	AUS	65	30 Jan
50.64	Plamen	Nyagin	BUL	71	3 Jul
50.66	Mohamed Hamed	Al-Bishi	SAU	75	7 Apr
50.67	Helio	Reis	POR	72	16 Jul
50.68	Carlos	Silva	POR	74	2 Jul
50.69	Jeff	Jackson	USA	74	8 Apr
50.69	Patrick	Ottoz	ITA	71	2 Jul
50.69	David	Niaré	FRA	69	23 Jul
50.70	Thomas	Zverina	CAN	71	15 Apr
50.70	Noel	Levy	GBR	75	8 Jul
50.70	Andrey	Borovikov	RUS	68	15 Jul
50.71	Vladislav	Shirayev	RUS	73	16 Jul
50.71	Stéphane	Traversini	FRA	69	24 Jul
50.72	Mauro	Mendes	BRA	65	11 Jun
50.76	Pawel	Wozniak	POL	69	16 Sep
50.79	Marvin	James	JAM	75	21 Jul
50.81	Michael	Rose	JAM		22 May
	(150)				
50.81	Aldelhaq	Lahlali	MAR	71	11 Jul
50.82	Enzo	Franciosi	ITA	70	24 Jun
50.84A	Jaco	Jonker	RSA	75	13 May
50.85	Cliff	Alexander	USA	72	1 Jun
50.85A	Riwan	Ibrahim	NGR		18 Jun
50.85	Miklós	Roth	HUN	75	22 Jul
50.86	Kehinde	Aladefa	NGR	74	1 May
50.87	Sylvain	Moreau	FRA	66	12 Jun
50.88	Manesh	Pillay	AUS	72	11 Mar
50.88	Louis	Sales	USA	71	22 May
50.88A	Peter	Tanui	KEN	62	23 Jul
50.89	Franck	Grondin	FRA	69	12 Jun
50.92	El Hafni	Abdelmaksoud Ibrahim	EGY		11 Jul
50.93	Tony	Briggs	AUS	67	28 Jan
50.93A	Peter	Wamithi	KEN	72	8 Jul
50.94	Aaron	Lacy	USA	73	23 Apr
50.94		Yang Xianjun	CHN	72	2 Jun
50.95	Jon	Schmidt	NZL	69	13 Feb
50.95	Hendrik	Willems	GER	71	12 Jun
50.95	Róbert	Jarábek	SVK	75	22 Jul
50.96	Tsuyoshi	Yasuda	JPN	74	22 May
50.97	Anson	Watts	USA	73	23 Apr
50.98	Tony	Williams	GBR	72	12 Jun
50.98	Antoine	Colle	FRA	70	23 Jul
50.99	Norge	Bell	CUB	71	25 Jun
	(175)				

Low altitude best

49.50	Kinyor	3	CG	Victoria	26Aug
49.95	Bellino	2h4	NC	Napoli	2 Jul
	hand 49.7	1		Giaveno	9 Jul

Hand timing

49.2A	Gideon	Biwott	KEN	26.6.66	2		Nairobi	23 Jul
49.7	Ian	Weakley	JAM	24.2.74	1h1	JUCO	Odessa, TX	20 May
49.7A	Rere	Sang	KEN	72	3		Nairobi	23 Jul

50.4	Mohamed	Debbab	MAR	68	1 Jul
50.4	Vyacheslav	Orinchuk	UKR	70	30 Apr
50.5	Abdelhaq	Lahlali	MAR	71	1 Jul
50.8	Eugene	Swift	USA	64	2 Apr
50.8A	Llimi	Rivas	COL	68	11 Sep

Unconfirmed: 49.91 Antonio Smith VEN 67 17 Jul

Subsequent to positive drugs test: 50.31 Aleksey Bazarov ¶ ISR 63 7 Aug

HIGH JUMP

Mark	Name		Nat	Born	Pos	Meet	Venue	Date
2.42	Javier	Sotomayor	CUB	13.10.67	1		Sevilla	5 Jun
2.41		Sotomayor			1	NC	Habana	25 Jun
2.41		Sotomayor			1	TSB	London	15 Jul
2.40i		Sotomayor			1		Wuppertal	4 Feb
2.40i		Sotomayor			1	TSB	Birmingham	26 Feb
2.40		Sotomayor			1		Eberstadt	10 Jul
2.40		Sotomayor			1	Nik	Nice	18 Jul
2.40		Sotomayor			1	GWG	St Peterburg	29 Jul
2.40		Sotomayor			1	WCp	London	11 Sep
2.39i		Sotomayor			1		Madrid	11 Feb
2.38i	Steve	Smith	GBR	29.3.73	2		Wuppertal	4 Feb
2.38i		Sotomayor			1		Berlin	4 Mar
2.38i	Wolf-Hendrik	Beyer	GER	14.2.72	1		Weinheim	18 Mar
2.37i		Sotomayor			1		Frankfurt am Main	9 Feb
2.37i	Dalton	Grant	GBR	8.4.66	1	EI	Paris	13 Mar
2.37		Sotomayor			1	GGala	Roma	8 Jun
2.37		Sotomayor			1	Athl	Lausanne	6 Jul
2.37		Sotomayor			1		Madrid	6 Sep
2.36i	Steinar	Hoen	NOR	8.2.71	1		Balingen	12 Feb
2.36i		Beyer			2		Balingen	12 Feb
2.36i		Sotomayor			1		Liverpool	24 Feb
2.36i		Smith			2		Liverpool	24 Feb
2.36i	Troy	Kemp	BAH	18.3.66	2		Weinheim	18 Mar
2.36		Sotomayor			1	Banes	São Paulo	21 May
2.36		Sotomayor			1	ISTAF	Berlin	30 Aug
2.35i		Kemp			1		Pireas	28 Feb
2.35i	Jean-Charles	Gicquel	FRA	24.2.67	2	EI	Paris	13 Mar
2.35		Sotomayor			1	AmCp	Manaus	15 May
2.35		Sotomayor			1		Granada	1 Jun
2.35		Kemp			1		Caorle	16 Jul
2.35		Hoen			1	Bisl	Oslo	22 Jul
2.35		Hoen			1	EC	Helsinki	9 Aug
2.35		Sotomayor			1	TOTO	Tokyo	15 Sep
2.35		Sotomayor			1		Fukuoka	17 Sep
	(34/7)							
2.34i	Ralf	Sonn	GER	17.1.67	3		Balingen	12 Feb
2.33	Tim	Forsyth	AUS	17.8.73	1	NC	Sydney	13 Mar
2.33	Artur	Partyka	POL	25.7.69	2=	EC	Helsinki	9 Aug
	(10)							
2.33A	Gilmar	Mayo	COL	30.9.69	1		Pereira	17 Oct
2.32i	Hollis	Conway	USA	8.1.67	2		Spala	27 Jan
2.32i	Christian	Popescu	ROM	12.8.72	1	Balk	Pireas	20 Feb
2.32i	Brendan	Reilly	GBR	23.12.72	4		Liverpool	24 Feb
2.32i	Ray	Doakes	USA	12.8.73	1	SEC	Gainesville	27 Feb
2.32	Charles	Austin	USA	19.12.67	1		Waco	25 May
2.32		Lee Jin-taek	KOR	13.4.72	1	NC	Seoul	18 Jun
2.32	Dragutin	Topic	YUG	12.3.71	3	ASV	Köln	21 Aug
2.31i	Robert	Ruffini	SVK	26.1.67	2		Arnstadt	29 Jan
2.31i	Grigoriy	Fyodorkov	RUS	9.11.64	1	NC	Lipetsk	26 Feb
	(20)							
2.31i	Håkon	Särnblom	NOR	3.3.66	3		Pireas	28 Feb
2.31i	Randy	Jenkins	USA	18.9.70	1	NCAA	Indianapolis	11 Mar
2.31i	Leonid	Pumalainen	RUS	13.4.70	5	EI	Paris	13 Mar
2.31	Steve	Smith	USA	11.1.71	2	NCAA	Boise	2 Jun
2.31	Jaroslaw	Kotewicz	POL	16.3.69	1	Kuso	Lublin	4 Jun
2.31	Dimitrios	Kokotis	GRE	12.4.72	1		Khania	5 Jun
2.31	Geoff	Parsons	GBR	14.8.64	3	CG	Victoria	26 Aug
2.30i	Ruslan	Stipanov	UKR	19.9.71	2		Banská Bystrica	26 Jan
2.30i	Stevan	Zoric	YUG	25.5.71	2		Pireas	16 Feb
2.30i	Lambros	Papakostas	GRE	20.10.69	2		Pireas	20 Feb
	(30)							
2.30	Lochsley	Thomson	AUS	20.8.73	1	NEC	Melbourne	24 Feb
2.30	Jagan	Hames	AUS	31.10.75	2	NC	Sydney	13 Mar
2.30	Aleksey	Makurin	RUS	21.7.72	1	NC-23	Voronezh	18 Jun
2.30	Oleg	Zhukovskiy	BLR	15.2.70	1	v3N	Krakow	30 Jun
2.30	Sorin	Matei	ROM	8.7.63	1		Bucuresti	22 Jul
2.30	Tony	Barton	USA	17.10.69	1		Byrkjelo	24 Jul

Mark	Name		Nat	Born	Pos	Meet	Venue	Date
2.29	Gustavo	Becker	ESP	17.6.66	1		Barcelona	29 Jun
2.28i	Georgi	Dakov	BUL	21.10.67	6		Balingen	12 Feb
2.28i	Juha	Isolehto	FIN	6.6.68	1		Tampere	19 Feb
2.28i	Torsten	Marschner	GER	17.11.68	7		Berlin	4 Mar
	(40)							
2.28	Tray	Barley	USA	24.1.73	1		Tempe	2 Apr
2.28		Xu Yang	CHN	21.6.70	1		Hiroshima	30 Apr
2.28	Sergey	Kolesnik	UKR	31.5.69	1		Odessa	20 May
2.28	Roberto	Ferrari	ITA	24.3.67	1		Rieti	22 May
2.28	Chris	Olsen-O'Neil	USA	27.5.73	3	NCAA	Boise	2 Jun
2.28		Tao Xu	CHN	26.1.72	1	NC	Beijing	5 Jun
2.28	Yuriy	Sergiyenko	UKR	19.3.65	2		Lisboa	18 Jun
2.28	Wolfgang	Kreissig	GER	29.8.70	2	NC	Erfurt	3 Jul
2.28	Cory	Siermachesky	CAN	20.8.69	4	CG	Victoria	26 Aug
2.28i	Sergey	Klyugin	RUS	24.3.74	1		Kineshma	6 Nov
	(50)							
2.28	Chris	Anderson	AUS	6.4.68	1		Perth	17 Dec
2.27i	Kristofer	Lamos	GER	1.1.74	6		Weinheim	18 Mar
2.27	Steve	Parker	USA	4.7.72	2	DogwR	Knoxville	9 Apr
2.27	Robert	Kolodziejczyk	POL	3.8.70	2	v3N	Krakow	30 Jun
2.27		Bi Hongyong	CHN	16.11.74	1		Jinan	20 Aug
2.27	Takahisa	Yoshida	JPN	17.2.70	1	AsiG	Hiroshima	15 Oct
2.26i	Carlo	Thränhardt	GER	5.7.57	1		Otterberg	19 Feb
2.26i	Matti	Viitala	FIN	26.3.66	1	vSWE	Växjö	5 Mar
2.26	Marino	Drake	CUB	13.6.67	2	NC	La Habana	25 Jun
2.26	Konstantin	Isayev	RUS	7.7.73	1		Sotteville	26 Jun
	(60)							
2.26	Przemyslaw	Radkiewicz	POL	25.8.70	2	NC	Pila	26 Jun
2.26	Konstantinos	Liapis	GRE	1.5.73	2	Balk-g	Trikala	9 Jul
2.26	Jeff	Wylie	USA	28.12.68	4		Byrkjelo	24 Jul
2.26	Masaaki	Uno	JPN	13.12.72	1		Tokyo	11 Sep
2.26	Takahiro	Kimino	JPN	19.2.73	2		Fukuoka	17 Sep
2.26		Kim Tae-hee	KOR	3.9.73			Daeju	30 Oct
2.25i	Konstantin	Galkin	RUS	25.3.65	1		Moskva	14 Jan
2.25i	Sergey	Malchenko	RUS	2.11.63	4		Moskva	14 Jan
2.25i	Monterio	Holder	USA	17.10.70	1		Johnson City	22 Jan
2.25i	Vladimir	Zaboronok	BLR	11.11.68	1	NC	Minsk	5 Feb
	(70)							
2.25i	Vyacheslav	Tyrtyshnik	UKR	16.1.71	1		Zaporozhe	5 Feb
2.25i	Petar	Malesev	YUG	6.8.72	1		Lincoln	12 Feb
2.25	Eric	Taylor-Perry	USA	22.2.72	2		Tempe	2 Apr
2.25	Alex	Rosen	USA	2.6.73	1	PennR	Philadelphia	30 Apr
2.25	Richard	Duncan	CAN	25.12.73	2		Austin	7 May
2.25	Edgar	Garcia	PUR		1		Lafayette	14 May
2.25	Abe	Faust	USA	73	1		Raleigh	19 May
2.25	Ettore	Ceresoli	ITA	11.4.70	5	GGala	Roma	8 Jun
2.25	Alessandro	Canale	ITA	15.5.69	7	GGala	Roma	8 Jun
2.25	Brian	Stanton	USA	19.2.61	5=	NC	Knoxville	16 Jun
	(80)							
2.25	Koji	Fujishima	JPN	2.7.70	1		Hiratsuka	3 Jul
2.25	Nikolay	Moskalets	BLR	5.6.69	1	NC	Gomel	10 Jul
2.25	Aleksandr	Buglakov	BLR	16.4.72	2	NC	Gomel	10 Jul
2.25	Anton	Riepl	GER	28.2.69	1		Mallersdorf	18 Jul
2.25	Sergey	Dymchenko	UKR	23.8.67	2		Kiev	24 Jul
2.25	Charles	Lefrançois	CAN	19.12.72	2	NC	Victoria	30 Jul
2.25	Ian	Thompson	BAH	8.12.68	9	CG	Victoria	26 Aug
2.24i	Mark	Mandy	IRL	19.11.72	1		Birmingham	8 Jan
2.24i	Oleg	Muravyov	RUS	6.5.68	1		Moskva	27 Jan
2.24i	Andrey	Sankovich	BLR	15.7.66	8		Spala	27 Jan
	(90)							
2.24i	Pierre	Bernhard	FRA	15.2.68	1		Siegen	13 Feb
2.24i	Eric	Bishop	USA	7.6.76	1		Syracuse	13 Mar
2.24	Yoshiteru	Kaihoko	JPN	19.11.71	3		Mito	8 May
2.24	Jacob	Katonon	KEN	70	1		Kasarani	9 Jul
2.24	Luca	Zampieri	ITA	15.2.74	2	v2N23	Modena	16 Jul
2.23i	Alex	Zaliauskas	CAN	20.4.71	2	Mill	New York	4 Feb
2.23i	Jan	Janku	TCH	10.8.71	1		Pardubice	19 Feb
2.23i	Jordi	Rofes	ESP	24.9.76	1	NC	Sevilla	26 Feb
2.23	Jeremy	Fischer	USA	16.2.76	1		Santa Barbara	26 Mar

Mark	Name		Nat	Born	Pos	Meet	Venue	Date
2.23	Thad	Hathaway	USA	10.3.74	1		Eugene	16 Apr
	(100)							
2.23	Dillon	Phelps	USA	1.12.74	1		Tuscaloosa	23 Apr
2.23	Itai	Margalit	ISR	25.1.70	1		Lincoln	12 May
2.23	Tim	Suchan	USA	2.2.72	2		Wichita	19 May
2.23	Omar	Dixon	USA	23.1.74	2		Raleigh	19 May
2.23	Jon	Royce	USA	2.3.74	1		Ypsilanti	25 May
2.23		Cho Hyun-uk	KOR	15.3.70	2	NC	Seoul	18 Jun
2.23	Zoltán	Bakler	HUN	1.12.71	1		Vels	16 Jul
2.23	Roland	Stark	GER	10.10.75	1	NC-j	Ulm	31 Jul
2.23i	Ed	Broxterman	USA	28.11.73			Manhattan	9 Dec
	(109)							

Mark	Name		Nat	Born	Date
2.22i	Andréa	Liverani	ITA	64	30 Jan
2.22i	Benoit	Lapeyrie	FRA	68	30 Jan
2.22i	Satoru	Nonaka	JPN	63	7 Feb
2.22i	Peter	Herber	USA		18 Feb
2.22	Bruce	King	USA	73	19 Mar
2.22	Ken	Washington	USA	61	2 Apr
2.22	Vinton	Bennett	CAN	70	9 Apr
2.22	Simeon Kiprotich Ruto		KEN		30 Apr
2.22	Nick	Johannsen	USA	75	21 May
2.22	Kevin	Keane	IRL	70	25 May
2.22	Guo Yuanming		CHN	75	5 Jun
2.22	Djamel	Benhacine	ALG	70	12 Jun
2.22	Attila	Zsivótzky	HUN	77	25 Jun
2.22	Konstantin	Matusevich	UKR	71	26 Jun
2.22	Dimitar	Toychev	BUL	68	3 Jul
2.22	Jon	Utgardsløkken	NOR	73	24 Jul
2.22	Mika	Polku	FIN	75	27 Aug
2.22	Zhou Zhongge		CHN	67	31 Aug
2.22	Nick	Moroney	AUS	72	9 Sep
2.21i	Sheldon	Carpenter	USA	73	9 Jan
2.21i	Vladimir	Sokolov	RUS	63	22 Jan
2.21i	Igor	Kulikov	RUS	71	c23 Jan
2.21Ai	Jon	DeBerry	USA	71	4 Mar
2.21	Ivan	Wagner	USA	76	11 Mar
2.21	Mike	Pascuzzo	USA	61	2 Apr
2.21	Pierre	Vorster	RSA	69	23 Apr
2.21	Marcus	Jahn	GER	72	30 Apr
2.21	Stefano	Savietto	ITA	72	8 May
2.21	Shannon	King	USA	75	28 May
2.21	Lou Cwee Peng		MAL	68	29 May
2.21	Antoine	Burke	IRL	75	25 Jun
2.21	Bjørn	Olsson	NOR	75	3 Jul
2.21	Jake	Jacoby	USA	61	9 Jul
2.21	Ain	Evard	EST	62	17 Jul
2.21	Federico	Rodeghiero	ITA	71	22 Jul
2.21	Tomás	Janku	TCH	74	30 Jul
2.21	Normunds	Sietins	LAT	67	19 Aug
2.21	Oskari	Frösén	FIN	76	17 Sep
2.21	Michiya	Onoue	JPN	71	2 Oct
2.21	Shunichi	Kobayashi	JPN	76	31 Oct
	(150)				

Outdoors on built-up runway: 2.36 Sotomayor 1 Salgotarjan 12 Sep

Unconfirmed

Mark	Name		Nat	Born
2.24	Igor	Paklin	KGZ	15.6.63
2.24	Stanislav	Mingazov	KGZ	21.8.65

Best outdoor

Mark	Name	Pos	Meet	Venue	Date
2.35	Hoen	1	Bisl	Oslo	22 Jul
2.35	Kemp	1		Caorle	16 Jul
2.34	Grant	1	OD	Jena	3 Jun
2.33	Gicquel	4		Eberstadt	10 Jul
2.33	Smith GBR	2=	EC	Helsinki	9 Aug
2.31	Jenkins	1	NCAA	Boise	2 Jun
2.31	Beyer	4=	Nik	Nice	18 Jul
2.31	Särnblom	4	EC	Helsinki	9 Aug
2.30	Conway	1	Jen	San José	28 May
2.30	Papakostas	1		Thessaloniki	11 Jun
2.28	Doakes	1=	SEC	Fayetteville	15 May
2.28	Reilly	1		Loughborough	5 Jun
2.28	Sonn	3	NC	Erfurt	3 Jul
2.28	Fyodorkov	2	Athl	Lausanne	6 Jul
2.28	Pumalainen	1	NC	St Peterburg	16 Jul
2.28	Stipanov	1		Kiev	24 Jul
2.27	Lamos	1		Schwieberdingen	2 Jun
2.26	Klyugin	2	NC-23	Voronezh	17 Jun
2.25	Holder	1	Gator	Knoxville	23 Apr
2.25	Tyrtyshnik	2		Odessa	20 May
2.25	Galkin	2		Duisburg	12 Jun
2.25	Isolehto	1		Saarijärvi	25 Jun
2.25	Zoric	1	NC	Beograd	31 Jul
2.24	Popescu	2		Zalaegerszeg	5 Jun
2.24	Ruffini	2	ECpII	Istanbul	11 Jun
2.23	Sankovich	1		Cottbus	15 Jun

Mark	Name	Date
2.22	Malesev	23 Apr
2.22	Liverani	8 May
2.22	Popescu	7 Jun
2.22	Mandy	18 Jun
2.22	Nonaka	2 Jul
2.21	J Janku	11 Jun
2.21	Zaliauskas	24 Jun

POLE VAULT

Mark	Name		Nat	Born	Pos	Meet	Venue	Date
6.14A	Sergey	Bubka	UKR	4.12.63	1		Sestriere	31 Jul
6.05i		Bubka			1	Mast	Grenoble	6 Feb
6.05		Bubka			1	ISTAF	Berlin	30 Aug
6.00i		Bubka			1		Clermont-Ferrand	28 Jan
6.00		Bubka			1		Kuortane	25 Jun
6.00	Radion	Gataullin	RUS	23.11.65	1	EC	Helsinki	11 Aug
6.00		Bubka			1		Sapporo	27 Aug
5.97	Scott	Huffman	USA	30.11.64	1	NC	Knoxville	18 Jun
5.95		Bubka			1	Pre	Eugene	4 Jun
5.95		Bubka			1	VD	Bruxelles	19 Aug
5.94	Jean	Galfione	FRA	9.6.71	1		Dijon	12 Jun
5.92	Dean	Starkey	USA	27.3.67	1	Banes	São Paulo	21 May
5.90i	Maksim	Tarasov	RUS	2.12.70	1		Madrid	11 Feb

Mark	Name		Nat	Born	Pos	Meet	Venue	Date
5.90i		Gataullin			1		Liévin	13 Feb
5.90i		Galfione			2		Liévin	13 Feb
5.90i		Bubka			1		Donyetsk	20 Feb
5.90i	Pyotr	Bochkaryov	RUS	3.11.67	1	EI	Paris	12 Mar
5.90		Starkey			1	Athl	Lausanne	6 Jul
5.90		Bubka			1		Padova	10 Jul
5.90		Bubka			1	DNG	Stockholm	12 Jul
5.90		Bubka			1	Nik	Nice	18 Jul
5.90	Igor	Trandenkov	RUS	17.8.66	1	GWG	St Peterburg	25 Jul
5.90		Tarasov			1	Kuts	Moskva	31 Jul
5.90		Trandenkov			2	EC	Helsinki	11 Aug
5.90		Bubka			1	GPF	Paris	3 Sep
5.90	Okkert	Brits	RSA	22.8.73	1	WCp	London	10 Sep
5.90		Bubka			1	TOTO	Tokyo	15 Sep
5.89		Bubka			1	GP	St Denis	10 Jun
5.89		Trandenkov			2	GP	St Denis	10 Jun
5.88		Gataullin			1	ASV	Köln	21 Aug
5.86	Valeri	Bukrejev	EST	15.6.64	1		Somero	3 Jul
	(31/10)							
5.85	Kory	Tarpenning	USA	27.2.62	2	Pre	Eugene	4 Jun
5.85	Pat	Manson	USA	29.11.67	2	TOTO	Tokyo	15 Sep
5.83i	Jani	Lehtonen	FIN	11.8.68	1		Stockholm	8 Mar
5.83i	Lawrence	Johnson	USA	7.5.74	1	NCAA	Indianapolis	12 Mar
5.83A	Bill	Payne	USA	21.12.67	1		El Paso	29 May
5.81	Igor	Potapovich	KZK	6.9.67	3	Banes	São Paulo	21 May
5.80i	Aleksandr	Korchagin	KZK	25.1.72	1		Almaty	18 Feb
5.80	Gérald	Baudouin	FRA	15.11.72	4	BNP	Villeneuve d'Ascq	8 Jul
5.80	Denis	Petushinskiy	RUS	28.6.67	2	NC	St Peterburg	15 Jul
5.80	Philippe	Collet	FRA	13.12.63	4	EC	Helsinki	11 Aug
	(20)							
5.75i	Vasiliy	Bubka	UKR	26.11.60	2		Clermont-Ferrand	28 Jan
5.75	Danny	Krasnov	ISR	25.5.70	2	VD	Bruxelles	19 Aug
5.75	Konstantin	Semyonov	RUS	20.11.69	1		Rostov	26 Aug
5.72A	Paul	Benavides	MEX	5.11.64	1		El Paso	18 Jun
5.71	Andrey	Tiwontschik	GER	13.7.70	1		Oberkochen	18 Jun
5.71	Petri	Peltoniemi	FIN	6.3.70	1		Raahe	20 Jul
5.70i	Philippe	D'Encausse	FRA	24.3.67	3		Clermont-Ferrand	28 Jan
5.70i	Grigoriy	Yegorov	KZK	12.1.67	2		Moskva	1 Feb
5.70i	Brent	Burns	USA	2.5.69	1	Mill	New York	4 Feb
5.70i	Andrey	Skvortsov	RUS	2.12.68	1		Moskva	4 Feb
	(30)							
5.70i	István	Bagyula	HUN	2.1.69	4		Berlin	4 Mar
5.70	Doug	Fraley	USA	7.3.65	2		Modesto	14 May
5.70	Nick	Hysong	USA	9.12.71	1	NCAA	Boise	3 Jun
5.70	Bill	Deering	USA	20.7.71	2	NCAA	Boise	3 Jun
5.70	Viktor	Chistyakov	RUS	9.2.75	1		Leppävirta	7 Jun
5.70	Daniel	Martí	ESP	23.4.73	1		Lisboa	18 Jun
5.70	Igor	Yanchevskiy	RUS	11.3.68	2	Barth	Luxemburg	30 Jun
5.70	Valeriy	Ishutin	RUS	5.9.65	2	TSB	London	15 Jul
5.70A	Gianni	Iapichino	ITA	2.3.69	4		Sestriere	31 Jul
5.66i	Mark	Buse	USA	30.11.72	1		Bloomington	12 Feb
	(40)							
5.66	Patrik	Stenlund	SWE	11.10.68	1		Staffanstorp	12 Jun
5.65i	Yevgeniy	Bondarenko	RUS	8.10.66	1		Moskva	5 Jan
5.65	Mike	Holloway	USA	12.7.69	1		Baton Rouge	25 May
5.65	Gennadiy	Sidorov	BLR	13.3.67	1	ECp I	Valencia	12 Jun
5.65	Tim	Bright	USA	28.7.60	2	WG	Helsinki	29 Jun
5.63	Jeff	Hartwig	USA	25.9.67	1		Jonesboro	1 Jun
5.62	Brit	Pursley	USA	25.4.69	1		Austin	6 May
5.62	Daren	McDonough	USA	29.5.74	1	Big 10	Madison	21 May
5.61	Justin	Daler	USA	12.4.71	2	DogwR	Knoxville	9 Apr
5.61	Alberto	Manzano	CUB	22.9.72	1	NC	La Habana	25 Jun
	(50)							
5.61	Nuno	Fernandes	POR	1.4.69	2		Funchal	18 Jul
5.60i	Aleksandr	Chervonyi	UKR	26.3.70	1		Donyetsk	30 Jan
5.60i	Yuriy	Yeliseyev	RUS	27.5.75	1		Malmö	2 Feb
5.60i	Aleksey	Gladkikh	RUS	17.4.71	2		Moskva	4 Feb
5.60i	Sergey	Fomenko	UKR	7.6.67	1	NC	Kiev	13 Feb

Mark	Name		Nat	Born	Pos	Meet	Venue	Date
5.60i	Doug	Wood	CAN	30.1.66	1		Edmonton	12 Mar
5.60	Delko	Lesev	BUL	6.1.67	1		Sofia	22 May
5.60	Dan	Burton	USA	11.3.67	2		Champaign	25 May
5.60	Sergey	Yesipchuk	UKR	1.10.67	5	Slov	Bratislava	1 Jun
5.60	Javier	Garcia	ESP	22.7.66	1		San Cugat	4 Jun
	(60)							
5.60	Jean-Marc	Tailhardat	FRA	12.4.66	8		St Denis	10 Jun
5.60	Tim	Lobinger	GER	3.9.72	3	ECp	Birmingham	26 Jun
5.60	Alain	Andji	FRA	20.11.74	1		Dreux	10 Jul
5.60	Peter	Widén	SWE	2.7.67	4		Göteborg	28 Aug
5.57	Hideyuki	Takei	JPN	19.11.70	1		Shizuoka	16 Jul
5.55i	Werner	Holl	GER	28.1.70	1	NC	Dortmund	25 Feb
5.55	Riaan	Botha	RSA	8.11.70	1		Port Elizabeth	15 Apr
5.55	Asko	Peltoniemi	FIN	7.2.63	4	WG	Helsinki	29 Jun
5.55	Thierry	Moÿse	FRA	18.2.67	1		La Roche sur-Yon	14 Jul
5.55	Martin	Amann	GER	23.11.70	2		Schelklingen	22 Jul
	(70)							
5.54	David	Cox	USA	7.8.72	1eB		Modesto	14 May
5.54	Gennadiy	Sukharev	BLR	3.2.65	1		Recklinghausen	3 Jun
5.53i		Kim Chul-kyun	KOR	28.2.69	1		Toyota	20 Mar
5.53	Terry	Womack	USA	29.10.65	3		Abilene	12 May
5.52	Kevin	Brown	USA	15.8.71	1		Knoxville	2 Apr
5.52	J.J.	Miller	USA	8.4.73	1eA	TexR	Austin	8 Apr
5.52	Jon	Bazzoni	USA	25.12.70	2eA	TexR	Austin	8 Apr
5.52	Scott	Shaffer	USA	31.5.64	1eB	TexR	Austin	8 Apr
5.52	Tim	Mack	USA	15.9.72	3	DogwR	Knoxville	9 Apr
5.52	Scotty	Miller	USA	8.8.69	2		Austin	6 May
	(80)							
5.52	Wayne	Guidry	USA	24.11.73	3		Austin	6 May
5.52	Anthony	Curran	USA	27.6.59	1		Irvine	7 May
5.52	Martin	Voss	DEN	5.9.67	1		Bad Gandersheim	15 May
5.52	Heikki	Vääräniemi	FIN	21.12.69	3		Kuortane	25 Jun
5.52	Vitaliy	Stepanov	RUS	9.12.65	1		Nurmijärvi	2 Jul
5.52	Trond	Barthel	NOR	11.9.70	1	NC	Jessheim	21 Aug
5.50i	Tim	McMichael	USA	22.2.67	1		Saskatoon	8 Jan
5.50i	Domitien	Mestre	BEL	13.12.73	1		Dortmund	9 Jan
5.50i	Dmitriy	Markov	BLR	14.3.75	3		Moskva	14 Jan
5.50i	José Manuel	Arcos	ESP	19.1.73	1		Madrid	15 Jan
	(90)							
5.50i	Jean-Michel	Godard	FRA	19.1.71	P		Liévin	16 Jan
5.50i	Rich	Fulford	USA	29.4.69	2		Johnson City	22 Jan
5.50i	Andrea	Pegoraro	ITA	24.10.66	1		Busto Arsizio	23 Jan
5.50i	Martin	Eriksson	SWE	15.6.71	1		Ames	12 Feb
5.50i	Christos	Pallakis	GRE	9.10.71	1		Portland	13 Feb
5.50i	Jesús Gabriel	Concepcion	ESP	7.8.72	1		Sevilla	26 Feb
5.50	Jon	Kelley	USA	19.12.69	1		Cape Girardeau	8 Apr
5.50	Teruyasu	Yonekura	JPN	2.1.71	2		Shizuoka	5 May
5.50	Massimo	Allevi	ITA	23.11.69	1		Rieti	21 May
5.50	Maurilio	Mariani	ITA	22.4.73	1		Formia	28 May
	(100)							
5.50	John	Besmer	USA	66	1		Los Gatos	11 Jun
5.50	Francine	Thénault	FRA	72	1		Bourgoin-Jallieu	13 Jul
5.50	Neil	Winter	GBR	74	1		Crawley	6 Aug
5.50	James	Miller	AUS	74	1		Victoria	19 Aug
5.50	Mark	Lugenbühl	GER	66	3=		Zweibrücken	27 Aug
5.50	Chris	Tamminga	NED	74	1		Groningen	11 Sep
	(106)							

Mark	Name		Nat	Born	Date
5.47i	Tim	James	USA	71	30 Apr
5.47	Alberto	Ruiz	ESP	61	26 Jul
5.46A	Lance	White	USA	70	25 May
5.45	Thierry	Vigneron	FRA	60	16 Apr
5.45	Isaac	Molinero	ESP	73	15 Jul
5.45	Carl-Johan	Alm	SWE	69	28 Sep
5.44	Martin	Eriksson	SWE	71	21 May
5.43	Shaun	Downey	USA	70	25 May
5.43	Mike	Heath	USA	69	25 May
	5.48 unconfirmed				
5.43	Mike	Albright	USA		25 May
5.42	Adam	Smith	USA	71	2 Apr
5.42	Mike	Edwards	GBR	68	12 May
5.41i	Steve	Bridges	USA	70	18 Feb
5.41i	Martin	Kysela	TCH	74	22 Feb
5.41i	Zoltán	Farkas	HUN	70	26 Feb
5.41	John	Sommers	USA	70	9 Apr
5.41	Michael	Stolle	GER	74	7 Aug
5.40i	Sergey	Moiseyev	RUS	73	14 Jan
5.40Ai	Scott	Hennig	USA	69	22 Jan
5.40i	Richard	Havlásek	TCH	73	23 Jan
5.40i	Alan	De Naeyer	BEL	71	6 Feb
5.40i	Hiroshi	Terada	JPN	71	11 Feb
5.40i	Vyacheslav	Kalinichenko	UKR	73	18 Feb

Mark	Name		Nat	Born		Mark	Name		Nat	Born	Date
5.40A	Tim	Canfield	USA	63	25 Feb	5.40	Nick	Buckfield	GBR	73	6 Aug
5.40i	Helmar	Schmidt	GER	63	25 Feb	5.38	Chad	Harting	USA	72	30 Jul
5.40i	Andrey	Isakov	KZK	70	27 Feb	5.37	Garth	Willard	USA	69	17 Apr
5.40i	Mårten	Ulvsbäck	SWE	66	11 Mar	5.35i	Brad	Darr	USA	68	22 Jan
5.40	Simon	Arkell	AUS	66	19 Mar	5.35i	Roman	Bocharnikov	RUS	67	29 Jan
5.40	Jeff	Bray	USA	70	9 Apr	5.35	Adam	Steinhardt	AUS	69	13 Mar
5.40	Toshiyuki	Hashioka	JPN	64	29 Apr	5.35	Paul	Gibbons	NZL	71	13 Mar
5.40A	Angel	Garcia	CUB	67	1 May	5.35	Simeon	Anastasiadis	GRE	68	8 May
5.40	Erki	Nool	EST	70	8 May	5.35	Scott	Krupilski	USA	64	14 May
5.40	Laurens	Looije	NED	73	15 May	5.35	Shannon	Pope	USA	73	25 May
5.40	Sergey	Voronin	KZK	73	21 May	5.35	Volkmar	Reinecke	GER	65	28 Jun
5.40	Boguslaw	Kopkowski	POL	70	1 Jun	5.35	Olivier	Lelong	FRA	70	24 Jul
5.40	Ron	Johnson	USA	69	1 Jun	5.35	Benoit	Lestrade	FRA	71	24 Jul
5.40	Pavel	Burlachenko	RUS	76	7 Jun	5.35	Fabio	Pizzolato	ITA	75	2 Sep
5.40	Michael	Kühnke	GER	73	15 Jun	5.35	Fulvio	Andreini	ITA	67	2 Oct
5.40	Yevgeniy	Smiryagin	RUS	76	18 Jun	5.35	Robert	Hill	AUS	69	15 Dec
5.40	Florian	Wacker	GER	72	18 Jun		(170)				
5.40	Marc	Osenberg	GER	69	18 Jun	5.33	Joe	Dial	USA	62	2 Apr
5.40	Matej	Urban ¶	TCH	75	25 Jun	5.33	Jacob	Davis	USA	78	12 Apr
5.40	Aleksandrs	Matusevics	LAT	73	29 Jun	5.33	Mike	Thompson	USA		16 Apr
5.40	Alain	Blondel	FRA	72	3 Jul	5.33	Todd	Campbell	USA	72	16 Apr
	(150)					5.33	Drew	Fucci	USA	67	7 May
5.40	Vyacheslav	Aristov	BLR	65	10 Jul	5.32Ai	Brad	Schweyen	USA	68	26 Feb
5.40	Hermann	Fehringer	AUT	62	10 Jul	5.32	Tommy	Negrete	USA		6 May
5.40	Fabrice	LeMonnier	FRA	73	10 Jul	5.32	Mark	Mullins	USA	72	12 May
5.40	Photis	Stephani	CYP	71	3 Aug	5.31	Markus	Ellinger	GER	68	9 Aug
						5.31	Pál	Rohanszky	HUN	70	12 Sep

Outdoors on built-up runway

Mark	Name		Nat	Born	Pos	Venue	Date
5.86	Denis	Petushinskiy	RUS	28.6.67	1	Karlskrona	23 Jul
5.61	Peter	Widén	SWE	2.7.67	3	Karlskrona	23 Jul
5.61	Konstantin	Semyonov	BLR	20.11.69	1	Salgotarjan	12 Sep

Exhibition

Mark	Name		Nat	Born	Pos	Venue	Date
5.80	Gianni	Iapichino	ITA	2.3.69	1	Iglesias	11 Sep
5.70	Tim	Bright	USA	28.7.60	4	New Orleans	6 Aug
5.70	Andrea	Pegoraro	ITA	24.10.66	3	Iglesias	11 Sep
5.53	Trond	Barthel	NOR	11.9.70	1	Århus	8 Sep
5.40	Adam	Kolasa	POL	2.8.75	2	Sopot	29 Jul

Best outdoor

Mark	Name	Pos	Meet	Venue	Date	Mark	Name	Pos	Meet	Venue	Date
5.80	Johnson	1	SEC	Fayetteville	15 May	5.60	Korchagin	2		Lisboa	18 Jun
5.75	V.Bubka	2	Slov	Bratislava	1 Jun	5.50	D'Encausse	1		Tours	8 May
5.70	Yegorov	5	Banes	São Paulo	21 May	5.50	Bondarenko	4		Cottbus	15 Jun
5.70	Bochkaryov	3	Slov	Bratislava	1 Jun	5.50	Holl	2	NC	Erfurt	2 Jul
5.70	Lehtonen	1		Hamina	14 Jun		5.50	4	Exh?	Praha	15 Jun
5.70	Burns	3	NC	Knoxville	18 Jun	5.50	Pegoraro	1	NC	Napoli	3 Jul
5.70	Bagyula	1		Budapest	31 Jul	5.50	Markov	2	WJ	Lisboa	24 Jul
5.60	Buse	1		Champaign	25 May						

Mark	Name	Date	Mark	Name	Date	Mark	Name	Date
5.44	Eriksson	21 May	5.40	Yelisayev	7 Jun	5.40	Mestre	2 Oct
5.42	James	23 Apr	5.40	Kim Chuk-kyun	17 Jun	5.35	Fulford	22 Apr
5.40	Terada	10 Apr	5.40	De Naeyer	10 Jul	5.32	Bocharnikov	28 May
5.40	Pallakis	4 Jun	5.40	Wood	11 Jul	5.40exh	Kysela	26 Sep

LONG JUMP

Mark	Wind	Name		Nat	Born	Pos	Meet	Venue	Date
8.74A	2.0	Erick	Walder	USA	5.11.71	1		El Paso	2 Apr
8.66A	1.4	Carl	Lewis	USA	1.7.61	*		Sestriere	31 Jul
8.63	0.5	Kareem	Streete-Thompson	USA	30.3.73	1	GP II	Linz	4 Jul
8.58	0.2	Mike	Powell	USA	10.11.63	1	VD	Bruxelles	19 Aug
8.51	1.6		Powell			*	NC	Knoxville	18 Jun
8.51	1.8		Streete-Thompson			1	Athl	Lausanne	6 Jul
8.47	0.8	Roland	McGhee	USA	15.10.71	1		Rhede	29 Jul
8.43i	-	Stanislav	Tarasenko	RUS	22.7.66	1	Army	Moskva	26 Jan
8.43i	-		Walder			1	NCAA	Indianapolis	11 Mar
8.42A			Streete-Thompson			1		El Paso	16 Apr
8.39	0.9		Walder			2	GWG	St Peterburg	26 Jul
8.38	1.4		Powell			1	GP	St Denis	10 Jun
8.37	0.8		Lewis			*	NYG	New York	22 May
8.37	-1.0		Streete-Thompson			2	VD	Bruxelles	19 Aug
8.36	1.6	Konstandinos	Koukodimos	GRE	14.9.69	1		Khania	5 Jun
8.36	1.7		Powell			*	Athl	Lausanne	6 Jul
8.35	1.1		Koukodimos			1	NC	Athina	26 Jun

Mark	Wind	Name		Nat	Born	Pos	Meet	Venue	Date
8.34	0.0		Walder			1	NCAA	Boise	2 Jun
8.34	0.6		McGhee			2	NCAA	Boise	2 Jun
8.33i	-		Walder			1		Lincoln	5 Feb
8.33	1.5		Streete-Thompson			1		Innsbruck	7 Jun
8.33	-1.4		Powell			*	GWG	St Peterburg	26 Jul
8.33	0.5		Powell			1	WK	Zürich	17 Aug
8.32	0.2		Powell			2		Innsbruck	7 Jun
8.32	0.0		McGhee			1		Salamanca	22 Jul
8.32	0.7		Streete-Thompson			2	WK	Zürich	17 Aug
8.31	0.8		Powell			*	Bisl	Oslo	22 Jul
8.31	0.8		Streete-Thompson			2	Bisl	Oslo	22 Jul
8.30i	-	Ivailo	Mladenov	BUL	6.10.73	1		Pireas	28 Feb
8.29	0.1	Yevgeniy	Tretyak	RUS	18.7.71	1		Stavropol	28 May
8.29	0.8		Streete-Thompson			3	GWG	St Peterburg	26 Jul
8.28	0.3	Dion	Bentley	USA	26.8.71	2	GP II	Linz	4 Jul
		(32/10)							
8.26i	-	Ivan	Pedroso	CUB	17.12.72	2		Pireas	28 Feb
8.24A	1.3	Reggie	Jones	USA	8.5.71	2		El Paso	16 Apr
8.24	0.7	Dietmar	Haaf	GER	6.3.67	1	NC	Erfurt	3 Jul
8.23i	-	Dmitriy	Bagryanov	RUS	18.12.67	1		Moskva	14 Jan
8.23A		Rogelio	Saenz	MEX	8.6.68	1		El Paso	25 Jun
8.22	1.2	Obinna	Eregbu	NGR	9.11.69	Q	CG	Victoria	24 Aug
8.21	1.5	Vitaliy	Kirilenko	UKR	25.4.68	1		Kharkov	29 May
8.21	1.2	Aleksandr	Glovatskiy	BLR	2.5.70	1	Malin	Grudziadz	1 Jun
8.21	0.9	Nikolay	Antonov	BUL	17.8.68	1		Plovdiv	10 Jul
8.21	1.7	Christian	Thomas	GER	21.5.65	1		Germering	23 Jul
		(20)							
8.20A	1.0	Armen	Martirosyan	ARM	6.8.69	1		Leninakan	17 Jul
8.20A	1.8	Giovanni	Evangelisti	ITA	11.9.61	6		Sestriere	31 Jul
8.20	-0.5	Douglas	de Souza	BRA	6.8.72	1	NC	Rio de Janeiro	16 Sep
8.15	0.0		Huang Geng	CHN	10.7.70	1	NC	Beijing	2 Jun
8.14	0.7	Georg	Ackermann	GER	13.7.72	1		Bad Langensalza	28 May
8.13		James	Beckford	JAM	9.1.75	1	JUCO	Odessa, TX	20 May
8.13	-0.4	Milko	Campus	ITA	2.4.69	1		Formia	5 Jun
8.13	0.9	Jaime	Jefferson	CUB	17.1.62	1	NC	La Habana	23 Jun
8.12	1.8		Huang Baoting	CHN	27.5.74	2	AsiG	Hiroshima	11 Oct
8.12A	0.8	Francois	Fouche	RSA	5.6.63	1		Johannesburg	8 Dec
		(30)							
8.11i	-	Bogdan	Tudor	ROM	1.2.70	1	NC	Bucuresti	27 Feb
8.11	1.3	Roman	Orlik	TCH	29.5.72	1		Praha	29 Jun
8.10	0.3	Sheddric	Fields	USA	13.4.73	3	GP II	Linz	4 Jul
8.10	-0.2	Fred	Salle	GBR	10.9.64	1	WCp	London	9 Sep
8.10	1.4	Konstantin	Sarnatskiy	UZB	16.10.71	3	AsiG	Hiroshima	11 Oct
8.09i	-	Galin	Georgiev	BUL	23.3.70	1		Dobrich	5 Mar
8.09	1.7	Larry	Myricks	USA	10.3.56	3		Tempe	2 Apr
8.08		Ayodele	Aladefa	NGR	29.12.70	1		Bauchi	16 Apr
8.08A	0.0	Cheikh	Tidiane Touré	SEN	70	1		La Chaux de Fonds	21 Aug
8.07		Chris	Sanders	USA	8.5.72	1	FlaR	Gainesville	26 Mar
		(40)							
8.07	1.4	Dimitrios	Hatzopoulos	GRE	17.4.67	2	NC	Athina	26 Jun
8.07	1.1	Joe	Greene	USA	17.2.67	4	Bisl	Oslo	22 Jul
8.06i	-	Aston	Morgan	JAM	18.2.73	1		Lincoln	5 Mar
8.06		Marcus	Bailey	USA	16.6.72	1		Athens, GA	7 May
8.06	0.8	Nobuharu	Asahara	JPN	21.6.72	1	NC	Tokyo	11 Jun
8.06	1.9	Masaki	Morinaga	JPN	27.3.72	1		Sapporo	27 Aug
8.05i	-	Angel	Hernández	ESP	15.4.66	1		Madrid	19 Feb
8.05	1.7	Brian	Thomas	CAN	27.1.70	1	DrakeR	Des Moines	29 Apr
8.05	1.0	Aleksey	Buyvolov	RUS	20.4.72	2		Stavropol	28 May
8.05		Elmer	Williams	PUR	8.10.64	1		San Juan	25 Jun
		(50)							
8.05	0.3	Edrick	Floréal	CAN	5.10.66	4	GP II	Linz	4 Jul
8.05A	2.0	Lotfi	Khaida	ALG	20.12.68	10		Sestriere	31 Jul
8.05		Dennis	Harris	USA	23.3.68	*		Malles	20 Aug
8.04A	1.6	Tony	Walton	USA	3.6.69	3		El Paso	16 Apr
8.04	2.0	Yevgeniy	Semenyuk	UKR	11.12.68	2		Kiev	23 Jul
8.04	1.4	Milan	Gombala	TCH	29.1.68	2	EC	Helsinki	10 Aug
8.03	1.1	Erik	Nys	BEL	27.7.73	Q	EC	Helsinki	9 Aug
8.02		Craig	Hepburn	BAH	10.12.69	2		Athens, GA	7 May

Mark	Wind	Name		Nat	Born	Pos	Meet	Venue	Date
8.02	1.3	André	Müller	GER	15.11.70	3	NC	Erfurt	3 Jul
8.02		Konstantin	Krause	GER	8.10.67	5		Bad Cannstatt	10 Jul
		(60)							
8.02	1.9		Lang Yong	CHN	.4.73	1		Tangshan	28 Aug
8.02	0.8		Chao Chih-kuo	TPE	9.12.72	4	AsiG	Hiroshima	11 Oct
8.01	-0.4	Percy	Knox	USA	14.10.69	1	USOF	Edwardsville	9 Jul
8.01	2.0	Bogdan	Tarus	ROM	1.8.75	2	WJ	Lisboa	22 Jul
8.00	0.8	Alexander	Moshammer	AUT	30.5.72	1		Ebensee	28 May
8.00		Sinisa	Ergotic	CRO	14.9.68	1		Zagreb	7 Jun
8.00	1.1	Luis	Bueno	CUB	22.5.69	2	NC	La Habana	23 Jun
8.00	1.4	Robert	Emmiyan	ARM	15.2.65	1	FRACh	Annecy	24 Jul
8.00	1.8	Mattias	Sunneborn	SWE	27.9.70	1		Byrkjelo	24 Jul
8.00	2.0	Jón Arnar	Magnússon	ISL	28.7.69	1		Reykjavik	26 Aug
		(70)							
8.00	2.0	David	Culbert	AUS	17.3.67	2	CG	Victoria	26 Aug
7.99	0.7	Csaba	Almási	HUN	4.7.66	1		Budapest	3 Jun
7.99	1.1	Vladimir	Malyavin	TKM	4.3.73	2		Budapest	3 Jun
7.98		Bernhard	Kelm	GER	23.12.67	1		München	21 May
7.98	0.0		Tan Zhengze	CHN	.1.74	3	NC	Beijing	2 Jun
7.98	0.7	Jai	Taurima	AUS	27.10.73	2		Byrkjelo	24 Jul
7.97i	-	Mike	Francis	PUR	23.10.70	1		Fargo	11 Mar
7.97		Reggie	Torian	USA	22.4.75	1	Big10	Madison	21 May
7.97	0.8	Andrey	Ignatov	RUS	3.2.68	3		Stavropol	28 May
7.97		Andrew	Owusu	GHA	8.7.72	1	NC	Accra	25 Jun
		(80)							
7.97		Ron	Chambers	JAM	5.10.58	1	NC	Kingston	30 Jun
7.97	0.6	Frans	Maas	NED	13.7.64	5	GP II	Linz	4 Jul
7.97A		Benjamin	Koech	KEN	12.4.69	1		Nairobi	23 Jul
7.96	1.4	Kirill	Sosunov	RUS	1.11.75	1		Krasnodar	28 May
7.96	1.7	Erki	Nool	EST	25.6.70	D	ECp C	Tallinn	2 Jul
7.96	0.0	Yuriy	Naumkin	RUS	5.11.68	4		Tallinn	29 Jul
7.96	-0.4		Xu Bin	CHN	4.8.70	2		Tangshan	28 Aug
7.96	2.0		Sung Hee-joon	KOR	8.6.74	5	AsiG	Hiroshima	11 Oct
7.95	1.7	Gordon	Laine	USA	24.2.58	4	NYG	New York	22 May
7.95		Del	Smutherman	USA	21.4.72	1	NC-j	Tallahassee	25 Jun
		(90)							
7.94i	-	Marco	Delonge	GER	16.6.66	1		Hannover	6 Feb
7.94		Lee	Adkins	USA	31.8.72	2		Tempe	25 May
7.94	-0.4	Simone	Bianchi	ITA	27.1.73	2		Formia	5 Jun
7.94A		James	Sabulei	KEN	12.4.69	2		Nairobi	23 Jul
7.94	-0.5	Paulo Sergio	de Oliveira	BRA	1.12.69	2	NC	Rio de Janeiro	16 Sep
7.93	1.0	Aleksey	Petrukhov	RUS	72	4		Stavropol	28 May
7.92	1.2	Gregor	Cankar	SLO	25.1.75	1	ECpII/3	Ljubljana	11 Jun
7.92	0.6	Franck	Zio	BKF	14.8.71	1		Nogent sur Marne	12 Jun
7.92A		Shirak	Pogasyan	ARM	24.9.69	1		Artashat	24 Sep
7.91i	-	Tony	Barton	USA	17.10.69	3	NC	Atlanta	5 Mar
		(100)							
7.91i	-	Sean	Robbins	USA	9.10.72	2		Fargo	11 Mar
7.91		Volker	Mai	GER	3.5.66	2	FlaR	Gainesville	26 Mar
7.91	1.3	János	Uzsoki	HUN	9.9.72	1		Budapest	24 Jun
7.91	1.9	Juha	Kivi	FIN	26.1.64	*		Koski	1 Jul

Mark	Wind	Name		Nat	Born	Date
7.90		Neil	Chance	USA	73	22 Apr
7.90	2.0	Andrey	Sazykin	RUS	75	28 May
7.90	2.0	Tetsuya	Shida	JPN	71	29 May
7.90	-0.9	Roberto	Coltri	ITA	69	5 Jun
7.90	1.2	Kenneth	Kastrén	FIN	75	9 Jul
7.90	1.7	Barrington	Williams	GBR	55	20 Jul
7.90A		Jacob	Katonen	KEN	70	23 Jul
7.90	1.3		Nai Hui-fang	TPE	69	11 Oct
7.89i		Daniel	Barbulescu	ROM	71	27 Feb
7.89	0.7	Teddy	Steinmayr	AUT	64	28 May
7.89	1.2	Martin	Morkes	TCH	71	29 Jun
7.89		Andrey	Nikulin	BLR	68	30 Jun
7.89	1.5	Jarmo	Kärná	FIN	58	31 Jul
7.88i		Andrey	Lyagin	RUS	73	14 Jan
7.88A	0.8	Diatori	Gildersleeve	USA	70	16 Apr
7.88	0.8	Darius	Pemberton	USA	75	2 Jun
7.88	1.5	Yoelbi	Quesada	CUB	73	23 Jun
7.88		Vyacheslav	Bordukov	RUS	59	29 Jun
7.88	1.0	Christian	Plaziat	FRA	63	2 Jul
7.87i		Mika	Kahma	FIN	66	5 Mar
7.87	1.4	Gordon	McKee	USA	66	19 Mar
7.87	0.0	Vadim	Dalibov	RUS	73	28 May
7.87		Nelson	Ferreira Jr	BRA	73	16 Aug
7.86		Alan	Turner	USA	69	26 Mar
7.86	1.5	Stacey	Brown	USA	72	17 Apr
7.86		Viktor	Popko	UKR	68	30 Jun
7.86		Alexander	Bub	GER	67	23 Jul
7.85A		Juan Carlos	Garzon	CUB	74	7 May
7.85	1.8	Justin	N'Koumazok	FRA	75	12 Jun
7.85	1.7	Jesus	Olivan	ESP	68	28 Jun
7.84i	-	Tibor	Ordina	HUN	71	5 Feb
7.84	1.7	Nat	Sowell	USA	73	29 Apr
7.84	0.2	Mark	Malisov	ISR	69	29 May
7.84	1.4	Marco	Alberti	ITA	72	18 Jun
7.84	0.7	Gael	Ovois	FRA	72	29 Jun
7.84	2.0	Balázs	Marik	HUN	69	9 Jul
7.83		Marc	Kimbrough	USA	71	26 Mar
7.83	1.3	Bakri	Darouèche	FRA	74	17 Jul
7.83	-0.5	Yasutaka	Hattori	JPN	72	10 Sep
7.83	-1.3	Stefan	Schmid	GER	70	10 Sep

Mark	Wind	Name		Nat		Born		Pos	Meet	Venue	Date
7.82i		Ron	Jones	USA	72	28 Jan					
7.82i		Leonid	Voloshin	RUS	66	9 Feb					
7.82	1.7	Leonid	Safronnikov	BLR	71	c7 Apr					
7.82	1.3	Kader	Klouchi	FRA	69	18 Jun					
7.82	0.9	Shigeru	Tagawa	JPN	75	21 Jul					
7.82	1.5	Ian	James	CAN	63	26 Aug					
		(150)									
7.81i		Róbert	Michalík	TCH	74	26 Feb					
7.81i		Spyros	Vasdekis	GRE	70	28 Feb					
7.81i		Tyrone	Minor	USA	70	5 Mar					
7.81i		Jerome	Romain	DMN	71	11 Mar					
7.81		Keita	Cline	BVI	74	16 Apr					
7.81		Franck	Monnel	FRA	69	3 Jun					
7.81	0.5	Dan	O'Brien	USA	66	14 Jun					
7.81	0.4	Serge	Hélan	FRA	64	24 Jul					
7.81	0.5	Emmanuel	Laderrière	FRA	71	24 Jul					
7.80i		Dariusz	Bontruk	POL	70	27 Feb					
7.80	0.3	Ken	Nakajima	JPN	67	29 Apr					
		(162)									

Best at low altitude

Mark	Wind	Name	Pos	Meet	Venue	Date
8.01i		Walton	2	NC	Alanta	5 Mar
7.97	1.1	Jones	*		Gateshead	20 Jul
7.93		Walton	*	NC	Knoxville	18 Jun
7.92	0.0	Evangelisti	2		Rovereto	24 Jul
7.85	1.8	Koech				24 Aug
7.83	-0.1	Garzon				25 May
7.82	1.4	Ordina				3 Jun

Wind-assisted

Mark	Wind	Name		Nat	Born	Pos	Meet	Venue	Date
8.95A	3.9	Mike	Powell	USA	10.11.63	1		Sestriere	31 Jul
8.72A	3.9	Carl	Lewis	USA	1.7.61	2		Sestriere	31 Jul
8.68	4.1		Powell			1	NC	Knoxville	18 Jun
8.64	3.1		Powell			1		Modesto	14 May
8.64	3.5	Kareem	Streete-Thompson	USA	30.3.73	2	NC	Knoxville	18 Jun
8.58A	2.7		Streete-Thompson			3		Sestriere	31 Jul
8.50	3.7		Powell			1		Azusa	23 Apr
8.45	2.3		Lewis			1	NYG	New York	22 May
8.45	2.4		Powell			1	GWG	St Peterburg	26 Jul
8.40	3.4	Konstandinos	Koukodimos	GRE	14.9.69	1	ECp I	Valencia	11 Jun
8.39	2.5		Powell			2	Athl	Lausanne	6 Jul
8.37	2.1		Powell			1	Bisl	Oslo	22 Jul
8.35			McGhee			1	DogwR	Knoxville	9 Apr
8.35	2.9		Walder			1	SEC	Fayetteville	14 May
8.34	2.5		Streete-Thompson			2	NYG	New York	22 May
8.34	2.4		Huang Geng	CHN	10.7.70	1	AsiG	Hiroshima	11 Oct
8.31	4.9		Tarasenko			1		Nurmijärvi	2 Jul
8.31A	3.0	Milko	Campus	ITA	2.4.69	3		Sestriere	31 Jul
8.29	2.2	James	Beckford	JAM	9.1.75	1		Tempe	2 Apr
8.19A	2.6	Francois	Fouche	RSA	5.6.63	1		Pietersburg	18 Mar
8.17	3.3	Dennis	Harris	USA	23.3.68	1		Malles	20 Aug
8.15A	4.0	Simone	Bianchi	ITA	27.1.73	8		Sestriere	31 Jul
8.12	3.3	Darius	Pemberton	USA	10.5.75	2	SEC	Fayetteville	14 May
8.12	2.1	Csaba	Almási	HUN	4.7.66	1		Budapest	21 May
8.11		Sheddric	Fields	USA	13.4.73	1		Houston	5 Mar
8.10A	2.4	Jai	Taurima	AUS	27.10.73	9		Sestriere	31 Jul
8.09	2.2	Milan	Gombala	TCH	29.1.68	1		Praha	14 May
8.07		Tony	Walton	USA	3.6.69	1		Abilene	12 May
8.07	4.2	Thorsten	Heide	GER	4.5.69	2		Cannstatt	10 Jul
8.06		Andrew	Owusu	GHA	8.7.72	4	SEC	Fayetteville	14 May
8.04	3.3	Mattias	Sunneborn	SWE	27.9.70	1		Västerås	30 Jun
8.04	3.1	Gregor	Cankar	SLO	25.1.75	1	WJ	Lisboa	21 Jul
8.03	2.4	Tetsuya	Shida	JPN	27.6.71	2	NC	Tokyo	11 Jun
8.01	2.6	Andrey	Ignatov	RUS	3.2.68	2	NC	St Peterburg	15 Jul
7.99	2.5	Ryan	Moore	AUS	18.10.74	2	NC	Sydney	13 Mar
7.99		Neil	Chance	USA	14.2.73	1		Raleigh	19 May
7.98	3.2	Daisuke	Watanabe	JPN	29.5.75	1		Tokyo	22 May
7.97	3.1	Ken	Nakajima	JPN	2.6.67	3		Shizuoka	5 May
7.94	5.1	Juha	Kivi	FIN	26.1.64	1		Koski	1 Jul
7.93	2.7	Ian	James	CAN	17.7.63	3	CG	Victoria	26 Aug
7.92		Carlos	Johnson	USA	20.8.73	1		San Angelo	7 May

Mark	Wind	Name		Nat	Born	Date
7.91		Clarence	Russell	USA	74	23 Apr
7.91		Leon	Gordon	JAM	74	19 Mar
7.91		Jerome	Romain	DMN	71	14 May
7.91	4.6	Steve	Ingram	GBR	70	18 Jun
7.91	2.3	Kader	Klouchi	FRA	69	2 Jul
7.91	2.3	Otto	Kärki	FIN	71	9 Jul
7.90		Stacey	Brown	USA	72	7 May
7.90	2.3	Marion	Robinson	USA	72	28 May
7.90	2.2	Gordon	McKee	USA	66	18 Jun
7.89	5.9	Shane	Cassey	AUS	71	13 Mar
7.89		Steve	Phillips	GBR	72	4 May
7.89		David	Bennett	USA	71	25 May
7.88		Brett	Harris	USA		9 Apr
7.88	5.1	Francisco	Garcia	ESP	70	23 Jul
7.88	2.2	Serge	Hélan	FRA	64	24 Jul
7.86		Keita	Cline	BVI	74	25 May
7.86	3.8	Benjamin	Koech	KEN	69	1 Jul
7.85		Victor	Houston	BAR	74	19 Mar
7.85		Evins	Tobler	PUR	65	14 May
7.85	2.3	Marco	Alberti	ITA	72	18 Jun
7.85	2.2	Shigeru	Tagawa	JPN	75	21 Jul
7.85	3.6	Ian	Lowe	CAN	73	17 Sep
7.85	2.8	Philippe	Lami	FRA	71	17 Sep
7.84	2.3	Anthuan	Maybank	USA	69	29 Apr
7.84		Tony	Barton	USA	69	14 May
7.84	3.3	Steve	Fritz	USA	67	14 Jun
7.83	2.6	Oliver	Borderan	FRA	76	8 Aug
7.82	2.5	Romuald	Ducros	FRA	73	5 Jun
7.82		Alexandr	Zharkov	RUS	71	30 Jun
7.82	2.3	Dan	O'Brien	USA	66	22 Jul

Mark	Wind	Name		Nat	Born	Pos	Meet	Venue	Date
7.82	3.1	Craig	Furber	AUS	72				8 Sep
7.81		Enyinna	Chukukere	NGR	73				9 Apr
7.81	3.0	Vyacheslav	Taranov	RUS	75				26 Jun
7.80		Vernon	George	USA	64				19 Mar
7.80A		Ampie	de Beer	RSA	70				6 May

Best outdoor marks

Mark	Wind	Name	Pos	Meet	Venue	Date
8.25	1.6	Tarasenko	3	Athl	Lausanne	6 Jul
8.24	1.8	Mladenov	4	Athl	Lausanne	6 Jul
8.21	0.5	Bagryanov	1	NC	St Peterburg	14 Jul
8.16		Pedroso	2		Khania	5 Jun
7.99	1.7	Tudor	4	EC	Helsinki	10 Aug
7.95	1.4	Morgan	3	WG	Helsinki	29 Jun
7.94	2.0	Hernandez	*	ECCp	Malaga	28 May
7.88		Robbins				29 Apr
7.85		Kahma				5 Jun
7.84		Francis				11 Jun
7.82	1.4	Ordina				3 Jun
7.81A		Romain				2 Apr

Best at low altitude - wind assisted

Mark	Wind	Name	Pos	Meet	Venue	Date
8.15	2.4	Jones	1	vGBR	Gateshead	20 Jul
7.96	2.1	Hernández	2	ECCp	Malaga	28 May

Exhibition

Mark	Wind	Name		Nat	Born	Pos	Meet	Venue	Date
8.15		Milko	Campus	ITA	2.4.69	1		Iglesias	10 Sep
7.88		Andrea	Paoloni	ITA	74	3		Iglesias	11 Sep

TRIPLE JUMP

Mark	Wind	Name		Nat	Born	Pos	Meet	Venue	Date
17.77i	-	Leonid	Voloshin	RUS	30.3.66	1		Grenoble	6 Feb
17.68	-0.5	Mike	Conley	USA	5.10.62	1	GPF	Paris	3 Sep
17.62	0.4	Denis	Kapustin	RUS	5.10.70	1	EC	Helsinki	13 Aug
17.61	0.6	Yoelbi	Quesada	CUB	4.8.73	1	WCp	London	10 Sep
17.55	0.9	Serge	Hélan	FRA	24.2.64	2	EC	Helsinki	13 Aug
17.51	0.8		Conley			1	NC	Knoxville	16 Jun
17.47i	-		Kapustin			1	NC	Lipetsk	27 Feb
17.46	0.2		Conley			1	DNG	Stockholm	12 Jul
17.44i	-		Voloshin			1	EI	Paris	12 Mar
17.43	1.4	Vasiliy	Sokov	RUS	7.4.68	1	Slov	Bratislava	1 Jun
17.43	0.3	Kenny	Harrison	USA	13.2.65	1	GWG	St Peterburg	29 Jul
17.42	0.2		Quesada			1		Alcalá	2 Jul
17.42	-0.6		Sokov			1	NC	St Peterburg	16 Jul
17.41A		Brian	Wellman	BER	8.9.67	1		El Paso	16 Apr
17.39	1.9	Jonathan	Edwards	GBR	10.5.66	1	AAA	Sheffield	12 Jun
17.38	0.6		Conley			1	Banes	São Paulo	21 May
17.38	1.0	Gennadiy	Markov	RUS	12.3.66	1		Stavropol	29 May
17.37i	-		Sokov			2	NC	Lipetsk	27 Feb
17.36	-0.1		Wellman			1	BNP	Villeneuve d'Ascq	8 Jul
17.36	0.7		Conley			2	v Afr	Durham	13 Aug
17.35i	-	Pierre	Camara	FRA	10.9.65	2		Grenoble	6 Feb
17.35i	-		Kapustin			2	EI	Paris	12 Mar
17.35	1.9		Harrison			1		Hiroshima	30 Apr
17.35	0.9	Oleg	Sakirkin	KZK	23.1.66	1	Znam	Moskva	5 Jun
17.35			Quesada			1		Lisboa	18 Jun
17.34	1.9		Quesada			*	GP II	Sevilla	5 Jun
17.33	1.9		Sakirkin			3	DNG	Stockholm	12 Jul
17.32	1.1		Conley			1	TSB	London	15 Jul
17.31i	-		Sokov			3	EI	Paris	12 Mar
17.30	1.2	Maris	Bruziks	LAT	25.8.62	2		Lisboa	18 Jun
17.30	1.0		Kapustin			1	ECp	Birmingham	26 Jun
17.29	1.3	James	Beckford	JAM	9.1.75	1		Tempe	2 Apr
		(32/14)							
17.28		Yuriy	Sotnikov	RUS	10.3.69	1		Sochi	9 Sep
17.24i	-	Erick	Walder	USA	5.11.71	1	NCAA	Indianapolis	12 Mar
17.21	0.7	Vladimir	Melikhov	RUS	30.3.69	*		Sevilla	5 Jun
17.18		Andrius	Raizgys	LIT	4.4.69	1		Kaunas	4 Jun
17.15	1.9	Igor	Sautkin	RUS	72	1	NC-23	Voronezh	18 Jun
17.13	1.4	Edrick	Floréal	CAN	5.10.66	1		Gateshead	1 Jul
		(20)							
17.13	0.0	Dmitriy	Byzov	RUS	25.1.66	1		Krasnodar	20 Aug
17.12i	-	Aleksandr	Glovatskiy	BLR	2.5.70	1		Gomel	15 Jan
17.12	0.7	Aliacer	Urrutia	CUB	22.9.74	2	Barr	La Habana	26 May
17.10i	-	Ralf	Jaros	GER	13.12.65	1	NC	Dortmund	25 Feb
17.06A	0.6	Armen	Martirosyan	ARM	6.8.69	2	NC	Tsakhadzhor	2 Jul
17.06	0.9	Julian	Golley	GBR	12.9.71	2	WCp	London	10 Sep
17.05i	-	Oleg	Grokhovskiy	RUS	3.5.68	4		Grenoble	6 Feb
17.04	0.4	Anisio Souza	Silva	BRA	18.6.69	1	NC	Rio de Janeiro	17 Sep
17.02i	-	Aleksandr	Petrunin	RUS	29.1.67	4	NC	Lipetsk	27 Feb
17.00	0.5	Damir	Tashpulatov	UZB	29.1.64	2		Almaty	21 May
		(30)							
17.00	1.8	Andrey	Kayukov	RUS	12.4.64	3		Sochi	9 Sep
16.99	-0.4	Tord	Henriksson	SWE	13.4.65	2	ECp	Birmingham	26 Jun

Mark	Wind	Name		Nat	Born	Pos	Meet	Venue	Date
16.97	0.7	Vladimir	Kravchenko	UKR	22.12.69	1	NC	Kiev	27 May
16.97	0.8	Georges	Sainte-Rose	FRA	3.9.69	2	NC	Annecy	24 Jul
16.96	-0.2	Reggie	Jones	USA	8.5.71	3	NC	Knoxville	16 Jun
16.96	1.9	Arne	Holm	SWE	22.12.61	1	vFIN	Stockholm	27 Aug
16.95	0.2	Nikolay	Musiyenko	UKR	16.12.59	1	Kuso	Lublin	4 Jun
16.95	1.3	Francis	Agyepong	GBR	16.6.65	3	AAA	Sheffield	12 Jun
16.94	1.8-	LaMark	Carter	USA	23.8.70	4	NC	Knoxville	16 Jun
16.93A	0.5	Parkev	Grigoryan	ARM	1.5.65	1		Artashat	30 Apr
		(40)							
16.93	1.9	Garfield	Anselm	FRA	7.6.66	5		Dijon	12 Jun
16.93A		Shirak	Pogasyan	ARM	24.9.69	3	NC	Tsakhkadzor	2 Jul
16.93		Gennadiy	Glushenko	UKR	26.5.70			Dnepropetrovsk	10 Jul
16.91	1.9	Andrey	Kurennoy	RUS	72	2	NC-23	Voronezh	18 Jun
16.90	1.3		Duan Qifeng	CHN	20.1.73	1		Tangshan	30 Aug
16.89A	1.4	Wikus	Olivier	RSA	8.3.68	1		Pietersburg	18 Mar
16.88	1.2	Takashi	Komatsu	JPN	30.12.67	2	AsiG	Hiroshima	14 Oct
16.87	0.2	Vladimir	Inozemtsev	UKR	25.5.64	5	Kuts	Moskva	31 Jul
16.86	1.1	Stoiko	Tsonov	BUL	6.5.69	1		Stara Zagora	16 Jul
16.84	0.7	Sergey	Arzamasov	KZK	9.4.71	3		Almaty	21 May
		(50)							
16.84	0.1		Zou Sixin	CHN	8.5.67	2		Tangshan	30 Aug
16.82i	-	Jerome	Romain	DMN	12.6.71	1		Oklahoma City	12 Feb
16.82		Volker	Mai	GER	3.5.66	1		Athens, Ga.	2 Apr
16.82	1.3	Aleksandr	Aseledchenko	RUS	72	4	NC-23	Voronezh	18 Jun
16.81i	-	Lars	Hedman	SWE	6.4.67	1		Växjö	27 Feb
16.78		Milan	Mikulás	TCH	1.4.63	3		Dreux	2 Jul
16.78		Marios	Hadjiandreou	CYP	19.9.62	1		Thessaloniki	24 Jul
16.77	1.8	Daniel	Osorio	CUB	5.11.72	3	NC	La Habana	25 Jun
16.76	0.5	Andrew	Murphy	AUS	18.12.69	1		Canberra	20 Mar
16.76		Francis	Dodoo	GHA	13.4.60	1		Tuscaloosa	23 Apr
		(60)							
16.76	1.9	Ketill	Hanstveit	NOR	2.11.73	1		Tønsberg	20 Jul
16.73	0.6	Tyrell	Taitt	USA	19.4.71	3	NCAA	Boise	4 Jun
16.73	1.8		Park Min-soo	KOR	30.1.68	1	NC	Seoul	18 Jun
16.72	1.1	Vladislav	Yegorov	UKR	20.4.72	3	NC	Kiev	27 May
16.70	1.0-	Tosi	Fasinro	GBR	28.3.72	4		Gateshead	1 Jul
16.69		Lucian	Sfiea	ROM	10.9.63	1		Bucuresti	10 Jun
16.69		Lotfi	Khaida	ALG	20.12.68	1		La Roche-sur-Yon	14 Jul
16.69	1.5	Ndabazihle	Mdhlongwa	ZIM	30.5.73	Q	CG	Victoria	27 Aug
16.68i	-	Tyrone	Scott	USA	18.1.70	1	NC	Atlanta	5 Mar
16.67		Joe	Greene	USA	17.2.67	2	OD	Jena	3 Jun
		(70)							
16.66i	-	Karsten	Richter	GER	25.7.72	2	NC	Dortmund	25 Feb
16.66		Maurizio	Gifaldi	ITA	19.5.67	1		Formia	12 Jul
16.65	1.0	Leonard	Cobb	USA	20.1.75	2	WJ	Lisboa	24 Jul
16.64i	-	Toussaint	Rabenala	MAD	29.10.65	3	FRA Ch	Bordeaux	27 Feb
16.64	1.5	Pierre	Andersson	SWE	4.1.67	1		Göteborg	28 Jul
16.63		André	Ernst	GER	6.12.67	1		Hamburg	27 Jul
16.63		Redzinaldas	Stasaitis	LIT	5.4.67	2		Palanga	28 Aug
16.62	1.5	Rogel	Nachum	ISR	21.5.67	1	ECCp	Tel Aviv	29 May
16.62	1.3	Yoel	Garcia	CUB	25.11.73	4	NC	La Habana	25 Jun
16.62		Vyacheslav	Bordukov	RUS	1.1.59	5		Sochi	9 Sep
		(80)							
16.59	1.5	Juan M	López	CUB	7.4.67	1		La Habana	12 Feb
16.57	1.6	Takashi	Komatsu	JPN	30.12.67	4		Mito	8 May
16.57	0.5	Viktor	Popko	UKR	13.8.68	4	NC	Kiev	27 May
16.57	1.9	Heikki	Herva	FIN	2.2.63	1		Koski	1 Jul
16.56i	-	Cátalin	Barbu	ROM	2.7.67	1	NC	Bucuresti	27 Feb
16.56		Mohamed Karim	Sassi	TUN	68			Tunis	1 May
16.56		Wolfgang	Knabe	GER	12.7.59	1		Gladbeck	25 Jun
16.55	1.4	Rich	Thompson	USA	16.6.69	1	USOF	Edwardsville	8 Jul
16.55	2.0	Jacob	Katonon	KEN	70	Q	CG	Victoria	27 Aug
16.54		David	Nti-Berko	GHA	71	4	NCAA	Boise	4 Jun
		(90)							
16.54		Daniele	Buttiglione	ITA	10.3.66	1		Formia	26 Jul
16.54	-0.3	Sergey	Kochkin	RUS	70	1		Bryansk	7 Aug
16.53	2.0	Michel	Martinez	CUB	6.11.74	2		La Habana	11 Feb
16.53	0.9	Kotzo	Kostov	BUL	9.1.68	1	Balk	Trikala	9 Jul
19.92i		Viktor	Bulat	BLR	1.4.71	1		Gomel	15 Jan

Mark	Wind	Name		Nat	Born	Pos	Meet	Venue	Date
16.53	0.7	Onochie	Achike	GBR	31.1.75	*	WJ	Lisboa	24 Jul
16.52	-0.3	Paul	Nioze	SEY	19.3.67	1		Reduit	2 Oct
16.51i	-	Hrvoje	Verzi	GER	12.11.70	3	NCAA	Indianapolis	12 Mar
16.51		Frank	Rutherford	BAH	23.11.64	*	MSR	Walnut	17 Apr
16.51	0.9	Zsolt	Czingler	HUN	26.4.71	1	ECCp	Malaga	29 May
16.51	1.0	Germain	Martial	FRA	19.1.69	4	NC	Annecy	24 Jul
16.51	0.5	Julio	López	ESP	8.3.72	3	ECp23	Ostrava	31 Jul
		(101)							

Mark	Wind	Name		Nat	Born	Date
16.49			Zhang Jun	CHN	74	3 Jun
16.49	1.8	Alex	Norca	FRA	69	24 Jul
16.48	2.0	Jefferson	Ilario	BRA	72	13 Aug
16.48		Yevgeniy	Timofeyev	RUS	74	9 Sep
16.46	1.8	Andrey	Zirko	BLR	72	28 May
16.45i	-	Shigehisa	Matsumoto	JPN	68	11 Feb
16.45		Dmitry	Piterman	USA	63	25 May
16.45	0.5	Christos	Meletoglou	GRE	72	25 Jun
16.45A		Benson	Mugun	KEN	62	9 Jul
16.45	0.1	Krystian	Ciemala	POL	69	20 Aug
16.45	0.7	Piotr	Weremczuk	POL	66	10 Sep
16.44i		Kelsey	Nash	USA	71	19 Feb
16.44		Tutu Gogo	Peters	NGR	71	4 Jun
16.44	1.9	Meiram	Beispakov	KZK	74	17 Sep
16.44	1.1	Kenichi	Sumida	JPN	73	3 Nov
16.43i		Ivory	Angello	USA	73	29 Jan
16.41	0.2	Charlie	Simpkins	USA	63	15 Jun
16.40i		Mike	Harris	USA	67	15 Jan
16.40		César	Rizo	CUB	75	11 Feb
16.40		Vitaliy	Firsov	TJM	73	9 May
16.40	0.2	Spencer	Williams	USA	67	14 May
16.40	1.0	Eric	Lancelin	USA	71	4 Jun
16.40	2.0	Volker	Ehmann	GER	72	2 Jul
16.40	1.2	Sergey	Izmaylov	UKR	75	24 Jul
16.39		Djordje	Kozulj	CRO	63	22 May
16.38			Du Jiuhui	CHN		3 Jun
16.38	1.0	Ronald	Servius	FRA	76	23 Jul
16.37i		Ionel	Efteme	ROM	71	c6 Feb
16.37	2.0	Anzhel	Shikov	BUL	69	26 Jun
16.37		Nikolay	Zakharov	RUS	72	6 Aug
16.36i		Aleksey	Fatyanov	AZE	69	9 Feb
16.36i		Gary	Johnson	USA	69	12 Feb
16.36	-0.8	Ilya	Yashchuk	UKR	70	27 May
16.35		Salem Mouled	Al-Ahmadi	SAU	69	7 Apr
16.35	0.1	Igor	Naimit	RUS	71	29 May
16.35	0.3	Jörg	Friess	GER	68	2 Jul
16.35	1.7	Gyula	Pálóczi	HUN	62	10 Jul
16.35		Papa Ladji	Konaté	SEN	68	24 Jul
16.35		Vissen	Mooneegan	MRI	71	27 Aug
16.34		Sergey	Bykov	UKR	71	8 Apr
16.34	1.9	Andre	Scott	USA	75	15 Apr
16.34		George	Darko	GHA		21 May
16.34	-0.6	Yuriy	Osipenko	UKR	69	27 May
16.33	0.3	Clifton	Etheridge	USA	69	16 Jun
16.32		Aleksey	Pushkarskiy	UZB	59	29 May
16.31	-1.2	Charles	Friedek	GER	71	3 Jun
16.31	1.6	Kendrick	Morgan	USA	73	4 Jun
16.31	1.3	Kenny	Boudine	FRA	73	9 Jul
16.31	1.1	Igor	Kurduzov	RUS	69	27 Aug
		(150)				
16.30	0.9	Vladimir	Castaneda	CUB	73	12 Feb
16.30	1.8	Jari	Lamsa	FIN	68	6 Mar
16.30	1.8	Dave	Frazier	USA	71	4 Jun

Wind-assisted

Mark	Wind	Name		Nat	Born	Pos	Meet	Venue	Date
17.86	5.7	Denis	Kapustin	RUS	5.10.70	1		Sevilla	5 Jun
17.67	5.0		Conley			1		Salamanca	22 Jul
17.54	2.2		Conley			1	Jen	San José	28 May
17.49	4.5	Vladimir	Melikhov	RUS	30.3.69	2		Sevilla	5 Jun
17.49	3.4	Oleg	Sakirkin	KZK	23.1.66	1		Dijon	12 Jun
17.39	5.0		Quesada			3		Sevilla	5 Jun
17.38	2.7		Harrison			1	v Afr	Durham	13 Aug
17.35	4.8	Andrey	Kayukov	RUS	12.4.64	4		Sevilla	5 Jun
17.35	2.5		Wellman			2	DNG	Stockholm	12 Jul
17.34	2.5		Hélan			2		Dijon	12 Jun
17.19	4.3	Georges	Sainte-Rose	FRA	3.9.69	3		Dijon	12 Jun
17.17	3.7	Edrick	Floréal	CAN	5.10.66	2		Hiroshima	30 Apr
17.05	2.6	Jerome	Romain	DMN	12.6.71	Q	CG	Victoria	27 Aug
16.99		Francis	Dodoo	GHA	13.4.60	1		Tulane	16 Apr
16.91A	2.2	Wikus	Olivier	RSA	8.3.68	1	NC	Secunda	7 May
16.89		Mohamed Karim	Sassi	TUN	68	1		Tunis	13 May
16.88	2.6	Frank	Rutherford	BAH	23.11.64	1	MSR	Walnut	17 Apr
16.81	2.3	Alex	Norca	FRA	18.1.69	3	NC	Annecy	24 Jul
16.79	3.3	Milan	Mikulás	TCH	1.4.63	1		Praha	3 Sep
16.78		Lotfi	Khaida	ALG	20.12.68	4	Jen	San José	28 May
16.74	2.5	Tosi	Fasinro	GBR	28.3.72	1	ECp23	Ostrava	31 Jul
16.68		Zsolt	Czingler	HUN	26.4.71	1		Veszprém	24 Jul
16.67	3.6	Kotzo	Kostov	BUL	9.1.68	2		Stara Zagora	16 Jul
16.67	2.4	Onochie	Achike	GBR	31.1.75	1	WJ	Lisboa	24 Jul
16.61		Kendrick	Morgan	USA	28.10.73	1		Raleigh	14 May
16.61	3.0	Gyula	Pálóczi	HUN	13.9.62	1	NC	Debrecen	10 Jul
16.59		Eric	Lancelin	USA	13.5.71	1		Natchitoches	30 Apr
16.57		Ivory	Angello	USA	27.8.73	2	TexR	Austin	8 Apr
16.57	2.7	Vladimir	Chernikov	UZB	3.8.59	1		Taoyuan	28 May
16.55	2.3	Ronald	Servius	FRA	21.2.76	3	WJ	Lisboa	23 Jul

Mark	Wind	Name		Nat	Born	Date
16.49	4.3	Roberto	Garcinuño	ESP	72	9 Jul
16.48		Dante	McGrew	USA	72	21 May
16.47		Clifton	Etheridge	USA	69	23 Apr
16.46	2.3	Joseph	Taiwo	USA	59	17 Apr
16.46	2.4	Jamal	Bush	USA		27 May
16.42			Wang Baoying	CHN	72	4 Jun
16.42		Antonio	Santos	ANO	64	15 Jun
16.42	3.5	Sergey	Izmaylov	UKR	75	24 Jul
16.41		Desmond	Hunt	USA	71	21 May
16.41	2.6	Daniel	Roman	ESP	74	9 Jul
16.40			Du Jiuhui	CHN		4 Jun
16.38	3.9	Akira	Anzai	JPN	69	27 Aug

Mark	Wind	Name		Nat	Born	Pos	Meet	Venue	Date
16.37	2.2	David	Frazier	USA	71				4 Jun
16.34	4.3	Diego	Lamenti	ITA	72				31 Jul
16.33		Helmuts	Rodke	LAT	67				18 May
16.31	3.3	Jean-Pierre	Sarant	FRA	68				4 Jun
16.30		Jermaine	Johnson	JAM	72				25 May

Best outdoor

Mark	Wind	Name	Pos	Meet	Venue	Date
17.12A		Walder	1		El Paso	2 Apr
17.09	1.7	Sotnikov	3	Slov	Bratislava	1 Jun
16.95		Petrunin	3	Kuts	Moskva	31 Jul
16.92	0.0	Glovatskiy	2	Kuso	Lublin	4 Jun
16.89	-0.1	Jaros	1	OD	Jena	3 Jun
16.88	1.7	Camara	*		Dijon	12 Jun
16.79	0.8	Romain	2	NCAA	Boise	4 Jun
16.71	0.7	Hedman	2	vFIN	Stockholm	27 Aug
16.54	-0.3	Richter	3	v2N23	Modena	16 Jul
16.41		Rabenala				8 Apr
16.36		Angello				23 Apr
16.36		Nash				21 May
16.35	1.6	Grokhovskiy				5 Jun
16.34	1.8	Matsumoto				8 May
16.34	1.3	Harris				22 May
16.33		Johnson				25 May

Best outdoors, wind assisted: 16.93 2.2 Camara 6 Dijon 12 Jun

Best outdoors at low altitude

Mark	Wind	Name	Pos	Meet	Venue	Date
16.91	0.5	Walder	1	NCAA	Boise	4 Jun
16.84	0.7	Arzamasov	3		Almaty	21 May

SHOT

Mark	Name		Nat	Born	Pos	Meet	Venue	Date
21.25i	Kevin	Toth	USA	29.12.67	1	NC	Atlanta	5 Mar
21.09	Jim	Doehring	USA	27.1.62	1	NYG	New York	22 May
21.07		Toth			1	Jen	San José	28 May
21.05i	Alexandr	Bagach	UKR	21.11.66	1		Kiev	1 Mar
21.01		Toth			1	GGala	Roma	8 Jun
20.97i		Bagach			1	NC	Kiev	13 Feb
20.94	C.J.	Hunter	USA	14.12.68	1		Boulder	15 May
20.94	Yevgeniy	Palchikov	RUS	12.10.68	1		Irkutsk	29 May
20.89	Gregg	Tafralis	USA	9.4.58	1	vGBR	Gateshead	20 Jul
20.88		Doehring			1	OD	Jena	3 Jun
20.86Ai		Hunter			1		Air Academy	29 Jan
20.82A	Randy	Barnes	USA	16.6.66	1		El Paso	16 Apr
20.82		Hunter			1	NC	Knoxville	17 Jun
20.81		Toth			1	Owens	Columbus	8 May
20.79		Hunter			2	v GBR	Gateshead	20 Jul
20.78	Alexandr	Klimenko	UKR	27.3.70	1	EC	Helsinki	13 Aug
20.76		Barnes			2	NC	Knoxville	17 Jun
20.75		Hunter			2	Jen	San José	28 May
20.75		Barnes			1	v Afr	Durham	12 Aug
20.73		Toth			2	NYG	New York	22 May
20.68	Paolo	Dal Soglio	ITA	29.7.70	1		Modena	5 Oct
20.67	Brent	Noon	USA	29.8.71	1	NCAA	Boise	4 Jun
20.66i		Bagach			1	EI	Paris	11 Mar
20.64i	Dragan	Peric	YUG	8.5.64	1		Sremska Mitrovica	19 Mar
20.64		Bagach			1	NC	Kiev	27 May
20.62i		Toth			1	v GBR	Glasgow	12 Feb
20.62		Klimenko			1		Kiev	24 Jul
20.60		Doehring			1		Nurmijärvi	2 Jul
20.60		Barnes			1	GPF	Paris	3 Sep
20.58i		Hunter			2	NC	Atlanta	5 Mar
20.57		Peric			3	Jen	San José	28 May
20.57		Hunter			1		Tallinn	29 Jul
	(32/11)							
20.44	Pétur	Gudmundsson	ISL	9.3.62	1		Santo Antonio	28 May
20.44	Oliver-Sven	Buder	GER	23.6.66	1	NC	Erfurt	2 Jul
20.29	Saulius	Kleiza	LIT	2.4.64	1		Vilnius	1 Jul
20.24	Sergey	Nikolayev	RUS	12.11.66	1		Moskva	11 Jun
20.22	Markus	Koistinen	FIN	1.5.70	1		Elimäki	18 Jun
20.16	Manuel	Martínez	ESP	7.12.74	1		San Sebastián	28 May
20.15	Arne	Pedersen	NOR	19.4.61	1		Athens, GA	7 May
20.13	Jonny	Reinhardt	GER	28.6.68	2	OD	Jena	3 Jun
20.12	Mikhail	Kostin	BLR	10.5.59	1		Minsk	28 Apr
	(20)							
20.07	Kjell Ove	Hauge	NOR	20.2.69	2	NCAA	Boise	4 Jun
20.04	Chris	Volgenau	USA	30.3.69	1		Tallahassee	2 Apr
20.03i	John	Godina	USA	31.5.72	1	NCAA	Indianapolis	11 Mar
20.02	Kent	Larsson	SWE	10.6.63	4	NYG	New York	22 May
20.01	Sergey	Smirnov	RUS	17.9.60	2	NC	St Peterburg	15 Jul
20.01	Thorsten	Herbrand	GER	9.4.70	1		Konstanz	4 Sep
20.00	Roman	Virastyuk	UKR	20.4.68			Lvov	9 Sep
19.94	Paul	Edwards ¶	GBR	16.2.59	1		College Station	21 May
19.94	Sören	Tallhem	SWE	16.2.64	1		Fåker	8 Aug
19.93i	Mika	Halvari	FIN	13.2.70	2	DNG	Stockholm	8 Mar
	(30)							

MEN 1994

Mark	Name		Nat	Born	Pos	Meet	Venue	Date
19.92i	Viktor	Bulat	BLR	1.4.71	1		Gomel	15 Jan
19.88	Dmitriy	Goncharuk	BLR	10.9.70	1	NC	Gomel	9 Jul
19.74	Kristian	Pettersson	SWE	5.10.71	1		Kuortane	25 Jun
19.74	Henrik	Wennberg	SWE	11.3.66	1		Stockholm	25 Jul
19.67	Jenö	Kóczián	HUN	5.4.67	4	GP II	Linz	4 Jul
19.65	Corrado	Fantini	ITA	7.2.67	2		Modena	5 Oct
19.64	Gert	Weil	CHL	3.1.60	1		Santiago de Chile	12 Oct
19.60i	Vyacheslav	Lykho	RUS	16.1.67	3	NC	Lipetsk	27 Feb
19.56i	Gheorge	Guset ¶	ROM	28.5.68	1		Bucuresti	6 Feb
19.56	Janne	Ronkainen	FIN	5.2.63	2		Hamina	14 Jun
	(40)							
19.52	Roar	Hoff	NOR	21.5.65	1		Drammen	1 Jun
19.50	Sergey	Rubtsov	KZK	4.9.65	1		Almaty	16 Sep
19.49	Matt	Simson	GBR	28.5.70	1	CG	Victoria	28 Aug
19.48	Andrey	Nemchaninov	UKR	27.11.66	4	NC	Kiev	27 May
19.46	Aleksandr	Klimov	BLR	26.5.69	2		Minsk	28 Apr
19.46	Piotr	Perzylo #	POL	15.11.61	1		Bielsko Biala	15 May
19.45	Courtney	Ireland	NZL	12.1.72	4	NCAA	Boise	4 Jun
19.36i	Martin	Bílek	TCH	7.1.73	1		Jablonec	29 Jan
19.36	Helmut	Krieger	POL	17.7.58	1	v3N	Krakow	30 Jun
19.27	Michael	Mertens	GER	27.12.65	2		Duisburg	12 Jun
	(50)							
19.26	Thomas	Hammarsten	SWE	31.12.66	1		Kingsville	23 Apr
19.26	Chima	Ugwu	NGR	72	2	CG	Victoria	28 Aug
19.26		Liu Hao	CHN	19.11.68	1	AsiG	Hiroshima	14 Oct
19.25i	Antero	Paljakka	FIN	1.8.69	2	vSWE	Växjö	5 Mar
19.20	Steve	Albert	USA	1.4.64	1		Springfield	7 May
19.11	Vladimir	Yaryshkin	RUS	28.2.63	1	Army	Rostov	24 Aug
19.07	Jeff	Brandenburg	USA	10.2.72	1		Kalamazoo	7 May
19.06	Burger	Lambrechts	RSA	3.4.73	1		Pretoria	13 Apr
19.04	Joe	Bailey	USA	30.3.71	2		Salinas	25 May
19.02	Bilal	Saad Mubarak	QAT	18.12.72			Kiev	26 Jun
	(60)							
19.00	Radoslav	Despotov	BUL	8.8.68	1		Sofia	21 May
18.99	Christian	Nebl	AUT	21.4.64	1		Kapfenberg	4 Jun
18.98	Petri	Torniainen	FIN	8.3.65	1		Jalasjärvi	16 Aug
18.94	David	Rodely	USA	7.6.68	1		Springfield	2 Apr
18.92	Dagfinn	Schikora	NOR	7.9.64	2		Drammen	1 Jun
18.91		Xie Shengying	CHN	18.4.71	1		Tangshan	28 Aug
18.91	Dirk	Urban	GER	14.1.69			Neumünster	1 Oct
18.90i	Oliver	Dück	GER	10.2.67	1		Karlsruhe	6 Feb
18.90i	Scott	Peterson	USA	9.11.72	3		Gainesville	26 Feb
18.88	Jaroslav	Zitnansky	SVK	18.2.71	1		Antwerp	21 Jul
	(70)							
18.87	Giorgio	Venturi	ITA	23.6.66	1		Novara	1 Aug
18.84	Randy	Heisler	USA	7.8.61	1		Indianapolis	14 May
18.81	Viktor	Kapustin	RUS	28.4.72	4	NC	St Peterburg	15 Jul
18.80	Elias	Louca	CYP	23.7.74	1		Nicosia	6 Jul
18.79	John	Minns	AUS	31.5.67	1		Prince George	13 Aug
18.78	Paul	Miller	USA	12.7.67	1		Napervile	20 May
18.78	Shakti	Singh	IND	14.5.62	1		Mandya	18 Jun
18.77	Pete	Kaligis	USA	1.6.71	1		Los Angeles Ww	7 May
18.77	Milan	Haborák	SVK	11.1.73	1	v4N	Nitra	13 Jul
18.74i	Kiril	Valchanov	BUL	1.3.74	1	NC	Sofia	12 Feb
	(80)							
18.74	Antti	Harju	FIN	18.3.74	1		Alajärvi	4 Aug
18.72i	José Luis	Martinez	ESP	25.8.70	1		San Sebastián	29 Jan
18.72	Yuriy	Belonog	UKR	9.3.74	1	ECp23	Lillehammer	30 Jul
18.72	Adilson	Oliveira	BRA	4.1.64	1	NC	Rio de Janeiro	17 Sep
18.71	Stefan	Pöhn	GER	30.12.73	1	v2N23	Modena	16 Jul
18.69i	Marco	Dodoni	ITA	5.9.72	1		Genova	16 Feb
18.67	Dmitriy	Latukhin	RUS	18.7.70	3		St Peterburg	28 Jun
18.66	Jeff	Teach	USA	14.4.72	1	Big10	Madison	22 May
18.66	Pavel	Muzhikov	RUS	71	3	Army	Rostov	24 Aug
18.64i	Jon	Ogden	USA	31.7.74	5	NCAA	Indianapolis	11 Mar
	(90)							
18.63	Andrés	Gudmundsson	ISL	65	1		Vanná	19 May
18.63	Anders	Axlid	SWE	1.5.66	2		Gävle	15 Jul
18.61	Ron	Willis	USA	6.12.71	1		Columbia	16 Apr

Mark	Name		Nat	Born	Pos	Meet	Venue	Date
18.60	Jorge	Montenegro	CUB	21.9.68	1		La Habana	7 Jun
18.60	Miroslav	Menc	TCH	16.3.71	1	NC	Jablonec	10 Jul
18.59i	Jan	Bártl	TCH	23.3.67	2		Jablonec	29 Jan
18.58i	Rob	Carlson	USA	27.8.71	1		Johnson City	22 Jan
18.56	Dennis	Black	USA	4.7.73	1		Eugene	16 Apr
18.55	Carel	le Roux	RSA	31.8.72	2		Albisola	16 Jul
18.53	Sergey (100)	Kot	UZB	7.1.60	1		Tashkent	18 Sep

Mark	Name		Nat	Born	Date
18.49	Carlos	Fandiño	CUB	69	8 May
18.47	Brad	Mears	USA	70	22 Apr
18.46	Rod	Chronister	USA	68	23 Apr
18.46	Joe	Hicks	USA	71	14 May
18.46	Vladimir	Chernysh	UKR	68	9 Jul
18.45	Yoav	Sharf	ISR	66	17 Dec
18.44	Andrey	Golivets	UKR	72	7 May
18.43	Shawn	Schleizer	USA	70	4 Jun
18.42i	Andy	Meyer	USA	70	26 Feb
18.42i	Merab	Kurashvili	GEO	71	11 Mar
18.40	Kobus	Botes	RSA	65	20 Mar
18.39i	Matt	Spears	USA		21 Jan
18.39i	Mauri	Lindstedt	SWE	64	5 Mar
18.39	Frits	Potgieter	RSA	74	7 May
18.38i	Igor	Palchikov	RUS	60	29 May
18.37		Wen Jili	CHN	73	17 Mar
18.37	Avtar	Singh	IND	74	19 Sep
18.36	Scott	Cappos	CAN	69	25 May
18.34	Adam	Nelson	USA	75	23 Jul
18.33Ai	Mark	Parlin	USA	73	5 Feb
18.31	Andy	Bloom	USA	73	4 Jun
18.30	Giovanni	Tubini	ITA	64	4 Sep
18.29i	Mark	Lacy	USA	70	15 Jan
18.29	Ari	Uusitalo	FIN	68	28 Jul
18.25	Dwight	Johnson	USA	69	5 Feb
18.25	Ralf	Kahles	GER	73	2 Jul
18.23	Alessandro	Andrei	ITA	59	5 Jun
18.22	Gary	Kirchhoff	USA	72	20 May
18.20	Cui Guangyuan		CHN	69	30 Aug
18.19	Edson (130)	Miguel	BRA	65	5 Nov
18.16i	Clint	Moore	USA		4 Mar
18.15	Mark	Proctor	GBR	63	22 Jun
18.10		Li Wenbiao	CHN	71	29 Apr

Unconfirmed: 19.08 Giorgio Venturi ITA 23.6.66 1 Kiembaum 23 Jan

Best outdoor

Mark	Name	Pos	Meet	Venue	Date
20.01	Godina	1		Long Beach	9 Jun
19.87	Halvari	1		Reykjavik	18 Jun
19.84	Virastyuk	2	NC	Kiev	27 May
19.62	Bulat	1		Pune	13 Sep
19.12	Paljakka	2		Leppävirta	7 Jun
18.87	Peterson	1		Baton Rouge	25 May
18.77	Bílek	1		Praha	29 Jun
18.77	Dück	3	NC	Erfurt	2 Jul
18.61	Valchanov	2		Sofia	21 May
18.59	Dodoni	3		Vicenza	22 Jun

Mark	Name	Date
18.40	Bártl	12 Jun
18.32	Ogden	14 May
18.27	Lindstedt	2 Jun
18.26	Parlin	1 May
18.20	Lacy	25 May
18.19	Martinez	22 Jan
18.14	Spears	25 May

Drugs disqualification

Mark	Name		Nat	Born	Pos	Meet	Venue	Date
20.61	Kálmán	Konya ¶	HUN	27.10.61	1		Budapest	19 Jun
19.97	Gheorge	Guset ¶	ROM	28.5.68	1	NC	Bucuresti	17 Jun

DISCUS

Mark	Name		Nat	Born	Pos	Meet	Venue	Date
68.58	Attila	Horváth	HUN	28.7.67	1		Budapest	24 Jun
66.88		Horváth			1		Szombathely	18 Jun
66.08	Jürgen	Schult	GER	11.5.60	1		Halle	14 May
66.08	Lars	Riedel	GER	28.6.67	1	OD	Jena	3 Jun
66.00	Nick	Sweeney	IRL	26.3.68	1		Helsingborg	9 Jul
65.98		Horváth			1		Szombathely	16 Apr
65.80	Vladimir	Dubrovshchik	BLR	7.1.72	1		Minsk	21 Jul
65.70		Riedel			1		Cottbus	15 Jun
65.64		Riedel			1		Nurnberg	10 Jun
65.64	Sergey	Lyakhov	RUS	1.3.68	1		Moskva	4 Jul
65.62		Schult			1		Rhede	29 Jul
65.58		Lyakhov			2		Cottbus	15 Jun
65.50		Riedel			1	NC	Erfurt	3 Jul
65.46		Horváth			1		Budapest	3 Jun
65.30A		Lyakhov			1		Pietersburg	18 Mar
65.18		Riedel			1		Lindau	31 Jul
65.16		Riedel			1		Falkenstein	4 Jun
65.04	Mike	Gravelle	USA	13.4.65	1		Salinas	25 May
64.92		Lyakhov			1		Duisburg	12 Jun
64.92	Vesteinn	Hafsteinsson	ISL	12.12.60	1		Helsingborg	1 Oct
64.90	Vladimir	Zinchenko	UKR	25.7.59	2		Duisburg	12 Jun
64.80		Hafsteinsson			1		Reykjavik	19 Jun
64.80		Riedel			2		Rhede	29 Jul
64.78		Dubrovshchik			1	EC	Helsinki	14 Aug
64.74	Dmitriy	Shevchenko	RUS	13.5.68	1	ECp	Birmingham	26 Jun
64.74		Sweeney			1		Helsingborg	6 Jul
64.68		Shevchenko			1	GWG	St Peterburg	25 Jul
64.64		Riedel			1		Chemnitz	18 Jun

Mark	Name		Nat	Born	Pos	Meet	Venue	Date
64.56		Schult			3		Cottbus	15 Jun
64.56		Shevchenko			2	EC	Helsinki	14 Aug
64.54		Dubrovshchik			1	WCp	London	10 Sep
	(31/10)							
64.40	Vitaliy	Sidorov	UKR	23.3.70	1		Kiev	24 Jul
64.20	Virgilijus	Alekna	LIT	13.2.72	1		Kaunas	14 May
64.18	Jim	Seifert	USA	26.11.62	1		King's Point	26 Apr
64.18	Anthony	Washington	USA	16.1.66	1		Tucson	7 May
64.08	Carsten	Kufahl	GER	14.11.67	1		Dortmund	25 Jun
63.94	Viktor	Baraznovskiy	BLR	23.1.68	1		Gomel	14 May
63.84	Gennadiy	Pronko	BLR	27.2.70	2		Gomel	14 May
63.78	Mickael	Conjungo	CAF	6.5.68	1		Sorgues	7 Jul
63.76	Dag	Solhaug	SWE	11.1.64	1		Västerås	30 Jun
63.68	Costel	Grasu	ROM	5.7.67	1	NC	Bucuresti	18 Jun
	(20)							
63.66	Svein-Inge	Valvik	NOR	20.9.56	1		Spikkestad	8 Oct
63.58	Andrey	Kokhanovskiy	UKR	11.1.68	1		San Marcos	30 Apr
63.00	Werner	Reiterer	AUS	27.1.68	1		Melbourne	15 Dec
62.74	Alexis	Elizalde	CUB	19.9.67	1		La Coruña	12 Jul
62.58	Kristian	Pettersson	SWE	5.10.71	2		Västerås	30 Jun
62.56A	Henrik	Wennberg	SWE	11.3.66	1		Boulder	28 Oct
62.54	Kevin	Fitzpatrick	USA	26.9.69	3		Salinas	25 May
62.46	Aleksandr	Borichevskiy	RUS	25.6.70	1	vFRA	Sotteville	26 Jun
62.46	Adewale	Olukoju	NGR	27.7.68	2	CG	Victoria	26 Aug
62.24	John	Godina	USA	31.5.72	1		San Diego	26 Mar
	(30)							
62.22	Andreas	Seelig	GER	6.7.70	2		Halle	14 May
62.08	Adam	Setliff	USA	15.12.69	4		Salinas	25 May
61.84	Yuriy	Seskin	RUS	7.7.66	1		St Peterburg	12 May
61.80	Valeriy	Yagovdik	BLR	16.9.63	3		Gomel	14 May
61.78	Randy	Heisler	USA	7.8.61	1		Indianapolis	30 Jul
61.72	Shakti	Singh	IND	14.5.62	1		Bangalore	25 Jun
61.64	Kari	Pekola	FIN	27.9.65	1		Ikaalinen	24 Jun
61.24A	Frits	Potgieter	RSA	13.3.74	2		Pietersburg	18 Mar
61.22	Imrich	Bugár	TCH	14.4.55	1		Praha	16 Jun
61.20	Tero	Lehtiö	FIN	24.8.63	2		Ikaalinen	24 Jun
	(40)							
61.16	Timo	Sinervo	FIN	5.8.75	3		Ikaalinen	24 Jun
61.06	Robert	Weir	GBR	4.2.61	1		Corby	31 Jul
61.00	Roberto	Moya	CUB	11.2.65	2		Las Tunas	3 Apr
60.90	Mike	Buncic	USA	25.7.62	6		Salinas	25 May
60.68	Marcel	Tîrle	ROM	19.10.66	2		Budapest	3 Jun
60.66	Lars	Sundin	SWE	21.7.61	1		Mora	10 Aug
60.60	David	Martínez	ESP	31.1.67	1		Barcelona	21 May
60.58	Kjell Ove	Hauge	NOR	20.2.69	1		Fresno	20 May
60.50A	Martin	Swart	RSA	28.9.69	3		Pietersburg	18 Mar
60.50	Sergey	Lukashok	ISR	20.6.58	1		Dortmund	23 Jul
	(50)							
60.48	Jamie	Presser	USA	28.11.70	1eB		Salinas	25 May
60.48	Christos	Papadopoulos	GRE	16.3.65	1		Iraklio	17 Jul
60.42	Ramón	Jiménez	PAR	10.4.69	1	IbAm	Mar del Plata	27 Oct
60.30	Ajit	Bhaduria	IND	1.1.69	1		Bangalore	30 Jun
60.26	Jaroslav	Zitnansky	SVK	18.2.71	1		Dubnica	16 Jul
60.08	Carlos	Scott	USA	2.7.60	2	vGBR	Gateshead	20 Jul
60.00	Frédéric	Selle	FRA	15.3.57	2		Abbeville	11 Jun
59.96	Nikolay	Orekhov	RUS	20.6.73	2	vFRA	Sotteville	26 Jun
59.84	Dmitriy	Kovtsun	UKR	29.9.55	2		Belaya Tserkov	18 Jul
59.78	Glen	Smith	GBR	21.5.72	1		Loughborough	5 Jun
	(60)							
59.78	Martti	Halmesmäki	FIN	25.10.66	1		Espoo	10 Sep
59.68	Diego	Fortuna	ITA	14.2.68	1		Bologna	28 May
59.42	Brett	Murray	USA	15.11.71	1		Columbia	16 Apr
59.42	Frank	Vicet	CUB	13.11.71	1		La Habana	17 Jun
59.24	Igor	Avrunin	ISR	16.7.57	2		Tel Aviv	30 Apr
59.22	Marcelo	Pugliese	ARG	2.9.68	1		Buenos Aires	18 Sep
59.20	João Joaquim	dos Santos	BRA	9.9.61	2	IbAm	Mar del Plata	27 Oct
59.16	Zdenek	Kohout	TCH	14.5.67	1		Praha	1 May
59.16	Jean-Claude	Retel	FRA	11.2.68	1		Salon de Provence	11 May
59.16	Steve	Muse	USA	27.1.66	5	Jen	San José	28 May
	(70)							

Mark	Name		Nat	Born	Pos	Meet	Venue	Date
59.06	Eggert	Bogason	ISL	19.7.60	2		Reykjavik	19 Jul
59.02	David	Rodely	USA	7.6.68	1		Springfield	2 Apr
59.02	Martin	Bílek	TCH	7.1.73	1		Olomouc	7 May
58.98		Ma Wei	CHN	1.7.66	1	NC	Beijing	3 Jun
58.98	Harri	Uurainen	FIN	20.12.61	1		Lahti	16 Aug
58.96	Gregg	Hart	USA	21.8.70	1		Indianapolis	7 May
58.96	Stanislav	Kovár	TCH	6.5.64	2		Olomouc	7 May
58.96	Thomas	Rosvold	NOR	21.7.67			Dallas	16 Jul
58.96	Vadim	Popov	UZB	18.12.71	1		Tashkent	16 Sep
58.90	Olav	Jenssen	NOR	11.5.62	1		Bergen	23 Apr
	(80)							
58.86	Marek	Majkrzak	POL	12.10.65	2		Jablonec	4 Jun
58.78		Zhang Cunbiao	CHN	11.2.69	1	AsiG	Hiroshima	14 Oct
58.76	Jason	Tunks	CAN	7.5.75	1		Kingston	14 Jul
58.74	Vyacheslav	Demakov	RUS	8.11.68	1	NC-w	Sochi	19 Feb
58.68	Luis M	Delis	CUB	6.12.57	4	NC	La Habana	25 Jun
58.68	Kevin	Brown	GBR	10.9.64	2		Victoria	19 Aug
58.64	Jean-Marc	David	FRA	2.9.57	2		Sorgues	7 Jul
58.58A	Christo	Kruger	RSA	21.6.71	3		Germiston	13 May
58.58	Chima	Ugwu	NGR	72	7		Rhede	29 Jul
58.54	Bernd	Kniessler	GER	13.9.62	4		Halle	14 May
	(90)							
58.52A	Frantz	Kruger	RSA	22.5.75	3		Pretoria	18 Apr
58.52		Han Jun	CHN	13.11.72	1		Beijing	12 Aug
58.42	Joachim	Tidow	GER	4.2.69	5	NC	Erfurt	2 Jul
58.38	Viaceslav	Pacinas	LIT	16.7.63	1	NC	Vilnius	2 Jul
58.38	Igor	Primc	SLO	8.1.66	1	NC	Velenje	9 Jul
58.34	Lee	Newman	GBR	1.5.73	1		Bromley	9 Jun
58.32	Simon	Williams	GBR	17.10.67	2	TexR	Austin	9 Apr
58.32	Vasiliy	Kaptyukh	BLR	26.6.67	2		Lapinlahti	26 Jun
58.28	Olaf	Többen	GER	19.12.62	1		Medelby	24 Sep
58.26	Michael	Mollenbeck	GER	12.12.69	1		Scheessel	22 May
	(100)							

Mark	Name		Nat	Yr	Date	Mark	Name		Nat	Yr	Date
58.24	Mike	Berwanger	USA	71	21 May	57.88	Marco	Jakobs	GER	74	21 Aug
58.24	Mika	Muuka	FIN	66	2 Jul	57.86	Markus	Tschiers	GER	72	3 Jun
58.18		Li Shaojie	CHN	75	27 Apr	57.80	Julio	Piñero	ARG	75	21 Jul
58.18	John	Wirtz	USA	69	25 May	57.78	Jean	Pons	FRA	57	27 Feb
58.10	Andris	Smocs	LAT	68	28 Aug	57.76	Pekka	Kerala	FIN	72	17 May
58.06	Raymond	Lazdins	CAN	64	19 Aug	57.76	Leonid	Cherevko	BLR	74	21 Jul
58.04	Cristian	Ponton	ITA	72	21 May	57.74	Libor	Malina	TCH	73	16 Jun
58.00	Róbert	Fazekas	HUN	75	24 Jun	57.72	Darrin	Morris	GBR	67	11 May
58.00	Vasiliy	Petrov	UKR	66	18 Jul	57.66	Brad	Cooper	BAH	57	16 Jun

Unsanctioned: 64.98 Erik de Bruin ¶ NED 25.5.63 Dublin 2 Apr

Unconfirmed: 58.36 Sergey Kot UZB 7.1.60

MEN 1994

HAMMER

Mark	Name		Nat	Born	Pos	Meet	Venue	Date
83.36	Andrey	Abduvaliyev	TJK	30.6.66	1		Budapest	3 Jun
83.24		Abduvaliyev			1	WK	Zürich	17 Aug
83.14	Igor	Astapkovich	BLR	4.1.63	1	GGala	Roma	8 Jun
83.00		Astapkovich			1	GP II	Sevilla	5 Jun
82.50	Lance	Deal	USA	21.8.61	1	NC	Knoxville	17 Jun
82.42		Abduvaliyev			1		Tallinn	2 Aug
82.02	Vasiliy	Sidorenko	RUS	1.5.61	2	WK	Zürich	17 Aug
81.72	Andrey	Skvaryuk	UKR	9.3.67	1	NC	Kiev	27 May
81.72		Abduvaliyev			1	WCp	London	10 Sep
81.52		Abduvaliyev			1		Szombathely	27 May
81.46		Abduvaliyev			1	GPF	Paris	3 Sep
81.40		Astapkovich			1		Staiki	28 Apr
81.20		Abduvaliyev			1	Znam	Moskva	5 Jun
81.20	Heinz	Weis	GER	14.7.63	1		Dortmund	24 Sep
81.18		Abduvaliyev			1A		Rehlingen	23 May
81.14A		Deal			1		El Paso	16 Apr
81.14		Deal			2	WCp	London	10 Sep
81.10		Sidorenko			1	EC	Helsinki	11 Aug
81.04		Abduvaliyev			1	ISTAF	Konigs Wusterhausen	28 Aug
80.96	Aleksandr	Seleznyov	RUS	25.1.63	2		Sevilla	5 Jun
80.84		Weis			1		Rhede	29 Jul
80.78	Aleksandr	Krasko	BLR	18.9.72	1		Minsk	22 Jul

Mark	Name		Nat	Born	Pos	Meet	Venue	Date
80.72		Astapkovich			1	GP II	Linz	4 Jul
80.72		Abduvaliyev			1		Tallinn	29 Jul
80.68	Vitaliy	Alisevich	BLR	15.6.67	2		Minsk	22 Jul
80.66		Sidorenko			2	Znam	Moskva	5 Jun
80.62		Astapkovich			2	ISTAF	Konigs Wusterhausen	28 Aug
80.52		Astapkovich			2		Szombathely	27 May
80.50		Astapkovich			3	WK	Zürich	17 Aug
80.40		Astapkovich			2	EC	Helsinki	11 Aug
80.32		Weis			3	WCp	London	10 Sep
80.26		Astapkovich			2		Budapest	3 Jun
80.26		Abduvaliyev			1	Nik	Nice	18 Jul
80.22	Tibor	Gécsek	HUN	22.9.64	1		Szombathely	3 Aug
80.20		Deal			1	GWG	St Peterburg	24 Jul
	(35/10)							
80.14	Yuriy	Sedykh	RUS	11.6.55	1		Versailles	22 May
79.62	Vadim	Kolesnik	UKR	29.4.69	1		Dnepropetrovsk	9 Jul
79.20	Christophe	Épalle	FRA	23.1.69	1		Montgeron	14 May
79.20	Igor	Nikulin	RUS	14.8.60	1		Nurmijärvi	2 Jul
79.18	Sergey	Gavrilov	RUS	22.5.70	1		Bryansk	28 May
79.02	Aleksey	Krykun	UKR	12.12.68	2	NC	Kiev	27 May
78.54	Gilles	Dupray	FRA	2.1.70	1	v2N	Cagliari	17 Sep
78.30	Ilya	Konovalov	RUS	14.3.71	3	Znam	Moskva	5 Jun
78.06	Jüri	Tamm	EST	5.2.57	1		Sevilla	30 Apr
77.74	Balázs	Kiss	HUN	21.3.72	1		Veszprém	3 Sep
	(20)							
77.68	Claus	Dethloff	GER	24.9.68	1		Lübeck	9 Sep
77.58	Sean	Carlin	AUS	29.11.67	1		Adelaide	11 Feb
77.38	Jaroslav	Chmyr	UKR	29.11.66	4	NC	Kiev	27 May
77.14	Vadim	Grabovoy	UKR	5.4.73	2		Kiev	23 Jul
76.78	Vadim	Khersontsev	RUS	8.7.74	1		St Peterburg	11 May
76.74	Yuriy	Chernega	RUS	18.2.67	3	GGala	Roma	8 Jun
76.70	Sergey	Alay	BLR	11.6.65	3		Adler	23 Feb
76.66	Andrey	Budykin	RUS	14.4.71	4	Znam	Moskva	5 Jun
76.64	Frédéric	Kuhn	FRA	10.7.68	1		Meutreuil-sous-Bois	16 Jun
76.46	Tore	Gustafsson	SWE	11.2.62	1		Rimbo	27 Jul
	(30)							
76.44	Savas	Saritzoglou	GRE	19.7.71	1		Athina	28 May
76.40	Enrico	Sgrulletti	ITA	24.4.65	1		Rieti	1 May
76.30	Karsten	Kobs	GER	16.9.71	2		Dortmund	24 Sep
76.28	Zoltán	Fábián	HUN	22.4.69	1		Budapest	25 Jun
76.20	József	Vida	HUN	9.1.63	2		Tapolca	20 Aug
76.16	Konstantin	Astapkovich	BLR	23.10.70	3		Minsk	28 Apr
76.14	Alberto	Sánchez	CUB	3.2.73	1	Barr	La Habana	26 May
76.04	Marko	Wahlman	FIN	6.4.69	1		Pori	5 Jun
75.96	Pavel	Sedlácek	TCH	5.4.68	1		Praha	21 May
75.84	Valeriy	Gubkin	BLR	3.9.67	2	NC	Gomel	10 Jul
	(40)							
75.38	Sergey	Litvinov	RUS	23.1.58	6		Sevilla	5 Jun
75.22	Mika	Laaksonen	FIN	21.3.68	1	NC	Tuusula	9 Jul
75.02	Nicolas	Rougetet	FRA	27.7.70	1		Dijon	22 May
74.96	Lech	Kowalski	POL	17.1.61	1		Mielec	29 May
74.66	Andrés	Charadia	ARG	10.7.66	1	NC	Córdoba	9 Oct
74.60	Sergey	Vorobyov	RUS	29.1.64	2		St Peterburg	11 May
74.60	Nikolay	Lysenko	RUS	14.7.66	1		Stavropol	29 May
74.54	Per	Karlsson	SWE	21.4.67	1		Saarijärvi	25 Jun
74.48	Vladislav	Filippov	RUS	72	2		Stavropol	29 May
74.36	Scott	McGee	USA	1.10.68	2	Jer	Port Coquitlam	28 May'
	(50)							
74.26	Andrey	Sukhanov	UKR	3.8.70			Dnepropetrovsk	13 May
74.18	Dmitriy	Varich	UKR	28.3.72	3		Kiev	7 May
73.94	Valeriy	Yevdokimov	RUS	73	1	NC-23	Voronezh	17 Jun
73.86	Walter	Ciofani	FRA	17.2.62	2		Angers	11 Jun
73.74	Aleksandros	Papadimitrou	GRE	18.6.73	1		Thessaloniki	11 Jun
73.68	Vladimir	Bykov	RUS	70	3		Stavropol	29 May
73.66	Vladislav	Piskunov ¶	UKR	7.6.78	1		Kiev	11 Jun
73.60	Mikhail	Popel	BLR	25.5.66	4	NC	Gomel	10 Jul
73.52	László	Redei	HUN	17.7.70	2eA		Budapest	25 Jun
73.50	Albert	Sinka	HUN	22.11.62	5		Tapolca	20 Aug
	(60)							

Mark	Name		Nat	Born	Pos	Meet	Venue	Date
73.50	David	Chaussinaud	FRA	19.4.73	1		Aix-les-Bains	22 Oct
73.44	Hakim	Toumi	ALG	30.1.61	1		Alger	4 Jul
73.32	Giovanni	Sanguin	ITA	14.5.69	1		Padova	21 Jun
73.30	Jim	Driscoll	USA	15.8.65	2	NC	Knoxville	17 Jun
73.14	Zsolt	Németh	HUN	9.11.71	6		Tapolca	20 Aug
73.10	Angus	Cooper #	NZL	7.5.64	1		Hamilton	23 Jan
73.08	Rumen	Koprivichin	BUL	2.10.62	1		Johannesburg	9 Mar
73.08	Viktor	Baygush	UKR	16.12.63	7	NC	Kiev	27 May
73.04	Christos	Polichroniou	GRE	31.3.72	2		Athina	28 May
73.04	Brian	Murer	USA	6.5.72	2	Pre	Eugene	4 Jun
	(70)							
73.04	Ruslan	Dikiy	BLR	17.3.72	5	NC	Gomel	10 Jul
72.94	Andrey	Yevgenyev	RUS	17.2.73	1		Enskede	6 Jun
72.74	Sergey	Kirmasov ¶	RUS	25.3.70	3		Sochi	18 Feb
72.70	Emilio	Calabro'	ITA	4.2.69	1		Formia	5 Jun
72.64	Nikolaos	Gentekos	GRE	9.7.66	1		Iraklio	17 Jul
72.56	Adrián	Annus	HUN	28.6.74	2eB		Budapest	25 Jun
72.48	Szymon	Ziolkowski	POL	1.7.76	1		Warszawa	11 Jun
72.46		Bi Zhong	CHN	5.9.68	1	NC	Beijing	2 Jun
72.42	Tomas	Sjöström	SWE	27.2.70	2		Rimbo	27 Jul
72.38	Roman	Linscheid	IRL	29.12.70	3	NCAA	Boise	1 Jun
	(80)							
72.32	Raphaël	Piolanti	FRA	14.11.67	1		Troyes	15 May
72.16	Marcel	Kunkel	GER	19.10.72	1		Alzey	23 Apr
72.14	Sergey	Vasilyev	RUS	23.6.75	3		St Peterburg	28 Jun
72.10	Sergey	Domrachov	UKR	27.3.68	9	NC	Kiev	27 May
72.00	Loris	Paoluzzi	ITA	14.5.74	1		Rieti	22 May
72.00	Andrey	Vikhrov	RUS	73	4		Stavropol	29 May
71.94	Alexander	Sporrer	GER	20.1.71	1		Neulussheim	18 Jun
71.80	Vadim	Burakov	BLR	22.10.74	2	v2N23	Lvov	3 Sep
71.78	Nicola	Vizzoni	ITA	4.11.73	1		Pescara	18 Jun
71.78	Plamen	Minev	BUL	28.4.65	1		Sofia	2 Jul
	(90)							
71.72	Kevin	McMahon	USA	26.5.72	3	NC	Knoxville	17 Jun
71.68	Juha	Packalén	SWE	5.8.59	1		Rimbo	13 Jul
71.66	Igor	Tugay	UKR	22.3.75	1	v2N-j	Dôle	6 Aug
71.32	Andrey	Gurskiy	RUS	72	5		Stavropol	29 May
71.22	Vladimír	Maska	TCH	6.2.73	2	NC	Jablonec	10 Jul
71.16	Darren	Zaylor	USA	2.12.68	1		Akron	13 May
71.16	Paul	Head	GBR	1.7.65	1		Crawley	6 Aug
71.08	József	Verebes	HUN	25.2.69	1		Pécs	27 Apr
71.08	Imre	Szitás	HUN	4.9.61	2		Szombathely	17 May
71.06	Thomas	Neumann	GER	7.8.71	2		Erlangen	7 May
	(100)							

Mark	Name		Nat	Born	Date
70.80	Peter	Vivian	GBR	70	12 Jun
70.50	Georgios	Naltsatziadis	GRE	69	23 Apr
70.50	Bengt	Johansson	SWE	73	27 Jul
70.48	Vasiliy	Yakovich	UKR	71	27 May
70.46	Albert	Petukhov	UKR	74	27 May
70.28	Yosvany	Suárez	CUB	73	26 May
70.22	Eladio	Hernández	CUB	63	24 Jun
70.18	David	Loshonkohl	USA	73	1 Jun
70.14	Alex	Malachenko	BEL	67	17 Apr
70.10	Jan	Bielecki	DEN	71	7 May
70.10	Stefan	Jönsson	SWE	64	6 Jun
70.04	Konstantinos	Drakopoulos	GRE	68	9 Apr
69.94	Håkan	Åberg	SWE	63	4 Jun
69.90	Oliver	Sack	SUI	65	28 May
69.86	Dave	Popejoy	USA	72	20 May
69.74	Jacek	Dreger	POL	65	14 May
69.74	Ralf	Jossa	GER	66	5 Jun
69.64	Norbert	Radefeld	GER	62	4 Jun
69.62	Pavel	Milinevskiy	UKR		24 Jul
69.60	Victor	da Costa	POR	74	24 Jul
69.56	Kjell	Bystedt	SWE	60	23 Jul
69.54	Koji	Murofushi	JPN	74	27 Aug
69.52	Lou	Chisari	USA	68	26 Apr
69.48	Jörn	Hübner	GER	66	3 Jul
69.28	Ioannis	Mylonas	GRE	71	24 Apr
69.24	Guillermo	Guzman	MEX	64	7 Aug
69.16	Konstantin	Balandin	RUS	76	28 Jun
69.14	Samir	Haouam	ALG	68	27 Aug
69.10	Paul	Carlin	AUS	70	3 Aug
69.08	João	Reis	POR	68	20 Mar
69.08	Hector	Bontempi	ARG	73	28 May
69.00	Dmitriy	Marinin	BLR	72	28 Apr
68.98	Anton	Godall	ESP	66	9 Jan
68.86	Nikolay	Davydov	RUS	70	30 Jan
68.86	Milan	Horák	TCH	72	2 May
68.80	John	Walker	USA	67	28 May
68.70	Mario	Tschierschwitz	GER	62	23 Apr
68.70	Michel	André	FRA	70	22 May
68.68	Michael	Jones	GBR	63	2 Jul
68.62	Taisto	Vierimaa	FIN	65	2 Jun
68.58	Franck	Kuhn	FRA	65	15 Jun
68.54	Jean Fr.	Gregoire	FRA	68	14 May
68.48	Adrian	Marzo	ARG	68	9 Oct
68.42	Demetrios	Dionisopoulos	AUS	71	24 Jan
68.34	Scott	Sargeant	USA	69	17 Jun
68.34	Kai	Maybach	GER	72	6 Aug
68.30	Steve	Dering	USA	69	4 Jun
	(147)				

Drugs disqualification: 79.20 Sergey Kirmasov ¶ RUS 25.3.70 2 Rehlingen 24 May

Mark	Name		Nat	Born	Pos	Meet	Venue	Date
JAVELIN								
91.82	Jan	Zelezny	TCH	16.6.66	1	McD	Sheffield	4 Sep
91.68		Zelezny			1	GP	Gateshead	1 Jul
91.50		Zelezny			1	Kuso	Lublin	4 Jun
91.28		Zelezny			1	BNP	Villeneuve d'Ascq	8 Jul
90.06	Raymond	Hecht	GER	11.11.68	1		Eschenbach	12 Feb
89.98		Zelezny			1		Auckland	29 Mar
89.92		Zelezny			1	iDAG	Göteborg	24 Aug
89.06		Hecht			1		St Denis	10 Jun
88.54		Hecht			1		Luzern	29 Jun
88.34		Zelezny			1	VD	Bruxelles	19 Aug
88.04		Zelezny			1	WG	Helsinki	29 Jun
87.34	Andrey	Moruyev	RUS	6.5.70	1	ECp	Birmingham	25 Jun
87.22		Zelezny			1		Jablonec	6 Sep
87.06		Zelezny			1		Fukuoka	17 Sep
86.76	Patrik	Bodén	SWE	30.6.67	2	iDAG	Göteborg	24 Aug
86.36	Mike	Hill	GBR	22.10.64	1		Lahti	5 Jun
86.34		Zelezny			1	TOTO	Tokyo	15 Sep
86.24		Bodén			1	NC	Göteborg	30 Jul
86.06		Moruyev			2		Sheffield	4 Sep
85.88		Hecht			1	NC	Erfurt	3 Jul
85.72		Hecht			1		Duisburg	12 Jun
85.66		Moruyev			1		Dijon	12 Jun
85.54	Juha	Laukkanen	FIN	6.1.69	2		Lahti	5 Jun
85.46	Gavin	Lovegrove	NZL	21.10.67	3		Lahti	5 Jun
85.46	Harri	Hakkarainen	FIN	16.10.69	1		Leppävirta	7 Jun
85.44		Lovegrove			1		Wellington	19 Jan
85.42		Zelezny			1		Praha	21 May
85.42		Bodén			1		Karlstad	19 Jun
85.40		Hecht			2	ECp	Birmingham	25 Jun
85.28	Donald	Sild	EST	3.10.68	2		St Denis	10 Jun
85.28		Hill			3	ECp	Birmingham	25 Jun
85.22	Seppo	Räty	FIN	27.4.62	1		Lappeenranta	26 Jul
85.20	Steve	Backley	GBR	12.2.69	1	EC	Helsinki	8 Aug
	(33/11)							
84.36	Dag	Wennlund	SWE	9.10.63	1	Herc	Monaco	2 Aug
84.00	Vladimir	Parfyonov	UZB	17.6.70	1		Tashkent	16 Sep
83.82	Kostas	Gatsioudis	GRE	17.12.73	1	ECp 23	Ostrava	30 Jul
83.38	Ari	Pakarinen	FIN	14.5.69	1	v2N	Cagliari	18 Sep
83.38		Zhang Lianbiao	CHN	25.1.69	1	AsiG	Hiroshima	16 Oct
83.14	Vladimir	Sasimovich	BLR	14.9.68	2	Bisl	Oslo	22 Jul
82.96	Yuriy	Rybin	RUS	5.3.63	1	NC	St Peterburg	16 Jul
82.90	Andrey	Shevchuk	RUS	8.3.70	1	GWG	St Peterburg	28 Jul
82.56	Peter	Blank	GER	10.4.62	2	NC	Erfurt	3 Jul
	(20)							
82.54	Sergey	Makarov	RUS	73	2	ECp 23	Ostrava	30 Jul
82.44	Ed	Kaminski	USA	26.3.68	1		Emporia	14 May
82.32	Tom	Pukstys	USA	28.5.68	1		Nurmijärvi	2 Jul
82.14	Terry	McHugh	IRL	22.8.63	Q	EC	Helsinki	7 Aug
82.08	Ivan	Mustapic	CRO	9.7.66	1	NC		
82.02	Boris	Henry	GER	14.12.73	1		Gengenbach	4 Sep
81.62	Sami	Saksio	FIN	28.4.69	2		Lapua	12 Jul
81.34A	Phillip	Spies	RSA	21.5.70	1		Germiston	13 May
81.30	Todd	Riech	USA	24.10.70	1	NCAA	Boise	3 Jun
81.28	Jari	Hartikainen	FIN	28.4.67	3	v2N	Cagliari	18 Sep
	(30)							
81.12	Milos	Steigauf	TCH	5.12.69	3		Auckland	29 Mar
81.10	Andreas	Linden	GER	20.2.65	2		Gengenbach	4 Sep
80.92	Marcis	Shtrobinders	LAT	12.6.66	2	GWG	St Peterburg	28 Jul
80.84	Andrew	Currey	AUS	7.2.71	2		Wellington	19 Jan
80.78	Sigurdur	Einarsson	ISL	28.9.62	1		Reykjavik	18 Jun
80.74	Miroslaw	Witek	POL	24.4.67	1	NC	Pila	25 Jun
80.38	Nigel	Bevan	GBR	3.1.68	4	CG	Victoria	28 Aug
79.76	Vladimir	Ovchinnikov	RUS	2.8.70	2		Khania	5 Jun
79.76	Peter	Borglund	SWE	29.1.64	1		Sundsvall	23 Jul
79.46	Christian	Benninger	GER	15.3.71	1		Passau	4 Jun
	(40)							

Mark	Name		Nat	Born	Pos	Meet	Venue	Date
79.44	Ilkka	Kontinaho	FIN	16.9.64	1		Pattijoki	28 Jun
79.34	Kimmo	Kinnunen	FIN	31.3.68	1		Äänekoski	16 Jun
79.26	Mika	Parviainen	FIN	19.12.70	3		Lappeenranta	26 Jul
79.20	Viktor	Zaitsev	UZB	6.6.66	1		Almaty	21 May
79.16	Colin	Mackenzie #	GBR	30.6.63	3	AAA	Sheffield	12 Jun
79.12	Andrey	Maznichenko	UKR	29.9.66	1		Kiev	24 Jul
78.94	Louis	Fouche	RSA	21.3.70	1		Potchefstroom	11 Mar
78.94	Mathias	Hold	GER	21.1.73	3		Kassel	25 May
78.90	Aleksey	Shchepin	RUS	3.4.72	1	NC-23	Voronezh	18 Jun
78.84	Jorma	Markus	FIN	28.11.52	1		Kempele	21 Jun
	(50)							
78.82	Mark	Roberson	GBR	13.3.67	2		London	26 Jun
78.76	Rajmund	Kolko	POL	1.3.71	1		Bydgoszcz	10 Jun
78.76	Aki	Parviainen	FIN	26.10.74	4		Pihtipudas	17 Jul
78.74	Marek	Kaleta	EST	17.12.61	1		Tallinn	28 May
78.66	Dariusz	Trafas	POL	5.6.72	2	NCAA	Boise	3 Jun
78.42 ??	Dirk	Pollakowski	GER	24.2.70	2		Bydgoszcz	10 Jun
78.38	Håvard	Johansen	NOR	23.1.68	1		Byrkjelo	24 Jul
78.38	Alain	Storaci	FRA	5.6.67	4	v2N	Cagliari	18 Sep
78.18	Emeterio	González	CUB	11.4.73	3		Madrid	6 Sep
78.12	Yevgeniy	Stankevich	RUS	73	1		Sochi	10 Sep
	(60)							
78.10	Stefan	König	GER	25.8.66	Q	NC	Erfurt	3 Jul
77.98	Oliver	Zschunke	GER	29.4.70	1		Karlstadt	13 Jul
77.98	Marius	Corbett	RSA	26.9.75	1	WJ	Lisboa	24 Jul
77.86	Jens	Reimann	GER	21.3.69	2		Ludweiler	7 May
77.80	Johan	van Lieshout	NED	8.3.69	1		Amersfoort	19 Jun
77.80	Karl-Friedrich	Michel	GER	9.5.65	2		Müllheim	4 Sep
77.68	Kazuhiro	Mizoguchi	JPN	18.3.62	1		Hamamatsu	13 Nov
77.46	Tomasz	Damszel	POL	25.3.72	1		Aix les Bains	8 May
77.40A	Hennes	de Wet	RSA	13.12.67	2		Germiston	13 May
77.22	Roald	Bradstock	GBR	24.4.62	1		Los Angeles (Ww)	9 Apr
	(70)							
77.02	Jarkko	Heimonen	FIN	6.3.72	9		Lahti	5 Jun
76.94	Mike	Barnett	USA	21.5.61	4	NC	Knoxville	18 Jun
76.86	Jarkko	Kinnunen	FIN	21.4.70	2		Äänekoski	16 Jun
76.70	Nery	Kennedy	PAR	28.5.73	1	Odesur	Valencia	23 Nov
76.62		Sun Fuhai	CHN	.7.72	2	NC	Beijing	5 Jun
76.60	Aleksandr	Fingert	ISR	1.5.65	1	v3N	Istanbul	21 May
76.60	Joakim	Nilsson	SWE	30.3.71	1		Helsingborg	10 Jul
76.58	Peter	Esenwein	GER	7.12.67	1		Lage	28 May
76.50	Julian	Sotelo	ESP	5.7.65	1		Madrid	4 Jun
76.50		Sun Fei	CHN	24.1.68	3	NC	Beijing	5 Jun
	(80)							
76.50	Rodrigo	Zelaya	CHI	12.6.68	2	Odesur	Valencia	23 Nov
76.46	Marko	Hyytiäinen	FIN	27.11.66	3		Elimäki	18 Jun
76.36	József	Belák ¶	HUN	13.8.58	1		Budapest	29 Apr
76.28	Nick	Nieland	GBR	31.1.72	1	U23Int	King's Lynn	9 Jul
76.20	Arne	Indrebø	NOR	6.8.69	2		Byrkjelo	24 Jul
76.16	Takahiro	Yamada	JPN	20.4.68	1		Hiratsuka	20 Mar
76.14	Matti	Närhi	FIN	17.8.75	2		Viitasaari	14 Jun
76.08	Kenneth	Petersen	DEN	18.12.65	1		Lyngby	20 Aug
75.98	Vladimír	Novácek	TCH	23.6.68	1		Innsbruck	26 Jun
75.96	Tommi	Huotilainen	FIN	17.11.67	4		Keuruu	24 Jun
	(90)							
75.94	Jim	Connolly	USA	24.3.62	2		Edwardsville	8 Jul
75.92	Robert	Srovnal	TCH	13.6.75	1		Praha	16 Jun
75.90	Tadayuki	Tsuchiya	JPN	7.4.73	1		Hiratsuka	26 Jun
75.80	Emil	Tsvetanov	BUL	14.3.63	1		Plovdiv	5 Mar
75.64	Mikko	Anttonen	FIN	5.7.63	5		Keuruu	24 Jun
75.60A	Tom	Petranoff	RSA	8.4.58	5		Pietersburg	18 Mar
75.56	Aleksandr	Khrichenko	KZK	72	1		Tucson	5 Feb
75.56	Art	Skipper	USA	31.7.70	1		Monmouth	7 May
75.54A	Luis	Lucumi	COL	25.10.58	1		Pereira	17 Oct
75.52	Viktor	Yevsyukov	KZK	6.10.56	2		Almaty	21 May
	(100)							
75.52		Chen Junlin	CHN	31.5.67	4	NC	Beijing	5 Jun
75.50	Garrett	Noel	USA	22.1.70	1		Flagstaff	14 May
75.50	Moreno	Belletti	ITA	10.8.70	1		Pesaro	15 May

Mark		Name	Nat	Born	Date	Mark		Name	Nat	Born	Date
75.48	Ari	Weckström	FIN	67	1 Jun	74.78		Li Rongxiang	CHN	72	2 Apr
75.48	Pascal	Lefèvre	FRA	65	23 Jul	74.64		?	CHN		18 Oct
75.42	Ty	Sevin	USA	71	3 Jun	74.64	Mika	Kainulainen	FIN	73	4 Sep
75.32		Kim Ki-hoon	KOR	68	28 Oct	74.58	Eduard	Budnik	UKR	61	24 Jul
75.30	Fikret	Özsoy	TUR	65	11 Jun	74.58	Franck	Pasquelin	FRA	73	30 Jul
75.12	Grégory	Wiesner	SUI	71	11 Jul	74.54	Knut	Hempel	GER	65	27 Jul
75.10	Michel	Bertimon	FRA	57	12 Jun		(126)				
75.10	Juha	Karjalainen	FIN	62	23 Aug	74.46	Goran	Bosnjak	YUG	70	20 Aug
75.08	Pietari	Skyttä	FIN	76	20 Aug	74.30	Myles	Cottrell	GBR	70	12 Jun
75.00	Petr	Novák	TCH	73	16 Jun	74.22	Jari-Pekka	Huttunen	FIN	70	16 Jun
75.00	Gregor	Högler	AUT	72	30 Jul	74.18	Georgiy	Shapkin	RUS	66	18 Feb
74.92	Lee Wook-jong		KOR	66	11 May	74.14	Carlo	Sonego	ITA	72	7 Jul
74.90	Diggery	Brooke	NZL	69	22 Jan	74.12	Vladimir	Ponomarenko	RUS	70	15 Jul
74.88		Miao Lianqin	CHN	75	30 Apr	74.12	Kota	Suzuki	JPN	68	30 Jul
74.88	Andrey	Uglov	UKR	73	13 Sep	74.10	Ramón	González	CUB	65	13 May
74.86	Edgar	Baumann	PAR	70	25 May	74.10	Pal	Fagernes	NOR	74	26 May
74.82	Ralph	Willinski	GER	67	5 Jun	74.10	Johan	Kloeck	BEL	75	27 Jul

Disqualified on positive drugs test

Mark		Name	Nat	Born	Pos	Venue	Date
80.82	Colin	Mackenzie #	GBR	30.6.63	1	Rovereto	24 Jul

PENTATHLON

Mark							Name	Nat	Born	Pos	Venue	Date
3826	6.31	63.08	22.53	42.72	4:16.37	Roland	Clauss	GER	16.4.70	1	Wiesbaden	14 May
3821	7.28	54.30	22.4	44.22	4:34.3	Thomas	Görz	GER	10.3.72	1	Kreutzal	30 Apr
3777	6.65	58.50	22.73	44.54	4:27.33	Alexander	Clauss	GER	16.4.70	2	Wiesbaden	14 May
3748	7.09	59.72	22.44	42.42	4:48.84	Martin	Otte	GER	3.5.67	1	Baunatal	24 Sep
3688	6.83	57.04	22.3	38.86	4:29.0	Tapio	Linnemöller	GER	31.12.71	1	Herford	30 Apr
3616	7.21	53.58	22.4	39.84	4:49.4	Søren	Johansson	DEN	26.8.71	1	Svendborg	3 Sep
3504	7.03	48.40	21.9	36.26	4:43.2	Dieter	Göhring	GER	14.11.67	1	Bad Mergentheim	30 Jul
3461	6.61	56.60	23.0	41.08	4:52.9	Gerald	Bayer	GER	4.1.70	1	Treuchtlingen	9 Oct
3455	6.60	51.80	23.0	35.88	4:25.3	Niels	Uth	DEN	19.10.74	2	Svendborg	3 Sep
3444	6.96	63.52	23.7	46.00	5:37.4	Miroslav	Rucky	TCH	24.3.68	1	Prerov	1 May
3441	6.87w	58.58	24.30	38.30	4:45.51	Georg	Werthner	AUT	7.4.56	1	Wattens	7 May

DECATHLON

Mark		Name	Nat	Born	Pos	Meet	Venue	Date										
8735	Eduard	Hämäläinen	BLR	21.1.69	1		Götzis	29 May	10.50/+2.1	7.26/+1.0	16.05	2.11	47.63	13.82/-3.0	49.70	4.90	60.32	4:35.09
8715	Dan	O'Brien	USA	18.7.66	1	GWG	St Peterburg	29 Jul	10.49/-0.3	7.81/+1.4	15.70	2.20	47.73	13.81/+0.6	48.10	4.90	62.20	5:10.9
8710		O'Brien			1		Talence	11 Sep	10.43/-0.8	7.75/-0.3	15.81	2.06	48.06	13.91/-0.6	48.88	5.20	59.56	4:56.58
8707		O'Brien			1	NC	Knoxville	15 Jun	10.31/+2.6	7.81/+0.5	15.87	2.17	48.19	13.98/-1.4	46.34	5.15	62.28	5:16.42
8548	Steve	Fritz	USA	1.11.67	2	NC	Knoxville	15 Jun	10.63/+2.6	7.84/+3.3	14.37	2.05	48.70	14.27/-1.4	46.76	4.95	64.58	4:43.09
8505	Christian	Plaziat	FRA	28.10.63	1	ECp A	Vénissieux	3 Jul	10.94/-0.2	7.88/+1.0	14.88	2.10	48.34	14.20/-1.9	44.54	5.10	57.32	4:39.32
8459		Hämäläinen			2		Talence	11 Sep	10.69/-0.8	681/-0.3	15.40	2.09	47.69	14.00/-0.6	52.20	4.80	55.00	4:32.01
8453	Alain	Blondel	FRA	7.12.62	1	EC	Helsinki	13 Aug	11.12/+0.6	7.50/+3.2	13.78	1.99	48.91	14.18/+0.9	45.08	5.40	60.64	4:20.48
8439		Blondel			3		Talence	11 Sep	11.07/-0.8	7.53/-0.6	13.58	1.94	48.21	14.29/-0.6	46.42	5.00	65.18	4:15.64
8403	Henrik	Dagård	SWE	7.8.69	4		Talence	11 Sep	10.82/-0.8	7.37/-0.2	14.80	1.97	47.25	14.24/-0.6	43.24	5.00	66.34	4:39.91
8362		Dagård			2	EC	Helsinki	13 Aug	10.69/+1.0	7.45/+0.9	14.93	1.93	46.71	14.15/+0.9	44.36	4.80	62.52	4:40.49
8359		Dagård			2		Götzis	29 May	10.45/+2.1	7.35/+3.2	14.44	1.99	47.44	14.27/-3.0	45.64	4.50	64.12	4:35.50
8347		Dagård			2	ECp A	Vénissieux	3 Jul	10.65/-0.2	7.45/+1.5	14.88	1.98	47.31	14.31/-1.9	42.94	4.90	64.08	4:47.15
8343		Fritz			5		Talence	11 Sep	10.92/-0.8	7.50/+0.8	14.68	2.00	49.68	14.20/-0.6	44.70	4.90	67.46	4:38.91
8326	Mike	Smith	CAN	16.9.67	1	CG	Victoria	24 Aug	11.00/+0.8	6.94/+1.3	16.22	1.98	48.85	14.82/+0.5	48.62	5.10	67.98	4:47.38
8313	Tomás	Dvorák	TCH	11.5.72	3	ECp A	Vénissieux	3 Jul	10.83/-0.2	7.75/+0.8	15.52	2.04	48.36	14.20/-1.9	41.04	4.40	62.16	4:32.67
8309	Stefan	Schmid	GER	6.5.70	6		Talence	11 Sep	11.01/-0.8	7.83/-1.3	13.55	2.00	49.15	14.46/-0.5	39.84	4.80	71.68	4:31.4

Mark	Name		Nat	Born	Pos	Meet	Venue	Date
8287	Kip	Janvrin	USA	8.7.65	3	NC	Knoxville	15 Jun
	10.73/+2.5 6.99/-0.2 13.52 1.90 47.57 14.82/-2.0 46.04 5.25 60.14 4:18.13							
8281	Sheldon	Blockburger	USA	19.9.64	4	NC	Knoxville	15 Jun
	10.83/+2.6 7.54/+3.2 15.06 2.14 50.31 14.97/-2.0 45.26 4.55 68.08 4:44.82							
8257	Vitaliy	Kolpakov	UKR	2.2.72	1	ECp B	Bressanone	3 Jul
	11.29/-0.5 7.62/+1.3 15.19 2.16 48.43 14.40/+1.3 44.50 4.70 57.38 4:44.00							
8248		Blondel			4	ECp A	Vénissieux	3 Jul
	11.01/+0.4 7.17/-0.8 13.83 1.92 49.04 14.74/-1.9 43.40 5.40 64.48 4:22.48							
8234	Paul	Foxson	USA	16.4.71	1		Sacramento	16 Apr
	11.00/+0.6 7.52/+0.6 14.56 2.06 48.58 15.12/+1.7 47.22 4.80 58.30 4:33.6							
8224	William	Motti	FRA	25.7.64	7		Talence	11 Sep
	11.62/+0.8 7.13/+0.5 16.33 2.12 51.09 15.01/-0.5 51.88 4.90 68.92 4:55.11							
8219	Dave	Johnson	USA	7.4.63	1	MSR	Azusa	15 Apr
	11.20 7.29 14.27 1.99 49.87 14.57 47.02 4.90 68.46 4:36.55							
8201		Schmid			3		Götzis	29 May
	10.76/+3.9 7.25/+1.2 14.31 1.96 48.69 14.75/-2.5 43.38 4.70 66.34 4:28.35							
8201	Lev	Lobodin	UKR	1.4.69	3	EC	Helsinki	13 Aug
	10.86/+1.0 7.30/+1.9 15.34 1.99 48.78 14.31/+0.9 45.50 5.00 50.14 4:31.80							
8199		Plaziat			8		Talence	11 Sep
	11.14/+0.8 7.46/-0.1 14.70 2.06 49.18 14.31/-0.6 43.98 5.00 56.08 4:38.31							
8191		Smith			4		Götzis	29 May
	10.83/+3.9 7.02/+3.7 15.27 1.93 49.70 14.64/-1.0 48.84 4.90 65.74 4:44.11							
8179w		Janvrin			1	DogwR	Knoxville	7 Apr
	10.79/+6.8 7.13 14.19 1.98 49.53 14.80/-1.5 40.94 5.00 62.12 4:17.74							
8177		Fritz			2	GWG	St Peterburg	29 Jul
	10.83/-0.3 7.37/+0.4 14.54 2.05 52.58 14.04/+0.6 47.38 4.90 67.32 5:01.72							
8176		Lobodin			2	ECp B	Bressanone	3 Jul
	10.87/+0.7 7.37/+0.9 14.64 2.04 48.94 14.17/+0.6 43.62 5.00 54.44 4:44.12							
	(32/11)							
8160w	Antonio	Peñalver	ESP	1.12.68	1	NC	Alhama	5 Jun
	11.00/+3.4 7.39/+4.3 16.52 2.03 50.59 14.48/+4.6 40.42 4.40 60.76 4:43.54							
8112	Thorsten	Dauth	GER	11.3.68	1		Aachen	10 Jul
	10.87/0.0 7.20/+0.5 15.52 1.98 48.91 14.43/+0.5 47.40 4.40 56.70 4:31.97							
8106	Ramil	Ganiyev	UZB	23.9.68	1		Wien	26 Jun
	10.80/+2.7 7.49/+0.9 14.21 2.12 49.91 14.65/+0.7 44.44 5.00 50.60 4:46.72							
8105	Sébastien	Levicq	FRA	25.6.71	5		Götzis	29 May
	11.18/+2.0 7.28/+1.9 13.75 1.93 51.43 14.89/-2.7 47.96 5.20 64.44 4:31.96							
8105	Drew	Fucci	USA	26.5.67	5	NC	Knoxville	15 Jun
	10.81/+1.3 7.54/+1.0 11.90 2.08 48.68 14.35/-1.4 41.26 5.25 52.72 4:42.34							
8105	Igor	Matsanov	BLR	13.4.70	1		Gomel	24 Aug
	10.85 7.16 15.34 2.08 50.69 14.28 46.80 4.70 52.22 4:36.40							
8093	Eugenio	Balanque	CUB	20.12.68	1	NC	La Habana	24 Jun
	10.75/-2.3 7.12/+1.2 13.54 2.08 47.53 14.87/-0.5 40.54 5.00 56.30 4:38.32							
8093	Erki	Nool	EST	25.6.70	1	ECp C	Tallinn	3 Jul
	10.68/+1.8 7.96/+1.7 14.26 1.94 49.02 15.49/+1.3 36.72 5.30 58.58 4:45.16							
8078	Alex	Kruger	GBR	18.11.63	7		Götzis	29 May
	11.22/+0.4 7.45/+2.0 14.63 2.14 50.04 15.09/-2.5 43.44 4.80 57.08 4:34.86							
	(20)							
8074	Peter	Winter	AUS	17.1.71	2	CG	Victoria	24 Aug
	10.79 7.65 13.68 1.95 47.95 14.47 41.08 4.90 60.40 4:54.94							
8071	Sándor	Munkácsi	HUN	24.7.69	6	EC	Helsinki	13 Aug
	11.14/+1.7 7.65/+2.0 13.02 1.93 48.38 14.24/+1.2 42.00 4.70 56.94 4:20.27							
8070	Yevgeniy	Dudakov	RUS	69	1		Krasnodar	18 May
	10.9 7.62 13.67 2.14 50.4 14.8 46.36 5.00 48.52 4:33.8							
8070	Dirk-Achim	Pajonk	GER	27.3.69	2		Aachen	10 Jul
	10.97/0.0 7.39/+0.3 14.48 1.98 48.75 14.71/+0.5 42.56 4.50 56.92 4:18.07							
8043	Muhammad	Oliver	USA	12.3.69	6	NC	Knoxville	15 Jun
	10.70/+1.3 7.37/+1.6 13.12 2.14 49.20 14.21/-1.4 38.84 4.55 58.26 4:41.06							
8038	Indrek	Kaseorg	EST	16.12.67	1		Laces	4 Sep
	11.34/-2.4 7.38/+2.4 13.79 2.06 48.77 14.48/-1.2 38.20 4.60 64.02 4:26.01							
8034w	Francisco	Benet	ESP	25.3.68	2	NC	Alhama	5 Jun
	11.15/+3.4 7.31/+3.8 13.25 1.97 49.87 14.33/+4.6 44.10 4.70 62.96 4:47.80							
8033	Dmitriy	Sukhomazov	BLR	10.3.71	2		Gomel	24 Aug
	11.10 7.19 13.82 2.14 50.28 14.68 40.90 4.90 60.62 4:39.47							
8023w	Frank	Müller	GER	18.6.68	10		Götzis	29 May
	10.87/+5.1 7.37/+3.9 13.94 1.99 49.53 14.67/-3.4 44.52 4.60 59.68 4:36.06							
7997	Rob	Muzzio	USA	25.6.64	7	NC	Knoxville	15 Jun
	11.04/+2.5 6.91/+0.5 15.59 1.96 49.19 15.02/-2.0 45.22 4.65 61.38 4:32.72							
	(30)							

Mark	Name		Nat	Born	Pos	Meet	Venue	Date
7996	Aric	Long	USA	15.4.70	1	vGER	San Luis Obispo	7 Aug
	11.47/-0.1 7.13/+0.7 15.58 2.08 50.37 14.90/+1.5 48.18 5.00 55.10 4:49.38							
7995	Dezsö	Szabó	HUN	4.9.67	8	EC	Helsinki	13 Aug
	11.02/+0.6 7.39/+1.8 12.87 1.93 48.63 14.68/+0.9 40.38 5.20 50.06 4:17.23							
7992	Valeriy	Belousov	RUS	22.1.70	1	NC	Vladimir	17 Jun
	10.95 7.22 13.32 2.05 50.32 14.54 41.30 5.00 55.84 4:31.49							
7980	Simon	Shirley	GBR	3.8.66	3	CG	Victoria	24 Aug
	10.89 7.11 14.16 2.04 48.90 14.87 38.38 4.60 63.80 4:32.34							
7979	Alvaro	Burrell	ESP	29.4.69	7	ECp A	Vénissieux	3 Jul
	10.88/-0.2 6.81/-1.5 14.91 2.07 47.54 14.62/-1.6 43.18 4.50 48.58 4:23.93							
7957	Brian	Schweyen	USA	17.2.68	8	NC	Knoxville	15 Jun
	11.08/+1.8 7.12/+0.1 12.78 2.17 51.10 14.91/-2.1 48.14 5.05 55.28 4:52.30							
7945	Cédric	Lopez	FRA	13.2.73	1		Bad Oeynhausen	7 Aug
	10.94/+1.3 7.19/+1.1 13.72 2.00 48.98 15.16/+0.3 41.08 4.30 71.34 4:35.74							
7941	Chris	Wilcox	USA	6.1.68	2		Sacramento	16 Apr
	10.89/+0.6 7.34/+2.2 14.69 2.09 49.85 14.47/+1.7 44.82 4.50 53.94 4:54.00							
7938	Frank	Busemann	GER	26.2.75	1		Zeven	2 Oct
	10.68 7.37 13.08 2.03 50.41 14.34 39.84 4.40 63.00 4:37.31							
7933w/7914	Mirko	Spada	SUI	26.1.69	1	NC	Winterthur	19 Jun
	11.06/+2.0 7.22/+4.4 (7.14/+3.3) 15.25 1.83 49.45 14.34/+1.0 43.98 4.50 61.22 4:32.34							
	(40)							
7926	Dean	Smith	AUS	1.11.67	4	CG	Victoria	24 Aug
	10.87 7.49 14.84 1.95 51.20 15.71 45.96 4.70 61.48 4:40.93							
7919	Norbert	Demmel	GER	10.5.63	1	NC	Vaterstetten	3 Sep
	11.40/0.0 6.88/-0.6 16.59 1.94 51.84 15.11 53.26 4.70 61.78 4:47.79							
7913	Raul	Duany	CUB	4.1.75	2	Barr	La Habana	26 May
	11.50 7.13 13.99 2.10 49.70 14.77 37.76 4.50 65.58 4:24.03							
7906	Mikhail	Medved	UKR	30.1.64	2		Laces	4 Sep
	11.43/-2.4 7.38/+2.7 15.10 2.03 51.79 15.09/-1.2 49.20 4.90 59.98 4:59.54							
7903w	Brian	Brophy	USA	6.1.69	1		Lynchburg	16 Apr
	11.07/+6.3 7.02/+6.3 14.55 2.02 49.52 14.83 51.60 4.95 49.02 4:57.26							
7899	Rolf	Schläfli	SUI	15.3.71	2	NC	Winterthur	19 Jun
	11.05/-0.4 7.34/+0.9 14.22 2.01 48.27 14.62/+1.0 40.78 4.30 57.82 4:33.93							
7896	Jón Arnar	Magnusson	ISL	28.7.69	12		Götzis	29 May
	10.80/+2.1 7.63/+1.9 14.31 1.99 50.28 14.73/-3.4 45.80 4.70 52.16 4:57.33							
7896w	Marcel	Dost	NED	28.9.69	1	NC	Eindhoven	5 Jun
	10.8/W 7.43 13.71 1.98 50.00 14.77 44.46 4.90 53.74 4:43.68							
7894	Andrey	Nazarov	EST	9.1.65	11	EC	Helsinki	13 Aug
	10.99/+1.7 7.22/+1.4 13.14 2.02 49.65 14.31/+1.2 43.54 4.80 54.02 4:42.10							
7882	Peter	Neumaier	GER	30.6.67	2		Brescia	15 May
	11.07/-0.9 7.12/0.0 13.98 2.00 47.80 15.39/+1.6 41.08 4.60 58.30 4:28.61							
	(50)							
7876	Jan	Podrebadsky	TCH	1.3.74	9	ECp A	Vénissieux	3 Jul
	10.83/+0.4 7.14/+1.5 13.52 1.92 46.92 14.64/-1.9 39.32 4.40 48.14 4:07.20							
7871	Ricky	Barker	USA	14.11.69	2	vGER	San Luis Obispo	7 Aug
	10.98/-0.1 7.23/-0.3 14.00 2.14 49.32 14.71/+0.9 36.56 5.00 54.66 4:56.42							
7870	Enoch	Borozinski	USA	2.7.71	1	NCAA	Boise	4 Jun
	10.82/+0.9 7.03/+2.7 14.43 2.01 50.92 15.30/+2.6 43.30 4.60 60.58 4:33.21							
7864	Doug	Pirini	NZL	6.9.69	1		Auckland	9 Jan
	10.72 7.62 12.71 1.89 48.60 14.90 42.02 4.70 54.06 4:36.26							
7853	Munehiro	Kaneko	JPN	6.6.68	1		Matto	17 Jul
	11.19 7.18 14.48 1.99 50.17 14.73 46.22 4.70 58.50 4:51.36							
7850		Cai Min	CHN	8.5.68	1	NC	Beijing	5 Jun
	10.56 7.73 14.48 1.90 49.16 14.35 41.74 4.40 55.08 5:02.42							
7843	Jarko	Finni	FIN	19.2.72	10	ECp A	Vénissieux	3 Jul
	11.09/+0.4 7.35/+1.4 14.63 1.98 51.08 15.45/-1.8 41.16 4.80 64.84 4:45.97							
7837	Rob	Pendergist	USA	12.7.70	2	NCAA	Boise	4 Jun
	11.04/+1.8 7.33/+2.9 12.95 2.01 50.05 14.99/+1.5 39.04 4.60 59.34 4:23.34							
7830	Rojs	Piziks	LAT	12.2.71	1		Murjani	15 May
	11.74 7.02 13.94 2.10 52.70 15.20 46.98 4.80 62.34 4:30.88							
7830	Helge	Günther	GER	10.4.69	4		Aachen	10 Jul
	11.31/0.0 6.95/+0.9 14.60 1.98 49.55 14.71/+0.5 43.08 4.50 62.40 4:36.23							
	(60)							
7799w	Aleksandr	Bogdanov	UKR	29.4.70	15		Götzis	29 May
	10.92/+3.9 7.00/+5.2 13.61 1.99 48.81 14.55/-3.0 43.94 4.60 52.10 4:40.13							
7789	Pierre-Alexandre	Vial	FRA	25.5.75	1		St Etienne	1 May
	10.82 7.29 12.90 1.86 48.98 14.61 42.98 4.60 54.04 4:30.41							
7786	Darrin	Steele	USA	20.3.69	4		Laces	4 Sep
	11.01/-2.4 7.00/+2.2 14.27 1.97 48.89 14.71/-1.2 46.02 4.50 61.32 5:04.22							

Mark	Name		Nat	Born	Pos	Meet	Venue	Date
7783	Udo	Jacobasch	GER	30.8.70	16		Götzis	29 May
	11.12/+2.0	7.34/+1.7	14.50 1.99	50.18		14.82/-3.4	44.94 4.80 49.96 4:49.77	
7778w	Brad	Swanson	USA	15.7.69	2		Pella	14 May
	10.7W	7.38W	13.26 2.03	49.9		14.8w	41.14 4.15 65.74 4:44.1	
7768	Christian	Mandrou	FRA	24.6.65	19		Götzis	29 May
	11.15/+2.0	6.96/+2.9	12.78 1.89	49.89		14.61/-2.7	40.68 4.60 62.80 4:26.94	
7768	Nikolay	Afanasyev	RUS	11.8.65	7	ECp B	Bressanone	3 Jul
	11.40/-0.5	7.27/-0.1	14.00 2.04	50.52		14.45/+0.6	38.42 4.70 57.08 4:37.79	
7764	Matt	Shelton	USA	3.6.69	1		Knoxville	23 May
	10.67	7.34/+0.8	13.41 2.01	48.32		14.52/0.0	41.16 4.00 55.90 4:46.66	
7761	Philipp	Huber	SUI	18.2.74	3	NC	Winterthur	19 Jun
	11.14/-0.4	7.07/+3.1	13.90 1.86	48.57		14.83/+1.1	41.58 4.60 53.72 4:19.25	
7760 h	Rick	Schwieger	USA	17.6.69	2		College Station	18 Mar
	10.92	7.07	13.42 2.11	50.6		14.89	41.98 4.70 50.44 4:38.54	
	(70)							
7756	Michael	Kohnle	GER	3.5.70	2	NC	Vaterstetten	3 Sep
	10.97/0.0	7.11/-0.4	12.98 2.00	51.04		14.76	43.08 5.00 59.96 4:59.97	
7753	Mike	Bennett	USA	22.9.68	1		Goleta	22 May
	10.99/+1.6	7.05/+0.2	13.15 1.88	49.56		14.16/+3.7	40.98 4.90 51.00 4:31.27	
7737	Stefan	Schneider	SUI	21.2.64	21		Götzis	29 May
	11.31/-1.0	7.28/+1.4	12.68 2.02	50.40		15.00/-2.7	40.20 4.60 56.40 4:21.15	
7724	Benjamin	Jensen	NOR	13.4.75	1	Sca-j	Hyvinkää	3 Aug
	11.15/+1.4	7.09/+1.0	11.77 1.96	49.44		14.46/+1.0	34.56 5.30 52.00 4:26.37	
7717	Sebastian	Chmara	POL	21.11.71	4		Brescia	15 May
	11.61/-0.5	7.18/+1.3	14.33 2.06	49.59		14.91/+1.6	40.76 4.80 46.90 4:28.20	
7715	Brendan	Tennant	AUS	22.4.72	2	NC	Canberra	18 Mar
	11.13	7.53	13.90 1.87	49.27		15.53	41.30 4.50 59.80 4:35.27	
7704	Tommy	Richards	USA	14.7.70	1		San Angelo	16 Apr
	11.26	6.87	13.07 2.03	50.48		14.70	43.56 5.10 56.18 4:57.24	
7702	Oleg	Veretelnikov	UZB	22.1.72	2	AsiG	Hiroshima	15 Oct
	11.23	7.16	12.40 1.94	49.36		15.02	37.40 4.50 62.90 4:19.50	
7701	Miguel	Valle	CUB	29.9.68	2	NC	La Habana	24 Jun
	11.01/-2.3	7.09/-1.3	14.38 1.96	50.56		14.66/-0.5	40.10 4.60 56.50 4:42.06	
7694	Bernhard	Floder	GER	17.4.73	3		Emmelshausen	29 May
	11.09	7.18	13.46 1.94	49.79		14.31	38.74 4.60 53.20 4:32.51	
	(80)							
7693	Gerard	Williams	USA	28.1.72	1		Tucson	15 Jul
	10.90/+0.6	7.35/+0.5	14.59 2.04	50.24		14.87/+0.4	42.22 4.60 57.20 5:21.60	
7692		Zhang Hongxin	CHN	23.2.72	2	NC	Beijing	4 Jun
	10.94	7.36	13.92 1.90	49.52		15.03	39.74 4.40 65.38 4:48.65	
7685	Gerald	Bayer	GER	4.1.70	5	NC	Vaterstetten	3 Sep
	11.13/0.0	6.74/-1.1	14.85 1.91	50.15		14.99	44.10 4.50 59.54 4:37.04	
7670w	Jamel	Bourmada	FRA	4.10.71	6		Brescia	15 May
	11.35/-0.5	7.52/+4.2	12.49 2.00	49.58		14.93/+0.1	35.14 4.60 53.06 4:18.05	
7670	Mikko	Valle	FIN	11.5.70	15	EC	Helsinki	13 Aug
	11.09/+1.7	7.04/+0.2	11.82 1.90	49.67		15.21/+1.4	40.82 5.00 67.80 4:53.75	
7666	Tomokazu	Sugama	JPN	13.12.71	3	AsiG	Hiroshima	15 Oct
	11.21	6.68	13.05 1.91	48.87		15.68	40.42 4.80 70.00 4:41.13	
7663	Rafer	Joseph	GBR	21.7.68	6	CG	Victoria	24 Jul
	11.06	6.80	13.04 1.95	50.50		15.08	48.30 4.70 54.64 4:40.48	
7662	Martin	Otte	GER	3.5.67	6	NC	Vaterstetten	3 Sep
	11.37/-0.1	7.11/-0.6	13.75 2.03	51.31		15.09/0.0	44.60 4.60 60.56 4:51.57	
7660	Kiril	Damasek	TCH	22.9.73	2		Praha	29 May
	11.35/-0.1	7.28/+0.8	13.42 2.01	48.52		15.27/+0.8	39.70 4.40 56.24 4:34.03	
7652	Prodromos	Korkizoglou	GRE	10.4.75	1		Thessaloniki	7 Aug
	10.88	7.41	12.86 2.06	50.26		14.92	40.38 4.50 53.36 4:53.00	
	(90)							
7649		Kim Tae-keun	KOR	18.4.71	4	AsiG	Hiroshima	15 Oct
	11.28	7.00	12.35 2.00	51.00		14.70	41.80 4.60 59.76 4:32.97	
7648	Aleksandr	Zhdanovich	BLR	15.11.69	7		Brescia	15 May
	11.29/-0.9	6.82/+1.9	13.35 2.00	50.70		15.35/+1.6	38.26 4.90 57.82 4:24.23	
7644	Grzegorz	Strominski	POL	19.5.70	8		Brescia	15 May
	11.53/-0.5	7.14/+0.9	13.25 1.94	49.64		14.82/+0.1	43.50 4.50 55.76 4:29.41	
7637	Bobby	Tonker	USA	15.5.71	3	NCAA	Boise	4 Jun
	11.21/+1.8	7.11/+2.0	12.77 2.04	53.22		14.96/+2.6	43.84 4.60 66.58 4:54.16	
7637	Patrik	Andersson	SWE	11.2.71	15	ECp A	Vénissieux	3 Jul
	11.20/+0.4	6.97/+0.6	15.47 1.98	49.90		14.82/-1.9	42.76 4.60 49.88 4:49.67	
7636w	Xavier	Brunet	ESP	5.2.71	4	NC	Alhama	5 Jun
	11.17/+3.4	6.73/+4.2	12.72 2.15	50.08		14.45/+4.6	41.56 4.70 47.94 4:41.96	

Mark	Name		Nat	Born	Pos	Meet	Venue	Date
7634	Matt	Zuber	USA	30.9.66	3		Sacramento	16 Apr
	11.17/-0.6 7.57/+2.5 12.98 2.00 51.40				14.54/+0.4 37.02 4.90 58.70 5:05.1			
7631	Andrey	Chernyavskiy	RUS	25.6.70	2		Krasnodar	18 May
	11.1 7.29 13.68 2.02 50.5				14.5 41.40 4.70 48.60 4:39.3			
7627w	Shawn	Wilbourn	USA	22.7.67	2		Goleta	22 May
	11.03/+0.7 6.66/+0.5 13.62 1.88 51.03				14.58/+4.4 47.32 4.60 62.04 4:53.99			
7625A	Danie	van Dyk	RSA	30.11.70	1		Pretoria	13 Apr
	11.18 6/90 13.66 2.02 50.02				15.12 40.74 4.60 53.08 4:32.10			

(100)

Mark	Name		Nat	Yr	Date
7612	Valter	Külvet	EST	64	29 Jul
7611	Steve	Rowland	USA	69	16 Apr
7610	Simon	Poelman	NZL	63	26 Jun
7610	Sergey	Nikitin	RUS	73	7 Aug
7610	Jamie	Quarry	GBR	72	24 Aug
7606	Mike	Maczey	GER	72	29 May
7604	Zsolt	Kürtösi	HUN	71	3 Sep
7603	Terry	Simpson	USA	70	7 May
7596	Alper	Kasapoglu	TUR	66	27 May
7595	Beniamino	Poserina	ITA	70	15 May
7592	Gvido	Einbergs	LAT	71	24 Aug
7590	Perry	Donnafield	USA		13 Aug
7570	Bill	Schuffenhaur	USA	73	18 Mar
7567	Klaus	Isekenmeier	GER	75	15 May
7541	Richard	Harrison	USA	73	18 Mar
7534	Pekka	Lahtinen	FIN	70	29 May
7532	Maxim	Marinenko	BLR	73	24 Aug
7531	Mario	Sategna	USA	72	4 Jun
7524	Wilfrid	Boulineau	FRA	70	23 Jul
7517	Michael	Hoffer	SWE	72	18 May
7515	Maurizio	Sferruzzi	ITA	66	15 May
7502	Glenn	Håkansson	SWE	66	3 Jul
7498	Mark	Ivanov	USA	67	6 May
7494	Thomas	Stewens	GER	66	3 Sep
7492	David	Cook	CAN	71	27 Apr
7492	Chad	Smith	USA		23 May
7491	Victor	Houston	BAR	74	7 Apr
7490	Aivar	Hommik	EST	66	17 May
7489	Christian	Savoia	GER	72	17 Jul
7488	Fernando	Benet	ESP	68	5 Jun
7487	Louis	Hinshaw	USA		22 May
7487w	Mark	Kallick	USA		22 May
7482	Hans Christian	Groninger	GER	70	3 Sep
7481	Peter	Soldos	TCH	73	3 Jul
7476	Alain	Schetty	SUI	73	7 Aug
7473	James	Dunkleberger	USA	73	22 May
7472	Sebastien	Denis	FRA	71	23 Jul
7470	Jack	Hoyt	USA	64	15 Jul
7465		Guo Jin	CHN	70	4 Jun
7463	Yuriy	Baranovskiy	BLR	71	5 Jun
7464	Michalis	Simitzis	GRE	71	22 May
7459	Gerhard	Roser	AUT	68	29 May
7458	Barry	Thomas	GBR	72	19 Jun
7451	Karl	Loss	EST	67	3 Jul
7450	Thomas	Lehmann	SUI	71	19 Jun
7447	Csaba	Fábián	HUN	67	3 Jul
7444	Sergey	Kolmakov	RUS	69	18 May
7441	Ryan	Werner	USA	71	20 May
7438	Sebastian	Siukonen	FIN	71	3 Jul
7434	David	Bigham	GBR	71	19 Jun
	(150)				
7431	Mario	Anibal	POR	72	29 Oct
7423	Remco	Van Velthuizen	NED	73	3 Jul
7403	Todd	Pettyjohn	USA		20 May
7402	Leonhard	Hudec	AUT	73	4 Sep

Best non wind assisted

Mark	Name	Pos	Meet	Venue	Date
8084	Peñalver	6	ECp A	Vénissieux	3 Jul
	11.11/+0.4 7.41/+0.2 16.52 2.01 51.00 14.88/-1.9 48.04 4.60 59.48 4:43.68				
7877	Spada	13		Götzis	29 May
	11.46/-1.0 7.12/+2.8 15.19 1.87 50.30 14.60/-1.0 48.56 4.60 60.72 4:35.76				
7865	Muller	3		Aachen	10 Jul
	11.21/0.0 7.03/-0.5 14.41 2.01 49.43 14.73/+0.5 44.18 4.90 60.68 4:59.51				
7836	Benet	12	EC	Helsinki	13 Aug
	11.36/+1.7 7.07/+0.7 12.78 1.87 49.34 14.40/+1.4 43.80 4.80 63.28 4:31.34				
7834	Brophy	14		Götzis	29 May
	11.14/+3.9 7.14/+0.8 15.15 2.05 49.33 15.69/-3.4 49.56 4.80 53.56 5:02.95				
7771	Bogdanov	6	ECp B	Bressanone	3 Jul
	10.98/-0.3 7.36/+1.1 13.96 2.01 48.67 14.38/+1.0 39.42 4.50 50.64 4:44.37				

4 X 100 METRES RELAY

Mark	Team	Pos	Meet	Venue	Date
37.79	USA - Santa Monica TC Marsh, Burrell, Heard, Lewis	1	MSR	Walnut	17 Apr
37.82	World All-Stars Drummond/USA, Jarrett/GBR, Regis/GBR, Mitchell/USA	2	MSR	Walnut	17 Apr
37.89	Santa Monica TC (USA) Marsh, Burrell, Heard, Lewis	1	TexR	Austin	9 Apr
38.29	SMTC (USA) Marsh, Burrell, Heard, Lewis	1	APM	Hengelo	4 Jun
38.30	SMTC (USA) Marsh, Burrell, S, Jefferson, Lewis	1	GWG	St Peterburg	29 Jul
38.39	CAN Bailey, Chambers, Gilbert, Surin	1	CG	Victoria	28 Aug
38.42	SMTC (USA) Marsh, Burrell, Heard, Lewis	1		Tempe	2 Apr
38.46	GBR Braithwaite, Jarrett, Regis, Christie	1	WCp	London	10 Sep
38.57	FRA Lomba, Sangouma, Trouabal, Perrot	1	EC	Helsinki	13 Aug
38.59	SMTC (USA) Marsh, Burrell, Heard, Lewis	1		Houston	19 Mar
38.63	CAN Bailey, Gilbert, Chambers, Surin	1h2	CG	Victoria	27 Aug
38.64	GBR John, Braithwaite, Regis, Christie	1	TSB	London	15 Jul
38.72	GBR John, Wariso, Regis, Christie	1	ECp	Birmingham	25 Jun
38.72	NGR - Africa Nwankpa, Effiong, Kayode, Adeniken	1	USA	Durham	12 Aug
38.76	CUB Simon, Lamela, Garcia, Prevot	2	GWG	St Peterburg	29 Jul
38.77	FRA Lomba, Sangouma, Trouabal, Perrot	1h2	EC	Helsinki	13 Aug

Mark	Name	Nat	Born	Pos	Meet	Venue	Date
38.79	UKR Osovich, Vanyaykin, Kramarenko, Dologodin			2	ECp	Birmingham	25 Jun
38.81	GER H Blume, Görmer, Huke, M Blume			3	ECp	Birmingham	25 Jun
38.83	Nike LA (USA) Miller, Bridgewater, R Lewis, J Williams			3	MSR	Walnut	17 Apr
38.88	USOC West (USA) B Lewis, R Lewis, Bowen, Carrigan			1	USOF	Edwardsville	8 Jul
38.88	AUS Naylor, Jackson, Henderson, Marsh			2	CG	Victoria	28 Aug
38.92	RUS Fedoriv, Parkhomovskiy, Fatun, Grigoryev			3	GWG	St Peterburg	29 Jul
	(22/10)						
38.99	ITA Madonia, Nettis, Marras, Floris			3	EC	Helsinki	13 Aug
39.05	SWE Karlsson, Ghansah, Hedner, T Eriksson			4	EC	Helsinki	13 Aug
39.18	GRE Genovelis, Panagiotopoulos, Alexopoulos, Terzian			1		Rhede	29 Jul
39.30	NOR Lorenzen, Sivle, Moen, Okeke			1		Tønsberg	20 Jul
39.33	JAM Robinson, W Johnson, Mair, Gordon			1h1	CG	Victoria	27 Aug
39.37	JPN Nakamura, Y Ito, Inoue, K Ito			1	AsiG	Hiroshima	16 Oct
39.38	CIV Lagazane, Zirignon, Waota, Meité			2	FrancG	Bondoufle	13 Jul
39.45	CHN Ye Hu, Chen Wenzhong, Huang Danwei, Haung Geng			2	AsiG	Hiroshima	16 Oct
39.58	GHA Owusu, Amegatcher, Boateng, Tuffour			2		Rhede	29 Jul
39.58	FIN Juusela, Ridanpaa, Pakarinen, Purola			5h2	EC	Helsinki	13 Aug
	(20)						
39.66	THA Jnrs Natenee, Seeharwong, Vechaprutti, Namwong			1	AsiC-j	Jakarta	20 Sep
39.67	CHI Almeida, Keitel, Moreno, Rocah			1	Odesur	Valencia	27 Nov
39.70	QAT Al-Sheib, Mufteh, Mansour, Khamis			1		Doha	7 Apr
39.76	BRA Botasso, Quirino, Brivilatti, Ferreira			2	Odesur	Valencia	27 Nov
39.77	TPE Tsen H-S, Hu Wen-Yu, Tsai Yi-Chen, Tao Wu-Shiun			4	AsiG	Hiroshima	16 Oct
39.78	ESP Turon, Parra, Trapero, Nolet			2		Salamanca	22 Jul
39.82	SUI Dubois, Widmer, Thurnherr, Burkart			1		Luzern	29 Jun
39.83	KOR			1		Taipeh	29 May
39.85	HUN Sámi, Karaffa, Alexa, Rezák			5	GGala	Roma	8 Jun
39.87	INA Sulistiono. Lestari, Witarsa, Juntasi			2		Singapore	4 Sep
	(30)						

39.88	NED	4 Jun	40.23	SEN	12 Jul	40.32	COL	27 Nov	40.49	BUL	11 Jun
39.93	POL	11 Jun	40.25A	RSA Transvaal Jnrs	8 Apr	40.34	BLR	11 Jun	40.57	LAT	11 Jun
39.95	TOG	12 Jul	40.31	ROM	18 Jun	40.39	NZL	19 Jan	40.59	DEN	11 Jun
40.14	GAB	12 Jul	40.32	SIN	28 Apr	40.39	TCH	11 Jun	40.64	BEL	29 May
40.22A	KEN	8 Jul				40.44	CYP	11 Jun	40.98	SVK	11 Jun
									40.98	AUT	11 Jun

Hand timed: 39.8A MEX 15 May **Disqualified**: 39.71 SLE 27 Aug

4 X 200 METRES RELAY

Mark	Name	Pos	Meet	Venue	Date
1:18.68	USA - Santa Monica TC Marsh, Burrell, Heard, Lewis	1	MSR	Walnut	17 Apr
1:19.10	World All-Stars Drummond/USA, Mitchell/USA, Bridgewater/USA, Regis/GBR	2	MSR	Walnut	17 Apr
1:20.53	UTEP Thompson/BAR, Mallard, Stephen/TRI, Tynes/BAH	1	Drake	Des Moines	29 Apr
1:20.60	Nike LA (USA) Bridgewater, Rouser, Drummond, Johnson	1	PennR	Philadelphia	30 Apr
1:21.17	Middle Tennessee (USA) Lloyd, McGhee, Gupton, Otis	1	PennR	Philadelphia	30 Apr
1:21.45	Blinn JC (USA) Montgomery, Lewis, Greenidge, Hill	1		Tempe	2 Apr
1:21.53	UTEP Thompson/BAR, Mallard, Stephen/TRI, Tynes/BAH	1h2	Drake	Des Moines	29 Apr
1:21.60	Wells International Regis/GBR, Stewart/JAM, Adeniken/NGR, Mitchell/USA	2		Tempe	2 Apr

4 X 400 METRES RELAY

Mark	Name	Pos	Meet	Venue	Date
2:59.13	GBR McKenzie, Whittle, Black, Ladejo	1	EC	Helsinki	14 Aug
2:59.42	USA Mills, Valmon, Rouser, Johnson	1	GWG	St Peterburg	29 Jul
3:01.11	FRA Hilaire, Rapnouil, Farraudière, Diagana	2	EC	Helsinki	14 Aug
3:01.26	Baylor (USA) Williams, Miller, Howard, Minor	1h1	NCAA	Boise	2 Jun
3:01.34	GBR McKenzie, Ladejo, Baulch, Black	1	WCp	London	11 Sep
3:01.38	USA C Jones, C Davis, Miller, Rouser	1	v GBR	Gateshead	20 Jul
3:01.70	USA C Davis, Watts, Terry, Rouser	1	v Afr	Durham	12 Aug
3:01.75	Georgia Tech (USA) Terry, Motiejunas, Nichols, Mills	1	NCAA	Boise	1 Jun
3:01.87	CUB Mena, Garcia, Crusellas, Tellez	2	GWG	St Peterburg	29 Jul
3:01.89	Blinn JC Whyte/JAM, Hill, Busby, E Thomas (each USA)	1	JUCO	Odessa	21 May
3:01.92	Africa Kemboi/KEN, Bada/NGR, Ochieng/KEN, Kitur/KEN	2	v Afr	Durham	12 Aug
3:02.02	Baylor (USA) Williams, Miller, Howard, Minor	2	NCAA	Boise	1 Jun
3:02.14	England (GBR) McKenzie, Crampton, Patrick, Ladejo	1	CG	Victoria	28 Aug
3:02.22	Blinn JC (USA) Busby, Hill, Stevens, Thomas	1		Tempe	2 Apr
3:02.28	UTEP Thompson/BAR, Stephen/TRI, Tynes/BAH, Mallard	1	TexR	Austin	9 Apr
3:02.32	JAM Taylor, Blake, Laird, Robinson	1	CG	Victoria	28 Aug
3:02.36	Georgia Tech (USA) Terry, Motiejunas, Nichols, Mills	1h2	NCAA	Boise	2 Jun
3:02.39	Illinois (USA) Green, Jones, Beyers, Turner	2h1	NCAA	Boise	2 Jun
3:02.50	GBR Ladejo, Patrick, Whittle, Black	1	ECp	Birmingham	26 Jun

Mark	Name	Nat	Born	Pos	Meet	Venue	Date
3:02.5A	KEN Air Force			1	NC	Nairobi	8 Jul
	(20/6)						
3:02.70	RUS Golovastov, Vdovin, Bey, Kosov			3	GWG	St Peterburg	29 Jul
3:02.78	TRI Delice, De Silva, Stephen, Morris			2	CG	Victoria	28 Aug
3:03.06	NGR Alohan, Adeniken, Okoli, Bada			4	CG	Victoria	28 Aug
3:03.46	ITA Vaccari, Grossi, Saber, Aimar			4	EC	Helsinki	14 Aug
	(10)						
3:03.46	AUS Hollingsworth, Joubert, Callaghan, Greene			5	CG	Victoria	28 Aug
3:03.87	RSA De Jager, Malherbe, Dempers, Phiri			6	CG	Victoria	28 Aug
3:04.15	GER Bittner, Karsten, Becker, Itt			4	EC	Helsinki	14 Aug
3:04.22	POL Rysukiewicz, Mackowiak, Kotlarski, Czubak			6	EC	Helsinki	14 Aug
3:04.55	FIN Pinomäki, Yli-Tuomi, Louramo, Pihlavisto			7	EC	Helsinki	13 Aug
3:05.34	SWE Rasmusson, Wallenlind, Nylander, Ekman			4	ECp	Birmingham	26 Jun
3:05.73	SEN Wade, Diarra, Dia, N'Daiye			1	FrancG	Bondoufle	13 Jul
3:06.00	SUI Jelinek, Rusterholz, Felder, Simasotchi			2		Chemnitz	18 Jun
3:06.10	JPN - Hosei University Suzuki, Ono, Inagaki, Hayashi			1		Tokyo	22 May
3:06.16	BRA - Funilense Parrela, Nunes, Rocha, Sena			1		São Paulo	13 Aug
	(20)						
3:06.36	KOR Shon Ju-il, Kim Soon-hyung, Kim Yong-hwan, Lee Jin-il			1		Seoul	18 Jun
3:06.6	GHA			1	NC	Accra	25 Jun
3:06.67	MAR Debbab, Lahlafi, Belkaïd, Lahlou			2	FrancG	Bondoufle	13 Jul
3:06.92	CHI Moreno, Squella, Roach, Keitel			1	Odesur	Valencia, VEN	27 Nov
3:07.17	NZL Taylor, Farrell, Keddell, Cowan			4	AusC	Sydney	13 Mar
3:07.50	ZIM Payne, Ngighi, Muyaba, Harnden			6h1	CG	Victoria	27 Aug
3:07.69	ESP Burrel, Cornet, Sabate, Sánchez			2	ECp I	Valencia	12 Jun
3:07.71	CAN Wilson, Crerar, Isaac, Goodwin			3	FrancG	Bondoufle	13 Jul
3:07.75	MEX Escalante, Vallin, Toledo, Cardenas			2	IbAm	Mar del Plata	29 Oct
3:07.84	COL Rivas, Vega, Pinto, Mayo			2	Odesur	Valencia	27 Nov
	(30)						

3:08.36	QAT	3 Jul	3:09.32	BUL	12 Jun	3:09.76	IRL	12 Jun	3:10.19	KOR	16 Oct
3:08.92	UKR	29 Jul	3:09.36	HUN	31 Jul	3:09.97	BEL	12 Jun	3:10.33	THA	16 Oct
3:08.83	AUT	12 Jun	3:09.43	IND	23 Aug	3:10.19	BLR	12 Jun	3:10.46	TCH	12 Jun
									3:10.84	SVK	12 Jun

4 X 800 METRES RELAY

Mark	Name	Pos	Meet	Venue	Date
7:15.28	JAM George Mason University Bowen, Cornwall, Vernon-Watson, Morgan	1	PennR	Philadelphia	30 Apr
7:15.32	USA - Seton Hall Un. Perez, Bell, Ayers, Royster	2	PennR	Philadelphia	30 Apr
7:18.94	Georgia Tech (USA) Atlee, Hayes, Krummenacker, Nichols	3	PennR	Philadelphia	30 Apr
7:19.57	Florida State (USA) Grey, Reid, Hampton, Middlekoop	4	PennR	Philadelphia	30 Apr
7:19.95	FIN - Lapin Lukko R Laaksonen, Keskitalo, Kokkola, Parpala	1	NC	Iisalmi	16 Jul

4 X 1500 METRES RELAY

Mark	Name	Pos	Meet	Venue	Date
14:52.81	Arkansas Un. Bunston, Baker, Bruton/IRL, Hood/CAN	1	PennR	Philadelphia	30 Apr
15:04.07	Providence Un. Healy, Jackson, Wedlake, Keith/GBR	2	PennR	Philadelphia	30 Apr
15:10.51	USA - Auburn Un. Rademacher, Gibbs, McClemon, Borden	3	PennR	Philadelphia	30 Apr
15:12.56	Mississippi Un . Manogin, Pérez/ESP, Waller, George	4	PennR	Philadelphia	30 Apr
15:13.06	FRA - Stade Sotteville Lemmonier, R Chekhemani, Dehornoy, K Chekhemani	1		Bondoufle	9 Oct

3000 METRES WALK

Mark	First name	Name	Nat	Born	Pos	Meet	Venue	Date
11:23.2	Steve	Beecroft	AUS	14.3.71	1		Melbourne	13 Jan
11:33.1	Andreas	Erm	GER	12.3.76	1		Berlin	6 May
11:44.1	Gintaras	Andriuskevicius	LIT	6.7.75	1		Hildesheim	19 Jul
11:49.2	Robert	Korzeniowski	POL	30.7.68	1		Sopot	23 Jul
11:49.6	Stanislav	Stosik	POL	26.3.72	2		Sopot	23 Jul
Indoors								
11:23.9	Axel	Noack	GER	23.9.61	1		Berlin	15 Jan
11:27.14	Allen	James	USA	14.4.64	1		Boston	22 Jan
11:29.87	Jonathan	Matthews	USA	2.7.56	2		Boston	22 Jan

5000 METRES WALK

Mark	First name	Name	Nat	Born	Pos	Meet	Venue	Date
18:55.42	Nick	A'Hern	AUS	6.1.69	6		Sydney	19 Feb
19:10.0+	Bernardo	Segura	MEX	11.2.70	1	SGP	Fana	7 May
19:11.99		A'Hern			1		Sydney	12 Mar
19:14.04	Robert	Korzeniowski	POL	30.7.68	1		Montgéron	15 May
19:20.9	Jirí	Malysa	TCH	10.8.66	2		Montgéron	15 May
19:21.49	Denis	Langlois	FRA	10.10.68	1		Arras	26 Jun
19:21.74	Sergey	Korepanov	KZK	3.5.64	1	Slov	Bratislava	1 Jun
	(7/6)							

Mark	Name		Nat	Born	Pos	Meet	Venue	Date
19:25.51	Ján	Záhoncík	SVK	23.4.65	2	Slov	Bratislava	1 Jun
19:25.55	Andrey	Makarov	RUS	2.6.71	2		Arras	26 Jun
19:26.44	Jean-Claude	Corre	FRA	14.9.61	1		Aix-les-Bains	8 May
19:27.3	Hirofumi	Sakai	JPN	10.2.65	1		Machida	25 Jun
19:30.0	Roman	Mrázek	SVK	21.1.62	1		Banská Bystrica	27 Aug
19:32.4	Robert	Valicek	SVK	10.3.69	2		Banská Bystrica	27 Aug
19:34.13	Tomás	Kratochvíl	TCH	19.12.71	1		Praha	8 Aug
19:34.4+	Stanislaw	Stosik	POL	26.3.72	2+		Sopot	23 Jul
19:35.7	Satoshi	Yanagisawa	JPN	19.1.71	2		Machida	25 Jun
Questionable								
18:40.75	Hatem	Ghoula	TUN	7.6.73			Leutkirch	26 Aug
Indoors								
18:32.0	Frants	Kostyukevich	BLR	4.4.63	1	NC	Minsk	4 Feb
18:34.32	Mikhail	Shchennikov	RUS	24.12.67	1	EI	Paris	13 Mar
18:40.0	Yevgeniy	Misyulya	BLR	9.3.64	2	NC	Minsk	4 Feb
18:40.32	Ronald	Weigel	GER	8.8.59	2	EI	Paris	13 Mar
18:43.20	Denis	Langlois	FRA	10.10.68	3	EI	Paris	13 Mar
18:45.97		Shchennikov			1		Moskva	4 Feb
18:47.02		Shchennikov			1	NC	Lipetsk	27 Feb
18:48.13	Vladimir	Andreyev	RUS	7.9.66	2	NC	Lipetsk	27 Feb
18:49.08	Grigoriy	Kornev	RUS	14.3.61	3	NC	Lipetsk	27 Feb
18:50.48	Jean-Claude	Corre	FRA	14.9.61	1		Paris	30 Jan
18:51.12		Kornev			2		Moskva	4 Feb
18:53.76		Weigel			1	NC	Dortmund	26 Feb
18:54.03		Corre			1	NC	Paris	27 Feb
18:54.72	Mikhail	Orlov	RUS	25.6.67	4	NC	Lipetsk	27 Feb
18:56.05	Sandor	Urbanik	HUN	15.12.64	1	NC	Budapest	5 Feb
18:56.28		Orlov			3		Moskva	4 Feb
18:56.8		Corre			1		Nogent-sur-Oise	13 Feb
	(17/10)							
19:01.0	Jirí	Malysa	TCH	10.8.66	1		Ostrava	8 Jan
19:01.03	Michele	Didoni	ITA	7.3.74	4	EI	Paris	12 Mar
19:02.36	Igor	Kollár	SVK	25.6.65	1		Wien	29 Jan
19:03.2	Mikhail	Khmelnitskiy	BLR	24.6.69	3	NC	Minsk	4 Feb
19:05.1	Oleg	Troshin	RUS	1.8.64	2		Moskva	28 Jan
19:05.85	Axel	Noack	GER	23.9.61	2	NC	Dortmund	26 Feb
19:06.81	Stefan	Johansson	SWE	11.4.67	2h1	EI	Paris	12 Mar
19:07.5	Tomás	Kratochvíl	TCH	2.6.71	1		Praha	23 Jan
19:07.83	Giovanni	De Benedictis	ITA	8.1.68	1	NC	Genova	12 Feb
19:09.05	Pavol	Blazek	SVK	9.7.58	2		Wien	29 Jan
19:11.37	Anatoliy	Kozlov	UKR	2.10.67	1	NC	Kiev	13 Feb
19:14.23	Vladimir	Druchik	UKR	26.6.65	2	NC	Kiev	13 Feb
19:15.2	Dmitriy	Golos	BLR	13.7.70	4	NC	Minsk	4 Feb
19:19.04	Sergey	Tyulenev	RUS	14.3.71	3		Moskva	4 Feb
19:19.18	Dmitriy	Dolnikov	RUS	19.11.72	5	NC	Lipetsk	27 Feb
19:19.69	Vyacheslav	Fedchuk	MOL	11.2.73	3	UKR Ch	Kiev	13 Feb
19:20.80	Karol	Repasky	SVK	3.1.69	3		Wien	29 Jan
19:20.91	Giovanni	Perricelli	ITA	25.8.67	1		Genova	5 Feb
19:21.0	Andrey	Makarov	RUS	2.6.71	4		Moskva	28 Jan
19:25.80	Ilya	Markov	RUS	19.6.72	6	NC	Lipetsk	27 Feb
19:26.38	Nikolay	Matyukhin	RUS	13.12.68	7	NC	Lipetsk	27 Feb
19:28.20	Stefan	Malík	SVK	11.2.66	4		Wien	29 Jan
19:29.91	Jean-Olivier	Brosseau	FRA	23.6.67	3	NC	Bordeaux	27 Feb
19:30.66	Andrey	Stadnichuk	RUS	.73	9	NC	Lipetsk	27 Feb
19:31.0	Aleksandr	Potashov	BLR	12.3.62	5	NC	Minsk	4 Feb
19:32.0	Aleksey	Kronin	RUS	.70	5		Moskva	28 Jan
19:33.77	Enrico	Lang	ITA	31.3.72	3	NC	Genova	12 Feb
19:33.96	Nikolay	Yamshchikov	UKR	19.5.61	4	NC	Kiev	13 Feb
19:34.7	Andrey	Popov	RUS	28.4.62	6		Moskva	28 Jan
19:35.07	Yuriy	Andronov	RUS	71	10	NC	Lipetsk	27 Feb
19:35.66	Gyula	Dudás	HUN	10.8.66	3		Budapest	5 Feb
19:36.17	Pietro	Fiorini	ITA	11.3.67	1		Firenze	19 Jan
19:36.8	Stanislav	Ustimenko	RUS	8.5.69	7		Moskva	28 Jan
19:36.85	Vittorio	Colombini	ITA	72	4		Genova	12 Feb
19:38.84	Sergio	Spagnulo	ITA	7.10.62	2		Firenze	19 Jan
19:39.47	Costica	Balan	ROM	25.8.69	1	Balk	Pireas	20 Feb

10,000 METRES WALK (Track)

Mark	Name		Nat	Born	Pos	Meet	Venue	Date
38:24 0+	Bernardo	Segura	MEX	11.2.70	1	SGP	Fana	7 May
39:00.14	Robert	Korzeniowski	POL	30.7.68	1		Sopot	23 Jul
39:33.12	Giovanni	Perricelli	ITA	25.8.67	1		Formia	4 Jun
39:52.33	Stefan	Johansson	SWE	11.4.67	1	vFIN	Stockholm	28 Aug
40:09.7	Yuriy	Kuko	BLR	23.1.68	1		Staiki	28 Apr
40:12.63	Valentin	Kononen	FIN	7.3.69	1		Stockholm	28 Aug
40:13.11	Yevgeniy	Shmalyuk	RUS	14.1.76	1		St Peterburg	28 May
40:13.40	Giovanni	De Benedictis	ITA	8.1.68	2		Formia	4 Jun
40:14.68	Arturo	Di Mezza	ITA	16.7.69	3		Formia	4 Jun
	(10)							
40:18.35	Stanislav	Stosik	POL	26.3.72	2		Sopot	23 Jul
40:26.93	Jorge	Segura	MEX	23.4.75	1	WJ	Lisboa	21 Jul
40:29.0	Jan	Holender	POL	12.3.64	2		Sopot	3 May
40:31.1	Aigars	Fadejevs	LAT	27.12.75	1		Valmiera	3 Sep
40:35.52	Artur	Meleshvekich	BLR	11.4.75	3	WJ	Lisboa	21 Jul
40:37.8	Vitaliy	Gordey	BLR	11.7.73	2		Staiki	28 Apr

Mark	Name		Nat	Born	Date
40:42.26	Magnus	Morenius	SWE	69	28 Aug
40:44.89	Pietro	Fiorini	ITA	67	7 May
40:46.42	Mariusz	Ornoch	POL	69	18 Jun
40:48.78	Andrey	Popov	RUS	62	28 May
40:48.78	Aleksandr	Yakimchuk	RUS	72	28 May
40:48.9	René	Piller	FRA	65	20 Mar
40:53.1	Dmitriy	Dolnikov	RUS	72	16 Jul
40:54.32	Walter	Arena	ITA	64	7 May
40:57.76	Jan	Staaf	SWE	62	28 Aug
40:58.46	Sebastiano	Catania	ITA	75	21 Jul

Unconfirmed

Mark	Name		Nat	Born	Pos	Meet	Venue	Date
40:16.2	Hatem	Ghoula	TUN	73			Tunis	6 Mar

Indoors

Mark	Name		Nat	Born	Pos	Meet	Venue	Date
39:42.50	Vladimir	Andreyev	RUS	7.9.66	1		Moskva	26 Jan
39:43.90	Mikhail	Orlov	RUS	25.6.67	2		Moskva	26 Jan
40:31.21	Andrey	Makarov	RUS	2.6.71	3		Moskva	26 Jan

Mark	Name		Nat	Born	Date
40:52.24	Oleg	Troshin	RUS	64	26 Jan
40:54.77	Viktor	Osipov	RUS	65	26 Jan

20 KILOMETRES WALK

t = track walk

Mark	Name		Nat	Born	Pos	Meet	Venue	Date
1:17:25.6t	Bernardo	Segura	MEX	11.2.70	1	SGP	Fana	7 May
1:18:04		Bo Lingtang	CHN	12.8.70	1	NC	Beijing	7 Apr
1:18:45	Mikhail	Shchennikov	RUS	24.12.67	1	EC	Helsinki	8 Aug
1:18:46		Tan Mingjun	CHN	17.7.70	2	NC	Beijing	7 Apr
1:19:16		Chen Shaoguo	CHN	20.1.71	3	NC	Beijing	7 Apr
1:19:22	Yevgeniy	Misyulya	BLR	9.3.64	2	EC	Helsinki	8 Aug
1:19:32		Shchennikov			1		La Coruña	21 May
1:19:38	Mikhail	Khmelnitskiy	BLR	24.6.69	1		Novopolotsk	21 May
1:20:02		Li Mingcai	CHN	22.8.71	4	NC	Beijing	7 Apr
1:20:06		Zhou Yongshen	CHN	15.10.72	5	NC	Beijing	7 Apr
1:20:12	Aleksandr	Potashov (10)	BLR	12.3.62	2		Novopolotsk	21 May
1:20:26		Shchennikov			1		Barcelona	10 Apr
1:20:33	Daniel	Garcia	MEX	28.10.71	1		Eisenhüttenstadt	15 May
1:20:33	Valentin	Massana	ESP	5.7.70	3	EC	Helsinki	8 Aug
1:20:35	Yuriy	Kuko	BLR	23.1.68	3		Novopolotsk	21 May
1:20:39	Giovanni	De Benedictis	ITA	8.1.68	4	EC	Helsinki	8 Aug
1:20:45		Massana			2		La Coruña	21 May
1:20:54		Massana			1		Livorno	12 Jun
1:20:55	Robert	Korzeniowski	POL	30.7.68	3		La Coruña	21 May
1:20:55.2		Li Mingcai			1		Fuxin	17 Sep
1:20:56		Zhao Yongsheng	CHN	.3.71	1		Fuxin	??? 7 Apr
1:20:56		Misyulya			2		Barcelona	10 Apr
1:21:00		Tian Niantang	CHN	.3.72	6	NC	Beijing	7 Apr
1:21:01	Mikhail	Orlov	RUS	25.6.67	5	EC	Helsinki	8 Aug
1:21:05		Korzeniowski			1		Hildesheim	28 Aug
1:21:14	Robert	Ihly	GER	5.5.63	2		Hildesheim	28 Aug
1:21:15		Chen Shaoguo			1	AsiG	Hiroshima	10 Sep
1:21:19.32t		Garcia			1	IbAm	Mar del Plata	23 Oct
1:21:20	Thierry	Toutain	FRA	14.2.62	2		Livorno	12 Jun
1:21:24		Misyulya			2		Eisenhüttenstadt	15 May
	(30/20)							
1:21:25		Jiao Baozhong	CHN	28.3.73	7	NC	Beijing	7 Apr
1:21:26		Hao Huanquan	CHN		8	NC	Beijing	7 Apr
1:21:27		Gao Yunbing	CHN	.10.75	9	NC	Beijing	7 Apr
1:21:35	Miguel	Rodriguez	MEX	15.5.62		NC	Jalapa	7 Aug
1:21:35	Aleksey	Kronin	RUS	70	1		Izhevsk	26 Aug

Mark	Name		Nat	Born	Pos	Meet	Venue	Date
1:21:37		Wang Libin	CHN		10	NC	Beijing	7 Apr
1:21:37.2t	Querubin	Moreno	COL	29.12.59	2	IbAm	Mar del Plata	29 Oct
1:21:39.4t	Viktoras	Meshauskas	LIT	4.11.70	1		Birstonas	7 May
1:21:40	Carlos	Mercenario	MEX	3.5.67		NC	Jalapa	7 Aug
	(30)							
1:21:42	Giovanni	Perricelli	ITA	25.8.67	3		Livorno	12 Jun
1:21:42	Gyula	Dudás	HUN	10.8.66	1		Szeged	2 Jul
1:21:44	Michele	Didoni	ITA	7.3.74	4		Livorno	12 Jun
1:21:49.9t	Héctor	Moreno	COL	8.6.63	3	IbAm	Mar del Plata	29 Oct
1:21:53	Vladimir	Andreyev	RUS	7.9.66	1	NC	Yaroslavl	22 May
1:21:54	Frants	Kostyukevich	BLR	4.4.63	5		Novopolotsk	21 May
1:21:54	Daniel	Plaza	ESP	3.7.66	2	NC	San Sebastián	17 Jul
1:21:55	Viktor	Ginko	BLR	7.12.65	3		Eisenhüttenstadt	15 May
1:21:55	Sándor	Urbánik	HUN	15.12.64	5		Livorno	12 Jun
1:21:57	Aleksandr	Rakovic	YUG	13.4.68	1	NC	Jagodina	12 May
	(40)							
1:22:00	Igor	Lyubomirov	RUS	9.11.61	2		Izhevsk	26 Aug
1:22:05	Dmitriy	Golos	BLR	13.7.70	6		Novopolotsk	21 May
1:22:05	Valentin	Kononen	FIN	7.3.69	1	NC	Helsinki	11 Jun
1:22:06	Valeriy	Borisov	KZK	10.9.66	2		Yaroslavl	22 May
1:22:11	Igor	Kollár	SVK	26.6.65	3		L'Hospitalet	10 Apr
1:22:11	Andrey	Makarov	RUS	2.6.71	3		Izhevsk	26 Aug
1:22:14.0t	Claudio	Bertolino	BRA	31.3.63	4	IbAm	Mar del Plata	29 Oct
1:22:14	Vitaliy	Gordey	BLR	11.7.73	7		Novopolotsk	21 May
1:22:14	Rinat	Shafikov	RUS	23.1.70	3	NC	Yaroslavl	22 May
1:22:18	Magnus	Morenius	SWE	20.3.69	1		Eschborn	6 Jun
	(50)							
1:22:24	Jean-Claude	Corre	FRA	14.9.61	8		Livorno	12 Jun
1:22:24	Vyacheslav	Cherepanov	RUS	2.11.64	4		Izhevsk	26 Aug
1:22:27	Stanislaw	Stosik	POL	26.3.72	1		Mielec	29 Jul
1:22:30	Grigoriy	Kornev	RUS	14.3.61	5		Izhevsk	26 Aug
1:22:30	Milos	Holusa	TCH	2.5.65	3		Hildesheim	27 Aug
1:22:33	Fernando	Vázquez	ESP	4.5.71	9		Livorno	12 Jun
1:22:37	Stefan	Johansson	SWE	11.4.67	10		Livorno	12 Jun
1:22:44	Rogelio	Sanchez	MEX	73	4		Eisenhüttenstadt	15 May
1:22:46	Miguel	Solis	MEX	70		NC	Jalapa	7 Aug
1:22:48.5t	Jiri	Malysa	TCH	14.8.66	2	SGP	Fana	7 May
	(60)							
1:22:53	Robert	Valicek	SVK	10.3.69	1		Borsky Mikulás	4 Jun
1:22:54	Satoshi	Yanagisawa	JPN	19.1.71	1		Takahata	6 Nov
1:22:55.6t	René	Piller	FRA	23.4.65	1		Héricourt	20 Mar
1:22:57	Pavol	Blazek	SVK	9.7.58	6		Eisenhüttenstadt	15 May
1:23:03	Hubert	Sonnek	TCH	12.10.62	1	NC	Olomouc	19 Jun
1:23:07	Nick	A'Hern	AUS	6.1.69	6		L'Hospitalet	10 Apr
1:23:11	Ronald	Weigel	GER	8.8.59	11		Livorno	12 Jun
1:23:14	Aleksandr	Voyevodin	RUS	4.3.70	5	NC	Yaroslavl	22 May
1:23:19	Denis	Langlois	FRA	10.10.68	13		Livorno	12 Jun
1:23:27	Jefferson	Pérez	ECU	1.1.74	2		Puebla	17 Apr
	(70)							
1:23:27	Yuriy	Gordeyev	RUS	64	6		Izhevsk	26 Aug
1:23:33.8t	Modris	Liepins	LAT	3.8.66	1	NC	Ventspils	16 Jul
1:23:35	Sergey	Tyulenev	RUS	14.3.71	6	NC	Yaroslavl	22 May
1:23:37 ?	Vladimir	Ostrovskiy	ISR	12.12.66	1		Budapest	28 Mar
	1:24:12				2		Olomouc	19 Jun
1:23:41	Aigars	Fadejevs	LAT	27.12.75	1		Alitus	24 Sep
1:23:41.3t	Hirofumi	Sakai	JPN	10.2.65	1		Matto	5 Jun
1:23:55	Anatoliy	Kozlov	UKR	2.10.67	1		Makachevo ?	22 May
1:23:56	Stefan	Malík	SVK	11.2.66	1		Dubnica	24 Apr
1:23:56	Anatoliy	Grigoryev	RUS	60	7	NC	Yaroslavl	22 May
1:23:56.0t	Martial	Fesselier	FRA	9.10.61	1		Caen	19 Jun
1:23:57	Valdas	Kaslauskas	LIT	23.2.58	4		Hildesheim	28 Aug
	(80)							
1:24:00	Rodrigo	Serrano	MEX	68	4	NC	Jalapa	7 Aug
1:24:01	Tomás	Kratochvíl	TCH	19.12.71	8		Eisenhüttenstadt	15 May
1:24:01	Ruslan	Shafikov	RUS	27.6.75	1	U23	Izhevsk	26 Aug
1:24:02	Justus	Kavulanya	KEN	64	1	NC	Nairobi	8 Jul
1:24:07	Ilya	Markov	RUS	19.6.72	14		Livorno	12 Jun
1:24:08	Pavel	Vasilyev	RUS	2.7.70	8	NC	Yaroslavl	22 May
1:24:09	Steve	Partington	GBR	17.9.65	1		Dublin	24 Sep

Mark	Name		Nat	Born	Pos	Meet	Venue	Date
1:24:14	Dimitris	Orfanopoulos	GRE	9.5.64	1		Ruse	9 Apr
1:24:14	Jan	Holender	POL	12.3.64	11		Eisenhüttenstadt	15 May
1:24:16	Giuseppe (90)	De Gaètano	ITA	4.10.66	1	NC	Molfetta	3 Sep
1:24:18	Fedosey	Chumachenko	UKR	27.1.73	2		Makachevo ?	22 May
1:24:22	Dmitriy	Yesipchuk	RUS	17.11.74	9	NC	Yaroslavl	22 May
1:24:25	Axel	Noack	GER	23.9.61	1	NC	Erfurt	2 Jul
1:24:26	Arturo	Di Mezza	ITA	16.7.69	2	NC	Molfetta	3 Sep
1:24:26.9t	Allen	James	USA	14.4.64	4	SGP	Fana	7 May
1:24:37	Sergio	Galdino	BRA	7.5.69	1		Blumenáu	12 Jun
1:24:38	Vladimir	Druchik	UKR	25.6.65	13		Eisenhüttenstadt	15 May
1:24:45	Aleksandr	Shapovalov	UKR	7.6.70	3		Makachevo ?	22 May
1:24:46	Nichan	Tsamonikian	KZK	19.7.67	1		Offenburg	1 May
1:24:48	Pavel (100)	Andrienko	UKR	30.7.74	3		Balassagyarmat	19 Jul

Mark	Name		Nat	Born	Date
1:24:49	Aleksey	Kravchik ?	RUS	70	19 Jul
1:24:49	Jorge	Segura	MEX	75	7 Aug
1:24:55	Anatoliy	Gorshkov	UKR	58	22 May
1:24:55.8t		Liu Haiming	CHN		17 Sep
1:24:56	Ignacio	Zamudio	MEX	71	7 Aug
1:24:57	Zoltán	Czukor	HUN	62	19 Jul
1:24:57.0t		Mao Xinjuan	CHN	71	17 Sep

Questionable

Mark	Name		Nat	Born	Pos	Meet	Venue	Date
1:22:51.9t	Hatem	Ghoula	TUN	73			Leutkitch	8 Sep

Best track times

Mark	Name		Nat	Born	Pos	Meet	Venue	Date
1:23:20.3	Stefan	Johansson	SWE	11.4.67	3	SGP	Fana	7 May
1:23:28.90	Rinat	Shafikov	RUS	23.1.70	2	GWG	St Peterburg	24 Jul
1:24:07.60		Jiao Baozhong	CHN	28.3.73	3	GWG	St Peterburg	24 Jul

30 KILOMETRES WALK

Mark	Name		Nat	Born	Pos	Meet	Venue	Date
2:07:53	Nick	A'Hern	AUS	6.1.69	1	CG	Victoria	25 Aug
2:08:14	Mikhail	Shchennikov	RUS	24.12.67	1		Sesto S.Giovanni	1 May
2:08:22	Giovanni	Perricelli	ITA	25.8.67	2		Sesto S.Giovanni	1 May
2:08:22	Tim	Berrett	CAN	23.1.65	2	CG	Victoria	25 Aug
2:09:10	Scott	Nelson	NZL	10.10.69	3	CG	Victoria	25 Aug
2:10:17	Valentin	Massana	ESP	5.7.70	1		Badalona	20 Feb
2:11:02	Jesús	Garcia	ESP	17.10.69	2		Badalona	20 Feb
2:11:30	Darrell	Stone	GBR	2.2.68	4	CG	Victoria	25 Aug
2:11:52	Daniel	Plaza	ESP	3.7.66	3		Badalona	20 Feb
2:12:31	Sándor	Urbanik	HUN	15.12.64	3		Sesto S.Giovanni	1 May
2:12:40.4t+	René	Piller	FRA	23.4.65	1=	In 50k	Fana	7 May
2:12:40.4t+		Zhao Yongshen	CHN	15.10.72	1=	In 50k	Fana	7 May

35 KILOMETRES WALK

12 Jun, Livorno: 1. Jesús Garcia ESP 2:31:06, 2. Valeriy Spitsyn RUS 2:32:01, 3. René Piller FRA 2:32:04, 4. Arturo Di Mezza 2:33:03, 5. Stefan Malik SVK 2:33:04, 6. Giuseppe De Gaetano 2:33:28, 7. Alain Lemercier FRA 2:34:44, 8. Peter Tichy SVK 2:35:37, 9. Basilio Labrador ESP 2:35:50, 10. Miguel Rodriguez MEX 2:36:24, 11. Gyula Dudás HUN 2:36:33, 12. Paolo Bianchi 2:36:36, 13. Andrey Plotnikov RUS 2:37:55, 14. Zoltán Czukor HUN 2:38:13, 15. Pavol Blazek SVK 2:38:29.
7 May, Fana (t): René Piller 2:34:22.9
13 Aug, Helsinki: In 50km: 1, Thiery Toutain FRA, Jesús Angel Garcia ESP 2:35:04; Valeriy Spitsyn RUS 2:35:05, German Skurygin RUS 2:35:24, Valentin Kononen FIN 2:36:32, Robert Korzeniowski POL 2:36:53, Axel Noack GER 2:37:01

50 KILOMETRES WALK

Mark	Name		Nat	Born	Pos	Meet	Venue	Date
3:38:43	Valentin	Massana	ESP	5.7.70	1	NC	Orense	20 Mar
3:41:07	Valeriy	Spitsyn	RUS	5.12.65	1	EC	Helsinki	13 Aug
3:41:28	Jesus	Garcia	ESP	17.10.69	2	NC	Orense	20 Mar
3:41:28.2t	René	Piller	FRA	23.4.65	1	SGP	Fana	7 May
3:43:16		Zhou Yongshen	CHN	15.10.72	1	NC	Beijing	10 Apr
3:43:52	Thierry	Toutain	FRA	14.2.62	2	EC	Helsinki	13 Aug
3:43:55	Giovanni	Perricelli	ITA	25.8.67	3	EC	Helsinki	13 Aug
3:45:24.2t		Toutain			1	NC	Franconville	3 Apr
3:45:25		Garcia			4	EC	Helsinki	13 Aug
3:45:34	Viktor	Ginko	BLR	7.12.65	1		Podrebrady	23 Apr
3:45:35	Nikolay	Matyukhin	RUS	13.12.68	1		Izhevsk	27 Aug
3:45:57	Robert	Korzeniowski (10)	POL	30.7.68	5	EC	Helsinki	13 Aug
3:46:30	German	Skurygin	RUS	23.12.63	6	EC	Helsinki	13 Aug
3:47:14	Valentin	Kononen	FIN	7.3.69	7	EC	Helsinki	13 Aug
3:47:43	Andrey	Plotnikov	RUS	12.8.67	8	EC	Helsinki	13 Aug
3:48:10		Skurygin			1	NC	Kaliningrad	23 Apr

Mark	Name		Nat	Born	Pos	Meet	Venue	Date
3:48:13.7		Zhao Yongsheng	CHN	.3.71	2	SGP	Fana	7 May
3:49:00	Aleksandr	Potashov	BLR	12.3.62	2		Podrebrady	23 Apr
3:49:29.7t	Alain	Lemercier	FRA	11.1.57	2	NC	Franconville	3 Apr
3:49:44	Pavol	Blazek	SVK	9.7.58	9	EC	Helsinki	13 Aug
3:49:50		Plotnikov			2	NC	Kaliningrad	23 Apr
3:50:16	Giovanni	De Benedictis	ITA	8.1.68	1	NC	Pescara	20 Mar
3:50:32	Axel	Noack	GER	23.9.61	10	EC	Helsinki	13 Aug
3:51:25	Zoltán	Czukor (20)	HUN	18.12.62	11	EC	Helsinki	13 Aug
3:51:53		Perricelli			2	NC	Pescara	20 Mar
3:52:06	Carlos	Mercenario	MEX	3.5.67	1	PAmCp	Atlanta	24 Sep
3:52:06	Miguel	Rodríguez	MEX	15.5.67	2	PAmCp	Atlanta	24 Sep
3:52:14	Andrés	Marin	ESP	18.7.61	12	EC	Helsinki	13 Aug
3:52:16	Artur	Shumak	BLR	19.10.63	3		Podrebrady	23 Apr
3:52:20	Giuseppe	De Gaetano	ITA	4.10.66	3	NC	Pescara	20 Mar
3:52:20		Jin Guohong	CHN	5.2.72	2	NC	Beijing	10 Apr
	(31/26)							
3:52:30	Yuriy	Andronov	RUS	71	2		Izhevsk	27 Aug
3:52:36	Aleksandr	Voyevodin	RUS	4.3.70	3	NC	Kaliningrad	23 Apr
3:52:56	Ronald	Weigel	GER	8.8.59	1	NC	Offenburg	1 May
3:53:29	Fumio	Imamura	JPN	5.11.66	1	NC	Wajima	17 Apr
	(30)							
3:53:49		Jiao Baozhong	CHN	28.3.73	3	NC	Beijing	10 Apr
3:53:54	Sergey	Katurayev	RUS	29.9.67	4	NC	Kaliningrad	23 Apr
3:54:04		Shen Weiquan	CHN		4	NC	Beijing	10 Apr
3:54:05	Oleg	Merkulov	RUS	70	3		Izhevsk	27 Aug
3:54:29	Stefan	Malik	SVK	11.2.66	2		Dudince	27 Mar
3:54:37	Sergey	Korepanov	KZK	9.5.64	1	AsiG	Hiroshima	15 Oct
3:55:23	Gyula	Dudás	HUN	10.8.66	1	NC	Békescsaba	17 Apr
3:55:34	Spyros	Kastanis	GRE	23.9.64	1	NC	Athina	13 Mar
3:55:38	Basilio	Labrador	ESP	29.3.67	3	NC	Orense	20 Mar
3:55:39	Allen	James	USA	14.4.64	1	NC	Palo Alto	13 Mar
	(40)							
3:55:45		Yang Yongjian	CHN		5	NC	Beijing	10 Apr
3:56:00	Germán	Sánchez	MEX	15.9.66	1		Chapultepec	10 Apr
3:56:00	Arturo	Di Mezza	ITA	16.7.69	14	EC	Helsinki	13 Aug
3:56:03	Roman	Bilek	TCH	29.9.67	3		Dudince	27 Mar
3:56:36	Tadahiro	Kosaka	JPN	10.2.60	2	NC	Wajima	17 Apr
3:56:55	Peter	Tichy	SVK	12.3.69	15	EC	Helsinki	13 Aug
3:57:00		Han Wei	CHN	71	6	NC	Beijing	10 Apr
3:57:20	Paolo	Bianchi	ITA	7.10.70	4	NC	Pescara	20 Mar
3:57:24	Milos	Holusa	TCH	2.5.65	16	EC	Helsinki	13 Aug
3:57:56	Daniel	Plaza	ESP	3.7.66	4	NC	Orense	20 Mar
	(50)							
3:58:10	Robert	Ihly	GER	5.5.63	2	NC	Offenburg	1 May
3:58:32		Xu Congxian	CHN	4.12.72	7	NC	Beijing	10 Apr
3:58:38	Stanislav	Ustimenko	RUS	8.5.69	6	NC	Kaliningrad	23 Apr
3:58:40	Thomas	Wallstab	GER	29.1.68	3	NC	Offenburg	1 May
3:58:46	Modris	Liepins	LAT	3.8.66	1	NC	Ogre	3 Jul
3:59:11	Andrey	Popov	RUS	28.4.62	7	NC	Kaliningrad	23 Apr
3:59:13	Dmitriy	Savoitan	BLR	26.8.71	4		Podrebrady	23 Apr
3:59:41.7t	Christophe	Cousin	FRA	22.5.65	3	NC	Franconville	3 Apr
3:59:48	Sergey	Semin	RUS	71	5		Izhevsk	27 Aug
4:00:04		Hao Huanquan	CHN		8	NC	Beijing	10 Apr
	(60)							
4:00:17	Daniel	Garcia	MEX	28.10.71	2	AmCp	Chapultepec	10 Apr
4:00:18	Stefan	Johansson	SWE	11.4.67	18	EC	Helsinki	13 Aug
4:00:52	Orazio	Romanzi	ITA	16.9.70	5	NC	Pescara	20 Mar
4:00:52.3t	Thierry	Nuttin	FRA	11.10.62	4	NC	Franconville	3 Apr
4:01:05	Roman	Mrázek	SVK	21.1.62	5		Podébrady	23 Apr
4:01:17	Aleksandr	Rakovic	YUG	13.4.68	19	EC	Helsinki	13 Aug
4:01:31	Pavel	Vasilyev	RUS	2.7.70	8	NC	Kaliningrad	23 Apr
4:01:36		Zhang Hong —	CHN		9	NC	Beijing	10 Apr
4:01:38	Vladimir	Boydachenko	RUS	70	6		Izhevsk	27 Aug
4:02:17	Mike	Harvey	AUS	5.12.62	1		Melbourne	18 Dec
	(70)							
4:02:18	Aigars	Fadejevs	LAT	27.12.75	2	NC	Ogre	3 Jul
4:02:25	Pascal	Charrière	SUI	14.11.64	20	EC	Helsinki	13 Aug
4:02:27		Mao Xinyuan	CHN	2.7.71	2		Fuxin	16 Sep

Mark	Name		Nat	Born	Pos	Meet	Venue	Date
4:02:37		Zhang Jiangpo	CHN	5.5.75	3		Fuxin	16 Sep
4:02:45	Theodoris	Stamatopoulos	GRE	24.4.70	2	NC	Athina	13 Mar
4:02:52		Wang Wei	CHN		4		Fuxin	16 Sep
4:02:55.6t	Pascal	Kieffer	FRA	6.5.61	5	NC	Franconville	3 Apr
4:02:59	Jonathan	Matthews	USA	2.7.56	2	NC	Palo Alto	13 Mar
4:03:38	Alessandro	Mistretta	ITA	16.9.70	6	NC	Pescara	20 Mar
4:03:43	Antero (80)	Lindman	FIN	25.12.64	1	Nordic	Stockholm	10 Sep
4:03:51	Bernardo	Segura	MEX	11.2.70	3	AmCp	Chapultepec	10 Apr
4:03:52	Koji	Hoga	JPN	22.11.69	4	NC	Wajima	17 Apr
4:04:03	Rogelio	Sánchez	MEX	73	4	AmCp	Chapultepec	10 Apr
4:04:19	Aleksandr	Artsybashev	RUS	70	7		Izhevsk	27 Aug
4:04:23	Herman	Nelson	USA	20.9.61	3	NC	Palo Alto	13 Mar
4:04:35	Filiberto	Pantoja	MEX	69	5	AmCp	Chapultepec	10 Apr
4:04:37	Sylvain	Caudron	FRA	10.9.69	3		Saran	25 Sep
4:04:38	Aldo	Bertoldi	SUI	5.3.61	1		La Tour-de-Peilz	1 May
4:04:46		Fu Youliang	CHN		5		Fuxin	16 Sep
4:04:56	Risto (90)	Nurmi	FIN	24.11.69	2	NC	Lapinlahti	7 May
4:04:58	Vitaliy	Popovich	UKR	22.10.62	1		Makachovo	22 May
4:05:01		Wang Lifeng	CHN		6		Fuxin	16 Sep
4:05:02	Juha	Kinnunen	FIN	4.3.72	3	NC	Lapinlahti	7 May
4:05:37	Jaime	Barroso	ESP	15.5.68	6	NC	Orense	20 Mar
4:05:48	Sergey	Dvoretskiy	RUS	69	9	NC	Kaliningrad	23 Apr
4:05:52	Slawomir	Cielica	POL	9.7.70	1	NC	Mielec	22 Sep
4:05:54	Didier	Menou	FRA	1.8.61			Saran	25 Sep
4:06:02		Wang Aiguo	CHN		7		Fuxin	16 Sep
4:06:14	Peter	Zanner	GER	19.7.68	4	NC	Offenburg	1 May
4:06:14	Matti (100)	Heikkilä	FIN	17.3.64	4	NC	Lapinlahti	7 May

Mark	Name		Nat	Born	Date
4:06:19	Faustino	Ruiz	ESP	65	20 Mar
4:06:42	Rodrigo	Serrano	MEX	68	10 Apr
4:06:42	Thomas	Prophet	GER	72	1 May
4:06:43	Yang Yongjian		CHN		16 Sep
4:06:45	Oscar	Font	ESP	66	20 Mar
4:07:06	Edel	Oliva	CUB	65	27 Feb
4:07:11	Ervin	Leczki	HUN	69	23 Apr
4:07:47	Bruno	Penocchio	ITA	62	20 Mar
4:07:48	Andrzej	Chylinski	USA	60	13 Mar
4:08:01	Károly	Kirszt	HUN	69	22 Oct
4:08:15	Paul	Wick	USA	62	13 Mar
4:08:21	Julio	Urias	GUA	72	22 Jan
4:08:26	Alfons	Schwarz	GER	54	1 May
4:08:59	Josef	Smola	TCH	64	27 Mar

Best track times

Mark	Name		Nat	Born	Pos	Meet	Venue	Date
3:57:36.9		Jin Guohong	CHN	5.2.72	3	SGP	Fana	7 May
3:59:46.4	Modris	Liepins	LAT	3.8.66	4	SGP	Fana	7 May

Questionable

Mark	Name		Nat	Born	Pos	Meet	Venue	Date
4:05:54	André	Toussaint	FRA	24.4.52	2		Bar-le-Duc	11 Nov

100 KILOMETRES WALK

Mark	Name		Nat	Born	Pos	Meet	Venue	Date
9:30:53	Denis	Terraz	FRA	5.2.58	1		Roubaix	9 Oct
9:35:04	Vladimoir	Boydachenko	RUS	3.10.55	2		Roubaix	9 Oct
9:35:24	André	Touissaint	FRA	24.4.52	3		Roubaix	9 Oct

WORLD JUNIOR MEN'S LISTS 1994

100 Metres

Mark	Wind	Name		Nat	Born	Pos	Meet	Venue	Date
10.08A	1.9	Obadele	Thompson	BAR	30.3.76	3		El Paso	16 Apr
		10.27				4q4	CG	Victoria	22 Aug
10.11	2.0	Tim	Montgomery	USA	28.1.75	3h3	NC	Knoxville	15 Jun
		10.15	0.9			2r2	Athl	Lausanne	6 Jul
		10.20	1.2					Fayetteville	23 Apr
10.17		Deji	Aliu	NGR	22.11.75	1	NC-j	Benin City	28 May
		10.17	??			1		Port Harcourt	18 Mar
		10.21	1.2			1	WJ	Lisboa	21 Jul
		10.23	0.6			1h4	CG	Victoria	22 Aug
10.24	0.4	Kazuhiro	Takahashi	JPN	27.7.76	1		Toyama	2 Aug
10.25	1.2	Jason	Gardener	GBR	17.9.75	2	WJ	Lisboa	21 Jul
10.26	1.2	Deworski	Odom	USA	11.4.77	3	WJ	Lisboa	21 Jul
10.29	1.6	Ibrahim	Meité	IVC	18.11.76	4		Noisy-le-Grand	2 Jul
10.30	1.2	Carlton	Chambers	CAN	27.6.75	5	WJ	Lisboa	22 Jul
10.31	0.0	Bryan	Howard	USA	7.10.76	1h2	N.Sch	Raleigh	18 Jun
10.33		Okechukwu	Ejiogu	NGR	76			Port Harcourt	18 Mar
10.33	1.1	Eric	Frempong	CAN	1.10.75	1	NC-j	Ottawa	2 Jul
10.34		Sylvester	Omodiale	NGR	5.9.77	2	NC-j	Benin City	28 May
10.37	0.0	Pat	Johnson	USA	10.8.76	1h3	N.Sch	Raleigh	18 Jun
10.37	0.6	Takahiro	Mazuka	JPN	29.6.76	2		Nagoya	30 Oct
10.38		Cyril	Oriala	NGR	75	2s1	NC-j	Benin City	27 May
10.39	0.9	David	Tomlin	CAN	25.5.76	2		Kitchener	22 Jun
10.40		Udo	Obong	NGR		1q3	NC-j	Benin City	27 May
10.42		Cyril	Obar	NGR		2s2	NC-j	Benin City	27 May
10.43	1.5	Julian	Golding	GBR	17.2.75	1h5	WJ	Lisboa	20 Jul
10.43	1.5	Erland	Sæterstøl	NOR	7.1.75	2h8	WJ	Lisboa	20 Jul
10.43	1.2	Worasit	Vechaprutti	THA	13.11.76	1	AsiC-j	Djarkata	18 Sep

Wind assisted

Mark	Wind	Name		Nat	Born	Pos	Meet	Venue	Date
10.19		Dion	Miller	USA	26.2.75	1		Lubbock	26 Mar
10.26		Stacy	Mitchell	USA	16.10.75	1		Dallas	2 Apr
10.27	3.8	Carlton	Chambers	CAN	27.6.75	1		Victoria	29 Jul
10.29	3.7	Trevor	Cameron	GBR	25.11.75	6	NC	Sheffield	11 Jun
10.30	3.0	David	Tomlin	CAN	25.5.76	1h1		Kitchener	22 Jun
10.34	3.5	Julian	Golding	GBR	17.2.75	1		Bedford	17 Sep
10.35	4.1	Toya	Jones	USA	28.10.76	1		Austin	14 May
10.36		Ben	Singleton	USA	26.5.75	1h4		Hampton	3 Jun
10.37		Ali	Evans	USA	9.9.75	1		Sacramento	27 May
10.40	7.2	Wayne	McGarity	USA	75	1h4		Austin	8 Apr
10.41		Tyron	Wilson	USA		1		Dallas	16 Apr
10.41		Maurice	Greene	USA	23.7.75	1		Lawrence	23 Apr

Hand timing

Mark	Wind	Name		Nat	Born	Pos	Meet	Venue	Date
10.0		Deji	Aliu	NGR	22.11.75			Bauchi	15 Apr
10.0	0.3	Obadele	Thompson	BAR	30.3.76	1	CAC-j	Port of Spain	8 Jul

Wind assisted

Mark	Wind	Name		Nat	Born	Pos	Meet	Venue	Date
10.1		Chad	Burnett	USA	75	1		Austin	13 Apr
10.1		John	George	USA	7.7.75	1		Lafayette	22 Apr
10.1		Claude	Toukene-Guébogo	CMR	75			Garoua	21 Aug

Track 4cm short & incorrect wind gauge position

Mark	Wind	Name		Nat	Born	Pos	Meet	Venue	Date
9.96	1.7	Tim	Montgomery	USA	28.1.75	1	JUCO	Odessa, Tx	20 May
		10.11	1.3			1s2	JUCO	Odessa, Tx	20 May
		10.24				1h4	JUCO	Odessa, Tx	20 May

200 Metres

Mark	Wind	Name		Nat	Born	Pos	Meet	Venue	Date
20.47	1.5	Tony	Wheeler	USA	19.1.75	1	USOF	Edwardsville	10 Jul
		20.52	1.6			1		Raleigh	23 Apr
		20.55	0.5			1s1	NCAA	Boise	3 Jun
		20.62	1.7			1	WJ	Lisboa	23 Jul
		20.67	-0.1			1	NC-j	Tallahassee	25 Jun
20.57	0.5	Kazuhiro	Takahashi	JPN	27.7.76	1		Osaka	19 Jun
20.61		Deji	Aliu	NGR	22.11.75	1		Bauchi	16 Apr
20.64	0.4	Ibrahim	Meité	CIV	18.11.76	2		Narbonne	19 Jun
20.65	1.8	Eric	Frempong	CAN	1.10.75	1	NC-j	Ottawa	3 Jul
20.71		Obadele	Thompson	BAR	30.3.76	1		Bridgetown	3 Apr
20.72	2.0	Tim	Montgomery	USA	28.1.75	1		Austin	13 Apr
20.76	-2.7	Bryan	Howard	USA	7.10.76	1		Long Beach	21 May

Mark		Name		Nat	Born	Pos	Meet	Venue	Date
20.83	0.0	Pat	Johnson	USA	10.8.76	1h1	Nat Sch	Raleigh	19 Jun
20.86A	1.3	Riaan	Dempers	RSA	4.3.77	1		Boksburg	9 Mar
20.91	1.9	Ian	Mackie	GBR	27.2.75	1s1	WJ	Lisboa	23 Jul
20.94	1.8	Carlton	Chambers	CAN	27.6.75	2	NC-j	Ottawa	3 Jul
21.00		Martavious	Houston	USA	75	1h1		Gainesville	14 May
21.01	1.8	David	Tomlin	CAN	25.5.76	3	NC-j	Ottawa	3 Jul
21.02	0.7	Todd	Blythe	NZL	8.1.75	1		Hamilton	5 Mar
21.02A	1.1	Ettienne	Roux	RSA	8.5.76	1	NC-j	Bloemfontein	8 Apr
21.02	-0.3	Takahiro	Mazuka	JPN	20.6.76	1		Gifu	26 Jun
21.02	1.7	Julian	Golding	GBR	17.2.75	1	NC-j	Bedford	3 Jul
21.02	1.8	Mark	Keddell	NZL	13.2.75	1q3	WJ	Lisboa	22 Jul
Wind assisted									
20.30	2.6	Tony	Wheeler	USA	19.1.75	3	NCAA	Boise	4 Jun
		20.61	2.1			2h1	NCAA	Boise	1 Jun
		20.4 hand	2.9			1	vCAN-j	Buffalo	15 Jul
20.73	2.8	Julian	Golding	GBR	17.2.75	1		Bedford	17 Sep
20.80		Pat	Johnson	USA	10.8.76	1		Long Beach	9 Jul
20.88	3.2	Isaac	Harvin	USA	75	1h		Gainesville	13 May
20.88	3.2	Trevor	Cameron	GBR	25.11.76	4	NC	Sheffield	12 Jun
20.94	3.9	Mark	Keddell	NZL	13.2.75	1		Christchurch	12 Nov
20.98		Ali	Evans	USA	9.9.75	1		Sacramento	26 May
21.00		Robert	Staten	USA	19.5.77	1		Dallas	2 Apr
21.01	2.7	Toya	Jones	USA	28.10.75	1		Austin	14 May
Hand timing									
20.7	0.6	Pat	Johnson	USA	10.8.76	1h		Riverside	26 Mar
20.7		Francis	Obikwelu	NGR	78			Bauchi	15 Apr
20.5w	2.9	Eric	Frempong	CAN	1.10.75	2	vUSA-j	Buffalo	15 Jul
20.6w		Jerod	Douglas	USA		1		San Antonio	16 Apr
20.8w	2.9	David	Tomlin	CAN	25.5.76	4	vUSA-j	Buffalo	15 Jul

300 Metres

Mark	Name		Nat	Born	Pos	Meet	Venue	Date
32.9	Mark	Hylton	GBR	24.9.76	1		Basingstoke	21 Aug

400 Metres

Mark	Name		Nat	Born	Pos	Meet	Venue	Date
45.15A	Riaan	Dempers	RSA	4.3.77	1	NC	Secunda	6 May
	45.98				1		Durban	23 Apr
45.46A	Leonard	Byrd	USA	17.3.75	1		Albuquerque	30 Apr
	45.70				3h2	NCAA	Boise	2 Jun
45.77	Desmond	Johnson	USA	6.4.77	1	NC-j	Tallahassee	25 Jun
45.82	Ramon	Clay	USA	29.6.75	2	NC-j	Tallahassee	25 Jun
	45.94				3	USOF	Edwardsville	9 Jul
45.83	Michael	McDonald	JAM	17.3.75	1	WJ	Lisboa	22 Jul
46.09	Milton	Campbell	USA	15.5.76	1		Winter Park	28 May
46.17	Rohan	McDonald	JAM	28.8.77	1	NC-j	Kingston	2 Jul
46.21A	Dirk	Pretorius	RSA	21.1.76	4	NC	Secunda	6 May
46.31	Jerome	Young	JAM	14.8.76	1	US Sch	Raleigh	18 Jun
46.31	Sean	Farrell	NZL	5.3.75	3	WJ	Lisboa	22 Jul
46.34	Michael	Granville	USA	14.2.78	3	Nat Sch	Raleigh	18 Jun
46.35A	Moses	Mabaso	RSA	28.5.77	2	NC-j	Bloemfontein	8 Apr
46.37	Mark	Hylton	GBR	24.9.76	4	WJ	Lisboa	22 Jul
46.41	Mario	Watts	JAM	21.5.75	1	NAIA	Naperville	28 May
46.61	Davian	Clarke	JAM	30.4.76	2	NC-j	Kingston	2 Jul
46.68	Keith	Black	USA	8.9.75	1r3		Austin	14 May
46.72	Arthur	Reece	USA	75	2r3		Austin	14 May
46.74	Mohamed Hamed	Al-Bishi	SAU	29.10.75	3h1	AsiG	Hiroshima	11 Oct
46.77	Guy	Bullock	GBR	15.10.75	3		Hengelo	4 Jun
46.79	Francis	Obikwelu	NGR	22.11.78	5s1	WJ	Lisboa	21 Jul
Hand timing								
45.6	Michael	McDonald	JAM	17.3.75	1		Kingston	12 Mar
46.6	Lorenzo	Robinson	JAM	27.3.75	2		Kingston	12 Mar

800 Metres

Mark	Name		Nat	Born	Pos	Meet	Venue	Date
1:46.97	Alain	Miranda	CUB	19.10.75	2		Maia	16 Jul
1:47.0A	Peter	Biwott	KEN	22.8.76	1		Nairobi	5 Jul
1:47.21	Paul	Byrne	AUS	29.1.76	5		Canberra	28 Jan
1:47.32	Julius	Achon	UGA	12.12.76	2h3	CG	Victoria	23 Aug
1:47.6A	Japhet	Kimutai	KEN	20.12.75	2		Nairobi	5 Jul
1:47.63	Abd. Hassan	Abdulrahman	QAT	3.7.77	7		Linz	4 Jul
1:47.66	Reyes	Estévez	ESP	2.8.76	1B		Mataro	3 Aug

Mark	Name		Nat	Born	Pos	Meet	Venue	Date
1:47.68	David	Krummenacker	USA	24.5.75	2rA		Atlanta	21 May
1:47.98A	Pieter	van Tonder	RSA	6.1.75	5		Pretoria	18 Apr
1:48.32	André	Bucher	SUI	19.10.76	1		Zofingen	2 Jul
1:48.43A	Clyde	Colenso	RSA	11.5.77	1		Pretoria	18 Apr
1:48.43	Bekele	Banbore	ETH	75	1		Alger	7 Jul
1:48.46	Roberto	Parra	ESP	6.4.76	1		Toledo	4 Jun
1:48:56	Ali	Hakimi	TUN	24.4.76			Ochsenhausen	10 Sep
1:48.63	Kipruto	Maru	KEN	77	2		Alger	7 Jul
1:48.70	Heath	Fitzpatrick	AUS	17.8.75	8		Brisbane	5 Feb
1:48.87	Andrea	Longo	ITA	26.7.75	2		Conegliano	22 May
1:48.90	Brian	Klein	USA	17.3.75	1		Houston	24 Apr
1:48.93	Edward	King	GBR	26.11.75	3	NC-j	Bedford	3 Jul
1:48.94	José	Azevedo	POR	20.7.75	7		Maia	16 Jul
1:48.98	Michael	Granville	USA	14.2.78	1		Long Beach	21 May

1000 Metres

Mark	Name		Nat	Born	Pos	Meet	Venue	Date
2:20.25	Reyes	Estévez	ESP	2.8.76	1	WK	Zürich	17 Aug
2:20.5	Paul	Byrne	AUS	29.1.76	1		Melbourne	6 Jan
2:21.09	André	Bucher	SUI	19.10.76	2	WK	Zürich	17 Aug

1500 Metres

Mark	Name		Nat	Born	Pos	Meet	Venue	Date
3:39.28	Reyes	Estévez	ESP	2.8.76	9	VD	Bruxelles	19 Aug
3:39.78	Julius	Achon	UGA	12.12.76	1	WJ	Lisboa	24 Jul
3:40.11	Ali	Hakimi	TUN	24.4.76	1		Konstanz	4 Sep
3:40.46	André	Bucher	SUI	19.10.76	2	WJ	Lisboa	24 Jul
3:41.09	Philip	Mosima	KEN	2.1.76	3	WJ	Lisboa	24 Jul
3:41.31	Bashir Ahmed	Boushra	QAT	23.3.77	4rB	ASV	Köln	21 Aug
3:43.09	Ivan	Pérez	ESP	23.4.76	2		Gijón	2 Jul
3:43.43	Daniel	Njenga	KEN	7.5.76	1		Toyama	1 Aug
3:43.86	Michael	Power	AUS	9.5.76	5	WJ	Lisboa	24 Jul
3:43.91		Song Mingyou	CHN	9.1.75	1h	NC	Beijing	4 Jun
3:43.96	Alexandru	Vasile	ROM	26.10.75	4		Bucuresti	17 Jun
3:44.06	Mauro	Casagrande	ITA	8.3.75	3		Bologna	2 Sep
3:44.2	Iván	Manjón	ESP	8.5.77	1		Gijón	24 Apr
3:44.30	Othman Ahmed	Suleiman	QAT	10.3.78	7rB	ASV	Köln	21 Aug
3:44.64	Paul	Cleary	AUS	28.4.76	6	WJ	Lisboa	24 Jul
3:44.90	Nasser	Suleiman	QAT	78	9rB		Hechtel	30 Jul
3:44.93	Pablo	Olmedo	MEX	8.5.75	9		Port Alberni	1 Jun
3:44.94	Sami	Ylihärsilä	FIN	14.6.75	1		Lapua	12 Jul
3:45.01	Fernando	Felipe	ESP	6.7.75	9		Baracaldo	18 Jun
3:45.08	Ciprian	Bolintinescu	ROM	30.3.76			Bucuresti	17 Jun
3:45.11	Bruno	Witchalls	GBR	22.3.75	8	WJ	Lisboa	24 Jul

1 Mile

Mark	Name		Nat	Born	Pos	Meet	Venue	Date
4:00.64	Michael	Power	AUS	9.5.76	4	NEC	Melbourne	24 Feb
4:01.87	Paul	Cleary	AUS	28.4.76	7	NEC	Melbourne	24 Feb

3000 Metres

Mark	Name		Nat	Born	Pos	Meet	Venue	Date
7:45.27	Ismael	Kirui	KEN	20.2.75	7	Nik	Nice	18 Jul
	7:48.46				3	Slov	Bratislava	1 Jun
8:00.7	Giuliano	Battocletti	ITA	1.8.75	1		Palermo	11 Sep
8:01.26	Darius	Burrows	GBR	8.8.75	3		Solihull	21 Aug
8:04.72	Simon	Zanon	ITA	3.5.75	4		Trento	25 Sep
8:05.46	Luciano	Di Pardo	ITA	3.2.75	1		Guilianova	8 May
8:08.8	Michael	Power	AUS	9.5.76	4		Canberra	18 Jan
8:09.71	Sergey	Lebedj	UKR	15.7.75	1	vFRA-j	Dôle	7 Aug
8:10.35A	Meck	Mothuli	RSA	12.4.76	1		Secunda	19 Mar
8:11:10	Salah	El Ghazi	MAR	75			Meknès	19 Mar
8:12.21	Mauro	Casagrande	ITA	8.3.75	9		Trento	25 Sep
8:13.27+	Daniel	Komen	KEN	17.5.76	1+	WJ	Lisboa	24 Jul
8:13.76	Samuli	Vasala	FIN	29.11.76	1	vSWE-j	Stockholm	28 Aug

5000 Metres

Mark	Name		Nat	Born	Pos	Meet	Venue	Date
13:14.46	Ismael	Kirui	KEN	20.2.75	1	DNG	Stockholm	12 Jul
	13:23.04				1		Hechtel	30 Jul
	13:24.45				10	GPF	Paris	3 Sep
	13:24.84				4	Herc	Monaco	2 Aug
	13:24.88				8	WK	Zürich	17 Aug
	13:26.33				8	Bisl	Oslo	22 Jul
	13:32.90i				2	DNG	Stockholm	8 Mar

Mark	Name		Nat	Born	Pos	Meet	Venue	Date
13:24.07	Philip	Mosima	KEN	2.1.76	5	CG	Victoria	24 Aug
	13:29.37				1h2	CG	Victoria	22 Aug
13:31.10	Daniel	Komen	KEN	17.5.76	1		Alger	8 Jul
13:35.2	Kenji	Takao	JPN	23.3.75	2rA		Nobeoka	28 May
	13:38.04				4	NC	Tokyo	12 Jun
13:42.43	Pablo	Olmedo	MEX	8.5.75	2	MSR	Walnut	16 Apr
13:43.92A	Habte	Jifar	ETH	76	2		Nairobi	18 Jun
13:51.11	Julius	Gitahi	KEN	29.4.78	1		Sendai	7 Oct
13:51.16	Giuliano	Battocletti	ITA	1.8.75	3	WJ	Lisboa	24 Jul
13:51.34	Benoit	Zwierchlewski	FRA	19.8.76	1		Lübeck	12 Aug
13:52.0	Meck	Mothuli	RSA	12.4.76	1		Welkom	17 Apr
13:53.1	Salah	El Ghazi	MAR	75			Rabat	4 Jun
13:54.45	Mohamed	Amyn	MAR	76			Alger	8 Jul
13:55.3	Samir	Moussal	ALG	15.5.75			Alger	25 May
13:56.8A	David	Chelule	KEN	7.7.77	2		Nairobi	5 Jul
13:57.66	Simone	Zanon	ITA	30.5.75	3		Conegliano	24 Jun
13:57.83	John	Maitai	KEN	22.4.76	1h1		Sendai	29 May
13:58.3	Muneyuki	Ojima	JPN	25.9.75	3		Kitakyushu	11 Jun
13:59.6	Michitane	Noda	JPN	25.3.75	1		Hachioji	10 Apr
13:59.80	Ivan	Pérez	ESP	23.4.76	16		Pontevedra	9 Jun
14:01.7	Yasuhiro	Karasu	JPN	19.12.75	6		Kitakyushu	11 Jun

10000 Metres

Mark	Name		Nat	Born	Pos	Meet	Venue	Date
28:20.78	Kenji	Takao	JPN	22.3.75	6rA		Kobe	24 Apr
28:29.74	Daniel	Komen	KEN	17.5.76	1		Lisboa	20 Jul
28:39.64	Daniel	Njenga	KEN	7.5.76	1		Konosu	1 Oct
28:43.27	Michitane	Noda	JPN	25.3.75	3		Tokyo	20 May
28:43.96	Julius	Gitahi	KEN	29.4.78	2		Konosu	1 Oct
28:51.7	Muneyuki	Ojima	JPN	25.9.75	3		Nobeoka	22 Oct
28:53.39	Makoto	Nakayama	JPN	7.4.77	11		Fukushima	24 Sep
28:57.60	John	Maitai	KEN	22.4.76	5		Konosu	1 Oct
28:58.6	Futayasu	Taguchi	JPN	12.1.75	5r2		Hachioji	27 Nov
29:04.57	Habte	Jifar	ETH	76	4	WJ	Lisboa	20 Jul
29:06.03	Tekalegn	Shewaye	ETH	75	5	WJ	Lisboa	20 Jul
29:06.3	Mamoru	Kawagoe	JPN	7.10.75			Nobeoka	22 Oct
29:06.54	Benoit	Zwierchlewski	FRA	19.8.76	1		Mol	20 Aug
29:14.54		Yang Guocai	CHN	6.2.75	3	NC	Beijing	5 Jun
29:17.23		Ko Jung-won	KOR	21.1.75	6	WJ	Lisboa	20 Jul
29:19.6	Kuniaki	Kanno	JPN	14.5.75	1		Saitama	24 Sep
29:20.01A	Meck	Mothuli	RSA	12.4.76	2	NC	Secunda	7 May
29:20.2	Wataru	Kobayashi	JPN	20.8.75	1r3		Hachioji	27 Nov
29:21.00	Simone	Zanon	ITA	30.5.75	7	WJ	Lisboa	20 Jul
29:22.0A	Mark	Bett	KEN	15.7.76	2		Nairobi	5 Jul

3000 Metres Steeplechase

Mark	Name		Nat	Born	Pos	Meet	Venue	Date
8:19.21	Daniel	Njenga	KEN	7.5.76	1	JPN Ch	Tokyo	12 Jun
8:31.51	Paul	Chemase	KEN	24.8.76	1	WJ	Lisboa	23 Jul
8:33.64	Julius	Chelule	KEN	25.12.78	2	WJ	Lisboa	23 Jul
8:34.42	Yarba	Lakhal	MAR	12.2.75	3	WJ	Lisboa	23 Jul
8:43.67	Wordofa	Lemma	ETH	77	3		Alger	7 Jul
8:46.56	Luciano	Di Pardo	ITA	3.2.75	8		Bologna	2 Sep
8:47.81	Naotaka	Takahashi	JPN	28.6.76	1		Nagoya	1 Nov
8:48.44	Takeyuki	Ojima	JPN	22.11.76	2		Nagoya	1 Nov
8:49.85	Jose Luis	Blanco	ESP	3.6.75	6	WJ	Lisboa	23 Jul
8:49.99	Christian	Knoblich	GER	1.10.76	7	WJ	Lisboa	23 Jul
8:51.5	Gustavo	de Paulo	BRA	24.10.75	1		Rio de Janeiro	26 Jun
8:52.45	César	Pérez	ESP	7.4.75	8	WJ	Lisboa	23 Jul
8:52.80	Domenico	D'Ambrosio	ITA	18.7.75	1rA		Pescara	19 Jun
8:54.5A	Daniel	Komen	KEN	17.5.76			Iten	12 Jun
8:55.2A	David	Chelule	KEN	7.7.77			Iten	12 Jun
8:55.63	Konstantin	Tomskiy	RUS	16.3.75	6	Znam	Moskva	11 Jun
8:55.90	Carlos	Suarez	ESP	25.9.75	10		Baracaldo	18 Jun
8:56.38	Hiroyuki	Yamamoto	JPN	21.9.76	2	AsiC-j	Djakarta	17 Sep
8:56.40	Chrisovaladios	Athanassiou	GRE	21.4.75	1		Piraeus	19 Jun
8:56.41	Aleksey	Potapov	RUS	10.8.75	1	v3N-j	Warszawa	18 Jun

110 Metres Hurdles

Mark	Wind	Name		Nat	Born	Pos	Meet	Venue	Date
13.56	0.5	Frank	Busemann	GER	26.2.75	1h2		Mannheim	4 Jun
		13.58	0.9			2		Scheessel	21 May

Mark		Name		Nat	Born	Pos	Meet	Venue	Date
Busemann		13.66	1.0			3s1	NC	Erfurt	7 Jul
		13.69	1.7			1h4	WJ	Lisboa	21 Jul
		13.70	-0.3			3		Duisburg	12 Jun
		13.71	1.3			1	v3N-j	Warszawa	18 Jun
		13.73	2.0			1		Mannheim	4 Jun
13.79	0.5	Dudley	Dorival	USA	1.9.75	1	NC-j	Tallahassee	25 Jun
13.84	1.8	Emerson	Perin	BRA	17.3.75	1	NC-j	Sao Leopoldo	27 Aug
13.90		Khary	Burnley	USA	28.7.75	1		Ypsilanti	25 May
13.91		Anier	Garcia	CUB	9.3.76	3		La Habana	18 Feb
13.93	1.1	Darius	Pemberton	USA	10.5.75	3	SEC	Fayetteville	15 May
14.03	1.6	Andrey	Kislikh	RUS	24.11.75	2h3	WJ	Lisboa	21 Jul
14.05		Reggie	Payton	USA	17.9.75	1		Athens, Ga.	2 Apr
14.06	1.4	Filip	Bickel	GER	12.2.75	1h2	WJ	Lisboa	21 Jul
14.06	1.9	Sven	Pieters	BEL	5.6.76	2s1	WJ	Lisboa	21 Jul
14.08	1.9	Chris	Aikens	USA	22.4.75	2		Villanova	8 May
14.15	1.7	Andrey	Vinitskiy	UKR	23.12.77	2h4	WJ	Lisboa	21 Jul
14.15	0.9	Nobuto	Watanabe	JPN	20.10.76	1h		Nagoya	1 Nov
14.17		Reggie	Torian	USA	22.4.75	2		Madison	22 May
14.18	1.9	James	Archampong	GBR	14.3.76	5s1	WJ	Lisboa	21 Jul
14.18	0.3	Philippe	Lamine	FRA	4.10.76	1	vUKR-j	Dôle	7 Aug
14.20	1.7	Yoel	Hernández	CUB	12.12.77	3h4	WJ	Lisboa	21 Jul
14.21	1.9	Robert	Kronberg	SWE	15.8.76	6s1	WJ	Lisboa	21 Jul
14.22		Promodos	Kantsantonis	CYP	21.10.75	1		Nicosia	6 Jul
Probably born 1973									
13.79		William	Erese	NGR	(76)	1	NC-j	Benin City	26 May
Hand timing									
13.9		Darius	Pemberton	USA	10.5.75	1		Knoxville	2 Apr
13.9		Andrey	Vinitskiy	UKR	23.12.77	1			30 Apr
13.9		Andrey	Kislikh	RUS	24.11.75			Krasnodar	28 May
Wind assisted									
13.47	2.1	Frank	Busemann	GER	26.2.75	1	WJ	Lisboa	22 Jul
		13.70w	2.1			1h2	WJ	Lisboa	21 Jul
13.65	2.1	Dudley	Dorival	USA	1.9.75	2	WJ	Lisboa	22 Jul
14.00	2.1	Sven	Pieters	BEL	5.6.76	4	WJ	Lisboa	22 Jul

400 Metres Hurdles

Mark	Name		Nat	Born	Pos	Meet	Venue	Date
50.56	Gennadiy	Gorbenko	UKR	22.9.75	1	WJ	Lisboa	22 Jul
50.58	Hadi Soua'an	Al-Somaily	SAU	30.12.76	6	AsiG	Hiroshima	11 Oct
50.66	Mohamed Hamed	Al-Bishi	SAU	29.10.75	1		Doha	7 Apr
50.70	Noel	Levy	GBR	22.6.75	6	TSB	Edinburgh	8 Jul
50.79	Kevin	James	JAM	7.2.75	1s2	WJ	Lisboa	21 Jul
50.84A	Jaco	Jonker	RSA	5.2.75	4		Germiston	13 May
50.85	Miklós	Roth	HUN	4.6.75	2	WJ	Lisboa	22 Jul
50.95	Róbert	Jarábek	SVK	29.7.75	4	WJ	Lisboa	22 Jul
51.01	Corey	Murdock	USA	3.3.75	1	NC-j	Tallahassee	25 Jun
51.04	Lukás	Soucek	TCH	10.7.75	2		Praha	2 Aug
51.08	Radoslav	Holúbek	SVK	28.11.75	1		Banská Bystrica	12 Jun
51.19	Edward	Clarke	JAM	7.2.75	1		Kingston	26 Mar
51.21	Khassif	Mubarak Sultan	QAT	74???	1	AsiC-j	Djakarta	19 Sep
51.31	Hamad Mubarak	Al Dosari	QAT	7.4.77	3h2	AsiG	Hiroshima	10 Oct
51.42	Aaron	Haynes	USA	1.11.75	2	NC-j	Tallahassee	25 Jun
51.45	Constantin	Budeanu	ROM	5.8.75	3		Bucuresti	18 Jun
51.45	Marcel	Schelbert	SUI	26.2.76	2h1	WJ	Lisboa	20 Jul
51.50	Nobuyuki	Suzuki	JPN	1.7.75	1h		Nagoya	1 Nov
51.57	Coke	Edmon	USA	76	1h2		Tallahassee	24 Jun
51.61	Naoto	Ichijima	JPN	5.2.75	1		Amagasaki	27 Oct
Hand timing								
51.1	Edward	Clarke	JAM	7.2.75	1	CAC-j	Port of Spain	10 Jul

High Jump

Mark	Name		Nat	Born	Pos	Meet	Venue	Date
2.30	Jagan	Hames	AUS	31.10.76	2	NC	Sydney	13 Mar
	2.24				1		Canberra	28 Jan
	2.24				3		Brisbane	5 Feb
2.24i	Eric	Bishop	USA	7.6.76	1		Syracuse	13 Mar
2.23i	Jordi	Rofes	ESP	24.9.76	1		Sevilla	26 Feb
	2.19				1		Barcelona	1 May
2.23	Jeremy	Fischer	USA	17.2.76	1		Santa Barbara	26 Mar
2.23	Roland	Stark	GER	10.7.75	1	NC-j	Ulm	31 Jul
2.22	Nick	Johannsen	USA	3.11.75	2	Big*	Lawrence	21 May

Mark		Name		Nat	Born	Pos	Meet	Venue	Date
2.22			Gao Yuanming	CHN	22.11.75	2	NC	Beijing	5 Jun
2.22		Attila	Zsivótzky	HUN	29.4.77	1	NC-j	Budapest	25 Jun
2.22		Mika	Polku	FIN	19.7.75	1	vSWE	Stockholm	27 Aug
2.21		Ivan	Wagner	USA	17.12.76	1		San Antonio	11 Mar
2.21		Shannon	King	USA	75	1		Charleston	28 May
2.21		Antoine	Burke	IRL	29.7.75	1		Cork City	25 Jun
2.21		Bjørn	Olsson	NOR	10.8.75	1		Oslo	3 Jul
2.21		Oskari	Frösén	FIN	24.1.76	2=	2N	Cagliari	17 Sep
2.21		Shunichi	Kobayashi	JPN	23.4.76	1		Nagoya	31 Oct
2.20		Michael	Majchrowicz	POL	29.9.75	1	v3N-j	Warszawa	18 Jun
2.20		Jörg	Lammerich	GER	28.1.75	1		Remscheid	26 Jun
2.20		Jarrod	Pozzi	AUS	29.7.75	1		Vilvoorde	26 Jun
2.20		Nikolay	Skorokhod	UKR	3.3.76	3=	NC	Kiev	27 May
2.19A		Kevin	Dotson	USA	26.2.78	1		Albuquerque	13 May

PoleVault

Mark		Name		Nat	Born	Pos	Meet	Venue	Date
5.70		Viktor	Chistyakov	RUS	9.2.75	1		Leppävirta	7 Jun
		5.70				3		Rieti	28 Aug
		5.65				2	ECp23	Ostrava	31 Jul
		5.60i				4	NC	Lipetsk	27 Feb
		5.60				6		Bratislava	1 Jun
		5.60				2		Lahti	5 Jun
		5.60				1	NC-j	Yekaterinburg	24 Jun
		5.60				1	WJ	Lisboa	22 Jul
5.60i		Yuriy	Yeliseyev	RUS	27.5.75	1		Malmö	2 Feb
		5.40				2		Leppävirta	7 Jun
5.50i		Dmitriy	Markov	BLR	14.3.75	2		Moskva	6 Jan
		5.50				2	WJ	Lisboa	22 Jul
5.40		Pavel	Burlachenko	RUS	76	1		Moskva	7 Jun
5.40		Yevgeniy	Smiryagin	RUS	17.5.76	1	v3N-j	Warszawa	18 Jun
5.40		Matej	Urban ¶	TCH	23.1.75	1		Praha	25 Jun
5.35		Fabio	Pizzolato	ITA	16.3.75	3		Bologna	2 Sep
5.33		Jacob	Davis	USA	29.4.78	1		Orangefield	12 Apr
5.30i		Adam	Kolasa	POL	2.8.75	2		Spala	26 Feb
		5.40 exh				2		Sopot	29 Jul
5.30		Andrea	Giannini	ITA	18.12.76	1		Pescara	19 Jun
5.30		Vesa	Rantanen	FIN	2.12.75	1		Ikaalinen	24 Jun
5.30		Jussi	Autio	FIN	5.4.75	5		Somero	3 Jul
5.30		Martin	Lorenci	SLO	7.2.75	2		Budapest	2 Jul
5.30		Taoufik	Lachheb	FRA	16.1.75	3	WJ	Lisboa	22 Jul
5.30		Przemyslaw	Gurin	POL	17.2.75	4	WJ	Lisboa	22 Jul
5.30		Eric	Boxley	USA	7.3.75	5	WJ	Lisboa	22 Jul
5.30		Benjamin	Jensen	NOR	13.4.75	D	Sca-j	Hyvinkää	3 Aug
5.30		Zdenek	Safár	TCH	28.2.75	3		Praha	3 Sep
5.25		Jussi	Autio	FIN	5.4.75	1		Nivala	20 Aug
5.23		Ariel	Mäki-Soini	FIN	23.7.75	3		Raahe	20 Jul

Long Jump

Mark		Name		Nat	Born	Pos	Meet	Venue	Date
8.13		James	Beckford	JAM	9.1.75	1	JUCO	Odessa, Tx	20 May
		8.12	1.1			*		Tempe	2 Apr
8.01	2.0	Bogdan	Tarus	ROM	1.8.75	2	WJ	Lisboa	21 Jul
7.97		Reggie	Torian	USA	22.4.75	1	Big10	Madison	21 May
7.96	1.4	Kirill	Sosunov	RUS	1.11.75	1		Krasnodar	28 May
7.92	1.2	Gregor	Cankar	SLO	25.1.75	1	ECpII/3	Ljubljana	11 Jun
7.90	2.0	Andrey	Sazykin	RUS	6.9.75	2		Krasnodar	28 May
7.90	1.2	Kenneth	Kastrén	FIN	8.11.75	2	NC	Tuusula	9 Jul
7.88	0.8	Darius	Pemberton	USA	10.5.75	6	NCAA	Boise	2 Jun
7.85	1.8	Justin	N'Koumazok	FRA	21.4.75	2		Nogent-sur-Marne	11 Jun
7.82	0.9	Shigeru	Tagawa	JPN	22.11.75	*	WJ	Lisboa	21 Jul
7.79	0.8	Olivier	Borderan	FRA	20.2.76	1		Versailles	22 May
7.77i	-	Troy	Twillie	USA	75	1		Decateur	Feb
7.77		Maurice	Wignall	JAM	75	1		Kingston	26 Mar
7.77	1.9		Chen Jing	CHN	10.3.75	2	Asi-J	Djarkata	18 Sep
7.76	0.3	Andrej	Benda	SVK	25.9.75	Q	WJ	Lisboa	20 Jul
7.73	1.4	Abdulrahman	Sultan Al-Nobi	QAT	79	*	Asi-J	Djarkata	18 Sep
7.72	1.8	Vyacheslav	Taranov	RUS	20.3.75	3		Krasnodar	28 May
7.72		Randy	Sedoc	HOL	8.9.75				
7.69i		Marvin	Forde	TRI	30.7.75	3		Gainesville	26 Feb
7.69	?w ok	Leonard	Cobb	USA	20.1.75	4	JUCO	Odessa, Tx	20 May

Mark		Name		Nat	Born	Pos	Meet	Venue	Date
Wind assisted									
8.29	2.3	James	Beckford	JAM	9.1.75	1		Tempe	2 Apr
		8.17w	2.7			2		Modesto	14 May
		8.15w				1	TexR	Austin	9 Apr
8.12	3.3	Darius	Pemberton	USA	10.5.75	2	SEC	Fayetteville	14 May
8.04	3.1	Gregor	Cankar	SLO	25.1.75	1	WJ	Lisboa	21 Jul
7.98	3.2	Daisuke	Watanabe	JPN	29.5.75	1		Tokyo	22 May
7.85	2.2	Shigeru	Tagawa	JPN	22.11.75	3	WJ	Lisboa	21 Jul
7.83	2.6	Olivier	Borderan	FRA	20.2.76	2		Reims	8 Jun
7.81	3.0	Vyacheslav	Taranov	RUS	20.3.75	1	NC-j	Yekaterinburg	26 Jun
7.79	2.3	Andrew	Channer	CAN	25.11.75	4	WJ	Lisboa	21 Jul
7.79	2.1	Abdulrahman	Sultan Al-Nobi	QAT	79	1	AsiC-j	Djakarta	18 Sep
7.78	2.1	Carlos	Calado	POR	5.10.75	1		Lisboa	9 Jul
7.71		Jerome	Wagner	USA					25 Apr
7.69A		Francois	Coetzee	RSA	30.7.75	1	NC-j	Bloemfontein	8 Apr

Triple Jump

Mark		Name		Nat	Born	Pos	Meet	Venue	Date
17.29	1.3	James	Beckford	JAM	9.1.75	1		Tempe	2 Apr
		17.11				1	JUCO	Odessa, Tx	21 May
		16.90w				1		Modesto	14 May
		16.63i				1		Manhattan, Ks	4 Mar
		16.62				1	TexR	Austin	8 Apr
16.65	1.0	Leonard	Cobb	USA	20.1.75	2	WJ	Lisboa	24 Jul
16.53	0.7	Onochie	Achike	GBR	31.1.75	*	WJ	Lisboa	24 Jul
16.40	1.5	César J	Rizo	CUB	8.10.75	4		La Habana	11 Feb
16.40	1.2	Sergey	Izmaylov	UKR	1.5.75	*	WJ	Lisboa	24 Jul
16.38	1.0	Ronald	Servius	FRA	21.2.76	Q	WJ	Lisboa	23 Jul
16.28i	-	Olivier	Borderan	FRA	20.2.76	1		Liévin	20 Feb
16.20		Alexander	Tumanov	TKM	29.8.75			Askhabad	24 Apr
16.16			Li Wanlong	CHN	12.10.76	1	MC-j	Nanchang	27 Apr
16.15	0.6	Vyacheslav	Taranov	RUS	20.3.75	1	v3N-j	Warszawa	18 Jun
16.10		Andrey	Sazykin	RUS	6.9.75	1		Krasnodar	24 Apr
16.09	1.0	Carlos	Calado	POR	5.10.75	*	WJ	Lisboa	23 Jul
16.08			Yan Xueying	CHN		2	NC-j	Nanchang	27 Apr
16.00	0.5	Luis Enrique	Ferrer	CUB	31.10.75	4		La Habana	18 Feb
15.98			Chen Chung-Chien	TPE	19.12.75	1		Taichung	24 Apr
15.97		Oluyeme	Sule	NGR	75			Port Harcourt	18 Mar
15.97	1.9	Pawel	Zdrajkowski	POL	27.9.76	1		Lodz	29 May
15.96	0.4	Angel	Cabrera	CUB	75	4		La Habana	25 Feb
15.96		Walter	Landry	USA	13.2.75	2		Lafayette	15 May
15.96	0.6	Jason	Wight	AUS	20.7.75	8	WJ	Lisboa	24 Jul
Wind assisted									
16.67	2.4	Onochie	Achike	GBR	31.1.75	1	WJ	Lisboa	24 Jul
16.55	2.3	Ronald	Servius	FRA	21.2.76	3	WJ	Lisboa	24 Jul
16.42	3.5	Sergey	Izmaylov	UKR	1.5.75	4	WJ	Lisboa	24 Jul
16.14	3.2	Carlos	Calado	POR	5.1.75	6	WJ	Lisboa	24 Jul

Shot

Mark		Name		Nat	Born	Pos	Meet	Venue	Date
18.34		Adam	Nelson	USA	7.7.75	1	WJ	Lisboa	23 Jul
		18.22				1	vCAN-j	Buffalo	15 Jul
17.95		Andreas	Gustafsson	SWE	2.7.75	2	WJ	Lisboa	23 Jul
17.90		Ville	Tiisanoja	FIN	24.12.75	3	WJ	Lisboa	23 Jul
17.89		Leif Dolonen	Larsen	NOR	3.4.75	3		Oslo	14 May
17.38		Jagbir	Singh	IND	75	3		Lucknow	25 Aug
17.32		Pavol	Pankuch	SVK	20.2.75	4		Praha	14 May
17.08		Róbert	Fazekas	HUN	18.8.75				
17.08		Conny	Karlsson	FIN	30.12.75	6	WJ	Lisboa	23 Jul
17.04		Vitaliy	Chuba	UKR	9.2.75				
17.02		Carlos	Geronés	ESP	7.6.75	1		Sevilla	9 Jul
16.97		Emmanuel	Hostache	FRA	18.7.75	2		Tours	8 May
16.95		Gunnar	Pfingsten	GER	24.3.75	7	WJ	Lisboa	23 Jul
16.74		Andrey	Mikhnevich	BLR	12.7.76	1	NC	Gomel	10 Jul
16.73		Bradley	Snyder	CAN	8.1.76	4	NC	Victoria	28 Jul
16.73		Yuriy	Fedorikh	UKR	20.6.75				
16.70		Felix	Hyde	GHA	7.8.76			Accra	11 Jun
16.68i		Vyacheslav	Kurchanskiy	BLR	3.9.76	1		Moskva	19 Feb
16.65		Gurpreet	Singh	IND	75	5		Taoyuan	28 May
16.64		Jason	Tunks	CAN	7.5.75	2	vUSA-j	Buffalo	15 Jul
16.63		Christian	Nehme	GER	13.7.75	8	WJ	Lisboa	23 Jul

Mark	Name		Nat	Born	Pos	Meet	Venue	Date

Discus

Mark	Name		Nat	Born	Pos	Meet	Venue	Date
61.16	Timo	Sinervo	FIN	5.8.75	3		Ikaalinen	24 Jun
	59.40				1		Ikaalinen	17 May
	58.58				4	vSWE	Stockholm	28 Aug
58.76	Jason	Tunks	CAN	7.5.75	1		Kingston, Ont.	14 Jul
58.52	Frantz	Kruger	RSA	22.5.75	3		Pretoria	18 Apr
58.18		Li Shaojie	CHN	26.1.75	1	NC-j	Nanchang	27 Apr
58.00	Róbert	Fazekas	HUN	18.8.75	2		Budapest	24 Jun
57.80	Julio César	Piñero	ARG	4.6.75	2	WJ	Lisboa	21 Jul
55.68	Andrzej	Krawczyk	POL	11.4.76	4	WJ	Lisboa	21 Jul
55.28	Doug	Reynolds	USA	11.8.75	2		Tucson	23 Apr
54.36	Mikhail	Korovin	RUS	29.1.75	2		Moskva	4 Sep
	57.36 ?				1		Yekaterinburg	24 Jun
54.10	Stéphane	Nativel	FRA	4.4.75			Martiques	11 Jun
54.10	Ville	Tiisanoja	FIN	24.12.75	3	NC20	Nivala	20 Aug
54.08	Linus	Bernhult	SWE	3.8.75	2		Västerås	27 Jul
53.50	Zoltán	Bango	HUN	31.12.75			Budapest	24 Jun
53.42	Rajiv	Kumar Singh	IND	75	3		Bangalore	30 Jun
53.30	Athanasios	Koukouzikis	GRE	15.1.75	1		Trikala	9 Apr
53.28	Alexis F	Paumier	CUB	21.1.75	1		Sevilla	9 Jul
53.22	Scott	McPherren	USA	10.4.76	q	WJ	Lisboa	20 Jul
53.12	Velijko	Cegar	YUG	30.7.75	3		Trikala	10 Jul
52.36	Justin	Anlezark	AUS	14.8.77	1	NC-j	Sydney	12 Mar
53.06	Alexander	Forst	GER	11.6.75			Schwerte-Ergste	13 Aug

Hammer

Mark	Name		Nat	Born	Pos	Meet	Venue	Date
73.66	Vladislav	Piskunov ¶	UKR	7.6.78	1		Kiev	11 Jun
	71.66 drugs dq				(1)	WJ	Lisboa	22 Jul
72.48	Szymon	Ziolkowski	POL	1.7.76	1		Warszawa	11 Jun
	71.82				2	NC	Pila	25 Jun
72.14	Sergey	Vasilyev	RUS	23.6.75	3		St Peterburg	28 Jun
71.66	Igor	Tugay	UKR	22.3.75	1	vFRA-j	Dôle	7 Aug
69.16	Konstantin	Valandin	RUS	25.1.76	4		St Peterburg	28 Jun
67.48	Norbert	Horváth	HUN	13.3.75	6		Budapest	24 Sep
67.20	Vadim	Devatovskiy	BLR	20.3.77	5		Minsk	28 Apr
66.62	Juan	Cerra	ARG	16.10.76	1	SAm-j	Santa Fé	4 Sep
66.54	Steve	Harnapp	GER	30.7.75	1		Mannheim	4 Jun
65.32	Vasiliy	Shevchenko	UKR	12.5.76				
65.30	Yosmel	Monte	CUB	26.6.77	1		La Habana	17 Jun
65.30	Karl	Andrews	GBR	21.3.75	1	NC-j	Bedford	2 Jul
65.26	Maciej	Palyszko	POL	2.1.78	4	NC	Pila	25 Jun
65.16	Dimitriy	Khuriyev	RUS	75	2	v3N-j	Warszawa	18 Jun
65.08	Tapio	Kolunsarka	FIN	27.3.75	5	WJ	Lisboa	23 Jul
64.90	Aleksey	Borisov	RUS	76	2		Moskva	29 May
64.86	Andrey	Karelin	RUS	75	3		Moskva	29 May
64.44	Ivan	Thon	BLR	4.6.76	1		Gomel	10 Jul
64.06	Aleksandr	Kukharenko	BLR	20.3.75			Gomel	10 Jul
63.76		He Xiuqan	CHN	75	1	NC-j	Nanchang	27 Apr
63.76	Kalle	Lehmusvuori	FIN	17.6.75	3		Vilppula	28 Jun

Javelin

Mark	Name		Nat	Born	Pos	Meet	Venue	Date
77.98	Marius	Corbett	RSA	26.9.75	1	WJ	Lisboa	24 Jul
76.14	Matti	Närhi	FIN	17.8.75	2		Viltasaari	14 Jun
	75.74				3		Äänekoski	16 Jun
75.92	Robert	Srovnal	TCH	13.6.75	1		Praha	16 Jun
75.08	Pietari	Skyttä	FIN	24.5.76	1	NC-j	Espoo	20 Aug
74.88		Miao Lianjin	CHN	7.1.75	1	NC-j	Nanchang	30 Apr
74.10	Johann	Kloek	BEL	4.12.75	1		Aartselaar	27 Jul
73.80	Christian	Nicolay	GER	4.3.76	1		Gegenbach	4 Sep
73.32	Esko	Mikkola	FIN	14.2.75	1		Huddinge	3 Sep
72.92	Sergey	Voynov	UZB	23.4.77	q	WJ	Lisboa	22 Jul
72.90	Isbel	Luaces	CUB	20.7.75	3	NC	La Habana	23 Jun
72.74		Wang Yichun	CHN		1	AsiC-j	Djakarta	17 Sep
72.10	Heilo	Väät	EST	25.8.75			Palanga	27 Aug
72.02	Hendrik	Fuhrmann	GER	17.2.75	1	NC-j	Ulm	31 Jul
72.02	Harri	Haatainen	FIN	5.1.78	1		Orimattila	10 Sep
71.88		Hu Sung-min	KOR	15.7.75	2	AsiC-j	Djakarta	17 Sep
71.82	Toru	Ue	JPN	25.6.75	q	WJ	Lisboa	22 Jul

Mark	Name		Nat	Born	Pos	Meet	Venue	Date
71.72	Kyoshi	Ishiba	JPN	9.7.76	q	WJ	Lisboa	22 Jul
71.52	Ali Saleh	Al Jadani	SAU	30.5.77	1		Damascus	25 Mar
71.38	Petri	Kuplainen	FIN	19.4.75	1		Kitee	1 Sep
71.36	Petteri	Piironen	FIN	10.12.76	1		Ikaalinen	17 May
71.32	Shane	Wyle	AUS	30.4.76	1	NC-j	Sydney	11 Mar

Decathlon

Mark	Name		Nat	Born	Pos	Meet	Venue	Date
7938	Frank	Busemann	GER	26.2.75	1		Zeven	2 Oct
	10.68 7.37	13.08 2.03 50.41			14.34 39.84 4.40 63.00 4:37.31			
7913	Raul	Duany	CUB	4.1.75	2	Barr	La Habana	26 May
	11.50 7.13	13.99 2.10 49.70			14.77 37.76 4.50 65.58 4:24.03			
7789	Pierre-Alexander	Vial	FRA	25.5.75	1		St Etienne	1 May
	10.82 7.29	12.90 1.86 48.98			14.61 42.98 4.80 54.04 4:30.41			
7724	Benjamin	Jensen	NOR	13.4.75	1	Sca-j	Hyyvinkää	3 Aug
	11.15 7.09	11.77 1.96 49.44			14.46 34.56 5.30 52.00 4:26.37			
7652	Prodomos	Korkizoglu	GRE	27.2.75	1		Thessaloniki	7 Aug
	10.88 7.41	12.86 2.06 50.26			14.92 40.38 4.50 53.36 4:53.00			
7567	Klaus	Isekenmeier	GER	14.4.75	1		Lage	15 May
	11.31w 6.98w	13.87 2.00 50.87			15.50 42.32 4.30 60.84 4:34.92			
7385		Sun Zhaohui	CHN	22.1.75	1	NC-j	Nanchang	27 Apr
	11.54 6.84	11.04 2.05 51.55			16.05 39.74 4.40 52.62 4:22.40			
7327w/7312	Ginés	Hidalgo	ESP	30.1.75	7		Alhama	5 Jun
	10.93w 7.32W/7.26w	12.80 1.85 49.44			15.62w 38.56 4.20 54.28 4:43.55			
7288	Glenn	Lindqvist	FIN	21.4.76	3	WJ	Lisboa	21 Jul
	11.54 6.78	12.30 1.85 50.64			15.32 40.62 4.60 56.82 4:31.60			
7267	Tage	Petersen	USA	18.3.75	3	NAIA	Azusa	26 May
	11.04 7.40	11.96 2.06 50.86			16.09 37.08 4.39 49.42 4:48.01			
7257	Alf-Gerrit	Christiansen	GER	30.3.75	2		Lage	15 May
	11.48w 7.06w	12.39 2.06 52.04			15.21 34.76 4.50 50.34 4:33.34			
7249	Thomas	Naubert	GER	11.6.76	2		Bernhausen	26 Jun
	11.08 6.91	13.93 1.82 51.19			14.67 36.82 4.40 49.18 4:38.80			
7217	Matej	Méhes	SVK	9.9.75	1		Nitra	31 May
	11.17w 7.31w	13.16 2.06 51.81			15.30w 37.26 3.60 57.90 4:53.35			
7173	Filip	Pejic	GER	26.2.75	3		Bernhausen	26 Jun
	10.84w 6.84	12.88 1.85 49.95			15.37 35.98 4.60 48.56 4:51.82			
7161	Alexander	Yurkov	UKR	21.7.75	2	NC	Kiev	27 May
	11.31 6.59	13.46 1.77 51.83			15.54 46.74 4.50 50.40 4:40.44			
7160	Yoelvis	Aguila	CUB	75	2		Santiago de Cuba	11 Dec
	10.9 7.18	12.10 2.00 50.5			14.9 39.14 3.30 56.42 4:40.4			
7155	Mikhail	Merzlikin	RUS	5.6.76	4		Krasnodar	17 Jun
	11.2 6.80	14.12 2.14 51.5			15.2 38.34 3.80 50.48 4:48.6			
7149	Jochen	Hegewald	GER	20.2.75	1	v3N-j	Bad Oeynhausen	7 Aug
	11.12 6.72	10.72 1.91 50.26			14.78 31.10 4.70 51.94 4:34.76			
7147	Gennadiy	Sitkevich	BLR	19.3.75	1		Gomel	11 Jun
	11.0 6.65	13.34 1.83 51.5			14.9 35.14 4.40 59.00 4:41.3			
7139	Pierre-Alain	Menneron	FRA	6.4.75	2		Saint Etienne	1 May
	10.63 7.26	12.41 1.86 49.54			14.96 34.52 4.00 46.00 4:50.31			

10000 Metres Walk (Track)

Mark	Name		Nat	Born	Pos	Meet	Venue	Date
40:13.11	Yevgeniy	Shmalyuk	RUS	14.1.76	1		St Peterburg	28 May
	40:32.72				2	WJ	Lisboa	21 Jul
40:26.93	Jorge	Segura	MEX	23.4.75	1	WJ	Lisboa	21 Jul
40:31.1	Aigars	Fadejevs	LAT	27.12.75	1		Valmiera	3 Sep
40:35.72	Artur	Meleshkevich	BLR	11.4.75	3	WJ	Lisboa	21 Jul
40:58.46	Sebastiano	Catania	ITA	13.4.75	4	WJ	Lisboa	21 Jul
41:01.97	Daisuke	Ikejima	JPN	30.1.75	5	WJ	Lisboa	21 Jul
41:05.63	Vitaliy	Stetsishchin	UKR	31.7.78	1		Kiev	12 Jun
41:23.35	Andreas	Erm	GER	12.3.76	1	v3N-j	Warszawa	18 Jun
41:28.14	Alejandro	López	MEX	9.2.75	6	WJ	Lisboa	21 Jul
41:46.30	Oleg	Ishutkin	RUS	22.7.75	7	WJ	Lisboa	21 Jul
41:50.0	Toshihito	Fujinohara	JPN	19.9.75	1		Matto	5 Jun
41:50.70	Dion	Russell	AUS	8.5.75	8	WJ	Lisboa	21 Jul
42:06.32	Lukasz	Szela	POL	10.2.75	1		Mielec	21 May
42:25.1A?	Stephen	Serg	KEN	75	1		Gusii	2 Jul
42:26.03	Marcos	Carracedo	ESP	29.12.75	10	WJ	Lisboa	21 Jul
42:26.17	João	Viera	POR	20.2.76	11	WJ	Lisboa	21 Jul
42:28.55	Peter	Barto	SVK	1.5.75	12	WJ	Lisboa	21 Jul
42:31.92	Lorenzo	Civallero	ITA	8.8.75	1		Livorno	9 Oct
42:35.67	Tobias	Persson	SWE	26.7.75	13	WJ	Lisboa	21 Jul

Mark	Name		Nat	Born	Pos	Meet	Venue	Date
42:47.62	Alejandro	Cambil	ESP	25.1.75	14	WJ	Lisboa	21 Jul
Road performance if better								
40:03	Artur	Meleshkevich	BLR	11.4.75	1		Novopolotsk	21 May
40:10unc	Jorge	Segura	MEX	23.4.75				
40:26	Aigars	Fadejevs	LAT	27.12.75	1		Eisenhüttenstadt	15 May
40:32	Andreas	Erm	GER	12.3.76	1		Eilenburg	1 Oct
40:40	Ivan	Trotskiy	BLR	27.5.76	2		Novopolotsk	21 May
41:42	Tobias	Persson	SWE	26.7.75				
41:46+	Toshihito	Fujinohara	JPN	19.9.75		In20k	Takahata	6 Jun
42:04	Silviu	Casandra	ROM	27.10.75	1		Ruse	9 Nov
42:20	Erik	Kalina	SVK	25.9.75	8		Trnava	28 May
42.39	Pavel	Alukayev	RUS	75			Esyevsk	26 Aug
42:43	Sergey	Melyentyev	RUS	76			Esyevsk	26 Aug
42:45	Aleksandr	Mironov	RUS	77			Esyevsk	26 Aug

20 Kilometres Walk

Mark	Name		Nat	Born	Pos	Meet	Venue	Date
1:21:27	Gao Yunbing		CHN	.10.75	9	NC	Beijing	7 Apr
1:23.41	Aigars	Fadejevs	LAT	27.12.75	1		Alitus	24 Sep
1:24:01	Ruslan	Shafikov	RUS	27.6.75	1	U23	Izhevsk	26 Aug
1:24:49	Jorge	Segura	MEX	23.4.75	5	NC	Xalapa	7 Aug
1:25:19	Daisuke	Ikeshima	JPN	30.1.75	4		Takahata	6 Nov
1:26.41	Andreas	Erm	GER	12.3.76	1		Offenburg	1 May
1:26.50	Artur	Meleshkevich	BLR	11.4.75	4		Brest	26 Mar

4x100 Metres

Mark	Nat	Team	Pos	Meet	Venue	Date
39.60	GBR	Gardener, Golding, Mackie, Cameron	1	WJ	Lisboa	24 Jul
39.66	THA	Natanee, Seeharwang, Vechaprutti, Namwong	1	AsiC-j	Djakarta	20 Sep
39.76	USA	Odom, Wheeler, P Johnson, T Jones	2	WJ	Lisboa	24 Jul
39.90	CAN	Chambers, Tomlin, Robinson, Frempong	3	WJ	Lisboa	24 Jul
40.03	JPN	Narita, Ebisawa, Arima, Imori	4	WJ	Lisboa	24 Jul
40.17	RSA	- Transvaal Roux, de Lange, Nel, Louw	1	NC-j	Bloemfontein	8 Apr
40.18	GHA		1		Cotonou	3 Apr
40.38	FRA	Baetz, Patros, Rubio, Jamain	5	WJ	Lisboa	24 Jul
40.46	JAM	- Vere TC	1		Philadelphia	30 Apr
40.54	UKR	Seniv, Dovgal, A Streltsov, Zamostyanik	1	vFRA-j	Dôle	7 Aug
40.85	ESP	Sabata, Quintana, Landa, José	3		Ciudad Réal	25 Jun
40.89	HUN		1		Zofingen	3 Jul
40.99	NOR	Venholen, Frabrot, Saeterstoel, Ertzgaard	4h2	WJ	Lisboa	23 Jul
41.06	MAS	Mahd, Nyambek, bin Saed, Ibrahim	3	AsiC-j	Djakarta	20 Sep
41.07	POL	Szymkowiak, Wrotek, Balcerzak, Krzywanski	3	v3N-j	Warszawa	18 Jun
41.09	GRE	Pavlakakis, Abatzopoulos, Hoidu, Korkizoglou	1h1	WJ	Lisboa	23 Jul
41.12	NZL	Blythe, Coad, Wise, Farrell	2		Walsdorf	10 Jul
41.13	SWE	U18 Eklund, Jansson, Olofsson, Hemström	1		Stockholm	27 Aug
41.26	TPE	Wu Ho-chin, Huang Hsiu-Ping, Wang Hsiong-Yi, Chen Chung-Hsiong	4h1	AsiC-j	Jakarta	20 Sep
41.33	SUI	Clerc, Grand, Dutoit, Tonazzi	1		Genéve	25 Jun

4x400 Metres

Mark	Nat	Team	Pos	Meet	Venue	Date
3:03.32	USA	Johnson, Wheeler, Campbell, Clay	1	WJ	Lisboa	24 Jul
3:04.12	JAM	R McDonald, D Clarke, Watts, M McDonald	2	WJ	Lisboa	24 Jul
3:06.17A	RSA	- Transvaal	1	NC	Secunda	7 May
3:06.59	GBR	Bullock, Budden, Levy, Hylton	3	WJ	Lisboa	24 Jul
3:07.25	NZL	Armstrong, Keddell, Donaldson, Farrell	4	WJ	Lisboa	24 Jul
3:08.06	JPN	Hattori, Tsukada, Okumura, Taga	5	WJ	Lisboa	24 Jul
3:08.77	GER	Krause, Schnorrenberger, Regenärmel, Seidler	6	WJ	Lisboa	24 Jul
3:09.68	NGR	Adejuyigbe, Omodiale, Ogbeide, Obikwelu	7	WJ	Lisboa	24 Jul
3:10.30	CUB	Vera, González, Benet, Miranda	8	WJ	Lisboa	24 Jul
3:11.36	FRA	Loubli, Lucea, Saticouche, Ravenet	3h2	WJ	Lisboa	23 Jul
3:11.29	FIN	Nordman, Hartonen, Lönnqvist, Pohjonen	1		Turku	1 Jul
3:11.61	UKR	Gorin, Kochenko, Zikharniy?, Gorbenko	1	v2N-j	Dôle	7 Aug
3:11.98	RUS	Bugayev, Urazov, Piankov, Schieglov	2	v3N-j	Warszawa	18 Jun
3:12.39	AUS	Gallagher, S Travis, Beckenham, P Travis	5h3	WJ	Lisboa	23 Jul
3:12.42	IND	Prodhan, Kumar, Aiyappa, Basak	2	AsiC-j	Djakarta	19 Sep
3:12.51	GRE	Iakovakis, Sarris, Mantelidis, Batsikas	3h1	WJ	Lisboa	23 Jul
3:12.6	SAU	Al-Seardan, Al-Bishi, Marzouk, Al-Somaily	1		Tunis	12 Aug
3:12.70	POL	Kuznicki, Bocian, Trelka, Grumant 3:10.70	4	v3N-j	Warszawa	18 Jun
3:13.37	NOR		3		Huddinge	4 Sep
3:13.65	ITA		2		Sevilla	9 Jul

WOMEN'S WORLD LISTS 1994

100 METRES

Mark	Wind	Name		Nat	Born	Pos	Meet	Venue	Date
10.77	0.9	Irina	Privalova	RUS	12.11.68	1rA	Athl	Lausanne	6 Jul
10.78	0.4	Merlene	Ottey	JAM	10.5.60	1	GPF	Paris	3 Sep
10.82	0.4	Gwen	Torrence	USA	12.6.65	2	GPF	Paris	3 Sep
10.83	0.0		Torrence			1	VD	Bruxelles	19 Aug
10.85	0.9		Torrence			2A	Athl	Lausanne	6 Jul
10.87	0.0		Torrence			1	Herc	Monaco	2 Aug
10.87	0.0		Torrence			1	v Afr	Durham	13 Aug
10.89	0.4		Torrence			1A	GP II	Linz	4 Jul
10.90	1.9		Privalova			1	DNG	Stockholm	12 Jul
10.92	0.0		Ottey			2	VD	Bruxelles	19 Aug
10.95	0.9		Ottey			3A	Athl	Lausanne	6 Jul
10.95	0.5		Torrence			1	GWG	St Peterburg	24 Jul
10.95	0.1		Torrence			1	ASV	Köln	21 Aug
10.98	0.5		Privalova			2	GWG	St Peterburg	24 Jul
10.99	0.4	Zhanna	Tarnopolskaya	UKR	6.7.72	2A	GP II	Linz	4 Jul
11.00	0.5		Tarnopolskaya			1		Kiev	28 May
11.00	0.0		Privalova			1	BNP	Villeneuve d'Ascq	8 Jul
11.01	0.9	Juliet	Cuthbert	JAM	9.4.64	4A	Athl	Lausanne	6 Jul
11.01	0.9		Tarnopolskaya			1q2	EC	Helsinki	7 Aug
11.02	0.3		Tarnopolskaya			1s		Kiev	28 May
11.02	0.1		Ottey			1	WG	Helsinki	29 Jun
11.02	0.6		Privalova			1	EC	Helsinki	8 Aug
11.02	0.4		Privalova			3	GPF	Paris	3 Sep
11.02	0.0		Privalova			1		Madrid	6 Sep
11.03	2.0	Holli	Hyche	USA	6.9.71	1s1	NCAA	Boise	3 Jun
11.03	0.0		Privalova			2	Herc	Monaco	2 Aug
11.03	0.1		Privalova			2	ASV	Köln	21 Aug
11.03	1.5	Mary	Onyali	NGR	3.2.68	1s2	CG	Victoria	23 Aug
11.05	1.1		Torrence			1		Luzern	29 Jun
11.06	0.0		Onyali			2	v USA	Durham	13 Aug
11.06	0.2		Onyali			1	CG	Victoria	23 Aug
		(31/7)							
11.07	1.8	Cheryl	Taplin	USA	2.9.72	1		Baton Rouge	25 May
11.11	1.1	Patricia	Girard	FRA	8.4.68	1s1	FranG	Bondoufle	11 Jul
11.12	2.0	D'Andre	Hill	USA	19.4.73	2s1	NCAA	Boise	3 Jun
		(10)							
11.12	0.9-	Gail	Devers	USA	19.11.66	1	NC	Knoxville	16 Jun
11.12	1.7	Melanie	Paschke	GER	29.6.70	1s1	NC	Erfurt	1 Jul
11.12A	1.9	Melinda	Gainsford	AUS	1.10.71	1		Sestriere	31 Jul
11.12	0.4	Carlette	Guidry	USA	4.9.68	4	GPF	Paris	3 Sep
11.14	0.0	Liliana	Allen	CUB	24.6.70	2		Madrid	6 Sep
11.15	1.0-	Marina	Trandenkova	RUS	7.1.67	2s1	NC	St Peterburg	14 Jul
11.15	1.5	Paula	Thomas	GBR	3.12.64	2s2	CG	Victoria	23 Aug
11.19	1.5	Christy	Opara-Thompson	NGR	2.5.70	3s2	CG	Victoria	23 Aug
11.21	1.1	Yekaterina	Leshcheva	RUS	21.4.74	1h1	NC	St Peterburg	14 Jul
11.23	-0.1	Petja	Pendareva	BUL	20.1.71	1s2		Sofia	14 May
		(20)							
11.24	1.1	Cathy	Freeman	AUS	16.2.73	1		Brisbane	5 Feb
11.25	0.3	Desislava	Dimitrova	BUL	19.6.72	2	NC	Sofia	2 Jul
11.25	1.2	Mary	Tombiri	NGR	23.7.72	1s1	CG	Victoria	23 Aug
11.26	0.2	Sheila	Echols	USA	2.10.64	2		Kingston	7 May
11.27	-0.7	Natalya	Anisimova	RUS	4.3.73	2s2	NC	St Peterburg	14 Jul
11.27	0.0	Jacqueline	Poelman	NED	5.10.73	1		Hechtel	30 Jul
11.27	0.8		Liu Xiaomei	CHN	11.1.72	1	AsiG	Hiroshima	14 Oct
11.28	0.9	Olga	Bogoslovskaya ¶	RUS	20.5.64	2	APM	Hengelo	4 Jun
11.29	1.5	Hermin	Joseph	DMN	13.4.64	4s2	CG	Victoria	23 Aug
11.30	-0.7	Yelena	Dubtsova	RUS	6.5.71	3s2	NC	St Peterburg	14 Jul
		(30)							
11.30	1.6	Sandra	Myers	ESP	9.1.61	1		La Laguna	11 Sep
11.31	1.3	Dedra	Davis	BAH	17.7.73	1		Knoxville	2 Apr
11.32	1.0	Wenda	Vereen	USA	24.4.66	1	MSR	Walnut	17 Apr
11.32	1.6	Inger	Miller	USA	12.12.72	2s2	NCAA	Boise	3 Jun
11.32	0.0	Dahlia	Duhaney	JAM	20.7.70	1	NC	Kingston	1 Jul

Mark	Wind	Name		Nat	Born	Pos	Meet	Venue	Date
11.32	-0.1	Chryste	Gaines	USA	14.9.70	1	USOF	Edwardsville	9 Jul
11.33	0.3	Dannette	Young	USA	6.10.64	2		Clemson	14 May
11.33	1.6	Merlene	Frazer	JAM	27.12.73	3s2	NCAA	Boise	3 Jun
11.33	0.3	Anelia	Nuneva	BUL	30.6.62	2q3	EC	Helsinki	7 Aug
11.34	0.9	Katharine	Merry	GBR	21.9.74	2	ECp	Birmingham	25 Jun
		(40)							
11.34	1.2	Stephanie	Douglas	GBR	22.1.69	3s1	CG	Victoria	23 Aug
11.35	1.3	Mercy	Nku	NGR	17.7.76	1s2	NC-j	Benin City	26 May
11.35	-1.1	Oksana	Dyachenko	RUS	26.11.74	1h1		Budapest	3 Jun
11.35	2.0	Faith	Idehen	NGR	5.2.73	3s1	NCAA	Boise	3 Jun
11.35	0.2	Nelli	Cooman	NED	6.6.64	1h4	EC	Helsinki	7 Aug
11.36	1.3	Sue	Walton	USA	21.8.72	2		Knoxville	2 Apr
11.36	1.6	Melinda	Sergent	USA	72	4s1	NCAA	Boise	3 Jun
11.36A	-0.1	Aspen	Burkett	USA	8.3.76	1		Denver	11 Jun
11.36	2.0	Sabrina	Herring-Kelly	USA	20.8.75	1	WJ	Lisboa	21 Jul
11.36	2.0	Sanna	Hernesniemi	FIN	9.3.71	1	NC	Tuusula	9 Jul
		(50)							
11.37	2.0		Chen Zhaojing	CHN	5.4.69	1	AsiG	Hiroshima	29 Apr
11.37	1.7	Natalya	Voronova #	RUS	9.7.65	5	Banes	São Paulo	21 May
11.37	1.0	Pauline	Davis	BAH	9.7.66	1		Budapest	3 Jun
11.37	2.0	Odiah	Sidibé	FRA	13.1.70	1s2	FranG	Bondoufle	11 Jul
11.38	0.4	Heike	Drechsler	GER	16.12.64	7A	GP II	Linz	4 Jul
11.38	1.1	Lalao	Ravaonirina	MAD	8.11.63	2s1	FranG	Bondoufle	11 Jul
11.38	-1.0	Natalya	Merzlyakova	RUS	65	3h1	NC	St Peterburg	14 Jul
11.39	1.6	Heather	Samuel	ANT	6.7.70	5s2	NCAA	Boise	3 Jun
11.39	1.3	Silke	Knoll	GER	21.2.67	2		Duisburg	12 Jun
11.39	-0.8	Bettina	Zipp	GER	29.4.72	1s2	NC	Erfurt	1 Jul
		(60)							
11.39	-0.1	Sabine	Tröger	AUT	7.7.67	1	NC	Linz	8 Jul
11.39	0.8	Philomina	Mensah	GHA	11.5.75	1s1	WJ	Lisboa	21 Jul
11.40	0.4	Flirtisha	Harris	USA	21.2.72	3	PennR	Philadelhia	30 Apr
11.40	1.9		Huang Xiaoyan	CHN	3.12.69	h	NC	Beijing	3 Jun
11.40	2.0	Marion	Jones	USA	12.10.75	4s1	NCAA	Boise	3 Jun
11.40		Michele	Collins	USA	12.2.71	1		Rovereto	24 Jul
11.41	-0.4	Maya	Azarashvili	GEO	12.4.64	2		Duisburg	12 Jun
11.41	0.2	Irina	Pukha	UKR	10.1.73	1		Kiev	24 Apr
11.41	0.6	Maguy	Nestoret	FRA	28.7.69	1		La Chaux-de-Fonds	21 Aug
11.41	1.0		Chen Yan	CHN	27.11.73	1		Tangshan	30 Aug
		(70)							
11.41	0.8		Wang Huei-chen	TPE	21.2.70	2	AsiG	Hiroshima	14 Oct
11.42	0.9	Kwajalein	Butler	USA	23.7.76	1		Baton Rouge	7 May
11.42	0.8	Richelle	Webb	USA	8.10.71	1	Big10	Madison	22 May
11.42	0.3	Savathea	Fynes	BAH	17.10.74	1h3	NAIA	Azusa	26 May
11.42	1.4	Galina	Malchugina	RUS	17.12.62	4B	Athl	Lausanne	6 Jul
11.42	1.4	Odile	Singa	FRA	29.12.67	1h1	NC	Annecy	23 Jul
11.42	2.0	Damarayanthi	Darsha	SRI	13.2.75	1	AsiC-j	Jakarta	18 Sep
11.43		Keisha	Criswell	USA	73	2		Fresno	21 May
11.43	0.3	Zlatka	Georgieva	BUL	20.7.69	3	NC	Sofia	2 Jul
11.43	1.3	Ekaterini	Thanou	GRE	1.2.75	2s2	WJ	Lisboa	21 Jul
		(80)							
11.43	1.8	Olga	Voronova	RUS	23.2.68	2		St Peterburg	2 Aug
11.43	1.2	Kàtia	Santos	BRA	31.12.67	1		São Paulo	13 Aug
11.43		Rachita	Panda	IND	4.3.74	1		Lucknow	25 Aug
11.44	1.5	Shantel	Twiggs	USA	4.10.72	1h2	Drake	Des Moines	29 Apr
11.45	1.8	Twilet	Malcolm	JAM	5.2.69	2		Baton Rouge	25 May
11.45		Endurance	Ojokolo	NGR	27.5.77	2	NC-j	Benin City	28 May
11.45	1.2	Donna	Smith	USA	7.9.72	5h1	NCAA	Boise	2 Jun
11.45	1.9		Wang Jing	CHN	16.1.75	2h	NC	Beijing	3 Jun
11.45	1.3	Nicole	Mitchell	JAM	5.6.74	3		Duisburg	12 Jun
11.45	-1.4	Nadezhda	Roshchupkina	RUS	14.6.63	4s1	NC	St Peterburg	14 Jul
		(90)							
11.46	1.3	Ekaterini	Koffa	GRE	10.4.69	1		Athina	28 May
11.46	1.2	Marcia	Richardson	GBR	10.2.72	2h3	AAA	Sheffield	11 Jun
11.46	0.0	Regula	Anliker-Aebi	SUI	12.11.65	1		Genève	18 Jun
11.47	0.7	Beverley	McDonald	JAM	15.2.70	7	Banes	São Paulo	21 May
11.47	-0.6	Elinda	Vorster	RSA	8.9.65	1		Ingolstadt	17 Jul
11.47	0.2	Oksana	Levenets	UKR	6.6.72	2		Kiev	23 Jul
11.47	1.5	Simmone	Jacobs	GBR	5.9.66	6s2	CG	Victoria	23 Aug
11.48	1.8	Zundra	Feagin	USA	12.7.73	3		Baton Rouge	25 May

Mark	Wind	Name		Nat	Born	Pos	Meet	Venue	Date
11.48		Chinedu	Odozor	NGR	77	3	NC-j	Benin City	28 May
11.48	2.0	Ndèye Binta (100)	Dia	SEN	8.4.73	2s2	FranG	Bondoufle	11 Jul
11.48	-3.7	Yelena	Mizera	RUS	22.2.66	4s2	NC	St Peterburg	14 Jul
11.48	2.0	Debbie	Ferguson	BAH	16.1.76	5	WJ	Lisboa	21 Jul
11.48A	1.9	Laura	Ardissone	ITA	7.2.69	2		Sestriere	31 Jul

Mark	Wind	Name		Nat	Born	Date
11.49		Omegia	Keeys	USA	75	23 Apr
11.49	-0.1	Iva	Prandzheva	BUL	72	14 May
11.49	0.8		Lee Young-suk	KOR	65	17 Jun
11.49	-0.1	Frédérique	Bangué	FRA	76	18 Jun
11.49	-0.7	Tina	Schönmetzler	GER	71	23 Jul
11.49	1.8	Zoya	Sokolova	RUS	70	2 Aug
11.49	2.0	Susanthika	Jayasinghe	SRI	75	18 Sep
11.50	1.7	Andrea	Philipp	GER	71	1 Jul
11.50	1.3	Dainelky	Pérez	CUB	76	21 Jul
11.50	1.4	Valérie	Jean-Charles	FRA	69	23 Jul
11.51	1.1	Monque	Miers	AUS	70	5 Feb
11.51	0.7	Cleide	Amaral	BRA	67	21 May
11.51	-0.8	Silke	Lichtenhagen	GER	73	1 Jul
11.51	0.2	Lyudmila	Antonova	UKR	70	23 Jul
11.51	0.5	Michelle	Seymour	NZL	65	22 Aug
11.51	0.4	Felipa	Palacios	COL	75	24 Nov
11.52	0.6	Éva	Barati	HUN	68	19 Jun
11.52	1.5	Sara	Wüest	SUI	69	19 Jun
11.52	1.0	Marie-Joëlle	Dogbo	FRA	75	2 Jul
11.52	0.8	Mireille	Donders	SUI	74	16 Jul
11.52	0.8	Kerry-Ann	Richards	JAM	76	21 Jul
11.52	1.1		Ou Yanlan	CHN	74	28 Jul
11.52	0.0		Qi Hong	CHN	69	30 Aug
11.53	2.0	Dawn	Bowles	USA	68	2 Apr
11.53	0.6	Lucrécia	Jardim	POR	71	29 May
11.53	0.3	Monika	Gachevska	BUL	74	2 Jul
11.53		Zhanna	Levashova	RUS	70	9 Sep
11.54	1.9	Lesa	Parker	USA	74	26 Mar
11.54	1.5	Andria	Lloyd	JAM	71	15 May
11.54		Yelena	Vinogradova	BLR	64	29 May
11.54	0.3	Giada	Gallina	ITA	73	8 Jun
11.54	0.3	Calister	Uba	NGR	73	9 Jun
11.54		Eldece	Clarke	BAH	65	18 Jun
11.54	1.3	Ingvild	Larsen	NOR	76	8 Jul
11.54	2.0		Gao Chunxia	CHN		19 Sep
11.55A	1.7	Celena	Mondie-Milner	USA	68	16 Apr
11.55	1.4	Kay	Iheagwam	NGR	68	21 May
11.55	0.8	Tonya	Williams	USA	74	22 May
11.55	0.0	Michelle	Christie	JAM	73	28 May
11.55	1.1	Erika	Suchovská	TCH	67	1 Jun
11.55	0.3	Vyara	Georgieva	BUL	77	2 Jul
11.55	0.9	Natalya	Yudakova	RUS	65	9 Jul
11.55	0.7	Catherine	Lenoir	BEL	73	9 Jul
11.55	1.1	Larisa	Dolmatova	RUS	71	14 Jul
11.55	1.4	Marina	Zhirova	RUS	63	14 Jul
11.56	1.2	Zenia	Ayrton	IND	72	16 Apr
11.56	1.0	Teresa (150)	Neighbors	USA	67	17 Apr
11.56	0.2	Anzhelika	Shevchuk	UKR	69	24 Jul
11.56	0.1	Michelle	Freeman	JAM	69	29 Jul
11.56	0.9	Irina	Slyusar	UKR	63	31 Jul
11.56	0.5	Doris	Manu	GHA		22 Aug
11.57	0.0	Andrea	Anderson	USA	77	9 Apr
11.57	0.2	Lou Ann	Williams	TRI	72	7 May
11.57	-2.1		Chen Shu-Chen	TPE	75	28 May
11.57	1.2	Dee	Bradley	USA	74	2 Jun
11.57	2.0	Hanitriniain	Rakotondrabe	MAD	67	11 Jul
11.58	1.3	Heather	Sumpter	USA	77	3 Jun
11.58	1.7	Violetta	Lapierre	FRA	63	17 Jun
11.58	1.3	Karen	Clarke	CAN	67	29 Jul
11.58	1.8	Yelena	Kuzina	RUS	66	2 Aug
11.58			Chan Sau Ying	HKG	70	13 Aug
11.58	0.8	Toshie	Kitada	JPN	69	14 Oct
11.59		Olga	Robinson	JAM		9 Apr
11.59		She She	Crawford	USA	70	16 Apr
11.60	1.0	Keisha	Owens	USA	73	29 Apr
11.60	1.7	Kim	Baldwin	USA	75	22 May
11.60		Tisha	Prather	USA	71	22 May
11.60	0.4		Chen Shu-Chen	TPE	75	28 May
11.60	1.4	Dionne	Wright	CAN	66	30 Jun
11.60	0.8		Huang Mei	CHN	75	21 Jul
11.60A	1.9	Annarita	Balzani	ITA	67	31 Jul
11.60	0.6	Muriel	Leroy	FRA	68	21 Aug
11.60	1.2	Danaa	Myhill	GBR	70	22 Aug

Track 4cm short and wind gauge illegally placed

Mark	Wind	Name		Nat	Born	Pos	Meet	Venue	Date
11.33	1.1	Sabrina	Herring-Kelly	USA	20.8.75	1	JUCO	Odessa, Tx	20 May
11.40	1.1	Dana	Collins	USA	23.7.73	2	JUCO	Odessa, Tx	20 May
11.43	1.1	Christian	Robertson	USA	27.10.74	3	JUCO	Odessa, Tx	20 May
11.56		Hydie Ann	Harper	TRI					

Drugs disqualification

Mark	Wind	Name		Nat	Born	Pos	Meet	Venue	Date
11.13	-1.0	Natalya	Voronova #	RUS	9.7.65	1s1	NC	St Peterburg	14 Jul
11.21	1.8	Olga	Bogoslovskaya ¶	RUS	20.5.64	1		Cottbus	15 Jun

Wind assisted

Mark	Wind	Name		Nat	Born	Pos	Meet	Venue	Date
10.77	2.3	Gail	Devers	USA	19.11.66	1	Jen	San José	28 May
10.97	2.3	Carlette	Guidry	USA	4.9.68	2	Jen	San José	28 May
10.97	2.2		Ottey	JAM		1		København	28 Aug
10.99	4.0	Cheryl	Taplin	USA	2.9.73	1	TexR	Austin	8 Apr
10.99	7.9	Inger	Miller	USA	12.6.72	1		Las Vegas	9 Apr
10.99		Chryste	Gaines	USA	14.9.70	1		Abilene	12 May
11.02	2.8		Privalova			1		Rieti	28 Aug
11.04	2.3		Cuthbert			3	Jen	San José	28 May
11.13	2.3	Sheila	Echols	USA	2.10.64	2	Jen	San José	28 May
11.15	3.8	Cathy	Freeman	AUS	16.2.73	2		Perth	13 Feb
11.15	4.0	Zlatka	Georgieva	BUL	20.7.69	1		Stara Zagora	16 Jul
11.18	3.2	Petja	Pendareva	BUL	20.1.71	1A		Dijon	12 Jun
11.18	4.0	Anelia	Nuneva	BUL	30.6.62	2		Stara Zagora	16 Jul
11.20	3.8	Shantel	Twiggs	USA	4.10.72	2		Wichita	20 May
11.22	3.2	Michelle	Collins	USA	12.2.71	1		Houston	7 May
11.22	2.3	Dahlia	Duhaney	JAM	20.7.70	5	Jen	San José	28 May
11.22	3.7	Maya	Azarashvili	GEO	6.4.64	1		Nurmijärvi	2 Jul
11.23		Sophia	Brown	JAM	73	1		Stillwater	2 Apr
11.23	4.0	Desislava	Dimitrova	BUL	19.6.72	3		Stara Zagora	16 Jul

Mark	Wind	Name		Nat	Born	Pos	Meet	Venue	Date
11.23	3.6		Liu Xiaomei	CHN	11.1.72	1h1	AsiG	Hiroshima	12 Oct
11.26	4.1	Andrea	Philip	GER	29.7.71	1		Rostock	4 Jun
11.27	2.9	Katharine	Merry	GBR	21.9.74	1	AAA	Sheffield	11 Jun
11.28	2.2	Pauline	Davis	BAH	9.7.66	2		Austin	7 May
11.30	2.4	Frédérique	Bangué	FRA	31.12.76	1B		Dijon	12 Jun
11.34	3.7	Elinda	Vorster	RSA	8.9.65	2		Nurmijärvi	2 Jul
11.35	5.0	Anita	Howard	USA	22.3.69	2		San Marcos	30 Apr
11.35	2.8		Wang Huei-chen	TPE	21.2.70	1h3	AsiG	Hiroshima	12 Oct
11.36	2.6	Kwani	Stewart	USA	9.10.72	1h2		Lawrence	21 May
11.36	3.5	Lucrécia	Jardim	POR	28.1.71	1	ECp I	Valencia	11 Jun
11.37	2.9	Simmone	Jacobs	GBR	5.9.66	3	AAA	Sheffield	11 Jun
11.37	2.4	Fabienne	Ficher	FRA	25.4.66	2B		Dijon	12 Jun
11.38	2.2	Michelle	Freeman	JAM	5.5.69	4		Austin	7 May
11.39	2.2	Twilet	Malcolm	JAM	5.2.69	5		Austin	7 May
11.39	2.9	Marcia	Richardson	GBR	10.2.72	4	AAA	Sheffield	11 Jun
11.39	2.8		Lee Young-suk	KOR	16.12.65	2h3	AsiG	Hiroshima	12 Oct
11.40	3.5	Giada	Gallina	ITA	1.3.73	2	ECp I	Valencia	11 Jun
11.40	3.5	Erika	Suchovská	TCH	27.7.67	3	ECp I	Valencia	11 Jun
11.42	3.4	Michelle	Seymour	NZL	21.12.65	1	NC	Hamilton	4 Mar
11.42		Savathea	Fynes	BAH	17.10.74	1		Baton Rouge	19 Mar
11.42	2.4	Violetta	Lapierre	FRA	15.10.63	3B		Dijon	12 Jun
11.43	3.2	Crystal	Braddock	USA	13.12.70	1A		Austin	6 May
11.43	2.6	Kathy	Travis	USA	12.3.73	2		Lawrence	21 May
11.43	5.2	Donna	Smith	USA	7.9.72	1h2		Waco	25 May
11.43	3.5	Sara	Wüest	SUI	4.8.69	5	ECp I	Valencia	11 Jun
11.44	4.2	Lesa	Parker	USA	8.1.74	2h4	TexR	Austin	8 Apr
11.44	5.6	Michelle	Christie	JAM	73	2		Des Moines	16 Apr
11.44		Natasha	Shafer	USA	22.2.73	1	KansR	Lawrence	23 Apr
11.47		Dawn	Bowles	USA	12.11.68	2		Baton Rouge	19 Mar
11.47		She She	Crawford	USA	28.12.70	3		Abilene	12 May
11.47	2.4	Delphine	Combe	FRA	6.12.74	4B		Dijon	12 Jun

Mark	Wind	Name		Nat	Born	Date
11.48		LaKeisha	Backus	USA	76	6 May
11.48	2.8	Toshie	Kitada	JPN	69	12 Oct
11.49		Gwen	Clardy	USA	73	1 Apr
11.49	3.2	Teresa	Neighbors	USA	67	7 May
11.49	2.3	Andria	Lloyd	JAM	71	14 May
11.49	3.7	Anu	Pirttimaa	FIN	72	2 Jul
11.50		Kenya	Alex	USA	74	5 Mar
11.50	4.1	Rebecca	Drummond	GBR	78	9 Jul
11.51	5.1	Aline	André	FRA	73	4 Jun
11.51	2.9	Geraldine	McLeod	GBR	71	11 Jun
11.51	2.9	Marie-Joëlle	Dogbo	FRA	75	26 Jun
11.52	3.1	Margarita	Molchan	BLR	66	30 Jun
11.53	5.0	Hydie Ann	Harper	TRI		8 Apr
11.53	3.3	Dee	Bradley	USA	74	6 May
11.53	3.2	Vonda	Newhouse	USA	74	7 May
11.53	2.3	Simone	Tomlinson	CAN	76	29 Jul
11.54	2.4	Muriel	Leroy	FRA	68	12 Jun
11.54	2.3	Karen	Clarke	CAN	67	29 Jul
11.55	3.8	Kathy	Sambell	AUS	63	13 Feb
11.56	2.2	Passion	Richardson	USA	75	8 Apr
11.56	3.3	Aileen	McGillivary	GBR	70	25 Jun
11.57	2.3	Regina	Frye	USA	72	14 May
11.58		Nicole	Green	USA	71	23 Apr
11.58	2.9	Kim	Baldwin	USA	75	21 May
11.58	2.9	Danaa	Myhill	GBR	70	11 Jun
11.58	2.1	Dionne	Wright	CAN	66	19 Jun
11.58		Kelly	Perryman	USA	77	10 Jul
11.59	3.8	Nicole	Vassella	AUS	69	13 Feb
11.59	2.7	Kim	McGruder	USA	77	30 Apr
11.59	2.6	Tanja	Reid	CAN	72	30 Jun

Best at low altitude

Mark	Wind	Name	Pos	Meet	Venue	Date
11.25	-0.2	Gainsford	1	NEC	Melbourne	24 Feb
11.38	1.3	Burkett	1s2	WJ	Lisboa	21 Jul
11.56		Mondie-Milner				23 Apr

Wind assisted

Mark	Wind	Name	Pos	Meet	Venue	Date
11.12	3.8	Gainsford	1		Perth	13 Feb

Doubtful

Mark	Wind	Name		Nat	Born	Pos	Meet	Venue	Date
11.42A		Mirtha	Brack	COL	9.4.70	1	NC	Cali	29 Jul
11.52A		Patricia	Rodriguez	COL	25.10.70	2	NC	Cali	29 Jul

Hand timed

Mark	Wind	Name		Nat	Born	Pos	Meet	Venue	Date
10.8		Svetlana	Goncharenko	RUS	28.5.71	1		Stavropol	28 May
10.9A		Liliana	Allen	CUB	24.6.70	1		Cali	9 Apr
11.0		Heather	Samuel	ANT	6.7.70	1		Murray	23 Apr
11.0	2.0	Nadezhda	Roshchupkina	RUS	14.6.63	1		Bryansk	28 May
11.0	2.0	Oksana	Khreskina	RUS	21.6.72	2		Bryansk	28 May
11.0	0.4	Tulia	Robinson	JAM	4.2.79	1	CAC17	Port of Spain	8 Jul
11.0	0.7	Yelena	Dubtsova	RUS	6.5.71	1		Bryansk	6 Aug
11.1		Natalya	Shatalova	RUS	73	2		Stavropol	28 May
11.1		Hydie Ann	Harper	TRI		1	NC	Port of Spain	11 Jun
11.1		Natalya	Anisimova	RUS	4.3.73	1h	NC-23	Voronezh	18 Jun
11.1	1.8	Debbie	Ferguson	BAH	16.1.76	1	CAC-j	Port of Spain	8 Jul
11.1	1.8	Beverley	Langley	JAM	16.12.76	2	CAC-j	Port of Spain	8 Jul
11.1	0.7	Yelena	Kuzina	RUS	66	2		Bryansk	6 Aug
11.1	0.7	Olga	Voronova	RUS	23.2.68	3		Bryansk	6 Aug
11.2	1.9	Chryste	Gaines	USA	14.9.70	1		San Luis Obispo	19 Mar

Mark	Wind	Name		Nat	Born	Pos	Meet	Venue	Date
11.2		Tatyana	Tereshchuk	UKR	11.10.69	1		Lugansk	12 May
11.2		Geraldine	McLeod	GBR	24.9.71	1		Los Angeles	21 May
11.2		Olga	Povtaryova	RUS	73	3		Stavropol	28 May
11.2		Oksana	Dyachenko	RUS	26.11.74	h	NC-23	Voronezh	18 Jun
11.2		Yekaterina	Leshchova	RUS	21.4.74	h	NC-23	Voronezh	18 Jun
11.2	1.8	Kerry-Ann	Richards	JAM	22.4.76	3	CAC-j	Port of Spain	8 Jul
11.2	1.7	Aspen	Burkett	USA	8.3.76	1	v CAN	Buffalo	14 Jul

Mark	Wind	Name		Nat	Born	Date
11.3	0.4	Ayana	Hutchinson	TRI	78	8 Jul
11.3	1.4	Merlene	Frazer	JAM	73	24 Apr
11.3		Oksana	Levenets	UKR	72	13 May
11.3	0.3	Anzhelika	Shevchuk	UKR	69	14 May
11.3		.	Ignatova	RUS		28 May
11.3		Yelena	Kuzina	RUS	66	28 May
11.3		Yulia	Timofeyeva	RUS	72	18 Jun
11.3	0.4	Ayana	Hutchinson	TRI	78	10 Jul
11.3	1.7	Sabrina	Herring-Kelly	USA	75	14 Jul
11.3	1.7	Simone	Tomlinson	CAN	76	14 Jul

Wind assisted

Mark	Wind	Name		Nat	Born	Pos	Meet	Venue	Date
11.2		Savathea	Fynes	BAH	17.10.74	1		Prairie View	25 Mar
11.2		Latasha	Gilliam	USA	19.2.76	1			Mar

Mark	Wind	Name		Nat	Born	Date
11.3		Sonya	Shepherd	USA	73	25 Mar
11.3		Chantel	Rolle	BAH	73	26 Mar
11.3	3.8	Lakeisha	Backus	USA	76	14 May
11.3	6.4	Jodi	Lambert	AUS	70	12 Nov

Wind and doubtful Oct 17, Pereira (A?): 1. Mirtha Brack COL 9.4.70 11.0; 2. Felipa Palacios COL 1.12.75 11.2; 3. Patricia Rodriguez COL 25.10.70 11.3.

200 METRES

Mark	Wind	Name		Nat	Born	Pos	Meet	Venue	Date
21.85	-0.8	Gwen	Torrence	USA	12.6.65	1	v Afr	Durham	12 Aug
21.94			Torrence			1	Bisl	Oslo	22 Jul
22.02	0.5	Irina	Privalova	RUS	12.11.68	1	DNG	Stockholm	12 Jul
22.04	0.5		Torrence			2	DNG	Stockholm	12 Jul
22.07	0.4	Merlene	Ottey	JAM	10.5.60	1A	ISTAF	Berlin	30 Aug
22.09	0.7		Torrence			1	GWG	St Peterburg	25 Jul
22.15	1.0		Privalova			1A	WK	Zürich	17 Aug
22.15	0.4		Torrence			2A	ISTAF	Berlin	30 Aug
22.16	1.0		Torrence			2A	WK	Zürich	17 Aug
22.19	0.9		Privalova			2	Bisl	Oslo	22 Jul
22.21	1.5		Privalova			1		Rieti	28 Aug
22.21			Ottey			1		Pune	13 Sep
22.22	0.0		Privalova			1	VD	Bruxelles	19 Aug
22.23	0.7		Privalova			2	GWG	St Peterburg	25 Jul
22.23	1.7		Ottey			1	WCp	London	9 Sep
22.24	0.3		Torrence			1	TOTO	Tokyo	15 Sep
22.25	1.3	Cathy	Freeman	AUS	16.2.73	1	CG	Victoria	26 Aug
22.29	0.9	Galina	Malchugina	RUS	17.12.62	1	NC	St Peterburg	16 Jul
22.29	-0.8	Dannette	Young	USA	6.10.64	2	v Afr	Durham	12 Aug
22.32	-0.5	Melinda	Gainsford	AUS	1.10.71	1		Hobart	26 Feb
22.32	0.9		Freeman			3	Bisl	Oslo	22 Jul
22.32	0.2		Privalova			1	EC	Helsinki	11 Aug
22.33	1.5		Torrence			1		Luzern	29 Jun
22.35	1.3	Mary	Onyali	NGR	3.2.68	2	CG	Victoria	26 Aug
22.37	0.4		Privalova			3A	ISTAF	Berlin	30 Aug
22.38	0.8	Carlette	Guidry	USA	4.9.68	3	v Afr	Durham	12 Aug
22.39	1.0		Young			1A	DogwR	Knoxville	8 Apr
22.40	0.8		Torrence			1	Drake	Des Moines	30 Apr
22.40	0.0		Guidry			2	VD	Bruxelles	19 Aug
22.41	1.3	Holli	Hyche	USA	6.9.71	1h1	NCAA	Boise	1 Jun
22.41	1.0		Ottey			3A	WK	Zürich	17 Aug
		(31/10)							
22.45	1.4	Melanie	Paschke	GER	29.6.70	1	NC	Erfurt	3 Jul
22.52	2.0	Pauline	Davis	BAH	9.7.66	1		Austin	7 May
22.55	1.4	Silke-Beate	Knoll	GER	21.2.67	2	NC	Erfurt	3 Jul
22.61	0.7	Marie-José	Pérec	FRA	9.5.68	1		St Denis	10 Jun
22.65	0.6	Merlene	Frazer	JAM	27.12.73	1s2	NCAA	Boise	3 Jun
22.66	0.5	Zhanna	Tarnopolskaya	UKR	6.7.72	6	DNG	Stockholm	12 Jul
22.69	1.3	Paula	Thomas	GBR	3.12.64	4	CG	Victoria	26 Aug
22.72	1.6	Liliana	Allen	CUB	24.6.70	1	NC	La Habana	24 Jun
22.73	-0.1	Inger	Miller	USA	12.12.72	1	MSR	Walnut	17 Apr
22.73	1.4	Silke	Lichtenhagen	GER	20.11.73	3	NC	Erfurt	3 Jul
		(20)							
22.74	1.9	Michelle	Collins	USA	12.2.71	1		Houston	7 May
22.74	0.9	Anna	Koshelyova	RUS	11.11.68	2	NC	St Peterburg	16 Jul
22.78	1.3	Marina	Trandenkova	RUS	7.1.67	2	Slov	Bratislava	1 Jun
22.80		Dahlia	Duhaney	JAM	20.7.70	2		Kingston	7 May
22.81	0.7	Viktoria	Fomenko	UKR	2.10.70	1	NC	Kiev	27 May

Mark	Wind	Name		Nat	Born	Pos	Meet	Venue	Date
22.83	0.9	Yekaterina	Leshcheva	RUS	21.4.74	3	NC	St Peterburg	16 Jul
22.84	-1.1	Heike	Drechsler	GER	16.12.64	H		Talence	10 Sep
22.85	1.1	Stacy	Bowen	CAN	17.12.69	1	SEC	Fayetteville	15 May
22.85	0.7	Petja	Pendareva	BUL	20.1.71	1s2		Sofia	15 May
22.85	0.6	Katharine	Merry	GBR	21.9.74	1	AAA	Sheffield	12 Jun
		(30)							
22.85	-0.7	Juliet	Cuthbert	JAM	9.4.64	6	GWG	St Peterburg	25 Jul
22.86	0.3	Maya	Azarashvili	GEO	6.4.64	1		Arnhem	9 Jul
22.88	1.7	Cheryl	Taplin	USA	2.9.72	1h2	NCAA	Boise	1 Jun
22.89	0.9	Yelena	Mizera	RUS	20.2.66	4	NC	St Peterburg	16 Jul
22.94	1.2	Sue	Walton	USA	21.8.72	1		Knoxville	2 Apr
22.97	-0.3		Chen Zhaojing	CHN	5.4.69	1	NC	Beijing	2 Jun
22.97	1.1	Flirtisha	Harris	USA	21.2.72	1	USOF	Edwardsville	10 Jul
22.97	0.2	Elinda	Vorster	RSA	8.12.65	2		Ingolstadt	17 Jul
23.03A	0.7	Yolanda	Steyn	RSA	22.8.72	1	NC	Secunda	7 May
23.05	-0.1	Wenda	Vereen	USA	24.4.66	3	MSR	Walnut	17 Apr
		(40)							
23.05	1.2		Qi Hong	CHN	.3.69	1		Tangshan	28 Aug
23.08		Omegia	Keeys	USA	25.6.75	1		Terre Haute	23 Apr
23.08A	0.7	Adri	de Jongh	RSA	13.7.70	2	NC	Secunda	7 May
23.08	1.1	D'Andre	Hill	USA	19.4.73	4	SEC	Fayetteville	15 May
23.08	0.2	Vera	Sychugova	RUS	13.10.63	1		Moskva	11 Jun
23.08	-0.7	Regula	Anliker-Aebi	SUI	12.11.65	1	NC	Lausanne	31 Jul
23.10	0.9	Yelena	Dubtsova	RUS	6.5.71	5	NC	St Peterburg	16 Jul
23.13	1.1	Zundra	Feagin	USA	12.7.73	5	SEC	Fayetteville	15 May
23.13	1.3	Oksana	Dyachenko	RUS	26.11.74	4	Slov	Bratislava	1 Jun
23.13	1.1	Richelle	Webb	USA	8.10.71	2	USOF	Edwardsville	10 Jul
		(50)							
23.14	-0.6	Sanna	Hernesniemi	FIN	9.3.71	1	NC	Tuusula	10 Jul
23.15	1.6	Julia	Duporty	CUB	9.2.71	2	NC	La Habana	24 Jun
23.15	0.7	Lucrecia	Jardim	POR	28.1.71	1	NC	Lisboa	10 Jul
23.16	0.2	Fatima	Yusuf	NGR	2.5.71	3		Ingolstadt	17 Jul
23.16	0.9	Susanthika	Jayasinghe	SRI	17.12.75	1	AsiC-j	Jakarta	20 Sep
23.17	0.6	Stephanie	Douglas	GBR	22.1.69	2	AAA	Sheffield	12 Jun
23.17	0.2	Jacqueline	Poelman	NED	5.10.73	1		Heiloo	19 Jun
23.18	1.3	Erika	Suchovská	TCH	27.7.67	5	Slov	Bratislava	1 Jun
23.18	1.2		Liu Xiaomei	CHN	11.1.72	2		Tangshan	28 Aug
23.19		Maicel	Malone	USA	12.6.69	1		Gainesville	1 May
		(60)							
23.19A	0.7	Esmari	Le Roux	RSA	27.1.76	3	NC	Secunda	7 May
23.20		Heather	Samuel	ANT	6.7.70	1		Atlanta	22 May
23.21	1.0	Andria	Lloyd	JAM	10.8.71	4s1	NCAA	Boise	3 Jun
23.21	1.4	Lakeisha	Backus	USA	15.12.76	1		Norwalk	4 Jun
23.21	1.4	Bettina	Zipp	GER	29.4.72	4	NC	Erfurt	3 Jul
23.22A	0.7	Heidi	Seyerling	RSA	19.8.76	4	NC	Secunda	7 May
23.22	0.6	Natalya	Voronova #	RUS	9.7.65	3	Banes	São Paulo	21 May
23.23	-0.5	Aminah	Haddad	USA	13.9.78	1		Long Beach	21 May
23.24	-0.6	Jearl	Miles	USA	4.9.66	1		Chapel Hill	15 May
23.24	0.9	Damarayanthi	Darsha	SRI	13.2.75	2	AsiC-j	Jakarta	20 Sep
		(70)							
23.26	1.5	Zlatka	Georgieva	BUL	20.7.69	1	NC	Sofia	3 Jul
23.26	0.3	Fabienne	Ficher	FRA	25.4.66	1h1	FranG	Bondoufle	12 Jul
23.26	-0.7	Sara	Wüest	SUI	4.8.69	2	NC	Lausanne	31 Jul
23.27	-0.8	Birgit	Rockmeier	GER	29.11.73	1		Germering	18 Jun
23.27	-0.8	Ximena	Restrepo	COL	10.3.69	1		Santiago de Chile	5 Nov
23.28	1.6	Kwani	Stewart	USA	9.10.72	2h3	NCAA	Boise	1 Jun
23.28	2.0	Natalya	Khrushchelyova	RUS	20.5.73	1		Voronezh	18 Jun
23.29	2.0	Michelle	Freeman	JAM	5.5.69	4		Austin	7 May
23.29		Celena	Mondie-Milner	USA	6.8.68	2		Atlanta	22 May
23.29	1.4	Angelika	Haggenmüller	GER	1.3.69	5	NC	Erfurt	3 Jul
		(80)							
23.29	1.5	Giada	Gallina	ITA	1.12.73	3		Rieti	28 Aug
23.30	1.2	Eldece	Clarke	BAH	13.2.65	1h3	Barr	La Habana	26 May
23.31	0.4	Nicole	Green	USA	28.10.71	1		Norman	16 Apr
23.31	0.5	Rochelle	Stevens	USA	8.9.66	1A	MSR	Walnut	17 Apr
23.31	0.6	Kim	Graham	USA	26.3.71	4	Banes	São Paulo	21 May
23.32		Debbie	Ferguson	BAH	16.1.76	1h2	Carif	Bridgetown	4 Apr
23.32	2.0	Chryste	Gaines	USA	14.9.70	5		Austin	7 May

Mark	Wind	Name		Nat	Born	Pos	Meet	Venue	Date
23.32	0.6	Marion	Jones	USA	12.10.75	3s2	NCAA	Boise	3 Jun
23.32	0.2	Yelena	Ruzina	RUS	3.4.64	2		Moskva	11 Jun
23.32	-1.5	Calista	Uba	NGR	15.11.73	2	NC	Lagos	11 Jun
		(90)							
23.32	0.6	Sabine	Tröger	AUT	7.7.67	1h	NC	Linz	10 Jul
23.34	-0.8		Wang Huei-chen	TPE	21.2.70	1	AsiG	Hiroshima	11 Oct
23.35	1.9	Vonda	Newhouse	USA	27.8.74	2		Houston	7 May
23.35	1.1	Shantel	Twiggs	USA	4.10.72	3	USOF	Edwardsville	10 Jul
23.35	0.6	Delphine	Combe	FRA	6.12.74	2	FranG	Bondoufle	12 Jul
23.36A		Aspen	Burkett	USA	8.3.76	1		Denver	14 May
23.36		Melinda	Sergent	USA	72	1		Fresno	21 May
23.37	1.5	Monika	Gachevska	BUL	30.10.74	2	NC	Sofia	3 Jul
23.38	2.0	Savathea	Fynes	BAH	17.10.74	2s2	NAIA	Azusa	27 May
23.38	0.9	Marina	Zhirova	RUS	6.6.63	2h4	NC	St Peterburg	15 Jul
23.38	1.1	Antonina	Slyusar	UKR	19.3.63	1		Kiev	24 Jul
		(101)							

Mark	Wind	Name		Nat	Yr	Date
23.39	2.0	Odile	Singa	FRA	67	3 Jul
23.41	0.0	Astia	Walker	JAM	75	21 May
23.44	0.5	Renee	Poetschka	AUS	71	26 Feb
23.44	1.2		Sun Yanshi	CHN	71	28 Aug
23.46	1.6	Janeen	Jones	USA	72	23 Apr
23.46	0.0	Michelle	Christie	JAM	73	28 May
23.47	2.1	Nicole	Mitchell	JAM	74	18 Jun
23.47	1.2	Geraldine	McLeod	GBR	71	24 Aug
23.47	1.5	Idalmis	Bonne	CUB	71	28 Aug
23.48A	0.7	Cindy	Bousema	RSA	74	7 May
23.48	1.8	Tatyana	Tkalich	UKR	75	22 May
23.48	1.7	Kim	Baldwin	USA	75	1 Jun
23.48	1.8	Jana	Schönenberger	GER	71	18 Jun
23.48	0.8	Simmone	Jacobs	GBR	66	26 Jun
23.48	0.3	Muriel	Leroy-Gallardo	FRA	68	12 Jul
23.48	1.2	Solvi	Meinseth	NOR	67	20 Jul
23.49	1.6	Treshell	Mayo	USA	74	23 Apr
23.49	1.2	Kate	Iheagwam	NGR		14 May
23.50A	0.7	Tammy	Sawyer	RSA	77	7 May
23.50	-1.1	Mireille	Donders	SUI	74	19 Jun
23.50	1.5	Nancy	McLeon	CUB	71	28 Aug
23.51	0.1		Zhang Henyun	CHN	74	12 Aug
23.53	1.9	D'Angelia	Johnson	USA	73	7 May
23.53	1.7	Margarita	Molchan	BLR	66	30 Jun
23.54		Jane	Flemming	AUS	65	28 May
23.54	-1.9	Sandra	Myers	ESP	61	5 Jun
23.54	1.4	Zhanna	Levashova	RUS	70	26 Jun
23.55	0.2	Evette	de Klerk	RSA	65	25 Feb
23.55	2.0	Twilet	Malcolm	JAM	69	7 May
23.55	1.3	Karen	Boone	USA	75	1 Jun
23.55	0.2	Oksana	Khreskina	RUS	72	11 Jun
23.55	0.6	Marcia	Richardson	GBR	72	12 Jun
23.56	1.6	Sheryl	Covington	USA	71	23 Apr
23.56		Vonetta	Jeffrey	USA	73	20 May
23.56	0.1	Svetlana	Moskalets	RUS	69	16 Jun
23.56	0.9	LaTasha	Colander	USA	76	19 Jun
23.56	1.4	Andrea	Philipp	GER	71	3 Jul
23.57	0.0	Beverley	Grant	JAM	70	8 Apr
23.57		Kendra	Mackey	USA	69	7 May
23.57	1.5	Maguy	Nestoret	FRA	69	17 Jul
23.58	0.0	Hermin	Joseph	DMN	64	28 May
23.58	0.0	Svetlana	Goncharenko	RUS	71	28 Aug
23.59	2.0	Anita	Howard	USA	69	7 May
23.59	1.9	Katerina	Koffa	GRE	69	29 May
23.61	1.0	Keisha	Owens	USA	73	15 May
23.61	0.0	Aileen	McGillivary	GBR	70	3 Jul
23.62	1.2	Faith	Idehen	NGR	73	23 Apr
23.62	0.3	Latasha	Gilliam	USA	76	28 May
23.62	-0.3	Ionela	Tîrlea	ROM	76	30 Jul
		(150)				
23.63	1.9	Yulia	Sotnikova	RUS	70	7 Jun
23.63	1.4	Christina	Hormann	GER	72	3 Jul
23.63	1.9	Natalya	Maurina	UKR	71	24 Jul
23.64	0.2	Donna	Smith	USA	72	23 Apr
23.64	0.8	Lyudmila	Mikhailova	RUS	69	28 May
23.64	0.7	Melanie	Neef	GBR	70	3 Jul
23.64	1.6	Aline	André	FRA	73	10 Jul
23.64	0.6	Anu	Pirttimaa	FIN	72	10 Jul
23.64	1.3	Fabé	Dia	FRA	77	10 Jul
23.64	0.9	Sandra	Cheri Zecote	FRA	73	24 Jul
23.65	0.9	Michelle	Mundey	USA	78	19 Jun
23.66	-0.2	Éva	Barati	HUN	68	16 Jun
23.66	0.8	Yulia	Timofeyeva	RUS	72	16 Jul
23.66	1.6	Karin	Janke	GER	63	23 Jul
23.67		Paula	Cohen	GBR	71	25 Jun
23.68	1.3	Michelle	Seymour	NZL	65	6 Mar
23.68	0.5	Sophia	Smith	GBR	72	9 Jul
23.68	1.9	Lyudmila	Antonova	UKR	70	24 Jul
23.68	0.8	Jackie	Joyner-Kersee	USA	62	25 Jul
23.69	2.4	Kathy	Sambell	AUS	63	13 Mar
23.69	0.0	Juliet	Campbell	JAM	70	14 May
23.69	1.9	Anzhela	Balakhonova	UKR	72	24 Jul
23.69	1.2	Kylie	Hanigan	AUS	71	26 Nov
23.70	1.6	Catherine	Lenoir	BEL	73	3 Jul
23.70		Yelena	Kuzina	RUS	66	15 Jul
		(175)				

Wind gauge illegally placed (on outside of track)

Mark	Wind	Name		Nat	Born	Pos	Meet	Venue	Date
23.34	1.2	Heide Ann	Harper	TRI		1	JUCO	Odessa	21 May

Mark	Wind	Name		Nat	Yr	Date
23.65	1.2	Sabrina	Herring-Kelly	USA	75	21 May
23.67	1.2	Shenita	Wilson	USA		21 May
23.69	1.2	Dana	Collins	USA	73	21 May

Wind-assisted

Mark	Wind	Name		Nat	Born	Pos	Meet	Venue	Date
21.82	3.1	Irina	Privalova	RUS	12.11.68	1	Athl	Lausanne	6 Jul
22.16	3.1	Dannette	Young	USA	6.10.64	2	Athl	Lausanne	6 Jul
22.33	3.1	Mary	Onyali	NGR	3.2.68	3	Athl	Lausanne	6 Jul
22.47	5.6	Inger	Miller	USA	12.12.72	1		Las Vegas	9 Apr
22.49	2.1	Merlene	Frazer	JAM	27.12.73	1	NCAA	Boise	4 Jun
22.67	2.6		Chen Zhaojing	CHN	5.4.69	1		Hiroshima	30 Apr
22.70	3.8	Regula	Anliker-Aebi	SUI	12.11.65	1		La Chaux de Fonds	21 Aug
22.74	2.7	Juliet	Cuthbert	JAM	9.4.64	1		Dijon	12 Jun
22.80	3.1	Cheryl	Taplin	USA	2.9.72	1h2	SEC	Fayetteville	14 May
22.80	2.2	Heidi	Seyerling	RSA	19.8.76	1	WJ	Lisboa	23 Jul
22.86	2.1	D'Andre	Hill	USA	19.4.73	3	NCAA	Boise	4 Jun
22.86	2.2	Lakeisha	Backus	USA	15.12.76	2	WJ	Lisboa	23 Jul
22.89	4.8	Yelena	Dubtsova	RUS	6.5.71	1h5	NC	St Peterburg	15 Jul
22.90	2.1	Richelle	Webb	USA	8.10.71	1		Madison	22 May

Mark	Wind	Name		Nat	Born	Pos	Meet	Venue	Date
22.91A	4.1	Lucrecia	Jardim	POR	28.1.71	1		Soria	8 Jul
23.00	4.8	Vera	Sychugova	RUS	8.4.63	2h5	NC	St Peterburg	15 Jul
23.02	3.1	Beverley	McDonald	JAM	15.2.70	1		Dallas	26 Mar
23.04	4.8	Oksana	Dyachenko	RUS	26.11.74	3h5	NC	St Peterburg	15 Jul
23.07		Andrea	Lloyd	JAM	10.8.71	2h2	SEC	Fayetteville	14 May
23.07	4.4	Ximena	Restrepo	COL	10.3.69	1	IbAm	Mar del Plata	30 Oct
23.10	2.2	Savathea	Fynes	BAH	17.10.74	1	NAIA	Azusa	28 May
23.12	3.9	Shantel	Twiggs	USA	4.10.72	1		Ames	23 Apr
23.13	3.1	Rochelle	Stevens	USA	8.9.66	5	Athl	Lausanne	6 Jul
23.14	4.7	Erika	Suchovská	TCH	27.7.67	1	ECp I	Valencia	12 Jun
23.21	4.0	Fabienne	Ficher	FRA	25.4.66	1B		Dijon	12 Jun
23.21	3.8	Muriel	Leroy-Gallardo	FRA	7.7.68	2		La Chaux-de-Fonds	21 Aug
23.22	2.2	Beverley	Grant	JAM	25.9.70	2	NAIA	Azusa	28 May
23.24A	2.2	Melinda	Sergent	USA	72	3A		El Paso	16 Apr
23.27	3.8	Maguy	Nestoret	FRA	28.7.69	3		La Chaux-de-Fonds	21 Aug
23.28	4.8	Nadezhda	Roshchupkina	RUS	14.6.63	4h5	NC	St Peterburg	15 Jul
23.30	2.1	Sandra	Myers	ESP	9.1.61	3		Lisboa	18 Jun
23.30	2.4	Natalya	Yudakova	RUS	25.3.65	2		Noisy-le-Grand	2 Jul
23.30	2.4	Lalao	Ravaonirina	MAD	8.11.63	3		Noisy-le-Grand	2 Jul
23.33	3.8	Deon	Hemmings	JAM	9.10.68	1		San Marcos	30 Apr
23.35	2.2	Tatyana	Tkalich	UKR	30.5.75	3	WJ	Lisboa	23 Jul
23.38	3.8	Anita	Howard	USA	22.3.69	2		San Marcos	30 Apr

Mark	Wind	Name		Nat	Born	Date
23.42	2.1	Karen	Boone	USA	75	25 May
23.42	3.0	Aileen	McGillivary	GBR	70	23 Jul
23.45		De'Angelia	Johnson	USA	73	26 Mar
23.45	5.6	Trevaia	Williams	USA	68	9 Apr
23.48	5.1	Andrea	Anderson	USA	77	9 Apr
23.49	?		Huang Mei	CHN	75	30 Apr
23.53	2.9	Claudia	Volk	GER	73	23 May
23.53	2.6	France	Gareau	CAN	67	24 Aug
23.54	3.9	Karin	Solbakken	NOR	67	30 Jun
23.55	2.4	Donna	Smith	USA	72	19 Mar
23.55		Faith	Idehen	NGR	73	14 May
23.58	2.1	Regina	Frye	USA	72	22 May
23.61	4.0	Violetta	Lapierre	FRA	63	12 Jun
23.61	2.2	Sylviane	Felix	FRA	77	23 Jul
23.62	3.5	Brigitte	Mullen	AUS	66	17 Dec
23.63	2.7	Marlene	Poole	USA		17 Apr
23.64	2.5	Patricia	Rodriguez	COL	70	26 May
23.65		Michelle	Bookman	USA	71	14 May
23.66	4.1	Nanceen	Perry	USA	75	14 May
23.68	2.7	Kathy	Travis	USA	73	21 May
23.69	3.9	Heather	Brown	USA		23 Apr
23.69	4.9	Lisette	Rondon	CHI	74	30 Oct

Best at low altitude

Mark	Wind	Name	Pos	Meet	Venue	Date
23.36	0.2	Seyerling	1s1	WJ	Lisboa	23 Jul
23.54	0.3	Burkett				25 Jun
23.54	0.7	de Jongh				10 Jul

Hand timed

Mark	Wind	Name		Nat	Born	Pos	Meet	Venue	Date
22.6	1.0	Svetlana	Goncharenko	RUS	28.5.71	1		Stavropol	29 May
22.8	1.2	Zlatka	Georgieva	BUL	20.7.69	1		Sofia	26 Jun
22.9		Rhonda	Forbes	TRI	74	1		Port of Spain	14 May
22.9		Astia	Walker	JAM	4.4.75	1h	CAC-j	Port of Spain	10 Jul
23.1		Heather	Samuel	ANT	6.7.70	1		Murray	23 Apr
23.1	1.5	Claudete	Alves Pina	BRA	19.4.71	1		Americana	30 Apr
23.1	1.2	Monika	Gachevska	BUL	30.10.74	1		Sofia	26 Jun
23.1		Debbie	Ferguson	BAH	16.1.76	h	CAC-j	Port of Spain	10 Jul
23.1		Renée	Poetschka	AUS	1.5.71	1		Perth	10 Dec

Mark	Wind	Name		Nat	Born	Date
23.2		Tatyana	Kotelnikova	UZB	75	13 May
23.3A		Idalmis	Bonne	CUB	71	16 Apr
23.3	1.8	Oksana	Khreskina	RUS	72	29 May
23.3		Nadezhda	Roshchupkina	RUS	63	
23.3A		Patricia	Rodriguez	COL	70	11 Sep
23.4A		Gwen	Clardy	USA	73	30 Apr
23.4		Monique	Hennagan	USA	76	12 May
23.4	1.1	Michelle	Bookman	USA	71	15 May
Wind assisted						
23.3		LaTasha	Colander	USA	76	23 Apr

Indoors

Mark	Wind	Name		Nat	Born	Pos	Meet	Venue	Date
22.16	-		Privalova			1A		Liévin	13 Feb
22.41	-		Malchugina			1	EI	Paris	13 Mar
22.84		Natalya	Voronova #	RUS	23.2.68	1B		Liévin	13 Feb
23.25		Dahlia	Duhaney	JAM	20.7.70	5	US Ch	Atlanta	5 Mar
23.47		Maria	Staafgård	SWE	8.6.69	1h4	EI	Paris	12 Mar

After positive drugs test

Mark	Wind	Name		Nat	Born	Pos	Meet	Venue	Date
22.82	-0.7	Natalya	Voronova #	RUS	9.7.65	5	GWG	St Peterburg	25 Jul
22.8	hand	Natalya	Voronova #	RUS	23.2.68	1		Moskva	27 Jan

300 METRES

Mark	Name		Nat	Born	Pos	Meet	Venue	Date
36.85	Kim	Graham	USA	26.3.71	1	TSB	Edinburgh	8 Jul
36.97	Natasha	Kaiser-Brown	USA	14.5.67	2	TSB	Edinburgh	8 Jul
37.06	Sally	Gunnell	GBR	29.7.66	3	TSB	Edinburgh	8 Jul
37.15	Deon	Hemmings	JAM	9.10.68	4	TSB	Edinburgh	8 Jul
37.33	Melanie	Neef	GBR	26.5.70	5	TSB	Edinburgh	8 Jul
37.39	Rochelle	Stevens	USA	8.9.66	6	TSB	Edinburgh	8 Jul
37.47	Phylis	Smith	GBR	29.9.65	7	TSB	Edinburgh	8 Jul

Mark	Name		Nat	Born	Pos	Meet	Venue	Date
Indoors								
36.81	Svetlana	Goncharenko	RUS	28.5.71	1		Moskva	4 Feb
37.50	Vera	Sychugova	RUS	8.4.63	2		Moskva	4 Feb
37.78	Tatyana	Alekseyeva	RUS	7.10.63	1B		Grenoble	6 Feb
37.94	Yelena	Ruzina	RUS	3.4.64	2B		Grenoble	6 Feb
37.96	Marina	Zhirova	RUS	6.6.63	2		St Peterburg	30 Jan

400 METRES

Mark	Name		Nat	Born	Pos	Meet	Venue	Date
49.77	Marie-José	Pérec	FRA	9.5.68	1	GPF	Paris	3 Sep
50.04	Cathy	Freeman	AUS	16.2.73	2	GPF	Paris	3 Sep
50.05	Maicel	Malone	USA	12.6.69	1	Athl	Lausanne	6 Jul
50.11	Jearl	Miles	USA	4.9.66	2	Athl	Lausanne	6 Jul
50.18		Freeman			2	Herc	Monaco	2 Aug
50.19	Renee	Poetschka	AUS	1.5.71	1	NC	Sydney	12 Mar
50.20	Gwen	Torrence	USA	12.6.65	1	BNP	Villeneuve d'Ascq	8 Jul
50.23		Freeman			3	Athl	Lausanne	6 Jul
50.24		Malone			1s2	NC	Knoxville	17 Jun
50.33		Pérec			1	EC	Helsinki	11 Aug
50.33		Malone			3	GPF	Paris	3 Sep
50.33	Sandra	Myers	ESP	9.1.61	1		Madrid	6 Sep
50.37		Miles			4	GPF	Paris	3 Sep
50.38	Natasha	Kaiser-Brown	USA	14.5.67	4	Athl	Lausanne	6 Jul
50.38		Freeman			1	CG	Victoria	23 Aug
50.45		Ma Yuqin	CHN	11.9.72	1	NC	Beijing	4 Jun
50.46	Pauline	Davis	BAH	9.7.66	5	Athl	Lausanne	6 Jul
50.53	Fatima	Yusuf	NGR	2.2.71	2	CG	Victoria	23 Aug
50.57		Malone			3	Herc	Monaco	2 Aug
50.58		Miles			4	Herc	Monaco	2 Aug
50.59		Pérec			1	NYG	New York	22 May
50.59		Davis			1	GGala	Roma	8 Jun
50.60		Miles			1	GWG	St Peterburg	26 Jul
50.60		Malone			2	GWG	St Peterburg	26 Jul
50.61	Julia	Duporty	CUB	9.2.71	2		Madrid	6 Sep
50.62	Irina	Privalova	RUS	12.11.68	1	WCp	London	11 Sep
50.65		Pérec			1	Jen	San José	28 May
50.68		Miles			2	NYG	New York	22 May
50.69	Sandie	Richards	JAM	6.11.68	3	CG	Victoria	23 Aug
50.71		Malone			1	v Afr	Durham	12 Aug
	(30/13)							
50.73		Miles			2s2	NC	Knoxville	17 Jun
50.73		Kaiser-Brown			1	NC	Knoxville	18 Jun
50.73		Kaiser-Brown			3	GWG	St Peterburg	26 Jul
51.00	Svetlana	Goncharenko	RUS	28.5.71	2	GGala	Roma	8 Jun
51.00	Nancy	McLeon	CUB	1.5.71	3		Madrid	6 Sep
51.04	Sally	Gunnell	GBR	29.7.66	1	v USA	Gateshead	20 Jul
51.16	Uta	Rohländer	GER	30.6.69	1		Lindau	31 Jul
51.19	Michelle	Collins	USA	12.2.71	2	v GBR	Gateshead	20 Jul
51.21	Francine	Landre	FRA	26.7.70	1	NC	Annecy	24 Jul
51.29	Dannette	Young	USA	6.10.64	2rA	GP II	Linz	4 Jul
	(20)							
51.30	Yelena	Andreyeva	RUS	9.5.69	5	GWG	St Peterburg	26 Jul
51.30	Phylis	Smith	GBR	29.9.65	3	EC	Helsinki	11 Aug
51.31	Ximena	Restrepo	COL	10.3.69	1	Odesur	Valencia	24 Nov
51.37	Maria	Mutola	MOZ	27.10.72	8	Herc	Monaco	2 Aug
51.41	Yelena	Golesheva	RUS	12.7.66	1h1	NC	St Peterburg	14 Jul
51.42	Tatyana	Zakharova	RUS	18.4.69	1h3	NC	St Peterburg	14 Jul
51.42	Anja	Rücker	GER	20.12.72	1	ECp23	Ostrava	30 Jul
51.43	Kim	Graham	USA	26.3.71	4	NC	Knoxville	18 Jun
51.45	Deon	Hemmings	JAM	9.10.68	1		Austin	6 May
51.45	Rochelle	Stevens	USA	8.9.66	3s2	NC	Knoxville	17 Jun
	(30)							
51.47	Janeen	Jones	USA	19.8.72	1r1		Atlanta	21 May
51.51	Carlette	Guidry	USA	4.9.68	1	MSR	Walnut	17 Apr
51.52	Evelyn	Elien	FRA	24.3.64	2	NC	Annecy	24 Jul
51.52		Cao Chunying	CHN	5.2.72	1		Tangshan	30 Aug
51.57	Ellen	Grant	JAM	17.10.74	1	JUCO	Odessa	21 May
51.61		Zhang Hengyun	CHN	26.11.74	2	NC	Beijing	4 Jun
51.65	Flirtisha	Harris	USA	21.2.72	1	NCAA	Boise	4 Jun

Mark	Name		Nat	Born	Pos	Meet	Venue	Date
51.65	Juliet	Campbell	JAM	17.3.70	1rB	GP II	Linz	4 Jul
51.67	Norfalia	Carabali	COL	21.1.67	3		Granada	1 Jun
51.73	Natalya	Khrushchelyova	RUS	30.5.73	1	NC-23	Voronezh	17 Jun
	(40)							
51.75		Lu Xifang	CHN	16.12.73	1		Beijing	12 Aug
51.81	Vera	Sychugova	RUS	8.4.63	1		Moskva	6 Jun
51.85	Sheryl	Covington	USA	3.3.71	1		Austin	7 May
51.85	Karin	Janke	GER	14.10.63	3		Lindau	31 Jul
51.90	Silke-Beate	Knoll	GER	21.2.67	1		Arnsberg	29 May
51.97	Bisi	Afolabi	NGR	31.10.75	1	WJ	Lisboa	22 Jul
52.01	Revoli	Campbell	JAM	4.7.72	2	NC	Kingston	2 Jul
52.02	Idalmis	Bonne	CUB	2.2.71	4		Madrid	6 Sep
52.04	Yelena	Ruzina	RUS	3.4.64	7A	GP II	Linz	4 Jul
52.06	Kylie	Hanigan	AUS	18.11.71	2		Canberra	28 Jan
	(50)							
52.09	Melanie	Neef	GBR	26.5.70	6	CG	Victoria	23 Aug
52.12	Omolade	Akinremi	NGR	13.9.64	3	NC	Lagos	11 Jun
52.14	Debbie-Ann	Parris	JAM	24.3.73	1		Baton Rouge	25 May
52.14	Regula	Anliker-Aebi	SUI	12.11.65	1h1		La Chaux-de-Fonds	21 Aug
52.15	Audrea	Sterling	JAM	1.7.68	2	NAIA	Azusa	27 May
52.15	Viviane	Dorsile	FRA	1.6.67	3	NC	Annecy	24 Jul
52.16	Nicole	Green	USA	28.10.71	3	NCAA	Boise	4 Jun
52.17	Michelle	Lock	AUS	29.3.67	1		Brisbane	8 Jan
52.19	Monique	Hennagan	USA	26.5.76	1	NC-j	Tallahasee	25 Jun
52.19	Claudine	Williams	JAM	8.1.76	3	NC	Kingston	2 Jul
	(60)							
52.21	Shiny	Wilson	IND	8.5.65	1		Lucknow	18 Sep
52.25	Daniela	Spasova	BUL	22.9.69	7	EC	Helsinki	11 Aug
52.27	Inez	Turner	JAM	3.12.72	5		Kingston	7 May
52.27	Avis	Morgan	JAM		2	JUCO	Odessa	21 May
52.27	Charmaine	Crooks	CAN	8.8.62	1B	GP II	Linz	4 Jul
52.28	Stacey	Bowen	CAN	17.12.69	4	NCAA	Boise	4 Jun
52.29	Tatyana	Chebykina	RUS	22.11.68	3h1	NC	St Peterburg	14 Jul
52.32	Lyudmila	Kashchey	UKR	30.1.68	1	NC	Kiev	27 May
52.32	Crystal	Irving	USA	26.5.70	4s2	NC	Knoxville	17 Jun
52.34	Yekaterina	Kulikova	RUS	7.11.68	4h1	NC	St Peterburg	14 Jul
	(70)							
52.35	Magdalena	Nedelcu ¶	ROM	12.5.74	1		Bucuresti	14 May
52.36	Heike	Meissner	GER	29.1.70	2		Chemnitz	18 Jun
52.37	Surella	Morales	CUB	16.6.63	4	NC	La Habana	23 Jun
52.42	Jana	Schönenberger	GER	28.11.71	3	NC	Erfurt	2 Jul
52.48	Tamara	Kupriyanovich	BLR	26.9.64	1		Gomel	14 May
52.48	Keisha	Caine	USA	13.7.73	1		Fairfax	22 May
52.49	Solvi	Meinseth	NOR	27.3.67	4h3	EC	Helsinki	8 Aug
52.49		Bai Xiaoyun	CHN	15.6.73	3		Tangshan	30 Aug
52.50	Revoli	Campbell	JAM	4.7.72	1r1	MSR	Walnut	16 Apr
52.53	Marie-Lyne	Scholent	FRA	11.5.66	4	NC	Annecy	24 Jul
	(80)							
52.55	Luciana	Mendes	BRA	26.7.71	1		Americana	30 Apr
52.55		Liu Weiwei	CHN	11.5.71	h	NC	Beijing	3 Jun
52.56	Terri	Dendy	USA	8.5.65	5s2	NC	Knoxville	17 Jun
52.57	Yelena	Nasonkina	UKR	11.8.62	2	NC	Kiev	27 May
52.47	Kalawati	Saramma	IND	25.2.71	2	Lucknow	18	Sep
52.59	Ludmila	Formanovå	TCH	2.1.74	3	ECp 23	Ostrava	30 Jul
52.60	Hana	Benesová	TCH	19.4.75	3	WJ	Lisboa	22 Jul
52.61	Tanya	Dooley	USA	8.5.72	3h1	NC	Knoxville	16 Jun
52.61	Anita	Howard	USA	22.3.69	2h2	NC	Knoxville	16 Jun
52.62		Li Yajun	CHN	21.7.77	4	WJ	Lisboa	22 Jul
	(90)							
52.65	Michelle	Brown	USA	12.3.75	1	Gator	Knoxville	23 Apr
52.65	Diana	Pitts	USA	22.1.72	1		Fairfax	14 May
52.65	Shanequa	Campbell	USA	1.9.72	6	NCAA	Boise	4 Jun
52.67	Charlotta	Johansson	SWE	14.12.70	1	NC	Göteborg	30 Jul
52.67	Linda	Kisabaka	GER	9.4.69	4		Lindau	31 Jul
52.69	Natalya	Anisimova	RUS	4.3.73	3		Duisburg	12 Jun
52.72A	Adri	de Jongh	RSA	13.7.70	1		Germiston	13 May
52.73	Angela	Joseph	TRI	14.10.65	6		Kingston	7 May
52.75	Nadezda	Kostovalová	TCH	10.9.71	5h2	EC	Helsinki	8 Aug
52.76	Inger	Miller	USA	12.6.72	1		Los Angeles	26 Mar

Mark	Name		Nat	Born	Pos	Meet	Venue	Date
52.76	Jackie	Gayle	JAM	73	1		Tempe	2 Apr
52.76	Anita	Protti	SUI	4.8.64	5		Madrid	6 Sep
	(102)							

Mark	Name		Nat	Born	Date
52.80	Emily	Odoemenam	NGR	70	11 Jun
52.83	Yulia	Tarasenko	RUS	68	11 May
52.86	Kendra	Mackey	USA	69	22 May
52.86	Elzbieta	Kilinska	POL	63	25 Jun
52.86	Lee	Naylor	AUS	71	13 Aug
52.90	Tamsyn	Lewis	AUS	78	20 Feb
52.91	Trevaia	Williams	USA	68	5 Jun
52.92	Silvia	Rieger	GER	70	29 May
52.93	Drexel	Long	USA	72	24 Apr
52.93	Valérie	Jaunâtre	FRA	69	21 Aug
52.94	Beverley	Grant	JAM	70	14 May
52.94	Nelrae	Pasha	USA	70	16 Jun
52.94	Lency	Montelier	CUB	71	23 Jun
52.95	Anna	Knoroz	RUS	70	12 Jun
52.95	Linda	Keough	GBR	63	8 Aug
52.98	Rosey	Edeh	CAN	66	3 Jun
52.98	Yana	Burtasenkova	MOL	73	12 Jun
52.98		Jiang Lanying	CHN		30 Aug
52.99	Ebony	Robinson	USA	74	15 May
52.99	Elena	Vizitiu	ROM	72	18 Jun
52.99	Patricia	Djaté	FRA	71	21 Aug
53.00	Tracy	Barnes	JAM	76	2 Jul
53.00	Yelena	Afanasyeva	RUS	66	6 Jun
53.01	Caroline	Avbobede	NGR	71	11 Jun
53.02	Juliette	Mato	FRA	67	2 Jul
53.04	Svetlana	Tverdokhleb	UKR	72	30 Jun
53.06	Florence	Ekpo Umoh	NGR	77	21 May
53.06	Marina	Zhirova	RUS	63	29 May
53.06	Ina	Cordes	GER	68	22 Jul
53.06	Maria	Figueiredo	BRA	63	17 Sep
53.09	Celena	Mondie-Milner	USA	68	22 May
53.09	Marina	Khripankova	RUS	69	14 Jul
53.10	Judy	Fraser	CAN	73	2 Jun
53.10	Tonja	Buford	USA	70	7 Jul
53.11	Yana	Manuilova	UKR	71	28 Aug
53.14	Joetta	Clark	USA	62	15 May
53.15	Cicely	Scott	USA	75	25 Jun
53.17	Laura	Itcou	ROM	72	10 Jun
53.18A	Marinda	Fourie	RSA	68	18 Apr
53.18	Faith	Idehen	NGR	73	21 May
53.18	Youlanda	Warren	USA	72	16 Jun
53.19	Marie-Louise	Bévis	FRA	72	23 Jul
53.20A	Yolanda	Venter	RSA	78	8 Apr
53.21	Susan	Francis	TRI		22 May
53.24	Vonda	Newhouse	USA	74	24 Apr
53.24	Kathrin	Lüthi	SUI	69	17 Aug
53.24		Hsu Pei-Ching	TPE	73	25 Oct
53.26	Gretha	Tromp	NED	64	17 Jul
	(150)				
53.28	Barbara	Grzywocz	POL	66	30 Jun
53.29	Holli	Hyche	USA	71	23 Apr
53.29		Liuan Yanping	CHN	70	4 Jun
53.29	Natalya	Sharova	RUS	72	17 Jun
53.29	Angelika	Haggenmüller	GER	69	29 Jul
53.30	Nicole	Bartley	GUY	74	14 May
53.31	Lorraine	Graham	USA		21 May
53.32	Danielle	Perpoli	ITA	68	21 May
53.32	Anna	Kozak	BLR	74	10 Jul
53.32	Alimata	Koné	CIV	65	13 Jul
53.34	Sandra	Douglas	GBR	67	3 Jul
53.35	Omegia	Keeys	USA	75	19 May
53.35	Stacey	Milligan	USA	75	25 May
53.35	Nina	Arnst	RUS	69	10 Sep
53.36	Ester	Goossens	NED	72	15 May
53.36	Heidi	Suomi	FIN	75	9 Jul
53.38	Viktoria	Miloserdova	UKR	70	28 Aug
53.39	Donna	Adamson	AUS	74	20 Feb
53.40	Heather	Van Norman	USA	70	19 Mar
53.40	Charlene	Maulseed	CAN?		7 May
53.40	Shelly	Beckford	JAM		28 May
53.40	Saidat	Onanuga	NGR	74	11 Jun
53.40	Mónika	Mádai	HUN	68	13 Jul
	(176)				
53.43	Charlynna	Foster	USA	80	31 Jul
53.44	Magalie	Blondel	FRA	72	10 Jul
53.44	Donna	Fraser	GBR	72	13 Jul
53.46A	Evette	De Klerk	RSA	65	25 Feb
53.47	Eusheka	Bartley	GUY	74	21 May
53.47	Althea	Tyndall	GUY	74	21 May
53.48	Meredith	Rainey	USA	68	14 May
53.49	Argentina	Paulino	MOZ	73	2 Apr
53.49	Patrizia	Spuri	ITA	73	21 May
53.49	Camile	Noel	CAN	74	21 May
53.50	Marie	Womplou	CIV	69	4 Apr
53.50	Esther	Lahoz	ESP	66	18 Jun
53.50	Lucie	Rangassamy	FRA	74	23 Jul

Indoors

Mark	Name		Nat	Born	Pos	Meet	Venue	Date
51.77	Tatyana	Alekseyeva	RUS	7.10.63	2	EI	Paris	13 Mar
51.92	Viviane	Dorsile	FRA	1.6.67	3	EI	Paris	13 Mar
52.34A	Trevaia	Williams	USA	7.9.68	1		Reno	29 Jan
52.34	Magdalena	Nedelcu ¶	ROM	12.5.74	1		Pireas	28 Feb
52.75	Regula	Zürcher	SUI	5.1.69	1	NC	Magglingen	24 Feb

Mark	Name		Nat	Born	Date
52.77	Ionella	Tîrlea	ROM	76	5 Feb
53.05	LaDonna	Antoine	CAN	74	12 Feb

Disqualified - ran inside lane: 49.95 Pérec (1) Herc Monaco 2 Aug

Hand timed

Mark	Name		Nat	Born	Pos	Meet	Venue	Date
52.2	Mercy	Addy	GHA	2.5.63	1	NC	Accra	25 Jun
52.3	Dalia	Matusevicienė ¶	LIT	7.12.61	1		Palanga	27 Aug
52.5	Viktoriya	Fomenko	UKR	2.10.70	1		Kharkov	28 Apr

Mark	Name		Nat	Born	Date
52.7	Nabiama	Salifu	GHA		25 Jun
52.8	Lee	Naylor	AUS	71	6 Aug
52.9	Nezha	Bidouane	MAR	69	16 Jul
52.9	Noodang	Phimphoo	THA	68	3 Sep
53.0	Sandra	Douglas	GBR	67	18 Jun
53.1	Tracy-Ann	Barnes	JAM	75	12 Mar
53.2	Lyudmila	Khodasevich	UKR	59	9 Jul
53.3	Tanya	Jarrett	JAM	77	26 Mar
53.3	Marina	Kakarova	UKR	73	9 Jul
53.4	Nadezhda	Loboyko	RUS	61	29 May
53.4	Tatyana	Molchan	UKR	70	9 Jul
53.4	Zoya	Maurina	UKR	71	9 Jul

800 METRES

Mark	Name		Nat	Born	Pos	Meet	Venue	Date
1:55.19	Maria	Mutola	MOZ	27.10.72	1	WK	Zürich	17 Aug
1:56.53	Lyubov	Gurina	RUS	6.8.57	1		Hechtel	30 Jul
1:57.0 mx		Mutola			1		Eugene	24 Jun
1:57.58		Mutola			1	ASV	Köln	21 Aug
1:57.63		Mutola			1	GWG	St Peterburg	28 Jul
1:57.87	Natalya	Dukhnova	BLR	16.7.66	2	WK	Zürich	17 Aug
1:58.07	Patricia	Djaté	FRA	3.1.71	3	WK	Zürich	17 Aug
1:58.10		Gurina			2	ASV	Köln	21 Aug
1:58.15		Mutola			1	v USA	Durham	12 Aug
1:58.27	Luciana	Mendes	BRA	26.7.71	2		Hechtel	30 Jul
1:58.27		Mutola			1	WCp	London	10 Sep
1:58.29		Dukhnova			1	WG	Helsinki	29 Jun
1:58.39	Joetta	Clark	USA	1.8.62	4	WK	Zürich	17 Aug
1:58.43	Lyudmila	Rogachova	RUS	30.10.66	2	GWG	St Peterburg	28 Jul
1:58.55		Gurina			1	EC	Helsinki	10 Aug
1:58.55		Dukhnova			2	EC	Helsinki	10 Aug
1:58.69		Rogachova			3	EC	Helsinki	10 Aug
1:58.81	Yelena	Zavadskaya	UKR	24.12.64	1	NC	Kiev	29 May
1:58.83		Clark			3	ASV	Köln	21 Aug
1:58.84		Dukhnova			4	ASV	Köln	21 Aug
1:58.88		Dukhnova			1		Madrid	6 Sep
1:58.90		Clark			2	v Afr	Durham	12 Aug
1:59.02	Suzy	Hamilton	USA	8.8.68	5	WK	Zürich	17 Aug
1:59.07	Irina	Samorokova	RUS	15.4.64	3	GWG	St Peterburg	28 Jul
1:59.12	Malgorzata	Rydz	POL	18.1.67	4	EC	Helsinki	10 Aug
1:59.23		Samorokova			1	NC	St Peterburg	15 Jul
1:59.25	Yekaterina	Podkopayeva	RUS	11.6.52	1		Luxembourg	30 Jun
1:59.25		Podkopayeva			1	Barth	Luxembourg	30 Jun
1:59.37		Qu Yunxia	CHN	25.12.72	1	NC	Beijing	3 Jun
1:59.39	Carla	Sacramento	POR	10.12.71	5	ASV	Köln	21 Aug
1:59.43	Kelly	Holmes	GBR	19.4.70	1	TSB	London	15 Jul
1:59.47	Lyubov	Kremlyova	RUS	21.12.62	1	Kuts	Moskva	31 Jul
	(32/15)							
1:59.81	Ann	Griffiths	GBR	20.8.65	5	EC	Helsinki	10 Aug
1:59.83	Tatyana	Grigoryeva	RUS	11.3.72	1h4	NC	St Peterburg	14 Jul
1:59.89	Ellen	van Langen	NED	9.2.66	2	TSB	London	15 Jul
1:59.90	Meredith	Rainey	USA	15.10.68	5	GWG	St Peterburg	28 Jul
1:59.95		Liu Li	CHN	12.3.71	2	NC	Beijing	3 Jun
	(20)							
1:59.98	Regina	Jacobs	USA	28.8.63	1		Caorle	16 Jul
2:00.02		Zhang Yumei	CHN	25.11.71	3	NC	Beijing	3 Jun
2:00.05	Ester	Goossens	NED	21.2.72	3		Hechtel	30 Jul
2:00.33	Yvonne	Graham	JAM	22.8.65	3		Madrid	6 Sep
2:00.41	Anna	Brzezinska	POL	9.1.71	8	EC	Helsinki	10 Aug
2:00.47	Violeta	Beclea	ROM	26.3.65	1	NC	Bucuresti	18 Jun
2:00.48		Yan Wei	CHN	12.10.71	4	NC	Beijing	3 Jun
2:00.52	Yelena	Afanasyeva	RUS	27.5.65	1h2	NC	St Peterburg	14 Jul
2:00.60	Amy	Wickus	USA	25.6.72	2	NC	Knoxville	18 Jun
2:00.61	Liliana	Salageanu	ROM	24.3.71	3	NC	Bucuresti	18 Jun
	(30)							
2:00.61	Hassiba	Boulmerka	ALG	10.7.68	1	TOTO	Tokyo	15 Sep
2:00.68	Stella	Jongmans	NED	17.5.71	6	WK	Zürich	17 Aug
2:00.69	Sonia	O'Sullivan	IRL	28.11.69	7	GWG	St Peterburg	28 Jul
2:00.71	Tina	Paulino	MOZ	7.7.73	1		Durban	23 Apr
2:00.73	Anneke	Matthijs	BEL	8.3.69	4		Hechtel	30 Jul
2:00.80	Kati	Kovacs	GER	7.9.73	7	ASV	Köln	21 Aug
2:00.8	Alla	Krasnoslobodskaya	RUS	20.10.70	1		Voronezh	27 Aug
2:00.82	Ella	Kovacs #	ROM	11.12.64	3	NYG	New York	22 May
2:00.84	Tamara	Kupriyanovich	BLR	26.9.64	1		Victoria	4 Jun
2:00.84	Natalya	Betekhtina	RUS	8.9.61	1		Moskva	11 Jun
	(40)							
2:00.94	Dalia	Matuseviciené ¶	LIT	12.11.62	1		Stockholm	2 Aug
2:00.97	Karen	Gydesen	DEN	3.6.67	3	WG	Helsinki	29 Jun
2:01.06	Irina	Podyalovskaya	RUS	9.10.59	4	Barth	Luxemburg	30 Jun
2:01.12	Rita	Paulaviciené	LIT	14.12.61	1		Port Alberni	1 Jun
2:01.13	Diane	Modahl ¶	GBR	17.6.66	4	APM	Hengelo	4 Jun

Mark	Name		Nat	Born	Pos	Meet	Venue	Date
2:01.13	Jane	Brooker	USA	10.5.64	4	NC	Knoxville	18 Jun
2:01.14	Carmen	Stanciu	ROM	5.1.70	1		Bucuresti	12 Jun
2:01.18	Olga	Burkanova	RUS	29.9.69	4	NC	St Peterburg	15 Jul
2:01.19	Simone	Weidner	GER	30.9.69	7	WK	Zürich	17 Aug
2:01.23	Maria	Akraka	SWE	7.7.66	2		Stockholm	2 Aug
	(50)							
2:01.25	Yelena	Storchovaya	UKR	23.6.66	1	Znam	Moskva	5 Jun
2:01.28	Laura	Itcou	ROM	13.2.72	4	NC	Bucuresti	18 Jun
2:01.31	Ines	Turner	JAM	1.3.72	3	Kuts	Moskva	31 Jul
2:01.33	Malin	Ewerlöf	SWE	2.6.72	1		Gävle	4 Jul
2:01.35	Irina	Stasenko	RUS	27.3.66	3h4	NC	St Peterburg	14 Jul
2:01.44		Liu Wanjie #	CHN	.11.75	5	NC	Beijing	3 Jun
2:01.53	Olga	Kuznetsova	RUS	23.10.67	2		Port Alberni	1 Jun
2:01.56	Larisa	Chzhao	RUS	4.2.72	2h1	NC	St Peterburg	14 Jul
2:01.6	Jyotirmoy	Sikdar	IND	11.12.69	1		Lucknow	25 Aug
2:01.66	Nekita	Beasley	USA	29.3.69	5	NC	Knoxville	18 Jun
	(60)							
2:01.69	Tosha	Woodward	USA	28.4.71	6	NC	Knoxville	18 Jun
2:01.7	Svetlana	Miroshnik	UKR	3.6.68	1		Dnepropetrovsk	18 Jul
2:01.77	Jasmin	Jones	USA	13.10.69	1	WG	Byrkjelo	24 Jul
2:01.78	Charmaine	Crooks	CAN	8.8.62	2	TOTO	Tokyo	15 Sep
2:01.80	Nadezhda	Loboyko	RUS	7.9.61	1		Madras	5 Feb
2:01.84	Christine	Wachtel	GER	6.1.65	6s1	EC	Helsinki	8 Aug
2:01.88	Marjo	Piipponen	FIN	29.5.71	6	WG	Helsinki	29 Jun
2:01.9	Shiny	Wilson	IND	8.5.65	2		Lucknow	25 Aug
2:01.91	Yelena	Goncharova	RUS	27.3.63	4		Moskva	11 Jun
2:01.94	Satu	Jääskeläinen	FIN	4.4.70	2		Lahti	5 Jun
	(70)							
2:02.1	Lisa	O'Connell	AUS	3.12.66	1		Sydney	5 Feb
2:02.16	Viviane	Dorsile	FRA	1.6.67	6		Hechtel	30 Jul
2:02.17	Sarah	Thorsett	USA	18.3.70	8	WG	Helsinki	29 Jun
2:02.22	Cécile	Clarinval	BEL	16.9.68	7		Hechtel	30 Jul
2:02.30	Sonya	Bowyer	GBR	18.9.72	5		Gateshead	1 Jul
2:02.39	Letitia	Vriesde	SUR	5.10.64	3		Kerkrade	28 May
2:02.4	Yelena	Bychkovskaya	BLR	4.3.72	2		Minsk	28 Apr
2:02.45		Chen Xuehui	CHN	.7.69	6	NC	Beijing	3 Jun
2:02.47	Lesley	Noll-Mayne	USA	22.5.67	1	USOF	Edwardsville	10 Jul
2:02.49	Sandra	Dawson	AUS	2.11.70	4		Stockholm	2 Aug
	(80)							
2:02.5	Yelena	Konchits	BLR	6.7.69	3		Minsk	28 Apr
2:02.52	Lorrieann	Adams	GUY	2.10.69	1		Austin	7 May
2:02.54	Ludmila	Formanová	TCH	2.1.74	3	Slov	Bratislava	1 Jun
2:02.54	Larisa	Mikhailova	RUS	69	1h3	NC	St Peterburg	14 Jul
2:02.6	Inna	Nedelenko	UKR	15.1.76	2		Dnepropetrovsk	18 Jul
2:02.63	Severine	Foulon	FRA	8.12.73	2	NC	Annecy	24 Jul
2:02.65	Daniela	Antipov	ROM	11.5.70	6	NC	Bucuresti	18 Jun
2:02.66	Monica	Westén	SWE	15.3.66	4	DNG	Stockholm	8 Mar
2:02.67	Olga	Maryina	RUS	64	3		Victoria	4 Jun
2:02.70	Yekaterina	Fedotova	RUS	4.11.75	5	Znam	Moskva	11 Jun
	(90)							
2:02.7	Yelena	Martson	UKR	16.11.72	3		Dnepropetrovsk	18 Jul
2:02.73	Diana	Pitts	USA	22.1.72	1		Fairfax	22 May
2:02.8	Alla	Kovpak	UKR	23.10.62	1		Nikolayev	10 Jul
2:02.83	Aisling	Molloy	IRL	12.6.64	4		La Celle-St Cloud	4 Jul
2:02.83	Lyudmila	Derevyankina	RUS	66	3h2	NC	St Peterburg	14 Jul
2:02.88	Antonia	Babushkina	RUS	28.12.64	8		Hechtel	30 Jul
2:03.00	Mitica	Constantin	ROM	18.8.52	6	NYG	New York	22 May
2:03.0A	Selina	Kosgei	KEN	17.1.76	1		Nairobi	5 Jul
2:03.0	Margaret	Crowley	AUS	24.5.67	1		Kamloops	10 Aug
2:03.02	Barbara	Gourdet	FRA	29.8.65	3		Narbonne	19 Jun
2:03.02	Olga	Sidorova	UKR	8.4.73	2		Kiev	23 Jul
	(101)							

Mark	Name		Nat	Born	Date
2:03.03	Melanie	Collins	AUS	67	28 Jan
2:03.04	Yekaterina	Dedkova	RUS	72	25 Aug
2:03.12	Gladys	Wamuyu	KEN	72	26 Aug
2:03.15	Galina	Reznikova	RUS	61	14 Jul
2:03.17	Irina	Kuzina	RUS	64	14 Jul
2:03.17	Cathy	Dawson	GBR	66	26 Aug
2:03.19	Kristen	Seabury	USA	69	29 Jun
2:03.21	Andrea	Suldesová	TCH	75	10 Jul
2:03.23	Inna	Yevseyeva	UKR	64	27 May
2:03.27	Joanna	Latimer	GBR	71	29 Jun
2:03.3	Angela	Chalmers	CAN	63	22 Jun
2:03.35	Fabia	Trabaldo	ITA	72	11 Jun
2:03.4	Svetlana	Romanovskaya	UKR	66	18 Jul
2:03.43	Kim	Toney	USA	72	17 Apr

Mark	Name		Nat		Date	Mark	Name		Nat		Date
2:03.52	Ellen	Kiessling	GER	68	12 Jun	2:04.0	Kari	Sleivert	CAN	63	10 Aug
2:03.54	Jennifer	Buckley	USA	74	3 Jun	2:04.00	Petya	Strashilova	BUL	65	24 May
2:03.54	Lynn	Gibson	GBR	69	3 Jul	2:04.00	Paula	Schnurr	CAN	64	16 Jul
2:03.55	Marie-Christ	Dampa	FRA	65	24 Jul	2:04.0	mxVicki	Freeborn	AUS	75	26 Feb
2:03.61	Toril	Hatling	NOR	67	2 Aug	2:04.05	Ivonne	Teichmann	GER	77	4 Jun
2:03.67		Lu Yi	CHN	74	3 Jun	2:04.06	Lyudmila	Vasilyeva	RUS	67	12 Jun
2:03.67	Angela	Davies	GBR	70	21 Aug	2:04.07	Jackline	Maranga	KEN	77	21 Jul
2:03.69	Lynda	Keough	GBR	63	5 Jun	2:04.1	Rosa	Kutty	IND	64	25 Aug
2:03.70	Martine	Meersman	BEL	67	30 Jul	2:04.11	Janice	Nichols	USA	74	17 Apr
2:03.7	Larisa	Ivanitskaya	UKR	69	10 Jul	2:04.20	Amaia	Andrés	ESP	66	5 Jun
2:03.73	Anna	Jakubczak	POL	73	25 Jun	2:04.20	Natalya	Knyazkova	RUS	63	11 Jun
2:03.75	Dawn	Gandy	GBR	65	12 Jun		(150)				
2:03.78	Tanya	Blake	GBR	71	17 Apr	2:04.2	Marina	Makarova	UKR		unc.
2:03.79	Karen	Bennett	JAM	72	21 May	2:04.26	Natalya	Tsyganova	UKR	71	11 Jun
2:03.79	Vicky	Lynch	CAN	70	3 Jun	2:04.30	Birte	Bruhns	GER	70	28 May
2:03.79	Irina	Platonova	RUS	73	4 Jul	2:04.32	Helen	Daniel	GBR	63	12 Jun
2:03.8	Fàtima	dos Santos	BRA	73	17 Sep	2:04.4	Leah	Pells	CAN	64	10 Aug
2:03.85	Anne	Bruns	GER	74	3 Jul	2:04.40	Benita	Willis	AUS	79	11 Dec
2:03.87	Aurica	Mitrea	ROM	61	18 Jun	2:04.44	Camilla	Spires	RSA	69	23 Apr
2:03.88	Julia	Sakala	ZIM	69	5 Apr	2:04.46	Julie	Speights	USA	70	23 Apr
2:03.93	Galina	Misiruk	UKR	70	28 Aug	2:04.48	Svetlana	Marchuk	UKR		27 May
2:03.94	Michelle	DiMuro	USA	67	4 Jul	2:04.49	Lotta	Bryggare	FIN	65	26 Jul
2:03.94	Munira	Gabbasova	RUS	67	14 Jul	2:04.50	Abby	Hunte	GBR	71	22 May
2:03.96	Mayte	Zuñiga	ESP	64	6 Sep		(160)				

Drugsdisqualification

Mark	Name		Nat	Born	Pos	Meet	Venue	Date
1:59.85	Diane	Modahl ¶	GBR	17.6.66	4	GWG	St Peterburg	28 Jul
2:00.52	Ella	Kovacs #	ROM	11.12.64	2	Rom IC	Bucuresti	18 Jun

Indoors

Mark	Name		Nat	Born	Pos	Meet	Venue	Date
1:59.30	Violeta	Beclea	ROM	26.3.65	1		Grenoble	6 Feb
1:59.34		Dukhnova			2		Grenoble	6 Feb
1:59.43	Ella	Kovacs #	ROM	11.12.64	1		Bucuresti	6 Feb
2:01.14	Mitica	Constantin	ROM	18.8.62	2		Karlsruhe	1 Mar
2:01.53	Letitia	Vriesde	SUR	5.10.64	2		Gent	9 Feb
2:02.66	Monica	Westén	SWE	15.3.66	4	DNG	Stockholm	8 Mar
2:02.94	Amaia	Andrés	ESP	26.6.66	2		San Sebastián	3 Mar
2:04.47	Regula	Zürcher	SUI	69				28 Jan

1000 METRES

Mark	Name		Nat	Born	Pos	Meet	Venue	Date
2:33.02	Maria	Mutola	MOZ	27.10.72	1	iDAG	Göteborg	24 Aug
2:33.33		Mutola			1	Pre	Eugene	4 Jun
2:34.99	Angela	Chalmers	CAN	6.9.63	1		Victoria	19 Aug
2:35.03	Regina	Jacobs	USA	28.8.63	2	iDAG	Göteborg	24 Aug
2:35.43	Lyubov	Gurina	RUS	6.8.57	1		Noisy-le-Grand	2 Jul
2:35.79	Yvonne	Graham	JAM	22.8.65	3	iDAG	Göteborg	24 Aug
2:36.16	Yekaterina	Podkopayeva	RUS	11.6.52	1		Nancy	14 Sep
2:37.47	Patricia	Djaté	FRA	3.1.71	2		Nancy	14 Sep
2:38.70	Maria	Akraka	SWE	7.7.66	4	iDAG	Göteborg	24 Aug
2:38.74	Julia	Sakala	ZIM	12.7.69	2		Noisy-le-Grand	2 Jul

Mark	Name		Nat		Date	Mark	Name		Nat		Date
2:40.06	Malin	Ewerlöf	SWE	72	24 Aug	2:41.3	Lisa	O'Connell	AUS	66	6 Jan
2:40.10	Luciana	Mendes	BRA	71	2 Jul	2:41.43	Anna	Jakubczak	POL	73	17 Aug
2:40.18	Tatyana	Grigoryeva	RUS	72	17 Aug	2:41.51	Sarah	Thorsett	USA	70	24 Aug
2:40.63	Ellen	Kiessling	GER	68	24 Aug	2:41.52	Blandine	Bitzner	FRA	65	2 Jul
2:40.70	Kari	Bertrand	USA	70	4 Jun	2:42.12	Donata	Sobiesiak	POL	70	17 Aug
2:41.11	Kati	Kovacs	GER	63	17 Aug						

Indoors

Mark	Name		Nat	Born	Pos	Meet	Venue	Date
2:36.84	Natalya	Dukhnova	BLR	16.7.66	1		Liévin	13 Feb
2:37.00		Podkopayeva			2		Liévin	13 Feb
2:37.26	Ludmila	Rogachova	RUS	10.10.66	3		Liévin	13 Feb

Mark	Name		Nat		Date	Mark	Name		Nat		Date
2:40.91	Letitia	Vriesde	SUR	64	23 Jan	2:42.11	Stella	Jongmans	NED	71	4 Feb
2:40.97	Sandra	Gasser	SUI	62	4 Feb	2:42.44	Anna	Brzezinska	POL	71	4 Feb

1500 METRES

Mark	Name		Nat	Born	Pos	Meet	Venue	Date
3:59.10	Sonia	O'Sullivan	IRL	28.11.69	1	Nik	Nice	18 Jul
3:59.78	Yekaterina	Podkopayeva	RUS	11.6.52	2	Nik	Nice	18 Jul
4:00.06		O'Sullivan			1	Bisl	Oslo	22 Jul
4:00.34		Qu Yunxia	CHN	4.10.72	1	NC	Beijing	5 Jun
4:01.05	Lyubov	Kremlyova	RUS	21.12.62	2	Herc	Monaco	2 Aug
4:00.46		O'Sullivan			1	DNG	Stockholm	12 Jul

Mark	Name		Nat	Born	Pos	Meet	Venue	Date
4:00.89		Podkopayeva			1	Herc	Monaco	2 Aug
4:01.05	Hassiba	Boulmerka	ALG	10.7.68	1	WCp	London	9 Sep
4:01.41	Kelly	Holmes	GBR	19.4.70	1	AAA	Sheffield	12 Jun
4:01.44	Yvonne	Murray	GBR	4.10.64	2	AAA	Sheffield	12 Jun
4:01.50		Podkopayeva			2	DNG	Stockholm	12 Jul
4:01.58		Podkopayeva			1	ASV	Köln	21 Aug
4:01.61	Angela	Chalmers	CAN	6.9.63	1	GPF	Paris	3 Sep
4:01.73		Chalmers			2	WCp	London	9 Sep
4:01.85		Boulmerka			2	GPF	Paris	3 Sep
4:01.86		Kremlyova			2	ASV	Köln	21 Aug
4:01.92		Podkopayeva			3	GPF	Paris	3 Sep
4:02.10	Olga	Churbanova	RUS	16.7.65	3	ASV	Köln	21 Aug
4:02.12		Chalmers			1		Abbotsford	6 Aug
4:02.15	Regina	Jacobs	USA	28.8.63	3	Herc	Monaco	2 Aug
4:02.27		Boulmerka			4	ASV	Köln	21 Aug
4:02.38		Chalmers			3	DNG	Stockholm	12 Jul
4:02.40	Lyudmila	Rogachova	RUS	30.10.66	1	NC	St Peterburg	16 Jul
4:02.47	Lyubov	Gurina	RUS	6.8.67	4	Herc	Monaco	2 Aug
4:02.52		Holmes			4	DNG	Stockholm	12 Jul
4:02.73		Rogachova			3	Nik	Nice	18 Jul
4:03.26		Boulmerka			1	WK	Zürich	17 Aug
4:03.40		Yan Wei	CHN	12.10.71	2	NC	Beijing	5 Jun
4:03.54		O'Sullivan			5	Herc	Monaco	2 Aug
4:03.64		Murray			2	Bisl	Oslo	22 Jul
4:03.70		Gurina			4	Nik	Nice	18 Jul
	(31/10)							
4:03.76	Viorica	Beclea	ROM	26.2.65	6	Herc	Monaco	2 Aug
4:03.78	Malgorzata	Rydz	POL	18.1.67	7	Herc	Monaco	2 Aug
4:04.19	Alison	Wyeth	GBR	26.5.64	5	Nik	Nice	18 Jul
4:04.35	Yvonne	Graham	JAM	22.8.65	1	VD	Bruxelles	19 Aug
4:04.41	Anna	Brzezinska	POL	9.1.71	2		Rieti	28 Aug
4:04.57	Suzy	Hamilton	USA	8.8.68	2	v GBR	Gateshead	20 Jul
4:04.72	Blandine	Bitzner	FRA	1.12.65	6	Nik	Nice	18 Jul
4:05.66	Lyudmila	Borisova	RUS	3.8.66	2	NC	St Peterburg	16 Jul
4:05.75	Lynn	Gibson	GBR	6.7.69	3	v USA	Gateshead	20 Jul
4:06.05	Carla	Sacramento	POR	10.12.71	6	GPF	Paris	3 Sep
	(20)							
4:06.97	Ellen	van Langen	NED	9.2.66	4	Athl	Lausanne	6 Jul
4:07.2	Svetlana	Miroshnik	UKR	3.6.68	1		Dnepropetrovsk	9 Jul
4:07.40	Gwen	Griffiths	RSA	30.8.67	11	Herc	Monaco	2 Aug
4:07.83	Ellen	Kiessling	GER	17.2.68	6	ASV	Köln	21 Aug
4:07.92	Yelena	Romanova	RUS	20.3.63	5	Athl	Lausanne	6 Jul
4:07.94	Paula	Schnurr	CAN	15.1.64	2	NC	Victoria	30 Jul
4:08.11	Farida	Fatès	FRA	2.2.62	1		Mulhouse	10 Jul
4:08.63	Maria	Akraka	SWE	7.7.66	9	VD	Bruxelles	19 Aug
4:08.63	Mayte	Zuñiga	ESP	28.12.64	10	VD	Bruxelles	19 Aug
4:08.66	Leah	Pells	CAN	9.11.64	3	NC	Victoria	30 Jul
	(30)							
4:08.71	Ann	Griffiths	GBR	20.8.65	3	AAA	Sheffield	12 Jun
4:08.77	Gina	Procaccio	USA	19.7.64	1	Jen	San José	28 May
4:08.79	Kathy	Franey	USA	25.12.67	3	NC	Knoxville	18 Jun
4:09.00	Frédérique	Quentin	FRA	22.12.69	2		Narbonne	19 Jun
4:09.1	Zoya	Kaznovskaya	UKR	22.9.66	2		Dnepropetrovsk	9 Jul
4:09.12	Robin	Meagher	CAN	17.6.67	4	NC	Victoria	30 Jul
4:09.29	Angela	Davies	GBR	21.10.70	5	vUSA	Gateshead	20 Jul
4:09.59	Marina	Bastos	POR	7.7.71	1	NC	Lisboa	9 Jul
4:09.6	Irina	Samorokova	RUS	6.12.64	1		Irkutsk	28 May
4:09.83	Yelena	Kaledina	RUS	3.10.68	1		Moskva	11 Jun
	(40)							
4:10.16	Geraldine	Nolan	IRL	11.4.74	4		Rieti	28 Aug
4:10.24	Sarah	Thorsett	USA	18.3.70	4	NC	Knoxville	18 Jun
4:10.32	Lynne	Robinson	GBR	21.6.69	3		Hechtel	30 Jul
4:10.47	Julie	Speights	USA	13.5.70	5	Jen	San José	28 May
4:10.54	Fernanda	Ribeiro	POR	23.6.69	2	NC	Lisboa	9 Jul
4:10.56	Elena	Fidatov	ROM	24.7.60	1		Bucuresti	29 Jul
4:10.69	Jasmin	Jones	USA	13.10.69	3	PennR	Philadelphia	30 Apr
4:10.73	Grete	Koens	NED	26.5.67	4		Hechtel	30 Jul
4:10.94		Zhang Yumei	CHN	25.11.71	1		Hiroshima	29 Apr

Mark	Name		Nat	Born	Pos	Meet	Venue	Date
4:10.97	Kristen	Seabury	USA	14.4.69	6	NC	Knoxville	18 Jun
	(50)							
4:11.01	Lyudmila	Vasilyeva	RUS	20.10.69	1		Fukuoka	24 Sep
4:11.04	Bev	Hartigan	GBR	10.6.67	4	AAA	Sheffield	12 Jun
4:11.10	Harumi	Hiroyama	JPN	2.9.68	2		Hiroshima	29 Apr
4:11.20		Wang Junxia	CHN	9.1.73	3	NC	Beijing	5 Jun
4:11.36	Julia	Sakala	ZIM	12.7.69	2		La Celle-St-Cloud	4 Jul
4:11.48	Margaret	Crowley	AUS	24.5.67	5	CG	Victoria	28 Aug
4:11.54	Liliana	Salageanu	ROM	24.3.71	2	NC	Bucuresti	17 Jun
4:11.56	Melanie	Choinière	CAN	.72	2		Abbotsford	6 Aug
4:11.57	Katharina	Orthaber	SUI	9.9.63	3		Cottbus	15 Jun
4:11.69	Hilde	Stavik	NOR	6.9.62	9	DNG	Stockholm	12 Jul
	(60)							
4:11.92	Alta	Lohann	RSA	9.3.68	5		Narbonne	16 Jun
4:11.94	Natalya	Dukhnova	BLR	16.7.66	1		Lapinlahti	26 Jun
4:12.05	Natalya	Betekhtina	RUS	8.9.61	4	Znam	Moskva	5 Jun
4:12.09	Simone	Weidner	GER	30.9.69	1		Nürnberg	10 Jun
4:12.10	Molly	Chacko	IND	15.5.69	1		Lucknow	25 Aug
4:12.12+	Ceci	St.Geme	USA	13.4.63	5	Bisl	Oslo	22 Jul
4:12.20	Sonia	McGeorge	GBR	2.11.64	2	TSB	London	15 Jul
4:12.20	Sinead	Delahunty	IRL	12.2.71	8h2	EC	Helsinki	12 Aug
4:12.27	Margarita	Maruseva	RUS	18.10.67	3	NC	St Peterburg	16 Jul
4:12.3	Olga	Sidorova	UKR	8.4.73			Dnepropetrovsk	9 Jul
	(70)							
4:12.31	Elisa	Rea	ITA	23.3.68	2		Nürnberg	10 Jun
4:12.48	Luminita	Zaituc	ROM	9.10.68	1		Minden	10 Aug
4:12.54	Yelena	Bychkovskaya	BLR	4.3.72	9h1	EC	Helsinki	12 Aug
4:12.55	Kelly	Rabush	USA	22.10.67	7	Jen	San José	28 May
4:12.62	Tudorita	Chidu	ROM	17.10.67	3	NC	Bucuresti	18 Jun
4:12.70	Camilla	Spires	RSA	29.10.69	3		La Celle-St-Cloud	4 Jul
4:12.72	Daniela	Bran	ROM	13.4.68	4	NC	Bucuresti	17 Jun
4:12.82	Joetta	Clark	USA	1.8.62	5	PennR	Philadelhia	30 Apr
4:12.84	Jackline	Maranga	KEN	16.12.77	6	CG	Victoria	28 Aug
4:12.91	Marina	Chirila	ROM	7.9.64	5	NC	Bucuresti	17 Jun
	(80)							
4:12.94	Kari	Bertrand	USA	11.11.70	7	NC	Knoxville	18 Jun
4:12.98	Andrea	Karhoff	GER	20.5.74	3		Nürnberg	10 Jun
4:13.15	Laurence	Vivier	FRA	21.11.67	4		La Celle-St Cloud	4 Jul
4:13.22	Angela	Raines-White	AUS	22.3.74	1		Melbourne	20 Nov
4:13.26	Yelena	Storchevaya	UKR	23.6.66	1	NC	Kiev	28 May
4:13.30	Cristina	Misaros	ROM	1.1.69	6	NC	Bucuresti	18 Jun
4:13.32	Antje	Beggerow	GER	10.12.73	4		Nürnberg	10 Jun
4:13.38	Laurence	Duquénoy	FRA	29.9.69	6		Hechtel	30 Jul
4:13.50	Debbie	Gunning	GBR	31.8.65	7	AAA	Sheffield	12 Jun
4:13.60	Zola	Pieterse	RSA	26.5.66	3		Luzern	29 Jun
	(90)							
4:13.64	Mitica	Constantin	ROM	18.8.62	7	NC	Bucuresti	17 Jun
4:13.71	Marjo	Piipponen	FIN	29.5.71	10h2	EC	Helsinki	12 Aug
4:13.74	Viorica	Niga	ROM	22.11.68	8	NC	Bucuresti	17 Jun
4:13.79	Susie	Power	AUS	26.3.75	2		Melbourne	20 Nov
4:13.84		Zhang Lirong	CHN	4.6.73	h	NC	Beijing	4 Jun
4:13.90	Larisa	Mikhailova	RUS	69	4	NC	St Peterburg	16 Jul
4:13.91	Olga	Kuznyetsova	RUS	23.10.67	4		Dijon	12 Jun
4:13.92	Vera	Norkina	RUS	20.8.68	5	NC	St Peterburg	16 Jul
4:13.93	Maria	Mutola	MOZ	27.12.72	1		Eugene	16 Apr
4:13.97		Zhang Linli	CHN	6.3.73	h	NC	Beijing	4 Jun
4:13.97	Anita	Weyermann	SUI	8.12.77	1	WJ	Lisboa	24 Jul
	(101)							

Mark	Name		Nat	Born	Date
4:14.12	Sarah	Howell	CAN	69	29 May
4:14.15	Cheri	Goddard	USA	70	2 Jul
4:14.23	Carmen	Wüstenhagen	GER	73	21 Aug
4:14.31		Lu Yi	CHN	74	4 Jun
4:14.43		Liu Wanjie#	CHN	75	5 Jun
4:14.43	Gabriela	Szabo	ROM	75	5 Jun
4:14.43	Silvia	Sommaggio	ITA	69	16 Jun
4:14.44	Darcy	Arreola	USA	68	28 May
4:14.54		Liu Li	CHN	71	5 Jun
4:14.56	Cindy	O'Krane	CAN	63	30 Jul
4:14.56	Atsumi	Yashima	JPN	75	24 Sep
4:14.59	Marta	Dominguez	ESP	75	24 Jul
4:14.60	Merima	Denboba	ETH	74	25 Jun
4:14.62	Susan	Parker	GBR	70	12 Jun
4:14.72	Anna	Jakubczak	POL	73	20 Aug
4:14.75	Mariya	Pantyukhova	RUS	74	24 Aug
4:14.84	Serenella	Sbrissa	ITA	67	2 Jul
4:14.86	Anne	Cross	AUS	65	24 Feb
4:14.89	Anita	Philpott	IRL	69	24 Jul
4:14.92	Klara	Kashapova	RUS	70	28 Jun
4:14.96	Yoshiko	Ichikawa	JPN	76	11 Jun
	(122)				

Mark	Name		Nat	Born	Pos	Meet	Venue	Date
Indoors								
4:07.85	Tudorita	Chidu	ROM	17.10.67	1		Budapest	5 Feb
4:08.96	Liliana	Salageanu	ROM	24.3.71	2		Budapest	5 Feb
4:10.30	Fernanda	Ribeiro	POR	23.6.69	2	NC	Braga	20 Feb
4:10.92	Mitica	Constantin	ROM	18.8.62	1		Stuttgart	6 Feb
4:12.44	Sarah	Howell	CAN	11.9.69	2		Hamilton	14 Jan
4:12.73	Sandra	Gasser	SUI	27.7.62	3		Stuttgart	6 Feb
4:12.87	Olga	Kuznyetsova	RUS	23.10.67	3	NC	Lipetsk	27 Feb

Mark	Name		Nat	Born	Date	Mark	Name		Nat	Born	Date
4:14.4	Luminita	Gogirlea	ROM	71	15 Jan	4:14.62	Ravilya	Agletdinova	BLR	66	6 Feb

1 MILE

Mark	Name		Nat	Born	Pos	Meet	Venue	Date
4:17.25	Sonia	O'Sullivan	IRL	28.11.69	1	Bisl	Oslo	22 Jul
4:22.09	Hassiba	Boulmerka	ALG	10.7.68	1	WK	Zürich	17 Aug
4:22.64	Yvonne	Murray	GBR	4.10.64	2	Bisl	Oslo	22 Jul
4:22.95		O'Sullivan			1		Cork	25 Jun
4:23.14		O'Sullivan			2	WK	Zürich	17 Aug
4:23.88	Lyudmila	Rogachova	RUS	30.10.66	3	WK	Zürich	17 Aug
4:24.64	Yvonne	Graham	JAM	22.8.65	4	WK	Zürich	17 Aug
4:25.1 +		O'Sullivan			1k	TSB	Edinburgh	8 Jul
4:25.2 +		Murray			2k	TSB	Edinburgh	8 Jul
4:25.77		O'Sullivan			1	GP	Gateshead	1 Jul
	(10/5)							
4:27.56	Lyubov	Kremlyova	RUS	21.12.62	5	WK	Zürich	17 Aug
4:27.66	Anna	Brzezinska	POL	9.1.71	6	WK	Zürich	17 Aug
4:27.78	Regina	Jacobs	USA	28.8.63	3	Bisl	Oslo	22 Jul
4:28.17	Angela	Chalmers	CAN	6.9.63	2		Gateshead	1 Jul
4:28.39	Malgorzata	Rydz	POL	18.1.67	4	Bisl	Oslo	22 Jul
	(10)							
4:29.34	Gina	Procaccio	USA	19.7.64	4		Gateshead	1 Jul
4:29.65	Carla	Sacramento	POR	10.12.71	7	WK	Zürich	17 Aug
4:30.20	Kathy	Franey	USA	25.12.67	5		Gateshead	1 Jul
4:30.24	Alison	Wyeth	GBR	26.5.64	6		Gateshead	1 Jul
4:30.62	Paula	Schnurr	CAN	15.1.64	7		Gateshead	1 Jul
4:31.17	Lynn	Gibson	GBR	6.7.69	8		Gateshead	1 Jul
4:31.26	Bev	Hartigan	GBR	10.6.67	9		Gateshead	1 Jul
4:31.59	Ceci	St Geme	USA	13.4.63	5	Bisl	Oslo	22 Jul
4:31.64	Blandine	Bitzner	FRA	1.12.65	8	WK	Zürich	17 Aug
4:31.83	Angela	Davies	GBR	21.10.70	10	GP	Gateshead	1 Jul
	(20)							
4:33.12	Sonia	McGeorge	GBR	2.11.64	11		Gateshead	1 Jul
4:33.33	Stela	Apetre	ROM	25.2.72	1		Bucuresti	29 May
4:34.29	Gwen	Griffiths	RSA	30.8.67	12		Gateshead	1 Jul
4:34.39	Hilde	Stavik	NOR	6.9.62	6	Bisl	Oslo	22 Jul
4:34.77	Sarah	Howell	CAN	11.9.69	13		Gateshead	1 Jul
Indoors								
4:34.48	Leslie	Lehane	USA	21.3.63	1		Boston	20 Feb
4:35.02	Jasmin	Jones	USA	13.10.69	4		Fairfax	6 Feb

2000 METRES

Mark	Name		Nat	Born	Pos	Meet	Venue	Date
5:25.36	Sonia	O'Sullivan	IRL	28.11.69	1	TSB	Edinburgh	8 Jul
5:26.93	Yvonne	Murray	GBR	4.10.64	2	TSB	Edinburgh	8 Jul
5:34.49	Angela	Chalmers	CAN	6.9.63	1	McD	Sheffield	4 Sep
5:37.6+		O'Sullivan			1+	TSB	London	15 Jul
5:37.7+		Murray			2+	TSB	London	15 Jul
5:38.33		Murray			2	McD	Sheffield	4 Sep
5:38.42	Regina	Jacobs	USA	28.8.63	3	TSB	Edinburgh	8 Jul
	(7/4)							
5:42.86	Suzy	Hamilton	USA	8.8.68	1	Pre	Eugene	4 Jun
5:42.90	Annette	Peters	USA	31.5.65	4	TSB	Edinburgh	8 Jul
5:43.13	Alison	Wyeth	GBR	26.5.64	3	McD	Sheffield	4 Sep
5:43.59	Libbie	Johnson	USA	17.2.65	5	TSB	Edinburgh	8 Jul
5:44.07	Lyubov	Kremlyova	RUS	21.12.62	4	McD	Sheffield	4 Sep
5:45.89	Robin	Meagher	CAN	17.6.67	5	McD	Sheffield	4 Sep
	(10)							

Mark	Name		Nat	Born	Date	Mark	Name		Nat	Born	Date
5:46.59	Lyudmila	Borisova	RUS	66	4 Sep	5:49.31	Gwen	Griffiths	RSA	67	4 Mar
5:47.14	Carla	Sacramento	POR	71	4 Sep	5:49.58+	Catherina	McKiernan	IRL	69	18 Jul
5:47.74	Yvonne	Graham	JAM	65	4 Sep	5:50.47	Susie	Power	AUS	75	4 Sep
5:47.76	Maria	Akraka	SWE	66	4 Sep	5:51.22	Polly	Plumer	USA	64	4 Jun
5:48.03	Zola	Pieterse	RSA	66	4 Mar						

3000 METRES

Mark	Name		Nat	Born	Pos	Meet	Venue	Date
8:21.64	Sonia	O'Sullivan	IRL	28.11.69	1	TSB	London	15 Jul
8:29.60	Yvonne	Murray	GBR	4.10.64	2	TSB	London	15 Jul
8:31.84		O'Sullivan			1	EC	Helsinki	10 Aug
8:32.17	Angela	Chalmers	CAN	5.9.63	1	CG	Victoria	23 Aug
8:36.48		Murray			2	EC	Helsinki	10 Aug
8:38.42		Chalmers			1	NC	Victoria	27 Jul
8:38.72		Chalmers			3	GP	London	15 Jul
8:40.08	Gabriela	Szabo	ROM	14.11.75	3	EC	Helsinki	10 Aug
8:40.48	Olga	Churbanova	RUS	16.7.64	4	EC	Helsinki	10 Aug
8:41.06	Yelena	Romanova	RUS	20.3.63	1	GWG	St Peterburg	24 Jul
8:41.71	Lyudmila	Borisova	RUS	3.8.66	5	EC	Helsinki	10 Aug
8:41.97	Annette	Peters	USA	31.5.65	4	TSB	London	15 Jul
8:42.13	Fernanda	Ribeiro	POR	23.6.69	2	GWG	St Peterburg	24 Jul
8:43.65		Peters			3	GWG	St Peterburg	24 Jul
8:43.70		Romanova			1	Nik	Nice	18 Jul
8:44.85		Peters			2	Nik	Nice	18 Jul
8:45.59	Robyn	Meagher	CAN	17.6.67	2	CG	Victoria	23 Aug
8:45.76	Alison	Wyeth	GBR	26.5.64	6	EC	Helsinki	10 Aug
8:45.80		Churbanova			1	Kuts	Moskva	31 Jul
8:45.87	Yvonne	Graham	JAM	22.8.65	3	Nik	Nice	18 Jul
8:46.04	Kathy	Franey	USA	25.12.67	1	WG	Helsinki	29 Jun
8:46.04	Farida	Fatès	FRA	2.2.62	7	EC	Helsinki	10 Aug
8:46.40		Fatès			4	Nik	Nice	18 Jul
8:46.42		Wyeth			2	WG	Helsinki	29 Jun
8:47.35		Romanova			1		Maia	16 Jul
8:47.40		Szabo			1	WJ	Lisboa	22 Jul
8:47.47	Hilde	Stavik	NOR	6.9.62	5	GP	London	15 Jul
8:47.50		Ribeiro			2	Kuts	Moskva	31 Jul
8:47.98		Wyeth			3	CG	Victoria	23 Aug
8:48.77		Borisova			4	GWG	St Peterburg	24 Jul
	(30/15)							
8:49.10	Gina	Procaccio	USA	19.7.64	3	WG	Helsinki	29 Jun
8:49.42	Nadia	Dandolo	ITA	11.9.62	8	EC	Helsinki	10 Aug
8:49.62	Roberta	Brunet	ITA	20.5.65	1	GGala	Roma	8 Jun
8:49.69	Cristina	Misaros	ROM	1.1.69	9	EC	Helsinki	10 Aug
8:49.92		Wang Xiaoxia	CHN	21.8.76	1	NC	Beijing	2 Jun
	(20)							
8:50.05		Zhang Linli	CHN	6.3.73	2	NC	Beijing	2 Jun
8:50.07	Kathrin	Wessel	GER	14.8.67	4	GGala	Roma	8 Jun
8:50.30	Silvia	Sommagio	ITA	20.11.69	5	GGala	Roma	8 Jun
8:50.40	Harumi	Hiroyama	JPN	2.9.68	5	WG	Helsinki	29 Jun
8:50.51		Zhang Lirong	CHN	3.3.73	3	NC	Beijing	2 Jun
8:50.61	Libbie	Johnson	USA	17.2.65	6	TSB	London	15 Jul
8:50.62		Ma Ningning	CHN	20.9.76	4	NC	Beijing	2 Jun
8:50.68		Wang Xiuting	CHN	16.2.65	1	JapC	Tokyo	12 Jun
8:50.79		Wang Junxia	CHN	9.1.73	5	NC	Beijing	2 Jun
8:51.55	Sonia	McGeorge	GBR	2.11.64	11	EC	Helsinki	10 Aug
	(30)							
8:51.57	Gwen	Griffiths	RSA	30.8.67	6	GGala	Roma	8 Jun
8:51.67	Catherina	McKiernan	IRL	30.11.69	5	Nik	Nice	18 Jul
8:51.96		Lin Jianying	CHN	19.11.71	6	NC	Beijing	2 Jun
8:52.06	Michiko	Shimizu	JPN	22.9.70	3	NC	Tokyo	12 Jun
8:52.24	Annemari	Sandell	FIN	2.1.77	7	WG	Helsinki	29 Jun
8:52.33	Olga	Bondarenko	RUS	2.6.60	2	NC	St Peterburg	14 Jul
8:52.54	Merami	Denboba	ETH	21.8.74	8	WG	Helsinki	29 Jun
8:53.01	Grete	Koens	NED	26.5.67	9	WG	Helsinki	29 Jun
8:53.27		Dong Li	CHN	9.12.73	7	NC	Beijing	2 Jun
8:53.40	Sally	Barsosio	KEN	21.3.78	1	Afr-J	Alger	8 Jul
	(40)							
8:54.40	Zahra	Ouaziz	MAR	20.12.69	1		Rabat	4 Jun
8:54.59	Maria	Guida	ITA	23.1.66	7	GGala	Roma	8 Jun
8:54.74	Derartu	Tulu	ETH	21.3.72	1	OD	Jena	3 Jun
8:54.79	Anita	Philpott	IRL	24.7.69	12	EC	Helsinki	10 Aug
8:55.38	Regina	Cistjakova	LIT	7.11.61	2	OD	Jena	3 Jun
8:55.56	Zoya	Kaznovskaya	UKR	22.9.66	3	Kuts	Moskva	31 Jul
8:55.65	Anna	Brzezinska	POL	9.1.71	2	APM	Hengelo	4 Jun

Mark	Name		Nat	Born	Pos	Meet	Venue	Date
8:55.89	Silvia	Botticelli	ITA	14.3.68	8	GGala	Roma	8 Jun
8:56.03mx	Zola	Pieterse	RSA	26.5.66	mx		Dübendorf	7 Jul
	9:00.00				6	GP II	Linz	4 Jul
8:56.39	Chikako	Suzuki	JPN	1.9.69	4	NC	Tokyo	12 Jun
	(50)							
8:56.40	Olga	Kovpotina	RUS	10.1.68	4	APM	Hengelo	4 Jun
8:56.43	Yelena	Kaledina	RUS	3.10.68	3	NC	St Peterburg	14 Jul
8:56.51	Elly	Van Hulst	NED	9.6.59	9	GGala	Roma	8 Jun
8:56.71	Gunhild	Halle	NOR	1.6.72	10	WG	Helsinki	29 Jun
8:56.79	Andrea	Karhoff	GER	20.5.74	5	APM	Hengelo	4 Jun
8:56.93	Susie	Power	AUS	26.3.75	2	WJ	Lisboa	22 Jul
8:56.94	Mahomi	Muranaka	JPN	31.10.66	5	NC	Tokyo	12 Jun
8:56.99	Päivi	Tikkanen	FIN	19.1.60	4h2	EC	Helsinki	7 Aug
8:57.13	Daria	Nauer	SUI	21.5.66	2	GP II	Linz	4 Jul
8:57.18	Kay	Gooch	NZL	2.5.72	1	MSR	Walnut	16 Apr
	(60)							
8:57.45	Kari	Bertrand	USA	11.11.70	11	WG	Helsinki	29 Jun
8:57.81	Mariko	Hara	JPN	27.12.70	9	TSB	London	15 Jul
8:58.19	Marina	Rodchenkova	RUS	30.7.61	6	JPNCh	Tokyo	12 Jun
8:58.23	Luminita	Zaituc	ROM	9.10.68	10	TSB	London	15 Jul
8:58.26	Patrizia	Di Napoli	ITA	27.9.69	10	GGala	Roma	8 Jun
8:58.30	Polly	Plumer	USA	14.10.64	12	WG	Helsinki	29 Jun
8:58.34	Masako	Saito	JPN	24.10.74	2	NC	Kumamoto	23 Oct
8:58.38	Claudia	Lokar	GER	9.2.64	3	OD	Jena	3 Jun
8:58.61	Getenesh	Urge	ETH	30.8.70	1		Padova	10 Jul
8:58.68		Lu Ou	CHN	10.4.74	2	AsiG	Hiroshima	11 Oct
	(70)							
8:58.74	Marina	Bastos	POR	7.7.71	1		Maia	26 Jun
8:58.75	Brynhild	Synstnes	NOR	20.4.71	6h	EC	Helsinki	7 Aug
8:59.11	Marina	Chirila	ROM	7.9.64	2	NC	Bucuresti	10 Jun
8:59.19	Helen	Kimaiyo	KEN	8.9.68	6	APM	Hengelo	4 Jun
8:59.2	Lynn	Jennings	USA	10.7.60	2	Jen	San José	28 May
8:59.23	Julia	Sakala	ZIM	12.7.69	1		Durban	23 Apr
8:59.30	Katy	McCandless	USA	22.6.70	13	GGala	Roma	8 Jun
8:59.37	Junko	Kataoka	JPN	13.6.70	11	TSB	London	15 Jul
8:59.79	Elisa	Rea	ITA	23.3.68	4		Padova	10 Jul
8:59.88	Tatyana	Pentukova	RUS	23.6.65	4	Kuts	Moskva	31 Jul
	(80)							
9:00.0	Gwyn	Coogan	USA	21.8.65	1		Dedham	4 Jun
9:00.09	Geraldine	Hendricken	IRL	19.4.70	2		Montreal	27 Jun
9:00.41	Viktoria	Nenasheva	RUS	26.6.70	3		Reims	8 Jun
9:00.5 mx	Christine	Toonstra	NED	22.6.66	-	mix	Amsterdam	5 Aug
	9:07.02				13	GP II	Linz	4 Jul
9:00.54	Estela	Estévez	ESP	24.2.65	1	NC	San Sebastián	17 Jul
9:00.82	Margarita	Maruseva	RUS	27.11.67	4	OD	Jena	3 Jun
9:00.89	Rose	Cheruiyot	KEN	21.7.76	6	CG	Victoria	23 Aug
9:01.14	Conceição	Ferreira	POR	13.3.62	2		Maia	26 Jun
9:01.16	Leah	Pells	CAN	9.11.64	3		Montreal	27 Jun
9:01.84	Nina	Byelikova	RUS	1.10.61	5	Kuts	Moskva	31 Jul
	(90)							
9:01.92	Alta	Lohann	RSA	9.3.68	6	OD	Jena	3 Jun
9:01.95	Renata	Sobiesiak	POL	14.6.70	12h1	EC	Helsinki	7 Aug
9:01.98	Anikó	Javos	HUN	14.1.71	9h2	EC	Helsinki	7 Aug
9:02.22		Wang Xiujie	CHN	20.11.73		NC	Beijing	2 Jun
9:02.28	Cheri	Goddard	USA	23.12.70	4		Montreal	28 Jun
9:02.30	Luminita	Gogîrlea	ROM	5.11.71	3	NC	Bucuresti	10 Jun
9:02.37	Delirde	Bernardi	BRA	27.4.69	8	GP II	Linz	4 Jul
9:02.38	Julia	Vaquero	ESP	18.9.70	2	NC	San Sebastián	17 Jul
9:02.43	Elana	Meyer	RSA	10.10.66	9	Nik	Nice	18 Jul
9:02.47	Laura	Adam	GBR	28.2.65	8	APM	Hengelo	4 Jun
	(100)							

Mark	Name		Nat	Born	Date
9:02.74	Milka	Mikhailova	BUL	72	7 Aug
9:02.86		Wu Mei	CHN	73	2 Jun
9:03.05	Yasuko	Kimura	JPN	76	1 Nov
9:03.21	Yuko	Kawakami	JPN	75	1 Nov
9:03.40	Klara	Kashapova	RUS	70	19 Jun
9:03.56	Wang Dongmei		CHN	73	11 Sep
9:03.62	Anne	Hare	NZL	64	6 Aug
9:04.21	Blandine	Bitzner	FRA	65	8 Jun
9:04.30	Yuko	Kubota	JPN	74	30 Apr
9:04.31	Esther	Wanjiru	KEN	77	12 Jun
9:04.35	Maria	Akraka	SWE	66	28 Aug
9:04.56	Khin Khin Htwe		MYA	67	11 Oct
9:04.64	Atsumi	Yashima	JPN	75	25 Sep
9:04.65	Isabel	Juárez	MEX	66	4 Jun
9:04.90	Minori	Hayakari	JPN	72	12 Jun
9:04.95	Carol	Montgomery	CAN	66	27 Jul

Mark	Name		Nat	Born	Pos	Meet	Venue	Date

Mark	First name	Surname	Nat	Born	Date
9:05.02	Rosario	Murcia	FRA	64	8 Jun
9:05.16	Elena	Cosovanu	ROM	74	10 Jun
9:05.17	Alena	Peterková	TCH	60	3 Sep
9:05.29	Yelena	Baranova	RUS	70	14 Jul
9:05.29	Lieve	Slegers	BEL	65	3 Sep
9:05.4	Anne	Cross	AUS	65	16 Jun
9:05.69	Claudia	Stalder	SUI	72	11 Jun
9:05.70	Miwa	Sugawara	JPN	76	29 May
9:06.0A	Pamela	Chepchumba	KEN	79	5 Jul
9:06.06	Lizanne	Bussières	CAN	61	10 Jul
9:06.21	Mariya	Pantyukhova	RUS	74	25 Aug
9:06.42	Molly	Chacko	IND	69	11 Oct
9:06.49	Tatyana	Belovol	UKR	69	25 Jun
9:06.49	Marzia	Gazzetta	ITA	67	8 Jun
9:06.7A	Eunice	Sagero	KEN	75	2 Jul
9:06.78	Laurence	Duquénoy	FRA	69	11 Jul
9:07.04	Joan	Nesbit	USA	62	14 May
9:07.04	Serap	Aktas	TUR	71	7 Aug
9:07.17	Laurence	Vivier	FRA	67	18 Jul
9:07.18	Maiken	Sørum	NOR	68	19 Aug
9:07.30	Cathy	Palacios	USA	68	9 Jul
9:07.40	Lauren	Gubicza	USA	71	4 Jul
9:07.47	Fran	ten Bensel	USA	69	27 Jun
9:07.65	Nela	Avramescu/Vlad	ROM	66	10 Jun
9:07.86	Els	Peiren	BEL	69	9 Jul
9:08.1	Angela	Raines-White	AUS	74	16 Jun
9:08.10+	Tecla	Lorupe	KEN	71	30 Aug
9:08.28	Kate	Fonshell	USA	69	28 Jun
9:08.38	Desana	Sourková	TCH	70	4 Jul
9:08.54	Rie	Ueno	JPN	76	23 Oct
9:08.68	Michelle	Dillon	AUS	73	28 Jan
9:08.86	Flavia	Gaviglio	ITA	63	8 Jun
9:09.2	Claudia	Metzner	GER	66	15 Jun
9:09.2	Cindy	O'Krane	CAN	63	23 Jul
	(150)				
9:09.28	Rosanna	Martin	ITA	73	10 Jul
9:09.63	Akiko	Hagiwara	JPN	69	12 Jun
9:09.94	Nadia	Bernard-Prasad	FRA	67	4 Jul
9:09.78	Lidia	Vasilevskaya	RUS	73	17 Jun
9:09.78	Ana	Dias	POR	74	16 Jul
9:09.94	Nadia	Bernard	FRA	67	4 Jul

Indoors

Mark	First name	Surname	Nat	Born	Pos	Meet	Venue	Date
8:55.58	Yelena	Lipsnis	RUS	20.3.68	1		St.Peterburg	20 Feb
8:55.61	Margareta	Keszeg	ROM	31.8.65	2	EI	Paris	11 Mar
8:57.49	Christina	Mai	GER	3.9.61	4	EI	Paris	11 Mar
8:58.30	Svetlana	Bulbanovich	RUS	8.4.70	2		St.Peterburg	20 Feb
8:59.95	Laurence	Vivier	FRA	21.11.67	5	EI	Paris	11 Mar
9:02.5	Tudorita	Chidu	ROM	17.10.67	1		Budapest	23 Jan

Mark	First name	Surname	Nat	Born	Date
9:07.4	Iulia	Ionescu	ROM	65	23 Jan
9:09.7	Matalia	Azpiazu	ESP	66	22 Jan

5000 METRES

Mark	First name	Surname	Nat	Born	Pos	Meet	Venue	Date
15:05.94	Yelena	Romanova	RUS	20.3.63	1	DNG	Stockholm	12 Jul
15:06.18	Sonia	O'Sullivan	IRL	28.11.69	1	ASV	Köln	21 Aug
15:06.91	Fernanda	Ribeiro	POR	23.6.69	1	TOTO	Tokyo	15 Sep
15:09.10	Catherina	McKiernan	IRL	30.11.69	2	DNG	Stockholm	12 Jul
15:10.38	Alison	Wyeth	GBR	26.5.64	1	ISTAF	Berlin	30 Aug
15:10.84	Kathrin	Wessel	GER	14.8.67	2	ISTAF	Berlin	30 Aug
15:12.94		O'Sullivan			1	GPF	Paris	3 Sep
15:13.07		McKiernan			3	ISTAF	Berlin	30 Aug
15:13.27	Lyudmila	Borisova	RUS	3.8.66	2	ASV	Köln	21 Aug
15:13.67	Yvonne	Graham	JAM	22.8.65	3	ASV	Köln	21 Aug
15:13.93	Daria	Nauer	SUI	21.5.66	4	ISTAF	Berlin	30 Aug
15:14.23	Nadia	Dandolo	ITA	11.9.62	5	ISTAF	Berlin	30 Aug
15:14.61		Borisova			2	GPF	Paris	3 Sep
15:15.42	Annette	Peters	USA	31.5.65	4	ASV	Köln	21 Aug
15:15.45		Wyeth			3	GPF	Paris	3 Sep
15:16.00		Wessel			5	ASV	Köln	21 Aug
15:16.41	Farida	Fatès	FRA	2.2.62	6	ASV	Köln	21 Aug
15:16.92	Claudia	Lokar	GER	9.2.64	6	ISTAF	Berlin	30 Aug
15:18.25		Graham			4	GPF	Paris	3 Sep
15:19.4	Yasuko	Kimura	JPN	6.1.76	1		Toyonaka	21 Dec
15:19.58	Lieve	Slegers	BEL	6.4.65	7	ISTAF	Berlin	30 Aug
15:19.94		Peters			3	DNG	Stockholm	12 Jul
	(22/15)							
15:22.54	Tecla	Lorupe	KEN	5.5.71	8	ASV	Köln	21 Aug
15:23.20	Roberta	Brunet	ITA	20.5.65	9	ASV	Köln	21 Aug
15:23.36	Miki	Igarashi	JPN	22.8.71	3	TOTO	Tokyo	15 Sep
15:23.38	Hilde	Stavik	NOR	6.9.62	1		København	28 Aug
15:24.05	Tatyana	Pentukova	RUS	23.6.65	10	ASV	Köln	21 Aug
	(20)							
15:25.59+	Elana	Meyer	RSA	10.10.66	1	WCp	London	10 Sep
15:26.14	Junko	Kataoka	JPN	13.6.70	5	DNG	Stockholm	12 Jul
15:26.3	Atsumi	Yashima	JPN	28.6.75	2		Toyonaka	21 Dec
15:27.55	Klara	Kashapova	RUS	29.1.70	1	NC	St Peterburg	16 Jul
15:28.03	Margaret	Kagiri	KEN	64	9	ISTAF	Berlin	30 Aug
15:28.70	Maria Conceição	Ferreira	POR	13.3.62	6	DNG	Stockholm	12 Jul
15:30.04	Gunhild	Halle	NOR	1.6.72	2		København	28 Aug
15:33.53	Harumi	Hiroyama	JPN	2.9.68	7	DNG	Stockholm	12 Jul

Mark	Name		Nat	Born	Pos	Meet	Venue	Date
15:33.88	Gitte	Karlshøj	DEN	14.5.59	3	GWG	St Peterburg	29 Jul
15:34.57	Angela	Chalmers	CAN	5.9.63	1		Seattle	7 Jun
	(30)							
15:35.81	Katy	McCandless	USA	22.6.70	4	GWG	St Peterburg	29 Jul
15:36.01	Michiko	Shimizu	JPN	22.9.70	5	TOTO	Tokyo	15 Sep
15:37.37		Zhong Huandi	CHN	17.1.68	1		Shizuoka	5 May
15:37.43	Alla	Shumakova	RUS	69	5	GWG	St Peterburg	29 Jul
15:38.00	Masako	Saito	JPN	24.10.74	6	TOTO	Tokyo	15 Sep
15:38.39	Gwen	Griffiths	RSA	30.8.67	9	GPF	Paris	3 Sep
15:38.41	Lynn	Jennings	USA	10.7.60	1	PennR	Philadelphia	28 Apr
15:38.64	Cathy	Palacios	USA	6.11.68	2	PennR	Philadelphia	28 Apr
15:38.85	Esther	Wanjiru	KEN	27.3.77	8	TOTO	Tokyo	15 Sep
15:39.79	Viktoria	Nenasheva	RUS	28.6.70	1	Slov	Bratislava	1 Jun
	(40)							
15:40.0		Wang Xiuting	CHN	16.2.65	2		Nobeoka	28 May
15:40.29	Derartu	Tulu	ETH	21.3.72	1	GP II	Sevilla	5 Jun
15:40.37	Anikó	Javos	HUN	14.1.71	2	Slov	Bratislava	1 Jun
15:40.86		Tian Mei	CHN	27.11.71	6	GWG	St Peterburg	29 Jul
15:40.96	Maria	Guida	ITA	23.1.66	4		København	28 Aug
15:40.99	Machiko	Tanaka	JPN	15.12.74	9	TOTO	Tokyo	15 Sep
15:41.23	Claudia	Dreher	GER	2.5.71	12	ISTAF	Berlin	30 Aug
15:41.46	Trina	Painter	USA	24.6.66	2		Eugene	14 May
15:41.47	Milka	Mihailova	BUL	23.5.72	3	Slov	Bratislava	1 Jun
15:42.45	Sally	Barsosio	KEN	21.3.78	13	ISTAF	Berlin	30 Aug
	(50)							

Mark	Name		Nat	Born	Date
15:42.5	Ai	Mitsukawa	JPN	74	3 Dec
15:42.67	Yuko	Kubota	JPN	74	5 May
15:43.10	Cristina	Misaros	ROM	69	12 May
15:43.37	Anne Marie	Letko	USA	69	28 Apr
15:44.05	Rose	Cheruiyot	KEN	76	1 Jun
15:44.10	Kathy	Franey	USA	67	28 Apr
15:46.01	Chiemi	Takahashi	JPN	76	15 Sep
15:46.5	Tonoko	Morigaki	JPN	76	23 Oct
15:46.79	Sammie	Gdowski	USA	67	14 May
15:46.93	Zola	Pieterse	RSA	66	23 Feb
	(60)				
15:47.57	Lidia	Vasilevskaya	RUS	73	1 Jun
15:47.59	Simona	Viola	ITA	71	22 May
15:47.70	Renata	Sobiesiak	POL	70	23 Jul
15:48.84+	Gwyn	Coogan	USA	65	25 Jul
15:49.24	Mahomi	Muranaka	JPN	66	5 May
15:49.42	Yuko	Kawakami	JPN	75	1 Oct
15:49.43+	Mariko	Hara	JPN	70	25 Jul
15:50.01	Angelina	Kanana	KEN	65	1 Jun
15:50.1	Zahra	Ouaziz	MAR	69	1 Jul
15:50.28	Ceci	St.Geme	USA	63	29 Jul
15:50.29	Claudia	Metzner	GER	66	5 Aug
15:50.65	Isabel	Juárez	MEX	66	1 Jun
15:50.7	Rie	Ueno	JPN	76	17 Dec
15:51.20	Yukiko	Okamoto	JPN	74	1 Oct
15:51.27	Catherine	Kirui	KEN	76	12 Jul
15:51.7		Wang Mingxia	CHN	71	28 May
15:51.7	Nicole	Lévêque	FRA	51	18 Jun
15:51.79	Liz	Wilson	USA	68	14 May
15:51.89	Kayumi	Morigami	JPN	69	1 Oct
15:52.04	Helen	Kimaiyo	KEN	68	28 May
15:52.20	Laura	LaMena-Coll	USA	66	14 May
15:52.2	Tomomi	Kozuma	JPN	77	17 Dec
15:52.41	Chikako	Suzuki	JPN	69	15 Sep
15:52.82	Grete	Koens	NED	67	28 May
15:52.89	Carole	Zajac	USA	72	12 Jul
15:53.09	Alena	Peterková	TCH	60	17 Sep
15:53.85	.Naomi	Sakashita	JPN	75	27 Aug
15:53.9	Noriko	Wada	JPN	75	17 Dec
15:53.99	Rosanna	Munerotto	ITA	62	8 May
15:54.01	Marleen	Renders	BEL	68	30 Jul
15:54.18	Mineko	Yamanouchi	JPN	72	15 Sep
15:54.23	Bernadette	Mitchell	USA	69	28 May
15:54.46	Silvia	Sommaggio	ITA	69	5 Jun
15:55.3	Mari	Yoshiawa	JPN	75	17 Dec
15:55.7	Mika	Adachi	JPN	76	17 Dec
15:55.88	Miwa	Sugawara	JPN	76	1 Oct
15:55.91	Martha	Ernstdóttir	ISL	64	30 Jul
15:56.6	Sanae	Mitsuhata	JPN	74	21 Dec
15:56.72	Margarita	Marusova	RUS	67	1 Jun
15:56.73	Anne-Marie	Danneels	BEL	62	30 Jul
	(100)				
15:56.83	Suzanne	Rigg	GBR	63	30 Jul
15:56.93	Christine	Toonstra	NED	66	28 May
15:57.29	Carol	Greenwood	GBR	66	1 Jun
15:57.50	Lyudmila	Afonyushkina	RUS	67	28 May
15:57.58	Nina	Belikova	RUS	61	24 Aug
15:57.9	Chiaki	Shigaki	JPN	74	28 May
15:58.7	Miyoko	Asahina	JPN	69	29 Apr
15:58.91	Flavia	Gaviglio	ITA	63	8 May
15:59.07	Eri	Yamaguchi	JPN	73	15 Oct
15:59.13+	Elena	Murgoci	ROM	60	25 Jul
15:59.30	Anne	Hare	NZL	64	5 Feb
15:59.6	Ayami	Sato	JPN	70	28 May
15:59.79		Wang Yongmei	CHN	68	5 May

Unconfirmed: 15:49.99 Elena Fidatov ROM 60

10,000 METRES

Mark	Name		Nat	Born	Pos	Meet	Venue	Date
30:50.34		Wang Junxia	CHN	9.1.73	1	AsiG	Hiroshima	15 Oct
30:52.51	Elana	Meyer	RSA	10.10.66	1	WCp	London	10 Sep
31:04.25	Fernanda	Ribeiro	POR	23.6.69	2	WCp	London	10 Sep
31:08.75		Ribeiro			1	EC	Helsinki	13 Aug
31:19.11	Catherina	McKiernan	IRL	30.11.69	1	ECp II	Dublin	12 Jun
31:31.08		Dong Li	CHN	9.12.73	2	AsiG	Hiroshima	15 Oct
31:32.11	Conceição	Ferreira	POR	13.3.62	1	vESP	Braga	9 Apr
31:32.82		Ferreira			2	EC	Helsinki	13 Aug
31:35.96	Daria	Nauer	SUI	21.5.66	3	EC	Helsinki	13 Aug

Mark	Name		Nat	Born	Pos	Meet	Venue	Date
31:38.17		Wang Junxia			1	NC	Beijing	5 Jun
31:38.75	Kathrin	Wessel	GER	14.8.67	4	EC	Helsinki	13 Aug
31:41.03	Cristina	Misaros	ROM	1.1.69	5	EC	Helsinki	13 Aug
31:42.14	Maria	Guida	ITA	23.1.66	6	EC	Helsinki	13 Aug
31:43.69		Zhong Huandi	CHN	28.6.67	1		Fukuoka	15 May
31:45.82	Miki	Igarashi	JPN	22.8.71	3	AsiG	Hiroshima	15 Oct
31:47.11	Lisa	Ondieki	AUS	12.5.60	1	Zat	Melbourne	15 Dec
31:48.93	Derartu	Tulu	ETH	21.3.72	1		St Denis	10 Jun
31:49.87		Dong Li			2	NC	Beijing	5 Jun
31:52.39	Tecla	Lorupe	KEN	5.5.71	1	GWG	St Peterburg	25 Jul
31:53.12	Fernanda	Marques	POR	15.4.66	7	EC	Helsinki	13 Aug
31:54.65		Ferreira			1	ECp I	Valencia	12 Jun
31:55.99	Klara	Kashapova	RUS	29.1.70	8	EC	Helsinki	13 Aug
31:56.97	Yvonne	Murray	GBR	4.10.64	1	CG	Victoria	24 Aug
31:59.45		Zhong Huandi			1	JapC	Tokyo	10 Jun
32:01.57	Mariko	Hara	JPN	27.12.70	2	NC	Tokyo	10 Jun
32:01.8		Marques			1		Braga	26 Jul
32:01.91	Junko	Kataoka	JPN	13.6.70	1		Fukuoka	23 Sep
32:02.95	Naomi	Yoshida	JPN	14.4.69	3	NC	Tokyo	10 Jun
32:03.42	Olga	Appell	USA	2.8.63	1	MSR	Walnut	16 Apr
32:05.42		Kashapova			2	GWG	St Peterburg	25 Jul
	(30/22)							
32:06.02		Meyer			2	CG	Victoria	24 Aug
32:06.42	Hiromi	Suzuki	JPN	6.12.68	4	NC	Tokyo	10 Jun
32:08.51	Mahomi	Muranaka	JPN	31.10.66	5	NC	Tokyo	10 Jun
32:08.74	Claudia	Lokar	GER	8.9.64	9	EC	Helsinki	13 Aug
32:08.77	Gwyn	Coogan	USA	21.8.65	3	GWG	St Peterburg	25 Jul
32:09.1	Manuela	Machado	POR	9.8.63	1		Maia	20 Jul
32:11.18	Marleen	Renders	BEL	24.12.68	10	EC	Helsinki	13 Aug
32:12.07	Nicole	Lévêque	FRA	27.1.51	11	EC	Helsinki	13 Aug
32:13.01	Jane	Omoro	KEN	12.9.74	3	CG	Victoria	24 Aug
	(30)							
32:16.50	Merami	Denboba	ETH	21.8.74	2		St Denis	10 Jun
32:16.72	Helen	Kimaiyo	KEN	8.9.68	3		St Denis	10 Jun
32:18.68	Lieve	Slegers	BEL	6.4.65	1		Heverlee	21 Sep
32:19.33		Zhang Linli	CHN	6.3.73	3	NC	Beijing	5 Jun
32:19.96	Tatyana	Pentukova	RUS	23.6.65	1	NC-23	Voronezh	18 Jun
32:22.93	Rocio	Rios	ESP	13.3.69	1		Baracaldo	18 Jun
32:23.25	Esther	Wanjiru	KEN	27.3.77	2		Mito	8 May
32:23.64	Krishna	Stanton	AUS	18.5.66	2	Jer	Coquitlam	28 May
32:24.96	Nadia	Bernard-Prasad	FRA	6.10.67	2	NC	St Maur	13 Jul
32:26.25	Gitte	Karlshøj	DEN	14.5.59	12	EC	Helsinki	13 Aug
	(40)							
32:26.58	Iulia	Negura	ROM	26.1.67	5	GP	St Denis	10 Jun
32:26.78	Carol	Montgomery	CAN	.8.65	3	Jer	Coquitlam	28 May
32:27.66	Ana Paula	Oliveira	POR	24.3.70	6		St Denis	10 Jun
32:28.05		Wang Dongmei	CHN	3.12.73	7	JPN Ch	Tokyo	10 Jun
32:29.17	Yasuko	Kimura	JPN	6.1.76	1		Amagasaki	28 Oct
32:29.33	Monica	Gama	POR	8.3.70	7		St Denis	10 Jun
32:29.86	Claudia	Metzner	GER	5.5.66	8		St Denis	10 Jun
32:31.35	Stefania	Statkuviene	LIT	5.9.62	1		Lebbeke	9 Sep
32:31.4	Anne	Hare	NZL	7.6.64	1		Wellington	16 Feb
32:31.4	Rosario	Murcia	FRA	23.9.64	1		La Flèche	16 Apr
	(50)							
32:33.03		Wang Xiaoxia	CHN	21.8.76	4	NC	Beijing	5 Jun
32:34.11	Yoko	Yamazaki	JPN	25.7.75	1	WJ	Lisboa	24 Jul
32:34.46	Helen	Moros	NZL	2.11.67	2	Zat	Melbourne	15 Dec
32:34.73	Sumie	Yamaguchi	JPN	9.11.73	3		Kobe	24 Apr
32:36.77		Wang Mingxia	CHN	6.6.71	3		Fukushima	23 Sep
32:37.94		Wei Li	CHN	.1.72	3	WCp	London	10 Sep
32:38.74	Sue	Hobson	AUS	13.3.58	1	NC	Sydney	12 Mar
32:41.67	Anne Marie	Letko	USA	7.3.69	3	NC	Knoxville	17 Jun
32:41.89	Izumi	Maki	JPN	10.12.68	4		Fukushima	23 Sep
32:43.73	Midori	Fumoto	JPN	18.12.71	5		Fukushima	23 Sep
	(60)							
32:43.92	Ai	Mitsukawa	JPN	2.12.74	2		Amagasaki	28 Oct
32:44.00	Ana Isabel	Alonso	ESP	16.8.63	1	NC	San Sebastián	17 Jul
32:46.12	Carmen	Fuentes	ESP	7.6.65	2	vPOR	Braga	9 Apr

Mark	Name		Nat	Born	Pos	Meet	Venue	Date
32:46.4mx	Michelle	Dillon	AUS	25.5.73	mx		Brisbane	15 Jul
32:47.10	Tamara	Koba	UKR	24.2.57	1		Kiev	23 Jul
32:47.40	Martha	Ernstdóttir	ISL	22.12.64	4	ECp II	Dublin	12 Jun
32:47.72	Tami	Yada	JPN	31.5.72	1		Himeji	21 May
32:47.88	Eriko	Asai	JPN	20.10.59	4		Kobe	24 Apr
32:48.02	Noriko	Nasuhara	JPN	4.10.70	1		Hiratsuka	20 May
32:48.24	Ulla	Marquette	CAN	28.1.58	4	Jer	Vancouver	29 May
	(70)							
32:48.40	Machiko	Tanaka	JPN	15.12.72	6		Fukushima	23 Sep
32:49.00	Margaret	Kagiri	KEN	64	9	GP	St Denis	11 Jun
32:49.86	Yuko	Kubota	JPN	5.10.74	1		Fukuoka	15 May
32:51.1	Monika	Schäfer	GER	6.10.59	1		Straubing	25 Mar
32:51.33	Elena	Murgoci	ROM	20.5.60	5	GWG	St Peterburg	25 Jul
32:52.04	Mitsuyo	Yoshida	JPN	29.10.66	2		Himeji	21 May
32:53.61	Kerryn	McCann	AUS	2.5.67	3	Zat	Melbourne	15 Dec
32:54.06	Claudia	Dreher	GER	2.5.71	10		St Denis	10 Jun
32:54.20	Nina	Kovrizhkina	UKR	5.2.65	2		Kiev	23 Jul
32:55.24	Annemari	Sandell	FIN	2.1.77	1	NC	Tuusula	8 Jul
	(80)							
32:55.73	Milka	Mikhailova	BUL	23.5.72	16	EC	Helsinki	13 Aug
32:56.45	Anne	Cross	AUS	16.4.65	4	Zat	Melbourne	15 Dec
32:56.86	Tsugumi	Fukuyama	JPN	10.4.68	3		Himeji	21 May
32:56.93	Estela	Estévez	ESP	24.2.65	3	vPOR	Braga	9 Apr
32:57.68	Kirsi	Rauta	FIN	17.3.62	3	ECp I	Valencia	12 Jun
32:57.85	Yukiko	Kiyomiya	JPN	4.3.69	8		Fukushima	23 Sep
32:58.65	Paivi	Tikkanen	FIN	19.1.60	1	v SWE	Stockholm	27 Aug
32:59.55	Trina	Painter	USA	25.6.66	2	MSR	Walnut	16 Apr
32:59.76	Serap	Aktas	TUR	25.9.71	17	EC	Helsinki	13 Aug
32:59.99	Miyoko	Asahina	JPN	24.9.69	4		Mito	8 May
	(90)							
33:00.03	Teresa	Recio	ESP	7.7.63	2		Baracaldo	18 Jun
33:01.02	Vicki	Mitchell	USA	12.6.69	1	PennR	Philadelhia	28 Apr
33:01.40	Suzanne	Rigg	GBR	29.11.63	4	CG	Victoria	24 Aug
33:01.66	Annick	Clouvel	FRA	15.10.63	3	NC	St Maur	13 Jul
33:02.74	Vikki	McPherson	GBR	1.6.71	5	CG	Victoria	24 Aug
33:03.21	Yumi	Akao	JPN	27.12.73	4		Himeji	21 May
33:04.09	Marjan	Freriks	NED	13.12.61	5	ECp II	Dublin	12 Jun
33:05.05	Carole	Zajac	USA	24.3.72	1	PennR	Philadelhia	28 Apr
33:05.53	Ayumi	Sato	JPN	27.7.70	9		Fukushima	23 Sep
33:05.78	Yoko	Nomura	JPN	1.7.70	10		Fukushima	23 Sep
	(100)							

Mark	First	Last	Nat	Born	Date
33:06.07	Alina	Tecuta	ROM	71	9 Jul
33:06.88	Clare	Carney	AUS	74	15 Dec
33:06.89	Ritva	Lemettinen	FIN	60	27 Aug
33:07.17		Wang Yongmei	CHN	68	10 Jun
33:07.33	Shelley	Smathers	USA	71	28 Apr
33:09.25		Tian Mei	CHN	71	5 Jun
33:10.43	Sara	Rome	SWE	61	27 Aug
33:10.57	Rosa	Oliveira	POR	66	9 Apr
33:11.35	Yuka	Terumuma	JPN	68	24 Apr
33:11.4	Fatima	Neves	POR	63	20 Jul
33:14.2A	Jackline	Okemwa	KEN	78	5 Jul
33:14.4	Nathalie	Tejera-Bernard	FRA	68	16 Apr
33:14.40	Heather	Turland	AUS	60	15 Dec
33:14.6A	Chepkemoi	Barsosio	KEN	77	5 Jul
33:15.15		Dong Chaoxia	CHN	72	5 Jun
33:15.93	Lucia	Mendiola	MEX	68	29 May
33:16.01	Raewyn	Rodger	NZL	61	6 Mar
33:16.02	Nyla	Carroll	NZL	65	6 Mar
33:16.39	Katrin	Dörre-Heinig	GER	61	14 May
33:16.68	Laura	LaMena-Coll	USA	66	16 Apr
33:16.80	Sue	Malaxos	AUS	61	15 Dec
33:16.8	Doris	Grossert	GER	61	5 Oct
33:17.16	Lucia	Rendon	MEX	69	16 Apr
33:18.18		Chen Xiuying	CHN	73	5 Jun
33:18.30	Hiroko	Tamagawa	JPN	72	15 May
33:18.5A	Edina	Kwambai	KEN	75	5 Jul
33:18.53	Emma	Carney	AUS	71	15 Dec
33:18.58		Wang Kaheki	CHN		20 May
33:19.01	Michelle	Dillon	AUS	73	24 Aug
33:19.05	Barbara	Moore	NZL	65	12 Mar
33:19.09	Michiyo	Ando	JPN	72	24 Apr
33:20.04	Alena	Peterková	TCH	60	12 Jun
33:20.05	Mayumi	Morigami	JPN	69	23 Sep
33:20.34	Chiaki	Shigaki	JPN	74	10 Jun
33:20.37	Jane	Salumäe	EST	68	12 Jun
33:20.43	Lyudmila	Alexeeff	CAN	65	28 Jul
33:20.78	Jacqueline	Mota	POR	66	9 Apr
33:20.90	Ana	Nanu	ROM	73	28 May
33:22.83		Ma Ningning	CHN	76	5 Jun
33:22.97	Angela	Raines-White	AUS	74	15 Dec
33:23.25	Zahara	Hyde	GBR	63	12 Jun
33:23.96	Midde	Hamrin	SWE	57	27 Aug
33:24.3A	Lucia	Subano	KEN		21 May
33:24.4	Kaori	Hosokawa	JPN	75	22 Oct
33:24.78		Jung Young-im	KOR	75	28 Oct
33:24.82		Kwak Hye-soon	KOR	74	28 Oct
33:25.62	Nadezhda	Gallyamova	RUS	59	26 Jun
33:25.65	Marina	Rodchenkova	RUS	61	8 May
33:25.71	Sonia	Betancourt	MEX	68	29 May
33:25.80	Mineko	Yamanouchi	JPN	72	20 May
	(150)				
33:26.43		Lee Mi-kyung	KOR	75	18 Jun
33:27.06	Megumi	Setoguchi	JPN	68	15 May
33:27.40	Emiko	Mizuno	JPN	69	23 Sep
33:27.59	Mari	Yoshiawa	JPN	75	23 Sep
33:28.20	Takako	Kobayashi	JPN	69	23 Sep

Mark	Name		Nat	Born	Date
33:28.36	Kayoko	Ogiwara	JPN	71	23 Sep
33:28.99	Albina	Lental	RUS	69	18 Jun
33:29.08	Manuela	Dias	POR	63	9 Apr
33:29.09	Kozue	Matsumoto	JPN	74	24 Apr
33:29.14	Hiromi	Goto	JPN	71	23 Sep
33:29.42	Lisa	Harvey	CAN	70	28 Jul
33:29.60	Silvana	Pereira	BRA	65	28 Oct
33:29.70	Kang Soon-duk		KOR		28 Oct
33:30.01	Hwang Keum-yeon		KOR		28 Oct
33:30.25	Fumiyo	Shinogi	JPN	73	23 Sep
33:31.14	Hiromi	Sato	JPN		23 Sep
33:33.31	Akemi	Hirai	JPN	73	23 Sep
33:34.85	Karen	Macleod	GBR	58	10 Jun
33:34.9	Rosie	Lamb	IRL	59	26 Jun
33:34.96	Carol	Greenwood	GBR	66	12 Jun
33:35.34	Tomoko	Kanno	JPN	68	23 Sep
33:35.82	Carmen	Brunet	ESP	63	18 Jun
33:35.93	May	Allison	CAN	64	28 Jul
33:35.98	Jebiwott	Keitany	KEN	78	23 Jul
33:36.42	Melanie	Kraus	GER	74	26 Aug
33:37.87	Luzia	Dias	POR	70	9 Apr
33:38.05	Carolyn	Schuwalow	AUS	65	15 Dec
33:38.18	Mineko	Watanabe	JPN	72	15 May
33:38.45	Hiroe	Tanikawa	JPN	68	23 Sep
33:39.62A	Catherine	Kirui	KEN	76	8 Jul
33:39.97	Nobuko	Fujimura	JPN	65	21 May
	(176)				

1 HOUR

Mark	Name		Nat	Born	Pos	Meet	Venue	Date
17.952m	Junko	Kataoka	JPN	13.6.70	1		Tokyo	1 Oct
17,693	Izumi	Maki	JPN	10.12.68	1		Amagasaki	1 Oct
17,692	Midori	Fumoto	JPN	18.12.71	2		Amagasaki	1 Oct
17,454	Takako	Kobayashi	JPN	13.8.69	3		Amagasaki	1 Oct
17,453	Naomi	Sakashita	JPN	25.5.75	4		Amagasaki	1 Oct
17,311	Junko	Asari	JPN	22.9.69	5		Amagasaki	1 Oct

10 KILOMETRES ROAD

Mark	Name		Nat	Born	Pos	Meet	Venue	Date
31:16	Yelena	Vyazova	UKR	18.4.60	1		Leipzig	8 Oct
31:38	Nadia	Bernard-Prasad	FRA	6.10.67	1		Chula Vista	16 Oct
31:39	Elana	Meyer	RSA	10.10.66	1	US Ch	Boston	10 Oct
31:46	Olga	Appell	USA	2.8.63	2		Chula Vista	16 Oct
31:48	Lynn	Jennings	USA	1.7.60	2	1 NC	Boston	10 Oct
31:50	Delilah	Asiago	KEN	24.2.72	3	USCh	Boston	10 Oct
31:52	Anne Marie	Letko	USA	7.3.69	1		New York	4 Jun
31:53	Jane	Omoro	KEN	12.9.74	4		Boston	10 Oct
31:55	Margaret	Kagiri	KEN	64	1		Naumburg	1 May
31:55		Letko			5		Boston	10 Oct
31:59	Conceição	Ferreira	POR	13.3.62	2		New York	4 Jun
31:59		Kagiri			1		Zoetermeer	18 Sep
32:03	Carmen	de Oliveira	BRA	17.8.65	3		New York	4 Jun
32:03	Laura	Mykytok	USA	17.9.68	1		Columbia	12 Feb
	(14/12)							
32:12	Celsa	Kidman	USA	66	1		San Diego	12 Jun
32:20	Ingrid	Kristiansen	NOR	21.3.56	1		Oslo	24 Apr
32:20	Izabela	Zatorska	POL	6.10.62	2		Olesnica	18 Sep
32:23	Tecla	Lorupe	KEN	5.5.71	4		New York	4 Jun
32:24	Colleen	de Reuck	RSA	13.4.64	1		Torrance	13 Mar
32:26	Judy	St Hilaire	USA	5.9.59	1	Cres	New Orleans	16 Apr
32:26	Trina	Painter	USA	24.6.66	4		Chula Vista	16 Oct
32:26	Joice	Chepchumba	KEN	70	1		Barnsley	5 Nov
	(20)							
32:30	Lisa	Ondieki	AUS	12.5.60	1		Phoenix	20 Mar
32:30	Lyudmila	Afonyushkina	RUS	67	1		Gent	23 May
32:30	Katrin	Dörre	GER	6.10.61	2		Leipzig	8 Oct
32:31	Heather	Heasman	GBR	27.9.63	2		Barnsley	6 Oct
32:33	Gitte	Karlshøj	DEN	14.5.59	1		Plant City	5 Mar
32:35	Marjan	Freriks	NED	13.12.61	1		Brunsumm	10 Apr
32:36	Regina	Chistyakova	LIT	7.11.61	2		Naumburg	1 May
32:38	Liz	McColgan	GBR	24.5.64	1	G.Mid	Coventry	16 Oct
32:39	Carla	Beurskens	NED	10.2.52	2		Brunsumm	10 Apr
32:40	Grazyna	Kowina	POL	6.5.62	3		Naumburg	1 May
	(30)							
32:40	Claudia	Dreher	GER	2.5.71	1		Dresden	26 Mar
32:40	Beatrice	Omwansa	KEN		2		Gent	23 May
32:42	Cristina	Misaros	ROM	1.1.69	1		Heidelberg	15 May
32:42	Maria Luisa	Servin	MEX	25.8.62	2		San Diego	12 Jun
32:43	Misti	Demko	USA	67	2		Washington	17 Apr
32:45	Esther	Wanjiru	KEN	27.3.77	1		Nara	20 Mar
32:46	Carol	Montgomery	CAN	.8.65	3		San Diego	12 Jun
32:47	Kathrin	Wessel	GER	14.8.67	2		Dresden	26 Mar
32:49	Nicole	Lévêque	FRA	27.1.51	1		Angers	23 May

Mark	Name		Nat	Born	Pos	Meet	Venue	Date
32:50	Gina	Procaccio	USA	19.7.64	3		Washington	17 Apr
	(40)							
32:51	Cathy	O'Brien	USA	10.7.67	4	Peach	Atlanta	4 Jul
32:52	Laurie	Henes	USA	16.4.70	7	NC	Boston	10 Oct
32:52	Sally	Barsosio	KEN	21.3.78	2	Cres	New Orleans	16 Apr
32:53	Anita	Håkenstad	NOR	19.2.68	1		Kodal	27 Aug
32:55	Karolina	Szabó	HUN	17.1.61	1		Mobile	26 Mar
32:55	Christine	Toonstra	NED	22.6.66	3		Brunsumm	10 Apr
32:55	Daria	Nauer	SUI	21.5.66	1		Vancouver	17 Apr
32:55	Lucy	Nusrala	USA	4.10.70	6	Peach	Atlanta	4 Jul
32:55	Marion	Sutton	GBR	7.10.63	1	G.Welsh	Cardiff	31 Jul
32:56	Linda	Somers	USA	7.5.61	1		Redondo Beach	30 Jan
	(50)							
32:56	Alison	Wyeth	GBR	26.5.64	1		Eastleigh	20 Mar
32:57	Irma	Heeren	NED	16.4.67	2		Zoetermeer	18 Sep
32:57	Zohra	Ouaziz	MAR	20.12.69			Wittenheim	9 Oct
32:58	Anne	Hare	NZL	7.6.64	2		Northport	17 Sep
32:58	Olga	Bondarenko	RUS	2.6.60	1		Edinburgh	2 Oct
32:59	Olga	Markova	RUS	6.8.68	1		Charlotte	8 Jan
Downhill								
31:02	Laura	Mykytok	USA	17.9.68	1		Pittsburgh	25 Sep
31:04A	Olga	Appell	USA	2.8.63	1		Salt Lake City	25 Jul
31:06	Jane	Omoro	KEN	12.9.74	2		Pittsburgh	25 Sep
32:00	Anne	Hare	NZL	7.6.64	3		Pittsburgh	25 Sep
32:20	Danuta	Bartoszak	CAN	19.8.61	1		Vancouver	1 May
32:32A	Jody	Hawkins	USA		2		Salt Lake City	25 Jul
32:34	Laurie	Henes	USA	16.4.70	4		Pittsburgh	25 Sep
32:44	Lyudmila	Alexeeff	CAN	16.7.65	2		Toronto	1 May
32:52A	Kellie	Archuletta	USA	24.11.61	3		Salt Lake City	25 Jul
Unconfirmed distance								
32:32	Stella	Castro	COL	24.3.62	1		Girardot	10 Jan

Note Ekiden Relay legs: Litochoro 16 Apr: Derartu Tulu ETH 32:26, Albina Gallyamova RUS 32:59 Yokohama 28 Feb: Anuta Catuna ROM 32:24, Nadezhda Gallyamova RUS 32:35, Alina Tecuta ROM 32:47, Tatyana Dzhabrailova UKR 32:48, Florina Pana ROM 32:51, Tatyana Pentukova RUS 32:55

15 KILOMETRES ROAD

Mark	Name		Nat	Born	Pos	Meet	Venue	Date
48:11	Elana	Meyer	RSA	10.10.66	1	Gasp	Tampa	26 Feb
48:38	Carmen	de Oliveira	BRA	17.8.65	2	Gasp	Tampa	26 Feb
48:43	Anne Marie	Letko	USA	7.3.69	3	Gasp	Tampa	26 Feb
48:46	Fernanda	Ribeiro	POR	23.6.69	1		La Courneuve	29 May
48:59	Delilah	Asiago	KEN	24.2.72	1		Tulsa	29 Oct
49:13	Colleen	de Reuck	RSA	13.4.64	4	Gasp	Tampa	26 Feb
49:27		Letko			1	NC	Jacksonville	12 Mar
49:33	Iulia	Negura	ROM	26.1.67	2		La Courneuve	29 May
49:36	Lisa	Ondieki	AUS	12.5.60	5	Gasp	Tampa	26 Feb
49:39	Olga	Bondarenko	RUS	2.6.60	3		La Courneuve	29 May
49:40	Angelina	Kanana	KEN	65	4		La Courneuve	29 May
49:41	Katrin	Dörre	GER	6.10.61	5		La Courneuve	29 May
49:44	Annette	Peters	USA	31.5.65	6	Gasp	Tampa	26 Feb
49:54	Laura	Mykytok	USA	17.9.68	7	Gasp	Tampa	26 Feb
49:55	Nicole	Lévêque	FRA	27.1.51	6		La Courneuve	29 May
49:56	Natalya	Galushko	BLR	18.9.71	1		Pila	10 Sep
49:56	Liz	McColgan	GBR	24.5.64	1		Nijmegen	20 Nov
49:58	Lynn	Jennings	USA	1.7.60	2		Tulsa	29 Oct
	(18/17)							
50:12	Joice	Chepchumba	KEN	70	2		Nijmegen	20 Nov
50:19	Anuta	Catuna	ROM	1.1.68	7		La Courneuve	29 May
50:21	Valentina	Yegorova	RUS	14.2.64	8	Gasp	Tampa	26 Feb
	(20)							
50:28	Ramilya	Burangulova	RUS	11.7.61	8		La Courneuve	29 May
50:30	Jody	Hawkins	USA		4		Tulsa	29 Oct
50:39	Gitte	Karlshøj	DEN	14.5.59	9	Gasp	Tampa	26 Feb
50:41	Albertina	Dias	POR	26.4.65	1	EClubs	Caserta	2 Oct
50:52	Izabela	Zatorska	POL	6.10.62	2		Pila	10 Sep
50:54	Stefania	Statkuviene	LIT	5.9.62	9		La Courneuve	29 May
50:57	Lisa	Weidenbach	USA	13.12.61	10	Gasp	Tampa	26 Feb

10 MILES ROAD

Mark		Name		Nat	Born	Pos	Meet	Venue	Date
52:23		Helen	Kimaiyo	KEN	8.9.68	1		Zaandam	18 Sep
52:43		Tecla	Lorupe	KEN	9.5.71	2		Zaandam	10 Apr
53:42		Anne Marie	Letko	USA	7.3.69	1		Flint	27 Aug
53:46		Yelena	Vyazova	UKR	18.4.60	2		Flint	27 Aug
53:54		Simona	Staicu	ROM	5.5.71	1		Den Haag	18 Dec
53:55		Joice	Chepchumba	KEN	70	3		Zaandam	18 Sep
54:02		Cathy	O'Brien	USA	19.7.67	3		Flint	27 Aug
54:05		Helen	Chepngeno	KEN	2.8.67	1		Washington	10 Apr
54:06		Jane	Omoro	KEN	12.9.74	2		Washington	10 Apr
54:21		Delilah	Asiago	KEN	24.2.72	4		Flint	27 Aug
54:27		Conceição	Ferreira	POR	13.3.62	4		Zaandam	18 Sep

HALF-MARATHON

Mark		Name		Nat	Born	Pos	Meet	Venue	Date
67:59		Uta	Pippig	GER	7.9.65	1		Kyoto	20 Mar
68:36		Elana	Meyer	RSA	10.10.66	1	WCh	Oslo	24 Sep
68:41		Junko	Kataoka	JPN	13.6.70	1		Tokyo	23 Jan
68:58		Nadezhda	Ilyina	RUS	2.4.64	1		Chelyabinsk	18 Jun
69:04			Meyer			2		Tokyo	23 Jan
69:08		Firaya	Sultanova	RUS	29.4.61	2		Chelyabinsk	18 Jun
69:14		Olga	Appell	USA	2.8.63	3		Tokyo	23 Jan
69:15		Iulia	Negura	ROM	26.1.67	2	WCh	Oslo	24 Sep
69:27		Tecla	Lorupe	KEN	5.5.71	1		Lisboa	13 Mar
69:29		Marleen	Renders	BEL	24.12.68	1		Hasselt	2 Oct
69:31		Carmen	de Oliveira	BRA	17.8.65	2		Lisboa	13 Mar
69:32		Yelena	Paramanova	RUS		3		Chelyabinsk	18 Jun
69:35		Anuta	Catuna	ROM	1.1.68	3	WCh	Oslo	24 Sep
69:57		Albertina	Dias	POR	26.4.65	4	WCh	Oslo	24 Sep
70:03		Anne Marie	Letko	USA	7.3.69	1		Philadelphia	18 Sep
70:10		Jane	Salumäe	EST	17.1.68	1		Den Haag	27 Mar
70:13		Elena	Fidatov	ROM	24.7.60	5	WCh	Oslo	24 Sep
70:19		Monica	Gama	POR	8.3.70	3		Lisboa	13 Mar
70:19		Maria	Guida	ITA	23.1.66	1	Stra	Milano	16 Apr
70:20			Guida			4		Lisboa	13 Mar
70:21		Izumi	Maki	JPN	10.12.68	1		Surfers Paradise	17 Jul
70:21		Hilde	Stavik	NOR	6.9.62	6	WCh	Oslo	24 Sep
70:29		Brynhild	Synstnes	NOR	20.4.71	7	WCh	Oslo	24 Sep
70:35		Päivi	Tikkanen	FIN	19.1.60	1		Stockholm	3 Sep
70:37		Olga	Bondarenko	RUS	2.6.60	1		St Peterburg	12 Jun
70:38		Delilah	Asiago	KEN	24.2.72	2		Philadelphia	18 Sep
70:38		Adriana	Barbu	ROM	17.1.61	9	WCh	Oslo	24 Sep
70:38			Lorupe			1		Grevenmacher	25 Sep
70:43		Mari	Tanigawa	JPN	27.10.62	10	WCh	Oslo	24 Sep
70:47			Lorupe			1		Paris	27 Mar
70:47		Kathrin	Wessel	GER	14.8.67	1		Berlin	10 Apr
		(31/26)							
70:49		Fatuma	Roba	ETH	73	11	WCh	Oslo	24 Sep
70:54		Maura	Viceconte	ITA	3.10.67	1		Gargnano	25 Sep
70:59		Nadia	Bernard-Prasad	FRA	6.10.67	3		Philadelphia	18 Sep
71:00		Natalya	Galushko	BLR	18.9.71	12	WCh	Oslo	24 Sep
		(30)							
71:01		Lieve	Slegers	BEL	6.4.65	2		Hasselt	2 Oct
71:02	?	Conceição	Ferreira	POR	13.3.62	1		Setúbal	24 Apr
71:02		Alena	Peterková	TCH	13.11.60	13	WCh	Oslo	24 Sep
71:04		Marina	Belyayeva	RUS	58	2		Grevenmacher	25 Sep
71:05		Angelina	Kanana	KEN	65	2		Berlin	10 Apr
71:06		Ritva	Lemettinen	FIN	9.9.60	5		Lisboa	13 Mar
71:08		Marzanna	Helbik	POL	11.9.61	6		Lisboa	13 Mar
71:08		Maria	Curatolo	ITA	12.10.63	2	Stra	Milano	16 Apr
71:11		Ramila	Burangulova	RUS	11.7.61	2		St Peterburg	12 Jun
71:11		Rosa	Mota	POR	29.6.58	1		Uster	17 Sep
		(40)							
71:16		Alla	Zhilyayeva	RUS	68	14	WCh	Oslo	24 Sep
71:20		Klara	Kashapova	RUS	29.1.70	3		St Peterburg	12 Jun
71:23		Rocio	Rios	ESP	13.3.69	1	NC	Igualada	4 Sep
71:26			Wang Mingxia	CHN	6.6.71	1		Yamaguchi	21 Mar
71:29		Rosanna	Munerotto	ITA	3.12.62	1	GNR	South Shields	18 Sep

Mark	Name		Nat	Born	Pos	Meet	Venue	Date
71:30	Susanna	Ciric	YUG	12.7.69	4		Philadelphia	18 Sep
71:31	Claudia	Lokar	GER	8.9.64	4		Grevenmacher	25 Sep
71:34	Fatima	Neves	POR	13.2.63	5		Paris	27 Mar
71:34	Andrea	Wallace	GBR	22.11.66	2	GNR	South Shields	18 Sep
71:35	Midori	Fumoto	JPN	18.12.71	2		Surfers Paradise	17 Jul
	(50)							
71:35	Nicole	Lévêque	FRA	27.1.51	1		Auray-Vennes	11 Sep
71:37	Yumi	Akao	JPN	27.12.73	2		Yamaguchi	21 Mar
71:37	Kirsi	Rauta	FIN	17.3.62	1		Forssa	18 Jun
71:38	Mineko	Watanabe	JPN	24.7.72	3		Yamaguchi	21 Mar
71:38	Franziska	Moser	SUI	17.8.66	2		Uster	17 Sep
71:41	Heléna	Barocsi	HUN	9.7.66	4		St Peterburg	12 Jun
71:42	Stefania	Statkuviene	LIT	5.9.62	5		Paris	27 Mar
71:42	Noriko	Nasuhara	JPN	4.10.70	4		Yamaguchi	21 Mar
71:43	Merima	Denboba	ETH	21.8.74	1		Canals	16 Apr
71:45	Lidia	Slavuteanu	ROM	4.9.73	6		Grevenmacher	25 Sep
	(60)							
71:47	Jody	Hawkins	USA		5		Philadelphia	18 Sep
71:48	Sachiko	Seiyama	JPN	6.11.72	5		Yamaguchi	21 Mar
71:48	Manuela	Machado	POR	9.8.63	3	GNR	South Shields	18 Sep
71:49	Rosario	Murcia	FRA	23.9.64	1		Lyon	15 May
71:55	Joice	Chepchumba	KEN	70	1		Griesheim	16 Oct
71:58	Hiroko	Tanagawa	JPN	24.6.72	6		Yamaguchi	21 Mar
72:00	Naoko	Yamagishi	JPN	28.8.70	7		Yamaguchi	21 Mar
72:01	Nadezhda	Ilyina	RUS	2.4.64	5		St Peterburg	12 Jun
72:01	Martha	Ernstdóttir	ISL	22.12.64	1		Reykjavik	21 Aug
72:02	Helen	Kimaiyo	KEN	8.9.68	7		Grevenmacher	25 Sep
	(70)							
72:04	Shizuoka	Oka	JPN	23.7.70	4		Surfers Paradise	17 Jul
72:05	Megumi	Setoguchi	JPN	14.7.68	1		Okayama	4 Dec
72:06	Malgorzata	Sobanska	POL	25.4.69	10		Lisboa	13 Mar
72:06	Mari	Yoshiawa	JPN	5.1.75	5		Surfers Paradise	17 Jul
72:06	Simona	Staicu	ROM	5.5.71	1		Budapest	23 Oct
72:07	Elena	Murgoci	ROM	20.5.60	7		Paris	27 Mar
72:08	Makomi	Muranaka	JPN	31.10.66	8		Yamaguchi	21 Mar
72:08	Junko	Nishi	JPN	11.8.74	9		Yamaguchi	21 Mar
72:10	Madina	Biktagirova	BLR	20.9.64	6		Philadelphia	18 Sep
72:13	Mineko	Yamanouchi	JPN	10.12.72	2		Okayama	4 Dec
	(80)							
72:14	Janete	Mayal	BRA	19.7.63	11		Lisboa	13 Mar
72:15	Lisa	Weidenbach	USA	13.12.61	2		Kyoto	20 Mar
72:15	Lyudmila	Korchagina	RUS		4		Chelyabinsk	18 Jun
72:18	Nadezhda	Tatarenkova	RUS	11.8.68	6		St Peterburg	13 Jun
72:19	Hiromi	Suzuki	JPN	6.12.68	3		Kyoto	20 Mar
72:21	Yukari	Komatsu	JPN	13.2.74	1		Matsue	13 Mar
72:21	Solange	de Souza	BRA	5.2.69	1		Buenos Aires	4 Sep
72:21		Kwak Hye-soon	KOR	12.5.74			Okayama	4 Dec
72:23	Stella	Castro	COL	24.3.62	18	WCh	Oslo	24 Sep
72:25	Claudia	Metzner	GER	5.5.66	1		Frankfurt	6 Mar
	(90)							
72:26	Carla	Beurskens	NED	10.2.52	3		Den Haag	27 Mar
72:28	Ana	Nanu	ROM	24.6.73	2	NC	Buzau	20 Aug
72:29	Lidia	Camberg	POL	31.1.62	2		Gragano	25 Sep
72:30	Emi	Yamaoka	JPN	15.11.74	4		Okayama	4 Dec
72:31	Albina	Gallyamova	RUS	8.5.64	3		Lyon	15 May
72:32	Aniela	Nikiel	POL	1.11.65	5		Okayama	4 Dec
72:34	Nives	Curti	ITA	1.9.69	3	Stra	Milano	16 Apr
72:34	Alevtina	Naumova	RUS	16.1.61	1	GScot	Glasgow	22 Aug
72:34	Antonina	Andronaki	RUS	.59	1		Lille	3 Sep
72:34	Trina	Painter	USA	24.6.66	7		Philadelphia	18 Sep
72:34	Tatyana	Pozdnyakova	UKR	4.3.56	1		St Denis	6 Nov
	(101)							

Mark	Name		Nat	Born	Date
72:35	Albina	Gallyamova	RUS	64	13 Jun
72:35	Isabelle	Guillot	FRA	61	13 Mar
72:37	Jackline	Maranga	KEN	77	2 Oct
72:41	Rosa	Oliveira	POR	66	24 Apr
72:43	Maria Manuela	Dias	POR	63	24 Sep
72:43	Lucia	Rendon	MEX	69	9 Oct
72:44	Marina	Rodchenkova	RUS	61	23 Jan
72:45	May	Allison	CAN	64	25 Sep
72:46	Yelena	Vyazova	UKR	60	8 Apr
72:46	Grete	Kirkeberg	NOR	64	24 Sep
72:48	Cathy	Shum	IRL	61	28 Aug
72:50	Berhane	Adere	ETH	73	16 Apr
72:52	Sue	Mahony	AUS	65	23 Jan
72:52	Garifa	Kuku	KZK	59	24 Sep

Mark	Name		Nat	Born	Date
72:53	Patrizia	Ritondo	ITA	74	16 Apr
72:53	Lyutsia	Belyayeva	RUS	57	13 Jun
72:54	Floria	Pana	ROM	73	23 Apr
72:55	Ana Isabel	Alonso	ESP	63	16 Apr
72:56	Alina	Ivanova	RUS	69	13 Jun
72:58	Mariana	Chirila	ROM	64	25 Sep

Uncertain course measurement

Mark	Name		Nat	Born	Date
72:43A	Lucia	Rendon	MEX	69	9 Oct

Downhill

Mark	Name		Nat	Born	Pos	Meet	Venue	Date
69:05	Nadia	Bernard-Prasad	FRA	67	1		Las Vegas	5 Feb

MARATHON

Note Boston times both downhill overall (139m) and strongly wind-aided - next bests are shown if to standard.

Mark	Name		Nat	Born	Pos	Meet	Venue	Date
2:21:45 dh	Uta	Pippig	GER	7.9.65	1		Boston	18 Apr
2:23:33 dh	Valentina	Yegorova	RUS	16.2.64	2		Boston	18 Apr
	2:30:09				1		Tokyo	20 Nov
2:25:15 dh	Elana	Meyer	RSA	10.10.66	3		Boston	18 Apr
2:25:15	Katrin	Dörre-Heinig	GER	6.10.61	1		Berlin	25 Sep
2:25:19 dh	Alena	Peterková	TCH	13.11.60	4		Boston	18 Apr
	2:31:43				1	NC	Pardubice	15 May
2:25:52	Miyoko	Asahina	JPN	24.9.69	1		Rotterdam	17 Apr
2:26:09	Tomoe	Abe	JPN	13.8.71	1		Osaka	30 Jan
2:26:09	Nobuko	Fujimura	JPN	18.12.65	2		Osaka	30 Jan
2:26:10	Junko	Asari	JPN	22.9.69	3		Osaka	30 Jan
2:26:26	Mitsuyo	Yoshida	JPN	29.10.66	4		Osaka	30 Jan
2:27:37	Tecla	Lorupe	KEN	5.5.71	1		New York	6 Nov
2:27:41 dh	Carmen	de Oliveira	BRA	17.8.65	5		Boston	18 Apr
	2:32:15				4		Tokyo	20 Nov
2:27:44	Franziska	Moser	SUI	17.8.66	1		Frankfurt	23 Oct
2:27:51		Asahina			5		Osaka	30 Jan
2:27:55	Mari	Tanigawa	JPN	27.10.62	1		Paris	24 Apr
2:28:08	Noriko	Kawaguchi	JPN	24.4.69	6		Osaka	29 Jan
2:28:12	Olga	Appell	USA	2.8.63	1		Los Angeles	6 Mar
2:28:26	Yuka	Terunuma	JPN	27.1.68	7		Osaka	30 Jan
2:28:58	Rocio	Rios	ESP	13.3.69	2		Berlin	25 Sep
2:29:06	Malgorzata	Sobanska	POL	25.4.69	8		Osaka	30 Jan
2:29:16	Ritva	Lemettinen	FIN	9.9.60	2		Rotterdam	17 Apr
2:29:21	Adriana	Barbu	ROM	17.1.61	1		Marrakesh	30 Jan
2:29:32		Zhong Huandi	CHN	28.6.67	1	AsiG	Hiroshima	9 Oct
2:29:36 dh	Monica	Pont	ESP	3.6.69	6		Boston	18 Apr
2:29:39	Anuta	Catuna	ROM	1.1.68	2		Marrakesh	30 Jan
2:29:43	Carla	Beurskens	NED	10.2.52	3		Rotterdam	17 Apr
2:29:54	Manuela	Machado	POR	9.8.63	1	EC	Helsinki	7 Aug
2:29:59	Angelina	Kanana	KEN	65	1		Hamburg	24 Apr
2:30:00		Sobanska			3		Berlin	25 Sep
2:30:00	Madina	Biktagirova	BLR	20.9.64	2		New York	6 Nov
	(30/28)							
2:30:12 dh	Martha	Tenorio	ECU	6.8.66	7		Boston	18 Apr
2:30:19	Anne Marie	Letko	USA	7.3.69	3		New York	6 Nov
	(30)							
2:30:30	Eriko	Asai	JPN	20.10.59	1		Nagoya	13 Mar
2:30:30	Sachiyo	Seiyama	JPN	6.11.72	2		Tokyo	20 Nov
2:30:33	Maria	Curatolo	ITA	12.10.63	2	EC	Helsinki	7 Aug
2:30:41	Carole	Rouillard	CAN	15.3.60	1	CG	Victoria	27 Aug
2:31:01	Lisa	Ondieki	AUS	12.5.60	3		Tokyo	20 Nov
2:31:07	Lizanne	Bussières	CAN	20.8.61	2	CG	Victoria	27 Aug
2:31:11		Wang Junxia	CHN	9.1.73	1		Beijing	30 Oct
2:31:12	Ramila	Burangulova	RUS	11.7.61	2		Nagoya	13 Mar
2:31:20		Pan Jinhong	CHN	18.8.73	2		Beijing	30 Oct
2:31:21.	Yuko	Yamazoe	JPN	4.5.73	9		Osaka	29 Jan
	(40)							
2:31:23	Kirsi	Rauta	FIN	17.3.62	4		Berlin	25 Sep
2:31:34	Kristy	Johnston	USA	3.6.65	1		Chicago	30 Oct
2:31:35	Sonja	Krolik	GER	24.2.73	5		Berlin	25 Sep
2:31:43	Anna	Rybicka	POL	23.9.63	3		Nagoya	13 Mar
2:31:45	Laura	Fogli	ITA	5.10.59	1		Torino	24 Apr
2:31:46 dh	Kim	Jones	USA	2.5.58	8		Boston	18 Apr
2:31:47	Claudia	Lokar	GER	9.2.64	5		New York	6 Nov
2:31:53 dh	Colleen	de Reuck	RSA	13.4.64	9		Boston	18 Apr
2:31:57	Omella	Ferrara	ITA	17.4.68	4	EC	Helsinki	7 Aug
2:31:57	Gitte	Karlshøj	DEN	14.5.59	2		Chicago	30 Oct
	(50)							

Mark	Name		Nat	Born	Pos	Meet	Venue	Date
2:32:01		Li Yemei	CHN	1.2.66	4		Rotterdam	17 Apr
2:32:01		Qu Yunxia	CHN	25.12.72	3		Beijing	30 Oct
2:32:02	Aiko	Magome	JPN	13.11.72	4		Nagoya	13 Mar
2:32:15		Zhang Linli	CHN	6.3.73	4		Beijing	30 Oct
2:32:22	Olga	Markova	RUS	6.8.68	10		Osaka	30 Jan
2:32:22	Stefania	Statkuviene	LIT	5.9.62	1		Reims	23 Oct
2:32:24	Yvonne	Danson	GBR	22.5.59	3	CG	Victoria	27 Aug
2:32:25	Elaine	Van Blunk	USA	11.9.64	3		Chicago	30 Oct
2:32:30		Ma Ningning	CHN	20.9.76	5		Beijing	30 Oct
2:32:32	Judit	Nagy	HUN	9.12.65	1		Orlando	16 Jan
	(60)							
2:32:38	Lidia	Slavuteanu	ROM	4.9.73	1		Kastoria	27 Apr
2:32:57	Sue	Hobson	AUS	13.3.58	1		Canberra	10 Apr
2:33:00	Olga	Loginova	RUS	18.12.69	2		Paris	24 Apr
2:33:00	Suzana	Ciric	YUG	12.7.69	1		Hannover	29 May
2:33:01	Elisabeth	Krieg	SUI	14.3.61	2		Hannover	29 May
2:33:07	Cristina	Pomacu	ROM	15.9.73	1		Beograd	23 Apr
2:33:09	Jane	Salumäe	EST	17.1.68	5		Rotterdam	17 Apr
2:33:12	Linda	Milo	BEL	9.7.60	3		Paris	24 Apr
2:33:16	Karen	Macleod	GBR	24.4.58	4	CG	Victoria	27 Aug
2:33:16	Aura	Buia	ROM	16.2.70	6		Berlin	25 Sep
	(70)							
2:33:18	Ana Isabel	Alonso	ESP	16.8.63	1	NC	Sevilla	27 Feb
2:33:21 dh	Albertina	Dias	POR	26.4.65	10		Boston	18 Apr
	2:34:14				8		New York	6 Nov
2:33:28	Elzbieta	Nadolna	POL	16.8.71	7		Berlin	25 Sep
2:33:36 dh	Emma	Scaunich	ITA	1.3.54	11		Boston	18 Apr
	2:37:05				2		Los Angeles	6 Mar
2:33:41	Yelena	Rasdrogina	RUS	25.8.69	6		Paris	24 Apr
2:33:42	Linda	Somers	USA	7.5.61	1		Duluth	18 Jun
2:33:49	Nadezhda	Ilyina	RUS	2.4.64	1		Omsk	6 Aug
2:33:56	Danuta	Bartoszak	CAN	19.8.61	2		Toronto	15 May
2:33:58	Josefa	Cruz	ESP	12.3.58	3		Sevilla	27 Feb
2:34:01	Anita	Håkenstad	NOR	19.2.68	2		Frankfurt	23 Oct
	(80)							
2:34:03	Nyla	Carroll	NZL	24.11.65	5	CG	Victoria	20 Aug
2:34:08	Kerryn	McCann	AUS	2.5.67	11		Osaka	30 Jan
2:34:08	Zinaida	Semyonova	RUS	.62	1		Valencia	6 Feb
2:34:12	Fatima	Neves	POR	13.2.63	8		Paris	24 Apr
2:34:15	Albertina	Machado	POR	25.12.61	6		Rotterdam	17 Apr
2:34:21	Janete	Mayal	BRA	17.7.63	3		London	17 Apr
2:34:23	Aniela	Nikiel	POL	1.11.65	3		Reims	23 Oct
2:34:23	Alina	Ivanova	RUS	16.3.69	6		Tokyo	20 Nov
2:34:29	Tani	Ruckle	AUS	25.6.62	5		Nagoya	13 Mar
2:34:32	Rosanna	Munerotto	ITA	3.12.62	8	EC	Helsinki	7 Aug
	(90)							
2:34:39	Chiharu	Sato	JPN	13.4.70	8		Tokyo	20 Nov
2:34:40	Antonina	Andronaki	MOL	.59	1		St Dizier	18 Sep
2:34:46	Anna	Villani	ITA	21.6.66	9	EC	Helsinki	7 Aug
2:34:47	Alevtina	Naumova	RUS	16.1.61	1		Houston	16 Jan
2:34:50	Yuki	Tamura	JPN	21.4.67	12		Osaka	30 Jan
2:34:50	Helena	Javornik	SLO	26.3.66	2		Valencia	6 Feb
2:34:55	May	Allison	CAN	29.10.64	1		Detroit	16 Oct
2:34:57	Marzanna	Helbik	POL	11.9.61	9		Paris	24 Apr
2:35:05	Alla	Dudayeva	RUS	.69	2		Lake Buena Vista	16 Jan
2:35:07	Maria	Rebelo	FRA	29.1.56	10		Paris	24 Apr
	(100)							

Mark	First name	Name	Nat	Born	Date
2:35:09	Tatyana	Pozdnyakova	UKR	56	16 Jan
2:35:10	Marjan	Freriks	NED	61	17 Apr
2:35:11	Cristina	Burca	ROM	73	23 Apr
2:35:11	Galina	Goranova	BUL	63	23 Apr
2:35:15	Maura	Viceconte	ITA	67	6 Nov
2:35:20	Nao	Otani	JPN	71	20 Nov
2:35:21	Trina	Painter	USA	66	30 Oct
2:35:24	Krystyna	Kuta	POL	67	25 Sep
2:35:25	Fatuma	Roba	ETH	73	24 Apr
2:35:39	Hayley	Nash	GBR	63	27 Aug
2:35:40	Lorraine	Davis	AUS	68	24 Jul
2:35:44		Lee Mi-kyung	KOR	75	20 Mar
2:35:46	Ana	Nanu	ROM	73	23 Apr
2:35:48	Maria Luisa	Muñoz	ESP	59	20 Nov
2:35:50	Sue	Mahony	AUS	65	17 Apr
2:35:55	Gabrielle	O'Rourke	NZL	67	5 Mar
2:35:57	Marie-Hélène	Ohier	FRA	61	24 Apr
2:35:58	Lidia	Camberg	POL	62	30 Jan
2:35:59		Ren Xiujuan	CHN		23 Oct
2:36:07	Irina	Lagodina	UKR	64	23 Apr
2:36:07	Simona	Viola	ITA	71	23 Oct
2:36:13	Lyubov	Klochko	UKR	59	15 May
2:36:17	Sissel	Grottenberg	NOR	56	10 Apr
2:36:19	Kayoko	Nishiyama	JPN	69	30 Jan

Mark	Name		Nat	Born	Date
2:36:19	Jennifer	Martin	USA	61	4 Dec
2:36:24		Jung Young-im	KOR	75	20 Mar
2:36:24		Cong Li	CHN		30 Oct
2:36:27		Zhang Lirong	CHN	73	9 Oct
2:36:29	Maryse	Le Gallo	FRA	60	24 Apr
2:36:29	Danielle	Sanderson	GBR	62	7 Aug
2:36:29	Kathrin	Wessel	GER	67	23 Oct
2:36:30	Solange	de Souza	BRA	69	16 Jan
2:36:32		Tian Mei	CHN	71	30 Oct
2:36:33	Emiko	Kawata	JPN	73	13 Mar
2:36:35	Lisa	Weidenbach	USA	61	30 Oct
2:36:40	Teresa	Dyer	GBR	59	17 Apr
2:36:44	Mariya	Vilesova	RUS	69	23 Apr
2:36:50	Firiya	Sultanova	RUS	61	7 Aug
2:36:51	Yelena	Tolstoguzova	RUS	62	23 Apr
2:36:53dh	Irina	Bondarchuk	RUS	52	18 Apr
2:36:55	Tatyana	Zuyeva	MOL	58	10 Apr
2:36:55	Antonella	Bizioli	ITA	57	24 Apr
2:36:58	Debbie	Kilpatrick	USA	63	2 Oct
2:36:59		Yun Seon-suk	KOR	72	20 Mar
2:37:01dh	Mary-Lynn	Currier	USA	64	18 Apr
2:37:02	Marina	Belyayeva	RUS	59	24 Apr
2:37:06	Sally	Ellis	GBR	58	17 Apr
2:37:06	Gergana	Voynova	BUL	69	27 Apr
2:37:08	Fumiko	Okada	JPN	69	30 Jan
2:37:08	Sally	Eastall	GBR	63	17 Apr
	(150)				
2:37:08	Polina	Grigorenko	BLR	58	23 Apr
2:37:09	Joan	Samuelson	USA	57	30 Oct
2:37:10	Rosario	Murcia	FRA	64	24 Apr
2:37:14	Tammy	Slusser	USA	65	1 May
2:37:25	Maria	Trujillo	USA	59	30 Oct
2:37:27		Wang Dongmei	CHN	73	13 Mar
2:37:29		Chung Mi-ja	KOR	70	20 Mar
2:37:37	Birgit	Schuckmann	GER	60	25 Sep
2:37:43	Franca	Fiacconi	ITA	65	5 Jun
2:37:46	Marian	Sutton	GBR	63	30 Jan
2:37:49	Yelena	Sipatova	RUS	55	2 Oct
2:37:51		Wang Mingxia	CHN	71	20 Nov
2:37:56		Hwang Keum-yeon	KOR		20 Mar
2:37:58	Sylvia	Renz	GER	69	17 Apr
2:38:02		Kim Kyung-hee	KOR	73	20 Mar
2:38:08	Kellie	Archuletta	USA	61	18 Jun
2:38:12	Megumi	Setoguchi	JPN	68	13 Mar
2:38:16	Karolina	Szabó	HUN	61	15 May
2:38:17	Sigrid	Wulsch	GER	53	24 Apr
2:38:21	Stayka	Gandurova	BUL	67	27 Apr
2:38:21	Svetlana	Nechayeva	RUS	61	2 Oct
2:38:21	Grete	Kirkeberg	NOR	64	23 Oct
2:38:28	Françoise	Bonnet	FRA	57	24 Apr
2:38:29	Irena	Czuta	POL	66	23 Oct
2:38:30	Irina	Bogacheva	KGZ	61	15 May
2:38:32/39	Sally	Goldsmith	GBR	61	23 Oct
2:38:32	Valentina	Yenatskiy	RUS	66	27 Nov
2:38:45	Junko	Tsukamoto	JPN	73	30 Jan
2:38:46dh	Veronica	Kanga	KEN	72	18 Apr
2:38:48	Romy	Lindner	GER	67	23 Oct
2:38:50	Lidia	Panciu	ROM	69	10 Oct
2:38:51	Tatyana	Titova	RUS	65	24 Apr
2:38:57	Jillian	Costley	NZL	61	30 Apr
2:38:59	Vera	Sukhova	RUS	63	18 Sep
2:39:00	Martha	Ernstdóttir	ISL	64	23 Oct
	(185)				

Uncertain distance: 30 Oct, Poitiers: 1. Valentina Yenatskiy RUS 66 2:33:22, 2. Olga Loginova RUS 69 2:33:27

100 KILOMETRES

Mark	Name		Nat	Born	Pos	Meet	Venue	Date
7:22:18	Valentina	Lyakhova	RUS	24.6.58	1	IAU	Amiens	24 Sep
7:30:32	Maria	Bak	GER	3.1.59	1	IAU	Kalisz	8 Oct
7:33:46	Donna	Perkins	USA		1	IAU NC	Sacramento	12 Feb
7:34:27	Alcira	Portela Lario	POR	.57	1	IAU	Torhout	17 Jun
7:34:58	Valentina	Shatyayeva	RUS	.63	1	IAU WC	Saroma	26 Jun
7:36:39		Lyakhova			1	IAU EC	Winschoten	3 Sep
7:38:14	Birgit	Lennartz	GER	22.11.65	1	IAU NC	Kiel	24 Sep
7:42:17	Trudi	Thomson	GBR	18.1.59	2	IAU WC	Saroma	26 Jun
7:45:04	Mary	Morgan	AUS		1	IAU	Kurow	31 Jan
7:46:35	Irina	Petrova	RUS	13.2.74	3	IAU WC	Saroma	26 Jun
7:47:43	Yelena	Maskina (10)	RUS	14.4.64	4	IAU WC	Saroma	26 Jun
7:48:13		Morgan			1	IAU	Victoria	31 Aug
7:51:58	Linda	Meadows	AUS	10.3.59	2	IAU	Kurow	31 Jan
7:52:59	Nurzia	Bagmanova	RUS	8.6.63	2	IAU EC	Winschoten	3 Sep
7:53:12	Anni	Lønstad	DEN	19.8.53	1	IAU	Rodenbach	16 Apr
7:53:22	Jutta	Philippin	GER	14.4.60	2	IAU NC	Kiel	24 Sep
7:55:49	Isabelle	Olive	FRA	19.5.60	5	IAU WC	Saroma	26 Jun
7:55:55	Kristine	Clark-Setnes	USA	28.12.59	2	IAU NC	Sacramento	12 Feb
7:56:33	Mariya	Ostrovskaya	UKR	.55	2	IAU	Kalisz	8 Oct
7:56:39	Rae	Bisschoff	RSA		6	IAU WC	Saroma	26 Jun
7:56:57	Chrissy	Duryea	USA	12..8.60	7	IAU WC	Saroma	26 Jun
7:57:12		Shatyayeva			1	IAU	Santa Cruz de Bezana	1 Oct
7:58:12		Bak			2	IAU	Rodenbach	16 Apr
7:58:23		Bak			8	IAU WC	Saroma	26 Jun
	(24/19)							
8:02:07	Anke	Drescher	GER	14.12.67	3	IAU NC	Kiel	24 Sep
	(20)							
8:02:23	Huguette	Jouault	FRA	8.7.51	9	IAU WC	Saroma	26 Jun
8:02:59	Ashley	Evans	CAN	15.4.64	3	IAU	Sacramento	12 Feb
8:05:20	Carolyn	Hunter-Rowe	GBR	25.1.64	10	IAU WC	Saroma	26 Jun
8:07:22	Beatrice	Reymann	FRA	.55	1	IAU NC	Rognonas	3 Apr

Mark	Wind	Name		Nat	Born	Pos	Meet	Venue	Date
8:07:28		Marta	Vass	HUN	6.7.62	2	IAU	Amiens	24 Sep
8:07:55		Danielle	Geffroy	FRA	14.5.45	12	IAU WC	Saroma	26 Jun
8:09:57		Patricia	Lithgow	RSA	16.11.55	13	IAU WC	Saroma	26 Jun
8:12:07		Anni	Floris	FRA	.61	5	IAU EC	Winschoten	3 Sep
8:13:49		Nicole	Duchemin	FRA	10.10.46	1		Chevagnes	14 May
8:14:36		Katharina	Janicke	GER	29.12.53	3	IAU	Rodenbach	16 Apr
		(30)							
8:14:58		Michelle	Jacquemin	FRA	10.6.49	3	IAU NC	Rognonas	3 Apr
8:15:16		Sanet	Beukes	RSA	.55	2	IAU	Santa Cruz de Bezana	1 Oct
8:18:45		Ellen	McCurtin	USA	6.2.67	16	IAU WC	Saroma	26 Jun
8:19:56		Sigrid	Lomsky	GER	16.1.42	4	IAU	Rodenbach	16 Apr
8:21:50		Eiko	Endo	JPN	15.1.50	17	IAU WC	Saroma	26 Jun
Marks made on courses not checked by calibrated bicycle									
7:22:55		Irina	Petrova	RUS	13.2.74	1		Kalingrad	9 Apr
7:38:57		Yelena	Maskina	RUS	14.4.64	2		Kalingrad	9 Apr
7:47:05		Larisa	Golovacheva	RUS	.69	3		Kalingrad	9 Apr

24 HOURS

Mark	Name		Nat	Born	Pos	Meet	Venue	Date
Track races								
213.491km	Helen	Stenger	AUS		1		Wollongong	26 Mar
212,840	Rimma	Paltseva	RUS	.48	1		Odessa	22/23 Oct
204.674	Sharon	Gayter	GBR	1.4.49	1	NC	London (TB)	22/23 Oct
202.204	S	Savoshkina	RUS		1	NC	Moskva	21/22 May
201.229	Yelena	Siderenkova	RUS	.66	1		Podolsk	27 Aug
200,925	Marianne	Savage	GBR	26.1.49	2	NC	London (TB)	22/23 Oct
Road races								
231.510	Marie	Bertrand	FRA	29.7.57	1	NC	Courcon	17/18 Sep
231.482	Sigrid	Lomsky	GER	16.1.42	1	IAU EC	Szeged	21 May
220.125	Sue Ellen	Trapp	USA	4.3.46	1	NC	Sylvania	17/18 Sep
215.363	Susen	Olsen	USA		2	NC	Sylvania	17/18 Sep
214.927	Monika	Peter	GER	5.7.50	1	IAU	Apeldoorn	13/14 May
211.608	Pascale	Mahe	FRA	.32	2	NC	Courcon	17/18 Sep
207.099	Helga	Backhaus	GER	19.1.53	2	IAU	Apeldoorn	13/14 May
202.825	Martina	Hausmann	GER	13.1.60	1	IAU	Torhout	13/14 Aug
202.276	Rimma	Paltseva	RUS	.48	2	IAU EC	Szeged	21 May
201.850	Gisela	Fricke	GER	13.5.53	3	IAU EC	Szeged	21 May
201.168	Kathy	Welch	USA		1		Sacramento	12/13 Nov
Indoors								
210.661	Nadezhda	Tarasova	RUS	.52	1		Podolsk	26/27 Feb
205.739	Rimma	Paltseva	RUS	.48	2		Podolsk	26/27 Feb

2000 METRES STEEPLECHASE

Mark	Name		Nat	Born	Pos	Meet	Venue	Date
6:11.84	Marina	Pluzhnikova	RUS	25.2.63	1	GWG	St Peterburg	25 Jul
6:21.71		Pluzhnikova			1	NC	St Peterburg	15 Jul
6:25.12	Olga	Kozal	UKR	25.3.70	1	NC	Kiev	27 May
6:25.19	Svetlana	Pospyelova	RUS	70	2	GWG	St Peterburg	25 Jul
6:25.72		Pospyelova			2	NC	St Peterburg	15 Jul
6:25.89	Vera	Ragulina	UKR	19.4.68	2		Kiev	27 May
6:26.76	Lyudmila	Kuropatkina	RUS	66	3	GWG	St Peterburg	25 Jul
6:27.4		Pospyelova			1		Rostov	26 Aug
6:29.20		Kuropatkina			3	NC	St Peterburg	15 Jul
	(9/5)							

Mark	Name		Nat	Born	Date	Mark	Name		Nat	Born	Date
6:31.49	Natalya	Cherepanova	RUS	67	15 Jul	6:37.81	Olimpia	Pop	ROM	76	6 Aug
6:33.59	Tatyana	Babik	UKR	75	24 Jul	6:38.31	Valentina	Sukhanova	RUS	76	15 Jul
6:37.64	Rimma	Ulyanova	RUS	74	15 Jul		(10)				

100 METRES HURDLES

Mark	Wind	Name		Nat	Born	Pos	Meet	Venue	Date
12.53	0.2	Tatyana	Reshetnikova	RUS	14.10.66	1rA	GP II	Linz	4 Jul
12.53	-0.4	Svetla	Dimitrova	BUL	27.1.70	1	Herc	Stara Zagora	16 Jul
12.53	0.0		Dimitrova			1	Herc	Monaco	2 Aug
12.56	1.0	Yordanka	Donkova	BUL	28.9.61	1	NC	Sofia	3 Jul
12.60	0.4		Dimitrova			1s1	EC	Helsinki	9 Aug
12.61	1.5		Dimitrova			1A	WK	Zürich	17 Aug
12.62	1.1	Yulia	Graudyn	RUS	13.11.70	1A	ISTAF	Berlin	30 Aug
12.63	0.0		Graudyn			2	Herc	Monaco	2 Aug
12.64	0.3		Dimitrova			1	GGala	Roma	8 Jun
12.64	1.3		Donkova			1A	Athl	Lausanne	6 Jul
12.65	0.7		Dimitrova			1	GP II	Sevilla	5 Jun
12.66	1.3		Reshetnikova			2A	Athl	Lausanne	6 Jul

Mark	Wind	Name		Nat	Born	Pos	Meet	Venue	Date
12.66	0.5		Dimitrova			1	GPF	Paris	3 Sep
12.67	0.9		Dimitrova			1	ASV	Köln	21 Aug
12.68	1.1		Donkova			2A	ISTAF	Berlin	30 Aug
12.69	1.0		Dimitrova			1		Sofia	24 May
12.69	0.7		Donkova			2	GP II	Sevilla	5 Jun
12.69	2.0	Jackie	Joyner-Kersee	USA	3.3.62	1	USOF	Edwardsville	8 Jul
12.70	0.0		Donkova			1	Nik	Nice	18 Jul
12.72	0.3		Donkova			2	GGala	Roma	8 Jun
12.72	0.8		Dimitrova			1h2	EC	Helsinki	8 Aug
12.72	1.7		Dimitrova			1	EC	Helsinki	9 Aug
12.73	1.7	Nadezhda	Bodrova	UKR	13.7.61	1h1		Kiev	23 Jul
12.73	0.9		Graudyn			2	ASV	Köln	21 Aug
12.73	0.1		Dimitrova			1	TOTO	Tokyo	15 Sep
12.74	0.9		Reshetnikova			1s1	NC	St Peterburg	16 Jul
12.74	0.0	Aliuska	López	CUB	29.8.69	3	Herc	Monaco	2 Aug
12.74	1.1		Reshetnikova			3A	ISTAF	Berlin	30 Aug
12.75	0.0		Graudyn			1	BNP	Villeneuve d'Ascq	8 Jul
12.75	0.0		Reshetnikova			2	Nik	Nice	18 Jul
12.75	1.1		López			4A	ISTAF	Berlin	30 Aug
		(31/7)							
12.76	0.6	Anne	Piquereau	FRA	15.6.64	1	NC	Annecy	24 Jul
12.77	0.0	Brigita	Bukovec	SLO	21.5.70	4	Herc	Monaco	2 Aug
12.78	0.9	Olga	Shishigina	KZK	23.12.68	1	Kuts	Moskva	31 Jul
		(10)							
12.82	-0.4	Julie	Baumann	SUI	17.6.64	3s1	EC	Helsinki	9 Aug
12.86	0.2	LaVonna	Martin	USA	18.11.66	2rA	GP II	Linz	4 Jul
12.86	-1.2		Zhang Yu	CHN	8.4.71	1		Tangshan	28 Aug
12.87	-2.0		Zhou Hongyan	CHN	5.4.70	2	AsiG	Hiroshima	11 Oct
12.88	0.2	Dawn	Bowles	USA	12.11.68	4rA	GP II	Linz	4 Jul
12.89		Natalya	Yudakova	RUS	25.3.65	1h		Moskva	29 May
12.90	1.6	Alena	Sukhorchenko	UKR	12.1.73	2		Kiev	23 Jul
12.91	1.4	Natalya	Tochilova	RUS	21.5.64	1		Sotteville	26 Jun
12.93	1.4	Jackie	Agyepong	GBR	5.1.69	2rB	Athl	Lausanne	6 Jul
12.93	1.0	Patricia	Girard	FRA	8.4.68	1h2	NC	Annecy	24 Jul
		(20)							
12.93	0.5	Michelle	Freeman	JAM	5.5.69	2		Tallinn	29 Jul
12.94	1.5	Marina	Azyabina	RUS	15.6.63	3		Reims	8 Jun
12.94	1.4	Kristin	Patzwahl	GER	16.7.65	3rB	Athl	Lausanne	6 Jul
12.97	0.5	Gillian	Russell	JAM	28.9.73	1s2	NCAA	Boise	3 Jun
12.97	1.1	Carla	Tuzzi	ITA	2.6.67	1	ECp I	Valencia	12 Jun
12.98	1.5	Caren	Jung	GER	18.1.68	1		Schriesheim	18 Jun
12.99	-1.2		Luo Bin	CHN	7.1.70	3	NC	Beijing	2 Jun
12.99	1.1	Aleksandra	Paskhina	RUS	14.8.71	1		Gävle	4 Jul
13.00	1.3	Lynda	Goode	USA	3.10.67	2rB	Bisl	Oslo	22 Jul
13.04	1.9	Yelizaveta	Chernyshova	RUS	26.1.58	1		Wipperfürth	19 Jun
		(30)							
13.04	-1.6	Svetlana	Laukhova	RUS	7.5.73	4	NC	St Peterburg	16 Jul
13.04	-0.4	Clova	Court	GBR	10.2.60	5s1	EC	Helsinki	9 Aug
13.07	0.9	Yelena	Sinyutina	RUS	12.5.64	4s2	NC	St Peterburg	16 Jul
13.08	0.2	Jane	Flemming	AUS	14.4.65	1	NEC	Melbourne	24 Feb
13.08	1.5	Monique	Tourret	FRA	11.7.67	6		Reims	8 Jun
13.08	0.4	Samantha	Farquharson	GBR	15.12.69	1rB	GP II	Linz	4 Jul
13.09	0.5	Sally	Gunnell	GBR	29.7.66	2	AAA	Sheffield	11 Jun
13.09	1.4	Donalda	Duprey	CAN	1.3.67	6rB	Athl	Lausanne	6 Jul
13.09	1.3	Monica	Grefstad	NOR	12.10.64	3rB	Bisl	Oslo	22 Jul
13.11	0.6	Nicole	Ramalalanirina	MAD	5.3.72	3	FraCh	Annecy	24 Jul
		(40)							
13.12	0.0	Allison	Williams	USA	1.6.71	1	PennR	Philadelphia	30 Apr
13.13	1.6	Jamie	McNeair	USA	26.6.69	1		Indianapolis	14 May
13.13	0.0	Cheryl	Dickey	USA	12.12.66	3		Rovereto	24 Jul
13.13	1.9	Dionne	Rose	JAM	7.11.69	1		Jakarta	30 Jul
13.14A	1.1	Tonja	Buford	USA	13.12.70	1		El Paso	16 Apr
13.14	0.0		Chan Sau Ying	HKG	30.8.70	1	MSR	Walnut	17 Apr
13.14	0.7	Lidia	Yurkova	BLR	15.1.67	1		Gomel	10 Jul
13.14	0.6	Nadege	Joseph	FRA	12.8.73	4	NC	Annecy	24 Jul
13.17	0.8	Natalya	Shekhodanova	RUS	29.12.71	2h1	NC	St Peterburg	15 Jul
13.18	1.9		Xie Liuying	CHN	.1.67	h	NC	Beijing	1 Jun
		(50)							

Mark	Wind	Name		Nat	Born	Pos	Meet	Venue	Date
13.19	1.8	Urszula	Wlodarczyk	POL	22.12.65	H	ECp	Vénissieux	2 Jul
13.20	0.8	Svetlana	Moskalets	RUS	22.1.69	H	NC	Vladimir	16 Jun
13.20	1.7	Natalya	Kolovanova	UKR	1.8.64	2h1		Kiev	23 Jul
13.21	-0.6	Odalys	Adams	CUB	31.7.67	2	NC	La Habana	23 Jun
13.22		Oraidis	Ramirez	CUB	11.11.73	1h		La Habana	24 Feb
13.22	0.5	Anjanette	Kirkland	USA	24.2.74	2s2	NCAA	Boise	3 Jun
13.23	0.8	Yekaterina	Gorbatova	RUS	13.6.68	2h2	NC	St Peterburg	15 Jul
13.23	0.2	Maria Jose	Mardomingo	ESP	27.1.69	1	NC	San Sebastián	17 Jul
13.24	0.4	Sharon	Couch	USA	13.9.69	11		Fresno	10 Jun
13.24	1.2	Melissa	Morrison	USA	9.7.71	2h1	NC	Knoxville	16 Jun
		(60)							
13.24	1.9	Keri	Maddox	GBR	4.7.72	1h2		Stoke-on-Trent	16 Jul
13.25	0.0		Sun Xue	CHN	3.3.72	h	NC	Beijing	1 Jun
13.25	1.1	Diane	Allahgreen	GBR	21.2.75	1s2	WJ	Lisboa	21 Jul
13.25	1.9	Sriyani	Kulawansa	SRI	1.3.70	2		Jakarta	30 Jul
13.26	0.5	Kirsten	Bolm	GER	4.3.75	1	WJ	Lisboa	22 Jul
13.26	0.4	Heike	Tillack	GER	6.1.68	1		Konstanz	23 Jul
13.26	1.6	Tatyana	Sableva	UKR	21.8.67	3		Kiev	23 Jul
13.26	0.8		Yu Qing	CHN	22.5.72	h		Tangshan	27 Aug
13.27	0.9	Monifa	Taylor	USA	3.3.71	1B		Austin	7 May
13.27		Irina	Mylnikova	BLR	14.6.65	1		Stargard	30 Jul
		(70)							
13.29	1.8	Sherlese	Taylor	USA	27.11.70	1		Durham	9 Apr
13.29	1.1	Doris	Williams	USA	30.6.63	1h		Long Beach	25 May
13.29		Svetlana	Buraga	BLR	3.9.65	H		Götzis	28 May
13.29	0.4	Yelena	Ovcharova	UKR	17.8.76	1h3	WJ	Lisboa	21 Jul
13.30		Marsha	Guialdo	USA	12.7.70	1		San Luis Obispo	2 Apr
13.30	0.8	Irina	Tyukhay	RUS	14.1.67	H	NC	Vladimir	16 Jun
13.30	1.0	LaTasha	Colander	USA	23.8.76	1s1	WJ	Lisboa	21 Jul
13.30	1.7	Yelena	Politika	UKR	24.8.64	3h1		Kiev	23 Jul
13.31	0.4	Jackie	Humphrey	USA	30.9.65	2A	DogwR	Knoxville	8 Apr
13.31	0.4	Sabine	Braun	GER	19.6.65	2	NC	Erfurt	3 Jul
		(80)							
13.31	1.6	Svetlana	Zavgorodnaya	UKR	20.9.66	4		Kiev	23 Jul
13.31	0.5	Remigija	Nazaroviene	LIT	2.6.67	5		Tallinn	29 Jul
13.32	1.3	Jayne	Moyes	AUS	25.1.66	2		Sydney	30 Jan
13.32		Kim	McKenzie	USA	21.3.61	1		Atlanta	22 May
13.32	1.0	Kim	Carson	USA	12.3.74	3s1	NCAA	Boise	3 Jun
13.32	0.2	Bettina	Stähli	SUI	5.11.73	2h1		Bellinzona	25 Jun
13.32	2.9	Angela	Thorp	GBR	7.12.72	1		Kings Lynn	9 Jul
13.32	0.4	Erica	Nicolae	ROM	21.9.73	1	Balk	Trikala	9 Jul
13.32	1.0		Chen Zhenghong	CHN	30.9.76	2s1	WJ	Lisboa	21 Jul
13.32	0.2	Bettine	Stähli	SUI	5.11.73	2h1	Athl	Lausanne	6 Jul
		(90)							
13.32	0.7	Maria	Kamrowska	POL	11.3.66	1	DEN Ch	Esbjerg	23 Jul
13.33	1.0	Ayo	Atterberry	USA	30.4.72	4s1	NCAA	Boise	3 Jun
13.34	1.2	Joyce	Melendez	PUR	7.4.70	3		Rhede	29 Jul
13.34	1.9		Zhou Jing	CHN	.2.73	h	NC	Beijing	1 Jun
13.34	-0.3	Heike	Drechsler	GER	16.12.64	H		Talence	10 Sep
13.36	1.0	Elisabeta	Pavlovska	MKD	24.9.72	2		Sofia	24 May
13.37	1.2	Keri	Hinderlie	USA	73	1h2		Fairfax	21 May
13.37		Trina	Murden	USA	69	3		Atlanta	22 May
13.37	0.9	Lyudmila	Mikhailova	RUS	12.4.69	H		Götzis	28 May
13.37		Yasmina	Azzizi	ALG	25.2.66	1h1		Barcelona	21 Jun
13.37	0.6	Sylvia	Dethier	BEL	20.5.65	1		Bruxelles	17 Jul
13.37	1.0	Astia	Walker	JAM	4.4.75	3s1	WJ	Lisboa	21 Jul
		(102)							

Mark	Wind	Name		Nat	Born	Date
13.38	0.4	Monica	Missick	USA	72	10 Jun
13.38	0.4	Keturah	Anderson	CAN	68	30 Jun
13.38	2.0	Manuela	Marxer	LIE	65	17 Jul
13.38	0.6	Angela	Atiede	NGR		19 Aug
13.39	1.7	Sonia	Paquette	CAN	72	9 Jul
13.40	1.0	Alethea	Antoine	USA	72	3 Jun
13.40	1.2	Kwani	Stewart	USA	72	16 Jun
13.40	1.8	Peggy	Beer	GER	69	2 Jul
13.40	0.6	Cristine	Hurtlin	FRA	67	24 Jul
13.40	1.0	Leshley	Tashlin	CAN	69	26 Aug
13.41	1.3	Nikki	Inglis	USA	72	21 May
13.41	1.2	Ine	Langenhuizen	NED	68	5 Jun
13.41	0.1	Ayumi	Sasaki	JPN	67	15 Sep
13.42	0.6	Lesley-Ann	Skeete	GBR	67	17 Jul
13.43		Irina	Polyakova	RUS	74	30 May
13.43	1.1	Dawn	Burrell	USA	73	2 Jun
13.44	1.1	Tonya	Williams	USA	74	23 Apr
13.44	1.2	Akiko	Morimoto	JPN	77	17 Jun
13.44	1.5	Zita	Bálint	HUN	71	19 Jun
13.44	0.6	Annette	Simon	FRA	71	24 Jul
13.44	0.8	Sandra	Barreiro	POR	71	8 Aug
13.44	0.4		Hsu Hsiu-Ying	TPE	73	25 Oct
13.45	0.5	Isabel	Pereira	POR	73	10 Jul
13.46	0.6	Naoko	Kobayashi	JPN	68	29 Apr
13.46	0.0	Rosa	Baker	USA	70	30 Apr
13.46	1.2	Caroline	Delplancke	BEL	67	5 Jun

Mark	Wind	Name		Nat	Born	Date	
13.46	0.5	Sharon	Hanson	USA	65	14	Jun
13.46	0.4	Natalya	Timofeyeva	RUS	72	16	Jun
13.46	0.4	Katrin	Blankenburg	GER	71	3	Jul
13.47	0.6	Trecia	Roberts	USA	71	23	Apr
13.47		Liliana	Nastase	ROM	62	14	May
13.47	2.7	Kim	Blair	USA	72	22	May
13.47	1.9		Tang Xiaoyue	CHN		2	Jun
13.47	0.3	Mona	Steigauf	GER	70	18	Jun
13.47	1.5	Irina	Matyusheva	UKR	65	2	Jul
13.47	1.5	Denise	Lewis	GBR	72	2	Jul
13.48	-1.2		Liu Jing	CHN		28	Aug
13.48	0.2	Lyudmila	Khristosenko	UKR	66	28	Aug
13.49	0.7	Karen	van der Veen	RSA	66	25	Mar
13.49	1.1	Le'Gretta	Hinds	USA	74	25	May
13.49	1.1	Iveta	Rudová	TCH	69	12	Jun
13.49		Ludmila	Olijare	LAT	58	17	Jul
13.49	1.1	Jutta	Kemila	FIN	72	8	Aug
13.49	1.4	Iina	Pekkola	FIN	73	27	Aug
13.50A	1.1	Gudrun	Arnardóttir	ISL	71	16	Apr
13.50	1.1	Carmen	Banks	USA	76	24	Jun
13.51	1.4	Petra	Hassinger	GER	66	22	May
13.51	0.7	Chelsa	Istre	USA	72	28	May
		(150)					
13.51	1.6	Ireina	Omelchenko	UKR	71	23	Jul
13.52	1.0	Jenny	Laurendet	AUS	62	26	Feb
13.52		Gudrun	Lattner	GER	59	30	Apr
13.52	0.3	Elisa	Andretti	ITA	70	3	Jul
13.52	0.7	Sharon	Jaklofsky	NED	68	30	Jul
13.53	1.2	Birgit	Gautzsch	GER	67	5	Jun
13.53	0.8	Angela	Coon-Francis	CAN	66	27	Jul
13.53	1.4	Michaelle	Deverell	AUS	70	11	Sep
13.54	1.7	Iwona	Konrad	POL	74	19	Jun
13.54	1.8	Leslie	Estwick	CAN	60	16	Jul
13.54	1.4	Helena	Fernström	SWE	69	27	Aug
13.55	0.2	Claudine	Robinson	USA	71	23	Apr
13.55	0.5	Kym	Carter	USA	64	14	Jun
13.56	0.1	Naomi	Hashioka	JPN	68	11	Jun
13.56	1.1	Tamika	Higgins-Francis	USA	71	16	Jun
13.57	0.7	Nadezhda	Novikova	RUS	66	16	Jun
13.57	1.5	Aldona	Fogiel	POL	72	31	Jul
13.58	2.0	Véronique	Storme	BEL	67	17	Jul
13.59	0.7	Nadine	Grouwels	BEL	73	30	Jul
		(169)					

Low altitude best: 13.53 0.8 Arnardottir 8 Aug

Wind gauge incorrectly placed

13.59 1.2 Samem Anderson USA 21 May

Wind assisted

Mark	Wind	Name		Nat	Born	Pos	Meet	Venue	Date
12.49	5.0	Yordanka	Donkova	BUL	28.9.61	1		Dijon	12 Jun
12.50	2.7	Svetla	Dimitrova	BUL	27.1.70	1		St Denis	10 Jun
12.51A	3.3	Yulia	Graudyn	RUS	13.11.70	1		Sestriere	31 Jul
12.52	5.0		Dimitrova	BUL		2		Dijon	12 Jun
12.55	3.8		Reshetnikova			1		Lyon	11 Jun
12.59A	3.3	Brigita	Bukovec	SLO	21.5.70	2		Sestriere	31 Jul
12.64	5.0	Anne	Piquereau	FRA	15.6.64	3		Dijon	12 Jun
12.65	2.7		Reshetnikova			1h4	NC	St Peterburg	15 Jul
12.69	2.7		Donkova			2		St Denis	10 Jun
12.71	2.9		Reshetnikova			1		Cottbus	15 Jun
12.73	2.7		Graudyn			3	GP	St Denis	10 Jun
12.74	2.9	Michelle	Freeman	JAM	5.5.69	1	Jen	San José	28 May
12.74	2.8	Marina	Azyabina	RUS	15.6.63	1s2	NC	St Peterburg	16 Jul
12.75	2.9		Joyner-Kersee			2	Jen	San José	28 May
12.75	5.0		López			4		Dijon	12 Jun
12.87	4.7	Aleksandra	Paskhina	RUS	14.8.71	1		Nurmijärvi	2 Jul
12.90	2.9	Lynda	Goode	USA	3.10.67	3	Jen	San José	28 May
12.91	2.6	Svetlana	Laukhova	RUS	7.5.73	2h3	NC	St Peterburg	15 Jul
12.96	5.0	Monique	Tourret	FRA	11.7.67	5		Dijon	12 Jun
13.03	2.9	Cheryl	Dickey	USA	12.12.66	4	Jen	San José	28 May
13.03	2.8	Yelizaveta	Chernyshova	RUS	26.1.58	4s1	NC	St Peterburg	16 Jul
13.06	5.5		Chan Sau Ying	HKG	30.8.70	1		Las Vegas	9 Apr
13.06	2.1	Dionne	Rose	JAM	7.11.69	2h2	CG	Victoria	26 Aug
13.08	2.8	Natalya	Shekhodanova	RUS	29.12.71	5s1	NC	St Peterburg	16 Jul
13.11	2.7	Debbie Ann	Parris	JAM	24.3.73	1	SEC	Fayetteville	15 May
13.16	2.8	Marina	Slushkina	RUS	2.8.60	6s2	NC	St Peterburg	16 Jul
13.21	5.0	Cristine	Hurtlin	FRA	29.9.67	6		Dijon	12 Jun
13.25	2.5	Ine	Langenhuizen	NED	27.10.68	1		Leiden	25 Jun
13.26	2.8	Doris	Williams	USA	30.6.68	1		Azusa	23 Apr
13.26	2.7	Gudrun	Arnardóttir	ISL	24.9.71	2	SEC	Fayetteville	15 May
13.26	4.2	Maria	Kamrowska	POL	11.3.66	1H		Alhama	4 Jun
13.29	4.2	Irina	Matyusheva	UKR	5.6.65	2H		Alhama	4 Jun
13.34	5.5	Trevaia	Williams	USA	7.9.68	2		Las Vegas	9 Apr
13.37	2.8	Donna	Waller	USA	6.4.64	2		Azusa	23 Apr

Mark	Wind	Name		Nat	Born	Date	
13.38	4.5	Sandra	Barreiro	POR	71	26	Jun
13.39	2.4	Sharon	Jaklofsky	NED	68	17	Jul
13.39	2.4	Naoko	Kobayashi	JPN	68	27	Aug
13.41	5.0	Annette	Simon	FRA	71	12	Jun
13.43	4.7	Jutta	Kemila	FIN	72	2	Jul
13.43	2.8	Lyubov	Prytkova	RUS	66	16	Jul
13.44A	2.2	Karen	van der Veen	RSA	66	15	Jan
13.45A	3.3	Annamaria	Di Terlizzi	ITA	73	31	Jul
13.49	2.9	Iveta	Rudová	TCH	69	15	Jun
13.49	2.7	Iina	Pekkola	FIN	73	2	Jul
13.50	2.2	Chelsa	Istre	USA	72	9	Apr
13.50	3.5+	Nichole	Belcher	USA	74	19	May
13.51	2.1	Leslie	Estwick	CAN	60	26	Aug
13.52	5.5	Felice	Lipscomb	USA	72	9	Apr
13.52A	3.1	Angeles	Guerra	ESP	69	8	Jul
13.52	2.4	Naomi	Hashioka	JPN	68	27	Aug
13.55	3.4	Claudine	Robinson	USA	71	16	Apr
13.55	2.3	Rhonda	Colvin	USA	69	14	May
13.56	2.3		Liu Bo	CHN	72	25	Jul
13.57	2.5	Valerie	Manning	USA		6	May
13.58	2.8	Monica	Pellegrinelli	SUI	65	8	Jul
13.59	2.6	Sophie	Marrot	FRA	75	2	Jul

Hand timed

Mark	Wind	Name		Nat	Born	Pos	Meet	Venue	Date
12.6		Yekaterina	Gorbatova	RUS	13.6.68	1		Moskva	12 May
12.7			Gorbatova			1h		Moskva	12 May

Mark	Wind		Name	Nat	Born	Pos	Meet	Venue	Date
12.8	1.9	Carla	Tuzzi	ITA	2.6.67	1		Rieti	30 Apr
13.0		Damarys	Anderson	CUB	24.10.74	1		La Habana	3 Feb
13.0		Svetlana	Zavgorodnaya	UKR	20.8.66	2		Dnepropetrovsk	9 Jul
13.1		Doris	Williams	USA	30.6.63	1		Los Angeles	21 May
13.1		Lyubov	Prytkova	RUS	5.7.66	1		Bryansk	28 May
13.1	0.4	Yelena	Ovcharova	UKR	17.8.76	1		Belaya Tserkov	9 Jul
13.1		Tatyana	Sableva	UKR	21.8.67			Dnepropetrovsk	9 Jul
13.2A	0.2	Karen	Van der Veen	RSA	66				16 Apr
13.2	0.2	Yelena	Politika	UKR	64				26 May
13.2		Yasmina	Azzizi	ALG	66				16 Jun
13.3	0.3	Lyudmila	Khristosenko	UKR	66				26 May
13.3	1.2	Isabel	Pereira	POR	73				18 Jul
No flash: 12.9		Samantha	Farquharson	GBR	15.12.69	1		Barry ?	18 May
Wind assisted									
12.7	2.4		Chan Sau Ying	HKG	30.8.70	1		San Luis Obispo	19 Mar
12.9	2.7	Jane	Flemming	AUS	14.4.65	1		Canberra	18 Jan
12.9	2.5	Kim	McKenzie	USA	21.3.61	2		Austin	7 May
13.0	2.6	Jayne	Moyes	AUS	25.1.66	1		Perth	8 Jan
13.0	2.4	Carolin	Sterling	JAM	17.3.70	2		San Luis Obispo	19 Mar
13.0	2.5	Monifa	Taylor	USA	3.3.71	3		Austin	7 May
13.1		Anjanette	Kirkland	USA	24.2.74	1		Abilene	12 May
13.2	2.4	Monica	Missick	USA	72				19 Mar
13.2	2.4	Astia	Walker	JAM	75				19 Mar
13.2	2.5	Jackie	Humphrey	USA	65				7 May

400 METRES HURDLES

Mark		Name	Nat	Born	Pos	Meet	Venue	Date
53.33	Sally	Gunnell	GBR	29.7.66	1	EC	Helsinki	12 Aug
53.51		Gunnell			1	GWG	St Peterburg	24 Jul
53.72	Kim	Batten	USA	29.3.69	1	Nik	Nice	18 Jul
53.91		Gunnell			2	Nik	Nice	18 Jul
54.04		Gunnell			1	GP	London	15 Jul
54.06		Gunnell			1	Athl	Lausanne	6 Jul
54.11	Anna	Knoroz	RUS	30.7.70	3	Nik	Nice	18 Jul
54.22		Batten			2	GP	London	15 Jul
54.22		Batten			2	GWG	St Peterburg	24 Jul
54.28		Knoroz			1	NC	St Peterburg	15 Jul
54.47		Batten			1	ASV	Köln	21 Aug
54.48	Deon	Hemmings	JAM	9.10.68	2	Athl	Lausanne	6 Jul
54.51		Batten			1	NC	Knoxville	17 Jun
54.51		Gunnell			1	CG	Victoria	26 Aug
54.52	Heike	Meissner	GER	29.1.70	1	NC	Erfurt	3 Jul
54.60		Gunnell			1s2	EC	Helsinki	10 Aug
54.62		Gunnell			1	ECp	Birmingham	25 Jun
54.62		Hemmings			4	Nik	Nice	18 Jul
54.67		Knoroz			3	GWG	St Peterburg	24 Jul
54.68	Silvia	Rieger	GER	14.11.70	2	EC	Helsinki	12 Aug
54.68		Knoroz			3	EC	Helsinki	12 Aug
54.69		Gunnell			1	GP	Gateshead	1 Jul
54.74		Gunnell			1	Slov	Bratislava	1 Jun
54.75		Knoroz			3	Athl	Lausanne	6 Jul
54.75		Knoroz			1	Herc	Monaco	2 Aug
54.78		Batten			1	DNG	Stockholm	12 Jul
54.78		Knoroz			1	iDAG	Göteborg	24 Aug
54.79		Meissner			4	EC	Helsinki	12 Aug
54.80		Gunnell			1	WCp	London	9 Sep
54.82	Olga	Nazarova	RUS	28.2.62	4	Athl	Lausanne	6 Jul
54.82		Knoroz			2s2	EC	Helsinki	10 Aug
	(31/7)							
54.92	Vera	Ordina	RUS	4.6.68	3	NC	St Peterburg	16 Jul
54.96	Tatyana	Tereshchuk	UKR	11.10.69	1	NC	Kiev	27 May
55.10	Donalda	Duprey	CAN	1.3.67	1	FranG	Bondoufle	12 Jul
	(10)							
55.15	Rosey	Edeh	CAN	13.8.66	2	Banes	São Paulo	21 May
55.17	Debbie Ann	Parris	JAM	24.3.73	4	Herc	Monaco	2 Aug
55.18	Tatyana	Kurochkina	BLR	15.9.67	5	EC	Helsinki	12 Aug
55.19	Nezha	Bidouane	MAR	18.9.69	2	FranG	Bondoufle	12 Jul
55.26	Tonja	Buford	USA	13.12.70	5	GWG	St Peterburg	24 Jul
55.26		Leng Xueyan	CHN	11.1.72	1	AsiG	Hiroshima	14 Oct
55.75		Hsu Pei-Ching	TPE	24.10.73	2	AsiG	Hiroshima	14 Oct
55.76	Gesine	Schmidt	GER	26.6.71	3	NC	Erfurt	3 Jul
55.78	Gowry	Retchakan	GBR	21.6.60	3s1	EC	Helsinki	10 Aug
55.81	Natalya	Torshina	KZK	4.10.68	3	AsiG	Hiroshima	14 Oct
	(20)							

Mark	Name		Nat	Born	Pos	Meet	Venue	Date
55.92	Monica	Westén	SWE	15.3.66	1	NC	Göteborg	31 Jul
55.93	Monika	Warnicka	POL	26.4.69	1	NC	Pila	26 Jun
55.96	Anita	Protti	SUI	4.8.64	1	NC	Lausane	31 Jul
55.98	Tonya	Williams	USA	5.10.74	1	USOF	Edinburgh	10 Jul
56.01	Lyudmila	Khodasevich	UKR	7.4.59	1	v3N	Krakow	30 Jun
56.05	Ximena	Restrepo	COL	10.3.69	1	Odesur	Valencia	27 Nov
56.06	Lauren	Poetschka	AUS	22.10.74	1	NC	Sydney	13 Mar
56.09	Frida	Johansson	SWE	5.1.70	2	NC	Göteborg	31 Jul
56.11	Maya	Shemchishina	UKR	6.5.72	1		Kiev	24 Jul
56.14	Lency	Montelier	CUB	13.2.71	4	Banes	São Paulo	21 May
	(30)							
56.21	Trevaia	Williams	USA	7.9.68	2		Tempe	2 Apr
56.25	Ionela	Tîrlea	ROM	9.2.76	1	WJ	Lisboa	22 Jul
56.25	Reawadee	Watanasin	THA	11.8.67	4	AsiG	Hiroshima	14 Oct
56.29	Nadia	Zétouani	MAR	3.1.70	1		Limoges	9 Jul
56.34	Michèle	Schenk	SUI	8.3.74	2	NC	Lausanne	31 Jul
56.35	Alla	Shilkina	UKR	15.11.68	2		Kiev	24 Jul
56.39	Marie	Womplou	CIV	20.12.69	3	FranG	Bondoufle	12 Jul
56.41	Jacqui	Parker	GBR	15.10.66	4	Slov	Bratislava	1 Jun
56.42	Sylwia	Pachut	POL	21.7.70	2	NC	Pila	26 Jun
56.45	Connie	Ellerbe	USA	24.6.68	2	USOF	Edwardsville	10 Jul
	(40)							
56.51	Nicoleta	Carutasu	ROM	14.2.64	5	Slov	Bratislava	1 Jun
56.56		Li Xiumei	CHN	.6.68	2	NC	Beijing	3 Jun
56.57	Catherine	Scott-Pomales	JAM	27.8.73	1	NAIA	Azusa	28 May
56.58	Karlene	Haughton	JAM	72	3	NC	Kingston	1 Jul
56.61	Carole	Nelson	FRA	27.1.71	1	NC	Annecy	24 Jul
56.62	Keisha	Marvin	USA	19.2.71	2	NCAA	Boise	3 Jun
56.63	Yulia	Tarasenko	RUS	28.3.68	6	Znam	Moskva	5 Jun
56.66	Sandra	Cummings-Glover	USA	30.12.68	3	USOF	Edwardsville	10 Jul
56.74	Natalya	Ignatyuk	BLR	28.12.63	1	NC	Gomel	10 Jul
56.79A	Karen	van der Veen	RSA	7.1.66	1		Pretoria	18 Apr
	(50)							
56.79	Virna	De Angeli	ITA	27.2.76	1	NC	Napoli	3 Jul
56.89	Birgit	Wolf	GER	11.9.69	2h1		Pfungstadt	19 Jun
56.90	Rebecca	Russell	USA	8.10.70	1		Atlanta	22 May
56.90	Yekaterina	Bakhvalova	RUS	8.3.72	5	Znam	Moskva	5 Jun
57.00	Svetlana	Starkova	RUS	68	4	NC	St Peterburg	15 Jul
57.04	Tonya	Lee	USA	6.11.69	5s1	NC	Knoxville	16 Jun
57.05	Lade	Akinremi	NGR	13.9.74	1		Pullman	21 May
57.09	Maria	Usifo	NGR	1.8.64	1	NC	Lagos	11 Jun
57.10	Inna	Nepluyeva	UKR	17.3.71	4		Kiev	24 Jul
57.13	Ester	Goossens	NED	21.2.72	1	NC	Assen	16 Jul
	(60)							
57.14	Corinne	Pierre-Joseph	FRA	27.10.66	1		Tarare	13 Jul
57.17	Anne	Renaud	FRA	24.3.70	1		Vénissieux	22 May
57.21	Tracy	Mattes	USA	13.12.68	1		Tallahassee	25 May
57.22	Debbie	Houseman	RSA	11.6.67	1		Durban	23 Apr
57.22	Petra	Stenman	FIN	12.3.74	1	v SWE	Stockholm	28 Aug
57.23	Emma	Holmqvist	SWE	26.3.75	3	WJ	Lisboa	22 Jul
57.27	Natasha	Reynolds	USA	7.6.72	6s1	NC	Knoxville	16 Jun
57.27	Stefanie	Zotter	AUT	8.12.71	1		Pfungstadt	19 Jun
57.27	Yelena	Znamenskaya	RUS	2.6.66	2h3	NC	St Peterburg	14 Jul
57.27		Wu Hongjie	CHN	13.4.71	2		Tangshan	29 Aug
	(70)							
57.34	Kathrin	Lüthi	SUI	7.10.69	2h1		Bellinzona	25 Jun
57.36	Yekaterina	Nikishova	RUS	73	2	ECp 23	Ostrava	30 Jul
57.39		Zheng Liyuan	CHN	1.4.74	3	NC	Beijing	3 Jun
57.40	Countess	Comadore	USA	27.1.67	4s2	NC	Knoxville	16 Jun
57.46	Rebecca	Campbell	AUS	23.1.76	2		Canberra	28 Jan
57.46	Lana	Uys	RSA	9.12.68	2		Durban	23 Apr
57.46	Isabelle	Dherbecourt	FRA	15.5.73	4	NC	Annecy	24 Jul
57.47	Kim	Blair	USA	12.3.72	3	NCAA	Boise	3 Jun
57.53	Sylvie	Birba	FRA	11.8.71	6	NC	Annecy	24 Jul
57.54	Yelena	Pavlova	UKR	3.2.69	5		Kiev	24 Jul
	(80)							
57.56	Yelena	Kardash	RUS	15.11.74	2	NC-23	Voronezh	18 Jun
57.65	Svetlana	Bordukova	RUS	1.5.65	1		St Peterburg	23 Jun
57.66	Esther	Lahoz	ESP	2.5.63	2	ECCp	Schwechat	29 May

Mark	Name		Nat	Born	Pos	Meet	Venue	Date
57.71	Maria Luisa	Cilimbini	ITA	25.10.67	2	NC	Napoli	3 Jul
57.73	Daniela	Graiani	GER	7.9.70	4	NC	Erfurt	3 Jul
57.73	Françoise	Dethier	BEL	20.5.65	1		Nivelles	23 Jul
57.75	Judit	Szekeres	HUN	18.11.66	1	NC	Debrecen	10 Jul
57.75	Irina	Omelchenko	UKR	12.5.71	6		Kiev	24 Jul
57.76	Vickie	Hudson	USA	17.10.71	3		Atlanta	22 May
57.78	Georgia	Harrison	JAM		2	NCAA II	Raleigh	28 May
	(90)							
57.81	Iina	Pekkola	FIN	23.3.73	6h1	EC	Helsinki	9 Aug
57.82	Le'Gretta	Hinds	USA	13.1.74	1		Long Beach	25 May
57.86	Pam	Brooks	USA	15.1.72	5	NCAA	Boise	3 Jun
57.86	Sahoko	Jodo	JPN	11.6.72	5	AsiG	Hiroshima	14 Oct
57.88	Winsome	Cole	JAM	30.5.74	2	NAIA	Azusa	28 May
57.89	Vanessa	Jack	NZL	9.11.70	3	AusC	Sydney	13 Mar
57.89	Odalys	Hernández	CUB	4.9.66	1	IbAm	Mar del Plata	30 Oct
57.94	Lana	Jekabsone	LAT	16.10.74	2	ECp II/3	Ljubljana	11 Jun
57.98	Charlynna	Foster	USA	2.1.80	1	NCj	Tallahassee	25 Jun
57.98	Miriam	Alonso	ESP	6.6.70	1		Vitoria	3 Jul
	(100)							

Mark	Name		Nat	Born	Date
58.01	Nioka	Gray	AUS	73	13 Mar
58.02	Cécile	Clarinval	BEL	68	3 Jul
58.03	Angela	Martin	USA	74	22 May
58.04	Yelena	Goncharova	RUS	63	26 Jun
58.04	Clare	Bleasdale	GBR	71	16 Jul
58.06	Tanya	Jarrett	JAM	77	28 Apr
58.06	Melanie	Moreels	BEL	73	16 Jul
58.06	Tiia	Eeskivi	EST	69	9 Aug
58.07	Louise	Brunning	GBR	72	21 Jul
58.09	Stephanie	McCann	GBR	65	12 Jun
58.10		Zhou Wei	CHN	75	22 Jul
58.10	Céline	Jeannet	SUI	68	21 Aug
58.13		Jiang Limei	CHN	77	29 Aug
58.17	Maria José	Santos	BRA	59	13 Aug
58.19	Maja	Gorjup	SLO	73	11 Jun
58.23	Sandrine	Robin	FRA	71	12 Jul
58.24	Nadia	Schmiedt	CAN	76	22 Jun
58.25	Erica	Peterson	CAN	73	21 May
58.27	Ulrike	Urbansky	GER	77	30 Jul
58.30A	Adri	van der Merwe	RSA	76	9 Apr
58.31	Eusheka	Bartley	GUY	74	28 Apr
58.33		Chen —hong	CHN		2 Jun
58.36	Saidat	Onanuga	NGR	74	21 May
58.36	Anabella	von Kesselstatt	ARG	69	21 May
58.37	Lydie	Deniau	FRA	71	9 Jul
58.40	Sharifa	Cox	USA	73	30 Apr
58.41	Eva	Paniagua	ESP	74	4 Jun
58.42	Mari	Bjone	NOR	70	26 Jul
58.43	Carla	Barbarino	ITA	67	25 Jun
58.43	Jane	Low	GBR	60	24 Aug
58.45	Elzbieta	Zaborowska	POL	72	25 Jun
58.47	Michelle	Johnson	USA	74	25 May
58.47	Natalya	Chistyakova	RUS	70	14 Jul
58.47	Ikiko	Yamagata	JPN	75	11 Oct
58.51A	Carolina	Kola	KEN	66	23 Jul
58.54	Elma	Muros-Posadas	PHI	67	29 May
58.55	Sabine	Gründel	GER	70	18 Jun
58.57	Stacy	Hudson	USA	71	1 Jun
58.58	Stephanie	Love	USA		21 May
58.59	Maud	Respaud	FRA	71	9 Jul
58.59	Ivana	Sekyrová	TCH	71	10 Jul
58.60	Oksana	Kochetkova	UKR	74	24 Jul
58.62	Mayte	Urcelaya	ESP	72	26 Jun
58.63	Kim	Townes	USA	74	15 May
58.63	Radhiya	Teagle	USA	74	25 May
58.63	Carmen	Nistor	ROM	71	18 Jun
58.63	Anfisa	Kosacheva	RUS	65	14 Jul
58.66	Glynis	Nunn-Cearns	AUS	60	20 Feb
58.66	Lynn	Massey	NZL	62	6 Mar
58.66	Monika	Niederstatter	ITA	74	19 Jun
	(150)				
58.66	Monique	Lopez	FRA	62	23 Jul
58.67	Danielle	Blackburn	RSA	75	23 Apr
58.68	Anna	Ambraziene	LIT	55	11 Jun
58.70	Telisa	Young	USA	71	8 Apr
58.71	Andrea	Giscombe	JAM		21 May
58.75	Andrea	Blackett	BAR	76	24 Apr
58.75	Maryam	Meyer	FRA	62	23 Jul

Hand timed

Mark	Name		Nat	Born	Pos	Meet	Venue	Date
55.0	Donalda	Duprey	CAN	1.3.67	1	AmCp	Manaus	15 May
56.7	Tatyana	Grigoryeva	RUS	11.3.72	1		Bryansk	7 Aug
57.3	Yelena	Goncharova	RUS	27.3.63	2		Bryansk	7 Aug
57.8A	Pam	Brooks	USA	15.1.72	1		Mexico	14 May
57.8	Glynis	Nunn-Cearns	AUS	4.12.60	1		Brisbane	15 Jul

Mark	Name		Nat	Born	Date
58.1	Natalya	Dorogina	UZB	70	16 Sep
58.3	Anabella	Von Kesselstat	ARG	69	24 Apr
58.4	Anna	Ambraziene	LIT	55	12 Jul

Best at low altitude

58.62 van der Merwe 23 Apr

Drugs disqualification

Mark	Name		Nat	Born	Pos	Meet	Venue	Date
54.74		Han Qing ¶	CHN	4.3.70	1	AsiG	Hiroshima	14 Oct

HIGH JUMP

Mark	Name		Nat	Born	Pos	Meet	Venue	Date
2.02i	Alina	Astafei	ROM	7.6.69	1		Berlin	4 Mar
2.01i		Astafei			1		Otterberg	19 Feb
2.00i	Yelena	Gulyayeva	RUS	14.8.67	1	Army	Moskva	27 Jan
2.00i	Britta	Bilac	SLO	4.12.68	1		Frankfurt am Main	9 Feb
2.00i	Stefka	Kostadinova	BUL	25.3.65	1	DNG	Stockholm	8 Mar
2.00	Silvia	Costa	CUB	4.5.64	1	NC	La Habana	24 Jun
2.00	Inga	Babakova	UKR	27.6.67	1	Kuts	Moskva	31 Jul
2.00		Bilac			1	EC	Helsinki	14 Aug
1.98i	Antonella	Bevilacqua	ITA	15.10.71	1		Pireas	28 Feb

Mark	Name		Nat	Born	Pos	Meet	Venue	Date
1.98i	Hanne	Haugland	NOR	14.12.67	2		Pireas	28 Feb
1.98i		Bilac			3		Pireas	28 Feb
1.98i	Angie	Bradburn	USA	4.9.68	1	NC	Atlanta	5 Mar
1.98i		Kostadinova			1	EI	Paris	12 Mar
1.98		Gulyayeva			1	Znam	Moskva	5 Jun
1.98	Yevgenia	Zhdanova	RUS	21.7.66	2	Znam	Moskva	5 Jun
1.98	Alison	Inverarity	AUS	12.8.70	1		Ingolstadt	17 Jul
1.97i		Astafei			1		Arnstadt	29 Jan
1.97i		Astafei			2		Frankfurt am Main	9 Feb
1.97i		Bevilacqua			1	NC	Genova	12 Feb
1.97i		Kostadinova			1	Balk	Pireas	20 Feb
1.97	Ioamnet	Quintero	CUB	18.9.72	2	NC	La Habana	24 Jun
1.97		Inverarity			1	TSB	Edinburgh	8 Jul
1.97	Yelena	Topchina	RUS	28.9.66	1	NC	St Peterburg	14 Jul
1.97		Haugland			1	Bisl	Oslo	22 Jul
1.97		Bilac			1	Herc	Monaco	2 Aug
1.97		Haugland			2	Herc	Monaco	2 Aug
1.97		Inverarity			1		Prince George	13 Aug
	(27/13)							
1.96i	Irina	Mikhalchenko	UKR	20.1.72	1		Banská Bystrica	26 Jan
1.96i	Tisha	Waller	USA	1.12.70	1		Fairfax	6 Feb
1.96i		Bilac			1		Grenoble	6 Feb
1.96i		Kostadinova			1		Maebashi	13 Feb
1.96i		Bilac			1		Pireas	16 Feb
1.96i		Kostadinova			2		Pireas	16 Feb
1.96i		Haugland			2		Berlin	4 Mar
1.96i	Desislava	Aleksandrova	BUL	27.10.75	2	EI	Paris	12 Mar
1.96i	Sigrid	Kirchmann	AUT	29.3.66	3	EI	Paris	12 Mar
1.96i	Tatyana	Shevchik	BLR	11.6.69	4	EI	Paris	12 Mar
1.96		Waller			1	MSR	Walnut	17 Apr
1.96		Kostadinova			1		Sofia	15 May
1.96	Tatyana	Motkova	RUS	26.10.68	1		Bryansk	28 May
1.96		Zhdanova			1		Sotteville	26 Jun
1.96	Nele	Zilinskiene	LIT	29.12.69	1	NC	Vilnius	2 Jul
	(20)							
1.96		Topchina			1		Lignano Sabbiadoto	7 Jul
1.96		Shevchik			1	NC	Gomel	10 Jul
1.96		Shevchik			2		Ingolstadt	17 Jul
1.96		Zhdanova			1		Halle	31 Jul
1.96		Gulyayeva			2	EC	Helsinki	14 Aug
1.96 performances: also 3 by Kostadinova, 2 Bilac, Zhdanova; 1 Haugland, Waller, Topchina, Gulyayeva								
1.95	Yelena	Yelesina	RUS	5.4.70	1		Moskva	4 Jul
1.95	Heike	Henkel	GER	5.5.64	2		Norderney	30 Jul
1.95	Heike	Balck	GER	19.8.70	3		Norderney	30 Jul
1.94i	Sabrina	De Leeuw	BEL	19.8.74	1	NC	Gent	6 Feb
1.94i	Marion	Hellmann	GER	6.4.67	3		Frankfurt	9 Feb
1.94i	Svetlana	Leseva	BUL	18.3.67	4		Pireas	16 Feb
1.94i	Olga	Bolshova	MOL	16.6.68	5		Pireas	28 Feb
1.94	Inna	Gliznutsa	MOL	18.4.73	1		Budapest	3 Jun
1.94	Zuzana	Kovácиková	TCH	16.4.73	1	ECp I	Valencia	12 Jun
1.94	Valentina	Gotovska	LAT	3.9.65	1		Nurmijärvi	2 Jul
	(30)							
1.94	Charmaine	Weavers	RSA	27.2.64	2	CG	Victoria	27 Aug
1.93	Yelena	Panikarovskikh	RUS	4.12.59	2		Dijon	12 Jun
1.93	Viktoria	Fyodorova	RUS	9.5.73	4	NC	St Peterburg	14 Jul
1.93i	Gwen	Wentland	USA	29.4.72	1P		Manhattan, Ks	9 Dec
1.92i	Svetlana	Bogomaz	UKR	16.7.74	1		Donetsk	1 Mar
1.92	Larisa	Serebryanskaya	UKR	15.9.63	1	v3N	Krakow	30 Jun
1.92	Donata	Wawrzyniak	POL	17.6.69	2	v3N	Krakow	30 Jun
1.92	Sandrine	Fricot	FRA	4.6.68	1	NC	Annecy	24 Jul
1.92	Sieglinde	Cadusch	SUI	28.8.67	1		Moutier	6 Aug
1.92	Svetlana	Munkova	UZB	23.6.65	1	AsiG	Hiroshima	14 Oct
	(40)							
1.91i	Yelena	Ivanova	RUS	23.1.71	2		Banská Bystrica	26 Jan
1.91i	Niki	Bakogianni	GRE	9.6.68	1	NC	Pireas	11 Feb
1.91	Andrea	Hughes	AUS	12.12.73	2		Perth	13 Feb
1.91	Desiré	du Plessis	RSA	20.5.65	1		Johannesburg	9 Mar
1.91	Viktoriya	Palamar	UKR	12.10.77	1		Odessa	23 Apr

Mark	Name		Nat	Born	Pos	Meet	Venue	Date
1.91	Iwona	Kielan	POL	5.7.66	1		Poznan	28 May
1.91	Eleonora	Milousheva	BUL	8.4.73	4	Slov	Bratislava	1 Jun
1.91	Maryse	Maury	FRA	4.9.64	3		Dijon	12 Jun
1.91	Monika	Iagar	ROM	1.4.73	2	ECp	Birmingham	26 Jun
1.91	Yuliya	Agapova	RUS	25.12.74	7	NC	St Peterburg	14 Jul
	(50)							
1.91	Debbie	Marti	GBR	14.5.68	3	CG	Victoria	27 Aug
1.91	Tania	Dixon	NZL	3.10.70	4	CG	Victoria	27 Aug
1.90i	Manuela	Aigner	GER	26.3.73	1B		Arnstadt	29 Jan
1.90i	Sabine	Braun	GER	19.6.65	4		Wuppertal	4 Feb
1.90	Tatyana	Khramova	BLR	1.2.70	1		Staiki	28 Apr
1.90	Galina	Isachenko	BLR	4.3.65	2		Gomel	15 May
1.90	Natalya	Popykina	RUS	11.12.70	1		Novosibirsk	28 May
1.90	Katarzyna	Majchrzak	POL	25.6.67	1	Kuso	Lublin	4 Jun
1.90	Yelena	Gribanova	RUS	2.3.72	1	NC-23	Voronezh	17 Jun
1.90	Birgit	Kähler	GER	14.8.70	1		Troisdorf	18 Jun
	(60)							
1.90	Irina	Matyusheva	UKR	5.6.65	H	ECp	Vénissieux	2 Jul
1.90	Lenka	Riháková	SVK	17.10.75	1	NC	Bratislava	2 Jul
1.90	Venelina	Veneva	BUL	13.6.74	1		Stara Zagora	16 Jul
1.90	Yulia	Lyakhova	RUS	77	1		Dzherzhinsk	5 Aug
1.90	Kajsa	Bergqvist	SWE	12.10.76	1	NC18	Luleå	7 Aug
1.90	Chinami	Sadahiro	JPN	17.8.72	1		Nagoya	2 Nov
1.89i	Svetlana	Zalevskaya	KZK	14.6.73	1		Moskva	4 Feb
1.89i	Sárká	Nováková	TCH	21.2.62	2		Wien	6 Feb
1.89i	Nicole	Hudson	USA	27.8.70	3=	NC	Atlanta	5 Mar
1.89i	Amy	Acuff	USA	14.7.75	1	NCAA	Indianapolis	12 Mar
	(70)							
1.89	Sue	Rembao	USA	15.5.62	1		Stanford	26 Mar
1.89	Yoko	Ota	JPN	14.1.75	1		Shizuoka	5 May
1.89	Clare	Look-Jaeger	USA	17.6.66	1		Los Angeles	21 May
1.89	Olga	Kaliturina	RUS	9.3.76	1		Krasnodar	28 May
1.89	Gai	Kapernick	AUS	20.9.70	1	NCAA	Boise	4 Jun
1.89	Julia	Bennett	GBR	26.3.70	1	AAA	Sheffield	11 Jun
1.89	Isabelle	Jeanne-Chevalier	FRA	31.5.67	6		Dijon	12 Jun
1.89	Laura	Sharpe	IRL	10.3.69	1		Dublin	3 Jul
1.89	Erzsébet	Fazekas	HUN	8.4.71	1	NC	Budapest	15 Jul
1.88i	Natalya	Golodnova	KZK	14.4.67	2		Moskva	14 Jan
	(80)							
1.88i	Barbara	Mencik	FRA	22.12.70	1		Gent	15 Jan
1.88i	Vasiliki	Xenou	GRE	5.5.74	1		Pireas	30 Jan
1.88i	Wiebke	Schwart	GER	13.12.73	1		Hannover	6 Feb
1.88i	Megumi	Sato	JPN	13.9.66	2		Osaka	11 Feb
1.88	Tracey	Phillips	NZL	8.1.68	2	AusC	Sydney	12 Mar
1.88	Irina	Vostrikova	RUS	30.8.70	H		Krasnodar	17 May
1.88	Melinda	Boice	USA	29.12.74	1		Fresno	21 May
1.88	Connie	Teaberry	USA	15.8.70	1		Atlanta	22 May
1.88	Kerstin	Schlawitz	GER	30.8.70	1B		Wörrstadt	28 May
1.88	Lucienne	N'Da-Bamba	CIV	6.7.65	1		Abidjan	5 Jun
	(90)							
1.88	Nathalie	Lefébvre	FRA	2.9.71	1		Aix-les-Bains	18 Jun
1.88	Yekaterina	Aleksandrova	RUS	3.6.77	1	NC-j	Yekaterinburg	24 Jun
1.88	Alica	Javad	SVK?	26.6.69	1		Gladbeck	25 Jun
1.88	Oana	Musunoi	ROM	17.9.72	1		Bucuresti	10 Jul
1.88	Tatyana	Ivanova	RUS	22.1.76	1		Krasnodar	19 Aug
1.88	Viktoriya	Seryogina	RUS	73	2		Rostov	26 Aug
1.88	Lea	Haggett	GBR	9.5.72	5=	CG	Victoria	27 Aug
1.88	Pia	Zinck	DEN	4.5.71	2		København	28 Aug
1.88		Zhang Liwen	CHN	29.1.73	1		Tangshan	30 Aug
	(99)							

Mark	Name		Nat	Born	Date
1.87i	Mila	Froberg	GER	64	18 Jan
1.87i	Emelie	Färdigh	SWE	77	29 Jan
1.87i	Andrea	Baumert	GER	67	4 Feb
1.87i	Yolanda	Henry	USA	64	6 Feb
1.87i	Maria	Lindholm	SWE	67	8 Mar
1.87i	Rita	Ináncsi	HUN	71	11 Mar
1.87i	J.C.	Broughton	USA	70	12 Mar
1.87i	Sherry	Gould	USA	67	12 Mar
1.87i	Corissa	Yasen	USA	73	12 Mar
1.87	Paula	Maree	RSA	69	13 May
1.87	Claudia	Ellinger	SUI	69	29 May
1.87	Kym	Carter	USA	64	14 Jun
1.87	Svetlana	Moskalets	RUS	69	2 Jul
1.87	Larisa	Teteryuk	UKR	70	2 Jul
1.87	Marie	Colonvillé	FRA	73	2 Jul
1.87	Tanya	Hughes	USA	72	9 Jul

Mark		Name	Nat	Born	Pos	Meet	Venue	Date
1.87	Natalie	Jonckheere	BEL	70				5 Aug
1.87	Miki	Imai	JPN	75				2 Nov
1.86i	Viktoriya	Styopina	UKR	76				5 Jan
1.86	Joanne	Jennings	GBR	69				22 Jan
1.86i	Larisa	Turchinskaya	RUS	65				4 Feb
1.86i	Helen	Sanzenbacher	GER	75				12 Feb
1.86	Judit	Hegyi	HUN	69				15 May
1.86	Hanne	Skei Andersen	NOR	70				4 Jun
1.86	Beata	Holub	POL	70				4 Jun
1.86i	Tatyana	Nikolayeva	UKR	76				30 Jan
1.86	Karol	Damon	USA	69				17 Jun
1.86	Beatrice	Landès	FRA	67				24 Jul
1.86	Roberta	Bugarini	ITA	69				30 Jul
1.86	Krisztina	Solti	HUN	68				31 Jul
1.86	Catherine	Bond-Mills	CAN	67				22 Aug
1.86		-??	CHN	72				25 Nov
1.85i	Urszula	Wlodarczyk	POL	65				27 Jan
1.85i	Larisa	Grigorenko	UKR	70				27 Jan
1.85	Jane	Millington	AUS	76				13 Feb
1.85i	Monika	Csapó	HUN	71				26 Feb
1.85	Svetlana	Lozova	KZK	66				21 May
1.85		Guan Weihua	CHN	75				2 Jun
1.85		Wang Wei	CHN	70				2 Jun
1.85	Dania	Fernández	CUB	78				24 Jun
1.85	Maria Mar	Martinez	ESP	69				26 Jun
1.85	Monika	Gollner	AUT	74				4 Jul
1.85	Julie	Major	GBR	70				8 Jul
1.85	Tatyana	Gulevich	BLR	71				10 Jul
1.85	Zhanna	Dyatlovskaya	BLR	73				10 Jul
1.85	Katell	Courgeon	FRA	72				11 Jul
1.85	Judit	Kovács	HUN	69				15 Jul
1.85	Leslie	Estwick	CAN	60				23 Aug
1.85	Sara	McGladdery	CAN	69				23 Aug
1.85	Corinna	Wolf	CAN	73				23 Aug
1.85	Ingela	Sandqvist	SWE	67				28 Aug
	(150)							
1.85	Luciane	Dambacher	BRA	76				9 Oct
1.90?		Guan Weihua	CHN	75			Beijing	28 Jul

Best outdoor

Mark	Name	Pos	Meet	Venue	Date
1.96	Waller	1	MSR	Walnut	17 Apr
1.96	Kostadinova	1		Sofia	15 May
1.96	Shevchik	2		Ingolstadt	17 Jul
1.95	Bradburn	1		Wörrstadt	28 May
1.95	Mikhalchenko	1		Kiev	23 Jul
1.94	Bolshova	3		Madrid	6 Sep
1.93	Kirchmann	3	Slov	Bratislava	1 Jun
1.93	Leseva	1		Caorle	16 Jul
1.92	Bevilacqua	1		Formia	4 Jun
1.91	Bogomaz	2	Kuts	Moskva	31 Jul
1.90	Hellmann			Duisburg	12 Jun
1.90	Bakogianni	1		Thessaloniki	30 Jul
1.89	Zalevskaya	1		Almaty	21 May
1.89	Acuff	2	NCAA	Boise	4 Jun
1.89	Wentland	3=		Lucerne	29 Jun
1.88	Y Ivanova	9	NC	St Peterburg	14 Jul
1.88	Aigner	5	ECp 23	Ostrava	31 Jul

Mark	Name	Date
1.87	Aleksandrova	26 May
1.87	Froberg	28 May
1.87	Braun	28 May
1.87	Ellinger	29 May
1.87	Färdigh	1 Jun
1.87	Nováková	16 Jun
1.87	Ináncsi	8 Aug
1.86	Nikolayeva	11 Jun
1.86	Henry	17 Jun
1.86	Xenou	25 Jun
1.86	Schwart	6 Aug
1.86	Styopina	24 Sep
1.85	Hudson	14 Apr
1.85	Sanzenbacher	23 Jul

POLE VAULT

Mark		Name	Nat	Born	Pos	Meet	Venue	Date
4.12		Sun Caiyun #	CHN	21.3.73	1		Guangzhou	22 Oct
4.12		Sun Caiyun			1		Guangzhou	24 Nov
4.08i	Nicole	Rieger	GER	5.2.72	1		Karlsruhe	1 Mar
4.02i		Rieger			1	NC	Dortmund	26 Feb
4.01i		Rieger			1		Landau	20 Feb
4.01	Marina	Andreyeva	RUS	73	1	NC-23	Voronezh	18 Jun
4.01		Cai Weiyan	CHN	25.10.73	1		Hefei	3 Aug
4.00i		Rieger			1		Clermont-Ferrand	28 Jan
4.00i	Andrea	Müller	GER	29.6.74	1		Sindelfingen	6 Mar
4.00i		Rieger			2		Sindelfingen	6 Mar
4.00		Rieger			1		Duisburg	12 Jun
4.00		Sun Caiyun			1	GWG	St Peterburg	24 Jul
4.00		Sun Caiyun			1		Tangshan	29 Aug
4.00		Cai Weiyan			2		Tangshan	29 Aug
3.96i	Gabriela	Mihalcea	ROM	27.1.64	1		Bucuresti	6 Feb
3.96		Rieger			1		Bad Bergzabern	2 Jun
3.96		Müller			1		Worms	5 Jun
3.95i		Rieger			1		Zweibrücken	29 Jan
3.95		Müller			2		Duisburg	12 Jun
3.95		Müller			1	NC	Erfurt	3 Jul
	(20/6)							
3.91	Caroline	Ammel	FRA	22.11.73	1		La Roche sur Yon	14 Jul
3.90i	Svetlana	Abramova	RUS	27.10.70	1	NC	Donyetsk	20 Feb
3.90	Carmen	Haage	GER	10.9.71	2		Worms	5 Jun
3.90	Christine	Adams	GER	28.2.74	2	NC	Erfurt	3 Jul
	(10)							
3.90	Daniela	Köpernick	GER	25.7.73	2		Ahlen	6 Aug
3.90	Tanja	Cors	GER	22.4.71	1		Lehrte	4 Sep
3.85	Janet	Zach	GER	19.6.75	3		Ahlen	6 Aug
3.80		Zhong Guiqing	CHN	75	1		Guangzhou	26 Mar
3.80	Natalya	Mekhanoshina	RUS	10.8.72	1		Moskva	11 Jun
3.75i	Daniela	Bártová	TCH	6.5.74	2		Praha	22 Feb

Mark	Wind	Name		Nat	Born	Pos	Meet	Venue	Date
3.71		Nastja	Ryshich	GER	19.9.77	1		Jablonec	16 Jul
3.70i		Marion	Meyer	GER	9.7.75	1	NC-j	Sindelfingen	12 Feb
3.70			Peng Xiaoyun	CHN		3		Guangzhou	26 Mar
3.70		Galina	Yenvarenko	RUS	70	2	NC	St Peterburg	14 Jul
		(20)							
3.65		Karin	Hecht	GER	27.10.77	2		Mannheim	3 Jun
3.65		Kate	Staples	GBR	2.11.65	1	AAA	Sheffield	11 Jun
3.63i		Sophie	Zubiolo	BEL	15.1.73	1		Oreye	20 Feb
3.60			Wu Weili	CHN	20.4.70	4	NC	Bejing	4 Jun
3.60		Gianina	Rusu	ROM	7.12.74	2	NC	Bucuresti	17 Jun

Mark	Name		Nat	Born	Date
3.55	Ariane	Knoll	GER	77	3 Jun
3.55	Maria Carla	Bresciani	ITA	73	25 Sep
3.51	Melissa	Price	USA	77	13 Jul
3.50i	Jana	Kábová	TCH	74	23 Jan
3.50		Yang Xie	CHN	71	4 Jun
3.50	Silke	Baumann	GER	76	5 Jun
3.50	Sabine	Schulte	GER	76	31 Jul
3.50	Pascale	Bourguignon	FRA	72	6 Jul
3.50	Sarelle	Verkade	NZL	76	12 Nov

Best outdoors

Mark	Name	Pos	Meet	Venue	Date
3.90	Abramova	2	GWG	St Peterburg	24 Jul
3.89	Mihalcea	1		Iasi	19 Jul
3.70	Bártová	4		Praha	16 Jun
3.60	Meyer	2	NC-j	Ulm	31 Jul
3.60	Zubiolo	1		Bruxelles	6 Aug

Drugs disqualification: 4.08i Sun Caiyun # 2 Karlsruhe 1 Mar

LONG JUMP

Mark	Wind	Name		Nat	Born	Pos	Meet	Venue	Date
7.49	1.3	Jackie	Joyner-Kersee	USA	3.3.62	1	NYG	New York	22 May
7.49A	1.7		Joyner-Kersee			1		Sestriere	31 Jul
7.30	0.7		Joyner-Kersee			1	Jen	San José	28 May
7.29	0.9	Heike	Drechsler	GER	16.12.64	2	Bisl	Oslo	22 Jul
7.26	1.4		Joyner-Kersee			*	Bisl	Oslo	22 Jul
7.25A	1.3		Drechsler			*		Sestriere	31 Jul
7.23	0.2		Drechsler			1	OD	Jena	3 Jun
7.21	0.7		Joyner-Kersee			1	GPF	Paris	3 Sep
7.20	0.7	Irina	Mushayilova	RUS	6.1.67	1	NC	St Peterburg	14 Jul
7.19i	-		Drechsler			1		Sindelfingen	6 Mar
7.15i	-		Drechsler			1		Maebashi	13 Feb
7.15	0.8		Drechsler			1		Ingolstadt	17 Jul
7.15	0.5		Drechsler			1	Herc	Monaco	2 Aug
7.14	0.7		Drechsler			1	EC	Helsinki	12 Aug
7.13i	-		Drechsler			1		Stuttgart	6 Feb
7.13i	-		Joyner-Kersee			1	NC	Atlanta	5 Mar
7.12	1.3		Drechsler			1	BNP	Villeneuve d'Ascq	8 Jul
7.12	1.0		Drechsler			1	GWG	St Peterburg	28 Jul
7.11			Drechsler			*	NC	Erfurt	2 Jul
7.11	0.0		Joyner-Kersee			1	VD	Bruxelles	19 Aug
7.10	-0.1		Joyner-Kersee			1	ASV	Köln	21 Aug
7.09	1.5	Ljudmila	Ninova	AUT	25.6.60	1	GP II	Sevilla	5 Jun
7.09	0.8	Inessa	Kravets	UKR	5.10.66	1	WK	Zürich	17 Aug
7.06i	-		Drechsler			1		Karlsruhe	1 Mar
7.06i	-		Drechsler			1	EI	Paris	11 Mar
7.05i	-		Drechsler			1	NC	Dortmund	25 Feb
7.04	1.2		Drechsler			*		Chemnitz	18 Jun
7.04	1.1		Drechsler			1	DNG	Stockholm	12 Jul
7.03	0.5	Yelena	Khlopotnova	UKR	4.8.63	1		Kharkov	30 May
7.01	0.3		Drechsler			1	GGala	Roma	8 Jun
7.01	0.4		Drechsler			2	WK	Zürich	17 Aug
7.01	0.1		Drechsler			2	VD	Bruxelles	19 Aug
7.00	1.1		Drechsler			2	ASV	Köln	21 Aug
7.00	0.6		Kravets			1	WCp	London	11 Sep
		(34/6)							
6.96	2.0	Renata	Nielsen	DEN	18.5.66	*	GP II	Sevilla	5 Jun
6.95A	1.5	Fiona	May	ITA	12.12.69	*		Sestriere	31 Jul
6.91	0.9		Yao Weili	CHN	6.5.68	1	AsiG	Hiroshima	15 Oct
6.89i	-	Larisa	Berezhnaya	UKR	28.2.61	2		Sindelfingen	6 Mar
		(10)							
6.89	1.4	Agata	Karczmarek	POL	29.11.63	1	ECp	Valencia	12 Jun
6.84	1.1	Vera	Olenchenko	RUS	21.3.59	1		Moskva	11 Jun
6.82i	-	Daphne	Saunders	BAH	18.12.71	1		Gainesville	26 Feb
6.82	1.6	Svetlana	Moskalets	RUS	1.11.69	2	GWG	St Peterburg	28 Jul
6.80	1.5	Larisa	Kuchinskaya	BLR	9.2.74	1		Minsk	6 May
6.80	0.0		Li Jing	CHN	21.10.69	1	NC	Beijing	5 Jun

Mark	Wind	Name		Nat	Born	Pos	Meet	Venue	Date
6.80A	1.7	Valentina	Uccheddu	ITA	26.10.66	*		Sestriere	31 Jul
6.79	-0.6	Yelena	Semiraz	UKR	21.11.65	1	NC	Kiev	26 May
6.78	1.4	Rita	Ináncsi	HUN	6.1.71	1H		Götzis	29 May
6.78	1.8	Lyudmila	Galkina	RUS	20.5.72	4	Bisl	Oslo	22 Jul
		(20)							
6.77	0.9	Iva	Prandzheva	BUL	15.2.72	*		Sofia	15 May
6.77			Zhang Yinlan	CHN	14.2.70	Q	NC	Beijing	4 Jun
6.77	0.2	Yelena	Sinchukova	RUS	23.1.61	2		Moskva	11 Jun
6.76		Olga	Rublyova	RUS	28.10.74	1	NC-23	Voronezh	17 Jun
6.75	1.8	Marion	Jones	USA	12.10.75	2	NCAA	Boise	1 Jun
6.74	1.3	Niki	Xanthou	GRE	11.10.73	1	NC23	Ioannina	17 Jul
6.73	1.6	Olyinka	Idowu	GBR	25.2.72	2	CG	Victoria	27 Aug
6.71i	-	Dedra	Davis	BAH	17.7.73	2	NCAA	Indianapolis	11 Mar
6.71	1.3	Niurka	Montalvo	CUB	4.6.68	*		Sevilla	5 Jun
6.69i	-	Mirela	Dulgheru	ROM	5.10.66	1		Bucuresti	6 Feb
		(30)							
6.69i	-	Ana	Biryukova	RUS	27.9.67	1	DNG	Stockholm	8 Mar
6.68	0.7	Viktoria	Vershinina	UKR	11.6.71	2	NC	Kiev	27 May
6.67		Olga	Vasilyeva	KZK	25.2.71	1		Tashkent	7 Jun
6.67	1.9	Sabine	Braun	GER	19.1.65	2	NC	Erfurt	2 Jul
6.67A	1.4	Nicole	Boegman	AUS	5.3.67	*		Sestriere	31 Jul
6.67		Galina	Chistyakova	RUS	26.7.62	1		Bratislava	25 Aug
6.66		Sheila	Echols	USA	2.10.64	1		Baton Rouge	23 Apr
6.66	1.7	Christy	Opara-Thompson	NGR	2.5.70	3	WCp	London	11 Sep
6.65i	-	Susen	Tiedtke-Greene	GER	23.1.69	2	DNG	Stockholm	8 Mar
6.65	2.0	Tatyana	Lebedyeva	RUS	21.7.76	1	NC-j	Yekaterinburg	24 Jun
		(40)							
6.63		Dionne	Rose	JAM	7.11.69	4	NCAA	Boise	1 Jun
6.63	2.0	Virge	Naeris	EST	12.12.69	*		Pärnu	30 Jun
6.63	1.9	Chantal	Brunner	NZL	5.11.70	6	CG	Victoria	27 Aug
6.62		Diane	Guthrie	JAM	24.10.71	1		Fairfax	21 May
6.62	1.7	Vonetta	Jeffrey	USA	29.10.73	1	USOF	Edwardsville	10 Jul
6.61	1.6	Yolanda	Chen	RUS	26.7.61	4	GP II	Sevilla	5 Jun
6.61	0.9	Yelena	Volf	RUS	2.3.69	H	NC	Vladimir	17 Jun
6.60i	-	Marieta	Ilcu	ROM	16.10.62	1		Budapest	23 Jan
6.60i	-	Yelena	Rupasova	RUS	68	1		Perm	23 Jan
6.60	0.4	Iolanta	Khropach	UKR	22.9.74	2		Kharkov	13 May
		(50)							
6.60	2.0	Helga	Radtke	GER	16.5.62	3	NC	Erfurt	2 Jul
6.60	-0.4	Nina	Perevedentseva	RUS	64	6	NC	St Peterburg	14 Jul
6.59i	-	Larisa	Turchinskaya	RUS	29.4.65	P	NC	Lipetsk	5 Feb
6.59	0.8	Natalya	Popykina	RUS	11.12.70	H	NC	Vladimir	17 Jun
6.58		Yulia	Shirokova	RUS	1.10.74	1		Moskva	20 May
6.58	-1.1		Feng Jie	CHN		2		Tangshan	30 Aug
6.58	1.9	Andrea	Avila	ARG	4.4.70	1	IbAm	Mar del Plata	29 Oct
6.57i	-	Vera	Maloletneva	RUS	6.1.66	1		Ryazan	23 Jan
6.57i	-	Yana	Kuznetsova	RUS	72	2		Perm	23 Jan
6.56	1.7	Denise	Lewis	GBR	27.8.72	2	AAA	Sheffield	12 Jun
		(60)							
6.55	0.5	Kirsten	Bolm	GER	4.3.75	1		Mannheim	4 Jun
6.55	0.9	Paraskevi	Patoulidou	GRE	29.3.65	2		Khania	5 Jun
6.55	0.8	Claudia	Gerhardt	GER	18.1.66	3	NC	Duisburg	12 Jun
6.55	1.1	Tatyana	Zhuravlyova	RUS	19.12.67	H		Vladimir	17 Jun
6.54	1.8	Sharon	Couch	USA	13.9.69	1		Modesto	14 May
6.54	-0.7	Tatyana	Ter-Mesrobian	RUS	12.5.68	1		St Peterburg	28 Jun
6.53	0.6	Terri	Hairston	USA	19.7.63	2	MSR	Walnut	17 Apr
6.53	0.8	Tatyana	Dyatlova	BLR	12.1.75	2		Minsk	6 May
6.53		Monica	Toth	ROM	7.3.70	3		Khania	5 Jun
6.52	0.9	Olga	Roslyakova	BLR	14.6.67	2		Gomel	14 May
		(70)							
6.52	1.7		Peng Fengmei	CHN	2.7.79	2	NC	Beijing	5 Jun
6.52	0.4	Antonella	Capriotti	ITA	4.2.62	2		Formia	5 Jun
6.52			Zhang Yan	CHN	.6.72	Q	NC	Beijing	4 Jun
6.52		Silvija	Babic	CRO	12.12.68	1		Zagreb	7 Jun
6.52	1.2	Irina	Tyukhay	RUS	14.1.67	H	NC	Vladimir	17 Jun
6.52	0.9	Irina	Vostrikova	RUS	30.8.70	H	NC	Vladimir	17 Jun
6.52	1.2	Sheila	Hudson-Strudwick	USA	30.6.67	5	NC	Knoxville	18 Jun
6.52	1.2	Anastasia	Mahob	FRA	28.7.72	*		Lillehammer	31 Jul
6.51i	-	Nadezhda	Novikova	RUS	66	P	NC	Lipetsk	4 Feb

Mark	Wind	Name		Nat	Born	Pos	Meet	Venue	Date
6.51	0.8	Rita	Schönenberger	SUI	3.12.62	1		Genève	18 Jun
		(80)							
6.51	0.5	Nadine	Caster	FRA	15.10.65	2		Sotteville	26 Jun
6.51		Lyudmila	Mikhailova	RUS	12.4.69	1		Noisy-le-Grand	2 Jul
6.50		Flora	Hyacinth	ISV	30.3.66	1		Tuscaloosa	27 Mar
6.50	0.3		Yang Fang	CHN	15.10.71	3	NC	Beijing	5 Jun
6.50	1.8	Cynthea	Rhodes	USA	30.9.67	*	NC	Knoxville	18 Jun
6.50	1.6	Sharon	Jaklofsky	NED	30.9.68	H	ECpl	Bressanone	3 Jul
6.49i		Lucena	Golding	JAM	24.3.75	1	JUCO	Manhattan	4 Mar
6.48i		Liliana	Nastase	ROM	1.8.62	P	NC	Bucuresti	5 Feb
6.48		Jacqui	Brown	USA	12.8.72	1		Indianapolis	14 May
6.48	1.1	Yelena	Selina	KZK	11.7.64	1		Temirtau	12 Aug
		(90)							
6.47		Najuma	Fletcher	GUY	31.5.74	1		Durham	9 Apr
6.47	1.6	Ringa	Ropo	FIN	16.2.66	3		Leppavirta	7 Jun
6.47	1.0	Muriel	Leroy	FRA	7.7.68	2	NC	Annecy	23 Jul
6.46	1.9	Joanne	Henry	NZL	2.10.71	*	NC	Hamilton	5 Mar
6.46	0.0	Svetlana	Buraga	BLR	4.9.65	H		Brescia	15 May
6.46	1.8	Dawn	Burrell	USA	1.11.73	2	USOF	Edwardsville	10 Jul
6.45i		Corinne	Hérigault	FRA	8.10.70	1	NC	Bordeaux	26 Feb
6.45		Oluchi	Elechi	NGR	24.6.68	1	NCAA II	Raleigh	27 May
6.45	0.7	Yelena	Lysak ¶	RUS	19.10.75	*	WJ	Lisboa	23 Jul
6.45	1.6	Natalya	Sorokina	UKR	24.3.75	1	vFRA-j	Dôle	6 Aug
6.45	-0.6		Xu Pin	CHN	.10.70	3		Tangshang	30 Aug
		(101)							

Mark	Wind	Name		Nat	Born	Date
6.44i		Lyubov	Borisova	RUS	66	4 Feb
6.44		Carolyn	Sterling	JAM	70	9 Apr
6.44		Natalya	Kuzina	RUS	70	24 Jul
6.44	0.8	Zhanna	Budilovskaya	UKR	72	24 Jul
6.43	1.8	Eleni	Karambesini	GRE	72	22 May
6.43	1.9	Tünde	Vaszi	HUN	72	28 May
6.43		Natalya	Kayukova	RUS	66	28 May
6.43	0.4	Marina	Slushkina	RUS	60	14 Jul
6.42			Li Hua	CHN		4 Jun
6.42	1.0	Heli	Koivula	FIN	75	27 Aug
6.41A	1.8	Karen	Botha	RSA	67	7 May
6.41	1.1	Beatrice	Mau-Repnak	GER	71	29 May
6.41	1.4		Xiong Yan	CHN		5 Jun
6.41		Sandrine	Hennart	BEL	72	15 Aug
6.41	2.0	Jackie	Edwards	BAH	71	27 Aug
6.41	-0.6	Elma	Muros-Posadas	PHI	67	15 Oct
6.40		Anzhela	Atroshchenko	BLR	70	28 May
		6.42 ??				28 Apr
6.40	0.8	Urszula	Wlodarczyk	POL	65	3 Jul
6.40		Trecia-Kaye	Smith	JAM	75	10 Jul
6.40		Cristina	Nicolau	ROM	77	6 Aug
6.40	-1.7	Dorota	Brodowska	POL	72	10 Sep
6.39i		Yurka	Khristova	BUL	68	12 Feb
6.39		Joanna	Koscielny	POL	74	15 May
6.39	1.6	Angee	Henry	USA	25	24 Jun
6.39	0.6	Ingvild	Larsen	NOR	75	31 Jul
6.38i		Veronika	Ryzhova	RUS	68	4 Feb
6.38	1.4	Vickie	Hudson	USA	73	29 Apr
6.38			Ding Ying	CHN	76	30 Apr
6.38	1.9	Zhasmina	Nikolova	BUL	77	15 May
6.38	2.0	Anna	Mironova	RUS	75	24 Jun
6.38	1.0	Ulrike	Holzner	GER	68	17 Jul
6.38		Luciana	dos Santos	BRA	70	13 Aug
6.37		Regina	Frye	USA	72	14 May
6.37	0.6	Cynthia	Tylor	USA	71	14 May
6.37		Ksenija	Predikaka	SLO	70	21 May
6.36		Yelena	Stakhova	BLR	69	17 Jun
6.36		Yolanda	Rodriguez	ESP	74	23 Jul
6.36	0.9	Sarah	Gautreau	FRA	77	6 Aug
6.36		Yelena	Lebedyenko	RUS		9 Sep
6.35i	-	Tonya	McKelvey	USA	71	12 Feb
6.35i	-	Vladka	Lopatic	SLO	68	12 Feb
6.35		Yelena	Pershina	KZK	63	9 Sep
6.34		Jane	Flemming	AUS	65	29 Apr
6.33i	-	Tamara	Cuffee	USA	71	15 Jan
6.33i	-	Marieke	Veltman	USA	71	5 Mar
6.33	-0.7	Miladys	Portuondo	CUB	72	26 May
6.33		Vera	Stenhouse	USA	69	28 May
6.33	0.9	Nicole	Devonish	CAN	73	2 Jun
6.33	-0.3	Elisa	Andretti	ITA	70	5 Jun
		(150)				
6.33		Daniela	Kirsch	GER	68	5 Jun
6.33	-0.4	Marika	Demestiha	GRE	76	26 Jun
6.33	1.0	Michaela	Frank	GER	69	2 Jul

Best outdoors

Mark	Wind	Name	Pos	Meet	Venue	Date
6.69		Davis	*	SEC	Fayetteville	14 May
6.66		Berezhnaya	7	BNP	Vill. d'Ascq	8 Jul
6.64	-0.8	Biryukova	6	WK	Zurich	17 Aug
6.62	1.8	Dulgheru	1		Hiroshima	29 Apr
6.54		Tiedtke-Greene	*	MSR	Walnut	17 Apr
6.50	1.2	Novikova	H	NC	Vladimir	17 Jun
6.49	1.6	Turchinskaya	2H	GWG	S.Peterburg	26 Jul
6.47		Golding	1	NC	Kingston	1 Jul
6.46		Saunders	6	NCAA	Boise	1 Jun

Mark	Wind	Name	Date
6.42		Ilcu	17 Jun
6.40	1.5	Kuznetsova	26 Aug
6.38		Ryzhova	9 Sep
6.37	0.6	Hérigault	5 Jun

Best at low altitude

Mark	Wind	Name	Pos	Meet	Venue	Date
6.90	-0.7	May	3	EC	Helsinki	12 Aug
6.67		Boegman	3	Herc	Monaco	2 Aug
6.69i	-	Uccheddu	4	EI	Paris	11 Mar
		6.62 0.2	2		Oristano	20 Sep

Wind-assisted

Mark	Wind	Name		Nat	Born	Pos	Meet	Venue	Date
7.39A	3.3	Heike	Drechsler	GER	16.12.64	2		Sestriere	31 Jul
7.33	3.3		Joyner-Kersee			1	Bisl	Oslo	22 Jul
7.20	2.3		Drechsler			1		Chemnitz	18 Jun
7.14	2.3		Joyner-Kersee			1	NC	Knoxville	18 Jun
7.13	2.3		Drechsler			1	NC	Erfurt	2 Jul
7.09	2.9	Renata	Nielsen	DEN	18.5.66	2		Sevilla	5 Jun
7.00A	2.1	Fiona	May	ITA	12.12.69	3		Sestriere	31 Jul
6.96A	3.0	Valentina	Uccheddu	ITA	26.10.66	4		Sestriere	31 Jul

Mark	Wind	Name		Nat	Born	Pos	Meet	Venue	Date
6.95	3.0	Iva	Prandzheva	BUL	15.2.72	1		Sofia	15 May
6.90	2.2	Viktoria	Vershinina	UKR	11.6.71	2		Duisburg	12 Jun
6.85	2.3	Dedra	Davis	BAH	17.7.73	1	NCAA	Boise	1 Jun
6.82A	2.2	Nicole	Boegman	AUS	5.3.67	5		Sestriere	31 Jul
6.81	2.6	Susen	Tiedtke-Greene	GER	23.1.69	1	MSR	Walnut	17 Apr
6.78	2.3	Niurka	Montalvo	CUB	4.6.68	3	GP II	Sevilla	5 Jun
6.75		Diane	Guthrie	JAM	24.10.71	3	NCAA	Boise	1 Jun
6.72	2.9	Helga	Radtke	GER	16.5.62	2		Chemnitz	18 Jun
6.72	4.5	Yelena	Lysak ¶	RUS	19.10.75	1	WJ	Lisboa	23 Jul
6.72	2.5	Christy	Opara-Thompson	NGR	2.5.70	3	CG	Victoria	27 Aug
6.70		Terri	Hairston	USA	19.7.63	1		Houston	19 Mar
6.70		Marsha	Henry	USA	22.12.71	1		Jamaica	14 May
6.68	3.3	Cynthea	Rhodes	USA	30.9.68	1	v GBR	Gateshead	20 Jul
6.68	2.4	Jackie	Edwards	BAH	14.4.71	4	CG	Victoria	27 Aug
6.66		Kwani	Stewart	USA	9.10.72	1	Big8	Lawrence	21 May
6.66	2.9	Virge	Naeris	EST	12.12.69	1		Pärnu	30 Jun
6.65	3.8	Joanne	Henry	NZL	2.10.71	5	CG	Victoria	27 Aug
6.64	3.2	Heli	Koivula	FIN	27.6.75	2	WJ	Lisboa	23 Jul
6.64	2.3	Anastasia	Mahob	FRA	28.7.72	1		Lillehammer	31 Jul
6.63	4.2	Ringa	Ropo	FIN	16.2.66	4	ECp I	Valencia	12 Jun
6.60	2.5	Sharon	Jaklofsky	NED	30.9.68	1	NC	Assen	17 Jul
6.59	2.4	Flora	Hyacinth	ISV	30.3.66	4	Jen	San José	28 May
6.58	2.3	Nadine	Caster	FRA	15.10.65	1	FranG	Bondoufle	12 Jul
6.57	3.4	Claudia	Gerhardt	GER	18.1.66	3		Waldshut-Tiengen	14 May
6.57	3.7	Sharon	Couch	USA	13.9.69	2	v GBR	Gateshead	20 Jul
6.55	2.8	Dawn	Burrell	USA	1.11.73	1		Houston	7 May
6.54		Chandra	Sturrup	BAH	12.9.71	1		Raleigh	25 Mar
6.53	4.7	Cynthia	Tylor	USA	10.1.71	5	NCAA	Boise	2 Jun
6.53		Shana	Williams	USA	7.4.72	1		Albany	16 Jul
6.52		Regina	Frye	USA	18.8.72	1		Indianapolis	2 Apr
6.52		Kim	Roland	USA	3.4.72	2		Lawrence	20 May
6.49		Lacena	Golding	JAM	24.3.75	1		Lafayette	26 Mar
6.48		Diana	Leftridge	USA		1		Ames	23 Apr
6.48		Sonya	Shepherd	USA	13.8.73	1		Houston	7 May
6.48	4.1	Catherine	Bond-Mills	CAN	20.9.67	H		Götzis	29 May
6.48	3.0	Anna	Mironova	RUS	15.10.75	2	NC-j	Yekaterinburg	24 Jun
6.47	2.3	Vickie	Hudson	USA	17.10.73	2	SEC	Fayetteville	15 May
6.47		Isabel	Pereira	POR	20.2.73	1		Maia	25 Jun
6.46		Nicole	Devonish	CAN	24.8.73	1		Waco	25 May
6.46	3.4	Tünde	Vaszi	HUN	18.4.72	2	NC	Debrecen	10 Jul
6.45	3.1	Ingvild	Larsen	NOR	3.10.75	1	NC-j	Drammen	9 Jul

Mark	Wind	Name		Nat	Born	Date
6.44		Da Jie		CHN	77	30 Apr
6.43	4.4	Irina	Melnikova I	RUS	74	26 May
6.43		Linda	Ferga	FRA	76	May
6.41	5.1	Irina	Matyusheva	UKR	65	5 Jun
6.41	3.9	Urszula	Wlodarczyk	POL	65	9 Aug
6.34	2.1	Peggy	Beer	GER	69	19 Jun
6.40	2.1	Maho	Hanaoka	JPN	76	18 Jun
6.39	3.5	Magdalena	Khristova	BUL	77	23 Jul
6.39	3.2	Erica	Johansson	SWE	74	30 Jul
6.38	3.3	Miladys	Portuondo	CUB	72	25 Jun
6.38		Ann	Brooks	GBR	71	7 Aug

TRIPLE JUMP

Mark	Wind	Name		Nat	Born	Pos	Meet	Venue	Date
14.98	1.8	Sofia	Bozhanova ¶	BUL	4.10.67	1		Stara Zagora	16 Jul
14.94	0.2	Inna	Lasovskaya	RUS	17.12.69	1	Slov	Bratislava	1 Jun
14.91	1.4	Inessa	Kravets	UKR	5.10.66	2	Slov	Bratislava	1 Jun
14.90i			Lasovskaya			1		Liévin	13 Feb
14.89	1.1	Anna	Biryukova	RUS	27.9.67	1	EC	Helsinki	8 Aug
14.88i			Lasovskaya			1	EI	Paris	13 Mar
14.81	0.4		Lasovskaya			1	GP II	Linz	4 Jul
14.78i			Lasovskaya			1		Moskva	27 Jan
14.74	0.6		Lasovskaya			1	NC	St Peterburg	16 Jul
14.72i	-		Biryukova			2	EI	Paris	13 Mar
14.71	1.0		Bozhanova			1	ECp II	Istanbul	11 Jun
14.70	0.8		Kravets			1		Luzern	29 Jun
14.70	1.5		Biryukova			1		Sheffield	4 Sep
14.67i	-		Lasovskaya			1		Grenoble	6 Feb
14.66	0.1		Biryukova			1	TOTO	Tokyo	15 Sep
14.65i	-		Lasovskaya			1		Madrid	11 Feb
14.63	0.2		Lasovskaya			1	Banes	São Paulo	21 May
14.62	0.2		Biryukova			3	Slov	Bratislava	1 Jun

Mark	Wind	Name		Nat	Born	Pos	Meet	Venue	Date
14.62	0.1		Kravets			2	TOTO	Tokyo	15 Sep
14.61i	-		Lasovskaya			1		Moskva	14 Jan
14.61	1.4		Kravets			1		Padova	10 Jul
14.60	0.7	Niurka	Montalvo	CUB	4.6.68	1	NC	La Habana	24 Jun
14.58	1.2	Yolanda	Chen	RUS	26.7.61	2	DNG	Stockholm	12 Jul
14.58	1.3		Chen			2	NC	St Peterburg	16 Jul
14.58	0.0		Kravets			1	Nik	Nice	18 Jul
14.57	0.6		Lasovskaya			2		Luzern	29 Jun
14.57	1.3		Biryukova			1	GWG	St Peterburg	24 Jul
14.53	1.8		Kravets			*	DNG	Stockholm	12 Jul
14.52i	-		Bozhanova			3	EI	Paris	13 Mar
14.51i	-		Biryukova			2		Grenoble	6 Feb
		(30/6)							
14.47	0.?	Rodica	Petrescu	ROM	13.3.71	1	NC	Bucuresti	18 Jun
14.47		Natalya	Kayukova	RUS	12.12.66	1		Sochi	10 Sep
14.46i	-	Sárka	Kasparková	TCH	20.5.71	4	EI	Paris	13 Mar
14.46	1.0	Helga	Radtke	GER	16.5.62	1	NC	Erfurt	3 Jul
		(10)							
14.38i	-	Iva	Prandzheva	BUL	15.2.72	5	EI	Paris	13 Mar
14.36	0.0		Ren Ruiping	CHN	1.2.76	1	NC	Beijing	1 Jun
14.32	-0.1	Yelena	Lysak ¶	RUS	19.10.75	1	NC-23	Voronezh	18 Jun
14.31	1.6	Lyudmila	Dubkova	RUS	27.2.68	3	NC	St Peterburg	16 Jul
14.30	1.8	Concepcion	Paredes	ESP	19.7.70	1		Segovia	28 Jun
14.23	1.0	Sheila	Hudson-Strudwick	USA	30.6.67	1	NC	Knoxville	16 Jun
14.22	0.2	Eloina	Echevarria	CUB	23.8.61	2	NC	La Habana	24 Jun
14.22	0.4	Yelena	Govorova	UKR	18.9.73	1	ECp 23	Lillehammer	30 Jul
14.22		Ashia	Hansen	GBR	5.12.71	1		Welwyn	29 Aug
14.21i	-	Galina	Chistyakova	RUS	26.7.62	4		Grenoble	6 Feb
		(20)							
14.16	1.4	Maria	Sokova	RUS	2.9.70	4	NC	St Peterburg	16 Jul
14.10	0.8	Petra	Laux-Schneider	GER	24.1.67	2	NC	Erfurt	3 Jul
14.10	0.5	Natalya	Kuzina	RUS	19.7.70	5	NC	St Peterburg	16 Jul
14.08	0.7	Michelle	Griffith	GBR	6.10.71	1	AAA	Sheffield	11 Jun
14.06	0.2		Liu Jingming	CHN	1.2.72	2	NC	Beijing	1 Jun
14.03i	-	Tanja	Bormann	GER	11.4.70	2	NC	Dortmund	26 Feb
14.03	0.9	Diana	Orrange	USA	9.8.67	2	NC	Knoxville	16 Jun
14.01		Ionela	Gogoase	ROM	4.2.71	1		Bucuresti	29 Jul
14.00	-0.6	Laiza	Carillo	CUB	27.11.68	3	NC	La Habana	24 Jun
13.98	1.2		Li Jing	CHN	21.10.69	3	NC	Beijing	1 Jun
		(30)							
13.96	0.9	Ramona	Molzan	GER	1.8.71	Q	EC	Helsinki	7 Aug
13.95	1.8	Olga	Cepero	CUB	4.2.75	1		La Habana	11 Feb
13.94	0.0	Cynthea	Rhodes	USA	30.9.68	2	PennR	Philadelphia	30 Apr
13.94	1.0	Irina	Mushayilova	RUS	6.1.67	*	DNG	Stockholm	12 Jul
13.94	-0.5		Zhang Yan	CHN	.6.72	1		Tangshan	27 Aug
13.92	0.7	Yamile	Aldama	CUB	14.8.72	4	NC	La Habana	24 Jun
13.92	1.6	Betty	Lise	FRA	5.9.72	1	NC	Annecy	22 Jul
13.89	-0.1	Tatyana	Matyashova	RUS	2.8.73	2	NC-23	Voronezh	18 Jun
13.88	-0.5	Nkechi	Madubuko	GER	28.3.72	2		Düsseldorf	21 May
13.86	1.7	Monica	Toth	ROM	7.3.70	2		Budapest	3 Jun
		(40)							
13.86	?	Yelena	Stakhova	BLR	4.1.69	1		Minsk	21 Jul
		13.74				3	ROMCh	Bucuresti	18 Jun
13.85	1.8	Valérie	Guiyoule	FRA	3.8.72	4		Reims	8 Jun
13.84	1.5	Viktoria	Vershinina	UKR	11.6.71	5	Slov	Bratislava	1 Jun
13.84	0.8	Barbara	Lah	ITA	24.3.72	1		Pescara	19 Jun
13.83	-0.6	Virge	Naeris	EST	12.12.69	1		Tallinn	29 Jul
13.82	1.1	Sandrine	Domain	FRA	6.9.71	2		Sotteville	26 Jun
13.82	0.6	Yelena	Khlusovich	UKR	31.5.72	2		Kiev	24 Jul
13.80	-1.6	Irina	Babakova	UKR	5.11.65	1	Mal	Grudziadz	1 Jun
13.79	1.1	Elena	Dumitrascu	ROM	14.5.74	2	ECp23	Ostrava	30 Jul
13.78	1.5	Irina	Myelnikova II	RUS	14.5.75	1		Krasnodar	29 May
		(50)							
13.77	1.6	Nadia	Morandini	ITA	12.12.73	3	ECp23	Ostrava	30 Jul
13.75	0.0		Zhang Jing	CHN	.3.70	5	NC	Beijing	1 Jun
13.74	1.6	Natalya	Klimovets	BLR	22.5.74	1	v3N	Krakow	30 Jun
13.71	1.7	Nicola	Martial	GUY	74	1	NCAA	Boise	3 Jun
13.70	2.0	Isabel	Aldecoa	CUB	21.6.71	3		La Habana	12 Feb

Mark	Wind	Name		Nat	Born	Pos	Meet	Venue	Date
13.69	-0.1	Tatyana	Lebedyeva	RUS	21.7.76	3	NC-23	Voronezh	18 Jun
13.69	-1.0	Tatyana	Fyodorova	RUS	67	6	NC	St Peterburg	16 Jul
13.69		Andrea	Avila	ARG	4.4.70	1		Córdoba	2 Oct
13.68	0.1	Irina	Melnikova I	RUS	19.1.74	4	NC-23	Voronezh	18 Jun
13.68	1.1	Carla	Shannon	USA	13.2.68	3	NC	Knoxville	16 Jun
		(60)							
13.67	1.4	Roshanda	Glenn	USA	13.11.71	4	NC	Knoxville	16 Jun
13.67	0.4	Angela	Barylla	GER	6.1.71	4	NC	Erfurt	3 Jul
13.66i	-	Agnieszka	Stanczyk ¶	POL	20.1.71	1		Spala	27 Feb
13.66	1.0		Zhao Tianhui	CHN	.2.73	7	NC	Beijing	1 Jun
13.64	1.1	Rachel	Kirby	GBR	18.5.69	Q	EC	Helsinki	7 Aug
13.61	1.5	Marika	Salminen	FIN	10.5.71	1	NC	Tuusula	10 Jul
13.60	1.5	Madelin	Martinez	CUB	10.2.76	4		La Habana	11 Feb
13.56	1.7	Hanne	Haugland	NOR	14.12.67	1	NC	Jessheim	21 Aug
13.54i	-	Daphne	Saunders	BAH	18.12.71	1		Baton Rouge	29 Jan
13.54	-0.5	Caroline	Honoré	FRA	29.4.70	3	NC	Annecy	22 Jul
		(70)							
13.54	1.6	Carina	Kjellman	FIN	3.9.63	1	v SWE	Stockholm	28 Aug
13.53	0.4	Telisa	Young	USA	17.1.71	2	NCAA	Boise	3 Jun
13.52	-0.5	Ksenija	Predikaka	SLO	11.3.70	3	ECCp	Schwechat	29 May
13.52	0.0		Zhou Xiuluan	CHN	.11.70	8	NC	Beijing	1 Jun
13.51	1.0	Olga	Ukolova	RUS	72	2		Stavropol	29 May
13.51	-1.0	Marina	Goryacheva	RUS	74	5	NC-23	Voronezh	18 Jun
13.51			Chen Hioqiang	CHN		1		Singapore	4 Sep
13.50	0.0		Wang Xiangrong	CHN	.2.76	9	NC	Beijing	1 Jun
13.50		Kathrin	Feuerbach	GER	8.3.66	1		Hamburg	27 Jul
13.48	0.9	Antonella	Capriotti	ITA	4.2.62	2		Formia	4 Jun
		(80)							
13.46		Suzette	Lee	JAM	6.3.75	1	JUCO	Odessa, Tx	20 May
13.45i	-	Natalya	Telepnyeva	RUS	27.5.66	3		Moskva	12 Feb
13.43i	-	Chukwuete	Olomina	SWE	28.4.78	1	v FIN	Växjö	6 Mar
13.40i	-	Olga	Skrebneyva	BLR	7.11.74	2	NC	Minsk	5 Feb
13.40	0.5	Jelena	Blazhevica	LAT	11.5.70	4		Tallinn	29 Jul
13.40	1.0	Maria	de Sousa	BRA	5.9.71	1	NC	Rio de Janeio	18 Sep
13.39	0.7	Magalys	Pedroso	CUB	3.6.72	2		La Habana	4 Feb
13.39	1.0	Yelena	Panferova	KZK	26.1.74	1		Almaty	22 May
13.35i	-	Urszula	Wlodarczyk	POL	22.12.65	Q	EI	Paris	12 Mar
13.35	0.7	Kathleem	Gutjahr	GER	27.7.75	1	NC-j	Ulm	31 Jul
		(90)							
13.34	0.5	Yulia	Baranova	UKR	12.8.72	8	Slov	Bratislava	1 Jun
13.34	-0.3	Anja	Vokuhl	GER	17.8.73	7		Duisburg	12 Jun
13.33	1.0		Luo Jun	CHN	75	1	AsiC-j	Jakarta	20 Sep
13.32	0.3	Olga	Rublyova	RUS	28.10.74	8	ECp	Birmingham	25 Jun
13.31	1.5	Connie	Henry	GBR	15.4.72	1		Kings Lynn	9 Jul
13.30i	-	Coamina	Boaje	ROM	20.7.77	1	NC-j	Bucuresti	11 Feb
13.30	1.9	Elizabeth	Machado	CUB	2.1.78	6		La Habana	11 Feb
13.29	1.2	Renata	Nielsen	DEN	18.5.66	1	ECp II	Dublin	11 Jun
13.28	-2.5	Christine	Gray	USA	17.8.71	1		Houston	19 Mar
13.28	1.0	Yulia	Lomakina	RUS	76	3	NC-j	Yekaterinburg	26 Jun
		(100)							
13.28	1.3	Natascha	Schmidt	GER	27.6.65	2		Hamburg	27 Jul

Mark	Wind	Name		Nat	Born	Date
13.27	0.7	Loredana	Rossi	ITA	67	4 Jun
13.27	0.7	Robyne	Johnson	USA	63	16 Jun
13.27		Olga	Boyko	UKR	75	10 Jul
13.26		Hasna	Atiallah	MAR		28 May
13.25i	-	Olga	Vasdeki	GRE	73	13 Feb
13.25i	-	Mariya	Kozlovskaya	RUS	78	26 Feb
13.25	2.0	Rene	Woodward	USA	71	3 Jun
13.25	0.9	Lene	Espegren	NOR	71	21 Aug
13.25	-0.2		Guo ??	CHN		27 Aug
13.24i	-	Dagmar	Urbánková	TCH	62	23 Jan
13.24	-0.5	Lazara	Morfa	CUB	67	24 Jun
13.23i	-	Olga	Voronina	UZB	75	26 Feb
13.23	0.6	Tereza	Marinova	BUL	77	21 May
13.22i	-	Vera	Olenchenko	RUS	59	28 Jan
13.22	0.0	Martha	Koulorizou	GRE	74	7 Aug
13.21i	-	Annie	Moelo	FRA	62	15 Jan
13.21	0.8	Yoko	Morioka	JPN	68	30 Apr
13.21	1.8	Eva	Medovárszky	HUN	69	3 Jun
13.21		Daniela	Bologa	ROM	76	7 Aug
13.20	0.2	Ariadne	Godinez	CUB	75	22 Apr
13.20	0.4	Heli	Koivula	FIN	75	20 Aug
13.19i	-	Petra	Franke	GER	71	26 Jan
13.17	1.1	Paraskevi	Tsiamita	GRE	72	30 Jul
13.17		Melinda	Marton	ROM	76	7 Aug
13.16		Shandi	Boyd-Pleasant	USA	74	22 May
13.16	0.9	Andreja	Ribac	SLO	76	8 Jul
13.15i	-	Lisa	Austin	USA	73	19 Feb
13.15	0.4	Karyn	Smith	USA	72	16 Jun
13.15	-1.2	Ilona	Pazola	POL	69	10 Sep
13.14i		Muriel	Glovil	FRA	68	27 Feb
13.14	0.7	Tania	Dixon	NZL	70	6 Mar
13.14	1.0	Luciana	dos Santos	BRA	70	18 Sep
13.13i		Gundega	Sproge	LAT	72	23 Jan
13.13		Jacqui	Brown	USA	72	8 Apr
13.13	0.6	Mónica	Jofresa	ESP	72	28 May
13.13	1.5	Helle	Aro	FIN	60	10 Jul
13.12	0.1	Anna	Rodivich	UKR	76	12 Jun
13.11	1.4	Anni	Paananen	FIN	71	1 Jul
13.11		Madalina	Coman	ROM	76	22 Jul
13.10i		Luisa	Celesia	ITA	63	5 Feb

Mark	Wind		Name	Nat	Born	Date
13.10		Najuma	Fletcher	GUY	74	22 May
13.10		Miheala	Gîndila	ROM	74	10 Jun
13.10	0.3	Christina	Öppinger	AUT	73	12 Jun
13.09			Lim Suk-hyun	KOR	73	18 Jun
13.09	0.1	Lada	Kalinovskaya	UKR	74	28 May
13.08	0.1	Olesya	Likhatkova	KZK	75	3 Jul
13.06i		Olga	Kontsevaya	RUS	72	22 Jan
13.06i		Claudia	Gerhardt	GER	66	26 Feb
		(150)				
13.06		Yana	Yesenova	RUS	76	24 Apr

Wind-assisted

Mark	Wind		Name	Nat	Born	Pos	Meet	Venue	Date
14.85	2.4		Kravets			1	DNG	Stockholm	12 Jul
14.85	3.1		Lasovskaya			2	EC	Helsinki	8 Aug
14.67	2.1		Kravets			3	EC	Helsinki	8 Aug
14.43	2.7	Yelena	Lysak ¶	RUS	19.10.75	1	EJ	Lisboa	21 Jul
13.98	6.0	Monica	Toth	ROM	7.3.70	2		Gateshead	1 Jul
13.98	2.1	Irina	Mushayilova	RUS	6.1.67	5	DNG	Stockholm	12 Jul
13.61	3.4	Urszula	Wlodarczyk	POL	22.12.65	2	ECp I	Valencia	11 Jun
13.51	2.6	Tereza	Marinova	BUL	25.9.77	1		Sofia	26 Jun
13.48	2.4	Lene	Espegren	NOR	8.5.71	2	NC	Jessheim	21 Aug
13.43		Jelena	Blazhevica	LAT	11.5.70	1		Riga	27 May
13.40	4.0	Andreja	Ribac	SLO	14.1.76	1		Zalaegerszeg	28 May
13.38		Hedvika	Korosak ¶	SLO	24.5.70	1		Ljubljana	6 May
13.36	3.0	Yoko	Morioka	JPN	17.7.68	1		Hiroshima	30 Apr
13.31		Christine	Gray	USA	17.8.71	1	SWAC	Houston	7 May

Mark	Wind		Name	Nat	Born	Date
13.27	2.9	Anni	Paananen	FIN	71	10 Jul
13.25		Inara	Curko	LAT	66	17 Jul
13.23		Amanda	Banks	USA	67	22 May
13.20	2.4	Sari	Kulmala	FIN	74	10 Jul
13.19		Tiombe	Hurd	USA	63	23 Apr
13.18		Najuma	Fletcher	GUY	74	22 May
13.16	6.3	Christina	Öppinger	AUT	73	11 Jun
13.15	4.5	Sanni	Suhonen	FIN	69	11 Feb
13.12		Ronalee	Davis	JAM	76	3 Apr
13.06		Leonie	Codrington	JAM	76	22 May

Best outdoors

14.14 -0.6 Kaspárková 1 Praha 21 May | 13.86 0.9 Prandzheva 3 Reims 8 Jun
14.12 0.7 Chistyakova 1 Kosice 10 Sep | 13.58 Borrmann 1 Baden Baden 20 May
13.23 Kozlovskaya 6 Aug | 13.16 1.5 Wlodarczyk 26 Jun | 13.08 1.3 Olomina 28 Aug
13.18 0.8 Skrebneva 14 May | 13.12 0.9 Voronina 22 May | 13.07 1.1 Boaje 21 Jul

wind assisted

14.20 2.1 Kasparková 4 Slov Bratislava 1 Jun
13.15 2.8 Olomina 28 Aug 13.14 3.2 Voronina 22 May 13.08 Sproge 27 May

Drugs disqualification

Mark	Wind		Name	Nat	Born	Pos	Meet	Venue	Date
14.58	1.1		Bozhanova			(4)	EC	Helsinki	8 Aug
13.48	1.8	Hedvika	Korosak ¶	SLO	24.5.70	(2)	ECp II/3	Ljubljana	11 Jun

SHOT

Mark		Name	Nat	Born	Pos	Meet	Venue	Date
20.79i	Valentina	Fedyushina	UKR	18.2.65	1		Brovary	1 Mar
20.74		Sui Xinmei	CHN	29.1.65	1		Beijing	29 Apr
20.56		Fedyushina			1		Kiev	26 May
20.54		Zhang Liuhong	CHN	16.1.69	1	NC	Beijing	5 Jun
20.45		Sui Xinmei			1	AsiG	Hiroshima	15 Oct
20.15		Sui Xinmei			2	NC	Beijing	5 Jun
20.15		Sui Xinmei			1	GWG	St Peterburg	29 Jul
20.08		Huang Zhihong	CHN	7.5.65	2	GWG	St Peterburg	29 Jul
20.06i		Fedyushina			1		Zaporozhye	30 Jan
20.06	Astrid	Kumbernuss	GER	5.2.70	1	OD	Jena	3 Jun
20.02		Sui Xinmei			1		Beijing	14 Apr
20.02		Cheng Xiaoyan	CHN	20.11.75	3	NC	Beijing	5 Jun
20.00i	Larisa	Peleshenko	RUS	29.2.64	1		St Peterburg	19 Feb
20.00		Huang Zhihong			1		Hechtel	30 Jul
19.93		Kumbernuss			1		Weiler	18 Jun
19.90i	Mihaela	Oana	ROM	11.11.68	1		Bucuresti	5 Feb
19.89	Kathrin	Neimke	GER	18.7.66	1		Lindau	31 Jul
19.85	Stephanie	Storp	GER	28.11.68	2		Weiler	18 Jun
19.84		Neimke			1		Halle	14 May
19.81		Peleshenko			1	Znam	Moskva	5 Jun
19.81	Irina	Khudorozhkina	RUS	13.10.68	1	NC	St Peterburg	15 Jul
19.79		Neimke			2	OD	Jena	3 Jun
19.79		Storp			1	NC	Erfurt	3 Jul
19.76		Fedyushina			2	Znam	Moskva	5 Jun
19.75	Anna	Romanova	RUS	9.3.68	2	NC	St Peterburg	15 Jul
19.74	Svetla	Mitkova	BUL	17.6.64	3	GWG	St Peterburg	29 Jul
19.72		Storp			3	OD	Jena	3 Jun
19.71		Cheng Xiaoyan			1	NC-j	Nanchang	30 Apr
19.71		Huang Zhihong			1		Papendal	9 Jul
19.65		Neimke			3		Weiler	18 Jun
19.65		Huang Zhihong			1	TOTO	Tokyo	15 Sep
	(31/13)							

Mark	Name		Nat	Born	Pos	Meet	Venue	Date
19.63		Kumbernuss			1	ECp	Birmingham	25 Jun
19.61	Viktoriya	Pavlysh	UKR	15.1.69	1	EC	Helsinki	7 Aug
19.60	Connie	Price-Smith	USA	3.6.62	1	NC	Knoxville	18 Jun
19.42	Grit	Hammer	GER	4.6.66	2		Halle	14 May
19.36i	Jana	Ciobanu	ROM	12.11.68	2		Bucuresti	5 Feb
19.23	Krystyna	Danilczyk	POL	14.1.68	1		Mielec	29 May
19.23		Wu Xianchun	CHN	.2.72	4	NC	Beijing	5 Jun
	(20)							
19.22	Irina	Zhuk	UKR	15.1.66	2		Kiev	7 May
19.14i	Ines	Wittich	GER	14.11.69	1		Bad Segerburg	29 Jan
19.07	Belsy	Laza	CUB	5.6.67	2	WCp	London	10 Sep
18.98		Zhen Wenhua	CHN	.2.67	2		Tangshan	27 Aug
18.85	Danguole	Urbikiene	LIT	10.12.62	1	NC	Vilnius	1 Jul
18.78	Ramona	Pagel	USA	10.11.61	1	MSR	Walnut	17 Apr
18.78	Yumeleisis	Cumba	CUB	4.2.75	1	NC-j	Camaguey	10 Jun
18.68	Judy	Oakes	GBR	14.2.58	1	v4N	Nitra	13 Jul
18.60		Zhang Zhiying	CHN	19.7.73	5	NC	Beijing	5 Jun
18.59		Dong Bo	CHN	.3.71	2		Beijing	26 Mar
	(30)							
18.36	Irina	Korzhanenko	RUS	10.5.74	1	ECp 23	Ostrava	31 Jul
18.35i		Yu Juan	CHN	21.1.74	1		Shanghai	26 Feb
18.32i	Livia	Mehes	ROM	6.3.65	3		Bucuresti	5 Feb
18.31		Xie Hongxia	CHN	5.4.70	1		Chengdu	9 Jun
18.30	Eileen	Vanisi	USA	28.3.72	1		Waco	25 May
18.15	Corrie	de Bruin	NED	26.10.76	1		Arnhem	19 Jun
18.12	Heike	Hopfer	GER	28.2.71	1		Berlin	23 Apr
18.12	Valeyta	Althouse	USA	7.1.74	1		Salinas	25 May
18.10	Natasha	Erjavec	SLO	15.5.68	1		Nova Gorica	14 May
17.93	Karolina	Lundahl	FIN	30.6.68	1		Tampere	21 Jun
	(40)							
17.86	Dawn	Dumble	USA	25.2.72	2		Long Beach	9 Jun
17.82	Margarita	Ramos	ESP	26.6.66	1		Léon	11 Jun
17.80	Danijela	Curovic	YUG	7.3.74	1		Ulcinj	Jan
17.68i	Nadezhda	Lukyniv	UKR	14.5.68	3	NC	Kiev	12 Feb
17.64	Myrtle	Augee	GBR	4.2.65	2	CG	Victoria	24 Aug
17.58i	Agnese	Maffeis	ITA	9.3.65	1		Genova	5 Feb
17.54	Marika	Tuliniemi	FIN	19.7.74	1		Hämeenkyrö	30 Jun
17.52	Herminia	Fernández	CUB	4.11.67	5	NC	La Habana	24 Jun
17.44	Nadine	Kleinert	GER	20.10.75	7	NC	Erfurt	3 Jul
17.34	Elvira	Urusova	GEO	2.2.66	1		Tbilisi	2 Jul
	(50)							
17.23	Alexandra	Amaro	BRA	20.12.72	1		Brasilia	26 Jul
17.22i	Claudia	Mues	GER	3.1.75	2		Bad Segerburg	29 Jan
17.20 ?	Elena	Hila	ROM	22.5.74	2		Bucuresti	12 Jun
	17.01						Bucuresti	22 Jul
17.14	Linda-Marie	Mårtensson	SWE	22.6.71	1		Kvarnsveden	14 Jun
17.13		Bao Dongying	CHN	13.4.73	1		Bangkok	30 Apr
17.13	Atanaska	Angelova	BUL	21.9.72	3		Sofia	24 May
17.11i	Kathrin	Koch	GER	23.4.68	2		Johnson City	21 Jan
17.07		Li Xiaoyun	CHN	10.7.71	2		Hiroshima	29 Apr
17.03i	Danyel	Mitchell	USA	16.9.72	2	NCAA	Indianapolis	12 Mar
17.02i	Stevanie	Wadsworth	USA	19.3.72	3	NCAA	Indianapolis	12 Mar
	(60)							
17.00	Natalya	Gurskaya	BLR	15.1.72	3	v3N	Krakow	30 Jun
16.98	Jacqueline	Goormachtigh	NED	28.2.70	1	ECp II	Dublin	12 Jun
16.96i	Maria	Tranchina	ITA	10.2.68	2		Genova	5 Feb
16.95		Lee Myong-sun	KOR	12.2.76	1		Seoul	13 May
16.90		Shang Xiaoli	CHN	10.4.75	2	NC-j	Nanchang	27 Apr
16.87	Peggy	Pollock	USA	60	4	USOF	Edwardsville	10 Jul
16.87	Manuela	Torazza	ITA	27.6.68	1		Novara	1 Aug
16.79	Katarina	Sederholm	FIN	19.6.68	1		Drammen	1 Jun
16.78i	Greet	Meulemeester	BEL	5.9.69	1		Hoboken	13 Feb
16.78	Monika	Raizgiene	LIT	14.4.65	1		Vilnius	7 May
	(70)							
16.77	Elizangela	Adriano	BRA	27.7.72	2	IbAC	Mar del Plata	29 Oct
16.76	Noelvis	Balanten	CUB	24.6.72	4	NC	La Habana	24 Jun
16.74	Teresa	Machado	POR	22.7.69	1		San Jacinto	17 Apr
16.74	Paulette	Mitchell	USA	2.12.72	1		Knoxville	23 Apr
16.69	Kaliopi	Ouzouni	GRE	8.3.73	1		Thessaloniki	18 May

Mark	Name		Nat	Born	Pos	Meet	Venue	Date
16.69	Mara	Rosolen	ITA	27.7.65	1		Riva del G.	3 Aug
16.66	Lyudmila	Sechko	RUS	27.11.74	1		St Peterburg	9 Jun
16.65	Alina	Pupo	CUB	9.3.75	1		La Habana	10 Feb
16.63	Georgette	Reed	CAN	26.1.67	1		Tucson	7 May
16.61	Lisa	Vizaniari	AUS	14.12.71	3	CG	Victoria	24 Aug
	(80)							
16.58	Eha	Rünne	EST	25.5.63	1		Tallinn	28 May
16.57	Kris	Kuehl	USA	30.7.70	1		Minneapolis	16 Apr
16.57	Margaret	Lynes	GBR	19.2.63	6	v USA	Gateshead	20 Jul
16.55	Edith	Krauss	GER	1.7.64	1		Ottobrunn	30 Jul
16.52	Olga	Ryabinkina	RUS	24.9.76	1		Krasnodar	28 May
16.51Ai	Melisa	Weis	USA	22.5.71	1		Pocatello	5 Feb
16.48i	Anelia	Yordanova	BUL	27.4.72	2		Sofia	5 Feb
16.43	Yvonne	Hanson-Nortey	GBR	18.2.64	1		Bournemouth	19 Jun
16.41	Renata	Katewicz	POL	2.5.65	2	NC	Pila	25 Jun
16.41	Nathalie	Ganguillet	SUI	21.8.67	1		Moutier	6 Aug
	(90)							
16.40i	Yekaterina	Shishchenko	UKR	24.12.71	4	NC	Kiev	12 Feb
16.40	Larisa	Lapa	UKR	9.4.72	4		Kiev	23 Jul
16.39	Asta	Ovaska	FIN	29.7.63	1		Ruotsinphytaa	12 Jun
16.38	Irina	Zakharova	RUS	2.2.74	3	Army	Rostov	24 Aug
16.35		Kim Jung-min	KOR	19.2.73	2	NC	Seoul	17 Jun
16.33i	Alice	Matejková	TCH	11.1.69	1	NC	Jablonec	26 Feb
16.32	Fabienne	Locuty	FRA	6.3.68	1		Nancy	8 May
16.31	Ilona	Zakharchenko	UKR	16.6.67	2		Belaya Tserkov	9 Jul
16.31	Yelena	Klochikhina	RUS	20.4.76	4	Army	Rostov	24 Aug
16.28	Rica	Brown	USA	3.4.69	3		Azusa	23 Apr
	(100)							

Mark	Name		Nat	Born	Date
16.27	Irina	Korotayeva	RUS	74	28 May
16.27	Christine	King	NZL	64	24 Aug
16.24	Fotini	Kyriakidou	GRE	71	9 Apr
16.24	Sunisa	Yooyao	THA	73	15 Oct
16.22	Pam	Dukes	USA	64	5 Feb
16.18	Linda	Tukkers	NED	71	7 May
16.17	Daniela	Costian	AUS	65	26 Feb
16.16	Elena	Tapîrlan	ROM	74	22 Jul
16.12	Larisa	Turchinskaya	RUS	65	25 Jul
16.11i	Beth	Bunge	USA	64	19 Feb
16.11	Yulia	Zaginay	RUS	63	15 Jul
16.09	Birgit	Petsch	GER	63	19 Jun
16.07	Kym	Carter	USA	64	14 Jun
16.07	Anna	Söderberg	SWE	73	7 Aug
16.01	Zdena	Silhavá	TCH	64	29 May
16.00	Yanina	Korolchik	BLR	76	1 Jul
15.96i	Laverne	Eve	BAH	65	4 Mar
15.89Ai	Collinus	Newsome	USA	76	22 Jan
15.88	Marie-France	Best	FRA	73	31 May
15.88	Mirella	Berger	GER	73	5 Jun
15.88	Leone	Bertimon	FRA	50	6 Jul
15.85i	Alison	Grey	GBR	73	12 Feb
	(122)				

Best outdoors

Mark	Name	Pos	Meet	Venue	Date
18.52	Wittich	3		Lindau	31 Jul
18.26	Oana	1		Bucuresti	27 May
18.08	Ciobanu	2		Sofia	21 May
17.24	Mehes	1		Bucuresti	10 Jun
17.11	Mues	8	NC	Erfurt	3 Jul
17.02	Lukyniv	4	NC	Kiev	26 May
16.95	Wadsworth	3	NCAA	Boise	4 Jun
16.81	Tranchina	1		Palermo	7 May
16.69	Koch	2	DogwR	Knoxville	9 Ap
16.62	Mitchell	1		Baton Rouge	25 May
16.48	Yordanova	2		Sofia	25 Jun
16.46	Weis	1	Big 8	Lawrence	21 May

16.02 Bunge 16 Apr 15.88 Matejková 21 Jun 15.86 Meulemeester 21 Jul 15.82 Eve 23 Apr

DISCUS

Mark	Name		Nat	Born	Pos	Meet	Venue	Date
68.72	Daniela	Costian	AUS	30.4.65	1		Auckland	22 Jan
68.72	Ilke	Wyludda	GER	28.3.69	1	EC	Helsinki	10 Aug
68.36		Wyludda			1	ECp	Birmingham	25 Jun
67.50		Li Qiumei	CHN	.9.74	1		Beijing	10 May
67.44	Ellina	Zvereva	BLR	16.11.60	1	VD	Bruxelles	19 Aug
67.32		Costian			1		Brisbane	5 Feb
66.82		Zvereva			1		Byrkjelo	24 Jul
66.68		Costian			1		Wellington	19 Jan
66.60		Qiu Qiaoping ¶	CHN	31.10.71	1		Hiroshima	30 Apr
66.58		Zvereva			1	WK	Zürich	17 Aug
66.46	Mette	Bergmann	NOR	9.11.62	1		Vasteras	30 Jun
66.42		Bergmann			1		Tonsberg	20 Jul
66.32		Wyludda			1		Halle	14 May
66.26		Bergmann			1		Hechtel	30 Jul
66.26		Min Chunfeng	CHN	17.3.69	1		Beijing	12 Aug
66.16		Costian			2	VD	Bruxelles	19 Aug
66.12		Wyludda			1	Herc	Monaco	2 Aug
66.10		Costian			1	NEC	Melbourne	24 Feb
66.08		Wyludda			1		Chemnitz	18 Jun

Mark	Name		Nat	Born	Pos	Meet	Venue	Date
66.06		Costian			1	ISTAF	Berlin	30 Aug
66.00	Olga	Chernyavskaya	RUS	17.9.63	1		Adler	23 Feb
66.00	Olga	Nikishina	UKR	29.4.66	1		Odessa	20 May
65.90		Wyludda			Q	EC	Helsiinki	9 Aug
65.84		Wyludda			1	GPF	Paris	3 Sep
65.72	Renata	Katewicz	POL	2.5.65	1		Chania	5 Jun
65.66		Qiu Qiaoping			1	NC	Beijing	4 Jun
65.64		Zvereva			1	v3N	Krakow	30 Jun
65.64		Bergmann			3	VD	Bruxelles	19 Aug
65.62	Barbara	Hechavarría	CUB	6.8.66	1	Banes	São Paulo	21 May
65.60		Costian			1		Brisbane	20 Feb
65.60		Chernyavskaya			4	VD	Bruxelles	19 Aug
65.52		Wyludda			1	GP II	Linz	4 Jul
	(32/11)							
64.40	Nicoleta	Grasu	ROM	17.9.71	1		Bucuresti	22 Jul
64.04	Manuela	Tîrneci	ROM	26.2.69	1	GGala	Roma	8 Jun
63.84	Lyudmila	Filiminova	BLR	22.3.71	1	NC	Gomel	10 Jul
63.30	Austrute	Mikelyte	LIT	5.5.69	1		Vilnius	6 May
62.92	Atanaska	Angelova	BUL	21.9.72	1		Plovdiv	4 May
62.76	Franka	Dietzsch	GER	22.1.68	2		Chemnitz	18 Jun
62.70	Jana	Lauren	GER	28.6.70	2		Halle	14 May
62.32	Katerina	Vogoli	GRE	30.10.70	1		Rethymno	21 May
62.32	Connie	Price-Smith	USA	3.6.62	3	Banes	São Paulo	21 May
	(20)							
62.12	Natalya	Sadova	RUS	7.2.72	3	Znam	Moskva	5 Jun
62.08	Larisa	Korotkevich	RUS	3.1.67	4	Znam	Moskva	5 Jun
62.00	Teresa	Machado	POR	22.7.69	1		São Jacinto	17 Apr
61.86	Vladimira	Malátová ¶	TCH	15.5.67	1		Praha	21 May
61.40	Marie-Paul	Geldhof	BEL	27.2.69	1		Eeklo	30 Apr
61.24		Cao Qi	CHN	.1.74	1		Tangshan	30 Aug
61.20	Anja	Gündler	GER	18.3.72	3		Chemnitz	18 Jun
61.18	Ilona	Zakharchenko	UKR	16.6.67	3		Odessa	20 May
61.12	Alice	Matejková	TCH	11.1.69	1	NC	Jablonec	9 Jul
61.12		Hu Honglian	CHN		2		Tangshan	30 Aug
	(30)							
61.04		Bao Dongying	CHN	13.4.73	4	NC	Beijing	4 Jun
60.98		Luan Zhili	CHN	6.1.73	1		Jinan	28 Apr
60.88	Zdenka	Silhavá	TCH	15.6.54	1		Ceska Budejovice	18 Jun
60.80	Antonina	Patoka	RUS	12.1.64	1		Fana	26 May
60.76	Valentina	Ivanova	RUS	1.5.63	1	NC-w	Sochi	19 Feb
60.66	Agnese	Maffeis	ITA	9.3.65	1		Tirrenia	6 Mar
60.56	Angeles	Barreiro	ESP	26.7.63	1		Ferrol	10 Jun
60.50	Anastasia	Kelesidou	GRE	28.11.72	1		Thessaloniki	11 May
60.22	Lacy	Barnes-Mileham	USA	23.12.64	1		Modesto	14 May
60.22	Maricela	Bristec	CUB	17.12.71	2	NC	La Habana	23 Jun
	(40)							
60.16	Ursula	Kreutel	GER	14.9.65	2		Nürnberg	10 Jun
59.84	Agnes	Teppe	FRA	4.5.68	1		Salon de Provence	11 May
59.80	Yelena	Antonova	UKR	16.6.72	1		Dnepropetrovsk	13 May
59.78	Svetla	Mitkova	BUL	17.6.64	2		Sofia	21 May
59.70	Cristina	Boit	ROM	14.5.68	3	NC	Bucuresti	17 Jun
59.64	Danijela	Curovic	YUG	7.3.74	2		Modesto	14 May
59.58	Joanna	Wisniewska	POL	24.5.72	1		Wroclaw	22 May
59.56		Yu Qingmei	CHN	20.5.75	1	NC-j	Nanchang	30 Apr
59.54	Kristin	Kuehl	USA	30.7.70	1		Minneapolis	16 Apr
59.36		Cheng Xianhong	CHN	.10.68	1		Beijing	29 Apr
	(50)							
59.24	Danyel	Mitchell	USA	16.9.72	1	SEC	Fayetteville	14 May
59.20	Dawn	Dumble	USA	25.2.72	1		Salinas	25 May
59.20	Irina	Grachova	RUS	11.1.63	1		Sochi	9 Sep
59.12	Simone	Schmitt	GER	5.12.71	1		Ludwigsburg	23 Apr
59.12	Jacqueline	Goormachtigh	NED	28.2.70	1		Vlaardingen	29 Jun
58.74	Anna	Söderberg	SWE	11.6.73	1	NC	Göteborg	30 Jul
58.56	Jackie	McKernan	GBR	1.7.65	1		Loughborough	22 Jun
58.56	Karin	Colberg	SWE	19.4.67	1		Kuortane	25 Jun
58.38	Isabelle	Devaluez	FRA	17.3.66	1		Viry-Chatillon	8 May
58.08	Maria	Urrutia	COL	25.3.65	1	Odesur	Valencia	27 Nov
	(60)							
58.00	Pam	Dukes	USA	15.5.64	4		Modesto	14 May

Mark	Name		Nat	Born	Pos	Meet	Venue	Date
57.94	Beatrice	Faumuina	NZL	23.10.74	1		Auckland	22 Jan
57.72	Eha	Rünne	EST	25.5.63	1		Tallinn	18 May
57.70	Liliana	Martineli	ARG	20.5.70	1		Buenos Aires	17 Oct
57.60	Corrie	de Bruin	NED	26.10.76	1		Zierikzee	10 Sep
57.42	Oksana	Andrusina	RUS	1.3.73	1		Krasnodar	20 Aug
57.40	Alison	Lever	AUS	13.10.72	2	NEC	Melbourne	24 Feb
57.40	Suzy	Powell	USA	3.9.76	1		Modesto	20 May
57.12	Ivona	Holubová	SVK	24.10.72	1		Bratislava	18 May
56.98	Stella	Tsikouna	GRE	19.10.72	2	NC	Athina	26 Jun
	(70)							
56.94	Zoubida	Laayouni	MAR	5.2.56	1		Meknès	20 Mar
56.94	Edie	Boyer	USA	21.2.66	1		St Paul	23 Apr
56.90	Maria	Vavilova	RUS	73	1		Bryansk	29 May
56.76	Sabine	Sievers	GER	3.3.75	1		Hagen	11 Jun
56.72	Amélia	Moreira	BRA	30.7.65	1		Campinas	15 Oct
56.54	Carla	Garrett	USA	31.7.67	5	NC	Knoxville	17 Jun
56.48	Sonia	Godall	ESP	28.3.68	1		Barcelona	14 Jun
56.48	Katalin	Csöke-Tóth	HUN	26.1.57	1		Tata	30 Jul
56.24	Sharon	Andrews	GBR	4.7.67	2	AAA	Sheffield	12 Jun
56.16	Annika	Larsson	SWE	10.7.70	1		Gävle	13 Aug
	(80)							
55.78	Kathrin	Koch	GER	23.4.68	3	PennR	Philadelphia	29 Apr
55.74	Marlene	Sánchez	CUB	12.10.71	2		Cali	9 Apr
55.74	Lizette	Etsebeth	RSA	3.5.63	3	CG	Victoria	23 Aug
55.66	Deborah	Callaway	GBR	15.7.64	1		Bracknell	2 May
55.66	Monique	Kuenen	NED	9.4.71	1		Eindhoven	5 Jun
55.56	Lisa	Vizaniari	AUS	14.12.71	1		Prince George	13 Aug
55.52	Natalya	Ampleyeva	BLR	25.9.72	2	NC	Gomel	10 Jul
55.36	Melisa	Weis	USA	22.5.71	7		Modesto	14 May
55.34	Sarah	Andrews	USA	4.11.71	2		Salinas	25 May
55.30		Zhang Yaqing	CHN	15.1.77	2	NC-j	Nanchang	30 Apr
	(90)							
55.28	Elizangela	Adriano	BRA	27.7.72	1		São Paulo	3 Sep
55.26	Candy	Roberts	USA	16.4.71	3		Salinas	25 May
55.24	Kirsi	Lindfors	FIN	9.12.75	1		Alavieska	14 Jul
55.20	Janet	Hill	USA	28.8.70	2		Fresno	9 Apr
55.20	Billur	Dulkadir	TUR	1.6.69	1		Istanbul	14 May
55.14	JoJo	Harris	USA	25.4.73	1		Baton Rouge	25 May
55.12	Ingrid	Hantho	USA	13.6.71	1		Raleigh	22 Apr
55.10	Marie-Luise	Rütz	GER	28.5.74	1		Heilbronn	12 Jun
55.04	Lorraine	Shaw	GBR	2.4.68	1		Cheltenham	15 May
55.02	Larisa	Zakorko	UKR	21.2.64	1		Dnepropetrovsk	9 Jul
	(100)							

Mark	Name		Nat	Born	Date
54.94	Areti	Abatzi	GRE	74	6 Aug
54.84	Martina	Greithanner	GER	74	12 May
54.84	Alana	Preston	USA	73	14 May
54.70	Lyudmila	Starovoitova	BLR	74	24 May
54.68	Katalin	Divos	HUN	74	29 Apr
54.62	Olga	Tsander	BLR	76	1 Jul
54.60	Felicity	Johnston	AUS	71	13 Mar
54.60	Latifa	Allam	MAR	70	4 Jun
54.60	Shelley	Drew	GBR	73	29 Aug
54.58	Dagmar	Galler	GER	61	12 May
54.50		Qin Lei	CHN		30 Apr
54.44	Angelika	Nilsson	SWE	74	6 Jun
54.42	Diana	Back	FIN	71	14 Jul
54.40	Alice	Meyer	FRA	72	11 Jun
54.38	Marzana	Wysocka	POL	69	1 Jun
54.38	Kati	Siltovuori	FIN	71	7 Jun
54.22	Nathalie	Ganguillet	SUI	67	3 Sep
54.12	Melinda	Wirtz	USA	74	25 May
54.10	Carol	Finsrud	USA	57	30 Apr
54.06	Monia	Kari	TUN	71	16 Jun
54.02	Maria	Marello	ITA	61	28 May
54.00	Kristy	Andrews	USA	71	25 May
53.94	Sonja	Spendelhofer	AUT	67	7 May
53.94	Rita	Lora	ESP	73	30 Jul
53.92	Ikuko	Kitamori	JPN	63	14 Oct
	(125)				

Drugs disqualification

Mark	Name		Nat	Born	Pos	Meet	Venue	Date
63.66	Vladimira	Malátová ¶	TCH	15.5.67	1	ECCp	Schwechat	29 May

Mark	Name		Nat	Born	Pos	Meet	Venue	Date
67.34	Svetlana	Sudak	BLR	17.11.71	1		Minsk	5 Jun
66.84	Olga	Kuzenkova	RUS	4.10.70	1		Sochi	23 Feb
65.48	Mihaela	Melinte	ROM	27.3.75	1		Bucuresti	25 Feb
65.14		Kuzenkova			1	Army	Rostov	26 Aug
65.04		Melinte			1		Bucuresti	10 Jun
64.40		Kuzenkova			1	NC	St Peterburg	16 Jul
63.56		Sudak			1		Gomel	9 Jul
63.44		Melinte			1	NC	Bucuresti	18 Jun
63.28		Kuzenkova			1	Army	Moskva	26 Jan

Mark	Name		Nat	Born	Pos	Meet	Venue	Date
63.20		Kuzenkova			1		Staiki	28 Apr
63.00		Kuzenkova			1	NC-w	Sochi	18 Feb
62.98		Melinte			1	Balk-j	Ankara	2 Jul
62.38	Debbie	Sosimenko	AUS	5.4.74	1		Sydney	19 Feb
62.22	Marina	Pirog	UKR	28.8.74	1		Kiev	23 Jul
62.16		Sosimenko			1	NEC	Melbourne	24 Feb
61.94		Sosimenko			1		Sydney	20 Feb
61.84	Alla	Fyodorova	RUS	66	1		Moskva	3 Jul
61.78		Fyodorova			1		Moskva	12 May
61.68	Lyubov	Karpova	RUS	14.8.57	1		Moskva	4 Sep
61.46		Sosimenko			1		Sydney	12 Feb
61.34		Sudak			2		Staiki	28 Apr
61.34	Viktoria	Polyanskaya	RUS	71	1		Krasnodar	19 Aug
61.18		Sosimenko			1		Hobart	26 Feb
60.94		Melinte			1	NC-j	Bucuresti	4 Jun
60.84		Sosimenko			1	NC	Sydney	11 Mar
60.74		Fyodorova			1		Sochi	9 Sep
60.68		Sosimenko			1		Hobart	27 Feb
60.36		Pirog			1	NC	Klev	27 May
60.30		Sosimenko			1		Sydney	29 Jan
60.14	Aya	Suzuki	JPN	18.11.67	1		Mito	8 May
	(30/10)							
59.92	Lorraine	Shaw	GBR	2.4.68	1		Colindale	1 Apr
59.50	Tatyana	Konstantinova	RUS	70	2	Army	Moskva	26 Jan
59.02	Simone	Mathes	GER	13.5.75	1		Rehlingen	23 May
58.68	Sonja	Fitts	USA	4.10.70	1		Jamaica, N.Y.	14 May
58.36	Livia	Mehes	ROM	6.3.65	2	NC	Bucuresti	17 Jun
58.02	Olga	Malakhova	UKR	25.8.71	2	NC	Kiev	27 May
57.80	Irina	Lungu	ROM	5.4.75	2		Bucuresti	10 Jun
57.62	Kirsten	Münchow	GER	21.1.77	1		Dortmund	25 Jun
57.58	Lyudmila	Gubkina	BLR	28.5.72	2	NC	Gomel	10 Jul
57.44	Natalya	Panarina	RUS	6.5.75	2		Krasnodar	19 Aug
	(20)							
57.42	Alexandra	Earl-Givan	USA	25.4.70	2	NC	Knoxville	15 Jun
56.82	Liz	Legault	USA	4.5.70	1	PennR	Philadelphia	30 Apr
56.78	Veronika	Ushakova	RUS	8.11.77	1	v3N-j	Warszawa	18 Jun
56.62	Natalya	Vasilenko	UKR	30.10.74	3	NC	Kiev	27 May
56.56	Theresa	Findlay	USA	11.1.74	1		Dedham	11 Jun
56.52	Tatyana	Lishchuk	UKR	18.1.73	4		Kiev	7 May
56.12	Inga	Beyer	GER	7.2.74	1		Bremen	23 Jul
56.10	Angelika	Lindemann	GER	5.9.71	1		Wiesbaden	5 Jun
56.06	Tina	Schäfer	GER	27.12.77	2		Rehlingen	23 May
56.04	Irina	Kuznetsova	RUS	75	2		Moskva	4 Sep
	(30)							
55.76	Bonnie	Edmondson	USA	17.3.64	3	NC	Knoxville	15 Jun
55.70	Marion	Große-Rammelkamp	GER	27.12.68	3		Rehlingen	23 May
55.70	Maria	Villamizar	COL	30.8.70	1	IbAm	Mar del Plata	30 Oct
55.44	Lyn	Sprules	GBR	11.9.75	1		Haslemere	19 Jul
55.38	Oksana	Lobtsova	RUS	74	1		Moskva	6 Jun
55.14	Crystal	Corbeil	USA	4.12.71	1		Worcester	23 Apr
55.12	Denise	Passmore	AUS	11.6.74	2	NC-j	Sydney	10 Mar
54.88	Svetlana	Papu	UKR	13.3.77	5	NC	Kiev	27 May
54.82	Natalya	Ignatova	RUS	74	2	NC-j	Yekaterinburg	25 Jun
54.80	Alice	Meyer	FRA	19.5.72	1		Montreuil	6 Jul
	(40)							
54.42	Andrea	Bunjes	GER	5.2.76	2		Ahlen	6 Aug
54.38	Mariya	Lobanova	RUS	77	2		Bryansk	20 Jun
54.36	Natalya	Zlydennaya	UKR	12.12.78	1		Odessa	23 Apr
54.34	Debbie	Templeton	USA	31.10.72	1	MSR	Walnut	17 Apr
54.34	Theresa	Brick	CAN	4.5.65	1		Suresnes	7 Jul
54.16	Yelena	Antonova	UKR	16.6.72	6	NC	Kiev	27 May
54.06	Natalya	Kunitskaya	UKR	17.8.71	7	NC	Kiev	27 May
53.84	Brenda	McNaughton	AUS	7.5.76	2		Sydney	3 Sep
53.72	Katalin	Divos	HUN	5.5.74	1		Szombathely	30 Apr
53.70	Caroline	Fournier	MRI	7.5.75	1		Montreuil-sous-Bois	21 Jun
	(50)							
53.68	Leslie	Coons	USA	16.7.73	5	NC	Knoxville	15 Jun
53.50	Cécile	Lignot	FRA	19.11.71	1		Clermont-Ferrand	29 Jun

Mark	Name		Nat	Born	Date
53.34	Diana	Holden	GBR	75	13 Aug
53.30	Tracey	Phillips	AUS	69	26 Nov
53.18	Susana	Reguela	ESP	71	8 Oct
52.52	Sandy	Sparrow	USA	74	26 Mar
52.50	Bettina	Gabler	GER	71	2 Jul
52.46	Maureen	Magnan	USA	67	15 Apr
52.38	Irina	Martynenko	UKR	76	23 Jul
52.30	Natalya	Samusenkova	RUS	79	4 Jul
52.10	Kiza	Brunner	USA	72	28 Apr
52.06	Carina	Moya	ARG	73	29 Nov

JAVELIN

Mark	Name		Nat	Born	Pos	Meet	Venue	Date
71.40	Natalya	Shikolenko	BLR	1.8.64	1	GP II	Sevilla	5 Jun
71.40		Shikolenko			1	GP	London	15 Jul
71.32	Trine	Hattestad	NOR	18.4.66	1	Bisl	Oslo	22 Jul
71.08		Hattestad			2	GP	London	15 Jul
70.44		Hattestad			1	ASV	Köln	21 Aug
69.96		Hattestad			1	WG	Helsinki	29 Jun
69.58		Shikolenko			1	Athl	Lausanne	6 Jul
69.20	Karen	Forkel	GER	24.9.70	2	Bisl	Oslo	22 Jul
69.00		Shikolenko			1	ECp	Birmingham	26 Jun
68.68		Forkel			1		Lehrte	4 Sep
68.62		Shikolenko			2	ASV	Köln	21 Aug
68.60		Shikolenko			1		Gomel	14 May
68.26		Shikolenko			1	GPF	Paris	3 Sep
68.16		Shikolenko			3	Bisl	Oslo	22 Jul
68.00		Hattestad			1	EC	Helsinki	12 Aug
67.94		Hattestad			1		Byrkjelo	24 Jul
67.88		Hattestad			1	DNG	Stockholm	12 Jul
67.72		Forkel			1	NC	Erfurt	3 Jul
67.10		Shikolenko			1	Banes	São Paulo	21 May
67.04		Hattestad			2	GPF	Paris	3 Sep
66.98		Shikolenko			1	BNP	Villeneuve d'Ascq	8 Jul
66.96		Shikolenko			1		Dijon	12 Jun
66.84		Shikolenko			1		Duisburg	12 Jun
66.82		Hattestad			2	Athl	Lausanne	6 Jul
66.80		Shikolenko			2	WG	Helsinki	29 Jun
66.56	Claudia	Isaila	ROM	17.7.73	3	GPF	Paris	3 Sep
66.48		Hattestad			1	WCp	London	9 Sep
66.44		Forkel			3	Athl	Lausanne	6 Jul
66.44		Forkel			1		Rhede	29 Jul
66.40	Felicia	Tilea	ROM	29.9.67	3	GP	London	15 Jul
66.22		Tilea			4	Bisl	Oslo	22 Jul
66.10		Forkel			2	EC	Helsinki	12 Aug
	(32/5)							
65.96	Sueli	Pereira Santos	BRA	8.1.65	1	IbAm	Mar del Plata	28 Oct
65.32	Louise	McPaul	AUS	24.1.69	1		Sydney	2 Jul
64.94	Tatyana	Shikolenko	BLR	10.5.68	4	Athl	Lausanne	6 Jul
64.90	Jette	Jeppesen	DEN	14.3.64	1	ECp II	Dublin	12 Jun
64.62	Oksana	Yarygina	UZB	24.12.72	1	AsiG	Hiroshima	15 Oct
	(10)							
64.32	Nadine	Auzeil	FRA	19.8.64	2		Dijon	12 Jun
64.26		Liu Cui	CHN	.8.71	1		Chengdu	9 Jun
64.24	Tanja	Damaske	GER	16.11.71	2	NC	Erfurt	3 Jul
64.04	Yekaterina	Ivakina	RUS	4.12.64	1	Slov	Bratislava	1 Jun
63.98		Ha Xiaoyan	CHN	30.1.72	1		Shizuoka	5 May
63.44		Li Lei	CHN	4.5.74	1		Tangshan	29 Aug
63.40	Kinga	Zsigmond	HUN	19.4.64	1		Budapest	29 Apr
63.38	Terese	Nekrosaité	LIT	19.10.61	1		Ventspils	29 May
62.90	Silke	Gast	GER	30.4.72	4	EC	Helsinki	12 Aug
62.74	Isel	López	CUB	11.7.70	1		Montreal	29 Jun
	(20)							
62.52	Kirsten	Hellier	NZL	6.10.69	1		Auckland	22 Jan
62.44	Xiomara	Rivero	CUB	22.12.68	1		Las Tunas	3 Apr
62.40	Joanna	Stone	AUS	4.10.72	1	NC	Sydney	12 Mar
62.30		Lee Young-sun	KOR	21.2.74	2	AsiG	Hiroshima	15 Oct
62.14	Päivi	Alafrantti	FIN	8.5.64	2		Hamina	14 Jun
62.06	Rita	Ramanauskaité	LIT	22.2.70	1		Karlstad	19 Jun
61.78	Taina	Uppa	FIN	24.10.76	1	v SWE	Stockholm	27 Aug
61.74	Renata	Strasek	SLO	8.4.72	1		Celje	21 May
61.68	Heli	Rantanen	FIN	26.2.70	1		Pihtipudas	17 Jul
61.60	Genowefa	Patla	POL	17.10.62	1	ECp I	Valencia	12 Jun
	(30)							

Mark	Name		Nat	Born	Pos	Meet	Venue	Date
61.60	Nathalie	Teppe	FRA	22.5.72	4		Dijon	12 Jun
61.50	Donna	Mayhew	USA	20.6.60	1	v GBR	Gateshead	20 Jul
61.42	Sonia	Vicet	CUB	1.4.71	2	Barr	La Habana	26 May
61.42	Martine	Bègue	FRA	22.12.69	5		Dijon	12 Jun
61.40		Zhao Yuhong	CHN	15.5.73			Beijing	1 Apr
61.34		Zhang Li	CHN	26.6.61	1	NC	Beijing	3 Jun
61.02	Antoaneta	Selenska	BUL	8.6.63	1		Stara Zagora	16 Jul
60.94	Irina	Kostyuchenko	UKR	11.5.61	1	NC	Kiev	27 May
60.92	Sonya	Radicheva	BUL	8.6.68	1		Sofia	22 May
60.72	Dörte	Barby	GER	21.6.73	1	v2N23	Arzignano	16 Jul
	(40)							
60.70	Kate	Farrow	AUS	6.5.67	3		Byrkjelo	24 Jul
60.32	Claudia	Coslovich	ITA	26.4.72	1	NC	Napoli	2 Jul
60.06	Maria C.	Alvárez	CUB	30.8.75	1		Santiago de Cuba	9 Dec
60.02	Ingrid	Thyssen	GER	9.1.56	1		Leverkusen	13 Aug
59.88	Julianne	Hoffmann	GER	13.12.73	3	OD	Jena	3 Jun
59.88	Oksana	Ovchinnikova	RUS	27.7.71	1		Sotteville	26 Jun
59.86		Tang Lishuang	CHN	25.2.66	3	NC	Beijing	3 Jun
59.80	Kaye	Nordstrom	NZL	30.5.68	3		Auckland	22 Jan
59.50	Yelena	Medvedeva	RUS	9.7.65	1		Halle	14 May
59.42	Elisabet	Wahlander	SWE	14.3.60	4	v FIN	Stockholm	27 Aug
	(50)							
59.34	Akiko	Miyajima	JPN	17.9.66	3		Shizuoka	5 May
59.08	Susanne	Riewe	GER	26.5.70	1		Rostock	18 May
58.96	Doreen	Karasiewicz	GER	21.7.74	1		Potsdam	4 Jun
58.86	Tatyana	Sudarikova	RUS	28.5.73	1		Luumäki	12 Jun
58.70	Mikaela	Ingberg	FIN	29.7.74	2		Lahti	5 Jun
58.62	Sue	Howland	AUS	4.9.60	2		Sydney	20 Feb
58.58	Venera	Mustakayeva	UKR	27.2.71	1		Kharkov	28 Apr
58.54		Fan Yuyan	CHN	.72			Beijing	26 Mar
58.54	Kim	Hyatt	USA	11.12.68	1		Boise	9 Apr
58.52	Olga	Ivankova	UKR	7.1.73	2	NC	Kiev	27 May
	(60)							
58.46	Tatyana	Alisevich	BLR	22.1.69	H		Valladolid	8 May
58.44	Ágnes	Preisinger	HUN	3.8.73	1		Zalaegerszeg	1 Oct
58.42	Natalya	Yermolovich	BLR	29.4.64	2	v3N	Krakow	30 Jun
58.38	Manuela	Alizadeh	GER	29.1.63	4	NC	Erfurt	3 Jul
58.28		Zhao Guiyan	CHN	25.4.77	1	NC-j	Nanchang	30 Apr
58.22	Lada	Chernova	RUS	70	1		Tolgattiy	12 Jun
58.20	Sharon	Gibson	GBR	31.12.61	3	CG	Victoria	26 Aug
58.18	Evi	Völker	GER	10.5.72	1		Bad Windsheim	30 Apr
58.18	Anna	Makhmutova	RUS	69	1		Sochi	10 Sep
58.12		Wang Lianyun	CHN	.10.69	3		Tangshan	29 Aug
	(70)							
58.08	Paula	Berry	USA	18.2.69	1		Portland	22 May
57.96	Laverne	Eve	BAH	16.6.65	1		Baton Rouge	25 May
57.96	Nadezhda	Kobrin	UKR	21.1.72	1		Kiev	24 Jul
57.86	Nicole	Carroll	USA	18.4.68	2	v GBR	Gateshead	20 Jul
57.80	Mari	Uusitalo	FIN	11.5.73	2		Keuruu	24 Jun
57.70	Ewa	Rybak	POL	22.12.74	1		Warszawa	22 May
57.28	Odeymis	Palma	CUB	18.12.71	4		La Habana	7 May
57.26	Valerie	Tulloch	CAN	13.7.72	5	CG	Victoria	26 Aug
57.20	Mirela	Manjani	ALB	21.12.76	1	Balk-j	Ankara	3 Jul
57.08	Shelley	Holroyd	GBR	17.5.73	1	AAA	Sheffield	11 Jun
	(80)							
57.04	Angeliki	Tsialakoudi	GRE	10.5.76	1		Athina	29 May
57.00	Valentina	Borovaya	BLR	6.3.70	2		Gomel	14 May
56.98		Xiang Zhengfeng	CHN		6	NC	Beijing	3 Jun
56.90A	Rhona	Dwinger	RSA	28.6.71	1		Pretoria	12 Apr
56.90	Yvonne	Reichardt	GER	5.2.73	1		Gengenbach	4 Sep
56.88	Silke	Renk	GER	30.6.67	5	OD	Jena	3 Jun
56.86	Tatyana	Khersontseva	RUS	25.5.73	1		St Peterburg	12 May
56.86	Rose-May	Poilagi	FRA	9.2.72	1	ECp/23	Lillehammer	31 Jul
56.84	Vijitha	Amarasekera	SRI	10.12.61	1	NCAA II	Raleigh	28 May
56.82	Valentina	Belaic	CRO	17.10.72	1		Split	2 Jul
	(90)							
56.68	Nikola	Tomecková	TCH	25.6.74	4	ECCp	Schwechat	29 May
56.52	Vera	Ináncsi	HUN	26.1.76	2	NC	Debrecen	9 Jul
56.46	Cinzia	Dallona	ITA	16.3.74	1		Lecco	10 Jul

Mark	Name		Nat	Born	Pos	Meet	Venue	Date
56.38	Liezel	Roux	RSA	25.5.67	1		Port Elizabeth	25 Mar
56.36	Lena	Åström	SWE	5.11.64	1		Oslo	24 Jul
56.32	Helena	Gouveia	POR	24.4.72	1		Braga	9 Apr
56.04	Yelena	Fedotova	RUS	29.5.67	2		Sochi	19 Feb
56.02	Tatyana	Nikishova	RUS	16.7.74	2		Stavropol	28 May
56.02	Carla	Bispo	BRA	29.7.66	2	NC	Rio de Janeiro	18 Sep
56.00	Nora	Bicet	CUB	29.10.77	3		La Habana	10 Feb
	(100)							

Mark	Name		Nat	Born	Date
55.90	Anna	Stroppolo	ITA	75	17 Sep
55.88	Réka	Kovács	HUN	76	22 Jul
55.84	Dörte	Patzschke	GER	76	14 May
55.84	Jaana	Paananen	FIN	66	5 Jun
55.84	Silvana	Koren	SLO	73	19 Jun
55.80	Odeyme	Palma	CUB	75	11 Jun
55.76	Shinobu	Deguchi	JPN	75	14 May
55.76		Chu Chunxia	CHN	78	20 May
55.76	Cindy	Herceg	USA	70	25 May
55.70	Christina	Scherwin	DEN	76	22 Jul
55.68	Marjo	Bus	NED	63	11 Jun
55.56	Yelena	Svezhentseva	UZB	68	21 May
55.56	Lynda	Lipson	USA	71	18 Jun
55.46	Erica	Wheeler	USA	67	16 Jun
55.46	Zuleima	Araméndiz	COL	75	25 Nov
55.32	Diane	Royle	GBR	59	7 May
55.30	Irina	Solodkaya	UKR	69	24 Jul
55.28	Katalin	Antal	HUN	75	8 May
55.24	Chizuru	Mizuno	JPN	67	27 Aug
55.22A	Ansi	Rogers	RSA	64	6 May
55.20	Lyudmila	Konon	RUS	69	29 Jun
54.96	Antigon	Vourdoli	GRE	75	9 Apr
54.86	Nancy	Rahmsdorff	GER	75	7 May
54.80	Isabelle	Surprenant	CAN	69	29 Jun
54.78	Kim	Engel	USA	68	22 May
54.76	Iveta	Locmele	LAT	73	29 May
54.74	Idoia	Mariezkurrena	ESP	70	18 Sep
54.72	Natalya	Shklyaravskaya	UKR	69	27 May
54.68	Jen	McCormick	USA	70	20 May
54.68	Karen	Wilkinson	CAN	71	29 Jun
54.62	Heli	Tolkkinen	FIN	73	23 Aug
54.62	Lorna	Jackson	GBR	74	4 Sep
54.60	Yanuris	LaMontana	CUB	75	13 May
54.50	Karen	Costello	GBR	68	11 Jun
54.40	Efi	Karatopouzi	GRE	68	24 Jul
54.38		Wang Yang	CHN	75	30 Apr
54.36	Belen	Palacios	ESP	69	4 Jun
54.22	Kaija	Kumpula	FIN	72	16 Jun
54.14	Oksana	Kovtun	UKR	72	7 May
54.08	Anne Grete	Bærass	NOR	63	17 Ju
54.08	Yuko	Kojima	JPN	73	3 Nov
54.06	Maret	Kalviste	EST	55	5 Jul
54.02	Delphine	Colinmaire	FRA	68	9 Oct
	(143)				

HEPTATHLON

Mark	Name		Nat	Born	Pos	Meet	Venue	Date
6741	Heike	Drechsler	GER	16.12.64	1		Talence	11 Sep
	13.34/-0.3 1.84 13.58 22.84/-1.1 6.95/+1.0 40.64 2:11.53							
6665	Sabine	Braun	GER	19.1.65	1		Götzis	29 May
	13.39/+1.3 1.87 14.57 24.31/+1.7 6.63/+3.1 49.68 2:18.39							
6606	Jackie	Joyner-Kersee	USA	3.3.62	1	GWG	St Peterburg	26 Jul
	12.77/+2.3 1.84 14.02 23.68/-0.8 6.96/-1.0 42.64 2:26.76							
6598	Svetlana	Moskalets	RUS	1.11.69	1	NC	Vladimir	17 Jun
	13.20/+0.8 1.82 13.78 23.56/+0.1 6.74/+0.8 42.48 2:14.54							
6596	Larisa	Turchinskaya	RUS	29.4.65	2		Götzis	29 May
	13.64/+0.9 1.84 15.35 24.24/+2.5 6.43/+2.1 49.30 2:17.13							
6573	Rita	Ináncsi	HUN	6.1.71	3		Götzis	29 May
	13.66/+2.0 1.84 13.94 24.20/+2.5 6.78/+1.4 46.28 2:16.02							
6507		Moskalets			1	ECp A	Vénissieux	3 Jul
	13.26/+1.5 1.87 13.20 23.75/-2.6 6.70/+1.3 40.10 2:16.84							
6498		Moskalets			4		Gotzis	29 May
	13.40/+1.3 1.84 13.64 23.98/+0.8 6.77/+1.2 40.50 2:15.97							
6492		Turchinskaya			2	GWG	St. Peterburg	26 Jul
	13.66/+2.3 1.84 1.6.12 24.92/-0.8 6.49/+1.6 45.02 2:18.91							
6419		Braun			1	EC	Helsinki	9 Aug
	13.33/+0.9 1.84 14.02 24.60/+0.7 6.32/+1.2 48.54 2:20.66							
6412	Irina	Tyukhay	RUS	14.1.67	2	NC	Vladimir	17 Jun
	13.30/+0.8 1.79 14.67 24.42/+0.1 6.52/+1.2 43.20 2:18.57							
6404		Ináncsi			2	EC	Helsinki	9 Aug
	13.80/+1.9 1.87 14.14 25.05/+0.7 6.48/+1.9 46.48 2:17.92							
6396	Nathalie	Teppe	FRA	22.5.72	2	ECp A	Vénissieux	3 Jul
	13.76/+1.8 1.81 13.41 25.84/-1.1 6.15/+1.9 59.78 2:15.90							
6379	Irina	Vostrikova	RUS	30.8.70	3	NC	Vladimir	17 Jun
	13.77 1.85 14.98 25.40 6.52/+0.9 43.16 2:16.24							
6371	Kym	Carter	USA	12.3.64	1	NC	Knoxville	15 Jun
	13.55 1.87 1.6.07 24.16 6.10 32.88 2:10.85							
6362	Peggy	Beer	GER	15.9.69	3	ECp A	Vénissieux	3 Jul
	13.40/+1.8 1.78 13.56 24.87/-2.6 6.21/-0.3 51.26 2:15.89							
6361		Vostrikova			1		Krasnodar	18 May
	13.6 1.88 15.09 25.3 6.25 45.38 2:15.9							
6361	Ghada	Shouaa	SYR	9.10.73	3	GWG	St Peterburg	26 Jul
	14.56/+2.3 1.81 13.77 24.48/-0.8 6.16/-1.4 53.62 2:12.65							

Mark	Name		Nat	Born	Pos	Meet	Venue	Date
6361		Teppe			2		Talence	11 Sep
	13.77/+0.4 1.78 13.54 25.84/+0.5 6.18/+1.0 59.26 2:16.06							
6360		Shouaa			1	AsiG	Hiroshima	11 Oct
	14.55 1.81 14.33 24.67 6.24 51.92 2:13.59							
6349	Beatrice	Mau-Repnak	GER	20.2.71	5		Götzis	29 May
	13.86/-0.3 1.75 13.53 24.57/+2.5 6.41/+1.1 50.34 2:14.46							
6325	Denise	Lewis	GBR	27.8.72	1	CG	Victoria	23 Aug
	13.66/+1.5 1.74 13.22 25.11/+0.6 6.44 53.68 2:17.60							
6323	Jamie	McNeair	USA	26.6.69	2	NC	Knoxville	15 Jun
	13.54 1.81 12.67 24.37 6.12 48.50 2:13.13							
6322	Urszula	Wlodarczyk	POL	22.12.65	3	EC	Helsinki	9 Aug
	13.26/+0.9 1.81 13.35 24.25/+0.7 6.41/+3.9 42.12 2:18.00							
6317	Jane	Flemming	AUS	14.4.65	2	CG	Victoria	23 Aug
	13.32/+1.5 1.77 14.10 24.06/+0.6 6.29 39.76 2:13.07							
6311		Turchinskaya			4	EC	Helsinki	9 Aug
	13.62/+1.9 1.78 15.42 24.70/-0.2 6.37/+0.8 44.44 2:21.53							
6308		Moskalets			5	EC	Helsinki	9 Aug
	13.37/+0.9 1.84 12.96 23.77/+0.7 6.44/+1.4 37.94 2:21.88							
6294		Turchinskaya			3		Talence	11 Sep
	14.01/-0.3 1.78 14.90 25.11/-1.1 6.22/+1.3 49.54 2:17.02							
6292		Carter			4	GWG	St Peterburg	26 Jul
	13.70/+2.3 1.81 15.50 24.36/-0.8 6.06/+1.2 35.82 2:08.63							
6290	Tatyana	Zhuravlyova	RUS	19.12.67	4	NC	Vladimir	17 Jun
	13.93 1.79 14.01 24.36 6.55/+1.1 39.62 2:13.67							
	(30/18)							
6284	Svetlana	Buraga	BLR	4.9.65	1		Brescia	15 May
	13.55/-1.9 1.78 14.43 24.74/-3.3 6.46/0.0 39.50 2:14.37							
6274	Larisa	Teteryuk	UKR	24.6.70	4	ECp	Vénissieux	3 Jul
	14.38/+1.8 1.87 13.93 24.76/-1.1 6.08/-0.9 49.20 2:16.95							
	(20)							
6262	Remigija	Nazaroviene	LIT	2.6.67	7	EC	Helsinki	9 Aug
	13.42/+0.2 1.75 14.11 24.58/+0.8 6.14/+1.0 46.64 2:16.66							
6241	Tina	Rättyä	FIN	12.11.68	8	EC	Helsinki	9 Aug
	13.78/+0.2 1.72 13.58 24.55/+0.8 6.08/+0.3 48.60 2:11.01							
6230	Monika	Steigauf	GER	17.1.70	7		Götzis	29 May
	13.54/+2.0 1.84 12.33 24.34/+1.7 6.25/+1.8 42.26 2:15.37							
6207w	Irina	Matyusheva	UKR	5.9.65	1		Alhama	5 Jun
	13.29/+4.2 1.82 13.07 24.81/-0.7 6.41/+5.1 33.46 2:09.87							
6206w	Catherine	Bond-Mills	CAN	20.9.67	8		Götzis	29 May
	13.88/+0.9 1.84 12.68 24.66/+1.5 6.48/+4.1 40.26 2:15.58							
	6193				3	CG	Victoria	23 Aug
	13.79 1.86 13.57 24.64 6.22 37.62 2:14.04							
6202h	Tamara	Moshicheva	RUS	29.8.62	1		Bryansk	7 Aug
	13.9 1.71 15.05 24.5 5.98 48.80 2:12.8							
6200		Zhang Xiaohui	CHN	23.3.71	1	NC	Beijing	2 Jun
	13.73 1.68 13.82 24.45 6.25 42.72 2:08.53							
6198	Maria	Kamrowska	POL	11.3.66	7	ECp	Vénissieux	3 Jul
	13.35/+1.5 1.63 15.53 24.57/-2.6 5.85/+0.5 45.56 2:10.74							
6189	DeDee	Nathan	USA	20.4.68	3	NC	Knoxville	15 Jun
	13.77 1.78 14.61 24.75 6.09 45.36 2:19.27							
6155	Lyudmila	Mikhailova	RUS	12.4.69	9		Götzis	29 May
	13.37/+2.0 1.78 12.06 23.64/+0.8 6.45/+1.3 32.42 2:11.85							
	(30)							
6146w	Anzhela	Atroshchenko	BLR	14.10.70	2		Alhama	5 Jun
	13.61/+5.4 1.76 13.01 23.99/-0.1 6.32/+2.6 34.52 2:10.13							
6138		Mu Lianjuan	CHN	28.6.73	2	NC	Beijing	2 Jun
	13.55 1.77 12.38 24.68 6.47 34.16 2:07.65							
6123	Marina	Shcherbina	UKR	5.1.68	1		Kiev	24 Jul
	13.99 1.74 14.46 24.88 5.85 45.22 2:11.32							
6121	Joanne	Henry	NZL	2.10.71	4	CG	Victoria	23 Aug
	14.12/+1.5 1.80 12.78 25.23/+0.6 6.46/+1.8 40.08 2:11.72							
6117	Ines	Krause	GER	10.7.65	10		Götzis	29 May
	13.70/-0.3 1.69 13.58 24.44/+1.5 6.27/+2.5 40.50 2:11.84							
6109	Birgit	Clarius	GER	18.3.65	1	NC	Vaterstetten	3 Sep
	14.32/-1.1 1.78 15.26 25.42/+1.1 5.61/-0.8 48.10 2:11.72							
6104	Natalya	Popykina	RUS	11.12.70	5	NC	Vladimir	17 Jun
	13.95 1.79 12.33 24.35 6.59/+0.8 35.96 2:14.72							
6096	Zhanna	Budilovskaya	UKR	6.4.72	2		Kiev	24 Jul
	14.48/+2.3 1.74 12.12 24.45/+1.2 6.44/+0.8 45.28 2:13.28							

Mark	Name		Nat	Born	Pos	Meet	Venue	Date
6095		Liu Bo	CHN	12.3.72	3	NC	Beijing	2 Jun
	13.52 1.77 13.49 25.08		6.03 37.10 2:07.79					
6094	Bettina	Oberdorf	GER	15.11.65	11		Götzis	29 May
	14.34/+2.0 1.81 13.09 23.90/+1.7		6.11/+3.1 40.54 2:15.35					
	(40)							
6093	Liliana	Nastase	ROM	1.8.62	4		Brescia	15 May
	13.47/-1.9 1.72 13.68 25.02/-3.3		6.31/0.0 39.04 2:14.09					
6093	Manuela	Marxer	LIE	6.8.65	12		Götzis	29 May
	13.45/0.9 1.72 13.03 24.14/1.5		6.07/3.1 40.38 2:13.49					
6083		Wang Wenxiang	CHN	.3.73	4	NC	Beijing	2 Jun
	14.17 1.83 15.19 25.48		5.89 36.84 2:09.45					
6083	Odile	Lesage	FRA	28.6.69	11	ECp A	Vénissieux	3 Jul
	13.85/+0.8 1.81 13.93 26.02/+1.5		6.08/+0.4 45.34 2:17.05					
6076	Magalys	Garcia	CUB	23.1.71	1	NC	La Habana	24 Jun
	13.77/-1.7 1.73 13.11 24.32/0.0		5.86/-0.8 51.46 2:22.19					
6071	Kathleen	Gutjahr	GER	27.7.75	1		Bernhausen	26 Jun
	14.14/+0.6 1.81 12.66 25.07/+1.5		6.14/+0.8 47.46 2:19.37					
6068	Sharon	Jaklofsky	NED	30.9.68	2	ECp B	Bressanone	3 Jul
	13.66/-0.6 1.75 13.24 25.14/-2.9		6.50/-1.6 40.12 2:19.43					
6047w	Tatyana	Alisevich	BLR	22.1.69	5		Alhama	5 Jun
	13.99/+5.4 155 14.08 24.09/-0.4		5.96/+4.6 53.40 2:17.72					
6046	Marcela	Podracká	SVK	13.3.70	11	EC	Helsinki	9 Aug
	14.56/-1.9 1.81 13.58 25.33/+0.2		5.76/-0.3 50.68 2:15.85					
6042	Tiia	Hautala	FIN	3.4.72	1		Kangasala	24 Jul
	13.93/+2.9 1.81 13.57 25.47/+2.4		6.18/+3.8 43.70 2:20.95					
	(50)							
6032	Diane	Guthrie	JAM	24.10.71	1	NCAA	Boise	2 Jun
	14.32 1.79 13.23 25.03		6.48 45.50 2:27.02					
6018	Nadezhda	Novikova	RUS	66	6	NC	Vladimir	17 Jun
	13.57 1.67 13.60 24.34		6.50/+1.2 33.58 2:14.96					
6001w	Sharon	Hanson	USA	24.9.65	1	DogwR	Knoxville	7 Apr
	13.53/W 1.67 13.09 25.12		5.95/W 44.62 2:11.86					
5996	Svetlana	Tkachova	RUS	14.4.70	1		Volgograd	20 Aug
	13.8 1.82 13.28 25.2		5.60 45.88 2:13.0					
5995	Marie	Collonvillé	FRA	23.11.73	16	ECp A	Vénissieux	3 Jul
	14.06/+1.7 1.87 11.55 25.32/-2.6		6.06/+1.1 41.60 2:14.30					
5992		Ding Ying	CHN	28.9.76	1	NC-j	Nanchang	30 Apr
	14.15 1.80 13.22 25.63		6.38 44.54 2:24.69					
5984	Giuliana	Spada	ITA	18.4.71	4	ECpI	Bressanone	3 Jul
	14.00/-0.9 1.72 12.93 25.08/0.0		6.23/+0.5 42.50 2:15.27					
5963	Yelena	Lebedenko	RUS	71	1	Army	Rostov	25 Aug
	13.73/+1.6 1.71 14.12 25.07/-1.2		6.26/+1.4 41.10 2:24.31					
5961	Helle	Aro	FIN	9.12.60	18	ECp A	Vénissieux	3 Jul
	14.05/+0.8 1.69 13.09 25.44/+1.5		6.00/+2.5 47.76 2:14.45					
5952	Birgit	Gautzsch	GER	14.12.67	8		Talence	11 Sep
	13.81/+0.4 1.78 12.37 24.67/-1.1		6.01 39.24 2:15.53					
	(60)							
5934	Karin	Periginelli	ITA	5.2.70	5	1 NC	Brescia	15 May
	14.20/-1.4 1.75 12.20 25.08/+2.3		6.21/+0.6 39.44 2:11.50					
5931	Natalya	Toropchina	RUS	25.2.71	7	NC	Vladimir	17 Jun
	13.83 1.70 13.82 25.66		6.05 41.54 2:14.35					
5929h	Yelena	Volf	RUS	2.3.69	2		Volgograd	20 Aug
	13.8 1.79 14.30 24.8		6.38 34.60 2:24.5					
	5913				8	NC	Vladimir	17 Jun
5907	Kelly	Blair	USA	24.11.70	4	NC	Knoxville	15 Jun
	13.74 1.78 11.65 24.58		6.15 41.28 2:22.74					
5876		Shi Guiqing	CHN	19.4.68	5	NC	Beijing	2 Jun
	13.83 1.77 12.67 24.88		6.23 37.50 2:22.65					
5871	Yolaida	Pompa	CUB	10.1.72	2	NC	La Habana	24 Jun
	14.31/-1.7 1.79 13.07 25.57/0.0		5.76/-0.9 48.70 2:22.39					
5844	Natalya	Kulikova	RUS	9.8.74	1	NC-23	Vladimir	17 Jun
	14.48 1.73 12.36 25.32		6.16 41.44 2:14.23					
5841	Yelena	Kovalyova	RUS	28.2.73	1		Krasnodar	18 May
	14.2 1.73 14.52 25.3		6.03 39.50 2:17.9					
5834	Regla	Cardenas	CUB	21.1.75	2	WJ	Lisboa	23 Jul
	13.92/+0.3 1.76 13.49 24.61/+0.3		6.06/+0.8 33.86 2:20.64					
5826	Jennifer	Kelly	GBR	20.6.70	19	ECp A	Vénissieux	3 Jul
	14.46/+0.8 1.75 14.36 24.70/-0.3		6.02/-0.2 39.50 2:25.62					
	(70)							

Mark	Name		Nat	Born	Pos	Meet	Venue	Date
5803	Ingrid	Didden	BEL	27.6.68	6	ECpl	Bressanone	3 Jul
	14.35/-0.6 1.72 13.39 26.20/-2.9		5.83/0.0 50.04 2:21.55					
5801	Yelena	Bolkun	UKR	26.2.67	2		Simferopol	8 May
	13.8 1.75 12.48 24.1		5.89 37.94 2:19.5					
5795 w	Marjolijn	Van Elk	NED	2.9.69	2	NC	Eindhoven	5 Jun
	14.30 1.71 14.52 26.35		5.82/W 50.80 2:27.45					
5786		Ma Chun-ping	TPE	3.8.71	3	AsiG	Hiroshima	11 Oct
	14.32 1.84 12.57 25.42		5.86 41.78 2:24.19					
5779	Karin	Specht	GER	23.6.74	21	ECp A	Vénissieux	3 Jul
	13.82/+1.7 1.78 11.87 25.14/+1.5		5.86/-0.3 41.46 2:22.27					
5770	Natalya	Sazanovich	BLR	15.8.73	7	ECpl	Bressanone	3 Jul
	14.42/-1.0 1.72 13.89 25.01/-0.4		6.11/+0.3 36.24 2:20.24					
5770	Svetlana	Kazanina	KZK	31.10.71	1	NC	Almaty	17 Sep
	14.97 1.83 12.81 26.50		6.02 45.10 2:20.43					
5766	Anoek	van Diessen	NED	20.2.73	8	ECpl	Bressanone	3 Jul
	14.34/0.0 1.84 11.77 25.28/+0.1		5.73/+0.6 38.88 2:15.54					
5757	Natalya	Timofeyeva	RUS	72	2		Krasnodar	18 May
	13.3 1.76 10.98 24.6		6.08 34.54 2:17.7 =5760					
5753		Wu Shuzhen	CHN	27.8.73	7	NC	Beijing	2 Jun
	14.04 1.71 13.21 25.75		5.65 41.28 2:13.29					
	(80)							
5753	Veronika	Ryzhova	RUS	3.2.68	9	NC	Vladimir	17 Jun
	13.72 1.76 14.27 25.30		6.32 27.46 2:24.93					
5750	Najuma	Fletcher	GUY	31.5.74	3	NCAA	Boise	2 Jun
	13.84 1.79 10.91 24.39		6.23 32.36 2:21.14					
5746	Yelena	Nikolyuk	UKR	2.10.72	3		Simferopol	8 May
	14.2 1.81 13.10 24.5		5.80 33.00 2:16.4					
5746	Clare	Look-Jaeger	USA	17.6.66	6	NC	Knoxville	15 Jun
	13.53 1.84 11.85 25.88		5.74 41.12 2:14.96					
5745	Sigrid	Kirchmann	AUT	29.3.66	1	NC	Ried	4 Sep
	14.71 190 12.48 26.61		5.92 50.18 2:34.99					
5734		Fu Xiuhong	CHN	6.5.70	8	NC	Beijing	2 Jun
	14.13 1.77 13.36 26.04		5.92 35.82 2:16.22					
5729	Guilaine	Belpérin	FRA	5.3.71	22	ECp A	Vénissieux	3 Jul
	13.94/+1.5 1.84 11.86 25.11/-0.3		5.85/+0.8 34.66 2:20.66					
5724	Astrid	Retzke	GER	13.7.73	1		Bad Oeynhausen	7 Aug
	14.32/+0.5 1.72 12.78 25.48/+3.2		5.87/-1.0 45.08 2:23.24					
5723	Patricia	Nadler	SUI	13.2.69	18		Götzis	29 May
	14.24/-0.3 1.66 11.60 25.32/+1.5		6.16/+3.6 41.52 2:15.59					
5722	Tatyana	Gordeyeva	RUS	3.6.73	2	NC-23	Vladimir	17 Jun
	14.11 1.70 12.56 25.27		6.04 42.30 2:23.93					
	(90)							
5710	Yurka	Khristova	BUL	19.1.68	1	Balk	Trikala	10 Jul
	14.19 1.81 11.91 25.48		6.12 38.66 2:26.08					
5710	Svetlana	Mikhailova	KZK	18.1.74	2	NC	Almaty	17 Sep
	14.48 1.80 12.50 25.87		6.16 39.40 2:24.64					
5694	Sabine	Smieja	GER	23.6.71	1		Illertissen	17 Jul
	14.39/-2.0 1.76 11.15 25.51/0.0		5.95/-0.8 41.30 2:16.61					
5693A	Chrisna	Oosthuizen	RSA	1.3.71	1	NC	Secunda	7 May
	14.44/-1.3 1.60 12.98 25.08/-1.1		6.09/+1.9 48.24 2:26.92					
5683	Elzbieta	Raczka	POL	19.11.70	23	ECp A	Vénissieux	3 Jul
	14.11/+1.7 1.78 12.20 25.52/-1.1		5.86/+2.0 42.92 2:29.97					
5671	Vikki	Schofield	GBR	29.12.72	24	ECp A	Vénissieux	3 Jul
	14.06/+1.8 1.72 11.84 25.04/-1.1		6.07/+1.6 38.16 2:22.83					
5665 w	Oluchi	Elechi	NGR	24.6.68	1	NCAA II	Raleigh	27 May
5656	Inga	Michailova	LIT	6.3.66	4		Valladolid	8 May
	14.00/-2.4 1.80 12.33 25.27/+2.7		6.12/+3.4 37.54 2:23.61					
5651	Terry	Roy	USA	26.1.73	2	USOF	Edwardsville	9 Jul
	15,12 1.74 14.10 25.76		5.58 42.90 2:17.55					
5650	Alena	Vlasova	KZK	2.12.69	1		Almaty	22 May
	14.40 1.62 14.83 24.62		5.93 34.30 2:19.50					
5650	Kylie	Coombe	AUS	22.12.67	19		Götzis	29 May
	13.97/+0.9 1.69 12.75 24.81/+2.5		5.61/+1.6 38.88 2:19.38					
	(101)							

Mark	Name		Nat	Born	Date
5641	Kim	Vanderhoek	CAN	70	13 Jul
5635	Silke	Knut	GER	72	3 Sep
5630	Zita	Bálint	HUN	71	3 Jul
5623	Laris	Tarasyuk	RUS	70	17 Jun
5620 w	Peggy	Odita	USA	68	29 May
5616	Diana	Koritskaya	RUS	75	23 Jul
5614	Gesine	Schmidt	GER	71	3 Sep
5613	Yelena	Nikolyuk	UKR	72	28 May

Mark	Name		Nat	Born	Date
5609	Maryse	Maury	FRA	64	29 May
5604	Deborah	den Boer	NED	75	23 Jul
5597A	Maralize	Visser	RSA	74	7 May
5596	Vera	Ináncsi	HUN	75	23 Jul
5587	Pila	Peltosaari	FIN	73	3 Jul
5586	Deborah	Feltrin	ITA	76	3 Jul
5586	Gertrud	Bacher	ITA	71	4 Sep
5576	Galina	Nikanorova	RUS	73	17 Jun
5567	Nicole	Hudson	USA	70	15 Apr
5567	Marvena	Almond	USA	73	9 Jul
5564	Annelies	De Meester	BEL	76	21 Aug
5563	Crystal	Young	USA	65	25 May
5560	Immaculada	Clopes	ESP	68	3 Jul
5560	Tatyana	Shutayeva	UKR	71	24 Jul
5557	Dagmar	Urbánková	TCH	62	3 Jul
5543	Gabriela	Groth	GER	75	14 May
5540	Francesca	Delon	ITA	73	26 Jun
5530	Helena	Vinarová	TCH	74	3 Jul
5527	Carmel	Corbett	NZL	72	22 May
5526	Birgit	Bauer	GER	70	17 Jul
5512	Rebecca	Grube	USA	72	26 Mar
5512		Wang Xiu	CHN	—	5 May
5501	Åsa	Hallström	SWE	72	3 Jul
	(132)				
Auto timed best					
5613	Yelena	Nikolyuk	UKR	72	28 May
5613	Yelena	Bolkun	UKR	67	5 Jun

4 X 100 METRES RELAY

Mark	Team	Pos	Meet	Venue	Date
42.45	USA Gaines, Guidry, Taplin, Young	1	vAFR	Durham	13 Aug
42.90	GER Paschke, Zipp, Knoll, Lichtenhagen	1	EC	Helsinki	13 Aug
42.92	NGR (Africa) Idehen, Tombiri, Opara-Thompson, Onyali	1	WCp	London	11 Sep
42.93	All-Stars Bowles/USA, Echols/USA, McDonald/JAM, Duhaney/USA	1		Tempe	2 Apr
42.94	GER Paschke, Zipp, Knoll, Lichtenhagen	1h1	EC	Helsinki	13 Aug
42.96	RUS Anisimova, Malchugina, Trandenkova, Privalova	2	EC	Helsinki	13 Aug
42.98	USA Taplin, Young, Collins, Torrence	1	GWG	St Peterburg	29 Jul
42.99	NGR Idehen, Tombiri, Opara-Thompson, Onyali	1	CG	Victoria	28 Aug
43.00	BUL D Dimitrova, Nuneva, S Dimitrova, Pendareva	3	EC	Helsinki	13 Aug
43.09	NGR (Africa) Idehen, Tombiri, Opara-Thompson, Onyali	2	vUSA	Durham	13 Aug
43.22	GER Philipp, Lichtenhagen, Knoll, Paschke	2	WCp	London	11 Sep
43.25	Louisiana State Un (USA) Parris/JAM, Hill, Feagin, Taplin	1	TexR	Austin	9 Apr
43.26	Louisiana State Un (USA) Parris/JAM, Hill, Feagin, Taplin	1	NCAA	Boise	3 Jun
43.35	USA Twiggs, Vereen, Harris, Gaines	1	vGBR	Gateshead	20 Jul
43.36	RUS Anisimova, Malchugina, Trandenkova, Leshcheva	1h2	EC	Helsinki	13 Aug
43.36	Oceania Miers, Freeman, Gainsford/AUS, Seymour/NZL	3	WCp	London	11 Sep
43.37	CUB Ferrer, López, Duporty, Allen	2	GWG	St Peterburg	29 Jul
43.38	UKR I Slyusar, Fomenko, Kravchenko, Tarnopolskaya	1	ECp	Birmingham	25 Jun
43.43	AUS Miers, Freeman, Gainsford, Sambell	2	CG	Victoria	28 Aug
43.46	GBR Douglas, Merry, Jacobs, Thomas	2	ECp	Birmingham	25 Jun
43.46	England (GBR) Douglas, McLeod, Jacobs, Thomas	3	CG	Victoria	28 Aug
	(21/8)				
43.51	JAM Freeman, Rose, Frazer, Duhaney	4	CG	Victoria	28 Aug
43.63	CHN Chen Yan, Liu Xiaomei, Chen Zhaojing, Huang Xiaoyan	4	WCp	London	11 Sep
	(10)				
43.65	FRA Girard, Sidibé, Ficher, Combe	1	FraG	Bondoufle	13 Jul
43.81	NED Elissen, Poelman, de Lange, Bogaards	6	EC	Helsinki	13 Aug
43.96	FIN Pirttimaa, Leveelahti, Hernesniemi, Salmela	7	EC	Helsinki	13 Aug
44.36	ITA Tuzzi, Ardissone, Balzani, Gallina	5h2	EC	Helsinki	13 Aug
44.39	SUI Donders, Haug, Wüest, Anliker-Aebi	1		Luzern	29 Jun
44.46	THA Suajongprue, Dokduang, Chommuak, Incharoen	2	AsiG	Hiroshima	16 Oct
44.57	JPN Ito, Kitada, Kakinuma, Kaneko	3	AsiG	Hiroshima	16 Oct
44.58	TPE Kao Yuh-Chuan, Chen Shu-Chen, Hsu Pei-chin, Wang Huei-Chen	4	AsiG	Hiroshima	16 Oct
44.63	AUT Hölzl, Tröger, Auer, Knoll-Mayr	2	GP II	Linz	4 Jul
44.64	BLR Zhuk, Vinogradova, Starinskaya, Molchan	5	ECp	Birmingham	25 Jun
	(20)				
44.67	GRE Tsoni, Patsou, Vasarmidou, Koffa	1	ECp II/1	Dublin	11 Jun
44.77	TCH Musinská, Klapácová, Nemcová, Suchovská	3	ECp I	Valencia	11 Jun
44.81	IND Usha, Panda, Saramma, Shyla	5	AsiG	Hiroshima	16 Oct
44.87	COL Mera, Restrepo, Rodriguez, Brack	1	IbAm	Mar del Plata	27 Oct
44.88	KZK Gridasova, Vyazova, Serdyuk, Shishigina	4	GWG	St Peterburg	29 Jul
44.89	BAH Clarke, Ferguson, D Davis, P Davis	5	CG	Victoria	28 Aug
44.91	NOR Miller, Brunner, Wise, Seymour	2	ECp II	Istanbul	11 Jun
44.97	SRI Samandeepika, Dharsha, Jayasinghe, Kulawansa	6	AsiG	Hiroshima	16 Oct
44.98	NZL	2		Hobart	26 Feb
45.01	SWE Kronberg, Staafgård, Olofsson, Johansson	2	vFIN	Stockholm	27 Aug
	(30)				

Mark	Team	Date
45.05	POL	11 Jun
45.09	CAN	13 Jul
45.11	ESP	13 Aug
45.18A	RSA (Transvaal Juniors)	7 May
45.22	MAD	13 Jul
45.25	BRA (Funilense)	13 Aug
45.46	SLO	11 Jun
45.55	HUN (Honved Budapest)	19 Jun
45.60	IRL	11 Jun
45.72	ROM u23	30 Jul
45.72	GHA	28 Aug
45.81	POR	12 Jun
45.81	CIV	29 Jun
Hand timed:		
45.3	GHA	25 Jun

Mark		Name	Nat	Born	Pos	Meet	Venue	Date

4 X 200 METRES RELAY

Mark	Nat	Name	Pos	Meet	Venue	Date
1:30.97		All-Stars Bowles, E chols, McDonald/JAM, Duhaney/JAM	1		Tempe	2 Apr
1:32.55		Louisiana State Un. (USA) D Hill, Boone, Hall, Taplin	1r2	PennR	Philadelphia	30 Apr
1:33.10		Arizona State Un. T Akinremi/NGR, Campbell/USA, C Akinremi/NGR, Parker/USA	2		Tempe	2 Apr
Other national tems						
1:33.20i	SWE	Johansson, Holmqvist, Cronberg, Staafgård	1	v FIN	Vaxjö	6 Mar
1:33.33i	RUS	Malchugina, Voronova, Bogoslovskaya, Ruzina	1	v GBR	Glasgow	29 Jan

4 X 400 METRES RELAY

Mark	Nat	Name	Pos	Meet	Venue	Date
3:22.27	USA	Kaiser-Brown, Malone, Miles, Collins	1	GWG	St Peterburg	29 Jul
3:22.34	FRA	Landre, Dorsile, Elien, Pérec	1	EC	Helsinki	14 Aug
3:24.06	RUS	Khrushchelyova, Andreyeva, Zakharova, Goncharenko	2	EC	Helsinki	14 Aug
3:24.10	GER	Janke, Rohländer, Meissner, Rücker	3	EC	Helsinki	14 Aug
3:24.14	GBR	Neef, Keough, Smith, Gunnell	4	EC	Helsinki	14 Aug
3:25.00	RUS	Andreyeva, Golesheva, Ruzina, Zakharova	2	GWG	St Peterburg	29 Jul
3:26.35	CUB	Bonne, Duporty, Morales, McLeon	3	GWG	St Peterburg	29 Jul
3:26.63	USA	Graham, Buford, Collins, Kaiser-Brown	1	vAFR	Durham	12 Aug
3:26.99	USA	T Williams, Stevens, Malone, Kaiser-Brown	1	vGBR	Gateskhead	20 Aug
3:27.06	GBR	(England) Smith, Goddard, Keough, Gunnell	1	CG	Victoria	28 Aug
3:27.25	GBR	Neef, Keough, Smith, Gunnell	1h1	EC	Helsinki	14 Aug
3:27.33	GBR	Neef, Goddard, Smith, Gunnell	1	ECp	Birmingham	26 Jun
3:27.36	GBR	Smith, Keough, Neef, Gunnell	1	WCp	London	9 Sep
3:27.50	GER	Janke, Rohländer, Kisabaka, Rücker	2h1	EC	Helsinki	13 Aug
3:27.59	GER	Janke, Rohländer, Meissner, Rücker	2	WCp	London	9 Sep
3:27.63	Africa	Afolabi/NGR, Paulino/MOZ, Bidouane/MAR, Yusuf/NGR	2	vUSA	Durham	12 Aug
3:27.63	JAM	R Campbell, Hemmings, Turner, Richards	2	CG	Victoria	28 Aug
3:27.78	GER	Schönenberger, Rohländer, Hagenmüller, Meissner	2	ECp	Birmingham	26 Jun
3:27.91	Americas	McLeon/CUB, Richards/JAM, Bonne/JAM, Duporty/JAM	3	WCp	London	9 Sep
3:27.95	TCH	Kostoválová, Benesová, Suchovská, Formanová	5	EC	Helsinki	14 Aug
	(20/8)					
3:28.78	SUI	Anliker-Aebi, Lüthi, Grossenbacher, Protti	6	EC	Helsinki	14 Aug
3:29.11	CHN	Leng Xueyan, Zhang Hengyun, Cao Chunying, Ma Yuqin	1	AsiG	Hiroshima	16 Oct
	(10)					
3:29.75	POL	Grzywocz, Warnicka, Pachut, Kilinska	7	EC	Helsinki	14 Aug
3:31.05	UKR	Manuilova, Miloserdova, Koshchey, Nasonkina	4	ECp	Birmingham	26 Jun
3:31.63	AUS	(Oceania) Naylor, Collins, Hanigan, Freeman	7	WCp	London	10 Sep
3:31.78	FIN	Halkkonen, Suomi, Jääskeläinen, Finell	4h1	EC	Helsinki	13 Aug
3:32.36	SWE	Westén, Holmqvist, Staafgård, Johansson	4h2	EC	Helsinki	13 Aug
3:32.52	CAN	Yakiwchuk, Bowen, Duprey, Crooks	3	CG	Victoria	28 Aug
3:33.25	BLR	Kozak, Ignatyuk, Kurochkina, Kuprianovich	6	ECp	Birmingham	26 Jun
3:33.26	IND		1		Pune	13 Sep
3:33.31	ITA	Carbone, Spuri, De Angeli, Perpoli	5h2	EC	Helsinki	13 Aug
3:33.39	ROM	Carutasu, Itcou, Vizitiu, Nedelcu	7	ECp	Birmingham	26 Jun
	(20)					
3:35.35	COL	Rodriguez, Mera, Robledo, Restrepo	1	IbAm	Mar del Plata	30 Oct
3:36.53	BAH	Ferguson, Williams, Sear, Rolle	2	Carif	Bridgetown	4 Apr
3:36.74	LIT	Minina, Matuseviciene, Mracinevici, Ambraziene	5	ECp I	Valencia	12 Jun
3:37.76	THA	Srimek, Watanasin, Sang-Nguen, Phimphoo	3	AsiG	Hiroshima	16 Oct
3:37.82A	RSA		1	NC	Secunda	7 May
3:37.91	NED	Pieck, Bogaards, de, Vries, Goossens	1	ECp II	Dublin	12 Jun
3:38.17	HUN	Szekeres, Dóczi, Kurucz, Mádai	2	EP-B	Ljubljana	12 Jun
3:38.18	SLO	Perc, Lopatic, Langerholc, Gorjup	3	EP-B	Ljubljana	12 Jun
3:38.20	ESP	Lacambra, Lluch, Reyes, Lahoz	8	ECp	Birmingham	26 Jun
3:38.61	BRA	Figueiredo, Souza, Lima, Castro	2	IbAm	Mar del Plata	30 Oct
	(30)					

3:39.43BUL	12 Jun	3:40.97BEL	12 Jun	3:42.54BAR	24 Apr	3:44.79NZL	6 Mar
3:39.53NOR	12 Jun	3:41.40CHI	30 Oct	3:43.32TRI	24 Apr	3:44.83AUT	12 Jun
3:39.74GRE	10 Jul	3:41.48CIV	13 Jul	3:43.69INA	19 Sep	3:44.99DEN	12 Jun
3:40.74JPN	16 Oct	3:41.54TPE		3:44.70NGR	10 Jun		

Disqualified for baulking opponents

Mark	Nat	Name	Pos	Meet	Venue	Date
3:26.84	AUS	Naylor, Hanigan, Poetschka, Freeman	(1)	CG	Victoria	28 Aug

4 X 800 METRES RELAY

Mark	Nat	Name	Pos	Meet	Venue	Date
8:18.71	RUS	Zaytseva, Kuznyetsova, Afanasyeva, Podkopayeva	1		Moskva	4 Feb
8:23.36	RUS B	Goncharova, Maryina, Betekhtina, Vasilevskaya	2		Moskva	4 Feb

4 X 1500 METRES RELAY

Mark	Name	Pos	Venue	Date
17:37.51	Villanova Un. Zajac/USA, Rhines/USA, Molley/IRL, Spies/USA	1	PennR Philadelphia	29 Apr
17:40.43	Michigan Un. Harvey/CAN, McClimon, Szabo, Babcock/CAN	2	PennR Philadelphia	29 Apr
17:54.37	USA (Reebok Enclave) Stanmeyer, Rabush, Goddard, Speights	1	Raleigh	26 Mar

3000 METRES WALK

Mark	Name		Nat	Born	Pos	Meet	Venue	Date
12:01.71	Kerry	Saxby-Junna	AUS	2.6.61	1		Brisbane	5 Feb
12:02.35		Saxby-Junna			1	NEC	Melbourne	24 Feb
12:02.74	Sari	Essayah	FIN	21.2.67	1		Viitarsaari	14 Jun
12:07.00		Essayah			1		Kouruu	24 Jun
12:14.62		Essayah			1		Luumäki	12 Jun
12:15.48	Elisabeta	Perrone	ITA	9.7.68	1		Bologna	2 Sep
	(6/3)							
12:22.09	Gabrielle	Blythe	AUS	9.3.69	2	NEC	Melbourne	24 Feb
12:23.0+	Beate	Gummelt	GER	4.2.68	1	NC	Erfurt	2 Jul
12:26.61	Annarita	Sidoti	ITA	25.7.69	2		Bologna	2 Sep
12:26.87	Anne	Manning	AUS	13.11.59	3	NEC	Melbourne	24 Feb
12:28.80	Ileana	Salvador	ITA	16.1.62	3		Bologna	2 Sep
12:29.10+	Olimpiada	Ivanova	RUS	5.5.70	1	GWG	St Peterburg	26 Jul
12:29.44+	Yelena	Sayko	RUS	24.12.67	2	GWG	St Peterburg	26 Jul
	(10)							
12:31.65	Michaela	Hafner	ITA	2.8.73	4		Bologna	2 Sep

Mark	Name		Nat	Born	Date
12:35.57+	Katarzyna	Radtke	POL	69	23 Jul
12:38.92+	Tamara	Kovalenko	RUS	64	26 Jul
12:39.34+		Kong Yan	CHN	75	26 Jul
12:41.33	Ruta	Schwoche	GER	70	19 Jul
12:41.52+	Yulia	Odzilyayeva	RUS	70	26 Jul
12:41.93+	Nadezhda	Ryashkina	RUS	67	26 Jul
12:45.08	Yelena	Arshintseva	RUS	71	2 Sep
12:45.41	Rimma	Makarova	RUS	63	12 Jun
12:47.44+	Lidiya	Fesenko	RUS	62	26 Jul
12:48.56	Yelena	Panfilova	RUS	60	27 May
12:49.7	Simone	Thust	GER	71	6 May

Indoors

Mark	Name		Nat	Born	Pos	Meet	Venue	Date
11:54.32	Annarita	Sidoti	ITA	25.7.69	1	EI	Paris	12 Mar
11:56.01	Beate	Gummelt	GER	4.2.68	2	EI	Paris	12 Mar
11:57.48	Yelena	Arshintseva	RUS	5.4.71	3	EI	Paris	12 Mar
11:57.49	Yelena	Nikolayeva	RUS	1.2.66	4	EI	Paris	12 Mar
12:01.41		Sidoti			1	NC	Genova	12 Feb
12:01.81		Arshintseva			1	NC	Lipetsk	26 Feb
12:02.25		Nikoleyeva			2	NC	Lipetsk	26 Feb
12:04.46	Leonarda	Yukhnevich	BLR	3.10.63	5	EI	Paris	12 Mar
12:06.24		Gummelt			1		Liévin	13 Feb
12:08.13		Arshintseva			1		Moskva	4 Feb
12:11.07	Yelena	Sayko	RUS	24.12.67	2		Moskva	4 Feb
12:11.45		Sayko			3	NC	Lipetsk	26 Feb
12:12.80		Essayah			6	EI	Paris	12 Mar
12:13.37		Gummelt			1	NC	Dortmund	26 Feb
12:14.6		Yukhnevich			1	NC	Minsk	5 Feb
12:14.35		Nikolayeva			2		Liévin	13 Feb
12:15.48	Olga	Leonenko	UKR	13.2.70	1	NC	Kiev	13 Feb
12:16.71		Perrone			1		Genova	5 Feb
12:16.83	Olimpiada	Ivanova	RUS	5.5.70	3		Moskva	4 Feb
12:17.91		Essayah			1		Jyväskylä	26 Feb
	(20/10)							
12:20.90	Tatyana	Ragozina	UKR	3.9.64	2	NC	Kiev	13 Feb
12:21.07	Larisa	Ramazanova	RUS	27.9.71	4		Moskva	4 Feb
12:21.63	Kathrin	Boyde	GER	4.12.70	8	EI	Paris	12 Mar
12:21.7	Susana	Feitor	POR	28.1.75	1	NC	Braga	19 Feb
12:24.04	Norica	Cimpean	ROM	22.3.72	9	EI	Paris	12 Mar
12:24.3	Valentina	Tsybulskaya	BLR	19.2.68	2	NC	Minsk	5 Feb
12:25.2	Irina	Stankina	RUS	25.3.77	1	NC-j	Chelyabinsk	4 Feb
12:30.24	Kamila	Holpuchová	TCH	27.9.73	5h1	EI	Paris	11 Mar

Mark	Name		Nat	Born	Date
12:35.32	Rossella	Giordano	ITA	72	12 Feb
12:36.17	Rimma	Makarova	RUS	63	19 Feb
12:38.71	Olga	Kuznetsova	RUS	71	19 Feb
12:39.08	Lidiya	Fesenko	RUS	61	26 Feb
12:40.48	Mária	Rosza	HUN	67	5 Feb
12:42.43	Nadezhda	Ryashkina	RUS	67	26 Feb
12:42.68	Yuko	Sato	JPN	71	11 Feb
12:42.99	Tamara	Kovalenko	RUS	64	4 Feb
12:43.5	Natalya	Misyulya	BLR	66	5 Feb
12:43.95	Natalya	Trofimova	RUS	75	19 Feb
12:45.01	Yuka	Mitsumori	JPN	72	11 Feb
12:45.77	Cristiana	Pellino	ITA	70	12 Feb
12:46.24	Yuka	Kamioka	JPN	75	11 Feb
12:47.80	Maria	Artynyuk	RUS	66	20 Feb
12:49.00	Emi	Hayashi	JPN	72	11 Feb

Mark	Name		Nat	Born	Pos	Meet	Venue	Date

5000 METRES WALK

Mark	Name		Nat	Born	Pos	Meet	Venue	Date
20:28.62	Sari	Essayah	FIN	21.2.67	1	NC	Tuusula	9 Jul
20:34.76		Essayah			1		Kokemäki	3 Jul
20:40.06	Kerry	Saxby-Junna	AUS	2.6.61	1		Sydney	20 Feb
20:45.03		Saxby-Junna			1	NC	Sydney	11 Mar
20:46.9	Annarita	Sidoti	ITA	25.7.69	1		Messina	16 Apr
20:49.39	Elsabetta	Perrone	ITA	9.7.68	1	NC	Napoli	3 Jul
20:54.39		Perrone			1		Formia	4 Jun
20:56.10+	Olimpiada	Ivanova	RUS	5.5.70	1	GWG	St Peterburg	26 Jul
20:59.82+	Yelena	Sayko	RUS	24.12.67	2	GWG	St Peterburg	26 Jul
21:05.41	Irina	Stankina	RUS	25.3.77	1	WJ	Lisboa	23 Jul
21:05.53	Katarzyna	Radtke	POL	31.8.69	1	NC	Sopot	23 Jul
21:06.0	Susana	Feitor	POR	28.1.75	1	SGP	Fana	7 May
21:06.44+		Saxby-Junna			3	GWG	St Peterburg	26 Jul
21:06.76		Essayah			4	GWG	St Peterburg	26 Jul
21:07.32		Perrone			1		Vigevano	21 May
21:12.87		Feitor			2	WJ	Lisboa	23 Jul
21:15.8 +		Gu Yan	CHN	17.3.74	1	SGP	Fana	7 May
21:17.0+		Perrone			2+	SGP	Fana	7 May
21:19.00	Beate	Gummelt	GER	4.2.68	1	NC	Erfurt	2 Jul
21:23.20+		Kong Yan	CHN	5.4.71	5	GWG	St Peterburg	26 Jul
	(20/12)							
21:24.71	Natalya	Trofimova	RUS	17.1.75	3	WJ	Lisboa	23 Jul
21:25.6mx	Anne	Manning	AUS	13.11.59	1	mix	Sydney	12 Feb
	21:46.43				2	NC	Sydney	11 Mar
21:25.62+	Tamara	Kovalenko	RUS	5.6.64	6	GWG	St Peterburg	26 Jul
21:30.9mx	Ileana	Salvador	ITA	16.1.62	1	mix	Canberra	18 Jan
	22:17.91					v2N	Cagliari	18 Sep
21:30.96	Cristiana	Pellino	ITA	21.9.70	2		Formia	4 Jun
21:34.20+	Nadezhda	Ryashkina	RUS	22.1.67	7	GWG	St Peterburg	26 Jul
21:36.74+	Yulia	Odzhilayeva	RUS	.70	8	GWG	St Peterburg	26 Jul
21:37.0 +		Liu Hongyu	CHN	1.12.75	3	SGP	Fana	7 May
	(20)							
21:41.2	Rimma	Makarova	RUS	25.2.63	1		St Peterburg	12 May
21:41.47	Maria	Vascó	ESP	26.12.75	4	WJ	Lisboa	23 Jul
21:43.2	Kathrin	Boyde	GER	4.12.70	1		Bad Rappenau	28 May
21:50.0mx	Gabrielle	Blythe	AUS	9.3.69	2	mx	Canberra	18 Jan
	22:07.27				3	NC	Sydney	11 Mar
21:51.0	Yelena	Panfilova	RUS	9.10.60	1		St Peterburg	28 May
21:51.72+	Lidia	Fesenko	RUS	25.11.61	9	GWG	St Peterburg	26 Jul
21:52.5	Larisa	Matureyeva	RUS	7.3.71	2		St Peterburg	28 May
21:52.96	Rossella	Giordano	ITA	1.12.72	3		Formia	4 Jun
21:53.86	Emi	Hayashi	JPN	9.7.72	1		Tokyo	21 May
21:58.64+	Leonarda	Yukhnevich	BLR	3.10.63	10	GWG	St Peterburg	26 Jul
	(30)							
22:02.2	Olga	Leonenko	UKR	13.2.70	1		Alushta	1 Mar
22:02.75	Michaela	Hafner	ITA	2.8.73	2	NC	Napoli	3 Jul
22:03.6	Grazia	Orsani	ITA	11.6.69	1		Portici	13 Jul
22:03.69		Song Lijuan	CHN	9.2.75	5	WJ	Lisboa	23 Jul
22:05.23	Yuka	Mitsumori	JPN	8.1.72	2		Nagoya	2 Nov
22:05.48	Valentina	Savchuk	UKR	19.1.75	1	v2N23	Lvov	4 Sep
22:05.76	Tatyana	Gudkova	RUS	23.12.77	1	v3N-j	Warszawa	18 Jun
22:06.47	Yuka	Kamioka	JPN	28.5.75	6	WJ	Lisboa	23 Jul
22:07.83	Veronica	Budileanu	ROM	27.2.76	2	v2N23	Lvov	4 Sep
22:08.0 *	Jane	Saville	AUS	12.2.74	mx		Sydney	12 Feb
	22:36.72				3		Sydney	20 Feb
	(40)							
22:11.6	Maribel	Rebollo	MEX	14.3.76	1	CAC-j	Port of Spain	8 Jul
22:14.52	Olga	Panferova	RUS	21.8.77	2	NC-j	Yaroslavl	21 May
22:15.5	Jane	Barbour	AUS	27.7.66	1		Adelaide	16 Feb
22:16.78	Michelle	Rohl	USA	12.11.65	11	GWG	St Peterburg	26 Jul
22:17.13	Yuko	Sato	JPN	22.11.71	3		Nagoya	2 Nov
22:17.46	Miwako	Tsukada	JPN	1.6.73	4		Nagoya	2 Nov
22:17.6	Larisa	Matveyeva	RUS	71	2		St Peterburg	12 May
22:17.8	Tatyana	Ragozina	UKR	13.2.70	2		Alushta	1 Mar
22:19.7	Jenny	Billington	AUS	20.4.67	mx		Brisbane	20 Feb
22:20.93	Teresa	Letherby	AUS	5.4.72	4	NC	Sydney	11 Mar
	(50)							

Mark	First	Name	Nat	Born	Pos	Meet	Venue	Date
22:22.64	Kjersti	Tysse	NOR	18.1.72	1	NC	Jessheim	21 Aug
22:23.31	Eva	Pérez	ESP	18.7.75	7	WJ	Lisboa	23 Jul
22:24.62	Tanoko	Uchida	JPN	6.8.72	4		Nagoya	2 Nov
22:24.79	Mónika	Pesti	HUN	27.6.75	9	WJ	Lisboa	23 Jul
22:25.39	Marta	Zukowska	POL	4.6.72	1		Slubice	18 Jun
22:30.29	Erica	Alfridi	ITA	22.2.68	4	NC	Napoli	3 Jul
22:33.9	Sandy	Leddin	GER	1.11.70	1		Erfurt	4 Jun
22:35.0	Yelena	Veremeychuk	UKR	13.10.59	1			9 Jul
22:36 +	Rosario	Sánchez	MEX	.71	4=	SGP	Fana	7 May
22:36 +	Eva	Machuka	MEX	14.1.70	4=	SGP	Fana	7 May
	(60)							
22:37.0 *	Wendy	Muldoon	AUS	27.5.71	mx		Melbourne	1 Dec
22:37.31	Doreen	Sellenriek	GER	20.8.73	3	NC	Erfurt	2 Jul
22:40.0	Lisa	Langford	GBR	15.3.67	1		Coventry	19 Jul

Mark	First	Name	Nat	Born	Date
22:41.94	Hanne	Liland	NOR	69	21 Aug
22:44.0	Alison	Baker	CAN	64	18 Jan
22:44.01	Santa	Compagnoni	ITA	63	3 Jul
22:47.2	Simone	Wolowiec	AUS	74	3 Feb
	22:50.82				11 Mar
22:47.64	Miki	Itakura	JPN	75	23 Apr
22:48.00	Sofia	Avoila	POR	76	23 Jul
22:48.24	Yelena	Alekseyeva	RUS	77	21 May
	21:59.8 ?				16 Apr
22:48.38	Rie	Mitsumori	JPN	74	22 May
22:48.42	Natalie	Saville	AUS	78	23 Jul
22:49.04	Jana	Weidemann	GER	76	23 Jul
22:50.6	Ruta	Schwoche	GER	70	4 Jun
22:54.8	Cheryl	Webb	AUS	76	12 Feb
22:54.92	Hidoko	Sakai	JPN	65	2 Nov

Indoors

Mark	First	Name	Nat	Born	Pos	Meet	Venue	Date
21:51.60	Nadezhda	Ryashkina	RUS	22.1.67	2		Moskva	26 Jan
22:07.57	Zinaida	Sviridenko	RUS	24.12.68	4		Moskva	26 Jan
22:30.07	Tatyana	Mironova	RUS	31.12.68	7		Moskva	26 Jan

5 km walk - road - where superior to track times

Mark	First	Name	Nat	Born	Pos	Meet	Venue	Date
20:48	Yelena	Nikolayeva	RUS	1.2.66	1		L'Hospitalet	29 May
21:45	Ruta	Schwoche	GER	27.2.70	1		Eisenach	11 Jun
21:46+	Yelena	Arshintseva	RUS	5.4.71	3		Yaroslavl	22 May
21:53	Tatyana	Gudkova	RUS	23.12.77	3		Livorno	12 Jun
21:54+	Natalya	Misyulya	BLR	12.2.66	8=	EC	Helsinki	9 Aug
21:54+	Tatyana	Ragozina	UKR	3.9.64	8=	EC	Helsinki	9 Aug
21:54+	Kjersti	Tysse	NOR	18.1.72	8=	EC	Helsinki	9 Aug
21:56+	Valentina	Tsybulskaya	BLR	9.2.68	14	EC	Helsinki	9 Aug
21:58	Encarnacion	Granados	ESP	30.1.72	1		El Prat	17 Apr
22:05	Mónika	Pesti	HUN	27.6.75	5		Livorno	12 Jun
22:09	Olga	Panferova	RUS	21.8.77	6		Livorno	12 Jun
22:10	Janice	McCaffrey	CAN	20.10.59	4		L'Hospitalet	29 May
22:12	Tina	Poitras	CAN	5.10.70	5		L'Hospitalet	29 May
22:19+	Miki	Itakura	JPN	1.8.75	1=	In 10k	Wajima	17 Apr
22:19+	Rie	Mitsumori	JPN	26.10.74	1=	In 10k	Wajima	17 Apr
22:24	Jana	Weidemann	GER	27.6.76	7		Livorno	12 Jun
22:28	Rosario	Sánchez	MEX	.71			L'Hospitalet	29 May
22:29	Dana	Pinkert	GER	26.1.76	8		Livorno	12 Jun
22:31	Maya	Sazanova	KZK	28.5.68	1		Trnava	28 May

Mark	First	Name	Nat	Born	Date
22:42+	Emilia	Cano	ESP	68	9 Aug
22:43	Alison	Baker	CAN	64	29 May
22:43	Yvonne	Anders	GER	76	12 Jun
22:45	Ivana	Brozmanová	SVK	69	28 May
22:45+	Vicky	Lupton	GBR	72	25 Aug
22:45+	Verity	Snook	GBR	70	25 Aug
22:47	Kamila	Holpuchová	TCH	73	23 Apr
22:48	Venera	Vasilyeva	RUS	76	26 Aug

10 KILOMETRES WALK

Mark	First	Name	Nat	Born	Pos	Meet	Venue	Date
41:38		Gao Hongmiao	CHN	8.7.72	1	NC	Beijing	7 Apr
41:46	Annarita	Sidoti	ITA	25.7.69	1		Livorno	12 Jun
42:15	Elisabeta	Perrone	ITA	9.7.68	2		Livorno	12 Jun
42:20		Gu Yan	CHN	17.3.74	2	NC	Beijing	7 Apr
42:30.31t	Olympiada	Ivanova	RUS	5.5.70	1	GWG	St Peterburg	26 Jul
42:31	Larisa	Ramazanova	RUS	27.9.71	3		Livorno	12 Jun
42:36	Beate	Gummelt	GER	4.2.68	4		Livorno	12 Jun
42:37	Sari	Essayah	FIN	21.2.67	1	EC	Helsinki	9 Aug
42:40	Yulia	Odzilyayeva	RUS	70	5		Livorno	12 Jun
42:43		Sidoti			2	EC	Helsinki	9 Aug
42:43	Yelena	Nikolayeva (10)	RUS	1.2.66	3	EC	Helsinki	9 Aug
42:43.23t	Yelena	Sayko	RUS	24.12.67	2	GWG	St Peterburg	26 Jul
42:45		Sidoti			1		Sesto S Giovanni	1 May
42:45.04t		Essayah			3	GWG	St Peterburg	26 Jul
42:49		Liu Hongyu	CHN	1.12.75	3	NC	Beijing	7 Apr
42:50	Tamara	Kovalenko	RUS	5.6.64	6		Livorno	12 Jun

Mark	Name		Nat	Born	Pos	Meet	Venue	Date
42:51.0t		Gu Yan			1	SGP	Fana	7 May
42:52		Nikolayeva			2		Sesto S Giovanni	1 May
42:53	Mária	Rosza	HUN	12.2.67	7		Livorno	12 Jun
42:55	Cristina	Pellino	ITA	21.9.70	8		Livorno	12 Jun
43:01		Li Chunxiu	CHN	.8.69	4	NC	Beijing	7 Apr
43:01	Yelena	Arshintseva	RUS	5.4.71	1	NC	Yaroslavl	22 May
43:03		Kong Yan	CHN	5.4.71	5	NC	Beijing	7 Apr
43:07		Arshintseva			9		Livorno	12 Jun
43:09		Nikolayeva			1		La Coruña	21 May
43:09		Kovalenko			2	NC	Yaroslavl	22 May
43:09	Kerry	Junna-Saxby	AUS	2.6.61	10		Livorno	12 Jun
43:10		Essayah			1		Eisenhüttenstadt	15 May
43:16	Katarzyna	Radtke	POL	31.8.69	2		Eisenhüttenstadt	15 May
43:16	Valentina	Tsybulskaya	BLR	17.3.68	1		Novopolotsk	21 May
	(30/21)							
43:26		Zhang Qinghua	CHN	6.2.73	6	NC	Beijing	7 Apr
43:29	Natalya	Misyulya	BLR	12.2.66	2		Novopolotsk	21 May
43:30	Susana	Feitor	POR	28.1.75	1		Grandola	15 Jan
43:41		Li Jingxue	CHN	10.2.70	7	NC	Beijing	7 Apr
43:41	Kathrin	Boyde	GER	4.10.70	11		Livorno	12 Jun
44:00		Feng Haixia	CHN	73	8	NC	Beijing	7 Apr
44:15	Tatyana	Ragozina	UKR	3.9.64	10	EC	Helsinki	9 Aug
44:15.76t	Nadezhda	Ryashkina	RUS	22.1.67	7	GWG	St Peterburg	26 Jul
44:17	Anikó	Szebenszky	HUN	12.8.65	2		Hildesheim	28 Aug
	(30)							
44:18	Natalya	Trofimova	RUS	17.1.75	1	NC 23	Yaroslavl	22 May
44:20	Rossella	Giordano	ITA	1.12.72	12		Livorno	12 Jun
44:25		Wei Linkun	CHN	.12.75	9	NC	Beijing	7 Apr
44:25	Ruta	Schwoche	GER	27.2.70	3		Hildesheim	28 Aug
44:35	Encarna	Granados	ESP	30.1.72	13		Livorno	12 Jun
44:37	Anne	Manning	AUS	13.11.59	2	CG	Victoria	25 Aug
44:38	Olga	Leonenko	UKR	13.2.70	2		Makachevo	22 May
44:41.42t	Lidiya	Fesenko	RUS	25.11.61	8	GWG	St Peterburg	26 Jul
44:41.87t	Michelle	Rohl	USA	12.11.65	9	GWG	St Peterburg	26 Jul
44:44	Yuko	Sato	JPN	23.1.68	1		Wajima	17 Apr
	(40)							
44:44	Simone	Thust	GER	22.9.71	14		Livorno	12 Jun
44:46	Emi	Hayashi	JPN	9.7.72	2		Wajima	17 Apr
44:50	Kamila	Holpuchová	TCH	27.9.73	3		Dudince	27 Mar
44:51	Michaela	Hafner	ITA	2.8.73	15		Livorno	12 Jun
44:51	Ileana	Salvador	ITA	16.1.62	11	EC	Helsinki	9 Aug
44:53	Miki	Itakura	JPN	1.8.75	3		Wajima	17 Apr
44:53.0t	Rosario	Sánchez	MEX	.71	4	SGP	Fana	7 May
44:53	Ildikó	Ilyés	HUN	3.7.66	16		Livorno	12 Jun
44:54	Janice	McCaffrey	CAN	20.10.59	3	CG	Victoria	25 Aug
44:59.5t	Eva	Machuca	MEX	14.1.70	5	SGP	Fana	8 May
	(50)							
45:01.46t	Teresa	Vaill	USA	20.11.62	1	NC	Knoxville	16 Jun
45:04.3t		Li Na	CHN		3		Fuxin	16 Sep
45:1046:10?	Irina	Tolstik	BLR	4.12.65	3		Novopolotsk	21 May
45:10.4t	Norica	Cîmpean	ROM	22.3.72	1	Balk	Trikala	10 Jul
45:10.5		Mu Lan	CHN		5		Fuxin	16 Sep
45:14	Emilia	Cano	ESP	4.3.68	13	EC	Helsinki	9 Aug
45:15.6		Chen Yueling	CHN	24.12.69	7		Fuxin	16 Sep
45:16	Marta	Zukowska	POL	4.6.72	3		Eisenhüttenstadt	15 May
45:18		Song Lijuan	CHN	9.2.75	8		Fuxin	30 Apr
45:23	Graciela	Mendoza	MEX	23.3.63	10		Eisenhüttenstadt	15 May
	(60)							
45:29	Sonata	Milusauskaité	LIT	31.8.73	4		Novopolotsk	21 May
45:32	Yelena	Veremeychuk	UKR	13.10.59	3		Makachevo	22 May
45:36	Rie	Mitsumori	JPN	26.10.74	4		Wajima	17 Apr
45:39	Yuka	Mitsumori	JPN	8.1.72	1		Takahata	6 Nov
45:43	Holly	Gerke	CAN	.64	4	CG	Victoria	25 Aug
45:47.18t	Leonarda	Yukhnevich	BLR	3.10.63	10	GWG	St Peterburg	26 Jul
45:48	Vicky	Lupton	GBR	17.4.72	5	CG	Victoria	25 Aug
45:51	Maya	Sazonova	KZK	28.5.68	7	RUSCh	Yaroslavl	22 May
45:53	Valérie	Nadaud	FRA	16.3.68	18		Livorno	12 Jun
45:53.39	Rimma	Makarova	RUS	18.7.63	1		St Peterburg	29 Jun
	(70)							

Mark	Name		Nat	Born	Pos	Meet	Venue	Date
45:54	Maria Luz	Colin	MEX	7.3.66	3		Takahata	6 Nov
45:58	Ute	Vollmann	GER	29.12.73	19		Livorno	12 Jun
46:01	Lisa	Langford	GBR	15.3.67	6	CG	Victoria	25 Aug
46:02	Tomoko	Uchida	JPN	6.8.72	4		Takahata	6 Nov
46:04	Jane	Saville	AUS	5.11.74	3		Runaway Bay	24 Apr
46:06	Natalya	Serbinyenko	UKR	27.1.59	12		Eisenhüttenstadt	15 May
46:06	Sandy	Leddin	GER	1.11.70	21		Livorno	12 Jun
46:06	Verity	Snook-Larby	GBR	13.11.70	7	CG	Victoria	25 Aug
46:10	Kjersti	Tysse	NOR	18.1.72	16	EC	Helsinki	9 Aug
46:10	Wendy	Muldoon	AUS	27.5.71	1		Melbourne	18 Dec
	(80)							
46:11	Doreen	Sellenriek	GER	20.8.73	1		Eisenbach	11 Jun
46:12	Hanne	Liland	NOR	7.8.69	1		Kyrksäteröta	27 Aug
46:12.02t	Irina	Savinova	RUS	.72	10	GWG	St Peterburg	26 Jul
46:12.1t	Alison	Baker	CAN	6.8.64	6	SGP	Fana	7 May
46:13	Isilda	Gonçalves	POR	11.11.69	2		Lisbon	27 Feb
46:15	Yelena	Kiselyova	RUS	73	2	NC-23	Yaroslavl	22 May
46:17.91t	Pascal	Grand	CAN	12.8.67	7	SGP	Fana	7 May
46:26	Santa	Compagnoni	ITA	13.11.63	22		Livorno	12 Jun
46:26.9mx	Jane	Barbour	AUS	27.7.66	mx		Adelaide	20 Feb
	46:29				23		Livorno	12 Jun
46:27	Vera	Kozhomina	RUS	70	8	NC	Yaroslavl	22 May
	(90)							
46:28	Svetlana	Bliznyukova	BLR	12.6.71	4		Novopolotsk	21 May
46:28	Francisca	Martinez	MEX	4.10.66	3	PAmCp	Atlanta	23 Sep
46:31	Teresa	Letherby	AUS	5.4.72	4		Runaway Bay	24 Apr
46:33	Svetlana	Tolstaya	KZK	9.8.71	1		Shuchinsk	10 Sep
46:35	Ivana	Brozmanová	SVK	15.3.69	7		Dudince	27 Mar
46:35	Tina	Poitras	CAN	5.10.70	6		La Coruña	21 May
46:36	Siguta	Zagarskiene	LIT	11.2.65	5		Hildesheim	28 Aug
46:38	Yuka	Kamioka	JPN	28.5.75	5		Wajima	17 Apr
46:38	Yelena	Panfilova	RUS	9.10.60	9	NC	Yaroslavl	22 May
46:41	Gabriele	Blythe	AUS	9.3.69	3		Canberra	28 Jan
	(100)							

Mark	Name		Nat	Born	Date	Mark	Name		Nat	Born	Date
46:44	Stefania	Pessina	ITA	74	1 May	46:56	Alfiya	Galiullina	RUS	72	22 May
46:49	Takako	Taura	JPN	68	6 Nov	46:56.28t	Debora	Van Orden	USA	59	8 Jul
46:51	Beata	Betlej	POL	68	21 May	46:58.43t	Nina	Alyushenko	RUS	68	26 Jul
46:54	Bertha	Vera	ECU	74	17 Apr	46:59	Lynda	Brubaker	USA	57	1 Oct
46:54	Larisa	Matveyeva	RUS	71	22 May						

Unconfirmed: Yaroslavl 19 May: 1. Ramazonova 42:31, 2. Arshintseva 42:38

Best track times

Mark	Name		Nat	Born	Pos	Meet	Venue	Date
43:27.6	Elisabetta	Perrone	ITA	9.7.68	2	SGP	Fana	7 May
43:39.39		Kong Yan	CHN	5.4.71	4	GWG	St Peterburg	26 Jul
43:45.80	Yulia	Odzilyayeva	RUS	70	5	GWG	St Peterburg	26 Jul
44:00.49	Tamara	Kovalenko	RUS	5.6.64	6	GWG	St Peterburg	26 Jul
44:45.4		Liu Hongyu	CHN	1.12.75	3	SGP	Fana	7 May
44:49.0	Rossella	Giordano	ITA	1.12.72	1		Formia	16 Apr
45:17.7	Suzana	Feitor	POR	28.1.75	1		Lisboa	28 May
45:38.06	Janice	McCaffrey	CAN	20.10.59	1	FranG	Bondoufle	13 Jul
46:01.77	Valérie	Nadaud	FRA	16.3.68	2	FranG	Bondoufle	13 Jul
46:12.05		Li Chunxiu	CHN	13.8.69	12	GWG	St Peterburg	26 Jul
46:38.6t	Hanne	Liland	NOR	7.8.69	1		Stockholm	10 Sep

Mark	Name		Nat	Born	Date	Mark	Name		Nat	Born	Date
46:44.0	Kjersti	Tysse	NOR	72	16 Sep	47:01.80	Francisca	Martinez	MEX	66	28 Oct
46:45.6	Wendy	Muldoon	AUS	71	22 May	47:01.83	Miriam	Ramon	ECU	73	28 Oct
46:46.9	Tina	Poitras	CAN	70	7 May	47:02.8	Michaela	Hafner	ITA	73	16 Apr
46:50.05	Vera	Kozhomina	RUS	70	26 Jul	47:06.76	Liliana	Bormeo	COL	69	28 Oct
46:50.21	Yelena	Veremeychuk	UKR	59	24 Jul	47:07.66	Maria	Colin	MEX	66	28 Oct

20 KILOMETRES WALK

Mark	Name		Nat	Born	Pos	Meet	Venue	Date
1:31:56	Yelena	Gruzinova	RUS	67	1		Izhevsk	27 Aug
1:31:59	Lyudmila	Savinova	RUS	72	1	U23	Izhevsk	27 Aug
1:32:08		Gu Yan	CHN	17.3.74	1		Fuxin	18 Sep
1:32:31	Yevgeniya	Guryeva	RUS	12.6.69	2		Izhevsk	27 Aug
1:33:36	Katarzyna	Radtke	POL	31.8.69	1		Zamosc	25 Sep
1:33:53		Gao Hongmiao	CHN	8.7.72	1		Beijing	Apr
1:34:02		Song Lijuan	CHN	1.2.76	2		Beijing	Apr
1:34:28		Kong Yan	CHN	4.5.75	3		Beijing	Apr
1:34:41	Irena	Putintseva	RUS	8.5.69	3		Izhevsk	27 Aug
1:34:55	Nadezhda	Ryashkina	RUS	22.1.67	4		Izhevsk	27 Aug
	(10)							

Mark		Name	Nat	Born	Pos	Meet	Venue	Date
1:35:09		Wang Liping	CHN		2		Fuxin	18 Sep
1:35:18		Liu Hongyu	CHN	1.12.75	3		Fuxin	18 Sep
1:35:27	Anne	Manning	AUS	13.11.59	1		Adelaide	10 Jul
1:35:35	Venera	Vasilyeva	RUS	17.3.76	2	U23	Izhevsk	27 Aug
1:35:36	Yelena	Kiselyova	RUS	73	3	U23	Izhevsk	27 Aug
1:35:36		Pan Hailian	CHN		4		Fuxin	18 Sep
1:35:43	Nina	Alyushenko	RUS	68	5		Izhevsk	27 Aug
1:35:49	Olga	Bychkova	RUS	69	6		Izhevsk	27 Aug
1:35:53		Feng Haixia	CHN	.1.73	4		Beijing	Apr
1:36:17	Vera	Kozhomina	RUS	70	7		Izhevsk	27 Aug
	(20)							
1:36:22		Wei Linkun	CHN	.12.75	5		Beijing	Apr
1:36:27		Sun Chunfang	CHN		6		Beijing	Apr
1:36:58		Niu Hongyan	CHN		7		Beijing	Apr
1:37:05	Yelena	Alekseyeva	RUS	3.5.77	4	U23	Izhevsk	27 Aug
1:37:08		Tang Yinghua	CHN	18.5.73	6		Fuxin	18 Sep
1:37:19	Maria	Artynyuk	RUS	5.3.66	8		Izhevsk	27 Aug
1:37:24		Wang Yan	CHN	3.5.71	7		Fuxin	18 Sep
1:37:52		Zhang Qinghua	CHN	6.2.73	8		Fuxin	18 Sep
1:38:02	Olga	Sergeyeva	RUS	67	9		Izhevsk	27 Aug

WORLD LIST TRENDS - 10th and 100th world list performance levels

Event	*1985*	*1986*	*1987*	*1988*	*1989*	*1990*	*1991*	*1992*	*1993*	*1994*
Women 10th Bests										
100m	11.11	11.08	11.01	**10.92**	11.12	11.10	11.09	11.07	11.12	11.12
200m	22.55	22.39	22.40	**22.24**	22.53	22.42	22.58	22.44	22.37	22.41
400m	50.38	50.29	50.41	49.90	51.05	50.59	50.30	50.30	50.83	50.53
800m	1:57.42	1:58.11	1:57.46	**1:56.91**	1:58.84	1:57.82	1:58.67	1:57.93	1:57.63	1:59.12
1500m	4:02.05	4:02.92	4:01.20	4:01.02	4:04.98	4:04.56	4:05.04	4:01.23	4:00.05	4:03.40
3000m	8:42.19	8:39.25	8:42.16	8:37.70	8:45.04	8:46.86	8:42.02	8:42.09	**8:36.45**	8:45.59
10000m	32:25.62	31:56.59	31:46.61	31:42.02	32:14.65	31:55.80	31:45.95	**31:28.06**	31:29.70	31:42.14
Marathon	2:28:38	2:29:51	2:29:56	2:28:40	2:28:45	2:28:56	2:27:43	2:27:42	**2:26:26**	**2:26:26**
100mh	12.85	12.75	12.80	**12.73**	12.77	**12.73**	12.81	12.76	12.78	12.78
400mh	54.95	54.76	55.05	**54.49**	55.03	55.18	54.88	54.70	54.53	55.10
HJ	1.96	1.97	1.97	**1.98**	**1.98**	1.97	1.96	1.96	1.97	**1.98**
LJ	7.00	7.01	7.01	**7.07**	6.88	6.92	6.89	6.92	6.90	6.89
TJ				13.07	13.68	13.80	13.83	14.07	14.23	**14.46**
SP	20.39	20.60	**20.85**	20.81	20.02	20.12	19.74	19.78	19.90	19.85
DT	67.52	67.92	67.90	70.34	66.50	66.94	65.72	67.08	65.14	65.72
JT	68.20	67.80	67.64	**68.42**	65.54	66.10	65.32	65.02	65.18	64.62
Heptathlon	6368	6403	6364	**6540**	6361	6359	6370	6460	6406	6371

Other peaks: 400m 49.74 (1984), 1500m 3:59.82 (1982), DT 68.56 (1984)

Event	*1985*	*1986*	*1987*	*1988*	*1989*	*1990*	*1991*	*1992*	*1993*	*1994*
Women 100th Bests										
100m	11.44	11.51	11.48	**11.43**	11.53	11.54	11.53	11.45	11.46	11.48
200m	23.58	23.36	23.35	**23.32**	23.49	23.53	23.48	23.36	23.40	23.38
400m	52.89	52.50	52.64	**52.50**	52.81	53.00	53.03	52.60	52.66	52.76
800m	2:02.43	2:02.04	2:01.79	2:01.66	2:02.67	2:02.72	2:02.60	2:02.80	2:02.77	2:03.02
1500m	4:12.30	4:12.00	4:11.59	4:11.70	4:13.32	4:12.89	4:12.60	4:11.80	4:12.93	4:13.97
3000m	9:05.94	9:04.04	9:03.64	9:01.60	9:05.75	9:06.05	9:01.70	9:01.83	**9:00.65**	9:02.47
10000m	33:59.39	33:29.46	33:19.20	33:11.31	33:23.91	33:28.44	33:05.13	33:05.80	**33:00.88**	33:05.78
Marathon	2:38:17	2:37:58	2:37:06	2:35:29	2:37:04	2:36:48	2:35:40	2:36:14	**2:35:04**	2:35:07
100mh	13.48	13.47	13.45	13.39	13.47	13.42	13.41	**13.35**	13.38	13.37
400mh	58.00	57.89	57.87	57.50	57.79	57.88	57,72	**57.58**	58.02	57.98
HJ	1.87	**1.88**	**1.88**	**1.88**	1.87	1.87	1.87	**1.88**	**1.88**	1.87
LJ	6.48	6.48	6.46	**6.53**	6.45	6.42	6.44	6.45	6.44	6.45
TJ							12.98	13.16	13.26	**13.28**
SP	116.92	17.12	**17.19**	16.95	16.30	16.60	16.52	16.40	16.33+	16.28+
DT	57.14	57.48	57.78	57.40	56.48	56.02	55.78	56.20	55.74	55.02
JT	57.44	57.20	57.82	**58.12**	56.80	56.48	56.08	56.36	56.54	56.00
Heptathlon	5566	5654	5701	**5741**	5696	5703	5671	5661	5636	5650

Other peaks: 800m 2:01.50 (1984), 1500m 4:10.22 (1984), DT 58.50 (1984)

All-time record levels indicated in bold

WORLD JUNIOR WOMEN'S LISTS 1994

100 Metres

Mark		Name		Nat	Born	Pos	Meet	Venue	Date
11.35	1.3	Mercy	Nku	NGR	17.7.76	1s2	NC-j	Benin City	27 May
11.36A	-0.1	Aspen	Burkett	USA	8.3.76	1		Denver	11 Jun
		11.38	1.3			1s2	WJ	Lisboa	21 Jul
11.36	2.0	Sabrina	Herring-Kelly	USA	20.8.75	1	WJ	Lisboa	21 Jul
11.39	0.8	Philomina	Mensah	GHA	11.5.75	1s1	WJ	Lisboa	21 Jul
11.40	2.0	Marion	Jones	USA	12.10.75	4s1	NCAA	Boise	3 Jun
11.42	0.9	Kwajalein	Butler	USA	23.7.76	1		Baton Rouge	7 May
11.42	2.0	Damayanthi	Darsha	SRI	13.2.75	1	AsiC-j	Jakarta	18 Sep
11.43	1.3	Ekaterini	Thanou	GRE	1.1.75	2s2	WJ	Lisboa	21 Jul
11.45		Endurance	Ojokolo	NGR	27.5.77	2	NC-j	Benin City	26 May
11.45	1.9		Wang Jing	CHN	16.1.75	2h	NC	Beijing	3 Jun
11.48		Chinedu	Odozor	NGR	75	3	NC-j	Benin City	26 May
11.48	2.0	Debbie	Ferguson	BAH	16.1.76	6	WJ	Lisboa	22 Jul
11.49		Omegia	Keeys	USA	25.6.75	1		Terre Haute	23 Apr
11.49	-0.1	Frédérique	Bangue	FRA	31.12.76	2		Genève	18 Jun
11.49	2.0	Susanthika	Jayasinghe	SRI	17.12.75	2	AsiC-j	Jakarta	18 Sep
11.50	1.3	Dainelky	Pérez	CUB	6.1.76	3s2	WJ	Lisboa	21 Jul
11.51		Felipa	Palacios	COL	75	1		Valencia	22 Nov
11.52	1.1	Marie-Joëlle	Dogbo	FRA	13.2.75	3		Noisy-le-Grand	2 Jul
11.52	0.8	Kerry Ann	Richards	JAM	22.4.76	4s1	WJ	Lisboa	21 Jul
11.54	1.3	Ingvild	Larsen	NOR	3.10.75	1	NC-j	Drammen	8 Jul
11.54	2.0		Gao Chunxia	CHN		3	AsiC-j	Jakarta	18 Sep
Unconfirmed: 11.44		Astia	Walker	JAM	4.4.75	1		Long Beach	May
Track 4cm short and wind gauge illegally placed									
11.33	1.1	Sabrina	Herring-Kelly	USA	20.8.75	1	JUCO	Odessa, Tx	20 May
Wind assisted									
11.30	2.4	Frédérique	Bangue	FRA	31.12.76	1B		Dijon	12 Jun
11.48		LaKeisha	Backus	USA	15.12.75	1		Long Beach	6 May
11.50	4.1	Rebecca	Drummond	GBR	18.4.78	1	N.Sch	Telford	8 Jul
11.51	2.9	Marie-Joëlle	Dogbo	FRA	13.2.75	1		Sotteville	26 Jun
11.53	2.3	Simone	Tomlinson	CAN	26.9.76	1	NC	Victoria	29 Jul
Hand timing									
11.0	0.4	Tulia	Robinson	JAM	4.2.79	1	CAC17	Port of Spain	8 Jul
11.1	1.8	Debbie	Ferguson	BAH	16.1.76	1	CAC-j	Port of Spain	8 Jul
11.1	1.8	Beverley	Langley	JAM	16.12.76	2	CAC-j	Port of Spain	8 Jul
11.2	1.8	Kerry-Ann	Richards	JAM	22.4.76	3	CAC-j	Port of Spain	8 Jul
11.2	1.7	Aspen	Burkett	USA	8.3.76	1	v CAN	Buffalo	14 Jul
11.3	0.4	Ayana	Hutchinson	TRI	18.2.78	2	CAC17	Port of Spain	8 Jul
11.3	1.7	Sabrina	Herring-Kelly	USA	20.8.75	2	v CAN	Buffalo	14 Jul
11.3	1.7	Simone	Tomlinson	CAN	26.9.76	3	v USA	Buffalo	14 Jul
Wind assisted									
11.2		Latasha	Gilliam	USA	19.2.76	1			Mar
11.2A		Aspen	Burkett	USA	8.3.76	1		Denver	7 Apr
11.3	3.8	LaKeisha	Backus	USA	15.12.75	1		Long Beach	14 May
Doubtful timing: 11.2A		Felipa	Palacios	COL	1.12.75	2		Pereira	17 Oct

200 Metres

Mark		Name		Nat	Born	Pos	Meet	Venue	Date
23.08		Omegia	Keeys	USA	25.6.75	1		Terre Haute	23 Apr
23.16	0.9	Susanthika	Jayasinghe	SRI	17.12.75	1	AsiC-j	Jakarta	20 Sep
23.19A	0.7	Esmari	le Roux	RSA	27.1.76	3	NC	Secunda	7 May
23.21	1.4	Lakeisha	Backus	USA	15.12.76	1		Norwalk	4 Jun
23.22A	0.7	Heidi	Seyerling	RSA	19.8.76	4	NC	Secunda	7 May
		23.36	0.2 best low altitude			1s1	WJ	Lisboa	23 Jul
23.23	-1.0	Aminah	Haddad	USA	13.9.78	1		Long Beach	21 May
23.24	0.9	Damayanthi	Darsha	SRI	13.2.75	2	AsiC-j	Jakarta	20 Sep
23.32		Debbie	Ferguson	BAH	16.1.76	1h2	Carif	Bridgetown	4 Apr
23.32	0.6	Marion	Jones	USA	12.10.75	3s2	NCAA	Boise	3 Jun
23.36A		Aspen	Burkett	USA	8.3.76	1		Denver	14 May
		23.54	0.3 best low altitude			1	NC-j	Tallahassee	25 Jun
23.41	0.0	Astia	Walker	JAM	4.4.75	1		Cerritos	21 May
23.48	1.8	Tatyana	Tkalich	UKR	30.5.75	1		Schwechat	22 May
23.48	1.7	Kim	Baldwin	USA	30.4.75	4h2	NCAA	Boise	1 Jun
23.50A	0.7	Tamaryn	Sawyer	RSA	8.6.77	6	NC	Secunda	7 May
23.55	1.3	Karen	Boone	USA	8.1.75	4h1	NCAA	Boise	1 Jun
23.56	0.9	LaTasha	Colander	USA	23.8.76	1	Nat Sch	Raleigh	19 Jun

Mark		Name		Nat	Born	Pos	Meet	Venue	Date
23.62	0.3	Latasha	Gilliam	USA	19.2.76	1		Berkeley	28 May
23.62	-0.3	Ionela	Tîrlea	ROM	9.2.76	2	ECp23	Ostrava	31 Jul
23.64	1.3	Fabé	Dia	FRA	14.2.77	1r2	NC-j	Dreux	10 Jul
23.65	0.9	Michelle	Mundey	USA	27.5.78	2		Raleigh	19 Jun
Wind assisted									
22.80	2.2	Heidi	Seyerling	RSA	19.8.76	1	WJ	Lisboa	23 Jul
22.86	2.2	Lakeisha	Backus	USA	15.12.76	2	WJ	Lisboa	23 Jul
23.35	2.2	Tatyana	Tkalich	UKR	30.5.75	3	WJ	Lisboa	23 Jul
23.42	2.1	Karen	Boone	USA	8.1.75	2r1		Baton Rouge	25 May
23.48	5.1	Andrea	Anderson	USA	17.9.77	1		Arcadia	9 Apr
23.49	?		Huang Mei	CHN	15.4.75	h	NC-j	Nanchang	30 Apr
23.61	2.2	Sylviane	Félix	FRA	31.10.77	5	WJ	Lisboa	23 Jul
Disqualified									
23.19w		Astia	Walker	JAM	4.4.75		WJ	Lisboa	23 Jul
Hand Timing									
22.9		Astia	Walker	JAM	4.4.75	1h	CAC-j	Port of Spain	10 Jul
23.1		Debbie	Ferguson	BAH	16.1.76	h	CAC-j	Port of Spain	10 Jul
23.2		Tatyana	Kotelnikova	UZB	23.8.75	1		Tashkent	13 May
23.4		Monique	Hennagan	USA	26.5.76	1		Columbia	12 May
23.3w		LaTasha	Colander	USA	23.8.76	1		Newport	23 Apr

400 Metres

Mark	Name		Nat	Born	Pos	Meet	Venue	Date
51.97	Bisi	Afolabi	NGR	31.11.75	1	WJ	Lisboa	22 Jul
	52.21				7	CG	Victoria	23 Jul
	52.25				4	AvUSA	Durham	12 Aug
	52.27				1s2	WJ	Lisboa	21 Jul
52.19	Monique	Hennagan	USA	26.5.76	1	NC-j	Tallahassee	25 Jun
	52.25				2	WJ	Lisboa	22 Jul
	52.41				1		Columbia	12 May
52.19	Claudine	Williams	JAM	6.1.76	3	NC	Kingston	2 Jul
	52.43				1s1	WJ	Lisboa	21 Jul
52.60	Hana	Benesová	TCH	19.4.75	3	WJ	Lisboa	22 Jul
52.62		Li Yajun	CHN	21.7.77	4	WJ	Lisboa	22 Jul
52.65	Michelle	Brown	USA	12.3.75	1	Gator	Knoxville	23 Apr
52.90	Tamsyn	Lewis	AUS	20.7.78	1		Melbourne	20 Feb
53.00	Tracy	Barnes	JAM	28.6.76	5	NC	Kingston	2 Jul
53.06	Florence	Ekpo Umoh	NGR	27.12.77			Lagos	21 May
53.15	Cicely	Scott	USA	10.9.75	2	NC-j	Tallahassee	25 Jun
53.20A	Yolande	Venter	RSA	16.8.78	1	NC-17	Bloemfontein	8 Apr
53.35	Omegia	Keeys	USA	25.6.75	1h1		Wichita	19 May
53.35	Stacey	Milligan	USA	30.6.75	2		Waco	25 May
53.36	Heidi	Suomi	FIN	2.1.75	1	NC	Tuusala	9 Jul
53.43	Charlynna	Foster	USA	2.1.80	1		Gainesville	31 Aug
53.55	Vernetta	Rolle	BAH	9.1.76	1		Bridgetown	4 Apr
53.55	Cindy	Ega	FRA	26.8.78	1	vUKR-j	Dôle	6 Aug
53.58	Natalya	Matukh	UKR	24.1.75	2	vFRA-j	Dôle	6 Aug
53.59	Rebecca	Campbell	AUS	23.1.76	1		Perth	26 Feb
53.66	Zenita	Davis	USA		4		Houston	24 Apr
Indoors								
52.77	Ionella	Tîrlea	ROM	19.2.76	2		Budapest	5 Feb
Hand timing								
53.1	Tracy-Ann	Barnes	JAM	28.6.75	1		Kingston	12 Mar
53.3	Tanya	Jarrett	JAM	18.9.77	1		Kingston	26 Mar

800 Metres

Mark	Name		Nat	Born	Pos	Meet	Venue	Date
2:01.44		Liu Wanjie #	CHN	27.11.75	5	NC	Beijing	5 Jun
2:02.6	Inna	Nedelenko	UKR	15.1.76	2		Dnepropetrovsk	18 Jul
2:02.70	Yekaterina	Fedotova	RUS	4.11.75	5	Znam	Moskva	11 Jun
2:03.0A	Salina	Kosgei	KEN	17.1.76	1		Nairobi	5 Jul
2:03.21	Andrea	Suldesová	TCH	11.2.75	2		Jablonec	10 Jul
2:04.0mx	Vicki	Freeborn	AUS	23.5.75	mx		Adelaide	26 Feb
	2:05.95				2	GBR-j	Bedford	3 Jul
2:04.05	Ivonne	Teichmann	GER	11.4.77	1		Mannheim	4 Jun
2:04.07	Jackline	Maranga	KEN	16.12.77	1s2	WJ	Lisboa	21 Jul
2:04.2	Marina	Makarova	UKR		unconfirmed			
2:04.53	Mariko	Ikeda	JPN	17.2.76	2	NC	Tokyo	12 Jun
2:04.73	Eleanora	Berlanda	ITA	6.4.76	1		Pescara	17 Jun
2:04.73	Miaora	Cosulianu	ROM	31.1.76	2s2	WJ	Lisboa	21 Jul
2:04.84	Ulrike	Urbansky	GER	11.4.77			Magdeburg	26 Jun

Mark	Name		Nat	Born	Pos	Meet	Venue	Date
2:04.96	Regina	Ehmer	GER	27.6.76			Magdeburg	26 Jun
2:05.11		Huang Lixing	CHN	77	1	AsiC-j	Jakarta	17 Sep
2:05.14	Anita	Weyermann	SUI	8.12.77	1	v2N	Bulle	10 Sep
2:05.17	Kuture	Delecha	ETH	78	3	WJ	Lisboa	22 Jul
2:05.19	Kumiko	Okamoto	JPN	19.3.76	3s2	WJ	Lisboa	21 Jul
2:05.28	Romana	Sanigová	TCH	10.3.75	1		Jablonec	4 Jun
2:05.29	Grazyna	Penc	POL	10.9.75	2		Pila	25 Jun
2:05.44	Lyudmila	Voronitsheva	RUS	5.10.77	2	v3N-j	Warszawa	18 Jun

1000 Metres

Mark	Name		Nat	Born	Pos	Meet	Venue	Date
2:42.54	Grazyna	Penc	POL	10.9.75	3		Sopot	17 Aug
2:42.89	Lidia	Chojecka	POL	30.1.77	3		Sopot	17 Aug
2:43.89	Anita	Weyermann	SUI	8.12.77	4	WK	Zürich	17 Aug

1500 Metres

Mark	Name		Nat	Born	Pos	Meet	Venue	Date
4:12.84	Jackline	Maranga	KEN	16.12.77	6	CG	Victoria	28 Aug
4:13.79	Susie	Power	AUS	16.3.75	2		Melbourne	22 Nov
4:13.97	Anita	Weyermann	SUI	8.12.77	1	WJ	Lisboa	24 Jul
4:14.43		Liu Wanjie #	CHN	27.11.75	4	NC	Beijing	5 Jun
4:14.43	Gabriele	Szabo	ROM	14.11.75	1	NC-j	Bucuresti	5 Jun
4:14.56	Atsumi	Yashima	JPN	28.6.75	3		Fukushima	24 Sep
4:14.59	Marta	Dominguez	ESP	3.11.75	2	WJ	Lisboa	24 Jul
4:14.96	Yoshiko	Ichikawa	JPN	18.4.76	2	NC	Tokyo	11 Jun
4:15.59	Kuture	Delecha	ETH	78	1h2	WJ	Lisboa	23 Jul
4:16.41	Rose	Cheruiyot	KEN	21.7.76	4h2	WJ	Lisboa	23 Jul
4:16.61	Sally	Barsosio	KEN	21.3.78	1		Alger	8 Jun
4:17.6	Heather	DeGeest	CAN	25.3.77	4		Seattle	7 Jun
4:18.20	Grazyna	Penc	POL	10.9.75	2		Lillehammer	31 Jul
4:18.2A	Helen	Mutai	KEN	18.12.77	1		Nairobi	5 Jul
4:18.47	Irina	Nedelenko	UKR	15.1.76	6	WJ	Lisboa	24 Jul
4:18.70	Lidia	Chojecka	POL	30.1.77	7	WJ	Lisboa	24 Jul
4:18.8+	Annemari	Sandell	FIN	2.1.77	1		Turku	8 Jun
4:19.04	Angela	Froese	CAN	16.11.76	6		Port Alberni	1 Jun
4:19.1	Natalya	Chernyshova	UKR	30.6.75	1			9 Jul
4:19.24		Korchnikova			1		Budapest	18 Jun

1 Mile

Mark	Name		Nat	Born	Pos	Meet	Venue	Date
4:38.20	Annemari	Sandell	FIN	2.1.77	1		Turku	8 Jun

2000 Metres

Mark	Name		Nat	Born	Pos	Meet	Venue	Date
5:50.47	Susie	Power	AUS	26.3.75	10	McD	Sheffield	4 Sep

3000 Metres

Mark	Name		Nat	Born	Pos	Meet	Venue	Date
8:40.08	Gabriela	Szabo	ROM	14.11.75	3	EC	Helsinki	12 Aug
	8:47.40				1	WJ	Lisboa	23 Jul
	8:47.96				2	GGala	Roma	8 Jun
8:49.92		Wang Xiaoxia	CHN	21.8.76	1	NC	Beijing	2 Jun
8:50.62		Ma Ningning	CHN	20.9.76	4	NC	Beijing	2 Jun
8:52.24	Annemari	Sandell	FIN	2.1.77	7	WG	Helsinki	29 Jun
8:53.40	Sally	Barsosio	KEN	2.10.78	1	Afr-J	Alger	6 Jul
8:56.93	Susie	Power	AUS	26.3.75	2	WJ	Lisboa	22 Jul
9:00.89	Rose	Cheruiyot	KEN	21.7.76	6	CG	Victoria	23 Aug
9:03.05	Yasuko	Kimura	JPN	6.1.76	1		Nagoya	1 Nov
9:03.21	Yuko	Kawakami	JPN	1.8.75	2		Nagoya	1 Nov
9:04.31	Esther	Wanjiru	KEN	27.3.77	8	JPN Ch	Tokyo	12 Jun
9:04.64	Atsumi	Yashima	JPN	28.6.75	3		Fukushima	25 Sep
9:05.70	Miwa	Sugawara	JPN	5.9.76	1		Sendai	29 May
9:06.0A	Pamela	Chepchumba	KEN	28.3.79	1		Nairobi	5 Jul
9:06.7A	Eunice	Sagero	KEN	75	2		Nairobi	5 Jul
9:08.54	Rie	Ueno	JPN	11.6.76	5		Kumamoto	23 Oct
9:10.47	Berhane	Dagne	ETH	7.10.77	3	Afr-J	Alger	6 Jul
9:11.70	Chiemi	Takahashi	JPN	16.2.76	13	NC	Tokyo	12 Jun
9:12.61	Naomi	Sakashita	JPN	25.5.75	7		Fukushima	25 Sep
9:13.33	Kazuko	Kusakabe	JPN	15.2.75	3		Nagoya	1 Nov
9:13.96	Azumi	Miyazaki	JPN	3.3.75	5		Hiroshima	30 Apr
9:13.97	Olivera	Jevtic	YUG	24.7.77	4h1	WJ	Lisboa	21 Jul

5000 Metres

Mark		Name		Nat	Born	Pos	Meet	Venue	Date
15:19.4		Yasuko	Kimura	JPN	6.1.76	1		Toyonaka	21 Dec
		15:24.1				1		Toyonaka	3 Dec
		15:36.9				1		Kyoto	23 Oct
15:26.3		Atsumi	Yashima	JPN	28.6.75	2		Toyonaka	21 Dec
15:38.85		Esther	Wanjiru	KEN	27.3.77	8	TOTO	Tokyo	15 Sep
15:42.45		Sally	Barsosio	KEN	21.3.78	13	ISTAF	Berlin	30 Aug
15:44.05		Rose	Cheruiyot	KEN	21.7.76	5	Slov	Bratislava	1 Jun
15:46.01		Chiemi	Takahashi	JPN	16.2.76	10	TOTO	Tokyo	15 Sep
15:46.5		Tomoko	Morigaki	JPN	4.9.76	2		Kyoto	23 Oct
15:49.42		Yuko	Kawakami	JPN	1.8.75	1		Amagasaki	1 Oct
15:50.7		Rie	Ueno	JPN	11.6.76			Kumamoto	17 Dec
15:51.27		Catherine	Kirui	KEN	1.3.76	12	DNG	Stockholm	12 Jul
15:52.2		Tomomi	Kozuma	JPN	4.2.77			Kumamoto	17 Dec
15:52.41		Madoka	Suzuki	JPN	1.1.75	11	TOTO	Tokyo	15 Sep
15:53.85		Naomi	Sakashita	JPN	25.5.75	4		Sapporo	27 Aug
15:53.9		Noriko	Wada	JPN	24.5.75			Kumamoto	17 Dec
15:55.3		Mari	Yoshikawa	JPN	5.1.75			Kumamoto	17 Dec
15:55.7		Mika	Adachi	JPN	14.1.76			Kumamoto	17 Dec
15:55.88		Miwa	Sugawara	JPN	5.9.76	1		Konosu	1 Oct
16:01.1		Masako	Chiba	JPN	18.7.76	2		Kameoka	12 Nov
16:01.7		Atsuko	Morigaki	JPN	4.9.76	3		Kameoka	12 Nov
16:02.1		Hiromi	Kasai	JPN	24.3.77	4		Kameoka	12 Nov

10000 Metres

Mark		Name		Nat	Born	Pos	Meet	Venue	Date
32:23.25		Esther	Wanjiru	KEN	27.3.77	2		Mito	8 May
		32:50.30				9	JPN Ch	Tokyo	10 Jun
32:29.17		Yasuke	Kimura	JPN	6.1.76	1		Amagasaki	28 Oct
32:33.03			Wang Xiaoxia	CHN	21.8.76	4	NC	Beijing	5 Jun
32:34.11		Yoko	Yamazaki	JPN	25.7.75	1	WJ	Lisboa	23 Jul
32:55.24		Annemari	Sandell	FIN	2.1.77	1	NC	Tuusula	8 Jul
33:14.2A		Jackline	Okemwa	KEN	12.5.78	1		Nairobi	5 Jul
33:14.6A		Chepkemoi	Barsosio	KEN	77	2		Nairobi	5 Jul
33:18.5A		Edina	Kwambai	KEN	75	3		Nairobi	5 Jul
33:22.83			Ma Ningning	CHN	20.9.76	9	NC	Beijing	5 Jun
33:24.4		Kaori	Hosokawa	JPN	21.9.75	1		Nobeoka	22 Oct
33:24.8			Jung Young-im	KOR	5.1.75	1		Daeju	28 Oct
33:26.43			Lee Mi-kyung	KOR	26.5.75	1	NC	Seoul	18 Jun
33:27.59		Mari	Yoshikawa	JPN	5.1.75	14		Fukushima	23 Sep
33:31.14		Hiromi	Sato	JPN		20		Fukushima	23 Sep
33:35.98		Jebiwott	Keitany	KEN	25.12.78	3	WJ	Lisboa	23 Jul
33:39.62A		Catherine	Kirui	KEN	1.3.76	2		Nairobi	7 Aug
33:45.25		Yoshiko	Imura	JPN	6.3.75	6		Himeji	21 May
33:49.10		Berhane	Dagne	ETH	7.10.77	1		Algers	8 Jul
33:49.19		Mari	Singeorzan	ROM	23.10.77	4	WJ	Lisboa	23 Jul
34:06.44		Olga	Nikolayeva	RUS	?				

Marathon

Mark		Name		Nat	Born	Pos	Meet	Venue	Date
2:32:30			Ma Ningning	CHN	20.9.76	5		Beijing	30 Oct
2:35:44			Lee Mi-kyung	KOR	26.5.75	1		Kyongju	20 Mar
2:36:24			Jung Young-im	KOR	5.1.75	2		Kyongju	20 Mar

2000 Metres Steeplechase

Mark		Name		Nat	Born	Pos	Meet	Venue	Date
6:33.59		Tatyana	Babik	UKR	17.4.75	1		Kiev	24 Jul
6:37.81		Olimpia	Pop	ROM	25.2.76	1		Bucuresti	6 Aug
6:38.31		Valentina	Sukhanova	RUS	76	6	NC	St Peterburg	15 Jul

100 Metres Hurdles

Mark		Name		Nat	Born	Pos	Meet	Venue	Date
13.25	1.1	Diane	Allahgreen	GBR	21.2.75	1s2	WJ	Lisboa	22 Jul
		13.31	0.5			3	WJ	Lisboa	22 Jul
13.26	0.5	Kirsten	Bolm	GER	4.3.75	1	WJ	Lisboa	22 Jul
		13.28	1.4			2		Scheesel	22 May
		13.27w	2.3			1		Mannheim	4 Jun
13.29	0.4	Yelena	Ovcharova	UKR	17.8.76	1h3	WJ	Lisboa	21 Jul
13.30	1.0	LaTasha	Colander	USA	23.8.76	1s1	WJ	Lisboa	21 Jul
		13.30	0.5			2	WJ	Lisboa	22 Jul
13.32	1.0		Chen Zhenghong	CHN	30.9.76	2s1	WJ	Lisboa	21 Jul
13.37	1.0	Astia	Walker	JAM	4.4.75	3s1	WJ	Lisboa	21 Jul
13.44	1.2	Akiko	Morimoto	JPN	17.2.77	1		Utsonomiya	17 Jun

Mark		Name		Nat	Born	Pos	Meet	Venue	Date
13.50	1.1	Carmen	Banks	USA	26.5.76	1h1	NC-j	Tallahassee	24 Jun
13.66	0.5	Ingvild	Larsen	NOR	3.10.75	5	WJ	Lisboa	22 Jul
13.67	1.1	Nikola	Spinová	TCH	10.2.76	4s2	WJ	Lisboa	21 Jul
13.70A	-3.6	Adri	van der Merwe	RSA	17.6.76	1	NC	Secunda	6 May
13.70		Chinyere	Odita	NGR				Houston	14 Jun
13.70	1.0	Katia	Brito	CUB	78	5s1	WJ	Lisboa	21 Jul
13.71A	1.4	Domingué	Calloway	USA	19.7.78	2		Provo	25 May
13.71	1.2	Claudia	Ruge	GER	14.8.75	2r1		Mannheim	3 Jun
13.72	1.2	Desiree	McQueen	USA	15.9.78	1		Fairfax	24 Jul
13.74	1.2	Akiko	Kondo	JPN	17.2.77	2		Utsonomiya	17 Jun
13.74	1.0	Rachel	Links	AUS	26.1.75	7s1	WJ	Lisboa	21 Jul
13.76	0.9	Sakiko	Miyamoto	JPN	12.7.76	2		Toyama	1 Aug
13.79A	0.6	Nadene	Fensham	RSA	9.10.76	2	NC-j	Bloemfontein	9 Apr
Wind assisted									
13.59	2.6	Sophie	Marrot	FRA	13.2.75			Durango	2 Jul
13.60	2.9	Nikola	Spinová	TCH	10.2.76	3h4	WJ	Lisboa	21 Jul
13.61A	0.6	Nadene	Fensham	RSA	9.10.76	1h	NC-j	Bloemfontein	8 Apr
13.66	2.9	Vanina	Fouet	FRA	23.11.75	4h4	WJ	Lisboa	21 Jul
13.67	4.0	Vanessa	Koslowski	GER	19.1.75	2	NC-j	Ulm	30 Jul
13.69	2.9	Rachel	Links	AUS	26.1.75	5h4	WJ	Lisboa	21 Jul
13.73	3.9	Daveetta	Shepherd	USA	15.1.79	1		Norwalk	4 Jun
13.76	3.9	Bisa	Grant	USA	10.7.76	2		Norwalk	4 Jun
13.76	3.4	Natasha	Danvers	GBR	19.9.77	1		London (He)	27 Aug
13.79	4.0	Anja	Haesecke	GER	21.12.76	3	NC-j	Ulm	30 Jul
Hand timed									
13.1	0.4	Yelena	Ovcharova	UKR	17.8.76	1		Belaya Tserkov	9 Jul
13.2w	2.4	Astia	Walker	JAM	4.4.75	4		San Luis Obispo	19 Mar

400 Metres Hurdles

Mark	Name		Nat	Born	Pos	Meet	Venue	Date
56.25	Ionela	Tîrlea	ROM	9.2.76	1	WJ	Lisboa	22 Jul
	56.98				1	NC	Bucuresti	18 Jun
56.79	Virna	De Angeli	ITA	27.2.76	1	NC	Napoli	3 Jul
	56.93				2	WJ	Lisboa	22 Jul
57.23	Emma	Holmqvist	SWE	26.3.75	3	WJ	Lisboa	22 Jul
57.46	Rebecca	Campbell	AUS	23.1.76	2		Canberra	28 Jan
57.98	Charlynna	Foster	USA	2.1.80	1	NC-j	Tallahassee	25 Jun
58.06	Tanya	Jarrett	JAM	18.9.77	1	PennR	Philadelphia	28 Apr
58.10		Zhou Wei	CHN	10.12.75	4	WJ	Lisboa	22 Jul
58.13		Jiang Limei	CHN	.3.77	3		Tangshan	29 Aug
58.24	Nadia	Schmiedt	CAN	20.10.76	1		Kitchener	22 Jun
58.27	Ulrike	Urbansky	GER	6.4.77	1	NC-j	Ulm	30 Jul
58.30A	Adri	van der Merwe	RSA	17.6.76	1	NC-j	Bloemfontein	9 Apr
	58.62				3		Durban	23 Apr
58.47	Ikiko	Yamagata	JPN	3.1.75	4h1	AsiG	Hiroshima	11 Oct
58.67	Danielle	Blackburn	RSA	19.6.75	4		Durban	23 Apr
58.75	Andrea	Blackett	JAM	.76	2		Houston	24 Apr
58.79A	Ronelle	Ulrich	RSA	9.2.75	2	NC-j	Bloemfontein	9 Apr
58.79	Angela	Harris	USA	5.3.76	1		Gainesville	31 Jul
58.82	Claudia	Salvarini	ITA	8.3.75	4h3	WJ	Lisboa	21 Jul
58.88	Yvonne	Harrison	USA	2.12.75	2	NC-j	Tallahassee	25 Jun
58.92	Mayuko	Hiro	JPN	20.5.76	2	NC	Tokyo	12 Jun
59.12	Joanna	Hayes	USA	23.12.76	2		Gainesville	31 Jul
Hand timed								
58.1	Tatyana	Dorogina	UZB	75	1		Tashkent	16 Sep

High Jump

Mark	Name		Nat	Born	Pos	Meet	Venue	Date
1.96i	Desislava	Aleksandrova	BUL	27.10.75	2	EI	Paris	12 Mar
	1.94i				6		Piraeus	28 Feb
	1.90i				1		Sofia	29 Jan
	1.90i				2	Balk	Piraeus	20 Feb
	1.87				1		Schwechat	26 May
1.91	Viktoriya	Palamar	UKR	12.10.77	1		Odessa	23 Apr
1.90	Lenka	Riháková	SVK	17.10.75	1	NC	Bratislava	2 Jul
1.90	Yuliya	Lyakhova	RUS	77	1		Dzerzhinsk	5 Aug
1.90	Kajsa	Bergqvist	SWE	12.10.76	1	NC-18	Luleå	7 Aug
1.89i	Amy	Acuff	USA	14.7.75	1	NCAA	Indianapolis	12 Mar
	1.89				2	NCAA	Boise	4 Jun
1.89	Yoko	Ota	JPN	14.1.75	1		Shizuoka	5 May
1.89	Olga	Kaliturina	RUS	9.3.76	1		Krasnodar	28 May

Mark	Name		Nat	Born	Pos	Meet	Venue	Date
1.88	Yekaterina	Aleksandrova	RUS	3.6.77	1	NC-j	Yekaterinburg	24 Jun
1.88	Tatyana	Ivanova	RUS	22.1.76	1		Krasnodar	19 Aug
1.87i	Emelie	Färdigh	SWE	13.9.77	1		Göteborg	29 Jan
	1.87				7		Bratislava	1 Jun
1.87	Miki	Imai	JPN	30.5.75	2		Nagoya	2 Nov
1.86i	Viktoriya	Styopina	UKR	21.2.76	2		Zaporozhe	5 Jan
	1.86				1		Warsawa	24 Sep
1.86i	Helen	Sanzenbacher	GER	28.10.75	1	NC-j	Sindelfingen	12 Feb
	1.85				5	WJ	Lisboa	23 Jul
1.86i	Tatyana	Nikolayeva	UKR	26.2.76	1		Donetsk	30 Jan
	1.86						Kiev	11 Jun
1.85	Jane	Millington	AUS	16.7.76	3		Perth	13 Feb
1.85		Guan Weihua	CHN	14.6.75	2	NC	Beijing	2 Jun
	1.90 ?						Beijing	28 Jul
1.85	Luciane	Dambacher	BRA	10.5.76	1		Buenos Aires	-2 Oc
1.84	Dora	Gwörfy	HUN	23.2.78	1		Budapest	24 Jun

Pole Vault

Mark	Name		Nat	Born	Pos	Meet	Venue	Date
3.85	Janet	Zach	GER	19.6.75	3		Ahlen	6 Aug
	3.81				1	NC-j	Ulm	30 Jul
	3.80				1		Bad Köstritz	25 Jun
	3.75				1		Mannheim	3 Jun
	3.75				4	NC	Erfurt	3 Jul
	3.74				1		Holzminden	10 Sep
3.80		Zhong Guiqing	CHN	75	1		Guangzhou	26 Mar
	3.80				1	NC-j	Nanchang	30 Apr
	3.80				1		Guangzhou	May
	3.80				2	NC	Beijing	3 Jun
3.71	Nastja	Ryshich	GER	19.9.77	1		Jablonec	16 Jul
3.70i	Marion	Meyer	GER	9.7.75	1	NC-j	Sindelfingen	12 Feb
	3.60				2	NC-j	Ulm	31 Jul
3.70		Peng Xiaoyun	CHN		3		Guangzhou	26 Mar
3.65	Karin	Hecht	GER	27.10.77	2		Mannheim	3 Jun
3.55	Ariane	Knoll	GER	1.7.77	3		Mannheim	3 Jun
3.51	Melissa	Price	USA	20.9.77	1		Fresno	13 Jul
3.50	Silke	Baumann	GER	18.11.76	4		Worms	5 Jun
3.50	Sabine	Schulte	GER	29.1.76	3	NC-j	Ulm	31 Jul
3.50	Sarelle	Verkade	NZL	19.5.76	1		Auckland	12 Nov
3.45	Melina	Hamilton	NZL	15.6.76	1		Hamilton	19 Mar
3.45	Sonja	Baumann	GER	18.11.76	7		Ahlen	6 Aug
3.44	Clare	Ridgley	GBR	11.9.77	5		Holzminden	10 Sep
3.42	Denise	Birkelbach	GER	6.10.77	1		Minden	10 Aug
3.40i	Judith	Ruppert	GER	.78	4		Karlsruhe	5 Feb
3.40	Veronika	Göbel	GER	9.6.75			Berlin	25 May
3.40	Veronika	Mempel	GER	9.1.77	1		Königsbrunn	12 Jun
3.40	Wiebke	Decker	GER	20.4.77	4	NC-j	Ulm	31 Jul
3.40	Shannon	Walker	USA	75	1		Stoke-on-Trent	31 Jul
3.40	Vala	Flosadóttir	ISL	16.2.78			Lund	20 Sep

Long Jump

Mark	Wind	Name		Nat	Born	Pos	Meet	Venue	Date
6.75	1.8	Marion	Jones	USA	12.10.75	2	NCAA	Boise	1 Jun
		6.68				1		Raleigh	14 May
6.65	2.0	Tatyana	Lebedyeva	RUS	21.7.76	1	NC-j	Yekaterinburg	24 Jun
6.58	-1.1		Feng Jie	CHN		2		Tangshan	30 Aug
6.55	0.5	Kirsten	Bolm	GER	4.3.75	1		Mannheim	4 Jun
6.53	0.8	Tatyana	Dyatlova	BLR	12.1.75	2		Minsk	6 May
6.52	1.7		Peng Fengmei	CHN	2.7.79	2	NC	Beijing	5 Jun
6.49i		Lacena	Golding	JAM	24.3.75	1	JUCO	Manhattan, Ks	4 Mar
		6.48				1		Houston	2 Apr
6.45	0.7	Yelena	Lysak ¶	RUS	19.10.75	*	WJ	Lisboa	23 Jul
6.45	1.6	Natalya	Sorokina	UKR	24.3.75	1	vFRA-j	Dôle	6 Aug
6.42	1.0	Heli	Koivula	FIN	27.6.75	*	vSWE	Stockholm	27 Aug
6.40		Trecia-Kaye	Smith	JAM	5.11.75	1	CAC-j	Port of Spain	-10 Jul
6.40		Cristina	Nicolau	ROM	9.8.77	1		Bucuresti	6 Aug
6.39	1.6	Angee	Henry	USA	21.12.75	1	NC-j	Tallahassee	24 Jun
6.39	0.6	Ingvild	Larsen	NOR	3.10.75	*	ECp23	Lillehammer	31 Jul
6.38			Ding Ying	CHN	28.9.76	H	NC-j	Nanchang	30 Apr
6.38	1.9	Zhasmina	Nikolova	BUL	5.3.77	2		Sofia	15 May
6.38	2.0	Anna	Mironova	RUS	15.10.75	*	NC-j	Yekaterinburg	24 Jun

Mark		Name		Nat	Born	Pos	Meet	Venue	Date
6.36	0.9	Sarah	Gautreau	FRA	21.6.77	2	vUKR-j	Dôle	7 Aug
6.33	-0.4	Marika	Demesticha	GRE	29.2.76	2	NC	Athinai	26 Jun
6.32	1.2	Franziska	Hofmann	SUI	20.4.75	6	WJ	Lisboa	23 Jul
Wind assisted									
6.72	4.5	Yelena	Lysak ¶	RUS	19.10.75	1	WJ	Lisboa	23 Jul
6.64	3.2	Heli	Koivula	FIN	27.6.75	2	WJ	Lisboa	23 Jul
6.49		Lacena	Golding	JAM	24.3.75	1		Lafayette	26 Mar
6.48	3.0	Anna	Mironova	RUS	15.10.75	2	NC-j	Yekaterinburg	24 Jun
6.45	3.1	Ingvild	Larsen	NOR	3.10.75	1	NC-j	Drammen	9 Jul
6.44			Da Jie	CHN	25.3.77	3	NC-j	Nanchang	-25 Apr
6.43		Linda	Ferga	FRA	24.12.76	1		Bonneuil	May
6.40	2.1	Mano	Hanaoka	JPN	3.8.76	1		Utsonomiya	18 Jun
6.39	3.5	Magdalena	Khistova	BUL	25.2.77	4	WJ	Lisboa	23 Jul
6.32		Angela	Brown	USA	15.5.76	1		Sacramento	11 Jun

Triple Jump

Mark		Name		Nat	Born	Pos	Meet	Venue	Date
14.36	0.0		Ren Ruiping	CHN	1.2.76	1	NC	Beijing	1 Jun
		14.36w 2.3, 14.34 1.7				2	WJ	Lisboa	21 Jul
		13.97	0.6			1		Jinan	22 Apr
		13.84	0.6			3	WCp	London	9 Sep
14.32	-0.1	Yelena	Lysak ¶	RUS	19.10.75	1		Voronezh	18 Jun
		14.31	0.9			*	WJ	Lisboa	21 Jul
		13.91i	-			1		Moskva	4 Feb
		13.84				Q	WJ	Lisboa	20 Jul
		13.88	-0.1 drugs disqualification			1	ECp23	Ostrava	30 Jul
13.95	1.8	Olga Lidia	Cepero	CUB	4.2.75	1		La Habana	11 Feb
		13.82	0.2			1	NC-j	Camaguey	10 Jun
13.78	1.5	Irina	Myelnikova	RUS	14.5.75	1		Krasnodar	29 May
13.69	-0.1	Tatyana	Lebedyeva	RUS	21.7.76	3	NC-23	Voronezh	18 Jun
13.60	1.5	Madelin	Martinez	CUB	10.2.76	4		La Habana	11 Feb
13.50	0.0		Wang Xiangrong	CHN	.2.76	9	NC	Beijing	1 Jun
13.46		Suzette	Lee	JAM	6.3.75	1	JUCO	Odessa, Tx	21 May
13.43i	-	Chukwuete	Olomina	SWE	28.4.78	1	vFIN	Vaxjö	6 Mar
13.35	0.7	Kathleen	Gutjahr	GER	27.7.75	1	NC-j	Ulm	31 Jul
13.33	1.0		Luo Jun	CHN	75	1	AsiC-j	Jakarta	20 Sep
13.30	1.9	Elizabeth	Machado	CUB	2.1.78	6		La Habana	11 Feb
13.30i	-	Coamine	Boaje	ROM	20.7.77	1	NC-j	Bucuresti	11 Feb
13.28	1.0	Yulia	Lomakina	RUS	76	3	NC-j	Yekaterinburg	25 Jun
13.27		Olga	Boyko	UKR	6.7.75	1		Dnepropetrovsk	10 Jul
13.25i	-	Mariya	Kozlovskaya	RUS	78			St Peterburg	26 Feb
		13.23				1		Dzerdzhinsk	5 Aug
13.23i	-	Olga	Voronina	UZB	31.3.75	1		Tashkent	26 Feb
13.23	0.6	Tereza	Marinova	BUL	25.9.77	*		Sofia	21 May
13.21		Daniela	Bologa	ROM	7.4.76	1		Bucuresti	7 Aug
13.20	0.2	Ariadne	Godinez	CUB	16.8.75	1		Santa Clara	22 Apr
13.20	0.4	Heli	Kolvula	FIN	27.6.75	Q	NC20	Nivala	20 Aug
Wind assisted									
14.43	2.7	Yelena	Lysak ¶	RUS	19.10.75	1	WJ	Lisboa	21 Jul
13.51	2.6	Tereza	Marinova	BUL	25.9.77	1		Sofia	26 Jun
13.40	4.0	Andreja	Ribac	SLO	14.1.76	1		Zalaegerszeg	28 May

Shot

Mark	Name		Nat	Born	Pos	Meet	Venue	Date
20.02		Cheng Xiaoyan	CHN	20.11.75	3	NC	Beijing	5 Jun
	19.71				1	NC-j	Nanchang	27 Apr
	19.23				1		Beijing	Mar
	19.13				1		Beijing	May
	18.76				1	WJ	Lisboa	21 Jul
18.78	Yumileidi	Cumba	CUB	4.2.75	1	NC-j	Camaguey	10 Jun
	18.35				2		Ciudad México	7 May
	18.27				2		Ciudad México	1 May
18.15	Corrie	de Bruin	NED	26.10.76	1		Arnhem	19 Jun
17.44	Nadine	Kleinert	GER	20.10.75	7	NC	Erfurt	3 Jul
17.22i	Claudia	Mues	GER	3.1.75	2		Bad Segerberg	29 Jan
	17.11				8	NC-j	Erfurt	3 Jul
16.95		Lee Myung-sun	KOR	12.2.76	1		Seoul	13 May
16.90		Shen Xiaoli	CHN	10.4.75	2	NC-j	Nanchang	27 Apr
16.65	Alina	Pupo	CUB	9.3.75	1		La Habana	10 Feb
16.52	Olga	Ryabinkina	RUS	24.9.76	1		Krasnodar	28 May
16.31	Yelena	Klochikina	RUS	20.4.76	4	Army	Rostov	24 Aug

Mark	Name		Nat	Born	Pos	Meet	Venue	Date
16.00	Yanina	Korolchik	BLR	26.12.76	1		Grodno	1 Jul
15.89i	Collinus	Newsome	USA	5.4.76	2		Boulder	22 Jan
	15.59				1		Provo	25 May
15.76	Martina	de la Puente	ESP	4.4.75	1		Pamplona	30 Apr
15.76i	Anna	Rauhala	FIN	26.3.75	3		Jyväskylä	26 Feb
	15.71				8	WJ	Lisboa	22 Jul
15.73	Kristen	Heaston	USA	23.11.75	1		Davis	9 Apr
15.68	Teri	Steer	USA	3.10.75	1		Denton	16 Apr
15.68	Katarzyna	Zakowicz	POL	12.5.75	3		Pila	25 Jun
15.63i	Tabitha	Polk	USA	26.87.75	2		Baton Rouge	4 Mar
15.62i	Agnieszka	Ptaszkiewicz	POL	19.2.76	2		Brzeszcze	6 Feb
15.62	Amy	Christiansen	USA	20.4.75	1	NC-j	Tallahassee	24 Jun

Discus

Mark	Name		Nat	Born	Pos	Meet	Venue	Date
59.56		Yu Qingmei	CHN	20.5.75	1	NC-j	Nanchang	30 Apr
57.60	Corrie	de Bruin	NED	26.10.76	1		Zierikzee	10 Sep
57.40	Suzy	Powell	USA	3.9.76	1		Modesto	20 May
56.76	Sabine	Sievers	GER	3.3.75	1		Hagen	11 Jun
55.30		Zhang Yaqing	CHN	15.1.77	2	NC-j	Nanchang	30 Apr
55.24	Kirsi	Lindfors	FIN	9.12.75	1		Alavieska	14 Jul
54.62	Olga	Tsander	BLR	18.5.76	1		Grodno	1 Jul
54.50		Qin Lei	CHN		3	NC-j	Nanchang	30 Apr
53.80	Claudia	Mues	GER	3.1.75	2	v3N-j	Warszawa	18 Jun
53.54	Tilna	Kankaanpää	FIN	16.8.76	1		Seinäjoki	30 Jun
52.54	Veerle	Blondeel	BEL	14.1.75	1		Melle	6 Aug
52.42		Liu Weying	CHN		1		Nicosia	20 May
52.18	Alison	Morgan	USA	23.10.75	1		Champaign	25 May
51.86	Disa	Salander	USA	11.3.76	1		Grand Forks	16 May
51.62	Sonia	O'Farrill	CUB	9.3.75	2		La Habana	17 Jun
51.52	Olga	Ryabinkina	RUS	24.9.76	Q		Bryansk	5 Jul
51.46	Grete	Etholm	NOR	25.1.76	1		Spikkestad	28 Jun
51.26	Oksana	Yesipchuk	RUS	13.12.76	Q		Bryansk	20 Jun
51.24	Tatyana	Kozlova	BLR	26.3.76	1		Bryansk	4 Jul
50.92	Anna	Rusakova	RUS	17.5.75	1		Krasnodar	29 May

Hammer

Mark	Name		Nat	Born	Pos	Meet	Venue	Date
65.48	Mihaela	Melinte	ROM	27.3.75	1		Bucuresti	25 Feb
	65.04				1		Bucuresti	10 Jun
	63.44				1	NC	Bucuresti	17 Jun
	62.98				1	Balk-j	Ankara	2 Jul
	60.94				1	NC-j	Bucuresti	5 Jun
59.02	Simone	Mathes	GER	13.5.75	1		Rehlingen	23 May
	58.96				1		Ahlen	6 Aug
	58.46							16 Jul
	58.34				1	NC	Erfurt	2 Jul
57.80	Irina	Lungu	ROM	5.4.75	2		Bucuresti	10 Jun
57.62	Kirsten	Münchow	GER	21.1.77	1		Dortmund	25 Jun
57.44	Natalya	Panarina	RUS	6.5.75	2		Krasnodar	19 Aug
56.78	Veronika	Ushakova	RUS	8.11.77	1	v3N-j	Warszawa	18 Jun
56.06	Tina	Schäfer	GER	27.12.77	2		Rehlingen	23 May
56.04	Irina	Kuznetzova	RUS	75	2		Moskva	4 Sep
55.44	Lyn	Sprules	GBR	11.9.75	1		Haslemere	19 Jul
54.88	Svetlana	Lapu	UKR	13.3.77	5	NC	Kiev	27 May
54.42	Andrea	Bunjes	GER	5.2.76	2		Ahlen	6 Aug
54.38	Mariya	Lobanova	RUS	77	2		Bryansk	20 Jun
54.36	Natalya	Zlydennaya	UKR	12.12.78	1		Odessa	23 Apr
53.84	Brenda	McNaughton	AUS	7.5.76	2		Sydney	3 Sep
53.70	Caroline	Fournier	MRI	7.5.75	1		Montreuil-sous-Bois	21 Jun
53.34	Diane	Holden	GBR	12.2.75	1		Feltham	13 Aug
52.38	Irina	Martynenko	UKR	19.10.76	6		Kiev	-24 Jul
52.30	Natalya	Samusenkova	RUS	79	1		Bryansk	4 Jul
51.94	Lyndelle	Taylor	AUS	29.1.78	1		Brisbane	9 Dec
51.80	Cristina	Fechita	ROM	76			Bucuresti	5 Jun

Javelin

Mark	Name		Nat	Born	Pos	Meet	Venue	Date
61.78	Taina	Uppa	FIN	24.10.76	1	vSWE	Stockholm	27 Aug
	61.06				1		Jyväskylä	2 Aug
	60.22				1		Reykjavik	18 Jun
	59.92				5	WG	Helsinki	29 Jun
	59.60				1		Lahti	5 Jun

Mark	Name		Nat	Born	Pos	Meet	Venue	Date
	59.02				1	WJ	Lisboa	22 Jul
	58.50				2	NC	Tuusula	9 Jul
	58.32				Q	NC-j	Espoo	19 Aug
60.06	Maria C	Alvárez	CUB	30.8.75	1		Santiago de Cuba	9 Dec
	58.26				2	WJ	Lisboa	22 Jul
58.28		Zhao Guiyan	CHN	25.4.77	1	NC-j	Nanchang	27 Apr
57.20	Mirela	Manjani	ALB	21.12.76	1	Balk-j	Ankara	3 Jul
57.04	Ageliki	Tsialakoudi	GRE	10.5.76	1		Athina	29 May
56.52	Vera	Ináncsi	HUN	21.7.75	2	NC	Debrecen	9 Jul
56.00	Nora	Bicet	CUB	29.10.77	3		La Habana	10 Feb
55.90	Anna	Stroppolo	ITA	4.1.75	4	v2N	Cagliari	17 Sep
55.88	Réka	Kovács	HUN	26.1.76	3	WJ	Lisboa	22 Jul
55.84	Dörte	Patzschke	GER	16.8.76	1		Halle	14 May
55.80	Odalis	Palma	CUB	11.6.75	2	NC-j	Camaguey	11 Jun
55.76	Shinobu	Deguchi	JPN	5.5.75	1		Nagoya	14 May
55.76		Chu Chunxia	CHN	78	1		Nicosia	20 May
55.70	Christina	Scherwin	DEN	11.7.76	5	WJ	Lisboa	22 Jul
55.46	Zuleina	Araméndez	COL	23.9.75	1	Odesur	Valencia	24 Nov
55.28	Katalin	Antal	HUN	28.11.75	2		Budapest	8 May
54.96	Antigon	Vourdoli	GRE	4.4.75	1		Alexandroupoli	9 Apr
54.86	Nancy	Rahmsdorf	GER	11.10.75	1B		Ludweiler	7 May
54.60	Yanuris	La Montana	CUB	29.8.75	5		La Habana	13 May
54.38		Wang Yan	CHN	11.10.75	2	NC-j	Nanchang	30 Apr

Heptathlon

Mark	Name		Nat	Born	Pos	Meet	Venue	Date
6071	Kathleen	Gutjahr	GER	27.7.75	1		Bernhausen	26 Jun
	14.14 1.81 12.66 25.07		6.14 47.46 2:19.36					
	5918				1	WJ	Lisboa	23 Jul
	13.99 1.79 12.29 25.19		6.02 43.04 2:16.72					
	5889				17		Götzis	30 May
	13.97 1.75 12.07 25.07		6.03 42.88 2:17.23					
5992		Ding Ying	CHN	28.9.76	1	NC-j	Nanchang	30 Apr
	14.15 1.80 13.22 25.63		6.38 44.54 2:24.69					
	5804				6	NC	Beijing	2 Jun
	14.35 1.80 13.47 25.63		5.99 40.70 2:23.16					
	5785				3	WJ	Lisboa	23 Jul
	13.90 1.70 13.24 25.19		6.19 37.60 2:22.71					
	5684				2		Tangshan	27 Aug
	14.24 1.79 13.19 25.94		6.03 40.08 2:29.18					
5834	Regula	Cardenas	CUB	21.1.75	2	WJ	Lisboa	23 Jul
	13.92 1.76 13.49 24.61		6.06 33.86 2:20.64					
5616	Diana	Koritskaya	RUS	22.2.75	4	WJ	Lisboa	23 Jul
	14.21 1.70 11.79 25.49		5.99 38.20 2:18.49					
5604	Deborah	den Boer	HOL	18.4.75	5	WJ	Lisboa	23 Jul
	13.86 1.70 11.21 24.99		6.01 42.16 2:30.05					
5596	Vera	Ináncsi	HUN	21.7.75	6	WJ	Lisboa	23 Jul
	15.06 1.76 12.98 26.62		5.44 51.94 2:23.00					
5586	Deborah	Feltrin	ITA	10.3.76	10	ECpI	Bressanone	3 Jul
	14.60 1.75 11.57 26.38		6.14 40.06 2:20.51					
5564	Annelies	De Meester	BEL	30.1.76	1		Vught	21 Aug
	14.50 1.73 11.85 25.34		5.75 38.88 2:19.02					
5543	Gabriela	Groth	GER	22.6.75	1		Lage	15 May
	14.27 1.66 12.58 25.28		5.88 43.66 2:30.72					
5495	Tiffany	Lott	USA	1.8.75	9	WJ	Lisboa	23 Jul
	14.39 1.70 11.80 25.60		6.00 36.96 2:21.56					
5490	Katerina	Nekolná	TCH	23.6.75	17	ECp I	Bressanone	23 Jul
	15.16 1.78 11.93 26.28		5.77 42.02 2:21.67					
5468	Jane	Jamieson	AUS	23.6.75	10	WJ	Lisboa	23 Jul
	14.44 1.73 12.47 25.61		5.22 39.94 2:18.08					
5457	Sophie	Marrot	FRA	13.2.75	1		Versailles	26 Jun
	14.01 1.69 10.70 25.55		5.80 35.90 2:18.19					
5419	Angela	Andrukevich	BLR	25.6.75	1	NC	Gomel	10 Jul
	14.8 1.76 11.44 24.7		5.88 37.50 2:28.88					
5411	Galina	Granik	BLR	27.1.75	1		Gomel	28 Aug
	14.81 1.72 12.88 25.42		5.78 34.88 2:25.88					
5401	Clare	Thompson	AUS	28.12.77	1	NC18	Hobart	27 Mar
	14.22 1.69 11.78 24.98		5.81 31.38 2:30.98					
5385w	Lacena	Golding	JAM	20.3.75	1		Austin	7 Apr
	5346	6.10						

Mark	Name		Nat	Born	Pos	Meet	Venue	Date
5349	Stefanie	Rombach	GER	2.4.76	3		Bernhausen	26 Jun
	14.54 1.69 11.96 25.41		5.70 35.94 2:25.75					
5335	Annu	Montell	FIN	7.5.76	11	WJ	Lisboa	23 Jul
	14.56 1.61 12.17 25.62		5.79 39.86 2:26.83					
5332	Yelizabeta	Shalygina	RUS	77	1		Bryansk	5 Jul
	14.67 1.72 13.47 26.38		5.74 31.02 2:23.49					

4x100 Metres Relay

Mark	Nat	Team	Pos	Meet	Venue	Date
44.01	JAM	Robinson, Langley, Richards, Walker	1	WJ	Lisboa	24 Jul
44.75	CHN	Gao, Yen, Feng, Wang	1	AsiC-j	Jakarta	20 Sep
44.78	GER	Roos, Becker, Görigk, Möller	2	WJ	Lisboa	24 Jul
45.08	GBR	Allahgreen, Williams, Dudgeon, Drummond	3	WJ	Lisboa	24 Jul
45.18A	RSA - Transvaal	Greyling, Pretorius, Ullrich, Hartman	1	NC	Secunda	7 May
45.63	RSA	Sawyer, le Roux, Fensham, Seyerling	1h2	WJ	Lisboa	23 Jul
45.22	BUL	Vasileva, Ivaova, Georgieva, Khristova	4	WJ	Lisboa	24 Jul
45.48	ITA	Bettio, Giolli, Cuccia, Sieni	5	WJ	Lisboa	24 Jul
45.57	NZL	Miller, Wise, Hunt Arnott	6	WJ	Lisboa	24 Jul
45.62	UKR	Octaficuk, Kartashova, Shcherbina, Tkalich	2	vFRA-j	Dôle	6 Aug
45.66	BAH	Williams, Cherubim, Wright, Ferguson	2	Carif	Bridgetown	4 Apr
45.74	ESP	Rodriguez, Ruipérez, Marin, Cacho	3h1	WJ	Lisboa	23 Jul
45.90	Long Beach Poly USA		1		Arcadia	9 Apr
45.90	TCH	Klapácova, Volná, Válková, Beránková	1		Zofingen	3 Jul
45.94	THA	Serbsoonthorn, Incharoen, Srichurot, Prasumsin	2	AsiC-j	Jakarta	20 Sep
45.96	POL	Dybowska, Rambuszek, Glowacka, Cisela	2	v3N-j	Warszawa	18 Jun
46.00	RUS		2		Nicosia	20 May
46.21	TPE	Chin Yu-Ping, Chen Shu-Chen, Yang Pei-Fang, Yang Hui-Ching	3	AsiC-j	Jakarta	20 Sep
46.24	JPN - Ichimura HS	Suzuki, Hiro, Kuchida, Shimazaki	1		Mizuho	9 Jul
46.27	CUB	Diaz, Brito, Pernia, Pérez	3h2	WJ	Lisboa	23 Jul
46.28	SRI	De Zoysa, Dharsa, Rasanthi, Jayasinghe	4	AsiC-j	Jakarta	20 Sep
Hand timing						
44.2	USA	Burktt, Backus, Colander, Kelly	1	vCAN-j	Buffalo	14 Jul
45.2	CAN	Twumasi, Benyarku, Tomlinson, Rejouis	2	vUSA-j	Buffalo	14 Jul

4x400 Metres Relay

Mark	Nat	Team	Pos	Meet	Venue	Date
3:32.08	USA	Scott, Hennagan, Brown, McMullen	1	WJ	Lisboa	24 Jul
3:34.00	JAM	Ballentine, Berth, Howell, Barnes	1	CAC-j	Port-of-Spain	10 Jul
3:36.53	BAH	Ferguson, Williams, Sears, Rolle,	2	Carif	Bridgetown	4 Apr
3:36.59	ROM	Mircea, Miroiu, Burlacu, Tirlea	1	WJ	Lisboa	24 Jul
3:36.65	GER	Merkel, Angerhausen, Teichmann, Urbanski	3	WJ	Lisboa	24 Jul
3:37.41	RUS	Kotlyarova, Golovko, Voronicheva, Bolenok	4	WJ	Lisboa	24 Jul
3.37.55	FIN	Karkäs, Niemelä, Kemppainen, Suomi	5	WJ	Lisboa	24 Jul
3:37.93	RSA	Venter, Henning, van der Merwe, Ullrich	6	WJ	Lisboa	24 Jul
3:37.95	CUB	Diaz, Fuentes, Torres, Pernia	7	WJ	Lisboa	24 Jul
3:38.70	GBR	Eustace, Sloane, Curbishley, Thorne	4h2	WJ	Lisboa	23 Jul
3:39.35	CHN		1	NC-j	Nanchang	30 Apr
3:40.36	AUS	Watkins, Campbell, Andrews, Bradley	6h2	WJ	Lisboa	23 Jul
3:41.02	ITA	Caddeo, Selis, Salvarani, De Angeli	5h1	WJ	Lisboa	23 Jul
3:41.71	POL	Konieczna, Guziak, Kopankiewicz, Pskit	3	v3N-j	Warszawa	18 Jun
3:42.54	BAR	Sealy, Howard, Brackett, Straker	3	Carif	Bridgetown	4 Apr
3:43.28	SWE	Melin, Stuhrmann, Welin, Ahlepil	1	vFIN18	Stockholm	28 Aug
3:43.32	TRI		4	Carif	Bridgetown	4 Apr
3:43.38	THA	Meekaew, Tinnawon, Nokdilde, Conpang	2	AsiC-j	Jakarta	20 Sep
3:43.69	IND	Pardhan, Kaur, Vanaja, Beenamol	3	AsiC-j	Jakarta	20 Sep
3:43.88	BEL	Velghe, Buysse, Van der Plaetse, Stals	1		Oerdegem	9 Jul

5000 Metres Walk

Mark	Name		Nat	Born	Pos	Meet	Venue	Date
21:05.41	Irina	Stankina	RUS	25.3.77	1	WJ	Lisboa	24 Jul
	21:32.99				1	NC-j	Yaroslavl	21 May
21:06.0	Susana	Feitor	POR	28.1.75	1	SGP	Fana	8 May
	21:33.05				1	NC-j	Maia	3 Jul
21:24.71	Natalya	Trofimova	RUS	17.1.75	3	WJ	Lisboa	24 Jul
21:37.0+		Liu Hongyu	CHN	1.12.75	3	SGP	Fana	8 May
21:41.47	Maria	Vascó	ESP	26.12.75	4	WJ	Lisboa	24 Jul
22:03.69		Song Lijuan	CHN	9.2.75	5	WJ	Lisboa	24 Jul
22:05.48	Valentina	Savchuk	UKR	19.1.75	1	v2N23	Lvov	4 Sep
22:05.76	Tatyana	Gudkova	RUS	23.12.77	1	v3N-j	Warszawa	18 Jun
22:06.47	Yuka	Kamioka	JPN	28.5.75	6	WJ	Lisboa	23 Jul
22:07.83	Veronika	Budileanu	ROM	27.2.76	2	v2N23	Lvov	4 Sep

Mark	Name		Nat	Born	Pos	Meet	Venue	Date
22:11.6	Maribel	Rebollo	MEX	14.3.76	1	CAC-j	Port of Spain	8 Jul
22:14.52	Olga	Panferova	RUS	21.8.77	2	NC-j	Yaroslavl	21 May
22:23.31	Eva	Pérez	ESP	18.7.75	7	WJ	Lisboa	24 Jul
22:24.79	Mónika	Pesti	HUN	27.6.75	9	WJ	Lisboa	24 Jul
22:47.64	Miki	Itakura	JPN	1.8.75	1		Tokyo	23 Apr
22:48.00	Sofia	Avoila	POR	30.7.76	10	WJ	Lisboa	24 Jul
22:48.24	Yelena	Alekseyeva	RUS	3.5.77	4		Yaroslav	21 May
	21:59.8 ?				1		Kaliningrad	16 Apr
22:48.42	Natalie	Saville	AUS	7.9.78	11	WJ	Lisboa	23 Jul
22:49.04	Jana	Weidemann	GER	27.6.76	12	WJ	Lisboa	23 Jul
22:54.8 mx	Cheryl	Webb	AUS	3.10.76	mx		Sydney	12 Feb
	22:59.81				2		Sydney	21 Feb
Road performances, under 21:45 and where superior to track								
21:24		Stankina			1			1 May
	21:30				1	Int	Livorno	12 Jun
21:33		Trofimova			2	Int	Livorno	12 Jun
21:53	Tatyana	Gudkova	RUS	23.12.77	3	Int	Livorno	12 Jun
22:05	Mónika	Pesti	HUN	27.6.75	5	Int	Livorno	12 Jun
22.09	Olga	Panferova	RUS	21.8.77	6	Int	Livorno	12 Jun
22:19+	Miki	Itakura	JPN	1.8.75	+		Wajima	17 Apr
22:24	Jana	Weidemann	GER	27.6.76	7	Int	Livorno	12 Jun
22:29	Dana	Pinkert	GER	26.1.76	8	Int	Livorno	12 Jun
22:43	Yvonne	Anders	GER	14.5.76	9	Int	Livorno	12 Jun
22:48	Venera	Vasilyeva	RUS	17.3.76	1		Ishevsk	26 Aug
22:53	Lyudmila	Dedekina	RUS	78	2		Ishevsk	26 Aug

10 Kilometres Walk

Mark	Name		Nat	Born	Pos	Meet	Venue	Date
42:49		Liu Hongyu	CHN	1.12.75	3	NC	Beijing	7 Apr
	44:45.4t				3	SGP	Fana	8 May
43:30	Susana	Feitor	POR	28.1.75	1		Grandola	15 Jan
	43:47				8	EC	Helsinki	9 Aug
	44:16				1		Podébrady	23 Apr
	44:24				1		Rio Maior	9 Apr
	45:17.7				1		Lisboa	28 May
44:18	Natalya	Trofimova	RUS	17.1.75	1	NC 23	Yaroslavl	22 May
	47:24.6				5		Rostov	24 Aug
44:25	Wei	Linkun	CHN	.12.75	9		Beijing	7 Apr
44.53	Miki	Itakura	JPN	1.8.75	3		Wajima	17 Apr
45:18		Song Lijuan	CHN	9.2.75	8		Fuxin	30 Apr
46.38	Yuka	Kamioka	JPN	28.5.75	5		Wajima	17 Apr
47.05	Maria	Vasco	ESP	26.12.75	1		Badalona	20 Feb
47.06	Monica	Pesti	HUN	27.6.75	5		Podébrady	23 Apr
47:13	Jane	Weidemann	GER	27.6.76	1		Offenburg	1 May

SUPPLEMENTARY BIOGRAPHIES

Athletes showing top class form in early 1995

Hicham EL GUERROUJ (Mar)
b. 14 Sep 1974 1.76m 58kg.
At 1500m: WI: '95- 1. At 5000m: WJ: '92- 3. Ran on winning World Road Relay team 1994.
Progression at 1500m: 1994- 3:33.61, 1995- 3:35.70i. pbs: 1M 3:53.71 '94, 3000m 7:49.84 '94, 5000m 13:46.79 '92.
Great breakthrough in 1994 to run 3:33.61 for 1500m at Nice with no known form at this event before.

Darnell HALL (USA)
b. 26 Sep 1971 Detroit 1.83m 88kg. Reebok RC.
At 400m/4x400mR: OG: '92- gold R (ran heat); WI: '93- 1R, '95- 1.
Progression at 400m: 1990- 46.55, 1991- 45.38, 1992- 44.95, 1993- 45.22, 1994- 45.14. pb 300m 32.57 '92.

Mika HALVARI (Fin)
b. 13 Feb 1970 1.90m 140kg.
At SP: WI: '95- 1; EC: '94- 4; WJ: '88- 7; EJ: '89- 5. Finnish champion 1994.
Progression at SP: 1987- 16.06, 1988- 17.62, 1989- 17.96, 1990- 18.66, 1991- 18.71, 1992- 18.60i/18.45, 1993- 20.08, 1994- 19.93i/19.87, 1995- 20.83i.

Lambros PAPAKOSTAS (Gre)
b. 20 Oct 1969 Karditsa 1.93m 75kg. G S Karditsas.
At HJ: OG: '92- dnq 19=; WI: '95- 2; WJ: '86- 8, '88- 2; EC: '90- dnq, '94- 8. Balkan champion 1994, Greek 1991-3.
Two Greek high jump records 1992.
Progression at HJ: 1985- 2.11, 1986- 2.15, 1988- 2.26, 1989- 2.21, 1990- 2,24, 1991- 2.25i/2.22, 1992- 2.36, 1993- 2.29i/2.26, 1994- 2.30, 1995- 2.35i.

Tatyana MOTKOVA (Rus)
b. 26 Oct 1968 Yaroslavl 1.75m 68kg. Yaroslavl SA.
At HJ: WI: '95- 4.
Progression at HJ: 1989- 1.78, 1990- 1.83, 1991- 1.89, 1992- 1.86i, 1993- 1.92, 1994- 1.96, 1995- 2.00i.

Malgorzata SOBANSKA (Pol)
b. 25 Apr 1969 1.65m 50kg.
Progression at Mar: 1991- 2:35:50, 1992- 2:34:54, 1993- 2:29:21, 1994- 2:29:06. pbs: 1500m 4:20.74 '89, 3000m 9:14.98 '91, 5000m 16:04.18 '92, 10000m 33:29.39 '91.
Won London marathon 1995. Third Berlin 1993 and 1994.

Maria SOKOVA (Rus)
b. 2 Sep 1970 Moskva 1.70m 58kg. née Kochetova. Moskva SA.
At TJ: WI: '95- 5.
Progression at TJ: 1993- 13.00, 1994- 14.16, 1995- 14.54i. pbs: 60m 7.36i '95, LJ 6.49i '95.
Has a daughter.

Late Amendments to 1994 Lists

Women
10000m: 33:19.01 Dillon associate with mixed race best of 32:46.4, **100mh**: 13.53 Miachelle Deverell, **LJ**: 6.75w 2.8 Guthrie
Junior Women
800m: 2:05.05mx Selena Roberts AUS 13.10.76 Brisbane 26 Nov; **400mh**: 58.75 Blackett 24.11.76

Additional Dope Test failure

See Page 13

Einari Thor Einarsson ICE	3 Jul	4y
Kevin Braunskill USA	22 May	
Geirmundur Vilhjalmsson ICE	26 Aug	4y
Dias Redroso POR	6 Jun	4y
Marie-Paule Geldhof BEL	Jul	

Name		Nat	Born	Ht/Wt	Event	1994 Mark	Pre-1994 Best

MEN'S INDEX 1994

This index includes men listed in the top 100 of all standard events and in shorter lists for world record distances such as 1000m and 3000m, but excludes other lists such as 300m, half marathon, pentathlon and 3000m walk.

** indicates athletes included in the biographies section.*

Name		Nat	Born	Ht/Wt	Event	1994 Mark	Pre-1994 Best
Abdellah	Abdelhak	MAR	13 Aug 68		1500	3:38.37	3:38.65 -93
* Abduvaliyev	Andrey	TJK	30 Jun 66	186/112	HT	83.36	83.46 -90
Abrahams	Sean	RSA	4 Jul 70		800	1:46.86	1:47.23 -92
Abrantes	Arnaldo	POR	15 May 68	176/68	800	1:46.34	1:46.57 -88
Achike	Onochie	GBR	31 Jan 75	188/73	TJ	16.53, 16.67w	16.49 -93
Achon	Julius	UGA	12 Dec 76		1500	3:39.78	
Achour	Chaouki	ALG	8 Apr 65		Mar	2:11:51	2:13:05 -93
Ackermann	Georg	GER	13 Jul 72	191/75	LJ	8.14	8.02 -93
Adam	Alexander	GER	10 May 68	184/76	800	1:46.76	1:46.59 -90
Adán	José Carlos	ESP	22 Jul 67	166/57	5k	13:28.50	13:19.71 -93
					10k	28:12.36	27:59.49 -93
Adegbite	Steve	USA	23 May 72	186/77	110h	13.78w	13.9 -93
Aden	Jama	SOM	62	180/68	1000	2:19.26	2:20.30 -93
Aden	Yayeh	DJI	67		10k	28:28.83	28:56.23 -93
* Adeniken	Olapade	NGR	19 Aug 69	186/78	100	9.95A, 10.03	9.97 -92
					200	20.28, 20.23w	20.11, 20.00Aw -92
* Adkins	Derrick	USA	2 Jul 70	188/80	400h	47.70	48.39 -93
Adkins	Lee	USA	31 Aug 72	183/74	LJ	7.94	7.69 -92
Afanasyev	Nikolay	RUS	11 Aug 65	187/80	Dec	7768	8090m -85
Aguiar	Henry	VEN	15 Aug 66		400	45.93uc	46.21 -90
Aguilera	Jorge	CUB	16 Jan 66	172/64	100	10.26A	10.30 -86, 10.22w -93
* Aguta	Lameck	KEN	10 Oct 71		Mar	2:10:41	2:17:36 -93
Agyepong	Francis	GBR	16 Jun 65	178/71	TJ	16.95	16.88, 17.00w -92
A'Hern	Nick	AUS	6 Jan 69	170/60	20kW	1:23:07	1:19:33 -93, 1:20:13t -93
Aimar	Alessandro	ITA	5 Jun 67	178/68	400	45.98A	45.76A -93
* Akonay	Boay	TAN	3 Jan 70	168/62	Mar	2:08:35dh	2:13:46 -93
Akutsu	Kozo	JPN	11 Nov 60	162/50	Mar	2:11:31	
Aladefa	Ayodele	NGR	29 Dec 70	185/73	LJ	8.08	7.99 -90, 8.05w -93
Aladefa	Kehinde	NGR	19 Sep 71	193/89	110h	13.81	14.12, 13.77w -93
* Al-Asmari	Sa'ed Shaddad	SAU	24 Sep 68	165/60	3kSt	8:15.95	8:29.38 -93
* Alay	Sergey	BLS	11 Jun 65	184/98	HT	76.70	82.00 -92
Albert	Steve	USA	1 Apr 64	180/114	SP	19.20	19.11 -92
Albihn	Claes	SWE	12 May 71	190/83	110h	13.68	13.61 -92
Alekna	Virgilijus	LIT	13 Feb 72	200/120	DT	64.20	62.84 -93
Ali	Ahmed	GHA	15 Oct 72		400	45.87	46.61 -93
* Alisevich	Vitaliy	BLS	15 Jun 67	186/112	HT	80.68	82.16 -88
Aliu	Deji	NGR	22 Nov 75	187/75	100	10.17, 10.0	10.64 -93
					200	20.61	21.24 -92
Allevi	Massimo	ITA	23 Nov 69	181/72	PV	5.50	5.50i -92, 5.50 -93
Allison	Chris	JAM	27 Jul 73		100	10.20wdt	10.5, 10.66 -92
Almási	Csaba	HUN	4 Jul 66	176/68	LJ	7.99, 8.12w	8.14 -89
Almeida	Vitor	POR	6 Mar 70		3kSt	8:30.49	8:29.04 -93
Alohan	Omokaro	NGR	18 Sep 71	180/70	400	45.65A, 45.67	45.80 -93
Al-Qahtani	Alyan Sultan	SAU	23 Aug 71	168/60	5k	13:24.68	13:29.67 -93
Amegatcher	Solomon	GHA	20 Dec 70	180/70	400	45.94	45.42 -92, 45.1A -93
Amann	Martin	GER	23 Nov 70	188/77	PV	5.55	5.60 -93
Amin	Mohammed	PAK	69	190/80	400h	49.90	51.29 -93
Amos	Brian	USA	26 Dec 71	188/82	110h	13.41, 13.37w	13.43, 13.42w -93
Anderson	Chris	AUS	6 Apr 68	189/75	HJ	2.28	2.26 -93
Anderson	Tyler	USA	27 Apr 70	185/75	200	20.69Aw	20.93 -92, 20.74Aw -93
Anderson	Ubeja	USA	30 Mar 74	180/69	110h	13.49	13.52 -93
Andersson	Patrik	SWE	11 Feb 71		Dec	7637	7416 -91
Andersson	Pierre	SWE	4 Jan 67		TJ	16.64	16.54 -93
Andji	Alain	FRA	20 Nov 74	187/89	PV	5.60	5.20 -93
Andreyev	Vladimir	RUS	7 Sep 66		20kW	1:21:53	1:19:17 -91
Andrienko	Pavel	UKR	30 Jul 74	179/68	20kW	1:24:48	
Andronov	Yuriy	RUS	71		50kW	3:52:30	3:59:28 -93
Angello	Ivory	USA	27 Aug 73	190/79	TJ	16.57w	16.15 -92
Annus	Adrián	HUN	28 Jun 73	194/100	HT	72.56	69.26 -93
Anselm	Garfield	FRA	7 Jun 66	174/63	TJ	16.93	16.62 -93
Ansley	Kevin	USA	23 Oct 72	183/79	400	45.68	46.26 -92
* Antón	Abel	ESP	24 Oct 62	179/63	5k	13:15.17	13:17.48 -93
					10k	28:06.03	28:09.04 -93

Name		Nat	Born	Ht/Wt	Event	1994 Mark	Pre-1994 Best
Antonov	Nikolay	BUL	17 Aug 68	194/86	LJ	8.21	8.15 -93
Anttonen	Mikko	FIN	5 Jul 63	181/83	JT	75.64	78.14 -93
Anusim	Nnamdi	NGR	11 Jul 72	170/64	100	10.17	10.38, 10.29w -90
Arconada	José	ESP	18 Jan 64	192/76	800	1:46.94	1:45.02 -90
Arcos	José Manuel	ESP	19 Jan 73	176/76	PV	5.50i	5.62i, 5.55 -93
Argudin	Alejandro	CUB	10 Mar 74	174/65	400h	49.74	50.00 -93
Artsybashev	Alekandr	RUS	70		50kW	4:04:19	4:12:14 -93
Arzamasov	Sergey	KZK	9 Apr 71	189/77	TJ	16.84	17.27?w, 16.90 -93
Asahara	Nobuhara	JPN	21 Jun 72	179/68	200	20.61w	20.81 -93
					LJ	8.06	8.13 -93
Aseledchenko	Aleksandr	RUS	72		TJ	16.82	
Asinga	Tommy	SUR	20 Nov 68	188/71	800	1:46.93	1:46.74 -92
Assefa	Abreham	ETH	9 Dec 72	165/51	5k	13:33.39	13:40.19 -90
Assemat	Jean-Luc	FRA	23 Apr 63	177/60	Mar	2:12:29	2:11:49 -91
* Astapkovich	Igor	BLS	4 Jan 63	191/118	HT	83.14	84.62 -92
Astapkovich	Konstantin	BLS	23 Oct 70	185/120	HT	76.16	78.20 -93
Atnafu	Adugna	ETH	28 Oct 74		Mar	2:11:37	
* Austin	Charles	USA	19 Dec 67	184/77	HJ	2.32	2.40 -91
Avrunin	Igor	ISR	16 Jul 57	195/119	DT	59.24	67.14 -84
Axlid	Anders	SWE	1 May 66		SP	18.63	18.51 -90
Azkueta	Jon	ESP	2 Jul 67	170/56	3kSt	8:30.30	8:27.91 -91
* Backley	Steve	GBR	12 Feb 69	196/95	JT	85.20	91.46 -92
* Bada	Sunday	NGR	22 Jun 69	188/79	400	44.96	44.63 -93
Badhouria	Ajit	IND	1 Jan 69		DT	60.30	56.12 -93
Baek	Seung-do	KOR	16 Jun 68	172/56	Mar	2:12:54	2:10:07 -92
* Bagach	Aleksandr	UKR	21 Nov 66	194/125	SP	21.05i, 20.64	21.42 -89
* Bagryanov	Dmitriy	RUS	18 Dec 67	188/78	LJ	8.23i, 8.21	8.35 -92
* Bagyula	István	HUN	2 Jan 69	185/76	PV	5.70i, 5.70	5.92 -91
* Bailey	Donovan	CAN	16 Dec 67	183/82	100	10.03	10.36 -93
					200	20.76, 20.39w	20.88 -93
Bailey	Joe	USA	30 Mar 71	193/127	SP	19.04	18.66i, 18.56 -93
Bailey	Marcus	USA	16 Jun 72	185/75	LJ	8.06	7.60 -93
Bakler	Zoltán	HUN	1 Dec 71		HJ	2.23	2.10 -93
Balanque	Eugenio	CUB	20 Dec 68	188/75	Dec	8093	7908 -92
Baldini	Stefano	ITA	25 May 71	176/58	5k	13:34.81	13:39.37 -92
					10k	27:57.86	28:25.98 -93
Baltus	Tonny	HOL	28 Dec 65	188/74	800	1:45.88	1:45.50 -89
Balzer	Falk	GER	14 Dec 73	189/80	110h	13.76	13.96 -93
Baraznovskiy	Viktor	BLS	23 Jan 68	200/123	DT	63.94	63.90 -90
* Barbosa	José Luiz	BRA	27 May 61	184/68	800	1:44.75	1:43.08 -91
					1000	2:18.73	2:17.36 -85
Barbu	Cátalin	ROM	13 Oct 69	189/78	TJ	16.56i	16.63 -93
Barkaoui	Moussa	MAR	71		1500	3:38.18	3:43.2 -93
Barker	Ricky	USA	14 Nov 69	190/77	Dec	7871	7931 -91
Barley	Tray	USA	24 Jan 73		HJ	2.28	2.20i -93
Barmao	Barnaba	KEN	10 Dec 69	173/55	3kSt	8:28.12	8:38.0A -93
Barmasai	Bernard	KEN	69	173/55	3kSt	8:14.18	
* Barnes	Randy	USA	16 Jun 66	194/137	SP	20.82	23.12 -90
Barnett	Mike	USA	21 May 61	186/104	JT	76.94	82.06 -87
* Barngetuny	Eliud	KEN	20 May 73	175/58	3kSt	8:10.84	8:28.85 -93
* Barrios	Arturo	MEX	12 Dec 62	174/60	Mar	2:08:28dh	2:12:21 -93
Barroso	Jaime	ESP	15 May 68	165/55	50kW	4:05:37	3:48:08 -92
Barthel	Trond	NOR	11 Sep 70	189/86	PV	5.52, 5.53ex	5.45 -93
Bártl	Jan	TCH	23 Mar 67	195/122	SP	18.59i	19.06idq, 18.72 -93
* Barton	Tony	USA	17 Oct 69	190/74	HJ	2.30	2.32 -92
					LJ	7.91i	8.12 -93
Bartoszak	Michal	POL	21 Jun 70	180/68	3k	7:49.56	7:47.68 -93
					3kSt	8:34.42	-0-
Barzhagi	Luca	ITA	1 Jun 68		Mar	2:12:52	2:10:53 -93
Batle	Erik	CUB	10 Dec 74		110h	13.78	13.95, 13.84Aw -93
* Baudouin	Gérald	FRA	15 Nov 72	183/79	PV	5.80	5.70 -92
Bauermeister	Kim-Lars	GER	20 Nov 70	170/56	3kSt	8:23.19	8:27.96 -93
* Baumann	Dieter	GER	9 Feb 65	178/62	1500	3:38.49	3:33.54 -87
					3k	7:34.69	7:33.91 -91
					5k	13:12.47	13:09.03 -92
					10k	28:20.66	29:03.33 -89
Bayer	Gerald	GER	4 Jan 70	183/78	Dec	7685	7763 -91
Baygush	Viktor	UKR	16 Dec 63	182/110	HT	73.08	78.10 -88

Name		Nat	Born	Ht/Wt	Event	1994 Mark	Pre-1994 Best
* Bayissa	Fita	ETH	15 Dec 72	179/52	3k	7:40.06	7:55.50 -92
					5k	13:07.70	13:05.40 -93
					10k	27:51.56	27:14.26 -92
Bazarov ¶	Aleksey	ISR	14 Oct 63	184/75	400h	50.31dq, 50.38	49.33 -88
Bazzoni	Jon	USA	25 Dec 70	188/80	PV	5.52	5.35 -93
Beck	Marty	USA	2 Mar 70	190/77	400h	49.53	49.59 -92
Becker	Gustavo	ESP	17 Jun 66	184/70	HJ	2.29	2.30 -92
Beckford	James	JAM	9 Jan 75	183/73	LJ	8.13, 8.29w	7.53 -93
					TJ	17.29	15.70 -93
Béhar	Noureddine	MAR	8 Apr 66	170/56	1500	3:38.12	3:37.30 -93
Béhar	Abdellah	FRA	5 Jul 63	170/55	2k	5:01.36	5:09.10 -92
					3k	7:39.29	7:44.34 -92
					5k	13:16.70	13:25.62 -92
Bekele	Tesfaye	ETH	5 Feb 71		Mar	2:12:24	2:13:57 -93
Belabbés	Mohamed	ALG	11 Mar 66		5k	13:28.57	13:40.4 -93
Belák ¶	József	HUN	13 Aug 58	188/89	JT	76.36	75.76 -90
Belaout	Aïssa	ALG	12 Aug 68	170/63	3k	7:47.90i	7:38.70 -93
					5k	13:25.90	13:08.03 -93
Belghazi	Ali	ALG	22 Sep 62	176/60	3kSt	8:30.59	8:32.98 -93
Belikhov	Aleksandr	RUS	27 Dec 72	190/74	400h	49.97	49.47 -92
Belkacem	Henri	FRA	16 Mar 64	172/61	3kSt	8:34.49	8:39.14 -93
Belkessam	Ahmed	ALG	27 Mar 62	175/70	800	1:46.65	1:45.43 -90
Bellino	Paolo	ITA	19 Aug 69	185/79	400h	49.65A	49.39 -91
Belokon	Vladimir	UKR	13 Feb 69	188/84	110h	13.40	13.48 -93
Belonog	Yuriy	UKR	9 Mar 74	198/110	SP	18.72	19.02 -92
Belousov	Valeriy	RUS	22 Jan 70		Dec	7992	7657 -92
Benavides	Paul	MEX	5 Nov 64	188/78	PV	5.72	5.71 -93
Benet	Francisco	ESP	25 Mar 68	186/82	Dec	8034w, 7836	7854w, 7842 -92
Benfarès	Samir	FRA	6 Jun 68	183/63	1500	3:35.99	3:37.47 -93
Bennett	Mike	USA	22 Sep 68	190/86	Dec	7753	7636 -91
Bennici	Francesco	ITA	3 Oct 71	171/50	5k	13:33.5	13:29.41 -92
Benninger	Christian	GER	15 Mar 71	193/90	JT	79.46	77.54 -93
Benoy	Richard	USA	14 Jul 68	193/90	110h	13.55	
* Bentley	Dion	USA	26 Aug 71	193/86	LJ	8.28	8.39 -93
* Benvenuti	Andrea	ITA	13 Dec 69	183/70	800	1:44.08	1:43.92 -92
Benzine	Réda	ALG	71	180/63	5k	13:34.52	13:26.3 -93
Bergna	Andrea	ITA	20 Aug 68	180/75	110h	13.81Aw	13.91 -93
Berkeley	Noel	IRL	28 Nov 64		5k	13:32.59	13:51.90 -93
					10k	28:22.41	27:55.82 -92
Bernhard	Pierre	FRA	15 Feb 68	183/70	HJ	2.24i	2.26 -91
Bertoldi	Aldo	SUI	5 Mar 61	176/69	50kW	4:04:38	4:03:58 -92
Bertolino	Claudio	BRA	31 Mar 63	174/65	20kW	1:22:13.94t	1:23:41 -93
Besmer	John	USA	16 Sep 66		PV	5.50	5.21 -93
* Bettiol	Salvatore	ITA	28 Nov 61	178/57	Mar	2:09:40	2:10:08 -89
Bevan	Nigel	GBR	3 Jan 68	186/92	JT	80.38	81.70 -92
* Beyer	Wolf-Hendrik	GER	14 Feb 72	199/85	HJ	2.38i, 2.31	2.36i, 2.33 -93
Bi Hongyong		CHN	16 Nov 74		HJ	2.27	2.28 -93
Bi Zhong		CHN	5 Sep 68	188/110	HT	72.46	77.04 -89
Bianchi	Paolo	ITA	7 Oct 70	178/62	50kW	3:57:20	4:00:04 -93
Bianchi	Simone	ITA	27 Jan 73	183/75	LJ	7.94, 8.15Aw	8.06 -93
Bicet	Frank	CUB	13 Nov 71		DT	59.42	58.14 -91
* Bile	Abdi	SOM	28 Dec 62	185/75	800	1:46.01	1:43.60 -89
					1500	3:33.63	3:30.55 -89
					Mile	3:50.67	3:49.40 -88
					3k	7:42.18	7:52.23 -89
Bilek	Roman	TCH	29 Sep 67	174/61	50kW	3:56:03	4:28:47 -93
Bílek	Martín	TCH	7 Jan 73	194/112	SP	19.36i, 18.77	18.45 -93
					DT	59.02	56.94 -93
Billaudaz	Alexandre	FRA	3 Mar 72	173/61	1500	3:38.69	3:41.04 -93
* Birir	Jonah	KEN	12 Dec 71	168/52	1000	2:19.40	-0-
					1500	3:35.65	3:33.36 -92
* Birir	Matthew	KEN	5 Jul 72	172/62	1500	3:38.84	
					3kSt	8:14.68	8:08.84 -92
Bishop	Eric	USA	7 Jun 76	188/84	HJ	2.24i	2.21 -93
Bitok	Cleophas	KEN	73		1500	3:38.47	3:40.7A -91
Bitok	Ezequiel	KEN	15 Feb 66		Mar	2:12:45dh	-0-
* Bitok	Paul	KEN	26 Jun 70	173/57	2k	5:02.0+	5:04.5+ -92
					3k	7:34.36	7:33.28 -92
					5k	13:07.30	13:08.68 -93

Name		Nat	Born	Ht/Wt	Event	1994 Mark	Pre-1994 Best
Bittner	Daniel	GER	7 Mar 71	180/68	400	46.05	46.43 -93
Biwott	Gideon	KEN	26 Jun 66	176/68	400h	49.43	49.27, 49.2A -93
Biwott	Sammy	KEN	23 Jul 74	183/65	400h	50.01	50.23 -93
Bjørkli	Frank	NOR	30 Jan 65	180/61	Mar	2:12:20	2:12:23 -93
Black	Dennis	USA	4 Jul 73	183/122	SP	18.56	18.86 -92
* Black	Roger	GBR	31 Mar 66	190/79	400	44.78	44.59 -86
Blake	Arthur	USA	19 Aug 66	180/68	110h	13.74, 13.46w	13.24 -88
							13.20w, 13.2 -90
Blank	Peter	GER	10 Apr 62	194/93	JT	82.56	82.82R -90, 81.12 -92
* Blazek	Pavol	SVK	9 Jul 58	168/58	20kW	1:22:57	1:18:13 -90
					50kW	3:49:44	3:47:31 -88
Blockburger	Sheldon	USA	19 Sep 64	188/84	Dec	8281	8301w -90, 8296 -93
* Blondel	Alain	FRA	7 Dec 62	186/78	Dec	8453	8444 -93
Blume	Marc	GER	28 Dec 73	180/68	100	10.20, 10.19w	10.30 -93
Bo Lingtang		CHN	12 Aug 70	168/54	20kW	1:18:04	1:19:49 -93
* Bochkaryov	Pyotr	RUS	3 Nov 67	186/76	PV	5.90i, 5.70	5.85i, 5.85 -92
* Bodén	Patrik	SWE	30 Jun 67	188/102	JT	86.76	89.10S -90
Bogason	Eggert	ISL	19 Jul 60	191/115	DT	59.06	63.18 -86
Bogdanov	Aleksandr	UKR	29 Apr 70	190/88	Dec	7799w	7767 -93
Boit	Wilson	KEN	72		3kSt	8:27.90A	8:39.0A -93
* Boldon	Ato	TRI	30 Dec 73	175/75	100	10.07	10.22 -92
					200	20.53	20.63, 20.4 -92
Bondarenko	Yevgeniy	RUS	8 Oct 66	190/82	PV	5.65i, 5.50	5.70 -88
Bordukov	Vyacheslav	RUS	1 Jan 59	184/72	TJ	16.62	17.37 -84, 17.39w -87
Borglund	Peter	SWE	29 Jan 64	183/85	JT	79.76	84.76S -89, 87.00R -91
Borichevskiy	Aleksandr	RUS	25 Jun 70		DT	62.46	60.78 -93
Borisov	Valeriy	KZK	18 Sep 66		20kW	1:22:06	1:20:58 -88
Bormann	Helge	GER	21 Aug 67	198/86	400h	49.63	51.60 -93
* Boroi	Georg	ROM	26 Aug 64	182/71	110h	13.46	13.34 -93
Borozinski	Enoch	USA	2 Jul 71	185/86	Dec	7870	7671 -93
* Boru	Atoi	KEN	25 Oct 73	160/55	1500	3:34.12	3:34.61 -93
Botha	Johan	RSA	10 Jan 74		800	1:46.37	1:46.79A -93
					1500	3:39.96	3:50.02 -93
Botha	Riaan	RSA	8 Nov 70		PV	5.55	5.42 -92
* Boulami	Khalid	MAR	7 Aug 69		5k	13:12.95	13:33.77 -93
Bourgeois	Joel	CAN	25 Apr 71		3kSt	8:31.19	8:30.77 -93
Bourmada	Jamel	FRA	4 Oct 71		Dec	7670	7476 -93
Boutayeb	Brahim	MAR	15 Aug 67	171/60	3k	7:48.13	7:38.39 -91
					5k	13:21.64	13:10.44 -91
Boutayeb	Hammou	MAR	56	173/60	10k	27:57.05	27:25.48 -90
Bowen	Terry	USA	15 Sep 71	175/64	100	10.16	10.28w -91
					200	20.68	20.82A -93
Box	Toby	GBR	9 Sep 72	190/80	100	10.07w	10.34, 10.25w -93
					200	20.72	20.89A, 20.82w -93
Boydachenko	Vladimir	RUS	3 Oct 70		50kW	4:01:38	
Brace	Steve	GBR	7 Jul 61	178/68	Mar	2:12:23	2:10:57 -91
Bradley	Aki	USA	7 Feb 71	175/66	100	10.17w	10.30 -93
					200	20.44, 20.27w	20.69 -93
Bradstock	Roald	GBR	24 Apr 62	180/95	JT	77.22	83.84 -87
Brahmi	Azzedine	ALG	13 Sep 66	178/72	3kSt	8:36.18	8:11.27 -92
Braithwaite	Darren	GBR	20 Jan 69	188/76	100	10.26	10.28, 10.25w -90
Branch	Terrence	USA	11 Mar 71		400	45.52, 45.5	
* Brand	Steffen	GER	10 Mar 65	176/66	3kSt	8:23.75	8:15.33 -93
Brandenburg	Jeff	USA	10 Feb 72	190/136	SP	19.07	
* Braunskill	Kevin #	USA	31 Mar 69	170/70	100	10.24, 10.13Aw	10.29 -90, 10.11w -93
					200	20.22A, 20.40	20.45, 19.9 -90
							20.21w -91
Bremer ¶	Martin	GER	19 Mar 70	173/57	5k	13:33.57	14:00.65 -91
					10k	28:12.50	-0-
Bridgewater	Bryan	USA	7 Sep 70	178/75	100	10.25	10.08 -93
					200	20.50	20.11 -93
* Bright	Tim	USA	28 Jul 60	188/79	PV	5.65, 5.70ex	5.82 -90
Brimacombe	Steve	AUS	7 May 71	180/75	100	10.29, 10.17w	10.32 -93
					200	20.58A, 20.68, 20.22w	20.99 -92
* Brits	Okkert	RSA	22 Aug 73	198/82	PV	5.90	5.71 -93
Bronson	Bryan	USA	9 Sep 72	183/75	200	20.53	20.28 -92
					400h	49.72	49.07 -93
Brophy	Brian	USA	6 Jan 69	188/96	Dec	7903w	8276 -92
Brown	Jon	GBR	27 Feb 71	172/57	5k	13:23.96	13:19.78 -93

Name		Nat	Born	Ht/Wt	Event	1994 Mark	Pre-1994 Best
Brown	Kevin	USA	15 Aug 71	183/77	PV	5.52	5.52 -92
Brown	Kevin	GBR	10 Sep 64	176/114	DT	58.68	59.20 -91
Brunet	Xavier	ESP	5 Feb 71	178/74	Dec	7636w	7621 -92
Brusseau	Thierry	FRA	22 Jul 64	182/63	3kSt	8:27.98	8:22.22 -91
Bruton	Niall	IRL	27 Oct 71	180/69	1500	3:36.23	3:37.16 -93
					Mile	3:55.10	3:59.23 -91
Bruwier	Jean-Paul	BEL	18 Feb 71	185/70	400h	49.70	49.83 -93
* Bruziks	Maris	LAT	25 Aug 62	185/70	TJ	17.30	17.56 -88
* Bubka	Sergey	UKR	4 Dec 63	183/82	PV	6.14	6.15i -93, 6.13 -92
* Bubka	Vasiliy	UKR	26 Nov 60	184/79	PV	5.75i, 5.75	5.86 -88
Buchleitner	Michael	AUT	14 Oct 69	180/70	Mile	3:54.28i	-0-
					3kSt	8:29.45	8:24.44 -92
Buckner	Tom	GBR	16 Apr 63	182/67	3kSt	8:29.84	8:25.50 -92
* Buder	Oliver-Sven	GER	23 Jun 66	200/125	SP	20.44	21.06 -90
Budykin	Andrey	RUS	14 Apr 71	184/100	HT	76.66	77.68 -93
Bueno	Luis	CUB	22 May 69	174/67	LJ	8.00	8.28 -88
Bufuku	Clinton	ZAM	6 Feb 72	167/60	100	10.26, 10.121w	10.34, 10.28w -92
Bugár	Imrich	TCH	14 Apr 55	190/120	DT	61.22	71.26 -85
Buglakov	Aleksandr	BLS	16 Apr 72		HJ	2.25	2.28i, 2.25 -93
Bukhanov	Vladimir	UKR	1 Oct 61	174/57	Mar	2:12:27	2:13:14 -92
* Bukrejev	Valeri	EST	15 Jun 64	186/82	PV	5.86	5.81, 5.86ex -93
Bulat	Viktor	BLS	1 Apr 71	192/105	SP	19.92i, 19.62	20.06i -93, 19.63 -92
Buldov	Dmitriy	RUS	2 Jul 68	191/79	110h	13.83, 13.49w	13.59 -91, 13.4 -90
* Bulkovskiy	Andrey	UKR	22 Jul 72	184/64	1500	3:36.99	3:37.51 -93
					Mile	3:55.28	-0-
* Buncic	Mike	USA	25 Jul 62	193/113	DT	60.90	69.36 -91
Bundo	Pau	ESP	13 Oct 70		3kSt	8:33.88	8:34.65 -93
Bunney	Elliot	GBR	11 Dec 66	182/80	100	10.20w	10.20 -86
Burakov	Vadim	BLS	22 Oct 74		HT	71.80	70.16 -93
Burns	Brent	USA	2 May 69	193/88	PV	5.70i, 5.70	5.70 -92
Burrell	Alvaro	ESP	29 Apr 69	191/84	Dec	7979	8005 -92
* Burrell	Leroy	USA	21 Feb 67	183/82	100	9.85	9.88 -91. 9.85w -93
					200	20.05w	20.12 -92, 19.61w -90
Burton	Dan	USA	11 Mar 67	185/75	PV	5.60	5.60i -91, 5.53 -93
Busby	Kempa	USA	9 Oct 73	188/77	400	45.63	46.91 -93
Buse	Mark	USA	30 Nov 72	191/77	PV	5.66i, 5.60	5.60 -93
Busemann	Frank	GER	26 Feb 75	191/80	110h	13.56, 13.47w	14.06 -93
					Dec	7938	-0-
Buttiglione	Daniele	ITA	10 Mar 66		TJ	16.54	16.54, 16.68Aw -89
Buyvolov	Aleksey	RUS	20 Apr 72		LJ	8.05	7.77 -93
Bykov	Vladimir	RUS	70		HT	73.68	75.08 -92
Byrd	Leonard	USA	17 Mar 75	178/64	400	45.46A, 45.70	46.75 -93
Byzov	Dmitriy	RUS	25 Jan 66	183/75	TJ	17.13	16.92 -93
* Cacho	Fermin	ESP	16 Feb 69	175/63	800	1:46.94	1:45.37 -91
					1000	2:19.23	2:16.13 -93
					1500	3:35.27	3:32.01 -93
Cadogan	Gary	GBR	8 Oct 66	190/85	400h	49.07	49.25 -93
Cadoni	Davide	ITA	4 May 73	183/80	800	1:45.24	1:46.63 -93
Cai Min		CHN	8 May 68	184/82	Dec	7850	7824 -93
Calabro'	Emilio	ITA	4 Feb 69	186/115	HT	72.70	74.06 -93
Callaghan	Brett	AUS	5 Oct 73		400	45.8	47.1 -93
* Camara	Pierre	FRA	10 Sep 65	181/74	TJ	17.35i, 16.88	17.34 -92, 17.59i -93
Cameron	Trevor	GBR	25 Nov 76	183/73	100	10.29w	10.72, 10.57w -93
Campus	Milko	ITA	2 Apr 69	175/62	LJ	8.13, 8.15ex, 8.31Aw	8.06, 8.08Aw -90
Canale	Alessandro	ITA	15 May 69		HJ	2.25	2.15 -88
Cankar	Gregor	SLO	25 Jan 75		LJ	7.92, 8.04w	7.60, 7.68w -93
Cañellas	Mateo	ESP	27 Apr 72	179/66	1500	3:39.15	3:39.87 -92
* Capobianco	Dean	AUS	11 May 70	180/76	100	10.25w	10.25, 10.17w -93
					400	45.47	45.76 -92
Carlier	Jacky	FRA	8 Nov 61	182/66	5k	13:25.14	13:28.27 -93
* Carlin	Sean	AUS	29 Nov 67	198/110	HT	77.58	77.12 -92
Carlson	Rob	USA	27 Aug 71	196/114	SP	18.58i	18.93 -93
* Carosi	Angelo	ITA	20 Jan 64	182/66	3k	7:50.52	7:49.91 -93
					3kSt	8:14.02	8:17.48 -90
Carrat	Sébastien	FRA	20 May 74		100	10.24Aw	10.62 -92
Carrigan	Ricky	USA	6 Jul 73	178/70	100	10.24	10.22, 10.17w -92
					200	20.59, 20.4	20.56 -92
Carroll	Mark	IRL	15 Jan 72	168/60	Mile	3:56.44i	4:00.81i -92

Name		Nat	Born	Ht/Wt	Event	1994 Mark	Pre-1994 Best
Carroll	Pat	AUS	17 Aug 61		Mar	2:11:51	2:10:44 -88
Carter	Brashant	USA	30 Nov 73	183/75	200	20.48	20.95, 20.83w -93
Carter	LaMark	USA	23 Aug 70	180/75	TJ	16.94	16.78, 16.83w -93
Carter	Marcel	USA	26 Mar 71	170/66	100	10.25w	10.29, 10.22w -92
					200	20.55, 20.41w	20.34 -93
Cascabelo	Marcello	ARG	6 Feb 64	174/65	3kSt	8:32.16	8:25.63 -89
* Cason	Andre	USA	20 Jan 69	170/70	100	9.98	9.92, 9.79w -93
Castillo	Maurilio	MEX	1 Dec 62	175/65	Mar	2:11:13	2:10:47 -91
Castro	Artur de Freitas	BRA	12 Nov 67	172/52	Mar	2:12:44	2:10:06 -93
Castro	Orlando	ESP	1 Dec 70	185/69	800	1:46.87	1:47.69 -93
* Castro	Domingos	POR	22 Nov 63	167/56	3k	7:47.87	7:43.32 -89
					5k	13:17.33	13:14.41 -89
					10k	28:27.14	27:34.53 -93
					Mar	2:12:49	-0-
Caudron	Sylvain	FRA	10 Sep 69	186/73	50kW	4:04:37	4:05:02 -93
Ceresoli	Ettore	ITA	11 Apr 70		HJ	2.25	2.25 -93
Cerezo	José Manuel	ESP	23 Jun 73	180/57	800	1:46.02	1:48.23 -93
* Ceron	Dionicio	MEX	9 Oct 65	173/54	Mar	2:08:53	2:08:36 -92
Chaïb	Rezki	ALG	23 Jun 72	175/60	3kSt	8:33.96	8:55.93 -93
Chambers	Ron	JAM	5 Oct 58	182/84	LJ	7.97	8.18 -90
Chance	Neil	USA	14 Feb 73	193/91	LJ	7.99w	8.01i, 8.20w -93
Chao Chih-kuo		TPE	9 Dec 72	178/70	LJ	8.02	8.09 -93
Charadia	Andrés	ARG	10 Jul 66	192/100	HT	74.66	74.38 -92
Charrière	Pascal	SUI	14 Nov 64	184/68	50kW	4:02:25	4:04:03 -92
Chaston	Justin	GBR	4 Nov 68	178/64	3kSt	8:23.90	8:32.67 -93
Chaussinaud	David	FRA	19 Apr 73	193/93	HT	73.50	73.42 -92
Chege	Laban	KEN	67		2k	5:06.64+	-0-
					3k	7:48.45	
					5k	13:27.58	
					3kSt	8:29.59	8:43.3A -92
Chékhémani	Abdelkader	FRA	18 Jul 71	178/70	1500	3:36.73	3:39.51 -93
Chelule	Julius	KEN	25 Dec 78		3kSt	8:33.64	-0-
Chemase	Paul	KEN	24 Aug 76	170/59	3kSt	8:31.51	8:46.7A -93
* Chemoiywo	Simon	KEN	28 Apr 68	170/60	5k	13:07.57	13:09.68 -93
Chen Junlin		CHN	31 May 67		JT	75.52	77.82 -91
Chen Shaoguo		CHN	20 Jan 71	171/50	20kW	1:19:16	1:19:43 -93
Chen Yanhao		CHN	2 Jan 72	182/70	110h	13.39	13.59 -93
Chepkwony	Julius	KEN	69		400	45.77A	46.1A -93
Cherepanov	Vyacheslav	RUS	2 Nov 64		20kW	1:22:24	1:19:52 -93
Chernega	Yuriy	RUS	18 Feb 67		HT	76.74	79.64 -93
Chernikov	Vladimir	UZB	3 Aug 59	188/74	TJ	16.57w	17.36 -88
Chernyavskiy	Andrey	RUS	25 Jun 70	183/78	Dec	7631	7744 -93
Chervonyi	Aleksandr	UKR	26 Mar 70	187/81	PV	5.60i?, 5.50i	5.60i, 5.60ex -93
* Chesang	Reuben	KEN	66	170/55	1500	3:36.70	3:39.88 -93
Chesire	Joseph	KEN	12 Nov 57	167/57	2k	5:02.5+	5:14.07+ -91
Chikhachev	Aleksey	UKR	1 Jan 71	180/76	200	20.76	20.84 -93
Chimusasa	Tendai	ZIM	28 Jan 71	180/60	5k	13:33.51i	13:29.46 -93
Chirchir	Gideon	KEN	24 Feb 66	178/67	3kSt	8:15.25	8:19.34 -93
Chirchir	Robert	KEN			800	1:45.5A	
Chistyakov	Viktor	RUS	9 Feb 75	203/90	PV	5.70	5.35 -93
Chmara	Sebastian	POL	21 Nov 71	188/76	Dec	7717	7608 -93
Chmyr	Jaroslav	UKR	29 Nov 66	189/100	HT	77.38	80.90 -90
Cho Myong-hak		KOR	10 Oct 72		Mar	2:10:41	2:11:47 -92
Cho Hyun-Uk		KOR	15 Mar 70	180/70	HJ	2.23	2.28 -92
Choumassi	Mohamed	MAR	2 Dec 69	171/62	1500	3:38.71	3:41.04 -93
					2k	5:01.0+	5:15+ -91
					3k	7:43.76	7:42.66 -91
					5k	13:25.17	13:22.44 -91
* Christie	Linford	GBR	2 Apr 60	189/82	100	9.91	9.87 -93
					200	20.67, 20.56i	20.09 -88
Chronister	Rod	USA	26 Feb 68	193/122	SP	18.46	18.03 -93
Chumashchenko	Fedosey	UKR	27 Jan 73	171/66	20kW	1:24:18	
Cielica	Slawomir	POL	16 Sep 70	164/61	50kW	4:05:52	3:53:03 -93
Ciofani	Walter	FRA	17 Feb 62	185/110	HT	73.86	78.50 -85
Clarico	Vincent	FRA	8 Jan 66	184/79	110h	13.60	13.68 -90, 13.64w -93
Clark	Cletus	USA	20 Jan 62	193/88	110h	13.58w	13.30 -88
Clark	Darren	AUS	6 Sep 65	180/80	400	45.49	44.38 -88
Clark	Ron	USA	1 Nov 69	185/75	100	10.21	10.35 -91, 10.15w -93
					200	20.47	20.49 -93, 20.3w -90

Name		Nat	Born	Ht/Wt	Event	1994 Mark	Pre-1994 Best
Clay	Ramon	USA	29 Jun 75	186/77	400	45.82	
Coates	David	USA	25 Feb 70		400	46.00	
Cobb	Leonard	USA	20 Jan 75		TJ	16.65	14.49 -93
Coghlan	Eamonn	IRL	21 Nov 52	178/63	Mile	3:58.15i	3:49.78i, 3:51.39 -83
Cojocaru	Daniel	ROM	27 May 69	188/76	100	10.21	10.24 -93
					200	20.75	20.79 -93
* Collet	Philippe	FRA	13 Dec 63	177/76	PV	5.80	5.94i -90, 5.85 -86
Concepción	Jesús Gabriel	ESP	7 Aug 72	189/75	PV	5.50i	5.55i, 5.50 -93
Conjungo	Mickael	CAF	6 May 68	194/94	DT	63.78	59.92 -93
* Conley	Mike	USA	5 Oct 62	185/77	TJ	17.68	17.87 -87, 18.17w -92
Connolly	Jim	USA	24 Mar 62	185/86	JT	75.94	75.38 -91
* Conway	Hollis	USA	8 Jan 67	183/68	HJ	2.32i, 2.30	2.40i -91, 2.39 -89
Coombs	Eswort	STV	26 Nov 72	187/74	400	45.54	46.99 -93
Cooper #	Angus	NZL	7 May 64	188/100	HT	73.10	73.96 -89
Cooper	David	AUS	10 Aug 72		110h	13.80	13.92 -93
Cooper	Obadiah	USA	8 Mar 70	173/75	100	10.22	10.35w -93
Corbett	Marius	RSA	26 Sep 75		JT	77.98	73.00 -91
Cordero	Domingo	PUR	17 Oct 65	188/73	400h	49.33	49.12 -91
Cornette	Frédéric	FRA	29 Jun 67	172/63	800	1:46.69	1:45.82 -92
Corre	Jean-Claude	FRA	14 Sep 61	172/58	20kW	1:22:24	1:22:07 -89
Cortés	Javier	ESP	26 Oct 71	172/60	10k	28:26.61	28:47.92 -93
Coupland	Steve	GBR	15 Jun 65	181/76	400h	50.19	50.63 -92
Cousin	Christophe	FRA	22 May 65	179/66	50kW	3:59:41.7t	4:09:05 -93
Couto	Fernando	POR	4 Dec 59	165/59	Mar	2:12:15	2:11:18 -93
Cowan	Lloyd	GBR	8 Jul 62	193/76	110h	13.75	13.91 -90
Cox	David	USA	7 Aug 72	180/77	PV	5.54	5.52 -93
Crampton	Peter	GBR	4 Jun 69	190/82	400h	49.26	50.34 -93
* Crear	Mark	USA	2 Oct 68	186/79	110h	13.07	13.26, 13.22w, 12.9w -93
* Creighton	Shaun	AUS	14 May 67	180/65	3k	7:43.99	7:46.10 -93
					10k	28:02.13	-0-
					3kSt	8:30.56	8:16.22 -93
Crepaldi	Gianni	ITA	19 Oct 68	182/65	3kSt	8:30.18	8:27.35 -93
* Croghan	Mark	USA	8 Jan 68	175/60	1500	3:39.05	3:43.6 -91
					3kSt	8:10.56	8:09.76 -93
Crook	Zeba	CAN	28 Dec 66		3kSt	8:34.46	8:31.2 -91
Crosio	Roberto	ITA	15 Jun 66		Mar	2:12:04	2:13:51 -93
Cruz	Joaquim	BRA	12 Mar 63	187/74	800	1:46.96	1:41.77 -84
					1500	3:38.99	3:34.63 -88
Csillag	Levente	HUN	22 Mar 73	188/76	110h	13.75	14.01, 13.81w-rs -93
Culbert	David	AUS	17 Mar 67	191/85	LJ	8.00	8.13 -88, 8.33w -89
Cunha	Luis	POR	5 Dec 64	175/65	100	10.25w	10.36A -88
Curran	Anthony	USA	27 Jun 59	183/80	PV	5.52	5.70 -92
Currey	Andrew	AUS	7 Feb 71	193/95	JT	80.84	80.48 -93
Cushing-murray	Christian	USA	18 Oct 67	180/66	1500	3:38.03	3:37.94 -92
					Mile	3:57.05	3:57.70 -91
Czingler	Zsolt	HUN	26 Apr 71	186/76	TJ	16.51, 16.68w	16.87, 17.25w -93
Czubak	Tomas	POL	16 Dec 73	180/62	400	45.89	46.58 -92
Czukor	Zoltán	HUN	18 Dec 62	187/68	20kW	1:24:57	1:26:51 -91
					50kW	3:51:25	3:55:15 -90
da Costa	Ronaldo	BRA	7 Jun 70	167/55	10k	28:18.26	28:35.8 -93
da Silva	Carlos	BRA	23 Jan 69		Mar	2:12:39	2:14:54 -93
* da Silva	Robson	BRA	4 Sep 64	187/74	200	20.66A, 20.71	19.96, 19.7A -89
* Dagård	Henrik	SWE	7 Aug 69	183/79	Dec	8403	8052 -90
Dailey	Mark	USA	11 Dec 68	186/73	1500	3:38.86	3:37.31 -93
Dakov	Georgi	BUL	21 Oct 67	196/80	HJ	2.28i	2.36 -90
Dakshevich	Gennadiy	RUS	15 Mar 66	178/75	110h	13.72, 13.54w	13.55 -93, 13.4 -87
* Dal Soglio	Paolo	ITA	29 Jul 70	188/107	SP	20.68	20.65i, 20.43 -93
Daler	Justin	USA	12 Apr 71	192/89	PV	5.61	5.60 -92
Damasek	Kamil	TCH	22 Sep 73	195/91	Dec	7660	7507 -93
Damian	Mickaël	FRA	9 Nov 69	170/66	1500	3:38.4i+	3:38.6 -93
					Mile	3:55.76i	-0-
Damszel	Tomasz	POL	25 Mar 72	186/82	JT	77.46	77.60 -93
Danielson	Jonny	SWE	4 Sep 64	191/74	5k	13:30.67	13:20.29 -88
Dauth	Thorsten	GER	11 Mar 68	201/102	Dec	8112	8156 -91
David	Jean-Marc	FRA	2 Sep 57	184/102	DT	58.64	60.48 -85
Davis	Calvin	USA	2 Apr 72	183/79	400	45.20	45.04 -93
* Davis	Marc	USA	17 Dec 69	183/64	1500	3:36.31	3:37.12 -93
					3k	7:42.8+	7:43.62 -93
					2M	8:12.74	8:31.85i -91
					3kSt	8:14.30	8:14.26 -93

Name		Nat	Born	Ht/Wt	Event	1994 Mark	Pre-1994 Best
Davis	Terril	USA	21 Apr 68	183/64	800	1:46.84	1:44.44 -92
* De Benedictis	Giovanni	ITA	8 Jan 68	180/58	20kW	1:20:39	1:20:29 -91
					50kW	3:50:16	-0-
de Bruin ¶	Erik	HOL	25 May 63	186/110	DT	64.98us	68.12 -91
De Gaetano	Giuseppe	ITA	4 Oct 66	186/72	20kW	1:24:16	1:24:59 -92
					50kW	3:52:20	3:51:54 -93
de Jager	Herman	RSA	16 Mar 71		400	45.49A	46.15A -93
de la Torre	Carlos	ESP	18 May 66	170/58	10k	27:58.20	27:59.77 -92
de la Torre	Elisardo	ESP	10 Oct 71	175/65	3kSt	8:28.18	8:32.67 -93
de Oliveira	Edgar	BRA	11 Nov 67	180/67	1000	2:18.90	
					1500	3:37.61	3:34.80 -91
					Mile	3:57.35	3:58.38 -91
De Silva	Neil	TRI	15 Nov 69	175/75	400	45.96	45.40 -93
* de Souza	Douglas	BRA	6 Aug 72	191/80	LJ	8.20	7.61 -93
* De Teresa	Tomás	ESP	5 Sep 68	179/66	800	1:45.89	1:44.99 -90
de Wet	Hennes	RSA	13 Dec 67		JT	77.40	81.02 -90
* Deal	Lance	USA	21 Aug 61	188/116	HT	82.50	81.08 -92
Deering	Bill	USA	20 Jul 71	183/82	PV	5.70	5.60 -92
* Dees	Anthony	USA	6 Aug 63	193/95	110h	13.40	13.05 -91
Dehmel	Joachim	GER	27 Jun 69	190/72	800	1:46.53	1:45.27 -91
Delice	Patrick	TRI	12 Nov 67	184/77	400	45.68	44.58 -93
Delis	Luis	CUB	6 Dec 57	185/96	DT	58.68	71.06 -83
Delonge	Marco	GER	16 Jun 66	194/81	LJ	7.94i	8.27 -87
Demakov	Vyacheslav	RUS	8 Nov 68	191/100	DT	58.74	63.92 -92
Demmel	Norbert	GER	10 May 63	191/86	Dec	7919	8152 -89
Dempers	Riaan	RSA	4 Mar 77	184/75	400	45.15A, 45.98	46.56A -93
D'Encausse	Philippe	FRA	24 Mar 67	184/77	PV	5.70i, 5.50	5.75i -93, 5.70 -88
* Denmark	Robert	GBR	23 Nov 68	171/60	3k	7:42.62	7:39.55 -93
					5k	13:22.40	13:10.24 -92
					10k	28:03.34	-0-
Despotov	Radoslav	BUL	8 Aug 68	190/130	SP	19.00	20.13 -88
Dethloff	Claus	GER	24 Sep 68	187/97	HT	77.68	77.46 -92
Di Lello	Luigi	ITA	31 May 68		Mar	2:12:41	2:12:08 -93
di Mezza	Arturo	ITA	16 Jul 69	170/60	20kW	1:24:26	1:23:06 -93
					50kW	3:56:00	4:00:47 -92
* Di Napoli	Gennaro	ITA	5 Mar 68	180/60	1000	2:19.10	2:17.28 -91
					1500	3:34.42	3:32.78 -90
					3k	7:50.33	7:42.68 -93
* Diagana	Stéphane	FRA	23 Jul 69	184/75	400	45.49	45.18 -92
					400h	48.22	47.64 -93
Diarra	Ousmane	FRA	10 Feb 64	182/63	800	1:45.93	1:45.45 -90
Dias	José	POR	4 Feb 68		10k	28:07.4	-0-
Díaz	Andrés	ESP	12 Jul 69	187/71	800	1:46.80	1:46.84 -92
Didoni	Michele	ITA	7 Mar 74		20kW	1:21:44	1:24:19 -93
* Diemer	Brian	USA	10 Oct 61	176/64	3kSt	8:33.07	8:13.16 -84
Dikiy	Ruslan	BLS	17 Mar 72	189/94	HT	73.04	76.42 -91
Dixon	Marcus	USA	6 Jul 70	193/77	110h	13.75	13.63 -91
Dixon	Omar	USA	23 Jan 74	180/74	HJ	2.23	2.13 -93
Doakes	Ray	USA	12 Aug 73	203/82	HJ	2.32i, 2.28	2.28 -93
Dobler	Konrad	GER	27 Apr 57	178/63	Mar	2:12:57	2:11:57 -91
Dodoni	Marco	ITA	5 Sep 72		SP	18.69i, 18.59	18.22 -93
Dodoo	Francis	GHA	13 Apr 60	186/75	TJ	16.76, 16.99w	16.78, 17.12A -87
* Doehring	Jim	USA	27 Jan 62	183/120	SP	21.09	21.60 -92
Doka	Ali Ismail	QAT	2 Aug 73	182/74	400h	49.56	50.44 -93
Dolgushev	Pavel	RUS	11 Jul 68		800	1:46.69	1:48.36 -92
Dollé	David	SUI	30 May 69	192/80	100	10.22w	10.25 -93
					200	20.69	20.43 -93
* Dollendorf	Marc	BEL	7 Feb 66	192/84	400h	49.05	49.82 -93
* Dologodin	Vladislav	UKR	23 Feb 72	188/83	100	10.18, 9.9	10.32 -93
					200	20.36	20.38 -93
Domrachov	Sergey	UKR	27 Mar 68	196/103	HT	72.10	75.18 -92
Donati	Paolo	ITA	22 Jan 62		5k	13:26.97	13:34.50 -88
					10k	28:06.70	28:46.40 -92
Döring	Mirco	GER	21 Jul 71	173/59	Mile	3:57.50i	-0-
Dorival	Dudley	USA	1 Sep 75	185/77	110h	13.79, 13.65w	-0-
dos Santos	Valdenor	BRA	21 Dec 69		Mar	2:10:15	2:10:20 -93
dos Santos	João Joaquim	BRA	9 Sep 61		DT	59.20	59.12 -91
dos Santos	Luis	BRA	6 Sep 64		Mar	2:10:39dh	2:12:15 -93
Dost	Marcel	HOL	28 Sep 69	195/82	Dec	7896w	7883 -93

Name		Nat	Born	Ht/Wt	Event	1994 Mark	Pre-1994 Best
* Douglas	Atle	NOR	9 Jun 68	193/80	800	1:44.16	1:44.74 -93
Douglas	Troy	BER	30 Nov 62	173/71	200	20.60	20.69 -93, 20.3 -90
					400	45.80	45.37 -92
Dove-Edwin ¶	Horace	SLE	10 Feb 67	182/84	100	10.02dq	10.34, 10.16w -91
Downes	John	GBR	21 Jul 67		5k	13:29.91	13:57.56 -92
* Doyle	Simon	AUS	9 Nov 66	185/74	1500	3:36.21	3:31.96 -91
					Mile	3:55.11	3:49.91 -91
					3k	7:44.65	7:46.62 -92
Drahonovsky	Milan	TCH	18 Jun 66	180/65	1500	3:39.91	3:39.24 -89
Drake	Marino	CUB	13 Jun 67	193/73	HJ	2.26	2.34 -91
Driscoll	Jim	USA	15 Aug 65	183/109	HT	73.30	74.58 -92
Druchik	Vladimir	UKR	25 Jun 65	179/67	20kW	1:24:38	1:20:48 -91
* Drummond	Jon	USA	9 Sep 68	175/72	100	9.99	10.03, 9.92w -93
Duan Qifeng		CHN	20 Jan 73		TJ	16.90	16.96 -93
Duany	Raul	CUB	4 Jan 75	179/79	Dec	7913	7715 -93
* Dubrovshchik	Vladimir	BLS	7 Jan 72	193/115	DT	65.80	63.26 -93
* Dubus	Éric	FRA	28 Feb 66	182/70	1500	3:34.75	3:37.03 -93
					Mile	3:54.16i	-0-
					2k	5:03.88i	5:02.05 -92
					3k	7:49.91i	7:48.37 -91
Dudakov	Yevgeniy	RUS	69		Dec	8070	7902 -93
Dudás	Gyula	HUN	10 Aug 66	175/68	20kW	1:21:42	1:21:16 -91
					50kW	3:55:23	3:53:47 -91
Duncan	Richard	CAN	25 Dec 73	190/77	HJ	2.25	2.10 -93
Dupray	Gilles	FRA	2 Jan 70	186/102	HT	78.54	77.18 -93
* D'Urso	Giuseppe	ITA	15 Sep 69	178/56	800	1:44.20	1:44.83 -93
					1500	3:36.03	3:43.15 -92
Duval	Spencer	GBR	5 Jan 70	178/63	3kSt	8:28.33	8:32.77 -93
Dück	Oliver	GER	10 Feb 67	213/138	SP	18.90i, 18.77	18.93 -90
* Dvorák	Tomás	TCH	11 May 72	186/83	Dec	8313	8054 -93
Dvoretskiy	Sergey	RUS	69		50kW	4:05:48	
Dydalin #	Andrey	RUS	7 Jun 66	190/90	110h	13.72	13.50 -92
Dymchenko	Sergey	UKR	23 Aug 67	202/82	HJ	2.25	2.37 -90
Dyomin	Konstantin	RUS	3 Feb 74	182/70	200	20.74	21.45 -93
Ebner	Thomas	AUT	17 Nov 71	180/65	800	1:46.90	1:48.59 -93
Edler-Muhr	Werner	AUT	4 Feb 69	174/56	1500	3:38.46	3:39.38 -93
* Edorh	Claude	GER	27 Feb 72	183/82	110h	13.41	13.73, 13.69w -93
Edwards	Devon	USA	17 Feb 73	183/73	400	45.67	45.56 -93
* Edwards	Jonathan	GBR	10 May 66	180/74	TJ	17.39	17.44, 17.70w -93
Edwards ¶	Paul	GBR	16 Feb 59	186/133	SP	19.94	20.33 -91
* Effiong	Daniel	NGR	17 Jun 72	187/79	100	10.08, 9.98ig, 9.94w	9.98, 9.97w -93
					200	20.10	20.15 -93
Einarsson	Sigurdur	ISL	28 Sep 62	188/100	JT	80.78	84.94R -91, 83.32 -92
Ekpeyong	Udeme	NGR	28 Mar 73	179/68	400	45.26, 45.2	46.30 -93
El Ahmadi	Mustapha	MAR	68		1500	3:38.28	3:42.02 -93
* El Basir	Rachid	MAR	4 Oct 68	180/61	1500	3:35.84	3:34.40 -92
** El Guerrouj	Hicham	MAR	14 Sep 74	176/58	1500	3:33.61	
					Mile	3:53.71	-0-
					3k	7:49.84	
* El Khattabi	Larbi	MAR	16 May 67	174/68	3kSt	8:16.18	8:16.60 -93
* Elizarde	Alexis	CUB	19 Sep 67	192/110	DT	62.74	64.12 -93
Ellis	Kevin	USA	29 Jun 73	185/77	110h	13.81w	14.20, 13.87w -93
Emmiyan	Robert	ARM	15 Feb 65	178/69	LJ	8.00	8.86A -87, 8.61 -86
* Epalle	Christophe	FRA	23 Jan 69	194/110	HT	79.20	79.98 -93
Erease	William	NGR	73		110h	13.79	14.28 -91
* Eregbu	Obinna	NGR	9 Nov 69	183/76	LJ	8.22	8.18, 8.32w -93
Ereng	Paul	KEN	22 Aug 67	188/69	800	1:46.48, 1:46.19i	1:43.16 -89
Ergotic	Sinisa	CRO	14 Sep 68	179/63	LJ	8.00	8.00, 8.04w -90
Eriksson	Martin	SWE	15 Jun 71		PV	5.50i	5.61 -93
Eriksson	Niklas	SWE	22 Feb 69		110h	13.62	13.80 -92
					400h	50.06	50.56 -93
Ermili	Saïd	MAR	63		Mar	2:10:57	2:11:56 -91
Ernst	André	GER	6 Dec 67	186/72	TJ	16.63	16.59 -90
Esenwein	Peter	GER	7 Dec 67	188/85	JT	76.58	78.26 -93
Esmie	Robert	CAN	5 Jul 72	175/64	100	10.18A, 10.20w	10.23 -93
					200	20.70	21.22 -92
* Espinosa	Andrés	MEX	4 Feb 63	167/55	Mar	2:07:19dh	2:10:00 -91
Essaid	Mustapha	FRA	20 Jan 70	179/62	5k	13:22.34	13:23.94 -93
Estévez	Reyes	ESP	2 Aug 76	187/70	1500	3:39.28	3:42.36 -93

Name		Nat	Born	Ht/Wt	Event	1994 Mark	Pre-1994 Best
Evangelisti	Giovanni	ITA	11 Sep 61	179/70	LJ	8.20A, 7.92	8.43 -87
Evans	Randall	USA	26 Oct 70	180/79	100	10.13	10.20, 10.19w -93
					200	20.61	20.50 -93
* Everett	Mark	USA	2 Sep 68	183/70	400	45.81	44.59 -91
					800	1:44.36	1:43.40 -92
Eyestone	Ed	USA	15 Jun 61	185/61	Mar	2:11:51	2:10:59 -90
* Ezinwa	Davidson	NGR	22 Nov 71	184/82	100	9.94	9.96, 9.91dwr -92
					200	20.43	20.25 -92, 19.9 -89
Ezinwa	Osmond	NGR	22 Nov 71	182/79	100	10.10	10.09 -92, 9.8dt -90
					200	20.75	20.83 -90, 20.6 -89
Ezzher	Mohamed	FRA	26 Apr 60	176/58	5k	13:23.82	13:42.47 -90
					10k	27:57.87	29:10.36 -92
Fábián	Zoltán	HUN	22 Apr 69	183/91	HT	76.28	72.98 -91
Fadeyevs	Aigars	LAT	27 Dec 75	170/59	20kW	1:23:41	1:36:19 -93
					50kW	4:02:18	-0-
Fantini	Corrado	ITA	7 Feb 67	191/120	SP	19.65	19.10 -93
Farraudière	Jacques	FRA	27 Jan 66	188/81	400	45.71	46.01 -93
Fasinro	Tosi	GBR	28 Mar 72	188/83	TJ	16.70, 16.74w	17.21, 17.30w -93
Fatun	Oleg	RUS	23 Mar 59	181/78	200	20.68, 20.5	20.41A -87, 20.65 -89
Faust	Abe	USA	73	190/80	HJ	2.25	2.23 -93
Faye	Ibou	SEN	69		400h	50.25	51.29 -93
Fedoriv	Andrey	RUS	11 Aug 63	177/80	100	10.26	10.21 -87, 10.19w -93
					200	20.56	20.53 -86
Fell	Graeme	CAN	19 Mar 59	190/75	3kSt	8:23.28	8:12.58 -85
* Fenner	Mike	GER	24 Apr 71	186/80	110h	13.42	13.64 -93
Fernandes	Nuño	POR	1 Apr 69	182/78	PV	5.61	5.45 -92
Ferrari	Roberto	ITA	24 Mar 67	185/72	HJ	2.28	2.30 -93
Ferrin	Wenceslão	COL	3 Oct 69		400	45.84A	
Fesselier	Martial	FRA	9 Oct 61	168/61	20kW	1:23:56.0t	1:23:43.1t -91
Fields	Sheddric	USA	13 Apr 73	190/77	LJ	8.10, 8.11w	8.14 -91
Filippov	Vladislav	RUS	72		HT	74.48	68.08 -93
Finch	Rodney	GBR	5 Aug 67	184/60	1500	3:38.80	3:37.97 -93
Fingert	Aleksandr	ISR	1 May 65	198/100	JT	76.60	80.18 -89
Finnerty	Cormac	IRL	14 Jan 70		10k	28:26.95	-0-
Finni	Jarko	FIN	19 Feb 72	191/86	Dec	7843	7517 -93
Fischer	Andreas	GER	11 Apr 68	182/60	3kSt	8:36.20	8:27.46 -90
Fischer	Jeremy	USA	17 Feb 76	175/68	HJ	2.23	2.18 -93
Fitzpatrick	Kevin	USA	26 Sep 69	193/105	DT	62.54	61.68 -92
* Fíz	Martin	ESP	3 Mar 63	167/56	Mar	2:10:21dh, 2:10:31	2:12:47 -93
Flint	Mark	GBR	19 Oct 63	163/58	Mar	2:12:07	2:19:04 -93
Floder	Bernhard	GER	17 Apr 73		Dec	7694	7397 -92
Floréal	Edrick	CAN	5 Oct 66	190/82	LJ	8.05	8.20 -91, 8.39w -89
					TJ	17.13, 17.17w	17.23 -90, 17.29A -89
Flowers	Ross	USA	10 Aug 71	183/77	110h	13.81, 13.69w	13.84, 13.80w -93
Fomenko	Sergey	UKR	7 Jun 67	188/82	PV	5.60i	5.70i -91, 5.65 -92
Fonseca	Peter	CAN	5 Oct 66	172/55	Mar	2:12:14	2:12:07 -90
Font	Oscar	ESP	30 Dec 66	174/62	50kW	4:06:45	3:57:25 -91
Forbes	Brad	JAM	72		100	10.21w	10.64 -92
* Forsyth	Tim	AUS	17 Aug 73	196/73	HJ	2.33	2.35 -93
Fortuna	Diego	ITA	14 Feb 68		DT	59.68	60.02 -93
* Foster	Greg	USA	4 Aug 58	190/88	110h	13.26, 13.22w	13.03 -81, 13.0 -79
Foster #	Robert	JAM	12 Jul 70	190/88	110h	13.53	13.77 -93, 13.4, 13.65w -92
Fouche	Francois	RSA	5 Jun 63	191/80	LJ	8.12A, 8.19Aw	8.21A -90
							8.03, 8.32Aw -89
Fouche	Louis	RSA	21 Mar 70		JT	78.94	79.64 -93
Fox	Chris	USA	22 Oct 58	185/57	10k	28:22.48	28:27.28 -88
Foxson	Paul	USA	16 Apr 71	193/93	Dec	8234	7878w/7817 -92
Fraley	Doug	USA	7 Mar 65	185/82	PV	5.70	5.80 -92
Francis	Mike	PUR	23 Oct 70	183/79	LJ	7.97i	8.13 -93
Francis	Mitchell	JAM	13 Jun 72	185/81	400h	49.86	49.89 -93
Frangi	Eugenio	ITA	6 Aug 71		3kSt	8:36.7	8:37.25 -93
* Franke	Stephane	GER	12 Feb 64	178/58	3k	7:40.75	7:40.11 -93
					5k	13:14.68	13:13.17 -93
					10k	28:07.95	27:57.98 -93
* Fredericks	Frank	NAM	2 Oct 67	180/73	100	10.04, 10.00w	9.95, 9.89w -91
					200	19.97A, 19.97	19.85 -93
* Freigang	Stephan	GER	27 Sep 67	177/64	10k	28:06.32	27:59.72 -93
Frempong	Eric	CAN	1 Oct 75	186/75	200	20.65, 20.5w	20.99 -93
Frinolli	Giorgio	ITA	12 Jul 70	184/73	400h	49.43	49.22 -93

Name		Nat	Born	Ht/Wt	Event	1994 Mark	Pre-1994 Best
* Fritz	Steve	USA	1 Nov 67	191/86	Dec	8548	8324 -93
Fritz	Wolfgang	AUT	3 Apr 68	180/65	3kSt	8:30.29	8:32.17 -92
Fucci	Drew	USA	26 May 67	188/84	Dec	8105	8079 -91
Fujishima	Koji	JPN	2 Jul 70	183/65	HJ	2.25	2.24 -93
Fulford	Rich	USA	29 Apr 69	183/79	PV	5.50i	5.60 -91
Fyodorkov	Grigoriy	RUS	9 Nov 64	198/82	HJ	2.31i, 2.28	2.31 -90
Gajdus	Grzegorz	POL	16 Jan 67	181/70	Mar	2:09:49	2:11:07 -93
* Galfione	Jean	FRA	9 Jun 71	181/82	PV	5.94	5.93 -93
Galkin	Konstantin	RUS	25 Mar 65	189/71	HJ	2.25i, 2.25	2.28 -93
Galkin	Pavel	RUS	9 Oct 68	186/79	100	10.20	10.27 -90, 10.12w -92
					200	20.5	21.24 -89
Ganiyev	Ramil	UZB	23 Sep 68	186/80	Dec	8106	8160 -92
Gao Junbing		CHN			20kW	1:21:37	1:24:02.5t -92
Gao Yunbin		CHN	Oct 75		20kW	1:21:27	1:25:17 -93
Gao Shuhai		CHN	18 Oct 68	175/60	3kSt	8:31.56	8:33.60 -93
* Garcia	Daniel	MEX	28 Oct 71	164/55	20kW	1:20:33	1:19:42 -93
					50kW	4:00:17	3:53:23 -93
* Garcia	Diego	ESP	12 Oct 61	172/62	Mar	2:10:46	2:10:30 -92
Garcia	Edgar	PUR			HJ	2.25	2.08 -93
Garcia	Ivan	CUB	29 Feb 72	182/68	200	20.60	20.65, 20.53w -93
Garcia	Javier	ESP	22 Jul 66	177/71	PV	5.60	5.77i -92, 5.75 -90
* Garcia	Jesus Angel	ESP	17 Oct 69	170/55	50kW	3:41:28	3:41:41 -93
Garcia	Joel	CUB	25 Nov 73		TJ	16.62	16.39 -93
Garcia	José M.	ESP	24 Jan 66	178/65	10k	28:11.06	28:36.21 -92
Garcia	Ruben	MEX	29 Dec 70	169/53	3kSt	8:36.81	8:33.2 -92
Gardener	Jason	GBR	17 Sep 75	178/66	100	10.25	10.62, 10.46w -93
Gariba	Salaam	GHA	23 Jan 69	172/71	100	10.27A	10.27, 9.9 -91
Garin	Gabriel	ESP	13 Aug 69	176/60	3kSt	8:32.45	8:38.99 -91
Gaskin	Wendell	USA	7 Jan 73	183/75	100	10.25ig	10.21 -93
					400	45.29	46.76 -93
* Gataullin	Radion	RUS	23 Nov 65	189/78	PV	6.00	6.02i, 6.00 -89
Gats	Carlos	ARG	11 Dec 69	181/73	100	10.25	10.42 -92
					200	20.51, 20.4w	21.06 -90, 20.5w -93
Gatsioudis	Kostas	GRE	17 Dec 73	188/86	JT	83.82	80.30 -92
Gavela	Rodrigo	ESP	5 Jan 66	173/60	Mar	2:11:34	2:10:27 -93
Gavrilov	Sergey	RUS	22 May 70		HT	79.18	75.76 -93
* Gebrselassie	Haile	ETH	18 Apr 73	160/54	1500	3:37.04	?
					2k	5:01.6+	-0-
					3k	7:37.49	7:47.8u+ -93
					5k	12:56.96	13:03.17 -93
					10k	27:15.00	27:30.17 -93
Gebrselassie	Tekeye	ETH	16 Oct 70		Mar	2:11:45	2:13:52 -93
* Gécsek	Tibor	HUN	22 Sep 64	184/100	HT	80.22	81.68 -88
Gendekos	Nikos	GRE	9 Jul 66	186/100	HT	72.64	70.70 -92
Georgiev	Galin	BUL	23 Mar 70	184/78	LJ	8.09i	8.20 -92
Ghirma	Daba	ETH	71		Mar	2:12:07	-0-
Ghoula	Hatem	TUN	7 Jun 63		20kW	1:22:51.84t	1:33:24 -93
* Gicquel	Jean-Charles	FRA	24 Feb 67	200/80	HJ	2.35i, 2.33	2.30 -90
Gilbert	Glenroy	CAN	31 Aug 68	183/79	100	10.10	10.16, 10.01w -93
					200	20.5	20.37 -93
Gilpan	Rory	JAM	15 Apr 72		100	10.24wdt	
Ginko	Viktor	BLS	7 Dec 65	186/76	20kW	1:21:55	1:20:03 -93
					50kW	3:45:34	3:48:42 -92
Giocondi	Andrea	ITA	17 Jan 69	180/70	800	1:45.43	1:45.97 -92
					1500	3:38.90	3:40.56 -92
* Gitonga	Charles	KEN	5 Oct 71	175/65	400	45.00	45.1A -93
Giusto	Matt	USA	25 Oct 66	178/62	1500	3:39.36	3:38.06 -90
					3k	7:46.96	7:41.60 -93
Gladkikh	Aleksey	RUS	17 Apr 71		PV	5.60i	5.40i -92
Glovatskiy	Aleksandr	BLS	2 May 70	185/72	LJ	8.21	8.10 -90
					TJ	17.12i, 16.92	16.28i -92
Glushenko	Gennadiy	UKR	26 May 70	186/74	TJ	16.77	16.65i -93
Godard	Jean-Michel	FRA	19 Jan 71	194/85	PV	5.50i	5.50 -93
Godina	John	USA	31 May 72	193/118	SP	20.03i, 20.01	20.03 -93
					DT	62.24	61.52 -92
Göhler	Sven	GER	25 Feb 74	187/74	110h	13.66	13.75 -92
Golding	Julian	GBR	17 Feb 75	184/69	200	20.73w	21.59, 21.48w -93
* Golley	Julian	GBR	12 Sep 71	185/80	TJ	17.06	16.95 -92
Golos	Dmitriy	BLS	13 Jul 70		20kW	1:22:05	1:20:42 -93

Name		Nat	Born	Ht/Wt	Event	1994 Mark	Pre-1994 Best
Golovastov	Dmitriy	RUS	14 Jul 71	191/72	400	45.62	45.65 -93
Golyas	Vladimir	RUS	25 Jan 71	182/63	3kSt	8:32.97	8:28.66 -92
Gombala	Milan	TCH	29 Jan 68	187/75	LJ	8.04, 8.09w	8.11, 8.42Aw, 8.18i.ir-pit -92
Goncharuk	Dmitriy	BLS	10 Sep 70		SP	19.88	19.25 -91
Gonzalez	Luis Javier	ESP	17 Jun 69	181/63	800	1:46.60, 1:46.35i	1:44.84 -93
González	Emeterio	CUB	11 Apr 73		JT	78.18	74.14 -93
Gordey	Vitaliy	BLS	11 Jul 73		20kW	1:22:14	1:22:14 -93
Gordeyev	Yuriy	RUS	64		20kW	1:23:27	1:19:53 -93
Gordon	Leon	JAM	1 Jul 74	172/75	100	10.24ig	10.4 -93
Görmer	Steffen	GER	28 Jul 68	178/80	100	10.24w	10.28 -89
Gorshenin	Aleksandr	RUS	11 May 69		110h	13.70, 13.49w	14.08 -93
Gorshkov	Anatoliy	UKR	4 Aug 58	176/62	20kW	1:24:55	1:20:04 -87
Grabovoy	Vadim	UKR	5 Apr 73	191/97	HT	77.14	73.98 -92
* Graham	Winthrop	JAM	17 Nov 65	178/72	400h	48.05	47.60 -93
Granat	Marko	SWE	7 Jan 66		400h	50.12	50.8, 51.32 -92
* Grant	Dalton	GBR	8 Apr 66	186/73	HJ	2.37i, 2.34	2.36 -91
Grant	Travis	USA	31 Aug 72	178/73	100	10.26A, 10.16w	10.37 -93
					200	20.72A, 20.59w	20.80, 20.65w -92
* Grasu	Costel	ROM	5 Jul 67	191/105	DT	63.68	67.08 -92
Grava	Jean-Marc	FRA	2 Dec 71	186/70	110h	13.81w	14.05 -93
Gravelle #	Mike	USA	13 Apr 65	196/111	DT	65.04	65.24 -91
* Gray	Johnny	USA	19 Jun 60	190/76	800	1:43.73	1:42.60 -85
Gray	Paul	GBR	25 May 69	184/79	110h	13.53	13.97 -88
Green	André	GER	21 Apr 73	182/65	3kSt	8:35.88	8:43.38 -93
* Green	Michael	JAM	7 Nov 70	176/73	100	10.05, 10.04w	10.09 -93, 10.02w -91
Green	Stephen	GBR	18 Feb 71	172/59	1500	3:39.19	3:42.43 -93
Greene	Joe	USA	17 Feb 67	183/68	LJ	8.07	8.38, 8.66Aw -92
					TJ	16.67	16.88 -89, 16.93w -90
Greene	Paul	AUS	9 Dec 72	184/78	400	45.50	45.61 -91
Greenidge	Ricardo	CAN	12 Feb 71	186/82	200	20.61ig	20.93 -93
Grifaldi	Maurizio	ITA	19 May 67		TJ	16.66	16.32i, 16.20 -93
Griffin	Roshaan	USA	21 Feb 74	175/64	200	20.58, 20.40ig	20.72 -93
Grigoryan	Parkev	ARM	1 May 65	186/74	TJ	16.93A	17.01 -92
Grigoryev	Anatoliy	RUS	60		20kW	1:23:56	1:20:50 -90
Grokhovskiy	Oleg	RUS	3 May 68	188/72	TJ	17.05i	17.40 -91
Grossard	Hubert	BEL	28 Mar 68	183/70	110h	13.67	13.47 -93
Grossi	Fabio	ITA	3 Sep 67	185/72	400	45.92	45.93 -91
Guba	Vladislav	UKR	17 Dec 71	186/70	110h	13.68, 13.42w	13.71 -93
Gubkin	Valeriy	BLS	3 Sep 67	190/93	HT	75.84	78.62 -93
Gudmundsson	Andrés	ISL	65		SP	18.63	17.35 -93
* Gudmundsson	Pétur	ISL	9 Mar 62	193/124	SP	20.44	21.26 -90
Guerra	Francisco	ESP	13 Dec 57	170/59	10k	28:29.75	28:17.81 -92
* Guerra	Paulo	POR	21 Aug 70	173/57	5k	13:25.13	13:42.35 -93
					10k	27:52.44	28:11.14 -93
Guerra	Silvio	ECU	18 Sep 68	158/49	5k	13:32.31	13:30.69 -92
Guidry	Wayne	USA	24 Nov 73	183/79	PV	5.52	5.30 -93
Guldberg	Mogens	DEN	2 Aug 63	184/65	1500	3:38.11	3:35.03 -90
					3k	7:49.84	7:43.78 -89
Gundersen	Gaute	NOR	13 Jun 72	187/83	110h	13.68	13.87 -92
Gurny	Slawomir	POL	2 Sep 64	181/68	Mar	2:12:31	2:10:38 -93
Gurskiy	Andrey	RUS	72		HT	71.32	69.06 -90
Guset ¶	Gheorge	ROM	28 May 68	185/110	SP	19.56i, 19.97dq	20.33 -91
Gustafsson	Tore	SWE	11 Feb 62	183/105	HT	76.46	80.14 -89
Guy	Robert	TRI	21 Feb 64	188/79	400	45.87	46.27 -93
Günther	Helge	GER	10 Apr 69	192/87	Dec	7830	7719w -90, 7702 -91
* Haaf	Dietmar	GER	6 Mar 67	173/67	LJ	8.24	8.25i -89, 8.25 -90, 8.30Aw -91
* Haapakoski	Antti	FIN	6 Feb 71	187/74	110h	13.45, 13.26Aw	13.55 -92
Haborák	Milan	SVK	11 Jan 73		SP	18.77	17.97 -92
Hacini	Amar	ALG	18 Nov 71	175/70	400	46.04	46.12 -93
Hacksteiner	Markus	SUI	18 Nov 64	186/72	3kSt	8:25.33	8:31.57 -93
Hadjiandreou	Marios	CYP	19 Sep 62	183/76	TJ	16.78	17.13 -91
* Hafsteinsson	Vesteinn	ISL	12 Dec 60	190/113	DT	64.92	67.64 -89
Haïda	Mahjoub	MAR	1 Jul 70	180/75	800	1:45.02	1:44.97 -93
* Hakkarainen	Harri	FIN	16 Oct 69	191/91	JT	85.46	84.36 -93
Hall	Darnell	USA	26 Sep 71	183/78	400	45.14	44.95 -92
Hall	Kenny	USA	25 Jan 67	187/79	400h	50.02	50.29 -89
Halmesmäki	Martti	FIN	25 Oct 66	188/91	DT	59.78	61.02 -92
** Halvari	Mika	FIN	13 Feb 70	190/140	SP	19.93i, 19.87	20.08 -93
* Hämäläinen	Eduard	BLS	21 Jan 69	192/88	110h	13.82	13.57 -93
					Dec	8735	8724 -93

Name		Nat	Born	Ht/Wt	Event	1994 Mark	Pre-1994 Best
Hamed	Zaid Abou	SYR	22 Apr 70	182/75	400h	49.98	49.09 -93
Hämeenniemi	Ismo	FIN	1 Jun 70	181/70	400h	49.94	50.67 -92
Hames	Jagan	AUS	31 Oct 75	190/80	HJ	2.30	2.25 -93
Hammarsten	Thomas	SWE	31 Dec 66		SP	19.26	18.97 -92
Han Wei		CHN	26 Dec 71		50kW	3:57:00	3:57:00 -92
Han Jun		CHN	13 Nov 72		DT	58.52	59.44 -93
Hanada	Katsuhiko	JPN	12 Jun 71	175/58	5k	13:34.35	13:28.73 -93
					10k	28:17.81	28:11.60 -93
Hanigan	Brendan	AUS	19 Mar 73	185/72	800	1:45.03	1:47.26 -92
Hanlon	Tom	GBR	20 May 67	183/67	3kSt	8:20.04	8:12.58 -91
* Hanneck	Phillimon	ZIM	12 May 71	170/59	3k	7:46.71	7:42.06 -92
					5k	13:14.50	13:14.76 -93
Hanstveit	Ketill	NOR	2 Nov 73	177/65	TJ	16.76	16.71 -93
Hao Huanquan		CHN			20kW	1:21:26	1:26:19 -93
					50kW	4:00:04	
Haraguchi	Junji	JPN	22 Jun 67	175/56	10k	28:24.24	28:29.76 -92
Harden	Tim	USA	27 Jan 74	175/66	100	10.14, 10.03w	10.32 -93
					200	20.54, 20.38w	20.83 -93
Harju	Antti	FIN	18 Mar 74	183/113	SP	18.74	18.40 -93
Harnden	Ken	ZIM	31 Mar 73	196/89	400h	49.89	
Harrington	Larry	USA	24 Nov 70	194/84	110h	13.65	13.60, 13.4 -92, 13.49w -93
* Harris	Danny	USA	7 Sep 65	183/77	400h	48.18sus	47.38 -92
Harris	Dennis	USA	23 Mar 68	187/79	LJ	8.05, 8.17w	8.15 -92
* Harrison	Kenny	USA	13 Feb 65	178/75	TJ	17.43	17.93 -90
Hart	Gregg	USA	21 Aug 70	193/111	DT	58.96	60.42 -93
Hartikainen	Jari	FIN	28 Apr 67	183/81	JT	81.28	78.84 -93
Hartwig	Jeff	USA	25 Sep 67	190/82	PV	5.63	5.60i, 5.50 -92
Harvey	Mike	AUS	5 Dec 62	175/68	50kW	4:02:17	3:57:20 -93
Hathaway	Thad	USA	10 Mar 74	185/63	HJ	2.23	
Hatungimana	Arthémon	BUR	21 Jan 74	178/63	800	1:45.02	1:46.42 -93
Hatzopoulos	Dimitrios	GRE	17 Apr 67	185/75	LJ	8.07	7.92 -87, 8.08w -89
Hauge	Kjell Ove	NOR	20 Feb 69	198/107	SP	20.07	18.52 -92, 18.64i -93
					DT	60.58	58.18 -93
* Haughton	Greg	JAM	10 Nov 73	185/79	400	44.93	44.78 -93
Hautala	Ville	FIN	19 Nov 68	174/59	3kSt	8:35.87	8:29.00 -93
* Hawkins	Courtney	USA	11 Jul 67	185/75	110h	13.27	13.25 -93
Hayata	Toshiyuki	JPN	2 May 68	176/61	Mar	2:10:19	2:11:04 -93
					10k	28:11.28	28:17.63 -91
Hayden	Ryan	USA	13 Mar 71	189/79	400h	50.04	51.15 -92
Head	Paul	GBR	1 Jul 65	193/115	HT	71.16	74.02 -90
Heard	Floyd	USA	24 Mar 66	178/71	200	20.67, 20.55w	19.95 -87
* Hecht	Raymond	GER	11 Nov 68	190/90	JT	90.06	90.84R -91, 88.90 -93
Hedman	Lars	SWE	6 Apr 67		TJ	16.81i, 16.71	16.44i, 16.66w -92
Hedner	Lars	SWE	27 May 67	188/78	100	10.21w	10.55 -92
Heide	Thorsten	GER	4 May 69	180/73	LJ	8.07w	8.08 -93
Heikkilä	Matti	FIN	17 Mar 64	178/63	50kW	4:06:14	4:08:10 -86
Heimonen	Jarkko	FIN	6 Mar 72	181/77	JT	77.02	77.40 -90
Heisler	Randy	USA	7 Aug 61	190/111	SP	18.84	19.97i -88, 19.46 -87
					DT	61.78	67.62 -87
* Hélan	Serge	FRA	24 Feb 64	176/70	TJ	17.55	17.45 -91
Hellebuyck	Eddy	BEL	22 Jan 61		Mar	2:11:50	2:12:16 -89
Henderson	Kevin	USA	4 Feb 65	185/77	400h	49.52	48.68 -88
Henderson	Paul	AUS	13 May 71	184/81	200	20.4w	20.63, 20.36w -93
Henderson	Vincent	USA	20 Oct 72	175/66	100	10.13	10.11 -93
					200	20.62, 20.50w	20.81 -93
Hendrix	Jason	USA	24 Oct 72	183/75	200	20.68	20.25 -93
Henriksson	Tord	SWE	13 Apr 65	189/83	TJ	16.99	17.26i -91, 17.21 -93
Henry	Boris	GER	14 Dec 73	193/98	JT	82.02	84.12 -93
Henry	Paul	JAM	15 Oct 72	178/74	400	45.94	46.76 -93
Hense	Olaf	GER	19 Nov 67	187/74	400h	49.19	48.48 -93
Hepburn	Craig	BAH	10 Dec 69	175/67	LJ	8.02	8.41 -93
Herbrand	Thorsten	GER	9 Apr 70	189/94	SP	20.01	18.84 -92
Hernández	Angel	ESP	15 Apr 66	179/73	LJ	8.05i, 7.94	8.18 -92
Hernández	Juan	CUB	16 Sep 68	185/72	400h	50.34	50.03 -92
* Herold	Jens-Peter	GER	2 Jun 65	176/64	1500	3:35.44	3:32.77 -92
					Mile	3:55.85, 3:53.74i	3:49.22 -88
Herrador	Antonio	ESP	21 Nov 66	178/62	1500	3:38.85	3:38.62 -93
Herrington	Terrance	USA	31 Jul 66	180/62	800	1:46.76	1:46.38 -88
					1500	3:36.82	3:35.77 -91
					Mile	3:55.38	3:49.12 -91

Name		Nat	Born	Ht/Wt	Event	1994 Mark	Pre-1994 Best
Herva	Heikki	FIN	2 Feb 63	193/80	TJ	16.57	16.51 -89
Herwig	Torsten	GER	19 Oct 68	179/60	3kSt	8:35.71	8:28.01 -93
Hicks	Joe	USA	71	183/97	SP	18.46	17.84 -93
Hilaire	Pierre-Marie	FRA	19 Nov 65	183/75	400	45.92	45.90 -93
Hill	Duane	USA	9 Jan 73		400	45.79, 45.7	46.98 -91
* Hill	Mike	GBR	22 Oct 64	190/95	JT	86.36	86.94 -93
Hiratsuka	Jun	JPN	8 Jan 69	167/54	5k	13:26.80	13:32.54 -92
					10k	28:18.10	27:59.91 -93
* Hissou	Salah	MAR	72	176/62	3k	7:38.14	7:59.94+ -91
					5k	13:04.93	13:37.40 -91
					10k	27:21.75	28:31.62 -92
Hobbs	Justin	GBR	12 Mar 69	184/64	10k	28:17.00	-0-
* Hoen	Steinar	NOR	8 Feb 71	193/77	HJ	2.36i, 2.35	2.32 -93
Hoff	Roar	NOR	21 May 65	188/118	SP	19.52	19.22 -91
Hoga	Koji	JPN	22 Nov 69	176/57	50kW	4:03:52	-0-
Hoki	Yoshiaki	JPN	26 Nov 70	185/75	110h	13.76	13.93, 13.88w -93
Hold	Mathias	GER	21 Jan 73	198/96	JT	78.94	77.54 -93
Holder	Monterio	USA	17 Oct 70	188/77	HJ	2.25i, 2.25	2.27 -93
Holender	Jan	POL	12 Mar 64	175/72	20kW	1:24:14	1:24:59 -92
Holl	Werner	GER	28 Jan 70	185/75	PV	5.55i, 5.50	5.80i -93
Hollingsworth	Simon	AUS	9 May 72	190/75	400h	49.68	49.72 -92
Holloway	Mike	USA	12 Jul 69	196/86	PV	5.65	5.70 -92
Holm	Arne	SWE	22 Dec 61	186/82	TJ	16.96	17.05 -87, 17.16w -86
* Holman	Steve	USA	2 Mar 70	186/66	800	1:46.13	1:47.54 -92
					1500	3:34.96	3:34.95 -92
					Mile	3:50.91	3:52.73 -93
Holusa	Milos	TCH	2 May 65	174/62	20kW	1:22:30	1:24:21 -92
					50kW	3:57:24	3:54:13 -92
Hong Bo		CHN	Oct 73		5k	13:32.28	13:32.46 -93
Honkawa	Kazumi	JPN	12 Jan 72	170/52	10k	28:28.1	28:36.91 -92
Hood	Graham	CAN	2 Apr 72	186/69	800	1:45.70	1:45.99 -92
					1500	3:36.54	3:35.27 -92
Horton	Maurice	USA	10 Nov 69	188/82	400h	49.72	50.17 -92
* Horváth	Attila	HUN	28 Jul 67	194/117	DT	68.58	67.06 -91
Howard	Bryan	USA	7 Oct 76	180/75	200	20.76	21.14 -93
Howard	Raoul	USA	11 Mar 74	188/80	400	45.91	45.91 -93
Hu Gangjun #		CHN	4 Dec 70		Mar	2:10:28dq/2:10:56	2:10:57 -93
* Huang Geng		CHN	10 Jul 70	179/72	LJ	8.15, 8.34w	8.30 -93
Huang Baoting		CHN	27 May 74	175/70	LJ	8.12	8.06 -93
Huber	Philipp	SUI	18 Feb 74		Dec	7761	7440 -92
Hudspith	Mark	GBR	19 Jan 69		Mar	2:12:52	-0-
* Huffman	Scott	USA	30 Nov 64	175/75	PV	5.97	5.85 -92
Huke	Michael	GER	30 Mar 69	183/72	200	20.60	20.62 -93
* Hunter	C.J.	USA	14 Dec 68	186/135	SP	20.94	20.82 -93
Huotilainen	Tommi	FIN	17 Nov 67	182/80	JT	75.96	76.46 -92
* Hwang Yung-cho		KOR	22 Mar 70	168/57	Mar	2:08:09dh	2:08:47 -92
Hysong	Nick	USA	9 Dec 71	183/77	PV	5.70	5.57i -93, 5.52 -92
Hyytiäinen	Marko	FIN	27 Nov 66	191/88	JT	76.46	83.40 -90
Iapichino	Gianni	ITA	2 Mar 69	185/75	PV	5.70, 5.80ex	5.60i, 5.60 -92, 5.62ex -93
Ibrahim Warsama	Ahmed	QAT	4 Feb 66	180/60	1500	3:35.38	3:39.61 -93
Idda	Gianpiero	ITA	27 Jun 69		400h	49.89	53.18 -92
Ignatov	Andrey	RUS	3 Feb 68	182/72	LJ	7.97, 8.01w	8.11 -90
* Ihly	Robert	GER	5 May 63	174/64	20kW	1:21:14	1:19:59 -92
					50kW	3:58:10	4:00:23 -90
Imamura	Fumio	JPN	5 Nov 66	178/63	50kW	3:53:29	3:56:17 -93
Imo ¶	Chidi	NGR	27 Aug 63	188/77	100	10.28	10.00 -86, 9.92Aw -87
Impens	Christoph	BEL	9 Dec 69	184/70	1500	3:38.41	3:36.63 -93
					3k	7:49.85i	7:53.70 -91
Inagaki	Seiji	JPN	28 Apr 73	175/65	400	45.84	46.36 -92
Indrebo	Arne	NOR	6 Aug 69		JT	76.20	76.04 -92
Inozemtsev	Vladimir	UKR	25 May 64	185/75	TJ	16.87	17.90 -90
Ionescu	Florian	ROM	3 Feb 71	179/66	3kSt	8:35.62	8:34.93 -93
Ireland	Courtney	NZL	12 Jan 72	193/110	SP	19.45	19.30 -93
Irvin	Brian	USA	30 Jul 70	180/68	200	20.71	20.51 -93
Isayev	Konstantin	RUS	7 Jul 73	188/73	HJ	2.26	2.26 -93
Ishutin	Valeriy	RUS	5 Sep 65	186/76	PV	5.70	5.75i -89, 5.70 -87
Ismail	Ibrahim	QAT	10 May 72	178/70	400	44.93	44.85 -93
Isolehto	Juha	FIN	6 Jun 68	191/74	HJ	2.28i, 2.25	2.29 -90
* Issangar	Mohamed	MAR	12 Dec 64	178/62	5k	13:12.13	13:08.51 -90

Name		Nat	Born	Ht/Wt	Event	1994 Mark	Pre-1994 Best
Ito	Koji	JPN	29 Jan 70	180/72	200	20.44	20.87 -93
Ito	Yoshitaka	JPN	23 Jun 70	184/64	100	10.25, 10.22w	10.38 -92
					200	20.70	21.18 -93
* Itt	Edgar	GER	8 Jun 67	186/75	400h	48.48	48.65 -88
* Jabbour	Brahim	MAR	1 Jan 70	178/56	2k	5:02.6+	5:06+ -93
					3k	7:43.92	7:36.54 -93
					5k	13:17.55	13:08.86 -93
* Jackson	Colin	GBR	18 Feb 67	183/75	110h	12.98, 12.94Aw	12.91 -93
Jackson	Jeff	USA	14 Mar 74	183/73	110h	13.56, 13.53w	13.81 -93
Jackson	Tim	AUS	4 Jul 69	185/80	100	10.24	10.26 -93, 10.00w, 10.0 -89
Jacobasch	Udo	GER	30 Aug 70	196/92	Dec	7783	7742 -93
James	Allen	USA	14 Apr 64	190/82	20kW	1:24:26.9t	1:25:01 -92
					50kW	3:55:39	-0-
James	Ian	CAN	17 Jul 63	178/73	LJ	7.93w	8.09 -86, 8.11w -87
Janku	Jan	TCH	10 Aug 71	195/78	HJ	2.23i	2.20 -93
Janssen	Miquel	HOL	5 Sep 70	186/77	200	20.59	21.22 -93
Januszewski	Pawel	POL	2 Jan 72	179/64	400h	49.95	51.71 -92
Janvrin	Kip	USA	8 Jul 65	183/84	Dec	8287	8052 -93, 8113w -90
* Jaros	Ralf	GER	13 Dec 65	193/85	TJ	17.10i, 16.89	17.66 -91
* Jarrett	Tony	GBR	13 Aug 68	188/82	110h	13.22, 13.1	13.00 -93
Jean-Joseph	Jimmy	FRA	15 Oct 72	181/65	800	1:46.23	1:47.09 -93
* Jefferson	Jaime	CUB	17 Jan 62	189/78	LJ	8.13	8.53 -90
* Jefferson	Sam	USA	19 Apr 71	168/69	100	10.12, 10.08Aw	10.13, 10.05w -93
Jefferson	Thomas	USA	8 Jun 62	183/79	200	20.67, 20.55Aw	20.21 -91
Jenkins	Randy	USA	18 Sep 70	190/86	HJ	2.31i, 2.31	2.30 -91
Jensen	Benjamin	NOR	13 Apr 75		Dec	7724	7311 -93
Jenssen	Olav	NOR	11 May 62		DT	58.90	66.28 -89
Jesus	José	POR	19 Nov 68	170/65	3kSt	8:29.76	8:29.19 -92
Jett	Rod	USA	28 Oct 66	183/80	110h	13.74	13.43 -92
Jiao Baozhong		CHN	28 Mar 73		20kW	1:21:25	
					50kW	3:53:49	4:02:35 -93
Jimenez	Ramon	PAR	10 Apr 69	191/107	DT	60.42	64.30 -92
Jiménez	Anacleto	ESP	24 Feb 67	179/57	1500	3:37.24	3:40.11 -92
					3k	7:47.88, 7:42.54i	7:46.79 -89
					5k	13:18.05	13:26.33 -92
Jin Guohong		CHN	5 Feb 72		50kW	3:52:20	3:55:08 -93
Jitsui	Kenjiro	JPN	16 Dec 68	166/54	Mar	2:11:10	2:14:14 -93
Johansen	Håvard	NOR	23 Jan 68		JT	78.38	74.10 -91
Johansson	Stefan	SWE	11 Apr 67	181/72	20kW	1:22:37	1:18:35.21t -92
					50kW	4:00:18	3:58:56 -92
Johansson	Torbjörn	SWE	23 Jan 70		800	1:46.25	1:47.69 -91
					1000	2:18.71	2:22.29 -91
John	Jason	GBR	17 Oct 71	185/75	100	10.23, 10.08w	10.30, 10.12w -93
* Johnson	Allen	USA	1 Mar 71	178/70	110h	13.25, 13.23Aw	13.47, 13.34w -93
Johnson	Carlos	USA	20 Aug 73		LJ	7.92w	7.76 -93
* Johnson	Dave	USA	7 Apr 63	190/91	Dec	8219	8727w/8705 -92
Johnson	Desmond	USA	6 Apr 77	188/70	400	45.77	46.20 -93
Johnson	Ferdana	USA	6 Oct 72	183/69	400	45.66	45.81 -93
Johnson	Lawrence	USA	7 May 74	183/83	PV	5.83i, 5.80	5.71 -93
* Johnson	Michael	USA	13 Sep 67	185/78	100	10.09	10.12 -93
					200	19.94	19.79 -92
					400	43.90	43.65 -93
Johnson	Warren	JAM	7 Nov 73	172/62	100	10.29, 10.03ig	10.60 -92
Johnston	Robbie	NZL	21 Aug 67		2k	5:05.83	-0-
					5k	13:28.97	13:25.11 -92
					10k	27:58.51	28:15.48 -93
Jones	Anthony	USA	12 Dec 71	180/76	100	10.10	10.57, 10.38w -93
					200	20.62	21.48 -91
Jones	Carleton	USA	20 Dec 65	188/62	Mile	3:57.43	4:00.26 -93
Jones	Chris	USA	8 Oct 73	181/79	400	45.11	45.23 -93
Jones	Reggie	USA	8 May 71	185/80	LJ	8.24A, 7.97	8.07A, 8.05, 8.35Aw -93
					TJ	16.96	17.12 -92
Jones	Rob	USA	11 Nov 70	188/75	110h	13.58	
Jonker	Johan	RSA	19 Mar 70		400h	50.25A	49.53 -91
Joseph	Rafer	GBR	21 Jul 68	196/92	Dec	7663	7300 -91
Jouÿs	Mathieu	FRA	13 Feb 72	184/78	110h	13.77	13.79, 13.67w -93
Junqueira	João	POR	24 Jun 65	174/58	3k	7:47.26	8:03.4 -93
					5k	13:22.3	13:27.88 -87
					10k	27:53.74	28:15.94 -93

Name		Nat	Born	Ht/Wt	Event	1994 Mark	Pre-1994 Best
Juzdado	Alberto	ESP	20 Aug 66	172/61	10k	28:06.36	28:26.87 -93
					Mar	2:11:18	2:11:39 -92
Kagwe	John	KEN	9 Jan 69		Mar	2:11:52dh	
Kähkonen	Jyrki	FIN	5 Jun 67	187/76	110h	13.65	13.97 -88
Kaihoko	Yoshiteru	JPN	19 Nov 71	183/69	HJ	2.24	2.24 -90
Kairouani	Khalid	MAR	66		5k	13:34.0	
Kaiser	Eric	GER	7 Mar 71	182/77	110h	13.58	13.48 -93
Káldy	Zoltán	HUN	7 Jan 69	176/56	10k	28:22.00	28:01.88 -91
Kaleta	Marek	EST	17 Dec 61	183/94	JT	78.74	83.80 -90
Kaligis	Pete	USA	1 Jun 71		SP	18.77	17.20 -93
Kamau	Charles	KEN			400h	50.01A	
Kaminski	Ed	USA	26 Mar 68	190/97	JT	82.44	80.36 -93
Kandie	Phillip	KEN			1500	3:38.38	3:44.8A -93
Kaneko	Munehiro	JPN	6 Jun 68	182/79	Dec	7853	7995 -93
Kapinski	Slawomir	POL	14 Apr 66	180/68	10k	28:30.15	29:00.56 -93
Kapkory	Josephat	KEN	2 Jan 67	175/57	5k	13:27.00	13:44.37 -93
					10k	28:20.64	28:22.4 -92
					3kSt	8:25.63	8:42.8 -92
Kaptyukh	Vasiliy	BLS	26 Jun 67	197/117	DT	58.32	66.18 -93
* Kapustin	Denis	RUS	5 Oct 70	188/83	TJ	17.62, 17.86w	17.54 -93
Kapustin	Viktor	RUS	28 Apr 72		SP	18.81	19.04 -93
Karatayev	Andrey	UKR	6 Mar 66	188/71	110h	13.60, 13.48w	13.62 -88
Kariuki	James	KEN	72		5k	13:17.78	13:18.57 -92
* Kariuki	Julius	KEN	12 Jun 61	181/62	3kSt	8:22.64	8:05.51 -88
Karlsson	Per	SWE	21 Apr 67	182/99	HT	74.54	73.36 -93
Karlsson	Peter	SWE	23 Nov 70	175/70	100	10.25	10.40 -93
Karube	Shunji	JPN	8 May 69	184/69	400h	49.13	48.75 -93
Kaseorg	Indrek	EST	16 Dec 67	194/86	Dec	8038	7966 -93
Kashayev	Vener	RUS	16 Mar 74	178/63	5k	13:31.93	13:53.73 -93
Kaslauskas	Valdas	LIT	23 Feb 58	178/68	20kW	1:23:57	1:23:30 -92
Kasprzyk	Jacek	POL	27 Aug 70	181/70	Mar	2:11:52	2:17:38 -92
Kastanis	Spiros	GRE	23 Sep 64	175/65	50kW	3:55:34	3:58:13 -91
Katonon	Jacob	KEN	70		HJ	2.24	2.24 -92
					TJ	16.55	16.50 -92
Katurayev	Sergey	RUS	29 Sep 67	182/70	50kW	3:53:54	3:58:41 -91
Kaul	Michael	GER	25 Jul 67	186/75	400h	49.55	49.76 -92
Kavulanya	Justus	KEN	64		20kW	1:24:02	1:24:40 -93
Kawamura	Hideaki	JPN	15 Sep 74	175/67	400h	50.05	51.10 -93
Kawashima	Shinji	JPN	4 Jun 66	166/53	Mar	2:11:55dh	2:10:41 -93
Kayode	Oluyemi	NGR	7 Jul 68	180/75	200	20.39	20.22 -92
Kayukov	Andrey	RUS	12 Apr 64	187/75	TJ	17.00, 17.35w	17.23 -88
* Kazanov	Igor	LAT	24 Sep 63	186/81	110h	13.54, 13.52w	13.26 -93, 13.14w -86
Keanchan	Chanond	THA	24 Jan 70	169/64	400h	49.89	50.46 -93
Kearns	Thomas	IRL	2 Jun 66	190/82	110h	13.60	13.63 -92, 13.6 -90
Kebede	Gemechu	ETH	73		Mar	2:12:34	2:17:29sc -92
Keitel	Sebastian	CHI	14 Feb 73	175/65	200	20.43, 20.1A	20.96 -93
					400	46.01A, 46.03	47.61 -93
Keith	Andy	GBR	25 Dec 71	185/63	1500	3:39.44	3:39.06 -93
					Mile	3:56.29i	3:57.7i -93
					3k	7:49.83i	-0-
Kelile	Chala	ETH	7 Oct 66		5k	13:18.32	13:47.17 -91
					10k	28:12.88	28:11.73 -91
Kelley	Jon	USA	19 Dec 69	180/73	PV	5.50	5.50 -92
Kelm	Bernhard	GER	23 Dec 67	173/62	LJ	7.98	8.02 -93, 8.11w -92
Kemboi	Simon	KEN	1 Mar 67	178/74	400	45.89, 45.5A	44.94, 44.7A -93
Kemei	David	KEN	70		3kSt	8:26.99	8:33.76 -93
* Kemp	Troy	BAH	18 Jun 66	187/69	HJ	2.36i, 2.35	2.37 -93
Kempainen	Bob	USA	18 Jun 66	183/70	Mar	2:08:47dh	2:11:03 -93
Kenneally	Dean	AUS	8 Mar 67	189/76	800	1:46.82	1:46.54 -92
* Kennedy	Bob	USA	18 Aug 70	183/66	1500	3:38.74	3:38.32 -91
					Mile	3:56.21	3:56.71 -93
					2k	5:02.6+	5:07+ -93
					3k	7:35.33	7:38.45 -93
					5k	13:02.93	13:14.91 -93
Kennedy	Nery	PAR	28 May 73	183/90	JT	76.70	68.08 -93
Kennison	Eddie	USA	20 Jan 73	185/82	200	20.76A, 20.76	21.30 -91
Kersh	George	USA	3 Jul 68	185/72	800	1:46.98	1:44.00 -92
* Keter	Joseph	KEN	13 Jun 69	178/64	3kSt	8:15.86	8:21.04 -93
Khaida	Lotfi	ALG	20 Dec 68	180/75	LJ	8.05A	7.97 -92
					TJ	16.69, 16.78w	16.92 -93

Name		Nat	Born	Ht/Wt	Event	1994 Mark	Pre-1994 Best
Khayatti	Fadhel	TUN	18 Jan 65	185/78	400h	49.52	49.83 -90
Khersontsev	Vadim	RUS	8 Jul 74		HT	76.78	72.72 -93
Khmelnitskiy	Mikhail	BLS	24 Jun 69	171/62	20kW	1:19:38	1:20:25 -93
* Kibet	David	KEN	24 Nov 63	189/68	1500	3:35.35	3:32.13 -92
					Mile	3:52.48	3:51.80 -91
Kibet	Robert	KEN	15 Dec 65	173/64	800	1:46.75	1:43.70 -89
Kibor	Joseph	KEN	22 Dec 72	178/60	5k	13:32.68	13:40.5A -92
Kido	Hasaki	JPN	10 Dec 70	169/55	10k	28:24.07	
Kieffer	Pascal	FRA	6 May 61	171/66	50kW	4:02:55.6t	4:02:11 -93
* Kim Jae-ryong		KOR	25 Apr 66	172/60	Mar	2:09:42	2:09:30 -92
Kim Chul-kyun		KOR	28 Feb 69	182/74	PV	5.53i	5.52 -92
Kim Chung-yong		KOR	10 Mar 69		Mar	2:11:54	2:13:06 -92
Kim Wan-ki		KOR	8 Jul 68		Mar	2:08:34	2:09:31 -92
Kim Yonghwan		KOR	20 Jun 71	181/65	800	1:46.50	1:47.67 -91
Kimani	Joseph	KEN	Sep 72		5k	13:26.44	
Kimino	Takahiro	JPN	19 Feb 73	176/62	HJ	2.26	2.32 -93
* Kingdom	Roger	USA	26 Aug 62	185/91	110h	13.39	12.92, 12.87w -89
Kinnunen	Jarkko	FIN	21 Apr 70	176/75	JT	76.86	79.70 -90
Kinnunen	Juha	FIN	4 Mar 72		50kW	4:05:02	4:14:19 -93
* Kinnunen	Kimmo	FIN	31 Mar 68	186/88	JT	79.34	90.82R -91, 84.78 -93
Kinyor	Barnabas	KEN	3 Aug 61	176/67	400h	49.07A, 49.50	48.90 -92, 48.7A -93
Kipkemboi	Simeon	KEN	15 Apr 60	190/74	400	45.89A, 45.8A	44.93 -90
* Kipketer	Wilson	KEN	12 Dec 70	172/62	800	1:43.29	1:45.46 -93
Kipkiai	Michael	KEN	27 Dec 68		Mar	2:10:08	
* Kipkoech	Johnstone	KEN	20 Dec 68	173/65	3k	7:48.26	7:53.27 -93
					3kSt	8:14.72	8:18.59 -91
Kipkoech	Julius	KEN	68		1500	3:38.10	
Kiplagat (Andersen)	Robert	KEN/ (DEN)	12 Dec 72	185/66	1500	3:39.41	3:43.6 -91
					2k	5:06.93	-0-
Kipngok	Jackson	KEN	16 Aug 66		Mar	2:08:08dh	
* Kiprotich	Nixon	KEN	4 Dec 62	185/68	800	1:44.48	1:43.31 -92
					1500	3:39.07	3:38.76 -89
Kipserem	Samuel	KEN	68		800	1:45.94	1:48.0A -93
					1500	3:37.99	
* Kiptanui	Moses	KEN	10 Oct 71	175/60	1500	3:34.44	3:34.0A -92
					Mile	3:57.71i	3:52.06 -91
					2k	5:01.3+	4:52.53 -92
					3k	7:35.23	7:28.96 -92
					2M	8:09.01	8:16.18i -92
					5k	13:10.76	13:00.93 -92
					3kSt	8:08.80	8:02.08 -92
* Kiptoo Singoei	David	KEN	26 Jun 67	175/68	800	1:44.07	1:45.64 -93
* Kiptum	William	KEN	30 Mar 71	168/55	5k	13:29.66	
					10k	27:17.20	
* Kirilenko	Vitaliy	UKR	25 Apr 68	192/80	LJ	8.21	8.21 -93
Kirmasov ¶	Sergey	RUS	25 Mar 70		HT	72.74, 79.20dq	82.54 -93
* Kirui	Ismael	KEN	20 Feb 75	160/55	3k	7:45.27	7:39.82 -93
					5k	13:14.46	13:02.75 -93
Kiss	Balázs	HUN	21 Mar 72	188/109	HT	77.74	77.18 -93
* Kitur	Samson	KEN	25 Feb 66	186/77	400	44.32	44.18 -92
Kivi	Juha	FIN	26 Jan 64	189/75	LJ	7.91, 7.94w	8.02 -89
Kjensli	Kennet	NOR	12 Mar 69	174/68	100	10.26	10.52 -91
Kleiza	Saulius	LIT	2 Apr 64	184/125	SP	20.29	20.91 -87
* Klimenko	Aleksandr	UKR	27 Mar 70	194/115	SP	20.78	20.84 -92
Klimov	Aleksandr	BLS	26 May 69	190/112	SP	19.46	19.91 -93
Klyugin	Sergey	RUS	24 Mar 74	184/77	HJ	2.28i, 2.26	2.27 -91
Knabe	Wolfgang	GER	12 Jul 59	183/75	TJ	16.56	16.81 -83
Kneissler	Bernd	GER	13 Sep 62	198/125	DT	58.54	61.86 -86
Knight	Derek	USA	11 Oct 67	180/73	110h	13.56w	13.71 -92
Knox	Percy	USA	14 Oct 69	172/75	LJ	8.01	8.11 -93
Kobayashi	Masayuki	JPN	4 Apr 74	175/62	10k	28:22.82	-0-
Kobs	Karsten	GER	16 Sep 71	196/109	HT	76.30	75.94 -93
Kochkin	Sergey	RUS	70		TJ	16.54	16.52 -93
Kocuvan	Miro	SLO	15 Jun 71	182/69	400h	50.30	49.71 -93
Kóczián	Jenö	HUN	5 Apr 67	176/102	SP	19.67	19.57 -93
Koech	Benjamin	KEN	23 Jun 69		LJ	7.97A	8.00A -92, 8.08w -90
* Koech	Benson	KEN	10 Nov 74	176/65	800	1:43.17	1:44.77 -92
					1500	3:34.72	3:36.47 -93
Koech	Jonah	KEN	2 Feb 68	172/59	5k	13:26.27	13:10.88 -92

Name		Nat	Born	Ht/Wt	Event	1994 Mark	Pre-1994 Best
Koers	Marko	HOL	3 Nov 72	192/77	800	1:45.99	1:44.84 -93
					1500	3:38.85	3:38.05 -93
Kohnle	Michael	GER	3 May 70	191/84	Dec	7756	8289 -90
Kohout	Zdenek	TCH	14 May 67	188/100	DT	59.16	60.52 -89
Köhrbrück	Carsten	GER	26 Jun 66	184/71	400h	50.10	48.89 -90
Koistinen	Markus	FIN	1 May 70	198/130	SP	20.22	20.31 -93
Kokhanovskiy	Andrey	UKR	11 Jan 68	193/125	DT	63.58	65.66 -92
Kokkola	Jarmo	FIN	31 May 68	192/74	800	1:45.91	1:47.25 -91
Kokotis	Dimitrios	GRE	12 Apr 72	190/70	HJ	2.31	2.25i, 2.24 -93
Kolesnichenko	Dmitriy	UKR	28 Feb 72	187/80	110h	13.67, 13.49w	13.66 -93
Kolesnik	Sergey	UKR	31 May 69	199/73	HJ	2.28	2.25 -93
Kolesnik	Vadim	UKR	29 Jan 69	187/112	HT	79.62	79.44 -93
Kolko	Rajmund	POL	1 Mar 71	186/83	JT	78.76	78.14 -93
Kollár	Igor	SVK	25 Jun 65	175/62	20kW	1:22:11	1:20:37 -90
Kolodziejczyk	Robert	POL	3 Aug 70	201/75	HJ	2.27	2.24 -93
* Kolpakov	Vitaliy	UKR	2 Feb 72	195/92	Dec	8257	8297 -93
Komar	Ivan	BLS	18 Mar 70	186/73	800	1:46.76i	1:45.73 -93
Komatsu	Takashi	JPN	30 Dec 67	181/70	TJ	16.88	16.76 -92
Komen	Daniel	KEN	17 May 76	170/55	5k	13:31.10	13:58.30 -93
					10k	28:29.74	-0-
Konchellah	Billy	KEN	20 Oct 61	188/74	800	1:46.2A	1:43.06 -87
* Konchellah	Patrick	KEN	63	185/70	800	1:44.24	1:45.71 -93
Konczylo	Bruno	FRA	26 Aug 68	182/72	800	1:45.60	1:50.73i -93
König	Stefan	GER	25 Aug 66	183/90	JT	78.10	80.40 -92
Konno	Yoshito	JPN	7 Apr 71	178/65	800	1:46.22	1:47.49 -93
* Kononen	Valentin	FIN	7 Mar 69	181/69	20kW	1:22:05	1:22:22.6t -93
					50kW	3:47:14	3:42:02 -93
Konovalov	Ilya	RUS	14 Mar 71	192/100	HT	78.30	77.04 -92
Kontinaho	Ilkka	FIN	16 Sep 64		JT	79.44	78.34 -93
Konya ¶	Kalman	HUN	27 Oct 61	192/115	SP	20.61dq	20.55 -93
Koprivichin	Rumen	BUL	2 Oct 62	190/110	HT	73.08	75.54 -89
Korchagin	Aleksandr	KZK	25 Jan 72	193/81	PV	5.80i, 5.60	5.70 -93
Korepanov	Sergey	KZK	9 May 64	170/61	50kW	3:54:37	3:52:50 -93
Korir	Julius	KEN	5 Dec 63	170/57	5k	13:26.84	13:22.07 -91
					10k	28:17.63	27:34.96 -91
Korkizoglou	Prodromos	GRE	10 Apr 75	190/84	Dec	7652	6793 -93
Kornelyuk	Sergey	BLS	1 May 69		100	10.27	10.45 -91, 10.2 -93
Kornev	Grigoriy	RUS	14 Mar 61	183/70	20kW	1:22:30	1:18:56 -90
* Kororia	Kibyego	KEN	25 Dec 71	180/64	5k	13:16.17	13:11.89 -93
					10k	28:28.56	27:52.11 -92
Kororia	Shem	KEN	27 Aug 72		5k	13:27.96	
					10k	28:21.21	
Korving	Robin	HOL	29 Jul 74	188/81	110h	13.83	13.85 -93
* Korzeniowski	Robert	POL	30 Jul 68	168/60	20kW	1:20:55	1:19:14 -92
					50kW	3:45:57	3:44:44 -93
Kosaka	Tadahiro	JPN	10 Feb 60	178/65	50kW	3:56:36	3:58:39 -91
* Kosgei	Richard	KEN	29 Dec 70	170/55	3kSt	8:10.20	8:12.68 -93
Koskei	Christopher	KEN	14 Aug 74		3kSt	8:33.2A	8:24.58 -93
Kosov	Dmitriy	RUS	28 Sep 68	187/80	400	45.55, 45.5	45.80 -93
Kostin	Mikhail	BLS	10 May 59	194/125	SP	20.12	21.96 -86
Kostov	Kotzo	BUL	9 Jan 68	187/72	TJ	16.53, 16.67w	16.58i, 16.77w -93
Kostyukevich	Frants	BLS	4 Apr 63	182/73	20kW	1:21:54	1:18:51 -90
Koszewski	Dietmar	GER	26 Jul 67	193/89	110h	13.56	13.41, 13.39w -90
Kot	Sergey	UZB	7 Jan 60	197/130	SP	18.53	20.55 -86
					DT	58.36uc	60.62 -88
Kotewicz	Jaroslaw	POL	16 Mar 69	195/73	HJ	2.31	2.30 -91
Kotlarski	Piotr	POL	5 Jun 69	188/76	400h	49.75	50.24 -93
Kotov	Vladimir	BLS	21 Feb 58	168/57	Mar	2:11:43	2:10:58 -80
Kotze	Jurgens	RSA	4 Nov 73		800	1:46.53	1:47.64 -93
* Koukodimos	Konstandinos	GRE	14 Sep 69	186/78	LJ	8.36, 8.40w	8.26 -91
Kovác	Igor	SVK	12 May 69	183/70	110h	13.50, 13.48w	13.52 -93, 13.3w -91
Kovács	Dusan	HUN	31 Jul 71	182/76	400h	50.01	49.92 -93
Kovár	Stanislav	TCH	6 May 64	196/105	DT	58.96	61.12 -88
Kovtsun	Dmitriy	UKR	29 Sep 55	191/120	DT	59.84	68.64 -84
Kowalski	Lech	POL	17 Jan 61	188/98	HT	74.96	75.98 -92
Kozlov	Anatoliy	UKR	2 Oct 67	175/63	20kW	1:24:07	1:22:44 -90
Kranchik	Aleksey	RUS	70		20kW	1:24:49	
Krasko	Aleksandr	BLS	18 Sep 72		HT	80.78	79.86 -93
* Krasnov	Danny	ISR	25 May 70	183/77	PV	5.75	5.65 -93

Name		Nat	Born	Ht/Wt	Event	1994 Mark	Pre-1994 Best
Kratochvíl	Tomás	TCH	19 Dec 71	175/70	20kW	1:24:01	1:26:10 -92
Krause	Konstantin	GER	8 Oct 67	189/79	LJ	8.02	8.09 -93
Kravchenko	Vladimir	UKR	22 Dec 69	185/75	TJ	16.97	16.65i -93
Kreissig	Wolfgang	GER	29 Aug 70	193/73	HJ	2.28	2.25 -93
Krichenko	Oleg	RUS	1 Mar 72	183/89	JT	75.56	74.02 -93
Krieger	Helmut	POL	17 Jul 58	196/137	SP	19.36	21.30 -86
Krykun	Aleksey	UKR	12 Dec 68	194/110	HT	79.02	80.36 -93
Kroeker	Tim	CAN	25 May 71	186/87	110h	13.57A, 13.62	13.71, 13.51w -93
Kronin	Aleksey	RUS	70		20kW	1:21:35	1:22:50 -93
Kruger	Alex	GBR	18 Nov 63	193/86	Dec	8078	7986 -93
Kruger	Christo	RSA	21 Jun 71		DT	58.58	58.38 -93
Kruger	Frantz	RSA	22 May 75		DT	58.52	58.28 -93
Kucej	Jozef	SVK	23 Mar 65	181/72	400h	49.68	48.94 -89
Kuchmuradov	Anvar	UZB	5 Jan 70	175/76	100	9.9	10.38 -90
Kufahl	Carsten	GER	14 Nov 67	203/125	DT	64.08	66.22 -90
Kuhn	Frédéric	FRA	10 Jul 68	180/105	HT	76.64	76.80 -92
Kuko	Yuriy	BLS	23 Jan 68	173/65	20kW	1:20:35	1:19:08 -93
Kunkel	Marcel	GER	19 Oct 72	188/93	HT	72.16	72.42 -92
Kurabayashi	Toshiaki	JPN	29 Apr 66	170/56	Mar	2:11:28	2:16:00 -93
Kurennoy	Andrey	RUS	72		TJ	16.91	16.20i, 16.29w -93
Kushibe	Seiji	JPN	11 Nov 71	174/58	10k	28:28.17	
Kuznetsov	Andrey	RUS	27 Jan 57	165/55	Mar	2:12:55	2:17:34 -92
Kwizera	Dieudonné	BUR	6 Jun 67	184/60	1500	3:38.56	3:37.05 -89
Kyllönen	Kai	FIN	30 Jan 65	185/75	110h	13.52	13.60 -91
Laaksonen	Mika	FIN	21 Mar 68	190/88	HT	75.22	74.44 -93
Labbe	Grady	USA	4 Jan 71		200	20.46w	
* Labrador	Basilio	ESP	29 Mar 67	165/62	50kW	3:55:38	3:46:46 -93
Lack	Alexander	GER	4 Jun 72	188/85	200	20.70	20.72 -92
* Ladejo	Du'aine	GBR	14 Feb 71	186/83	400	44.94	45.25 -92
Laheurta	Alfredo	ESP	21 Mar 64	170/60	800	1:46.49	1:46.39 -89
* Lahlafi	Brahim	MAR	15 Apr 68	172/62	3k	7:40.31	-0-
					2M	8:16.12	7:50.01 -93
					5k	13:03.36	13:15.85 -93
Laine	Gordon	USA	24 Feb 58	183/75	LJ	7.95	8.28 -91, 8.31w -88
Laird	Linval	JAM	69	185/77	400	46.01	46.49 -92
Lakhal	Yarba	MAR	12 Feb 75		3kSt	8:34.42	
Lambrechts	Burger	RSA	3 Apr 73		SP	19.06	18.43 -93
* Lambruschini	Alessandro	ITA	7 Jan 65	178/63	1500	3:36.62	3:35.27 -87
					3kSt	8:17.62	8:08.78 -93
Lamela	Joel	CUB	29 Jan 71	172/70	200	20.3A	20.94 -93
Lamos	Kristofer	GER	1 Jan 74	190/77	HJ	2.27i, 2.27	2.20 -92
Lancelin	Eric	USA	13 May 71	193/79	TJ	16.59w	16.23 -93
Landsman	Johan	RSA	12 May 64	178/62	1500	3:37.60	3:33.56 -93
Lang Yong		CHN	Apr 73		LJ	8.02	7.90 -93
Langat	Kipkemboi	KEN	25 Mar 68	172/66	800	1:45.51	1:48.1 -93
* Langat	Sammy	KEN	24 Jan 70	168/57	800	1:44.46	1:44.06 -93
Langlois	Denis	FRA	10 Oct 68	173/60	20kW	1:23:19	1:22:27.9t -92
Laros	Marcel	HOL	10 Oct 71	182/64	3kSt	8:29.12	8:34.66 -93
Larsson	Kent	SWE	10 Jun 63	180/102	SP	20.02	20.03 -93
Latukhin	Sergey	RUS	70		SP	18.67	17.91i -93
* Laukkanen	Juha	FIN	6 Jan 69	186/86	JT	85.54	88.22 -92
Lawson	Kevin	TRI	4 Mar 70	178/75	100	10.27w	10.35w -91
Lawyer	Kerry	USA	3 Nov 72	183/79	100	10.21w	10.33 -93, 10.31w -91
Laynes	Jeff	USA	3 Oct 70	178/84	100	10.27	10.17 -93, 10.08w -91
Le Roux	Carel	RSA	31 Aug 72		SP	18.55	18.86 -93
Lee Bong-ju		KOR	68		Mar	2:09:57dh	2:13:16 -93
* Lee Jin-il		KOR	12 Jan 73	183/68	800	1:44.14	1:46.34 -92
Lee Jin-Taek		KOR	13 Apr 72	189/65	HJ	2.32	2.30 -93
Lefou	Judex	MRI	24 Jun 66	194/85	400h	50.06	50.08 -89
Lefrançois	Charles	CAN	19 Dec 72		HJ	2.25	2.21 -93
Lehtiö	Tero	FIN	24 Aug 63	203/101	DT	61.20	58.72 -93
Lehtonen	Jani	FIN	11 Aug 68	179/72	PV	5.83i, 5.70	5.82 -93
Lelei	Sammy	KEN	14 Aug 62	160/52	Mar	2:12:24	2:12:12 -93
Lemercier	Alain	FRA	11 Jan 57	174/66	50kW	3:49:29.7t	3:50:00.2t -92
Lemora	Shannon	USA	24 Mar 70	172/58	Mile	3:57.47	4:01.33i -93
Lesov	Delko	BUL	6 Jan 67	181/69	PV	5.60	5.75i -92, 5.70 -91
Levicq	Sebastien	FRA	25 Jun 71	186/81	Dec	8105	7874 -93
Lewis	Brian	USA	5 Dec 74		100	10.27	10.37w -93
					200	20.70	21.36 -92, 21.13w -93

Name		Nat	Born	Ht/Wt	Event	1994 Mark	Pre-1994 Best
* Lewis	Carl	USA	1 Jul 61	188/80	100	10.04	9.86 -91, 9.78w -88
					LJ	8.66A, 8.72Aw	8.87, 8.91w -91
Lewis	Rodney	USA	17 Jul 66	187/81	100	10.06	10.23A -92
* Lewis	Steve	USA	16 May 69	188/84	400	44.68A, 44.73	43.87 -88
Li Mingcai		CHN	22 Aug 71	169/58	20kW	1:20:02	1:20:00 -93
* Li Tong		CHN	6 May 67	190/84	110h	13.25	13.26, 13.0w -93
Liapis	Konstantinos	GRE	1 May 73	189/72	HJ	2.26	2.22 -93
Liepins	Modris	LAT	3 Aug 66	178/68	20kW	1:23:33.8t	1:25:11 -91
					50kW	3:58:46	3:48:27 -90
Lima	Wanderley de	BRA	11 Aug 69		Mar	2:11:06	
Linden	Andreas	GER	20 Feb 65	185/90	JT	81.10	84.46 -91
Lindman	Antero	FIN	25 Dec 64		50kW	4:03:43	3:59:57 -93
Linscheid	Roman	IRL	29 Dec 70	180/90	HT	72.38	66.44 -89
Litvinov	Sergey	RUS	23 Jan 58	180/100	HT	75.38	86.04 -86
Liu Haiming		CHN			20kW	1:24:55.8t	
Liu Hao		CHN	19 Nov 68	185/120	SP	19.26	19.78 -93
Lobinger	Tim	GER	3 Sep 72	193/80	PV	5.60	5.55 -93
Lobodin	Lev	UKR	1 Apr 69	188/84	Dec	8201	8156 -93
Loginov	Andrey	RUS	27 Nov 72	183/63	800	1:45.71	1:46.08 -92
Lomba	Hermann	FRA	11 Oct 60	180/69	100	10.24	10.34 -82
Long	Aric	USA	15 Apr 70	190/92	Dec	7996	8237 -92
Lopes	João	POR	67		5k	13:34.3	13:48.15 -93
					10k	28:27.4	
Lopez	Cédric	FRA	13 Feb 73	185/78	Dec	7945	7451 -93
Lopez	Danny	USA	25 Sep 68	175/63	3kSt	8:31.86	8:16.88 -92
Lopez	Jose	USA	4 Oct 72		400h	50.36	
López	Juan	CUB	7 Apr 67	189/81	TJ	16.59	17.28 -88
López	Julio	ESP	8 Mar 72	194/68	TJ	16.51	16.38, 16.65w -93
Löser	Dominique	GER	21 Jan 73	176/69	1500	3:37.21	3:39.62 -93
Lotik	Thomas	KEN			1500	3:38.76	
					3k	7:49.50	
Lough	Gary	GBR	6 Jul 70	184/71	1500	3:35.83	3:40.48 -93
Louka	Elias	CYP	23 Jul 74	179/115	SP	18.80	18.75 -93
Loum	Omar	SEN	31 Dec 73	184/79	100	10.19	10.33 -93
					200	20.42	20.58 -93
* Lovegrove	Gavin	NZL	21 Oct 67	187/95	JT	85.46	86.14 -92
Lucumi	Luis	COL	25 Dec 58	192/90	JT	75.54	77.80 -89
Lugenbühl	Mark	GER	17 Jun 66	193/82	PV	5.50	5.55 -92
Lukashok	Sergey	ISR	20 Jun 58	202/128	DT	60.50	66.64 -83
* Lyakhov	Sergey	RUS	1 Mar 68	195/105	DT	65.64	66.64 -92
* Lykho	Vyacheslav	RUS	16 Jan 67	196/120	SP	19.60i	21.20 -87
Lyles	Kevin	USA	23 Jul 73	185/75	400	45.50	45.73 -93
Lynch	Lawrence	GBR	1 Nov 67	186/75	400h	50.24	50.19 -91
Lysenko	Nikolay	RUS	14 Jul 66	185/100	HT	74.60	80.32 -88
Lyubomirov	Igor	RUS	9 Nov 61		20kW	1:22:00	1:20:10 -88
Ma Wei		CHN	10 Mar 69	191/120	DT	58.98	60.62 -93
Maas	Frans	HOL	13 Jul 64	196/89	LJ	7.97	8.07, 8.11i -89, 8.27Aw -88
Maazouzi	Driss	MAR	69		1500	3:37.04	3:43.3 -93
Maccarone	Gabriele	ITA	10 Apr 69		110h	13.6	14.23 -92
MacDonald	Michael	JAM	17 Mar 75	188/79	400	45.83, 45.6	46.86 -93
Mächler	Arnold	SUI	11 May 64	188/70	10k	28:25.35	28:40.49 -93
Machuka	Josephat	KEN	12 Dec 73	160/55	5k	13:33.56	13:28.85 -92
Mack	Tim	USA	15 Sep 72	188/78	PV	5.52	5.36 -93
Mackenzie #	Colin	GBR	30 Jun 63	186/90	JT	79.16, 80.82dq	82.38 -93, 82.60R -91
Madonia	Ezio	ITA	7 Aug 66	175/70	100	10.26Aw	10.26 -90, 10.24w -91
Maffei	Giuseppe	ITA	28 Jan 74		3kSt	8:32.34	9:04.63 -92
Magnusson	Jon	ISL	28 Jul 69		LJ	8.00	7.36 -93
					Dec	7896	
Magut	Joseph	KEN	65		400	45.79A	45.6A -93
Mahorn	Atlee	CAN	27 Oct 65	187/80	200	20.72	20.17 -91
Mai	Volker	GER	3 May 66	194/75	LJ	7.91	8.04 -85
					TJ	16.82	17.50 -85
Mair	John	JAM	20 Nov 63	175/74	100	10.21	10.18 -92, 10.14w -93
Majid	Nur Herman	MAL	2 Aug 69		110h	13.73	14.04 -93
Majkrzak	Marek	POL	12 Oct 65	198/116	DT	58.86	61.54 -92
Makarov	Andrey	RUS	2 Jun 71	181/72	20kW	1:22:11	1:21:33 -93
Makarov	Sergey	RUS	73		JT	82.54	76.08 -92
Makoena	Johannes	RSA	25 Sep 69		800	1:46.86A	1:46.4 -93

Name		Nat	Born	Ht/Wt	Event	1994 Mark	Pre-1994 Best
Makurin	Aleksey	RUS	21 Jul 72	192/79	HJ	2.30	2.25 -92
Malakwen	Vincent	KEN	19 Jul 74	175/65	800	1:46.07	1:46.06 -93
Malchenko	Sergey	RUS	2 Nov 63	190/74	HJ	2.25i	2.38 -88
Malchugin	Viktor	RUS	16 Jan 61	189/86	100	10.29, 10.0	10.38 -87
Malesev	Petar	YUG	6 Aug 72	199/76	HJ	2.25i	2.25 -91
Malherbe	Arnaud	RSA	20 Nov 72	187/75	400	45.49A	46.21A -93
Malik	Stefan	SVK	4 Feb 66	183/69	20kW	1:24:54	1:23:40 -93
					50kW	3:54:29	3:59:10 -90
Mallard	Milton	USA	24 Nov 73	183/77	200	20.44A	20.77, 20.5w -92
					400	45.75A, 45.86	45.94 -92
Malyavin	Vladimir	TKM	4 Mar 73	188/73	LJ	7.99	7.92 -93
Malysa	Jiri	TCH	10 Aug 66	180/71	20kW	1:22:48.5t	1:25:35 -93
Mandrou	Christian	FRA	24 Jun 65	177/77	Dec	7768	7842 -92
Mandy	Mark	IRL	19 Nov 72	197/83	HJ	2.24i	2.24 -93
Mann	Pat	USA	24 Apr 66	180/79	400h	50.05	49.80 -87
* Manson	Pat	USA	29 Nov 67	178/72	PV	5.85	5.75 -93
* Mansour	Talal	QAT	8 May 64	180/73	100	10.17	10.14, 9.9w -92
					200	20.41	20.62 -92
Manzano	Alberto	CUB	22 Sep 72	185/75	PV	5.61	5.60 -92
Mao Xinyuan		CHN	2 Jul 71	170/61	20kW	1:24:57t	1:20:35.4t -92
					50kW	4:02:27	3:53:36 -92
Mapstone	Rod	AUS	19 Nov 69	176/76	100	9.9w	10.35 -92
Maravilha	Alberto	POR	27 Dec 65	174/67	10k	28:20.50	28:17.69 -93
Maremane	Johannes	RSA	65		Mar	2:12:10dh	2:14:44 -93
Margalit	Itai	ISR	25 Jan 70	190/72	HJ	2.23	2.26i, 2.25 -93
Mariani	Maurilio	ITA	22 Apr 73	183/72	PV	5.50	5.40 -92
Marin	Andrés	ESP	18 Jul 61	162/50	50kW	3:52:14	3:52:16 -87
Maritim	Joseph	KEN	22 Oct 68	184/68	400h	49.90A	49.33A -87, 49.50 -88
Maritim	Samwel	KEN	64	167/55	Mar	2:12:59	
Markin	Aleksandr	RUS	8 Sep 62	188/77	110h	13.65, 13.55w	13.20 -88
Markoullides	Anninos	CYP	8 Feb 71	185/79	100	10.28w	10.49 -90
Markov	Dmitriy	BLS	14 Mar 75		PV	5.50i, 5.50	5.42 -93
* Markov	Gennadiy	RUS	15 Jun 67	182/75	TJ	17.38	17.06 -93
Markov	Ilya	RUS	19 Jun 72	173/66	20kW	1:24:07	1:20:19 -93
Markus	Jorma	FIN	28 Nov 52	178/86	JT	78.84	82.62 -90
Marquez	Jorge	MEX	19 Mar 67		10k	28:24.03	
					Mar	2:12:55	
Marras	Giorgio	ITA	15 Oct 71	178/65	200	20.48A, 20.62	20.66 -93
Marschner	Torsten	GER	17 Nov 68	194/75	HJ	2.28i	2.30i -89, 2.28 -88
Marseille	Wagner	HAI	13 Sep 70		110h	13.82	13.80 -92, 13.71w -93
* Marsh	Damien	AUS	28 Mar 71	185/79	100	10.16	10.19 -93
					200	20.43, 20.40w	20.49, 20.29w -93
* Marsh	Michael	USA	4 Aug 67	178/68	100	10.00	9.93 -92
					200	20.48	19.73 -92
					400	45.46	45.53 -93
Marti	Daniel	ESP	23 Apr 73	184/74	PV	5.70	5.65 -93
Martial	Germain	FRA	19 Jan 69	180/73	TJ	16.51	16.42 -92
Martin	Eamonn	GBR	9 Oct 58	183/67	Mar	2:11:05	2:10:50 -93
Martin	Eliseo	ESP	5 Nov 73	173/62	3kSt	8:32.89	8:45.77 -93
Martin	Fred	AUS	4 Oct 66	181/76	100	10.0w	10.35w -85
Martinez	David	ESP	31 Jan 67	194/105	DT	60.60	65.46 -92
Martinez	José	ESP	25 Aug 70	182/115	SP	18.72i	18.55 -93
Martinez	Manuel	ESP	7 Dec 74	187/120	SP	20.16	19.53 -93
Martinez	Michel	CUB	6 Nov 74		TJ	16.53	16.77 -93
Martínez	Andrés Miguel	ESP	9 Dec 68		1500	3:39.43	3:39.78 -91
Martins	Antonio	FRA	23 Aug 63	169/58	5k	13:24.46	13:14.47 -92
					10k	28:23.87	27:22.78 -92
Martirosyan	Armen	ARM	6 Aug 69		LJ	8.20A	
					TJ	17.05A	17.05 -92
Masai	Andrew	KEN	13 Dec 60		Mar	2:11:01	2:13:05 -93
Mashchenko	Ruslan	RUS	11 Nov 71	186/75	400h	49.43	51.11 -93
Maska	Vladimír	TCH	6 Feb 73	190/106	HT	71.22	66.94 -93
* Massana	Valentin	ESP	5 Jul 70	162/50	20kW	1:20:33	1:19:25 -92
					50kW	3:38:43	3:46:11 -93
* Masya	Benson	KEN	14 May 70	167/60	Mar	2:12:35dh	2:14:19 -92
Mateescu	Mugur	ROM	13 Jun 69	181/65	400h	49.76	49.98 -89
* Matei	Sorin	ROM	8 Jul 63	184/71	HJ	2.30	2.40 -90
* Matete	Samuel	ZAM	27 Jul 68	183/81	400	46.04	44.88 -91
					400h	47.90	47.10 -91

Name		Nat	Born	Ht/Wt	Event	1994 Mark	Pre-1994 Best
* Matias	Manuel	POR	30 Mar 62	172/58	10k	28:21.67	28:31.9 -88
					Mar	2:08:33	2:08:38 -92
Matilu	Abednigo	KEN	21 Nov 68	175/73	400	45.09A, 45.38	45.59, 44.9A -93
Matsanov	Igor	BLS	13 Apr 70	191/87	Dec	8105	7991 -92
Matsue	Noriaki	JPN	17 Jul 71	178/65	400h	50.24	50.12 -93
Matsuhisa	Takahiro	JPN	10 Apr 68	189/71	110h	13.76	13.93 -93
Matthews	David	IRL	9 Apr 74		800	1:45.57	1:48.35 -93
Matthews	Jonathan	USA	2 Jul 56	185/75	50kW	4:02:59	4:01:36 -93
Matyukhin	Nikolay	RUS	13 Dec 68		50kW	3:45:35	-0-
Maurizi	Mauro	ITA	12 Oct 68	175/68	400h	50.34	50.63 -93
Mayaka	Stephen	KEN	16 Nov 72	166/52	10k	28:22.16	28:18.29 -93
* Maybank	Anthuan	USA	30 Dec 69	185/75	200	20.59, 20.55w	20.70 -92
					400	45.76	44.99 -93
Maye	Sean	USA	24 Jun 69	190/72	400	45.83	46.10 -91, 45.98A -93
* Mayo	Gilmar	COL	30 Sep 69		HJ	2.33	2.20 -91
Mayock	John	GBR	26 Oct 70	177/66	1500	3:37.20	3:36.45 -93
Maznichenko	Andrey	UKR	29 Sep 66	188/94	JT	79.12	83.92 -91
Mbaye	Hamadou	SEN	21 Apr 60	183/75	400h	49.92	50.05 -93
McCall	Tony	USA	16 Jun 74	173/72	100	10.20	10.31 -93
					200	20.73w	21.09 -93
McCloy	Paul	CAN	6 Nov 63	187/70	10k	28:29.81	27:56.8 -86
McCray	Danny	USA	11 Mar 74	183/84	200	20.41w	20.70, 20.55w -93
					400	45.69	45.74 -92, 45.4 -93
McDonough	Daren	USA	29 May 74	183/78	PV	5.62	5.26 -92
McFarlane	Danny	JAM	14 Feb 72	183/75	400	45.74	45.82 -93
McGee	Scott	USA	1 Oct 68	185/104	HT	74.36	
McGhee	Pat	USA	24 Jun 66	192/79	110h	13.74w	13.56 -90, 13.50Aw -89
					400h	50.29	48.83A -88, 48.89 -89
* McGhee	Roland	USA	15 Oct 71	180/70	100	10.0	10.3 -93
					200	20.4w	20.99 -93
					LJ	8.47	8.38 -93
McGuirk	Matt	USA	15 Aug 64	185/75	3kSt	8:36.54	8:26.10 -92
McHugh	Terry	IRL	22 Aug 63	191/97	JT	82.14	84.54R -91, 80.98 -93
McKay	Kevin	GBR	9 Feb 69	178/62	1500	3:37.86	3:35.94 -92
					Mile	3:53.64	3:54.45 -92
McKean	Tom	GBR	27 Oct 63	183/71	800	1:46.20	1:43.88 -89
McKennie	Tony	USA	26 Oct 67	178/73	400h	49.92	49.38 -92
McKenzie	David	GBR	3 Sep 70	183/83	400	45.47	45.75 -93
* McKoy	Mark	AUT	10 Dec 61	182/77	110h	13.14	13.08 -93, 13.06w -92
McMahon	Kevin	USA	26 May 72	183/98	HT	71.72	69.76 -93
McMichael	Tim	USA	22 Feb 67	173/65	PV	5.50i	5.65 -89
Mdhlongwa	Ndabazihle	ZIM	30 May 73	176/69	TJ	16.69	16.57 -92
Mears	Brad	USA	24 Dec 70	193/127	SP	18.47	
Medved	Mikhail	UKR	30 Jan 64	199/89	Dec	7906	8330 -88
Mehlich	Ronald	POL	26 Sep 69	189/85	110h	13.70	13.62 -93
Meité	Ibrahim	CIV	18 Nov 76	183/75	100	10.29	10.32, 10.27w -93
					200	20.64	21.7 -92
* Mekonnen	Abebe	ETH	9 Jan 64	158/59	Mar	2:09:17	2:07:35 -88
* Melikhov	Vladimir	RUS	30 Mar 69	186/76	TJ	17.21, 17.49w	17.28 -93
Melnikov	Sergey	RUS	8 Nov 68	184/62	1500	3:38.78	3:37.58 -92
					2k	5:05.18i	5:01.15 -92
Memedov	Chary	TKM			DT	60.62	
Mena	Omar	CUB	13 Oct 66	172/70	400	45.9	46.18 -93
Menc	Miroslav	TCH	16 Mar 71	197/115	SP	18.60	18.63 -93
Menou	Didier	FRA	1 Aug 61	172/65	50kW	4:05:54	4:08:50 -91
Mensah	Frank	USA	11 May 74	183/79	110h	13.77w	14.17 -93
* Mercenario	Carlos	MEX	23 May 67	175/63	20kW	1:21:40	1:19:24 -87
					50kW	3:52:06	3:42:03 -91
Merkulov	Oleg	RUS	70		50kW	3:54:05	
Mertens	Michael	GER	27 Dec 65	191/105	SP	19.27	19.47 -92
Meshauskas	Viktoras	LIT	4 Nov 70	170/60	20kW	1:21:39.4t	1:21:44 -91
Mestre	Domitien	BEL	13 Dec 73	183/68	PV	5.50i	5.40 -92
Metcalf	Greg	USA	16 Oct 69	178/66	3kSt	8:36.63	8:41.39 -93
Mezegebu	Ayele	ETH	6 Jan 73	175/55	5k	13:21.21	
Michalík	Róbert	TCH	23 Jan 74	184/77	LJ	7.91i	7.55i -93
Michel	Karl-Friedrich	GER	9 May 65	180/93	JT	77.80	78.84 -87
Mikulás	Milan	TCH	1 Apr 63	193/79	TJ	16.78, 16.79w	17.53 -88
Milesi	Davide	ITA	27 Dec 64		Mar	2:12:44	2:14:31 -92
Miller	Dion	USA	26 Feb 75	165/73	100	10.19w	10.2w -93

Name		Nat	Born	Ht/Wt	Event	1994 Mark	Pre-1994 Best
Miller	James	AUS	4 Jun 74	188/79	PV	5.50	5.55 -93
Miller	J.J.	USA	8 Apr 73	185/78	PV	5.52	5.41 -93
Miller	Paul	USA	12 Jul 67	178/109	SP	18.78	
Miller	Scotty	USA	8 Aug 69	178/80	PV	5.52	5.60 -92
Miller	Tony	USA	12 Feb 71	193/85	400	45.27	45.48 -92
Millon	Yann	FRA	26 Mar 70	182/61	3kSt	8:32.31	
* Mills	Derek	USA	9 Jul 72	175/68	400	44.59A, 44.62	44.62 -93
Mills	Keevan	USA	10 Jul 72	188/86	110h	13.83	13.96, 13.72w -93
Minev	Plamen	BUL	28 Apr 65	192/120	HT	71.78	82.40 -91
Mingazov	Stanislav	KGZ	21 Aug 65	194/78	HJ	2.24	2.25 -91
Minns	John	AUS	31 May 67	188/120	SP	18.79	19.64 -89
Minor	Deon	USA	22 Jan 73	193/82	400	45.35	44.75 -92
Miranda	Alain	CUB	19 Oct 75		800	1:46.97	1:47.05 -93
Mistretta	Alessandro	ITA	6 Mar 71		50kW	4:03:38	4:02:52 -93
* Misyulya	Yevgeniy	BLS	9 Mar 64	177/68	20kW	1:19:22	1:19:56 -93
* Mitchell	Dennis	USA	20 Feb 66	174/69	100	9.94	9.91 -91, 9.85w -93
					200	20.63	20.09A -89, 20.20 -92
Mitchell	Maurice	USA	14 May 71	196/86	400h	49.84	49.66A, 49.75 -93
Mitchell	Stacy	USA	16 Oct 75		100	10.26w	10.3w -93
Miyajima	Seiichi	JPN	27 Sep 69	170/54	10k	28:19.17	28:43.91 -93
Mizoguchi	Kazuhiro	JPN	18 Mar 62	181/90	JT	77.68	87.60 -89
* Mladenov	Ivailo	BUL	6 Oct 73	184/73	LJ	8.30i, 8.24	8.27, 8.35w -93
Modica	Vincenzo	ITA	2 Mar 71	168/53	5k	13:30.31	13:35.35 -93
					10k	28:01.65	28:16.1 -93
* Moen	Geir	NOR	26 Jun 69	189/85	100	10.17	10.48 -92, 10.30w -93
					200	20.30	21.11 -91
Molina	Enrique	ESP	25 Feb 68	174/63	3k	7:41.90i	7:42.38 -93
* Moneghetti	Steve	AUS	26 Sep 62	176/60	10k	28:03.48	27:47.69 -92
					Mar	2:08:55	2:08:16 -90
Monreal	Iñigo	ESP	26 Sep 74	191/85	400h	50.38	51.14 -93
Monteiro	Carlos	POR	14 Dec 65	178/59	5k	13:30.37	13:22.70 -92
Montenegro	Jorge	CUB	21 Sep 68	190/105	SP	18.60	19.55 -90
Montgomery	Tim	USA	28 Jan 75	178/69	100	10.11, 9.96ig	10.61, 10.3 -93
					200	20.72	21.3 -93
Montiel	José Esteban	ESP	20 Sep 62	172/56	Mar	2:12:48	2:11:04 -90
Monye	Jude	NGR	16 Nov 73	188/75	400	45.41	46.93 -93
Moore	Ryan	AUS	18 Oct 74		LJ	7.99w	7.80, 7.84w -93
Moqhali	Thabiso	LES	7 Dec 67		Mar	2:11:40dh	2:10:55 -92
* Morceli	Noureddine	ALG	28 Feb 70	172/62	800	1:44.89	1:44.79 -91
					1500	3:30.61	3:28.86 -92
					Mile	3:48.67	3:49.12 -91
					2k	5:01.3+	4:58.21 -92
					3k	7:25.11	7:29.24 -93
					5k	13:03.85	13:25.20 -90
Morenius	Magnus	SWE	20 Mar 69		20kW	1:22:18	1:22:17 -93
Moreno	Héctor	COL	8 Jun 63	162/53	20kW	1:21:49.90t	1:22:20.8t -92
Moreno	Querubin	COL	29 Dec 59		20kW	1:21:37.17t	1:20:19 -87
Morgan	Alex	JAM	27 Dec 72	183/66	800	1:46.95	1:48.40 -93
Morgan #	Aston	JAM	18 Feb 69	175/70	100	10.28, 10.14w, 10.0w	
					LJ	8.06i, 7.95	7.78i -93
Morgan	Kendrick	USA	28 Oct 73	183/78	TJ	16.61	16.30 -93
Morgan	Marco	USA	14 Apr 71	181/75	400h	49.72	49.94 -93
Mori	Fabrizio	ITA	28 Jun 69	175/68	400h	49.24	48.92 -91
Morinaga	Masaki	JPN	27 Mar 72	175/70	LJ	8.06	8.25 -92
Morinière	Max	FRA	16 Feb 64	183/82	100	10.29	10.09 -87
* Moruyev	Andrey	RUS	6 May 70	185/90	JT	87.34	86.20 -93
Moshammer	Alexander	AUT	30 May 72	183/74	LJ	8.00	7.56 -93
Mosima	Philip	KEN	2 Jan 76	168/55	5k	13:24.07	13:43.77 -93
Moskalev	Nikolay	BLS	5 Jun 69		HJ	2.25	2.20 -93
* Motchebon	Nico	GER	13 Nov 69	186/82	800	1:44.61	1:45.67 -93
Motiejunas	Jonas	USA	7 Dec 74		400	45.69	46.75 -92
* Motti	William	FRA	25 Jul 64	198/95	Dec	8224	8327w -87, 8306 -85
Mou Weiguo		CHN	9 May 72		800	1:46.44	1:49.27 -93
Moura	Wander	BRA	22 Feb 69	181/62	3kSt	8:27.66	8:26.65 -93
* Moya	Roberto	CUB	11 Feb 65	196/120	DT	61.00	65.68 -90
Moyse	Thierry	FRA	18 Feb 67	184/78	PV	5.55	5.50 -89
Mrázek	Roman	TCH	21 Jan 62	168/55	50kW	4:01:05	3:50:46 -88
Mtolo	Willie	RSA	5 May 64	178/62	Mar	2:10:17	2:08:15 -86
Mubarak	Bilal Saad	QAT	3 Oct 72	189/110	SP	19.02	18.99 -93

Name		Nat	Born	Ht/Wt	Event	1994 Mark	Pre-1994 Best
Munkácsi	Sándor	HUN	24 Jul 69	184/81	Dec	8071	8021 -92
Muravyov	Oleg	RUS	6 May 68		HJ	2.24i	2.26i -93
Murer	Brian	USA	6 May 72	181/95	HT	73.04	68.96 -93
Murphy	Andrew	AUS	18 Dec 69	185/77	TJ	16.76	17.18 -89
Murray	Brett	USA	15 Nov 71	193/114	DT	59.42	55.82 -93
Muse	Steve	USA	27 Jan 66	185/100	DT	59.16	61.44 -93
Musiyenko	Nikolay	UKR	16 Dec 59	183/76	TJ	16.95	17.78 -86
Mustapic	Ivan	CRO	9 Jul 66	196/106	JT	82.08	82.70 -92
Musyoka	Kisilu	KEN			400	45.99A, 45.6A	
Muturi	Patrick	KEN			Mar	2:12:56	
Mutwol	William	KEN	10 Oct 67	160/55	5k	13:24.39	13:22.15 -91
					3kSt	8:11.52	8:10.74 -92
Muyaba	Fabian	ZIM	30 Sep 70	180/67	100	10.20A	10.15, 10.14w -91
Muzhikov	Pavel	RUS	71		SP	18.66	18.42 -93
Muzzio	Rob	USA	25 Jun 64	188/91	Dec	7997	8237 -93
Müller	André	GER	15 Nov 70	188/78	LJ	8.02	8.11 -90
Müller	Frank	GER	18 Jun 68	193/80	Dec	8023w	8256 -90
Münzer	Oliver	AUT	16 Feb 70	182/66	800	1:46.73	1:46.87 -93
Myricks	Larry	USA	10 Mar 56	187/84	LJ	8.09	8.74 -88
Naaji	Atiq	FRA	21 Nov 66	176/59	3k	7:39.12	7:49.7 -90
					5k	13:23.09	13:34.35 -92
Nachum	Rogel	ISR	21 May 67	181/71	TJ	16.62	17.20 -92, 17.31w -91
Nadolski	Zbigniew	POL	14 Jan 67	178/63	Mar	2:11:57	2:13:37 -93
Nakajima	Ken	JPN	2 Jun 67	177/62	LJ	7.97w	7.86 -93
Nakamura	Akira	JPN	26 Jun 67	160/53	10k	28:23.12	28:40.16 -93
					3kSt	8:29.54	8:28.98 -92
Nakamura	Shingo	JPN	4 Aug 63	178/55	Mar	2:12:15	
Nakatomi	Hajime	JPN	24 Aug 68	167/53	Mar	2:11:28	
Napier	Dino	USA	24 Nov 69	178/64	200	20.48	20.37A -89, 20.61 -92
Närhi	Matti	FIN	17 Aug 75	187/90	JT	76.14	73.18 -93
Natsume	Katsuya	JPN	1 Dec 66	169/55	10k	28:22.94	28:52.8 -93
Naumkin	Yuriy	RUS	5 Nov 68		LJ	7.96	8.04 -93
Naylor	Shane	AUS	3 Nov 67	173/83	100	10.26w	10.31 -91, 10.24w -90
Nazarov	Andrey	EST	9 Jan 65	190/80	Dec	7894	8322 -87
Nazhipov	Mukhamet	RUS	10 Sep 64	178/64	Mar	2:11:35	2:12:15 -93
* N'Deti	Cosmas	KEN	24 Nov 71	168/57	Mar	2:07:15dh	2:09:33 -93
Ndorori	Patrick	KEN	72		400	45.4A	-0-
Neal	Henry	USA	18 Oct 70	170/78	100	10.25	10.09, 10.07w -92
Nebl	Christian	AUT	21 Apr 64	180/112	SP	18.99	19.66 -93
Nedeau	Erik	USA	30 Aug 71	180/70	800	1:46.97	1:46.19 -92
					1500	3:38.31	3:42.87 -92
Negere	Tena	ETH	5 Oct 72		Mar	2:10:50	2:09:04 -92
* Nelloms	Chris	USA	14 Aug 71	175/74	200	20.70, 20.57i	20.23 -93, 19.94w -92
Nelson	Herman	USA	20 Sep 61	183/77	50kW	4:04:23	4:04:24t -89
Nemchaninov	Andrey	UKR	27 Nov 66	188/105	SP	19.48	20.95i -88, 20.60 -92
Németh	Zsolt	HUN	9 Nov 71		HT	73.14	71.14 -92
* Nerurkar	Richard	GBR	6 Jan 64	177/61	Mar	2:11:56	2:10:03 -93
Neumaier	Peter	GER	30 Jun 67	187/77	Dec	7882	7958 -90
Neumann	Thomas	GER	7 Aug 71	189/93	HT	71.06	72.42 -93
Newman	Lee	GBR	1 May 73	183/92	DT	58.34	53.14 -93
Nghidi	Savieri	ZIM	3 Feb 68	175/64	800	1:46.06	1:46.50 -92
Nieland	Nick	GBR	31 Jan 72		JT	76.28	74.50 -93
Niewoudt	Whaddon	RSA	6 Jan 70	178/62	1500	3:37.93	3:35.65 -93
					Mile	3:57.21	3:58.24 -93
Nijs	Erik	BEL	27 Jul 73	186/75	LJ	8.03	7.85 -93
Nikolayev	Sergey	RUS	12 Nov 66	189/122	SP	20.24	21.35 -89
* Nikulin	Igor	RUS	14 Aug 60	191/100	HT	79.20	84.48 -90
Nilsson	Joakim	SWE	30 Mar 71	178/79	JT	76.60	76.02 -93
Ning Limin		CHN	9 Apr 72		Mar	2:12:54	2:14:29 -93
* Niyongabo	Vénuste	BUR	9 Dec 73	170/55	800	1:45.13	1:46.15 -93
					1000	2:15.91	-0-
					1500	3:30.66	3:36.30 -93
					Mile	3:48.94	3:54.71 -93
					3k	7:49.22i	-0-
* Nizigama	Aloÿs	BUR	18 Jun 66	168/55	2k	5:01.6+	
					3k	7:35.08	7:42.42 -92
					5k	13:14.66	13:12.14 -93
					10k	27:20.51	27:47.77 -93
Njenga	Daniel	KEN	7 May 76	175/60	3kSt	8:19.21	8:41.46 -93

Name		Nat	Born	Ht/Wt	Event	1994 Mark	Pre-1994 Best
Nkazamyampi	Charles	BUR	1 Nov 64	184/68	800	1:45.85	1:44.24 -93
Nketia	Augustine	NZL	30 Dec 70	181/73	100	10.11	10.43 -93
Nnamdi	Anusim	NGR	11 Jul 72	178/68	100	10.24	10.29w -90
* Noack	Axel	GER	23 Sep 61	182/74	20kW	1:24:25	1:19:12 -87
					50kW	3:50:32	3:43:50 -93
Nogales	Benito	ESP	1 Aug 65	182/67	3kSt	8:33.30	8:23.52 -90
Nool	Erki	EST	25 Jun 70	183/78	LJ	7.96	7.77i -91, 8.17w -93
					Dec	8093	8001 -92
* Noon	Brent	USA	29 Aug 71	188/123	SP	20.67	20.48 -93
Norca	Alex	FRA	18 Jan 69	185/90	TJ	16.49, 16.81w	16.82 -92, 17.04w -91
Novácek	Vladimir	TCH	23 Jun 68	186/92	JT	75.98	77.40 -93
N'senga	Jonathan	BEL	21 Apr 73	186/79	110h	13.56	13.76 -93
* Ntawulikura	Mathias	RWA	14 Jul 64	171/63	5k	13:25.27	13:11.29 -92
					10k	27:36.15	27:47.59 -93
Nti-Berko	David	GHA	71	175/68	TJ	16.54	16.47, 16.67w -93
Ntirampéba	Hilaire	BUR			3kSt	8:36.19	8:57.0 -92
N'Tyamba	João	ANO	20 Mar 68	178/58	1000	2:18.82	2:22.67 -92
Nunes	Eronildo	BRA	31 Dec 70	183/75	400h	48.88	49.10 -92
Nunige	Guy	FRA	11 Feb 66	178/62	1500	3:39.56	3:36.94 -92
Nurmi	Risto	FIN	24 Nov 69	186/70	50kW	4:04:56	4:05:15 -92
Nuti	Andrea	ITA	4 Aug 67	185/74	400	46.05A	45.35A -93, 45.50 -92
Nuttall	John	GBR	11 Jan 67	176/58	5k	13:23.54	13:24.26 -92
Nuttin	Thierry	FRA	11 Oct 62	186/70	50kW	4:00:52.3t	4:04:58 -89
Nwankpa	Frank	NGR	26 May 73	172/73	100	10.27, 10.14w	10.42 -92, 10.39w -93
Nyambaso	Zacharia	KEN	71		Mar	2:12:12	
Nyangincha	Sammy	KEN	10 Nov 62		Mar	2:08:50	2:14:09 -92
* Nylander	Sven	SWE	1 Jan 62	193/85	400h	48.22	48.37 -87
Oaks	David	USA	12 May 72	178/70	100	10.04w	10.14A -93
					200	20.63, 20.24w	20.34 -93
					400	45.80	45.36 -93
* O'Brien	Dan	USA	18 Jul 66	189/84	110h	13.81	13.93 -93, 13.89w -89
					Dec	8715	8891 -92
Ochieng	Kennedy	KEN	30 Dec 71	183/73	400	45.20	44.82, 44.5A -93
Odegård	Tor Öyvind	NOR	28 Feb 69		800	1:45.55	1:46.67 -93
Odom	Deworski	USA	11 Apr 77	183/73	100	10.26	10.69 -93
Odom	Ed	USA	24 Feb 73		400	45.35	46.22 -92
O'Donoghue	Peter	AUS	1 Oct 61	185/68	5k	13:24.09	13:23.31 -93
Ogden	Jon	USA	31 Jul 74	203/140	SP	18.64i	17.97 -93
Ogilvie	Peter	CAN	2 May 72	178/70	200	20.69A	20.46 -92
Ogino	Sumito	JPN	2 Apr 73	167/53	3kSt	8:36.55	8:45.07 -93
Ogola	Francis	UGA	1 Jul 73	183/74	400	45.47	45.87 -92
Oiada	Mircea	ROM	20 Feb 69	189/75	110h	13.68	13.54 -92
Okawa	Hisayuki	JPN	71	166/54	10k	28:20.38	28:46.1 -93
Okeke ¶	Aham	NOR	19 Aug 69	172/76	100	10.26, 10.19dq,	10.40 -87
						10.16ig, 10.10wdt	10.27w -93
Okoli	Emmanuel	NGR	13 Nov 73		400	45.92	46.67 -93
Ole Marai	Stephen	KEN	11 Nov 62	184/65	800	1:46.64	1:44.3A -89
Oliveira	Adilson Ramos	BRA	4 Jan 64	188/110	SP	18.72	18.61 -87
Oliveira	Paulo Sergio	BRA	1 Dec 69		LJ	7.94	7.89 -91
Oliver	Muhammad	USA	12 Mar 69	179/80	Dec	8043	8087 -92
Olivier	Wikus	RSA	8 Mar 68		TJ	16.89A, 16.91Aw	16.64A, 16.71Aw -93
Olsen-O'Neil	Chris	USA	27 May 73		HJ	2.28	
Olteanu	Ovidiu	ROM	6 Aug 70	183/69	1500	3:38.73	3:40.79 -93
					Mile	3:58.18	-0-
					2k	5:02.47	-0-
					5k	13:33.80	13:50.08 -93
* Olukoju	Adewale	NGR	27 Jul 68	193/115	DT	62.46	67.80 -91
O'Mara	Frank	IRL	17 Jul 60	176/61	3k	7:45.74	7:40.41 -89
					5k	13:26.67	13:13.02 -87
Omelyusik	Vasiliy	BLS	17 Mar 65		3kSt	8:33.73	8:34.4 -93
* Ondieki	Yobes	KEN	21 Feb 61	168/55	2k	5:06.8+	5:01.6 -89
					3k	7:43.75	7:34.18 -92
					5k	13:13.80	13:01.82 -91
Ongeta	Henry	KEN	68		800	1:46.6A	1:47.2A -93
Ono	Tomonari	JPN	7 Feb 74	185/73	800	1:46.18	1:47.28 -93
Orekhov	Nikolay	RUS	20 Jun 73		DT	59.96	57.78 -93
Orfanopoulos	Dimitris	GRE	9 May 64	170/64	20kW	1:24:14	1:24:11 -88
Orlík	Roman	TCH	29 May 72	182/71	LJ	8.11	7.87 -92, 7.94i -93
* Orlov	Mikhail	RUS	25 Jun 67	175/68	20kW	1:21:01	1:20:07 -90

Name		Nat	Born	Ht/Wt	Event	1994 Mark	Pre-1994 Best
Osagiobare	Bode	NGR	1 Dec 70	175/70	100	10.01A	10.33 -93, 10.21w -90
					200	20.49A, 20.66, 20.50w	20.89 -93
Osawa	Yoshuke	JPN	7 Sep 67	173/58	10k	28:23.56	28:09.06 -92
Osei	Kennedy	GHA	21 Oct 66	178/68	800	1:45.13	1:45.62 -93
Osorio	Daniel	CUB	5 Nov 72	184/77	TJ	16.77	17.02 -93
* Osoro	Ondoro	KEN	3 Dec 67	168/63	3k	7:50.47	7:43.20 -93
					5k	13:16.39	13:11.77 -91
					10k	27:28.36	27:24.24 -93
Osovich	Sergey	UKR	16 Dec 73	181/73	100	10.26, 10.0w	10.58 -92
					200	20.58	21.00 -93
Ostrovskiy	Vladimir	ISR	12 Dec 66	168/56	20kW	1:23:37	1:21:32 -90
* O'Sullivan	Marcus	IRL	22 Dec 61	176/61	1500	3:34.96	3:34.57 -92
					Mile	3:53.86	3:51.64 -89
					2k	5:01.2+	4:58.08 -88
Otte	Martin	GER	3 May 67		Dec	7662	7386 -93
Ottoz	Laurent	ITA	10 Apr 70	180/63	110h	13.42, 13.32Aw	13.51 -92
Ouhrouch	Hassan	MAR	2 Jun 64		3kSt	8:33.79	8:36.58 -91
* Ovchinnikov	Vladimir	RUS	2 Aug 70	190/90	JT	79.76	82.12 -90
Owen	Neil	GBR	18 Oct 73	193/74	110h	13.80	14.01, 13.99w -93
Owusu	Andrew	GHA	8 Jul 72	180/75	LJ	7.97, 8.06w	7.83i, 7.88w -93
Pachin	Vyacheslav	LIT	16 Jul 63	188/100	DT	58.38	60.46 -92
Packalén	Juha	FIN	5 Aug 59		HT	71.68	70.18 -91
Pajonk	Dirk-Achim	GER	27 Mar 69	190/80	Dec	8070	7942 -92
* Pakarinen	Ari	FIN	14 May 69	182/90	JT	83.38	84.00 -92
Paklin	Igor	KGZ	15 Jun 63	191/72	HJ	2.24	2.41 -85
* Palchikov	Yevgeniy	RUS	12 Oct 68	198/110	SP	20.94	20.86 -93
Paljakka	Antero	FIN	1 Aug 69	201/117	SP	19.25i, 19.12	19.84 -93
Pallakis	Christos	GRE	9 Oct 71	191/78	PV	5.50i	5.49 -92
Palóczi	Gyula	HUN	13 Sep 62	185/67	TJ	16.61w	16.87, 16.94w -93
Panagiotopoulos	Georgios	GRE	12 Aug 69	185/75	200	20.52	20.90 -92
Pancorbo	Manuel	ESP	7 Jul 66	178/60	1500	3:38.01	3:34.37 -92
* Panetta	Francesco	ITA	10 Jan 63	175/64	3k	7:46.48	7:42.73 -87
					3kSt	8:23.55	8:08.57 -87
Pantoja	Filiberto	MEX	69		50kW	4:04:35	4:10:19 -93
Paoluzzi	Loris	ITA	14 May 74	191/105	HT	72.00	69.38 -93
Papadimitrou	Aleksandros	GRE	18 Jun 73	183/105	HT	73.74	70.16 -93
Papadopoulos	Christos	GRE	16 Mar 65	186/100	DT	60.48	60.96 -92
Papakostas	Lambros	GRE	20 Oct 69	193/78	HJ	2.30i, 2.30	2.36 -92
Paredes	Benjamin	MEX	30 Apr 62		Mar	2:10:40	2:14:23 -93
Parfyonov	Vladimir	UZB	17 Jun 70	198/105	JT	84.00	80.64 -93
Park Min-soo		KOR	30 Jan 68	181/73	TJ	16.73	16.69 -93
Parker	Andrew	JAM	11 Jan 65	190/77	110h	13.76	13.51 -87, 13.5 -86
Parker	Steve	USA	4 Jul 72	192/79	HJ	2.27	2.23 -92
Parpala	Esko	FIN	2 Jul 65	180/67	800	1:45.99	1:45.24 -89
Parrilla	Jose	USA	31 Mar 72	172/65	400	45.76	45.84 -92
					800	1:46.01	1:43.97 -92
Parsons	Geoff	GBR	14 Aug 64	203/80	HJ	2.31	2.30i -86, 2.30 -90
Partington	Stephen	GBR	17 Sep 65		20kW	1:24:09	1:24:18 -90
* Partyka	Artur	POL	25 Jul 69	192/69	HJ	2.33	2.37i -91, 2.37 -93
Parviainen	Aki	FIN	26 Oct 74	190/86	JT	78.76	80.94 -92
Parviainen	Mika	FIN	19 Dec 70	195/105	JT	79.26	80.26 -92
Patricio	Carlos	POR	9 Jan 64	176/59	Mar	2:11:42	2:11:00 -93
Patrick	David	USA	12 Jun 60	183/72	400h	49.92	47.75 -88
Patrick	Paul	AUS	15 Sep 71	183/63	5k	13:34.02	13:33.21 -93
Patserin	Aleksey	UKR	16 May 67	178/66	3kSt	8:33.78	8:33.87 -89
Patterson	Tiberia	USA	26 Jan 71	185/74	110h	13.67	13.90, 13.82w -92, 13.6 -93
Payne	Arnold	ZIM	17 Oct 72	182/72	400	46.00	
Payne	Bill	USA	21 Dec 67	188/77	PV	5.83	5.86 -91
Paynter	Julian	AUS	15 Jul 70	183/71	5k	13:30.18	13:36.09 -93
Pechenkin	Yevgeniy	RUS	9 Oct 73	192/82	110h	13.81w	13.60 -93
Pedersen	Arne	NOR	19 Apr 61	191/115	SP	20.15	20.24 -86, 20.92dq -87
* Pedroso	Ivan	CUB	17 Dec 72	176/70	LJ	8.26i, 8.16	8.53, 8.79w -92
Pegoraro	Andrea	ITA	24 Oct 66	186/74	PV	5.50i, 5.50, 5.70ex	5.65, 5.70ex -92
Pegoretti	Massimo	ITA	16 Jul 74		1500	3:39.99	3:43.94 -93
Pekola	Kari	FIN	27 Sep 65	187/99	DT	61.64	58.76 -93
Peltoniemi	Asko	FIN	7 Feb 63	187/77	PV	5.55	5.72 -91
Peltoniemi	Petri	FIN	6 Mar 70	178/68	PV	5.71	5.70 -93
Pemberton	Darius	USA	10 May 75	185/77	LJ	8.12w	7.21 -93
* Peñalver	Antonio	ESP	1 Dec 68	194/90	Dec	8160w, 8084	8534w/8478 -92

Name		Nat	Born	Ht/Wt	Event	1994 Mark	Pre-1994 Best
Pendergist	Rob	USA	12 Jul 70	183/79	Dec	7837	7875 -92
Pérez	Andrés	ESP	27 Nov 69	175/65	10k	28:20.22	28:27.59 -93
Pérez	António	ESP	23 Mar 66	191/77	10k	28:26.36	29:17.98 -92
Pérez	Jefferson	ECU	1 Jan 74		20kW	1:23:27	
Pérez	José	CUB	19 Mar 71	184/73	400h	49.39	49.28A, 49.34 -93
* Peric	Dragan	YUG	8 May 64	188/110	SP	20.64i, 20.57	21.26 -93
* Perricelli	Giovanni	ITA	25 Aug 67	170/67	20kW	1:21:42	1:21:37 -91
					50kW	3:43:55	3:49:40 -91
Perrot	Eric	FRA	26 Aug 69	180/75	100	10.29rsw	10.37 -93
Perszke	Wieslaw	POL	18 Feb 60	172/60	Mar	2:11:52dh	2:11:15 -93
Perzylo #	Piotr	POL	15 Nov 61	186/118	SP	19.46	20.23 -86
Pesava	Jan	TCH	14 Jan 72	174/54	10k	28:10.73	28:56.89 -93
Petersen	Kenneth	DEN	18 Dec 65	195/98	JT	76.08	81.22 -89
Peterson	Scott	USA	9 Nov 72	187/118	SP	18.90i, 18.87	18.92 -93
Petranoff	Tom	RSA	8 Apr 58	186/105	JT	75.60	89.16S -91
Petrov	German	RUS	26 Mar 67	184/70	400h	49.91	49.40 -88
Petrunin	Aleksandr	RUS	29 Jan 67		TJ	17.02i, 16.95	16.83 -93
Petrunov	Aleksey	RUS	72		LJ	7.93	7.67 -92
Pettersson	Kristian	SWE	5 Oct 71		SP	19.74	18.03 -93
					DT	62.58	54.72 -91
* Pettigrew	Antonio	USA	3 Nov 67	183/70	200	20.38	20.70, 20.62w -89
					400	44.43	44.27 -89
* Petushinskiy	Denis	RUS	28 Jun 67	188/77	PV	5.80, 5.86br	5.90 -93
Peula	Antonio	ESP	21 Mar 66	171/67	3kSt	8:28.28	8:23.47 -90
Phelps	Dillon	USA	1 Dec 74	188/72	HJ	2.23	2.21 -93
* Philibert	Dan	FRA	6 Aug 70	183/77	110h	13.43	13.33 -91
Philipp	Peter	SUI	18 Feb 72		1500	3:39.58	3:46.72 -93
Phillips	Chris	USA	24 Jul 72	183/77	110h	13.61, 13.4	13.58 -93
Phiri	Bobang	RSA	5 May 68	179/72	400	45.26A, 45.45	45.27 -92
* Pierce	Jack	USA	23 Sep 62	185/84	110h	13.48, 13.41Aw	13.06 -91
Pieterse	Ferrins	RSA	22 Mar 67		400h	49.70A	49.48A -91
Pihlavisto	Vesa-Pekka	FIN	15 Apr 65	182/69	400h	49.69	50.12 -90
Pilkington	Paul	USA	12 Oct 58	172/60	Mar	2:12:13	2:11:13 -90
* Piller	René	FRA	23 Apr 65	168/56	20kW	1:22:55.6t	1:22:15.0t -92
					50kW	3:41:28.2t	3:48:57 -93
Pinheiro	Joaquim	POR	20 Dec 60	164/57	10k	27:55.0	28:08.49 -88
* Pinto	António	POR	22 Mar 66	165/59	5k	13:21.1	13:25.35 -92
					10k	27:48.1	28:01.00 -88
					Mar	2:08:31	2:10:02 -92
Piñera	Pedro	CUB	20 Dec 71	173/63	400h	50.19	49.97 -92
Piolanti	Raphael	FRA	14 Nov 67	184/95	HT	72.32	79.68 -92
Pirini	Doug	NZL	6 Sep 69		Dec	7864	7862 -93
Piskunov ¶	Vladislav	UKR	7 Jun 78	183/90	HT	73.66	68.96 -93
Pitayo	Martin	MEX	10 Nov 60	173/55	Mar	2:10:58	2:09:41 -90
Pitcher	Tim	USA	11 Oct 70	183/68	1500	3:39.23	3:41.24 -93
Pitillas	Oscar	ESP	16 Oct 71	185/62	400h	50.26	50.32 -92
Piziks	Rojs	HUN	12 Feb 71	195/90	Dec	7830	7699 -93
Plasencia	Steve	USA	28 Oct 56	180/66	Mar	2:12:51	2:14:14 -92
* Plaza	Daniel	ESP	3 Jul 66	181/63	20kW	1:21:54	1:20:42 -92
					50kW	3:57:56	3:49:31 -92
* Plaziat	Christian	FRA	28 Oct 63	191/87	Dec	8505	8574 -90
Plotnikov	Andrey	RUS	12 Aug 67	186/77	50kW	3:47:43	3:40:07 -90
Podrebadsky	Jan	TCH	1 Mar 74	186/78	Dec	7876	7396 -93
Podrez	Sergey	RUS	26 Feb 71		400h	49.90	50.3, 51.45 -93
Pogosyan	Shirak	ARM	24 Sep 69		LJ	7.92A	7.98 -89
Pöhn	Stefan	GER	30 Dec 73		SP	18.71	17.70 -93
Polichroniou	Christos	GRE	31 Mar 72	185/102	HT	73.04	73.16 -93
Pollakowski	Dirk	GER	24 Feb 70		JT	78.42 ??	71.36 -93
Popel	Mikhail	BLS	25 May 66	192/100	HT	73.60	79.10 -87
Popescu	Eugen	ROM	12 Aug 62	194/78	HJ	2.32i, 2.24	2.32 -88
Popko	Viktor	UKR	13 Aug 68	188/75	TJ	16.57	16.61i -93
Popov	Andrey	RUS	28 Apr 62	185/68	50kW	3:59:11	
Popov	Vadim	UZB	18 Dec 71	193/105	DT	58.96	54.32 -92
* Porkhomovskiy	Aleksandr	RUS	12 Aug 72	174/68	100	10.12	10.16 -93
					200	20.35	20.80 -93
Portuondo	Omar	CUB	1 May 70	184/72	110h	13.77, 13.4A	13.88 -89, 13.75A -93
Potapovich	Igor	KZK	6 Sep 67	185/75	PV	5.81	5.92 -92
* Potashov	Aleksandr	BLS	12 Mar 62	187/80	20kW	1:20:12	1:21:21 -80
					50kW	3:49:00	3:40:02 -90

Name		Nat	Born	Ht/Wt	Event	1994 Mark	Pre-1994 Best
Potgieter	Frits	RSA	13 Mar 74	195/110	DT	61.24	59.12 -93
Potts	Richard	NZL	13 Jul 71	186/72	1500	3:38.25	3:44+ -93
Powell	Donovan	JAM	13 Jun 71	183/79	100	10.22, 10.19w	10.31, 10.21w -93
* Powell	Mike	USA	10 Nov 63	188/77	LJ	8.58, 8.95Aw	8.95 -91
Pratt	Shane	USA	7 Nov 73	173/66	400	46.04	47.41 -93
Presser	Jamie	USA	28 Nov 70	197/109	DT	60.48	56.34 -92
Prevot	Leonardo	CUB	13 Jun 71	168/71	200	20.61, 20.4A	21.13 -90
Pride	Brad	USA	7 Jun 74	175/76	400	45.29	47.06 -92
Primc	Igor	SLO	66		DT	58.38	58.10 -90
Pronin	Vladimir	RUS	27 May 69	186/70	3kSt	8:26.33	8:32.03 -93
Pronko	Gennadiy	BLS	27 Feb 70		DT	63.84	60.66 -92
Prophet	Thomas	GER	22 May 72		50kW	4:06:42	4:06:05 -93
Pugliese	Marcelo	ARG	2 Sep 68	191/105	DT	59.22	53.08 -92
* Pukstys	Tom	USA	28 May 68	188/91	JT	82.32	85.70 -93
Pumalainen	Leonid	RUS	13 Apr 70	191/73	HJ	2.31i, 2.28	2.25 -90
Pursley	Brit	USA	25 Apr 69	183/79	PV	5.62	5.61i -93, 5.50 -89
Pusterla	Umberto	ITA	21 Oct 67		5k	13:26.94	13:35.40 -92
					10k	28:08.55	29:24.2 -92
Pyrah	Jason	USA	6 Apr 69	172/64	800	1:46.83	1:48.04 -92
					1500	3:38.20	3:39.22 -92
Quénéhervé	Gilles	FRA	17 May 66	183/74	100	10.17	10.29 -90
					200	20.64	20.16 -87
* Quesada	Yoelbi	CUB	4 Aug 73	180/73	TJ	17.61	17.68 -93
* Quintanilla	Armando	MEX	19 Apr 68	175/56	5k	13:33.48	13:30.66 -92
					10k	27:18.59	27:49.24 -92
Quintero	Reinaldo	CUB	7 Oct 69	186/74	110h	13.75	13.91 -88
Rabenala	Toussaint	MAD	29 Oct 65	178/71	TJ	16.64i, 16.49	17.05 -89, 17.21w -93
Radkiewicz	Przemyslaw	POL	25 Aug 70	194/75	HJ	2.26	2.28 -93
Raizgys	Andrius	LIT	4 Apr 69	185/80	TJ	17.18	17.22 -93
Rakipov	Azat	BLS	25 Nov 68	174/56	Mile	3:57.88	-0-
Rakovic	Aleksandr	YUG	13 Apr 68		20kW	1:24:19/1:21:57sc	1:23:37 -93
					50kW	4:01:17	
Ramos	José	POR	28 Jul 68		5k	13:24.50	13:47.08 -93
					10k	28:16.27	
Ramsey	Marlon	USA	11 Sep 74	175/66	400	45.36	46.35 -92
* Räty	Seppo	FIN	27 Apr 62	188/105	JT	85.22	96.96R -91, 90.60 -92
* Reading	Robert	USA	9 Jun 67	193/82	110h	13.34, 13.18w	13.42A, 13.44, 13.19Aw -89
Redei	Lászlo	HUN	17 Jul 70	182/85	HT	73.52	73.08 -93
Redwine	Stanley	USA	10 Apr 61	190/77	800	1:46.18	1:44.87 -84
Reed	Marcus	USA	17 Jul 72	179/70	100	10.18	10.37 -92
					200	20.57, 20.56w	21.03 -92
Reese	Dan	USA	15 Oct 63	173/55	3kSt	8:31.4	8:25.72 -91
Reese	Terry	USA	20 Jun 67	183/79	110h	13.72, 13.71w	13.74A, 13.62Aw -89
* Regis	John	GBR	13 Oct 66	181/94	100	10.10Aw, 10.23w	10.20, 10.07w -90
					200	19.87A, 20.01	19.94 -93
Reilly	Brendan	GBR	23 Dec 72	195/77	HJ	2.32i, 2.28	2.31 -92
Reimann	Jens	GER	21 Mar 69	198/100	JT	77.86	79.78 -90
Reina	Reuben	USA	16 Nov 67	170/51	3k	7:49.94	7:43.02 -91
Reinhardt	Jonny	GER	28 Jun 68	198/120	SP	20.13	20.07 -93
* Reiterer	Werner	AUS	27 Jan 68	193/112	DT	63.00	65.62 -87
Retel	Jean-Claude	FRA	11 Feb 68	193/102	DT	59.16	60.32 -93
* Reynolds	Butch	USA	8 Jun 64	190/80	400	45.18	43.29 -88
Rhymer	Greg	USA	22 Feb 72	178/68	800	1:46.98	1:47.70 -93
Riad	Mohamed	MAR	71		5k	13:26.6	13:44.10 -92
Ribeiro	Juvenal	POR	9 Mar 64	174/60	10k	28:15.6	28:15.25 -93
					Mar	2:12:52	2:13:03 -93
Richard	Thierry	FRA	22 Sep 61	184/78	110h	13.71A	13.77 -89
Richards	Clarence	JAM	15 Apr 71	183/80	400	45.94	47.5i -93
Richards	Tommy	USA	14 Jul 70	188/79	Dec	7704	7635 -91, 7702w -93
Richter	Karsten	GER	25 Jul 72	194/80	TJ	16.66i, 16.54	16.95 -93
Rico	Isidro	MEX	15 May 61		Mar	2:09:14	2:09:28 -92
Riech	Todd	USA	24 Oct 70	188/95	JT	81.30	74.64 -92
* Riedel	Lars	GER	28 Jun 67	198/110	DT	66.08	68.66 -92
Riepl	Anton	GER	28 Feb 69	175/63	HJ	2.25	2.26 -93
Riley	Phil	USA	24 Sep 72	183/77	110h	13.71	13.83 -92, 13.73w -91
Ritter	Daniel	SUI	28 Dec 65	184/72	400h	49.95	50.35 -91
Robbins	Sean	USA	9 Oct 72	188/84	100	10.28w	
					LJ	7.91i	7.74i -93
Roberson	Mark	GBR	13 Mar 67	194/100	JT	78.82	80.92 -88

Name		Nat	Born	Ht/Wt	Event	1994 Mark	Pre-1994 Best
Roberts	Grant	RSA	22 May 71		400h	50.22A	50.07A -92, 50.28 -93
Robinson	Garth	JAM	11 Oct 70	173/72	200	20.66, 20.61w	
Robinson	Rohan	AUS	15 Nov 71	191/80	400h	49.53	49.35 -91
* Rodal	Vebjörn	NOR	16 Sep 72	185/76	800	1:43.50	1:45.33 -92
Rodely	David	USA	7 Jun 68	190/104	SP	18.94	18.90 -92
					DT	59.02	57.22 -91
Rodrigues	António	POR	14 Jun 63	177/61	Mar	2:12:43	2:11:18 -93
* Rodrigues	Pedro	POR	8 Jul 71	181/72	400h	48.77	49.46 -92
Rodriguez	Javier	ESP	22 Feb 74	176/62	3kSt	8:35.03	8:47.21 -93
Rodriguez	Miguel	MEX	15 May 62	173/66	20kW	1:21:35	1:20:59 -93
					50kW	3:52:06	3:50:55 -92
Rodriguez	Rene	USA	6 Apr 74	180/80	400	45.85	47.4 -92
Rofes	Jordi	ESP	24 Sep 76	194/77	HJ	2.23i	2.21 -93
Romain	Jerome	DMN	12 Jun 71	183/76	TJ	16.82i, 16.79, 17.05w	16.98 -93
Romanzi	Orazio	ITA	16 Sep 70		50kW	4:00:52	4:12:55 -92
Roney	Jerry	USA	5 Jan 70	183/80	110h	13.59, 13.52w, 13.2	13.52 -92
Ronkainen	Janne	FIN	5 Feb 63	191/110	SP	19.56	20.75 -90
Rono	Simeon	KEN	9 Apr 72		5k	13:30.99	14:04.1A -90
					3kSt	8:20.98	8:37.4 -93
Rosen	Alex	USA	2 Jun 73	196/70	HJ	2.25	2.24 -93
Ross	Duane	USA	5 Dec 72	183/79	110h	13.48	13.74 -93, 13.62w -92
Rosswess	Michael	GBR	11 Jun 65	186/73	100	10.29, 10.07w	10.15 -91
Rosvold	Thomas	NOR	21 Jul 67		DT	58.96	58.82 -90
Rothell	John	USA	29 Mar 72	183/73	400h	49.81	50.45 -93
Rougetet	Nicolas	FRA	27 Jul 70	196/120	HT	75.02	73.98 -93
Rouser	Jason	USA	22 Mar 70	198/80	200	20.47	20.45 -91
Rouser	Jason	USA	22 Mar 70	198/80	400	45.19	44.82 -92
* Rousseau	Vincent	BEL	29 Jul 62	176/60	5k	13:32.06	13:10.99 -93
					10k	27:47.79	27:23.18 -93
					Mar	2:07:51	2:09:13 -93
* Rowland	Mark	GBR	7 Mar 63	183/68	3k	7:50.30	7:46.22i -90
					3kSt	8:22.20	8:07.96 -88
Royce	Jon	USA	2 Mar 74		HJ	2.23	2.20 -93
Rubtsov	Sergey	UZB	4 Sep 65	190/140	SP	19.50	20.68 -88
Rudolph	Clyde	USA	15 Feb 72	170/70	200	20.54, 20.40w	20.59 -93
Ruffini	Robert	SVK	26 Jan 67	185/70	HJ	2.31i, 2.24	2.34 -88
Ruiz	Faustino	ESP	20 Sep 65	178/65	50kW	4:06:19	3:57:25 -91
Ruiz	Marc	ESP	5 Feb 74	184/73	3kSt	8:35.13	8:56.71 -93
Russell	Wes	USA	3 Mar 71	183/73	400	45.64	45.22 -93
* Rusterholz	Matthias	SUI	16 Aug 71	184/70	400	45.43	46.20 -93
Rutherford	Frank	BAH	23 Nov 64	185/82	TJ	16.51, 16.88w	17.41 -92
Ruto	Gilbert	KEN	3 Mar 66		Mar	2:12:36	
Ruto	Paul	KEN	23 Nov 63	184/68	800	1:45.41A	1:43.92 -93
Ryabukhin	Mikhail	RUS	25 Mar 67	188/71	110h	13.75, 13.54w	13.64 -91, 13.5 -88
Ryans	Larry	USA	28 Jul 71	181/83	110h	13.81	13.76 -91, 13.61w -92
Rybin	Yuriy	RUS	5 Mar 63	186/85	JT	82.96	84.54S -91
Saber	Ashraf	ITA	2 Apr 73	185/75	400h	49.70	49.71 -93
Sabulei	James	KEN	12 Apr 69	172/65	LJ	7.94A	8.00A -91, 7.99 -93
Saddler	Greg	USA	29 Jun 74	172/73	100	10.20, 10.11w	10.25w -93
					200	20.56	20.84 -93
Saenz	Rogelio	MEX	8 Jun 68	185/74	LJ	8.23A	7.67, 8.01uc -93
* Sahere	Abdelaziz	MAR	18 Sep 67	183/63	3kSt	8:11.11	8:12.21 -91
Saho	Nozomi	JPN	6 Mar 73	170/53	10k	28:17.32	27:58.47 -93
Sainte-Rose	Georges	FRA	3 Sep 69	184/66	TJ	16.97, 17.19w	17.24, 17.48w -91
* Saito	Yoshihiko	JPN	12 Feb 72	177/63	400h	49.13	48.68 -93
Sakhri	Sid-Ali	ALG	20 Dec 61	173/67	10k	28:28.11	28:34.31 -93
					Mar	2:11:44	2:11:09 -93
* Sakirkin	Oleg	KZK	23 Jan 66	182/72	TJ	17.35, 17.49w	17.58 -89
Saksio	Sami	FIN	28 Apr 69	190/95	JT	81.62	80.30 -93
Salah	Ahmed	DJI	31 Dec 56	180/60	Mar	2:11:19	2:07:07 -88
Salle	Fred	GBR	10 Sep 64	188/84	LJ	8.10	7.97 -86
Samoei	Barnabas	KEN	65		800	1:46.41A	1:48.1A -91
Sánchez	Alberto	CUB	3 Feb 73	180/92	HT	76.14, 76.60li	75.86 -93
Sánchez	Alexis	CUB	3 Mar 71	187/77	110h	13.71	13.63 -92, 13.58w -91
* Sánchez	German	MEX	15 Sep 66	173/65	50kW	3:56:00	3:51:02 -92
Sánchez	Rogelio	MEX	73		20kW	1:22:44	
					50kW	4:04:03	
Sanders	Chris	USA	8 May 72	183/82	200	20.42	20.76w -92
					LJ	8.07	8.17i, 8.05 -92

Name		Nat	Born	Ht/Wt	Event	1994 Mark	Pre-1994 Best
Sanders	Larry	USA	26 Apr 70	180/73	400h	49.99	49.24 -93
* Sang	Patrick	KEN	11 Apr 64	177/64	3kSt	8:12.16	8:06.03 -89
Sang	Rere	KEN	72	173/64	400h	49.75A	51.4A -93
Sangouma	Daniel	FRA	7 Feb 65	187/84	200	20.56	20.20 -89
Sanguin	Giovanni	ITA	14 May 69	180/90	HT	73.32	72.36 -93
Sankovich	Andrey	BLS	15 Jul 65		HJ	2.24i, 2.23	2.34 -93
Santos	Gilmar	BRA	16 Dec 70	185/78	800	1:46.90	1:45.88 -93
Santos	José	POR	20 Dec 70		10k	28:16.2	
Santos	Raimundo	POR	22 Aug 67		10k	28:22.29	29:17.39 -93
Saritzoglou	Savas	GRE	19 Jul 71	188/109	HT	76.44	76.12 -93
Sarnatskiy	Konstantin	UZB	16 Oct 71	174/73	LJ	8.10	7.69 -92
* Särnblom	Håkon	NOR	3 Mar 66	194/77	HJ	2.31i, 2.31	2.28 -91
* Sasimovich	Vladimir	BLS	14 Sep 68	178/86	JT	83.14	87.08 -91
Sassi	Mohamed Karim	TUN	68		TJ	16.56, 16.89w	16.32 -93
Sautkin	Igor	RUS	72		TJ	17.15	16.71w -93
Savaitin	Dmitriy	BLS	26 Aug 71		50kW	3:59:13	
Savin	Vitaliy	KZK	23 Jan 66	180/86	100	10.25	10.08, 9.94w -92
Scammell	Pat	AUS	15 Apr 61	189/67	1500	3:37.74	3:34.61 -88
					Mile	3:56.89	3:53.58 -91
Scherer	John	USA	3 Nov 66	185/72	10k	28:20.33	28:16.24 -90
Schikora	Dagfinn	NOR	7 Sep 64		SP	18.92	17.99 -90
Schläfli	Rolf	SUI	15 Mar 71		Dec	7899	7350 -93
* Schmid	Stefan	GER	6 May 70	186/78	Dec	8309	8061 -93
Schneider	Stefan	SUI	21 Feb 64	186/80	Dec	7737	7681 -90
* Schult	Jürgen	GER	11 May 60	193/110	DT	66.08	74.08 -86
* Schwarthoff	Florian	GER	7 May 68	201/82	110h	13.16	13.13 -92
Schweyen	Brian	USA	17 Feb 68	196/86	Dec	7957	7024 -89
Schwieger	Rick	USA	17 Jun 69	196/84	Dec	7760	7877 -92
Scott	Carlos	USA	2 Jul 60	193/165	DT	60.08	63.74 -83
Scott	Tyrone	USA	18 Jan 70	186/77	TJ	16.68i	17.03 -92
* Sediki	Azzeddine	MAR	21 May 70	171/55	1500	3:32.71	3:41.01 -93
					Mile	3:55.67	-0-
Sedlácek	Pavel	TCH	5 Apr 68	198/105	HT	75.96	76.46 -92
* Sedykh	Yuriy	RUS	11 Jun 55	185/106	HT	80.14	86.74 -86
Seelig	Andreas	GER	6 Jul 70	200/120	DT	62.22	61.90 -93
* Segura	Bernardo	MEX	11 Feb 70	179/61	20kW	1:17:25.5t	1:19:39 -93
					50kW	4:03:51	
Segura	Jorge	MEX	23 Apr 75		20kW	1:24:49	
Seifert	Jim	USA	26 Nov 62	188/114	DT	64.18	66.14 -92
Gebrselassie	Tekeye	ETH	16 Oct 70		Mar	2:11:45	2:13:52 -93
Seleznyov	Aleksandr	RUS	25 Jan 63	182/97	HT	80.96	81.70 -93
Selle	Frédéric	FRA	15 Mar 57	198/125	DT	60.00	62.96 -89
Semenyuk	Yevgeniy	UKR	11 Dec 68	175/65	LJ	8.04	8.13 -93
Semin	Sergey	RUS	71		50kW	3:59:48	
Semyonov	Konstantin	BLS	20 Nov 69	190/80	PV	5.75	5.70 -91
Sena	Inaldo	BRA	18 Jun 71	181/76	400	45.02	45.25 -92
* Sepeng	Hezekiel	RSA	30 Jun 74	178/58	800	1:45.32	1:45.46 -93
Serem	William	KEN	71	173/63	800	1:45.67	1:45.8A -93
Sergiyenko	Yuriy	UKR	19 Mar 65	190/73	HJ	2.28	2.34i, 2.31 -85
Serrano	Antonio	ESP	8 Mar 65	179/65	5k	13:31.21	13:22.40 -91
					10k	27:56.99	27:47.33 -93
					Mar	2:09:13	-0-
Serrano	Rodrigo	MEX	68		20kW	1:24:00	
					50kW	4:06:42	4:03:02 -92
Servius	Ronald	FRA	21 Feb 76	186/75	TJ	16.55w	15.24 -93
Seskin	Yuriy	RUS	7 Jul 66	196/100	DT	61.84	64.58 -88
Setliff	Adam	USA	15 Dec 69	193/122	DT	62.08	64.08 -93
Sfiea	Lucian	ROM	10 Sep 63	177/67	TJ	16.69	17.07 -91
Sghir	Smail	MAR	16 Mar 72	163/50	3k	7:42.15	7:57.82 -93
					5k	13:13.47	14:05.03 -93
Sgrulletti	Enrico	ITA	24 Apr 65	182/100	HT	76.40	79.80 -93
Shabunin	Vyacheslav	RUS	27 Sep 69	171/56	800	1:46.82	1:50.58 -92
					1500	3:38.61	3:36.59 -93
					Mile	3:53.54	-0-
Shaffer	Scott	USA	31 May 64	188/77	PV	5.52	5.72i -90, 5.67 -88
Shafikov	Rinat	RUS	23 Jan 70		20kW	1:22:14	1:22:10 -91
Shafikov	Ruslan	RUS	27 Jun 75		20kW	1:23:28.90t	
Shannon	Thaddeus	USA	6 Aug 73	165/68	100	10.16ig	10.55 -93
Shapovalov	Aleksandr	UKR	7 Jun 70	172/61	20kW	1:24:45	

Name		Nat	Born	Ht/Wt	Event	1994 Mark	Pre-1994 Best
* Shchennikov	Mikhail	RUS	24 Dec 67	182/70	20kW	1:18:45	1:18:33 -93
Shchepin	Aleksey	RUS	3 Apr 72	183/82	JT	78.90	80.18 -93
Shelton	Matt	USA	3 Jun 69	188/84	Dec	7764	7870 -92
Shen Weiquan		CHN			50kW	3:54:04	
* Shevchenko	Dmitriy	RUS	13 May 68	198/125	DT	64.74	67.30 -92
Shevchuk	Andrey	RUS	8 Mar 70		JT	82.90	85.70 -93
Shida	Tetsuya	JPN	27 Jun 71	181/70	LJ	8.03w	7.80, 7.98w -93
Shields	Brett	USA	24 Aug 70	184/75	110h	13.60	13.92 -93, 13.82w -91
Shirley	Simon	GBR	3 Aug 66	190/90	Dec	7980	8036 -88
Shishkin	Vladimir	RUS	12 Jan 64	193/77	110h	13.62w	13.21, 13.0 -88
Shon Ju-il		KOR	6 Oct 69	175/65	400	45.37	46.43 -91
Shtrobinders	Marcis	LAT	12 Jun 66	186/100	JT	80.92	81.78 -93
Shumak	Artur	BLS	19 Oct 63	179/70	50kW	3:52:16	3:49:58 -84
Shvetsov	Leonid	RUS	69		Mar	2:12:21	2:14:07 -93
Siba	Lahoussine	MAR	15 Feb 73	173/58	1500	3:39.47	3:39.48 -93
* Sidorenko	Vasiliy	RUS	1 May 61	190/100	HT	82.02	82.54 -92
Sidorov	Gennadiy	BLS	13 Mar 67		PV	5.65	5.60 -92
Sidorov	Vitaliy	UKR	23 Mar 70	195/120	DT	64.40	60.46 -93
Siermachesky	Cory	CAN	20 Aug 69		HJ	2.28	2.25 -92
Sierra	Pablo	ESP	13 May 69	175/61	Mar	2:11:35	-0-
* Sigei	William	KEN	11 Oct 69	178/57	5k	13:06.72	13:07.35 -93
					10k	26:52.23	27:16.81 -93
* Sild	Donald-Aik	EST	3 Oct 68	200/107	JT	85.28	80.90 -93
Silio	Antonio	ARG	9 May 66	172/67	5k	13:34.9	13:19.64 -91
					10k	28:02.40	27:38.72 -93
* Silva	Anisio Sousa	BRA	18 Jun 69	186/81	TJ	17.04	17.32 -93
Silva	Arnaldo	BRA	26 Mar 64	174/71	100	10.23w	10.12A,10.23 -88, 10.06w -85
					200	20.71	20.59 -85
* Silva	German	MEX	9 Jan 68	160/60	Mar	2:09:18	-0-
Silva	Joaquim	POR	13 Jan 61		Mar	2:10:42	2:17:30 -93
Silva	Marcelo Briv.	BRA	19 Feb 66	180/75	200	20.69	20.98 -93
Simatei	Ben	KEN	68		3kSt	8:30.30	8:29.47 -92
Simson	Matt	GBR	28 May 70	197/125	SP	19.49	19.23 -91
Sinclair	Winston	JAM	11 Oct 71	180/70	400h	49.77	50.76 -93
Sinervo	Timo	FIN	5 Aug 75	190/100	DT	61.16	55.56 -93
Singh	Shakti	IND	14 May 62	185/100	SP	18.78	17.86 -93
					DT	61.72	57.70 -89
Sinka	Albert	HUN	22 Nov 62	187/95	HT	73.50	81.18 -88
Sinque	Zithulele	RSA	9 Jun 63		Mar	2:12:01	2:08:04 -86
Sjöström	Tomas	SWE	27 Feb 70		HT	72.42	67.70 -93
* Skah	Khalid	MAR	29 Jan 67	170/60	3k	7:36.76	7:37.09 -90
					2M	8:12.92	8:12.17 -93
					5k	13:00.54	13:04.67 -93
					10k	27:38.74	27:17.74 -93
					3kSt	8:19.30	8:44.17 -90
Skipper	Art	USA	31 Jul 70	190/91	JT	75.56	76.70 -92, 79.22qm -93
* Skurygin	German	RUS	23 Dec 63	169/65	50kW	3:46:30	3:50:25 -92
* Skvaruk	Andrey	UKR	9 Mar 67	187/100	HT	81.72	80.80 -93
Skvortsov	Andrey	RUS	2 Dec 68		PV	5.70i	5.72 -93
Slimani	Abdelhamid	ALG	70		1500	3:39.58	3:44.1 -93
* Smirnov	Sergey	RUS	17 Sep 60	192/126	SP	20.01	22.24 -86
Smith	Antonio	VEN	1 Mar 67	186/70	400h	49.91uc	49.18 -91
Smith	Arthur	USA	16 May 69	186/84	110h	13.5	13.72 -92, 13.69w -91
Smith	Calvin	USA	8 Jan 61	178/69	100	10.22	9.93A, 9.97 -83, 9.87w -88
Smith	Dean	AUS	1 Nov 67	182/82	Dec	7926	7964 -92
Smith	Glen	GBR	21 May 72	190/102	DT	59.78	57.82 -92
Smith	Lamont	USA	11 Dec 72	188/73	400	45.99	45.30 -93
* Smith	Mike	CAN	16 Sep 67	196/96	Dec	8326	8549 -91
Smith	Steve	USA	11 Jan 71	190/66	HJ	2.31	2.27 -91
* Smith	Steve	GBR	29 Mar 73	185/70	HJ	2.38i, 2.33	2.37 -92
Smutherman	Del	USA	21 Apr 72	185/79	LJ	7.95	8.00 -92
Söderman	Mikael	FIN	5 Nov 65	183/72	800	1:45.20	1:46.22 -93
* Sokov	Vasiliy	RUS	7 Apr 68	186/73	TJ	17.43	17.59 -93, 17.73w -89
Solhaug	Dag	SWE	11 Jan 64	200/124	DT	63.76	60.04 -93
Solis	Miguel	MEX	70		20kW	1:22:46	
* Sonn	Ralf	GER	17 Jan 67	197/85	HJ	2.34i, 2.28	2.39i -91, 2.34 -93
Sonnek	Hubert	TCH	12 Oct 62	182/65	20kW	1:23:03	1:21:59 -91
Sorensen	Kåre	DEN	4 Apr 67	188/70	3kSt	8:35.20	8:41.84 -92
Sosunov	Kiril	RUS	1 Nov 75		LJ	7.96	7.66 -93

Name		Nat	Born	Ht/Wt	Event	1994 Mark	Pre-1994 Best
Sotelo	Julian	ESP	5 Jul 65	195/100	JT	76.50	78.78 -92
Sotnikov	Yuriy	RUS	10 Mar 69	189/75	TJ	17.28	17.14 -93
Soto	Miguel	PUR	8 Dec 67		110h	13.83, 13.5A	13.92 -93
* Sotomayor	Javier	CUB	13 Oct 67	195/82	HJ	2.42	2.45 -93
Sousa	Mario	POR	3 Nov 61	168/54	Mar	2:12:12	2:12:43 -92
Spada	Mirko	SUI	26 Jan 69	192/86	Dec	7933w/7914	7813 -93
Spears	Derek	USA	11 Apr 74	183/76	110h	13.81w	13.82 -93
					400h	50.18	50.49 -93
Spies	Phillip	RSA	21 May 70	188/87	JT	81.34	80.90 -93
* Spitsyn	Valeriy	RUS	5 Dec 65	178/67	50kW	3:41:07	3:42:50 -93
* Spivey	Jim	USA	7 Mar 60	180/63	1500	3:36.80	3:31.01 -88
					3k	7:39.65	7:37.04 -93
					5k	13:15.86	13:19.24 -83
Sporrer	Alexander	GER	20 Jan 71		HT	71.94	69.22 -93
Srovnal	Robert	TCH	13 Jun 75	187/77	JT	75.92	72.62 -93
St Julian	Jahshawn	USA	8 Aug 68		200	20.68	
Staines	Gary	GBR	3 Jul 63	186/63	10k	28:25.60	27:48.73 -91
Stamatopoulos	Theodoris	GRE	24 Apr 70	182/70	50kW	4:02:45	4:11:36 -91
Staniszewski	Mariusz	POL	17 Oct 70	178/70	3kSt	8:34.51	8:38.15 -91
Stankevich	Yevgeniy	RUS	73		JT	78.12	69.92 -92
Stanton	Brian	USA	19 Feb 61	198/87	HJ	2.25	2.33 -88
Stark	Roland	GER	10 Oct 75	191/73	HJ	2.23	2.18 -93
* Starkey	Dean	USA	27 Mar 67	188/77	PV	5.92	5.91 -92
Stasaitis	Redzinaldas	LIT	5 Apr 67	183/71	TJ	16.63	16.47 -91
Steele	Darrin	USA	20 Mar 69	188/88	Dec	7786	7982w -93
Steele	Martin	GBR	30 Sep 62	170/66	800	1:46.13	1:43.84 -93
Stefko	Róbert	SVK	28 May 68		3k	7:48.73	7:57.50 -93
					5k	13:28.03	13:37.69 -92
					10k	27:57.42	28:34.08 -93
Steigauf	Milos	TCH	5 Dec 69	195/98	JT	81.12	80.32 -93
Stenlund	Patrik	SWE	11 Oct 68	194/79	PV	5.66	5.62 -93
Stenzel	Rüdiger	GER	16 Apr 68	180/65	1000	2:18.82	2:20.56 -89
					1500	3:36.12	3:36.08 -93
					Mile	3:55.83	-0-
Stepanov	Hristo	BUL	21 Dec 70	170/58	10k	28:24.47	29:16.74 -93
Stepanov	Vitaliy	RUS	9 Dec 65	186/76	PV	5.52	5.50 -90
Stephen	Hayden	TRI	9 Jan 72	188/77	400	45.83	45.70A -93
Stevens	Patrick	BEL	31 Jan 68	183/73	100	10.29	10.32, 10.29A -90, 10.26w -93
					200	20.67, 20.64w	20.59, 20.41w -92
* Stewart	Raymond	JAM	18 Mar 65	178/73	100	10.21, 10.09w	9.96 -91, 9.89w, 9.8w -87
					200	20.63w	20.41 -88, 20.31w -87
Steynberg	Johan	RSA	6 Jun 72		400h	49.98A	50.51 -93
Stipanov	Ruslan	UKR	19 Sep 71	192/76	HJ	2.30i, 2.28	2.27 -93
Stokes	Marcus	USA	24 Dec 74	183/77	200	20.74w	20.8 -93
Storaci	Alain	FRA	5 Jun 67	194/88	JT	78.38	80.00 -93
Stosik	Stanislaw	POL	26 Mar 72	175/64	20kW	1:22:27	1:24:59 -93
Strang	David	GBR	13 Dec 68	175/70	1500	3:36.53	3:39.72 -93
					Mile	3:54.30	3:56.86 -93
* Streete-Thompson	Kareem	USA	30 Mar 73	183/84	100	10.21A, 10.29	10.30, 10.19w -93
					LJ	8.63, 8.64w	8.36A, 8.31 -93
							8.46w -91
Strege	Martin	GER	21 Feb 66	178/63	3kSt	8:25.87	8:21.24 -93
Strizhakov	Oleg	RUS	18 Jul 63	179/61	10k	28:27.69	28:16.15 -90
					Mar	2:12:24	-0-
Strominski	Grzegorz	POL	19 May 70	186/82	Dec	7644	7686 -93
Struganov	Sergey	RUS	5 Apr 66	171/60	Mar	2:12:12	2:15:24 -93
Stubbs	Ali	BAH	73	179/73	100	10.25	10.88 -92
Suchan	Tim	USA	2 Feb 72	193/86	HJ	2.23	2.16 -91
Sugama	Tomokazu	JPN	13 Dec 71	180/80	Dec	7666	7254 -92
Suhonen	Ari	FIN	19 Dec 65	185/65	800	1:45.79	1:44.10 -89
Sukhanov	Andrey	UKR	3 Aug 70	193/120	HT	74.26	74.52 -93
Sukharev	Gennadiy	BLS	3 Feb 65		PV	5.54	5.73 -87
Sukhomashov	Dmitriy	BLS	10 Mar 71		Dec	8033	7590 -92
* Suleiman	Mohamed	QAT	23 Nov 69	170/60	800	1:46.82	1:47.31 -93
					1500	3:32.73	3:33.29 -93
					Mile	3:51.32	3:57.05i -93
					3k	7:44.83	7:38.20 -93
Sullivan	Kevin	CAN	20 Mar 74	180/68	1500	3:36.78	3:39.11 -92
					Mile	3:58.00i	4:06.21i -93

Name		Nat	Born	Ht/Wt	Event	1994 Mark	Pre-1994 Best
Sun Fei		CHN	24 Jan 68		JT	76.50	78.36 -91
Sun Fuhai		CHN	Jul 72		JT	76.62	74.20 -93
Sun Ripeng		CHN	25 Jan 74	180/68	3kSt	8:31.73	8:24.87 -93
Sunada	Takahiro	JPN	19 Jan 73	166/54	10k	28:27.0	
Sundin	Lars	SWE	21 Jul 61	193/107	DT	60.66	65.42 -87
Sung Hee-joon		KOR	8 Jun 74	189/77	LJ	7.96	7.74 -93
Sunneborn	Mattias	SWE	27 Sep 70	187/82	LJ	8.00, 8.04w	8.05i, 8.06w -92, 8.18ex -93
* Surin	Bruny	CAN	12 Jul 67	180/81	100	10.08	10.02 -93, 10.01w -91
					200	20.63	20.48 -93
Suzuki	Kenichi	JPN	6 Apr 67	174/64	Mar	2:11:05dh	2:11:56 -93
Svenøy	Jim	NOR	22 Apr 72	186/70	3kSt	8:28.12	8:28.51 -93
Swanson	Brad	USA	15 Jul 69		Dec	7778w	7400 -93
Swart	Martin	RSA	28 Sep 69		DT	60.50	60.76 -92
* Swartbooi	Lucketz	NAM	7 Feb 66		Mar	2:09:08dh	2:09:57 -93
* Sweeney	Nick	IRL	26 Mar 68	195/121	DT	66.00	63.26 -93
* Swift	Eugene	USA	14 Sep 64	180/75	110h	13.23	13.49 -91
Swinton	Jacob	USA	26 Dec 71	173/68	100	10.20	10.66 -93
* Szabó	Dezsö	HUN	4 Sep 67	184/82	Dec	7995	8436 -90
Szitás	Imre	HUN	4 Sep 61	184/105	HT	71.08	80.60 -88
Tadessa	Belayneh	ETH	24 Apr 66		Mar	2:11:30	2:13:09 -91
Tadesse	Becho	ETH	68		Mar	2:11:21	2:10:27 -93
* Tafralis	Gregg	USA	9 Apr 58	183/129	SP	20.89	21.98 -92
Tailhardat	Jean-Marc	FRA	12 Apr 66	178/66	PV	5.60	5.70 -91
Taitt	Tyrell	USA	19 Apr 71	178/75	TJ	16.73	16.62i, 16.91w -93
Tajiri	Yuichi	JPN	23 May 71	181/60	5k	13:34.4	13:53.77 -93
					10k	27:59.97	28:33.11 -93
Takahashi	Kazuhiro	JPN	27 Jul 76	162/55	100	10.24	10.57 -93
					200	20.57	21.51 -93
Takao	Kenji	JPN	23 Mar 75	170/53	10k	28:20.78	29:39.9 -93
Takaoka	Toshinari	JPN	24 Sep 70	186/64	5k	13:33.31	13:20.43 -92
					10k	27:59.72	28:28.1 -93
Takei	Hideyuki	JPN	19 Nov 70	167/58	PV	5.57	5.50 -91
Takeuchi	Kenichiro	JPN	12 Feb 64	168/55	Mar	2:11:39	2:15:09 -92
Tako	Hiroshi	JPN	10 Sep 68	168/54	Mar	2:11:35dh	-0-
Tallhem	Sören	SWE	16 Feb 64	192/110	SP	19.94	20.91, 21.24i -85
* Tamm	Jüri	EST	5 Feb 57	193/120	HT	78.06	84.40 -84
Tamminga	Chris	HOL	30 Apr 74		PV	5.50	5.40 -93
Tan Zhengze		CHN	Jan 74		LJ	7.98	7.81 -91
Tan Mingjun		CHN	17 Jul 70		20kW	1:18:46	1:20:41 -93
* Taniguchi	Hiromi	JPN	5 Apr 60	171/55	Mar	2:10:46	2:07:40 -88
Tanui	Kirwa	KEN			3kSt	8:36.4A	8:55.2A -93
* Tanui	Moses	KEN	20 Aug 65	165/55	3k	7:44.87	7:41.87 -93
					5k	13:29.30	13:17.80 -92
					10k	28:06.76	27:18.32 -93
					Mar	2:09:40dh	2:15:36 -93
Tanui	Samson	KEN			10k	28:20.1A	
* Tanui	William	KEN	22 Feb 64	183/70	800	1:44.18	1:43.30 -91
					1500	3:36.56	3:34.25 -90
					Mile	3:56.34	3:53.80 -93
Tao Rui		CHN	26 Jan 73		HJ	2.28	2.25 -93
* Tarasenko	Stanislav	RUS	22 Jul 66	185/79	LJ	8.43i, 8.25	8.24 -93
* Tarasov	Maksim	RUS	2 Dec 70	194/80	PV	5.90i, 5.90	5.90 -92
Tarazona	Carlos	VEN	14 Aug 65		Mar	2:12:49dh	2:13:37 -93
* Tarpenning	Kory	USA	27 Feb 62	180/76	PV	5.85	5.89 -88
Tarus	Bogdan	ROM	1 Aug 75		LJ	8.01	7.65 -93
Tashpulatov	Damir	UZB	29 Jan 64	188/74	TJ	17.00	16.84 -90
Taurima	Jai	AUS	27 Oct 73	190/75	LJ	7.98, 8.10Aw	7.57 -93
Taylor-Perry	Eric	USA	22 Feb 72	183/86	HJ	2.25	2.27 -91
Teach	Jeff	USA	14 Apr 72	183/111	SP	18.66	18.28i, 18.09 -93
Teape	Hugh	GBR	26 Dec 63	178/73	110h	13.76	13.44 -92
Teixeira	Everson	BRA	23 Nov 74	178/70	400h	49.76	52.16 -92
Tellez	Norberto	CUB	23 Dec 72	180/73	400	45.27	45.51 -93
Tengelei	Joseph	KEN	8 Dec 72	173/64	800	1:44.44	1:44.48 -93
Tennant	Brendan	AUS	22 Apr 72		Dec	7715	7459 -93
* Tergat	Paul	KEN	17 Jun 69	183/61	5k	13:15.07	13:20.16 -93
					10k	27:23.89	27:18.43 -93
Terry	Glenn	USA	10 Feb 71	193/82	110h	13.55, 13.46w	13.35, 13.24w -93
* Terry	Octavius	USA	7 Nov 72	189/74	400h	49.03	49.71 -92
Terzian	Alex	GRE	24 Jun 68	180/74	100	10.25, 10.16Aw	10.20 -93
					200	20.72	20.83 -93

MEN'S INDEX

Name		Nat	Born	Ht/Wt	Event	1994 Mark	Pre-1994 Best
Thenault	François	FRA	4 May 72	175/72	PV	5.50	5.40 -93
Thibault	Sébastien	FRA	25 Jul 70	183/74	110h	13.66	13.45, 13.44w -92
Thiébaut	Pascal	FRA	6 Jun 59	175/60	2k	5:00.61	4:56.70 -87
					5k	13:24.83	13:14.60 -87
Thigpen	Aaron	USA	18 Sep 64	170/71	100	10.28w	10.28 -91, 10.02Aw -86
					200	20.72	20.53 -92, 20.45Aw -86
Thomas	Brian	CAN	27 Jan 70	178/75	LJ	8.05	8.04 -92
Thomas	Christian	GER	21 May 65	186/73	LJ	8.21	8.13 -89, 8.16w -90
Thomas	Eric	USA	1 Dec 73	190/88	400h	49.29	49.83 -93
Thomas	Iwan	GBR	5 Jan 74	183/79	400	45.98	47.37 -92
Thompson	Derrick	USA	24 Feb 73	175/73	100	10.20w	9.9w -93
					200	20.76, 20.60w	20.59, 20.35w -93
Thompson	Ian	BAH	8 Dec 68		HJ	2.25	2.28 -92
Thompson	Mark	JAM	2 Aug 67	185/82	400h	49.87	49.37 -92
Thompson	Obadele	BAR	30 Mar 76	175/67	100	10.08A, 10.28, 10.0	10.71, 10.30Aw -93
					200	20.71	21.18 -93
Thompson	Rich	USA	16 Jun 69	188/82	TJ	16.55	16.34 -93
Thompson	Scott	USA	24 Jul 73	190/81	110h	13.69	
Thomson	Lochsley	AUS	20 Aug 73	183/67	HJ	2.30	2.31 -92
Thorne	Ronald	BAR	18 Mar 71		800	1:46.66	
Thränhardt	Carlo	GER	5 Jul 57	199/85	HJ	2.26i	2.42i -88, 2.37 -84
Thymes	Derrick	USA	14 Jan 72	183/79	400	45.93	46.03 -91
Tian Niantang		CHN	Mar 72		20kW	1:21:00	1:20:50.0t -92
Tichy	Peter	SVK	12 Mar 69	177/67	50kW	3:56:55	4:14:22 -89
Tidiane Touré	Cheikh	SEN	70		LJ	8.08A	7.88 -93
Tidow	Joachim	GER	4 Feb 69	198/100	DT	58.42	62.26 -91
Timofeyev	Yevgeniy	RUS	22 Feb 74		TJ	16.48	17.00 -93
Tirelli	Davide	ITA	12 Aug 66	178/65	1500	3:37.85	3:34.61 -92
Tîrle	Marcel	ROM	19 Oct 66	195/109	DT	60.68	64.62 -91
Tiwontschik	Andrej	GER	13 Jul 70	187/76	PV	5.71	5.65 -93
Toerien	Mario	RSA	19 Apr 72		400h	50.31A	52.42 -93
Tolbert	Rod	USA	11 Jun 67	185/75	200	20.64	20.38 -92
Tolstikov	Yakov	RUS	20 May 59	165/58	Mar	2:12:55	2:09:17 -91
Tonker	Bobby	USA	15 May 71	188/84	Dec	7637	7440 -93
* Topic	Dragutin	YUG	12 Mar 71	197/77	HJ	2.32	2.37 -90
Torian	Reggie	USA	22 Apr 75	190/82	LJ	7.97	7.50, 7.54w -93
Torkelsson	Patrik	SWE	24 Apr 73		110h	13.83, 13.74w	14.31 -93
Torniainen	Petri	FIN	8 Mar 65	184/100	SP	18.98	19.13 -92
* Toth	Kevin	USA	29 Dec 67	193/127	SP	21.25i, 21.07	21.29 -93
Toumi	Hakim	ALG	30 Jan 61	180/105	HT	73.44	74.02 -93
* Toutain	Thierry	FRA	14 Feb 62	182/75	20kW	1:21:20	1:20:56 -91
					50kW	3:43:52	3:47:38 -93
Trafas	Dariusz	POL	5 Jun 72	188/87	JT	78.66	77.38 -93
* Trandenkov	Igor	RUS	17 Aug 66	191/80	PV	5.90	5.90 -92
Treacy	Brian	GBR	29 Jul 71	176/61	1500	3:38.93	3:40.68 -90
Tretyak	Yevgeniy	RUS	18 Jul 71	184/75	LJ	8.29	7.68 -91
* Trouabal	Jean-Charles	FRA	20 May 65	187/77	100	10.26	10.19 -93
					200	20.39, 20.35w	20.20 -93
Tyrtyshnik	Vyacheslav	UKR	16 Jan 71	186/75	HJ	2.25i	2.23 -93
Tsamonikian	Nichan	RUS	19 Jul 67		20kW	1:24:46	
Tsonov	Stoiko	BUL	6 May 69	180/76	TJ	16.86	16.53 -92
Tsuchiya	Tadayuki	JPN	7 Apr 73	177/84	JT	75.90	74.46 -92
Tsvetanov	Emil	BUL	14 Mar 63	175/83	JT	75.80	80.12 -89
Tudor	Bogdan	ROM	1 Feb 70	174/66	LJ	8.11i, 7.99	8.09i -93, 8.06 -91
Tuffour	Emmanuel	GHA	2 Dec 66	180/70	100	10.07	10.12 -91
					200	20.55	20.44 -93
Tugay	Igor	UKR	22 Mar 75	183/90	HT	71.66	67.72 -93
Tukhbatullin	Eduard	RUS	13 Oct 71		Mar	2:12:58	2:13:02 -93
Tulloch	Andrew	GBR	1 Apr 67	183/75	110h	13.52	13.59 -93
Tunks	Jason	CAN	7 May 75		DT	58.76	51.52 -93
Turay	Sanusi	SLE	14 Apr 68	181/84	100	10.28	10.34 -91
Turbo	Tumo	ETH	70		Mar	2:10:24	2:10:31 -93
* Tverdokhleb	Oleg	UKR	3 Nov 69	184/70	400h	48.06	48.62 -93
Twillie	Troy	USA	75		LJ	7.96w	7.53 -93
Tynes	Andrew	BAH	13 Feb 72	193/82	100	10.21	10.24Aw -93
					200	20.25, 20.20w	20.22A, 20.48 -93
Tyrtyshnik	Vyacheslav	UKR	16 Jan 71	186/75	HJ	2.25	2.25 -92
Tyulenev	Sergey	RUS	14 Mar 71	177/58	20kW	1:23:35	1:21:31 -93
Uchikoshi	Tadao	JPN	30 Oct 65	168/52	Mar	2:12:52	2:13:45 -93

Name		Nat	Born	Ht/Wt	Event	1994 Mark	Pre-1994 Best
Uchitomi	Yasunori	JPN	29 Oct 72	173/64	3kSt	8:33.04	8:44.15 -93
Ugwu	Chima	NGR	72	190/115	SP	19.26	19.06 -92
					DT	58.58	47.78 -92
Ulmala	Risto	FIN	7 May 63	184/63	3k	7:49.76	7:44.5 -91
					5k	13:28.80	13:21.90 -91
					10k	27:57.01	27:53.00 -91
Uno	Masaki	JPN	13 Dec 72	180/63	HJ	2.26	2.28 -93
Urainen	Harri	FIN	20 Dec 61		DT	58.98	56.84 -93
Urban	Dirk	GER	14 Jan 69	188/101	SP	18.91	19.34i -93
* Urbanik	Sándor	HUN	15 Dec 64	172/56	20kW	1:21:55	1:20:55 -92
Urge	Girma	ETH	65		Mar	2:11:40	2:20:08A -90
Urrutia	Aliacer	CUB	22 Sep 74		TJ	17.12	16.59 -92, 17.27w -93
Urrutia	Robinson	COL	19 Feb 69	176/80	100	10.29A, 10.20Awdt	10.56 -89
Ustimenko	Stanislav	RUS	8 May 69	185/75	50kW	3:58:38	
Uzsoki	János	HUN	9 Sep 72	180/69	LJ	7.91	7.43 -93
Vääräniemi	Heikki	FIN	21 Dec 69	187/74	PV	5.52	5.63 -93
Valchanov	Kiril	BUL	1 Mar 74	186/102	SP	18.74i, 18.61	17.29 -93
Valente	José Mauro	BRA	1 Jul 69		1500	3:38.07	3:38.25 -92
Valicek	Robert	SVK	10 Mar 69		20kW	1:22:53	1:22:53 -93
Valin	Juan	MEX	7 Sep 69	185/72	400h	50.08A, 50.31	49.5 -90, 50.00A -93
* Valle	Emilio	CUB	21 Apr 67	182/70	110h	13.33	13.19 -93
Valle	Miguel	CUB	29 Sep 68	181/81	Dec	7701	7798 -92
Valle	Mikko	FIN	11 May 70	181/73	Dec	7670	7764 -93
* Valmon	Andrew	USA	1 Jan 65	186/78	400	44.97	44.28 -93
Valvik	Svein-Inge	NOR	20 Sep 56	190/112	DT	63.66	68.00 -82
* van Dijck	William	BEL	24 Jan 61	180/59	3kSt	8:19.92	8:10.01 -86
van Heerden	Marius	RSA	8 Sep 74	179/67	800	1:46.92	1:46.38A -93
van Helden	Rob	HOL	6 Feb 65	180/73	800	1:46.91i	1:45.17 -88
van Hest	Greg	HOL	3 Jun 73		10k	28:29.67	29:22.60 -93
van Lieshout	Johan	HOL	8 Mar 69	197/96	JT	77.80	79.16 -90
van Rensburg	Francois	RSA	2 Aug 70		2k	5:05.45A	5:08.5A -92
					3k	7:48.35	8:00.48 -92
van Vlaanderen	Bert	HOL	25 Nov 64	180/60	Mar	2:10:49	2:11:53 -92
Vandegrift	Paul	USA	16 May 69	186/70	1500	3:37.22	3:38.21 -92
					Mile	3:57.88i	3:59.60 -92
* Vander-Kuyp	Kyle	AUS	30 May 71	192/76	110h	13.45, 13.27Aw, 13.2	13.48 -93
Varich	Dmitriy	UKR	28 Feb 72	180/96	HT	74.06	74.06 -93
Vasilyev	Pavel	RUS	2 Jul 70	174/63	20kW	1:24:08	1:24:28 -92
					50kW	4:01:31	
Vasilyev	Sergey	RUS	23 Jun 75		HT	72.14	66.80 -93
Vasquez	Fernando	ESP	4 May 71	173/58	20kW	1:22:33	1:23:46 -93
Vdovin	Mikhail	RUS	15 Jan 67	182/73	400	45.66	45.89 -93
Venter	Johann	RSA	30 Dec 71	181/73	200	20.68A	21.19A -93
Venturi	Giorgio	ITA	23 Jun 66	187/102	SP	18.87	19.27 -93
Vera	Ricardo	URU	16 Sep 62	186/71	3kSt	8:25.53	8:23.02 -92
Vera	Rolando	ECU	27 Apr 65	155/47	Mar	2:11:15	2:10:46 -90
Verebes	János	HUN	25 Feb 69	188/106	HT	71.08	71.30 -93
Veretelnikov	Oleg	UZB	22 Jan 72	187/81	Dec	7702	7601 -93
Versteeg	Marcel	HOL	20 Aug 65	193/75	5k	13:33.93	13:26.29 -92
Verzi	Hrvoje	GER	12 Nov 70	183/78	TJ	16.51i	16.03 -92
Vetrov	Sergey	RUS	8 May 68	186/80	110h	13.68, 13.64w	13.66 -92
Vial	Pierre-Alexandre	FRA	25 May 75	180/73	Dec	7789	7618 -93
Viali	Tonino	ITA	16 Sep 60	179/70	1500	3:39.13	3:37.94 -93
* Viciosa	Isaac	ESP	26 Dec 69	175/68	1500	3:36.01	3:34.75 -93
					Mile	3:52.72	-0-
					3k	7:41.46i	7:57.65i -93
Vida	József	HUN	9 Jan 63	192/115	HT	76.20	79.06 -84
Viitala	Matti	FIN	26 Mar 66	190/78	HJ	2.26i	2.25 -90
Vikhrov	Andrey	RUS	73		HT	72.00	
Virastyuk	Roman	UKR	20 Apr 68	190/120	SP	20.00	20.04i -91, 20.03 -90
Vizzoni	Nicola	ITA	4 Nov 73	193/114	HT	71.78	70.76 -93
Volgenau	Chris	USA	30 Mar 69	188/111	SP	20.04	19.54 -93
* Voloshin	Leonid	RUS	30 Mar 66	180/74	TJ	17.77i	17.75 -91
Vorobyov	Sergey	RUS	29 Jan 64	184/91	HT	74.60	77.08 -90
Voss	Martin	DEN	5 Sep 67	188/76	PV	5.52	5.50 -93
Voyevodin	Aleksandr	RUS	4 Mar 70	179/64	20kW	1:23:14	
					50kW	3:52:36	4:04:44 -93
Vroemen	Simon	HOL	11 May 69		1500	3:39.19	3:39.71 -91
					3kSt	8:36.61	-0-

Name		Nat	Born	Ht/Wt	Event	1994 Mark	Pre-1994 Best
Wade	Larry	USA	22 Nov 74		110h	13.74w	
Wagner	Rich	USA	1 Nov 73		200	20.66	
Wahlman	Marko	FIN	6 Apr 69	194/104	HT	76.04	72.80 -93
* Walder	Erick	USA	5 Nov 71	186/77	LJ	8.74A	8.53 -93, 8.58w -92
					TJ	17.24i, 17.12A	16.88i -92, 16.87 -93
Walker	Colin	GBR	29 Oct 62	173/61	3kSt	8:27.78	8:25.15 -92
Walker	Doug	GBR	28 Jul 73	187/77	200	20.71	21.51 -92
* Wallenlind	Niklas	SWE	21 Nov 68	185/75	400h	49.31	48.35 -92
Wallstab	Thomas	GER	29 Jan 68	178/64	50kW	3:58:40	3:59:59 -93
Walton	Tony	USA	3 Jun 69	172/66	LJ	8.04A, 7.93, 8.07w	8.16 -93
Wang Aiguo		CHN			50kW	4:06:02	
Wang Lifeng		CHN			50kW	4:05:01	
Wang Wei		CHN			50kW	4:02:52	
Ward	Nick	AUS	18 Jan 70	184/75	400h	49.49	51.77 -93
Wariso #	Solomon	GBR	11 Nov 66	180/73	200	20.51	21.14 -91
* Washington	Anthony	USA	16 Jan 66	186/109	DT	64.18	67.88 -92
Washington	Riley	USA	31 Jul 73		100	10.25	10.30 -92
Watanabe	Daisuke	JPN	29 May 75	185/72	LJ	7.98w	7.85, 7.89w -93
Watanabe	Yasuyuki	JPN	8 Jun 73	176/59	5k	13:26.53	13:39.87 -93
					10k	28:07.94	28:17.26 -93
Watkins	Slip	USA	29 Sep 67	177/80	100	10.26, 10.24w	10.15, 10.08w -89
					200	20.69	20.40 -89
* Watts	Quincy	USA	19 Jun 70	190/88	400	45.03	43.50 -92
Weakley	Ian	JAM	24 Feb 74	180/68	400h	49.73, 49.7	51.66 -93
Weber	Christian	CAN	22 Apr 66		10k	28:30.17	
* Weigel	Ronald	GER	8 Aug 59	176/63	20kW	1:23:11	1:19:18.3t -90
					50kW	3:52:56	3:38:17 -86
* Weil	Gert	CHL	3 Jan 60	197/122	SP	19.64	20.90 -86
Weir	Robert	GBR	4 Feb 61	187/124	DT	61.06	62.50 -84
* Weis	Heinz	GER	14 Jul 63	193/110	HT	81.20	82.84 -89
* Wellman	Brian	BER	8 Sep 67	175/73	TJ	17.41A	17.27i -93, 17.25 -92, 17.41w -91
Wells	Renward	BAH	23 Feb 70	173/72	100	10.19w , 10.0w	10.39 -93
					200	20.60, 20.06w	21.09 -93
Wennberg	Henrik	SWE	11 Mar 66	192/122	SP	19.74	19.98 -92
					DT	62.56	60.16 -93
* Wennlund	Dag	SWE	9 Oct 63	188/97	JT	84.36	82.64S -87, 85.52R -91
* Wheeler	Tony	USA	19 Jan 75	180/70	200	20.47, 20.30w	21.48 -93
White	Kevin	USA	16 Aug 74	188/77	110h	13.52, 13.2	13.81,13.75w -93
Whitted	Alvis	USA	4 Sep 74	188/79	100	10.13	10.67 -93
Whittle	Brian	GBR	24 Apr 64	190/77	400	45.46	45.22 -88
Whyte	Wayne	JAM	4 May 74		400h	49.93	51.44 -93
Widén	Peter	SWE	2 Jul 67	183/74	PV	5.60, 5.61br	5.75 -91
Wilcox	Chris	USA	6 Jan 68	183/84	Dec	7941	8032 -92
Williams	Bryant	USA	25 Mar 71	184/68	100	10.25w	10.26 -92
					200	20.62A	20.92i, 20.60w -93
Williams	Elmer	PUR	8 Oct 64	180/68	LJ	8.05	8.19A -89, 8.05 -92
* Williams	Jeff	USA	31 Dec 64	183/68	100	10.19	10.21, 10.16w -91
					200	20.19	20.27, 20.25Aw -92
Williams	Jeromy	USA	28 Jan 72		Dec	7643	7178Aw -93
Williams	Shante	USA	21 Dec 73		400	46.01	47.98 -92
Williams	Simon	GBR	17 Oct 67	189/110	DT	58.32	61.14 -92
Williams	Terry	GBR	15 Nov 68	183/75	100	10.23, 10.19w	10.27 -92
					200	20.50	21.56 -92
Williams ¶	Tim	USA	27 May 63	186/79	100	10.26w	10.25 -89
					200	20.59dq	20.30 -92
Willis	Ron	USA	6 Dec 71	198/136	SP	18.61	18.36 -93
Winrow	Craig	GBR	22 Dec 71	179/71	800	1:46.54	1:47.5 -92
Winter	Neil	GBR	21 Mar 74	187/83	PV	5.50	5.50 -92
Winter	Peter	AUS	17 Jan 71	183/83	Dec	8074	7600 -93
Witek	Miroslaw	POL	24 Apr 67	183/91	JT	80.74	79.12 -88
Witherspoon	Mark	USA	3 Sep 63	190/85	100	10.19	10.04, 9.91w -87
					200	20.66	20.12 -89
Wittman	David	USA	4 Jul 69	183/66	Mile	3:58.05	
Womack	Terry	USA	29 Oct 65	193/95	PV	5.53	5.51 -86
Wood	Doug	CAN	30 Jan 66	182/78	PV	5.60i	5.65i -92, 5.61 -91
* Worku	Bikila	ETH	70	176/60	3k	7:48.69	7:47.6u+ -93
					5k	13:08.62	13:06.64 -93
Wyatt	Jonathan	NZL	20 Dec 72	175/62	5k	13:33.72	
Wylie	Jeff	USA	28 Dec 68	193/75	HJ	2.26	2.26 -93

Name	Nat	Born	Ht/Wt	Event	1994 Mark	Pre-1994 Best
Xu Bin	CHN	4 Aug 70		LJ	7.96	8.19 -92
Xie Shengying	CHN	18 Apr 71	190/120	SP	18.91	19.48 -90
Xu Congxian	CHN	4 Dec 72		50kW	3:58:32	4:00:07 -92
Xu Yang	CHN	21 Jun 70	188/62	HJ	2.28	2.31 -93
Yagovdik Valeriy	BLS	16 Sep 63		DT	61.80	62.24 -93
Yamada Takahiro	JPN	20 Apr 68	177/81	JT	76.16	76.30 -89
Yamazaki Kazuhiko	JPN	10 May 71	174/66	400h	49.29	49.08 -93
Yanchevskiy Igor	RUS	11 Mar 68	188/77	PV	5.70	5.70 -92
Yang Yongjian	CHN			50kW	3:55:45	4:10:07 -92
Yanigasawa Satoshi	JPN	19 Jan 71	170/60	20kW	1:22:54	1:27:48.6 -92
Yaryshkin Vladimir	RUS	28 Feb 63		SP	19.11	20.80 -86
* Yates Matthew	GBR	4 Feb 69	190/70	1500	3:35.32	3:34.00 -91
Yawa Xolile	RSA	29 Sep 62	169/50	Mar	2:11:54	2:10:57 -93
* Yegorov Grigoriy	KZK	12 Jan 67	184/75	PV	5.70i, 5.70	5.90i -90, 5.90 -93
Yegorov Vladislav	UKR	20 Mar 72	194/83	TJ	16.72	16.42 -91
Yeliseyev Yuriy	RUS	27 May 75		PV	5.60i	5.50 -93
Yesipchuk Dmitriy	RUS	17 Nov 74	173/57	20kW	1:24:22	-0-
Yesipchuk Sergey	UKR	1 Oct 67	192/80	PV	5.60	5.55 -90
Yevdokimov Valeriy	RUS	73		HT	73.94	73.52 -93
Yevgenyev Andrey	RUS	17 Feb 73	182/100	HT	72.94	75.64 -93
Yevsyukov Viktor	KZK	6 Oct 56	190/95	JT	75.52	85.16 -87
Yonekura Teruyasu	JPN	2 Jan 71	177/65	PV	5.50	5.40 -93
Yoo Young-hoon	KOR	27 Feb 72		Mar	2:10:12	2:13:03 -92
Yoshida Takahisa	JPN	17 Feb 70	180/67	HJ	2.27	2.31 -93
Young Curt	USA	18 Jan 74	193/86	110h	13.81w	13.90 -93
				400h	50.35	-0-
* Young Kevin	USA	16 Sep 66	193/82	400h	49.70	46.78 -92
Yudakov Timur	RUS	12 Jul 66		110h	13.59	13.68 -92
Zaboronok Vladimir	BLS	11 Nov 68		HJ	2.25i	2.28 -93
Zadoinov Vadim	MOL	24 May 69	187/74	400h	49.30	48.61 -90
Zaitsev Viktor	UZB	6 Jun 66	198/92	JT	79.20	87.20 -92
Zakrzewski Jan	POL	70		3kSt	8:36.53	
Zaliauskas Alex	CAN	20 Apr 71	193/73	HJ	2.23i	2.31 -91
Zampieri Luca	ITA	15 Feb 74		HJ	2.24	2.18 -93
Zamuda Ignacio	MEX	71		20kW	1:24:56	1:24:33 -91
Zang Jiangpo	CHN	5 May 75		50kW	4:02:37	4:09:02 -93
Zanner Peter	GER	19 Jul 68	191/78	50kW	4:06:14	4:10:10 -93
Zaylor Darren	USA	2 Dec 68	190/111	HT	71.16	65.60 -93
Zelaya Rodrigo	CHL	12 Jun 68	183/82	JT	76.50	76.20ui -93
* Zelezny Jan	TCH	16 Jun 66	186/77	JT	91.82	95.66 -93
Zellner Torrance	USA	6 Jan 70	187/75	400h	49.07	48.97 -93
Zhang Cunbiao	CHN	11 Feb 69	183/100	DT	58.78	62.06 -93
Zhang Fukui	CHN	27 Jan 70	170/51	Mar	2:11:56	2:11:10 -93
Zhang Hongxin	CHN	23 Feb 72		Dec	7692	7430 -93
Zhang Jiangbao	CHN	75		50kW	4:01:36	4:09:02 -93
Zhang Jun	CHN	Jan 74		TJ	16.49	16.61 -93
Zhang Lianbiao	CHN	10 Apr 69	193/110	JT	83.38	82.76 -93
Zhao Yongshen	CHN	Mar 71		50kW	3:48:13.7t	4:02:23 -92
Zhdanovich Aleksandr	BLS	15 Nov 69	184/80	Dec	7648	8035 -92
Zhelonkin Aleksey	RUS	21 Jan 66	170/53	Mar	2:12:22	2:10:44 -93
Zhou Yongshen	CHN	15 Oct 72		20kW	1:20:06	1:20:50.0t -92
				50kW	3:43:16	3:58:07 -93
Zhukovskiy Oleg	BLS	15 Feb 70	196/76	HJ	2.30	2.31 -93
* Zinchenko Vladimir	UKR	25 Jul 59	192/115	DT	64.90	68.88 -88
Zio Franck	BKF	14 Aug 71	186/80	LJ	7.92	7.77, 8.04us -92
Ziolkowski Szymon	POL	1 Jul 76	188/103	HT	72.48	67.34 -93
Zithansky Jaroslav	SVK	18 Feb 72		SP	18.88	17.24 -93
				DT	60.26	55.40 -93
Zitouna Abderrahim	MAR	70		5k	13:33.76	13:45.62 -93
Zoric Stevan	YUG	25 May 71	199/75	HJ	2.30i, 2.25	2.31i 91, 2.30 -93
* Zorko Branko	CRO	1 Jul 67	180/73	1500	3:34.84	3:35.09 -93
Zou Sixin	CHN	8 May 67	178/76	TJ	16.84	17.31 -90
Zschunke Oliver	GER	29 Apr 70		JT	77.98	75.66 -93
Zuber Matt	USA	30 Sep 66	185/86	Dec	7634	7686 -93

WORLD LIST TRENDS - 10th and 100th world list performance levels

Event	*1985*	*1986*	*1987*	*1988*	*1989*	*1990*	*1991*	*1992*	*1993*	*1994*
Men 10th Bests										
100m	10.11	10.10	10.09	10.06	10.11	10.10	10.07	10.07	10.06	**10.03**
200m	20.32	20.33	20.23	20.18	20.25	20.33	20.30	**20.15**	20.16	20.35
400m	44.91	44.72	44.72	44.61	44.89	44.91	44.88	**44.52**	44.62	44.96
800m	1:44.15	1:44.59	1:44.72	1:44.10	1:44.20	1:44.77	1:44.27	1:44.33	1:44.30	1:44.20
1500m	3:33.91	3:34.01	**3:33.66**	3:34.61	3:34.53	3:34.10	3:34.10	3:33.80	3:34.61	3:34.72
5000m	113:18.47	13:15.86	13:17.44	13:17.48	13:16.90	13:14.17	13:17.25	13:10.47	13:08.03	**13:07.70**
10000m	227:49.36	27:45.45	27:45.05	27:40.36	27:49.69	27:42.65	27:37.36	27:45.46	**27:30.17**	27:38.74
Marathon	2:09:05	2:09:57	2:10:34	2:08:49	2:09:40	2:10:10	2:10:08	2:09:30	2:10:06	**2:08:05**
3000mSt	8:18.02	8:16.59	8:16.46	8:16.04	8:17.64	8:15.95	8:14.41	**8:13.65**	8:15.33	8:14.30
110mh	13.46	13.40	13.39	13.36	13.37	13.28	13.37	13.33	**13.26**	13.33
400mh	49.03	48.71	48.56	48.65	48.79	48.61	48.92	48.60	48.73	48.88
HJ	2.35	2.34	2.34	**2.36**	2.34	2.35	2.34	2.34	2.35	2.33
PV	5.80	5.80	5.80	5.80	5.80	5.81	5.81	5.85	5.81	**5.86**
LJ	8.23	8.24	8.25	**8.31**	8.23	8.24	8.25	8.28	8.30	8.28
TJ	**17.48**	17.43	17.39	17.43	17.29	17.33	17.43	17.30	17.32	17.38
SP	21.32	21.49	21.22	21.16	21.02	20.86	20.43	20.93	20.84	20.67
DT	67.36	67.02	67.22	67.38	66.46	65.80	66.36	66.64	66.12	64.74
HT	80.20	80.68	80.74	81.88	79.38	80.90	80.56	80.46	80.80	80.20
JT (Old 85)	(91.56)	81.86	83.24	82.70	83.90	94.80	**86.32**	85.74	85.10	85.22
Decathlon	8317	8302	8304	8387	8182	8275	8267	8237	8297	8219

Other peaks: 800m 1:43.93 (1984), SP 21.63 (1984), DT: 68.20 (1982), Dec 8491 (1984), note roughened tailed javelins were in use in 1991

Event	*1985*	*1986*	*1987*	*1988*	*1989*	*1990*	*1991*	*1992*	*1993*	*1994*
Men 100th Bests										
100m	10.35	10.36	10.34	10.34	10.36	10.34	10.33	10.32	10.32	**10.27**
200m	20.80	20.79	20.75	20.79	20.85	20.84	20.83	20.78	20.80	**20.72**
400m	45.99	46.01	46.00	45.99	46.22	46.31	46.13	**45.98**	46.08	46.01
800m	1:47.17	1:47.12	1:46.94	**1:46.91**	1:47.14	1:47.32	1:47.10	1:46.95	1:47.12	1:46.98
1500m	3:40.32	3:39.88	3:39.52	3:39.46	3:39.88	3:39.70	3:39.51	3:39.11	3:39.62	3:39.58
5000m	13:38.50	13:35.34	13:37.31	13:37.20	13:36.60	13:37.88	13:37.40	**13:31.44**	13:33.40	13:34.3
10000m	28:39.20	28:329.41	28:333.77	28:27.28	28:34.18	28:30.52	**28:24.70**	28:30.42	28:32.19	28:30.15
Marathon	2:13:39	2:13:38	2:13:34	2:13:08	2:13:37	2:13:30	2:13:13	2:13:22	2:12:50	**2:12:24**
3000mSt	8:35.95	8:35.65	8:37.20	8:35.24	8:36.95	8:35.93	8:35.40	**8:34.43**	8:36.20	8:36.61
110mh	13.94	13.90	13.86	13.83	13.93	13.85	13.86	**13.78**	13.85	13.83
400mh	50.65	50.41	50.54	50.52	50.55	50.45	50.68	50.50	50.45	**50.30**
HJ	**2.24**	2.23	**2.24**	**2.24**	**2.24**	2.23	2.23	**2.24**	**2.24**	2.23
PV	5.40	**5.50**	5.44	**5.50**	**5.50**	5.45	5.45	**5.50**	**5.50**	**5.50**
LJ	7.89	7.90	7.92	**7.93**	7.90	7.90	**7.93**	**7.93**	7.92	7.91
TJ	16.51	16.52	16.50	**16.60**	16.55	16.55	16.54	16.59	16.55	16.51
SP	19.34	19.33	19.09	19.17	18.94	18.79	18.57	18.79	18.50	18.53
DT	60.54	60.96	60.40	60.84	60.18	59.74	59.28	59.80	58.58	58.26
HT	72.96	72.36	72.00	72.34	71.50	71.26	70.20	70.70	70.46	71.06
JT	(81.40)	75.30	76.68	76.48	76.72	76.82	**77.14**	76.40	75.90	75.52
Decathlon	7676	7686	7631	**7702**	7553	7594	7585	7567	7564	7625

Note other peaks: 1500m 3:38.89 (1984), HJ 2.24 (1984), SP 19.48 (1984), DT 60.96 (1984), HT 73.08 (1984)

All-time record levels indicated in bold

WOMEN'S INDEX 1994

Name		Nat	Born	Ht/Wt	Event	1994 Mark	Pre-1994 Best
Abatzi	Areti	GRE	14.5.74	183/76	DT	54.94	54.50 -93
* Abe	Tomoe	JPN	13.8.71	150/38	Mar	2:26:09	2:26:27 -93
Abramova	Svetlana	RUS	27.10.70		PV	3.90i, 3.90	3.90 -93
Acuff	Amy	USA	14.7.75	180/59	HJ	1.89i, 1.89	1.93 -93
Adachi	Mika	JPN	14.1.76	161/52	5k	15:55.7	15:59.4 -93
Adam	Laura	GBR	28.2.65	164/52	3k	9:02.47	9:05.33 -92
Adams	Christine	GER	28.2.74		PV	3.90	3.80 -93
Adams	Lorrie Ann	GUY	2.10.69		800	2:02.52	2:04.53 -93
Adams	Odalys	CUB	1.8.66	171/59	100h	13.21	12.86, 12.8 -89
Addy	Mercy	GHA	2.5.63	174/52	400	52.2	52.08, 51.0 -89
Adriano	Elizangela	BRA	27.7.72	180/92	SP	16.77	17.36 -92
					DT	55.28	53.94 -93
Afanasyeva	Yelena	RUS	1.3.67	164/51	800	2:00.52	1:57.77 -88
Afolabi	Olabisi	NGR	31.10.75	171/59	400	51.97	53.42 -93
Agapova	Yulia	RUS	25.12.74		HJ	1.91	1.83 -91
* Agyepong	Jackie	GBR	5.1.69	172/63	100h	12.93	13.03, 13.01w -93
Aigner	Manuela	GER	26.3.73	183/63	HJ	1.90i, 1.88	1.93 -92
Akao	Yumi	JPN	27.12.73	157/45	10k	33:03.21	
					HMar	71:37	
Akinremi	Lade	NGR	13.9.74	158/60	400	52.12	52.24 -93
					400h	57.05	56.84 -92
Akraka	Maria	SWE	7.7.66	170/55	800	2:01.23	2:00.50 -91
					1500	4:08.63	4:08.92, 4:07.74i -92
Aktas	Serop	TUR	25.9.71		10k	32:59.76	33:43.2 -93
Alafrantti	Paivi	FIN	8.5.64	178/82	JT	62.14	67.68 -90
Aldama	Yanilet	CUB	14.8.72	171/59	TJ	13.92	0
Aldecoa	Isabel	CUB	21.6.71		TJ	13.70	13.82 -92
Aleksandrova	Desislava	BUL	27.10.75	176/55	HJ	1.96i, 1.88	1.92 -93
* Alekseyeva	Tatyana	RUS	7.10.63	170/56	400	51.77i	50.49 -93
Alisevich	Tatyana	BLR	22.1.69		JT	58.46	59.04 -87
					Hep	6047	6073 -93
Alizadeh	Manuela	GER	29.1.63	172/78	JT	58.38	65.34 -88
Allahgreen	Diane	GBR	21.2.75		100h	13.25	13.42 -93
* Allen	Liliana	CUB	24.5.70	170/62	100	11.14	11.10 -92
					200	22.72	22.98 -92, 22.90w -93
							22.7w -89
Allison	May	CAN	29.10.64		Mar	2:34:55	
Alonso	Ana Isabel	ESP	16.8.63	154/44	10k	32:44.00	32:28.7 -88
					Mar	2:31:47	2:31:46 -93
Alonso	Miriam	ESP	6.6.70	164/54	400h	57.98	56.87 -92
Althouse	Valeyta	USA	7.1.74	175/102	SP	18.12	16.71 -93
Alvárez	Maria C.	CUB	30.8.75	165/62	JT	60.06	57.00 -93
Amarasekera	Vijitha	SRI	10.12.61	170/64	JT	56.84	56.10 -92
Amaro	Alexandra Borges	BRA	20.12.72	176/73	SP	17.23	
Ammel	Caroline	FRA	22.11.73		PV	3.91	3.40 -93
Ampleyeva	Natalya	BLR	25.9.72		DT	55.52	57.40 -92
Anderson	Damarys	CUB	24.10.74	175/68	100h	13.0	13.38 -93
Andres	Amaya	ESP	26.6.66	165/52	800	2:02.94i	2:02.33 -92
Andrews	Sharon	GBR	4.7.67	172/86	DT	56.24	55.14 -93
Andrews	Sarah	USA	4.11.71		DT	55.34	51.70 -93
Andreyeva	Marina	RUS	.73		PV	4.01	3.50 -93
Andreyeva	Yelena	RUS	9.5.69		400	51.30	52.24 -92
Andronaki	Antonina	RUS	.59		HMar	72:34	74:20 -93
Andrusina	Oksana	RUS	1.3.73	187/82	DT	57.42	54.18 -92
Angelova	Atanaska	BUL	21.9.72	176/75	SP	17.13	15.80 -93
					DT	62.92	59.68 -93
Anisimova	Natalya	RUS	4.3.73	172/65	100	11.27, 11.1	11.57 -93
					400	52.69	
Anliker-Aebi	Regula	SUI	12.11.65	170/58	100	11.46	11.46 -89
					200	23.08, 22.70w	22.88 -88
					400	52.14	53.22 -89
Antipov	Daniela	ROM	31.5.70	177/59	800	2:02.65	2:01.48 -91
Antonova	Yelena	UKR	16.6.72	180/80	DT	59.80	61.94 -92
* Appell	Olga	USA	2.8.63	173/59	10k	32:03.42	32:09.6 -92
					HMar	69:14	68:34 -93
					Mar	2:28:12	2:28:56 -93
Arnardóttir	Gudrun	ISL	24.9.71	168/57	100h	13.26w	13.39 -93

Name		Nat	Born	Ht/Wt	Event	1994 Mark	Pre-1994 Best
Aro	Helle	FIN	9.12.60	175/66	Hep	5961	6106 -93
* Arshintseva	Yelena	RUS	5.4.71	163/58	10kW	43:01	42:03 -93
* Asahina	Miyoko	JPN	24.9.69	171/52	10k	32:59.99	32:14.65 -89
(now Takahashi)					Mar	2:25:52	2:30:48 -92
Asai	Eriko	JPN	20.10.59	158/40	10k	32:47.88	32:22.18 -93
					Mar	2:30:30	2:28:22 -93
Asari	Junko	JPN	22.9.69	164/44	Mar	2:26:10	2:26:26 -93
* Asiago	Delilah	KEN	24.2.72	164/50	HMar	70:38	69:05 -91
* Astafei	Alina (now GER)	ROM	7.6.69	181/60	HJ	2.02i	2.00 -88
Astrom	Lena	SWE	5.11.64	173/78	JT	56.36	56.18 -91
Atroshchenko	Anzhela	BLR	14.10.70	178/68	Hep	6146	6339 -93
Atterberry	Ayo	USA	30.4.72	168/59	100h	13.33	13.62, 13.45w -93
Augee	Myrtle	GBR	4.2.65	173/96	SP	17.64	19.03 -90
Auzeil	Nadine	FRA	19.8.64	176/60	JT	64.32	63.30 -88
Avila	Andrea	ARG	4.4.70	171/55	LJ	6.58	6.61 -93
					TJ	13.69	13.91 -93
Azarashvili	Maya	GEO	12.4.64	170/60	100	11.41, 11.22w	11.08, 10.9 -88
					200	22.86	22.24 -88
* Azyabina	Marina	RUS	15.6.63	172/62	100h	12.94, 12.74w	12.47 -93
Azzizi	Yasmina	ALG	25.2.66	176/67	100h	13.37	13.02 -92
* Babakova	Inga	UKR	27.6.67	180/58	HJ	2.00	2.02 -91
Babakova	Irina	UKR	14.9.65	172/60	TJ	13.80	13.92 -90
Babic	Silvija	CRO	12.12.68	171/52	LJ	6.52	6.68 -90
Babushkina	Antonia	RUS	28.12.64	168/52	800	2:02.88	2:00.44 -92
Backus	Lakeisha	USA	15.12.76		200	23.21, 22.86w	23.96, 23.95w -93
Bai	Xiaoyun	CHN	15.6.73		400	52.49	52.07 -93
Baker	Alison	CAN	6.8.64	172/62	10kW	46:12.1	44:30.1 -92
Bakhvalova	Yekaterina	RUS	8.3.72		400h	56.90	60.00 -93
Bakogianni	Niki	GRE	9.6.68	170/58	HJ	1.91i, 1.90	1.94 -92
Balanten	Noelvis	CUB	24.6.72		SP	16.76	17.54 -93
* Balck	Heike	GER	19.8.70	180/57	HJ	1.95	2.01 -89
Bálint	Zita	HUN	25.1.71	178/64	Hep	5630	5891 -90
Bangue	Frédérique	FRA	31.12.76	179/61	100	11.30w	11.68 -93
Bao	Dongying	CHN	13.4.73	178/85	SP	17.13	
					DT	61.04	62.64 -93
Baranova	Yulia	UKR	12.8.72	180/58	TJ	13.34	13.40 -93
Barbour	Jane	AUS	27.7.66		10kW	46:26.9	46:58 -93
* Barbu	Adriana	ROM	17.1.61	161/53	HMar	70:38	71:52 -93
					Mar	2:29:21	2:34:38 -93
Barby	Dörte	GER	21.6.73	174/68	JT	60.72	61.56 -93
Barnes-Mileham	Lacy	USA	23.12.64	168/75	DT	60.22	62.98 -89
Barocsi	Helen	HUN	9.7.66	162/48	HMar	71:41	70:01 -92
Barreiro	Angeles	ESP	26.7.63	170/75	DT	60.56	59.22 -92
* Barsosio	Sally	KEN	21.3.78	165/46	3k	8:53.40	8:59.70 -93
					5k	15:42.45	15:43.6 -93
Bartoszek	Danuta	CAN	19.8.61	168/52	Mar	2:33:56	2:34:33 -93
Bártová	Daniela	TCH	6.5.74		PV	3.75i, 3.70	3.57 -93
Barylla	Angela	GER	6.1.71	177/68	TJ	13.67	13.50 -93
Bastos	Marina	POR	7.7.71	165/50	1500	4:09.59	4:08.92
					3k	8:58.74	9:08.71 -92
* Batten	Kim	USA	29.3.69	170/57	400h	53.72	53.84 -93
* Baumann	Julie	SUI	17.6.64	165/56	100h	12.82	12.76 -91
Beasley	Nekita	USA	29.3.69	162/52	800	2:01.66	2:02.00 -91
* Beclea	Violeta	ROM	26.3.65	166/50	800	1:59.30i, 2:00.47	1:58.7 -86
					1500	4:03.76	3:59.35 -93
* Beer	Peggy	GER	15.9.69	176/66	Hep	6362	6531 -90
Beggerow	Antje	GER	10.12.73	169/54	1500	4:13.32	4:11.98 -93
Bègue	Martine	FRA	22.12.69	170/61	JT	61.42	64.46 -93
Belaic	Valentin	CRO	17.10.72		JT	56.82	55.68 -93
Belikova	Nina	RUS	1.10.61		3k	9:01.84	9:07.7 -93
Belpérin	Guilaine	FRA	5.3.71	180/64	Hep	5729	5595 -93
Belyayeva	Marina	RUS	15.8.58	159/50	HMar	71:04	73:33 -93
Benesová	Hana	TCH	19.4.75	170/58	400	52.60	52.88 -93
Bennett	Julia	GBR	26.3.70	178/62	HJ	1.89	1.92i, 1.86 -90
* Berezhnaya	Larisa	UKR	28.2.61	178/66	LJ	6.89i, 6.66	7.24 -91
* Bergmann	Mette	NOR	9.11.62	174/80	DT	66.46	63.12 -89
Bergqvist	Kajsa	SWE	12.10.76		HJ	1.90	1.84 -93
Bernard	Nadia	FRA	6.10.67		10k	32:24.96	33:24.96 -93
(- Prasad)					HMar	69:05	71:59 -93

Name		Nat	Born	Ht/Wt	Event	1994 Mark	Pre-1994 Best
Bernardi	Delirde	BRA	27.4.69		3k	9:02.37	9:34.1 -91
Berry	Paula	USA	18.2.69	176/75	JT	58.08	61.60 -91
Bertrand	Kari	USA	11.11.70	162/47	1500	4:12.94	4:22.30 -91
					3k	8:57.45	9:25.2 -91
Betekhtina	Natalya	RUS	8.9.61		800	2:00.84	2:00.7 -88
					1500	4:12.05	4:06.25 -88
Beurskens	Carla	NED	10.2.52	165/46	HMar	72:26	70:04 -90
					Mar	2:29:43	2:26:34 -87
* Bevilacqua	Antonella	ITA	15.10.71	171/54	HJ	1.98i, 1.92	1.95 -92
Beyer	Inga	GER	7.2.74		HT	56.12	37.42 -93
Bicet	Nora	CUB	29.10.77		JT	56.00	52.86 -93
Bidouane	Nezha	MAR	18.9.69	174/65	400h	55.19	55.08 -92
Biktagirova	Madina	RUS	20.9.64	158/50	Mar	2:30:00	2:26:23 -92
* Bilac	Britta	SLO	4.12.68	181/61	HJ	2.00i, 2.00	1.97i -93, 1.94 -92
Birba	Sylvie	FRA	11.8.71	162/57	400h	57.53	59.01 -93
* Biryukova	Anna	RUS	27.9.67	174/60	LJ	6.69i, 6.64	6.89 -90
					TJ	14.89	15.09 -93
Bispo	Carla M Souza	BRA	29.7.66	177/69	JT	56.02	60.88 -93
Bitzner	Blandine	FRA	1.12.65	165/50	1500	4:04.72	4:07.17 -93
					Mile	4:31.64	4:36.65 -93
Blair	Kim	USA	12.3.72		400h	57.47	59.30 -91
Blair	Kelly	USA	24.11.70	181/62	Hep	5907	6038 -93
Blazevica	Jelena	LAT	11.5.70	170/54	TJ	13.40, 13.43w	13.57 -93
Bliznyukova	Svetlana	BLR	12.6.71		10kW	46:28	
Blythe	Gabriele	AUS	9.3.69	173/58	5000W	21:50.0	21:46.0 -93
					10kW	46:41	44:12.0 -93
Boaje	Cosmina	ROM	20.7.77		TJ	13.30i	12.81 -93
Bodrova	Nadezhda	UKR	13.7.61	170/58	100h	12.73	12.81 -91, 12.7 -90
* Boegman	Nicole	AUS	5.3.67	174/65	LJ	6.67, 6.82w	6.87 -88
Bogomaz	Svetlana	UKR	16.7.74	174/53	HJ	1.92i, 1.91	1.88 -93
Bogoslovskaya ¶	Olga	RUS	20.5.64	166/54	100	11.21dq	11.07 -92, 10.96w -89
Boice	Melinda	USA	29.12.74		HJ	1.88	1.84 -93
Boit	Cristina	ROM	14.5.68	170/80	DT	59.72	64.58 -88
Bolm	Kirsten	GER	4.3.75	181/69	100h	13.26, 13.23w	13.42 -92
					LJ	6.55	6.52 -93
Bolshova	Olga	MOL	16.6.68	174/60	HJ	1.94i, 1.94	1.97 -93
Bond-Mills	Catherine	CAN	20.9.67	180/69	LJ	6.48w	6.24 -93
					Hep	6206	6058
Bondarenko	Olga	RUS	2.6.60	155/41	3k	8:52.33	8:33.99 -86
					HMar	70:37	72:32 -93
Bonne	Idalmis	CUB	2.2.71	168/62	200	23.3	23.26, 23.22w -93
					400	52.02	52.98, 52.3 -93
Bordukova	Svetlana	RUS	1.5.65	173/65	400h	57.65	57.33 -92
* Borisova	Lyudmila	RUS	3.8.66	172/57	1500	4:05.66	4:03.66 -92
					3k	8:41.71	8:40.78 -93
					5k	15:13.27	0
Borovaya	Valentina	BLR	6.3.70		JT	57.00	53.62 -92
Borrmann	Tanja	GER	11.4.70	184/63	TJ	14.03i, 13.58	13.88 -93
Botticelli	Silvia	ITA	14.3.68	162/48	3k	8:55.89	9:00.32 -93
* Boulmerka	Hassiba	ALG	10.7.68	158/49	800	2:00.61	1:58.72 -91
					1500	4:01.05	3:55.30 -92
					Mile	4:22.09	4:20.79 -91
Bowen	Stacy	CAN	17.12.69	169/51	200	22.85	23.16 -93
					400	52.28	54.04 -93
* Bowles	Dawn	USA	12.11.68	168/52	100	11.47w	11.56 -92
					100h	12.88	12.82, 12.70w -91
Bowyer	Sonya	GBR	18.9.72	173/52	800	2:02.30	2:05.85 -93
Boyde	Kathrin	GER	4.12.70	172/62	5000W	21:43.2	21:20.97 -91
					10kW	43:41	44:05 -90
Boyer	Edie	USA	21.2.66	183/84	DT	56.94	59.36 -92
* Bozhanova ¶	Sofia	BUL	4.10.67	172/52	TJ	14.98	14.08 -91
Brack	Mirtha	COL	9.4.70		100	11.42wdt, 11.0w	11.93 -93
Bradburn	Angie	USA	4.9.68	178/61	HJ	1.98i, 1.95	1.96i -92, 1.94 -93
Braddock	Crystal	USA	13.12.70	170/57	100	11.43w	11.52 -92, 11.34w -93
Bran	Daniela	ROM	13.3.68	170/52	1500	4:12.72	4:08.2 -90
* Braun	Sabine	GER	19.6.65	174/62	100h	13.31	13.02 -92
					HJ	1.90i	1.94 -92
					LJ	6.67	6.73 -85
					Hep	6665	6985 -92

Name		Nat	Born	Ht/Wt	Event	1994 Mark	Pre-1994 Best
Bristel	Maricela	CUB	17.12.71		DT	60.22	55.52 -91
Brooker	Jane	USA	10.5.64	168/52	800	2:01.13	2:03.40 -92
Brooks	Pam	USA	15.1.72	175/59	400h	57.8, 57.86	57.39 -93
Brown	Jacqui	USA	12.8.72		LJ	6.48	6.13 -91
Brown	Michelle	USA	12.3.75		400	52.65	
Brown	Rica	USA	3.4.69	183/97	SP	16.28	17.40 -93
Brown	Sophia	JAM	.73		100	11.23w	11.55 -93
Brozmánová	Ivana	SVK	15.3.69	169/63	10kW	46:35	46:27 -91
Brunet	Roberta	ITA	20.5.65	168/55	3k	8:49.62	8:42.64 -91
					5k	15:23.20	15:16.93 -93
Brunner	Chantal	NZL	5.11.70	165/58	LJ	6.63	6.37 -93
Brzezinska	Anna	POL	9.1.71	171/58	800	2:00.41	2:01.67 -93
					1500	4:04.41	4:07.15 -93
					Mile	4:27.66	4:23.08 -93
					3k	8:55.63	8:55.52 -93
Budilovskaya	Zhanna	UKR	6.4.72	175/59	Hep	6096	5936 -93
* Buford	Tonja	USA	13.12.70	176/62	100h	13.14	13.07, 12.94w -92
					400h	55.26	54.38 -93
Buia	Aura	ROM	16.2.70	161/52	Mar	2:33:16	2:31:48 -93
* Bukovec	Brigita	SLO	21.5.70	168/57	100h	12.77, 12.59w	12.98, 12.89w -93
Bulbanovich	Svetlana	RUS	8.4.70		3k	8:58.30i	
* Buraga	Svetlana	BLR	4.9.65	168/56	100h	13.29	12.86, 12.8 -88
					LJ	6.46	6.79i, 6.63 -87
					Hep	6284	6635 -93
Burangulova	Ramilya	RUS	11.7.61	154/50	HMar	71:11	
					Mar	2:31:12	2:28:03 -93
Burca	Cristina	ROM	6.2.73	161/50	Mar	2:35:10	2:36:32 -93
Burkanova	Olga	RUS	29.9.69	177/61	800	2:01.18	2:00.28 -92
Burkett	Aspen	USA	8.3.76		100	11.36, 11.2	
					200	23.36	
Burrell	Dawn	USA	1.11.73	175/58	LJ	6.46, 6.55w	6.16i -91
Bussières	Lizanne	CAN	20.8.61	159/51	Mar	2:31:07	2:30:57 -88
Butler	Kwajalein	USA	23.7.76		100	11.42	
Bychkovskaya	Yelena	BLR	4.3.72		800	2:02.4	2:03.2 -92
					1500	4:12.54	
Cadusch	Sieglinde	SUI	28.8.67	180/56	HJ	1.92	1.91i -93, 1.90 -92
Cai	Weiyan	CHN	25.10.73		PV	4.01	4.00 -92
Caine	Keisha	USA	13.7.73	168/54	400	52.48	53.94 -93
Callaway	Debbie	GBR	15.7.64	170/91	DT	55.66	54.74 -93
Campbell	Juliet	JAM	17.3.70	176/62	400	51.65	50.11 -93
Campbell	Revoli	JAM	4.7.72	168/62	400	52.01	52.95 -93
Campbell	Rebecca	AUS	23.1.76		400h	57.46	57.06 -93
Campbell	Shanequa	USA	1.9.72	163/52	400	52.65	51.77 -93
Cano	Emilia	ESP	4.3.68	163/54	10kW	45:14	45:15 -92
Cao	Chunying	CHN	5.2.72	170/57	400	51.52	52.28 -93
Cao	Qi	CHN	.1.74		DT	61.24	66.08 -93
Capriotti	Antonella	ITA	4.2.62	162/55	LJ	6.52	6.72i, 6.70 -93, 6.79w -92
					TJ	13.48	14.18 -93
Carabali	Norfalia	COL	21.1.67	163/51	400	51.67	51.06 -92
Cardeñas	Regla	CUB	21.1.75	184/68	Hep	5834	5840 -93
Carney	Clare	AUS	6.2.74		10k	33:06.88	0
Carrillo	Laiza	CUB	27.11.68	170/63	TJ	14.00	13.77 -93
Carroll	Nicole	USA	18.4.68	168/68	JT	57.86	54.72 -93
Carroll	Nyla	NZL	24.11.65		Mar	2:34:03	
Carson	Kim	USA	12.3.74	170/56	100h	13.32	13.29 -93
* Carter	Kym	USA	12.3.64	188/77	Hep	6371	6357 -93
Carutasu	Nicoleta	ROM	14.2.64	173/64	400h	56.51	54.94 -93
Caster	Nadine	FRA	15.10.65	174/64	LJ	6.51, 6.58w	6.47 -92
Castro	Stella	COL	.62		HMar	72:23	72:07 -93
* Catuna	Anuta	ROM	1.1.68	152/48	HMar	69:35	69:22 -93
					Mar	2:29:39	2:37:02 -93
Cepero	Olga	CUB	4.5.75	178/66	TJ	13.95	13.68 -93
Chacko	Molly	IND	15.5.69		1500	4:12.10	4:20.98 -93
* Chalmers	Angela	CAN	6.9.63	172/56	1500	4:01.61	4:02.11 -92
					Mile	4:28.17	4:24.91 -91
					3k	8:32.17	8:38.38 -90
					5k	15:34.57	0
Chan	Sau Ying	HKG	30.8.70	170/60	100h	13.14, 13.06w, 12.7w	13.27 -93
Chebykina	Tatyana	RUS	22.11.68		400	52.29	52.62 -93

Name		Nat	Born	Ht/Wt	Event	1994 Mark	Pre-1994 Best
Chen	Huoqiang	CHN	.		TJ	13.51	13.01 -92
Chen	Xuehui	CHN	.7.69		800	2:02.45	1:58.48 -93
Chen	Yan	CHN	27.11.73	160/47	100	11.41	11.27 -93
* Chen	Yolanda	RUS	26.7.61	170/58	LJ	6.61	7.16 -88
					TJ	14.58	14.97 -93
Chen	Yueling	CHN	24.12.69	159/50	10kW	45:15.6	42:46.7 -92
Chen	Zhaojing	CHN	5.4.69	177/68	100	11.37	11.28 -92
					200	22.97, 22.67w	22.56 -93
Chen	Zhenhong	CHN	30.9.76		100h	13.32	
Cheng	Xiaoyan	CHN	20.11.75	174/100	SP	20.02	18.00 -93
Cheng	Xianhong	CHN	, 10.68		DT	59.36	62.32 -93
Chepchumba	Joyce	KEN	.70		HMar	71:55	75:17 -93
Chernova	Lada	RUS	.70		JT	58.22	58.02 -91
* Chernyavskaya	Olga	RUS	17.9.63	184/85	DT	65.60	68.38 -92
Chernyshova	Yelizaveta	RUS	26.1.58	168/60	100h	13.04, 13.03w	12.68 -89
Cheruiyot	Rose	KEN	21.7.76		3k	9:00.89	9:13.46 -93
					5k	15:44.06	
Chidu	Tudorita	ROM	17.10.67	170/54	1500	4:12.62, 4:07.85i	4:05.69 -90
					3k	9:02.5i	8:52.4i -92
Chirila	Mariana	ROM	7.9.64	168/52	1500	4:12.91	4:04.69 -86
					3k	8:59.11	8:38.83 -86
* Chistyakova	Galina	RUS	26.7.62	169/53	LJ	6.67	7.52 -88
					TJ	14.21i, 14.12	14.62 -92
Choinière	Melanie	CAN	.72		1500	4:11.56	4:14.72 -93
Christie	Michelle	JAM	.73		100	11.44w	
* Churbanova	Olga	RUS	16.7.65	170/53	1500	4:02.10	4:10.10 -93
					3k	8:40.48	8:53.63 -93
Chzhao	Larisa	RUS	4.2.72		800	2:01.56	2:01.33 -93
Cilimbini	Maria Luisa	ITA	25.10.67	164/52	400h	57.71	57.05 -88
Cîmpean	Norica	ROM	22.3.72	164/53	10kW	45:10.4	45:42 -93
Ciobanu	Jana	ROM	12.11.68	176/102	SP	19.36i, 18.08	19.23 -88
Ciric	Suzana	YUG	12.7.69	164/47	HMar	71:30	73:19 -91
					Mar	2:33:00	2:33:26 -93
Cistjakova	Regina	LIT	7.11.61	166/49	3k	8:55.38	8:39.25 -86
Clarinval	Cécile	BEL	16.9.68		800	2:02.22	2:05.39 -93
* Clarius	Birgit	GER	18.3.65	176/65	Hep	6109	6500 -93
* Clark	Joetta	USA	1.8.62	172/55	800	1:58.39	1:58.06 -92
					1500	4:12.82	4:14.3 -93
Clarke	Eldece	BAH	13.2.65	162/43	200	23.30	
Clouvel	Annick	FRA	15.10.63	170/54	10k	33:01.66	33:05.30 -93
Colander	LaTasha	USA	23.8.76		200	23.3	23.99 -93
					100h	13.30	13.84, 13.76w -93
Colberg	Karin	SWE	19.4.67	180/78	DT	58.56	55.30 -91
Cole	Wynsome	JAM	30.5.74	175/61	400h	57.88	58.74 -93
Colin	Maria	MEX	7.3.66	163/55	10kW	45:54	45:11 -93
Collins	Dana	USA	23.7.73	155/53	100	11.40x	11.30 -93
Collins	Michele	USA	12.2.71	178/61	100	11.40, 11.22w	11.36, 11.26w -92
					200	22.74	22.80 -92
					400	51.19	51.59 -93
Collins	Melanie	AUS	28.10.67		800	2:03.03	2:03.50 -93
Collonvillé	Marie	FRA	23.11.73	163/51	Hep	5995	5638
Comadore	Countess	USA	27.1.67	165/56	400h	57.40	56.18 -92
Combe	Delphine	FRA	6.12.74	168/59	100	11.47w	11.64, 11.55w -93
					200	23.35	23.54 -93
Compagnoni	Santa	ITA	13.11.63		10kW	46:26	50:17 -93
Constantin	Mitica	ROM	18.8.62	174/56	800	2:01.14i, 2:03.00	1:57.87 -86
					1500	4:10.92i, 4:13.64	4:03.04 -87
Coogan	Gwyn	USA	21.8.65	153/50	3k	9:00.0	9:01.10 -91
					5k	15:48.84	15:39.20 -91
					10k	32:08.77	32:27.5 -92
Cooman	Nelli	NED	6.6.64	159/60	100	11.35	11.08 -86
Coombe	Kylie	AUS	22.12.67		Hep	5650	5895w -89
Cors	Tanja	GER	22.4.71	171/60	PV	3.90	3.93 -93
Coslovich	Claudia	ITA	26.4.72	170/70	JT	60.32	53.88 -93
* Costa	Silvia	CUB	4.5.64	179/60	HJ	2.00	2.04 -89
Costescu	Denisa	ROM	26.1.75		3k	9:02.27	9:00.27 -93
* Costian	Daniela	AUS	30.4.65	181/87	DT	68.72	73.84 -88
Couch	Sharon	USA	13.9.69	172/63	100h	13.24	13.38 -91
					LJ	6.54, 6.57w	6.68 -92

Name		Nat	Born	Ht/Wt	Event	1994 Mark	Pre-1994 Best
Court	Clova	GBR	10.2.60	175/66	100h	13.04	13.26, 13.13w -93
Covington	Sheryl	USA	3.3.71	170/50	400	51.85	53.19 -92
Crawford	She She	USA	28.12.70	165/57	100	11.47w	11.34, 11.29w -92
Criswell	Keisha	USA	.		100	11.43	
Crooks	Charmaine	CAN	8.8.62	175/64	400	52.27	50.45 -84
					800	2:01.78	1:58.52 -90
Cross	Anne	AUS	16.4.64		10k	32:56.45	0
Crowley	Margaret	AUS	24.5.67		800	2:03.0	2:03.29 -93
					1500	4:11.48	4:12.67 -93
Cruz	Josefa	ESP	12.3.58	158/52	Mar	2:33:58	2:36:31 -93
Csöke	Katalin	HUN	26.1.57	173/79	DT	56.48	63.20 -80
Cumba	Yumileidis	CUB	11.2.75	185/85	SP	18.78	17.70 -93
Cummings-Glover	Sandra	USA	30.12.68	170/55	400h	56.66	55.77 -92
* Curatolo	Maria	ITA	12.10.63	147/40	HMar	71:08	
					Mar	2:30:33	2:30:14 -88
Curovic	Danijela	YUG	7.3.74	184/98	SP	17.80	18.02 -93
					DT	59.64	58.40 -93
Curti	Nives	ITA	1.9.69	167/49	HMar	72:34	
* Cuthbert	Juliet	JAM	9.4.64	160/54	100	11.01	10.83 -92
					200	22.85, 22.74w	21.75 -92
Dallona	Cinzia	ITA	16.3.74		JT	56.46	53.16 -93
* Damaske	Tanja	GER	16.11.71	177/69	JT	64.24	61.06 -90
Dandolo	Nadia	ITA	11.9.62	169/60	3k	8:49.42	8:44.36 -91
					5k	15:14.23	15:11.64 -90
Danchinova	Anastasia	RUS	.73		HMar	72:06	
Danilczyk	Krystyna	POL	14.1.68	183/88	SP	19.23	19.42 -92
Danson	Yvonne	GBR	22.5.59	151/39	Mar	2:32:24	2:32:42 -93
Darsha	Damaryanthi	SRI	13.2.75	165/55	100	11.42	11.52 -93
					200	23.24	23.29 -93
Davies	Angela	GBR	21.10.70	166/52	1500	4:09.29	4:15.35 -93
					Mile	4:31.83	0
Davis	Dedra	BAH	17.7.73	168/62	100	11.31	11.33 -93
					LJ	6.71i, 6.69, 6.85w	6.72, 6.76w -93
* Davis	Pauline	BAH	9.7.66	168/57	100	11.37, 11.28w	11.14, 10.9 -89
					200	22.52	22.44 -92, 22.1w -87
					400	50.46	50.05 -90
Dawson	Sandra	AUS	2.11.70		800	2:02.49	2:02.23 -93
De Angeli	Virna	ITA	27.2.76	170/54	400h	56.79	58.04 -93
de Bruin	Corrie	NED	26.10.76	179/80	SP	18.15	18.12 -93
					DT	57.60	56.48 -92
de Jongh	Adri	RSA	13.7.70		200	23.08	24.36 -93
					400	52.72	54.42 -93
De Leeuw	Sabrina	BEL	19.8.74	182/63	HJ	1.94i	1.93 -93
de Reuck	Colleen	RSA	13.4.64	164/47	Mar	2:31:53	2:31:21 -92
Delahunty	Sinead	IRL	12.2.71		1500	4:12.20	4:19.5i -92
Denboba	Merima	ETH	21.8.74	170/56	3k	8:52.54	9:14.48 -93
					5k	15:47.85	
					10k	32:16.50	33:57.21 -92
					HMar	71:43	
Dendy	Terri	USA	8.5.65	168/55	400	52.56	51.45 -88
Derevyankina	Lyudmila	KGZ	.66		800	2:02.83	1:58.85 -88
Dethier	Françoise	BEL	20.5.65		400h	57.73	58.02 -93
Dethier	Sylvie	BEL	20.5.65	164/55	100h	13.37	12.98 -91
Devaluez	Isabelle	FRA	17.3.66	180/75	DT	58.38	59.50 -93
* Devers	Gail	USA	19.11.66	163/52	100	11.12, 10.77w	10.82 -92
Devonish	Nicole	CAN	24.8.73	179/68	LJ	6.46w	6.46, 6.55w -93
Dherbecourt	Isabelle	FRA	15.5.73	168/54	400h	57.46	58.34 -92
Di Napoli	Patrizia	ITA	27.9.69		3k	8:58.26	9:14.85 -93
* Dias	Albertina	POR	26.4.65	163/48	HMar	69:57	70:40 -92
					Mar	2:33:21	2:26:49 -93
Dias	Manuela	POR	19.6.63	160/45	HMar	72:43	71:23 -93
Dickey	Cheryl	USA	12.12.66	165/61	100h	13.13	12.97 -92, 12.91w -93
					100h	13.03w	12.8w -90
Didden	Ingrid	BEL	27.6.68	179/64	Hep	5803	6056 -91
* Dietzsch	Franka	GER	22.1.68	183/96	DT	62.76	68.26 -89
Dillon	Michelle	AUS	25.5.73		10k	32:46.4	32:35.40 -93
Dimitrova	Desislava	BUL	19.6.72	165/50	100	11.25, 11.23w	11.36 -93
* Dimitrova	Svetla	BUL	27.1.70	170/57	100h	12.53, 12.50w	12.71 -93
Ding	Ying	CHN	28.9.76		Hep	5992	5838 -93

Name		Nat	Born	Ht/Wt	Event	1994 Mark	Pre-1994 Best
Dixon	Tania	NZL	3.10.70	172/57	HJ	1.91	1.91 -91
* Djaté	Patricia	FRA	3.1.71	173/58	800	1:58.07	2:00.75 -93
Domain	Sandrine	FRA	6.9.71	176/63	TJ	13.82	13.42 -91, 13.59w -93
Dong	Bo	CHN	.3.71		SP	18.59	18.77 -93
* Dong	Li	CHN	9.12.73	164/55	3k	8:53.27	9:00.62 -93
					10k	31:31.08	31:52.29 -93
* Donkova	Yordanka	BUL	28.9.61	175/67	100h	12.56, 12.49w	12.21 -88, 12.0w -86
Dooley	Tanya	USA	8.5.72	168/55	400	52.61	52.83 -93
* Dörre-Heinig	Katrin	GER	6.10.61	170/56	Mar	2:25:15	2:25:24 -87
Dorsile	Viviane	FRA	1.6.67	170/51	400	52.15, 51.92i	52.02 -92
					800	2:02.16	1:59.29 -92
Douglas	Stephanie	GBR	22.1.69	166/59	100	11.34	11.27 -91
					200	23.17	23.30 -91
Dreher	Claudia	GER	2.5.71	169/52	5k	15:41.23	15:33.83
					10k	32:54.06	32:44.41 -91
* Drechsler	Heike	GER	16.12.64	181/68	100	11.38	10.91, 10.80w -86
					200	22.84	21.71 -86
					100h	13.34	14.12 -80
					LJ	7.29, 7.39w	7.48 -88, 7.63w -92
					Hep	6741	5812 -81
Dubkova	Lyudmila	RUS	27.2.68		TJ	14.31	14.00 -93
Dubtsova	Yelena	RUS	6.5.71		100	11.30, 11.0	11.51 -90
					200	23.10, 22.89w	23.52 -93
Dudayeva	Alla	RUS	.69		Mar	2:35:05	2:35:05 -91
Duhaney	Dahlia	JAM	20.7.70	168/56	100	11.32, 11.22w	11.22 -93
					200	22.80	22.80 -92, 22.79w -93
Dukes	Pam	USA	15.5.64	183/85	DT	58.00	61.14 -92
* Dukhnova	Natalya	BLR	16.7.66	176/64	800	1:57.87	1:58.03 -93
					1500	4:11.94	4:11.19 -93
* Dulgheru	Mirela	ROM	5.10.66	172/62	LJ	6.69i, 6.62	7.14 -92
Dumble	Dawn	USA	25.2.72	173/80	SP	17.86	17.36i -92, 17.36 -93
					DT	59.20	57.42 -93
Dumitrascu	Elena	ROM	14.5.74	176/68	TJ	13.79	13.39i -93, 13.32 -91
du Plessis	Desiré	RSA	20.5.65	184/64	HJ	1.91	2.01 -86
* Duporty	Julia	CUB	9.2.71	171/63	200	23.15	23.31 -93
					400	50.61	51.81 -93
Duprey	Donalda	CAN	1.3.67	172/56	100h	13.09	13.20 -93
					400h	55.10, 55.0	55.80 -93
Duquenoy	Laurence	FRA	29.9.69	160/46	1500	4:13.38	4:24.43 -93
Dwinger	Rhona	RSA	28.6.71		JT	56.90	55.98 -92
Dyachenko	Oksana	RUS	26.11.74	172/55	100	11.35, 11.2	11.66 -93
					200	23.13, 23.04w	23.25 -93
Dyatlova	Tatyana	BLR	12.1.75		LJ	6.53	6.36 -93
Earl-Givan	Alexandria	USA	25.4.70	176/73	HT	57.42	55.26 -92
* Edeh	Rosey	CAN	13.8.66	173/54	400h	55.15	54.53 -93
Edmondson	Bonnie	USA	17.3.64	176/73	HT	55.76	54.56 -92
Edwards	Jackie	BAH	14.4.71	172/64	LJ	6.68w	6.69 -92
Echevarría	Eloina	CUB	23.8.61	168/63	TJ	14.22	14.07 -92
* Echols	Sheila	USA	2.10.64	165/52	100	11.26, 11.13w	10.83 -88
					LJ	6.66	6.94 -87
Elechi	Oluchi	NGR	24.6.68		LJ	6.45	6.31 -91
					Hep	5665	5320 -91
Elien	Evelyne	FRA	24.3.64	160/50	400	51.52	51.79 -88
Ellerbe	Connie	USA	24.6.68	173/55	400h	56.45	55.87 -92
Erjavec	Natasa	SLO	15.5.68	179/105	SP	18.10	17.53 -93
Ernstdóttir	Martha	ISL	22.12.64	160/46	5k	15:55.91	15:53.5 -92
					10k	32:47.40	33:10.93 -91
					HMar	72:01	72:33 -93
Espegren	Lene	NOR	8.5.71		TJ	13.48w	13.54, 13.56w -93
* Essayah	Sari	FIN	21.2.67	162/58	5000W	20:28.62	20:38.65 -93
					10kW	42:37	42:37.0 -93
Estévez	Estela	ESP	24.2.65	161/47	3k	9:00.54	8:55.58 -92
					10k	32:56.93	33:13.62 -93
Etsebeth	Lizette	RSA	3.5.63	185/92	DT	55.74	56.28 -91
Eve	Laverne	BAH	16.6.65	179/77	JT	57.96	54.78 -89
Ewerlöf	Malin	SWE	2.6.72	178/61	800	2:01.33	2:02.86 -92
Fan	Yuyan	CHN	.72		JT	58.54	
Farquharson	Samantha	GBR	15.12.69	162/53	100h	13.08, 12.9nf	13.28 -92
Farrow	Kate	AUS	6.5.67	176/70	JT	60.70	58.98 -90

Name		Nat	Born	Ht/Wt	Event	1994 Mark	Pre-1994 Best
Fatès	Farida	FRA	2.2.62	166/49	1500	4:08.11	4:08.90 -90
					3k	8:46.04	8:51.33 -93
					5k	15:16.41	0
Faumuina	Beatrice	NZL	23.10.74	180/98	DT	57.94	55.20 -93
Fazekas	Erzsebet	HUN	8.4.71	174/60	HJ	1.89	1.88 -92
Feagin	Zundra	USA	12.7.73	163/57	200	23.13	23.13 -90
Fedotova	Yekaterina	RUS	4.11.75		800	2:02.70	2:07.81 -93
Fedotova	Yelena	RUS	29.5.67		JT	56.04	59.34 -90
* Fedyushina	Valentina	UKR	10.2.65	190/90	SP	20.79i, 20.56	21.08 -88
* Feitor	Susana	POR	25.1.75	159/52	5000W	21:06.0	21:01.8 -93
					10kW	43:30	43:44 -93
Feng	Haixia	CHN	.73		10kW	44:00.0	46:10 -92
Feng	Jie	CHN	.		LJ	6.58	
Ferguson	Debbie	BAH	16.1.76		100	11.1	
					200	23.32, 23.1	23.82, 23.32w -93
Fernández	Herminia	CUB	4.11.67	170/80	SP	17.52	18.60 -93
Ferrara	Ornella	ITA	17.4.68	153/40	Mar	2:31:57	2:35:08 -93
* Ferreira	M Conceição	POR	13.3.62	148/40	3k	9:01.14	8:53.27 -91
					5k	15:28.70	15:54.01 -86
					10k	31:32.11	31:16.42 -92
					HMar	71:02	70:07 -93
Fesenko	Lidia	RUS	5.10.62		5000W	21:51.72	
					10kW	44:41.42	42:52 -91
Feuerbach	Kathrin	GER	.66		TJ	13.50	12.90 -93
* Fidatov	Elena	ROM	24.7.60	168/52	1500	4:10.56	4:04.55 -92
					5k	15:49.99 unc	15:41.83 -86
					HMar	70:13	
Ficher	Fabienne	FRA	25.4.66	175/68	100	11.37w	11.77 -93
					200	23.26, 23.21w	23.19 -90
Filimonova	Lyudmila	BLR	22.3.71	184/76	DT	63.84	62.62 -93
Findlay	Theresa	USA	11.1.74		HT	56.56	48.62 -93
Fitts	Sonja	USA	4.10.70	173/81	HT	58.68	56.18 -93
* Flemming	Jane	AUS	14.4.65	168/56	100h	13.08, 12.9w	12.98 -93
					Hep	6317	6695 -90
Fletcher	Najuma	GUY	31.5.74	178/59	LJ	6.47	
					Hep	5750	5413 -93
Fogli	Laura	ITA	5.10.59	168/50	Mar	2:31:44	2:27:49 -88
Fomenko	Viktoria	UKR	2.10.71	170/60	200	22.81	23.16 -93
Forbes	Rhonda	TRI	.74		200	22.9	25.22 -93
* Forkel	Karen	GER	24.9.70	172/64	JT	69.20	70.20 -91
Formanová	Ludmila	TCH	2.1.74	167/60	400	52.59	53.04 -93
					800	2:02.54	2:03.78 -93
Foster	Char	USA	2.1.80		400h	57.98	0
Foulon	Severine	FRA	8.12.73	170/55	800	2:02.63	2:02.85 -93
Franey	Kathy	USA	25.12.67	163/54	1500	4:08.79	4:12.18 -93
					Mile	4:30.20	4:35.16i -93
					3k	8:46.03	8:58.50 -93
					5k	15:44.10	15:35.05 -93
Frazer	Merlene	JAM	27.12.73	172/57	100	11.33	11.24 -93
					200	22.65, 22.49w	22.91 -93
* Freeman	Cathy	AUS	16.2.73	164/52	100	11.24, 11.15w	11.43 -93, 11.42w -89
					200	22.25	22.37 -93
					400	50.04	51.14 -92
* Freeman	Michelle	JAM	5.5.69	170/63	100	11.38w	11.16, 11.13w -92
					200	23.29	22.87 -92
					100h	12.93, 12.74w	12.75 -92
Freriks	Marjan	NED	13.12.61	180/65	10k	33:04.09	32:23.0 -90
					Mar	2:35:10	2:39:45 -93
Fricot	Sandrine	FRA	4.6.68	180/57	HJ	1.92	1.93 -92
Frye	Regina	USA	18.8.72	157/61	LJ	6.52w	6.35 -93
Fu	Xiuhong	CHN	6.5.70		Hep	5734	5854 -93
Fuentes	Carmen	ESP	7.6.65	158/47	10k	32:46.12	33:12.92 -91
* Fujimura	Nobuko	JPN	18.12.65	163/48	Mar	2:26:09	2:30:03 -93
Fukuyama	Tsugumi	JPN	10.4.68	162/46	10k	32:56.86	0
Fumoto	Midori	JPN	18.12.71	160/43	10k	32:43.73	32:04.40 -92
					HMar	71:34	69:37 -92
Fynes	Savathea	BAH	17.10.74	165/68	100	11.42, 11.2w	11.55 -93
					200	23.38, 23.10w	23.43 -93
Fyodorova	Alla	RUS	.66		HT	61.84	64.44 -91

Name		Nat	Born	Ht/Wt	Event	1994 Mark	Pre-1994 Best
Fyodorova	Tatyana	RUS	.67		TJ	13.69	13.81i -93, 13.74 -89
Fyodorova	Viktoria	RUS	9.5.73	179/56	HJ	1.93	1.83 -93
Gachevska	Monika	BUL	30.10.74		200	23.37, 23.1	24.13 -93
Gaines	Chryste	USA	14.9.70	170/57	100	11.32, 10.99w	11.16, 10.90w -92
						11.2	
					200	23.32	22.81 -93
* Gainsford	Melinda	AUS	1.10.71	175/63	100	11.12	11.22, 11.15w -93
					200	22.32	22.49 -93
* Galkina	Lyudmila	RUS	20.5.72	174/56	LJ	6.78	6.75 -93
Gallina	Giada	ITA	1.12.73	165/54	100	11.40w	11.56 -91
					200	23.29	23.72 -92, 23.60w -93
Gallyamova	Albina	RUS	8.5.64		HMar	72:31	
Galushko	Natalya	BLR	18.9.71	160/46	HMar	71:00	72:08 -93
Gama	Monica	POR	9.3.70	165/52	10k	32:29.33	32:26.41 -89
					HMar	70:19	
Ganguillet	Nathalie	SUI	21.8.67		SP	16.41	16.49 -87
* Gao	Hongmiao	CHN	17.3.72	162/51	10kW	41:37.9	42:49.7 -92
Garcia	Magalys	CUB	23.10.71	173/70	Hep	6076	5903 -93
Garrett	Carla	USA	31.7.67	172/114	DT	56.54	60.54 -92
Gasser	Sandra	SUI	27.7.62	169/52	1500	4:12.73i	3:59.06 -87
Gast	Silke	GER	30.4.72	184/70	JT	62.90	60.06 -93
Gautzsch	Birgit	GER	14.12.67	180/68	Hep	5952	6425 -89
Gayle	Jackie	JAM	.73		400	52.76	52.67 -93
Gdowski	Sammie	USA	1.1.67	165/51	5k	15:46.79	15:45.29 -90
Geldhof	Marie Paule #	BEL	27.2.59	172/72	DT	61.40	60.30 -91
Georgieva	Zlatka	BUL	20.7.69		100	11.43, 11.15w	11.40 -92
					200	23.26, 22.8	23.00 -92
Gerhardt	Claudia	GER	18.1.66	176/63	LJ	6.55, 6.57w	6.57i -91, 6.57 -93
Gerke	Holly	CAN	.64		10kW	45:43	47:02 -91
Gibson	Lynn	GBR	6.7.69	167/55	1500	4:05.75	4:12.12 -93
					Mile	4:31.17	0
Gibson	Sharon	GBR	31.12.61	168/77	JT	58.20	62.32 -87
Gilliam	Latasha	USA	19.2.76		100	11.2w	
Giordano	Rossella	ITA	1.12.72	172/52	5000W	21:52.96	21:45.52 -93
					10kW	44:20	45:28.1 -93
* Girard	Patricia	FRA	8.4.68	162/48	100	11.11	11.20 -93
					100h	12.93	12.91 -92
Glenn	Roshanda	USA	13.11.71	173/55	TJ	13.67	13.35 -93
Gliznutsa	Inna	MOL	12.4.73	184/63	HJ	1.94	1.91 -93
Godall	Sonia	ESP	28.3.68	172/65	DT	56.48	57.14 -92
Goddard	Cheri	USA	23.12.70	173/55	3k	9:02.28	9:10.30 -91
Gogirlea	Luminita	ROM	5.11.71	159/49	3k	9:02.30	9:13.89 -93
					HMar	71:34	74:08 -93
Gogoase	Ionela	ROM	4.2.70	175/62	TJ	14.01	13.70 -93
Golding	Lacena	JAM	24.3.75		LJ	6.49i, 6.47	6.34 -93
					TJ	13.99	12.27 -93
Golesheva	Yelena	RUS	12.7.66	167/60	400	51.41	51.28 -89
Golodnova	Natalya	KZK	14.4.67	179/58	HJ	1.88i	1.95 -87
Gonçalves	Isilda	POR	11.11.69	157/48	10kW	46:13	46:24 -93
* Goncharenko	Svetlana	RUS	28.5.71	176/60	100	10.8	11.48 -92
					200	22.6	23.40 -93
					400	51.00	54.00 -93
Goncharova	Yelena	RUS	27.3.63	179/66	800	2:01.91	2:00.13 -92
					400h	57.3	
Gooch	Kay	NZL	2.5.72	157/55	3k	8:57.18	9:20.34 -92
					3k		9:12.53i -93
Goormachtigh	Jacqueline	NED	28.2.70	179/84	SP	16.98	17.77 -93
					DT	59.12	60.80 -92
Goossens	Ester	NED	21.2.72	175/65	800	2:00.05	2:04.07 -93
					400h	57.13	57.51 -93
Gorbatova	Yekaterina	RUS	13.6.68		100h	13.23, 12.6	13.16, 13.0 -93
Gordeyeva	Tatyana	RUS	3.6.73		Hep	5722	5450 -93
Goryacheva	Marina	RUS	.74		TJ	13.51	12.79 -93
Gotovska	Valentina	LAT	3.9.65	176/59	HJ	1.94	1.97 -90
Gourdet	Barbara	FRA	29.8.65	168/52	800	2:03.02	2:01.31 -88
Gouveia	Helena	POR	24.4.72	167/52	JT	56.32	53.04 -92
Govorova	Yelena	UKR	18.9.73	177/59	TJ	14.22	13.43 -92
Graham	Kim	USA	26.3.71	163/58	200	23.31	22.98 -93
					400	51.43	51.88 -93

Name		Nat	Born	Ht/Wt	Event	1994 Mark	Pre-1994 Best
* Graham	Yvonne	JAM	22.8.65	167/55	800	2:00.33	1:58.32 -90
					1500	4:04.35	4:02.69 -90
					Mile	4:24.64	4:22.97 -90
					3k	8:45.87	8:49.97 -89
					5k	15:13.67	0
Grachova	Irina	RUS	11.3.63		DT	59.20	60.54 -93
Graiani	Daniela	GER	7.9.70	168/51	400h	57.73	58.35 -89
* Granados	Encarnacion	ESP	30.1.72	168/50	10kW	44:35	43:21 -93
Grand	Pascale	CAN	12.8.67	169/48	10kW	46:17.9	45:53 -90
Grant	Beverley	JAM	25.9.70		200	23.22w	
Grant	Ellen	JAM	17.10.74		400	51.57	53.11 -93
Grasu	Nicoleta	ROM	11.9.71	176/68	DT	64.40	65.66 -92
* Graudyn	Yulia	RUS	13.11.70	171/59	100h	12.62, 12.51w	12.82 -93
Gray	Christine	USA	17.8.71	173/61	TJ	13.31w	13.11 -93
Gray	Nioka	AUS	30.4.73		400h	58.01	58.31 -92
Green	Nicole	USA	28.10.71	164/57	200	23.31	23.78 -93
					400	52.16	53.67 -91
Grefstad	Monica	NOR	12.10.64	173/63	100h	13.09	13.26 -93
Gribanova	Yelena	RUS	2.3.72	189/66	HJ	1.90	1.97 -93, 1.96 -92
Griffith	Michelle	GBR	6.10.71	173/64	TJ	14.08	13.75, 13.93w -93
Griffiths	Ann	GBR	20.8.65	183/60	800	1:59.81	1:59.88 -91
					1500	4:08.71	4:07.59 -92
Griffiths	Gwen	RSA	30.8.67	174/50	1500	4:07.40	4:04.73 -93
					3k	8:51.57	8:49.48 -92
					5k	15:38.39	16:12.55 -91
Grigoryeva	Tatyana	RUS	11.3.72		800	1:59.83	2:03.46 -92
					400h	56.7	
Grosse-Rammelkamp	Marion	GER	27.12.68		HT	56.00	53.64 -93
Gu	Yan	CHN	6.6.73	164/54	5000W	21:15.8	21:56.6 -91
					10kW	42:19.2	42:50 -93
Gubkina	Lyudmila	BLR	28.5.73	170/52	HT	57.58	59.62
Guialdo	Marsha	USA	12.7.70	165/54	100h	13.30	13.08, 12.89w -93
Guida	Maria	ITA	23.1.66	160/49	3k	8:54.59	8:58.35 -93
					5k	15:40.96	15:36.98 -93
					10k	31:42.14	32:10.29 -92
					HMar	70:19	
* Guidry (- White)	Carlette	USA	4.9.68	168/50	100	11.12, 10.97w	10.94, 10.91w -91
					200	22.38	22.24 -92
					400	51.51	52.46 -90
Guillot	Isabelle	FRA	25.10.61	155/46	HMar	72:35	74:04 -93
Guiyoule	Valérie	FRA	3.8.72	174/60	TJ	13.85	13.14 -93
* Gulyayeva	Yelena	RUS	14.8.67	181/62	HJ	2.00i, 1.98	1.99 -91
* Gummelt	Beate	GER	4.2.68	169/54	5000W	21:19.00	20:07.52 -90
					10kW	42:36	42:11.5 -92
* Gündler	Anja	GER	18.3.72	184/85	DT	61.20	62.92 -93
* Gunnell	Sally	GBR	29.7.66	167/58	400	51.04	51.11 -91
					100h	13.09	12.92, 12.80w -88
					400h	53.33	52.74 -93
Gunning	Debbie	GBR	31.8.65	157/49	1500	4:13.50	4:12.69 -90
* Gurina	Lyubov	RUS	6.8.57	166/57	800	1:56.53	1:55.56 -87
					1500	4:02.47	4:03.32 -92
Gurskaya	Natalya	BLR	15.1.72	175/74	SP	17.00	17.81i -93, 17.23 -92
Guthrie	Diane	JAM	24.10.71	174/66	LJ	6.62, 6.75w	6.78 -92
					Hep	6032	6040 -92
Gutjahr	Kathleen	GER	27.7.75	176/65	TJ	13.35	12.90 -92
					Hep	6071	5678 -93
Gydesen	Karen	DEN	3.6.67	165/60	800	2:00.97	2:05.74 -92
Ha	Xiaoyan	CHN	30.1.72	176/73	JT	63.98	65.44 -93
Haage	Carmen	GER	10.9.71		PV	3.90	3.90 -92
Haddad	Aminah	USA	13.9.78		200	23.23	23.67, 23.48w -93
Hafner	Michaela	ITA	2.8.73	176/67	10kW	44:51	48:13.6 -93
Haggenmüller	Angelika	GER	1.3.69	168/58	200	23.29	23.44 -93
Haggett	Lea	GBR	9.5.72	173/56	HJ	1.88	1.91 -91
Hairston	Terri	USA	19.7.63	178/64	LJ	6.53, 6.70w	6.74 -87
Håkenstad	Anita	NOR	19.2.68		Mar	2:34:01	0
Halle	Gunhild	NOR	1.6.72	166/47	3k	8:56.71	9:02.66 -93
					5k	15:30.04	0
* Hamilton	Suzy	USA	8.8.68	160/48	800	1:59.02	1:59.11 -90
					1500	4:04.57	4:04.53 -92

Name		Nat	Born	Ht/Wt	Event	1994 Mark	Pre-1994 Best
Hammer	Grit	GER	4.6.66	180/93	SP	19.42	20.72
Han ¶	Qing	CHN	14.3.70	170/55	400h	54.74 dq	53.96 -93
Hanigan	Kylie	AUS	18.11.71	169/56	400	52.06	52.26 -93
Hansen	Ashia	GBR	5.12.71		TJ	14.22	13.48i, 13.55w -93
Hanson	Sharon	USA	24.9.65	169/63	Hep	6001	6123 -91
Hanson-Nortey	Yvonne	GBR	18.2.64	185/91	SP	16.43	17.45 -89
Hantho	Ingrid	USA	13.6.71		DT	55.12	49.00 -93
Hara	Mariko	JPN	27.12.70	165/51	3k	8:57.81	8:57.37 -93
					5k	15:49.43	15:36.78 -93
					10k	32:01.57	32:25.89 -92
Hare	Anne	NZL	7.6.64	167/55	10k	32:31.4	32:42.86 -93
Harper	Hydie Ann	TRI	.		200	23.34x	23.1 -93
Harris	Flirtisha	USA	21.2.72	155/52	100	11.40	11.38 -93
					200	22.97	23.02, 22.56w -93
					400	51.65	53.09i -93
Harris	JoJo	USA	25.4.73	176/86	DT	55.14	49.14 -93
Harrison	Georgia	JAM	.		400h	57.78	
Hartigan	Bev	GBR	10.6.67	156/45	1500	4:11.04	4:05.66 -90
					Mile	4:31.26	4:26.52 -92
* Hattestad	Trine	NOR	18.4.66	173/75	JT	71.32	72.12 -93
Haughton	Karlene	JAM	.72		400h	56.58	58.00 -93
* Haugland	Hanne	NOR	14.12.67	183/65	HJ	1.98i, 1.97	1.96i, 1.94 -89
					TJ	13.56	12.94 -93
Hautala	Tiia	FIN	3.4.72	170/57	Hep	6042	5606 -92
Hayashi	Emi	JPN	9.7.72	169/55	10kW	44:46	46:02 -93
Hechavarría	Barbara	CUB	6.8.66	174/94	DT	65.62	67.18 -92
Hecht	Karin	GER	27.10.77		PV	3.65	3.31 -93
Helbik	Marzena	POL	11.9.61	157/46	HMar	71:08	
					Mar	2:34:57	2:39:45 -93
Hellier	Kirsten	NZL	6.10.69	174/73	JT	62.52	62.52 -93
Hellmann	Marion	GER	6.4.67	184/62	HJ	1.94i, 1.90	1.94 -92
* Hemmings	Deon	JAM	9.10.68	176/61	200	23.33w	
					400	51.45	51.77 -93
					400h	54.48	54.12 -93
Hendricken	Geraldine	IRL	19.4.70	165/53	3k	9:00.09	9:00.34 -93
* Henkel	Heike	GER	5.5.64	182/63	HJ	1.95	2.07 -92
Hennagan	Monique	USA	26.5.76	173/55	400	52.19	52.30 -93
Hennart	Sandrine	BEL	12.12.72	172/62	LJ	6.48	6.61 -93
Henry	Connie	GBR	15.4.72		TJ	13.31	12.72 -92, 13.03w -93
Henry	Joanne	NZL	2.10.71	173/60	LJ	6.46, 6.65w	6.54 -92
					Hep	6121	6278 -91
Hérigault	Corinne	FRA	8.10.70	165/53	LJ	6.45i	6.54 -93
Hernández	Odalys	CUB	4.9.66	178/63	400h	57.89	56.90 -87
Hernesniemi	Sanna	FIN	9.3.71	170/53	100	11.36	11.40 -93, 11.26w -92
					200	23.14	23.01, 22.98w -93
Herring-Kelly	Sabrina	USA	20.8.75	160/58	100	11.36, 11.33x	11.52 -91
Hila	Elena	ROM	20.5.74	179/95	SP	17.20	16.76 -93
Hill	D'Andre	USA	19.4.73	165/56	100	11.12	11.77, 11.71w -90
					200	23.08, 22.86w	24.25 -90
Hill	Janet	USA	28.8.70	176/82	DT	55.20	57.82 -93
Hinderlie	Keri	USA	.		100h	13.37	
Hinds	Le'Gretta	USA	13.1.74		400h	57.82	
Hiroyama	Harumi	JPN	2.9.68	160/50	1500	4:11.10	4:12.39 -92
					3k	8:50.40	9:01.62 -93
					5k	15:33.53	15:30.78 -93
Hobson	Sue	AUS	13.3.58	170/55	10k	32:38.74	32:05.47 -91
					Mar	2:32:57	0
Hoffmann	Juliane	GER	13.12.73	175/65	JT	59.88	58.70 -92
* Holmes	Kelly	GBR	19.4.70	163/55	800	1:59.43	1:58.64 -93
					1500	4:01.41	4:17.3 -93
Holmqvist	Emma	SWE	26.3.75	173/59	400h	57.23	0
Holpuchová	Kamila	TCH	27.9.73	170/52	10kW	44:50	44:20 -93
Holroyd	Shelley	GBR	17.5.73	177/66	JT	57.08	60.10 -93
Holubová	Ivona	SVK	24.1.72	185/80	DT	57.12	56.74 -93
Honoré	Caroline	FRA	29.4.70	171/56	TJ	13.54	13.65 -93
Hopfer	Heike	GER	28.2.71	179/87	SP	18.12	18.13 -91
Houseman	Debbie	RSA	11.6.67		400h	57.22	56.25 -91
Howard	Anita	USA	22.3.69	162/59	100	11.35w	11.14 -89
					200	23.38w	22.85 -89
					400	52.61	51.01 -92

Name		Nat	Born	Ht/Wt	Event	1994 Mark	Pre-1994 Best
Howell	Sarah	CAN	11.9.69	163/55	1500	4:12.44i	4:09.36 -93
Howland	Sue	AUS	4.9.60	180/80	JT	58.62	69.80 -86
Hsu	Pei-Ching	TPE	24.10.73	169/53	400h	55.75	57.93 -92
Hu	Honglian	CHN	.		DT	61.12	58.48 -93
Huang	Xiaoyan	CHN	23.2.69	167/55	100	11.40	11.31 -93
* Huang	Zhihong	CHN	7.5.65	174/100	SP	20.08	21.52 -90
Hudson	Nicole	USA	27.8.70	178/61	HJ	1.89i	1.86 -90
Hudson	Vickie	USA	17.10.71	165/	400h	57.76	58.08 -93
					LJ	6.47w	6.20w -92
* Hudson-Strudwick	Sheila	USA	30.6.67	160/58	LJ	6.52	6.73 -90
					TJ	14.23	14.23 -92
Hughes	Andrea	AUS	12.12.73	185/67	HJ	1.91	1.89 -93
Humphrey	Jackie	USA	30.9.65	163/60	100h	13.31	12.83 -88
Hurtlin	Cristine	FRA	29.9.67	176/66	100h	13.21w	12.83 -90
Hyacinth	Flora	ISV	30.3.66	172/62	LJ	6.50, 6.59w	6.71 -92
Hyatt	Kim	USA	11.12.68	170/73	JT	58.54	55.06 -93
* Hyche	Holli	USA	6.9.71	165/52	100	11.03	11.12, 10.93w, 10.9w -93
					200	22.41	22.34 -93
Iagar	Monica	ROM	1.4.73	187/62	HJ	1.91	1.78 -92, 1.87i -93
Idehen	Faith	NGR	5.2.73	163/	100	11.35	11.27 -93
Idowu	Oluyinka	GBR	25.2.72	178/65	LJ	6.73	6.73 -93
Igarashi	Miki	JPN	22.8.71	154/44	5k	15:23.36	15:27.47 -91
					10k	31:45.82	32:01.04 -91
Ignatyuk	Natalya	BLR	28.12.63		400h	56.74	55.28 -91
* Ilcu	Marieta	ROM	16.10.62	173/65	LJ	6.60i	7.08 -89
Ilyés	Ildiko	HUN	3.7.66	158/52	10kW	44:53	44:36 -92
Ilyina	Nadezhda	RUS	2.4.64	160/45	HMar	68:58	70:58 -92
* Ináncsi	Rita	HUN	6.1.71	190/70	LJ	6.78	6.62 -93
					Hep	6573	6263 -93
Ináncsi	Vera	HUN	21.7.75	185/69	JT	56.52	51.24 -93
Ingberg	Mikaela	FIN	29.7.74	173/69	JT	58.70	58.26 -93
* Inverarity	Alison	AUS	12.8.70	181/80	HJ	1.98	1.97i -93, 1.96 -92
Irving	Crystal	USA	26.5.70	175/65	400	52.32	51.71 -92
Isachenko	Galina	BLR	4.3.65	176/60	HJ	1.90	1.96 -92
* Isaila	Claudia	ROM	17.7.73	167/62	JT	66.56	63.04 -92
Itakura	Miki	JPN	1.8.75	158/44	10kW	44:53	45:16 -92
Itcou	Laura	ROM	13.2.72	171/54	800	2:01.28	2:01.39 -93
* Ivakina	Yekaterina	RUS	7.12.64	168/68	JT	64.04	65.36 -93
Ivankova	Olga	UKR	7.1.73	173/62	JT	58.52	56.66 -93
Ivanova	Alina	RUS	16.3.69	163/52	Mar	2:34:23	2:35:16 -93
* Ivanova	Olimpiada	RUS	5.5.70		5000W	20:56.10	21:39.3 -93
					10kW	42:30.31	45:15 -87
Ivanova	Tatyana	RUS	22.1.76		HJ	1.88	1.78 -93
Ivanova	Valentina	RUS	1.5.63		DT	60.76	63.16 -89
Ivanova	Yelena	RUS	23.1.71	173/67	HJ	1.91i, 1.88	1.89i, 1.88 -93
Jääskeläinen	Satu	FIN	4.4.70	165/52	800	2:01.94	2:01.77 -93
Jack	Vanessa	NZL	9.11.70		400h	57.89	58.52 -93
* Jacobs	Regina	USA	28.3.63	168/51	800	1:59.98	1:59.36 -87
					1500	4:02.15	4:00.46 -88
					Mile	4:27.78	4:29.40 -86
Jacobs	Simmone	GBR	5.9.66	155/51	100	11.47,11.37w	11.31 -88,11.26w -84
Jaklofsky	Sharon	NED	30.9.68	173/60	LJ	6.50, 6.60w	6.36 -90, 6.51w -92
					Hep	6068	6118w -89
Janke	Karin	GER	14.10.63	178/63	400	51.85	50.64 -90
Jardim	Lucrécia	POR	28.1.71	159/49	100	11.36w	11.39 -93
					200	23.15, 22.91w	23.09 -92
Javad	Alica	SVK?	26.6.69	183/64	HJ	1.88	1.86 -88
Javornik	Elena	SLO	26.3.66	163/50	Mar	2:34:50	2:37:27 -93
Javos	Aniko	HUN	14.1.71	169/59	3k	9:01.98	9:06.29 -90
					5k	15:40.37	0
Jayasinghe	Susanthika	SRI	17.12.75	160/54	200	23.16	24.56 -93
Jeanne-Chevallier	Isabelle	FRA	31.5.67	176/56	HJ	1.89	1.91 -91
Jeffrey	Vonetta	USA	29.10.73	170/64	LJ	6.62	6.34 -93
Jekabsone	Lana	LAT	16.10.74	175/50	400h	57.94	58.07 -93
* Jennings	Lynn	USA	1.7.60	165/51	3k	8:59.2	8:44.60, 8:40.45i -90
					5k	15:38.41	15:07.92 -90
Jeppesen	Jette	DEN	14.3.64	173/72	JT	64.90	62.30 -93
Jodo	Sahoko	JPN	11.6.72	162/50	400h	57.86	59.12 -93
Johansson	Charlotta	SWE	14.12.70	177/65	400	52.67	54.72 -91

Name		Nat	Born	Ht/Wt	Event	1994 Mark	Pre-1994 Best
Johansson	Frida	SWE	5.1.70	167/57	400h	56.09	55.36 -91
Johnson	Libbie	USA	17.2.65	168/52	3k	8:50.61	9:04.41 -93
Johnston	Kristy	USA	3.6.65	165/50	Mar	2:31:34	2:29:05 -93
Jones	Janeen	USA	19.8.72	170/52	400	51.47	52.35 -93
Jones	Jasmin	USA	13.10.69	170/57	800	2:01.77	2:00.24 -90
					1500	4:10.69	4:09.34 -92
Jones	Kim	USA	2.5.58	170/52	Mar	2:31:46	2:26:40 -91
Jones	Marion	USA	12.10.75	178/64	100	11.40	11.14 -92, 11.12w -91
					200	23.32	22.58 -92
					LJ	6.75	6.71, 6.75w -93
Jongmans	Stella	NED	17.5.71	174/59	800	2:00.68	1:58.61 -92
Joseph	Angela	TRI	14.10.65		400	52.73	52.40 -89
Joseph	Hermin	DMN	13.4.64	155/52	100	11.29	11.39, 11.13w, 11.1w -93
Joseph	Nadège	FRA	12.8.73	173/59	100h	13.14	13.21 -93
* Joyner-Kersee	Jackie	USA	3.3.62	178/68	100h	12.69	12.61 -92
					LJ	7.49	7.45 -87
					Hep	6606	7291 -88
Juárez	Isabel	MEX	10.9.66	155/43	5k	15:50.65	
Jung	Caren	GER	18.1.68	169/55	100h	12.98	13.05 -92
Kagiri	Margaret	KEN	.64		5k	15:28.03	15:27.39 -93
					10k	32:49.00	0
Kähler	Birgit	GER	14.8.70	180/60	HJ	1.90	1.94 -91
* Kaiser-Brown	Natasha	USA	14.5.67	175/59	400	50.38	50.17 -93
Kaledina	Yelena	RUS	18.5.66	175/64	1500	4:09.83	4:11.4 -93
					3k	8:56.43	8:55.42 -93
Kaliturina	Olga	RUS	9.3.76	180/60	HJ	1.89	1.86 -93
Kamioka	Yuka	JPN	28.5.75	154/47	10kW	46:38	45:18 -93
Kamrowska	Maria	POL	11.3.66	178/65	100h	13.32, 13.26w	12.86 -93
					Hep	6198	6279w -91
Kanana	Angelina	KEN	.65		5k	15:50.01	17:12.1 -91
					HMar	71:05	70:00 -93
					Mar	2:29:59	0
Kapernick	Gai	AUS	20.9.70	183/65	HJ	1.89	1.95 -91
Karasiewicz	Doreen	GER	21.7.74	178/78	JT	58.96	57.60 -93
Karczmarek	Agata	POL	29.11.63	172/62	LJ	6.89	6.97 -88
Kardash	Yelena	RUS	15.11.74		400h	57.56	59.10 -93
Karhoff	Andrea	GER	20.5.74	174/52	1500	4:12.98	4:32.11 -92
					3k	8:56.79	9:25.92 -93
Karlshøj	Gitte	DEN	14.5.59	171/56	5k	15:33.88	15:22.95 -93
					10k	32:26.25	32:29.24 -92
					Mar	2:31:57	0
Karpova	Lyubov	RUS	14.8.57	174/84	HT	61.68	61.80 -91
Kashapova	Klara	RUS	29.1.70	158/47	5k	15:27.55	0
					10k	31:55.99	0
					HMar	71:20	72:24 -93
Kashchey	Lyudmila	UKR	30.1.68	165/56	400	52.32	52.76 -89
* Kaspárková	Sárka	TCH	20.5.71	185/68	TJ	14.46i, 14.14	14.16 -93
Kataoka	Junko	JPN	13.6.70	158/45	3k	8:59.37	8:59.10 -93
					5k	15:26.14	15:27.76 -93
					10k	32:01.91	32:15.47 -93
					HMar	68:41	72:18 -92
* Katewicz	Renata	POL	2.5.65	180/95	SP	16.41	17.27 -87
					DT	65.72	66.18 -88
Kawaguchi	Noriko	JPN	24.4.69	154/41	Mar	2:28:08	2:35:45 -93
Kawakami	Yuko	JPN	1.8.75	152/45	5k	15:49.42	16:13.4 -93
Kayukova	Natalya	RUS	10.12.66	175/66	TJ	14.47	14.21i -92, 14.09 -91
Kazanina	Svetlana	KZK	31.10.71	174/56	Hep	5770	5758 -93
Kaznovskaya	Zoya	UKR	22.9.66	172/62	1500	4:09.1	4:08.8 -88
					3k	8:55.56	8:58.36 -93
Keeys	Omegia	USA	25.6.75		200	23.08	
Kelesidou	Anastasia	GRE	28.11.72	190/83	DT	60.50	57.44 -93
Kelly	Jennifer	GBR	20.6.70	167/73	Hep	5826	5765 -90
* Keszeg	Margareta	ROM	31.8.65	165/51	3k	8:55.61i	8:39.94 -92
Khersontseva	Tatyana	RUS	25.5.73		JT	56.86	51.84 -92
* Khlopotnova	Yelena	UKR	4.8.63	172/64	LJ	7.03	7.31 -85
Khlusovich	Yelena	UKR	31.5.72	175/58	TJ	13.82	13.20 -93
Khodasevich	Lyudmila	UKR	7.4.59	170/59	400h	56.01	55.99 -90
Khramova	Tatyana	BLR	1.2.70	178/58	HJ	1.90	1.95 -93
Khreskina	Oksana	RUS	21.6.72		100	11.0	11.75 -93
					200	23.3	23.67 -92

Name		Nat	Born	Ht/Wt	Event	1994 Mark	Pre-1994 Best
Khristova	Yurka	BUL	19.1.68	171/64	Hep	5710	6028 -93
Khropach	Iolanta	UKR	22.9.74	168/55	LJ	6.60	6.46 -93
Khrushchelyova	Natalya	RUS	20.5.73	172/55	200	23.28	
					400	51.73	53.56 -92
Khudorozhkina	Irina	RUS	13.10.68	182/98	SP	19.81	19.16 -93
Kielan	Iwona	POL	5.7.66	184/58	HJ	1.91	1.93 -91
Kiessling	Ellen	GER	17.2.68	163/48	1500	4:07.83	4:04.44 -89
Kim	Jung-min	KOR	19.2.73	178/120	SP	16.35	15.33 -91
* Kimaiyo	Helen	KEN	8.9.68	163/50	3k	8:59.19	8:55.05 -92
					5k	15:52.04	15:19.20 -92
					10k	32:16.72	31:38.91 -92
					HMar	72:02	72:15 -93
Kimura	Yasuko	JPN	6.1.76	163/47	5k	15:19.4	
					10k	32:29.17	
King	Chris	NZL	29.8.64		SP	16.27	16.00 -93
Kirby	Rachel	GBR	18.5.69	172/58	TJ	13.64	13.60 -93, 13.64w -91
* Kirchmann	Sigrid	AUT	29.3.66	181/63	HJ	1.96i, 1.93	1.97 -93
					Hep	5745	5944 -85
Kirkland	Anjanette	USA	24.2.74	173/66	100h	13.22, 13.1w	13.49 -93
Kirui	Catherine	KEN	1.3.76		5k	15:51.27	
Kisabaka	Linda	GER	9.4.69	166/51	400	52.67	52.01 -92
Kiselyova	Yelena	RUS	.73		10kW	46:15	46:25 -93
Kiyomiya	Yukiko	JPN	4.3.69	153/43	10k	32:57.85	33:01.57 -93
Kjellman	Carina	FIN	3.9.63	172/57	TJ	13.54	13.40 -91
Kleinert	Nadine	GER	20.10.75	190/78	SP	17.44	17.07 -92
Klimovets	Natalya	BLR	22.5.74		TJ	13.74	13.65 -93
Klochikhina	Yelena	RUS	20.4.76		SP	16.31	14.45 -93
* Knoll	Silke-Beate	GER	21.2.67	163/52	100	11.39	11.17 -92
					200	22.55	22.29 -92
					400	51.90	52.06 -90
* Knoroz	Anna	RUS	30.7.70	163/54	400h	54.11	54.42 -93
Knut	Silke	GER	27.7.72	168/53	Hep	5635	5685 -93
Koba	Tamara	UKR	24.2.57	165/53	10k	32:47.10	32:34.95 -92
Kobrin	Nadezhda	UKR	21.1.72	166/63	JT	57.96	56.64 -93
Koens	Grete	NED	26.5.67	182/63	1500	4:10.73	4:13.16 -93
					3k	8:53.01	9:01.0 -93
					5k	15:52.82	0
Koffa	Katerina	GRE	10.4.69	177/63	100	11.46	11.60 -92
Koch	Kathrin	GER	23.4.68	183/88	SP	17.11i, 16.69	17.53 -92
					DT	55.78	59.04 -93
Koivula	Heli	FIN	27.6.75	173/58	LJ	6.64w	6.42 -92
Kolovanova	Natalya	UKR	1.8.64	175/62	100h	13.20	12.81 -92
Komatsu	Yukari	JPN	13.2.74	163/44	HMar	72:21	76:11 -93
Kong	Yan	CHN	5.4.71	161/46	5000W	21:23.20	44:30.4 -89
					10kW	43:02.3	43:28 -93
Konchits	Yelena	BLR	6.7.69		800	2:02.5	2:01.8 -93
Konstantinova	Tatyana	RUS	.70		HT	59.50	57.42 -90
Köpernick	Daniela	GER	25.7.73	168/59	PV	3.90	3.80 -92
Korchagina	Yelena	RUS	.69		HMar	72:15	
Korosak ¶	Hedvika	SLO	24.5.70	168/58	TJ	13.48 dq, 13.38w	12.98 -93
Korotayeva	Irina	RUS	27.7.74		SP	16.27	15.50 -93
* Korotkevich	Larisa	RUS	3.1.67	180/88	DT	62.08	71.30 -92
Korzhanyenko	Irina	RUS	16.5.74		SP	18.36	17.92i, 17.02 -93
Kosgei	Selina	KEN	17.6.76		800	2:03.0	2:04.4 -93
Koshelyeva	Anna	RUS	12.8.68		200	22.74	23.25 -93
* Kostadinova	Stefka	BUL	25.3.65	180/60	HJ	2.00i, 1.96	2.09 -87
Kostovalová	Nadezda	TCH	10.9.71	167/60	400	52.75	52.69 -93
Kostyuchenkova	Irina	UKR	11.5.61	171/72	JT	60.94	67.00 -88
Kotelnikova	Tatyana	UZB	23.8.75		200	23.2	
Kováciková	Zuzana	TCH	16.4.73	178/60	HJ	1.94	1.89 -93
* Kovacs #	Ella	ROM	11.12.64	167/55	800	1:59.43i, 2:00.52dq	1:55.68 -85
Kovacs	Kati	GER	7.9.73	173/55	800	2:00.80	2:04.08 -93
Kovalenko	Tamara	RUS	5.6.64		5000W	21:25.62	21:04 -88
					10kW	42:50	42:46 -92
Kovalyova	Yelena	RUS	28.2.73	173/61	Hep	5841	5675 -93
Kovpotina	Olga	RUS	10.1.68		3k	8:56.40	8:56.15i -93, 9:09.65 -91
Kovrizhkina	Nina	UKR	5.2.65	164/54	10k	32:54.20	33:53.56 -93
Kozhomina	Vera	RUS	.70		10kW	46:27	44:21 -91
Kozuma	Tomomi	JPN	4.2.77	158/45	5k	15:52.2	16:12.7 -93

Name		Nat	Born	Ht/Wt	Event	1994 Mark	Pre-1994 Best
Krasnoslobodskaya	Alla	RUS	20.10.70		800	2:00.8	2:02.01 -93
Krause	Ines	GER	10.7.65	177/64	Hep	6117	6660 -88
Krauss	Edith	GER	1.7.64		SP	16.55	16.59 -90
* Kravets	Inessa	UKR	5.10.66	178/60	LJ	7.09	7.37 -92
					TJ	14.91	14.95 -91
					1500	4:01.05	3:58.71 -92
					Mile	4:27.56	4:22.46 -93
Kreutel	Ursula	GER	14.9.65	174/83	DT	60.16	65.32 -90
Krieg-Ruprecht	Elisabeth	SUI	14.3.61	173/53	Mar	2:33:01	2:37:33 -93
Krolik	Sonja	GER	24.2.73		Mar	2:31:35	2:38:02 -93
Kubota	Yuko	JPN	5.10.74	157/44	5k	15:42.67	15:52.02 -93
					10k	32:49.86	0
Kuehl	Kris	USA	30.7.70	183/90	SP	16.57	14.71 -93
					DT	59.54	60.16 -93
Kuenen	Monique	NED	9.4.71		DT	55.66	53.58 -93
Kuchinskaya	Larisa	BLR	9.2.74		LJ	6.80	
Kulawansa	Sriyani	SRI	1.3.70	168/53	100h	13.25	13.38 -93
Kulikova	Natalya	RUS	9.8.74		Hep	5844	5462 -93
Kulikova	Yekaterina	RUS	7.11.68		400	52.34	54.01 -93
* Kumbernuss	Astrid	GER	5.2.70	186/90	SP	20.06	20.77 -90
Kuprianovich	Tamara	BLR	26.9.64	182/67	400	52.48	51.76 -91
					800	2:00.84	2:00.63 -93
Kurochkina	Tatyana	BLR	15.9.67	174/62	400h	55.18	54.39 -88
* Kuzenkova	Olga	RUS	4.10.70		HT	66.84	65.40 -92
Kuzina	Natalya	RUS	19.7.70		TJ	14.10	13.16 -91, 13.31w -92
Kuznyetsova	Irina	RUS	.75		HT	56.04	52.90 -93
Kuznyetsova	Olga	RUS	23.10.67		800	2:01.53	2:01.19 -92
					1500	4:12.87i, 4:13.91	4:13.42 -92
Kuznyetsova	Yana	RUS	.72		LJ	6.57i	6.44i -93, 6.40 -90
Laayouni	Zoubida	MAR	5.2.56		DT	56.94	55.14 -90
Lah	Barbara	ITA	24.3.72	180/60	TJ	13.84	13.38, 13.50w -93
Lahoz	Esther	ESP	2.5.63	175/57	400h	57.66	58.32 -89
LaMena-Coll	Laura	USA	10.10.66	163/50	5k	15:52.20	16:08.06 -90
Landre	Francine	FRA	26.7.70	164/50	400	51.21	51.92 -93
Langenhuizen	Ine	NED	27.10.68	176/72	100h	13.25w	13.28 -93
Langford	Lisa	GBR	15.3.67	175/57	10kW	46:01	45:42 -87
Langley	Beverley	JAM	16.12.76	152/50	100	11.1	11.89, 11.0w -93
Lapa	Larisa	UKR	9.4.72	176/92	SP	16.40	16.34 -93
Lapierre	Violetta	FRA	15.10.63	164/53	100	11.42w	11.55 -87, 11.43w -93
Larsen	Ingvild	NOR	3.10.75	179/65	LJ	6.45w	6.32 -92, 6.53w -93
Larsson	Annika	SWE	10.7.70		DT	56.16	53.92 -92
Lasota	Elzbieta	POL	19.11.70	178/63	Hep	5683	5426 -93
* Lasovskaya	Inna	RUS	17.12.69	177/67	TJ	14.94	14.70 -93
Laukhova	Svetlana	RUS	7.5.73	168/56	100h	13.04, 12.91w	13.39 -93
* Lauren	Jana	GER	28.6.70	183/82	DT	62.70	66.30 -89
Laux	Petra	GER	24.1.67	180/66	TJ	14.10	13.77 -93
* Laza	Belsy	CUB	5.6.67	174/96	SP	19.07	20.96 -92
Le Roux	Esmari	RSA	27.1.76		200	23.19	24.27, 24.16w -93
Lebedyenko	Yelena	RUS	.71		Hep	5963	5703 -90
Lebedyeva	Tatyana	RUS	21.7.76		LJ	6.65	6.17 -93
					TJ	13.69	13.13i, 12.94 -93
Leddin	Sandy	GER	1.11.70	166/54	10kW	46:06	46:42 -93
Lee	Myong-sun	KOR	12.2.76	167/81	SP	16.95	16.08 -93
Lee	Suzette	JAM	6.3.75	180/70	TJ	13.46	13.04 -93
Lee	Tonya	USA	6.11.69	170/56	400h	57.04	55.78 -91
Lee	Young-suk	KOR	16.12.65	164/60	100	11.39w	11.77 -91
Lee	Young-sun	KOR	21.2.74	165/65	JT	62.30	63.32 -92
Lefébvre	Nathalie	FRA	2.9.71	183/61	HJ	1.88	1.90 -93
Leftridge	Dianna	USA	.		LJ	6.48w	
Legault	Liz	USA	4.5.70	170/77	HT	56.82	53.58 -93
Lemettinen	Ritva	FIN	9.9.60	171/53	HMar	71:06	72:58 -93
					Mar	2:29:16	2:33:18 -93
Leng	Xueyan	CHN	14.2.72	175/60	400h	55.26	54.52 -93
Leonenko	Olga	UKR	13.2.70	169/55	5000W	22:02.2	21:38.86 -92
					10kW	44:39	44:18 -92
Leroy-Gallardo	Muriel	FRA	7.7.68	170/55	200	23.21w	23.19 -88
					LJ	6.47	6.38 -91
Lesage	Odile	FRA	28.6.69	178/65	Hep	6083	6141 -92
* Leseva	Svetlana	BUL	18.3.67	176/60	HJ	1.94i, 1.93	2.00 -87

Name		Nat	Born	Ht/Wt	Event	1994 Mark	Pre-1994 Best
Leshcheva	Yekaterina	RUS	21.4.74	176/68	100	11.21, 11.2	11.55 -93
					200	22.83	23.25 -93
Letherby	Teresa	AUS	5.4.72		10kW	46:31	46:41 -93
* Letko	Anne Marie	USA	7.3.69	168/48	5k	15:43.37	15:54.31 -93
					10k	32:41.67	31:37.26 -93
					HMar	70:03	
					Mar	2:30:19	0
Levenets	Oksana	UKR	6.6.72	160/69	100	11.47	11.5 -92
Lévêque	Nicole	FRA	27.1.51	156/45	5k	15:51.7	17:25.62 -93
					10k	32:12.07	35:10.4 -93
					HMar	71:35	
Lever	Alison	AUS	13.10.72		DT	57.40	55.22 -93
Lewis	Denise	GBR	27.8.72	173/64	LJ	6.56	6.25, 6.30w -93
					Hep	6325	5812 -92
* Li	Chunxiu	CHN	13.8.69	171/63	10kW	43:00.3	42:47.6 -92
Li	Jing	CHN	10.7.69	170/56	LJ	6.88	6.77 -92
					TJ	13.98	13.97 -90
Li	Jingxue	CHN	10.2.70		10kW	43:40.3	43:48 -89
Li	Lei	CHN	.73		JT	63.44	54.80 -92
Li	Na	CHN	.		10kW	45:04.3	
Li	Qiumei	CHN	.9.74		DT	67.50	58.90 -93
Li	Xiaoyun	CHN	10.7.71	179/87	SP	17.07	18.17 -93
Li	Xiumei	CHN	1.1.68		400h	56.56	56.46 -92
Li	Yajun	CHN	21.7.77		400	52.62	
Li	Yemei	CHN	1.2.71		Mar	2:32:01	2:30:36 -93
Lightfoot -O'Connell	Lisa	AUS	3.12.66		800	2:02.1	2:04.64 -93
Lichtenhagen	Silke	GER	20.11.73	174/54	200	22.73	23.54 -92, 23.33w -93
Liland	Hanne	NOR	7.8.69	179/66	10kW	46:12, 46:38.6	
Lindemann	Angelika	GER	5.9.71		HT	56.10	51.34 -93
Lindfors	Kirsi	FIN	9.12.75	179/90	DT	55.24	54.18 -93
Lipsnis	Yelena	RUS	20.3.68		3k	8:55.58i	
Lise	Betty	FRA	5.9.72	187/70	TJ	13.92	13.22 -92
Lishchuk	Tatyana	UKR	13.1.73	164/72	HT	56.52	53.10 -93
Liu	Bo	CHN	12.3.72		Hep	6095	6205 -93
Liu	Cui	CHN	7.8.71		JT	64.26	60.45 -90
Liu	Hongyu	CHN	1.12.75	158/54	5000W	21:37.0	21:55 -93
					10kW	42:47	43:49.5 -93
Liu	Jianying	CHN	19.11.71		3k	8:51.96	8:52.7 -91
Liu	Jingmin	CHN	1.2.72	169/48	TJ	14.06	14.03 -93
* Liu	Li	CHN	15.3.71	167/55	800	1:59.95	1:56.96 -93
Liu ¶	Wanjie	CHN	27.11.75		800	2:01.44	2:01.36 -93
Liu	Weiwei	CHN	11.5.71		400	52.55	51.53 -93
Liu	Xiaomei	CHN	11.1.72	168/57	100	11.27, 11.23w	11.02 -93
					200	23.18	22.70 -93
Lloyd	Andria	JAM	10.8.71	170/	200	23.21, 23.07w	23.35 -91, 23.19w -90
Loboyko	Nadezhda	RUS	7.9.61	165/54	800	2:01.80	1:56.64 -90
Lock	Michelle	AUS	29.3.67		400	52.17	50.78 -92
Locuty	Fabienne	FRA	6.3.68	171/84	SP	16.32	15.93i, 15.90 -93
Loginova	Olga	RUS	18.12.69		Mar	2:33:00	2:35:25 -93
Lohann	Alta	RSA	9.3.68		1500	4:11.92	4:28.09 -93
					3k	9:01.92	9:20.68 -93
Lokar	Claudia	GER	9.2.64	160/47	3k	8:58.38	8:51.35 -93
					5k	15:16.92	15:16.16 -93
					10k	32:08.74	32:05.33 -93
					HMar	71:31	
					Mar	2:31:47	0
Look-Jaeger	Clare	USA	17.6.66	174/64	HJ	1.89	1.87 -93
					Hep	5746	5670 -93
* López	Aliuska	CUB	29.8.69	169/53	100h	12.74	12.73 -90
* López	Isel	CUB	11.7.70	174/76	JT	62.74	66.18 -90
* Lorupe	Tecla	KEN	5.5.71	156/48	5k	15:22.54	15:08.03-
					10k	31:52.39	31:21.20 -93
					HMar	69:27	70:12 -93
					Mar	2:27:37	0
Lu	Ou	CHN	10.4.74	170/60	3k	8:58.68	8:19.78 -93
Lu	Xifang	CHN	16.12.73		400	51.75	52.66 -93
Luan	Zhili	CHN	6.1.73		DT	60.98	64.62 -93
Lukyniv	Nadezhda	UKR	14.5.68	180/105	SP	17.68i, 17.02	18.01-78

Name		Nat	Born	Ht/Wt	Event	1994 Mark	Pre-1994 Best
Lundahl	Karoliina	FIN	30.6.68	172/81	SP	17.93	16.76 -93
Lungu	Irina	ROM	5.4.75	165/69	HT	57.80	54.32 -93
Luo	Bin	CHN	7.1.70	166/49	100h	12.99	12.97 -90
Luo	Jun	CHN	.75		TJ	13.33	
Lupton	Vicky	GBR	17.4.72	160/57	10kW	45:48	45:28 -93
Lüthi	Kathrin	SUI	7.10.69	175/59	400h	57.34	57.69 -93
Lyakhova	Yulia	RUS	.77		HJ	1.90	
Lynes	Maggie	GBR	19.2.63	167/76	SP	16.57	16.55 -89
* Lysak ¶	Yelena	RUS	19.10.75	175/55	LJ	6.45, 6.72w	6.40 -93
					TJ	14.32, 14.43w	13.86 -93
Ma	Chun-ping	TPE	3.8.71	176/62	Hep	5786	5636 -93
Ma	Ningning	CHN	20.9.76	159/51	3k	8:50.62	8:36.45 -93
					Mar	2:32:30	0
* Ma	Yuqin	CHN	10.9.72	165/57	400	50.45	19.81 -93
Macleod	Karen	GBR	24.4.58	168/50	Mar	2:33:16	2:34:30 -93
Maddox	Keri	GBR	4.7.72	170/62	100h	13.24	13.24, 13.20w -93
Madubuko	Nkechi	GER	28.3.72	173/62	TJ	13.88	13.22, 13.53w -93
Maffeis	Agnese	ITA	9.3.65	187/81	SP	17.58i	17.73i -93, 17.56 -92
					DT	60.66	62.54 -93
Magome	Aiko	JPN	13.11.72	159/47	Mar	2:32:02	
Mahob	Anastasia	FRA	28.7.72		LJ	6.52, 6.64w	
Machado	Albertina	POR	25.12.61	167/56	Mar	2:34:15	0
Machado	Elizabeth	CUB	2.1.78		TJ	13.30	12.82 -93
* Machado	Manuela	POR	9.8.63	161/52	10k	32:09.1	32:24.07 -91
					HMar	71:48	73:27 -93
					Mar	2:29:54	2:27:42 -92
Machado	Teresa	POR	22.7.69	170/80	SP	16.74	16.76 -93
					DT	62.00	63.70 -93
Machuca	Eva	MEX	14.1.70	154/45	10kW	44:59.5	44:53 -93
Mai	Christina	GER	3.9.61	159/46	3k	8:57.49i	8:54.16 -91
Majchrzak	Katarzyna	POL	25.6.67	186/67	HJ	1.90	1.92 -92
Makarova	Rimma	RUS	18.7.63	168/62	5000W	21:41.2	21:32.70i -93, 21:46 -89
					10kW	45:53.39	43:54 -93
Makhmutova	Anna	RUS	.69		JT	58.18	62.68 -91
Maki	Izumi	JPN	10.12.68	161/43	10k	32:41.89	31:40.30 -92
					HMar	70:21	72:38 -93
Malakhova	Olga	UKR	25.8.71	174/76	HT	58.92	54.84 -93
Malátová ¶	Vladimira	TCH	15.5.67	178/79	DT	63.66dq	63.92 -93
Malcolm	Twilet	JAM	5.2.69	163/60	100	11.45, 11.39w	11.40, 11.17w -93
* Malchugina	Galina	RUS	17.12.62	168/62	100	11.42	10.96 -92, 10.8 -88
					200	22.29	22.22 -92
Maloletnyeva	Vera	RUS	6.1.66	176/61	LJ	6.57i	6.46i, 6.52w -92
* Malone	Maicel	USA	12.6.69	176/61	200	23.19	22.91 -91
					400	50.05	50.33 -92
Manjani	Mirela	ALB	21.12.76		JT	57.20	54.86 -93
Manning	Anne	AUS	13.11.59		5000W	21:25.6	21:55.5 -93
					10kW	44:37	46:15.6 -93
Maranga	Jackline	KEN	16.12.77	155/47	1500	4:12.84	4:08.79 -92
Mardomingo	Maria José	ESP	27.1.69	165/56	100h	13.23	13.19 -91
Marinova	Tereza	BUL	25.9.77		TJ	13.51w	12.18 -93
* Markova	Olga	RUS	6.8.68	163/47	Mar	2:32:22	2:23:43 -92
Marques	Fernanda	POR	15.4.66	163/50	10k	31:53.12	32:10.57 -91
Marquette	Ulla	CAN	28.6.58		10k	32:48.24	32:55.02 -91
Märtensson	Linda-Marie	SWE	22.6.71	185/81	SP	17.14	16.27 -93
Marti	Debbie	GBR	14.5.68	171/53	HJ	1.91	1.94i -91, 1.93 -92
Martial	Nicola	GUY	.74		TJ	13.71	12.94 -93
* Martin-Floreal	LaVonna	USA	18.11.66	170/66	100h	12.86	12.69 -92
Martinelli	Liliana	ARG	20.5.70	172/99	DT	57.70	55.04 -93
Martínez	Francesca	MEX	4.10.66	157/52	10kW	46:28	46:08 -90
Martínez	Madelin	CUB	10.2.76		TJ	13.60	13.07 -93
Maruseva	Margarita	RUS	18.10.67	170/60	1500	4:12.27	4:17.81i -93
					3k	9:00.82	8:52.16 -93
					5k	15:56.72	16:01.72 -93
Marvin	Keisha	USA	19.2.71	173/61	400h	56.62	58.34 -93
Marxer	Manuela	LIE	6.8.65	172/60	Hep	6093	5924 -92
Maryina	Olga	RUS	.64		800	2:02.67	2:01.26 -92
Matejková	Alice	TCH	11.1.69	180/74	SP	16.33i	15.94 -93
					DT	61.12	60.52 -93
Mathes	Simone	GER	13.3.75	171/75	HT	59.02	55.42 -93

Name		Nat	Born	Ht/Wt	Event	1994 Mark	Pre-1994 Best
Mattes	Tracy	USA	13.12.68	172/54	400h	57.21	56.35 -92
Matthijs	Anneke	BEL	8.3.69	172/59	800	2:00.73	2:02.14 -92
Matusevicienė ¶	Dalia	LIT	7.1.61	167/52	400	52.3	51.12 -84
					800	2:00.94	1:56.7 -88
Matveyeva	Larisa	RUS	7.3.71	179/53	5000W	21:52.5	22:10 -92
Matyashova	Tatyana	RUS	2.8.73	182/62	TJ	13.89	13.85 -91
Matyusheva	Irina	UKR	5.6.65	179/62	100h	13.29w	13.20 -88
					HJ	1.90	1.90 -85
					Hep	6207	6424 -88
Mau-Repnak	Beatrice	GER	20.2.71	174/66	Hep	6349	6267 -92
Maury	Maryse	FRA	4.9.64	178/61	HJ	1.91	1.96 -85
* May	Fiona	ITA	12.12.69	181/60	LJ	6.95 7.00w	6.88 -90, 6.98w -89
Mayal	Janete	BRA	19.7.63	163/48	HMar	72:14	70:46 -92
					Mar	2:34:21	2:31:27 -91
Mayhew	Donna	USA	20.6.60	162/68	JT	61.50	63.66 -88
McCaffrey	Janice	CAN	20.10.59	163/47	10kW	44:54	45:06 -92
McCandless	Katy	USA	22.6.70	173/52	3k	8:59.30	8:56.00 -93
					5k	15:35.81	15:34.93 -93
McCann	Kerryn	AUS	2.5.67		10k	32:53.61	33:05.60 -93
					Mar	2:34:08	2:40:09 -93
McDonald	Beverly	JAM	15.2.70	165/59	100	11.47	11.22 -93, 11.2 -87
					200	23.02w	22.67 -93
McGeorge	Sonia	GBR	2.11.64	170/53	1500	4:12.20	4:10.75 -90
					3k	8:51.55	8:51.33 -90
McKenzie	Kim	USA	21.3.61	165/58	100h	13.32, 12.9w	12.77 -92
McKernan	Jackie	GBR	1.7.65	178/73	DT	58.56	60.72 -93
* McKiernan	Catherina	IRL	30.11.69	165/48	3k	8:51.67	8:51.33 -92
					5k	15:09.10	0
					10k	31:19.11	32:14.74 -93
McLeod	Geraldine	GBR	24.9.71	170/57	100	11.2	11.58, 11.46w -93
					200	23.47	23.88 -92, 23.4 -93
McLeon	Nancy	CUB	1.5.71	167/55	400	51.00	52.15, 51.5 -93
McNeair	Jamie	USA	26.6.69	170/59	100h	13.13	13.20 -91
					Hep	6323	6016 -90
* McPaul	Louise	AUS	24.1.69	173/64	JT	65.32	63.34 -91
McPherson	Vikki	GBR	1.6.71	167/54	10k	33:02.74	32:32.42 -93
* Meagher	Robyn	CAN	17.6.67	168/54	1500	4:09.12	4:06.0 -92
					3k	8:45.59	8:43.71 -92
Medvedyeva	Yelena	RUS	9.7.65	160/57	JT	59.50	65.68 -95
Mehes	Livia	ROM	6.3.65	174/90	SP	18.32i, 17.24	19.61 -86
					HT	58.36	57.96 -93
Meinseth	Sølvi	NOR	27.3.67	170/62	400	52.49	52.45 -91
* Meissner	Heike	GER	29.1.70	172/57	400	52.36	52.46 -92
					400h	54.52	54.64 -93
Mekhanoshina	Natalya	RUS	10.8.72	174/58	PV	3.80	0
Melendez	Joyce	PUR	7.4.70	165/48	100h	13.34	13.22, 13.20w -93
* Melinte	Mihaela	ROM	27.3.75	174/81	HT	65.48	62.52 -93
Melnikova I	Irina	RUS	19.1.74	170/57	TJ	13.68	13.68 -90
Melnikova II	Irina	RUS	14.5.75		TJ	13.78	13.12 -93
Mencik	Barbara	FRA	22.12.70	174/57	HJ	1.88i	1.90i -90, 1.90 -91
* Mendes	Luciana	BRA	26.7.71	170/55	400	52.55	52.36 -93
					800	1:58.27	2:00.37 -93
Mendoza	Graciela	MEX	22.3.63	158/48	10kW	45:23	44:03 -91
Mensah	Philomina	GHA	11.5.75		100	11.39	11.58, 11.3 -93
* Merry	Katharine	GBR	21.9.74	170/52	100	11.34, 11.27w	11.52 -92, 11.40w -93
					200	22.85	23.20 -93
Merzlyakova	Natalya	RUS	.65		100	11.38	11.43 -88
Metzner	Claudia	GER	5.5.66	173/51	5k	15:50.29	15:54.3 -93
					10k	32:29.86	32:30.8 -92
					HMar	72:25	71:19 -93
Meulemeester	Greet	BEL	5.9.69		SP	16.78i	16.10 -92
* Meyer	Elana	RSA	10.10.66	158/45	3k	9:02.43	8:32.00 -91
					5k	15:25.59	14:44.15 -92
					10k	30:52.51	30:52.51 -93
					HMar	68:36	67:22 -93
					Mar	2:25:15	0
Meyer	Marion	GER	9.7.75		PV	3.70i	3.60 -93
Mihalcea	Gabriela	ROM	27.1.64	174/63	PV	3.96i, 3.89	3.70 -93
Michailova	Inga	LIT	6.3.66	177/57	Hep	5656	6200 -92

Name		Nat	Born	Ht/Wt	Event	1994 Mark	Pre-1994 Best
Mihailova	Milka	BUL	23.5.72	163/48	3k	9:02.74	9:07.10 -93
					5k	15:41.47	0
					10k	32:55.73	0
Mikelyté	Austra	LIT	5.5.69	185/92	DT	63.30	64.14 -91
Mikhailova	Larisa	RUS	.69		800	2:02.54	
					1500	4:13.90	
Mikhailova	Lyudmila	RUS	12.4.69	174/62	100h	13.37	13.52 -93
					LJ	6.51	6.83 -93
					Hep	6155	6308 -93
Mikhailova	Svetlana	KZK	18.1.74		Hep	5710	5369 -93
Mikhalchenko	Irina	UKR	20.1.72	174/58	HJ	1.96i, 1.95	1.93 -92
* Miles	Jearl	USA	4.9.66	170/59	200	23.24	23.29, 23.19w -93
					400	50.11	19.82 -93
Miller	Inger	USA	12.6.72	163/55	100	11.32, 10.99w	11.11 -93, 11.09w -92
					200	22.73, 22.47w	22.33 -93
					400	52.76	0
Milo	Linda	BEL	9.7.60		Mar	2:33:12	2:34:12 -93
Milousheva	Eleonora	BUL	8.4.73	174/54	HJ	1.91	1.91 -92
Milusauskaité	Sonata	LIT	31.8.73	163/51	10kW	45:29	45:50 -93
* Min	Chunfeng	CHN	17.3.69	175/82	DT	66.26	66.76 -91
Mironova	Anna	RUS	15.10.75		LJ	6.48w	6.42 -93
Miroshnik	Svetlana	UKR	3.6.68	162/52	800	2:01.7	2:02.56 -93
					1500	4:07.2	4:09.45 -93
Misaros	Cristina	ROM	1.1.69	173/59	1500	4:13.30	4:06.85 -87
					3k	8:49.69	9:02.61 -92
					5k	15:43.10	0
					10k	31:41.03	0
* Misyulya	Natalya	BLR	12.2.66	157/47	10kW	43:29	43:15 -93
Mitchell	Danyel	USA	16.9.72	178/93	SP	17.03i, 16.62	16.91i, 16.49 -93
					DT	59.24	57.04 -93
Mitchell	Nicole	JAM	5.6.74	168/60	100	11.45	11.18, 11.02w -93, 11.1 -92
Mitchell	Paulette	USA	2.12.72	178/86	SP	16.74	16.24 -92
Mitchell	Vicki	USA	6.12.69	176/52	5k	15:54.23	16:16.2 -91
					10k	33:01.02	33:09.70 -93
* Mitkova	Svetla	BUL	17.6.64	178/97	SP	19.74	20.91 -87
					DT	59.78	69.42 -87
Mitsuhata	Sanae	JPN	17.6.74	152/39	5k	15:56.6	
Mitsukawa	Ai	JPN	2.12.74	152/39	5k	15:42.5	
					10k	32:43.92	33:39.29 -91
Mitsumori	Rie	JPN	26.10.74	158/45	10kW	45:36	45:48 -93
Mitsumori	Yuka	JPN	8.1.72	160/45	10kW	45:39	45:05 -93
Miyajima	Akiko	JPN	17.9.66	162/59	JT	59.34	59.48 -91
Mizera	Yelena	RUS	20.2.66	162/56	200	22.89	22.49 -90
Modahl ¶	Diane	GBR	17.6.66	170/56	800	1:59.85dq, 2:01.13	1:58.65 -90
Molloy	Aisling	IRL	12.6.64	170/51	800	2:02.83	2:01.14 -90
Molzan	Ramona	GER	1.8.71	168/54	TJ	13.96	13.19 -92, 13.43w -93
Mondie-Milner	Celena	USA	6.8.68	169/57	200	23.29	22.66 -90
* Montalvo	Niurka	CUB	4.6.68	170/53	LJ	6.71, 6.78w	6.88 -92
					TJ	14.60	14.51 -93
Montelier	Lency	CUB	13.2.71	163/55	400h	56.14	56.79 -92
Montgomery	Carole	CAN	9.12.66		10k	32:26.78	33:58.84 -92
Morales	Surella	CUB	.63		400	52.37	53.06 -93
Morandini	Nadia	ITA	12.12.73	168/49	TJ	13.77	12.98 -92
Moreira	Amélia	BRA	30.7.65	175/70	DT	56.72	55.74 -93
Morgan	Avis	JAM	.		400	52.27	53.89 -93
Morigaki	Tomoko	JPN	4.9.76	156/39	5k	15:46.5	16:07.3 -93
Morigami	Mayumi	JPN	12.1.69	162/47	5k	15:51.89	16:07.9 -93
Morioka	Yoko	JPN	17.7.68	168/54	TJ	13.36w	13.15, 13.24w -93
Moros	Helen	NZL	2.11.67	165/48	10k	32:34.46	32:32.24 -93
Morrison	Melissa	USA	9.7.71	163/50	100h	13.24	13.24, 13.2 -93
Moser	Franziska	SUI	17.8.66	175/50	HMar	71:38	73:13 -92
					Mar	2:27:44	2:33:09 -92
* Moskalets	Svetlana	RUS	22.1.69	172/62	100h	13.20	13.40 -93
					LJ	6.82	6.77 -93
					Hep	6598	6510 -93
Mota	Rosa	POR	29.6.58	157/45	HMar	71:11	69:33 -90
Motkova	Tatyana	RUS	26.10.68		HJ	1.96	1.92 -93
Mou	Lianjuan	CHN	23.9.73	180/70	Hep	6138	6154 -93
Moyes	Jayne	AUS	25.1.66		100h	13.32, 13.0w	13.34 -93, 13.1w -92

Name		Nat	Born	Ht/Wt	Event	1994 Mark	Pre-1994 Best
Mu	Lan	CHN	.		10kW	45:10.5	
Mues	Claudia	GER	3.1.75	192/77	SP	17.22i, 17.11	16.66 -93
Muldoon	Wendy	AUS	27.5.71		10kW	46:10	47:20 -93
Muller	Andrea	GER	29.6.74	164/57	PV	4.00i, 3.96	3.60 -93
Munerotto	Rosanna	ITA	3.12.62	169/53	5k	15:53.99	15:36.62 -93
					HMar	71:29	69:38 -92
					Mar	2:34:32	2:29:34 -92
Münchow	Kirsten	GER	21.1.77		HT	57.62	50.96 -93
Munkova	Svetlana	UZB	23.5.65	175/59	HJ	1.92	1.94 -88
Muranaka	Mahomi	JPN	31.10.66	162/45	3k	8:56.94	9:02.04 -90
					5k	15:49.24	15:31.01 -93
					10k	32:08.51	32:19.85 -93
					HMar	72:08	
Murcia	Rosario	FRA	23.9.64	158/46	10k	32:31.4	31:42.83 -92
					HMar	71:49	72:54 -93
Murden	Trina	USA	17.12.69		100h	13.37	13.47 -91
Murgoci	Elena	ROM	20.5.60	165/50	10k	32:51.33	32:08.60-
					HMar	72:17	70:13 -93
* Murray	Yvonne	GBR	4.10.64	172/50	1500	4:01.44	4:01.20 -87
					Mile	4:22.64	4:23.06 -86
					3k	8:29.60	8:29.02 -88
					10k	31:56.97	0
* Mushayilova	Irina	RUS	6.1.67	164/56	LJ	7.20	7.02 -93
					TJ	13.94, 13.98w	14.79 -93
Mustakayeva	Venera	UKR	27.2.71	170/70	JT	58.58	56.92 -92
Musunoi	Oana	ROM	17.9.72	175/50	HJ	1.88	1.94 -92
* Mutola	Maria	MOZ	27.12.72	167/50	400	51.37	51.44 -93
					800	1:55.19	1:55.43 -93
					1500	4:13.93	4:02.60 -92
* Myers	Sandra	ESP	9.1.61	168/58	100	11.30	11.06 -91
					200	23.30w	22.38 -90
					400	50.33	49.67 -91
Mylnikova	Irina	BLR	14.6.65		100h	13.27	13.08, 13.0 -86
N'Da-Bamba	Lucienne	CIV	6.7.65	174/60	HJ	1.88	1.95 -92
Nadaud	Valérie	FRA	16.3.68	157/45	10kW	45:53	46:41 -90
Nadler	Patricia	SUI	13.2.69	175/58	Hep	5723	5699 -91
Nadolna	Elzbieta	POL	16.8.71	164/50	Mar	2:33:28	0
Naeris	Virge	EST	12.12.69	178/63	LJ	6.63, 6.66w	6.41 -93
					TJ	13.83	12.56 -93
Nagy	Judit	HUN	9.12.65	168/56	Mar	2:32:32	2:32:07 -93
Nanu	Ana	ROM	24.6.73	150/40	HMar	72:28	72:15 -93
Nasonkina	Yelena	UKR	11.8.62	167/58	400	52.57	52.43 -93
* Nastase	Liliana	ROM	1.6.62	170/67	LJ	6.48i	6.78 -89
					Hep	6093	6619 -92
Nasuhara	Noriko	JPN	4.10.70	164/47	10k	32:48.02	33:01.97 -93
					HMar	71:42	
Nathan	DeDee	USA	20.4.68	180/75	Hep	6189	6162 -92
* Nauer	Daria	SUI	21.5.66	168/48	3k	8:57.13	8:54.53 -93
					5k	15:13.93	15:18.00 -93
					10k	31:35.96	0
Naumova	Alevtina	RUS	16.1.61	158/50	HMar	72:34	71:51 -93
					Mar	2:34:47	2:29:49 -88
* Nazarova	Olga	RUS	28.2.62	177/63	400h	54.82	55.08 -93
* Nazaroviene	Remigija	LIT	2.6.67	178/70	100h	13.31	13.18, 12.9 -89
					Hep	6262	6604 -89
Nedelcu #	Magdalena	ROM	12.5.74	167/56	400	52.35, 52.34i	50.87 -92
Neef	Melanie	GBR	26.5.70	166/54	400	52.09	54.14 -93
* Negura	Iulia	ROM	26.1.67	166/56	10k	32:26.58	31:52.58 -91
					HMar	69:15	70:59 -92
* Neimke	Kathrin	GER	18.7.66	180/95	SP	19.89	21.21 -87
Nekrosaité	Terese	LIT	19.10.61	172/74	JT	63.38	67.64 -92
Nelson	Carole	FRA	22.1.71	162/51	400h	56.61	56.61 -92
Nenasheva	Viktoria	RUS	26.6.70	160/50	3k	9:00.41	8:54.88 -92
					5k	15:39.79	15:36.28 -92
Nepluyeva	Inna	UKR	17.3.71	178/63	400h	57.10	57.10 -93
Nestoret	Maguy	FRA	28.7.69	165/55	100	11.41	11.36 -91
					200	23.27w	23.15, 22.95w -91
Neves	Fatima	POR	13.2.63	163/50	HMar	71:34	71:22 -93
					Mar	2:34:12	2:36:15 -93

Name		Nat	Born	Ht/Wt	Event	1994 Mark	Pre-1994 Best
Newhouse	Vonda	USA	27.8.74	163/46	200	23.35	24.47 -90
Niculae	Erica	ROM	21.9.73	171/57	100h	13.32	13.45 -92
* Nielsen	Renata	DEN	18.5.66	176/63	LJ	6.96 7.09w	6.86 -91
Niga	Viorica	ROM	22.11.68	159/52	1500	4:13.74	4:09.00 -89
Nikiel	Aniela	POL	1.11.65	157/49	Mar	2:34:23	2:38:31 -93
* Nikishina	Olga	UKR	29.4.66	172/86	DT	66.00	63.54 -90
Nikishova	Tatyana	RUS	16.7.74		JT	56.02	51.94 -92
Nikishova	Yekaterina	RUS	.73		400h	57.36	
* Nikolayeva	Yelena	RUS	1.2.66	168/60	5kW	20:48	21:08.8 -91
					10kW	42:43	42:40 -92
* Ninova	Ljudmila	AUT	25.6.60	175/61	LJ	7.09	7.06 -93
Nishi	Junko	JPN	11.8.74	161/47	HMar	72:08	
Nku	Mercy	NGR	17.7.76		100	11.35	12.20 -93
Nolan	Geraldine	IRL	11.4.74		1500	4:10.16	4:24.98 -92
Noll-Mayne	Lesley	USA	22.5.67	163/56	800	2:02.47	2:02.67 -90
Nomura	Yoko	JPN	1.7.70	157/48	10k	33:05.78	
Nordstrom	Kaye	NZL	30.5.68	163/74	JT	59.80	60.84 -92
Norkina	Vera	RUS	20.8.68		1500	4:13.92	4:14.67 -93
Nováková	Sarka	TCH	21.2.71	185/62	HJ	1.89i	1.95 -92
Novikova	Nadezhda	RUS	.66		LJ	6.51i, 6.50	6.56 -93
					Hep	6018	5754 -92
* Nuneva	Anelia	BUL	30.6.62	167/57	100	11.33, 11.10w	10.85 -88
Nunn-Cearns	Glynis	AUS	4.12.60	168/58	400h	57.8	57.23 -83
Oakes	Judy	GBR	14.2.58	163/79	SP	18.68	19.38 -88
Oana	Mihaela	ROM	11.11.68	176/86	SP	19.90i, 18.26	19.51 -93
Oberdorf	Bettina	GER	15.11.65	176/66	Hep	6094	6083 -93
Odzilyayeva	Yulia	RUS	.70		5000W	21:36.74	
					10kW	42:40	44:42 -93
Ojokolo	Endurance	NGR	27.5.77		100	11.45	11.99 -93
Oka	Shizuka	JPN	23.7.70	166/53	HMar	72:05	
Okamoto	Yukiko	JPN	29.11.74		5k	15:51.20	16:01.21 -93
Olenchenko	Vera	RUS	21.3.59		LJ	6.84	6.92 -85
Oliveira	Ana Paula	POR	19.3.70	160/43	10k	32:27.66	33:25.4 -88
Oliveira	Carmen de	BRA	17.8.65	160/46	HMar	69:31	
					Mar	2:27:41	2:31:18 -93
Oliveira	Rosa	POR	25.7.66	171/59	HMar	72:41	71:53 -93
Olomina	Chukwuete	SWE	28.4.78		TJ	13.43i	11.66 -93
Omoro	Jane	KEN	12.9.74		10k	32:13.01	
* Ondieki	Lisa	AUS	12.5.60	168/48	10k	31:47.11	31:11.72 -92
					Mar	2:31:01	2:23:51 -88
* Onyali	Mary	NGR	3.2.68	165/52	100	11.03	10.97 -93, 10.9 -91
					200	22.35, 22.33w	22.32 -93
Oosthuizen	Chrisna	RSA	1.3.72		Hep	5693	5339 -93
Opara-Thompson	Christy	NGR	2.5.70	170/60	100	11.19	11.28 -92
					LJ	6.66, 6.72w	6.72 -92
* Ordina	Vera	RUS	4.6.68	172/56	400h	54.92	54.37 -92
Orrange	Diana	USA	9.8.67	178/59	TJ	14.03	13.63, 13.71w -90
Orthaber	Katharina	SUI	9.9.63	176/56	1500	4:11.57	4:10.63 -91
* O'Sullivan	Sonia	IRL	28.11.69	173/53	800	2:00.69	2:03.39 -92
					1500	3:59.10	3:59.60 -93
					Mile	4:17.25	4:22.94 -93
					2000	5:25.36	5:41.22 -91
					3k	8:21.64	8:28.74 -93
					5k	15:06.18	14:45.92 -93
Ota	Yoko	JPN	14.1.75	173/53	HJ	1.89	1.93 -93
* Ottey	Merlene	JAM	10.5.60	173/59	100	10.78	10.78 -90
					200	22.07	21.64 -91
Ouaziz	Zohra	MAR	20.12.69	166/50	3k	8:54.40	9:00.55 -93
					5k	15:50.1	16:19.03 -92
Ouzouni	Kaliopi	GRE	8.3.73	182/78	SP	16.69	15.86 -93
Ovaska	Asta	FIN	29.7.63	185/105	SP	16.39	18.57 -89
Ovcharova	Yelena	UKR	17.8.76	175/57	100h	13.29, 13.1	13.98 -93
Ovchinnikova	Oksana	RUS	21.7.71	176/69	JT	59.88	52.98 -93
Pagel	Ramona	USA	10.11.61	182/82	SP	18.78	21.18 -88
Pachut	Sylwia	POL	21.7.70	168/58	400h	56.42	56.18 -93
Painter	Trina	USA	24.6.66	165/50	5k	15:41.46	15:50.28 -92
					10k	32:59.55	32:19.79 -93
Palacios	Cathy	USA	6.11.68	172/56	5k	15:38.64	0
Palacios	Felipa	COL	.75		100	11.2w	
Palamar	Vita	UKR	12.10.77		HJ	1.91	1.83 -93

Name		Nat	Born	Ht/Wt	Event	1994 Mark	Pre-1994 Best
Palma	Odeymis	CUB	18.12.71	170/70	JT	57.28	56.70 -91
Pan	Jinhong	CHN	18.8.73		Mar	2:31:20	2:36:48 -92
Panarina	Natalya	RUS	6.5.75		HT	57.44	59.06 -93
Panda	Rachita	IND	4.3.74		100	11.43	12.04 -93
Panferova	Yelena	KZK	26.1.74		TJ	13.39	12.16 -93
Panfilova	Yelena	RUS	9.10.60	166/48	5000W	21:51.0	21:57 -90
					10kW	46:38	44:39.0 -90
Pang	Xiaoyue	CHN	.		PV	3.70	
Panikarovskikh	Yelena	RUS	4.12.59	172/64	HJ	1.93	1.98i -90, 1.95 -87
Paramonova	Yelena	RUS	.		HMar	69:32	
Paredes	Concepción	ESP	19.7.70	175/67	TJ	14.30	14.11, 14.16w -93
Parker	Jacqui	GBR	15.10.66	163/54	400h	56.41	56.15 -91
Parker	Lesa	USA	8.1.74	165/	100	11.44w	11.57 -93
* Parris	Debbie Ann	JAM	24.3.73	162/48	400	52.14	52.84 -93
					100h	13.11w	13.51 -93
					400h	55.17	55.80 -93
* Paschke	Melanie	GER	29.6.70	168/54	100	11.12	11.23 -93
					200	22.45	23.43, 22.97w -93
Paskhina	Alexandra	RUS	14.8.71		100h	12.99, 12.87w	13.13, 13.1, 13.07w -93
Patla	Genowefa	POL	17.10.62	175/73	JT	61.60	65.96 -91
Patoka	Antonina	RUS	12.1.64	182/95	DT	60.80	67.12 -89
Patoulidou	Paraskevi	GRE	29.3.65	168/61	LJ	6.55	6.14 -86
* Patzwahl	Kristin	GER	16.7.65	169/60	100h	12.94	12.80 -90
Paulavicienė	Rita	LIT	14.12.61	169/64	800	2:01.10	1:59.83 -92
* Paulino	Argentina	MOZ	7.7.73	166/59	800	2:00.71	1:56.62 -93
Pavlova	Yelena	UKR	3.2.69	162/52	400h	57.54	58.10 -93
Pavlovska	Elizabeta	MKD	24.9.72	170/62	100h	13.36	13.82 -93
* Pavlysh	Viktoria	UKR	15.1.69	175/80	SP	19.61	19.66 -92
Pedroso	Magalys	CUB	3.6.72		TJ	13.39	13.42 -93
Pekkola	Iina	FIN	23.3.73	173/60	400h	57.81	61.49 -93
* Peleshenko	Larisa	RUS	29.2.64	187/95	SP	20.00i, 19.81	20.99 -87
Pellino	Cristiana	ITA	21.9.70	164/49	5000W	21:30.96	22:04.26 -93
					10kW	42:55	45:17 -93
Pells	Leah	CAN	9.11.64	170/55	1500	4:08.68	4:05.11 -89
					3k	9:01.16	8:53.05 -91
Pendareva	Petya	BUL	20.1.71	162/50	100	11.23, 11.18w	11.14 -93
					200	22.85	22.78 -93
Peng	Fenghai	CHN	2.7.79		LJ	6.52	
Pentukova	Tatyana	RUS	23.6.65	176/53	3k	8:59.88	8:55.98 -93
					5k	15:24.05	15:44.18 -93
					10k	32:19.96	33:10.47 -87
* Pérec	Marie-José	FRA	9.5.68	180/60	200	22.61	21.99 -93
					400	49.77	48.83 -92
Pereira	Isabel	POR	20.2.73		LJ	6.47w	6.15 -92
Perevedentseva	Nina	RUS	.64		LJ	6.60	6.66 -88
Periginelli	Karin	ITA	5.2.70	176/63	Hep	5934	5780 -92
* Perrone	Elisabetta	ITA	9.7.68	168/68	5000W	20:49.39	20:53.71 -93
					10kW	42:15	41:56 -93
Pessina	Stefania	ITA	26.5.74		10kW	46:44	
Peterková	Alena	TCH	13.11.60	167/53	5k	15:53.09	0
					HMar	71:02	72:17 -93
					Mar	2:25:19	2:30:36 -91
* Peters	Annette	USA	31.5.65	165/50	3k	8:41.97	8:42.09 -93
					5k	15:15.42	14:56.07 -93
Petrescu	Rodica	ROM	13.3.71		TJ	14.47	
Philipp	Andrea	GER	29.7.71	165/54	100	11.26w	11.36 -90, 11.34w -92
Phillips	Tracey	NZL	8.1.68		HJ	1.88	1.88 -90
Philpott	Anita	IRL	24.7.69		3k	8:54.79	9:12.45 -93
Pierre-Joseph	Corinne	FRA	27.10.66	166/57	400h	57.14	56.86 -89
Pieterse	Zola	RSA	9.5.66	164/48	1500	4:13.60	3:59.96 -85
					3k	8:56.03 mx, 9:00.00	8:28.83 -85
					5k	15:46.93	15:01.83 -83
Piipponen	Marjo	FIN	29.5.71	167/56	800	2:01.88	2:02.93 -93
					1500	4:13.71	4:18.09 -93
Pina	Claudete Alves	BRA	18.4.71	166/47	200	23.1	23.34 -91, 22.9 -92
* Pippig	Uta	GER	7.9.65	167/55	HMar	67:59	70:35 -91
					Mar	2:21:45	2:26:24 -93
* Piquereau	Anne	FRA	15.6.64	171/65	100h	12.76, 12.64w	12.74 -93
Pirog	Marina	UKR	28.8.74	180/67	HT	62.22	58.24 -93

Name		Nat	Born	Ht/Wt	Event	1994 Mark	Pre-1994 Best
Pitts	Diana	USA	22.1.72	165/56	400	52.65	54.14 -93
					800	2:02.73	2:06.17 -92
Plumer	Polly	USA	14.10.64	164/50	3k	8:58.30	9:09.28 -87
* Podkopayeva	Yekaterina	RUS	11.6.52	164/54	800	1:59.25	1:55.96 -83
					1500	3:59.78	3:56.65 -84
Podracká	Marcela	SVK	13.3.70	177/69	Hep	6046	6034 -89
Podyalovskaya	Irina	RUS	19.10.59	165/52	800	2:01.06	1:55.69 -84
Poelman	Jacqueline	NED	5.10.73	171/65	100	11.27	11.41 -93
					200	23.17	23.28 -92
Poetschka	Lauren	AUS	22.10.74		400h	56.06	57.5 -93
* Poetschka	Renee	AUS	1.5.71	174/56	200	23.1	23.68, 23.5w -93
					400	50.19	51.00 -93
Poilagi	Rose-May	FRA	9.2.72	166/62	JT	56.86	57.22 -93
Poitras	Tina	CAN	5.10.70	165/52	10kW	46:35	45:30.7 -92
Politika	Yelena	UKR	24.8.64	172/70	100h	13.30, 13.2	12.71 -86, 12.66w -88
Pollock	Peggy	USA	1.5.60	178/91	SP	16.87	17.79i -87, 17.58 -86
Polyanskaya	Viktoria	RUS	.71		HT	61.34	58.16 -93
Pomacu	Cristina	ROM	15.9.73	164/46	Mar	2:33:09	2:37:47 -93
Pompa	Yolaida	CUB	10.1.72	171/62	Hep	5871	5723 -92
Pont	Monica	ESP	3.6.69	161/48	Mar	2:29:36	2:31:21 -93
Popykina	Natalya	RUS	11.12.70	174/66	HJ	1.90	1.84i -93
					LJ	6.59	6.58 -93
					Hep	6104	6008 -93
Povtaryova	Olga	RUS	.73		100	11.2	11.97, 11.7 -92
Powell	Suzy	USA	3.9.76	181/70	DT	57.40	55.06 -93
Power	Susie	AUS	26.3.75	175/53	1500	4:13.79	4:14.46 -93
					3k	8:56.93	8:59.71 -93
Pozdnyakova	Tatyana	UKR	4.3.56	164/59	HMar	72:34	71:22 -93
					Mar	2:35:09	0
* Prandzheva	Iva	BUL	15.2.72	174/57	LJ	6.77, 6.95w	6.62 -92
					TJ	14.38i, 13.86	14.23, 14.32w -93
Predikaka	Ksenija	SLO	11.3.70		TJ	13.52	13.41 -93
Preisinger	Agnes	HUN	3.8.73	177/62	JT	58.44	56.04 -93
* Price-Smith	Connie	USA	3.6.62	190/95	SP	19.60	19.34 -91
					DT	62.32	64.82 -87
* Privalova	Irina	RUS	12.11.68	174/60	100	10.77	10.82, 10.81w -92
					200	22.02, 21.82w	21.88 -93
					400	50.62	49.89 -93
Procaccio	Gina	USA	19.7.64	160/50	1500	4:08.77	4:06.6 -92
					Mile	4:29.34	4:24.85 -90
					3k	8:49.10	8:54.45 -93
* Protti	Anita	SUI	4.8.64	170/56	400	52.76	51.32 -90
					400h	55.96	54.25 -91
Prytkova	Lyubov	RUS	5.7.66		100h	13.1	13.40 -93
Pukha	Irina	UKR	10.1.73	168/60	100	11.41	11.46 -93, 11.2 -92
Pupo	Alina	CUB	9.3.75		SP	16.65	16.33 -93
Qi	Hong	CHN	.3.69		200	23.05	22.87 -93
Qiu ¶	Qiaoping	CHN	31.10.71	180/92	DT	66.60	66.08 -92
* Qu	Yunxia	CHN	25.12.72	172/57	800	1:59.37	1:56.24 -93
					1500	4:00.34	3:50.46 -93
					Mar	2:32:01	2:24:32 -93
Quentin	Frédérique	FRA	22.12.69	173/58	1500	4:09.00	4:10.45 -92
* Quintero	Ioamnet	CUB	18.9.72	178/62	HJ	1.97	2.01i, 2.00 -93
Rabush	Kelly	USA	22.10.67	168/56	1500	4:12.55	4:15.7 -93
Radicheva	Sonya	BUL	8.6.68	170/65	JT	60.92	60.00 -93
* Radtke	Helga	GER	16.5.62	171/64	LJ	6.60, 6.72w	7.21 -84
					TJ	14.46	14.30, 14.44w -92
Radtke	Katarzyna	POL	31.8.69	161/45	5000W	21:05.53	20:51.96 -93
					10kW	43:16	42:55 -93
Ragozina	Tatyana	UKR	3.9.64	162/51	10kW	44:15	44:13 -90
Raines-White	Angela	AUS	22.3.74	161/44	1500	4:13.22	4:14.2 -93
* Rainey	Meredith	USA	15.10.68	168/55	800	1:59.90	1:57.63 -93
Raizgiene	Monika	LIT	14.4.65		SP	16.78	18.43 -89
Ramalalanirina	Nicole	MAD	5.3.72	164/57	100h	13.11	13.11, 12.92w -93
Ramanauskaité	Rita	LIT	22.2.70		JT	62.06	58.84 -93
Ramazanova	Larisa	RUS	23.9.71	173/60	5kW	21:52	22:40.82 -93
					10kW	42:31	42:47 -93
Ramirez	Oraidis	CUB	11.11.73	171/65	100h	13.22	13.27, 13.0, 13.04w -93
Ramos	Margarita	ESP	26.6.66	178/72	SP	17.82	17.71 -91

Name		Nat	Born	Ht/Wt	Event	1994 Mark	Pre-1994 Best
Rantanen	Heli	FIN	26.2.70	174/72	JT	61.68	64.66 -91
Rättyä	Tina	FIN	12.11.68	181/63	Hep	6241	6086 -91
Rauta	Kirsi	FIN	17.3.62	170/55	10k	32:57.68	33:08.12 -90
					HMar	71:37	72:41 -92
					Mar	2:31:23	2:32:31 -92
Ravaonirina	Lalao	MAD	8.11.63	165/58	100	11.38	11.32 -91, 11.22w -88
					200	23.30w	23.26 -89
Razdrogina	Yelena	RUS	25.8.69		Mar	2:33:41	2:38:20 -93
Rea	Elisa	ITA	23.3.68	164/50	1500	4:12.31	4:11.03 -92
					3k	8:59.79	0
Rebelo	Maria	FRA	29.1.56	158/45	Mar	2:35:07	2:29:04 -91
Recio	Teresa	ESP	7.7.63	145/38	10k	33:00.03	33:35.38 -93
Reed	Georgette	CAN	26.1.67	178/89	SP	16.63	16.64 -92
Reichardt	Yvonne	GER	5.2.73	170/65	JT	56.90	61.74 -89
Rembao	Sue	USA	15.5.62	177/59	HJ	1.89	1.96 -91
* Ren	Ruiping	CHN	1.2.76		TJ	14.36	14.29 -93
Renaud	Anne	FRA	24.3.70	173/58	400h	57.17	0
Renders	Marleen	BEL	24.12.68	166/41	5k	15:54.01	15:40.1 -87
					10k	32:11.18	32:04.2 -91
					HMar	69:29	
Rendon	Lucia	MEX	.69		HMar	72:43	
* Renk	Silke	GER	30.6.67	173/75	JT	56.88	71.00 -88
* Reshetnikova	Tatyana	RUS	14.10.66	171/66	100h	12.53	12.73 -92
* Restrepo	Ximena	COL	10.3.69	175/58	200	23.27, 23.07w	22.92 -92
					400	51.31	49.64 -92
					400h	56.05	59.1 -89
* Retchakan	Gowry	GBR	21.6.60	158/45	400h	55.78	54.63 -92
Retzke	Astrid	GER	13.7.73	178/61	Hep	5724	5694 -91
Reynolds	Natasha	USA	7.6.72	155/48	400h	57.27	56.96 -93
Rhodes	Cynthea	USA	30.9.68	168/58	LJ	6.50, 6.68w	6.18 -91
					TJ	13.94	13.68 -93
Ribac	Andreja	SLO	14.1.76		TJ	13.30, 13.40w	12.90 -93
* Ribeiro	Fernanda	POR	23.6.69	161/48	1500	4:10.54, 4:10.80i	4:12.90 -91
					3k	8:42.13	8:51.91 -93
					5k	15:06.91	0
					10k	31:04.25	31:40.51 -93
* Rieger	Nicole	GER	5.2.72	168/53	PV	4.08i, 4.00	3.92 -92
* Rieger	Silvia	GER	14.11.70	175/55	400h	54.68	54.90 -93
Riewe	Susanne	GER	26.5.70	171/70	JT	59.08	63.46 -92
Rigg	Suzanne	GBR	29.11.63	168/52	10k	33:01.40	32:44.06 -93
Riháková	Lenka	SVK	17.10.75		HJ	1.90	1.81 -93
Richards	Kerry-Ann	JAM	22.4.76		100	11.2	11.72, 11.59w -93
* Richards	Sandie	JAM	6.11.68	170/62	400	50.69	50.19 -92
Richardson	Marcia	GBR	10.2.72	171/56	100	11.46, 11.39w	11.45 -93
Rios	Rocio	ESP	13.3.69	152/45	10k	32:22.93	32:51.72 -93
					HMar	71:23	74:07 -93
					Mar	2:29:00	2:31:33 -93
Rivero	Xiomara	CUB	22.12.68	177/73	JT	62.44	64.56 -86
Roba	Fatuma	ETH	.73	160/49	HMar	70:49	70:28 -92
Roberts	Candy	USA	16.4.71	176/76	DT	55.26	51.10 -89
Robertson	Christian	USA	27.10.74		100	11.43x	
Robinson	Lynne	GBR	21.6.69	158/46	1500	4:10.32	4:12.03 -93
Robinson	Tulia	JAM	4.2.79		100	11.0	12.00, 11.7w -93
Rockmeier	Birgit	GER	29.11.73	173/53	200	23.27	23.45 -93
Rodchenkova	Marina	RUS	30.7.61	164/50	3k	8:58.19	8:45.69 -88
Rodriguez	Patricia	COL	.70		200	23.3	23.46 -93
* Rogachova	Lyudmila	RUS	30.10.66	166/57	800	1:58.43	1:56.82 -88
					1500	4:02.40	3:56.91 -92
					Mile	4:23.88	4:21.30 -92
Rohl	Michelle	USA	12.11.65	150/41	10kW	44:41.87	46:45 -92
Rohländer	Uta	GER	30.6.69	173/58	400	51.16	51.39 -90
Roland	Kim	USA	3.4.72		LJ	6.52w	642w -93
* Romanova	Anna	RUS	9.3.68	180/87	SP	19.75	20.24 -93
* Romanova	Yelena	RUS	20.3.63	163/51	1500	4:07.92	4:00.91 -92
					3k	8:41.06	8:30.45 -88
					5k	15:05.94	14:59.70 -91
Ropo	Ringa	FIN	16.2.66	177/60	LJ	6.47, 6.63w	6.85 -90, 6.93w -92
Roshchupkina	Nadezhda	RUS	14.6.63	164/57	100	11.45, 11.0	11.22-00, 11.1, 11.0w -90
					200	23.3, 23.28w	23.15 -90, 22.8 -88

Name		Nat	Born	Ht/Wt	Event	1994 Mark	Pre-1994 Best
Rose	Dionne	JAM	7.11.69	168/52	100h	13.13, 13.06w	13.03 -92
					LJ	6.63	6.63 -93, 6.70w -92
Roslyakova	Olga	BLR	14.6.67		LJ	6.52	6.57 -92
Rosolen	Mara	ITA	27.7.65	175/80	SP	16.69	17.40i -93, 17.12 -92
Rósza	Maria	HUN	12.2.67	165/54	10kW	42:53	43:21 -93
Rouillard	Carole	CAN	15.3.60	153/44	Mar	2:30:41	2:31:33 -92
Roux	Liezel	RSA	25.5.67		JT	56.38	55.98 -91
Roy	Terry	USA	26.1.73	173/65	Hep	5651	5644 -93
Rublyova	Olga	RUS	28.10.74	175/62	LJ	6.76	6.74 -93
					TJ	13.32	12.95 -92
Rücker	Anja	GER	20.12.72	174/56	400	51.42	51.33 -92
Ruckle	Tani	AUS	25.6.62	162/52	Mar	2:34:29	2:31:19 -88
Rünne	Eha	EST	25.5.63	182/84	SP	16.58	17.61i -88, 17.01 -86
					DT	57.72	63.18 -88
Rupasova	Yelena	RUS	.68		LJ	6.60i	6.31 -93
* Russell	Gillian	JAM	28.9.73	167/56	100h	12.97	13.00 -93
Russell	Rebecca	USA	8.10.70	168/52	400h	56.90	56.86 -92
Rutz	Marie-Luise	GER	28.5.74	190/80	DT	55.10	52.58 -93
Ruzina	Yelena	RUS	3.4.64	172/58	200	23.32	22.73 -88
					400	52.04	50.65 -90
Ryabinkina	Olga	RUS	24.9.76		SP	16.52	15.61 -93
Ryashkina	Nadezhda	RUS	22.1.67	160/47	5000W	21:51.60i	20:44 -91
					10kW	44:15.76	41:56.23 -90
Rybak	Ewa	POL	22.12.74	174/67	JT	57.70	55.88 -93
Rybicka	Anna	POL	23.9.63	173/56	Mar	2:31:43	2:31:43 -93
* Rydz	Malgorzata	POL	18.1.67	165/52	800	1:59.12	2:00.68 -91
					1500	4:03.78	4:01.91 -92
					Mile	4:28.39	4:33.54 -90
Ryshich	Nastja	GER	19.9.77		PV	3.71	3.50 -93
Ryzhova	Veronika	RUS	3.2.68	174/68	Hep	5753	6254 -91
Sableva	Tatyana	UKR	21.8.67	163/55	100h	13.26, 13.1	13.11 -88
* Sacramento	Carla	POR	10.12.71	168/53	800	1:59.39	1:59.42 -93
					1500	4:06.05	4:04.10 -92
					Mile	4:29.65	4:31.05 -92
Sadahiro	Chinami	JPN	17.8.72	174/55	HJ	1.90	1.89 -93
Sadova	Natalya	RUS	15.6.72	178/83	DT	62.12	58.14 -93
Saito	Masako	JPN	24.10.74	157/45	3k	8:58.34	9:06.36 -93
					5k	15:38.00	
Sakala	Julia	ZIM	12.7.69	169/55	1500	4:11.36	
					3k	8:59.23	8:57.69 -93
Sakashita	Naomi	JPN	25.5.75	158/42	5k	15:53.85	16:14.4 -92
Salagean	Liliana	ROM	24.3.71	172/55	800	2:00.61	1:59.17 -92
					1500	4:11.54, 4:08.96i	4:09.98 -93
Salminen	Marika	FIN	10.5.71	172/56	TJ	13.61	13.44 -93
Salumäe	Jane	EST	17.1.68	169/52	HMar	70:10	72:30 -93
					Mar	2:33:09	
* Salvador	Ileana	ITA	16.1.62	163/52	5000W	21:30.9	20:28 -89
					10kW	44:51	41:30 -93
Samorokova	Irina	RUS	15.4.64	165/55	800	1:59.07	2:01.55 -91
					1500	4:09.6	4:18.9 -93
Samuel	Heather	ANT	6.7.70	160/59	100	11.39, 11.0	11.20 -93
					200	23.20, 23.1	23.32 -93
Sandell	Annemari	FIN	2.1.77	170/49	3k	8:52.24	8:51.22 -93
					10k	32:55.24	0
Sánchez	Marlen	CUB	12.10.71		DT	55.74	57.92 -93
Sánchez	Rosario	MEX	.71		10kW	44:53.0	46:24.3 -92
Santos	Kàtia	BRA	31.12.67		100	11.43	11.62 -93
* Santos #	Sueli Pereira	BRA	8.1.65	165/63	JT	65.96	63.74 -93
Saramma	Kalawati	IND	25.2.71	151/44	400	52.57	52.83 -93
Sato	Ayumi	JPN	21.7.70	159/52	10k	33:05.53	
Sato	Chiharu	JPN	13.4.70	155/40	Mar	2:34:39	2:35:00 -92
Sato	Megumi	JPN	13.9.66	178/54	HJ	1.88i	1.95 -87
Sato	Yuko	JPN	23.1.68	170/53	10kW	44:44	44:53 -93
Saunders	Daphne	BAH	18.12.71	176/68	LJ	6.82i, 6.46	6.77, 6.86w -93
						13.54i	13.01, 13.20w -93
Saville	Jane	AUS	5.11.74	164/53	10kW	46:04	46:02 -92
Savinova	Lyudmila	RUS	.72		10kW	46:12.02	44:54 -93
* Saxby-Junna	Kerry	AUS	2.6.61	163/57	5000W	20:40.06	20:17.19 -90
					10kW	43:09	41:57.22 -90

Name		Nat	Born	Ht/Wt	Event	1994 Mark	Pre-1994 Best
* Sayko	Yelena	RUS	24.12.67	161/48	5000W	20:59.82	21:19.81 -92
					10kW	42:43.23	42:04 -93
Sazanova	Maya	KZK	28.5.68		10kW	45.51	45:00 -93
Sazanovich	Natalya	BLR	15.8.73	178/63	Hep	5770	6036 -92
Scaunich	Emma	ITA	10.3.54	163/48	Mar	2:33:36	2:29:46 -88
Schäfer	Monika	GER	6.10.59	177/56	10k	32:51.1	32:27.2 -91
Schäfer	Tina	GER	27.12.77		HT	56.06	50.64 -93
Schenk	Michele	SUI	8.3.74	176/52	400h	56.34	58.95 -92
Schlawitz	Kerstin	GER	30.8.70	182/56	HJ	1.88	1.89 -92
Schmidt	Gesine	GER	26.6.71	184/65	400h	55.76	56.03 -93
Schmidt	Natascha	GER	27.6.65		TJ	13.31	13.16i -92
Schmitt	Simone	GER	5.12.71	182/85	DT	59.12	60.80 -93
Schnurr	Paula	CAN	15.1.64	160/54	1500	4:07.94	4:04.80 -92
					Mile	4:30.62	4:31.75 -92
Schofield	Vikki	GBR	29.12.72	163/60	Hep	5671	5268 -93
Scholent	Marie-Line	FRA	11.5.66	175/64	400	52.53	53.86 -93
Schönenberger	Jana	GER	28.11.71	167/55	400	52.42	52.77 -93
Schönenberger	Rita	SUI	3.12.62	165/54	LJ	6.51	6.59 -85
Schwart	Wiebke	GER	13.12.73	184/64	HJ	1.88i	1.86 -92
Schwoche	Ruta	GER	27.2.70		5kW	21:45	21:45 -92
(Erlingkite)					10kW	44:25	45:09 -92
Scott-Pomales	Catherine	JAM	27.8.73		400h	56.57	0
Seabury	Kristen	USA	14.4.69	168/57	1500	4:10.97	4:16.40 -93
Sederholm	Katarina	FIN	19.6.68	174/78	SP	16.79	15.83 -92
Sechko	Lyudmila	RUS	27.11.74		SP	16.66	15.27i -93
Seiyama	Sachiyo	JPN	6.11.72	155/45	HMar	71:48	72:49 -93
					Mar	2:30:30	2:42:23 -93
Selenska	Antoaneta	BUL	8.6.63	170/75	JT	61.02	71.88 -81
Selina	Yelena	KZK	11.7.64	156/54	LJ	6.48	6.54 -88
Sellenriek	Doreen	GER	20.4.73	170/54	10kW	46:11	49:13 -93
Semiraz	Yelena	UKR	21.11.65	168/57	LJ	6.79	6.86 -88
Semyonova	Zinaida	RUS	.62	150/42	Mar	2:34:08	2:37:20 -93
Serbinenko	Natalya	UKR	27.1.59	161/53	10kW	46:06	43:46 -89
Serebryanskaya	Larisa	UKR	15.9.63	183/58	HJ	1.92	1.92 -93
Sergent	Melinda	USA	.72		100	11.36	11.43 -93
					200	23.36, 23.24w	23.55 -93
Seryogina	Viktoria	RUS	.73		HJ	1.88	1.75 -92
Setoguchi	Megumi	JPN	14.7.68	153/37	HMar	72:05	72:31 -93
Seyerling	Heidi	RSA	19.8.76	167/52	200	23.22, 22.82w	24.08, 23.94w -93
Seymour	Michelle	NZL	21.12.65	162/58	100	11.42w	11.32 -93
Shafer	Natasha	USA	22.2.73	155/	100	11.44w	11.67 -93, 11.58w -92
Shang	Xiaoli	CHN	10.4.75		SP	16.90	
Shannon	Carla	USA	13.2.68	169/57	TJ	13.68	13.52 -91
Sharpe	Laura	IRL	10.3.69		HJ	1.89	1.85i -93
Shatalova	Natalya	RUS	.73		100	11.1	12.10 -92
Shaw	Lorraine	GBR	2.4.68	170/86	DT	55.04	50.82 -93
					HT	59.92	56.56 -93
Shekhodanova	Natalya	RUS	29.12.71	169/55	100h	13.17, 13.08w	13.14 -93, 13.0 -92
Shemchishina	Maya	UKR	6.5.72	174/58	400h	56.11	59.38 -92
Shepherd	Sonya	USA	13.8.73		LJ	6.48w	5.80 -92, 6.16w -93
* Shevchik	Tatyana	BLR	11.6.69	178/59	HJ	1.96i, 1.96	2.00 -93
Shcherbina	Marina	UKR	5.1.68	181/65	Hep	6123	6192 -89
Shi	Guiqing	CHN	19.4.68		Hep	5876	6188 -93
* Shikolenko	Natalya	BLR	1.8.64	182/80	JT	71.40	70.36 -92
* Shikolenko	Tatyana	BLR	10.5.68	175/79	JT	64.94	65.18 -93
Shilkina	Alla	UKR	15.11.68	168/55	400h	56.35	58.22 -87
Shimizu	Michiko	JPN	22.9.70	164/46	3k	8:52.06	9:09.58 -93
					5k	15:36.01	15:39.71 -93
Shirokova	Yulia	RUS	1.10.74		LJ	6.58	6.23i, 6.12 -93
Shishchenko	Yekaterina	UKR	24.12.71	180/90	SP	16.40i	17.23 -91
* Shishigina	Olga	KZK	23.12.68	162/54	100h	12.78	13.29 -93
* Shouaa	Ghada	SYR	10.9.72	178/65	Hep	6361	6260 -93
Shumakova	Alla	RUS	28.8.69		5k	15:37.43	
Sidibe	Odiah	FRA	13.1.70	176/64	100	11.37	11.24 -89
* Sidoti	Annarita	ITA	25.7.69	150/40	5000W	20:46.9	21:30.5 -90
					10kW	41:46	42:41 -93
Sievers	Sabine	GER	3.3.75	182/67	DT	56.76	53.48 -93
Sikdar	Jyotirmoy	IND	11.12.69		800	2:01.80	2:06.7 -93
Silhavá	Zdenka	TCH	15.6.54	178/84	DT	60.88	74.56 -84

Name		Nat	Born	Ht/Wt	Event	1994 Mark	Pre-1994 Best
Singa	Odile	FRA	29.12.67	162/52	100	11.42	11.46 -89
* Sinchukova	Yelena	RUS	23.1.61	173/67	LJ	6.77	7.20 -91
Sinyutina	Yelena	RUS	12.5.64	169/56	100h	13.07	12.91 -97, 12.9 -90
Skrebnyeva	Olga	BLR	7.11.74		TJ	13.40i	13.68 -93
Slavuteanu	Lidia	ROM	4.9.73	160/44	HMar	71:45	73:57 -93
					Mar	2:32:38	
Slegers	Lieve	BEL	6.4.65	163/51	5k	15:19.58	15:27.10 -90
					10k	32:18.68	31:43.36 -92
					HMar	71:01	
Slushkina	Marina	RUS	2.8.60	169/61	100h	13.16w	12.89 -90
Slyusar	Antonina	UKR	19.3.63	161/54	200	23.38	22.97 -90
Smieja	Sabine	GER	23.6.71		Hep	5694	5647 -93
Smith	Donna	USA	7.9.72	168/58	100	11.45, 11.43w	11.62 -93
* Smith	Phylis	GBR	29.9.65	168/62	400	51.30	50.40 -92
Snook-Larby	Verity	GBR	13.11.70	162/55	10kW	46:06	47:01 -93
** Sobanska	Malgorzata	POL	25.4.69	165/50	HMar	72:06	
					Mar	2:29:06	2:29:21 -93
Sobiesak	Renata	POL	14.6.70	165/50	3k	9:01.95	9:01.40 -93
					5k	15:47.70	16:08.52 -93
Söderberg	Anna	SWE	11.6.73	177/74	DT	58.74	55.30 -91
Sokova	Maria	RUS	2.9.70		TJ	14.16	13.00 -93
Somers	Linda	USA	7.5.61	163/46	Mar	2:33:42	2:33:37 -89
Sommaggio	Silvia	ITA	20.11.69	170/53	3k	8:50.30	9:08.65 -92
					5k	15:54.46	0
Song	Lijuan	CHN	.2.76	166/54	10kW	43:11	43:07 -93
Sorokina	Natalya	RUS	.75		LJ	6.45	6.23 -91
* Sosimenko	Debbie	AUS	5.4.74		HT	62.38	58.90 -93
Sousa	Maria de	BRA	5.9.71		TJ	13.40	13.13 -93
Sousa	Solange de	BRA	5.2.69	156/43	HMar	72:21	
Spada	Giuliana	ITA	18.4.71	172/63	Hep	5984	5991w -92
Spasova	Daniela	BUL	22.9.69	166/54	400	52.25	52.46 -88
Specht	Karin	GER	23.6.74	176/60	Hep	5779	5591 -93
Speights	Julie	USA	13.5.70	168/56	1500	4:10.47	4:12.43 -93
Spires	Camilla	RSA	29.10.69		1500	4:12.70	4:14.37 -92
St Geme	Ceci	USA	13.4.63	165/49	1500	4:12.12	4:11.72 -92
					Mile	4:31.59	4:27.0 -93
					5k	15:50.28	16:24.3 -82
Stähli	Bettina	SUI	5.11.73		100h	13.32	13.86 -92
Staicu	Simona	ROM	5.5.71	164/48	HMar	72:06	
Stakhova	Yelena	BLR	4.1.69		TJ	13.86	13.46 -91
Stanciu	Carmen	ROM	5.1.70	167/53	800	2:01.14	2:01.40 -93
Stanczyk ¶	Agnieszka	POL	20.1.71	168/55	TJ	13.66i	14.05 -93
Stankina	Irina	RUS	25.3.77	165/45	5000W	21:05.41	21:49.65 -93
Stanton	Krishna	AUS	18.5.66	171/56	10k	32:23.64	32:17.37 -91
Staples	Kate	GBR	2.11.65		PV	3.65	3.56 -93
Starkova	Svetlana	RUS	.68		400h	57.00	56.40 -93
Stasenko	Irina	RUS	27.3.66	177/70	800	2:01.35	2:01.35 -93
Statkuviene	Stefania	LIT	5.9.62	166/57	10k	32:31.35	33:05.52 -93
					HMar	71:42	73:07 -93
					Mar	2:32:22	0
Stavik	Hilde	NOR	6.9.62	173/58	1500	4:11.69	4:10.51 -92
					3k	8:47.47	8:58.24 -93
					5k	15:23.38	16:31.6 -88
					HMar	70:21	72:31 -92
Steigauf	Mona	GER	17.1.70	178/59	Hep	6230	6195 -93
Stenman	Petra	FIN	12.3.74	170/54	400h	57.22	59.84 -93
Sterling	Audrea	JAM	1.7.68	169/59	400	52.15	52.33 -93
Sterling	Carolin	JAM	17.3.70	173/59	100h	13.0w	13.18 -92
* Stevens	Rochelle	USA	8.9.66	172/58	200	23.31, 23.13w	22.84 -87
					400	51.45	50.06 -92
Stewart	Kwani	USA	9.10.72	183/61	100	11.36w	11.52 -93, 11.45w -92
					200	23.28	
					LJ	6.66w	6.26 -92
Steyn	Yolanda	RSA	22.8.72	170/59	200	23.03	23.04 -93
Stone	Joanna	AUS	1.10.72		JT	62.40	57.92 -93
Storchevaya	Yelena	UKR	23.6.66	165/51	800	2:01.25	1:59.09 -92
					1500	4:13.26	4:12.95 -90
* Storp	Stephanie	GER	28.11.68	194/95	SP	19.85	20.34 -90
Strasek	Renata	SLO	8.4.72	165/63	JT	61.74	63.60 -92

Name		Nat	Born	Ht/Wt	Event	1994 Mark	Pre-1994 Best
Sturrup	Chandra	BAH	12.9.71	159/52	LJ	6.54w	6.25, 6.48w -93
Sudak	Svetlana	BLR	17.11.71		HT	67.34	63.70 -93
Sudarikova	Tatyana	RUS	28.5.73	189/79	JT	58.86	61.18 -93
Sugawara	Miwa	JPN	5.9.76	154/41	5k	15:55.88	
Suchovská	Erika	TCH	27.7.67	177/59	100	11.40w	11.51 -93
					200	23.18, 23.14w	23.24 -92
* Sui	Xinmei	CHN	29.1.65	174/90	SP	20.74	21.66 -90
Sukhoruchenko	Alena	UKR	12.1.73	173/60	100h	12.90	13.78 -93, 13.6 -92
Sultanova	Firia	RUS	29.4.61	163/52	HMar	69:08	72:50 -93
* Sun #	Caiyun	CHN	21.3.73		PV	4.12	4.11 -93
Sun	Xue	CHN	3.3.72		100h	13.25	13.28 -93
Suzuki	Aya	JPN	18.11.67	168/75	HT	60.14	60.90 -93
Suzuki	Chikako	JPN	1.9.69	164/44	3k	8:56.39	9:14.89 -92
		JPN	1.9.69	164/44	5k	15:52.41	15:48.90 -93
Suzuki	Hiromi	JPN	6.12.68	155/43	10k	32:06.42	32:02.41 -92
Suzuki	Harumi	JPN	6.12.68	155/43	HMar	72:19	72:17 -93
Sychugova	Vera	RUS	8.4.63	173/66	200	23.08, 23.00w	22.85 -87
					400	51.81	51.64 -88
Synstnes	Brynhild	NOR	20.4.71	173/56	3k	8:58.75	9:14.71 -93
					HMar	70:29	0
* Szabo	Gabriela	ROM	14.11.75	160/42	3k	8:40.08	8:48.28 -92
Szebenszky	Anikó	HUN	12.8.65	169/58	10kW	44:17	44:54 -90
Szekeres	Judit	HUN	18.11.66	168/55	400h	57.75	57.44 -92
Takahashi	Chiemi	JPN	16.2.76	160/43	5k	15:46.01	
Tamagawa	Hiroko	JPN	24.6.72	155/40	HMar	71:52	
Tamura	Yuki	JPN	21.4.67	154/43	Mar	2:34:50	
Tanaka	Machiko	JPN	15.12.72	154/45	5k	15:40.99	16:06.6 -93
					10k	32:48.40	
Tang	Lishuang	CHN	25.2.66		JT	59.86	59.62 -88
* Tanigawa	Mari	JPN	27.10.62	160/44	HMar	70:43	70:09 -93
					Mar	2:27:55	2:28:22 -93
* Taplin	Cheryl	USA	2.9.73	165/56	100	11.07, 10.99w	11.23, 11.08w -93
					200	22.88, 22.80w	23.04 -93
Tarasenko	Yulia	RUS	28.3.68	182/62	400h	56.63	56.27 -92
* Tarnopolskaya	Zhanna	UKR	6.7.72	166/58	100	10.99	11.08 -93, 11.0 -91
					200	22.66	22.79 -93
Tatarenkova	Nadezhda	RUS	11.8.68	170/20	HMar	72:18	
Taura	Takako	JPN	22.7.68	156/41	10kW	46:49	46:42 -89
Taylor	Monifa	USA	3.3.71	169/61	100h	13.27, 13.0w	12.80 -92
Taylor	Sherlese	USA	27.11.70		100h	13.29	13.62, 13.24w -93
Teaberry	Connie	USA	15.8.70	179/63	HJ	1.88	1.92 -93
Tecuta	Alina	ROM	10.11.71	165/47	10k	33:06.07	32:15.96 -93
Telepnyeva	Natalya	RUS	27.5.66		TJ	13.45i	13.90i -92, 13.40 -91
Tenorio	Martha	ECU	8.6.66	154/43	Mar	2:30:12	0
Teppe	Agnès	FRA	4.5.68	182/78	DT	59.84	60.14 -92
* Teppe	Nathalie	FRA	22.5.72	183/61	JT	61.60	61.36 -89
					Hep	6396	6256 -93
Ter-Mesrobian	Tatyana	RUS	12.5.68	178/59	LJ	6.54	6.74 -90
* Tereshchuk	Tatyana	UKR	11.10.69	174/61	400h	54.96	57.19 -91
Terunuma	Yuka	JPN	27.1.68	161/45	Mar	2:28:26	2:37:42 -93
Teteryuk	Larisa	UKR	24.12.70	171/63	Hep	6274	5725w -92
Thanou	Katerina	GRE	1.2.75	165/53	100	11.43	12.09 -93
Thomas	Paula	GBR	3.12.64	157/46	100	11.15	11.24 -89, 11.13w -88
					200	22.69	22.79 -88
Thorp	Angela	GBR	7.12.72	171/60	100h	13.32	13.28 -93
Thorsett	Sarah	USA	18.3.70		800	2:02.17	2:03.49 -93
					1500	4:10.24	4:19.25 -93
Thust	Simone	GER	22.9.71	176/63	10kW	44:44	16:11 -93
Thyssen	Ingrid	GER	9.1.56	171/72	JT	60.02	69.68 -87
Tian	Mei	CHN	27.11.71		5k	15:40.86	16:17.60 -91
* Tiedtke-Greene	Susen	GER	23.1.69	175/56	LJ	6.65i, 6.81w	7.00 -91, 7.19w -92
Tikkanen	Päivi	FIN	19.1.60	164/50	3k	8:56.99	8:41.30 -91
					10k	32:58.65	31:45.02 -92
					HMar	70:35	71:22 -92
* Tilea	Felicia	ROM	29.9.67	167/74	JT	66.40	65.62 -93
Tillack	Heike	GER	6.1.68	171/60	100h	13.26	13.10 -86
Timofeyeva	Natalya	RUS	.72		Hep	5757	
Tîirlea	Ionela	ROM	9.2.76	165/48	400h	56.25	56.30 -93
Tîrneci	Manuela	ROM	26.2.69	171/83	DT	64.04	66.16 -92

Name		Nat	Born	Ht/Wt	Event	1994 Mark	Pre-1994 Best
Tkachova	Svetlana	RUS	14.4.70		Hep	5996	5677 -90
Tkalich	Tatyana	UKR	30.5.75	161/50	200	23.35w	24.29 -93
Tochilova	Natalya	RUS	21.5.64		100h	12.91	12.87 -88, 12.7 -90
* Tolbert-Goode	Lynda	USA	3.10.67	164/54	100h	13.00,12.90w	12.67 -93,12.66w -92
Tolstaya	Svetlana	KZK	9.8.71		10kW	46:33	
Tolstik	Irina	BLR	4.12.65		10kW	45:10	43:52 -90
Tombiri	Mary	NGR	23.7.72	160/56	100	11.25	11.38, 11.27w -93
Tomecková	Nikola	TCH	25.6.74	178/75	JT	56.68	59.78 -92
Toonstra	Christine	NED	22.6.66	171/53	3k	9:00.5	8:45.96 -92
* Topchina	Yelena	RUS	28.9.66	178/59	HJ	1.97	1.99 -93
Torazza	Manuela	ITA	27.6.68	170/73	SP	16.87	16.43 -93
Toropchina	Natalya	RUS	25.2.71		Hep	5931	5688 -93
* Torrence	Gwen	USA	12.6.65	172/57	100	10.82	10.86 -92, 10.78w -88
					200	21.85	21.72 -92
					400	50.20	49.64 -92
Torres	Lidurka	CUB	.77		400	52.44	
Torshina	Natalya	KZK	4.10.68	172/57	400h	55.81	54.53 -93
Toth	Monika	ROM	7.3.70	178/64	LJ	6.53	6.48 -92
					TJ	13.86, 13.98w	13.93, 13.96w -93
* Tourret	Monique	FRA	11.7.67	173/62	100h	13.08, 12.96w	12.56 -90
Trandenkova	Marina	RUS	7.1.67	170/58	100	11.15	11.08 -92
					200	22.78	22.50 -92
Tranchina	Maria	ITA	10.2.68	168/75	SP	16.96i, 16.81	16.65i, 16.62 -93
Travis	Kathy	USA	12.3.73	174/59	100	11.43w	11.57, 11.50w -92
Trofimova	Natalya	RUS	17.1.75	164/55	5000W	21:24.71	21:39.75 -93
					10kW	44:18	0
Tröger	Sabine	AUT	7.7.67	171/56	100	11.39	11.28 -93
					200	23.32	23.12 -92
Tsialakoudi	Angeliki	GRE	10.5.76	172/66	JT	57.04	58.42 -93
Tsikouna	Stella	GRE	19.10.72	171/75	DT	56.98	56.48 -92
Tsybulskaya	Valentina	BLR	19.2.68		10kW	43:16	43:50 -93
Tuliniemi	Marika	FIN	19.7.74	188/113	SP	17.54	17.93 -93
Tulloch	Valerie	CAN	13.7.72	168/	JT	57.26	58.26 -92
* Tulu	Derartu	ETH	21.3.72	155/45	3k	8:54.74	9:01.04 -91
					5k	15:40.29	15:21.29 -91
					10k	31:48.93	31:06.02 -92
Turchinskaya	Larisa	RUS	29.4.65	177/70	LJ	6.59i, 6.49	6.75 -89
					Hep	6596	7007 -89
Turner	Inez	JAM	3.12.72	170/56	400	52.27	51.64 -93
					800	2:01.31	2:04.14 -93
Tuzzi	Carla	ITA	2.6.67	162/57	100h	12.97, 12.8	13.08 -88
Twiggs	Shantel	USA	4.10.72	165/57	100	11.44, 11.20w	11.50, 11.32w -93
					200	23.35, 23.12w	23.66, 22.9w -93
Tylor	Cynthia	USA	10.1.71	163/56	LJ	6.53w	6.41 -93
Tysse	Kjersti	NOR	18.1.72	173/58	10kW	46:10	45:45 -92
* Tyukhay	Irina	RUS	14.1.67	168/64	100h	13.30	13.32, 13.0 -88
					LJ	6.52	6.71i, 6.60 -93, 6.73w -92
		RUS	14.1.67	168/60	Hep	6412	6478 -92
Uba	Calister	NGR	15.11.73		200	23.32	24.01 -93
Uccheddu	Valentina	ITA	26.10.66	166/45	LJ	6.80, 6.96w	6.77 -91, 6.83w -93
Ueno	Rie	JPN	11.6.76	163/49	5k	15:50.7	16:11.3 -93
Uchida	Tomoko	JPN	8.6.72	156/45	10kW	46:02	46:14 -93
Ukolova	Olga	RUS	.72		TJ	13.51	13.74 -93
Uppa	Taina	FIN	24.10.76	172/68	JT	61.78	54.78 -92
Urbikiene	Danguole	LIT	10.12.62	184/82	SP	18.85	20.27 -87
Urge	Getenesh	ETH	30.8.70	157/52	3k	8:58.61	9:03.32 -92
Urrutia	Maria Isabel	COL	25.3.65	170/78	DT	58.08	58.50 -92
Urusova	Elvira	GEO	2.2.66		SP	17.34	17.63-
Ushakova	Veronika	RUS	8.11.77		HT	56.78	52.16 -93
Usifo	Maria	NGR	1.8.64	174/63	400h	57.09	55.16 -86
Uusitalo	Mari	FIN	11.5.73	176/71	JT	57.80	56.36 -92
Uys	Lana	RSA	9.12.68	172/62	400h	57.46	56.23 -93
Vaill	Teresa	USA	20.11.62	163/54	10kW	45:01.46	45:16 -92
Van Blunk	Elaine	USA	11.9.64	162/48	Mar	2:32:25	0
van der Veen	Karen	RSA	7.1.66		400h	56.79	55.99 -88
van Diessen	Anoek	NED	20.2.73	183/71	Hep	5766	5490 -93
van Elk	Marjolijn	NED	2.9.69	178/67	Hep	5795	5669 -92
van Hulst	Elly	NED	9.6.59	177/56	3k	8:56.51	8:33.97 -88
					3k		8:33.82i -89

Name		Nat	Born	Ht/Wt	Event	1994 Mark	Pre-1994 Best
* van Langen	Ellen	NED	9.2.66	172/54	800	1:59.89	1:55.54 -92
					1500	4:06.97	4:06.92 -92
Vanderhoek	Kim	CAN	30.11.70		Hep	5641	5935 -92
Vanisi	Eileen	USA	28.3.72	178/129	SP	18.30	17.60 -91
Vaquero	Julia	ESP	18.9.70	160/47	3k	9:02.38	8:55.27 -93
Vascó	Maria	ESP	23.12.75	158/47	5000W	21:41.47	22:28 -92
Vasilenko	Natalya	UKR	30.10.74	167/68	HT	56.62	59.80 -93
Vasilevskaya	Lidia	RUS	1.4.73		5k	15:47.57	0
Vasilyeva	Lyudmila	RUS	20.10.67	170/54	1500	4:11.01	4:15.19 -93
Vasilyeva	Olga	KZK	25.2.71	176/68	LJ	6.67	6.31 -93
Vaszi	Tunde	HUN	18.4.72		LJ	6.46w	6.22 -92
Vavilova	Maria	RUS	.73		DT	56.90	55.42 -93
Veneva	Venelina	BUL	13.6.74	177/56	HJ	1.90	1.93i -90, 1.91 -91
Vereen	Wenda	USA	24.4.66	160/56	100	11.32	11.17 -83, 11.07w -93
					200	23.05	22.63 -93
Veremeychuk	Yelena	UKR	13.10.59	162/52	10kW	45:32	44:21 -88
Vershinina	Viktoria	UKR	11.6.71	177/58	LJ	6.68, 6.90w	6.62 -92
					TJ	13.84	13.25, 13.54w -93
Viceconte	Maura	ITA	3.10.67		HMar	70:54	
Vicet	Sonia	CUB	1.4.71	171/69	JT	61.42	59.52 -93
Villamizar	Maria	COL	30.8.70		HT	55.70	47.18 -93
Villani	Anna	ITA	21.6.66	153/42	Mar	2:34:46	2:31:06 -91
Viola	Simona	ITA	18.11.71		5k	15:47.59	16:58.34 -93
Vivier	Laurence	FRA	21.11.67	167/52	1500	4:13.15	4:13.69 -93
					3k	8:59.95i	8:56.92 -93
Vizaniari	Lisa	AUS	14.12.71	173/93	SP	16.61	16.14 -88
					DT	55.58	60.44 -90
Vlasova	Alena	KZK	2.12.69		Hep	5650	5819 -93
Vogoli	Katerina	GRE	30.1.70	175/87	DT	62.32	59.70 -93
Vokuhl	Anja	GER	17.8.73	177/61	TJ	13.34	13.92i, 13.87 -93
Volf	Yelena	RUS	2.3.69		LJ	6.61	6.53 -88
					Hep	5929	5975w -89
Volker	Evi	GER	10.5.72	178/74	JT	58.18	58.34 -93
Vollmann	Ute	GER	29.12.73	162/52	10kW	45:58	47:04 -93
* Voronova #	Natalya	RUS	9.7.65	170/60	100	11.13dq, 11.37	10.98 -88
					200	22.82dq, 23.22, 22.8i	22.35 -93
Voronova	Olga	RUS	23.2.68	173/58	100	11.43, 11.1	11.36, 11.32w -88
Vorster	Elinda	RSA	8.9.65	167/54	100	11.47, 11.34w	11.22 -90
					200	22.97	22.58 -90
Vostrikova	Irina	RUS	30.8.70	177/64	HJ	1.88	1.86 -93
					LJ	6.52	6.40 -93
					Hep	6379	6066 -93
Voverytė	Jurgita	LIT	29.12.74		HJ	1.88	1.86 -93
Vriesde	Letitia	SUR	5.10.64	159/50	800	2:02.39	1:57.96 -92
					800	2:01.53i	1:57.96 -92
Wada	Noriko	JPN	24.5.75	163/48	5k	15:53.9	15:56.0 -93
Wadsworth	Stevanie	USA	19.3.72	170/86	SP	17.02i, 16.95	17.19 -93
Wahlander	Elisabeth	SWE	14.3.60	170/67	JT	59.42	63.18 -92
Wachtel	Christine	GER	6.1.65	166/56	800	2:01.84	1:55.32 -87
Walker	Astia	JAM	4.4.75		100	11.44	11.91, 11.4w -93
					200	22.9, 23.19 dq	23.65 -93
					100h	13.37	13.75, 13.6 -93
Wallace	Andrea	GBR	22.11.66	170/47	HMar	71:34	69:39 -93
Waller	Donna	USA	6.4.64	167/57	100h	13.37w	13.01, 12.94w -92
Waller	Tisha	USA	1.12.70	183/60	HJ	1.96i, 1.96	1.94 -93
Walton	Sue	USA	21.8.72	167/51	100	11.36	11.64 -91, 11.24w -92
					200	22.94	23.41, 22.93w -92
Wamuyu	Gladys	KEN	23.12.72	167/63	800	2:03.00	2:00.0 -93
Wang	Dongmei	CHN	3.12.73	164/45	10k	32:28.05	31:50.39 -93
Wang	Huei-chen	TPE	21.2.71	171/55	100	11.41, 11.35w	11.29, 11.2 -91
					200	23.34	22.56 -92
Wang	Jing	CHN	16.1.75		100	11.45	11.39 -93
* Wang	Junxia	CHN	9.1.73	160/48	1500	4:11.20	3:51.92 -93
					3k	8:50.79	8:06.11 -93
					10k	30:50.34	29:31.78 -93
					Mar	2:31:11	2:24:07 -93
Wang	Lianyun	CHN	, 10.69		JT	58.12	63.92 -93
Wang	Mingxia	CHN	6.6.71	156/46	5k	15:51.7	15:54.48 -92
					10k	32:36.77	32:30.96 -92
					HMar	71:26	

Name		Nat	Born	Ht/Wt	Event	1994 Mark	Pre-1994 Best
Wang	Wenxiang	CHN	.3.73		Hep	6083	5935 -93
Wang	Xiangrong	CHN	.2.76		TJ	13.50	13.74, 14.07w -93
Wang	Xiaoxia	CHN	20.9.76	159/51	10k	32:33.03	
Wang	Xiujie	CHN	20.11.73		3k	9:02.22	8:47.89 -93
* Wang	Xiuting	CHN	16.2.65	158/45	3k	8:50.68	8:50.68 -87
					5k	15:40.0	15:23.58 -92
Wang	Xiuxie	CHN	21.8.76		3k	8:49.92	9:15.42 -93
Wanjiru	Esther	KEN	27.3.77	162/42	5k	15:38.85	
					10k	32:23.25	34:38.05 -92
Warnicka	Monika	POL	26.4.69	178/62	400h	55.93	55.82 -93
Watanabe	Mineko	JPN	24.7.72	161/45	HMar	71:38	
Watanasin	Reawadee	THA	11.8.67	168/59	400h	56.25	56.78 -91
Wawrzyniak (Jancewicz)	Donata	POL	17.6.69	189/68	HJ	1.92	1.93 -92
* Weavers	Charmaine	RSA	27.2.64	178/65	HJ	1.94	2.00 -85
Webb	Richelle	USA	8.10.71		100	11.42	
					200	23.13, 22.90w	
Wei	Li	CHN	.1.72		10k	32:37.94	31:28.83 -93
Wei	Linkun	CHN	, 12.75		10kW	44:25.0	43:34 -93
Weidenbach	Lisa	USA	13.12.61	178/57	HMar	72:15	71:44 -93
Weidner	Simone	GER	30.9.69	173/55	800	2:01.19	2:02.45 -93
					1500	4:12.09	4:10.26 -93
Weis	Melisa	USA	22.5.71	176/80	SP	16.51i, 16.46	16.79 -92
					DT	55.36	55.86 -92
Wentland	Gwen	USA	29.4.72	178/64	HJ	1.93i, 1.89	1.92 -93
* Wessel	Kathrin	GER	14.8.67	172/52	3k	8:50.07	8:44.81 :41.79i -88
					5k	15:10.84	14:58.71 -91
					10k	31:38.75	31:03.62 -91
					HMar	70:47	0
Westén	Monica	SWE	15.3.66	175/62	800	2:03.0	2:01.86 -93
					800	2:02.66i	2:01.86 -91
					400h	55.92	54.69 -90
Wickus	Amy	USA	25.6.72	163/55	800	2:00.60	2:00.07 -93
Williams	Allison	USA	21.6.71	160/55	100h	13.12	13.16 -93
Williams	Claudine	JAM	8.1.76	175/62	400	52.19	51.66 -92
Williams	Doris	USA	30.6.63	172/64	100h	13.29, 10.26w, 13.1	13.18, 13.14w -93
Williams	Shana	USA	7.4.72	178/57	LJ	6.53w	6.63 -93
Williams	Trevaia	USA	7.9.68	183/64	400	52.34i	52.79 -93
					100h	13.34w	13.67 -91
					400h	56.21	55.94 -92
Williams	Tonya	USA	5.10.74	165/54	400h	55.98	56.48 -93
Wilson	Liz	USA	9.6.68	165/54	5k	15:51.79	16:10.42 -90
Wilson	Shiny	IND	8.5.65	167/53	400	52.41	53.46, 5, 3.2 -91
					800	2:01.90	2:01.90 -92
Wisniewska	Joanna	POL	24.5.72	178/82	DT	59.58	57.56 -93
Wittich	Ines	GER	14.11.69	188/90	SP	19.14i, 18.52	19.48 -87
* Wlodarczyk	Urszula	POL	22.12.65	180/67	100h	13.19	13.31 -92
					TJ	13.35i, 13.61w	13.98 -93
					Hep	6322	6425 -91
Wolf	Birgit	GER	11.9.69	175/58	400h	56.89	55.91 -93
Womplou	Marie	CIV	20.12.69	161/46	400h	56.39	56.52 -92
Woodward	Tosha	USA	28.4.71	168/48	800	2:01.69	2:05.03 -93
Wu	Hongjie	CHN	13.4.71		400h	57.27	56.86 -93
Wu	Shuzhen	CHN	27.8.73		Hep	5753	6249 -93
Wu	Xianchun	CHN	1.2.72		SP	19.23	19.35 -92
Wüest	Sara	SUI	4.8.69	170/56	100	11.43w	11.46 -92
					200	23.26	23.32 -92
* Wyeth	Alison	GBR	26.5.64	178/56	1500	4:04.19	4:03.17 -93
					Mile	4:30.24	4:24.87 -91
					3k	8:45.76	8:43.93 -92
					5k	15:10.38	15:47.97 -89
* Wyludda	Ilke	GER	28.3.69	185/97	DT	68.72	74.56 -89
Xanthou	Niki	GRE	11.10.73	174/56	LJ	6.74	6.60 -92
Xenou	Vasiliki	GRE	5.5.74	175/56	HJ	1.88i	1.80 -93
Xiang	Zhengfeng	CHN	.		JT	56.98	
Xie	Hongxia	CHN	5.4.70		SP	18.31	19.22 -93
Xie	Liuying	CHN	.1.67		100h	13.18	12.75 -93
Xu	Pin	CHN	, 10.70		LJ	6.45	
Yada	Tami	JPN	31.5.72		10k	32:47.72	

Name		Nat	Born	Ht/Wt	Event	1994 Mark	Pre-1994 Best
Yamagishi	Naoko	JPN	28.8.70	167/50	HMar	72:00	
Yamaguchi	Sumie	JPN	9.11.73	157/43	10k	32:34.73	
Yamanouchi	Mineko	JPN	10.12.72	161/45	5k	15:54.18	15:47.86 -93
					HMar	72:13	
Yamaoka	Emi	JPN	15.11.74	160/50	HMar	72:30	73:59 -93
Yamazaki	Yoko	JPN	25.7.75	154/38	10k	32:34.11	
Yamazoe	Yuko	JPN	4.5.73	158/46	Mar	2:31:21	
Yan	Wei	CHN	12.10.71	164/52	800	2:00.48	2:00.49 -93
					1500	4:03.40	4:01.69 -93
Yang	Fang	CHN	15.10.71	173/63	LJ	6.50	
Yao	Weili	CHN	6.5.68	172/57	LJ	6.91	7.01 -93
Yarygina	Oksana	UZB	24.12.72	170/65	JT	64.62	59.90 -92
Yashima	Atsumi	JPN	28.6.75	149/44	5k	15:26.3	
* Yegorova	Valentina	RUS	16.2.64	156/52	Mar	2:23:33	2:26:40 -93
* Yelesina	Yelena	RUS	4.4.70	184/56	HJ	1.95	2.02 -90
Yenvarenko	Galina	RUS	.70		PV	3.70	3.80 -93
Yermolovich	Natalya	BLR	29.4.64	175/80	JT	58.42	69.86 -85
Yordanova	Anelia	BUL	27.4.72	174/74	SP	16.48i, 16.48	16.01 -91
Yoshiawa	Mari	JPN	5.1.75	154/38	5k	15:55.3	
					HMar	72:06	
Yoshida	Mitsuyo	JPN	29.10.66	172/50	10k	32:52.04	
					Mar	2:26:26	2:29:16 -93
Yoshida	Naomi	JPN	14.4.69	160/44	10k	32:02.95	32:24.19 -92
* Young	Dannette	USA	3.10.64	170/57	100	11.33	11.10 -88
					200	22.29, 22.16w	22.23 -88, 22.19w -90
					400	51.29	50.46 -92
Young	Telisa	USA	17.1.71	165/55	TJ	13.53	13.14 -93
Yu	Juan	CHN	21.1.74		SP	18.35i	17.53 -93
Yu	Qing	CHN	22.5.72		100h	13.26	13.32 -93
Yu	Qingmei	CHN	20.5.75		DT	59.56	54.50 -93
Yudakova	Natalya	RUS	25.3.65		200	23.30w	
					100h	12.89	13.42 -86
Yukhnevich	Leonarda	BLR	3.10.63		5000W	21:58.64	22:11.2 -92
					10kW	45:47.18	44:02 -93
Yurkova	Lidia	BLR	15.1.67	168/60	100h	13.14	12.66 -90, 12.5 -88
* Yusuf	Fatima	NGR	2.5.71	178/64	200	23.16	22.84 -91
					400	50.53	50.41 -91
Zagarskiene	Danute	LIT	13.10.70		10kW	46:36	
Zach	Janet	GER	19.6.75		PV	3.85	3.50i, 3.50 -93
Zaituc	Luminita	ROM	9.10.68	163/47	1500	4:12.48	4:10.42 -93
					3k	8:58.23	8:51.54 -93
Zajac	Carole	USA	24.3.72	163/46	5k	15:52.89	15:56.36 -92,15:53.78i -93
					10k	33:05.05	32:22.97 -92
Zakharchenko	Ilona	UKR	16.6.67	178/85	DT	61.18	64.80 -92
Zakharova	Irina	RUS	2.2.74		SP	16.38	15.35 -93
Zakharova	Tatyana	RUS	18.4.69	181/65	400	51.42	53.44 -93
Zalevskaya	Svetlana	KZK	14.6.73	188/65	HJ	1.89i, 1.89	1.94 -93
Zavadskaya	Yelena	UKR	24.12.64	171/60	800	1:58.81	1:59.36 -92
Zavgorodnaya	Svetlana	UKR	20.8.66	162/55	100h	13.31, 13.0	13.69 -93
Zetouani	Nadia	MAR	3.1.70	166/59	400h	56.29	56.76 -93
Zhang	Hengyun	CHN	25.10.74	170/58	400	51.61	51.25 -93
Zhang	Jing	CHN	10.3.70	170/60	TJ	13.75	13.92 -93
Zhang	Li	CHN	26.6.61	170/85	JT	61.34	70.42 -90
* Zhang	Linli	CHN	6.3.73	161/52	3k	8:50.05	8:16.50 -93
					10k	32:19.33	31:16.28 -93
					Mar	2:32:15	2:24:42 -93
* Zhang	Lirong	CHN	3.3.73	156/48	1500	4:13.84	3:59.70 -93
					3k	8:50.51	8:21.84 -93
* Zhang	Liuhong	CHN	16.1.69	180/86	SP	20.54	19.90 -93
Zhang	Liwen	CHN	29.1.73		HJ	1.88	1.82 -93
Zhang	Qinghua	CHN	6.2.73		10kW	43:25.2	42:57 -93
Zhang	Xiaohui	CHN	23.3.71	176/66	Hep	6200	6092 -93
Zhang	Yan	CHN	.6.72		LJ	6.52	
					TJ	13.94	14.28 -93
Zhang	Yaqing	CHN	15.1.77		DT	55.30	
Zhang	Yinlan	CHN	14.2.70		LJ	6.77	6.65 -92, 6.74w -93
* Zhang	Yu	CHN	8.4.71	176/60	100h	12.86	12.64 -93
Zhang	Yumei	CHN	25.11.71		800	2:00.02	1:58.63 -93
					1500	4:10.94	

Name		Nat	Born	Ht/Wt	Event	1994 Mark	Pre-1994 Best
Zhang	Zhiying	CHN	19.7.73	174/80	SP	18.60	19.77 -93
Zhao	Guiyan	CHN	25.4.77		JT	58.28	
Zhao	Tianhui	CHN	.2.73		TJ	13.66	13.31 -91, 13.55w -93
Zhao	Yuhong	CHN	15.5.73	169/75	JT	61.40	64.16 -93
* Zhdanova	Yevgenia	RUS	21.7.66	175/53	HJ	1.98	1.95i, 1.94 -93
Zhen	Wenhua	CHN	8.3.67		SP	18.98	20.06 -91
Zheng	Liyuan	CHN	.4.74		400h	57.39	55.72 -93
Zhilyayeva	Alla	RUS	.68		HMar	71:16	
Zhirova	Marina	RUS	6.6.63	170/58	200	23.38	22.46 -85
Zhong	Guiqing	CHN	.75		PV	3.80	
* Zhong	Huandi	CHN	20.9.67	155/43	5k	15:37.37	15:05.69 -93
					10k	31:43.69	30:13.37 -93
					Mar	2:29:32	2:25:36 -93
Zhou	Hongyang	CHN	5.4.70	170/55	100h	12.87	12.90 -93
Zhou	Jing	CHN	.2.73		100h	13.34	13.15 -93
Zhou	Xiulian	CHN	.11.70		TJ	13.52	13.91 -93
Zhuk	Irina	UKR	15.1.66	184/104	SP	19.22	17.94 -92
Zhuravlyova	Tatyana	RUS	19.12.67	183/74	LJ	6.55	6.60 -93
					Hep	6290	6370 -91
Zilinskiene	Nele	LIT	29.12.69	177/61	HJ	1.96	1.95 -93
Zinck	Pia	DEN	4.5.71	170/58	HJ	1.88	1.84 -92
Zipp	Bettina	GER	29.4.72	168/59	100	11.39	11.46 -91
					200	23.21	24.17 -93
Znamenskaya	Yelena	RUS	2.6.66	180/66	400h	57.27	56.57 -92
Zotter	Stefanie	AUT	8.12.71	180/65	400h	57.27	59.97 -90
Zsigmond	Kinga	HUN	19.4.64	172/68	JT	63.40	63.90 -92
Zubiolo	Sophie	BEL	15.1.73		PV	3.63i. 3.60	
Zukowska	Marta	POL	4.6.72	154/54	10kW	45:16	46:50 -93
* Zuñiga	Teresa	ESP	28.12.64	167/56	1500	4:08.63	4:00.59 -92
Zürcher	Regula	SUI	5.1.69	165/55	400	52.75i	52.19 -93
* Zvereva	Ellina	BLR	16.11.60	182/90	DT	67.44	71.58 -88

1995 WORLD INDOOR LISTS

\# Oversized track (over 200m/220y), @ suspect timing

MEN

50 Metres

Mark	Athlete	Pl	Venue	Date
5.63A	Henry Neal USA	1	Reno	10 Feb
5.64	Bruny Surin CAN	1	Moskva	27 Jan

55 Metres

Mark	Athlete	Pl	Venue	Date
6.12	Tim Harden USA	1	Indianapolis	11 Mar
6.13	Philip Riley USA	1	Gainesville	22 Jan

60 Metres

Mark	Athlete	Pl	Venue	Date
6.46	Bruny Surin CAN	1	Barcelona	10 Mar
6.47	Linford Christie GBR	1	Liévin	19 Feb
6.51	Darren Braithwaite GBR	2	Barcelona	10 Mar
6.52	Frank Fredericks NAM	2	Liévin	19 Feb
6.52@	Andrey Grigoryev RUS	1	Volgograd	26 Feb
6.52	Donovan Bailey CAN	2	Singelfingen	4 Mar
6.54	Tim Harden USA	1	Atlanta	4 Mar
6.54	Michael Green JAM	1s1	Atlanta	4 Mar
6.55	Robert Esmie CAN	2	Saskatoon	18 Feb
6.56	Henry Neal USA	1	Cleveland	17 Feb
6.56	Dmitriy Bartenyev RUS	h	Volgograd	26 Feb
6.56	Michael Marsh USA	3	Atlanta	4 Mar
6.57	Olapade Adeniken NGR	3	Liévin	19 Feb
6.57	Vitaliy Savin KZK	4	Liévin	19 Feb
6.57	Dennis Mitchell USA	4	Atlanta	4 Mar
6.58	Colin Jackson GBR	1	Birmingham	28 Jan
6.58@	Yevgeniy Mizera RUS	2	Volgograd	26 Feb
6.59	Gus Nketia NZL	2h3	Barcelona	10 Mar
6.59	Maurice Greene USA	4	Barcelona	10 Mar

100 Metres

Mark	Athlete	Pl	Venue	Date
10.13	Oladape Adeniken NGR	1	Johnson C	29 Jan
10.14	Michael Green JAM	2	Johnson C	29 Jan

200 Metres

Mark	Athlete	Pl	Venue	Date
20.25	Linford Christie GBR	1r1	Liévin	19 Feb
20.26	Frank Fredericks NAM	2r1	Liévin	19 Feb
20.48	John Regis GBR	1	Stuttgart	5 Feb
20.51	Geir Moen NOR	1r2	Liévin	19 Feb
20.54	Olapade Adeniken NGR	2r2	Liévin	19 Feb
20.66	Patrick Stevens BEL	1r3	Liévin	19 Feb
20.75	Tod Long USA	1	Atlanta	4 Mar
20.77	Vladislav Dologodin UKR	2r3	Liévin	19 Feb
20.78	Dave Dopek USA	1r2	Indianapolis	10 Mar
20.80	Antonio Pettigrew USA	2	Atlanta	4 Mar
20.81	Brad Fields USA	3	Atlanta	4 Mar
20.82	Donovan Bailey CAN	1	Sindelfingen	4 Mar
20.84	Solomon Wariso GBR	2	Birmingham	28 Jan
20.84	Rod Tolbert USA	4	Atlanta	4 Mar
20.86	Derrick Thompson USA	1r1	Indianapolis	10 Mar
20.87	Darren Braithwaite GBR	1	Birmingham	1 Jan

400 Metres

Mark	Athlete	Pl	Venue	Date
44.63	Michael Johnson USA	1	Atlanta	4 Mar
45.59	Derek Mills USA	2	Atlanta	4 Mar
45.61	Darnell Hall USA	3	Atlanta	4 Mar
45.66	Greg Haughton JAM	1r2	Boston	11 Feb
45.98	Charles Gitonga KEN	2	Liévin	19 Feb
46.00	Deon Minor USA	1r2	Indianapolis	11 Mar
46.05	Mark Everett USA	2h3	Atlanta	4 Mar
46.16	Kevin Lyles USA	3r2	Indianapolis	11 Mar
46.17	Ryan Hayden USA	1	Indianapolis	11 Mar
46.31	Karsten Just GER	2	Stuttgart	5 Feb
46.38	Sunday Bada NGR	2	Barcelona	12 Mar
46.42	Dorian Green USA	1B	Champaign	26 Feb
46.46	Andrew Valmon USA	1	Boston	21 Jan
46.47	Marlin Cannon USA	2	Indianapolis	11 Mar
46.57	Calvin Davis USA	2	Fairfax	25 Feb
45.94#	Jude Monye NGR	1	Lexington	4 Feb

800 Metres

Mark	Athlete	Pl	Venue	Date
1:44.88	Nico Motchebon GER	1	Stuttgart	5 Feb
1:46.35	Joachim Dehmel GER	2	Stuttgart	5 Feb
1:46.38	Pavel Soukup TCH	1	Ludwigshafen	25 Jan
1:46.61	Andrey Loginov RUS	1	Stockholm	27 Feb
1:46.67	Benson Koech KEN	1	Budapest	29 Jan
1:46.70	Joseph Tengelei KEN	1	Atlanta	4 Mar
1:46.76	Marco Chiavarini ITA	1	Genoa	28 Jan
1:46.79	Ivan Komar BLR	1	Birmingham	25 Feb
1:47.24	Kennedy Osei GHA	2	Birmingham	25 Feb
1:47.24	Jose Parrilla USA	2	Atlanta	4 Mar
1:47.30	Tor Øyvind Ødegård NOR	2	Stockholm	27 Feb
1:47.30	Clive Terrelonge JAM	1	Barcelona	12 Mar
1:47.37	Torbjörn Johansson SWE	3	Stockholm	27 Feb
1:47.45	Andrea Giocondi ITA	2	Gent	12 Feb
1:47.46	Andrés Diaz ESP	2	Valencia	14 Mar

1000 Metres

Mark	Athlete	Pl	Venue	Date
2:15.62	Vénuste Niyongabo BUR	1	Stockholm	27 Feb

1500 Metres

Mark	Athlete	Pl	Venue	Date
3:34.29	Noureddine Morceli ALG	1	Grenoble	29 Jan
3:35.70	Hicham El Guerrouj MAR	1	Stuttgart	5 Feb
3:36.33	Vénuste Niyongabo BUR	1	Sindelfingen	4 Mar
3:36.61	Fermin Cacho ESP	1	Sevilla	17 Feb
3:37.99	Mateo Cañellas ESP	2	Sevilla	17 Feb
3:38.21	Moses Kiptanui KEN	2	Stuttgart	5 Feb
3:40.74	Jens-Peter Herold GER	3	Stuttgart	5 Feb
3:41.06	Massimo Pegoretti ITA	3	Sevilla	17 Feb
3:41.19	Patrik Johansson SWE	4	Sevilla	17 Feb
3:41.28	Tony Whiteman GBR	2	Birmingham	25 Feb
3:41.66	Éric Dubus FRA	1	Glasgow	11 Feb
3:41.74	Rüdiger Stenzel GER	1	Sindelfingen	26 Feb
3:42.10	Victor Rojas ESP	5	Sevilla	17 Feb
3:42.23	Dominique Löser GER	4	Stuttgart	5 Feb
3:42.41	Ignasi Taló ESP	6	Sevilla	17 Feb

1 Mile

Mark	Athlete	Pl	Venue	Date
3:55.33	Kevin Sullivan CAN	1	Indianapolis	11 Mar
3:55.72	Graham Hood CAN	2	Indianapolis	11 Mar
3:56.48	Marcus O'Sullivan IRL	1	Fairfax	25 Feb
3:56.89	Terrance Herrington USA	2	Fairfax	25 Feb
3:57.23	Jason Pyrah USA	3	Fairfax	25 Feb
3:57.28	Erik Nedeau USA	4	Fairfax	25 Feb
3:57.34#	Paul McMullen USA	2	Notre Dame	4 Feb
3:58.21		3	Indianapolis	11 Mar
3:57.76	Vyacheslav Shabunin RUS	1	Moskva	14 Feb
3:57.99	Andrey Loginov RUS	2	Moskva	14 Feb
3:58.14	Niall Bruton IRL	3	New York	3 Feb
3:58.77	Passmore Furusa ZIM	4	Indianapolis	11 Mar
3:59.16	Brian Hyde USA	5	Indianapolis	11 Mar
3:59.99#	Buck Jones USA	1	Moscow, Id	17 Feb

2000 Metres

Mark	Athlete	Pl	Venue	Date
5:03.61	Mateo Cañellas ESP	1	Valencia	14 Mar
5:03.70	Anacleto Jiménez ESP	2	Valencia	14 Mar

3000 Metres

Mark	Athlete	Pl	Venue	Date
7:35.15	Moses Kiptanui KEN	1	Gent	12 Feb
7:37.51	Dieter Baumann GER	1	Karlsruhe	12 Feb
7:37.82	Vénuste Niyongabo BUR	1	Birmingham	25 Feb
7:41.94	Gennaro Di Napoli ITA	2	Liévin	19 Feb
7:42.66	Stephane Franke GER	3	Liévin	19 Feb
7:43.44	Éric Dubus FRA	2	Stuttgart	5 Feb
7:45.25	Smail Sghir MAR	2	Stockholm	27 Feb
7:45.34	Bob Kennedy USA	1	Fairfax	25 Feb
7:45.69	Brahim Jabbour MAR	4	Stuttgart	5 Feb
7:45.69	Mohamed Suleiman QAT	3	Stockholm	27 Feb
7:46.06	Anacleto Jiménez ESP	1	Sevilla	17 Feb
7:46.61	Todd Williams USA	2	Fairfax	25 Feb

7:46.80 John Mayock GBR 3 Birmingham 25 Feb
7:47.41 Richard Kosgei KEN 4 Stockholm 27 Feb
7:50.46 Khalid Kaiourani MAR 3 Fairfax 25 Feb
7:50.96 Ovidio Olteanu ROM 4 Gent 12 Feb
7:51.42 Réda Benzine ALG 5 Stuttgart 5 Feb
7:51.80 Eliud Barngetuny KEN 4 Fairfax 25 Feb
7:52.04 Isaac Viciosa ESP 3 Sevilla 17 Feb

50 Metres Hurdles

6.39 Mark McKoy AUT 1 Moskva 27 Jan
6.41A Mark Crear USA 1 Reno 10 Feb
6.47 Allen Johnson USA 2 Grenoble 29 Jan
6.48 Greg Foster USA 2 Moskva 27 Jan
6.51 Igor Kazankov LAT 2h1 Moskva 27 Jan
6.51A Jack Pierce USA 2 Reno 10 Feb
6.52 Mike Fenner GER 1 Leipzig 21 Jan
6.52 Aleksandr Markin RUS 3 Moskva 27 Jan

55 Metres Hurdles

7.01 Courtney Hawkins USA 1 Boston 21 Jan
7.08 Terry Reese USA 1 Fairfax 11 Feb
7.09 Anthony Dees USA 1 Johnson C 28 Jan
7.09 Allen Johnson USA 2 Boston 21 Jan
7.10 Philip Riley USA 1 Indianapolis 10 Mar

60 Metres Hurdles

7.38 Allen Johnson USA 1 Karlsruhe 12 Feb
7.39 Colin Jackson GBR 1 Glasgow 11 Feb
7.41 Courtney Hawkins USA 2 Barcelona 12 Mar
7.42 Tony Jarrett GBR 2 Liévin 19 Feb
7.46 Mark McKoy AUT 4 Barcelona 12 Mar
7.49 Mark Crear USA 2 Atlanta 4 Mar
7.52@ Yevgeniy Pechonkin RUS 1 Moskva 26 Jan
7.52 Jack Pierce USA 3 Fairfax 25 Feb
7.52@ Aleksandr Markin RUS 1s3 Volgograd 26 Feb
7.54 Anthony Dees USA 3 Madrid 9 Feb
7.54 Frank Busemann GER 1 Moskva 11 Feb
7.55 Mike Fenner GER 2 Berlin 10 Feb
7.56 Igor Kazanov LAT 5 Liévin 19 Feb
7.58 George Boroi ROM 6 Liévin 19 Feb
7.59@ Gennadiy Dakshevich RUS 2 Moskva 26 Jan
7.59 Sven Göhler GER 2 Sindelfingen 25 Feb
7.59 Antti Haapakoski FIN 1 Kuopip 5 Mar
7.61 Emilio Valle CUB 4s2 Barcelona 12 Mar
7.63 Vladimir Belokon UKR 1 Kiev 12 Feb
7.57 rs Greg Foster USA 1 Cleveland 17 Feb

110 Metres Hurdles

13.34 Allen Johnson USA 1 Moskva 14 Feb
13.38 Mark McKoy AUT 2 Moskva 14 Feb

High Jump

2.38 Javier Sotomayor CUB 1 Liévin 19 Feb
2.38 Sorin Matei ROM 1 Wuppertal 3 Feb
2.37 Artur Partyka POL 1 Balingen 11 Feb
2.36 Steinar Hoen NOR 1 Berlin 3 Mar
2.35 Lambros Papakostas GRE 2 Barcelona 12 Mar
2.34 Troy Kemp BAH 2 Wuppertal 3 Feb
2.34 Charles Austin USA 3 Balingen 11 Feb
2.34 Håkon Särnblom NOR 4 Balingen 11 Feb
2.33 Cristian Popescu ROM 2 B Bystrica 8 Feb
2.33 Oleg Zhukovskiy BLR 3 B Bystrica 8 Feb
2.33 Toni Riepl GER 1 Siegen 12 Feb
2.32 Ralf Sonn GER 4 Wuppertal 3 Feb
2.32 Dalton Grant GBR 6 Wuppertal 3 Feb
2.32 Tony Barton USA 3 Barcelona 12 Mar
2.30 Sergey Kolesnik UKR 5 B Bystrica 8 Feb
2.29A Rick Noji USA 2 Reno 10 Feb
2.28 Gustavo Becker ESP 1 S Sebastián 5 Feb
2.28 Patrik Sjöberg SWE 7 Balingen 11 Feb
2.28 Hendrik Beyer GER 8= Balingen 11 Feb
2.28 Petar Malesev YUG 1 Cleveland 17 Feb
2.28 Stevan Zoric YUG 6 Barcelona 12 Mar
2.28 Steve Smith USA 7 Barcelona 12 Mar
2.28 Ettore Ceresoli ITA 8 Barcelona 12 Mar

Pole Vault

6.00 Sergey Bubka UKR 1 Liévin 19 Feb
5.86 Radion Gataullin RUS 1 Moskva 14 Feb
5.85 Igor Trandenkov RUS 2 Donetsk 12 Feb
5.85 Nick Hysong USA 1 Atlanta 4 Mar
5.80 Pyotr Bochkaryov RUS 1 Grenoble 29 Jan
5.80 Viktor Chistyakov RUS 2 Grenoble 29 Jan
5.80A Bill Payne USA 1 Reno 10 Feb
5.80A Pat Manson USA 2 Reno 10 Feb
5.80 Maksim Tarasov RUS 2 Moskva 14 Feb
5.80 Andrej Tiwontschik GER 2 Berlin 3 Mar
5.80 Tim Bright USA 2 Atlanta 4 Mar
5.75 Vadim Strogalyov RUS 2 Volgograd 26 Feb
5.75 Okkert Brits RSA 3= Barcelona 11 Mar
5.72 Martin Voss DEN 1 Malmö 25 Feb
5.70 Pedro Arcos ESP 1 Zaragoza 28 Jan
5.70 Igor Potapovich KZK 3= Grenoble 29 Jan
5.70 Kory Tarpenning USA 3= Grenoble 29 Jan
5.70 Patrik Stenlund SWE 1 Skellefteå 11 Feb
5.70 Tim Lobinger GER 1 Sindelfingen 4 Mar
5.70 Dean Starkey USA 3 Atlanta 4 Mar
5.70 István Bagyula 4 Atlanta 4 Mar
5.70 Bill Deering USA 7 Atlanta 4 Mar

Long Jump

8.51 Ivan Pedroso CUB 1 Barcelona 11 Mar
8.28 ? Yuriy Naumkin RUS 1 Shakhti 21 Jan
8.28 Roland McGhee USA 1 New York 3 Feb
8.25 Anthuan Maybank USA 1 Ames 28 Jan
8.23 Joe Greene USA 1 Boston 21 Jan
8.21 Kareem Streete-Thompson USA 1 Fort Worth 17 Feb
8.20 Mattias Sunneborn SWE 2 Barcelona 11 Mar
8.15 Bogdan Tudor ROM 1 Bucuresti 12 Feb
8.14 Erick Walder USA 3 Barcelona 11 Mar
8.13 Milan Gombala TCH 1 Praha 5 Feb
8.13 Angel Hernández ESP 2 Madrid 9 Feb
8.11 Yevgeniy Tretyak RUS 1 Shatkti 21 Jan
8.09 Ivaylo Mladenov BUL 3 Madrid 9 Feb
8.08 Erik Nijs BEL 1 Gent 12 Feb
8.07 Percy Knox USA 1 Johnson C 26 Jan
8.06 Darius Pemberton USA 1 Baton Rouge 25 Feb
8.00 Kostas Koukodimos GRE 1 Pireas 12 Feb
8.00 Gregor Cankar SLO 1 Ljubljana 25 Feb

Triple Jump

17.72 Brian Wellman BER 1 Barcelona 12 Mar
17.62 Yoelvis Quesada CUB 2 Barcelona 12 Mar
17.16 Serge Hélan FRA 1 Liévin 26 Feb
17.06 Oleg Sakirkin KZK 2 Grenoble 29 Jan
17.06 Dmitriy Byzov RUS 1 Volgograd 26 Feb
17.05A Kenny Harrison USA 1 Reno 10 Feb
17.03 Andrius Raizgys LIT 1 Panevezys 26 Feb
17.00 Gennadiy Markov RUS 1 Birmingham 28 Jan
16.99 Edrick Floreal CAN 1 Johnson C 29 Jan
16.99 James Beckford JAM 1 Manhattan 4 Mar
16.95 Denis Kapustin RUS 2 Moskva 27 Jan
16.93 Vasiliy Sokov RUS 2 Moskva 14 Feb
16.92 Sergey Arzamasov KZK 3 Moskva 14 Feb
16.92 Maris Bruziks LAT 2 Liévin 19 Feb
16.92 LaMark Carter USA Q Barcelona 10 Mar
16.90 Arne Holm SWE 1 Malmö 26 Feb
16.88 Andrey Kayukov RUS 2 Volgograd 25 Feb
16.86 Stoyko Tsonev BUL 1 Sofia 11 Feb
16.86 Vladimir Kravchenko UKR 1 Kiev 12 Feb
16.86 Garfield Anselm FRA 2 Liévin 26 Feb
16.86 Lars Hedman SWE 4 Barcelona 12 Mar
16.74 Francis Agyepong GBR 7 Barcelona 12 Mar

Shot

21.22	C J Hunter USA	1	Air Academy	5 Feb
21.17	Kevin Toth USA	1	Cleveland	17 Feb
20.83	Mika Halvari FIN	1	Tampere	25 Feb
20.53	John Godina USA	1	Baton Rouge	28 Jan
20.53	Randy Barnes USA	1	Maebashi	5 Feb
20.38	Paolo Dal Soglio ITA	1	Genoa	22 Jan
20.36	Dragan Peric YUG	3	Barcelona	10 Mar
20.24	Saulius Kleiza LIT	1	Panevys	17 Feb
20.19	Brent Noon USA	1	Baton Rouge	25 Feb
19.97	Manuel Martínez ESP	4	Barcelona	10 Mar
19.92	Saulis Kleiza LIT	1	Panevezys	25 Feb
19.89	Yevgeniy Palchikov RUS	1	Volgograd	26 Feb
19.87	Oliver-Sven Buder GER	1	Sindelfingen	25 Feb
19.80	Gregg Tafralis USA	1	Sassnitz	11 Feb
19.74	Yuriy Belonog UKR	5	Barcelona	10 Mar
19.67	Petur Gudmundsson ISL	6	Barcelona	10 Mar
19.64	Thorsten Herbrand GER	1	Erfurt	15 Feb

35 Lb Weight

25.86	Lance Deal USA	1	Atlanta	4 Mar
23.48	Lou Chisari USA	2	New York	3 Feb
22.75	Scott McGee USA	3	Atlanta	4 Mar
22.22	Alex Papadimitriou GRE	1	Air Academy	24 Feb
21.95	Brian Murer USA	1	Lincoln	10 Feb

Heptathlon

6246	Christian Plaziat FRA	1	Barcelona	12 Mar
6169	Tomas Dvorák TCH	2	Barcelona	12 Mar
6142	Henrik Dagård SWE	3	Barcelona	12 Mar
6120	Ricky Barker USA	4	Barcelona	12 Mar
6035#	Sheldon Blockburger USA	1	Moscow, Id	11 Feb
6026#	Petri Keskitalo FIN	1	Kuopio	12 Feb
5978	Alex Kruger GBR	5	Barcelona	12 Mar
5953	Yevgeniy Dudakov RUS	1	Chelyabinsk	4 Feb
5939	Antonio Peñalver ESP	6	Barcelona	12 Mar
5939#	Erki Nool EST	2	Kuopio	12 Feb
5885	Michael Kohnle GER	1	Frankfurt	29 Jan
5880	Zsolt Kürtösi HUN	1	Budapest	4 Feb
5877	Anthony Brannen GBR	1	Birmingham	5 Feb
5876	Jan Podebradsky TCH	1	Praha	5 Mar
5870	Sebastien Levicq FRA	8	Barcelona	12 Mar
5858	Dmitriy Sukhomazov BLR	1	Gomel	28 Jan

5000 Metres Walk

18:07.08	Mikhail Shchennikov RUS	1	Moskva	14 Feb
18:56.9	Aigars Fadejevs LAT	1	Riga	18 Feb
19:03.93	Axel Noack GER	1	Sindelfingen	25 Feb
19:04.29	Grigoriy Kornev RUS	2	Moskva	14 Feb
19:04.52	Costica Balan ROM	1	Bucuresti	24 Feb
19:09.8	Mikhail Orlov RUS	2	Moskva	24 Jan

10,000 Metres Walk

39:10.6	Mikhail Khmelnitskiy BLR	1	Minsk	4 Feb
39:34.0	Frants Kostyukevich BLR	1	Minsk	4 Feb

WOMEN

50 Metres

5.96+	Irina Privalova RUS	1	Madrid	9 Feb
6.12	Anelia Nuneva BUL	1	Moskva	27 Jan
6.15+	Zhanna Tarnopolskaya UKR	2=	Madrid	9 Feb
6.15+	Juliet Cuthbert JAM	2=	Madrid	9 Feb
6.16	Christy Opara-Thompson NGR	2	Moskva	27 Jan

55 Metres

6.60	Gwen Torrence USA	1	Johnson C	28 Jan
6.67	Carlette Guidry USA	2	Johnson C	28 Jan
6.67	Sevatheda Fynes BAH	1	Lincoln	11 Feb

60 Metres

6.92	Irina Privalova RUS	1	Madrid	9 Feb
6.97	Merlene Ottey JAM	2	Liévin	19 Feb
7.04	Gwen Torrence USA	1	Atlanta	4 Mar
7.04	Carlette Guidry USA	2	Atlanta	4 Mar
7.08@	Nadezhda Roshchupkina RUS	1	Volgograd	24 Feb
7.08@	Yekat. Leshcheva RUS	2	Volgograd	24 Feb
7.10	Melanie Paschke GER	2	Barcelona	10 Mar
7.11@	Irina Pukha UKR	1s	Kiev	11 Feb
7.12	Zhanna Tarnopolskaya UKR	2	Madrid	9 Feb
7.12	Juliet Cuthbert JAM	3	Madrid	9 Feb
7.13	Liliana Allen CUB	2s1	Barcelona	10 Mar
7.15	Anelia Nuneva BUL	1h1	Madrid	9 Feb
7.15@	Natalya Merzlyakova RUS	3	Volgograd	24 Feb
7.15	Chryste Gaines USA	2s1	Atlanta	4 Mar
7.16	Patricia Girard FRA	1h	Liévin	25 Feb
7.16@	Svetlana Goncharenko RUS	4	Volgograd	24 Feb
7.16	Bev McDonald JAM	5	Barcelona	10 Mar
7.16	Sheila Echols USA	3s1	Atlanta	4 Mar
7.17	Nelli Cooman NED	7	Barcelona	10 Mar

200 Metres

22.10	Irina Privalova RUS	1	Liévin	19 Feb
22.60	Juliet Cuthbert JAM	2	Liévin	19 Feb
22.64	Melinda Gainsford AUS	1	Barcelona	11 Mar
22.68	Pauline Davis BAH	2	Barcelona	11 Mar
22.73	Carlette Guidry USA	1	Atlanta	4 Mar
22.80	Natalya Voronova RUS	1	Stuttgart	5 Feb
22.80A	Gwen Torrence USA	1	Reno	10 Feb
22.83	Dannette Young USA	2	Atlanta	4 Mar
22.96	Silke Lichtenhagen GER	1	Sindelfingen	26 Feb
23.00	Yekat. Leshchova RUS	1	Volgograd	26 Feb
23.03	Zlatka Georgieva BUL	2s2	Barcelona	10 Mar
23.05	Heike Drechsler GER	2	Sindelfingen	4 Mar
23.06	Silke Knoll GER	1	Dortmund	11 Feb
23.07	Maya Azarashvili GEO	2	Stuttgart	5 Feb
23.12	Oksana Dyachenko RUS	2	Moskva	26 Jan
23.14	Merlene Frazer JAM	1r2	Indianapolis	10 Mar
23.15	Svetlana Goncharenko RUS	3	Moskva	14 Feb
23.16	Bev McDonald JAM	1	Sevilla	17 Feb
23.16	Juliet Campbell JAM	1h2	Atlanta	4 Mar
23.19	Galina Malchugina RUS	2A	Budapest	29 Jan
22.85#	Carlette Guidry USA	1	Johnson C	29 Jan

400 Metres

50.23	Irina Privalova RUS	1	Barcelona	12 Mar
50.99	Jearl Miles USA	1	Atlanta	4 Mar
51.38	Sandie Richards JAM	2	Barcelona	12 Mar
51.57	Svetlana Goncharenko RUS	1	Gent	12 Feb
51.64	Yelena Andreyeva RUS	1	Stuttgart	5 Feb
51.74	Daniela Georgieva BUL	1	Sofia	4 Feb
51.92	Maicel Malone USA	2	Atlanta	4 Mar
52.01	Deon Hemmings JAM	4	Barcelona	12 Mar
52.03	Sandra Myers ESP	1	Valencia	26 Feb
52.27	Helena Dziurová TCH	1	Praha	26 Feb
52.27	Kim Graham USA	4	Atlanta	4 Mar
52.33	Rochelle Stevens USA	5	Atlanta	4 Mar
52.35	Tatyana Chebykina RUS	1	Moskva	26 Jan
52.39	Youlanda Warren USA	1	Indianapolis	11 Mar
52.40	Linda Kisabaka GER	2	Stuttgart	5 Feb

800 Metres

1:57.62	Maria Mutola MOZ	1	Barcelona	12 Mar
1:59.61	Meredith Rainey USA	2	Atlanta	4 Mar
1:59.79	Yelena Afanasyeva RUS	2	Barcelona	12 Mar
1:59.85	Joetta Clark USA	3	Atlanta	4 Mar
2:00.36	Ellen van Langen NED	1	Liévin	19 Feb
2:00.36	Letitia Vriesde SUR	3	Barcelona	12 Mar
2:00.43	Irina Samorokova RUS	4	Barcelona	12 Mar
2:00.44	Lyudmila Rogachova RUS	1	Budapest	29 Jan
2:00.81	Carla Sacramento POR	1	Sevilla	17 Feb
2:01.14	Stella Jongmans NED	5	Barcelona	12 Mar
2:01.54	Lyubov Kremlyova RUS ¶	1	Moskva	26 Jan
2:01.71	Yelena Afanasyeva RUS	2	Moskva	14 Feb

2:01.93	Violeta Beclea ROM	3	Stockholm	27 Feb
2:02.00	Inez Turner JAM	6	Barcelona	12 Mar
2:02.07	Yelena Zavadskaya UKR	3	Liévin	19 Feb
2:02.10	Ludmila Formanová TCH	1	Wien	12 Feb

1000 Metres

2:34.41	Lyubov Kremlyova RUS ¶	1	Erfurt	15 Feb
2:34.89	Violeta Beclea ROM	2	Erfurt	15 Feb

1500 Metres

4:10.41	Lyubov Kremlyova RUS ¶	1	Moskva	26 Jan
4:12.61	Regina Jacobs USA	1	Barcelona	12 Mar
4:13.02	Carla Sacramento POR	2	Barcelona	12 Mar
4:13.15	Yvonne van der Kolk NED	1	Den Haag	19 Feb
4:13.46	Violeta Beclea ROM	2	Karlsruhe	12 Feb
4:13.91	Mayte Zuñiga ESP	3	Karlsruhe	12 Feb
4:14.74	Ann Griffiths GBR	1	Birmingham	28 Jan
4:14.91	Carmen Wüstenhagen GER	1	Berlin	22 Jan

1 Mile

4:26.54	Regina Jacobs USA	1	Atlanta	4 Mar
4:31.66	Angela Chalmers CAN	1	New York	3 Feb
4:33.58	Kristen Seabury USA	1	Boston	19 Feb
4:33.78	Hassiba Boulmerka ALG	2	Indianapolis	4 Mar
4:33.97	Lynn Jennings USA	2	Fairfax	25 Feb
4:34.24	Kathy Franey USA	3	Fairfax	25 Feb
4:34.60	Debbie Marshall USA	1	Boston	21 Jan

3000 Metres

8:52.49	Lynn Jennings USA	1	Boston	19 Feb
8:54.50	Gabriela Szabo ROM	1	Barcelona	11 Mar
8:56.08	Joan Nesbit USA	3	Barcelona	11 Mar
8:56.21	Elisa Rea ITA	4	Barcelona	11 Mar
8:56.72	Lyudmila Borisova RUS	1	Berlin	10 Feb
8:58.28	Lidiya Vasilevskaya RUS	5	Barcelona	11 Mar
8:58.33	Sinead Delahunty IRL	2	Atlanta	4 Mar
9:00.90	Olga Kovpotina RUS	2	Erfurt	15 Feb
9:01.27	Kathrin Wessel GER	2	Berlin	10 Feb
9:01.72	Viktoria Nenasheva RUS	1	St Peterburg	9 Jan
9:01.79	Marta Dominguez ESP	6	Barcelona	11 Mar
9:02.59	Maria Pantyukova RUS	1	Volgograd	26 Feb
9:03.60	Marina Bastos POR	1	Braga	19 Feb
9:03.84	Zahra Ouaziz MAR	7	Barcelona	11 Mar
9:04.03	Annette Sergent-Palluy FRA	8	Barcelona	11 Mar

50 Metres Hurdles

6.67A	Jackie Joyner-Kersee USA	1	Reno	10 Feb
6.73	Yulia Graudyn RUS	1	Moskva	27 Jan
6.77	Olga Shishigina KZK	2	Moskva	27 Jan
6.77A	Michelle Freeman JAM	2	Reno	10 Feb
6.80	Brigita Bukovec SLO	2	Grenoble	29 Jan
6.85	Aleksandra Pashkina RUS	3	Moskva	27 Jan
6.86	Julie Baumann SUI	4	Moskva	27 Jan

55 Metres Hurdles

7.46	Michelle Freeman JAM	1	Johnson C	28 Jan
7.48	Gillian Russell JAM	1	Fairfax	4 Feb
7.51	Angie Coon CAN	2	Johnson C	28 Jan
7.57	Dione Rose JAM	3	Johnson C	28 Jan
7.57	LaTasha Colander USA	2	Indianapolis	10 Mar

60 Metres Hurdles

7.84	Patricia Girard FRA	1	Liévin	26 Feb
7.85	Olga Shishigina KZK	1	Liévin	19 Feb
7.87	Jackie Joyner-Kersee USA	1	Fairfax	25 Feb
7.90	Brigita Bukovec SLO	1	Madrid	9 Feb
7.91	Aliuska López CUB	1s1	Barcelona	11 Mar
7.93	Lynda Goode USA	1	Atlanta	4 Mar
7.97	Julie Baumann SUI	3	Liévin	19 Feb
7.98	Tatyana Reshetnikova RUS	3	Madrid	9 Feb
7.98	Michelle Freeman JAM	2	Atlanta	4 Mar
7.98	Monique Tourret FRA	4	Barcelona	11 Mar
7.99	Nicole Ramalalanirina MAD	2	Liévin	26 Feb
8.01	Jacqui Agyepong GBR	5	Barcelona	11 Mar
8.03	Aleksandra Paskhina RUS	1	Moskva	26 Jan
8.03	Cheryl Dickey USA	4s1	Barcelona	11 Mar
8.04@	Marina Slushkina RUS	1s1	Volgograd	25 Feb
8.04	Dionne Rose JAM	5s1	Barcelona	11 Mar
8.06	Svetlana Laukhova RUS	h	Stuttgart	5 Feb
8.06	Dawn Bowles USA	3	Fairfax	25 Feb

High Jump

2.04	Alina Astafei GER	1	Berlin	3 Mar
2.00	Tatyana Motkova RUS	1	B Bystrica	8 Feb
2.00	Hanne Haugland NOR	1	Spala	17 Feb
1.99	Yelena Gulyayeva RUS	2	Berlin	3 Mar
1.99	Inga Babakova UKR	3	Berlin	3 Mar
1.99	Britta Bilac SLO	2	Barcelona	11 Mar
1.99	Heike Henkel GER	3	Barcelona	11 Mar
1.97	Monica Iager ROM	2	B Bystrica	8 Feb
1.97	Amy Acuff USA	1	Indianapolis	11 Mar
1.96	Yevgeniya Zhdanova RUS	1	Gent	12 Feb
1.96	Gwen Wentland USA	1	Atlanta	4 Mar
1.96	Tisha Waller USA	2	Atlanta	4 Mar
1.96	Tatyana Shevchik BLR	6	Barcelona	11 Mar
1.95	Angela Bradburn USA	1	New York	3 Feb
1.95	Olga Kaliturina RUS	3	Gent	12 Feb
1.95	Natalja Jonckheere BEL	4	Gent	12 Feb
1.95	Yelena Topchina RUS	4	Moskva	14 Feb
1.95	Sigrid Kirchmann AUT	1	Vienna	18 Feb
1.94	Yelena Panikarovskikh RUS	3	B Bystrica	8 Feb
1.94	Venelina Veneva BUL	1	Sofia	18 Feb

Pole Vault

4.15	Sun Caiyun CHN	1	Erfurt	15 Feb
4.09	Daniela Bartová TCH	1	Praha	26 Feb
4.06	Marina Andreyeva RUS	1	Volgograd	26 Feb
4.05	Andrea Müller GER	3	Zweibrücken	27 Jan
4.03	Cai Weiyan CHN	2	Karlsruhe	12 Feb
4.00	Christine Adams GER	2	Erfurt	15 Feb
4.00	Gabriela Mihalcea ROM	1	Landau	17 Feb
4.00	Tanja Cors GER	1	Sindelfingen	26 Feb
3.95	Nicole Rieger GER	5	Erfurt	15 Feb
3.91	Svetlana Abramova RUS	4	Pulheim	3 Feb
3.85	Daniela Köpernick GER	3	Landau	17 Feb
3.81	Janet Zach GER	6	Pulheim	3 Feb
3.80	Kate Staples GBR	1	Birmingham	4 Feb
3.80	Sophie Zubiolo BEL	1	Gent	5 Feb
3.71	Melissa Price USA	1	Los Angeles	11 Feb

Long Jump

7.09	Heike Drechsler GER	1	Liévin	19 Feb
6.95	Lyudmila Galkina RUS	1	Barcelona	12 Mar
6.90	Irina Mushayilova RUS	2	Barcelona	12 Mar
6.90	Susen Tiedtke-Greene GER	3	Barcelona	12 Mar
6.86	Inessa Kravets UKR	2	Liévin	19 Feb
6.85	Larisa Berezhnaya UKR	1	Kiev	6 Jan
6.84	Jackie Joyner-Kersee USA	2	New York	3 Feb
6.84	Svetlana Moskalets RUS	1	Moskva	25 Jan
6.81	Yelena Sinchukova RUS	2	Moskva	25 Jan
6.81	Nicole Boegman AUS	4	Barcelona	12 Mar
6.77	Renata Nielsen DEN	5	Barcelona	12 Mar
6.75	Iva Prandzheva BUL	4	Liévin	19 Feb
6.72	Marieta Ilcu ROM	1	Bacau	21 Jan
6.71	Niki Xanthou GRE	1	Pireas	25 Feb
6.70	Olga Rublyova RUS	Q	Volgograd	24 Feb
6.68	Paraskevi Patoulidou GRE	1	Pireas	11 Fb
6.65	Anna Biryukova RUS	3	Grenoble	29 Jan
6.65	Agata Karczmarek POL	2	Karlsruhe	12 Feb
6.65	Claudia Gerhardt GER	6	Barcelona	12 Mar

Triple Jump

15.03	Yolanda Chen RUS	1	Barcelona	11 Mar
14.75	Anna Biryukova RUS	1	Moskva	14 Feb
14.71	Iva Prandzheva BUL	2	Barcelona	11 Mar
14.67	Inessa Kravets UKR	1	Moskva	27 Jan
14.54	Maria Sokova RUS	1	Volgograd	26 Feb
14.47	Inna Lasovskaya RUS	2	Moskva	27 Jan
14.46	Irina Mushayilova RUS	2	Volgograd	26 Feb
14.37	Ren Ruiping CHN	3	Barcelona	11 Mar
14.30	Rodica Petrescu ROM	1	Bucuresti	4 Feb
14.29	Ashia Hansen GBR	2	Birmingham	25 Feb
14.25	Sarka Kasparková TCH	4	Barcelona	11 Mar
14.23	Sheila Hudson-Strudwick USA	1	Atlanta	4 Mar
14.12	Natalya Kayukova RUS	1	Moskva	25 Jan
14.09	Galina Chistyakova RUS	2	Moskva	25 Jan
14.08	Yelena Govorova UKR	1	Kiev	12 Feb
14.04	Niurka Montalvo CUB	6	Barcelona	11 Mar
14.02	Concepción Paredes ESP	1	Valencia	26 Feb
14.00	Tatyana Matyashova	1	Moskva	11 Feb

Shot

19.93	Larisa Peleshenko RUS	1	Barcelona	11 Mar
19.42	Grit Hammer GER	1	Sassnitz	11 Feb
19.40	Kathrin Neimke GER	2	Barcelona	11 Mar
19.37	Mihaela Oana ROM	1	Bucuresti	12 Feb
19.29	Irina Korzhanenko RUS	1	Moskva	25 Jan
19.24	Valentina Fedyushina RUS	1	Zaporozhye	2 Feb
19.21	Astrid Kumbernuss GER	4	Sassnitz	11 Feb
19.12	Connie Price-Smith USA	3	Barcelona	11 Mar
18.84	Zhang Liuhong CHN	5	Barcelona	11 Mar
18.83	Huang Zhihong CHN	1	Maebashi	5 Feb
18.81	Sui Xinmei CHN	6	Barcelona	11 Mar
18.68	Ramona Pagel USA	1	Atlanta	4 Mar
18.64	Anna Romanova RUS	2	Volgograd	25 Feb
18.45	Irina Khudorozhkina RUS	4	Volgograd	25 Feb
18.24	Cheng Xiaoyan CHN	1	Yokohama	4 Mar
18.16	Viktoria Pavlysh UKR	2	Moskva	19 Feb
18.06	Corrie de Bruin HOL	1	Den Haag	12 Feb

Pentathlon

4867	Svetlana Moskalets RUS	1	Chelyabinsk	4 Feb
4696#	Kym Carter USA	1	Moscow, Id	10 Feb
	4633	2	Barcelona	10 Mar
4639	Irina Tyukhay RUS	2	Chelyabinsk	4 Feb
4604	Irina Vostrikova RUS	3	Chelyabinsk	4 Feb
4585	Yelena Lebedenko RUS	4	Chelyabinsk	4 Feb
4528	Nadezhda Novikova RUS	5	Chelyabinsk	4 Feb
4520	Anzhela Atroshchenko BLR	1	Gomel	27 Jan
4487	Svetlana Buraga BLR	2	Gomel	27 Jan
4450	Veronika Ryzhova RUS	6	Chelyabinsk	4 Feb
4449	Yelena Volf RUS	7	Chelyabinsk	4 Feb
4447	Liliana Nastase ROM	5	Barcelona	10 Mar
4445	Mona Steigauf GER	6	Barcelona	10 Mar
4444	Lyudmila Mikhaylova RUS	8	Chelyabinsk	4 Feb
4440	Tatyana Gordayeva RUS	1	Chelyabinsk	3 Feb
4434	Sharon Jaklofsky NED	8	Barcelona	10 Mar
4409	Jamie McNeair USA	2	Moscow, Id	11 Feb

3000 Metres Walk

12:17.57	Beate Gummelt GER	1	Erfurt	15 Feb
12:36.37	Simone Thust GER	2	Sindelfingen	26 Feb

5000 Metres Walk

21:33.22	Valentina Tsbulskaya BLR	1	Minsk	4 Feb
21:39.05	Olga Kardopoltseva	2	Minsk	4 Feb

IAAF WORLD INDOOR CHAMPIONSHIPS

Barcelona, Spain, 10-12 March 1995

Triple jumpers starred as Yolanda Chen spanned 15.03 for the only world record of the meeting, while in the men's event Brian Wellman produced the third longest ever jump of 17.72 to withstand the onslaught of Yoelbi Quesada (17.62).

Other highlights of a championships avoided by too many of the top performers who had been competing indoors in the preceding two months included Cuba's two jumping golds, as Ivan Pedroso leapt into second place on the indoor all-time list for long jump with 8.51 and Javier Sotomayor had a good attempt at a world record 2.44. Sergey Bubka added to his collection of titles, Alina Astafei cleared 2.01 for victory in her first appearance for Germany and Lyudmila Galkina's long jump success indicated that she will be the world's next 7m performer.

The track events were patchy, as usual at major indoor championships, but the sprints were good as championship records were established by Bruny Surin with 6.46 for 60m, Allen Johnson with 7.39 for the hurdles and Irina Privalova with 50.23 in her first indoor 400m event. Other high quality marks included a 6.97 60m by Merlene Ottey and a 1:57.62 800m by Maria Mutola.

The most successful teams were Russia with six gold medals, the USA with four and Cuba with three; in terms of total medals the USA came out on top with 15 as against 12 by Russia and six by Germany.

Results of finals, (day of competition in parentheses)
* = national record, # = area record.

MEN

60 METRES (10)
1. Bruny Surin CAN 6.46 Ch rec
2. Darren Braithwaite GBR 6.51
3. Robert Esmie CAN 6.55
4. Maurice Greene USA 6.59
5. Marc Blume GER 6.59
6. Gus Nketia NZL 6.63
7. Patrick Strenius SWE 6.64
8. Vitaliy Savin KZK 6.65

200 METRES (11)
1. Geir Moen NOR 20.58
2. Troy Douglas BER 20.94
3. Sebastian Keitel CHI 20.98*
4. Donovan Bailey CAN 21.08

dns, Sergey Osovich UKR & John Regis GBR

400 METRES (12)
1. Darnell Hall USA 46.17
2. Sunday Bada NGR 46.38
3. Mikhail Vdovin RUS 46.65
4. Carlos Silva POR 46.87*
5. Son Ju-il KOR 46.90 #
6. Calvin Davis USA 47.19

800 METRES (12)
1. Clive Terrelonge JAM 1:47.30 #
2. Benson Koech KEN 1:47.51
3. Pavel Soukup TCH 1:47.74
4. Ter Øyvind Ødegård NOR 1:48.34
5. Mahjoub Haïda MAR 1:48.63
6. Joseph Tengelei KEN 1:49.22

1500 METRES (11)
1. Hicham El Guerrouj MAR 3:44.54
2. Mateo Cañellas ESP 3:44.85
3. Eric Nedeau USA 3:44.91
4. Niall Bruton IRL 3:45.05
5. Vyacheslav Shabunin RUS 3:45.40
6. Fermin Cacho ESP 3:45.46
7. Rüdiger Stenzel GER 3:45.64
8. Dominique Löser GER 3:46.09

3000 METRES (12)
1. Gennaro Di Napoli ITA 7:50.89
2. Anacleto Jiménez ESP 7:50.98
3. Brahim Jabbour MAR 7:51.42
4. Mohamed Suleiman QAT 7:51.73
5. John Mayock GBR 7:51.86
6. Reuben Reina USA 7:53.86
7. Shaun Creighton AUS 7:54.46
8. Isaac Viciosa ESP 8:01.00

60 METRES HURDLES (12)
1. Allen Johnson USA 7.39 Ch rec
2. Courtney Hawkins USA 7.41
3. Tony Jarrett GBR 7.42
4. Mark McKoy AUT 7.46*
5. Emilio Valle CUB 7.67
6. Antti Haapakoski FIN 7.70
7. Frank Busemann GER 7.70
8. Kyle Vander-Kuyp 7.73 = #

HIGH JUMP (12)
1. Javier Sotomayor CUB 2.38
2. Lambros Papakostas GRE 2.35*
3. Tony Barton USA 2.32
4. Steinar Hoen NOR 2.32
5. Ralf Sonn GER 2.28
6. Stevan Zoric YUG 2.28
7. Steve Smith USA 2.28

8=. Dalton Grant GBR 2.28
8=. Ettore Ceresoli ITA 2.28

POLE VAULT (11)
1. Sergey Bubka UKR 5.90
2. Igor Potapovich KZK 5.80

3=. Okkert Brits RSA 5.75 #
3= Andrej Tiwontschik GER 5.75
5= Nick Hysong USA 5.70
5= José Manuel Arcos ESP 5.70
7=. Javier Garcia ESP 5.60
7= Maksim Tarasov RUS 5.60

LONG JUMP (11)
1. Ivan Pedroso CUB 8.51 # Ch rec
2. Mattias Sunneborn SWE 8.20*
3. Erick Walder USA 8.14
4. Joe Greene USA 8.12
5. Bogdan Tudor ROM 8.11
6. Milan Gombala TCH 7.95
7. Erik Nijs BEL 7.88
8. Huang Geng CHN 7.83

TRIPLE JUMP (12)
1. Brian Wellman BER 17.72 # Ch rec
2. Yoelvis Quesada CUB 17.62*
3. Serge Hélan FRA 17.06
4. Lars Hedman SWE 16.86
5. Arne Holm SWE 16.81
6. Lamark Carter USA 16.80
7. Francis Agyepong GBR 16.74
8. Garfield Anselm FRA 16.51

SHOT (10)
1. Mika Halvari FIN 20.74
2. C J Hunter USA 20.58
3. Dragan Peric YUG 20.36
4. Manuel Martinez ESP 19.97
5. Yuriy Belonog UKR 19.74
6. Petur Gudmundsson ISL 19.67
7. Paolo Dal Soglio ITA 19.44

HEPTATHLON (11/12)
1. Christian Plaziat FRA 6246 Ch rec (6.96. 7.52. 14.92. 2.04. 7.85. 5.10. 2:44.56)
2. Tomas Dvorák TCH 6169*
3. Henrik Dagård SWE 6142
4. Ricky Barker USA 6120
5. Alex Kruger GBR 5978*
6. Antonio Peñalver ESP 5939
7. Erki Nool EST 5887
8. Sebastien Levicq FRA 5870

4 x 400 METRES RELAY (12)
1. USA 3:07.37 (Rod Tolbert 47.33. Calvin Davis 46.16. Tod Long 47.50. Frankie Atwater 46.38)
2. ITA 3:09.12 (Grossi 48.08. Nuti 46.73. Mazzoleni 47.87. Saber 46.44)
3. JPN 3:09.73 (Kan 47.27. Inagaki 47.93. Ono 47.30. Hayashi 47.23)
4. GBR 3:10.89

WOMEN

60 METRES (10)
1. Merlene Ottey JAM 6.97
2. Melanie Paschke GER 7.10
3. Carlette Guidry USA 7.11
4. Liliana Allen CUB 7.13
5. Beverly McDonald JAM 7.16
6. Nelli Fiere-Cooman NED 7.17
7. Chryste Gaines USA 7.22
8. Lalao Ravaonirina MAD 7.28

200 METRES (11)
1. Melinda Gainsford AUS 22.64 =#
2. Pauline Davis BAH 22.68*
3. Natalya Voronova RUS 23.01
4. Silke Lichtenhagen GER 23.23
5. Zlatka Georgieva BUL 23.36
6. Juliet Cuthbert JAM 23.43

400 METRES (12)
1. Irina Privalova RUS 50.23* Ch rec
2. Sandie Richards JAM 51.38
3. Daniela Georgieva BUL 51.78
4. Deon Hemmings JAM 52.01
5. Jearl Miles USA 52.01
6. Marie-Louise Bévis FRA 53.27

800 METRES (12)
1. Maria Mutola MOZ 1:57.62
2. Yelena Afanasyeva RUS 1:59.79
3. Letitia Vriesde SUR 2:00.36 #
4. Irina Samorokova RUS 2:00.43
5. Stella Jongmans NED 2:01.14
6. Inez Turner JAM 2:02.00 #

1500 METRES (12)
1. Regina Jacobs USA 4:12.61
2. Carla Sacramento POR 4:13.02
3. Lyubov Kremlyova RUS 4:13.19
4. Violeta Beclea ROM 4:16.32
5. Maite Zuñiga ESP 4:16.63
6. Kristen Seabury USA 4:16.77
7. Yvonne van der Kolk NED 4:17.00
8. Paula Schnurr CAN 4:19.26

3000 METRES (11)
1. Gabriela Szabo ROM 8:54.50
2. Lynn Jennings USA 8:55.23
3. Joan Nesbit USA 8:56.08
4. Elisa Rea ITA 8:56.21
5. Lidia Vasilevskaya RUS 8:58.28
6. Marta Dominguez ESP 9:01.79*
7. Zahra Ouaziz MAR 9:03.84*
8. Annette Sergent-Palluy FRA 9:04.03

60 METRES HURDLES (12)
1. Aliuska López CUB 7.92
2. Olga Shishigina KZK 7.92
3. Brigita Bukovec SLO 7.93
4. Monique Tourret FRA 7.98
5. Jacqui Agyepong GBR 8.01*
6. Cheryl Dickey USA 8.19
7. Michelle Freeman JAM 8.21

Patricia Girard FRA dnf

HIGH JUMP (11)
1. Alina Astafei GER 2.01
2. Britta Bilac SLO 1.99
3. Heike Henkel GER 1.99
4. Tatyana Motkova RUS 1.96
5. Yelena Gulyayeva RUS 1.96
6. Tatyana Shevchik BLR 1.96
7. Tisha Waller USA 1.93
8. Sigrid Kirchmann AUT 1.93

LONG JUMP (12)
1. Lyudmila Galkina RUS 6.95
2. Irina Mushayilova RUS 6.90
3. Susen Tiedtke-Greene GER 6.90
4. Nicole Boegman AUS 6.81#
5. Renata Nielsen DEN 6.77*
6. Claudia Gerhardt GER 6.65
7. Yao Weili CHN 6.57
8. Marieta Ilcu ROM 6.52

TRIPLE JUMP (11)
1. Yolanda Chen RUS 15.03 WR
2. Iva Prandzheva BUL 14.71*
3. Ren Ruiping CHN 14.37 #WJR
4. Sarka Kaspárková TCH 14.25
5. Maria Sokova RUS 14.22
6. Niurka Montalvo CUB 14.04 #
7. Yelena Govorova UKR 14.04
8. Sheila Hudson-Strudwick USA 13.88

SHOT (11)
1. Larisa Peleshenko RUS 19.93
2. Kathrin Neimke GER 19.40
3. Connie Price-Smith USA 19.12
4. Grit Hammer GER 19.02
5. Zhang Liuhong CHN 18.84
6. Sui Xinmei CHN 18.81
7. Valentina Fedyushina UKR 18.48
8. Mihaela Oana ROM 18.07

PENTATHLON (10)
1. Svetlana Moskalets RUS 4834 (8.20. 1.88. 14.41. 6.55. 2:19.78)
2. Kym Carter USA 4632*
3. Irina Tyukhay RUS 4622
4. Svetlana Buraga BLR 4466
5. Liliana Nastase ROM 4447
6. Mona Steigauf GER 4445
7. Anzhela Atroshchenko BLR 4441
8. Sharon Jaklofsky NED 4434

4 x 400 METRES RELAY (12)
1. RUS 3:29.29* (Tatyana Chebykina 52.67. Yelena Ruzina 52.68. Yekaterina Kulikova 51.62. Svetlana Goncharenko 51.32)
2. TCH 3:30.27* (Kostoválová 53.19. Dziurová 52.71. Benesová 52.40. Formánová 51.97)
3. USA 3:31.43 (Pasha 54.11. Dooley 52.58. Graham 52.78. Harris 51.96)
4. GBR 3:35.39
5. CHN 3:39.76 #

WORLD CROSS COUNTRY CHAMPIONSHIPS

At Durham. GBR
25 March 1995.

ALTHOUGH they lost three of their four individual titles. Kenya succeeded - as in 1991 and 1993 - in capturing all four team titles. The African domination of this championship continued: the first non-African among the junior men finished 13th in the junior women's race nine of the first 11 places went to Africans. while in the senior events nine of the top 12 men and eight of the top 12 women came from Africa.

Senior Men (12.02k)

1. Paul Tergat KEN	34:05
2. Ismael Kirui KEN	34:13
3. Salah Hissou MAR	34:14
4. Haile Gebrselassie ETH	34:26
5. Brahim Lahlafi MAR	34:34
6. Paulo Guerra POR	34:38
7. James Songok KEN	34:41
8. Simon Chemoiywo KEN	34:46
9. Todd Williams USA	34:47
10. Martin Fiz ESP	34:50
11. Larbi Khattabi MAR	34:55
12. Abdelaziz Sahere MAR	35:00
13. José Garcia ESP	35:01
14. Bob Kennedy USA	35:02
15. J Ondieki KEN	35:02
16. Mustapha Essaïd FRA	35:03
17. Abdellah Béhar FRA	35;03
18. José Carlos Adan ESP	35:05
19. Antonio Serrano ESP	35:07
20. Andrew Pearson GBR	35:07
21. Ayele Mezgebu ETH	35:11
22. António Pinto POR	35:11
23. Domingos Castro POR	35:14
24. José Regalo POR	35:16
25. Shaun Creighton AUS	35:19

214 starters.

Teams

1. KEN	62
2. MAR	111
3. ESP	120
4. POR	139
5. ETH	169
6. USA	310
7. ITA	325
8. RSA	326
9. GBR	354
10. FRA	422

Junior Men (8.47k)

1. Assefa Mezgebu ETH	24:12
2. Dejene Lidetu ETH	24:14
3. David Chelule KEN	24:16
4. Andrew Panga TAN	24:19
5. Philip Mosima KEN	24:23
6. Abreham Tsige ETH	24:40
7. Hezron Otwori KEN	24:43
8. Mark Bett KEN	24:48
9. Sammy Kipruto KEN	24:58
10. Christopher Lelong KEN	25:02
11. John Morapedi RSA	25:04
12. Marco Hhawu TAN	25:04
13. Hideaki Haraguchi JPN	25:09
14. Benoit Zwierzchlewski FRA	25:10
15. Mohammed El Hattab MAR	25:14

148 starters

Teams

1. KEN	23
2. ETH	25
3. MAR	72
4. JPN	84
5. ALG	150
6. RSA	156
7. ESP	164
8. FRA	182
9. USA	227
10. YEM	261

Senior Women (6.47k)

1. Derartu Tulu ETH	20:21
2. Catherina McKiernan IRL	20:29
3. Sally Barsosio KEN	20:39
4. Margaret Ngotho KEN	20:40
5. Gete Wami ETH	20:49
6. Joan Nesbit USA	20:50
7. Merima Denboba ETH	20:53
8. Rose Cheruiyot KEN	20:54
9. Albertina Dias POR	20:56
10. Gabriela Szabo ROM	20:57
11. Catherine Kirui KEN	20:58
12. Zahra Ouaziz MAR	21:06
13. Olga Bondarenko RUS	21:06
14. Olga Appell USA	21:07
15. Yukiko Okamoto JPN	21:07
16. Julia Vaquero ESP	21:12
17. Helen Kimaiyo KEN	21:13
18. Paula Radcliffe GBR	21:14
19. Annette Sergent-Palluy FRA	21:15
20. Kanako Haginaga JPN	21:17
21. Carmen Fuentes ESP	21:18
22. Tudorita Chidu ROM	21:19
23. Eelena Fidatov ROM	21:20
24. Bev Hartigan GBR	21:21
25. Askale Bereda ETH	21:22

135 starters

Teams

1. KEN	26
2. ETH	38
3. ROM	84
4. JPN	102
5. USA	111
6. RUS	116
7. ESP	133
8. FRA	151
9. GBR	164
10. POR	175.

Junior Women (4.47k)

1. Annemari Sandell FIN	14:04
2. Jebiwot Keitany KEN	14:09
3. Nancy Kipron KEN	14:17
4. Jepkorir Aiyabei KEN	14:21
5. Berhane Dagne ETH	14:25
6. Anita Weyermann SUI	14:25
7. Alemitu Bekele ETH	14:26
8. Yimenashu Taye ETH	14:27
9. Elizabeth Cheptanui KEN	14:28
10. Pamela Chepchumba KEN	14:31
11. Ayelech Worku ETH	14:33
12. Chiemi Takahashi JPN	14:39
13. Miwa Sugawara JPN	14:39
14. Helen Kimutai KEN	14:40
15. Yoshiko Ichikawa JPN	14:42

109 starters.

Teams

1. KEN	18
2. ETH	31
3. JPN	56
4. USA	113
5. ROM	120
6. GBR	133
7. ESP	183
8. BEL	208
9. CAN	219
10. RSA	219

IAAF World Cross Challenge:

Final Standings

Men

1. Ismael Kirui KEN	135pts
2. Paulo Guerra POR	130
3. Salah Hissou MAR	117
4. Paul Tergat KEN	97
5. James Kariuki KEN	72
6. Martin Fíz ESP	63
7. Umberto Pusterla ITA	60
8. Domingos Castro POR	57
9. Shem Kororia KEN	56
10. Haile Gebrselassie ETH	53

Women

1. Catherina McKiernan IRL	135
2. Rose Cheruiyot KEN	126
3. Catherine Kirui KEN	100
4. Gabriela Szabo ROM	97
5. Derartu Tulu ETH	92
6. Albertina Dias POR	88
7. Elena Fidatov ROM	77
8. Helen Kimaiyo KEN	75
9. Sally Barsosio KEN	74
10= Fernanda Ribeiro POR	69
10= Joyce Koech KEN	69